19th Edition
Toys
& Prices

Mark Bellomo

Published by

Krause Publications, a division of F+W Media, Inc.
700 East State Street • Iola, WI 54990-0001
715-445-2214 • 888-457-2873
www.krausebooks.com

To order books or other products call toll-free 1-800-258-0929
or visit us online at www.krausebooks.com

ISBN-13: 978-1-4402-3501-6
ISBN-10: 1-4402-3501-5

Cover Design by Jim Butch/Sandi Carpenter
Designed by Sandi Carpenter
Edited by Paul Kennedy

Printed in the United States of America

Contents

Acknowledgments 4

Introduction 5

How To Use This Book 6

Action Figures 7

Advertising Toys 157

Barbie 167

Battery-Operated Toys 228

Character Toys 235

Fisher-Price 306

Games 320

G.I. Joe 363

Guns 415

Lunch Boxes 425

Marx Play Sets 445

PEZ 455

Robots 470

Rock 'n' Roll 481

Sci-Fi and Space Toys 483

Star Wars 501

TV Toys 565

Vehicles 584

    Buddy L 585

    Corgi 601

    Deluxe Reading 635

    Dinky 636

    Doepke 650

    Eldon 651

    Gay Toys 652

    Hot Wheels Redlines 654

    Japanese Tin Cars 668

    Johnny Lightning (Topper) 678

    Matchbox King Size 680

    Matchbox Regular Wheels 683

    Matchbox Superfast 706

    Midgetoy 726

    Nylint 727

    Processed Plastic 732

    Remco 734

    Smith Miller 735

    Structo 738

    Tonka 762

    Tootsietoy 777

View-Master 786

Western Toys 801

Acknowledgements

Acknowledgements

I'd like to once again thank my beautiful, patient, saintly wife, Jessica Rivers-Bellomo, for her endless support: I adore her – I still can't write without her physically sitting by my side every single minute; I don't know what I'd do without her empathy. I'm indebted to her for not only allowing me to compile a collection of nearly 50,000 toys and 125,000+ comic books, but for shooing away my faithful cats – Pea Pod and Reverend James Caldwell Ignatoswki ("Iggy") – before they began tearing into the myriad boxes and Jenga-like stacks of toys in our living room, dining room, bedroom(s), kitchen, basement, attic, and garage. Thanks to my mom and dad for never forcing me to "stop collecting those stupid toys," regardless what their friends, extended family or co-workers said: like my acquisitions editor, Paul Kennedy, my parents always trusted that I knew what I was doing (even if I didn't really know myself [!]). And a final thanks should go out to my mentor/hector Dr. H.R. Stoneback, who – like my industrious mother and father – showed me that working 16-18 hours-a-day for twenty years pays off in ways most folks couldn't begin to imagine.

Mark W. Bellomo

Many things go into the making of Toys & Prices. A book of this scope and magnitude is dependent upon the talents and passion of some of the finest and most dedicated people in the field. This is a work built on the shoulders of giants, and those who have helped along the way, we say thank you.

Let's start with you, our loyal readers. We've been creating this book for 20 years. The letters, emails and phone calls we have received from you throughout the years are greatly appreciated. You help keep us up-to-date with the latest happenings in the hobby. This project would not be possible without the continued support of the toy-collecting community. We love hearing from you. Thank you all, and keep it up!

It has been my great pleasure to have known and worked with Mark Bellomo, the editor and leading force of this project, for some 10 years. He is without doubt one of the brightest and most knowledgeable toy experts in the country. He has written outstanding references on G.I. Joe and Transformers. His book, *Totally Tubular '80s Toys*, is a great nostalgic trip. Mark is one of the best. But more than that, he is a good guy. It's great working with you Mark. Thank you.

As I mentioned early, this book is dependent on the work of many contributors, most of them the finest source of toy information in their field. In no particular order, thanks to: Bruce Fox, Mark Rich, Justin Pinchot, Leo Rishty, Mary Ann Sell, Shawn Peterson, Randy Prasse, Karen O'Brien, Justin Moen, Dr. Douglas Sadecky, Joe Soucy, Ron Smith, George Newcomb, Mike Zarnock and Tom Larson. Through the years these fine folks have helped shape this work in untold ways. Thank you.

The staff at Krause Publications continues to do a magnificent job of putting this title together. Thanks to intern Steve Zahurones for his dogged determination to get the job done. Steve's work ethic portends to a bright future. Thanks also to designer Sandi Carpenter whose resolve and sense of purpose is surpassed only by her good cheer.

And finally, to the child in all of us. Play on!

Paul Kennedy
Editorial Director
Krause Publications

Introduction

By Mark W. Bellomo

Throw the key words "collectibles program," "storage space show," or "auction TV" into a Google Search, and you will not only realize how many current television programs are based on these themes, but you'll also witness an overwhelming amount of Americans who—based on testimonials they've plastered all over the World Wide Web (from blogs to YouTube to personal web sites, etc.)—are turning to pawn shops, flea markets, collectible stores, garage and estate sales, storage unit auctions, and the classified adverts of Craigslist (the *largest* garage sale of all…) to buy and sell items and collectible artifacts. More and more, everyday folks are becoming better-educated about the secondary market, and are joining the once-hallowed ranks of diehard collectors, eschewing traditional retail shops and foregoing visits to brick-and-mortar stores in favor of pursuing non-traditional modes of shopping.

In this economy, every dollar is important: if you can make a few bucks over "guide price" selling that mint condition Aladdin *Buck Rogers in the 25th Century* lunchbox that's been lurking in your attic for 30+ years, then do so; if you can find Coleco's talking Alf plush, a stuffed animal that takes you back to the happy days of yesteryear for a marvelously low price, then do so. In both of these examples, consumers act shrewdly: they maximize their revenue in the first instance, and minimize the amount they're willing to spend in the second instance.

This is the climate that the new edition of *Toys & Prices* is released: a more knowledgeable, involved readership comprised of economically-minded people that simply do NOT want to pay full price for the collectibles and antiques they desire—yet these same folks are desperate to reap ample rewards when selling the items they wish to part with from their own collections—it's a precarious balance that most fans of collectibles must strike. And I can't say that I blame them: I myself am in the same boat. During a down economy, if I can persuade a retailer, dealer, or seller to part with an item for ANY percentage less than the marked price, I'll do it… of course. Everyone is looking for a deal. Simply put: many consumers refuse to purchase a collectible if there is no discount given by the dealer, regardless of the rarity of the item.

For instance, in a recent story drafted by Anne D'Innocenzio titled "Deal Junkies Hurt Stores Profits," the AP Retail Writer evinces this new philosophy. D'Innocenzio's highly informative article reflects upon this current trend of American consumers to save money—regardless of the item; modern American consumers are savvy customers who've become so preoccupied with obtaining lower prices that they *refuse* to patronize any store that isn't hosting a sale. We're swimming in the wake of a global financial crisis so deep and resounding that "…it has bred a group of *deal junkies* that won't shop unless they see '70 percent [off]' signs or yellow clearance stickers [on merchandise]."

So then, if you're a seller of antiques and collectibles who is remiss to discount any of your wares regardless of the country's economic climate, my advice to you is delineated as follows: the artifacts you own are worth only what people will pay for them, *regardless of what they've sold for in the past.* You may feel free to hearken back to a better-vanished time (the 90s, the early 00s), when "red-carded" Star Wars figures were an easy sale at four-for-$20. Please enjoy reminiscing about the time you sold Depression-era glassware for 200% of guide. This simply isn't the case anymore.

There's a distinct difference between high nostalgia value and high retail value. Just because you paid "X" for something that you dearly love and fiercely believe will one day yield an increase in revenue, doesn't mean you'll ever be able to sell it over again—one, two, five, ten, fifteen—years later for a profit. Predicting trends is quite difficult. This is true with stocks and commodities, and it holds true with comic books and collectibles as well. If we were all gurus and prognosticators, we'd all be quite wealthy. Simply look at the lack of secondary market value for two fads of the mid-1990s—pogs and Beanie Babies—that everyone was buying up for an investment and you'll see what I mean: for every one truly successful idea (the Slinky, Transformers, or Barbie fashion dolls), there are hundreds upon thousands of failures.

Today, toys that aren't in demand languish in retail aisles and gather dust on the pegs of secondary store walls, while it appears that many higher-end collectibles (essentially anything valued at more than $225 [run a "Completed Items" search on eBay in ANY category and you'll see what I mean]) meet considerable resistance from buyers; these items just aren't getting the bids they used to receive.

Over the past few years one positive aspect of the hobby is becoming apparent: more people are becoming acquainted with toys, collectibles, and their values than at any other point in American history, thanks to the exposure our beloved hobby has garnered from the myriad collectible-based reality programs broadcast on cable television stations such as The History Channel, Travel Channel, A&E, truTV, Discovery Channel, Syfy, NatGeo, HGTV, AMC, and even America's most-trusted public network, PBS, who has captured our attention with its two seminal productions that feature the appraisal of *objets d'art*, curios, and collector's items from bygone eras: *Antiques Roadshow* (1997-present) and the British broadcast that started it all, *Antiques Roadshow UK* (1979-present). Of course, it's not just one program about collectibles whose name falls trippingly off of my tongue—there are literally dozens of these shows, among these: *American Pickers*, *Auctioneer$*, *Auction Hunters*, *Auction Kings*, *Auction Packed*, *Cajun Pawn Stars*, *Cash & Cari*, *Collection Intervention*, *Comic Book Men*, *Hardcore Pawn*, *History Detectives*, *It's Worth What?*, *Pawn Stars*, *Storage Wars*, *Toy Hunter*, and *What the Sell?*

Regularly watching one of these popular shows may even be the reason you're picking up Toys & Prices. Congratulations on your purchase, because the best weapon in the battle for equitable prices for toys and collectibles is obtaining an education: acquiring knowledge of the item and its back-story, knowing its manufacturer and the collectible's date-of-production, as well as the artifact's value and importance in the realm of popular culture is all very useful. Yes, this book will assist you in determining a value for the item you're appraising (of course), but remember that a price guide is just that: a guide. The prices given in this book are estimates based upon what an item has sold for in the past and what an expert believes the item is currently worth. As a consultant for one of these collectible shows, I am very careful at assigning value to an item. I do this only after consulting with the top experts in the collectible industry, after contacting the largest collect-ible dealers in different regions of the United States, and furthermore (and most importantly), by utilizing closed auctions on eBay to determine a piece's end price (when scouring a Completed Items Search on eBay, we must take their additional shipping and handling costs into consideration). However, based on my 20+ years in the industry, I've concluded that assigning value to a collectible is much like assigning blame—there's always plenty of value to go around. Plenty of different opinions, as it were. The values in Toys & Prices are not scripture, nor are they meant to be: they are simply an average value based on our contributors' expertise combined with a bevy of empirical data.

In conclusion, I'll leave you with a final note. As many different consumers have recently discovered the subtle-ties of the collectible world and have begun to embrace this subculture, more people than ever are bringing items to the secondary market: often at the same time (!). Thousands more items are hitting eBay, Craigslist, and local flea markets. This gives the educated and informed collector a much larger base to pick from to fill their collections. Take advantage of the economic clime if you can—this is the single best time to buy collectibles since the early 1980s. We may never witness a period so ripe for picking again in our lifetimes.

Toys & Prices is organized alphabetically by chapter. The tabs on the side of pages indicate the chapter. The headers at the top of each page have the chapter title followed by the section.

As a general rule, individual chapters override a character name. If there is a chapter devoted to the type of toy you're looking for, check there first. For example, if you're looking up a Batman and Robin lunch box, look first in the Lunch Boxes chapter. Overlap is the nature of the beast with toy classification. For example, space-related action figures are most likely to be listed in the Action Figures chapter, but you may also find some listed in the Sci-Fi and Space Toys chapter.

Condition is Everything

When estimating the value of a toy, you must first evaluate its condition. Mint toys in mint packaging command higher prices than well played with toys whose boxes disappeared with the wrapping paper on Christmas Day. Mint is a rare condition indeed as toys were meant to be played with by children. Realistic evaluation of condition is essential, as grading standards do vary from class to class. Grading a 1960s G.I. Joe is a different task than grading a Mattel Fanner 50 cap pistol.

Ultimately, the market is driven by buyers, and the bottom line final value of a toy is often the last price at which it is sold.

Common Abbreviations

MIB or MIP (Mint in Box, Mint in Package, C10): Just like new, in the original package, preferably still sealed. Boxes may have been opened, but any packages inside (as with model kits) remain unopened. Blister cards should be intact, undamaged, and unopened. Factory-sealed boxes should be unopened and command higher prices.

MNP or MNB (Mint no Package, Mint no Box, C10): A toy typically produced in the 1960s or later in Mint condition with all of its pieces, but missing its original package. A toy outside its original package is often referred to as "loose."

NM (Near Mint, C9): A toy that is complete and appears like new but exhibits very minor wear and may or may not have the original box. An exception would be a toy that came in kit form. A kit in Near Mint condition would be expected to have the original box, but the box would display some wear.

EX (Excellent, C8): Toy is complete and shows signs of minor wear. Very clean and well cared for.

VG (Very Good, C6): Toy obviously has been played with and shows general overall wear. Paint chipping is readily apparent. In metal toys, some minor rust may be evident. Some minor pieces may be missing.

GD or G (Good, C4): A toy with evidence of heavy play, dents, chips, and possibly moderate rust. The toy may be missing a major replaceable component or may be in need of repair. In sets, several pieces may be missing.

Action Figures

Action Figures

By Mark Bellomo

The 1960s

The production of action figures in the United States can be traced back to the nascent origins of Hasbro's G.I. Joe, "America's Moveable Fighting Man," in early 1964. Hoping to build on the overwhelming success of Mattel's Barbie doll (launched in 1959), Hasbro was approached by a designer who concocted the idea of crafting a foot-tall, fully articulated, military-themed toy soldier to American boys. Hasbro loved the idea, and developed what would be called the G.I. Joe line, and thus the 11-1/2" toy was born. G.I. Joe was a huge hit for Hasbro, who labeled the toy an "action figure" in order to differentiate and dissociate it from Barbie and other female fashion dolls on the market, knowing full well that young boys would not play with dolls.

Due to the success of G.I. Joe, other companies entered into the action figure market. Realizing that poseable male action figures tapped into a heretofore-unknown aspect of a young boy's imagination, A.C. Gilbert, Marx, and Ideal also forayed into the field. As a result, boys were treated to new action figures based on James Bond, Secret Agent (A.C. Gilbert, 1965), D.C. Comics and Marvel Comics super hero costumes for Captain Action (Ideal, 1966-68), and Western heroes and knights in Marx's Best of the West (1965-75) and Noble Knights (1968) lines, respectively.

The 1970s

The '70s saw action figure companies building on the strong foundation of the 1960s. Clever designers and executives realized that licensing popular characters from motion pictures and television could lead to huge revenues. A leader in the push for the use of licensed toy properties is the now defunct but legendary Mego Corporation (1971-1983), a '70s business juggernaut that captured a wealth of different film and TV licenses. An abbreviated list of Mego's licenses reads like a summation of '70s popular culture: *C.H.I.P.S., Planet of the Apes, The Black Hole, Captain & Tennille, The Love Boat, Dukes of Hazzard, Happy Days, Laverne & Shirley, James Bond, KISS,* and a wealth of others. Perhaps Mego's most famous product was the company's Official World's Greatest Super Heroes (1972-1978), which are, to this day considered to be some of the most popular and desirable of all comic book action figures. Expect prices of Mint on Card and Mint in Box Mego figures (particularly the aforementioned super heroes) to be extraordinarily high.

Although Mego's Micronauts (1976-1980) and Comic Action Heroes (1975-1978) were among the very first 3 ¾" action figures, Kenner's stellar line of *Star Wars* figures, vehicles, creatures, and playsets took America by storm in 1977. *Star Wars* revolutionized play for a whole generation of American children with this new scale of action figures, and the franchise's success spans three decades.

With the triumph of the *Star Wars* line, toy manufacturers began looking at action figures in a new light, understanding the wealth of possibilities that could be explored in this new 3 ¾" format. What once was a shoebox full of 2" tall hard-plastic little green army men in the 1950s, in the 1970s became a colorful carrying case chock full of 4" tall, fully poseable, distinctly different characters with a slew of different weapons and accessories.

The 1980s

Although the 1970s ushered in a new format (and era) of action figure collecting, it wasn't until the 1980s (and Ronald Reagan's deregulation of children's television) that licensed properties *exploded* into children's toy rooms. The 1980s are considered by many collectors to be a renaissance for action figures, as Reagan's deregulation allowed companies to provide children with—in essence—24-minute long animated toy commercials. These animated programs were so popular that they volleyed into syndication, some cable channels showing a block of toy cartoons for hours on end, every day of the week. As a result, the characters from these action figure lines of the '80s permeated the American collective consciousness for an entire generation, and many toy lines that were born in the '80s are still über popular to this day: G.I. Joe: A Real American Hero, Transformers, He-Man and the Masters of the Universe, Thundercats, Voltron, M.A.S.K., Dungeons & Dragons, The Real Ghostbusters, Indiana Jones, Robotech, She-Ra Princess of Power, the World Wrestling Federation, and those plucky Teenage Mutant Ninja Turtles.

Many casual fans don't recognize what any conscientious collector of 1980s action figures knows: these '80s toys are worth quite a bit of money in good condition, whether the toy is Mint Loose and Complete, or even better, Mint in Package (Mint in Box or Mint on Card). Of course, casual fans are well aware that "big" G.I. Joes (the 11 ½" figures from 1964-1976) are worth a considerable amount of money, and that vintage Star Wars figures will command a good price at auction, but in recent years, even secondary and tertiary toy lines from the 1980s have caught steam (i.e. M.A.S.K., She-Ra Princess of Power, etc.).

The 1990s

With the introduction of many new super hero toy lines from novice toy maker Toy Biz (DC Super Heroes, Marvel Super Heroes, Batman, X-Men, and Spider-Man), the 1990s started with a bang.

Toy Biz would fizzle for a bit due to criticism of their poor sculpting, terrible action features, and inferior plastics, but the company would come back strong in the new millennium with their stunning Marvel Legends line (2002-present, with the license now owned by Hasbro).

New toy lines sprung up seemingly out of nowhere. Licensed properties were being utilized to the max, from the *Aliens* franchise to *Austin Powers*, from Playmate's *Star Trek: The Next Generation* (among their many other *Star Trek* offerings) to *Tim Burton's Nightmare Before Christmas*. A few toy lines truly stand out from this decade. Todd MacFarlane's line of expertly crafted *Spawn* (1994-present) action figures based on his No. 1 selling Image comic book, and Playmate's revolutionary *Simpsons* (1999-2004) line of figures and play sets dominated toy shelves. With the vast amount of different product offered, it seemed that collectors couldn't get enough of the wide variety. Unfortunately, the secondary market prices of many of these '90s toys have declined. The action figure market, however, is based on the value of popular lines increasing across the board on the secondary market after eight to fifteen years have passed.

The 2000s

The last decade produced many advances in action figure production: improved articulation (*Star Wars*, G.I. Joe), better paint applications and sculpting (McFarlane Toys), and even "Real Scan Technology" (World Wrestling Entertainment). "Real Scan Technology" (pioneered by Jakks Pacific) allowed an actual human face to be scanned and grafted into the mold of an action figure. Only time will tell which of the many toy lines of the new millennium will be prized as collectibles, determined by supply-and-demand and the desire of passionate aficionados who control the secondary market.

Action Figure Trends

Adrienne Appell, Senior Public Relations Manager of the Toy Industry Association (the important folks who organize the annual International Toy Show [TIA]) identified the following "toy trends" for the current fiscal year, suggesting that the following six dispositions are presently resonating within children's contemporary culture:

- "Products that work with an app or smart devices and products that are based upon an app or web property but have no digital tie-in" (e.g. web-enhanced play).

- "Toys that rely on a glow component to drive the play experience and toys that are equally enjoyable in the light of day as they are in the dark" (e.g. [the return of] glow-in-the-dark toys).

- "Infant to pre-school toys and games that educate and challenge and educational toys targeted to children of all ages" (e.g. [once again,] educational toys).

- "Toys that combine multiple play patterns (i.e. active play, role play, game play, etc.) and customizable toys (playthings become a unique reflection of a child's individuality)" (e.g. toys that can "grow" with a child's formative development).

- "'The Big Ask'/ impressive toys (at higher prices) and collectibles/expanded lines (at affordable prices)" (e.g. foregoing the purchase of three-or-more low-to-mid quality/play-value toys in favor of higher-priced toys with superior play value).

- "Toys for young kids that teach music basics and toys for older kids that let them emulate their favorite pop stars" (e.g. role-play items that allow kids to create music or emulate rock idols from pop culture).

So then… where does this leave action figures? Is the hobby impacted and affected by the above trends? Somewhat. Action figure collecting is like comic book collecting: no matter what the manufacturers of these collectibles throw at consumers, the aficionados of these artifacts are purists at heart. Sure, you can incorporate glow-in-the-dark features into action figures and you can link them to my smart phone's applications. You can construct the latest Star Wars lightsaber as a customizable, interactive, immersive experience unique to each child who purchases the item, or develop a Transformer that functions in an educational manner to preschoolers. But what ultimately sells an action figure is: (1) Does the figure look "cool" (are the paint applications accurate and well-rendered, does the figure's aesthetics "speak" to the collector, does the figure have a "wow factor"?), (2) Is the figure fully poseable? (How many points-of-articulation does the figure have? Anything less than six, and it's back to the drawing board for the designers…), (3) Are the action figure's accessories either perfectly appropriate to the character— or plentiful/abundant? (Wolverine needs his adamantium claws and not much else, but the Punisher or a Star Wars Clone Trooper had best come equipped with a doggone arsenal…), and most importantly, (4) Is the figure an accurate representation of the character in question? (If the character is derived from the pages of a comic book, did the toy's designer make the translation truthfully? If the figure is taken from a CGI film, live action movie, or animated program, does the toy perfectly capture scale: is the character's likeness—both face and body—expertly captured in the toy's design?).

I find that if a toy company follows these four design aspects, they'll usually—9 times out of 10—have a product that won't miss, as long as there's media support to sustain sales (e.g. a television program, film, comic book, or even Internet clips [!]). Two modern action figure lines that exemplify the abovementioned four categories are Toy Biz's magnificent Marvel Legends (2002-2006) toys which were supported by many different media types: comics, cartoons, and films, and Palisades Toys' Muppets line (2002-2004). And the ridiculously-high secondary market prices for these action figures underscores why it's so profoundly important for newly-released franchises to hit all four of these aspects. Collectors and pundits should look to Mattel's brilliantly promoted Monster High action figures (fashion dolls?) for the best example I've seen of this system in many, many years.

But what about the vintage action figure market? What's "hot" and what's "not"? The global economic crisis has indeed adversely affected the secondary market: this much is true. Due to the poor economy, there are many good deals to be found—particularly in toys produced from the 1990s onward: if the toy line in question has been a relatively low-demand franchise during the last few years (i.e. collecting dust on the shelves of secondary stores), then in the past twelve months these artifacts have taken a nose dive; toy lines such as *Babylon 5* (except for the hard-to-find piece, the Shadow Sentient), Playmates' *Star Trek: The Next Generation* and the company's other *Star Trek* sub-lines (nearly all pieces apart from Tapestry Picard, Yesterday's Enterprise Yar, and the few other "limited edition" figures), the Playmates' Simpsons line (with a few exceptions), Hasbro's Stargate toys, the many 90s Toy Biz WCW and Jakks Pacific WWF Wrestling assortments (yet NOT the highly-collectible, hard-plastic Hasbro WWF line), and McFarlane Toys' Spawn line (again, with few exceptions).

For example, I recently witnessed an enormous lot of 101 *Star Trek: The Next Generation* Playmates figures sell for $232.50 (+$30 shipping & handling). That runs $2.60 per figure; a few dollars less than these figures sold for at retail (!). Another recent lot of 86 Mint in Sealed Package (MISP) Spawn figures sold for $225.00 (plus $75 shipping & handling [due to the size of the toys' large clamshell packages]), which averages out at $3.49 per figure—a full one-third to one-quarter of what these action figures originally retailed for when they were first released. In yet another spectacular deal, a massive eBay auction of 170 Simpsons figures (including the super-rare Radioactive Homer) and 35 Simpsons interactive environment playsets ended at $450 (add another whopping $100 for shipping & handling due to the playsets' size). That means each individual Simpsons piece, whether figure or deluxe playset, was purchased by some lucky buyer for the pittance of $2.68 each. We must remember that these deals are just a few of MANY that can currently be had on eBay; it presently remains a buyer's market.

Batman: The Animated Series, and the late-80s/ early 90s Toy Biz lines of DC and Marvel Comics Super Heroes have all made a bit of a comeback, but it's the licensed action figure lines of the 1980s that are in HUGE demand. From the Real Ghostbusters to the Adventures of Indiana Jones, from the ThunderCats to Teenage Mutant Ninja Turtles, the values of the toys within these 80's lines have remained relatively steady, except for the rarest specimens—those pristine, Mint in Sealed Box samples—which continue to slowly rise every year. However, it's those tertiary and quaternary lines of the 80s, the curious little franchises which only lasted a year or less, that many folks passed over (and over, and over…) in order to hunt for specimens of the "Big Five" toy lines (Star Wars, Marvel & DC Super Heroes, Transformers, G.I. Joe, and He-Man & the Masters of the Universe) which have garnered the most attention in recent months. You see, the rarest pieces within the "Big Five" action figure lines will *always* hold steady in terms of both price and demand. But when it comes to the smaller 80s toy lines—those tertiary and quaternary franchises that were produced in 1/10th to 1/100th the numbers of these larger lines that have skyrocketed in price within the past twelve months.

Action figure fans should watch for deals from ANY of the following toy lines since their values have jumped in recent months: Air Raiders, Bionic Six, Blackstar, Bravestarr, Centurions, Dino-Riders*, Dungeons & Dragons, Schaper/Tyco's "Filmation's Ghostbusters," He-Man (the 2nd series from 1989-1992), Inhumanoids, Princess of Power (She-Ra), Rambo & the Forces of Freedom, Silverhawks, and the vintage Tron line as well.

Finally, super hero action figure sales remain steady, with Marvel Legends (whether Toy Biz or Hasbro) and Mattel's DC Universe Classics leading the way. Die-hard collectors should pay careful attention to Mego's Official World's Greatest Super-Heroes line as well as their Comic Action Super-Heroes and Pocket Super-Heroes since these celebrated toy properties saw renewed interest—if not a renewed price increase: remember folks, these are creeping up toward their 40th anniversary (!), elevating the lines toward "antique" status. Folks are re-discovering these toys once again, affording these iconic super hero figures the reverence they so richly deserve. Even Toy Biz's much-maligned Amazing Spider-Man, Fantastic Four, X-Force, and Uncanny X-Men figures based upon Marvel Comics' many animated series of the 90's have garnered interest to die-hard "Marvel Zombies" (the slang term for a fan of Marvel Comics).

The **Top 10 ACTION FIGURES** in mint condition

1. Captain Action, Spider-Man Costume, Ideal, 1967	$9,200
2. Captain Action, Green Hornet Costume, Ideal, 1967	$6,800
3. Batgirl, Comic Heroine Posin' Dolls, Ideal, 1967	$5,300
4. Supergirl, Comic Heroine Posin' Dolls, Ideal, 1967	$5,100
5. Wonder Woman, Comic Heroine Posin' Dolls, Ideal, 1967	$5,100
6. Mera, Comic Heroine Posin' Dolls, Ideal, 1967	$4,600
7. Captain Action, Dr. Evil Gift Set, 1967	$3,700
8. Captain Action, Action Boy Superboy Costume, 1967	$3,100
9. Captain Action, Dr. Evil Sanctuary, 1967	$2,800
10. Captain Action, Silver Streak Vehicle, 1967	$2,000

3D Animation from Japan (McFarlane, 2000)

AKIRA

Kaneda w/Motorcycle, 2000, McFarlane
NM $3   MIP $10

Tetsuo, 2000, McFarlane
NM $3   MIP $10

TENCHI MUYO!

Ryoko, 2000, McFarlane
NM $3   MIP $15

TRIGUN

Vash w/Stampede, 2000, McFarlane
NM $3   MIP $13

Action Jackson (Mego, 1974)

8" FIGURES

Action Jackson, 1974, Mego, blond, brown, or black hair
NM $15   MIP $40

Action Jackson, 1974, Mego, blond, brown, or black beard
NM $15   MIP $40

Action Jackson, 1974, Mego, black version
NM $35   MIP $75

ACCESSORIES

Fire Rescue Pack, 1974, Mego
NM $5   MIP $15

Parachute Plunge, 1974, Mego
NM $5   MIP $15

Strap-On Helicopter, 1974, Mego
NM $5   MIP $15

Water Scooter, 1974, Mego
NM $5   MIP $15

OUTFITS

Air Force Pilot, 1974, Mego
NM $7   MIP $12

Army Outfit, 1974, Mego
NM $7   MIP $12

Aussie Marine, 1974, Mego
NM $7   MIP $12

Baseball, 1974, Mego
NM $7   MIP $12

Fisherman, 1974, Mego
NM $7   MIP $12

Football, 1974, Mego
NM $7   MIP $12

Frog Man, 1974, Mego
NM $7   MIP $12

Hockey, 1974, Mego
NM $7   MIP $12

Jungle Safari, 1974, Mego
NM $7   MIP $12

Karate, 1974, Mego
NM $7   MIP $12

Navy Sailor, 1974, Mego
NM $7   MIP $12

Rescue Squad, 1974, Mego
NM $7   MIP $12

Scramble Cyclist, 1974, Mego
NM $7   MIP $12

Secret Agent, 1974, Mego
NM $7   MIP $12

Ski Patrol, 1974, Mego
NM $7   MIP $12

Snowmobile Outfit, 1974, Mego
NM $7   MIP $12

Surf and Scuba Outfit, 1974, Mego
NM $7   MIP $12

Western Cowboy, 1974, Mego
NM $7   MIP $12

PLAY SETS

Jungle House, 1974, Mego
NM $120   MIP $300

Lost Continent Play Set, 1974, Mego
NM $200   MIP $475

VEHICLES

Adventure Set, 1974, Mego
NM $40   MIP $100

Campmobile, 1974, Mego
NM $40   MIP $90

Dune Buggy, 1974, Mego
NM $30   MIP $60

Formula Racer, 1974, Mego
NM $30   MIP $75

Mustang, 1974, Mego
NM $30   MIP $100

Rescue Helicopter, 1974, Mego
NM $40   MIP $90

Safari Jeep, 1974, Mego
NM $40   MIP $100

Scramble Cycle, 1974, Mego
NM $20   MIP $50

Snowmobile, 1974, Mego
NM $15   MIP $40

Addams Family (Playmates, 1992)

FIGURES

Gomez, 1992, Playmates
NM $2   MIP $6

Granny, 1992, Playmates
NM $2   MIP $6

Lurch, 1992, Playmates
NM $2   MIP $6

Morticia, 1992, Playmates
NM $2   MIP $6

Pugsley, 1992, Playmates
NM $2   MIP $6

Uncle Fester, 1992, Playmates
NM $2   MIP $6

Addams Family (Remco, 1964)

FIGURES

Lurch, 1964, Remco
NM $200   MIP $475

Morticia, 1964, Remco
NM $180   MIP $525

Uncle Fester, 1964, Remco
NM $180   MIP $525

Alien (Kenner, 1979)

18" FIGURE

Alien, 1979, Kenner, this is the ultimate figure for Alien collectors, to be complete it must have the plastic headpiece
NM $210   MIP $500

Aliens (Kenner, 1992-94)

ACCESSORIES

Evac Fighter, 1992-94, Kenner
NM $10   MIP $22

Hovertread, 1992-94, Kenner
NM $6   MIP $16

Power Loader, 1992-94, Kenner
NM $10   MIP $18

Stinger XT-37, 1992-94, Kenner
NM $6   MIP $16

SERIES 1, 1992

Apone, 1992, Kenner
  NM $3   MIP $5

Bishop, 1992, Kenner, Gatlin gun,
  body breaks into two parts
  NM $3   MIP $5

Bull Alien, 1992, Kenner
  NM $3   MIP $5

Drake, 1992, Kenner
  NM $3   MIP $5

Gorilla Alien, 1992, Kenner
  NM $3   MIP $5

Hicks, 1992, Kenner
  NM $3   MIP $5

Queen Alien, 1992, Kenner
  NM $3   MIP $5

Ripley, 1992, Kenner, w/Turbo Torch
  NM $3   MIP $5

Scorpion Alien, 1992, Kenner
  NM $3   MIP $5

SERIES 2, 1993

Alien vs. Predator, 1993, Kenner,
  billed as the "ultimate battle
  between beast and hunter"
  NM $7   MIP $20

Flying Queen Alien, 1993, Kenner
  NM $3   MIP $10

Queen Face Hugger, 1993, Kenner
  NM $3   MIP $10

Snake Alien, 1993, Kenner
  NM $3   MIP $10

SERIES 3, 1994

Arachnid Alien, 1994, Kenner
  NM $4   MIP $10

Atax, 1994, Kenner
  NM $4   MIP $10

Clan Leader Predator, 1994, Kenner
  NM $4   MIP $10

Cracked Tusk Predator, 1994, Kenner
  NM $4   MIP $10

Hudson (foreign release), 1994, Kenner
  NM $4   MIP $10

Invisible Predator (mail-in), 1994,
  Kenner
  NM $3   MIP $10

Kill Krab Alien, 1994, Kenner
  NM $3   MIP $10

King Alien, 1994, Kenner
  NM $3   MIP $10

Lasershot Predator (electronic),
  1994, Kenner
  NM $3   MIP $10

Lava Predator, 1994, Kenner
  NM $3   MIP $10

Mantis Alien, 1994, Kenner
  NM $3   MIP $10

Night Cougar Alien, 1994, Kenner
  NM $3   MIP $10

Night Storm Predator, 1994, Kenner
  NM $3   MIP $10

O'Malley (foreign release), 1994,
  Kenner
  NM $3   MIP $12

Panther Alien, 1994, Kenner
  NM $3   MIP $10

Rhino Alien, 1994, Kenner
  NM $3   MIP $10

Spiked Tail Predator, 1994, Kenner
  NM $3   MIP $10

Stalker Predator, 1994, Kenner
  NM $3   MIP $10

Swarm Alien (electronic), 1994,
  Kenner
  NM $3   MIP $10

Vasquez (foreign release), 1994,
  Kenner
  NM $3   MIP $10

Wild Boar Alien, 1994, Kenner
  NM $3   MIP $10

Alpha Fight
(Toy Biz, 1999)

5" FIGURES

Northstar & Aurora, 1999
  NM $6   MIP $10

Sasquatch & Vindicator, 1999
  NM $6   MIP $10

Snowbird & Puck, 1999
  NM $6   MIP $12

American West
(Mego, 1973)

8" FIGURES

Buffalo Bill Cody, 1973, Mego, carded
  NM $35   MIP $100

Buffalo Bill Cody, 1973, Mego, boxed,
  shirt, pants, belt, two boots, rifle,
  hat, gun, holster
  NM $35   MIP $75

Cochise, 1973, Mego, carded
  NM $30   MIP $100

Cochise, 1973, Mego, boxed
  NM $30   MIP $75

Davy Crockett, 1973, Mego, carded
  NM $55   MIP $140

Davy Crockett, 1973, Mego, boxed
  NM $55   MIP $110

Shadow (horse), 1973, Mego, boxed
  NM $60   MIP $140

Sitting Bull, 1973, Mego, carded
  NM $35   MIP $125

Sitting Bull, 1973, Mego, boxed
  NM $35   MIP $90

Wild Bill Hickok, 1973, Mego, carded
  NM $35   MIP $125

Wild Bill Hickok, 1973, Mego, boxed
  NM $35   MIP $75

Wyatt Earp, 1973, Mego, carded
  NM $35   MIP $125

Wyatt Earp, 1973, Mego, boxed
  NM $35   MIP $75

PLAY SETS

Dodge City Play Set, 1973, Mego, vinyl
  NM $150   MIP $300

Angel (Moore Action Collectibles, 2002-04)

SERIES 1

Angel, Moore Action Collectibles
  NM $6   MIP $12

Cordelia, Moore Action Collectibles,
  summer show exclusive, red shirt
  w/short hair
  NM $6   MIP $15

Cordelia, Moore Action Collectibles
  NM $6   MIP $15

Faith, Moore Action Collectibles,
  Action Figure Express exclusive,
  leather jacket
  NM $6   MIP $15

Faith, Moore Action Collectibles
  NM $6   MIP $15

Slave Cordelia, Moore Action Collectibles, Suncoast exclusive, carded

    NM $5   **MIP** $10

Slave Cordelia, Moore Action Collectibles, ToyFare exclusive, boxed

    NM $5   **MIP** $10

Vampire Angel, Moore Action Collectibles, M.A.C. Collector's Club exclusive, leather jacket

    NM $6   **MIP** $15

Vampire Angel, Moore Action Collectibles, Diamond exclusive

    NM $6   **MIP** $15

SERIES 2

Lorne, Moore Action Collectibles, white jacket

    NM $5   **MIP** $15

Lorne, Moore Action Collectibles, red suit chase figure; "There's No Place Like Glrb"

    NM $6   **MIP** $15

Lorne, Moore Action Collectibles, Vegas: "The House Always Wins;" Time and Space Toys Wizard World Chicago exclusive

    NM $6   **MIP** $15

Wesley, Moore Action Collectibles, unpainted, Wizard World Philadelphia exclusive

    NM $4   **MIP** $12

Wesley, Moore Action Collectibles, "Waiting in the Wings;" Tower Records exclusive

    NM $4   **MIP** $12

Wesley, Moore Action Collectibles, "Season Four"

    NM $4   **MIP** $12

Wesley, Moore Action Collectibles, "Rain of Fire;" Time and Space Toys exclusive

    NM $4   **MIP** $12

Wesley, Moore Action Collectibles, "Parting Gifts;" ToyFare exclusive

    NM $4   **MIP** $12

Wesley, Moore Action Collectibles, "Bad Girls;" Diamond exclusive

    NM $4   **MIP** $12

SERIES 3

Angel, Moore Action Collectibles, "Graduation Day;" Suncoast exclusive

    NM $4   **MIP** $12

Angel, Moore Action Collectibles, "The Ring;" Action Figure Express exclusive

    NM $4   **MIP** $12

Angel, Moore Action Collectibles, "Season Five"

    NM $4   **MIP** $12

Fred, Moore Action Collectibles, "Season Three"

    NM $4   **MIP** $12

Illyria, Moore Action Collectibles, "Shells"

    NM $4   **MIP** $12

Illyria, Moore Action Collectibles, Diamond exclusive

    NM $4   **MIP** $12

Pylean Demon Angel, Moore Action Collectibles, Time and Space Toys exclusive

    NM $4   **MIP** $12

Vampire Angel w/Baby Connor, Moore Action Collectibles, Tower Records exclusive

    NM $4   **MIP** $12

Archies (Marx, 1975)

FIGURES

Archie, 1975, Marx, shown w/Jughead

    NM $15   **MIP** $60

Betty, 1975, Marx

    NM $15   **MIP** $50

Jughead, 1975, Marx

    NM $15   **MIP** $60

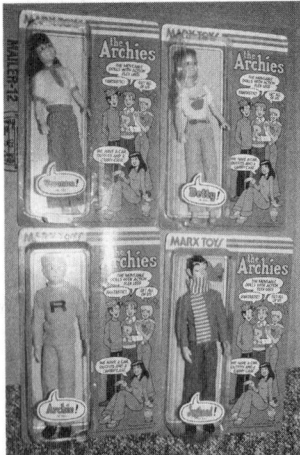

Veronica, 1975, Marx, shown w/Betty, Archie, Jughead

    NM $15   **MIP** $50

Army of Darkness (Sideshow Toys, 1998-Present)

12" FIGURES

Bruce Campbell as Ash, 1998, Sideshow Toys, #1301

    NM n/a   **MIP** $40

Evil Ash, 1998, Sideshow Toys, #1302

    NM n/a   **MIP** $40

Astronauts (Marx, 1969)

FIGURES

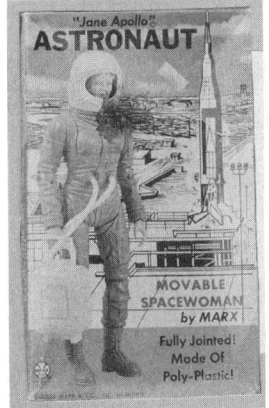

Jane Apollo Astronaut, 1969, Marx, movable, includes helmet and a variety of plastic accessories, much in the style of the "Best of the West" series

    NM $65   **MIP** $125

Johnny Apollo Astronaut, 1969, Marx, movable

    NM $125   **MIP** $200

Kennedy Space Center Astronaut, 1969, Marx, movable

    NM $65   **MIP** $140

A-Team (Galoob, 1984)

12" FIGURES

Mr. T, non-talking, 1984, Galoob

    NM $20   **MIP** $40

Mr. T, talking, 1984, Galoob

    NM $35   **MIP** $60

3-3/4" FIGURES AND ACCESSORIES

Armored Attack Adventure w/B.A. Figure, 1984, Galoob, vehicle w/3-3/4" figure

    NM $25   **MIP** $55

A-Team Four Figure Set, 1984, Galoob, 3-3/4" figures

    NM $22   **MIP** $42

Bad Guys Figure Set: Viper, Rattler, Cobra, Python, 1984, Galoob, 3-3/4" figures on card
    NM $18   MIP $35

Combat Attack Gyrocopter w/Murdock, 1984, Galoob, vehicle w/3-3/4" figure
    NM $20   MIP $45

Combat Headquarters w/four A-Team figures, 1984, Galoob, 3-3/4" figures
    NM $50   MIP $125

Corvette w/Face Figure, 1984, Galoob, vehicle and 3-3/4" figure
    NM $20   MIP $45

Motorized Patrol Boat, 1984, Galoob
    NM $15   MIP $35

Tactical Van Play Set, 1984, Galoob
    NM $75   MIP $100

6-1/2" FIGURES AND ACCESSORIES

Amy Allen, 1984, Galoob
    NM $30   MIP $60

B.A. Baracus, 1984, Galoob
    NM $15   MIP $40

Cobra, 1984, Galoob
    NM $12   MIP $20

Combat Attack Gyrocopter, 1984, Galoob
    NM $15   MIP $35

Face, 1984, Galoob
    NM $15   MIP $35

Hannibal, 1984, Galoob
    NM $15   MIP $40

(KP Photo, Karen O'Brien collection)

Murdock, 1984, Galoob
    NM $15   MIP $35

Off Road Attack Cycle, 1984, Galoob
    NM $8   MIP $20

Python, 1984, Galoob
    NM $12   MIP $25

Rattler, 1984, Galoob
    NM $12   MIP $25

Viper, 1984, Galoob
    NM $12   MIP $25

Avengers (Toy Biz, 1997-2000)
6" FIGURES

Iron Man, 1997, Toy Biz, w/"Power Converter"
    NM $4   MIP $8

Loki, 1997, Toy Biz
    NM $4   MIP $8

Scarlett Witch, 1997, Toy Biz
    NM $4   MIP $8

(Lenny Lee)

The Mighty Thor, 1997, Toy Biz, w/hammer
    NM $6   MIP $12

AVENGERS: UNITED THEY STAND

Ant-Man, 1999, Toy Biz
    NM $4   MIP $8

Captain America, 1999, Toy Biz
    NM $4   MIP $8

Ultron, 1999, Toy Biz
    NM $4   MIP $8

Vision, 1999, Toy Biz
    NM $4   MIP $8

Wasp, 1999, Toy Biz
    NM $4   MIP $8

SERIES II, 5" FIGURES

Falcon, 1999, Toy Biz
    NM $4   MIP $8

Hawkeye, 1999, Toy Biz
    NM $4   MIP $8

Kang, 1999, Toy Biz
    NM $4   MIP $8

Tigra, 1999, Toy Biz
    NM $4   MIP $8

Wonder Man, 1999, Toy Biz
    NM $4   MIP $8

SERIES III, 5" FIGURES

Ant-Man, 1999, Toy Biz
    NM $4   MIP $8

Hawkeye, 1999, Toy Biz
    NM $4   MIP $8

Iron Man, 1999, Toy Biz
    NM $4   MIP $8

Remnant I, 1999, Toy Biz
    NM $4   MIP $8

Thor, 1999, Toy Biz
    NM $4   MIP $8

SHAPE SHIFTERS

Ant-Man transforms into Armored Ant, 2000, Toy Biz
    NM $2   MIP $6

Captain America transform into American Eagle, 2000, Toy Biz
    NM $2   MIP $6

Hawykeye transforms into Armored Hawk, 2000, Toy Biz
    NM $2   MIP $6

Thor transforms into Flying Horse, 2000, Toy Biz
    NM $2   MIP $6

TEAM GIFT PACK

Hulk, Iron Man, Thor, Ant-Man/Giant Man, The Wasp, 1999, Toy Biz
    NM $8   MIP $30

Babylon 5 (Exclusive Toy Products, 1997)
6" FIGURES

Ambassador Delenn, 1997, Exclusive, Series I
    NM $3   MIP $7

Ambassador Delenn w/Minbari Flyer, Diamond Exclusive, 1997, Exclusive, Series I
    NM $3   MIP $7

Ambassador Juphar Trkider, 1997, Exclusive, Series IV
    NM $3   **MIP** $7

Ambassador Kosh, 1997, Exclusive, Series II
    NM $3   **MIP** $7

Ambassador Londo Mollari, 1997, Exclusive, Series I
    NM $3   **MIP** $7

Ambassador She'Lah, 1997, Exclusive, Series IV
    NM $3   **MIP** $17

Ambassador Vlur/Nhur, 1997, Exclusive
    NM $3   **MIP** $7

Captain Elizabeth Lochley, 1997, Exclusive, Series IV
    NM $3   **MIP** $7

Captain John Sheridan, 1997, Exclusive, Series I
    NM $3   **MIP** $7

Chief Garibaldi, 1997, Exclusive, Series III
    NM $3   **MIP** $7

G'Kar, 1997, Exclusive, Series I
    NM $3   **MIP** $7

G'Kar, green outfit, Diamond Exclusive, 1997, Exclusive, Series I
    NM $3   **MIP** $7

Lennier, 1997, Exclusive, Series III
    NM $4   **MIP** $7

Lyta Alexander, 1997, Exclusive, Series III
    NM $4   **MIP** $7

(KP Photo, Karen O'Brien collection)

Marcus Cole, 1997, Exclusive, Series II, w/White Star
    NM $3   **MIP** $7

PSI Cop Bester, 1997, Exclusive, Series IV
    NM $3   **MIP** $7

Shadow Sentient, Diamond Exclusive, 1997, Exclusive, Series III
    NM $5   **MIP** $15

Stephen Franklin, 1997, Exclusive, Series III
    NM $3   **MIP** $7

Susan Ivanova, 1997, Exclusive, Series II, w/Starfury
    NM $3   **MIP** $7

Susan Ivanova, White's Collecting Figures Exclusive, 1997, Exclusive, Series II
    NM $3   **MIP** $7

Vir Cotto, 1997, Exclusive, Series II
    NM $3   **MIP** $7

Vorlon Visitor, Diamond Exclusive, 1997, Exclusive, Series II
    NM $3   **MIP** $7

9" FIGURES

Ambassador Delenn, 1997, Exclusive, Series II
    NM $4   **MIP** $15

Ambassador G'Kar, 1997, Exclusive, Series II
    NM $4   **MIP** $15

Ambassador G'Kar, Diamond Exclusive, 1997, Exclusive, Series II
    NM $4   **MIP** $18

Ambassador Londo Mollari, 1997, Exclusive, gray hair, gold outfit
    NM $4   **MIP** $15

Chief Michael Garibaldi, 1997, Exclusive, Series III
    NM $4   **MIP** $15

John Sheridan, 1997, Exclusive, Series II
    NM $4   **MIP** $15

Lennier, Diamond Exclusive, 1997, Exclusive, Series I
    NM $4   **MIP** $15

Londo, 1997, Exclusive, Series III
    NM $4   **MIP** $15

Marcus Cole, 1997, Exclusive, Series I
    NM $4   **MIP** $15

Michael Garibaldi, 1997, Exclusive
    NM $4   **MIP** $15

Susan Ivanova, 1997, Exclusive, Series III
    NM $4   **MIP** $15

Vir Cotto, 1997, Exclusive, Series I
    NM $4   **MIP** $15

Banana Splits (Sutton, 1970)

FIGURES

Bingo the Bear, 1970, Sutton
    NM $75   **MIP** $150

Drooper the Lion, 1970, Sutton
    NM $75   **MIP** $150

Fleagle Beagle, 1970, Sutton
    NM $75   **MIP** $150

Snorky the Elephant, 1970, Sutton
    NM $75   **MIP** $150

Batman (Mattel, 2003-04)

FIGURES

Arctic Shield Batman, 2004, Mattel, w/arctic shield, axe launcher
    NM $3   **MIP** $12

Battle Armor Batman, 2003, Mattel, w/combat blade and battle armor
    NM $3   **MIP** $12

Battle Board Robin, 2003, Mattel, w/disc missile and battle board
    NM $3   **MIP** $12

Battle Board Robin - repaint, 2004, Mattel, green vest version
    NM $3   **MIP** $12

Battle Spike Batman, 2004, Mattel, spike gauntlets, battle armor
    NM $3   **MIP** $12

Croc Armor Batman, 2004, Mattel, wing blades, claws, armor
    NM $3   **MIP** $12

Drill Cannon Batman, 2004, Mattel, cannon, six missiles, battle wings, claw
    NM $3   **MIP** $12

Electro-Net Batman, 2004, Mattel, two disks, launcher, green armor
    NM $3   **MIP** $12

Hydro-Suit Batman, 2003, Mattel, w/dive pack, breathing mask, missile launcher
    NM $3   **MIP** $12

Ice Cannon Mr. Freeze, 2004, Mattel, w/ice cannon; version w/out goggles doubles value
    NM $3   **MIP** $12

Killer Croc, 2003, Mattel, bendable tail
    NM $3   **MIP** $12

Martial Arts Batman, 2003, Mattel, w/dual axe staff and hand blade
    NM $3   **MIP** $12

Night Patrol Batman, 2003, Mattel, deluxe figure w/shield and batarang launcher
    NM $3   **MIP** $12

Quick Fire Joker, 2003, Mattel, w/cane and gun
    NM $3   **MIP** $12

Sky Strike Batman, 2004, Mattel, deluxe, wing pack, net missile
    NM $3   **MIP** $12

Sling Strike Nightwing, 2004, Mattel, green costume
    NM $3   **MIP** $12

Snare Strike Batman, 2004, Mattel, retractable snare rope, missile launcher
    NM $3   **MIP** $12

Stealth Armor Batman, 2003, Mattel, deluxe, w/stealth armor, missile launcher, jet boots
    NM $3   **MIP** $12

Tech Armor Batman, 2003, Mattel, deluxe figure w/laser cannon, claw arm, disc missile launcher
    NM $3   **MIP** $12

(KP Photo, Karen O'Brien collection)

Zipline Batman, 2003, Mattel, w/zipline and batarang
    NM $3   **MIP** $15

MULTI-PACKS

Attack of the Penguin, 2004, Mattel, animated, Batman, Penguin, Nightwing, Batgirl
    NM $10   **MIP** $20

Batman and Nightwing, 2003, Mattel, new sculpt
    NM $5   **MIP** $8

Batman and Nightwing, 2003, Mattel, animated
    NM $4   **MIP** $10

Batman and Robin, 2003, Mattel, animated
    NM $4   **MIP** $10

Batman and Superman, 2003, Mattel, new sculpt
    NM $4   **MIP** $10

Batman vs. Joker, 2003, Mattel, animated
    NM $4   **MIP** $10

Battle Armor Batman & Quick Fire Joker, 2004, Mattel, combat blade, cane, quick-fire gun
    NM $4   **MIP** $10

Battle Scars, Batman vs. Catwoman, 2003, Mattel, animated
    NM $4   **MIP** $10

Gotham City Figures, 2004, Mattel, Batman, Robin, Nightwing, exclusive silver Batgirl
    NM $12   **MIP** $25

Gotham City Figures, Series 2, 2004, Mattel, Batman, Joker, Catwoman, Two-Face
    NM $12   **MIP** $25

Tech Suit Batman vs. Two-Face, 2003, Mattel, Animated
    NM $4   **MIP** $10

Zipline Batman & Battle Board Robin, 2004, Mattel, batarang, zipline, missile, battle board
    NM $4   **MIP** $10

VEHICLES

Batcopter, 2003, Mattel, fixed Batman figure
    NM $7   **MIP** $15

Batcycle, 2003, Mattel, fixed Batman figure
    NM $7   **MIP** $15

Batjet, 2003, Mattel, Batman figure, two missiles, retractable wing
    NM $12   **MIP** $20

Batmobile, 2003, Mattel, w/detachable Robin Cycle, recalled
    NM $35   **MIP** $65

Batplane, 2003, Mattel, Batman figure, two missiles
    NM $12   **MIP** $25

Batman & Robin (Kenner, 1997-98)

12" FIGURES

Batgirl, 1997-98, Kenner
    NM $10   **MIP** $25

Batman, 1997-98, Kenner
    NM $15   **MIP** $30

Batman and Poison Ivy, 1997-98, Kenner, two-pack, cloth outfits
    NM $12   **MIP** $20

(Kenner)

Ice Battle Batman (WB Exclusive), 1997-98, Kenner, includes Batarang and Bat Laser
    NM $4   **MIP** $10

Mr. Freeze, 1997-98, Kenner
    NM $8   **MIP** $15

Robin, 1997-98, Kenner
    NM $8   **MIP** $20

Ultimate Batman, 1997-98, Kenner
    NM $6   **MIP** $15

Ultimate Robin, 1997-98, Kenner
    NM $6   **MIP** $12

5" FIGURES

Bane, 1997, Kenner, Series 1, w/double-attack axe and colossial crusher gauntlet
    NM $3   **MIP** $5

Batgirl, 1997, Kenner, w/battle blade blaster and strike scythe
    NM $3   **MIP** $5

Batman, Ambush Attack, 1998, Kenner, Series 2, w/Arsenal Cape and Restraint Rockets
    NM $3   **MIP** $5

Batman, Battle Board w/Ring, 1997-98, Kenner
    NM $3   **MIP** $5

Batman, Heat Scan, 1997, Kenner, Series 1, w/opti-scope launcher and laser ray emitters
    NM $3   **MIP** $5

Batman, Hover Attack, 1997, Kenner, Series 1, w/Blasting battle sled and sickle shields
    NM $3   **MIP** $5

Batman, Ice Blade, 1997-98, Kenner
    NM $3   **MIP** $5

Batman, Ice Blade w/Ring, 1997-98, Kenner
    NM $3   **MIP** $5

Batman, Laser Cape w/Ring, 1997-98, Kenner

  NM $3 MIP $5

Batman, Mail Away from Fuji, 1997-98, Kenner

  NM $3 MIP $5

Batman, Neon Armor, 1997-98, Kenner

  NM $2 MIP $4

Batman, Neon Armor w/Ring, 1997-98, Kenner

  NM $2 MIP $4

Batman, Rotoblade w/Ring, 1997-98, Kenner

  NM $3 MIP $5

Batman, Sky Assault w/Ring, 1997-98, Kenner

  NM $3 MIP $5

Batman, Snow Tracker, 1997-98, Kenner

  NM $3 MIP $5

Batman, Thermal Shield w/Ring, 1998, Kenner, Series 2, w/Heatblast cape and flying disc blaster

  NM $3 MIP $5

Batman, Wing Blast, 1997-98, Kenner

  NM $3 MIP $5

Batman, Wing Blast w/Ring, 1997-98, Kenner

  NM $3 MIP $5

Bruce Wayne, Battle Gear, 1997, Kenner, Series 1, w/ice block armor suit and cryo claw shooter

  NM $3 MIP $5

Frostbite, 1997-98, Kenner

  NM $3 MIP $5

Jungle Venom Poison Ivy, 1997, Kenner, on the left, Batgirl on right; Series 1, w/toxic spray venom cannon and entanglement vines

  NM $3 MIP $5

Mr. Freeze, Ultimate Armor w/Ring, 1997, Kenner, Series 2, w/freeze-on missile

  NM $3 MIP $5

Robin, Attack Wing w/Ring, 1998, Kenner, Series 2, w/vertical assault cape

  NM $3 MIP $5

Robin, Blade Blast, 1998, Kenner, Series 2, w/rapid deploy vine slicers and blasting battle spear

  NM $3 MIP $5

Robin, Iceboard, 1997-98, Kenner

  NM $3 MIP $5

Robin, Razor Skate, 1997, Kenner, Series 1, w/chopping blade launcher and ice battle armor

  NM $3 MIP $5

Robin, Talon Strike, 1998, Kenner, Series 2, w/twin capture claws and roto blade

  NM $3 MIP $5

Robin, Talon Strike w/Ring, 1997-98, Kenner

  NM $3 MIP $5

Robin, Triple Strike, 1997-98, Kenner

  NM $3 MIP $5

Robin, Triple Strike w/Ring, 1997-98, Kenner

  NM $3 MIP $5

ACCESSORIES

Batmobile, 1998, Kenner

  NM $8 MIP $20

Batmobile, Sonic, 1998, Kenner

  NM $8 MIP $15

Cryo Freeze Chamber, 1998, Kenner

  NM $3 MIP $7

Ice Fortress, 1998, Kenner

  NM $5 MIP $7

Ice Hammer, 1998, Kenner

  NM $8 MIP $15

Iceglow Bathammer, 1997, Kenner

  NM $8 MIP $15

Jet Blade, 1998, Kenner

  NM $6 MIP $15

NightSphere, 1998, Kenner

  NM $12 MIP $25

Wayne Manor Batcave, 1998, Kenner

  NM $23 MIP $53

DELUXE FIGURES, 1997

Batgirl w/Icestrike Cycle, 1997, Kenner, w/snow assault mode and razor wheel launcher

  NM $8 MIP $12

Batman, 1998, Kenner

  NM $3 MIP $5

Batman, Blast Wing, 1997, Kenner, w/ice chopper hover pack and freeze-seeker missile

  NM $3 MIP $5

Batman, Rooftop Pursuit, 1997, Kenner

  NM $3 MIP $5

Mr. Freeze, Ice Terror, 1997, Kenner

  NM $3 MIP $5

Robin, 1998, Kenner

  NM $3 MIP $5

Robin, Blast Wing, 1997, Kenner

  NM $3 MIP $5

Robin, Glacier Battle, 1997, Kenner, Tandem Assault Snow Skiff and Stinger Missile

  NM $3 MIP $5

Robin, Redbird Cycle, 1997, Kenner, w/Night strike missile and ice slice blades

  NM $8 MIP $18

FIGURES

Aerial Combat Batman, 1997, Kenner

  NM $3 MIP $5

Mr. Freeze, Iceblast, 1997, Kenner, Series 1, w/Ice ray cannon and rocket thrusters

  NM $3 MIP $6

Mr. Freeze, Jet Wing w/Ring, 1998, Kenner, Series 2, w/Glacier assault wing and ice blaster

  NM $3 MIP $6

TWO-PACK FIGURES, 1998

A Cold Night At Gotham, 1998, Kenner

  NM $5 MIP $8

Batman vs. Poison Ivy, 1998, Kenner

  NM $10 MIP $22

Brain vs. Brawn, 1998, Kenner, Batman and Bane

  NM $5 MIP $8

Challengers Of The Night, 1998, Kenner

  NM $5 MIP $10

Guardians Of Gotham, 1998, Kenner, Batman and Robin

  NM $5 MIP $8

Night Hunter Robin vs. Evil Entrapment Poison Ivy, 1998, Kenner

  NM $5 MIP $8

Batman 100th Edition Figure

FIGURES

Batman, 1996, Hasbro, w/diorama display stand
NM $2 **MIP** $9

Batman 200th Edition Figure

FIGURES

Batman, 2001, Hasbro, Batman Beyond figure w/cloth wings
NM $12 **MIP** $25

Batman Beyond (Hasbro, 1999-01)

ACCESSORIES

Street-to-Sky Batmobile, 1999-01, Hasbro
NM $10 **MIP** $22

FIGURES

Ballistic Blade Batman, 1999-01, Hasbro, w/Batarang Disc Barrage
NM $5 **MIP** $10

Bat Hang Batman, 1999-01, Hasbro, w/covert Cape and Upside-down action
NM $5 **MIP** $10

Blight, 1999-01, Hasbro, w/Radiation Blaster and Plasma Missile
NM $8 **MIP** $15

Covert Batman, 1999-01, Hasbro, w/Shield Cape and Retriever Missile
NM $5 **MIP** $10

Energy Strike Batman, 1999-01, Hasbro, w/Lightning Cape and Neutron Weapons
NM $5 **MIP** $10

Future Knight Batman, 1999-01, Hasbro, w/Glide Wings and Electro Swords
NM $5 **MIP** $10

Hydro-Force Batman, 1999-01, Hasbro, w/Aqua Torpedo and Propulsion Armor
NM $5 **MIP** $10

J's Gang Power Throw, 1999-01, Hasbro, Happy tosses Smirk!
NM $5 **MIP** $10

Laser Batman, 1999-01, Hasbro, w/Hyper Flight gear and Pulse Missile
NM $5 **MIP** $10

Lightning Storm Batman, 1999-01, Hasbro, w/Forcefields and Lightning Weapons
NM $5 **MIP** $10

Manta Racer Batman, 1999-01, Hasbro, w/Surf Sled and Stinger Tail
NM $5 **MIP** $10

Neon Camo Batman, 1999-01, Hasbro, Deluxe figure w/Pump Action Launcher and combat ready canine
NM $5 **MIP** $10

Power Armor Batman, 1999-01, Hasbro, w/Anti-Gravity and Strike R.O.B.I.N.
NM $5 **MIP** $10

Power Cape Batman, 1999-01, Hasbro, w/Jet Thrusters and Sual Batarang
NM $5 **MIP** $10

Sonar Strike Batman, 1999-01, Hasbro, w/Ramjet Rocket Pack and Dual Wing Blast
NM $5 **MIP** $10

Strato Defense Batman, 1999-01, Hasbro, Deluxe figure w/Knight hunter patrol jet and Thermal disc blaster
NM $5 **MIP** $10

Strikecycle Batman, 1999-01, Hasbro, Deluxe figure
NM $5 **MIP** $10

Surface-to-Air Batman, 1999-01, Hasbro, w/Converting mobile assault cape
NM $5 **MIP** $10

The Jokerz, 1999-01, Hasbro, w/Assault Hover Cycle
NM $5 **MIP** $10

Tomorrow Armor Batman, 1999-01, Hasbro, deluxe figure
NM $5 **MIP** $10

Batman Beyond: Batlink (Hasbro 2000-01)

ACCESSORIES

Net Escape Play Set, 2000-01, Hasbro
NM $8 **MIP** $15

Netrunner Batmobile, 2000-01, Hasbro
NM $10 **MIP** $15

Virtual Bat, 2000-01, Hasbro, vehicle lights up Batlink figures
NM $5 **MIP** $10

FIGURES

Circutry Storm Batman, 2000-01, Hasbro
NM $3 **MIP** $7

Codebuster Batman, 2000-01, Hasbro, w/Optical Disk Phaser
NM $3 **MIP** $7

Energy Surge Batman, 2000-01, Hasbro, w/Batlink story on CD-ROM
NM $3 **MIP** $7

Firewall Robin, 2000-01, Hasbro, w/Anti-virus Blaster
NM $3 **MIP** $7

Mainframe Attack Batman, 2000-01, Hasbro
NM $3 **MIP** $7

Particle Burst Batman, 2000-01, Hasbro, w/Quantimizer Batarang
NM $3 **MIP** $7

Power Grid Batman, 2000-01, Hasbro, w/five-finger Booster Shield
NM $3 **MIP** $7

Search Engine Batman, 2000-01, Hasbro, w/Cyberscope vision
NM $3 **MIP** $7

Virtual Joker, 2000-01, Hasbro, w/Virus-tech lasers and Byte mouth
NM $3 **MIP** $7

Batman Beyond: Return of the Joker (Hasbro, 2000)

FIGURES

Arkham Assault Joker, 2000, Hasbro, w/secret image card launcher
NM $3 **MIP** $7

Golden Armor Batman, 2000, Hasbro
NM $3 **MIP** $7

Gotham Defender Batman, 2000, Hasbro
NM $3 **MIP** $7

Gotham Knight Batman, 2000, Hasbro, w/Jet-Booster Cape and Ion Swords
NM $3 **MIP** $7

Rapid Switch Bruce Wayne, 2000, Hasbro, w/Quick change outfit and Disk launcher
NM $3 **MIP** $7

Batman Forever (Kenner, 1995)

ACCESSORIES

Batboat, 1995, Kenner
NM $15 **MIP** $25

Batcave, 1995, Kenner, play set
 NM $25   **MIP** $50

Batmobile, 1995, Kenner, remote control
 NM $20   **MIP** $40

Batwing, 1995, Kenner
 NM $10   **MIP** $25

Robin Cycle, 1995, Kenner, vehicle only, no figure
 NM $7   **MIP** $12

Triple Action Vehicle Set, 1995, Kenner, Batmobile, Batwing, Batboat
 NM $20   **MIP** $40

Wayne Manor, 1995, Kenner, play set
 NM $25   **MIP** $50

FIGURES

Attack Wing Batman, 1995, Kenner, deluxe figure
 NM $4   **MIP** $10

Batarang Batman, 1995, Kenner, Series 2
 NM $3   **MIP** $7

Blast Cape Batman, 1995, Kenner, Series 1, w/assault blades and launching attack cape
 NM $3   **MIP** $7

Bruce Wayne/Batman, 1996, Kenner, Target Exclusive, w/snap-on crimefighting armor and side swords
 NM $3   **MIP** $7

Fireguard Batman, 1995, Kenner, Series 1, w/spinning attack cape
 NM $3   **MIP** $7

Hydro Claw Robin, 1995, Kenner, Series 1, w/aqua attack launcher and diving gear
 NM $3   **MIP** $7

Ice Blade Batman, 1995, Kenner, Series 2
 NM $3   **MIP** $7

Laser Disc Batman, 1995, Kenner, deluxe figure
 NM $3   **MIP** $7

Lightwing Batman, 1995, Kenner, deluxe figure w/electra-glow wings and lightning launcher
 NM $3   **MIP** $7

Manta Ray Batman, 1995, Kenner, Series 1, w/firing sea sled and pop-out breathing gear
 NM $3   **MIP** $7

Martial Arts Robin, 1995, Kenner, deluxe figure
 NM $3   **MIP** $7

Neon Armor Batman, 1995, Kenner, Series 2
 NM $3   **MIP** $7

Night Flight Batman, 1995, Kenner, w/winged backpack
 NM $3   **MIP** $7

Night Hunter Batman, 1995, Kenner, Series 1
 NM $3   **MIP** $7

Power Beacon Batman, 1995, Kenner, Series 2
 NM $3   **MIP** $7

Recon Hunter Batman, 1995, Kenner, Series 2, w/missile firing surveillance drone
 NM $3   **MIP** $7

Skyboard Robin, 1995, Kenner, Series 2, w/missile blasting pursuit vehicle
 NM $3   **MIP** $7

Solar Shield Batman, 1995, Kenner, Series 2
 NM $3   **MIP** $7

Sonar Sensor Batman, 1995, Kenner, Series 1, w/flying disc blaster and pop-up sonar scope
 NM $3   **MIP** $7

Street Biker Robin, 1995, Kenner, Series 1, w/launching grappling hooks and battle staff
 NM $3   **MIP** $7

Street Racer Batman, 1995, Kenner, Series 2
 NM $3   **MIP** $7

The Riddler, 1995, Kenner, Target Exclusive, w/brain drain helmet, green figure w/silver trim
 NM $3   **MIP** $7

The Riddler w/Brain Drain, 1995, Kenner, Series 1, w/brain drain helmet, green figure w/black trim
 NM $3   **MIP** $7

The Riddler w/Question Mark Bazooka, 1995, Kenner, Series 2, w/question mark gun, black figure w/green trim
 NM $3   **MIP** $7

The Talking Riddler, 1995, Kenner, deluxe figure, says three movie phrases
 NM $3   **MIP** $7

Tide Racer Robin, 1995, Kenner, Target Exclusive, w/deep dive gear and sea claw launcher
 NM $3   **MIP** $7

Transforming Bruce Wayne, 1995, Kenner, Series 1, Target Exclusive
 NM $3   **MIP** $7

Transforming Dick Grayson, 1995, Kenner, Series 1, w/crime fighting suit and sudden reveal mask
 NM $3   **MIP** $7

Triple Strike Robin, 1995, Kenner, Series 2
 NM $3   **MIP** $7

Two-Face, 1995, Kenner, Series 1, w/coin
 NM $3   **MIP** $7

Wing Blast Batman, 1995, Kenner, Series 2, w/sudden alert bio wings
 NM $3   **MIP** $7

MULTI-PACKS

Batman v. The Riddler, 1995, Kenner, Batman, Riddler
 NM $6   **MIP** $12

Guardians of Gotham City, 1995, Kenner, Batman and Robin
 NM $8   **MIP** $16

Riddler and Two-Face, 1995, Kenner
 NM $6   **MIP** $14

Batman Movie Collection (Kenner, 1997)

FIGURES

Batman v. Catwoman, 1997, Kenner, Batman Returns, Toys R Us
 NM $10   **MIP** $20

Batman v. Joker, 1997, Kenner, Batman movie, Toys R Us
 NM $10   **MIP** $20

Batman v. Riddler, 1997, Kenner, Batman Forever, Toys R Us
 NM $10   **MIP** $20

Batman Returns (Kenner, 1992-94)

FIGURES

Aerostrike Batman, 1993, Kenner, Series 1
 NM $3   **MIP** $7

Air Attack Batman, 1992, Kenner, Series 1, w/camouflage artillary gear
 NM $3   **MIP** $7

Arctic Batman, 1992, Kenner, Series 1
 NM $3   **MIP** $7

Batman, 16", 1992-94, Kenner
 NM $10   **MIP** $25

Bola Strike Batman, 1992, Kenner, Toys R Us Exclusive boxed figure
 NM $3   **MIP** $7

Bruce Wayne, 1992, Kenner, Series 1, w/quick change Batman armor
 NM $3   **MIP** $7

Catwoman, 1992, Kenner, Series 1, w/whipping arm action and taser gun
 NM $3   **MIP** $7

Claw Climber Batman, 1992, Kenner, Toys R Us Exclusive boxed figure
    NM $3   MIP $7

Crime Attack Batman, 1992, Kenner, Series 1
    NM $3   MIP $7

Deep Dive Batman, 1992, Kenner, Series 1, w/torpedo launching scuba gear
    NM $3   MIP $7

Firebolt Batman, 1992, Kenner, Toys R Us Exclusive boxed electronic figure
    NM $5   MIP $10

Glider Batman, 1992-94, Kenner
    NM $3   MIP $7

High Wire Batman, 1992-94, Kenner
    NM $3   MIP $7

Hydrocharge Batman, 1994, Kenner, Series 2, w/water blast missile
    NM $3   MIP $7

Jungle Tracker Batman, 1994, Kenner, Series 2, w/shoulder mount launcher
    NM $3   MIP $7

Laser Batman, 1992, Kenner, Series 1
    NM $3   MIP $7

Night Climber Batman, 1994, Kenner, Series 2
    NM $3   MIP $7

Penguin, 1992, Kenner, Series 1
    NM $3   MIP $7

Penguin Commandos, 1992, Kenner, Series 1, w/mind control gear and missiles
    NM $3   MIP $7

Polar Blast Batman, 1992, Kenner, Toys R Us Exclusive boxed figure
    NM $3   MIP $7

Powerwing Batman, 1992, Kenner, Series 1, wing fires missile
    NM $3   MIP $7

Robin, 1992, Kenner, Series 1, on the left, shown here w/Catwoman; w/launching grappling hook
    NM $3   MIP $7

Rocket Blast Batman, 1992, Kenner, Toys R Us Exclusive, boxed electronic figure
    NM $3   MIP $7

Shadow Wing Batman, 1992, Kenner, Series 1
    NM $3   MIP $7

Sky Winch Batman, 1992, Kenner, Series 1
    NM $3   MIP $7

Thunder Strike Batman, 1992-94, Kenner
    NM $3   MIP $7

Thunder Whip Batman, 1992, Kenner, Series 1
    NM $3   MIP $7

VEHICLES

All-Terrain Batskiboat, 1992, Kenner
    NM $18   MIP $30

Bat Cycle, 1992, Kenner
    NM $5   MIP $15

Batcave Command Center, 1992, Kenner
    NM $25   MIP $65

Batmissile Batmobile, 1992, Kenner, removable sides reveal Batmissile
    NM $45   MIP $80

Batmobile, 1992, Kenner
    NM $20   MIP $65

Bat-Signal Jet, 1992, Kenner
    NM $4   MIP $12

Bruce Wayne Custom Coupe, 1992, Kenner
    NM $10   MIP $22

Camo Attack Batmobile, 1994, Kenner
    NM $22   MIP $60

Penguin Umbrella Jet, 1992, Kenner, w/two umbrella bombs
    NM $8   MIP $18

Robin Jetfoil, 1992, Kenner
    NM $6   MIP $18

Sky Blade, 1992, Kenner
    NM $15   MIP $35

Sky Drop, 1992, Kenner, airship w/hidden compartment
    NM $10   MIP $20

Batman: Crime Squad (Kenner, 1995-96)

ACCESSORIES

Batcycle, 1995, Kenner, Series 1 vehicle
    NM $10   MIP $20

Triple Attack Jet, 1995, Kenner, Series 1, Batman: The Animated Series card
    NM $8   MIP $20

FIGURES

Air Assault Batman, 1995, Kenner, Series 1, Batman: The Animated Series card
    NM $5   MIP $12

Bomb Control Batman, 1996, Kenner, Series 2, The Adventures of Batman and Robin card
    NM $5   MIP $12

Disaster Control Batman, 1996, Kenner, Series 2, The Adventures of Batman and Robin card
    NM $5   MIP $12

Fast Pursuit Batman, 1996, Kenner, Series 2, The Adventures of Batman and Robin card
    NM $5   MIP $12

Land Strike Batman, 1995, Kenner, Series 1, Batman: The Animated Series card
    NM $5   MIP $12

Piranha Blade Batman, 1995, Kenner, Series 1, Batman: The Animated Series card
    NM $5   MIP $12

Sea Claw Batman, 1995, Kenner, Series 1, Batman: The Animated Series card
    NM $5   MIP $12

Ski Blast Robin, 1995, Kenner, Series 1, Batman: The Animated Series card
    NM $5   MIP $12

Skycopter Batman, 1996, Kenner, Series 2, deluxe figure, Batman: The Adventures of Batman and Robin
    NM $5   MIP $12

Stealthwing Batman, 1995, Kenner, Series 1, Batman: The Animated Series card
    NM $5   MIP $12

Supersonic Batman, 1996, Kenner, Series 2, The Adventures of Batman and Robin card
    NM $5   MIP $12

Torpedo Batman, 1995, Kenner, Series 1, Batman: The Animated Series card
    NM $5   MIP $12

Tri-Wing Batman, 1996, Kenner, Series 2, deluxe figure, Batman: The Adventures of Batman and Robin, w/Techno-glide backpack
    NM $5   MIP $12

Batman: Knight Force Ninjas (Hasbro, 1998-99)

FIGURES

Arsenal Cape Batman, 1999, Kenner, Series 3
    NM $3   MIP $8

Batman Ally Azrael, 1998, Kenner, Series 2
    NM $3   MIP $8

Batman vs. The Joker, 1998, Kenner, Series 1

NM $5   **MIP** $10

Fist Fury Batman, 1998, Kenner, Series 2

NM $3   **MIP** $8

Hyper Crush Robin, 1999, Kenner, Series 3

NM $3   **MIP** $8

Karate Chop Batman, 1998, Kenner, Series 1

NM $3   **MIP** $8

Knight Blade Batman, 1999, Kenner, Series 3

NM $3   **MIP** $8

Multi-Blast Batman, 1998, Kenner, rare

NM $3   **MIP** $8

Power Kick Batman, 1998, Kenner, Series 1

NM $3   **MIP** $8

Side Strike Robin, 1998, Kenner, Series 1

NM $3   **MIP** $8

Tail Whip Killer Croc, 1998, Kenner, Series 1

NM $3   **MIP** $8

Thunder Kick Batman, 1998, Kenner, Series 2

NM $3   **MIP** $8

Tornado Blade Riddler, 1998, Kenner, Series 2

NM $3   **MIP** $8

VEHICLES

Knight Force Batmobile, 1998, Kenner

NM $8   **MIP** $18

Batman: Legends of Batman (Kenner 1994-96)

12" FIGURES

Batman vs. Catwoman, 1994-96, Kenner, figures in cloth costumes

NM $20   **MIP** $40

ACCESSORIES

Batcycle, 1994, Kenner, w/Batman rider

NM $10   **MIP** $25

Batmobile, 1994-96, Kenner, w/missile detonator and quick lift canopy

NM $10   **MIP** $22

Sky Bat, 1994-96, Kenner, w/wing mount missile and menacing jaw attack

NM $12   **MIP** $30

FIGURES

Buccaneer Batman, 1996, Kenner, Series 3, w/slamming mace actions and pirate sword

NM $3   **MIP** $8

Catwoman, 1994, Kenner, Series 1, w/quick climb claw and capture net

NM $3   **MIP** $8

Crusader Batman, 1994, Kenner, Series 1, w/punching action

NM $3   **MIP** $8

Crusader Robin, 1995, Kenner, Series 2, w/firing crossbow and battle shield

NM $3   **MIP** $8

Cyborg Batman, 1994, Kenner, Series 1, w/light-up eye and laser weapon

NM $3   **MIP** $8

Dark Rider Batman, 1994, Kenner, Series 1, featuring battle stallion

NM $7   **MIP** $14

Dark Warrior Batman, 1995, Kenner, Series 2, w/slamming mace attack

NM $3   **MIP** $8

Desert Knight Batman, 1995, Kenner, Series 2, deluxe figure w/whirling scimitar swords and double battle axes

NM $3   **MIP** $8

First Mate Robin, 1996, Kenner, Series 3, blasting cannon and cutlass sword

NM $3   **MIP** $8

Flightpak Batman, 1995, Kenner, Series 2, deluxe figure w/battle ready jet-wing

NM $3   **MIP** $8

Future Batman, 1994, Kenner, Series 1, w/pop-up aero-power wings

NM $3   **MIP** $8

Gladiator Batman, 1996, Kenner, Series 3, w/spear launcher

NM $3   **MIP** $8

Knightquest Batman, 1994, Kenner, Series 1, Azrael w/Battle wings and blazing missile

NM $3   **MIP** $8

Knightsend Batman, 1995, Kenner, Series 2, Jean-Paul Valley w/Arial torpedo launcher

NM $3   **MIP** $8

Long Bow Batman, 1995, Kenner, Series 2, w/arrow slinging assault

NM $3   **MIP** $8

Nightwing, 1994, Kenner, Series 1, w/super-strike rocket launcher

NM $3   **MIP** $8

Power Guardian Batman, 1994, Kenner, Series 1, w/real sword fighting action and shield

NM $3   **MIP** $8

Samuri Batman, 1995, Kenner, Series 2, w/slashing sword and banner

NM $3   **MIP** $8

Silver Knight Batman, 1995, Kenner, Series 2, deluxe figure w/smashing battle axe and slashing sword

NM $3   **MIP** $8

The Joker, 1994, Kenner, Series 1, w/snapping jaw

NM $3   **MIP** $8

The Laughing Man Joker, 1996, Kenner, Series 3, w/gatling gun, pirate outfit

NM $3   **MIP** $8

The Riddler, 1995, Kenner, Series 2, w/firing question mark ammo

NM $3   **MIP** $8

Ultra Armor Batman, 1996, Kenner, Series 3, Azrael w/blasting battle cannon

NM $3   **MIP** $8

Viking Batman, 1995, Kenner, Series 2, w/battle axe and shield

NM $3   **MIP** $8

MULTI-PACKS

Egyptian Batman and Egyptian Catwoman, 1994-96, Kenner

NM $3   **MIP** $10

Pirate Batman vs. Pirate Two-Face, 1994-96, Kenner

NM $3   **MIP** $10

Batman: Legends of the Dark Knight (Kenner, 1996-98)

ACCESSORIES

Skywing Street Bike, 1996, Kenner, w/Batman figure

NM $8   **MIP** $15

FIGURES

Assault Gauntlet Batman, 1996, Kenner, w/neural pumped power and Spike strike missile gloves

NM $3   **MIP** $10

Bat Attack Batman, 1997, Kenner

NM $3   **MIP** $8

Batgirl, 1998, Kenner, w/Knightscan wings and Batarang

NM $3   **MIP** $8

Batman The Dark Knight, 1998, Kenner, blue and gray costume

NM $4   **MIP** $10

Batman The Dark Knight, 1998, Kenner, black costume re-issue

NM $6   **MIP** $12

Clayface, 1996-98, Kenner, Internet exclusive

NM $4   **MIP** $12

Dark Knight Detective Batman, 1996-98, Kenner, Internet exclusive
    NM $6   **MIP** $14

Dive Claw Robin, 1996, Kenner, w/Blast Attack Missile and Power Glide Wings
    NM $3   **MIP** $8

Glacier Shield Batman, 1997, Kenner
    NM $3   **MIP** $8

Jungle Rage Robin, 1998, Kenner, w/Battle Staff and Utility Gauntlet
    NM $3   **MIP** $8

Laughing Gas Joker, 1997, Kenner
    NM $3   **MIP** $8

Lava Fury Batman, 1998, Kenner, w/Solar arrary wings, fire swallower blast shield
    NM $3   **MIP** $8

Lethal Impact Bane, 1996-98, Kenner, w/venom-powered punch and stinger gauntlet
    NM $3   **MIP** $8

Man-Bat, 1998, Kenner
    NM $3   **MIP** $8

Neutral Claw Batman, 1996, Kenner
    NM $3   **MIP** $8

Panther Prowl Catwoman, 1997, Kenner, w/Battle panther exoskeleton
    NM $3   **MIP** $8

Penguin, 1998, Kenner, w/Spinning Attack Umbrella
    NM $3   **MIP** $8

Shatter Blade Batman, 1996-98, Kenner, w/Assault cape and arm swords
    NM $3   **MIP** $8

Spline Cape Batman, 1996, Kenner
    NM $3   **MIP** $8

Twister Strike Scarecrow, 1996, Kenner, w/Scythe Slash attack and Nightmare glow eyes
    NM $3   **MIP** $8

Underwater Assault Batman, 1998, Kenner
    NM $3   **MIP** $8

Batman: Mask of the Phantasm (Kenner, 1994)

FIGURES

Decoy Batman, 1994, Kenner
    NM $4   **MIP** $8

Jet Pack Joker (green face), 1994, Kenner
    NM $4   **MIP** $8

Jet Pack Joker (white face), 1994, Kenner
    NM $4   **MIP** $8

Phantasm, 1994, Kenner
    NM $4   **MIP** $8

Rapid Attack Batman, 1994, Kenner, also released on Batman: The Animated Series card
    NM $4   **MIP** $8

Retro Batman, 1994, Kenner
    NM $4   **MIP** $8

Tornado Batman, 1994, Kenner, also released on Batman: The Animated Series card
    NM $4   **MIP** $8

(Mark Bellomo collection)

Total Armor Batman, 1994, Kenner
    NM $4   **MIP** $8

Batman: Mission Masters (Hasbro, 1997-2002)

SERIES 1 FIGURES

Anti-Blaze Batman, 1997-2002, Hasbro, Series 1
    NM $3   **MIP** $7

Arctic Blast Robin, 1997-2002, Hasbro, Series 1
    NM $3   **MIP** $7

Cave Climber Batman, 1997-2002, Hasbro, Series 1
    NM $3   **MIP** $7

Desert Attack Batman, 1997-2002, Hasbro, Series 1
    NM $3   **MIP** $7

Glider Strike Batman, 1997-2002, Hasbro, Series 1
    NM $3   **MIP** $7

Insect-Body Mr.Freeze, 1997-2002, Hasbro, Series 1, head detaches from body, attaches to insect legs
    NM $3   **MIP** $7

Jungle Tracker Batman, 1997-2002, Hasbro, Series 1
    NM $3   **MIP** $7

Mr. Freeze, 1997-2002, Hasbro, Series 1
    NM $5   **MIP** $7

Rumble Ready Riddler, 1997-2002, Hasbro, Series 1
    NM $6   **MIP** $15

Slalom Racer Batman, 1997-2002, Hasbro, Series 1
    NM $3   **MIP** $7

Speedboat Batman, 1997-2002, Hasbro, Series 1
    NM $3   **MIP** $7

SERIES 2 FIGURES

Arctic Ambush Robin, 1997-2002, Hasbro, Series 2
    NM $3   **MIP** $7

Desert Attack Batman, 1997-2002, Hasbro, Series 2
    NM $3   **MIP** $7

Hydro Assault Joker, 1997-2002, Hasbro, Series 2
    NM $3   **MIP** $7

Knight Strike Batman, 1997-2002, Hasbro, Series 2
    NM $3   **MIP** $7

Land Strike Batman, 1997-2002, Hasbro, Series 2
    NM $3   **MIP** $7

Radar Batman, 1997-2002, Hasbro, Series 2, deluxe figure
    NM $3   **MIP** $7

Sea Claw Batman, 1997-2002, Hasbro, Series 2
    NM $3   **MIP** $7

Skychopper Batman, 1997-2002, Hasbro, Series 2, deluxe figure
    NM $3   **MIP** $7

SERIES 3 FIGURES

Capture Cape Batman, 1997-2002, Hasbro, Series 3
    NM $3   **MIP** $7

Firewing Batman, 1997-2002, Hasbro, Series 3
    NM $3   **MIP** $7

Freestyle Skate Batman, 1997-2002, Hasbro, Series 3
    NM $3   **MIP** $7

Gotham Crusader Batman, 1997-2002, Hasbro, Series 3
    NM $3   **MIP** $7

Ground Pursuit Batman, 1997-2002, Hasbro, Series 3
    NM $3   **MIP** $7

Highwire Zip Line Batman, 1997-2002, Hasbro, Series 3
    NM $3   **MIP** $7

Inferno Extinction Batman, 1997-2002, Hasbro, Series 3
    NM $3   **MIP** $7

Knight Assault Batman, 1997-2002, Hasbro, Series 3
    NM $3   **MIP** $7

Mountain Pursuit Batman, 1997-2002, Hasbro, Series 3
    NM $3   **MIP** $7

Quick Attack Batman, 1997-2002, Hasbro, Series 3
    NM $3   **MIP** $7

Sky Attack Batman, 1997-2002, Hasbro, Series 3
    NM $3   **MIP** $7

Virus Attack Mr. Freeze, 1997-2002, Hasbro, Series 3
    NM $3   **MIP** $7

Virus Delete Batman, 1997-2002, Hasbro, Series 3
    NM $3   **MIP** $7

SERIES 4 ACCESSORIES

B.A.T.V., 1997-2002, Hasbro, Batman all-terrain vehicle and projectile launcher w/Batman figure
    NM $10   **MIP** $15

Team Batcycle, 1997-2002, Hasbro, w/Batman and Nightwing
    NM $10   **MIP** $15

SERIES 4 FIGURES

Attack Wing Batman, 1997-2002, Hasbro, deluxe figure w/flight mechanized wings
    NM $3   **MIP** $7

Battle Staff Batman, 1997-2002, Hasbro, w/Hover Jet
    NM $3   **MIP** $7

Jet Wing Batman, 1997-2002, Hasbro, w/Rocket Strike Blaster
    NM $3   **MIP** $7

Lunar Force Batman, 1997-2002, Hasbro, w/Night Attack Wing
    NM $3   **MIP** $7

Midnight Hunter Batman, 1997-2002, Hasbro
    NM $3   **MIP** $7

Midnight Pursuit Batman, 1997-2002, Hasbro, w/Night Assault Jet
    NM $3   **MIP** $7

Midnight Rescue Batman, 1997-2002, Hasbro, w/Strike Wing
    NM $3   **MIP** $7

Night Assault Batman, 1997-2002, Hasbro, deluxe figure w/Land Runner
    NM $3   **MIP** $7

Night Fury Robin, 1997-2002, Hasbro, w/Triple Bolo Striker
    NM $3   **MIP** $7

Night Shadow Batman, 1997-2002, Hasbro
    NM $3   **MIP** $7

Night Spark Joker, 1997-2002, Hasbro, w/Wildcard Launcher
    NM $4   **MIP** $12

Photon Armor Batman, 1997-2002, Hasbro, w/Shadow Blast Cape
    NM $3   **MIP** $7

Rocket Blast Mr. Freeze, 1997-2002, Hasbro, w/Ice Disk Launcher
    NM $4   **MIP** $7

Shadow Blast Batman, 1997-2002, Hasbro, deluxe figure w/Night Charge Hoverpack
    NM $3   **MIP** $7

Shadow Copter Batman, 1997-2002, Hasbro, deluxe figure w/Night Sting Missile
    NM $3   **MIP** $7

Tunnel Racer Batman, 1997-2002, Hasbro, w/Lightning Luge and Homing Batarang
    NM $3   **MIP** $7

Turbo Force Nightwing, 1997-2002, Hasbro, deluxe figure w/Dual Mode Action Craft
    NM $4   **MIP** $7

Velocity Storm Batman, 1997-2002, Hasbro, w/High Speed Glider
    NM $3   **MIP** $7

SERIES 4 MULTI-PACKS

Night Shadow Batman and Night Fury Robin, 1997-2002, Hasbro, w/Hyper-Speed Stun Rockets and Triple Bolo Striker
    NM $8   **MIP** $18

Batman: Spectrum of the Bat (Hasbro, 2000-01)

FIGURES

Fractal Armor Batman, 2000-01, Hasbro
    NM $2   **MIP** $5

Gamma Blast Batman, 2000-01, Hasbro
    NM $2   **MIP** $5

Infared Armor Batman, 2000-01, Hasbro
    NM $2   **MIP** $5

Signal Hacker Batman, 2000-01, Hasbro
    NM $2   **MIP** $5

Sonic Stun Batgirl, 2000-01, Hasbro
    NM $4   **MIP** $8

Sub-Frequency Armor Batman, 2000-01, Hasbro
    NM $2   **MIP** $5

Sub-Pulse Detonator Robin, 2000-01, Hasbro
    NM $2   **MIP** $5

Technocast Catwoman, 2000-01, Hasbro
    NM $2   **MIP** $5

Technocast Jervis Tetch, 2000-01, Hasbro, a.k.a. the Mad Hatter
    NM $2   **MIP** $5

Terrorcast Joker, 2000-01, Hasbro
    NM $2   **MIP** $5

Ultra-Frequency Armor Batman, 2000-01, Hasbro
    NM $2   **MIP** $5

Ultraviolet Ambush Batman, 2000-01, Hasbro
    NM $2   **MIP** $5

X-Ray Assailant Robin, 2000-01, Hasbro
    NM $2   **MIP** $5

Batman: The Adventures of Batman and Robin (Kenner, 1996-97)

DUO FORCE

Air Strike Robin, 1996, Kenner, Series 1
    NM $3   **MIP** $7

Cycle Thruster Batman, 1997, Kenner, Series 2
    NM $3   **MIP** $7

Hydro Storm Robin, 1997, Kenner, Series 2
    NM $3   **MIP** $7

Mr. Freeze, 1996, Kenner, Series 1
    NM $3   **MIP** $7

The Riddler Roto Chopper, 1997, Kenner, Series 2
    NM $3   **MIP** $7

Turbo Surge Batman, 1996, Kenner, Series 1
    NM $3   **MIP** $7

Vector Wing Batman, 1996, Kenner, Series 1
    NM $3   **MIP** $7

Wind Blitz Batgirl, 1997, Kenner, Series 2 Sky Glider and Wave Racer
    NM $3   **MIP** $7

MULTI-PACKS

Rogues Gallery, 1997, Kenner, Figure 8-pack w/Catwoman, Killer Croc, Man-Bat, Poison Ivy, Scarecrow, Joker, Phantasm, and Clayface
    NM $18   **MIP** $40

SERIES 1

Bane, 1996, Kenner, w/body slam arm action and venom tube
NM $3   **MIP** $7

Hover Jet Batman, 1996, Kenner
NM $3   **MIP** $7

Paraglide Batman, 1996, Kenner, w/Dive Bomb Sky Wing
NM $3   **MIP** $7

Pogo Stick Joker, 1996, Kenner, w/Power Launcher
NM $3   **MIP** $7

Ra's Al Ghul, 1996, Kenner, w/Strike Shooter and Combat Sword
NM $15   **MIP** $25

Rocketpack Batman, 1996, Kenner
NM $3   **MIP** $7

SERIES 1 ACCESSORIES

Nightsphere, 1996, Kenner, w/Batman figure
NM $12   **MIP** $20

SERIES 2

Bola Trap Robin, 1997, Hasbro, also released in Batman: The Animated Series figures
NM $3   **MIP** $7

Harley Quinn, 1997, Kenner, w/Knockout Punching Glove and Trick Pistol
NM $4   **MIP** $8

Joker Machine Gun, 1997, Kenner, w/Machine Gun and Joke-A-Matic Time Bomb
NM $3   **MIP** $7

Batman: The Animated Series (Kenner, 1992-95)

ACCESSORIES

AeroBat, 1992, Kenner
NM $10   **MIP** $20

B.A.T.V. Vehicle, 1992, Kenner
NM $8   **MIP** $18

Batcave, 1993, Kenner, play set
NM $35   **MIP** $70

Batcycle, 1992, Kenner, w/Batman figure
NM $8   **MIP** $18

Batcycle, 1992, Kenner, w/Nightwing
NM $8   **MIP** $18

Batmobile, 1992, Kenner
NM $45   **MIP** $100

Bat-Signal Jet, 1992, Kenner
NM $8   **MIP** $18

Crime Stalker, 1992, Kenner
NM $8   **MIP** $18

Hoverbat Vehicle, 1992, Kenner
NM $4   **MIP** $12

Ice Hammer, 1994, Kenner
NM $8   **MIP** $12

Joker Mobile, 1992, Kenner
NM $15   **MIP** $30

Robin Dragster, 1992, Kenner, very rare
NM $80   **MIP** $200

Street Jet, 1993, Kenner
NM $8   **MIP** $15

Turbo Batplane, 1992, Kenner
NM $50   **MIP** $90

FIGURES

Anti-Freeze Batman, 1994, Kenner, Series 3, w/Firing Shield and Blaster
NM $4   **MIP** $7

(Lenny Lee)

Bane, 1995, Kenner, Series 4, w/"Body Slam" action and venom tube
NM $3   **MIP** $7

Battle-Helmet Batman, 1995, Kenner, mail-order figure
NM $10   **MIP** $20

Bola Trap Robin, 1994, Kenner, Series 3
NM $4   **MIP** $7

Bruce Wayne, 1993, Kenner, Series 2
NM $4   **MIP** $12

Catwoman, 1993, Kenner, Series 2, w/whipping arm action and Claw Hook
NM $6   **MIP** $16

Clayface, 1994, Kenner, Series 3
NM $8   **MIP** $15

Combat Belt Batman, 1992, Kenner, Series 1
NM $25   **MIP** $50

Cyber Gear Batman, 1995, Kenner, Series 4
NM $4   **MIP** $7

Dick Grayson/Robin, 1994, Kenner, Series 3
NM $5   **MIP** $10

Glider Robin, 1995, Kenner, Series 4, w/Winged Jet Pack and Firing Claw
NM $4   **MIP** $7

Ground Assault Batman, 1994, Kenner, Deluxe figure w/motorized turbo-powered ground jet
NM $4   **MIP** $7

High-Wire Batman, 1994, Kenner, Deluxe figure w/Quick Escape Cable Wire and Cable-Riding Action
NM $8   **MIP** $25

Infrared Batman, 1993, Kenner, Series 2 w/Launching Bat-Signal Disks
NM $4   **MIP** $15

Joker, 1993, Kenner, Series 2 w/laughing gas spray gun
NM $5   **MIP** $12

Killer Croc, 1994, Kenner, Series 3 w/power punch arm and pet crocodile
NM $5   **MIP** $10

Knight Star Batman, 1994, Kenner, Series 3 w/Star Blade Rocket Launcher
NM $4   **MIP** $7

Lightning Strike Batman, 1994, Kenner, Series 3 w/Transforming Cape Glider
NM $4   **MIP** $7

Manbat, 1993, Kenner, Series 2
NM $5   **MIP** $10

Mech-Wing Batman, 1994, Kenner, Deluxe figure w/Mechanized Soaring Wings and pop-out wing action
NM $4   **MIP** $7

Mr. Freeze, 1994, Kenner, Series 3 w/Firing Ice Blaster
NM $4   **MIP** $10

Ninja Robin, 1993, Kenner, Series 2 w/chopping arm action and ninja weapons
NM $4   **MIP** $7

Penguin, 1992, Kenner, Series 1
NM $10   **MIP** $25

Poison Ivy, 1994, Kenner, Series 3, w/crossbow and Venus Flytrap weapon

    NM $8   **MIP** $14

Power Vision Batman, 1994, Kenner, Deluxe figure w/electric light up eyes, firing missile

    NM $4   **MIP** $7

Radar Scope Batman, 1995, Kenner, Series 4

    NM $4   **MIP** $7

Rapid Attack Batman, 1994, Kenner, Series 3 w/Escape Hook and Utility Belt

    NM $4   **MIP** $7

Riddler, 1992, Kenner, Series 1 w/Question mark launcher

    NM $8   **MIP** $14

Robin, 1992, Kenner, Series 1 w/Turbo Glider

    NM $4   **MIP** $8

Scarecrow, 1993, Kenner, Series 2

    NM $6   **MIP** $10

Sky Dive Batman, 1993, Kenner, Series 2 w/working parachute

    NM $4   **MIP** $7

Tornado Batman, 1994, Kenner, Series 3 w/Whirling Weapon

    NM $4   **MIP** $7

Turbojet Batman, 1992, Kenner, Series 1 w/Firing Wrist Rocket and Pivoting Engines

    NM $4   **MIP** $10

Two Face, 1992, Kenner, Series 1

    NM $6   **MIP** $12

Ultimate Batman (16"), 1994, Kenner

    NM $18   **MIP** $40

MULTI-PACKS

Ninja Batman and Robin, 1994, Kenner, w/duo-power Ninja weapons

    NM $8   **MIP** $18

Batman: The Dark Knight Collection (Kenner, 1990-91)

ACCESSORIES

Batcycle, 1990-91, Kenner

    NM $10   **MIP** $20

Batjet, 1990, Kenner

    NM $25   **MIP** $45

Batmobile, 1990-91, Kenner

    NM $30   **MIP** $60

Batwing, 1990-91, Kenner

    NM $20   **MIP** $55

Bola Bullet, 1991, Kenner

    NM $15   **MIP** $25

The Joker Cycle, 1990-91, Kenner

    NM $8   **MIP** $15

FIGURES

Blast Shield Batman, 1990-91, Kenner, deluxe figure, boxed

    NM $7   **MIP** $15

Bruce Wayne, 1990, Kenner, Series 1, w/quick change suit

    NM $7   **MIP** $15

Claw Climber Batman, 1990-91, Kenner, deluxe figure, boxed

    NM $7   **MIP** $15

Crime Attack Batman, 1990, Kenner, Series 1, w/batarang and claw

    NM $7   **MIP** $15

Iron Winch Batman, 1990, Kenner, Series 1, w/batarang winch

    NM $7   **MIP** $15

Knockout Joker, 1991, Kenner, Series 2

    NM $7   **MIP** $15

Night Glider Batman, 1990-91, Kenner, deluxe figure, boxed

    NM $7   **MIP** $15

Power Wing Batman, 1991, Kenner, Series 2

    NM $7   **MIP** $15

Shadow Wing Batman, 1990, Kenner, Series 1, w/cape spreading pop-up arms and handcuffs

    NM $7   **MIP** $15

Sky Escape Joker, 1990, Kenner, Series 1, w/whirling copter pack

    NM $7   **MIP** $15

Tec-Shield Batman, 1990, Kenner, Series 1, w/flight pack and gold shield suit

    NM $7   **MIP** $15

Thunder Whip Batman, 1991, Kenner, Series 2

    NM $7   **MIP** $15

Wall Scaler Batman, 1990, Kenner, Series 1, w/climbing action pack

    NM $7   **MIP** $15

Batman: The New Batman Adventures (Hasbro, 1997-2000)

ACCESSORIES

Batmobile, 1997-2000, Hasbro, fits Batman, Robin or Nightwing figure

    NM $22   **MIP** $38

Joker Toxic Lab, 2000, Hasbro

    NM $15   **MIP** $30

FIGURES

Crime Fighter Robin, 1997, Hasbro

    NM $3   **MIP** $7

Crime Solver Nightwing, 1997, Hasbro

    NM $3   **MIP** $7

Detective Batman, 1997, Hasbro

    NM $3   **MIP** $7

Force Shield Nightwing, 1998, Hasbro

    NM $3   **MIP** $7

Heavy Artillery Batman, 1998, Hasbro

    NM $3   **MIP** $7

Hydrojet Nightwing, 1998, Hasbro, deluxe figure

    NM $3   **MIP** $7

Knight Glider Batman, 1998, Hasbro

    NM $3   **MIP** $7

Mad Hatter, 1997, Hasbro

    NM $3   **MIP** $7

Shatter Blade Batman, 1998, Hasbro

    NM $3   **MIP** $7

Silver Defender Batman, 1998, Hasbro, deluxe figure

    NM $3   **MIP** $7

Street Strike Batman, 1998, Hasbro

    NM $3   **MIP** $7

The Creeper, 1998, Hasbro

    NM $3   **MIP** $7

Undercover Bruce Wayne, 1998, Hasbro

    NM $3   **MIP** $7

Wildcard Joker, 1998, Hasbro

    NM $3   **MIP** $7

MULTI-PACKS

Arkham Asylum Escape (four-pack): Batman, Two-Face, Poison Ivy, Harley Quinn, 1997-2000, Hasbro

    NM $18   **MIP** $35

Arkham Asylum Escape: Batman vs. Two-Face, 2000, Hasbro
NM $4   MIP $10

Batman and Robin, 2000, Hasbro, Wal-Mart Exclusive
NM $4   MIP $10

Batman and Superman, 2000, Hasbro, Wal-Mart Exclusive
NM $4   MIP $10

Batman Figure (four-pack): Batman, Robin, Alfred, Clayface, 1997-2000, Hasbro
NM $30   MIP $50

Batman vs. Joker, 2000, Hasbro, Wal-Mart Exclusive
NM $4   MIP $10

Knight Force (four-pack): Batman, Robin, Nightwing, Batgirl, 1997-2000, Hasbro
NM $12   MIP $25

World's Finest: Batman and Superman, 2001, Hasbro, Wal-Mart Exclusive
NM $4   MIP $10

Batman: The New Batman Adventures (Hasbro, 1998-99)

12" FIGURES

Batgirl, 1998-99, Hasbro
NM $10   MIP $20

Batman, 1998-99, Hasbro, the most valuable figure in this series
NM $12   MIP $30

Harley Quinn, 1998-99, Hasbro, Mr. J's favorite henchperson
NM $8   MIP $15

Joker, 1998-99, Hasbro
NM $10   MIP $20

Nightwing, 1998-99, Hasbro
NM $10   MIP $20

Robin, 1998-99, Hasbro
NM $10   MIP $20

Batman: World of Batman (Hasbro, 2001)

FIGURES

Aqua Sled Batman, 2001, Hasbro, w/sub-marine assault sled and scuba armor
NM $3   MIP $7

Hover Jet Batman, 2001, Hasbro, w/blasting battle sled
NM $3   MIP $7

Plasma Glow Joker, 2001, Hasbro
NM $3   MIP $7

Quick Change Bruce Wayne, 2001, Hasbro
NM $3   MIP $7

Radar Scope Batman, 2001, Hasbro, w/pulse-scan blaster
NM $3   MIP $7

Rapid Attack Robin, 2001, Hasbro
NM $3   MIP $7

MULTI-PACKS

Batman Two-Pack, 2001, Hasbro, Gotham City Adventures Batman and Knight Watch Batman
NM $8   MIP $10

Battlestar Galactica (Mattel, 1978-79)

12" FIGURES

Colonial Warrior, 1979, Mattel
NM $30   MIP $70

Cylon Centurian, 1979, Mattel, silver armor
NM $30   MIP $75

3-3/4" FIGURES, SERIES 1, 1978

Commander Adama, 1978, Mattel, w/cloth robe and laser pistol, shown w/Starbuck
NM $15   MIP $40

Cylon Centurian, 1978, Mattel
NM $15   MIP $40

Daggit (brown), 1978, Mattel
NM $15   MIP $30

Daggit (tan), 1978, Mattel, shown w/Imperious Leader
NM $15   MIP $30

Imperious Leader, 1978, Mattel, w/red-purple cloth robe
NM $12   MIP $23

Ovion, 1978, Mattel
NM $12   MIP $35

Starbuck, 1978, Mattel
NM $15   MIP $40

3-3/4" FIGURES, SERIES 2, 1979

Baltar, 1979, Mattel
NM $40   MIP $80

Boray, 1979, Mattel
NM $40   MIP $80

Cylon Commander, 1979, Mattel
NM $55   **MIP** $110

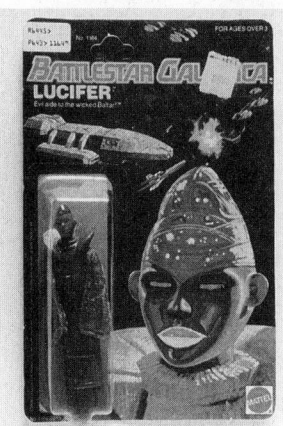

Lucifer, 1979, Mattel
NM $40   **MIP** $90

ACCESSORIES

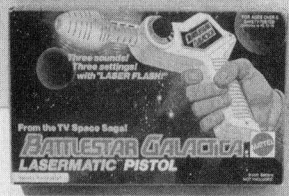

Lasermatic Pistol, 1978, Mattel, barrel lights up when fired, has three different laser-firing sounds
NM $35   **MIP** $75

VEHICLES

Colonial Scarab, 1978-79, Mattel, 1978 versions came w/red missiles, 1979 versions didn't
NM $25   **MIP** $75

Colonial Stellar Probe, 1978-79, Mattel, 1978 versions came w/red missiles, 1979 versions didn't
NM $30   **MIP** $80

Colonial Viper, 1978-79, Mattel, 1978 editions came w/red missiles, 1979 editions didn't
NM $25   **MIP** $75

Cylon Raider, 1978-79, Mattel, 1978 editions came w/red missiles, 1979 editions didn't
NM $25   **MIP** $70

Beavis & Butthead (Moore, 1998)

FIGURES

Beavis, 1998, Moore
NM $8   **MIP** $15

Butthead, 1998, Moore
NM $8   **MIP** $15

Cornholio, 1998, Moore
NM $5   **MIP** $12

Beetlejuice (Kenner, 1989-90)

ACCESSORIES

Creepy Cruiser, 1989-90, Kenner
NM $3   **MIP** $10

Gross Out Meter, 1990, Kenner
NM $3   **MIP** $10

Phantom Flyer, 1989-90, Kenner
NM $4   **MIP** $8

Snake Mask, 1989-90, Kenner
NM $4   **MIP** $8

Vanishing Vault, 1989-90, Kenner
NM $4   **MIP** $8

FIGURES

Adam Maitland, 1989-90, Kenner
NM $2   **MIP** $5

(Lenny Lee)

Exploding Beetlejuice, 1989-90, Kenner, body flies apart to reveal bug, also includes smaller dragon figure
NM $2   **MIP** $5

Harry the Haunted Hunter, 1989-90, Kenner
NM $2   **MIP** $5

Old Buzzard, 1989-90, Kenner
NM $2   **MIP** $5

Otho the Obnoxious, 1989-90, Kenner
NM $2   **MIP** $5

Shipwreck Beetlejuice, 1989-90, Kenner
NM $2   **MIP** $5

Shish Kabab Beetlejuice, 1989-90, Kenner
NM $2   **MIP** $5

Showtime Beetlejuice, 1989-90, Kenner
NM $2   **MIP** $5

Spinhead Beetlejuice, 1989-90, Kenner
NM $2   **MIP** $5

Street Rat, 1989-90, Kenner
NM $2   **MIP** $5

Talking Beetlejuice, 1989-90, Kenner
NM $8   **MIP** $20

Teacher Creature, 1989-90, Kenner
NM $2   **MIP** $5

Best of the West (Marx, 1965-75)

ACCESSORIES

Buckboard w/Horse & Harness, 1967-75, Marx, #4424, w/Thunderbolt
NM $105   MIP $235

Buckskin Horse, 1967, Marx, #2036, for 12" figures, head nods and neck bends
NM $65   MIP $110

Circle X Ranch Play Set, 1967, Marx, #5275, 22 pieces, cardboard, rare
NM $210   MIP $325

Comanche Horse, 1967, Marx, #1861, for 12" figures, head and leg articulation
NM $65   MIP $125

Covered Wagon, 1967-75, Marx, #4434, w/horse and harness
NM $120   MIP $240

Flame Horse, 1966, Marx, #2081, for 12" figures, legs in trotting pose
NM $65   MIP $130

Fort Apache Play Set, 1967, Marx, #1875, scaled for 12" figures
NM $210   MIP $400

Pancho Pony, 1967, Marx, #1061, for 7-1/2" figures, brown w/off-white mane and tail, includes black plastic saddle and bridle
NM $50   MIP $80

Storm Cloud Horse, 1967, Marx, #2071, originally "Pinto," brown w/white spots
NM $60   MIP $125

Thunderbolt Horse, 1965-75, Marx, #2061, most common horse produced, black version rarest
NM $75   MIP $135

Thundercolt Horse, 1967-69, Marx, #2031a, for use w/ranch and corral sets
NM $30   MIP $60

FIGURES

Bill Buck, 1967, Marx, #1868, Fort Apache Fighters Series
NM $325   MIP $500

Captain Tom Maddox, 1967, Marx, #1865, Fort Apache Fighters, blue body, brown hair
NM $80   MIP $175

Chief Cherokee, 1965, Marx, includes headdress, rifle, spear, Bowie knife, ceremonial mask, pipe and more
NM $150   MIP $210

Daniel Boone, 1965, Marx, #2060, limited articulation
NM $155   MIP $250

Davy Crockett, 1960s, Marx
NM $180   MIP $260

Fighting Eagle, 1967, Marx, #1864, fully poseable, includes spear, Bowie knife, hatchet, bear claw necklace, pouch, and more
NM $175   MIP $260

General Custer, 1967, Marx, #1866, blue molded uniform, w/yellow and dark blue plastic accessories
NM $110   MIP $200

Geronimo, 1967, Marx, #1863, w/tan molded buckskin uniform, darker brown, yellow and medium brown plastic accessories, including Bowie knife, headband, mask, spear, rifle and more
NM $100   MIP $150

Geronimo and Pinto, 1967-75, Marx, #2087, mail-order set
NM $160   MIP $240

Geronimo w/Storm Cloud, 1967-75, Marx, figure and horse in colored box
NM $100   MIP $210

Jamie West, 1967, Marx, #1062A, body molded in carmel, light blue, or black in Canada
    NM $65   MIP $115

Jane West, 1966, Marx, #2067, includes white plastic clothes and accessories
    NM $70   MIP $130

Jane West w/Flame, 1967-75, Marx, mail-order figure and horse
    NM $115   MIP $195

Janice West, 1967, Marx, #1067b, turquoise body, short black hair
    NM $65   MIP $120

Jay West, 1967, Marx, #1062b, carmel body, blond hair
    NM $65   MIP $110

Jed Gibson, 1975, Marx, #2057c, African-American cavalry soldier, teal body, rare
    NM $500   MIP $1000

Johnny West, 1965, Marx, #2062, straight hands in 1965, curved hands 1966-75, carmel body, brown hair
    NM $80   MIP $160

Johnny West w/Comanche, 1967, Marx, fully jointed
    NM $95   MIP $150

Johnny West w/Thunderbolt, 1967-75, Marx, #2062, mail-order figure and horse
    NM $90   MIP $175

Josie West, 1967, Marx, #1067a, turquoise body, blonde hair
    NM $65   MIP $110

Princess Wildflower, 1974, Marx, #2097, includes 22 accessories and gear
    NM $110   MIP $180

Sam Cobra, 1972, Marx, #2072, black molded-plastic clothing and accessories
    NM $125   MIP $250

Sam Cobra w/Thunderbolt, 1975, Marx, #4959075, mail-order figure and horse
    NM $90   MIP $250

Sheriff Garrett, 1973, Marx, #2085, blue-molded clothing w/white and blue plastic clothing and accessories included
    NM $165   MIP $200

Sheriff Garrett w/horse, 1967-75, Marx, mail-order figure and horse, rare
    NM $180   MIP $310

Zeb Zachary, 1967-69, Marx, #1862, Fort Apache Fighters, blue body, black hair
    NM $210   MIP $325

Big Jim
(Mattel, 1971-77)

ACCESSORIES

Baja Beast, 1973, Mattel
    NM $40   MIP $130

Boat and Buggy Set, 1973, Mattel
    NM $40   MIP $140

Camping Tent, 1973, Mattel
    NM $30   MIP $80

Devil River Trip, 1974, Mattel
    NM $35   MIP $80

Jungle Truck, 1974, Mattel
    NM $40   MIP $90

Motorcross Honda, 1973, Mattel
    NM $55   MIP $75

Olympic Basketball Player, 1975, Mattel, Olympic series, #7374
    NM $20   MIP $60

Olympic Boxer, 1975, Mattel, Olympic series, #7348
    NM $25   MIP $90

Olympic Karate, 1975, Mattel, Olympic series, #7344
    NM $20   MIP $50

Olympic Ski Run Play Set, 1975, Mattel, Olympic series, #7369
    NM $60   MIP $150

Olympic Skier, 1975, Mattel, Olympic series, #7350
    NM $20   MIP $35

Rescue Rig, 1973, Mattel
    NM $75   MIP $175

Rugged Rider and Cycle Set, 1973, Mattel
    NM $25   MIP $65

Sky Commander, 1974, Mattel
    NM $80   MIP $175

Sport Camper, 1973, Mattel
    NM $40   MIP $80

FIGURES

Big Jack, 1973, Mattel
    NM $50   MIP $210

Big Jeff, 1973, Mattel
    NM $50   MIP $210

Big Jim, 1971-77, Mattel, window box
    NM $65   MIP $190

Big Josh, 1973, Mattel
    NM $50   MIP $150

Dr. Steel, 1975, Mattel
    NM $60   MIP $165

Gold Medal Big Jack, 1975, Mattel, Olympic series
    NM $45   MIP $130

Gold Medal Big Jim, 1975, Mattel, Olympic series
    NM $75   MIP $180

Gold Medal Big Jim Olympic Boxing Match, 1975, Mattel, Olympic series, #7425
    NM $100   MIP $275

Big Jim's P.A.C.K.
(Mattel, 1974-77)

ACCESSORIES

Beast, 1976-77, Mattel
    NM $60   MIP $150

BlitzRig, 1976-77, Mattel
    NM $125   MIP $220

Frogman, 1974-77, Mattel, Double Trouble Disguise
    NM $28   **MIP** $70

Hard Hat Gunner, 1974-77, Mattel, Double Trouble Adventure Sets
    NM $20   **MIP** $60

Howler, 1976-77, Mattel
    NM $30   **MIP** $60

LazerVette, 1976-77, Mattel
    NM $55   **MIP** $110

Martial Arts, 1974-77, Mattel, Double Trouble Disguise
    NM $7   **MIP** $20

Motocross, 1974-77, Mattel, Double Trouble Disguise
    NM $7   **MIP** $20

S.W.A.T., 1974-77, Mattel, Double Trouble Adventure Sets
    NM $10   **MIP** $40

Secret Spy, 1974-77, Mattel, Double Trouble Adventure Sets
    NM $25   **MIP** $60

Ski Patrol, 1974-77, Mattel, Double Trouble Disguise
    NM $7   **MIP** $40

Swamp Patrol, 1974-77, Mattel, Sears Exclusive
    NM $100   **MIP** $200

The Whip's Dune Buggy, 1974-77, Mattel, dune buggy vehicle
    NM $40   **MIP** $75

Underworld Gunner, 1974-77, Mattel, Double Trouble Adventure Sets
    NM $25   **MIP** $60

FIGURES

Big Jim, Window Box, 1974-77, Mattel, Series 2, #9258, a.k.a. "The Gold Commander," gold pants, black shirt
    NM $45   **MIP** $160

Big Jim, Window Box, 1974-77, Mattel, Series 1, #9092, a.k.a. "The Blue Commander," white pants, blue shirt
    NM $60   **MIP** $225

Double Trouble Commander, 1974-77, Mattel, Series 2, #9287, face changes
    NM $80   **MIP** $210

Dr. Steel, Window Box, 1974-77, Mattel, Series 1, #7367, w/pipe
    NM $35   **MIP** $130

Torpedo Fist, 1974-77, Mattel, Series 2, #9289, eye patch, hat
    NM $125   **MIP** $250

Warpath, Window Box, 1974-77, Mattel, Series 1, #9059, w/bow, quiver, two arrows
    NM $45   **MIP** $160

Whip, The, Window Box, 1974-77, Mattel, Series 1, #9060, w/bull whip, bolos, shinai stick, boomerangs
    NM $45   **MIP** $160

Zorak, 1974-77, Mattel, Series 2
    NM $50   **MIP** $160

Bill & Ted's Excellent Adventure (Kenner, 1991)

ACCESSORIES

Phone Booth, 1991, Kenner
    NM $40   **MIP** $85

Wild Stallyns Speaker and Tape, 1991, Kenner
    NM $3   **MIP** $10

FIGURES

Abe Lincoln, 1991, Kenner
    NM $4   **MIP** $12

Bill, 1991, Kenner
    NM $9   **MIP** $18

Bill & Ted Jam Session, two pack, 1991, Kenner
    NM $15   **MIP** $30

Billy The Kid, 1991, Kenner
    NM $4   **MIP** $12

Genghis Khan, 1991, Kenner
    NM $4   **MIP** $12

Grim Reaper, 1991, Kenner
    NM $4   **MIP** $12

Rufus, 1991, Kenner
    NM $4   **MIP** $12

Ted, 1991, Kenner
    NM $9   **MIP** $18

Bionic Six (LJN, 1986)

ACCESSORIES

Dirt Bike, 1986, LJN
    NM $15   **MIP** $30

Flying Laser Throne, 1986, LJN
    NM $5   **MIP** $20

Laser Aero Chair, 1986, LJN
    NM $5   **MIP** $20

M.U.L.E.S. Van, 1986, LJN
    NM $40   **MIP** $80

Quad Runner, 1986, LJN, 4x4
    NM $15   **MIP** $30

Secret Headquarters, 1986, LJN, Super Hi-Tech Bionic Laboratory
    NM $160   **MIP** $275

FIGURES

Bunji, 1986
    NM $15   **MIP** $40

Chopper, 1986
    NM $6   **MIP** $12

Dr. Scarab, 1986
    NM $10   **MIP** $20

(KP Photo, Karen O'Brien collection)

Eric, 1986
    NM $10   **MIP** $25

F.L.U.F.F.I., 1986
    NM $20   **MIP** $40

(KP Photo, Karen O'Brien collection)

Glove, 1986
    NM $6   **MIP** $12

Helen, 1986
    NM $6   **MIP** $12

J.D., 1986
    NM $15   **MIP** $35

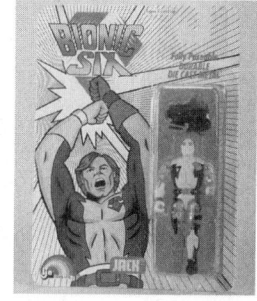

(KP Photo, Karen O'Brien collection)

Jack, 1986
    NM $15   **MIP** $30

Klunk, 1986
    NM $6   **MIP** $12

Madame O, 1986
     NM $6   **MIP** $12

Mechanic, 1986
     NM $6   **MIP** $12

Meg, 1986
     NM $6   **MIP** $12

Bionic Woman (Kenner, 1976-77)

12" FIGURES

Fembot, 1977
     NM $100+   **MIP** $300+

Jamie Sommers, 1976, w/purse
     NM $50   **MIP** $250

Jamie Sommers, 1976, in jogging suit, white top, navy pants
     NM $40   **MIP** $160

ACCESSORIES

Beauty Salon, 1976
     NM $30   **MIP** $75

Carriage House, 1977
     NM $350+   **MIP** $700+

Classroom, 1976-77
     NM $125+   **MIP** $250+

Dome House, 1976-77
     NM $75   **MIP** $360

Sports Car, 1976
     NM $45   **MIP** $100

FASHIONS

Designer Budget Fashions, 1976, Kenner, red evening gown w/red shoes
     NM $15   **MIP** $30

Designer Budget Fashions, 1976, Kenner, green dress w/white shoes
     NM $15   **MIP** $30

Designer Collection, 1976, Kenner, floral party dress w/platform shoes
     NM $12   **MIP** $25

Designer Collection, 1976, Kenner, "Peach Dream," peach evening dress w/peach shoes
     NM $12   **MIP** $25

Designer Collection, 1976, Kenner, light blue two-piece pant outfit w/white shoes
     NM $25   **MIP** $45

Designer Collection, 1976, Kenner, calico dress red/yellow w/apron
     NM $12   **MIP** $25

Black Hole (Mego, 1979-80)

12" FIGURES

Captain Holland, 1979, Mego, shown w/other figures from the Black Hole
     NM $40   **MIP** $75

Dr. Alex Durant, 1979, Mego
     NM $40   **MIP** $75

Dr. Hans Reinhardt, 1979, Mego
     NM $40   **MIP** $75

Harry Booth, 1979, Mego
     NM $45   **MIP** $90

Kate McCrae, 1979, Mego
     NM $50   **MIP** $100

Pizer, 1979, Mego
     NM $40   **MIP** $80

3-3/4" FIGURES

Captain Holland, 1979, Mego, shown w/other figures from the Black Hole
     NM $15   **MIP** $40

Dr. Alex Durant, 1979, Mego
     NM $15   **MIP** $40

Dr. Hans Reinhardt, 1979, Mego
     NM $15   **MIP** $40

Harry Booth, 1979, Mego
     NM $15   **MIP** $40

Humanoid, 1980, Mego
     NM $600+ **MIP** $1000+

Kate McCrae, 1979, Mego
     NM $15   **MIP** $40

Maximillian, 1979, Mego
     NM $40   **MIP** $70

Old B.O.B., 1980, Mego
     NM $90   **MIP** $225

Pizer, 1979, Mego
     NM $20   **MIP** $60

S.T.A.R., 1980, Mego
     NM $150   **MIP** $400

Sentry Robot, 1980, Mego
     NM $45   **MIP** $110

V.I.N.cent., 1979, Mego
     NM $45   **MIP** $110

Blackstar (Galoob, 1984)

ACCESSORIES

Ice Castle, 1984
     NM $90   **MIP** $175

Triton, 1984
     NM $60   **MIP** $150

Warlock Dragon Mount, 1984
     NM $60   **MIP** $150

FIGURES

Blackstar, 1984
     NM $70   **MIP** $150

Blackstar w/Laser Light, 1984
     NM $25   **MIP** $65

Devil Knight w/Laser Light, 1984
     NM $25   **MIP** $75

(Mark Bellomo collection)

Gargo, 1984
     NM $20   **MIP** $50

Gargo w/Laser Light, 1984
     NM $25   **MIP** $65

Kadray, 1984
     NM $20   **MIP** $55

Kadray w/Laser Light, 1984
     NM $25   **MIP** $65

Klone w/Laser Light, 1984
     NM $20   **MIP** $65

Lava Loc w/Laser Light, 1984
     NM $25   **MIP** $65

Mara, 1984
  NM $45   MIP $85
Meuton, 1984
  NM $20   MIP $65
Neptul, 1984
  NM $20   MIP $75
Overlord, 1984
  NM $22   MIP $75
Overlord w/Laser Light, 1984
  NM $30   MIP $100
Palace Guard, 1984
  NM $25   MIP $75
Palace Guard w/Laser Light, 1984
  NM $35   MIP $90
Togo, 1984
  NM $20   MIP $65
Togo w/Laser Light, 1984
  NM $25   MIP $70
Vizir w/Laser Light, 1984
  NM $20   MIP $30
White Knight, 1984
  NM $25   MIP $65

Blade (Toy Biz, 1998)

6" FIGURES

Blade, 1998, Toy Biz
  NM $5   MIP $12
Deacon Frost, 1998, Toy Biz
  NM $5   MIP $12
Vampire Blade, 1998, Toy Biz
  NM $5   MIP $12
Whistler, 1998, Toy Biz
  NM $5   MIP $12

Blade Vampire Hunter (Toy Biz, 1998)

FIGURES

Blade, 1998
  NM $2   MIP $7
Deacon Frost, 1998
  NM $2   MIP $7
Vampire Blade, 1998
  NM $2   MIP $7
Whistker, 1998
  NM $2   MIP $7

Bob & Doug McKenzie (McFarlane, 2000)

FIGURES

Bob McKenzie w/half of Great White North stage set, 2000, McFarlane
  NM $5   MIP $15
Doug McKenzie w/half of Great White North stage set, 2000, McFarlane
  NM $5   MIP $15

Bonanza (American Character, 1966)

ACCESSORIES

4 in 1 Wagon, 1966
  NM $50   MIP $140
Ben's Palomino, 1966
  NM $40   MIP $125
Hoss' Stallion, 1966
  NM $40   MIP $125
Little Joe's Pinto, 1966
  NM $40   MIP $125

FIGURES

Ben, 1966
  NM $50   MIP $160
Ben w/Palomino, 1966
  NM $80   MIP $250
Hoss, 1966
  NM $70   MIP $160
Hoss w/Stallion, 1966
  NM $70   MIP $250

Little Joe, 1966
  NM $50   MIP $160
Little Joe w/Pinto, 1966
  NM $70   MIP $250
Outlaw, 1966
  NM $50   MIP $160

BraveStarr (Mattel, 1986)

FIGURES

BraveStarr and Thirty/Thirty, two-pack, 1986, Mattel
  NM $110   MIP $250
Col. Borobot, 1986, Mattel
  NM $18   MIP $35
Deputy Fuzz, 1986, Mattel
  NM $20   MIP $35
Handle Bar, 1986, Mattel
  NM $12   MIP $35
Laser-Fire BraveStarr, 1986, Mattel
  NM $25   MIP $45
Laser-Fire Tex Hex, 1986, Mattel
  NM $20   MIP $45
Marshal BraveStarr, 1986, Mattel
  NM $15   MIP $40
Outlaw Skuzz, 1986, Mattel
  NM $18   MIP $35
Sand Storm, 1986, Mattel
  NM $10   MIP $30
Skull Walker, 1986, Mattel
  NM $20   MIP $50
Tex Hex, 1986, Mattel
  NM $18   MIP $40
Thunder Stick, 1986, Mattel
  NM $40   MIP $75

Bruce Lee (Sideshow Toys, 1999)

8" FIGURES

(KP Photo)

Bruce Lee, bare chested, 1999, w/stand, nunchaku and staff
  NM $4   MIP $10
Bruce Lee, traditional outfit, 1999
  NM $4   MIP $10

Buck Rogers (Mego, 1979)

12" FIGURES

Buck Rogers, 1979, Mego
    NM $22   MIP $50

Doctor Huer, 1979, Mego
    NM $22   MIP $45
Draco, 1979, Mego
    NM $18   MIP $40
Draconian Guard, 1979, Mego,
w/brown and silver uniform
    NM $20   MIP $50
Killer Kane, 1979, Mego
    NM $20   MIP $50

Tiger Man, 1979, Mego, w/tattooed
face and head and tiger-skin vest
and clothing
    NM $32   MIP $70
Twiki, 1979, Mego
    NM $15   MIP $35

3-3/4" FIGURES

Ardella, 1979, Mego
    NM $8   MIP $15
Buck Rogers, 1979, Mego
    NM $20   MIP $40
Doctor Huer, 1979, Mego
    NM $5   MIP $15

Draco, 1979, Mego
    NM $5   MIP $15
Draconian Guard, 1979, Mego
    NM $5   MIP $15
Killer Kane, 1979, Mego
    NM $5   MIP $12
Tiger Man, 1979, Mego
    NM $5   MIP $15
Twiki, 1979, Mego
    NM $15   MIP $30
Wilma Deering, 1979, Mego
    NM $15   MIP $28

3-3/4" PLAY SETS

Star Fighter Command Center, 1979,
Mego
    NM $70   MIP $160

3-3/4" VEHICLES

Draconian Marauder, 1979, Mego
    NM $40   MIP $90
Land Rover, 1979, Mego
    NM $55   MIP $90
Laserscope Fighter, 1979, Mego
    NM $30   MIP $70
Star Fighter, 1979, Mego
    NM $125+   MIP $200+
Star Searcher, 1979, Mego
    NM $175+   MIP $300+

Buffy the Vampire Slayer (Diamond Select, 1999)

FIGURES

Prophecy Girl Buffy, 1999, Diamond
Select
    NM $5   MIP $15
Vampiric Angel, 1999, Diamond
Select
    NM $5   MIP $15
Willow, 1999, Diamond Select
    NM $5   MIP $15

Buffy the Vampire Slayer (Moore Action Collectibles, 1999-Present)

SERIES I

Angel, 1999, Moore Action Collectibles
    NM $5   MIP $18
Buffy, 1999, Moore Action
Collectibles, blue shirt and black
pants, crossbow, stakes, dagger,
Moore Action Collectibles Exclusive
    NM $5   MIP $15
Buffy, 1999, Moore Action Collectibles
    NM $5   MIP $15

Master, The, 1999, Moore Action
Collectibles
    NM $5   MIP $15
Willow, 1999, Moore Action Collectibles
    NM $5   MIP $18

SERIES II

Three-Pack, 2000, Moore Action
Collectibles, Buffy, Giles, Oz
    NM $5   MIP $15
Buffy, red leather pants, 2000
    NM $3   MIP $15
Exclusive Entertainment Earth Oz,
2000, Moore Action Collectibles
    NM $5   MIP $15
Exclusive MAC's Fiesta Giles, 2000,
Moore Action Collectibles
    NM $5   MIP $15
Exclusive Spike, 2000, Moore Action
Collectibles
    NM $5   MIP $15
Exclusive Toy Fare Season 2 Hair Buffy,
2000, Moore Action Collectibles
    NM $5   MIP $15
Exclusive Vampire Spike, 2000,
Moore Action Collectibles
    NM $6   MIP $15
Exclusive Werewolf Oz, 2000, Moore
Action Collectibles
    NM $5   MIP $15
Giles, 2000
    NM $4   MIP $12
Oz, 2000
    NM $4   MIP $12

(KP Photo)

Spike, 2000, Moore Action
Collectibles, in black trenchcoat,
includes gravesite stand
    NM $4   MIP $12

SERIES III

Three-Pack, 2001, Moore Action
Collectibles, Cordelia, Xander,
Cheerleader Cordelia
    NM $10   MIP $18

Cordelia, 2001, Moore Action Collectibles

    NM $5   MIP $15

Exclusive Cheerleader Cordelia, 2001, Moore Action Collectibles

    NM $5   MIP $15

Exclusive Cordelia T1, 2001, Moore Action Collectibles, Summer Show Special

    NM $5   MIP $15

Exclusive Military Xander, 2001, Moore Action Collectibles

    NM $5   MIP $15

Xander, 2001, Moore Action Collectibles

    NM $3   MIP $12

SERIES IV

Drusilla, 2002, Moore Action Collectibles

    NM $5   MIP $14

Exclusive Bunny Anya, 2002, Moore Action Collectibles

    NM $6   MIP $12

Exclusive Vampire Drusilla, 2002, Moore Action Collectibles

    NM $5   MIP $15

Geltleman #2, 2002, Moore Action Collectibles, tilted head

    NM $5   MIP $14

Gentleman #1, 2002, Moore Action Collectibles, straight head

    NM $5   MIP $14

Buffy the Vampire Slayer (Sideshow Toys, 1998-Present)

12" FIGURES

Angel, 2004, Sideshow Toys, #2006, "Becoming"

    NM $20   MIP $65

Buffy Summers, 1998, Sideshow Toys, #2001, from the television series

    NM $15   MIP $25

Buffy Summers, 2004, Sideshow Toys, #2005, "Graduation Day"

    NM $15   MIP $30

Buffy/Gentlemen, 1998, Sideshow Toys, #2000, four figures from "Hush" Season 4

    NM $100   MIP $275

Gentlemen, 1998, Sideshow Toys, #20002R, three Gentlemen figures from "Hush"

    NM $20   MIP $55

Bug's Life, A (Mattel, 1998)

FIGURES

Enemy Hopper, 1998, Mattel

    NM $2   MIP $5

Enemy Molt, 1998, Mattel

    NM $2   MIP $5

Francis & Slim, 1998, Mattel

    NM $2   MIP $5

Hang Glider Flik, 1998, Mattel

    NM $2   MIP $5

Inventor Flik, 1998, Mattel

    NM $2   MIP $5

Princess Atta, 1998, Mattel

    NM $2   MIP $5

Tuck & Roll, 1998, Mattel

    NM $2   MIP $5

Warrior Flik, 1998, Mattel

    NM $2   MIP $5

Butch and Sundance: The Early Days (Kenner, 1979)

ACCESSORIES AND VEHICLES

Bluff, Butch's Horse, 1979, Kenner

    NM $20   MIP $55

Mint Wagon, 1979, Kenner

    NM $25   MIP $70

Saloon Play Set, 1979, Kenner

    NM $45   MIP $120

Spurs, Sundance's Horse, 1979, Kenner

    NM $20   MIP $55

FIGURES

Butch Cassidy, 1979, Kenner

    NM $12   MIP $25

Marshall LeFors, 1979, Kenner

    NM $12   MIP $25

O.C. Hanks, 1979, Kenner

    NM $12   MIP $25

Sheriff Bledsoe, 1979, Kenner

    NM $18   MIP $35

Sundance Kid, 1979, Kenner

    NM $12   MIP $25

Captain & Tennille (Mego, 1977)

FIGURES

Daryl Dragon (Captain), 1977, Mego, Model No. 7501

    NM $20   MIP $45

Toni Tennille, 1977, Mego, features a stand and "fully washable hair…wash and blow dry on cool setting"

    NM $20   MIP $45

Captain Action (Ideal, 1966-68)

12" FIGURES

Captain Action, 1966, Ideal, w/red-shirted Lone Ranger on box

    NM $210   MIP $575

Captain Action, 1966, Ideal, w/blue-shirted Lone Ranger on box

    NM $210   MIP $575

Captain Action, 1966, Ideal, photo box

    NM $300   MIP $925

Captain Action, 1967, Ideal, parachute offer on box

    NM $275   MIP $725

Dr. Evil, 1967, Ideal, photo box

    NM $250   MIP $460

Dr. Evil, Lab Set Display Box, 1967, Ideal, all Dr. Evil accessories plus white lab coat, blue/red thought-control helmet, reducer wand w/prism, gun, hypnotic eye (eyelid often missing), Dr. Ling mask

    NM $1100   MIP $3700

Dr. Evil, Mailer box version of lab set, 1968, Ideal

    NM $1100   MIP $2800

9" FIGURES

Action Boy, 1967, Ideal

    NM $275   MIP $925

Action Boy, 1968, Ideal, w/space suit

    NM $350   MIP $1200

ACCESSORIES

Action Cave Carrying Case, 1967, Ideal, vinyl

    NM $400   MIP $710

Directional Communicator Set, 1966, Ideal

    NM $110   **MIP** $320

Dr. Evil Sanctuary, 1967, Ideal

    NM $2700   **MIP** $4000

Jet Mortar, 1966, Ideal, two shells

    NM $110   **MIP** $310

Parachute Pack, 1966, Ideal, silver boots, orange helmet, working (sometimes) parachute

    NM $100   **MIP** $250

Power Pack, 1966, Ideal, jet pack w/handles; silver helmet, gloves and boots, CA belt w/out slit for sword

    NM $125   **MIP** $250

Quick Change Chamber, 1967, Ideal, Sears Exclusive, cardboard

    NM $760   **MIP** $910

Silver Streak Amphibian, 1967, Ideal

    NM $900   **MIP** $2000

Silver Streak Garage, 1966-68, Ideal, Sears Exclusive, w/Silver Streak Vehicle

    NM $2000   **MIP** $3000

Survival Kit, 1967, Ideal, 20 pieces; orange vest

    NM $130   **MIP** $280

Vinyl Headquarters Carrying Case, 1967, Ideal, Sears Exclusive

    NM $210   **MIP** $525

Weapons Arsenal, 1966, Ideal, 10 pieces

    NM $90   **MIP** $175

ACTION BOY COSTUMES

Aqualad, 1967, Ideal

    NM $275   **MIP** $950

Robin, 1967, Ideal, included gloves, batarangs, boots, uniform, face mask, suction cups for climbing buildings

    NM $350   **MIP** $2800

Superboy, 1967, Ideal

    NM $375+   **MIP** $3100

CAPTAIN ACTION COSTUMES

Aquaman, 1966, Ideal, costume, mask, yellow flippers, trident, seashell w/strap, yellow belt, lance-like sword, yellow/silver knife; photo shows Batman, Captain America, Aquaman, and Superman

    NM $200   **MIP** $950

Aquaman, 1967, Ideal, w/flasher ring, 1966 accessories

    NM $250   **MIP** $1050

Batman, 1966, Ideal, costume, two-piece mask, batarang, blue cape, utility belt and boots, blue flashlight w/hook, drill, rope w/reel and hook

    NM $235   **MIP** $950

Batman, 1967, Ideal, w/flasher ring, 1966 accessories

    NM $265   **MIP** $1200

Buck Rogers, 1967, Ideal, w/flasher ring, silver suit, mask, black boots and gloves, black belt/shoulder harness, two blue rocket packs, blue helmet, canteen, raygun, flashlight

    NM $450   **MIP** $2700

Captain America, 1966, Ideal, red, white, blue costume, mask, red boots, white belt w/gun holster,

laser pistol, laser rifle, shield (red, white and blue w/star in middle)

    NM $260   **MIP** $1000

Captain America, 1967, Ideal, w/flasher ring, 1966 accessories

    NM $275   **MIP** $1300

Flash Gordon, 1966, Ideal, white spacesuit w/helmet, silver boots, space pistol, propellant gun, belt and mask

    NM $200   **MIP** $600

Flash Gordon, 1967, Ideal, w/flasher ring, 1966 accessories

    NM $225   **MIP** $800

Green Hornet, 1967, Ideal, w/flasher ring, green trench coat, mask, black pants, white scarf, black hat w/green band, yellow gas mask, shoulder holster, pistol, TV w/phone, gold pocket watch, black cane w/removable handle

    NM $1700   **MIP** $6800

Lone Ranger, 1966, Ideal, red shirt, black pants, white hat, mask, black belt w/two holsters, two silver pistols, rifle, black boots w/spurs

    NM $200   **MIP** $550

Lone Ranger, 1967, Ideal, blue shirt (1967 only), w/flasher ring, 1966 accessories

    NM $500   **MIP** $2000

Phantom, 1966, Ideal, purple uniform, black boots, knife, rifle, two pistols, double-rig holster, mask, brass knuckles

    NM $150   **MIP** $600

Phantom, 1967, Ideal, w/flasher ring, 1966 accessories

    NM $175   **MIP** $950

Sgt. Fury, 1966, Ideal, camo uniform, bearded mask, moustache mask, clean-shaven mask, black boots, helmet, walkie-talkie, bandolier, machine gun, three grenades, .45 pistol

    NM $265   **MIP** $1000

Spider-Man, 1967, Ideal, w/flasher ring, red/blue uniform, spider mask, red boots, yellow spider, web fluid tank w/shoulder strap and hoses, "web" sword, flashlight, grappling hook

    NM $675   **MIP** $9200

Steve Canyon, 1966, Ideal, green flight suit, black boots, mask, blue cap, white flight helmet, parachute pack, oxygen mask, green belt/holster, pistol, knife

    NM $250   **MIP** $875

Steve Canyon, 1967, Ideal, w/flasher ring, 1966 accessories

    NM $250   **MIP** $900

Superman, 1966, Ideal, costume, mask, red boots, yellow belt, green Kryptonite, yellow shackles and chain, Krypto, Phantom Zone Projector

    NM $150   **MIP** $950

Superman, 1967, Ideal, w/flasher ring, 1966 accessories

    NM $180   **MIP** $1250

Tonto, 1967, Ideal, w/flasher ring, brown costume, headband w/feather, moccasins, brown belt, brown quiver and boe, gun, knife, four arrows (each has different color feather: red, blue, yellow, green), Taka the eagle

    NM $200   **MIP** $950

Captain Action (Playing Mantis, 1998-99)

FIGURES AND COSTUMES

Captain Action, 1998-99, Playing Mantis

    NM $15   **MIP** $25

Dr. Evil, 1998-99, Playing Mantis

    NM $15   **MIP** $30

Flash Gordon, 1998-99, Playing Mantis

    NM $15   **MIP** $25

Green Hornet, 1998-99, Playing Mantis, Kay-Bee Exclusive

    NM $15   **MIP** $25

Kabai Singh, 1999, Playing Mantis, outfit only, for Dr. Evil

    NM $10   **MIP** $25

Kato, 1998-99, Playing Mantis, Kay-Bee Exclusive

    NM $15   **MIP** $20

(Playing Mantis)

Lone Ranger, 1998-99, Playing Mantis, photo shows Lone Ranger and Tonto

    NM $15   **MIP** $25

Ming the Merciless, 1998-99, Playing Mantis

    NM $15   **MIP** $25

The Phantom, 1999, Playing Mantis

    NM $10   **MIP** $25

Tonto, 1998-99, Playing Mantis

    NM $15   **MIP** $20

Captain Power and the Soldiers of the Future (Mattel, 1987-88)

ACCESSORIES

Dread Stalker, 1988, Mattel

    NM $25   **MIP** $60

Interlocker Throne, 1987, Mattel

    NM $14   **MIP** $25

Magna Cycle, 1988, Mattel

    NM $12   **MIP** $25

Phantom Striker, 1987, Mattel

    NM $20   **MIP** $35

Power Base, 1987, Mattel

    NM $150   **MIP** $250

Power Jet XT-7, 1987, Mattel

    NM $30   **MIP** $45

Power on Energizer w/figure, 1987, Mattel

    NM $12   **MIP** $25

Trans-Field Base Station, 1988, Mattel

    NM $30   **MIP** $60

Trans-Field Communication Station, 1988, Mattel

    NM $20   **MIP** $45

Wind-Up Soaron Beam Deflector, 1988, Mattel

    NM $15   **MIP** $55

FIGURES, SERIES I

Blastarr Ground Guardian, 1987, Mattel

    NM $8   **MIP** $14

Captain Power, 1987, Mattel

    NM $8   **MIP** $18

Lord Dread, 1987, Mattel

    NM $8   **MIP** $18

Lt. Tank Ellis, 1987, Mattel

    NM $8   **MIP** $14

Major Hawk Masterson, 1987, Mattel

    NM $5   **MIP** $12

Soaron Sky Sentry, 1987, Mattel

    NM $14   **MIP** $22

FIGURES, SERIES II

Col. Stingray Johnson, 1988, Mattel

    NM $22   **MIP** $30

Cpl. Pilot Chase, 1988, Mattel

    NM $6   **MIP** $14

Dread Commander, 1988, Mattel

    NM $25   **MIP** $65

Dread Trooper, 1988, Mattel

    NM $30   **MIP** $80

Sgt. Scout Baker, 1988, Mattel

    NM $6   **MIP** $16

Tritor, 1988, Mattel

    NM $30   **MIP** $40

Captain Scarlett (Pedigree, 1967)

12" FIGURE

Captain Scarlet, 1967, Pedigree

    NM $550   **MIP** $1300

Captain Scarlett (Vivid Imaginations, 1993-94)

12" FIGURES

Captain Black, 1993-94
NM $15   MIP $35

Captain Scarlett, 1993-94
NM $15   MIP $35

3-3/4" FIGURES

Captain Black, 1993-94
NM $2   MIP $5

Captain Blue, 1993-94
NM $2   MIP $5

Captain Scarlett, 1993-94
NM $2   MIP $5

Colonel White, 1993-94
NM $2   MIP $5

Destiny Angel, 1993-94
NM $2   MIP $5

Lieutenant Green, 1993-94
NM $2   MIP $5

Centurions (Kenner, 1986)

ACCESSORIES

Power Pack, 1986, Kenner, Series 1
NM $10   MIP $20

FIGURES

Ace McCloud, 1986, Kenner, Series 1, air operations expert
NM $35   MIP $60

Dr. Terror, 1986, Kenner, Series 1, evil genius
NM $32   MIP $50

Hacker, 1986, Kenner, Series 1, Dr. Terror's Henchman
NM $32   MIP $50

Jake Rockwell, 1986, Kenner, Series 1, land operations expert
NM $40   MIP $70

Max Ray, 1986, Kenner, Series 1, sea operations expert
NM $35   MIP $65

Traumatizer, 1986, Kenner, Series 2
NM $80+   MIP $200+

VEHICLES

Detonator, 1986, Kenner, Series 1
NM $25   MIP $80

Skybolt, 1986, Kenner, Series 1
NM $35   MIP $100

Strafer, 1986, Kenner, Series 1
NM $20   MIP $45

Tidal Blast, 1986, Kenner, Series 1
NM $20   MIP $55

Wild Weasel, 1986, Kenner, Series 1
NM $22   MIP $65

Chaos! (Moore Action Collectibles, 1997-1999)

SERIES I, 12" FIGURES

Lady Death, 1997-99
NM $3   MIP $7

Royal Lady Death, 1997-99
NM $3   MIP $7

SERIES I, FIGURES

Evil Ernie, 1997-99
NM $2   MIP $5

Evil Ernie, glow in the dark, 1997-99
NM $2   MIP $5

Lady Death, 1997-99
NM $2   MIP $5

Lady Death, chrome, 1997-99
NM $2   MIP $5

Lady Death, glow in the dark, 1997-99
NM $2   MIP $5

Lady Demon, 1997-99
NM $2   MIP $5

Lady Demon, glow in the dark, 1997-99
NM $2   MIP $5

Purgatori, 1997-99
NM $2   MIP $5

Purgatori, metallic, 1997-99
NM $2   MIP $5

SERIES II, FIGURES

Cremator, 1997-99
NM $2   MIP $5

Cremator, 1997-99
NM $2   MIP $5

Lady Death in Battle Armor, 1997-99
NM $2   MIP $5

Lady Death, Azure, 1997-99
NM $2   MIP $5

Lady Death, bronze, 1997-99
NM $2   MIP $5

Charlie's Angels (Hasbro, 1977)

8-1/2" FIGURES

Jill — Farrah Fawcett, 1977, Hasbro
NM $25   MIP $45

Kelly — Jaclyn Smith, 1977, Hasbro
NM $25   MIP $65

Kris — Cheryl Ladd, 1977, Hasbro
NM $20   MIP $40

Sabrina — Kate Jackson, 1977, Hasbro
NM $18   MIP $45

Sabrina, Kris, and Kelly Gift Set, 1977, Hasbro
NM $60   MIP $180

ACCESSORIES

Adventure Van, 1977, Hasbro, "Headquarters on Wheels"
NM $25   MIP $75

Charlie's Angels (JAKKS Pacific, 2000)

FIGURES

Alex, 2000, JAKKS Pacific, played by Lucy Liu in "Charlie's Angels"
NM $6   MIP $15

(KP Photo)

Dylan Saunders, 2000, JAKKS Pacific, model of Drew Barrymore's character in "Charlie's Angels" movie
NM $6   MIP $15

Natalie, 2000, JAKKS Pacific, played by Cameron Diaz in "Charlie's Angels"
NM $6   MIP $15

CHiPs (Mego, 1979)
3-3/4" FIGURES AND ACCESSORIES

Jimmy Squeaks, 1979, Mego
NM $6   MIP $11
Jon, 1979, Mego
NM $10   MIP $16
Launcher w/Motorcycle, 1979, Mego
NM $24   MIP $42
Motorcycle, boxed, 1979, Mego
NM $15   MIP $32
Ponch, 1979, Mego
NM $12   MIP $16
Sarge, 1979, Mego
NM $10   MIP $65
Wheels Willie, 1979, Mego
NM $6   MIP $11

8" FIGURES AND ACCESSORIES

Jon, 1979, Mego
NM $18   MIP $32
Motorcycle, 1979, Mego
NM $22   MIP $65
Ponch, 1979, Mego
NM $18   MIP $26
Sarge, 1979, Mego
NM $22   MIP $40

Chuck Norris Karate Kommandos (Kenner, 1986-87)
6" FIGURES

Chuck Norris Battle Gear, 1986, Kenner
NM $12   MIP $35
Chuck Norris Kung Fu Training, 1986, Kenner
NM $10   MIP $20
Chuck Norris Undercover Agent, 1986, Kenner
NM $10   MIP $18
Kimo, 1986, Kenner
NM $6   MIP $15
Ninja Master, 1986, Kenner
NM $8   MIP $18
Ninja Serpent, 1986, Kenner
NM $8   MIP $18

Ninja Warrior, 1986, Kenner
NM $8   MIP $20
Super Ninja, 1986, Kenner
NM $8   MIP $18
Tabe, 1986, Kenner
NM $6   MIP $12

VEHICLES
Karate Corvette, 1986, Kenner
NM $10   MIP $20

Clash of The Titans (Mattel, 1980)
FIGURES

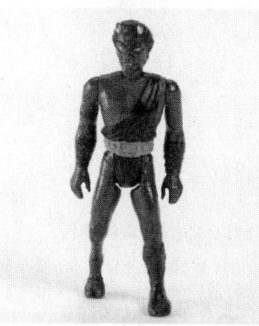
(KP Photo, Karen O'Brien collection)

Calibos, 1980, Mattel, Lord of the Marsh
NM $24   MIP $70
Charon, 1980, Mattel, Ferryman of the River Styx
NM $15   MIP $40
Kraken, 1980, Mattel, Sea Monster
NM $105   MIP $250
Pegasus, 1980, Mattel
NM $35   MIP $65

(KP Photo, Karen O'Brien collection)

Perseus, 1980, Mattel, Hero Son of Zeus
NM $22   MIP $55
Perseus and Pegasus, two-pack, 1980, Mattel
NM $65   MIP $150
Thallo, 1980, Mattel, Captain of the Guard
NM $12   MIP $35

Comic Action Heroes (Mego, 1975-78)
3-3/4" FIGURES

Aquaman, 1975, Mego
NM $35   MIP $90
Batman, 1975, Mego
NM $32   MIP $110
Captain America, 1975, Mego
NM $32   MIP $110
Green Goblin, 1975, Mego
NM $40   MIP $160
Hulk, 1975, Mego
NM $25   MIP $65
Joker, 1975, Mego
NM $30   MIP $90

Penguin, 1975, Mego, shown here w/Robin
NM $35   MIP $90

Robin, 1975, Mego, shown here w/The Penguin, many of the components of Mego action figures were interchangeable, allowing the company to release almost limitless variations of popular figures
NM $30   MIP $75
Shazam, 1975, Mego
NM $30   MIP $110
Spider-Man, 1975, Mego
NM $25   MIP $250
Superman, 1975, Mego
NM $30   MIP $120

Wonder Woman, 1975, Mego
　　　NM $30　　MIP $80

ACCESSORIES

Batcopter, 1975-78, Mego, w/Batman figure
　　　NM $150　　MIP $325

Batmobile, 1975-78, Mego, w/Batman and Robin figures
　　　NM $100　　MIP $225

Collapsing Tower (w/Invisible Plane & Wonder Woman), 1975, Mego
　　　NM $150　　MIP $325

Exploding Bridge w/Batmobile, 1975, Mego
　　　NM $125　　MIP $325

Fortress of Solitude w/Superman, 1975, Mego
　　　NM $125　　MIP $325

Mangler, 1975, Mego
　　　NM $155　　MIP $375

Spidercar, 1975-78, Mego, w/Spider-Man and Green Goblin figures
　　　NM $125　　MIP $325

Comic Heroine Posin' Dolls (Ideal, 1967)

12" BOXED FIGURES

(KP Photo, Joe Desris collection)

Batgirl, 1967, Ideal, Purple gloves, boots, cape and mask
　　　NM $1800　　MIP $5300

Mera, 1967, Ideal
　　　NM $1600　　MIP $4600

Supergirl, 1967, Ideal
　　　NM $1450　　MIP $5100

Wonder Woman, 1967, Ideal
　　　NM $1250　　MIP $5100

Commander Power (Mego, 1975)

FIGURE W/VEHICLE

Commander Power w/Lightning Cycle, 1975, Mego
　　　NM $20　　MIP $40

Commando (Diamond, 1985)

18" FIGURES

Arnold Schwarzenegger, black box, 1985
　　　NM $40　　MIP $125

Arnold Schwarzenegger, red box, 1985
　　　NM $40　　MIP $190

3-3/4" FIGURES

Blaster, 1985
　　　NM $8　　MIP $15

Chopper, 1985
　　　NM $8　　MIP $15

Lead Head, 1985
　　　NM $8　　MIP $15

Matrix, 1985
　　　NM $12　　MIP $35

Psycho, 1985
　　　NM $8　　MIP $15

Sawbones, 1985
　　　NM $8　　MIP $15

Spex, 1985
　　　NM $8　　MIP $15

Stalker, 1985
　　　NM $8　　MIP $15

6" FIGURES

Blaster, 1985
　　　NM $6　　MIP $20

Chopper, 1985
　　　NM $6　　MIP $20

Lead Head, 1985
　　　NM $6　　MIP $20

Matrix, 1985
　　　NM $12　　MIP $35

Pyscho, 1985
　　　NM $6　　MIP $20

Sawbones, 1985
　　　NM $6　　MIP $20

Spex, 1985
　　　NM $6　　MIP $20

Stalker, 1985
　　　NM $6　　MIP $20

Conan (Hasbro, 1994)

FIGURES, ASST. I

Conan the Adventurer w/Star Metal Slash, 1994, Hasbro
　　　NM $5　　MIP $10

Conan the Warrior w/Slashing Battle Action, 1994, Hasbro
　　　NM $5　　MIP $10

Wrath-Amon w/Serpent Slash, 1994, Hasbro
　　　NM $5　　MIP $10

Zulu w/Dart Firing Crossbow, 1994, Hasbro
　　　NM $5　　MIP $10

FIGURES, ASST. II

Conan the Exlporer w/Two-Fisted Chopping Action, 1994, Hasbro
　　　NM $5　　MIP $10

Greywolf w/Cyclone Power Punch, 1994, Hasbro
　　　NM $5　　MIP $10

Ninja Conan w/Katana Chop, 1994, Hasbro
　　　NM $5　　MIP $10

Skulkur w/Zombie Tornado Slash, 1994, Hasbro
　　　NM $5　　MIP $10

Conan (Remco, 1984)

FIGURES

Conan The Warrior, 1984, Remco
　　　NM $175　　MIP $250

Devourer Of Souls, 1984, Remco
　　　NM $100　　MIP $175

Jewel Man, 1984, Remco
　　　NM $100　　MIP $175

Throth Amon, 1984, Remco
NM $60   MIP $150

Coneheads (Playmates, 1995)

FIGURES

(Playmates Toys)

Agent Seedling, 1998, Playmates, shown here w/group of figures in the series
NM $2   MIP $4

Beldar in flight uniform, 1998, Playmates
NM $2   MIP $4

Beldar in street clothes, 1998, Playmates
NM $2   MIP $4

Connie, 1998, Playmates
NM $2   MIP $4

Prymaat in flight uniform, 1998, Playmates
NM $2   MIP $4

Prymaat in street clothes, 1998, Playmates
NM $2   MIP $4

Congo (Kenner, 1995)

FIGURES

(KP Photo)

Amy, 1995, Kenner, shown here w/a group of Congo figures
NM $3   MIP $5

(KP Photo)

Blastface, 1995, Kenner, shown here w/Congo figure group
NM $3   MIP $5

Bonecrucher, Deluxe, 1995, Kenner
NM $4   MIP $6

Kahega, 1995, Kenner
NM $2   MIP $4

Karen Ross, 1995, Kenner
NM $2   MIP $4

Mangler, 1995, Kenner
NM $2   MIP $4

Monroe, 1995, Kenner
NM $2   MIP $4

Monroe, Deluxe, 1995, Kenner
NM $4   MIP $8

Peter Elliot, 1995, Kenner
NM $2   MIP $4

VEHICLES

Net Trap Vehicle, 1995, Kenner
NM $4   MIP $8

Trail Hacker Vehicle, 1995, Kenner
NM $4   MIP $8

Danger Girl (McFarlane, 1999)

FIGURES

Abbey Chase, 1999, McFarlane
NM $4   MIP $8

Major Maxim, 1999, McFarlane
NM $3   MIP $7

Natalia Kassle, 1999, McFarlane
NM $4   MIP $8

Sydney Savage, 1999, McFarlane
NM $4   MIP $8

DC Comics Super Heroes (Toy Biz, 1989)

FIGURES

Aquaman, 1989, Toy Biz
NM $3   MIP $8

Batman, 1989, Toy Biz
NM $3   MIP $8

Bob The Goon, 1989, Toy Biz
NM $3   MIP $8

Flash, 1989, Toy Biz
NM $3   MIP $8

Flash II w/Turbo Platform, 1989, Toy Biz
NM $3   MIP $8

Green Lantern, 1989, Toy Biz
NM $4   MIP $12

Hawkman, 1989, Toy Biz
NM $4   MIP $12

Joker, no forehead curl, 1989, Toy Biz
NM $3   MIP $12

Joker, w/forehead curl, 1989, Toy Biz
NM $3   MIP $12

Lex Luthor, 1989, Toy Biz
NM $3   MIP $10

Mr. Freeze, 1989, Toy Biz
NM $3   MIP $8

Penguin, long missile, 1989, Toy Biz
NM $5   MIP $12

Penguin, short missile, 1989, Toy Biz
NM $5   MIP $12

Penguin, umbrella-firing, 1989, Toy Biz
NM $3   MIP $8

Riddler, 1989, Toy Biz
NM $3   MIP $8

Superman, 1989, Toy Biz
NM $15   MIP $32

Two Face, 1989, Toy Biz
NM $3   MIP $8

Wonder Woman, 1989, Toy Biz
NM $6   MIP $15

Defenders of the Earth (Galoob, 1985)

FIGURES

Flash Gordon, 1985, Galoob, Model No. 5100
NM $5   MIP $12

Garaz, 1985, Galoob
NM $4   MIP $10

Lothar, 1985, Galoob
NM $4   MIP $10

Mandrake, 1985, Galoob
NM $5   MIP $12

Ming, 1985, Galoob
NM $4   MIP $12

Phantom, The, 1985, Galoob
NM $5   MIP $12

VEHICLES

Claw Copter, 1985, Galoob
NM $5   MIP $15

Flash Swordship, 1985, Galoob
NM $6   MIP $20

Garax Swordship, 1985, Galoob
NM $6   MIP $20

Phantom Skull Copter, 1985, Galoob
NM $8   MIP $22

Dick Tracy (Playmates, 1990)

FIGURES, LARGE

Breathless Mahoney, 1990, Playmates, based on the movie, shown here w/the Dick Tracy figure
NM $10   MIP $12

Dick Tracy, 1990, Playmates
NM $10   MIP $15

FIGURES, SMALL

Al "Big Boy" Caprice, 1990, Playmates, photo w/The Blank, Dick Tracy, Influence, Lips Manlis, and Sam Catchem
NM $2   MIP $5

Blank, The, 1990, Playmates
NM $78   MIP $225

Brow, The, 1990, Playmates, Photo w/Mumbles, Flattop, Shoulders
NM $2   MIP $5

Dick Tracy, 1990, Playmates
NM $3   MIP $7

Flattop, 1990, Playmates, includes Tommy gun and bullwhip
NM $2   MIP $5

Influence, 1990, Playmates
NM $2   MIP $5

Itchy, 1990, Playmates
NM $2   MIP $5

Lips Manlis, 1990, Playmates
NM $2   MIP $5

Mumbles, 1990, Playmates
NM $2   MIP $5

Pruneface, 1990, Playmates
NM $2   MIP $5

Rodent, The, 1990, Playmates
NM $2   MIP $5

Sam Catchem, 1990, Playmates
NM $2   MIP $5

Shoulders, 1990, Playmates
NM $2   MIP $5

Steve the Tramp, 1990, Playmates
NM $2   MIP $5

Die-Cast Super Heroes (Mego, 1979)

6" FIGURES

Batman, 1979, Mego
NM $30   MIP $125

Hulk, 1979, Mego
NM $25   MIP $75

Spider-Man, 1979, Mego
NM $30   MIP $125

Superman, 1979, Mego
NM $30   MIP $100

Doctor Who (Dapol, 1988-95)

FIGURES

Ace w/bat and pack, 1988-95, Dapol
NM $4   MIP $10

Cyberman, 1988-95, Dapol
NM $4   MIP $14

Dalek, black and gold, w/friction drive, 1988-95, Dapol
NM $10   MIP $20

Dalek, black and silver, w/friction drive, 1988-95, Dapol
NM $10   MIP $20

Dalek, gold, w/friction drive, 1988-95, Dapol
NM $10   MIP $20

Dalek, gray and black, w/friction drive, 1988-95, Dapol
NM $10   MIP $20

Dalek, gray and black, w/friction drive, 1988-95, Dapol
NM $10   MIP $20

Dalek, red and black, w/friction drive, 1988-95, Dapol
NM $10   MIP $20

Dalek, red and gold, w/friction drive, 1988-95, Dapol
NM $10   MIP $20

Dalek, white and gold, w/friction drive, 1988-95, Dapol
NM $10   MIP $20

Doctor Who (2nd) Pat Troughton, 1988-95, Dapol
NM $10   MIP $20

Doctor Who (3rd), Jon Pertwee, 1988-95, Dapol
NM $8   MIP $20

Doctor Who (4th), Tom Baker, 1988-95, Dapol
NM $12   MIP $25

Doctor Who (7th) w/brown coat, 1988-95, Dapol
NM $8   MIP $20

Doctor Who (7th) w/gray coat, 1988-95, Dapol
NM $8   MIP $20

Early Cybermen, 1988-95, Dapol
NM $6   MIP $18

Ice Warrior, 1988-95, Dapol
NM $4   MIP $10

K9 w/motor action, 1988-95, Dapol
NM $4   MIP $12

Master, The, 1988-95, Dapol
NM $4   MIP $10

Mel, blue shirt, 1988-95, Dapol

> NM $4   MIP $10

Mel, pink shirt, 1988-95, Dapol

> NM $4   MIP $10

Melkur, 1988-95, Dapol

> NM $4   MIP $10

Sea Devil w/cloth outfit, 1988-95, Dapol

> NM $4   MIP $10

Silurian, 1988-95, Dapol

> NM $4   MIP $10

Silurian, armored, 1988-95, Dapol

> NM $4   MIP $10

Sontaran Captain w/helmet, 1988-95, Dapol

> NM $4   MIP $10

Tetrap, 1988-95, Dapol

> NM $4   MIP $10

Time Lords, brown, 1988-95, Dapol

> NM $4   MIP $10

Time Lords, burgundy, 1988-95, Dapol

> NM $4   MIP $10

Time Lords, gray, 1988-95, Dapol

> NM $4   MIP $10

Time Lords, off-white, 1988-95, Dapol

> NM $4   MIP $10

PLAY SETS

Anniversary Play Set, 1988-95, Dapol

> NM $30   MIP $70

Doctor Who (3rd) Play Set, 1988-95, Dapol

> NM $20   MIP $60

Doctor Who Play Set w/Console, 1988, Dapol

> NM $100   MIP $200

VEHICLES AND ACCESSORIES

Dalek Play Set, 1988-95, Dapol, four figures

> NM $20   MIP $40

Tardis w/flashing light, 1988-95, Dapol

> NM $25   MIP $50

Doctor Who (Denys Fisher, 1976)

FIGURES

(Corey LeChat)

Cyberman, 1976, Denys Fisher, very 1930s-looking robotic figure from the BBC-TV series, called "The Threat from the Outerworld" on the box

> NM $250   MIP $500

Dalek, 1976, Denys Fisher

> NM $225   MIP $590

Doctor Who (4th), 1976, Denys Fisher

> NM $100   MIP $250

(Corey LeChat)

Giant Robot, 1976, Denys Fisher, gray plastic robot from the BBC-TV series

> NM $125   MIP $290

(Corey LeChat)

K-9, 1976, Denys Fisher, looking much like today's toy robot dogs, this Talking K-9 could say a variety of phrases by pressing the control panel on his back

> NM $140   MIP $295

Leela, 1976, Denys Fisher

> NM $180   MIP $295

VEHICLES

(Corey LeChat)

Tardis Play Set, 1976, Denys Fisher, plastic model of the time-travelling police call box as seen in the popular BBC-TV series

> NM $175   MIP $350

Doctor Who (Palitoy, 1976)

FIGURES

(Corey LeChat)

Dalek, Talking, 1976, Palitoy, shown on the right

> NM $110   MIP $160

(Corey LeChat)

K-9, Talking, 1976, Palitoy

> NM $160   MIP $260

Dukes of Hazzard (Mego, 1981-82)

3-3/4" CARDED FIGURES

Bo Duke, 1981-82, Mego
NM $6   MIP $14

Boss Hogg, 1981-82, Mego
NM $8   MIP $22

Cletus, 1981-82, Mego
NM $15   MIP $50

Cooter, 1981-82, Mego
NM $12   MIP $45

Coy Duke, 1981-82, Mego
NM $15   MIP $35

Daisy Duke, 1981-82, Mego
NM $12   MIP $35

Luke Duke, 1981-82, Mego
NM $9   MIP $28

Rosco Coltrane, 1981-82, Mego
NM $16   MIP $38

Uncle Jesse, 1981-82, Mego
NM $15   MIP $30

Vance Duke, 1981-82, Mego
NM $15   MIP $35

3-3/4" FIGURES W/VEHICLES

Boss Hogg's Cadillac, 1981, Mego, w/Boss Hogg figure
NM $55   MIP $110

Daisy Jeep w/Daisy, 1981, boxed, 1981-82, Mego
NM $30   MIP $70

General Lee Car w/Bo and Luke, 1981, boxed, 1981-82, Mego
NM $50   MIP $90

Police Car, 1981, Mego, w/Sheriff Roscoe P. Coltrane
NM $50   MIP $100

8" CARDED FIGURES

Bo Duke, 1981-82, Mego
NM $15   MIP $30

Boss Hogg, 1981-82, Mego
NM $20   MIP $40

Coy Duke (card says Bo), 1981-82, Mego
NM $25   MIP $50

Daisy Duke, 1981-82, Mego
NM $25   MIP $50

(Lenny Lee)

Luke Duke, 1981-82, Mego
NM $18   MIP $35

Vance Duke (card says Luke), 1981-82, Mego
NM $25   MIP $50

Dune (LJN, 1984)

FIGURES

Baron Harkonnen, 1984, LJN
NM $15   MIP $30

Feyd, 1984, LJN
NM $15   MIP $30

Paul Atreides, 1984, LJN
NM $15   MIP $30

Rabban, 1984, LJN
NM $15   MIP $30

Sardauker Warrior, 1984, LJN
NM $18   MIP $35

Stilgar the Freman, 1984, LJN
NM $15   MIP $30

VEHICLES

Sand Crawler, 1984, LJN
NM $15   MIP $30

Sand Tracker, 1984, LJN
NM $15   MIP $30

Sandworm, 1984, LJN
NM $25   MIP $50

Spice Scout, 1984, LJN
NM $20   MIP $45

Dungeons & Dragons (LJN, 1983-84)

MONSTERS

Dragonne, 1983, LJN
NM $25   MIP $75

Hook Horror, 1983, LJN
NM $20   MIP $45

Tiamat, 1983, LJN
NM $155   MIP $500

MOUNTS

Bronze Dragon, 1983, LJN
NM $20   MIP $60

Destrier, 1983, LJN
NM $18   MIP $45

Nightmare, 1983, LJN
NM $18   MIP $50

PLAY SETS

Fortress of Fangs, 1983, LJN
NM $125   MIP $300

SERIES I, 3-3/4" FIGURES, 1983

Elkhorn, 1983, LJN
NM $15   MIP $30

Kelek, 1983, LJN
NM $15   MIP $30

Melf, 1983, LJN
NM $15   MIP $40

Mercion, 1983, LJN
NM $18   MIP $40

Peralay, 1983, LJN
NM $15   MIP $40

Ringlerun, 1983, LJN
NM $12   MIP $28

Strongheart, 1983, LJN
NM $15   MIP $30

Warduke, 1983, LJN
NM $15   MIP $30

Zarak, 1983, LJN
NM $15   MIP $30

SERIES I, 5" FIGURES, 1983

Northlord, 1983, LJN
NM $20   MIP $50

Ogre King, 1983, LJN
NM $20   MIP $45

Young Male Titan, 1983, LJN
NM $12   MIP $30

SERIES II, 3-3/4" FIGURES, 1984

Bowmarc, 1984, LJN, w/"Battle-Matic Action"
NM $40   MIP $100

Deeth, 1984, LJN, w/"Battle-Matic Action"
NM $75   MIP $160

Drex, 1984, LJN, w/"Battle-Matic Action"
NM $55   MIP $120

Elkhorn, 1984, LJN, w/"Battle-Matic Action"
NM $35   MIP $250

Grimsword, 1984, LJN, w/"Battle-Matic Action"
NM $30   MIP $180

Hawkler, 1984, LJN, w/"Battle-Matic Action"
    NM $60   **MIP** $140

Strongheart, 1984, LJN, w/"Battle-Matic Action"
    NM $25   **MIP** $175

Warduke, 1984, LJN, w/"Battle-Matic Action"
    NM $25   **MIP** $175

Zarak, 1984, LJN, w/"Battle-Matic Action"
    NM $40   **MIP** $250

Zorgar, 1984, LJN, w/"Battle-Matic Action"
    NM $60   **MIP** $135

SERIES II, 5" FIGURES, 1984

Mandoom, 1984, LJN
    NM $100   **MIP** $175

Mettaflame, 1984, LJN
    NM $110   **MIP** $175

Northlord, 1984, LJN
    NM $125   **MIP** $225

Ogre King, 1984, LJN
    NM $175   **MIP** $350

Young Male Titan, 1984, LJN
    NM $150   **MIP** $300

E.T. the Extra-Terrestrial (LJN, 1982-83)

FIGURES

E.T and Elliot w/bike, 1982-83, LJN
    NM $8   **MIP** $15

E.T. w/dress and hat, 1982-83, LJN
    NM $6   **MIP** $12

E.T. w/robe, 1982-83, LJN
    NM $6   **MIP** $12

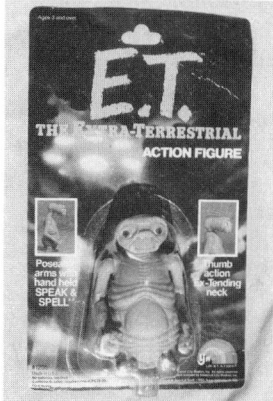

E.T. w/Speak and Spell, 1982-83, LJN, thumb-operated switch on E.T.'s back extends neck
    NM $6   **MIP** $12

E.T., talking, 1982-83, LJN, w/phone, flower, Speak 'n Spell, can
    NM $12   **MIP** $24

E.T., talking, 1982-83, LJN
    NM $12   **MIP** $30

E.T., walking, 1982-83, LJN
    NM $8   **MIP** $22

Earthworm Jim (Playmates, 1995)

FIGURES

Bob, 1995, Playmates
    NM $3   **MIP** $7

Earthworm Jim w/Battle Damage, 1995, Playmates
    NM $5   **MIP** $10

(Playmates Toys)

Earthworm Jim w/Pocket Rocket, 1995, Playmates, figure w/small turbo-driven vehicle (looks a bit like a Gee-Bee racer)
    NM $3   **MIP** $7

Earthworm Jim w/Snott, 1995, Playmates
    NM $3   **MIP** $7

Hench Rat w/Evil Cat, 1995, Playmates
    NM $3   **MIP** $7

Monstrous Peter Puppy, 1995, Playmates
    NM $3   **MIP** $7

Peter Puppy, 1995, Playmates
    NM $3   **MIP** $7

Princess What's-Her-Name, 1995, Playmates
    NM $3   **MIP** $7

Psycrow w/Major Mucus, 1995, Playmates
    NM $3   **MIP** $7

Emergency (LJN, 1973)

FIGURES

John, 1973, LJN
    NM $35   **MIP** $75

Roy, 1973, LJN
    NM $35   **MIP** $75

PLAY SETS

Fire House Play Set, 1973, LJN
    NM $80   **MIP** $200

VEHICLES

Rescue Truck, 1973, LJN
    NM $85   **MIP** $250

Evel Knievel (Ideal, 1973-74)

FIGURES

(Mark Bellomo collection)

Evel Knievel, 1973-74, Ideal, red suit
    NM $30   **MIP** $75

Robby Knievel, 1973-74, Ideal
    NM $30   **MIP** $75

VEHICLES AND ACCESSORIES

Arctic Explorer Set, 1973-74, Ideal
    NM $40   **MIP** $80

Canyon Stunt Cycle, 1973-74, Ideal
    NM $40   **MIP** $80

Chopper, 1973-74, Ideal
    NM $35   **MIP** $80

Dragster, 1973-74, Ideal
    NM $50   **MIP** $120

Explorer Set, 1973-74, Ideal
    NM $25   **MIP** $75

Racing Set, 1973-74, Ideal
    NM $25   **MIP** $75

Rescue Set, 1973-74, Ideal
    NM $25   **MIP** $70

Road and Trail Set, 1973-74, Ideal
    NM $55   **MIP** $135

Scramble Van, 1973-74, Ideal
    NM $55   **MIP** $130

Skull Canyon Play Set, 1973-74, Ideal
    NM $65   **MIP** $150

Stunt and Crash Car, 1973-74, Ideal
    NM $40   **MIP** $100

Stunt Cycle, 1973-74, Ideal
    NM $55   **MIP** $200

Stunt Stadium, 1973-74, Ideal
    NM $35   **MIP** $100

Tail Bike, 1973-74, Ideal
    NM $35   **MIP** $60

ExoSquad (Playmates, 1993-95)

EXOCONVERTING SERIES

J.T. Marsh w/Exoconverting E-frame, 1993-94, Playmates
    NM $10   **MIP** $20

EXOWALKING SERIES

Marsala w/ExoWalking E-frame, 1993-94, Playmates
    NM $10   **MIP** $20

GENERAL PURPOSE E-FRAMES W/FIGURE, ORIGINAL SERIES

(KP Photo, Brian Brogaard collection)

Alec DeLeon w/Field Communications, 1993-95, Playmates
    NM $10   **MIP** $20

J.T. Marsh w/Aerial Attack E-Frame, 1993-95, Playmates
    NM $10   **MIP** $20

Pheaton w/Command E-Frame, 1993-95, Playmates
    NM $10   **MIP** $20

Typhonus w/High Speed Stealth E-Frame, 1993-95, Playmates
    NM $10   **MIP** $20

GENERAL PURPOSE E-FRAMES W/FIGURE, SECONDARY SERIES

Draconis w/Interrogator E-frame, 1994, Playmates
    NM $10   **MIP** $20

Jinx Madison w/Fire Warrior E-frame, 1994, Playmates
    NM $10   **MIP** $20

Jonas Simbacca w/Pirate Captain E-frame, 1994, Playmates
    NM $10   **MIP** $20

Nara Burns w/Reconnaissance E-frame, 1994, Playmates
    NM $10   **MIP** $20

Peter Tanaka w/Samurai E-frame, 1994, Playmates
    NM $10   **MIP** $20

(KP Photo, Brian Brogaard collection)

Rita Torres w/Field Sergeant E-frame, 1994, Playmates
    NM $10   **MIP** $20

Sean Napier w/Police Enforcer E-frame, 1994, Playmates
    NM $10   **MIP** $20

Wolf Bronski w/Ground Assault E-frame, 1994, Playmates
    NM $10   **MIP** $20

GENERAL PURPOSE E-FRAMES W/FIGURE, THIRD SERIES

(KP Photo, Brian Brogaard collection)

J.T. Marsh w/Gridiron Command E-frame, 1995, Playmates
    NM $10   **MIP** $20

Kaz Takagi w/Gorilla E-frame, 1995, Playmates
    NM $10   **MIP** $20

Marsala w/Sub-Sonic Scout E-frame, 1995, Playmates
    NM $10   **MIP** $20

Wolf Bronski w/Medieval Knight E-frames, 1995, Playmates
    NM $10   **MIP** $20

JUMPTROOPS

Captain Avery Butler, 1993-94, Playmates
    NM $6   **MIP** $12

Gunnery Sergeant Ramon Longfeather, 1993-94, Playmates
    NM $6   **MIP** $12

Lance Corporal Vince Pelligrino, 1993-94, Playmates
    NM $6   **MIP** $12

Lieutenant Colleen O'Reilly, 1993-94, Playmates
    NM $6   **MIP** $12

LIGHT ATTACK E-FRAMES

Livanus w/Troop Transport E-frame, 1993-94, Playmates
    NM $16   **MIP** $32

Maggie Weston w/Field Repair E-frame, 1993-94, Playmates
    NM $16   **MIP** $32

(KP Photo, Brian Brogaard collection)

Marsala w/Rapid Assault E-frame, 1993-94, Playmates
    NM $16   **MIP** $32

Shiva w/Amphibious Assault E-frame, 1993-94, Playmates
    NM $50   **MIP** $110

MINI EXO-COMMAND BATTLE SETS

Alec DeLeon and Phaeton w/Vesta Space Port Battleset, 1995, Playmates
    NM $6   **MIP** $12

J.T. Marsh and Typhonus w/Resolute II Hangar Battleset, 1995, Playmates
    NM $6   **MIP** $12

Phaeton and J.T. Marsh w/Olympus Mons Command Ship Bridge Battleset, 1995, Playmates
    NM $6   **MIP** $12

NEO WARRIORS

Neo Cat, 1993-94, Playmates
NM $6   MIP $12

Neo Lord, 1993-94, Playmates
NM $6   MIP $12

ROBOTECH SERIES, 3" FIGURES

Excaliber, 1995, Playmates
NM $3   MIP $5

Gladiator, 1995, Playmates
NM $3   MIP $5

RaidarX, 1995, Playmates
NM $3   MIP $5

Spartan, 1995, Playmates
NM $3   MIP $5

ROBOTECH SERIES, 7" FIGURES

Excaliber MK VI, 1995, Playmates
NM $7   MIP $12

Gladiator Destroid, 1995, Playmates
NM $7   MIP $12

RaidarX, 1995, Playmates
NM $7   MIP $12

Spartan Destroid, 1995, Playmates
NM $7   MIP $12

Zentraedi Power Armor Botoru Battalion, 1995, Playmates
NM $7   MIP $12

Zentraedi Power Armor Quadrono Battalion, 1995, Playmates
NM $7   MIP $12

ROBOTECH SERIES, VEHICLES

VeriTech Hover Tank, 1995, Playmates
NM $22   MIP $42

VF-IS Veritech Fighter, 1995, Playmates
NM $32   MIP $75

SPACE SERIES

Exocarrier Resolute II, 1993-94, Playmates, w/Mini E-frames
NM $15   MIP $30

Kaz Takagi, 1993-94, Playmates, w/ExoFighter Space E-frame
NM $15   MIP $30

Thrax, 1993-94, Playmates, w/NeoFighter Space E-frame
NM $15   MIP $30

SPECIAL MISSION E-FRAMES

Alec DeLeon, 1993-94, Playmates, w/All-Terrain Special Mission E-frame
NM $10   MIP $18

J.T. Marsh, 1993-94, Playmates, w/Deep Space Special Mission E-frame
NM $10   MIP $18

Typhonus, 1993-94, Playmates, w/Deep Submergence Special Mission E-frame
NM $10   MIP $18

Wolf Ronski, 1993-94, Playmates, w/Subterranean Special Mission E-frame
NM $10   MIP $18

Extreme Ghostbusters (Trendmasters, 1997-98)

FIGURES

Eduardo, 1997, Trendmasters
NM $3   MIP $7

Eduardo, Deluxe Edition, 1997, Trendmasters
NM $4   MIP $7

Egon, 1997, Trendmasters
NM $5   MIP $12

Egon, Deluxe Edition, 1997, Trendmasters
NM $4   MIP $7

House Ghost, 1997, Trendmasters
NM $3   MIP $7

Kylie, 1997, Trendmasters
NM $3   MIP $7

Kylie, Deluxe Edition, 1997, Trendmasters
NM $4   MIP $7

Mouth Critter, 1997, Trendmasters
NM $3   MIP $7

Roland, 1997, Trendmasters
NM $3   MIP $7

Roland, Deluxe Edition, 1997, Trendmasters
NM $4   MIP $7

Sam Hain, 1997, Trendmasters
NM $4   MIP $10

Slimer, 1997, Trendmasters
NM $4   MIP $10

VEHICLES AND ACCESSORIES

Ecto 1, 1997, Trendmasters
NM $40   MIP $75

Eduardo w/Motorcycle, 1998, Trendmasters
NM $5   MIP $10

Roland and Gyro-Copter, 1998, Trendmasters
NM $5   MIP $10

Fantastic Four (Toy Biz, 1995)

10" BOXED FIGURES

Dr. Doom, 1995, Toy Biz
NM $4   MIP $10

Human Torch, 1995, Toy Biz
NM $4   MIP $10

Silver Surfer, 1995, Toy Biz
NM $4   MIP $10

The Thing, 1995, Toy Biz
NM $4   MIP $10

5" FIGURES

Annihilus, 1995, Toy Biz
NM $2   MIP $5

Attuma, 1995, Toy Biz
NM $2   MIP $5

Black Bolt, 1995, Toy Biz
NM $2   MIP $5

Blastaar, 1995, Toy Biz
NM $2   MIP $5

Dr. Doom, 1995, Toy Biz
NM $2   MIP $5

Dragon Man, 1995, Toy Biz
NM $2   MIP $5

Firelord, 1995, Toy Biz
NM $2   MIP $5

Gorgon, 1995, Toy Biz
NM $2   MIP $5

Human Torch, 1995, Toy Biz
NM $2   MIP $5

Invisible Woman, 1995, Toy Biz
NM $2   MIP $5

Mole Man, 1995, Toy Biz
NM $2   MIP $5

Mr. Fantastic, 1995, Toy Biz
NM $2   MIP $5

Namor the Sub-Mariner, 1995, Toy Biz
NM $2   MIP $5

Silver Surfer, 1995, Toy Biz
NM $2   MIP $5

Super Skrull, 1995, Toy Biz
NM $2   MIP $5

Terrax, 1995, Toy Biz
NM $2   MIP $5

Thanos, 1995, Toy Biz
NM $2   MIP $5

Thing, 1995, Toy Biz
NM $2   MIP $5

Thing II, 1995, Toy Biz
NM $2   MIP $5

Triton, 1995, Toy Biz
NM $2   MIP $5

ELECTRONIC 14" FIGURES

Galactus, 1995, Toy Biz
    NM $10   **MIP** $20

Talking Thing, 1995, Toy Biz
    NM $4   **MIP** $8

VEHICLES

Fantasticar, 1995, Toy Biz
    NM $20   **MIP** $40

Mr. Fantastic Sky Shuttle, 1995, Toy Biz
    NM $8   **MIP** $20

The Thing's Sky Cycle, 1995, Toy Biz
    NM $5   **MIP** $15

Flash Gordon (Mego, 1976)

9" FIGURES

Dale Arden, 1976, Mego
    NM $45   **MIP** $120

Dr. Zarkow, 1976, Mego
    NM $40   **MIP** $100

Flash Gordon, 1976, Mego
    NM $75   **MIP** $175

Ming the Merciless, 1976, Mego
    NM $60   **MIP** $150

PLAY SETS

Flash Gordon Play Set, 1976, Mego
    NM $40   **MIP** $80

Flash Gordon (Mattel, 1979)

FIGURE SETS

Bad Guys Set, 1979, Mattel, three figures: Ming, Lizard Woman, Beastman, JCPenny Exclusive
    NM $50   **MIP** $135

Sears Set #1, 1979, Mattel, four figures: Dr. Zarkhov, Ming, Vultan, Beastman, #59353, Sears Exclusive
    NM $50   **MIP** $135

Sears Set #2, 1979, Mattel, four figures: Flash, Thun, Arak, Lizard Woman, #59357, Sears Exclusive
    NM $50   **MIP** $120

FIGURES

Beastman, 1979, Mattel, Series 2, no accessories
    NM $20   **MIP** $45

Captain Arak, 1979, Mattel, Series 3, no accessories
    NM $20   **MIP** $50

Dr. Zarkhov, 1979, Mattel, Series 2, no accessories
    NM $8   **MIP** $20

Flash Gordon, 1979, Mattel, Series 1, white gun
    NM $13   **MIP** $25

Lizard Woman, 1979, Mattel, Series 1, white staff
    NM $15   **MIP** $30

Ming the Merciless, 1979, Mattel, Series 1, white gun
    NM $12   **MIP** $22

Thun, the Lion Man, 1979, Mattel, Series 1, white staff
    NM $15   **MIP** $30

Vultan, 1979, Mattel, Series 3, detachable wings
    NM $40   **MIP** $75

VEHICLES

Ming's Shuttle, 1979, Mattel, plastic, scarce, includes blue cannon
    NM $30   **MIP** $65

Rocket Ship, 1979, Mattel, plastic inflatable ship, detachable cockpit, orange nose cone cannon
    NM $40   **MIP** $75

Flintstones (Mattel, 1994)

FIGURES

Betty and Bamm Bamm, 1994, Mattel
    NM $1   **MIP** $2

Big Shot Fred, 1994, Mattel
    NM $1   **MIP** $2

Evil Cliff Vandercave, 1994, Mattel
    NM $1   **MIP** $2

Filling Station Barney, 1994, Mattel
    NM $1   **MIP** $2

Hard Hat Fred, 1994, Mattel
    NM $1   **MIP** $2

Lawn Bowling Barney, 1994, Mattel
    NM $1   **MIP** $2

Licking Dino, 1994, Mattel
    NM $1   **MIP** $2

Wilma and Pebbles, 1994, Mattel
    NM $1   **MIP** $2

Gargoyles (Kenner, 1995-96)

ACCESSORIES

Night Striker, 1995, Kenner
    NM $6   **MIP** $12

Rippin' Rider Cycle, 1995, Kenner
    NM $4   **MIP** $10

FIGURES

Battle Goliath, 1995, Kenner, Series 2
    NM $4   **MIP** $10

Broadway, 1995, Kenner, Series 1, w/Power Slam Arms
    NM $4   **MIP** $10

Broadway, 1996, Hasbro, Hard Wired
    NM $6   **MIP** $12

Bronx, 1995, Kenner, Series 1
    NM $4   **MIP** $10

Brooklyn, 1995, Kenner, Series 1, w/Striking Horns and Snapping Jaw
    NM $4   **MIP** $10

Castle Play Set, 1995, Hasbro
    NM $50   **MIP** $100

Claw Climber Goliath, 1995, Kenner, Series 1
    NM $4   **MIP** $12

Coldstone, 1996, Hasbro, Hard Wired
    NM $4   **MIP** $12

Demona, 1995, Kenner, Series 1, w/Firing Stungun and Wingflap Attack
    NM $4   **MIP** $10

(Mark Bellomo collection)

Elisa Maza, 1995, Hasbro, Series 1
    NM $5   **MIP** $12

Flamestorm Goliath, 1996, Hasbro
    NM $5   **MIP** $12

Goliath, 1996, Hasbro, Hard Wired
    NM $5   **MIP** $12

Lexington, 1995, Kenner, Series 1, w/Firing Stinging Crossbow
    NM $4   **MIP** $10

Mighty Roar Goliath, 1995, Kenner
    NM $4   **MIP** $10

Power Wing Goliath, 1995, Kenner
    NM $4   **MIP** $10

Quick Strike Goliath, 1995, Kenner, Series 1, w/Springing Attack Action
    NM $4   **MIP** $10

Steel Clan Robot, 1995, Kenner, Series 1, w/Exploding Body Power
    NM $4   **MIP** $10

Stone Armor Goliath, 1995, Kenner, Series 1, w/Breaking Away Stone Plates and Flapping Wings
    NM $4   **MIP** $10

Stone Camo Broadway, 1996, Hasbro, Series 2
    NM $4   **MIP** $12

Stone Camo Lexington, 1996, Hasbro, Series 2
    NM $4   **MIP** $12

Strike Hammer Macbeth, 1995, Kenner, Series 1
    NM $4   **MIP** $10

Xanatos, 1995, Kenner, Series 1, w/Gargoyles Disguise Armor and Battle Wings

NM $4   MIP $10

Xanatos, 1996, Hasbro, Series 2

NM $4   MIP $12

Generation X (Toy Biz, 1995-96)

FRESHMAN, 5" FIGURES

Chamber, 1995

NM $2   MIP $4

Emplate, 1995, Toy Biz

NM $2   MIP $4

Jubilee, 1995, Toy Biz

NM $2   MIP $4

Penance, 1995, Toy Biz

NM $2   MIP $4

Phalanx, 1995, Toy Biz

NM $2   MIP $4

Skin, 1995, Toy Biz

NM $2   MIP $4

SOPHOMORE, 5" FIGURES

Banshee, 1996, Toy Biz

NM $3   MIP $5

Marrow, 1996, Toy Biz

NM $3   MIP $4

Mondo, 1996, Toy Biz

NM $3   MIP $4

Protector, The, 1996, Toy Biz

NM $3   MIP $4

White Queen, 1996, Toy Biz

NM $4   MIP $8

Ghost Rider (Toy Biz, 1995-96)

10" FIGURES

Blaze, 1995

NM $2   MIP $5

Ghost Rider, 1995

NM $2   MIP $5

Vengence, 1995

NM $2   MIP $5

5" FIGURES

Armored Blaze, 1996, Toy Biz

NM $2   MIP $5

Blackout, 1995

NM $2   MIP $5

Blaze, 1995

NM $2   MIP $5

Ghost Rider, 1995

NM $2   MIP $5

Ghost Rider II, 1996, Toy Biz, w/transforming action

NM $2   MIP $5

Outcast, 1996, Toy Biz

NM $2   MIP $5

Skinner, 1995, w/Extending Rib action

NM $2   MIP $5

Vengence, 1995

NM $2   MIP $5

Zarathos, 1995

NM $2   MIP $5

FLAMIN' STUNT CYCLES W/MOLDED-ON FIGURES

Blaze, 1995

NM $4   MIP $8

Ghost Rider, 1995

NM $4   MIP $8

Vengeance, 1995

NM $4   MIP $8

PLAY SETS

Ghost Rider Play Set, 1995

NM $4   MIP $10

SPIRIT OF VENGEANCE MOTORCYCLES AND FIGURES

Blaze, 1995, Toy Biz

NM $6   MIP $12

Ghost Rider, 1995, Toy Biz

NM $8   MIP $20

Vengeance, 1995

NM $6   MIP $12

Ghostbusters (Kenner, 1986-91)

1986

Bad to the Bone Ghost, Kenner

NM $7   MIP $15

Banshee Bomber Gooper Ghost w/Ecto-Plazm, Kenner

NM $22   MIP $45

Bug-Eye Ghost, Kenner

NM $8   MIP $25

Ecto-1, Kenner

NM $50   MIP $150

Egon Spengler & Gulper Ghost, Kenner, 5-1/4" tall

NM $35   MIP $140

Firehouse Headquarters, Kenner

NM $100   MIP $250

Ghost Popper, Kenner

NM $30   MIP $65

Ghost Zapper, Kenner

NM $30   MIP $65

Gooper Ghost Sludge Bucket, Kenner

NM $20   MIP $60

Gooper Ghost Squisher w/Ecto-Plazm, Kenner

NM $20   MIP $30

Green Ghost w/Pizza, Kenner

NM $20   MIP $50

H2 Ghost, Kenner

NM $10   MIP $20

Peter Venkman & Grabber Ghost, Kenner

NM $35   MIP $125

Proton Pack, Kenner

NM $85   MIP $140

Ray Stantz & Wrapper Ghost, Kenner

NM $25   MIP $120

Slimer Plush Figure, Kenner

NM $20   MIP $35

Stay-Puft Marshmallow Man, Kenner

NM $18   MIP $70

Stay-Puft Marshmallow Man Plush, Kenner, plush

NM $45   MIP $100

Winston Zeddmore & Chomper Ghost, Kenner

NM $22   MIP $100

1988

Brain Blaster Ghost Haunted Human, Kenner

NM $20   MIP $40

Ecto-2 Helicopter, Kenner

NM $20   MIP $50

Fright Feature Egon, Kenner

NM $8   MIP $25

Fright Feature Janine Melnitz, Kenner

NM $8   MIP $25

Fright Feature Peter, Kenner

NM $8   MIP $25

Fright Feature Ray, Kenner

NM $8   MIP $25

Fright Feature Winston, Kenner

NM $8   MIP $25

Granny Gross Haunted Human, Kenner

NM $7   MIP $15

Hard Hat Horror Haunted Human, Kenner

NM $7   MIP $15

Highway Haunter, Kenner

NM $15   MIP $35

Mail Fraud Haunted Human, Kenner

NM $7   MIP $15

Mini Ghost Mini-Gooper, Kenner

NM $7   MIP $40

Mini Ghost Mini-Shooter, Kenner

NM $7   MIP $12

Mini Ghost Mini-Trap, Kenner

NM $7   MIP $12

Pull Speed Ahead Ghost, Kenner
NM $7　　MIP $15

Terror Trash Haunted Human, Kenner
NM $7　　MIP $15

Tombstone Tackle Haunted Human,
Kenner
NM $7　　MIP $15

X-Cop Haunted Human, Kenner
NM $7　　MIP $15

1989

Dracula, Kenner
NM $12　　MIP $25

Ecto-3, Kenner
NM $12　　MIP $25

Fearsome Flush, Kenner
NM $10　　MIP $22

Frankenstein, Kenner
NM $10　　MIP $22

Hunchback, Kenner
NM $10　　MIP $22

Mummy, Kenner
NM $10　　MIP $22

Screaming Hero Egon, Kenner
NM $10　　MIP $25

Screaming Hero Janine Melnitz, Kenner
NM $10　　MIP $25

Screaming Hero Peter, Kenner
NM $10　　MIP $25

Screaming Hero Ray, Kenner
NM $10　　MIP $25

Screaming Hero Winston, Kenner
NM $10　　MIP $25

Slimer w/Proton Pack, red or blue,
Kenner, red or blue
NM $20　　MIP $50

Super Fright Egon w/Slimy Spider,
Kenner
NM $10　　MIP $25

**Super Fright Janine w/Boo Fish
Ghost,** Kenner
NM $10　　MIP $25

**Super Fright Peter Venkman & Snake
Head,** Kenner
NM $10　　MIP $25

Super Fright Ray, Kenner
NM $10　　MIP $25

**Super Fright Winston Zeddmore &
Meanie Wienie,** Kenner
NM $10　　MIP $25

Wolfman, Kenner
NM $10　　MIP $25

Zombie, Kenner
NM $10　　MIP $25

1990

Ecto Bomber w/Bomber Ghost, Kenner
NM $60　　MIP $200

Ecto-1A w/Ambulance Ghost, Kenner
NM $50　　MIP $125

Ghost Sweeper, Kenner, vehicle in box
NM $12　　MIP $30

Gobblin' Goblin Nasty Neck, Kenner
NM $20　　MIP $35

Gobblin' Goblin Terrible Teeth,
Kenner, boxed action figure
NM $20　　MIP $35

Gobblin' Goblin Terror Tongue,
Kenner, boxed action figure
NM $20　　MIP $35

Slimed Hero Egon, Kenner
NM $20　　MIP $45

**Slimed Hero Louis Tully & Four Eyed
Ghost,** Kenner
NM $20　　MIP $40

**Slimed Hero Peter Venkman & Tooth
Ghost,** Kenner
NM $20　　MIP $45

**Slimed Hero Ray Stantz & Vapor
Ghost,** Kenner
NM $20　　MIP $45

Slimed Hero Winston, Kenner, boxed
action figure
NM $20　　MIP $40

1991

Ecto-Glow Egon, Kenner
NM $18　　MIP $50

Ecto-Glow Louis Tully, Kenner
NM $14　　MIP $40

Ecto-Glow Peter, Kenner
NM $18　　MIP $45

Ecto-Glow Ray, Kenner
NM $18　　MIP $50

Ecto-Glow Winston Zeddmore, Kenner
NM $14　　MIP $40

Ghostbusters, Filmation (Schaper, 1986)

FIGURES

Belfry and Brat-A-Rat, 1986, Schaper
NM $10　　MIP $15

Bone Troller, 1986, Schaper
NM $10　　MIP $15

Eddie, 1986, Schaper
NM $10　　MIP $15

Fangster, 1986, Schaper
NM $10　　MIP $15

Fib Face, 1986, Schaper
NM $10　　MIP $15

Futura, 1986, Schaper
NM $10　　MIP $15

Ghost Popper Ghost Buggy, 1986,
Schaper
NM $20　　MIP $40

Haunter, 1986, Schaper
NM $10　　MIP $15

Jake, 1986, Schaper
NM $10　　MIP $15

Jessica, 1986, Schaper
NM $10　　MIP $15

Mysteria, 1986, Schaper
NM $10　　MIP $15

Prime Evil, 1986, Schaper
NM $12　　MIP $18

Scare Scooter Vehicle, 1986, Schaper
NM $10　　MIP $20

Scared Stiff, 1986, Schaper
NM $6　　MIP $15

Tracy, 1986, Schaper
NM $10　　MIP $15

VEHICLES

Time Hopper Vehicle, 1986, Schaper
NM $10　　MIP $15

Godzilla (Trendmasters, 1998-99)

FIGURES

Baby X Baby Godzilla, 1998-99
NM $3　　MIP $8

Capture Net Phillipe, 1998-99
NM $2　　MIP $8

Claw Slashing Baby Godzilla, 1998-99
NM $3　　MIP $6

Combat Claw Godzilla, 1998-99
NM $8　　MIP $12

Double Blast O'Neil, 1998-99
NM $3　　MIP $7

Fang Bite Godzilla, 1998-99
NM $3　　MIP $7

Grapple Gear Nick, 1998-99
NM $3　　MIP $7

**Hammer Tail Baby Godzilla
Hatchling,** 1998-99
NM $3　　MIP $7

Living Godzilla, 1998-99
NM $8　　MIP $20

**Monster Claw Baby Godzilla
Hatching,** 1998-99
NM $3　　MIP $7

Nuclear Strike Godzilla vs. Hornet Jet,
1998-99
NM $3　　MIP $7

Power Shield Jean-Luc, 1998-99
NM $3　　MIP $7

Razor Bite Godzilla, 1998-99
NM $8　　MIP $20

Razor Fang Baby Godzilla, 1998-99
NM $3　　MIP $7

Shatter Blast Godzilla vs. Rocket
Launcher, 1998-99
NM $3   MIP $7

Shatter Tail Godzilla, 1998-99
NM $7   MIP $15

Spike Jaw Baby Godzilla Hatchling,
1998-99
NM $3   MIP $7

Supreme Godzilla, 1998-99
NM $12   MIP $25

Tail Thrasher Baby Godzilla, 1998-99
NM $3   MIP $7

Thunder Tail Godzilla, 1998-99
NM $7   MIP $15

Ultimate Godzilla, 1998-99
NM $12   MIP $30

Ultra Attack Animal, 1998-99
NM $3   MIP $7

VEHICLES

All-Terrain Vehicle w/figure, 1998-99
NM $7   MIP $15

Apache Attack Copter, 1998-99
NM $10   MIP $20

Battle Bike w/figure, 1998-99
NM $7   MIP $15

Battle Blaster w/figure, 1998-99
NM $7   MIP $15

Combat Cannon w/figure, 1998-99
NM $7   MIP $15

Thunderblast Tank, 1998-99
NM $7   MIP $15

Godzilla Wars
(Trendmasters, 1996)

FIGURES

Battra, 1996
NM $4   MIP $8

Biollante, 1996
NM $4   MIP $8

Gigan, 1996
NM $4   MIP $8

Moguera, 1996
NM $4   MIP $8

Space Godzilla, 1996
NM $4   MIP $8

Supercharged Godzilla, 1996
NM $4   MIP $8

Godzilla:
King of the Monsters
(Trendmasters, 1995)

10" FIGURES

Ghidorah, 1995
NM $4   MIP $10

Ghidorah, walking, 1995
NM $6   MIP $12

Godzilla, 1995
NM $4   MIP $10

Godzilla, walking, 1995
NM $7   MIP $15

Mecha-Ghidora, 1995
NM $6   MIP $12

Mecha-Godzilla, 1995
NM $6   MIP $12

Mothra, 1995
NM $8   MIP $16

Rodan, 1995
NM $4   MIP $10

4-6" FIGURES

Battra, 1995
NM $4   MIP $8

Biollante, 1995
NM $4   MIP $8

Ghidorah, boxed, 1995
NM $4   MIP $8

Ghidorah, carded, 1995
NM $5   MIP $10

Gigan, 1995
NM $5   MIP $10

Godzilla, boxed, 1995
NM $4   MIP $8

Mecha-Ghidorah, boxed, 1995
NM $4   MIP $8

Mecha-Ghidorah, carded, 1995
NM $3   MIP $6

Mecha-Godzilla, boxed, 1995
NM $4   MIP $8

Mecha-Godzilla, carded, 1995
NM $3   MIP $6

Moguera, 1995
NM $4   MIP $10

Mothra, boxed, 1995
NM $5   MIP $10

Mothra, carded, 1995
NM $4   MIP $8

Rodan, boxed, 1995
NM $4   MIP $8

Rodan, carded, 1995
NM $3   MIP $6

Greatest
American Hero, The
(Mego, 1981)

VEHICLES

Convertible Bug w/Ralph and Bill
figures, 1981, Mego
NM $175   MIP $520

Happy Days
(Mego, 1978)

FIGURES

(KP Photo, Karen O'Brien collection)

Fonzie, boxed, 1978, Mego
NM $25   MIP $100

Fonzie, carded, 1978, Mego
NM $25   MIP $60

Potsie, carded, 1978, Mego
NM $15   MIP $40

(Lenny Lee)

Ralph, carded, 1978, Mego
NM $15   MIP $40

Richie, carded, 1978, Mego
NM $15   MIP $40

PLAY SETS

Fonzie's Garage Play Set, 1978, Mego
NM $160+   MIP $325+

VEHICLES

Fonzie's Jalopy, 1978, Mego
NM $50   MIP $100

Fonzie's Motorcycle, 1978, Mego
NM $45   MIP $100

He-Man 2nd Animated Series (Mattel, 1989-1992)

ACCESSORIES

Electronic Terror Punch, 1992, Mattel
NM $10   MIP $25

Electronic Thunder Punch, 1992, Mattel
NM $10   MIP $25

Power Sword, 1989, Mattel
NM $40   MIP $80

Rocket Disk Power Pack, 1989, Mattel
NM $10   MIP $25

Sagitar (Tharkus), 1991, Mattel, creature
NM $20   MIP $40

Skull Staff, 1991, Mattel
NM $35   MIP $70

Turbo Tormentor, 1989, Mattel
NM $10   MIP $20

FIGURES

Artilla (Weaponstronic), 1991, Mattel, Series 3
NM $12   MIP $25

Battle Blade Skeletor, 1992, Mattel, Series 4
NM $20   MIP $40

Battle Punching He-Man, 1990, Mattel, Series 2
NM $40   MIP $90

Butthead, 1991, Mattel, Series 3
NM $15   MIP $30

Disk of Doom Skeletor, 1990, Mattel, Series 2
NM $15   MIP $30

Flipshot (Icarius), 1989, Mattel, Series 1
NM $12   MIP $30

Flogg (Brakk), 1989, Mattel, Series 1
NM $12   MIP $30

He-Man, 1989, Mattel, Series 1
NM $14   MIP $30

He-Man w/Flogg, 1989, Mattel, Series 1
NM $25   MIP $75

He-Man w/Skeletor, 1989, Mattel, Series 1
NM $40   MIP $125

He-Man w/Slush Head, 1989, Mattel, Series 1
NM $25   MIP $75

Hoove, 1990, Mattel, Series 2
NM $12   MIP $20

Hydron, 1989, Mattel, Series 1
NM $14   MIP $30

Kalamarr, 1989, Mattel, Series 1
NM $10   MIP $25

Karatti, 1991, Mattel, Series 3
NM $10   MIP $20

Kayo (Tartarus), 1990, Mattel, Series 2
NM $10   MIP $22

Lizorr, 1990, Mattel, Series 2
NM $12   MIP $25

Missile Armor Flipshot Hook 'em Flogg, 1992, Mattel
NM $150   MIP $225

Nocturna, 1990, Mattel, Series 2
NM $12   MIP $25

Optikk, 1990, Mattel, Seires 2, Model No. 3262
NM $10   MIP $20

Quakke (Earthquake), 1991, Mattel, Series 3
NM $10   MIP $20

Skeletor, 1989, Mattel, Series 1
NM $20   MIP $35

Slush Head (Kalamarr), 1989, Mattel, Series 1
NM $14   MIP $28

Spin-Fist Hydron, 1992, Mattel, Series 4
NM $60   MIP $150

Spinwit (Tornado), 1991, Mattel, Series 3
NM $12   MIP $22

Staghorn, 1991, Mattel, Series 3
NM $12   MIP $25

Thunder Punch He-Man, 1992, Mattel, Series 4
NM $30   MIP $60

Too-Tall Hoove, 1992, Mattel, Series 4
NM $18   MIP $35

Tuskador (Insyzor), 1991, Mattel, Series 3
NM $10   MIP $22

Vizar, 1990, Mattel, Series 2
NM $10   MIP $20

PLAY SETS

Nordor, 1990, Mattel
NM $100   MIP $175

Starship Eternia, 1989, Mattel
NM $75   MIP $145

VEHICLES

Astrosub, 1989, Mattel
NM $8   MIP $15

Battle Bird, 1991, Mattel
NM $120   MIP $250

Bolajet, 1989, Mattel
NM $10   MIP $20

Doomcopter (Skullcopter), 1991, Mattel
NM $15   MIP $38

Dreadwing (Shuttlepod), 1989, Mattel
NM $15   MIP $35

Sagitar, 1989-91, Mattel
NM $6   MIP $14

Terrorclaw (Terrapod), 1989, Mattel
NM $5   MIP $15

Terrortread (Dreadtread), 1991, Mattel
NM $8   MIP $15

He-Man Reissues (Mattel, 2000-01)

ACCESSORIES

He-Man w/Battle Cat, 2000, Mattel, Series 1
NM $30   MIP $70

Skeletor w/Panthor, 2000, Mattel, Series 1
NM $28   MIP $55

FIGURES

Battle Armor He-Man, 2001, Mattel, Series 2
NM $8   MIP $20

Battle Armor Skeletor, 2001, Mattel, Series 2
NM $8   MIP $20

Beast Man, 2000, Mattel, Series 1
NM $5   MIP $15

Buzz Off, 2001, Mattel, Series 2
NM $8   MIP $25

Clawful, 2001, Mattel, Series 2
NM $6   MIP $20

Evil-Lyn, 2000, Mattel, Series 1
NM $5   MIP $20

Faker, 2000, Mattel, Series 1
NM $7   MIP $20

He-Man, 2000, Mattel, Series 1
NM $12   MIP $38

Man-At-Arms, 2000, Mattel, Series 1
NM $5   MIP $25

Mer-Man, 2000, Mattel, Series 1
NM $5   MIP $19

Skeletor, 2000, Mattel, Series 1
NM $12   MIP $30

Stratos, 2001, Mattel, Series 2
NM $10   MIP $25

Teela, 2000, Mattel, Series 1
NM $6   MIP $22

Trap Jaw, 2000, Mattel, Series 1
NM $8   MIP $25

Tri-Klops, 2000, Mattel, Series 1
NM $5   MIP $18

Zodac, 2001, Mattel, Series 2
NM $6   MIP $20

GIFTSETS

Figure 10-pack, JC Penney Exclusive, 2001, Mattel, Series 2
NM $125   MIP $400

Figure five-pack w/exclusive Moss Man, 2001, Mattel, Series 2
NM $40   MIP $110

Figure five-pack w/exclusive Prince Adam, 2001, Mattel, Series 2
NM $65   MIP $160

Hercules: The Legend Continues (Toy Biz, 1995-97)

DELUXE 10" FIGURES

Hercules and Xena, 1995-97, Toy Biz
NM $10   MIP $25

FIGURES

Ares, Detachable Weapons of War, 1995-97, Toy Biz
NM $2   MIP $4

Centaur, Bug Horse Kick, 1995-97, Toy Biz
NM $2   MIP $4

Hercules I, Iron Spiked Spinning Mace, 1995-97, Toy Biz
NM $2   MIP $4

Hercules II, Archery Combat Set, 1995-97, Toy Biz
NM $2   MIP $4

Hercules III, Herculean Assault Blades, 1995-97, Toy Biz
NM $2   MIP $4

Hercules w/Chain Breaking Strength, 1995-97, Toy Biz
NM $2   MIP $4

Hercules, Swash Buckling, 1995-97, Toy Biz
NM $2   MIP $4

Iolaus, Catapult Battle Gear, 1995-97, Toy Biz
NM $2   MIP $4

Minotaur, Immobilizing Sludge Mask, 1995-97, Toy Biz
NM $2   MIP $4

Mole-Man, Exploding Body, 1995-97, Toy Biz
NM $2   MIP $4

She-Demon, Stone Strike Tail, 1995-97, Toy Biz
NM $2   MIP $4

Xena, Warrior Princess Weaponry, 1995-97, Toy Biz
NM $2   MIP $4

MONSTERS

Cerberus, 1995-97, Toy Biz
NM $2   MIP $4

Echidna, 1995-97, Toy Biz
NM $2   MIP $4

Graegus, 1995-97, Toy Biz
NM $2   MIP $4

Hydra, 1995-97, Toy Biz
NM $2   MIP $4

Labyrinth Snake, 1995-97, Toy Biz
NM $2   MIP $4

Stymphalian Bird, 1995-97, Toy Biz
NM $2   MIP $4

PLAY SETS

Hercules Tower of Power Play Set, 1995-97, Toy Biz
NM $4   MIP $5

Hercules: The Legendary Journeys (Toy Biz, 1995-97)

DELUXE 10" FIGURES

Hercules w/bladed shield and sword dagger, 1997, Toy Biz
NM $5   MIP $10

Xena w/two sets of body armor, 1997, Toy Biz
NM $5   MIP $10

LEGENDARY WARRIOR TWIN PACKS, 5" FIGURES

Hercules and Iolaus, 1997, Toy Biz
NM $3   MIP $8

Hercules and Xena, 1997, Toy Biz
NM $3   MIP $8

Xena and Gabrielle, 1997, Toy Biz
NM $3   MIP $8

LEGENDARY WARRIORS, 5" FIGURES

Hercules, Mace Hurling Hercules, 1997, Toy Biz
NM $2   MIP $4

Iolaus, Catapult Back-pack Iolaus, 1997, Toy Biz
NM $2   MIP $4

Nessus, Leg Kicking Centaur, 1997, Toy Biz
NM $2   MIP $4

Xena, Temptress Costume Xena, 1997, Toy Biz
NM $2   MIP $4

MONSTERS, 6" FIGURES

Cerberus, 1997, Toy Biz
NM $2   MIP $4

Graegus, 1997, Toy Biz
NM $2   MIP $4

Hydra, 1997, Toy Biz
NM $2   MIP $4

MT. OLYMPUS GAMES, 5" FIGURES

Atlanta, Spear Shooting Weaponry Rack, 1997, Toy Biz
NM $2   MIP $4

Hercules, Discus Launcher, 1997, Toy Biz
NM $2   MIP $4

Mesomorph, Shield Attack Action, 1997, Toy Biz
NM $2   MIP $4

Salmoneus, Light-up Olympic Torch, 1997, Toy Biz
NM $2   MIP $4

Heroes of the American Revolution (Bonanza, 1970s)

FIGURES

Benjamin Franklin, Bonanza
NM $5   MIP $12

Daniel Boone, Bonanza
NM $5   MIP $12

George Washington, Bonanza
NM $5   MIP $12

John Paul Jones, Bonanza
NM $5   MIP $12

Marquis de Lafayette, Bonanza
NM $5   MIP $12

Nathan Hale, Bonanza
NM $5   MIP $12

Patrick Henry, Bonanza
NM $5   MIP $12

Paul Revere, Bonanza
NM $5   MIP $12

Thomas Jefferson, Bonanza
NM $5   MIP $12

Honey West (Gilbert, 1965)

ACCESSORIES

Formal Outfit, 1965
NM $45   MIP $90

Honey West Accessory Set, 1965, Gilbert, telephone purse, lipstick, handcuffs and telescope
NM $45   MIP $90

Honey West Accessory Set, 1965, Gilbert, cap-firing pistol, binoculars, shoes and glasses
    NM $40   MIP $85

Karate Outfit, 1965, Gilbert
    NM $45   MIP $95

Pet Set w/Ocelot, 1965, Gilbert
    NM $45   MIP $95

Secret Agent Outfit, 1965, Gilbert
    NM $45   MIP $95

FIGURES

Honey West Doll, 1965, Gilbert
    NM $145   MIP $310

Hook (Mattel, 1991-92)

5" FIGURES

Captain Hook, Multi-blade, 1991-92, Mattel
    NM $2   MIP $4

Captain Hook, Swiss Army, 1991-92, Mattel
    NM $2   MIP $4

Captain Hook, Tall Terror, 1991-92, Mattel
    NM $2   MIP $4

Lost Boy Ace, 1991-92, Mattel
    NM $2   MIP $4

Lost Boy Ruffio, 1991-92, Mattel
    NM $2   MIP $4

Lost Boy Thud Butt, 1991-92, Mattel
    NM $2   MIP $4

Peter Pan, Air Attack, 1991-92, Mattel
    NM $2   MIP $4

Peter Pan, Battle Swing, 1991-92, Mattel
    NM $2   MIP $4

Peter Pan, Food Fighting, 1991-92, Mattel
    NM $2   MIP $4

Peter Pan, Swashbuckling, 1991-92, Mattel
    NM $2   MIP $4

Pirate Bill Jukes, 1991-92, Mattel
    NM $2   MIP $4

Pirate Smee, 1991-92, Mattel
    NM $2   MIP $4

DELUXE FIGURES

Captain Hook, Skull Armor, 1991-92, Mattel
    NM $3   MIP $8

Lost Boy Attack Croc, 1991-92, Mattel
    NM $3   MIP $8

Pete Pan, Learn to Fly, 1991-92, Mattel
    NM $3   MIP $8

VEHICLES

Lost Boy Attack Raft, 1991-92, Mattel
    NM $4   MIP $10

Lost Boy Strike Tank, 1991-92, Mattel
    NM $4   MIP $10

Incredible Hulk, The (Toy Biz, 1996-97)

6" FIGURES

Abomination, Toxic Blaster, 1996
    NM $3   MIP $5

Gray Hulk Battle Damaged, 1996
    NM $3   MIP $5

Leader, Anti-Hulk Armor, 1996
    NM $3   MIP $5

Savage Hulk, Transforming Action, 1996
    NM $3   MIP $5

She Hulk, Gamma Cross Bow, 1996
    NM $3   MIP $5

OUTCASTS, 5" FIGURES

Battle Hulk, Mutant Outcast, 1997
    NM $3   MIP $5

Chainsaw, Gamma Outcast Bat, 1997
    NM $3   MIP $5

Leader-Hulk Metamorphosized, Gargoyle Sidekick, 1997
    NM $3   MIP $5

Two-Head, Gamma Outcast Kangaroo-Rat, 1997
    NM $3   MIP $5

Wendingo, Gamma Outcast Rattlesnake, 1997
    NM $3   MIP $5

PLAY SETS

Gamma Ray Trap, 1997
    NM $3   MIP $6

Steel Body Trap, 1997
    NM $3   MIP $6

SMASH AND CRASH, 5" FIGURES

Battle-Damaged Hulk w/Restraints and Smash Out Action, 1997
    NM $3   MIP $6

Doc Samson, Omega w/Missile Firing Action, 1997
    NM $3   MIP $6

Incredible Hulk, Crash out Action, 1997
    NM $3   MIP $6

Leader, Evil Robot Drone w/Missile Firing Action, 1997
    NM $3   MIP $6

Zzzax w/Energy Trap, 1997
    NM $3   MIP $6

TRANSFORMATIONS, 6" FIGURES

(KP Photo)

Absorbing Man, Breakaway Safe and Wrecking Ball, 1997, includes accessories
    NM $3   MIP $6

Hulk 2099, Futuristic Clip-on Weapons, 1997
    NM $3   MIP $6

(KP Photo)

Maestro, Fallen Hero Armor, 1997, includes Captain America's broken shield, and a belt featuring the masks of Iron Man and other Marvel characters
    NM $3   MIP $6

Smart Hulk, Gamma Blaster Backpack, 1997
    NM $3   MIP $6

Independence Day (Trendmasters, 1996)

FIGURES

Alien Attacker Pilot, 1996, Trendmasters
    NM $5   MIP $10

Alien in Bio Chamber, 1996, Trendmasters
    NM $8   MIP $12

Alien Science Officer, 1996, Trendmasters
>   NM $5   MIP $10

Alien Shock Trooper, 1996, Trendmasters
>   NM $5   MIP $10

Alien Supreme Commander, 1996, Trendmasters
>   NM $6   MIP $14

David Levinson, 1996, Trendmasters
>   NM $2   MIP $4

President Thomas Whitmore, 1996, Trendmasters
>   NM $2   MIP $4

Steve Hiller, 1996, Trendmasters
>   NM $2   MIP $4

Ultimate Alien Commander, 1996, Trendmasters, FAO Schwarz Exclusive
>   NM $6   MIP $12

Weapons Expert, 1996, Trendmasters
>   NM $2   MIP $4

Zero Gravity, 1996, Trendmasters
>   NM $2   MIP $4

Indiana Jones (Toys McCoy, 1999)

12" FIGURES

Arabian Horse, 1999
>   NM $150   MIP $450

Indiana Jones, 1999
>   NM $250   MIP $650

Indiana Jones and The Temple of Doom (LJN, 1984)

FIGURES

Giant Thugee, 1984, LJN, on the right
>   NM $50   MIP $120

Indiana Jones, 1984, LJN, shown in the center
>   NM $105   MIP $225

Mola Ram, 1984, LJN, on the left, these figures didn't enjoy as much popularity at the time, probably reflecting the public's mood about the film
>   NM $65   MIP $150

Indiana Jones, The Adventures of (Kenner, 1982-1983)

12" FIGURES

Indiana Jones, 12", 1982-83, Kenner, includes leather jacket, fedora, bullwhip and pistol, Model No. 46000
>   NM $70   MIP $150

4" FIGURES

Belloq, 1982-83, Kenner
>   NM $20   MIP $45

Belloq in Ceremonial Robe, mail away, 1982-83, Kenner
>   NM $15   MIP $30

Cairo Swordsman, 1982-83, Kenner
>   NM $15   MIP $30

German Mechanic, 1982-83, Kenner
>   NM $20   MIP $35

Indiana Jones in German Uniform, 1982-83, Kenner
>   NM $25   MIP $75

Indiana Jones w/whip, 1982-83, Kenner, includes fedora, leather jacket and pistol, too, Model No. 46060
>   NM $80   MIP $225

(Lenny Lee)

Marion Ravenwood, 1982-83, Kenner, includes small monkee
>   NM $110   MIP $325

Sallah, 1982-83, Kenner
>   NM $25   MIP $55

(Lenny Lee)

Toht, 1982-83, Kenner, fully poseable, black plastic overcoat and hat, packaging has mail-in offer for ceremonial Beloq figure
>   NM $18   MIP $35

PLAY SETS

Map Room Play Set, 1982-83, Kenner
>   NM $68   MIP $115

Streets of Cairo Play Set, 1982-83, Kenner
>   NM $52   MIP $75

Well of Souls Play Set, 1982-83, Kenner
>   NM $65   MIP $125

VEHICLES AND ACCESSORIES

Arabian Horse, 1982-83, Kenner
NM $65   MIP $150

Convoy Truck, 1982-83, Kenner
NM $75   MIP $150

Inhumanoids (Hasbro, 1986)

EARTH CORPS

Auger, 1986, Hasbro, helmet, drill
NM $16   MIP $25

Dr. Derek Bright, 1986, Hasbro, helmet, movable claws
NM $16   MIP $25

Herc Armstrong, 1986, Hasbro, helmet, grappling hook arm
NM $16   MIP $25

Liquidator, 1986, Hasbro, helmet, water shooting backpack
NM $16   MIP $25

INHUMANOIDS

D.Compose, 1986, Hasbro, opening ribcage
NM $85   MIP $190

Metlar, 1986, Hasbro, inhumanoid leader
NM $32   MIP $60

Tendrill, 1986, Hasbro, movable tentacles
NM $55   MIP $85

MUTORES, GRANITES

Granites, 1986, Hasbro, rock-like, tan
NM $15   MIP $30

Granok, 1986, Hasbro, rock-like, gray
NM $15   MIP $30

MUTORES, REDWOODS

Redlen, 1986, Hasbro, tree-like, yellow
NM $12   MIP $25

Redsun, 1986, Hasbro, tree-like, orange-brown
NM $12   MIP $25

The Redwoods, 1986, Hasbro, tree-like, gray
NM $12   MIP $25

MUTROES, MAGNOKOR

Magnokor, 1986, Hasbro, splits into Crygen and Pyre
NM $14   MIP $30

VEHICLES

Terrascout, 1986, Hasbro, movable gun, scanner
NM $18   MIP $35

Trappeur, 1986, Hasbro, movable claw, grapping hook, hovercraft
NM $25   MIP $45

Inspector Gadget (Galoob, 1984)

12" FIGURE

Inspector Gadget, 1984, Galoob
NM $80   MIP $175

Inspector Gadget (Tiger Toys, 1992)

FIGURES

Dr. Claw, 1992, Tiger Toys
NM $18   MIP $40

Inspector Gadget that Falls Apart, 1992, Tiger Toys
NM $5   MIP $15

Inspector Gadget that Squirts Water, 1992, Tiger Toys
NM $5   MIP $15

Inspector Gadget w/Expanding Arms, 1992, Tiger Toys
NM $4   MIP $12

Inspector Gadget w/Expanding Legs, 1992, Tiger Toys
NM $5   MIP $15

Inspector Gadget w/Snap Open Hat, 1992, Tiger Toys
NM $5   MIP $15

Inspector Gadget w/Telescopic Neck, 1992, Tiger Toys
NM $5   MIP $15

MAD Agent w/Bazooka, 1992, Tiger Toys
NM $8   MIP $20

Penny and Brain, 1992, Tiger Toys
NM $15   MIP $30

VEHICLES

Gadgetmoile, 1992, Tiger Toys
NM $35   MIP $70

Iron Man (Toy Biz, 1995-96)

5" FIGURES, 1995

Blacklash, Nunchaku and Whip-cracking Action, 1995
NM $3   MIP $8

Blizzard, Ice-Fist Punch, 1995
NM $3   MIP $8

Century, Cape and Battle Staff, 1995
NM $3   MIP $8

Dreadknight, Firing Lance Action, 1995
NM $3   MIP $8

Grey Gargoyle, Stone Hurling Action, 1995
NM $3   MIP $8

Hawkeye, Bow and Arrow, 1995
NM $3   MIP $8

Hulkbuster Iron Man, Removable Armor, 1995
NM $3   MIP $8

Iron Man Arctic Armor, Removable Armor and Launching Claw Action, 1995
NM $3   MIP $8

Iron Man Hologram, 1995, Toy Biz
NM $3   MIP $8

Iron Man Space Armor, Power-lift Space Pack, 1995, Toy Biz
NM $3   MIP $8

Iron Man Stealth Armor, 1995, Toy Biz
NM $3   MIP $8

Iron Man, Hydro Armor, 1995
NM $3   MIP $8

Iron Man, Plasma Cannon Missile Launcher, 1995
NM $3   MIP $8

Mandarin, Light-up Power Rings, 1995
NM $3   MIP $8

Modok, Energy Brain Blasts, 1995, Toy Biz
NM $3   MIP $8

Spider-Woman, Psisonic Web Hurling Action, 1995
NM $3   MIP $8

Titanium Man, Retractable Blade Action, 1995
NM $3   MIP $8

Tony Stark, Armor Carrying Suitcase, 1995
NM $3   MIP $8

U.S. Agent, Firing Shield Action, 1995
NM $12   MIP $30

War Machine, Shoulder-Mount Cannons, 1995
NM $3   MIP $8

Whirlwind, Whirling Battle Action, 1995
NM $3   MIP $8

5" FIGURES, 1996

Crimson Dynamo, 1996
NM $3   MIP $8

Iron Man Inferno Armor, 1996
NM $3   MIP $8

Iron Man Lava Armor, 1996
NM $3   MIP $8

Iron Man Magnetic Armor, 1996
NM $3   MIP $8

Iron Man Radiation Armor, 1996
NM $3   MIP $8

Iron Man Samurai Armor, 1996
NM $3   MIP $8

Iron Man Subterranean Armor, 1996
NM $3   MIP $8

War Machine 2, 1996
    NM $3   **MIP** $8

DELUXE 10" FIGURES

Iron Man, 1995
    NM $3   **MIP** $10

Mandarin, 1995
    NM $3   **MIP** $10

War Machine, 1995
    NM $3   **MIP** $10

DELUXE DRAGONS

Argent, 1995
    NM $3   **MIP** $6

Aureus, 1995
    NM $3   **MIP** $6

FinFang Foom, 1995
    NM $3   **MIP** $6

James Bond Secret Agent 007 (Gilbert, 1965)

12" FIGURES

James Bond, 1965, Gilbert, Sean Connery likeness from "Dr. No.," white shirt, swimming trunks, goggles, snorkel, fins, gun
    NM $160   **MIP** $375

Odd Job, 1965, Gilbert, in white judo outfit w/blackbelt and headband, bowler hat
    NM $130   **MIP** $300

4" FIGURES

Domino, 1965, Gilbert, light blue shirt, blue pants
    NM $10   **MIP** $22

Dr. No, 1965, Gilbert, in white lab coat
    NM $10   **MIP** $22

Goldfinger, 1965, Gilbert
    NM $10   **MIP** $27

James Bond #1, 1965, Gilbert, in white tuxedo w/gun
    NM $10   **MIP** $22

James Bond #2, 1965, Gilbert, in black scuba outfit, Model No. 16503
    NM $10   **MIP** $22

James Bond Casual, 1965, Gilbert, in blue shirt, blue pants
    NM $10   **MIP** $22

Largo, 1965, Gilbert
    NM $10   **MIP** $22

M, 1965, Gilbert
    NM $10   **MIP** $22

Moneypenny, 1965, Gilbert
    NM $10   **MIP** $22

Odd Job, 1965, Gilbert, throwing bowler
    NM $10   **MIP** $22

ACCESSORIES

Action Toys Dr. No's Dragon Tank and Largo's Hydrofoil/Yacht, 1965, Gilbert, Model No. 16543
    NM $15   **MIP** $30

Secret Agent Gun Case and Bullet Shield "M"s Desk, 1965, Gilbert, both in one package, Model No. 16543
    NM $12   **MIP** $24

Spy Wrist Watch w/Decoder, 1965, Gilbert, w/Secret Sighting lenses and World Time Guide
    NM $75   **MIP** $135

FIGURE SETS

Action Toy Set #5, 1965, Gilbert, includes M, Moneypenny, Bond in tux
    NM $25   **MIP** $50

Movie Characters Set, 1965, Gilbert, 10 characters
    NM $300   **MIP** $600

VEHICLES

Aston Martin DB5, 1965, Gilbert, battery-operated, working ejection seat, 11" long
    NM $160   **MIP** $275

James Bond: Moonraker (Mego, 1979)

12" FIGURES

Drax, 1979, Mego
    NM $85   **MIP** $125

Holly, 1979, Mego
    NM $85   **MIP** $125

James Bond, 1979, Mego
    NM $60   **MIP** $75

James Bond, deluxe version, 1979, Mego
    NM $250   **MIP** $400

Jaws, 1979, Mego
    NM $300   **MIP** $500

Johnny Hero (Rosko, 1965-68)

13" FIGURES

Johnny Hero, 1965-68
    NM $65   **MIP** $100

Johnny Hero, Olympic Hero, 1965-68
    NM $65   **MIP** $100

Outfits, 1965-68
    NM $40   **MIP** $75

Jonny Quest (Galoob, 1996)

ACCESSORIES

Cyber Copter, 1996, Galoob
    NM $3   **MIP** $6

Quest Porpoise w/Deep Sea Jonny, 1996, Galoob
    NM $3   **MIP** $6

Quest Rover, 1996, Galoob
    NM $3   **MIP** $6

QUEST WORLD FIGURES

Cyber Cycle Jonny Quest, 1996, Galoob
    NM $3   **MIP** $6

Cyber Jet Race, 1996, Galoob
    NM $3   **MIP** $6

Cyber Suit Hadji, 1996, Galoob
    NM $3   **MIP** $6

Cyber Trax Surd, 1996, Galoob
    NM $3   **MIP** $6

REAL WORLD FIGURES

Deep Sea Race Bannon & Hadji, 1996, Galoob
    NM $3   **MIP** $6

Jungle Commando Dr. Quest & Ezekiel Rage, 1996, Galoob
    NM $3   **MIP** $6

Night Stryker Jonny Quest & Jessie, 1996, Galoob
    NM $3   **MIP** $6

Shuttle Pilot Jonny Quest & Race Bannon, 1996, Galoob
    NM $3   **MIP** $6

X-Treme Action Jonny Quest & Hadji, 1996, Galoob
    NM $3   **MIP** $6

KISS (McFarlane, 1997)

6" FIGURES

(McFarlane Toys)

Ace Frehley w/album, 1997, McFarlane, Series 1, shown w/his other bandmates
    NM $4   **MIP** $12

Ace Frehley w/letter stand, 1997, McFarlane, Series 1
    NM $4   **MIP** $10

Gene Simmons w/album, 1997, McFarlane, Series 1
NM $4   **MIP** $12

Gene Simmons w/letter base, 1997, McFarlane, Series 1
NM $4   **MIP** $10

Paul Stanley w/album, 1997, McFarlane, Series 1
NM $4   **MIP** $12

Paul Stanley w/letter stand, 1997, McFarlane, Series 1
NM $4   **MIP** $10

Peter Criss w/album, 1997, McFarlane, Series 1
NM $4   **MIP** $12

Peter Criss w/letter stand, 1997, McFarlane, Series 1
NM $4   **MIP** $10

KISS (Mego, 1978)

12" BOXED FIGURES

Ace Frehley, 1978, Mego
NM $95   **MIP** $250

Gene Simmons, 1978, Mego, w/accurate face make-up and realistic "wild" hair
NM $95   **MIP** $250

Paul Stanley, 1978, Mego, another in Mego's series—they wisely made

the boxes interchangeable, the package shown appears to have been autographed, face make-up is accurate, and figure also features realistic "wild" hair
NM $90   **MIP** $250

Peter Criss, 1978, Mego
NM $90   **MIP** $250

KISS: Alive (McFarlane, 2000)

FIGURES

(KP Photo)

Ace, 2000, McFarlane, Series 4, figure includes guitar and amp
NM $8   **MIP** $15

(KP Photo)

Gene, 2000, McFarlane, Series 4, includes figure, amp, guitar and candelabra
NM $8   **MIP** $15

(KP Photo)

Paul, 2000, McFarlane, Series 4, includes guitar and amp
NM $8   **MIP** $15

(KP Photo)

Peter, 2000, McFarlane, Series 4, includes drumkit
NM $8   **MIP** $15

KISS: Alive (McFarlane, 2000)

FIGURES

Deluxe Boxed Set, 2000, McFarlane
NM $45   **MIP** $100

KISS: KISS Creatures (McFarlane, 2002)

FIGURES

Deluxe Boxed Set, 2002, McFarlane, included full drum kit
NM $45   **MIP** $115

Space Ace, 2002, McFarlane
NM $10   **MIP** $25

The Demon, 2002, McFarlane
NM $5   **MIP** $15

The Fox, 2002, McFarlane
NM $5   **MIP** $15

The Starchild, 2002, McFarlane
NM $5   **MIP** $15

KISS: Psycho Circus (McFarlane, 1998)

FIGURES

(McFarlane Toys)

Ace Frehley w/Stiltman, 1998, McFarlane, Series 2, includes two figures, Stiltman w/base and skull-topped stilts
NM $3   **MIP** $7

(McFarlane Toys)

Gene Simmons w/Ring Master, 1998, McFarlane, Series 2, each poseable figure includes staff

NM $3   MIP $7

(McFarlane Toys)

Paul Stanley w/The Jester, 1998, McFarlane, Series 2

NM $3   MIP $7

(McFarlane Toys)

Peter Criss w/Animal Wrangler, 1998, McFarlane, Series 2

NM $3   MIP $7

KISS: Psycho Circus Tour (McFarlane, 1999)

FIGURES

Ace Frehley, 1999, McFarlane, Series 3

NM $3   MIP $6

(McFarlane Toys)

Gene Simmons, 1999, McFarlane, Series 3, fierce-looking Gene w/black bass guitar

NM $3   MIP $6

(McFarlane Toys)

Paul Stanley, 1999, McFarlane, Series 3, Paul includes flying-V guitar

NM $3   MIP $6

Peter Criss, 1999, McFarlane, Series 3

NM $3   MIP $6

Lara Croft (Playmates, 1999)

FIGURES

Lara in Area 51 Outfit, 1999, Playmates

NM $6   MIP $12

Lara in Jungle Outfit, 1999, Playmates

NM $6   MIP $12

Lara in Wet Suit, 1999, Playmates

NM $6   MIP $12

talking Lara, 1999, Playmates

NM $10   MIP $20

Laverne and Shirley (Mego, 1978)

12" BOXED FIGURES

Laverne and Shirley, 1978, Mego

NM $40   MIP $70

Lenny and Squiggy, 1978, Mego

NM $35   MIP $70

Legends of the West (Excel Toy Co., 1974)

FIGURES

Buffalo Bill Cody, 1974, Excel Toy Co., hat, gun, and holster

NM $10   MIP $35

Cochise, 1974, Excel Toy Co., rifle

NM $10   MIP $35

Davy Crockett, 1974, Excel Toy Co.

NM $10   MIP $35

Deadwood Dick, 1974, Excel Toy Co., rarest figure in series

NM $15   MIP $45

Jesse James, 1974, Excel Toy Co.

NM $10   MIP $35

Wild Bill Hickok, 1974, Excel Toy Co., gun, holster

NM $10   MIP $35

Wyatt Earp, 1974, Excel Toy Co., gun, holster

NM $10   MIP $35

Lone Ranger (Hubley, 1973)

FIGURES

Lone Ranger, 1973, Hubley, w/hat, mask, two guns and holster rig, scarf, Model No. 23620

NM $60   MIP $140

Silver, 1973, Hubley, w/stand, saddle, halter, bit, reins, martingale, girth, stirrups, poseable and rears up, No. 27625, Model No. 23625

NM $35   MIP $60

Tonto, 1973, Hubley

NM $50   MIP $130

Lone Ranger Rides Again (Gabriel, 1979)

FIGURES

Butch Cavendish, 1979, Gabriel, figure shown here w/Smoke, Butch's horse
    NM $45   **MIP** $80

Dan Reid, 1979, Gabriel
    NM $42   **MIP** $90

Little Bear w/Hawk, 1979, Gabriel
    NM $40   **MIP** $90

Lone Ranger, 1979, Gabriel, figure includes revolvers, hat, mask, scarf, shown here w/Silver
    NM $60   **MIP** $140

Red Sleeves, 1979, Gabriel
    NM $50   **MIP** $90

Tonto, 1979, Gabriel, includes buckskin cloth outfit, shown here w/Scout, the horses in this series were fully poseable and included stands
    NM $50   **MIP** $130

Lone Ranger, Legend of (Gabriel, 1982)

FIGURES

Buffalo Bill Cody, 1982, Gabriel
    NM $15   **MIP** $30

Butch Cavendish, 1982, Gabriel
    NM $14   **MIP** $28

General Custer, 1982, Gabriel
    NM $15   **MIP** $35

Lone Ranger, 1982, Gabriel
    NM $25   **MIP** $40

Lone Ranger w/Silver, 1982, Gabriel
    NM $35   **MIP** $90

Scout, 1982, Gabriel
    NM $20   **MIP** $40

Silver, 1982, Gabriel
    NM $22   **MIP** $45

Smoke, 1982, Gabriel
    NM $15   **MIP** $30

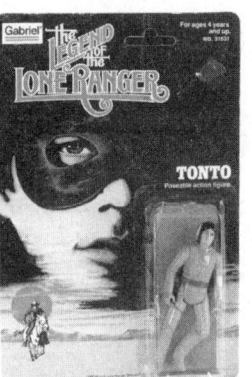

(KP Photo, Karen O'Brien collection)

Tonto, 1982, Gabriel
    NM $20   **MIP** $35

Tonto w/Scout, 1982, Gabriel
    NM $20   **MIP** $65

Lord of the Rings (Toy Vault, 1998-99)

FIGURES

Earth Balrog, Toy Vault, sword, fire whip
    NM $2   **MIP** $6

(KP Photo)

Frodo in Lorien, Toy Vault, w/dagger, belt, pack walking stick, and cloak
    NM $2   **MIP** $6

(KP Photo)

Frodo in the Barrow Downs, Toy Vault, in white ceremonial cloak w/gold highlights
    NM $2   **MIP** $6

Frodo the Hobbit, Toy Vault, w/cloak, sword, pack, belt and blanket
    NM $2   **MIP** $6

(KP Photo)

Gandalf the Wizard, Toy Vault, in gray cloth robe w/hat, food pouch, pipeweed pouch, staff, belt, sword, and scabbard

    NM $2   **MIP** $6

Gimli in Battle, Toy Vault, w/helmet, shield, battle axe

    NM $2   **MIP** $6

Gimli in Lorien, Toy Vault, w/cloth blindfold, cloth Lorien cloak, helmet, pipe

    NM $2   **MIP** $6

Gimli of the Fellowship, Toy Vault, w/dragon helmet, battle axe, pipe, hexagonal stand

    NM $2   **MIP** $6

Gollum, Toy Vault

    NM $2   **MIP** $6

Gollum the Fisherman, Toy Vault

    NM $2   **MIP** $6

(KP Photo)

Ugluk at War, Toy Vault, Fierce Orc w/sword, helmet, dagger and shield

    NM $2   **MIP** $6

(KP Photo)

Ugluk on the Hunt, Toy Vault, w/bow, arrows, quiver, medicine bottle

    NM $2   **MIP** $6

Ugluk the Orc, Toy Vault, figure in gold armor w/medicine bottle, sword, dagger, and helmet

    NM $2   **MIP** $6

Lord of the Rings (Knickerbocker, 1979)

CREATURES

Charger of the Ringwraith, 1979, Knickerbocker

    NM $150+   **MIP** $325+

Frodo's Horse, 1979, Knickerbocker

    NM $160+   **MIP** $275+

Ringwraith the Black Rider, 1979, Knickerbocker, sword, axe

    NM $255+   **MIP** $450+

FIGURES

Aragorn, 1979, Knickerbocker, sword

    NM $75+   **MIP** $175+

Frodo, 1979, Knickerbocker, sword

    NM $70+   **MIP** $200+

Gandalf, 1979, Knickerbocker, staff, hat

    NM $90+   **MIP** $170+

Gollum, 1979, Knickerbocker

    NM $45+   **MIP** $160+

Samwise, 1979, Knickerbocker

    NM $70+   **MIP** $160+

Lost (McFarlane, 2006-07)

SERIES 1

Charlie, 2006, McFarlane, hood up, seated on wreckage writing "FATE" on his finger bandages, Drive Shaft ring, sing it w/me: "You all, everybody!"

    NM $30   **MIP** $65

Hurley, 2006, McFarlane, "Island Open" base, winning lottery ticket

    NM $10   **MIP** $20

Jack, 2006, McFarlane, in suit, plane crash base

    NM $20   **MIP** $40

Kate, 2006, McFarlane, toy plane, jungle base w/tall reeds

    NM $10   **MIP** $20

Locke, 2006, McFarlane, hunting knife, water bottle, Walkabout brochure, hatch base

    NM $15   **MIP** $30

Shannon, 2006, McFarlane, in red bikini sunning herself among the wreckage

    NM $10   **MIP** $20

The Hatch Boxed Set, 2006, McFarlane, Locke, Jack, Kate, Hurley at the partially excavated hatch, lights up from within

    NM $25   **MIP** $50

SERIES 2

Jin, 2007, McFarlane, from Season 2 Episode 2 "Adrift," arms tied behind him, Jin races on the beach to warn

Sawyer and Michael "Others," says four phrases

    NM $10   **MIP** $20

Mr. Eko, 2007, McFarlane, from Season 2 Episode 10 "The 23rd Psalm," says three phrases

    NM $6   **MIP** $20

Sawyer, 2007, McFarlane, from Season 2 Episode 20 "Born to Run," says four phrases

    NM $20   **MIP** $45

Sun, 2007, McFarlane, from Season 1 Episode 15 "In Translation," Sun asserts her independence by wearing a bikini on the beach, says four phrases

    NM $10   **MIP** $20

Lost In Space (Trendmasters, 1998)

9" CLASSIC FIGURES

Cyclops, 1998, Trendmasters

    NM $20   **MIP** $43

Don West, 1998, Trendmasters

    NM $10   **MIP** $20

Dr. Smith, 1998, Trendmasters

    NM $20   **MIP** $40

Judy Robinson, 1998, Trendmasters

    NM $10   **MIP** $20

Robot B9, 1998, Trendmasters

    NM $18   **MIP** $38

Tybo the Carrot Man, 1998, Trendmasters

    NM $18   **MIP** $35

Will Robinson, 1998, Trendmasters

    NM $12   **MIP** $25

FIGURES

(Lenny Lee)

Battle Armor Don West, 1998, Trendmasters, includes blaster rifle and magnet attack micro-spider

    NM $3   **MIP** $6

Cryo Chamber Judy Robinson, 1998, Trendmasters
  NM $3   **MIP** $6

(Lenny Lee)

Cryo Chamber Will Robinson, 1998, Trendmasters, w/chamber, camera and magnet attack micro-spiders
  NM $3   **MIP** $6

(Lenny Lee)

Cryo-Suit Dr. Judy Robinson, 1998, Trendmasters, w/accessories and magnet attack micro-spider
  NM $3   **MIP** $6

Cyclops, 1998, Trendmasters
  NM $12   **MIP** $35

(Lenny Lee)

Dr. Smith, sabotage action, 1998, Trendmasters, includes rifle, magnet attack micro-spider and accessories
  NM $4   **MIP** $8

Future Smith, 1998, Trendmasters
  NM $3   **MIP** $6

Judy Robinson, 1998, Trendmasters
  NM $4   **MIP** $8

(Lenny Lee)

Proteus Armor Dr. Smith, 1998, Trendmasters, w/rifle, and magnet attack micro-spider
  NM $3   **MIP** $6

(Lenny Lee)

Proteus Armor John Robinson, 1998, Trendmasters, includes micro-spider and accessories
  NM $3   **MIP** $6

Will Robinson, 1998, Trendmasters
  NM $4   **MIP** $8

PLAY SETS

(Lenny Lee)

Bubble Fighter, 1998, Trendmasters, fighter ship as seen in the beginning of the movie, features: swiveling cockpit, missile launchers, ejecting bubble section and breakaway battle damage
  NM $8   **MIP** $15

Classic Jupiter 2 Play Set, 1998, Trendmasters
  NM $8   **MIP** $15

(Lenny Lee)

Jupiter 2 Play Set, 1998, Trendmasters, ship fits action figure in cockpit and features: pop-out hyperspace struts, missile launchers, "battle damage" and more magnet-attack micro spiders
  NM $8   **MIP** $15

Lost World of The Warlord (Remco, 1983)

ACCESSORIES AND TEAMS

Warpult, 1983, Remco
  NM $20   **MIP** $45

Warteam w/Arak, 1983, Remco
  NM $30   **MIP** $80

Warteam w/Deimos, 1983, Remco
  NM $30   **MIP** $80

Warteam w/Manchitse, 1983, Remco
  NM $30   **MIP** $80

Warteam w/Mikola, 1983, Remco
  NM $30   **MIP** $80

FIGURES

Arak, 1983, Remco
  NM $15   **MIP** $35

Deimos, 1983, Remco
NM $18   MIP $45

Hercules, 1983, Remco
NM $15   MIP $35

Manchiste, 1983, Remco
NM $18   MIP $45

Mikola, 1983, Remco
NM $18   MIP $45

Warlord, 1983, Remco
NM $12   MIP $32

Love Boat (Mego, 1982)

4" FIGURES

Captain Stubing, 1982, Mego
NM $8   MIP $18

Doc, 1982, Mego
NM $8   MIP $18

Gopher, 1982, Mego
NM $8   MIP $18

Isaac, 1982, Mego
NM $8   MIP $18

Julie, 1982, Mego
NM $10   MIP $20

Vicki, 1982, Mego
NM $10   MIP $20

ACCESSORIES

Love Boat Play Set, 1982, Mego
NM $150   MIP $300

M*A*S*H (Durham, 1973)

8" FIGURES

Hawkeye, 1973, Durham, 8"
NM $15   MIP $30

Hot Lips, 1973, Durham, 8"
NM $15   MIP $30

M*A*S*H (Tristar, 1982)

3-3/4" FIGURES AND VEHICLES

B.J., 1982, Tristar, 3-3/4" tall
NM $6   MIP $14

Base Play Set, 1982, Tristar
NM $100   MIP $180

Colonel Potter, 1982, Tristar, 3-3/4" figure on car
NM $6   MIP $20

Father Mulcahy, 1982, Tristar, 3-3/4" figure on car
NM $6   MIP $14

GI w/Ambulance, 1982, Tristar
NM $25   MIP $40

GI w/Helicopter, 1982, Tristar
NM $28   MIP $60

GI w/Jeep, 1982, Tristar
NM $20   MIP $40

Hawkeye, 1982, Tristar, 3-3/4" figure on car
NM $6   MIP $20

Hot Lips, 1982, Tristar, 3-3/4" figure on car
NM $6   MIP $20

Klinger, 1982, Tristar, 3-3/4" figure on car
NM $6   MIP $20

Klinger in Drag, 1982, Tristar, 3-3/4" figure on car
NM $10   MIP $25

M*A*S*H Figures Collectors Set, 1982, Tristar
NM $40   MIP $80

Winchester, 1982, Tristar, 3-3/4" tall
NM $6   MIP $15

M.A.S.K. (Kenner, 1985-88)

ADVENTURE PACKS

Coast Patrol, 1986
NM $18   MIP $40

Jungle Challenge, 1986
NM $20   MIP $50

Rescue Mission, 1986
NM $20   MIP $50

T-Bob, 1986
NM $20   MIP $50

Venom's Revenge, 1986
NM $18   MIP $40

M.A.S.K. VEHICLES

Billboard Blast w/Dusty Hayes, 1987, Series 3
NM $20   MIP $45

Bulldog w/Boris Bushkin, 1987, Series 3
NM $60   MIP $150

Bullet w/Ali Bombay, 1987, Series 3
NM $32   MIP $55

Buzzard w/Miles Mayhem and Maximus Mayhem, 1987, Series 3
NM $55   MIP $110

Collector, 1987, Kenner, Series 3
NM $22   MIP $70

(Mark Bellomo collection)

Condor w/Brad Turner, 1985, Series 1
NM $25   MIP $65

Firecracker w/Hondo Mac Lean, 1985, Series 1
NM $30   MIP $125

Firefly w/Julio Lopez, 1986, Series 2
NM $20   MIP $60

Gator w/Dusty Hayes, 1985, Series 1
NM $25   MIP $65

Goliath w/Matt Tracker, 1987, Series 3
NM $110   MIP $220

Hurricane w/Hondo Mac Lean, 1986, Series 2
NM $25   MIP $75

Iguana w/Lester Sludge, 1987, Series 3
NM $20   MIP $55

Manta w/Vanessa Warfield, 1987, Series 3
NM $50   MIP $145

Meteor w/Ace Riker, 1987, Series 3
NM $40   MIP $160

Pit Stop Catapult w/Sly Rax, 1987, Series 3
NM $20   MIP $40

Raven w/Calhoun Burns, 1986, Series 2
NM $25   MIP $90

Razorback w/Brad Turner, 1987, Series 3
NM $45   MIP $150

Rhino w/Bruce Sato and Matt Tracker, 1985, Series 1
NM $65   MIP $125

Slingshot w/Ace Riker, 1986, Series 2
NM $32   MIP $110

Thunder Hawk w/Matt Tracker, 1985, Series 1
NM $40   MIP $135

Volcano w/Matt Tracker and Jacques LaFleur, 1986, Series 2
NM $52   MIP $100

Wildcat w/Clutch Hawks, 1987, Series 3
NM $50   MIP $120

MYSTERY ADVENTURE PACKS (UK ONLY)

Arctic Assault, 1988, Kenner
NM $42   MIP $82

Glider Strike, 1988, Kenner
NM $42   MIP $82

Racing Arena, 1988, Kenner
NM $42   MIP $90

Sea Attack, 1988, Kenner
NM $35   MIP $70

PLAY SETS

Boulder Hill Play Set, 1985, Series 1
NM $65   MIP $175

SPLIT SECONDS
M.A.S.K. VEHICLES

Afterburner w/Dusty Hanes, 1988, Series 4
    NM $50   **MIP** $100

Detonator, 1988, Series 4
    NM $60   **MIP** $115

Dynamo w/Bruce Sato, 1988, Series 4
    NM $15   **MIP** $40

Fireforce, 1988, Series 4
    NM $150   **MIP** $270

Jackal w/Bruno Shepherd, 1988, Kenner, Series 4
    NM $35   **MIP** $70

Skybolt, 1988, Kenner, Series 4
    NM $100   **MIP** $210

Stiletto, 1988, Kenner, Series 4
    NM $55   **MIP** $165

Wolfbeast w/Miles Mayhem, 1988, Kenner, Series 4
    NM $110   **MIP** $210

SPLIT SECONDS
V.E.N.O.M. VEHICLES

Barracuda w/Bruno Shepherd, 1988, Series 4
    NM $40   **MIP** $90

Vandal w/Floyd Malloy, 1988, Series 4
    NM $28   **MIP** $60

V.E.N.O.M. VEHICLES

Jackhammer w/Cliffhanger, 1985, Series 1
    NM $35   **MIP** $75

Outlaw w/Miles Mayhem and Nash Gorey, 1986, Series 2
    NM $65   **MIP** $150

Piranha w/Sly Rax, 1985, Series 1
    NM $25   **MIP** $50

Stinger w/Bruno Shepherd, 1986, Series 2
    NM $38   **MIP** $70

Switchblade w/Miles Mayhem, 1985, Series 1
    NM $60   **MIP** $125

Vampire w/Floyd Malloy, 1986, Series 2
    NM $18   **MIP** $40

Mad Monster Series
(Mego, 1974)

8" FIGURES

The Dreadful Dracula, 1974, Mego
    NM $80   **MIP** $200

The Horrible Mummy, 1974, Mego
    NM $50   **MIP** $175

The Human Wolfman, 1974, Mego
    NM $75   **MIP** $175

The Monster Frankenstein, 1974, Mego, w/glow-in-the-dark eyes and hands
    NM $50   **MIP** $175

ACCESSORIES

Mad Monster Castle, vinyl, 1974, Mego
    NM $300   **MIP** $600

Major Matt Mason
(Mattel, 1967-70)

FIGURES

Callisto, 1967, Mattel, #6331, friend from Jupiter
    NM $110   **MIP** $260

Captain Lazer, 1967, Mattel, #6330, blue plastic w/silver trim, friend from Mars
    NM $150   **MIP** $380

Doug Davis, 1967, Mattel, yellow figure
    NM $110   **MIP** $310

(Corey LeChat)

Jeff Long, 1967, Mattel, blue figure
    NM $175   **MIP** $560

Major Matt Mason, 1967, Mattel, white figure
    NM $100   **MIP** $320

Scorpio, 1970, Mattel, rare
    NM $360   **MIP** $875

Sergeant Storm, 1967, Mattel, red figure
    NM $110   **MIP** $410

Space Mission Team, 1969, Mattel, four-pack w/MMM, Callisto, Doug Davis, and Sgt. Storm
    NM $360   **MIP** $650

VEHICLES AND
ACCESSORIES

Astro Trac Missile Convoy Set, 1968, Mattel, #6327, Sears Exclusive set
    NM $275   **MIP** $550

Astro-Trak, 1967, Mattel, #6302, vehicle
    NM $50   **MIP** $150

Doug Davis w/Cat Trac, 1968, Mattel, #6333, figure w/red/orange vehicle
    NM $80   **MIP** $150

Firebolt Space Cannon, 1968, Mattel, #6340, accessory
    NM $75   **MIP** $200

Firebolt Space Cannon Super Action Set, 1968, Mattel, #6341, w/Major Matt Mason, Sgt. Storm, and Captain Lazer
    NM $45   **MIP** $150

Gamma Ray-Gard Pak, 1969, Mattel, #6342, accessory
    NM $30   **MIP** $100

Jeff Long w/Cat Trac, 1968, Mattel, #6332, figure w/white vehicle
    NM $150   **MIP** $240

Lunar Base Command Set, 1969, Mattel, #6353, largest boxed set of the series
    NM $300   **MIP** $600

Major Matt Mason w/Cat Trac, 1968, Mattel, #6318, figure w/red/orange vehicle
    NM $80   **MIP** $160

Major Matt Mason w/Moonsuit, 1967, Mattel, #6303, w/jet pack, space sled, moon suit and tools
    NM $125   **MIP** $400

Mobile Launch Pad, 1968, Mattel, #6328, Sears Exclusive
    NM $35   **MIP** $100

Moon Suit Pak, 1967, Mattel, #6301, accessory
    NM $55   **MIP** $135

Reconojet Pak, 1968, Mattel, #6320, accessory
    NM $25   **MIP** $100

Rocket Launch Pak, 1967, Mattel, #6305, accessory
    NM $25   **MIP** $110

Satellite Launch Pak, 1968, Mattel, #6306, accessory
    NM $25   **MIP** $110

Satellite Locker, 1968, Mattel, #6322, carry case
    NM $30   **MIP** $90

Sgt. Storm w/Cat Trac, 1968, Mattel, #6319, figure w/white vehicle
    NM $110   **MIP** $220

Space Bubble, 1969, Mattel, #6345, vehicle
    NM $80   **MIP** $150

Space Crawler, 1967, Mattel, #6304, vehicle, battery-operated
    NM $100   **MIP** $210

Space Crawler Action Set, 1967, Mattel, #6311, w/MMM, Space Crawler, jet pack, and space sled
    NM n/a   **MIP** n/a

Space Discovery Set, 1969, Mattel, #6355, w/Doug Davis, Callisto, Space Crawler, Space Bubble, Space Power Suit
    NM n/a   **MIP** n/a

Space Power Suit, 1969, Mattel, #6336, accessory
    NM $30   **MIP** $110

Space Power Suit Pak, 1969, Mattel, #6344, accessory
    NM $35   **MIP** $110

Space Probe Pak, 1967, Mattel, #6307, accessory
    NM $35   **MIP** $110

Space Shelter Pak, 1968, Mattel, #6321, accessory
    NM $25   **MIP** $75

Space Station & Space Crawler Deluxe Action Set, 1967, Mattel, #6310, play set
    NM n/a   **MIP** n/a

Space Station Set, 1967, Mattel, #6308, play set, three decks
    NM $200   **MIP** $420

Space Travel Pak, 1969, Mattel, #6347, w/jet propulsion pack, space sled, rifle, chemical tanks
    NM n/a   **MIP** n/a

Spaceship Carry Case, 1967, Mattel, #6316, accessory
    NM $25   **MIP** $50

Star Seeker, 1970, Mattel, #6357, vehicle
    NM $85   **MIP** $180

Star Seeker Walk in Space Set, 1970, Mattel, #6386, space walk feature
    NM n/a   **MIP** n/a

Super Power Set, 1970, Mattel, #6379, MMM figure, Cat Trac, Space Power Suit, Supernaut Power Limbs, rare set
    NM n/a   **MIP** n/a

Supernaut Power Limbs Pak, 1968, Mattel, #6343, accessory
    NM $30   **MIP** $110

Talking Command Console, 1969, Mattel, #5157, accessory, says nine commands
    NM $80   **MIP** $150

Talking Flying Major Matt Mason, 1970, Mattel, #6378, figure, talking jet pack, XRG-1 Reentry Glider
    NM **$210**   **MIP** $318

Talking Major Matt Mason, 1970, Mattel, #6362, figure w/talking jet pack
    NM $150   **MIP** $305

Uni-Tred & Space Bubble, 1969, Mattel, #6339, vehicle
    NM $95   **MIP** $175

Uni-Tred Space Hauler, 1969, Mattel, #6346, vehicle set
    NM n/a   **MIP** n/a

XRG-1 Reentry Glider, 1969, Mattel, #6360, vehicle
    NM $150   **MIP** $395

XRG-1 Reentry Glider w/Major Matt Mason, 1969, Mattel, #6361, glider w/figure
    NM n/a   **MIP** n/a

Man from U.N.C.L.E. (Gilbert, 1965)

FIGURES

Illya Kuryakin, 1965, black sweater, pants and shoes, spring loaded arm
    NM $200   **MIP** $400

Napoleon Solo, 1965, plastic, white shirt, black pants and shoes, spring loaded arm to shoot pistol
    NM $145   **MIP** $325

Mars Attacks! (Trendmasters, 1997)

FIGURES

Martian Ambassador, 1997, Trendmasters
    NM $4   **MIP** $10

Martian Leader, 1997, Trendmasters
    NM $4   **MIP** $10

Martian Spy Girl, 1997, Trendmasters, talking version
    NM $15   **MIP** $30

Martian Spy Girl, 1997, Trendmasters
    NM $15   **MIP** $30

Martian Trooper, 1997, Trendmasters
    NM $4   **MIP** $10

Marvel Famous Covers (Toy Biz, 1997-98)

8" FIGURES

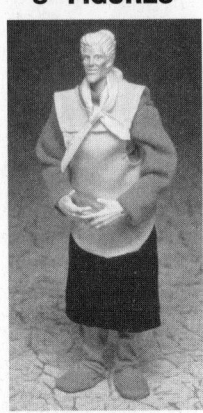

Aunt May, 1997, Toy Biz, mail-away exclusive, w/tied bandana around neck
> NM $7   MIP $12

Captain America, 1998, Toy Biz
> NM $7   MIP $12

Cyclops, 1999, Toy Biz
> NM $7   MIP $12

Dark Phoenix, 1998, Toy Biz
> NM $7   MIP $12

Dr. Doom, 1998, Toy Biz
> NM $7   MIP $12

Green Goblin, 1997, Toy Biz
> NM $7   MIP $12

Magneto, 1999, Toy Biz
> NM $7   MIP $12

Nightcrawler, 1999, Toy Biz
> NM $7   MIP $12

Rogue, 1999, Toy Biz
> NM $7   MIP $12

Spider-Man, red and black costume, 1997, Toy Biz
> NM $9   MIP $15

Storm, 1997, Toy Biz
> NM $7   MIP $12

Thor, 1998, Toy Biz
> NM $7   MIP $12

Wolverine, 1997, Toy Biz
> NM $8   MIP $15

MARVEL MILESTONE, 8" FIGURES

Black Widow, 1998, Toy Biz
> NM $3   MIP $8

Daredevil, 1998, Toy Biz
> NM $3   MIP $8

Falcon, 1998, Toy Biz
> NM $3   MIP $8

Mr. Sinister, 1998, Toy Biz
> NM $3   MIP $8

Marvel Famous Covers (Toy Biz, 1997-98)

8" FIGURES

Gambit, 1998, Toy Biz
> NM $10   MIP $25

Marvel Famous Covers Avengers Assemble (Toy Biz, 1999)

8" FIGURES

Hawkeye, 1999, Toy Biz
> NM $6   MIP $12

Hulk, 1999, Toy Biz
> NM $5   MIP $10

Iron Man, 1999, Toy Biz
> NM $10   MIP $20

Vision, 1999, Toy Biz
> NM $6   MIP $12

Marvel Gold (Toy Biz, 1998)

FIGURES

Black Panther, 1998, Toy Biz
> NM $3   MIP $5

Captain Marvel, 1998
> NM $3   MIP $5

Iron Fist, 1998
> NM $3   MIP $5

Marvel Girl, 1998, Toy Biz
> NM $3   MIP $5

Moon Knight, 1998, Toy Biz
> NM $3   MIP $5

Power Man, 1998, Toy Biz
> NM $3   MIP $5

Vision, 1998, Toy Biz
> NM $3   MIP $5

Marvel Legends (2007-Present)

FANTASTIC FOUR "RONAN THE ACCUSER" SERIES (OCTOBER 2007)

Doctor Doom, 2007, Hasbro, unmasked version; chase variant
> NM $20   MIP $35

Doctor Doom, 2007, Hasbro, w/Ronan's cape
> NM $10   MIP $20

Human Torch, 2007, Hasbro, w/Ronan's right leg
> NM $6   MIP $16

Invisible Woman, 2007, Hasbro, w/Ronan's torso
> NM $15   MIP $40

Mole Man, 2007, Hasbro, w/Ronan's left arm
> NM $8   MIP $25

Mr. Fantastic, 2007, Hasbro, w/Ronan's hammer
> NM $8   MIP $20

Namor the Sub-Mariner, 2007, Hasbro, w/Ronan's right arm
> NM $25   MIP $40

Ronan, 2007, Hasbro, "Build-A-Figure"; assembled
> NM $100   MIP n/a

Silver Surfer, 2007, Hasbro, w/Ronan's left leg
> NM $12   MIP $25

Thing, 2007, Hasbro, w/Ronan's head and helmet
> NM $8   MIP $25

HULK SERIES (JULY 2008)

Absorbing Man, 2008, Hasbro, w/Fin Fang Foom's right leg
> NM $10   MIP $20

Doc Samson, 2008, Hasbro, w/Fin Fang Foom's lower torso
> NM $12   MIP $25

Fin Fang Foom, 2008, Hasbro, "Build-A-Figure"; assembled; very large figure
> NM $130   MIP n/a

Hulk, 2008, Hasbro, "The End" version; w/Fin Fang Foom's right wing and arm
> NM $35   MIP $70

King Hulk, 2008, Hasbro, "World War Hulk" version; w/Fin Fang Foom's tail
> NM $40   MIP $75

Savage Grey Hulk, 2008, Hasbro, classic green hulk variant; w/Fin Fang Foom's left leg
> NM $18   MIP $30

Savage Grey Hulk, 2008, Hasbro, w/Fin Fang Foom's left leg
> NM $15   MIP $30

Shaar, Son of Hulk, 2008, Hasbro, w/Fin Fang Foom's upper torso
> NM $10   MIP $16

She-Hulk, 2008, Hasbro, "Savage" version; w/Fin Fang Foom's head and neck
> NM $25   MIP $38

Wendigo, 2008, Hasbro, w/Fin Fang Foom's left wing and arm
> NM $14   MIP $22

SERIES 1 ("ANNIHILUS" SERIES; JANUARY 2007)

"Planet Hulk," 2007, Hasbro, green left arm
> NM $20   MIP $30

"Planet Hulk," 2007, Hasbro, silver left arm, later updated to the correct green w/head of Annihilus
> **NM** $22   **MIP** $40

Annihilus, 2007, Hasbro, "Build-A-Figure"; corrected armor; assembled
> **NM** $35   **MIP** n/a

Annihilus, 2007, Hasbro, "Build-A-Figure"; pastel armor; assembled
> **NM** $30   **MIP** n/a

Banshee, 2007, Hasbro, w/right wing of Annihilus
> **NM** $3   **MIP** $8

Emma Frost, 2007, Hasbro, w/right arm and leg of Annihilus
> **NM** $4   **MIP** $8

Hercules, 2007, Hasbro, w/left wing of Annilihus
> **NM** $6   **MIP** $8

Ultimate Iron Man, 2007, Hasbro, "facemask off"; chest variant
> **NM** $5   **MIP** $8

Ultimate Iron Man, 2007, Hasbro, w/chest and torso of Annihilus
> **NM** $5   **MIP** $8

X-Men: The Last Stand Beast, 2007, Hasbro, w/left arm and leg of Annihilus
> **NM** $3   **MIP** $7

SERIES 2 ("BLOB" SERIES; APRIL 2007)

Blob, 2007, Hasbro, "Build-A-Figure"; assembled
> **NM** $45   **MIP** n/a

Lord of Asgard Thor, 2007, Hasbro, w/Blob's head
> **NM** $8   **MIP** $15

Quicksilver, 2007, Hasbro, first appearance green costume version; chase variant
> **NM** $5   **MIP** $12

Quicksilver, 2007, Hasbro, silver costume; w/Blob's left arm
> **NM** $3   **MIP** $8

She-Hulk, 2007, Hasbro, w/Blob's upper torso
> **NM** $6   **MIP** $8

Ultimate Wolverine, 2007, Hasbro, w/Blob's lower torso
> **NM** $4   **MIP** $8

X-Men: The Last Stand Jean Grey, 2007, Hasbro, Dark Phoenix version; chase variant
> **NM** $3   **MIP** $8

X-Men: The Last Stand Jean Grey, 2007, Hasbro, w/Blob's right arm
> **NM** $3   **MIP** $8

X-Men: The Last Stand Juggernaut, 2007, Hasbro, w/Blob's hands
> **NM** $6   **MIP** $10

Xorn, 2007, Hasbro, w/Blob's left leg
> **NM** $6   **MIP** $10

Yellowjacket, 2007, Hasbro, gold cotume; chase variant
> **NM** $5   **MIP** $10

Yellowjacket, 2007, Hasbro, w/Blob's right leg
> **NM** $5   **MIP** $8

SERIES 3 ("BROOD QUEEN" SERIES; NOVEMBER 2007)

Black Knight, 2007, Hasbro, w/Brood Queen's legs
> **NM** $7   **MIP** $12

Brood Queen, 2007, Hasbro, "Build-A-Figure"; assembled
> **NM** $30   **MIP** n/a

Bucky, 2007, Hasbro, Golden Age version; w/Brood Queen's tail
> **NM** $7   **MIP** $12

Captain America, 2007, Hasbro, Golden Age version; w/Brood Queen's legs
> **NM** $6   **MIP** $12

Cyclops, 2007, Hasbro, Astonishing X-Men version; w/Brood Queen's head
> **NM** $8   **MIP** $15

Danger, 2007, Hasbro, Astonishing X-Men version; w/Brood Queen's wings
> **NM** $4   **MIP** $8

HYDRA Soldier, 2007, Hasbro, opened mouth variant; w/Brood Queen's front leg
> **NM** $5   **MIP** $10

HYDRA Soldier, 2007, Hasbro, closed mouth; w/Brood Queen's front leg
> **NM** $5   **MIP** $10

Marvel Girl, 2007, Hasbro, "powered-up" chase variant; w/Brood Queen's torso
> **NM** $9   **MIP** $14

Marvel Girl, 2007, Hasbro, Rachel Summers version
> **NM** $3   **MIP** $8

X-Men: The Last Stand Colossus, 2007, Hasbro, chrome paint; chase variant
> **NM** $5   **MIP** $10

X-Men: The Last Stand Colossus, 2007, Hasbro, w/Brood Queen's front leg
> **NM** $4   **MIP** $8

SPIDER-MAN: THE MOVIE (TRILOGY)

"SANDMAN" SERIES (OCTOBER 2007)

Dr. Octopus, 2007, Hasbro, w/Sandman's right arm
> **NM** $15   **MIP** $32

Green Goblin, 2007, Hasbro, w/Sandman's leg
> **NM** $18   **MIP** $32

Mary Jane Watson, 2007, Hasbro, w/Sandman's torso
> **NM** $12   **MIP** $32

New Goblin, 2007, Hasbro, w/Sandman's head
> **NM** $32   **MIP** $60

Sandman, 2007, Hasbro, "Build-A-Figure"; assembled
> **NM** $40   **MIP** n/a

Sandman, 2007, Hasbro, w/Sandman's left foot
> **NM** $20   **MIP** $35

Spider-Man, 2007, Hasbro, red and blue costume; w/Sandman's right foot
> **NM** $22   **MIP** $45

Spider-Man, 2007, Hasbro, black costume; w/Sandman's leg
> **NM** $15   **MIP** $32

Venom, 2007, Hasbro, w/Sandman's left arm
> **NM** $15   **MIP** $32

Marvel Legends (Toy Biz, 2002-Present)

SERIES 1 (MAY 2002)

Captain America, 2002, Toy Biz
> **NM** $16   **MIP** $30

Hulk, 2002, Toy Biz, Wal-Mart Exclusive, removable white shirt
> **NM** $8   **MIP** $16

Hulk, 2002, Toy Biz, non-articulated hands
> **NM** $12   **MIP** $25

Hulk, 2002, Toy Biz, bendable fingers
> **NM** $8   **MIP** $12

Iron Man, 2002, Toy Biz, Wal-Mart Exclusive, stealth armor
> **NM** $32   **MIP** $60

Iron Man, 2002, Toy Biz, gold armor
> **NM** $35   **MIP** $55

Iron Man, 2002, Toy Biz
> **NM** $15   **MIP** $22

Toad, 2002, Toy Biz
> **NM** $22   **MIP** $35

SERIES 2 (SEPTEMBER 2002)

Doctor Doom, 2002, Toy Biz
> **NM** $5   **MIP** $12

Doombot, 2002, Toy Biz, chase variant
NM $6 MIP $16

Human Torch, 2002, Toy Biz, w/out "4" on chest (corrected release)
NM $5 MIP $10

Human Torch, 2002, Toy Biz, w/"4" on chest (early release)
NM $5 MIP $10

Namor, 2002, Toy Biz
NM $8 MIP $15

Thing, 2002, Toy Biz
NM $4 MIP $10

Thing, 2002, Toy Biz, Wal-Mart Exclusive, removable trench coat
NM $6 MIP $12

SERIES 3 (DECEMBER 2002)

Daredevil, 2002, Toy Biz, film version; w/or w/out beard
NM $5 MIP $10

Ghost Rider, 2002, Toy Biz, Dan Ketch version
NM $25 MIP $40

Magneto, 2002, Toy Biz
NM $16 MIP $26

Thor, 2002, Toy Biz
NM $12 MIP $26

Wolverine, 2002, Toy Biz, unmasked version; chase variant
NM $15 MIP $35

Wolverine, 2002, Toy Biz, yellow-and-blue costume
NM $8 MIP $12

SERIES 4 (JUNE 2003)

Beast, 2003, Toy Biz
NM $8 MIP $14

Elektra, 2003, Toy Biz
NM $6 MIP $12

Gambit, 2003, Toy Biz
NM $16 MIP $25

Goliath, 2003, Toy Biz, w/Ant-Man and Wasp
NM $18 MIP $35

Punisher, 2003, Toy Biz, white or gray belt
NM $8 MIP $14

SERIES 5 (NOVEMBER 2003)

Blade, 2003, Toy Biz, film version
NM $18 MIP $26

Colossus, 2003, Toy Biz
NM $20 MIP $28

Mister Fantastic, 2003, Toy Biz
NM $8 MIP $18

Nick Fury, 2003, Toy Biz
NM $14 MIP $22

Red Skull, 2003, Toy Biz, chase variant
NM $25 MIP $40

Sabertooth, 2003, Toy Biz
NM $15 MIP $30

Silver Surfer, 2003, Toy Biz, w/out Howard the Duck
NM $12 MIP $30

Silver Surfer, 2003, Toy Biz, w/Howard the Duck
NM $12 MIP $20

SERIES 6 (SEPTEMBER 2004)

Cable, 2004, Toy Biz, brown costume; chase variant
NM $35 MIP $60

Cable, 2004, Toy Biz, blue costume
NM $20 MIP $35

Dark Phoenix, 2004, Toy Biz, red costume; chase variant
NM $20 MIP $38

Deadpool, 2004, Toy Biz
NM $40 MIP $60

Juggernaut, 2004, Toy Biz
NM $35 MIP $55

Phoenix, 2004, Toy Biz, green costume
NM $12 MIP $22

Punisher, 2004, Toy Biz, film version
NM $10 MIP $15

Wolverine, 2004, Toy Biz, brown costume
NM $8 MIP $16

Wolverine Unmasked, 2004, Toy Biz, chase variant (Series III re-release)
NM $20 MIP $50

SERIES 7 (NOVEMBER 2004)

Apocalypse, 2004, Toy Biz
NM $20 MIP $35

Ghost Rider, 2004, Toy Biz, chase "phasing" variant
NM $20 MIP $35

Ghost Rider, 2004, Toy Biz, Johnny Blaze version
NM $25 MIP $40

Goliath, 2004, Toy Biz, w/Ant-Man and Wasp; chase variant (Series IV re-release)
NM $22 MIP $40

Hawkeye, 2004, Toy Biz, standard-issue regular bow
NM $40 MIP $60

Hawkeye, 2004, Toy Biz, bow w/"knuckle guard"
NM $45 MIP $65

Iron Man, 2004, Toy Biz, Silver Centurion armor
NM $10 MIP $20

Vision, 2004, Toy Biz, chase "phasing" variant
NM $8 MIP $18

Vision, 2004, Toy Biz
NM $8 MIP $18

Wolverine, 2004, Toy Biz, Weapon X version
NM $4 MIP $10

SERIES 8 (DECEMBER 2004)

Black Widow, 2004, Toy Biz, blonde hair, chase variant
NM $8 MIP $30

Black Widow, 2004, Toy Biz, red hair
NM $10 MIP $18

Classic Captain America, 2004, Toy Biz, chase variant
NM $25 MIP $38

Doctor Octopus, 2004, Toy Biz
NM $12 MIP $22

Doombot, 2004, Toy Biz, chase variant (Series II re-release)
NM $6 MIP $12

Iceman, 2004, Toy Biz
NM $15 MIP $22

Iron Man, 2004, Toy Biz, modern armor
NM $18 MIP $30

Man-Thing, 2004, Toy Biz
NM $6 MIP $12

Storm, 2004, Toy Biz, Mohawk version, chase variant
NM $7 MIP $20

Storm, 2004, Toy Biz
NM $9 MIP $20

Ultimate Captain America, 2004, Toy Biz
NM $22 MIP $32

SERIES 9 ("GALACTUS SERIES" BUILD-A-FIGURE; FEBRUARY 2005)

Bullseye, 2005, Toy Biz, chase variant; gritting teeth, gray costume
NM $5 MIP $10

Bullseye, 2005, Toy Biz, w/Galactus' left leg
NM $5 MIP $10

Deathlok, 2005, Toy Biz, w/Galactus' upper torso
NM $5 MIP $10

Doctor Strange, 2005, Toy Biz, w/Galactus' right arm
NM $6 MIP $15

Galactus, 2005, Toy Biz, "Build-A-Figure"; assembled
NM $45 MIP n/a

Hulk, 2005, Toy Biz, first appearance, green; chase variant
NM $5 MIP $10

Hulk, 2005, Toy Biz, first appearance, gray; w/Galactus' left arm
    NM $5   **MIP** $10

Nightcrawler, 2005, Toy Biz, w/Galactus' lower torso
    NM $8   **MIP** $20

Professor X, 2005, Toy Biz, w/Galactus' head
    NM $12   **MIP** $18

War Machine, 2005, Toy Biz, w/Galactus' right leg
    NM $15   **MIP** $30

SERIES 10 ("SENTINEL SERIES" BUILD-A-FIGURE; SEPTEMBER 2005)

Angel, 2005, Toy Biz, blue costume; chase variant
    NM $8   **MIP** $20

Angel, 2005, Toy Biz, red costume; w/Sentinel's left leg
    NM $6   **MIP** $15

Black Panther, 2005, Toy Biz, w/Sentinel's right arm
    NM $20   **MIP** $40

Cyclops, 2005, Toy Biz, X-Factor costume; chase variant
    NM $6   **MIP** $12

Cyclops, 2005, Toy Biz, w/Sentinel's left arm
    NM $5   **MIP** $10

Mister Sinister, 2005, Toy Biz, w/Sentinel's right leg
    NM $10   **MIP** $20

Mystique, 2005, Toy Biz, w/Sentinel's torso
    NM $6   **MIP** $12

Omega Red, 2005, Toy Biz, also w/Sentinel's torso
    NM $12   **MIP** $18

Sentinel, 2005, Toy Biz, "Build-A-Figure"; assembled
    NM $65   **MIP** n/a

Spider-Man, 2005, Toy Biz, first appearance; w/Sentinel's head/upper torso
    NM $15   **MIP** $40

SERIES 11 (LEGENDARY RIDERS SERIES; NOVEMBER 2005)

Iron Man, 2005, Toy Biz, Hulkbuster armor w/Rocket Wing Glider
    NM $28   **MIP** $40

Scarlet Witch, 2005, Toy Biz, w/Hover Platform
    NM $5   **MIP** $10

Taskmaster, 2005, Toy Biz, w/Hover Bike
    NM $10   **MIP** $14

Thing, 2005, Toy Biz, first appearance; w/Sky Cycle
    NM $3   **MIP** $6

Ultron, 2005, Toy Biz, w/Cyber Glider
    NM $5   **MIP** $10

Vengeance, 2005, Toy Biz, w/motorcycle
    NM $5   **MIP** $10

Wolverine/Logan, 2005, Toy Biz, w/motorcycle; younger version w/cowboy hat; chase variant
    NM $15   **MIP** $25

Wolverine/Logan, 2005, Toy Biz, w/motorcycle; "Days of Future Past" version
    NM $8   **MIP** $12

Wonder Man, 2005, Toy Biz, w/Wonder Bike and Yellowjacket; translucent "Ionic" chase variant
    NM $6   **MIP** $10

Wonder Man, 2005, Toy Biz, w/Wonder Bike and Yellowjacket
    NM $5   **MIP** $10

SERIES 12 ("APOCALYPSE SERIES" BUILD-A-FIGURE; DECEMBER 2005)

Apocalypse, 2005, Toy Biz, "Build-A-Figure"; assembled; black color
    NM $65   **MIP** n/a

Apocalypse, 2005, Toy Biz, "Build-A-Figure"; assembled; standard blue color
    NM $38   **MIP** n/a

Bishop, 2005, Toy Biz, bald-head; chase version
    NM $6   **MIP** $12

Bishop, 2005, Toy Biz, w/Apocalypse's lower torso
    NM $5   **MIP** $10

Hulk, 2005, Toy Biz, "Maestro" version; w/Apocalypse's left arm
    NM $5   **MIP** $10

Iron Fist, 2005, Toy Biz, red costume; chase variant
    NM $5   **MIP** $10

Iron Fist, 2005, Toy Biz, green costume; w/Apocalypse's right leg
    NM $5   **MIP** $10

Sasquatch, 2005, Toy Biz, white fur; chase variant
    NM $7   **MIP** $14

Sasquatch, 2005, Toy Biz, orange fur; w/Apocalypse's right arm
    NM $4   **MIP** $10

Wolverine, 2005, Toy Biz, astonishing X-Men; unmasked version; chase variant
    NM $12   **MIP** $28

Wolverine, 2005, Toy Biz, astonishing X-Men version; w/Apocalypse's left leg
    NM $14   **MIP** $32

X-23, 2005, Toy Biz, black costume; chase variant
    NM $4   **MIP** $10

X-23, 2005, Toy Biz, purple costume; w/Apocalypse's head/upper torso
    NM $4   **MIP** $10

SERIES 13 ("ONSLAUGHT" SERIES; MAY 2006)

Abomination, 2006, Toy Biz, melted face; chase variant
    NM $8   **MIP** $12

Abomination, 2006, Toy Biz, w/the left arm of Onslaught
    NM $8   **MIP** $12

Blackheart, 2006, Toy Biz, w/left leg of Onslaught
    NM $4   **MIP** $8

Green Goblin, 2006, Toy Biz, unmasked version; chase variant
    NM $8   **MIP** $14

Green Goblin, 2006, Toy Biz, w/right leg of Onslaught
    NM $5   **MIP** $12

Lady Deathstrike, 2006, Toy Biz, w/upper torso of Onslaught
    NM $3   **MIP** $6

Loki, 2006, Toy Biz, "Crown of Lies" version; chase variant
    NM $4   **MIP** $10

Loki, 2006, Toy Biz, w/right arm of Onslaught
    NM $4   **MIP** $8

Onslaught, 2006, Toy Biz, "Build-A-Figure"; assembled
    NM $25   **MIP** n/a

Pyro, 2006, Toy Biz, w/lower torso of Onslaught
    NM $4   **MIP** $8

SERIES 14 ("MOJO" SERIES; AUGUST 2006)

Baron Zemo, 2006, Toy Biz, unmasked; chase variant
    NM $4   **MIP** $8

Baron Zemo, 2006, Toy Biz, w/Mojo's head and upper torso
    NM $4   **MIP** $8

Falcon, 2006, Toy Biz, newer costume; chase variant
    NM $4   **MIP** $10

Falcon, 2006, Toy Biz, w/Mojo's stomach/lower torso
NM $4   **MIP** $8

Iron Man, 2006, Toy Biz, first appearance; gold armor; chase variant
NM $10   **MIP** $18

Iron Man, 2006, Toy Biz, first appearance; w/Mojo's back tentacles
NM $6   **MIP** $10

Longshot, 2006, Toy Biz, w/Mojo's lower right mechanical legs
NM $4   **MIP** $8

Luke Cage, 2006, Toy Biz, black pants; chase variant
NM $5   **MIP** $10

Luke Cage, 2006, Toy Biz, blue pants; w/Mojo's lower left mechanical legs
NM $4   **MIP** $8

Mojo, 2006, Toy Biz, "Build-A-Figure"; assembled
NM $16   **MIP** n/a

Psylocke, 2006, Toy Biz, w/Mojo's back/lower torso
NM $7   **MIP** $12

SERIES 15 (M.O.D.O.K. SERIES; OCTOBER 2006)

Beta Ray Bill, 2006, Toy Biz, w/M.O.D.O.K.'s hover base
NM $5   **MIP** $10

Captain Marvel, 2006, Toy Biz, "Genis-vell" version; chase variant
NM $12   **MIP** $25

Captain Marvel, 2006, Toy Biz, w/M.O.D.O.K.'s control panel
NM $4   **MIP** $8

Destroyer, 2006, Toy Biz, Iron-Man chase variant
NM $25   **MIP** $40

Iron Man, 2006, Toy Biz, Thor-Buster version; w/M.O.D.O.K.'s right arm
NM $5   **MIP** $12

M.O.D.O.K., 2006, Toy Biz, "Build-A-Figure"; assembled
NM $40   **MIP** n/a

Moon Knight, 2006, Toy Biz, silver costume version; chase variant
NM $18   **MIP** $38

Moon Knight, 2006, Toy Biz, w/M.O.D.O.K.'s left arm
NM $15   **MIP** $28

Spider-Woman, 2006, Toy Biz, Julia Carpenter version; chase variant
NM $17   **MIP** $35

Spider-Woman, 2006, Toy Biz, Jessica Drew version; w/M.O.D.A.K.'s head
NM $5   **MIP** $10

Wasp, 2006, Toy Biz, red costume; chase variant
NM $8   **MIP** $14

Wasp, 2006, Toy Biz, black costume; w/M.O.D.O.K.'s legs
NM $4   **MIP** $8

Marvel Legends Boxed Sets

FANTASTIC FOUR (NOVEMBER 2004)

Doctor Doom, 2004
NM $4   **MIP** n/a

Fantastic Four, 2004
NM $22   **MIP** $35

Franklin Richards, 2004
NM $5   **MIP** n/a

H.E.R.B.I.E. the Robot, 2004
NM $5   **MIP** n/a

Human Torch, 2004
NM $4   **MIP** n/a

Invisible Woman, 2004
NM $4   **MIP** n/a

Mr. Fantastic, 2004
NM $4   **MIP** n/a

Thing, 2004
NM $4   **MIP** n/a

FANTASTIC FOUR (VARIANT SET; NOVEMBER 2004)

Fantastic Four, 2004
NM $22   **MIP** $35

Franklin Richards, 2004
NM $5   **MIP** n/a

H.E.R.B.I.E. the Robot, 2004
NM $5   **MIP** n/a

Human Torch, 2004, translucent variant
NM $4   **MIP** n/a

Invisible Woman, 2004, vanishing/translucent variant
NM $4   **MIP** n/a

Mr. Fantastic, 2004
NM $4   **MIP** n/a

Thing, 2004
NM $4   **MIP** n/a

HOUSE OF M (NOVEMBER 2006)

House of M, 2006
NM $35   **MIP** $65

Hulk, 2006
NM $22   **MIP** n/a

Iron Man, 2006
NM $20   **MIP** n/a

The Inhuman Torch, 2006
NM $13   **MIP** n/a

The It, 2006
NM $15   **MIP** n/a

MARVEL MONSTERS (MAY 2006)

Dracula, 2006
NM $12   **MIP** n/a

Frankenstein's Monster, 2006
NM $10   **MIP** n/a

Marvel Monsters, 2006
NM $22   **MIP** $38

Werewolf by Night, 2006
NM $12   **MIP** n/a

Zombie, 2006
NM $10   **MIP** n/a

SPIDER-MAN & THE SINISTER SIX (SEPTEMBER 2004)

Black Cat, 2004, exclusive
NM $15   **MIP** n/a

Doctor Octopus, 2004
NM $15   **MIP** n/a

Electro, 2004, exclusive
NM $18   **MIP** n/a

Green Goblin, 2004
NM $15   **MIP** n/a

Kraven the Hunter, 2004, new head
NM $10   **MIP** n/a

Spider-Man, 2004
NM $22   **MIP** n/a

Spider-Man & The Sinister Six, 2004
NM $65   **MIP** $132

Venom, 2004, exclusive
NM $22   **MIP** n/a

SPIDER-MAN: FEARSOME FOES (SEPTEMBER 2005)

Carnage, 2005
NM $28   **MIP** n/a

Lizard, 2005
NM $15   **MIP** n/a

Rhino, 2005
NM $25   **MIP** n/a

Spider-Man, 2005
NM $30   **MIP** n/a

Spider-Man: Fearsome Foes, 2005
NM $65   **MIP** $125

Vulture, 2005
NM $25   **MIP** n/a

URBAN LEGENDS (SEPTEMBER 2003)

Daredevil, 2003
NM $12   **MIP** n/a

Elektra, 2003, white costume repaint of Series IV figure
NM $14   **MIP** n/a

Punisher, 2003
NM $14   MIP n/a
Spider-Man, 2003
NM $12   MIP n/a
Urban Legends, 2003
NM $18   MIP $30

X-MEN LEGENDS
(SEPTEMBER 2003)

Beast, 2003, w/added glasses and lab coat
NM $15   MIP n/a
Gambit, 2003, w/added vinyl trench coat
NM $20   MIP n/a
Megneto, 2003, new head sculpt
NM $20   MIP n/a
Rogue, 2003, exclusive
NM $32   MIP n/a
Wolverine, 2003, unmasked version; yellow-and-blue costume
NM $15   MIP n/a
X-Men Legends, 2003
NM $58   MIP $82

YOUNG AVENGERS
(MAY 2006)

Asgardian, 2006
NM $8   MIP n/a
Hulking, 2006
NM $12   MIP n/a
Iron Lad, 2006
NM $8   MIP n/a
Patriot, 2006
NM $8   MIP n/a
Young Avengers, 2006
NM $22   MIP $30

Marvel Legends
Target Exclusives

HASBRO

Adam Warlock, 2008, Hasbro, w/left leg of Red Hulk
NM $12   MIP $25
Fantastic Four: Rise of the Silver Surfer: Movie Silver Surfer, Hasbro
NM $14   MIP $25
Movie Edition Hulk (May 2008), 2008, Hasbro
NM $12   MIP $22
Red Hulk, 2008, Hasbro, "Build-A-Figure"; assembled
NM $80   MIP n/a
Silver Savage, 2008, Hasbro, "Planet Hulk" version; w/right leg of Red Hulk
NM $22   MIP $42
Spider-Man, 2008, Hasbro, black costume; w/left arm of Red Hulk
NM $16   MIP $30

Spiral, 2008, Hasbro, gold weapons; chase variant
NM $15   MIP $35
Spiral, 2008, Hasbro, w/head of Red Hulk
NM $15   MIP $35
Union Jack, 2008, Hasbro, w/torso of Red Hulk
NM $18   MIP $30
Wolverine, 2008, Hasbro, black costume; chase variant
NM $12   MIP $28
Wolverine, 2008, Hasbro, yellow and blue costume; w/right arm of Red Hulk
NM $30   MIP $42

Marvel Legends:
Two-Packs

SERIES 1

Forge and Wolverine, Hasbro
NM $15   MIP $25
Mr. Fantastic and the Thing, Hasbro
NM $12   MIP $20
Ronin and Skrull Elektra, Hasbro, red uniform, chase variant
NM $15   MIP $22
Ronin and Skrull Elektra, Hasbro, orange uniform
NM $15   MIP $22
Ultimate Captain America and Ultimate Nick Fury, Hasbro, green costume, chase variant
NM $15   MIP $25
Ultimate Captain America and Ultimate Nick Fury, Hasbro, black costume
NM $15   MIP $25

Marvel Legends
Two-Packs

TOY BIZ: FACE OFF
SERIES

Captain America (unmasked) vs. Baron Strucker (chase variant), 2006, Toy Biz
NM $18   MIP $32
Captain America vs. Red Skull, 2006, Toy Biz
NM $65   MIP $90
Daredevil (unmasked) vs. Kingpin (black suit) (chase variant), 2006, Toy Biz
NM $12   MIP $22
Daredevil vs. Kingpin (white suit), 2006, Toy Biz
NM $16   MIP $30
First Appearance Wolverine (open-mouthed) vs. Sabertooth (open-

mouthed), 2006, Toy Biz, chase variant
NM $22   MIP $38
First Appearance Wolverine vs. Sabertooth, 2006, Toy Biz
NM $20   MIP $30
Hulk (screaming) vs. Leader (classic version), 2006, Toy Biz, chase variant
NM $28   MIP $40
Hulk vs. Leader (modern version), 2006, Toy Biz
NM $32   MIP $45
Iron Man vs. Mandarin (green costume), 2006, Toy Biz
NM $20   MIP $35
Punisher (classic) vs. Jigsaw (Punisher costume), 2006, Toy Biz
NM $15   MIP $25
Punisher (modern) vs. Jigsaw (suit), 2006, Toy Biz, chase variant
NM $30   MIP $40
War Machine vs. Mandarin (red costume), 2006, Toy Biz, chase variant
NM $32   MIP $50

Marvel Legends
Wal*Mart Exclusives

HASBRO

Ares, 2008, Hasbro, "Build-A-Figure"; assembled
NM $150   MIP n/a
Cable and Marvel Girl (October 2007), 2007, Hasbro
NM $7   MIP $11
Cannonball and Domino (October 2007), 2007, Hasbro
NM $8   MIP $12
Crossbones, 2008, Hasbro, w/Ares' left leg
NM $65   MIP $100
Guardian, 2008, Hasbro, w/Ares' lower torso
NM $25   MIP $50
Heroes Reborn Iron Man, 2008, Hasbro, w/Ares' helmet and sword
NM $6   MIP $12
Human Torch, 2008, Hasbro, semi-translucent; chase variant, w/Ares' left arm
NM $15   MIP $22
Human Torch, 2008, Hasbro, w/Ares' left arm
NM $8   MIP $15
Kang, 2008, Hasbro, w/Ares' upper torso
NM $20   MIP $45
Scarlet Spider, 2008, Hasbro, chase variant; w/Ares' right arm
NM $6   MIP $15

Scarlet Spider, 2008, Hasbro, w/Ares' right arm
    NM $8   MIP $15

Ultimate War Machine, 2008, Hasbro, w/Ares' head
    NM $8   MIP $15

Vision, 2008, Hasbro, w/Ares' right leg
    NM $20   MIP $40

TOY BIZ

Age of Apocalypse Sabertooth, 2006, Toy Biz, w/Giant Man's left foot
    NM $6   MIP $12

Age of Apocalypse Weapon X, 2006, Toy Biz, burnt face; chase variant, w/Giant Man's left hand
    NM $6   MIP $10

Age of Apocalypse Weapon X, 2006, Toy Biz, w/Giant Man's right foot
    NM $7   MIP $12

Ant Man, 2006, Toy Biz, w/Giant Man's right arm
    NM $25   MIP $45

Captain Britain, 2006, Toy Biz, w/Giant Man's right leg
    NM $15   MIP $25

Fantastic Four Box Set, 2004, Toy Biz
    NM $20   MIP $28

Giant-Man, 2006, Toy Biz, "Build-A-Figure"; assembled
    NM $115   MIP n/a

Havok, 2006, Toy Biz, w/Giant Man's left leg
    NM $12   MIP $22

Human Torch, 2004, Toy Biz
    NM $6   MIP n/a

Invisible Woman, 2004, Toy Biz, Heroes Reborn costume
    NM $6   MIP n/a

Kitty Pryde, 2006, Toy Biz, w/Giant Man's upper torso and head
    NM $20   MIP $32

Mr. Fantastic, 2004, Toy Biz, Heroes Reborn costume
    NM $6   MIP n/a

Sentry, 2006, Toy Biz, bearded w/long hair; chase variant, NOTE: Sentry would ship in two different-color uniform variations: tan and light blue, and yellow and dark blue.
    NM $6   MIP $10

Sentry, 2006, Toy Biz, cut hair and clean face; w/Giant Man's left arm
    NM $6   MIP $10

Thing, 2004, Toy Biz
    NM $6   MIP n/a

Thor, 2006, Toy Biz, w/Giant Man's right hand
    NM $20   MIP $40

Warbird, 2006, Toy Biz, w/Giant Man's lower torso
    NM $18   MIP $30

Marvel Legends: Icons

HASBRO

Cyclops, Hasbro
    NM $12   MIP $30

Doctor Doom, Hasbro
    NM $12   MIP $30

Human Torch, Hasbro, "flame on" version; chase variant
    NM $12   MIP $30

Human Torch, Hasbro
    NM $12   MIP $30

Magneto, Hasbro
    NM $12   MIP $30

Punisher, Hasbro
    NM $12   MIP $30

Silver Surfer, Hasbro
    NM $12   MIP $30

Thor, Hasbro
    NM $18   MIP $35

Wolverine, Hasbro, repaint (Toy Biz Series I)
    NM $18   MIP $35

TOY BIZ

Beast, Toy Biz, blue fur; chase variant
    NM $7   MIP $12

Beast, Toy Biz, gray fur
    NM $7   MIP $12

Captain America, Toy Biz, unmasked; chase variant
    NM $15   MIP $30

Captain America, Toy Biz
    NM $55   MIP $85

Hulk, Toy Biz, gray; chase variant
    NM $60   MIP $85

Hulk, Toy Biz, green version
    NM $60   MIP $85

Iron Man, Toy Biz, gold; chase variant
    NM $20   MIP $35

Iron Man, Toy Biz
    NM $12   MIP $25

Spider-Man, Toy Biz, unmasked; chase variant
    NM $12   MIP $25

Spider-Man, Toy Biz
    NM $30   MIP $65

Venom, Toy Biz, unmasked; chase variant
    NM $14   MIP $30

Venom, Toy Biz
    NM $14   MIP $30

Wolverine, Toy Biz, unmasked; chase variant
    NM $20   MIP $32

Wolverine, Toy Biz
    NM $32   MIP $50

Marvel Shape Shifters (Toy Biz, 1999)

7" FIGURES

Hulk forms into Dino Beast, 1999
    NM $3   MIP $7

Rhino forms into Racing Rhino, 1999
    NM $3   MIP $7

Sabretooth forms into Sabretooth Tiger, 1999
    NM $3   MIP $7

Spider Sense Spider-Man forms into Spider-Bat, 1999
    NM $3   MIP $7

Marvel Shape Shifters II (Toy Biz, 1999)

7" FIGURES

Captain America forms into American Eagle, 1999
    NM $3   MIP $7

Colossus forms into Cyborg Gorilla, 1999
    NM $3   MIP $7

Kraven forms into Mighty Lion, 1999
    NM $3   MIP $7

Thor forms into Winged Stallion, 1999
    NM $3   MIP $7

Marvel Shape Shifters Weapons (Toy Biz, 1999)

DELUXE FIGURES

Apocalypse forms into Gattling Gun, 1999
    NM $3   MIP $7

Iron Man forms into Battle Axe, 1999
    NM $3   MIP $7

Punisher forms into Power Pistol, 1999
    NM $3   MIP $7

Spider-Man forms into Wrist Blaster, 1999
    NM $3   MIP $7

Marvel Special Edition Series (Toy Biz, 1998)

12" FIGURES

Dr. Octopus, 1998
    NM $6   MIP $12

Punisher, 1998
    NM $6   MIP $12

Spider-Woman, 1998
    NM $6   MIP $12

Marvel Super Heroes (Toy Biz, 1990-92)

SERIES 1, 1990

Captain America, Toy Biz
NM $6   MIP $15

Daredevil, Toy Biz
NM $4   MIP $10

Doctor Doom, Toy Biz
NM $4   MIP $8

Doctor Octopus, Toy Biz
NM $4   MIP $8

Hulk, Toy Biz
NM $3   MIP $7

Punisher (cap firing), Toy Biz
NM $3   MIP $5

Silver Surfer, Toy Biz
NM $4   MIP $8

Spider-Man (suction cups), Toy Biz
NM $3   MIP $10

SERIES 2, 1991

Green Goblin (back lever), Toy Biz
NM $3   MIP $12

Green Goblin (no lever), Toy Biz
NM $3   MIP $12

Iron Man, Toy Biz
NM $3   MIP $10

Punisher (machine gun sound), Toy Biz
NM $3   MIP $10

Spider-Man (web climbing), Toy Biz
NM $3   MIP $10

Spider-Man (web shooting), Toy Biz
NM $3   MIP $10

Thor (back lever), Toy Biz
NM $3   MIP $10

Thor (no lever), Toy Biz
NM $3   MIP $10

Venom, Toy Biz
NM $3   MIP $10

SERIES 3, 1992

Annihilus, Toy Biz
NM $3   MIP $10

Deathlok, Toy Biz
NM $3   MIP $10

Human Torch, Toy Biz
NM $3   MIP $10

Invisible Woman, catapult
NM $3   MIP $10

Invisible Woman, vanishing, Toy Biz, turns from color uniform to translucent
NM $8   MIP $15

Mister Fantastic, Toy Biz
NM $3   MIP $10

Silver Surfer (chrome), Toy Biz
NM $3   MIP $10

Spider-Man (ball joints), Toy Biz
NM $3   MIP $10

Spider-Man (web tracer), Toy Biz
NM $3   MIP $10

Thing, Toy Biz
NM $3   MIP $10

Venom (tongue flicking), Toy Biz
NM $3   MIP $10

TALKING HEROES

Cyclops, 1990-92, Toy Biz
NM $2   MIP $5

Hulk, 1990-92, Toy Biz
NM $2   MIP $5

Magneto, 1990-92, Toy Biz
NM $2   MIP $5

Punisher, 1990-92, Toy Biz
NM $2   MIP $5

Spider-Man, 1990-92, Toy Biz
NM $2   MIP $5

Venom, 1990-92, Toy Biz
NM $2   MIP $5

Wolverine, 1990-92, Toy Biz
NM $2   MIP $5

Marvel Super Heroes Cosmic Defenders (Toy Biz, 1992-93)

FIGURES

Annihilus, 1992-93, Toy Biz
NM $2   MIP $8

Deathlok, 1992-93, Toy Biz
NM $2   MIP $5

Human Torch, 1992-93, Toy Biz
NM $2   MIP $8

Invisible Woman, vanishing color action, 1992-93, Toy Biz
NM $5   MIP $12

Mr. Fantastic, 1992-93, Toy Biz
NM $2   MIP $12

Silver Surfer, 1992-93, Toy Biz
NM $2   MIP $8

Spider-Man, enemy tracking tracer, 1992-93, Toy Biz
NM $2   MIP $8

Spider-Man, multi-jointed, 1992-93, Toy Biz
NM $2   MIP $8

Marvel Super Heroes Secret Wars (Mattel, 1984-85)

4" FIGURES

Baron Zemo, 1984-85, Mattel
NM $12   MIP $25

Captain America & Doctor Doom, Two-Figure Set, 1984-85, Mattel
NM $25   MIP $85

(Lenny Lee)

Captain America, w/Secret Shield, 1984-85, Mattel, includes figure, shield and mini comic book
NM $15   MIP $45

Constrictor (foreign release), 1984-85, Mattel
NM $110   MIP $200

Daredevil, 1984-85, Mattel
NM $15   MIP $35

(Lenny Lee)

Doctor Doom, 1984-85, Mattel, shown at left w/Kang

　　　NM $10　　　MIP $20

(Lenny Lee)

Doctor Octopus, 1984-85, Mattel, Spidey's nemesis w/mechanical arms and shield

　　　NM $10　　　MIP $20

Electro (foreign release), 1984-85, Mattel

　　　NM $120　　　MIP $215

Falcon, 1984-85, Mattel

　　　NM $22　　　MIP $50

Hobgoblin, 1984-85, Mattel

　　　NM $45　　　MIP $95

Ice Man (foreign release), 1984-85, Mattel

　　　NM $95　　　MIP $205

Iron Man, 1984-85, Mattel

　　　NM $12　　　MIP $25

(Lenny Lee)

Kang, 1984-85, Mattel, shown at right

　　　NM $8　　　MIP $12

Magneto, 1984-85, Mattel

　　　NM $8　　　MIP $12

Spider-Man, black outfit, 1984-85, Mattel

　　　NM $20　　　MIP $45

Spider-Man, red and blue outfit, 1984-85, Mattel

　　　NM $12　　　MIP $30

Three-Figure Set, 1984-85, Mattel, includes DareDevil, Spidey (in black costume) and Captain America

　　　NM $55　　　MIP $100

Wolverine, black claws, 1984-85, Mattel

　　　NM $25　　　MIP $80

Wolverine, silver claws, 1984-85, Mattel

　　　NM $15　　　MIP $40

ACCESSORIES

Secret Messages Pack, 1984-85, Mattel

　　　NM $3　　　MIP $6

Tower of Doom, 1984-85, Mattel

　　　NM $25　　　MIP $60

VEHICLES

Doom Copter, 1984-85, Mattel

　　　NM $20　　　MIP $55

Doom Copter w/Doctor Doom, 1984-85, Mattel

　　　NM $30　　　MIP $100

Doom Cycle, 1984-85, Mattel

　　　NM $10　　　MIP $20

Doom Cycle w/Doctor Doom, 1984-85, Mattel

　　　NM $16　　　MIP $35

Doom Roller, 1984-85, Mattel

　　　NM $10　　　MIP $20

Doom Star Glider w/Kang, 1984-85, Mattel

　　　NM $25　　　MIP $40

Freedom Fighter, 1984-85, Mattel

　　　NM $10　　　MIP $30

Star Dart w/Spider-Man (black outfit), 1984-85, Mattel

　　　NM $40　　　MIP $75

Turbo Copter, 1984-85, Mattel

　　　NM $15　　　MIP $60

Turbo Cycle, 1984-85, Mattel

　　　NM $12　　　MIP $25

Marvel's Most Wanted (Toy Biz, 1998)

6" FIGURES

Blink, 1998

　　　NM $2　　　MIP $5

Spat and Grovel, 1998

　　　NM $2　　　MIP $5

X-Man, 1998

　　　NM $2　　　MIP $5

Masters of The Universe (Mattel, 1981-1988)

12" FIGURES (ITALIAN)

Megator, 1987

　　　NM $950　　　MIP $1400

Tytus, 1987

　　　NM $1050　　　MIP $1500

ACCESSORIES

Battle Bones Carrying Case, 1984

　　　NM $10　　　MIP $25

Battle Cat, 1982

　　　NM $20　　　MIP $60

Battle Cat w/Battle Armor He-Man, 1984

　　　NM $70　　　MIP $175

Battle Cat w/He-Man, 1982

　　　NM $50　　　MIP $175

Beam Blaster and Artillery, 1987

　　　NM $32　　　MIP $70

Bionatops, 1987, Mattel, creature

　　　NM $25　　　MIP $85

He-Man and Wind Raider, 1982, Mattel

　　　NM $22　　　MIP $125

Jet Sled, 1986

　　　NM $12　　　MIP $25

Mantisaur, 1986

　　　NM $22　　　MIP $60

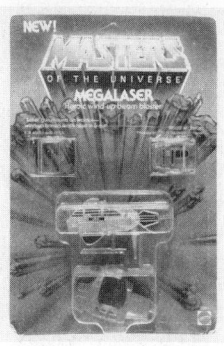

Megalaser, 1986, while this weapon didn't fire any projectiles, it had a blast-effect action and fit warriors in the series
NM $5   **MIP** $15

(Lenny Lee)

Monstroid Creature (The Evil Horde), 1986, Mattel, creature grabs warriors in pincers and whirls them around
NM $30   **MIP** $52

Night Stalker, 1984
NM $12   **MIP** $30

Night Stalker w/Jitsu, 1984
NM $40   **MIP** $75

Panthor, 1983
NM $20   **MIP** $50

Panthor w/Battle Armor Skeletor, 1984
NM $35   **MIP** $125

Panthor w/Skeletor, 1983
NM $42   **MIP** $175

Road Ripper w/Battle Armor He-Man, 1984, Mattel
NM $20   **MIP** $65

Screech, 1983
NM $15   **MIP** $40

Screech w/Skeletor, 1983
NM $40   **MIP** $70

Screeech w/Battle Armor Skeletor, 1984, Mattel
NM $22   **MIP** $60

Slime Vat, 1986, Mattel
NM $3   **MIP** $6

Stilt Stalkers, 1986
NM $5   **MIP** $20

Stridor (Armored Horse), 1984
NM $10   **MIP** $30

Stridor w/Fisto, 1984
NM $30   **MIP** $75

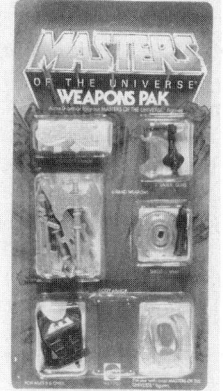

(Lenny Lee)

Weapons Pak, 1984, included laser guns, body armor, battle axe, shield, sword and more
NM $5   **MIP** $15

Zoar, 1983
NM $15   **MIP** $30

Zoar w/Teela, 1983
NM $40   **MIP** $120

FIGURES

Battle Armor He-Man, 1984
NM $16   **MIP** $60

Battle Armor Skeletor, 1984
NM $14   **MIP** $45

Beast Man, 1982
NM $12   **MIP** $80

Blade, 1987
NM $35   **MIP** $75

(KP Photo)

Blast-Attak, 1987, limbs actually fly off the figure during battle
NM $20   **MIP** $55

Buzz-Off, 1984
NM $8   **MIP** $42

Buzz-Saw Hordak (The Evil Horde), 1987
NM $35   **MIP** $120

Clamp Champ, 1987
NM $35   **MIP** $110

Clawful, 1984
NM $9   **MIP** $40

Dragon Blaster Skeletor, 1985
NM $35   **MIP** $75

(KP Photo)

Dragstor (The Evil Horde), 1986, Mattel, ripcord (like the SST's series) makes this "transforming evil warrior vehicle" pursue the good guys
NM $14   **MIP** $60

Evil-Lyn, 1983
NM $14   **MIP** $90

(KP Photo)

Extendar, 1986, w/extending arms, legs, head and torso
NM $20   **MIP** $60

Faker, 1983, Mattel
NM $35   MIP $550
Faker (reissue), 1987
NM $18   MIP $80
Fisto, 1984
NM $12   MIP $40
Flying Fists He-Man, 1986
NM $20   MIP $75
Grizzlor (The Evil Horde), 1985
NM $12   MIP $40
Grizzlor, black face, 1985
NM $40   MIP $125
Gwildor, 1987, figure from Masters of the Universe movie
NM $15   MIP $50
He-Man, original, 1982, 1983
NM $22   MIP $375
Hordak (The Evil Horde), 1985
NM $15   MIP $50
Horde Trooper, 1986
NM $40   MIP $140
Hurricane Hordak, 1986
NM $29   MIP $65
Jitsu, 1984
NM $10   MIP $40
King Hiss (Snake Men), 1986
NM $12   MIP $62

(KP Photo)

King Randor, 1987, w/scepter and mini comic book
NM $42   MIP $200
Kobra Kahn (Snake Men), 1984, 1986
NM $10   MIP $50
Leech (The Evil Horde), 1985
NM $8   MIP $40
Man-At-Arms, 1982, Mattel
NM $10   MIP $100
Man-E-Faces, 1983
NM $8   MIP $100
Man-E-Faces, five extra weapons, 1983
NM $35   MIP $1000+

Mantenna (The Evil Horde), 1985
NM $12   MIP $40
Mekaneck, 1983
NM $8   MIP $50
Mer-Man, 1982
NM $20   MIP $120
Modulok (The Evil Horde), 1985
NM $12   MIP $40
Mosquitor (The Evil Horde), 1987
NM $22   MIP $95
Moss Man, 1985
NM $8   MIP $32
Multi-Bot (The Evil Horde), 1986
NM $32   MIP $65
Ninjor, 1987
NM $50   MIP $200

(KP Photo, Karen O'Brien collection)

Orko, 1984
NM $35   MIP $100
Prince Adam, 1984
NM $28   MIP $115
Ram-Man, 1983
NM $12   MIP $70

Rattlor (Snake Men), 1986, w/translucent plastic "snake staff" and mini comic book
NM $10   MIP $42

(Lenny Lee)

Rio Blast, 1986, Mattel, an "old West" warrior w/hidden weapons, includes comic book
NM $20   MIP $80
Roboto, 1985
NM $8   MIP $35
Rokkon (Comet Warrior), 1986
NM $12   MIP $32
Rotar (Energy Zoids), 1987
NM $75   MIP $160
Saurod, 1987, figure from Masters of the Universe movie
NM $35   MIP $150
Scare Glow, 1987
NM $60   MIP $250
Skeletor, original, 1982, 1983
NM $30   MIP $210
Snake Face (Snake Men), 1987
NM $35   MIP $160
Snout Spout, 1986
NM $20   MIP $70
Sorceress, 1987
NM $40   MIP $200
Spikor, 1985
NM $10   MIP $40

(KP Photo)

Sssqueeze (Snake Men), 1987, Mattel, traps warriors in "slither-hold" grip, includes serpent
NM $20   MIP $160

Stinkor, 1985
NM $8   MIP $40

Stonedar (Comet Warriors), 1986
NM $12   MIP $40

Stratos, 1982, Mattel
NM $13   MIP $120

Sy-klone, 1985
NM $8   MIP $40

Teela, 1982
NM $15   MIP $80

Terror Claws Skeletor, 1986
NM $32   MIP $85

Thunder Punch He-Man, 1985, Mattel
NM $12   MIP $85

Trap Jaw, 1983
NM $15   MIP $75

Tri-Klops, 1983
NM $10   MIP $60

Tung Lashor (Snake Men), 1986
NM $10   MIP $45

Twistoid (Energy Zoids), 1987
NM $85   MIP $160

Two-Bad, 1985
NM $10   MIP $40

Webstor, 1984
NM $12   MIP $40

Whiplash, 1984
NM $10   MIP $35

Zodac, 1982, Mattel
NM $12   MIP $130

GIFT SETS

Battle for Eternia, 1983, Mattel, Skeletor, Panthor, Man-E-Faces
NM $58   MIP $250

Evil Horde, 1986, Mattel, Hordak, Leech, Mantenna
NM $60   MIP $210

Evil Warriors, 1983, Mattel, Skeletor, Beast Man, Faker
NM $60   MIP $210

Evil Warriors, 1984, Mattel, Battle Armor Skeletor, Webstor, Mer-Man
NM $55   MIP $210

Evil Warriors, 1985, Mattel, Stinkor, Webstor, Whiplash
NM $40   MIP $210

Flying Fist He-Man and Terror Claws Skeletor, 1986, Mattel
NM $70   MIP $240

Heroic Warriors, 1983, Mattel, He-Man, Teela, Ram-Man
NM $45   MIP $210

Heroic Warriors, 1984, Mattel, Battle Armor He-Man, Man-At-Arms, Man-E-Faces
NM $45   MIP $210

Heroic Warriors, 1985, Mattel, Mekaneck, Buzz-Off, Moss-Man
NM $30   MIP $160

Jet Sled w/He-Man, 1986, Mattel
NM $45   MIP $85

Mantisaur w/Hordak, 1986, Mattel
NM $35   MIP $75

GRAYSKULL DINOSAUR SERIES

Bionatops, 1987, Mattel
NM $42   MIP $85

Turbodaltyl, 1987, Mattel
NM $45   MIP $160

Tyrantisaurus Rex, 1987, Mattel
NM $75   MIP $175

LASER FIGURES

Laser Light Skeletor, 1988, Mattel
NM $260   MIP $925

Laser Power He-Man, 1988, Mattel
NM $375   MIP $1200

MAIL AWAY FIGURES

Savage He-Man, 1982, Mattel
NM $275   MIP $1000

METEORBS

Astro Lion, 1987, Mattel
NM $32   MIP $70

Comet Cat, 1987, Mattel
NM $40   MIP $75

Cometroid, 1987, Mattel
NM $15   MIP $30

Crocobite, 1987, Mattel
NM $15   MIP $30

Dinosorb, 1987, Mattel
NM $15   MIP $30

Gore-illa, 1987, Mattel
NM $15   MIP $30

Orbear, 1987, Mattel
NM $20   MIP $40

Rhinorb, 1987, Mattel
NM $15   MIP $30

Tuskor, 1987, Mattel
NM $30   MIP $60

Ty-Gyr, 1987, Mattel
NM $32   MIP $65

OVERSEAS ACCESSORIES

Cliff Climber, 1987, Mattel
NM $42   MIP $125

Scubattack, 1987, Mattel
NM $45   MIP $125

Tower Tools, 1987, Mattel
NM $42   MIP $125

PLAY SETS

Castle Grayskull, 1982, Mattel
NM $110   MIP $400

Eternia, 1986, Mattel
NM $800   MIP $1400

Fright Zone, 1985, Mattel
NM $50   MIP $175

(Lenny Lee)

Slime Pit, 1986, Mattel, slime oozes from top of pit to trap warriors, the set included real Slime, which actually must have made for a very cool effect on the figures
NM $25   MIP $70

Snake Mountain, 1984, Mattel, Snake Pit went quite well w/the Slime Pit for play value.
NM $60   MIP $350

VEHICLES

Attak Trak, 1983, Mattel
NM $16   MIP $45

Bashasaurus, 1985, Mattel
NM $12   MIP $42

Battle Ram, 1982, Mattel
NM $15   MIP $42

Blaster Hawk, 1986, Mattel
NM $50   MIP $110

(Lenny Lee)

Dragon Walker, 1984, Mattel, open-cockpit vehicle that sideways "walks"
    NM $10   **MIP** $40

Fright Fighter, 1986, Mattel
    NM $55   **MIP** $95

Hordak w/Grizzlor, 1985, Mattel
    NM $20   **MIP** $75

Land Shark, 1985, Mattel
    NM $12   **MIP** $25

Land Shark w/Battle Armor Skeletor, 1985, Mattel
    NM $12   **MIP** $40

Laser Bolt, 1986, Mattel
    NM $12   **MIP** $35

Point Dread and Talon Fighter, 1983, Mattel
    NM $32   **MIP** $75

(KP Photo)

Road Ripper, 1983, Mattel, He-Man's motorcycle-type vehicle, ripcord-powered
    NM $10   **MIP** $25

Roton, 1984, Mattel
    NM $10   **MIP** $25

Spydor, 1985, Mattel
    NM $25   **MIP** $75

Wind Raider, 1982, Mattel
    NM $14   **MIP** $50

Masters of the Universe (Mattel, 2002-03)

ACCESSORIES

Bat Fight-Pack, 2003, Mattel
    NM $2   **MIP** $4

Battle Cat, 2002, Mattel
    NM $4   **MIP** $10

Battle Raptor, 2003, Mattel
    NM $4   **MIP** $10

Eagle Fight-Pack, 2003, Mattel
    NM $2   **MIP** $4

He-Man's Sword, 2002, Mattel
    NM $4   **MIP** $10

Panthor, 2002, Mattel
    NM $4   **MIP** $10

Samurai Battlecat, 2003, Mattel
    NM $4   **MIP** $10

DELUXE FIGURES

Battle Sound He-Man, 2002, Mattel, Series 1
    NM $3   **MIP** $6

Battle Sound Skeletor, 2002, Mattel, Series 1
    NM $3   **MIP** $6

Samauri Man-At-Arms, 2003, Mattel
    NM $2   **MIP** $5

Samurai He-Man, 2003, Mattel
    NM $2   **MIP** $5

Samurai Skeletor, 2003, Mattel
    NM $2   **MIP** $5

FIGURES

Battle Glove Man-At-Arms, 2003, Mattel, Series 4
    NM $2   **MIP** $8

Beast Man, 2002, Mattel, Series 1
    NM $4   **MIP** $10

Buzz-Off, 2003, Mattel, Series 4
    NM $4   **MIP** $10

Evil-Lyn, 2003, Mattel, Series 3
    NM $6   **MIP** $12

Faker, 2003, Mattel, Toy Fare Exclusive
    NM $28   **MIP** $42

Fire Armor Skeletor, 2003, Mattel, Series 3
    NM $2   **MIP** $5

He-Man, 2002, Mattel, Series 1
    NM $2   **MIP** $5

Ice Armor He-Man, 2003, Mattel, Series 4
    NM $2   **MIP** $4

Jungle Attack He-Man, 2002, Mattel, Series 2
    NM $2   **MIP** $4

Makaneck, 2002, Mattel, Series 2
    NM $2   **MIP** $10

Man-At-Arms, 2002, Mattel, Series 1
    NM $4   **MIP** $8

Man-E-Faces, 2003, Mattel, Series 4
    NM $2   **MIP** $10

Martial Arts He-Man, 2003, Mattel, Series 4
    NM $2   **MIP** $4

Mega-Punch He-Man, 2003, Mattel, Series 4
    NM $2   **MIP** $4

Mer-Man, 2002, Mattel, Series 1
    NM $5   **MIP** $10

Orko, 2003, Mattel, Series 3
    NM $4   **MIP** $12

Prince Adam, 2003, Mattel, Series 4
    NM $4   **MIP** $12

Ram Man, 2002, Mattel, Series 2
    NM $4   **MIP** $8

Skeletor, 2002, Mattel, Series 1
    NM $4   **MIP** $10

Smash Blade He-Man, 2003, Mattel, Series 3
    NM $2   **MIP** $6

Spin Blade Skeletor, 2003, Mattel, Series 2
    NM $2   **MIP** $6

Stratos, 2002, Mattel, Series 1
    NM $4   **MIP** $10

Sy-Klone, 2003, Mattel, Series 4
    NM $4   **MIP** $10

Teela, 2003, Mattel, Series 3
    NM $4   **MIP** $12

Trapjaw, 2003, Mattel, Series 2
    NM $4   **MIP** $10

Tri-Klops, 2003, Mattel, Series 2
    NM $4   **MIP** $10

Two-Bad, 2003, Mattel, Series 3
    NM $4   **MIP** $10

Whiplash, 2003, Mattel, Series 3
    NM $4   **MIP** $10

GIFT SETS

Armor Skeletor, 2003, Mattel
    NM $4   **MIP** $10

He-Man vs. Skeletor, 2002, Mattel, figure two-pack
    NM $8   **MIP** $14

Wolf Armor He-Man & Snake, 2003, Mattel
    NM $5   **MIP** $12

MINI FIGURES

He-Man, 2002, Mattel
    NM $1   **MIP** $3

Heroes vs. Villians Giftpack, 2002, Mattel, w/exclusive Beastman
    NM $4   **MIP** $10

Man-At-Arms, 2002, Mattel
    NM $1   **MIP** $3

Mekaneck, 2002, Mattel
    NM $1   **MIP** $3

Mer-Man, 2002, Mattel
    NM $1   **MIP** $3

Skeletor, 2002, Mattel
    NM $1   **MIP** $3

Stratos, 2002, Mattel

    NM $1   **MIP** $3

PLAY SETS

Castle Grayskull, 2002, Mattel

    NM $25   **MIP** $60

VEHICLES

Attack Squid, 2003, Mattel

    NM $4   **MIP** $8

Bashin' Beetle, 2002, Mattel

    NM $2   **MIP** $6

Battle Hawk, 2002, Mattel

    NM $2   **MIP** $6

Battle Ram Chariot, 2002, Mattel

    NM $4   **MIP** $8

Battle Tank, 2002, Mattel

    NM $5   **MIP** $10

Terrordactyl, 2002, Mattel

    NM $4   **MIP** $10

War Whale, 2003, Mattel

    NM $4   **MIP** $15

Masters of the Universe (Mattel, 2002-03)

FIGURES

Moss-Man, 2003, Mattel, mail-away

    NM $12   **MIP** $18

Matrix, The (McFarlane, 2003)

SERIES 1 FIGURES

(KP Photo, Brian Brogaard Collection)

Morpheus, 2003, McFarlane, w/gun and sword

    NM $5   **MIP** $12

(KP Photo, Brian Brogaard collection)

Neo, 2003, McFarlane

    NM $5   **MIP** $10

Neo in Chateau, 2003, McFarlane, deluxe boxed set

    NM $10   **MIP** $17

(KP Photo, Brian Brogaard collection)

Trinity, 2003, McFarlane

    NM $5   **MIP** $10

(KP Photo, Karen O'Brien collection)

Twin 1, 2003, McFarlane

    NM $5   **MIP** $12

(KP Photo, Karen O'Brien collection)

Twin 2, 2003, McFarlane

    NM $5   **MIP** $12

SERIES 2 FIGURES

A.P.U. Deluxe Boxed Set, 2003, McFarlane, w/Mifune

    NM $8   **MIP** $15

Agent Smith, fight scene, 2003, McFarlane, in suit

    NM $5   **MIP** $12

(KP Photo, Brian Brogaard collection)

Morpheus, seated, 2003, McFarlane, w/red chair, telephone stand and phone

    NM $5   **MIP** $12

Neo, fight scene, 2003, McFarlane, backdrop of Smiths

    NM $5   **MIP** $12

(KP Photo, Brian Brogaard collection)

Neo, real world, 2003, McFarlane, w/different heads

    NM $5   **MIP** $12

Niobe, 2003, McFarlane

    NM $5   **MIP** $12

Sentinel Deluxe Boxed Set, 2003, McFarlane, fully articulated tentacles

    NM $8   **MIP** $17

(KP Photo, Karen O'Brien collection)

Trinity, 2003, McFarlane, falling scene

    NM $5   **MIP** $12

McFarlane Music (McFarlane, 1999-02)

FIGURES

Alice Cooper, 2000, McFarlane

    NM $4   **MIP** $10

Angus Young, 2001, McFarlane, AC/DC guitarist

    NM $15   **MIP** $30

Beatles, The, McFarlane, Paul

    NM $8   **MIP** $20

Beatles, The, McFarlane, John

    NM $18   **MIP** $35

Beatles, The, McFarlane, George

    NM $8   **MIP** $20

Beatles, The, McFarlane, Ringo

    NM $20   **MIP** $50

Iron Maiden's Eddie: from "Killers," 2002, McFarlane, based on the album artwork

    NM $12   **MIP** $22

Iron Maiden's Eddie: from "Peace of Mind," 2002, McFarlane, "the Trooper," based on the album artwork

    NM $18   **MIP** $35

Janis Joplin, 2000

    NM $15   **MIP** $25

Jerry Garcia, 2001, McFarlane

    NM $6   **MIP** $12

Jim Morrison, 2001, McFarlane

    NM $20   **MIP** $40

Metallica: Boxed Set, 2001, McFarlane, pose from "And Justice for All"

    NM $82   **MIP** $160

Metallica: James Hetfield, 2001, McFarlane, pose from "And Justice for All"

    NM $6   **MIP** $15

Metallica: Jason Newsted, 2001, McFarlane, pose from "And Justice for All"

    NM $6   **MIP** $15

Metallica: Kirk Hammett, 2001, McFarlane, pose from "And Justice for All"

    NM $6   **MIP** $15

Metallica: Lars Ulrich, 2001, McFarlane, pose from "And Justice for All"

    NM $6   **MIP** $15

(KP Photo)

Ozzie Osbourne, 1999, McFarlane, fairly buff Ozzy figure holding cross and dead bat w/dead bats and doves at his feet, includes church window diorama backdrop

    NM $4   **MIP** $12

(KP Photo)

Rob Zombie, 2000, figure w/mechanical arms includes "Zombie" base

    NM $5   **MIP** $15

Metal Gear Solid (McFarlane, 1998)

FIGURES

(McFarlane Toys)

Liquid Snake, 1998, McFarlane, w/pistol and machine gun rifle

    NM $4   **MIP** $14

(McFarlane Toys)

Meryl Silverburgh, 1998, McFarlane, w/pistol, bayonet, grappling hook and machine gun

    NM $4   **MIP** $12

(McFarlane Toys)

Ninja, 1998, McFarlane, multi-colored figure w/sword

NM $4   **MIP** $12

(McFarlane Toys)

Psycho Mantis, 1998, McFarlane, includes bust, vase, crystal ball and detailed figure

NM $4   **MIP** $10

(McFarlane Toys)

Revolver Ocelot, 1998, McFarlane, detailed gunslinger figure includes two pistols

NM $4   **MIP** $10

(KP Photo)

Sniper Wolf, 1998, McFarlane, w/rifle and snarling wolf figure

NM $4   **MIP** $12

(McFarlane Toys)

Solid Snake, 1998, McFarlane, includes a variety of weapons and accessories; rifle, pistol, infra-red goggles and more

NM $6   **MIP** $14

(McFarlane Toys)

Vulcan Raven, 1998, McFarlane, w/multi-barreled weapon and barrel-shaped pack

NM $4   **MIP** $10

Micronauts (Mego, 1976-80)

ACCESSORIES

Karrio, 1979, Mego, carrying case

NM $10   **MIP** $20

ALIEN INVADERS CARDED

Antron, 1979, Mego

NM $40   **MIP** $210

Centaurus, 1980, Mego, also a foreign release

NM $50   **MIP** $275

Kronos, 1980, Mego, also a foreign release

NM $100   **MIP** $300

Lobros, 1980, Mego, also a foreign release

NM $150   **MIP** $350

Membros, 1979, Mego

NM $35   **MIP** $125

Repto, 1979, Mego

NM $25   **MIP** $125

ALIEN INVADERS VEHICLES

Alphatron, 1979, Mego, vehicle w/figure

NM $8   **MIP** $30

Betatron, 1979, Mego, vehicle w/figure

NM $8   **MIP** $30

Gammatron, 1979, Mego, vehicle w/figure

NM $10   **MIP** $40

Hornetroid, 1979, Mego, vehicle for Antron

NM $60   **MIP** $130

Hydra, 1976, Mego

NM $20   **MIP** $60

Mobile Exploration Lab, 1976, Mego, largest of the vehicles

NM $20   **MIP** $75

Solarion, 1978, Mego, rare

NM $20   **MIP** $65

Star Searcher, 1978, Mego

NM $20   **MIP** $75

Taurion, 1978, Mego

NM $25   **MIP** $70

Terraphant, 1979, Mego, vehicle for Membros

NM $25   **MIP** $100

BOXED FIGURES

Andromeda, 1977, Mego

NM $10   **MIP** $25

Baron Karza, 1977, Mego

NM $35   **MIP** $100

Biotron, 1976, Mego

NM $10   **MIP** $25

Force Commander, 1977, Mego

NM $25   **MIP** $75

Giant Acroyear, 1977, Mego

NM $20   **MIP** $70

Megas, 1981, Mego, foreign release

NM $20   **MIP** $75

Microtron, 1976, Mego

NM $20   **MIP** $85

Nemesis Robot, 1978, Mego

NM $35   **MIP** $65

Oberon, 1977, Mego
NM $25   MIP $55

Phobos Robot, 1978, Mego
NM $45   MIP $75

Red Falcon, 1976, Mego
NM $38   MIP $160

CARDED FIGURES

Acroyear, 1976, Mego, red, blue, orange
NM $30   MIP $70

Acroyear II, 1977, Mego, red, blue, orange
NM $30   MIP $75

Galactic Defender, 1978, Mego, white, yellow
NM $15   MIP $45

Galactic Warrior, 1976, Mego, red, blue, orange
NM $12   MIP $40

Pharoid w/Time Chamber, 1977, Mego, blue, red, gray
NM $25   MIP $55

Space Glider, 1976, Mego, blue, green, orange
NM $20   MIP $50

(Mark Bellomo collection)

Time Traveler, 1976, Mego, solid plastic, yellow, orange
NM $20   MIP $50

Time Traveler, 1976, Mego, opaque plastic, yellow, orange
NM $25   MIP $100

MICROPOLIS PLAY SETS

Galactic Command Center, 1978, Mego
NM $45   MIP $110

Interplanetary Headquarters, 1978, Mego
NM $60   MIP $120

Mega City, 1978, Mego, largest of the micro cities, 500+ pieces
NM $45   MIP $110

Microrail City, 1978, Mego
NM $60   MIP $130

PLAY SETS

Astro Station, 1976, Mego
NM $25   MIP $65

Rocket Tubes, 1978, Mego, two versions, deluxe and standard
NM $45   MIP $110

Stratstation, 1976, Mego
NM $30   MIP $80

VEHICLES

Aquatron, 1977, Mego, two pontoons, detachable motor
NM $15   MIP $50

Battle Cruiser, 1977, Mego, Model No. 71054
NM $40   MIP $75

Crater Cruncher w/Figure, 1976, Mego, Time Traveler included
NM $20   MIP $60

Galactic Cruiser, 1976, Mego
NM $20   MIP $60

Hydro Copter, 1976, Mego
NM $25   MIP $50

Neon Orbiter, 1977, Mego
NM $12   MIP $40

Photon Sled, 1976, Mego
NM $12   MIP $35

Rhodium Orbiter, 1977, Mego
NM $12   MIP $45

Thorium Orbiter, 1977, Mego
NM $12   MIP $40

Ultronic Scooter w/Figure, 1976, Mego, Time Traveler included
NM $20   MIP $60

Warp Racer w/Figure, 1976, Mego, Time Traveler included
NM $15   MIP $45

Mighty Morphin Power Rangers (Bandai, 1993-95)

3" FIGURES

Black Ranger, 1995, Bandai
NM $4   MIP $10

Blue Ranger, 1995, Bandai
NM $4   MIP $10

Pink Ranger, 1995, Bandai
NM $4   MIP $10

Red Ranger, 1995, Bandai
NM $4   MIP $10

Yellow Ranger, 1995, Bandai
NM $4   MIP $10

5" FIGURES W/THUNDER BIKES

Black Ranger, 1995, Bandai
NM $3   MIP $10

Blue Ranger, 1995, Bandai
NM $3   MIP $10

Pink Ranger, 1995, Bandai
NM $3   MIP $10

Red Ranger, 1995, Bandai
NM $3   MIP $10

Yellow Ranger, 1995, Bandai
NM $3   MIP $10

8" ALIENS, 1993

Baboo, 1993, Bandai
NM $4   MIP $10

Bones, 1993, Bandai
NM $4   MIP $10

Finster, 1993, Bandai
NM $4   MIP $10

Goldar, 1993, Bandai
NM $4   MIP $10

King Sphinx, 1993, Bandai
NM $4   MIP $10

Putty Patrol, 1993, Bandai
NM $4   MIP $10

Squatt, 1993, Bandai
NM $4   MIP $10

8" FIGURES, 1993

Black Ranger, 1993, Bandai
NM $7   MIP $20

Blue Ranger, 1993, Bandai
NM $7   MIP $20

Pink Ranger, 1993, Bandai
NM $10   MIP $20

Red Ranger, 1993, Bandai
NM $5   MIP $20

Yellow Ranger, 1993, Bandai
NM $10   MIP $20

8" MOVIE FIGURES, 1995

Black Ranger, 1995, Bandai, metallic
NM $2   MIP $5

Blue Ranger, 1995, Bandai, metallic
NM $2   MIP $5

Pink Ranger, 1995, Bandai, metallic
NM $2   MIP $5

Red Ranger, 1995, Bandai, metallic
NM $2   MIP $5

White Ranger, 1995, Bandai, metallic
NM $2   MIP $5

Yellow Ranger, 1995, Bandai, metallic
NM $2   MIP $5

ACTION FEATURE EVIL SPACE ALIENS, 5-1/2" FIGURES, 1994

Dark Knight, 1994, Bandai
NM $3   MIP $10

Eye Guy, 1994, Bandai
NM $3   MIP $10

Minotar, 1994, Bandai
NM $3   MIP $10

Mutaytus, 1994, Bandai
NM $3   MIP $10

Pudgy Pig, 1994, Bandai
NM $3   MIP $10

Rita Repulsa, 1994, Bandai
NM $3   MIP $10

Snizard Lips, 1994, Bandai
NM $3   MIP $10

Spidertron, 1994, Bandai
NM $3   MIP $10

AUTO-MORPHIN POWER RANGERS, 5-1/2" FIGURES, 1994

Black Ranger, 1994, Bandai
NM $3   MIP $12

Blue Ranger, 1994, Bandai
NM $3   MIP $12

Green Ranger, 1994, Bandai
NM $3   MIP $12

Pink Ranger, 1994, Bandai
NM $3   MIP $12

Red Ranger, 1994, Bandai
NM $2   MIP $12

Yellow Ranger, 1994, Bandai
NM $3   MIP $12

DELUXE EVIL SPACE ALIENS, 8" FIGURES, 1994

Evil Eye, 1994, Bandai
NM $3   MIP $7

Goo Fish, 1994, Bandai
NM $3   MIP $7

Guitardo, 1994, Bandai
NM $3   MIP $7

Lord Zedd, 1994, Bandai
NM $3   MIP $7

Pirantus Head, 1994, Bandai
NM $3   MIP $7

Pudgy Pig, 1994, Bandai
NM $3   MIP $7

Putty Patrol, 1994, Bandai
NM $3   MIP $7

Rhino Blaster, 1994, Bandai
NM $3   MIP $7

Socaddillo, 1994, Bandai
NM $3   MIP $7

KARATE ACTION FIGURES, 1994

Black Ranger, 1994, Bandai
NM $4   MIP $7

Blue Ranger, 1994, Bandai
NM $4   MIP $7

Pink Ranger, 1994, Bandai
NM $8   MIP $12

Red Ranger, 1994, Bandai
NM $4   MIP $7

Yellow Ranger, 1994, Bandai
NM $4   MIP $7

POWER RANGERS FOR GIRLS

Kimberly, 1995, Bandai
NM $4   MIP $10

Kimberly/Trini Set, 1995, Bandai
NM $10   MIP $20

Trini, 1995, Bandai
NM $4   MIP $10

ZORDS, 1993

Dragon Dagger, 1993, Bandai
NM $65   MIP $100

Dragon Zord w/Green Ranger, 1993, Bandai
NM $60   MIP $130

MegaZord, 1993, Bandai
NM $35   MIP $80

MegaZord Deluxe, 1993, Bandai
NM $65   MIP $155

Titanus the Carrier Zord, 1993, Bandai
NM $40   MIP $135

ZORDS, 1994

MegaZord, black/gold, limit. ed., 1994, Bandai
NM $60   MIP $120

Power Cannon, 1994, Bandai
NM $10   MIP $25

Power Dome Morphin Set, 1994, Bandai
NM $40   MIP $100

Red Dragon Thunder Zord, 1994, Bandai
NM $25   MIP $50

Saba (White Sword), 1994, Bandai
NM $15   MIP $35

Thunder Zord Assault Team, 1994, Bandai
NM $25   MIP $75

TOR the Shuttle Zord, 1994, Bandai
NM $30   MIP $75

Ultra Thunder Zord, 1994, Bandai
NM $40   MIP $100

White Tiger Zord w/White Ranger, 1994, Bandai
NM $30   MIP $90

Modern Horror Classics (Sideshow Toys, 2003)

12" FIGURES

Freddy Krueger, 2003, Sideshow Toys, #7302
NM $35   MIP $90

Furnace Environment, 2003, Sideshow Toys, #6606
NM $35   MIP $75

Furnace/ Freddy Combo Pack, 2003, Sideshow Toys, #6606R, Freddy and the Furnace
NM $40   MIP $150

Jason Voorhees, 2003, Sideshow Toys, #7301
NM $35   MIP $100

Leatherface - Texas Chainsaw Massacre, 2003, Sideshow Toys, #7303
NM $20   MIP $65

Michael Myers - Halloween, 2003, Sideshow Toys, #7304
NM $70   MIP $150

Monsters (McFarlane, 1997-2002)

FIGURES

Dracula, 2002, McFarlane
NM $3   MIP $8

Frankenstein, 2002, McFarlane
NM $3   MIP $8

Mummy, 2002, McFarlane
NM $3   MIP $8

Sea Creature, 2002, McFarlane
NM $3   MIP $8

VooDoo Queen, 2002, McFarlane
NM $3   MIP $8

Werewolf, 2002, McFarlane
NM $3   MIP $8

SERIES 1, PLAY SETS W/4" FIGURES

Dracula and Bat, 1997, McFarlane, includes Dracula, coffin, masouleum, "bat" figure and accessories
NM $4   MIP $12

Frankenstein and Igor, 1997, McFarlane, Hunchbacked Igor in lab coat and monster figure on upright table
NM $3   MIP $8

(McFarlane Toys)

Yellow Ranger, 1994, Bandai
NM $4   MIP $7

Hunchback, Quasimodo and Gargoyle, 1997, McFarlane, includes catapult-topped bell tower and two figures

NM $3 MIP $8

Werewolf and Victim, 1997, McFarlane

NM $3 MIP $8

SERIES 2, PLAY SETS W/4" FIGURES

Dr. Frankenstein, 1998, McFarlane, set includes re-animation bed, gruesome Frankenstein monster figure, Dr. F in lab coat, includes various lab instruments

NM $3 MIP $8

The Mummy, 1998, McFarlane, includes sarcophogus, Anubis figure, jars, and Mummy

NM $3 MIP $8

The Phantom of the Opera, 1998, McFarlane, great detail--includes pipe organ, inspector and phantom figures

NM $3 MIP $8

The Sea Creature, 1998, McFarlane, set includes diver in old-fashioned dive suit and attacking sea creature

NM $3 MIP $8

Mork and Mindy (Mattel, 1980)

FIGURES

Mindy, 1980, Mattel

NM $6 MIP $18

Mork from Ork w/Egg, 1980, Mattel

NM $8 MIP $30

Mork w/Talking Spacepack, upside down, 1980, Mattel, talking Mork says, "Nano, Nano," and seven other crazy things

NM $12 MIP $30

Movie Maniacs (McFarlane, 1998-2004)

18" FIGURES

(KP Photo, Merry Dudley collection)

Ash, 2001, McFarlane, from Army of Darkness

NM $12 MIP $30

Edward Scissorhands, 2002, McFarlane

NM $18 MIP $60

Freddy Krueger, 2000, McFarlane, from "A Nightmare on Elm Street"

NM $10 MIP $25

Leatherface, 2001, McFarlane, from "Texas Chainsaw Massacre"

NM $18 MIP $40

Michael Myers, 2000, McFarlane, "Halloween"

NM $20 MIP $75

SERIES 1

Eve, "Species II," 1998, McFarlane

NM $4 MIP $8

(McFarlane Toys)

Freddy Krueger, "Nightmare on Elm Street," 1998, McFarlane, Classic

Freddy w/red-striped sweater, fedora and extended claws

NM $6 MIP $20

Freddy Krueger, gory, "Nightmare on Elm Street," 1998, McFarlane

NM $6 MIP $20

Jason, "Friday the 13th," 1998, McFarlane

NM $6 MIP $15

(McFarlane Toys)

Jason, gory, "Friday the 13th," 1998, McFarlane, detailed figure includes machete

NM $7 MIP $20

Leatherface, "The Texas Chainsaw Massacre," 1998, McFarlane

NM $8 MIP $20

Leatherface, gory, "The Texas Chainsaw Massacre," 1998, McFarlane

NM $8 MIP $25

Patrick, "Species II," 1998, McFarlane

NM $4 MIP $8

SERIES 2

Chucky and Tiffany, "Bride of Chucky," 1999, McFarlane

NM $12 MIP $20

Chucky, "Child's Play," 1999, McFarlane

NM $8 MIP $15

(KP Photo)

Eric Draven, "The Crow," 1999, McFarlane, w/black guitar and crow figure

NM $6   **MIP** $8

(KP Photo)

Ghostface, "Scream," 1999, McFarlane, detailed Scream figure w/knife and cellphone, movie-poster stand

NM $8   **MIP** $15

(KP Photo)

Michael Myers, "Halloween," 1999, McFarlane, Michael Myers figure w/knife and movie-poster stand

NM $5   **MIP** $12

(KP Photo)

Norman Bates, "Psycho," 1999, McFarlane, Norman in "mother" outfit and wig w/knife, includes movie-poster stand

NM $3   **MIP** $8

(KP Photo)

Pumkinhead, "Pumpkinhead," 1999, McFarlane, figure includes movie-poster stand

NM $3   **MIP** $10

SERIES 3

(KP Photo)

Ash, "Army of Darkness," 2000, McFarlane, great Bruce Campbell likeness w/chainsaw hand, rifle and movie-poster stand

NM $3   **MIP** $8

(KP Photo)

Blair Monster, "The Thing," 2000, McFarlane, highly detailed figure w/movie stand

NM $2   **MIP** $6

(KP Photo)

Edward Scissorhands, "Edward Scissorhands," 2000, McFarlane, very detailed likeness w/movie-poster stand

NM $2   **MIP** $6

(KP Photo)

Fly, The, "The Fly," 2000, McFarlane, brindle-pattern figure w/movie-poster stand

NM $2   **MIP** $5

King Kong, "King Kong," 2000, McFarlane, deluxe figure

NM $6   **MIP** $14

(KP Photo)

Norris Creature w/Spider, "The Thing," 2000, McFarlane

NM $2   **MIP** $5

Shaft, "Shaft," 2000, McFarlane, figures w/"The Thing" movie-poster stand

NM $2   **MIP** $5

(KP Photo)

Snake Plissken, "Escape From L.A.," 2000, McFarlane, figure w/rifle and movie-poster stand

NM $2   **MIP** $5

SERIES 4

Blair Witch, "Blair Witch Project," 2001, McFarlane

NM $2   **MIP** $5

Candyman, 2001, McFarlane
NM $2   MIP $5

(KP Photo, Brian Brogaard collection)

Evil Ash, 2001, McFarlane, from
"Army of Darkness"
NM $2   MIP $5

Freddy Krueger, 2001, McFarlane,
from "Nightmare on Elm Street"
NM $4   MIP $10

Jaws Deluxe Boxed Set, 2001,
McFarlane
NM $70   MIP $120

T-1000, 2001, McFarlane, T2
NM $5   MIP $15

T-800, 2001, McFarlane, T2
NM $5   MIP $15

SERIES 5

Alien and Predator Deluxe Boxed Set,
2002, McFarlane
NM $15   MIP $35

Djinn, 2002, McFarlane, from
"Wishmaster"
NM $3   MIP $8

Jason X, 2002, McFarlane
NM $12   MIP $30

Lord of Darkness, 2002, McFarlane,
from "Legend"
NM $12   MIP $20

Sarah Connor, 2002, McFarlane
NM $4   MIP $12

T-800 Endoskeleton, 2002, McFarlane
NM $5   MIP $15

(KP Photo, Brian Brogaard collection)

Tooth Fairy, 2002, McFarlane, from
"Darkness Falls"
NM $2   MIP $5

SERIES 6

(KP Photo, Brian Brogaard collection)

Alien Queen, 2003, McFarlane, large
set, w/Ripley
NM $20   MIP $42

Dog Alien, 2003, McFarlane
NM $15   MIP $30

Predator, 2003, McFarlane
NM $20   MIP $40

Predator the Hunter, 2003, McFarlane
NM $12   MIP $30

Warrior Alien, 2003, McFarlane
NM $12   MIP $35

SERIES 7

12" Leatherface, 2004, McFarlane,
from Texas Chainsaw Massacre
NM $10   MIP $30

Colonial Marine Corporal Hicks,
2004, McFarlane, from Aliens
NM $3   MIP $7

Erin, 2004, McFarlane, from Texas
Chainsaw Massacre
NM $3   MIP $7

Leatherface, 2004, McFarlane, from
Texas Chainsaw Massacre
NM $3   MIP $10

Old Monty, 2004, McFarlane, from
Texas Chainsaw Massacre
NM $3   MIP $7

Robocop, 2004, McFarlane, from film
NM $12   MIP $30

Sherrif Hoyt, 2004, McFarlane, from
Texas Chainsaw Massacre
NM $3   MIP $7

Muppets
(Palisades, 2002-04)

12" FIGURES

Mega Animal, 2003, Palisades
NM $12   MIP $25

Mega Beaker, 2003, Palisades
NM $12   MIP $25

Mega Gonzo, 2004, Palisades, in tuxedo
NM $12   MIP $25

EXCLUSIVES

(KP Photo, Merry Dudley collection)

"Invisible Spray" Fozzie, Palisades,
2002 San Diego Comic-Con
exclusive; from Muppets in Space
NM $7   MIP $15

(KP Photo, Karen O'Brien collection)

Animal Tour 2003, Palisades,
convention special, didn't come
w/drumsticks
NM $15   MIP $30

PLAY SETS

Electric Mayhem, 2002, Palisades,
w/Animal
NM $40   MIP $85

Muppet Labs, 2002, Palisades, w/Beaker
NM $25   MIP $50

Pigs in Space, 2002, Palisades
NM $18   MIP $30

Swedish Kitchen, 2002, Palisades,
w/the Swedish Chef
NM $40   MIP $60

SERIES 01 FIGURES

Dr. Bunsen Honeydew, 2002, Palisades
NM $15   MIP $38

Dr. Teeth, 2002, Palisades
NM $12   MIP $32

Kermit the Frog, 2002, Palisades
    NM $8   **MIP** $18

Miss Piggy, 2002, Palisades
    NM $6   **MIP** $15

SERIES 02 FIGURES

Crazy Harry, 2002, Palisades
    NM $6   **MIP** $12

Floyd Pepper, 2002, Palisades
    NM $12   **MIP** $25

Fozzie Bear, 2002, Palisades
    NM $15   **MIP** $30

Gonzo the Great, 2002, Palisades
    NM $6   **MIP** $12

SERIES 03 FIGURES

Lew Zealand, 2002, Palisades
    NM $8   **MIP** $15

Rowlf, 2002, Palisades
    NM $20   **MIP** $40

Scooter, 2002, Palisades
    NM $14   **MIP** $30

Zoot, 2002, Palisades
    NM $32   **MIP** $70

SERIES 04 FIGURES

Dr. Strangepork, 2002, Palisades
    NM $8   **MIP** $18

Link Hogthrob, 2002, Palisades
    NM $13   **MIP** $22

(KP Photo, Merry Dudley collection)

Mr. Samuel Arrow, 2002, Palisades
    NM $8   **MIP** $15

Rizzo the Rat, 2002, Palisades
    NM $16   **MIP** $28

SERIES 05 FIGURES

Gonzo & Camilla, 2003, Palisades
    NM $15   **MIP** $25

Janice, 2003, Palisades
    NM $15   **MIP** $30

Muppet Newsman, 2003, Palisades
    NM $8   **MIP** $16

Pepe, 2003, Palisades
    NM $6   **MIP** $13

SERIES 06 FIGURES

Clifford, 2003, Palisades
    NM $4   **MIP** $10

Patrol Bear, 2003, Palisades
    NM $7   **MIP** $15

Statler, 2003, Palisades
    NM $26   **MIP** $40

Waldorf, 2003, Palisades
    NM $18   **MIP** $30

SERIES 07 FIGURES

Beauregard, 2004, Palisades
    NM $5   **MIP** $10

Captain Smollet & Polly, 2004, Palisades, Kermit as sea captain
    NM $4   **MIP** $10

Frog Scout Robin, 2004, Palisades
    NM $10   **MIP** $18

Johnny Fiama, 2004, Palisades, available w/three different jacket colors, silver, pinstripe, maroon
    NM $4   **MIP** $12

SERIES 08 FIGURES

Dr. Phil Van Neuter, 2004, Palisades
    NM $3   **MIP** $7

Marvin Suggs, 2004, Palisades
    NM $12   **MIP** $35

Movie Usher Scooter, 2004, Palisades
    NM $5   **MIP** $10

Sam the Eagle, 2004, Palisades
    NM $20   **MIP** $35

SERIES 09 FIGURES

Classic Swedish Chef, 2004, Palisades
    NM $20   **MIP** $35

Lips, 2004, Palisades
    NM $60   **MIP** $120

Pops, 2004, Palisades
    NM $22   **MIP** $35

Steppin' Out Fozzie (Tuxedo Fozzie), 2004, Palisades, w/Chucky, the dummy
    NM $8   **MIP** $15

Nightmare Before Christtmas (Hasbro, 1993)

FIGURES

Behemoth, 1993, Hasbro
    NM $35   **MIP** $80

Evil Scientist, 1993, Hasbro
    NM $50   **MIP** $150

Jack Skellington, 1993, Hasbro
    NM $40   **MIP** $100

Jack Skellington as Santa, 1993, Hasbro
    NM $35   **MIP** $80

Lock, Shock and Barrel, 1993, Hasbro
    NM $75   **MIP** $250

Mayor, 1993, Hasbro
    NM $45   **MIP** $125

Oogie Boogie, 1993, Hasbro
    NM $75   **MIP** $250

Sally, 1993, Hasbro
    NM $40   **MIP** $100

Santa, 1993, Hasbro
    NM $75   **MIP** $250

Werewolf, 1993, Hasbro, tombstone, bone
    NM $40   **MIP** $100

Noble Knights (Marx, 1968)

FIGURES

Black Knight, Sir Cedric, 1968, Marx, #2082, w/removeable helmet, shield and accessories, a UK figure
NM $250   **MIP** $550

Gold Knight, Sir Gordon, 1968, Marx, #5366, like the black knight, this figure had molded-on armor, but included a variety of plastic accessories such as shield, helmet and sword, Sir Percival in UK
NM $75   **MIP** $150

(KP Photo, Karen O'Brien collection)

Silver Knight, Sir Stuart, 1968, Marx, #5364, Sir Roland in UK, shown here w/most (not all) of his accessories
NM $75   **MIP** $150

HORSES

Bravo Armor Horse, 1968, Marx, #5371, Gold Knight's horse, chestnut color, Victor in UK
NM $75   **MIP** $150

Valiant Armor Horse, 1968, Marx, Black Knight's horse, gray color, UK only
NM $200   **MIP** $400

Valor Armor Horse, 1968, Marx, #5391, Silver Knight's horse, palomino color, Valour in UK, Big Valor on 1970 packaging
NM $75   **MIP** $150

Noble Knights (Marx, 1968)

HORSES

Castle Play Set, 1968, Marx
NM $180   **MIP** $350

One Million B.C. (Mego, 1976)

FIGURES

Dimetrodon, 1976, Mego, boxed
NM $100   **MIP** $250

Grok, 1976, Mego, carded
NM $25   **MIP** $50

Hairy Rhino, 1976, Mego, boxed
NM $125   **MIP** $300

Mada, 1976, Mego, carded
NM $25   **MIP** $50

Orm, 1976, Mego, carded
NM $25   **MIP** $50

Trag, 1976, Mego, carded
NM $25   **MIP** $50

Tribal Lair, 1976, Mego, boxed
NM $100   **MIP** $200

Tribal Lair Gift Set (five figures), 1976, Mego, boxed
NM $200   **MIP** $400

Tyrannosaur, 1976, Mego, boxed
NM $125   **MIP** $300

Zon, 1976, carded, 1976, Mego, carded
NM $25   **MIP** $50

Outer Space Men (Colorforms, 1968)

FIGURES

Alpha 7/Man from Mars, 1968, Colorforms
NM $150   **MIP** $450

Astro-Nautilus/Man from Neptune, 1968, Colorforms,
NM $300   **MIP** $750

Colossus Rex/Man from Jupiter, 1968, Colorforms
NM $300   **MIP** $800

Commander Comet/Man from Venus, 1968, Colorforms
NM $200   **MIP** $500

Electron/Man from Pluto, 1968, Colorforms, a flexible figure that packs heat, and by the looks of things, can shoot lightning from his head
NM $200   **MIP** $500

Orbitron/Man from Uranus, 1968, Colorforms, an unfortunately-named, but neat toy nonetheless, looking very much like the Metaluna Mutant in "This Island Earth," Orbitron was a bendable figure that included a blaster pistol

NM $200   MIP $600

Xodiac/Man from Saturn, 1968, Colorforms

NM $200   MIP $500

(KP Photo, Kris Manty collection)

Pee-Wee's Playhouse (Matchbox, 1988)

16" FIGURES

(KP Photo, Kris Manty collection)

Billy Baloney, 1988, Matchbox, his eyes and mouth move

NM $20   MIP $50

5" FIGURES

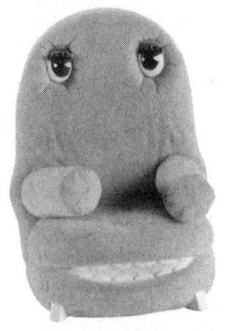

(KP Photo, Kris Manty collection)

Chairry, 1988, Matchbox

NM $5   MIP $20

Conky, 1988, Matchbox

NM $5   MIP $20

Cowboy Curtis, 1988, Matchbox

NM $4   MIP $20

(KP Photo, Kris Manty collection)

Globey, 1988, Matchbox, packaged w/Randy

NM $5   MIP $18

Jambi and Puppetland Band, 1988, Matchbox

NM $12   MIP $25

King of Cartoons, 1988, Matchbox

NM $6   MIP $15

Magic Screen, 1988, Matchbox

NM $5   MIP $12

Miss Yvonne, 1988, Matchbox

NM $6   MIP $15

(KP Photo, Kris Manty collection)

Pee-Wee Herman, 1988, Matchbox

NM $10   MIP $20

Pee-Wee Herman w/Scooter, 1988, Matchbox

NM $12   MIP $25

(KP Photo, Kris Manty collection)

Pterri, 1988, Matchbox

NM $5   MIP $15

(KP Photo, Kris Manty collection)

Randy, 1988, Matchbox, packaged w/Globey

NM $5   MIP $15

Reba, 1988, Matchbox

NM $5   MIP $15

Ricardo, 1988, Matchbox

NM $5   MIP $15

PLAY SETS

Pee-Wee's Playhouse, 1988, Matchbox, w/Scooter, Floory, Clockey, Mr. Window, Dancing Flowers; working front door, fridge, swinging wall; includes platform, island couch, TV console, kitchen table and bench

NM $60   MIP $125

Planet of the Apes (Hasbro, 1998-99)

12" FIGURES

Cornelius, 1999, Hasbro

NM $8   MIP $20

Dr. Zaius, 1999, Hasbro

NM $8   MIP $20

Dr. Zira, 1998, Hasbro

NM $10   MIP $20

General Ursus, 1999, Hasbro
    NM $8   **MIP** $20

Gorilla Sergeant, 1998, Hasbro
    NM $10   **MIP** $20

Gorilla Soldier, 1998, Hasbro, Diamond Previews Exclusive
    NM $15   **MIP** $30

Taylor, 1998, Hasbro
    NM $10   **MIP** $20

7" FIGURES

Commander Taylor, 1999, Hasbro
    NM $2   **MIP** $6

Cornelius, 1999, Hasbro
    NM $2   **MIP** $6

Dr. Zaius, 1999, Hasbro
    NM $2   **MIP** $6

Gorilla Sergeant, 1999, Hasbro
    NM $2   **MIP** $6

Gorilla Soldier, 1999, Hasbro
    NM $2   **MIP** $6

Zira, 1999, Hasbro
    NM $2   **MIP** $6

Planet of the Apes (Mego, 1973-75)

8" FIGURES

Astronaut, 1973, Mego, boxed
    NM $50   **MIP** $250

Astronaut, 1975, Mego, carded
    NM $50   **MIP** $100

Astronaut Burke, 1975, Mego, carded
    NM $50   **MIP** $100

Astronaut Burke, 1975, Mego, boxed
    NM $50   **MIP** $250

Astronaut Verdon, 1975, Mego, boxed
    NM $50   **MIP** $250

Astronaut Verdon, 1975, Mego, carded
    NM $50   **MIP** $125

Cornelius, 1973, Mego, boxed
    NM $40   **MIP** $200

Cornelius, 1975, Mego, carded
    NM $40   **MIP** $100

Dr. Zaius, 1973, Mego, boxed
    NM $40   **MIP** $200

Dr. Zaius, 1975, Mego, carded
    NM $40   **MIP** $100

Galen, 1975, Mego, carded
    NM $40   **MIP** $100

Galen, 1975, Mego, boxed
    NM $40   **MIP** $200

General Urko, 1975, Mego, boxed
    NM $50   **MIP** $250

General Urko, 1975, Mego, carded
    NM $50   **MIP** $250

General Ursus, 1975, Mego, boxed
    NM $50   **MIP** $250

General Ursus, 1975, Mego, carded
    NM $50   **MIP** $250

Soldier Ape, 1973, Mego, boxed
    NM $50   **MIP** $250

Soldier Ape, 1975, Mego, carded
    NM $50   **MIP** $200

Zira, 1973, Mego, boxed
    NM $30   **MIP** $200

Zira, 1975, Mego, carded
    NM $30   **MIP** $100

ACCESSORIES

Action Stallion, 1975, Mego, brown, motorized, remote-controlled
    NM $50   **MIP** $100

Battering Ram, 1975, Mego, boxed
    NM $20   **MIP** $40

Dr. Zaius' Throne, 1975, Mego, boxed
    NM $20   **MIP** $40

Jail, 1975, Mego, boxed
    NM $20   **MIP** $40

PLAY SETS

Forbidden Zone Trap, 1975, Mego, boxed
    NM $90   **MIP** $230

Fortress, 1975, Mego, boxed
    NM $85   **MIP** $230

Treehouse, 1975, Mego, boxed
    NM $75   **MIP** $230

Village, 1975, Mego, boxed
    NM $110   **MIP** $275

VEHICLES

Catapult and Wagon, 1975, Mego, boxed
    NM $45   **MIP** $75

Pocket Super Heroes (Mego, 1976-79)

3-3/4" FIGURES

Aquaman, white card, 1976, Mego
    NM $65   **MIP** $150

Batman, red card, 1976, Mego
    NM $35   **MIP** $110

Batman, white card, 1976, Mego
    NM $35   **MIP** $150

Captain America, white card, 1976, Mego
    NM $50   **MIP** $150

General Zod, red card, 1979, Mego
    NM $8   **MIP** $25

Green Goblin, white card, 1976, Mego
    NM $75   **MIP** $250

Hulk, 1976, white card, 1976, Mego
    NM $15   **MIP** $50

Hulk, 1979, red card, 1979, Mego, shown on right w/Robin
    NM $15   **MIP** $65

Jor-El (Superman), red card, 1979, Mego
    NM $10   **MIP** $25

Lex Luthor (Superman), red card, 1979, Mego
    NM $10   **MIP** $25

Robin, red card, 1979, Mego, shown on left w/Hulk
    NM $25   **MIP** $85

Robin, white card, 1976, Mego
    NM $25   **MIP** $180

Spider-Man, red card, 1979, Mego
    NM $18   **MIP** $85

Spider-Man, white card, 1976, Mego
    NM $18   **MIP** $130

Superman, red card, 1979, Mego
    NM $15   **MIP** $110

Superman, white card, 1976, Mego
    NM $15   **MIP** $125

Wonder Woman, white card, 1979, Mego
    NM $25   **MIP** $110

ACCESSORIES

Batcave, 1981, Mego
    NM $120   **MIP** $300

VEHICLES

Batmachine, 1979, Mego
    NM $75   **MIP** $210

Batmobile, 1979, Mego, w/Batman and Robin
　NM $80　　MIP $200

Spider-Car, 1979, Mego, w/Spider-Man and Hulk
　NM $45　　MIP $125

Spider-Machine, 1979, Mego
　NM $75　　MIP $210

Power Rangers in Space (Bandai, 1998)

ACTION ZORDS

Astro Megaship, 1998, Bandai
　NM $20　　MIP $40

Astro Megazord, 1998, Bandai
　NM $45　　MIP $78

Delta Megazord, 1998, Bandai
　NM $20　　MIP $50

Mega Tank, 1998, Bandai
　NM $10　　MIP $20

Mega Winger, 1998, Bandai
　NM $10　　MIP $20

ASTRO RANGER, 5" FIGURES

Black Ranger, 1998, Bandai
　NM $10　　MIP $20

Pink Ranger, 1998, Bandai
　NM $10　　MIP $20

Red Ranger, 1998, Bandai
　NM $10　　MIP $20

Red Ranger, 1998, Bandai
　NM $10　　MIP $20

Silver Ranger, 1998, Bandai
　NM $10　　MIP $20

Yellow Ranger, 1998, Bandai
　NM $10　　MIP $20

BATTLIZED POWER RANGERS, 5" FIGURES

Black Ranger, 1998, Bandai
　NM $3　　MIP $10

Blue Ranger, 1998, Bandai
　NM $3　　MIP $10

Red Ranger, 1998, Bandai
　NM $3　　MIP $10

Silver, 1998, Bandai
　NM $3　　MIP $10

EVIL SPACE ALIENS, 5" FIGURES

Craterite, 1998, Bandai
　NM $2　　MIP $6

Ecliptor, 1998, Bandai
　NM $2　　MIP $6

STAR POWER RANGERS IN SPACE, 5" FIGURES

Blue Ranger, 1998, Bandai
　NM $2　　MIP $6

Green Ranger, 1998, Bandai
　NM $2　　MIP $6

Pink Ranger, 1998, Bandai
　NM $2　　MIP $6

Red Ranger, 1998, Bandai
　NM $2　　MIP $6

Yellow Ranger, 1998, Bandai
　NM $2　　MIP $6

Power Rangers Turbo (Bandai, 1997)

EVIL SPACE ALIENS, 5" FIGURES

Amphibitor, 1997, Bandai
　NM $2　　MIP $6

Chromite, 1997, Bandai
　NM $2　　MIP $6

Divatox, 1997, Bandai
　NM $4　　MIP $20

Elgar, 1997, Bandai
　NM $2　　MIP $6

Griller, 1997, Bandai
　NM $2　　MIP $6

Hammeron, 1997, Bandai
　NM $2　　MIP $6

Rygog, 1997, Bandai
　NM $2　　MIP $6

Visceron, 1997, Bandai
　NM $2　　MIP $6

REPEAT TURBO RANGERS, 5" FIGURES

Blue Ranger, 1997, Bandai
　NM $2　　MIP $6

Green Ranger, 1997, Bandai
　NM $2　　MIP $6

Pink Ranger, 1997, Bandai
　NM $2　　MIP $6

Red Ranger, 1997, Bandai
　NM $2　　MIP $6

Yellow Ranger, 1997, Bandai
　NM $2　　MIP $6

TURBO CARTS W/4" FIGURE

Cart w/Blue Turbo Ranger, 1997, Bandai
　NM $3　　MIP $8

Cart w/Green Turbo Ranger, 1997, Bandai
　NM $3　　MIP $8

Cart w/Pink Turbo Ranger, 1997, Bandai
　NM $3　　MIP $8

Cart w/Red Turbo Ranger, 1997, Bandai
　NM $3　　MIP $8

Cart w/Yellow Turbo Ranger, 1997, Bandai
　NM $3　　MIP $8

TURBO RANGERS, 5" FIGURES, EACH ACTIVATED W/KEY

Blue Turbo Ranger, 1997, Bandai
　NM $2　　MIP $6

Green Turbo Ranger, 1997, Bandai
　NM $2　　MIP $6

Pink Turbo Ranger, 1997, Bandai
　NM $2　　MIP $6

Red Turbo Ranger, 1997, Bandai
　NM $2　　MIP $6

Yellow Turbo Ranger, 1997, Bandai
　NM $2　　MIP $6

TURBO SHIFTER, 5" FIGURES

Blue Ranger, 1997, Bandai
　NM $2　　MIP $6

Green Ranger, 1997, Bandai
　NM $2　　MIP $6

Pink Ranger, 1997, Bandai
　NM $2　　MIP $6

Red Ranger, 1997, Bandai
　NM $2　　MIP $6

Yellow Ranger, 1997, Bandai
　NM $2　　MIP $6

Power Rangers Zeo (Bandai, 1996)

AUTO MORPHIN, 5-1/2" FIGURES

Blue, 1996, Bandai
　NM $2　　MIP $6

Gold Warrior, 1996, Bandai
　NM $2　　MIP $6

Green, 1996, Bandai
　NM $2　　MIP $6

Pink, 1996, Bandai
　NM $2　　MIP $6

Red, 1996, Bandai
　NM $2　　MIP $6

Yellow, 1996, Bandai
　NM $2　　MIP $6

EVIL SPACE ALIENS, 5-1/2" FIGURES

Cogs, 1996, Bandai
　NM $2　　MIP $6

Drill Master, 1996, Bandai
　NM $2　　MIP $6

Mechanizer, 1996, Bandai
　NM $2　　MIP $6

Quadfighter, 1996, Bandai

NM $2   MIP $6

Silo, 1996, Bandai

NM $2   MIP $6

ZEO JET CYCLES W/FIGURE

Cycle w/Blue Zeo Ranger III, 1996, Bandai

NM $2   MIP $6

Cycle w/Gold Zeo Ranger, 1996, Bandai

NM $2   MIP $6

Cycle w/Green Zeo Ranger IV, 1996, Bandai

NM $2   MIP $6

Cycle w/Pink Zeo Ranger I, 1996, Bandai

NM $2   MIP $6

Cycle w/Red Zeo Ranger V, 1996, Bandai

NM $2   MIP $6

Cycle w/Yellow Zeo Ranger II, 1996, Bandai

NM $2   MIP $6

ZEO POWER ZORDS, 5-1/2" FIGURES

1-2 Punching Action Red Battlezord, 1996, Bandai

NM $2   MIP $6

Auric the Conqueror Zord, 1996, Bandai

NM $2   MIP $6

Power Sword Action Zeo Megazord, 1996, Bandai

NM $2   MIP $6

Pyramidas, 1996, Bandai

NM $2   MIP $6

Super Zeo Megazord, 1996, Bandai

NM $2   MIP $6

Warrior Wheel, 1996, Bandai

NM $2   MIP $6

ZEO RANGERS, 5-1/2" FIGURES

Blue Zeo Ranger III, 1996, Bandai

NM $2   MIP $6

Gold Zeo Ranger, 1996, Bandai

NM $2   MIP $6

Green Zeo Ranger IV, 1996, Bandai

NM $2   MIP $6

Pink Zeo Ranger I, 1996, Bandai

NM $2   MIP $6

Red Zeo Ranger V, 1996, Bandai

NM $2   MIP $6

Yellow Zeo Ranger II, 1996, Bandai

NM $2   MIP $6

ZEO RANGERS, 8" FIGURES

Blue Zeo Ranger III, 1996, Bandai

NM $3   MIP $8

Gold Zeo Ranger, 1996, Bandai

NM $3   MIP $8

Green Zeo Ranger IV, 1996, Bandai

NM $3   MIP $8

Pink Zeo Ranger I, 1996, Bandai

NM $3   MIP $8

Red Zeo Ranger V, 1996, Bandai

NM $3   MIP $8

Yellow Zeo Ranger II, 1996, Bandai

NM $3   MIP $8

Pulsar (Mattel, 1976)

FIGURES

Hypnos, 1976, Mattel, no circulatory system, spinning disk in chest

NM $45   MIP $125

Pulsar the Ultimate Man of Adventure, 1976, Mattel, exposed chest shows veins w/"blood" pumping through

NM $30   MIP $80

PLAY SET

Life Systems Center Play Set, 1976, Mattel

NM $25   MIP $50

Puppetmaster (Full Moon Toys, 1997-98)

FIGURES

Blade, 1997-98, Full Moon Toys

NM $8   MIP $20

Blade, blood splattered, 1997-98, Full Moon Toys

NM $25   MIP $85

Blade, bullet-eyed (Troll & Joad), 1997-98, Full Moon Toys

NM $15   MIP $40

Blade, gold, 1997-98, Full Moon Toys

NM $8   MIP $20

Blade, red Japanese Exclusive, 1997-98, Full Moon Toys

NM $15   MIP $40

Jester, 1997-98, Full Moon Toys

NM $3   MIP $12

Jester, gold, 1997-98, Full Moon Toys

NM $8   MIP $20

Jester, Japanese Exclusive, Carse of Jester, 1997-98, Full Moon Toys

NM $3   MIP $12

Jester, Previews Exclusive, 1997-98, Full Moon Toys

NM $8   MIP $20

Leech Woman, 1997-98, Full Moon Toys

NM $3   MIP $12

Leech Woman, gold, 1997-98, Full Moon Toys

NM $8   MIP $20

Leech Woman, Japanese Exclusive, Geisha Leech Woman, 1997-98, Full Moon Toys

NM $3   MIP $12

Leech Woman, Previews Exclusive, 1997-98, Full Moon Toys

NM $8   MIP $20

Mephisto, 1997-98, Full Moon Toys

NM $3   MIP $12

Mephisto, clear, 1997-98, Full Moon Toys

NM $5   MIP $15

Mephisto, Japanese Exclusive, death Mephisto, 1997-98, Full Moon Toys

NM $8   MIP $20

Mephisto, Previews Exclusive, 1997-98, Full Moon Toys

NM $8   MIP $20

Pinhead, 1997-98, Full Moon Toys

NM $3   MIP $12

Pinhead, gold, 1997-98, Full Moon Toys

NM $8   MIP $20

Pinhead, Halloween 1999, 1997-98, Full Moon Toys

NM $8   MIP $20

Pinhead, Japanese Exclusive, Pinhead in the Dark, 1997-98, Full Moon Toys

NM $8   MIP $25

Pinhead, Previews Exclusive, 1997-98, Full Moon Toys

NM $8   MIP $20

Sixshooter, 1997-98, Full Moon Toys

NM $8   MIP $20

Sixshooter, gold, 1997-98, Full Moon Toys

NM $8   MIP $20

Sixshooter, Japanese Exclusive, DOA Sixshooter, 1997-98, Full Moon Toys

NM $10   MIP $30

Sixshooter, Troll & Joad Edition, 1997-98, Full Moon Toys

NM $10   MIP $30

Torch, 1997-98, Full Moon Toys

NM $3   MIP $12

Torch, gold, 1997-98, Full Moon Toys

NM $8   MIP $20

Torch, Japanese Exclusive, Camouflage Torch, 1997-98, Full Moon Toys

NM $8   MIP $25

Torch, Previews Exclusive, 1997-98, Full Moon Toys

NM $8   MIP $20

Totem, 1997-98, Full Moon Toys
    NM $3   MIP $12

Totem, 1998 San Diego Comic-Con, 1997-98, Full Moon Toys
    NM $15   MIP $45

Totem, gold, 1997-98, Full Moon Toys
    NM $5   MIP $15

Totem, Japanese Exclusive, Evil Spirit Totem, 1997-98, Full Moon Toys
    NM $10   MIP $35

Totem, Preview Exclusive, 1997-98, Full Moon Toys
    NM $8   MIP $20

Tunneler, 1997-98, Full Moon Toys
    NM $3   MIP $12

Tunneler, Australian Exclusive, 1997-98, Full Moon Toys
    NM $15   MIP $45

Tunneler, gold, 1997-98, Full Moon Toys
    NM $8   MIP $20

Tunneler, Japanese Exclusive, Cruel Sgt. Tunneler, 1997-98, Full Moon Toys
    NM $15   MIP $45

Tunneler, Previews Exclusive, 1997-98, Full Moon Toys
    NM $8   MIP $20

Rambo (Coleco, 1985)

FIGURES

Black Dragon, 1985, Coleco, Series 1
    NM $22   MIP $35

Chief, 1985, Coleco, Series 2
    NM $70   MIP $210

Colonel Troutman, 1985, Coleco, Series 1
    NM $18   MIP $30

Dr. Hyde, 1985, Coleco, Series 2
    NM $125   MIP $325

General Warhawk, 1985, Coleco, Series 1
    NM $15   MIP $25

Gripper, 1985, Coleco, Series 1
    NM $12   MIP $25

K.A.T., 1985, Coleco, Series 1
    NM $22   MIP $45

Mad Dog, 1985, Coleco, Series 2
    NM $20   MIP $35

Nomad, 1985, Coleco, Series 1
    NM $15   MIP $25

Rambo, 1985, Coleco, Series 1
    NM $15   MIP $30

Rambo w/Fire Power, 1985, Coleco, Series 2
    NM $15   MIP $30

Sergeant Havoc, 1985, Coleco, Series 1
    NM $12   MIP $25

Snakebite, 1985, Coleco, Series 2
    NM $65   MIP $225

T.D. Jackson, 1985, Coleco, Series 2
    NM $65   MIP $250

Turbo, 1985, Coleco, Series 1
    NM $13   MIP $25

White Dragon, 1985, Coleco, Series 1
    NM $18   MIP $35

X-Ray, 1985, Coleco, Series 2
    NM $210   MIP $400

PLAY SETS

S.A.V.A.G.E. Strike Headquarters, 1985, Coleco, Series 1
    NM $50   MIP $125

VEHICLES

Defender 6 x 6, 1985, Coleco, Series 1
    NM $30   MIP $50

S.A.V.A.G.E. Strike Cycle, 1985, Coleco, Series 1
    NM $12   MIP $30

Skyfire Assault Copter, 1985, Coleco, Series 1
    NM $20   MIP $30

Skywolf Assault Jet, 1985, Coleco, Series 1
    NM $22   MIP $35

Swamp Dog, 1985, Coleco, Series 1
    NM $12   MIP $25

Resident Evil (Toy Biz, 1998)

5" FIGURES

Chris Redfield and Cerberus, 1998
    NM $5   MIP $15

Hunter and Chimera, 1998
    NM $3   MIP $8

Jill Valentine and Web Spinner, 1998
    NM $3   MIP $8

Maggot Zombie and Forrest Speyer, 1998
    NM $3   MIP $8

Tyrant, 1998
    NM $3   MIP $8

Resident Evil (Palisades, 2002)

SERIES II

(KP Photo)

Alexia, 2002, Palisades, bug-winged figure w/"leafy" hair
    NM $3   MIP $7

(KP Photo)

Claire Redfield, 2002, Palisades, figure includes dagger and pistol
    NM $3   MIP $7

(KP Photo)

Mr. X, 2002, Palisades, black jacket and uniform, dark gray skin, glowing eyes

    NM $4   **MIP** $8

(KP Photo)

Zombie Cop, 2002, Palisades, mauled policeman w/terrifying ? on a leash…

    NM $4   **MIP** $8

Robin Hood and His Merry Men (Mego, 1974)

FIGURES

Friar Tuck, 1974, Mego
    NM $35   **MIP** $65

Little John, 1974, Mego
    NM $70   **MIP** $165

Robin Hood, 1974, Mego
    NM $100   **MIP** $310

Will Scarlett, 1974, Mego
    NM $80   **MIP** $285

Robin Hood Prince of Thieves (Kenner, 1991)

ACCESSORIES

Battle Wagon, 1991, Kenner
    NM $25   **MIP** $45

Bola Bomber, 1991, Kenner
    NM $8   **MIP** $15

Net Launcher, 1991, Kenner
    NM $8   **MIP** $15

Sherwood Forest Play Set, 1991, Kenner
    NM $50   **MIP** $110

FIGURES

Azeem, 1991, Kenner
    NM $3   **MIP** $5'

(Lenny Lee)

Friar Tuck, w/Battle Staff, 1991, Kenner, w/fabric road
    NM $3   **MIP** $5

(KP Photo, Karen O'Brien collection)

Little John, 1991, Kenner
    NM $3   **MIP** $5

Robin Hood, Crossbow, 1991, Kenner
    NM $3   **MIP** $5

Robin Hood, Crossbow, Costner Head, 1991, Kenner
    NM $3   **MIP** $5

Robin Hood, Long Bow, 1991, Kenner
    NM $3   **MIP** $5

Robin Hood, Long Bow, Costner Head, 1991, Kenner
    NM $3   **MIP** $5

Sheriff of Nottingham, 1991, Kenner
    NM $3   **MIP** $5

The Dark Warrior, 1991, Kenner
    NM $3   **MIP** $5

Will Scarlett, 1991, Kenner
    NM $3   **MIP** $5

RoboCop and the Ultra Police (Kenner, 1989-90)

FIGURES

Ace Jackson, 1989-90, Kenner
    NM $3   **MIP** $10

Anne Lewis, 1989-90, Kenner
    NM $3   **MIP** $10

Birdman Barnes, 1989-90, Kenner
    NM $3   **MIP** $10

Chainsaw, 1989-90, Kenner
    NM $3   **MIP** $10

Claw Callahan, 1989-90, Kenner
    NM $3   **MIP** $10

Dr. McNamara, 1989-90, Kenner
    NM $3   **MIP** $10

Ed-260, 1989-90, Kenner
    NM $35   **MIP** $70

Headhunter, 1989-90, Kenner
    NM $6   **MIP** $12

Nitro, 1989-90, Kenner
    NM $6   **MIP** $12

RoboCop, 1989-90, Kenner
    NM $20   **MIP** $40

RoboCop Night Fighter, 1989-90, Kenner
    NM $15   **MIP** $30

RoboCop, Gatlin' Gun, 1989-90, Kenner
    NM $20   **MIP** $40

Scorcher, 1989-90, Kenner
    NM $6   **MIP** $12

Sgt. Reed, 1989-90, Kenner
    NM $6   **MIP** $10

Toxic Waster, 1989-90, Kenner
    NM $6   **MIP** $12

Wheels Wilson, 1989-90, Kenner
    NM $3   **MIP** $10

VEHICLES

Robo-1, 1989-90, Kenner
    NM $20   **MIP** $40

Robo-Command w/figure, 1989-90, Kenner, w/figure
    NM $20   **MIP** $45

Robo-Copter, 1989-90, Kenner
    NM $5   **MIP** $12

Robo-Cycle, 1989-90, Kenner
    NM $5   **MIP** $5

Robo-Hawk, 1989-90, Kenner
    NM $5   **MIP** $15

Robo-Jailer, 1989-90, Kenner
    NM $5   **MIP** $15

Robo-Tank, 1989-90, Kenner
    NM $12   **MIP** $30

Skull-Hog, 1989-90, Kenner
    NM $3   **MIP** $15

Vandal-1, 1989-90, Kenner
    NM $3   **MIP** $15

Robotech
(Matchbox, 1986)

11-1/2" FIGURES

Dana Sterling, 1986
        NM $10   MIP $18

Lisa Hayes, 1986
        NM $10   MIP $15

Lynn Minmei, 1986
        NM $10   MIP $20

Rick Hunter, 1986
        NM $12   MIP $30

3-3/4" FIGURES

Bioroid Terminator, 1986
        NM $5   MIP $15

Corg, 1986
        NM $8   MIP $20

Dana Sterling, 1986
        NM $12   MIP $30

Lisa Hayes, 1986, Matchbox
        NM $7   MIP $12

Lisa Hayes, 1986, center figure,
    shown w/Roy Fokker and Zor Prime
        NM $8   MIP $20

Lunk, 1986
        NM $10   MIP $50

Max Sterling, 1986
        NM $8   MIP $20

Micronized Zentraedi, 1986, Matchbox
        NM $12   MIP $18

Miriya, black, 1986
        NM $25   MIP $65

Miriya, red, 1986
        NM $8   MIP $20

Rand, 1986
        NM $5   MIP $12

Rick Hunter, 1986
        NM $15   MIP $30

Robotech Master, 1986
        NM $5   MIP $12

Rook Bartley, 1986
        NM $20   MIP $50

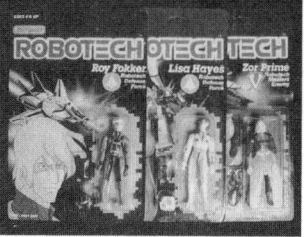

Roy Fokker, 1986, at left, shown
    w/Lisa Hayes and Zor Prime
        NM $12   MIP $30

Scott Bernard, 1986
        NM $20   MIP $45

Zor Prime, 1986, Matchbox, at right,
    shown w/Lisa Hayes and Roy Fokker
        NM $8   MIP $15

6" FIGURES

Breetai, 1986
        NM $8   MIP $12

Dolza, 1986
        NM $6   MIP $12

Exedore, 1986
        NM $6   MIP $12

Khryon, 1986
        NM $6   MIP $12

Miriya, 1986
        NM $6   MIP $12

8" FIGURES

Armoured Zentraedi Warrior, 1986
        NM $8   MIP $20

VEHICLES AND
ACCESSORIES

Armoured Cyclone, 1986
        NM $10   MIP $50

Bioroid Hover Craft, 1986
        NM $10   MIP $25

Bioroid Invid Fighter, 1986, Matchbox
        NM $20   MIP $40

Dana's Hover Cycle, 1986
        NM $50   MIP $110

Excaliber MkVI, 1986, Matchbox
        NM $25   MIP $45

Gladiator, 1986, Matchbox
        NM $20   MIP $40

Invid Scout Ship, 1986
        NM $30   MIP $50

Invid Shock Trooper, 1986, Matchbox
        NM $30   MIP $50

Raidar X, 1986, Matchbox
        NM $20   MIP $40

SDF-1 Play Set, 1986, Matchbox
        NM $750   MIP $1500

Spartan, 1986, Matchbox
        NM $20   MIP $40

Tactical Battle Pod, 1986
        NM $45   MIP $85

Veritech Fighter, 1986
        NM $45   MIP $125

Veritech Hover Tank, 1986
        NM $50   MIP $90

Zentraedi Officer's Battle Pod, 1986
        NM $50   MIP $90

Zentraedi Powered Armor, 1986,
    Matchbox, Botoru or Quadrono
    Battalion
        NM $25   MIP $45

Sea Devils
(Mattel, 1970)

FIGURES

Commander Chuck Carter, 1970,
    Mattel, orange wetsuit, mask,
    diving gear, sea jet, motor
        NM $80   MIP $150

Kretar and Zark, 1970, Mattel, sea
    creature and shark
        NM $80   MIP $150

Rick Riley, 1970, Mattel, black wetsuit,
    mask, diving gear, sea jet, motor
        NM $80   MIP $150

SET

Search and Rescue Set, 1970, Mattel,
    Commander Carter, Aqualander,
    sea jet, motor, diving gear
        NM $100   MIP $200

Sectaurs (Coleco, 1984)

FIGURE SETS

Genral Spydrax and Spiderflyer,
    1984, Coleco
        NM $40   MIP $75

Mantor w/Rapplor, 1984, Coleco
        NM $14   MIP $25

Night-Fighting Dargon w/Parafly, 1984,
    Coleco, night-vision trinoculars, gun,
    knife, double holsters
        NM $25   MIP $40

Pinsor and Battle Beetle, 1984,
    Coleco, weapons belt, pistol,
    sword, axe, shield
        NM $30   MIP $65

Prince Dargon and Dragonflyer, 1984, Coleco, two pistols w/holsters, sword, shield, bag, Slazor
NM $30   MIP $50

Skito w/Toxcid, 1984, Coleco, gun, sword, holster, shield
NM $15   MIP $25

Skulk and Trancula, 1984, Coleco
NM $35   MIP $75

Waspax w/Wingid, 1984, Coleco
NM $18   MIP $30

Zak and Bitaur, 1984, Coleco, gun, Slazor, holster, shield
NM $18   MIP $30

PLAY SET

The Hyve, Forbidden Fortress, 1984, Coleco
NM $150   MIP $275

She-Ra Princess of Power (Mattel, 1984-86)

CREATURES

Arrow, 1984, Mattel, #9721, Bow's horse, blue
NM $22   MIP $40

Clawdeen, 1985, Mattel, #9627, Catra's large cat
NM $30   MIP $50

Crystal Moonbeam, 1985, Mattel, #2434
NM $30   MIP $65

Crystal Sun Dancer, 1985, Mattel, #2435
NM $30   MIP $60

Crystal Swift Wind, 1985, Mattel, #2433
NM $30   MIP $65

Enchanta, 1984, Mattel, #9681, She-Ra's swan
NM $25   MIP $50

Royal Swift Wind, 1986, Mattel, #3050
NM $80   MIP $160

Sea Harp, 1985, Mattel, #2902, She-Ra's Sea Horse
NM $25   MIP $50

Silver Storm, 1986, Mattel, #3150
NM $80   MIP $160

Storm, 1984, Mattel, #9722, Catra's horse
NM $25   MIP $45

Swift Wind, 1984, Mattel, #9191, She-Ra's horse, pink
NM $35   MIP $60

FASHIONS

Blue Lightning, 1986, Mattel, #2833
NM $50   MIP $160

Colorful Secret, 1986, Mattel, #2837
NM $50   MIP $115

Deep Blue Secret, 1984, Mattel, #2836
NM $10   MIP $20

Fit To Be Tied, 1984, Mattel, #2825
NM $5   MIP $12

Flight of Fancy, 1984, Mattel, #2828
NM $5   MIP $12

Flower Power, 1984, Mattel, #2835
NM $5   MIP $12

Frosty Fur, 1986, Mattel, #2831
NM $72   MIP $200

Heart of Gold, 1986, Mattel, #2838
NM $50   MIP $110

Hidden Gold, 1986, Mattel, #2832
NM $50   MIP $110

Hold on to Your Hat, 1984, Mattel, #2826
NM $5   MIP $12

Ready in Red, 1984, Mattel, #2827
NM $5   MIP $12

Reflections in Red, 1986, Mattel, #2834
NM $45   MIP $140

Rise and Shine, 1984, Mattel, #2824
NM $5   MIP $12

Secret Messanger, 1986, Mattel, #2830
NM $25   MIP $65

Veils of Mystery, 1984, Mattel, #2829
NM $5   MIP $12

Windy Jumper, 1986, Mattel, #2839
NM $60   MIP $125

FIGURE SETS

Bow and Arrow, 1984, Mattel, #9817
NM $25   MIP $100

Catra and Clawdeen, 1985, Mattel, #2746
NM $25   MIP $100

Catra and Storm, 1984, Mattel, #5047
NM $25   MIP $100

Defenders of Good, 1985, Mattel, #1052, She-Ra, Perfuma, and Sweet Bee
NM $60   MIP $200

Peekablue and Moonbeam, 1985, Mattel, #2900
NM $25   MIP $110

She-Ra and Swift Wind, 1984, Mattel
NM $50   MIP $200

Starburst She-Ra and Crystal Swift Wind, 1985, Mattel, #2898
NM $100   MIP $400

Sweet Bee and Crystal Sundancer, 1985, Mattel, #2901
NM $100   MIP $300

FIGURES

Angella, 1984, Mattel, #9186
NM $25   MIP $50

Bow, 1984, Mattel, #9183, bow, shield
NM $20   MIP $35

Bubble Power She-Ra, 1986, Mattel, #3023
NM $210   MIP $350

Castaspella, 1984, Mattel, #9187
NM $25   MIP $65

Catra, 1984, Mattel, #9184, tail, mask, shield
NM $22   MIP $50

Double Trouble, 1984, Mattel, #9185
NM $25   MIP $62

Entrapta, 1985, Mattel, #2636
NM $28   MIP $48

Flutterina, 1985, Mattel, #2453
NM $40   MIP $75

Frosta, 1984, Mattel, #9189
NM $30   MIP $58

Glimmer, 1984, Mattel, #9188
NM $18   MIP $45

Kowl, 1984, Mattel, #9190
NM $40   MIP $80

Loo-Kee, 1986, Mattel, #1969
NM $180   MIP $325

Mermista, 1985, Mattel, #2454
NM $40   MIP $80

Netossa, 1986, Mattel, #1835
NM $75   MIP $135

Peekablue, 1985, Mattel, #2452
NM $35   MIP $78

Perfuma, 1985, Mattel, #2455
NM $35   MIP $60

Scratchin' Sound Catra, 1985, Mattel, #2451
NM $25   MIP $58

She-Ra, 1984, Mattel, #9182, helmet, shield, sword
NM $20   MIP $50

Shower Power Catra, 1986, Mattel, #3021
NM $210   MIP $350

Spinnerella, 1986, Mattel, #3053, very rare!
NM $1000   MIP $2100

Starburst She-Ra, 1985, Mattel, #2450
NM $20   MIP $55

Sweet Bee, 1985, Mattel, #2635
NM $25   MIP $62

PLAY SETS

Crystal Castle, 1984, Mattel, #9193, 30+ pieces
NM $125   MIP $300

Crystal Falls, 1985, Mattel, #2456
NM $38   MIP $110

Shogun Warriors (Mattel, 1979)

24" FIGURES

Daimos, 1979, Mattel, #2988, shooting fist, calf missile launchers
NM $105   MIP $210

Dragun, 1979, Mattel, #9858, fires shurikan and axes
NM $90   MIP $165

Gaiking, 1979, Mattel, eye launchers, shooting fist
NM $75   MIP $150

Godzilla, 1979, Mattel, fire tongue, shooting fist
NM $130   MIP $200

Godzilla (second figure), 1979, Mattel, fire tongue, shooting fist
NM $150   MIP $210

Great Mazinga, 1979, Mattel, #9860, swords, missile fingers
NM $95   MIP $160

Raydeen, 1979, Mattel, #9859, shield, shooting fist, missiles
NM $85   MIP $150

Rodan, 1979, 38" wingspan
NM $275+   MIP $450+

2-IN-1 FIGURES

Daimos, 1979, Mattel, #2992, die-cast, leg cannons, shooting fists
NM $125   MIP $195

Danguard, 1979, Mattel, #2729, die-cast, para-wing, shooting arms and head
NM $90   MIP $250

Gaiking, 1979, Mattel, #2728, die-cast
NM $110   MIP $280

Grandizer, 1979, Mattel, #2994, die-cast, shooting fists, sickles
NM $100   MIP $270

Raydeen, 1979, Mattel, #2727, die-cast
NM $120   MIP $350

Voltus V, 1979, Mattel, #2993, die-cast, changes to battle tank
NM $100   MIP $325

3" FIGURES

17, 1979, Mattel, #2997, Series 2
NM $18   MIP $40

Combattra, 1979, Mattel, #2512, Series 1
NM $18   MIP $40

Dangard, 1979, Mattel, #2995, Series 2
NM $18   MIP $40

Dragun, 1979, Mattel, #2515, Series 1
NM $18   MIP $40

Gaiking, 1979, Mattel, #2514, Series 1
NM $18   MIP $40

Grandizer, 1979, Mattel, #2517, Series 1
NM $18   MIP $40

Great Mazinga, 1979, Mattel, #2516, Series 1
NM $18   MIP $40

Leopaldon, 1979, Mattel, #2996, Series 2
NM $18   MIP $40

Poseidon, 1979, Mattel, #2513, Series 1
NM $18   MIP $40

Voltez V, 1979, Mattel, #2994, Series 2
NM $18   MIP $40

5" FIGURES

Dragun, 1979, Mattel, #2106, die-cast, w/three axes
NM $75   MIP $175

Dragun (second figure), 1979, Mattel, #2106, die-cast, w/two axes
NM $75   MIP $150

Great Mazinga, 1979, Mattel, #2103, die-cast, knees bend
NM $85   MIP $175

Great Mazinga (second figure), 1979, Mattel, #2103, die-cast, knees don't bend much
NM $75   MIP $150

Poseidon, 1979, Mattel, #2104, die-cast, moveable shins
NM $75   MIP $150

Poseidon (second figure), 1979, Mattel, #2104, die-cast, shins don't move
NM $75   MIP $125

Poseidon (third figure), 1979, Mattel, #2105, die-cast, four yellow safety missiles
NM $75   MIP $125

Raider, 1979, Mattel, #2105, die-cast, knees bend
NM $75   MIP $150

Raider (second figure), 1979, Mattel, #2105, die-cast, knees don't bend
NM $75   MIP $125

VEHICLES

Bazoler, 1979, Mattel, #2690
NM $30   MIP $55

Combatra Vehicle #3 Battle Tank, 1979, Mattel, #2622
NM $70   MIP $140

Daimos Truck, 1979, Mattel, #2990
NM $125   MIP $275

Dangard Launcher, 1979, Mattel, #2699
NM $30   MIP $55

Grand Car, 1979, Mattel, #2696
NM $30   MIP $55

Grandizer Saucer, 1979, Mattel, #8998, European release
NM $75   MIP $135

Heli-Capter, 1979, Mattel, #2695
NM $35   MIP $60

Jetcar, 1979, Mattel, #2698
NM $30   MIP $55

Kargosaur, 1979, Mattel, #2694, rare
NM $175   MIP $310

Kondar, 1979, Mattel, #2693
NM $30   MIP $55

Liabe, 1979, Mattel, #2734
NM $100   MIP $200

Nessar, 1979, Mattel, #2691
NM $25   MIP $50

Rydoto, 1979, Mattel, #2900
NM $25   MIP $55

Schicon Jet, 1979, Mattel, #2732
NM $40   MIP $80

Shigcon Tank, 1979, Mattel, #2731
NM $40   MIP $85

Sky Arrow, 1979, Mattel, #2733
NM $40   MIP $80

Sky Jet, 1979, Mattel, #2697
NM $25   MIP $50

Solar Saucer, 1979, Mattel, #2520
NM $50   MIP $95

Varitank, 1979, Mattel, #2519
NM $25   MIP $50

Vertilift, 1979, Mattel, #2521
NM $25   MIP $50

Silver Surfer (Toy Biz, 1997-98)

COSMIC POWER ALIEN FIGHTERS

Adam Warlock w/Cosmic Skull Space Racer, 1998
NM $2   MIP $5

Cosmic Silver Surfer and Pip the Troll, 1998
NM $2   MIP $5

Galactus w/Silver Surfer in Cosmic Orb, 8" Figure, 1998
NM $3   MIP $7

Ivar and Ant Warrior w/Alien Annihilator, 1998
NM $2   MIP $5

Molten Lava Silver Surfer w/Eyeball Alien Space Racer, 1998
NM $2   MIP $5

Ronan the Accussor w/Tree Root Space Racer, 1998
NM $2   MIP $5

Solar Silver Surfer & Draconian Warrior, 1998
NM $2   MIP $5

Super Nova w/Flaming Bird, 1998
NM $2   MIP $5

FIGURES

Beta Ray Bill, Thunder Hammer, 1997
    NM $2   **MIP** $5

Classic Silver Surfer w/Cosmic Surf Board, 1997
    NM $2   **MIP** $5

Meegan Alien, Galactic Weapon Seeker, 1997
    NM $2   **MIP** $5

Nova, Poseable Flaming Hair, 1997
    NM $2   **MIP** $5

INFINITY GAUNTLET SERIES, 10" FIGURE

Silver Surfer, 1997
    NM $4   **MIP** $8

Silverhawks (Kenner, 1987)

ACCESSORIES

Super Attack Bird Sky-Shadow, 1987, Kenner, 20" wingspan
    NM $25   **MIP** $50

Super Attack Bird Stronghold, 1987, Kenner, 20" wingspan
    NM $20   **MIP** $40

Super Attack Bird Tallyhawk, 1987, Kenner, 25" wingspan
    NM $25   **MIP** $50

FIGURES

Bluegrass, 1988, Kenner, w/Hot Licks, guitar transforms, new uniform
    NM $15   **MIP** $30

Condor, 1988, Kenner, w/Jet Stream
    NM $12   **MIP** $25

Hardware, 1988, Kenner, w/Prowler
    NM $10   **MIP** $22

Moon Stryker, 1988, Kenner, w/Tail-Spin
    NM $10   **MIP** $22

Quicksilver, 1988, Kenner, w/Tallyhawk, black uniform
    NM $150   **MIP** $350

Steelwill, 1988, Kenner, w/Steamer
    NM $14   **MIP** $30

Windhammer, 1988, Kenner, w/Tuning Fork
    NM $12   **MIP** $25

FIGURES, BAD

Buzz Saw, 1987, Kenner, w/Shredator
    NM $12   **MIP** $25

Mo-Lec-U-Lar, 1987, Kenner, w/Volt-Ure
    NM $20   **MIP** $45

Mon-Star, 1987, Kenner, w/Sky Shadow
    NM $20   **MIP** $35

Mumbo-Jumbo, 1987, Kenner, w/Airshock
    NM $14   **MIP** $30

FIGURES, GOOD

Bluegrass, 1987, Kenner, w/Side Man, converts from hawk to guitar
    NM $18   **MIP** $50

Copper Kidd, 1987, Kenner, w/May-Day
    NM $30   **MIP** $80

Flashback, 1987, Kenner, w/Backlash
    NM $22   **MIP** $65

Hotwing, 1987, Kenner, w/Gyro
    NM $22   **MIP** $30

Quicksilver, 1987, Kenner, w/Tallyhawk
    NM $30   **MIP** $150

Stargazer, 1987, Kenner, w/Sly-Bird
    NM $12   **MIP** $25

Steelheart, 1987, Kenner, w/Rayzor
    NM $40   **MIP** $100

Steelwill, 1987, Kenner, w/Stronghold
    NM $25   **MIP** $80

VEHICLES

Copper Racer, 1988, Kenner, friction motor, for Copper Kidd
    NM $12   **MIP** $22

Maraj, 1987, Kenner, holds five figures
    NM $85   **MIP** $150

Sky-Runner, 1988, Kenner, for Mon-Star
    NM $70   **MIP** $110

Sprinthawk, 1988, Kenner, for Quicksilver
    NM $35   **MIP** $90

Simpsons (Mattel, 1990)

FIGURES

Bart, 1990, Mattel
    NM $5   **MIP** $10

Bartman, 1990, Mattel
    NM $5   **MIP** $10

Homer, 1990, Mattel
    NM $5   **MIP** $10

Lisa, 1990, Mattel
    NM $5   **MIP** $10

Maggie, 1990, Mattel
    NM $5   **MIP** $10

Marge, 1990, Mattel
    NM $5   **MIP** $10

Nelson, 1990, Mattel
    NM $5   **MIP** $6

Sofa Set, 1990, Mattel
    NM $5   **MIP** $12

Simpsons (Playmates, 1999-2004)

ALL STAR VOICES

Brad Goodman, 2002, Playmates, by Albert Brooks
    NM $4   **MIP** $8

Fat Tony, 2002, Playmates, by Joe Mantegna
    NM $4   **MIP** $8

Herb Powell, 2002, Playmates, by Danny DeVito
    NM $4   **MIP** $8

Lionel Hutz, 2002, Playmates, by Phil Hartman
    NM $4   **MIP** $8

Troy McClure, 2002, Playmates, by Phil Hartman
    NM $4   **MIP** $8

ENVIRONMENTS

Aztec Theater, 2003, Playmates, w/McBain
    NM $6   **MIP** $12

Bart's Treehouse, 2003, Playmates, w/Military Bart
    NM $8   **MIP** $22

Bowl-A-Rama, 2001, Playmates, w/Pin Pal Apu
    NM $6   **MIP** $12

Burns Manor, 2002, Playmates, w/P.J. Burns
    NM $6   **MIP** $12

Comic Book Shop, 2001, Playmates, w/Comic Book Guy
    NM $6   **MIP** $12

Court Room, 2002, Playmates, w/Judge Snyder
    NM $5   **MIP** $10

Doctor's Office, 2002, Playmates, w/Dr. Nick Riviera
    NM $6   **MIP** $18

First Church of Springfield, 2001, Playmates, w/Reverend Lovejoy
    NM $5   **MIP** $10

Krusty Burger, 2002, Playmates, w/Pimply Faced Teen
    NM $5   **MIP** $10

Krustylu Studios, 2001, Playmates, w/Sideshow Bob
    NM $5   **MIP** $10

Kwik-E-Mart, 2000, Playmates, w/Apu
  NM $5   **MIP** $10
Living Room, 2000, Playmates, w/Marge and Maggie
  NM $5   **MIP** $10
Military Antique Shop, 2003, Playmates, w/Herman
  NM $5   **MIP** $10
Noiseland Arcade, 2001, Playmates, w/Jimbo Jones
  NM $5   **MIP** $10
Nuclear Power Plant, 2000, Playmates, w/Homer
  NM $8   **MIP** $16
Nuclear Power Plant Lunch Room, 2004, Playmates, w/Frank Grimes
  NM $8   **MIP** $16
Police Station, 2002, Playmates, w/Officer Eddie
  NM $5   **MIP** $10
Retirement Castle, 2002, Playmates, w/Jasper
  NM $5   **MIP** $10
Simpson's Family Kitchen, 2002, Playmates, w/Muumuu Homer
  NM $5   **MIP** $10
Springfield DMV, 2002, Playmates, w/Selma Bouvier
  NM $5   **MIP** $10
Springfield Elementary, 2000, Playmates, w/Principal Skinner
  NM $5   **MIP** $10
Springfield Elementary School Cafeteria, 2002, Playmates, w/Lunchlady Doris
  NM $5   **MIP** $10
Town Hall, 2001, Playmates, w/Mayor Quimby
  NM $5   **MIP** $10

EXCLUSIVES

All-Star Voices 2-Pack #1, 2002, Playmates, Toys R Us, Lurleen Lumpkin, Colonel Homer
  NM $5   **MIP** $10
All-Star Voices 2-Pack #2, 2002, Playmates, Toys R Us, Jacques, Bowling Marge
  NM $5   **MIP** $10
Barney Gumble, 2002, Playmates, Target, Wave 2
  NM $3   **MIP** $8
Be-Sharp Apu, 1999-2004, Playmates, Playmates mail-in
  NM $10   **MIP** $15
Be-Sharp Barney, 1999-2004, Playmates, Playmates mail-in
  NM $10   **MIP** $15
Be-Sharp Homer, 1999-2004, Playmates, Playmates mail-in
  NM $13   **MIP** $20

Be-Sharp Skinner, 1999-2004, Playmates, Playmates mail-in
  NM $10   **MIP** $15
Bongo Comics Three-Pack, 1999-2004, Playmates, Homer as Ingestible Bulk, Edna Krabappel as Vampiredna, Apu as Captain Kwik
  NM $6   **MIP** $15
Boxing Homer, 2001, Playmates, ToyFare
  NM $5   **MIP** $10
Convention Comic Book Guy, 2001, Playmates, ToyFare
  NM $6   **MIP** $13
Cooder, 1999-2004, Playmates, Playmates mail-in
  NM $10   **MIP** $20
Family Christmas, 2001, Playmates, Toys R Us
  NM $12   **MIP** $22
Family New Years, 2002, Playmates, Toys R Us
  NM $12   **MIP** $22
High School Prom, 2002, Playmates, Diamond, Homer and Marge
  NM $6   **MIP** $12
Homer Simpson, 2002, Playmates, Target, Wave 1
  NM $3   **MIP** $8
KBBL Radio, 2002, Playmates, Diamond
  NM $4   **MIP** $10
Llewellyn Sinclair, 1999-2004, Playmates, Playmates mail-in
  NM $10   **MIP** $20
Lunar Base Environment, 2001, Playmates, Diamond
  NM $4   **MIP** $10
Mainstreet Environment, 2002, Playmates, Toys R Us
  NM $18   **MIP** $35
Moe Szyslak, 2002, Playmates, Target, Wave 2
  NM $4   **MIP** $8
Moe's Tavern Environment, 2003, Playmates, Diamond
  NM $4   **MIP** $10
Mr. Burns, 2002, Playmates, Target, Wave 1
  NM $4   **MIP** $8
Pin Pal Moe, 2001, Playmates, ToyFare
  NM $5   **MIP** $15
Pin Pal Mr. Burns, 2001, Playmates, ToyFare
  NM $5   **MIP** $15

(Mark Bellomo collection)

Radio Active Homer, 2000, Playmates, ToyFare Exclusive, w/radioactive plate of donuts, glow, helmet, glowing tongs
  NM $40   **MIP** $125
Treehouse of Horror I, 2000, Playmates, Toys R Us, Springfield Cemetary
  NM $20   **MIP** $45
Treehouse of Horror II, 2001, Playmates, Toys R Us, Alien Ship
  NM $20   **MIP** $45
Treehouse of Horror III, 2002, Playmates, Toys R Us, Ironic Punishment
  NM $22   **MIP** $40
Treehouse of Horror IV, 2003, Playmates, Toys R Us, Collector's Lair; Bart as Stretch Dude, Lisa as Clobber Girl, Comic Book Guy as The Collector, Lucy Lawless as Xena
  NM $10   **MIP** $20
Treehouse of Horrors, 2000, Playmates, Toys R Us Exclusive
  NM $25   **MIP** $75

SERIES 01 FIGURES

Bart, 1999, Playmates, Series 1
  NM $4   **MIP** $8
Grandpa, 1999, Playmates, Series 1
  NM $3   **MIP** $6
Homer, 1999, Playmates, Series 1
  NM $4   **MIP** $8
Krusty, 1999, Playmates, Series 1
  NM $4   **MIP** $8
Lisa, 1999, Playmates, Series 1
  NM $3   **MIP** $6
Mr. Burns, 1999, Playmates, Series 1
  NM $4   **MIP** $8

SERIES 02 FIGURES

Barney, 2000, Playmates, Series 2
  NM $4   **MIP** $8
Chief Wiggum, 2000, Playmates, Series 2
  NM $3   **MIP** $6
Ned Flanders, 2000, Playmates, Series 2
  NM $3   **MIP** $6

Pin Pal Homer, 2000, Playmates, Series 2

    NM $4   **MIP** $8

Smithers, 2000, Playmates, Series 2

    NM $4   **MIP** $8

Sunday Best Bart, 2000, Playmates, Series 2

    NM $2   **MIP** $5

SERIES 03 FIGURES

Kamp Krusty Bart, 2000, Playmates, Series 3

    NM $2   **MIP** $5

Milhouse, 2000, Playmates, Series 3

    NM $3   **MIP** $6

Moe, 2000, Playmates, Series 3

    NM $4   **MIP** $8

Nelson, 2000, Playmates, Series 3

    NM $2   **MIP** $5

Otto, 2000, Playmates, Series 3

    NM $2   **MIP** $5

Sunday Best Homer, 2000, Playmates, Series 3

    NM $2   **MIP** $5

SERIES 04 FIGURES

Casual Homer, 2001, Playmates, Series 4

    NM $2   **MIP** $5

Groundskeeper Willie, 2001, Playmates, Series 4

    NM $4   **MIP** $8

Itchy and Scratchy, 2001, Playmates, Series 4

    NM $10   **MIP** $14

Lenny, 2001, Playmates, Series 4

    NM $2   **MIP** $5

Patty, 2001, Playmates, Series 4

    NM $2   **MIP** $5

Ralph Wiggum, 2001, Playmates, Series 4

    NM $3   **MIP** $6

SERIES 05 FIGURES

Bartman, 2001, Playmates, Series 5

    NM $3   **MIP** $6

Bumble Bee Man, 2001, Playmates, Series 5

    NM $2   **MIP** $5

Captain McCallister, 2001, Playmates, Series 5

    NM $2   **MIP** $5

Kent Brockman, 2001, Playmates, Series 5

    NM $2   **MIP** $5

Martin, 2001, Playmates, Series 5

    NM $2   **MIP** $5

Sideshow Mel, 2001, Playmates, Series 5

    NM $2   **MIP** $5

SERIES 06 FIGURES

Bleeding Gums Murphy, 2001, Playmates, Series 6

    NM $2   **MIP** $5

Carl, 2001, Playmates, Series 6

    NM $2   **MIP** $5

Dr. Hibbert, 2001, Playmates, Series 6

    NM $2   **MIP** $5

Isotopes Mascot Homer, 2001, Playmates, Series 6

    NM $2   **MIP** $5

Professor Frink, 2001, Playmates, Series 6

    NM $2   **MIP** $5

Snake, 2001, Playmates, Series 6

    NM $2   **MIP** $5

SERIES 07 FIGURES

Cletus, 2001, Playmates, Series 7

    NM $3   **MIP** $6

Dolph, 2001, Playmates, Series 7

    NM $2   **MIP** $5

Hans Moleman, 2001, Playmates, Series 7

    NM $2   **MIP** $5

Mrs. Krabappel, 2001, Playmates, Series 7

    NM $2   **MIP** $5

Officer Lou, 2001, Playmates, Series 7

    NM $2   **MIP** $5

Officer Marge, 2001, Playmates, Series 7

    NM $2   **MIP** $5

SERIES 08 FIGURES

Daredevil Bart, 2002, Playmates, Series 8

    NM $2   **MIP** $5

Kearney, 2002, Playmates, Series 8

    NM $2   **MIP** $5

Ragin' Willie, 2002, Playmates, Series 8

    NM $3   **MIP** $6

Sherri and Terri, 2002, Playmates, Series 8

    NM $2   **MIP** $5

Superintendent Chalmers, 2002, Playmates, Series 8

    NM $3   **MIP** $6

Uter, 2002, Playmates, Series 8

    NM $2   **MIP** $5

SERIES 09 FIGURES

Busted Krusty the Clown, 2002, Playmates, Series 9

    NM $2   **MIP** $5

Disco Stu, 2002, Playmates, Series 9

    NM $3   **MIP** $7

Prison Sideshow Bob, 2002, Playmates, Series 9

    NM $2   **MIP** $5

Rod and Todd Flanders, 2002, Playmates, Series 9

    NM $3   **MIP** $7

Sunday Best Grandpa, 2002, Playmates, Series 9

    NM $2   **MIP** $5

SERIES 10 FIGURES

Hank Scorpio, 2002, Playmates, Series 10

    NM $2   **MIP** $5

Marvin Monroe, 2002, Playmates, Series 10

    NM $2   **MIP** $5

Resort Smithers, 2002, Playmates, Series 10

    NM $2   **MIP** $5

Scout Leader Flanders, 2002, Playmates, Series 10

    NM $2   **MIP** $5

Stonecutter Homer, 2002, Playmates, Series 10

    NM $2   **MIP** $5

Sunday Best Marge and Maggie, 2002, Playmates, Series 10

    NM $2   **MIP** $5

Wendell, 2002, Playmates, Series 10

    NM $2   **MIP** $5

SERIES 11 FIGURES

Blue Haired Lawyer, 2002, Playmates, Series 11

    NM $2   **MIP** $5

Gil, 2002, Playmates, Series 11

    NM $2   **MIP** $5

Kirk VanHouten, 2002, Playmates, Series 11

    NM $2   **MIP** $5

Larry Burns, 2002, Playmates, Series 11

    NM $2   **MIP** $5

Plow King Barney, 2002, Playmates, Series 11

    NM $2   **MIP** $5

Rainier Wolfcastle, 2002, Playmates, Series 11

    NM $2   **MIP** $5

SERIES 12 FIGURES

Database, 2003, Playmates, Series 12

    NM $2   **MIP** $5

Don Vittorio, 2003, Playmates, Series 12

    NM $2   **MIP** $5

Luann VanHouten, 2003, Playmates, Series 12
    NM $2   MIP $5

Moe, 2003, Playmates, Series 12, re-release
    NM $2   MIP $5

Mr. Burns, 2003, Playmates, Series 12, re-release
    NM $2   MIP $5

Mr. Largo, 2003, Playmates, Series 12
    NM $2   MIP $5

Mr. Plow Homer, 2003, Playmates, Series 12
    NM $2   MIP $5

Number 1, 2003, Playmates, Series 12
    NM $2   MIP $5

SERIES 13 FIGURES

Dr. Stephen Hawking, 2003, Playmates, Series 13
    NM $25   MIP $50

Freddy Quimby, 2003, Playmates, Series 13
    NM $2   MIP $5

Helen Lovejoy, 2003, Playmates, Series 13
    NM $2   MIP $5

Legs, 2003, Playmates, Series 13
    NM $2   MIP $5

Princess Kashmir, 2003, Playmates, Series 13
    NM $2   MIP $5

Tuxedo Krusty the Clown, 2003, Playmates, Series 13
    NM $2   MIP $5

SERIES 14 FIGURES

Groundskeeper Willie in Kilt, 2003, Playmates, Series 14
    NM $5   MIP $10

Louie, 2003, Playmates, Series 14
    NM $2   MIP $5

Luigi, 2003, Playmates, Series 14
    NM $2   MIP $5

Miss Botz, 2003, Playmates, Series 14
    NM $2   MIP $5

Miss Hoover, 2003, Playmates, Series 14
    NM $2   MIP $5

Sarcastic Man, 2003, Playmates, Series 14
    NM $2   MIP $5

SERIES 15 FIGURES

Brandine, 2004, Playmates, Series 15
    NM $2   MIP $5

Comic Book Guy, 2004, Playmates, Series 15, re-release
    MIP $5

Deep Space Homer, 2004, Playmates, Series 15
    NM $2   MIP $5

Handsome Moe, 2004, Playmates, Series 15, re-release
    NM $2   MIP $5

Manjula, 2004, Playmates, Series 15
    NM $2   MIP $5

Octuplets, 2004, Playmates, Series 15
    NM $2   MIP $5

SERIES 16 FIGURES

Agnes Skinner, 2004, Playmates, Series 16
    NM $2   MIP $5

Artie Ziff, 2004, Playmates, Series 16
    NM $2   MIP $5

Benjamin and Gary, 2004, Playmates, Series 16
    NM $2   MIP $5

Brain Freeze Bart, 2004, Playmates, Series 16
    NM $2   MIP $5

Doug, 2004, Playmates, Series 16
    NM $4   MIP $5

Evil Homer, 2004, Playmates, Series 16, also called Devil Homer
    NM $15   MIP $25

VEHICLES

Elementary School Bus, 2002, Playmates, interactive
    NM $12   MIP $25

Family Car, 2001, Playmates
    NM $15   MIP $30

Six Million Dollar Man (Kenner, 1975-78)

ACCESSORIES

Back Pack Radio, 1975-78, Kenner, working crystal radio needs no batteries, white radio, white helmet for Steve and earpiece so you can listen to the radio
    NM $15   MIP $50

Bionic Cycle, 1975-78, Kenner
    NM $20   MIP $70

Bionic Mission Vehicle, 1975-78, Kenner
    NM $40   MIP $100

Bionic Transport, 1975-78, Kenner
    NM $50   MIP $125

Bionic Video Center, 1975-78, Kenner
    NM $40   MIP $140

Critical Assignment Arms, 1975-78, Kenner
    NM $20   MIP $50

Critical Assignment Legs, 1975-78, Kenner
    NM $20   MIP $50

Dual Launch Drag Set w/4" Steve Austin Bionic Bigfoot Figure, 1975-78, Kenner
    NM $150   MIP $300

Flight Suit, 1975-78, Kenner
    NM $25   MIP $150

Mission Control Center, 1975-78, Kenner
    NM $45   MIP $150

Mission to Mars Space Suit, 1975-78, Kenner
    NM $25   MIP $45

OSI Headquarters, 1975-78, Kenner
    NM $110   MIP $190

OSI Undercover Blue Denims, 1975-78, Kenner
    NM $35   MIP $60

Porta-Communicator, 1975-78, Kenner, Steve wears the backpack speaker, you talk into a battery-operated walkie and voice is amplified out of the backpack
    NM $20   MIP $50

Tower & Cycle Set, 1975-78, Kenner
    NM $100   MIP $250

Venus Space Probe, 1975-78, Kenner, very rare
    NM $550+   MIP $850+

FIGURES

Bionic Bigfoot, 1975-78, Kenner, must have the chestplate to be complete
    NM $130   MIP $375+

Maskatron, 1975-78, Kenner, three faces, two arms

    NM $80   **MIP** $260

Oscar Goldman, 1975-78, Kenner, wearing familiar checkered jacket and carrying exploding briefcase, should Steve Austin's secrets fall into the wrong hands

    NM $55   **MIP** $140

Steve Austin w/biosonic arm, 1975-78, Kenner

    NM $200+   **MIP** $400+

Steve Austin w/engine block, 1975-78, Kenner

    NM $60   **MIP** $225

Steve Austin w/girder, 1975-78, Kenner

    NM $50   **MIP** $200

Slap Shot (McFarlane, 2000)

FIGURES

(KP Photo)

Jack Hanson, 2000, McFarlane Toys, from movie "Slap Shot," includes detailed figure and rink diorama

    NM $5   **MIP** $10

Jeff Hanson, 2000, McFarlane Toys, detailed figure w/hockey rink base and background

    NM $5   **MIP** $10

Steve Hanson, 2000, McFarlane Toys, part of the trio of figures from the movie "Slap Shot"

    NM $5   **MIP** $10

Sleepy Hollow (McFarlane, 1999)

FIGURES

Crone, 1999, McFarlane Toys

    NM $3   **MIP** $7

Headless Horseman, 1999, McFarlane Toys

    NM $3   **MIP** $7

Headless Rider and Horse Box Set, 1999, McFarlane Toys

    NM $8   **MIP** $15

Ichabod Crane, 1999, McFarlane Toys

    NM $3   **MIP** $7

Space:1999 (Mattel, 1976)

FIGURES

(Corey LeChat)

Commander Koenig, 1976, Mattel, shown at center w/Bergman and Russell

    NM $30   **MIP** $65

Dr. Russell, 1976, Mattel

    NM $30   **MIP** $65

Professor Bergman, 1976, Mattel

    NM $30   **MIP** $65

Zython Alien, 1976, Mattel

    NM $100   **MIP** $275

PLAY SETS

Eagle Play Set w/three 3" figures, 1976, Mattel

    NM $160   **MIP** $325

Moonbase Alpha Deluxe Play Set w/three figures, 1976, Mattel

    NM $80   **MIP** $210

Moonbase Alpha Play Set, 1976, Mattel

    NM $35   **MIP** $85

Space:1999 (Palitoy, 1975)

FIGURES

Alan Carter, 1975, Palitoy

    NM $200   **MIP** $425

Captain Koenig, 1975, Palitoy

    NM $150   **MIP** $250

Captain Zantor, 1975, Palitoy

    NM $75   **MIP** $160

Mysterious Alien, 1975, Palitoy

    NM $75   **MIP** $160

Paul Morrow, 1975, Palitoy

    NM $175   **MIP** $300

Spawn (McFarlane, 1994-present)

13" FIGURES

Angela, 1996, McFarlane

    NM $5   **MIP** $10

Medieval Spawn, Kay Bee Exclusive, 1997, McFarlane

    NM $5   **MIP** $10

Spawn, 1996, McFarlane

    NM $5   **MIP** $10

ACCESSORIES

Spawn Alley Play Set, 1994-96, McFarlane

    NM $4   **MIP** $10

Spawnmobile, 1994-96, McFarlane

    NM $6   **MIP** $12

Violator Monster Rig, 1994-96, McFarlane

    NM $6   **MIP** $12

MCFARLANE TOYS COLLECTOR'S CLUB EXCLUSIVES

Cogliosto, 1994, McFarlane

    NM $3   **MIP** $6

Spawn, Club Exclusive, blue body, 1997, McFarlane

    NM $2   **MIP** $5

Spawn, Club Exclusive, green body, 1997, McFarlane

    NM $2   **MIP** $5

Terry Fitzgerald, 1994, McFarlane

    NM $3   **MIP** $6

Todd the Artist, 1994, McFarlane

    NM $2   **MIP** $5

Wanda and Cyan, 2000, McFarlane

    NM $2   **MIP** $5

SERIES 01, 1994 (TODD TOYS PACKAGING)

Clown, clown head, 1994, McFarlane
NM $2 **MIP** $4

Clown, Kay Bee Exclusive, 1994, McFarlane
NM $2 **MIP** $4

Clown, monster head, 1994, McFarlane
NM $2 **MIP** $4

Medieval Spawn, black armor, 1994, McFarlane
NM $2 **MIP** $5

Medieval Spawn, blue armor, 1994, McFarlane
NM $2 **MIP** $5

Medieval Spawn, Kay Bee Exclusive, 1994, McFarlane
NM $2 **MIP** $5

Overtkill, dark green, 1994, McFarlane
NM $2 **MIP** $5

Overtkill, Kay Bee Exclusive, 1996, McFarlane
NM $2 **MIP** $5

Overtkill, turquoise, 1994, McFarlane
NM $2 **MIP** $5

Spawn, Diamond Exclusive, 1994, McFarlane
NM $5 **MIP** $20

Spawn, full mask, 1994, McFarlane
NM $2 **MIP** $5

Spawn, Kay Bee Exclusive, 1995, McFarlane
NM $2 **MIP** $5

Spawn, Spawn No. 50 premium (Worm Head), 1996, McFarlane
NM $5 **MIP** $20

Spawn, unmasked (Hamburger Head), first card, 1994, McFarlane
NM $2 **MIP** $10

Tremor, dark green costume, 1994, McFarlane
NM $2 **MIP** $5

Tremor, Kay Bee Exclusive, 1996, McFarlane
NM $2 **MIP** $5

Tremor, orange skin, 1994, McFarlane
NM $2 **MIP** $5

Violator, 1994, McFarlane
NM $2 **MIP** $5

Violator, chrome card, 1994, McFarlane
NM $2 **MIP** $5

Violator, club version, 1997, McFarlane
NM $2 **MIP** $5

Violator, green card, 1994, McFarlane
NM $2 **MIP** $5

Violator, Kay Bee Exclusive, 1996, McFarlane
NM $2 **MIP** $5

Violator, mail-order, 1995, McFarlane
NM $3 **MIP** $10

Violator, red card, 1994, McFarlane
NM $2 **MIP** $5

SERIES 02, 1995

Angela, 1995, McFarlane
NM $2 **MIP** $5

Angela, Club Exclusive, blue, 1997, McFarlane
NM $5 **MIP** $12

Angela, Club Exclusive, pewter, 1997, McFarlane
NM $5 **MIP** $15

(KP Photo)

Angela, gold headpiece w/gold and purple costume, 1995, McFarlane, includes sword, belt and accessories
NM $5 **MIP** $20

Angela, Kay Bee Exclusive, 1997, McFarlane
NM $2 **MIP** $5

Angela, McFarlane Toy Collector's Club Exclusive, 1996, McFarlane
NM $5 **MIP** $10

Angela, silver headpiece w/silver and blue costume, 1995, McFarlane
NM $5 **MIP** $10

Badrock, blue, 1995, McFarlane, w/firing missiles
NM $2 **MIP** $5

Badrock, red pants, 1995, McFarlane
NM $2 **MIP** $5

Chapel, blue/black pants, 1995, McFarlane, includes gun and jagged-edge sword
NM $2 **MIP** $5

Chapel, green khaki pants, 1995, McFarlane
NM $2 **MIP** $5

(McFarlane Toys)

Commando Spawn, 1995, McFarlane, black and red uniform, includes weapons and headset
NM $2 **MIP** $5

Malebolgia, 1995, McFarlane, highly-detailed figure
NM $5 **MIP** $10

Pilot Spawn, black costume, 1995, McFarlane, black uniform w/red highlights, includes jet pack and dagger
NM $3 **MIP** $5

Pilot Spawn, Kay Bee Toys, 1997, McFarlane
NM $2 **MIP** $5

Pilot Spawn, white "Astronaut Spawn," 1995, McFarlane
NM $3 **MIP** $5

SERIES 03, 1995

Cosmic Angela, 1995, McFarlane
NM $3 **MIP** $5

Cosmic Angela, McFarlane Collector's Club Exclusive, 1997, McFarlane
NM $3 **MIP** $6

Cosmic Angela, No. 62 Spawn and No. 9 Curse of Spawn, Diamond Exclusive, 1997, McFarlane
NM $10 **MIP** $25

Curse, The, 1995, McFarlane
NM $2 **MIP** $6

Curse, The, McFarlane Collector's Club Exclusive, 1997, McFarlane
NM $3 **MIP** $6

Ninja Spawn, 1995, McFarlane
NM $2 **MIP** $5

Ninja Spawn, McFarlane Collector's Club Exclusive, 1997, McFarlane
NM $3 **MIP** $6

Redeemer, 1995, McFarlane
NM $2 **MIP** $5

Redeemer, McFarlane Collector's Club Exclusive, 1997, McFarlane
NM $3 **MIP** $6

Spawn II, 1995, McFarlane
NM $2 **MIP** $5

Spawn II, McFarlane Collector's Club
Exclusive, 1997, McFarlane
NM $3   **MIP** $6

Vertebreaker, 1995, McFarlane
NM $2   **MIP** $5

Vertebreaker, gray or black body,
Exclusive available through
various store, 1996, McFarlane
NM $2   **MIP** $5

Vertebreaker, McFarlane Collector's
Club Exclusive, 1997, McFarlane
NM $3   **MIP** $6

Violator II, 1995, McFarlane
NM $2   **MIP** $5

Violator II, McFarlane Collector's
Club Exclusive, 1997, McFarlane
NM $3   **MIP** $6

SERIES 04, 1996

Clown II, black guns, 1996, McFarlane
NM $2   **MIP** $5

Clown II, neon orange guns, 1996,
McFarlane
NM $2   **MIP** $5

Cy-Gor, gold trim, 1996, McFarlane
NM $2   **MIP** $5

Cy-Gor, purple trim, 1996, McFarlane
NM $2   **MIP** $5

Cy-Gor, Target Exclusive, 1996,
McFarlane
NM $2   **MIP** $5

Exo-Skeleton Spawn, black and gray
exo-skeleton, 1996, McFarlane
NM $2   **MIP** $5

Exo-Skeleton Spawn, Target
Exclusive, 1997, McFarlane
NM $2   **MIP** $5

Exo-Skeleton Spawn, white and light
gray bones and white costume,
1996, McFarlane
NM $2   **MIP** $5

Future Spawn, red trimmed, 1996,
McFarlane
NM $2   **MIP** $5

Maxx, The, FAO Schwarz Exclusive,
1996, McFarlane
NM $6   **MIP** $15

Maxx, The, w/black Isz, 1996,
McFarlane
NM $4   **MIP** $12

Maxx, The, w/white Isz, 1996,
McFarlane
NM $4   **MIP** $10

Shadowhawk, black w/silver trim,
1996, McFarlane
NM $1   **MIP** $3

Shadowhawk, gold w/gray trim,
1996, McFarlane
NM $1   **MIP** $3

She-Spawn, black mask, 1996,
McFarlane
NM $2   **MIP** $5

She-Spawn, red face mask, 1996,
McFarlane
NM $2   **MIP** $5

SERIES 05, 1996

Nuclear Spawn, green skin, 1996,
McFarlane
NM $2   **MIP** $5

Nuclear Spawn, orange skin, 1996,
McFarlane
NM $2   **MIP** $5

Overkill II, flesh colored w/gray trim,
1996, McFarlane
NM $2   **MIP** $5

Overkill II, silver w/gold trim, 1996,
McFarlane
NM $2   **MIP** $5

Tremor II, orange w/red blood, 1996,
McFarlane
NM $2   **MIP** $5

Tremor II, purple w/green blood,
1996, McFarlane
NM $2   **MIP** $5

Vandalizer, FAO Schwarz Exclusive,
1996, McFarlane
NM $2   **MIP** $5

Vandalizer, gray skinned w/black
trim, 1996, McFarlane
NM $2   **MIP** $5

Vandalizer, tan skinned w/brown
trim, 1996, McFarlane
NM $2   **MIP** $5

Viking Spawn, 1996, McFarlane
NM $2   **MIP** $5

Widow Maker, black and red w/flesh-
colored body, 1996, McFarlane
NM $2   **MIP** $5

Widow Maker, purple and rose outfit,
gray body, 1996, McFarlane
NM $2   **MIP** $5

SERIES 06, 1996

Alien Spawn, black w/white, 1996,
McFarlane
NM $2   **MIP** $5

Alien Spawn, white w/black, 1996,
McFarlane
NM $2   **MIP** $5

Battleclad Spawn, black costume,
1996, McFarlane
NM $2   **MIP** $5

Battleclad Spawn, tan sections,
1996, McFarlane
NM $2   **MIP** $5

Chameleon Spawn, 1996, McFarlane
NM $2   **MIP** $5

Freak, The, purplish flesh w/brown and
silver weapons, 1996, McFarlane
NM $2   **MIP** $5

Freak, The, tan flesh, 1995, McFarlane
NM $2   **MIP** $5

Sansker, black and yellow, 1996,
McFarlane
NM $2   **MIP** $5

Sansker, brown and tan, 1996,
McFarlane
NM $2   **MIP** $5

Superpatriot, metallic blue arms and
legs, 1996, McFarlane
NM $2   **MIP** $5

Superpatriot, silver arms and legs,
1996, McFarlane
NM $4   **MIP** $7

Tiffany the Amazon, green trim,
1996, McFarlane
NM $4   **MIP** $8

Tiffany the Amazon, McFarlane
Collector's Club Exclusive, 1998,
McFarlane
NM $5   **MIP** $10

Tiffany the Amazon, red trim, 1996,
McFarlane
NM $4   **MIP** $8

SERIES 07, 1997

Crutch, green goatee, 1977, McFarlane
NM $2   **MIP** $5

Crutch, purple goatee, 1997,
McFarlane
NM $2   **MIP** $5

Mangler, The, 1997, McFarlane,
figure includes skull-topped staff
NM $2   **MIP** $5

No-Body, 1997, McFarlane, detailed
robotic figure containing smaller
"No-Body" inside
NM $1   **MIP** $3

(McFarlane Toys)

Sam and Twitch, 1997, McFarlane, Sam
w/donut and pistol, Twitch w/rifle
NM $6   **MIP** $10

Scourge, 1997, McFarlane
NM $2   **MIP** $5

Spawn III, w/owl and bat, 1997, McFarlane
   NM $2   MIP $5

Spawn III, w/wolf and bat, 1997, McFarlane, figure also includes "spring up action cape"
   NM $8   MIP $25

Zombie Spawn, tan skin w/red tunic, 1997, McFarlane, figure includes chainsaw and large machine-gun rifle
   NM $2   MIP $5

SERIES 08, 1997

Curse of the Spawn, 1997, McFarlane
   NM $3   MIP $7

Gate Keeper, 1997, McFarlane
   NM $3   MIP $7

Grave Digger, 1997, McFarlane
   NM $3   MIP $7

Renegade, tan flesh, 1997, McFarlane
   NM $3   MIP $7

Rotarr, 1997, McFarlane
   NM $3   MIP $7

Sabre, 1997, McFarlane
   NM $3   MIP $7

SERIES 09, 1997

Goddess, The, 1997, McFarlane
   NM $3   MIP $7

Manga Clown, 1997, McFarlane
   NM $3   MIP $7

Manga Curse, 1997, McFarlane
   NM $3   MIP $7

Manga Ninja Spawn, 1997, McFarlane
   NM $3   MIP $7

Manga Spawn, 1997, McFarlane
   NM $3   MIP $7

Manga Violator, 1997, McFarlane
   NM $3   MIP $7

SERIES 10, MANGA 2, 1998

Cybertooth, 1998, McFarlane
   NM $3   MIP $7

Manga Cyber Violator, 1998, McFarlane
   NM $3   MIP $7

Manga Dead Spawn, 1998, McFarlane
   NM $3   MIP $7

Manga Freak, 1998, McFarlane
   NM $3   MIP $7

Manga Overkill, 1998, McFarlane
   NM $3   MIP $7

Manga Samurai Spawn, 1998, McFarlane
   NM $3   MIP $7

SERIES 11, DARK AGES, 1998

Horrid, The, 1998, McFarlane, two figures; one winged human-type (larger) and the other, a small skeletal figure w/weapon
   NM $3   MIP $7

(KP Photo)

Ogre, The, 1998, McFarlane, large Ogre figure controlled by smaller figure riding on shoulders, also includes war club
   NM $3   MIP $7

Raider, The, 1998, McFarlane, Centaur figure w/battle armor, double-edged pike/axe, string of defeated skulls
   NM $3   MIP $7

(KP Photo)

Skull Queen, The, 1998, McFarlane, Figure includes battle axes, flying skeletal warrior
   NM $3   MIP $7

Spawn The Black Knight, 1998, McFarlane
   NM $3   MIP $7

Spellcaster, The, 1998, McFarlane, includes battle axe, shield and helmet
   NM $3   MIP $7

SERIES 12, 1998

BottomLine, 1998, McFarlane
   NM $3   MIP $7

Creech, The, 1998, McFarlane
   NM $3   MIP $7

Cy-Gor II, 1998, McFarlane, deluxe boxed figure
   NM $3   MIP $7

Heap, The, 1998, McFarlane
   NM $3   MIP $7

Re-Animated Spawn, 1998, McFarlane
   NM $3   MIP $7

Spawn IV, 1998, McFarlane
   NM $4   MIP $10

TopGun, 1998, McFarlane
   NM $3   MIP $7

SERIES 13, CURSE OF THE SPAWN, 1999

Curse of the Spawn II, 1999, McFarlane
   NM $3   MIP $7

Desiccator, 1999, McFarlane, deluxe boxed figure
   NM $3   MIP $7

Hatchet, 1999, McFarlane
   NM $3   MIP $7

Medusa, 1999, McFarlane
   NM $4   MIP $8

Priest and Mr. Obersmith, 1999, McFarlane
   NM $4   MIP $8

Raenius, 1999, McFarlane
   NM $4   MIP $8

Zeus, 1999, McFarlane
   NM $4   MIP $8

SERIES 14, DARK AGES 2, 1999

Iguantus and Tuskadon, 1999, McFarlane
   NM $4   MIP $8

Mandarin Spawn the Scarlet Edge, 1999, McFarlane, a double-edged sword that is twice the size of the figure
   NM $4   MIP $8

Necromancer, 1999, McFarlane
   NM $4   MIP $8

Spawn the Black Heart, 1999, McFarlane
   NM $4   MIP $8

Tormentor, 1999, McFarlane
   NM $4   MIP $8

Viper King, 1999, McFarlane
   NM $4   MIP $8

SERIES 15, TECHNO SPAWN, 1999

Code Red, 1999, McFarlane
   NM $4   MIP $8

Cyber Spawn, 1999, McFarlane
   NM $4   MIP $8

Gray Thunder, 1999, McFarlane
   NM $4   MIP $8

Iron Express, 1999, McFarlane
    NM $4   MIP $8
Steel Trap, 1999, McFarlane
    NM $4   MIP $8
Warzone, 1999, McFarlane
    NM $3   MIP $7

SERIES 16, NITRO RIDERS, 2000

Spawn: After Burner, 2000, McFarlane, 5-1/4" figure and 9" x 4-1/4"cycle
    NM $3   MIP $7
Spawn: Eclipse 5000, 2000, McFarlane, 5-1/2" figure and 9-1/2" x 5-1/2" cycle
    NM $3   MIP $7
Spawn: Flash Point, 2000, McFarlane, 5-1/4" figure and 9" x 4-1/2" cycle
    NM $3   MIP $7
Spawn: Green Vapor, 2000, McFarlane, 5-1/4" figure and 9-1/2" x 5-1/2" cycle
    NM $3   MIP $7

SERIES 17, SPAWN CLASSIC, 2001

Al Simmons, 2001, McFarlane, includes stand, machine gun, pistol and accessories
    NM $3   MIP $7
Clown III, 2001, McFarlane, includes wrapped body and stretcher
    NM $3   MIP $7

(KP Photo)

Malebogia II, 2001, McFarlane
    NM $3   MIP $7

(KP Photo)

Medieval Spawn II, 2001, McFarlane, includes chain, sword and accessories
    NM $5   MIP $7

(KP Photo)

Spawn V, 2001, McFarlane, w/stand
    NM $5   MIP $7
Tiffany II, 2001, McFarlane, includes swords, knives, pike, battle staff, accessories, and stand
    NM $5   MIP $7

SERIES 18, INTERLINK 6, 2001

(KP Photo)

HD-1, 2001, McFarlane
    NM $3   MIP $10
LA-6, 2001, McFarlane
    NM $3   MIP $10

(KP Photo)

LL-4, 2001, McFarlane
    NM $3   MIP $10

(KP Photo)

RA-5, 2001, McFarlane
    NM $3   MIP $10
RL-3, 2001, McFarlane
    NM $3   MIP $10
TS-2, 2001, McFarlane
    NM $3   MIP $10

SERIES 19, DARK AGES SPAWN: THE SAMURAI WARS, 2001

Dojo, 2001, McFarlane
    NM $5   MIP $10
Jackyl Assassin, 2001, McFarlane
    NM $5   MIP $10
Jyaaku the Nightmare, 2001, McFarlane, deluxe boxed figure
    NM $7   MIP $12
Lotus the Angel Warrior, 2001, McFarlane
    NM $5   MIP $10

(KP Photo, Brian Brogaard collection)

Samurai Spawn, 2001, McFarlane
    NM $5   MIP $10
Scorpion Assassin, 2001, McFarlane
    NM $5   MIP $12

SERIES 20, SPAWN CLASSIC 2, 2001

Clown IV, 2001, McFarlane
    NM $4   MIP $8
Domina, 2001, McFarlane
    NM $4   MIP $8

Medieval Spawn III, 2001, McFarlane
NM $8   MIP $12

Overkill III, 2001, McFarlane
NM $4   MIP $8

Spawn VI, 2001, McFarlane
NM $4   MIP $8

Violator III, 2001, McFarlane
NM $4   MIP $8

SERIES 21, ALTERNATE REALITIES, 2002

Alien Spawn, 2002, McFarlane
NM $7   MIP $12

Pirate Spawn, 2002, McFarlane
NM $7   MIP $12

Raven Spawn, 2002, McFarlane
NM $7   MIP $12

She Spawn, 2002, McFarlane
NM $7   MIP $12

Spawn VII, 2002, McFarlane
NM $7   MIP $12

Wings of Redemption Spawn, 2002, McFarlane
NM $8   MIP $18

SERIES 22, DARK AGES SPAWN: THE VIKING AGE, 2002

Berserker the Troll, 2002, McFarlane
NM $7   MIP $12

Bluetooth, 2002, McFarlane
NM $7   MIP $12

Dark Raider, 2002, McFarlane
NM $7   MIP $12

Skullsplitter, 2002, McFarlane
NM $7   MIP $12

Spawn the Bloodaxe, 2002, McFarlane
NM $7   MIP $12

Spawn the Bloodaxe and Thunderhoof, 2002, McFarlane, deluxe boxed set
NM $9   MIP $18

Valkerie, 2002, McFarlane
NM $7   MIP $12

SERIES 23, MUTATIONS, 2003

Al Simmons, 2003, McFarlane
NM $4   MIP $8

Kin, 2003, McFarlane
NM $4   MIP $8

Malebolgia, 2003, McFarlane
NM $4   MIP $8

Spawn, 2003, McFarlane
NM $4   MIP $8

Warrior Lilith, 2003, McFarlane
NM $4   MIP $8

SERIES 23.5, SPAWN REBORN

Clown IV, 2003, McFarlane, from Series 20
NM $4   MIP $8

Curse of the Spawn II, 2003, McFarlane, from Series 13
NM $4   MIP $8

Domina, 2003, McFarlane, from Series 20
NM $4   MIP $8

(KP Photo, Brian Brogaard collection)

Raven Spawn, 2003, McFarlane, from Series 21
NM $4   MIP $8

Redeemer, 2003, McFarlane, from Series 03
NM $4   MIP $8

Wings of Redemption Spawn, 2003, McFarlane, from Series 21
NM $5   MIP $10

SERIES 24, THE CLASSIC COMIC COVERS, 2003

Hellspawn i.001, 2003, McFarlane
NM $5   MIP $10

Spawn i.039, 2003, McFarlane
NM $5   MIP $10

Spawn i.043, 2003, McFarlane
NM $12   MIP $18

Spawn i.064, 2003, McFarlane
NM $5   MIP $10

Spawn i.088, 2003, McFarlane
NM $5   MIP $10

Spawn i.109, 2003, McFarlane
NM $5   MIP $10

SERIES 25, CLASSIC COMIC COVERS 2

Creech Cl.001, 2004, McFarlane
NM $6   MIP $12

Redeemer I.117, 2004, McFarlane
NM $6   MIP $12

Sam and Twitch STI.022, 2004, McFarlane
NM $6   MIP $12

Spawn HSI.005, 2004, McFarlane
NM $12   MIP $20

Spawn HSI.011, 2004, McFarlane
NM $6   MIP $12

Spawn I.095, 2004, McFarlane
NM $6   MIP $12

SERIES 26, ART OF SPAWN

Curse 2, 2004, McFarlane, Spawn Bible art
NM $7   MIP $13

Spawn the Black Knight, 2004, McFarlane, Dark Ages Issue 1 cover art
NM $5   MIP $10

Spawn v. Cy-Gor, 2004, McFarlane, Issue 57 cover art
NM $5   MIP $10

Spawn, Issue 7, 2004, McFarlane
NM $5   MIP $10

Spawn, Issue 8, 2004, McFarlane
NM $9   MIP $15

Tiffany 3, 2004, McFarlane, Issue 45 art
NM $5   MIP $10

Tremor 3, 2004, McFarlane, Spawn Bible art
NM $5   MIP $10

SERIES 27, ART OF SPAWN

Clown 5, 2005, McFarlane, original art
NM $4   MIP $8

Spawn v. Al Simmons, 2005, McFarlane, deluxe boxed setfd
NM $8   MIP $20

Spawn, Issue 119, 2005, McFarlane, interior art
NM $12   MIP $18

Spawn, Issue 131, 2005, McFarlane, cover art
NM $5   MIP $10

Spawn, Issue 85, 2005, McFarlane, cover art
NM $5   MIP $10

Vandalizer 2, 2005, McFarlane, original art
NM $5   MIP $10

Wanda 2, 2005, McFarlane, Issue 65 interior art
NM $3   MIP $6

SERIES 28, REGENERATED

Commando Spawn 2, 2005, McFarlane
NM $10   MIP $28

Cyber Spawn 2, 2005, McFarlane
NM $8   MIP $12

Grave Digger 2, 2005, McFarlane
NM $5   MIP $10

Lotus Warrior Angel 2, 2005, McFarlane
NM $5   MIP $10

Mandarin Spawn 2, 2005, McFarlane
NM $7   MIP $12

Spawn v. Urizen, 2005, McFarlane, deluxe boxed set
NM $7   MIP $15

Zombie Spawn 2, 2005, McFarlane
NM $8   MIP $16

SERIES 29, EVOLUTIONS, 2006

Disciple, 2006, McFarlane
NM $5   MIP $10

Man of Miracles, 2006, McFarlane
NM $5   MIP $10

Ninja Swawn 2, 2006, McFarlane
NM $8   MIP $15

Spawn 9, 2006, McFarlane
NM $5   MIP $10

Thamuz, 2006, McFarlane
NM $5   MIP $10

Zera, 2006, McFarlane
NM $5   MIP $10

SERIES 30, THE ADVENTURES OF SPAWN, 2006

Codename: Cy-Gor, 2006, McFarlane
NM $3   MIP $6

Omega Spawn, 2006, McFarlane
NM $3   MIP $6

Overtkill The Destroyer, 2006, McFarlane
NM $3   MIP $6

Spawn X, 2006, McFarlane
NM $3   MIP $6

The Redeemer, 2006, McFarlane
NM $3   MIP $6

Tiffany the Amazon, 2006, McFarlane
NM $3   MIP $6

SERIES 31, OTHER WORLDS

Goddess Llyra, 2007, McFarlane
NM $6   MIP $12

Lord Covenant, 2007, McFarlane
NM $6   MIP $12

Necro Cop, 2007, McFarlane
NM $6   MIP $12

Nightmare Spawn, 2007, McFarlane
NM $12   MIP $30

Spawn 11, 2007, McFarlane
NM $6   MIP $12

Spawn the Maurader, 2007, McFarlane
NM $6   MIP $12

SERIES 32, THE ADVENTURES OF SPAWN SERIES 2

Agent 8, 2007, McFarlane
NM $2   MIP $6

Commando Spawn, 2007, McFarlane
NM $2   MIP $6

Creech, 2007, McFarlane
NM $2   MIP $6

Omega Squadron, 2007, McFarlane
NM $2   MIP $6

Raven Spawn, 2007, McFarlane
NM $2   MIP $6

Spawn X (Blue), 2007, McFarlane
NM $2   MIP $6

Tremor, 2007, McFarlane
NM $2   MIP $6

Spawn: The Movie (McFarlane, 1997)

DELUXE FIGURES

Attack Spawn, 1997, McFarlane
NM $4   MIP $10

(McFarlane Toys)

Malebolgia, 1997, McFarlane, detailed figure includes skull-topped staff
NM $3   MIP $7

Violator, 1997, McFarlane, from the Spawn Deluxe Boxed Set, highly-detailed figure
NM $3   MIP $7

FIGURES

Al Simmons, 1997, McFarlane, w/rifle and mobile rocket launcher
NM $2   MIP $5

Burnt Spawn, 1997, McFarlane, w/rifle and femur-bone handled shovel
NM $2   MIP $5

Clown, 1997, McFarlane
NM $2   MIP $5

(McFarlane Toys)

Jason Wynn, 1997, McFarlane, w/rifle, headset and accessories
NM $2   MIP $5

(McFarlane Toys)

Jessica Priest, 1997, McFarlane, w/rifle and accessories
NM $2   MIP $5

PLAY SETS

(McFarlane Toys)

Final Battle, 1997, McFarlane, Spawn w/creature crashing through house diorama
NM $3   MIP $8

(McFarlane Toys)

Graveyard, 1997, McFarlane, includes two figures and open grave

    NM $3   **MIP** $8

(McFarlane Toys)

Spawn Alley, 1997, McFarlane, includes Spawn, alley backdrop and creature

    NM $2   **MIP** $7

Spider-Man Electro-Spark (Toy Biz, 1997)

5" FIGURES

Captain America, 1997, Toy Biz

    NM $3   **MIP** $10

Electro, 1997, Toy Biz

    NM $2   **MIP** $5

Electro-Shock Spidey, 1997, Toy Biz

    NM $2   **MIP** $5

Electro-Spark Spider-Man, 1997, Toy Biz

    NM $2   **MIP** $5

Steel-Shock Spider-Man, 1997, Toy Biz

    NM $2   **MIP** $5

Spider-Man Sneak Attack (Toy Biz, 1998)

BUG BUSTERS, 5" FIGURES

Jack O'Lantern and Bug Eye Blaster, 1998, Toy Biz

    NM $3   **MIP** $5

Silver Sable and Beetle Basher, 1998, Toy Biz

    NM $3   **MIP** $5

Spider-Man and Spider Stinger, 1998, Toy Biz

    NM $3   **MIP** $5

Vulture and Jaw Breaker, 1998, Toy Biz

    NM $3   **MIP** $5

SHAPE SHIFTERS, 7" FIGURES

Lizard forms into Mutant Alligator, 1998, Toy Biz

    NM $2   **MIP** $5

Spider-Man forms into Monster Spider, 1998, Toy Biz

    NM $2   **MIP** $5

Venom forms into Three-Headed Serpent, 1998, Toy Biz

    NM $2   **MIP** $5

STREET WARRIORS, 5" FIGURES

Scarecrow w/Pitchfork Projectile, 1998, Toy Biz

    NM $2   **MIP** $4

Spider-Sense Peter Parker, 1998, Toy Biz

    NM $2   **MIP** $4

Street War Spider-Man, 1998, Toy Biz

    NM $2   **MIP** $4

Vermin w/Rat-firing Fire Hydrant, 1998, Toy Biz

    NM $2   **MIP** $4

WEB FLYERS, 5" FIGURES

Carnage, 1998, Toy Biz

    NM $2   **MIP** $4

Copter Spider-Man, 1998, Toy Biz

    NM $2   **MIP** $4

Hobgoblin, 1998, Toy Biz

    NM $2   **MIP** $4

Spider-Man, 1998, Toy Biz

    NM $2   **MIP** $4

Spider-Man Special Edition Series (Toy Biz, 1998)

12" FIGURES

Black Cat, 1998, Toy Biz

    NM $4   **MIP** $10

Spider-Man, 1998, Toy Biz

    NM $4   **MIP** $10

Venom, 1998, Toy Biz

    NM $4   **MIP** $10

Spider-Man Spider Force (Toy Biz, 1997)

5" FIGURES

Beetle w/Transforming Beetle Armor, 1997, Toy Biz

    NM $2   **MIP** $5

Cybersect Spider-Man w/Transforming Cyber Spider, 1997, Toy Biz

    NM $2   **MIP** $4

Swarm w/Transforming Bee Action, 1997, Toy Biz

    NM $2   **MIP** $4

Tarantula w/Transforming Tarantula Armor, 1997, Toy Biz

    NM $2   **MIP** $5

Wasp w/Transforming Wasp Armor, 1997, Toy Biz

    NM $2   **MIP** $4

Spider-Man Spider Power (Toy Biz, 1999)

SERIES I, 5" FIGURES

Slime Shaker Venom, 1999, Toy Biz

    NM $2   **MIP** $4

Spider Sense Spider-Man, 1999, Toy Biz

    NM $2   **MIP** $4

Street Warrior Spider-Man, 1999, Toy Biz

    NM $2   **MIP** $4

Triple Threat Spider-Man, 1999, Toy Biz

    NM $2   **MIP** $4

SERIES II, 5" FIGURES

Doctor Octopus, 1999, Toy Biz

    NM $2   **MIP** $4

Flip and Swing Spider-Man, 1999, Toy Biz

    NM $2   **MIP** $4

J. Jonah Jameson, 1999, Toy Biz

    NM $2   **MIP** $4

Spider Sense Peter Parker, 1999, Toy Biz

    NM $2   **MIP** $4

Spider-Man Vampire Wars (Toy Biz, 1996)

5" FIGURES

Air-Attack Spider-Man, 1997, Toy Biz

    NM $2   **MIP** $4

Anti-Vampire Spider-Man, 1997, Toy Biz

    NM $2   **MIP** $4

Blade-The Vampire Hunter, 1997, Toy Biz

    NM $3   **MIP** $6

Morbius Unbound, 1997, Toy Biz

    NM $3   **MIP** $6

Vampire Spider-Man, 1997, Toy Biz

    NM $2   **MIP** $4

Spider-Man Venom (Toy Biz, 1996-97)

ALONG CAME A SPIDER, 6" FIGURES

Bride of Venom and Vile the Spider, 1997, Toy Biz

    NM $3   **MIP** $7

Phage and Pincer the Spider, 1997, Toy Biz

NM $3   MIP $7

Spider-Carnage and Spit the Spider, 1997, Toy Biz

NM $3   MIP $7

Venom the Symbiote and Riper the Spider, 1997, Toy Biz

NM $3   MIP $7

PLANET OF THE SYMBIOTES, 6" FIGURES

Hybrid, Pincer Wing Action, 1997, Toy Biz

NM $8   MIP $15

Lasher, Tentacle Whipping Action, 1997, Toy Biz

NM $8   MIP $15

Riot, Launching Attack Arms, 1997, Toy Biz

NM $8   MIP $15

Venom the Madness, Surprise Attack Heads, 1997, Toy Biz

NM $12   MIP $25

PLANET OF THE SYMBIOTES, DELUXE 6" FIGURES

Hybrid, Pincer Wing Action, 1996, Toy Biz

NM $3   MIP $8

Lasher, Tentacle Whipping Action, 1996, Toy Biz

NM $3   MIP $8

Riot, Launcing Attack Arms, 1996, Toy Biz

NM $3   MIP $8

Scream, Living Tendril Hair, 1996, Toy Biz

NM $3   MIP $8

Venom the Madness, Surprise Attack Heads, 1996, Toy Biz

NM $3   MIP $8

Spider-Man Web Force (Toy Biz, 1997)

5" FIGURES

Daredevil, Transforming Web Tank Armor, 1997, Toy Biz

NM $2   MIP $4

Lizard, Transforming Swamp Rider, 1997, Toy Biz

NM $2   MIP $4

Vulture, Transforming Vuture-Bot, 1997, Toy Biz

NM $2   MIP $4

Web Commando Spidey, Transforming Web Copter, 1997, Toy Biz

NM $2   MIP $4

Web Swamp Spidey, Transforming Web Swamp Seeker Armor, 1997, Toy Biz

NM $2   MIP $4

Spider-Man Web Traps (Toy Biz, 1997)

5" FIGURES

Future Spider-Man w/Snapping Cocoon Trap, 1997, Toy Biz

NM $2   MIP $4

Monster Spider-Man w/Grappling Spider Sidekick, 1997, Toy Biz

NM $2   MIP $4

Rhino w/Rotating Web Snare, 1997, Toy Biz

NM $2   MIP $4

Scorpion w/Whipping Tail Attacker Trap, 1997, Toy Biz

NM $3   MIP $5

Spider-Man w/Pull-String Web Trap, 1997, Toy Biz

NM $2   MIP $4

Spider-Man: The New Animated Series (Toy Biz, 1994-96)

15" TALKING FIGURES

Spider-Man, 1994-96, Toy Biz

NM $6   MIP $12

Venom, 1994-96, Toy Biz

NM $6   MIP $12

2-1/2" DIE-CAST FIGURES

Spider-Man vs. Carnage, 1994-96, Toy Biz

NM $2   MIP $4

Spider-Man vs. Dr. Octopus, 1994-96, Toy Biz

NM $2   MIP $4

Spider-Man vs. Hobgoblin, 1994-96, Toy Biz

NM $2   MIP $4

Spider-Man vs. Venom, 1994-96, Toy Biz

NM $2   MIP $4

5" FIGURES

Alien Spider Slayer, 1994-96, Toy Biz

NM $2   MIP $5

Battle-Ravaged Spider-Man, 1994-96, Toy Biz

NM $2   MIP $5

Cameleon, 1994-96, Toy Biz

NM $3   MIP $7

Carnage, 1994-96, Toy Biz

NM $7   MIP $22

Carnage II, 1994-96, Toy Biz

NM $7   MIP $20

Dr. Octopus, 1994-96, Toy Biz

NM $3   MIP $10

(KP Photo, Brian Brogaard collection)

Green Goblin, 1994-96, Toy Biz

NM $3   MIP $10

Hobgoblin, 1994-96, Toy Biz

NM $3   MIP $10

Kingpin, 1994-96, Toy Biz

NM $3   MIP $10

Kraven, 1994-96, Toy Biz

NM $3   MIP $10

Lizard, 1994-96, Toy Biz

NM $3   MIP $10

Man-Spider, 1996, Toy Biz, Series 6

NM $2   MIP $5

Morbius, 1994-96, Toy Biz

NM $3   MIP $10

(KP Photo, Brian Brogaard collection)

Mysterio, 1994-96, Toy Biz, Series 4

NM $3   MIP $10

Nick Fury, 1994-96, Toy Biz, Series 5

NM $3   MIP $8

Peter Parker, 1994-96, Toy Biz

NM $3   MIP $10

Prowler, 1994-96, Toy Biz

NM $3   MIP $10

Punisher, 1994-96, Toy Biz, the recognizable man in black (and white)

NM $3   MIP $10

Rhino, 1994-96, Toy Biz

NM $3   MIP $10

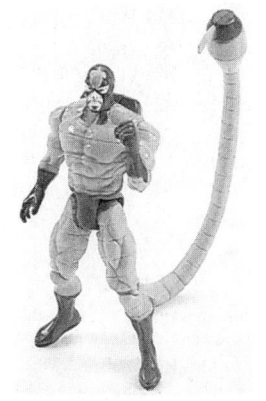

(KP Photo, Brian Brogaard collection)

Scorpion, 1994-96, Toy Biz

NM $7   MIP $17

Shocker, 1994-96, Toy Biz

NM $3   MIP $10

Smythe, 1994-96, Toy Biz

NM $2   MIP $5

Spider-Man 2099, 1996, Toy Biz, Series 7

NM $3   MIP $7

(KP Photo, Brian Brogaard collection)

Spider-Man in Black Costume, 1994-96, Toy Biz

NM $3   MIP $10

Spider-Man Octo, 1996, Toy Biz, Series 6

NM $2   MIP $5

(KP Photo, Brian Brogaard collection)

Spider-Man Six Arm, 1994-96, Toy Biz

NM $2   MIP $5

Spider-Man w/Parachute Web, 1994-96, Toy Biz

NM $2   MIP $5

Spider-Man w/Spider Armor, 1994-96, Toy Biz

NM $2   MIP $4

Spider-Man w/Web Cannon, 1996, Toy Biz, Series 6

NM $2   MIP $5

Spider-Man w/Web Racer, 1994-96, Toy Biz

NM $2   MIP $5

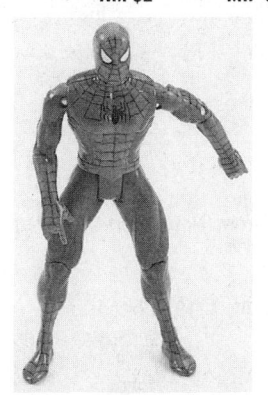

(KP Photo, Brian Brogaard collection)

Spider-Man w/Web Shooter, 1994-96, Toy Biz

NM $2   MIP $5

Spider-Man, multi-jointed, 1994-96, Toy Biz

NM $2   MIP $5

Spider-Sense Spider-Man, 1994-96, Toy Biz

NM $2   MIP $5

Symbiotic Venom Attack, 1994-96, Toy Biz

NM $4   MIP $10

Tombstone, 1996, Toy Biz, Series 6

NM $4   MIP $10

Venom, 1994-96, Toy Biz

NM $4   MIP $10

Venom II, 1994-96, Toy Biz

NM $3   MIP $8

Vulture, 1994-96, Toy Biz

NM $4   MIP $10

ACCESSORIES

Daily Bugle Play Set, 1994-96, Toy Biz

NM $12   MIP $20

DELUXE 10" FIGURES

Carnage, 1994-96, Toy Biz

NM $6   MIP $15

Dr. Octopus, 1994-96, Toy Biz

NM $3   MIP $8

Hobgoblin, 1994-96, Toy Biz

NM $3   MIP $8

Kraven, 1994-96, Toy Biz

NM $3   MIP $8

Lizard, 1994-96, Toy Biz

NM $3   MIP $8

Myserio, 1994-96, Toy Biz

NM $3   MIP $8

Punisher, 1994-96, Toy Biz

NM $3   MIP $8

Spider-Man Spider Sense, 1994-96, Toy Biz

NM $3   MIP $7

Spider-Man w/Suction Cups, 1994-96, Toy Biz

NM $3   MIP $7

Spider-Man, Armor, 1994-96, Toy Biz

NM $3   MIP $6

Spider-Man, Sensational, 1994-96, Toy Biz

NM $3   MIP $6

Spider-Man, Silver Web, 1994-96, Toy Biz

NM $3   MIP $6

Spider-Man, Spider Armor, 1994-96, Toy Biz

NM $3   MIP $6

Spider-Man, Super Posable, 1994-96, Toy Biz

NM $3   MIP $6

Spider-Man, Wall Hanging, 1994-96, Toy Biz

NM $3   MIP $6

Venom, 1994-96, Toy Biz

NM $4   MIP $8

Venom, Dark Blue, 1994-96, Toy Biz

NM $3   MIP $10

Vulture, 1994-96, Toy Biz

NM $4   MIP $8

PROJECTORS

Hobgoblin, 1994-96, Toy Biz

NM $2   MIP $4

Lizard, 1994-96, Toy Biz

    NM $2   **MIP** $4

Spider-Man, 1994-96, Toy Biz

    NM $2   **MIP** $4

Venom, 1994-96, Toy Biz

    NM $2   **MIP** $4

VEHICLES

Hobgoblin Wing Bomber, 1994-96, Toy Biz

    NM $3   **MIP** $10

Smythe Battle Chair Attack Vehicle, 1994-96, Toy Biz

    NM $3   **MIP** $7

Spider-Man Wheelie Cycle, 1994-96, Toy Biz

    NM $3   **MIP** $7

Spider-Man's Cycle (radio-controlled), 1994-96, Toy Biz

    NM $3   **MIP** $7

Tri-Spider Slayer, 1994-96, Toy Biz

    NM $3   **MIP** $7

Star Trek (Mego, 1974-80)

CARDED FIGURES

Andorian, 1976, Mego

    NM $250   **MIP** $550

Captain Kirk, 1974, Mego

    NM $20   **MIP** $60

Cheron, 1975, Mego, black and white face and uniform

    NM $85   **MIP** $180

(Karen O'Brien collection)

Dr. McCoy, 1974, Mego, medical tricorder pack

    NM $25   **MIP** $50

Gorn, 1975, Mego

    NM $80   **MIP** $180

(Corey LeChat)

Klingon, 1974, Mego, black boots, brown plastic body armor, brown tunic

    NM $25   **MIP** $50

Lt. Uhura, 1974, Mego

    NM $30   **MIP** $80

(Karen O'Brien collection)

Mr. Spock, 1974, Mego, tricorder, communicator, phaser, belt

    NM $20   **MIP** $50

Mugato, 1976, Mego

    NM $250   **MIP** $450

Neptunian, 1975, Mego

    NM $100   **MIP** $215

Romulan, 1976, Mego

    NM $550   **MIP** $1200

Scotty, 1974, Mego

    NM $30   **MIP** $60

Talos, 1976, Mego

    NM $250   **MIP** $450

The Keeper, 1975, Mego

    NM $75   **MIP** $250

PLAY SETS

Mission to Gamma VI, 1974-80, Mego, w/four generic aliens, rare

    NM $300   **MIP** $725

U.S.S. Enterprise Bridge, 1974-80, Mego, captain's chair, navigation console, two crew seats, three double-sided cards for screen, Model No. 51210

    NM $50   **MIP** $160

U.S.S. Enterprise Gift Set, 1975, Mego, bridge set w/five figures Kirk, Spock, McCoy, Mr. Scott, and Klingon, rare

    NM $125   **MIP** $375

Star Trek Alien Combat (Playmates, 1999)

FIGURES

Borg Drone, 1999, Playmates

    NM $10   **MIP** $20

Klingon Warrior, 1999, Playmates

    NM $10   **MIP** $20

Star Trek Collector Assortment (Playmates, 1999)

FIGURES

Andorian Ambassador, 1999, Playmates

    NM $5   **MIP** $10

Captain Janeway, 1999, Playmates

    NM $5   **MIP** $10

Counselor Troi, 1999, Playmates

    NM $5   **MIP** $10

Dr. McCoy, 1999, Playmates

    NM $5   **MIP** $10

Ensign Chekov, 1999, Playmates

    NM $5   **MIP** $10

Geordi LaForge, 1999, Playmates
NM $5   MIP $10

Gorn Captain, 1999, Playmates
NM $5   MIP $10

Khan, 1999, Playmates
NM $5   MIP $10

Lieutenant Sulu, 1999, Playmates
NM $5   MIP $10

Lieutenant Uhura, 1999, Playmates
NM $5   MIP $10

Locutus of Borg, 1999, Playmates
NM $5   MIP $10

Mr. Spock, 1999, Playmates
NM $5   MIP $10

Mugatu, 1999, Playmates
NM $5   MIP $10

Q, 1999, Playmates
NM $5   MIP $10

Scotty, 1999, Playmates
NM $5   MIP $10

Seven of Nine, 1999, Playmates
NM $5   MIP $10

Star Trek Collector Series (Playmates, 1994-95)

9-1/2" BOXED FIGURES

Borg, 1995, Playmates, #6069
NM $5   MIP $12

Captain Benjamin Sisko, 1995, Playmates, #16188
NM $5   MIP $12

Captain Benjamin Sisko (Command Edition), 1994, Playmates, #6067
NM $5   MIP $12

Captain Jean-Luc Picard (Command Edition), 1994, Playmates, #6066
NM $5   MIP $12

Captain Jean-Luc Picard (Movie Edition), 1994, Playmates, #6288
NM $5   MIP $12

Captain Jean-Luc Picard, Dress Uniform, 1995, Playmates, #6289
NM $5   MIP $12

Captain Kirk (Command Edition), 1994, Playmates, #6068
NM $5   MIP $12

Captain Kirk (Movie Edition), 1994, Playmates, #6288
NM $5   MIP $12

Captian Christopher Pike, 1995, Playmates, #16183
NM $5   MIP $12

Chief Miles O'Brien, 1995, Playmates, #16182
NM $5   MIP $12

Commander Riker, 1995, Playmates, #6285
NM $5   MIP $12

Data (Movie Edition), 1995, Playmates, #6284
NM $5   MIP $12

Dr. Beverly Crusher, 1995, Playmates, #6282
NM $5   MIP $12

Dr. Leonard McCoy, 1995, Playmates, #6292
NM $5   MIP $12

Ensign Pavel Chekov, 1995, Playmates, #16185
NM $5   MIP $12

Geordi La Forge (Movie Edition), 1994, Playmates, #6287
NM $5   MIP $12

Guinan, 1995, Playmates, #6283
NM $5   MIP $12

Lt. Cmdr. Deanna Troi, 1995, Playmates, #6281
NM $5   MIP $12

Lt. Cmdr. Montgomery Scott, 1995, Playmates, #6293
NM $5   MIP $12

Lt. Cmdr. Worf in DS9 Uniform, 1995, Playmates, #6295
NM $5   MIP $12

Lt. Hikaur Sulu, 1995, Playmates, #16184
NM $5   MIP $12

Lt. Jadzia Dax, 1995, Playmates, #16186
NM $5   MIP $12

Lt. Uhura, 1995, Playmates, #6294
NM $5   MIP $12

Lt. Worf in Ritual Klingon Attire, 1995, Playmates, #6286
NM $5   MIP $12

Major Kira Nerys, 1995, Playmates, #16189
NM $5   MIP $12

Mr. Spock, 1995, Playmates, #6291
NM $5   MIP $12

Q in Judges Robes, 1995, Playmates, #16187
NM $5   MIP $12

Romulan Commander, 1995, Playmates, #16181
NM $5   MIP $12

Star Trek Electronic Display Assortment (Playmates, 1999)

FIGURES

Captain Kirk, 1999, Playmates
NM $20   MIP $40

Captain Picard, 1999, Playmates
NM $20   MIP $40

Commander Riker, 1999, Playmates
NM $20   MIP $40

Lieutenant Commander Data, 1999, Playmates
NM $20   MIP $40

Lieutenant Worf, 1999, Playmates
NM $20   MIP $40

Mr. Spock, 1999, Playmates
NM $20   MIP $40

Star Trek Millennium Collector's Set (Playmates, 1999)

FIGURES

Captain Janeway/Commander Chakotay, 1999, Playmates
NM $10   MIP $20

Captain Kirk/Mr. Spock, 1999, Playmates
NM $10   MIP $20

Captain Picard/Commander Riker, 1999, Playmates
NM $10   MIP $20

Captain Sisko/Kira Nerys, 1999, Playmates
NM $10   MIP $20

Star Trek V (Galoob, 1989)

BOXED FIGURES

Captain Kirk, 1989, Galoob
NM $4   MIP $10

Dr. McCoy, 1989, Galoob
NM $4   MIP $10

Klaa, 1989, Galoob
NM $4   MIP $10

Mr. Spock, 1989, Galoob
NM $4   MIP $10

Sybok, 1989, Galoob
NM $4   MIP $10

Star Trek: Classic Movie Figures (Playmates, 1995)

FIGURES

Admiral Kirk, 1995, Playmates, #6451, "ST:TMP"
NM $2   MIP $5

Cmdr. Kruge, 1995, Playmates, #6459, "STIII:TSFS"
NM $2   MIP $5

Cmdr. Spock, 1995, Playmates, #6452, "ST:TMP"
NM $2   MIP $5

Dr. McCoy, 1995, Playmates, #6453, "ST:TMP"

    NM $2   **MIP** $5

General Chang, 1995, Playmates, #6458, "STVI:TUC"

    NM $2   **MIP** $5

Khan, 1995, Playmates, #6456, "STII:TWOK"

    NM $2   **MIP** $5

Lt. Saavik, 1995, Playmates, #6460, "STII:TWOK," Kirstie Alley likeness

    NM $2   **MIP** $5

Lt. Sulu, 1995, Playmates, #6454, "ST:TMP"

    NM $2   **MIP** $5

Lt. Uhura, 1995, Playmates, #6455, "ST:TMP"

    NM $2   **MIP** $5

Martia, 1995, Playmates, #6457, "STVI:TUC"

    NM $2   **MIP** $5

Star Trek: Deep Space Nine (Playmates, 1994-95)

SERIES 1

Chief Miles O'Brien, 1994, Playmates, #6204

    NM $2   **MIP** $5

Cmdr. Benjamin Sisko, 1994, Playmates, #6201

    NM $2   **MIP** $5

Cmdr. Gul Ducat, 1994, Playmates, #6207

    NM $2   **MIP** $5

Dr. Julian Bashir, 1994, Playmates, #6208

    NM $2   **MIP** $5

Lt. Jadzia Dax, 1994, Playmates, #6205

    NM $2   **MIP** $5

Major Kira Nerys, 1994, Playmates, #6206

    NM $2   **MIP** $5

(KP Photo, Karen O'Brien collection)

Morn, 1994, Playmates, #6210

    NM $2   **MIP** $5

Odo, 1994, Playmates, #6202

    NM $2   **MIP** $5

Quark, 1994, Playmates, #6203

    NM $2   **MIP** $5

SERIES 2

Captain Jean-Luc Picard, 1995, Playmates, #6245, DS9 uniform

    NM $2   **MIP** $5

Chief Miles O'Brien, dress uniform, 1995, Playmates, #6226

    NM $2   **MIP** $5

Chief Miles O'Brien, duty uniform, 1995, Playmates, #6244

    NM $2   **MIP** $5

Cmdr. Benjamin Sisko, dress uniform, 1995, Playmates, #6220

    NM $2   **MIP** $5

Dr. Julian Bashir, duty uniform, 1995, Playmates, #6243

    NM $2   **MIP** $5

Jake Sisko, 1995, Playmates, #6235

    NM $2   **MIP** $5

Lt. Jadzia Dax, duty uniform, 1995, Playmates, #6242

    NM $2   **MIP** $5

Lt. Thomas Riker, 1995, Playmates, #6246, DS9 uniform

    NM $2   **MIP** $5

Q, 1995, Playmates, #6247, DS9 uniform

    NM $2   **MIP** $5

Rom w/Nog, 1995, Playmates, #6241

    NM $2   **MIP** $5

Tosk, 1995, Playmates, #6237

    NM $2   **MIP** $5

Vedek Bareil, 1995, Playmates, #6236

    NM $2   **MIP** $5

Star Trek: First Contact (Playmates, 1996)

6" FIGURES

Borg, 1996, Playmates, #16108

    NM $2   **MIP** $5

Captain Jean-Luc Picard, 1996, Playmates, #16101

    NM $2   **MIP** $5

Captain Jean-Luc Picard in space suit, 1996, Playmates, #16115

    NM $2   **MIP** $5

Cmdr. Deanna Troi, 1996, Playmates, #16106

    NM $2   **MIP** $5

(KP Photo, Karen O'Brien collection)

Cmdr. William T. Riker, 1996, Playmates, #16102

    NM $2   **MIP** $5

Dr. Beverly Crusher, 1996, Playmates, #16107

    NM $2   **MIP** $5

Lily, 1996, Playmates, #16110

    NM $2   **MIP** $5

Lt. Cmdr. Data, 1996, Playmates, #16104

    NM $2   **MIP** $5

Lt. Cmdr. Geordi LaForge, 1996, Playmates, #16103

    NM $2   **MIP** $5

Lt. Cmdr. Worf, 1996, Playmates, #16105

    NM $2   **MIP** $5

Zefram Cochrane, 1996, Playmates, #16109

    NM $2   **MIP** $5

9" FIGURES

Data, 1996, Playmates, #16133

    NM $4   **MIP** $8

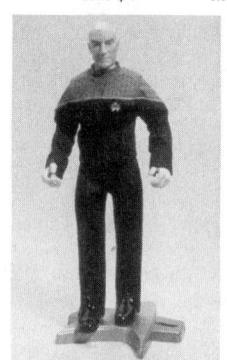

Jean-Luc Picard, 1996, Playmates, #16131

    NM $4   **MIP** $10

Jean-Luc Picard in 21st century outfit, 1996, Playmates, #16153

    NM $4   **MIP** $10

William Riker, 1996, Playmates, #16132

    NM $4   MIP $10

Zefram Cochrane, 1996, Playmates, #16134

    NM $4   MIP $10

Star Trek: Generations (Playmates: 1995)

5" FIGURES

Admiral James T. Kirk, 1995, Playmates, #6911

    NM $2   MIP $5

B'Etor, 1995, Playmates, #6928

    NM $2   MIP $5

Captain James T. Kirk in spacesuit, 1995, Playmates, #6930

    NM $2   MIP $5

Captain Jean-Luc Picard, 1995, Playmates, #6918

    NM $2   MIP $5

Cmdr. Deanna Troi, 1995, Playmates, #6920

    NM $2   MIP $5

Dr. Beverly Crusher, 1995, Playmates, #6924

    NM $2   MIP $5

Dr. Soran, 1995, Playmates, #6925

    NM $2   MIP $5

Guinan, 1995, Playmates, #6927

    NM $2   MIP $5

Lt. Cmdr. Data, 1995, Playmates, #6921

    NM $2   MIP $5

Lt. Cmdr. Geordi LaForge, 1995, Playmates, #6923

    NM $2   MIP $5

Lt. Cmdr. William Riker, 1995, Playmates, #6919, should be a Commander

    NM $2   MIP $5

Lt. Cmdr. Worf, 1995, Playmates, #6922

    NM $2   MIP $5

Lt. Cmdr. Worf in 19th century outfit, 1995, Playmates, #6931

    NM $2   MIP $5

Lursa, 1995, Playmates, #6929

    NM $2   MIP $5

Montgomery Scott, 1995, Playmates, #6914

    NM $2   MIP $5

Pavel A. Chekov, 1995, Playmates, #6916

    NM $2   MIP $5

9" FIGURES

Captain James T. Kirk, 1995, Playmates, #6142

    NM $4   MIP $12

Captain Jean-Luc Picard, 1995, Playmates, #6141

    NM $4   MIP $12

Lt. Cmdr. Data, 1995, Playmates, #6143

    NM $4   MIP $12

Lt. Cmdr. Geordi LaForge, 1995, Playmates, #6144

    NM $4   MIP $12

Star Trek: Insurrection (Playmates, 1998)

12" FIGURES

Captain Picard, 1998, Playmates, #65071

    NM $4   MIP $10

Data, 1998, Playmates, #65074

    NM $4   MIP $10

Geordi LaForge, 1998, Playmates, #65504

    NM $4   MIP $10

William Riker, 1998, Playmates, #65072

    NM $4   MIP $10

Worf, 1998, Playmates, #65073

    NM $4   MIP $10

9" FIGURES

Anji, 1998, Playmates, #65358

    NM $5   MIP $10

Counselor Troi, 1998, Playmates, #65355

    NM $5   MIP $10

Data, 1998, Playmates, #65356

    NM $5   MIP $10

Geordi LaForge, 1998, Playmates, #65354

    NM $5   MIP $10

Jean-Luc Picard, 1998, Playmates, #65351

    NM $5   MIP $10

Ru' Afo, 1998, Playmates, #65357

    NM $5   MIP $10

William Riker, 1998, Playmates, #65352, clean shaven

    NM $5   MIP $10

Worf, 1998, Playmates, #65353

    NM $5   MIP $10

Star Trek: Mixed Sets (Playmates, 1996-97)

SERIES 1

Captain Jean Luc Picard, 1996, Playmates, #6442, "Tapestry," limited to 1701 figures

    NM $115   MIP $275

Christine Chapel, 1996, Playmates, #6447

    NM $2   MIP $5

Cmdr. Benjamin Sisko, 1996, Playmates, #6445, "Crossover"

    NM $2   MIP $5

Grand Negus Zek, 1996, Playmates, #6444

    NM $2   MIP $5

Janice Rand, 1996, Playmates, #6449

    NM $2   MIP $5

Worf, Governor of H'Atoria, 1996, Playmates, #6437, "All Good Things"

    NM $2   MIP $5

SERIES 2

Admiral William Riker, 1996, Playmates, #16034, "All Good Things"

    NM $2   MIP $5

Captain Kirk, casual, 1996, Playmates, #16031

    NM $2   MIP $5

Jem Haddar, 1996, Playmates, #16032

    NM $2   MIP $5

Lt. Cmdr. Worf, 1996, Playmates, #16033, DS9 Strategic Operations Officer

    NM $2   MIP $5

Lt. Natasha Yar, 1996, Playmates, #16043, "Yesterday's Enterprise," limited to 1701 figures

    NM $60   MIP $145

Security Chief Odo, 1996, Playmates, #6446, "Necessary Evil"

    NM $2   MIP $5

SERIES 3

Captain Christopher Pike, 1996, Playmates, #6448, "The Cage"

    NM $2   MIP $5

Elim Garak, 1996, Playmates, #16035, DS9 Tailor

    NM $2   MIP $5

Lt. Reginald Barclay, 1996, Playmates, #16044, "Projections," limited to 3000 figures

    NM $15   MIP $60

Mr. Spock, 1996, Playmates, #16038, "The Cage"

    NM $2   MIP $5

Talosian Keeper, 1996, Playmates, #16039, "The Cage"

    NM $2   MIP $5

Vina, The Orion Slave Girl, 1996, Playmates, #16040, "The Cage"

    NM $2   MIP $5

SERIES 4

Captain Benjamin Sisko, 1997, Playmates, #16021, bald head

    NM $2   MIP $5

Captain Kurn, 1997, Playmates, #16020, "Sons of Mogh"

    NM $2   MIP $5

Dr. Beverly Crusher, 1997, Playmates, #16047, movie "Generations," limited to 10,000 figures

> NM $6   MIP $12

Gorn Captain, 1997, Playmates, #16041, "Arena"

> NM $2   MIP $5

Seska as Cardassian, 1997, Playmates, #16022, ST:Voy "Maneuvers"

> NM $2   MIP $5

Tom Paris Mutated, 1997, Playmates, #16023, ST:Voy "Threshold"

> NM $2   MIP $5

SERIES 5

Captain Kirk in Environmental Suit, 1997, Playmates, #16048, "The Tholian Web"

> NM $2   MIP $5

Dr. McCoy in dress uniform, 1997, Playmates, #16155, "Journey to Babel," limited to 10,000 figures

> NM $4   MIP $5

Harry Mudd, 1997, Playmates, #16154, "I, Mudd" and "Mudd's Women"

> NM $2   MIP $5

Professor Data, 1997, Playmates, #16152, "All Good Things"

> NM $2   MIP $5

The Mugatu, 1997, Playmates, #16042, "A Private Little War"

> NM $2   MIP $5

Star Trek: Space Talk Series (Playmates, 1995)

SPACE TALK SERIES

Borg, 1995, Playmates

> NM $3   MIP $5

Picard, 1995, Playmates

> NM $3   MIP $5

Q, 1995, Playmates

> NM $3   MIP $5

Riker, 1995, Playmates

> NM $3   MIP $5

Star Trek: Starfleet Academy (Playmates, 1996)

FIGURES

Cadet Geordi LaForge, 1996, Playmates, #16004, radiation repair suit

> NM $3   MIP $5

Cadet Jean-Luc Picard, 1996, Playmates, #16001, flight training suit

> NM $3   MIP $5

(KP Photo, Karen O'Brien collection)

Cadet William Riker, 1996, Playmates, #16002, geo-hazard suit

> NM $3   MIP $5

Cadet Worf, 1996, Playmates, #16005, night reconnaissance suit

> NM $3   MIP $5

Star Trek: The Motion Picture (Mego, 1979-81)

12" BOXED FIGURES

Arcturian, 1979, Mego

> NM $60   MIP $150

Captain Kirk, 1979, Mego

> NM $40   MIP $75

Decker, 1979, Mego

> NM $45   MIP $115

Ilia, 1979, Mego

> NM $40   MIP $75

Klingon, 1979, Mego

> NM $40   MIP $125

Mr. Spock, 1979, Mego

> NM $40   MIP $75

3-3/4" CARDED FIGURES

Acturian, 1980, Mego, Series 2, light tan uniform

> NM $40   MIP $110

Betelgeusian, 1980, Mego, Series 2

> NM $40   MIP $110

Captain Kirk, 1979, Mego, Series 1

> NM $8   MIP $20

(Mark Bellomo collection)

Decker, 1979, Mego, Series 1

> NM $4   MIP $15

Dr. McCoy, 1979, Mego, Series 1, white shirt, gray pants

> NM $10   MIP $25

Ilia, 1979, Mego, Series 1

> NM $8   MIP $15

Klingon, 1980, Mego, Series 2

> NM $50   MIP $120

Megarite, 1980, Mego, Series 2

> NM $50   MIP $120

Mr. Spock, 1979, Mego, Series 1, dark gray uniform as seen in movie

> NM $10   MIP $20

Rigellian, 1980, Mego, Series 2

> NM $50   MIP $120

Scotty, 1979, Mego, Series 1

> NM $10   MIP $30

Zatanite, 1980, Mego, Series 2

> NM $60   MIP $120

PLAY SETS

U.S.S. Enterprise Bridge, 1980, Mego

> NM $35   MIP $110

Star Trek: The Next Generation (Galoob, 1988-89)

ACCESSORIES

Enterprise, 1989, Galoob, die-cast vehicle

> NM $8   MIP $20

Ferengi Fighter, 1989, Galoob, vehicle

> NM $12   MIP $35

Galileo Shuttle, 1989, Galoob, vehicle

> NM $8   MIP $25

Phaser, 1989, Galoob, role playing toy

> NM $10   MIP $25

SERIES 1 FIGURES

(KP Photo, Karen O'Brien collection)

Commander William Riker, 1988, Galoob, w/phaser and tricorder
NM $3   MIP $7

Data, blue face, 1988, Galoob
NM $3   MIP $7

Data, brown face, 1988, Galoob
NM $3   MIP $7

Data, flesh face, 1988, Galoob
NM $3   MIP $7

Data, spotted face, 1988, Galoob
NM $3   MIP $7

Geordi La Forge, 1988, Galoob
NM $3   MIP $7

Jean-Luc Picard, 1988, Galoob
NM $3   MIP $7

(KP Photo, Karen O'Brien collection)

Lt. Tasha Yar, 1988, Galoob, w/phaser and tricorder
NM $3   MIP $7

Lt. Worf, 1988, Galoob
NM $3   MIP $7

SERIES 2 FIGURES

Antican, 1989, Galoob
NM $10   MIP $25

Ferengi, 1989, Galoob
NM $10   MIP $25

Q, 1989, Galoob
NM $10   MIP $25

Selay, 1989, Galoob
NM $10   MIP $25

SERIES 1

Borg, 1992, Playmates, #6055
NM $2   MIP $5

(KP Photo, Karen O'Brien collection)

Captain Jean-Luc Picard, 1992, Playmates, #6011
NM $2   MIP $5

(KP Photo, Karen O'Brien collection)

Commander Riker, 1992, Playmates, #6014
NM $2   MIP $5

Counselor Deanna Troi, 1992, Playmates, #6016
NM $2   MIP $5

(KP Photo, Karen O'Brien collection)

Ferengi, 1992, Playmates, #6052
NM $2   MIP $5

Gowron the Klingon, 1992, Playmates, #6053
NM $2   MIP $5

(KP Photo, Karen O'Brien collection)

Lt. Commander Data, 1992, Playmates, #6012
NM $2   MIP $5

Lt. Commander Geordi LaForge, 1992, Playmates, #6015
NM $2   MIP $5

Lt. Worf, 1992, Playmates, #6013
NM $2   MIP $5

Romulan, 1992, Playmates, #6051
NM $2   MIP $5

SERIES 2

Admiral McCoy, 1993, Playmates, #6028, w/card or space cap
NM $2   MIP $5

Ambassador Spock, 1993, Playmates, #6027, w/card or space cap
NM $2   MIP $5

Benzite, 1993, Playmates, #6057, w/card or space cap
NM $2   MIP $5

Borg, 1993, Playmates, #6077, w/card or space cap
NM $2   MIP $5

(KP Photo, Karen O'Brien collection)

Cadet Wesley Crusher, 1993, Playmates, #6021, w/card or space cap

> **NM** $2   **MIP** $5

Captain Jean-Luc Picard, 1993, Playmates, #6071, w/card or space cap

> **NM** $2   **MIP** $5

Captain Scott (Scotty), 1993, Playmates, #6029, w/card or space cap

> **NM** $2   **MIP** $5

Commander Sela, 1993, Playmates, #6056, w/card or space cap

> **NM** $2   **MIP** $5

(KP Photo, Karen O'Brien collection)

Commander William Riker, 1993, Playmates, #6074, w/card or space cap

> **NM** $2   **MIP** $5

Counselor Deanna Troi, 1993, Playmates, #6076, w/card or space cap, second season uniform

> **NM** $2   **MIP** $5

Dathon, 1993, Playmates, #6060, w/card or space cap

> **NM** $2   **MIP** $5

Dr. Beverly Crusher, 1993, Playmates, #6019, w/card or space cap

> **NM** $2   **MIP** $5

Guinan, 1993, Playmates, #6020, w/card or space cap

> **NM** $2   **MIP** $5

K'Ehleyr, 1993, Playmates, #6059, w/card or space cap

> **NM** $2   **MIP** $5

Klingon Warrior Worf, 1993, Playmates, #6024, w/card or space cap

> **NM** $2   **MIP** $5

Locutus, 1993, Playmates, #6023, w/card or space cap

> **NM** $2   **MIP** $5

Lore, 1993, Playmates, #6022, w/card or space cap

> **NM** $2   **MIP** $5

Lt. Cmdr. Geordi LaForge in Dress Uniform, 1993, Playmates, #6026, w/card or space cap

> **NM** $2   **MIP** $5

Lt. Commander Data, 1993, Playmates, #6072, w/card or space cap

> **NM** $2   **MIP** $5

Lt. Geordi LaForge, 1993, Playmates, #6075, w/card or space cap

> **NM** $2   **MIP** $5

Lt. Worf, 1993, Playmates, #6073, w/card or space cap

> **NM** $2   **MIP** $5

Q, red shirt, 1993, Playmates, #6058, w/card or space cap

> **NM** $2   **MIP** $5

Vorgon, 1993, Playmates, #6061, w/card or space cap

> **NM** $2   **MIP** $5

SERIES 3

Ambassador Sarek, 1994, Playmates, #6042, Canadian release

> **NM** $2   **MIP** $5

(KP Photo, Karen O'Brien collection)

Captain Jean-Luc Picard as Dixon Hill, 1994, Playmates, #6050

> **NM** $2   **MIP** $5

(KP Photo, Karen O'Brien collection)

Captain Picard as Romulan, 1994, Playmates, #6032

> **NM** $2   **MIP** $5

(KP Photo, Karen O'Brien collection)

Captain Picard, red duty uniform, 1994, Playmates, #6942

> **NM** $2   **MIP** $5

(KP Photo, Karen O'Brien collection)

Commander Riker, Malcorian, 1994, Playmates, #6034, 7th season episode

NM $2 **MIP** $5

Dr. Noonian Soong, 1994, Playmates, #6038

NM $2 **MIP** $5

Ensign Ro, 1994, Playmates, #6044

NM $2 **MIP** $5

Ensign Wesley Crusher, 1994, Playmates, #6943

NM $2 **MIP** $5

(Lenny Lee)

Esoqq, 1994, Playmates, #6049, fearsome-looking alien includes; knife, food ration, communicator, collector card

NM $4 **MIP** $8

Gowron in Ritual Klingon Attire, 1994, Playmates, #6945

NM $2 **MIP** $5

Hugh Borg, 1994, Playmates, #6037

NM $2 **MIP** $5

Lt. Barclay, 1994, Playmates, #6045

NM $2 **MIP** $5

(KP Photo, Karen O'Brien collection)

Lt. Cmdr. Data as Romulan, 1994, Playmates, #6031

NM $2 **MIP** $5

Lt. Cmdr. Data, dress uniform, 1994, Playmates, #6941

NM $2 **MIP** $5

Lt. Cmdr. Data, red "Redemption" outfit, 1994, Playmates, #6947, JC Penney Exclusive, rare

NM $2 **MIP** $5

Lt. Cmdr. Deanna Troi, 1994, Playmates, #6035, 6th season uniform, includes a stand, laptop computer, tricorder, PADD and accessories

NM $2 **MIP** $5

(KP Photo, Karen O'Brien collection)

Lt. Cmdr. Geordi La Forge as Tarchannen III Alien, 1994, Playmates, #6033

NM $2 **MIP** $5

Lt. Thomas Riker, 1994, Playmates, #6946

NM $10 **MIP** $25

(KP Photo, Karen O'Brien collection)

Lt. Worf in Starfleet Rescue Outfit, 1994, Playmates, #6036

NM $2 **MIP** $5

Lwaxana Troi, 1994, Playmates, #6041, Canadian release

NM $2 **MIP** $5

Q in Judge's Robe, 1993, Playmates, #6042, Q as he appears in "Encounter at Farpoint," Next Gen's first episode, and "All Good Things," its last, includes scroll, scepter, lion statue and gavel

NM $2 **MIP** $5

SERIES 4

Ambassador Sarek, 1995, Playmates, #6968

NM $2 **MIP** $5

Captain Jean-Luc Picard as Locutus, 1995, Playmates, #6986, Supernova Series

NM $2 **MIP** $5

Captain Jean-Luc Picard in "All Good Things," 1995, Playmates, #6974, Picard is older

NM $2 **MIP** $5

Dr. Beverly Crusher, duty uniform, 1994, Playmates, #6961

NM $2 **MIP** $5

(KP Photo, Karen O'Brien collection)

Dr. Noonian Soong, 1995, Playmates, #6982

NM $2 **MIP** $5

Ensign Ro Laren, 1995, Playmates, #6981

    NM $2   **MIP** $5

Lt. Cmdr. Data in 1940s Attire, 1995, Playmates, #6979, Holodeck Series

    NM $2   **MIP** $5

Lt. Cmdr. Data in movie uniform, 1995, Playmates, #6962

    NM $2   **MIP** $5

Lt. Cmdr. Geordi LaForge in movie uniform, 1995, Playmates, #6960

    NM $2   **MIP** $5

(KP Photo, Karen O'Brien collection)

Lt. Natasha Yar, 1994, Playmates, #6965

    NM $2   **MIP** $5

Lt. Worf in Ritual Klingon Attire, 1995, Playmates, #6985, Supernova Series

    NM $2   **MIP** $5

Lwaxana Troi, 1995, Playmates, #6967, 7th Season

    NM $2   **MIP** $5

Nausicaan, 1994, Playmates, #6969, "Tapestry"

    NM $2   **MIP** $5

SERIES 5

Borg, 1995, Playmates, #6441, Interstellar Action Series

    NM $2   **MIP** $5

Captain Picard, 1995, Playmates, #6442, "Tapestry" one of the show's finest episodes, Picard discovers what his world would have been like if he had been less reckless in his youth, only 1701 produced

    NM $115   **MIP** $275

Commander Benjamin Sisko, 1995, Playmates, #6445, "Crossover"

    NM $2   **MIP** $5

Counselor Troi as Durango, 1995, Playmates, #6438, "A Fist Full of Datas"

    NM $2   **MIP** $5

Dr. Beverly Crusher in 1940s Attire, 1995, Playmates, #6435, "The Big Goodbye"

    NM $2   **MIP** $5

Dr. Katherine Pulaski, 1995, Playmates, #6428

    NM $2   **MIP** $5

Geordi LaForge, 1995, Playmates, #6433, "All Good Things"

    NM $2   **MIP** $5

Governor Worf of H'Atoria, 1995, Playmates, #6437, "All Good Things"

    NM $2   **MIP** $5

Grand Nagus Zek, 1995, Playmates, #6444

    NM $2   **MIP** $5

Lt. Geordi LaForge, 1995, Playmates, #6443, Interstellar Action Series

    NM $2   **MIP** $5

Lt. Jadzia Dax, 1995, Playmates, #6440, "Blood Oath" in ritual Klingon attire

    NM $2   **MIP** $5

Picard as Galen, 1995, Playmates, #6432, "The Gambit"

    NM $2   **MIP** $5

Sheriff Worf, 1995, Playmates, #6434, "A Fist Full of Datas"

    NM $2   **MIP** $5

The Hunter of Tosk, 1995, Playmates, #6439

    NM $2   **MIP** $5

The Traveler, 1995, Playmates, #6436

    NM $2   **MIP** $5

(KP Photo, Karen O'Brien collection)

Vash, 1995, Playmates, #6429

    NM $2   **MIP** $5

SERIES 6

Admiral William T. Riker, 1996, Playmates, #16034, "All Good Things"

    NM $2   **MIP** $5

Captain Christopher Pike, 1996, Playmates, #6448, "The Cage"

    NM $2   **MIP** $5

Captain James T. Kirk, 1996, Playmates, #16031, in casual attire, green shirt

    NM $2   **MIP** $5

Elim Garak, 1996, Playmates, #16035

    NM $2   **MIP** $5

Jem'Hadar, 1996, Playmates, #16032

    NM $2   **MIP** $5

Lt. Commander Worf, 1996, Playmates, #16033, in DS9 uniform

    NM $2   **MIP** $5

Lt. Natasha Yar, 1996, Playmates, #16043, "Yesterday's Enterprise," another great episode, only 1701 produced

    NM $75   **MIP** $160

Lt. Reginald Barclay, 1996, Playmates, #16044, ST:VOY "Projections," only 3,000 produced

    NM $2   **MIP** $5

Mr. Spock, 1996, Playmates, #16038, "The Cage"

    NM $2   **MIP** $5

Nurse Christine Chapel, 1996, Playmates, #6447

    NM $2   **MIP** $5

Security Chief Odo, 1996, Playmates, #6446, "Necessary Evil"

    NM $2   **MIP** $5

The Talosian Keeper, 1996, Playmates, #16039, "The Cage"

    NM $2   **MIP** $5

Vina the Orion Animal Woman, 1996, Playmates, #16040, "The Cage"

    NM $2   **MIP** $5

Yeoman Janice Rand, 1996, Playmates, #6449

    NM $2   **MIP** $5

SERIES 7

Beverly Crusher, 1997, Playmates, #16047, as seen in "Star Trek:Generations"

    NM $2   **MIP** $5

Captain Benjamin Sisko, 1997, Playmates, #16021, bald w/goatee

    NM $2   **MIP** $5

Captain Kirk in Environmental Suit, 1997, Playmates, #16048, "The Tholian Web"

    NM $2   **MIP** $5

Captain Kurn, 1997, Playmates, #16020, ST:DS9 "Sons of Mogh"

    NM $2   **MIP** $5

Dr. McCoy in Dress Uniform, 1997, Playmates, #16155, "Journey to Babel"

    NM $2   **MIP** $5

Gorn Captain, 1997, Playmates, #16041, "Arena," one of the best opponents Capt. Kirk ever faced

    NM $2   **MIP** $5

(KP Photo, Karen O'Brien collection)

Harry Mudd, 1997, Playmates, #16154, "Mudd's Women," and "I, Mudd"

NM $2   **MIP** $5

(KP Photo, Karen O'Brien collection)

Professor Data, 1997, Playmates, #16152, "All Good Things"

NM $2   **MIP** $5

Seska as a Cardassian, 1997, Playmates, #16022, ST:VOY "Maneuvers"

NM $2   **MIP** $5

(KP Photo, Karen O'Brien collection)

The Mugato, 1997, Playmates, #16042, "A Private Little War"

NM $2   **MIP** $5

Tom Paris Mutated, 1997, Playmates, #16023, ST:VOY "Maneuvers"

NM $2   **MIP** $5

Star Trek: Transporter Series (Playmates, 1997)

EXCLUSIVES

Ensign Pavel Chekov, 1998, Playmates, #65231, Target Exclusive

NM $3   **MIP** $8

Lt. Hikaru Sulu, 1998, Playmates, #65232, Target Exclusive

NM $3   **MIP** $8

Nurse Christine Chapel, 1998, Playmates, #65441, Target Exclusive

NM $3   **MIP** $8

Yeoman Janice Rand, 1998, Playmates, #65442, Target Exclusive

NM $3   **MIP** $8

SERIES 1

Captain James T. Kirk, 1998, Playmates, #65401, yellow shirt

NM $3   **MIP** $8

Dr. McCoy, 1998, Playmates, #65403

NM $3   **MIP** $8

Lt. Scott, 1998, Playmates, #65405

NM $3   **MIP** $8

Lt. Uhura, 1998, Playmates, #65404

NM $3   **MIP** $8

Mr. Spock, 1998, Playmates, #65402

NM $3   **MIP** $8

SERIES 2

Captain Jean Luc Picard, 1998, Playmates, #65422

NM $3   **MIP** $8

Cmdr. William T. Riker, 1998, Playmates, #65432

NM $3   **MIP** $8

Lt. Cmdr. Data, 1998, Playmates, #65421

NM $3   **MIP** $8

Lt. Cmdr. Geordi LaForge, 1998, Playmates, #65433

NM $3   **MIP** $8

Lt. Worf, 1998, Playmates, #65423

NM $3   **MIP** $8

Star Trek: Voyager (Playmates, 1995-96)

SERIES 1

Captain Kathryn Janeway, 1996, Playmates, #6481

NM $2   **MIP** $5

Cmdr. Chakotay, 1996, Playmates, #6482

NM $2   **MIP** $5

Doctor, 1996, Playmates, #6486

NM $2   **MIP** $5

En. Harry Kim, 1996, Playmates, #6484

NM $2   **MIP** $5

Kes the Ocampa, 1996, Playmates, #6488

NM $2   **MIP** $5

Lt. B'Elanna Torres, 1996, Playmates, #6485

NM $2   **MIP** $5

Lt. Tom Paris, 1996, Playmates, #6483

NM $2   **MIP** $5

Lt. Tuvok, 1996, Playmates, #6487

NM $2   **MIP** $5

Neelix the Telaxian, 1996, Playmates, #6489

NM $2   **MIP** $5

SERIES 2

Chakotay the Maquis, 1996, Playmates, #16466

NM $2   **MIP** $5

En. Seska, 1996, Playmates, #16460

NM $2   **MIP** $5

Kazon, 1996, Playmates, #16462

NM $2   **MIP** $5

Lt. Carey, 1995, Playmates, #16461

NM $2   **MIP** $5

Torres as Klingon, 1995, Playmates, #16465

NM $2   **MIP** $5

Vidiian, 1995, Playmates, #16463

NM $2   **MIP** $5

VEHICLES

U.S.S. Voyager, 1995, Playmates, #6479

NM $75   **MIP** $160

Star Trek: Warp Factor (Playmates, 1997-98)

COMBAT ACTION SERIES 1

Borg, 1997, Playmates, #16234, spring-firing arm

NM $4   **MIP** $8

Captain Jean-Luc Picard, 1997, Playmates, #16251, fencing action

NM $4   **MIP** $8

Cmdr. William T. Riker, 1997, Playmates, #16252, phaser drawing action

NM $4   **MIP** $8

Lt. Cmdr. Worf, 1997, Playmates, #16253, bat'leth slashing action

NM $4   **MIP** $8

Q, 1997, Playmates, #16255, fencing action

NM $4   **MIP** $8

COMBAT ACTION SERIES 2

Captain Benjamin Sisko, 1998, Playmates, #16258
NM $4 MIP $8

Cardassian Soldier, 1998, Playmates, #16256
NM $4 MIP $8

Chief Miles O'Brien, 1998, Playmates, #16266
NM $4 MIP $8

Jem'Hadar Soldier, 1998, Playmates, #16257
NM $4 MIP $8

Lt. Cmdr. Jadzia Dax, 1998, Playmates, #16260
NM $4 MIP $8

SERIES 1

Captain Benjamin Sisko, 1997, Playmates, #65107, DS9 "Trials and Tribbleations"
NM $3 MIP $6

Captain Koloth, 1997, Playmates, #65111, DS9 "Trials and Tribbleations"
NM $3 MIP $6

Chief Miles O'Brien, 1997, Playmates, #65106, DS9 "Trials and Tribbleations," limited to 10,000
NM $3 MIP $6

Constable Odo, 1997, Playmates, #65109, DS9 "Trials and Tribbleations"
NM $3 MIP $6

Dr. Julian Bashir, 1997, Playmates, #65110, DS9 "Trials and Tribbleations"
NM $3 MIP $6

Lt. Cmdr. Jadzia Dax, 1997, Playmates, #65108, DS9 "Trials and Tribbleations"
NM $3 MIP $6

SERIES 2

Captain Beverly Picard, 1997, Playmates, #65112, "All Good Things"
NM $3 MIP $6

Ilia Probe, 1997, Playmates, #65102, ST:TMP
NM $3 MIP $6

Leeta the Dabo Girl, 1997, Playmates, #65102, DS9
NM $3 MIP $6

Sisko as a Klingon, 1997, Playmates, #65101, DS9 "Apocalypse Rising"
NM $3 MIP $6

Swarm Alien, 1997, Playmates, #65104, ST:YOY "The Swarm"
NM $3 MIP $6

SERIES 3

Cadet Beverly Howard Crusher, 1997, Playmates, #65117
NM $3 MIP $6

Cadet Data, 1997, Playmates, #65116
NM $3 MIP $6

Cadet Deanna Troi, 1997, Playmates, #65115
NM $3 MIP $6

(KP Photo, Karen O'Brien collection)

Edith Keeler, 1997, Playmates, #65114, "City on the Edge of Forever"
NM $3 MIP $6

Mr. Spock, 1997, Playmates, #65105, "Mirror, Mirror"
NM $3 MIP $6

SERIES 4

Andorian, 1998, Playmates, #65120, "Whom Gods Destroy"
NM $3 MIP $6

Intendant Kira, 1998, Playmates, #65124, DS9 "Crossover"
NM $3 MIP $6

Kang, 1998, Playmates, #65123, DS9 "Blood Oath"
NM $3 MIP $6

Keiko O'Brien, 1998, Playmates, #65121
NM $3 MIP $6

Trelane, 1998, Playmates, #65122, "The Squire of Gothos"
NM $3 MIP $6

SERIES 5

Borg Queen, 1998, Playmates, #65130, ST:FC
NM $4 MIP $8

James Kirk, 1998, Playmates, #65128, "City on the Edge of Forever"
NM $3 MIP $6

Mr. Spock, 1998, Playmates, #65129, "City on the Edge of Forever"
NM $3 MIP $6

Seven of Nine, 1998, Playmates, #65131, ST:VOY "The Gift"
NM $3 MIP $6

Stargate (Hasbro, 1994)

FIGURES

Anubis, 1998, Hasbro
NM $2 MIP $4

(Lenny Lee)

Col. O'Neil, 1998, Hasbro, group shot
NM $2 MIP $4

Daniel Jackson, 1994, Hasbro
NM $2 MIP $5

Horus, Attack Pilot, 1998, Hasbro
NM $2 MIP $4

Horus, Palace Guard, 1998, Hasbro
NM $2 MIP $4

Lt. Kawalsky, 1998, Hasbro
NM $2 MIP $4

Ra, 1998, Hasbro
NM $2 MIP $4

Skaara, 1998, Hasbro
NM $2 MIP $4

Starsky and Hutch (Mego, 1976)

FIGURES

Captain Dobey, 1976, Mego
NM $25 MIP $50

Chopper, 1976, Mego, in cable-knit sweater and dark pants
NM $25 MIP $45

Huggy Bear, 1976, Mego
NM $25 MIP $50

Hutch, 1976, Mego
NM $25 MIP $55

Starsky, 1976, Mego
NM $25 MIP $55

VEHICLES

Car, 1976, Mego
NM $85 MIP $195

Strawberry Shortcake (Kenner, 1979-85)

SERIES 1

Apple Dumplin' and Tea Time Turtle, Kenner
NM $22　　MIP $45

Apricot and Hopsalot, Kenner
NM $22　　MIP $50

Blueberry Muffin, Kenner
NM $22　　MIP $45

Huckleberry Pie, Kenner
NM $25　　MIP $65

Lemon Meringue, Kenner
NM $22　　MIP $45

Orange Blossom, Kenner
NM $22　　MIP $50

Purple Pieman and Cackle, Kenner
NM $24　　MIP $45

Raspberry Tart, Kenner
NM $22　　MIP $45

Strawberry Shortcake, Kenner
NM $26　　MIP $80

SERIES 2

Almond Tea and Marza Panda, Kenner
NM $25　　MIP $60

Angel Cake and Souffl'e, Kenner
NM $20　　MIP $50

Apple Dumplin' and Tea Time Turtle, Kenner
NM $20　　MIP $45

Apricot and Hopsalot, Kenner
NM $20　　MIP $45

Blueberry Muffin and Cheesecake, Kenner
NM $30　　MIP $50

Butter Cookie and Jelly Bear, Kenner
NM $15　　MIP $38

Café Ole' and Burrito, Kenner
NM $30　　MIP $40

Cherry Cuddler and Gooseberry, Kenner
NM $20　　MIP $40

Crepe Suzette and Éclair, Kenner
NM $35　　MIP $60

Huckleberry pie and Pupcake, Kenner
NM $25　　MIP $50

Lem n' Ada and Sugarwoofer, Kenner
NM $35　　MIP $50

Lemon Meringue and Frappe, Kenner
NM $30　　MIP $50

Lime Chiffon and Parfait, Kenner
NM $25　　MIP $50

Mint Tulip and Marsh Mallard, Kenner
NM $35　　MIP $55

Orange Blossom and Marmalade, Kenner
NM $22　　MIP $45

Purple Pieman and Cackle, Kenner
NM $24　　MIP $45

Raspberry Tart and Rhubarb Doll, Kenner
NM $22　　MIP $50

Sour Grapes and Dregs the Snake, Kenner
NM $25　　MIP $60

Strawberry Shortcake and Custard, Kenner
NM $25　　MIP $50

SERIES 3

Almond Tea and Marza Panda Doll, Kenner, Party Pleasers
NM $65　　MIP $100

Angel Cake and Souffl'e, Kenner, Party Pleasers
NM $65　　MIP $100

Apple Dumplin' and Tea Time Turtle, Kenner, Party Pleasers
NM $65　　MIP $100

Café O'le and Burrito, Kenner, Party Pleasers
NM $50　　MIP $90

Cherry Cuddler and Gooseberry, Kenner, Party Pleasers
NM $100　　MIP $150

Mint Tulip and Marsh Mallard, Kenner, Party Pleasers
NM $120　　MIP $165

Orange Blossom and Marmalade, Kenner, Party Pleasers
NM $65　　MIP $100

Peach Blush and Melonie Belle, Kenner, Party Pleasers
NM $110　　MIP $150

Plum Puddin' and Elderberry Owl, Kenner, Party Pleasers
NM $90　　MIP $150

Strawberry Shortcake and Custard, Kenner, Party Pleasers
NM $50　　MIP $85

SERIES 4

Banana Twirl, Kenner, Berrykins
NM $270　　MIP $375

Mint Tulip, Kenner, Berrykins
NM $350　　MIP $525

Orange Blossom, Kenner, Berrykins
NM $200　　MIP $325

Peach Blush, Kenner, Berrykins
NM $375　　MIP $500

Plum Puddin', Kenner, Berrykins
NM $225　　MIP $325

Strawberry Shortcake, Kenner, Berrykins
NM $125　　MIP $250

Street Fighter (Hasbro, 1994)

12" FIGURES

Blanka, 1994, Hasbro
NM $15　　MIP $25

Colonel Guile, 1994, Hasbro
NM $15　　MIP $25

General Bison, 1994, Hasbro
NM $15　　MIP $25

Ryu Hoshi, 1994, Hasbro
NM $15　　MIP $25

Super Hero Bend 'n Flex (Mego, 1974-75)

5" FIGURES

Aquaman, 1974-75, Mego
NM $30　　MIP $120

Batgirl, 1974-75, Mego
NM $50　　MIP $120

Batman, 1974-75, Mego
NM $35　　MIP $90

Captain America, 1974-75, Mego
NM $35　　MIP $90

Catwoman, 1974-75, Mego
NM $70　　MIP $175

Joker, 1974-75, Mego
NM $40　　MIP $150

Mr. Mxyzptlk, 1974-75, Mego
NM $40　　MIP $125

Penguin, 1974-75, Mego
NM $40　　MIP $150

Riddler, 1974-75, Mego
NM $60　　MIP $150

Robin, 1974-75, Mego
NM $30　　MIP $75

Shazam, 1974-75, Mego
NM $50　　MIP $125

Spider-Man, 1974-75, Mego
NM $50　　MIP $125

Supergirl, 1974-75, Mego
NM $70　　MIP $175

Superman, 1974-75, Mego
NM $30　　MIP $75

Tarzan, 1974-75, Mego
NM $25　　MIP $60

Wonder Woman, 1974-75, Mego
NM $50　　MIP $100

ACCESSORIES

Carry Case, 1974-75, Mego, red vinyl case w/red plastic handle, "World's Greatest Super Heroes" logo
NM $40　　MIP $85

Super Powers (Kenner, 1984-86)

5" FIGURES

Aquaman, 1984, Kenner
NM $10   MIP $60

(KP Photo, Karen O'Brien collection)

Batman, 1984, Kenner
NM $50   MIP $110

(Lenny Lee)

Braniac, 1984, Kenner, chrome plastic figure, includes free mini comic book
NM $18   MIP $32

Clark Kent, mail-in figure, 1986, Kenner
NM $40   MIP $65

Cyborg, 1986, Kenner
NM $150   MIP $290

Cyclotron, 1986, Kenner
NM $20   MIP $50

Darkseid, 1985, Kenner, gray and blue figure w/"Power Action Raging Motion"
NM $12   MIP $25

Desaad, 1985, Kenner
NM $12   MIP $25

Dr. Fate, 1985, Kenner
NM $22   MIP $60

Firestorm, 1985, Kenner
NM $15   MIP $35

(Lenny Lee)

Flash, 1984, Kenner, figure has power action legs that simulate the Flash's lightning-speed running style
NM $8   MIP $20

Golden Pharaoh, 1986, Kenner
NM $45   MIP $80

Green Arrow, 1985, Kenner, w/bow
NM $40   MIP $70

Green Lantern, 1984, Kenner, w/lantern
NM $30   MIP $70

Hawkman, 1984, Kenner
NM $25   MIP $60

Joker, 1984, Kenner
NM $15   MIP $30

Kalibak, 1985, Kenner
NM $12   MIP $25

(Lenny Lee)

Lex Luthor, 1984, Kenner, has "Power Action Nuclear Punch"
NM $10   MIP $20

(Lenny Lee)

Mantis, 1985, Kenner, figure has "Power Action Pincer Thrust" and includes a free comic book
NM $12   MIP $25

Martian Manhunter, 1985, Kenner
NM $20   MIP $45

Mister Miracle, 1986, Kenner
NM $70   MIP $130

Mr. Freeze, 1986, Kenner
NM $25   MIP $65

(Lenny Lee)

Orion, 1986, Kenner, w/"Power Action Astro Punch"

NM $20 **MIP** $45

(Lenny Lee)

Parademon, 1985, Kenner, includes mini-comic book

NM $18 **MIP** $28

(Lenny Lee)

Penguin, 1984, Kenner

NM $20 **MIP** $50

(Lenny Lee)

Plastic Man, 1986, Kenner

NM $55 **MIP** $110

Red Tornado, 1985, Kenner

NM $25 **MIP** $50

Robin, 1984, Kenner

NM $15 **MIP** $50

Samurai, 1986, Kenner

NM $55 **MIP** $90

Shazam (Captain Marvel), 1986, Kenner, bright-colored figure, very "cartoony" look

NM $55 **MIP** $120

Steppenwolf, in mail-in bag, 1985, Kenner

NM $10 **MIP** $18

Steppenwolf, on card, 1985, Kenner

NM $10 **MIP** $80

(KP Photo, Karen O'Brien collection)

Superman, 1984, Kenner

NM $25 **MIP** $50

Tyr, 1986, Kenner, w/yellow attached "Power Action Rocket Launcher"

NM $25 **MIP** $50

(Lenny Lee)

Wonder Woman, 1984, Kenner

NM $22 **MIP** $60

ACCESSORIES

Collector's Case, 1984, Kenner, 11-1/4" x 10" x 3-3/4"

NM $20 **MIP** $40

PLAY SETS

Hall of Justice, 1984, Kenner

NM $110 **MIP** $210

VEHICLES

Batcopter, 1986, Kenner

NM $55 **MIP** $150

Batmobile, 1984, Kenner

NM $50 **MIP** $150

Darkseid Destroyer, 1985, Kenner

NM $25 **MIP** $50

Delta Probe One, 1985, Kenner

NM $15 **MIP** $30

Justice Jogger, wind-up, 1986, Kenner

NM $12 **MIP** $30

Kalibak Boulder Bomber, 1985, Kenner

NM $12 **MIP** $25

Lex-Soar 7, 1984, Kenner

NM $15 **MIP** $30

Supermobile, 1984, Kenner

NM $25 **MIP** $50

Superman: Man of Steel (Kenner, 1995-96)

FIGURES

Blast Hammer Steel, 1995, Kenner, Deluxe

NM $3 **MIP** $7

Conduit, 1995, Kenner

NM $2 **MIP** $5

Laser Superman, 1995, Kenner
  NM $3   MIP $7
Lex Luthor, 1995, Kenner
  NM $6   MIP $15
Power Flight Superman, 1995, Kenner
  NM $3   MIP $7
Solar Suit Superman, 1995, Kenner
  NM $3   MIP $7
Steel, 1995, Kenner
  NM $3   MIP $7
Street Guardian Superman, 1995, Kenner
  NM $3   MIP $7
Superboy, 1995, Kenner
  NM $3   MIP $7
Ultra Heat Vision Superman, 1995, Kenner
  NM $3   MIP $7
Ultra Shield Superman, 1995, Kenner
  NM $3   MIP $7

MULTI-PACKS

Cyber-Link Superman & Cyber-Link Batman, 1995, Kenner, Wal-Mart Exclusive
  NM $6   MIP $12
Hunter-Prey Superman v. Doomsday, 1995, Kenner
  NM $7   MIP $14
Superman v. Massacre, 1995, Kenner
  NM $6   MIP $12

VEHICLES

Kryptonian Battle Suit, 1995, Kenner
  NM $3   MIP $10
Superboy VTOL Cycle, 1995, Kenner
  NM $3   MIP $10
Superman Matrix Conversion Coupe, 1995, Kenner, Silver w/Clark Kent
  NM $3   MIP $10

Superman: The Animated Series (Kenner, 1995-96)

FIGURES

Anti-Kryptonite Superman, 1995, Kenner, Series 3
  NM $3   MIP $7
Brainiac, 1995, Kenner, Series 1
  NM $3   MIP $7
Capture Claw Superman, 1995, Kenner, Series 2
  NM $3   MIP $7
Capture Net Superman, 1995, Kenner, Series 1
  NM $3   MIP $7
City Camo Superman, 1995, Kenner, Deluxe
  NM $3   MIP $7

Cyber Crunch Superman, 1996, Kenner, European release
  NM $3   MIP $7
Darkseid, 1995, Kenner, Series 2
  NM $10   MIP $25
Deep Dive Superman, 1995, Kenner, Series 1
  NM $3   MIP $7
Electro Energy Superman, 1995, Kenner, Series 2
  NM $3   MIP $7
Evil Bizzaro, 1995, Kenner, Series 3
  NM $4   MIP $15
Flying Superman, 1995, Kenner, Deluxe, a glider
  NM $3   MIP $7
Fortress of Solitude Superman, 1995, Kenner
  NM $3   MIP $7
Kryptonite Escape Superman, 1995, Kenner, Deluxe
  NM $3   MIP $7
Lex Luthor, 1995, Kenner, Series 1
  NM $3   MIP $10
Metallo, 1995, Kenner, Series 3, Diamond
  NM $4   MIP $12
Mission Masters 3: Quick Change Superman, 1999, Hasbro, Wal-Mart exclusive
  NM $3   MIP $7
Neutron Star Superman, 1995, Kenner, Series 1
  NM $3   MIP $7
Power Swing Superman, 1995, Kenner, Series 3
  NM $3   MIP $7
Quick Change Superman, 1995, Kenner, Series 1
  NM $3   MIP $7
Strong Arm Superman, 1995, Kenner, Series 3
  NM $3   MIP $7
Supergirl, 1995, Kenner, Series 3, Diamond
  NM $4   MIP $10
Tornado Force Superman, 1995, Kenner, Series 3
  NM $3   MIP $7
Ultra Shield Superman, 1995, Kenner
  NM $3   MIP $7
Vision Blast Superman, 1995, Kenner, Deluxe
  NM $3   MIP $7
X-Ray Vision Superman, 1995, Kenner
  NM $3   MIP $7

MULTI-PACKS

Battle for Metropolis, 1999, Kenner, Toys R Us Exclusive, Superman, Lois Lane, Lex Luthor, Brainiac
  NM $12   MIP $30
Super Heroes v. Super Villians, 1995, Kenner, Superman, Supergirl, Bizzaro, Metallo
  NM $12   MIP $25

PLAY SETS

Metropolis Bank, 1995, Kenner, w/Superman figure, foreign release
  NM $35   MIP $75

VEHICLES

Superman Conversion Coupe, 1995, Kenner, Red w/Clark Kent
  NM $10   MIP $20

Teenage Mutant Ninja Turtles (Playmates, 1988-92)

GIANT TURTLES, 1991

Donatello, 1991, Playmates
  NM $40   MIP $80
Leonardo, 1991, Playmates
  NM $40   MIP $80
Michelangelo, 1991, Playmates
  NM $40   MIP $80
Raphael, 1991, Playmates
  NM $40   MIP $80

GIANT TURTLES, 1992

Bebop, 1992, Playmates
  NM $30   MIP $60
Movie Don, 1992, Playmates
  NM $30   MIP $60
Movie Leo, 1992, Playmates
  NM $30   MIP $60
Movie Mike, 1992, Playmates
  NM $30   MIP $60
Movie Raph, 1992, Playmates
  NM $30   MIP $60
Rocksteady, 1992, Playmates
  NM $20   MIP $40

SERIES 01, 1988

April O'Neil, no stripe, 1988, Playmates
  NM $30   MIP $75
Bebop, 1988, Playmates
  NM $15   MIP $30
Donatello, 1988, Playmates
  NM $18   MIP $40
Donatello, w/fan club form, 1988, Playmates
  NM $22   MIP $55

Foot Soldier, 1988, Playmates
NM $13   MIP $35

Leonardo, 1988, Playmates
NM $18   MIP $40

Leonardo, w/fan club form, 1988, Playmates
NM $22   MIP $55

Michelangelo, 1988, Playmates
NM $18   MIP $40

Michelangelo, w/fan club form, 1988, Playmates
NM $22   MIP $55

Raphael, 1988, Playmates
NM $18   MIP $40

Raphael, w/fan club form, 1988, Playmates
NM $22   MIP $55

Rocksteady, 1988, Playmates
NM $15   MIP $35

Shredder, 1988, Playmates
NM $15   MIP $40

Splinter, 1988, Playmates
NM $15   MIP $25

SERIES 02, 1989

Ace Duck, hat off, 1989, Playmates
NM $6   MIP $18

Ace Duck, hat on, 1989, Playmates
NM $6   MIP $12

April O'Neil, blue stripe, 1989, Playmates
NM $10   MIP $20

Baxter Stockman, 1989, Playmates, a man who had a nasty run-in with a bug
NM $8   MIP $20

Genghis Frog, black belt, 1989, Playmates
NM $4   MIP $12

Genghis Frog, black belt, bagged weapons, 1989, Playmates
NM $5   MIP $30

Genghis Frog, yellow belt, 1989, Playmates
NM $20   MIP $60

Krang, 1989, Playmates
NM $6   MIP $12

SERIES 03, 1989

Casey Jones, 1989, Playmates
NM $14   MIP $30

General Traag, 1989, Playmates
NM $6   MIP $16

Leatherhead, 1989, Playmates, way too much sun for this guy
NM $12   MIP $30

Metalhead, 1989, Playmates, carded
NM $8   MIP $22

Rat King, 1989, Playmates
NM $6   MIP $14

Usagi Yojimbo, 1989, Playmates
NM $8   MIP $16

SERIES 04, 1990

Mondo Gecko, 1990, Playmates
NM $6   MIP $15

Muckman and Joe Eyeball, 1990, Playmates
NM $6   MIP $15

Scumbag, 1990, Playmates
NM $6   MIP $12

Wingnut & Screwloose, 1990, Playmates
NM $6   MIP $12

SERIES 05, 1990

Fugitoid, 1990, Playmates
NM $5   MIP $15

Slash, black belt, 1990, Playmates
NM $3   MIP $15

Slash, purple belt, red "S," 1990, Playmates
NM $15   MIP $40

Triceraton, 1990, Playmates
NM $8   MIP $18

SERIES 06, 1990

Mutagen Man, 1990, Playmates
NM $18   MIP $35

Napoleon Bonafrog, 1990, Playmates
NM $5   MIP $12

Panda Khan, 1990, Playmates
NM $5   MIP $12

SERIES 07, 1991

April O'Neil, 1991, Playmates
NM $25   MIP $100

April O'Neil, "Press," 1991, Playmates
NM $5   MIP $15

Pizza Face, 1991, Playmates
NM $5   MIP $10

Ray Fillet, purple body, red "V," 1991, Playmates, purple torso, red V
NM $10   MIP $25

Ray Fillet, red body, maroon "V," 1991, Playmates, red torso, maroon V
NM $10   MIP $30

Ray Fillet, yellow body, blue "V," 1991, Playmates, yellow torso, blue V
NM $8   MIP $12

SERIES 08, 1991

Don The Undercover Turtle, 1991, Playmates
NM $5   MIP $10

Leo the Sewer Samurai, 1991, Playmates
NM $5   MIP $10

Mike the Sewer Surfer, 1991, Playmates
NM $5   MIP $10

Raph the Space Cadet, 1991, Playmates
NM $5   MIP $10

SERIES 09, 1991

Chrome Dome, 1991, Playmates, carded
NM $5   MIP $12

Dirt Bag, 1991, Playmates, carded
NM $6   MIP $15

Ground Chuck, 1991, Playmates
NM $15   MIP $30

Storage Shell Don, 1991, Playmates
NM $5   MIP $10

Storage Shell Leo, 1991, Playmates
NM $5   MIP $10

Storage Shell Michelangelo, 1991, Playmates
NM $5   MIP $10

Storage Shell Raphael, 1991, Playmates
NM $5   MIP $10

SERIES 10, 1991

Grand Slam Raph, 1991, Playmates
NM $5   MIP $10

Hose 'em Down Don, 1991, Playmates
NM $5   MIP $10

Lieutenant Leo, 1991, Playmates
NM $5   MIP $10

Make My Day Leo, 1991, Playmates
NM $5   MIP $10

Midshipman Mike, 1991, Playmates
NM $5   MIP $10

Pro Pilot Don, 1991, Playmates
NM $5   MIP $10

Raph the Green Teen Beret, 1991, Playmates
NM $5   MIP $10

Slam Dunkin' Don, 1991, Playmates
NM $5   MIP $10

Slapshot Leo, 1991, Playmates
NM $5   MIP $10

T.D. Tossin' Leonardo, 1991, Playmates
NM $5   MIP $10

SERIES 11, 1992

Rahzar, black nose, 1992, Playmates
NM $5   MIP $12

Rahzar, red nose, 1992, Playmates
NM $8   MIP $25

Skateboard'n Mike, 1992, Playmates
NM $5   MIP $10

Super Shredder, 1992, Playmates
NM $18   MIP $34

Tokka, brown trim, 1992, Playmates
NM $9   MIP $25

Tokka, gray trim, 1992, Playmates
NM $6   MIP $15

SERIES 12, 1992

Movie Don, 1992, Playmates
NM $7   MIP $15

Movie Leo, 1992, Playmates
NM $7   MIP $15

Movie Mike, 1992, Playmates
NM $7   MIP $15

Movie Raph, 1992, Playmates
NM $7   MIP $15

Movie Splinter, no tooth, 1992, Playmates
NM $7   MIP $15

Movie Splinter, w/tooth, 1992, Playmates
NM $25   MIP $75

VEHICLES AND ACCESSORIES

Flushomatic, 1988-92, Playmates
NM $14   MIP $30

Foot Cruiser, 1988-92, Playmates
NM $38   MIP $100

Foot Ski, 1988-92, Playmates
NM $10   MIP $30

Mega Mutant Killer Bee, 1988-92, Playmates
NM $22   MIP $40

Mega Mutant Needlenose, 1988-92, Playmates
NM $20   MIP $35

Mike's Pizza Chopper Backpack, 1988-92, Playmates
NM $4   MIP $10

Mutant Sewer Cycle w/Sidecar, 1988-92, Playmates
NM $8   MIP $30

Ninja Newscycle, 1988-92, Playmates
NM $12   MIP $20

Oozey, 1988-92, Playmates
NM $12   MIP $25

Pizza Powered Sewer Dragster, 1988-92, Playmates
NM $12   MIP $40

Pizza Thrower, 1988-92, Playmates
NM $40   MIP $70

Psycho Cycle, 1988-92, Playmates
NM $15   MIP $30

Raph's Sewer Dragster, 1988-92, Playmates
NM $6   MIP $16

Raph's Sewer Speedboat, 1988-92, Playmates
NM $10   MIP $30

Retrocatapult, 1988-92, Playmates
NM $7   MIP $30

Retromutagen Ooze, 1988-92, Playmates
NM $20   MIP $45

Sewer Seltzer Cannon, 1988-92, Playmates
NM $8   MIP $20

Sludgemobile, 1988-92, Playmates
NM $10   MIP $20

Technodrome, 1988-92, Playmates
NM $145   MIP $260

Toilet Taxi, 1988-92, Playmates
NM $12   MIP $35

Turtle Blimp, green vinyl, 1988-92, Playmates, green vinyl
NM $75   MIP $225

Turtle Party Wagon, 1988-92, Playmates
NM $65   MIP $100

Turtle Trooper Parachute, 1988-92, Playmates
NM $12   MIP $30

Turtlecopter, 1988-92, Playmates
NM $35   MIP $75

WACKY ACTION, 1991

Breakfightin' Raphael, 1988-92, Playmates
NM $5   MIP $10

Creepy Crawlin' Splinter, 1988-92, Playmates
NM $5   MIP $10

Headspinnin' Bebop, 1988-92, Playmates
NM $5   MIP $10

Machine Gunnin' Rocksteady, 1988-92, Playmates
NM $5   MIP $10

Rock & Roll Michelangelo, 1988-92, Playmates
NM $5   MIP $10

Sewer Swimmin' Don, 1988-92, Playmates
NM $5   MIP $10

Slice 'n Dice Shredder, 1988-92, Playmates
NM $10   MIP $20

Sword Slicin' Leonardo, 1988-92, Playmates
NM $5   MIP $10

Wacky Walkin' Mouser, 1988-92, Playmates
NM $8   MIP $18

Terminator 3 (McFarlane, 2003)

FIGURES

12" T-850 Terminator, 2003, McFarlane, w/sound chip
NM $15   MIP $38

T-850 Terminator, 2003, McFarlane
NM $7   MIP $15

T-850 Terminator w/Coffin, 2003, McFarlane
NM $7   MIP $15

T-850 vs. T-X, 2003, McFarlane, Deluxe Boxed Set
NM $15   MIP $30

T-X Terminatrix, 2003, McFarlane
NM $7   MIP $15

T-X Terminatrix Endoskeleton, 2003, McFarlane
NM $7   MIP $15

This is Spinal Tap (Sideshow Toys, 2000)

FIGURES

David St. Hubbins, 2000
NM $15   MIP $35

Derek Smalls, 2000
NM $15   MIP $35

Nigel Tufnel, 2000
NM $15   MIP $35

Thundercats (LJN, 1985-87)

6" FIGURES

Ben-Gali, 1985-87, LJN
    NM $100   MIP $575

Capt. Cracker, 1985-87, LJN
    NM $35   MIP $10

Capt. Shiner, 1985-87, LJN
    NM $15   MIP $85

Cheetara, 1985-87, LJN
    NM $32   MIP $150

Cheetara and Wilykit, 1985-87, LJN
    NM $28   MIP $175

Grune the Destroyer, 1985-87, LJN
    NM $20   MIP $60

Hachiman, 1985-87, LJN
    NM $20   MIP $65

Jackalman, 1985-87, LJN
    NM $20   MIP $65

Jaga, 1986, LJN, Series 3, w/Sword of Omens and Helmet, rare
    NM $85   MIP $290

Lion-O, 1985-87, LJN
    NM $48   MIP $350

Lion-O and Snarf, 1985-87, LJN
    NM $52   MIP $290

Lynx-O, 1985-87, LJN
    NM $75   MIP $355

Mongor, 1985-87, LJN
    NM $65   MIP $125

Monkian, 1985-87, LJN
    NM $32   MIP $70

Mumm-ra, 1985-87, LJN
    NM $30   MIP $175

Panthro, 1985-87, LJN
    NM $35   MIP $150

(Mark Bellomo collection)

Pumyra, 1985-87, LJN
    NM $60   MIP $195

Ratar-O, 1985-87, LJN
    NM $20   MIP $65

Safari Joe, 1985-87, LJN
    NM $48   MIP $110

Snowman of Hook Mountain, 1985-87, LJN
    NM $18   MIP $70

S-S-Slithe, 1985-87, LJN
    NM $12   MIP $60

(KP Photo, Karen O'Brien collection)

Tuska Warrior, 1985-87, LJN
    NM $20   MIP $60

Tygra, 1985-87, LJN
    NM $40   MIP $125

Tygra and Wilykat, 1985-87, LJN
    NM $42   MIP $135

Vultureman, 1985-87, LJN
    NM $18   MIP $55

ACCESSORIES

Astral Moat Monster, 1986, LJN
    NM $295   MIP $575

Laser Sabers Backpacks, 1986, LJN, evil, red pack w/black strap
    NM $25   MIP $50

Laser Sabers Backpacks, 1986, LJN, evil, black pack w/red strap
    NM $25   MIP $50

Laser Sabers Backpacks, 1986, LJN, good, orange pack w/blue strap
    NM $25   MIP $50

Laser Sabers Backpacks, 1986, LJN, good, blue pack w/red strap
    NM $25   MIP $50

Luna-Lasher, 1986, LJN
    NM $25   MIP $45

Stilt Runner, 1986, LJN
    NM $20   MIP $35

Sword of Omens, 1986, LJN, role playing toy for kids
    NM $125   MIP $400

Thunder Wings, 1986, LJN
    NM $50   MIP $140

Tongue-A-Saurus, 1986, LJN
    NM $120   MIP $250

BERSERKERS

Cruncher, 1985-87
    NM $20   MIP $60

Hammerhead, 1985-87
    NM $20   MIP $60

Ram-Bam, 1985-87
    NM $20   MIP $60

Top-Spinner, 1985-87
    NM $20   MIP $60

COMPANIONS

Berbil Belle, 1985-87
    NM $22   MIP $75

Berbil Bert, 1986, LJN
    NM $22   MIP $75

Berbil Bill, 1985-87
    NM $22   MIP $75

Ma-Mut, 1985-87
    NM $29   MIP $80

Snarf, 1985-87
    NM $22   MIP $80

Wilykat, 1985-87
    NM $35   MIP $100

Wilykit, 1985-87
    NM $35   MIP $100

DELUXE FIGURES

Luna-Laser Mumm-Ra, 1986, LJN
    NM $500   MIP $1800

Thunderwings Lion-O, 1986, LJN
    NM $600   MIP $1800

PLAY SETS

Cat's Lair, 1986, LJN
    NM $300   MIP $800

Mumm-Ra's Tomb Fortress, 1986, LJN, w/Mumm-Ra
    NM $175   MIP $350

RAM-PAGERS

Driller, the, 1985-87
    NM $175   MIP $300

Stinger, The, 1985-87
    NM $275   MIP $450

VEHICLES

Hovercat, 1986, LJN
    NM $40   MIP $85

Mutant Fistpounder, 1986, LJN
    NM $35   MIP $80

Mutant Nose Diver, 1986, LJN
    NM $30   MIP $60

Mutant Skycutter, 1986, LJN
    NM $28   MIP $55

Thunderclaw, 1986, LJN
    NM $25   MIP $55

Thundertank, 1986, LJN
    NM $70   MIP $265

Thundercats: Miniatures (Kid Works, 1986)

ACCESSORIES

Mutant Four-Pack, 1986, LJN, four figures
    NM $30   MIP $70

Snowman and Snowmeow, 1986, LJN
    NM $18   MIP $25

Thundercats Four-Pack, 1986, LJN, four figures
    NM $25   MIP $75

Weapons Pack, 1986, LJN
    NM $7   MIP $15

FIGURES

Cheetara, 1986, LJN
    NM $7   MIP $14

Grune, 1986, LJN
    NM $7   MIP $14

Hachiman, 1986, LJN
    NM $6   MIP $12

Jackalman, 1986, LJN
    NM $6   MIP $12

Lion-O, 1986, LJN
    NM $7   MIP $14

Monkian, 1986, LJN
    NM $5   MIP $10

Mumm-Ra, 1986, LJN
    NM $6   MIP $12

Panthro, 1986, LJN
    NM $6   MIP $12

Ratar-O, 1986, LJN
    NM $5   MIP $10

Reptilian, 1986, LJN
    NM $5   MIP $10

S-S-Slithe, 1986, LJN
    NM $5   MIP $10

Tuska Warrior, 1986, LJN
    NM $5   MIP $10

Tygra, 1986, LJN
    NM $6   MIP $12

Vulturman, 1986, LJN
    NM $5   MIP $10

PLAY SETS

Cat's Lair, 1986, LJN
    NM $30   MIP $60

Eye of Thundera, 1986, LJN
    NM $10   MIP $20

Mumm-Ra's Crypt, 1986, LJN
    NM $30   MIP $70

Tick, The (Bandai, 1994-95)

ACCESSORIES

(Bandai)

Steel Box, 1994, Bandai, figure-sized box w/"Really, Really Dangerous!" and "Unsafe" in yellow type
    NM $8   MIP $15

SERIES I, FIGURES

Bounding Tick, 1994, Bandai
    NM $2   MIP $5

Death Hug Dean, 1994, Bandai
    NM $2   MIP $5

Exploding Dyne-Mole, 1994, Bandai
    NM $2   MIP $5

Fluttering Arthur, 1994, Bandai
    NM $3   MIP $6

Grasping El Seed, 1994, Bandai
    NM $3   MIP $6

Growing Dinosaur Neil, 1994, Bandai
    NM $3   MIP $6

(KP Photo)

Man Eating Cow, 1994, Bandai, brown and white cow w/moving jaw (and a set of teeth!)
    NM $8   MIP $12

Pose Striking Die Fledermaus, 1994, Bandai
    NM $8   MIP $12

Projectile Human Bullet, 1994, Bandai
    NM $3   MIP $6

Sewer Spray Sewer Urchin, 1994, Bandai
    NM $3   MIP $6

SERIES II, FIGURES

Color Changing Chameleon, 1995, Bandai
    NM $3   MIP $6

Hurling Stop Sign Tick, 1995, Bandai
    NM $2   MIP $5

Propellerized Skippy the Dog, 1995, Bandai
    NM $2   MIP $5

Sliming Mucus Tick, 1995, Bandai
    NM $3   MIP $6

Thrakkorzog, 1995, Bandai
    NM $3   MIP $6

Twist and Chop American Maid, 1995, Bandai
    NM $3   MIP $7

Tomb Raider (Playmates, 1999)

12" FIGURE

Talking Lara Croft, 1999, Playmates
    NM $8   MIP $25

9" FIGURES

Lara Croft in Area 51 outfit w/hand guns and an M-16, on base, 1999
    NM $8   MIP $20

Lara Croft in jungle outfit w/two guns, on base, 1999
    NM $8   MIP $20

(Playmates Toys)

Lara Croft in wet suit w/harpoon and two pistols, on base, 1999, detailed figure w/stand
    NM $8   MIP $20

ADVENTURES OF LARA CROFT, 6" FIGURES

Lara Croft escapes a Bengal, on diorama base, 1999
    NM $3   MIP $10

Lara Croft escapes the yeti, on diorama base, 1999
    NM $3   MIP $10

Lara Croft faces a Bengal, on diorama
base, 1999

    NM $3   MIP $10

Total Chaos
(McFarlane, 1996-97)

SERIES 1, FIGURES

Al Simmons, 1996, McFarlane

    NM $5   MIP $15

Al Simmons, blue uniform, 1996

    NM $3   MIP $12

**Al Simmons, red uniform w/"Spawn"
on visor, available through
convention**, 1997

    NM $15   MIP $45

Conqueror, 1996

    NM $5   MIP $15

**Dragon Blade vs. Conqueror, Puzzle
Zoo Exclusive**, 1997

    NM $6   MIP $18

Dragon Blade, black tunic, 1996

    NM $4   MIP $12

Dragon Blade, white tunic, 1996,
McFarlane

    NM $5   MIP $15

(KP Photo)

Gore, 1996, McFarlane, w/harpoon-
launching arm and bomb-dropping
parrot figure

    NM $5   MIP $15

Hoof, black body w/khaki armor, 1996

    NM $3   MIP $12

(Lenny Lee)

Hoof, gray body w/brown armor,
1996, McFarlane, w/rotating and
firing missile launcher

    NM $5   MIP $15

Thorax, black and yellow, 1996

    NM $3   MIP $12

Thorax, green and red, 1996,
McFarlane

    NM $4   MIP $12

Thresher, light blue skin, 1996,
McFarlane

    NM $5   MIP $15

Thresher, violet skin, 1996

    NM $3   MIP $10

SERIES 2, FIGURES

Blitz, 1997

    NM $3   MIP $10

Brain Drain, 1997

    NM $3   MIP $10

Corn Boy, 1997

    NM $3   MIP $10

Poacher, 1997

    NM $3   MIP $10

Quartz, 1997

    NM $3   MIP $10

Smuggler, 1997

    NM $3   MIP $10

Total Justice
(Kenner, 1996)

FIGURES

Aquaman, black armor, 1996, Kenner

    NM $5   MIP $8

**Aquaman, w/Hydro-Blasting Spear,
gold armor**, 1996, Kenner

    NM $7   MIP $8

(Kenner)

Batman, 1996, Kenner, w/flight armor
and glider cape

    NM $3   MIP $7

Batman, Fractal Armor, 1986, Kenner

    NM $2   MIP $7

Black Lightning, 1996, Kenner

    NM $2   MIP $7

Darkseid, 1996, Kenner, w/omega-
effect capture claw

    NM $2   MIP $7

Despero, 1996, Kenner, w/galactic
body blow attack

    NM $2   MIP $7

Flash, The, 1996, Kenner, w/velocity
power suit

    NM $2   MIP $7

Green Arrow, 1996, Kenner

    NM $2   MIP $7

(Kenner)

Green Lantern, 1996, Kenner

    NM $2   MIP $7

Hawkman, 1996, Kenner, w/talon

    NM $2   MIP $5

Huntress, 1996, Kenner

    NM $3   MIP $7

Parallax, 1996, Kenner

    NM $3   MIP $7

(Kenner)

Robin, 1996, Kenner, w/spinning razor disc and battle staff
    NM $3   **MIP** $7

(Kenner)

Superman, 1996, Kenner, w/shield and kryptonite ray emitter
    NM $3   **MIP** $7

Toy Story (Thinkway, 1996)

5" FIGURES

Alien, 1996, Thinkway
    NM $5   **MIP** $15

Boxer Buzz, 1996, Thinkway
    NM $4   **MIP** $8

Crawling Baby Face, 1996, Thinkway
    NM $3   **MIP** $9

Fighting Woody, 1996, Thinkway
    NM $3   **MIP** $9

Flying Buzz (Rocket), 1996, Thinkway
    NM $4   **MIP** $8

Hamm, 1996, Thinkway
    NM $4   **MIP** $8

Karate Buzz, 1996, Thinkway
    NM $4   **MIP** $8

Kicking Woody, 1996, Thinkway
    NM $4   **MIP** $8

Quick-Draw Woody, 1996, Thinkway
    NM $4   **MIP** $8

Rex, 1996, Thinkway
    NM $4   **MIP** $8

Super Sonic Buzz, 1996, Thinkway
    NM $3   **MIP** $9

LARGE FIGURES

Talking Buzz Lightyear, 1996, Thinkway
    NM $15   **MIP** $50

Talking Woody, 1996, Thinkway
    NM $15   **MIP** $60

Toys R Us Exclusives

25th Anniversary Wolverine (March 2007), 2007, Toy Biz, silver version of Toy Biz Series 6
    NM $4   **MIP** $8

Black Queen (October 2007), 2007
    NM $6   **MIP** $12

Diamond Emma Frost (March 2007), 2007, Hasbro, clear plastic version of Hasbro Series I
    NM $4   **MIP** $8

Transformers (Hasbro, 1984-1995)

GENERATION 1, SERIES 1, 1984

Bluestreak, silver, 1984, Hasbro
    NM $85   **MIP** $600

Brawn, 1984, Hasbro
    NM $12   **MIP** $70

Bumblebee, red, 1984, Hasbro
    NM $22   **MIP** $110

Bumblebee, yellow, 1984, Hasbro
    NM $24   **MIP** $110

Bumblejumper, 1984, Hasbro
    NM $75   **MIP** $350

Cliffjumper, red, 1984, Hasbro
    NM $25   **MIP** $85

Cliffjumper, yellow, 1984, Hasbro
    NM $22   **MIP** $85

Frenzy & Laserbeak, 1984, Hasbro
    NM n/a   **MIP** $150

Gears, 1984, Hasbro
    NM $12   **MIP** $80

Hound, 1984, Hasbro
    NM $55   **MIP** $300

Huffer, 1984, Hasbro
    NM $12   **MIP** $70

Ironhide, 1984, Hasbro
    NM $65   **MIP** $275

Jazz, 1984, Hasbro
    NM $75   **MIP** $350

(Lenny Lee)

Megatron, 1984, Hasbro, deception leader turns from handgun to robot
    NM $100   **MIP** $275

Mirage, 1984, Hasbro
    NM $75   **MIP** $275

Optimus Prime w/gray or blue roller, 1984, Hasbro
    NM $100   **MIP** $275

Prowl, 1984, Hasbro
    NM $85   **MIP** $275

Ratchet w/cross, 1984, Hasbro
    NM $65   **MIP** $275

Ratchet w/out cross, 1984, Hasbro
    NM $65   **MIP** $250

Rumble & Ravage, 1984, Hasbro
    NM n/a   **MIP** $175

Sideswipe, 1984, Hasbro
    NM $65   **MIP** $375

Skywarp, 1984, Hasbro
    NM $70   **MIP** $210

Soundwave and Buzzsaw, 1984, Hasbro
    NM $75   **MIP** $250

Starscream, 1984, Hasbro
    NM $80   **MIP** $310

Sunstreaker, 1984, Hasbro
    NM $75   **MIP** $400

Thundercracker, 1984, Hasbro
    NM $60   **MIP** $200

Trailbreaker, 1984, Hasbro
    NM $65   **MIP** $300

Wheeljack, 1984, Hasbro
    NM $70   **MIP** $275

Windcharger, 1984, Hasbro
    NM $12   **MIP** $70

GENERATION 1, SERIES 2, 1985

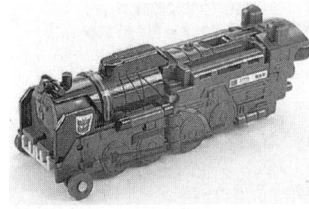

(KP Photo, Karen O'Brien collection)

Astrotrain, 1985, Hasbro, triple changer
NM $50   MIP $210

Barrage, 1985, Hasbro
NM $35   MIP $75

Beachcomber, 1985, Hasbro
NM $14   MIP $110

Blaster, 1985, Hasbro
NM $60   MIP $120

Blitzwing, 1985, Hasbro
NM $50   MIP $200

Bombshell, 1985, Hasbro
NM $15   MIP $40

Bonecrusher, 1985, Hasbro
NM $15   MIP $65

Brawn, 1985, Hasbro
NM $12   MIP $70

Brawn w/Minispy, 1985, Hasbro
NM $18   MIP $110

Bumblebee w/Minispy, yellow, 1985, Hasbro
NM $28   MIP $125

Bumblebee, red, 1985, Hasbro
NM $22   MIP $100

Bumblebee, yellow, 1985, Hasbro
NM $24   MIP $100

Chop Shop, 1985, Hasbro
NM $30   MIP $65

Cliffjumper w/Minispy, red, 1985, Hasbro
NM $32   MIP $100

Cliffjumper, red, 1985, Hasbro
NM $25   MIP $75

Cliffjumper, yellow, 1985, Hasbro
NM $22   MIP $85

Cosmos, 1985, Hasbro
NM $12   MIP $35

Dirge, 1985, Hasbro
NM $55   MIP $155

Gears, 1985, Hasbro
NM $12   MIP $65

Gears w/Minispy, 1985, Hasbro
NM $20   MIP $90

Grapple, 1985, Hasbro
NM $70   MIP $200

(Lenny Lee)

Grimlock, 1985, Hasbro
NM $75   MIP $180

Hoist, 1985, Hasbro
NM $65   MIP $200

Hook, 1985, Hasbro
NM $15   MIP $60

Huffer, 1985, Hasbro
NM $12   MIP $50

Huffer w/Minispy, 1985, Hasbro
NM $20   MIP $70

Inferno, 1985, Hasbro
NM $75   MIP $225

(Lenny Lee)

Jetfire, 1985, Hasbro, red and white pieces transform from folding-wing jet bomber to robot
NM $160   MIP $375

Kickback, 1985, Hasbro
NM $15   MIP $40

Long Haul, 1985, Hasbro
NM $15   MIP $60

Mixmaster, 1985, Hasbro
NM $15   MIP $60

Omega Supreme, 1985, Hasbro
NM $210   MIP $350

Perceptor, 1985, Hasbro
NM $60   MIP $180

Powerglide, 1985, Hasbro
NM $12   MIP $40

Ramjet, 1985, Hasbro
NM $55   MIP $200

Ransack, 1985, Hasbro
NM $25   MIP $65

Red Alert, 1985, Hasbro
NM $55   MIP $225

Roadbuster, 1985, Hasbro
NM $100   MIP $300

Scavenger, 1985, Hasbro
NM $15   MIP $60

Scrapper, 1985, Hasbro
NM $15   MIP $60

Seaspray, 1985, Hasbro
NM $8   MIP $40

Shockwave, 1985, Hasbro
NM $120   MIP $325

Shrapnel, 1985, Hasbro
NM $25   MIP $100

Skids, 1985, Hasbro
NM $65   MIP $300

Slag, 1985, Hasbro
NM $60   MIP $225

Sludge, 1985, Hasbro
NM $60   MIP $250

Smokescreen, 1985, Hasbro
NM $75   MIP $225

Snarl, 1985, Hasbro
NM $60   MIP $270

Thrust, 1985, Hasbro
NM $55   MIP $225

Topspin, 1985, Hasbro
NM $20   MIP $75

Tracks, 1985, Hasbro
NM $65   MIP $225

Twin Twist, 1985, Hasbro
NM $20   MIP $75

Venom, 1985, Hasbro
NM $35   MIP $110

Warpath, 1985, Hasbro
NM $12   MIP $50

Whirl, 1985, Hasbro
NM $70   MIP $250

Windcharger, 1985, Hasbro
NM $10   MIP $70

Windcharger w/Minispy, 1985, Hasbro
NM $20   MIP $85

GENERATION 1, SERIES 3, 1986

Air Raid, 1986, Hasbro
NM $15   MIP $55

Air Raid w/Patch, 1986, Hasbro
NM $18   MIP $60

Beachcomber, 1986, Hasbro
NM $10   MIP $30

Beachcomber w/Patch, 1986, Hasbro
 NM $12 **MIP** $35

Blades, 1986, Hasbro
 NM $13 **MIP** $50

Blades, plastic chest, 1986, Hasbro
 NM $10 **MIP** $45

Blast Off, metal treads, 1986, Hasbro
 NM $22 **MIP** $60

Blast Off, plastic chest, 1986, Hasbro
 NM $10 **MIP** $55

Blurr, 1986, Hasbro
 NM $45 **MIP** $200

Blurr w/Poster, 1986, Hasbro
 NM $55 **MIP** $225

Brawl, metal treads, 1986, Hasbro
 NM $14 **MIP** $50

Brawl, plastic treads, 1986, Hasbro
 NM $12 **MIP** $45

Breakdown, 1986, Hasbro
 NM $15 **MIP** $55

Breakdown w/Patch, 1986, Hasbro
 NM $18 **MIP** $60

Broadside, 1986, Hasbro
 NM $45 **MIP** $130

Broadside w/Poster, 1986, Hasbro
 NM $32 **MIP** $75

Bumblebee, 1986, Hasbro
 NM $22 **MIP** $70

Bumblebee w/Patch, 1986, Hasbro
 NM $25 **MIP** $75

Cosmos, 1986, Hasbro
 NM $10 **MIP** $30

Cosmos w/Patch, 1986, Hasbro
 NM $13 **MIP** $32

Cyclonus, 1986, Hasbro
 NM $65 **MIP** $230

Dead End, 1986, Hasbro
 NM $15 **MIP** $55

Dead End w/Patch, 1986, Hasbro
 NM $18 **MIP** $60

Divebomb w/Poster, plastic body, 1986, Hasbro
 NM $45 **MIP** $85

Divebomb, metal body, 1986, Hasbro
 NM $55 **MIP** $175

Divebomb, plastic body, 1986, Hasbro
 NM $40 **MIP** $175

Drag Strip, 1986, Hasbro
 NM $15 **MIP** $55

Drag Strip w/Patch, 1986, Hasbro
 NM $18 **MIP** $60

Eject & Ramhorn, 1986, Hasbro
 NM n/a **MIP** $140

Fireflight, 1986, Hasbro
 NM $15 **MIP** $55

Fireflight w/Patch, 1986, Hasbro
 NM $18 **MIP** $60

First Aid, 1986, Hasbro
 NM $15 **MIP** $60

First Aid, plastic chest, 1986, Hasbro
 NM $12 **MIP** $55

Frenzy & Ratbat, 1986, Hasbro
 NM n/a **MIP** $180

Galvatron, 1986, Hasbro, City Commander
 NM $70 **MIP** $275

Gnaw, 1986, Hasbro
 NM $50 **MIP** $175

Groove, 1986, Hasbro
 NM $15 **MIP** $50

Groove, silver chest, 1986, Hasbro
 NM $18 **MIP** $60

Headstrong, metal body, 1986, Hasbro
 NM $55 **MIP** $175

Headstrong, plastic body, 1986, Hasbro
 NM $45 **MIP** $175

Hot Rod w/poster, plastic toes, 1986, Hasbro
 NM $65 **MIP** $350

Hot Rod, metal toes, 1986, Hasbro
 NM $75 **MIP** $360

Hot Spot, 1986, Hasbro
 NM $40 **MIP** $150

Hubcap, 1986, Hasbro
 NM $12 **MIP** $40

Hubcap w/Patch, 1986, Hasbro
 NM $14 **MIP** $42

Kup, plastic tires and wheels, 1986, Hasbro
 NM $30 **MIP** $210

Kup, rubber tires and metal wheels, 1986, Hasbro
 NM $35 **MIP** $225

Metroplex, 1986, Hasbro
 NM $95 **MIP** $400

Motormaster, 1986, Hasbro
 NM $40 **MIP** $200

Octane, 1986, Hasbro
 NM $50 **MIP** $200

Octane w/Poster, 1986, Hasbro
 NM $55 **MIP** $210

Onslaught, 1986, Hasbro
 NM $35 **MIP** $150

Outback, 1986, Hasbro
 NM $15 **MIP** $55

Outback w/Patch, 1986, Hasbro
 NM $18 **MIP** $60

Pipes, 1986, Hasbro
 NM $10 **MIP** $45

Pipes w/Patch, 1986, Hasbro
 NM $13 **MIP** $48

Powerglide, 1986, Hasbro
 NM $12 **MIP** $35

Powerglide w/Patch, 1986, Hasbro
 NM $15 **MIP** $45

Rampage, metal body, 1986, Hasbro
 NM $55 **MIP** $175

Rampage, plastic body, 1986, Hasbro
 NM $45 **MIP** $175

Ranamuck, 1986, Hasbro
 NM $12 **MIP** $45

Razorclaw, metal body, 1986, Hasbro
 NM $60 **MIP** $175

Razorclaw, plastic body, 1986, Hasbro
 NM $55 **MIP** $175

Reflector, 1986, Hasbro
 NM $225 **MIP** $375

Rewind & Steeljaw, 1986, Hasbro
 NM n/a **MIP** $140

Rodimus Prime, metal toes, 1986, Hasbro
 NM $70 **MIP** $175

Rodimus Prime, plastic toes, 1986, Hasbro
 NM $62 **MIP** $175

Runabout, 1986, Hasbro
 NM $12 **MIP** $45

Sandstorm, metal or plastic toes, 1986, Hasbro
 NM $38 **MIP** $130

Scourge, 1986, Hasbro
 NM $48 **MIP** $230

Seaspray, 1986, Hasbro
 NM $10 **MIP** $30

Seaspray w/Patch, 1986, Hasbro
 NM $13 **MIP** $42

Silverbolt, 1986, Hasbro
 NM $40 **MIP** $220

Sky Lynx, 1986, Hasbro
 NM $95 **MIP** $350

Skydive, 1986, Hasbro
 NM $15 **MIP** $55

Skydive w/Patch, 1986, Hasbro
 NM $18 **MIP** $60

Slingshot, 1986, Hasbro
 NM $15 **MIP** $55

Slingshot w/Patch, 1986, Hasbro
 NM $18 **MIP** $60

Springer, metal or plastic front, 1986, Hasbro
 NM $55 **MIP** $210

Streetwise, 1986, Hasbro
 NM $15 **MIP** $50

Swerve, 1986, Hasbro
 NM $10 **MIP** $45

Swerve w/Patch, 1986, Hasbro
          NM $13   MIP $50

Swindle, gray plastic chest, 1986, Hasbro
          NM $12   MIP $50

Swindle, metal treads, 1986, Hasbro
          NM $14   MIP $55

Tailgate, 1986, Hasbro
          NM $10   MIP $50

Tailgate w/Patch, 1986, Hasbro
          NM $13   MIP $55

Tantrum w/Poster, plastic body, 1986, Hasbro
          NM $45   MIP $80

Tantrum, metal body, 1986, Hasbro
          NM $50   MIP $125

Tantrum, plastic body, 1986, Hasbro
          NM $40   MIP $125

Trypticon, 1986, Hasbro, battery-operated, walks
          NM $135   MIP $500

Ultra Mangus, 1986, Hasbro
          NM $75   MIP $160

Vortex, metal treads, 1986, Hasbro
          NM $22   MIP $65

Vortex, plastic chest, 1986, Hasbro
          NM $18   MIP $60

Warpath, 1986, Hasbro
          NM $10   MIP $45

Warpath w/Patch, 1986, Hasbro
          NM $13   MIP $52

Wheelie, 1986, Hasbro
          NM $10   MIP $45

Wheelie w/Patch, 1986, Hasbro
          NM $13   MIP $58

Wildrider, 1986, Hasbro
          NM $15   MIP $55

Wildrider w/Patch, 1986, Hasbro
          NM $18   MIP $60

Wreck-gar, 1986, Hasbro
          NM $40   MIP $160

Wreck-gar w/Poster, 1986, Hasbro
          NM $45   MIP $180

GENERATION 1, SERIES 4, 1987

Afterburner, 1987, Hasbro
          NM $20   MIP $50

Afterburner w/Decoy, 1987, Hasbro
          NM $24   MIP $60

Air Raid, 1987, Hasbro
          NM $15   MIP $45

Air Raid w/Decoy, 1987, Hasbro
          NM $20   MIP $55

Apeface, 1987, Hasbro
          NM $65   MIP $175

Battletrap, 1987, Hasbro
          NM $35   MIP $45

Blades w/Decoy, plastic chest, 1987, Hasbro
          NM $13   MIP $55

Blades, plastic chest, 1987, Hasbro
          NM $13   MIP $50

Blast Off w/Decoy, plastic chest, 1987, Hasbro
          NM $25   MIP $60

Blot w/Decoy, 1987, Hasbro
          NM $12   MIP $45

Blurr Targetmaster, 1987, Hasbro
          NM $85   MIP $325

Brainstorm, 1987, Hasbro
          NM $75   MIP $175

Brawl w/Decoy, plastic treads, 1987, Hasbro
          NM $16   MIP $50

Breakdown w/Decoy, 1987, Hasbro
          NM $20   MIP $60

Chase, 1987, Hasbro
          NM $12   MIP $30

Chase w/Decoy, 1987, Hasbro
          NM $14   MIP $35

Chromedome, 1987, Hasbro
          NM $70   MIP $160

Cloudraker & Fastlane, 1987, Hasbro
          NM $50   MIP $110

(KP photo, Karen O'Brien collection)

Computron Gift Set, 1987, Hasbro, all five Technobots in one boxed set
          NM $210   MIP $550

Crosshairs, 1987, Hasbro
          NM $65   MIP $135

Cutthroat w/Decoy, 1987, Hasbro
          NM $12   MIP $45

Cyclonus, 1987, Hasbro
          NM $160   MIP $450

Dead End w/Decoy, 1987, Hasbro
          NM $20   MIP $60

Doublecross, 1987, Hasbro
          NM $50   MIP $100

Drag Strip w/Decoy, 1987, Hasbro
          NM $20   MIP $60

Fireflight, 1987, Hasbro
          NM $15   MIP $55

Fireflight w/Decoy, 1987, Hasbro
          NM $20   MIP $65

First Aid w/Decoy, plastic chest, 1987, Hasbro
          NM $22   MIP $60

First Aid, plastic chest, 1987, Hasbro
          NM $15   MIP $55

Flywheels, 1987, Hasbro
          NM $35   MIP $45

Fortess Maximus, 1987, Hasbro
          NM $600   MIP $1800

Freeway, 1987, Hasbro
          NM $10   MIP $30

Freeway w/Decoy, 1987, Hasbro
          NM $12   MIP $35

Goldbug, 1987, Hasbro
          NM $10   MIP $55

Goldbug w/Decoy, 1987, Hasbro
          NM $14   MIP $60

Groove w/Decoy, silver chest, 1987, Hasbro
          NM $14   MIP $60

Groove, silver chest, 1987, Hasbro
          NM $15   MIP $55

Grotusque, 1987, Hasbro
          NM $45   MIP $110

Hardhead, 1987, Hasbro
          NM $60   MIP $160

Highbrow, 1987, Hasbro
          NM $70   MIP $180

Hot Rod Targetmaster, 1987, Hasbro
          NM $210   MIP $575

Hun-Grrr, 1987, Hasbro
          NM $50   MIP $125

Kup Targetmaster, 1987, Hasbro
          NM $85   MIP $300

Lightspeed, 1987, Hasbro
          NM $20   MIP $50

Lightspeed w/Decoy, 1987, Hasbro
          NM $24   MIP $55

Mindwipe, 1987, Hasbro
          NM $60   MIP $150

Misfire, 1987, Hasbro
          NM $70   MIP $225

Nosecone, 1987, Hasbro
          NM $12   MIP $45

Nosecone w/Decoy, 1987, Hasbro
          NM $16   MIP $50

Overkill & Slugfest, 1987, Hasbro
          NM n/a   MIP $150

Pointblank, 1987, Hasbro
          NM $60   MIP $135

Punch/Counterpunch, 1987, Hasbro
          NM $60   MIP $120

Repugnus, 1987, Hasbro
          NM $50   MIP $120

Rippersnapper w/Decoy, 1987, Hasbro
NM $14   MIP $45

Rollbar, 1987, Hasbro
NM $10   MIP $30

Rollbar w/Decoy, 1987, Hasbro
NM $13   MIP $34

Scattershot, 1987, Hasbro
NM $40   MIP $135

Scorponok, 1987, Hasbro
NM $210   MIP $550

Scourge & Targetmaster, 1987, Hasbro
NM $225   MIP $600

Searchlight, 1987, Hasbro
NM $10   MIP $30

Searchlight w/Decoy, 1987, Hasbro
NM $14   MIP $35

Sinnertwin w/Decoy, 1987, Hasbro
NM $12   MIP $45

Sixshot, 1987, Hasbro
NM $70   MIP $200

Skullcruncher, 1987, Hasbro
NM $60   MIP $125

Skydive, 1987, Hasbro
NM $15   MIP $55

Skydive w/Decoy, 1987, Hasbro
NM $18   MIP $60

Slingshot, 1987, Hasbro
NM $15   MIP $55

Slingshot w/Decoy, 1987, Hasbro
NM $18   MIP $60

Slugslinger, 1987, Hasbro
NM $75   MIP $225

Snapdragon, 1987, Hasbro
NM $75   MIP $200

Strafe, 1987, Hasbro
NM $20   MIP $55

Strafe w/Decoy, 1987, Hasbro
NM $24   MIP $60

Streetwise, 1987, Hasbro
NM $18   MIP $50

Streetwise w/Decoy, 1987, Hasbro
NM $22   MIP $55

Sureshot, 1987, Hasbro
NM $65   MIP $125

Swindle w/Decoy, gray plastic chest, 1987, Hasbro
NM $12   MIP $50

Triggerhappy, 1987, Hasbro
NM $75   MIP $225

Vortex w/Decoy, plastic chest, 1987, Hasbro
NM $22   MIP $65

Weirdwolf, 1987, Hasbro
NM $60   MIP $125

Wideload, 1987, Hasbro
NM $10   MIP $30

Wideload w/Decoy, 1987, Hasbro
NM $14   MIP $35

Wildrider w/Decoy, 1987, Hasbro
NM $20   MIP $60

Wingspan & Pounce, 1987, Hasbro
NM $50   MIP $125

GENERATION 1, SERIES 5, 1988

Backstreet, 1988, Hasbro
NM $12   MIP $35

Beastbox & Squawktalk, 1988, Hasbro
NM n/a   MIP $150

Bomb-Burst, 1988, Hasbro
NM $60   MIP $120

Bugly, 1988, Hasbro
NM $55   MIP $110

Carnivac, 1988, Hasbro
NM $65   MIP $110

Catilla, 1988, Hasbro
NM $60   MIP $100

Chainclaw, 1988, Hasbro
NM $55   MIP $100

Cindersaur, 1988, Hasbro
NM $10   MIP $40

Cloudburst, clear insert, 1988, Hasbro
NM $55   MIP $110

Crankcase, 1988, Hasbro
NM $12   MIP $35

Darkwing, 1988, Hasbro
NM $70   MIP $150

Dogfight, 1988, Hasbro
NM $15   MIP $35

Doubledealer, 1988, Hasbro
NM $75   MIP $135

Dreadwind, 1988, Hasbro
NM $70   MIP $150

Fangry, 1988, Hasbro
NM $60   MIP $115

Finback, 1988, Hasbro
NM $55   MIP $110

Fizzle, 1988, Hasbro
NM $12   MIP $45

Flamefeather, 1988, Hasbro
NM $12   MIP $40

Getaway, 1988, Hasbro
NM $60   MIP $150

Grand Slam & Raindance, 1988, Hasbro
NM n/a   MIP $125

Groundbreaker, 1988, Hasbro
NM $95   MIP $175

Gunrunner, 1988, Hasbro
NM $45   MIP $100

Guzzle, 1988, Hasbro
NM $12   MIP $45

Horri-Bull, 1988, Hasbro
NM $55   MIP $115

Hosehead, 1988, Hasbro
NM $60   MIP $165

Iguanus, 1988, Hasbro
NM $50   MIP $110

Joyride, 1988, Hasbro
NM $60   MIP $150

Landfill, 1988, Hasbro
NM $25   MIP $85

Landmine, clear insert, 1988, Hasbro
NM $55   MIP $110

Nautilator, 1988, Hasbro
NM $30   MIP $65

Needlenose, 1988, Hasbro
NM $40   MIP $150

Nightbeat, 1988, Hasbro
NM $65   MIP $175

Overbite, 1988, Hasbro
NM $30   MIP $65

Override, 1988, Hasbro
NM $15   MIP $35

Powermaster Optimus Prime, 1988, Hasbro
NM $60   MIP $150

Quake, 1988, Hasbro
NM $30   MIP $100

Quickmix, 1988, Hasbro
NM $25   MIP $85

Quickswitch, 1988, Hasbro
NM $45   MIP $120

Roadgrabber, 1988, Hasbro
NM $45   MIP $110

Ruckus, 1988, Hasbro
NM $18   MIP $35

Scoop, 1988, Hasbro
NM $25   MIP $85

Seawing, 1988, Hasbro
NM $25   MIP $60

Siren, 1988, Hasbro
NM $65   MIP $165

Sizzle, 1988, Hasbro
NM $12   MIP $45

Skalor, 1988, Hasbro
NM $30   MIP $65

Skullgrin, clear insert, 1988, Hasbro
NM $55   MIP $110

Sky High, 1988, Hasbro
NM $75   MIP $175

Slapdash, 1988, Hasbro
NM $65   MIP $150

Snaptrap, 1988, Hasbro
NM $70   MIP $150

Snarler, 1988, Hasbro
NM $55   MIP $110

Sparkstalker, 1988, Hasbro
NM $12   MIP $40

Spinister, 1988, Hasbro
NM $35   MIP $110

Splashdown, 1988, Hasbro
NM $55   MIP $110

Squeezeplay, 1988, Hasbro
NM $55   MIP $115

Submarauder, 1988, Hasbro
NM $50   MIP $110

Tentakil, 1988, Hasbro
NM $35   MIP $65

Waverider, 1988, Hasbro
NM $45   MIP $100

Windsweeper, 1988, Hasbro
NM $15   MIP $35

GENERATION 1, SERIES 6, 1989

Air Strike Patrol, 1989, Hasbro
NM $12   MIP $30

Airwave, 1989, Hasbro
NM $18   MIP $35

Battle Patrol, 1989, Hasbro
NM $12   MIP $30

Birdbrain, 1989, Hasbro
NM $30   MIP $75

Bludgeon, 1989, Hasbro
NM $75   MIP $175

Bomb-Burst, 1989, Hasbro
NM $40   MIP $70

Bristleback, 1989, Hasbro
NM $30   MIP $75

Bumblebee, pretender, 1989, Hasbro
NM $40   MIP $70

Cloudburst, 1989, Hasbro
NM $40   MIP $75

Countdown, 1989, Hasbro
NM $80   MIP $110

Crossblades, 1989, Hasbro
NM $80   MIP $125

Doubleheader, 1989, Hasbro
NM $40   MIP $90

Erector, 1989, Hasbro
NM $18   MIP $30

Flattop, 1989, Hasbro
NM $18   MIP $30

Greasepit, 1989, Hasbro
NM $18   MIP $35

Grimlock, pretender, 1989, Hasbro
NM $40   MIP $75

Groundshaker, 1989, Hasbro
NM $40   MIP $65

Hot House, 1989, Hasbro
NM $18   MIP $30

Icepick, 1989, Hasbro
NM $35   MIP $65

Ironworks, 1989, Hasbro
NM $18   MIP $30

Jazz, pretender, 1989, Hasbro
NM $40   MIP $60

Landmine, 1989, Hasbro
NM $40   MIP $60

Longtooth, 1989, Hasbro
NM $40   MIP $90

Octopunch, 1989, Hasbro
NM $40   MIP $90

Off Road Patrol, 1989, Hasbro
NM $18   MIP $30

Overload, 1989, Hasbro
NM $18   MIP $30

Pincher, 1989, Hasbro
NM $40   MIP $90

Race Car Patrol, 1989, Hasbro
NM $14   MIP $30

Rescue Patrol, 1989, Hasbro
NM $14   MIP $30

Roadblock, 1989, Hasbro
NM $70   MIP $110

Roughstuff, 1989, Hasbro
NM $18   MIP $30

Scowl, 1989, Hasbro
NM $30   MIP $75

Skullgrin, 1989, Hasbro
NM $40   MIP $70

Skyhammer, 1989, Hasbro
NM $40   MIP $75

Skyhopper, 1989, Hasbro
NM $40   MIP $60

Skystalker, 1989, Hasbro
NM $60   MIP $80

Slog, 1989, Hasbro
NM $30   MIP $75

Sports Car Patrol, 1989, Hasbro
NM $14   MIP $30

Starscream, pretender, 1989, Hasbro
NM $25   MIP $60

Stranglehold, 1989, Hasbro
NM $30   MIP $80

Submarauder, 1989, Hasbro
NM $35   MIP $70

Thunderwing, 1989, Hasbro
NM $90   MIP $200

Vroom, 1989, Hasbro
NM $110   MIP $160

Waverider, 1989, Hasbro
NM $40   MIP $70

Wildfly, 1989, Hasbro
NM $30   MIP $70

GENERATION 1, SERIES 7, 1990

Air Patrol, 1990, Hasbro
NM $18   MIP $35

Anti-Aircraft Base, 1990, Hasbro
NM $55   MIP $80

Astro Squad, 1990, Hasbro
NM $18   MIP $40

Axer, 1990, Hasbro
NM $45   MIP $65

Banzai-Tron, 1990, Hasbro
NM $18   MIP $30

Battle Squad, 1990, Hasbro
NM $18   MIP $40

Battlefield Headquarters, 1990, Hasbro
NM $75   MIP $125

Blaster, action master, 1990, Hasbro
NM $18   MIP $25

Bumblebee, action master, 1990, Hasbro
NM $14   MIP $22

Cannon Transport, 1990, Hasbro
NM $50   MIP $60

Construction Patrol, 1990, Hasbro
NM $18   MIP $35

Constructor Squad, 1990, Hasbro
NM $18   MIP $30

Devastator, action master, 1990, Hasbro
NM $20   MIP $60

Erector, 1990, Hasbro
NM $14   MIP $30

Flattop, 1990, Hasbro
NM $18   MIP $30

Grimlock, action master, 1990, Hasbro
NM $20   MIP $30

Gutcruncher, 1990, Hasbro
NM $70   MIP $100

Hot Rod Patrol, 1990, Hasbro
NM $18   MIP $35

Inferno, action master, 1990, Hasbro
NM $18   MIP $25

Jackpot, 1990, Hasbro
NM $14   MIP $20

Jazz, action master, 1990, Hasbro
NM $18   MIP $35

Kick-Off, 1990, Hasbro
NM $18   MIP $20

Krok, 1990, Hasbro
NM $18   MIP $20

Mainframe, 1990, Hasbro
NM $14   MIP $20

Megatron, action master, 1990, Hasbro
NM $100   MIP $200

Metro Squad, 1990, Hasbro
NM $18   MIP $35

Military Patrol, 1990, Hasbro
  NM $25   MIP $40

Missile Launcher, 1990, Hasbro
  NM $55   MIP $85

Monster Trucks Patrol, 1990, Hasbro
  NM $18   MIP $40

Optimus Prime, action master, 1990, Hasbro
  NM $100   MIP $250

Overload, 1990, Hasbro
  NM $18   MIP $25

Over-Run, 1990, Hasbro
  NM $45   MIP $55

Prowl, action master, 1990, Hasbro
  NM $50   MIP $70

Race Track Patrol, 1990, Hasbro
  NM $15   MIP $35

Rad, 1990, Hasbro
  NM $14   MIP $25

Rollout, 1990, Hasbro
  NM $14   MIP $22

Roughstuff, 1990, Hasbro
  NM $18   MIP $30

Shockwave, action master, 1990, Hasbro
  NM $18   MIP $30

Skyfall, 1990, Hasbro
  NM $15   MIP $20

Snarl, action master, 1990, Hasbro
  NM $15   MIP $25

Soundwave, action master, 1990, Hasbro
  NM $20   MIP $30

Sprocket, 1990, Hasbro
  NM $55   MIP $75

Starscream, action master, 1990, Hasbro
  NM $50   MIP $70

Tanker Truck, 1990, Hasbro
  NM $55   MIP $85

Treadshot, 1990, Hasbro
  NM $12   MIP $30

Wheeljack, action master, 1990, Hasbro
  NM $55   MIP $75

GENERATION 2, SERIES 1, 1993

Afterburner, 1993, Hasbro
  NM $3   MIP $12

Bonecrusher, orange, 1993, Hasbro
  NM $5   MIP $17

Bonecrusher, yellow, 1993, Hasbro
  NM $3   MIP $12

Bumblebee, 1993, Hasbro
  NM $5   MIP $15

Deluge, changes colors, 1993, Hasbro
  NM $5   MIP $15

Drench, changes colors, 1993, Hasbro
  NM $5   MIP $15

Eagle Eye, 1993, Hasbro
  NM $3   MIP $12

Gobots, changes colors, 1993, Hasbro
  NM $5   MIP $15

Grimlock, dark blue, 1993, Hasbro
  NM $20   MIP $45

Grimlock, silver, 1993, Hasbro
  NM $25   MIP $75

Grimlock, turquoise, 1993, Hasbro
  NM $40   MIP $120

Hook, orange, 1993, Hasbro
  NM $5   MIP $15

Hook, yellow, 1993, Hasbro
  NM $3   MIP $12

Hubcap, 1993, Hasbro
  NM $5   MIP $15

Inferno, 1993, Hasbro
  NM $15   MIP $40

Jazz, 1993, Hasbro
  NM $40   MIP $120

Jetstorm, changes colors, 1993, Hasbro
  NM $5   MIP $15

Long Haul, orange, 1993, Hasbro
  NM $5   MIP $15

Long Haul, yellow, 1993, Hasbro
  NM $3   MIP $12

Mixmaster, orange, 1993, Hasbro
  NM $5   MIP $15

Mixmaster, yellow, 1993, Hasbro
  NM $3   MIP $12

Ramjet, missiles grouped, 1993, Hasbro
  NM $15   MIP $45

Ramjet, missiles separate, 1993, Hasbro
  NM $20   MIP $55

Rapido, 1993, Hasbro
  NM $3   MIP $12

Scavenger, orange, 1993, Hasbro
  NM $5   MIP $15

Scavenger, yellow, 1993, Hasbro
  NM $3   MIP $12

Scrapper, orange, 1993, Hasbro
  NM $5   MIP $15

Scrapper, yellow, 1993, Hasbro
  NM $5   MIP $15

Seaspray, 1993, Hasbro
  NM $5   MIP $15

Sideswipe, 1993, Hasbro
  NM $35   MIP $65

Skram, 1993, Hasbro
  NM $5   MIP $15

Slag, green, 1993, Hasbro
  NM $20   MIP $60

Slag, red, 1993, Hasbro
  NM $25   MIP $75

Slag, silver, 1993, Hasbro
  NM $35   MIP $80

Snarl, green, 1993, Hasbro
  NM $20   MIP $60

Snarl, red, 1993, Hasbro
  NM $15   MIP $75

Snarl, silver, 1993, Hasbro
  NM $20   MIP $80

Starscream, missiles grouped, 1993, Hasbro
  NM $15   MIP $45

Starscream, missiles separate, 1993, Hasbro
  NM $20   MIP $55

Terradive, 1993, Hasbro
  NM $5   MIP $15

Turbofire, 1993, Hasbro
  NM $5   MIP $15

Windbreaker, 1993, Hasbro
  NM $5   MIP $15

Windrazor, 1993, Hasbro
  NM $5   MIP $15

GENERATION 2, SERIES 2, 1994

Air Raid, 1994, Hasbro
  NM $5   MIP $15

Blast Off, 1994, Hasbro
  NM $5   MIP $15

Brawl, 1994, Hasbro
  NM $8   MIP $20

Electro, 1994, Hasbro
  NM $5   MIP $15

Fireflight, 1994, Hasbro
  NM $5   MIP $15

Jolt, 1994, Hasbro
  NM $5   MIP $15

Leadfoot, 1994, Hasbro
  NM $3   MIP $12

Manta Ray, 1994, Hasbro
  NM $3   MIP $12

Megatron, purple and black camouflage, 1994, Hasbro
  NM $30   MIP $55

Onslaught, 1994, Hasbro
  NM $10   MIP $40

Optimus Prime, red and white, 1994, Hasbro
  NM $35   MIP $80

Powerdive, black rotors, 1994, Hasbro
  NM $8   MIP $20

Powerdive, red rotors, 1994, Hasbro
NM $3   **MIP** $12

Ransack, black rotors, 1994, Hasbro
NM $8   **MIP** $20

Ransack, red rotors, 1994, Hasbro
NM $3   **MIP** $12

Silverbolt, 1994, Hasbro, blue and red body
NM $15   **MIP** $40

Sizzle, 1994, Hasbro
NM $5   **MIP** $15

Skydive, 1994, Hasbro
NM $5   **MIP** $15

Slingshot, 1994, Hasbro
NM $5   **MIP** $15

Swindle, 1994, Hasbro
NM $5   **MIP** $15

Volt, 1994, Hasbro
NM $5   **MIP** $15

Vortex, 1994, Hasbro
NM $5   **MIP** $15

GENERATION 2, SERIES 3, 1995

Air Raid, 1995, Hasbro
NM $2   **MIP** $6

Blowout, 1995, Hasbro
NM $3   **MIP** $10

Bumblebee, 1995, Hasbro
NM $3   **MIP** $10

Dirtbag, 1995, Hasbro
NM $3   **MIP** $12

Double Clutch, 1995, Hasbro
NM $3   **MIP** $10

Firecracker, 1995, Hasbro
NM $3   **MIP** $10

Frenzy, 1995, Hasbro
NM $3   **MIP** $10

Gearhead, clear, 1995, Hasbro
NM $3   **MIP** $10

Gearhead, solid, 1995, Hasbro
NM $3   **MIP** $10

High Beam, 1995, Hasbro
NM $3   **MIP** $10

Hooligan, 1995, Hasbro
NM $2   **MIP** $6

Ironhide, 1995, Hasbro
NM $3   **MIP** $10

Jetfire, 1995, Hasbro
NM $2   **MIP** $6

Megatron, 1995, Hasbro
NM $3   **MIP** $10

Mirage, 1995, Hasbro
NM $3   **MIP** $10

Motormouth, clear, 1995, Hasbro
NM $3   **MIP** $10

Motormouth, solid, 1995, Hasbro
NM $3   **MIP** $10

Optimus Prime, 1995, Hasbro
NM $20   **MIP** $45

Roadblock, 1995, Hasbro
NM $3   **MIP** $12

Sideswipe, 1995, Hasbro
NM $3   **MIP** $10

Skyjack, 1995, Hasbro
NM $2   **MIP** $6

Soundwave, 1995, Hasbro
NM $3   **MIP** $10

Space Case, 1995, Hasbro
NM $2   **MIP** $6

Strafe, 1995, Hasbro
NM $2   **MIP** $6

Transformers: Beast Wars (Hasbro, 1996-1999)

BASIC BEAST, 1996

Airazor, 1996, Hasbro
NM $10   **MIP** $30

Armordillo, 1996, Hasbro
NM $5   **MIP** $15

Claw Jaw, 1996, Hasbro
NM $8   **MIP** $25

Drill Bit, 1996, Hasbro
NM $8   **MIP** $25

Iguanus, 1996, Hasbro
NM $10   **MIP** $30

Insecticon, 1996, Hasbro
NM $5   **MIP** $15

Lazorbeak, 1996, Hasbro
NM $8   **MIP** $25

Rattrap, 1996, Hasbro
NM $15   **MIP** $50

Razorbeast, 1996, Hasbro
NM $15   **MIP** $45

Razorclaw, 1996, Hasbro
NM $10   **MIP** $30

Snapper, 1996, Hasbro
NM $8   **MIP** $20

Snarl, 1996, Hasbro
NM $8   **MIP** $25

Terrorsaur, 1996, Hasbro
NM $15   **MIP** $50

BASIC BEAST, 1997

Powerpinch, 1997, Hasbro
NM $8   **MIP** $25

Spittor, 1997, Hasbro
NM $8   **MIP** $25

BASIC FUZORS, 1998

Air Hammer, 1998, Hasbro
NM $5   **MIP** $15

Bantor, 1998, Hasbro
NM $3   **MIP** $8

Buzzclaw, 1998, Hasbro
NM $3   **MIP** $8

Noctorro, 1998, Hasbro
NM $3   **MIP** $8

Quickstrike, 1998, Hasbro
NM $5   **MIP** $15

Terragator, 1998, Hasbro
NM $4   **MIP** $12

BASIC TRANSMETAL 2, 1999

Optimus Minor, 1999, Hasbro
NM $8   **MIP** $25

Scarem, 1999, Hasbro
NM $3   **MIP** $8

Sonar, 1999, Hasbro
NM $3   **MIP** $8

Spittor, 1999, Hasbro
NM $3   **MIP** $10

COMIC 2-PACK, 1996

Megatron, 1996, Hasbro
NM $15   **MIP** $50

Optimus Primal, 1996, Hasbro
NM $15   **MIP** $50

DELUXE BEAST, 1996

Blackarachnia, 1996, Hasbro
NM $40   **MIP** $115

Bonecrusher, 1996, Hasbro
NM $15   **MIP** $50

Buzz Saw, 1996, Hasbro
NM $25   **MIP** $75

Cheetor, blue eyes, 1996, Hasbro
NM $50   **MIP** $150

Cheetor, red eyes, 1996, Hasbro
NM $40   **MIP** $120

Cybershark, 1996, Hasbro
NM $30   **MIP** $90

Dinobot, 1996, Hasbro
NM $40   **MIP** $110

Jetstorm, 1996, Hasbro
NM $15   **MIP** $45

Rhinox, 1996, Hasbro
NM $40   **MIP** $110

Tarantulas, 1996, Hasbro
NM $40   **MIP** $125

Tigatron, 1996, Hasbro
NM $30   **MIP** $100

Waspinator, 1996, Hasbro
NM $40   **MIP** $125

Wolfang, 1996, Hasbro
NM $40   **MIP** $110

DELUXE BEAST, 1997

Grimlock, 1997, Hasbro
NM $25   MIP $75

K-9, 1997, Hasbro
NM $8   MIP $25

Manterror, 1997, Hasbro
NM $15   MIP $50

Retrax, 1997, Hasbro
NM $8   MIP $25

DELUXE FUZORS, 1998

Injector, 1998, Hasbro
NM $4   MIP $12

Silverbolt, 1998, Hasbro
NM $8   MIP $25

Sky Shadow, 1998, Hasbro
NM $4   MIP $12

Torca, 1998, Hasbro
NM $3   MIP $10

DELUXE TRANSMETAL 2, 1999

Iguanus, 1999, Hasbro
NM $3   MIP $10

Jawbreaker, 1999, Hasbro
NM $3   MIP $10

Ramulus, 1999, Hasbro
NM $5   MIP $15

Scourge, 1999, Hasbro
NM $4   MIP $12

DELUXE TRANSMETALS, 1998

Airazor, 1998, Hasbro
NM $8   MIP $20

Cheetor, 1998, Hasbro
NM $8   MIP $25

Rattrap, 1998, Hasbro
NM $10   MIP $30

Rhinox, 1998, Hasbro
NM $15   MIP $35

Tarantulas, 1998, Hasbro
NM $8   MIP $20

Terrorsaur, 1998, Hasbro
NM $5   MIP $15

Waspinator, 1998, Hasbro
NM $8   MIP $25

MEGA BEAST, 1996

B'Boom, 1996, Hasbro
NM $12   MIP $30

Polar Claw, 1996, Hasbro
NM $25   MIP $70

Scorponok, 1996, Hasbro
NM $18   MIP $60

MEGA BEAST, 1997

Inferno, 1997, Hasbro
NM $18   MIP $50

Transquito, 1997, Hasbro
NM $8   MIP $20

MEGA TRANSMETAL 2, 1999

Blackarachnia, 1999, Hasbro
NM $15   MIP $45

Cybershark, 1999, Hasbro
NM $5   MIP $15

MEGA TRANSMETALS, 1998

Megatron, 1998, Hasbro
NM $8   MIP $20

Optimus Primal, 1998, Hasbro
NM $8   MIP $25

Scavenger, 1998, Hasbro
NM $5   MIP $15

SUPER BEAST, 1998

Optimal Optimus, 1998, Hasbro
NM $20   MIP $50

ULTRA BEAST, 1996

Megatron, 1996, Hasbro
NM $15   MIP $50

Optimus Primal, 1996, Hasbro
NM $20   MIP $60

ULTRA TEAM, 1997

Magnaboss (Maximal Team)—Ironhide, Silverbolt, Prowl, 1997, Hasbro
NM $20   MIP $35

Tripredacus (Predacon Team)-Ram Horn, Sea Clamp, Cicadacon, 1997, Hasbro
NM $20   MIP $50

ULTRA TRANSMETAL 2, 1999

Megatron, 1999, Hasbro
NM $25   MIP $70

Tigerhawk, 1999, Hasbro
NM $20   MIP $55

ULTRA TRANSMETALS, 1998

Depth Charge, 1998, Hasbro
NM $15   MIP $40

Rampage, 1998, Hasbro
NM $8   MIP $20

VIDEO PACK-IN, 1998

Airazor, 1998, Hasbro
NM $8   MIP $25

Razorclaw, 1998, Hasbro
NM $8   MIP $25

Tron (Tomy, 1981)

FIGURES

Flynn, 1981, Tomy, disk
NM $20   MIP $50

Sark, 1981, Tomy, red figure w/disk
NM $20   MIP $50

Tron, 1981, Tomy, disk
NM $20   MIP $65

Warrior, 1981, Tomy, red figure w/staff
NM $22   MIP $55

VEHICLES

Light Cycle, 1981, Tomy, red or yellow
NM $35   MIP $95

Universal Monsters (Remco, 1979)

8" FIGURES

Creature From the Black Lagoon, 1979
NM $80   MIP $210

Dracula, 1979
NM $50   MIP $125

Frankenstein, 1979
NM $30   MIP $60

Mummy, The, 1979
NM $30   MIP $60

Phantom of the Opera, 1979
NM $120   MIP $275

Wolfman, The, 1979
NM $65   MIP $150

Universal Monsters (Sideshow Toys, 1998-Present)

1/4 SCALE

Frankenstein, 2004, Sideshow Toys, #7102, limited to 1,000
NM n/a   MIP $225

Vampyre - Count Orlock, 1998, Sideshow Toys, #7101R, limited to 700
NM n/a   MIP $150

12" FIGURES

Bela Lugosi as Bela the Gypsy, 1998, Sideshow Toys, #4412
NM $12   MIP $35

Bela Lugosi as Dracula, 1998, Sideshow Toys, #4405
NM $22   MIP $55

Bela Lugosi as Frankenstein, 1998, Sideshow Toys, #4410
NM $10   MIP $20

Bela Lugosi as Murder Legendre, 1998, Sideshow Toys, #7002
NM $10   MIP $20

Boris Karloff as the Monster from Bride of Frankenstein, 1998, Sideshow Toys, #4413
NM $15   MIP $30

Boris Karloff as The Mummy, 1998, Sideshow Toys, #4418R

NM $45 **MIP** $80

Creature from the Black Lagoon, 2003, Sideshow Toys, #4423

NM $70 **MIP** $110

Dwight Frye as Fritz, 1998, Sideshow Toys, #4406, from Frankenstein

NM $10 **MIP** $15

Dwight Frye as Renfield, 1998, Sideshow Toys, #4411

NM $10 **MIP** $15

Elsa Lanchester as Bride of Frankenstein, 1998, Sideshow Toys, #4414

NM $15 **MIP** $30

Frankenstein Monster, 1998, Sideshow Toys, #4416R, Son of Frankenstein

NM $22 **MIP** $50

Glenn Strange as Frankenstein, 1998, Sideshow Toys, #4409

NM $10 **MIP** $20

Henry Hill as Werewolf of London, 1998, Sideshow Toys, #4421R

NM $20 **MIP** $45

Lon Chaney as Frankenstein, 1998, Sideshow Toys, #4408

NM $12 **MIP** $25

Lon Chaney as the Vampire, 1998, Sideshow Toys, #4404, London After Midnight

NM $10 **MIP** $20

Lon Chaney Jr. as Larry Talbot, 1998, Sideshow Toys, #4407

NM $10 **MIP** $20

Lon Chaney Sr. as Phantom, 1998, Sideshow Toys, #4403

NM n/a **MIP** $40

Max Schreck as Vampyre, 1998, Sideshow Toys, #7001

NM $22 **MIP** $55

Phantom of the Opera Mask of the Red Death, 1998, Sideshow Toys, #4415R

NM $10 **MIP** $25

The Creature from The Creature Walks Among Us, 1998, Sideshow Toys, #4419R

NM $12 **MIP** $25

The Mole Man from The Mole People, 1998, Sideshow Toys, #4422R

NM $20 **MIP** $50

Wolfman, The, 2000, Sideshow Toys

NM $22 **MIP** $52

SERIES I, 8" FIGURES

(KP Photo)

Creature from the Black Lagoon, special edition, 2001, Sideshow Toys, fully poseable translucent figure

NM $4 **MIP** $8

Frankenstein, 1998-99, Sideshow Toys

NM $4 **MIP** $8

Mummy, The, 1998-99, Sideshow Toys

NM $4 **MIP** $8

Wolfman, The, 1998-99, Sideshow Toys, w/log base and trap, packaged in movie-poster style box

NM $4 **MIP** $8

SERIES II, 8" FIGURES

Bride of Frankenstein, 1998-99, Sideshow Toys, detailed figure w/stand

NM $4 **MIP** $8

(KP Photo)

Creature from the Black Lagoon, 1998-99, Sideshow Toys, realistic-looking gilled Creature w/stand (showing abandoned harpoon gun)

NM $4 **MIP** $8

(KP Photo)

Phantom of the Opera, 1998-99, Sideshow Toys, highly-detailed figure w/stand

NM $4 **MIP** $8

SERIES III, 8" FIGURES

Hunchback of Notre Dame, 1998-99, Sideshow Toys, detailed figure w/purple cloak, scepter and green crown

NM $4 **MIP** $8

Invisible Man, 1998-99, Sideshow Toys

NM $4 **MIP** $8

(KP Photo)

Metaluna Mutant, 1998-99, Sideshow Toys, blue-gray detailed alien from "This Island Earth," a neat figure

NM $4 **MIP** $8

SERIES IV, 8" FIGURES

Mole People, The, 2000, Sideshow Toys, fun-looking figure

NM $4 **MIP** $8

Son of Frankenstein, 2000, Sideshow Toys, figure w/fabric outer garment and replaceable arm

NM $4 **MIP** $8

Werewolf of London, 2000, Sideshow Toys, w/cap, scarf and flower

NM $4 **MIP** $8

SILVER SCREEN EDITION

Boris Karloff as Frankenstein, 1998, Sideshow Toys, #44012R
    NM $6   MIP $15

Frankenstein, 2000, Sideshow Toys, Series 1
    NM $6   MIP $15

Lon Chaney as Phantom of the Opera, 1998, Sideshow Toys, #44032R
    NM $6   MIP $15

Lon Chaney in London After Midnight, 1998, Sideshow Toys, #44042R
    NM $6   MIP $15

Lon Chaney Jr. as The Wolf Man, 1998, Sideshow Toys, #44022R
    NM $6   MIP $15

Max Schreck as Vampyre, 1998, Sideshow Toys, #70012R
    NM $6   MIP $15

Mummy, The, 2000, Sideshow Toys, Series 1
    NM $6   MIP $15

Wolfman, The, 2000, Sideshow Toys, Series 1
    NM $6   MIP $15

Universal Monsters: Hasbro Signature Series (Hasbro, 1998)

FIGURES

Bride of Frankenstein, The, 1998, Hasbro
    NM $10   MIP $25

Creature from the Black Lagoon, 1998, Hasbro, Series 2
    NM $10   MIP $20

Frankenstein, 1998, Hasbro
    NM $10   MIP $25

Mummy, The, 1998, Hasbro
    NM $10   MIP $25

Phantom of the Opera, 1998, Hasbro, Series 2
    NM $10   MIP $20

Son of Dracula, 1998, Hasbro, Series 2
    NM $10   MIP $20

The Invisible Man, 1998, Hasbro, Series 2
    NM $10   MIP $20

Wolf Man, The, 1998, Hasbro
    NM $10   MIP $25

Vault, The (Toy Biz, 1998)

6" FIGURES

Stegron, 1998, Marvel
    NM $2   MIP $4

Typhoid Mary, 1998, Marvel
    NM $2   MIP $4

Ultron, 1998, Marvel
    NM $2   MIP $4

Vikings (Marx, 1960s)

FIGURES

Brave Erik the Viking, 1970-72, Marx, #5430, lime-green outfit, blond hair, blue eyes - like many Marx figures, this too had a molded uniform w/other plastic accessories and clothing included in the package
    NM $125   MIP $300

Mighty Viking Horse, 1970-72, Marx, #5381, Palomino for Erik, Brown for Odin, 11-piece vinyl tack set, wheels in hooves, nodding heads
    NM $125   MIP $300

Odin the Viking Chieftan, 1970-72, Marx, #5440, molded carmel outfit, brown hair, full beard
    NM $125   MIP $300

Voltron (Matchbox, 1984)

FIGURES

Battling Black Lion, 1984, LJN
    NM $7   MIP $30

Black Lion, 1984, LJN, Motorized Lion Force
    NM $7   MIP $20

Blue Lion & Red Lion, 1984, LJN, Motorized Lion Force
    NM $7   MIP $20

Green Lion & Yellow Lion, 1984, LJN, Motorized Lion Force
    NM $7   MIP $20

Lion Force Fortress, 1984, LJN
    NM $15   MIP $35

Radio-Controlled Voltron, 1984, LJN
    NM $10   MIP $20

Voltron Assembler - Lion Force, 1984, LJN, disassembles
    NM $7   MIP $15

Voltron Assembler - Vehicle Team, 1984, LJN, disassembles
    NM $7   MIP $15

Voltron Assembler Gift Set, 1984, LJN, both Lion Force and Vehicle Team assemblers
    NM $10   MIP $20

Voltron Motorized, 1984, LJN, w/Motorized Black, Blue, Red, Green, and Yellow Lions
    NM $20   MIP $40

Voltron (Panosh Place, 1985-86)

3-3/4" FIGURES

Doom Commander, 1985-86
    NM $10   MIP $20

Haggar the Witch, 1985-86
    NM $12   MIP $25

Hunk, 1985-86
    NM $15   MIP $30

Keith, 1985-86
    NM $15   MIP $35

King Zarkon, 1985-86
    NM $10   MIP $25

Lance, 1985-86
    NM $15   MIP $40

Pidge, 1985-86
    NM $15   MIP $30

Prince Lotor, 1985-86
    NM $18   MIP $30

Princess Allura, 1985-86
    NM $15   MIP $30

Robeast Mutilor, 1985-86
    NM $10   MIP $20

Robeast Scorpious, 1985-86
    NM $10   MIP $20

Skull Scavenger, 1985-86, pilot of the Skull Tank
    NM $10   MIP $20

Voltron Robot, 1985-86
    NM $14   MIP $32

GIFT SETS

Deluxe Gift Set I, 1985-86, Warrior
    NM $85   MIP $210

Deluxe Gift Set II, 1985-86, Gladiator
    NM $75   MIP $190

Deluxe Gift Set III, 1985-86, Lion
    NM $85   MIP $220

MINIATURES

Voltron I, 1985-86, die-cast
    NM $15   MIP $30

Voltron II, 1985-86, die-cast
    NM $15   MIP $30

Voltron III, 1985-86, die-cast
NM $15   MIP $30

VEHICLES

Castle of Lions, 1985-86
NM $150   MIP $400

Coffin of Darkness, 1985-86
NM $12   MIP $25

Coffin of Doom, 1985-86
NM $12   MIP $25

Doom Blaster, 1985-86
NM $14   MIP $30

Skull Tank, 1985-86
NM $20   MIP $35

Zarkon Zapper, 1985-86
NM $20   MIP $40

Waltons (Mego, 1975)

8" FIGURES

Grandma and Grandpa, 1975, Mego
NM $18   MIP $40

John Boy and Ellen, 1975, Mego
NM $22   MIP $40

Mom and Pop, 1975, Mego
NM $22   MIP $40

ACCESSORIES

Barn, 1975, Mego
NM $30   MIP $70

Country Store, 1975, Mego
NM $35   MIP $75

Truck, 1975, Mego
NM $25   MIP $50

PLAY SETS

Farm House, 1975, Mego
NM $50   MIP $100

Farm House w/Six Figures, 1975, Mego
NM $125   MIP $250

Warrior Beasts, The (Remco, 1983)

FIGURES

Craven, 1983
NM $15   MIP $50

Gecko, 1983
NM $15   MIP $60

Guana, 1983
NM $15   MIP $50

Hydraz, 1983
NM $15   MIP $60

Ramar, 1983
NM $15   MIP $50

Skullman, 1983
NM $25   MIP $90

Snake Man, 1983
NM $25   MIP $90

Stegos, 1983
NM $15   MIP $50

Wolf Warrior, 1983
NM $30   MIP $90

Zardus, 1983
NM $15   MIP $50

WCW Bash at the Beach (Toy Biz, 2000)

6" FIGURES

Bret Hart, 2000, Toy Biz
NM $8   MIP $18

Diamond Dallas Page, 2000, Toy Biz
NM $6   MIP $12

Goldberg, 2000, Toy Biz
NM $5   MIP $12

Hulk Hogan, 2000, Toy Biz
NM $5   MIP $12

Lex Luger, 2000, Toy Biz
NM $5   MIP $12

Sting, 2000, Toy Biz
NM $10   MIP $30

WCW Cyborg Wrestlers (Toy Biz, 2000)

6" FIGURES

Bret Hart, 2000, Toy Biz
NM $2   MIP $4

Goldberg, 2000, Toy Biz
NM $2   MIP $4

Kevin Nash, 2000, Toy Biz
NM $2   MIP $4

Sid Vicious, 2000, Toy Biz
NM $2   MIP $4

Sting, 2000, Toy Biz
NM $2   MIP $4

WCW Nitro Active Wrestlers (Toy Biz, 2000)

6" FIGURES

Buff Bagwell, 2000, Toy Biz
NM $2   MIP $4

Goldberg, 2000, Toy Biz
NM $2   MIP $4

Jeff Jarrett, 2000, Toy Biz
NM $2   MIP $4

Sid Vicious, 2000, Toy Biz
NM $2   MIP $4

Vampiro, 2000, Toy Biz
NM $2   MIP $4

WCW Power Slam Wrestlers I (Toy Biz, 2000)

6" FIGURES

Goldberg, 2000, Toy Biz
NM $2   MIP $5

Hak, 2000, Toy Biz
NM $2   MIP $5

Hulk Hogan, 2000, Toy Biz
NM $2   MIP $5

Rodman, 2000, Toy Biz
NM $2   MIP $5

Sid Vicious, 2000, Toy Biz
NM $2   MIP $5

WCW Power Slam Wrestlers II (Toy Biz, 2000)

6" FIGURES

Buff Bagwell, 2000, Toy Biz
NM $2   MIP $5

Kanyon, 2000, Toy Biz
NM $2   MIP $5

Kevin Nash, 2000, Toy Biz
NM $2   MIP $5

Roddy Piper, 2000, Toy Biz
NM $2   MIP $5

Sting, 2000, Toy Biz
NM $2   MIP $5

WCW S.L.A.M. Force (Toy Biz, 2000)

6" FIGURES

Benoit w/comic book, 2000, Toy Biz
NM $2   MIP $5

Bret Hart w/comic book, 2000, Toy Biz
NM $2   MIP $5

Goldberg w/comic book, 2000, Toy Biz
NM $2   MIP $5

Kevin Nash w/comic book, 2000, Toy Biz
NM $2   MIP $5

Sting w/comic book, 2000, Toy Biz
NM $2   MIP $5

WCW Signature Series (Toy Biz, 2000)

12" FIGURES

Goldberg, 2000, Toy Biz
NM $3   MIP $8

Hulk Hogan, 2000, Toy Biz
NM $3   MIP $8

Sting, 2000, Toy Biz
NM $3   MIP $8

WCW Thunder Slam Twin Packs (Toy Biz, 2000)

6" FIGURES

Bam Bam Bigelow and Goldberg, 2000, Toy Biz
    NM $3   MIP $10

Kevin Nash and Scott Hall, 2000, Toy Biz
    NM $3   MIP $10

Sting and Bret Hart, 2000, Toy Biz
    NM $3   MIP $10

WCW World Championship Wrestling Ring Fighters (Toy Biz, 1999)

6" FIGURES

Booker T, 1999
    NM $2   MIP $5

Bret Hart, 1999
    NM $2   MIP $5

Chris Benoit, 1999
    NM $2   MIP $5

Scott Steiner, 1999
    NM $2   MIP $5

WCW World Championship Wrestling Smash'nSlam (Toy Biz, 1999)

6" FIGURES

Hollywood Hogan, 1999
    NM $2   MIP $5

Kevin Nash, 1999
    NM $2   MIP $5

Macho Man Randy Savage, 1999
    NM $2   MIP $5

Scott Hall, 1999
    NM $2   MIP $5

WCW World Championship Wrestling Smash 'n Slam II (Toy Biz, 1999)

6" FIGURES

D.D.P., 1999
    NM $2   MIP $5

Giant & Rey Mysterio Jr., 1999
    NM $2   MIP $5

Goldberg & Masked Wrestler, 1999
    NM $2   MIP $5

Lex Luger, 1999
    NM $2   MIP $5

Sting, 1999
    NM $2   MIP $5

WCW/NWO Ring Masters (Toy Biz, 1998)

6" FIGURES

Bret Hart, 1999
    NM $3   MIP $6

Chris Jericho, 1999
    NM $3   MIP $6

Goldberg, 1999
    NM $3   MIP $6

Lex Luger, 1999
    NM $3   MIP $6

WCW/NWO Slam 'n Crunch (Toy Biz, 1998)

6" FIGURES

Buff Bagwell, 1999
    NM $2   MIP $5

Goldberg, 1999
    NM $2   MIP $5

Konnan, 1999
    NM $2   MIP $5

Sting, 1999
    NM $2   MIP $5

WCW/NWO Two Packs (Toy Biz, 1999)

BATTLE OF THE GIANTS, 6" FIGURES

Giant vs. Kevin Nash, 1999
    NM $3   MIP $7

CLASH OF THE CHAMPIONS, 6" FIGURES

Sting vs. Hollywood Hogan, 1999
    NM $3   MIP $7

GRIP 'N FLIP WRESTLERS II, 6" FIGURES

Kevin Nash vs. Bret Hart, 1999
    NM $3   MIP $7

Scott Steiner vs. Rick Steiner, 1999
    NM $3   MIP $7

Sting vs. Lex Luger, 1999
    NM $3   MIP $7

GRIP 'N FLIP WRESTLERS, 6" FIGURES

Chris Jericho vs. Dean Malenko, 1999, Toy Biz
    NM $2   MIP $5

Goldberg vs. Hollywood Hogan, 1999, Toy Biz
    NM $2   MIP $5

Raven vs. Diamond Dallas Page, 1999
    NM $2   MIP $5

POWER AND BEAUTY, 6" FIGURES

Macho Man & Elizabeth, 1999
    NM $2   MIP $5

Welcome Back, Kotter (Mattel, 1976)

FIGURES

Barbarino, 1976
    NM $8   MIP $20

Epstein, 1976
    NM $8   MIP $20

Horshback, 1976
    NM $8   MIP $20

Mr. Kotter, 1976
    NM $8   MIP $20

Washington, 1976
    NM $8   MIP $20

PLAY SETS

Welcome Back Kotter Play Set, Deluxe, 1976
    NM $50   MIP $150

Welcome Back, Kotter Play Set, 1976, classroom shown here w/all five figures
    NM $35   MIP $90

Wetworks (McFarlane, 1995-96)

SERIES 1

Dane, 1995
    NM $2   MIP $4

Dozer, 1995
    NM $2   MIP $4

Grail, 1995
    NM $2   MIP $4

Mother-One, 1995
    NM $2   MIP $4

Vampire, dark green, 1995
    NM $2   MIP $4

Vampire, gray, 1995
    NM $2   MIP $4

Werewolf, light blue, 1995
 NM $2   MIP $4
Werewolf, reddish-brown, 1995
 NM $2   MIP $4

SERIES 2

Assasin One, blue, 1996
 NM $2   MIP $4
Assasin One, red, 1996
 NM $2   MIP $4
Blood Queen, all black, 1996
 NM $2   MIP $4
Blood Queen, all black w/red trim, 1996
 NM $2   MIP $4
Delta Commander, flesh tones, 1996
 NM $2   MIP $4
Delta Commander, gold, 1996
 NM $2   MIP $4
Frankenstein, brown, 1996
 NM $2   MIP $4
Frankenstein, green, 1996
 NM $2   MIP $4
Mendoza, flesh colored, 1996
 NM $2   MIP $4
Mendoza, half gold, 1996
 NM $2   MIP $4
Pilgrim, flesh tones, 1996
 NM $2   MIP $4
Pilgrim, gold, 1996
 NM $2   MIP $4

Where the Wild Things Are (McFarlane, 2000)
FIGURES

Aaron, 2000
 NM $8   MIP $16
Bernard, 2000
 NM $8   MIP $16
Emil, 2000
 NM $9   MIP $20
Max and Goatboy, 2000
 NM $10   MIP $30
Moishe, 2000
 NM $10   MIP $25
Tzippy, 2000
 NM $8   MIP $15

Witchblade (Moore Action Collectibles)
SERIES I, FIGURES

Ian Nottingham
 NM $2   MIP $4
Kenneth Irons
 NM $2   MIP $4
Medieval Witchblade
 NM $2   MIP $4
Sara Pezzini/Witchblade
 NM $2   MIP $4

SERIES II, FIGURES

Aspen Mathews/Fathom, a ripped dude w/a mutant right hand
 NM $2   MIP $4
Sara Pezzini, in red dress, w/matching boots
 NM $2   MIP $4

Wizard of Oz (Mego, 1974)
4" BOXED FIGURES

Munchkin Dancer, 1974, Mego
 NM $75   MIP $150
Munchkin Flower Girl, 1974, Mego
 NM $75   MIP $150
Munchkin General, 1974, Mego
 NM $75   MIP $150
Munchkin Lollipop Kid, 1974, Mego
 NM $75   MIP $150
Munchkin Mayor, 1974, Mego
 NM $75   MIP $150

8" BOXED FIGURES

Cowardly Lion, 1974, Mego
 NM $25   MIP $60
Dorothy w/Toto, 1974, Mego
 NM $25   MIP $60
Glinda the Good Witch, 1974, Mego
 NM $25   MIP $60
Scarecrow, 1974, Mego
 NM $25   MIP $60
Tin Woodsman, 1974, Mego
 NM $25   MIP $60
Wicked Witch, 1974, Mego
 NM $50   MIP $100
Wizard of Oz, 1974, Mego
 NM $35   MIP $250

PLAY SETS

Emerald City, 1974, Mego, play set w/seven 8" figures
 NM $125   MIP $400
Emerald City w/Wizard of Oz, 1974, Mego, play set w/Wizard of Oz
 NM $45   MIP $100
Munchkin Land, 1974, Mego
 NM $150   MIP $300
Witch's Castle, Sears Exclusive, 1974, Mego
 NM $275   MIP $550

Wonder Woman Series (Mego, 1977-80)
FIGURES

Major Steve Trevor, 1978, Mego, left, in white suit
 NM $42   MIP $140

Nubia, 1978, Mego
 NM $110   MIP $275
Queen Hippolyte, 1978, Mego
 NM $80   MIP $190

(KP Photo, Karen O'Brien collection)

Wonder Woman w/Diana Prince Outfit, 1978, Mego
 NM $110   MIP $290
Wonder Woman w/Fly Away Action, 1978, Mego
 NM $85   MIP $300

World's Greatest Super Knights (Mego, 1975)
8" FIGURES

Black Knight, 1975
 NM $75   MIP $320

Ivanhoe, 1975, in full body armor
NM $55   MIP $250
King Arthur, 1975
NM $50   MIP $200
Sir Galahad, 1975
NM $60   MIP $275
Sir Lancelot, 1975
NM $60   MIP $285

World's Greatest Super Pirates (Mego, 1974)

FIGURES

Blackbeard, 1974
NM $160   MIP $425
Captain Patch, 1974
NM $125   MIP $275
Jean Lafitte, 1974
NM $200   MIP $500
Long John Silver, 1974
NM $200   MIP $500

World's Greatest Super-Heroes (Mego, 1972-78)

12-1/2" FIGURES

Amazing Spider-Man, **1978**, 1972-78, Mego
NM $40   MIP $100
Batman, **1978**, 1972-78, Mego, magnetic
NM $100   MIP $250
Batman, **1978**, 1972-78, Mego
NM $60   MIP $125
Captain America, **1978**, 1972-78, Mego
NM $75   MIP $210
Hulk, **1978**, 1972-78, Mego
NM $30   MIP $100
Robin, magnetic, **1978**, 1972-78, Mego
NM $125   MIP $260

Spider-Man, 1972-78, Mego, web shooting
NM $75   MIP $150

Superman, 1972-78, Mego
NM $50   MIP $135

8" FIGURES

Aquaman, 1972, Mego, carded
NM $50   MIP $165

Aquaman, 1972, Mego, solid box, no window
NM $50   MIP $800

Aquaman, 1972, Mego, boxed
NM $50   MIP $150

Batgirl, 1973, Mego, boxed
NM $125   MIP $325

Batgirl, 1973, Mego, carded
NM $125   MIP $300

Batman, 1972, Mego, removable mask, Kresge card only
NM $200   MIP $775

Batman, 1972, Mego, painted mask, boxed
NM $60   MIP $150

Batman w/removable cowl, 1972, Mego, solid box, no window
NM $125   MIP $1000

Batman, fist fighting, 1975, Mego, boxed
NM $150   MIP $450

Batman, painted mask, 1972, Mego, carded
NM $60   MIP $150

Batman, removable mask, 1972, Mego, boxed
NM $200   MIP $610

Bruce Wayne, 1974, Mego, boxed, Montgomery Ward Exclusive
NM $1200   MIP $2000

Captain America, 1972, Mego, carded
NM $60   MIP $160

Captain America, 1972, Mego, boxed
NM $60   MIP $250

Catwoman, 1973, Mego, boxed
NM $150   MIP $350
Catwoman, 1973, Mego, carded
NM $150   MIP $2000
Clark Kent, 1974, Mego, boxed, Montgomery Ward Exclusive
NM $1200   MIP $2000
Conan, 1975, Mego, boxed
NM $150   MIP $400
Conan, 1975, Mego, carded
NM $150   MIP $525
Dick Grayson, 1974, Mego, boxed, Montgomery Ward Exclusive
NM $1200   MIP $2000

Falcon, 1974, Mego, boxed
NM $60   MIP $150
Falcon, 1974, Mego, carded
NM $60   MIP $1500
Green Arrow, 1973, Mego, boxed, w/hat, belt and bow and arrow accessories
NM $150   MIP $450
Green Arrow, 1973, Mego, carded
NM $150   MIP $2000

Green Goblin, 1974, Mego, boxed
NM $90   MIP $325

Green Goblin, 1974, Mego, carded
NM $90   MIP $2000

Human Torch, Fantastic Four, 1975, Mego, boxed
NM $25   MIP $90

Human Torch, Fantastic Four, 1975, Mego, carded
NM $25   MIP $55

Incredible Hulk, 1974, Mego, carded
NM $20   MIP $55

Incredible Hulk, 1974, Mego, boxed
NM $40   MIP $150

Invisible Girl, Fantastic Four, 1975, Mego, boxed
NM $30   MIP $150

Invisible Girl, Fantastic Four, 1975, Mego, carded
NM $30   MIP $60

Iron Man, 1974, Mego, boxed
NM $75   MIP $125

Iron Man, 1974, Mego, carded
NM $75   MIP $475

Isis, 1976, Mego, boxed
NM $75   MIP $250

Isis, 1976, Mego, carded
NM $75   MIP $125

Joker, 1973, Mego, boxed
NM $60   MIP $200

Joker, 1973, Mego, carded
NM $60   MIP $150

Joker, fist fighting, 1975, Mego, boxed
NM $150   MIP $600

Lizard, 1974, Mego, carded
NM $100   MIP $2000

Lizard, 1974, Mego, boxed
NM $75   MIP $200

Mr. Fantastic, Fantastic Four, 1975, Mego, boxed
NM $30   MIP $140

Mr. Fantastic, Fantastic Four, 1975, Mego, carded
NM $30   MIP $60

Mr. Mxyzptlk, open mouth, 1973, Mego, boxed
NM $50   MIP $75

Mr. Mxyzptlk, open mouth, 1973, Mego, carded
NM $50   MIP $150

Mr. Mxyzptlk, smirk, 1973, Mego, boxed
NM $60   MIP $150

Penguin, 1973, Mego, carded
NM $60   MIP $125

Penguin, 1973, Mego, boxed
NM $60   MIP $150

Peter Parker, 1974, Mego, boxed, Montgomery Ward Exclusive
NM $1200   MIP $2000

Riddler, 1973, Mego, carded
NM $100   MIP $2000

Riddler, 1973, Mego, boxed
NM $100   MIP $250

Riddler, 1975, Mego, fist fighting, boxed
NM $150   MIP $600

Robin, 1972, Mego, painted mask, boxed
NM $60   MIP $150

Robin, 1972, Mego, painted mask, carded
NM $60   MIP $90

Robin, 1972, Mego, removable mask, boxed
NM $250   MIP $750

Robin, 1972, removable mask, solid box
NM $250   MIP $1500

Robin, 1975, Mego, fist fighting, boxed
NM $125   MIP $450

Shazam, 1972, Mego, boxed
NM $75   MIP $200

Shazam, 1972, Mego, carded
NM $75   MIP $150

Spider-Man, 1972, Mego, boxed
NM $20   MIP $100

Spider-Man, 1972, Mego, carded
NM $20   MIP $55

Supergirl, 1973, Mego, boxed
NM $300   MIP $550

Supergirl, 1973, Mego, carded
NM $300   MIP $450

Superman, 1972, Mego, boxed
NM $50   MIP $200

Superman, 1972, Mego, carded
NM $50   MIP $125

Superman, 1972, Mego, solid box, no window
NM $50   MIP $800

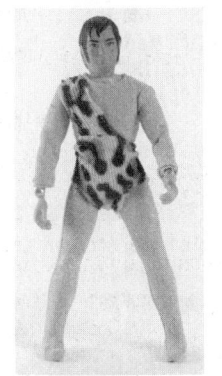

(KP Photo, Karen O'Brien collection)

Tarzan, 1972, Mego, boxed
NM $50   MIP $150

Tarzan, 1976, Mego, Kresge card only
NM $60   MIP $225

Thing, Fantastic Four, 1975, Mego, carded
NM $40   MIP $60

Thing, Fantastic Four, 1975, Mego, boxed
NM $40   MIP $350

Thor, 1975, Mego, boxed
NM $150   MIP $400

Thor, 1975, Mego, carded
NM $150   MIP $475

Wonder Woman, 1972-78, Mego, boxed
NM $100   MIP $400

Wonder Woman, 1972-78, Mego, Kresge card only
NM $100   MIP $475

ACCESSORIES

Super Hero Carry Case, 1973, Mego
NM $40   MIP $100

Supervator, 1974, Mego
NM $60   MIP $120

PLAY SETS

Aquaman vs. the Great White Shark, 1978, Mego, rare
NM $500   MIP $1000

Batcave Play Set, 1974, Mego, vinyl
NM $150   MIP $300

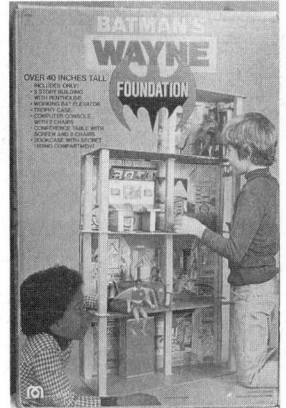

Batman's Wayne Foundation Penthouse, 1977, Mego, fiberboard
NM $600   MIP $1000

Hall of Justice, 1976, Mego, vinyl
NM $125   MIP $250

SUPERMAN SERIES

General Zod, 1978, Mego
  NM $50   MIP $100
Jor-El, 1978, Mego
  NM $50   MIP $100
Lex Luthor, 1978, Mego
  NM $50   MIP $100

(KP Photo, Karen O'Brien collection)
Superman, 1978, Mego
  NM $55   MIP $135

TEEN TITANS, 6-1/2" FIGURES

Aqualad, 1976, Mego
  NM $175   MIP $350
Kid Flash, 1976, Mego
  NM $175   MIP $450

Speedy, 1976, Mego
  NM $310   MIP $525
Wondergirl, 1976, Mego
  NM $210   MIP $500

VEHICLES

Batcopter, 1974, Mego, on display card
  NM $55   MIP $125
Batcopter, 1974, Mego, boxed
  NM $75   MIP $160
Batcycle, 1974, Mego, blue, carded
  NM $75   MIP $135
Batcycle, 1974, Mego, blue, boxed
  NM $75   MIP $170
Batcycle, 1975, Mego, black, carded
  NM $60   MIP $150
Batcycle, 1975, Mego, black, boxed
  NM $75   MIP $185
Batmobile, 1974, Mego, photo box
  NM $75   MIP $400
Batmobile, 1974, Mego, carded
  NM $50   MIP $120
Batmobile, 1974, artwork box
  NM $75   MIP $325
Batmobile and Batman, 1972-78, Mego
  NM $40   MIP $100
Captain Americar, 1976, Mego
  NM $125   MIP $275
Green Arrowcar, 1976, Mego
  NM $175   MIP $360
Jokermobile, 1976, Mego
  NM $150   MIP $410
Mobile Bat Lab, 1975, Mego
  NM $125   MIP $410
Spidercar, 1976, Mego
  NM $50   MIP $125

WWF (Jakks Pacific, 1997-present)

2-TUFF, SERIES 1
D.O.A.
  NM $3   MIP $6
Goldust and Marlena
  NM $3   MIP $6
HHH and Chyna
  NM $3   MIP $6
Truth Commission
  NM $3   MIP $6

2-TUFF, SERIES 2
Brian Christopher and Jerry Lawler
  NM $3   MIP $6
D-Lo Brown and Kama
  NM $3   MIP $6
Kurrgan and Jackyl
  NM $3   MIP $6

New Age Outlaws
  NM $3   MIP $6

2-TUFF, SERIES 3
Kane and Mankind
  NM $3   MIP $6
Legion of Doom 2000
  NM $3   MIP $6
Rocky Maivia (The Rock) and Owen Hart
  NM $3   MIP $6
Stone Cold Steve Austin/Undertaker
  NM $3   MIP $6

2-TUFF, SERIES 4
Billy Gunn and Val Venis
  NM $3   MIP $6
Mankind and The Rock
  NM $3   MIP $6
Stone Cold Steve Austin and Big Bossman
  NM $3   MIP $6
Undertaker and Kane
  NM $3   MIP $6

2-TUFF, SERIES 5
Debra and Jarrett
  NM $3   MIP $6
Road Dogg and Billy Gunn
  NM $3   MIP $6
Stone Cold Steve Austin and The Rock
  NM $3   MIP $6
Undertaker and Viscera
  NM $3   MIP $6

BEST OF 1997, SERIES 1
Ahmed Johnson
  NM $3   MIP $7
Bret Hart
  NM $3   MIP $7
British Bulldog
  NM $3   MIP $7
Owen Hart
  NM $3   MIP $7
Stone Cold Steve Austin
  NM $3   MIP $7
Undertaker
  NM $3   MIP $7

BEST OF 1997, SERIES 2
Crush
  NM $3   MIP $7
Goldust
  NM $3   MIP $7
HHH
  NM $3   MIP $7
Ken Shamrock
  NM $3   MIP $7
Marc Mero
  NM $3   MIP $7

Rocky Maivia (The Rock)
| | NM $3 | MIP $7 |

Shawn Michaels
| | NM $3 | MIP $7 |

Undertaker
| | NM $3 | MIP $7 |

BEST OF 1998, SERIES 1

8-Ball
| | NM $3 | MIP $7 |

Blackjack Bradshaw
| | NM $3 | MIP $7 |

Brian Christopher
| | NM $3 | MIP $7 |

Chyna
| | NM $3 | MIP $7 |

Shawn Michaels
| | NM $3 | MIP $7 |

Skull
| | NM $3 | MIP $7 |

Stone Cold Steve Austin
| | NM $3 | MIP $7 |

Vader
| | NM $3 | MIP $7 |

BEST OF 1998, SERIES 2

Dan Severn
| | NM $3 | MIP $7 |

Dude Love
| | NM $3 | MIP $7 |

HHH
| | NM $3 | MIP $7 |

Jeff Jarrett
| | NM $3 | MIP $7 |

Ken Shamrock
| | NM $3 | MIP $7 |

Mark Henry
| | NM $3 | MIP $7 |

Stone Cold Steve Austin
| | NM $3 | MIP $7 |

Undertaker
| | NM $3 | MIP $7 |

BONE CRUNCHIN' BUDDIES, SERIES 1

Dude Love
| | NM $10 | MIP $20 |

Shawn Michaels
| | NM $12 | MIP $25 |

Stone Cold Steve Austin
| | NM $15 | MIP $30 |

Undertaker
| | NM $15 | MIP $30 |

BONE CRUNCHIN' BUDDIES, SERIES 2

Animal
| | NM $10 | MIP $20 |

Hawk
| | NM $15 | MIP $30 |

Rock, The
| | NM $15 | MIP $30 |

Stone Cold Steve Austin
| | NM $15 | MIP $30 |

Undertaker
| | NM $15 | MIP $30 |

BONE CRUNCHIN' BUDDIES, SERIES 3

HHH
| | NM $15 | MIP $30 |

Kane
| | NM $12 | MIP $20 |

Rock, The
| | NM $12 | MIP $30 |

Stone Cold Steve Austin in shirt and pants
| | NM $12 | MIP $25 |

Stone Cold Steve Austin in tights and vest
| | NM $12 | MIP $25 |

Undertaker
| | NM $12 | MIP $30 |

FULLY LOADED, SERIES 1

Al Snow
| | NM $3 | MIP $6 |

Billy Gunn
| | NM $3 | MIP $6 |

Hunter Hearst Hemsley
| | NM $3 | MIP $6 |

Kane
| | NM $3 | MIP $6 |

Road Dog Jesse James
| | NM $3 | MIP $6 |

Rocky Maivia (The Rock)
| | NM $3 | MIP $6 |

FULLY LOADED, SERIES 2

Road Dog Jesse James
| | NM $3 | MIP $6 |

Rock, The
| | NM $3 | MIP $6 |

Shane McMahon
| | NM $3 | MIP $6 |

Stone Cold Steve Austin
| | NM $3 | MIP $6 |

Test
| | NM $3 | MIP $6 |

X Pac
| | NM $3 | MIP $6 |

GRUDGE MATCH

Brian Christopher vs. TAKA
| | NM $4 | MIP $10 |

Dan Severn vs. Ken Shamrock
| | NM $4 | MIP $10 |

HHH vs. Owen Hart
| | NM $4 | MIP $10 |

HHH vs. HBK
| | NM $4 | MIP $10 |

Jeff Jarrett vs. X Pac
| | NM $4 | MIP $10 |

Kane vs. Undertaker
| | NM $4 | MIP $10 |

Marc Mero vs. Steve Blackman
| | NM $4 | MIP $10 |

Mark Henry vs. Vader
| | NM $4 | MIP $10 |

McMahon vs. Stone Cold Steve Austin
| | NM $4 | MIP $10 |

Road Dog Jesse James vs. Al Snow
| | NM $4 | MIP $10 |

Sable vs. Luna Vachon
| | NM $4 | MIP $10 |

Shamrock vs. Billy Gunn
| | NM $4 | MIP $10 |

Shawn Michaels vs. Stone Cold Steve Austin
| | NM $4 | MIP $10 |

Stone Cold Steve Austin vs. The Rock
| | NM $4 | MIP $10 |

LEGENDS, SERIES 1

Andre the Giant
| | NM $2 | MIP $5 |

Captian Lou Albano
| | NM $2 | MIP $5 |

Classie Freddie Blassie
| | NM $2 | MIP $5 |

Jimmy Snuka
| | NM $2 | MIP $5 |

LIVEWIRE, SERIES 1

Chyna
| | NM $2 | MIP $4 |

Ken Shamrock
| | NM $2 | MIP $4 |

Mankind
| | NM $2 | MIP $4 |

Stone Cold Steve Austin
| | NM $2 | MIP $4 |

Undertaker
| | NM $2 | MIP $4 |

Vader
| | NM $2 | MIP $4 |

LIVEWIRE, SERIES 2

Marc Mero
| | NM $2 | MIP $4 |

Mark Henry
| | NM $2 | MIP $4 |

Rock, The
NM $2   MIP $4

Shawn Michaels
NM $2   MIP $4

Val Venis
NM $2   MIP $4

X Pac
NM $2   MIP $4

MANAGER, SERIES 1

Backlund and Sultan
NM $2   MIP $3

Bearer and Mankind
NM $2   MIP $3

Mason and Crush
NM $2   MIP $3

Sable and Mero
NM $2   MIP $3

MAXIMUM SWEAT, SERIES 1

HHH
NM $3   MIP $6

Kane
NM $3   MIP $6

Rock, The
NM $3   MIP $6

Shawn Michaels
NM $3   MIP $6

Stone Cold Steve Austin
NM $3   MIP $6

Undertaker
NM $3   MIP $6

MAXIMUM SWEAT, SERIES 2

Billy Gunn
NM $3   MIP $6

Edge
NM $3   MIP $6

Ken Shamrock
NM $3   MIP $6

Road Dogg Jesse James
NM $3   MIP $6

Stone Cold Steve Austin
NM $3   MIP $6

Undertaker
NM $3   MIP $6

MAXIMUM SWEAT, SERIES 3

Big Bossman
NM $3   MIP $6

Billy Gunn
NM $3   MIP $6

Gangrel
NM $3   MIP $6

Mankind
NM $3   MIP $6

Rock, The
NM $3   MIP $6

Stone Cold Steve Austin
NM $3   MIP $6

RINGSIDE, SERIES 1

Referee
NM $3   MIP $5

Sable
NM $3   MIP $5

Sunny
NM $3   MIP $5

Vince McMahon
NM $3   MIP $5

RINGSIDE, SERIES 2

Honky Tonk Man
NM $3   MIP $6

Jim Cornette
NM $3   MIP $6

Jim Ross
NM $3   MIP $6

Referee
NM $3   MIP $6

Sgt. Slaughter
NM $3   MIP $6

Vince McMahon
NM $3   MIP $6

RIPPED AND RUTHLESS, SERIES 1

Goldust
NM $3   MIP $6

Mankind
NM $3   MIP $6

Stone Cold Steve Austin
NM $3   MIP $6

Undertaker
NM $3   MIP $6

RIPPED AND RUTHLESS, SERIES 2

HHH
NM $3   MIP $6

Kane
NM $3   MIP $6

Sable
NM $3   MIP $6

Shawn Michaels
NM $3   MIP $6

S.T.O.M.P., SERIES 1

Ahmed Johnson
NM $3   MIP $6

Brian Pillman
NM $3   MIP $6

Crush
NM $3   MIP $6

Ken Shamrock
NM $3   MIP $6

Stone Cold Steve Austin
NM $3   MIP $6

Undertaker
NM $3   MIP $6

S.T.O.M.P., SERIES 2

Chyna
NM $3   MIP $6

Mosh
NM $3   MIP $6

Owen Hart
NM $3   MIP $6

Rocky Maivia (The Rock),
Jakks Pacific
NM $3   MIP $6

Stone Cold Steve Austin
NM $3   MIP $6

Thrasher
NM $3   MIP $6

S.T.O.M.P., SERIES 3

Animal
NM $3   MIP $6

Hawk
NM $3   MIP $6

Kane
NM $3   MIP $6

Marc Mero
NM $3   MIP $6

Sable
NM $3   MIP $6

Undertaker
NM $3   MIP $6

S.T.O.M.P., SERIES 4

Billy Gunn
NM $3   MIP $6

Chyna
NM $3   MIP $6

HHH
NM $3   MIP $6

Road Dog Jesse James
NM $3   MIP $6

Stone Cold Steve Austin
NM $3   MIP $6

X Pac
NM $3   MIP $6

SHOTGUN SATURDAY NIGHT, SERIES 1

Animal
NM $3   MIP $6

Hawk
NM $3   MIP $6

Henry O. Godwinn
NM $3   MIP $6

Phineas I. Godwinn
NM $3   MIP $6

Rocky Maivia (The Rock)
NM $3   MIP $6

Savio Vega
NM $3   MIP $6

Stone Cold Steve Austin
NM $3   MIP $6

Undertaker
NM $3   MIP $6

SHOTGUN SATURDAY NIGHT, SERIES 2

Billy Gunn
NM $3   MIP $6

Jeff Jarrett
NM $3   MIP $6

Kane
NM $3   MIP $6

Road Dog Jesse James
NM $3   MIP $6

Sable
NM $3   MIP $6

Shawn Michaels
NM $3   MIP $6

SIGNATURE, SERIES 1

Animal
NM $3   MIP $6

Goldust
NM $3   MIP $6

Hawk
NM $3   MIP $6

Hunter Hearst Hemsley
NM $3   MIP $6

Mankind
NM $3   MIP $6

Stone Cold Steve Austin
NM $3   MIP $6

SIGNATURE, SERIES 2

Billy Gunn
NM $3   MIP $6

Dude Love
NM $3   MIP $6

Kane
NM $3   MIP $6

Road Dog Jesse James
NM $3   MIP $6

Shawn Michaels
NM $3   MIP $6

Undertaker
NM $3   MIP $6

SIGNATURE, SERIES 3

Edge
NM $3   MIP $6

HHH
NM $3   MIP $6

Jackie
NM $3   MIP $6

Rock, The
NM $3   MIP $6

Stone Cold Steve Austin
NM $3   MIP $6

Undertaker
NM $3   MIP $6

SUNDAY NIGHT HEAT

Billy Gunn
NM $3   MIP $6

Road Dog Jesse James
NM $3   MIP $6

Rock, The
NM $3   MIP $6

Sable
NM $3   MIP $6

Stone Cold Steve Austin
NM $3   MIP $6

Undertaker
NM $3   MIP $6

SUPERSTARS, SERIES 1

Bret Hart
NM $3   MIP $7

Diesel
NM $3   MIP $7

Goldust
NM $3   MIP $7

Razor Ramon
NM $3   MIP $7

Shawn Michaels
NM $3   MIP $7

Undertaker
NM $3   MIP $7

SUPERSTARS, SERIES 2

Bret Hart
NM $3   MIP $7

Owen Hart
NM $3   MIP $7

Shawn Michaels
NM $3   MIP $7

Ultimate Warrior
NM $3   MIP $7

Undertaker
NM $3   MIP $7

Vader
NM $3   MIP $7

SUPERSTARS, SERIES 3

Ahmed Johnson
NM $3   MIP $7

Bret Hart
NM $3   MIP $7

British Bulldog
NM $3   MIP $7

Diesel, reissue
NM $3   MIP $7

Goldust, reissue
NM $3   MIP $7

Mankind
NM $3   MIP $7

Shawn Michaels
NM $3   MIP $7

Sycho Sid
NM $3   MIP $7

SUPERSTARS, SERIES 4

Farooq
NM $3   MIP $7

Hunter Hearst Hemsley
NM $3   MIP $7

Jerry The King Lawler
NM $3   MIP $7

Justin Hawk Bradshaw
NM $3   MIP $7

Stone Cold Steve Austin
NM $3   MIP $7

Vader
NM $3   MIP $7

SUPERSTARS, SERIES 5

Flash Funk
NM $3   MIP $7

Ken Shamrock
NM $3   MIP $7

Rocky Maivia
NM $3   MIP $7

Savio Vega
NM $3   MIP $7

Stone Cold Steve Austin
NM $3   MIP $7

Sycho Sid
NM $3   MIP $7

SUPERSTARS, SERIES 6

HHH
NM $3   MIP $7

Jeff Jarrett
NM $3   MIP $7

Marc Mero
NM $3   MIP $7

Mark Henry
NM $3   MIP $7

Owen Hart, Jakks Pacific
NM $3   MIP $7

Steve Blackman

NM $3	MIP $7

SUPERSTARS, SERIES 7

Dr. Death Steve Williams

NM $3	MIP $7

Edge

NM $3	MIP $7

Stone Cold Steve Austin

NM $3	MIP $7

Undertaker

NM $3	MIP $7

Val Venis

NM $3	MIP $7

X Pac

NM $3	MIP $7

SUPERSTARS, SERIES 8

Big Boss Man

NM $3	MIP $7

Ken Shamrock

NM $3	MIP $7

Rock, The

NM $3	MIP $7

Shane McMahon

NM $3	MIP $7

Shawn Michaels

NM $3	MIP $7

SUPERSTARS, SERIES 9

Bob Holly

NM $3	MIP $7

Christian

NM $3	MIP $7

Gangrel

NM $3	MIP $7

Paul Wright

NM $3	MIP $7

Undertaker w/Robe

NM $3	MIP $7

Vince McMahon

NM $3	MIP $7

TAG TEAM, SERIES 1

Godwinns

NM $3	MIP $7

Headbangers

NM $3	MIP $7

Legion of Doom

NM $3	MIP $7

New Blackjacks

NM $3	MIP $7

TITAN TRON LIVE

Kane

NM $3	MIP $7

Mankind

NM $3	MIP $7

Road Dogg Jesse James

NM $3	MIP $7

Rock, The

NM $3	MIP $7

Stone Cold Steve Austin

NM $3	MIP $7

Undertaker

NM $3	MIP $7

WWF World Wrestling Federation (Hasbro, 1990-94)

FIGURES

1-2-3 Kid, 1994, Hasbro

NM $20	MIP $40

Adam Bomb, 1994, Hasbro

NM $10	MIP $18

Akeem, 1990, Hasbro

NM $15	MIP $26

Andre the Giant, 1990, Hasbro

NM $25	MIP $60

Ax, 1990, Hasbro

NM $5	MIP $12

Bam Bam Bigelow, 1994, Hasbro

NM $6	MIP $15

Bart Gunn, 1994, Hasbro

NM $10	MIP $18

Berzerker, 1993, Hasbro

NM $3	MIP $8

Big Bossman w/Jailhouse Jam, 1992, Hasbro

NM $4	MIP $8

Big Bossman, 1990, Hasbro

NM $4	MIP $25

Billy Gunn, 1994, Hasbro

NM $10	MIP $18

Bret "Hitman" Hart w/Hart Attack, 1992, Hasbro

NM $5	MIP $13

Bret Hart, 1993 mail-in, 1993, Hasbro

NM $38	MIP n/a

Bret Hart, 1994, Hasbro

NM $4	MIP $8

British Bulldog w/Bulldog Bash, 1992, Hasbro

NM $4	MIP $8

Brutus "The Barber" Beefcake w/Beefcake Flattop, 1992, Hasbro

NM $6	MIP $13

Brutus the Barber, 1990, Hasbro

NM $6	MIP $13

Bushwackers, two-pack, 1990-94, Hasbro

NM $5	MIP $25

Butch Miller, 1994, Hasbro

NM $3	MIP $8

Crush, 1993, 1993, Hasbro

NM $6	MIP $13

(Hasbro)

Crush, 1994, Hasbro

NM $5	MIP $15

Demolition, two-pack, 1990-94, Hasbro

NM $10	MIP $40

Doink the Clown, 1994, Hasbro

NM $4	MIP $8

Dusty Rhodes, 1991, Hasbro

NM $63	MIP $250

Earthquake, 1991, Hasbro

NM $8	MIP $15

Earthquake w/Aftershock, 1992, Hasbro

NM $4	MIP $13

El Matador, 1993, Hasbro

NM $3	MIP $8

Fatu, 1994, Hasbro

NM $3	MIP $8

Giant Gonzales, 1994, Hasbro

NM $3	MIP $8

Greg "the Hammer" Valentine w/Hammer Slammer, 1992, Hasbro

NM $5	MIP $15

Hacksaw Jim Duggan, 1991, Hasbro

NM $3	MIP $8

Hacksaw Jim Duggan, 1994, Hasbro

NM $3	MIP $8

Honky Tonk Man, 1991, Hasbro

NM $13	MIP $25

Hulk Hogan w/Hulkaplex, 1992, Hasbro

NM $5	MIP $10

Hulk Hogan, 1990, Hasbro

NM $6	MIP $13

Hulk Hogan, 1991, Hasbro

NM $5	MIP $10

Hulk Hogan, mail-in, 1993, Hasbro

NM $100	MIP $160

Hulk Hogan, no shirt, 1993, Hasbro

NM $5	MIP $10

I.R.S., 1993, Hasbro

NM $4	MIP $8

Jake the Snake Roberts, 1990, Hasbro
NM $5   MIP $10

Jim Neidhart, 1993, Hasbro
NM $3   MIP $8

Jimmy Superfly Snuka, 1991, Hasbro
NM $6   MIP $13

Kamala, 1993, Hasbro
NM $5   MIP $13

Koko B. Ware w/Bird Man Bounce, 1992, Hasbro
NM $10   MIP $30

Legion of Doom, two-pack, 1990-94, Hasbro
NM $10   MIP $20

Lex Luger, 1994, Hasbro
NM $8   MIP $15

Ludwig Borga, 1994, Hasbro
NM $20   MIP $35

Luke Williams, 1994, Hasbro
NM $5   MIP $15

Macho Man Randy Savage w/Macho Masher, 1992, Hasbro
NM $15   MIP $35

Macho Man, 1990, Hasbro
NM $12   MIP $25

Macho Man, 1991, Hasbro
NM $15   MIP $35

Macho Man, 1993, Hasbro
NM $7   MIP $15

Marty Jannetty, 1994, Hasbro
NM $5   MIP $15

Mountie, 1993, Hasbro
NM $6   MIP $15

Mr. Perfect w/Perfect Plex, 1992, Hasbro
NM $8   MIP $20

Mr. Perfect w/Texas Twister, 1992, Hasbro
NM $15   MIP $35

Mr. Perfect, 1994, Hasbro
NM $12   MIP $25

Nailz, 1993, Hasbro
NM $12   MIP $25

Nasty Boys, two-pack, 1990-94, Hasbro
NM $10   MIP $20

Owen Hart, 1993, Hasbro
NM $12   MIP $30

Papa Shango, 1993, Hasbro
NM $7   MIP $25

Razor Ramon, 1993, Hasbro
NM $15   MIP $30

(Hasbro)

Razor Ramon, 1994, Hasbro
NM $8   MIP $15

Repo Man, 1993, Hasbro
NM $7   MIP $15

Ric Flair, 1993, Hasbro
NM $7   MIP $15

Rick Martel, 1993, Hasbro
NM $5   MIP $15

Rick Rude, 1990, Hasbro
NM $15   MIP $30

Rick Steiner, 1994, Hasbro
NM $9   MIP $18

Ricky "The Dragon" Steamboat w/Steamboat Springer, 1992, Hasbro
NM $7   MIP $15

Rockers, two-pack, 1990-94, Hasbro
NM $10   MIP $20

Rowdy Roddy Piper, 1991, Hasbro
NM $15   MIP $30

Samu, 1994, Hasbro
NM $5   MIP $15

Scott Steiner, 1994, Hasbro
NM $8   MIP $18

Sgt. Slaughter w/Sgt.'s Salute, 1992, Hasbro
NM $15   MIP $30

Shawn Michaels, 1993, Hasbro
NM $10   MIP $25

(KP Photo)

Shawn Michaels, 1994, Hasbro, shown here w/group of figures from the series
NM $6   MIP $15

Sid Justice, 1993, Hasbro
NM $6   MIP $15

Skinner, 1993, Hasbro
NM $6   MIP $15

Smash, 1990, Hasbro
NM $12   MIP $25

Tatanka, 1993, Hasbro
NM $7   MIP $15

Tatanka, 1994, Hasbro
NM $7   MIP $15

Ted Diabiase, 1990, Hasbro
NM $10   MIP $20

Ted Diabiase, 1991, Hasbro
NM $7   MIP $15

Ted Diabiase, 1994, Hasbro
NM $7   MIP $15

Texas Tornado w/Texas Twister, 1992, 1992, Hasbro
NM $10   MIP $40

Typhoon w/Tidal Wave, 1992, Hasbro
NM $15   MIP $30

Ultimate Warrior w/Warrior Wham, 1992, Hasbro
NM $20   MIP $40

Ultimate Warrior, 1990, Hasbro
NM $12   MIP $25

Ultimate Warrior, 1991, Hasbro
NM $10   MIP $20

Undertaker w/Graveyard Smash, 1992, Hasbro
NM $9   MIP $18

Undertaker, mail-in, 1993, Hasbro
NM $25   MIP $50

Undertaker, 1994, Hasbro
NM $15   MIP $25

Virgil, 1993, Hasbro
NM $7   MIP $15

Warlord, 1993, Hasbro
NM $6   MIP $15

Yokozuna, 1994, Hasbro
NM $15   MIP $30

Xena Warrior Princess (Toy Biz, 1998-99)

6" FIGURES

Callisto Warrior Goddess w/Hope, 1999
NM $5   MIP $12

Grieving Gabrielle, 1999
NM $5   MIP $12

Xena Conqueror of Nations, 1999
NM $5   MIP $12

Xena Warrior Huntress, 1999
NM $5   MIP $12

SERIES I, 12" FIGURES

Callisto, 1998
NM $7   MIP $20

Gabrielle, 1998
NM $7   MIP $20

Xena, 1998

    NM $7   **MIP** $20

SERIES II, 12" FIGURES

Ares, 1999

    NM $7   **MIP** $20

Gabrielle Amazon Princess, 1999

    NM $7   **MIP** $20

Roman Xena, 1999

    NM $7   **MIP** $20

Warlord Xena, 1999

    NM $7   **MIP** $20

SERIES III, 12" FIGURES

Empress Gabrielle, 1999

    NM $14   **MIP** $30

Shamaness Xena, 1999

    NM $14   **MIP** $30

Xena the Evil Warrior, 1999

    NM $14   **MIP** $30

X-Files
(McFarlane, 1998)

FIGURES

Fireman w/Cryolitter, 1998, McFarlane

    NM $3   **MIP** $6

Mulder in Arctic Wear, 1998, McFarlane

    NM $3   **MIP** $6

Mulder w/Docile Alien, 1998, McFarlane

    NM $3   **MIP** $6

Mulder w/Human Host and Cryopod Chamber, 1998, McFarlane

    NM $3   **MIP** $6

Mulder w/Victim, 1998, McFarlane

    NM $3   **MIP** $6

Primitive Man w/Attack Alien, 1998, McFarlane

    NM $3   **MIP** $6

Scully in Arctic Wear, 1998, McFarlane

    NM $3   **MIP** $6

Scully w/Docile Alien, 1998, McFarlane

    NM $3   **MIP** $6

(Lenny Lee)

Scully w/Human Host and Cryopod Chamber, 1998, McFarlane, Agent Scully in parka, bases of human hosts snap together to form a row--just like in the movie

    NM $3   **MIP** $6

Scully w/Victim, 1998, McFarlane

    NM $3   **MIP** $6

X-Men
(Toy Biz, 1991-96)

FIGURES

Ahab, 1994, Toy Biz

    NM $2   **MIP** $5

Apocalypse I, 1991, Toy Biz

    NM $2   **MIP** $5

Apocalypse I, 1993, Toy Biz

    NM $2   **MIP** $5

Apocolypse, 1996, Toy Biz

    NM $2   **MIP** $5

Archangel, 1991, Toy Biz

    NM $2   **MIP** $5

Archangel, 1996, Toy Biz

    NM $2   **MIP** $5

Archangel II, 1995, Toy Biz

    NM $2   **MIP** $5

Banshee I, 1992, Toy Biz

    NM $2   **MIP** $5

Battle Ravaged Wolverine, 1995, Toy Biz

    NM $2   **MIP** $5

Beast, 1994, Toy Biz

    NM $2   **MIP** $5

Bishop II, 1993, Toy Biz

    NM $2   **MIP** $5

Bishop II, 1996, Toy Biz

    NM $2   **MIP** $5

Blob, 1995, Toy Biz

    NM $2   **MIP** $5

Cable Cyborg, 1995, Toy Biz

    NM $2   **MIP** $5

Caliban, 1995, Toy Biz

    NM $2   **MIP** $5

Cameron Hodge, 1995, Toy Biz

    NM $2   **MIP** $5

Captive Sabretooth, 1995, Toy Biz

    NM $2   **MIP** $5

Colossus, 1991, Toy Biz

    NM $2   **MIP** $5

Colossus, 1993, Toy Biz

    NM $2   **MIP** $5

Colossus, 1996, Toy Biz

    NM $2   **MIP** $5

Corsair, 1995, Toy Biz

    NM $2   **MIP** $5

Cyclops, 1996, Toy Biz

    NM $2   **MIP** $5

Cyclops I, blue, 1991, Toy Biz

    NM $2   **MIP** $5

Cyclops I, stripes, 1991, Toy Biz

    NM $2   **MIP** $5

Cyclops II, 1993, Toy Biz

    NM $2   **MIP** $5

Deadpool, 1995, Toy Biz

    NM $2   **MIP** $5

Domino, 1995, Toy Biz

    NM $2   **MIP** $5

Forge, 1992, Toy Biz

    NM $2   **MIP** $5

Gambit, 1992, Toy Biz

    NM $2   **MIP** $5

Gambit, 1993, Toy Biz

    NM $2   **MIP** $5

Gladiator, 1995, Toy Biz

    NM $2   **MIP** $5

Havok, 1995, Toy Biz

    NM $2   **MIP** $5

Ice Man, 1992, Toy Biz

    NM $2   **MIP** $5

Ice Man II, 1995, Toy Biz

    NM $2   **MIP** $5

Juggernaut, 1991, Toy Biz

    NM $2   **MIP** $5

Juggernaut, 1993, Toy Biz

    NM $2   **MIP** $5

Lady Deathstrike, 1996, Toy Biz

    NM $2   **MIP** $5

Magneto, 1996, Toy Biz

    NM $2   **MIP** $5

Magneto I, 1991, Toy Biz

    NM $2   **MIP** $5

Magneto II, 1992, Toy Biz

    NM $2   **MIP** $5

Morph, 1994, Toy Biz

    NM $2   **MIP** $5

Morph II, Toy Biz, Toyfare mail-away

    NM $2   **MIP** $5

Mr. Sinister, 1992, Toy Biz

    NM $2   **MIP** $5

Nightcrawler, 1993, Toy Biz

    NM $2   **MIP** $5

Nimrod, 1995, Toy Biz

    NM $2   **MIP** $5

Omega Red, 1993, Toy Biz

    NM $2   **MIP** $5

Omega Red II, 1996, Toy Biz

    NM $2   **MIP** $5

Phoenix, 1995, Toy Biz

    NM $2   **MIP** $5

Polaris, 1996, Toy Biz

    NM $2   **MIP** $5

Professor X, 1993, Toy Biz

    NM $2   **MIP** $5

Raza, 1994, Toy Biz
NM $2 MIP $5

Sabretooth, 1996, Toy Biz
NM $2 MIP $5

Sauron, 1992, Toy Biz
NM $2 MIP $5

Savage Land Wolverine, 1996, Toy Biz
NM $2 MIP $5

Spiral, 1995, Toy Biz
NM $2 MIP $5

Storm, 1991, Toy Biz
NM $2 MIP $5

Strong Guy, 1993, Toy Biz
NM $2 MIP $5

Sunfire, 1995, Toy Biz
NM $2 MIP $5

Trevor Fitzroy, 1994, Toy Biz
NM $2 MIP $5

Tusk, 1992, Toy Biz
NM $2 MIP $5

Warstar, 1995, Toy Biz
NM $2 MIP $5

Weapon X, 1996, Toy Biz
NM $2 MIP $5

Wolverine, 1996, Toy Biz
NM $2 MIP $5

Wolverine Fang, 1995, Toy Biz
NM $2 MIP $5

Wolverine I, 1991, Toy Biz
NM $2 MIP $5

Wolverine I, 1993, Toy Biz
NM $2 MIP $5

Wolverine II, 1992, Toy Biz
NM $2 MIP $5

Wolverine III, 1992, Toy Biz
NM $2 MIP $5

Wolverine V, 1993, Toy Biz
NM $2 MIP $5

Wolverine, space armor, 1995, Toy Biz
NM $2 MIP $5

Wolverine, street clothes, 1994, Toy Biz
NM $2 MIP $5

X-Cutioner, 1995, Toy Biz
NM $2 MIP $5

X-Men
(Toy Biz, 1996-98)

AGE OF APOCALYPSE, 5" FIGURES, 1996

Apocalypse, Removable Armor and Transforming Limbs, 1996
NM $3 MIP $6

Cyclops, Cybernetic Guardian and Laser Blaster, 1996
NM $3 MIP $6

Gambit, Blast-throwing Action, 1996
NM $3 MIP $6

Magneto, Removable Helmet and Shrapnel, 1996
NM $3 MIP $6

Sabretooth, Wild Child Sidekick Figure, 1996
NM $3 MIP $6

Weapon X, Interchangeable Weaponry, 1996
NM $3 MIP $6

CLASSICS, LIGHT-UP WEAPONS, 5" FIGURES, 1996

Gambit, Light-Up Plasma Energy Weapon, 1996
NM $3 MIP $7

Juggernaut, Light-Up Jewel Weapon, 1996
NM $3 MIP $7

Nightcrawler, Light-Up Sword, 1996
NM $3 MIP $7

Psylock, light-Up Psychic Knife, 1996
NM $3 MIP $7

Wolverine Stealth, Light-Up Plasma Weapon, 1996
NM $3 MIP $7

MISSLE FLYERS, 5" FIGURES, 1997

Apocalypse, Trap-Door Chest, 1997
NM $2 MIP $7

Bishop, Fold-Out Armor Wing Blasters, 1997
NM $2 MIP $7

Cable, Attack Wings, 1997
NM $2 MIP $7

Shard, Spring Loaded Firing Wing Extensions, 1997
NM $2 MIP $7

Wolverine, Head Launching Bird of Prey, 1997
NM $2 MIP $7

MONSTER ARMOR, 5" FIGURES, 1997

Cyclops w/Snap-On Cyclaw Armor, 1997
NM $2 MIP $6

Mr. Sinister w/Snap-On Cyber Tech Armor, 1997
NM $2 MIP $6

Mystique w/Snap-On She-Beast Armor, 1997
NM $2 MIP $6

Rogue w/Snap-On Leech Bat Armor, 1997
NM $2 MIP $6

Wolverine w/Snap-On Fangor Armor, 1997
NM $2 MIP $6

NEW MUTANTS, 5" FIGURES, 1998

Magik, 1998
NM $2 MIP $6

Warlock, 1998
NM $2 MIP $6

Wolfsbane, 1998
NM $2 MIP $6

NINJA FORCE, 5" FIGURES, 1997

Dark Nemesis w/Spear Shooting Staff, 1997
NM $2 MIP $5

Ninja Sabretooth w/Clip-on Claw Armor, 1997
NM $2 MIP $5

Ninja Wolverine w/Warrior Assault Gear, 1997
NM $2 MIP $5

Psylocke w/Extending Power Sword, 1997
NM $2 MIP $5

Space Ninja Deathbird w/Fold-Out Ninja Wings, 1997
NM $2 MIP $5

ONSLAUGHT, 6" FIGURES, 1997

Apocalypse Rising, Ozymandias, 1997
NM $2 MIP $5

Jean Grey, Psychic Claw, 1997
NM $2 MIP $5

Onslaught, Ultimate Power Armor, 1997
NM $2 MIP $5

Wolverine Unleashed, Franklin Richards, 1997
NM $2 MIP $5

ROBOT FIGHTERS, 5" FIGURES, 1997

Cyclops, Apocalypse Droid w/Gattling Gun Arm, 1997
NM $2 MIP $5

Gambit, Attack Robot Droid w/Projectile Missile, 1997
NM $2 MIP $5

Jubilee, Grabbing Sentinel Hand w/Projectile Finger, 1997
NM $2 MIP $5

Storm, Spinning Weather Station w/Lightning Projectile, 1997
NM $2 MIP $5

Wolverine, Slashing Sabretooth Droid w/Missile Claw, 1997
NM $2 MIP $5

SAVAGE LAND, 5" FIGURES, 1997

Angel w/Wing Flapping Sauron-Dino, 1997

NM $2   MIP $5

Kazar w/Jumping Zabu Tiger, 1997

NM $2   MIP $5

Magneto w/Water Spitting Amphibious, 1997

NM $2   MIP $5

Savage Storm w/Head Ramming Colossus Dino, 1997

NM $2   MIP $5

Savage Wolverine w/Jaw Chomping Crawler-Rex, 1997

NM $2   MIP $5

SECRET WEAPON FORCE BATTLE BASES, 5" FIGURES, 1998

Cyclops w/War Tank Blaster, 1998

NM $2   MIP $5

Jean Grey w/Catapult Tank Blaster, 1998

NM $2   MIP $5

Magneto Battle Base, 1998

NM $2   MIP $5

Omega w/Spinning Rocket Blaster, 1998

NM $2   MIP $5

Wolverine Battle Base, 1998

NM $2   MIP $5

Wolverine w/Claw Cannon Blaster, 1998

NM $2   MIP $5

SECRET WEAPON FORCE FLYING FIGHTERS, 5" FIGURES, 1998

Cyclops w/High-Flying Hazard Gear, 1998

NM $2   MIP $5

Jean Grey w/Fire Bird Flyer, 1998

NM $2   MIP $5

Maggot w/Expanding Assault Wings, 1998

NM $2   MIP $5

Mr. Sinister w/Bio-Tech Attack Wings, 1998

NM $2   MIP $5

SECRET WEAPON FORCE POWER SLAMMERS, 5" FIGURES, 1998

Gambit w/Rapid Fire Card Cannon Slammer, 1998

NM $2   MIP $4

Master Mold w/Rapid Fire Sentinels, 1998

NM $2   MIP $4

Rogue w/Double Barrel Slammer, 1998

NM $2   MIP $4

Wolverine w/Rapid Fire Disk Slammer, 1998

NM $2   MIP $4

SECRET WEAPON FORCE SHAPE SHIFTERS, 7" FIGURES, 1998

Juggernaut forms into Titanic Tank, 1998

NM $2   MIP $6

Morph forms into Mega Missile, 1998

NM $2   MIP $6

Wolverine forms into Mutant Wolf, 1998

NM $2   MIP $6

SECRET WEAPON FORCE SUPER SHOOTER, 5" FIGURES, 1998

Apocalypse, 1998

NM $3   MIP $10

Beast, 1998

NM $3   MIP $8

Colossus, 1998

NM $3   MIP $8

Wolverine, 1998

NM $3   MIP $8

SHATTERSHOT, 5" FIGURES, 1996

Age of Apocalypse Beast, Wind-up Chain Saw, 1996

NM $2   MIP $6

Archangel, Wing-flapping Action, 1996

NM $2   MIP $6

Colossus, Super Punch Gauntlets, 1996

NM $2   MIP $6

Lady Death Strike, Transforming Reaver Armor, 1996

NM $2   MIP $6

Patch Wolverine, Total Assault Arsenal, 1996

NM $2   MIP $6

SPECIAL EDITION SERIES, 12" FIGURES, 1998

Gambit, 1998

NM $8   MIP $25

Storm, 1998

NM $8   MIP $25

Wolverine, 1998

NM $8   MIP $25

X-Men 2099 (Toy Biz, 1996)

5" FIGURES

Bloodhawk, 1996

NM $2   MIP $5

Breakdown, Dominick Sidekick Figure, 1996

NM $2   MIP $5

Brimstone Love, 1996

NM $2   MIP $5

Halloween Jack, 1996

NM $2   MIP $5

Junkpile, Snap-on Battle Armor, 1996

NM $2   MIP $5

La Lunatica, Futuristic Jai-Lai, 1996

NM $2   MIP $5

Meanstreak, 1996

NM $2   MIP $5

Metalhead, 1996

NM $2   MIP $5

Shadow Dancer, 1996

NM $2   MIP $5

Skullfire, Glowing Fire Skeleton, 1996

NM $2   MIP $5

X-Men vs. Street Fighter (Toy Biz, 1998)

5" FIGURES

Apocalypse vs. Dhalism, 1998

NM $6   MIP $15

Cyclops vs. M. Bison, 1998

NM $4   MIP $12

Gambit vs. Cammy, 1998

NM $4   MIP $12

Juggernaut vs. Chun-Li, 1998

NM $6   MIP $15

Magneto vs. Ryu, 1998

NM $5   MIP $12

Rogue vs. Zangief, 1998

NM $4   MIP $12

Sabretooth vs. Ken, 1998

NM $6   MIP $15

Wolverine vs. Akuma, 1998

NM $5   MIP $12

X-Men/X-Force (Toy Biz, 1991-96)

DELUXE 10" FIGURES

Cable, 1995

NM $3   MIP $8

Kane, 1995

NM $3   MIP $8

Shatterstar, 1995

NM $3   MIP $8

FIGURES

Arctic Armor Cable, 1996, Toy Biz

NM $2   MIP $4

Avalanche, 1995, Toy Biz

NM $2   MIP $4

Black Tom, 1994, Toy Biz

NM $2   MIP $4

Black Tom, 1995, Toy Biz
NM $2   MIP $4

Blob, The, 1995, Toy Biz
NM $2   MIP $4

Bonebreaker, 1994, Toy Biz
NM $2   MIP $4

Bridge, 1992, Toy Biz
NM $2   MIP $4

Brood, 1993, Toy Biz
NM $2   MIP $4

Cable Cyborg, 1995, Toy Biz
NM $2   MIP $4

Cable I, 1992, Toy Biz
NM $2   MIP $4

Cable II, 1993, Toy Biz
NM $2   MIP $4

Cable III, 1993, Toy Biz
NM $2   MIP $4

Cable IV, 1994, Toy Biz
NM $2   MIP $4

Cable Stealth, 1996, Toy Biz
NM $2   MIP $4

Cable V, 1994, Toy Biz
NM $2   MIP $4

(KP Photo)

Cannonball, pink, 1993, Toy Biz
NM $2   MIP $4

Cannonball, purple, 1993, Toy Biz
NM $2   MIP $4

Commando, 1995, Toy Biz
NM $2   MIP $4

Deadpool, 1992, Toy Biz
NM $4   MIP $12

Deadpool, 1995, Toy Biz
NM $4   MIP $12

Domino, 1995, Toy Biz
NM $2   MIP $4

Exodus, 1995, Toy Biz
NM $2   MIP $4

Forearm, 1992, Toy Biz
NM $2   MIP $4

Genesis, 1995, Toy Biz
NM $2   MIP $4

Gideon, 1992, Toy Biz
NM $2   MIP $4

Grizzly, 1993, Toy Biz
NM $2   MIP $4

Kane I, 1992, Toy Biz
NM $2   MIP $4

Kane II, 1993, Toy Biz
NM $2   MIP $4

Killspree, 1994, Toy Biz
NM $2   MIP $4

Killspree II, 1996, Toy Biz
NM $2   MIP $4

Krule, 1993, Toy Biz
NM $2   MIP $4

Kylun, 1994, Toy Biz
NM $2   MIP $4

Longshot, 1994, Toy Biz
NM $2   MIP $4

Mojo, 1995, Toy Biz
NM $2   MIP $4

Nimrod, 1995, Toy Biz
NM $2   MIP $4

Pyro, 1994, Toy Biz
NM $2   MIP $4

Quark, 1994, Toy Biz
NM $2   MIP $4

Random, 1994, Toy Biz
NM $2   MIP $4

Rictor, 1994, Toy Biz
NM $2   MIP $4

Rogue, 1994, Toy Biz
NM $2   MIP $4

Sabretooth I, 1992, Toy Biz
NM $2   MIP $4

Sabretooth II, 1994, Toy Biz
NM $2   MIP $4

Shatterstar I, 1992, Toy Biz
NM $2   MIP $4

Shatterstar II, 1994, Toy Biz
NM $2   MIP $4

Shatterstar III, 1996, Toy Biz
NM $2   MIP $4

Silver Samurai, 1994, Toy Biz
NM $2   MIP $4

Slayback, 1994, Toy Biz
NM $2   MIP $4

Stryfe, 1992, Toy Biz
NM $2   MIP $4

Sunspot, 1994, Toy Biz
NM $2   MIP $4

Urban Assault, 1995, Toy Biz
NM $2   MIP $4

Warpath I, 1992, Toy Biz
NM $2   MIP $4

Warpath II, 1994, Toy Biz
NM $2   MIP $4

X-Treme, 1994, Toy Biz
NM $2   MIP $4

X-Men: Evolution (Toy Biz, 2001-02)

5" FIGURES

Battle Ravaged Wolverine, 2001-02, Toy Biz, Series 3, w/Sabretooth
NM $4   MIP $8

Cyclops, 2001-02, Toy Biz, Series 1
NM $4   MIP $12

Juggernaut, 2001-02, Toy Biz, Series 3
NM $4   MIP $8

Logan, 2001-02, Toy Biz, w/hat and "X" base
NM $4   MIP $8

Magneto, 2001-02, Toy Biz, Series 3
NM $4   MIP $12

Nightcrawler, 2001-02, Toy Biz, Series 1
NM $4   MIP $8

Nightcrawler II, 2001-02, Toy Biz, Series 3
NM $4   MIP $8

Ninja Wolverine, 2001-02, Toy Biz, Series 2
NM $4   MIP $8

Sabretooth, 2001-02, Toy Biz, Series 1
NM $4   MIP $8

Spyke, 2001-02, Toy Biz, Series 2
NM $4   MIP $8

Storm, 2001-02, Toy Biz, Series 2
NM $4   MIP $8

The Blob, 2001-02, Toy Biz, Series 2
NM $4   MIP $8

Toad, 2001-02, Toy Biz, Series 1
NM $4   MIP $8

Wolverine, 2001-02, Toy Biz, Series 1
NM $4   MIP $8

8" FIGURES

Cyclops, 2001-02, Toy Biz
NM $4   MIP $8

Toad, 2001-02, Toy Biz
NM $4   MIP $8

Wolverine, 2001-02, Toy Biz
NM $4   MIP $8

VEHICLES

Logan Battle Cycle, 2001-02, Toy Biz, w/Logan
NM $5   MIP $10

Sabretooth Battle Cycle, 2001-02, Toy Biz, w/Sabretooth
NM $5   MIP $10

Wolverine Battle Cycle, 2001-02, Toy Biz, w/Wolverine
NM $5   MIP $10

X-Men: The Movie (Toy Biz, 2000)

FIGURES

Cyclops, 2000, Toy Biz
NM $2   MIP $4

Jean Grey, 2000, Toy Biz
NM $2   MIP $4

Logan, 2000, Toy Biz
NM $2   MIP $4

Magneto, 2000, Toy Biz
NM $2   MIP $4

Mystique, 2000, Toy Biz
NM $2   MIP $4

Professor X, 2000, Toy Biz
NM $2   MIP $4

Rogue, 2000, Toy Biz
NM $2   MIP $4

Sabretooth, 2000, Toy Biz
NM $2   MIP $4

Storm, 2000, Toy Biz
NM $2   MIP $4

Toad, 2000, Toy Biz
NM $2   MIP $4

Wolverine, 2000, Toy Biz
NM $2   MIP $4

TWO PACKS

Logan and Rogue, 2000, Toy Biz
NM $2   MIP $4

Magneto and Logan, 2000, Toy Biz
NM $2   MIP $4

Wolverine and Sabre, 2000, Toy Biz
NM $2   MIP $4

X-Men: X2, X-Men United (Toy Biz, 2003)

12" FIGURES

Nightcrawler, 2003, Toy Biz
NM $4   MIP $8

Wolverine, 2003, Toy Biz
NM $4   MIP $8

5" FIGURES

Cyclops, 2003, Toy Biz, Series 2
NM $4   MIP $7

Cyclops, 2003, Toy Biz, Series 1
NM $4   MIP $7

Iceman, 2003, Toy Biz, Series 2
NM $4   MIP $7

Logan, 2003, Toy Biz, Series 2
NM $4   MIP $10

Logan, 2003, Toy Biz, Series 1
NM $4   MIP $10

Magneto, 2003, Toy Biz, Series 2
NM $4   MIP $7

Nightcrawler, 2003, Toy Biz, Series 1
NM $4   MIP $7

Wolverine, 2003, Toy Biz, Series 2
NM $5   MIP $10

Wolverine, 2003, Toy Biz, Series 1
NM $5   MIP $12

VEHICLES

X-Jet, 2003, Toy Biz, w/Wolverine figure
NM $12   MIP $25

Yellow Submarine (McFarlane, 1999-2004)

SERIES 1, 1999

George w/Yellow Submarine, 1999, McFarlane
NM $3   MIP $10

John w/Jeremy, 1999, McFarlane
NM $3   MIP $10

Paul w/Capt in Fred, 1999, McFarlane
NM $3   MIP $10

Paul w/Glove and Love Base, 1999, McFarlane
NM $4   MIP $12

Ringo w/Blue Meanie, 1999, McFarlane
NM $3   MIP $10

SERIES 2, SGT. PEPPER'S LONELY HEARTS CLUB BAND, 2000

George w/Snapping Turk, 2000, McFarlane
NM $3   MIP $8

(McFarlane Toys)

John w/Bulldog, 2000, McFarlane
NM $3   MIP $8

(McFarlane Toys)

Paul w/Sucking Monster, 2000, McFarlane
NM $3   MIP $9

(McFarlane Toys)

Ringo w/Apple Bonker, 2000, McFarlane
NM $3   MIP $8

SERIES 3, 2004

George w/Blue Meanie, 2004, McFarlane
NM $3   MIP $10

John w/Love and Glove Base, 2004, McFarlane
NM $3   MIP $10

Paul w/Jeremy, 2004, McFarlane
NM $3   MIP $10

Ringo w/Yellow Submarine, 2004, McFarlane
NM $3   MIP $10

Zorro (Gabriel, 1982)

FIGURES

Amigo, 1982, Gabriel
NM $12   MIP $30

Captain Ramon, 1982, Gabriel
NM $12   MIP $27

Picaro, 1982, Gabriel, horse
NM $20   MIP $55

Sergeant Gonzales, 1982, Gabriel
NM $12   MIP $24

Tempest, 1982, Gabriel, horse
NM $20   MIP $60

Zorro, 1982, Gabriel
NM $15   MIP $35

Zorro (Playmates, 1997)

FIGURES

Barbed Wire Zorro, 1997, Playmates
NM $2   MIP $4

Chain Mail Zorro, 1997, Playmates
NM $2   MIP $4

Don Diego, 1997, Playmates
NM $2   MIP $4

Evil Ramon, 1997, Playmates
NM $2   MIP $4

Zorro w/Tornado, 1997, Playmates, figure and horse
NM $2   MIP $4

Advertising Toys

by Justin Moen

In advertising the primary objective, of course, is to effectively sell a company's product. And there is no better way of doing that than by creating unique, lovable mascot-like characters to help make the product more appealing.

These charming characters are found everywhere, from carefully packaged products at stores to TV ads, radio spots, print ads, online ads, and billboards, representing anything from food to car insurance.

This is a practice that has existed for well over a century. And over that time some of these characters have overshadowed the products they sell to become pop culture icons. Examples include: Energizer Bunny (Energizer Batteries), Tony the Tiger (Kellogg's Frosted Flakes), Charlie the Tuna (Starkist), Aunt Jemima (Aunt Jemima Syrup), and Speedy (Alka-Seltzer) just to name a few.

The best advertising characters are those that promote fun, excitement, and education for both children and adults. This often leads to "pester power," often among children, who continually bug their parents to the point where the parent finally gives in and buys the product the child wants. Who is going to say "no" to Ernie the Keebler Elf, right?

In recent years this form of product advertising has generated controversy in the fast-food industry due to the growing concern of child obesity in this country, but the fact remains that characters like Ronald McDonald and The Burger King have been effective in bringing parents and children into the restaurants.

In today's market food-related characters are generally the most popular among collectors. Characters like Mr. Peanut, Elsie the Cow, Aunt Jemima, Vegetable Man, and Charlie the Tuna still stand the test of time, and only get sweeter with age. But there are several non-food-related characters that are just as popular like Speedy, The Michelin Man, Reddy Kilowatt, and the Energizer Bunny.

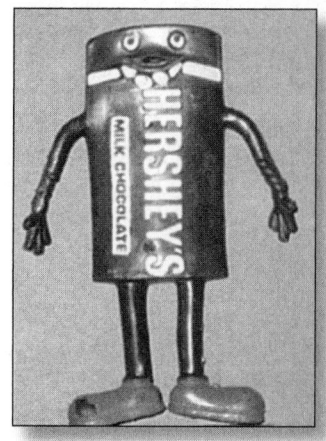

The **Top 10 ADVERTISING TOYS** in mint condition

1. Quisp Bank, Quaker Oats, 1960s $850
2. Reddy Kilowatt Bobbin' Head, Reddy Communications, 1960s $450
3. Quisp Powered Sugar Space Gun, Quaker Oats. $400
4. Esky Store Display, Esquire Magazine, 1940s $375
5. Mr. Peanut Figure, Planters Peanuts, 1930s $375
6. Speedy Figure, Alka-Seltzer, 1963. . . . . $360
7. Elsie the Cow Cookie Jar, Borden's, 1950s. $350
8. Vegetable Man Bank, Kraft, 1970s $280
9. Vegetable Man Display, Kraft, 1980. . . . . $280
10. Barnum's Animal Crackers Cookie Jar, Nabisco, 1972 . . . . $275

7-Eleven

Big Bite Figures, 1987, 3-1/2" hot dog men holding snacks
EX $10   NM $15   MIP $25

7-Up

Fresh Up Freddie, 1959, 9" tall, vinyl figure, red hair, white shirt, holding bottle of 7-Up
EX $45   NM $100   MIP $150

Spot, 1988, 4" tall, wind-up walking figure of the red "spot" w/sunglasses
EX $5   NM $10   MIP $15

Spot Wind-Up, 1990, 3" red circular figure w/sunglasses
EX $8   NM $12   MIP $15

Air India

Air India Man Figure, 1973, 4-1/2" statue of man wearing turban standing on flying carpet
EX $15   NM $25   MIP $40

Alka-Seltzer

Speedy, 2003, Wacky Wobbler, #6012, 8"
EX $3   NM $7   MIP $12

Speedy Figure, 1963, 5-1/2" vinyl boy holding Alka-Seltzer figure
EX $280   NM $310   MIP $360

Alpo

Alpo Winross Semi, 1976, 1:64-scale die-cast truck
EX $8   NM $15   MIP $25

Dan the Dog Cookie Jar, 1980s, 7" ceramic gray and white sheep dog
EX $40   NM $55   MIP $75

Dan the Dog Wind-Up, 1979, 3" wind-up figure of shaggy gray dog walking on his front paws
EX $10   NM $15   MIP $25

American Home Food Products

Marky Maypo Figure, 1960, 9" vinyl figure
EX $45   NM $60   MIP $85

Aunt Jemima Syrup

Aunt Jemima Doll, 1950s, 13" cloth doll wearing red checkered dress
EX $75   NM $90   MIP $110

Salt & Pepper Shakers, Aunt Jemima and Uncle Mose, plastic
EX $35   NM $45   MIP $65

Baskin Robbins

Pinky the Spoon Figure, 1993, 5" bendable figure
EX $6   NM $8   MIP $12

Bazooka

Bazooka Joe, 2003, Wacky Wobbler, #6028, 8"
EX $3   NM $7   MIP $12

Bazooka Joe Doll, 1973, 19" plush boy pirate
EX $30   NM $35   MIP $45

Beatrice Foods

Clark Bar Figure, 1960s, 8-1/2" vinyl boy holding a Clark bar wearing a striped shirt
EX $200   NM $225   MIP $275

Beech-Nut

Fruit Stripe Gum Figure, 1967, 7-1/2" bendable man shaped like a pack of gum riding a motorcycle
EX $150   NM $200   MIP $225

Bob's Big Boy

Big Boy, Wacky Wobbler, 8"
EX $5   NM $10   MIP $15

Big Boy Bank, bank w/black or blue shoes, 8"
EX $15   NM $20   MIP $30

Big Boy Cloth Doll, 1970s, 14" tall, smiling Big Boy w/hands holding suspenders
EX $50   NM $100   MIP $150

Big Boy Night Light, 1960s, 6-3/4" tall, vinyl, electric night light
EX $50   NM $100   MIP $150

Dolly Doll, 1978, 14" cloth girl doll w/Dolly nametag
EX $15   NM $25   MIP $30

Nodder, 1960s
EX $15   NM $30   MIP $45

Nugget Doll, 1978, 10" cloth dog doll w/"Nugget" on collar
EX $20   NM $30   MIP $40

Borden's

Elsie the Cow Cookie Jar, 1950s, 12" Elsie w/her head popping out of barrel
EX $275   NM $300   MIP $350

Elsie the Cow Doll, 1950s, 12" plush cow that moos when shaken
EX $55   NM $80   MIP $90

Elsie the Cow Lamp, 1947, electric lamp, ceramic
EX $150   NM $175   MIP $225

Bradford House Restaurants

Bucky Bradford Figure, 1960s, 9-1/2" blond pilgrim boy holding dish that reads "It's Yum Yum Time"
EX $35   NM $40   MIP $50

Burger King

Burger King Doll, 1980, "Magical Burger King," 20"
EX $10   NM $20   MIP $40

Burger King Stuffed Toy, 1972, smiling, beardless, 15"
EX $10   NM $18   MIP $35

Burger King Stuffed Toy, 1977, hands on hips, w/beard, 13"
EX $15   NM $25   MIP $35

Campbell

Campbell's Kid Doll, 1950s, 9-1/2" vinyl jointed cheerleader wearing a white shirt w/"C" in middle
EX $45   NM $65   MIP $80

Campbell's Kid Doll, 1973, 16" blonde girl w/red hair
EX $35   NM $45   MIP $50

Campbell's Kid Figure, 1950s, 7" boy chef doll w/"C" on hat and spoon in his hand
EX $50   NM $60   MIP $75

Campbell's Kid Figure, 1970s, 7" vinyl Campbell boy w/blue overalls
EX $35   NM $50   MIP $65

Christmas Ornament, 1989, ball ornament w/picture of Campbell Kid dressed as Santa
EX $5   NM $10   MIP $15

Wizard of O's Figure, 1978, 7-1/2" vinyl wizard w/Spaghetti O's on his hat and bow tie
EX $35   NM $45   MIP $55

Champion Auto Stores

Champ Man Figure, 1991, 6" bendable man; head is a flag
EX $7   NM $10   MIP $15

Chicken Delight International

Chicken Delight Bank, 1960s, 6" yellow and red chicken holding a tray of biscuits
EX $85   NM $125   MIP $150

Chiquita

Chiquita Banana Doll, 1974, 16" plush dancing banana w/fruit on its head
EX $20   NM $25   MIP $30

Coca-Cola

Sprite - Lucky Lymon, 1990, 7-1/2", vinyl, talking doll
EX $25   NM $35   MIP $45

Sprite Boy, 2003, Wacky Wobbler, #5065, 8"
EX $5   NM $10   MIP $15

Cracker Jack

Cracker Jack and Bingo, 1996, 16" doll, 100th anniversary of Cracker Jack
EX $25   NM $30   MIP $45

Cracker Jack and Bingo, 2000, Wacky Wobbler, 8"
EX $3   NM $12   MIP $25

Cracker Jack Doll, 1974, 15" plush sailor holding small box of Cracker Jacks snacks
EX $25   NM $35   MIP $45

Cracker Jack Doll, 1980, vinyl and cloth
EX $7   NM $20   MIP $40

Crest Toothpaste

Sparkle Telephone, 1980s, 11" blue and silver snowman-type character
EX $30   NM $40   MIP $45

Curad

Taped Crusader Figure, 1977, 7-1/2" male cartoon superhero
EX $65   NM $75   MIP $85

Curity

Miss Curity Display, 1950s, 18" plastic store display of a nurse on a base
EX $125   NM $150   MIP $185

Del Monte

Big Top Bonanza Clown Bank, 1985, colorful, smiling clown
EX $6   NM $11   MIP $22

Cobbie Corn, 1984, stuffed ear of corn, Yumkins
EX $8   NM $16   MIP $24

Juicie Pineapple, 1984, 11" stuffed pineapple, Country Yumkin, tan w/green leaves
EX $10   NM $20   MIP $30

Lushy Peach, 1984, stuffed peach, Yumkins
EX $8   NM $16   MIP $24

Precious Pear, 1984, stuffed pear, Yumkins
EX $8   NM $16   MIP $24

Reddie Tomato, 1984, stuffed tomato, Yumkins
EX $8   NM $16   MIP $24

Shoo-Shoo Scarecrow, 1983, 14" stuffed scarecrow, Country Yumkin, white shirt, blue coveralls
EX $10   NM $20   MIP $30

Sweetie Pea, 1984, stuffed pea, Yumkins
EX $8   NM $16   MIP $24

Yumkins Christmas Ornaments, 1984, set of six Yumkins mini characters
EX $6   NM $12   MIP $20

Domino's Pizza

Noid Plush Doll, 1988, 11" plush toy
EX $5   NM $10   MIP $15

Douglas Oil Co.

Freddy Fast Figure, 1976, 7" freckled face boy; hat says "Freddy Fast"
EX $90   NM $110   MIP $130

Dow Brands

Scrubbing Bubble Brush, 1980s, 3-1/2" light blue scrub brush
EX $12   NM $15   MIP $18

Scrubbing Bubbles Bank, 1990s, ceramic bubble character bank
EX $5   NM $12   MIP $22

Scrubbing Bubbles Bathroom Shelf, 1992, 6" x 4" x 2-1/2" shelf w/characters
EX $5   NM $10   MIP $15

Scrubbing Bubbles Character, 1989, vinyl bubble character, floats
EX $5   NM $10   MIP $15

Scrubbing Bubbles Shower Radio,
1980s, transistor radio, waterproof,
3-1/2" x 7" w/hook for use in shower
EX $5   NM $10   MIP $15

Esquire Magazine

Esky Store Display, 1940s, 11" old
man dressed in a tuxedo standing
on an Esquire magazine
EX $300   NM $350   MIP $375

Esso

Esso Tiger Figure, 1960s, 8-1/2"
plastic tiger
EX $25   NM $30   MIP $35

Esso Tiger Garbage Can, 1970s,
10" metal garbage can w/picture of
the Esso tiger
EX $15   NM $20   MIP $30

Little Oil Drop Bank, 1958, plastic, red
or white, 6-1/2"
EX $25   NM $50   MIP $100

Tiger Mug, 1960s, Fire King/Anchor
Hocking, ceramic mug w/Esso
Tiger image
EX $3   NM $7   MIP $12

Eveready Batteries

Energizer Bunny Plush, 1996, 22"
plush
EX $17   NM $42   MIP $68

Eveready Cat Bank, 1981, black cat
w/Eveready battery on side
EX $10   NM $15   MIP $20

Facit Adding Machines

Facit Man Figure, 1964, 4" man
wearing yellow outfit w/black
wizard hat
EX $25   NM $35   MIP $45

Florida Citrus Department

Florida Orange Bird Hat, 1970s,
child's-size hat w/visor, pictures
Orange Bird on front and back
EX $10   NM $15   MIP $20

Florida Orange Bird Nodder, 1970s,
7" plastic
EX $50   NM $60   MIP $75

Florida Orange Bird Stick Pin, 1980s,
metal, depicts the Florida Orange
Bird
EX $5   NM $10   MIP $15

Frito Lay

Chester Cheese, 1998, Cheetos'
mascot in a 10" tall plush figure
EX $10   NM $20   MIP $30

Funny Face Drink

Choo Choo Cherry Ramp Walker,
1971, 3" round, red figure
w/conductor's hat
EX $73   NM $95   MIP $120

Freezer Molds, 1977, mold of each
character w/spoon, color
variations, value for each
EX $4   NM $8   MIP $12

Funny Face Mugs, 1969, 3" mugs of
Funny Face characters, each
EX $9   NM $13   MIP $17

Goofy Grape Pitcher, 1973, 10"
pitcher of smiling, purple character
wearing lime green captain's hat
EX $75   NM $95   MIP $125

Lefty Lemon Frisbee, 1980s, plastic
w/picture of Lefty Lemon
EX $5   NM $10   MIP $12

Pillows, 1970s, one for each
character, sizes from 11" to 15",
value for each
EX $20   NM $40   MIP $60

General Mills

Boo Berry Bank, bank, no moving
parts, 8"
EX $3   NM $7   MIP $15

Boo Berry Figure, 1975, 7-1/2" white
and light blue ghost w/hat and bow
tie
EX $78   NM $97   MIP $124

Cereal Card Game, 1981, card game
w/different cereal characters
EX $10   NM $15   MIP $20

Chex Party Mix Snoopy, 1990s,
plastic bank, Snoopy on doghouse
w/stickers "Chex Pary Mix and
Peanuts 40 Years of Tradion"
EX $5   NM $10   MIP $15

Count Chocula, 2000, Wacky
Wobbler, 8"
EX $3   NM $7   MIP $15

Count Chocula Figure, 1975, 7-1/2"
vinyl vampire
EX $70   **NM** $85   **MIP** $110

Count Chocula Plush, 1997, 9" plush
figure
EX $5   **NM** $10   **MIP** $15

Franken Berry, 2000, Wacky Wobbler,
8"
EX $3   **NM** $7   **MIP** $15

Frankenberry Figure, 1975, 8" vinyl
pink Frankenstein
EX $72   **NM** $100   **MIP** $140

Frankenberry Premium, 1970s, small
plastic Frankenberry, cereal
premium
EX $2   **NM** $4   **MIP** $8

Frankenberry Toothbrush Holder,
1970s, small plastic for single
toothbrush
EX $2   **NM** $4   **MIP** $6

Fruit Brute Figure, 1975, 8" vinyl
werewolf w/striped shirt
EX $75   **NM** $90   **MIP** $120

Lucky Charms, 2000, Wacky Wobbler,
8"
EX $3   **NM** $7   **MIP** $15

Lucky Charms Leprechaun Doll,
1978, 17" plush
EX $25   **NM** $35   **MIP** $40

Lucky Charms Plush, 1997, 9" plush
figure
EX $5   **NM** $10   **MIP** $15

Monster Cereal Pencil Case, 1980s,
8" x 5", vinyl case featuring Count
Chocula, Frankenberry and Boo
Berry
EX $10   **NM** $15   **MIP** $20

Monster Cereals Puppets, 1970s,
plastic puppets of Count Chocula,
Frankenberry, Boo Berry
EX $4   **NM** $8   **MIP** $12

Trix Rabbit, 2000, Wacky Wobbler, 8"
EX $3   **NM** $7   **MIP** $12

Trix Rabbit Figure, 1977, 9" vinyl
white rabbit
EX $32   **NM** $44   **MIP** $56

Gerber Products

Gerber Boy figure, 1985, 8" vinyl boy
w/baseball cap turned sideways
that reads "I'm a Gerber Kid"
EX $25   **NM** $30   **MIP** $35

Good Humor

Good Humor Bar, 1975, 8" vinyl ice
cream bar w/a bite out of it
EX $200   **NM** $225   **MIP** $325

Grandma's Cookies

Grandma Bank, 1988, 7-1/2" hard plastic
Grandma wearing a blue dress
EX $25   **NM** $30   **MIP** $35

H.P. Hood

Harry Hood Figure, 1981, 7-1/2"
delivery man w/"Hood" inscription
on chest
EX $55   **NM** $70   **MIP** $80

Hershey's

Hershey's Chocolate Figure, 1987,
4-1/2" bendable candy bar shaped
like a man
EX $8   **NM** $12   **MIP** $20

Hostess

Hostess Twinkie Bake Set, 1990s,
bake your own Twinkies, non-stick
pan, spatula
EX $8   **NM** $15   **MIP** $25

Twinkie Holder, 1990s, plastic
Twinkie the Kid holds one Twinkie
inside
EX $2   **NM** $5   **MIP** $10

Twinkie the Kid, 2000, Wacky
Wobbler, 8"
EX $3   **NM** $7   **MIP** $12

Twinkie the Kid All American Yo-Yo,
1970s, white w/sticker "All
American Yo-Yo"
EX $10   **NM** $20   **MIP** $30

Hush Puppies

Hush Puppies Figure, 1970s, 8" tan
and brown basset hound
EX $30   **NM** $35   **MIP** $45

ICEE

ICEE Bear Figure, 1970s, 8" vinyl polar
bear drinking an ICEE
EX $35   **NM** $45   **MIP** $55

Insty-Prints

Insty-Prints Wizard Figure, 1980s, 9"
vinyl figure of wizard dressed in red
outfit w/moons and stars
EX $75   **NM** $100   **MIP** $135

Kahn's Wieners

Beefy Frank Figure, 1980, 5-1/2" vinyl
figural hot dog mustard dispenser
EX $18   **NM** $20   **MIP** $30

Keebler Co.

Ernie the Keebler Elf Figure, 1974,
7" figure of Ernie wearing orange
and yellow hat and green jacket
EX $30   **NM** $40   **MIP** $55

Ernie the Keebler Elf Mug, 1972, 3"
plastic figural mug
EX $8   NM $12   MIP $15

Kellogg's

Coppertone, 1998, Coppertone Beach
Set: Coppertone girl, black dog,
drawstring tote, suntan lotion,
towel, radio and umbrella; Madame
Alexander, the set
EX $25   NM $50   MIP $100

Dig 'Em Bendy Figure, 1970, 3-1/2"
bendable frog figure w/"Dig 'Em" on
shirt
EX $10   NM $15   MIP $25

Dig 'Em Doll, 1973, 16" smiling frog
w/baseball hat wearing shirt that
reads "Dig 'Em"
EX $15   NM $20   MIP $30

Dig 'Em Slide Puzzle, 1979, 4" plastic
squares that make a scene when put
together
EX $8   NM $10   MIP $15

Milton The Toaster Figure, 1980, 5"
white, smiling toaster
EX $50   NM $70   MIP $90

Newton the Owl License Plate, 1973,
5" x 7" plastic license plate w/Newton
the Owl; made in several colors
EX $5   NM $8   MIP $10

Rice Krispie Dolls, 1998, Snap,
Crackle and Pop, the set
EX $100   NM $150   MIP $200

Rice Krispies Dolls, 1998, 8" Snap,
Crackle, Pop; Madame Alexander,
each
EX $20   NM $40   MIP $65

Rice Krispies Towel, 1972, 20" x 38"
towel featuring Snap, Crackle and
Pop!
EX $10   NM $20   MIP $25

Snap, Crackle and Pop Figures,
1975, 7-1/2" vinyl, arms at side,
each
EX $30   NM $40   MIP $46

Snap, Crackle and Pop Figures,
1975, 7-1/2" vinyl, arms extended,
each
EX $25   NM $30   MIP $35

**Snap, Crackle and Pop Hand
Puppets,** 1950s, cloth body and
vinyl head, each
EX $25   NM $35   MIP $40

Snap, Crackle and Pop Vinyl Figures,
1984, 5"
EX $12   NM $20   MIP $30

Tony the Tiger Bank, 1970s, plastic,
8-1/2"
EX $15   NM $25   MIP $35

Tony the Tiger Cookie Jar, 1968,
7" plastic
EX $70   NM $95   MIP $125

Tony the Tiger Figure, 1974, 7-1/2"
vinyl tiger
EX $45   NM $60   MIP $75

Tony the Tiger Plush Toy, 1990, 12"
plush toy, orange kerchief,
EX $8   NM $17   MIP $25

Tony the Tiger Stuffed Doll, 1973, 14"
EX $10   NM $20   MIP $30

Tony Tiger, 2003, Wacky Wobbler,
#6009, 8"
EX $3   NM $7   MIP $12

Toucan Sam Backpack, 1983, 12" blue
backpack that pictures Toucan Sam
sitting on a schoolhouse
EX $15   NM $20   MIP $25

Toucan Sam Figure, 1984, 3" plastic
jointed figure w/blue body and
multi-colored beak
EX $12   NM $15   MIP $20

Toucan Sam Wallet, 1984, plastic
w/picture of Toucan Sam
EX $10   NM $15   MIP $20

Kendall Co.

Curad Taped Crusader Figure, 1977,
7-1/2" vinyl figure, green outfit,
orange cape and hair
EX $50   NM $75   MIP $100

Ken-L-Ration

Ken-L-Ration Wall Pockets, 1960s,
3" pair of plastic wall pockets; cat's
head and a dog's head
EX $40   NM $50   MIP $65

Kentucky Fried Chicken

Colonel Sanders, Wacky Wobbler, 8"
EX $3   NM $7   MIP $15

Colonel Sanders Bank, 1965, vinyl,
12-1/2"
EX $35   NM $45   MIP $65

Colonel Sanders Bank, 1977, plastic,
red, 8"
EX $10   NM $20   MIP $30

Colonel Sanders Nodder, 1960s,
7" plastic nodder of Colonel holding
bucket of chicken
EX $70   NM $85   MIP $100

Kiddie City Toy Store

Kaycee Kangaroo Figure, 1980s,
vinyl kangaroo w/baby in pouch
EX $40   NM $55   MIP $65

Kraft

Cheesasaurus Rex Figure, 1990s,
5-1/2" orange dinosaur figures
wearing different outfits
EX $4   NM $7   MIP $10

Mr. Wiggle Hand Puppet, 1966, 6" red
rubber
EX $150   NM $185   MIP $225

Vegetable Man Bank, 1970s,
8" vegetable man w/tomato for a
head and a celery body
EX $205   NM $260   MIP $280

Vegetable Man Display, 1980, 3" plastic vacuuform store display of Vegetable Man
EX $155   **NM** $230   **MIP** $280

Labatt's Brewery

Labatt's Beer Man Figure, 1972, 6" man standing next to wood barrel
EX $35   **NM** $45   **MIP** $65

Magic Chef

Magic Chef Figure, 1980s, 7" chef dressed in tuxedo and chef's hat
EX $20   **NM** $25   **MIP** $35

McDonald's

Big Mac Hand Puppet, 1973, 12"
EX $7   **NM** $14   **MIP** $25

Big Mac Vinyl Doll, 1976, 6-1/2"
EX $10   **NM** $20   **MIP** $30

Collector Series Glasses, 1975-76, six in series: Big Mac, Hamburglar, Mayor McCheese, Ronald McDonald, Grimmace, Captain Crook
EX $6   **NM** $10   **MIP** $15

Hamburglar Stuffed Doll, 1971, removable cape, 16"
EX $12   **NM** $18   **MIP** $30

Hamburglar Stuffed Doll, 1972, removable cape, 17"
EX $12   **NM** $18   **MIP** $30

Ronald McDonald Stuffed Doll, 1971, 16"
EX $15   **NM** $25   **MIP** $35

Ronald McDonald Stuffed Doll, 1977, 13"
EX $10   **NM** $18   **MIP** $25

Michelin Tires

Mr. Bib Figure, 1980s, 12" plastic figure w/Michelin sash across chest
EX $35   **NM** $45   **MIP** $55

Miscellaneous

Nauga, 1960s, 11" tall x 15-1/2" wide, monster, naugahyde promotional piece
EX $30   **NM** $60   **MIP** $110

RCA Silverama Repairman Bank, mid-1950s, 5" plastic,
EX $6   **NM** $14   **MIP** $27

Mister Softee

Mister Softee, 2000, Wacky Wobbler, vanilla, chocolate, strawberry, 8"
EX $3   **NM** $7   **MIP** $15

Mohawk Carpet Co.

Mohawk Tommy Doll, 1970, 16" stuffed doll of a little boy marked "Mohawk Tommy" across front
EX $10   **NM** $15   **MIP** $20

Nabisco

Barnum's Animal Crackers Cookie Jar, 1972, ceramic, shaped like a box of animal crackers
EX $175   **NM** $225   **MIP** $275

Chips Ahoy Girl Figure, 1983, 4-1/2" vinyl figure of girl w/Chips Ahoy cookie on her head and in her hand
EX $15   **NM** $18   **MIP** $20

Fig Newton Girl Figure, 1983, 4-1/2" girl w/Fig Newton on her head
EX $17   **NM** $21   **MIP** $25

Nabisco Thing, 1996, 5" multi-colored bendable figure w/Nabisco logo for its head
EX $5   **NM** $10   **MIP** $15

Oreo Cookie Girl Figure, 1983, 4-1/2" vinyl figure of girl w/Oreo Cookie on head and in her hand
EX $15   **NM** $18   **MIP** $20

Nestle's

Milky Bar Kid, 2000s, 8" plush toy, mascot of the U.K. white chocolate "Milky Bar" since the 1960s, plush toy is of recent varitey
EX $5   **NM** $10   **MIP** $15

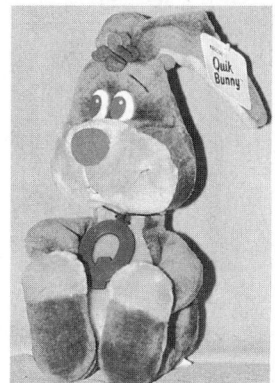

Quik Bunny Doll, 1976, 24" plush rabbit w/letter "Q" on his chest
EX $27   **NM** $38   **MIP** $44

Quik Bunny Figure, 1991, 6" bendable brown and tan rabbit w/the letter "Q" hanging from his neck
EX $3   **NM** $7   **MIP** $10

Novotel Hotel

Dophi Figure, 1990s, 4-1/2" bendable dolphin figures; set of four produced each year
EX $5   **NM** $8   **MIP** $10

Oscar Mayer Foods

Hot Wheels Wienermobile, die-cast Wienermobile
EX $10 **NM** $12 **MIP** $15

Little Oscar Puppet, thin plastic, theme song on back
EX $5 **NM** $8 **MIP** $10

Wienermobile, 1950s, 11" car; Little Oscar pops up when car is rolled
EX $150 **NM** $175 **MIP** $225

Wienermobile Bank, 1984, plastic
EX $15 **NM** $25 **MIP** $45

Wienermobile Beanbag, 1998, 7" plush beanbag
EX $3 **NM** $5 **MIP** $8

Pepperidge Farm

Goldfish Plush, 1970s, 16" plush figure
EX $15 **NM** $20 **MIP** $25

Pillsbury

Biscuit the Cat Puppet, 1974, 2-1/2" vinyl cat finger puppet
EX $18 **NM** $25 **MIP** $30

Grandpopper & Grandmommer Figures, 1974, 5" vinyl pair of figures
EX $85 **NM** $128 **MIP** $155

Green Giant Stuffed Doll, 1966, 16"
EX $35 **NM** $50 **MIP** $75

Jolly Green Giant Figure, 1970s, 9-1/2" vinyl green man wearing loincloth of leaves
EX $110 **NM** $125 **MIP** $150

Little Sprout Figure, 1970s, 6-1/2" vinyl green figure w/leaves on head and body
EX $10 **NM** $15 **MIP** $25

Little Sprout Inflatable Figure, 1976, 24" vinyl
EX $25 **NM** $30 **MIP** $35

Little Sprout Salt and Pepper Shakers, 1988, 3" ceramic figural shakers
EX $25 **NM** $30 **MIP** $35

Poppie Fresh Figure, 1971, vinyl, all white, 5"
EX $10 **NM** $12 **MIP** $15

Poppin' Fresh Doll, 1972, white velour doll w/hat and scarf
EX $20 **NM** $25 **MIP** $30

Poppin' Fresh Figure, 1971, 6-1/2" vinyl white baker w/blue eyes and blue dot on hat
EX $15 **NM** $18 **MIP** $25

Sprout Stuffed Doll, 1970, small eyes, 10"
EX $7 **NM** $15 **MIP** $25

Sprout Vinyl Doll, 1996, w/Pasta Accents sash, 6-1/2"
EX $7 **NM** $12 **MIP** $20

Pizza Hut

Pizza Hut Pete Bank, 1969, 7-1/2" plastic
EX $20 **NM** $35 **MIP** $50

Pizza Time Theatre

Chuck E. Cheese Bank, 1980s, 6-1/2" plastic
EX $12 **NM** $15 **MIP** $18

Planters Peanuts

Mr. Peanut Bank, plastic, rare, orange, hat twists off to get to coins
EX $30 **NM** $70 **MIP** $155

Mr. Peanut Bank, plastic, tan, hat twists off to get to coins
EX $10 **NM** $20 **MIP** $45

Mr. Peanut Bank, 1950s, plastic, pink, 8-1/2" tall, hat twists off to get to coins
EX $15 **NM** $30 **MIP** $50

Mr. Peanut Bank, 1991, 75th Birthday edition; black, yellow, white; base says "Mr. Peanut"
EX $10 **NM** $15 **MIP** $25

Mr. Peanut Doll, 1967, 21" pillow doll
EX $15 **NM** $20 **MIP** $35

Mr. Peanut Figure, 1930s, 8-1/2" painted wood figure w/hat and cane
EX $275 **NM** $300 **MIP** $375

Mr. Peanut Figure, 1992, 8-1/2" yellow and black plastic
EX $20 **NM** $25 **MIP** $35

Mr. Peanut Lamp, 1950s, plastic figure of Mr. Peanut, bulb fits inside
EX $30   NM $60   MIP $125

Mr. Peanut Pinback Button, celluloid
EX $15   NM $30   MIP $45

Mr. Peanut Wind-Up, 1984, 3" yellow peanut man w/traditional hat and cane
EX $20   NM $25   MIP $30

Mr. Peanut Wind-Up Walker, 1950s, black and yellow plastic, 8-1/2" tall, wind-up motor
EX $25   NM $75   MIP $150

Mr. Peanut Wind-Up Walker, 1950s, red plastic, 8-1/2" tall, wind-up motor
EX $25   NM $75   MIP $150

Mr. Peanut's Peanut Wagon, 1950s, plastic, 2-1/8" tall, premium, red and yellow
EX $30   NM $75   MIP $150

Stake Truck, 1950s, plactic, 1-1/2" tall, premium, red, blue and yellow
EX $25   NM $65   MIP $115

Post Cereal

California Raisins PVC Figure, 1987, 2" male raisin playing drums
EX $10   NM $12   MIP $18

California Raisins Wind-Up, 1987, 4" female raisin w/tambourine
EX $5   NM $7   MIP $10

Sugar Bear Doll, 1970s, 12" plush brown bear w/blue "Sugar Bear" shirt
EX $20   NM $25   MIP $35

Sugar Bear Doll, 1988, 12" plush bear w/blue "Sugar Bear" shirt
EX $15   NM $20   MIP $25

Proctor & Gamble

24-Hour Flu Bug, 1970s, 7" tall, vinyl bank, spotted green bug
EX $40   NM $65   MIP $95

Hawaiian Punch Doll, 1983, 15" plush Punchy w/red hair and blue and white striped shirt
EX $20   NM $22   MIP $25

"PUNCHY"

Hawaiian Punch Radio, 1970s, 6" figural radio of Punchy
EX $25   NM $35   MIP $45

Mr. Clean Figure, 1961, 8" bald man wearing white clothes w/earring; arms are folded
EX $85   NM $100   MIP $135

Purina Chuck Wagon

Chuck Wagon, 1975, 8" vinyl team of horses and checker board covered wagon
EX $35   NM $45   MIP $55

Quaker Oats

Cap'n Crunch, Wacky Wobbler, 8"
EX $3   NM $7   MIP $15

Cap'n Crunch Bank, 1969, 8" vinyl captain wearing blue outfit and sword
EX $45   NM $65   MIP $85

Cap'n Crunch Stuffed Doll, 1978, 15"
EX $5   NM $10   MIP $20

Jean LaFoote Bank, 1975, 8" vinyl pirate wearing green suit and purple hat
EX $60   NM $85   MIP $125

Quake Cereal Doll, 1965, 9" man w/raised arms and letter "Q" across chest
EX $85   NM $95   MIP $125

Quaker Oats Figure Mug, plastic, 4"
EX $25   NM $35   MIP $45

Quisp, Wacky Wobbler, 8"
EX $3   NM $7   MIP $15

Quisp Bank, 1960s, 6-1/2" papier-mâché
EX $500   NM $750   MIP $850

Quisp Cereal Doll, 1965, 10" doll w/pink body, green clothes and letter "Q" across stomach
EX $70   NM $85   MIP $125

Quisp Powered Sugar Space Gun, 7" long, red, mail away premium
EX $150   NM $250   MIP $400

R.J. Reynolds

Joe Camel Can Cooler, 1991, 4" vinyl
EX $10   NM $15   MIP $22

Raid

Raid Bug, 1989, plush green bug
EX $22   NM $30   MIP $40

Raid Bug Radio, 1980s, Raid bug in standing position w/clock on one side and radio on the other
EX $70   NM $200   MIP $135

Raid Bug Wind-Up, 1983, 4" yellow and green angry bug
EX $40   NM $50   MIP $70

Ralston Purina

Meow Mix Cat, 1976, 4-1/2" vinyl yellow cat w/black stripes
EX $20   NM $25   MIP $30

Reckitt & Colman

Mr. Bubble Figure, 1990, 8" pink vinyl
EX $20   NM $30   MIP $35

Reddy Communications

Reddy Kilowatt, 2000, Wacky Wobbler, 8"
EX $3   NM $7   MIP $15

Reddy Kilowatt Bobbin' Head, 1960s, 6-1/2" Reddy wearing cowboy outfit
EX $225   NM $275   MIP $450

Reddy Kilowatt Figure, 1961, 6" plastic figure w/lightbulb for head and lightning bolts for body
EX $150   NM $185   MIP $225

Ritalin

Ritalin Man Statue, 1970s, 7" smiling plastic statue w/hat

EX $58   **NM** $67   **MIP** $78

Sea Host

Clem the Clam Push Puppets, 1969, 4" fish push puppets; four different fish were issued

EX $15   **NM** $30   **MIP** $40

Shop Rite

Scrunchy Bear Doll, 1970s, 16" plush bear w/Shop-Rite shirt

EX $20   **NM** $25   **MIP** $30

Smith Kline & French Lab

Tagamet Figure, 1989, 2-1/2" bendable pink figure standing on base

EX $15   **NM** $20   **MIP** $25

Sony

Sony Boy Figure, 1960s, 4" vinyl boy wearing yellow "Sony" shirt

EX $150   **NM** $200   **MIP** $225

Squirt Beverage

Squirt Doll, 1961, 17" vinyl boy w/blond hair and removable clothing; "Squirt" written across shirt

EX $100   **NM** $150   **MIP** $175

Starkist

Charlie the Tuna Doll, 1970, 15" pull string talking doll

EX $40   **NM** $50   **MIP** $80

Charlie the Tuna Figure, 1973, 7-1/2" vinyl Charlie; arms pointed down

EX $60   **NM** $75   **MIP** $110

Charlie the Tuna Radio, 1970, 6" radio

EX $50   **NM** $60   **MIP** $90

Charlie the Tuna Scale, 1972, oval shaped bathroom scale w/Charlie the Tuna

EX $50   **NM** $65   **MIP** $80

Charlie Tuna, Wacky Wobbler, 8"

EX $3   **NM** $7   **MIP** $15

Sterling Drug

Diaparene Baby Doll, 1980, 5" baby w/movable arms and legs; baby wears diaper

EX $35   **NM** $40   **MIP** $50

Tastykake

Tastykake Baker Doll, 1974, 13" pillow doll wearing chef outfit

EX $15   **NM** $20   **MIP** $25

Tony's Pizza

Mr. Tony Figure, 1972, 8" vinyl Italian pizza chef

EX $40   **NM** $50   **MIP** $65

Toys 'R Us

Geoffrey Doll, 1967, 2-1/2" plush Geoffrey wearing red and white striped shirt

EX $20   **NM** $25   **MIP** $50

Geoffrey Flashlight, 1989, 8-1/2" plastic figural flashlight of Geoffrey the Giraffe

EX $8   **NM** $10   **MIP** $12

Travelodge

Sleepy Bear Squeeze Toy, 1970s, 5-1/2" bear wearing pajamas

EX $25   **NM** $30   **MIP** $35

Tropicana

Tropic-Ana Doll, 1977, 17" pillow doll of Hawaiian girl

EX $15   **NM** $20   **MIP** $25

U.S. Forestry Department

Smokey the Bear Bank, ceramic, 6" tall, Smokey sitting w/hand on hat

EX n/a   **NM** $10   **MIP** $22

Smokey the Bear Bank, 1980s, plastic, 8"

EX $7   **NM** $14   **MIP** $25

Smokey the Bear Bendy, 1967, bendable Smokey

EX n/a   **NM** $5   **MIP** $10

Smokey the Bear Boxcar, 60th anniversary boxcar rolling stock, #52334

EX n/a   **NM** $55   **MIP** $85

Smokey the Bear Comic Book, 1960, "The True Story of Smokey the Bear," first edition 1960

EX n/a   **NM** $7   **MIP** $14

Smokey the Bear Figure, 1976, plastic, w/shovel, 8"

EX $40   **NM** $50   **MIP** $65

Smokey the Bear Little Golden Book, 1955, cover reads, "Smokey the Bear"

EX n/a   **NM** $10   **MIP** $15

Smokey the Bear Nodder, 1960s, 6"

EX $30   **NM** $65   **MIP** $100

Smokey the Bear Pinback Button, 1970s, brown & yellow, reads, "Join Smokey's Campaign, Prevent Forest Fires"

EX n/a   **NM** $7   **MIP** $15

Smokey the Bear Puppet, 1960s

EX n/a   **NM** $10   **MIP** $20

Smokey the Bear Soaky, 1965, 9-1/2"

EX $10   **NM** $20   **MIP** $30

Smokey the Bear Stuffed Animal, 1960s, 12"

EX $25   **NM** $50   **MIP** $75

Smokey the Bear Stuffed Animal, 1960s, Smokey in coveralls

EX n/a   **NM** $10   **MIP** $20

Smokey the Bear Stuffed Animal, 1972, 6-3/4" tall; box reads, "The Official Smokey Bear"

EX n/a   **NM** $10   **MIP** $20

Smokey the Bear Stuffed Animal, 1985, 9-1/2" tall, Model No. SB-12-1

EX n/a   **NM** $10   **MIP** $25

Woodsy Owl Bank, 1970s, 8-1/2" ceramic figural bank

EX $100   **NM** $125   **MIP** $150

U.S. Postal Service

Mr. ZIP Statue, 1960s, 6-1/2" wood statue w/mailbag and pop-up hat

EX $150   **NM** $180   **MIP** $225

Wonder Bread

Fresh Guy Figure, 1975, 4" smiling loaf of bread w/polka dots, smiling face and "Wonder" on side

EX $100   **NM** $150   **MIP** $175

Barbie

by Justin Moen

Her full name is Barbara Millicent Roberts. We know her better as Barbie doll. She's been a cheerleader, princess, rocker, movie star, and career woman. Most importantly, she's been an all-time toy icon for millions of little girls worldwide, capturing the essence of their imaginations and dreams.

More than 50 years after her debut, more than 1 billion Barbie dolls have been sold in more than 150 countries at a rate of three dolls per second, according to Mattel. Observation breeds inspiration, and it was Mattel co-founder Ruth Handler's observation of her daughter (Barbara) playing with her paper dolls and giving them roles as career women that inspired her to create a three-dimensional fashion doll that would encourage little girls to dream of a bright future.

Initially, Handler's idea of an adult-bodied doll was met with skepticism by her husband and co-founder Elliot, as well as Mattel's directors. Ironically, Elliot would be met with the same skepticism several years later when he proposed the idea of Hot Wheels cars.

But Handler was determined to make her vision a reality. On March 9, 1959, Barbie doll (named after Ruth Handler's daughter) made her debut at the American International Toy Fair in New York City. This date is also recognized as Barbie's official birthday.

Barbie was marketed as the "Teen-Age Fashion Model." She stood 11-1/2 inches tall, with her clothing created by Mattel fashion designer Charlotte Johnson. The first Barbie dolls were made in Japan, with nearly 350,000 dolls sold during the first year of production.

There was no doubt that Barbie was distinctive from the baby/toddler dolls on the market at the time. Indeed, Barbie had an adult appearance—almost too adult for some parents, who were not happy with the size of Barbie's breasts, or the fact that Barbie had breasts at all.

Regardless, Barbie dolls realized strong sales thanks in large part to extensive advertising on TV. In fact, Barbie dolls were one of the first toys that had a marketing strategy devoted greatly to TV advertising.

Over the years Barbie has successfully reinvented herself in order to keep up with the times. Barbie has also evolved from just a doll with great outfits and accessories to books, fashion items, series of animated films, and video games.

While Barbie has faced competition from the Bratz dolls line in recent years, she's still number one in the hearts of millions of girls all over the world who see her as a companion to help them build their dreams, and collectors who keep her as a reminder of their childhood.

Trends

Collectors covet both vintage and newer, collector-edition Barbie dolls today. But it is the vintage dolls from 1959 and the early-60s that command the highest prices, thanks in large part to the difficulty of finding vintage dolls in mint-in-package condition. Such examples generally command hundreds, if not thousands, of dollars each.

The original 1959 Ponytail Barbie dolls, both blonde and brunette numbers one and two, are at the very top, with prices ranging anywhere from $5,000-25,000, depending on condition. However, in September 2006, a 1965 Barbie in Midnight Red sold at auction at Christie's in London for an astonishing $17,000. But this is a rare and rather unusual occurrence.

Investment-savvy collectors focus on dolls from the early-60s, as these dolls have a history of appreciating more in value than the newer dolls, mainly because pristine condition dolls from the early 60s are hard to find. Any damaged, loose, or unclothed Barbie dolls from the 70s-present for the most part have very little or no collectible value.

Other vintage Barbie dolls to pay close attention to include the 1966 Color Magic dolls, Swirl Ponytails, and any early African-American doll. But there are modern Barbie dolls that have also seen a rise in popularity in recent years. Some limited-edition series, like the 1996 Harley-Davidson series featuring Barbie and Ken, have seen consistent growth over the years.

The Fashion Model collection (made from a durable Silkstone material), released in 2000, has also generated enormous popularity in the last few years. The cancellation of the Lingerie series in 2003 due to nationwide protests about the doll's risqué appear-

The **Top 10 BARBIES** in mint condition

1. Ponytail Barbie #2, brunette, Mattel, 1959	$7,000
2. Ponytail Barbie #1, brunette, Mattel, 1959	$5,500
3. Ponytail Barbie #1, blonde, Mattel, 1959	$5,000
4. Ponytail Barbie #2, blonde, Mattel, 1959	$5,000
5. Roman Holiday, Barbie Vintage Fashions, Mattel, 1959-66	$4,800
6. Gay Parisienne, Barbie Vintage Fashions, Mattel, 1959-66	$4,000
7. Pan Am Stewardess, Barbie Vintage Fashions, Mattel, 1959-66	$4,000
8. Easter Parade, Barbie Vintage Fashions, Mattel, 1959-66	$4,000
9. Barbie's Sport Plane, Barbie vehicles, Mattel, 1964	$3,500
10. Barbie's Airplane, Barbie vehicles, Mattel, 1964	$3,500

ance has only heightened the desire for these dolls.

Please note: As with any collectible on the market, not every Barbie doll in a series is popular among collectors. And not every Barbie series will maintain its popularity.

Tips for Collecting

Although many Barbie dolls increase in value, others do not. Here are some tips for smart collecting:

• Avoid regular issue dolls (also known as pink box dolls or play dolls). These dolls generally retail in toy stores for less than $15. These have limited investment potential. Buy them because you like them, not because you expect them to increase in value.

• Look for limited-edition exclusives. Certain dolls are "exclusives" because they are made only for one retail outlet, like Target or FAO Schwarz. Many of these dolls have increased in value; others, however, show less success. Harley-Davidson Barbie, exclusive to Toys R Us, for example, was next to impossible to find in stores. Its secondary market prices immediately soared to $250 or more.

• Look for dolls in the best possible condition. Dolls in top condition command higher prices than dolls in poor condition. And watch for original boxes, apparel, and even tiny accessories. They can all add value to a doll.

• Dig carefully through big boxes of loose dolls. Loose, unclothed, or damaged vintage Barbie dolls from the 1970s-present have very little or no collectible value. Dolls from the 1960s in the same condition may be worth something to collectors; for example, even an unclothed or slightly damaged Color Magic or Miss Barbie doll from the 1960s could

bring $100 or more.

• Don't be fooled by dates! Barbie dolls have distinct markings on their buttocks, but remember that the date on a doll is likely the date the doll's body style was copyrighted, NOT necessarily the date the doll was made. Therefore, dolls with a 1960s date may actually be made in the 1990s. Plenty of books exist with photos of dolls and markings, making it more accurate to identify your doll.

• Don't overlook licensed Barbie products. Mattel licenses the Barbie name to companies which make paper dolls, clothing, cases, watches, lunch boxes, and other collectibles. Anything with the Barbie name is collectible but not necessarily valuable.

• Buy the less-than-obvious choices. Lots of collectors are looking for dolls and fashions. Look for the more disposable items bearing the Barbie name: think boxes of bandages or Jell-O or other items meant to be consumed and discarded. The packaging will be a great find years down the road.

To the non-collector, the first Ponytail Barbie dolls all look similar. There are, however, subtle and important differences. Below are characteristics of the first Barbie (1959) known to collectors as Ponytail Barbie #1.

Looking Out for #1
- holes in the bottom of the feet with copper tubes inside the legs
- zebra-stripe one-piece swimsuit
- blonde or brunette hair with soft curly bangs
- red fingernails, toenails, and lips
- gold hoop earrings
- white irises and severely pointed black eyebrows
- heavy, black facial paint
- pale, almost white, ivory skin tone
- body markings: Barbie T.M./Pats.Pend./ [copyright mark] MCMLVIII/by/Mattel/Inc.

Clubs

Literally hundreds of clubs, ranging from local and regional to national and international, exist to serve avid collectors. It's unknown if a complete and up-to-date list has ever been compiled, but the other Barbie resources listed on this page are the best bets for locating other collectors and clubs. For more information on Mattel's official Barbie Collector's Club, visit their Web site at www.barbiecollector.com or call (800)-491-7514.

Web Sites

This list could be endless, especially with all the dealer, retail, secondary market, and fan sites out there. The best bet for surfing through the sites more suc-cessfully is to search the Internet under the keywords "Barbie," "Barbie doll [or dolls]," "Barbie collectibles," "Mattel's Barbie," or other appropriate terms.

Mattel Toys / Barbie Collectibles
www.barbiecollector.com

Fashion Doll Guide
www.fashion-doll-guide.com

Sandi Holder's Doll Attic
www.dollattic.com

Books

Books on America's favorite fashion doll are plentiful as well. A library search or visit to www.bn.com or www.amazon.com will also reveal more complete lists of Barbie books.

The Ultimate Barbie Doll Book
Barbie Doll: A Rare Beauty
Barbie and Her Mod, Mod, Mod, Mod World of Fashion Barbie: All Dolled Up (Celebrating 50 Years of Barbie)
The Collectible Barbie Doll
Barbie Fashion Volume I
Barbie: The First 30 Years -- 1959 through 1989
Warman's Barbie Doll Field Guide, 2nd Edition

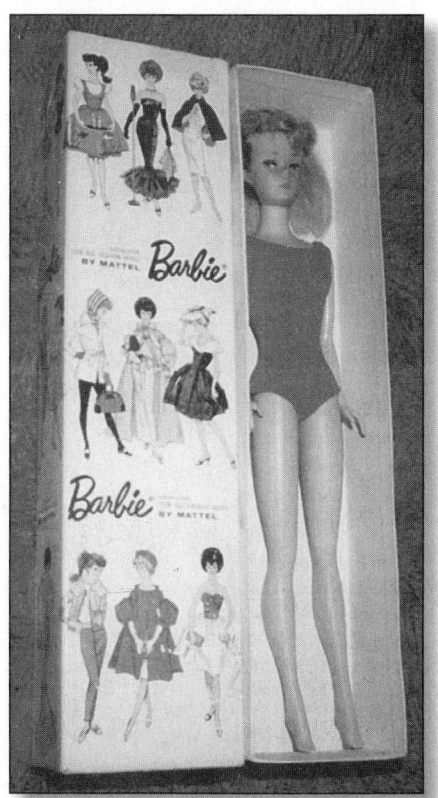

Accessories

COLORFORMS SETS

Barbie Make-Up Kit, 1989, Colorforms, Barbie make-up face w/stand, four easy wipe-off styling crayons, wipe-off cloth, 42 Colorforms Fashion Jewelry accessories
MNP $7   MIP $15

Barbie Sport Fashion, 1975, Colorforms
MNP $4   MIP $8

Barbie's 3-D Fashion Theatre, 1970, Colorforms
MNP $9   MIP $20

Baywatch Barbie, 1995, Colorforms
MNP $7   MIP $15

Dress-Up Kit New Living Barbie, 1970, Colorforms
MNP $10   MIP $38

Malibu Barbie, 1972, Colorforms
MNP $7   MIP $20

Western Barbie, 1982, Colorforms, Barbie and horse
MNP $6   MIP $12

MISCELLANEOUS

Barbie & Ken Wipe Away Cloths, 1964
MNP $100   MIP $280

Barbie and Ken Hangers, 1960s, SPP, plastic hangers in bag w/cardboard backing
MNP $20   MIP $35

Barbie Beauty Kit, 1961, Roclar
MNP $100   MIP $200

Barbie Bubble Bath, 1961, Roclar
MNP $45   MIP $100

Barbie Carry-All Wallet, 1963, SPP
MNP $145   MIP $255

Barbie Disco Record Player, 1976
MNP $85   MIP $160

Barbie Dresser Accessories, 1962
MNP $175   MIP $300

Barbie Ge-Tar, 1963, Mattel
MNP $200   MIP $400

Barbie Hair Fair, 1966, Mattel
MNP $75   MIP $145

Barbie Mattel-A-Phone, 1968
MNP $100   MIP $175

Barbie Nurse Kit, 1962, Pressman, tin litho box
MNP $100   MIP $275

Barbie Powder Mitt, 1961
MNP $75   MIP $140

Barbie Pretty Up Time, 1960s, brush/comb/mirror set
MNP $50   MIP $125

Barbie Record, 1965, Columbia Records
MNP $70   MIP $120

Barbie Store Display, 1980, Mattel
MNP $10   MIP $30

Barbie Wig Wardrobe, 1960s, Mattel, doll head w/three wigs
MNP $75   MIP $150

Barbie, Ken, Midge Pencil Case, 1964, SPP
MNP $100   MIP $260

Barbie's Dog Snowball, 1990s, Arco/Mattel
MNP $10   MIP $15

Francie Electric Drawing Table, 1966
MNP $65   MIP $130

Jack and Jill Magazine Advertisements, 1960s
MNP $15   MIP $35

Jigsaw Puzzle, 1963-65, Whitman
MNP $30   MIP $60

Jumbo Trading Cards, 1962, Dynamic, complete set
MNP $225   MIP $365

Record Player, 1961, Emenee
MNP $700   MIP $950

Record Tote, 1961, Ponytail, vinyl, several colors
MNP $75   MIP $180

Vanity Fair Transistor Radio, 1962, Vanity Fair
MNP $700   MIP $1350

Wine Set, 1986
MNP $40   MIP $75

PAPER DOLLS

Barbie and Ken Cut-Outs, 1962, Whitman, pink cover, Model No. 1971
MNP $50   MIP $135

Barbie and Ken Paper Dolls, 1970, Whitman, Model No. 1986
MNP $25   MIP $45

Barbie and Skipper, 1964, Whitman, Model No. 1957
MNP $35   MIP $100

Barbie Costume Dolls, 1964, Whitman, Model No. 1976
MNP $60   MIP $125

Barbie Cut-Outs, 1962, Model No. 1963
MNP $55   MIP $125

Barbie Doll Cut-Outs, 1963, Whitman, Model No. 1962
MNP $45   MIP $95

Barbie Dolls and Clothes, 1969, Model No. 1976
MNP $35   MIP $50

Barbie Has a New Look Paper Dolls, 1967, Whitman, Model No. 1996
MNP $40   MIP $85

Barbie Paper Dolls, Boxed, 1967, Whitman, Model No. 4701
MNP $20   MIP $50

Barbie, Christie and Stacey, 1968, Whitman, Model No. 1978
MNP $35   MIP $65

Barbie, Ken and Midge Paper Dolls, 1963, Whitman, Model No. 1976
MNP $50   MIP $75

Barbie, Two Magic Dolls w/Stay-On Clothes, 1969, Model No. 4763
MNP $30   MIP $50

Barbie's Travel Wardrobe, Boxed, 1964, Model No. 4616
MNP $50   MIP $100

Francie and Casey Paper Dolls, 1967, Whitman, Model No. 1986
MNP $30   MIP $50

Francie Paper Dolls, 1967, Whitman, Model No. 1094
MNP $40   MIP $70

Malibu Barbie Paper Dolls, 1972, Whitman, Model No. 1994
MNP $20   MIP $35

Meet Francie Paper Dolls, 1966, Whitman, Model No. 1980
MNP $35   MIP $70

Midge Cut-Outs, 1963, Whitman, Model No. 1962
MNP $45   MIP $65

P.J. Cover Girl Paper Dolls, 1971, Whitman, Model No. 1981
MNP $20   MIP $40

Skipper Paper Dolls, 1965, Whitman, Model No. 1984
MNP $25   MIP $45

Skooter Paper Dolls, 1965, Whitman, Model No. 1985
MNP $35   MIP $75

Tutti, Boxed, 1967, Model No. 4622
MNP $30   MIP $45

Twiggy Paper Dolls, 1967, Whitman, Model No. 1999
MNP $25   MIP $40

STRUCTURES

Barbie and Ken Little Theatre, 1964, Mattel, Model No. 4090
MNP $175   MIP $250

Barbie Café Today, 1971, Mattel, Model No. 4973
MNP $150   MIP $225

Barbie Fashion Stage, 1971, Mattel,
Model No. 1148
MNP $50   MIP $75

Barbie Goes to College, 1964, Mattel,
Model No. 4093
MNP $200   MIP $350

Barbie's Dream House, 1962, Mattel,
Model No. 816
MNP $50   MIP $150

Barbie's Dream Kitchen, 1965,
Mattel, Model No. 4095
MNP $300   MIP $400

Barbie's New Dream House, 1964,
Mattel, Model No. 4092
MNP $75   MIP $200

Fashion Shop, 1962, Mattel, Model
No. 817
MNP $150   MIP $275

Francie and Casey Studio House,
1967, Mattel, Model No. 1026
MNP $50   MIP $75

Francie House, 1966, Mattel, Model
No. 3302
MNP $40   MIP $75

Jamie's Penthouse (Sears), 1971,
Mattel, Model No. 31122
MNP $200   MIP $425

Quick Curl Boutique, 1973, Mattel,
Model No. 8665
MNP $40   MIP $80

Skipper's Dream Room, 1965, Mattel,
Model No. 4094
MNP $200   MIP $350

Skipper's Schoolroom, 1965, Mattel
MNP $250   MIP $350

Tutti Ice Cream Stand, 1967, Model
No. 3363
MNP $75   MIP $175

Tutti's and Todd's Playhouse, 1966
MNP $75   MIP $125

TIMEPIECES

Barbie Personal Photo Clock, 1964,
Bradley/Elgin
MNP $500   MIP $600

Barbie Starbright Boudoir Clock,
1964, Bradley/Elgin
MNP $600   MIP $700

Broken Heart Wristwatch, 1964,
Bradley/Elgin
MNP $300   MIP $400

Brokn' Heart Pendant, 1965,
Bradley/Elgin
MNP $400   MIP $500

Curly Bangs Pendant, 1963-64,
Bradley/Elgin
MNP $150   MIP $400

Curly Bangs Wristwatch, 1963-64,
Bradley/Elgin
MNP $125   MIP $300

Midge Wristwatch, 1964, Bradley/Elgin
MNP $300   MIP $450

Skipper Wristwatch, 1964, Bradley/
Elgin
MNP $300   MIP $450

Swirl Ponytail Wristwatch, 1964,
Bradley/Elgin
MNP $150   MIP $300

VEHICLES

Allan's Mercedes Roadster, 1964,
Irwin, Model No. 5348
MNP $150   MIP $575

**Barbie and Ken and Midge
Convertible,** 1964, Irwin
MNP $125   MIP $150

Barbie's Airplane, 1964, Irwin
MNP $1000   MIP $3500

Barbie's Austin-Healey, 1964, Irwin,
lavender, Montgomery Wards
exclusive
MNP $800   MIP $1000

Barbie's Austin-Healey Convertible,
1962, Irwin, coral
MNP $65   MIP $250

(KP Photo)

Barbie's Speedboat, 1964, Irwin,
shown w/Ken at the helm
MNP $100   MIP $1800

Barbie's Sport Plane, 1964, Irwin
MNP $1800   MIP $3500

Ken's Hot Rod, 1963, Irwin, blue
MNP $125   MIP $275

Skipper's Speedboat, 1965, Irwin
MNP $1450   MIP $1850

Skipper's Sports Car, 1965, Irwin
MNP $175   MIP $400

VINYL CASES

Barbie & Francie Case, 1967, SPP
MNP $20   MIP $40

Barbie & Skipper Case, 1964, Mattel,
assorted colors - blue or gold most
common
MNP $10   MIP $25

Barbie & Stacey Sleep & Keep Case,
1969, Sears Exclusive, Model
No. 5023
MNP $50   MIP $75

Barbie Double Case, 1961, Ponytail,
various illustrations/colors
MNP $5   MIP $10

Barbie Double Case, 1963, SPP,
various illustrations/colors
MNP $5   MIP $15

Barbie Goes Travelin' Case, 1965, SPP
MNP $100   MIP $325

Barbie Single Case, 1961, Ponytail,
various illustrations/colors
MNP $5   MIP $15

Barbie Single Case, 1963, SPP,
various illustrations/colors
MNP $7   MIP $15

Barbie Train Case, 1961, SPP
MNP $45   MIP $70

Fashion Queen Case, 1963, SPP
MNP $50   MIP $100

Hatbox-Style Cases, 1961, Mattel,
assorted styles
MNP $20   MIP $50

Ken Cases (U.S. versions), 1961,
Ponytail
MNP $5   MIP $10

Midge Cases (U.S. versions), 1963
MNP $5   MIP $10

Miss Barbie Case, 1964, SPP
MNP $75   MIP $125

Skipper Cases (U.S. versions), 1964
MNP $7   MIP $15

Dolls

BARBIE & FRIENDS

Aine Legends of Ireland, 2008,
Mattel, Model No. L9638
MNP $40   MIP $80

All American Barbie, 1991, Mattel,
Model No. 9423
MNP $4   MIP $10

All American Christie, 1991, Mattel,
Model No. 9425
MNP $4   MIP $10

All American Ken, 1991, Mattel,
Model No. 9424
MNP $4   MIP $10

All American Kira, 1991, Mattel,
Model No. 9427
MNP $4   MIP $12

All American Teresa, 1991, Mattel,
Model No. 9426
MNP $4   MIP $12

All Star Ken, 1981, Mattel, Model
No. 3553
MNP $5   MIP $10

All Stars Barbie, 1989, Mattel, Model
No. 9099
MNP $5   MIP $10

All Stars Christie, 1989, Mattel, Model
No. 9352
MNP $5   MIP $10

All Stars Ken, 1989, Mattel, Model
No. 9361
MNP $5   MIP $10

All Stars Midge, 1989, Mattel, Model
No. 9360
MNP $5   MIP $10

All Stars Teresa, 1989, Mattel, Model No. 9353

    MNP $5   **MIP** $10

(KP Photo)

Allan, Bendable Leg, 1965, Mattel, Model No. 1010

    MNP $95   **MIP** $175

Allan, Straight Leg, 1964, Mattel, Model No. 1000

    MNP $20   **MIP** $65

American Beauties Mardi Gras Barbie, 1988, Mattel, Model No. 4930

    MNP $10   **MIP** $25

American Beauty Queen, 1991, Mattel, Model No. 3137

    MNP $5   **MIP** $10

American Beauty Queen, Black, 1991, Mattel, Model No. 3245

    MNP $5   **MIP** $10

Angel Face Barbie, 1982, Mattel, Model No. 5640

    MNP $8   **MIP** $30

Animal Lovin' Barbie, Black, 1989, Mattel, Model No. 4828

    MNP $5   **MIP** $10

Animal Lovin' Barbie, White, 1989, Mattel, Model No. 1350

    MNP $5   **MIP** $10

Animal Lovin' Ken, 1989, Mattel, Model No. 1351

    MNP $5   **MIP** $10

Animal Lovin' Nikki, 1989, Mattel, Model No. 1352

    MNP $7   **MIP** $10

Astronaut Barbie, Black, 1985, Mattel, Model No. 1207

    MNP $15   **MIP** $20

Astronaut Barbie, White, 1985, Mattel, Model No. 2449

    MNP $15   **MIP** $25

Babysitter Courtney, 1991, Mattel, Model No. 9434

    MNP $4   **MIP** $10

Babysitter Skipper, 1991, Mattel, Model No. 9433

    MNP $4   **MIP** $10

Babysitter Skipper, Black, 1991, Mattel, Model No. 1599

    MNP $4   **MIP** $8

Baggie Casey, Blond, 1975, Mattel, (sold in plastic bag), Model No. 9000

    MNP $75   **MIP** $200

Ballerina Barbie on Tour, Gold, 1st Version, 1976, Mattel, Model No. 9613

    MNP $45   **MIP** $65

Ballerina Barbie, 1st Version, 1976, Mattel, Model No. 9093

    MNP $20   **MIP** $40

Ballerina Cara, 1976, Mattel, Model No. 9528

    MNP $25   **MIP** $50

Barbie & Her Fashion Fireworks, 1976, Mattel, Model No. 9805

    MNP $20   **MIP** $60

Barbie & the Beat, 1990, Mattel, Model No. 3751

    MNP $5   **MIP** $10

Barbie & the Beat Christie, 1990, Mattel, Model No. 2752

    MNP $5   **MIP** $10

Barbie & the Beat Midge, 1990, Mattel, Model No. 2754

    MNP $6   **MIP** $10

Barbie Hair Happenings (department store exclusive, red hair), 1971, Mattel, Model No. 1174

    MNP $275   **MIP** $800

(KP Photo)

Barbie w/Growin' Pretty Hair, 1971, Mattel, Model No. 1144

    MNP $75   **MIP** $300

Bathtime Fun Barbie, 1991, Mattel, Model No. 9601

    MNP $3   **MIP** $10

Bathtime Fun Barbie, Black, 1991, Mattel, Model No. 9603

    MNP $3   **MIP** $10

Beach Blast Barbie, 1989, Mattel, Model No. 3237

    MNP $3   **MIP** $10

Beach Blast Christie, 1989, Mattel, Model No. 3253

    MNP $4   **MIP** $10

Beach Blast Ken, 1989, Mattel, Model No. 3238

    MNP $4   **MIP** $10

Beach Blast Miko, 1989, Mattel, Model No. 3244

    MNP $4   **MIP** $10

Beach Blast Skipper, 1989, Mattel, Model No. 3242

    MNP $4   **MIP** $10

Beach Blast Steven, 1989, Mattel, Model No. 3251

    MNP $4   **MIP** $10

Beach Blast Teresa, 1989, Mattel, Model No. 3249

    MNP $5   **MIP** $10

Beautiful Bride Barbie, 1978, Mattel, Model No. 9907

    MNP $40   **MIP** $65

Beauty Secrets Barbie, 1st Issue, 1980, Mattel, Model No. 1290

    MNP $12   **MIP** $65

Beauty Secrets Christie, 1980, Mattel, Model No. 1295

    MNP $12   **MIP** $65

Beauty, Barbie's Dog, 1979, Mattel, Model No. 1018

    MNP $12   **MIP** $30

(KP Photo)

Bendable Leg "American Girl" Barbie, Short Hair, 1965, Mattel, Model No. 1070

    MNP $250   **MIP** $1100

Bendable Leg "American Girl" Barbie, Color Magic Face, 1966, Mattel, Model No. 1070

    MNP $700   **MIP** $1500

Bendable Leg "American Girl" Barbie, Long Hair, 1965, Mattel, Model No. 1070

    MNP $700   **MIP** $1500

Bendable Leg "American Girl" Barbie, Side-Part Long Hair, 1966, Mattel, Model No. 1070

    MNP $1700   **MIP** $2500

Bendable Leg "American Girl" Barbie, Swirl Ponytail or Bubblecut Hairstyle, 1965, Mattel, Model No. 1070

    MNP $1000   **MIP** $2800

Benetton Barbie, 1991, Mattel, Model No. 9404

    MNP $5   **MIP** $15

Benetton Christie, 1991, Mattel, Model No. 9407

    MNP $5   **MIP** $15

Benetton Marina, 1991, Mattel, Model No. 9409

    MNP $5   **MIP** $15

(KP Photo)

Black Barbie, 1980, Mattel, Model No. 1293

    MNP $20   **MIP** $45

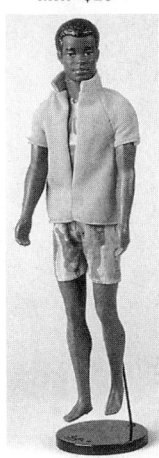

(KP Photo)

Brad, Bendable Leg, 1970, Mattel, Model No. 1142

    MNP $65   **MIP** $175

Brad, Talking, 1970, Mattel, Model No. 1114

    MNP $65   **MIP** $200

Bubblecut Barbie Sidepart, All Hair Colors, 1961, Mattel, Model No. 850

    MNP $425   **MIP** $900

Bubblecut Barbie, Blonde, Brunette, Titian, 1962, Mattel, Model No. 850

    MNP $50   **MIP** $150

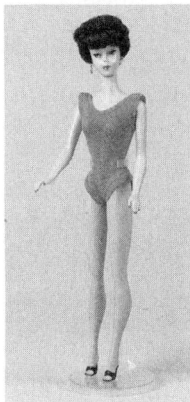

(KP Photo)

Bubblecut Barbie, Brownette, 1961, Mattel, Model No. 850

    MNP $500   **MIP** $850

Bubblecut Barbie, White Ginger, 1962, Mattel, Model No. 850

    MNP $250   **MIP** $600

Busy Barbie, 1971, Mattel, Model No. 3311

    MNP $75   **MIP** $175

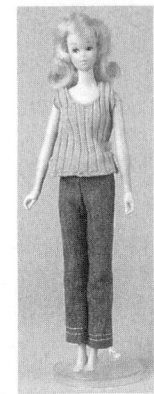

(KP Photo)

Busy Francie, 1971, Mattel, Model No. 3313

    MNP $125   **MIP** $300

(KP Photo)

Busy Ken, 1971, Mattel, Model No. 3314

    MNP $60   **MIP** $145

(KP Photo)

Busy Steffie, 1971, Mattel, Model No. 3312
MNP $85   MIP $200

Calgary Olympic Skating Barbie, 1987, Mattel, Model No. 4547
MNP $25   MIP $45

California Dream Barbie, 1988, Mattel, Model No. 4439
MNP $5   MIP $10

California Dream Christie, 1988, Mattel, Model No. 4443
MNP $6   MIP $10

California Dream Ken, 1988, Mattel, Model No. 4441
MNP $8   MIP $10

California Dream Midge, 1988, Mattel, Model No. 4442
MNP $3   MIP $10

California Dream Skipper, 1988, Mattel, Model No. 4440
MNP $13   MIP $10

California Dream Teresa, 1988, Mattel, Model No. 4403
MNP $15   MIP $10

Carla, European Exclusive, 1976, Mattel, Model No. 7377
MNP $65   MIP $120

Casey, Twist and Turn, 1967, Mattel, Model No. 1180
MNP $60   MIP $250

Chris, Titian, Blond, Brunette (Tutti's friend), 1967, Mattel, Model No. 3570
MNP $50   MIP $200

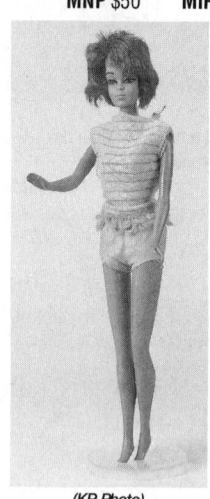

(KP Photo)

Christie, Talking, 1970, Mattel, Model No. 1126
MNP $70   MIP $300

Christie, Twist N Turn, 1970, Mattel, Model No. 1119
MNP $70   MIP $300

Coach Ken & Tommy, White or Black, 2000, Mattel
MNP $7   MIP $10

(KP Photo)

Color Magic Barbie, Golden Blonde, 1966, Mattel, Model No. 1150
MNP $350   MIP $1500

Color Magic Barbie, Midnight Black, 1966, Mattel, Model No. 1150
MNP $1100   MIP $2500

Cool City Blues: Barbie, Ken, Skipper, 1989, Mattel, Model No. 4893
MNP $5   MIP $15

Cool Shavin' Ken, 1996, Mattel, Model No. 15469
MNP $5   MIP $10

Cool Times Barbie, 1989, Mattel, Model No. 3022
MNP $5   MIP $10

Cool Times Christie, 1989, Mattel, Model No. 3217
MNP $5   MIP $10

Cool Times Ken, 1989, Mattel, Model No. 3219
MNP $5   MIP $10

Cool Times Midge, 1989, Mattel, Model No. 3216
MNP $7   MIP $10

Cool Times Teresa, 1989, Mattel, Model No. 3218
MNP $5   MIP $10

Cool Tops Courtney, 1989, Mattel, Model No. 7079
MNP $7   MIP $10

Cool Tops Kevin, 1989, Mattel, Model No. 9351
MNP $5   MIP $10

Cool Tops Skipper, Black, 1989, Mattel, Model No. 5441
MNP $5   MIP $10

Cool Tops Skipper, White, 1989, Mattel, Model No. 4989
MNP $7   MIP $10

Corduroy Cool Barbie, 2000, Mattel, Model No. 24658
MNP $5   MIP $10

Costume Ball Barbie, Black, 1991, Mattel, Model No. 7134
MNP $6   MIP $10

Costume Ball Barbie, White, 1991, Mattel, Model No. 7123
MNP $6   MIP $10

Costume Ball Ken, Black, 1991, Mattel, Model No. 7160
MNP $6   MIP $10

Costume Ball Ken, White, 1991, Mattel, Model No. 7154
MNP $6   MIP $10

Crystal Barbie, Black, 1984, Mattel, Model No. 4859
MNP $10   MIP $25

Crystal Barbie, White, 1984, Mattel, Model No. 4598
MNP $10   MIP $25

Crystal Ken, Black, 1983, Mattel, Model No. 9036
MNP $15   MIP $25

Crystal Ken, White, 1983, Mattel, Model No. 4898
MNP $8   MIP $25

Dance Club Barbie, 1989, Mattel, Model No. 3509
MNP $5   MIP $15

Dance Club Devon, 1989, Mattel, Model No. 3513
MNP $5   MIP $15

Dance Club Kayla, 1989, Mattel, Model No. 3512
MNP $5   MIP $15

Dance Club Ken, 1989, Mattel, Model No. 3511
MNP $5   MIP $15

Dance Magic Barbie, 1990, Mattel, Model No. 4836
MNP $7   MIP $15

Dance Magic Barbie, Black, 1990, Mattel, Model No. 7080
MNP $7   MIP $15

Dance Magic Ken, 1990, Mattel, Model No. 7081
MNP $6   MIP $10

Dance Magic Ken, Black, 1990, Mattel, Model No. 7082
MNP $6   MIP $10

Day-to-Night Barbie, Black, 1985, Mattel, Model No. 7945
MNP $10   MIP $40

Day-to-Night Barbie, Hispanic, 1985, Mattel, Model No. 7944
MNP $17   MIP $45

Day-to-Night Barbie, White, 1985, Mattel, Model No. 7929
    MNP $10   **MIP** $45

(KP Photo)

Day-to-Night Ken, Black, 1984, Mattel, Model No. 9018
    MNP $8   **MIP** $35

Day-to-Night Ken, White, 1984, Mattel, Model No. 9019
    MNP $8   **MIP** $35

Dentist Barbie, 1997, Mattel, Model No. 17255
    MNP $15   **MIP** $15

Doctor Barbie, 1988, Mattel, Model No. 3850
    MNP $8   **MIP** $15

Doctor Ken, 1988, Mattel, Model No. 4118
    MNP $5   **MIP** $15

Dolls of the World Amazonia, 2009, Mattel, Model No. P4754
    MNP $25   **MIP** $50

Dolls of the World Carnaval, 2006, Mattel, Model No. J0927
    MNP $35   **MIP** $70

Dolls of the World Cinco de Mayo, 2006, Mattel, Model No. K7921
    MNP $35   **MIP** $70

Dolls of the World France, 2009, Mattel, Model No. N4972
    MNP $15   **MIP** $35

Dolls of the World Italian, 2009, Mattel, Model No. P3488
    MNP $15   **MIP** $30

Dolls of the World Kwanzaa, 2006, Mattel, Model No. J0945
    MNP $60   **MIP** $125

Dolls of the World Princess of Ancient Greece, 2004, Mattel
    MNP $10   **MIP** $20

Dolls of the World Princess of Ancient Mexico, 2004, Mattel, Model No. C2203
    MNP $45   **MIP** $90

Dolls of the World Princess of Cambodia, 2004, Mattel
    MNP $10   **MIP** $20

(Mattel Photo)

Dolls of the World Princess of China, 2002, Mattel, Model No. 53368
    MNP $70   **MIP** $145

Dolls of the World Princess of England (Tudor Rose), 2004, Mattel
    MNP $10   **MIP** $20

Dolls of the World Princess of Imperial Russia, 2005, Mattel, Model No. G5861
    MNP $25   **MIP** $50

Dolls of the World Princess of India, 2000, Mattel, Model No. 28374
    MNP $100   **MIP** $200

Dolls of the World Princess of Ireland, 2002, Mattel, Model No. 53367
    MNP $10   **MIP** $15

(Mattel Photo)

Dolls of the World Princess of South Africa, 2003, Mattel, Model No. 56218
    MNP $35   **MIP** $70

Dolls of the World Princess of the Danish Court, 2003, Mattel, Model No. 56216
    MNP $25   **MIP** $50

Dolls of the World Princess of the French Court, 2000, Mattel, Model No. 28372
    MNP $8   **MIP** $15

Dolls of the World Princess of the Incas, 2000, Mattel, Model No. 28373
    MNP $8   **MIP** $15

Dolls of the World Princess of the Korean Court, 2005, Mattel
    MNP $25   **MIP** $50

Dolls of the World Princess of the Navajo, 2004, Mattel
    MNP $10   **MIP** $50

(Mattel Photo)

Dolls of the World Princess of the Nile, 2002, Mattel, Model No. 53369
    MNP $10   **MIP** $15

Dolls of the World Princess of the Pacific Islands, 2005, Mattel, Model No. G8056
    MNP $45   **MIP** $95

Dolls of the World Princess of the Portuguese Empire, 2003, Mattel, Model No. 56217
    MNP $10   **MIP** $15

Dolls of the World Princess of the Renaissance, 2005, Mattel, Model No. G5860
    MNP $60   **MIP** $125

Dolls of the World Russia, 2009, Mattel, Model No. R4488
    MNP $15   **MIP** $30

Dolls of the World Scotland, 2009, Mattel, Model No. N4973
    MNP $15   **MIP** $35

Dolls of the World Spain, 2007, Mattel, Model No. L9583
MNP $15   MIP $30

Dolls of the World Sumatra Indonesia, 2007, Mattel, Model No. L9582
MNP $15   MIP $30

Dolls of the World/International Arctic, 1997, Mattel, Model No. 16495
MNP $20   MIP $25

Dolls of the World/International Australian, Two Box Variations, 1993, Mattel, Model No. 3626
MNP $10   MIP $20

Dolls of the World/International Austrian, 1999, Mattel, Model No. 21553
MNP $15   MIP $20

Dolls of the World/International Brazilian, 1990, Mattel, Model No. 9094
MNP $15   MIP $25

Dolls of the World/International Canadian, 1988, Mattel, Model No. 4928
MNP $15   MIP $35

Dolls of the World/International Chilean, 1998, Mattel, Model No. 18559
MNP $10   MIP $15

Dolls of the World/International Chinese, 1994, Mattel, Model No. 11180
MNP $10   MIP $15

Dolls of the World/International Czechoslovakian, 1991, Mattel, Model No. 7330
MNP $20   MIP $30

Dolls of the World/International Dutch, 1994, Mattel, Model No. 11104
MNP $10   MIP $20

Dolls of the World/International English, 1992, Mattel, Model No. 4973
MNP $12   MIP $25

Dolls of the World/International Eskimo, 1982, Mattel, Model No. 3898
MNP $30   MIP $40

Dolls of the World/International Eskimo, 1991, Mattel, Model No. 9844
MNP $8   MIP $20

Dolls of the World/International French, 1997, Mattel, Model No. 16499
MNP $20   MIP $40

Dolls of the World/International German, 1987, Mattel, Model No. 3188
MNP $15   MIP $25

Dolls of the World/International German, 1995, Mattel, Model No. 12598
MNP $10   MIP $20

Dolls of the World/International Ghanaian, 1996, Mattel, Model No. 15303
MNP $15   MIP $20

Dolls of the World/International Gift Set (Chinese, Dutch, Kenyan), 1994, Mattel, Model No. 12043
MNP $30   MIP $70

Dolls of the World/International Gift Set (Irish, German, Polynesian), 1995, Mattel, Model No. 13939
MNP $30   MIP $65

Dolls of the World/International Gift Set (Japanese, Indian, Norwegian), 1996, Mattel, Model No. 15283
MNP $30   MIP $60

Dolls of the World/International Greek, 1986, Mattel, Model No. 2997
MNP $30   MIP $45

Dolls of the World/International Iceland, 1987, Mattel, Model No. 3189
MNP $30   MIP $45

Dolls of the World/International Indian, 1982, Mattel, Model No. 3897
MNP $30   MIP $45

Dolls of the World/International Indian, 1995, Mattel, Model No. 14451
MNP $12   MIP $20

(KP Photo)

Dolls of the World/International Irish, 1984, Mattel, Model No. 7517
MNP $20   MIP $40

Dolls of the World/International Irish, 1995, Mattel, Model No. 12998
MNP $10   MIP $20

(KP Photo)

Dolls of the World/International Italian, 1980, Mattel, Model No. 1601
MNP $65   MIP $95

Dolls of the World/International Italian, 1993, Mattel, Model No. 2256
MNP $10   MIP $25

Dolls of the World/International Jamaican, Silver Earrings, 1992, Mattel, Model No. 4647
MNP $12   MIP $20

(KP Photo)

Dolls of the World/International Japanese, 1984, Mattel, Model No. 9481
MNP $25   MIP $35

Dolls of the World/International Japanese, 1996, Mattel, Model No. 14163
MNP $10   MIP $20

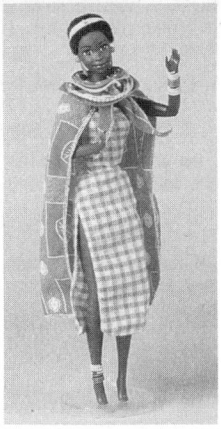

(KP Photo)

(KP Photo)

Dolls of the World/International Puerto Rican, 1997, Mattel, Model No. 16754

    MNP $15   MIP $20

(KP Photo)

Dolls of the World/International Kenyan, 1994, Mattel, Model No. 11181

    MNP $10   MIP $20

Dolls of the World/International Korean, 1988, Mattel, Model No. 4929

    MNP $15   MIP $30

Dolls of the World/International Malaysian, 1991, Mattel, Model No. 7329

    MNP $10   MIP $25

Dolls of the World/International Mexican, 1989, Mattel, Model No. 1917

    MNP $45   MIP $90

Dolls of the World/International Mexican, 1995, Mattel, Model No. 14449

    MNP $10   MIP $15

Dolls of the World/International Moroccan, 1999, Mattel, Model No. 21507

    MNP $15   MIP $20

Dolls of the World/International Native American #1, Two Box Versions, 1993, Mattel, Model No. 1753

    MNP $12   MIP $30

Dolls of the World/International Native American #2, 1994, Mattel, Model No. 11609

    MNP $10   MIP $20

Dolls of the World/International Native American #3, 1995, Mattel, Model No. 12699

    MNP $10   MIP $15

Dolls of the World/International Nigerian, 1990, Mattel, Model No. 7376

    MNP $15   MIP $20

Dolls of the World/International Norwegian, Pink flowers, Limited to 3,000, 1996, Mattel, Model No. 14450

    MNP $12   MIP $50

Dolls of the World/International NW Coast Native American Barbie, 2000, Mattel, Model No. 24671

    MNP $12   MIP $15

Dolls of the World/International Oriental, 1981, Mattel, Model No. 3262

    MNP $35   MIP $50

Dolls of the World/International Parisian, 1980, Mattel, Model No. 1600

    MNP $50   MIP $45

Dolls of the World/International Parisian, 1991, Mattel, Model No. 9843

    MNP $25   MIP $50

Dolls of the World/International Peruvian, 1986, Mattel, Model No. 2995

    MNP $15   MIP $30

Dolls of the World/International Peruvian, 1999, Mattel, Model No. 21506

    MNP $10   MIP $20

Dolls of the World/International Polish, 1998, Mattel, Model No. 18560

    MNP $15   MIP $20

Dolls of the World/International Polynesian, 1995, Mattel, Model No. 12700

    MNP $10   MIP $20

Dolls of the World/International Royal, 1980, Mattel, Model No. 1602

    MNP $50   MIP $65

Dolls of the World/International Russian, 1989, Mattel, Model No. 1916

    MNP $10   MIP $20

Dolls of the World/International Russian, 1997, Mattel, Model No. 16500

    MNP $10   MIP $30

Dolls of the World/International Scottish, 1981, Mattel, Model No. 3263

    MNP $50   MIP $70

Dolls of the World/International Scottish, 1991, Mattel, Model No. 9845

    MNP $8   MIP $30

Dolls of the World/International Spanish, 1983, Mattel, Model No. 4031

    MNP $40   MIP $45

Dolls of the World/International Spanish, 1992, Mattel, Model No. 4963

    MNP $25   MIP $50

Dolls of the World/International Spanish, 2000, Mattel, Model No. 24670

    MNP $12   MIP $20

Dolls of the World/International Swedish, 1983, Mattel, Model No. 4032

    MNP $25   MIP $40

Dolls of the World/International Swedish, 2000, Mattel, Model No. 24672

    MNP $12   MIP $20

Dolls of the World/International Swiss, 1984, Mattel, Model No. 7451

MNP $30   MIP $45

Dolls of the World/International Thai, 1998, Mattel, Model No. 18561

MNP $10   MIP $25

Dramatic New Living Barbie, 1970, Mattel, Model No. 1116

MNP $65   MIP $175

Dramatic New Living Skipper, 1970, Mattel, Model No. 1117

MNP $40   MIP $125

Dream Bride, 1992, Mattel, Model No. 1623

MNP $10   MIP $25

Dream Date Barbie, 1983, Mattel, Model No. 5868

MNP $10   MIP $20

Dream Date Ken, 1983, Mattel, Model No. 4077

MNP $10   MIP $20

Dream Glow Barbie, Black, 1986, Mattel, Model No. 2242

MNP $12   MIP $30

Dream Glow Barbie, Hispanic, 1986, Mattel, Model No. 1647

MNP $25   MIP $50

Dream Glow Barbie, White, 1986, Mattel, Model No. 2248

MNP $12   MIP $40

Dream Glow Ken, Black, 1986, Mattel, Model No. 2421

MNP $13   MIP $20

Dream Glow Ken, White, 1986, Mattel, Model No. 2250

MNP $13   MIP $15

Dream Time Barbie, Pink, 1985, Mattel, Model No. 9180

MNP $10   MIP $20

Earring Magic Barbie, Blonde, 1993, Mattel, Model No. 7014

MNP $10   MIP $15

(KP Photo)

Earring Magic Ken, 1993, Mattel, Model No. 2290

MNP $10   MIP $20

Earring Magic Midge, 1993, Mattel

MNP $10   MIP $15

Fabulous Fur Barbie, 1983, Mattel, Model No. 7093

MNP $20   MIP $50

Fashion Jeans Barbie, 1981, Mattel, Model No. 5313

MNP $15   MIP $50

Fashion Jeans Ken, 1982, Mattel, Model No. 5316

MNP $12   MIP $25

Fashion Photo Barbie, two versions, 1978, Mattel, Model No. 2210

MNP $20   MIP $60

Fashion Photo Christie, 1978, Mattel, Model No. 2324

MNP $20   MIP $60

Fashion Photo P.J., 1978, Mattel, Model No. 2323

MNP $35   MIP $70

Fashion Play Barbie, 1983, Mattel, Model No. 7193

MNP $5   MIP $15

Fashion Play Barbie, 1987, Mattel, Model No. 4835

MNP $5   MIP $15

Fashion Play Barbie, 1990, Mattel, Model No. 9429

MNP $2   MIP $15

Fashion Play Barbie, 1991, Mattel, Model No. 9629

MNP $2   MIP $15

Fashion Play Barbie, Black, 1991, Mattel, Model No. 5953

MNP $2   MIP $15

Fashion Play Barbie, Hispanic, 1990, Mattel, Model No. 5954

MNP $2   MIP $15

Fashion Queen Barbie, 1963, Mattel, Model No. 870

MNP $65   MIP $275

Feelin' Fun Barbie, two versions, White, 1st Issue, 1988, Mattel, Model No. 1189

MNP $5   MIP $10

Festivals of the World Chinese New Year, 2006, Mattel, Model No. J0928

MNP $60   MIP $125

Flight Time Barbie, Black, 1990, Mattel, Model No. 9916

MNP $5   MIP $10

Flight Time Barbie, White, 1990, Mattel, Model No. 9584

MNP $5   MIP $15

Flight Time Ken, 1990, Mattel, Model No. 9600

MNP $5   MIP $10

Fluff, 1971, Mattel, Model No. 1143

MNP $100   MIP $225

Francie w/Growin' Pretty Hair, 1971, Mattel, Model No. 1129

MNP $65   MIP $175

Francie, Bendable Leg, Blonde, Brunette, 1966, Mattel, Model No. 1130

MNP $85   MIP $350

Francie, Hair Happenins, 1970, Mattel, Model No. 1122

MNP $95   MIP $350

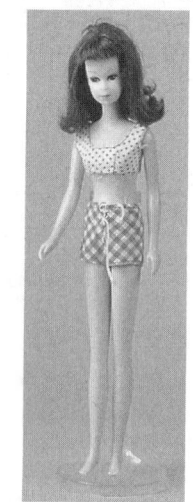

(KP Photo)

Francie, Straight Leg, Brunette, Blonde, 1966, Mattel, Model No. 1140

MNP $85   MIP $350

Francie, Twist N Turn, "Black Francie" 1st Issue, Red Hair, 1967, Mattel, Model No. 1100
MNP $650   MIP $1150

Francie, Twist N Turn, "Black Francie" 2nd Issue, Black Hair, Mattel, Model No. 1100
MNP $650   MIP $1500

(KP Photo)

Francie, Twist N Turn, Blonde or Brunette, "No Bangs," 1967, Mattel, Model No. 1170
MNP $650   MIP $1300

Francie, Twist N Turn, Blonde or Brunette, Long Hair w/Bangs, 1969, Mattel, Model No. 1170
MNP $75   MIP $375

Francie, Twist N Turn, Blonde or Brunette, Short Hair, 1969, Mattel, Model No. 1170
MNP $75   MIP $425

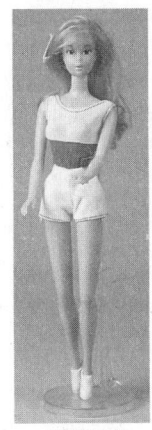

(KP Photo)

Free Moving Barbie, 1974, Mattel, Model No. 7270
MNP $45   MIP $100

Free Moving Cara, 1974, Mattel, Model No. 7283
MNP $50   MIP $125

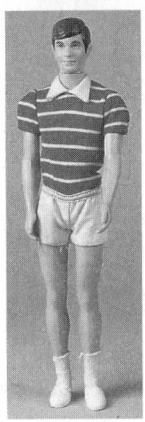

(KP Photo)

Free Moving Ken, 1974, Mattel, Model No. 7280
MNP $40   MIP $75

Free Moving P.J., 1974, Mattel, Model No. 7281
MNP $45   MIP $85

Funtime Barbie, Black, 1987, Mattel, Model No. 1739
MNP $5   MIP $10

Funtime Barbie, White, 1987, Mattel, Model No. 1738
MNP $5   MIP $10

Funtime Ken, 1987, Mattel, Model No. 7194
MNP $7   MIP $10

Garden Party Barbie, 1989, Mattel, Model No. 1953
MNP $8   MIP $15

Gift Giving Barbie, 1986, Mattel, Model No. 1922
MNP $5   MIP $15

Gift Giving Barbie, 1989, Mattel, Model No. 1205
MNP $5   MIP $15

Gold Medal Olympic Barbie Skater, 1975, Mattel, Model No. 7262
MNP $20   MIP $75

Gold Medal Olympic Barbie Skier, 1975, Mattel, Model No. 7264
MNP $20   MIP $75

Gold Medal Olympic P.J. Gymnast, 1975, Mattel, Model No. 7263
MNP $20   MIP $85

Gold Medal Olympic Skier Ken, 1975, Mattel, Model No. 7261
MNP $20   MIP $65

Gold Medal Olympic Skipper, 1975, Mattel, Model No. 7274
MNP $20   MIP $65

Golden Dreams Barbie, two versions, 1981, Mattel, Model No. 1974
MNP $15   MIP $50

Golden Dreams Christie, 1981, Mattel, Model No. 3249
MNP $15   MIP $50

Great Shapes Barbie, Black, 1984, Mattel, Model No. 7834
MNP $5   MIP $10

Great Shapes Barbie, w/Walkman, 1984, Mattel, Model No. 7025
MNP $12   MIP $15

Great Shapes Barbie, White, 1984, Mattel, Model No. 7025
MNP $5   MIP $10

Great Shapes Ken, 1984, Mattel, Model No. 7310
MNP $5   MIP $10

Great Shapes Skipper, 1984, Mattel, Model No. 7417
MNP $5   MIP $10

Groom Todd, 1982, Mattel, Model No. 4253
MNP $15   MIP $45

Growin' Pretty Hair Barbie, 1971, Mattel, Model No. 1144
MNP $150   MIP $350

Growing Up Ginger, 1977, Mattel, Model No. 9222
MNP $30   MIP $125

(KP Photo)

Growing Up Skipper, 1977, Mattel, Model No. 7259
MNP $30   MIP $100

Happy Birthday Barbie, 1981, Mattel, Model No. 1922
MNP $8   MIP $15

Happy Birthday Barbie, 1984, Mattel, Model No. 1922
MNP $8   MIP $20

Happy Birthday Barbie, 1991, Mattel, Model No. 9561
MNP $8   MIP $15

Happy Birthday Barbie, Black, 1991, Mattel, Model No. 9561

    MNP $8   **MIP** $10

Hawaiian Barbie, 1975, Mattel, Model No. 7470

    MNP $25   **MIP** $60

Hawaiian Barbie, 1977, Mattel, Model No. 7470

    MNP $30   **MIP** $70

Hawaiian Fun Barbie, 1991, Mattel, Model No. 5040

    MNP $3   **MIP** $10

Hawaiian Fun Christie, 1991, Mattel, Model No. 5044

    MNP $3   **MIP** $10

Hawaiian Fun Jazzie, 1991, Mattel, Model No. 9294

    MNP $3   **MIP** $10

Hawaiian Fun Ken, 1991, Mattel, Model No. 5041

    MNP $3   **MIP** $10

Hawaiian Fun Kira, 1991, Mattel, Model No. 5043

    MNP $3   **MIP** $10

Hawaiian Fun Skipper, 1991, Mattel, Model No. 5042

    MNP $3   **MIP** $10

Hawaiian Fun Steven, 1991, Mattel, Model No. 5045

    MNP $3   **MIP** $10

Hawaiian Ken, 1979, Mattel, Model No. 2960

    MNP $13   **MIP** $50

Hawaiian Ken, 1984, Mattel, Model No. 7495

    MNP $7   **MIP** $30

High School Chelsie, 1989, Mattel, Model No. 3698

    MNP $5   **MIP** $20

High School Dude, Jazzie's Boyfriend, 1989, Mattel, Model No. 3600

    MNP $5   **MIP** $20

High School Jazzie, 1989, Mattel, Model No. 3635

    MNP $5   **MIP** $20

High School Stacie, 1989, Mattel, Model No. 3636

    MNP $5   **MIP** $20

(KP Photo)

Hispanic Barbie, 1980, Mattel, Model No. 1292

    MNP $15   **MIP** $65

Hollywood Nails Barbie, White or Black, 1999, Mattel

    MNP $7   **MIP** $10

Hollywood Nails Christie, 1999, Mattel

    MNP $7   **MIP** $10

Hollywood Nails Teresa, White or Black, 1999, Mattel

    MNP $7   **MIP** $10

Home Pretty Barbie, 1990, Mattel, Model No. 2249

    MNP $8   **MIP** $15

Homecoming Queen Skipper, Black, 1988, Mattel, Model No. 2390

    MNP $8   **MIP** $10

Homecoming Queen Skipper, White, 1988, Mattel, Model No. 1952

    MNP $12   **MIP** $10

Horse Lovin' Barbie, 1983, Mattel, Model No. 1757

    MNP $10   **MIP** $20

Horse Lovin' Ken, 1983, Mattel, Model No. 3600

    MNP $8   **MIP** $15

Horse Lovin' Skipper, 1983, Mattel, Model No. 5029

    MNP $8   **MIP** $15

Hot Stuff Skipper, 1984, Mattel, Model No. 7927

    MNP $5   **MIP** $10

Ice Capades Barbie, 50th Anniversary, Black, 1990, Mattel, Model No. 7348

    MNP $5   **MIP** $15

Ice Capades Barbie, 50th Anniversary, White, 1990, Mattel, Model No. 7365

    MNP $5   **MIP** $20

Ice Capades Ken, 1990, Mattel, Model No. 7375

    MNP $5   **MIP** $15

Inline Skating Barbie, 1996, Mattel, Model No. 15473

    MNP $5   **MIP** $15

Inline Skating Ken, 1996, Mattel, Model No. 15474

    MNP $5   **MIP** $15

Inline Skating Midge, 1996, Mattel, Model No. 15475

    MNP $5   **MIP** $15

Island Fun Barbie, 1988, Mattel, Model No. 4061

    MNP $3   **MIP** $10

Island Fun Christie, 1988, Mattel, Model No. 4092

    MNP $3   **MIP** $10

Island Fun Ken, 1988, Mattel, Model No. 4060

    MNP $3   **MIP** $10

Island Fun Skipper, 1988, Mattel, Model No. 4064

    MNP $3   **MIP** $10

Island Fun Steven, 1988, Mattel, Model No. 4093

    MNP $3   **MIP** $10

Island Fun Teresa, 1988, Mattel, Model No. 4117

    MNP $3   **MIP** $10

Jazzie Workout, 1989, Mattel, Model No. 3633

    MNP $5   **MIP** $10

Jewel Girl Barbie, Christie, Teresa (new body style, belly button), 2000, Mattel

    MNP $5   **MIP** $15

Jewel Secrets Barbie, Black, two box versions, 1987, Mattel, Model No. 1756

    MNP $6   **MIP** $25

Jewel Secrets Barbie, White, two box versions, 1987, Mattel, Model No. 1737

    MNP $6   **MIP** $25

Jewel Secrets Ken, Black, 1987, Mattel, Model No. 3232

    MNP $6   **MIP** $15

Jewel Secrets Ken, Rooted Hair, 1987, Mattel, Model No. 1719

    MNP $6   **MIP** $15

Jewel Secrets Skipper, 1987, Mattel, Model No. 3133

    MNP $6   **MIP** $15

Jewel Secrets Whitney, 1987, Mattel, Model No. 3179

    MNP $8   **MIP** $20

Julia, Talking, First Issue w/Straight Hair, 1969, Mattel, Model No. 1128
    MNP $75   **MIP** $250

Julia, Talking, Second Issue, Afro Hair, 1969, Mattel, Model No. 1128
    MNP $75   **MIP** $250

Julia, Twist N Turn, One-Piece Nurse Dress, 2nd Issue, 1969, Mattel, Model No. 1127
    MNP $100   **MIP** $250

Julia, Twist N Turn, Two-Piece Nurse Outfit, 1st Issue, 1969, Mattel, Model No. 1127
    MNP $125   **MIP** $300

Ken, Bendable Leg, Brunette, Blond, 1965, Mattel, Model No. 750
    MNP $125   **MIP** $275

Ken, Flocked Hair, Brunette, Blond, 1961, Mattel, Model No. 750
    MNP $45   **MIP** $85

Ken, Painted Hair, Brunette, Blond, 1962, Mattel, Model No. 750
    MNP $40   **MIP** $85

Ken, Talking, 1970, Mattel, Model No. 1124
    MNP $50   **MIP** $125

Kevin, 1991, Mattel, Model No. 9325
    MNP $5   **MIP** $10

(KP Photo)

Kissing Barbie, 1979, Mattel, Model No. 2597
    MNP $8   **MIP** $30

Kissing Christie, 1979, Mattel, Model No. 2955
    MNP $10   **MIP** $30

Lights & Lace Barbie, 1991, Mattel, Model No. 9725
    MNP $4   **MIP** $10

Lights & Lace Christie, 1991, Mattel, Model No. 9728
    MNP $4   **MIP** $10

Lights & Lace Teresa, 1991, Mattel, Model No. 9727
    MNP $4   **MIP** $10

(KP Photo)

Live Action Barbie, 1970, Mattel, Model No. 1155
    MNP $60   **MIP** $150

Live Action Barbie on Stage, 1970, Mattel, Model No. 1152
    MNP $75   **MIP** $250

Live Action Christie, 1970, Mattel, Model No. 1175
    MNP $60   **MIP** $350

Live Action Ken, 1970, Mattel, Model No. 1159
    MNP $55   **MIP** $150

Live Action Ken on Stage, 1970, Mattel, Model No. 1172
    MNP $40   **MIP** $150

Live Action P.J., 1970, Mattel, Model No. 1156
    MNP $65   **MIP** $250

Live Action P.J. on Stage, 1970, Mattel, Model No. 1153
    MNP $75   **MIP** $175

Lovin' You Barbie, 1983, Mattel, Model No. 7072
    MNP $20   **MIP** $40

Magic Curl Barbie, Black, 1982, Mattel, Model No. 3989
    MNP $8   **MIP** $15

Magic Curl Barbie, White, 1982, Mattel, Model No. 3856
    MNP $10   **MIP** $20

Magic Moves Barbie, Black, 1985, Mattel, Model No. 3137
    MNP $15   **MIP** $20

Magic Moves Barbie, White, 1985, Mattel, Model No. 2126
    MNP $15   **MIP** $20

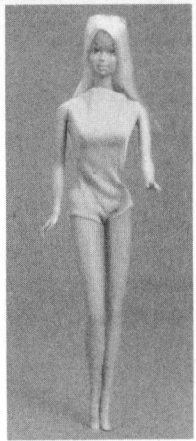

(KP Photo)

Malibu Barbie, 1971, Mattel, Model No. 1067
    MNP $15   **MIP** $50

Malibu Barbie (Sunset), 1975, Mattel, Model No. 1067
    MNP $15   **MIP** $30

Malibu Christie, 1975, Mattel, Model No. 7745
    MNP $10   **MIP** $50

Malibu Francie, 1971, Mattel, Model No. 1068
    MNP $15   **MIP** $50

Malibu Ken, 1976, Mattel, Model No. 1088
    MNP $8   **MIP** $25

Malibu P.J., 1975, Mattel, Model No. 1087
    MNP $5   **MIP** $50

Malibu Skipper, 1977, Mattel, Model No. 1069
    MNP $8   **MIP** $40

Midge, Bendable Leg, Blonde, Brunette, Titian, 1965, Mattel, Model No. 1080
    MNP $175   **MIP** $425

Midge, Straight Leg, Blonde, Brunette, Titian, 1963, Mattel, Model No. 860
    MNP $35   **MIP** $115

Miss Barbie (sleep eyes), 1964, Mattel, Model No. 1060
    MNP $300   **MIP** $1200

(KP Photo)

Mod Hair Ken, 1972, Mattel, Model No. 4224
MNP $45   MIP $65

Music Lovin' Barbie, 1985, Mattel, Model No. 9988
MNP $10   MIP $20

Music Lovin' Ken, 1985, Mattel, Model No. 2388
MNP $10   MIP $20

Music Lovin' Skipper, 1985, Mattel, Model No. 2854
MNP $10   MIP $20

My First Barbie, 1991, Mattel, Model No. 9942
MNP $5   MIP $20

My First Barbie, Aqua and Yellow Dress, 1981, Mattel, Model No. 1875
MNP $5   MIP $15

My First Barbie, Black, 1990, Mattel, Model No. 9943
MNP $5   MIP $15

My First Barbie, Hispanic, 1991, Mattel, Model No. 9944
MNP $3   MIP $15

My First Barbie, Pink Checkered Dress, 1983, Mattel, Model No. 1875
MNP $5   MIP $15

My First Barbie, Pink Tutu, Black, 1987, Mattel, Model No. 1801
MNP $5   MIP $15

My First Barbie, Pink Tutu, White, 1987, Mattel, Model No. 1788
MNP $5   MIP $15

My First Barbie, White, 1990, Mattel, Model No. 9942
MNP $4   MIP $15

My First Barbie, White Dress, Black, 1984, Mattel, Model No. 9858
MNP $7   MIP $15

My First Barbie, White Dress, White, 1984, Mattel, Model No. 1875
MNP $5   MIP $15

My First Barbie, White Tutu, Black, 1988, Mattel, Model No. 1281
MNP $6   MIP $10

My First Barbie, White Tutu, Hispanic, 1988, Mattel, Model No. 1282
MNP $6   MIP $10

My First Barbie, White Tutu, White, 1988, Mattel, Model No. 1280
MNP $5   MIP $10

My First Ken, 1st Issue, 1989, Mattel, Model No. 1389
MNP $4   MIP $15

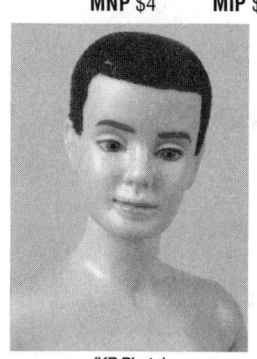

(KP Photo)

My First Ken, Prince, 1990, Mattel, Model No. 9940
MNP $4   MIP $15

New Look Ken, 1976, Mattel, Model No. 9342
MNP $23   MIP $65

Newport Barbie, two versions, 1974, Mattel, Model No. 7807
MNP $25   MIP $125

Nurse Whitney, 1987, Mattel, Model No. 4405
MNP $15   MIP $30

Ocean Friends Barbie, 1996, Mattel, Model No. 15430
MNP $5   MIP $10

Ocean Friends Ken, 1996, Mattel, Model No. 15430
MNP $5   MIP $10

Ocean Friends Kira, 1996, Mattel, Model No. 15431
MNP $5   MIP $10

Olympic Gymnast, Blond, 1996, Mattel, Model No. 15123
MNP $7   MIP $15

P.J., Talking, 1970, Mattel, Model No. 1113
MNP $65   MIP $250

P.J., Twist N Turn, 1970, Mattel, Model No. 1118
MNP $65   MIP $275

Party Treats Barbie, 1989, Mattel, Model No. 4885
MNP $8   MIP $20

Peaches n' Cream Barbie, Black, 1984, Mattel, Model No. 9516
MNP $8   MIP $30

Peaches n' Cream Barbie, White, 1984, Mattel, Model No. 7926
MNP $8   MIP $30

Perfume Giving Ken, Black, 1989, Mattel, Model No. 4555
MNP $6   MIP $15

Perfume Giving Ken, White, 1989, Mattel, Model No. 4554
MNP $6   MIP $15

Perfume Pretty Barbie, Black, 1989, Mattel, Model No. 4552
MNP $8   MIP $15

Perfume Pretty Barbie, White, 1989, Mattel, Model No. 4551
MNP $8   MIP $15

Perfume Pretty Whitney, 1987, Mattel, Model No. 4557
MNP $8   MIP $15

Pink 'n Pretty Barbie, 1982, Mattel, Model No. 3551
MNP $12   MIP $45

Pink 'n Pretty Christie, 1982, Mattel, Model No. 3554
MNP $10   MIP $40

Playtime Barbie, 1984, Mattel, Model No. 5336
MNP $5   MIP $10

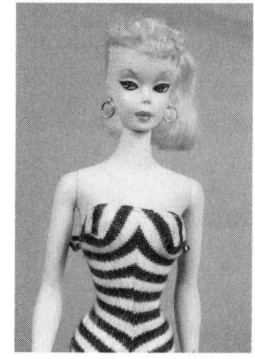

(KP Photo)

Ponytail Barbie #1, Blonde, 1959, Mattel, Model No. 850
MNP $2000   MIP $5000

(KP Photo)

Ponytail Barbie #1, Brunette, 1959, Mattel, Model No. 850

    MNP $2500   **MIP** $5500

Ponytail Barbie #2, Blonde, 1959, Mattel, Model No. 850

    MNP $2500   **MIP** $5000

Ponytail Barbie #2, Brunette, 1959, Mattel, Model No. 850

    MNP $3000   **MIP** $7000

Ponytail Barbie #3, Blonde, 1960, Mattel, Model No. 850

    MNP $325   **MIP** $850

Ponytail Barbie #3, Brunette, 1960, Mattel, Model No. 850

    MNP $375   **MIP** $900

Ponytail Barbie #4, Blonde, 1960, Mattel, Model No. 850

    MNP $175   **MIP** $400

Ponytail Barbie #4, Brunette, 1960, Mattel, Model No. 850

    MNP $275   **MIP** $450

Ponytail Barbie #5, Blonde, 1961, Mattel, Model No. 850

    MNP $125   **MIP** $350

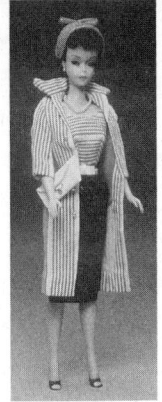

(KP Photo)

Ponytail Barbie #5, Brunette, 1961, Mattel, Model No. 850

    MNP $200   **MIP** $400

Ponytail Barbie #5, Titian, 1961, Mattel, Model No. 850

    MNP $225   **MIP** $500

Ponytail Barbie #6, Blonde, 1962, Mattel, Model No. 850

    MNP $125   **MIP** $350

(KP Photo)

Ponytail Barbie #6, Brunette, 1962, Mattel, Model No. 850

    MNP $125   **MIP** $350

Ponytail Barbie #6, Titian, 1962, Mattel, Model No. 850

    MNP $125   **MIP** $350

Ponytail Swirl Style Barbie, Blonde, 1964, Mattel, Model No. 850

    MNP $275   **MIP** $600

Ponytail Swirl Style Barbie, Brunette, 1964, Mattel, Model No. 850

    MNP $275   **MIP** $600

Ponytail Swirl Style Barbie, Platinum, 1964, Mattel, Model No. 850

    MNP $500   **MIP** $1200

Ponytail Swirl Style Barbie, Titian, 1964, Mattel, Model No. 850

    MNP $275   **MIP** $600

Pose 'n Play Skipper (baggie), 1973, Mattel, Model No. 1117

    MNP $20   **MIP** $55

Pretty Changes Barbie, 1978, Mattel, Model No. 2598

    MNP $8   **MIP** $30

Pretty Party Barbie, 1983, Mattel, Model No. 7194

    MNP $12   **MIP** $25

(KP Photo)

Quick Curl Barbie, 1972, Mattel, Model No. 4220

    MNP $20   **MIP** $65

Quick Curl Cara, 1974, Mattel, Model No. 7291

    MNP $20   **MIP** $60

Quick Curl Deluxe Barbie, 1976, Mattel, Model No. 9217

    MNP $20   **MIP** $65

Quick Curl Deluxe Cara, 1976, Mattel, Model No. 9219

    MNP $20   **MIP** $60

Quick Curl Deluxe P.J., 1976, Mattel, Model No. 9218

    MNP $20   **MIP** $50

Quick Curl Deluxe Skipper, 1976, Mattel, Model No. 9428

    MNP $20   **MIP** $50

Quick Curl Francie, 1972, Mattel, Model No. 4222

    MNP $20   **MIP** $55

Quick Curl Kelley, 1972, Mattel, Model No. 4221

    MNP $20   **MIP** $75

(KP Photo)

Quick Curl Miss America, Blonde, 1974, Mattel, Model No. 8697
    MNP $35   **MIP** $75

Quick Curl Miss America, Brunette, 1973, Mattel, Model No. 8697
    MNP $45   **MIP** $125

Quick Curl Skipper, 1974, Mattel, Model No. 4223
    MNP $20   **MIP** $50

(KP Photo)

Ricky, 1965, Mattel, Model No. 1090
    MNP $55   **MIP** $125

Rocker Barbie, 1st Issue, 1986, Mattel, Model No. 1140
    MNP $7   **MIP** $25

(KP Photo)

Rocker Barbie, 2nd Issue, 1987, Mattel, Model No. 3055
    MNP $7   **MIP** $20

Rocker Dana, 1st Issue, 1986, Mattel, Model No. 1196
    MNP $7   **MIP** $25

Rocker Dana, 2nd Issue, 1987, Mattel, Model No. 3158
    MNP $7   **MIP** $15

Rocker Dee-Dee, 1st Issue, 1986, Mattel, Model No. 1141
    MNP $7   **MIP** $25

Rocker Dee-Dee, 2nd Issue, 1987, Mattel, Model No. 3160
    MNP $7   **MIP** $15

Rocker Derek, 1st Issue, 1986, Mattel, Model No. 2428
    MNP $7   **MIP** $25

Rocker Derek, 2nd Issue, 1987, Mattel, Model No. 3173
    MNP $7   **MIP** $15

Rocker Diva, 1st Issue, 1986, Mattel, Model No. 2427
    MNP $7   **MIP** $25

Rocker Diva, 2nd Issue, 1987, Mattel, Model No. 3159
    MNP $7   **MIP** $15

Rocker Ken, 1st Issue, 1986, Mattel, Model No. 3131
    MNP $7   **MIP** $25

Roller Skating Barbie, 1980, Mattel, Model No. 1880
    MNP $8   **MIP** $35

Roller Skating Ken, 1980, Mattel, red shirt, blue shorts, jacket, skates, Model No. 1881
    MNP $8   **MIP** $30

Safari Barbie, 1983, Mattel, Model No. 4973
    MNP $8   **MIP** $15

Scott, 1979, Mattel, Model No. 1019
    MNP $15   **MIP** $60

Sea Lovin' Barbie, 1984, Mattel, Model No. 9109
    MNP $8   **MIP** $15

Sea Lovin' Ken, 1984, Mattel, Model No. 9110
    MNP $8   **MIP** $15

Secret Messages Barbie, White or Black, 2000, Model No. 26422
    MNP $7   **MIP** $10

Sensations Barbie, 1987, Mattel, Model No. 4931
    MNP $5   **MIP** $10

Sensations Becky, 1987, Mattel, Model No. 4977
    MNP $5   **MIP** $10

Sensations Belinda, 1987, Mattel, Model No. 4976
    MNP $5   **MIP** $10

Sensations Bobsy, 1987, Mattel, Model No. 4967
    MNP $5   **MIP** $10

Sit 'n Style Barbie, 2000, Mattel, Model No. 23421
    MNP $7   **MIP** $10

Ski Fun Barbie, 1991, Mattel, Model No. 7511
    MNP $6   **MIP** $15

Ski Fun Ken, 1991, Mattel, Model No. 7512
    MNP $6   **MIP** $15

Ski Fun Midge, 1991, Mattel, Model No. 7513
    MNP $6   **MIP** $25

(KP Photo)

Skipper, Bendable Leg, Brunette, Blonde, Titian, 1965, Mattel, Model No. 1030
    MNP $60   **MIP** $150

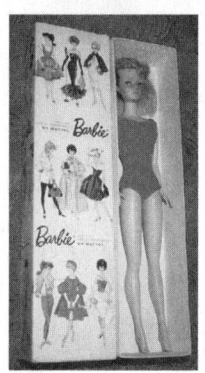

Skipper, Straight Leg, Brunette, Blonde, Titian, 1964, Mattel, Model No. 950
    MNP $30   **MIP** $125

Skipper, Straight Leg, Reissues,
Brunette, Blonde, Titian, 1971,
Mattel, Model No. 950
    MNP $125   **MIP** $350

Skipper, Twist N Turn, Blonde or
Brunette, Curl Pigtails, 1969,
Mattel, Model No. 1105
    MNP $75   **MIP** $225

Skipper, Twist N Turn, Blonde,
Brunette, Red Hair, Long Straight
Hair, 1968, Mattel, Model No. 1105
    MNP $75   **MIP** $200

(KP Photo)

Skooter, Bendable Leg, Brunette,
Blonde, Titian, 1966, Mattel,
Model No. 1120
    MNP $75   **MIP** $275

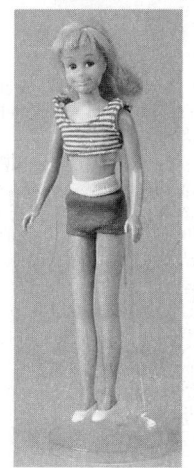

Skooter, Straight Leg, Brunette,
Blonde, Titian, 1965, Mattel,
Model No. 1040
    MNP $30   **MIP** $125

Snowboard Barbie, 1996, Mattel,
Model No. 15408
    MNP $10   **MIP** $15

Sparkle Barbie, 1996, Mattel, Model
No. 15419
    MNP $10   **MIP** $15

Sport 'n Shave Ken, 1980, Mattel,
Model No. 1294
    MNP $8   **MIP** $30

Stacey, Talking, Blonde or Red Hair,
Side Ponytail, 1968, Mattel, Model
No. 1125
    MNP $175   **MIP** $400

Stacey, Twist N Turn, Blonde or Red
Hair, Long Ponytail w/Spit Curls,
1968, Mattel, Model No. 1165
    MNP $125   **MIP** $400

Stacey, Twist N Turn, Blonde or Red
Hair, Short Rolled Flip, 1969,
Mattel, Model No. 1165
    MNP $125   **MIP** $400

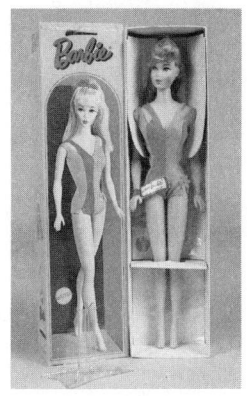

(KP Photo)

Standard Barbie, Blonde, Brunette,
Long Straight Hair w/Bangs, 1967,
Mattel, Model No. 1190
    MNP $150   **MIP** $425

Standard Barbie, Centered Eyes,
1971, Mattel, Model No. 1190
    MNP $300   **MIP** $475

Standard Barbie, Titian, Long
Straight Hair w/Bangs, 1967,
Mattel, Model No. 1190
    MNP $225   **MIP** $450

Stars & Stripes Air Force Barbie,
1990, Mattel, Model No. 3360
    MNP $5   **MIP** $10

(KP Photo)

Stars & Stripes Army Barbie, White
or Black, 1993, Mattel, Model
No. 1234/5618
    MNP $10   **MIP** $20

Stars & Stripes Marine Corps Barbie,
White or Black, 1992, Mattel,
Model No. 7549/7594
    MNP $10   **MIP** $20

(KP Photo)

Stars & Stripes Navy Barbie, White
or Black, 1991, Mattel, Model
No. 9693/9694
    MNP $10   **MIP** $20

Stars 'n Stripes Air Force Ken, White
or Black, 1994, Mattel, Model
No. 11554/11555
    MNP $15   **MIP** $20

Stars 'n Stripes Air Force
Thunderbirds Barbie, White or
Black, 1994, Mattel, Model
No. 11552/11553
    MNP $15   **MIP** $20

Stars 'n Stripes Army Ken, White or
Black, 1993, Mattel, Model
No. 1237/5619
    MNP $15   **MIP** $20

Stars 'n Stripes Marine Corps Ken, Black or White, 1992, Mattel, Model No. 5352/7574
MNP $20   MIP $20

Style Magic Barbie, 1989, Mattel, Model No. 1283
MNP $5   MIP $20

Style Magic Christie, 1989, Mattel, Model No. 1288
MNP $5   MIP $10

Style Magic Skipper, 1989, Mattel, Model No. 1915
MNP $5   MIP $10

Style Magic Whitney, 1989, Mattel, Model No. 1290
MNP $5   MIP $10

Summit Barbie, Asian, 1990, Mattel, Model No. 7029
MNP $10   MIP $15

Summit Barbie, Black, 1990, Mattel, Model No. 7028
MNP $12   MIP $15

Summit Barbie, Hispanic, 1990, Mattel, Model No. 7030
MNP $10   MIP $15

Summit Barbie, White, 1990, Mattel, Model No. 7027
MNP $8   MIP $15

Sun Gold Malibu Barbie, Black, 1983, Mattel, Model No. 7745
MNP $5   MIP $15

Sun Gold Malibu Barbie, Hispanic, 1985, Mattel, Model No. 4970
MNP $3   MIP $20

Sun Gold Malibu Barbie, White, 1983, Mattel, Model No. 1067
MNP $5   MIP $15

Sun Gold Malibu Ken, Black, 1983, Mattel, Model No. 3849
MNP $3   MIP $15

Sun Gold Malibu Ken, Hispanic, 1985, Mattel, Model No. 4971
MNP $3   MIP $20

Sun Gold Malibu Ken, White, 1983, Mattel, Model No. 1088
MNP $3   MIP $15

Sun Gold Malibu P.J., 1983, Mattel, Model No. 1187
MNP $5   MIP $15

Sun Gold Malibu Skipper, 1983, Mattel, Model No. 1069
MNP $5   MIP $15

Sun Lovin' Malibu Barbie, 1978, Mattel, Model No. 1067
MNP $5   MIP $20

Sun Lovin' Malibu Ken, 1978, Mattel, Model No. 1088
MNP $5   MIP $20

Sun Lovin' Malibu P.J., 1978, Mattel, Model No. 1187
MNP $5   MIP $20

Sun Lovin' Malibu Skipper, 1978, Mattel, Model No. 1069
MNP $5   MIP $20

Sun Valley Barbie, 1974, Mattel, Model No. 7806
MNP $20   MIP $115

Sun Valley Ken, 1974, Mattel, Model No. 7809
MNP $20   MIP $95

Sunsational Malibu Barbie, 1982, Mattel, Model No. 1067
MNP $6   MIP $25

Sunsational Malibu Barbie, Hispanic, 1982, Mattel, Model No. 4970
MNP $8   MIP $25

Sunsational Malibu Christie, 1982, Mattel, Model No. 7745
MNP $6   MIP $20

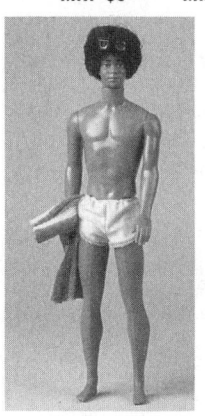

(KP Photo)

Sunsational Malibu Ken, Black, 1981, Mattel, Model No. 3849
MNP $15   MIP $35

Sunsational Malibu P.J., 1982, Mattel, Model No. 1187
MNP $6   MIP $30

Sunsational Malibu Skipper, 1982, Mattel, Model No. 1069
MNP $5   MIP $35

Sunset Malibu Christie, 1973, Mattel, Model No. 7745
MNP $20   MIP $65

Sunset Malibu Francie, 1971, Mattel, Model No. 1068
MNP $25   MIP $65

Sunset Malibu Ken, 1972, Mattel, Model No. 1088
MNP $15   MIP $50

Sunset Malibu P.J., 1971, Mattel, Model No. 1187
MNP $10   MIP $50

Sunset Malibu Skipper, 1971, Mattel, Model No. 1069
MNP $20   MIP $50

Super Hair Barbie, Black, 1987, Mattel, Model No. 3296
MNP $8   MIP $15

Super Hair Barbie, White, 1987, Mattel, Model No. 3101
MNP $8   MIP $15

Super Sport Ken, 1982, Mattel, Model No. 5839
MNP $8   MIP $15

Super Talk Barbie, 1994, Mattel, Model No. 12290
MNP $10   MIP $15

Super Teen Skipper, 1978, Mattel, Model No. 2756
MNP $7   MIP $15

(KP Photo)

Supersize Barbie, 1977, Mattel, Model No. 9828
MNP $45   MIP $125

Supersize Bride Barbie, 1977, Mattel, Model No. 9975
MNP $100   MIP $250

Supersize Christie, 1977, Mattel, Model No. 9839
MNP $75   MIP $225

Supersize Super Hair Barbie, 1979, Mattel, Model No. 2844
MNP $85   MIP $125

Superstar Ballerina Barbie, 1976, Mattel, Model No. 4983
MNP $20   MIP $50

Superstar Barbie, 1977, Mattel, Model No. 9720
MNP $15   MIP $60

Superstar Barbie, 1988, Mattel, Model No. 1604
MNP $45   MIP $95

Superstar Barbie 30th Anniversary, Black, 1989, Mattel, Model No. 1605

     MNP $6   MIP $25

Superstar Barbie 30th Anniversary, White, 1989, Mattel, Model No. 1604

     MNP $8   MIP $20

Superstar Christie, 1977, Mattel, Model No. 9950

     MNP $20   MIP $50

Superstar Ken, 1978, Mattel, Model No. 2211

     MNP $17   MIP $50

Superstar Ken, Black, 1989, Mattel, Model No. 1550

     MNP $5   MIP $25

Superstar Ken, White, 1989, Mattel, Model No. 1535

     MNP $7   MIP $40

Superstar Malibu Barbie, 1977, Mattel, Model No. 1067

     MNP $10   MIP $35

(KP Photo)

Sweet 16 Barbie, 1974, Mattel, Model No. 7796

     MNP $25   MIP $100

Sweet Roses P.J., 1983, Mattel, Model No. 7455

     MNP $15   MIP $40

Swimming Champion Barbie, 2000, Mattel, Model No. 24590

     MNP $7   MIP $15

Talk w/Me Barbie, 1997, Mattel, w/software, Model No. 17350

     MNP $15   MIP $30

Talking Barbie, Chignon w/Nape Curls, Blonde, Brunette, Titian, 1970, Mattel, Model No. 1115

     MNP $150   MIP $500

(KP Photo)

Talking Barbie, Side Ponytail w/Spit Curls, Blonde or Brunette, 1968, Mattel, Model No. 1115

     MNP $100   MIP $400

(KP Photo)

Talking Busy Barbie, 1972, Mattel, Model No. 1195

     MNP $100   MIP $300

Talking Busy Ken, 1972, Mattel, Model No. 1196

     MNP $70   MIP $140

(KP Photo)

Talking Busy Steffie, 1972, Mattel, Model No. 1186

     MNP $150   MIP $350

Talking Ken, 1969, Mattel, Model No. 1111

     MNP $60   MIP $150

Teacher Barbie, Painted on Panties, Black, 1996, Mattel, Model No. 13915

     MNP $10   MIP $15

(KP Photo)

Teacher Barbie, Painted on Panties, White, 1996, Mattel, Model No. 13914

     MNP $10   MIP $15

Teen Dance Jazzie, 1989, Mattel, Model No. 3634

     MNP $7   MIP $20

Teen Fun Skipper Cheerleader, 1987, Mattel, Model No. 5893

     MNP $5   MIP $10

Teen Fun Skipper Party Teen, 1987, Mattel, Model No. 5899

     MNP $5   MIP $10

Teen Fun Skipper Workout, 1987, Mattel, Model No. 5889
MNP $5 MIP $10

Teen Jazzie (Teen Dance), 1989, Mattel, Model No. 3634
MNP $4 MIP $35

Teen Looks Jazzie Cheerleader, 1989, Mattel, Model No. 3631
MNP $4 MIP $20

Teen Looks Jazzie Workout, 1989, Mattel, Model No. 3633
MNP $4 MIP $20

Teen Scene Jazzie, two box versions, 1991, Mattel, Model No. 5507
MNP $5 MIP $35

Teen Sweetheart Skipper, 1988, Mattel, Model No. 4855
MNP $5 MIP $10

(KP Photo)

Teen Talk Barbie, 1992, Mattel, Model No. 5745
MNP $10 MIP $20

Teen Talk Barbie, "Math is Tough" variation, 1992, Mattel, Model No. 5745
MNP $50 MIP $275

Teen Time Courtney, 1988, Mattel, Model No. 1950
MNP $5 MIP $10

Teen Time Skipper, 1988, Mattel, Model No. 1951
MNP $5 MIP $10

Tennis Barbie, 1986, Mattel, Model No. 1760
MNP $5 MIP $15

Tennis Ken, 1986, Mattel, Model No. 1761
MNP $5 MIP $15

(KP Photo)

Todd, 1967, Mattel, Model No. 3590
MNP $70 MIP $200

Tracy Bride, 1983, Mattel, Model No. 4103
MNP $8 MIP $45

Tropical Barbie, Black, 1986, Mattel, Model No. 1022
MNP $3 MIP $10

Tropical Barbie, White, 1986, Mattel, Model No. 1017
MNP $3 MIP $10

Tropical Ken, Black, 1986, Mattel, Model No. 1023
MNP $3 MIP $10

Tropical Ken, White, 1986, Mattel, Model No. 4060
MNP $3 MIP $10

Tropical Miko, 1986, Mattel, Model No. 2056
MNP $3 MIP $10

Tropical Skipper, 1986, Mattel, Model No. 4064
MNP $3 MIP $10

Truly Scrumptious, Standard, 1969, Mattel, Model No. 1107
MNP $175 MIP $400

Truly Scrumptious, Talking, 1969, Mattel, Model No. 1108
MNP $175 MIP $450

Tutti, All Hair Colors, Floral Dress w/Yellow Ribbon, 1967, Mattel, Model No. 3580
MNP $45 MIP $150

(KP Photo)

Tutti, All Hair Colors, Pink, White Gingham Suit, Hat, 1966, Mattel, Model No. 3550
MNP $50 MIP $170

Tutti, Germany, 1978, Mattel, Model No. 8128
MNP $40 MIP $125

Twiggy, 1967, Mattel, Model No. 1185
MNP $95 MIP $300

Twirley Curls Barbie, Black, 1983, Mattel, Model No. 5723
MNP $10 MIP $20

Twirley Curls Barbie, Hispanic, 1982, Mattel, Model No. 5724
MNP $10 MIP $20

Twirley Curls Barbie, White, 1982, Mattel, Model No. 5579
MNP $10 MIP $20

Twist N Turn Barbie, Blonde, Brunette, Red Hair w/Centered Eyes, 1971, Mattel, Model No. 1160
MNP $175 MIP $575

Twist N Turn Barbie, Flip Hair, Blonde or Brunette, 1969, Mattel, Model No. 1160
MNP $95 MIP $450

Twist N Turn Barbie, Light Blonde, Blonde, Light Brown, Brunette, 1967, Mattel, Model No. 1160
MNP $90 MIP $450

Twist N Turn Barbie, Long Straight Hair w/Bangs, Red Hair, 1967, Mattel, Model No. 1160
    MNP $175   **MIP** $550

UNICEF Barbie, Asian, 1989, Mattel, Model No. 4774
    MNP $5   **MIP** $10

UNICEF Barbie, Black, 1989, Mattel, Model No. 4770
    MNP $5   **MIP** $10

UNICEF Barbie, Hispanic, 1989, Mattel, Model No. 4782
    MNP $5   **MIP** $10

UNICEF Barbie, White, 1989, Mattel, Model No. 1920
    MNP $5   **MIP** $10

University Barbie, 1997, Mattel, many schools offered
    MNP $8   **MIP** $15

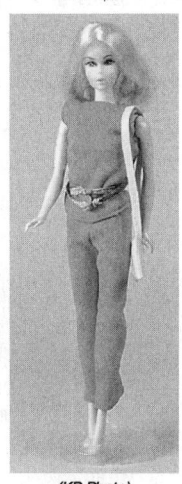

(KP Photo)

Walk Lively Barbie, 1971, Mattel, Model No. 1182
    MNP $75   **MIP** $200

Walk Lively Ken, 1971, Mattel, Model No. 1184
    MNP $40   **MIP** $150

Walk Lively Miss America Barbie, Brunette, 1971, Mattel, Model No. 3200
    MNP $95   **MIP** $200

Walk Lively Steffie, 1971, Mattel, Model No. 1183
    MNP $75   **MIP** $300

Walking Jamie, 1970, Mattel, Model No. 1132
    MNP $175   **MIP** $400

Wedding Fantasy Barbie, Black, 1989, Mattel, Model No. 7011
    MNP $7   **MIP** $20

Wedding Fantasy Barbie, White, 1989, Mattel, Model No. 2125
    MNP $7   **MIP** $20

Wedding Party Allan, 1991, Mattel, Model No. 9607
    MNP $7   **MIP** $20

Wedding Party Barbie, 1991, Mattel, Model No. 9608
    MNP $7   **MIP** $20

Wedding Party Kelly & Todd, 1991, Mattel, Model No. 9852
    MNP $15   **MIP** $25

Wedding Party Ken, 1991, Mattel, Model No. 9609
    MNP $7   **MIP** $20

Wedding Party Midge, 1991, Mattel, Model No. 9606
    MNP $7   **MIP** $15

(KP Photo)

Western Barbie, 1980, Mattel, Model No. 1757
    MNP $8   **MIP** $25

Western Fun Barbie, Black, 1989, Mattel, Model No. 2930
    MNP $5   **MIP** $15

Western Fun Barbie, White, 1989, Mattel, Model No. 9932
    MNP $5   **MIP** $15

Western Fun Ken, 1989, Mattel, Model No. 9934
    MNP $5   **MIP** $15

Western Fun Nia, 1989, Mattel, Model No. 9933
    MNP $5   **MIP** $15

Western Ken, 1981, Mattel, Model No. 3600
    MNP $7   **MIP** $25

Western Skipper, 1982, Mattel, Model No. 5029
    MNP $8   **MIP** $20

Wet 'n Wild Barbie, 1990, Mattel, Model No. 4103
    MNP $8   **MIP** $15

Wet 'n Wild Christie, 1989, Mattel, Model No. 4121
    MNP $3   **MIP** $10

Wet 'n Wild Ken, 1989, Mattel, Model No. 4104
    MNP $3   **MIP** $10

Wet 'n Wild Kira, 1989, Mattel, Model No. 4120
    MNP $3   **MIP** $10

Wet 'n Wild Skipper, 1989, Mattel, Model No. 4138
    MNP $3   **MIP** $10

Wet 'n Wild Steven, 1989, Mattel, Model No. 4137
    MNP $3   **MIP** $10

Wet 'n Wild Teresa, 1989, Mattel, Model No. 4136
    MNP $3   **MIP** $10

Wig Wardrobe Midge, 1965, Mattel, Model No. 1009
    MNP $200   **MIP** $500

Working Woman Barbie, Black or White, 1999, Mattel
    MNP $7   **MIP** $10

COLLECTORS' EDITIONS, STORE EXCLUSIVES, GIFT SETS

1 Modern Circle Barbie, 2003, Mattel
    MNP $15   **MIP** $20

1 Modern Circle Barbie (Evening Wear), 2004, Mattel
    MNP $15   **MIP** $20

1 Modern Circle Ken, 2003, Mattel
    MNP $15   **MIP** $20

1 Modern Circle Ken (Evening Wear), 2004, Mattel
    MNP $15   **MIP** $20

1 Modern Circle Melody, 2003, Mattel
    MNP $15   **MIP** $20

1 Modern Circle Melody (Evening Wear), 2004, Mattel
    MNP $15   **MIP** $20

1 Modern Circle Simone, 2003, Mattel
    MNP $15   **MIP** $20

1 Modern Circle Simone (Evening Wear), 2004, Mattel
    MNP $15   **MIP** $20

2008 Holiday Barbie, African-American, 2008, Mattel, Model No. L9644
    MNP $20   **MIP** $45

2008 Holiday Barbie, Caucasian, 2008, Mattel, Model No. L9643
    MNP $20   **MIP** $45

40th Anniversary Barbie, White or Black, 1999, Mattel, Model No. 21384/22336
    MNP $45   **MIP** $85

40th Anniversary Gala, 1999, Mattel, "bumblebee"
    MNP $30   **MIP** $90

40th Anniversary Ken, Black, 2001, Mattel, Model No. 52967
    MNP $45   **MIP** $85

40th Anniversary Ken, White, 2001, Mattel, Model No. 50722
    MNP $45   **MIP** $85

50th Anniversary Barbie, African-American, 2009, Mattel, Model No. N5860
    MNP $30   **MIP** $60

50th Anniversary Wedding Doll Set, 2009, Mattel, Model No. P6750
    MNP $65   **MIP** $130

Alice in Wonderland, Alice, 2007, Mattel
    MNP n/a   **MIP** $30

Alice in Wonderland, Mad Hatter, 2007, Mattel
    MNP n/a   **MIP** $30

Alice in Wonderland, Queen of Hearts, 2007, Mattel
    MNP n/a   **MIP** $30

All American Barbie & Starstepper, 1991, Mattel, Model No. 3712
    MNP $12   **MIP** $35

American Favorites: Harley-Davidson, 2009, Mattel, Model No. N6590
    MNP $20   **MIP** $45

American Stories #1 American Indian, 1996, Mattel, Model No. 14612
    MNP $7   **MIP** $10

American Stories #2 American Indian, 1997, Mattel, Model No. 17313
    MNP $7   **MIP** $10

American Stories Civil War Nurse, 1996, Mattel, Model No. 14612
    MNP $7   **MIP** $10

American Stories Colonial Barbie, 1995, Mattel, Model No. 12578
    MNP $7   **MIP** $10

American Stories Patriot Barbie, 1997, Mattel, Model No. 17312
    MNP $7   **MIP** $10

American Stories Pilgrim Barbie, 1995, Mattel, Model No. 12577
    MNP $7   **MIP** $10

American Stories Pioneer Barbie, 1995, Mattel, Model No. 12680
    MNP $7   **MIP** $10

American Stories Pioneer Shopkeeper, 1996, Mattel, Model No. 14756
    MNP $7   **MIP** $10

Ames Country Looks Barbie, 1993, Mattel, Model No. 5854
    MNP $8   **MIP** $15

Ames Denim 'N Lace Barbie, 1992, Mattel, Model No. 2452
    MNP $5   **MIP** $20

Ames Hot Looks Barbie, 1992, Mattel, Model No. 5756
    MNP $5   **MIP** $15

Ames Ice Cream Barbie, 1998, Mattel, Model No. 19280
    MNP $8   **MIP** $15

Ames Lady Bug Fun Barbie, 1997, Mattel, Model No. 17695
    MNP $5   **MIP** $15

Ames Party in Pink, 1991, Mattel, Model No. 2909
    MNP $5   **MIP** $15

Ames Strawberry Party Barbie, 1999, Mattel, Model No. 22895
    MNP $8   **MIP** $10

Angel Lights Barbie, 1993, Mattel
    MNP $40   **MIP** $65

Angels of Music Harpist Angel, Black or White, 1998, Mattel
    MNP $35   **MIP** $50

Angels of Music Heartstring Angel, Black or White, 1999, Mattel
    MNP $40   **MIP** $50

Anna Sui Boho Barbie, 2006, Mattel
    MNP n/a   **MIP** $130

Anne Klein Barbie, 1997, Mattel, Model No. 17603
    MNP $35   **MIP** $75

Applause Barbie Holiday, 1991, Mattel, Model No. 3406
    MNP $20   **MIP** $20

Applause Style Barbie, 1990, Mattel, Model No. 5313
    MNP $10   **MIP** $20

Armani Barbie, 2003, Mattel
    MNP $75   **MIP** $150

Artist Series, Reflections of Light Barbie, Renoir, 1999, Mattel, Model No. 23884
    MNP $40   **MIP** $60

Artist Series, Sunflower Barbie, Van Gogh, 1998, Mattel, Model No. 19366
    MNP $40   **MIP** $60

Artist Series, Water Lily Barbie, Monet, 1997, Mattel, Model No. 17783
    MNP $50   **MIP** $60

Avon Blushing Bride Barbie, White or Black, 2000, Mattel
    MNP $10   **MIP** $20

Avon Exotic Intrigue, 2004, Mattel, blonde, Hispanic, black
    MNP $10   **MIP** $20

Avon Fruit Fantasy Barbie, Blonde, 1999, Mattel
    MNP $10   **MIP** $20

Avon Fruit Fantasy Barbie, Brunette, 1999, Mattel
    MNP $15   **MIP** $20

Avon Lemon-Lime Barbie, 1999, Mattel, Model No. 20318
    MNP $10   **MIP** $20

Avon Mrs. P.F.E. Albee, 1997, Mattel, Model No. 17690
    MNP $15   **MIP** $35

Avon Mrs. P.F.E. Albee #2, 1998, Mattel, Model No. 20330
    MNP $15   **MIP** $30

Avon Representative Barbie, Black, White, Hispanic, 1999, Mattel
    MNP $20   **MIP** $50

Avon Snow Sensation, Black or White, 1999, Mattel
    MNP $10   **MIP** $25

Avon Spring Blossom, Black, 1996, Mattel, Model No. 15202
    MNP $5   **MIP** $10

Avon Spring Blossom, White, 1996, Mattel, Model No. 15201
    MNP $5   **MIP** $10

Avon Spring Petals Barbie, Black, 1997, Mattel, Model No. 16871
    MNP $5   **MIP** $10

Avon Spring Petals Barbie, Blonde or Brunette, 1997, Mattel, Model No. 10746/16872
    MNP $5   **MIP** $10

Avon Spring Tea Party Barbie, Black, Mattel
    MNP $10   **MIP** $20

Avon Spring Tea Party Barbie, Blonde or Brunette, Mattel, Model No. 18658
    MNP $10   **MIP** $20

Avon Strawberry Sorbet Barbie, 1999, Mattel, Model No. 20317
    MNP $5   **MIP** $15

Avon Timeless Silhouette Barbie, White or Black, 2001, Mattel
    MNP $10   **MIP** $20

Avon Victorian Skater Barbie, White or Black, 2000, Mattel
    MNP $10   **MIP** $30

Avon Winter Rhapsody Barbie, Black, Mattel, Model No. 16354
    MNP $15   **MIP** $30

Avon Winter Rhapsody Barbie, Blonde or Brunette, Mattel, Model No. 16353/16873
MNP $15   MIP $30

Avon Winter Splendor Barbie, Black, 1998, Mattel, Model No. 19358
MNP $20   MIP $40

Avon Winter Splendor Barbie, White, 1998, Mattel, Model No. 19357
MNP $15   MIP $35

Avon Winter Velvet, Black, 1996, Mattel, Model No. 15587
MNP $10   MIP $25

Avon Winter Velvet, White, 1996, Mattel, Model No. 15571
MNP $10   MIP $25

B Mine Barbie, 1993, Mattel, Model No. 11182
MNP $7   MIP $10

Back To School, 1993, Mattel, Model No. 3208
MNP $15   MIP $35

Back to School, 1997, Mattel
MNP $5   MIP $10

Badgley Mischka Barbie, 2006, Mattel
MNP $40   MIP $90

Badgley Mischka Bride, 2004, Mattel
MNP $40   MIP $95

Ballerina Barbie as Juliet, 2004, Mattel
MNP $20   MIP $45

Ballerina Barbie as Titania, 2004, Mattel
MNP $20   MIP $45

Ballerina Barbie Peppermint Candy Cane, 2003, Mattel
MNP $10   MIP $20

Ballerina Dreams Barbie, 2000, Mattel, Model No. 20676
MNP $5   MIP $12

Ballerina on Tour Gift Set, 1976, Mattel, Model No. 9613
MNP $25   MIP $125

Ballet Lessons Barbie, Black or White, 2000, Mattel
MNP $5   MIP $12

Ballroom Beauties, Midnight Waltz, 1996, Mattel, Model No. 15685
MNP $25   MIP $40

Ballroom Beauties, Moonlight Waltz Barbie, 1997, Mattel, Model No. 17763
MNP $25   MIP $40

Ballroom Beauties, Starlight Waltz Barbie, 1995, Mattel, Model No. 14070
MNP $75   MIP $150

Barbie 2000, White or Black, 2000, Mattel, Model No. 27409/27410
MNP $35   MIP $75

Barbie 2001, Black or White, 2001, Mattel, Model No. 50842/50841
MNP $35   MIP $75

Barbie 2002, White or Black, 2002, Mattel, Model No. 53975/53976
MNP $35   MIP $75

Barbie 2003, White or Black, 2003, Mattel
MNP $35   MIP $75

Barbie 2009 Convention 50th Anniversary Gala Tribute Gift Set, 2009, Mattel
MNP $200   MIP $400

Barbie and Curious George, 2001, Mattel, Model No. 28798
MNP $25   MIP $50

Barbie and Friends: Ken, Barbie, P.J., 1983, Mattel, Model No. 4431
MNP $25   MIP $75

Barbie and Ken as Arwen & Aragorn in Lord of the Rings: Return of the King, 2004, Mattel
MNP $40   MIP $125

Barbie and Ken Camping Out, 1983, Mattel
MNP $25   MIP $65

Barbie and Ken Tennis Gift Set, 1962, Mattel, Model No. 892
MNP $400   MIP $900

Barbie and Krissy Magical Mermaids, Black or White, 2000, Mattel
MNP $15   MIP $30

Barbie as Aphrodite, 2009, Mattel, Model No. N5020
MNP $95   MIP $195

Barbie as DC Comics Bat Girl, 2004, Mattel
MNP $10   MIP $20

Barbie as DC Comics Catwoman, 2004, Mattel, comic book store exclusive
MNP $20   MIP $110

Barbie as DC Comics Catwoman, 2004, Mattel, Model No. B5838
MNP $25   MIP $50

Barbie as DC Comics Super Girl, 2004, Mattel
MNP $10   MIP $20

Barbie as DC Comics Supergirl, 2003, Mattel, Model No. B5837
MNP $45   MIP $90

Barbie as DC Comics Supergirl, 2008, Mattel, Model No. L9639
MNP $30   MIP $60

Barbie as Elle Woods from Legally Blonde 2, 2003, Mattel
MNP $15   MIP $24

Barbie as Galadriel in Lord of the Rings: Fellowship of the Ring, 2004, Mattel
MNP $10   MIP $25

Barbie as Mary Jane Watson from Spider-Man, 2006, Mattel
MNP n/a   MIP $15

Barbie as Sue Storm, Invisible Woman from Fantastic Four, 2006, Mattel
MNP n/a   MIP $15

Barbie Beautiful Blues Gift Set, 1967, Mattel, Model No. 3303
MNP $1600   MIP $3000

Barbie Collector's Club Café Society, 1998, Mattel, Model No. 18892
MNP $50   MIP $125

Barbie Collector's Club Club Couture, 2000, Mattel, Model No. 26068
MNP $25   MIP $65

Barbie Collector's Club Embassy Waltz, 1999, Mattel, Model No. 23386
MNP $45   MIP $100

Barbie Collector's Club French Quarter Barbie Fashion, 2003, Mattel
MNP $15   MIP $25

Barbie Collector's Club Grand Premiere, 1997, Mattel, Model No. 16498
MNP $100   MIP $200

Barbie Collector's Club Holiday Treasures 1999, 1999, Mattel
MNP $75   MIP $125

Barbie Collector's Club Holiday Treasures 2000, 2000, Mattel, Model No. 27673
MNP $35   MIP $75

Barbie Collectors Club Hollywood Divine Blonde, 2004, Mattel, LE 3000 pcs
MNP $10   MIP $50

Barbie Collectors Club Hollywood Divine Brunette, 2004, Mattel, LE 4000 pcs, Model No. B3426
MNP $110   MIP $225

Barbie Collectors Club Melrose Morning Fashion, 2004, Mattel
MNP $10   MIP $25

Barbie Collector's Club Midnight Tuxedo, White or Black, 2001, Mattel
MNP $25   MIP $65

Barbie Collectors Club Nod for Mod, 2004, Mattel
MNP $10   MIP $40

Barbie Collector's Club Noir et Blanc Barbie, Black, 2003, Mattel
MNP $40   MIP $60

Barbie Collector's Club Noir et Blanc Barbie, White, 2003, Mattel
MNP $40   MIP $60

Barbie Fan Club 2006 Rhapsody in New York, 2006, Mattel
MNP n/a   MIP $50

Barbie Millicent Roberts Matinee Today, 1996, Mattel, Model No. 16079
MNP $22   MIP $60

Barbie Millicent Roberts Perfectly Suited, 1997, Mattel, Model No. 17567
MNP $30   MIP $45

Barbie Millicent Roberts Pinstripe Power Barbie, 1998, Mattel, Model No. 19791
MNP $30   MIP $50

Barbie's Round the Clock Gift Set, Bubblecut, 1964, Mattel, Model No. 1013
MNP $1000   MIP $2500

Barbie's Sparkling Pink Gift Set, Bubblecut, 1964, Mattel, Model No. 1011
MNP $1000   MIP $2400

Barbie's Wedding Party Gift Set, 1964, Mattel, Model No. 1017
MNP $1000   MIP $2400

Bathing Suit Barbie, 2009, Mattel, Model No. P6508
MNP $10   MIP $20

Beauty Secrets Barbie Pretty Reflections Gift Set, 1979, Mattel, Model No. 1702
MNP $40   MIP $100

Best Buy Detective Barbie, 2000, Mattel, Model No. 24189
MNP $8   MIP $17

Best Models on Location Milan, Black, 2006, Mattel
MNP n/a   MIP $35

Best Models on Location Monte Carlo, Brunette, 2006, Mattel
MNP n/a   MIP $35

Best Models on Location South Beach, Blonde, 2006, Mattel
MNP n/a   MIP $35

Bill Blass Barbie, 1997, Mattel, Model No. 17040
MNP $20   MIP $40

(KP Photo)

Billions of Dreams Barbie, 1997, Mattel, Model No. 17641
MNP $150   MIP $275

(KP Photo)

Billy Boy Feelin' Groovy Barbie, 1986, Mattel, Model No. 3421
MNP $75   MIP $125

(KP Photo)

Billy Boy Le Nouveau Theatre de la Mode Barbie, 1985, Mattel, Model No. 6279
MNP $100   MIP $200

Birds of Beauty #1 Peacock Barbie, 1998, Mattel, Model No. 19365
MNP $32   MIP $50

Birds of Beauty #2 Flamingo Barbie, 1999, Mattel, Model No. 22957
MNP $75   MIP $150

Birds of Beauty #3 Swan Barbie, 2000, Mattel, Model No. 27682
MNP $40   MIP $50

Birthday Fun at McDonald's Gift Set, 1994, Mattel, Model No. 11589
MNP $15   MIP $35

Birthday Wishes #1, Black or White, 1999, Mattel, Model No. 21128/21509
MNP $15   MIP $35

Birthday Wishes #2, Black or White, 2000, Mattel, Model No. 24667/24668
MNP $20   MIP $40

Birthday Wishes #3, Black or White, 2001, Mattel
MNP $10   MIP $35

Birthday Wishes 2005, 2005, Mattel, peach or blue dress, Model No. G8059
MNP $25   MIP $50

Birthday Wishes Barbie, Black, 2004, Mattel
MNP $25   MIP $50

Birthday Wishes Barbie Blonde, 2004, Mattel, Model No. C6228
MNP $25   MIP $50

Birthday Wishes Barbie Brunette, 2004, Mattel
MNP $25   MIP $50

Birthday Wishes Barbie Redhead, 2004, Mattel
MNP $25   MIP $50

Birthstone Beauty Collection (Jan-Dec), 2007, Mattel
MNP n/a   MIP $25

Birthstone Beauty Collection (Jan-Dec), Black, 2007, Mattel
MNP n/a   MIP $25

BJ's Fantastica Barbie, 1993, Mattel, Model No. 3196
MNP $10   MIP $25

BJ's Festiva, 1993, Mattel
MNP $10   MIP $25

BJ's Golden Waltz, Blond or Red, 1999, Mattel
MNP $10   MIP $25

BJ's Rose Bride Barbie, 1996, Mattel, Model No. 15987
MNP $15   MIP $20

BJ's Sparkle Beauty, 1997, Mattel
MNP $15   MIP $20

Bloomingdale's Barbie at Bloomingdale's, 1996, Mattel, Model No. 16290
MNP $15   MIP $35

Bloomingdale's Calvin Klein Barbie, 1996, Mattel
MNP $20   MIP $35

Bloomingdale's Donna Karan, Blonde, 1995, Mattel, Model No. 14452
MNP $25   MIP $45

Bloomingdale's Donna Karan, Brunette, 1996, Mattel, Model No. 14452
MNP $25   MIP $45

Bloomingdale's Oscar de la Renta,
1998, Mattel, Model No. 20376
>**MNP** $20   **MIP** $45

Bloomingdale's Ralph Lauren, 1997,
Mattel, Model No. 15950
>**MNP** $30   **MIP** $45

**Bloomingdale's Savvy Shopper,
Nicole Miller,** 1994, Mattel, Model
No. 12152
>**MNP** $25   **MIP** $35

Bob Mackie 45th Anniversary Barbie,
2004, Mattel, white or black, Model
No. B3452
>**MNP** $50   **MIP** $100

Bob Mackie 45th Anniversary Barbie,
2004, Mattel, white, black hair,
LE 1000 pcs
>**MNP** $25   **MIP** $100

**Bob Mackie Couture Confection
Bride,** 2007, Mattel
>**MNP** n/a   **MIP** $100

**Bob Mackie Couture Confection Bride
Barbie,** 2006, Mattel
>**MNP** n/a   **MIP** $125

Bob Mackie Designer Gold, 1990,
Mattel, Model No. 5405
>**MNP** $245   **MIP** $495

Bob Mackie Empress Bride, 1992,
Mattel, Model No. 4247
>**MNP** $425   **MIP** $950

**Bob Mackie Fantasy Goddess of
Africa,** 1999, Mattel, Model
No. 22044
>**MNP** $100   **MIP** $175

(KP Photo)

Bob Mackie Fantasy Goddess of Asia,
1998, Mattel, Model No. SA415
>**MNP** $160   **MIP** $325

**Bob Mackie Fantasy Goddess of the
Americas,** 2000, Mattel, Model
No. 25859
>**MNP** $160   **MIP** $325

**Bob Mackie Fantasy Goddess of the
Arctic,** 2001, Mattel, Model
No. 50840
>**MNP** $195   **MIP** $395

(KP Photo)

Bob Mackie Goddess of the Moon,
1996, Mattel, Model No. 14105
>**MNP** $95   **MIP** $195

Bob Mackie Goddess of the Sun,
1995, Mattel, Model No. 14056
>**MNP** $95   **MIP** $195

Bob Mackie Golden Legacy Barbie,
2009, Mattel, Model No. N6610
>**MNP** $150   **MIP** $325

**Bob Mackie Jewel Essence Amethyst
Aura,** 1997, Mattel, Model
No. 15522
>**MNP** $60   **MIP** $125

**Bob Mackie Jewel Essence Diamond
Dazzle,** 1997, Mattel, Model
No. 15519
>**MNP** $60   **MIP** $125

**Bob Mackie Jewel Essence Emerald
Embers,** 1997, Mattel, Model
No. 15521
>**MNP** $60   **MIP** $125

**Bob Mackie Jewel Essence Ruby
Radiance,** 1997, Mattel, Model
No. 15520
>**MNP** $60   **MIP** $125

**Bob Mackie Jewel Essence Sapphire
Splendor,** 1997, Mattel, Model
No. 15523
>**MNP** $60   **MIP** $125

Bob Mackie Madame du Barbie,
1997, Mattel, Model No. 17934
>**MNP** $260   **MIP** $525

Bob Mackie Masquerade Ball, 1993,
Mattel, Model No. 10803
>**MNP** $125   **MIP** $250

(KP Photo)

Bob Mackie Neptune Fantasy, 1992,
Mattel, Model No. 4248
>**MNP** $375   **MIP** $750

Bob Mackie Platinum, 1991, Mattel,
Model No. 2703
>**MNP** $225   **MIP** $450

(KP Photo)

Bob Mackie Queen of Hearts, 1994,
Mattel, Model No. 12046
>**MNP** $70   **MIP** $150

**Bob Mackie Red Carpet, Brunette
Brilliance,** 2003, Mattel, Model
No. B0585
>**MNP** $120   **MIP** $245

**Bob Mackie Red Carpet, Radiant
Redhead,** 2002, Mattel, Model
No. 55501
>**MNP** $100   **MIP** $125

Bob Mackie Starlight Splendor, 1991,
Mattel, Model No. 2704
>**MNP** $150   **MIP** $250

Bowling Champ Barbie, 2000, Mattel, Model No. 25871
MNP $15   MIP $30

Bridal Collection Millennium Wedding, White, Black or Hispanic, 2000, Mattel, Model No. 27674
MNP $75   MIP $150

Bridal Collection, Vera Wang Barbie, 2008, Mattel, Model No. L9652
MNP $75   MIP $150

Burberry Barbie, 2001, Mattel, Model No. 29421
MNP $25   MIP $40

Byron Lars Ayako Jones Barbie, 2009, Mattel, Model No. N6614
MNP $95   MIP $195

Byron Lars Chapeaux Collection Sugar, 2006, Mattel
MNP n/a   MIP $100

Byron Lars Chapeaux Collection, Coco, 2007, Mattel
MNP n/a   MIP $100

Byron Lars Cinnabar Sensation, Black or White, 1999, Mattel, Model No. 19848
MNP $60   MIP $125

Byron Lars In the Limelight, 1997, Mattel, Model No. 17031
MNP $100   MIP $225

Byron Lars Indigo Obsession, 2000, Mattel, Model No. 26935
MNP $25   MIP $65

Byron Lars Moja Barbie, 2001, Mattel, Model No. 50826
MNP $40   MIP $175

Byron Lars Nne, 2004, Mattel
MNP $10   MIP $80

Byron Lars Plum Royale, 1998, Mattel, Model No. 23478
MNP $40   MIP $95

Byron Lars Tatu, 2003, Mattel
MNP $50   MIP $80

Byron Lars, Pepper Barbie, 2008, Mattel, Model No. L9601
MNP $80   MIP $160

Carolina Herrera Bridal Doll, 2005, Mattel, Model No. B9797
MNP $175   MIP $350

Caroling Fun Barbie, 1995, Mattel, Model No. 13966
MNP $8   MIP $10

Casey Goes Casual Gift Set, 1967, Mattel, Model No. 3304
MNP $800   MIP $1650

Celebration Barbie 2000, White or Black, 2000, Mattel
MNP $45   MIP $95

Celebrity Kelly Grease Gift Set, 2008, Mattel, Model No. N2688
MNP $10   MIP $25

Celebrity Kelly Lucy/Ethel Paris Gown Gift Set, 2008, Mattel, Model No. N2690
MNP $10   MIP $25

Celebrity Lucy L.A. at Last, 2003, Mattel
MNP $25   MIP $40

Celestial Collection #1 Evening Star, 2000, Mattel, Model No. 27690
MNP $10   MIP $25

Celestial Collection #2 Morning Sun, 2000, Mattel, Model No. 27688
MNP $10   MIP $25

Celestial Collection #3 Midnight Moon Princess, 2000, Mattel, Model No. 27689
MNP $10   MIP $25

Charlie's Angles Kelly Gift Set, 2010, Mattel, Model No. N6583
MNP $15   MIP $30

Cher 1970s, 2007, Mattel
MNP n/a   MIP $35

Cher 1980s, 2007, Mattel
MNP n/a   MIP $35

Cher 1990s, Platinum Edition, 2007, Mattel
MNP n/a   MIP $200

Children's Collector Series Belle (Beauty and the Beast), 2000, Mattel, Model No. 24673
MNP $15   MIP $30

Children's Collector Series Cinderella, 1997, Mattel, Model No. 16900
MNP $15   MIP $25

Children's Collector Series Little Bo Peep, 1995, Mattel, Model No. 14960
MNP $30   MIP $50

Children's Collector Series Rapunzel, 1995, Mattel, Model No. 13016
MNP $15   MIP $25

Children's Collector Series Sleeping Beauty, 1998, Mattel
MNP $15   MIP $25

Children's Collector Series Snow White, 1999, Mattel, Model No. 21130
MNP $15   MIP $25

Chocolate Obsession Barbie, 2005, Mattel
MNP $15   MIP $40

Chocolate Obsession Barbie, 2006, Mattel, Model No. G8878
MNP $85   MIP $175

Christian Dior 50th Anniversary, 1997, Mattel, The New Look, Model No. 16013
MNP $35   MIP $125

Christian Dior Barbie, 1995, Mattel, Model No. 13168
MNP $25   MIP $50

Christian Louboutin Barbie, 2009, Mattel, Model No. N6599
MNP $70   MIP $145

Chuck E. Cheese Barbie, 1996, Mattel, Model No. 14615
MNP $15   MIP $30

Citrus Obsession Barbie, 2006, Mattel, Model No. J0933
MNP $50   MIP $100

Citrus Obsession Barbie, Platinum Pink Grapefruit Edition, 2006, Mattel
MNP n/a   MIP $200

Citrus Obsession Barbie, Regular Edition, 2006, Mattel
MNP n/a   MIP $35

City Seasons Autumn in London, 1999, Mattel, Model No. 22257
MNP $18   MIP $25

City Seasons Autumn in Paris, 1998, Mattel, Model No. 19367
MNP $18   MIP $25

(KP Photo)

City Seasons Spring in Tokyo, 1999, Mattel, Model No. 19430
MNP $30   MIP $65

City Seasons Spring in Tokyo, Internet Exclusive, 1999, Mattel, Model No. 23499
MNP $18   MIP $30

(KP Photo)

City Seasons Summer in Rome,
1999, Mattel, Model No. 19431

   MNP $18   **MIP** $25

City Seasons Winter in Montreal,
1999, Mattel, Model No. 22258

   MNP $18   **MIP** $25

(KP Photo)

City Seasons Winter in New York,
1998, Mattel, Model No. 19429

   MNP $18   **MIP** $25

Classic Ballet Flower Ballerina,
2001, Mattel, Model No. 28375

   MNP $10   **MIP** $25

Classic Ballet Marzipan, 1999,
Mattel, Model No. 20581

   MNP $15   **MIP** $25

(Mattel Photo)

**Classic Ballet Peppermint Candy
Cane,** 2003, Mattel, Model
No. 57578

   MNP $10   **MIP** $25

Classic Ballet Snowflake, 2000,
Mattel, Model No. 25642

   MNP $15   **MIP** $25

(KP Photo)

Classic Ballet Sugar Plum Fairy,
1997, Mattel, Model No. 17056

   MNP $15   **MIP** $30

Classic Ballet Swan Ballerina, 2002,
Mattel, Model No. 53867

   MNP $10   **MIP** $25

**Classic Ballet Swan Lake, Black or
White,** 1998, Mattel, Model
No. 18509/18510

   MNP $15   **MIP** $25

Classique Benefit Ball Barbie, 1992,
Mattel, Model No. 1521

   MNP $40   **MIP** $70

Classique City Style Barbie, 1993,
Mattel, Model No. 10149

   MNP $25   **MIP** $40

Classique Evening Extravaganza,
1994, Mattel, Model No. 11622

   MNP $35   **MIP** $75

**Classique Evening Extravaganza,
Black,** 1994, Mattel, Model
No. 11638

   MNP $40   **MIP** $80

Classique Evening Sophisticate,
1998, Mattel, Model No. 19361

   MNP $18   **MIP** $35

Classique Midnight Gala, 1995,
Mattel, Model No. 12999

   MNP $25   **MIP** $40

Classique Opening Night Barbie,
1993, Mattel, Model No. 10148

   MNP $30   **MIP** $45

Classique Romantic Interlude Barbie,
1997, Mattel, Model No. 17136

   MNP $15   **MIP** $30

**Classique Romantic Interlude
Barbie, Black,** 1997, Mattel, Model
No. 17137

   MNP $15   **MIP** $30

Classique Starlight Dance, 1996,
Mattel, Model No. 15461

   MNP $20   **MIP** $35

Classique Starlight Dance, Black,
1996, Mattel, Model No. 15819

   MNP $75   **MIP** $150

Classique Uptown Chic Barbie, 1994,
Mattel, Model No. 11623

   MNP $25   **MIP** $40

Coca-Cola #5 (majorette), 2002,
Mattel, Model No. 53974

   MNP $35   **MIP** $75

Coca-Cola Barbie #1, Carhop, 1999,
Mattel, Model No. 22831

   MNP $20   **MIP** $65

Coca-Cola Barbie #2, 2000, Mattel,
Model No. 24637

   MNP $25   **MIP** $59

Coca-Cola Barbie #3, Cheerleader,
2001, Mattel

   MNP $15   **MIP** $50

**Coca-Cola Fashion Classic #1, Soda
Fountain Sweetheart,** 1996, Mattel

   MNP $50   **MIP** $125

**Coca-Cola Fashion Classic #2, After
the Walk,** 1997, Mattel, Model
No. 17341

   MNP $46   **MIP** $60

**Coca-Cola Fashion Classic #3,
Summer Daydreams,** 1998,
Mattel, Model No. 19739

   MNP $85   **MIP** $175

Coca-Cola Ken, 2000, Mattel, Model
No. 25678

   MNP $100   **MIP** $175

Coca-Cola Party, 1999, Mattel, Model
No. 22964

   MNP $5   **MIP** $15

Coca-Cola Picnic, 1998, Mattel,
Model No. 19626

   MNP $5   **MIP** $15

Coca-Cola Splash, 2000, Mattel,
Model No. 22590
MNP $5   MIP $15

**Coca-Cola, Disney Teddy & Doll
Convention, Brunette, Limited to
1,500,** Mattel
MNP $45   MIP $95

Collector Ferrari Barbie, 2005,
Mattel, Model No. H6466
MNP $85   MIP $170

**Collector's Request All That Jazz
Vintage Repro Barbie, Regular
Edition,** 2006, Mattel
MNP n/a   MIP $50

**Collector's Request All That Jazz
Vintage Repro Barbie, Sanai
Japanese,** 2006, Mattel, brunette
MNP n/a   MIP $200

**Collector's Request Color Magic
Barbie Giftset,** 2004, Mattel
MNP $10   MIP $25

Collector's Request Commuter Set,
1999, Mattel, Model No. 21510
MNP $25   MIP $65

**Collector's Request Evening
Splendour Barbie,** 2005, Mattel
MNP $15   MIP $40

Collector's Request Gay Parisienne,
2003, Mattel, Model No. 57610
MNP $25   MIP $40

Collector's Request Gold 'N Glamour,
2002, Mattel, Model No. 54185
MNP $20   MIP $50

**Collector's Request Made for Each
Other Vintage Repro Barbie,** 2006,
Mattel
MNP n/a   MIP $50

**Collector's Request Open Road
Barbie,** 2004, Mattel
MNP $20   MIP $65

**Collector's Request Plantation
Barbie,** 2004, Mattel
MNP $15   MIP $65

**Collector's Request Sophisticated
Lady,** 1999, Mattel, Model No. 24930
MNP $75   MIP $150

**Collector's Request Suburban
Shopper,** 2000, Mattel
MNP $15   MIP $45

**Collector's Request Twist N Turn
Smasheroo, Brunette,** 1998,
Mattel, Model No. 18941
MNP $25   MIP $40

**Collector's Request Twist N Turn
Smasheroo, Red Hair,** 1998,
Mattel, Model No. 23258
MNP $25   MIP $50

Cool Collecting Barbie, 2000, Mattel,
Nostalgic Toys, Model No. 25525
MNP $60   MIP $125

Corvette Barbie, 2009, Mattel, red,
Model No. P5247
MNP $25   MIP $50

Corvette Barbie, 2009, Mattel, yellow,
Model No. N4984
MNP $25   MIP $50

**Couture Collection Portrait in Taffeta
Barbie,** 1996, Mattel, Model
No. 15528
MNP $80   MIP $165

**Couture Collection Serenade in Satin
Barbie,** 1997, Mattel, Model
No. 17572
MNP $50   MIP $75

**Couture Collection Symphony in
Chiffon,** 1998, Mattel, Model
No. 21295
MNP $80   MIP $165

**Cracker Barrel Country Charm
Barbie,** 2001, Mattel
MNP $5   MIP $15

Cut My Favorite Barbie Gift Set, 2009,
Mattel, Model No. N4975
MNP $20   MIP $45

Cynthia Rowley Barbie, 2005, Mattel
MNP $15   MIP $60

Dance Club Barbie Gift Set, 1989,
Mattel, Model No. 4917
MNP $25   MIP $60

Dance Magic Gift Set Barbie & Ken,
1990, Mattel, Model No. 5409
MNP $15   MIP $35

Dance Sensation Barbie Gift Set,
1984, Mattel, Model No. 9058
MNP $15   MIP $40

**David's Bridal Romance Barbie,
African-American,** 2007, Mattel
MNP n/a   MIP $45

**David's Bridal Romance Barbie,
Blonde,** 2007, Mattel
MNP n/a   MIP $45

**David's Bridal Romance Barbie,
Brunette,** 2007, Mattel
MNP n/a   MIP $45

David's Bridal Unforgettable Barbie,
2004, Mattel, blonde, Hispanic,
African American
MNP $15   MIP $45

**David's Bridal, Perfect Pair Tommy
and Kelly,** 2005, Mattel, Model
No. H7548
MNP $25   MIP $50

**Democratic National Convention
Delegate Barbie,** 2000, Mattel
MNP $25   MIP $150

Designer Katiana Jimenez, 2003,
Mattel, Model No. B0836
MNP $60   MIP $125

**Designer Spotlight by Heather
Fonesca,** 2004, Mattel
MNP $20   MIP $40

Designer Spotlight, Katiana Jimenez,
2003, Mattel, Model No. B0836
MNP $20   MIP $35

Diahann Carroll as Julia Gift Set,
2009, Mattel, Model No. N5017
MNP $25   MIP $50

Diane Von Furstenburg Barbie, 2006,
Mattel
MNP n/a   MIP $100

Diva Collection, All that Glitters,
2002, Mattel, Model No. 55426
MNP $20   MIP $40

**Diva Collection, Gone Platinum,
White or Black,** 2002, Mattel,
Model No. 52739/53868
MNP $20   MIP $40

(Mattel Photo)

**Diva Collection, Red Hot, White or
Black,** 2003, Mattel, Model
No. 56707/56708
MNP $35   MIP $70

Doone & Bourke #2, 2007, Mattel
MNP n/a   MIP $35

Dooney & Bourke Barbie, 2006, Mattel
MNP n/a   MIP $35

Dream Seasons I Dream of Autumn,
2006, Mattel, Toys R Us Exclusive
MNP n/a   MIP $30

Dream Seasons I Dream of Spring,
2006, Mattel, Toys R Us Exclusive
MNP n/a   MIP $30

Dream Seasons I Dream of Summer,
2006, Mattel, Toys R Us Exclusive
MNP n/a   MIP $30

Dream Seasons I Dream of Winter,
2006, Mattel, Toys R Us Exclusive
MNP n/a   MIP $30

Dressmaker Details La Rondine,
2008, Mattel, Model No. 0528
MNP $45   MIP $91

**Drug/Grocery Store Halloween Hip
Barbie,** 2006, Mattel
MNP n/a   MIP $20

Drugstore/Grocery Halloween Charm Barbie, African-American, 2007, Mattel

MNP n/a MIP $15

Drugstore/Grocery Halloween Charm Barbie, Blonde, 2007, Mattel

MNP n/a MIP $15

Duchess Emma Barbie, 2004, Mattel

MNP $10 MIP $80

Easter Magic Barbie, 2003, Mattel

MNP $8 MIP $15

Empress of the Golden Blossom, 2008, Mattel, Model No. L9660

MNP $125 MIP $255

Empress Sissy, Barbie as, 1996, Mattel, Model No. 15846

MNP $35 MIP $60

Enchanted Mermaid, 2002, Mattel, Model No. 53978

MNP $100 MIP $250

Enchanted Seasons #1 Snow Princess, 1994, Mattel, Model No. 11875

MNP $30 MIP $75

Enchanted Seasons #2 Spring Bouquet, 1995, Mattel, Model No. 12989

MNP $30 MIP $50

Enchanted Seasons #3 Autumn Glory, 1996, Mattel, Model No. 15204

MNP $30 MIP $50

Enchanted Seasons #4 Summer Splendor, 1997, Mattel, Model No. 15683

MNP $30 MIP $50

Enchanted World of Fairies, Fairy of the Forest, 2000, Mattel, Model No. 25639

MNP $25 MIP $45

Enchanted World of Fairies, Fairy of the Garden, 2001, Mattel

MNP $15 MIP $40

Escada Barbie, 1996, Mattel, Model No. 15948

MNP $40 MIP $65

(KP Photo)

Essence of Nature #1 Water Rhapsody, 1998, Mattel, Model No. 19847

MNP $60 MIP $125

Essence of Nature #2 Whispering Wind, 1999, Mattel, Model No. 22834

MNP $40 MIP $80

Essence of Nature #3 Dancing Fire, 2000, Mattel, Model No. 26327

MNP $35 MIP $80

Ethereal Princess Barbie, 2006, Mattel

MNP n/a MIP $40

Fab Girl, 2009, Mattel, Model No. P6883

MNP $10 MIP $20

(Mattel Photo)

FAO Schwarz American Beauty, Barbie as George Washington, 1996, Mattel, Model No. 17557

MNP $35 MIP $65

(Mattel Photo)

FAO Schwarz American Beauty, Statue of Liberty, 1996, Mattel, Model No. 14684

MNP $40 MIP $65

FAO Schwarz Barbie & Ken Tango Gift Set, 2002, Mattel

MNP $40 MIP $85

FAO Schwarz Barbie Fashion Model Collection Chantaine, 2003, Mattel, LE 600 pcs

MNP $400 MIP $600

FAO Schwarz Bob Mackie Lady Liberty, 2000, Mattel, limited to 15,000

MNP $75 MIP $125

FAO Schwarz Bob Mackie Le Papillon, 1999, Mattel, Model No. 23276

MNP $70 MIP $175

FAO Schwarz Circus Star Barbie, 1995, Mattel, Model No. 13257

MNP $35 MIP $70

FAO Schwarz City Seasons Summer in San Francisco, Blond, 1998, Mattel, Model No. 19363

MNP $40 MIP $95

FAO Schwarz City Seasons Summer in San Francisco, Red Hair, Mattel

MNP $200 MIP $750

FAO Schwarz Exclusive Joyeux Barbie, 2004, Mattel, LE redheaded

MNP $200 MIP $300

FAO Schwarz Fashion Model Fashion Designer Barbie, 2002, Mattel

MNP $50 MIP $85

FAO Schwarz Fashion Model Fashion Editor, 2000, Mattel

MNP $50 MIP $90

FAO Schwarz Floral Signature #1 Antique Rose, 1996, Mattel, limited to 10,000, Model No. 15814

MNP $50 MIP $150

FAO Schwarz Floral Signature #2 Lily Barbie, 1997, Mattel, limited to 10,000, Model No. 17556

MNP $50 MIP $145

FAO Schwarz Golden Greetings Barbie, 1989, Mattel, Model No. 7734

MNP $50 MIP $95

FAO Schwarz Golden Hollywood Barbie, White or Black, 1999, Mattel

MNP $35 MIP $60

FAO Schwarz Jeweled Splendor (125th Anniversary), 1995, Mattel, Model No. 14061

MNP $75 MIP $125

FAO Schwarz Madison Ave. Barbie, 1992, Mattel, Model No. 1539

MNP $75 MIP $100

FAO Schwarz Mann's Chinese Theatre Barbie, White or Black, 2000, Mattel, Model No. 24636/24998

MNP $35 MIP $50

FAO Schwarz Night Sensation, 1991, Mattel, Model No. 2921

MNP $25 MIP $50

(KP Photo)

FAO Schwarz Phantom of the Opera Gift Set, 1998, Mattel, Model No. 20377
  MNP $50   **MIP** $85

FAO Schwarz Rockettes Barbie, 1993, Mattel, Model No. 2017
  MNP $50   **MIP** $85

FAO Schwarz Shopping Spree, 1994, Mattel, Model No. 12749
  MNP $5   **MIP** $15

FAO Schwarz Silver Screen Barbie, 1994, Mattel, Model No. 11652
  MNP $65   **MIP** $100

FAO Schwarz Winter Fantasy, 1990, Mattel, Model No. 5946
  MNP $45   **MIP** $70

FAO Schwarz, Barbie at FAO, 1997, Mattel, Model No. 17298
  MNP $12   **MIP** $25

Fashion Model 45th Anniversary Barbie & Ken Gift Set, 2004, Mattel, Model No. C4656
  MNP $70   **MIP** $140

Fashion Model A Model Life Gift Set, 2003, Mattel
  MNP $50   **MIP** $85

Fashion Model Capucine Barbie, 2003, Mattel
  MNP $50   **MIP** $95

Fashion Model Chinoiserie Red Midnight, Fan Club Exclusive, 2004, Mattel
  MNP $10   **MIP** $225

Fashion Model Chinoiserie Red Moon, 2004, Mattel
  MNP $40   **MIP** $80

Fashion Model Collection 45th Anniversary Barbie, African American, 2004, Mattel
  MNP $10   **MIP** $50

Fashion Model Collection 45th Anniversary Barbie, Blonde, 2004, Mattel
  MNP $10   **MIP** $50

Fashion Model Collection A Day at the Races Barbie, 2006, Mattel
  MNP n/a   **MIP** $60

Fashion Model Collection Capucine, 2003, Mattel, Model No. B0146
  MNP $75   **MIP** $150

Fashion Model Collection Chinoiserie Red Sunset, Barbie Bazaar Exclusive, 2004, Mattel
  MNP $10   **MIP** $150

Fashion Model Collection Continental Holiday Gift Set, 2002, Mattel, Model No. J5497
  MNP $85   **MIP** $175

Fashion Model Collection Dahlia, 2006, Mattel, U.S. Dealers Exclusive
  MNP n/a   **MIP** $500

Fashion Model Collection Delphine Barbie, 2000, Mattel, Model No. 26929
  MNP $35   **MIP** $65

Fashion Model Collection Dusk to Dawn, 2001, Mattel, Model No. 29654
  MNP $50   **MIP** $125

Fashion Model Collection High Stepping Fashion, 2006, Mattel
  MNP n/a   **MIP** $50

Fashion Model Collection High Tea and Savories Barbie Giftset, 2006, Mattel
  MNP n/a   **MIP** $90

Fashion Model Collection Highland Fling, 2006, Mattel
  MNP n/a   **MIP** $90

Fashion Model Collection In The Pink, 2001, Mattel, Model No. 27683
  MNP $75   **MIP** $200

Fashion Model Collection Ken Fashion Insider Gift Set, 2003, Mattel
  MNP $50   **MIP** $95

Fashion Model Collection Lady of the Manor Barbie, 2006, Mattel
  MNP n/a   **MIP** $150

Fashion Model Collection Lingerie #1, Blonde, 2000, Mattel, Model No. 26930
  MNP $60   **MIP** $175

Fashion Model Collection Lingerie #2, Brunette, 2000, Mattel, Model No. 26931
  MNP $60   **MIP** $175

Fashion Model Collection Lingerie #3, Black Hair, 2001, Mattel, Model No. 29651
  MNP $125   **MIP** $250

Fashion Model Collection Lingerie #4, 2002, Mattel, Model No. 55498
  MNP $60   **MIP** $125

(Mattel Photo)

Fashion Model Collection Lingerie #5, Black, 2002, Mattel, Model No. 56120
  MNP $60   **MIP** $125

Fashion Model Collection Lingerie #6, Redhead, 2003, Mattel, Model No. 56948
  MNP $45   **MIP** $95

Fashion Model Collection Lisette, 2001, Mattel, Model No. 29650
  MNP $45   **MIP** $70

Fashion Model Collection Maria Therese, Bride, 2002, Mattel, Model No. 55496
  MNP $150   **MIP** $275

Fashion Model Collection Midnight Mischief Fashion, 2003, Mattel
  MNP $15   **MIP** $50

Fashion Model Collection New England Escape Gift Set, 2004, Mattel, fashion, Model No. B3433
  MNP $70   **MIP** $140

Fashion Model Collection Pajama #2 Suite Retreat, 2005, Mattel
  MNP $15   **MIP** $40

Fashion Model Collection Pretty Pleats Barbie, 2006, Mattel
  MNP n/a   **MIP** $80

Fashion Model Collection Provencale, 2002, Mattel, Model No. 50829
  MNP $50   **MIP** $120

Fashion Model Collection Silkstone, 50th Anniversary Barbie, 2009, Mattel, Model No. N5006
  MNP $30   **MIP** $60

Fashion Model Collection Silkstone, BFMC 1959 Barbie, 2009, Mattel, Model No. N5007
  MNP $30   **MIP** $60

Fashion Model Collection Silkstone, BFMC Dealer Exclusive Parisienne Party, 2009, Mattel, Model No. N6594
  MNP $65   **MIP** $130

Fashion Model Collection Silkstone, BFMC Southern Belle, 2009, Mattel, Model No. N5009
MNP $35   MIP $75

Fashion Model Collection Silkstone, BFMC Stunning in the Spotlight, 2009, Mattel, Model No. N6603
MNP $80   MIP $160

Fashion Model Collection Silkstone, Country Bound, 2002, Mattel, Model No. 55499
MNP $40   MIP $80

Fashion Model Collection Silkstone, Fashion Insider, 2005, Mattel, Model No. 56706
MNP $65   MIP $130

Fashion Model Collection Silkstone, Happy Go Lightly, 2005, Mattel, Model No. G8889
MNP $65   MIP $130

Fashion Model Collection Silkstone, Je Ne Sais Quoi, 2008, Mattel, Model No. L9598
MNP $40   MIP $80

Fashion Model Collection Silkstone, Joyeux Barbie, 2004, Mattel, Model No. B3430
MNP $95   MIP $195

Fashion Model Collection Silkstone, Model Life, 2004, Mattel, Model No. B0147
MNP $65   MIP $130

Fashion Model Collection Silkstone, Prime Ballerina, 2009, Mattel, Model No. P4753
MNP $60   MIP $125

Fashion Model Collection Silkstone, Stolen Magic, 2005, Mattel, Model No. G8072
MNP $100   MIP $225

Fashion Model Collection Silkstone, The Artist - Japan/Singapore Exclusive, 2008, Mattel, Model No. M4973
MNP $85   MIP $175

Fashion Model Collection Silkstone, The Shopgirl, 2008, Mattel, Model No. M4971
MNP $85   MIP $170

Fashion Model Collection Silkstone, The Showgirl, 2008, Mattel, U.S. Exclusive, Model No. L9597
MNP $45   MIP $80

Fashion Model Collection Silkstone, Tout De Suite, 2008, Mattel, Model No. L9596
MNP $35   MIP $70

Fashion Model Collection Silkstone, Trace of Lace, 2005, Mattel, Model No. G7212
MNP $65   MIP $130

Fashion Model Collection Sunday Best Barbie, African American, 2003, Mattel
MNP $30   MIP $60

Fashion Model Collection The French Maid, 2006, Mattel, Canadian Exclusive
MNP n/a   MIP $75

Fashion Model Collection The Nurse Barbie, 2006, Mattel, European/Australian Exclusive
MNP n/a   MIP $200

Fashion Model Collection The Nurse Barbie, African-American, 2006, Mattel, Fan Club Exclusive
MNP n/a   MIP $250

Fashion Model Collection The Spa Getaway Gift Set, 2004, Mattel
MNP $10   MIP $125

Fashion Model Collection The Stewardess, 2006, Mattel, Japanese Exclusive
MNP n/a   MIP $175

Fashion Model Collection The Teacher, 2006, Mattel, Singapore Exclusive, Model No. J4257
MNP n/a   MIP $150

Fashion Model Collection The Waitress, 2006, Mattel, U.S. Exclusive, Model No. J8763
MNP n/a   MIP $125

Fashion Model Collection Trend Setter Barbie, 2004, Mattel, Model No. B3442
MNP $65   MIP $130

Fashion Model Collection True Brit Accessories, 2006, Mattel, Model No. J0914
MNP n/a   MIP $70

Fashion Model Collection Tweed Indeed Barbie, 2006, Mattel
MNP n/a   MIP $60

Fashion Model Collection Violette, 2006, Mattel, U.S. Dealers Exclusive
MNP n/a   MIP $500

Fashion Model Collection, Hollywood Bound, 2007, Mattel, Barbie Fan Club Exclusive
MNP n/a   MIP $70

Fashion Model Collection, Hollywood Hostess, 2007, Mattel, Model No. K7900
MNP n/a   MIP $110

Fashion Model Collection, Honey in Hollywood Accessory Pack, 2007, Mattel
MNP n/a   MIP $60

Fashion Model Collection, Movie Mixer, 2007, Mattel
MNP n/a   MIP $80

Fashion Model Collection, Red Hot Reviews, 2007, Mattel
MNP n/a   MIP $60

Fashion Model Collection, The Ingenue, 2007, Mattel
MNP n/a   MIP $40

Fashion Model Collection, The Interview, 2007, Mattel, Model No. K7964
MNP n/a   MIP $100

Fashion Model Collection, The Secretary, 2007, Mattel, International exclusive, Model No. L7322
MNP n/a   MIP $110

Fashion Model Collection, The Siren, 2007, Mattel
MNP n/a   MIP $90

Fashion Model Collection, The Soiree, 2007, Mattel
MNP n/a   MIP $140

Fashion Model Collection, The Usherette, 2007, Mattel, Dealer's exclusive, Model No. K8668
MNP n/a   MIP $90

Fashion Queen Barbie & Her Friends, 1964, Mattel, Model No. 863
MNP $1000   MIP $2400

Fashion Queen Barbie & Ken Trousseau Gift Set, 1964, Mattel, Model No. 864
MNP $1200   MIP $2800

Fashion Savvy #1 Tangerine Twist, 1997, Mattel, Model No. 17860
MNP $14   MIP $45

Fashion Savvy #2 Uptown Chic, 1998, Mattel, Model No. 19632
MNP $20   MIP $45

Fashionista, 2009, Mattel, Model No. R9879-R9882
MNP $10   MIP $20

Ferrari Barbie #1, Scuderia, Racing Outfit, 2001, Mattel, Model No. 25636
MNP $30   MIP $65

Ferrari Barbie #2, Red Dress, 2001, Mattel, Model No. 29608
MNP $15   MIP $45

Festivals of the World Carnaval Barbie, 2006, Mattel
MNP n/a   MIP $20

Festivals of the World Chinese New Year Barbie, 2006, Mattel
MNP n/a   MIP $20

Festivals of the World Diwali Barbie,
2006, Mattel
MNP n/a   MIP $40

Festivals of the World Kwanzaa Barbie, 2006, Mattel
MNP n/a   MIP $20

Festivals of the World Oktoberfest Barbie, 2006, Mattel
MNP n/a   MIP $20

Festivals of the World, Cinco de Mayo, 2007, Mattel
MNP n/a   MIP $25

Festivals of the World, Irish Dance, 2007, Mattel
MNP n/a   MIP $25

Festive Season, 1998, Mattel
MNP $5   MIP $15

Fire and Ice, White or Black, 2002, Mattel, Model No. 53511/53863
MNP $20   MIP $40

Flowers in Fashion Iris Barbie, 2002, Mattel, Model No. 53935
MNP $60   MIP $125

Flowers in Fashion Orchid Barbie, 2001, Mattel, Model No. 50319
MNP $25   MIP $65

Flowers in Fashion Rose Barbie, 2001, Mattel
MNP $25   MIP $65

Francie Rise n' Shine Gift Set, 1971, Mattel, Model No. 1194
MNP $600   MIP $1200

Francie Swingin' Separates Gift Set, 1966, Mattel, Model No. 1042
MNP $700   MIP $1500

Friends of the World, Europe Kelly, 2005, Mattel, Model No. G8063
MNP $15   MIP $30

Fun to Dress Barbie Gift Set, 1993, Mattel, Model No. 3826
MNP $5   MIP $10

Gap Barbie and Kelly Gift Set, 1997, Mattel, Model No. 18547
MNP $15   MIP $40

Gap Barbie and Kelly Gift Set, Black, 1997, Mattel, Model No. 18548
MNP $15   MIP $40

Gap Barbie, Black, 1996, Mattel, Model No. 16450
MNP $20   MIP $50

Gap Barbie, White, 1996, Mattel, Model No. 16449
MNP $30   MIP $50

Garden of Flowers Rose Barbie, 1999, Mattel, Model No. 22237
MNP $25   MIP $50

General Mills Winter Dazzle, Black, 1997, Mattel
MNP $5   MIP $20

General Mills Winter Dazzle, White, 1997, Mattel, Model No. 18456
MNP $5   MIP $20

Generations of Dreamz 50th Anniversary Barbie, 2009, Mattel, Model No. N6571
MNP $30   MIP $65

Givenchy Barbie, 2000, Mattel, Model No. 24635
MNP $40   MIP $80

Go For Red American Heart Association, 2007, Mattel
MNP n/a   MIP $25

Go For Red American Heart Association, African-American, 2007, Mattel
MNP n/a   MIP $25

Goddess of Beauty Barbie, 2000, Mattel, Model No. 27286
MNP $25   MIP $65

Goddess of Spring Barbie, 2000, Mattel, Model No. 28112
MNP $25   MIP $65

Goddess of Wisdom Barbie, 2001, Mattel
MNP $25   MIP $65

Golden Angel Barbie, 2006, Mattel
MIP $40

Golden Qi-Pao, 1998, Mattel, Model No. 20866
MNP $75   MIP $150

Gorgeous Greetings Birthday Angel, 2008, Mattel, Model No. N2439
MNP $10   MIP $25

Gorgeous Greetings Birthday Glamour, 2008, Mattel, Model No. N2440
MNP $10   MIP $25

Gorgeous Greetings Disco Celebration, Teresa, 2008, Mattel, Model No. N2441
MNP $10   MIP $25

Graduation Barbie Class of 1996, 1996, Mattel
MNP $5   MIP $15

Graduation Barbie Class of 1997, 1997, Mattel
MNP $5   MIP $10

Graduation Barbie Class of 1998, White or Black, 1998, Mattel
MNP $5   MIP $10

Graduation Barbie Class of 2000, black box, 2000, Mattel
MNP $5   MIP $15

Graduation Barbie Class of 2000, blue box, 2000, Mattel
MNP $5   MIP $15

Grand Entrance Barbie, White or Black, 2001, Mattel
MNP $25   MIP $65

Grand Entrance Barbie, White or Black, 2002, Mattel, Model No. 53841/53842
MNP $20   MIP $50

Grand Ole Opry #1 Country Rose Barbie, 1997, Mattel, Model No. 17782
MNP $40   MIP $80

Grand Ole Opry #2 Rising Star Barbie, 1998, Mattel, Model No. 17864
MNP $40   MIP $80

Grand Ole Opry Barbie and Kenny Country Duet, 1999, Mattel, Model No. 23498
MNP $55   MIP $75

Grease Barbie 2 as Sandy Olsson, 2004, Mattel
MNP $10   MIP $30

Grease Barbie as Sandy Olsson, 2003, Mattel
MNP $20   MIP $40

Great Eras #01, Gibson Girl, 1993, Mattel, Model No. 3702
MNP $40   MIP $80

Great Eras #02, Flapper, 1993, Mattel, Model No. 4063
MNP $25   MIP $60

(Mattel Photo)

Great Eras #03, Egyptian Queen, 1994, Mattel, Model No. 11397
MNP $20   MIP $55

Great Eras #04, Southern Belle, 1994, Mattel, Model No. 11478
MNP $20   MIP $55

Great Eras #05, Medieval Lady, 1995, Mattel, Model No. 12791
MNP $50   MIP $100

Great Eras #06, Elizabethan Queen, 1995, Mattel, Model No. 12792
MNP $50   MIP $100

Great Eras #07, Grecian Goddess, 1996, Mattel, Model No. 15005

    MNP $50   **MIP** $100

Great Eras #08, Victorian Lady, 1996, Mattel, Model No. 14900

    MNP $50   **MIP** $100

Great Eras #09, French Lady, 1997, Mattel, Model No. 16707

    MNP $75   **MIP** $150

Great Eras #10, Chinese Empress, 1997, Mattel, Model No. 16708

    MNP $50   **MIP** $100

Great Fashions of the 20th Century #1, Promenade in the Park, 1998, Mattel, 1910s, Model No. 18630

    MNP $20   **MIP** $50

Great Fashions of the 20th Century #2, Dance 'til Dawn, 1998, Mattel, 1920s, Model No. 19631

    MNP $30   **MIP** $40

Great Fashions of the 20th Century #3, Steppin Out Barbie, 1999, Mattel, 1930s, Model No. 21531

    MNP $60   **MIP** $125

Great Fashions of the 20th Century #4, Fabulous Forties, 2000, Mattel, 1940s, Model No. 22162

    MNP $25   **MIP** $40

(KP Photo)

Great Fashions of the 20th Century #5, Nifty Fifties, 2000, Mattel, 1950s, Model No. 27675

    MNP $25   **MIP** $50

(KP Photo)

Great Fashions of the 20th Century #6, Groovy Sixties, 2000, Mattel, 1960s, Model No. 27676

    MNP $65   **MIP** $135

Great Fashions of the 20th Century #7, Peace & Love 70s Barbie, 2000, Mattel, 1970s, Model No. 27677

    MNP $15   **MIP** $40

Groliers Book Club The Front Window Barbie, 2000, Mattel, Model No. 27968

    MNP $10   **MIP** $35

Hallmark Fair Valentine Barbie, 1998, Mattel

    MNP $20   **MIP** $40

Hallmark Holiday Memories Barbie, 1995, Mattel, Model No. 14108

    MNP $15   **MIP** $20

Hallmark Holiday Sensation Barbie, 1999, Mattel, Model No. 19792

    MNP $15   **MIP** $20

Hallmark Holiday Traditions Barbie, 1997, Mattel, Model No. 17094

    MNP $15   **MIP** $20

Hallmark Holiday Voyage Barbie, 1998, Mattel

    MNP $15   **MIP** $20

Hallmark Sentimental Valentine Barbie, 1997, Mattel

    MNP $15   **MIP** $20

Hallmark Sweet Valentine Barbie, 1996, Mattel, Model No. 14880

    MNP $15   **MIP** $20

Hallmark Victorian Elegance Barbie, 1994, Mattel, Model No. 12579

    MNP $20   **MIP** $40

Hallmark Yuletide Romance Barbie, 1996, Mattel, Model No. 15621

    MNP $15   **MIP** $20

Halloween Enchantress Barbie, 2004, Mattel

    MNP $10   **MIP** $20

Halloween Glow Barbie, White or African American, 2002, Mattel

    MNP $10   **MIP** $25

Halloween Maskerade Barbie, 2004, Mattel

    MNP $10   **MIP** $20

Hanae Mori Barbie, 2000, Mattel

    MNP $70   **MIP** $140

Happy Birthday Barbie Gift Set, 1985, Mattel

    MNP $20   **MIP** $40

Happy Holiday 2005 Barbie, 2005, Mattel

    MIP $40

Happy Holiday 2005 Barbie, Black, 2005, Mattel

    MIP $40

Happy Holiday 2006 Barbie, 2006, Mattel

    MIP $40

Happy Holiday 2006 Barbie, African-American, 2006, Mattel

    MIP $40

(KP Photo)

Happy Holidays 1988, 1988, Mattel, Model No. 1703

    MNP $75   **MIP** $350

(KP Photo)

Happy Holidays 1989, 1989, Mattel, Model No. 3253

    MNP $50   **MIP** $125

(KP Photo)

Happy Holidays 1990, 1990, Mattel, Model No. 4098

    MNP $25   **MIP** $70

Happy Holidays 1990, Black, 1990, Mattel, Model No. 4543

    MNP $20   **MIP** $55

(KP Photo)

Happy Holidays 1991, 1991, Mattel, Model No. 1871

    MNP $40   **MIP** $70

Happy Holidays 1991, Black, 1991, Mattel, Model No. 2696

    MNP $40   **MIP** $60

(KP Photo)

Happy Holidays 1992, 1992, Mattel, Model No. 1429

    MNP $30   **MIP** $50

Happy Holidays 1992, Black, 1992, Mattel, Model No. 2396

    MNP $30   **MIP** $50

(KP Photo)

Happy Holidays 1993, 1993, Mattel, Model No. 10824

    MNP $30   **MIP** $60

Happy Holidays 1993, Black, 1993, Mattel, Model No. 10911

    MNP $30   **MIP** $40

(KP Photo)

Happy Holidays 1994, 1994, Mattel, Model No. 12155

    MNP $30   **MIP** $65

Happy Holidays 1994, Black, 1994, Mattel, Model No. 12156

    MNP $30   **MIP** $45

(KP Photo)

Happy Holidays 1995, 1995, Mattel, Model No. 14123

    MNP $20   **MIP** $40

Happy Holidays 1995, Black, 1995, Mattel, Model No. 14124

    MNP $15   **MIP** $30

(KP Photo)

Happy Holidays 1996, White or Black, 1996, Mattel, Model No. 15646

    MNP $15   **MIP** $30

(KP Photo)

Happy Holidays 1997, 1997, Mattel, Model No. 17832

    MNP $45   **MIP** $95

Happy Holidays 1997, Black, 1997, Mattel, Model No. 17833

    MNP $5   **MIP** $20

(KP Photo)

Happy Holidays 1998, White or Black, 1998, Mattel, Model No. 20200/ 20201

    MNP $10   **MIP** $15

Hard Rock Café #4, Blond, 2007, Mattel
MNP n/a MIP $35

Hard Rock Café #4, Brunette, 2007, Mattel, Hard Rock Exclusive
MNP n/a MIP $90

Hard Rock Café Barbie, 2003, Mattel
MNP $25 MIP $125

Hard Rock Café Barbie, 2007, Mattel, black, Model No. K7946
MNP $75 MIP $150

Hard Rock Café Barbie #3, 2006, Mattel
MNP n/a MIP $75

Hard Rock Café Barbie 2, 2004, Mattel
MNP $25 MIP $75

Harrods/Hamleys West End Barbie, 1996, Mattel, Model No. 17590
MNP $20 MIP $40

Harvey Nichols Special Edition (limited to 250), 1995, Mattel, Model No. 0175
MNP $500 MIP $700

Hello Kitty Barbie, 2007, Mattel
MNP n/a MIP $35

Hello Kitty Barbie, 2008, Mattel, Model No. M9958
MNP $35 MIP $75

Hershey's Barbie, 2009, Mattel, Model No. N5004
MNP $35 MIP $70

Hills Blue Elegance Barbie, 1992, Mattel, Model No. 1879
MNP $12 MIP $25

Hills Evening Sparkle, 1990, Mattel, Model No. 3274
MNP $10 MIP $20

Hills Moonlight Rose, 1991, Mattel, Model No. 3549
MNP $7 MIP $20

Hills Party Lace Barbie, 1989, Mattel, Model No. 4843
MNP $15 MIP $20

Hills Polly Pocket Barbie, 1994, Mattel, Model No. 12412
MNP $12 MIP $20

Hills Sea Pearl Mermaid Barbie, 1995, Mattel, Model No. 13940
MNP $8 MIP $20

Hills Sidewalk Chalk Barbie, 1998, Mattel, Model No. 19784
MNP $10 MIP $20

Hills Teddy Fun Barbie, 1996, Mattel, Model No. 15684
MNP $10 MIP $20

Holiday Angel #1, Black, 2000, Mattel, Model No. 28080
MNP $20 MIP $50

Holiday Angel #1, White, 2000, Mattel, Model No. 26914
MNP $20 MIP $50

Holiday Angel #2, Black, 2001, Mattel, Model No. 29770
MNP $60 MIP $125

Holiday Angel #2, White, 2001, Mattel, Model No. 29769
MNP $60 MIP $125

Holiday Barbie 2007, 2007, Mattel, Model No. K7958
MNP n/a MIP $45

Holiday Barbie 2007, African-American, 2007, Mattel, Model No. K7959
MNP n/a MIP $45

Holiday Barbie 2009, African-American, 2009, Mattel, Model No. N6557
MNP $30 MIP $60

Holiday Barbie 2009, Caucasian, 2009, Mattel, Model No. N6556
MNP $30 MIP $60

Holiday Celebration Barbie 2002, 2002, Mattel
MNP $30 MIP $50

Holiday Celebration Barbie 2004, 2004, Mattel, blonde or black
MNP $10 MIP $40

Holiday Dreams Barbie, 1994, Mattel, Model No. 12192
MNP $10 MIP $20

Holiday Hostess Barbie, 1993, Mattel, Model No. 10280
MNP $20 MIP $30

Holiday Season, 1996, Mattel, Model No. 15581
MNP $5 MIP $10

Holiday Singing Sisters Gift Set, 2000, Mattel
MNP $15 MIP $40

Holiday Surprise Barbie, White or Black, 2000, Mattel
MNP $5 MIP $10

Holiday Treasures 1999, 1999, Mattel, Model No. 24669
MNP $75 MIP $150

Holiday Treats Barbie, 1997, Mattel
MNP $5 MIP $10

Holiday Wishes Barbie 2007, 2007, Mattel, Model No. J9207
MNP $10 MIP $25

Hollywood Hair Deluxe Gift Set, 1993, Mattel, Model No. 10928
MNP $15 MIP $35

Hollywood Legends Dorothy (Wizard of Oz), 1995, Mattel, Model No. 12701
MNP $20 MIP $60

Hollywood Legends Eliza Doolittle (My Fair Lady), Green Coat, 1996, Mattel, Model No. 15498
MNP $75 MIP $150

Hollywood Legends Eliza Doolittle (My Fair Lady), Lace Ball Gown, 1996, Mattel, Model No. 15500
MNP $30 MIP $65

Hollywood Legends Eliza Doolittle (My Fair Lady), Pink, 1996, Mattel, Model No. 15501
MNP $30 MIP $50

Hollywood Legends Eliza Doolittle (My Fair Lady), White Lace Gown w/Parasol, 1996, Mattel, Model No. 15497
MNP $30 MIP $75

Hollywood Legends Glinda (Wizard of Oz), 1996, Mattel, Model No. 14901
MNP $35 MIP $50

Hollywood Legends Ken as Cowardly Lion (Wizard of Oz), 1996, Mattel, Model No. 16573
MNP $35 MIP $45

Hollywood Legends Ken as Henry Higgins (My Fair Lady), 1996, Mattel, Model No. 15499
MNP $75 MIP $150

Hollywood Legends Ken as Rhett Butler, 1994, Mattel, Gone With the Wind, Model No. 12741
MNP $25 MIP $30

Hollywood Legends Ken as Scarecrow (Wizard of Oz), 1996, Mattel, Model No. 16497
MNP $35 MIP $40

Hollywood Legends Ken as Tin Man (Wizard of Oz), 1996, Mattel, Model No. 14902
MNP $15 MIP $25

Hollywood Legends Maria (Sound of Music), 1995, Mattel, Model No. 13676
MNP $20 MIP $50

Hollywood Legends Marilyn Monroe, Pink, 1997, Mattel, Gentlemen Prefer Blondes, Model No. 17451
MNP $20 MIP $45

Hollywood Legends Marilyn Monroe, Red, 1997, Mattel, Gentlemen Prefer Blondes, Model No. 17452
MNP $20 MIP $45

Hollywood Legends Marilyn Monroe, White, 1997, Mattel, Seven Year Itch, Model No. 17155
MNP $20 MIP $45

Hollywood Legends Scarlett O'Hara, Black/White Dress, 1993, Mattel, Gone With the Wind, Model No. 13254
MNP $60 MIP $125

(KP Photo)

Hollywood Legends Scarlett O'Hara, Green Velvet Curtain, 1994, Mattel, Gone With the Wind, Model No. 12045

MNP $25   MIP $50

Hollywood Legends Scarlett O'Hara, Green/White Silk Dress, 1995, Mattel, Gone With the Wind, Model No. 12997

MNP $60   MIP $125

Hollywood Legends Scarlett O'Hara, Red Velvet Dress, 1994, Mattel, Gone With the Wind, Model No. 12815

MNP $60   MIP $125

(KP Photo)

Hollywood Movie Star, Between Takes, 2000, Mattel, Model No. 27684

MNP $15   MIP $25

Hollywood Movie Star, By the Pool, 2000, Mattel, Model No. 27684

MNP $15   MIP $25

Hollywood Movie Star, Day in the Sun, 2000, Mattel, Model No. 2000

MNP $15   MIP $25

Hollywood Movie Star, Hollywood Cast Party, 2001, Mattel, Model No. 50825

MNP $45   MIP $95

Hollywood Movie Star, Hollywood Premiere, 2000, Mattel, Model No. 26914

MNP $40   MIP $85

Hollywood Movie Star, Publicity Tour, 2001, Mattel

MNP $15   MIP $25

Home Shopping Club Evening Flame, 1991, Mattel, Model No. 1865

MNP $70   MIP $125

Home Shopping Club Golden Allure Barbie, 1999, Mattel

MNP $5   MIP $30

Home Shopping Club Premiere Night, 1999, Mattel

MNP $5   MIP $30

I Dream of Jeannie Barbie, 2001, Mattel

MNP $15   MIP $45

Japanese Living Eli, 1970, Mattel, Foreign

MNP $700   MIP $1400

Jazz Baby Collection, Cabaret Dancer, 2007, Mattel, redhead, Model No. L6250

MNP $35   MIP $75

Jazz Baby Collection, Cabaret Dancer, 2007, Mattel, brunette, Model No. L6251

MNP $35   MIP $75

JCPenney Enchanted Evening, 1991, Mattel, Model No. 2702

MNP $20   MIP $40

JCPenney Evening Elegance, 1990, Mattel, Model No. 7057

MNP $20   MIP $40

JCPenney Evening Enchantment, 1998, Mattel, Model No. 19783

MNP $25   MIP $40

JCPenney Evening Majesty, 1997, Mattel, Model No. 17235

MNP $10   MIP $25

JCPenney Evening Sensation, 1992, Mattel, Model No. 1278

MNP $12   MIP $35

JCPenney Golden Winter, 1993, Mattel, Model No. 10684

MNP $12   MIP $35

JCPenney Night Dazzle, 1994, Mattel, Model No. 12191

MNP $15   MIP $35

JCPenney Original Arizona Jean Co. Barbie #1, 1996, Mattel, Model No. 15441

MNP $12   MIP $25

JCPenney Original Arizona Jean Co. Barbie #2, 1997, Mattel, Model No. 18020

MNP $12   MIP $25

JCPenney Original Arizona Jean Co. Barbie #3, 1998, Mattel, Model No. 19873

MNP $12   MIP $25

JCPenney Royal Enchantment, 1995, Mattel, Model No. 14010

MNP $25   MIP $35

JCPenney Winter Renaissance, 1996, Mattel, Model No. 15570

MNP $10   MIP $25

JCPenney/Sears Evening Recital Barbie, Stacie, Kelly and Tommy, 2000, Mattel, Model No. 27954

MNP $15   MIP $42

Jubilee Series, Crystal Jubilee, Limited to 20,000, 1999, Mattel, Model No. 21923

MNP $150   MIP $275

Jubilee Series, Gold Jubilee, Limited to 5,000, 1994, Mattel, Model No. 12009

MNP $300   MIP $500

Jubilee Series, Pink Jubilee, Limited to 1,200, 1989, Mattel, Model No. 3756

MNP $800   MIP $2000

Jude Deveraux, The Raider, Barbie and Ken Gift Set, 2003, Mattel

MNP $40   MIP $80

Juicy Couture Gift Set, 2004, Mattel

MNP $20   MIP $60

Julia Simply Wow Gift Set, 1969, Mattel

MNP $400   MIP $1500

Just for You Barbie, 2003, Mattel, Model No. B0151

MNP $10   MIP $35

Kate Spade Barbie, 2004, Mattel

MNP $20   MIP $80

K-B Fantasy Ball Barbie, 1997, Mattel, Model No. 18594

MNP $10   MIP $20

K-B Fashion Avenue Barbie, 1998, Mattel, Model No. 20782

MNP $8   MIP $15

K-B Glamour Barbie, Black, 1997, Mattel

MNP $10   MIP $20

K-B Starlight Carousel Barbie, 1998, Mattel, Model No. 19708

MNP $10   MIP $20

Keepsake Treasures, Barbie and Curious George, 2001, Mattel

MNP $15   MIP $30

Keepsake Treasures, Barbie and the Tale of Peter Rabbit, 1998, Mattel, Model No. 19360

MNP $15   MIP $40

Keepsake Treasures, Peter Rabbit 100th Anniversary Barbie, 2002, Mattel, Model No. 53872
MNP $20 MIP $40

Kelly & Tommy as Alice and the Mad Hatter, 2003, Mattel
MNP $10 MIP $20

Kelly and Friends Wizard of Oz Gift Set, 2003, Mattel
MNP $15 MIP $30

Kelly as the Witches from Wizard of Oz, 2004, Mattel
MNP $10 MIP $30

Kelly Nostalgic Favorites Gift Set, 2003, Mattel
MNP $15 MIP $30

Kelly Princess of the World Collection, Dutch, Scottish, Spanish, 2005, Mattel
MNP $10 MIP $20

Ken as Legolas in the Lord of the Rings: Fellowship of the Ring, 2004, Mattel
MNP $10 MIP $25

Kentucky Derby Barbie, 2009, Mattel, Model No. P4755
MNP $40 MIP $80

Kimora Lee Simmons, 2007, Mattel, (Baby Phat)
MNP n/a MIP $60

Kissing Barbie Gift Set, 1978, Mattel, Model No. 2977
MNP $25 MIP $65

Kmart March of Dimes Walk America Barbie & Kelly Gift Set, 1999, Mattel, Model No. 20843
MNP $15 MIP $25

Kmart March of Dimes Walk America Barbie, Black or White, 1998, Mattel, Model No. 18506/18507
MNP $10 MIP $24

Kmart Peach Pretty Barbie, 1989, Mattel, Model No. 4870
MNP $10 MIP $30

Kmart Pretty in Purple, Black, 1992, Mattel, Model No. 3121
MNP $12 MIP $25

Kmart Pretty in Purple, White, 1992, Mattel, Model No. 3117
MNP $12 MIP $25

Kmart Route 66 Barbecue Bash, 2000, Mattel
MNP $8 MIP $25

Kmart Very Berry Barbie, White or Black, 2000, Mattel
MNP $5 MIP $10

Kool-Aid Barbie, 1996, Mattel
MNP $15 MIP $40

Kool-Aid Wacky Warehouse Barbie I, 1993, Mattel, Model No. 10309
MNP $25 MIP $60

Kool-Aid Wacky Warehouse Barbie II, 1994, Mattel, Model No. 11763
MNP $25 MIP $50

Kraft Treasures Barbie, 1992, Mattel
MNP $30 MIP $55

L.E. Festival Holiday Barbie (540 made), 1994, Mattel
MNP $500 MIP $900

Lady Camille Barbie, 2003, Mattel
MNP $45 MIP $80

Life Ball Barbie #1, Vivienne Westwood, 1998, Mattel
MNP $200 MIP $400

Life Ball Barbie #2, Christian LaCroix, 1999, Mattel
MNP $200 MIP $400

Little Debbie #1, 1993, Mattel, Model No. 10123
MNP $25 MIP $40

Little Debbie #2, 1996, Mattel, Model No. 14616
MNP $15 MIP $25

Little Debbie #3, 1998, Mattel, Model No. 16352
MNP $15 MIP $20

Little Debbie #4, 1999, Mattel, Model No. 24977
MNP $10 MIP $20

Living Barbie Action Accents Gift Set, 1970, Mattel, Model No. 1585
MNP $500 MIP $1500

Lounge Kitty, 2004, Mattel, black or white
MNP $10 MIP $40

Lounge Kitty, Latina, 2004, Mattel
MNP $10 MIP $60

Loving You Barbie Gift Set, 1983, Mattel, Model No. 7583
MNP $45 MIP $100

Lucy is Envious Kelly, 2009, Mattel, Model No. R4519
MNP $15 MIP $35

M.A.C. Barbie, 2007, Mattel, M.A.C. Cosmetics Exclusive
MNP n/a MIP $100

Macy's Anne Klein Barbie, 1997, Mattel, Model No. 17603
MNP $25 MIP $35

Macy's City Shopper, Nicole Miller, 1996, Mattel, Model No. 16289
MNP $25 MIP $30

Mademoiselle Isabelle Barbie, 2002, Mattel
MNP $45 MIP $80

Magic & Mystery, Morgan LeFay and Merlin, 2000, Mattel, Model No. 27287
MNP $50 MIP $75

Magic & Mystery, Tales of the Arabian Nights, 2001, Mattel, Model No. 50827
MNP $40 MIP $65

Maiko Barbie, 2006, Mattel
MNP n/a MIP $150

Major League Baseball Chicago Cubs, 1999, Mattel, Model No. 23883
MNP $20 MIP $35

Major League Baseball Los Angeles Dodgers, 1999, Mattel, Model No. 23882
MNP $20 MIP $11

Major League Baseball New York Yankees, 1999, Mattel, Model No. 23881
MNP $20 MIP $11

Make-A-Valentine Barbie, White or Black, 1999, Mattel
MNP $5 MIP $15

Malibu Barbie "The Beach Party," w/Case, 1979, Mattel, Model No. 1703
MNP $17 MIP $35

Malibu Ken Surf's Up Gift Set, 1971, Mattel, Model No. 1248
MNP $75 MIP $200

Marie Antoinette Barbie, 2003, Mattel
MNP $125 MIP $200

Masquerade Gala #1, Illusion, 1997, Mattel, Model No. 18667
MNP $85 MIP $175

Masquerade Gala #2, Rendezvous, 1998, Mattel, Model No. 20647
MNP $40 MIP $60

Masquerade Gala #3, Venetian Opulence, 2000, Mattel, Model No. 24501
MNP $30 MIP $50

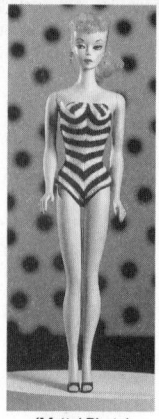

(Mattel Photo)

Mattel Festival 35th Anniversary (3,500 made), 1994, Mattel
MNP $50   MIP $150

Mattel Festival 35th Anniversary Gift Set (975 made), 1994, Mattel, Model No. 11591
MNP $70   MIP $100

Mattel Festival Banquet, Blond, 1994, Mattel
MNP $75   MIP $125

Mattel Festival Banquet, Brunette, 1994, Mattel
MNP $75   MIP $125

Mattel Festival Banquet, Red Hair, 1994, Mattel
MNP $75   MIP $125

Mattel Festival Doctor, Brunette (1,500 made), 1994, Mattel, Model No. 11160
MNP $35   MIP $60

Mattel Festival Gymnast (1,500 made), 1994, Mattel, Model No. 11921
MNP $35   MIP $60

Mattel Festival Happy Holiday, 1994, Mattel, Model No. 12155
MNP $200   MIP $450

Mattel Festival Haute Couture, Rainbow (500 made), 1994, Mattel
MNP $75   MIP $200

Mattel Festival Haute Couture, Red Velvet (480 made), 1994, Mattel
MNP $75   MIP $200

Mattel Festival Night Dazzle, Brunette (420 made), 1994, Mattel, Model No. 12191
MNP $100   MIP $300

Mattel Festival Snow Princess, Brunette (285 made), 1994, Mattel, Model No. 12905
MNP $500   MIP $1000

Meijers Hula Hoop, 1997, Mattel, Model No. 18167
MNP $10   MIP $20

Meijers Ice Cream, 1998, Mattel, Model No. 19820
MNP $10   MIP $20

Meijers Ladybug Fun, 1997, Mattel, Model No. 17695
MNP $10   MIP $20

Meijers Shopping Fun, 1993, Mattel, Model No. 10051
MNP $10   MIP $20

Meijers Something Extra, 1992, Mattel, Model No. 0863
MNP $10   MIP $20

Mervyns Ballerina Barbie, 1983, Mattel, Model No. 4983
MNP $30   MIP $75

Mervyns Fabulous Fur, 1986, Mattel, Model No. 7093
MNP $25   MIP $65

Midge's Ensemble Gift Set, 1964, Mattel, Model No. 1012
MNP $1200   MIP $3150

Millennium Bride, Limited to 10,000, 1999, Mattel, Model No. 24505
MNP $150   MIP $300

Mix n' Match Gift Set, 1962, Mattel, Model No. 857
MNP $800   MIP $1850

Model of the Moment Daria Celebutante, 2004, Mattel, blonde
MNP $10   MIP $50

Model of the Moment Fashion (Blonde) Shopping Queen, 2005, Mattel, Model No. G8081
MNP $20   MIP $40

Model of the Moment Marisa Pretty Young Thing, 2004, Mattel, Latina
MNP $10   MIP $50

Model of the Moment Nichelle Urban Hipster, 2004, Mattel, black
MNP $10   MIP $50

Monique Lhuillier Bride Barbie, 2006, Mattel
MNP n/a   MIP $110

Monique Lhuillier Bride Barbie, Platinum Edition, Blonde, 2006, Mattel
MNP n/a   MIP $140

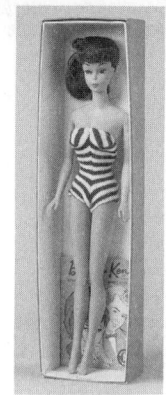

(KP Photo)

Montgomery Wards Barbie, Pink Box, 1972, Mattel, Model No. 3210
MNP $350   MIP $650

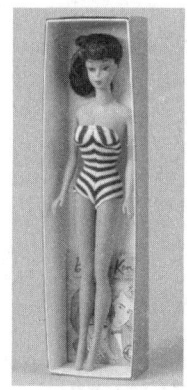

(KP Photo)

Montgomery Wards, Mail Order Box, 1972, Mattel, Model No. 3210
MNP $30   MIP $500

My Favorite Barbie, 1959 Gift Set, 2009, Mattel, Model No. N4974
MNP $20   MIP $45

My Favorite Barbie, Malibu Barbie, 2009, Mattel, Model No. N4977
MNP $20   MIP $45

My Favorite Barbie, Rockers, 2009, Mattel, Model No. N4979
MNP $20   MIP $45

My Favorite Barbie, Superstar, 2009, Mattel, Model No. N4978
MNP $20   MIP $45

My Favorite Barbie, Twist 'N Turn, 2009, Mattel, Model No. N4976
MNP $45   MIP $95

My Favorite Black Barbie, 2009, Mattel, Model No. R4468
MNP $20   MIP $45

My Favorite Career, Astronaut, 2009, Mattel, Model No. R4474
MNP $20   MIP $40

My Favorite Career, Nurse, 2009, Mattel, Model No. R4472
MNP $20   MIP $40

My Favorite Career, Pan Am Stewardess, 2010, Mattel, Model No. R4473
MNP $30   MIP $60

My Favorite Career, Teacher, 2009, Mattel, Model No. R4471
MNP $20   MIP $40

My Favorite Vintage Swirl, 2009, Mattel, Model No. T1373
MNP $20   MIP $45

My First Barbie Gift Set, 1991, Mattel, Model No. 2483
MNP $8   MIP $20

My First Barbie Gift Set, Pink Tutu, 1986, Mattel, Model No. 1979
MNP $15   MIP $35

My First Barbie Gift Set, Pink Tutu, 1987, Mattel, Model No. 5386
MNP $18   MIP $40

My First Barbie, Pink Tutu, Zayre's Hispanic, 1987, Mattel, Model No. 1875
MNP $8   MIP $45

NASCAR Barbie #1, Kyle Petty #44, 1998, Mattel, Model No. 20442
MNP $5   MIP $15

NASCAR Barbie #2, Bill Elliott #94, 1999, Mattel, Model No. 22954
MNP $5   MIP $20

NASCAR Dale Earnhardt Jr. Barbie, 2007, Mattel
MNP n/a   MIP $35

NASCAR Jeff Gordon Barbie, 2007, Mattel
MNP n/a   MIP $35

National Convention A Date w/Barbie Doll in Atlanta, 1998, Mattel
MNP $100   MIP $350

National Convention Barbie in the Old West, 2000, Mattel
MNP $85   MIP $225

National Convention We Girls Can Do Anything Right Barbie, 1999, Mattel
MNP $85   MIP $225

National Convention, Barbie and the Bandstand, 1996, Mattel, Pennsylvania
MNP $225   MIP $450

National Convention, Barbie Around the World Festival, 1985, Mattel, Michigan
MNP $125   MIP $300

National Convention, Barbie Convention 1980, 1980, Mattel, New York
MNP $125   MIP $350

National Convention, Barbie Forever Young, 1989, Mattel, California
MNP $125   MIP $300

National Convention, Barbie Loves a Fairytale, 1991, Mattel, Nebraska
MNP $150   MIP $250

National Convention, Barbie Loves New York, 1984, Mattel, New York
MNP $125   MIP $275

National Convention, Barbie Ole, 1995, Mattel, New Mexico
MNP $225   MIP $400

National Convention, Barbie Wedding Dreams, 1992, Mattel, New York
MNP $50   MIP $200

National Convention, Barbie's Pow Wow, 1983, Mattel, Arizona
MNP $125   MIP $350

National Convention, Barbie's Reunion, 1986, Mattel, Arizona
MNP $125   MIP $275

National Convention, Beach Blanket Barbie, 1997, Mattel, California
MNP $225   MIP $375

National Convention, Christmas w/Barbie, 1987, Mattel, Oklahoma
MNP $125   MIP $300

National Convention, Come Rain or Shine, 1988, Mattel, Washington
MNP $125   MIP $250

National Convention, Deep in the Heart of Texas, 1990, Mattel, Texas
MNP $125   MIP $250

National Convention, Michigan Entertains Barbie, 1982, Mattel, Michigan
MNP $125   MIP $275

National Convention, The Magic of Barbie, 1994, Mattel, Alabama
MNP $175   MIP $375

National Convention, We Are Family, 2004, 2004, Mattel
MNP $10   MIP $200

National Convention, You've Come a Long Way, 1993, Mattel, Maryland
MNP $225   MIP $450

New Lifestyles of the West Western Plains, 1999, Mattel, Model No. 23205
MNP $40   MIP $80

Nite Lightning Stacey, 2006, Mattel, Model No. J0964
MNP $50   MIP $100

Nolan Miller #1, Sheer Illusion, 1998, Mattel, Model No. 20662
MNP $95   MIP $195

Nolan Miller #2, Evening Illusion, 1999, Mattel, Model No. 23495
MNP $100   MIP $225

Nostalgic 35th Anniversary Gift Set, 1994, Mattel, Model No. 11591
MNP $50   MIP $75

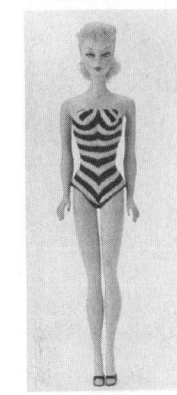

Nostalgic 35th Anniversary, Blonde, 1994, Mattel, Model No. 11590
MNP $25   MIP $40

Nostalgic 35th Anniversary, Brunette, 1994, Mattel, Model No. 11782
MNP $30   MIP $60

Nostalgic Reproductions, Busy Gal Barbie, 1995, Mattel, Model No. 13675
MNP $15   MIP $30

Nostalgic Reproductions, Enchanted Evening Barbie, Blonde, 1996, Mattel, Model No. 14992
MNP $10   MIP $20

Nostalgic Reproductions, Enchanted Evening, Brunette, 1996, Mattel, Model No. 15407
MNP $10   MIP $20

(KP Photo)

Nostalgic Reproductions, Fashion Luncheon, 1997, Mattel, Model No. 17382

    MNP $25   **MIP** $40

Nostalgic Reproductions, Francie Wild Bunch, 1997, Mattel, Model No. 17601

    MNP $20   **MIP** $50

(KP Photo)

Nostalgic Reproductions, Francie, 30th Anniversary, 1996, Mattel, Model No. 14808

    MNP $20   **MIP** $35

Nostalgic Reproductions, Silken Flame, Blonde or Brunette, 1998, Mattel

    MNP $15   **MIP** $25

Nostalgic Reproductions, Solo in the Spotlight, Blonde or Brunette, 1995, Mattel, Model No. 13534/13820

    MNP $12   **MIP** $20

Nostalgic Reproductions, Wedding Day, Blonde, 1997, Mattel

    MNP $10   **MIP** $20

Nursery Rhymes, Barbie Had a Little Lamb, 1999, Mattel, Model No. 21740

    MNP $20   **MIP** $40

Nutcracker Barbie, 1992, Mattel, Model No. 5472

    MNP $85   **MIP** $225

Ocean Friends Gift Set, 1996, Mattel, Model No. 16442

    MNP $20   **MIP** $45

Olympic Barbie Gift Set, 1996, Mattel, Model No. 16443

    MNP $15   **MIP** $30

On Location: Barcelona, 2007, Mattel, Target Exclusive

    MNP n/a   **MIP** $25

On Parade Gift Set, Barbie, Ken, Midge, 1964, Mattel, Model No. 1014

    MNP $800   **MIP** $2300

Osco Picnic Pretty, 1993, Mattel, Model No. 3803

    MNP $15   **MIP** $25

Oshagatsu Barbie, 1995, Mattel, Model No. 14024

    MNP $20   **MIP** $50

P.J.'s Swinging Silver Gift Set, 1970, Mattel, Model No. 1588

    MNP $700   **MIP** $1500

Pace Party Sensations Barbie, 1990, Mattel

    MNP $15   **MIP** $50

Pace Very Violet Barbie, 1992, Mattel

    MNP $15   **MIP** $50

Paint 'N Dazzle Deluxe Gift Set, 1993, Mattel, Model No. 10926

    MNP $17   **MIP** $35

Palm Beach Breeze Barbie, 2010, Mattel, Model No. R4484

    MNP $35   **MIP** $75

Palm Beach Coral Barbie, 2010, Mattel, Model No. R4535

    MNP $75   **MIP** $150

Palm Beach Swim Suit Barbie, 2010, Mattel, Model No. R4483

    MNP $25   **MIP** $50

Paul Frank Barbie, Blue Pajamas, 2004, Mattel

    MNP $10   **MIP** $60

Peaches and Cream Barbie, 2009, Mattel, Model No. R9525

    MNP $20   **MIP** $45

(Mattel Photo)

Peanuts, Barbie and Snoopy, 2002, Mattel, Model No. 55558

    MNP $15   **MIP** $25

Peppermint Obsession Barbie, 2006, Mattel, Model No. J1743

    MIP $150

Peppermint Princess Barbie, Winter Princess Collection, 1995, Mattel, Model No. 13598

    MNP $35   **MIP** $50

Picture Pockets Barbie, Christie, Kira or Teresa, 2000, Mattel

    MNP $5   **MIP** $11

Pink & Pretty Barbie Gift Set, 1982, Mattel, Model No. 5239

    MNP $35   **MIP** $90

Pink Hope, 2007, Mattel, International Heart Association

    MNP n/a   **MIP** $26

Pink Ribbon Barbie, 2006, Mattel

    MNP n/a   **MIP** $25

Pink Ribbon Barbie, African-American, 2006, Mattel

    MNP n/a   **MIP** $25

(KP Photo)

Pink Splendor, 1995, Mattel, Model No. 16091

    MNP $150   **MIP** $200

Pin-Up Girls Hula Honey, 2006, Mattel

    MNP n/a   **MIP** $40

Pin-Up Girls Lady Luck, 2006, Mattel

    MNP n/a   **MIP** $40

Pin-Up Girls Way Out West, 2006, Mattel, FAO Schwarz Exclusive, Blond

MNP n/a   MIP $225

Pin-Up Girls Way Out West, 2006, Mattel, regular edition, Model No. J0934

MNP n/a   MIP $125

Pivotal Body Jazz Baby, Blonde, 2007, Mattel

MNP n/a   MIP $50

Pivotal Body Jazz Baby, Brunette, 2007, Mattel

MNP n/a   MIP $50

Pivotal Body Jazz Baby, Redhead, 2007, Mattel

MNP n/a   MIP $50

Pivotal Body Mistress of Ceremonies, 2007, Mattel, Dealer's Exclusive

MNP n/a   MIP $50

Pivotal Mod Pop Life, 2009, Mattel, redhead, black, blond, Model No. N6595

MNP $25   MIP $55

Platinum Label, Joie De Vivre, African-American, 2008, Mattel, Model No. M0723

MNP $300   MIP $600

Poodle Parade, 1996, Mattel, Model No. 15280

MNP $25   MIP $40

Pop Culture Barbie as That Girl, 2003, Mattel

MNP $20   MIP $40

Pop Culture James Bond 007 Barbie & Ken Gift Set, 2003, Mattel

MNP $40   MIP $75

(KP Photo)

Pop Culture, Barbie & Ken as Morticia & Gomez Addams, 2000, Mattel, Model No. 27276

MNP $100   MIP $225

Pop Culture, Barbie and Ken as Lily and Herman Munster, 2001, Mattel, Model No. 50544

MNP $25   MIP $175

(Mattel Photo)

Pop Culture, Barbie as Samantha from Bewitched, 2002, Mattel, Model No. 53510

MNP $75   MIP $150

(Mattel Photo)

Pop Culture, Barbie as That Girl, 2003, Mattel, Model No. 56705

MNP $20   MIP $30

Pop Culture, Barbie as Wonder Woman, 2000, Mattel, Model No. 24638

MNP $25   MIP $40

Pop Culture, Barbie Loves Elvis Gift Set, 1997, Mattel, Model No. 17450

MNP $30   MIP $50

Pop Culture, Barbie Loves Frankie Sinatra Gift Set, 1999, Mattel, Model No. 22953

MNP $30   MIP $45

(Mattel Photo)

Pop Culture, James Bond 007 Ken and Barbie, 2003, Mattel, Model No. B0150

MNP $30   MIP $50

(Mattel Photo)

Pop Culture, Malibu Barbie, 2002, Mattel, Model No. 56061

MNP $10   MIP $20

(KP Photo)

Pop Culture, Star Trek Barbie and Ken, 1996, Mattel, Model No. 15006

MNP $30   MIP $65

(Mattel Photo)

Pop Culture, Starring Barbie in King Kong, 2003, Mattel, Model No. 56737

MNP $60   MIP $125

Pop Culture, X-Files Barbie and Ken, 1998, Mattel

MNP $20   MIP $50

Pretty Changes Barbie Gift Set, 1978, Mattel, Model No. 2598

MNP $35   MIP $75

Pretty Hearts Barbie, 1992, Mattel, Model No. 2901
MNP $7   MIP $15

Pretty Pairs Angie N' Tangie, 1970, Mattel, foreign, Model No. 1135
MNP $125   MIP $250

Pretty Pairs Lori N' Rori, 1970, Mattel, foreign, Model No. 1133
MNP $125   MIP $250

Pretty Pairs Nan N' Fran, 1970, Mattel, foreign, Model No. 1134
MNP $125   MIP $250

Princess and the Pea Barbie, 2001, Mattel, Model No. 28800
MNP $15   MIP $35

Princess Series, Rapunzel, 2002, Mattel, Model No. 53973
MNP $20   MIP $40

Queen Elizabeth I Barbie, 2004, Mattel
MNP $10   MIP $200

Radio Shack Earring Magic, 1991, Mattel, came w/software package, Model No. 25192
MNP $20   MIP $40

Red Romance Barbie, 1993, Mattel, Model No. 3161
MNP $7   MIP $15

Reem Acra Bride, 2007, Mattel, Model No. K7968
MNP n/a   MIP $230

Republican National Convention Delegate Barbie, 2000, Mattel
MNP $25   MIP $150

Romantic Bride Barbie, Black, 2001, Mattel, Model No. 29439
MNP $15   MIP $45

Romantic Bride Barbie, Blonde, 2001, Mattel, Model No. 29438
MNP $15   MIP $45

Royal Jewels Countess of Rubies, 2001, Mattel
MNP $40   MIP $100

Royal Jewels Duchess of Diamonds, 2001, Mattel
MNP $40   MIP $100

Royal Jewels Empress of Emeralds, 2000, Mattel, Model No. 25680
MNP $50   MIP $100

Royal Jewels Queen of Sapphires, 2000, Mattel, Model No. 24924
MNP $50   MIP $100

Russell Stover Easter, 1996, Mattel, Model No. 14956
MNP $10   MIP $25

Russell Stover Easter, 1997, Mattel, Model No. 17091
MNP $5   MIP $15

Russell Stover Easter (w/Easter basket), 1996, Mattel, Model No. 14617
MNP $10   MIP $25

Sam's Club 50s Fun Barbie, 1996, Mattel, Model No. 15820
MNP $10   MIP $30

Sam's Club 60s Fun Barbie, Blonde, 1997, Mattel, Model No. 17252
MNP $10   MIP $20

Sam's Club 60s Fun Barbie, Red Hair, 1997, Mattel, Model No. 17693
MNP $10   MIP $20

Sam's Club 70s Fun Barbie, Blonde, 1998, Mattel, Model No. 19928
MNP $10   MIP $20

Sam's Club 70s Fun Barbie, Brunette, 1998, Mattel, Model No. 19929
MNP $10   MIP $20

Sam's Club Barbie Sisters' Celebration, Barbie and Krissy, 2000, Mattel
MNP $10   MIP $25

Sam's Club Bronze Sensation Barbie, 1998, Mattel, Model No. 20022
MNP $25   MIP $40

Sam's Club Dinner Date Barbie, Blonde, 1998, Mattel, Model No. 19016
MNP $8   MIP $15

Sam's Club Dinner Date Barbie, Red Hair, 1998, Mattel, Model No. 19037
MNP $9   MIP $15

Sam's Club Jewel Jubilee Barbie, 1991, Mattel, Model No. 2366
MNP $20   MIP $40

Sam's Club Party Sensation Barbie, 1990, Mattel, Model No. 9025
MNP $20   MIP $40

Sam's Club Peach Blossom Barbie, 1992, Mattel, Model No. 7009
MNP $20   MIP $30

Sam's Club Season's Greetings Barbie, 1994, Mattel, Model No. 12384
MNP $25   MIP $40

Sam's Club Sweet Moments Barbie, 1997, Mattel, Model No. 17642
MNP $12   MIP $20

Sam's Club Wedding Fantasy Barbie Gift Set, 1993, Mattel, Model No. 10924
MNP $30   MIP $70

Sam's Club Winter Fantasy Barbie, Blonde or Brunette, 1997, Mattel, Model No. 17249/17666
MNP $10   MIP $20

Sam's Club Winter's Eve Barbie, 1995, Mattel, Model No. 13613
MNP $12   MIP $25

Scarlett Macaw, 2008, Mattel, Model No. L9659
MNP $85   MIP $175

School Spirit Barbie, 1996, Mattel
MNP $5   MIP $10

Schooltime Barbie 1995, 1995, Mattel
MNP $5   MIP $10

Schooltime Barbie 1998, 1998, Mattel
MNP $5   MIP $10

Sears 100th Celebration Barbie, 1986, Mattel, Model No. 2998
MNP $20   MIP $45

Sears Barbie Twinkle Town Set, 1969, Mattel, Model No. 1866
MNP $800   MIP $1600

Sears Blossom Beautiful Barbie, 1992, Mattel, Model No. 3817
MNP $100   MIP $275

Sears Blue Starlight, 1997, Mattel, Model No. 17125
MNP $10   MIP $20

Sears Dream Princess, 1992, Mattel, Model No. 2306
MNP $10   MIP $20

Sears Enchanted Princess, 1993, Mattel, Model No. 10292
MNP $10   MIP $20

Sears Evening Enchantment, 1989, Mattel, Model No. 3596
MNP $10   MIP $20

Sears Evening Flame, 1996, Mattel, Model No. 15533
MNP $10   MIP $20

Sears Holiday Celebration Barbie 2004 (red dress), 2004, Mattel, blond or black
MNP $10   MIP $40

Sears Lavender Surprise, 1990, Mattel, Model No. 9049
MNP $8   MIP $20

Sears Lavender Surprise, Black, 1990, Mattel, Model No. 5588
MNP $8   MIP $20

Sears Lilac and Lovely Barbie, 1988, Mattel, Model No. 7669
MNP $10   MIP $20

Sears Perfectly Plaid Gift Set, 1971, Mattel, Model No. 1193
MNP $800   MIP $1500

Sears Pink Reflections, 1998, Mattel, Model No. 19130
MNP $10   MIP $20

Sears Ribbons and Roses Barbie, 1995, Mattel, Model No. 13011
MNP $10   MIP $20

Sears Silver Sweetheart Barbie, 1994, Mattel, Model No. 12410
MNP $17   MIP $20

Sears Skooter Cut n' Button Gift Set, 1967, Mattel, Model No. 1036
MNP $150   MIP $650

Sears Southern Belle, 1991, Mattel, Model No. 2586
MNP $10   MIP $20

Sears Star Dream Barbie, 1987, Mattel, Model No. 4550
MNP $10   MIP $20

Sears Winter Sports, 1975, Mattel, Model No. 9042
MNP $65   MIP $115

Seasons Sparkle Barbie, 2003, Mattel
MNP $8   MIP $15

Secret Hearts Gift Set, 1993, Mattel, Model No. 10929
MNP $17   MIP $35

See's Candy Barbie, White or Black, 2000, Mattel
MNP $15   MIP $45

Service Merchandise Blue Rhapsody, 1991, Mattel, Model No. 1364
MNP $10   MIP $30

Service Merchandise City Sophisticate, 1994, Mattel, Model No. 12005
MNP $10   MIP $30

Service Merchandise Definitely Diamonds, 1998, Mattel, Model No. 20204
MNP $10   MIP $40

Service Merchandise Dream Bride, Black or White, 1997, Mattel, Model No. 17933/17153
MNP $10   MIP $25

Service Merchandise Evening Symphony, 1998, Mattel, Model No. 19777
MNP $10   MIP $25

Service Merchandise Ruby Romance, 1995, Mattel, Model No. 13612
MNP $15   MIP $35

Service Merchandise Satin Nights, two earring versions, 1992, Mattel, Model No. 1886
MNP $20   MIP $50

Service Merchandise Sea Princess, 1996, Mattel, Model No. 15531
MNP $10   MIP $20

Service Merchandise Sparkling Splendor, 1993, Mattel, Model No. 10994
MNP $10   MIP $20

Sharin Sisters Gift Set, 1992, Mattel, Model No. 5716
MNP $12   MIP $25

Sharin Sisters Gift Set, 1993, Mattel, Model No. 10143
MNP $12   MIP $25

Shopko/Venture Blossom Beauty, 1991, Mattel, Model No. 3142
MNP $10   MIP $20

Shopko/Venture Party Perfect, 1992, Mattel, Model No. 1876
MNP $12   MIP $20

Skipper Party Time Gift Set, 1964, Mattel, Model No. 1021
MNP $100   MIP $550

Skipper Swing 'a' Rounder Gym Gift Set, 1972, Mattel, Model No. 1172
MNP $100   MIP $400

Snap 'N Play Gift Set (Snap 'N Play Deluxe), 1992, Mattel, Model No. 2262
MNP $12   MIP $35

Society Hound Barbie, 2001, Mattel
MNP $20   MIP $40

(Mattel Photo)

Sophisticated Wedding, White or Black, 2002, Mattel, Model No. 53370/53371
MNP $20   MIP $50

Spiegel Golden Qi-Pao Barbie, 1998, Mattel, Model No. 20866
MNP $30   MIP $65

Spiegel Regal Reflections, 1992, Mattel, Model No. 4116
MNP $20   MIP $75

Spiegel Royal Invitation, 1993, Mattel, Model No. 10969
MNP $15   MIP $50

Spiegel Shopping Chic, 1995, Mattel, Model No. 14009
MNP $15   MIP $40

Spiegel Sterling Wishes, 1991, Mattel, Model No. 3347
MNP $30   MIP $75

Spiegel Summer Sophisticate, 1996, Mattel, Model No. 15591
MNP $10   MIP $25

Spiegel Theatre Elegance, 1994, Mattel, Model No. 12077
MNP $30   MIP $50

Spiegel Winner's Circle, 1997, Mattel, Model No. 17441
MNP $15   MIP $25

Splash 'N Color Barbie Gift Set, 1997, Mattel
MNP $10   MIP $20

Spring Bouquet Barbie, 1993, Mattel, Model No. 3477
MNP $10   MIP $20

Spring Parade Barbie, 1992, Mattel, Model No. 7008
MNP $15   MIP $25

Spring Parade Barbie, Black, 1992, Mattel, Model No. 2257
MNP $15   MIP $25

(Mattel Photo)

Storybook Favorites, Alice and Mad Hatter (Kelly and Tommy), 2003, Mattel, Model No. 57577
MNP $10   MIP $30

Storybook Favorites, Goldilocks and the Three Bears (Kelly), 2001, Mattel, Model No. 29605
MNP $8   MIP $25

Storybook Favorites, Hansel & Gretel (Kelly and Tommy), 2000, Mattel, Model No. 28535
MNP $5   MIP $25

(Mattel Photo)

Storybook Favorites, Little Red Riding Hood (Kelly and Tommy), 2002, Mattel, Model No. 52899
MNP $10   MIP $20

(Mattel Photo)

Storybook Favorites, Mickey and Minnie Mouse (Kelly and Tommy), 2002, Mattel, Model No. 55502

MNP $10 MIP $25

Storybook Favorites, Raggedy Ann and Andy (Kelly and Tommy), 2000, Mattel, Model No. 24639

MNP $5 MIP $25

Style Set Bohemian Glamour Barbie, 2003, Mattel

MNP $25 MIP $40

Style Set Exotic Beauty Barbie, 2002, Mattel

MNP $25 MIP $40

Style Set Exotic Beauty Barbie Limited Edition, 2002, Mattel, w/Treasure Hunt jewelry

MNP $35 MIP $65

Style Set, Society Girl, White or Black, 2002, Mattel, Model No. 56203/56204

MNP $20 MIP $50

Superman Returns Barbie as Lois Lane, 2006, Mattel

MNP n/a MIP $14

Superman Returns Ken as Superman, 2006, Mattel, Model No. J2096

MNP n/a MIP $15

Sweet Spring Barbie, 1992, Mattel, Model No. 3208

MNP $10 MIP $20

Sydney 2000 Olympic Pin Collector, Black or White, 2000, Mattel, Model No. 25644/26302

MNP $20 MIP $30

Target 35th Anniversary Barbie, Black, 1997, Mattel, Model No. 176608

MNP $10 MIP $24

Target 35th Anniversary Barbie, White, 1997, Mattel, Model No. 16485

MNP $10 MIP $20

Target Baseball Date Barbie, 1993, Mattel, Model No. 4583

MNP $10 MIP $30

Target City Style #1, 1996, Mattel, Model No. 15612

MNP $8 MIP $15

Target City Style #2, 1997, Mattel, Model No. 17237

MNP $10 MIP $20

Target Club Wedd Barbie, Black, 1998, Mattel, Model No. 20423

MNP $10 MIP $20

Target Club Wedd Barbie, Blonde or Brunette, 1998, Mattel, Model No. 19717/19718

MNP $10 MIP $20

Target Cute 'n Cool, 1991, Mattel, Model No. 2954

MNP $8 MIP $30

Target Dazzlin' Date Barbie, 1992, Mattel, Model No. 3203

MNP $10 MIP $25

Target Easter Bunny Fun Barbie & Kelly, 1999, Mattel, Model No. 21720

MNP $15 MIP $25

Target Easter Bunny Gia, 2007, Mattel, yellow suit

MNP n/a MIP $15

Target Easter Bunny Kelly, 2007, Mattel, pink suit

MNP n/a MIP $15

Target Easter Bunny Tori, 2007, Mattel, purple suit

MNP n/a MIP $15

Target Easter Egg Hunt, 1998, Mattel, Model No. 19014

MNP $15 MIP $25

Target Easter Egg Party, White or Black, 2000, Mattel

MNP $15 MIP $25

Target Easter Garden Hunt Barbie and Kelly, 2001, Mattel

MNP $10 MIP $25

Target Easter Garden Kelly as Bunny, 2003, Mattel

MNP $8 MIP $15

Target Easter Garden Melody as Flower, 2003, Mattel

MNP $8 MIP $15

Target Easter Garden Melody as Lamb, 2003, Mattel

MNP $8 MIP $15

Target Easter Garden Nikki as Chick, 2003, Mattel

MNP $8 MIP $15

Target Easter Garden Tamika as Chick, 2003, Mattel

MNP $8 MIP $15

Target Gold and Lace Barbie, 1989, Mattel, Model No. 7476

MNP $10 MIP $30

Target Golden Evening, 1991, Mattel, Model No. 2587

MNP $6 MIP $45

Target Golf Date Barbie, 1993, Mattel, Model No. 10202

MNP $10 MIP $25

Target Halloween 2006 Kelly as Pumpkin, 2006, Mattel

MNP n/a MIP $15

Target Halloween 2006 Kelly as Spider, 2006, Mattel

MNP n/a MIP $15

Target Halloween 2006 Kelly as Witch, 2006, Mattel

MNP n/a MIP $15

Target Halloween 2006 Kelly as Witch, African-American, 2006, Mattel

MNP n/a MIP $15

Target Halloween 2006 Tommy as Mummy, 2006, Mattel

MNP n/a MIP $15

Target Halloween Fortune Barbie, 2003, Mattel

MNP $10 MIP $25

Target Halloween Fun Barbie & Kelly, White or Black, 1999, Mattel, Model No. 23460

MNP $15 MIP $25

Target Halloween Fun Li'l Friends of Kelly, 1999, Mattel, Model No. 23796

MNP $15 MIP $25

Target Halloween Goo-tiful Barbie, 2004, Mattel

MNP $10 MIP $20

Target Halloween Kelly as Pumpkin, 2006, Mattel

MNP n/a MIP $10

Target Halloween Kelly as Spider, 2006, Mattel

MNP n/a MIP $10

Target Halloween Kelly as Witch, 2006, Mattel

MNP n/a MIP $10

Target Halloween Kelly as Witch, African-American, 2006, Mattel

MNP n/a MIP $10

Target Halloween Party Barbie & Ken, Pirates, 1998, Mattel, Model No. 19874

MNP $20 MIP $40

Target Halloween Party Belinda as Black Cat, 2003, Mattel

MNP $8 MIP $20

Target Halloween Party Deidre (Pumpkin), 2000, Mattel, Model No. 28310

MNP $5 MIP $15

Target Halloween Party Deirdre as Pumpkin, 2002, Mattel
MNP $8   MIP $15

Target Halloween Party Deirdre as Pumpkin, 2003, Mattel
MNP $8   MIP $15

Target Halloween Party Jenny (Pumpkin), 2000, Mattel, Model No. 28308
MNP $5   MIP $15

Target Halloween Party Jenny as Genie, 2002, Mattel
MNP $8   MIP $20

Target Halloween Party Jenny as Witch, 2003, Mattel
MNP $8   MIP $20

Target Halloween Party Kayla (Ghost), 2000, Mattel, Model No. 28307
MNP $5   MIP $15

Target Halloween Party Kelly (Alien), 2000, Mattel, Model No. 28306
MNP $5   MIP $15

Target Halloween Party Kelly as Pumpkin, 2002, Mattel
MNP $8   MIP $20

Target Halloween Party Kelly as Spider, 2003, Mattel
MNP $8   MIP $20

Target Halloween Party Kelly as Witch, 2004, Mattel, white or African American
MNP $10   MIP $10

Target Halloween Party Kerstie as Pumpkin, 2004, Mattel
MNP $10   MIP $10

Target Halloween Party Lorena as Witch, 2002, Mattel
MNP $8   MIP $20

Target Halloween Party Melody as Tiger, 2004, Mattel
MNP $10   MIP $10

Target Halloween Party Nikki as Pumpkin, 2003, Mattel
MNP $8   MIP $20

Target Halloween Party Nikkie as Ghost, 2004, Mattel
MNP $10   MIP $10

Target Halloween Party Tommy (Cowboy), 2000, Mattel, Model No. 28309
MNP $5   MIP $15

Target Halloween Party Tommy as Dragon, 2003, Mattel
MNP $8   MIP $20

Target Halloween Party Tommy as Scarecrow, 2002, Mattel
MNP $8   MIP $20

Target Halloween Party Tommy as Vampire, 2004, Mattel
MNP $10   MIP $10

Target Halloween Tommy as Mummy, 2006, Mattel
MNP n/a   MIP $10

Target Halloween Trick or Chic Barbie, 2006, Mattel
MNP n/a   MIP $15

(KP Photo)

Target Happy Halloween Barbie & Kelly, 1997, Mattel, Model No. 17238
MNP $30   MIP $60

Target Party Pretty Barbie, 1990, Mattel, Model No. 5955
MNP $6   MIP $25

Target Pet Doctor Barbie, Brunette, 1996, Mattel, Model No. 16458
MNP $15   MIP $30

Target Pretty in Plaid Barbie, 1992, Mattel, Model No. 5413
MNP $15   MIP $30

Target Purrfectly Halloween Barbie, 2002, Mattel
MNP $10   MIP $25

Target Soccer Kelly & Tommy, 1999, Mattel
MNP $8   MIP $20

Target Steppin' Out Barbie, 1995, Mattel, Model No. 14110
MNP $8   MIP $20

Target Valentine Barbie, 1996, Mattel, Model No. 15172
MNP $8   MIP $20

Target Valentine Date Barbie, 1998, Mattel, Model No. 18306
MNP $8   MIP $20

Target Valentine Kelly and Friend, 2001, Mattel
MNP $5   MIP $15

Target Valentine Lil Heart Kelly, Jenny or Balinda, 2003, Mattel
MNP $8   MIP $15

Target Valentine Romance Barbie, 1997, Mattel, Model No. 16059
MNP $8   MIP $20

Target Valentine Style Barbie, Black, 1999, Mattel, Model No. 22150
MNP $8   MIP $18

Target Valentine Style Barbie, White, 1999, Mattel, Model No. 20465
MNP $8   MIP $15

Target w/Love Barbie, 2000, Mattel
MNP $8   MIP $15

Target Wild Style Barbie, 1992, Mattel, Model No. 0411
MNP $10   MIP $24

Target Xhilaration Barbie, White or Black, 1999, Mattel
MNP $15   MIP $35

Tarina Tarantino Barbie, 2008, Mattel, Model No. L9602
MNP $35   MIP $75

Tennis Star Barbie & Ken, 1988, Mattel, Model No. 7801
MNP $18   MIP $40

The Pirate Barbie, 2008, Mattel, Model No. K7972
MNP $110   MIP $225

The Waltz Barbie & Ken Gift Set, 2003, Mattel
MNP $40   MIP $75

Tiff Pose N' Play, 1972, Mattel, foreign, Model No. 1199
MNP $125   MIP $350

Timeless Sentiments Angel of Hope, 1999, Mattel, Model No. 22955
MNP $60   MIP $125

Timeless Sentiments Angel of Joy, White or Black, 1998, Mattel, Model No. 19633/20929
MNP $60   MIP $125

Timeless Sentiments Angel of Peace, 1999, Mattel, Model No. 24240
MNP $60   MIP $125

Timeless Sentiments Angel of Peace, Black, 1999, Mattel, Model No. 24241
MNP $60   MIP $125

Titanic Rose, 2007, Mattel
MNP n/a   MIP $75

Todd Oldham (Designer), 1999, Mattel
MNP $35   MIP $70

(KP Photo)

Together Forever, Romeo & Juliet, 1998, Mattel, Model No. 19364

MNP $50   MIP $100

(KP Photo)

Together Forever, King Arthur and Queen Guinevere, 1999, Mattel, Model No. 23880

MNP $50   MIP $100

Tommy as Elvis, 2004, Mattel

MNP $10   MIP $25

Tooth Fairy Barbie, 2007, Mattel

MNP n/a   MIP $35

Top Model Barbie, 2007, Mattel

MNP n/a   MIP $25

Top Model Summer, Redhead, 2007, Mattel

MNP n/a   MIP $25

Top Model Teresa, Brunette, 2007, Mattel

MNP n/a   MIP $25

Toys R Us 101 Dalmatians Barbie, Black, 1999, Mattel, Model No. 17601

MNP $12   MIP $20

(KP Photo)

Toys R Us 101 Dalmatians Barbie, White, 1997, Mattel, Model No. 17248

MNP $15   MIP $28

Toys R Us 35th Anniversary Midge, Senior Prom, 1998, Mattel, Model No. 18976

MNP $25   MIP $40

Toys R Us Astronaut Barbie, Black, 1994, Mattel, Model No. 12150

MNP $10   MIP $20

Toys R Us Astronaut Barbie, White, 1994, Mattel, Model No. 12149

MNP $10   MIP $20

Toys R Us Barbie as DC Comics Bat Girl w/Batcycle, 2004, Mattel

MNP $10   MIP $30

(KP Photo)

Toys R Us Barbie for President, 1992, Mattel, Model No. 3722

MNP $17   MIP $45

Toys R Us Barbie for President, 2000, Mattel, Model No. 3940

MNP $5   MIP $18

Toys R Us Barbie Renaissance Rose Gift Set, 2000, Mattel, Model No. 28633

MNP $15   MIP $35

Toys R Us Bath Time Skipper, 1992, Mattel, Model No. 7970

MNP $12   MIP $25

Toys R Us Beauty Pageant Skipper, 1991, Mattel, Model No. 9342

MNP $10   MIP $25

Toys R Us Bicyclin' Barbie, Black or White, 1995, Mattel

MNP $15   MIP $25

Toys R Us Birthday Fun Kelly Gift Set, 1996, Mattel

MNP $15   MIP $28

Toys R Us Cool 'N Sassy, Black, 1992, Mattel, Model No. 4110

MNP $10   MIP $20

Toys R Us Cool 'N Sassy, White, 1992, Mattel, Model No. 1490

MNP $10   MIP $20

Toys R Us Crystal Splendor, Black, 1996, Mattel, Model No. 15137

MNP $10   MIP $25

Toys R Us Crystal Splendor, White, 1996, Mattel, Model No. 15136

MNP $12   MIP $25

Toys R Us Dream Date Barbie, 1982, Mattel, Model No. 9180

MNP $7   MIP $30

Toys R Us Dream Date Ken, 1982, Mattel, Model No. 4077

MNP $5   MIP $30

Toys R Us Dream Date P.J., 1982, Mattel, Model No. 5869

MNP $8   MIP $40

Toys R Us Dream Date Skipper, 1990, Mattel, Model No. 1075

MNP $10   MIP $25

Toys R Us Dream Time Barbie, 1988, Mattel, Model No. 9180

MNP $10   MIP $30

Toys R Us Dream Wedding Gift Set, Black, 1993, Mattel, Model No. 10713

MNP $22   MIP $45

Toys R Us Dream Wedding Gift Set, White, 1993, Mattel, Model No. 10712

MNP $20   MIP $45

Toys R Us Faerie Queen of Ireland, 2004, Mattel

MNP $10   MIP $30

Toys R Us Fashion Brights Barbie, White or Black, 1992, Mattel, Model No. 1882/4112

MNP $10   MIP $20

Toys R Us Fashion Fun Barbie Gift Set, 1999, Mattel

MNP $15   MIP $25

(KP Photo)

(KP Photo)

Toys R Us Firefighter Barbie, White or Black, 1995, Mattel, w/yellow uniform and hat and dalmatian puppy, Model No. 13553/13472

MNP $10   MIP $25

Toys R Us Gardening Fun Barbie & Kelly Gift Set, 1997, Mattel, Model No. 17242

MNP $12   MIP $23

Toys R Us Got Milk? Barbie, White or Black, 1996, Mattel, Model No. 15721/15122

MNP $8   MIP $20

Toys R Us Gran Gala Teresa, 1997, Mattel, Model No. 17239

MNP $8   MIP $15

Toys R Us Harley-Davidson Barbie #1, 1997, Mattel, Model No. 17692

MNP $150   MIP $325

Toys R Us Harley-Davidson Barbie #2, 1998, Mattel, Model No. 20441

MNP $75   MIP $150

Toys R Us Harley-Davidson Barbie #3, 1999, Mattel, Model No. 22256

MNP $25   MIP $60

Toys R Us Harley-Davidson Barbie #4, 2000, Mattel, Model No. 25637

MNP $25   MIP $45

Toys R Us Harley-Davidson Barbie #5, Black, 2001, Mattel, Model No. 29208

MNP $25   MIP $60

Toys R Us Harley-Davidson Barbie #5, White, 2001, Mattel, Model No. 29207

MNP $25   MIP $45

Toys R Us Harley-Davidson Ken #1, 1999, Mattel, Model No. 22255

MNP $25   MIP $60

Toys R Us Harley-Davidson Ken #2, 2000, Mattel, Model No. 25638

MNP $15   MIP $40

Toys R Us I'm A Toys R Us Kid Barbie, White or Black, 1998, Mattel, Model No. 18895/21040

MNP $15   MIP $30

Toys R Us International Pen Friend Barbie, 1995, Mattel, Model No. 13558

MNP $7   MIP $16

Toys R Us Love to Read Barbie, 1993, Mattel, Model No. 10507

MNP $12   MIP $40

Toys R Us Malt Shop Barbie, 1993, Mattel, Model No. 4581

MNP $10   MIP $25

Toys R Us Moonlight Magic Barbie, Black, 1993, Mattel, Model No. 10609

MNP $15   MIP $55

Toys R Us Moonlight Magic Barbie, White, 1993, Mattel, Model No. 10608

MNP $15   MIP $65

Toys R Us My Size Bride Barbie, Red Hair, 1995, Mattel, Model No. 15649

MNP $60   MIP $135

Toys R Us Native Spirit Barbie Spirit of the Sky, 2003, Mattel

MNP $20   MIP $50

Toys R Us Native Spirit Barbie Spirit of the Water, 2002, Mattel

MNP $25   MIP $50

Toys R Us Olympic Gymnast Barbie, Red Hair, box w/out Special Edition Marking, 1996, Mattel, Model No. 15725

MNP $15   MIP $30

Toys R Us Oreo Fun Barbie, 1997, Mattel, Model No. 18511

MNP $8   MIP $18

Toys R Us Paleontologist Barbie, White or Black, 1997, Mattel, Model No. 17240/17241

MNP $12   MIP $24

Toys R Us Party Time Barbie, White or Black, 1994, Mattel, Model No. 12243

MNP $10   MIP $20

Toys R Us Pepsi Spirit Barbie, 1989, Mattel, Model No. 4869

MNP $18   MIP $70

Toys R Us Pepsi Spirit Skipper, 1989, Mattel, Model No. 4867

MNP $15   MIP $65

Toys R Us POG Barbie, 1995, Mattel, Model No. 13239

MNP $7   MIP $15

(KP Photo)

Toys R Us Police Officer Barbie, Black, 1993, Mattel, Model No. 10689

MNP $15   MIP $65

Toys R Us Police Officer Barbie, White, 1993, Mattel, Model No. 10688

MNP $15   MIP $70

Toys R Us Purple Passion, Black, 1995, Mattel, Model No. 13554

MNP $10   MIP $30

Toys R Us Purple Passion, White, 1995, Mattel, Model No. 13555

MNP $10   MIP $30

Toys R Us Radiant in Red Barbie, Black, 1992, Mattel, Model No. 4113

MNP $12   MIP $55

Toys R Us Radiant in Red Barbie, White, 1992, Mattel, Model No. 1276

MNP $12   MIP $55

Toys R Us Sapphire Sophisticate, 1997, Mattel, Model No. 16692
MNP $12   MIP $25

Toys R Us School Fun, 1991, Mattel, Model No. 2721
MNP $6   MIP $40

Toys R Us School Spirit Barbie, Black, 1993, Mattel, Model No. 10683
MNP $10   MIP $30

Toys R Us School Spirit Barbie, White, 1993, Mattel, Model No. 10682
MNP $10   MIP $25

Toys R Us Share A Smile Barbie, 1997, Mattel, Model No. 17247
MNP $7   MIP $15

Toys R Us Share A Smile Becky, 1997, Mattel, Model No. 15761
MNP $15   MIP $28

Toys R Us Share A Smile Christie, 1997, Mattel, Model No. 17372
MNP $7   MIP $15

Toys R Us Show and Ride Barbie, 1988, Mattel, Model No. 7799
MNP $10   MIP $35

Toys R Us Sign Language Barbie, White or Black, 2000, Mattel
MNP $8   MIP $20

Toys R Us Society Style Emerald Elegance, 1994, Mattel, Model No. 12322
MNP $15   MIP $40

Toys R Us Society Style Emerald Enchantment, 1997, Mattel, Model No. 17443
MNP $25   MIP $50

Toys R Us Society Style Sapphire Dream, 1995, Mattel, Model No. 13256
MNP $50   MIP $70

Toys R Us Space Camp Barbie, White or Black, 1999, Mattel, Model No. 22435/22246
MNP $12   MIP $28

Toys R Us Spellbound Lover (Iseult), 2005, Mattel
MNP $15   MIP $30

Toys R Us Spirit of the Earth Barbie, 2001, Mattel
MNP $25   MIP $75

Toys R Us Spots 'N Dots Barbie, 1993, Mattel, Model No. 10491
MNP $12   MIP $35

Toys R Us Spots 'N Dots Teresa, 1993, Mattel, Model No. 10885
MNP $12   MIP $40

Toys R Us Spring Parade Barbie, White or Black, 1992, Mattel, Model No. 7008/2257
MNP $15   MIP $30

Toys R Us Sunflower Barbie, 1995, Mattel, Model No. 13488
MNP $9   MIP $20

Toys R Us Sunflower Teresa, 1995, Mattel, Model No. 13489
MNP $9   MIP $20

Toys R Us Sweet Romance, 1991, Mattel, Model No. 2917
MNP $8   MIP $30

Toys R Us Sweet Roses, 1989, Mattel, Model No. 7635
MNP $7   MIP $25

Toys R Us The Bard, 2004, Mattel
MNP n/a   MIP $10

Toys R Us Totally Hair Courtney, 1992, Mattel, Model No. 1433
MNP $10   MIP $25

Toys R Us Totally Hair Skipper, 1992, Mattel, Model No. 1430
MNP $10   MIP $25

Toys R Us Totally Hair Whitney, 1992, Mattel, Model No. 7735
MNP $20   MIP $40

Toys R Us Travelin' Sisters Gift Set, 1995, Mattel, Model No. 14073
MNP $30   MIP $65

Toys R Us Vacation Sensation Barbie, Blue, 1986, Mattel, Model No. 1675
MNP $10   MIP $40

Toys R Us Vacation Sensation Barbie, Pink, 1989, Mattel, Model No. 1675
MNP $12   MIP $48

Toys R Us Wedding Fantasy Barbie & Ken Gift Set, 1997, Mattel, Model No. 17243
MNP $20   MIP $45

Toys R Us Winter Fun Barbie, 1990, Mattel, Model No. 5949
MNP $10   MIP $40

Toys R Us/FAO Schwarz Sea Holiday Barbie #1, w/Lip Gloss, 1993, Mattel
MNP $15   MIP $30

Toys R Us/FAO Schwarz Sea Holiday Barbie #2, w/Lip Gloss, 1993, Mattel
MNP $15   MIP $24

Toys R Us/FAO/JCPenney, Winter Sports Barbie, 1995, Mattel
MNP $15   MIP $30

Toys R Us/FAO/JCPenney, Winter Sports Ken, 1995, Mattel
MNP $15   MIP $30

Trail Blazin' Barbie, 1991, Mattel, Model No. 2783
MNP $10   MIP $25

Tree Trimming Barbie, White or Black, 1999, Mattel
MNP $5   MIP $15

Trend Forecaster Barbie, 1999, Mattel, Model No. 22833
MNP $20   MIP $45

Tropical Barbie Deluxe Gift Set, 1985, Mattel, Model No. 2996
MNP $20   MIP $45

Tutti and Todd Sundae Treat Set, 1966, Mattel, Model No. 3556
MNP $150   MIP $350

Tutti Me n' My Dog, 1966, Mattel, Model No. 3554
MNP $150   MIP $350

Tutti Nighty Night Sleep Tight, 1965, Mattel, Model No. 3553
MNP $100   MIP $300

Twirley Curls Barbie Gift Set, 1982, Mattel, Model No. 4097
MNP $30   MIP $85

Twist and Turn Far Out Barbie, 1999, Mattel, Model No. 21911
MNP $20   MIP $40

Vera Wang #1, Bride, 1998, Mattel, Model No. 19788
MNP $125   MIP $250

Vera Wang #2, Lavender Dress, 1999, Mattel, Model No. 23027
MNP $55   MIP $140

Vera Wang, The Romanticist, 2009, Mattel, Model No. L9664
MNP $250   MIP $500

Versace Barbie, 2004, Mattel
MNP $50   MIP $75

Versus by Versace Barbie, 2004, Mattel
MNP $25   MIP $80

Very Violet Barbie, 1992, Mattel, Model No. 1859
MNP $10   MIP $20

Victorian Barbie w/Cedric Bear, 2000, Mattel
MNP $25   MIP $59

Vintage Reproduction 45th Anniversary Ken, 2006, Mattel
MNP n/a   MIP $25

Vintage Reproduction Barbie Learns to Cook, Blonde, 2007, Mattel
MNP n/a   MIP $50

Vintage Reproduction Barbie Learns to Cook, Brunette, 2007, Mattel, limited edition, 999 pieces
MNP n/a   MIP $200

Vintage Reproduction Campus Sweetheart, 2008, Mattel, Model No. L9600
MNP $25   MIP $50

Vintage Reproduction Career Girl, 2007, Mattel
MNP n/a MIP $50

Vintage Reproduction Evening Gala, 2007, Mattel
MNP n/a MIP $50

Vintage Reproduction Friday Night Dream Date Barbie & Ken Gift Set, 2006, Mattel
MNP n/a MIP $100

Vintage Reproduction Knitting Pretty Barbie & Skipper Gift Set, 2007, Mattel
MNP n/a MIP $100

Vintage Reproduction Most Mod Party Becky, 2009, Mattel, Model No. N5012
MNP $60 MIP $120

Vintage Reproduction Picnic Set Barbie, 2006, Mattel
MNP n/a MIP $50

Vintage Reproduction Red, White & Warm, Brunette, 2007, Mattel
MNP n/a MIP $50

Vintage Reproduction Red, White & Warm, Christie, 2007, Mattel, platinum edition
MNP n/a MIP $200

Vintage Reproduction Sleepytime Gal, 2007, Mattel
MNP n/a MIP $80

Vintage Reproduction Sparkling Pink Gift Set, 2009, Mattel, Model No. N6591
MNP $55 MIP $110

Vintage Reproduction Stacey Night Lightning, 2006, Mattel, Barbie Convention Exclusive, blond
MNP n/a MIP $150

Vintage Reproduction Stacey Nite Lightning, 2006, Mattel
MNP n/a MIP $60

Walking Jamie Strollin' in Style Gift Set, 1972, Mattel, Model No. 1247
MNP $300 MIP $600

Wal-Mart 25th Year Pink Jubilee Barbie, 1987, Mattel, Model No. 4589
MNP $20 MIP $50

Wal-Mart 35th Anniversary Barbie, Black or White, Mattel, Model No. 17616/17245
MNP $10 MIP $24

Wal-Mart 35th Anniversary Teresa, 1997, Mattel, Model No. 17617
MNP $12 MIP $25

Wal-Mart Anniversary Star Barbie, 1992, Mattel, Model No. 2282
MNP $15 MIP $30

Wal-Mart Ballroom Beauty, 1991, Mattel, Model No. 3678
MNP $8 MIP $30

Wal-Mart Bathtime Fun Barbie, 1991, Mattel, Model No. 9601
MNP $5 MIP $25

Wal-Mart Country Bride, 1995, Mattel, Model No. 13014
MNP $8 MIP $15

Wal-Mart Country Bride, Black, 1995, Mattel, Model No. 13015
MNP $8 MIP $15

Wal-Mart Country Bride, Hispanic, 1995, Mattel, Model No. 13016
MNP $8 MIP $15

Wal-Mart Country Western Star Barbie, Black or Hispanic, 1994, Mattel, Model No. 12096
MNP $12 MIP $30

Wal-Mart Country Western Star Barbie, White, 1994, Mattel, Model No. 12097
MNP $10 MIP $25

Wal-Mart Dream Fantasy, 1990, Mattel, Model No. 7335
MNP $8 MIP $35

Wal-Mart Exclusive Barbie 2007, African-American, 2007, Mattel
MNP n/a MIP $35

Wal-Mart Exclusive Barbie 2007, Blonde, 2007, Mattel
MNP n/a MIP $35

Wal-Mart Exclusive Zodiac Barbie, 2004, Mattel, Aries, Taurus, Gemini, Cancer, Leo, Virgo
MNP $25 MIP $50

Wal-Mart Exclusive Zodiac Barbie, 2005, Mattel, Aquarius, Sagittarius, Model No. C6251
MNP $25 MIP $50

Wal-Mart Frills and Fantasy Barbie, 1988, Mattel, Model No. 1374
MNP $7 MIP $45

Wal-Mart Jewel Skating Barbie, 1999, Mattel, Model No. 23239
MNP $6 MIP $12

Wal-Mart Lavender Look Barbie, 1989, Mattel, Model No. 3963
MNP $7 MIP $30

Wal-Mart Portrait in Blue Barbie, Black, 1998, Mattel, Model No. 19356
MNP $10 MIP $20

Wal-Mart Portrait in Blue Barbie, White, 1998, Mattel, Model No. 19355
MNP $8 MIP $18

Wal-Mart Pretty Choices Barbie, Black, 1997, Mattel, Model No. 18018
MNP $8 MIP $18

Wal-Mart Pretty Choices Barbie, Blonde or Brunette, 1997, Mattel, Model No. 17971/18019
MNP $8 MIP $18

Wal-Mart Puzzle Craze Barbie, White or Black, 1998, Mattel, Model No. 20164/20165
MNP $6 MIP $14

Wal-Mart Puzzle Craze Teresa, 1998, Mattel, Model No. 20166
MNP $6 MIP $14

Wal-Mart Shopping Time Barbie, Black or White, 1997, Mattel, Model No. 18231/18230
MNP $7 MIP $15

Wal-Mart Shopping Time Teresa, 1997, Mattel, Model No. 18232
MNP $7 MIP $15

Wal-Mart Skating Star Barbie, 1996, Mattel, Model No. 15510
MNP $10 MIP $15

Wal-Mart Star Skater Barbie, White or Black, 2000, Mattel
MNP $5 MIP $15

Wal-Mart Superstar Barbie, Black, 1993, Mattel, Model No. 10711
MNP $15 MIP $40

Wal-Mart Superstar Barbie, White, 1993, Mattel, Model No. 10592
MNP $15 MIP $30

Wal-Mart Sweet Magnolia Barbie, Black, White or Hispanic, 1996, Mattel, Model No. 15653/15652/15654
MNP $9 MIP $15

Wal-Mart the Birthstone Collection, 2003, Mattel, 12 different dolls
MNP $10 MIP $25

Wal-Mart Tooth Fairy #1, 1994, Mattel, Model No. 11645
MNP $7 MIP $20

Wal-Mart Tooth Fairy #2, 1995, Mattel, Model No. 11645
MNP $5 MIP $20

Wal-Mart Tooth Fairy #3, 1998, Mattel, Model No. 17246
MNP $6 MIP $14

Walt Disney World Animal Kingdom Barbie, White or Black, 1998, Mattel, Model No. 20363/20989
MNP $15 MIP $30

Walt Disney World Barbie 25th Anniversary, 1996, Mattel, Model No. 16525
MNP $15 MIP $30

Walt Disney World Disney Fun 1994, 1994, Mattel, Model No. 11650
MNP $15   MIP $50

Walt Disney World Disney Fun 1995, 1995, Mattel, Model No. 13533
MNP $15   MIP $40

Walt Disney World Disney Fun 1997, 1997, Mattel, Model No. 17058
MNP $8   MIP $20

Walt Disney World Millennium Barbie, White or Black, 2000, Mattel
MNP $5   MIP $15

Walt Disney World Resort Vacation Barbie, Ken, Tommy, Kelly, 1998, Mattel, Model No. 20315
MNP $35   MIP $80

Walt Disney World Toontown Stacie, 1994, Mattel, Model No. 11587
MNP $15   MIP $30

Warner Bros. Barbie Loves Tweety, 1999, Mattel, Model No. 21632
MNP $8   MIP $22

Warner Bros. Scooby-Doo Barbie, 2001, Mattel, Model No. 27966
MNP $5   MIP $15

Wedding Fantasy Gift Set, 1993, Mattel, Model No. 10924
MNP $50   MIP $125

Wedding Flower Blushing Orchid Bride, 1997, Mattel
MNP $100   MIP $200

Wedding Flower Romantic Rose Bride, 1996, Mattel
MNP $100   MIP $220

Wedding Party Gift Set, Six Dolls, 1991, Mattel, Model No. 9852
MNP $45   MIP $125

Wedgwood Barbie #1, Blue Dress, 2000, Mattel, Model No. 25641
MNP $40   MIP $80

Wedgwood Barbie #2, Pink Dress, Black, 2001, Mattel, Model No. 50824
MNP $30   MIP $85

Wedgwood Barbie #2, Pink Dress, White, 2001, Mattel, Model No. 50823
MNP $30   MIP $85

Wessco Carnival Cruise Barbie, 1997, Mattel, Model No. 15186
MNP $25   MIP $40

Wessco International Traveler #1, 1995, Mattel, Model No. 13912
MNP $35   MIP $60

Wessco International Traveler #2, 1996, Mattel, Model No. 16158
MNP $25   MIP $50

Western Chic Barbie, 2002, Mattel, Model No. 55487
MNP $20   MIP $50

Western Fun Gift Set Barbie & Ken, 1989, Mattel, Model No. 5408
MNP $12   MIP $30

Western Fun Gift Set Barbie & Ken, 1990, Mattel, Model No. 5408
MNP $12   MIP $30

Western Plains Barbie, 2000, Mattel, Model No. 23205
MNP $75   MIP $150

Wind Rider Barbie, 2006, Mattel
MNP n/a   MIP $150

Winn-Dixie Party Pink Barbie, 1989, Mattel, Model No. 7637
MNP $7   MIP $25

Winn-Dixie Pink Sensation, 1990, Mattel, Model No. 5410
MNP $6   MIP $20

Winn-Dixie Southern Beauty, 1991, Mattel, Model No. 3284
MNP $10   MIP $25

Winter Concert Barbie, 2002, Mattel
MNP $40   MIP $80

Winter Princess #1 Winter Princess, 1993, Mattel, Model No. 10655
MNP $35   MIP $175

Winter Princess #2 Evergreen Princess, 1994, Mattel, Model No. 12123
MNP $45   MIP $95

Winter Princess #3 Peppermint Princess, 1995, Mattel, Model No. 13598
MNP $35   MIP $175

Winter Princess #4 Jewel Princess, 1996, Mattel, Model No. 15826
MNP $40   MIP $80

Winter Princess #5 Midnight Princess, 1997, Mattel, Model No. 17780
MNP $35   MIP $175

Wizard of Oz Barbie, Cowardly Lion, 2009, Mattel, Model No. N6562
MNP $20   MIP $40

Wizard of Oz Barbie, Dorothy, 2009, Mattel, Model No. N6558
MNP $25   MIP $50

Wizard of Oz Barbie, Glinda, 2009, Mattel, Model No. N6558
MNP $20   MIP $40

Wizard of Oz Barbie, Scarecrow, 2009, Mattel, Model No. N6562
MNP $20   MIP $40

Wizard of Oz Barbie, Tin Man, 2009, Mattel, Model No. N6562
MNP $20   MIP $40

Wizard of Oz Barbie, Wicked Witch of the West, 2009, Mattel, Model No. N6561
MNP $20   MIP $40

Wizard of Oz, Cowardly Lion 2007, 2007, Mattel
MNP n/a   MIP $25

Wizard of Oz, Dorothy 2007, 2007, Mattel
MNP n/a   MIP $25

Wizard of Oz, Glinda 2007, 2007, Mattel
MNP n/a   MIP $25

Wizard of Oz, Munchkins 3-pak 2007, 2007, Mattel
MNP n/a   MIP $25

Wizard of Oz, Scarecrow 2007, 2007, Mattel
MNP n/a   MIP $25

Wizard of Oz, Tinman 2007, 2007, Mattel
MNP n/a   MIP $25

Wizard of Oz, Wicked Witch of the West, 2007, Mattel
MNP n/a   MIP $25

Wizard of Oz, Winkie Guard, 2007, Mattel, w/Flying Monkey, Toys R Us Exclusive
MNP n/a   MIP $40

Woolworth's Special Expressions, Black, Blue Dress, 1991, Mattel, Model No. 2583
MNP $4   MIP $10

Woolworth's Special Expressions, Black, Peach Dress, 1992, Mattel, Model No. 3200
MNP $5   MIP $30

Woolworth's Special Expressions, Black, Pink Dress, 1990, Mattel, Model No. 5505
MNP $4   MIP $10

Woolworth's Special Expressions, Black, White Dress, 1989, Mattel, Model No. 7326
MNP $5   MIP $20

Woolworth's Special Expressions, Blue Dress, Pastel Print, 1993, Mattel, Model No. 10048
MNP $5   MIP $15

Woolworth's Special Expressions, Pink Dress, 1990, Mattel, Model No. 5504
MNP $3   MIP $20

Woolworth's Special Expressions, White, 1989, Mattel, Model No. 4842
MNP $5   MIP $20

Woolworth's Special Expressions, White, Blue Dress, 1991, Mattel, Model No. 2582

MNP $4   MIP $15

Woolworth's Special Expressions, White, Peach Dress, 1992, Mattel, Model No. 3197

MNP $5   MIP $20

Woolworth's Sweet Lavender Barbie, Black or White, 1992, Mattel, Model No. 2523/2522

MNP $12   MIP $28

Workin' Out Barbie Gift Set, 1997, Mattel

MNP $10   MIP $25

XO Valentine Barbie, 2003, Mattel

MNP $8   MIP $15

XXXOOO Barbie Doll, 2000, Mattel

MNP $8   MIP $20

Zac Posen Barbie/Ken Gift Set, 2007, Mattel, FAO Schwarz and Dealer's Exclusive

MNP n/a   MIP $175

MATTEL DOLLS, NON-BARBIE

1970s Cher, 2007, Mattel, Model No. L3548

MNP $50   MIP $100

1980s Cher, 2007, Mattel, Model No. K7903

MNP $50   MIP $100

Audrey Hepburn, Breakfast At Tiffany's, black dress, 1998, Mattel

MNP $30   MIP $50

Audrey Hepburn, Pink Princess, 1998, Mattel

MNP $25   MIP $40

Barbra Streisand, 2010, Mattel, Model No. N6574

MNP $30   MIP $55

Betty Boop #1 Glamour Girl, 2001, Mattel, Model No. 29733

MNP $15   MIP $25

Bob Mackie Cher, 2001, Mattel, Model No. 29049

MNP $15   MIP $40

Buffy and Mrs. Beasley, 1968, Mattel, Model No. 3577

MNP $125   MIP $275

Carol Burnett, 2009, Mattel, Model No. N4986

MNP $25   MIP $50

Chatty Cathy, 1999 Reissue, 1999, Mattel, Model No. 23782

MNP $50   MIP $100

Chatty Cathy, Holiday, 1999, Mattel, Model No. 23783

MNP $50   MIP $125

(Mattel Photo)

Clark Gable as Rhett Butler, 2002, Mattel, Model No. 53854

MNP $30   MIP $70

Coca-Cola Holiday Series, Santa Claus, 1999, Mattel, Model No. 23288

MNP $25   MIP $60

Daytime Drama, Erica Kane #1, 1998, Mattel

MNP $20   MIP $50

Daytime Drama, Erica Kane #2, 1999, Mattel

MNP $20   MIP $45

Daytime Drama, Marlena Evans, 1999, Mattel

MNP $20   MIP $45

Destiny's Child Set of 3, 2005, Mattel, Beyonce, Kelly and Michelle, Model No. H7267

MNP $100   MIP $200

Diana Ross, 2004, Mattel

MNP $75   MIP $150

Elizabeth Taylor as Cleopatra, 1999, Mattel

MNP $35   MIP $60

Elizabeth Taylor in Father of the Bride, 2000, Mattel, Model No. 26836

MNP $30   MIP $70

Elvis and Pricilla, 2008, Mattel, Model No. L9632

MNP $40   MIP $85

Elvis Presley #1, 1998, Mattel, Model No. 20544

MNP $20   MIP $50

Elvis Presley #2 The Army Years, 1999, Mattel, Model No. 21912

MNP $20   MIP $50

(Mattel Photo)

Elvis Presley #4 King of Rock 'N Roll, 2002, Mattel, Model No. 53869

MNP $20   MIP $40

Elvis Presley, Jailhouse Rock, 2009, Mattel, Model No. R4156

MNP $20   MIP $45

Flapper Minnie Mouse, 2001, Mattel, Model No. 29734

MNP $30   MIP $60

Frank Sinatra The Recording Years, 2001, Mattel

MNP $15   MIP $35

Goldie Hawn, Blonde Ambition, 2009, Mattel, Model No. N8134

MNP $20   MIP $45

Grease, Cha Cha, 2008, Mattel, Model No. M7505

MNP $35   MIP $75

Grease, Frenchy Dance Off, 2008, Mattel, Model No. M3256

MNP $20   MIP $40

Grease, Frenchy Race Day, 2008, Mattel, Model No. M0682

MNP $20   MIP $40

Grease, Rizzo Dance Off, 2008, Mattel, Model No. M3255

MNP $20   MIP $40

Grease, Rizzo Race Day, 2008, Mattel, Model No. M0681

MNP $20   MIP $40

Grease, Sandy Dance Off, 2008, Mattel, Model No. M3254

MNP $20   MIP $40

Grease, Sandy Race Day, 2008, Mattel, Model No. M0683

MNP $20   MIP $40

Great Villains, Captain Hook (Peter Pan), 1999, Mattel

MNP $30   MIP $75

Great Villains, Cruella DeVil, Power in Pinstripes, 1996, Mattel, Model No. 16295
MNP $35   MIP $75

Great Villains, Cruella DeVil, Ruthless in Red, 1997, Mattel
MNP $35   MIP $75

Great Villains, Evil Queen (Snow White), 1998, Mattel, Model No. 18626
MNP $30   MIP $75

Great Villains, Maleficent (Sleeping Beauty), 1999, Mattel
MNP $25   MIP $75

Great Villains, Ursula (Little Mermaid), 1997, Mattel, Model No. 17575
MNP $30   MIP $75

Heidi Klum, 2009, Mattel, Model No. N8135
MNP $20   MIP $45

I Love Lucy Sales Resistance, 2004, Mattel, Model No. B3451
MNP $75   MIP $150

I Love Lucy, Ballet Doll, 2009, Mattel, Model No. N6566
MNP $20   MIP $45

I Love Lucy, Be a Pal, 2002, Mattel, Model No. 52737
MNP $20   MIP $40

I Love Lucy, Job Switching, 1999, Mattel, Model No. 21268
MNP $75   MIP $175

I Love Lucy, L.A. At Last, 2003, Mattel, Model No. B1078
MNP $75   MIP $150

I Love Lucy, Lucille Ball, 2008, Mattel, Model No. N2691
MNP $45   MIP $90

I Love Lucy, Lucy and Ricky 50th Anniversary Dolls, 2000, Mattel
MNP $25   MIP $75

(Mattel Photo)

I Love Lucy, Lucy Gets a Paris Gown, 2003, Mattel, Model No. B0313
MNP $20   MIP $40

I Love Lucy, Lucy Gets in the Movies, 2006, Mattel, Model No. J0878
MNP $65   MIP $130

I Love Lucy, Lucy the Operetta, 2005, Mattel, Model No. G8057
MNP $35   MIP $70

I Love Lucy, Lucy's Italian Movie, 2000, Mattel, Model No. 25527
MNP $75   MIP $125

I Love Lucy, The Audition, 2007, Mattel, Model No. L8808
MNP $45   MIP $90

I Love Lucy, Vitameatavegemin, 1998, Mattel
MNP $25   MIP $45

Jolly Holiday Mary Poppins, 2000, Mattel
MNP $20   MIP $40

Ladies of the 80s, Cyndi Lauper, 2010, Mattel, Model No. R4460
MNP $15   MIP $35

Ladies of the 80s, Debbie Harry, 2010, Mattel, Model No. R4459
MNP $15   MIP $35

Ladies of the 80s, Joan Jett, 2010, Mattel, Model No. R4461
MNP $15   MIP $35

Lucy and Ethel Gift Set, 2007, Mattel, Model No. K8670
MNP $65   MIP $130

Lucy and Ethel Gift Set, The Chocolate Factory, 2008, Mattel, Model No. L9585
MNP $30   MIP $65

Marilyn Monroe, 2002, Mattel, Model No. 53873
MNP $20   MIP $35

Marilyn Monroe, Blond Ambition, 2009, Mattel, Model No. N4987
MNP $25   MIP $50

Mary Poppins, Bert, 2007, Mattel, Model No. M0685
MNP $15   MIP $30

Mary Poppins, Mary, 2007, Mattel, Model No. M0672
MNP $15   MIP $30

Rosie O'Donnell, 1999, Mattel
MNP $10   MIP $25

Tinker Bell, 2001, Mattel, Model No. 29735
MNP $20   MIP $40

Twilight, Bella Swann, 2009, Mattel, Model No. R4162
MNP $15   MIP $30

Twilight, Edward Cullen, 2009, Mattel, Model No. R4161
MNP $15   MIP $30

Vivien Leigh Scarlett O'Hara #1 Barbecue at Twelve Oaks, 2001, Mattel, Model No. 29910
MNP $25   MIP $45

Vivien Leigh Scarlett O'Hara #2 Peachtree St. Drapery Dress, 2001, Mattel, Model No. 29771
MNP $25   MIP $45

PORCELAIN BARBIES

30th Anniversary Ken, 1991, Mattel, Model No. 1110
MNP $135   MIP $275

30th Anniversary Midge, 1993, Mattel, Model No. 7957
MNP $40   MIP $65

30th Anniversary Skipper, 1994, Mattel, Model No. 11396
MNP $125   MIP $250

Benefit Performance Barbie, 1988, Mattel, Model No. 5475
MNP $150   MIP $350

Blue Rhapsody, First Porcelain Barbie, 1986, Mattel, Model No. 1708
MNP $200   MIP $450

Blushing Orchid Bride Barbie, 1997, Mattel, Model No. 16962
MNP $80   MIP $160

Bob Mackie Celebration of Dance Charleston, 2001, Mattel
MNP $100   MIP $300

Bob Mackie Celebration of Dance Tango, 1999, Mattel, Model No. 23451
MNP $150   MIP $200

Crystal Rhapsody, Blond, Presidential Porcelain Barbie Collection, 1992, Mattel, Model No. 1553
MNP $100   MIP $300

Crystal Rhapsody, Brunette, Presidential Porcelain Barbie Collection, 1993, Mattel, Model No. 10201
MNP $100   MIP $600

Enchanted Evening Barbie, 1987, Mattel, Model No. 3415
MNP $125   MIP $200

Evening Pearl, Presidential Porcelain Collection, 1996, Mattel, Model No. 12825
MNP $150   MIP $300

Faberge Imperial Elegance Barbie, Limited to 15,000, 1999, Mattel, Model No. 19816
MNP $150   MIP $250

Gay Parisienne, Blond, 1991, Mattel, Model No. 9973
    MNP $225   **MIP** $400

Gay Parisienne, Brunette, 1991, Mattel, Model No. 9973
    MNP $75   **MIP** $125

Gay Parisienne, Red Hair, 1991, Mattel, Model No. 9973
    MNP $225   **MIP** $400

Gold Sensation, Gold and Silver Porcelain Barbie Set, 1993, Mattel, Model No. 10246
    MNP $175   **MIP** $350

Holiday Porcelain #1, Holiday Jewel, 1995, Mattel, Model No. 14311
    MNP $55   **MIP** $125

Holiday Porcelain #2, Holiday Caroler, 1996, Mattel, Model No. 15760
    MNP $60   **MIP** $100

Holiday Porcelain #3, Holiday Ball, 1997, Mattel, Model No. 18326
    MNP $50   **MIP** $100

Holiday Porcelain #4, Holiday Gift, 1998, Mattel, Model No. 20128
    MNP $50   **MIP** $100

Mattel's 50th Anniversary Barbie, 1995, Mattel, Model No. 14479
    MNP $75   **MIP** $150

Mint Memories, Victorian Tea Porcelain Collection, 1999, Mattel
    MNP $100   **MIP** $215

Plantation Belle, Blond, Porcelain Treasures Collection, 1992, Mattel, Model No. 7526
    MNP $100   **MIP** $300

Plantation Belle, Red, Porcelain Treasures Collection, 1992, Mattel, Model No. 5351
    MNP $50   **MIP** $125

Presidential Porcelain Evening Pearl Barbie, 1996, Mattel
    MNP $95   **MIP** $225

Romantic Rose Bride, 1995, Mattel, Model No. 14541
    MNP $65   **MIP** $135

Royal Splendor, Presidential Porcelain Collection, 1993, Mattel, Model No. 10950
    MNP $175   **MIP** $350

Silken Flame Barbie, Brunette, Porcelain Treasures Collection, 1993, Mattel, Model No. 1249
    MNP $100   **MIP** $200

Silken Flame, Blond, 1993, Mattel, Model No. 11099
    MNP $150   **MIP** $250

Silver Starlight, Gold and Silver Porcelain Barbie Set, 1994, Mattel, Model No. 11875
    MNP $175   **MIP** $350

Solo in the Spotlight, 1990, Mattel, Model No. 7613
    MNP $135   **MIP** $275

Sophisticated Lady, 1990, Mattel, Model No. 5313
    MNP $75   **MIP** $125

Star Lily Bride Barbie, Wedding Flower Collection, 1995, Mattel, Model No. 12953
    MNP $125   **MIP** $250

Victorian Tea Orange Pekoe Barbie, 2000, Mattel, Model No. 25507
    MNP $110   **MIP** $220

Wedding Day Barbie, 1989, Mattel, Model No. 2641
    MNP $150   **MIP** $250

(Mattel Photo)

Wizard of Oz Cowardly Lion, 2002, Mattel, Model No. 54180
    MNP $50   **MIP** $150

Wizard of Oz Dorothy, 2000, Mattel, Model No. 26834
    MNP $70   **MIP** $150

Wizard of Oz Scarecrow, 2001, Mattel, Model No. 29190
    MNP $50   **MIP** $150

Wizard of Oz Tin Man, 2001, Mattel, Model No. 29676
    MNP $50   **MIP** $150

Wizard of Oz Wicked Witch, 2000, Mattel, Model No. 26835
    MNP $70   **MIP** $150

Wizard of Oz Winged Monkey, 2001, Mattel, Model No. 29476
    MNP $50   **MIP** $150

Fashions

BARBIE VINTAGE FASHIONS 1959-1966

Aboard Ship, Mattel, Model No. 1631
    MNP $95   **MIP** $200

After Five, Mattel, Model No. 934
    MNP $40   **MIP** $75

American Airlines Stewardess, Mattel, Model No. 984
    MNP $30   **MIP** $175

Apple Print Sheath, Mattel, Model No. 917
    MNP $15   **MIP** $100

Ballerina, Mattel, Model No. 989
    MNP $30   **MIP** $150

Barbie Arabian Nights, Mattel, Model No. 0874
    MNP $75   **MIP** $275

Barbie Baby-Sits, 1963, Mattel, Model No. 953
    MNP $65   **MIP** $250

Barbie in Hawaii, Mattel, Model No. 1605
    MNP $65   **MIP** $225

Barbie in Holland, Mattel, Model No. 0823
    MNP $50   **MIP** $175

Barbie in Japan, Mattel, Model No. 0821
    MNP $100   **MIP** $400

Barbie in Mexico, Mattel, Model No. 0820
    MNP $95   **MIP** $200

Barbie in Switzerland, Mattel, Model No. 0822
    MNP $75   **MIP** $225

Barbie Learns to Cook, Mattel, Model No. 1634
    MNP $150   **MIP** $500

Barbie Skin Diver, Mattel, Model No. 1608
    MNP $15   **MIP** $100

Barbie-Q Outfit, Mattel, Model No. 962
    MNP $50   **MIP** $140

Beau Time, Mattel, Model No. 1651
    MNP $175   **MIP** $500

Beautiful Bride, Mattel, Model No. 1698
    MNP $400   **MIP** $2100

Benefit Performance, Mattel, Model No. 1667
    MNP $450   **MIP** $1375

(KP Photo)

(KP Photo)

Black Magic, Mattel, Model No. 1609
    MNP $60   **MIP** $250

Bride's Dream, Mattel, Model No. 947
    MNP $50   **MIP** $200

Brunch Time, Mattel, Model No. 1628
    MNP $110   **MIP** $350

Busy Gal, Mattel, Model No. 981
    MNP $95   **MIP** $250

Busy Morning, Mattel, Model No. 956
    MNP $125   **MIP** $275

Campus Sweetheart, Mattel, Model
No. 1616
    MNP $400   **MIP** $1600

Candy Striper Volunteer, Mattel,
Model No. 0889
    MNP $175   **MIP** $365

Career Girl, Mattel, Model No. 954
    MNP $60   **MIP** $225

Caribbean Cruise, Mattel, Model
No. 1687
    MNP $65   **MIP** $200

Cheerleader, Mattel, Model No. 0876
    MNP $50   **MIP** $170

Cinderella, Mattel, Model No. 0872
    MNP $100   **MIP** $425

Club Meeting, Mattel, Model No. 1672
    MNP $75   **MIP** $375

Coffee's On, Mattel, Model No. 1670
    MNP $70   **MIP** $150

Commuter Set, Mattel, Model No. 916
    MNP $500   **MIP** $1500

Country Club Dance, Mattel, Model
No. 1627
    MNP $115   **MIP** $400

Country Fair, Mattel, Model No. 1603
    MNP $45   **MIP** $165

Crisp 'n Cool, Mattel, Model No. 1604
    MNP $30   **MIP** $150

Cruise Stripes, Mattel, Model No. 918
    MNP $35   **MIP** $165

Dancing Doll, Mattel, Model No. 1626
    MNP $175   **MIP** $450

Debutante Ball, Mattel, Model No. 1666
    MNP $375   **MIP** $1200

Dinner At Eight, Mattel, Model No. 946
    MNP $60   **MIP** $225

Disc Date, Mattel, Model No. 1633
    MNP $125   **MIP** $295

Dog n' Duds, Mattel, Model No. 1613
    MNP $125   **MIP** $325

Dreamland, Mattel, Model No. 1669
    MNP $110   **MIP** $200

Drum Majorette, Mattel, Model
No. 0875
    MNP $50   **MIP** $200

Easter Parade, Mattel, shown on a
Ponytail #3 doll, Model No. 971
    MNP $950   **MIP** $4000

(KP Photo)

Enchanted Evening, Mattel, seen here
on a Bubblecut Barbie, Model
No. 983
    MNP $65   **MIP** $300

Evening Enchantment, Mattel, Model
No. 1695
    MNP $250   **MIP** $500

Evening Gala, Mattel, Model No. 1660
    MNP $110   **MIP** $350

Evening Splendor, Mattel, Model
No. 961
    MNP $60   **MIP** $300

Fabulous Fashion, Mattel, Model
No. 1676
    MNP $250   **MIP** $525

Fancy Free, Mattel, Model No. 943
    MNP $15   **MIP** $65

Fashion Editor, Mattel, Model No. 1635
    MNP $225   **MIP** $650

Fashion Luncheon, Mattel, Model No. 1656
MNP $450   MIP $1200

Fashion Shiner, Mattel, Model No. 1691
MNP $90   MIP $220

Floating Gardens, Mattel, Model No. 1696
MNP $175   MIP $500

Floral Petticoat, Mattel, Model No. 921
MNP $20   MIP $50

Formal Occasion, Mattel, Model No. 1697
MNP $150   MIP $500

Fraternity Dance, Mattel, Model No. 1638
MNP $175   MIP $575

Friday Night Date, Mattel, Model No. 979
MNP $50   MIP $225

Fun At The Fair, Mattel, Model No. 1624
MNP $95   MIP $285

Fun n' Games, Mattel, Model No. 1619
MNP $110   MIP $300

Garden Party, Mattel, Model No. 931
MNP $47   MIP $150

Garden Tea Party, Mattel, Model No. 1606
MNP $50   MIP $175

Garden Wedding, Mattel, Model No. 1658
MNP $195   MIP $650

(KP Photo)

Gay Parisienne, Mattel, shown here on a Ponytail #1, Model No. 964
MNP $1100   MIP $4000

Gold 'n Glamour, Mattel, Model No. 1647
MNP $600   MIP $1600

Golden Elegance, Mattel, Model No. 992
MNP $150   MIP $350

Golden Evening, Mattel, Model No. 1610
MNP $95   MIP $250

Golden Girl, Mattel, Model No. 911
MNP $65   MIP $150

Golden Glory, Mattel, Model No. 1645
MNP $175   MIP $425

Graduation, Mattel, Model No. 945
MNP $45   MIP $95

Guinevere, Mattel, Model No. 0873
MNP $100   MIP $300

Here Comes The Bride, Mattel, Model No. 1665
MNP $400   MIP $995

Holiday Dance, Mattel, Model No. 1639
MNP $250   MIP $595

Icebreaker, Mattel, Model No. 942
MNP $35   MIP $100

International Fair, Mattel, Model No. 1653
MNP $250   MIP $500

Invitation To Tea, Mattel, Model No. 1632
MNP $265   MIP $525

It's Cold Outside, Brown, Mattel, Model No. 0819
MNP $25   MIP $110

It's Cold Outside, Red, Mattel, Model No. 0819
MNP $30   MIP $165

Junior Designer, Mattel, Model No. 1620
MNP $150   MIP $350

Junior Prom, Mattel, Model No. 1614
MNP $275   MIP $600

Knit Hit, Mattel, Model No. 1621
MNP $125   MIP $225

Knit Separates, Mattel, Model No. 1602
MNP $70   MIP $160

Knitting Pretty, Blue, Mattel, Model No. 957
MNP $65   MIP $150

Knitting Pretty, Pink, Mattel, Model No. 957
MNP $75   MIP $300

Let's Dance, Mattel, Model No. 978
MNP $40   MIP $175

Little Red Riding Hood & The Wolf, Mattel, Model No. 0880
MNP $150   MIP $450

London Tour, Mattel, Model No. 1661
MNP $125   MIP $400

Lunch Date, Mattel, Model No. 1600
MNP $45   MIP $125

Lunch On The Terrace, Mattel, Model No. 1649
MNP $175   MIP $325

Lunchtime, Mattel, Model No. 1673
MNP $150   MIP $285

Magnificence, Mattel, Model No. 1646
MNP $350   MIP $595

Masquerade, Mattel, Model No. 944
MNP $40   MIP $175

Matinee Fashion, Mattel, Model No. 1640
MNP $320   MIP $525

Midnight Blue, Mattel, Model No. 1617
MNP $375   MIP $800

(KP Photo)

Miss Astronaut, Mattel, shown here w/re-constructed helmet, Model No. 1641
MNP $395   MIP $650

Modern Art, Mattel, Model No. 1625
MNP $300   MIP $550

Mood For Music, Mattel, Model No. 940
MNP $70   MIP $150

Movie Date, Mattel, Model No. 933
MNP $30   MIP $50

Music Center Matinee, Mattel, Model No. 1633
MNP $325   MIP $600

Nighty Negligee, Mattel, Model No. 965
MNP $30   MIP $75

On The Avenue, Mattel, Model No. 1644
MNP $200   MIP $525

(KP Photo)

Open Road, Mattel, the Mattel Road Map included w/this outfit is especially hard to find, Model No. 985

MNP $125   MIP $350

Orange Blossom, 1961, Mattel, Model No. 987

MNP $30   MIP $150

Outdoor Art Show, Mattel, Model No. 1650

MNP $195   MIP $500

Outdoor Life, Mattel, Model No. 1637

MNP $75   MIP $275

Pajama Party, Mattel, Model No. 1601

MNP $10   MIP $50

(KP Photo)

Pan Am Stewardess, Mattel, very rare fashion shown on American Girl doll, Model No. 1678

MNP $1500   MIP $4000

Party Date, Mattel, Model No. 958

MNP $85   MIP $175

Patio Party, Mattel, Model No. 1692

MNP $100   MIP $325

Peachy Fleecy, Mattel, Model No. 915

MNP $35   MIP $100

Photo Fashion, Mattel, Model No. 1648

MNP $125   MIP $375

Picnic Set, Mattel, Model No. 967

MNP $125   MIP $410

Pink Moonbeams, Mattel, Model No. 1694

MNP $85   MIP $300

Plantation Belle, Mattel, Model No. 966

MNP $150   MIP $350

Poodle Parade, Mattel, Model No. 1643

MNP $400   MIP $950

Pretty As A Picture, Mattel, Model No. 1652

MNP $175   MIP $450

Print Aplenty, Mattel, Model No. 1686

MNP $75   MIP $275

Rain Coat, Mattel, Model No. 949

MNP $20   MIP $75

Reception Line, Mattel, Model No. 1654

MNP $350   MIP $500

Red Flare, Mattel, Model No. 939

MNP $30   MIP $150

(KP Photo)

Registered Nurse, Mattel, seen here on Midge, Model No. 991

MNP $55   MIP $175

Resort Set, Mattel, Model No. 963

MNP $50   MIP $175

Riding In The Park, Mattel, Model No. 1668

MNP $175   MIP $595

(KP Photo)

Roman Holiday, Mattel, shown on Ponytail #4 Barbie doll, Model No. 968

MNP $750   MIP $4800

Satin n' Rose, Mattel, Model No. 1611

MNP $190   MIP $375

Saturday Matinee, Mattel, Model No. 1615

MNP $525   MIP $900

Senior Prom, Mattel, Model No. 951

MNP $50   MIP $200

Sheath Sensation, Mattel, Model No. 986

MNP $80   MIP $150

Shimmering Magic, Mattel, Model No. 1664

MNP $350   MIP $1600

Silken Flame, Mattel, Model No. 977

MNP $40   MIP $125

Singing In The Shower, Mattel, Model No. 988

MNP $65   MIP $130

Skater's Waltz, Mattel, Model No. 1629

MNP $125   MIP $395

Ski Queen, Mattel, Model No. 948

MNP $50   MIP $150

Sleeping Pretty, Mattel, Model No. 1636

MNP $85   MIP $350

Sleepytime Gal, Mattel, Model No. 1674

MNP $95   MIP $220

Slumber Party, Mattel, Model No. 1642

MNP $95   MIP $260

(KP Photo)

Solo In The Spotlight, Mattel, seen here on a Ponytail #4 doll, Model No. 982
MNP $75   MIP $300

Sophisticated Lady, Mattel, Model No. 993
MNP $125   MIP $300

Sorority Meeting, Mattel, Model No. 937
MNP $60   MIP $180

Sporting Casuals, Mattel, Model No. 1671
MNP $60   MIP $165

Stormy Weather, Mattel, Model No. 0949
MNP $50   MIP $95

(KP Photo)

Student Teacher, Mattel, Model No. 1622
MNP $235   MIP $400

Studio Tour, Mattel, Model No. 1690
MNP $110   MIP $250

Suburban Shopper, Mattel, Model No. 969
MNP $75   MIP $300

Sunday Visit, Mattel, Model No. 1675
MNP $175   MIP $450

Sunflower, Mattel, Model No. 1683
MNP $75   MIP $245

Sweater Girl, Mattel, Model No. 976
MNP $75   MIP $175

Sweet Dreams, Pink, Mattel, Model No. 973
MNP $200   MIP $425

Sweet Dreams, Yellow, Mattel, Model No. 973
MNP $25   MIP $125

Swingin' Easy, Mattel, Model No. 955
MNP $95   MIP $245

Tennis Anyone, Mattel, Model No. 941
MNP $35   MIP $150

Theatre Date (1963), 1963, Mattel, Model No. 1612
MNP $75   MIP $175

Theatre Date (1964), 1964, Mattel, Model No. 959
MNP $75   MIP $200

Travel Togethers, Mattel, Model No. 1688
MNP $75   MIP $240

Under Fashions, Mattel, Model No. 1655
MNP $175   MIP $500

Undergarments, Mattel, Model No. 919
MNP $25   MIP $65

Underprints, Mattel, Model No. 1685
MNP $55   MIP $225

Vacation Time, Mattel, Model No. 1623
MNP $95   MIP $240

Wedding Day Set, Mattel, Model No. 972
MNP $150   MIP $350

White Magic, Mattel, Model No. 1607
MNP $95   MIP $275

Winter Holiday, Mattel, Model No. 975
MNP $82   MIP $165

FRANCIE VINTAGE FASHIONS 1966

Checkmates, Mattel, Model No. 1259
MNP $65   MIP $140

Clam Diggers, Mattel, Model No. 1258
MNP $100   MIP $250

Concert In The Park, Mattel, Model No. 1256
MNP $75   MIP $250

Dance Party, Mattel, Model No. 1257
MNP $150   MIP $250

First Formal, Mattel, Model No. 1260
MNP $80   MIP $175

First Things First, Mattel, Model No. 1252
MNP $55   MIP $100

Fresh As A Daisy, Mattel, Model No. 1254
MNP $65   MIP $140

Fur Out, 1966, Mattel, Model No. 1262
MNP $195   MIP $400

Gad-About, Mattel, Model No. 1250
MNP $75   MIP $220

Go Granny Go, 1966, Mattel, Model No. 1267
MNP $85   MIP $200

Hip Knits, 1966, Mattel, Model No. 1265
MNP $100   MIP $200

It's A Date, Mattel, Model No. 1251
MNP $70   MIP $125

Leather Limelight, 1966, Mattel, Model No. 1269
MNP $125   MIP $255

Orange Cozy, 1966, Mattel, Model No. 1263
MNP $170   MIP $235

Polka Dots N' Raindrops, Mattel, Model No. 1255
MNP $35   MIP $100

Quick Shift, 1966, Mattel, Model No. 1266
MNP $90   MIP $180

Shoppin' Spree, Mattel, Model No. 1261
MNP $75   MIP $140

Style Setters, 1966, Mattel, Model No. 1268
MNP $95   MIP $260

Swingin' Skimmy, 1966, Mattel, Model No. 1264
    MNP $95   **MIP** $245

Tuckered Out, Mattel, Model No. 1253
    MNP $55   **MIP** $125

KEN VINTAGE FASHIONS 1961-1966

American Airlines Captain #1, Mattel, Model No. 0779
    MNP $175   **MIP** $300

Army and Air Force, Mattel, Model No. 797
    MNP $120   **MIP** $245

(KP Photo)

Best Man, Mattel, seen on Allan doll, Model No. 1425
    MNP $700   **MIP** $1100

Business Appointment, Mattel, Model No. 1424
    MNP $800   **MIP** $1150

Campus Corduroys, Mattel, Model No. 1410
    MNP $20   **MIP** $65

Campus Hero, Mattel, Model No. 770
    MNP $25   **MIP** $95

Casuals, Striped Shirt, Mattel, Model No. 0782
    MNP $70   **MIP** $100

Casuals, Yellow Shirt, Mattel, Model No. 782
    MNP $25   **MIP** $65

College Student, Mattel, Model No. 1416
    MNP $190   **MIP** $400

Country Clubbin', Mattel, Model No. 1400
    MNP $40   **MIP** $85

Dr. Ken, Mattel, Model No. 793
    MNP $55   **MIP** $130

Dreamboat, Mattel, Model No. 785
    MNP $40   **MIP** $95

Drum Major, Mattel, Model No. 0775
    MNP $75   **MIP** $175

Fountain Boy, Mattel, Model No. 1407
    MNP $230   **MIP** $325

Fraternity Meeting, Mattel, Model No. 1408
    MNP $25   **MIP** $55

Fun On Ice, Mattel, Model No. 791
    MNP $55   **MIP** $105

Going Bowling, Mattel, Model No. 1403
    MNP $20   **MIP** $35

Going Huntin', Mattel, Model No. 1409
    MNP $50   **MIP** $100

Graduation, Mattel, Model No. 795
    MNP $35   **MIP** $65

Here Comes The Groom, Mattel, Model No. 1426
    MNP $1000   **MIP** $1400

Hiking Holiday, Mattel, Model No. 1412
    MNP $100   **MIP** $210

Holiday, Mattel, Model No. 1414
    MNP $48   **MIP** $100

In Training, Mattel, Model No. 780
    MNP $30   **MIP** $50

Jazz Concert, Mattel, Model No. 1420
    MNP $135   **MIP** $250

(KP Photo)

Ken A Go Go, Mattel, this outfit even included a mod-hair wig to make the rather staid Ken look hip, Model No. 1423
    MNP $500   **MIP** $700

Ken Arabian Nights, Mattel, Model No. 0774
    MNP $100   **MIP** $200

Ken In Hawaii, Mattel, Model No. 1404
    MNP $100   **MIP** $195

Ken In Holland, Mattel, Model No. 0777
    MNP $155   **MIP** $250

Ken In Mexico, Mattel, Model No. 0778
    MNP $150   **MIP** $250

Ken In Switzerland, Mattel, Model No. 0776
    MNP $150   **MIP** $200

Ken Skin Diver, Mattel, Model No. 1406
    MNP $30   **MIP** $50

King Arthur, Mattel, Model No. 0773
    MNP $225   **MIP** $375

Masquerade (Ken), Mattel, Model No. 794
    MNP $60   **MIP** $145

Mountain Hike, Mattel, Model No. 1427
    MNP $150   **MIP** $300

Mr. Astronaut, Mattel, Model No. 1415
    MNP $395   **MIP** $650

Off To Bed, Mattel, Model No. 1413
    MNP $82   **MIP** $150

Play Ball, Mattel, Model No. 792
    MNP $55   **MIP** $110

Rally Day, Mattel, Model No. 788
    MNP $66   **MIP** $130

Roller Skate Date, w/Hat, Mattel, Model No. 1405
    MNP $40   **MIP** $125

Roller Skate Date, w/Slacks, Mattel, Model No. 1405
    MNP $40   **MIP** $150

Rovin' Reporter, Mattel, Model No. 1417
    MNP $175   **MIP** $295

Sailor, Mattel, Model No. 796
    MNP $65   **MIP** $120

Saturday Date, Mattel, Model No. 786
    MNP $40   **MIP** $105

Seein' The Sights, Mattel, Model No. 1421
    MNP $195   **MIP** $455

Ski Champion, Mattel, Model No. 798
    MNP $85   **MIP** $155

Sleeper Set, Blue, Mattel, Model No. 0781
    MNP $60   **MIP** $120

Sleeper Set, Brown, Mattel, Model No. 781
    MNP $25   **MIP** $70

Special Date, Mattel, Model No. 1401
    MNP $70   **MIP** $145

Sport Shorts, Mattel, Model No. 783
    MNP $20   **MIP** $55

Summer Job, Mattel, Model No. 1422
    MNP $290   **MIP** $475

Terry Togs, Mattel, Model No. 784
MNP $60   MIP $90

The Prince, Mattel, Model No. 0772
MNP $285   MIP $375

The Yachtsman, No Hat, Mattel,
Model No. 789
MNP $45   MIP $90

The Yachtsman, w/Hat, Mattel, Model
No. 0789
MNP $235   MIP $475

Time For Tennis, Mattel, Model No. 790
MNP $45   MIP $140

Time To Turn In, Mattel, Model No. 1418
MNP $80   MIP $175

Touchdown, Mattel, Model No. 799
MNP $55   MIP $125

Tuxedo, Mattel, Model No. 787
MNP $95   MIP $245

TV's Good Tonight, Mattel, Model
No. 1419
MNP $110   MIP $250

Victory Dance, Mattel, Model No. 1411
MNP $60   MIP $135

RICKY FASHIONS 1965-1966

Let's Explore, Mattel, Model No. 1506
MNP $35   MIP $85

Lights Out, Mattel, Model No. 1501
MNP $55   MIP $100

Little Leaguer, Mattel, Model No. 1504
MNP $65   MIP $95

Saturday Show, Mattel, Model No. 1502
MNP $45   MIP $70

Skateboard Set, Mattel, Model No. 1505
MNP $55   MIP $100

Sunday Suit, Mattel, Model No. 1503
MNP $45   MIP $65

SKIPPER VINTAGE FASHIONS 1964-1966

Ballet Class, Mattel, Model No. 1905
MNP $60   MIP $135

Can You Play?, Mattel, Model No. 1923
MNP $60   MIP $125

Chill Chasers, Mattel, Model No. 1926
MNP $55   MIP $100

Cookie Time, Mattel, Model No. 1912
MNP $85   MIP $150

Country Picnic, Mattel, Model No. 1933
MNP $300   MIP $450

Day At The Fair, Mattel, Model No. 1911
MNP $120   MIP $200

Dog Show, Mattel, Model No. 1929
MNP $190   MIP $300

Dreamtime, Mattel, Model No. 1909
MNP $60   MIP $125

Dress Coat, Mattel, Model No. 1906
MNP $60   MIP $80

Flower Girl, Mattel, Model No. 1904
MNP $80   MIP $150

Fun Time, Mattel, Model No. 1920
MNP $100   MIP $200

Happy Birthday, Mattel, Model No. 1919
MNP $355   MIP $500

Junior Bridesmaid, Mattel, Model
No. 1934
MNP $285   MIP $475

Land & Sea, Mattel, Model No. 1917
MNP $90   MIP $155

Learning To Ride, Mattel, Model
No. 1935
MNP $185   MIP $275

Let's Play House, Mattel, Model
No. 1932
MNP $125   MIP $250

Loungin' Lovelies, Mattel, Model
No. 1930
MNP $55   MIP $125

Masquerade (Skipper), Mattel, Model
No. 1903
MNP $80   MIP $155

Me N' My Doll, Mattel, Model No. 1913
MNP $150   MIP $260

Outdoor Casuals, Mattel, Model
No. 1915
MNP $85   MIP $135

Platter Party, Mattel, Model No. 1914
MNP $75   MIP $125

Rain Or Shine, Mattel, Model No. 1916
MNP $50   MIP $90

Rainy Day Checkers, Mattel, Model
No. 1928
MNP $155   MIP $300

Red Sensation, Mattel, Model
No. 1901
MNP $65   MIP $125

School Days, Mattel, Model No. 1907
MNP $60   MIP $130

School Girl, Mattel, Model No. 1921
MNP $200   MIP $295

Ship Ahoy, Mattel, Model No. 1918
MNP $155   MIP $275

Silk N' Fancy, Mattel, Model No. 1902
MNP $60   MIP $125

Skating Fun, Mattel, Model No. 1908
MNP $48   MIP $110

Sledding Fun, Mattel, Model No. 1936
MNP $155   MIP $275

Sunny Pastels, Mattel, Model No. 1910
MNP $60   MIP $125

Tea Party, Mattel, Model No. 1924
MNP $185   MIP $300

Town Togs, Mattel, Model No. 1922
MNP $95   MIP $170

Under-Pretties, Mattel, Model No. 1900
MNP $25   MIP $50

What's New At The Zoo?, Mattel,
Model No. 1925
MNP $50   MIP $120

TUTTI FASHIONS 1966

Puddle Jumpers, Mattel, Model
No. 3601
MNP $20   MIP $45

Sand Castles, Mattel, Model No. 3603
MNP $55   MIP $98

Ship Shape, Mattel, Model No. 3602
MNP $55   MIP $90

Skippin' Rope, Mattel, Model No. 3604
MNP $55   MIP $95

Battery-Operated Toys

by Leo Rishty

Battery-operated toys are the distant cousins of late 19th century automatons. Combining motion with bright tin lithography, quality craftsmanship, and prices the masses could afford, the battery-powered toys produced following World War II brought a new type of toy into American households—toys that moved under their own power.

Japanese companies that perfected tin lithography techniques prior to the war replaced wind-up and friction motors with the more reliable battery power source as postwar manufacturing resumed. The results were toys capable of complex and compound motions such as walking, lifting, drumming, and even dancing. The innovative designs and ingenuity employed in their creation make battery-operated toys valuable today for their motion, design, humorous outlook, and nostalgia.

Identifying the manufacturer of a particular toy without the box can be difficult. Many companies used only initials to mark toys, and others didn't mark them at all. Major manufacturers from the 40s-60s include: Marx, Linemar (Marx's Japanese subsidiary), Alps, Marusan, Yonezawa, Bandai, Ashai Toy, Toy Nomura, and Modern Toy. Marx is identified by a circle with an "X" containing the company name; Alps shows a mountain top with the name "Alps" underneath; Marusan used the initials "SAN"; Yonezawa used the initial "Y" in a leaf; Bandai used the initial "B" in a diamond; and Toy Nomura used the initials "TN."

Trends

When you think of battery-operated toys, your thoughts are of little toys for children. You are right when you consider the current run of modern toys. But when you consider battery-operated toys of the 50s and 60s, that's another story.

It's amazing the many actions of battery-operated toys of the 50s and 60s. Some of them as many as six or seven actions. The more the actions the greater the demand. And demand dictates market value.

Speaking of values, keep in mind that values have held up well despite recent economic struggles. The beautiful thing about toys as collectibles is: the entertainment factor, supply will never increase and, most obvious, condition of the toy and if the orginal box is available. It's quite possible that a number of toys from the 50s and 60s will become more rare and therefore more valuable.

Contributor: Leo Rishty is a long-time collector of battery-operated toys. He may be contacted in care of the editor at: Krause Publications, 700 E. State St., Iola, WI 54990.

The Top 10 BATTERY-OPERATED in mint condition

1. Smoking Popeye, Linemar, 1950s $3,775
2. Bubble Blowing Popeye, Linemar, 1950s $3,100
3. Mickey the Magician, Linemar, 1960s $2,775
4. Gypsy Fortune Teller, Ichida, 1950s $2,360
5. Smoking Spaceman, Linemar, 1950s $2,250
6. Drumming Mickey Mouse, Linemar, 1950s $1,900
7. Main Street, Linemar, 1950s $1,575
8. Nutty Nibs, Linemar, 1950s $1,500
9. Climbing Donald Duck on Friction Fire, Linemar, 1950s $1,500
10. Kooky-Spooky Whistling Tree, Marx, 1950s $1,475

Battery-Operated Toys

ABC Fairy Train, 1950s, MT, 14-1/2" long
EX $95   NM $135   MIP $190

Accordion Bear, 1950s, Alps, 11" tall, five actions
EX $250   NM $450   MIP $650

Accordion Player Bunny, 1950s, Alps, 12" tall, 9" long
EX $300   NM $450   MIP $600

Accordion Playing Hobo w/Chimp, 1950s, Alps, 10" tall, six actions, chimp plays cymbals
EX $325   NM $550   MIP $750

Air Cargo Prop-Jet Airplane, 1960s, Marx, Seaboard World Airlines, 12" long, 14-1/2" wingspan
EX $220   NM $350   MIP $465

Air Control Tower, 1960s, Bandai, 11" tall, 37" span, four actions
EX $275   NM $400   MIP $550

Air Defense Truck w/Pom-Pom Gun, 1950s, Linemar, 14" long
EX $170   NM $255   MIP $340

Air Mail Helicopter, 1960s, K-O, 10" long, seven actions
EX $100   NM $200   MIP $300

Aircraft Carrier, 1950s, Marx, 20" long, six actions
EX $350   NM $475   MIP $625

Alley, the Exciting New Roaring Stalking Alligator, 1960s, Marx, 17-1/2" long
EX $200   NM $275   MIP $400

American Airlines DC-7, 1960s, Linemar, 17-1/2" long, 19" wingspan
EX $215   NM $330   MIP $435

American Airlines Electra, 1950s, Linemar, 18" long, 19-1/2" wingspan
EX $215   NM $350   MIP $440

American Airlines Flagship Caroline, 1950s, Linemar, 18" long, 19-1/2" wingspan
EX $215   NM $350   MIP $440

Anti-Aircraft Unit No. 1, 1950s, Linemar, 12-1/2" long
EX $150   NM $235   MIP $310

Antique Gooney Car, 1960s, Alps, 9" long, four actions
EX $60   NM $100   MIP $150

Armored Knights Contest Set, 1950s, Bandai, 8" high, six actions
EX $125   NM $250   MIP $375

Army Radio Jeep—J1490, 1950s, Linemar, 7-1/4" long
EX $125   NM $175   MIP $225

(KP Photo)

Arthur A-Go-Go, 1960s, Alps, 10" tall, drum lights up, cymbals detach, six actions
EX $215   NM $335   MIP $430

Atomic Rocket X-1800, 1960s, MT, 9" long, three actions
EX $180   NM $275   MIP $370

B-58 Hustler Jet, 1950s, Marx, 21" long, 12" wingspan
EX $350   NM $525   MIP $700

Ball Blowing Clown, 1950s, TN, w/two balls and "mystery action"
EX $150   NM $200   MIP $270

Ball Playing Dog, 1950s, Linemar, 9"
EX $115   NM $175   MIP $230

Barber Bear, 1950s, Linemar, 9-1/2" tall
EX $325   NM $430   MIP $600

Barking Boxer Dog, 1950s, Marx, 7" long
EX $75   NM $100   MIP $150

Barney Bear Drummer, 1950s, Alps, 11" tall
EX $135   NM $205   MIP $265

Barnyard Rooster, 1950s, Marx, 10" tall
EX $100   NM $150   MIP $210

(KP Photo)

Bartender, 1960s, TN, six actions - shakes Martini, drinks, face turns

red, puckers lips, smoke shoots out ears, 11-1/2" tall
EX $75   NM $100   MIP $150

Bear the Cashier, 1950s, MT, 7-1/2" tall
EX $225   NM $325   MIP $450

Bengali—The Exciting New Growling, Prowling Tiger, 1961, Linemar, 18-1/2" long
EX $225   NM $300   MIP $375

Big John, 1960s, Alps, 12" tall
EX $95   NM $125   MIP $175

Big John the Indian Chief, 1960s, TN, 12-1/2" tall
EX $100   NM $150   MIP $200

Big Max & Conveyor, 1958, Remco, 7" tall
EX $135   NM $190   MIP $275

Bimbo the Clown, 1950s, Alps, 9-1/4" tall
EX $225   NM $340   MIP $460

Blushing Gunfighter, 1960s, Y Co., 11" tall
EX $100   NM $160   MIP $200

Blushing Willie, 1960s, Y Co., four actions - pours real water, drinks, eyes spin, hair stands up, 10" tall
EX $75   NM $110   MIP $150

Bobby the Drumming Bear, 1950s, Alps, 10" tall
EX $225   NM $350   MIP $475

Bongo Player, 1960s, Alps, 10" tall
EX $80   NM $120   MIP $165

(KP Photo)

Bongo the Drumming Monkey, 1960s, Alps, 9-1/2" tall
EX $80   NM $125   MIP $170

Brave Eagle, 1950s, TN, 11" tall
EX $125   NM $175   MIP $225

Brewster the Rooster, 1950s, Marx, 9-1/2" tall
EX $120   NM $175   MIP $250

Bubble Blowing Bear, 1950s, MT, 9-1/2" tall
EX $175   NM $255   MIP $350

Bubble Blowing Boy, 1950s, Y Co., 7" tall
EX $150 **NM** $225 **MIP** $300

(KP Photo)

Bubble Blowing Monkey, 1950s, Alps, five actions, 10" tall
EX $150 **NM** $200 **MIP** $300

Bubble Blowing Popeye, 1950s, Linemar, 11-3/4" tall
EX $1550 **NM** $2325 **MIP** $3100

Bubbling Bull, 1950s, Linemar, 8" tall
EX $100 **NM** $165 **MIP** $215

Bunny the Magician, 1950s, Alps, 14-1/2" tall
EX $350 **NM** $500 **MIP** $650

Burger Chef Dog, 1950s, Y Co., 9" tall, dog cooking w/frying pan
EX $175 **NM** $250 **MIP** $340

Busy Housekeeper, 1950s, Alps, 8-1/2" tall
EX $250 **NM** $350 **MIP** $450

Busy Secretary, 1950s, Linemar, 7-1/2" tall
EX $250 **NM** $375 **MIP** $475

Busy Shoe Shining Bear, 1950s, Alps, 10" tall
EX $155 **NM** $230 **MIP** $295

Cabin Cruiser w/Outboard Motor, 1950s, Linemar, 12" long
EX $135 **NM** $210 **MIP** $275

Calypso Joe, 1950s, Linemar, 11" tall
EX $300 **NM** $450 **MIP** $600

Camera Shooting Bear, 1950s, Linemar, 11" tall
EX $500 **NM** $750 **MIP** $1000

Cappy the Baggage Porter Dog, 1960s, Alps, 12" tall
EX $150 **NM** $225 **MIP** $300

Caterpillar, 1950s, Alps, 16" long
EX $60 **NM** $95 **MIP** $135

Central Choo Choo, 1960s, MT, 15" long
EX $50 **NM** $75 **MIP** $100

Charlie the Drumming Clown, 1950s, Alps, 9-1/2" tall
EX $155 **NM** $235 **MIP** $315

(KP Photo)

Charlie Weaver, 1962, TN, 12"
EX $85 **NM** $120 **MIP** $175

Charm the Cobra, 1960s, Alps, 6" tall
EX $130 **NM** $200 **MIP** $280

Chee Chee Chihuahua, 1960s, Mego, 8" tall
EX $45 **NM** $65 **MIP** $90

(KP Photo)

Chef Cook, 1960s, Y Co., 11-1/2" tall
EX $175 **NM** $275 **MIP** $350

Chippy the Chipmunk, 1950s, Alps, 12" long
EX $75 **NM** $125 **MIP** $165

Circus Elephant, 1950s, TN, w/ball and umbrella
EX $65 **NM** $110 **MIP** $155

Circus Fire Engine, 1960s, MT, 11" tall
EX $125 **NM** $205 **MIP** $265

Clancy the Great, 1960s, Ideal, 19-1/2" tall
EX $110 **NM** $175 **MIP** $235

Climbing Donald Duck on Friction Fire Engine, 1950s, Linemar, 12" long
EX $750 **NM** $1150 **MIP** $1500

Clown Circus Car, 1960s, MT, 8-1/2" long
EX $125 **NM** $200 **MIP** $260

Clown on Unicycle, 1960s, MT, 10-1/2" tall
EX $230 **NM** $365 **MIP** $475

Coney Island Penny Machine, 1950s, Remco, 13" tall
EX $125 **NM** $140 **MIP** $275

Coney Island Rocket Ride, 1950s, Alps, 13-1/2" tall
EX $500 **NM** $750 **MIP** $1000

Cragstan Two-Gun Sheriff, 1950s, Cragstan, remote control, two guns
EX $75 **NM** $125 **MIP** $175

Cragstan Beep Beep Greyhound Bus, 1950s, Cragstan, 20" long
EX $155 **NM** $230 **MIP** $285

(KP Photo)

Cragstan Crapshooter, 1950s, Y Co., 9-1/2" tall
EX $150 **NM** $200 **MIP** $250

Cragstan Crapshooting Monkey, 1950s, Alps, 9" tall
EX $150 **NM** $200 **MIP** $250

Cragstan Mother Goose, 1960s, Y Co., 8-1/4" tall
EX $110 **NM** $165 **MIP** $220

Cragstan Playboy, 1960s, Cragstan, 13" tall
EX $100 **NM** $175 **MIP** $225

Cragstan Roulette, A Gambling Man, 1960s, Y Co., 9" tall
EX $200 **NM** $275 **MIP** $345

Crawling Baby, 1940s, Linemar, 11" long

EX $40   NM $60   MIP $80

Daisy, the Jolly Drumming Duck, 1950s, Alps, 9" tall

EX $175   NM $260   MIP $350

(KP Photo)

Dancing Merry Chimp, 1960s, Kuramochi, 11" tall

EX $125   NM $175   MIP $250

Dandy, the Happy Drumming Pup, 1950s, Alps, 8-1/2" tall

EX $110   NM $165   MIP $230

Dennis the Menace, 1950s, Rosko, 9" tall, w/xylophone

EX $200   NM $300   MIP $375

Disney Acrobats, 1950s, Linemar, 9" tall; Mickey, Donald, and Pluto

EX $585   NM $890   MIP $1200

Disney Fire Engine, 1950s, Linemar, 11" long

EX $575   NM $830   MIP $1130

Disneyland Fire Engine, 1950s, Linemar, 18" long

EX $500   NM $750   MIP $1000

Dolly Dressmaker, 1950s, TN, 7-1/2" tall

EX $250   NM $350   MIP $510

Donald Duck, 1960s, Linemar, 8" tall

EX $275   NM $385   MIP $525

Doxie the Dog, 1950s, Linemar, 9" long

EX $35   NM $50   MIP $65

(KP Photo)

Drinking Captain, 1960s, S & E, 12" tall

EX $110   NM $165   MIP $220

Drummer Bear, 1950s, Alps, 10" tall

EX $150   NM $225   MIP $300

Drumming Mickey Mouse, 1950s, Linemar, 10" tall

EX $950   NM $1425   MIP $1900

Drumming Polar Bear, 1960s, Alps, 12"

EX $85   NM $125   MIP $170

Ducky Duckling, 1960s, Alps, 8"

EX $50   NM $80   MIP $110

El Toro, Cragstan Bullfighter, 1950s, TN, 9-1/2" long

EX $120   NM $190   MIP $270

Feeding Bird Watcher, 1950s, Linemar, 9" tall

EX $300   NM $465   MIP $625

Fido the Xylophone Player, 1950s, Alps, 8-3/4" tall

EX $150   NM $230   MIP $300

Flintstone Yacht, 1961, Remco, 17" long

EX $125   NM $175   MIP $225

Frankenstein Monster, 1960s, TN, 14" tall

EX $175   NM $250   MIP $330

Frankie the Rollerskating Monkey, 1950s, Alps, 12"

EX $150   NM $225   MIP $300

Fred Flintstone Bedrock Band, 1962, Alps, 9-1/2" tall

EX $400   NM $595   MIP $760

Fred Flintstone Flivver, 1960s, Marx, 7" long

EX $450   NM $700   MIP $900

Fred Flintstone on Dino, 1961, Marx, 22"

EX $600   NM $825   MIP $1000

Friendly Jocko, My Favorite Pet, 1950s, Alps, 8" tall

EX $115   NM $175   MIP $240

(KP Photo)

Gino, Neapolitan Balloon Blower, 1960s, Tomiyama, 10" tall

EX $150   NM $225   MIP $275

Girl w/Baby Carriage, 1960s, TN, 8" tall

EX $110   NM $165   MIP $215

Godzilla Monster, 1970s, Marusan, 11-1/2" tall

EX $190   NM $285   MIP $375

(KP Photo)

Good Time Charlie, 1960s, MT, 12" tall

EX $150   NM $200   MIP $250

Grandpa Panda Bear, 1950s, MT, 9" tall

EX $130   NM $205   MIP $275

(KP Photo)

Great Garloo, 1960s, Marx, 23" tall green monster

EX $400   NM $550   MIP $765

Green Caterpillar, 1950s, Daiya, 19-1/2" long

EX $125 NM $185 MIP $250

Gypsy Fortune Teller, 1950s, Ichida, 12" tall, 20 cards

EX $1200 NM $1775 MIP $2360

Happy & Sad Face Cymbal Clown, 1960s, Y Co., 10" tall

EX $175 NM $260 MIP $340

Happy Fiddler Clown, 1950s, Alps, 9-1/2" tall

EX $300 NM $425 MIP $550

Happy Naughty Chimp, 1960s, Daishin, 9-1/2" tall

EX $75 NM $110 MIP $155

Happy Santa One-Man Band, 1950s, Alps, 9" tall

EX $130 NM $205 MIP $275

Hippo Chef, 1960s, Y Co., 10" tall

EX $145 NM $230 MIP $315

Hobo Clown w/Accordion, 1950s, Alps, 10-1/2" tall

EX $325 NM $450 MIP $600

Hong Kong Rickshaw, 1960s, PMC Co., all plastic, made in Hong Kong

EX $55 NM $85 MIP $125

Hoop Zing Girl, 1950s, Linemar, 11-1/2" tall

EX $145 NM $225 MIP $300

Hoopy the Fishing Duck, 1950s, Alps, 10" tall

EX $275 NM $410 MIP $555

Hooty the Happy Owl, 1960s, Alps, 9" tall

EX $85 NM $125 MIP $170

Hungry Baby Bear, 1950s, Y Co., 9-1/2" tall

EX $225 NM $325 MIP $425

Hungry Cat, 1960s, Linemar, 9" tall

EX $350 NM $500 MIP $750

Hungry Hound Dog, 1950s, Y Co., 9-1/2" tall

EX $205 NM $310 MIP $405

Hy-Que, the "Speak no Evil, See No Evil, Hear No Evil" Monkey, 1960s, TN, six actions, shake his hand and he raises arms, 17" tall

EX $200 NM $285 MIP $430

Ice Cream Baby Bear, Vanilla, 1950s, MT, 9-1/2"

EX $225 NM $340 MIP $435

(KP Photo)

Indian Joe, 1960s, Alps, 12" tall

EX $100 NM $150 MIP $200

Jocko the Drinking Monkey, 1950s, Linemar, 11" tall

EX $125 NM $175 MIP $240

Jo-Jo the Flipping Monkey, 1970s, TN, 10" tall

EX $45 NM $70 MIP $100

Jolly Bambino, 1950s, Alps, 9" tall

EX $275 NM $410 MIP $540

Jolly Bear Peanut Vendor, 1950s, TN, 8" tall

EX $260 NM $375 MIP $510

Jolly Daddy, 1950s, Marusan, 8-3/4" tall

EX $165 NM $245 MIP $325

Jolly Drummer Chimpy, 1950s, Alps, 9" tall

EX $75 NM $115 MIP $150

Jolly Pianist, 1950s, Marusan, 8" tall

EX $110 NM $175 MIP $230

Jolly Santa on Snow, 1950s, Alps, 12-1/2" tall

EX $170 NM $265 MIP $350

Josie the Walking Cow, 1950s, Daiya, 14" long

EX $200 NM $250 MIP $375

Jumbo the Bubble Blowing Elephant, 1950s, Y Co., 7-1/4" tall

EX $100 NM $150 MIP $250

Jungle Jumbo [Elephant], 1950s, B-C Toy Co., walks and bellows, remote control

EX $85 NM $145 MIP $195

Jungle Trio, 1950s, Linemar, 8" tall

EX $485 NM $740 MIP $990

King Zor, 1962, Ideal, blue plastic dinosaur, 30" long

EX $325 NM $510 MIP $725

Kissing Couple, 1950s, Ichida, 10-3/4" long

EX $170 NM $225 MIP $340

Knitting Grandma, 1950s, TN, 8-1/2" tall

EX $185 NM $275 MIP $365

Kooky-Spooky Whistling Tree, 1950s, Marx, 14-1/4" tall

EX $775 NM $1135 MIP $1475

Lambo Elephant, 1950s, Alps, 16" long w/trailer

EX $230 NM $350 MIP $470

Linemar Music Hall, 1950s, Linemar, 8" tall

EX $125 NM $175 MIP $235

Lion, 1950s, Linemar, 9" long

EX $100 NM $150 MIP $200

Loop the Loop Clown, 1960s, TN, 10" tall

EX $70 NM $120 MIP $170

Mac the Turtle, 1960s, Y Co., 8" tall

EX $130 NM $195 MIP $265

Magic Man Clown, 1950s, Marusan, 11" tall

EX $225 NM $325 MIP $450

Magic Snowman, 1950s, MT, 11-1/4" tall

EX $150 NM $200 MIP $300

Main Street, 1950s, Linemar, 19-1/2" long

EX $775 NM $1175 MIP $1575

Major Tooty, 1960s, Alps, 14" tall

EX $110 NM $155 MIP $210

Mambo the Jolly Drumming Elephant, 1950s, Alps, 9-1/2" tall

EX $155 NM $230 MIP $315

Marching Bear, 1960s, Alps, 10" tall

EX $110 NM $165 MIP $225

(Don Hultzman)

Marshal Wild Bill, 1950s, Y Co., 10-1/2" tall

EX $200 NM $300 MIP $400

Marvelous Mike, 1950s, Saunders, 17" long

EX $170 NM $260 MIP $350

Maxwell Coffee-Loving Bear, 1960s, TN, 10" tall

EX $150 NM $225 MIP $350

(KP Photo)

McGregor, 1960s, Rosko, 12" tall
EX $155   NM $220   MIP $315

Mew-Mew Walking Cat, 1950s, MT, three actions, remote control
EX $70   NM $125   MIP $150

Mickey the Magician, 1960s, Linemar, 10" tall
EX $1375 NM $2050   MIP $2775

Mighty Kong, 1950s, Marx, 11" tall
EX $295   NM $430   MIP $575

Mischievous Monkey, 1950s, MT, 18" tall
EX $210   NM $315   MIP $430

Miss Friday the Typist, 1950s, TN, six actions, 8" tall
EX $250   NM $375   MIP $450

Motorcycle Cop, 1950s, Daiya, 10-1/2" long, 8-1/4" tall
EX $500   NM $750   MIP $1000

Mr. MacPooch, 1950s, Marusan, 8" tall
EX $155   NM $225   MIP $300

Mr. Traffic Policeman, 1950s, A-I, 1 4" tall
EX $235   NM $350   MIP $475

Mumbo Jumbo, 1960s, Alps, 9-3/4" tall
EX $130   NM $195   MIP $250

Musical Bear, 1950s, Linemar, 10" tall
EX $285   NM $425   MIP $575

Musical Jackal, 1950s, Linemar, 10" tall
EX $175   NM $315   MIP $700

(Don Hultzman)

Musical Jolly Chimp, 1960s, Daishin, 10-1/2" tall, plays cymbals, glares w/eyes, shows teeth and chatters
EX $50   NM $75   MIP $110

Musical Marching Bear, 1950s, Alps, 11" tall
EX $250   NM $385   MIP $550

NASA Space Capsule, 1950s, four actions
EX $200   NM $315   MIP $430

Nutty Mad Indian, 1960s, Marx, 12" tall
EX $150   NM $200   MIP $250

Nutty Nibs, 1950s, Linemar, 11-1/2" tall
EX $750   NM $1125   MIP $1500

Odd Ogg, 1962, Ideal, large plastic turtle-frog creature
EX $145   NM $225   MIP $365

Ol' Sleepy Head RIP, 1950s, Y Co., 9" tall
EX $190   NM $300   MIP $400

Panda Bear, 1970s, MT, 10" long
EX $55   NM $80   MIP $110

Pat the Roaring Elephant, 1950s, Y Co., 9" long
EX $155   NM $225   MIP $310

Peppermint Twist Doll, 1950s, Haji, 12" tall
EX $185   NM $285   MIP $375

Peppy Puppy, 1950s, Y Co., 8" long
EX $65   NM $95   MIP $120

Pet Turtle, 1960s, Alps, 7" long
EX $85   NM $130   MIP $175

Pete the Space Man, 1960s, Bandai, 5" tall
EX $75   NM $110   MIP $155

Peter the Drumming Rabbit, 1950s, Alps, 13" tall
EX $170   NM $250   MIP $335

Phantom Raider, 1963, Ideal, 33", freighter turned warship
EX $80   NM $135   MIP $200

(KP Photo)

Picnic Bear, 1950s, Alps, five actions - pours real water, 10" tall
EX $150   NM $200   MIP $265

Picnic Bunny, 1950s, Alps, 10" tall
EX $150   NM $185   MIP $240

Picnic Monkey, 1950s, Alps, 10" tall
EX $150   NM $185   MIP $240

Picnic Poodle, 1950s, STS, 7" long
EX $45   NM $70   MIP $95

Pierrot Monkey Cycle, 1950s, MT, 8" tall
EX $255   NM $370   MIP $500

Piggy Cook, 1950s, Y Co., 9-1/2" tall
EX $160   NM $240   MIP $325

Pinkee the Farmer, 1950s, MT, 9-1/2" long
EX $125   NM $190   MIP $250

Pipie the Whale, 1950s, Alps, 12" long
EX $175   NM $260   MIP $365

Pistol Pete, 1950s, Marusan, 10-1/4" tall
EX $275   NM $460   MIP $550

Playful Puppy w/Caterpillar, 1950s, MT, 5" tall
EX $115   NM $170   MIP $230

Polar Bear, 1970s, Alps, 8" long
EX $75   NM $110   MIP $150

Popcorn Eating Bear, 1950s, MT, 9" tall
EX $135   NM $200   MIP $265

Rambling Ladybug, 1960s, MT, 8" long
EX $70   NM $100   MIP $135

Reading Bear, 1950s, Alps, 9" tall
EX $165   NM $245   MIP $330

Rembrandt the Monkey Artist, 1950s, Alps, 8" tall
EX $215   NM $315   MIP $430

Ricki the Begging Poodle, 1950s, Rock Valley, 9" long
EX $40   NM $55   MIP $70

Roarin' Jungle Lion, 1950s, Marx, 16" long
EX $200   NM $275   MIP $350

Rock 'N Roll Monkey, 1950s, Rosko, 13" tall
EX $200   NM $300   MIP $400

Rocking Chair Bear, 1950s, MT, 10" tall
EX $135   NM $200   MIP $265

Roller Skater, 1950s, Alps, 12" tall
EX $200   NM $300   MIP $400

Root Beer Counter, 1960s, K Co., 8" tall
EX $155   NM $230   MIP $310

Sam the Shaving Man, 1960s, Plaything Toy, 11-1/2" tall
EX $155   NM $230   MIP $310

Sammy Wong the Tea Totaler, 1950s, TN, 10" tall
EX $155   NM $230   MIP $310

Santa Claus on Handcar, 1960s, MT, 10" tall
EX $140   NM $220   MIP $290

Santa Claus on Reindeer Sleigh, 1950s, MT, 17" long
EX $475 NM $675 MIP $875

Santa Claus on Scooter, 1960s, MT, 10" tall
EX $150 NM $225 MIP $300

Santa Copter, 1960s, MT, 8-1/2" high
EX $115 NM $170 MIP $225

Saxophone Playing Monkey, 1950s, Alps, 9-1/2" tall
EX $250 NM $385 MIP $510

Serpent Charmer, 1950s, Linemar, 7" tall
EX $345 NM $485 MIP $700

Shaggy the Friendly Pup, 1960s, Alps, 8" long
EX $30 NM $50 MIP $70

Shoe Maker Bear, 1960s, TN, 8-1/2" tall
EX $175 NM $250 MIP $350

Shoe Shine Bear, 1950s, TN, 9" tall
EX $175 NM $250 MIP $350

Shoe Shine Joe, 1950s, Alps, 11" tall, monkey w/pipe polishing a shoe
EX $175 NM $235 MIP $325

Shoe Shine Monkey, 1950s, TN, 9" tall
EX $175 NM $235 MIP $325

Shooting Gorilla, 1950s, MT, 12" tall
EX $250 NM $350 MIP $450

Shutterbug Photographer, 1950s, TN, 9" tall
EX $600 NM $850 MIP $1025

Skating Circus Clown, 1950s, TPS, 6" tall
EX $600 NM $850 MIP $1025

Skiing Santa, 1960s, MT, 12" tall
EX $175 NM $260 MIP $345

Skipping Monkey, 1960s, TN, 9-1/2" tall
EX $45 NM $65 MIP $90

Slalom Game, 1960s, TN, 15-1/4" long
EX $115 NM $175 MIP $235

Sleeping Baby Bear, 1950s, Linemar, 9" long
EX $300 NM $450 MIP $600

Sleepy Pup, 1960s, Alps, 9" long
EX $45 NM $75 MIP $100

Slurpy Pup, 1960s, TN, 6-1/2" long
EX $55 NM $80 MIP $110

Smoking Bunny, 1950s, Marusan, 10-1/2" tall
EX $125 NM $190 MIP $260

Smoking Elephant, 1950s, Marusan, 8-3/4" tall
EX $135 NM $200 MIP $250

Smoking Grandpa in Rocker, 1950s, Marusan, 8" tall, four actions
EX $200 NM $325 MIP $400

Smoking Popeye, 1950s, Linemar, 9" tall
EX $1875 NM $2625 MIP $3775

Smoking Spaceman, 1950s, Linemar, 12" tall
EX $1125 NM $1675 MIP $2250

Smoky Bear, 1950s, Marusan, 9" tall
EX $250 NM $335 MIP $500

Sneezing Bear, 1950s, Linemar, 9" tall
EX $190 NM $270 MIP $380

Snoopy Sniffer, 1960s, MT, 8" long
EX $45 NM $70 MIP $90

Spanking Bear, 1950s, Linemar, 9" tall
EX $190 NM $300 MIP $385

Struttin' Sam, 1950s, Haji, 10-1/2" tall
EX $250 NM $400 MIP $450

Sunday Driver, 1950s, MT, 10" long
EX $75 NM $115 MIP $155

Super Susie, 1950s, Linemar, 9" tall
EX $575 NM $860 MIP $1175

Suzette the Eating Monkey, 1950s, Linemar, 8-3/4" tall
EX $425 NM $585 MIP $800

Switchboard Operator, 1950s, Linemar, 7-1/2" tall
EX $500 NM $750 MIP $1000

Tarzan, 1966, Marusan, 13" tall
EX $625 NM $935 MIP $1250

Teddy Bear Swing, 1950s, TN, 17" tall
EX $325 NM $425 MIP $650

Teddy the Artist, 1950s, Y Co., 8-1/2" tall
EX $400 NM $600 MIP $800

Teddy the Boxing Bear, 1950s, Y Co., 9" tall
EX $150 NM $225 MIP $300

Teddy the Rhythmical Drummer, 1960s, Alps, 11" tall
EX $110 NM $170 MIP $230

Teddy-Go-Kart, 1960s, Alps, 10-1/2" long
EX $120 NM $180 MIP $225

(KP Photo)

Telephone Bear, 1950s, Linemar, 7-1/2" tall
EX $225 NM $315 MIP $425

Telephone Bear w/Rocking Chair, 1950s, MT, 10" tall
EX $250 NM $350 MIP $450

Television Spaceman, 1960s, Alps, 14-1/2" tall
EX $500 NM $875 MIP $1050

Tinkling Trolley, 1950s, MT, 10-1/2" long
EX $150 NM $225 MIP $300

Tom and Jerry Choo Choo, 1960s, MT, 10-1/4" long
EX $175 NM $250 MIP $325

Tom and Jerry Handcar, 1960s, MT, 7-3/4" long
EX $160 NM $270 MIP $350

Tom-Tom Indian, 1961, Y Co., 10-1/2" tall
EX $100 NM $150 MIP $185

Topo Gigio Playing the Xylophone, 1960s, TN
EX $350 NM $550 MIP $725

Traveler Bear, 1950s, Linemar, 8" tall
EX $150 NM $225 MIP $300

Trumpet Playing Bunny, 1950s, Alps, 10" tall
EX $200 NM $300 MIP $400

Trumpet Playing Monkey, 1950s, Alps, 9" tall
EX $200 NM $300 MIP $400

Tubby the Turtle, 1950s, Y Co., 7" long
EX $70 NM $110 MIP $140

Tumbles the Bear, 1960s, Yanoman, 8-1/2" tall
EX $95 NM $140 MIP $190

Twirly Whirly, 1950s, Alps, 13-1/2" tall
EX $400 NM $600 MIP $800

Walking Bear w/Xylophone, 1950s, Linemar, 10" tall
EX $270 NM $420 MIP $540

Walking Elephant, 1950s, Linemar, 8-1/2" tall
EX $100 NM $150 MIP $225

Walking Esso Tiger, 1950s, Marx, 11-1/2" tall
EX $200 NM $300 MIP $400

Walking Itchy Dog, 1950s, Alps, 9" long
EX $55 NM $85 MIP $110

Western Locomotive, 1950s, MT, 10-1/2" long
EX $45 NM $35 MIP $90

Character Toys

By Justin Moen

The Character Toys chapter is perhaps the most comprehensive and complex in this price guide, simply because any toy related to characters in movies, TV, and comic books can be placed in this chapter. The strong majority of these characters have become pop culture icons that have stood the test of time. Because of this, collectors do not limit their acquired treasures to just toys. Their collections include, but are not limited to: glasses, costumes, coloring books, and membership rings just to name a few.

Because this is such a massive category, most collectors limit their collections to specific characters like Superman, Mickey Mouse, or Batman. But even then collectors' shelves can fill rather quickly. The best advice for any novice in the character toy-collecting hobby is to limit your search to a character, or a couple characters, and the kind of collectibles you want in relation to that character or characters.

And it is in this category where you really need to do plenty of research and ask the right questions to avoid buying fakes that are sold as originals. With character toys, licenses were granted to manufacturers at an almost unlimited rate. Consequently, this has led to many similar toys featured on the market.

Again, it's all about doing research and asking the right questions. Try to find the manufacturers you are looking for and pay close attention to markings on the collectibles. Beware, not every seller has the sufficient amount of knowledge on the collectible they are trying to sell, which may lead to buyers getting burned by overpaying for an item that in reality has little or no collectible value.

In general, the older the character toy is, the better condition it's in, and the more popular the character is, the higher the value. Superman and Mickey Mouse toys are probably the best examples of this, especially the pristine condition pieces that are very difficult to find.

Excellent condition character toys produced on an exclusive basis over 50 years ago also command top dollar. Popeye toys are perfect examples of such pieces. Early postwar era character toys in general have remained quite steady in recent years, as baby boomers are still buying toys they played with as kids. As a result, TV character toys from the 50s have seen a nice boost in popularity and value.

Keep in mind that it is the character toys in top condition that realize the largest area of movement among collectors. These collectors typically start small before advancing their collections over time. Fortunately, every character has something at every price range. It's just a matter of what one wants to pay for an item.

The Top 10 **CHARACTER TOYS** in mint condition

1. Action Comics #1 (first appearance of Superman), 1938 . . . . $2,160,000
2. Detective Comics #27 (first appearance of Batman), 1939 . . . . $1,075,000
3. Superman Club Member Ring, 1940 . . . . $50,000
4. Superman Milk Defense Club Ring, 1941 . . . . $25,000
5. Little Orphan Annie Altascope Ring, Quaker, 1942 . . . . $20,000
6. Superman Trading Cards, Gum Inc., set of 72, 1940 . . . . $15,000
7. Batman Play Set, Ideal, 1966 . . . . $10,000
8. Mickey Mouse Lionel Circus Train, Lionel, 1935 . . . . $10,000
9. Superman Bubblegum Badge, Fo-Lee Gum Co., 1948 . . . . $10,000
10. Donald Duck Bicycle, Shelby, 1949 . . . . $8,000

101 Dalmatians

ACCESSORIES

101 Dalmatians Snow Dome, 1961, Marx, 3" x 5" x 3-1/2" tall
EX $35   NM $65   MIP $110

FIGURES

Dalmatian Pups Figures, 1960s, Enesco, 4-1/2" tall, set of three
EX $25   NM $50   MIP $160

Lucky Figure, 1960s, Enesco, 4" tall
EX $35   NM $65   MIP $100

TOY

101 Dalmatians Wind-Up, 1959, Linemar
EX $125   NM $250   MIP $500

Lucky Squeeze Toy, Dell, 7" tall, squeakers in the bottom
EX $10   NM $20   MIP $50

Alice in Wonderland

ACCESSORIES

Clock Radio, 1970s, General Electric, features characters on face
EX $20   NM $40   MIP $85

Film Viewer, 1950s, Tru-Vue, viewer and filmstrip
EX $30   NM $60   MIP $100

Handbag, 1950s, ACME Briefcase, child's red leather shoulder bag
EX $30   NM $80   MIP $120

Handbag, 1950s, Salient, child's pink vinyl shoulder bag, Alice w/rocking fly
EX $30   NM $80   MIP $120

Hatbox, 1950s, Neevel, Caterpillar or Tea Party graphics
EX $55   NM $100   MIP $150

Picture Frame, 1970s, Dexter-Mahnke, cloth picture frame, featuring Mad Tea Party
EX $20   NM $35   MIP $60

Record Player, 1951, RCA Victor, 45 rpm
EX $75   NM $225   MIP $400

School Bag, 1950s, ACME Briefcase, fabric and leather
EX $30   NM $100   MIP $150

Soap Set, 1951
EX $40   NM $120   MIP $250

Wall Decor, 1951, Dolly Toy, #260 contains Alice, Mad Hatter, March Hare and a lamp
EX $50   NM $100   MIP $200

Wall Plaque, 1974, Leisuramics, bisque, oval shape, featuring TweedleDee and TweedleDum
EX $20   NM $40   MIP $60

Wall Plaque, 1974, Leisuramics, bisque, oval shape, featuring Mad Hatter
EX $20   NM $40   MIP $75

BANK

Alice Bank, 1950s, Leeds, figural
EX $100   NM $200   MIP $275

BOOK

Alice in Wonderland and Cinderella Book, 1950s, Collins, Great Britain version
EX $25   NM $60   MIP $120

Alice in Wonderland Book, 1950s, Whitman, #2074 Cozy Corner Book, green endpapers
EX $30   NM $60   MIP $100

Alice in Wonderland Book, 1950s, Whitman, #10426, w/out gold backing
EX $30   NM $70   MIP $150

Alice in Wonderland Book, 1950s, Whitman, #10426, Big Golden Book, gold foil backing
EX $50   NM $100   MIP $175

Alice in Wonderland Book, 1951, Whitman, Sandpiper Book w/dust jacket
EX $50   NM $100   MIP $200

Alice in Wonderland Book, 1951, Dell Publishing, #331
EX $35   NM $75   MIP $175

Alice in Wonderland Book, 1951, Whitman, #426, Big Golden Book
EX $50   NM $100   MIP $175

Alice in Wonderland Classic Series w/Disney Book, 1950s, Whitman, #2140 Lewis Carroll text w/Disney dust jacket
EX $50   NM $100   MIP $200

Alice in Wonderland Paint Book, 1951, Whitman, #2167
EX $55   NM $110   MIP $225

Alice in Wonderland Punch-Out Book, 1951, Whitman, #2164
EX $80   NM $200   MIP $350

Alice in Wonderland Sticker Fun, 1950s, Whitman, #2193 stencil and coloring book
EX $30   NM $60   MIP $100

(KP Photo)

Alice Meets the White Rabbit Book, 1951, Whitman, #D-19, Little Golden Book
EX $15   NM $45   MIP $80

(KP Photo)

Mad Hatter's Tea Party Book, 1951, Whitman, #D-23 Little Golden Book
EX $15   NM $45   MIP $60

Unbirthday Party Book, The, 1974, Whitman, #22, Walt Disney Showcase
EX $8   NM $15   MIP $30

CANDY TIN

Candy Tin, 1950s, Edward Sharp and Sons, Great Britain English Toffee Tin
EX $125   NM $250   MIP $325

COLLECTIBLE

Alice Snow Dome, 1961, Marx, 3" tall featuring Alice and the White Rabbit in front of tree
EX $15   NM $35   MIP $100

Caterpillar Figure, 1956, Hagen-Renaker
EX $200   NM $400   MIP $600

Mad Hatter Snow Dome, 1980s, New England Collectors Society, crystal, Mad Hatter, St. Patrick's Day
EX $15   NM $25   MIP $50

Mad Hatter Teapot, 1950s, Regal
EX $500   NM $1000   MIP $1600

Pitcher, 1950s, Regal, King of Hearts
EX $200   NM $375   MIP $650

Plaque, 1970s, Disneyland, wooden, w/Alice and live flowers

EX $15   NM $25   MIP $50

Salt and Pepper Shakers, 1950s, Regal, featuring TweedleDee and TweedleDum

EX $150   NM $300   MIP $525

Salt and Pepper Shakers, 1950s, Regal, blue or white featuring Alice

EX $150   NM $300   MIP $500

Tea Cake Box, 1980s, TDL, w/a Mad Tea Party lid

EX $10   NM $15   MIP $30

Tea Cup and Saucer, 1986, TDL, ceramic, Mad Tea Party

EX $60   NM $120   MIP $200

Thimble, 1980s, New England Collectors Society, Mad Hatter and Alice

EX $5   NM $15   MIP $25

Vase, 1960s, Enesco, featuring Alice's head

EX $75   NM $150   MIP $250

White Rabbit Creamer, 1950s, Regal

EX $175   NM $350   MIP $500

White Rabbit Sugar Bowl, 1950s, Regal

EX $200   NM $400   MIP $600

COLORING BOOK

Alice in Wonderland Big Coloring Book, 1951, Whitman, #301 Big Golden, Model No. 301

EX $75   NM $150   MIP $225

Alice in Wonderland Coloring Book, 1974, Whitman, #1049

EX $5   NM $20   MIP $40

COOKIE JAR

Alice Cookie Jar, Regal, 13-1/2" tall

EX $375   NM $1000   MIP $1650

Alice Cookie Jar, 1950s, Leeds, printed in relief

EX $200   NM $325   MIP $425

Looking Glass Cookie Jar, Fred Roberts, raised characters on the body of the jar w/a mirror lid

EX $300   NM $500   MIP $725

COSTUMES

Alice Costume, 1950s, Ben Cooper, costume made until 1970s

EX $50   NM $100   MIP $200

Mad Hatter Costume, 1950s, Ben Cooper, costume made until 1970s

EX $30   NM $60   MIP $120

March Hare Costume, 1950s, Ben Cooper, costume made until 1970s

EX $30   NM $60   MIP $120

DOLLS

Alice Doll, 1950s, Gund, flat vinyl, stuffed

EX $50   NM $125   MIP $200

Alice Doll, 1951, Duchess, 12-1/2" tall

EX $100   NM $225   MIP $350

Alice Doll, 1951, Duchess, #739, 7-1/2" tall

EX $80   NM $200   MIP $300

Alice Doll, 1970s, Horsman, Alice has a castle on her apron

EX $20   NM $45   MIP $90

Alice Doll, 1970s, Pedigree, Great Britain

EX $20   NM $40   MIP $75

Alice Doll, 1970s, Horsman, #1071, Walt Disney Classics

EX $20   NM $35   MIP $75

Cheshire Cat Doll, 1970s, Disneyland, plush

EX $10   NM $25   MIP $60

Dormouse Doll, 1950s, Lars/Italy, stuffed

EX $160   NM $330   MIP $550

Mad Hatter Doll, 1950s, Gund, flat vinyl, stuffed

EX $40   NM $90   MIP $150

Mad Hatter Doll, 1950s, Gund, plush

EX $125   NM $275   MIP $425

March Hare Doll, 1950s, Gund, plush

EX $175   NM $350   MIP $600

March Hare Doll, 1950s, Gund, flat vinyl, stuffed

EX $50   NM $60   MIP $135

Queen of Hearts Doll, 1950s, Gund, flat vinyl, stuffed

EX $40   NM $80   MIP $150

TweedleDee and TweedleDum Dolls, 1950s, Gund, flat vinyl, stuffed, each

EX $75   NM $150   MIP $225

TweedleDee and TweedleDum Dolls, 1980s, TDL, plush, each

EX $15   NM $30   MIP $60

Walrus Doll, 1950s, Lars/Italy, stuffed

EX $200   NM $500   MIP $675

White Rabbit Doll, 1950s, Gund, flat vinyl, stuffed

EX $50   NM $125   MIP $175

White Rabbit Doll, 1950s, Gund

EX $110   NM $300   MIP $450

White Rabbit Doll, 1970s, Sears, plush w/waistcoat and umbrella

EX $12   NM $25   MIP $50

White Rabbit Doll, 1970s, Disneyland, large, plush w/yellow spectacles

EX $12   NM $25   MIP $50

White Rabbit Doll, 1970s, Disneyland, small w/black spectacles

EX $10   NM $20   MIP $40

White Rabbit Doll, 1974, Buena Vista/Disney, plush

EX $50   NM $100   MIP $150

White Rabbit Doll, 1980s, TDL, plush

EX $10   NM $25   MIP $50

FIGURES

Alice Figure, 1950s, Marx, painted w/"Holland" stamped on the bottom

EX $40   NM $75   MIP $120

Alice Figure, 1950s, Aldon Industries, plastic, cut-out standup

EX $50   NM $110   MIP $150

Alice Figure, 1951, Shaw

EX $120   NM $300   MIP $750

Alice Figure, 1956, Hagen-Renaker

EX $200   NM $400   MIP $625

Alice Figure, 1980s, Sears, Magic Kingdom Collection, bone china

EX $15   NM $25   MIP $35

Alice Figure, 1984, Bully, Germany, PVC, wearing a blue or red dress, each

EX $10   NM $15   MIP $20

Disneyland Figures Set, 1960s, United China, large set, each piece

EX $15   NM $30   MIP $60

Disneyland Figures Set, 1970s, United China, small figures, each piece

EX $10   NM $15   MIP $30

Dormouse Figure, 1951, Shaw

EX $130   NM $225   MIP $400

Mad Hatter Figure, 1950s, Marx, painted w/"Holland" stamped on the bottom

EX $20   NM $35   MIP $75

Mad Hatter Figure, 1950s, Sydney Pottery, large size, sold only in Australia

EX $250   NM $425   MIP $625

Mad Hatter Figure, 1951, Shaw

EX $65   NM $200   MIP $350

Mad Hatter Figure, 1956, Hagen-Renaker

EX $150   NM $300   MIP $450

Mad Hatter Figure, 1980s, Schmid, playing xylophone

EX $20   NM $40   MIP $75

Mad Hatter/March Hare Figure, 1980s, TDL, Mad Hatter, March Hare w/saxophone

EX $20   NM $40   MIP $60

March Hare Figure, 1950s, Sydney Pottery, large size, sold only in Australia

EX $200   NM $400   MIP $625

March Hare Figure, 1950s, Marx, painted w/"Holland" stamped on the bottom

EX $15   NM $30   MIP $60

March Hare Figure, 1951, Shaw
EX $170   NM $320   MIP $500

March Hare Figure, 1956, Hagen-Renaker
EX $110   NM $275   MIP $450

Queen of Hearts Figure, 1950s, Marx, painted w/"Holland" stamped on the bottom
EX $12   NM $25   MIP $50

Queen of Hearts Figure, 1980s, Sears, Magic Kingdom Collection, bone china
EX $15   NM $25   MIP $35

TweedleDee Figure, 1950s, Sydney Pottery, large size, sold only in Australia
EX $200   NM $400   MIP $600

TweedleDee Figure, 1951, Shaw
EX $70   NM $150   MIP $235

TweedleDum Figure, 1950s, Sydney Pottery, large size, sold only in Australia
EX $200   NM $400   MIP $600

TweedleDum Figure, 1951, Shaw
EX $70   NM $150   MIP $235

Walrus Figure, 1950s, Sydney Pottery, large size, sold only in Australia
EX $160   NM $375   MIP $575

Walrus Figure, 1951, Shaw
EX $110   NM $250   MIP $425

White Rabbit Figure, Italy, 5-1/2" tall, ceramic
EX $15   NM $35   MIP $60

White Rabbit Figure, 1950s, Marx, painted w/"Holland" stamped on the bottom
EX $12   NM $25   MIP $50

White Rabbit Figure, 1951, Shaw
EX $65   NM $140   MIP $250

White Rabbit Figure, 1980s, Sears, Magic Kingdom Collection, bone china
EX $12   NM $25   MIP $50

GAMES

Adventures in Costumeland Game, 1980s, Walt Disney World, created for Disney costume division members, game board and pieces in a small vinyl garment bag
EX $75   NM $150   MIP $200

Alice in Wonderland Card Game, 1980s, Thos. De LaRue
EX $10   NM $20   MIP $35

Bridge Card Game, 1950s, Whitman, two decks of cards
EX $35   NM $75   MIP $175

Canasta Card Game, 1950s, Whitman, two Canasta decks of White Rabbit cards
EX $50   NM $100   MIP $150

Queen of Hearts Card Game, 1975, Edu-Cards
EX $20   NM $35   MIP $65

GLASSWARE

Alice and White Rabbit Mug, 1991, TDL/Daiichi Seimei, promo piece
EX $25   NM $40   MIP $65

Alice Mug, 1970s, Disney
EX $12   NM $20   MIP $40

Glass, 1970s, Pepsi Cola, featuring Alice, part of Wonderful World of Disney set
EX $10   NM $20   MIP $35

Glasses, 1951, Libbey, eight styles released for film opening, each
EX $40   NM $60   MIP $120

Mad Tea Party/Cheshire Cat Mug, 1988, Applause, Cheshire Cat handle w/Tea Party on the mug
EX $12   NM $18   MIP $30

MUSIC BOX

Music Box, 1980s, Disneyland, wooden box features Alice and White Rabbit "I'm Late"
EX $30   NM $60   MIP $100

Music Box, 1980s, TDL, plastic, tea cup rotates
EX $45   NM $80   MIP $150

Music Box, 1980s, TDL, ceramic teacup
EX $45   NM $80   MIP $150

PAPER DOLLS

Alice Paper Dolls, 1972, Whitman, #4712
EX $25   NM $50   MIP $90

Alice Paper Dolls, 1976, Whitman, #1948
EX $20   NM $40   MIP $75

PAPER GOODS

Alice Stationery and Notepad, 1970s, Pak-Well, #77065 w/a fan card cover
EX $10   NM $20   MIP $35

Cheshire Cat Costume Pattern, 1951, McCall's
EX $25   NM $40   MIP $75

Fan Card, 1951, Walt Disney, premium sent to fans who wrote letters to studio
EX $30   NM $50   MIP $75

Fan Card, 1951, Walt Disney, original release w/1973 invitation to studio screening
EX $40   NM $60   MIP $80

Mad Hatter Costume Pattern, 1951, McCall's
EX $20   NM $35   MIP $55

March Hare Costume Pattern, 1951, McCall's
EX $20   NM $35   MIP $60

Poster, 1958, Disneyland, Alice attraction
EX $400   NM $700   MIP $1000

Poster, 1980s, Walt Disney World, costume division poster featuring Cheshire Cat
EX $20   NM $40   MIP $65

Ticket, 1970s, Disneyland, employee screening ticket featuring Cheshire Cat
EX $10   NM $15   MIP $25

PREMIUMS

Bread Labels, 1950s, NBC, 12 different styles, each
EX $25   NM $40   MIP $80

Bread Seal Poster, 1950s, NBC
EX $40   NM $60   MIP $100

Bread Stickers, 1974, Continental Baking/Wonder, five styles, each
EX $5   NM $10   MIP $15

Cards, 1951, Royal Desserts, 16 different cards on the back of dessert packages, each
EX $20   NM $35   MIP $70

Cereal Box w/Record, 1956, General Mills, Wheaties
EX $400   NM $500   MIP $650

Magic Picture Kit Set, 1974, Jiffy Pop, set of four
EX $12   NM $25   MIP $50

Poster, 1980, Kraft, Disneyland 25th Anniversary Family Reunion
EX $15   NM $30   MIP $65

RECORD

Record/Little Nipper Giant Storybook, 1951, RCA Victor, LY-437, 33, 45, or 78 rpm, each
EX $80   NM $120   MIP $160

TOY

Alice Disneykin, 1950s, Marx, unpainted, soft plastic
EX $10   NM $20   MIP $40

Alice Disneykin, 1950s, Marx, hard plastic
EX $10   NM $25   MIP $50

Alice Marionette, 1950s, Peter Puppet, comes in two different boxes, one "Alice in Wonderland" the other Peter Puppet Disney
EX $70   NM $225   MIP $450

Balloons, 1951, Oak Rubber, four different designs
EX $12   NM $20   MIP $50

Balloons, 1951, Eagle Rubber
EX $12   NM $20   MIP $50

Blocks, 1950s, Chad Valley, five cylindrical tin blocks w/color graphics
EX $75   NM $150   MIP $300

Child's Vanity, 1950s, Neevel, illustrated w/film scenes
EX $70   NM $120   MIP $200

Disneykin Play Set, 1950s, Marx
EX $200   NM $400   MIP $650

Jingle Ball, 1951, Vanguard
EX $12   NM $25   MIP $50

Mad Hatter Disneykin, 1950s, Marx, unpainted, soft plastic
EX $10   NM $16   MIP $30

Mad Hatter Disneykin, 1950s, Marx
EX $25   NM $45   MIP $85

Mad Hatter Hand Puppet, 1960s, hand puppet w/cloth body
EX $40   NM $75   MIP $100

Mad Hatter Marionette, 1950s, Peter Puppet
EX $100   NM $150   MIP $275

Mad Hatter Nodder, 1950s, Marx
EX $100   NM $250   MIP $375

Mad Hatter Snap Eeze, 1950s, Marx
EX $15   NM $30   MIP $50

Make-Up Kit, 1951, Hasbro
EX $25   NM $55   MIP $100

March Hare Disneykin, 1950s, Marx, unpainted and soft plastic
EX $12   NM $18   MIP $35

March Hare Marionette, 1950s, Peter Puppet
EX $100   NM $150   MIP $250

March Hare Snap Eeze, 1950s, Marx
EX $15   NM $20   MIP $50

March Hare Twistoy, 1950s, Marx
EX $15   NM $20   MIP $50

Molding Set, 1951, Model Craft
EX $50   NM $100   MIP $200

Molding Set, 1952, Great Britain, similar to Model Craft set
EX $60   NM $120   MIP $210

Puppet Theatre, 1950s, Peter Puppet
EX $125   NM $200   MIP $300

Puzzle, 1951, Jaymar, Alice and Rabbit
EX $50   NM $90   MIP $150

Puzzle, 1951, Jaymar, Alice under a tree
EX $50   NM $90   MIP $150

Puzzle, 1951, Jaymar, Croquet cast scene
EX $50   NM $90   MIP $150

Puzzle, 1951, Jaymar, Tea Party scene
EX $50   NM $90   MIP $150

Puzzle, 1979, Stafford/England, wooden, Great Britain Tea Party
EX $10   NM $25   MIP $40

Puzzle, 1980s, TDL, #18, Mad Tea Party and Cast
EX $5   NM $10   MIP $25

Queen of Hearts Disneykin, 1950s, Marx
EX $30   NM $55   MIP $85

Queen of Hearts Disneykin, 1950s, Marx, unpainted, soft plastic
EX $15   NM $20   MIP $35

Ramp Walker, 1950s, Marx, Mad Hatter and White Rabbit
EX $40   NM $80   MIP $100

Rubber Stamp Set, 1970s, Multiprint, Italy, #177
EX $20   NM $30   MIP $55

Rubber Stamp Set, 1989, All Night Media
EX $10   NM $15   MIP $25

(KP Photo)

Sewing Cards, 1951, Whitman
EX $40   NM $75   MIP $125

Sewing Kit, 1951, Hasbro, 7" sewing machine and 5" doll, all plastic
EX $50   NM $100   MIP $150

TV Scene, White Rabbit and March Hare, 1950s, Marx
EX $30   NM $65   MIP $100

View-Master Set, 1970s, GAF, three reels, Disney
EX $12   NM $25   MIP $40

Wallet, 1950s, Salient, vinyl, featuring Mad Tea Party
EX $30   NM $60   MIP $100

Wallet, 1950s, Salient, vinyl, featuring White Rabbit
EX $30   NM $60   MIP $100

White Rabbit Disneykin, 1950s, Marx
EX $30   NM $60   MIP $85

White Rabbit Disneykin, 1950s, Marx, unpainted and soft plastic
EX $10   NM $20   MIP $35

White Rabbit Ears, 1980s, TDL
EX $10   NM $20   MIP $35

White Rabbit Rolykin, 1950s, Marx
EX $20   NM $40   MIP $70

WATCH

Alice Wristwatch, 1950s, U.S. Time, Alice peeking through pink flowers and a plastic statue
EX $400   NM $750   MIP $1200

Alice Wristwatch, 1950s, U.S. Time, came w/ceramic statue
EX $400   NM $750   MIP $1000

Alice Wristwatch, 1990s, Alba, Japan, gold tone face
EX $15   NM $30   MIP $60

Tea Cup Wristwatch, 1950s, U.S. Time, picture of Mad Hatter w/an overlay
EX $450   NM $850   MIP $1300

Andy Gump

ACCESSORIES

Brush and Mirror, 4" diameter, red on ivory colored surface of brush
EX $65   NM $125   MIP $200

TOY

Chester Gump Playstone Funnies Mold Set, 1940s
EX $100   NM $150   MIP $200

Archies

ACCESSORIES

Archie Halloween Costume, 1969, Ben Cooper
EX $50   NM $75   MIP $100

TOY

Archies Paper Dolls, 1969, Whitman
EX $25   NM $50   MIP $100

Jalopy, 1975, Marx, 12", plastic
EX $80   NM $150   MIP $275

(KP Photo)

Puzzle, 1960s, Jaymar, "Swinging Malt Shop"
EX $40   NM $60   MIP $100

Atom Ant and Friends

TOY

Atom Ant Kite, 1960s, Roalex
EX $40   NM $80   MIP $150

Atom Ant Punch-Out Set, 1966, Whitman
EX $100 NM $175 MIP $325

Atom Ant Push Puppet, 1960s, Kohner
EX $40   NM $65   MIP $90

Atom Ant Puzzle, 1966, Whitman
EX $40   NM $80   MIP $100

Atom Ant Soaky, 1966, Purex
EX $35   NM $70   MIP $100

Morocco Mole Bubble Club Soaky, 1960s, Purex, 7" hard plastic
EX $35   NM $70   MIP $100

Squiddly Diddly Bubble Club Soaky, 1960s, Purex, 10-1/2" hard plastic
EX $35   NM $70   MIP $100

Winsome Witch Bubble Club Soaky, 1960s, Purex, 10-1/2" hard plastic
EX $35   NM $70   MIP $100

Babes in Toyland

DOLL

Cadet Doll, Gund, 15-1/2" tall, fabric
EX $35   NM $80   MIP $150

TOY

Babes in Toyland Go Mobile Friction Car, 1961, Linemar, 4" x 5" x 6"
EX $150 NM $300 MIP $450

Babes in Toyland Hand Puppets, Gund, Silly Dilly Clown, Soldier, or Gorgonzo, each
EX $50   NM $100 MIP $150

Babes in Toyland Twist 'N Bend Toy, 1963, Marx, 4" tall flexible toy w/Private Valiant holding a baton
EX $10   NM $25   MIP $55

Babes in Toyland Wind-Up Toy, 1950s, Linemar, tin
EX $200 NM $400 MIP $525

Puzzle, 1961, Jaymar
EX $20   NM $45   MIP $65

Bambi

ACCESSORIES

Bambi Prints, 1947, New York Graphic Society, 11" x 14" framed
EX $25   NM $50   MIP $100

Lamp, Bambi and Thumper
EX $150 NM $275 MIP $400

Throw Rug, 1960s, 21" x 39", Bambi and Thumper
EX $30   NM $60   MIP $100

Thumper Ashtray, 1950s, Goebel, 4" tall
EX $75   NM $150 MIP $200

Wristwatch, 1949, US Time
EX $150 NM $275 MIP $450

BANK

Flower Bank, 1940s, 5" x 5"x 7" tall, plaster
EX $75   NM $125 MIP $250

Thumper Bank, 1950s, Leeds, ceramic, figural
EX $75   NM $100 MIP $185

DOLL

Thumper Doll, 16" tall, plush
EX $15   NM $30   MIP $75

TOY

Bambi Soaky, Colgate-Palmolive
EX $20   NM $40   MIP $80

Thumper Soaky, 1960s, Colgate-Palmolive
EX $25   NM $60   MIP $100

Barney Google

FIGURE

Barney Google and Spark Plug Figurines, 3" x 3", bisque, on white bisque pedestal
EX $200 NM $350 MIP $475

TOY

Spark Plug Pull Toy, 10" x 8" tall, wood
EX $150 NM $250 MIP $400

Batman

ACCESSORIES

Batcoin Lot, 1966, Space Magic Limited, four 1-1/2" diameter metal coins, each depicting a scene featuring Batman and Robin battling villains
EX $30   NM $75   MIP $100

Batman and Robin Society Membership Button, 1966, Button World, full-color litho metal button featuring Batman and Robin and the words "Charter Member-Batman and Robin Society"
EX $15   NM $25   MIP $35

Batman Candy Box, 1966, Phoenix Candy, 2-1/2" x 3-1/2" x 1", several color scenes
EX $100 NM $150 MIP $250

Batman Cereal Box, 1966, Kellogg's, w/Yogi Bear on front
EX $700 NM $1500 MIP $2000

Batman Crazy Foam, 1974
EX $20   NM $40   MIP $100

Batman Dinner Set, 1966, ceramic; three pieces
EX $40   NM $70   MIP $175

Batman Fork, 1966, Imperial, 6" stainless steel w/embossed figure of Batman, w/"Batman" engraved towards the bottom
EX $15   NM $30   MIP $60

Batman Halloween Costume, 1965, Ben Cooper, plastic Halloween mask and purple and yellow cape, several versions, some feature logo on chest
EX $40   NM $75   MIP $150

(KP Photo)

Batman Helmet and Cape Set, 1966, Ideal, blue hard plastic cowl shaped helmet and soft blue vinyl cape w/drawstring
EX $250 NM $450 MIP $650

Batman Lamp, Vanity Fair, Made in Taiwan
EX $50   NM $100 MIP $220

(KP Photo)

Batman Pencil Box, 1966, Empire Pencil, gun-shaped pencil box w/set of Batman pencils
EX $30   NM $55   MIP $125

Batman Pillow, 1966, 10" x 12" w/1940s logo
EX $20   NM $40   MIP $75

Batman Wastepaper Basket, 1966, 10" tall, color tin litho
EX $30   NM $60   MIP $125

Batmobile AM Radio, 1970s, Bandai
EX $50   NM $100 MIP $225

Beach Towel, 1966, 34" x 58" white, Batman hitting a crook
EX $40   NM $95   MIP $180

Cake Decoration, 1960s, 2" hard plastic figure of Robin or Batman, each
EX $8   NM $15   MIP $30

Cake Decorations, 1966, Space Magic Limited, 4" plastic one dimensional figures of Batman, Robin and old 1940s Batman logo
EX $20   NM $40   MIP $70

Catwoman Iron-On Patch, 1966, Catwoman w/the words "Batkids Fan Club"
EX $20   NM $50   MIP $80

Charm Bracelet, 1966, on card
EX $50   NM $85   MIP $150

Child's Dinner Plate, 1966, Boontonware, 7" plastic w/image of Batman and Robin
EX $15   NM $30   MIP $60

Christmas Ornament, 1989, Presents
EX $5   NM $10   MIP $20

Coins, 1966, Transogram, plastic, set
EX $50   NM $75   MIP $120

Costume Patterns, 1960s, McCalls, patterns for making Batman, Robin, and Superman costumes, paper envelope, each
EX $15   NM $35   MIP $85

Inflatable TV Chair, 1982
EX $10   NM $20   MIP $35

Joker Cereal Bowl, 1966, Sun Valley, 5" hard plastic
EX $15   NM $30   MIP $55

Lapel Pin, 1966, Mamsell, 2" bat-shaped metal, black w/yellow eyes
EX $20   NM $35   MIP $60

Mug, 1966, 5" clear plastic; color wrap around sheet
EX $30   NM $60   MIP $100

Pennant, 1966, 11" x 29" white felt, illustration of the Dynamic Duo swinging on ropes w/the Bat-signal in the background
EX $80   NM $150   MIP $250

Robin Character Sponge, 1966, Epic, 5"
EX $10   NM $30   MIP $80

Robin Iron-on Patch, 1966, 2-1/2" diameter patch, Batkids Fan Club
EX $12   NM $35   MIP $60

Robin Ornament, 1989, Presents
EX $5   NM $13   MIP $20

Robin Placemat, 1966, 13" x 18" vinyl
EX $35   NM $80   MIP $110

Sip-A-Drink Cup, 1966, British, 6" tall, white plastic
EX $50   NM $100   MIP $200

(KP Photo)

Talking Alarm Clock, 1975, Janex, plastic clock w/Bat logo on face
EX $75   NM $100   MIP $180

ACTION FIGURES

Batman Bendy Figure, 1960s, Diener, on card
EX $35   NM $65   MIP $90

Batman Figure, 1966, Ideal, 3" yellow plastic, detachable gray plastic cape
EX $12   NM $25   MIP $50

(KP Photo)

Batman Figure, 1988, Applause, 15" tall w/stand
EX $15   NM $25   MIP $45

Batman Figure, 1989, Billiken, 8" on card
EX $8   NM $15   MIP $30

Batman Figure, 1989, Bully, 7" bendy
EX $8   NM $15   MIP $25

Batman Figure, 1989, Presents, 15-1/2" tall vinyl and cloth figure on base, 1970s logo, metal stand
EX $20   NM $40   MIP $75

Batman Figure, 1989, Takara/Japan
EX $40   NM $80   MIP $150

Batman Figure, 1989, Toy Biz, 5" w/retractable Batrope, speargun and Batarang, Model No. 4401
EX n/a   NM n/a   MIP n/a

Batman Figure and Parachute, 1966, CDC, 11" x 9" card, metallic blue figure of Batman and working parachute
EX $40   NM $75   MIP $150

Batman Flying Figure on String, 1973, Ben Cooper, 6" rubber figure of Batman w/rubber cape
EX $12   NM $25   MIP $55

Batman Inflated Gliding Figure, 1966, Ideal, 16" soft plastic inflatable Batman w/free flowing cape and hard plastic cable rail
EX $40   NM $60   MIP $125

Batman on a String Figure, 1966, Fun Things, 4" rubber, flexible arms, legs and removable cape
EX $20   NM $30   MIP $60

Joker Figure, Presents, 15" vinyl figure
EX $10   NM $20   MIP $40

Joker Figure, 1966, Ideal, 3" blue plastic
EX $20   NM $30   MIP $50

Joker Figure, 1988, Applause, vinyl w/stand
EX $10   NM $20   MIP $40

Robin Figure, Presents, cloth and vinyl, on base
EX $10   NM $20   MIP $35

Robin Figure, 1966, Ideal, 3" plastic, detachable yellow plastic cape
EX $15   NM $30   MIP $50

Robin Figure, 1970s, Palitoy, 8" figure on card
EX $20   NM $40   MIP $80

Robin Figure, 1988, Applause, vinyl w/stand
EX $10   NM $20   MIP $35

Robin on a String Figure, Ben Cooper, 4" tall, rubber
EX $10   NM $25   MIP $50

BANK

Batman Bank, 1966, 7" tall glazed china figural bank depicts Batman w/hands on hip
EX $90   NM $120   MIP $160

Batman Bank, 1989, figural bank given away w/Batman Cereal
EX $6   NM $12   MIP $25

Joker Bank, 1974, Mego, plastic
EX $30   NM $60   MIP $125

Robin Bank, 1966, ceramic bank depicts Robin removing mask, 7" tall
EX $80   NM $110   MIP $150

BOOK

Batman 3-D Comic Book, 1966, DC Comics, 9" x 11" comic w/3-D pages and glasses
EX $200 **NM** $500 **MIP** $1000

Batman Annual, 1965-66, 8" x 10" hardback annual contains reprinted stories from 1950s Batman and Detective Comics
EX $25 **NM** $50 **MIP** $85

Batman Comic Book and Record Set, 1966, Golden Records, 33-1/3 rpm record, full size Batman comic book, official Batman membership card w/secret Batman code on back
EX $60 **NM** $125 **MIP** $175

Batman vs. the Joker Book, 1966, Signet, 160-page paperback
EX $10 **NM** $20 **MIP** $30

Detective Comics #27, 1939, DC Comics, first appearance of Batman
EX $10 **NM** $75 **MIP** $500

Dot-To-Dot and Coloring Book, 1967, Vasquez Bros., Batman w/Robin the Boy Wonder, printed in the Phillipines, 20 pages
EX $30 **NM** $50 **MIP** $100

From Alfred to Zowie! Book, 1966, Golden Press
EX $10 **NM** $20 **MIP** $35

Paint-By-Number Book, 1966, Whitman
EX $20 **NM** $40 **MIP** $85

Sticker Fun w/Batman Book, 1966, Watkins-Strathmore, 8" x 11" softbound w/stickers
EX $15 **NM** $50 **MIP** $110

Three Villains of Doom Book, 1966, Signet, 160 pages
EX $10 **NM** $40 **MIP** $85

CLOTHING

Child's Belt, 1960s, elastic w/bronze logo buckle
EX $22 **NM** $40 **MIP** $90

Child's Mittens, 1973, children's blue plastic vinyl, raised illustration of Batman and logo
EX $12 **NM** $25 **MIP** $50

Child's Pajamas, 1966, Wormser, light blue, two-piece pajamas, full-color Batman logo on chest
EX $200 **NM** $450 **MIP** $900

FOOD PRODUCTS

Batman "Punch-O" Drink Mix, 1966, small paper packet
EX $25 **NM** $40 **MIP** $75

Batman Cereal Box, 1989, Ralston
EX $20 **NM** $30 **MIP** $60

Batman Crusader Sundae Fudgesicle, 1966, Popsicle, 7" white and brown paper wrapper
EX $10 **NM** $20 **MIP** $30

Bread Wrapper, 1966, New Century Bread, plastic
EX $25 **NM** $45 **MIP** $85

Candy Cigarettes, 1960s, made in England
EX $30 **NM** $60 **MIP** $90

Chocolate Milk Carton, 1966, Reiter and Hart, one-quart carton in yellow, red and brown, features front and back panels of Batman in action poses
EX $100 **NM** $200 **MIP** $400

Jelly Jar, 1966, W.H. Marvin, 5"-6" glass jar w/color label, "Bat" Pure Apple Jelly
EX $200 **NM** $400 **MIP** $600

Slam Bang Ice Cream Carton, 1966, Cabarrus Creamery, features Batman and Robin on side panels
EX $20 **NM** $45 **MIP** $65

GAMES

Batman Arcade Game, 1989, Bluebox, electronic
EX $75 **NM** $120 **MIP** $165

Batman Pinball Game, 1960s, Marx, tin litho w/plastic casing
EX $35 **NM** $90 **MIP** $175

Batman Target Game, 1966, Hasbro, tin litho target w/plastic revolver and rubber-tipped darts
EX $75 **NM** $100 **MIP** $200

GLASSWARE

Batman Drinking Glass, 1976, Pepsi, 7" tall glass tumbler, all Batman characters, each
EX $10 **NM** $20 **MIP** $30

Coffee Mug, 1966, Anchor-Hocking, milk glass, action pose of Batman on one side and the Bat logo on the opposite side
EX $15 **NM** $30 **MIP** $50

Drinking Glass, 1989, 5", made in France
EX $10 **NM** $25 **MIP** $40

MAGAZINE

Life Magazine, 1966, March 11, 1966 issue, Adam West as Batman on cover
EX $50 **NM** $70 **MIP** $125

TV Guide, 1966, TV Guide, March 26-April 1 issue, photo cover of Adam West as Batman
EX $120 **NM** $250 **MIP** $385

MODEL KIT

Catwoman Returns, 1990s, Horizon, vinyl model kit
EX $10 **NM** $20 **MIP** $40

Penguin Returns Model Kit, Horizon
EX $10 **NM** $20 **MIP** $40

PAINT SET

Batman Cast and Paint Set, 1960s, plaster casting mold and paint set
EX $50 **NM** $100 **MIP** $200

Batman Paint by Number Set, 1965, Hasbro, five pre-numbered sketches, 10 oil paint vials and brush
EX $50 **NM** $100 **MIP** $200

Batman Super Powers Stain and Paint Set, 1984
EX $15 **NM** $30 **MIP** $70

Sparkle Paint Set, 1966, Kenner, paint and six pre-numbered sketches of Batman
EX $50 **NM** $100 **MIP** $175

PAPER GOODS

Batman and Robin Valentine, 1966
EX $10 **NM** $30 **MIP** $60

Batman Lobby Display, 1989, Warner Bros., Michael Keaton cardboard stand up
EX $125 **NM** $200 **MIP** $250

Batman Lucky Charm Display Card, 1966, 4" x 4" paper display card used in bubble gum machines, card shows Bat logo and red "Be protected—Get your Batman lucky charm now"
EX $12 **NM** $35 **MIP** $70

Batman Postcards, 1966, Dexter Press, set of eight postcards w/Carmine Infantino artwork
EX $40 **NM** $100 **MIP** $160

Batman Postcards, 1966, Dexter Press, three full-color postcards, each taken from a comic panel from Batman comics, each
EX $8 **NM** $15 **MIP** $30

Batman Returns Display, 1992, Warner Bros.
EX $50 **NM** $90 **MIP** $160

Batman Returns Lobby Display, 1992, Warner Bros., Michael Keaton life-size cardboard stand up
EX $125 **NM** $200 **MIP** $325

Batmobile Display Sign, 1969, Burry's, 34" x 48" die-cut 3-D plastic story display, raised images of Batman, Robin, and Batmobile, bright orange w/yellow lettering
EX $600 **NM** $1000 **MIP** $1500

Button Display Card, 1966, full-color display card used in bubble gum machines which offered Batman buttons

EX $30   **NM** $60   **MIP** $100

Costume Store Poster, 1966, Ben Cooper, 12" x 24", yellow

EX $80   **NM** $160   **MIP** $220

Flicker Pictures Display Card, 1966, bubble gum machine display card

EX $10   **NM** $25   **MIP** $50

Glow-in-the Dark Poster, 1966, Ciro Art, 18" x 14" poster of Batman and Robin swinging across Gotham City

EX $50   **NM** $100   **MIP** $150

Official Bat-Signal Stickers, 1966, Alan-Whitney

EX $10   **NM** $20   **MIP** $35

Party Hat, 1972, Amscan/Canadian, 7" child's cardboard hat depicts Batman and Robin

EX $8   **NM** $15   **MIP** $30

PLAY SET

Batcave Play Set, 1974, Mego, vinyl

EX $200   **NM** $400   **MIP** $600

(KP photo, Karen O'Brien collection)

Batman and Robin Play Set, 1973, Ideal, "Fantastic Batcave, Gotham Museum, Wayne Manor," vinyl fold-over w/cardboard figures

EX $15   **NM** $30   **MIP** $55

(KP Photo)

Batman Play Set, 1966, Ideal, 11 pieces including characters and vehicles

EX $3000   **NM** $8000   **MIP** $12000

Batman Shaker Maker Play Set, 1974, Ideal, Batman, Robin and Joker: bodies included, head molds, shaker cup, molding compound, paints

EX $20   **NM** $40   **MIP** $60

(KP Photo)

Batman Switch and Go Play Set, 1966, Mattel, 9" plastic Batmobile, 40 feet of track, figures, etc.

EX $175   **NM** $450   **MIP** $750

Magic Magnetic Gotham City Play Set, 1966, Remco, cardboard city, character figures

EX $300   **NM** $700   **MIP** $1000

PUPPET

Batman and Robin Hand Puppets, 1966, Ideal, 12" soft vinyl head, plastic body, each

EX $100   **NM** $200   **MIP** $300

(KP Photo)

Batman Push Puppet, 1966, Kohner, 3" plastic w/push button on bottom

EX $25   **NM** $50   **MIP** $100

Batman String Puppet, 1977, Madison

EX $35   **NM** $75   **MIP** $160

Robin Push Puppet, 1966, Kohner, 3" plastic, push button on bottom

EX $40   **NM** $85   **MIP** $150

PUZZLE

(KP Photo)

Frame Tray Puzzle, 1966, Whitman, 11" x 14", Batman and Robin thwarting the Joker

EX $20   **NM** $40   **MIP** $80

RECORD

Batman and Superman Record Album, 1969-71, Wonderland, 45 rpm record Batman theme song from the 1966 television show and "The Superman Song"

EX $20   **NM** $75   **MIP** $100

Batman Record, 1966, SPC, 45 rpm, sleeve shaped like Batman's head; also available in Robin, Joker, Penguin, Riddler and Batmobile versions

EX $15   **NM** $50   **MIP** $100

Batman Soundtrack Record, 1966, 20th Century Fox, mono and stereo versions, each

EX $60   **NM** $150   **MIP** $275

Catwoman's Revenge Record, 1975, Power Records, 33-1/3 rpm story record

EX $10   **NM** $25   **MIP** $60

Joker Record, 1966, SPC, 45 rpm, sleeve shaped like Joker's head

EX $20   **NM** $50   **MIP** $90

RINGS

Bat Ring, 1966, yellow plastic, originally for a gumball machine

EX $10   **NM** $25   **MIP** $50

Batman/Robin Flicker-Flasher Ring, 1966, Vari-Vue, silver plastic base

EX $10   **NM** $20   **MIP** $25

Riddler/Batman Punching Riddler Flicker-Flasher Ring, 1966, Vari-Vue, silver plastic base

EX $10   **NM** $25   **MIP** $45

Robin/Dick Grayson Flicker-Flasher Ring, 1966, Vari-Vue, silver plastic base

EX $10   **NM** $25   **MIP** $45

TOY

Bat Bomb, 1966, Mattel

EX $75   **NM** $100   **MIP** $210

Batman Batarang Bagatelle, 1966, Marx, throw at targets

EX $15   **NM** $35   **MIP** $65

Batman Cartoon Kit, 1966, Colorforms
EX $25   NM $55   MIP $85

Batman Kite, 1982, Hiflyer
EX $8   NM $15   MIP $35

Batman Radio Belt and Buckle, 1966
EX $60   NM $125   MIP $200

Batman Superfriends Lite Brite Refill Pack, 1980, Hasbro
EX $5   NM $15   MIP $25

Batman Superhero Stamp Set, 1970s
EX $10   NM $25   MIP $60

(KP Photo)

Batman Trace-a-Graph, 1966, Emenee
EX $50   NM $100   MIP $200

(KP Photo)

Batman Utility Belt, 1960s, Ideal
EX $1500 NM $3500   MIP $5750

Batman Wind-Up, 1989, Billiken, tin litho
EX $25   NM $50   MIP $100

Batman Yo-Yo, 1989, SpectraStar
EX $10   NM $20   MIP $35

(KP Photo)

Batphone, 1966, Marx
EX $100   NM $175   MIP $350

Batscope Dart Launcher, 1966, Tarco
EX $25   NM $45   MIP $100

Bat-Troll Doll, 1966, Wish-Nik, vinyl, dressed in a blue felt Batman outfit w/cowl and cape
EX $125   NM $200   MIP $350

Cave Tun-L, 1966, New York Toy, 26" x 26" x 2" tunnel
EX $700   NM $1500   MIP $2350

Escape Gun, 1966, Lincoln, red plastic spring-loaded pistol w/Batman decal, two separate firing barrels
EX $75   NM $150   MIP $225

Give-A-Show Projector Cards, 1960s, Kenner, four slide cards in box
EX $10   NM $30   MIP $60

Gotham City Stunt Set, 1989, Tonka
EX $15   NM $55   MIP $85

(KP Photo)

Joker Wind-Up, 1989, Billiken, tin litho
EX $50   NM $100   MIP $185

Joker Yo-Yo, 1989, SpectraStar
EX $10   NM $20   MIP $45

Projector Gun, 1989, Toy Biz
EX $15   NM $30   MIP $70

Puppet Theater Stage, 1966, Ideal, marketed by Sears, 19" x 11" x 20" cardboard stage w/hand puppets
EX $200   NM $400   MIP $675

Ray Gun, 1960s, 7" long blue and black futuristic space gun w/bat sights and bats on handgrip
EX $125   NM $350   MIP $450

Rubber Stamp Set, 1966, Kellogg's, 2" x 5" hard black plastic case, set of six plastic stamps plus ink pad: Batman, Robin, Batmobile, Joker, Riddler, and Penguin
EX $60   NM $100   MIP $160

Shooting Arcade, 1970s, AHI, graphics of Joker, Catwoman and Penguin
EX $35   NM $100   MIP $175

VEHICLES

Bat Cycle, 1989, Toy Biz
EX $10   NM $30   MIP $60

Bat Machine, 1979, Mego
EX $30   NM $75   MIP $120

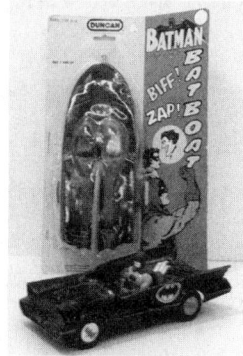

(KP Photo)

Batboat, 1987, Duncan
EX $10   NM $30   MIP $70

Batboat Pullstring Toy, Eidai, made in Japan
EX $60   NM $140   MIP $200

Batman Flying Copter, 1966, Remco, 12" plastic w/guide-wire control
EX $50   NM $120   MIP $210

Batman Road Race Set, 1960s, slot car racing set
EX $150   NM $300   MIP $550

Batman Slot Car, 1966, Magicar (England), 5" long Batmobile being driven by Batman and Robin in illustrated display window box
EX $150   NM $325   MIP $550

(KP Photo)

Batmobile, Apollo (Japan), radio-controlled
EX $60   NM $125   MIP $260

Batmobile, Matsushiro, radio-controlled
EX $60   NM $125   MIP $260

Batmobile, 1960s, Simms, plastic car on card
EX $25   NM $60   MIP $125

Batmobile, 1972, AHI, 11" long tin litho battery-operated mystery action car w/blinking light and jet engine noise
EX $75   NM $150   MIP $300

Batmobile, 1974, Azrak-Hamway, battery-operated
EX $50   NM $100   MIP $210

Batmobile, 1977, Duncan, 12" x 8" on card
EX $25   NM $50   MIP $100

Batmobile, 1980s, Aoshinu (Japan), motorized
EX $30   NM $60   MIP $150

Batmobile, 1980s, Bandai, pullback vehicle w/machine guns
EX $25   NM $60   MIP $135

Batmobile, 1989, Rich Man's Toys, remote control
EX $85   NM $160   MIP $350

Batmobile, 1989, Toy Biz, w/rocket launchers and two rockets
EX $15   NM $35   MIP $75

Batmobile, 1989, Ertl, 1/64-scale, die-cast, Model No. 1064
EX $5   NM $10   MIP $15

Batmobile, 1989, Ertl, 1/43-scale, die-cast, Model No. 2575
EX $10   NM $15   MIP $25

Batmobile, 1989, Toy Biz, remote control
EX $12   NM $30   MIP $65

Batmobile Motorized Kit, 1980s, Aoshinu (Japan), smaller snap kit
EX $20   NM $35   MIP $75

Batwing, 1980s, Toy Biz
EX $15   NM $30   MIP $60

Joker Van, 1989, Ertl, 1/64-scale, die-cast, Model No. 1532
EX $5   NM $10   MIP $15

(KP Photo)

Joker Van, 1989, Ertl, 1/43-scale, die-cast vehicle on card, Model No. 3494
EX $5   NM $20   MIP $40

Robin Shuttle, 1979, Mego, sized for British-made Mego figures, in box
EX $20   NM $40   MIP $90

Super Accelerator Batmobile, 1970s, AHI, on card
EX $25   NM $60   MIP $120

Turbine-Sound Batmobile, 1989, Toy Biz
EX $10   NM $15   MIP $25

WATCH

Batman Returns Watch, 1989, Consort, gray or yellow Bat logo
EX $20   NM $40   MIP $80

Batman Wristwatch, 1991, Quintel, digital
EX $10   NM $15   MIP $35

Catwoman Watch, 1991, Quintel, digital
EX $10   NM $20   MIP $50

Catwoman Watch, 1991, Consort, Batman Returns
EX $10   NM $20   MIP $60

Joker Wristwatch, 1980s, Fossil
EX $25   NM $65   MIP $120

Joker Wristwatch, 1989, Quintell, digital
EX $10   NM $20   MIP $60

Video Game Watch, 1989, Tiger, w/alarm
EX $8   NM $20   MIP $40

Betty Boop

DOLL

Betty Boop Doll, 1986, M-Toy, 12" vinyl jointed
EX $20   NM $30   MIP $70

Betty Boop Doll Clothing, 1986, M-Toy, outfits for 12" dolls high fashion boutique, each
EX $7   NM $15   MIP $30

FIGURE

Betty Boop Figure, 1980s, 3" PVC figure, eight different poses and outfits, each
EX $5   NM $10   MIP $20

Betty Boop Figure, 1988, NJ Croce, 9" bendy
EX $7   NM $20   MIP $30

TOY

Betty Boop Delivery Truck, 1990, Schylling, tin litho
EX $15   NM $30   MIP $60

Betty Boop Wacky Wobbler, 2000, Funko, nodder
EX $6   NM $12   MIP $25

Blondie and Dagwood

ACCESSORIES

Blondie Paint Set, 1946, American Crayon
EX $75   NM $150   MIP $275

Dagwood Marionette, 1945, 14"
EX $100   NM $225   MIP $375

Lucky Safety Card, 1953, 2" x 4" cards, Dagwood offers safety tips
EX $10   NM $55   MIP $80

BOOK

Blondie Paint Book, 1947, Whitman
EX $60   NM $150   MIP $250

DOLL

Blondie, 1985, Presents, released by Presents, a division of Tomy, plastic head and hands, red dress
EX $10   NM $20   MIP $30

Blondie Paper Dolls, 1955, Whitman
EX $40   NM $125   MIP $225

Dagwood, 1985, Presents, released by Presents, a division of Tomy, plastic head and hands, black pants, white shirt, red tie
EX $10   NM $20   MIP $30

FIGURE

Blondie Figure, 1940s, 2-1/2" tall, lead
EX $30   NM $75   MIP $150

Bugs Bunny

ACCESSORIES

Bugs Bunny Charm Bracelet, 1950s, brass charms of Bugs Bunny, Tweety, Sniffles, Fudd, etc.
EX $40   NM $80   MIP $125

Bugs Bunny Chatter Chum, 1982, Mattel
EX $10   NM $25   MIP $50

Bugs Bunny Clock, 1972, Litech, 12" x 14"
EX $35   NM $100   MIP $185

Bugs Bunny Mini Snow Dome, 1980s, Applause
EX $5   NM $15   MIP $35

Bugs Bunny Musical Ge-Tar, 1977, Mattel
EX $30   NM $70   MIP $110

Bugs Bunny Night Light, 1980s, Applause
EX $5   NM $10   MIP $15

Bugs Bunny Talking Alarm Clock, 1974, Janex, battery-operated
EX $50   NM $100   MIP $175

Bugs Bunny Wristwatch, 1978, Lafayette
EX $50   NM $120   MIP $180

BANK

Bugs Bunny Bank, 1940s, 5-3/4" x 5-1/2", pot metal, figure on base
EX $70   NM $140   MIP $260

Bugs Bunny Bank, 1971, Dakin, on a basket of carrots
EX $15   NM $30   MIP $60

COSTUME

Bugs Bunny Costume, 1960s, Collegeville, mask and costume
EX $25   NM $50   MIP $85

DOLL

Bugs Bunny Talking Doll, 1971, Mattel
EX $50   NM $110   MIP $180

FIGURE

Bugs Bunny Bendy, 1980s, Applause, 4" tall
EX $5   NM $15   MIP $30

Bugs Bunny Figure, 1971, Dakin, 10" tall
EX $10   NM $35   MIP $75

Bugs Bunny Figure, 1975, Warner Bros., 5-1/2" tall, ceramic, holding carrot
EX $30   NM $70   MIP $120

Bugs Bunny Figure, 1975, Warner Bros., 2-3/4" tall, ceramic
EX $15   NM $30   MIP $75

Bugs Bunny Figure, 1976, Dakin, yellow globes in "Cartoon Theater" box
EX $15   NM $35   MIP $75

Bugs Bunny in Uncle Sam Outfit, 1976, Dakin, distributed through Great America Theme Park, Illinois
EX $25   NM $70   MIP $110

TOY

Bugs Bunny Colorforms Set, 1958, Colorforms
EX $15   NM $50   MIP $100

Bugs Bunny Soaky, soft rubber
EX $10   NM $30   MIP $65

California Raisins

ACCESSORIES

California Raisins Chalkboard, 1988, Rose Art
EX $7   NM $15   MIP $40

California Raisins Clay Factory, 1988, Rose Art
EX $15   NM $45   MIP $75

California Raisins Crayon By Number, 1988, Rose Art
EX $15   NM $35   MIP $70

TOY

California Raisins Colorforms Play Set, 1987, Colorforms
EX $10   NM $30   MIP $65

California Raisins Wind-Up Walkers, 1987, Rasta
EX $6   NM $15   MIP $35

Captain America

FIGURE

Captain America Bendy Figure, 1966, Lakeside, 6", rubber
EX $50   NM $85   MIP $150

Powerized Captain America, 1980, Remco, plastic figure, wind-up shield spins
EX $10   NM $20   MIP $30

TOY

Captain America Rocket Racer, 1984, Buddy L, Secret Wars remote-controlled, battery-operated car
EX $75   NM $150   MIP $200

(KP Photo)

Captain America Scooter, 1967, Marx, 4", yellow plastic friction toy w/figure
EX $200   NM $350   MIP $475

Captain America Shooting Gallery, 1976, Larami, red dart gun, two darts, three duck targets, carded, Model No. 7068-0
EX $5   NM $10   MIP $20

Hand Puppet, 1960s, Ideal, box reads, "Super Hero TV Favorites"
EX $15   NM $30   MIP $65

Propeller Toy, 1968, Ohio Art, rubber band driven, fragile
EX $10   NM $20   MIP $30

Captain Marvel

ACCESSORIES

Adventures of Captain Marvel Ink Blotter/Ruler, 1940s, Republic/Fawcett, 6" blotter w/ruler advertises the 12-part serial, theatre premium
EX $200   NM $500   MIP $700

Captain Marvel Booklet, 1940s, Fawcett
EX $50   NM $100   MIP $350

Captain Marvel Button, 1940s, celluloid, pinback
EX $30   NM $95   MIP $150

Captain Marvel Club Felt Shoulder Patches, 1940s, Fawcett, Captain Marvel diving towards Earth, yellow
EX $200   NM $475   MIP $675

Captain Marvel Club Felt Shoulder Patches, 1940s, Fawcett, Captain Marvel diving towards Earth, blue
EX $50   NM $100   MIP $200

Captain Marvel Club Membership Card, 1940s, Fawcett
EX $50   NM $75   MIP $120

Captain Marvel Felt Pennant, 1940s, Fawcett, yellow, shows Captain Marvel flying
EX $100   NM $190   MIP $325

Captain Marvel Felt Pennant, 1940s, Fawcett, blue, shows Captain Marvel flying
EX $90   NM $110   MIP $175

Captain Marvel Film Viewer Gun, 1940s, gun-shaped movie viewer w/film strips from Paramount series
EX $125   NM $250   MIP $425

Captain Marvel Flannel Patch, 1940s, Fawcett
EX $50   NM $80   MIP $175

Captain Marvel Glow Pictures, 1940s, Fawcett, set of four
EX $350   NM $750   MIP $1000

Captain Marvel Iron-Ons, 1950s, Fawcett, sheet
EX $30   NM $60   MIP $100

Captain Marvel Jr. Wristwatch, 1940s, blue band, round dial w/blue costumed Jr., no box issued
EX $400   NM $850   MIP $1350

Captain Marvel Key Chain, 1940s, Fawcett
EX $60   NM $125   MIP $175

Captain Marvel Magic Dime Register Bank, 1948, Fawcett, available in three colors
EX $200   NM $425   MIP $650

Captain Marvel Magic Flute, 1940s, on die-cut card, shows Captain Marvel on side
EX $60   NM $100   MIP $160

(KP Photo)

Captain Marvel Magic Lightning Box, 1940s, Fawcett
EX $50   NM $100   MIP $150

Captain Marvel Magic Membership Card, 1940s, Fawcett
EX $40   NM $60   MIP $100

Captain Marvel Magic Picture, 1940s, Reed and Associates, paper, shows Billy Batson "transforming" into Captain Marvel
EX $50   NM $80   MIP $160

Captain Marvel Magic Whistle, 1948, Fawcett, seed company premium, picture of Captain Marvel on both sides, on card
EX $60   NM $120   MIP $175

Captain Marvel Neck Tie, 1940s, Fawcett
EX $60   NM $150   MIP $275

Captain Marvel Overseas Cap, 1940s, rare
EX $400   NM $800   MIP $1200

Captain Marvel Paint Set, 1940s, paint set w/five chalk figurines
EX $500   NM $1100   MIP $1750

Captain Marvel Paper Horn, 1940s, Fawcett
EX $20   NM $40   MIP $75

Captain Marvel Patch, 1940s, Fawcett
EX $30   NM $75   MIP $150

Captain Marvel Pinback Pattern, 1940s, Fawcett, pattern for original pinback
EX $15   NM $30   MIP $100

Captain Marvel Portrait, 1940s, Whiz Comics/Fawcett
EX $75   NM $125   MIP $250

Captain Marvel Portrait, 1940s, Republic, different version than Whiz Comics portrait
EX $75   NM $125   MIP $200

Captain Marvel Power Siren, 1940s, Fawcett
EX $60   NM $125   MIP $185

Captain Marvel Secret Code Sheet, 1940s, Fawcett
EX $15   NM $30   MIP $75

Captain Marvel Skull Cap, 1940s
EX $125   NM $400   MIP $600

Captain Marvel Soap, 1947, Fawcett, three illustrated bars in box
EX $300   NM $600   MIP $800

(KP Photo)

Captain Marvel Stationary, 1940s, Fawcett, paper and envelopes in box
EX $150   NM $250   MIP $400

Captain Marvel Suspenders, 1940s, Fawcett
EX $50   NM $125   MIP $185

Captain Marvel Sweater, 1940s, white or off-white, red Captain Marvel logo
EX $60   NM $300   MIP $400

Captain Marvel Tattoo Transfers, 1940s, Fawcett
EX $30   NM $110   MIP $200

Captain Marvel Tie Bar, 1940s, on card
EX $40   NM $65   MIP $150

Captain Marvel Wristwatch, 1948, in box, shows Captain Marvel holding an airplane
EX $400   NM $900   MIP $1350

Captain Marvel, Jr. Booklet, 1940s, Fawcett
EX $25   NM $50   MIP $100

(KP Photo)

Fawcett's Comic Stars Christmas Tree Ornaments, 1940s, Fawcett, metal star-shaped ornaments w/art of Captain Marvel and Hoppy
EX $25   NM $45   MIP $100

(KP Photo)

Mary Marvel Illustrated Soap, 1947, Fawcett, three soap bars in box
EX $300   NM $500   MIP $700

Mary Marvel Patch, 1940s, Fawcett
EX $150   NM $300   MIP $450

Mary Marvel Pin, 1940s, Fawcett, fiberboard
EX $50   NM $150   MIP $250

Mary Marvel Stationery, 1940s, Fawcett, boxed
EX $100   NM $200   MIP $400

(KP Photo)

Mary Marvel Wristwatch, 1948, in box
EX $400   NM $900   MIP $1300

Membership Secret Code Card, 1940s, Fawcett
EX $150   NM $250   MIP $400

Rocket Raider, 1940s, Fawcett, paper airplane in envelope
EX $20   NM $40   MIP $70

COMIC

Boy Who Never Heard of Captain Marvel Mini Comic, 1940s, Bond Bread
EX $40   NM $100   MIP $210

Captain Marvel and Billy's Big Game Mini Comic, 1940s
EX $90   NM $250   MIP $410

Captain Marvel Meets the Weatherman Mini Comic, 1940s, Bond Bread, Bond Bread premium
EX $50   NM $110   MIP $185

Giveaway Comics #1, Captain Marvel and the Lt. of Safety, 1950, Danger Flies a Kite
EX $400   NM $800   MIP $1300

Giveaway Comics #2, Captain Marvel and the Lt. of Safety, 1950, Danger Takes to Climbing
EX $400   NM $800   MIP $1300

Giveaway Comics #3, Captain Marvel and the Lt. of Safety, 1951, Danger Smashes Street Lights
EX $400   NM $800   MIP $1300

FIGURE

Captain Marvel Sirocco Figurine, 1940s, Fawcett
EX $1500   NM $3000   MIP $4000

Mary Marvel Figurine, 5"
EX $500   NM $1250   MIP $2000

PUZZLE

Captain Marvel Puzzle, 1940s, Reed and Associates, in envelope
EX $50   NM $350   MIP $425

TOY

Captain Marvel Beanbags, 1940s, Captain Marvel, Mary Marvel or Hoppy, each
EX $75   NM $175   MIP $325

Captain Marvel Beanie, 1940s, cap shows image of Captain Marvel flying toward word "Shazam," blue
EX $175   NM $300   MIP $500

Captain Marvel Beanie, 1940s, girls' cap shows image of Captain Marvel flying toward word "Shazam," pink, rare
EX $750   NM $1500   MIP $2000

(KP Photo)

Captain Marvel Buzz Bomb, 1950s, Fawcett, paper airplane in envelope
EX $25   NM $75   MIP $125

(KP Photo)

Captain Marvel Jr. Ski Jump, 1947, Reed and Associates, paper, in envelope
EX $10   NM $20   MIP $65

Captain Marvel Jr. Statuette, 1940s, Fawcett, hand-painted plastic
EX $500   NM $750   MIP $1500

Captain Marvel Lightning Race Cars, 1940s, Automatic Toy Co., set of four cars w/wind-up keys; green, yellow, orange or blue; rare
EX $2000   NM $3000   MIP $4500

Captain Marvel Statuette, 1940s, Fawcett, hand-painted plastic, shows Captain Marvel standing w/arms crossed, on base w/name engraved
EX $600   NM $800   MIP $1600

Mary Marvel Statuette, 1940s, Fawcett, hand-painted plastic
EX $500   NM $750   MIP $1500

Captain Midnight

ACCESSORIES

(KP Photo)

Captain Midnight Cup, plastic, 4" tall, "Ovaltine-The Heart of a Hearty Breakfast"
EX $30   NM $70   MIP $150

Captain Midnight Secret Society Decoder, 1949, w/key
EX $85   NM $180   MIP $375

Captain Midnight's Spy Scope, 1950s, Ovaltine, plastic telescope
EX $20   NM $40   MIP $60

Decoder, 1948, radio premium, copper disc w/signal mirror
EX $15   NM $30   MIP $75

Mug w/handle, 1952, Ovaltine, sticker says "Ovaltine-The Heart of a Hearty Breakfast"
EX $15   NM $30   MIP $60

Premium Ring, 1957, Ovaltine, Ovaltine premium, adjustable ring
EX $150   NM $300   MIP $500

Whistle, 1947, Code-A-Graph Decoder, radio premium
EX $15   NM $30   MIP $65

Cartoon/Comic Characters

ACCESSORIES

Beetle Bailey Comic Strip Stamper Set, 1981, Ja-Ru, seven stampers, book, crayon
EX $8   NM $25   MIP $60

Beetle Bailey Gun Set, 1981, Ja-Ru, cord gun and target
EX $10   NM $40   MIP $90

Daffy Dog Poster, 10" x 13", The Morning After
EX $10   NM $17   MIP $30

Doggie Daddy Metal Trivet, 1960s, says "You have to work like a dog to live like one."
EX $15   NM $35   MIP $70

Dudley Do-Right Jigsaw Puzzle, 1975, Whitman, Dudley and Snidley
EX $15   NM $35   MIP $75

Easy Show Movie Projector Films, 1965, Kenner, numerous cartoon characters, each film
EX $8   NM $15   MIP $30

Geoffrey Jack-in-the-Box, 1970s, Toys R Us, jack-in-the-box
EX $20   NM $40   MIP $80

Hair Bear Bunch Mug, 1978, Square Bear figural mug
EX $5   NM $13   MIP $20

Hair Bear Bunch Wristwatch, 1972, medium gold tone case, base metal back, articulated hands, red leather snap down band
EX $30   NM $70   MIP $150

Harold Teen Playstone Funnies Mold Set, 1940s
EX $40   NM $100   MIP $200

Herman and Katnip Punch Out Kite, 1960s, Saalfield, folds into a kite
EX $12   NM $30   MIP $75

Josie and the Pussycats Paper Doll Book, 1971, Whitman, Model No. 1982
EX $25   NM $50   MIP $110

Little Audrey Dress Designer Kit, 1962, Saalfield, die-cut doll and accessories in illustrated box
EX $60   NM $125   MIP $185

Little Audrey Shoulder Bag Leathercraft Kit, 1961, Jewel
EX $75   NM $150   MIP $200

Little Lulu Dish, 1940s, 5-1/2" hand-painted ceramic, pictures of Lulu, Tubby and her friends
EX $100   NM $200   MIP $350

Nancy Music Box, 1968, United Feature, ceramic
EX $80   NM $150   MIP $225

Supercar Molding Color Kit, 1960s, Sculptorcraft, set of rubber plaster casting models of vehicle and show characters, including Mike Mercury, Beaker and Popkiss, Jimmy and Mitch, Masterspy
EX $150   NM $300   MIP $445

Winnie Winkle Playstone Funnies Mold Set, 1940s
EX $30   NM $75   MIP $150

BANK

Andy Panda Bank, 1977, Walter Lantz, 7" tall, hard plastic
EX $15   NM $50   MIP $85

Little Lulu Bank, 8" tall hard plastic w/black fire hydrant
EX $60   NM $125   MIP $185

Scrappy Bank, 3" x 3-1/2" metal, embossed illustration of Scrappy and his dog
EX $150   NM $300   MIP $425

DOLL

Bloom County Opus Doll, 1986, 10" tall, plush, penguin Opus wearing a Santa Claus cap
EX $10   NM $30   MIP $75

Chilly Willy Doll, 1982, Walter Lantz, plush
EX $7   NM $25   MIP $60

Dudley Do-Right Doll, 1972, Wham-O, bendy
EX $20   NM $40   MIP $80

Hagar the Horrible Doll, 1983, 12" tall
EX $12   NM $22   MIP $70

King Leonardo Doll, 1960s, Holiday Fair, cloth plush dressed in royal robe
EX $75   NM $100   MIP $200

FIGURE

Alfred E. Neuman Figurine, 1960s, base says "What Me Worry?"
EX $70   NM $140   MIP $225

Cadbury the Butler Figure, 1981, DFC, 3-1/2" figure from Richie Rich
EX $7   NM $20   MIP $35

Wonder Woman Figure, Presents, 14" tall cloth and vinyl figure on base
EX $9   NM $25   MIP $50

PUZZLE

Little Lulu Puzzles, 1973, Whitman, four frame tray puzzles
EX $30   NM $60   MIP $100

TOY

Breezley Soaky, 1967, Purex, 9" tall, plastic
EX $25   NM $60   MIP $110

Henry on Trapeze Toy, G. Borgfeldt, 6" x 9", celluloid, wind-up, jointed Henry suspended from trapeze
EX $400   NM $700   MIP $1250

Mush Mouse Pull Toy, 1960s, Ideal, pull toy w/vinyl figure
EX $40   NM $100   MIP $180

Peter Potamus Soaky, 11" tall
EX $20   NM $40   MIP $90

Touche Turtle Soaky, 1960s, lying down
EX $15   NM $40   MIP $75

Touche Turtle Soaky, 1960s, standing
EX $25   NM $60   MIP $110

Yipee Pull Toy, 1960s, Ideal, w/vinyl figures of Yipee, Yapee and Yahoee
EX $40   NM $80   MIP $150

Casper the Friendly Ghost

ACCESSORIES

Casper Figure Lamp, 1950, Archlamp, 17" tall
EX $75   NM $175   MIP $275

Casper Light Shade, 1960s
EX $70   NM $100   MIP $175

Casper Night Light, 1975, Duncan, 6-1/2" tall
EX $15   NM $40   MIP $75

COSTUME

Casper Costume, Collegeville, "Ghostland" costume, #216
EX $45   NM $70   MIP $110

Casper Halloween Costume, 1960s, Collegeville, mask and costume
EX $20   NM $40   MIP $90

DOLL

Casper Doll, 7-3/4" tall squeeze doll holds black spotted puppy
EX $30   NM $65   MIP $125

Casper Doll, 1960s, 15" cloth
EX $30   NM $60   MIP $125

Casper Doll, 1972, Sutton and Sons, rubber squeeze doll w/logo
EX $20   NM $30   MIP $60

Casper the Friendly Ghost Talking Doll, 1961, Mattel, 15" tall, terry cloth, plastic head w/a pull string voice box
EX $75   NM $175   MIP $250

PUZZLE

Casper Jigsaw Puzzle, 1988, Ja-Ru
EX $4   NM $10   MIP $20

TOY

Casper Hand Puppet, 1960s, Commonwealth Toys, all fuzzy, ribbon says "Casper the Friendly Ghost"
EX $15   NM $30   MIP $60

Casper Hand Puppet, 1960s, 8" tall, cloth and plastic head
EX $20   NM $40   MIP $100

Casper Pull Toy, 1950s, red wheels, paper litho of cartoon Casper on wood, arms play xylophone when pulled
EX $50   NM $125   MIP $250

Casper Soaky, 1960s, Colgate-Palmolive, 10" tall
EX $20   NM $55   MIP $90

Casper Spinning Top, 1960s, blue top w/figure of Casper inside
EX $25   NM $60   MIP $90

Casper Wind-Up Toy, 1950s, Linemar, tin
EX $300   NM $500   MIP $850

Wacky Wobbler, 2001, Funko, nodder
EX $5   NM $10   MIP $25

Wendy the Good Witch Soaky, 1960s, Colgate-Palmolive
EX $20   NM $55   MIP $90

Charlie Chaplin

ACCESSORIES

Charlie Chaplin Pencil Case, 8" long
EX $50   NM $100   MIP $200

Charlie Chaplin Wristwatch, 1972, Bubbles/Cadeaux, Swiss, large chrome case, black and white dial, articulated sweep cane second hand, black leather band
EX $45   NM $100   MIP $225

Charlie Chaplin Wristwatch, 1985, Bradley, oldies series, quartz, large black plastic case and band, sweep seconds, shows Chaplin as Little Tramp
EX $20   NM $50   MIP $100

DOLL

Charlie Chaplin Cloth Doll, patterned fabric
EX $225   NM $375   MIP $475

Charlie Chaplin Doll, 11-1/2" tall, wind-up
EX $500   NM $1000   MIP $1500

FIGURE

Charlie Chaplin Figure, 2-1/2" tall, lead
EX $60   NM $175   MIP $325

Charlie Chaplin Figure, 8-1/2" tall, tin w/cast iron feet, wind-up
EX $600   NM $1100   MIP $1800

TOY

Charlie Chaplin Toy, 4" tall, spring mechanism tips his hat when string is pulled
EX $100 **NM** $175 **MIP** $300

Chipmunks

ACCESSORIES

Chipmunks Toothbrush, 1984, battery-operated
EX $10 **NM** $25 **MIP** $50

Chipmunks Wallet, 1959, vinyl
EX $40 **NM** $80 **MIP** $120

DOLL

Alvin Doll, 1963, Knickerbocker, 14" tall plush w/vinyl head
EX $30 **NM** $70 **MIP** $120

TOY

Chipmunks Bean Bags, 1998, three in set, talking
EX $20 **NM** $40 **MIP** $60

Chipmunks Soaky, 1960s, 10" tall, Alvin, Simon, or Theodore, each
EX $10 **NM** $40 **MIP** $80

Cinderella

ACCESSORIES

Cinderella Alarm Clock, Westclox, 2-1/2" x 4-1/2" x 4" tall
EX $70 **NM** $125 **MIP** $275

Cinderella Bank, 1950s, ceramic, Cinderella holding magic wand
EX $40 **NM** $75 **MIP** $150

Cinderella Charm Bracelet, 1950, golden brass link w/five charms, Cinderella, Fairy Godmother, slipper, pumpkin coach and Prince
EX $40 **NM** $80 **MIP** $150

Cinderella Molding Set, 1950s, Model Craft, set of character molds in illustrated box
EX $40 **NM** $100 **MIP** $200

Cinderella Musical Jewelry Box, mahogany music box plays "So This Is Love"
EX $20 **NM** $40 **MIP** $85

Cinderella Wristwatch, 1950, US Time
EX $225 **NM** $450 **MIP** $800

Cinderella Wristwatch, 1958, Timex, Cinderella and castle, pink leather band
EX $150 **NM** $350 **MIP** $700

Fairy Godmother Pitcher, 7" tall figural pitcher
EX $22 **NM** $50 **MIP** $100

Gus/Jaq Serving Set, 1960s, Westman, creamer, pitcher and sugar bowl
EX $50 **NM** $100 **MIP** $200

DOLL

Cinderella Doll, 11" tall, blue stain ballgown w/white bridal gown, glass slippers, holding Little Golden Book
EX $20 **NM** $40 **MIP** $120

Cinderella Doll, Horsman, 8" tall in illustrated box
EX $30 **NM** $75 **MIP** $175

Cinderella Paper Dolls, 1965, Whitman
EX $50 **NM** $100 **MIP** $185

Gus Doll, 1950s, Gund, 13" tall, gray doll w/dark red shirt and green felt hat
EX $75 **NM** $150 **MIP** $250

FIGURE

Cinderella Figurine, 5" tall, plastic
EX $10 **NM** $20 **MIP** $50

Cinderella Figurine, 5" tall, ceramic
EX $20 **NM** $40 **MIP** $100

PUZZLE

Cinderella Puzzle, 1960s, Jaymar
EX $15 **NM** $30 **MIP** $60

TOY

Cinderella Soaky, 1960s, 11" tall, blue
EX $15 **NM** $40 **MIP** $80

Cinderella Wind-Up Toy, 1950, Irwin, 5" tall, Cinderella and Prince dancing
EX $75 **NM** $225 **MIP** $350

Prince Charming Hand Puppet, 1959, Gund, 10" tall
EX $25 **NM** $50 **MIP** $100

Crusader Rabbit

ACCESSORIES

Crusader Rabbit Paint Set, 1960s, 13" x 19"
EX $90 **NM** $135 **MIP** $225

BOOK

Crusader Rabbit Book, 1958, Wonder Book
EX $30 **NM** $60 **MIP** $125

Crusader Rabbit in Bubble Trouble Book, 1960, Whitman
EX $30 **NM** $60 **MIP** $100

Crusader Rabbit Trace and Color Book, 1959, Whitman
EX $55 **NM** $110 **MIP** $185

TOY

Crusader Rabbit Soaky, 1960s, Purex
EX $50 **NM** $100 **MIP** $150

Danger Mouse

ACCESSORIES

Danger Mouse ID Set, 1985, Gordy
EX $10 **NM** $15 **MIP** $50

Danger Mouse Pendant Necklace, 1986, Gordy
EX $10 **NM** $15 **MIP** $50

DOLL

Danger Mouse Doll, 1988, Russ, 15" tall
EX $40 **NM** $60 **MIP** $100

TOY

Danger Mouse Bendy, 1986, Cosgrove, 5" tall, bendable
EX $7 **NM** $14 **MIP** $25

Dennis the Menace

ACCESSORIES

Giant Mischief Kit, 1950s, Hasbro
EX $60 **NM** $110 **MIP** $210

Paint Set, 1954, Pressman, paints, crayons, brush and trays
EX $40 **NM** $100 **MIP** $185

BOOK

Dennis the Menace and Ruff Book, 1959, Whitman, Little Golden Book
EX $10 **NM** $18 **MIP** $40

Dennis the Menace and Ruff Book Ends, 1974, ceramic
EX $30 **NM** $65 **MIP** $125

PUZZLE

TV Show Puzzle, 1960, Whitman
EX $20 **NM** $40 **MIP** $60

TOY

Colorforms Set, 1961, Colorforms
EX $15 **NM** $45 **MIP** $100

Doll, 1959, blue and white stripped shirt w/red overalls, 13" tall
EX $25 **NM** $50 **MIP** $70

Hand Puppet, 1950s, plastic head, cloth body
EX $10 **NM** $20 **MIP** $35

Plastic Figure, 1954, press his cowlick and he raises his right arm holding a gun
EX $10 **NM** $20 **MIP** $30

Tiddley Winks, 1961, Whitman
EX $25 **NM** $45 **MIP** $90

Deputy Dawg

DOLL

Deputy Dawg Doll, 1960s, Ideal, 14" tall, cloth w/plush arms and vinyl head
EX $75 **NM** $135 **MIP** $195

FIGURE

Deputy Dawg Figure, 1977, Dakin, 6" tall, plastic body w/vinyl head
EX $30   NM $55   MIP $100

TOY

Deputy Dawg Soaky, 1966, 9-1/2" tall, plastic
EX $15   NM $45   MIP $80

Dick Tracy

ACCESSORIES

Bonny Braids Store Contest Card, 1951, 5-1/2" x 5-1/2"
EX $25   NM $65   MIP $125

Candy Box, 1940s, Novel Package, box w/cartoons and story on back; comic strips on bottom
EX $150   NM $275   MIP $385

(KP Photo)

Dick Tracy Lamp, 1950s, painted ceramic bust of Tracy in black coat, yellow hat and red tie
EX $1500   NM $2000   MIP $3500

Dick Tracy Picture, 1940s, Pillsbury, part of set of eight, each 7" x 10" in mat, shows Tracy and Junior
EX $60   NM $130   MIP $250

Dinnerware Set, 1950s, Homer Laughlin, bowl, dinner plate, and mug
EX $70   NM $150   MIP $300

Dinnerware Set, 1980s, Zak Designs, plate, cup, bowl
EX $10   NM $15   MIP $30

Hat, 1940s, Miller Bros. Hat, wool fedora, blue/gray
EX $50   NM $100   MIP $175

Sparkle Plenty Christmas Tree Lights, 1940s, Mutual Equipment, seven-light set
EX $30   NM $65   MIP $125

Sparkle Plenty Christmas Tree Lights, 1940s, Mutual Equipment, 15-light set
EX $40   NM $90   MIP $175

Super 8 Color Film, 1965, Republic, b/w cartoon "Trick or Treat"
EX $10   NM $25   MIP $55

Wall Clock, 1990s, 16" x 20" battery power quartz, face shows Disney movie Tracy talking into wrist radio
EX $15   NM $20   MIP $40

Wallpaper Section, 1950s, shows comic strip scenes of Tracy and seven other characters
EX $15   NM $40   MIP $75

BADGE

Detective Club Crime Stoppers Badge, 1940s, Guild
EX $30   NM $60   MIP $100

Dick Tracy Crime Stopper Badge, 1960s, star shape giveaway badge from WGN "9 Official Dick Tracy Crimestopper" TV Badge
EX $30   NM $65   MIP $125

Dick Tracy Detective Club Belt Badge w/Belt, premium
EX $35   NM $150   MIP $350

BANK

(KP Photo)

Sparkle Plenty Bank, 1940s, Jayess, 12" tall, base features a medallion of Dick Tracy as Godfather
EX $150   NM $300   MIP $525

BOOK

Dick Tracy and the Bicycle Gang Book, 1948, Whitman, 288 pages, Big Little Book, hardcover
EX $60   NM $120   MIP $180

Dick Tracy and the Mad Killer Book, 1947, Whitman, 288 pages, Big Little Book, hardcover
EX $40   NM $90   MIP $150

Dick Tracy and the Tiger Lilly Gang Book, 1949, Whitman, 288 pages, Big Little Book, hardcover
EX $35   NM $80   MIP $140

Dick Tracy and the Wreath Kidnapping Case Book, 1945, Whitman, 432 pages, Big Little Book, hardcover
EX $40   NM $90   MIP $150

Dick Tracy and Yogee Yamma Book, 1946, Whitman, 352 pages, Big Little Book, hardcover
EX $35   NM $80   MIP $135

Dick Tracy Encounters Facey Book, 1967, Whitman, 260 pages, hardcover Big Little Book, cover price 39 cents
EX $10   NM $15   MIP $30

(KP Photo)

Dick Tracy Junior Detective Kit Book, 1962, Golden Press, punchout book of Tracy tools, including badges, revolver, wrist radio
EX $25   NM $50   MIP $100

Dick Tracy Little Golden Book, 1962, Golden Press, features characters from the TV show
EX $20   NM $30   MIP $60

BUTTON

Dick Tracy and Little Orphan Annie Button, Genung Promo
EX $1000   NM $2400   MIP $3000

Pep Flintheart Pin, 1945, Kellogg's, tin litho button
EX $10   NM $20   MIP $45

COMIC BOOK

Dick Tracy Comic Book, 1947, Popped Wheat Cereal, premium
EX $6   NM $10   MIP $20

Dick Tracy in 3-D Comic Book, 1986, Blackthorne, Ocean Death Trap
EX $4   NM $8   MIP $15

Motorola Presents Dick Tracy Comic Book, 1953, Motorola, premium comic book w/paper mask and vest
EX $50   NM $100   MIP $175

DOLL

Bonny Braids Doll, 1950s, 6" tall, plastic, walking wobble doll
EX $30   NM $75   MIP $150

Bonny Braids Doll, 1951, Ideal, 14" tall w/toothbrush
EX $90   NM $180   MIP $375

Bonny Braids Doll, 1952, Ideal, 8" tall, crawls when wound

EX $80 NM $170 MIP $325

Little Honey Moon Doll, 1965, Ideal, 16" space baby, bubble helmet and outfit w/white pigtails, doll sitting on half a moon w/stars in the background

EX $200 NM $350 MIP $500

Sparkle Plenty Doll, 1947, Ideal, 12" tall

EX $125 NM $250 MIP $450

FIGURES

B.O. Plenty Figure, 1950s, Marx, Famous Comic Figures series, waxy cream, pink, 60mm tall

EX $20 NM $40 MIP $65

Blank Figure, The, 1990, Playmates, figure w/gun and hat w/featureless face attached

EX $60 NM $100 MIP $150

Breathless Mahoney Figure, 1990, Applause, 14" tall

EX $5 NM $10 MIP $20

Dick Tracy Figure, 1940s, Professional Art, 7" unpainted, detailed white chalk figure or painted

EX $80 NM $200 MIP $375

Dick Tracy Figures, 1950s, Marx, Famous Comic Figures series, several characters, each

EX $40 NM $75 MIP $150

Dick Tracy Nodder, 1960s, 6-1/2" tall, ceramic nodding head bust

EX $350 NM $800 MIP $1200

Gravel Gertie Figure, 1950s, Marx, Famous Comic Figures series

EX $12 NM $20 MIP $40

Sparkle Plenty Figure, 1950s, Marx, Famous Comic Figures series

EX $10 NM $15 MIP $50

Steve the Tramp Figure, 1990, Playmates, discontinued

EX $10 NM $20 MIP $40

GAME

Dick Tracy Bingo, Lock Them Up in Jail and Harmonize w/Tracy Game, 1940s, object of each is to roll BBs into different holes on the face of a glass framed game card for points

EX $45 NM $90 MIP $160

Dick Tracy Crime Stopper Game, 1963, Ideal, workstation contains crime indicator dial, decoder knobs, criminal buttons, clue cards and holders and clue windows

EX $40 NM $90 MIP $180

Dick Tracy Pinball Game, 1967, Marx, 14" x 24", shows characters from TV show pilot

EX $40 NM $90 MIP $175

Dick Tracy Pop-Pop Game, 1980s, Ja-Ru, Diet Smith and Flattop are targets

EX $10 NM $15 MIP $25

GUN

.45 Special Water Handgun, 1950s, Tops Plastics, plastic

EX $50 NM $100 MIP $160

Automatic Target Range Gun, 1967, Marx, BB gun mounted in an enclosed plastic shooting gallery

EX $60 NM $125 MIP $300

Luger Water Gun, 1971, Larami

EX $15 NM $35 MIP $90

(KP Photo)

Power Jet Squad Gun, 1962, Mattel, 29" long cap and water rifle

EX $60 NM $120 MIP $220

Rapid Fire Tommy Gun, 1940s, Parker Johns, 20" long tommy gun w/Tracy on stock

EX $250 NM $400 MIP $600

Sub-Machine Gun, 1950s, Tops Plastics, 12" long, red, green or blue, water gun "holds over 500 shots on one filling," Dick Tracy decal on magazine

EX $100 NM $200 MIP $350

PIN

Bonny Braids Pin, 1951, Charmore, 1-1/4" figure plastic pin on full-color card

EX $20 NM $60 MIP $100

Pep B.O. Plenty Pin, 1945, Kellogg's, tin litho button

EX $20 NM $30 MIP $50

Pep Chief Brandon Pin, 1945, Kellogg's, tin litho button

EX $10 NM $15 MIP $30

Pep Dick Tracy Pin, 1945, Kellogg's, tin litho button

EX $25 NM $45 MIP $80

Pep Flattop Pin, 1945, Kellogg's, tin litho button

EX $20 NM $35 MIP $60

Pep Gravel Gertie Pin, 1945, Kellogg's, tin litho button

EX $20 NM $35 MIP $50

Pep Junior Tracy Pin, 1945, Kellogg's, tin litho button

EX $10 NM $20 MIP $40

Pep Pat Patten Pin, 1945, Kellogg's, tin litho button

EX $10 NM $20 MIP $35

Pep Tess Trueheart Pin, 1945, Kellogg's, tin litho button

EX $12 NM $20 MIP $35

RECORD

Dick Tracy Original Radio Broadcast Album, 1972, Coca-Cola, presents the cast from "The Case of the Firebug Murders" radio show

EX $20 NM $60 MIP $80

Flattop Story Double Record Set, 1947, Mercury Records, record, book, comics

EX $65 NM $125 MIP $225

RING

Dick Tracy Ring, 1940s, Miller Bros. Hat, enameled portrait

EX $60 NM $100 MIP $200

Dick Tracy Service Patrol Ring, 1966, premium

EX $20 NM $40 MIP $60

TOY

Auto Magic Picture Gun, 1950s, 6-1/2" x 9" metal picture gun and filmstrip

EX $30 NM $100 MIP $175

(KP Photo)

Automatic Police Station, 1950s, Marx, tin litho police station and car

EX $500 NM $800 MIP $1500

B.O. Plenty Walker, 1940s, Marx, holds Sparkle Plenty

EX $175 NM $300 MIP $500

B.O. Plenty Wind-Up, 1940s, Marx, 8-1/2" tall holding baby Sparkle, litho tin, walks, hat tips up and down when key is wound

EX $150 NM $300 MIP $700

(KP Photo)

Baby Sparkle Plenty Paper Dolls, 1948, Saalfield, #1510, on cover, Baby Sparkle is standing by a clothes line
EX $22   **NM** $75   **MIP** $175

Big Boy Figure, 1990, Playmates
EX $6   **NM** $12   **MIP** $25

Black Light Magic Kit, 1952, Stroward, ultra-violet bulb, cloth, invisible pen, brushes and fluorescent dyes
EX $75   **NM** $125   **MIP** $250

(KP Photo)

Bonny Braids Paper Dolls, 1951, Saalfield, #1559, Dick Tracy's new daughter and Tess
EX $50   **NM** $100   **MIP** $200

Bonny Braids Stroll Toy, 1951, Charmore, tin litho, Bonny doll in carriage
EX $35   **NM** $80   **MIP** $175

Camera Dart Gun, 1971, Larami, 8mm camera-shaped toy w/dart-shooting viewer
EX $30   **NM** $70   **MIP** $150

Coloring Set, 1967, Hasbro, six pre-sketched, numbered pictures to color, w/pencils
EX $30   **NM** $70   **MIP** $140

Crimestopper Club Kit, 1961, Chicago Tribune, premium kit containing badge, whistle, decoder, magnifying glass, fingerprinting kit, ID card, crimestopper textbook
EX $35   **NM** $60   **MIP** $100

(KP Photo)

Crimestopper Play Set, 1970s, Hubley, Dick Tracy cap gun, holster, handcuffs, wallet, flashlight, badge and magnifying glass
EX $35   **NM** $70   **MIP** $50

Crimestoppers Set, 1973, Larami, handcuffs, nightstick and badge
EX $12   **NM** $25   **MIP** $50

Decoder Card, Post Cereal, cereal premium, red or green
EX $30   **NM** $50   **MIP** $100

Dick Tracy Braces, 1940s, Deluxe, Chicago Tribune premium, suspenders on colorful card
EX $50   **NM** $100   **MIP** $185

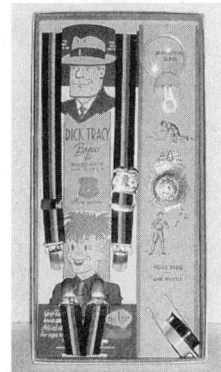

(KP Photo)

Dick Tracy Braces for Smart Boys and Girls, 1950s, Deluxe, Police badge, metal handcuffs, whistle, suspenders w/a Dick Tracy badge as a holder and magnifying glass
EX $50   **NM** $100   **MIP** $175

(KP Photo)

Dick Tracy Candid Camera, 1950s, Seymour Sales, w/50mm lens, plastic carrying case and 127 film
EX $60   **NM** $125   **MIP** $200

Dick Tracy Cartoon Kit, 1962, Colorforms
EX $20   **NM** $45   **MIP** $90

Dick Tracy Crime Lab, 1980s, Ja-Ru, click pistol, fingerprint pad, badge

and magnifying glass, available in orange and bright yellow
EX $8   **NM** $15   **MIP** $30

Dick Tracy Crime Stoppers Laboratory, 1955, Porter Chemical, 60 power microscope, fingerprint pack, glass slides and magnifying glass and textbook
EX $150   **NM** $250   **MIP** $450

Dick Tracy Detective Club Wrist Radios, 1945, Gaylord
EX $85   **NM** $180   **MIP** $375

Dick Tracy Figure, Lakeside, bendy
EX $15   **NM** $30   **MIP** $50

Dick Tracy Hand Puppet, 1961, Ideal, 10-1/2", fabric and vinyl, w/record
EX $35   **NM** $80   **MIP** $150

Dick Tracy Jr. Bombsight, 1940s, Miller Bros. Hat, cardboard
EX $50   **NM** $80   **MIP** $175

Dick Tracy Play Set, 1973, Ideal, contains 18 cardboard figures that measure 3-1/2" to 5" tall, w/carrying case
EX $50   **NM** $120   **MIP** $225

Dick Tracy Play Set, 1982, Placo, plastic dart gun, targets of different villians and a set of handcuffs
EX $10   **NM** $30   **MIP** $50

Dick Tracy Puzzle, 1952, 11" x 14" frame tray
EX $25   **NM** $85   **MIP** $150

Dick Tracy Soaky, 1965, Colgate-Palmolive, 10" tall
EX $25   **NM** $60   **MIP** $100

Dick Tracy Sparkle Paints, 1963, Kenner, paints, brushes and six pictures to paint
EX $25   **NM** $50   **MIP** $100

Dick Tracy Target Game, 1940s, Marx, 17" circular cardboard target, w/dart gun and box
EX $150   **NM** $300   **MIP** $425

(KP Photo)

Dick Tracy Target Set, 1969, Larami, red, green or blue; shoots rubber bands
EX $15   **NM** $35   **MIP** $75

Dick Tracy's Two-in-One Mystery Puzzle, 1958, Jaymar, one puzzle shows the crime and the other the solution

EX $30 **NM** $60 **MIP** $120

Film Strip Viewer, 1948, Acme, viewer and two films in colorful illustrated box

EX $100 **NM** $175 **MIP** $225

(KP Photo)

Film Strip Viewer, 1964, Acme, viewer w/two boxes of film, on card, jumbo movie style

EX $20 **NM** $45 **MIP** $90

Film Viewer, 1973, Larami, mini color televiewer w/two paper filmstrips

EX $10 **NM** $20 **MIP** $50

Flashlight, 1961, Bantam Lite, metal wrist light

EX $25 **NM** $55 **MIP** $150

Handcuffs, 1946, John Henry, metal toy handcuffs on display header card

EX $25 **NM** $55 **MIP** $110

Hemlock Holmes Hand Puppet, 1961, Ideal, includes record

EX $40 **NM** $90 **MIP** $175

Joe Jitsu Hand Puppet, 1961, Ideal, 10-1/2", fabric and vinyl, includes record

EX $45 **NM** $150 **MIP** $250

Mobile Commander, 1973, Larami, toy telephone w/plastic connecting tube, plastic gun and badge

EX $20 **NM** $40 **MIP** $100

Offical Holster Outfit, 1940s, Classy Products, leather holster w/painted Tracy profile

EX $150 **NM** $300 **MIP** $450

Police Whistle No. 64, Marx, tin

EX $20 **NM** $40 **MIP** $80

Puzzle, "Dick Tracy's New Daughter," 1951, Saalfield, tray puzzle of Bonny Braids

EX $22 **NM** $65 **MIP** $125

Puzzle, "The Bank Holdup," 1960s, Jaymar, triple-thick interlocking pieces featuring the TV cartoon

EX $20 **NM** $65 **MIP** $110

Shoulder Holster Set, 1950s, J. Hapern, leather holster w/Dick Tracy's profile

EX $45 **NM** $90 **MIP** $185

Sparkle Plenty Islander Ukette, 1950, Styron, musical instrument, junior size, w/instruction book

EX $60 **NM** $130 **MIP** $300

Sparkle Plenty Washing Machine, 1940s, Kalon Radio, 12" tall tin litho, pictured outside on tub is Gravel Gertie doing the wash as B.O. Plenty holds baby Sparkle

EX $125 **NM** $200 **MIP** $400

Talking Phone, 1967, Marx, green w/ivory handle, battery-operated w/10 different phrases

EX $35 **NM** $75 **MIP** $125

Transistor Radio Receivers, 1961, American Doll and Toy, shoulder holster and secret ear plug w/two transistor radio receivers

EX $40 **NM** $80 **MIP** $160

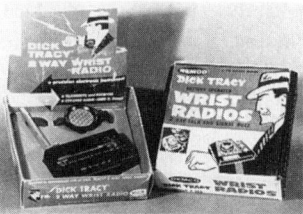

(KP Photo)

Two-Way Electronic Wrist Radios, 1950s, Remco, 2-1/2" x 9 1/2" x 13-1/2", plastic battery-operated wrist radios

EX $80 **NM** $150 **MIP** $275

Two-Way Wrist Radios, 1960s, American Doll and Toy, plastic w/power pack, battery-operated

EX $50 **NM** $100 **MIP** $185

Two-Way Wrist Radios, 1990, Ertl, battery-operated

EX $15 **NM** $20 **MIP** $30

Wrist Band AM Radio, 1976, Creative Creations, w/earphone and two mercury batteries; box shows Tracy and Flattop

EX $30 **NM** $65 **MIP** $150

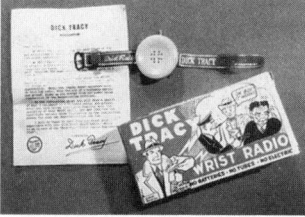

(KP Photo)

Wrist Radio, 1947, Da-Myco Products, crystal set w/receiver on a leather band, 30" wires and connectors for aerial and ground, no batteries, no tubes and no electric

EX $350 **NM** $500 **MIP** $750

Wrist TV, 1980s, Ja-Ru, paper roll of cartoon strips are threaded through the TV viewer

EX $10 **NM** $20 **MIP** $40

VEHICLE

(KP Photo)

Convertible Squad Car, 1948, Marx, 20", friction power w/flashing lights

EX $300 **NM** $450 **MIP** $800

Copmobile, 1963, Ideal, 24" long, white and blue plastic, battery-operated w/a microphone w/amplified speaker on top

EX $100 **NM** $200 **MIP** $400

Dick Tracy Car, 1950s, Marx, 6-1/2" long, light blue w/machine gun pointing out of the front window

EX $125 **NM** $275 **MIP** $475

Get Away Car, 1990, Playmates

EX $15 **NM** $25 **MIP** $50

(KP Photo)

Space Coupe, 1968, Aurora, assembly required, all plastic

EX $150 **NM** $350 **MIP** $600

WATCH

Dick Tracy Two-Way Wristwatch, 1990, Playmates, watch w/no radio function

EX $4 **NM** $7 **MIP** $20

Dick Tracy Wristwatch, 1959, Bradley

EX $50 **NM** $100 **MIP** $210

Dick Tracy Wristwatch, 1981, Omni, digital; police car box

EX $15 **NM** $40 **MIP** $90

Dick Tracy Wristwatch w/Animated Gun, 1951, New Haven

EX $200 **NM** $450 **MIP** $750

Disney

ACCESSORIES

Disney Figure Golf Balls, set of 12

EX $12 **NM** $23 **MIP** $35

Disney Filmstrips, 1940s, Craftman's Guild, 13 color filmstrips

EX $95 **NM** $180 **MIP** $275

Disney Tin Tray, Ohio Art, 8" x 10", pictures Mickey and Minnie Mouse,

Goofy, Horace, Pluto, Donald Duck
and Clarabelle
EX $25   NM $50   MIP $85

Disney World Globe, 1950s, Rand
McNally, 6-1/2" metal base,
8" diameter w/Disney characters
EX $60   NM $125   MIP $200

Disneyland Ashtray, 1950s, 5" diameter,
china, w/Tinker Bell and castle
EX $20   NM $65   MIP $150

Disneyland Electric Light, 1950s,
Econlite, picture of Disney characters
leaving a bus on a drum base
EX $45   NM $80   MIP $235

Disneyland Felt Banner, 1960s, Disney,
"The Magic Kingdom," 24-1/2"
red/white/blue coat of arms
EX $25   NM $60   MIP $90

(KP Photo)

**Disneyland Give-A-Show Projector
Color Slides,** 1960s, 112 color slides
EX $85   NM $140   MIP $250

Disneyland Metal Craft Tapping Set,
1950s, Pressman
EX $25   NM $40   MIP $100

Disneyland Miniature License Plates,
1966, Marx, 2" x 4" plates w/Mickey,
Minnie and Pluto, or Snow White,
Donald and Goofy, each
EX $12   NM $23   MIP $35

Disneyland Pen, 1960s, 6" long w/a
picture of a floating riverboat
EX $15   NM $25   MIP $40

Duck Tales Travel Tote, 1980s, travel
agency premium
EX $5   NM $20   MIP $35

Fantasia Musical Jewelry Box, 1990,
Schmid Bros., box features Mickey
and plays "The Sorcerer's Apprentice"
EX $30   NM $55   MIP $90

Figural Light Switch Plates, Monogram,
hand-painted switch plates: Goofy,
Donald, Mickey, on card, each
EX $6   NM $12   MIP $25

Happy Birthday/Pepsi Placemats,
1978, Pepsi, set of four mats
EX $15   NM $35   MIP $60

Lap Trays, 1960s, Hasko, set of four:
Donald, Goofy and Pluto, Peter Pan,
and the Seven Dwarfs
EX $35   NM $65   MIP $150

Silly Symphony Lights, Noma, set of
eight
EX $100   NM $150   MIP $375

BANK

Color Television Bank, 1950s, Linemar,
4" x 4-1/2", tin, Mickey or Donald on
side panels, litho screen rotates
EX $200   NM $400   MIP $600

Disneyland Haunted House Bank,
1960s, Japanese
EX $35   NM $65   MIP $225

Second National Duck Bank, Chein,
3-1/2" tall x 7" long
EX $100   NM $200   MIP $375

BOOK

Toby Tyler Circus Playbook, 1959,
Whitman, punch-out character
activity book
EX $25   NM $50   MIP $100

FIGURES

Aristocats Thomas O'Malley Figure,
1967, Enesco, 8" tall ceramic
EX $30   NM $65   MIP $125

Fantasia Figure, Vernon Kilns,
half-woman, half-zebra centaur
EX $85   NM $180   MIP $400

Fantasia Unicorn Figure, 1940s, Vernon
Kilns, ceramic black-winged unicorn
EX $75   NM $110   MIP $250

Johnny Tremain Figure and Horse,
1957, Marx, plastic, 9-1/2" tall
horse and 5-1/2" tall Johnny
EX $80   NM $120   MIP $225

Jose Carioca Figure, Marx, 2" tall, plastic
EX $30   NM $55   MIP $80

Jose Carioca Figure, 1960s, Marx,
5-1/2" tall plastic, wire arms and legs
EX $50   NM $110   MIP $200

GAME

Disneyland Bagatelle, 1970s,
Wolverine, large game w/Disneyland
graphics
EX $15   NM $25   MIP $100

**Walt Disney's Game/Parade/Academy
Award Winners,** American Toy
Works, 15 games for all ages
EX $60   NM $120   MIP $185

PUZZLE

Black Hole Puzzle, 1979, Whitman,
jigsaw puzzle, V.I.N.C.E.N.T. or
Cygnus
EX $15   NM $30   MIP $85

Disneyland Puzzle, 1956, Whitman,
frame tray
EX $20   NM $50   MIP $100

TOY

Carousel, Linemar, 7" tall w/3" figures,
wind-up
EX $200   NM $350   MIP $500

Casey Jr. Disneyland Express Train,
1950s, Marx, 12" long, tin, wind-up
EX $200   NM $300   MIP $550

Character Molding and Coloring Set,
1950s, red rubber molds of Bambi,
Thumper, Dumbo, Goofy, Flower and
Jose Carioca to make plaster figures
EX $35   NM $75   MIP $150

Disney Shooting Gallery, 1950s,
Welso Toys, 8" x 12" x 1-1/2" tin
target w/molded figures of Mickey,
Donald, Goofy and Pluto
EX $75   NM $150   MIP $300

Disney Treasure Chest Set, 1940s,
Craftman's Guild, red plastic film
viewer and filmstrips in blue box
designed like a chest
EX $70   NM $145   MIP $210

**Disneyland Auto Magic Picture Gun
and Theater,** 1950s, battery-
operated metal gun w/oval filmstrip
EX $50   NM $90   MIP $150

Disneyland F.D. Fire Truck, Linemar,
18" long, battery-operated,
moveable, Donald Duck fireman
climbs the ladder
EX $250   NM $400   MIP $600

Early Settlers Log Set, 1960s,
Halsam, log building set based on
Disneyland's Tom Sawyer's Island
EX $40   NM $75   MIP $150

Horace Horsecollar Hand Puppet,
1950s, Gund
EX $30   NM $75   MIP $150

Jose Carioca Wind-Up Toy, 1940s,
France, 3-1/2" x 5" x 7-1/2" tall
EX $100   NM $300   MIP $450

Nautilus Expanding Periscope, 1954,
Pressman, inspired by 20,000
Leagues Under the Sea, 19" long
EX $75   NM $160   MIP $250

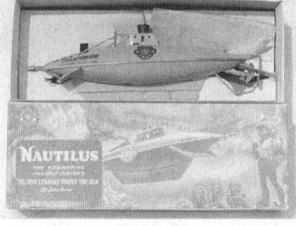

(KP Photo)

Nautilus Wind-Up Submarine,
1950s, Sutcliffe/England
EX $150   NM $250   MIP $475

Official Santa Fe and Disneyland R.R. Scale Model Train, 1966, Tyco, HO scale, electric
EX $200 NM $350 MIP $600

Pecos Bill Wind-Up Toy, 1950s, Marx, 10" tall, riding his horse Widowmaker and holding a metal lasso
EX $75 NM $200 MIP $400

Walt Disney Movie Viewer and Cartridge, 1972, Action Films, #9312 w/the cartridge "Lonesome Ghosts"
EX $10 NM $16 MIP $35

Walt Disney's Character Scramble, 1940s, Plane Facts, 10 cardboard figures, 6" tall
EX $30 NM $70 MIP $175

Walt Disney's Realistic Noah's Ark, 1940s, W.H. Greene, 6" x 7" x 18" Ark, 101 2" animals, and 4" human figures on cardboard
EX $150 NM $350 MIP $700

Walt Disney's Silly Symphony Bells, Noma, Christmas tree bells
EX $60 NM $125 MIP $275

Walt Disney's Snap-Eeze Set, 1963, Marx, 12-1/2" x 15" x 1" box w/12 flat plastic figures
EX $60 NM $115 MIP $275

Walt Disney's Television Car, Marx, 8" long, friction toy lights up a picture on the roof when motor turns
EX $500 NM $750 MIP $1500

Doc Savage

ACCESSORIES

Club Kit, 1975, comics premium; includes card, button and mailer
EX $40 NM $75 MIP $150

Donald Duck

ACCESSORIES

Donald Duck Alarm Clock, 1950s, Glen Clock/Scotland, 5-1/2" x 5-1/2" x 2", Donald pictured w/blue bird on his hand
EX $150 NM $300 MIP $675

Donald Duck Alarm Clock, 1960s, Bayard, 2" x 4-1/2" x 5"
EX $125 NM $275 MIP $600

Donald Duck Lamp, 1940s, 9" tall, china, Donald holding an axe standing next to a tree trunk
EX $150 NM $275 MIP $425

Donald Duck Lamp, 1970s, Dolly Toy, Donald on a tug boat
EX $75 NM $150 MIP $250

Donald Duck Light Switch Cover, 1976, Dolly Toy, plastic, Donald on a boat
EX $5 NM $10 MIP $25

Donald Duck Music Box, 1971, Anri, Donald w/guitar, plays "My Way"
EX $75 NM $100 MIP $200

Donald Duck Soap, Disney, figural castile soap
EX $40 NM $70 MIP $140

Donald Duck Toothbrush Holder, 1930s, bisque, figural
EX $200 NM $450 MIP $725

Donald Duck WWI Pencil Box, Dixon, 5" x 8-1/2" x 1-1/4" deep, Donald flying a plane, holding a tomahawk
EX $50 NM $125 MIP $250

Ludwig Von Drake Wonderful World of Color Pencil Box, 1961, Hasbro, box shows Ludwig and the nephews
EX $25 NM $55 MIP $85

Uncle Scrooge Wallet, 1970s, 3" x 4", Uncle Scrooge tossing coins
EX $20 NM $40 MIP $85

BANK

Donald Duck Bank, 1940s, 5-1/2" x 6" x 7-1/2" tall, china, Donald seated holding a coin in one hand
EX $75 NM $200 MIP $325

Donald Duck Bank, 1940s, 4-1/2" x 4-1/2" x 6-1/2" tall, ceramic, Donald holding a rope w/a large brown fish by his side
EX $50 NM $100 MIP $250

DOLL

Donald Duck Doll, 1976, Mattel, talking doll
EX $75 NM $250 MIP $425

Huey, Dewey and Louie Dolls, 1950s, Gund, set of three 8" tall dolls
EX $65 NM $125 MIP $350

Louie Doll, 1940s, Gund, 8" tall, white/light green plush
EX $40 NM $70 MIP $115

FIGURES

Donald Duck Figure, Seiberling, 6" tall, solid rubber w/movable head
EX $175 NM $260 MIP $500

Donald Duck Figure, Seiberling, 5" tall, rubber
EX $175 NM $260 MIP $500

Donald Duck Figure, 1950s, Dell, 7" tall, rubber
EX $75 NM $150 MIP $250

Donald Duck Nodder, 1960s, 5-1/2" tall on green base
EX $50 NM $150 MIP $200

Ludwig Von Drake Figure, 1961, Marx, 3" tall, from the "Snap-Eeze" collection
EX $10 NM $20 MIP $40

TOY

Crayon Box, 1946, Transogram, tin, pictures Donald and Mickey
EX $30 NM $55 MIP $150

Donald Duck and Pluto Car, Sun Rubber, 6-1/2" long, hard rubber, blue
EX $50 NM $125 MIP $375

Donald Duck Bicycle, 1949, Shelby
EX $2500 NM $4500 MIP $8000

Donald Duck Camera, 1950s, Herbert-George, 3" x 4" x 3"
EX $60 NM $150 MIP $300

Donald Duck Car, 1950s, Sun Rubber, 2-1/2" x 3-1/2" x 6-1/2", rubber
EX $40 NM $110 MIP $400

Donald Duck Driving Pluto Toy, 9" long, wind-up, celluloid
EX $500 NM $800 MIP $1600

Donald Duck Dump Truck, 1950s, Linemar
EX $150 NM $275 MIP $525

Donald Duck Marionette, 1950s, Peter Puppet, 6-1/2" tall
EX $50 NM $150 MIP $250

Donald Duck Projector, 1950s, Stephens, projector w/four films
EX $55 NM $125 MIP $250

Donald Duck Puppet, 1960s, Pelham Puppets, 10" tall, hollow composition
EX $40 NM $75 MIP $200

Donald Duck Push Puppet, 1950s, Kohner, sailor Donald
EX $30 NM $100 MIP $160

Donald Duck Push Toy, 1950s, Gong Bell
EX $35 NM $60 MIP $100

Donald Duck Puzzle, 1940s, Jaymar, frame tray
EX $50 NM $100 MIP $175

Donald Duck Ramp Walker, 1950s, Marx, 1-1/4" x 3-1/2" x 3" tall, Donald is pulling red wagon w/his nephews
EX $110 NM $175 MIP $325

Donald Duck Sand Pail, 1950s, Ohio Art, 3-1/2" tall, tin, Donald in life preserver fighting off seagulls
EX $65 NM $175 MIP $300

Donald Duck Scooter, 1960s, Marx, tin wind-up, 4" x 4" x 2"
EX $150 NM $250 MIP $350

Donald Duck Skating Rink Toy, 1950s, Mettoy, 4" diameter, Donald is skating while other Disney characters circle the rink
EX $40 NM $70 MIP $160

Donald Duck Snow Shovel, Ohio Art, wood, tin, litho
EX $60 NM $130 MIP $250

Donald Duck Soaky, 1950s, 7" tall
EX $15 NM $50 MIP $100

Donald Duck Squeeze Toy, 1960s, Dell, 8" tall, rubber
EX $15   NM $40   MIP $80

Donald Duck Tea Set, Ohio Art, 7-1/2" tray, 2-1/4" diameter cups, saucers
EX $100   NM $175   MIP $250

Donald Duck the Drummer, 1940s, Marx, 5" x 7" x 10" tall, Donald beats on a metal drum
EX $300   NM $500   MIP $725

Donald Duck Toy, Schuco, 5-1/2" tall, wind-up w/a bellows, quacking sound
EX $350   NM $700   MIP $1000

Donald Duck Toy Raft, 1950s, Ideal, 2" tall, blue plastic raft w/yellow sail w/Donald looking through a telescope
EX $400   NM $75   MIP $110

Donald Duck Trapeze Toy, Linemar, 5" tall, celluloid, wind-up
EX $60   NM $200   MIP $600

Donald Duck Wind-Up, 1972, Durham Plastic, 6-1/2" tall, hard plastic
EX $15   NM $40   MIP $85

Donald Tricycle Toy, 1950s, Linemar, tin
EX $500   NM $800   MIP $1200

Ludwig Von Drake in Go Cart, 1960s, Linemar, tin and plastic
EX $115   NM $250   MIP $500

Ludwig Von Drake Mug, 1961, 3-1/2" white china
EX $15   NM $20   MIP $50

Ludwig Von Drake Squeeze Toy, 1961, Dell, 8" tall, rubber
EX $10   NM $20   MIP $50

Ludwig Von Drake Tiddly Winks, 1961, Whitman
EX $10   NM $20   MIP $60

WATCH

Daisy Duck Wristwatch, 1948, US Time
EX $275   NM $550   MIP $875

Donald Duck Wristwatch, 1940s, US Time
EX $275   NM $550   MIP $950

Dr. Doolittle

FIGURES

Dr. Doolittle Figure, 1967, Mattel, 5" tall w/parrot
EX $15   NM $30   MIP $50

Dr. Doolittle Figure, 1967, Mattel, 7" tall
EX $15   NM $35   MIP $75

TOY

Dr. Doolittle Giraffe-in-the-Box, jack-in-the-box
EX $50   NM $100   MIP $200

Dr. Seuss

ACCESSORIES

Mattel-O-Phone, 1970, Mattel
EX $40   NM $75   MIP $225

DOLL

Cat in the Hat Doll, 1983, Coleco, plush
EX $10   NM $40   MIP $90

Grinch Doll, 1983, Coleco
EX $55   NM $110   MIP $300

Horton the Elephant Doll, 1983, Coleco
EX $25   NM $65   MIP $135

(KP Photo)

Lorax Doll, 1983, Coleco
EX $25   NM $65   MIP $135

Star-Bellied Sneetch Doll, 1983, Coleco
EX $40   NM $70   MIP $140

Talking Cat in the Hat Doll, 1970, Mattel
EX $60   NM $175   MIP $300

Talking Hedwig Doll, 1970, Mattel
EX $50   NM $125   MIP $250

Talking Horton Doll, 1970, Mattel
EX $60   NM $175   MIP $350

(KP Photo)

Thidwick the Moose Doll, 1983, Coleco
EX $15   NM $40   MIP $90

(KP Photo)

Yertle the Turtle Doll, 1983, Coleco, 12" plush
EX $15   NM $45   MIP $100

TOY

Cat in the Hat Ge-Tar, 1970, Mattel
EX $40   NM $110   MIP $220

Cat in the Hat Jack-in-the-Box, 1969, Mattel
EX $100   NM $180   MIP $310

Cat in the Hat Riding Toy, 1983, Coleco
EX $25   NM $50   MIP $135

Cat in the Hat Rocking Toy, 1983, Coleco
EX $25   NM $50   MIP $135

Cat in the Hat Talking Puppet, 1970, Mattel, vinyl head
EX $75   NM $125   MIP $300

Dumbo

ACCESSORIES

Dumbo Christmas Ornament, 2" porcelain bisque, 50th anniversary
EX $8   NM $15   MIP $35

Dumbo Milk Pitcher, 1940s, 6" tall
EX $65   NM $110   MIP $250

DOLL

Dumbo Doll, 12" plush
EX $10   NM $20   MIP $50

FIGURES

Dumbo Figure, Dakin
EX $12   NM $25   MIP $50

TOY

Dumbo Squeeze Toy, 1950s, Dell, 5" tall
EX $15   NM $30   MIP $75

Elmer Fudd

ACCESSORIES

Elmer Fudd Mini Snow Dome, 1980s, Applause
EX $10   NM $20   MIP $35

Elmer Fudd Mug, 1980s, Applause, figural
EX $5   NM $10   MIP $20

FIGURES

Elmer Fudd Figure, 1950s, metal 5", on green base w/his name embossed, Elmer in hunting outfit
EX $55   NM $125   MIP $275

Elmer Fudd Figure, 1968, Dakin, 8" tall
EX $20   NM $60   MIP $100

Elmer Fudd Figure, 1971, Dakin, in a red hunting outfit
EX $30   NM $70   MIP $125

Elmer Fudd Figure, 1977, Dakin, Fun Farm
EX $18   NM $33   MIP $65

TOY

Elmer Fudd Pull Toy, 1940s, Brice Toys, 9", wooden, Elmer in fire chief's car
EX $100   NM $225   MIP $400

Felix the Cat

ACCESSORIES

Felix Cartoon Lamp Shade, 6" tall
EX $75   NM $150   MIP $250

Felix Flashlight, 1960s, contains whistle
EX $50   NM $200   MIP $325

Felix Pencil Case, 1950s
EX $25   NM $75   MIP $120

Felix Sip-a-Drink Cup, 5" tall
EX $15   NM $25   MIP $60

TOY

Felix Punching Bag, 1960s, 11" tall inflatable bobber
EX $25   NM $60   MIP $110

Felix Soaky, 1960s, 10" tall, blue plastic
EX $20   NM $60   MIP $100

Felix Soaky, 1960s, 10" tall, red plastic
EX $20   NM $60   MIP $100

Felix Soaky, 1960s, 10" tall, black plastic
EX $15   NM $50   MIP $90

WATCH

Felix Wristwatch, 1960s
EX $65   NM $150   MIP $275

Ferdinand the Bull

BANK

Ferdinand Savings Bank, Crown Toy, 5" tall, wood composition w/silk flower w/metal trap door
EX $50   NM $100   MIP $250

FIGURES

Ferdinand Figure, 9" tall, plastic
EX $20   NM $35   MIP $150

Ferdinand Figure, 3-1/2" bisque
EX $15   NM $40   MIP $110

Ferdinand Figure, 1940s, Disney, composition
EX $125   NM $200   MIP $350

Flipper

TOY

Flipper Halloween Costume, 1964, Collegeville
EX $20   NM $40   MIP $125

Flipper Magic Slate, 1960s, Lowe
EX $12   NM $24   MIP $75

Flipper Model Kit, 1965, Revell
EX $17   NM $35   MIP $100

Flipper Puzzle, 1960s, Whitman, several variations, each
EX $12   NM $22   MIP $50

Flipper Ukelele, 1968, Mattel
EX $12   NM $22   MIP $60

Foghorn Leghorn

FIGURES

Foghorn Leghorn Figure, 1970, Dakin, 6-1/4" tall
EX $22   NM $45   MIP $100

Foghorn Leghorn Figure, 1980s, Applause, PVC
EX $3   NM $50   MIP $75

TOY

Foghorn Leghorn Hand Puppet, 1960s, 9", fabric w/vinyl head
EX $20   NM $75   MIP $150

Fontaine Fox

TOY

Toonerville Trolley, Nifty, miniature, 2" tall
EX $250   NM $350   MIP $525

Toonerville Trolley, 3" tall
EX $200   NM $350   MIP $450

Toonerville Trolley, 4" tall, red pot metal
EX $500   NM $800   MIP $1450

Garfield

BANK

Garfield Chair Bank, 1981, Enesco
EX $12   NM $25   MIP $80

Garfield Figure Bank, 1981, Enesco, 4-3/4"
EX $12   NM $24   MIP $70

FIGURES

Garfield Easter Figure, 1978, Enesco
EX $7   NM $20   MIP $50

Garfield Figure, 1978, Enesco, Garfield as graduate
EX $6   NM $12   MIP $40

MUSIC BOX

Garfield Music Box, 1981, Enesco, Garfield dancing
EX $50   NM $75   MIP $150

Gasoline Alley

ACCESSORIES

Uncle Walt and Skeezix Pencil Holder, F.A.S., 5" tall, bisque
EX $125   NM $200   MIP $325

FIGURES

Uncle Walt and Skeezix Figure Set, bisque, Uncle Walt, Skeezix, Herby and Smitty
EX $125   NM $250   MIP $400

Goofy

ACCESSORIES

Goofy Night Light, 1973, Horsman, green, figural
EX $16   NM $30   MIP $45

Goofy Toothbrush, 1970s, Pepsodent
EX $5   NM $10   MIP $40

DOLL

Goofy Doll, 1970s, 5" x 6" x 13" tall, fabric and vinyl, laughing doll
EX $50   NM $100   MIP $200

FIGURES

Goofy Figure, Marx, Snap-Eeze figure
EX $15   NM $35   MIP $50

Goofy Figure, Arco, bendy
EX $10   NM $15   MIP $25

Goofy Lil' Headbobber, Marx
EX $50   NM $100   MIP $160

Goofy Rolykin, Marx
EX $25   NM $50   MIP $75

Goofy Twist 'n Bend Figure, 1963, Marx, 4" tall
EX $11   NM $20   MIP $30

TOY

Goofy Car, Spain, vinyl head Goofy drives tin litho car
EX $50   NM $100   MIP $150

Goofy Safety Scissors, 1973, Monogram, on card
EX $5   NM $10   MIP $20

Goofy w/Bump 'n Go Action Lawn Mower, 1980s, Illfelder, 3-1/2" x 10" x 11", plastic figure pushing lawn mower w/silver handle
EX $40   NM $70   MIP $125

WATCH

Backwards Goofy Wristwatch, Pedre, silver case 2nd edition
EX $40   NM $75   MIP $225

Backwards Goofy Wristwatch, 1972, Helbros
EX $325   NM $650   MIP $1000

Gumby

ACCESSORIES

(KP Photo)

Gumby Adventure Costume, 1960s, Lakeside, fireman, cowboy, knight and astronaut, each
EX $25   NM $50   MIP $90

FIGURES

Gumby Figure, 1980s, large, foam rubber
EX $20   NM $40   MIP $100

Gumby Figure, 1980s, Applause, 12" tall, poseable
EX $10   NM $20   MIP $40

Gumby Figure, 1980s, Applause, 5-1/2" bendy, three styles
EX $5   NM $10   MIP $30

Pokey Figure, 1960s, Lakeside
EX $20   NM $40   MIP $95

TOY

Adventures of Gumby Electric Drawing Set, 1966, Lakeside
EX $22   NM $50   MIP $125

Gumby Colorforms Set, 1988, Colorforms
EX $8   NM $12   MIP $50

Gumby Hand Puppet, 1965, Lakeside, 9" tall w/vinyl head
EX $15   NM $40   MIP $90

Gumby Modeling Dough, 1960s, Chemtoy
EX $25   NM $50   MIP $90

Gumby's Jeep, 1960s, Lakeside, yellow tin litho, Gumby and Pokey's names are printed on seat
EX $150   NM $250   MIP $400

Pokey Modeling Dough, 1960s, Chemtoy
EX $25   NM $50   MIP $90

Happy Hooligan

TOY

Happy Hooligan Nesting Toys, Anri, 4" tall, wooden set of four nesting pieces
EX $100   NM $150   MIP $350

Heckle and Jeckle

BOOK

Heckle and Jeckle Story Book, 1957, Wonder Book
EX $30   NM $50   MIP $75

FIGURES

Heckle and Jeckle Figures, 7" soft foam figures
EX $25   NM $70   MIP $135

Little Roquefort Figure, 1959, 8-1/2" tall, wood
EX $20   NM $40   MIP $80

TOY

Heckle and Jeckle Skooz-It Game, 1963, Ideal, cylindrical container
EX $40   NM $80   MIP $125

Huckleberry Hound

BANK

Huckleberry Hound Bank, 1960, Knickerbocker, 10" tall, hard plastic figural
EX $30   NM $60   MIP $100

Huckleberry Hound Bank, 1980, Dakin, 5" tall figural bank of Huck sitting
EX $20   NM $40   MIP $80

DOLL

Huckleberry Hound Doll, 1959, Knickerbocker, 18" plush, vinyl hands and face
EX $60   NM $125   MIP $175

Mr. Jinks Doll, 1959, Knickerbocker, 13" tall, plush, vinyl face
EX $50   NM $110   MIP $230

Pixie and Dixie Dolls, 1960, Knickerbocker, 12" tall, each
EX $25   NM $45   MIP $100

FIGURES

Hokey Wolf Figure, 1961, Marx, TV-Tinykin
EX $15   NM $40   MIP $85

Hokey Wolf Figure, 1970, Dakin
EX $30   NM $75   MIP $150

Huckleberry Hound Figure, Dakin, 8" tall
EX $25   NM $50   MIP $90

Huckleberry Hound Figure, 1960s, 6" tall, glazed china
EX $20   NM $40   MIP $100

Huckleberry Hound Figure, 1961, Marx, TV-Tinykins
EX $15   NM $25   MIP $60

Huckleberry Hound Figure Set, 1961, Marx, TV-Tinykins
EX $50   NM $80   MIP $125

TOY

Huckleberry Hound Go-Cart, 1960s, Linemar, 6-1/2" tall, friction
EX $100   NM $200   MIP $375

Huckleberry Hound Wind-Up Toy, 1962, Linemar, 4" tall, tin
EX $175   NM $350   MIP $500

Mr. Jinks Soaky, 1960s, Purex, 10" tall, Pixie and Dixie, hard plastic
EX $15   NM $35   MIP $75

Pixie and Dixie Magic Slate, 1959
EX $30   NM $50   MIP $80

WATCH

Huckleberry Hound Wristwatch, 1965, Bradley, chrome case, wind-up mechanism, gray leather band, face shows Huck in full view
EX $100   NM $150   MIP $300

Humpty Dumpty

ACCESSORIES

Humpty Dumpty Bubble Bath, 1960s, Avon, figural plastic container
EX $7   NM $30   MIP $85

Humpty Dumpty Figural Soap, 1990s, Avon
EX $3   NM $6   MIP $20

Humpty Dumpty Magazine, 1960s
EX $3   NM $7   MIP $25

Humpty Dumpty Potato Chip Tin, 1990s, large blue and gold tin
EX $7   NM $15   MIP $40

FIGURE

Humpty Dumpty Figure, 1950s, Marx, Fairy Tale series, plastic
EX $5   NM $10   MIP $40

Humpty Dumpty Game, 1981, Orchard Toys, British matching game
EX $8   NM $15   MIP $50

PUZZLE

Humpty Dumpty Puzzle, 1970s, wood frame tray puzzles, several varieties
EX $5   NM $15   MIP $40

TOY

Humpty Dumpty Crib Toy, 1980s, Mattel, plastic, sits on crib rail
EX $4   **NM** $8   **MIP** $25

Humpty Dumpty Musical Toy, 1960s, Alladin Plastics, plastic, record inside toy
EX $15   **NM** $30   **MIP** $70

Humpty Dumpty Pull Toy, 1970s, Fisher-Price, plastic, several color variations
EX $5   **NM** $10   **MIP** $30

Indiana Jones

ACCESSORIES

Indiana Jones Backpack, Pepsi
EX $20   **NM** $45   **MIP** $90

Indiana Jones The Legend Mug
EX $5   **NM** $10   **MIP** $15

Last Crusade Button, Pepsi, retailer button
EX $5   **NM** $15   **MIP** $30

Patch, 1990
EX $10   **NM** $20   **MIP** $40

Temple of Doom Calendar
EX $5   **NM** $10   **MIP** $30

Temple of Doom Storybook, hardbound
EX $7   **NM** $20   **MIP** $30

TOY

(KP Photo)

Indiana Jones 3-D View-Master Gift Set, View-Master
EX $20   **NM** $35   **MIP** $75

James Bond

ACCESSORIES

007 Flicker Rings, 1967, set of 11
EX $75   **NM** $110   **MIP** $220

007 Video Disc Promo Kit, 1980s, RCA, disc, poster, pamphlet
EX $15   **NM** $30   **MIP** $60

Bond Golf Tees, 1987, British, six tees and pencil in leather pouch
EX $8   **NM** $15   **MIP** $30

James Bond Alarm Clock, painting of Roger Moore in center
EX $20   **NM** $40   **MIP** $100

James Bond B.A.R.K. Attache Case w/Box, 1965, Multiple Toys, 007 luger, missiles, hideaway pistol and rocket launching device, case and gun bears 007 logo
EX $1000 **NM** $1500   **MIP** $3000

James Bond Jr. Bath Towel
EX $10   **NM** $20   **MIP** $20

James Bond Parachute Set, 1984, Imperial, orange and green parachutist figures
EX $12   **NM** $35   **MIP** $80

James Bond Ring, 1964, glass oval w/photo of Sean Connery
EX $10   **NM** $25   **MIP** $40

James Bond Wall Clock, 1981, large clock w/painting of Roger Moore in action
EX $25   **NM** $45   **MIP** $100

View to a Kill Michelin Button, Bond on large size pinback w/Midas man
EX $5   **NM** $12   **MIP** $25

ACTION FIGURES

James Bond Jr. Action Ninja Figure, Hasbro
EX $8   **NM** $15   **MIP** $80

James Bond Jr. Buddy Mitchell Figure, Hasbro
EX $5   **NM** $10   **MIP** $30

James Bond Jr. Capt. Walker D. Plank Figure, Hasbro
EX $3   **NM** $6   **MIP** $20

James Bond Jr. Dr. Derange Figure, Hasbro
EX $3   **NM** $6   **MIP** $25

James Bond Jr. Dr. No. Figure, Hasbro
EX $3   **NM** $6   **MIP** $25

James Bond Jr. Figure, Hasbro, w/pistol
EX $3   **NM** $8   **MIP** $35

James Bond Jr. Figure, Hasbro, w/scuba gear
EX $3   **NM** $8   **MIP** $35

James Bond Jr. Gordo Leiter Figure, Hasbro
EX $4   **NM** $10   **MIP** $40

James Bond Jr. I.Q. Figure, Hasbro, w/weapon device
EX $3   **NM** $6   **MIP** $25

James Bond Jr. Jaws Figure, Hasbro
EX $5   **NM** $12   **MIP** $40

James Bond Jr. Odd Job Figure, Hasbro
EX $6   **NM** $15   **MIP** $50

BOOK

Bond Pocket Diary, 1988, British, leather bound
EX $5   **NM** $15   **MIP** $40

James Bond Jr. Sticker Book
EX $3   **NM** $6   **MIP** $20

COSTUME

James Bond Costume, 1966, Ben Cooper, tuxedo
EX $50   **NM** $100   **MIP** $200

Moonraker Halloween Costume, 1979, mask of Roger Moore and space suit costume
EX $30   **NM** $75   **MIP** $150

DOLL

(KP Photo)

Odd Job Action Figure, 1965, Gilbert, 12" doll in karate outfit, w/derby
EX $300 **NM** $550   **MIP** $750

FIGURES

Jaws Figure, 1979, Mego
EX $135 **NM** $300   **MIP** $600

GAME

Goldfinger II Role Playing Game
EX $6   **NM** $15   **MIP** $40

James Bond Computer Game "The Stealth Affair," 1990, based on Licence to Kill
EX $15   **NM** $30   **MIP** $70

James Bond Jr. Karate Punch Target Game, gun w/boxing glove and targets of villain
EX $8   **NM** $15   **MIP** $45

(KP Photo)

James Bond Secret Service Game, 1965, Spears
EX $150 **NM** $275   **MIP** $625

James Bond Tarot Game, 1973
EX $15   **NM** $30   **MIP** $70

James Bond Video Game, 1983, Coleco
EX $15   NM $25   MIP $60

Moonraker Spanish Card Game, 33 cards w/different color stills
EX $15   NM $30   MIP $70

The James Bond Box, 1965, rare game played w/dice
EX $50   NM $100   MIP $200

Thunderball Balloon Target Game, 1965
EX $40   NM $95   MIP $200

GUN

(KP Photo)

007 Dart Gun, 1984, Imperial, photo of Roger Moore
EX $15   NM $35   MIP $100

007 Submachine Gun, 1984, Imperial, photo of Roger Moore
EX $10   NM $30   MIP $100

007 Toy Pistol, Edgemark
EX $5   NM $15   MIP $50

(KP Photo)

James Bond Harpoon Gun (Thunderball), 1960s, Lone Star, box illustrated w/undersea fight scene graphics
EX $125   NM $250   MIP $400

James Bond Hideaway Pistol, 1985, Coibel
EX $40   NM $90   MIP $170

James Bond Sting Pistol, Coibel, eight-shot cap pistol and booklet from On Her Majesty's Secret Service
EX $20   NM $40   MIP $120

Living Daylights German Pistol, 1980s, Wicke, 25-shot cap gun
EX $12   NM $30   MIP $90

May Day Pistol, 1985
EX $12   NM $30   MIP $75

PUPPETS

Odd Job Puppet, Gilbert, plastic hand puppet
EX $250   NM $500   MIP $750

PUZZLE

Goldfinger Puzzle, 1965, Milton Bradley, Bond and Golden Girl
EX $25   NM $55   MIP $120

(KP Photo)

Goldfinger Puzzle, 1965, Milton Bradley, Bond's Bullets Blaze
EX $20   NM $40   MIP $95

Spy Who Loved Me Puzzle, Milton Bradley, several scenes, each
EX $20   NM $40   MIP $90

STICKERS

007 Bullet Hole Stickers, 1987, simulated bullet holes, magnetic license holder
EX $6   NM $15   MIP $40

TOY

007 Exploding Cigarette Lighter, Coibel
EX $12   NM $30   MIP $100

007 Exploding Coin, Coibel, on blister pack
EX $6   NM $20   MIP $50

007 Exploding Pen, Coibel, on blister pack
EX $6   NM $20   MIP $50

007 Exploding Spoon, Coibel, on blister pack
EX $6   NM $20   MIP $50

007 Radio Trap, 1966, Multiple Toys, radio w/secret business cards
EX $50   NM $105   MIP $220

(KP Photo)

Electric Drawing Set, 1965, Lakeside, plastic tracing board, pencils, sharpener, adventure sheets
EX $55   NM $110   MIP $250

James Bond Disguise Kit, 1965, Gilbert
EX $40   NM $85   MIP $200

James Bond Disguise Kit #2, 1965, Gilbert
EX $40   NM $85   MIP $200

James Bond Hand Puppet, 1965, Gilbert
EX $45   NM $100   MIP $175

James Bond Jr. CD Player/Weapons Kit, Hasbro
EX $10   NM $20   MIP $60

James Bond Jr. Crime Fighter Set, includes handcuffs, watch and walkie-talkie
EX $5   NM $15   MIP $50

James Bond Jr. Ninja Play Set, throw stars, nunchukas and badge
EX $8   NM $15   MIP $60

James Bond Jr. Ninja Wrist Weapon Set
EX $5   NM $10   MIP $50

(KP Photo)

James Bond Secret Attache Case, 1965, MPC, box is rare
EX $1250   NM $1750   MIP $3200

Spy Who Loved Me Jr. Set, Corgi, Lotus and Copter
EX $15   NM $40   MIP $95

(KP Photo)

Thunderball Puzzle, 1965, Milton Bradley, several pictures, each
EX $20   NM $45   MIP $95

Thunderball Set, 1965, Gilbert
EX $40   NM $105   MIP $220

Tuxedo Outfit, 1965, Gilbert
EX $50   NM $110   MIP $230

VEHICLES

James Bond Aston Martin, 1965, Gilbert, 12", battery-operated
EX $150   NM $300   MIP $575

James Bond Aston Martin Slot Car, 1965, Gilbert
EX $75   NM $150   MIP $325

James Bond Jr. Corvette, Hasbro
EX $15   NM $35   MIP $90

James Bond Jr. Scum Shark Mobile, Hasbro
EX $10   NM $15   MIP $40

James Bond Jr. Sub Cycle, Hasbro
EX $10   NM $15   MIP $40

James Bond Jr. Vehicles, Ertl, S.C.U.M. Helicopter, Bond's car and van; set of three
EX $20   NM $65   MIP $150

James Bond Roadrace Set, 1965, Gilbert, scenery tracks, Aston Martin and other cars
EX $350   NM $600   MIP $1000

Licence to Kill Car Set, Matchbox, jeep, seaplane, oil tanker, and copter
EX $25   NM $50   MIP $125

Living Daylights Record Mobile, 1980s
EX $5   NM $20   MIP $50

Moonraker Drax Copter, Corgi
EX $15   NM $40   MIP $85

Moonraker Jr. Set, Corgi, Aston Martin and Lotus
EX $25   NM $60   MIP $175

Moonraker Jr. Shuttle, Corgi
EX $15   NM $35   MIP $80

(KP Photo)

Moonraker Shuttle and Drax Copter Jr.'s, Corgi, set of two
EX $15   NM $35   MIP $80

Moonraker Space Shuttle, Corgi
EX $25   NM $50   MIP $150

Multi-Action Aston Martin, 1960s, friction-operated car for Agent 711
EX $90   NM $200   MIP $400

(KP Photo)

Octopussy Gift Set, Corgi, plane, truck and horse trailer
EX $35   NM $100   MIP $200

Spy Who Loved Me Helicopter Jr., Corgi
EX $10   NM $25   MIP $60

Stromberg Helicopter, Corgi
EX $25   NM $60   MIP $100

WATCHES

James Bond Pocket Watch, 1981, Roger Moore on face
EX $40   NM $80   MIP $175

Jungle Book

ACCESSORIES

Jungle Book Dinner Set, vinyl placemat, bowl, plate and cup
EX $10   NM $20   MIP $70

Jungle Book Utensils, fork and spoon w/melamine handles
EX $5   NM $12   MIP $50

DOLL

Baloo Doll, 12" tall, plush
EX $10   NM $50   MIP $120

FIGURES

Mowgli Figure, 1967, Holland Hill, 8", vinyl
EX $20   NM $40   MIP $90

Shere Kahn Figure, 1965, Enesco, 5" tall, ceramic
EX $20   NM $40   MIP $85

TOY

Jungle Book Carrying Case, 1966, Ideal, 5" x 14" x 8"
EX $25   NM $60   MIP $150

Jungle Book Fun-L Tun-L, 1966, New York Toy, 108" x 24"
EX $40   NM $70   MIP $150

Jungle Book Magic Slate, 1967, Watkins-Strathmore
EX $10   NM $25   MIP $75

Jungle Book Sand Pail and Shovel, 1966, Chein, tin litho, illustrated w/Jungle Book characters
EX $25   NM $60   MIP $120

Jungle Book Tea Set, 1966, Chein, tin litho, plates, saucers, tea cups and serving tray
EX $35   NM $75   MIP $140

Mowgli's Hut Mobile and Figures, 1968, Multiple Toymakers, 2" x 3" x 3" mobile w/Baloo and King Louis figures
EX $35   NM $100   MIP $150

WATCH

Mowgli/Baloo Wristwatch, digital, clear plastic band
EX $5   NM $10   MIP $30

Lady and the Tramp

DOLL

Lady Doll, 1955, Woolikin, 5" x 8" x 8-1/2", light tank w/burnt orange accents on face, ears, stomach and tail, plastic eyes, nose and a white silk ribbon around neck
EX $75   NM $150   MIP $325

Perri Doll, 1950s, Steiff, 6" tall, plush
EX $40   NM $85   MIP $175

Tramp Doll, 1955, Schuco, 8" tall, brown w/a white underside and face, hard plastic eyes and nose
EX $100   NM $175   MIP $400

FIGURES

Lady and Tramp Figures, 1955, Marx, Lady is 1-1/2" tall and white, Tramp is 2" tall and tan
EX $30   NM $75   MIP $150

TOY

Modeling Clay, 1955, Pressman
EX $30   NM $120   MIP $185

Puzzle, 1954, Whitman, 11" x 15", frame tray
EX $20   NM $35   MIP $75

Toy Bus, 1966, Modern Toys/Japan, 3-1/2" x 4" x 14" long
EX $20   NM $40   MIP $90

Laurel and Hardy

BANK

(KP Photo)

Oliver Hardy Bank, 1974, Play Pal, 13-1/2" tall, plastic
EX $15   NM $30   MIP $85

Stan Laurel Bank, 1972, 15" tall, vinyl figural bank
EX $22   NM $50   MIP $95

(KP Photo)

Stan Laurel Bank, 1974, Play Pal, 13-1/2" tall, plastic
EX $15　NM $30　MIP $85

FIGURES

Oliver Hardy Figure, 1974, Dakin, 7-1/2" tall
EX $60　NM $120　MIP $175

Stan Laurel Figure, 1974, Dakin, 8" tall
EX $60　NM $120　MIP $130

TOY

Laurel and Hardy Die-Cut Puppets, 1970s, Larry Harmon, moveable, each
EX $25　NM $125　MIP $275

Laurel and Hardy Die-Cut Puppets, 1982, Dell, soft vinyl, each
EX $20　NM $75　MIP $175

Laurel and Hardy TV Set, 1976, w/paper filmstrips
EX $25　NM $50　MIP $125

Oliver Hardy Doll, Dakin, 5" tall wind-up dancing/shaking vinyl doll
EX $35　NM $50　MIP $125

Little Mermaid

ACCESSORIES

Ariel Jewelry Box, 5-3/4" x 4-1/2", musical
EX $10　NM $16　MIP $40

Ariel Toothbrush, battery-operated w/holder
EX $10　NM $16　MIP $35

Flounder and Ariel Faucet Cover, plastic
EX $6　NM $10　MIP $30

Flounder Pillow, 14" x 24" shaped like Flounder
EX $8　NM $13　MIP $35

Little Mermaid Purse, 6" diameter, vinyl, canteen style purse
EX $6　NM $12　MIP $30

Little Mermaid Snow Globe, 4" water globe
EX $10　NM $16　MIP $40

Under the Sea Jewelry Box, 4" mahogany, musical
EX $20　NM $35　MIP $75

DOLL

Eric Doll, 9-1/2" tall in full dress uniform
EX $10　NM $16　MIP $35

Flounder Doll, 15" plush fish
EX $10　NM $16　MIP $35

Scuttle Doll, 15" seagull, plush
EX $12　NM $20　MIP $40

Sebastian Doll, 16" crab, plush
EX $10　NM $16　MIP $35

FIGURES

Little Mermaid Figures, Applause, several PVC characters, each
EX $2　NM $5　MIP $12

Little Orphan Annie

ACCESSORIES

Little Orphan Annie Altascope Ring, 1942, Quaker, premium, only eight known to exist
EX $6000　NM $10000　MIP $20000

Little Orphan Annie Music Box, 1970, N.Y. News, figural
EX $25　NM $60　MIP $100

BOOK

Little Orphan Annie and the Gooneyville Mystery Book, 1947, Whitman
EX $20　NM $100　MIP $180

DOLL

Annie Doll, 1982, Knickerbocker, 10" doll w/out locket
EX $2　NM $7　MIP $20

Annie Doll, 1982, Knickerbocker, 10" tall, w/two dresses and removable heart locket
EX $5　NM $12　MIP $30

Daddy Warbucks Doll, 1982, Knickerbocker
EX $10　NM $50　MIP $90

Little Orphan Annie Doll, 1973, Well Toy, 7" tall
EX $15　NM $20　MIP $60

Miss Hannigan Doll, 1982, Knickerbocker
EX $5　NM $10　MIP $30

Molly Doll, 1982, Knickerbocker
EX $5　NM $10　MIP $30

Punjab Doll, 1982, Knickerbocker
EX $5　NM $15　MIP $50

FIGURES

Annie Figures, 1982, Knickerbocker, six figures, 2" tall, each
EX $2　NM $5　MIP $10

Little Orphan Annie Figure, 1940s, 1-1/2" tall, lead
EX $20　NM $40　MIP $80

Sandy Figure, 1940s, 3/4" tall, lead
EX $20　NM $55　MIP $120

GAME

Little Orphan Annie Light Up the Candles Game, Ovaltine, 3-1/2" x 5", premium
EX $125　NM $175　MIP $350

TOY

Little Orphan Annie Colorforms Set, 1970s, Colorforms
EX $10　NM $20　MIP $50

Little Orphan Annie Cut-Outs, 1960s, Miller Toys, Sandy, Grunts the Pig, Pee Wee the Elephant
EX $50　NM $100　MIP $200

Pastry Set, 1950s, Transogram, Model No. 3993
EX $20　NM $40　MIP $75

Puzzle, Novelty Dist., Famous Comics
EX $35　NM $100　MIP $210

Looney Tunes

BANK

Daffy Duck Bank, 1980s, Applause, figural
EX $10　NM $20　MIP $50

(KP Photo)

Sylvester and Tweety Bank, 1972, vinyl
EX $15　NM $25　MIP $90

Tasmanian Devil Bank, 1980s, Applause
EX $10　NM $20　MIP $70

DOLL

Tasmanian Devil Doll, 1971, Mighty Star, 13" tall, plush
EX $20　NM $40　MIP $100

Tweety Doll, 1969, Dakin, 6", moveable head and feet
EX $10   NM $25   MIP $80

FIGURE

Daffy Duck Figure, 1968, Dakin, 8-1/2" tall
EX $15   NM $25   MIP $80

Daffy Duck Figure, 1970s, Dakin
EX $15   NM $30   MIP $90

Daffy Duck Figure, 1980s, Applause, 4" bendy
EX $10   NM $20   MIP $60

Sylvester Figure, 1971, Dakin, Sylvester on a fish crate
EX $15   NM $25   MIP $80

Sylvester Figure, 1976, Dakin, Cartoon Theater
EX $11   NM $22   MIP $60

FIGURES

Pepe Le Pew Figure, 1971, Dakin, 8" tall
EX $25   NM $50   MIP $100

Speedy Gonzales Figure, Dakin, 5", vinyl
EX $10   NM $20   MIP $60

Speedy Gonzales Figure, 1970, Dakin, 7-1/2" tall, vinyl
EX $15   NM $25   MIP $65

Sylvester and Tweety Figures, 1975, Warner Bros., 6" tall
EX $10   NM $16   MIP $50

Sylvester Figure, 1950, Oak Rubber, 6", rubber
EX $40   NM $80   MIP $135

Sylvester Figure, 1969, Dakin
EX $15   NM $25   MIP $70

Tasmanian Devil Figure, 1989, Superior, 7", plastic, on base
EX $5   NM $15   MIP $50

Tweety Figure, 1971, Dakin, on bird cage
EX $14   NM $25   MIP $70

Tweety Figure, 1971, Dakin, Goofy Gram, holding red heart
EX $15   NM $25   MIP $70

Tweety Figure, 1976, Dakin, Cartoon Theater
EX $15   NM $25   MIP $70

TOY

Bugs Bunny Hand Puppet, 1940s, Zany, rubber head
EX $60   NM $125   MIP $200

Elmer Fudd Hand Puppet, 1940s, Zany, rubber head
EX $30   NM $70   MIP $150

Foghorn Leghorn Hand Puppet, 1940s, Zany, rubber head
EX $45   NM $85   MIP $175

Pepe Le Pew Goofy Gram, 1971, Dakin
EX $25   NM $50   MIP $100

Sylvester Hand Puppet, 1940s, Zany, rubber head
EX $60   NM $125   MIP $200

Sylvester Soaky, Colgate
EX $10   NM $30   MIP $70

Tweety Hand Puppet, 1940s, Zany, rubber head
EX $60   NM $125   MIP $200

Tweety Soaky, 1960s, Colgate, 8-1/2", plastic
EX $10   NM $30   MIP $70

Magilla Gorilla

ACCESSORIES

Magilla Gorilla Cereal Bowl, MB Inc.
EX $10   NM $35   MIP $90

Magilla Gorilla Plate, 1960s, 8" diameter, plastic
EX $7   NM $20   MIP $50

BOOK

Magilla Gorilla Book, 1964, Golden, Big Golden Book
EX $12   NM $30   MIP $70

DOLL

Magilla Gorilla Doll, 1960s, 11" tall, cloth body, hard arms and legs, hard plastic head
EX $125   NM $225   MIP $425

Magilla Gorilla Doll, 1966, Ideal, 18-1/2" plush w/vinyl head
EX $135   NM $250   MIP $500

TOY

Droop-A-Long Coyote Soaky, 1960s, Purex, 12", plastic
EX $20   NM $45   MIP $90

Droop-A-Long Hand Puppet, Ideal, vinyl head
EX $25   NM $60   MIP $135

Magilla Gorilla Cannon, 1964, Ideal
EX $60   NM $90   MIP $200

Magilla Gorilla Pull Toy, 1960s, Ideal, w/vinyl figure
EX $75   NM $150   MIP $250

Magilla Gorilla Puppet, Ideal
EX $40   NM $110   MIP $210

Magilla Gorilla Push Puppet, 1960s, Kohner, brown plastic figure in pink shorts and shoes, yellow base
EX $25   NM $55   MIP $110

Punkin' Puss Soaky, 1960s, Purex, 11-1/2" tall, plastic
EX $20   NM $50   MIP $85

Ricochet Rabbit Hand Puppet, 1960s, Ideal, 11", vinyl head
EX $35   NM $65   MIP $125

Ricochet Rabbit Soaky, 1960s, Purex, 10-1/2" tall, plastic
EX $30   NM $70   MIP $140

Mary Poppins

ACCESSORIES

Mary Poppins Pencil Case, 1964, vinyl w/zipper top
EX $10   NM $22   MIP $60

DOLL

Mary Poppins Doll, 1964, Gund, 11-1/2" tall, bendable
EX $75   NM $150   MIP $300

FIGURES

Mary Poppins Figure, 8" tall, ceramic
EX $20   NM $40   MIP $90

PUZZLE

Mary Poppins Puzzle, 1964, Jaymar, frame tray
EX $8   NM $20   MIP $50

TOY

Mary Poppins Manicure Set, 1964, Tre-Jur
EX $20   NM $45   MIP $95

Mary Poppins Paper Dolls, 1973, Whitman, w/magic tote bag, Model No. 1977
EX $40   NM $75   MIP $120

Mary Poppins Tea Set, 1964, Chein, tin, creamer, plates, place settings, cups, serving tray
EX $60   NM $110   MIP $200

Mickey and Minnie Mouse

ACCESSORIES

Mickey and Donald Alarm Clock, 1960s, Jerger/Germany, 2-1/2" x 5" x 7"; metal case, dark brass finish, 3-D plastic figures of Mickey and Donald on either side
EX $70   NM $140   MIP $210

Mickey and Minnie and Donald Throw Rug, 26" x 41", Mickey and Minnie in an airplane w/Donald parachuting
EX $60   NM $120   MIP $210

Mickey and Minnie Carpet, 27" x 41", Peg Leg Pete is lassoed by Mickey; all characters in western outfits
EX $130   NM $225   MIP $360

Mickey and Minnie Snow Dome, 1970s, Monogram, 3" x 4" x 3" tall, Mickey and Minnie w/a pot of gold at the end of the rainbow
EX $12   NM $25   MIP $50

Mickey and Minnie Toothbrush Holder, 4-1/2" tall, bisque, toothbrush holes are located behind their heads
EX $120   NM $200   MIP $375

Mickey and Minnie Toothbrush Holder, 2-1/2" x 4" x 3-1/2", Mickey and Minnie on sofa w/Pluto at their feet
EX $130   NM $210   MIP $425

Mickey and Minnie Trash Can, 1970s, Chein, 13" tall tin litho, Mickey and Minnie fixing a flat tire on one side, other side shows Mickey feeding Minnie soup
EX $25   NM $80   MIP $160

Mickey and Pluto Ashtray, 3" x 4" x 3" tall, ceramic, Mickey and Pluto playing banjos while sitting on the edge of the ashtray
EX $250   NM $400   MIP $625

Mickey Mouse Alarm Clock, 1960s, Bayard, 2" x 4-1/2" x 4-1/2" tall, 1930s style Mickey w/movable head that ticks off the seconds
EX $100   NM $200   MIP $350

Mickey Mouse Alarm Clock, 1975, Bradley, travel alarm, large red cube case, shut off button on top, separate alarm wind, in sleeve box
EX $30   NM $55   MIP $100

Mickey Mouse Alarm Clock, 1988, House Martin, 5" x 7" x 2"
EX $11   NM $20   MIP $50

Mickey Mouse Ashtray, 3-1/2" tall, wood composition figure of Mickey
EX $75   NM $150   MIP $310

Mickey Mouse Beanie, 1950s, blue/yellow felt hat w/Mickey on front
EX $200   NM $350   MIP $500

Mickey Mouse Clock, 1970s, Elgin, 10" x 15" x 3", electric wall clock
EX $12   NM $25   MIP $50

Mickey Mouse Club Coffee Tin, 1950s, illustrated lid promotes the club, tin included MM badge
EX $50   NM $100   MIP $200

Mickey Mouse Club Mousketeer Handbag, Connecticut Leather, leather/vinyl crafting set
EX $45   NM $60   MIP $125

Mickey Mouse Club Plastic Plate, 1960s, Arrowhead, 9" diameter, clubhouse w/Goofy, Pluto and Donald wearing mouse ears and sweaters w/club emblems
EX $16   NM $30   MIP $45

Mickey Mouse Club Toothbrush, 1970s, Pepsodent
EX $4   NM $7   MIP $30

Mickey Mouse Cup, 1950s, Cavalier, 3" tall, silver-plated cup w/a 2-1/2" opening
EX $25   NM $50   MIP $100

Mickey Mouse Electric Table Radio, 1960s, General Electric, 4-1/2" x 10-1/2" x 6" tall
EX $50   NM $150   MIP $225

Mickey Mouse Pencil Sharpener, 3" tall, celluloid, sharpener located on base
EX $65   NM $125   MIP $250

Mickey Mouse Pencil Sharpener, 1960s, Hasbro, shape of Mickey's head, pencil goes into mouth
EX $12   NM $25   MIP $50

Mickey Mouse Radio, 1970s, Philgee
EX $20   NM $40   MIP $80

Mickey Mouse Record Player, 1970s, General Electric, playing arm is the design of Mickey's arm
EX $60   NM $125   MIP $175

Mickey Mouse Transistor Radio, 1950s, Gabriel, 6-1/2" x 7" x 1-1/2"
EX $40   NM $80   MIP $160

Mickey Mouse Wall Clock, 1978, Elgin, 9" diameter dial, 15" long, shaped like oversize watchband, "50 Happy Years" logo on dial
EX $30   NM $60   MIP $90

Minnie Mouse Alarm Clock, 1970s, Bradley, pink metal electric two-bell clock w/articulated hands
EX $25   NM $50   MIP $85

Minnie Mouse Clock, 1970s, Phinney-Walker, 8" deep, plastic, "Behind Every Great Man, There is a Woman!"
EX $40   NM $70   MIP $125

BANK

Mickey Mouse Band Leader Bank, Knickerbocker, 7-1/2" tall, plastic
EX $10   NM $25   MIP $50

Mickey Mouse Bank, 1950s, 5" x 5-1/2" x 6", china, shaped like Mickey's head w/slot between his ears
EX $30   NM $70   MIP $160

Mickey Mouse Bank, 1960s, Wolverine, 1-1/2" x 5-1/2" x 1" tall, plastic
EX $50   NM $60   MIP $125

Mickey Mouse Bank, 1970s, Transogram, 5" x 7-1/2" x 19" tall, plastic w/Mickey standing on a white chest
EX $15   NM $25   MIP $40

Mickey Mouse Bank, 1978, Fricke and Nacke, 3" x 5" x 7" tall, embossed image of Mickey in front, side panels have Minnie, Goofy, Donald and Pluto
EX $15   NM $25   MIP $175

Mickey Mouse Club Bank, 1970s, Play Pal Plastics, 4-1/2" x 6" x 11-1/2" tall, vinyl
EX $16   NM $30   MIP $60

Mickey Mouse Gumball Bank, 1968, Hasbro
EX $15   NM $40   MIP $90

BOOK

Mickey Mouse Club Fun Box, 1957, Whitman, box includes stamp book, club scrapbook, six coloring books and four small gameboards
EX $45   NM $85   MIP $175

DOLL

Mickey and Minnie Dolls, 1940s, Gund, 13" tall, each
EX $300   NM $500   MIP $1000

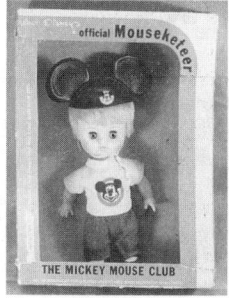

THE MICKEY MOUSE CLUB

(KP Photo)

Mickey Mouse Club Mouseketeer Doll, 1960s, Horsman, 8" tall, denim outfit
EX $35   NM $75   MIP $200

Mickey Mouse Doll, Knickerbocker, 5" x 7" x 12" tall, fabric, Mickey in checkered shorts and green jacket w/white felt flower stapled to it
EX $400   NM $650   MIP $1200

Mickey Mouse Doll, 1950s, Schuco, 10" tall
EX $110   NM $225   MIP $400

Mickey Mouse Doll, 1960s, Gund, 12", Mickey as fireman
EX $30   NM $55   MIP $90

Mickey Mouse Doll, 1970s, Hasbro, 4" x 5-1/2" x 7-1/2" tall, talks
EX $20   NM $40   MIP $60

Mickey Mouse Doll, 1972, Horsman, 3" x 10" x 12" tall, talking doll, says five different phrases
EX $20   NM $40   MIP $70

Minnie Mouse Doll, 1940s, Petz, 10" tall
EX $135   NM $260   MIP $500

FIGURES

Mickey Mouse Figure, 4" tall, bisque, dressed in a green nightshirt
EX $40   NM $80   MIP $140

Mickey Mouse Figure, composition, part of the Lionel Circus Train Set
EX $150   NM $200   MIP $375

Mickey Mouse Figure, 1970, Marx, 6" tall, vinyl
EX $10   NM $20   MIP $40

Minnie Mouse Figure, 1958, Ingersoll, 5-1/2" tall, plastic
EX $35   NM $60   MIP $125

GAME

Mickey Mouse Club Magic Divider, 1950s, Jacmar, arithmetic game
EX $30   NM $55   MIP $100

Mickey Mouse Club Magic Subtractor, 1950s, Jacmar, arithmetic game
EX $11   NM $20   MIP $60

MUSIC BOX

Mickey Mouse Music Box, 4-1/2" x 5" x 7", plays "It's a Small World," Mickey in conductor's uniform standing on cake
EX $20   NM $35   MIP $100

Mickey Mouse Music Box, Schmid, 3" x 6" x 7-1/2" tall, bisque, Spirit of '76, plays "Yankee Doodle"; Mickey, Goofy and Donald are dressed as Revolutionary War Minutemen
EX $60   NM $120   MIP $220

Mickey Mouse Music Box, 1970s, Schmid, 3-1/2" x 5-1/2", plays "Mickey Mouse Club March," ceramic, Mickey in western clothes standing next to a cactus
EX $35   NM $60   MIP $125

Mickey Mouse Music Box, 1970s, Japan, 4" x 6" tall, china, plays "Side by Side," Mickey is brushing a kitten in a washtub
EX $15   NM $25   MIP $90

Mickey Mouse Music Box, 1971, Anri, 5" x 3-1/2", plays "If I Were Rich Man"
EX $50   NM $90   MIP $180

Minnie Mouse Music Box, 1970s, Schmid, 3-1/2" diameter, plays "Love Story"
EX $25   NM $40   MIP $150

TOY

Crayons, 1946, Transogram
EX $30   NM $60   MIP $100

Mickey and Donald Jack-in-the-Box, 1966, Lakeside, Donald pops out
EX $100   NM $175   MIP $300

Mickey and Minnie Sand Pail, Ohio Art, 5" x 5", tin, Mickey, Minnie, Pluto and Donald in boat looking across water at castle, w/swivel handle
EX $100   NM $160   MIP $340

Mickey and Three Pigs Spinning Top, Lackawanna, 9" diameter, tin
EX $50   NM $100   MIP $200

Mickey Mouse Band Spinning Top, 9" diameter
EX $40   NM $80   MIP $175

Mickey Mouse Bump-N-Go Spaceship, 1980s, Matsudaya, battery operated tin litho w/clear dome, has six flashing lights, rotating antenna
EX $35   NM $65   MIP $150

Mickey Mouse Camera, 1960s, Ettelson, 3" x 3" x 5"
EX $18   NM $40   MIP $100

Mickey Mouse Camera, 1970s, Child Guidance, 4" x 7" x 7"
EX $12   NM $25   MIP $100

Mickey Mouse Camera, 1970s, Helm Toy, 2" x 5" x 4-1/2", Mickey in engineer's uniform riding on top of the train
EX $13   NM $25   MIP $85

Mickey Mouse Car, 1970s, Polistil, 2" x 4" x 1-1/2" tall plastic car w/rubber figure, Mickey in driver's seat
EX $30   NM $55   MIP $125

Mickey Mouse Cardboard House, 1930s, O.B. Andrews, 14" x 12" x 13" tall
EX $200   NM $350   MIP $500

Mickey Mouse Chatty Chums, 1979, Mattel
EX $8   NM $15   MIP $40

Mickey Mouse Club Magic Kit, 1950s, Mars Candy, two 8" x 20" punch-out sheets
EX $75   NM $100   MIP $160

Mickey Mouse Club Marionette, 1950s, 3" x 6-1/2" x 13-1/2" tall, composition figure of a girl w/black felt hat and mouse ears
EX $300   NM $425   MIP $600

Mickey Mouse Club Mousketeer Ears, Kohner, 7" x 12-1/2"
EX $11   NM $20   MIP $40

Mickey Mouse Club Newsreel w/Sound, 1950s, Mattel, 4" x 4-1/2" x 9" tall, orange box, plastic projector w/two short filmstrips, record, cardboard screen, cartoons "Touchdown Mickey" and "No Sail"
EX $100   NM $170   MIP $300

Mickey Mouse Club Rhythm Makers Set, Emenee
EX $100   NM $200   MIP $350

(KP Photo)

Mickey Mouse Colorforms Set, 1976, Colorforms, 8" x 12-1/2" x 1", Spirit of '76
EX $10   NM $30   MIP $75

Mickey Mouse Dominoes, Halsam, Mickey and Pluto on dominoes
EX $80   NM $100   MIP $180

Mickey Mouse Fire Engine, Sun Rubber, 7" long, rubber, push toy
EX $75   NM $150   MIP $275

(KP Photo)

Mickey Mouse Fire Truck w/Figure, Sun Rubber, 2-1/2" x 6-1/2" x 4", Mickey driving and mold-in image of Donald standing on the back holding onto his helmet
EX $75   NM $150   MIP $275

Mickey Mouse Jack-In-the-Box, 1970s, 5-1/2" square tin litho box shows Mickey, Pluto, Donald and Goofy, Mickey pops out
EX $25   NM $50   MIP $100

Mickey Mouse Lionel Circus Train, 1935, Lionel, five cars w/Mickey, 30" train, 84 inches of track, circus tent, Sunoco station, truck, tickets, Mickey composition statue
EX $5000   NM $7500   MIP $10000

Mickey Mouse Lionel Circus Train Handcar, Lionel, metal, 9" long w/6" tall composition/rubber figures of Mickey and Minnie
EX $600   NM $1000   MIP $1750

Mickey Mouse Magic Slate, 1950s, Watkins-Strathmore, 8-1/2" x 14" tall
EX $15   NM $30   MIP $90

Mickey Mouse Marbles, Monarch, marbles and Mickey bag, on card
EX $10   NM $20   MIP $60

Mickey Mouse Mechanical Robot, Gabriel
EX $70   NM $125   MIP $150

Mickey Mouse Mousegetar, 1960s, 10" x 30" x 2-1/2" black plastic
EX $40   NM $85   MIP $175

Mickey Mouse Movie-Fun Shows, 1940s, Mastercraft, 7-1/2" square by 4" deep, animated action movies
EX $106   NM $212   MIP $325

Mickey Mouse Musical Money Box, 1970s, 3" x 6", tin box w/Mickey, Pluto, Donald and Goofy
EX $30   NM $55   MIP $90

Mickey Mouse Old Timers Fire Engine, 1980s, Matsudaya, red, tin and plastic fire truck w/Mickey at the wheel
EX $40   NM $70   MIP $125

Mickey Mouse Picture Gun, 1950s, Stephens, 6-1/2" x 9-1/2" x 3", metal, lights to show filmstrips
EX $65   NM $125   MIP $250

Mickey Mouse Play Tiles, 1964, Halsam, 336 tiles
EX $15   NM $25   MIP $50

Mickey Mouse Pull Toy, Toy Kraft, 7" x 22" x 8" tall, horse cart drawn by wooden horses
EX $450   NM $600   MIP $1100

Mickey Mouse Puppet Forms, 1960s, Colorforms
EX $10   NM $25   MIP $60

Mickey Mouse Rodeo Rider, 1980s, Matsudaya, plastic wind-up, cowboy Mickey rides a bucking bronco
EX $25   NM $45   MIP $75

Mickey Mouse Rolykin, Marx, 1-1/2" tall, ball bearing action
EX $12   NM $20   MIP $70

Mickey Mouse Rub 'N Play Magic Transfer Set, 1978, Colorforms
EX $15   NM $30   MIP $80

Mickey Mouse Sand Shovel, Ohio Art, 10" long, tin
EX $35   NM $70   MIP $175

Mickey Mouse Scissors, Disney, 3" long, child's scissors w/Mickey figure
EX $20   NM $35   MIP $100

Mickey Mouse Serving Tray, 1960s, 11" diameter, tin
EX $11   NM $35   MIP $70

Mickey Mouse Sewing Cards, 1978, Colorforms, 7-1/2" x 12" cut-out card designs of Mickey, Minnie, Pluto, Clarabelle, Donald Duck, and Horace
EX $10   NM $20   MIP $85

Mickey Mouse Squeeze Toy, 1950s, Dell, rubber, Mickey as hitchhiking hobo
EX $35   NM $75   MIP $160

Mickey Mouse Squeeze Toy, 1950s, Sun Rubber, 10" tall, rubber
EX $25   NM $50   MIP $110

Mickey Mouse Squeeze Toy, 1960s, Dell, 8" tall
EX $15   NM $30   MIP $70

Mickey Mouse Steamboat, 1988, Matsudaya, wind-up plastic steamboat w/Mickey as Steamboat Willie, runs on floor as smokestacks go up and down, box says "60 Years w/You"
EX $30   NM $60   MIP $135

Mickey Mouse Tea Set, Wolverine, plastic
EX $50   NM $175   MIP $175

Mickey Mouse Tractor, Sun Rubber, 5" long, rubber
EX $85   NM $200   MIP $400

Mickey Mouse Twirling Tail Toy, 1950s, Marx, 3" x 5-1/2" x 5-1/2" tall, w/a built-in key, metal tail spins around as the toy vibrates
EX $120   NM $225   MIP $400

Mickey Mouse Utensils, 1947, Wm. Rogers and Son, 6" fork and 5-1/2" spoon
EX $75   NM $100   MIP $185

(KP Photo)

Mickey Mouse Viewer, 1940s, Craftsmen's Guild, film viewer w/12 films
EX $85   NM $150   MIP $300

Mickey Mouse Wash Machine, Ohio Art, 8" tin litho w/Mickey and Minnie Mouse pictured doing their wash
EX $150   NM $350   MIP $550

Mickey Mouse Water Globes, 1970s, 3" x 4-1/2" x 5" tall, three dimensional plastic figures of Mickey seated w/a plastic water globe between his legs
EX $25   NM $50   MIP $150

Mickey Mouse Wind-Up Musical Toy, 1970s, Illco, 6" tall, plays "Lullaby and Goodnight," 3-D figure of Mickey in red pants and yellow shirt
EX $25   NM $35   MIP $75

Mickey Mouse Wind-Up Toy, 1978, Gabriel, plastic transparent figure of Mickey w/visible metal gears
EX $10   NM $20   MIP $60

Mickey Mouse Wind-Up Trike, 1960s, Korean, tin litho trike w/plastic Mickey w/flag and balloon on handle, bell on back
EX $100   NM $175   MIP $300

Mickey's Air Mail Plane, 1940s, Sun Rubber, 3-1/2" x 6" long, 5" wingspan, rubber
EX $150   NM $300   MIP $500

Minnie Mouse Car, 1979, Matchbox
EX $5   NM $15   MIP $45

Minnie Mouse Choo-Choo Train Pull Toy, 1940s, Linemar, 3" x 8-1/2" x 7" tall, green metal base and green wooden wheels
EX $125   NM $250   MIP $450

Minnie Mouse Hand Puppet, 1940s, 11" tall, white on red polka-dot, fabric hard cover and a pair of black and white felt hands
EX $55   NM $135   MIP $225

Minnie Mouse Rocker, 1950s, Marx, tin wind-up, rocker moves back and forth w/gravity motion of her head and ears
EX $250   NM $480   MIP $720

Minnie w/Bump-n-Go Action Shopping Cart, 1980s, Illfelder, 4" x 9-1/2" x 11-1/2" tall, plastic, battery-operated Minnie pushing cart
EX $30   NM $55   MIP $80

Mouseketeer Cut-Outs, 1957, Whitman, figures and accessories
EX $60   NM $125   MIP $200

Mouseketeer Fan Club Typewriter, 1950s, lithographed tin
EX $75   NM $125   MIP $225

Puzzle, 1957, Whitman, Adventureland, 11" x 15" frame tray; Mickey, Minnie, Donald and his nephew in boat surrounded by jungle beasts
EX $15   NM $40   MIP $80

Puzzle, 1960s, Jaymar, Pluto's Wash and Scrub Service
EX $15   NM $40   MIP $80

Spinning Top, 1950s, Chein, tin litho, features Mickey in cowboy outfit and other characters
EX $60   NM $140   MIP $280

WATCH

50 Years w/Mickey Wristwatch, 1983, Bradley, small round chrome case, inscription and serial number on back
EX $45   NM $85   MIP $200

Mickey and Pluto Wristwatch, 1980, Bradley, LCD quartz, black vinyl band
EX $20   NM $45   MIP $110

Mickey Mouse Pocket Watch, 1970s, Bradley
EX $50   NM $100   MIP $250

Mickey Mouse Pocket Watch, 1976, Bradley, 3-1/2" x 4-1/2" x 3/4", Mickey in his Bicentennial outfit
EX $75   NM $175   MIP $300

Mickey Mouse Pocket Watch, 1988, Lorus, #2202, quartz, small gold bezel, gold chain and clip fob, articulated hands
EX $25   NM $50   MIP $100

Mickey Mouse Wristwatch, two-gun Mickey, saddle tan western style band
EX $25   NM $45   MIP $90

(KP Photo)

Mickey Mouse Wristwatch, 1958, Timex, electric
EX $140   NM $300   MIP $550

Mickey Mouse Wristwatch, 1960s, Timex, large round case, stainless back, articulated hands, red vinyl band
EX $50   NM $80   MIP $160

Mickey Mouse Wristwatch, 1970s, Bradley, white plastic case, watch on pendant, bubble crystal, articulated hands, gold chain
EX $25   NM $60   MIP $135

Mickey Mouse Wristwatch, 1970s, Bradley, 2-1/2" x 6" x 2-1/2", plastic case, white dial w/Mickey playing tennis, the second hand has a tennis ball on the end of it
EX $35   NM $75   MIP $175

Mickey Mouse Wristwatch, 1978, Bradley, commemorative edition
EX $65   NM $130   MIP $300

Mickey Mouse Wristwatch, 1983, Bradley, medium black octagonal case, articulated hands, no numbers on face, in plastic window box
EX $25   NM $260   MIP $400

Mickey Mouse Wristwatch, 1984, Bradley, medium white case, articulated hands, black face, sweep seconds, white vinyl band, in plastic window box
EX $20   NM $40   MIP $80

Minnie Mouse Wristwatch, 1958, Timex, small round chrome case, stainless back, articulated hands, yellow vinyl band
EX $75   NM $150   MIP $275

Minnie Mouse Wristwatch, 1978, Bradley, gold case, sweep seconds, red vinyl band, articulated hands
EX $16   NM $35   MIP $70

Mighty Mouse

ACCESSORIES

Charm Bracelet, 1950s, brass charms of Gandy Goose, Terry Bear, Mighty Mouse and other Terrytoon characters
EX $75   NM $125   MIP $200

(KP Photo)

Mighty Mouse Sneakers, 1960s, Randy Co., children's, graphics on box, picture on sneakers
EX $75   NM $125   MIP $200

DOLL

Mighty Mouse Doll, 1950s, Ideal, 14" tall, stuffed, cloth
EX $50   NM $100   MIP $250

FIGURES

Mighty Mouse Figure, 1950s, 9-1/2" rubber, squeaks
EX $20   NM $60   MIP $150

Mighty Mouse Figure, 1977, Dakin, hard and soft vinyl figure
EX $30   NM $60   MIP $125

Mighty Mouse Figure, 1978, Dakin, Fun Farm
EX $35   NM $70   MIP $135

GAME

Mighty Mouse Ball Game, 1981, Ja-Ru
EX $5   NM $12   MIP $50

TOY

Mighty Mouse Cinema Viewer, 1979, Fleetwood, w/four strips
EX $10   NM $30   MIP $75

Mighty Mouse Dynamite Dasher, 1981, Takara
EX $50   NM $110   MIP $275

Mighty Mouse Flashlight, 1979, Dyno, 3-1/2" figural light
EX $50   NM $80   MIP $120

Mighty Mouse Hit the Claw Target Set, Parks
EX $100   NM $150   MIP $275

Mighty Mouse Make-a-Face Sheet, 1958, Towne, w/dials to change face parts
EX $40   NM $80   MIP $160

Mighty Mouse Mighty Money, 1979, Fleetwood
EX $20   NM $55   MIP $85

Mighty Mouse Money Press, 1981, Ja-Ru, stampers, pads and money
EX $8   NM $15   MIP $30

Mighty Mouse Movie Viewer, 1980, Chemtoy
EX $10   NM $15   MIP $50

Mighty Mouse Picture Play Lite, 1983, Janex
EX $8   NM $15   MIP $40

Mighty Mouse Wallet, 1978, Larami
EX $15   NM $35   MIP $80

Puzzle, tray puzzle; Mighty Mouse and his TV Pals
EX $20   NM $35   MIP $80

Puzzle, 1979, Fleetwood, Mighty Mouse/Heckle and Jeckle
EX $45   NM $90   MIP $140

WATCH

Mighty Mouse Wristwatch, 1979, Bradley, chrome case
EX $40   NM $60   MIP $100

Miscellaneous Characters

ACCESSORIES

Amy Carter Paper Dolls, 1970s, Toy Factory, 14" cardboard doll w/accessories
EX $15   NM $30   MIP $60

Holly Hobbie Wristwatch, 1982, Bradley, small gold tone case, base metal back, yellow plastic band
EX $5   NM $10   MIP $50

Jimmy Carter Radio, peanut-shaped transistor radio
EX $20   NM $45   MIP $125

Kennedy Kards, 1960s, red, white, and blue playing cards w/cartoon artwork
EX $10   NM $20   MIP $50

Little King Lucky Safety Card, 1953, New York Journal, 2" x 4" cards, Little King warns of safety
EX $15   NM $30   MIP $75

Mr. Potato Head Ice Pops, 1950s, Hasbro, plastic molds for freezing treats, in box
EX $16   NM $35   MIP $80

Sandra Dee Paper Dolls, 1959, Saalfield, two cardboard dolls w/outfits
EX $30   NM $75   MIP $150

Tuesday Weld Paper Dolls, 1960, Saalfield, two cardboard dolls w/outfits
EX $30   NM $60   MIP $135

Uncle Don's "Puzzy and Sizzy" Membership Card, 1950s
EX $20   NM $50   MIP $75

BANK

Sir Reginald Play-N-Save Bank, 1960s, 7" tall plastic lion and hunter, on a 15" green plastic base, the hunter fires the coin into the lion's mouth
EX $45   NM $125   MIP $180

DOLL

Hardy Boys Dolls, 1979, Kenner, 12" tall Joe Hardy (Shaun Cassidy) or Frank Hardy (Parker Stevenson)
EX $20   NM $40   MIP $90

FIGURES

Bruce Lee Figure, 1986, Largo, 8" w/weapon
EX $20   NM $40   MIP $100

George Bush Figure, 7" tall
EX $8   NM $20   MIP $40

Lyndon Johnson Figure, 1960s, Remco
EX $17   NM $35   MIP $60

Patton Figure, Excel Toy, poseable doll w/clothing and accessories
EX $20   NM $40   MIP $80

Prince Charles of Wales Figure, 1982, Goldberger, 13" tall, dressed in palace guard uniform
EX $18   NM $35   MIP $70

Sylvester Stallone Rambo Figure, 1986, 18" tall, poseable figure
EX $10   NM $20   MIP $40

TOY

Bonzo Scooter Toy, 7" scooter w/6" Bonzo, wind-up
EX $185   NM $400   MIP $600

Daktari Puzzle, 1967, Whitman, 100 pieces
EX $10   NM $30   MIP $100

Evel Knievel Stunt Stadium, 1974, Ideal, large vinyl case w/accessories
EX $50   NM $100   MIP $200

Jimmy Carter Wind-Up Walking Peanut, 5" tall
EX $10   NM $22   MIP $50

Joan Palooka Stringless Marionette, 1952, Nat'l Mask and Puppet, 12-1/2" tall "daughter of Joe Palooka" doll comes w/pink blanket and birth certificate
EX $75   NM $110   MIP $235

Komic Kamera Film Viewer Set, 1950s, 5" long, Dick Tracy, Little Orphan Annie, Terry and the Pirates and The Lone Ranger
EX $40   NM $100   MIP $175

Mr. and Mrs. Potato Head Set, 1960s, Hasbro, cars, boats, shopping trailer, etc.
EX $25   NM $55   MIP $110

Mr. Potato Head Frankie Frank, 1966, Hasbro, companion to Mr. Potato Head, w/accessories
EX $20   NM $40   MIP $90

Mr. Potato Head Frenchy Fry, 1966, Hasbro, companion to Mr. Potato Head, w/accessories
EX $20   NM $40   MIP $90

Ringling Bros. and Barnum and Bailey Circus Play Set, 1970s, vinyl, w/animals, trapeze personnel, clowns and assorted circus equipment
EX $25   NM $50   MIP $125

Rin-Tin-Tin Magic Erasable Pictures, 1955, Transogram
EX $75   NM $135   MIP $260

Space Ghost Puzzle, 1967, Whitman
EX $20   NM $55   MIP $110

Moon Mullins

ACCESSORIES

Moon Mullins and Kayo Toothbrush Holder, 4" tall, bisque
EX $100   NM $150   MIP $250

Moon Mullins Playstone Funnies Mold Set, 1940s
EX $40   NM $80   MIP $160

FIGURE

Moon Mullins Figure Set, bisque, Uncle Willie, Kayo, Moon Mullins and Emmy, 2-1/4" to 3-1/2"
EX $150   NM $300   MIP $550

Mr. Magoo

ACCESSORIES

Mr. Magoo Drinking Glass, 1962, 5-1/2" tall
EX $10   NM $25   MIP $50

DOLL

Mr. Magoo Doll, 1962, Ideal, 5" tall, vinyl head w/cloth body
EX $75   NM $125   MIP $250

Mr. Magoo Doll, 1970, Ideal, 12" tall
EX $50   NM $75   MIP $120

FIGURES

Mr. Magoo Figure, Dakin, 7" tall
EX $40   NM $90   MIP $180

TOY

Mr. Magoo Car, 1961, Hubley, 7-1/2" x 9" long, metal, battery-operated
EX $350   NM $450   MIP $700

Mr. Magoo Hand Puppet, 1960s, vinyl head, cloth body
EX $35   NM $80   MIP $145

Mr. Magoo Puzzle, 1978, Warren, frame tray
EX $10   NM $20   MIP $50

Mr. Magoo Soaky, 1960s, Palmolive, 10" tall, vinyl and plastic
EX $20   NM $50   MIP $90

Mutt and Jeff

BANK

Mutt and Jeff Bank, 5" tall, cast iron, two-piece construction held together by screw in the back
EX $150   NM $200   MIP $325

BOOK

Big Little Book, Whitman, Mutt and Jeff, #1113
EX $35   NM $75   MIP $140

Nightmare Before Christmas

ACCESSORIES

Beach Towel, Fashion Victim
EX $22   NM $29   MIP $40

Brass Keychain, Disney, Jack Skellington's Tombstone
EX $3   NM $8   MIP $20

Buttons, set of 12 featuring logo, characters, etc.
EX $15   NM $20   MIP $75

Comforter, Wamsutta, twin size featuring Lock, Shock and Barrel
EX $45　　NM $55　　MIP $100

Drawstring Bag, Jack Skellington on front
EX $10　　NM $15　　MIP $25

Jack Soaky, glow head
EX $20　　NM $35　　MIP $75

Mug, Selandia, 16 ounces acrylic mug w/floating snowflakes and glitter
EX $5　　NM $10　　MIP $30

Mug, Selandia, 10 ounces acrylic mug w/floating snowflakes and glitter
EX $5　　NM $10　　MIP $30

Mylar Balloons, Anagram, five variations, each
EX $10　　NM $15　　MIP $35

Pencil, Whirly Sally or Whirly Jack
EX $4　　NM $10　　MIP $25

Purse, multi-compartment w/mirror
EX $10　　NM $25　　MIP $75

PVC Figure on Drinking Straws, Jack or Sally
EX $3　　NM $7　　MIP $10

Sunglasses, Jet Vision Limited
EX $12　　NM $15　　MIP $30

Tumbler, Selandia, seven-ounce, acrylic
EX $10　　NM $13　　MIP $20

BOOK

Pop-Up Book
EX $20　　NM $45　　MIP $90

CLOTHING

Bandanna, Fashion Victim, two styles: Jack or Lock, Shock and Barrel
EX $5　　NM $15　　MIP $45

Baseball Caps, Fashion Victim, three styles: Fishbone w/metal keychain; Lock, Shock and Barrel; or Jack "Bone Daddy"
EX $8　　NM $10　　MIP $20

Boxer Shorts, Stanley DeSantis, Lock, Shock and Barrel or Jack styles; cotton
EX $6　　NM $8　　MIP $12

Silk Necktie, many styles/patterns
EX $15　　NM $22　　MIP $45

Vest, Fashion Victim, Lock, Shock and Barrel or Jack styles
EX $12　　NM $15　　MIP $40

DOLL

Lock, Shock, and Barrel Dolls, Applause, set of three; 6" cloth and vinyl dolls
EX $25　　NM $60　　MIP $120

Oogie Boogie Doll, Applause, 16"; makes farting noise when squeezed
EX $15　　NM $40　　MIP $90

Sally Doll, Hasbro, removable limbs
EX $100　　NM $250　　MIP $425

(KP Photo)

Santa Claus Doll, Applause, 10" plush
EX $10　　NM $30　　MIP $60

Santa Puppet Doll, Hasbro
EX $25　　NM $50　　MIP $85

Talking Jack Doll, Hasbro
EX $50　　NM $130　　MIP $360

FIGURES

Glow Oogie Boogie Figure, Applause, PVC figure
EX $7　　NM $25　　MIP $45

Jack Figure, Hasbro, bendy on card
EX $6　　NM $20　　MIP $40

Jack in Coffin Figure, Applause, 12"
EX $30　　NM $100　　MIP $325

Lock, Shock and Barrel Figures, Applause, set of three, 3" PVC figures
EX $10　　NM $30　　MIP $60

Magic Action Figures, Applause, set of three; 4" figures has its own action when rolled
EX $20　　NM $30　　MIP $60

Mayor Figure, Hasbro, bendy on card
EX $10　　NM $30　　MIP $60

Sally Figure, Hasbro, bendy on card
EX $15　　NM $40　　MIP $80

Sally in Coffin Figure, Applause, 12"
EX $125　　NM $250　　MIP $500

Santa Jack Figure, Hasbro, bendy on card
EX $6　　NM $12　　MIP $25

MISCELLANEOUS

Cardboard Store Display, Applause, over 6" wide
EX $150　　NM $200　　MIP $300

Cookie Jar, Treasure Craft, ceramic; Jack on Tombstone
EX $100　　NM $250　　MIP $400

Handheld Video Game, Tiger
EX $25　　NM $35　　MIP $80

Kaleidoscope, C. Bennett Scopes
EX $20　　NM $35　　MIP $90

Mayor Wind-Up Music Box, Schmid, head spins while music plays "What's This?"
EX $60　　NM $125　　MIP $225

Pin, Oopsa Daisy, several character styles, pewter
EX $10　　NM $18　　MIP $30

Rhinestone Pin, Oopsa Daisy, red stones featuring Jack Skellington
EX $40　　NM $65　　MIP $100

Rhinestone Pin, white stones featuring Jack Skellington
EX $30　　NM $55　　MIP $85

Sky Floater Kite, Spectra Star
EX $5　　NM $15　　MIP $50

Temporary Tattoos, US Kids
EX $2　　NM $4　　MIP $10

Wooden Ornaments, Kurt S. Adler, set of 10; 4" to 6" tall; individually packaged
EX $20　　NM $65　　MIP $80

Wristwatch, Timex, six styles available, each
EX $10　　NM $40　　MIP $90

Yo-Yo, Spectra Star
EX $10　　NM $25　　MIP $45

PAPER GOODS

Bionic Airwalker Balloon, Anagram, featuring Jack Skellington; over 7" tall
EX $15　　NM $20　　MIP $50

Bookmarks, OSP Publishing, set of eight styles including wallet cards
EX $10　　NM $15　　MIP $30

Gift Bags, Cleo, five styles available
EX $6　　NM $10　　MIP $20

Greeting Cards, set of six featuring various characters
EX $15　　NM $35　　MIP $85

Notepad, Beach, 75-sheet pad featuring Lock, Shock and Barrel
EX $3　　NM $5　　MIP $20

Partyware, Beach, 65 pieces
EX $14　　NM $16　　MIP $35

Postcard Book, 30 full-color postcards
EX $5　　NM $20　　MIP $60

Stickers, Gibson, featuring movie characters
EX $2　　NM $6　　MIP $15

Video Release Poster, Touchstone, 24" x 36"
EX $15　　NM $50　　MIP $75

Peanuts

ACCESSORIES

Lucy Candlestick Holder, Hallmark, 7-1/4" figural composition
EX $15　　NM $21　　MIP $60

Snoopy Snippers Scissors, 1975, Mattel, plastic, Model No. 7410
EX $30   NM $45   MIP $70

Snoopy Toothbrush, 1972, Kenner, Snoopy on doghouse holder, Model No. 30301
EX $15   NM $30   MIP $50

Vaporizer/Humidifier, Milton Bradley, plastic, 13" x 16", Snoopy on doghouse
EX $45   NM $75   MIP $110

BANK

Peanuts Banks, 1970, United Features, set of five
EX $60   NM $100   MIP $200

Snoopy Bank, 1968, United Feature, 7" figural bank
EX $15   NM $35   MIP $90

BOOKS

Peanuts Projects, 1963, Determined, activity book
EX $30   NM $45   MIP $75

Peanuts Trace and Color, 1960s, Saalfield, five book set, Model No. 6122
EX $35   NM $50   MIP $125

Peanuts: A Book to Color, Saalfield, cover features Snoopy and Charlie Brown on skateboard, Model No. 4629
EX $25   NM $75   MIP $150

Speak Up, Charlie Brown Talking Storybook, 1971, Mattel, cardboard w/vinyl pages, Model No. 4812
EX $75   NM $150   MIP $200

COSTUMES

Charlie Brown Costume, Collegeville, w/mask
EX $15   NM $30   MIP $100

Snoopy as Flying Ace Costume, Collegeville, w/mask
EX $15   NM $30   MIP $100

Snoopy Costume, Collegeville, w/mask
EX $12   NM $25   MIP $100

Woodstock Costume, Collegeville, w/mask
EX $12   NM $25   MIP $75

DOLL

Peppermint Patty Doll, 14" tall, cloth
EX $10   NM $20   MIP $60

Tub Time Snoopy Doll, 1980s, Knickerbocker, rubber, Model No. 0539
EX $15   NM $35   MIP $70

DOLLS

Charlie Brown Doll, 1958, Hungerford Plastics, 8-1/2" plastic
EX $60   NM $125   MIP $250

Charlie Brown Doll, 1970s, Determined, plastic; wearing baseball gear
EX $60   NM $100   MIP $200

Charlie Brown Doll, 1976, Ideal, removable clothing, Model No. 1412-6
EX $30   NM $70   MIP $140

Charlie Brown Pocket Doll, 1968, Boucher, 7", Model No. 800
EX $20   NM $32   MIP $100

Dolls, 1960s, Simon Simple, 7-1/2", Charlie Brown, Lucy, or Linus
EX $20   NM $50   MIP $100

Dress Me Belle Doll, 1983, Knickerbocker, Belle wearing pink dress w/blue dots, Model No. 1581
EX $15   NM $40   MIP $70

Dress Me Snoopy Doll, 1983, Knickerbocker, Snoopy wearing blue jeans and red/yellow shirt, Model No. 1580
EX $15   NM $40   MIP $70

Linus Doll, 1958, Hungerford Plastics, 8-1/2" plastic
EX $50   NM $100   MIP $225

Linus Doll, 1976, Ideal, removable clothing, Model No. 1414-2
EX $55   NM $100   MIP $215

Linus Pocket Doll, 1968, Boucher, 7", Model No. 801
EX $15   NM $25   MIP $60

Lucy Doll, 1958, Hungerford Plastics, 8-1/2" plastic
EX $50   NM $90   MIP $175

Lucy Doll, 1976, Ideal, removable clothing, Model No. 1411-8
EX $30   NM $60   MIP $125

Lucy Pocket Doll, 1968, Boucher, 7" open mouth, Model No. 802
EX $15   NM $25   MIP $50

Lucy Pocket Doll, 1968, Boucher, 7" smiling, Model No. 802
EX $15   NM $30   MIP $60

Peppermint Patty Doll, 1976, Ideal, removable clothing, Model No. 1413-4
EX $30   NM $45   MIP $70

Pigpen Doll, 1958, Hungerford Plastics, 8-1/2" plastic
EX $65   NM $100   MIP $175

Playmate Snoopy Doll, 1971, Determined, 6" plush, Model No. 819
EX $10   NM $20   MIP $70

Sally Doll, 1958, Hungerford Plastics, 6-1/2" plastic
EX $65   NM $100   MIP $175

Schroeder and Piano Doll, 1958, Hungerford Plastics, 7" plastic
EX $175   NM $275   MIP $450

Snoopy as Astronaut Doll, Knickerbocker, 5" vinyl
EX $75   NM $150   MIP $225

Snoopy as Astronaut Doll, 1969, Determined, 9", rubber head, plastic body, Model No. 808
EX $75   NM $150   MIP $225

Snoopy as Astronaut Doll, 1977, Ideal, 14" plush w/helmet and space suit, Model No. 1441-5
EX $200   NM $300   MIP $400

Snoopy as Magician Doll, 1977, Ideal, 14" plush w/cape, hat, and moustache, Model No. 1448-0
EX $110   NM $180   MIP $250

Snoopy as Rock Star Doll, 1977, Ideal, 14" plush w/wig, shoes and microphone, Model No. 1446-4
EX $115   NM $200   MIP $280

Snoopy Autograph Doll, 1971, Determined, 10-1/2", Model No. 838
EX $20   NM $25   MIP $60

Snoopy Doll, Ideal, 7" rag doll
EX $8   NM $20   MIP $60

Snoopy Doll, 1958, Hungerford Plastics, 7" plastic
EX $60   NM $100   MIP $225

Snoopy Doll, 1970s, Determined, plastic jointed
EX $25   NM $40   MIP $90

Snoopy Doll, 1971, Determined, 15" plush, felt eyes, eyebrows, and nose; red tag around neck
EX $25   NM $45   MIP $95

Snoopy Paper Dolls, 1976, Determined, w/10 outfits
EX $20   NM $40   MIP $75

Snoopy Pocket Doll, 1968, Boucher, 7" w/Flying Ace outfit, Model No. 803
EX $20   NM $35   MIP $80

GAME

Lucy Tea Party Game, 1972, Milton Bradley, Model No. 4129
EX $25   NM $50   MIP $100

Snoopy Snack Attack Game, 1980, Gabriel, Model No. 70345
EX $25   NM $40   MIP $75

Snoopy's Pound-A-Ball Game, 1980, Gabriel/Child Guidance, Model No. 51702
EX $35   NM $65   MIP $90

Table Top Snoopy Game, 1980s, Nintendo, Model No. SM-73
EX $65 NM $125 MIP $160

Tabletop Hockey, 1972, Munro Games
EX $65 NM $125 MIP $160

Tell Us a Riddle, Snoopy Game, 1974, Colorforms, Model No. 2397
EX $20 NM $55 MIP $100

MUSIC BOX

Linus Music Box, Anri, wood, Linus in pumpkin patch on cover, plays "Who Can I Turn To?"
EX $100 NM $150 MIP $200

Lucy and Charlie Brown Music Box, 1971, Anri, 4", each character beside large mushroom, plays "Rose Garden," Model No. 81973
EX $100 NM $175 MIP $250

Lucy Music Box, 1969, Anri, 6-1/2", Lucy behind psychiatrist booth, plays "Try to Remember," Model No. 819400
EX $100 NM $250 MIP $325

Lucy Music Box, 1971, Anri, 5", Lucy w/mushrooms on ground, plays "Love Story," Model No. 81981
EX $100 NM $250 MIP $325

Peanuts Music Box, 1972, Schmid, 8" wooden ferris wheel box/bank, plays "Spinning Wheel," Model No. 277408
EX $175 NM $600 MIP $375

Peanuts Music Box, 1984, Schmid, 8", ceramic, characters revolve around Christmas tree, plays "Joy to the World," Model No. 253724
EX $100 NM $200 MIP $325

Peanuts Music Box, 1985, Schmid, ceramic, characters piled on car, "Clown Capers," plays "Be a Clown," Model No. 289052
EX $85 NM $120 MIP $200

Schroeder Music Box, 1971, Anri, 5", Schroeder at the piano, plays "Beethoven's Emperor's Waltz," Model No. 819030
EX $110 NM $150 MIP $275

Snoopy as Astronaut Music Box, 1970s, Schmid
EX $25 NM $40 MIP $100

Snoopy Music Box, 1974, Aviva, 6", Snoopy w/hobo pack w/Woodstock, plays "Born Free"
EX $30 NM $45 MIP $100

Snoopy Music Box, 1979, Aviva, 8", Snoopy on doghouse shaped box, roof is removable lid, plays "Candy Man," Model No. 214
EX $50 NM $90 MIP $150

Snoopy Music Box, 1982, Aviva, ceramic heart-shaped base w/Snoopy and

Woodstock hugging on top, plays "Love Makes the World Go Round," Model No. 215
EX $30 NM $60 MIP $100

Snoopy Music Box, 1984, Schmid, 7" ceramic, Snoopy and Woodstock on seesaw, plays "Playmates," Model No. 253709
EX $100 NM $125 MIP $175

Snoopy Music Box, 1984, Quantasia, ceramic Snoopy and musical note on base, plays "Fur Elise," Model No. 141017
EX $50 NM $65 MIP $85

Snoopy Music Box, 1985, Quantasia, plastic, Snoopy in boat inside waterglobe, plays "Blue Hawaii," Model No. 141020
EX $20 NM $40 MIP $75

Snoopy Music Box, 1986, Schmid, 6" ceramic, Snoopy as Lion Tamer, plays "Pussycat, Pussycat," Model No. 289053
EX $60 NM $85 MIP $150

Snoopy Music Box, 1986, Schmid, 7-1/2" ceramic, Snoopy next to Christmas tree, plays "O, Tannenbaum," Model No. 159101
EX $125 NM $175 MIP $250

PUZZLES

Puzzle, 1971, Determined, eight-panel cartoon strip, 1,000 pieces, Model No. 711-2
EX $15 NM $25 MIP $60

Puzzle, 1971, Determined, four "Love Is" scenes, 1,000 pieces, Model No. 711-4
EX $25 NM $40 MIP $80

Puzzle, 1973, Milton Bradley, Schroeder, Charlie Brown, Snoopy, and Lucy on baseball mound, Model No. 4383-3
EX $10 NM $22 MIP $60

Puzzle, 1979, Playskool, six pieces, Snoopy leaning on bat, Model No. 230-27
EX $5 NM $10 MIP $40

RADIOS

Snoopy and Woodstock Radio, 1970s, Determined, plastic, two-dimensional doghouse, Model No. 354
EX $30 NM $50 MIP $100

Snoopy Bank Radio, 1978, Concept 2000, plastic, Snoopy dancing, Model No. 4442
EX $65 NM $100 MIP $150

Snoopy Doghouse Radio, 1970s, Determined, plastic
EX $60 NM $85 MIP $140

Snoopy Hi-Fi Radio, 1977, Determined, three-dimensional Snoopy wearing headphones, plastic, Model No. 405
EX $60 NM $125 MIP $200

Snoopy Radio, 1970s, Determined, figural radio, Snoopy on green grass, plastic
EX $20 NM $40 MIP $85

Snoopy Radio, 1975, Determined, plastic two-dimensional, Model No. 351
EX $30 NM $65 MIP $150

Snoopy Radio, 1977, Determined, plastic square radio w/Snoopy pointing to dial
EX $30 NM $65 MIP $150

Snoopy, Woodstock, and Charlie Brown Radio, 1970s, Concept 2000, two-dimensional plastic, Model No. 4443
EX $20 NM $35 MIP $80

Snoopy's Spaceship AM Radio, 1978, Concept 2000, plastic, Model No. 4443
EX $75 NM $125 MIP $250

TOY

Batter-Up Snoopy Colorforms, 1979, Colorforms
EX $10 NM $35 MIP $60

Big Quart-O-Snoopy Bubbles, 1970s, Chemtoy
EX $9 NM $13 MIP $20

Camp Kamp Play Set, 1970s, Child Guidance, rubber camp building w/characters, Model No. 1683
EX $75 NM $100 MIP $150

Charlie Brown Deluxe View-Master Gift Pak, 1970s, GAF/View-Master, cylindrical container holds seven reels and viewer, Model No. 2380
EX $40 NM $75 MIP $100

(KP Photo)

Charlie Brown Nodder, 1960s, Japanese, 5-1/2" tall, bobbing head
EX $125 NM $200 MIP $350

Charlie Brown Punching Bag, 1970s, Determined
EX $15 NM $30 MIP $60

Charlie Brown Push Puppet, 1977, Ideal
EX $20   NM $45   MIP $85

Charlie Brown's All-Star Dugout Play Set, 1970s, Child Guidance, Model No. 1636
EX $20   NM $40   MIP $75

Charlie Brown's Backyard Play Set, 1970s, Child Guidance
EX $20   NM $40   MIP $80

Chirping Woodstock, 1977, Aviva, plastic w/electronic sound, Model No. 477
EX $18   NM $25   MIP $80

Electronic Snoopy Playmate, 1980, Romper Room/Hasbro, Model No. 830
EX $80   NM $125   MIP $200

Express Station Set, 1977, Aviva, Snoopy riding locomotive, Model No. 988
EX $40   NM $60   MIP $100

Joe Cool Punching Bag, 1976, Ideal, Model No. 5530-1
EX $20   NM $30   MIP $60

Joe Cool Push Puppet, 1977, Ideal
EX $20   NM $40   MIP $100

Kaleidorama, 1979, Determined, Model No. 4961
EX $20   NM $35   MIP $65

Lucy Nurse Push Puppet, 1977, Ideal
EX $20   NM $35   MIP $75

Lucy's Winter Carnival Colorforms, 1973, Colorforms, Model No. 7400
EX $20   NM $40   MIP $70

Official Peanuts Baseball, 1969, Wilson, illustrated w/characters
EX $40   NM $100   MIP $150

Parade Drum, 1969, Chein, large tin drum features characters in director's chairs, Model No. 1798
EX $100   NM $165   MIP $250

Peanuts Deluxe Play Set, 1975, Determined, includes Lucy's psychiatrist booth and three action figures, Model No. 575
EX $100   NM $200   MIP $300

Peanuts Drum, 1974, Chein, tin, features characters w/instruments, Model No. 1713
EX $85   NM $120   MIP $200

Peanuts Kindergarten Rhythm Set, 1972, Chein, four percussion instruments, Model No. 327
EX $100   NM $160   MIP $240

Peanuts Magic Catch Puppets, 1978, Synergistics, four characters w/Velcro balls
EX $10   NM $20   MIP $60

Peanuts Pelham Puppets, 1979, Pelham/Tiderider, 7"-8" Charlie Brown, Snoopy or Woodstock
EX $45   NM $90   MIP $180

Peanuts Puppets Display, 1979, Pelham/Tiderider, display theater
EX $350   NM $550   MIP $800

Peanuts Show Time Finger Puppets, 1977, Ideal, several rubber character puppets, Model No. 5379-3
EX $25   NM $35   MIP $70

Peanuts Skediddler Clubhouse Set, 1970, Mattel, three rubber skediddlers, Snoopy, Lucy, Charlie Brown, Model No. 3803
EX $125   NM $185   MIP $275

Peanuts Stackables, 1979, Determined, four hard rubber figures, Model No. 8642
EX $18   NM $25   MIP $35

Peanuts Tea Set, 1961, one tray, two plates, two cups, four small plates
EX $40   NM $60   MIP $100

Piano, 1960s, Ely, wood w/characters on top
EX $165   NM $275   MIP $425

Picture Maker, 1971, Mattel, plastic character stencils, Model No. 4153
EX $45   NM $65   MIP $90

Push and Play w/the Peanuts Gang, 1970s, Child Guidance, plastic w/rubber characters, Model No. 1700
EX $30   NM $50   MIP $100

Push 'N' Fly Snoopy, 1980, Romper Room/Hasbro, pull toy featuring Snoopy the Flying Ace, Model No. 824
EX $12   NM $20   MIP $60

Rowing Snoopy, 1981, Mattel, Model No. 3478
EX $20   NM $40   MIP $90

Schroeder's Piano, 1970s, Child Guidance, Model No. 1701
EX $75   NM $150   MIP $300

See 'N' Say Snoopy Says, 1969, Mattel, Model No. 4864
EX $40   NM $80   MIP $125

Snoopy Action Toys, 1977, Aviva, wind-up Snoopy as drummer or boxer
EX $25   NM $45   MIP $70

Snoopy and Charlie Brown Copter, 1979, Aviva/Hasbro, plastic, Model No. 600
EX $15   NM $25   MIP $50

Snoopy and his Flyin' Doghouse, 1974, Mattel, Model No. 8263
EX $60   NM $100   MIP $175

Snoopy Color 'N' Recolor, 1980, Avalon, Model No. 742
EX $30   NM $50   MIP $80

Snoopy Copter Pull Toy, 1980, Romper Room, sound and action toy, Model No. 822
EX $6   NM $10   MIP $25

Snoopy Deep Diver Submarine, 1980s, Knickerbocker, plastic, Model No. 0553
EX $35   NM $55   MIP $70

Snoopy Drive-In Movie Theater, 1975, Kenner, Model No. 39570
EX $95   NM $160   MIP $300

Snoopy Express, 1977, Aviva, mechanical wind-up train, wood, includes track, tunnel, and signs, Model No. 922
EX $20   NM $55   MIP $90

Snoopy Express, 1982, Aviva, mechanical wind-up train, plastic, Model No. 70911
EX $20   NM $35   MIP $50

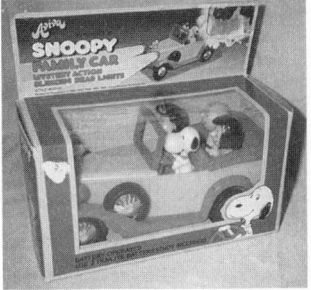

(KP Photo)

Snoopy Family Car, 1978, Aviva, Model No. 2700
EX $40   NM $70   MIP $90

Snoopy Gravity Raceway, 1977, Aviva, Model No. 990
EX $40   NM $70   MIP $120

Snoopy Gyro Cycle, 1982, Aviva/Hasbro, plastic friction toy, Model No. 70440
EX $20   NM $50   MIP $100

Snoopy High Wire Act, 1973, Monogram/Mattel, Model No. 6661
EX $25   NM $45   MIP $70

Snoopy in the Music Box, 1969, Mattel, metal jack-in-the-box, Model No. 4747
EX $15   NM $30   MIP $100

Snoopy is Joe Cool Model Kit, 1971, Monogram/Mattel, Snoopy rides surfboard, Model No. 7502
EX $40   NM $80   MIP $140

Snoopy Jack-in-the-Box, 1980, Romper Room/Hasbro, plastic doghouse jack-in-the-box, Model No. 818
EX $8   NM $15   MIP $40

Snoopy Magician Push Puppet, 1977, Ideal
EX $15   NM $35   MIP $80

Snoopy Marionette, 1979, Pelham/Tiderider, 27", Pelham Puppets, Model No. DP10

EX $300   **NM** $475   **MIP** $700

Snoopy Movie Viewer, 1975, Kenner, Model No. 35900

EX $15   **NM** $25   **MIP** $60

Snoopy Musical Ge-tar, 1969, Mattel, crank handle, Model No. 4715

EX $30   **NM** $60   **MIP** $120

Snoopy Musical Guitar, 1980, Aviva, plastic, crank handle, Model No. 444

EX $15   **NM** $35   **MIP** $70

Snoopy Nodder, 1960s, Japanese, 5-1/2" tall, bobbing head

EX $45   **NM** $100   **MIP** $225

Snoopy Paint-by-Number Set, 1980s, Craft House, 12" x 16"

EX $10   **NM** $20   **MIP** $50

Snoopy Phonograph, 1979, Vanity Fair, features picture of dancing Snoopy, Model No. 66

EX $100   **NM** $130   **MIP** $175

Snoopy Playhouse, 1977, Determined, plastic doghouse w/furniture, Snoopy, and Woodstock, Model No. 120

EX $50   **NM** $80   **MIP** $150

Snoopy Playland, 1978, Aviva, Snoopy in bus and six other characters, Model No. 888

EX $60   **NM** $80   **MIP** $125

Snoopy Radio-Controlled Doghouse, 1980, Aviva, Model No. 988

EX $35   **NM** $60   **MIP** $125

Snoopy Radio-Controlled Fire Engine, 1980, Aviva, w/Woodstock transmitter, Model No. 988

EX $50   **NM** $75   **MIP** $120

Snoopy Sheriff Push Puppet, 1977, Ideal

EX $20   **NM** $30   **MIP** $80

Snoopy Sign Mobile, 1970s, Avalon, Model No. 262

EX $50   **NM** $80   **MIP** $160

Snoopy Skediddler and His Sopwith Camel, 1969, Mattel, w/carrying case, Model No. 4954

EX $250   **NM** $400   **MIP** $500

Snoopy Slugger, 1979, Playskool, ball, bat and cap, Model No. 411

EX $20   **NM** $40   **MIP** $85

(KP Photo)

Snoopy Soaper, 1975, Kenner, gold soap dispenser w/Snoopy on top, Model No. 30700

EX $30   **NM** $50   **MIP** $85

Snoopy Tea Set, 1970, Chein, metal, features tray, plate, cups, and saucers, Model No. 276

EX $100   **NM** $175   **MIP** $250

Snoopy the Critic, 1977, Aviva, Snoopy and Woodstock on doghouse w/microphone, Model No. 222

EX $120   **NM** $250   **MIP** $300

Snoopy the Flying Ace Push Puppet, 1977, Ideal

EX $20   **NM** $30   **MIP** $90

(KP Photo)

Snoopy-Matic Instant Load Camera, 1970s, Helm Toy, uses 110 film, Model No. 975

EX $95   **NM** $150   **MIP** $225

Snoopy's Beagle Bugle, 1970s, Child Guidance, plastic, Model No. 1730

EX $55   **NM** $80   **MIP** $120

Snoopy's Bubble Blowing Bubble Tub, 1970s, Chemtoy

EX $20   **NM** $45   **MIP** $60

Snoopy's Dog House, 1978, Romper Room/Hasbro, Snoopy walks on roof, Model No. 815

EX $20   **NM** $40   **MIP** $90

Snoopy's Dream Machine, 1979, DCS, w/blinking lights

EX $95   **NM** $155   **MIP** $220

Snoopy's Dream Machine, 1980, DCS, small version, no blinking lights, laminated cardboard, Model No. 417-M

EX $55   **NM** $80   **MIP** $120

Snoopy's Fantastic Automatic Bubble Pipe, 1970s, Chemtoy, Model No. 126

EX $5   **NM** $12   **MIP** $30

Snoopy's Good Grief Glider, 1970s, Child Guidance, spring load launcher, Model No. 1775

EX $50   **NM** $75   **MIP** $120

Snoopy's 'Lectric Comb and Brush, 1975, Kenner, Model No. 30900

EX $35   **NM** $50   **MIP** $70

Snoopy's Pencil Sharpener, 1974, Kenner, Model No. 3550

EX $25   **NM** $50   **MIP** $100

Snoopy's Shape Register, 1980, Gabriel/Child Guidance, plastic cash register, Model No. 51740

EX $30   **NM** $60   **MIP** $90

Snoopy's Soft House, 1980, Knickerbocker, soft cloth house, Model No. 0573

EX $25   **NM** $40   **MIP** $75

Snoopy's Stunt Spectacular, 1978, Child Guidance, Snoopy on motorcycle, Model No. 1750

EX $35   **NM** $50   **MIP** $90

Snoopy's Swim and Sail Club, 1970s, Child Guidance, characters and water vehicles, Model No. 1710

EX $45   **NM** $75   **MIP** $120

Snoopy's Take-a-Part Doghouse, 1980, Gabriel/Child Guidance, Model No. 51705

EX $15   **NM** $30   **MIP** $60

Spinning Top, Ohio Art, 5", Snoopy and the Gang

EX $10   **NM** $30   **MIP** $80

Spinning Top, 1960s, Chein, faces of Snoopy, Charlie Brown, Lucy, and Linus, Model No. 263

EX $40   **NM** $75   **MIP** $150

Stack-Up Snoopy, 1980, Romper Room/Hasbro, Model No. 818

EX $10   **NM** $13   **MIP** $25

Super Cartoon Maker, 1970, Mattel, molds to make character figures, Model No. 4696

EX $80   **NM** $130   **MIP** $180

Swimming Snoopy, 1970s, Concept 2000, Model No. 106
EX $15   NM $40   **MIP** $80

Talking Peanuts Bus, 1967, Chein, metal, chracters seen in windows, Model No. 261
EX $300   NM $500   **MIP** $800

Tell Time Clock, 1980s, Concept 2000, three styles: Snoopy, Woodstock or Charlie Brown
EX $15   NM $25   **MIP** $60

Woodstock Climbing String Action, 1977, Aviva/Hasbro, plastic, Model No. 667
EX $15   NM $28   **MIP** $60

Yankee Doodle Snoopy, 1975, Colorforms, Model No. 756
EX $20   NM $35   **MIP** $70

VEHICLES

(Gary Hardin photo)

Charlie Brown Riding Kubota Tractor, 1950, Aviva, 2-1/2" long, Charlie Brown metal on bottom, rest is plastic, made in Japan, Model No. C10
EX $15   NM $30   **MIP** $60

Formula-1 Racing Car, 1978, Aviva, 11-1/2" plastic w/Woodstock or Snoopy, Model No. 950
EX $80   NM $125   **MIP** $185

Schroeder's Piano, Aviva
EX $30   NM $60   **MIP** $100

Snoopy and Woodstock in Wagon, Aviva, green die-cast w/white wheels, Model No. 72060
EX $10   NM $15   **MIP** $25

Snoopy and Woodstock on Skateboard, Aviva
EX $10   NM $15   **MIP** $25

Snoopy as Beagle Scout in Bus, 1983, Hasbro, die-cast
EX $4   NM $10   **MIP** $25

Snoopy as Flying Ace in Wagon, Aviva, yellow die-cast w/red wheels, Model No. 72057
EX $10   NM $20   **MIP** $45

Snoopy as Joe Cool in Wagon, Aviva, purple die-cast w/orange wheels, Model No. 72055
EX $10   NM $15   **MIP** $30

Snoopy Biplane, 1977, Aviva, die-cast, Snoopy as Flying Ace, Model No. 2024
EX $30   NM $50   **MIP** $90

Snoopy Emergency Set, Hasbro, Snoopy in three vehicles
EX $20   NM $50   **MIP** $90

Snoopy Family Car, 1977, Aviva, die-cast convertible, 2-1/4", Model No. 2028
EX $35   NM $55   **MIP** $90

Snoopy Handfuls, Hasbro, twin pack; characters in die-cast racers
EX $15   NM $35   **MIP** $60

(Gary Hardin photo)

Snoopy in Bi-Plane, 1958, Aviva, Snoopy metal on bottom, rest is plastic, made in Hong Kong, Model No. C26
EX $10   NM $20   **MIP** $35

Snoopy in Tow Truck, 1983, Hasbro, die-cast
EX $5   NM $10   **MIP** $30

Snoopy Racing Car Stickshifter, 1978, Aviva, Model No. 975
EX $90   NM $150   **MIP** $210

Snoopy Slot Car Racing Set, 1977, Aviva, Model No. XL500
EX $75   NM $120   **MIP** $220

Woodstock in Ice Cream Truck, Aviva, friction vehicle
EX $6   NM $9   **MIP** $15

WATCHES

Charlie Brown Wristwatch, 1970s, Determined, Charlie Brown in baseball gear, yellow face, black band
EX $65   NM $200   **MIP** $325

Lucy Wristwatch, 1970s, Timex, small chrome case, articulated arms, sweep seconds, white vinyl band
EX $35   NM $100   **MIP** $200

Lucy's Watch Wardrobe, 1970s, Determined, white face, comes w/blue, white, and pink bands
EX $60   NM $100   **MIP** $175

Snoopy Hero Time Watch, 1970s, Determined, Snoopy in dancing pose, red band
EX $75   NM $150   **MIP** $300

Snoopy Wristwatch, 1969, Determined, Snoopy in dancing pose, silver or gold case, various colors
EX $70   NM $140   **MIP** $275

Snoopy Wristwatch, 1970s, Lafayette Watch, Snoopy dancing, Woodstock is the second hand, silver case w/red face and black band
EX $70   NM $140   **MIP** $275

Snoopy Wristwatch, 1970s, Timex, gold bezel, tennis ball circles Snoopy on clear disk, articulated hands holding racket, denim background and band
EX $60   NM $90   **MIP** $175

Peter Pan

ACCESSORIES

Peter Pan Charm Bracelet, 1974
EX $30   NM $50   **MIP** $100

Peter Pan Map of Neverland, 1953, 18" x 24", collectors issue for users of Peter Pan Beauty Bar
EX $250   NM $400   **MIP** $600

Tinker Bell Pincushion, 1960s, w/1-1/2" tall Tinker Bell figure, in clear plastic display can
EX $25   NM $40   **MIP** $125

DOLL

Peter Pan Doll, 1953, Ideal, 18" tall
EX $100   NM $200   **MIP** $500

Peter Pan Doll, 1953, Duchess Doll, 11-1/2" tall, brown trim fabric shoes, green mesh stockings w/flocked outfit, hat w/a large red feather, shiny silver white metal dagger in belt, eyes, arms and head move
EX $175   NM $350   **MIP** $700

Tinker Bell Doll, 1953, Duchess Doll, 8" tall, flocked green outfit w/a pair of large white fabric wings w/gold trim, eyes open and close, jointed arms and head moves
EX $150   NM $300   **MIP** $600

Wendy Doll, 1953, Duchess Doll, 8" tall, full purple length skirt w/purple bow in back of dress, eyes open and close, jointed arms and head moves
EX $150   NM $275   **MIP** $525

FIGURES

Captain Hook Figure, 8" tall, plastic
EX $10   NM $20   **MIP** $50

Peter Pan Baby Figure, 1950s, Sun Rubber
EX $70   NM $125   **MIP** $250

Peter Pan Paper Dolls, 1952, Whitman, 11 die-cut cardboard figures
EX $100   NM $175   **MIP** $300

Tinker Bell Figure, 1960s, Sutton, 7" tall, plastic and rubber figure
EX $25   NM $50   MIP $100

TOY

Captain Hook Hand Puppet, 1950s, Gund, 9" tall
EX $35   NM $70   MIP $175

Peter Pan Hand Puppet, 1953, Oak Rubber, rubber
EX $30   NM $70   MIP $160

Peter Pan Nodder, 1950s, 6" tall
EX $125   NM $250   MIP $400

Peter Pan Push Puppet, 1950s, Kohner, 6" tall, green and flesh colored beads, plastic head, light green plastic hat
EX $25   NM $50   MIP $110

Peter Pan Sewing Cards, 1952, Whitman
EX $15   NM $30   MIP $70

Puzzle, 1950s, Jaymar, frame tray puzzle shows Peter, Wendy, John and Michael flying over Neverland
EX $20   NM $42   MIP $90

Phantom

ACCESSORIES

Oil Paint by Numbers Set, 1967, Hasbro
EX $225   NM $320   MIP $550

Phantom 2040 Rubber Ball, 1995, Unice
EX $12   NM $17   MIP $30

Phantom Binoculars, 1976, Larami
EX $120   NM $155   MIP $225

Phantom Candy Jar, 1996, KFS, plastic w/figural lid
EX $12   NM $22   MIP $70

Phantom Club Rubber Stamper Skull Ring, 1950s
EX $500   NM $800   MIP $1200

Phantom Costume, 1950s, Ben Cooper
EX $175   NM $225   MIP $350

Phantom Costume, 1970s, Collegeville
EX $70   NM $90   MIP $150

Phantom Puffy Magnet, 1975, Hanna-Barbera
EX $40   NM $50   MIP $70

Phantom Squirt Camera, 1976, Larami
EX $100   NM $120   MIP $225

Playing Cards, 1990, Bulls Dist., Swedish
EX $16   NM $25   MIP $60

Playing Cards, 1990, John Sands
EX $16   NM $25   MIP $60

Rub-On Transfer Set, 1967, Hasbro
EX $100   NM $120   MIP $200

BOOK

Phantom Giant Games Book, 1968, World Distributors
EX $80   NM $125   MIP $200

COSTUME

Phantom Costume, 1989, Character Costumes
EX $40   NM $55   MIP $80

FIGURE

Phantom Figure, 1980s, 6" dark blue PVC figure
EX $25   NM $35   MIP $60

Phantom Figure, 1990s, 6" purple PVC figure
EX $12   NM $30   MIP $60

Phantom Figure, 1996, Street Players, 4" action figure w/skull throne or horse
EX $10   NM $20   MIP $40

Phantom Figures, 1990, Spain, 3-1/2", two pieces, purple PVC
EX $10   NM $20   MIP $40

Syrocco Figure, 1944, Pillsbury Mills, brown
EX $700   NM $1000   MIP $1600

TOY

Phantom 2040 Carded Toys, 1995, Ja-Ru, sword, crossbow, gun or whistle light
EX $8   NM $12   MIP $30

Phantom Archery Set, 1976, Larami, bow, arrows, animals
EX $100   NM $125   MIP $220

Phantom Dagger Set, 1976, Larami, knife and sheath
EX $100   NM $120   MIP $250

Phantom Desert Survival Kit, 1976, Larami, canteen and Thermos bottle
EX $80   NM $120   MIP $200

Phantom Jungle Play Set, 1976, Larami, figure, palm trees, animals
EX $110   NM $160   MIP $325

Phantom Pathfinder Set, 1976, Larami, compass, canteen, binoculars, case
EX $80   NM $120   MIP $185

Phantom Pinback, 1940s, club member cello, Australia
EX $300   NM $750   MIP $1000

Phantom Safari Set, 1976, Larami, figure, truck, trailer, animals
EX $130   NM $180   MIP $275

Phantom Water Pistol, 1974, Nasta, w/holster
EX $70   NM $90   MIP $160

Phantom Water Pistol, 1974, Nasta
EX $80   NM $120   MIP $175

Pink Panther

ACCESSORIES

Pink Panther Memo Board, write on/wipe off memo board
EX $5   NM $10   MIP $25

BOOK

Pink Panther and The Fancy Party Book, Golden
EX $5   NM $10   MIP $30

Pink Panther and The Haunted House Book, Golden
EX $5   NM $10   MIP $35

Pink Panther at Castle Kreep Book, Whitman
EX $5   NM $10   MIP $35

Pink Panther at The Circus Sticker Book, 1963, Golden
EX $10   NM $20   MIP $50

Pink Panther Coloring Book, 1976, Whitman, cover shows Pink Panther roasting hot dogs
EX $10   NM $20   MIP $50

FIGURES

Pink Panther Figure, 1971, Dakin, 8" tall, w/legs open
EX $25   NM $50   MIP $100

Pink Panther Figure, 1971, Dakin, 8" tall, w/legs closed
EX $25   NM $50   MIP $100

GAME

Pink Panther Pool Game, 1980s, Ja-Ru
EX $10   NM $20   MIP $40

MUSIC BOX

Pink Panther Music Box, 1982, Royal Orleans, Christmas limited edition
EX $60   NM $80   MIP $150

Pink Panther Music Box, 1983, Royal Orleans, Christmas limited edition
EX $60   NM $80   MIP $150

Pink Panther Music Box, 1984, Royal Orleans, Christmas limited edition
EX $60   NM $80   MIP $150

TOY

Pink Panther Motorcycle, 2-1/2" plastic
EX $7   NM $15   MIP $50

Pink Panther One-Man Band, 1980, Illco, 10" tall, battery-operated, plush body w/vinyl head
EX $35   NM $70   MIP $100

Pink Panther Putty, 1970s, Ja-Ru
EX $4   NM $7   MIP $10

Pink Panther Wind-Up, 3" tall, plastic, walking wind-up w/trench coat and glasses
EX $20   NM $40   MIP $60

Puzzle, 1960s, Whitman, 100 pieces, several pictures available, each
EX $20   NM $35   MIP $60

Pinocchio and Jiminy Cricket

ACCESSORIES

Jiminy Cricket Toothbrush Set, 1950s, Dupont, plastic wall hanging Jiminy holds a toothbrush
EX $30   NM $55   MIP $90

Pinocchio Snow Dome, 1970s, Disney, 3" x 4-1/2" x 5" tall, Pinocchio holds plastic dome between hands and feet
EX $20   NM $50   MIP $100

BANK

Pinocchio Bank, 1960s, Play Pal Plastics, 11-1/2" tall, plastic
EX $15   NM $25   MIP $50

Pinocchio Bank, 1970s, Play Pal Plastics, 7" x 7" x 10" tall, vinyl, 3-D molded head of Pinocchio
EX $10   NM $20   MIP $50

DOLL

Pinocchio and Jiminy Cricket Dolls, 1962, Knickerbocker, 6" tall, vinyl, titled "Knixies," each
EX $40   NM $60   MIP $110

FIGURES

Figaro Figure, 1940s, Knickerbocker, composition, movable limbs and head
EX $120   NM $200   MIP $350

Gideon Figure, Multi-Wood Products, 5" tall
EX $40   NM $70   MIP $200

Honest John Figure, Multi-Wood Products, 2-1/2" x 3" base w/a 7" tall figure
EX $300   NM $400   MIP $500

Jiminy Cricket Figure, Marx, 3-1/2" x 4-3/4" tall, Snap-Eeze, white plastic base w/movable arms and legs
EX $30   NM $55   MIP $95

Jiminy Cricket Figure, 1940s, Ideal, wood jointed, hand painted
EX $200   NM $300   MIP $500

Pinocchio Figure, Crown Toy, 9-1/2" tall, jointed arms
EX $60   NM $110   MIP $275

MUSIC BOX

Pinocchio Music Box, plays "Puppet on a String"
EX $18   NM $35   MIP $85

TOY

Jiminy Cricket Hand Puppet, 1950s, Gund, 11" tall
EX $30   NM $60   MIP $140

Jiminy Cricket Marionette, 1950s, Pelham Puppets, 3" x 6" x 10" tall, dark green head w/large eyes, gray felt hat
EX $75   NM $160   MIP $350

Jiminy Cricket Ramp Walker, 1960s, Marx, 1" x 3" x 3" tall, pushing a bass fiddle
EX $80   NM $140   MIP $270

Jiminy Cricket Soaky, 7" tall bottle
EX $15   NM $50   MIP $80

Pinocchio and Jiminy Push Puppet, 1960s, Marx, 2-1/2" x 5" x 4" tall, double puppet
EX $30   NM $45   MIP $100

Pinocchio Color Box, Transogram, also known as paint box
EX $18   NM $35   MIP $80

Pinocchio Crayon Box, 1940s, Transogram, 4-1/2" x 5-1/2" x 1/2" deep, tin
EX $18   NM $35   MIP $85

Pinocchio Hand Puppet, Crown Toy, 9" tall, composition
EX $25   NM $45   MIP $70

Pinocchio Hand Puppet, 1950s, Gund, 10" tall, w/squeaker
EX $40   NM $75   MIP $150

Pinocchio Hand Puppet, 1962, Knickerbocker
EX $25   NM $50   MIP $85

Pinocchio Push Puppet, 1960s, Kohner, 5" tall
EX $15   NM $25   MIP $75

Pinocchio Soaky
EX $20   NM $40   MIP $85

Pinocchio Wind-Up Toy, Linemar, 6" tall, tin wind-up, arms and legs move
EX $200   NM $300   MIP $500

Puzzle, 1960s, Jaymar, 5" x 7", "Pinocchio's Expedition"
EX $12   NM $22   MIP $50

WATCH

Jiminy Cricket Wristwatch, 1948, US Time, Birthday Series
EX $250   NM $450   MIP $750

Pluto

ACCESSORIES

Pluto Alarm Clock, 1955, Allied, 4" x 5-1/2" x 10" tall, eyes and hands shaped like dog bones, glow in the dark
EX $100   NM $200   MIP $325

Pluto Purse, 1940s, Gund, 9" x 14" x 2"
EX $25   NM $55   MIP $100

BANK

Pluto Bank, 1940s, Disney, 4" x 4-1/2" x 6-1/2", ceramic
EX $60   NM $100   MIP $200

Pluto Bank, 1970s, Animal Toys Plus, 9" tall vinyl, Pluto standing in front of a doghouse
EX $20   NM $35   MIP $85

TOY

Pluto Hand Puppet, 1950s, Gund, 9" tall
EX $15   NM $35   MIP $80

Pluto Lantern Toy, 1950s, Linemar
EX $250   NM $350   MIP $500

Pluto Pop-A-Part Toy, 1965, Multiple Toymakers, 9" long, plastic
EX $20   NM $35   MIP $50

Pluto Rolykin, Marx, 1" x 1" x 1-1/2" tall, ball bearing action
EX $15   NM $35   MIP $70

Pluto Sports Car, Empire, 2" long
EX $10   NM $25   MIP $50

Pluto the Acrobat Trapeze Toy, Linemar, 10" tall, metal, celluloid, wind-up
EX $120   NM $250   MIP $350

Pluto the Drum Major, 1950s, Marx/Linemar, tin, mechanical
EX $300   NM $450   MIP $750

Popeye

ACCESSORIES

60th Anniversary Candle Box, 1989, Presents, metal, heart shaped, #P5979
EX $5   NM $12   MIP $30

Bell, 1980, Vandor, Popeye on top, ceramic
EX $15   NM $20   MIP $35

Belt Buckle, U.S. Spinach Growers, Strength thru Spinach
EX $8   NM $20   MIP $40

Belt Buckle, 1973, Pyramid Belt, Popeye w/sailor hat
EX $10   NM $20   MIP $50

Belt Buckle, 1980, Lee, Popeye w/spinach
EX $8   NM $15   MIP $35

Blinky Cup, Beacon Plastics
EX $8   NM $15   MIP $25

Bookends, 1980, Vandor, ceramic, Popeye and Brutus
EX $20   NM $45   MIP $100

Bowl, 1971, Deka, oval, plastic
EX $10   NM $20   MIP $50

Bowl, 1979, National Home Products, plastic
EX $6   NM $12   MIP $25

Bowl, 1980, Vandor, ceramic, 1 of 3
EX $8   NM $18   MIP $40

Cabinet, mirrored
EX $75   NM $100   MIP $175

Candy, 1980, Alberts, bonbons
EX $6   NM $10   MIP $15

Candy Box, 1960, Phoenix Candy, Popeye and his pals
EX $20   NM $50   MIP $100

Candy Cigarettes, 1959, Primrose Confectionery - England
EX $15   NM $35   MIP $100

Candy Sticks, 1989, Hearst, red box
EX $6   NM $15   MIP $30

Candy Sticks, 1990, World Candies, 48 count
EX $6   NM $15   MIP $25

Cereal Bowl, 1979, National Home Products
EX $8   NM $20   MIP $45

Cereal Box, 1987, Cocoa-Puffs, w/gum
EX $25   NM $50   MIP $75

Charm Bracelet, 1990, Peter Brams, silver or gold
EX $10   NM $20   MIP $40

Chocolate Mold, 1940s, metal, Popeye
EX $35   NM $90   MIP $150

Chocolate Mold, 1991, Turmic Plastics, plastic, Popeye
EX $3   NM $6   MIP $10

Christmas Ornament, 1981, Bully, Dufus
EX $8   NM $15   MIP $40

Christmas Ornament, 1981, Bully, Bluto
EX $8   NM $15   MIP $40

Christmas Ornament, 1987, Presents, Alice the Goon, Swee'Pea, Wimpy, Popeye, Olive Oyl or Brutus, each
EX $8   NM $15   MIP $40

Christmas Ornament, 1989, Presents, Season's Greetings
EX $8   NM $15   MIP $40

Circus Man Film, 1950s, Brumberger, 8mm
EX $20   NM $30   MIP $60

Color Markers, 1990, Sanrio, six
EX $2   NM $5   MIP $10

Comb and Brush, 1979, KFS
EX $8   NM $25   MIP $60

Cookie Jar, 1965, McCoy, ceramic white-suited Popeye
EX $200   NM $310   MIP $475

Cook's Catch-All, 1980, KFS, ceramic, Wimpy
EX $10   NM $20   MIP $50

Cup, 1940s, New Zealand, Popeye on skis, ceramic
EX $18   NM $40   MIP $80

Dice, 1990, w/Popeye head
EX $2   NM $5   MIP $15

Dish, 1940s, New Zealand, ceramic, Popeye and Olive Oyl
EX $30   NM $50   MIP $100

Dish Set, 1964, Boontonware, three piece plastic
EX $30   NM $45   MIP $90

Egg Cup, 1940s, Japan, Popeye sitting at table w/spinach
EX $30   NM $65   MIP $125

Egg Cup and Mug, 1989, Magna, Great Britain
EX $15   NM $40   MIP $75

Film Card, 1959, Tru-Vue, T-28
EX $8   NM $20   MIP $60

Freezicles, 1980, Imperial
EX $5   NM $15   MIP $20

Indian Fighter Film, Atlas Films, 8mm
EX $5   NM $10   MIP $20

Jackknife, 1940s, Imperial, green Popeye on pearl handle
EX $150   NM $250   MIP $350

Jeep Wall Plaque, ceramic
EX $6   NM $12   MIP $50

King of the Jungle Film, 1960s, Atlas Films, 8mm
EX $5   NM $10   MIP $30

Knapsack, 1979, Fabil
EX $10   NM $15   MIP $30

Kooky Straw, 1980, Imperial
EX $4   NM $10   MIP $20

Lamp, 1940s, boat w/Popeye light bulb
EX $500   NM $1000   MIP $1500

Life Raft, 1979, KFS, large, blue
EX $10   NM $20   MIP $40

Magic Eyes Film Card, 1962, Tru-Vue, set of three
EX $15   NM $25   MIP $60

Mini Hurricane Lamp, 1989, Presents, P5981-1993, 60th year
EX $4   NM $10   MIP $30

Mini Memo Board, 1980, Freelance
EX $5   NM $10   MIP $15

Mirror, 1978, Freelance, Popeye lifting weights
EX $7   NM $15   MIP $35

Mirror, 1979, Freelance, Olive w/mirror
EX $7   NM $15   MIP $35

Mirror Rattle, 1979, Cribmates
EX $8   NM $13   MIP $30

Mug, 1950s, Schmid, ceramic
EX $10   NM $20   MIP $40

Music Lovers Film, 1960s, Atlas Films, 8mm
EX $8   NM $15   MIP $20

Musical Mug, 1982, KFS, ceramic
EX $10   NM $20   MIP $35

Musical Rattle, 1979, Cribmates
EX $8   NM $15   MIP $30

(KP Photo)

Olive Oyl and Swee'Pea Hot Water Bottle, 1970, Duarry
EX $75   NM $100   MIP $200

Olive Oyl and Swee'Pea Snow Globe, 1989, Presents, several styles
EX $7   NM $15   MIP $40

Olive Oyl and Swee'Pea Telephone Shoulder Rest, 1982, Comvu
EX $6   NM $15   MIP $40

Olive Oyl and Swee'Pea Thermometer, 1981, KFS
EX $8   NM $13   MIP $20

Olive Oyl Cup, 1977, Coke, Coke Kollect-A-Set
EX $4   NM $10   MIP $30

Olive Oyl Hairbrush, 1979, Cribmates, musical
EX $8   NM $20   MIP $60

Olive Oyl Mug, 1950s, Schmid, musical ceramic
EX $15   NM $40   MIP $80

Olive Oyl Mug, 1980, Vandor, ceramic
EX $8   NM $15   MIP $25

Olive Oyl Wall Plaque, ceramic
EX $3   NM $7   MIP $20

Paper Party Blowouts, 1988, Gala/James River
EX $2   NM $4   MIP $10

Pencil Case, 1950s, Hassenfeld Bros., red
EX $35   NM $75   MIP $150

Pencil Case, 1990, Sanrio
EX $5   NM $10   MIP $20

Pig for a Friend Mug, 1980, Vandor, ceramic
EX $6   NM $12   MIP $50

Playing Cards, 1988, Presents, metal box, #P5998, two decks, 60th year
EX $4   NM $10   MIP $25

Popeye Alarm Clock, 1967, Smiths, British
EX $100   NM $180   MIP $320

Popeye and Cast Cigar Box
EX $25 NM $45 MIP $90

Popeye and Olive Oyl Suspenders, 1979, KFS, blue
EX $6 NM $12 MIP $25

Popeye and Swee'Pea Snow Globe, 1989, Presents, several varieties
EX $5 NM $10 MIP $25

Popeye Apron, 1990, Chester
EX $4 NM $8 MIP $15

Popeye Beach Set, 1950s, Peer Products/KFS, plastic rowboat, accessories
EX $25 NM $50 MIP $100

Popeye Charm, silver w/dangly parts
EX $20 NM $30 MIP $60

Popeye Charm, solid gold
EX $100 NM $150 MIP $200

Popeye Cup, 1979, Deca Plastics, plastic
EX $5 NM $10 MIP $25

Popeye Cup, 1989, Popeye Picnic, plastic
EX $1 NM $2 MIP $5

Popeye Glass, 1977, Coke, Coke Kollect-A-Set
EX $4 NM $10 MIP $25

Popeye Hot Water Bottle, 1970, Duarry
EX $40 NM $90 MIP $175

(KP Photo)

Popeye Lamp, 1940s, telescope w/Popeye at base
EX $225 NM $350 MIP $600

Popeye Lamp, 1959, Alan Jay, Popeye w/legs folded holding spinach
EX $75 NM $100 MIP $220

Popeye Night Light, Arrow Plastic
EX $8 NM $13 MIP $20

Popeye Picture, KFS-Sears, silver foil
EX $10 NM $20 MIP $40

Popeye Pin, Popeye at steering wheel, stick pin
EX $5 NM $12 MIP $35

Popeye Popcorn, 1949, Purity Mills, in can
EX $65 NM $100 MIP $150

Popeye Snow Globe, 1960s, KFS, Popeye holds globe between legs
EX $25 NM $45 MIP $100

Popeye Thimble, 1990
EX $4 NM $7 MIP $10

Popeye Toothbrush Holder, Vandor, 5" tall, figural
EX $10 NM $15 MIP $30

Popeye Toothbrush Set, 1980s, Nasta, holds two toothbrushes
EX $6 NM $15 MIP $25

Popeye Utensils, 1970s, Arrow Plastic, spoon and fork
EX $8 NM $15 MIP $30

Popeye Wall Hanging, 1979, Amscan, 42", jointed
EX $8 NM $13 MIP $20

Popeye/Olive Oyl/Swee'Pea Lamp Shade, 1950s
EX $50 NM $75 MIP $185

Punching Bag Film, 1950s, Brumberger, 8mm
EX $8 NM $15 MIP $30

Rain Boots, 1950s, KFS, spinach power
EX $15 NM $30 MIP $60

Record Player, 1960s, Emerson, Dynamite Music Machine
EX $50 NM $100 MIP $170

Secret Message Pen, 1981, Gordy
EX $6 NM $12 MIP $30

Sketchbook, 1960, Japan
EX $15 NM $25 MIP $60

Sleeping Bag, 1979, KFS
EX $15 NM $35 MIP $65

Soap Dispenser, 1970s, Woolfoam
EX $15 NM $25 MIP $35

Soap on a Rope, KFS, white, shaped like Popeye's head
EX $15 NM $25 MIP $60

Stationery, 1989, Presents, metal box, heart-shaped note paper, #P5976
EX $6 NM $10 MIP $20

Storage Box, 1990, Sanrio, smoke colored
EX $6 NM $10 MIP $15

Sunday Funnies Soda Can, 1970s, Flavor Valley
EX $8 NM $15 MIP $25

Suspenders, 1970s, red, white and blue w/plastic emblems
EX $10 NM $20 MIP $35

Swee'Pea Cup, 1977, Coke, Coke Kollect-A-Cup
EX $4 NM $7 MIP $12

Swee'Pea Egg Cup, 1980, Vandor, ceramic
EX $10 NM $20 MIP $35

Swee'Pea Night Light, 1978, Presents, bone china
EX $20 NM $30 MIP $60

Swee'Pea Snow Globe, 1989, Presents, several styles
EX $10 NM $15 MIP $30

Swee'Pea Wall Plaque, 1950s, ceramic
EX $12 NM $35 MIP $70

Swee'Pea's Lemonade Stand Television Film, 1950s, Zaboly
EX $12 NM $25 MIP $60

Training Cup, 1971, Deka
EX $8 NM $13 MIP $30

Transistor Radio, 1960s, Philgee
EX $35 NM $60 MIP $100

Trash Can, 1980s, KFS
EX $10 NM $30 MIP $50

Trinket Box, 1980, Vandor, Popeye laying on top, ceramic
EX $10 NM $16 MIP $30

Trinket Box, 1980, Vandor, Popeye's head in preserver, ceramic
EX $10 NM $18 MIP $35

TV Tray, 1979, KFS
EX $8 NM $15 MIP $30

Umbrella, 1979, KFS, blue and white
EX $20 NM $35 MIP $80

Wagon Works Film, 1960s, Atlas Films, 8mm
EX $6 NM $10 MIP $25

Wallet, 1978, Larami
EX $8 NM $20 MIP $50

Wallet, 1990, Sanrio
EX $6 NM $10 MIP $20

Wallet, 1991, Presents, P-5432, tri-fold
EX $6 NM $10 MIP $20

Whistle Candy, 1989, Alberts
EX $6 NM $10 MIP $20

Wimpy Cup, 1977, Coke, Coke Kollect-A-Set
EX $4 NM $7 MIP $10

Wimpy Magnet
EX $6 NM $10 MIP $15

Wimpy Thermometer, 1981, KFS
EX $10 NM $15 MIP $25

Write on/Wipe Off Board, 1979, Freelance
EX $10 NM $20 MIP $40

BADGE

Popeye and Swee'Pea Flicker Badge, 1960s, Varivue
EX $10 NM $20 MIP $50

Popeye and Wimpy Flicker Badge, 1960s, Varivue
EX $10 NM $20 MIP $50

BANK

60th Anniversary Bank, 1988, Presents, metal, P5988
EX $15   NM $30   MIP $60

Brutus Mini Bank, 1979, KFS
EX $10   NM $20   MIP $50

(KP Photo)

Daily Dime Bank, 1956, KFS
EX $60   NM $150   MIP $260

(KP Photo)

Daily Quarter Bank, 1950s, Kalon, 4-1/2" tall, metal
EX $150   NM $300   MIP $500

Olive Oyl Bank, 1940s, cast iron
EX $200   NM $300   MIP $500

Olive Oyl Mini Bank, 1979, KFS
EX $15   NM $30   MIP $60

Popeye Bank, ceramic, Popeye in light blue cap
EX $5   NM $10   MIP $30

Popeye Bank, 1940s, Popeye w/life preserver
EX $100   NM $150   MIP $300

Popeye Bank, 1940s, 9" cast iron
EX $175   NM $250   MIP $375

Popeye Bank, 1970s, Play Pal, plastic, Popeye sitting on rope
EX $10   NM $30   MIP $55

Popeye Bank, 1972, Play Pal, shape of Popeye's head, plastic
EX $15   NM $30   MIP $65

Popeye Bank, 1979, Renz, beige bust
EX $12   NM $25   MIP $60

Popeye Bank, 1980, Leonard, silver, Popeye sitting
EX $15   NM $30   MIP $60

Popeye Bank, 1980, Vandor, ceramic, Popeye sitting on rope
EX $12   NM $25   MIP $50

Popeye Bank, 1980, Vandor, ceramic
EX $130   NM $260   MIP $525

Popeye Bank, 1990, Sanrio, w/padlock
EX $5   NM $10   MIP $25

Popeye Bank, 1990, Mexico, ceramic bust
EX $20   NM $35   MIP $50

Popeye Bank, 1991, Presents, vinyl, Popeye w/removable pipe
EX $6   NM $12   MIP $25

Popeye Mini Bank, 1979, KFS
EX $10   NM $20   MIP $40

Spinach Can Bank, 1975, KFS, blue can w/raised characters
EX $20   NM $40   MIP $80

Swee'Pea Bank, 1980, Vandor, 6-1/2" figural
EX $80   NM $125   MIP $200

Swee'Pea Mini Bank, 1979, KFS
EX $20   NM $40   MIP $90

BOOK

60th Anniversary Collection Book, 1990, Hawk Books
EX $20   NM $40   MIP $60

Big Surprise Book, 1976, Wonder Books
EX $5   NM $15   MIP $40

Captain George Presents Popeye Book, 1970, Memory Lane
EX $10   NM $25   MIP $55

Danger Ahoy! Book, 1969, Whitman, Big Little Book
EX $5   NM $15   MIP $35

Deep Sea Danger Book, 1980, Whitman, Big Little Book
EX $2   NM $6   MIP $20

Fun Booklets, 1980, Spot-O-Gold, set of 10
EX $20   NM $40   MIP $80

Ghost Ship to Treasure Island Book, 1967, Whitman, Big Little Book
EX $8   NM $15   MIP $45

Giant 24 Big Picture Coloring Book, 1981, Merrigold Press
EX $6   NM $12   MIP $50

House that Popeye Built Book, 1960, Wonder Books
EX $8   NM $25   MIP $55

Jiffy Pop Fun 'N Games Booklet, 1980, Spot-O-Gold
EX $6   NM $12   MIP $30

Little Pops the Ghost Book, 1981, Random House
EX $5   NM $10   MIP $30

Little Pops the Magic Flute Book, 1981, Random House
EX $5   NM $10   MIP $30

Little Pops the Spinach Burgers Book, 1981, Random House
EX $5   NM $10   MIP $30

Little Pops the Treasure Hunt Book, 1981, Random House
EX $5   NM $10   MIP $30

Mix or Match Storybook, 1981, Random House
EX $8   NM $15   MIP $30

Olive Oyl and Swee'Pea Wash Up Book, 1980, Tuffy Books
EX $4   NM $10   MIP $25

Paint w/Water Book, 1981, Whitman
EX $3   NM $6   MIP $20

Painting and Crayon Book, 1960, England
EX $15   NM $25   MIP $80

Popeye Activity Pad, 1982, Merrigold Press
EX $3   NM $7   MIP $15

Popeye and Swee'Pea Coloring Book, 1970, Whitman, 1056-31
EX $7   NM $15   MIP $50

Popeye and the Pet Book, 1987, Peter Haddock, book three of four
EX $3   NM $5   MIP $25

Popeye and the Time Machine Book, 1990, Quaker, mini comic
EX $3   NM $5   MIP $25

Popeye Book, 1980, Random House, hardcover, based on movie
EX $4   NM $8   MIP $20

Popeye Climbs a Mountain Book, 1983, Wonder Books
EX $3   NM $7   MIP $20

Popeye Color and Recolor Book, 1957, Jack Built, color, wipe and color again
EX $25   NM $50   MIP $120

Popeye Learn and Play Activity Book, 1985, Allen Canning
EX $2   NM $5   MIP $10

Popeye on Rocket Coloring Book, 1980, Whitman - France
EX $8   NM $15   MIP $40

Popeye on Safari Book, 1990, Quaker, mini comic
EX $2   NM $4   MIP $8

Popeye Paint Coloring Book, 1951, Whitman
EX $25   NM $60   MIP $140

Popeye Pop-Up Book, 1981, Random House
EX $6   NM $12   MIP $40

Popeye Punch-Out Play Book, 1961, Whitman
EX $12   NM $22   MIP $45

Popeye Stay in Shape Book, 1980, Tuffy Books
EX $6   NM $10   MIP $20

Popeye Surprise Present Book, 1987, Peter Haddock
EX $6   NM $10   MIP $20

Popeye the Movie Book, 1980, Avon Printing
EX $6   NM $10   MIP $25

Popeye vs. Bluto the Bad Book, 1990, Quaker, mini comic
EX $2   NM $4   MIP $10

Popeye's Adventure Book, 1958, Purnell, England
EX $15   NM $30   MIP $80

Puzzle Party Book, 1979, Cinnamon House
EX $6   NM $12   MIP $25

Race to Pearl Peak Book, 1982, Golden
EX $6   NM $10   MIP $20

S.S. Funboat Coloring Book, 1981, Merrigold Press
EX $5   NM $10   MIP $40

Sailor and the Spinach Stalk Coloring Book, 1982, Whitman, 1150-1
EX $6   NM $15   MIP $30

Scott Fun 'N Games Booklet, 1980, Spot-O-Gold, set of five
EX $10   NM $20   MIP $40

The Outer Space Zoo Book, 1980, Golden
EX $6   NM $12   MIP $30

What! No Spinach? Book, 1981, Golden
EX $6   NM $10   MIP $25

Wimpy in Back to his First Love Book, eight pages
EX $6   NM $10   MIP $15

Wimpy What's Good to Eat? Book, 1980, Tuffy Books
EX $6   NM $12   MIP $30

BUTTON

Bluto Button, 1979, Lisa Frank, 2", Bluto getting socked
EX $2   NM $7   MIP $15

Brutus Button, 1980, Factors, 3", movie
EX $2   NM $5   MIP $10

Brutus Button, 1983, Mini Media, 1", "I'm Mean"
EX $2   NM $5   MIP $10

Brutus Button, 1985, Strand, 3", "Gonna Eat You for Breakfast"
EX $3   NM $6   MIP $12

Brutus Button, 1985, Strand, 3", "Ya Little Runt"
EX $2   NM $5   MIP $10

Button, 1983, Mini Media, 1", "No Wimps"
EX $3   NM $7   MIP $15

Olive Oyl Button, 1946, Pep
EX $8   NM $25   MIP $45

Olive Oyl Button, 1980, Factors, 3"
EX $2   NM $4   MIP $8

Olive Oyl Button, 1983, Mini Media, 1", "More than just a pretty face"
EX $2   NM $4   MIP $8

Popeye and Olive Oyl Button, 1970s, 1-1/2", "I Love You"
EX $5   NM $10   MIP $22

Popeye and Olive Oyl Button, 1980, Lisa Frank, 1", cowboy Popeye and Indian Olive
EX $5   NM $10   MIP $20

Popeye Button, 1946, Pep
EX $15   NM $35   MIP $65

Popeye Button, 1950s, KFS, 1", Famous Studios
EX $20   NM $40   MIP $100

(KP Photo)

Popeye Button, 1959, Lowe, sew-on card
EX $12   NM $20   MIP $60

Popeye Button, 1960s, KMOX TV, 1", S.S. Popeye
EX $5   NM $15   MIP $65

Popeye Button, 1980, Factors, 3", movie
EX $2   NM $4   MIP $10

Popeye Button, 1985, Strand, 3", several styles
EX $3   NM $6   MIP $20

Popeye Button, 1989, KFS, 3", marine conservation
EX $2   NM $4   MIP $10

Popeye Button, 1990, S. Cruz, 2", Santa Cruz boardwalk
EX $2   NM $4   MIP $10

Swee'Pea Button, 1980, Lisa Frank, 1", Swee'Pea w/Jeep
EX $2   NM $5   MIP $12

Wimpy Button, 1946, Pep
EX $10   NM $20   MIP $50

Wimpy Button, 1979, Lisa Frank, 2"
EX $3   NM $8   MIP $15

Wimpy Button, 1985, Strand, 3", "Must Go Home and Water the Ducks"
EX $3   NM $8   MIP $15

DOLL

Brutus Doll, 1985, Presents, small
EX $12   NM $25   MIP $75

Brutus Doll, 1985, Presents, large w/tag
EX $20   NM $50   MIP $120

Chimes Doll, 1950s, J. Swedlin, gray plush body, chimes
EX $20   NM $50   MIP $100

Jeep Doll, 1985, Presents, two sizes
EX $10   NM $25   MIP $80

Olive Oyl Doll, 9" vinyl sqeeze doll, Olive w/Swee'Pea
EX $15   NM $40   MIP $100

Olive Oyl Doll, 1950s, Rempel, small
EX $25   NM $50   MIP $120

Olive Oyl Doll, 1960s, Dakin, 8" tall
EX $25   NM $50   MIP $120

Olive Oyl Doll, 1970s, Dakin, Cartoon Theatre, in box
EX $25   NM $50   MIP $120

Olive Oyl Doll, 1970s, Dakin, hard plastic w/removable clothes
EX $20   NM $40   MIP $100

Olive Oyl Doll, 1979, Uneeda, removable clothing
EX $15   NM $30   MIP $80

Olive Oyl Doll, 1985, Presents, small
EX $10   NM $18   MIP $45

Olive Oyl Doll, 1985, Presents, Christmas, large
EX $14   NM $30   MIP $65

Olive Oyl Doll, 1990, Toy Toons
EX $4   NM $9   MIP $20

Olive Oyl Doll, 1990, Presents, small molded plastic, musical # P5948
EX $10   NM $20   MIP $40

Olive Oyl Doll, 1991, Presents, small molded plastic, # P5966
EX $4   NM $8   MIP $25

Olive Oyl Doll, 1991, Presents, Christmas, small
EX $8   NM $13   MIP $30

Poopdeck Pappy Doll, 1985, Presents, w/tag
EX $35   NM $75   MIP $200

Popeye Doll, 23" china
EX $200   NM $350   MIP $500

Popeye Doll, 1950s, Chicago Herald American
EX $30   NM $85   MIP $250

Popeye Doll, 1950s, Rempel, small
EX $20   NM $45   MIP $120

Popeye Doll, 1950s, Woolikin, white plush
EX $30   NM $65   MIP $180

Popeye Doll, 1950s, Chad Valley, 7" tall, squeaks
EX $20   NM $55   MIP $140

Popeye Doll, 1957, Sears/Cameo, 13" in box
EX $300   NM $600   MIP $1000

Popeye Doll, 1958, Gund, 20" tall
EX $55   NM $110   MIP $250

Popeye Doll, 1960s, Quaker, 12" cloth
EX $20   NM $40   MIP $100

Popeye Doll, 1960s, 9" vinyl squeeze doll, Popeye w/Swee'Pea
EX $15   NM $30   MIP $100

Popeye Doll, 1968, Lakeside, 12" tall, sponge rubber
EX $15   NM $30   MIP $100

Popeye Doll, 1970s, Dakin, Cartoon Theatre, in box
EX $30   NM $60   MIP $150

Popeye Doll, 1970s, Dakin, hard plastic w/removable clothes
EX $20   NM $60   MIP $150

Popeye Doll, 1974, Dakin, squeaks
EX $15   NM $30   MIP $85

Popeye Doll, 1979, Uneeda
EX $20   NM $40   MIP $90

Popeye Doll, 1979, Uneeda, 16" tall
EX $22   NM $45   MIP $100

Popeye Doll, 1983, Etone, 8" plush
EX $7   NM $15   MIP $40

Popeye Doll, 1985, Presents, small
EX $8   NM $13   MIP $40

Popeye Doll, 1985, Presents, small doll w/pipe molded into hand
EX $10   NM $15   MIP $45

Popeye Doll, 1990, Presents, small molded plastic, musical #P5949
EX $10   NM $15   MIP $35

Popeye Doll, 1990, Toy Toons
EX $7   NM $15   MIP $40

Sea Hag Doll, 1985, Presents
EX $30   NM $75   MIP $225

Swee'Pea Doll, 1979, Uneeda
EX $10   NM $20   MIP $70

Swee'Pea Doll, 1985, Presents, large
EX $15   NM $30   MIP $80

Swee'Pea Doll, 1985, Presents, small
EX $12   NM $25   MIP $60

Swee'Pea Doll, 1991, Presents, small molded plastic, # P5968
EX $10   NM $15   MIP $40

Swee'Pea Doll, 1991, Presents, Christmas, small
EX $10   NM $20   MIP $60

Wimpy Doll, 1950s, KFS, rubber
EX $40   NM $75   MIP $135

Wimpy Doll, 1985, Presents, holding a hamburger
EX $50   NM $100   MIP $200

FIGURES

Bluto Figure, Cristallerie Antonio, Italian crystal
EX $15   NM $35   MIP $85

Brutus Figure, 1962, Japan Olympics, wood, Brutus in barrel
EX $75   NM $180   MIP $350

Brutus Figure, 1981, Bully, pink shirt
EX $7   NM $15   MIP $30

Brutus Figure, 1984, Comic-Spain, Brutus w/club
EX $4   NM $7   MIP $15

Brutus Figure, 1990, Presents, PVC
EX $2   NM $3   MIP $10

Brutus Figure, 1991, KFS-Hearst, wood
EX $4   NM $7   MIP $12

Character Figures, 1980, Spoontiques, 2" figures: Popeye w/barbell, Popeye w/parrot, Olive walking, Popeye flexing muscles, Popeye w/spinach, each
EX $10   NM $20   MIP $40

Character Figures, 1980, Spoontiques, two 1" figures: Jeep lifting tail, Swee'Pea w/feet showing, each
EX $10   NM $25   MIP $50

Character Figures, 1981, Spoontiques, pewter, three 1" figures: Olive w/hands clasped, Popeye w/muscles, Jeep standing, each
EX $10   NM $25   MIP $50

Character Figures, 1991, Popeye's Chicken, blue plastic, several characters available
EX $2   NM $5   MIP $10

Dufus Figure, 1981, Bully, w/hand on stomach
EX $8   NM $15   MIP $28

Jeep Figure, 1991, KFS-Hearst, wood
EX $7   NM $20   MIP $50

Olive Oyl Figure, Cristallerie Antonio, Italian crystal
EX $10   NM $15   MIP $50

Olive Oyl Figure, 1940s, lead
EX $15   NM $30   MIP $100

Olive Oyl Figure, 1940s, 5" wooden jointed
EX $75   NM $165   MIP $400

Olive Oyl Figure, 1950s, Multiple Toymakers, 2" tall
EX $15   NM $40   MIP $75

Olive Oyl Figure, 1974, Ben Cooper, rubber
EX $20   NM $40   MIP $85

Olive Oyl Figure, 1980, KFS, arms clamped together, hanging figure
EX $5   NM $10   MIP $30

Olive Oyl Figure, 1980, Amscan, large bendy
EX $6   NM $12   MIP $30

Olive Oyl Figure, 1981, Bully, holding flower
EX $8   NM $15   MIP $30

Olive Oyl Figure, 1981, Bully, w/hands clasp
EX $8   NM $15   MIP $30

Olive Oyl Figure, 1984, Comics Spain, PVC, Olive w/flower
EX $6   NM $10   MIP $20

Olive Oyl Figure, 1986, Comics Spain, 6" bendy
EX $6   NM $10   MIP $20

Olive Oyl Figure, 1988, Jesco, small bendy
EX $2   NM $4   MIP $12

Olive Oyl Figure, 1988, Jesco, large bendy
EX $3   NM $6   MIP $18

Olive Oyl Figure, 1990, Presents, 3" tall, plastic
EX $2   NM $5   MIP $10

Olive Oyl Figure, 1990, Presents, PVC
EX $2   NM $5   MIP $10

Olive Oyl Figure, 1990, Chester, 10", Olive w/rolling pin
EX $10   NM $25   MIP $50

Olive Oyl Figure, 1990, Mexico, ceramic
EX $10   NM $25   MIP $50

Olive Oyl Figure, 1991, KFS-Hearst, wood
EX $5   NM $10   MIP $20

Popeye Figure, Cristallerie Antonio Imperatore, Italian crystal
EX $20   NM $30   MIP $60

Popeye Figure, Dakin, 8" tall w/spinach can
EX $22   NM $45   MIP $100

Popeye Figure, 1940s, celluloid w/wooden feet
EX $75   NM $125   MIP $225

Popeye Figure, 1940s, lead
EX $25   NM $50   MIP $100

Popeye Figure, 1950s, England, 7", bendy, yellow pants
EX $30   NM $60   MIP $170

Popeye Figure, 1950s, plastic, Popeye on four wheels w/telescope
EX $25   NM $50   MIP $130

Popeye Figure, 1950s, Japan, celluloid
EX $40   NM $75   MIP $150

Popeye Figure, 1960s, Combex, rubber, Popey w/a can of spinach
EX $20   NM $40   MIP $90

Popeye Figure, 1962, Japan Olympics, wood, Popeye at bat
EX $150   NM $325   MIP $550

Popeye Figure, 1968, Lakeside, miniflex
EX $10   NM $25   MIP $70

Popeye Figure, 1969, Lakeside, superflex
EX $10   NM $25   MIP $60

Popeye Figure, 1970, Duncan, 8" tall
EX $20   NM $40   MIP $70

Popeye Figure, 1970s, ceramic, removeable head Popeye
EX $30   NM $60   MIP $100

Popeye Figure, 1974, Ben Cooper, rubber
EX $8   NM $15   MIP $40

Popeye Figure, 1978, Bronco, bendy
EX $6   NM $10   MIP $25

Popeye Figure, 1979, Imperial
EX $6   NM $10   MIP $20

Popeye Figure, 1980, Amscan, small bendy
EX $4   NM $7   MIP $14

Popeye Figure, 1980, Amscan, large bendy
EX $6   NM $12   MIP $20

Popeye Figure, 1981, Bully, several variations
EX $9   NM $18   MIP $30

Popeye Figure, 1984, Comics Spain, PVC, Popeye w/spinach
EX $5   NM $10   MIP $20

Popeye Figure, 1986, Comics Spain, 6" bendy, white pants
EX $3   NM $6   MIP $20

Popeye Figure, 1988, Jesco, bendy
EX $6   NM $10   MIP $25

Popeye Figure, 1988, Jesco, small bendy
EX $2   NM $5   MIP $15

Popeye Figure, 1990, Mexico, ceramic
EX $7   NM $15   MIP $35

Popeye Figure, 1990, Presents, PVC
EX $1   NM $4   MIP $8

Popeye Figure, 1990, Presents, 3" tall, plastic
EX $2   NM $3   MIP $6

Popeye Figure, 1990, Chester, 10", ceramic, Popeye w/spinach
EX $6   NM $10   MIP $30

Popeye Figure, 1991, KFS-Hearst, wood
EX $8   NM $12   MIP $25

Popeye Galley Steward Figure, 1980, KFS, ceramic
EX $10   NM $22   MIP $50

Swee'Pea Figure, ceramic, one of five
EX $5   NM $15   MIP $45

Swee'Pea Figure, Cristallerie Antonio Imperatore, Italian crystal
EX $15   NM $30   MIP $50

Swee'Pea Figure, 1984, Comics Spain, PVC, Swee'Pea w/cake
EX $4   NM $8   MIP $20

Swee'Pea Figure, 1984, Presents, PVC
EX $2   NM $4   MIP $10

Swee'Pea Figure, 1990, Presents, 3" tall, plastic
EX $5   NM $10   MIP $20

Wimpy Figure, Cristallerie Antonio Imperatore, Italian crystal
EX $25   NM $40   MIP $75

Wimpy Figure, 1940s, lead
EX $15   NM $30   MIP $80

Wimpy Figure, 1950s, Buitoni, premium
EX $40   NM $70   MIP $150

Wimpy Figure, 1981, Bully, yellow hat
EX $6   NM $12   MIP $25

Wimpy Figure, 1984, Comics Spain, Wimpy w/hamburger
EX $7   NM $15   MIP $30

Wimpy Figure, 1990, Presents, PVC
EX $2   NM $5   MIP $10

GAME

Adventures of Popeye Game, 1957, Transogram
EX $50   NM $80   MIP $160

Boxing Game, 1981, Harmony
EX $7   NM $15   MIP $40

Jumbo Card Game, 1978, House of Games
EX $10   NM $20   MIP $35

Jumbo Trading Card Game, 1960s, Dynamic Toy
EX $15   NM $30   MIP $60

Magic Play Around Game, 1960s, Amsco
EX $20   NM $45   MIP $100

Pocket Pin Ball, 1983, Nintendo/Ja-Ru, cups
EX $5   NM $10   MIP $20

Pocket Pin Ball, 1983, Nintendo/Ja-Ru, holes
EX $5   NM $10   MIP $20

Popeye Arcade Game, 1980, Parker Bros., card game
EX $5   NM $10   MIP $25

(KP Photo)

Popeye Ball Toss Game, 1950s, KFS
EX $50   NM $75   MIP $160

Popeye Break-A-Plate Game, 1963, Combex
EX $30   NM $80   MIP $150

Popeye Fishing Game, 1962, Transogram, magnetic
EX $15   NM $30   MIP $80

Popeye Fishing Game, 1980, Fleetwood
EX $5   NM $10   MIP $25

Popeye Games, 1960s, Ed-U-Card, set of four games
EX $15   NM $30   MIP $60

Popeye Hammer Game, 1960s, Holgate
EX $70   NM $140   MIP $280

Popeye Mini Tennis Game, 1970s, Nordic
EX $10   NM $15   MIP $30

Popeye Nail-On Game, 1963, Colorforms
EX $20   NM $45   MIP $100

Popeye Pinball Game, 1983, Ja-Ru
EX $6   NM $10   MIP $25

Popeye Playing Card Game, 1983, Parker Bros.
EX $6   NM $10   MIP $30

Popeye Ring Toss Game, 1957, Transogram
EX $32   NM $65   MIP $135

Popeye Ring Toss Game, 1980, Fleetwood
EX $6   NM $10   MIP $25

Popeye Spinach Target Game, 1960s, Gardner
EX $40   NM $75   MIP $120

Popeye Video Game, 1983, Nintendo
EX $12   NM $20   MIP $30

Popeye/Olive Oyl/Wimpy Skill Games, 1965, Lido
EX $10   NM $16   MIP $40

Popeye's Gang Pinball Game, 1970s, MSS
EX $13   NM $25   MIP $50

Popeye's Sliding Boards and Ladders, 1958, Warren Built-Rite
EX $12   NM $25   MIP $80

Popeye's Spinach Hunt Game, 1976, Whitman
EX $11   NM $22   MIP $50

Popeye's Three Game Set, 1956, Built-Rite
EX $20   NM $40   MIP $90

Popeye's Tiddly Winks, 1948, Parker Bros.
EX $20   NM $40   MIP $100

Popeye's Treasure Map Game, 1977, Whitman
EX $12   NM $25   MIP $50

Popeye's Where's Me Pipe Game
EX $30   NM $50   MIP $90

Puzzle Game, 1978, Waddington's House of Games
EX $10   NM $20   MIP $40

Ring the Bell w/Hammer Game, 1960s, Harett-Gilmar
EX $25   NM $42   MIP $70

Ring Toss Stand-Up Game, 1958, Transogram
EX $15   NM $30   MIP $70

Roly Poly and Cork Gun Game, 1958, Knickbocker
EX $60   NM $120   MIP $210

Rub 'N Win Party Game, 1980, Spot-O-Gold
EX $5   NM $10   MIP $25

Skeet Shoot Game, 1950, Irwin
EX $75   NM $125   MIP $185

Skoozit Pick-A-Puzzle Game, 1966, Ideal
EX $15   NM $35   MIP $70

Water Ball Game, 1983, Nintendo, one basket
EX $6   NM $10   MIP $25

LUNCH BOX

Mini Lunch Box, 1990, Sanrio, plastic
EX $4   NM $10   MIP $25

MUSIC BOX

Brutus Music Box, 1980, KFS, Brutus dancing
EX $10   NM $15   MIP $40

Brutus Music Box, 1989, Presents, #P5984
EX $8   NM $17   MIP $45

Music Box, 1980, Vandor, revolving Popeye spanks Swee'Pea, ceramic
EX $20   NM $45   MIP $100

Music Box, 1980, Vandor, revolving Olive w/Popeye dancing, ceramic
EX $20   NM $45   MIP $100

Music Box, 1980, Vandor, Wimpy on top of hamburger, ceramic
EX $20   NM $45   MIP $100

Olive Oyl Music Box, 1980, KFS, Olive dancing
EX $8   NM $20   MIP $50

Olive Oyl Music Box, 1989, Presents, #P5983
EX $8   NM $20   MIP $50

Popeye and Olive Oyl Music Box, Schmid, 8-1/4" figural box
EX $50   NM $100   MIP $180

Swee'Pea Music Box, 1980, KFS, Swee'Pea dancing
EX $8   NM $15   MIP $50

Swee'Pea Music Box, 1989, Presents, #P5986
EX $8   NM $15   MIP $50

Wimpy Music Box, 1989, Presents, #P5985
EX $8   NM $15   MIP $40

RECORD

Fleas A Crowd Record, 1962, Peter Pan, 78 rpm
EX $10   NM $25   MIP $50

Olive Oyl on Troubled Waters Record, 1976, Peter Pan, 45 rpm
EX $7   NM $20   MIP $40

Original Radio Broadcasts Record, 1977, Golden Age, 33 rpm
EX $7   NM $25   MIP $60

Picture Disc Record, 1948, Record of America, 78 rpm
EX $25   NM $50   MIP $100

Picture Disc Record, 1982, Peter Pan, 33 rpm
EX $6   NM $10   MIP $25

Pollution Solution Record, 1970s, Peter Pan, 45 rpm
EX $5   NM $10   MIP $35

Popeye and Friends Record, 1981, Merry Records, 33 rpm
EX $3   NM $10   MIP $25

Popeye French Record, 1981, Polygram, 45 rpm
EX $7   NM $15   MIP $35

Popeye in the Movies Record, Peter Pan, 33 rpm w/book
EX $6   NM $15   MIP $35

Popeye Launches His New Song Hits Record, 1958, Peter Pan, 45 rpm
EX $15   NM $30   MIP $80

Popeye on Parade/Strike Me Pink Record, 1950s, Cricket, 45 rpm
EX $12   NM $25   MIP $60

Popeye Record, 1977, Peter Pan, 33 rpm, four stories, #1114
EX $6   NM $15   MIP $30

Popeye the Ladies Man Record, 33 rpm
EX $8   NM $15   MIP $35

Popeye the Movie Soundtrack Record, 1980, Paramount
EX $6   NM $15   MIP $30

Popeye the Sailor Man and His Friends Record, 1960s, Golden, 33 rpm
EX $8   NM $15   MIP $30

Popeye the Sailor Man Record, 1959, Golden, 45 rpm
EX $7   NM $15   MIP $30

Popeye the Sailor Man Record, 1960, Diplomat Records, 33 rpm
EX $7   NM $15   MIP $35

Popeye the Sailor Man Record, 1976, Peter Pan, 33 rpm
EX $7   NM $15   MIP $35

Popeye's Favorite Sea Shanties Record, 1960, RCA Camden
EX $10   NM $25   MIP $50

Popeye's Favorite Sea Songs Record, 1959, Peter Pan, 45 rpm
EX $10   NM $25   MIP $60

Popeye's Favorite Stories Record, 1960, RCA Camden, 33 rpm
EX $10   NM $20   MIP $40

Popeye's Songs About…… Record, 1961, Golden, 33 rpm
EX $8   NM $18   MIP $35

Six Popeye Songs Record, 1950s, Wonderland Records, 45 rpm
EX $8   NM $30   MIP $70

Song and Story Skin Diver Record, 1964, KFS
EX $10   NM $20   MIP $40

Songs of Health Record, 1960s, Golden, 45 rpm
EX $6   NM $10   MIP $25

Songs of Safety Record, 1960s, Golden, 45 rpm
EX $6   NM $10   MIP $25

Whale of a Tale Record, 1981, Peter Pan, 45 rpm
EX $6   NM $10   MIP $20

RING

Candy Rings, 1989, Alberts
EX $6   NM $15   MIP $25

Popeye and Oscar Flicker Ring, blue
EX $8   NM $20   MIP $35

Popeye and Swee'Pea Flicker Ring, blue
EX $8   NM $15   MIP $35

Popeye and Wimpy Flicker Ring, blue
EX $8   NM $15   MIP $35

TOY

Apprentice Printer, 1970s, MSS
EX $6   NM $20   MIP $40

Ball and Jacks Set, MSS
EX $6   NM $12   MIP $3035

Ball and Paddle, BC
EX $6   NM $15   MIP $35

Balloon Pump, 1957, inflato-pump
EX $40   NM $60   MIP $120

Barber Shop, 1970s, Larami
EX $5   NM $15   MIP $30

Baseball, 1983, Ja-Ru
EX $10   NM $20   MIP $40

Beach Boat, 1980, H.G. Industries, red or yellow
EX $5   NM $10   MIP $35

Biffbat-Fly Back Paddle, 1935
EX $75   NM $100   MIP $175

Billion Bubbles, 1984, Larami
EX $4   NM $8   MIP $15

Blackboard, 1962, Bar Zim
EX $20   NM $40   MIP $85

Bluto's Road Roller, 1980, Lesney/ Matchbox, CS-14, 2-3/4" x 2-7/8"
EX $8   NM $18   MIP $50

Bop Bag, 1981, Miner Industries
EX $8   NM $15   MIP $30

Boxing Gloves, 1960s, Everlast
EX $35   NM $60   MIP $150

Brutus Dog Toy, 1986, Petex
EX $6   NM $12   MIP $25

Brutus Figure Painting Kit, 1980, Avalon
EX $8   NM $15   MIP $35

Brutus Hand Puppet, 1960s, Gund
EX $25   NM $60   MIP $120

Brutus Hi-Pop Ball, 1981, Ja-Ru
EX $6   NM $10   MIP $20

Brutus Hookies, 1977, Tiger
EX $5   NM $18   MIP $50

Brutus in Jeep, 1950s, tiny plastic car
EX $15   NM $35   MIP $80

Brutus Jump-Up, 1970s, Imperial
EX $8   NM $20   MIP $40

Brutus Painting Kit, 1980, Avalon
EX $8   NM $15   MIP $25

Brutus Soaky, 1960s, Colgate-Palmolive
EX $15   NM $35   MIP $80

Brutus Sports Car, 1950s, tiny plastic car
EX $15   NM $35   MIP $75

Brutus Wind-Up Toy, 1980, Durham
EX $5   NM $10   MIP $25

Bubble Blower, 1958, Transogram
EX $15   NM $35   MIP $90

Bubble Blower Boat, 1984, Larami
EX $7   NM $15   MIP $40

Bubble Blowing Popeye, 1950s, Linemar
EX $550   NM $1000   MIP $1650

Bubble Blowing Train, 1970s, Hong Kong, pink
EX $10   NM $20   MIP $60

Bubble 'N Clean, 1960s, Woolfoam
EX $20   NM $45   MIP $75

Bubble Pipe, 1960s, KFS, yellow w/red end
EX $15   NM $30   MIP $80

Bubble Pipe, 1985, Ja-Ru
EX $5   NM $12   MIP $35

Bubble Shooter, 1980s, Ja-Ru, orange or yellow body
EX $5   NM $10   MIP $30

Bubbleblaster, 1980, Carlin Playthings
EX $10   NM $15   MIP $30

Bubbles Blaster, 1984, Larami
EX $5   NM $10   MIP $20

Bubbles w/Dip Pow Bubbles, 1986, MSS
EX $5   NM $10   MIP $20

Cap Gun, 1981, Ja-Ru
EX $10   NM $25   MIP $60

Chain Bubbles Maker, 1984, Larami, red Popeye
EX $6   NM $10   MIP $20

Change Purse, 1990, Sanrio
EX $5   NM $10   MIP $20

Checker Board, 1959, Ideal
EX $20   NM $35   MIP $90

Chinese Jump Rope, MSS
EX $4   NM $12   MIP $25

Colorforms Birthday Party Set, 1961, Colorforms
EX $25   NM $70   MIP $110

Colorforms Movie Version, 1980, Colorforms
EX $7   NM $15   MIP $30

Color-Me Stickers, 1983, Diamond Toymakers
EX $5   NM $12   MIP $25

Color-Vue Pencil-by-Numbers, 1979, Hasbro
EX $10   NM $20   MIP $35

Construction Trucks, 1981, Larami
EX $6   NM $15   MIP $30

Crayons, 1950s, American Crayon
EX $20   NM $35   MIP $80

Crayons, 1958, Dixon, 12 giant crayons
EX $20   NM $35   MIP $80

Dockside Presto Magix, 1980, APC
EX $3   NM $6   MIP $12

Double Action Water Gun Set, MSS
EX $10   NM $20   MIP $40

Drawing Board, 1978, KFS, slate w/rope attached
EX $8   NM $16   MIP $40

Drawing Desk, 1980, Carlin Playthings
EX $10   NM $25   MIP $60

Duck Shoot, 1980s, Ja-Ru
EX $5   NM $15   MIP $30

Erase-O-Board and Magic Screen Set, 1957, Hassenfeld Bros.
EX $50   NM $90   MIP $180

Film Projector, Cinexin-Spain, 8mm w/13 movies
EX $85   NM $140   MIP $250

Finger Puppet Family, 1960s, Denmark Plastics
EX $25   NM $50   MIP $100

Flashlight, 1960s, Bantam-Lite, three color, wrist light
EX $10   NM $20   MIP $40

Flashlight, 1983, Larami, blue, yellow, or red
EX $7   NM $15   MIP $30

Foto-Fun Printing Kit, 1958, Fun Bilt
EX $32   NM $65   MIP $130

Funny Color Foam, 1983, Creative Aerosol
EX $5   NM $15   MIP $60

(KP Photo)

Funny Face Maker, 1962, Jaymar
EX $15   NM $30   MIP $70

Funny Films Viewer, 1940s, Acme
EX $50   NM $75   MIP $120

(KP Photo)

Give-A-Show Projector, Kenner, projector w/slides
EX $75 NM $100 MIP $180

Gumball Dispenser, 1983, Superior Toys, pocket pack
EX $10 NM $20 MIP $40

Gumball Machine, 1968, Hasbro, 6", shape of Popeye's head
EX $30 NM $50 MIP $100

Gumball Machine, 1983, Superior Toys, Popeye gives Olive flowers
EX $10 NM $20 MIP $45

Gumball Machine, 1983, Superior Toys, Popeye eating spinach
EX $10 NM $20 MIP $45

Halloween Bucket, 1979, Renz, shaped like Popeye's head, red, yellow or blue
EX $10 NM $20 MIP $40

Harmonica, 1973, Larami
EX $15 NM $40 MIP $90

Hat and Pipe, 1950s, Empire Plastics
EX $40 NM $60 MIP $110

Holster Set, 1960s, Halco
EX $90 NM $150 MIP $250

Horseshoe Magnets, 1984, Larami
EX $5 NM $15 MIP $30

Hunting Knife, 1973, Larami
EX $20 NM $50 MIP $85

ID Set, 1982, Gordy
EX $5 NM $15 MIP $40

Jack-in-the-Box, 1961, Mattel
EX $60 NM $120 MIP $210

Jack-in-the-Box, 1979, Nasta
EX $25 NM $50 MIP $100

Jack-in-the-Box, 1983, Nasta
EX $20 NM $40 MIP $85

Kaleidoscope, 1979, Larami
EX $10 NM $25 MIP $85

Kazoo and Harmonica, 1979, Larami
EX $8 NM $20 MIP $35

Kazoo Pipe, 1960s, Peerless Playthings, yellow
EX $15 NM $30 MIP $60

Kite, 1980, Sky-Way, regular
EX $4 NM $8 MIP $25

Kite, 1980, Sky-Way, inflatable
EX $6 NM $12 MIP $25

Lantern, 1950s, Linemar, 7-1/2" tall, battery-operated, light in belly
EX $130 NM $275 MIP $525

Magic Glow Putty, FC Famous Toys
EX $6 NM $10 MIP $15

Magic Slate, 1959, Lowe
EX $20 NM $40 MIP $90

Magic Slate Paper Saver, 1981, Whitman
EX $4 NM $8 MIP $25

Marble, 1940s
EX $8 NM $20 MIP $50

Marble Set, 1980, Imperial
EX $12 NM $25 MIP $70

Marble Shooter, 1940s, milk glass container
EX $35 NM $50 MIP $100

Metal Tapping Set, 1950s, Carlton Dank
EX $25 NM $50 MIP $120

Metal Target Set, 1983, Ja-Ru
EX $8 NM $18 MIP $60

Metal Whistle, 1981, Ja-Ru
EX $5 NM $12 MIP $35

Micro-Movie, 1990, Fascinations, Popeye-Ali Baba
EX $4 NM $8 MIP $15

Miniature Train Set, 1980, Larami
EX $8 NM $15 MIP $60

Model Kit, 1970s, Carto, Popeye and Olive Oyl
EX $25 NM $60 MIP $120

Motor Friend, 1976, Nasta
EX $10 NM $20 MIP $50

Muscle Builder Bluto, 1980, Carlin Playthings
EX $6 NM $12 MIP $25

Muscle Builder Popeye, 1980, Carlin Playthings
EX $6 NM $12 MIP $30

My Popeye Coloring Kit, 1957, American Crayon
EX $50 NM $100 MIP $175

Official Popeye Pipe, 1958, 5" stem w/2" bowl, battery-operated, "It lites, it toots"
EX $45 NM $100 MIP $200

Old Time Wild West Train, 1984, Larami
EX $5 NM $20 MIP $70

Olive Oyl Bike Bobbers, 1960s, KFS
EX $15 NM $25 MIP $60

Olive Oyl Costume, 1950s, Collegeville
EX $40 NM $75 MIP $120

Olive Oyl Costume, 1976, Ben Cooper
EX $10 NM $20 MIP $70

Olive Oyl Figure Painting Kit, 1980, Avalon
EX $6 NM $12 MIP $20

Olive Oyl Foam Toy, 1979, Cribmates
EX $8 NM $15 MIP $35

Olive Oyl Hand Puppet, 1960s, Gund, comic strip body
EX $30 NM $75 MIP $150

Olive Oyl Hi-Pop Ball, 1981, Ja-Ru
EX $5 NM $10 MIP $40

Olive Oyl Hookies, 1977, Tiger
EX $4 NM $10 MIP $30

Olive Oyl in Airplane, 1970s, Corgi
EX $12 NM $30 MIP $70

Olive Oyl Jump-Up, Imperial
EX $5 NM $10 MIP $20

Olive Oyl Marionette, 1950s, Gund, 11-1/2" tall
EX $70 NM $120 MIP $210

Olive Oyl Painting Kit, 1980, Avalon
EX $5 NM $10 MIP $25

Olive Oyl Push Puppet, 1960s, Kohner, 4" tall, plastic
EX $15 NM $35 MIP $75

Olive Oyl Sports Car, 1950s, tiny plastic car
EX $15 NM $35 MIP $80

Olive Oyl Squeak Toy, 1979, Cribmates, on a stick
EX $5 NM $13 MIP $30

Olive Oyl Squeeze Toy, 1950s, Rempel, vinyl
EX $30 NM $60 MIP $120

Olive Oyl Swim Ring, 1979, Wet Set-Zee Toys
EX $5 NM $10 MIP $25

Olive Oyl Tiles, 1970s, Italy, 3" x 5" w/stand
EX $12 NM $25 MIP $50

Olive Oyl Toboggan, 1979, KFS
EX $6 NM $15 MIP $35

Olive Oyl's Convertible, 1980, Lesney/ Matchbox, CS-15, 2-3/4" x 2-7/8"
EX $12 NM $30 MIP $75

Paint 'N Puff Set, 1979, Art Award, two versions
EX $6 NM $12 MIP $35

Pick-Up Sticks, 1957, Lido
EX $20 NM $40 MIP $80

Pirate Island Presto Magix, 1980, American Pub.
EX $10 NM $20 MIP $25

Plane and Parachute, 1980, Fleetwood
EX $8 NM $15 MIP $35

Play Money, 1970, The Toy House
EX $5 NM $10 MIP $30

Pool Table, 1984, Larami
EX $5   NM $10   MIP $25

Pop Maker and Son, 1987, Ja-Ru
EX $2   NM $4   MIP $15

Pop Pistol, 1984, Larami
EX $4   NM $10   MIP $40

Popeye Air Mattress, 1979, Zee Toys
EX $8   NM $20   MIP $25

Popeye and Brutus Punch Me Bop Bag, 1960s, Dartmore
EX $15   NM $30   MIP $60

Popeye and Olive Oyl Sand Set, 1950s, Peer Products, bucket, shovel
EX $20   NM $50   MIP $125

Popeye and Olive Oyl Toy Watch, 1970s, Unknown, flicker
EX $6   NM $12   MIP $30

Popeye and Shark Swim Ring, 1960s, Laurel Star-Japan
EX $10   NM $25   MIP $35

Popeye and Wimpy Walk-A-Way Toy, 1964, Marx
EX $25   NM $50   MIP $120

Popeye Arcade, 1980, Fleetwood
EX $6   NM $12   MIP $25

Popeye at the Wheel, 1950s, Woolnough, musical
EX $150   NM $300   MIP $625

Popeye Ball, rubber kick ball
EX $7   NM $13   MIP $30

Popeye Bathtub Toy, 1960s, Stahlwood, floating boat
EX $20   NM $40   MIP $90

Popeye Bend-I-Face, 1967, Lakeside
EX $15   NM $35   MIP $65

Popeye Bingo, 1980, Nasta
EX $6   NM $10   MIP $20

Popeye Bubble Liquid, 1970s, M. Shimmel Sons, shaped like Popeye w/necktie similar to a sailor's knot
EX $8   NM $15   MIP $25

Popeye Car, 1980, Vandor, Popeye and Olive in blue or pink car
EX $20   NM $45   MIP $100

Popeye Carnival, 1965, Toymaster
EX $75   NM $100   MIP $250

Popeye Coloring Set, 1960s, Hasbro, numbered, w/pencils
EX $12   NM $30   MIP $70

Popeye Costume, 1950s, Collegeville
EX $40   NM $75   MIP $120

Popeye Costume, 1980s, Collegeville
EX $9   NM $18   MIP $40

Popeye Costume, 1984, Ben Cooper
EX $7   NM $15   MIP $35

Popeye Dog Toy, 1986, Petex
EX $3   NM $6   MIP $10

Popeye Figure Painting Kit, 1980, Avalon
EX $4   NM $8   MIP $20

Popeye Finger Rings, 1949, Post Toasties
EX $20   NM $50   MIP $125

Popeye Flicker Badge, 1960s, Varivue, Popeye eating spinach
EX $8   NM $15   MIP $35

Popeye Flickers, 1960s, Sonwell
EX $8   NM $15   MIP $35

Popeye Ge-tar, 1960s, Mattel, 14" long, shaped like Popeye's face, plays "I'm Popeye the Sailor Man"
EX $30   NM $60   MIP $125

Popeye Glow Putty, 1984, Larami
EX $3   NM $6   MIP $10

Popeye Goes Swimming Colorforms, 1963, Colorforms
EX $15   NM $35   MIP $75

Popeye Goes to School Television, 1950s, Zaboly
EX $30   NM $50   MIP $100

Popeye Hand Puppet, 1950s, Gund, plush
EX $15   NM $40   MIP $100

Popeye Hand Puppet, 1960s, Gund, Popeye's head on cloth body
EX $20   NM $50   MIP $120

Popeye Hi-Pop Ball, 1981, Ja-Ru
EX $4   NM $8   MIP $25

Popeye in Boat, 1970s, Corgi
EX $10   NM $20   MIP $60

Popeye Jump-Up, 1970s, Imperial
EX $8   NM $20   MIP $50

Popeye Magic Play Around, 1950s, Amsco, characters w/magnetic bases that slide across play set
EX $35   NM $70   MIP $150

Popeye Marionette, Create-Japan, wood
EX $100   NM $200   MIP $425

Popeye Marionette, 1950s, Gund, 11-1/2" tall
EX $75   NM $150   MIP $325

Popeye Mini Winder, 1980, Durham
EX $4   NM $10   MIP $30

Popeye Model Kit, 1964, Tokyo Plamo, #808
EX $60   NM $120   MIP $250

Popeye on Tricycle, Linemar, 4-1/2", tin wind-up w/celluloid arms and legs, bell rings behind Popeye
EX $350   NM $750   MIP $1000

Popeye One Man Band, 1980s, Larami
EX $6   NM $10   MIP $30

Popeye Paddle Ball, 1984, Larami, w/color photo of Popeye
EX $7   NM $15   MIP $40

Popeye Paint By Numbers, 1960s, Hasbro
EX $12   NM $25   MIP $75

Popeye Paint-By-Numbers, 1981, Hasbro
EX $8   NM $13   MIP $30

Popeye Painting Kit, 1980, Avalon
EX $6   NM $10   MIP $25

Popeye Pencil-By-Numbers, 1979, Hasbro
EX $10   NM $25   MIP $60

Popeye Peppy Puppet, 1970, Kohner
EX $12   NM $25   MIP $50

Popeye Pipe, 1940s, red wooden
EX $20   NM $40   MIP $100

Popeye Pipe, 1958, Micro-Lite-KFS
EX $12   NM $30   MIP $100

Popeye Pipe, 1970, Edmonton Pipe, figural head
EX $15   NM $25   MIP $60

Popeye Pipe, 1970s, MSS, plastic, white
EX $8   NM $20   MIP $50

Popeye Pipe, 1970s, KFS, plastic kazoo, red and blue
EX $6   NM $20   MIP $50

Popeye Pipe, 1980, Harmony
EX $6   NM $10   MIP $20

Popeye Pistol, Delcast, Super mini cap w/24 caps No. 807-BB
EX $15   NM $30   MIP $80

Popeye Play Set, 1979, Cribmates, Popeye, Olive Oyl, and Swee'Pea squeak toys, mirror, rattle and pillow
EX $15   NM $30   MIP $60

Popeye Presto Paints, 1961, Kenner
EX $15   NM $50   MIP $70

Popeye Pull Toy, 1950s, Metal Masters, 10-1/2" x 11-1/2", xylophone, wood w/paper litho labels, metal wheels
EX $150   NM $225   MIP $500

Popeye Puppet, Kohner, pull string, Popeye jumps
EX $10   NM $15   MIP $30

Popeye Push Puppet, 1960, Kohner, 4" tall

EX $20 NM $45 MIP $90

(KP Photo)

Popeye Sailboat, 1976, KFS

EX $9 NM $15 MIP $60

Popeye Service Station, 1979, Larami

EX $8 NM $25 MIP $70

Popeye Soaky, 1960s, Colgate-Palmolive

EX $15 NM $40 MIP $75

(KP Photo)

Popeye Soaky, 1987, KFS, British

EX $12 NM $20 MIP $45

Popeye Sparkler, 1959, Chein

EX $90 NM $125 MIP $200

Popeye Speed Boat, 1981, Harmony

EX $10 NM $16 MIP $40

Popeye Speedboard Pull Toy, 1960s

EX $175 NM $375 MIP $700

Popeye Sports Car, 1950s, Linemar

EX $225 NM $425 MIP $800

Popeye Squeeze Toy, 1950s, Rempel, 8" tall, vinyl

EX $25 NM $50 MIP $120

Popeye Squeeze Toy, 1979, Cribmates, Popeye on a stick

EX $8 NM $15 MIP $40

Popeye Supergyro, 1980s, Larami

EX $6 NM $10 MIP $25

Popeye the Pilot, 1940s, Chein, tin wind-up airplane, 8" long, 8" wingspan

EX $750 NM $1200 MIP $1600

Popeye the Weatherman Colorforms, 1959, Colorforms

EX $20 NM $50 MIP $120

Popeye Tiles, 1970s, Italy, 3" x 5" w/stand

EX $15 NM $35 MIP $70

Popeye Toboggan, 1979, KFS

EX $6 NM $10 MIP $30

Popeye Train Pull Toy, Larami

EX $150 NM $250 MIP $450

Popeye Train Set, 1973, Larami

EX $6 NM $15 MIP $50

Popeye Transit Co. Moving Van, 1950, Linemar, tin

EX $550 NM $900 MIP $1300

Popeye Tricky Trapeze, 1970, Kohner

EX $15 NM $35 MIP $80

Popeye Tricky Walker, 1960s, Jaymar, plastic

EX $10 NM $25 MIP $60

Popeye Tricycling, 1950s, Linemar

EX $400 NM $650 MIP $1000

Popeye Tug and Dingy Pull Toy, 1950s, Fisher-Price, wood

EX $135 NM $225 MIP $375

Popeye Tugboat, 1961, Ideal, inflatable

EX $15 NM $35 MIP $70

(KP Photo)

Popeye TV Cartoon Kit, 1966, Colorforms

EX $20 NM $40 MIP $80

Popeye TV Magic Putty, 1970s, MSS

EX $6 NM $10 MIP $15

Popeye Water Colors, 1933, American Crayon

EX $25 NM $60 MIP $110

Popeye Water Sprinkler, 1960s, KFS, w/rubbber head

EX $15 NM $25 MIP $40

Popeye's Official Wallet, 1959, KFS

EX $10 NM $30 MIP $70

Popeye's Spinach Wagon, 1980, Lesney/Matchbox, CS-13, 2-3/4" x 2-7/8"

EX $8 NM $15 MIP $40

Popeye's Submarine, 1973, Larami

EX $10 NM $30 MIP $60

Punch Ball, 1970s, National Latex

EX $10 NM $20 MIP $50

Punch'Em Talking Rattle Toy, 1950s, Sanitoy

EX $15 NM $35 MIP $85

Punching Bag, 1960s, Dartmore

EX $15 NM $30 MIP $60

Puppetforms, 1950s, Colorforms

EX $25 NM $40 MIP $80

Puzzle, 1945, Jaymar, 22" x 13-1/2", Popeye

EX $40 NM $100 MIP $200

Puzzle, 1959, England, 120 pieces, "What a Catch"

EX $25 NM $55 MIP $80

Puzzle, 1960s, Roalex, tile

EX $20 NM $35 MIP $50

Puzzle, 1962, Tower Press, wood, Popeye

EX $10 NM $16 MIP $30

Puzzle, 1973, Larami, magnetic

EX $6 NM $15 MIP $40

Puzzle, 1976, American Pub. Corp., 5-1/2" round can

EX $10 NM $20 MIP $35

Puzzle, 1977, Opera Mundi, tile, "Popeye's Riddle"

EX $11 NM $18 MIP $30

Puzzle, 1978, Waddington's House of Games, 27" x 18" floor puzzle

EX $8 NM $15 MIP $35

Puzzle, 1981, Ja-Ru, comic

EX $6 NM $12 MIP $30

Puzzle, 1987, Illco, 11 pieces, Olive 3-D

EX $6 NM $10 MIP $20

Puzzle, 1987, Illco, 11 pieces, Popeye 3-D

EX $6 NM $10 MIP $20

Puzzle, 1987, Ja-Ru, Popeye and Son TV show

EX $5 NM $10 MIP $20

Puzzle, 1989, Ja-Ru, "Birthday Cake and Ice Cream"

EX $6 NM $10 MIP $20

Puzzle, 1989, Ja-Ru, boating and dancing

EX $6 NM $10 MIP $20

Puzzle, 1991, Jaymar, 63 pieces, jumbo, Popeye's boat

EX $6 NM $12 MIP $25

Puzzle, 1991, Jaymar, 63 pieces, jumbo, Popeye rescues Olive
EX $6   NM $10   MIP $20

Puzzle, 1991, Jaymar, 63 pieces, Popeye blowing candles
EX $6   NM $10   MIP $20

Puzzle, 1991, Jaymar, 63 pieces, jumbo, Popeye and Olive surfing
EX $6   NM $10   MIP $20

Puzzle, 1991, Jaymar, Christmas scene, inlaid, 12 pieces
EX $6   NM $10   MIP $20

Puzzle, 1991, Jaymar, 12 pieces, Popeye holding turkey
EX $6   NM $10   MIP $20

Puzzle, 1991, Jaymar, 12 pieces, Popeye gang swimming
EX $6   NM $10   MIP $20

Race Set, 1989, Ja-Ru
EX $6   NM $12   MIP $35

Road Building Set, 1979, Larami
EX $6   NM $12   MIP $35

Roller Skating Popeye, 1950s, Linemar
EX $150   NM $225   MIP $350

Roly Poly Popeye, 1940s, w/beaded arms and celluloid
EX $100   NM $175   MIP $300

Sailboats, 1981, Larami
EX $6   NM $10   MIP $25

Sailor's Knife, 1981, Ja-Ru
EX $10   NM $20   MIP $45

Screen-A Show Projector, 1973, Denys Fisher
EX $35   NM $90   MIP $160

Sea Hag Hand Puppet, 1987, Presents
EX $15   NM $35   MIP $110

Shaving Kit, 1979, Larami
EX $6   NM $10   MIP $35

Sling Darts, KFS
EX $20   NM $35   MIP $70

Soapy Popeye Boat, 1950s, Kerk Guild
EX $200   NM $300   MIP $500

Squirt Face, 1981, Ja-Ru
EX $6   NM $10   MIP $20

Stitch-A-Story, KFS
EX $12   NM $20   MIP $35

Sun-Eze Pictures, 1962, Tillman Toy
EX $10   NM $25   MIP $60

Sunglasses, 1980s, Larami, red, yellow, or blue
EX $6   NM $10   MIP $20

Super Race w/Launcher, 1980, Fleetwood
EX $6   NM $12   MIP $25

Surf Rider, 1979, Wet Set-Zee Toys
EX $10   NM $25   MIP $65

Swee'Pea Bean Bag, 1974, Dakin
EX $10   NM $25   MIP $65

Swee'Pea Hand Puppet, 1960s, Gund, bonnet on head, cloth body decorated w/baby lambs
EX $15   NM $40   MIP $100

Swee'Pea Hand Puppet, 1987, Presents
EX $8   NM $25   MIP $70

Swee'Pea Hi-Pop Ball, 1981, Ja-Ru
EX $6   NM $12   MIP $30

Swee'Pea Squeak Toy, 1970s, frowning or smiling
EX $12   NM $25   MIP $75

Swirler Flying Barrel Toy, 1980, Imperial
EX $8   NM $15   MIP $30

Talking View-Master Set, 1962, GAF, old type
EX $12   NM $25   MIP $70

Tambourine, 1980s, Larami
EX $6   NM $10   MIP $20

Tambourine, 1990, Santa Cruz
EX $6   NM $10   MIP $20

Target Ball, 1981, Ja-Ru
EX $6   NM $10   MIP $20

Telephone, 1982, Comvu
EX $15   NM $30   MIP $70

Telescope, 1973, Larami
EX $10   NM $25   MIP $60

Thimble Theatre Cut-Outs, 1950s, Aldon
EX $50   NM $85   MIP $140

Toy Watch, 1987, Sekonda-Japan, comic strip band
EX $30   NM $50   MIP $100

Trace and Color, 1980, Fleetwood
EX $6   NM $10   MIP $20

Trumpet Bubble Blower, 1984, Larami, pink or yellow pan
EX $6   NM $12   MIP $25

Tube-A-Loonies, 1973, Larami, five small tubes on card
EX $6   NM $15   MIP $35

Turn-A-Scope, 1979, Larami
EX $6   NM $20   MIP $50

TV Set w/Three Film Scrolls, 1957
EX $12   NM $20   MIP $50

View-Master Set, 1959, Sawyers, three reels
EX $15   NM $30   MIP $80

View-Master Set, 1959, GAF, "The Fish Story"
EX $8   NM $15   MIP $40

View-Master Set, 1959, GAF, "The Hunting Bird"
EX $8   NM $15   MIP $40

View-Master Set, 1962, GAF, three pack
EX $8   NM $15   MIP $50

Whistling Flashlights, 1960s, Bantam-Lite, six w/display
EX $300   NM $500   MIP $800

Whistling Wing Ding, 1950s, Mego
EX $20   NM $40   MIP $80

Wimpy Dog Toy, 1986, Petex
EX $8   NM $13   MIP $25

Wimpy Hand Puppet, 1950s, Gund, fabric hand cover, vinyl squeaker head and voice
EX $15   NM $50   MIP $120

Wimpy Hand Puppet, 1960s, Gund, cloth body
EX $15   NM $40   MIP $80

Wimpy Hand Puppet, 1987, Presents
EX $8   NM $13   MIP $90

Wimpy Ring, 1949, Post Toasties
EX $12   NM $45   MIP $110

Wimpy Squeeze Toy, 1950s, Rempel, vinyl
EX $20   NM $40   MIP $80

Wimpy Squeeze Toy, 1979, Cribmates
EX $12   NM $20   MIP $40

Wimpy Tugboat, 1961, Ideal, inflatable
EX $20   NM $40   MIP $60

Wood Slate, 1983, Ja-Ru
EX $6   NM $15   MIP $40

WATCH

Popeye Wristwatch, 1964, Bradley, #308, green case
EX $115   NM $210   MIP $375

Popeye Wristwatch, 1979, Bradley
EX $60   NM $110   MIP $170

Popeye Wristwatch, 1987, Unique, Popeye's head pops open, digital
EX $12   NM $30   MIP $80

Popeye Wristwatch, 1990, KFS-Japan, Popeye in ship's wheel
EX $40   NM $80   MIP $130

Popeye Wristwatch, 1991, Armitron
EX $20   NM $35   MIP $80

Porky Pig

DOLL

Porky Pig Doll, 1950, Gund, 14" tall
EX $60   NM $120   MIP $225

Porky Pig Doll, 1960s, Mattel, 17", cloth, vinyl head
EX $15   NM $35   MIP $85

Porky Pig Doll, 1968, Dakin, 7-3/4" tall in black velvet jacket
EX $15   NM $35   MIP $85

FIGURES

Porky and Petunia Figures, 1975, Warner Bros., 4-1/2" tall

EX $9   NM $16   MIP $50

TOY

Porky Pig Soaky

EX $15   NM $35   MIP $75

Porky Pig Umbrella, 1940s, hard plastic 3" figure on end, Porky and Bugs printed in red cloth

EX $100   NM $150   MIP $200

Quick Draw McGraw

ACCESSORIES

Cereal Box, 1960, Kellogg's

EX $250   NM $400   MIP $650

BANK

Baba Looey Bank, 1960s, Knickerbocker, 9" tall, vinyl, plastic head

EX $16   NM $32   MIP $80

Quick Draw McGraw Bank, 1960, 9-1/2", plastic, orange, white, and blue

EX $40   NM $75   MIP $150

BOOK

Quick Draw McGraw Book, 1960, Whitman

EX $30   NM $45   MIP $90

DOLL

Auggie Doggie Doll, 1959, Knickerbocker, 10" tall, plush w/vinyl face

EX $40   NM $85   MIP $150

Baba Looey Doll, 1959, Knickerbocker, 20" tall, plush w/vinyl donkey ears and sombrero

EX $75   NM $125   MIP $250

Blabber Doll, 1959, Knickerbocker, 15" tall, plush w/vinyl face

EX $50   NM $100   MIP $180

Quick Draw McGraw Doll, 1959, Knickerbocker, 16", plush w/vinyl face, cowboy hat

EX $150   NM $300   MIP $450

Scooper Doll, 1959, Knickerbocker, 20", plush w/vinyl face

EX $75   NM $100   MIP $175

TOY

Auggie Doggie Soaky, 1960s, Purex, 10" tall, plastic

EX $15   NM $45   MIP $90

Blabber Soaky, 1960s, Purex, 10-1/2" tall, plastic

EX $18   NM $45   MIP $100

Quick Draw McGraw Moving Target Game, 1960s, Knickerbocker

EX $125   NM $175   MIP $300

Quick Draw Mold and Model Cast Set, 1960

EX $75   NM $100   MIP $150

Raggedy Ann and Andy

ACCESSORIES

Raggedy Ann/Andy Wastebasket, 1972, tin

EX $8   NM $20   MIP $60

BANK

Raggedy Andy Bank, Play Pal, 11"

EX $15   NM $20   MIP $50

Raggedy Ann Bank, 1974, Play Pal, 11"

EX $15   NM $20   MIP $50

BOOK

Raggedy Ann Coloring Book, 1968

EX $6   NM $12   MIP $50

Raggedy Ann/Andy Paper Doll Book, 1974, Whitman, #1962

EX $15   NM $25   MIP $75

FIGURES

Raggedy Andy Figure, 1970s, rubber/wire, 4" tall

EX $5   NM $10   MIP $35

TOY

Raggedy Andy Puppet, 1975, Dakin, cloth

EX $20   NM $35   MIP $70

Raggedy Ann Puppet, 1975, Dakin, cloth

EX $20   NM $35   MIP $70

Raggedy Ann/Andy Record Player, square, cardboard

EX $45   NM $100   MIP $175

Raggedy Ann/Andy Record Player, 1950s, plastic, heart shaped

EX $100   NM $150   MIP $275

Road Runner and Wile E. Coyote

ACCESSORIES

Road Runner and Coyote Lamp, 1977, 12-1/2", figures standing on base

EX $40   NM $100   MIP $250

Road Runner Costume, 1960s, Collegeville

EX $30   NM $50   MIP $100

Wile E. Coyote Night Light, 1980s, Applause

EX $20   NM $45   MIP $90

BANK

Road Runner Bank, standing on base

EX $8   NM $15   MIP $50

DOLL

Road Runner Doll, 1971, Mighty Star, 13" tall

EX $12   NM $30   MIP $90

Wile E. Coyote Doll, 1970, Dakin, on explosive box

EX $40   NM $75   MIP $150

Wile E. Coyote Doll, 1971, Mighty Star, 18" tall, plush

EX $40   NM $75   MIP $150

FIGURES

Road Runner Figure, Dakin, plastic, Cartoon Theater

EX $18   NM $50   MIP $125

Road Runner Figure, 1968, Dakin, 8-3/4" tall

EX $18   NM $50   MIP $125

Road Runner Figure, 1971, Dakin, Goofy Gram

EX $15   NM $50   MIP $125

Wile E. Coyote and Road Runner Figures, 1979, Royal Crown, 7" tall, each

EX $15   NM $30   MIP $85

Wile E. Coyote Figure, 1968, Dakin, 10" tall

EX $30   NM $75   MIP $180

Wile E. Coyote Figure, 1971, Dakin, Goofy Gram, fused bomb in right hand

EX $20   NM $50   MIP $125

Wile E. Coyote Figure, 1976, Dakin, Cartoon Theater

EX $18   NM $32   MIP $100

TOY

Road Runner Hand Puppet, 1970s, Japanese, 10", vinyl head

EX $8   NM $20   MIP $60

Wile E. Coyote Hand Puppet, 1970s, Japanese, 10", vinyl head

EX $10   NM $20   MIP $60

Rocky

DOLL

Apollo Creed Doll, 1983, Phoenix Toys, 8" tall

EX $5   NM $10   MIP $25

Clubber Lang Doll, 1983, Phoenix Toys, 8" tall

EX $6   NM $12   MIP $35

Rocky Balboa Doll, 1983, Phoenix Toys, 8" tall

EX $7   NM $15   MIP $35

Roger Rabbit

ACCESSORIES

Baby Herman and Roger Rabbit Mug, Applause
EX $5 NM $8 MIP $15

Jessica Zipper Pull
EX $5 NM $10 MIP $15

BOOK

Paint w/Water Book, Golden, #1702
EX $6 NM $12 MIP $30

Trace and Color Book, Golden, #2355
EX $5 NM $10 MIP $30

DOLL

Benny the Cab Doll, 1988, Applause, 6" long
EX $6 NM $12 MIP $30

Roger Rabbit Doll, Applause, 8-1/2" tall
EX $7 NM $15 MIP $60

Roger Rabbit Doll, Applause, 17" tall
EX $10 NM $30 MIP $125

FIGURES

Baby Herman Figure, 1987, LJN, 6" figure on card
EX $9 NM $20 MIP $35

Baby Herman Figure, 1988, LJN, ceramic
EX $9 NM $15 MIP $35

Boss Weasel Figure, 1988, LJN, 4" bendable
EX $4 NM $10 MIP $20

Eddie Valiant Figure, 1988, LJN, 4", flexible
EX $5 NM $10 MIP $20

Judge Doom Figure, 1988, LJN, 4" bendable
EX $4 NM $8 MIP $24

Roger Rabbit Figure, 1988, LJN, 4" bendable
EX $4 NM $10 MIP $30

Smart Guy Figure, 1988, LJN, flexible
EX $4 NM $8 MIP $15

GAME

Dip Flip Game, LJN
EX $8 NM $15 MIP $30

Who Framed Roger Rabbit Game, 1988, Milton Bradley, low production run
EX $75 NM $125 MIP $200

TOY

Animates, 1988, Doom, Roger, Eddie and Smart Guy, each
EX $5 NM $8 MIP $15

Benny the Cab, LJN
EX $20 NM $40 MIP $75

Eddie Valiant Animate, 1988, LJN, 6" tall, bendable
EX $4 NM $8 MIP $15

Jessica License Plate
EX $6 NM $12 MIP $20

Judge Doom Animate, 1988, LJN, 6" tall poseable
EX $6 NM $12 MIP $25

Paint-A-Cel Set, Benny the Cab and Roger pictures
EX $8 NM $15 MIP $60

Roger Rabbit Animate, 1988, LJN, 6" poseable
EX $4 NM $10 MIP $20

Roger Rabbit Blow-Up Buddy, 36" tall
EX $6 NM $12 MIP $30

Roger Wacky Head Puppets, Applause, hand puppets
EX $6 NM $12 MIP $50

Roger Wind-Up, 1988, Matsudaya
EX $18 NM $35 MIP $100

Talking Roger in Benny the Cab, 17" tall
EX $12 NM $35 MIP $100

WATCH

Roger Rabbit Bullet Hole Wristwatch, 1987, Shiraka, white case and leather band, in plastic display box
EX $40 NM $85 MIP $160

Roger Rabbit Silhouette Wristwatch, 1987, Shiraka, large gold case, black band
EX $35 NM $80 MIP $160

Rootie Kazootie

BOOK

Cut-Out Coloring Book, 1952, Western Publishing, Funtime Books, Rootie Kazootie, red cover - kids drawing, baseball bat and glove
EX $10 NM $20 MIP $30

Cut-Out Coloring Book, 1954, Western Publishing, Funtime Books, Rootie Kazootie and his Wonderful Games, green cover - pin the tail on the donkey
EX $10 NM $20 MIP $30

Little Golden Book, 1953, Simon & Schuster, Rootie Kazootie Detective
EX $10 NM $20 MIP $60

Little Golden Book, 1954, Simon & Schuster, Rootie Kazootie Baseball Star, #190
EX $10 NM $30 MIP $60

Little Golden Book, 1955, Simon & Schuster, Rootie Kazootie Joins the Circus
EX $10 NM $20 MIP $60

BUTTON

Rootie Kazootie Club Button, 1950s, 1" tin litho
EX $18 NM $42 MIP $80

TOY

Rootie Kazootie Doll, 1950s, Effanbee, cloth body, vinyl head and hands, baseball outfit
EX $75 NM $125 MIP $200

Rootie Kazootie Drum, 1950s, 8" diameter drum, Rootie on the drum head
EX $40 NM $75 MIP $150

Rootie Kazootie Fishing Tackle Box, 1950s, RK Inc., tin litho, bright graphics
EX $15 NM $30 MIP $70

Ruff and Reddy

BOOK

Ruff and Reddy Go To A Party Tell-A-Tale Book, 1958, Whitman
EX $15 NM $35 MIP $70

TOY

Ruff and Reddy Draw Cartoon Set Color, Wonder Art
EX $50 NM $85 MIP $175

Ruff and Reddy Magic Rub-Off Picture Set, 1958, Transogram
EX $45 NM $80 MIP $175

Secret Squirrel

TOY

Secret Squirrel Bubble Club Soaky, 1960s, Purex
EX $20 NM $35 MIP $90

Secret Squirrel Push Puppet, 1960s, Kohner, plastic figure in white coat, blue hat holding binoculars
EX $20 NM $40 MIP $80

Secret Squirrel Puzzle, 1967, frame tray
EX $15 NM $30 MIP $65

Secret Squirrel Ray Gun
EX $25 NM $50 MIP $100

Shirley Temple

ACCESSORIES

Doll Trunk, 18" tall w/"Our Little Girl" decal on the side, photo of Shirley
EX $100 NM $200 MIP $375

Doll Wardrobe Trunk, 20" heavy cardboard/wood steamer trunk for 18" doll, leather strap, metal latch w/lock and key, two drawers, and four cardboard hangers
EX $120 NM $200 MIP $375

Hanger, cardboard; picture of Shirley Temple, came w/all outfits
EX $15   NM $25   MIP $60

Pin, Reliable, "The World's Darling/Genuine Shirley Temple, A Reliable Doll"
EX $65   NM $80   MIP $100

Purse, 1950s, red, white, and black w/Shirley Temple lettering
EX $30   NM $40   MIP $80

Texas Ranger/Cowgirl Gun, came w/Texas Ranger outfit
EX $35   NM $70   MIP $200

BOOK

Shirley Temple Treasury Book, 1959, Random House
EX $20   NM $30   MIP $75

Shirley Temple's Busy Book, 1958, Saalfield, Activity book, #5326, Model No. 5326
EX $40   NM $50   MIP $80

DOLL

Captain January Doll, Ideal, 22", dark blue sailor suit w/white trim
EX $700   NM $910   MIP $1600

Captain January Doll, 1957, Ideal, 12", vinyl head, dark blond hair, plastic body, arms and legs
EX $175   NM $225   MIP $425

Heidi Doll, 1957, Ideal, 12", vinyl head, dark blonde hair and plastic body, arms and legs
EX $200   NM $285   MIP $425

Heidi Doll, 1960-61, 17"
EX $250   NM $325   MIP $475

Little Colonel Doll, 13", taffeta outfit, variations in the collar, ruffles and pantaloons
EX $775   NM $900   MIP $2200

Little Colonel Doll, Alexander, 13", pink hat w/ruffle, pink dress and bloomers
EX $475   NM $575   MIP $1750

Little Colonel Doll, 20", blue organdy, bonnet w/pink feather
EX $925   NM $1100   MIP $2400

Little Colonel Doll, 13", variations in pantaloons, bonnets and shoes
EX $775   NM $900   MIP $2200

Rebecca of Sunnybrook Farm Doll, 1957, 12" vinyl, blue bib overalls, blue polka dot blouse, straw hat
EX $125   NM $230   MIP $425

Rebecca of Sunnybrook Farm Doll, 1957, 12" vinyl, red felt jumper and plastic purse
EX $175   NM $230   MIP $425

Rebecca of Sunnybrook Farm Doll, 1957, 12" vinyl, blue bib overalls w/plaid blouse, black low shoes
EX $125   NM $185   MIP $325

Rebecca of Sunnybrook Farm Doll, 1957, Ideal, 12", vinyl head, dark blonde hair, plastic body, arms and legs
EX $175   NM $230   MIP $425

Shirley Temple Baby, 16", mohair wig, flirty eyes
EX $525   NM $800   MIP $2200

Shirley Temple Baby, 20", composition head, arms and legs, cloth body
EX $700   NM $975   MIP $2450

Shirley Temple Baby, Ideal, 18", painted hair, chubby toddler body w/dimpled cheeks, flirty eyes, dressed in pink organdy w/silk ribbons
EX $600   NM $925   MIP $2000

Shirley Temple Doll, Reliable (Ideal/Canada), 13", yellow organdy dress, silk ribbon
EX $460   NM $760   MIP $1600

Shirley Temple Doll, Made in Japan, 8" composition w/pink silk undies
EX $175   NM $210   MIP $425

Shirley Temple Doll, 27" composition w/pink taffeta, bonnet and pantaloons
EX $850   NM $1250   MIP $2750

Shirley Temple Doll, 22" composition w/facial molding
EX $600   NM $800   MIP $1600

Shirley Temple Doll, 20" composition w/facial molding
EX $500   NM $750   MIP $1600

Shirley Temple Doll, 18" composition w/facial molding
EX $525   NM $700   MIP $1500

Shirley Temple Doll, 16", black velveteen coat and hat
EX $180   NM $350   MIP $1500

Shirley Temple Doll, 16", light blue organdy w/pink hemstitching and silk ribbons
EX $275   NM $575   MIP $1500

Shirley Temple Doll, 13", pleated pique w/white applique
EX $275   NM $550   MIP $1450

Shirley Temple Doll, Ideal, 22" jointed, composition body, blonde mohair, hazel glass eyes, open mouth, red/white polka dot dress
EX $225   NM $500   MIP $1450

Shirley Temple Doll, Ideal, 19" vinyl, twinkle eyes, dressed in pink nylon, black purse
EX $180   NM $340   MIP $625

Shirley Temple Doll, 16" composition
EX $375   NM $675   MIP $1450

Shirley Temple Doll, 1957, 12", vinyl, molded hands and feet, synthetic rooted wig, pink slip trimmed w/lace
EX $125   NM $225   MIP $525

Shirley Temple Doll, 1957, 12" vinyl, molded hands and feet, synthetic rooted wig, two piece slip/undies
EX $110   NM $225   MIP $500

Shirley Temple Doll, 1957, 12" vinyl, pink/blue nylon dress w/daisy appliques, hat, purse
EX $125   NM $250   MIP $525

Shirley Temple Doll, 1958, 15" vinyl, red nylon dress w/floral detailing at collar, hair ribbon, purse
EX $110   NM $210   MIP $400

Shirley Temple Doll, 1958, Ideal, 15" vinyl, yellow nylon dress trimmed w/lace and ribbon around skirt
EX $175   NM $320   MIP $575

Shirley Temple Doll, 1958-59, Ideal, 17" vinyl, brown twinkle eyes, pink/blue dress
EX $210   NM $320   MIP $725

Shirley Temple Doll, 1960, 15" vinyl, blue jumper w/red/white gingham blouse and pocket facing
EX $100   NM $200   MIP $400

Shirley Temple Doll, 1960s, 17", yellow party dress, white purse w/Shirley Temple lettering
EX $225   NM $325   MIP $725

Shirley Temple Doll, 1960s, Ideal, 17", yellow nylon dress and Twinkle Eyes wrist tag
EX $210   NM $320   MIP $725

Shirley Temple Doll, 1972, Ideal/Hong Kong, 16", vinyl, red polka dot dress, Stand Up and Cheer
EX $155   NM $185   MIP $325

Shirley Temple Doll, 1972, Ideal/Hong Kong, 15" vinyl manufactured for Montgomery Ward's
EX $175   NM $210   MIP $400

Stand Up and Cheer Doll, 11" composition, short rayon dress w/blue polka dots
EX $675   NM $925   MIP $1700

Texas Ranger Doll, 17", plaid shirt, leather vest w/trim
EX $550   NM $700   MIP $1600

Texas Ranger Doll, 20", plaid shirt, leather vest w/trim, chaps, holster, and metal gun
EX $700   NM $950   MIP $2100

Texas Ranger/Cowgirl Doll, 11", plaid cotton shirt, leather vest, chaps, holster, metal gun, felt 10 gallon hat w/"Ride 'Em Cowboy" printed band
EX $450   NM $750   MIP $2100

Wee Willie Winkie Doll, 1957, Ideal, 12", vinyl head, dark blond hair, plastic body, arms and legs
EX $190   NM $250   MIP $500

DOLL CLOTHING

Ballerina Outfit, 1957-58, blue/green nylon and tulle, flower hair piece; fits 12" vinyl doll
EX $80   NM $85   MIP $120

Bright Eyes Outfit, white corduroy coat and hat w/original pin, fits 16" doll
EX $100   NM $150   MIP $250

Coat and Hat, velveteen coat and hat w/red buttons; fits 16" doll
EX $80   NM $90   MIP $130

Coat and Hat, 1958, Ideal, red corduroy coat and hat, fits 12" doll
EX $60   NM $70   MIP $95

Dress, 1958, Ideal, nylon w/loop details; fits 12" doll
EX $65   NM $80   MIP $110

Dress, Jacket, and Purse, 1959, nylon
EX $65   NM $75   MIP $100

Jumper and Blouse, 1959, Ideal, blue velveteen jumper w/floral applique, cotton blouse
EX $60   NM $70   MIP $100

Jumpsuit, red w/white flowers
EX $80   NM $85   MIP $120

Jumpsuit, red/white checkered
EX $35   NM $40   MIP $70

Littlest Rebel Outfit, checkered dress, rick rack ribbon on sleeves, lace collar and apron
EX $85   NM $110   MIP $475

Nightcoat and Cap, 1958-59, Ideal, flannel; fits 12" doll
EX $60   NM $70   MIP $100

Rain Cape and Umbrella, plaid red or blue rain cape w/hood and matching umbrella; fits 18" doll
EX $80   NM $100   MIP $195

Wool Coat, fits 18" dolls, from Little Miss Marker
EX $60   NM $90   MIP $200

PAPER DOLLS

Paper Doll Book, 1976, Whitman, #1986, Model No. 1986
EX $8   NM $15   MIP $50

Paper Dolls, 1958, Saalfield, #4435, Model No. 4435
EX $35   NM $50   MIP $180

Paper Dolls, 1959, Saalfield, 18" folding doll w/easel, costumes, and accessories, #5110, Model No. 5110
EX $10   NM $40   MIP $120

Shirley Temple Dolls and Dresses, 1960, Saalfield, two dolls

w/different outfits, #1789, Model No. 1789
EX $12   NM $20   MIP $50

PHOTOGRAPH

Promo Photo, 8" x 10" photo of Shirley w/facsimile autograph, came w/all composition dolls and outfits
EX $30   NM $45   MIP $75

Sleeping Beauty

ACCESSORIES

Sleeping Beauty Alarm Clock, 1950s, Phinney-Walker, 2-1/2" x 4" x 4-1/2" tall, Sleeping Beauty surrounded by three birds and petting a rabbit
EX $75   NM $125   MIP $250

Sleeping Beauty Doll Crib Mattress, 1960s, 9" x 17", Sleeping Beauty and the fairies
EX $15   NM $25   MIP $50

BOOK

Sleeping Beauty Sticker Fun Book, 1959, Whitman
EX $15   NM $30   MIP $75

TOY

Fairy Godmother Hand Puppets, 1958, set of three: 10-1/2" tall, Flora, Merryweather, and Fauna, each
EX $75   NM $125   MIP $250

King Huber/King Stefan Hand Puppets, 1956, Gund, 10" tall, molded rubber heads w/fabric hand cover
EX $30   NM $75   MIP $150

Puzzle, 1958, Whitman, 11-1/2" x 14-1/2", Three Good Fairies circling around a baby in a crib
EX $15   NM $35   MIP $80

Puzzle, 1958, Whitman, 11-1/2" x 14-1/2", Sleeping Beauty w/Prince Phillip and Three Good Fairies circling
EX $15   NM $35   MIP $80

Puzzle, 1958, Whitman, 11-1/2" x 14-1/2", Sleeping Beauty w/forest animals
EX $15   NM $35   MIP $80

Sleeping Beauty Jack-In-The-Box, 1980s, Enesco, Princess Aurora, wooden box, plays "Once Upon A Dream"
EX $65   NM $125   MIP $250

Sleeping Beauty Magic Paint Set, Whitman
EX $25   NM $50   MIP $90

Sleeping Beauty Squeeze Toy, 1959, Dell, 4" x 4" x 5" tall, rubber, Sleeping Beauty w/rabbit
EX $30   NM $60   MIP $90

Smokey Bear

BANK

Smokey Bank, 6" tall, china
EX $50   NM $100   MIP $175

BOOK

Smokey Bear and the Campers Book, 1961, Golden
EX $10   NM $20   MIP $50

Smokey Bear Coloring Book, 1958, Whitman
EX $25   NM $40   MIP $75

DOLL

Smokey Doll, 1950s, Ideal, 15" plush, vinyl face
EX $100   NM $175   MIP $350

FIGURES

Smokey Bobbing Head Figure, 1960s, 6-1/4" tall
EX $100   NM $250   MIP $450

Smokey Figure, 1971, Dakin, figure on a tree stump
EX $30   NM $75   MIP $185

TOY

Smokey Bear Record, Peter Pan, 45 rpm
EX $5   NM $15   MIP $35

Smokey Soaky, 1960s, 9" tall, plastic
EX $10   NM $25   MIP $60

WATCH

Smokey Wristwatch, 1960s, Hawthorne
EX $75   NM $150   MIP $300

Snow White and the Seven Dwarfs

ACCESSORIES

Dopey Lamp, 1940s, 9" tall, ceramic base w/Dopey
EX $125   NM $275   MIP $475

Pencil Box, Venus Pencil, 3" x 8" x 1"
EX $75   NM $125   MIP $200

Snow White Mirror, 1940s, 9-1/2", plastic handle
EX $30   NM $100   MIP $200

DOLL

Dopey Doll, Krueger, 14" tall
EX $100   NM $220   MIP $450

Sneezy Doll, Krueger, 14" tall
EX $125   NM $250   MIP $600

Snow White and the Seven Dwarfs Dolls, 1940s, Deluxe, 22" Snow White and 7" dwarfs
EX $1000   NM $1500   MIP $2500

Snow White Doll, Horsman, 8", in illustrated box
EX $25   NM $50   MIP $125

FIGURES

Dopey Figure, 1960s, ceramic figure and barrel
EX $15   NM $30   MIP $100

TOY

Dopey Rolykin, Marx, 2"
EX $35   NM $75   MIP $125

Dopey Soaky, 1960s, 10" tall
EX $11   NM $30   MIP $80

Happy Toy, YS Toys (Taiwan), battery-operated, Happy fries eggs
EX $50   NM $120   MIP $300

Ironing Board, Wolverine, tin board and cover
EX $15   NM $30   MIP $80

Puzzle, 1960s, Jaymar, 11" x 14"
EX $20   NM $35   MIP $65

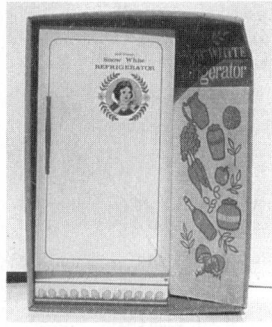

(KP Photo)

Refrigerator, 1970s, Wolverine, 15", tin, single door, white and yellow depicting Snow White
EX $25   NM $60   MIP $150

Snow White Sewing Set, 1940s, Ontex
EX $30   NM $100   MIP $200

Snow White Sink, 1960s, Wolverine, tin
EX $15   NM $30   MIP $75

Snow White Soaky
EX $15   NM $40   MIP $80

Tea Set, 1960s, Marx, teapot, five saucers, large plates and tea cups
EX $40   NM $70   MIP $175

Spider-Man

ACCESSORIES

Button, 1966, Button World, 3", "Superhero Club"
EX $15   NM $35   MIP $75

Crazy Foam, 1974, American Aerosol
EX $10   NM $30   MIP $50

BOOKS

Big Little Book, 1976, Whitman, Spider-Man Zaps Mr. Zodiak
EX $5   NM $10   MIP $15

Coloring Book, 1983, Marvel Books, oversized, "The Arms of Doctor Octopus"
EX $10   NM $20   MIP $50

TOY

Costume, 1972, Ben Cooper, plastic costume w/mask
EX $15   NM $30   MIP $45

Fisher-Price Cartoon Viewer, 1985, Fisher-Price, Spider-Man and His Amazing Friends, cartridge for viewer
EX $5   NM $10   MIP $15

Hand Puppet, 1976, Imperial, 9", vinyl head, plastic body
EX $15   NM $35   MIP $90

Mechanical Marvel Super Heroes Spider-Man, 1968, Marx, plastic, wind-up, made in Japan, Model No. 6257
EX $25   NM $60   MIP $100

Radio-Controlled Spider-Man Car, 1977, Marvel, battery-operated red racer w/Spidey driving, Model No. 6852
EX $25   NM $50   MIP $75

Super 8 Film, 1976, Marvel, Spider-Man in King Pinned
EX $7   NM $14   MIP $25

Talking View-Master Set, 1970s, GAF, talking View-Master, six reels w/Spider-Man, Captain America, and Thor
EX $15   NM $30   MIP $50

The Amazing Energized Green Goblin, 1978, Remco, w/Motorized action, web cutter, Goblin Ray gun
EX $50   NM $100   MIP $150

The Amazing Energized Spider-Man, 1978, Remco, w/Motorized Web Climber, plastic bodied Spidey w/raised left hand, no articulation, battery-operated, flashlight, net, clamp
EX $50   NM $100   MIP $150

The Amazing Energized Spider-Man Accessory Pack, 1978, Remco, for Energized Spider-Man, spider trap, spider ray gun, rocket camera, all attach to figure's belt
EX $15   NM $35   MIP $60

The Amazing Energized Spider-Man Copter, 1978, Remco, helicopter-like vehicle
EX $50   NM $125   MIP $175

TOYS

Spider-Man Friction Vehicle, 1968, Marx, tin litho w/Spider-Man figure at wheel
EX $150   NM $300   MIP $500

Sports

DOLL

Dorothy Hamill Doll, 1975, Ideal, 11-1/4" tall
EX $30   NM $55   MIP $100

Evel Knievel Doll, Ideal, 6" tall
EX $20   NM $35   MIP $100

Julius Erving (Dr. J) Doll, 1974
EX $20   NM $40   MIP $100

Wayne Gretzky Doll, Mattel, 12" tall
EX $25   NM $50   MIP $80

WATCH

Muhammed Ali Wristwatch, 1980, Bradley, chrome case, sweep seconds, brown leather band, face shows Ali in trunks and gloves, w/signature beneath
EX $100   NM $175   MIP $300

Steve Canyon

BOOK

Steve Canyon's Interceptor Station Punch Out, 1950s, Golden
EX $75   NM $100   MIP $160

TOY

Jet Helmet, 1959, Ideal, U.S. Air Force helmet w/sun visor and speaker mask
EX $40   NM $80   MIP $150

Steve Canyon Costume, 1959, Halco
EX $25   NM $60   MIP $185

Steve Canyon's Membership Card and Badge, 1/2" x 4" Milton Caniff membership card for the Airagers, Morse code on back, 3" tin litho color badge w/gold feathers w/Steve's face centered
EX $100   NM $150   MIP $220

Superheroes

ACCESSORIES

Aquaman Halloween Costume, 1967, Ben Cooper
EX $35   NM $55   MIP $100

Captain America Halloween Costume, 1967, Ben Cooper
EX $100   NM $200   MIP $375

Comic Book Tattoos, 1967, Topps, Aquaman, Wonder Woman, Superman, or Batman
EX $20   NM $30   MIP $80

Flash Glass, 1978, Pepsi
EX $20   NM $40   MIP $70

Green Lantern Halloween Costume, 1967, Ben Cooper
EX $100   NM $175   MIP $300

Hawkman Button, 1966, Button World, 3", "Hawkman Superhero Club"
EX $20   NM $30   MIP $60

Justice League of America Display Card, 1970, Fleer, cardboard display from inside gumball machine
EX $30   NM $45   MIP $85

Mr. Bubble Superfriends Box, 1984, bubble bath box features Superman, Wonder Woman, Batman, and Robin
EX $20   NM $30   MIP $85

Wonder Woman Glass, 1978, Pepsi, 6"
EX $10   NM $25   MIP $45

Wonder Woman Record, 1977, Peter Pan Records, 33-1/3" rpm record w/comic book
EX $10   NM $30   MIP $50

BOOKS

Aquaman Scourge of the Sea Book, 1968, Whitman, Big Little Book
EX $15   NM $30   MIP $65

GAMES

Marvel Superheroes Card Game, 1978, Milton Bradley
EX $20   NM $30   MIP $90

TOY

Aquaman Jigsaw Puzzle, 1968, Whitman, 100 pieces; Aquaman and Mera
EX $20   NM $40   MIP $70

Marvel Superheroes Colorforms Set, 1983, Colorforms
EX $10   NM $20   MIP $60

Marvel Superheroes Easy Show Projector, 1967, Kenner, projector and three cartridges
EX $150   NM $300   MIP $450

Marvel Superheroes Puzzle, 1967, Milton Bradley, 100 pieces
EX $40   NM $80   MIP $175

Marvel Superheroes Sparkle Paint Set, 1967, Kenner
EX $40   NM $80   MIP $175

Marvel World Adventure Play Set, 1975, Amsco, w/stand-up scenes and figures
EX $100   NM $200   MIP $350

Mechanical Marvel Super Heroes Captain America, 1968, Marx, plastic, wind-up, made in Japan
EX $25   NM $60   MIP $100

Mechanical Marvel Super Heroes Thor, 1968, Marx, plastic, wind-up, made in Japan
EX $25   NM $60   MIP $100

Thor Flashlight, 1976, Marvel, yellow plastic, image of Thor on side, battery-operated
EX $10   NM $20   MIP $30

Superman

ACCESSORIES

Children's Dish Set, 1966, Boonton-ware, 7" plate, 5-1/2" bowl, 3-1/2" cup, all white plastic w/Superman image
EX $50   NM $100   MIP $150

Fan Card, 1950s, National Comics, 5" x 7" promo b/w post card w/signature "Best Wishes, George Reeves"
EX $75   NM $150   MIP $200

Hair Brush, 1976, Avon, Superman handle, illustrated box
EX $15   NM $25   MIP $50

Junior Defense League of America Membership Certificate, 1940s, Superman, Inc., Superman Bread premium, red/blue print and Superman bust and logo on paper, "signed" by Clark Kent
EX $600   NM $1000   MIP $1250

Membership Certificate, 1965, last year of club
EX $175   NM $350   MIP $500

Original Radio Broadcasts Record, 1977, Nostalgia Lane, old Superman radio teleplays, in illustrated sleeve showing chain breaking pose in color and b/w strip panels
EX $10   NM $25   MIP $50

Patch, 1940s, 3-1/2" round patch shows chain breaking pose
EX $750   NM $2000   MIP $5000

Patch, 1970s, cloth diamond-shaped patch of "S" logo in gold/red, several sizes, each
EX $5   NM $10   MIP $20

Patch, 1970s, triangular orange cloth patch w/red border shows Superman flying over desert scene
EX $5   NM $10   MIP $20

Patch, 1970s, rectangular white patch w/green border shows full color Superboy running toward viewer
EX $20   NM $40   MIP $70

Patch, 1970s, rectangular white cloth patch w/green border shows full-color Supergirl flying
EX $5   NM $10   MIP $20

Patch, 1973, diamond-shaped cloth patch shows Superman standing against vertical red/white stripes, wide yellow border has stars and reads "Superman Junior Olympics"
EX $5   NM $10   MIP $20

Pen, 1947, Jaffe, red/blue pen on illustrated card
EX $300   NM $450   MIP $750

Pencil Box, 1966, Mattel
EX $25   NM $50   MIP $75

Pencil Holder, 1940s, Superman, Inc., hollow holder in shape of large pencil, illustrated on shaft w/red and blue on white images and Superman-Tim Club logos
EX $500   NM $850   MIP $1250

Pennant, 1940s, yellow pennant w/Superman image and raised logo
EX $500   NM $800   MIP $1500

Pennant, 1973, 35th anniversary item, felt pennant has Amazing World of Superman logo and reads "Metropolis, Illinois, Home of Superman," came in two sizes, each
EX $12   NM $25   MIP $85

Pillow, 1960s, 12" square felt pillow w/color art of flying Superman
EX $35   NM $65   MIP $100

Pin, 1940s, Kellogg's, 7/8" round pin w/black/red/blue bust of Superman, most common pin in Pep Cereal series of late 1940s
EX $12   NM $25   MIP $60

Record and Club Membership Kit, 1966, 33-1/3 rpm record of the original comic, Superman Club card, shoulder patch and 1" tin litho club button, in 12" square illustrated box
EX $100   NM $150   MIP $200

Super Candy and Toy, 1967, Phoenix Candy, boxed candy w/a small toy inside each box
EX $50   NM $75   MIP $135

Superman 3-D Cut-Out Picture, 1950s, Kellogg's, 4-1/2 x 6-1/2" premium framed cut-out of Superman from the back of cereal box, reads "Best Wishes From Your Friend Superman"
EX $60   NM $80   MIP $100

Superman Christmas Card, 1940s, 4" x 5", Superman Brings You Christmas Greetings, shows him flying w/small tree in hands
EX $50   NM $150   MIP $300

Superman Cigarette Lighter, 1940s, Dunhill, battery-operated table-top lighter has chrome finish figure standing on black base
EX $750   NM $1000   MIP $1500

Superman Crazy Foam, 1970s, American Aerosol, spray bath soap in full-color illustrated can
EX $25   NM $50   MIP $75

Superman Cup, 1984, Burger King, one of four in set w/figural handles, others are Batman, Wonder Woman and Darkseid
EX $5   **NM** $7   **MIP** $10

Superman Figurine, 1966, Ideal, 3" tall hard plastic painted or unpainted figure on base, removable cape, part of Justice League series
EX $35   **NM** $65   **MIP** $85

Superman Figurine, 1984, Craft Master, solid figurine and paint set, on illustrated card
EX $25   **NM** $50   **MIP** $80

Superman Hood Ornament, 1940s, Lee, chrome finish, shows Superman in stylized running pose w/box
EX $500   **NM** $2000   **MIP** $3000

Superman Junior Defense League Pin, 1940s, die-cut pin in shape of flying Superman holding banner aloft, gold finish pin w/red/white/blue detailing
EX $75   **NM** $150   **MIP** $250

Superman Krypto-Raygun Filmstrips, 1940s, Daisy, extra boxed films for Krypto-Raygun, each
EX $25   **NM** $50   **MIP** $100

Superman Mug, 1950s, left handed mug, shows Superman on front and name across cape in back, handle has arrow and star
EX $75   **NM** $150   **MIP** $250

Superman Mug, 1966, white glass, red and blue logo w/Superman image, reverse picture is Superman breaking chain
EX $20   **NM** $40   **MIP** $65

Superman of Metropolis Award Certificate, 1973, premium given out during Metropolis, Illinois' 1973 35th anniversary of Superman celebration
EX $20   **NM** $40   **MIP** $75

Superman Phone Booth Radio, 1978, Vanity Fair, battery-operated AM radio of green British-style booth has color bas-relief Superman exiting
EX $35   **NM** $75   **MIP** $175

Superman Planter, 1970s, 3" diameter painted ceramic
EX $5   **NM** $10   **MIP** $25

Superman Radio, 1973, transistor radio made in punch-out shape of Superman from waist up
EX $50   **NM** $75   **MIP** $200

Superman Record Player, 1978, latching box briefcase type record player illustrated on all sides in full color, also features b/w origin strip on back
EX $55   **NM** $100   **MIP** $200

Superman School Bag, 1950s, Acme, red/blue fold-over clasp vinyl bag, screened full color Superman figure, black plastic handle and shoulder strap
EX $100   **NM** $200   **MIP** $450

Superman Soaky, 1965, Colgate Palmolive, 10" soap bottle, shows him standing w/hands at sides
EX $20   **NM** $40   **MIP** $100

Superman Soaky, 1978, Avon, 9-1/2" bubble bath bottle, Superman stands atop building
EX $30   **NM** $40   **MIP** $65

Superman Song Record, 1950s, A.A. Records, 6" two-song, 45 rpm record in sleeve, other song is "Tarzan Song," Model No. 723
EX $25   **NM** $50   **MIP** $100

Superman Statue, 1940s, 15" tall, crude painted plaster carnival prize
EX $300   **NM** $450   **MIP** $600

Superman Telephone, 1979, ATE, plastic phone w/large figure of Superman in hands on hips pose standing over key pad, receiver hangs up into back of his cape, illustrated box
EX $150   **NM** $600   **MIP** $1000

Superman Toothbrush, 1970s, Janex, figural, battery-operated
EX $20   **NM** $35   **MIP** $65

Superman Towels, 1970s, G.H. Wood, children's sponge towels, illustrated
EX $14   **NM** $30   **MIP** $65

Superman Wall Clock, 1978, New Haven, plastic and cardboard battery-operated framed wall clock showing Superman fighting alien spaceship
EX $30   **NM** $60   **MIP** $150

Superman Wallet, 1950s, Croyden, brown, color embossed flying Superman and logo
EX $100   **NM** $175   **MIP** $375

Superman Wallet, 1960s, brown leather
EX $25   **NM** $40   **MIP** $70

Superman's Christmas Adventure Record, 1940s, Decca, set of three 78 rpm records in illustrated sleeves
EX $150   **NM** $500   **MIP** $900

Superman-Tim Club Membership Card, 1940s, Superman, Inc., blue/red or red/black card
EX $150   **NM** $200   **MIP** $325

Superman-Tim Club Press Card, 1940s, blue/red card for identifying self as an Official Reporter for club
EX $150   **NM** $225   **MIP** $350

Superman-Tim Club Redbacks, 1940s, Superman, Inc., red on white imprinted coupons styled to look like money, denominations of $1, $5 and $10 "redbacks," each
EX $10   **NM** $20   **MIP** $35

Superman-Tim Magazine, 1940s, 5" x 7" monthly store premium, each
EX $50   **NM** $75   **MIP** $160

Supermen of America Membership Certificate, 1948, 8-1/2" x 11", signed by "Clark Kent"
EX $75   **NM** $150   **MIP** $350

Utensil Set, 1966, Imperial Knife, stainless steel spoon and fork set w/Superman on the handles, on 4-1/2" x 10" illustrated card
EX $50   **NM** $100   **MIP** $200

Wall Banner, 1966, 16" x 25" w/hanging rod at top, shows large central picture of Superman in front of city skyline and two lower panels of him smashing rocks and flying through space
EX $40   **NM** $85   **MIP** $175

ACTION FIGURES

(KP Photo)

Energized Superman Figure, 1979, Remco, 12" tall battery-operated hard body figure, in box
EX $35   **NM** $65   **MIP** $190

Flying Superman, 1950s, Kellogg's, plastic premium, 5" x 6-1/2", toy only
EX $50   **NM** $100   **MIP** $200

Flying Superman, 1950s, Kellogg's, premium, 5" x 6-1/2", rubber band propelled, w/instruction sheet and mailer
EX $150   **NM** $200   **MIP** $350

Flying Superman, 1955, Transogram, 12-1/2" tall molded plastic figure propelled by "super flight launcher," a rubber band attached to a pistol grip holder, on illustrated card
EX $75   **NM** $125   **MIP** $250

Superman Figure, Chemtoy, rubber, three different poses, on card, each
EX $25   **NM** $40   **MIP** $55

Superman Figure, Fun Things, 6" rubber figure on card
EX $9   NM $16   MIP $35

Superman Figure, Palitoy, 8" figure on card
EX $35   NM $65   MIP $120

Superman Figure, 1979, Japan, plastic body w/soft vinyl head, movable arms and head, in illustrated window box
EX $40   NM $60   MIP $90

BANK

Superman Bank, 1949, 9-1/2" painted ceramic shows youthful looking Superman standing on a cloud
EX $300   NM $500   MIP $800

Superman Bank, 1974, bust of Superman
EX $50   NM $75   MIP $125

Superman Dime Register Bank, 1940s, 1/2" x 2-1/2" x 2-1/2" yellow tin, front shows full-color Superman breaking chains off chest, held $5 in dimes
EX $200   NM $300   MIP $525

BOOKS

Book and Record Set, 1947, Musette Records, The Magic Ring
EX $100   NM $150   MIP $200

Book and Record Set, 1947, Musette Records, The Flying Train
EX $40   NM $100   MIP $200

Book, w/Superman at the Gilbert Hall of Science, 1948, Gilbert, 32-page promo catalog for Gilbert's Erector Sets and other toys, illustrated w/Superman
EX $75   NM $100   MIP $175

Superman Book and Record Set, 1970s, Peter Pan, two stories w/record
EX $5   NM $10   MIP $18

Superman Paint-by-Number Book, 1966, Whitman, 11" x 13-1/2", 40 pictures plus coloring guide on back cover
EX $15   NM $50   MIP $100

Superman Pop-Up Book, 1979, Random House, hardcover, full color
EX $15   NM $30   MIP $60

Superman Press-Out Book, 1966, Whitman, punch out, assemble and hang scenes and characters
EX $20   NM $35   MIP $85

Superman To The Rescue Coloring Book, 1964, Whitman, cover shows Superman rescuing woman, Model No. 1001
EX $25   NM $50   MIP $100

Superman Workbook, 1940s, DC Comics, English grammar workbook
EX $200   NM $500   MIP $825

BUTTONS

Superman Button, 1966, WABC Radio, radio premium button for "It's a Bird, It's a Plane..." production, shows faceless Superman w/"WABC 77" across chest
EX $100   NM $150   MIP $300

Superman Club Button, 1966, 3-1/2" celluloid button, shows 3/4 profile thigh-up view of Superman in hands on hips pose, reads, "Official Member Superman Club"
EX $10   NM $20   MIP $30

Superman Muscle Building Club Button, 1954, Peter Puppets Playthings, part of Golden Muscle Building set, full-color bust in sunburst circle in white button, reads "Superman Muscle Building Club"
EX $50   NM $150   MIP $250

Superman-Tim Club Button, 1940s, Superman, Inc., two different, both say Superman-Tim Club and have red/blue lettering and images on white background
EX $50   NM $75   MIP $120

CLOTHING

Superman Beanie, 1940s, hat w/two-color Superman embossed images on brim
EX $750   NM $900   MIP $1650

Superman Belt, 1940s, Pioneer, clear plastic w/color images and round brass buckle in box
EX $300   NM $500   MIP $700

Superman Belt, 1940s, Pioneer, brown leather w/Superman images and rectangular buckle, in box
EX $300   NM $500   MIP $750

Superman Belt, 1950s, Kellogg's, 28" long red plastic, aluminum "S" symbol buckle in red/yellow
EX $100   NM $250   MIP $450

Superman Belt Buckle, 1940s, square metal buckle shows red/blue chain breaking pose
EX $100   NM $150   MIP $425

Superman Moccasins, 1940s, Penobscot Shoe, leather moccasins w/Superman chain breaking pose on toe upper
EX $350   NM $750   MIP $2200

Superman Necktie, 1940s
EX $100   NM $200   MIP $350

Superman Necktie Set, 1940s, boxed set of two ties, small tie shows Superman standing w/arms crosses, larger tie shows Superman landing
EX $500   NM $1000   MIP $1500

Superman Suspenders, 1948, Pioneer, elastic, illustrated box
EX $350   NM $500   MIP $900

COMIC BOOKS

3-D Adventures of Superman Comic Book, 1950s, DC Comics, w/3-D goggles
EX $150   NM $250   MIP $850

Action Comics #1, 1938, DC Comics, first appearance of Superman
EX $300,000   NM $1,000,000   MIP $1,500,000

Mini Comic Book, 1955, Kellogg's, cereal premium, #1, The Superman Time Capsule
EX $75   NM $100   MIP $225

Mini Comic Book, 1955, Kellogg's, cereal premium, #1-A, Duel in Space
EX $75   NM $100   MIP $210

Mini Comic Book, 1955, Kellogg's, cereal premium, #1-B, Supershow of Metropolis
EX $75   NM $100   MIP $200

DOLLS

Super Babe Doll, 1947, Imperial Crown Toy, 15" tall, rubber skin, movable arms and legs, sleep eyes, composition head
EX $1000   NM $1500   MIP $2750

Superman Doll, Knickerbocker, 20" tall plush in box
EX $12   NM $25   MIP $40

Superman Doll, 1977, Toy Works, 25-1/2" tall, cloth, w/cape
EX $12   NM $25   MIP $40

GAMES

Superman Action Game, 1940s, American Toy Works, wood and cardboard wartime game, Superman holds tottering bridge and kids shoot darts at tanks on bridge, Model No. 530
EX $1000   NM $1500   MIP $2500

Superman City Game, 1966, Remco, board game w/magnetic figures and buildings
EX $500   NM $750   MIP $1500

Superman Electronic Question and Answer Quiz Machine, 1966, Lisbeth Whiting Co., battery-operated quiz game in full color illustrated box
EX $50   NM $100   MIP $225

Superman Official Eight-Piece Junior Quoit Set, 1940s, game in illustrated box includes wood and rubber game pieces, instruction booklet and membership card for "Superman Official Sports Club"
EX $75   NM $100   MIP $150

Superman Pinball Game, 1978, Bally, full-sized arcade game
EX $500 NM $750 MIP $1000

Superman Tilt Track, 1966, Kohner, marble skill game, in illustrated window box
EX $65 NM $95 MIP $175

PUZZLES

Puzzle, 1966, Whitman, 150 pieces, 14" X 18", Superman
EX $12 NM $25 MIP $50

Puzzle, 1966, Whitman, two frame tray puzzles: one shows Superman fighting space robot, other shows him flying past manned rocket ship in outer space, each
EX $25 NM $50 MIP $85

Puzzle, 1973, APC
EX $10 NM $15 MIP $25

RINGS

Superman Crusader Ring, 1940s, brass or silver finish ring shows forward facing bust of Superman
EX $75 NM $120 MIP $250

Superman Member Ring, 1940, red paint on top of gold finish
EX $20000 NM $35000 MIP $50000

Superman Milk Defense Club Ring, 1941, gold finish hidden compartment ring, face is embossed milk companies initial, different initials known, lightning bolt and eyeball symbol, compartment shows Superman decal image
EX $5000 NM $15000 MIP $25000

Superman Milk Defense Club Ring, 1941, Different Milk Companies Sponsors, gold finish hidden compartment ring, face is embossed w/"S," lightning bolt and Superman bust, compartment shows Superman image, b/c of restrike none are found in MIP condition
EX $5000 NM $20000 MIP n/a

Superman Ring, 1978, Nestle's, premium ring, gold finish w/white circle center and yellow/red diamond "S" logo in middle
EX $20 NM $40 MIP $70

Superman-Tim Club Ring, 1940s, bronze finish metal ring w/embossed image of Superman in flight, w/initials S and T near his feet
EX $1500 NM $3000 MIP $4000

TOY

Bicycle Siren, 1970s, Empire
EX $10 NM $20 MIP $50

Bubble Gum Badge, 1948, Fo-Lee Gum Corp., shield-shaped brass finish badge shows a variant of the chain breaking pose inside a sun burst pattern ringed w/stars
EX $4000 NM $7000 MIP $10000

Crayon-by-Numbers Set, 1954, Transogram, 16 crayons and 44 action scenes
EX $100 NM $200 MIP $400

(KP Photo)

Daily Planet Jetcopter, 1979, Corgi, Model No. 929
EX $20 NM $40 MIP $75

Dangle Dandies Mobile, 1955, Kellogg's, set of eight cut outs on boxes of Rice Krispies and Corn Flakes
EX $75 NM $100 MIP $200

Film Viewer, 1947, 1-1/2" x 4" x 6-1/2" wide boxed set of hand-held viewer and six films
EX $350 NM $550 MIP $800

Film Viewer, 1947, Acme, 1-1/2" x 6-1/2" wide boxed set of hand-held viewer and two films
EX $200 NM $500 MIP $700

Film Viewer, 1965, plastic hand viewer w/two boxes of film, on illustrated card
EX $25 NM $40 MIP $85

Flying Noise Balloon, 1966, Van Dam, oversized balloon makes noise in flight, Superman illustration on balloon and card
EX $12 NM $23 MIP $50

Jumbo Movie Viewer, 1950s, Acme, blue/yellow plastic viewer w/35 mm "theatre size" film, on illustrated card, w/one filmstrip
EX $125 NM $200 MIP $350

Kryptonite Rock, 1970s, glow-in-the-dark rocks sold as kryptonite chunks, in illustrated box
EX $10 NM $15 MIP $25

Movie Viewer, 1947, Acme Plastics, black plastic viewer, white knob and two individually boxed Superman films, in red/blue die-cut box
EX $175 NM $450 MIP $675

Movie Viewer, 1948, Acme Plastics, red plastic viewer and three individually boxed Superman films, in small full color die-cut box
EX $150 NM $400 MIP $600

Movie Viewer, 1950s, Acme, black/red plastic viewer w/two individually boxed Superman films
EX $90 NM $150 MIP $300

Official Magic Kit, 1956, Bar-Zim, magic balls, disappearing cards, multiplying corks, vanishing trick, shell game, balancing belt and directions, in illustrated box
EX $350 NM $750 MIP $1500

Official Superman Costume, 1954, Ben Cooper, blue/red suit w/red/yellow monogram and belt, in box
EX $140 NM $260 MIP $425

Official Superman Playsuit, 1954, Funtime Playwear, rayon outfit, red cap w/screened Superman image, navy and red suit w/5" gold monogram and belt
EX $200 NM $400 MIP $625

Official Superman Playsuit, 1970, Ben Cooper, cloth suit in illustrated box
EX $20 NM $40 MIP $70

Official Superman Two-Piece Kiddie Swim Set, 1950s, set of rubber swim fins and goggles w/Superman's image or "S" symbol, in box
EX $50 NM $150 MIP $250

Paint-by-Numbers Watercolor Set, 1954, Transogram, 16 watercolors and 44 action scenes
EX $75 NM $200 MIP $375

(KP Photo)

Super Heroes String Puppets, 1978, Madison, string controlled cloth and vinyl marionette
EX $25 NM $75 MIP $150

Superman and Supergirl Push Puppets, 1968, Kohner, set of two: 5-1/4" on bases, in window box
EX $350 NM $600 MIP $1000

Superman Back-a-Wack, 1966, Dell, blue plastic paddle w/gold imprinted "S" logo and name, elastic string and red ball, on illustrated card, Model No. 1194
EX $50 NM $100 MIP $150

Superman Balloon, 1966, small balloon w/centered image
EX $5 NM $15 MIP $35

Superman Costume, 1950s, red pants and tie-on cape, blue shirt w/red,

blue and yellow "S" emblem on chest, yellow belt
EX $100 NM $300 MIP $425

Superman Figure, Presents, 15" vinyl/cloth figure on base
EX $25 NM $40 MIP $60

Superman Golden Muscle Building Set, 1954, Peter Puppets Playthings, handles, springs, hand grippers, jump rope, wall hooks, measuring tape, progress chart, membership certificate and button, illustrated box
EX $700 NM $1000 MIP $1600

(KP Photo)

Superman Hand Puppet, 1966, Ideal, 11", cloth body, vinyl head
EX $50 NM $75 MIP $120

Superman Junior Horseshoe Set, 1950s, Super Swim, four rubber horseshoes, two rubber bases and two wood pegs and Official Sports Club card and rules for sportsmanship
EX $75 NM $150 MIP $300

Superman Junior Swim Goggles, 1950s, Super Swim, plastic lenses, rubber goggles w/red strap, "S" logo and membership card for Superman Safety Swim Club
EX $50 NM $125 MIP $225

Superman Kite, 1966, Pressman
EX $50 NM $75 MIP $135

Superman Kite, 1984, Hiflyer
EX $5 NM $10 MIP $35

Superman Krypton Rocket, 1954, Kellogg's, 2" x 9" x 9-1/2" water powered rocket w/"Krypton generating pump," in mailer box
EX $150 NM $325 MIP $425

Superman Krypton Rocket, 1956, Park Plastics, 2" x 9" x 9-1/2" water powered rocket w/Krypton generating pump, reserve fuel tank and Krypton Rocket, in illustrated box, same as Kellogg's

rocket but in mass market packaging w/added fuel tank
EX $150 NM $325 MIP $425

Superman Paint Set, 1940s, American Toy Works, box shows Superman flying up toward upper right corner of box, w/pallet and brushes at lower right, "Paint Set" inside pallet
EX $400 NM $800 MIP $1250

Superman Paint Set, 1940s, American Toy Works, larger version, shows Superman in front of pallet background
EX $400 NM $800 MIP $1250

Superman Play Set, 1973, Ideal, self-contained vinyl covered full color snap-close case opens to three backdrops, Fortress of Solitude, Daily Planet and villain's hideout, for staging action scenes w/supplied color punch-outs
EX $50 NM $75 MIP $175

Superman Pogo Stick, 1977, 48" w/a vinyl bust on top
EX $50 NM $100 MIP $225

Superman Push Puppet, 1966, Kohner, 5-1/4" on base, in window box
EX $50 NM $75 MIP $110

Superman Roller Skates, 1975, Larami, plastic w/color bust of Superman shaped around front of each skate, in illustrated window box
EX $20 NM $50 MIP $100

Superman Rub-Ons, 1966, Hasbro, magic picture transfers in box illustrated w/picture of Superman flying
EX $50 NM $100 MIP $150

Superman Senior Rubber Horseshoe Set, 1950s, in box
EX $75 NM $125 MIP $200

Superman Senior Swim Goggles, 1950s, Super Swim, plastic lenses, rubber goggles w/red strap, "S" logo on bridge, membership card for Superman Safety Swim Club
EX $40 NM $80 MIP $175

Superman Sky Hero, 1977, Marx, rubber band glider w/color Superman image, on card, Model No. 9310
EX $25 NM $40 MIP $85

Superman Space Satellite Launcher Set, 1950s, Kellogg's, premium set of generic plastic gun w/firing "satellite wheel" and illustrated instruction sheet, in mailer box
EX $300 NM $500 MIP $750

Superman Stamp Set, 1965, set of six wood-backed character stamps
EX $25 NM $50 MIP $200

Superman Super Watch, 1967, Toy House, plastic toy watch w/moveable hands, watch "case" is large "S" chest symbol, on illustrated card
EX $25 NM $50 MIP $150

Superman Tank, 1958, Linemar, large battery-operated tin, 3-D Superman w/a cloth cape, in illustrated box
EX $1200 NM $2500 MIP $3500

Superman Utility Belt, 1979, Remco, illustrated window box, decoder glasses, kryptonite detector, nonworking watch, handcuffs, ring, decoder map, press card and secret message
EX $50 NM $150 MIP $275

Superman Water Gun, 1967, Multiple Toymakers, 6" plastic, Model No. 484
EX $50 NM $100 MIP $200

Toy Wristwatch, 1950s, Germany, non-working toy watch, blue plastic band, rectangular case w/full-color full-standing pose on white dial
EX $35 NM $65 MIP $200

Trick Picture Sun Camera, 1950s, Made in Japan, when left in the sun for two minutes, the camera "develops" a picture of Superman fighting a space monster
EX $75 NM $150 MIP $250

TRADING CARDS

Superman II Trading Cards, 1981, Costa Rican, set of 88 cards, complete set
EX $18 NM $35 MIP $50

Superman II Trading Cards, 1981, Topps, set of 88 cards, complete set
EX $20 NM $30 MIP $40

Superman III Trading Cards, 1983, Topps, set of 99 cards, complete set
EX $5 NM $10 MIP $15

Superman the Movie Trading Cards, 1978, Topps, set of 77 cards, first issue
EX $20 NM $40 MIP $65

Superman the Movie Trading Cards, 1979, Topps, set of 88 cards, second issue
EX $12 NM $25 MIP $35

Superman the Movie Trading Cards, 1979, French, set of 180 cards
EX $18 NM $35 MIP $50

Superman the Movie Trading Cards, 1979, OPC, set of 132 cards
EX $12 NM $25 MIP $35

Superman Trading Cards, 1940, Gum Inc., 2-1/2" x 3-1/4" cards, set of 72
EX $7500 NM $10000 MIP $15000

Superman Trading Cards, 1966, Topps, set of 66 cards, George Reeves TV series scenes
EX $90   NM $165   MIP $400

Superman Trading Cards, 1966, Topps, set of 66 cards, shows George Reeves TV series scenes, price per each card
EX $5   NM $10   MIP $15

Superman Trading Cards Display Box, 1966, Topps, 2" x 4" x 8" display box of 24 unopened packs, box shows George Reeves bust
EX $500   NM $750   MIP $1350

WATCHES

Superman Supertime Wristwatch, 1950s, National Comics, gray band, stamped red "S" logo, silver western style buckle, full-color hands on hips pose inside chrome finish case, second hand, even-hour numbers around face, in full color box
EX $750   NM $1750   MIP $3750

Superman Wristwatch, 1940s, New Haven Clock, squared-oval faced watch, leather band, dial shows Superman standing, hands on hips, in illustrated box
EX $2000   NM $3500   MIP $5000

Superman Wristwatch, 1959, Bradley, dial shows Superman flying over city, second hand, chrome finish case
EX $750   NM $1000   MIP $1750

Superman Wristwatch, 1977, gold bezel, stainless back, blue leather band, face shows Superman flying upward from below
EX $35   NM $65   MIP $200

Superman Wristwatch, 1986, Una-Donna, plastic case and band, several color and face illustrations, each
EX $10   NM $20   MIP $75

Tarzan

ACCESSORIES

Tarzan Flasher Ring, 1960s, Vari-Vue
EX $10   NM $20   MIP $50

Tarzan Party Set, 1977, Amscan
EX $10   NM $25   MIP $60

FIGURES

Figure, 1950s, 2-1/2" tall, celluloid, French
EX $750   NM $1000   MIP $1550

Kala Ape Figure, 1984, Dakin, 3" tall
EX $10   NM $15   MIP $30

Young Tarzan Figure, 1984, Dakin, 4", bendable
EX $10   NM $15   MIP $30

Three Little Pigs

TOY

Puzzle, 1940s, Jaymar, 7" x 10" x 2"
EX $100   NM $200   MIP $300

Three Little Pigs Soaky Set, 1960s, Drew Chemical, 8" tall each: Three Little Pigs and the Big Bad Wolf
EX $70   NM $125   MIP $275

Tom and Jerry

BANK

Tom and Jerry Bank, 1980, Gorham, 6" tall
EX $20   NM $35   MIP $80

FIGURES

Jerry Figure, 1973, Marx, 4" tall
EX $15   NM $25   MIP $70

Tom and Jerry Figure Set, 1975, walking, Tom, Jerry, and Droopy
EX $25   NM $50   MIP $125

Tom Figure, 1973, Marx, 6" tall
EX $15   NM $30   MIP $70

TOY

Puzzles, Whitman, four frame tray puzzles
EX $20   NM $35   MIP $90

Tom and Jerry Go Kart, 1973, Marx, plastic, friction drive
EX $50   NM $75   MIP $150

Tom and Jerry on Scooter, 1971, Marx, plastic, friction drive
EX $30   NM $50   MIP $100

WATCH

Tom and Jerry Wristwatch, 1985, Bradley, quartz, oldies series, small white plastic case and band, sweep seconds, face shows Tom squirting Jerry w/hose
EX $15   NM $35   MIP $90

Tony the Tiger

ACCESSORIES

Cookie Jar, 1960s, Kellogg's, plastic, figural
EX $25   NM $70   MIP $120

Radio, 1980s, plastic, figural
EX $20   NM $45   MIP $80

BANK

Figural Bank, 1967, Kellogg's
EX $30   NM $45   MIP $90

FIGURES

Inflatable Tiger, 1950s, Kellogg's
EX $7   NM $20   MIP $35

Plush Tiger, 1970s, Kellogg's
EX $10   NM $25   MIP $75

Top Cat

FIGURES

Top Cat Figure, 1961, Marx, TV-Tinykins, plastic
EX $20   NM $35   MIP $70

TOY

Top Cat Soaky, 1960s, 10" tall, vinyl
EX $25   NM $45   MIP $90

Viewmarx Micro-Viewer, 1963, Marx, plastic
EX $40   NM $60   MIP $120

Winnie the Pooh

ACCESSORIES

Lamp, 1964, Dolly Toy, 7" tall
EX $35   NM $90   MIP $200

Radio, 1970s, Thilgee, 5" x 6" x 1-1/2" tall
EX $45   NM $90   MIP $135

Winnie the Pooh Button, 1960s, 3-1/2", celluloid
EX $10   NM $25   MIP $60

Winnie the Pooh Snow Globe, 5-1/2", musical
EX $15   NM $35   MIP $80

DOLL

Winnie the Pooh and Christopher Robin Dolls, 1964, Horsman, Winnie the Pooh 3-1/2" tall and Christopher 11" tall, set
EX $100   NM $175   MIP $350

Winnie the Pooh Doll, 1960s, 12" tall
EX $40   NM $60   MIP $120

TOY

Jack-In-The-Box, 1960s, Carnival Toys
EX $40   NM $60   MIP $120

Kanga and Roo Squeak Toy, 1966, Holland Hill, vinyl
EX $20   NM $40   MIP $80

Magic Slate, 1965, Western Publishing, 8-1/2" x 13-1/2"
EX $30   NM $50   MIP $120

Puzzle, 1964, Whitman, frame tray
EX $10   NM $30   MIP $70

Wizard of Oz

ACCESSORIES

Christmas Ornaments, 1977, Bradford Novelty, 4-1/2" tall, Dorothy, Scarecrow, Tin Man, Cowardly Lion, each
EX $5   NM $10   MIP $30

Christmas Ornaments, 1989, Presents, cloth and vinyl: Dorothy, Scarecrow,

Tin Man, Cowardly Lion, Glinda and Wicked Witch, each

EX $8   **NM** $10   **MIP** $20

Cookie Jar, 1990, Clay Art, white w/relief figures of characters

EX $50   **NM** $100   **MIP** $175

Crayon Box, 1975, Cheinco, rectangular, metal

EX $5   **NM** $10   **MIP** $30

Erasers, 1989, Applause, set of six: figural, Scarecrow, Cowardly Lion, Dorothy, Wicked Witch, Tin Man, Glinda, set

EX $15   **NM** $20   **MIP** $40

Give-A-Show Projector Slides, 1968, Kenner, 35 color slides, five different shows

EX $20   **NM** $40   **MIP** $100

Magnets, 1987, Grynnen Barrett, six character magnets in box

EX $6   **NM** $10   **MIP** $15

Magnets, 1989, Vanderbilt Products, several characters available, each

EX $2   **NM** $3   **MIP** $5

Pails, 1950s, Swift and Company, Oz Peanut Butter, red and yellow and red, yellow and white tin

EX $25   **NM** $40   **MIP** $100

Scarecrow Night Light, 1989, Hamilton Gifts, 7", unpainted bone china

EX $10   **NM** $15   **MIP** $25

Snack 'N Sip Pals, 1989, Multi Toys, 12 red and white striped straws w/detachable character figures

EX $4   **NM** $7   **MIP** $25

Tin, 1989, Multi Toys, 8" x 10" x 2", illustrated w/Emerald City and characters

EX $8   **NM** $15   **MIP** $35

Trash Can, 1975, Chein, oval metal

EX $20   **NM** $35   **MIP** $70

Wall Decorations, 1967, Shepard Press, 20 punch-out decorations

EX $20   **NM** $35   **MIP** $65

BANK

Cowardly Lion Bank, 1960s, ceramic, red nose

EX $30   **NM** $75   **MIP** $160

Dorothy Bank, 1960s, ceramic, blue dress w/brown wicker basket

EX $30   **NM** $60   **MIP** $160

Scarecrow Bank, 1960s, ceramic

EX $30   **NM** $50   **MIP** $135

Tin Man Bank, 1960s, ceramic, silver

EX $30   **NM** $70   **MIP** $150

BOOK

Cut and Make Masks, 1982, Dover, eight cut-out color masks

EX $5   **NM** $10   **MIP** $30

Dorothy and Friends Visit Oz Book, 1967, Curtis Candy, candy premium

EX $8   **NM** $20   **MIP** $45

Dorothy Meets the Wizard Book, 1967, Curtis Candy, candy premium

EX $15   **NM** $30   **MIP** $65

Little Golden Book Series, 1951, The Road to Oz, The Emerald City of Oz, and The Tin Woodman of Oz, each

EX $8   **NM** $20   **MIP** $70

Mask Book, 1990, Watermill Press, four paper masks

EX $3   **NM** $10   **MIP** $30

Return To Oz Little Golden Books, 1985, Western, Dorothy Returns to Oz, Escape from the Witch's Castle, Dorothy in the Ornament Room, Dorothy Saves the Emerald City, each

EX $2   **NM** $5   **MIP** $10

Scarecrow and the Tin Man Book, 1904, G. W. Dillingham

EX $300   **NM** $600   **MIP** $875

Tales of the Wizard of Oz Coloring Book, 1962, Whitman, art from animated TV show

EX $15   **NM** $20   **MIP** $70

The Tin Woodsman and Dorothy Book, 1967, Curtis Candy, candy premium

EX $12   **NM** $40   **MIP** $80

The Wonderful Cut-Outs of Oz Book, 1985, Crown, 35 figures to cut out

EX $7   **NM** $15   **MIP** $50

Wizard of Oz Book, 1975, Western, #310-32, Little Golden Book

EX $5   **NM** $10   **MIP** $40

Wizard of Oz Christmas Book, 1968, Gimbel's, New York department store premium

EX $20   **NM** $50   **MIP** $100

Wizard of Oz Color-By-Number Book, 1962, Karas Publishing, #A-116, Twinkle Books series

EX $10   **NM** $30   **MIP** $70

Wizard of Oz Paper Dolls, 1976, Whitman

EX $7   **NM** $15   **MIP** $50

Wizard of Oz Sticker Fun Book, 1976, Whitman

EX $6   **NM** $12   **MIP** $35

COMIC BOOK

Tales of the Wizard of Oz Comic Book, 1962, Dell, #1306

EX $10   **NM** $15   **MIP** $50

Wizard of Oz Comic Book, 1956, Dell, Dell Junior Treasury, #5

EX $12   **NM** $40   **MIP** $100

Wizard of Oz Comic Book, 1957, Dell, Classic Illustrated Jr., #535

EX $6   **NM** $20   **MIP** $60

DOLL

Cowardly Lion Doll, 1971, M-D Tissue, cloth, light brown body w/white snout

EX $10   **NM** $20   **MIP** $40

Cowardly Lion Doll, 1984, Ideal, 9", Character Dolls series

EX $20   **NM** $40   **MIP** $90

Cowardly Lion Doll, 1988, Presents, vinyl

EX $20   **NM** $40   **MIP** $90

Cowardly Lion Doll, 1989, Largo Toys, rag doll

EX $8   **NM** $18   **MIP** $50

Dandy Lion Doll, 1962, Artistic, 14" tall, cloth and vinyl

EX $35   **NM** $85   **MIP** $175

Doodle Dolls, 1979, Whiting, three dolls: cardboard parts, yarn, styrofoam balls, fabric

EX $8   **NM** $20   **MIP** $40

Dorothy and Toto Doll, 1984, Ideal, 9", Character Dolls series

EX $20   **NM** $40   **MIP** $80

Dorothy Doll, 1971, M-D Tissue, cloth, stuffed, yellow hair, orange jumper

EX $10   **NM** $20   **MIP** $60

Dorothy Doll, 1984, Effanbee, 14-1/2" tall, vinyl, Judy Garland, blue dress and hair ribbons, ruby slippers, Legend Series

EX $45   **NM** $100   **MIP** $150

Dorothy Doll, 1988, Presents, vinyl, blue checkered jumper, white blouse, red slippers, yellow brick road base

EX $20   **NM** $35   **MIP** $80

Dorothy Doll, 1989, Largo Toys, Judy Garland

EX $8   **NM** $20   **MIP** $60

Dorothy Doll, 1991, Madame Alexander, 8", blue checked jumper w/white blouse, basket w/Toto and red shoes, Storyland Dolls series

EX $20   **NM** $40   **MIP** $80

Glinda Doll, 1989, Presents, vinyl, pink dress w/pink crown and wand, yellow brick road base

EX $20   **NM** $40   **MIP** $90

Lollipop Guild Boy Doll, 1989, Presents, vinyl, plaid shirt, green shorts and striped socks, on a yellow brick road base

EX $20   **NM** $40   **MIP** $80

Lullabye League Girl Doll, 1989, Presents, vinyl, pink ballerina dress and slippers w/hat on a yellow brick road base

EX $20   NM $40   MIP $80

Mayor of Munchkinland Doll, 1989, Presents, vinyl, black suit and shoes on a yellow brick road base

EX $20   NM $40   MIP $80

Rusty the Tin Man Doll, 1962, Artistic Toy Company, 14" tall, cloth and vinyl

EX $35   NM $60   MIP $150

Scarecrow Doll, 1971, M-D Tissue, cloth, stuffed, frowning, blue pants and red and white plaid jacket

EX $10   NM $15   MIP $45

Scarecrow Doll, 1984, Ideal, 9", Character Dolls series

EX $25   NM $40   MIP $75

Scarecrow Doll, 1988, Presents, vinyl, brown pants, green shirt, and black hat and shoes, on a yellow brick road base

EX $25   NM $40   MIP $85

Scarecrow Doll, 1989, Largo Toys, rag doll

EX $9   NM $15   MIP $60

Scarecrow Talkin' Patter Pillow Doll, 1968, Mattel, cloth, pull-string, says 10 phrases, dark blue pants and sleeves, white gloves, black boots

EX $50   NM $100   MIP $200

Socrates the Scarecrow Doll, 1962, Artistic, 14" tall, cloth and vinyl

EX $30   NM $70   MIP $160

Tin Man Doll, 1971, M-D Tissue, cloth, stuffed, gray body, blue eyes, red heart

EX $8   NM $20   MIP $50

Tin Man Doll, 1984, Ideal, 9", Character Dolls series

EX $20   NM $35   MIP $75

Tin Man Doll, 1988, Presents, vinyl, silver body w/a heart clock on chaint, on a yellow brick road base

EX $20   NM $35   MIP $75

Tin Man Doll, 1989, Largo Toys, rag doll

EX $10   NM $15   MIP $40

Toto Doll, 1988, Presents, 5-1/2" plush

EX $15   NM $30   MIP $75

Wicked Witch Doll, 1989, Presents, vinyl, black dress and hat, green face and hands holding broom on a yellow brick road base

EX $25   NM $40   MIP $100

Wizard of Oz Dolls, 1985, Effanbee, 11-1/2", Dorothy, Scarecrow, Tin Man, Cowardly Lion, each

EX $15   NM $22   MIP $70

Wizard of Oz Live! Dolls, Applause, cloth, three different sizes, each

EX $8   NM $15   MIP $40

FIGURES

Jack Pumpkinhead Figure, 1985, Heart and Heart, Return to Oz, 3"-4" tall, plastic jointed

EX $35   NM $55   MIP $100

Munchkins Figures, 1988, Presents, PVC, 1-3/4" to 2-3/4": Mayor, Lollipop Guild Boy, Sleepyhead Girl, Lady, Soldier and Ballerina, each

EX $5   NM $10   MIP $35

(KP Photo)

Oz-Kins Figures, 1967, Aurora, plastic Burry Biscuit premium: set of 10

EX $50   NM $100   MIP $220

Scarecrow Figure, 1968, 15", ceramic, painted or unpainted

EX $20   NM $50   MIP $110

Scarecrow Figure, 1984, Dalen Products, 6' inflatable

EX $12   NM $20   MIP $60

Scarecrow Figure, 1985, Heart and Heart, Return to Oz, 3"-4" tall, plastic jointed

EX $30   NM $45   MIP $100

Tik Tok Figure, 1985, Heart and Heart, Return to Oz, 3"-4" tall, plastic jointed

EX $35   NM $55   MIP $105

Tin Man Figure, 1968, 15", ceramic, painted or unpainted

EX $20   NM $30   MIP $80

Tin Man Figure, 1985, Return to Oz, 3"-4" tall, plastic jointed

EX $20   NM $35   MIP $100

Wizard of Oz Figures, 1967, Multiple Toymakers, 6" tall, bendy, several characters, on card

EX $16   NM $30   MIP $75

Wizard of Oz Figures, 1988, Presents, 3-3/4": Dorothy, Scarecrow, Tin Man, Cowardly Lion, Wicked Witch, Glinda, each

EX $4   NM $6   MIP $15

Wizard of Oz Figures, 1989, Presents, six figures on musical bases, each

EX $10   NM $12   MIP $25

Wizard of Oz Figures, 1989, Multi Toys, 4" poseable figures, set of six

EX $15   NM $25   MIP $50

Wizard of Oz Figures, 1989, Just Toys, several characters, bendy, each

EX $4   NM $6   MIP $15

GAME

Return to Oz Game, 1985, Golden Press

EX $8   NM $13   MIP $30

MUSIC BOX

Cowardly Lion Music Box, 1983, Schmid

EX $20   NM $35   MIP $60

Dorothy Music Box, 1983, Schmid, plays "Over the Rainbow"

EX $25   NM $40   MIP $65

Scarecrow Music Box, 1983, Schmid

EX $20   NM $35   MIP $60

Tin Man Music Box, 1983, Schmid

EX $20   NM $35   MIP $60

TOY

Cast 'N Paint Set, 1975, makes six 6" figures

EX $15   NM $25   MIP $75

Chalkboard, 1975, Roth American, wood frame, steel stand w/chalk, chalk holder and eraser

EX $16   NM $27   MIP $75

Cowardly Lion Costume, 1975, Ben Cooper, costume and mask

EX $15   NM $25   MIP $60

Cowardly Lion Costume, 1989, Collegeville, plastic mask and vinyl bodysuit

EX $10   NM $15   MIP $30

Cowardly Lion Costume, 1989, Collegeville, deluxe

EX $20   NM $40   MIP $75

Cowardly Lion Mask, 1983, Don Post Studios, rubber

EX $35   NM $55   MIP $90

Cowardly Lion Wind-Up, 1975, Durham Industries, on illustrated card

EX $20   NM $30   MIP $60

(KP Photo)

(KP Photo)

Decoupage Kit, 1975, two wooden plaques, scenes based on film
EX $15   NM $25   MIP $60

Dorothy Costume, 1975, Ben Cooper, costume and mask
EX $15   NM $25   MIP $70

Dorothy Costume, 1989, Collegeville, deluxe, includes red metallic glitter chips for shoes
EX $20   NM $40   MIP $85

Dorothy Costume, 1989, Collegeville, plastic mask and vinyl bodysuit
EX $8   NM $15   MIP $40

Fun Shades, 1989, Multi Toys, children's sunglasses w/character images
EX $5   NM $8   MIP $20

Glinda's Magic Wand, 1989, Multi Toys, battery-operated wand w/red glitter star on end, lights up, on illustrated card
EX $5   NM $10   MIP $30

Magic Picture Kit, 1968, Jiffy Pop Popcorn
EX $5   NM $25   MIP $70

Magic Slate, 1961, Lowe, art based on animated TV show
EX $12   NM $30   MIP $80

Magic Slate, 1976, Whitman
EX $6   NM $18   MIP $40

Magic Slate, 1985, Western, Return to Oz
EX $4   NM $10   MIP $35

Magic Slate, 1989, Western
EX $3   NM $6   MIP $30

Magic Story Cloth, 1978, Raco, 38" x 44" plastic sheet, eight crayons and sponge
EX $6   NM $12   MIP $35

Off to See the Wizard Colorforms, 1967, Colorforms
EX $25   NM $50   MIP $100

Off to See the Wizard Dancing Toys, 1967, Marx, mechanical, dancing Tin Man, the Cowardly Lion and the Scarecrow, Montgomery Ward's Exclusive, each
EX $100   NM $150   MIP $250

Off to See the Wizard Flasher Rings, 1967, Vari-Vue, gumball machine prizes, silver painted resin, gold painted, dark or light blue plastic, each
EX $10   NM $20   MIP $30

Off to See the Wizard Hand Puppet, 1968, Mattel, talking, four vinyl heads on finger tips, Toto and Cowardly Lion on thumb pad, 10 phrases
EX $30   NM $45   MIP $100

Paint by Number 'N Frame Set, 1969, Hasbro, 16" x 18", two plastic frames, 18 watercolors, brush and eight pictures to paint
EX $20   NM $30   MIP $90

Paint by Number Set, 1968, Craft Master, six paints, brush, picture of Tin Man, Cowardly Lion, or the Scarecrow
EX $20   NM $35   MIP $95

Paint by Number Set, 1973, Hasbro, six oil paint vials and brush
EX $6   NM $20   MIP $50

Paint by Number Set, 1979, Craft House, two 10" x 14" panels, 15 colors, brush and instructions
EX $10   NM $25   MIP $50

Paint by Number Set, 1989, Art Award, three different versions
EX $6   NM $10   MIP $20

Paint with Crayons Set, 1989, Art Award, four pictures based on MGM film characters, in illustrated box
EX $5   NM $10   MIP $20

Paper Dolls, 1975, The Toy Factory, Dorothy, Tin Man, Scarecrow, Cowardly Lion and Toto, clothes and accessories
EX $10   NM $20   MIP $60

Playing Cards, 1988, Presents, tin holds two decks
EX $5   NM $10   MIP $40

Puppet Theatre, 1965, Proctor and Gamble, cardboard theater designed for P and G puppets
EX $100   NM $175   MIP $300

Puzzle, 1960s, Haret-Gilmar, 10" x 14" puzzle in canister
EX $15   NM $30   MIP $70

Puzzle, 1976, Whitman, frame tray
EX $4   NM $8   MIP $35

Puzzle, 1976, American Puzzle Company, 200-piece puzzle in canister
EX $15   NM $30   MIP $50

Puzzle, 1984, Effanbee, in canister
EX $8   NM $15   MIP $40

Puzzle, 1985, Crisco Oil, Return to Oz, mail away premium, 200 piece puzzle
EX $30   NM $50   MIP $80

Puzzle, 1989, Western, frame tray, 100 pieces, Glinda and Dorothy in Munchkinland
EX $5   NM $10   MIP $35

Puzzle, 1990, Milton Bradley, 1000 piece jigsaw featuring the 1989 Norman James Company poster
EX $6   NM $15   MIP $30

Puzzles, 1960s, Jaymar, set of four, 100 pieces each, each
EX $15   NM $30   MIP $90

Puzzles, 1960s, Jaymar, frame tray
EX $10   NM $20   MIP $65

Puzzles, 1967, Whitman, set of three: Peter Pan, Alice in Wonderland and The Wizard of Oz, in box
EX $12   NM $18   MIP $60

Puzzles, 1977, Doug Smith, 17" x 22" each, frame tray
EX $10   NM $20   MIP $50

Puzzles, 1985, Golden Press, frame tray, Return to Oz characters
EX $3   NM $5   MIP $15

Return to Oz Hand Puppets, 1985, Welch's Jelly, Scarecrow, Gump, or Tik-Tok, Return to Oz promotion
EX $20   NM $40   MIP $60

Rubber Stamps, 1989, set of 11 characters in plastic case
EX $10   NM $15   MIP $30

Rubber Stamps, 1989, Multi Toys, 12 figural stampers
EX $4   NM $6   MIP $15

Rubber Stamps, 1989, 18 chracter stamps
EX $12   NM $20   MIP $35

Scarecrow Costume, 1967, Ben Cooper
EX $30   NM $40   MIP $75

Scarecrow Costume, 1968, Ben Cooper, battery-operated light-up mask
EX $30   NM $40   MIP $75

Scarecrow Costume, 1989, Collegeville, plastic mask and vinyl bodysuit
EX $6   NM $12   MIP $30

Scarecrow Costume, 1989, Collegeville, deluxe, includes straw
EX $20   NM $35   MIP $50

Scarecrow Mask, 1983, Don Post Studios, rubber
EX $40   NM $60   MIP $90

Scarecrow Wind-Up, 1975, Durham Industries, on illustrated card
EX $20   NM $30   MIP $75

Scarecrow-in-the-Box, 1967, Mattel, jack-in-the-box
EX $40   NM $60   MIP $120

Showboat Play Set, 1962, Remco, pink plastic showboat w/oversized central stage area, four different plays, scenery, players and scripts
EX $75   NM $100   MIP $175

Stand-Up Rub-Ons, 1968, Hasbro, three full-color transfer sheets, character outline sheets of 10 characters
EX $20   NM $30   MIP $75

Stitch a Story Set, 1973, Hasbro, two framed pictures, thread and embroidery needle
EX $10   NM $15   MIP $35

Tea Set, 1970s, Ohio Art, 30-piece set, red and yellow plastic
EX $40   NM $60   MIP $120

Tin Man Costume, 1961, Halco, costume and mask
EX $20   NM $35   MIP $90

Tin Man Costume, 1968, Ben Cooper
EX $20   NM $30   MIP $65

Tin Man Costume, 1975, Ben Cooper, costume and mask
EX $15   NM $25   MIP $55

Tin Man Costume, 1989, Collegeville, plastic mask and vinyl bodysuit
EX $6   NM $10   MIP $25

Tin Man Costume, 1989, Collegeville, deluxe
EX $20   NM $35   MIP $70

Tin Man Mask, 1983, Don Post Studios, rubber
EX $35   NM $55   MIP $85

Tin Man Robot, 1969, Remco, 21-1/2" tall, battery-operated, lifts legs and swings arms as he walks
EX $125   NM $200   MIP $325

Tin Man Wind-Up, 1975, Durham Industries
EX $25   NM $50   MIP $100

Toy Watch, 1940s, tin, Scarecrow and the Tin Man on either side of non-working dial
EX $75   NM $125   MIP $175

Vinyl Stick-On Play Set, 1989, Multi Toys, 10 vinyl stickers w/Emerald City background, on header card
EX $4   NM $6   MIP $10

Water Guns, 1976, Durham, heads of Scarecrow, Tin Man, or Cowardly Lion, water squirts out of nose, each
EX $15   NM $30   MIP $70

Wicked Witch Mask, 1975, Ben Cooper
EX $6   NM $12   MIP $25

Wizard of Oz Costume, 1961, Halco, costume and mask
EX $20   NM $35   MIP $75

Wizard of Oz Hand Puppets, 1965, Proctor and Gamble, plastic
EX $8   NM $20   MIP $40

Wizard of Oz Hand Puppets, 1989, Presents, several characters available, each
EX $8   NM $15   MIP $35

Wizard of Oz Hand Puppets, 1989, Multi Toys, set of six on blister cards, each
EX $6   NM $20   MIP $50

Wizard of Oz Wind-Ups, 1989, Multi Toys, 50th anniversary editions, several characters, each
EX $4   NM $12   MIP $25

WATCH

Oz Time Wristwatch, 1989, Macy's, 50th anniversary premium, round face w/Emerald City, black plastic band
EX $30   NM $50   MIP $100

Wizard of Oz Pocket Watch, 1980s, Westclock, silver finish case, four characters on dial
EX $20   NM $35   MIP $85

Wizard of Oz Wristwatch, 1989, EKO, child's LCD, red face in round yellow case, plastic band shows yellow brick road and Emerald City
EX $15   NM $25   MIP $60

Wizard of Oz Wristwatch, 1989, EKO, quartz, illustrated face showing Emerald City, black plastic band
EX $15   NM $25   MIP $60

Woody Woodpecker

ACCESSORIES

Alarm Clock, 1959, Columbia Time, Woody's Cafe
EX $100   NM $200   MIP $400

Lamp, 1971
EX $30   NM $60   MIP $135

Wrist Watch, 1940s, in box
EX $850   NM $1250   MIP $1750

BOOK

Woody Woodpecker's Fun-o-Rama Punch-Out Book, 1972
EX $20   NM $30   MIP $60

TOY

Paper Dolls, 1968, Saalfield, Woody Woodpecker and Andy Panda
EX $30   NM $50   MIP $90

Playing Cards, 1950s, two decks in a carrying case
EX $40   NM $65   MIP $100

Woody Woodpecker Hand Puppet, 1963, Mattel, pull-string voice box
EX $50   NM $90   MIP $135

Woody Woodpecker Nodder, 1950s
EX $75   NM $125   MIP $200

Yogi Bear

ACCESSORIES

Coat Rack, 1979, Wolverine, 48", red wood, Yogi and Boo Boo cut out in front, growth chart on back
EX $40   NM $70   MIP $100

Hot Water Bottle, 1966
EX $25   NM $50   MIP $75

Safety Scissors, 1973, Monogram, on card
EX $4   NM $7   MIP $15

BANK

Yogi Bear Bank, 1960s, Knickerbocker, 22", figural
EX $40   NM $75   MIP $150

Yogi Bear Bank, 1980, Dakin, 7", figural
EX $6   NM $15   MIP $50

BOOK

Snagglepuss Sticker Fun Book, 1963, Whitman
EX $15   NM $35   MIP $80

Yogi vs. Magilla for President Coloring Book, 1964, Whitman, Model No. 1144
EX $35   NM $70   MIP $125

DOLL

Boo Boo Doll, 1960s, Knickerbocker, 9-1/2" tall, plush
EX $30   NM $60   MIP $120

Cindy Bear Doll, 1959, Knickerbocker, 16", plush w/vinyl face
EX $40   NM $70   MIP $140

Yogi Bear Doll, 1959, Knickerbocker, 16" plush w/vinyl face
EX $75   NM $150   MIP $300

Yogi Bear Doll, 1959, Knickerbocker, 10" tall
EX $125   NM $250   MIP $400

Yogi Bear Doll, 1960s, Knickerbocker, 19" plush
EX $75   NM $150   MIP $300

Yogi Bear Doll, 1962, 6", soft vinyl w/movable arms and head
EX $75   NM $125   MIP $200

Yogi Bear Stuff and Lace Doll, 1959, Knickerbocker, items to make a 13" x 5" doll
EX $30   NM $60   MIP $125

Yogi Squeeze Doll, 1979, Sanitoy, 12", vinyl
EX $10   NM $35   MIP $75

FIGURES

Character Figures, 1960, 12" tall, Yogi, Boo Boo, and Ranger Smith, each
EX $30   NM $60   MIP $90

Snagglepuss Figure, 1970, Dakin
EX $30   NM $75   MIP $140

Yogi Bear Figure, 1960s, Knickerbocker, 9" tall, plastic
EX $25   NM $50   MIP $120

Yogi Bear Figure, 1961, Marx, TV-Tinykins
EX $20   NM $35   MIP $80

Yogi Bear Figure, 1970, Dakin, 7-3/4" tall
EX $20   NM $35   MIP $80

GAME

Yogi Bear and Pixie and Dixie Game Car, Whitman, 7-1/2" pile on game in car
EX $30   NM $60   MIP $120

Yogi Score-A-Matic Ball Toss Game, 1960, Transogram
EX $50   NM $100   MIP $150

TOY

Bubble Pipe, 1963, Transogram, Yogi Bear figural pipe
EX $20   NM $35   MIP $50

Magic Slate, 1963
EX $20   NM $40   MIP $75

Snagglepuss Soaky, 1960s, Purex, 9" tall, vinyl/plastic
EX $20   NM $40   MIP $90

Yogi Bear and Cindy Push Puppet Set, 1960s, Kohner, boxed set of two
EX $60   NM $125   MIP $250

Yogi Bear Cartoonist Stamp Set, 1961, Lido
EX $30   NM $70   MIP $100

Yogi Bear Friction Toy, 1960s, Yogi in yellow tie and green hat, illustrated red box
EX $100   NM $175   MIP $300

Yogi Bear Ge-Tar, 1960s, Mattel
EX $55   NM $100   MIP $160

Yogi Bear Hand Puppet, Knickerbocker
EX $20   NM $35   MIP $75

Yogi Bear Paint 'Em Pals, 1978, Craft Master, paint-by-number set
EX $15   NM $30   MIP $75

Yogi Bear Push Puppet, 1960s, Kohner
EX $35   NM $45   MIP $90

WATCH

Yogi Bear Wristwatch, 1963
EX $80   NM $125   MIP $250

Yogi Wristwatch, 1967, Bradley, medium base metal case, shows Yogi w/hobo sack on stick, black vinyl band
EX $80   NM $120   MIP $250

Yosemite Sam

ACCESSORIES

Mini Snow Dome, 1980s, Applause
EX $9   NM $16   MIP $25

Musical Snow Dome, 1980s, Applause
EX $15   NM $30   MIP $50

FIGURES

Yosemite Sam Figure, 1968, Dakin, 7" tall
EX $20   NM $40   MIP $80

Yosemite Sam Figure, 1971, Dakin, on treasure chest
EX $20   NM $40   MIP $80

Yosemite Sam Figure, 1978, Dakin, Fun Farm
EX $15   NM $25   MIP $60

TOY

Yosemite Sam Nodder, 1960s, 6-1/4", bobbing head and spring mounted head
EX $125   NM $175   MIP $350

Fisher-Price

By Bruce Fox

With their colorful paper lithography attached to sturdy wooden toys, Fisher-Price toys conjure up nostalgic images for four generations of collectors. These toys have been woven into the fabric of our childhood tapestry.

More than 80 years after the production of their first toys, Fisher-Price is still the first choice of parents and grandparents seeking safe, well-made toys for their loved ones.

Founded by Herman Fisher, Irving Price and Helen Schelle on Sept. 9, 1930 in East Aurora, N.Y., the company was determined to create toys with a matchless charm and unprecedented quality. Known as the "Sixteen Hopefuls," sixteen toys were introduced at Toy Fair in 1931. They included Doctor Doodle and Granny Doodle, a pair of whimsical ducks that initiated the use of animal characters as a staple in the Fisher-Price line.

The foundation of Fisher-Price Toys' long-term success has been the timeless application of the Fisher-Price Five-Point Creed introduced at Toy Fair 1931: Intrinsic Play Value; Ingenuity; Strong Construction; Good Value for The Money; and Action.

Most collectors are familiar with the look of vintage Fisher-Price toys with their crisp, colorful paper lithography glued onto Ponderosa pine. Fisher-Price quickly realized the value of licensing, and in 1935, the company issued the Walt DisneyMickey Mouse Band, featuring Mickey and Pluto.

This piece can command more than $2,000 in Mint Condition today. Other Disney characters and Popeye also became favorites and are very desirable in today's market. Musical toys, especially items featuring bells or xylophones, became perennial favorites.

The Fisher-Price Play Family first appeared in 1959 in the yellow wooden Safety School Bus. With bodies made of wood, the Play Family could be removed from their vehicles. Their body styles and compositions have changed over the years, and today, the Little People (trademarked in 1985) are larger, poseable, made of plastic, and have names like Eddy, Sonya Lee and Sarah Lynn.

Fisher-Price Brands, a division of Mattel, Inc., has grown from its simple beginnings in 1931 to become the largest preschool toy company in the world. The Fisher-Price Collector's Club is an excellent resource for collectors. Their Web site is: www.fpclub.org.

Some Fisher-Price toys had more than one variation, which may mean different values for vintage toys. The date on the toy is only a copyright date, which is earlier than the actual date of manufacture. Especially important to note is that the values are determined by rarity, desirability, and condition and prices noted include all original parts and accessories.

The recent downturn in the economy has created the opportunity to purchase hard-to-find Fisher-Price toys at reasonable prices. Of special note is the reduction in demand and value for Disney and comic character toys. Some vintage toys will always hold their value because of their rarity and desirability, especially with the original box.

Bruce Fox retired from Fisher-Price after 30 years of outstanding service, winning multiple sales awards during his career. He has co-authored two books on Fisher-Price history, including toy values. As the company's spokesperson for the 75th anniversary in 2005, he appeared on ABC television and hosted a satellite media tour. Through decades of searching, Fox has acquired the largest known private collection of vintage Fisher-Price toys, including the 1931 "Sixteen Hopefuls" and every company catalog.

Bruce lives in Northwest Arkansas with his lovely wife Becky. He can be reached through his website, www.FisherPriceAuthor.com.

The **Top 10 FISHER-PRICE** in mint condition

1. Push Cart Pete, 1936	$9,500
2. Skipper Sam, 1934	$6,500
3. Donald Duck Bak-Up, 1936	$6,000
4. Bunny Scoot, 1931	$5,500
5. Penelope Penguin, 1935	$5,000
6. Donald & Donna Duck, 1937	$5,000
7. Road Roller, 1934	$4,500
8. Raggedy Ann & Andy, 1941	$3,750
9. American Airline's Flagship, 1941	$3,500
10. Tricky Tommy, 1936	$3,500

Vintage

Allie Gator, 1960, w/plastic flippers on wooden wheels, Model No. 653
EX $45   **NM** $60   **M** $75

American Airlines Flagship, 1941, w/original tail, props, springs, wheels, Model No. 170
EX $1800 **NM** $2400 **MIP** $3500

Amusement Park, 1963, 20 pieces, chair ride, musical merry-go-round, play swing, choo-choo, play people and more, Model No. 932
EX $150   **NM** $225   **MIP** $400

Baby Chick Tandem Cart, 1953, Easter only, Model No. 50
EX $30   **NM** $50   **M** $70

Barky Buddy, 1934, blue and yellow military uniform, red hat, red wheels, Model No. 150
EX $900   **NM** $1400 **MIP** $1800

Barky Dog, 1958, black and white w/red wheels, Model No. 462
EX $50   **NM** $75   **MIP** $185

Barky Puppy, 1931, blue wheels, oilcloth ears, pipecleaner and wooden ball tail, Model No. 103
EX $550   **NM** $850   **MIP** $1500

Big Bill Pelican, 1961, opening bill, cardboard fish the first three years of release (add $25 if present), light blue feet, Model No. 794
EX $35   **NM** $50   **MIP** $75

Big Performing Circus, 1932, included nine figures, w/all parts, Model No. 250
EX $450   **NM** $800   **MIP** $1600

Blackie Drummer, 1939, bear in parade uniform strikes bass drum w/right arm and cymbal w/left arm, Model No. 785
EX $500   **NM** $750   **MIP** $1200

Bonny Bunny Wagon, 1959, Easter release, bunny pulling wagon, light blue wheels, Model No. 318
EX $30   **NM** $50   **M** $60

Boom Boom Popeye, 1937, Popeye and Sweatpea, two mallets hit litho drum, unpainted wheels, Model No. 491
EX $300   **NM** $500   **M** $750

Bossy Bell, 1959, bell, light blue wheels, yellow tail and horns, Model No. 656
EX $35   **NM** $50   **M** $70

Bouncing Bunny Wheelbarrow, 1939, bell on head, Model No. 727
EX $300   **NM** $450   **M** $600

Bouncy Racer, 1960, driver w/helmet bounces and arms move as pulled, large red plastic wheels, Model No. 8
EX $40   **NM** $60   **MIP** $90

Bruno Bak-Up, 1932, pushes wheelbarrow, Model No. 375
EX $850   **NM** $1300 **MIP** $1800

(John Murray, photo by Russ MacKeamin)

Bucky Burro, 1955, yellow burro that bucks, spring tail, driver w/sombrero, Model No. 166
EX $125   **NM** $200   **MIP** $300

Buddy Bronc, 1938, cowboy bounces on horse, Model No. 430
EX $200   **NM** $350   **MIP** $600

Buddy Bullfrog, 1959, offered w/checkered pants in last year, croaking noise, jumping action, top hat, Model No. 728
EX $60   **NM** $85   **MIP** $125

Bunny Basket Cart, 1957, woven basket, Model No. 301
EX $25   **NM** $35   **M** $50

Bunny Basket Cart, 1960, plastic basket, Model No. 303
EX $30   **NM** $45   **M** $60

Bunny Bell Cart, 1941, two mallets strike bell, yellow wheels, cart in front of bunny, Model No. 520
EX $100   **NM** $200   **M** $300

Bunny Bell Cart, 1954, two mallets strike bell, light blue wheels, cart behind bunny, Model No. 604
EX $40   **NM** $60   **M** $100

Bunny Cart, 1948, white bunny pulls cylindrical cart w/metal rim, Model No. 5
EX $30   **NM** $60   **M** $100

Bunny Drummer, 1942, two mallets hit painted wood disk or metal bell, yellow wagon in front of bunny, red wheels, Model No. 512
EX $100   **NM** $160   **M** $250

Bunny Drummer, 1946, two mallets hit metal bell, yellow cart in front of bunny, red wheels, Model No. 505
EX $100   **NM** $125   **M** $175

Bunny Egg Cart, 1949, new for 1949, forerunner of the No. 406 Bunny Cart, Model No. 404
EX $50   **NM** $75   **M** $100

Bunny Egg Cart, 1950, bunny pulling cart-sides are colorful eggs, dark blue/purple wheels, Model No. 28
EX $60   **NM** $90   **M** $125

Bunny Engine, 1954, train w/bell and bunny engineer, blue w/yellow wheels, Model No. 703
EX $45   **NM** $65   **M** $95

Bunny Push Cart, 1957, bunny pushes cart, six light blue wheels, Model No. 303
EX $40   **NM** $55   **M** $80

Bunny Racer, 1942, yellow and blue "racecar" w/red wood wheels, wooden axles during World War II, Model No. 474
EX $150   **NM** $200   **M** $300

BunnyScoot, 1931, yellow wheels, oilcloth ears, Model No. 105
EX $2500 **NM** $3500 **MIP** $5500

Busy Bunny Cart, 1936, bunny pulls 7" cart, Easter release, Model No. 719
EX $750   **NM** $1000 **M** $1500

Butch the Pup, 1951, yellow wheels, tail wags, felt ears, Model No. 333
EX $35   **NM** $50   **M** $75

Buzzy Bee, 1950, first use of acetate (form of plastic) in a Fisher-Price toy, two spring antennae, Model No. 325
EX $20   **NM** $40   **MIP** $50

Cackling Hen, 1958, Model No. 120
EX $30   **NM** $45   **M** $75

Campbell Kids Farm Truck, 1954, swayed back and forth, w/paper vegetable cut-outs, Model No. 845
EX $200   **NM** $350   **MIP** $500

Cash Register, 1960, three numbered coins, plastic keys pop up characters, Model No. 972
EX $50   **NM** $75   **MIP** $100

Chatter Monk, 1957, monkey w/jumping action, wooden hat, vinyl tail, chatter sound, Model No. 798
EX $50   **NM** $75   **MIP** $125

Chatter Telephone, 1962, same as the Talk-Back Telephone of 1961, red plastic handle, blue wheels, wooden wheels (through 1966), Model No. 747
EX $15   **NM** $25   **MIP** $50

Choo-Choo Local, 1936, push toy, 18" stick, six wheels, steel bell, Model No. 517
EX $750   **NM** $900   **MIP** $1500

Chubby Chief, 1932, elephant on scooter w/steel bell, Model No. 110
EX $750   **NM** $1300 **MIP** $2000

Chuggy Pop-Up, 1955, red train, yellow wheels, pop-up engineer, metal boiler, realistic sound, Model No. 616
EX $50   **NM** $75   **M** $100

Circus, 1962, w/all parts, Model No. 900
EX $75   **NM** $125   **MIP** $225

(John Murray, photo by Russ MacKearnin)

Circus Wagon, 1942, Ringmaster's arms move up and down and pipes play, blue wheels, Model No. 156
EX $350   **NM** $500   **MIP** $900

Coaster Boy, 1941, working w/original bell, Model No. 140
EX $600   **NM** $950   **MIP** $1400

Concrete Mixer Truck, 1959, mixing drum rotates and pops, plastic grille, lithographed sides, Model No. 926
EX $150   **NM** $225   **MIP** $350

Corn Popper, 1957, red and blue push toy, Model No. 785
EX $35   **NM** $60   **MIP** $100

Corn Popper, 1963, push toy, variations of this toy endured through 1990, Model No. 788
EX $10   **NM** $15   **MIP** $30

Cotton Tail Cart, 1940, upright bunny pulls red cart, legs rotate, clicking sound, yellow wheels, Model No. 525
EX $150   **NM** $200   **M** $300

Cowboy Chime, 1951, new version of 1936 Dandy Dobbin, western pony head and litho saddle graphics attached to stick, metal musical push chime base had cowboy and indian graphics, Model No. 700
EX $150   **NM** $200   **MIP** $350

(John Murray, photo by Russ MacKearnin)

Dandy Dobbin, 1941, 14-1/2" long, 12-1/4" high, riding horse w/red seat, green or yellow wheels, braided cord bridle, Model No. 765
EX $200   **NM** $300   **M** $400

Dapper Donald Duck w/Wings, 1936, Model No. 460
EX $200   **NM** $300   **M** $400

Dashing Dobbin, 1938, riding horse, blue or red versions, braided cord bridle, 150-pound capacity, Model No. 742
EX $225   **NM** $350   **M** $500

Ding Dong Duckey, 1949, Easter release, duck's head turned side to side and concealed wires played a tune as pulled, Model No. 724
EX $100   **NM** $150   **MIP** $200

Dinkey Engine, 1959, "chug-chug" sound, pistons moved, plastic cowcatcher and cab, Model No. 642
EX $30   **NM** $40   **M** $50

Dizzy Dino, 1931, Pop-Up Kritters, dinosaur on round paddle, pulley system used 50-pound test fish line, Model No. 407
EX $600   **NM** $900   **MIP** $1250

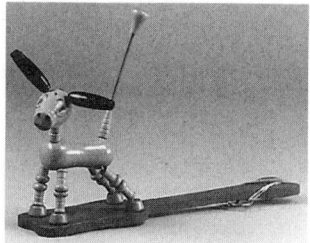

(John Murray, photo by Russ MacKearnin)

Dizzy Donkey, 1939, Pop-Up Kritters, donkey on blue paddle, black ears, Model No. 433
EX $65   **NM** $90   **MIP** $125

(John Murray, photo by Ross MacKearnin)

Doc & Dopey Dwarfs, 1938, each has hammer that hits stump, red wheels, Model No. 770
EX $550   **NM** $900   **MIP** $1600

Doctor Doodle, 1931, styled by Margaret Evans Price, blue wheels, black topcoat and hat, orange bill, Model No. 100
EX $1000   **NM** $1500   **MIP** $2000

Doctor Doodle, 1940, green wheels, waddle, lower bill moves w/clicker as quacking sound, Model No. 477
EX $100   **NM** $200   **M** $300

Dogcart Donald, 1936, Pluto pulls Donald in cart, Model No. 149
EX $600   **NM** $900   **MIP** $1500

Doggy Racer, 1942, black wheels, arms "turned" the steering wheel, Model No. 7
EX $125   **NM** $200   **M** $250

Donald & Donna Duck, 1937, w/original wings, Model No. 160
EX $2000   **NM** $3000   **MIP** $5000

(John Murray, photo by Ross MacKearnin)

Donald Duck & Nephews, 1941, w/two nephews Huey and Louie, red wheels, Model No. 479
EX $150   **NM** $225   **M** $375

Donald Duck Bak-Up, 1936, w/original wings, Model No. 358
EX $3500   **NM** $4500   **MIP** $6000

Donald Duck Cart, 1937, unpainted wheels, cart (three different colors) behind Donald, w/wings, Model No. 500
EX $325   **NM** $500   **M** $675

Donald Duck Cart, 1940, red wheels, blue base, Easter release, chick can behind Donald, Model No. 469
EX $250   **NM** $375   **M** $525

(John Murray, photo by Russ MacKearnin)

Donald Duck Cart, 1942, swinging arms, concealed voice, blue cart behind Donald in red outfit, red wheels, Model No. 544
EX $100   **NM** $150   **M** $200

Donald Duck Cart, 1954, orange flip-flop feet, quack-quack sound, flowers litho on blue and yellow cart behind Donald, Model No. 605
EX $75   **NM** $125   **M** $175

Donald Duck Choo Choo, 1937, Model No. 465
EX $200   **NM** $300   **M** $500

Donald Duck Choo-Choo, 1940, yellow wheels, blue base, red engineer's hat, steel bell, 9-1/2" long in 1940, 8-1/2" long in 1941, Model No. 450

EX $125   **NM** $200   **M** $350

(John Murray, photo by Ross MacKearnin)

Donald Duck Choo-Choo, 1942, yellow wheels, red base, blue engineer's hat, steel bell, Model No. 450

EX $65   **NM** $100   **M** $150

Donald Duck Delivery, 1936, long-billed Donald in front of pink cart w/blue wheels, Model No. 715

EX $350   **NM** $500   **M** $750

Donald Duck Drum Major, 1940, red wheels, green base, Donald holding green baton, Model No. 550/463

EX $125   **NM** $175   **M** $275

Donald Duck Drum Major, 1948, blue wheels, red base, Donald holding yellow baton, Model No. 432/532

EX $90   **NM** $140   **M** $175

Donald Duck Drummer, 1949, two mallets, arms move to strike red drum, red wheels, blue base, Model No. 454

EX $150   **NM** $200   **M** $250

Donald Duck Pop-Up, 1938, red paddle, rubber bill, w/oilcloth wings, Model No. 425

EX $300   **NM** $400   **M** $600

Donald Duck Xylophone, 1938, red wheels, blue base, blue hat, Model No. 185

EX $325   **NM** $475   **MIP** $775

(John Murray, photo by Ross MacKearnin)

Donald Duck Xylophone, 1946, red wheels, green base, blue hat (different from No. 185), Model No. 177

EX $250   **NM** $325   **MIP** $525

Dopey Dwarf, 1939, blue or yellow wheels, red base, two mallets hit drum when pulled, Model No. 770

EX $350   **NM** $600   **M** $850

Doughboy Donald, 1942, 13-3/4" long, soldier outfit, two mortars, Pluto pulling green base w/red wheels, Model No. 744

EX $650   **NM** $1000   **MIP** $1600

Drummer Bear, 1931, yellow wheels, blue base, black hat, Model No. 102

EX $450   **NM** $900   **MIP** $1700

Drummer Bear, 1932, yellow wheels, Model No. 102

EX $400   **NM** $750   **MIP** $1200

Ducky Cart, 1948, duck pulls cylinder-shaped cart w/red wheels, Model No. 6

EX $25   **NM** $50   **M** $75

Ducky Cart, 1950, litho yellow duck w/blue background, red wheels, Model No. 51

EX $35   **NM** $50   **M** $75

Ducky Daddles, 1941, yellow duck w/blue wheels, exclusive for F.W. Woolworth Co., Model No. 14

EX $40   **NM** $60   **M** $100

Ducky Daddles, 1942, predecessor of Snap Quack, waddle, movable feet, head turns side to side, quacks, Model No. 148

EX $100   **NM** $150   **MIP** $250

Ducky Flip-Flap, 1937, purple cart, Model No. 717

EX $225   **NM** $300   **M** $375

Ducky Transport, 1937, mom w/two ducklings, rubber feet, Model No. 799

EX $250   **NM** $325   **M** $425

Dumbo Circus Racer, 1941, rubber arms turn steering wheel, 10-3/4" long, Model No. 738

EX $600   **NM** $900   **MIP** $1500

Easter Bunny, 1936, pink and white, Model No. 490

EX $600   **NM** $800   **M** $1000

(John Murray, photo by Ross MacKearnin)

Elsie's Dairy Truck, 1948, F-P's second advertising toy, based on Borden's Elsie the Cow, truck driven by her son Beau-regard, movable arms struck nickel bell on grille, came w/two glass square bottles (add $50 for each bottle), Model No. 745

EX $150   **NM** $300   **MIP** $500

Farmer in Dell Music Box, 1962, formerly #764, red crank/handle on side, Model No. 763

EX $40   **NM** $65   **MIP** $100

Farmer in the Dell Music Box Barn, 1960, crank, strap, Swiss music box, Model No. 764

EX $40   **NM** $60   **MIP** $90

Farmer in the Dell TV Radio, 1963, spring anetnnae, white handle, Model No. 166

EX $15   **NM** $25   **MIP** $50

Ferdinand The Bull, 1939, Model No. 434

EX $350   **NM** $500   **M** $650

Fido Zilo, 1955, movable arms w/mallets to strike four nickel keys, red wheels, Model No. 707

EX $50   **NM** $75   **MIP** $125

Fire Truck, 1959, red truck w/yellow grille & ladder, driver bounces and turns when pulled, Model No. 630

EX $35   **NM** $50   **M** $75

Fred Flintstone Zilo, 1962, Sears exclusive, Model No. 712

EX $200   **NM** $250   **MIP** $500

(John Murray, photo by Russ MacKearnin)

Fuzzy Fido, 1941, spring wire tail, offset green wheels caused waddling, Model No. 444

EX $125   **NM** $175   **M** $250

Gabby Duck, 1952, blue wheels, yellow duck, orange bill opens, waddling motion, quacks, Model No. 767
EX $50   **NM** $75   **M** $100

Gabby Goofies, 1956, first version, red Daddy Goofy w/three ducklings, twirling acetate wings, Model No. 775
EX $20   **NM** $30   **MIP** $50

Gabby Goofies, 1963, final version, blue Mama Goofy w/three ducklings, Model No. 777
EX $15   **NM** $20   **MIP** $35

Gabby Goose, 1936, red wheels, sailor suit, concealed voice, Model No. 120
EX $250   **NM** $350   **MIP** $750

Galloping Horse & Wagon, 1948, horse pulling red wagon w/yellow wheels, Model No. 737
EX $100   **NM** $150   **MIP** $250

(John Murray, photo by Russ MacKearnin)

Gold Star Stagecoach, 1954, two horses pull stagecoach, driver sways side to side, two mail pouches, Model No. 175
EX $200   **NM** $325   **MIP** $475

Golden Gulch Express, 1961, red and green train, spring mounted indian on the tender, Model No. 191
EX $75   **NM** $100   **MIP** $150

Go'N Back Bruno, 1931, Model No. 355
EX $600   **NM** $1000   **MIP** $1600

Go'N Back Jumbo, 1931, Walky-Balky Back-Up Toys, wind up w/removable key, oilcloth ears, pipecleaner tail, styled by Margaret Evans Price, designed by Edward Savage, Model No. 360
EX $350   **NM** $600   **MIP** $900

Go'N Back Mule, 1931, Model No. 350
EX $350   **NM** $600   **MIP** $900

Goofy Gertie Pop-Up Critter, 1935, banjo paddle, Model No. 440
EX $60   **NM** $90   **MIP** $150

Granny Doodle, 1931, felt bonnet, orange wheels, orange bill, Model No. 101
EX $500   **NM** $750   **MIP** $1500

Granny Doodle & Family, 1933, duck followed by two baby ducks, green wheels, Model No. 101
EX $650   **NM** $1000   **MIP** $1750

Happy Helicopter, 1953, litho teddy bear pilot, yellow wheels and propellers, Model No. 498
EX $95   **NM** $135   **MIP** $200

Happy Hippo, 1962, vinyl ears, spring tail, storage inside for other toys, Model No. 151
EX $75   **NM** $130   **MIP** $175

Horse & Wagon, 1933, Model No. 605
EX $700   **NM** $1600   **MIP** $2400

Horse and Wagon, 1934, w/two wooden blocks, Model No. 610
EX $900   **NM** $1700   **MIP** $2500

Hot Diggety, 1934, wind-up, hat, painted face, heavy metal dancing feet, Model No. 800
EX $400   **NM** $650   **MIP** $1000

Hot Dog Wagon, 1938, Model No. 750
EX $125   **NM** $175   **M** $250

Hot Mammy, 1934, wind-up, hair and dress, painted face, heavy metal dancing feet
EX $400   **NM** $650   **MIP** $1000

Howdy Bunny, 1939, orange "running" legs, green base, red wheels, Model No. 757
EX $375   **NM** $600   **MIP** $900

Huckleberry Hound Zilo, 1961, Sears exclusive, Model No. 711
EX $200   **NM** $350   **MIP** $500

Huffy Puffy Train, 1958, engine, coal car, cattle car, caboose, yellow wheels, "chug-chug" sound, Model No. 999
EX $60   **NM** $90   **MIP** $125

Humpty Dump Truck, 1963, big yellow wheels, two characters, Model No. 145
EX $50   **NM** $75   **MIP** $100

Humpty Dumpty, 1957, smiling face one side, crying face on the other, bells for hands, could roll along on arms or feet, Model No. 757
EX $100   **NM** $150   **MIP** $200

Husky Dump Truck, 1961, big orange tires, two characters, Model No. 145
EX $45   **NM** $65   **MIP** $100

Ice Cream Wagon, 1940, Model No. 778
EX $325   **NM** $450   **M** $650

Jack-n-Jill TV Radio, 1959, Swiss music box, winding knob, spring aerial, Model No. 148
EX $30   **NM** $45   **MIP** $75

Jingle Giraffe, 1956, blue wheels, spring tail, nickeled bell, Model No. 472
EX $125   **NM** $175   **MIP** $250

Johnny Jumbo, 1933, circus elephant, w/or w/out bell, yellow wheels, Model No. 712
EX $750   **NM** $1500   **MIP** $2300

Jolly Jumper, 1954, red wheels w/green feet, googly eyes, Model No. 450
EX $30   **NM** $45   **M** $50

Jolly Jumper, 1963, green frog, big yellow wheels, mouth opens "croak" sound, Model No. 793
EX $25   **NM** $35   **MIP** $50

(John Murray, photo by Ross MacKearnin)

Juggling Jumbo, 1958, crank pops five colored wooden balls through circular acetate trunk, spring tail, vinyl ears, Model No. 735
EX $75   **NM** $125   **MIP** $200

Jumbo Jitterbug, 1940, Pop-Up Kritter, movable trunk and legs, oilcloth ears, blue paddle, Model No. 422
EX $100   **NM** $150   **MIP** $200

Jumbo Rolo, 1951, blue elephant pedals tricycle, six colored balls rattle in cage behind tricycle, Model No. 755
EX $100   **NM** $175   **MIP** $250

Junior Circus, 1963, 22 pieces in reusable container, Model No. 902
EX $100   **NM** $150   **MIP** $200

(John Murray, photo by Russ MacKearnin)

Katy Kackler, 1954, wings and feet move up and down, "cluck-cluck-squawk" sound, red wheels, first of three versions, Model No. 140

EX $45   NM $70   MIP $100

Kicking Donkey, 1937, large rubber ears, red wheels, rope tail, Model No. 175

EX $350   NM $500   MIP $800

Kiltie (Scotty) Dog, 1936, Model No. 450

EX $200   NM $350   MIP $850

(John Murray, photo by Ross MacKearnin)

Kitty Bell, 1950, cat's arms rotate ball that strikes bell, blue base, yellow wheels, Model No. 499

EX $60   NM $100   M $140

Lady Bug, 1961, two spring antennae, red shell, "twirp-twirp" sound, Model No. 658

EX $30   NM $45   M $60

Leo the Drummer, 1952, red base, yellow wheels, two spring "sticks" to strike drum, Model No. 480

EX $100   NM $150   M $200

Lofty Lizzy, 1931, giraffe on round paddle, Model No. 405

EX $1000   NM $1500   MIP $2000

Lookee Monk, 1931, hat w/tassel, Model No. 104

EX $500   NM $900   MIP $1600

(John Murray, photo by Ross MacKearnin)

Looky Chug-Chug, 1949, engine and coal car, red wheels, nickel bell, moving pistons, Model No. 161

EX $150   NM $200   MIP $300

(John Murray, photo by Ross MacKearnin)

Looky Fire Truck, 1950, three firemen, moving eyes, nickel bell, red truck w/yellow wheels, Model No. 7

EX $85   NM $125   MIP $175

Looky Push Car, 1962, Model No. 875

EX $50   NM $75   MIP $100

(John Murray, photo by Russ MacKearnin)

Lop-Ear Looie, 1934, Pop-Up Kritter, mouse, retailed for 25 cents; paddle in red, blue, yellow or green, Model No. 415

EX $100   NM $150   M $200

Lucky Monk, 1932, monkey in orange cart w/blue wheels, felt hat, sound, Model No. 109

EX $500   NM $900   MIP $1600

Merry Mousewife, 1962, red wheels, sweeps broom, yellow tail and hat, Model No. 662

EX $35   NM $50   MIP $75

Merry Mutt, 1949, red base, blue wheels, two nickel 3" xylophone keys, two spring mallets, Model No. 473

EX $45   NM $65   MIP $95

Mickey Mouse Band, 1935, first Disney-themed release, blue base, yellow wheels, Mickey and Pluto, push toy w/18" stick, Model No. 530

EX $750   NM $1200   MIP $2000

Mickey Mouse Choo-Choo, 1938, blue base, yellow wheels, Mickey w/long-billed red hat, nickel bell, Model No. 432

EX $300   NM $400   M $600

Mickey Mouse Drummer, 1937, pie-eyed version w/blue base, Model No. 795

EX $250   NM $375   M $600

Mickey Mouse Drummer, 1941, red base, blue wheels, Mickey's arms move and mallets hit metal-topped drum, Model No. 476

EX $125   NM $150   M $200

Mickey Mouse Puddle Jumper, 1953, yellow wheels, car sways, Mickey bounces side to side, Model No. 310

EX $75   NM $125   M $175

(John Murray, photo by Ross MacKearnin)

Mickey Mouse Safety Patrol, 1956, Mickey the motorcycle cop pulls cart, yellow wheels, hands swing reading "STOP" and "GO," Model No. 733

EX $125   NM $175   MIP $300

Mickey Mouse Xylophone, 1939, band outfit, blue base, yellow wheels, five-key xylophone, arms hold mallets, Model No. 798

EX $300   NM $400   MIP $750

Mickey Mouse Xylophone, 1942, w/out band outfit, Model No. 798

EX $250   NM $375   MIP $600

Mickey Mouse Zilo, 1963, last Sears exclusive xylophone, last Disney pull-toy, Mickey in band outfit, three xylophone keys, Model No. 714

EX $150   NM $200   MIP $400

Molly Moo-Moo, 1956, brown cow, head moves up and down, spring tail, Model No. 190

EX $60   NM $85   MIP $125

Moo-oo Cow, 1958, black and white cow, vinyl ears, pink wheels, spring tail, Model No. 155

EX $50   NM $75   MIP $110

Mother Goose, 1964, orange plastic wheels, blue scarf on head, Model No. 164

EX $25   NM $35   MIP $50

Mother Goose Music Cart, 1955, yellow goose pulls red cart, feet flip flop as pulled, Model No. 784

EX $35   NM $50   MIP $80

Music Box Sweeper, 1961, final version, Swiss music box, steel yoke, Model No. 131

EX $40   NM $60   MIP $90

Musical Duck, 1952, Model No. 795

EX $40   NM $60   MIP $90

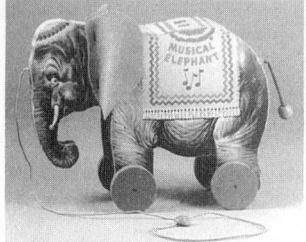

(John Murray, photo by Ross MacKearnin)

Musical Elephant, 1948, Model No. 145
 EX $150 **NM** $225 **MIP** $400

Musical Mutt, 1935, large wheels w/bell in between, Model No. 725
 EX $350 **NM** $500 **M** $600

Musical Push Chime, 1950, Model No. 722
 EX $25 **NM** $35 **MIP** $75

Musical Sweeper, 1950, Model No. 100
 EX $70 **NM** $100 **MIP** $150

Musical Sweeper, 1953, Model No. 225
 EX $45 **NM** $75 **MIP** $100

Musical Tick Tock Clock, 1962, Model No. 997
 EX $30 **NM** $45 **MIP** $60

(John Murray, photo by Ross MacKearnin)

Nifty Station Wagon, 1960, wooden car w/wood top and two plastic braces on top, w/four large straight wooden figures, blue dad, green mom, yellow cone-shaped boy, and a black dog w/white ears and a ribbed body, Model No. 234
 EX $175 **NM** $275 **MIP** $400

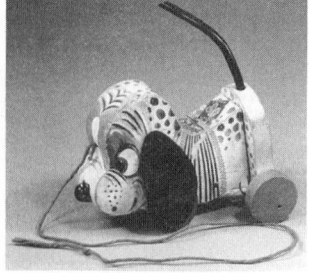

(John Murray, photo by Russ MacKearnin)

Nosey Pup, 1956, Model No. 445
 EX $35 **NM** $50 **M** $65

Patch Pony, 1963, Model No. 616
 EX $15 **NM** $25 **MIP** $35

Penelope Penguin, 1935, Model No. 345
 EX $3000 **NM** $4000 **MIP** $5000

Perky Pot, 1958, Model No. 686
 EX $50 **NM** $75 **M** $100

(John Murray, photo by Ross MacKearnin)

Peter Bunny Cart, 1939, Model No. 472
 EX $100 **NM** $150 **M** $250

Peter Bunny Engine, 1941, Model No. 715
 EX $110 **NM** $160 **MIP** $200

Peter Bunny Engine, 1949, Model No. 721
 EX $100 **NM** $140 **MIP** $200

Peter Pig, 1959, Model No. 479
 EX $25 **NM** $40 **M** $60

Pinky Pig, 1956, first version, wooden eyes, Model No. 695
 EX $35 **NM** $50 **M** $75

Pinky Pig, 1958, Model No. 695
 EX $50 **NM** $75 **M** $100

Pinocchio Express, 1939, Model No. 720
 EX $250 **NM** $350 **MIP** $650

Playful Puppy, 1961, Model No. 625
 EX $40 **NM** $55 **M** $70

Playland Express, 1962, Model No. 192
 EX $70 **NM** $90 **MIP** $145

(John Murray, photo by Ross MacKearnin)

Plucky Pinocchio, 1939, Model No. 494
 EX $200 **NM** $300 **M** $400

Pluto Pop-Up, 1936, Model No. 440
 EX $40 **NM** $75 **MIP** $125

Pony Chime, 1962, Model No. 137
 EX $35 **NM** $50 **MIP** $70

Pony Express, 1941, Model No. 733
 EX $125 **NM** $175 **MIP** $300

Poodle Zilo, 1962, Model No. 739
 EX $35 **NM** $60 **MIP** $100

Pop 'N Ring, 1959, Model No. 809
 EX $30 **NM** $50 **M** $75

Popeye, 1935, red base, yellow wheels, Model No. 700
 EX $600 **NM** $1000 **M** $1500

Popeye Cowboy, 1937, Model No. 705
 EX $350 **NM** $600 **M** $900

Popeye Spinach Eater, 1939, Model No. 488
 EX $300 **NM** $500 **M** $700

(John Murray, photo by Russ MacKearnin)

Popeye the Sailor, 1936, unpainted wheels, arms strike bell attached to steering wheel, green boat-shaped base, Model No. 703
 EX $400 **NM** $600 **M** $800

Prancing Horses, 1937, Model No. 766
 EX $500 **NM** $700 **M** $1000

Pudgy Pig, 1962, Model No. 478
 EX $25 **NM** $35 **M** $50

Puffy Engine, 1951, Model No. 444
 EX $35 **NM** $50 **MIP** $75

Pull-A-Tune Xylophone, 1957, Model No. 870
 EX $20 **NM** $40 **MIP** $75

Puppy Bak-Up, 1932, oilcloth ears, Model No. 365
 EX $350 **NM** $600 **MIP** $900

Push Cart Pete, 1936, Model No. 740
 EX $6000 **NM** $7500 **MIP** $9500

Pushy Bruno w/Stick, 1933, bell or parasol, Model No. 777
 EX $1300 **NM** $1900 **MIP** $2400

Pushy Doddle w/Stick, 1933, Model No. 507
 EX $900 **NM** $1300 **MIP** $1800

Pushy Drummer w/Stick, 1934, Model No. 520
 EX $550 **NM** $900 **MIP** $1500

Pushy Elephant w/Stick, 1934, Model No. 525

EX $1200   NM $1700   **MIP** $2000

Pushy Pat w/Stick, 1933, dog rings bell, Model No. 515

EX $600   NM $900   **MIP** $1400

Pushy Piggy w/Stick, 1932, first push toy, Model No. 500

EX $1200   NM $1600   **MIP** $2000

Quacko Duck, 1939, Model No. 300

EX $50   NM $80   **M** $120

Quacky Family, 1946, Model No. 799

EX $40   NM $60   **MIP** $100

(John Murray, photo by Russ MacKearnin)

Queen Buzzy Bee, 1950, Model No. 325

EX $25   NM $35   **M** $50

Rabbit Cart, 1950, Model No. 52

EX $35   NM $50   **M** $75

Racing Bunny Cart, 1938, checkered pants, Model No. 723

EX $125   NM $175   **M** $250

Racing Ponies, 1936, Model No. 760

EX $500   NM $750   **M** $1150

Racing Pony, 1933, Model No. 705

EX $550   NM $850   **MIP** $1300

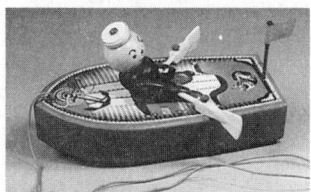

(John Murray, photo by Ross MacKearnin)

Racing Rowboat, 1952, Model No. 730

EX $125   NM $175   **M** $225

Raggedy Ann & Andy, 1941, 12" long, green base, red wheels, Model No. 711

EX $1250   NM $2500   **MIP** $3750

Rattle Ball, 1959, Model No. 682

EX $10   NM $15   **M** $20

Riding Horse, 1940, Model No. 254

EX $250   NM $350   **M** $500

Road Roller, 1934, Model No. 152

EX $2000   NM $3000   **MIP** $4500

Rock-A-Bye Bunny Cart, 1940, Model No. 788

EX $150   NM $200   **MIP** $350

Rock-A-Stack, 1960, Model No. 627

EX $20   NM $30   **MIP** $50

Roller Chime, 1953, Model No. 123

EX $35   NM $50   **MIP** $70

Rolling Bunny Basket, 1961, Model No. 310

EX $25   NM $35   **M** $50

Rooster Cart, 1938, Model No. 469

EX $250   NM $350   **MIP** $550

Rooster Pop-Up Critter, 1936, purple or yellow, Model No. 476

EX $2500   NM $3500   **MIP** $4000

Safety School Bus, 1959, first appearance of "Play Family" figures, Model No. 983

EX $200   NM $300   **MIP** $500

Safety School Bus, 1959, Model No. 983, first version and appearance of "Play Family" figures, yellow school bus w/stop sign on the driver's side and a flat nose; wooden top piece reads "Fisher-Price," six removable people w/litho on wooden bodies

EX $235   NM $400   **MIP** $550

Safety School Bus, 1960, Model No. 983, second version w/four removable people and two that are fixed in the back; as the bus moves the fixed people bounce up and down

EX $235   NM $400   **MIP** $550

Safety School Bus, 1961, yellow school bus w/stop sign on the drivers side and a flat nose, five tall wooden people, the people from this bus are similar in design to the people from the No. 990 Safety School Bus and the No. 234 Nifty Station wagon, Model No. 984

EX $200   NM $275   **MIP** $400

Safety School Bus, 1962, yellow school bus w/stop sign on the drivers side and a flat nose, five tall wooden people; the people from this bus and similar in design to the people from the No. 984 Safety School Bus and the No. 234 Nifty Station wagon, Model No. 990

EX $125   NM $175   **MIP** $225

Safety School Bus, 1962, Model No. 990

EX $125   NM $160   **MIP** $225

Scotty Dog, 1933, Model No. 710

EX $750   NM $1200   **MIP** $2100

Shaggy Zilo, 1960, Model No. 738

EX $35   NM $60   **MIP** $100

Skipper Sam, 1934, Model No. 155

EX $4000   NM $5000   **MIP** $6500

Sleepy Sue (Turtle), 1962, Model No. 495

EX $30   NM $40   **M** $60

Smokie Engine, 1960, Model No. 642

EX $25   NM $35   **M** $45

Snap Quack, 1947, designed by Lynn Bogue Hunt, Model No. 141

EX $125   NM $175   **MIP** $250

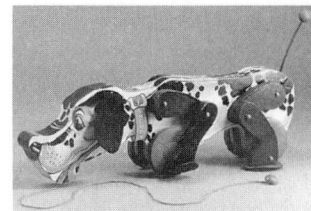

(John Murray, photo by Ross MacKearnin)

Snoopy Sniffer, 1938, Model No. 180

EX $100   NM $200   **MIP** $325

Snoopy Sniffer, 1955, Model No. 780

EX $60   NM $100   **MIP** $180

Snorky Fire Engine, 1960, four fireman figures included, Model No. 168

EX $125   NM $225   **MIP** $325

Sonny Duck Cart, 1941, Model No. 410

EX $100   NM $150   **M** $200

Space Blazer, 1953, Model No. 750

EX $250   NM $350   **M** $500

Sports Car, 1958, various colors and designs, Model No. 674

EX $50   NM $75   **M** $100

(John Murray, photo by Russ MacKearnin)

Squeaky the Clown, 1958, Model No. 777

EX $75   NM $125   **MIP** $200

Stake Truck, 1960, Model No. 649

EX $50   NM $75   **M** $100

Stoopy Storky, 1931, stork on round paddle, Model No. 410

EX $600   NM $900   **MIP** $1250

Streamline Express, 1935, Model No. 215

EX $750   NM $1000   **M** $1500

Strutter Donald Duck, 1941, Model No. 510

EX $100   NM $150   M $200

Struttin' Donald Duck, 1939, Model No. 900

EX $200   NM $300   MIP $500

Sunny Fish, 1955, Model No. 420

EX $125   NM $175   M $250

Super Jet, 1952, Model No. 415

EX $135   NM $190   M $250

Suzie Seal, 1961, Model No. 460

EX $25   NM $35   M $50

Tabby Ding Dong, 1939, Model No. 730

EX $250   NM $400   MIP $575

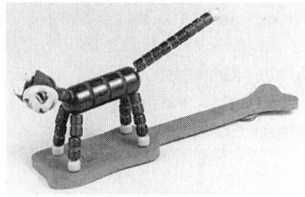

(David W Mapes, Inc.)

Tailspin Tabby, 1931, banjo w/instructions, Model No. 400

EX $50   NM $75   M $125

Tailspin Tabby Pop-Up, 1947, Model No. 600

EX $75   NM $110   MIP $150

Talk-Back Telephone, 1961, Model No. 747

EX $50   NM $110   MIP $175

(John Murray, photo by Ross MacKearnin)

Talking Donald Duck, 1955, Model No. 765

EX $100   NM $150   MIP $250

(John Murray, photo by Ross MacKearnin)

Talky Parrot, 1963, Model No. 698

EX $60   NM $90   M $125

Tawny Tiger, 1962, Model No. 654

EX $50   NM $75   M $90

Teddy Bear Parade, 1938, Model No. 195

EX $750   NM $1100   MIP $1600

Teddy Choo-Choo, 1937, Model No. 465

EX $225   NM $300   M $400

Teddy Drummer, 1936, Model No. 775

EX $325   NM $500   MI $650

Teddy Station Wagon, 1942, Model No. 480

EX $125   NM $175   M $225

Teddy Tooter, 1940, Model No. 150

EX $250   NM $400   MIP $700

Teddy Tooter, 1957, Model No. 712

EX $125   NM $175   MIP $250

Teddy Trucker, 1949, Model No. 711

EX $125   NM $175   MIP $300

Teddy Xylophone, 1948, Model No. 752

EX $75   NM $125   MIP $200

(John Murray, photo by Russ MacKearnin)

Teddy Zilo, 1950, Model No. 777

EX $60   NM $100   MIP $175

Ten Little Indians TV Radio, 1961, Model No. 159

EX $15   NM $25   MIP $50

This Little Pig, 1963, Model No. 910

EX $15   NM $25   MIP $50

Thumper Bunny, 1942, Model No. 533

EX $150   NM $250   M $350

Timber Toter, 1957, Model No. 810

EX $40   NM $60   MIP $90

Timmy Turtle, 1953, Model No. 150

EX $40   NM $60   MIP $100

Tiny Teddy, 1955, Model No. 634

EX $35   NM $50   M $75

Tiny Tim, 1957, Model No. 496

EX $25   NM $35   M $50

Tip-Toe Turtle, 1962, Model No. 773

EX $20   NM $30   MIP $45

Toot Toot Engine, 1962, Model No. 641

EX $25   NM $35   M $45

Tow Truck, 1960, Model No. 615

EX $50   NM $75   M $100

Toy Wagon, 1951, Model No. 131

EX $150   NM $225   MIP $300

Tricky Tommy, 1936, w/stick, Model No. 470

EX $1500   NM $2400   M $3500

Trotting Donald Duck, 1937, Model No. 741

EX $1000   NM $1600   M $2200

Tuggy Turtle, 1959, Model No. 139

EX $60   NM $90   MIP $125

Tumbling Tim, 1939, w/stick, Model No. 166

EX $300   NM $475   MIP $900

(John Murray, photo by Ross MacKearnin)

Uncle Timmy Turtle, 1956, Model No. 125

EX $40   NM $60   MIP $100

Waggy Woofy, 1942, Model No. 437

EX $100   NM $150   M $200

Walt Disney's Carnival, 1936, Model No. 483

EX $1100   NM $1800   MIP $2750

Walt Disney's Easter Parade, 1936, Model No. 475

EX $1000   NM $1700   MIP $2500

Walt Disney's Mickey Mouse, 1936, Model No. 209

EX $200   NM $300   M $400

Walt Disney's Pluto-the-Pup, 1936, Model No. 210

EX $200   NM $300   M $400

Wheel Horse, 1934, red wheels, horsehair tail, Model No. 200
EX $600   NM $900   M $1200

Wheel Horses, 1935-1942, various colors, all w/horsehair or wooden tails
EX $250   NM $350   M $500

Whistling Engine, 1957, Model No. 617
EX $60   NM $90   MIP $130

Wiggily Woofer, 1957, Model No. 640
EX $50   NM $90   MIP $150

Winky Blinky Fire Truck, 1954, Model No. 200
EX $45   NM $75   MIP $125

Woodsy Circus Wagon, 1933, clown, giraffe, lion, elephant, camel, pony, tickets, ticket booth, Model No. 202
EX $900   NM $1200 MIP $1800

Woodsy Wee Carts, 1932, five versions, Model No. 600
EX $2000   NM $2500   M $2900

Woodsy-Wee Zoo, 1931, five animals
EX $500   NM $900   MIP $1500

Woodsy-Wee Circus, 1931, Model No. 201
EX $800   NM $1300 MIP $2000

Woodsy-Wee Dog Show, 1932, Model No. 209
EX $750   NM $1200 MIP $1900

Woodsy-Wee Pets, 1931, four animals and a cart, Model No. 207
EX $650   NM $1000 MIP $1750

Woofy Wagger, 1947, Model No. 447
EX $90   NM $120   M $150

Woofy Wowser, 1940, Model No. 700
EX $125   NM $175   MIP $325

Ziggy Zilo, 1958, Model No. 737
EX $60   NM $90   MIP $130

Modern

ADVENTURE PEOPLE SETS

Aero-Marine Search Team, 1979, Model No. 323
EX $30   NM $45   MIP $70

Alpha Probe, 1980, Model No. 325
EX $45   NM $75   MIP $125

Alpha Recon, 1981, Model No. 359
EX $5   NM $10   MIP $20

Alpha Star, 1983, Model No. 326
EX $30   NM $55   MIP $85

Construction Workers, 1976, Model No. 352
EX $5   NM $10   MIP $20

Cycle Racing Team, 1977, Model No. 356
EX $5   NM $10   MIP $20

Daredevil Skydiver, 1976, Model No. 354
EX $5   NM $10   MIP $15

Daredevil Sport Van, 1978, Model No. 318
EX $45   NM $65   MIP $90

Deep Sea Diver, 1980, Model No. 358
EX $5   NM $10   MIP $20

Dune Buster, 1979, Model No. 322
EX $25   NM $40   MIP $65

Firestar 1, 1980, Model No. 357
EX $5   NM $10   MIP $20

Land Speed Racer, 1981, Model No. 359
EX $5   NM $10   MIP $20

Motocross Team, 1983, Model No. 335
EX $5   NM $10   MIP $20

Mountain Climbers, 1976, Model No. 351
EX $5   NM $10   MIP $20

Northwoods Trailblazer, 1977, Model No. 312
EX $45   NM $65   MIP $95

Rescue Copter, 1975, Model No. 305
EX $10   NM $30   MIP $60

Rescue Team, 1976, Model No. 350
EX $5   NM $10   MIP $20

Rescue Truck, 1975, Model No. 303
EX $10   NM $35   MIP $60

Safari, 1975, Model No. 304
EX $45   NM $75   MIP $100

Scuba Divers, 1976, Model No. 353
EX $5   NM $10   MIP $20

Sea Explorer, 1976, Model No. 310
EX $10   NM $30   MIP $50

Sea Shark, 1981, Model No. 334
EX $20   NM $35   MIP $60

Sky Surfer, 1977, Model No. 375
EX $50   NM $70   MIP $115

Sport Plane, 1975, Model No. 306
EX $10   NM $35   MIP $60

Super Speed Racer, 1976, Model No. 308
EX $5   NM $20   MIP $40

T.V. Action Team, 1977, Model No. 309
EX $65   NM $85   MIP $130

Wheelie Dragster, 1981, w/driver, Model No. 333
EX $5   NM $15   MIP $25

White Water Kayak, 1977, Model No. 355
EX $5   NM $10   MIP $20

Wilderness Patrol, 1976, Model No. 307
EX $40   NM $65   MIP $95

HUSKY PLAY SETS

Dozer Loader, 1980, Model No. 329
EX $10   NM $20   MIP $40

Farm Set, 1981, Model No. 331
EX $10   NM $20   MIP $45

Fire Pumper, 1983, Model No. 336
EX $15   NM $30   MIP $55

Firefighters, 1979, Model No. 321
EX $10   NM $20   MIP $40

Highway Dump Truck, 1980, Model No. 328
EX $10   NM $20   MIP $40

Hook & Ladder, 1979, Model No. 319
EX $10   NM $20   MIP $40

Load Master Dump, 1984, Model No. 327
EX $10   NM $20   MIP $35

Police Patrol Squad, 1981, Model No. 332
EX $15   NM $30   MIP $55

Power & Light Service Rig, 1983, Model No. 339
EX $15   NM $30   MIP $55

Power Tow Truck, 1982, Model No. 338
EX $15   NM $30   MIP $55

Race Car Rig, 1979, Model No. 320
EX $10   NM $20   MIP $40

Rescue Rig, 1981, Model No. 337
EX $15   NM $30   MIP $55

Rodeo Rig, 1980, w/figure and horses, Model No. 330
EX $10   NM $20   MIP $40

LITTLE PEOPLE

Airport, 1986, airport building, blue and yellow copter, large blue and yellow plane, four captain chairs, two orange coffee tables, green and white two-seat car w/luggage rack, one brown and one blue suitcase, three-car tram, tan bald man, short light blue blonde stewardess, short pilot, mom, boy and girl, Model No. 2502
EX $30   NM $45   MIP $65

Airport Crew, 1983, green pilot, black pilot w/blue body, and a tall light blue stewardess, Model No. 678
EX $5   NM $10   MIP $15

Beauty Salon, 1990, small beauty salon connects w/No. 2454 and No. 2455; set comes w/one pink and white car w/a luggage rack and a girl, Model No. 2453
EX $5   NM $10   MIP $20

Boat Rig, 1981, blue and white truck and trailer w/snap on gray boat holder, blue and white speedboat, one man w/white body and one dark blue worker, Model No. 345
EX $10   NM $15   MIP $25

Choo-Choo, 1963, small wood and plastic train engine w/three, three straight-sided Little People and Lucky the dog, Model No. 719

EX $10   **NM** $15   **MIP** $30

Circus Clowns, 1983, three different clowns, on card, Model No. 675

EX $5   **NM** $10   **MIP** $15

Construction Set, 1985, orange and yellow dump truck, scoop loader, bulldozer, two black barrels, one gold-cone barricade, one brown crate, two yellow w/black stripes road barricades, two white and one black construction workers, Model No. 2352

EX $5   **NM** $10   **MIP** $15

Crazy Clown Brigade, 1983, large clown car, two white crooked hoses, two white crooked ladders, white hose reel, and small green bathtub w/wheels, clown feet, tall blue clown w/white or yellow tie, and a short black clown w/a red fireman hat, Model No. 657

EX $25   **NM** $35   **MIP** $50

Cruise Boat, 1988, S.S. Tadpole, small ship, one-piece chair w/fishing pole, one yellow life preserver, short blue sea captain w/white beard, blond boy w/green base, Model No. 2524

EX $10   **NM** $15   **MIP** $25

Drive In Movie, 1990, small drive in movie building w/movie screen connects w/No. 2453 and No. 2455; set comes w/one white and yellow car w/a luggage rack and a boy, Model No. 2454

EX $5   **NM** $10   **MIP** $20

Dump Truckers, 1965, dumping station w/three slots for trucks, three trucks of different shape and color, three balls in wood or plastic, three light or dark blue straight-sided boys (one smiling, one frowning, and one w/freckles), Model No. 979

EX $40   **NM** $60   **MIP** $85

Express Train, 1987, three-car train, flat car, caboose, solid yellow one-seat car w/luggage rack, one yellow and one blue suitcase, dad, mom, light blue engineer and Lucky the dog, Model No. 2581

EX $10   **NM** $15   **MIP** $25

Farm, 1986, barn base w/mooing door, silo, four pieces of fence, tractor, cart, white harness, white trough, red chicken, white chicken, horse, cow, pig, jointed dog, sheep, dad

w/cowboy hat, mom, boy w/cowboy hat and a girl, Model No. 2501

EX $25   **NM** $35   **MIP** $50

Farm Family, 1983, dark red woman w/blonde hair, tall green dad w/white hat and yellow scarf, and a blue girl w/brown hair, Model No. 677

EX $5   **NM** $10   **MIP** $15

Farm Fun, 1985, green tractor w/yellow wheels, farmer, hay, dog, chicken, yellow trailer, Model No. 2448

EX $5   **NM** $10   **MIP** $15

Fire Pumper, 1983, long red fire engine w/two yellow braces, w/two firemen, Model No. 336

EX $20   **NM** $30   **MIP** $45

Fire Truck, 1989, large red and white truck w/cherry picker and attached yellow hose, red fire hydrant, two firemen and one dalmatian, Model No. 2361

EX $5   **NM** $10   **MIP** $15

Floating Marina, 1987, floating marina building w/two boats slips, orange seaplane, one yellow life preserver, detachable clear lighthouse dome, orange boat, red and white boat w/steering wheel, short blue captain w/white beard, boy and girl, Model No. 2582

EX $10   **NM** $15   **MIP** $25

Garage, 1986, two-story building, elevator and car ramps, fire hydrant, pay phone, gas pump, three single-seat cars, and three little boys and one little girl, Model No. 2504

EX $25   **NM** $35   **MIP** $55

Garage Squad, 1983, three workers, Model No. 679

EX $5   **NM** $10   **MIP** $15

Gas Station, 1990, small gas station building connects w/No. 2453 and No. 2454; set comes w/one red and white car w/a luggage rack and a boy, Model No. 2455

EX $5   **NM** $10   **MIP** $20

Goldilocks and the Three Bears, 1967, playhouse w/yellow key attached, w/mama bear, papa bear, baby bear, and blue girl w/blonde braids, Model No. 151

EX $45   **NM** $65   **MIP** $90

Helicopter Rig, 1981, green and white truck and trailer w/gray snap-on compass, gold one-seat helicopter, one tall blue pilot and one worker w/tan base, Model No. 344

EX $10   **NM** $15   **MIP** $25

Indy Race Rig, 1983, yellow and white truck w/trailer, red Indy-type

racecar, w/dad engineer and a driver w/a black body and helmet, Model No. 347

EX $10   **NM** $15   **MIP** $25

Jetliner, 1986, large yellow and blue plane, one blue and one brown suitcase, dad, mom, boy and girl, Model No. 2360

EX $15   **NM** $25   **MIP** $35

Little Mart, 1987, small shopping mart building, red tow truck w/orange hook, orange shopping cart, brown bag of groceries, two-seat car w/solid greenback, yellow pay phone, dad, mom, policewoman and Lucky the dog, Model No. 2580

EX $10   **NM** $15   **MIP** $25

Main Street, 1986, large building of main street w/a pull up background, two blue ramps, yellow two-seat taxi, blue mailbox, parking meter, pay phone, red fire hydrant, red stop sign, yellow turning stop light, yellow-and-black striped road diverter, mail truck, seven plastic letters, small one-seat fire truck, shopkeeper, fireman, mom, mailman, and a little girl, Model No. 2500

EX $25   **NM** $35   **MIP** $55

McDonald's, 1990, McDonald's restaurant w/pull-out playground, one blue and white two-seat car, one brown trash can, one McDonald's sign, french fry cart, Ronald McDonald, Hamburglar, mom, yellow boy w/black molded hair and girl, Model No. 2552

EX $55   **NM** $80   **MIP** $110

Neighborhood, 1989, pull apart two-piece building connected by tree, attached basketball hoop w/ball, yellow five-rung ladder, two twin beds w/teddy bear imprint, one bed w/quilt imprint, one lounge chair, modular kitchen insert, modular bathroom insert, two-seat car, turquoise pool, one round table, two captain chairs, dad, mom, boy, girl and Lucky the dog, Model No. 2551

EX $10   **NM** $15   **MIP** $30

Pampers Promotional, 1988 only, yellow mini bus w/family, green body boy and red cap exclusive to the set

EX $5   **NM** $10   **MIP** $30

Playground, 1986, green base playground w/spring rides and a slide, orange and yellow swing, orange and yellow merry-go-round, blue climbing cube, boy and girl, Model No. 2525

EX $5   **NM** $10   **MIP** $20

School, 1988, schoolhouse building w/pull-out playground, red stop sign, small school bus, yellow skateboard, white flag, chalk, orange and blue jump rope, white drum, red-bodied woman teacher w/glasses, boy, black girl, black boy, and orange-bodied girl w/glasses, Model No. 2550

EX $20   NM $30   MIP $50

Swimming Pool, 1986, swimming pool base, black stand-up grill, diving board, slide, lifeguard stand w/white life preserver, two lounge chairs (one orange and one yellow), umbrella table w/base shaped to fit in hole, boy, and a girl, Model No. 2526

EX $5   NM $10   MIP $20

PLAY FAMILY

3-Car Circus Train, 1979, three-car train, engine w/silver imprinted headlight, green or blue cage car w/lion litho, red caboose, light blue engineer, short ringmaster, and a red clown w/pointed yellow hat, Model No. 991

EX $15   NM $25   MIP $40

4-Car Circus Train, 1973, four-car train, engine w/paper headlight litho, blue or green car w/giraffe litho, blue or green flat car w/lion litho, red caboose, elephant, monkey, lion, giraffe, tan bear, short, light blue engineer, red clown w/pointed yellow hat, and a short ringmaster, Model No. 991

EX $20   NM $30   MIP $50

A-Frame, 1974, A-frame house w/removable door and sidewalk, three-rung white ladder, two sets of yellow bunk beds, two yellow lounge chairs, grill, two white picnic benches, white table w/steak litho, two yellow captain chairs, four-seat jeep, dad, mom, boy, girl and Lucky the dog, Model No. 990

EX $50   NM $75   MIP $100

Airport, 1972, large fold out airport base, white/turquoise jet, orange/yellow helicopter, four-car tram front car, two luggage cars, fuel car, two white/green two seat cars w/luggage rack, two green hat boxes, two yellow pieces of luggage, cardboard hanger parts box, dad, mom, boy, girl, stewardess, black pilot w/turquoise base, Model No. 996

EX $35   NM $60   MIP $85

Animal Circus, 1974, two yellow ladders, red hoop, yellow trapeze, blue tub (base w/clown on cardboard litho), yellow elephant stand, w/bear, monkey, lion, blue

elephant, giraffe, short ringmaster and red clown, Model No. 135

EX $10   NM $20   MIP $30

Bath and Utility Set, 1971, toilet, sink, tub, captains chair, sewing machine, washer, dryer, all wooden family consisting of a dad, mom, boy and a girl; many color variations exist, Model No. 725

EX $15   NM $20   MIP $35

Camper, 1972, green flatbed truck, white removable camper, green boat w/litho inside, boat sits on top of camper, yellow/red umbrella table, four red captain chairs, grill, yellow motorcycle, red table w/hot dog litho, toilet, sink, red ladder, dad, mom, boy, girl and Lucky the dog, Model No. 994

EX $30   NM $45   MIP $70

Car & Boat Set, 1968, car w/hook, boat w/two holes in bottom, v-shaped trailer, straight yellow body boy w/cap, and a straight-sided Lucky, Model No. 685

EX $30   NM $40   MIP $60

Car & Camper Set, 1968, car and trailer same as mini boat, wood camper marked "Fisher Price," straight yellow body boy w/cap, and a straight-sided Lucky the dog, Model No. 686

EX $30   NM $40   MIP $60

Car and Camper, 1980, 15 pieces, white and red four-seat SUV, white and red pop-up camper w/yellow canvas tent inside, yellow clam carrier w/litho on top, green and yellow boat that sits on top of jeep, two green lounge chairs, grill, green table w/steak litho, motorcycle, dad, mom, boy and girl, Model No. 992

EX $25   NM $35   MIP $60

Castle, 1974, 21 pieces, castle w/attached flag, pink dragon, one brown and one black horse, white or yellow horse armor, white or yellow scalloped horse harness, castle coach, two short red or yellow thrones, two tall red or yellow thrones, two red or yellow twin beds w/crown headboard, one red or yellow double bed w/crown headboard, one red or yellow round table w/medieval-style litho, plastic knight, woodsman, king, queen, prince, princess and a cardboard parts box; reissued in 1987 w/no flag and all plastic people, Model No. 993

EX $60   NM $100   MIP $165

Change-a-Tune Carousel, 1981, three records labeled A-B-C, two boys and a girl, Model No. 170

EX $20   NM $30   MIP $55

(KP Photo, Brent Frankenhoff collection)

Farm, 1968, barn base w/mooing door, silo, four pieces of fence, tractor, cart, white harness, white trough, red chicken, white chicken, horse, cow, pig, jointed dog, sheep, dad w/cowboy hat, mom, boy w/cowboy hat, and a girl; many variations exist, Model No. 915

EX $30   NM $40   MIP $60

Ferris Wheel, 1966, ferris wheel base winds up plays music, three Little People and Lucky the dog; first year versions come w/straight-sided Little People, Model No. 969

EX $25   NM $70   MIP $100

(Sean and Debbie Craig)

Ferry Boat, 1979, w/pull string and wheels, white and blue speed boat, two yellow life preservers, two two-seat cars, orange and black man w/out mustache, blue mom w/blonde hair, tall blue captain, Model No. 932

EX $20   NM $30   MIP $50

Fire Engine, 1969, wooden truck and a fireman, Model No. 720

EX $10   NM $15   MIP $30

Fire Station, 1980, fire house building, gray fire training tower, two yellow connecting ladders, two barricades, ambulance, fire truck w/ladder, fire chief car, two yellow truck braces, two black connecting fire hoses, two black rubber hoses, two yellow truck braces, three fireman and one dalmatian dog, Model No. 928

EX $30   NM $40   MIP $60

Fun Jet, 1970, plane w/red wings and tail, one green and one yellow suitcase, w/dad, mom, boy and a girl, Model No. 183

EX $25   **NM** $40   **MIP** $55

Garage, 1970, two-story building, elevator and car ramps, car grease rack, four single-seat cars in red, blue, green, yellow, and three little boys and one little girl, Model No. 930

EX $30   **NM** $45   **MIP** $75

Happy Hoppers, 1969, push toy play set w/three Little People that pop up and down as toy is pushed; value may fluctuate depending on version of Little People, Model No. 121

EX $15   **NM** $25   **MIP** $35

Hospital, Children's, 1976, building w/fold down door and elevator and white ambulance, turquoise plastic pieces include stretcher, x-ray, scale, two chairs, two beds, large sink, baby cradle; white plastic pieces include wheelchair, operating table, privacy screen; white baby w/out bib, white nurse w/white mask, doctor, black doctor, dad, mom and girl, Model No. 931

EX $45   **NM** $60   **MIP** $90

(Sean and Debbie Craig)

House, 1969, fold-open house w/yellow roof and attached garage, car w/hook, one double bed, two twin beds, four captain chairs, one round table, two lounge chairs, one coffee table, yellow stairs w/closet and litho, blue cardboard moving van parts box, dad, mom, boy, girl and Lucky the dog; complete w/moving van add $100-200 to total value, Model No. 952

EX $30   **NM** $45   **MIP** $70

House Decorator Set, 1970, double bed, two twin beds, T.V., checkerboard litho round table, two stuffed chairs, coffee table, all wooden family consisting of a dad, mom, boy and a girl; many color variations exist, Model No. 728

EX $20   **NM** $30   **MIP** $45

House Kitchen Set, 1970, 12 pieces, stove, sink, fridge, litho table, four captain chairs, all wooden family consisting of a dad, mom, boy and a girl; many color variations exist, Model No. 729

EX $15   **NM** $25   **MIP** $35

House w/Brown Roof, 1980, fold-open house w/a garage, green and

white car, one double bed, two twin beds, four captain chairs, one round table, two lounge chairs, one coffee table, dad, mom, boy, girl, and Lucky the dog, Model No. 952

EX $15   **NM** $25   **MIP** $45

Houseboat, 1972, blue base boat w/wheels and fold open lid, two yellow lounge chairs, two yellow life preservers, two red captain chairs, red lobster litho table, yellow grill, white/blue speedboat, white-bodied dad w/blue hat, mom, boy, girl and Lucky the dog, Model No. 985

EX $25   **NM** $30   **MIP** $60

Jetliner, 1981, green/white yellow plane, one brown and one blue suitcase, w/dad, mom, boy, and a girl, Model No. 182

EX $15   **NM** $25   **MIP** $35

Jetport, 1981, 22 pieces, airport building, blue and yellow copter, large blue and yellow plane, four captain chairs, two orange coffee tables, green and white two-seat car w/luggage rack, one brown and one blue suitcase, three-car tram, tan bald man, light blue short stewardess w/blonde hair, short pilot, mom, boy and girl, Model No. 933

EX $20   **NM** $30   **MIP** $60

Lacing Shoe, 1965, shoe w/mostly black litho and blue base, special lace, w/large all-wood mom wearing glasses, two-yellow triangle-shaped girls w/different faces, two square red boys w/different faces, and a dog w/marshmallow-shaped base, Model No. 136

EX $35   **NM** $45   **MIP** $80

Lacing Shoe, 1970, shoe w/mostly brown litho and wheels, special lace, mom wearing glasses w/regular shaped body, two yellow triangle-shaped girls w/different faces, two square red boys w/different faces, and a dog w/marshmallow-shaped base, Model No. 146

EX $25   **NM** $30   **MIP** $60

Lift & Load Depot, 1977, building, green and yellow dump truck, fork lift, scoop loader, yellow sling, four brown pallets, two brown crates, two gray crates, two black barrels, orange scoop bucket attached to building, and one black and two white workers w/light blue bodies and orange hardhats, Model No. 942

EX $20   **NM** $30   **MIP** $45

Lift & Load Lumber Yard, 1979, small lumber yard building w/yellow ramp, green and yellow lift truck, truck and

trailer, six pieces of wood lumber (two square, two long rectangular, two short rectangular), four brown pallets, one white and one black worker w/light blue bodies and orange hardhats, Model No. 944

EX $10   **NM** $15   **MIP** $30

Lift & Load Railroad, 1978, train depot building w/track section, seven-piece track (makes an oval), two-piece train (engine winds up), orange sling, two gray crates, two black barrels, four brown pallets, orange ramp, green/yellow lift truck, one white and one black worker w/light blue body and orange hardhats, tall light blue train engineer w/mustache, Model No. 943

EX $25   **NM** $40   **MIP** $65

Little Riders, 1976, plane, rocking horse, tricycle, wagon, train, w/boy and girl, Model No. 656

EX $20   **NM** $30   **MIP** $40

Merry-Go-Round, 1972, merry-go-round play set base, w/mom, two boys and a girl, Model No. 111

EX $45   **NM** $65   **MIP** $90

Mini Bus, 1970, w/five Little People: dad, mom, girl, boy, and a dog, Model No. 141

EX $15   **NM** $20   **MIP** $40

Mini Snowmobile, 1971, snowmobile w/detachable sled, turquoise boy red cap, turquoise girl w/red hair and Lucky the dog, Model No. 705

EX $25   **NM** $35   **MIP** $50

More Sesame Street Characters, 1977, boxed set showing Sesame Street scenes, comes w/Roosevelt Franklin, Grover, Sherlock Hemlock, Prairie Dawn, The Count, Harry Monster, and Snuffleupagus, Model No. 940

EX $45   **NM** $70   **MIP** $100

Music Box Lacing Shoe, 1964, wind-up musical shoe w/wheels and special lace, and three straight-sided people w/red bases, all w/different facial imprints (girl, two different boys), Model No. 991

EX $30   **NM** $45   **MIP** $75

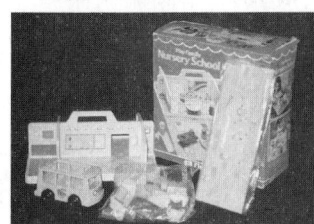

(Sean and Debbie Craig)

Nursery School, 1978, flat base w/dividing rooms and plastic edges, cardboard roof/play area, gold bus w/apple, double sink, stove, toilet, bathroom sink, slide, merry-go-round, blue easel, teeter totter, four captain chairs, round arts-and-craft table, dad, mom, black boy and two girls, Model No. 929

EX $20   **NM** $30   **MIP** $55

Nursery Sets, 1972, changing table, highchair, cradle, rocking horse, playpen, stroller, dad, mom, girl and a baby; many color variations exist, Model No. 761

EX $10   **NM** $15   **MIP** $30

Off-Shore Cargo Base, 1979, one large rectangular and square black floats, crane, tan cargo hold, helicopter landing pad, cargo hold cover, tug boat, helicopter, white and blue barge, two gold feed bags, two sections of pipe, two crates, mesh cargo net, two black tow chains, red diver, tall blue captain, and one white and one black worker w/light green bodies and yellow hardhats, Model No. 945

EX $20   **NM** $30   **MIP** $50

Patio Set, 1970, flowered umbrella table, pool w/imprint, four captain chairs, BBQ grill, all wooden family consisting of a dad, mom, boy and a girl; many color variations exist, Model No. 726

EX $20   **NM** $30   **MIP** $50

Rooms—Sears Exclusive, 1972, flat base w/divided rooms, yellow fridge, yellow double sink, yellow stove w/litho, green table w/formal setting, four green captain chairs, white tub, scale, toilet, sink, red or blue couch, two red or blue twin beds, red or blue T.V. w/litho puppet, red or blue coffeetable, red and blue stuffed chair, turquoise umbrella table, two yellow captain chairs, turquoise or yellow grill, white cotton drawstring bag, all wooden family consisting of a green bald man, blue mom w/blonde hair, orange bald boy, red girl w/blonde hair and Lucky the dog, Model No. 909

EX $100   **NM** $150   **MIP** $225

School, 1971, schoolhouse building w/bell and pull down sidewall w/chalkboard, four green or yellow student desks, one green or yellow teachers desk w/chair, green and yellow swing, merry-go-round, green or yellow slide, numbers tray, letter tray w/letters A-Z and extra P, S, T, N, R, I, and E letters, chalk box, eraser,

blue teacher w/blond hair, two boys and two girls, Model No. 923

EX $30   **NM** $45   **MIP** $70

School Bus, 1965, six wooden Little People kids, and one dog, there have been many variations of the School Bus over the years; all brown dog from first issue is worth $30-50 in excellent condition, Model No. 192

EX $55   **NM** $75   **MIP** $125

Sesame Street, 1975, brownstone fold-out building, Sesame Street lamppost, mailbox w/litho, garbage truck, five-rung white ladder, newsstand, fire hydrant on gray triangle, soda fountain stand, T.V. showing Grover, sofa, table w/pork chop litho, two captain chairs, two twin beds marked "B" and "E," chalk box, eraser, Big Bird's nest, coffeetable, Bert, Ernie, Mr. Hooper, Big Bird, Cookie Monster, Susan, Gordon, and Oscar in his can, Model No. 938

EX $55   **NM** $90   **MIP** $150

Sesame Street Characters, 1976, boxed set showing Sesame Street scenes comes w/Ernie, Bert, Cookie Monster, Susan, Gordon, Mr. Hooper, Big Bird and Oscar in his can, Model No. 939

EX $45   **NM** $70   **MIP** $100

Sesame Street Clubhouse, 1977, clubhouse w/bird nest and shaker board and attached tire swing, yellow slide, three barrels (red, blue, yellow), yellow cable drum, black and red jump rope, two-seat wagon, Big Bird, Roosevelt Franklin, Grover, The Count, Bert, and Ernie, Model No. 937

EX $55   **NM** $90   **MIP** $150

Snorkey Fire Engine, 1960, fire truck w/white base and blue wheels and yellow boom, w/four firemen w/green bases, red arms and hats, and a black dog exclusive to this set, Model No. 168

EX $150   **NM** $225   **MIP** $325

Snorkey Fire Engine, 1961, fire truck w/red base, black wheels and a yellow boom, w/four firemen w/white bases, red arms and hats, Model No. 169

EX $115   **NM** $190   **MIP** $300

Tow Truck and Car, 1969, tow truck, car w/hook, and a straight body yellow boy w/cap, Model No. 718

EX $15   **NM** $25   **MIP** $40

Village, 1973, large fold out village base, connecting bridge and traffic light, six letters, one yellow single bed, small fire engine, red and blue

police car, mail truck, four yellow captain chairs, umbrella table, green and white one-seat car w/luggage rack, white and green back-to-back two-seat car, phone booth, yellow grill, dentist chair, barber chair, yellow couch and coffeetable, black doctor, white doctor, fireman, mailman w/gray base, policewoman, mom, boy, girl and Lucky the dog, Model No. 997

EX $25   **NM** $40   **MIP** $65

Western Town, 1982, building w/shaker board, tan or green buckboard, tan or green stagecoach w/removable red top, one brown and one black horse, two brown harnesses, brown saddle, gray crate, green hatbox luggage, four-pieces fence, blue sheriff w/star badge on chest, red sodbuster man w/black hat and mustache, Native American w/chest markings on front, yellow lady w/green hat, Model No. 934

EX $25   **NM** $40   **MIP** $65

Westerners, 1983, tall ringmaster, Native American w/headdress, and a green cowboy w/10-gallon hat, on card, Model No. 676

EX $5   **NM** $10   **MIP** $20

Zoo, 1984, zoo base, tree, orange and yellow parrots, vulture, black and orange monkeys, orange cabaña, black seal, blue elephant, yellow lion cub, hippo, gorilla, mountain goat, four food trays, two green benches, one green table, three car tram, dad, mom, girl, boy, and a zookeeper w/safari-style hat, Model No. 916

EX $35   **NM** $50   **MIP** $75

Games

Board games are a peculiar bunch when it comes to collectible toys. If you had to hazard a guess as to which category of toys were most often played with in the entire toy category, board games would rank among the highest, if not the highest. Think about it—what kid didn't play some sort of board game growing up?

However, as much as nostalgia drives the toy market, you don't see the proportionate numbers of board game players become board game collectors, thus keeping values for games relatively low and easily affordable for everyone. This is due to a number of reasons. Most modern games were produced in massive numbers, thus taking scarcity out of the equation. Also, keeping all of the pieces together for games—one of the main drawing points in collecting—is a challenge. Collectors want Mint games, and that means not only having all of the pieces, but also having those pieces in good shape. Those chewed up by the family pet are not welcome here.

Trends

What people are looking for now, with the baby boomers having more time to collect and admire, are games from the 1950s and 60s in Excellent condition. Anyone can get nicely used games at any show or online venue. Most people already have that. Condition is key and collectors will pay to upgrade their collections.

For more information

Association of Games and Puzzle Collectors
www.agpc.org

The **Top 10 GAMES** in mint condition

1. Elvis Presley Game, Teen Age Games, 1957 .... $4,000
2. Challenge the Yankees, Hasbro, 1964 .... $1,800
3. Red Barber's Big League Baseball Game, G&R Anthony, 1950s $1,700
4. Munsters Masquerade Game, Hasbro, 1965 .... $1,000
5. Munsters Drag Race Game, Hasbro, 1965 .... $1,000
6. Munster Picnic Game, Hasbro, 1965 .... $1,000
7. Willie Mays "Say Hey," Toy Development, 1954 .... $700
8. Creature From the Black Lagoon, Hasbro, 1963 .... $600
9. Mickey Mouse Haunted Bagatelle, 1950s $550
10. Man From U.N.C.L.E. Target Game, 1966 .... $550

Postwar Games

BOARD GAMES

$10,000 Pyramid Game, The, 1974, Milton Bradley
EX $8   NM $15   MIP $20

$20,000 Pyramid Game, The, 1975, Milton Bradley
EX $8   NM $15   MIP $20

$25,000 Pyramid, 1980s, Cardinal Industries
EX $10   NM $15   MIP $25

$64,000 Question Quiz Game, 1955, Lowell
EX $12   NM $25   MIP $30

1-2-3 Game Hot Spot!, 1961, Parker Bros.
EX $6   NM $15   MIP $20

1863, Civil War Game, 1961, Parker Bros.
EX $10   NM $20   MIP $40

2 For The Money, 1955, Lowell
EX $10   NM $15   MIP $20

20,000 Leagues Under the Sea, 1950s, Gardner
EX $30   NM $55   MIP $50

221 B Baker Street, 1978, John Hansen
EX $2   NM $6   MIP $10

25 Ghosts, 1969, Lakeside
EX $15   NM $25   MIP $40

3 Up, 1972, Lakeside
EX $3   NM $7   MIP $12

300 Mile Race, 1955, Warren
EX $15   NM $20   MIP $40

36 Fits, 1966, Watkins-Strathmore
EX $12   NM $30   MIP $40

4 Alarm Game, 1963, Milton Bradley
EX $18   NM $40   MIP $65

4000 A.D. Interstellar Conflict Game, 1972, House of Games
EX $8   NM $20   MIP $35

(KP Photo)

77 Sunset Strip, 1960, Lowell
EX $30   NM $40   MIP $50

99, The Game of, 1969, Broman-Percepta Corp.
EX $8   NM $17   MIP $25

Abbott & Costello Who's On First?, 1978, Selchow & Righter
EX $5   NM $10   MIP $15

ABC Monday Night Football Roger Staubach Edition, 1973, Aurora
EX $15   NM $25   MIP $35

ABC Sports Winter Olympics, 1987, Mindscape
EX $10   NM $15   MIP $25

Acquire (plastic tiles), 1968, 3M
EX $12   NM $30   MIP $45

Acquire (wood tiles), 1963, 3M
EX $35   NM $75   MIP $100

Across the Board Horse Racing Game, 1975, MPH
EX $8   NM $20   MIP $35

Across the Continent (cars), 1960, Parker Bros.
EX $20   NM $30   MIP $40

Across the Continent (trains), 1952, Parker Bros.
EX $20   NM $30   MIP $40

Action Baseball, 1965, Pressman
EX $20   NM $30   MIP $40

Addams Family, 1965, Ideal
EX $65   NM $90   MIP $125

Addams Family, 1973, Milton Bradley
EX $15   NM $25   MIP $30

Admirals, 1973, Parker Bros. (U.K.)
EX $10   NM $25   MIP $35

Advance To Boardwalk, 1985, Parker Bros.
EX $5   NM $15   MIP $20

Adventure in Science, An, 1950, Jacmar
EX $20   NM $30   MIP $50

Agent Zero-M Spy Detector, 1964, Mattel
EX $30   NM $65   MIP $80

Aggravation, 1970, Lakeside
EX $5   NM $10   MIP $15

Air Assault on Crete, 1977, Avalon Hill
EX $3   NM $10   MIP $15

Air Charter, 1970, Waddington
EX $10   NM $25   MIP $35

Air Empire, 1961, Avalon Hill
EX $100   NM $200   MIP $250

Air Race Around the World, 1950s, Lido
EX $12   NM $30   MIP $50

Air Traffic Controller, 1974, Schaper
EX $12   NM $30   MIP $40

Airline, 1985, Mulgara Products
EX $4   NM $10   MIP $15

Airline: The Jet Age Game, 1977, MPH Games
EX $6   NM $16   MIP $25

Alfred Hitchcock "Why?," 1965, Milton Bradley
EX $10   NM $20   MIP $30

Alfred Hitchcock Presents Mystery Game "Why," 1958, Milton Bradley
EX $20   NM $35   MIP $55

(KP Photo)

Alien, 1979, Kenner
EX $15   NM $30   MIP $40

All American Football, 1969, Cadaco
EX $5   NM $10   MIP $20

(KP Photo)

All In The Family, 1972, Milton Bradley
EX $10   NM $20   MIP $30

All My Children, 1985, TSR
EX $5   NM $10   MIP $20

All Pro Baseball, 1969, Ideal
EX $20   NM $35   MIP $55

All Pro Basketball, 1969, Ideal
EX $10   NM $25   MIP $35

All Pro Football, 1967, Ideal
EX $10   NM $30   MIP $30

All Star Baseball, 1960s, Cadaco-Ellis
EX $30   NM $65   MIP $125

All Star Baseball, 1970s, Cadaco-Ellis
EX $10   NM $25   MIP $45

All Star Baseball, 1989, Cadaco
EX $5   NM $12   MIP $20

All Star Baseball Fame, 1962, Cadaco-Ellis
EX $15   NM $25   MIP $40

All Star Basketball, 1950s, Gardner
EX $55   NM $90   MIP $135

All Star Electric Baseball & Football, 1955, Harett-Gilmar
EX $35   NM $65   MIP $90

All Star Football, 1950, Gardner
EX $20   NM $45   MIP $65

All The King's Men, 1979, Parker Bros.
EX $6   NM $10   MIP $15

All Time Greats Baseball Game, 1971, Midwest Research
EX $15   NM $35   MIP $50

Alumni Fun, 1964, Milton Bradley
EX $8   NM $20   MIP $30

Amazing Dunninger Mind Reading Game, 1967, Hasbro
EX $12   NM $20   MIP $25

American Derby, The, 1951, Cadaco-Ellis
EX $15   NM $20   MIP $30

American Dream, The, 1979, Milton Bradley
EX $10   NM $25   MIP $35

Animal Crackers, 1970s, Milton Bradley
EX $4   NM $7   MIP $11

Annette's Secret Passage, 1958, Parker Bros.
EX $10   NM $20   MIP $30

Annie Oakley (larger), 1955, Milton Bradley
EX $20   NM $40   MIP $60

Annie Oakley (smaller game), 1950s, Milton Bradley
EX $12   NM $30   MIP $40

Annie, The Movie Game, 1981, Parker Bros.
EX $4   NM $6   MIP $10

Anti-Monopoly, 1973, Anti-Monopoly
EX $8   NM $20   MIP $30

APBA "Pro" League Football, 1980s, APBA
EX $12   NM $20   MIP $30

APBA Baseball Master Game, 1975, APBA
EX $20   NM $75   MIP $100

APBA Pro League Football, 1964, APBA
EX $25   NM $60   MIP $85

APBA Saddle Racing Game, 1970s, APBA
EX $15   NM $25   MIP $40

Apollo: A Voyage to the Moon, 1969, Tracianne
EX $12   NM $30   MIP $40

Apple's Way, 1974, Milton Bradley
EX $12   NM $20   MIP $30

Archies, The, 1969, Whitman
EX $15   NM $20   MIP $40

Arena, 1962, Lakeside
EX $6   NM $15   MIP $25

Arnold Palmer's Inside Golf, 1961, D.B. Remson
EX $30   NM $45   MIP $75

Around the World, 1962, Milton Bradley
EX $10   NM $25   MIP $35

Around The World in 80 Days, 1957, Transogram
EX $10   NM $20   MIP $30

Art Lewis Football Game, 1955, Morgantown Game
EX $70   NM $115   MIP $175

Art Linkletter's House Party, 1968, Whitman
EX $8   NM $20   MIP $30

As The World Turns, 1966, Parker Bros.
EX $12   NM $20   MIP $30

ASG Baseball, 1989, 3W (World Wide Wargames)
EX $15   NM $35   MIP $50

ASG Major League Baseball, 1973, Gerney Games
EX $35   NM $75   MIP $125

Assembly Line, 1953, Selchow & Righter
EX $18   NM $27   MIP $50

Astro Launch, 1963, Ohio Art
EX $18   NM $40   MIP $60

Astron, 1955, Parker Bros.
EX $25   NM $35   MIP $60

(KP Photo)

A-Team, 1984, Parker Bros.
EX $5   NM $15   MIP $15

Atom Ant Game, 1966, Transogram
EX $25   NM $60   MIP $90

Aurora Pursuit! Game, 1973, Aurora
EX $8   NM $25   MIP $40

Auto Dome, 1967, Transogram
EX $18   NM $40   MIP $60

Autograph Baseball Game, 1948, Philadelphia Inquirer
EX $110   NM $180   MIP $275

B.T.O. (Big Time Operator), 1956, Bettye-B
EX $20   NM $30   MIP $40

B-17 Queen of The Skies, 1983, Avalon Hill
EX $6   NM $10   MIP $15

(KP Photo)

Babes in Toyland, 1961, Whitman
EX $15   NM $27   MIP $35

Ballplayer's Baseball Game, 1955, Jon Weber
EX $30   NM $50   MIP $75

Bamboozle, 1962, Milton Bradley
EX $15   NM $20   MIP $30

Banana Tree, 1977, Marx
EX $10   NM $15   MIP $25

Bang, A Game of the Old West, 1956, Selchow & Righter
EX $35   NM $75   MIP $100

Bantu, 1955, Parker Bros.
EX $15   NM $22   MIP $30

Barbapapa Takes A Trip, 1977, Selchow & Righter
EX $3   NM $5   MIP $8

Barbie, Queen of The Prom, 1960, Mattel
EX $30   NM $60   MIP $85

Barbie's Little Sister Skipper Game, 1964, Mattel
EX $15   NM $40   MIP $60

(KP Photo)

Baretta, 1976, Milton Bradley
EX $30   NM $50   MIP $75

Bargain Hunter, 1981, Milton Bradley
EX $6   NM $15   MIP $25

(KP Photo)

Barnabas Collins Game, 1969, Milton Bradley
EX $20   NM $50   MIP $70

(KP Photo)

Barney Miller, 1977, Parker Bros.
EX $10   NM $15   MIP $25

Barnstormer, 1970s, Marx
EX $20   NM $35   MIP $55

Bart Starr Quarterback Game, 1960s
EX $175   NM $300   MIP $450

Bar-Teen Ranch Game, 1950s, Warren Built-Rite
EX $10   NM $25   MIP $35

Baseball Challenge, 1980, Tri-Valley Games
EX $15   **NM** $35   **MIP** $50

Baseball Game, Official, 1969, Milton Bradley
EX $50   **NM** $77   **MIP** $100

Baseball Game, The, 1988, Horatio
EX $12   **NM** $20   **MIP** $30

Baseball Strategy, 1973, Avalon Hill
EX $6   **NM** $15   **MIP** $25

Baseball, A Sports Illustrated Game, 1971-73, Time
EX $60   **NM** $150   **MIP** $200

Baseball, Football & Checkers, 1957, Parker Bros.
EX $20   **NM** $30   **MIP** $50

Basketball Strategy, 1974, Avalon Hill
EX $10   **NM** $15   **MIP** $25

(KP Photo)

Bat Masterson, 1958, Lowell
EX $20   **NM** $45   **MIP** $75

Batman, 1978, Hasbro
EX $15   **NM** $30   **MIP** $50

Batman and Robin Game, 1965, Hasbro
EX $30   **NM** $75   **MIP** $95

Batman Game, 1966, Milton Bradley
EX $25   **NM** $65   **MIP** $90

Batter Up, 1946, M. Hopper
EX $30   **NM** $50   **MIP** $75

Batter-Rou Baseball Game (Dizzy Dean), 1950s, Memphis Plastic
EX $100   **NM** $165   **MIP** $250

Battle Cry, 1962, Milton Bradley
EX $25   **NM** $40   **MIP** $85

(KP Photo)

Battle Line, 1964, Ideal
EX $25   **NM** $40   **MIP** $75

Battle Masters, 1992, Milton Bradley
EX $15   **NM** $40   **MIP** $60

(KP Photo)

Battle of the Planets, 1979, Milton Bradley
EX $15   **NM** $25   **MIP** $35

Battleboard, 1972, Ideal
EX $10   **NM** $25   **MIP** $35

Battleship, 1965, Milton Bradley
EX $10   **NM** $15   **MIP** $20

(KP Photo)

Battlestar Galactica, 1978, Parker Bros.
EX $10   **NM** $22   **MIP** $25

Battling Tops Game, 1968, Ideal
EX $30   **NM** $50   **MIP** $80

Bazaar, 1967, 3M
EX $12   **NM** $30   **MIP** $40

Bazaar, 1987, Discovery Toys
EX $8   **NM** $20   **MIP** $30

Beany & Cecil Match It, 1960s, Mattel
EX $30   **NM** $55   **MIP** $80

Beat Inflation, 1975, Avalon Hill
EX $8   **NM** $20   **MIP** $30

Beat the 8 Ball, 1975, Ideal
EX $10   **NM** $15   **MIP** $25

Beat The Buzz, 1958, Kenner
EX $10   **NM** $17   **MIP** $25

Beat The Clock, 1954, Lowell
EX $15   **NM** $35   **MIP** $50

Beat The Clock, 1960s, Milton Bradley
EX $6   **NM** $10   **MIP** $16

(KP Photo)

Beatles Flip Your Wig Game, 1964, Milton Bradley
EX $100   **NM** $150   **MIP** $275

Beetle Bailey, The Old Army Game, 1963, Milton Bradley
EX $20   **NM** $40   **MIP** $65

Behind the 8 Ball Game, 1969, Selchow & Righter
EX $8   **NM** $15   **MIP** $20

(KP Photo)

Ben Casey MD Game, 1961, Transogram
EX $15   **NM** $20   **MIP** $35

Bermuda Triangle, 1976, Milton Bradley
EX $10   **NM** $15   **MIP** $20

Betsy Ross and the Flag, 1950s, Transogram
EX $18   **NM** $45   **MIP** $70

Beverly Hillbillies Game, 1963, Standard Toykraft, "If you like the T.V. show… you'll love the game…"
EX $25   **NM** $40   **MIP** $50

Bewitched, 1965
EX $50   **NM** $75   **MIP** $100

Beyond the Stars, 1964, Game Partners
EX $20   **NM** $45   **MIP** $65

Bible Baseball, 1950s, Standard
EX $50   **NM** $75   **MIP** $150

Big Boggle, 1979, Parker Bros.
EX $10   **NM** $15   **MIP** $20

Big Foot, 1977, Milton Bradley
EX $5   **NM** $12   **MIP** $20

Big League Baseball, 1959, Saalfield
EX $20   **NM** $45   **MIP** $65

Big League Baseball Game, 1966, 3M
EX $15   **NM** $25   **MIP** $40

Big League Manager Football, 1965, BLM
EX $30   NM $75   MIP $100

Big Payoff, 1984, Payoff Enterprises
EX $6   NM $10   MIP $15

Big Six Sports Game, 1950s, Gardner
EX $125   NM $275   MIP $450

Big Time Colorado Football, 1983, B.J. Tall
EX $6   NM $10   MIP $15

Big Town, 1954, Lowell
EX $10   NM $20   MIP $40

Billionaire, 1973, Parker Bros.
EX $5   NM $10   MIP $15

Bing Crosby's Game, Call Me Lucky, 1954, Parker Bros.
EX $15   NM $35   MIP $50

Bingo-Matic, 1954, Transogram
EX $5   NM $10   MIP $15

(KP Photo)

Bionic Crisis, 1975, Parker Bros.
EX $6   NM $15   MIP $22

(KP Photo)

Bionic Woman, 1976, Parker Bros.
EX $6   NM $15   MIP $22

Bird Brain, 1966, Milton Bradley
EX $10   NM $25   MIP $40

Bird Watcher, 1958, Parker Bros.
EX $15   NM $35   MIP $50

Birdie Golf, 1964, Barris
EX $15   NM $35   MIP $50

Black Ball Express, 1957, Schaper
EX $8   NM $25   MIP $40

Black Beauty, 1957, Transogram
EX $15   NM $25   MIP $25

Black Box, 1978, Parker Bros.
EX $5   NM $10   MIP $15

Blade Runner, 1982
EX $25   NM $60   MIP $85

Blast Off, 1953, Selchow & Righter
EX $50   NM $100   MIP $125

Blast, The Game of, 1973, Ideal
EX $8   NM $20   MIP $35

Blitzkrieg, 1965, Avalon Hill
EX $4   NM $10   MIP $16

Blockhead, 1954, Russell
EX $5   NM $10   MIP $25

Blondie, 1970s, Parker Bros.
EX $6   NM $10   MIP $17

Blondie and Dagwood's Race for the Office, 1950, Jaymar
EX $20   NM $35   MIP $70

Blue Line Hockey, 1968, 3M
EX $10   NM $25   MIP $40

Bluff, 1964, Saalfield
EX $10   NM $25   MIP $40

BMX Cross Challenge Action Game, 1988, Cross Challenge
EX $6   NM $10   MIP $15

Bob Feller's Big League Baseball, 1949, Saalfield
EX $75   NM $100   MIP $150

Bobbsey Twins, 1957, Milton Bradley
EX $8   NM $15   MIP $20

Bobby Shantz Baseball Game, 1955, Realistic Games
EX $80   NM $150   MIP $235

Body Language, 1975, Milton Bradley
EX $2   NM $5   MIP $10

Boggle, 1976, Parker Bros.
EX $3   NM $8   MIP $12

(KP Photo)

Bonanza Michigan Rummy Game, 1964, Parker Bros.
EX $20   NM $35   MIP $40

Bonkers!, This Game is, 1978, Parker Bros.
EX $3   NM $10   MIP $15

Boom or Bust, 1951, Parker Bros.
EX $75   NM $150   MIP $200

Booth's Pro Conference Football, 1977, Sher-Co
EX $10   NM $15   MIP $25

(KP Photo)

Boots and Saddles, 1960, Chad Valley
EX $35   NM $65   MIP $100

Boris Karloff's Monster Game, 1965, Gems
EX $100   NM $150   MIP $250

Boston Marathon Game, Official, 1978, Perl Products
EX $15   NM $25   MIP $35

Bottoms Up, 1970s
EX $3   NM $5   MIP $8

Boundary, 1970, Mattel
EX $8   NM $20   MIP $30

Bowl & Score, 1974, Lowe
EX $6   NM $8   MIP $10

Bowl And Score, 1962, Lowe
EX $6   NM $10   MIP $15

Bowl Bound!, 1973, Sports Illustrated
EX $15   NM $25   MIP $40

Brain Waves, 1977, Milton Bradley
EX $6   NM $15   MIP $25

(KP Photo)

Branded, 1966, Milton Bradley
EX $25   NM $45   MIP $60

Brass Monkey Game, The, 1973, U.S. Game Systems
EX $2   NM $5   MIP $10

Break Par Golf Game, 1950s, Warren/Built-Rite
EX $8   NM $20   MIP $30

Break The Bank, 1955, Bettye-B
EX $12   NM $25   MIP $40

Breaker 1-9, 1976, Milton Bradley
EX $5   NM $10   MIP $15

Breakthru, 1965, 3M
EX $8   NM $20   MIP $35

Brett Ball, 1981, 9th Inning
EX $15   NM $20   MIP $30

Bride Bingo, 1957, Leister Game
EX $2   NM $5   MIP $8

Bride Game, The, 1971, Selchow & Righter
EX $12   NM $25   **MIP** $50

Broadside, 1962, Milton Bradley
EX $35   NM $75   **MIP** $100

Broadsides & Board Gameing Parties, 1984, Milton Bradley
EX $50   NM $125   **MIP** $175

Bruce Jenner Decathlon Game, 1979, Parker Bros.
EX $4   NM $7   **MIP** $11

Buck Fever, 1984, L & D Robton
EX $12   NM $20   **MIP** $30

Buck Rogers Game, 1979, Milton Bradley
EX $10   NM $25   **MIP** $40

Buck Rogers: Battle for the 25th Century, 1988, TSR
EX $18   NM $45   **MIP** $65

Buckaroo, 1947, Milton Bradley
EX $20   NM $35   **MIP** $45

Bucket Ball, 1972, Marx
EX $10   NM $15   **MIP** $25

Bug-A-Boo, 1968, Whitman
EX $6   NM $15   **MIP** $20

(KP Photo)

Bugaloos, 1971, Milton Bradley
EX $15   NM $35   **MIP** $50

Bugs Bunny Under the Cawit Game, 1972, Whitman
EX $15   NM $25   **MIP** $40

Building Boom, 1950s, Kohner
EX $10   NM $20   **MIP** $35

Built-Rite Swish Basketball Game, 1950s, Warren/Built-Rite
EX $10   NM $20   **MIP** $40

(KP Photo)

Bullwinkle Hide & Seek Game, 1961, Milton Bradley
EX $20   NM $45   **MIP** $90

Bullwinkle's Super Market Game, 1970s, Whitman
EX $15   NM $50   **MIP** $75

Buster Brown Game and Play Box, 1950s, Buster Brown Shoes
EX $40   NM $75   **MIP** $125

Buy and Sell, 1953, Whitman
EX $8   NM $15   **MIP** $20

Buy or Sell, 1967, KMS Industries
EX $5   NM $12   **MIP** $18

C&O/B&O, 1969, Avalon Hill
EX $20   NM $50   **MIP** $95

Cabbage Patch Kids, 1984, Parker Bros.
EX $5   NM $10   **MIP** $15

California Raisins Board Game, 1987, Decipher
EX $4   NM $16   **MIP** $25

Call it Golf, 1966, Strauss
EX $15   NM $25   **MIP** $40

Call My Bluff, 1965, Milton Bradley
EX $15   NM $20   **MIP** $30

Calling All Cars, 1930s-40s, Parker Bros.
EX $40   NM $50   **MIP** $75

Calling All Cars, 1950s, Parker Bros.
EX $10   NM $20   **MIP** $30

Calling Superman, 1955, Transogram
EX $45   NM $85   **MIP** $140

Calvin & The Colonel High Spirits, 1962, Milton Bradley
EX $12   NM $25   **MIP** $35

Camelot, 1955, Parker Bros.
EX $15   NM $20   **MIP** $25

Camouflage, 1961, Milton Bradley
EX $5   NM $20   **MIP** $35

Camp Granada Game, Allan Sherman's, 1965, Milton Bradley
EX $40   NM $70   **MIP** $100

Camp Runamuck, 1965, Ideal
EX $25   NM $45   **MIP** $55

Campaign, 1966, Campaign Game
EX $8   NM $25   **MIP** $40

Campaign, 1971, Waddington
EX $10   NM $30   **MIP** $45

Campaign: The American "Go" Game, 1961, Saalfield
EX $15   NM $45   **MIP** $65

Can You Catch It Charlie Brown?, 1976, Ideal
EX $10   NM $25   **MIP** $35

Candid Camera Game, 1963, Lowell
EX $15   NM $25   **MIP** $35

Candyland, 1949, Milton Bradley
EX $25   NM $50   **MIP** $75

Candyland, 1955, Milton Bradley
EX $20   NM $35   **MIP** $50

Cannonball Run, The, 1981, Cadaco
EX $4   NM $16   **MIP** $25

Can't Stop, 1980, Parker Bros.
EX $5   NM $12   **MIP** $20

Caper, 1970, Parker Bros.
EX $30   NM $70   **MIP** $100

Capital Punishment, 1981, Hammerhead
EX $20   NM $35   **MIP** $60

Captain America, 1966, Milton Bradley
EX $25   NM $50   **MIP** $75

Captain America, 1977, Milton Bradley
EX $10   NM $15   **MIP** $25

Captain Caveman and the Teen Angels, 1981, Milton Bradley
EX $8   NM $20   **MIP** $30

(KP Photo)

Captain Gallant Desert Fort Game, 1956, Transogram
EX $20   NM $40   **MIP** $65

(KP Photo)

Captain Kangaroo, 1956, Milton Bradley
EX $35   NM $45   **MIP** $100

(KP Photo)

Captain Video Game, 1952, Milton Bradley
EX $50   NM $75   **MIP** $125

Car Travel Game, 1958, Milton Bradley
EX $5   NM $10   **MIP** $15

Carapace, 1970, Plan B Corp.
EX $5   NM $16   **MIP** $25

Cardino, 1970, Milton Bradley
EX $10   NM $15   **MIP** $25

Careers, 1957, Parker Bros.
EX $8   **NM** $20   **MIP** $30

Careers, 1965, Parker Bros.
EX $15   **NM** $20   **MIP** $33

Cargoes, 1958, Selchow & Righter
EX $10   **NM** $25   **MIP** $50

Carl Hubbell Mechanical Baseball, 1950, Gotham
EX $65   **NM** $100   **MIP** $125

Carl Yastrzemski's Action Baseball, 1968, Pressman
EX $50   **NM** $75   **MIP** $125

Carrier Strike, 1977, Milton Bradley
EX $15   **NM** $25   **MIP** $35

Cars 'n Trucks Build-A-Game, 1961, Ideal
EX $15   **NM** $45   **MIP** $80

Cartel, 1974, Gamut of Games
EX $18   **NM** $45   **MIP** $65

Case of the Elusive Assassin, The, 1967, Ideal
EX $20   **NM** $30   **MIP** $50

Casey Jones, 1959, Saalfield
EX $20   **NM** $45   **MIP** $65

(KP Photo)

Casper the Friendly Ghost Game, 1959, Milton Bradley
EX $5   **NM** $10   **MIP** $15

Casper the Friendly Ghost Game, 1974, Schaper
EX $8   **NM** $18   **MIP** $30

Castle Risk, 1986, Parker Bros.
EX $15   **NM** $35   **MIP** $50

Cat & Mouse, 1964, Parker Bros.
EX $7   **NM** $15   **MIP** $20

Catchword, 1954, Whitman
EX $3   **NM** $5   **MIP** $10

Catfish Bend Storybook Game, 1978, Selchow & Righter
EX $15   **NM** $20   **MIP** $35

Cathedral, 1986, Mattel
EX $10   **NM** $25   **MIP** $35

Cattlemen, The, 1977, Selchow & Righter
EX $10   **NM** $15   **MIP** $25

Cavalcade, 1953, Selchow & Righter
EX $15   **NM** $25   **MIP** $35

Caveat Emptor, 1971, Plan B
EX $5   **NM** $16   **MIP** $25

Centipede, 1983, Milton Bradley
EX $6   **NM** $10   **MIP** $15

Century of Great Fights, 1969, Research Games
EX $40   **NM** $75   **MIP** $110

Challenge Golf at Pebble Beach, 1972, 3M
EX $6   **NM** $15   **MIP** $25

Challenge the Yankees, 1960s, Hasbro
EX $500 **NM** $1000   **MIP** $1800

Challenge Yahtzee, 1974, Milton Bradley
EX $7   **NM** $15   **MIP** $20

Championship Baseball, 1966, Championship Games
EX $8   **NM** $20   **MIP** $30

Championship Basketball, 1966, Championship Games
EX $8   **NM** $20   **MIP** $30

Championship Golf, 1966, Championship Games
EX $8   **NM** $20   **MIP** $30

Changeover: The Metric Game, 1976, John Ladell
EX $8   **NM** $20   **MIP** $30

Changing Society, 1981, Phil Carter
EX $5   **NM** $16   **MIP** $25

Chaos, 1965, Amsco Toys
EX $5   **NM** $16   **MIP** $25

Chaos, 1971, Lakeside
EX $8   **NM** $20   **MIP** $30

Charlie Brown's All Star Baseball Game, 1965, Parker Bros.
EX $18   **NM** $23   **MIP** $50

Charlie's Angels, 1977, Milton Bradley
EX $6   **NM** $10   **MIP** $20

(KP Photo)

Charlie's Angels (Farrah Fawcett box), 1977, Milton Bradley
EX $10   **NM** $20   **MIP** $35

Charlotte's Web Game, 1974, Hasbro
EX $10   **NM** $25   **MIP** $35

Chase, The, 1966, Cadaco
EX $12   **NM** $30   **MIP** $35

Chaseback, 1962, Milton Bradley
EX $5   **NM** $16   **MIP** $25

Checkpoint: Danger!, 1978, Ideal
EX $5   **NM** $16   **MIP** $25

Cherry Ames' Nursing Game, 1959, Parker Bros.
EX $50   **NM** $90   **MIP** $115

Chess, 1977, Milton Bradley
EX $3   **NM** $5   **MIP** $8

Chevyland Sweepstakes, 1968, Milton Bradley
EX $25   **NM** $50   **MIP** $100

Chex Ches Football, 1971, Chex Ches Games
EX $15   **NM** $25   **MIP** $40

Cheyenne, 1958, Milton Bradley
EX $25   **NM** $45   **MIP** $60

Chicago Sports Trivia Game, 1984, Sports Trivia
EX $6   **NM** $10   **MIP** $15

Chicken In Every Pot, A, 1980s, Animal Town Game
EX $20   **NM** $30   **MIP** $50

Children's Hour, The, 1946, Parker Bros.
EX $5   **NM** $10   **MIP** $15

CHiPs, 1981, Ideal
EX $7   **NM** $10   **MIP** $20

(KP Photo)

CHiPs Game, 1977, Milton Bradley
EX $4   **NM** $7   **MIP** $10

Chit Chat Game, 1963, Milton Bradley
EX $6   **NM** $10   **MIP** $15

Chopper Strike, 1976, Milton Bradley
EX $10   **NM** $15   **MIP** $20

Chug-A-Lug, 1969, Dynamic
EX $5   **NM** $16   **MIP** $25

Chute-5, 1973, Lowe
EX $5   **NM** $12   **MIP** $20

Chutes & Ladders, 1956, Milton Bradley
EX $10   **NM** $15   **MIP** $20

Chutzpah, 1967, Cadaco
EX $10   **NM** $20   **MIP** $30

Chutzpah, 1967, Middle Earth
EX $15   **NM** $20   **MIP** $40

Cimarron Strip, 1967, Ideal
EX $35   **NM** $75   **MIP** $90

Circle Racer Board Game, 1988, Sport Games USA
EX $6   **NM** $10   **MIP** $15

Cities Game, The, 1970, Psychology Today
EX $5   **NM** $16   **MIP** $25

Civil War, 1961, Avalon Hill
EX $15   NM $45   MIP $65

Civilization, 1982, Avalon Hill
EX $10   NM $17   MIP $28

Clash of the Titans, 1981, Whitman
EX $10   NM $25   MIP $45

Class Struggle, 1978, Bernard Ollman
EX $15   NM $25   MIP $50

(KP Photo)

Clean Sweep, 1960s, Schaper
EX $15   NM $20   MIP $35

Clean Water, 1972, Urban Systems
EX $8   NM $25   MIP $40

Cloak & Dagger, 1984, Ideal
EX $8   NM $25   MIP $40

(KP Photo)

Close Encounters of the Third Kind, 1977, Parker Bros.
EX $7   NM $15   MIP $20

Clue, 1949, Parker Bros.
EX $35   NM $50   MIP $75

Clue, 1972, Parker Bros.
EX $4   NM $7   MIP $11

Clue Master Detective, 1988, Parker Bros.
EX $20   NM $15   MIP $65

Clue: The Great Museum Caper, 1991, Parker Bros.
EX $8   NM $20   MIP $30

Code Name: Sector, 1977, Parker Bros.
EX $10   NM $30   MIP $45

Collector, The, 1977, Avalon Hill
EX $5   NM $16   MIP $25

College Basketball, 1954, Cadaco-Ellis
EX $10   NM $25   MIP $35

(KP Photo)

Columbo, 1973, Milton Bradley
EX $6   NM $10   MIP $15

Combat, 1963, Ideal
EX $25   NM $45   MIP $60

Comin' Round The Mountain, 1954, Einson-Freeman
EX $30   NM $50   MIP $80

Computer Baseball, 1966, Epoch Playtime
EX $25   NM $40   MIP $65

Computer Basketball, 1969, Electric Data
EX $10   NM $25   MIP $35

Computerized Pro Football, 1971, Data Prog.
EX $15   NM $25   MIP $40

Concentration (25th Anniversary Ed.), 1982, Milton Bradley
EX $6   NM $10   MIP $16

Concentration (3rd Ed.), 1960, Milton Bradley
EX $12   NM $15   MIP $20

Conestoga, 1964, Washburne Research
EX $25   NM $65   MIP $95

Coney Island, The Game of, 1956, Selchow & Righter
EX $20   NM $35   MIP $45

Conflict, 1960, Parker Bros.
EX $25   NM $35   MIP $50

Confucius Say, 1960s, Pressman
EX $10   NM $15   MIP $20

Conquer, 1979, Whitman
EX $8   NM $17   MIP $25

Conquest of the Empire, 1984, Milton Bradley
EX $50   NM $105   MIP $150

Consetta and Her Wheel of Fate, 1946, Selchow & Righter
EX $20   NM $50   MIP $65

Conspiracy, 1982, Milton Bradley
EX $4   NM $9   MIP $11

Containment, 1979, Shamus Gamus
EX $10   NM $25   MIP $35

Contigo, 1974, 3M
EX $7   NM $20   MIP $35

Cootie, 1949, Schaper
EX $10   NM $20   MIP $30

Count Coup, 1979, Marcian Chronicles
EX $10   NM $30   MIP $45

Count Down Space Game, 1960, Transogram
EX $15   NM $25   MIP $43

Countdown, 1967, Lowe
EX $15   NM $40   MIP $60

Counter Point, 1976, Hallmark
EX $10   NM $15   MIP $25

Cowboy Roundup, 1952, Parker Bros.
EX $10   NM $20   MIP $30

Cracker Jack Game, 1976, Milton Bradley
EX $5   NM $16   MIP $25

Creature Castle, 1975, Whitman
EX $12   NM $30   MIP $40

Creature Features, 1975, Athol
EX $20   NM $50   MIP $75

Creature From the Black Lagoon, 1963, Hasbro
EX $150   NM $410   MIP $600

Cribb Golf, 1980s, J.K. Games, Inc.
EX $10   NM $22   MIP $40

Crosby Derby, The, 1947, Fishlove
EX $25   NM $75   MIP $100

Cross Up, 1974, Milton Bradley
EX $2   NM $5   MIP $10

Crosswords, 1954, National Games
EX $12   NM $20   MIP $32

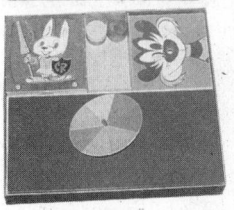

(KP Photo)

Crusader Rabbit TV Game, 1960s, Tryne
EX $50   NM $100   MIP $175

Cub Scouting, The Game of, 1987, Cadaco
EX $5   NM $16   MIP $25

Curious George Game, 1977, Parker Bros.
EX $4   NM $6   MIP $10

Curse of the Cobras Game, 1982, Ideal
EX $10   NM $25   MIP $35

Cut Up Shopping Spree Game, 1968, Milton Bradley
EX $8   NM $15   MIP $20

Dallas, 1980, Yaquinto
EX $10   NM $15   MIP $22

Dallas, 1985, Maruca Industries
EX $17   NM $35   MIP $55

Dallas (TV Role Playing), 1980, SPI
EX $4   NM $7   MIP $11

Danger Pass, 1964, Game Partners
EX $15   NM $45   MIP $65

Daniel Boone Trail Blazer, 1964, Milton Bradley
EX $20   NM $50   MIP $65

Dark Crystal Game, The, 1982, Milton Bradley
EX $7   NM $20   MIP $35

Dark Shadows Game, 1968, Whitman
EX $20   NM $40   MIP $60

Dark Tower, 1981, Milton Bradley
EX $125   NM $175   MIP $350

Dark World, 1992, Mattel
EX $12   NM $25   MIP $35

Dastardly and Muttley, 1969, Milton Bradley
EX $15   NM $25   MIP $40

Dating Game, The, 1967, Hasbro
EX $10   NM $20   MIP $25

Davy Crockett Adventure Game, 1956, Gardner
EX $45   NM $75   MIP $90

Davy Crockett Frontierland Game, 1955, Parker Bros.
EX $20   NM $50   MIP $65

Davy Crockett Radar Action Game, 1955, Ewing Mfg. & Sales
EX $40   NM $100   MIP $150

Davy Crockett Rescue Race Game, 1950s, Gabriel
EX $20   NM $50   MIP $60

Dawn of the Dead, 1978, SPI
EX $45   NM $95   MIP $135

Daytona 500 Race Game, 1989, Milton Bradley
EX $10   NM $25   MIP $35

Dead Pan, 1956, Selchow & Righter
EX $8   NM $10   MIP $15

Deadlock, 1972, American Greetings
EX $8   NM $20   MIP $30

Dealer's Choice, 1972, Parker Bros.
EX $10   NM $20   MIP $35

Dealer's Choice, 1974, Gamut of Games
EX $18   NM $45   MIP $65

Dear Abby, 1972, Ideal
EX $7   NM $20   MIP $35

Decathalon, 1972, Sports Illustrated
EX $10   NM $25   MIP $35

Decoy, 1956, Selchow & Righter
EX $12   NM $25   MIP $40

Deduction, 1976, Ideal
EX $5   NM $9   MIP $12

Deluxe Wheel of Fortune, 1986, Pressman
EX $5   NM $8   MIP $13

Dennis The Menace Baseball Game, 1960
EX $22   NM $50   MIP $70

Denny McLain Magnetik Baseball Game, 1968, Gotham
EX $115   NM $195   MIP $295

Deputy Dawg TV Lotto, 1961, Ideal
EX $15   NM $35   MIP $60

Deputy Game, The, 1960, Bell, "Starring Henry Fonda as Simon Fry"
EX $20   NM $50   MIP $75

Derby Day, 1959, Parker Bros.
EX $18   NM $35   MIP $50

Derby Downs, 1973, Great Games
EX $10   NM $30   MIP $45

(KP Photo)

Detectives Game, The, 1961, Transogram
EX $15   NM $30   MIP $40

Dick Tracy Crime Stopper, 1963, Ideal
EX $20   NM $30   MIP $40

(KP Photo)

Dick Tracy The Master Detective Game, 1961, Selchow & Righter
EX $25   NM $60   MIP $75

Dick Van Dyke Board Game, 1964, Standard Toykraft
EX $75   NM $150   MIP $200

Diet, 1972, Dynamic
EX $5   NM $16   MIP $25

Diner's Club Credit Card Game, The, 1961, Ideal
EX $15   NM $20   MIP $30

Dinosaur Island, 1980, Parker Bros.
EX $5   NM $16   MIP $25

Diplomacy, 1961, Games Research
EX $15   NM $25   MIP $40

Diplomacy, 1976, Avalon Hill
EX $15   NM $25   MIP $40

Direct Hit, 1950s, Northwestern Products
EX $40   NM $70   MIP $110

Dirty Water—The Water Pollution Game, 1970, Urban Systems
EX $8   NM $20   MIP $30

Disney Mouseketeer, 1964, Parker Bros.
EX $40   NM $65   MIP $100

(KP Photo)

Disneyland Game, 1965, Transogram
EX $25   NM $60   MIP $100

Dispatcher, 1958, Avalon Hill
EX $45   NM $70   MIP $125

Dobbin Derby, 1950, Cadaco-Ellis
EX $8   NM $25   MIP $40

(KP Photo)

Doctor Who, 1980s, Denys Fisher
EX $35   NM $75   MIP $125

Doctor, Doctor! Game, 1978, Ideal
EX $8   NM $20   MIP $30

(KP Photo)

Dogfight, 1962, Milton Bradley
EX $35   NM $45   MIP $65

Dollar A Second, 1955, Lowell
EX $12   NM $20   MIP $25

Dollars & Sense, 1946, Sidney Rogers
EX $100   NM $150   MIP $200

Domain, 1983, Parker Bros.
EX $2   NM $3   MIP $5

Domination, 1982, Milton Bradley
EX $8   NM $20   MIP $30

Don Carter's Strike Bowling Game, 1964, Saalfield
EX $20   NM $55   MIP $75

Donald Duck Big Game Box, 1979, Whitman
EX $10   NM $15   MIP $20

Donald Duck Pins & Bowling Game, 1955s, Pressman
EX $35   NM $50   MIP $70

Donald Duck Tiddley Winks Game, 1950s
EX $6   NM $10   MIP $15

Donald Duck's Party Game, 1950s, Parker Bros.
EX $10   NM $35   MIP $50

Dondi Potato Race Game, 1950s, Hasbro
EX $10   NM $20   MIP $35

Donkey Party Game, 1950, Saalfield
EX $4   NM $10   MIP $15

Donny & Marie Osmond TV Show Game, 1977, Mattel
EX $8   NM $25   MIP $40

Don't Miss the Boat, 1965, Parker Bros.
EX $12   NM $30   MIP $40

Doorways to Adventure VCR Game, 1986, Pressman
EX $6   NM $15   MIP $25

Doorways to Horror VCR Game, 1986, Pressman
EX $10   NM $25   MIP $35

Double Cross, 1974, Lakeside
EX $5   NM $16   MIP $25

Double Crossing, 1988, Lionel Games
EX $10   NM $25   MIP $35

Double Trouble, 1987, Milton Bradley
EX $3   NM $5   MIP $8

Doubletrack, 1981, Milton Bradley
EX $2   NM $7   MIP $12

(KP Photo)

Dr. Kildare, 1962, Ideal
EX $20   NM $25   MIP $35

(KP Photo)

Dracula Mystery Game, 1960s, Hasbro
EX $80   NM $160   MIP $250

Dracula's "I Vant To Bite Your Finger" Game, 1981, Hasbro
EX $10   NM $20   MIP $30

Dragnet, 1955, Transogram
EX $20   NM $40   MIP $80

Dragonlance, 1988, TSR
EX $15   NM $35   MIP $50

Dragon's Lair, 1983, Milton Bradley
EX $7   NM $10   MIP $20

Dream House, 1968, Milton Bradley
EX $15   NM $35   MIP $50

Driver Ed, 1973, Cadaco
EX $6   NM $10   MIP $20

Duell, 1976, Lakeside
EX $5   NM $16   MIP $25

(KP Photo)

Dukes of Hazzard, 1981, Ideal
EX $6   NM $15   MIP $25

Dunce, 1955, Schaper
EX $7   NM $20   MIP $35

Dune, 1984, Parker Bros.
EX $10   NM $20   MIP $35

Dune, Frank Herbert's, 1979, Avalon Hill
EX $20   NM $50   MIP $75

Dungeon Dice, 1977, Parker Bros.
EX $5   NM $8   MIP $15

Dungeon!, 1981, TSR
EX $10   NM $25   MIP $35

Dungeons & Dragons, Electronic, 1980, Mattel
EX $12   NM $30   MIP $40

Duplicate Ad-Lib, 1976, Lowe
EX $5   NM $10   MIP $15

Duran Duran Game, 1985, Milton Bradley
EX $45   NM $80   MIP $125

Dynomutt, 1977, Milton Bradley
EX $10   NM $15   MIP $25

E.T. The Extra-Terrestrial, 1982, Parker Bros.
EX $8   NM $12   MIP $20

Earl Gillespie Baseball Game, 1961, Wei-Gill
EX $25   NM $30   MIP $40

Earth Satellite Game, 1956, Gabriel
EX $30   NM $70   MIP $100

Easy Money, 1956, Milton Bradley
EX $10   NM $15   MIP $20

Ecology, 1970, Urban Systems
EX $7   NM $20   MIP $35

Egg and I, The, 1947, Capex
EX $30   NM $50   MIP $80

El Dorado, 1977, Invicta
EX $7   NM $20   MIP $35

Electra Woman and Dyna Girl, 1977, Ideal
EX $10   NM $25   MIP $50

Electric Sports Car Race, 1959, Tudor
EX $35   NM $60   MIP $90

(KP Photo)

Electronic Detective Game, 1970s, Ideal
EX $12   NM $30   MIP $40

Electronic Lightfight, 1981, Milton Bradley
EX $8   NM $20   MIP $30

Electronic Radar Search, 1967, Ideal
EX $10   NM $15   MIP $25

(KP Photo)

Eliot Ness and the Untouchables, 1961, Transogram
EX $30   NM $50   MIP $75

Ellsworth Elephant Game, 1960, Selchow & Righter
EX $30   NM $45   MIP $70

Elmer Wheeler's Fat Boys Game, 1951, Parker Bros.
EX $18   NM $25   MIP $30

Elvis Presley Game, 1957, Teen Age
Games
EX $1000 NM $2000 MIP $4000

Emenee Chocolate Factory, 1966
EX $6 NM $10 MIP $15

Emergency, 1974, Milton Bradley
EX $15 NM $25 MIP $40

Emily Post Popularity Game, 1970,
Selchow & Righter
EX $10 NM $25 MIP $40

Emperor of China, 1972, Dynamic
EX $10 NM $25 MIP $40

Empire Auto Races, 1950s, Empire
Plastics
EX $20 NM $30 MIP $50

Empire Builder (1st edition), 1982,
Mayfair Games
EX $20 NM $50 MIP $75

(KP Photo)

Empire Strikes Back, Hoth Ice World,
1977, Kenner
EX $10 NM $20 MIP $30

Encore, 1989, Parker Bros.
EX $8 NM $20 MIP $30

Enemy Agent, 1976, Milton Bradley
EX $8 NM $20 MIP $30

Energy Quest, 1977, Weldon
EX $5 NM $16 MIP $25

Engineer, 1957, Selchow & Righter
EX $8 NM $25 MIP $40

Entertainment Trivia Game, 1984,
Lakeside
EX $5 NM $10 MIP $15

Entre's Fun & Games In Accounting,
1988, Entrepreneurial Games
EX $4 NM $7 MIP $12

Ergo, 1977, Invicta
EX $5 NM $16 MIP $25

(KP Photo)

Escape From New York, 1980, TSR
EX $12 NM $20 MIP $30

Escape from the Casbah, 1975,
Selchow & Righter
EX $7 NM $20 MIP $35

Escape From the Death Star, 1977,
Kenner
EX $10 NM $20 MIP $30

Escort: Game of Guys and Gals, 1955,
Parker Bros.
EX $15 NM $20 MIP $25

Espionage, 1973, MPH
EX $6 NM $18 MIP $30

Events, 1974, 3M
EX $6 NM $15 MIP $25

Everybody's Talking!, 1967, Watkins-
Strathmore
EX $8 NM $25 MIP $40

Executive Decision, 1971, 3M
EX $5 NM $16 MIP $25

Exit, 1983, Milton Bradley
EX $2 NM $6 MIP $10

Expanse, 1949, Milton Bradley
EX $15 NM $20 MIP $30

Extra Innings, 1975, J. Kavanaugh
EX $30 NM $50 MIP $75

(KP Photo)

Eye Guess, 1960s, Milton Bradley
EX $15 NM $20 MIP $35

F.B.I., 1958, Transogram
EX $35 NM $55 MIP $70

F.B.I. Crime Resistance Game, 1975,
Milton Bradley
EX $12 NM $30 MIP $40

F/11 Armchair Quarterback, 1964,
James R. Hock
EX $15 NM $25 MIP $40

Fact Finder Fun, 1963, Milton Bradley
EX $10 NM $15 MIP $25

Fall Guy, The, 1981, Milton Bradley
EX $10 NM $15 MIP $25

(KP Photo)

Family Affair, 1967, Whitman
EX $25 NM $40 MIP $65

Family Feud, 1977, Milton Bradley
EX $4 NM $12 MIP $20

Family Ties Game, The, 1986, Apple
Street
EX $10 NM $15 MIP $20

Famous 500 Mile Race, 1988
EX $8 NM $13 MIP $20

Fang Bang, 1966, Milton Bradley
EX $12 NM $25 MIP $35

Fangface, 1979, Parker Bros.
EX $5 NM $8 MIP $13

Fantastic Voyage Game, 1968, Milton
Bradley
EX $15 NM $25 MIP $40

Fantasy Island Game, 1978, Ideal
EX $7 NM $20 MIP $35

Farming Game, The, 1979, Weekend
Farmer Co.
EX $8 NM $20 MIP $30

Fast 111s, 1981, Parker Bros.
EX $5 NM $16 MIP $25

Fastest Gun, The, 1974, Milton
Bradley
EX $10 NM $25 MIP $40

Fat Albert, 1973, Milton Bradley
EX $15 NM $25 MIP $40

Fearless Fireman, 1957, Hasbro
EX $45 NM $70 MIP $150

(KP Photo)

Felix the Cat Dandy Candy Game,
1957, Warren/Built-Rite
EX $10 NM $20 MIP $45

Felix the Cat Game, 1960, Milton
Bradley
EX $15 NM $25 MIP $45

Felix the Cat Game, 1968, Milton
Bradley
EX $8 NM $20 MIP $30

Feudal, 1967, 3M
EX $8 NM $20 MIP $30

Fighter Bomber, 1977, Cadaco
EX $15   NM $25   MIP $40

Finance, 1962, Parker Bros.
EX $10   NM $15   MIP $20

Finger Dinger Man, 1969, Mattel
EX $10   NM $25   MIP $35

Fingers Harry, 1967, Topper Toys
EX $20   NM $50   MIP $75

Fire Chief, 1957, Selchow & Righter
EX $10   NM $20   MIP $30

Fire Fighters!, 1957, Russell
EX $15   NM $25   MIP $40

Fire House Mouse Game, 1967,
Transogram
EX $10   NM $35   MIP $50

(KP Photo)

Fireball XL-5, 1963, Milton Bradley
EX $40   NM $75   MIP $100

First Class Farmer, 1965, F+W
Publishing
EX $7   NM $20   MIP $35

First Down, 1970, TGP Games
EX $50   NM $80   MIP $125

Fish Bait, 1965, Ideal
EX $20   NM $30   MIP $50

Fish Pond, 1950s, National Games
EX $10   NM $15   MIP $20

**Flagship Airfreight: The Airplane
Cargo Game,** 1946, Milton Bradley
EX $30   NM $55   MIP $80

Flash Gordon, 1977, Waddington/
House Of Games
EX $10   NM $25   MIP $35

**Flash: The Press Photographer
Game,** 1956, Selchow & Righter
EX $35   NM $60   MIP $100

Flight Captain, 1972, Lowe
EX $5   NM $16   MIP $25

Flintstones, 1971, Milton Bradley
EX $6   NM $15   MIP $25

Flintstones, 1980, Milton Bradley
EX $15   NM $20   MIP $35

**Flintstones Dino The Dinosaur
Game,** 1961, Transogram
EX $45   NM $75   MIP $100

**Flintstones Hoppy The Hopperoo
Game,** 1964, Transogram
EX $45   NM $75   MIP $120

Flintstones Mitt-Full Game, 1962,
Whitman
EX $25   NM $50   MIP $75

Flintstones Stone Age Game, 1961,
Transogram
EX $20   NM $45   MIP $65

Flip Flop Go, 1962, Mattel
EX $6   NM $10   MIP $15

Flip 'N Skip, 1971, Little Kennys
EX $5   NM $10   MIP $15

(KP Photo)

Flipper Flips, 1960s, Mattel
EX $30   NM $50   MIP $70

Flying Nun Game, The, 1968, Milton
Bradley
EX $15   NM $20   MIP $30

Fonz Game, The, 1976, Milton Bradley
EX $15   NM $20   MIP $30

Fooba-Roo Football Game, 1955,
Memphis Plastic
EX $15   NM $35   MIP $50

Football Fever, 1985, Hansen
EX $20   NM $35   MIP $50

Football Strategy, 1962, Avalon Hill
EX $8   NM $25   MIP $40

Football Strategy, 1972, Avalon Hill
EX $3   NM $10   MIP $15

Football, Baseball, & Checkers,
1948, Parker Bros.
EX $15   NM $25   MIP $40

Fore, 1954, Artcraft Paper
EX $20   NM $35   MIP $50

Forest Friends, 1956, Milton Bradley
EX $5   NM $12   MIP $18

Formula One Car Race Game, 1968,
Parker Bros.
EX $25   NM $40   MIP $50

Fortress America, 1986, Milton
Bradley, part of a series of intricate
strategy games developed by Milton
Bradley in the 1980s, two others in
the series were "Axis & Allies" and
"Conquest of the Empire"
EX $35   NM $75   MIP $100

Fortune 500, 1979, Pressman
EX $5   NM $16   MIP $25

Foto-Electric Baseball, 1951,
Cadaco-Ellis
EX $15   NM $25   MIP $40

(KP Photo)

Foto-Electric Football, 1965, Cadaco-
Ellis
EX $10   NM $15   MIP $20

Four Lane Road Racing, 1963,
Transogram
EX $15   NM $45   MIP $65

Fox & Hounds, Game of, 1948, Parker
Bros.
EX $10   NM $20   MIP $25

**Frank Cavanaugh's American
Football,** 1955, F. Cavanaugh
EX $25   NM $60   MIP $90

Frankenstein Game, 1962, Hasbro
EX $80   NM $160   MIP $250

Frantic Frogs, 1965, Milton Bradley
EX $10   NM $20   MIP $30

Frisky Flippers Slide Bar Game,
1950s, Warren/Built-Rite
EX $5   NM $10   MIP $15

Frontier Fort Rescue Game, 1956,
Gabriel
EX $10   NM $35   MIP $50

Frontier-6, 1980, Rimbold
EX $8   NM $25   MIP $40

F-Troop, 1965, Ideal
EX $50   NM $100   MIP $125

Fu Manchu's Hidden Hoard, 1967,
Ideal
EX $23   NM $50   MIP $75

(KP Photo)

Fugitive, 1966, Ideal
EX $30   NM $60   MIP $100

Fun City, 1987, Parker Bros.
EX $8   NM $20   MIP $30

Funky Phantom Game, 1971, Milton
Bradley
EX $10   NM $15   MIP $25

G.I. Joe, 1982, International Games
EX $15   NM $25   MIP $40

G.I. Joe Adventure, 1982, Hasbro
EX $20   NM $30   MIP $50

G.I. Joe Card Game, 1965, Whitman
EX $10   NM $15   MIP $25

G.I. Joe Marine Paratrooper, 1965, Hasbro
EX $20   NM $30   MIP $50

G.I. Joe Navy Frogman, 1965, Hasbro
EX $25   NM $60   MIP $75

Gambler, 1977, Parker Bros.
EX $6   NM $15   MIP $20

Gambler's Golf, 1975, Gammon Games
EX $4   NM $10   MIP $15

Games People Play Game, The, 1967, Alpsco
EX $7   NM $20   MIP $35

Gammonball, 1980, Fun-Time Products
EX $10   NM $16   MIP $25

Gang Way For Fun, 1964, Transogram
EX $25   NM $40   MIP $65

Gardner's Championship Golf, 1950s, Gardner
EX $10   NM $35   MIP $50

Garfield, 1981, Parker Bros.
EX $4   NM $6   MIP $10

Garrison's Gorillas, 1967, Ideal
EX $45   NM $75   MIP $120

Gay Puree, 1962
EX $25   NM $40   MIP $65

Gene Autry's Dude Ranch Game, 1950s, Warren/Built-Rite
EX $20   NM $25   MIP $50

General Hospital, 1974, Parker Bros.
EX $7   NM $15   MIP $20

General Hospital, 1980s, Cardinal
EX $15   NM $20   MIP $30

Generals, The, 1980, Ideal
EX $7   NM $20   MIP $35

Gentle Ben Animal Hunt Game, 1967, Mattel
EX $30   NM $70   MIP $100

Geo-Graphy, 1954, Cadaco-Ellis
EX $5   NM $15   MIP $20

George of the Jungle Game, 1968, Parker Bros.
EX $40   NM $80   MIP $100

Get Beep Beep: The Road Runner Game, 1975, Whitman
EX $15   NM $25   MIP $35

Get in That Tub, 1969, Hasbro
EX $15   NM $35   MIP $50

(KP Photo)

Get Smart Game, 1966, Ideal
EX $20   NM $30   MIP $50

Get That License, 1955, Selchow & Righter
EX $10   NM $15   MIP $25

Get the Message, 1964, Milton Bradley
EX $5   NM $15   MIP $25

Get the Picture, 1987, Worlds Of Wonder
EX $6   NM $10   MIP $15

Gettysburg, 1960, Avalon Hill
EX $5   NM $16   MIP $25

Ghosts, 1985, Milton Bradley
EX $8   NM $20   MIP $35

Giant Wheel Thrills 'n Spills Horse Race, 1958, Remco
EX $15   NM $20   MIP $30

Gil Hodges' Pennant Fever, 1970, Research Games
EX $35   NM $75   MIP $90

(KP Photo)

Gilligan, The New Adventures of, 1974, Milton Bradley
EX $15   NM $20   MIP $25

(KP Photo)

Gilligan's Island, 1965, Game Gems
EX $125   NM $250   MIP $400

Gingerbread Man, 1964, Selchow & Righter
EX $10   NM $35   MIP $50

Globetrotter Basketball, Official, 1950s, Meljak
EX $60   NM $100   MIP $150

Globe-Trotters, 1950, Selchow & Righter
EX $8   NM $25   MIP $35

Go For Broke, 1965, Selchow & Righter
EX $5   NM $7   MIP $10

Go for the Green, 1973, Sports Illustrated
EX $10   NM $25   MIP $40

Goal Line Stand, 1980, Game Shop
EX $12   NM $20   MIP $30

Godfather Game, The (violin case box), 1971, Family Games
EX $35   NM $50   MIP $75

Godfather, The (white box), 1971, Family Games
EX $8   NM $20   MIP $30

Godzilla, 1960s, Ideal
EX $100   NM $200   MIP $300

Godzilla, 1978, Mattel
EX $30   NM $50   MIP $80

Going to Jerusalem, 1955, Parker Bros.
EX $15   NM $20   MIP $25

Going, Going, Gone!, 1975, Milton Bradley
EX $6   NM $15   MIP $25

Gold!, 1981, Avalon Hill
EX $5   NM $16   MIP $25

Golden Trivia Game, 1984, Western
EX $6   NM $10   MIP $15

Goldilocks, 1955, Cadaco-Ellis
EX $8   NM $25   MIP $35

Goldilocks and the Three Bears, 1973, Cadaco
EX $2   NM $6   MIP $10

Gomer Pyle Game, 1960s, Transogram
EX $15   NM $20   MIP $30

Gong Show Game, 1975, Milton Bradley
EX $15   NM $25   MIP $40

Gong Show Game, 1977, American Publishing
EX $15   NM $25   MIP $40

Good Guys 'N Bad Guys, 1973, Cadaco
EX $5   NM $16   MIP $25

Good Ol' Charlie Brown Game, 1971, Milton Bradley
EX $8   NM $20   MIP $30

Goodbye Mr. Chips Game, 1969, Parker Bros.
EX $8   NM $20   MIP $25

Goofy's Mad Maze, 1970s, Whitman
EX $6   NM $10   MIP $15

Goonies, 1980s, Milton Bradley
EX $12   NM $30   MIP $40

Gooses Wild, 1966, CO-5
EX $2   NM $7   MIP $12

(KP Photo)

Gotham Professional Basketball,
1950s, Gotham
EX $35   NM $50   MIP $70

Grand Master of Martial Arts, 1986,
Hoyle
EX $6   NM $10   MIP $15

Gray Ghost, The, 1958, Transogram
EX $30   NM $50   MIP $80

Great Escape, The, 1967, Ideal
EX $8   NM $25   MIP $40

Great Grape Ape Game, The, 1975,
Milton Bradley
EX $15   NM $25   MIP $40

(KP Photo)

Green Acres Game, The, 1960s,
Standard Toykraft
EX $73   NM $100   MIP $200

(KP Photo)

Green Ghost Game, 1965, Transogram
EX $50   NM $90   MIP $125

Green Ghost Game (re-issue), 1997,
Marx
EX $15   NM $35   MIP $50

Green Hornet Quick Switch Game,
1966, Milton Bradley
EX $90   NM $225   MIP $300

Gremlins, 1984, International Games
EX $10   NM $15   MIP $25

Greyhound Pursuit, 1985, N/N Games
EX $8   NM $13   MIP $20

(KP Photo)

Grizzly Adams, 1978, Waddington's
House of Games
EX $15   NM $25   MIP $40

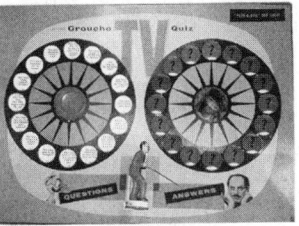

(KP Photo)

Groucho's TV Quiz Game, 1954,
Pressman
EX $40   NM $50   MIP $75

Groucho's You Bet Your Life, 1955,
Lowell
EX $25   NM $35   MIP $45

Group Therapy, 1969, Group Therapy
Assn.
EX $3   NM $12   MIP $20

**Guinness Book of World Records
Game, The,** 1979, Parker Bros.
EX $5   NM $9   MIP $15

Gulf Strike, 1983, Victory Games
EX $5   NM $16   MIP $25

(KP Photo)

Gunsmoke Game, 1950s, Lowell
EX $40   NM $65   MIP $90

Gusher, 1946, Carrom Industries
EX $50   NM $75   MIP $125

Half-Time Football, 1979, Lakeside
EX $5   NM $9   MIP $15

Handicap Harness Racing, 1978, Hall
of Fame Games
EX $15   NM $25   MIP $35

Hang On Harvey, 1969, Ideal
EX $15   NM $20   MIP $30

Hangman, 1976, Milton Bradley
EX $5   NM $8   MIP $15

Hank Aaron Baseball Game, 1970s,
Ideal
EX $50   NM $80   MIP $125

Hank Aaron Bases Loaded, 1976,
Twentieth Century Enterprises
EX $45   NM $70   MIP $100

Hank Bauer's "Be a Manager,"
1960s, Barco Games
EX $75   NM $125   MIP $170

Happiness, 1972, Milton Bradley
EX $12   NM $20   MIP $25

Happy Days, 1976, Parker Bros.
EX $8   NM $15   MIP $25

Happy Little Train Game, The, 1957,
Milton Bradley
EX $3   NM $12   MIP $20

(KP Photo)

**Hardy Boys Mystery Game, Secret of
Thunder Mountain,** 1978, Parker
Bros.
EX $7   NM $15   MIP $20

Hardy Boys Mystery Game, The,
1968, Milton Bradley
EX $6   NM $15   MIP $25

Hardy Boys Treasure, 1960, Parker
Bros.
EX $25   NM $35   MIP $50

Harlem Globetrotters Game, 1971,
Milton Bradley
EX $12   NM $30   MIP $40

**Harlem Globetrotters Official Edition
Basketball,** 1970s, Cadaco-Ellis
EX $45   NM $75   MIP $105

Harpoon, 1955, Gabriel
EX $20   NM $35   MIP $50

Harry Lorayne Memory Game, The,
1976, Reiss
EX $7   NM $20   MIP $35

Hashimoto San, 1963, Transogram
EX $20   NM $30   MIP $60

Haul the Freight, 1962, Bar-Zim
EX $25   NM $50   MIP $60

Haunted House Game, 1963, Ideal
EX $120   NM $250   MIP $400

Haunted Mansion, 1970s, Lakeside
EX $60   NM $150   MIP $200

Have Gun Will Travel Game, 1959,
Parker Bros.
EX $45   NM $65   MIP $85

Hawaii Five-O, 1960s, Remco
EX $30   NM $90   MIP $120

Hawaiian Eye, 1960, Transogram
EX $50   NM $120   MIP $200

Hawaiian Punch Game, 1978, Mattel
EX $5   NM $10   MIP $15

Hector Heathcote, 1963, Transogram
EX $35   NM $45   MIP $60

Hex: The Zig-Zag Game, 1950, Parker
Bros.
EX $10   NM $35   MIP $50

Hey Fatso, 1969, Hasbro
EX $15   NM $35   MIP $50

Hey Pa, There's a Goat on the Roof!,
1965, Parker Bros.
EX $40   NM $60   MIP $75

Hide 'N' Thief, 1965, Whitman
EX $7 NM $20 MIP $35

Hide-N-Seek, 1967, Ideal
EX $20 NM $50 MIP $75

High-Bid, 1965, 3M
EX $7 NM $20 MIP $35

Highway Traffic Game, 1957, John H Allison Jr.
EX $15 NM $35 MIP $50

Hi-Ho! Cherry-O, 1960, Whitman
EX $6 NM $10 MIP $15

Hijacked, 1973, Valley Games
EX $12 NM $30 MIP $40

Hip Flip, 1968, Parker Bros.
EX $6 NM $15 MIP $25

Hippety Hop, 1947, Corey Game
EX $20 NM $30 MIP $40

Hippopotamus, 1961, Remco
EX $8 NM $25 MIP $40

Hispaniola, The Game of, 1957, Schaper
EX $30 NM $70 MIP $100

Hit The Beach, 1965, Milton Bradley
EX $45 NM $50 MIP $60

Hobbit Game, The, 1978, Milton Bradley
EX $30 NM $60 MIP $85

Hock Shop, 1975, Whitman
EX $3 NM $12 MIP $20

Hocus Pocus, 1960s, Transogram
EX $40 NM $50 MIP $75

Hog Tied, 1981, Selchow & Righter
EX $3 NM $12 MIP $20

Hogan's Heroes Game, 1966, Transogram
EX $45 NM $85 MIP $120

Holiday, 1958, Replogle Globes
EX $40 NM $65 MIP $100

Holiday, 1973, RGI-Athol
EX $18 NM $40 MIP $60

Hollywood Awards Game, 1976, Milton Bradley
EX $8 NM $25 MIP $40

Hollywood Go, 1954, Parker Bros.
EX $10 NM $25 MIP $35

Hollywood Squares, 1974, Ideal
EX $6 NM $10 MIP $15

Hollywood Squares, 1980, Milton Bradley
EX $4 NM $6 MIP $10

Hollywood Stars, The Game of, 1955, Whitman
EX $8 NM $20 MIP $30

Home Court Basketball, 1954
EX $145 NM $250 MIP $380

Home Game, 1960s, Pressman
EX $30 NM $50 MIP $60

Home Stretch Harness Racing, 1967, Lowe
EX $15 NM $35 MIP $50

Home Team Baseball Game, 1957, Selchow & Righter
EX $18 NM $30 MIP $40

Honey West, 1965, Ideal
EX $35 NM $50 MIP $75

Honeymooners Game, The, 1986, TSR
EX $7 NM $12 MIP $20

Hoodoo, 1950, Tryne
EX $4 NM $10 MIP $15

Hookey Go Fishin', 1974, Cadaco
EX $8 NM $16 MIP $25

Hopalong Cassidy Chinese Checkers Game, 1950s
EX $20 NM $50 MIP $75

(KP Photo)

Hopalong Cassidy Game, 1950s, Milton Bradley
EX $50 NM $85 MIP $125

Horse Play, 1962, Schaper
EX $10 NM $35 MIP $50

Horseshoe Derby Game, 1950s, Built-Rite
EX $8 NM $20 MIP $30

Hot Property!, 1980s, Take One Games
EX $8 NM $25 MIP $40

Hot Rod, 1953, Harett-Gilmar
EX $15 NM $35 MIP $50

Hot Wheels Game, 1982, Whitman
EX $8 NM $13 MIP $20

Hot Wheels Wipe-Out Game, 1968, Mattel
EX $15 NM $35 MIP $60

Hotels, 1987, Milton Bradley
EX $20 NM $35 MIP $50

Houndcats Game, 1970s, Milton Bradley
EX $8 NM $15 MIP $25

House Party, 1968, Whitman
EX $10 NM $25 MIP $35

Houston Astros Baseball Challenge Game, 1980, Croque
EX $15 NM $25 MIP $35

How To Succeed In Business w/out Really Trying, 1963, Milton Bradley
EX $6 NM $10 MIP $15

Howard Hughes Game, The, 1972, Family Games
EX $10 NM $35 MIP $50

Howdy Doody Adventure Game, 1950s, Milton Bradley
EX $35 NM $50 MIP $60

Howdy Doody Quiz Show, 1950s, Multiple Products
EX $20 NM $40 MIP $50

Howdy Doody's Electric Carnival Game, Harrett-Gilmar
EX $20 NM $30 MIP $50

Howdy Doody's Own Game, 1949, Parker Bros.
EX $50 NM $60 MIP $75

Howdy Doody's Three Ring Circus, 1950, Harett-Gilmar
EX $35 NM $50 MIP $60

(KP Photo)

Howdy Doody's TV Game, 1950s, Milton Bradley
EX $50 NM $50 MIP $75

Huckleberry Hound, 1981, Milton Bradley
EX $10 NM $20 MIP $35

Huckleberry Hound Bumps, 1960, Transogram
EX $20 NM $50 MIP $75

Huckleberry Hound Spin-O-Game, 1959
EX $45 NM $75 MIP $120

Huckleberry Hound Tiddly Winks, 1959, Milton Bradley
EX $15 NM $30 MIP $60

Huckleberry Hound Western Game, 1959, Milton Bradley
EX $25 NM $35 MIP $50

Huff 'N Puff Game, 1968, Schaper
EX $6 NM $15 MIP $25

Huggermugger, 1989, Huggermugger Co.
EX $8 NM $20 MIP $30

(KP Photo)

Hullabaloo, 1965, Remco
EX $25 NM $65 MIP $75

Humor Rumor, 1969, Whitman
EX $10 NM $20 MIP $30

Humpty Dumpty Game, 1950s, Lowell
EX $25 NM $40 MIP $50

Hunch, 1956, Happy Hour
EX $7   NM $20   MIP $35

Hungry Ant, The, 1978, Milton Bradley
EX $5   NM $16   MIP $25

Hunt For Red October, 1988, TSR
EX $5   NM $15   MIP $25

Hurry Up, 1971, Parker Bros.
EX $5   NM $16   MIP $25

Hurry Waiter! Game, 1969, Ideal
EX $8   NM $20   MIP $30

Husker Du, 1970, Regina Products
EX $10   NM $25   MIP $40

I Dream of Jeannie Game, 1965, Milton Bradley
EX $35   NM $50   MIP $75

I Spy, 1965, Ideal
EX $35   NM $75   MIP $95

I Vant to Bite Your Finger, 1981, Hasbro
EX $12   NM $20   MIP $25

I Wanna Be President, 1983, J.R. Mackey
EX $5   NM $16   MIP $25

Ice Cube Game, The, 1972, Milton Bradley
EX $50   NM $125   MIP $175

(KP Photo)

Identipops, 1969, Playvalue
EX $75   NM $175   MIP $250

I'm George Gobel, And Here's The Game, 1955, Schaper
EX $12   NM $20   MIP $32

Image, 1972, 3M
EX $3   NM $12   MIP $20

Incredible Hulk, 1978, Milton Bradley
EX $6   NM $10   MIP $15

Indiana Jones: Raiders of The Lost Ark, 1981, Kenner
EX $15   NM $20   MIP $30

Indianapolis 500 75th Running Race Game, 1991, International Games
EX $8   NM $13   MIP $20

Input, 1984, Milton Bradley
EX $4   NM $7   MIP $15

Inside Moves, 1985, Parker Bros.
EX $3   NM $12   MIP $20

Inspector Gadget, 1983, Milton Bradley
EX $15   NM $25   MIP $40

Instant Replay, 1987, Parker Bros.
EX $8   NM $13   MIP $20

Intercept, 1978, Lakeside
EX $7   NM $20   MIP $35

International Airport Game, 1964, Magic Wand
EX $8   NM $20   MIP $30

International Grand Prix, 1975, Cadaco
EX $8   NM $20   MIP $30

Interpretation of Dreams, 1969, Hasbro
EX $7   NM $15   MIP $25

Interstate Highway, 1963, Selchow & Righter
EX $15   NM $30   MIP $40

(KP Photo)

Intrigue, 1954, Milton Bradley
EX $12   NM $30   MIP $40

Inventors, The, 1974, Parker Bros.
EX $10   NM $20   MIP $30

Ipcress File, 1966, Milton Bradley
EX $15   NM $25   MIP $35

(KP Photo)

Ironside, 1976, Ideal
EX $55   NM $75   MIP $100

(KP Photo)

Is the Pope Catholic?!, 1986, Crowley Connections
EX $10   NM $25   MIP $40

Isolation, 1978, Lakeside
EX $2   NM $7   MIP $12

It Takes Two, 1970, NBC-Hasbro
EX $5   NM $12   MIP $18

Itinerary, 1980, Xanadu Leisure
EX $3   NM $12   MIP $20

Jace Pearson's Tales of The Texas Rangers, 1955, E.E. Fairchild
EX $40   NM $60   MIP $75

Jack and The Beanstalk, 1946, National Games
EX $25   NM $45   MIP $50

Jack and The Beanstalk Adventure Game, 1957, Transogram
EX $25   NM $30   MIP $40

Jack Barry's Twenty One, 1956, Lowell
EX $20   NM $30   MIP $50

Jackie Gleason's and AW-A-A-A-Y We Go!, 1956, Transogram
EX $50   NM $75   MIP $125

Jackie Gleason's Story Stage Game, 1955, Utopia Enterprises
EX $50   NM $75   MIP $125

Jackpot, 1975, Milton Bradley
EX $7   NM $11   MIP $20

Jacmar Big League Electric Baseball, 1950s, Jacmar
EX $100   NM $175   MIP $250

James Bond 007 Goldfinger Game, 1966, Milton Bradley
EX $35   NM $60   MIP $75

James Bond 007 Thunderball Game, 1965, Milton Bradley
EX $35   NM $50   MIP $75

James Bond Message From M Game, 1966, Ideal
EX $1125   NM $250   MIP $400

James Bond Secret Agent 007 Game, 1964, Milton Bradley
EX $15   NM $30   MIP $45

James Bond You Only Live Twice, 1984, Victory Games, box shows helicopter chase
EX $5   NM $12   MIP $25

James Clavell's Noble House, 1987, FASA
EX $6   NM $15   MIP $25

James Clavell's Shogun, 1983, FASA
EX $6   NM $15   MIP $25

James Clavell's Tai-Pan, 1987, FASA
EX $6   NM $15   MIP $25

James Clavell's Whirlwind, 1986, FASA
EX $6   NM $15   MIP $25

Jan Murray's Charge Account, 1961, Lowell
EX $10   NM $15   MIP $20

Jan Murray's Treasure Hunt, 1950s, Gardner
EX $10   NM $25   MIP $35

JDK Baseball, 1982, JDK Baseball
EX $20   NM $45   MIP $65

Jeanne Dixon's Game of Destiny,
1968, Milton Bradley
EX $7   NM $10   MIP $15

Jeopardy, 1964, Milton Bradley
EX $10   NM $15   MIP $25

Jerry Kramer's Instant Replay, 1970,
EMD Enterprises
EX $15   NM $25   MIP $40

Jet World, 1975, Milton Bradley
EX $5   NM $16   MIP $25

Jetsons Fun Pad Game, 1963, Milton
Bradley
EX $40   NM $70   MIP $80

Jetsons Game, 1985, Milton Bradley
EX $5   NM $10   MIP $15

Jetsons Out of this World Game,
1963, Transogram
EX $40   NM $75   MIP $125

**Jimmy the Greek Oddsmaker
Football,** 1974, Aurora
EX $10   NM $20   MIP $35

Jockette, 1950s, Jockette
EX $25   NM $40   MIP $60

Jockey, 1976, Hallmark Games
EX $10   NM $25   MIP $35

Joe Palooka Boxing Game, 1950s,
Lowell
EX $75   NM $125   MIP $200

John Drake Secret Agent, 1966,
Milton Bradley
EX $15   NM $20   MIP $30

Johnny Ringo, 1959, Transogram
EX $40   NM $90   MIP $110

Johnny Unitas Football Game, 1970,
Pro Mentor
EX $15   NM $35   MIP $50

Joker's Wild, 1973, Milton Bradley
EX $5   NM $10   MIP $15

Jonathan Livingston Seagull, 1973,
Mattel
EX $8   NM $20   MIP $30

(KP Photo)

Jonny Quest Game, 1964, Transogram
EX $200   NM $350   MIP $500

**Jose Canseco's Perfect Baseball
Game,** 1991, Perfect Game
EX $8   NM $13   MIP $20

Jubilee, 1954, Cadaco-Ellis
EX $10   NM $25   MIP $35

Jumbo Jet, 1963, Jumbo
EX $18   NM $45   MIP $65

Jumpin', 1964, 3M
EX $7   NM $20   MIP $35

Jumping DJ, 1962, Mattel
EX $15   NM $50   MIP $75

Junior Bingo-Matic, 1968, Transogram
EX $6   NM $10   MIP $15

Junior Executive, 1963, Whitman
EX $7   NM $15   MIP $25

Junior Quarterback Football, 1950s,
Warren/Built-Rite
EX $7   NM $20   MIP $35

Junk Yard Game, 1975, Ideal
EX $8   NM $20   MIP $30

Jurisprudence, 1974, James Vail
EX $8   NM $20   MIP $30

Justice, 1954, Lowell
EX $25   NM $55   MIP $75

Justice League of America, 1967,
Hasbro
EX $70   NM $150   MIP $200

Ka Bala, 1965, Transogram
EX $40   NM $75   MIP $100

Karate, The Game of, 1964, Selchow
& Righter
EX $7   NM $20   MIP $35

Karter Peanut Shell Game, 1978,
Morey & Neely
EX $7   NM $20   MIP $35

Kar-Zoom, 1964, Whitman
EX $15   NM $20   MIP $35

Kennedys, The, 1962, Transogram
EX $35   NM $60   MIP $75

Kentucky Derby, 1960, Whitman
EX $25   NM $35   MIP $50

Kentucky Jones, 1964, T. Cohn
EX $20   NM $35   MIP $50

Keyword, 1954, Parker Bros.
EX $3   NM $6   MIP $10

Kick-Off Soccer, 1978, Camden
Products
EX $7   NM $20   MIP $35

King Kong Game, 1963, Ideal
EX $100   NM $200   MIP $325

(KP Photo)

King Kong Game, 1966, Milton Bradley
EX $8   NM $20   MIP $30

King Kong Game, 1976, Ideal
EX $8   NM $30   MIP $45

**King Leonardo and His Subjects
Game,** 1960, Milton Bradley
EX $18   NM $45   MIP $65

King of the Hill, 1965, Schaper
EX $35   NM $50   MIP $70

King of the Sea, 1975, Ideal
EX $8   NM $25   MIP $40

King Oil, 1974, Milton Bradley
EX $25   NM $55   MIP $70

King Tut's Game, 1978, Cadaco
EX $5   NM $16   MIP $25

(KP Photo)

King Zor, The Dinosaur Game, 1964,
Ideal
EX $55   NM $85   MIP $120

Kismet, 1971, Lakeside
EX $6   NM $15   MIP $25

KISS On Tour Game, 1978, Aucoin
EX $25   NM $60   MIP $100

Klondike, 1975, Gamma Two
EX $12   NM $30   MIP $40

Knight Rider, 1983, Parker Bros.
EX $7   NM $12   MIP $20

(KP Photo)

Kojak, 1975, Milton Bradley
EX $7   NM $12   MIP $35

Kommisar, 1960s, Selchow & Righter
EX $12   NM $20   MIP $30

Koo Koo Choo Choo, 1960s, Ohio Art
EX $12   NM $30   MIP $40

Kooky Carnival, 1969, Milton Bradley
EX $10   NM $35   MIP $50

Korg 70,000 BC, 1974, Milton Bradley
EX $7   NM $15   MIP $25

(KP Photo)

Kreskin's ESP, 1966, Milton Bradley
EX $4   NM $10   MIP $15

Krull, 1983, Parker Bros.
EX $6   NM $10   MIP $15

KSP Baseball, 1983, Koch Sports Products
EX $25   NM $60   MIP $85

Kukla & Ollie, 1962, Parker Bros.
EX $15   NM $25   MIP $50

Labyrinth (movie game), 1986, Golden
EX $25   NM $60   MIP $85

Lancer, 1968, Remco
EX $40   NM $90   MIP $135

(KP Photo)

Land of The Giants, 1968, Ideal
EX $75   NM $100   MIP $175

Land of The Lost, 1975, Milton Bradley
EX $10   NM $25   MIP $35

Landmarks, The Game of, 1962, Selchow & Righter
EX $6   NM $15   MIP $25

Landslide, 1971, Parker Bros.
EX $5   NM $16   MIP $20

Laramie, 1960, Lowell
EX $50   NM $100   MIP $150

Las Vegas Baseball, 1987, Samar Enterprises
EX $8   NM $13   MIP $20

Laser Attack Game, 1978, Milton Bradley
EX $7   NM $20   MIP $35

Lassie Game, 1965, Game Gems
EX $20   NM $35   MIP $75

Last Straw, 1966, Schaper
EX $5   NM $10   MIP $15

(KP Photo)

Laugh-In's Squeeze Your Bippy Game, 1968, Hasbro
EX $35   NM $75   MIP $100

Laurel & Hardy Game, 1962, Transogram
EX $20   NM $30   MIP $40

(KP Photo)

Laverne & Shirley Game, 1977, Parker Bros.
EX $9   NM $15   MIP $25

Leave It To Beaver Ambush Game, 1959, Hasbro
EX $20   NM $35   MIP $60

Leave It To Beaver Money Maker, 1959, Hasbro
EX $20   NM $35   MIP $60

(KP Photo)

Leave It To Beaver Rocket To The Moon, 1959, Hasbro
EX $20   NM $353   MIP $60

Lee vs Meade: Battle of Gettysburg, 1974, Gamut of Games
EX $7   NM $15   MIP $25

Legend of Jesse James Game, The, 1965, Milton Bradley
EX $30   NM $50   MIP $75

LeMans, 1961, Avalon Hill
EX $25   NM $60   MIP $85

Let's Bowl a Game, 1960, DMR
EX $5   NM $12   MIP $20

Let's Drive, 1969, Milton Bradley
EX $8   NM $20   MIP $30

Let's Go to the Races, 1987, Parker Bros.
EX $7   NM $20   MIP $35

Let's Make a Deal, 1964, Milton Bradley
EX $12   NM $30   MIP $40

Let's Make A Deal, 1970s, Ideal
EX $10   NM $15   MIP $25

Let's Play Golf "The Hawaiian Open," 1968, Burlu
EX $8   NM $20   MIP $30

(KP Photo)

Let's Play Safe Traffic Game, 1960s, X-Acto
EX $25   NM $50   MIP $90

Let's Play Tag, 1958, Milton Bradley
EX $5   NM $16   MIP $25

Let's Take a Trip, 1962, Milton Bradley
EX $8   NM $15   MIP $20

Leverage, 1982, Milton Bradley
EX $4   NM $6   MIP $10

LF Baseball, 1980, Len Feder
EX $18   NM $45   MIP $65

Lie Detector Game, 1961, Mattel
EX $20   NM $40   MIP $85

Lie Detector Game, 1987, Pressman
EX $8   NM $20   MIP $30

Lieutenant, The, 1963, Transogram
EX $20   NM $35   MIP $60

Life, The Game of, 1960, Milton Bradley
EX $8   NM $20   MIP $30

Limit Up, 1980, Willem
EX $6   NM $18   MIP $30

Line Drive, 1953, Lord & Freber
EX $18   NM $45   MIP $65

Linebacker Football, 1990, Linebacker
EX $12   NM $20   MIP $30

Linkup, 1972, American Greetings
EX $5   NM $16   MIP $25

Linus the Lionhearted Uproarious Game, 1965, Transogram
EX $50   NM $85   MIP $135

Linx, 1972, American Greetings
EX $6   NM $15   MIP $25

Lion and the White Witch, The, 1983, David Cook
EX $5   NM $16   MIP $25

(KP Photo)

Lippy the Lion Game, 1963, Transogram
EX $30   NM $45   MIP $70

Little Black Sambo, 1952, Cadaco-Ellis
EX $45   NM $90   MIP $175

Little Boy Blue, 1955, Cadaco-Ellis
EX $6   NM $18   MIP $30

Little Creepies Monster Game, 1974, Toy Factory
EX $6   NM $10   MIP $15

Little House On The Prairie, 1978, Parker Bros.
EX $12   NM $30   MIP $40

Little League Baseball Game, 1950s, Standard Toykraft
EX $20   NM $35   MIP $60

Little Orphan Annie, 1981, Parker Bros.
EX $10   NM $15   MIP $20

Little Red Schoolhouse, 1952, Parker Bros.
EX $10   NM $20   MIP $35

Lobby, 1949, Milton Bradley
EX $8   NM $20   MIP $30

Long Shot, 1962, Parker Bros.
EX $45   NM $75   MIP $125

Longball, 1975, Ashburn Industries
EX $35   NM $75   MIP $100

Look All-Star Baseball Game, 1960, Progressive Research
EX $35   NM $60   MIP $90

Looney Tunes Game, 1968, Milton Bradley
EX $20   NM $40   MIP $50

Lord of the Rings, The, 1979, Milton Bradley
EX $40   NM $85   MIP $125

Los Angeles Dodgers Baseball Game, 1964, Ed-U-Cards
EX $10   NM $25   MIP $35

Lost Gold, 1975, Parker Bros.
EX $7   NM $20   MIP $35

(KP Photo)

Lost In Space Game, 1965, Milton Bradley
EX $35   NM $60   MIP $100

Lost Treasure, 1982, Parker Bros.
EX $7   NM $20   MIP $35

Lottery Game, 1972, Selchow & Righter
EX $6   NM $18   MIP $30

Louie the Electrician, ca. 1960, Hasbro
EX $20   NM $50   MIP $70

Love Boat World Cruise, 1980, Ungame
EX $5   NM $15   MIP $20

Loving Game, The, 1987, R.J.E. Enterprises
EX $4   NM $6   MIP $10

Lucan, The Wolf Boy, 1977, Milton Bradley
EX $5   NM $10   MIP $15

Lucky Break, 1975, Gabriel
EX $10   NM $20   MIP $30

Lucky Strike, 1972, International Toy
EX $5   NM $10   MIP $15

Lucky Town, 1946, Milton Bradley
EX $15   NM $40   MIP $50

Lucy Show Game, The, 1962, Transogram
EX $60   NM $90   MIP $150

Lucy's Tea Party Game, 1971, Milton Bradley
EX $15   NM $25   MIP $50

Ludwig Von Drake Ball Toss Game, 1960
EX $6   NM $10   MIP $15

Luftwaffe, 1971, Avalon Hill
EX $3   NM $8   MIP $15

(KP Photo)

M Squad, 1958, Bell Toys
EX $35   NM $75   MIP $125

M*A*S*H Game, 1981, Milton Bradley
EX $15   NM $20   MIP $35

MacDonald's Farm, 1948, Selchow & Righter
EX $12   NM $20   MIP $30

(KP Photo)

MAD Magazine Game, The, 1979, Parker Bros.
EX $4   NM $12   MIP $20

MAD, What Me Worry?, 1987, Milton Bradley
EX $6   NM $10   MIP $15

Madame Planchette Horoscope Game, 1967, Selchow & Righter
EX $6   NM $18   MIP $30

Magic Miles, 1956, Hasbro
EX $10   NM $15   MIP $20

Magilla Gorilla, 1964, Ideal
EX $40   NM $65   MIP $100

Magnetic Flying Saucers, 1950s, Pressman
EX $21   NM $35   MIP $55

Magnificent Race, 1975, Parker Bros.
EX $10   NM $20   MIP $30

Mail Run, 1960, Quality Games
EX $35   NM $75   MIP $100

Main Street Baseball, 1989, Main St. Toy
EX $20   NM $35   MIP $55

Major League Baseball, 1965, Cadaco
EX $10   NM $20   MIP $30

Major League Baseball Magnetic Dart Game, 1958, Pressman
EX $20   NM $45   MIP $65

(KP Photo)

Man from U.N.C.L.E. Napoleon Solo Game, 1965, Ideal
EX $25   NM $45   MIP $60

Man from U.N.C.L.E. THRUSH Ray Gun Affair Game, 1966, Ideal
EX $50   NM $85   MIP $135

Manage Your Own Team, 1950s, Warren
EX $10   NM $30   MIP $40

Management, 1960, Avalon Hill
EX $10   NM $25   MIP $40

Mandinka, 1978, Lowe
EX $3   NM $12   MIP $20

Manhunt, 1972, Milton Bradley
EX $5   NM $16   MIP $20

Maniac, 1979, Ideal
EX $7   NM $15   MIP $20

Margie, The Game of Whoopie, 1961, Milton Bradley
EX $12   NM $20   MIP $30

Marlin Perkins' Zoo Parade, 1965, Cadaco-Ellis
EX $12   NM $30   MIP $40

Martin Luther King Jr., 1980, Cadaco
EX $6   NM $10   MIP $15

Mary Hartman, Mary Hartman, 1976, Reiss Games
EX $10   NM $25   MIP $35

(KP Photo)

Mary Poppins Carousel Game, 1964, Parker Bros.
EX $12   NM $20   MIP $30

Masquerade Party, 1955, Bettye-B
EX $25   NM $35   MIP $75

Mastermind, 1970s, Invicta
EX $5   NM $10   MIP $15

Masterpiece, The Art Auction Game, 1971, Parker Bros.
EX $8   NM $15   MIP $30

Match Game (3rd Ed.), The, 1963, Milton Bradley
EX $10   NM $20   MIP $60

Matchbox Traffic Game, 1960s, Bronner
EX $25   NM $45   MIP $70

(KP Photo)

McDonald's Game, The, 1975, Milton Bradley
EX $12   NM $30   MIP $40

(KP Photo)

McHale's Navy Game, 1962, Transogram
EX $20   NM $30   MIP $50

McMurtle Turtle, 1965, Cadaco-Ellis
EX $8   NM $25   MIP $40

Mechanic Mac, 1961, Selchow & Richter
EX $15   NM $35   MIP $50

Meet The Presidents, 1953, Selchow & Righter
EX $8   NM $15   MIP $20

Megiddo, 1985, Global Games
EX $8   NM $20   MIP $30

(KP Photo)

Melvin The Moon Man, 1960s, Remco
EX $30   NM $70   MIP $100

Men Into Space, 1960, Milton Bradley
EX $25   NM $60   MIP $90

Merger, 1965, Universal Games
EX $12   NM $30   MIP $40

(KP Photo)

Merry Milkman, 1955, Hasbro
EX $50   NM $85   MIP $125

Merv Griffin's Word For Word, 1963, Mattel
EX $5   NM $16   MIP $25

Miami Vice: The Game, 1984, Pepperlane
EX $10   NM $25   MIP $35

Mickey Mantle's Action Baseball, 1960, Pressman
EX $75   NM $125   MIP $200

(KP Photo)

Mickey Mantle's Big League Baseball, 1958, Gardner
EX $150   NM $225   MIP $325

Mickey Mouse, 1950, Jacmar
EX $35   NM $55   MIP $90

Mickey Mouse, 1976, Parker Bros.
EX $6   NM $10   MIP $15

Mickey Mouse Basketball, 1950s, Gardner
EX $55   NM $90   MIP $135

Mickey Mouse Lotto Game, 1950s, Jaymar
EX $10   NM $15   MIP $25

Mickey Mouse Pop Up Game, 1970s, Whitman
EX $7   NM $15   MIP $20

Mickey Mouse Slugaroo, 1950s
EX $20   NM $30   MIP $50

Mid Life Crisis, 1982, Gameworks
EX $5   NM $10   MIP $20

Mighty Comics Super Heroes Game, 1966, Transogram
EX $30   NM $70   MIP $100

(KP Photo)

Mighty Hercules Game, 1963, Hasbro
EX $125   NM $300   MIP $500

(KP Photo)

Mighty Heroes on the Scene Game, 1960s, Transogram
EX $35   NM $75   MIP $100

Mighty Mouse, 1978, Milton Bradley
EX $15   NM $20   MIP $30

(KP Photo)

Mighty Mouse Rescue Game, 1960s, Harett-Gilmar
EX $25   NM $50   MIP $75

(KP Photo)

Milton The Monster, 1966, Milton Bradley
EX $10   NM $20   MIP $30

Mind Over Matter, 1968, Transogram
EX $10   NM $15   MIP $25

Miss America Pageant Game, 1974, Parker Bros.
EX $10   NM $20   MIP $30

Miss Popularity Game, 1961, Transogram
EX $10   NM $20   MIP $50

Missing Links, 1964, Milton Bradley
EX $6   NM $18   MIP $35

Mission: Impossible, 1967, Ideal
EX $40   NM $80   MIP $135

(KP Photo)

Mission: Impossible, 1975, Berwick
EX $10   NM $15   MIP $25

Mister Ed Game, 1962, Parker Bros.
EX $20   NM $40   MIP $75

Mister Football, 1951, Alkay
EX $30   NM $75   MIP $100

Mob Strategy, 1969, NBC-Hasbro
EX $4   NM $10   MIP $15

Mod Squad Game, 1968, Remco
EX $45   NM $85   MIP $125

Monday Morning Quarterback, 1963, Zbinden
EX $8   NM $25   MIP $35

Money Card: Amer. Express Travel Game, 1972, Schaper
EX $8   NM $20   MIP $30

Money! Money! Money!, 1957, Whitman
EX $5   NM $15   MIP $25

(KP Photo)

Monkees Game, 1968, Transogram
EX $65   NM $100   MIP $150

Monkeys and Coconuts, 1965, Schaper
EX $6   NM $15   MIP $20

Monopoly (large maroon box), 1964, Parker Bros.
EX $15   NM $25   MIP $50

(KP Photo)

Monopoly (train cover), 1958, Parker Bros.
EX $50   NM $75   MIP $125

Monster Game, 1977, Ideal
EX $25   NM $60   MIP $85

Monster Game, The, 1965, Milton Bradley
EX $15   NM $25   MIP $40

Monster Mansion, 1981, Milton Bradley
EX $20   NM $50   MIP $75

Monster Squad, 1977, Milton Bradley
EX $10   NM $20   MIP $35

Monsters of the Deep, 1976, Whitman
EX $5   NM $16   MIP $25

Moon Blast-Off, 1970, Schaper
EX $12   NM $20   MIP $30

Moon Shot, 1960s, Cadaco
EX $15   NM $35   MIP $60

Moon Tag, Game of, 1957, Parker Bros.
EX $40   NM $60   MIP $100

(KP Photo)

Mork and Mindy, 1978, Milton Bradley
EX $6   NM $15   MIP $25

Mostly Ghostly, 1975, Cadaco
EX $8   NM $20   MIP $30

Movie Moguls, 1970, RGI
EX $15   NM $35   MIP $50

Movie Studio Mogul, 1981, International Mktg.
EX $8   NM $25   MIP $40

Mr. Bug Goes To Town, 1955, Milton Bradley
EX $10   NM $15   MIP $25

Mr. Doodle's Dog, 1940s, Selchow & Righter
EX $15   NM $25   MIP $40

Mr. Machine Game, 1961, Ideal
EX $60   NM $90   MIP $150

Mr. Magoo Maddening Misadventures Game, The, 1970, Transogram
EX $45   NM $75   MIP $120

Mr. Magoo Visits The Zoo, 1961, Lowell
EX $25   NM $45   MIP $70

Mr. President, 1967, 3M
EX $8   NM $25   MIP $40

Mr. Ree, 1957, Selchow & Righter
EX $15   NM $25   MIP $50

Mt. Everest, 1955, Gabriel
EX $18   NM $25   MIP $50

Mug Shots, 1975, Cadaco
EX $7   NM $12   MIP $20

Munsters Drag Race Game, 1965, Hasbro
EX $250   NM $600   MIP $1000

Munsters Masquerade Game, 1965, Hasbro
EX $250   NM $600   MIP $1000

Munsters Picnic Game, 1965, Hasbro
EX $200   NM $500   MIP $1000

(KP Photo)

Muppet Show, 1977, Parker Bros.
EX $6   NM $15   MIP $20

Murder on the Orient Express, 1967, Ideal
EX $20   NM $50   MIP $75

Murder She Wrote, 1985, Warren
EX $4   NM $6   MIP $10

Mushmouse & Punkin Puss, 1964, Ideal
EX $45   NM $75   MIP $120

MVP Baseball, The Sports Card Game, 1989, Ideal
EX $8   NM $13   MIP $20

My Fair Lady, 1960s, Standard Toykraft
EX $5   NM $10   MIP $20

(KP Photo)

My Favorite Martian, 1963, Transogram
EX $40   NM $50   MIP $75

(KP Photo)

My First (Walt Disney Character) Game, 1963, Gabriel
EX $20   NM $35   MIP $60

Mystery Checkers, 1950s, Creative Designs
EX $15   NM $20   MIP $30

Mystery Date, 1965, Milton Bradley
EX $75   NM $125   MIP $300

Mystery Date Game, 1972, Milton Bradley
EX $50   NM $70   MIP $125

Mystery Mansion, 1984, Milton Bradley
EX $10   NM $25   MIP $35

Mystic Skull The Game of Voodoo, 1965, Ideal
EX $15   NM $30   MIP $50

Mystic Wheel of Knowledge, 1950s, Novel Toy
EX $15   NM $20   MIP $30

Name That Tune, 1959, Milton Bradley
EX $12   NM $20   MIP $30

Names and Faces, 1960, Pressman
EX $6   NM $15   MIP $25

Nancy Drew Mystery Game, 1957, Parker Bros.
EX $35   NM $90   MIP $150

NASCAR Daytona 500, 1990, Milton Bradley
EX $10   NM $25   MIP $35

National Football League Quarterback, Official, 1965, Standard Toykraft
EX $12   NM $30   MIP $40

National Inquirer, 1991, Tyco
EX $10   NM $15   MIP $20

National Lampoon's Sellout, 1970s, Cardinal
EX $6   NM $15   MIP $25

National Pro Football Hall of Fame Game, 1965, Cadaco
EX $15   NM $25   MIP $40

National Pro Hockey, 1985, Sports Action
EX $15   NM $25   MIP $40

(KP Photo)

National Velvet Game, 1950s, Transogram
EX $15   NM $25   MIP $40

Naval Battle, 1954, Coronet Products
EX $25   NM $60   MIP $85

NBA Basketball Game, Official, 1970s, Gerney Games
EX $35   NM $75   MIP $100

NBC Game of the Week, 1969, Hasbro
EX $10   NM $25   MIP $35

NBC Peacock, 1966, Selchow & Righter
EX $20   NM $50   MIP $75

NBC Pro Playoff, 1969, Hasbro
EX $10   NM $25   MIP $35

NBC TV News, 1960, Dadan
EX $15   NM $35   MIP $50

Nebula, 1976, Nebula
EX $4   NM $6   MIP $10

Neck & Neck, 1981, Yaquinto
EX $8   NM $13   MIP $20

Negamco Basketball, 1975, Nemadji Game
EX $10   NM $16   MIP $25

New Avengers Shooting Game, 1976, Denys Fisher
EX $165   NM $275   MIP $440

New Frontier, 1962, Colorful Products
EX $30   NM $50   MIP $80

New York World's Fair, 1964, Milton Bradley
EX $15   NM $25   MIP $50

Newlywed Game (1st Ed.), 1967, Hasbro
EX $10   NM $15   MIP $20

(KP Photo)

Newlywed Game (2nd Ed.), 1967, Hasbro
EX $8   NM $15   MIP $20

Newtown, 1972, Harwell Associates
EX $15   NM $35   MIP $50

Next President, The, 1971, Reiss
EX $15   NM $35   MIP $50

NFL Armchair Quarterback, 1986, Trade Wind
EX $8   NM $13   MIP $20

NFL Franchise, 1982, Rohrwood
EX $10   NM $16   MIP $25

NFL Game Plan, 1980, Tudor
EX $6   NM $10   MIP $15

NFL Quarterback, 1977, Tudor
EX $8   NM $20   MIP $30

NFL Strategy, 1970, Tudor
EX $10   NM $20   MIP n/a

NFL Strategy, 1976, Tudor
EX $15   NM $25   MIP $50

NHL All-Pro Hockey, 1969, Ideal
EX $12   NM $30   MIP $40

NHL Strategy, 1976, Tudor
EX $10   NM $35   MIP $50

Nieuchess, 1961, Avalon Hill
EX $12   NM $40   MIP $60

Nightmare, 1991, Chieftain Products
EX $8   NM $20   MIP $30

Nightmare II, III, IV (add-ons, each), mid-1990s, Chieftain Products
EX $15   NM $35   MIP $50

Nightmare On Elm Street, 1989, Cardinal
EX $20   NM $30   MIP $45

Nile, 1967, Lowe
EX $6   NM $18   MIP $30

Nirtz, The Game is, 1961, Ideal
EX $8   NM $20   MIP $30

No Respect, The Rodney Dangerfield Game, 1985, Milton Bradley
EX $2　　NM $6　　MIP $8

No Time for Sergeants Game, 1964, Ideal
EX $12　　NM $20　　MIP $30

Noah's Ark, 1953, Cadaco-Ellis
EX $8　　NM $25　　MIP $40

Nok-Hockey, 1947, Carrom
EX $20　　NM $35　　MIP $55

Noma Party Quiz, 1947, Noma Electric
EX $10　　NM $15　　MIP $25

Northwest Passage, 1969, Impact
EX $5　　NM $10　　MIP $20

Number Please TV Quiz, 1961, Parker Bros.
EX $10　　NM $15　　MIP $20

Numble, 1968, Selchow & Righter
EX $4　　NM $10　　MIP $15

Numeralogic, 1973, American Greetings
EX $6　　NM $18　　MIP $30

Nurses, The, 1963, Ideal
EX $15　　NM $50　　MIP $60

Nuts to You, 1969, Hasbro
EX $15　　NM $35　　MIP $50

O.J. Simpson See-Action Football, 1974, Kenner
EX $50　　NM $125　　MIP $175

Obsession, 1978, Mego
EX $5　　NM $10　　MIP $15

Obstruction, 1979, Whitman
EX $4　　NM $10　　MIP $15

Octopus, 1954, Norton Games
EX $12　　NM $40　　MIP $60

Off To See The Wizard, 1968, Cadaco
EX $10　　NM $15　　MIP $25

Oh Magoo Game, 1960s, Warren
EX $10　　NM $20　　MIP $30

Oh What a Mountain, 1980, Milton Bradley
EX $5　　NM $16　　MIP $25

Oh, Nuts! Game, 1968, Ideal
EX $10　　NM $25　　MIP $35

Oh-Wah-Ree, 1966, 3M
EX $8　　NM $20　　MIP $30

Oil Power, 1980s, Antfamco
EX $20　　NM $45　　MIP $65

Old Shell Game, The, 1974, Selchow & Righter
EX $7　　NM $20　　MIP $35

Oldies But Goodies, 1987, Original Sound Records
EX $6　　NM $18　　MIP $30

On Guard, 1967, Parker Bros.
EX $6　　NM $10　　MIP $15

Oodles, 1992, Milton Bradley
EX $8　　NM $20　　MIP $30

(KP Photo)

Operation, 1965, Milton Bradley
EX $5　　NM $15　　MIP $25

Opinion, 1970, Selchow & Righter
EX $6　　NM $15　　MIP $25

Option, 1983, Parker Bros.
EX $2　　NM $7　　MIP $12

Orbit, 1959, Parker Bros.
EX $10　　NM $20　　MIP $30

Organized Crime, 1974, Koplow Games
EX $6　　NM $18　　MIP $30

Orient Express, 1985, Just Games
EX $5　　NM $16　　MIP $25

Original Home Jai-Alai Game, The, 1984, Design Origin
EX $15　　NM $25　　MIP $35

(KP Photo)

Oscar Robertson's Pro Basketball Strategy, 1969, Research Games
EX $50　　NM $72　　MIP $150

Our Gang Bingo, 1958
EX $30　　NM $50　　MIP $75

Outdoor Survival, 1972, Avalon Hill
EX $2　　NM $6　　MIP $10

Outer Limits, 1964, Milton Bradley
EX $80　　NM $180　　MIP $225

Outlaw & Posse, 1978, Milton Bradley
EX $8　　NM $20　　MIP $30

Outlaw Trail, 1972, Dynamic
EX $6　　NM $18　　MIP $30

Outwit, 1978, Parker Bros.
EX $5　　NM $10　　MIP $15

Over the Rainbow See-Saw, 1949, Milton Bradley
EX $12　　NM $20　　MIP $30

Overboard, 1978, Lakeside
EX $3　　NM $12　　MIP $18

Overland Trail Board Game, 1960, Transogram
EX $45　　NM $65　　MIP $80

Ozark Ike's Complete Three Game Set, 1956, Warren Built-Rite
EX $45　　NM $80　　MIP $110

P.T. Boat 109 Game, 1963, Ideal
EX $25　　NM $35　　MIP $50

Pac-Man, 1980, Milton Bradley
EX $5　　NM $15　　MIP $20

Pan American World Jet Flight Game, 1960, Hasbro
EX $10　　NM $20　　MIP $35

Panic Button, 1978, Mego
EX $7　　NM $15　　MIP $20

Panzer Blitz, 1970, Avalon Hill
EX $6　　NM $12　　MIP $20

Panzer Leader, 1974, Avalon Hill
EX $8　　NM $15　　MIP $25

Par '73, 1961, Big Top Games
EX $15　　NM $25　　MIP $40

Par Golf, 1950s, National Games
EX $35　　NM $40　　MIP $60

Parcheesi (Gold Seal Ed.), 1964, Selchow & Righter
EX $7　　NM $10　　MIP $15

Pari Horse Race Card Game, 1959, Pari Sales
EX $20　　NM $35　　MIP $50

Paris Metro, 1981, Infinity Games
EX $10　　NM $16　　MIP $25

Park and Shop, 1952, Traffic Game
EX $35　　NM $50　　MIP $75

Park and Shop Game, 1960, Milton Bradley
EX $75　　NM $100　　MIP $175

Parker Brothers Baseball Game, 1955, Parker Bros.
EX $25　　NM $50　　MIP $75

Parollette, 1946, Selchow & Righter
EX $18　　NM $40　　MIP $60

(KP Photo)

Partridge Family, 1974, Milton Bradley
EX $20　　NM $25　　MIP $50

Pass It On, 1978, Selchow & Righter
EX $3　　NM $12　　MIP $20

Pass the Buck, 1964, Transco Adult Games
EX $12   NM $30   MIP $40

(KP Photo)

Password, 1963, Milton Bradley
EX $6   NM $15   MIP $20

Pathfinder, 1977, Milton Bradley
EX $5   NM $15   MIP $20

Patty Duke Game, 1963, Milton Bradley
EX $18   NM $25   MIP $50

Paul Brown's Football Game, 1947, Trikilis
EX $110   NM $180   MIP $275

Payday, 1975, Parker Bros.
EX $5   NM $10   MIP $15

Payday: The People's Game, 1975, Payday Game Co/Barker
EX $12   NM $30   MIP $40

Paydirt, 1979, Avalon Hill
EX $12   NM $30   MIP $40

Paydirt!, 1973, Time, Inc., (Sports Illustrated)
EX $10   NM $25   MIP $35

Payoff Machine Game, 1978, Ideal
EX $5   NM $16   MIP $25

Pazaz, 1978, E.S.Lowe
EX $4   NM $10   MIP $15

Peanut Butter & Jelly Game, 1971, Parker Bros.
EX $12   NM $30   MIP $40

(KP Photo)

Peanuts: The Game of Charlie Brown And His Pals, 1959, Selchow & Righter
EX $20   NM $30   MIP $50

Pebbles Flintstone Game, 1962, Transogram
EX $20   NM $35   MIP $55

Pee Wee Reese Marble Game, 1956, Pee Wee Enterprises
EX $175   NM $295   MIP $450

Penetration, 1968, Crea-Tek
EX $8   NM $20   MIP $30

Pennant Chasers Baseball Game, 1946, Craig Hopkins
EX $25   NM $45   MIP $70

Pennant Drive, 1980, Accu-Stat Game
EX $8   NM $13   MIP $20

People Trivia Game, 1984, Parker Bros.
EX $7   NM $11   MIP $20

People's Court, The, 1986, Pressman
EX $4   NM $10   MIP $15

Per Plexus, 1976, Aladdin
EX $10   NM $25   MIP $35

Perils of Pauline, 1964, Marx
EX $40   NM $90   MIP $135

Perquackey, 1970, Lakeside
EX $4   NM $9   MIP $12

Perry Mason Case of The Missing Suspect Game, 1959, Transogram
EX $20   NM $30   MIP $45

Personalysis, 1957, Lowell
EX $15   NM $25   MIP $40

Pete the Plumber, c. 1960, Hasbro
EX $20   NM $50   MIP $75

Peter Gunn Detective Game, 1960, Lowell
EX $25   NM $35   MIP $50

Peter Pan, 1953, Transogram
EX $10   NM $15   MIP $20

Peter Potamus Game, 1964, Ideal
EX $30   NM $50   MIP $80

Peter Principle Game, 1973, Skor-Mor
EX $6   NM $18   MIP $30

Peter Principle Game, 1981, Avalon Hill
EX $5   NM $16   MIP $25

Petropolis, 1976, Pressman
EX $10   NM $25   MIP $40

Petticoat Junction, 1963, Standard Toykraft
EX $30   NM $50   MIP $85

Phalanx, 1964, Whitman
EX $10   NM $30   MIP $45

Phantom Game, The, 1965, Transogram
EX $50   NM $100   MIP $200

Phantom's Complete Three Game Set, The, 1955, Built-Rite
EX $30   NM $75   MIP $125

Phil Silvers' You'll Never Get Rich Game, 1955, Gardner
EX $25   NM $40   MIP $60

(KP Photo)

Philip Marlowe, 1960, Transogram
EX $10   NM $20   MIP $50

Phlounder, 1962, 3M
EX $6   NM $18   MIP $30

Pig in the Garden, 1960, Schaper
EX $20   NM $30   MIP $50

Pigskin Vegas, 1980, Jokari/US
EX $6   NM $10   MIP $15

Pilgrimage, 1984, Whitehall Games
EX $8   NM $20   MIP $30

Pinbo Sport-o-Rama, 1950s
EX $35   NM $60   MIP $90

Pinhead, 1959, Remco
EX $10   NM $35   MIP $50

Pink Panther Game, 1977, Warren
EX $8   NM $15   MIP $30

Pink Panther Game, 1981, Cadaco
EX $4   NM $7   MIP $12

Pinky Lee and the Runaway Frankfurters, 1950s, Lisbeth Whiting
EX $30   NM $40   MIP $60

Pinocchio, 1977, Parker Bros.
EX $5   NM $8   MIP $15

Pinocchio Board Game, Disney's, 1960, Parker Bros.
EX $10   NM $15   MIP $25

Pinocchio, The New Adventures of, 1961, Lowell
EX $25   NM $45   MIP $70

(KP Photo)

Pirate and Traveller, 1953, Milton Bradley
EX $10   NM $25   MIP $40

Pirate Raid, 1956, Cadaco-Ellis
EX $8   NM $25   MIP $40

Pirate's Cove, 1956, Gabriel
EX $15   NM $35   MIP $65

Pizza Pie Game, 1974, Milton Bradley
EX $5   NM $16   MIP $25

Plane Parade, 1950s, Harett-Gilmar Inc.
EX $25   NM $60   MIP $85

Planet of the Apes, 1974, Milton Bradley
EX $20   NM $45   MIP $65

Play Ball! A Baseball Game of Skill, 1940s, Rosebud Art
EX $50   NM $75   MIP $150

Play Basketball w/Bob Cousy, 1950s, National Games
EX $50   NM $100   MIP $150

Play Your Hunch, 1960, Transogram
EX $8   NM $25   MIP $40

Playoff Football, 1970s, Crestline
EX $20   NM $35   MIP $50

Plaza, 1947, Parker Bros.
EX $7   NM $20   MIP $35

Plot!, 1968, Cadaco
EX $10   NM $25   MIP $35

Ploy, 1970, 3M
EX $5   NM $16   MIP $25

Plus One, 1980, Milton Bradley
EX $6   NM $18   MIP $30

Pocket Size Bowling Card Game, 1950s, Warren/Built-Rite
EX $15   NM $25   MIP $40

Pocket Whoozit, 1985, Trivia
EX $4   NM $7   MIP $10

Point of Law, 1972, 3M
EX $4   NM $14   MIP $20

Pole Position, 1983, Parker Bros.
EX $8   NM $13   MIP $20

Police Patrol, 1955, Hasbro
EX $50   NM $80   MIP $125

Police State, 1974, Gameophiles Unltd.
EX $25   NM $60   MIP $85

Politics, Game of, 1952, Parker Bros.
EX $10   NM $25   MIP $50

Ponents, 1974, Dynamic
EX $6   NM $15   MIP $25

Pony Express, Game of, 1947, Polygon
EX $12   NM $40   MIP $60

Pooch, 1956, Hasbro
EX $10   NM $20   MIP $30

Pop Yer Top!, 1968, Milton Bradley
EX $15   NM $35   MIP $50

Popeye Spinach Flip, 1969, Whitman
EX $10   NM $25   MIP $35

Popeye, Adventures of, 1957, Transogram
EX $35   NM $60   MIP $100

Poppin Hoppies, 1968, Ideal
EX $10   NM $25   MIP $35

Population, 1970, Urban Systems
EX $6   NM $18   MIP $30

Pop-Up Store Game, 1950s, Milton Bradley
EX $25   NM $40   MIP $75

Post Office, 1968, Hasbro
EX $8   NM $20   MIP $30

Postman, 1957, Selchow & Righter
EX $8   NM $15   MIP $30

Pothole Game, The, 1979, Cadaco
EX $10   NM $25   MIP $40

Pow, The Frontier Game, 1955, Selchow & Righter
EX $12   NM $40   MIP $60

Power Four Car Racing Game, 1960s, Manning
EX $15   NM $50   MIP $75

Power Play Hockey, 1970, Romac
EX $12   NM $35   MIP $50

Power: The Game, 1981, Power Games
EX $10   NM $25   MIP $35

Prediction Rod, 1970, Parker Bros.
EX $5   NM $16   MIP $25

Presidential Campaign, 1979, John Hansen
EX $6   NM $18   MIP $30

Prince Caspian, 1983, David Cook
EX $5   NM $16   MIP $25

Prince Valiant (Harold Foster's), 1950s, Transogram
EX $20   NM $30   MIP $75

Prize Property, 1974, Milton Bradley
EX $8   NM $15   MIP $30

Pro Draft, 1974, Parker Bros.
EX $15   NM $35   MIP $45

Pro Football, 1980s, Strat-O-Matic
EX $10   NM $20   MIP $30

Pro Foto-Football, 1977, Cadaco
EX $6   NM $15   MIP $25

Pro Franchise Football, 1987, Rohrwood
EX $10   NM $16   MIP $25

Pro Golf, 1982, Avalon Hill
EX $7   NM $11   MIP $17

Pro Quarterback, 1964, Tod Lansing
EX $20   NM $30   MIP $50

Pro Soccer, 1968, Milton Bradley
EX $12   NM $30   MIP $40

Probe, 1964, Parker Bros.
EX $2   NM $7   MIP $12

Products and Resources, Game of, 1962, Selchow & Righter
EX $6   NM $18   MIP $30

Profit Farming, 1979, Foster Enterprises
EX $6   NM $18   MIP $30

Prospecting, 1953, Selchow & Righter
EX $20   NM $30   MIP $50

Prospector, The, 1980, McJay Game Co.
EX $8   NM $20   MIP $30

Public Assistance, 1980, Hammerhead
EX $20   NM $30   MIP $50

Pug-i-Lo, 1960, Pug-i-Lo Games
EX $55   NM $90   MIP $135

Pure Greed, 1971, Crea-Tek
EX $12   NM $30   MIP $40

Pursue the Pennant, 1984, Pursue the Pennant
EX $30   NM $70   MIP $100

Pursuit!, 1973, Aurora
EX $8   NM $25   MIP $40

Push Over, 1981, Parker Bros.
EX $3   NM $12   MIP $18

Put and Take, 1956, Schaper
EX $5   NM $16   MIP $20

Puzzling Pyramid, 1960, Schaper
EX $6   NM $18   MIP $30

Pyramid, 1978, Hasbro
EX $6   NM $15   MIP $25

Pyramid Power, 1978, Castle Toy
EX $8   NM $20   MIP $30

Q*Bert, 1983, Parker Bros.
EX $4   NM $10   MIP $15

Quad-Ominos, 1978, Pressman
EX $2   NM $6   MIP $10

Quarterback Football Game, 1969, Transogram
EX $25   NM $40   MIP $65

Qubic, 1965, Parker Bros.
EX $3   NM $10   MIP $15

Quest, 1962, Lakeside
EX $12   NM $30   MIP $40

Quest, 1978, Gametime/Heritage Models
EX $10   NM $25   MIP $35

Quick Draw McGraw Game, 1981, Milton Bradley
EX $5   NM $12   MIP $18

Quick Draw McGraw Private Eye Game, 1960
EX $15   NM $25   MIP $35

Quinto, 1964, 3M
EX $6   NM $18   MIP $30

Quiz Panel, 1954, Cadaco-Ellis
EX $6   NM $18   MIP $30

Race-A-Plane, 1947, Phon-O-Game
EX $12   NM $40   MIP $60

Race-O-Rama, 1960, Warren/Built-Rite
EX $10   NM $20   MIP $30

Raceway, 1950s, B & B Toy
EX $30   NM $50   MIP $75

Radaronics, 1946, ARC
EX $15   NM $30   MIP $40

Raggedy Ann, 1956, Milton Bradley
EX $10   NM $20   MIP $35

Raiders of the Lost Ark, 1981, Kenner
EX $8   NM $20   MIP $30

Rainy Day Golf, 1980, Bryad
EX $6   NM $18   MIP $30

Raise the Titanic, 1987, Hoyle
EX $12   NM $30   MIP $40

Rat Patrol Game, 1966, Transogram
EX $40   NM $70   MIP $100

Rawhide, 1959, Lowell
EX $125   NM $250   MIP $350

Raymar of The Jungle, 1952, Dexter Wayne
EX $30   NM $40   MIP $50

Razzle, 1981, Parker Bros.
EX $2   NM $6   MIP $10

Razzle Dazzle Football Game, 1954, Texantics Unlimited
EX $50   NM $80   MIP $125

React-Or, 1979
EX $15   NM $25   MIP $40

Real Action Baseball Game, 1966, Real-Action Games
EX $20   NM $35   MIP $50

Real Baseball Card Game, 1990, National Baseball
EX $110   NM $180   MIP $275

Real Ghostbusters, The, 1986, Milton Bradley
EX $6   NM $18   MIP $30

Real Life Basketball, 1974, Gamecraft
EX $20   NM $50   MIP $75

Realistic Football, 1976, Match Play
EX $15   NM $25   MIP $35

(KP Photo)

Rebel, The, 1961, Ideal
EX $50   NM $75   MIP $100

Rebound, 1971, Ideal
EX $5   NM $16   MIP $25

Record Game, The, 1984, The Record Game
EX $8   NM $25   MIP $40

Red Barber's Big League Baseball Game, 1950s, G & R Anthony
EX $450   NM $1200   MIP $1700

Red Herring, 1945, Cadaco-Ellis
EX $12   NM $40   MIP $60

Red Rover Game, The, 1963, Cadaco-Ellis
EX $5   NM $16   MIP $25

Reddy Clown Three-Ring Circus Game, 1952, Parker Bros.
EX $15   NM $30   MIP $45

Reese's Pieces Game, 1983, Ideal
EX $5   NM $8   MIP $15

Reflex, 1966, Lakeside
EX $5   NM $16   MIP $25

Regatta, 1946
EX $40   NM $70   MIP $110

Regatta, 1968, 3M
EX $10   NM $15   MIP $25

Replay Series Baseball, 1983, Bond Sports
EX $6   NM $10   MIP $15

Restless Gun, 1950s, Milton Bradley
EX $18   NM $35   MIP $50

Return To Oz Game, 1985, Western
EX $10   NM $15   MIP $25

Reward, 1958, Happy Hour
EX $10   NM $35   MIP $50

Rhyme Time, 1969, NBC-Hasbro
EX $6   NM $15   MIP $25

Rich Farmer, Poor Farmer, 1978, McJay Game
EX $5   NM $16   MIP $25

Rich Uncle The Stock Market Game, 1955, Parker Bros.
EX $10   NM $20   MIP $30

(KP Photo)

Rich Uncle, Game of, 1946, Parker Bros.
EX $20   NM $40   MIP $50

Richie Rich, 1982, Milton Bradley
EX $3   NM $5   MIP $10

Rickenbacker Ace Game, 1946, Milton Bradley
EX $50   NM $75   MIP $100

Ricochet Rabbit Game, 1965, Ideal
EX $45   NM $75   MIP $120

Rifleman Game, 1959, Milton Bradley
EX $30   NM $50   MIP $75

(KP Photo)

Rin Tin Tin Game, 1950s, Transogram
EX $30   NM $50   MIP $65

Ringmaster Circus Game, 1947, Cadaco-Ellis
EX $10   NM $15   MIP $20

Rio, The Game of, 1956, Parker Bros.
EX $10   NM $20   MIP $30

Ripley's Believe It Or Not, 1979, Whitman
EX $6   NM $10   MIP $15

Risk, 1959, Parker Bros.
EX $15   NM $30   MIP $60

Riverboat Game, 1950s, Parker Bros./Disney
EX $20   NM $35   MIP $55

Road Runner Game, 1968, Milton Bradley
EX $10   NM $25   MIP $35

Road Runner Pop Up Game, 1982, Whitman
EX $20   NM $30   MIP $50

Robert Schuller's Possibility Thinkers Game, 1977, Selchow & Righter
EX $3   NM $5   MIP $10

Robin Hood, 1955, Harett-Gilmar
EX $30   NM $40   MIP $55

Robin Hood Game, 1970s, Parker Bros.
EX $7   NM $15   MIP $30

Robin Hood, Adventures of, 1956, Bettye-B
EX $30   NM $40   MIP $50

Robin Roberts Sports Club Baseball Game, 1960, Dexter Wayne
EX $100   NM $165   MIP $250

Robocop VCR Game, 1988, Spinnaker
EX $7   NM $20   MIP $35

Robot Sam the Answer Man, 1950, Jacmar
EX $15   NM $25   MIP $30

Rock 'N' Roll Replay, 1984, Baron-Scott
EX $7   NM $20   MIP $35

Rock the Boat Game, 1978, Milton Bradley
EX $6   NM $18   MIP $30

Rock Trivia, 1984, Pressman
EX $5   NM $10   MIP $15

Rocket Race, 1958, Stone Craft
EX $30   NM $70   MIP $95

Rocket Race To Saturn, 1950s, Lido
EX $15   NM $20   MIP $30

Rodeo, The Wild West Game, 1957, Whitman
EX $12   NM $40   MIP $60

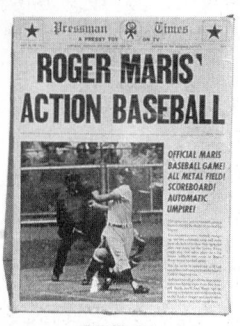
(KP Photo)

Roger Maris' Action Baseball, 1962, Pressman
EX $50   NM $80   MIP $100

Rol-A-Lite, 1947, Durable Toy & Novelty
EX $45   NM $75   MIP $120

Rol-It, 1954, Parker Bros.
EX $4   NM $12   MIP $20

Roll And Score Poker, 1977, Lowe
EX $3   NM $7   MIP $12

Roll-A-Par, 1964, Lowe
EX $8   NM $20   MIP $30

Roller Derby, 1974, Milton Bradley
EX $70   NM $150   MIP $225

Roman X, 1964, Selchow & Righter
EX $7   NM $20   MIP $35

Roscoe Turner Air Race Game, 1960, Southern Games
EX $40   NM $90   MIP $135

Rose Bowl, 1949, Keck Enterprises
EX $15   NM $35   MIP $50

Rose Bowl, 1966, E.S.Lowe
EX $15   NM $20   MIP $25

Roundup, 1952, Wales Game Systems
EX $10   NM $20   MIP $30

Route 66 Game, 1960, Transogram
EX $70   NM $100   MIP $160

Roy Rogers Game, 1950s
EX $20   NM $35   MIP $55

Rribit, Battle of the Frogs, 1982, Genesis Enterprises
EX $6   NM $18   MIP $30

Ruffhouse, 1980, Parker Bros.
EX $3   NM $10   MIP $15

Rules of the Road, 1977, Cadaco
EX $5   NM $16   MIP $25

Run to Win, 1980, Cabela
EX $6   NM $18   MIP $30

Russian Campaign, The, 1976, Avalon Hill
EX $3   NM $5   MIP $10

(KP Photo)

S.O.S., 1947, Durable Toy & Novelty
EX $65   NM $85   MIP $110

S.W.A.T., 1976, Milton Bradley
EX $5   NM $10   MIP $15

(KP Photo)

S.W.A.T. Game, 1970s, Milton Bradley
EX $10   NM $15   MIP $25

Sabotage, 1985, Lakeside
EX $2   NM $6   MIP $10

Saddle Racing Game, 1974, APBA
EX $20   NM $50   MIP $75

Safari, 1950, Selchow & Righter
EX $12   NM $25   MIP $40

Safecrack, 1982, Selchow & Righter
EX $4   NM $15   MIP $20

Sail Away, 1962, Howard Mullen
EX $12   NM $30   MIP $40

Salvo, 1961, Ideal
EX $15   NM $25   MIP $30

Samsonite Basketball, 1969, Samsonite
EX $15   NM $30   MIP $40

Samsonite Football, 1969, Samsonite
EX $12   NM $20   MIP $35

Sandlot Slugger, 1960s, Milton Bradley
EX $35   NM $60   MIP $75

Save the President, 1984, Jack Jaffe
EX $8   NM $20   MIP $30

Say When!, 1961, Parker Bros.
EX $6   NM $15   MIP $20

Scarne's Challenge, 1947, John Scarne Games
EX $10   NM $15   MIP $20

Scavenger Hunt, 1983, Milton Bradley
EX $3   NM $5   MIP $10

Scooby Doo and Scrappy Doo, 1983, Milton Bradley
EX $3   NM $8   MIP $16

Scooby-Doo, Where are You?, 1973, Milton Bradley
EX $20   NM $30   MIP $40

Scoop, 1956, Parker Bros.
EX $20   NM $35   MIP $45

Scoop: The Newspaper Game, 1976, Western Publishing
EX $18   NM $40   MIP $55

Score Four, 1968, Funtastic
EX $3   NM $10   MIP $15

Scotland Yard, 1985, Milton Bradley
EX $3   NM $10   MIP $15

Scrabble, 1953, Selchow & Righter
EX $5   NM $12   MIP $20

Scrabble for Juniors, 1968, Selchow & Righter
EX $2   NM $5   MIP $8

Scrabble RPM, 1971, Selchow & Righter
EX $8   NM $20   MIP $30

Screaming Eagles, 1987, Milton Bradley
EX $4   NM $15   MIP $20

Screwball The Mad Mad Mad Game, 1960, Transogram
EX $30   NM $40   MIP $60

Scribbage, 1963, Lowe
EX $3   NM $10   MIP $15

Scrimmage, 1973, SPI
EX $5   NM $15   MIP $25

Scruples, 1986, Milton Bradley
EX $5   NM $10   MIP $15

Scrutineyes, 1992, Hersch & Co./Mattel
EX $12   NM $30   MIP $40

Sea World Treasure Key, 1983, International Games
EX $4   NM $15   MIP $20

Sealab 2020 Game, 1973, Milton Bradley
EX $6   NM $10   MIP $15

Seance, 1972, Milton Bradley
EX $75   NM $100   MIP $225

Secrecy, 1965, Universal Games
EX $12   NM $30   MIP $40

Secret Agent Man, 1966, Milton Bradley
EX $25   NM $40   MIP $60

Secret of NIMH, 1982, Whitman
EX $15   NM $20   MIP $30

Secret Weapon, 1984, Selchow & Righter
EX $5   NM $16   MIP $25

Seduction, 1966, Createk
EX $10   NM $25   MIP $35

See New York 'Round the Town, 1964, Transogram
EX $50   NM $70   MIP $90

Sergeant Preston Game, 1950s, Milton Bradley
EX $15   NM $30   MIP $40

Set Point, 1971, XV Productions
EX $8   NM $20   MIP $30

Seven Keys, 1961, Ideal
EX $12   NM $20   MIP $30

(KP Photo)

Seven Seas, 1960, Cadaco-Ellis
EX $15   NM $25   MIP $40

(KP Photo)

Seven Up, 1960s, Transogram
EX $7   NM $12   MIP $20

Shadowlord!, 1983, Parker Bros.
EX $3   NM $10   MIP $15

Sha-ee, the Game of Destiny, 1963, Ideal
EX $20   NM $65   MIP $90

(KP Photo)

Shazam, Captian Marvel's Own Game, 1950s, Reed & Associates
EX $30   NM $60   MIP $95

Shenanigans, 1964, Milton Bradley
EX $15   NM $40   MIP $50

Sheriff of Dodge City, 1966, Parker Bros.
EX $8   NM $25   MIP $40

Sherlock Holmes, 1950s, National Games
EX $25   NM $50   MIP $65

Sherlock Holmes, 1980, Whitman
EX $5   NM $16   MIP $25

Sherlock Holmes Game, The, 1974, Cadaco
EX $6   NM $18   MIP $30

Shifty Checkers, 1973, Aurora
EX $8   NM $25   MIP $40

Shifty Gear Game, 1962, Schaper
EX $5   NM $16   MIP $25

Shindig, 1965, Remco
EX $30   NM $45   MIP $60

Shmo, 1960s, Remco
EX $10   NM $25   MIP $35

Shogun, 1976, Epoch Playthings
EX $6   NM $15   MIP $25

Shogun, 1986, Milton Bradley
EX $18   NM $45   MIP $75

Shopping, 1973, John Ladell
EX $5   NM $16   MIP $25

(KP Photo)

Shotgun Slade, 1960, Milton Bradley
EX $20   NM $45   MIP $65

Show-Biz, 1950s, Lowell
EX $15   NM $50   MIP $75

SI: The Sporting Word Game, 1961, Time
EX $10   NM $16   MIP $25

Siege Game, 1966, Milton Bradley
EX $20   NM $50   MIP $60

Silly Carnival, 1969, Whitman
EX $7   NM $12   MIP $20

Silly Safari, 1966, Topper
EX $30   NM $60   MIP $90

Silly Sidney, 1963, Transogram
EX $12   NM $30   MIP $40

Simpsons Mystery of Life, The, 1990, Cardinal
EX $5   NM $7   MIP $10

Sinbad, 1978, Cadaco
EX $20   NM $30   MIP $50

Sinking of The Titanic, The, 1976, Ideal
EX $15   NM $25   MIP $40

Sir Lancelot, Adventures of, 1960s, Lisbeth Whiting
EX $40   NM $70   MIP $110

Situation 4, 1968, Parker Bros.
EX $5   NM $16   MIP $20

Situation 7, 1969, Parker Bros.
EX $8   NM $25   MIP $40

Six Million Dollar Man, 1975, Parker Bros.
EX $10   NM $15   MIP $25

Skatebirds Game, 1978, Milton Bradley
EX $7   NM $20   MIP $35

Skatterbug, Game of, 1951, Parker Bros.
EX $30   NM $40   MIP $50

Skedaddle, 1965, Cadaco-Ellis
EX $8   NM $25   MIP $40

Ski Gammon, 1962, American Publishing
EX $8   NM $20   MIP $30

Skill-Drive, 1950s, Sidney Tarrson
EX $10   NM $35   MIP $40

Skins Golf Game, Official, 1985, O'Connor Hall
EX $12   NM $20   MIP $30

Skip-A-Cross, 1953, Cadaco
EX $3   NM $7   MIP $10

Skipper Race Sailing Game, 1949, Cadaco-Ellis
EX $25   NM $60   MIP $90

(KP Photo)

Skirmish, 1975, Milton Bradley
EX $30   NM $50   MIP $60

Skirrid, 1979, Kenner
EX $4   NM $15   MIP $20

Skudo, 1949, Parker Bros.
EX $8   NM $25   MIP $40

Skully, 1961, Ideal
EX $3   NM $5   MIP $10

Skunk, 1950s, Schaper
EX $7   NM $12   MIP $20

Sky Lanes, 1958, Parker Bros.
EX $15   NM $30   MIP $50

Sky's The Limit, The, 1955, Kohner
EX $15   NM $25   MIP $40

Sla-lom Ski Race Game, 1957, Cadaco-Ellis
EX $20   NM $50   MIP $75

Slap Trap, 1967, Ideal
EX $8   NM $25   MIP $40

Slapshot, 1982, Avalon Hill
EX $10   NM $25   MIP $35

Slip Disc, 1980, Milton Bradley
EX $5   NM $16   MIP $25

Smess, The Ninny's Chess, 1970, Parker Bros.
EX $30   NM $40   MIP $50

Smog, 1970, Urban Systems
EX $8   NM $20   MIP $30

Smokey: The Forest Fire Prevention Bear, 1961, Ideal
EX $30   NM $65   MIP $105

Smurf Game, 1984, Milton Bradley
EX $4   NM $7   MIP $12

Snafu, 1969, Gamescience
EX $7   NM $20   MIP $35

Snagglepuss Fun at the Picnic Game, 1961, Transogram
EX $40   NM $50   MIP $60

Snake Eyes, 1957, Selchow & Righter
EX $15   NM $20   MIP $30

Snakes & Ladders, 1974, Summmerville/Canada
EX $4   NM $7   MIP $10

Snake's Alive, Game of, 1967, Ideal
EX $12   NM $30   MIP $40

Snakes In The Grass, 1960s, Kohner
EX $10   NM $15   MIP $25

Snappet Catch Game w/Harmon Killebrew, 1960, Killebrew
EX $55   NM $90   MIP $135

Sniggle!, 1980, Amway
EX $4   NM $10   MIP $15

Snob, A Fantasy Shopping Spree, 1983, Helene Fox
EX $7   NM $20   MIP $35

Snoopy & The Red Baron, 1970, Milton Bradley
EX $15   NM $35   MIP $45

Snoopy Come Home Game, 1973, Milton Bradley
EX $10   NM $16   MIP $25

Snoopy Game, 1960, Selchow & Righter
EX $25   NM $35   MIP $50

Snoopy's Doghouse Game, 1977, Milton Bradley
EX $5   NM $16   MIP $25

(KP Photo)

Snow White and the Seven Dwarfs, 1970s, Cadaco
EX $6   NM $10   MIP $15

Snuffy Smith Game, 1970s, Milton Bradley
EX $15   NM $20   MIP $25

Society Scandals, 1978, E.S.Lowe
EX $6   NM $15   MIP $25

Sod Buster, 1980, Santee
EX $10   NM $16   MIP $25

Solar Conquest, 1966, Atech Enterprises
EX $15   NM $35   MIP $50

Solarquest, 1986, Western
EX $6   NM $10   MIP $15

Solid Gold Music Trivia, 1984, Ideal
EX $6   NM $10   MIP $15

Solitaire (Lucille Ball), 1973, Milton Bradley
EX $2   NM $5   MIP $10

Sons of Hercules Game, The, 1966, Milton Bradley
EX $30   NM $45   MIP $60

Soupy Sales Sez Go-Go-Go Game, 1960s, Milton Bradley
EX $35   NM $50   MIP $70

Southern Fast Freight Game, 1970, American Publishing
EX $8   NM $25   MIP $40

Space Angel Game, 1966, Transogram
EX $25   NM $65   MIP $85

Space Chase, 1967, United Nations Constructors
EX $15   NM $35   MIP $50

Space Game, 1953, Parker Bros.
EX $25   NM $65   MIP $85

Space Pilot, 1951, Cadaco-Ellis
EX $20   NM $45   MIP $60

Space Shuttle 101, 1978, Media-Ungame
EX $8   NM $20   MIP $30

Space Shuttle, The, 1981, Ungame
EX $8   NM $20   MIP $30

(KP Photo)

Space: 1999 Game, 1975, Milton Bradley
EX $10   NM $15   MIP $25

Special Agent, 1966, Parker Bros.
EX $10   NM $25   MIP $40

Special Detective/Speedway, 1959, Saalfield
EX $15   NM $40   MIP $60

Speedorama, 1950s, Jacmar
EX $30   NM $50   MIP $80

Speedway, Big Bopper Game, 1961, Ideal
EX $18   NM $40   MIP $60

Spider and the Fly, 1981, Marx
EX $12   NM $20   MIP $30

Spider-Man Game, The Amazing, 1967, Milton Bradley
EX $20   NM $45   MIP $85

(KP Photo)

Spider-Man w/The Fantastic Four, 1977, Milton Bradley
EX $10   NM $20   MIP $35

Spider's Web Game, The, 1969, Multiple Plastics
EX $7   NM $12   MIP $20

Spin Cycle Baseball, 1965, Pressman
EX $25   NM $40   MIP $65

Spin The Bottle, 1968, Hasbro
EX $8   NM $20   MIP $30

Spin Welder, 1960s, Mattel
EX $7   NM $12   MIP $20

Spiro T. Agnew American History Challenge Game, 1971, Gabriel
EX $20   NM $35   MIP $55

Splat!, 1990, Milton Bradley
EX $8   NM $20   MIP $30

Sporting News: Baseroll, 1986, Mundo Games
EX $8   NM $13   MIP $20

Sports Arena No. 1, 1954, Rennoc
Games & Toys
EX $35   NM $60   MIP $90

**Sports Illustrated All Time All Star
Baseball,** 1973, Sports Illustrated
EX $75   NM $175   MIP $250

Sports Illustrated Baseball, 1972,
Time, Inc. (Sports Illustrated)
EX $60   NM $120   MIP $175

Sports Illustrated College Football,
1971, Sports Illustrated
EX $8   NM $25   MIP $40

Sports Illustrated Decathlon, 1972,
Time
EX $8   NM $25   MIP $40

Sports Illustrated Handicap Golf,
1971, Sports Illustrated
EX $10   NM $25   MIP $35

Sports Illustrated Pro Football, 1970,
Time
EX $15   NM $25   MIP $40

Sports Trivia Game, 1984, Hoyle
EX $6   NM $10   MIP $15

Sports Yesteryear, 1977, Skor-Mor
EX $15   NM $25   MIP $35

Spot Cash, 1959, Milton Bradley
EX $7   NM $15   MIP $20

Spy vs. Spy, 1986, Milton Bradley
EX $10   NM $15   MIP $25

Square Mile, 1962, Milton Bradley
EX $15   NM $25   MIP $30

Square Off, 1972, Parker Bros.
EX $8   NM $20   MIP $30

Square-It, 1961, Hasbro
EX $5   NM $16   MIP $25

Squares, 1950s, Schaper
EX $4   NM $15   MIP $20

Squatter: The Australian Wool Game,
1960s, John Sands/Australia
EX $15   NM $25   MIP $45

**St. Louis Cardinals Baseball Card
Game,** 1964, Ed-U-Cards
EX $10   NM $25   MIP $35

Stadium Checkers, 1954, Schaper
EX $7   NM $12   MIP $20

Stagecoach West Game, 1961,
Transogram
EX $35   NM $45   MIP $60

Stampede, 1952, Wales Game Systems
EX $15   NM $35   MIP $40

Stampede, 1956, Gabriel
EX $8   NM $25   MIP $30

Star Reporter, 1950s, Parker Bros.
EX $85   NM $125   MIP $175

Star Team Battling Spaceships,
1977, Ideal
EX $8   NM $20   MIP $30

Star Trek, 1979, Milton Bradley
EX $18   NM $30   MIP $40

Star Trek Adventure Game, 1985,
West End Games
EX $8   NM $20   MIP $30

(KP Photo)

Star Trek Game, 1960s, Ideal
EX $35   NM $70   MIP $85

Star Trek: The Next Generation,
1993, Classic Games
EX $15   NM $25   MIP $50

Star Wars Adventures of R2D2 Game,
1977, Kenner
EX $12   NM $20   MIP $30

Star Wars Battle at Sarlacc's Pit,
1983, Parker Bros.
EX $10   NM $15   MIP $25

Star Wars Escape from Death Star,
1977, Kenner
EX $10   NM $15   MIP $25

Star Wars Monopoly, 1997, Parker Bros.
EX $15   NM $20   MIP $35

(KP Photo)

**Star Wars ROTJ Ewoks Save The
Trees,** 1984, Parker Bros.
EX $10   NM $15   MIP $25

Star Wars Wicket the Ewok, 1983,
Parker Bros.
EX $7   NM $12   MIP $20

Star Wars X-Wing Aces Target Game,
1978
EX $20   NM $30   MIP $50

Starship Troopers, 1976, Avalon Hill
EX $5   NM $16   MIP $25

Starsky & Hutch, 1977, Milton Bradley
EX $10   NM $16   MIP $25

State Capitals, Game of, 1952, Parker
Bros.
EX $4   NM $8   MIP $10

States, Game of the, 1975, Milton
Bradley
EX $4   NM $6   MIP $10

Statis Pro Football, 1970s, Statis-Pro
EX $25   NM $40   MIP $65

Stay Alive, 1971, Milton Bradley
EX $6   NM $15   MIP $25

Steps of Toyland, 1954, Parker Bros.
EX $20   NM $35   MIP $55

Steve Allen's Qubila, 1955, Lord &
Freber
EX $8   NM $25   MIP $40

Steve Canyon, 1959, Lowell
EX $20   NM $40   MIP $60

Steve Scott Space Scout Game, 1952,
Transogram
EX $30   NM $40   MIP $60

Stick the IRS!, 1981, Courtland
Playthings
EX $8   NM $12   MIP $15

Sting, The, 1976, Ideal
EX $10   NM $20   MIP $25

Stock Car Race, 1950s, Gardner
EX $25   NM $50   MIP $75

Stock Car Racing Game, 1956,
Whitman
EX $12   NM $25   MIP $35

**Stock Car Racing Game (w/Petty/
Yarborough),** 1981, Ribbit Toy
EX $17   NM $30   MIP $45

Stock Car Speedway, Game of, 1965,
Johnstone
EX $55   NM $90   MIP $135

Stock Market Game, 1955, Gabriel
EX $20   NM $30   MIP $40

Stock Market Game, 1963, 1968,
Whitman
EX $25   NM $45   MIP $60

Stock Market Game, 1970, Avalon Hill
EX $7   NM $12   MIP $20

Stock Market Specialist, 1983, John
Hansen
EX $6   NM $18   MIP $30

Stoney Burk, 1963, Transogram
EX $30   NM $60   MIP $80

Stop Thief, 1979, Parker Bros.
EX $15   NM $35   MIP $50

Straight Arrow, 1950, Selchow &
Righter
EX $25   NM $35   MIP $55

Straightaway, 1961, Selchow & Righter
EX $45   NM $60   MIP $90

Strata 5, 1984, Milton Bradley
EX $5   NM $16   MIP $25

Strategic Command, 1950s, Transogram
EX $15   NM $30   MIP $40

Stratego (plastic pieces), 1962-on, Milton Bradley
EX $6   NM $10   MIP $15

Stratego (wood pieces), 1961, Milton Bradley
EX $50   NM $75   MIP $90

Strategy Manager Baseball, 1967, McGuffin-Ramsey
EX $2   NM $6   MIP $12

Strato Tac-tics, 1972, Strato-Various
EX $8   NM $25   MIP $40

Strat-O-Matic Baseball, 1961, Strat-O-Matic
EX $125   NM $165   MIP $300

Strat-O-Matic College Football, 1976, Strat-O-Matic
EX $25   NM $55   MIP $75

Strat-O-Matic Hockey, 1978, Strat-O-Matic
EX $12   NM $30   MIP $50

Strat-O-Matic Sports "Know-How," 1984, Strat-O-Matic
EX $6   NM $10   MIP $15

Strato-O-Matic Baseball, 1970, Strat-O-Matic
EX $25   NM $50   MIP $70

Strato-O-Matic Baseball, 1980, Strat-O-Matic
EX $20   NM $35   MIP $50

Strato-O-Matic Baseball (varies by season of cards), 1960s, Strat-O-Matic
EX $80   NM $150   MIP $225

Strato-O-Matic Football (varies by season of cards), 1967-74, Strat-O-Matic
EX $50   NM $125   MIP $175

Strato-O-Matic Football (varies by season of cards), 1975-85, Strat-O-Matic
EX $25   NM $60   MIP $85

Strato-O-Matic Football (varies by season of cards), 1986-90s, Strat-O-Matic
EX $12   NM $30   MIP $40

Stretch Call, 1986, Sevedeo A. Vigil
EX $12   NM $20   MIP $30

Strike Three (Carl Hubbell's), 1948, Tone Products
EX $75   NM $150   MIP $200

Stuff Yer Face, 1982, Milton Bradley
EX $6   NM $20   MIP $35

Stump the Stars, 1962, Ideal
EX $8   NM $25   MIP $40

Sub Attack Game, 1965, Milton Bradley
EX $7   NM $20   MIP $35

Sub Search, 1973, Milton Bradley
EX $8   NM $45   MIP $50

Sub Search, 1977, Milton Bradley
EX $6   NM $18   MIP $30

Sudden Death!, 1978, Gabriel
EX $5   NM $16   MIP $25

Suffolk Downs Racing Game, 1947, Corey Game
EX $40   NM $90   MIP $135

Sugar Bowl, 1950s, Transogram
EX $20   NM $30   MIP $40

Summit, 1961, Milton Bradley
EX $15   NM $20   MIP $30

Sunken Treasure, 1948, Parker Bros.
EX $15   NM $20   MIP $30

Sunken Treasure, 1976, Milton Bradley
EX $7   NM $12   MIP $20

Super Coach TV Football, 1974, Coleco
EX $5   NM $12   MIP $20

Super Market, 1953, Selchow & Righter
EX $10   NM $20   MIP $35

Super Powers, 1984, Parker Bros.
EX $15   NM $25   MIP $40

Super Spy, 1971, Milton Bradley
EX $15   NM $25   MIP $40

(KP Photo)

Superboy Game, 1960s, Hasbro
EX $45   NM $75   MIP $135

Supercar Road Race, 1962, Standard Toykraft
EX $45   NM $100   MIP $140

(KP Photo)

Supercar to the Rescue Game, 1962, Milton Bradley
EX $25   NM $50   MIP $75

Superman & Superboy, 1967, Milton Bradley
EX $40   NM $65   MIP $105

Superman Game, 1965, Hasbro
EX $45   NM $75   MIP $120

Superman Game, 1966, Merry Manufacturing
EX $35   NM $55   MIP $90

Superman II, 1981, Milton Bradley
EX $10   NM $20   MIP $30

Superman III, 1982, Parker Bros.
EX $4   NM $12   MIP $20

Superman, Adventures of, 1940s, Milton Bradley
EX $125   NM $250   MIP $450

Superstar Baseball, 1966, Sports Illustrated
EX $30   NM $50   MIP $75

Superstar Pro Wrestling Game, 1984, Super Star Game
EX $8   NM $13   MIP $20

Superstar TV Sports, 1980, ARC
EX $6   NM $10   MIP $15

Superstition, 1977, Milton Bradley
EX $12   NM $20   MIP $30

Sure Shot Hockey, 1970, Ideal
EX $15   NM $25   MIP $40

(KP Photo)

Surfside 6, 1961, Lowell
EX $30   NM $50   MIP $75

Surprise Package, Your, 1961, Ideal
EX $25   NM $60   MIP $85

Survive!, 1982, Parker Bros.
EX $12   NM $30   MIP $40

Swahili Game, 1968, Milton Bradley
EX $8   NM $10   MIP $20

Swap, the Wheeler-Dealer Game, 1965, Ideal
EX $7   NM $20   MIP $35

Swat Baseball, 1948, Milton Bradley
EX $20   NM $35   MIP $50

(KP Photo)

Swayze, 1954, Milton Bradley
EX $10   NM $15   MIP $20

Swish, 1948, Jim Hawkers Games
EX $45   NM $75   MIP $115

Swoop, 1969, Whitman
EX $7   NM $12   MIP $20

Sword In The Stone Game, 1960s, Parker Bros.
EX $18   NM $40   MIP $60

Swords and Shields, 1970, Milton Bradley
EX $10   NM $35   **MIP** $50

Syncron-8, 1963, Transogram
EX $18   NM $40   **MIP** $60

T.V. Bingo, 1970, Selchow & Richter
EX $3   NM $5   **MIP** $10

Tabit, 1954, John Norton
EX $25   NM $35   **MIP** $75

Tactics II, 1984, Avalon Hill
EX $6   NM $10   **MIP** $15

Taffy's Party Game, 1960s, Transogram
EX $10   NM $15   **MIP** $25

Taffy's Shopping Spree Game, 1964, Transogram
EX $10   NM $25   **MIP** $35

Tagalong Joe, 1950, Wales Game Systems
EX $5   NM $10   **MIP** $15

Tales of Wells Fargo, 1959, Milton Bradley
EX $40   NM $65   **MIP** $105

Talking Baseball, 1971, Mattel
EX $35   NM $60   **MIP** $85

Talking Football, 1971, Mattel
EX $35   NM $50   **MIP** $75

Talking Monday Night Football, 1977, Mattel
EX $25   NM $30   **MIP** $50

Tally Ho!, 1950s, Whitman
EX $8   NM $20   **MIP** $30

Tangle, 1964, Selchow & Richter
EX $6   NM $18   **MIP** $30

Tank Battle, 1975, Milton Bradley
EX $15   NM $30   **MIP** $40

Tank Command, 1975, Ideal
EX $7   NM $20   **MIP** $35

Tantalizer, 1958, Northern Signal
EX $10   NM $20   **MIP** $30

Tarzan, 1984, Milton Bradley
EX $5   NM $10   **MIP** $15

(KP Photo)

Tarzan To The Rescue, 1976, Milton Bradley
EX $10   NM $15   **MIP** $25

Taxi!, 1960, Selchow & Righter
EX $20   NM $30   **MIP** $40

Tee Off by Sam Snead, 1973, Glenn Industries
EX $18   NM $40   **MIP** $60

Teed Off!, 1966, Cadaco
EX $6   NM $15   **MIP** $25

Teeko, 1948, John Scarne Games
EX $10   NM $15   **MIP** $20

Teen Time, 1960s, Warren-Built Rite
EX $6   NM $15   **MIP** $25

Telephone Game, The, 1982, Cadaco
EX $7   NM $20   **MIP** $35

Television, 1953, National Novelty
EX $35   NM $75   **MIP** $100

Tell It To The Judge, 1959, Parker Bros.
EX $20   NM $35   **MIP** $50

Temple of Fu Manchu Game, The, 1967, Pressman
EX $20   NM $30   **MIP** $50

Ten-Four, Good Buddy, 1976, Parker Bros.
EX $5   NM $7   **MIP** $12

Tennessee Tuxedo, 1963, Transogram
EX $75   NM $125   **MIP** $200

Tennis, 1975, Parker Bros.
EX $10   NM $16   **MIP** $25

Tension, 1970, Kohner
EX $7   NM $12   **MIP** $20

(KP Photo)

Terrytoons Hide N' Seek Game, 1960, Transogram
EX $30   NM $45   **MIP** $60

Test Driver Game, The, 1956, Milton Bradley
EX $45   NM $60   **MIP** $75

Texas Millionaire, 1955, Texantics
EX $25   NM $55   **MIP** $75

Texas Rangers, Game of, 1950s, All-Fair
EX $25   NM $50   **MIP** $75

That's Truckin', 1976, Showker
EX $7   NM $20   **MIP** $35

They're at the Post, 1976, MAAS Marketing
EX $12   NM $30   **MIP** $40

Thing Ding Robot Game, 1961, Schaper
EX $35   NM $75   **MIP** $100

Think Twice, 1974, Dynamic
EX $4   NM $15   **MIP** $20

Thinking Man's Football, 1969, 3M
EX $6   NM $15   **MIP** $25

Thinking Man's Golf, 1966, 3M
EX $5   NM $15   **MIP** $25

Think-Thunk, 1973, Milton Bradley
EX $6   NM $18   **MIP** $30

Third Man, 1969, Saalfield
EX $6   NM $15   **MIP** $25

Third Reich, 1974, Avalon Hill
EX $3   NM $8   **MIP** $15

Thirteen, 1955, Cadaco-Ellis
EX $3   NM $7   **MIP** $10

(KP Photo)

This Is Your Life, 1954, Lowell
EX $20   NM $30   **MIP** $35

Three Little Pigs, 1959, Selchow & Righter
EX $7   NM $20   **MIP** $35

Three Musketeers, 1958, Milton Bradley
EX $35   NM $50   **MIP** $70

Three On a Match, 1972, Milton Bradley
EX $10   NM $25   **MIP** $35

(KP Photo)

Three Stooges Fun House Game, 1950s, Lowell
EX $125   NM $275   **MIP** $400

Thunder Road, 1986, Milton Bradley
EX $10   NM $16   **MIP** $25

(KP Photo)

Thunderbirds Game, 1965, Waddington/England
EX $45   NM $75   **MIP** $100

Tic-Tac Dough, 1957, Transogram
EX $12   NM $20   **MIP** $25

Tiddle Flip Baseball, 1949, Modern Craft
EX $20   NM $35   **MIP** $50

Tiddle-Tac-Toe, 1955, Schaper
EX $3   NM $10   MIP $15

Tilt Score, 1964, Schaper
EX $4   NM $15   MIP $20

Time Machine, 1961, American Toy
EX $100   NM $150   MIP $200

(KP Photo)

Time Tunnel Game, The, 1966, Ideal
EX $90   NM $150   MIP $240

Time: The Game, 1983, Time/John Hansen
EX $2   NM $5   MIP $8

Tiny Tim Game of Beautiful Things, The, 1970, Parker Bros.
EX $20   NM $30   MIP $40

(KP Photo)

Tom & Jerry, 1977, Milton Bradley
EX $5   NM $15   MIP $20

Tom & Jerry Adventure In Blunderland, 1965, Transogram
EX $25   NM $45   MIP $70

Tom Seaver Game Action Baseball, 1969, Pressman
EX $50   NM $125   MIP $175

Tomorrowland Rocket To Moon, 1956, Parker Bros.
EX $20   NM $50   MIP $65

Toot! Toot!, 1964, Selchow & Righter
EX $8   NM $25   MIP $40

(KP Photo)

Tootsie Roll Train Game, 1969, Hasbro
EX $20   NM $30   MIP $50

Top Cat Game, 1962, Transogram
EX $50   NM $100   MIP $125

Top Cop, 1961, Cadaco-Ellis
EX $25   NM $40   MIP $55

Top Pro Basketball Quiz Game, 1970, Ed-U-Cards
EX $6   NM $15   MIP $25

Top Pro Football Quiz Game, 1970, Ed-U-Cards
EX $6   NM $15   MIP $25

Top Scholar, 1957, Cadaco-Ellis
EX $5   NM $16   MIP $25

Top Ten College Basketball, 1980, Top Ten Game
EX $30   NM $70   MIP $100

Top-ography, 1951, Cadaco-Ellis
EX $10   NM $15   MIP $20

Topper, 1962, Lakeside
EX $15   NM $35   MIP $50

Topple, 1979, Kenner
EX $4   NM $15   MIP $20

Tornado Bowl, 1971, Ideal
EX $5   NM $16   MIP $25

Tornado Rex, 1991, Parker Bros.
EX $10   NM $25   MIP $35

Total Depth, 1984, Orc Productions
EX $12   NM $30   MIP $40

Touche Turtle Game, 1964, Ideal
EX $45   NM $100   MIP $175

Town & Country Traffic Game, 1950s, Ranger Steel
EX $50   NM $90   MIP $125

Track Meet, 1972, Sports Illustrated
EX $10   NM $25   MIP $35

Trade Winds: The Caribbean Sea Pirate Treasure Hunt, 1960, Parker Bros.
EX $65   NM $100   MIP $150

Traffic Game, 1968, Matchbox
EX $35   NM $55   MIP $90

Traffic Jam, 1954, Harett-Gilmar
EX $15   NM $30   MIP $45

(KP Photo)

Trail Blazers Game, 1964, Milton Bradley
EX $20   NM $35   MIP $50

Trails to Tremble By, 1971, Whitman
EX $6   NM $18   MIP $30

Trap Door, 1982, Milton Bradley
EX $3   NM $10   MIP $15

Trap-em!, 1957, Selchow & Righter
EX $8   NM $25   MIP $40

Trapped (Ellery Queen's), 1956, Bettye-B
EX $30   NM $50   MIP $75

Traps, The Game of, 1950s, Traps
EX $75   NM $100   MIP $125

Travel America, 1950, Jacmar
EX $15   NM $25   MIP $40

Travel-Lite, 1946, Saxon Toy
EX $45   NM $75   MIP $120

Treasure Island, 1954, Harett-Gilmar
EX $15   NM $40   MIP $60

Tribulation, The Game of, 1981, Whitman
EX $3   NM $10   MIP $15

Tri-Ominoes, Deluxe, 1978, Pressman
EX $3   NM $5   MIP $10

Triple Play, 1978, Milton Bradley
EX $5   NM $10   MIP $15

Triple Yahtzee, 1972, Lowe
EX $4   NM $6   MIP $10

Tripoley Junior, 1962, Cadaco-Ellis
EX $5   NM $16   MIP $25

Trivial Pursuit, 1981, Selchow & Righter
EX $10   NM $15   MIP $20

Troke (Castle Checkers), 1961, Selchow & Righter
EX $6   NM $18   MIP $25

Tru-Action Electric Baseball Game, 1955, Tudor
EX $12   NM $30   MIP $50

Tru-Action Electric Sports Car Race, 1959, Tudor
EX $20   NM $50   MIP $75

True Colors, 1990, Milton Bradley
EX $20   NM $50   MIP $70

Trump, the Game, 1989, Milton Bradley
EX $5   NM $10   MIP $15

Trust Me, 1981, Parker Bros.
EX $5   NM $8   MIP $13

Truth or Consequences, 1955, Gabriel
EX $12   NM $40   MIP $60

Truth or Consequences, 1962, Lowell
EX $10   NM $35   MIP $50

TSG I: Pro Football, 1971, TSG
EX $35   NM $55   MIP $85

Tumble Bug, 1950s, Schaper
EX $6   NM $18   MIP $30

Turbo, 1981, Milton Bradley
EX $4   NM $15   MIP $20

(KP Photo)

TV Fun Kit, 1950s, Paul Winchell & Jerry Mahoney
EX $10   NM $20   MIP $30

TV Guide Game, 1984, Trivia
EX $8   NM $13   MIP $15

Twelve O'Clock High, 1965, Ideal
EX $35   NM $60   MIP $85

Twiggy, Game of, 1967, Milton Bradley
EX $30   NM $50   MIP $80

(KP Photo)

Twilight Zone Game, 1960s, Ideal
EX $75   NM $100   MIP $200

Twinkles Trip to the Star Factory, 1960, Milton Bradley
EX $45   NM $75   MIP $120

Twister, 1966, Milton Bradley
EX $15   NM $20   MIP $30

Twixt, 1962, 3M
EX $5   NM $16   MIP $25

Two For The Money, 1950s, Lowell
EX $10   NM $20   MIP $35

Tycoon, 1966, Parker Bros.
EX $12   NM $30   MIP $40

Tycoon, 1981, Wattson Games
EX $4   NM $10   MIP $15

Tycoon: The Real Estate Game, 1986, Ram Innovations
EX $6   NM $15   MIP $20

U.N. Game of Flags, 1961, Parker Bros.
EX $12   NM $20   MIP $25

U.S. Air Force, Game of, 1950s, Transogram
EX $25   NM $45   MIP $60

Ubi, 1986, Selchow & Righter
EX $6   NM $18   MIP $30

Ultimate Golf, 1985, Ultimate Golf
EX $6   NM $18   MIP $25

Uncle Milton's Ant Farm Game, 1969, Uncle Milton Industries
EX $20   NM $35   MIP $50

Uncle Wiggly, 1979, Parker Bros.
EX $8   NM $15   MIP $20

(KP Photo)

Undercover: The Game of Secret Agents, 1960, Cadaco-Ellis
EX $20   NM $30   MIP $40

Underdog, 1964, Milton Bradley
EX $20   NM $50   MIP $75

Underdog Save Sweet Polly, 1972, Whitman
EX $25   NM $45   MIP $70

Undersea World of Jacques Cousteau, 1968, Parker Bros.
EX $20   NM $35   MIP $50

Ungame, 1975, Ungame
EX $4   NM $6   MIP $10

United Nations, A Game about the, 1961, Payton Products
EX $12   NM $30   MIP $40

Universe, 1966, Parker Bros.
EX $6   NM $18   MIP $30

Up for Grabs, 1978, Mattel
EX $6   NM $15   MIP $20

Up! Against Time, 1977, Ideal
EX $4   NM $10   MIP $15

Ur, Royal Game of Sumer, 1977, Selchow & Righter
EX $3   NM $10   MIP $15

Uranium, 1950s, Saalfield
EX $18   NM $40   MIP $60

(KP Photo)

Uranium Rush, 1955, Gardner
EX $45   NM $60   MIP $80

USAC Auto Racing, 1980, Avalon Hill
EX $18   NM $45   MIP $65

Vagabondo, 1979, Invicta
EX $5   NM $16   MIP $25

Vallco Pro Drag Racing Game, 1975, Zyla
EX $15   NM $25   MIP $35

Valvigi Downs, 1985, Valvigi
EX $6   NM $18   MIP $30

Vaquero, 1952, Wales Game Systems
EX $15   NM $20   MIP $25

Varsity, 1955, Cadaco-Ellis
EX $12   NM $30   MIP $50

VCR Basketball Game, 1987, Interactive VCR Games
EX $6   NM $10   MIP $15

VCR Quarterback Game, 1986, Interactive VCR Games
EX $8   NM $13   MIP $20

(KP Photo)

Veda, The Magic Answer Man, 1960s, Pressman
EX $15   NM $20   MIP $25

Vegas, 1969, NBC-Hasbro
EX $6   NM $15   MIP $20

Vegas, 1974, Milton Bradley
EX $4   NM $15   MIP $20

Venture, 1970, 3M
EX $8   NM $20   MIP $30

Verbatim, 1985, Lakeside
EX $3   NM $10   MIP $15

Verdict, 1959, Avalon Hill
EX $15   NM $50   MIP $75

Verdict II, 1961, Avalon Hill
EX $12   NM $40   MIP $60

Verne Gagne World Champion Wrestling, 1950, Gardner
EX $40   NM $90   MIP $135

Vice Versa, 1976, Hallmark Games
EX $5   NM $16   MIP $25

Video Village, 1960, Milton Bradley
EX $15   NM $25   MIP $35

Vietnam, 1984, Victory Games
EX $10   NM $15   MIP $25

Vince Lombardi's Game, 1970, Research Games
EX $35   NM $65   MIP $85

Virginian, The, 1962, Transogram
EX $45   NM $75   MIP $90

Visit To Walt Disney World Game, 1970, Milton Bradley
EX $15   NM $20   MIP $35

Voice of The Mummy, 1960s, Milton Bradley
EX $75   NM $125   MIP $300

Voodoo Doll Game, 1967, Schaper
EX $12   NM $30   MIP $40

Voyage of the Dawn Treader, 1983, David Cook
EX $5   NM $16   MIP $25

Voyage to Cipangu, 1979, Heise-Cipangu
EX $25   NM $55   MIP $75

Voyage to the Bottom of the Sea, 1964, Milton Bradley, eight blue and eight red subs
EX $10   NM $20   MIP $30

Wackiest Ship In The Army, 1964, Ideal
EX $18   **NM** $25   **MIP** $35

Wacky Races Game, 1970s, Milton Bradley
EX $15   **NM** $25   **MIP** $40

(KP Photo)

Wagon Train, 1960, Milton Bradley
EX $25   **NM** $40   **MIP** $50

Wahoo, 1947, Zondine
EX $15   **NM** $20   **MIP** $30

Wally Gator Game, 1963, Transogram
EX $65   **NM** $85   **MIP** $130

Walt Disney's 101 Dalmatians, 1960, Whitman
EX $20   **NM** $35   **MIP** $55

Walt Disney's 20,000 Leagues Under The Sea, 1954, Jacmar
EX $45   **NM** $75   **MIP** $120

Walt Disney's Jungle Book, 1967, Parker Bros.
EX $15   **NM** $25   **MIP** $45

(KP Photo)

Walt Disney's Official Frontierland, 1950s, Parker Bros.
EX $15   **NM** $35   **MIP** $50

Walt Disney's Sleeping Beauty Game, 1958, Whitman
EX $30   **NM** $50   **MIP** $80

Walt Disney's Swamp Fox Game, 1960, Parker Bros.
EX $30   **NM** $40   **MIP** $60

(KP Photo)

Waltons, 1974, Milton Bradley
EX $15   **NM** $20   **MIP** $30

(KP Photo)

Wanted Dead or Alive, 1959, Lowell
EX $50   **NM** $75   **MIP** $125

War At Sea, 1976, Avalon Hill
EX $10   **NM** $20   **MIP** $30

War of the Networks, 1979, Hasbro
EX $6   **NM** $18   **MIP** $30

Watergate Scandal, The, 1973, American Symbolic
EX $8   **NM** $20   **MIP** $30

Waterloo, 1962, Avalon Hill
EX $10   **NM** $20   **MIP** $45

(KP Photo)

Weird-Ohs Game, The, 1964, Ideal
EX $85   **NM** $145   **MIP** $230

(KP Photo)

Welcome Back, Kotter, 1977, Ideal
EX $10   **NM** $20   **MIP** $25

Welfare, 1978, Jedco
EX $12   **NM** $40   **MIP** $60

(KP Photo)

Wendy, The Good Little Witch, 1966, Milton Bradley
EX $50   **NM** $75   **MIP** $100

West Point Story, The, 1950s, Transogram
EX $25   **NM** $40   **MIP** $60

What Shall I Be?, 1966, Selchow & Righter
EX $15   **NM** $35   **MIP** $45

What Shall I Wear?, 1969, Selchow & Righter
EX $15   **NM** $35   **MIP** $45

What's My Line Game, 1950s, Lowell
EX $20   **NM** $30   **MIP** $40

What's Up, Doc?, 1978, Milton Bradley
EX $6   **NM** $15   **MIP** $20

Whatzit?, 1987, Milton Bradley
EX $5   **NM** $16   **MIP** $25

Wheel of Fortune, 1985, Pressman
EX $5   **NM** $8   **MIP** $13

Where's The Beef?, 1984, Milton Bradley
EX $6   **NM** $10   **MIP** $15

Which Witch?, 1970, Milton Bradley
EX $45   **NM** $75   **MIP** $100

Whirl Out Game, 1971, Milton Bradley
EX $6   **NM** $18   **MIP** $30

Whirl-A-Ball, 1978, Pressman
EX $10   **NM** $15   **MIP** $25

Whirligig, 1963, Milton Bradley
EX $8   **NM** $20   **MIP** $30

Whirly Bird Play Catch, 1960s, Innovation Industries
EX $20   **NM** $35   **MIP** $50

White Shadow Basketball Game, The, 1980, Cadaco
EX $20   **NM** $25   **MIP** $35

Who Can Beat Nixon?, 1971, Dynamic
EX $10   **NM** $35   **MIP** $40

Who Framed Roger Rabbit?, 1987, Milton Bradley
EX $20   **NM** $35   **MIP** $55

Who What Or Where?, 1970, Milton Bradley
EX $5   **NM** $8   **MIP** $13

Who, Game of, 1951, Parker Bros.
EX $20   **NM** $30   **MIP** $40

Whodunit, 1972, Selchow & Righter
EX $10   **NM** $15   **MIP** $25

Whodunit?, 1959, Cadaco-Ellis
EX $8   **NM** $25   **MIP** $40

Whosit?, 1976, Parker Bros.
EX $6   **NM** $10   **MIP** $15

Wide World, 1957, 1962, Parker Bros.
EX $10   **NM** $15   **MIP** $20

Wide World of Sports Auto Racing, 1975, Milton Bradley
EX $12   **NM** $30   **MIP** $45

Wide World of Sports Golf, 1975, Milton Bradley
EX $12   **NM** $30   **MIP** $45

Wide World of Sports Tennis, 1975, Milton Bradley
EX $12   **NM** $30   **MIP** $45

Wide World Travel, 1957, Parker Bros.
EX $15   NM $35   MIP $50

Wil-Croft Baseball, 1971, Wil-Croft
EX $10   NM $16   MIP $25

(KP Photo)

Wild Bill Hickok, 1955, Built-Rite
EX $15   NM $25   MIP $35

Wild Kingdom Game, 1977, Teaching Concepts
EX $20   NM $35   MIP $50

Wild, Wild West, The, 1966, Transogram
EX $125   NM $350   MIP $500

Wildcatter, 1981, Kessler
EX $12   NM $30   MIP $40

Wildlife, 1971, Lowe
EX $15   NM $35   MIP $50

Willie Mays "Say Hey" Baseball, 1958, Centennial Games
EX $190   NM $295   MIP $450

Willie Mays "Say Hey," 1954, Toy Development
EX $200   NM $350   MIP $700

Willie Mays Push Button Baseball, 1965, Eldon
EX $175   NM $295   MIP $450

Willow, 1988, Parker Bros.
EX $10   NM $25   MIP $35

Win, Place & Show, 1966, 3M
EX $6   NM $20   MIP $30

Wine Cellar, 1971, Dynamic
EX $5   NM $16   MIP $25

Winko Baseball, 1940s, Milton Bradley
EX $25   NM $40   MIP $60

(KP Photo)

Winky Dink Official TV Game Kit, 1950s
EX $50   NM $100   MIP $125

Winnie The Pooh Game, 1959, Parker Bros.
EX $20   NM $30   MIP $40

Winnie The Pooh Game, 1979, Parker Bros.
EX $5   NM $8   MIP $13

Winning Ticket, The, 1977, Ideal
EX $6   NM $20   MIP $30

Wiry Dan's Electric Baseball Game, 1953, Harett-Gilmar
EX $8   NM $25   MIP $35

Wiry Dan's Electric Football Game, 1953, Harett-Gilmar
EX $8   NM $25   MIP $35

Wise Old Owl, 1950s, Novel Toy
EX $20   NM $30   MIP $40

Witch Pitch Game, 1970, Parker Bros.
EX $15   NM $25   MIP $40

Wit's End, Game of, 1948, Parker Bros.
EX $15   NM $35   MIP $50

Wizard of Oz Game, 1962, Lowe
EX $20   NM $30   MIP $50

(KP Photo)

Wizard of Oz Game, 1974, Cadaco
EX $15   NM $20   MIP $25

(KP Photo)

Wolfman Mystery Game, 1963, Hasbro
EX $80   NM $160   MIP $225

Woman & Man, 1971, Psychology Today
EX $4   NM $15   MIP $20

Women's Lib, 1970, Urban Systems
EX $12   NM $30   MIP $40

(KP Photo)

Wonder Woman Game, 1967, Hasbro
EX $20   NM $35   MIP $50

Wonderbug Game, 1977, Ideal
EX $8   NM $25   MIP $35

(KP Photo)

Woody Woodpecker Game, 1959, Milton Bradley
EX $15   NM $25   MIP $35

(KP Photo)

Woody Woodpecker, Travel w/, 1950s, Cadaco-Ellis
EX $35   NM $60   MIP $80

Woody Woodpecker's Crazy Mixed Up Color Factory, 1972, Whitman
EX $12   NM $20   MIP $30

Woody Woodpecker's Moon Dash Game, 1976, Whitman
EX $12   NM $20   MIP $30

Word War, 1978, Mattel
EX $6   NM $15   MIP $20

World Bowling Tour, 1979, World Bowling Tour
EX $7   NM $20   MIP $35

World Champion Wrestling Official Slam O' Rama, 1990, International Games
EX $5   NM $8   MIP $12

World of Micronauts, 1978, Milton Bradley
EX $10   NM $15   MIP $25

World of Wall Street, 1969, NBC-Hasbro
EX $4   NM $10   MIP $15

(KP Photo)

World's Fair Game, 1964, Milton Bradley

    EX $10   **NM** $20   **MIP** $35

World's Greatest Baseball Game, 1977, J. Woodlock

    EX $35   **NM** $75   **MIP** $100

Wrestling Superstars, 1985, Milton Bradley

    EX $8   **NM** $13   **MIP** $20

WWF Wrestling Game, 1991, Colorforms

    EX $5   **NM** $8   **MIP** $12

Wyatt Earp Game, 1958, Transogram

    EX $35   **NM** $60   **MIP** $75

Xaviera's Game, 1974, Dynamic

    EX $7   **NM** $20   **MIP** $35

X-Men Alert! Adventure Game, 1992, Pressman

    EX $5   **NM** $16   **MIP** $25

Yacht Race, 1961, Parker Bros.

    EX $45   **NM** $65   **MIP** $80

(KP Photo)

Yahtzee, 1956, Lowe

    EX $6   **NM** $10   **MIP** $15

(KP Photo)

Yertle, The Game of, 1960, Revell

    EX $30   **NM** $55   **MIP** $75

Yogi Bear Break A Plate Game, 1960s, Transogram

    EX $25   **NM** $40   **MIP** $60

Yogi Bear Cartoon Game, 1980, Milton Bradley

    EX $3   **NM** $5   **MIP** $10

Yogi Bear Game, 1971, Milton Bradley

    EX $8   **NM** $20   **MIP** $30

Yogi Bear Go Fly A Kite Game, 1961, Transogram

    EX $25   **NM** $40   **MIP** $60

Your America, 1970, Cadaco

    EX $2   **NM** $7   **MIP** $12

Yours For a Song, 1962, Lowell

    EX $20   **NM** $35   **MIP** $55

Zaxxon, 1982, Milton Bradley

    EX $6   **NM** $10   **MIP** $15

Zig Zag Zoom, 1970, Ideal

    EX $10   **NM** $20   **MIP** $30

Ziggy Game, A Day w/, 1977, Milton Bradley

    EX $4   **NM** $10   **MIP** $15

Zingo, 1950s, Empire Plastics

    EX $15   **NM** $20   **MIP** $30

(KP Photo)

Zip Code Game, 1964, Lakeside

    EX $40   **NM** $60   **MIP** $80

Zomax, 1988, Zomax

    EX $8   **NM** $25   **MIP** $40

Zoography, 1972, Amway

    EX $5   **NM** $16   **MIP** $25

Zorro Game, Walt Disney's, 1966, Parker Bros.

    EX $25   **NM** $40   **MIP** $65

Zorro Target Game w/Dart Gun, 1950s, Knickerbocker

    EX $20   **NM** $30   **MIP** $50

CARD GAMES

Addams Family, 1965, Milton Bradley

    EX $20   **NM** $30   **MIP** $60

(KP Photo)

Archie Bunker's Card Game, 1972, Milton Bradley

    EX $6   **NM** $10   **MIP** $15

Art Linkletter's People are Funny Party Game, 1954, Whitman

    EX $5   **NM** $16   **MIP** $20

Bali, 1954, I-S Unlimited

    EX $8   **NM** $20   **MIP** $30

Baseball Card All Star Game, 1987, Captoys

    EX $5   **NM** $12   **MIP** $15

Baseball Card Game, 1950s, Ed-U-Cards

    EX $8   **NM** $20   **MIP** $30

Baseball Card Game, Official, 1965, Milton Bradley

    EX $20   **NM** $40   **MIP** $50

Batman Card Game, 1966, Ideal

    EX $35   **NM** $75   **MIP** $95

Batter Up Card Game, 1949, Ed-U-Cards

    EX $8   **NM** $20   **MIP** $30

(KP Photo)

Beverly Hillbillies Game, "Set Back," 1963, Milton Bradley

    EX $10   **NM** $15   **MIP** $20

(KP Photo)

Bewitched Stymie Game, 1960s, Milton Bradley
EX $20 NM $50 MIP $60

Bible Quiz Lotto, 1949, Jack Levitz
EX $5 NM $12 MIP $20

Boston Red Sox Game, 1964, Ed-U-Cards
EX $15 NM $35 MIP $55

Bullwinkle Card Game, 1962, Ed-U-Cards
EX $10 NM $30 MIP $40

Charge It!, 1972, Whitman
EX $5 NM $15 MIP $25

Combat, 1964, Milton Bradley
EX $10 NM $15 MIP $20

Cowboys & Indians, 1949, Ed-U-Cards
EX $8 NM $20 MIP $35

Dallas Game, 1980, Mego
EX $3 NM $10 MIP $15

Daniel Boone Wilderness Trail, 1964, Transogram
EX $10 NM $40 MIP $65

Dragonmaster, 1981, Lowe
EX $8 NM $40 MIP $50

Fast Golf, 1977, Whitman
EX $8 NM $13 MIP $20

Flintstones Animal Rummy, 1960, Ed-U-Cards
EX $7 NM $18 MIP $25

Flintstones Cut-Ups Game, 1963, Whitman
EX $15 NM $45 MIP $60

Funny Bones Game, 1968, Parker Bros.
EX $5 NM $7 MIP $11

Gidget, 1966, Milton Bradley
EX $15 NM $35 MIP $50

Go Go Go, 1950s, Arco Playing Card
EX $6 NM $20 MIP $35

Gong Hee Fot Choy, 1948, Zondine Game
EX $20 NM $35 MIP $55

Grabitz, 1979, International Games
EX $2 NM $5 MIP $7

Harry's Glam Slam, 1962, Harry Obst
EX $35 NM $60 MIP $90

Howdy Doody Card Game, 1954, Russell
EX $5 NM $10 MIP $20

I Survived New York!, 1981, City Enterprises
EX $4 NM $7 MIP $12

James Bond Live and Let Die Tarot Game, 1973, US Games Systems
EX $25 NM $55 MIP $85

Kardball, 1946, Ajak
EX $20 NM $30 MIP $40

Know Your States, 1955, Garrard Press
EX $10 NM $25 MIP $45

Let's Play Basketball, 1965, D.M.R.
EX $12 NM $20 MIP $35

Li'l Abner's Spoof Game, 1950, Milton Bradley
EX $65 NM $95 MIP $135

Man from U.N.C.L.E. Illya Kuryakin Card Game, 1966, Milton Bradley
EX $15 NM $25 MIP $30

Match, 1953, Garrard Press
EX $10 NM $15 MIP $25

Mickey Mouse Canasta Jr., 1950, Russell
EX $20 NM $30 MIP $40

Mickey Mouse Jr. Royal Rummy, 1970s, Whitman
EX $5 NM $15 MIP $30

Mickey Mouse Library of Games, 1946, Russell
EX $30 NM $50 MIP $100

Mille Bornes, 1962, Parker Bros.
EX $10 NM $15 MIP $20

(KP Photo)

Monster Old Maid, 1964, Milton Bradley
EX $15 NM $40 MIP $55

Mr. T Game, 1983, Milton Bradley
EX $5 NM $15 MIP $25

Munsters Card Game, 1966, Milton Bradley
EX $20 NM $40 MIP $55

New York World's Fair Children's Game, 1964, Ed-U-Cards
EX $15 NM $35 MIP $55

Nuclear War, 1965, Douglas Malewicki
EX $25 NM $40 MIP $75

NY Mets Baseball Card Game, Official, 1961, Ed-U-Cards
EX $20 NM $45 MIP $65

Pro Baseball Card Game, 1980s, Just Games
EX $6 NM $10 MIP $15

Scan, 1970, Parker Bros.
EX $3 NM $10 MIP $15

Scott's Baseball Card Game, 1989, Scott's Baseball Cards
EX $12 NM $20 MIP $30

Skeeter, 1950s, Arco Playing Card
EX $6 NM $20 MIP $35

Strategy Poker Fine Edition, 1967, Milton Bradley
EX $5 NM $12 MIP $18

Superheroes Card Game, 1978, Milton Bradley
EX $15 NM $30 MIP $55

Superman Game, 1966, Whitman
EX $35 NM $75 MIP $110

Syllable, 1948, Garrard Press
EX $10 NM $15 MIP $25

Touch, 1970, Parker Bros.
EX $5 NM $16 MIP $25

Trail Drive, 1950s, Arco Playing Card
EX $15 NM $35 MIP $65

(KP Photo)

Twelve O'Clock High, 1966, Milton Bradley
EX $15 NM $25 MIP $35

Voyage to the Bottom of the Sea, 1964, Milton Bradley
EX $8 NM $15 MIP $25

Waterworks, 1972, Parker Bros.
EX $5 NM $12 MIP $20

Welcome Back, Kotter, 1976, Milton Bradley
EX $5 NM $16 MIP $25

SKILL GAMES

Call It!, 1978, Ideal
EX $5 NM $12 MIP $20

Chicken Lotto, 1965, Ideal
EX $8 NM $25 MIP $40

Chutes Away!, 1978, Gabriel
EX $15 NM $60 MIP $85

Clickety-Clak, 1950s, Milton Bradley
EX $10 NM $15 MIP $20

Clunk-A-Glunk, 1968, Whitman
EX $8 NM $25 MIP $40

Don't Break the Ice, 1960s, Schaper
EX $5   NM $16   MIP $25

Don't Spill the Beans, 1967, Schaper
EX $10   NM $16   MIP $25

Feed the Elephant!, 1952, Cadaco-Ellis
EX $10   NM $35   MIP $50

Gnip Gnop, 1971, Parker Bros.
EX $5   NM $10   MIP $15

Hoc-Key, 1958, Cadaco-Ellis
EX $10   NM $35   MIP $50

Hungry Henry, 1969, Ideal
EX $7   NM $15   MIP $25

Jack & Jill Target Game, 1948, Cadaco-Ellis
EX $7   NM $20   MIP $35

Jaws, The Game of, 1975, Ideal
EX $10   NM $16   MIP $20

Kick Back, 1965, Schaper
EX $5   NM $16   MIP $25

Leapin' Letters, 1969, Parker Bros.
EX $5   NM $16   MIP $25

Marblehead, 1969, Ideal
EX $5   NM $16   MIP $25

Mark "Three," 1972, Ideal
EX $6   NM $18   MIP $30

Mentor, 1960s, Hasbro
EX $18   NM $40   MIP $60

Mind Maze Game, 1970, Parker Bros.
EX $5   NM $16   MIP $25

Mr. Mad Game, 1970, Ideal
EX $12   NM $40   MIP $60

Nibbles 'N Bites, 1964, Schaper
EX $5   NM $16   MIP $25

On Target, 1973, Milton Bradley
EX $12   NM $40   MIP $60

Pitchin' Pal, 1952, Cadaco-Ellis
EX $7   NM $20   MIP $35

(KP Photo)

Poosh-em-up Slugger Bagatelle, 1946, Northwestern Products
EX $30   NM $50   MIP $75

Quick Shoot, 1970, Ideal
EX $6   NM $18   MIP $30

Sharpshooter, 1962, Cadaco-Ellis
EX $12   NM $20   MIP $25

Skip Bowl, 1955, Transogram
EX $6   NM $18   MIP $30

Slap Stick, 1967, Milton Bradley
EX $7   NM $20   MIP $35

Smack-A-Roo, 1964, Mattel
EX $6   NM $18   MIP $30

(KP Photo)

Tight Squeeze, 1967, Mattel
EX $7   NM $20   MIP $35

Tip-It, 1965, Ideal
EX $5   NM $16   MIP $20

Topple Chairs, 1962, Eberhard Faber
EX $6   NM $18   MIP $30

Wing-Ding, 1951, Cadaco-Ellis
EX $8   NM $25   MIP $40

SKILL/ACTION GAMES

Airways, 1950s, Lindstrom Tool & Toy
EX $25   NM $40   MIP $60

Angry Donald Duck Game, 1970s, Mexico
EX $40   NM $65   MIP $100

Bandu, 1991, Milton Bradley
EX $12   NM $30   MIP $40

Baseball, 1960s, Tudor
EX $20   NM $30   MIP $50

(KP Photo)

Bash!, 1967, Milton Bradley
EX $10   NM $15   MIP $25

Batman Batarang Toss, 1966, Pressman
EX $150   NM $250   MIP $400

Batman Pin Ball, 1966, Marx
EX $55   NM $95   MIP $150

Bats in the Belfry, 1964, Mattel
EX $35   NM $75   MIP $100

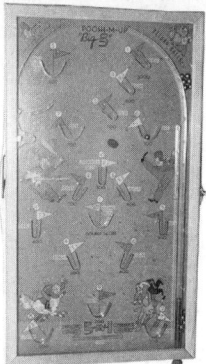

(KP Photo)

Big 5 Poosh-M Up, 1950s, Knickerbocker
EX $35   NM $40   MIP $50

Big Game Hunt, The, 1947, Carrom Industries
EX $15   NM $25   MIP $30

Big Sneeze Game, The, 1968, Ideal
EX $10   NM $25   MIP $40

Boob Tube Race, 1962, Milton Bradley
EX $2   NM $10   MIP $15

Booby Trap, 1965, Parker Bros.
EX $10   NM $10   MIP $15

Bop Bop 'N Rebop, 1979, Hasbro
EX $12   NM $30   MIP $40

Bop The Beetle, 1963, Ideal
EX $10   NM $20   MIP $30

Bowl-A-Matic, 1963, Eldon
EX $100   NM $250   MIP $350

Bugs Bunny Game (Bagatelle), 1975, Ideal
EX $15   NM $25   MIP $40

Candid Camera Target Shot, 1950s, Lindstrom Tool & Toy
EX $35   NM $50   MIP $65

Careful: The Toppling Tower, 1967, Ideal
EX $8   NM $20   MIP $30

Coney Island Penny Pitch, 1950s, Novel Toy
EX $33   NM $55   MIP $88

(KP Photo)

Crazy Clock Game, 1964, Ideal
EX $30   NM $40   MIP $50

Crazy Maze, 1966, 1975, Lakeside

    EX $8   **NM** $20   **MIP** $30

Deputy Dawg Hoss Toss, 1973

    EX $15   **NM** $25   **MIP** $40

(KP Photo)

Disney Dodgem Bagatelle, 1960s, Marx

    EX $30   **NM** $65   **MIP** $90

Don't Dump the Daisy, 1970, Ideal

    EX $10   **NM** $25   **MIP** $35

Dynamite Shack Game, 1968, Milton Bradley

    EX $10   **NM** $25   **MIP** $30

Facts In Five, 1967, 3M

    EX $3   **NM** $8   **MIP** $12

Fascination, 1962, Remco

    EX $15   **NM** $20   **MIP** $30

Fascination Pool, 1962, Remco

    EX $8   **NM** $20   **MIP** $30

Feeley Meeley Game, 1967, Milton Bradley

    EX $20   **NM** $50   **MIP** $75

Fireball XL-5 Magnetic Dart Game, 1963, Magic Wand

    EX $75   **NM** $125   **MIP** $200

Flea Circus Magnetic Action Game, 1968, Mattel

    EX $15   **NM** $25   **MIP** $40

Flintstones Brake Ball, 1962, Whitman

    EX $45   **NM** $60   **MIP** $75

Flintstones Mechanical Shooting Gallery, 1962, Marx

    EX $75   **NM** $125   **MIP** $200

Flying Nun Marble Maze Game, The, 1967, Hasbro

    EX $20   **NM** $30   **MIP** $50

(KP Photo)

G.I. Joe Bagatelle Gun Action Game, 1970s, Hasbro

    EX $7   **NM** $12   **MIP** $15

(KP Photo)

Gotham's Ice Hockey, 1960s, Gotham

    EX $35   **NM** $60   **MIP** $85

Grab A Loop, 1968, Milton Bradley

    EX $7   **NM** $12   **MIP** $15

Grand Slam Game, 1969, Ideal

    EX $8   **NM** $20   **MIP** $30

Hands Down, 1965, Ideal

    EX $10   **NM** $15   **MIP** $20

Hi Pop, 1946, Advance Games

    EX $20   **NM** $35   **MIP** $55

Hopalong Cassidy Bean Bag Toss Game, 1950s

    EX $20   **NM** $40   **MIP** $60

Hoppity Hooper Pin Ball Game, 1965, Lido

    EX $40   **NM** $75   **MIP** $115

Howdy Doody Dominoes Game, 1950s, Ed-U-Cards

    EX $50   **NM** $75   **MIP** $100

Huckleberry Hound's Huckle Chuck Target Game, 1961, Transogram

    EX $25   **NM** $50   **MIP** $100

(KP Photo)

Huggin' The Rail, 1948, Selchow & Righter

    EX $40   **NM** $50   **MIP** $60

I-Qubes, 1948, Capex

    EX $10   **NM** $15   **MIP** $25

Johnny Apollo Moon Landing Bagatelle, 1969, Marx

    EX $20   **NM** $35   **MIP** $55

KaBoom!, 1965, Ideal

    EX $10   **NM** $15   **MIP** $25

Ker-Plunk, 1967, Ideal

    EX $5   **NM** $10   **MIP** $15

Kimbo, 1950s, Parker Bros.

    EX $10   **NM** $25   **MIP** $70

King Arthur, 1950s, Northwestern Products

    EX $25   **NM** $40   **MIP** $65

King Pin Deluxe Bowling Alley, 1947, Baldwin Mfg.

    EX $10   **NM** $20   **MIP** $30

(KP Photo)

Knockout, Electronic Boxing Game, 1950s, Northwestern Products

    EX $75   **NM** $125   **MIP** $175

Krokay, 1955, Transogram

    EX $4   **NM** $10   **MIP** $15

Land of The Lost Pinball, 1975, Larami

    EX $10   **NM** $20   **MIP** $30

Lone Ranger and Tonto Spin Game, The, 1967, Pressman

    EX $15   **NM** $25   **MIP** $40

Loopin' Louie, 1992, Milton Bradley

    EX $10   **NM** $25   **MIP** $35

Magnetic Fish Pond, 1948, Milton Bradley

    EX $10   **NM** $20   **MIP** $30

Man from U.N.C.L.E. Pinball Game, 1966

    EX $80   **NM** $135   **MIP** $215

Man from U.N.C.L.E. Target Game, 1966, Marx

    EX $130   **NM** $275   **MIP** $550

Marathon Game, 1978, Sports Games

    EX $10   **NM** $20   **MIP** $35

(KP Photo)

Marx-O-Matic All Star Basketball, 1950s, Marx
EX $150   NM $250   MIP $400

(KP Photo)

Mechanical Shooting Gallery, 1950s, Wyandotte
EX $95   NM $135   MIP $195

(KP Photo)

Mickey Mouse Haunted House Bagatelle, 1950s
EX $210   NM $350   MIP $550

(KP Photo)

Mighty Mouse Target Game, 1960s, Parks
EX $30   NM $60   MIP $90

(KP Photo)

Monster Lab, 1964, Ideal
EX $225   NM $275   MIP $500

Mouse Trap, 1963, Ideal
EX $20   NM $30   MIP $50

NFL Football Game, Official, 1968, Ideal
EX $12   NM $30   MIP $40

Nixon Ring Toss, 1970s
EX $20   NM $30   MIP $50

Nutty Mads Bagatelle, 1963, Marx
EX $25   NM $45   MIP $85

(KP Photo)

Nutty Mads Target Game, 1960s, Marx
EX $35   NM $70   MIP $125

Par-A-Shoot Game, 1947, Baldwin
EX $15   NM $25   MIP $40

(KP Photo)

Pony Polo, 1960s, Remco
EX $10   NM $20   MIP $35

(KP Photo)

Pro Bowl Live Action Football, 1960s, Marx
EX $35   NM $65   MIP $95

Rat Patrol Spin Game, 1967, Pressman
EX $30   NM $65   MIP $85

(KP Photo)

Rocket Patrol Magnetic Target Game, 1950s, American Toy Products
EX $35   NM $65   MIP $100

(KP Photo)

Rocket Sock-It Rifle and Target Game, 1960s, Kenner
EX $20   NM $35   MIP $75

Saratoga: 1777, 1974, Gamut of Games
EX $10   NM $25   MIP $50

Simon, 1978, Milton Bradley
EX $6   NM $15   MIP $20

Space Strike, 1980, Ideal
EX $12   NM $30   MIP $40

Speed Circuit, 1971, 3M
EX $15   NM $30   MIP $45

Superman Spin Game, 1967, Pressman
EX $40   NM $65   MIP $105

Suspense, 1950s, Northwestern Products
EX $15   NM $20   MIP $30

Tickle Bee, 1956, Schaper
EX $10   NM $15   MIP $20

(KP Photo)

Time Bomb, 1965, Milton Bradley
EX $30   NM $60   MIP $80

Time Tunnel Spin-to-Win Game,
1967, Pressman
EX $60   NM $100   MIP $160

Tipp Kick, 1970s, Top Set
EX $15   NM $25   MIP $40

Tournament Labyrinth, 1980s,
Pressman
EX $10   NM $15   MIP $25

Tru-Action Electric Basketball, 1965,
Tudor
EX $25   NM $50   MIP $75

**Tru-Action Electric Harness Race
Game,** 1950s, Tudor
EX $15   NM $40   MIP $65

Try-It Maze Puzzle Game, 1965,
Milton Bradley
EX $7   NM $12   MIP $20

Tug Boat, 1974, Parker Bros.
EX $10   NM $30   MIP $40

Untouchables, The, 1950s, Marx
EX $95   NM $160   MIP $250

Whiplash, 1966, Lakeside
EX $10   NM $25   MIP $35

Wow! Pillow Fight For Girls Game,
1964, Milton Bradley
EX $12   NM $30   MIP $40

Yogi Berra Pitch Kit, 1963, Ross
Products
EX $35   NM $50   MIP $100

Zowie Horseshoe Game, 1947,
James L. Decker
EX $20   NM $35   MIP $55

Tabletop Games

AUTO RACING

No. 300 Electric Auto Racing, 1948-49,
Tudor
EX $50   NM $100   MIP n/a

**No. 530 Tru-Action Electric Sports
Car Race,** 1959-65, Tudor
EX $25   NM $55   MIP n/a

**No. 590 Mickey Mouse Electric
Treasure Hunt Game,** 1963-64,
Tudor
EX $40   NM $85   MIP n/a

BASEBALL

No. 550 Tru-Action Electric Baseball,
1950-58, Tudor
EX $30   NM $75   MIP n/a

No. 550 Tru-Action Electric Baseball,
1958-63, Tudor
EX $25   NM $60   MIP n/a

No. 555 Tru-Action Electric Baseball,
1964-88, Tudor, square field
EX $22   NM $50   MIP n/a

BASKETBALL

Gotham Pass 'N Shoot Basketball,
1968, Gotham Pressed Steel Co.
EX $20   NM $55   MIP n/a

Gotham Pro Basketball, 1950s,
Gotham Pressed Steel Co.
EX $15   NM $45   MIP n/a

No. 475 Magnetic Baseball, 1964-67,
Tudor
EX $20   NM $45   MIP n/a

No. 480 NBPA Game, 1968-70, Tudor
EX $30   NM $75   MIP n/a

No. 480 NBPA Game, 1971, Tudor
EX $15   NM $40   MIP n/a

**No. 575 Tru-Action Electric
Basketball,** 1957-58, Tudor
EX $30   NM $70   MIP n/a

**No. 575 Tru-Action Electric
Basketball,** 1959-63, Tudor
EX $25   NM $55   MIP n/a

No. G-660 Gotham All Star Basketball,
1947, Gotham Pressed Steel Co.
EX $20   NM $50   MIP n/a

FOOTBALL

G-890 Dick Butkus, 1972, Gotham
EX $30   NM $75   MIP n/a

No. G-1400, 1965-67, Gotham
EX $30   NM $60   MIP n/a

No. G-1440, 1962-64, Gotham
EX $35   NM $70   MIP n/a

No. G-1503, 1968, Gotham
EX $33   NM $70   MIP n/a

No. G-1503-S NFL Big Bowl, 1965-
67, Gotham
EX $50   NM $125   MIP n/a

No. G-1506 NFL Players Association,
Gotham
EX $25   NM $60   MIP n/a

No. G-1512 Super Dome, 1969-71,
Gotham
EX $45   NM $110   MIP n/a

**No. G-1550 Yankee Stadium
Grandstand,** 1962-64, Gotham
EX $40   NM $80   MIP n/a

No. G-812 Joe Namath, 1969-71,
Gotham
EX $35   NM $75   MIP n/a

No. G-812 Joe Namath, 1972, Gotham
EX $35   NM $85   MIP n/a

No. G-818 Roman Gabriel Model,
1969-71, Gotham
EX $25   NM $65   MIP n/a

No. G-818 Roman Gabriel Model,
1972, Gotham
EX $25   NM $55   MIP n/a

**No. G-880 Gotham All-Star Electric
Football,** 1956-58, Gotham
EX $30   NM $70   MIP n/a

**No. G-880 Gotham All-Star Electric
Football,** 1959-61, Gotham
EX $25   NM $50   MIP n/a

No. G-882, 1965-67, Gotham
EX $18   NM $50   MIP n/a

No. G-883, 1968, Gotham
EX $15   NM $40   MIP n/a

No. G-883, 1972, Gotham
EX $10   NM $20   MIP n/a

**No. G-890 Gotham Official NFL Electric
Football,** 1962-64, Gotham
EX $20   NM $45   MIP n/a

No. G-895 NFL Players Association,
1969-71, Gotham
EX $22   NM $50   MIP n/a

**No. G-940 Gotham Electro Magnetic
Football,** 1954-55, Gotham
EX $38   NM $80   MIP n/a

Tudor Electronic Football, 1965,
Tudor
EX $15   NM $35   MIP n/a

Tudor Tru-Action Electric Football,
1949, Tudor
EX $25   NM $40   MIP n/a

HOCKEY

Bobby Hull, 1960s, Munro
EX $125   NM $275   MIP n/a

Bobby Hull, 1970s, Munro
EX $75   NM $155   MIP n/a

Bobby Orr, late-1960s/early-1970s,
Munro
EX $125   NM $265   MIP n/a

Canadian, late-1960s, Eagle
EX $75   NM $145   MIP n/a

Canadian Hockey Master, 1963,
Munro, #976
EX $100   NM $225   MIP n/a

City Series, early-1970s, Coleco
EX $100   NM $210   MIP n/a

Foster Hewitt, 1950s, Reliable
EX $125   NM $235   MIP n/a

Hockey games, 1940s-50s, Cresta,
various games
EX $200   NM $500   MIP n/a

Hot Shot, late-1960s, Munro
EX $60   NM $125   MIP n/a

Hot Shot, mid-1960s, Munro
EX $75   NM $160   MIP n/a

National, early-1960s, Eagle
EX $125   NM $200   MIP n/a

NHL All-Pro Hockey, 1969, Tudor
EX $25   NM $60   MIP n/a

NHPLA, 1969, Tudor
EX $75   NM $135   MIP n/a

No. 5100 Pro Stars, mid-1960s/
early- 1970s, Coleco
EX $65   NM $125   MIP n/a

No. 5160-80 Pro Stars, late-1960s/
early-1970s, Coleco
EX $75   NM $165   MIP n/a

No. 730 NHL All-Star Hockey, 1968,
Tudor
EX $25   NM $50   MIP n/a

No. G1200, 1950s-1960s, Gotham
EX $75   NM $155   MIP n/a

No. G-200, 1930s-1950s, Gotham
EX $125   NM $350   MIP n/a

Official Hockey Night, early-1960s,
Eagle
EX $150   NM $325   MIP n/a

Official NHL, 1969-71, Coleco
EX $150   NM $500   MIP n/a

Olympic, 1964, Eagle
EX $200   NM $500   MIP n/a

Pee Wee, late-1950s, Eagle
EX $150   NM $260   MIP n/a

Playmaker, early-1960s, Eagle
EX $150   NM $250   MIP n/a

Playoff, early-1960s, Eagle
EX $125   NM $225   MIP n/a

Power Play, early-1960s, Eagle
EX $125   NM $200   MIP n/a

Power Play, late-1950s, Eagle
EX $125   NM $230   MIP n/a

Power Play, late-1960s, Coleco
EX $100   NM $185   MIP n/a

Pro Series, mid-1950s/early-1960s,
Eagle
EX $125   NM $225   MIP n/a

Stanley Cup, mid-1960s, Eagle
EX $150   NM $275   MIP n/a

Stanley Cup, Beliveau, late-1960s,
Coleco
EX $125   NM $235   MIP n/a

HORSE RACING

Horse and Harness Race Game,
1963-64, Tudor, combined game
EX $20   NM $50   MIP n/a

No. 525 Horse Race Game, 1950-58,
Tudor
EX $25   NM $65   MIP n/a

No. 525 Horse Race Game, 1959-61,
Tudor, grooved plastic track
EX $22   NM $55   MIP n/a

**No. 525 Tru-Action Electric Horse
Race Game,** 1962, Tudor, plastic
track, no grooves
EX $20   NM $40   MIP n/a

No. 526 Harness Race Game, 1962,
Tudor
EX $20   NM $45   MIP n/a

Tru-Action Races Game, 1965-67,
Tudor
EX $35   NM $75   MIP n/a

TRACK AND FIELD

No. 528 Track and Field Meet, 1963-64,
Tudor
EX $35   NM $85   MIP n/a

No. 528 Tru-Action Races, 1965-67,
Tudor
EX $35   NM $90   MIP n/a

G.I. Joe

by Mark Bellomo

The 1960s

The landscape of the world of boys' toys would be changed forever when designer Stan Weston concocted the idea of marketing a military themed, Barbie-inspired toy line to red-blooded American boys. After pitching the concept to Hasbro, Inc. (a conglomeration of the words "Hassenfeld Brothers" [Has+Bro]), Don Levine, the company's creative director, approved the idea wholeheartedly. The G.I. Joe line was developed in a short amount of time, and presented to toy buyers and the media on February 9, 1964. Released with a WWII theme, this 11-½" G.I. Joe "action figure" line received an overwhelmingly positive response when test marketed in New York City. Hasbro coined the term "action figures" (instead of *dolls*) to be associated with the G.I. Joe line, because they suspected young boys would not identify G.I. Joes as dolls, for what boy would play with a doll? We can speculate the myriad reasons why the G.I. Joe line was a roaring success: the figures were wonderfully poseable, with 21 points of articulation ("Move G.I. Joe into action positions," the box touted); the figures' accessories and uniforms were expertly crafted and admirably authentic; the military theme of the line appealed not only to testosterone filled boys, but to their fathers and grandfathers who were veterans of WWI, WWII, and

Korea; and further, these action figures may have built on the memory of moviegoers who popularized the critically praised film *The Story of G.I. Joe* (1945) starring Burgess Meredith and Robert Mitchum.

Regardless of conjecturing into the figures' appeal, it should be noted that each of the four initial action figures were generic soldiers assembled with enough difference to make them interesting and collectible. Hasbro accomplished this feat by constructing G.I. Joe figures to mimic the four branches of the U.S. Armed Forces: Action Soldier (Army); Action Sailor (Navy); Action Pilot (Air Force); and Action Marine (Marine Corps). Each G.I. Joe (where the "G.I." is suggested to mean "General Issue") was boxed individually with a basic, branch-specific uniform, a metal dog tag, and a molded plastic hat and boots. Extra uniforms and accessory sets were also available. Due to the scarcity of these 1964-1969 items in Mint condition, early pristine pieces command supremely high prices on today's secondary market: sometimes two or three times the value that price guides suggest. The initial military-themed run of G.I. Joe ended in 1968 with the escalation of the Vietnam War, as many parents refused to purchase a toy soldier for their child. Anti-war activists protested the G.I. Joe line as public sentiment turned against Hasbro's ingenious marketing scheme. In 1969 G.I. Joe toys—known for their military bent—were re-created as civilian men of action. Among Joe's new appellations were Adventurer (and Black Adventurer), Aquanaut, and Talking Astronaut. In 1969, Hasbro re-released accessories from the 1964-1968 run with many recycled pieces and concocted all-new exciting sets. "Danger of the Depths," "Fight for Survival," "Mouth of Doom," "Mysterious Explosion," and the popular "Secret Mission to Spy Island," were among those toys released under the new "Adventures of G.I. Joe" banner.

The 1970s

The "G.I. Joe Adventure Team" rose to prominence from 1970-1976. Among the new innovations to the 11 ½" figure line was the addition of Joe's "Life-Like" beard and hair thanks to the discovery of a flocking process by Hasbro's British licensee, Palitoy (the distributor of the British version of G.I. Joe: Action Man). Rounding out the basic figure assortment of the Adventure Team was: Land Adventurer, Sea Adventurer, Air Adventurer, the Man of Action, and the Black Adventurer. Replete with an "AT" dog tag (as the Adventure Team is referred to in collector's circles), shoulder holster and revolver, boots, and either a jumpsuit or combination of shirt and pants, these basic figure assortments were just what Hasbro needed to appeal to cautious shoppers. All-new accessory and equipment sets were also released in conjunction with the G.I. Joe Adventure Team, and none of these were military inspired. Some of the Adventure Team accessory sets would be the most fondly remembered in the duration of the 11-½" line, such as Danger of the Depths, White Tiger Hunt, Capture of the Pygmy Gorilla, Fantastic Freefall, and Hidden Missile Discovery. G.I. Joe even received a wide range of vehicles in the 1970s (there was a dearth of Joe vehicles in the1960s) such as the Mobile Support Vehicle, the Secret of the Mummy's Tomb vehicle, the Big Trapper, the Action Sea Sled, and Fate of the Troubleshooter to name a few. 1974 saw the invention and addition of one of the most famous action features in toy history: G.I. Joe with "Kung Fu Grip." Although primitive by modern standards (no buttons were pushed, no bells and whistles went off), the addition of the Kung Fu Grip capitalized on the 1970s martial arts fad, and Joe's hard-plastic hands, with him since 1964, were replaced by soft, pliable fingers that allowed the action figure to better hold weapons and accessories.

In 1975, Hasbro introduced their very first "named" G.I. Joe character: Mike Power—Atomic Man. The production of Mike Power allowed Hasbro to compete with Kenner's hugely popular Six Million Dollar Man toy line. With an atomic "flashing" right eye, atomic right arm with additional dial-spinning feature, atomic left leg (since Hasbro could not use the term "bionic" in their description), Mike Power's transparent limbs added an element of science-fiction to the G.I. Joe Adventure Team. A new "Life-Like" body was created for G.I. Joe in 1975-76 due to the OPEC oil embargo, as the cost of plastic was at a premium. Now G.I. Joe figures had a mere 15 points of articulation compared to the original 21. Yet another change was introduced during the same time: a new "Eagle Eye" feature. Available with three different figures, the Black Commando, Land Commander, and Man of Action, the "Eagle Eye" action

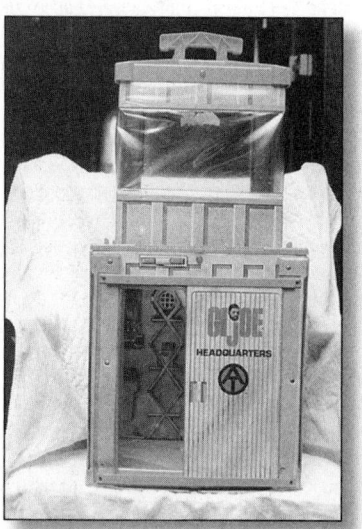

feature allowed the action figures to move their eyes from side-to-side with the movement of a lever. In 1976, another curious addition to the Adventure Team was Bulletman: The Human Bullet. With a chromed removable helmet, chromed arms, colorful tunic, belt, boots, and zip-line, Bulletman seemed to mimic the current action figure industry push to produce comic book superheroes (see Mego's The Official World's greatest Super-Heroes, 1972-1983), rather than continuing with the Adventure Team feel of G.I. Joe. Bulletman's advertising lauded him as being "faster than the speed of light, more powerful than a dynamo...capable of crashing through a brick wall with his steel arms." The Intruders ("Strongmen from Another World") were also introduced in 1976, to provide the Adventure Team with adversaries from outer space. With the outward appearance of armored cavemen, these Intruder figures had an action button on their backs that allowed them to grab Joes with their "Crusher Grip" arms. The final 11-½" G.I. Joe figures produced were The Defenders, a set of plastic-molded mannequins that simply couldn't replace the more sophisticated, more articulated G.I. Joe figures in collector's hearts. From 1977-78, G.I. Joe figures were scaled down to a more manageable 8" size when Hasbro introduced the Super Joe Adventure Team, and the company went "cosmic" with their toy line. Now G.I. Joe battled intergalactic villains such as Gor, Luminos, and Terron for the fate of the universe with all new equipment sets and a newly constructed command center. The line only lasted two years. The G.I. Joe line ceased production entirely in 1978.

The 1980s

While watching the overwhelming success of Kenner's *Star Wars* line of action figures (1977-1984), Hasbro decided to reintroduce G.I. Joe to the American toy marketplace in the early 1980s. Deciding to make G.I. Joe a *group* of specialists rather than an individual fighting soldier, the G.I. Joe team was launched in 1982, and nobody could have imagined the success this new incarnation would have on the toy market. Shrunk to 3 ¾" tall and originally pitched as an action vehicle line, the G.I. Joe team took the world by storm because of the toys' excellent design (the most articulation introduced at such a small scale [along with Mego's Micronauts]), interchangeable "snap on, stay on" accessories, beautiful packaging artwork, and expert characterization by Marvel comic book writer and toy biography author Larry Hama. As an added bonus, on the back of each figure package was a cut-out "Combat Command File Card" that helped to suspend children's beliefs—collectible biographies that made them consider that the toy they bought was truly a three-dimensional character that might exist as part of the real world. These file cards outlined a G.I. Joe team member's personality (or Cobra villain's persona), the character's military specialty, their personal and military

background, and their special code name, which was also provided. These file card dossiers were an important contribution to the process by which toys are marketed—and continue to be an industry standard today.

Originally consisting of 13 G.I. Joe team members and a mere three Cobra villains in 1982, over the course of the next 12 years, Hasbro produced more than 500 different 3-¾" action figures and nearly 300 vehicles and accessories. The success and endurance of the G.I. Joe line was maintained by a Marvel comic book tie-in (155 total issues), a syndicated cartoon program (first produced by Marvel/Sunbow, then by DIC), and television commercials that leapt from the small screen into children's living rooms. The characters introduced in the 1980s incarnation of G.I. Joe still endure: Snake Eyes, Storm Shadow, Duke, Cobra Commander, Scarlett, the Baroness, Shipwreck, Hawk, Destro, and many, many others.

The 1990s

The success of the 3-¾" G.I. Joe line waned in the early '90s as neon action figure colors and poorly designed vehicles dominated the retail shelves. Collectors lost interest in the toy line: it was cancelled in 1994. It wasn't until 1997 and 1998 that these fans would receive new 3-¾" offerings in the form of a few select Toys 'R Us Exclusives that were simple repaints of the original figures and vehicles. These figures sold fairly well, and allowed Hasbro to reintroduce the 3-¾" G.I. Joe line in a larger format in 2000. The 11 ½" G.I. Joe line experienced a renaissance in the 1990s, first with the introduction of 1991's Duke: Master Sergeant exclusive that sold quite briskly. Hasbro capitalized on Duke's success by introducing a "Hall of Fame" line of 11-½" figures based on the characters from the '80s G.I. Joe team. Although 1994 would mark the final year of production for the original run of 3-¾" Joes, Hasbro still celebrated the 30th Anniversary of the G.I. Joe (1964-1994) line by showing a series of "Commemorative Collection" figures at the 1994 International Toy Fair that were met with thunderous applause. Created in both scales—11 ½" and 3 ¾"—collectors were once again treated to the four original Joes from within their respective service branches.

Hasbro still felt that a smaller scale of action figures would be successful, yet 1995 saw the Sgt. Savage and his Screaming Eagles line fail, while 1996's G.I. Joe Extreme fell flat as well, lasting only two years. 1996 gave 11 ½" aficionados the Classic Collection of

"original" Joes, a line that built on the success of the original 1964-1968 run. The Classic Collection grew to incorporate many different figures that represented every branch of military service, and nearly every U.S. military conflict. In 1998, Hasbro released a Timeless Collection (1998-2003) of 11 ½" figures. These Target retail exclusives reproduced Joe figures from the 1960's with an assortment of expertly crafted equipment. In 1999, the G.I. Joe line turned 35, and fans were happy to welcome many celebrity 11 ½" figures: Teddy Roosevelt, Ted Williams, John F. Kennedy, and even astronaut Buzz Aldrin. In 2000, Hasbro concocted the Adventures of G.I. Joe, where new action sets were introduced to the marketplace: Save the Tiger, Challenge at Hawk River, and Peril of the Raging Inferno thrilled longtime fans. By 2000, the 11-½" Joe line was still chugging along.

The 2000s

The G.I. Joe Real American Hero Collection (2000-2002) gave Hasbro an opportunity to see how much demand there was for the "little Joes," and since it was modestly popular, the G.I. Joe vs. Cobra line was born in 2002 (sub lines: Spy Troops, Valor vs. Venom). Featuring all new sculpts and accessories, the 3 ¾" line met a great deal of success until 2005, when the 3 ¾:" line went Direct to Consumer as an Internet exclusive.

In 2007, Hasbro returned to its roots with the 3 ¾" line, producing a 25th Anniversary collection of action figures and vehicles, utilizing all-new figure sculpts, fully painted card and packaging artwork, and an eye for detail. These 25th Anniversary figures and vehicles command excellent prices on the secondary market. Although the 25th Anniversary label was dropped from packages, the line of 3 ¾" G.I. Joes continues to this day, fueled by the films *G.I. Joe: The Rise of Cobra* (2009) and *G.I. Joe: Retaliation* (2013).

Trends

Due to the delayed release of Paramount Pictures' *G.I. Joe: Retaliation* (*G.I. Joe 2*, the sequel to 2009's *G.I. Joe: The Rise of Cobra*) from June 29, 2012, to March 29, 2013, Hasbro Inc. lost *nine months' worth* of revenue from the many product assortments they had readied for release in 2012 and 2013, a fact that caused the entire G.I. Joe collecting community to hold their collective breath—and wallets—waiting for the movie to inject eagerly-anticipated new product onto retail shelves. Although Hasbro saved face with the overwhelming popularity of three other major current product lines (Star Wars, Transformers, and Marvel Comics Super Heroes [Marvel Legends + Marvel Universe]), they still lost money and squandered an opportunity to capitalize on the heralded resurrection of the G.I. Joe brand.

With the promise of more authentic uniforms for both the G.I. Joe team members and the agents of Cobra Command, a better (and stronger) narrative for the brand's most popular characters to negotiate (Cobra Commander, the Arashikage Red Ninja Clan, Roadblock, Duke, and Snake Eyes & Storm Shadow), as well as the inclusion of veteran A-list action heroes Dwayne "The Rock" Johnson and Bruce Willis (let's not forget rising star Channing Tatum), the potential revenue generated by Jon M. Chu's action-packed film would have helped sustain the growth of the brand.

It is unknown whether or not this contributed to Hasbro's poor performance in their quarterly yearly earnings for 2012 (particularly quarter two), but this news certainly didn't help. With a huge promotional push for the film in early 2012, the company and its affiliates may have dropped a considerable amount of capital to promote a movie that was delayed by *forces majeure* at the eleventh hour. Unfortunately, if we couple this film delay with the overall decline in sales for the vintage and modern 11 ½" lines, 2012 was a difficult year for G.I. Joe, and we hope that 2013 will indeed redeem the brand's image.

Speaking to this decline in interest for the original G.I. Joe brand (1964-1976), it is disconcerting to me and shaking the core of my being, that (as a lifelong devotee of the G.I. Joe franchise) there's a waning interest in the original

11 ½" scale of G.I. Joe figures—both modern and vintage. The reason why this comes as a shock to me? Hasbro Incorporated's coffers were filled, expanded, and refreshed on the back of G.I. Joe product in the '60s and '80s. The profits from G.I. Joe allowed the company to *build* other successful brands such as Transformers, and buy other lucrative *brands* such as Marvel Super Heroes and Star Wars; all of these successful Hasbro licenses owe their retail lives to G.I. Joe.

On a related note, for the past few years I have been a guest of the G.I. Joe Collectors Club at their fabulous annual event, the International G.I. Joe Convention, where I take note of the ups-and-downs of the hobby and speak at great length with some of the leading G.I. Joe action figure dealers in the country. At this four-day convention, I daily walk the sales floor to purchase hundreds of dollars of G.I. Joe merchandise (both vintage 3 ¾" and vintage 11 ½"), and have noticed an alarming trend over the past ten years: fewer and fewer vendors who attend the convention are there to sell vintage 11 ½" G.I. Joe product (!). There's such a

The **Top 10 G.I. Joe** in mint condition

1. G.I. Nurse, Hasbro, 1967. . . . .$5,400
2. Action Soldiers of the World Talking Adventure Pack, Hasbro, 1968 . . . .$5,250
3. Canadian Mounties Set, Sears Exclusive, Hasbro, 1967 . . . .$4,300
4. Flying Space Adventure Set, Hasbro, 1970 . . . .$3,750
5. Army Adventure Pack, Bivouac Equipment Set, Hasbro, 1968 . . . .$3,600
6. Crash Crew Fire Truck Set, Hasbro, 1967 . . . .$3,650
7. Talking Shore Patrol Set, Hasbro, 1968 . . . .$3,575
8. Dress Parade Adventure Pack, Hasbro, 1968 . . . .$3,575
9. Talking Landing Signal Officer Set, Hasbro, 1968. . . . .$3,575
10. Shore Patrol Equipment Set, Hasbro, 1967 . . . .$3,500

dearth of these original G.I. Joe figures from the military era of Joe (1964-1969) as well as from the Adventure Team Era (1970-1976), that at the 2012 convention, only FOUR booths out of the fifty total dealers were selling vintage 11 ½" product. Joe's lack of presence at this convention must feel quite discouraging for those diehard 11 ½" attendees. Yet, what is the reason for the decline of vintage 11 ½" dealers at the International G.I. Joe Convention? What's the reason for a declining interest in the 11 ½" franchise? There are many factors that have contributed to this problem.

Since these figures were released between 1964 and 1976, the target market for the vintage G.I. Joe action figure line was boys growing up at the *tail end* of the Baby Boomer era (those born between 1946-1964) and *before* Generation X (born between the early 1960s to the early 1980s). However, this target market of potential collectors seems to have let their interest in the line wane a bit; it appears that most of the G.I. Joe line's brand awareness is for the characters established in the 1980s (Duke, Cobra Commander, Snake-Eyes, etc.), not the Action Soldier, Action Sailor, Action Marine, and Action Pilot of the 1960s. Since

these four types of original G.I. Joe figures (representing the four service branches) did not have a media tie-in, and the '80s line did (television, comic book, film, etc.), the more recent '80's toy line has endured. Hasbro has established brand awareness for the '80s product and its related characters with recent animated programs, a blockbuster film, and five different IDW comic books per month. A media push does not exist for the original 11 ½" line.

This lack of brand awareness for the vintage 11 ½" G.I. Joe line is definitely hurting the hobby. Furthermore, modern American children are simply not replacing the aging fans of the "big Joes" who've retired, passed on, or have left the hobby because of the lack of disposable income and financial insolvency due to the global economic crisis. Diehard 11 ½" G.I. Joe fans simply must pass their love of the genre on to their children and grandchildren, since that's what caused the brand to succeed in the first place; fathers and grandfather who were veterans of WWI, WWII, and Korea who saw this magnificent, authentically-styled military line of action figures in their local department store and leapt at the chance to share their military experiences with their sons or grandsons. Due to these numerous obstacles, the prices of many pieces of 11 ½" vintage G.I. Joe memorabilia have certainly decreased; some pieces, quite dramatically.

However, the premiere pieces of the line have managed not only to keep their prices intact but also to generate interest and a resultant rise in value. Moreover, any vintage 11 ½" G.I. Joe toy that's Mint in Sealed Box (MISB) will cause quite a stir on eBay or other auction sites. The existence of any high grade sealed samples of product from 1964-1976 is almost negligible; if you find a sealed piece in a dead-mint condition package, more than likely you'll NEVER come across that treasure again. You see, most vintage 11 ½" product is found loose—usually in a worn footlocker or two—and the clothes, weapons, accessories, and other soft goods (tents, etc.) are rarely found in excellent condition, much less mint condition. The only method a collector may use to guarantee mint condition 11 ½" product? Buying sealed samples; a technique that quickly becomes inordinately expensive.

Where sealed samples of vintage 3 ¾" pieces from the 1980s are available on eBay or in secondary stores (perhaps not in abundance, but they're most certainly available for sale on a fairly regular basis), vintage MISB 11 ½" pieces are literally worth their weight in gold. If you can obtain them for a decent price, early high-grade samples of 1964-1969 military-era 11 ½" G.I. Joes are always an excellent investment.

Don't be caught off guard when the 2013 blockbuster *G.I. Joe: Retaliation* hits theaters. Expect figures based on the iconic 1980s characters utilized in the movie to become desirable once again. And hopefully, the 11 ½" line will follow suit…

Original Series and Adventure Team (1964-78)

ACTION GIRL SERIES
Figure Sets

G.I. Nurse, 1967, Hasbro, Red Cross hat and arm band, white dress, stockings, shoes, crutches, medic bag, stethoscope, plasma bottle, bandages and splints, Model No. 8060

EX $1850 **NM** $2300 **MIP** $5400

ACTION MARINE SERIES
Figure Sets

Action Marine, 1964, Hasbro, fatigues, green cap, boots, dog tags, insignias and manual, Model No. 7700

EX $135 **NM** $210 **MIP** $450

Marine Medic Series, 1967, Hasbro, Red Cross helmet, flag and arm bands, crutch, bandages, splints, first aid pouch, stethoscope, plasma bottle, stretcher, medic bag, belt w/ammo pouches, Model No. 90711

EX $310 **NM** $400 **MIP** $1400

Talking Action Marine, 1967, Hasbro, Model No. 7790

EX $175 **NM** $210 **MIP** $800

Talking Adventure Pack, 1968, Hasbro, w/Field Pack Equipment, Model No. 90712

EX $250 **NM** $310 **MIP** $1400

Talking Adventure Pack and Tent Set, 1968, Hasbro, Model No. 90711

EX $250 **NM** $300 **MIP** $1600

Uniform/Equipment Sets

Beachhead Assault Field Pack Set, 1964, Hasbro, M-1 rifle, bayonet, entrenching shovel and cover, canteen w/cover, belt, mess kit w/cover, field pack, flamethrower, first aid pouch, tent, pegs and poles, tent camo and camo, Model No. 7713

EX $75 **NM** $110 **MIP** $290

Beachhead Assault Tent Set, 1964, Hasbro, tent, flamethrower, pistol belt, first-aid pouch, mess kit w/utensils and manual, Model No. 7711

EX $75 **NM** $175 **MIP** $390

Beachhead Fatigue Pants, 1964, Hasbro, Model No. 7715

EX $15 **NM** $30 **MIP** $200

Beachhead Fatigue Shirt, 1964, Hasbro, Model No. 7714

EX $20 **NM** $30 **MIP** $225

Beachhead Field Pack, 1964, Hasbro, cartridge belt, rifle, grenades, field pack, entrenching tool, canteen and manual, Model No. 7712

EX $30 **NM** $60 **MIP** $135

Beachhead Flamethrower Set, 1964, Hasbro, Model No. 7718

EX $15 **NM** $30 **MIP** $125

Beachhead Flamethrower Set, 1967, Hasbro, reissue, Model No. 7718

EX $15 **NM** $30 **MIP** $225

Beachhead Mess Kit Set, 1964, Hasbro, Model No. 7716

EX $25 **NM** $40 **MIP** $275

Beachhead Rifle Set, 1964, Hasbro, bayonet, cartridge belt, hand grenades and M-1 rifle, Model No. 7717

EX $30 **NM** $50 **MIP** $150

Beachhead Rifle Set, 1967, Hasbro, reissue, Model No. 7717

EX $30 **NM** $50 **MIP** $225

Communications Field Radio/Telephone Set, 1967, Hasbro, reissue, Model No. 7703

EX $35 **NM** $60 **MIP** $275

Communications Field Set, 1964, Hasbro, Model No. 7703

EX $35 **NM** $50 **MIP** $175

Communications Flag Set, 1964, Hasbro, flags for Army, Navy, Air Corps, Marines and United States, Model No. 7704

EX $190 **NM** $210 **MIP** $425

Communications Poncho, 1964, Hasbro, Model No. 7702

EX $35 **NM** $50 **MIP** $250

Communications Post and Poncho Set, 1964, Hasbro, field radio and telephone, wire roll, carbine, binoculars, map, case, manual, poncho, Model No. 7701

EX $125 **NM** $175 **MIP** $475

Dress Parade Set, 1964, Hasbro, Marine jacket, trousers, pistol belt, shoes, hat, M-1 rifle, and manual, Model No. 7710

EX $150 **NM** $250 **MIP** $550

Dress Parade Set, 1968, Hasbro, reissue, Model No. 7710

EX $125 **NM** $225 **MIP** $750

Jungle Fighter Set, 1967, Hasbro, bush hat, jacket w/emblems, pants, flamethrower, field telephone, knife and sheath, pistol belt, pistol, holster, canteen w/cover and knuckle knife, Model No. 7732

EX $480 **NM** $800 **MIP** $1500

Jungle Fighter Set, 1968, Hasbro, reissue, Model No. 7732

EX $450 **NM** $700 **MIP** $1050

Marine Automatic M-60 Machine Gun Set, 1967, Hasbro, Model No. 7726

EX $35 **NM** $75 **MIP** $325

Marine Basics Set, 1966, Hasbro, Model No. 7722

EX $55 **NM** $85 **MIP** $275

Marine Bunk Bed Set, 1966, Hasbro, Model No. 7723

EX $55 **NM** $80 **MIP** $375

Marine Bunk Bed Set, 1967, Hasbro, reissue, Model No. 7723

EX $55 **NM** $175 **MIP** $350

Marine Demolition Set, 1966, Hasbro, mine detector and harness, land mine, Model No. 7730
EX $50   **NM** $100   **MIP** $350

Marine Demolition Set, 1968, Hasbro, reissue, Model No. 7730
EX $50   **NM** $145   **MIP** $400

Marine First Aid Set, 1964, Hasbro, first-aid pouch, arm band and helmet, Model No. 7721
EX $45   **NM** $85   **MIP** $125

Marine First Aid Set, 1967, Hasbro, reissue, Model No. 7721
EX $45   **NM** $85   **MIP** $225

Marine Medic Set, 1965, Hasbro, w/crutch, etc., Model No. 7720
EX $35   **NM** $60   **MIP** $150

Marine Medic Set, 1967, Hasbro, reissue, Model No. 7720
EX $35   **NM** $60   **MIP** $235

Marine Medic Set w/Stretcher, 1964, Hasbro, first-aid shoulder pouch, stretcher, bandages, arm bands, plasma bottle, stethoscope, Red Cross flag, and manual, Model No. 7719
EX $175   **NM** $300   **MIP** $850

Marine Mortar Set, 1967, Hasbro, Model No. 7725
EX $60   **NM** $80   **MIP** $350

Marine Weapons Rack Set, 1967, Hasbro, Model No. 7727
EX $75   **NM** $145   **MIP** $625

Paratrooper Camouflage Set, 1964, Hasbro, netting and foliage, Model No. 7708
EX $20   **NM** $35   **MIP** $65

Paratrooper Helmet Set, 1964, Hasbro, Model No. 7707
EX $20   **NM** $40   **MIP** $85

Paratrooper Parachute Pack, 1964, Hasbro, Model No. 7709
EX $30   **NM** $80   **MIP** $125

Paratrooper Small Arms Set, 1967, Hasbro, reissue, Model No. 7706
EX $30   **NM** $75   **MIP** $225

Tank Commander Set, 1967, Hasbro, includes faux leather jacket, helmet and visor, insignia, radio w/tripod, machine gun, ammo box, Model No. 7731
EX $355   **NM** $560   **MIP** $1400

Tank Commander Set, 1968, Hasbro, reissue, Model No. 7731
EX $325   **NM** $500   **MIP** $1200

ACTION PILOT SERIES

Figure Sets

Action Pilot, 1964, Hasbro, orange jumpsuit, blue cap, black boots, dog tags, insignias, manual, catalog and club application, Model No. 7800
EX $145   **NM** $170   **MIP** $510

Talking Action Pilot, 1967, Hasbro, Model No. 7890
EX $200   **NM** $255   **MIP** $1500

Uniform/Equipment Sets

Air Academy Cadet Set, 1967, Hasbro, deluxe set w/figure, dress jacket, shoes, and pants, garrison cap, saber and scabbard, white M-1 rifle, chest sash and belt sash, Model No. 7822
EX $220   **NM** $450   **MIP** $1100

Air Academy Cadet Set, 1968, Hasbro, reissue, Model No. 7822
EX $210   **NM** $410   **MIP** $900

Air Force Basics Set, 1966, Hasbro, Model No. 7814
EX $30   **NM** $55   **MIP** $200

Air Force Basics Set, 1967, Hasbro, reissue, Model No. 7814
EX $30   **NM** $55   **MIP** $275

Air Force Mae West Air Vest & Equipment Set, 1967, Hasbro, Model No. 7816
EX $85   **NM** $125   **MIP** $325

Air Force Police Set, 1965, Hasbro, Model No. 7813
EX $70   **NM** $150   **MIP** $250

Air Force Police Set, 1967, Hasbro, reissue, Model No. 7813
EX $70   **NM** $150   **MIP** $325

Air Force Security Set, 1967, Hasbro, Air Security radio and helmet, cartridge belt, pistol and holster, Model No. 7815
EX $290   **NM** $375   **MIP** $610

Air/Sea Rescue Set, 1967, Hasbro, includes black air tanks, rescue ring, buoy, depth gauge, face mask, fins, orange scuba outfit, Model No. 7825
EX $310   **NM** $500   **MIP** $1450

Air/Sea Rescue Set, 1968, Hasbro, reissue, Model No. 7825
EX $310   **NM** $500   **MIP** $1450

Astronaut Set, 1967, Hasbro, helmet w/visor, foil space suit, booties, gloves, space camera, propellant gun, tether cord, oxygen chest pack, silver boots, white jumpsuit and cloth cap, Model No. 7824
EX $120   **NM** $210   **MIP** $2800

Astronaut Set, 1968, Hasbro, reissue, Model No. 7824
EX $85   **NM** $230   **MIP** $800

Communications Set, 1964, Hasbro, Model No. 7812
EX $55   **NM** $100   **MIP** $225

Crash Crew Set, 1966, Hasbro, fire proof jacket, hood, pants and gloves, silver boots, belt, flashlight, axe, pliers, fire extinguisher, stretcher, strap cutter, Model No. 7820
EX $135   **NM** $250   **MIP** $450

Dress Uniform Jacket Set, 1964, Hasbro, Model No. 7804
EX $40   **NM** $65   **MIP** $250

Dress Uniform Pants, 1964, Hasbro, Model No. 7805
EX $20   **NM** $35   **MIP** $200

Dress Uniform Set, 1964, Hasbro, Air Force jacket, trousers, shirt, tie, cap and manual, Model No. 7803
EX $225   **NM** $550   **MIP** $1650

Dress Uniform Shirt & Equipment Set, 1964, Hasbro, Model No. 7806
EX $25   **NM** $40   **MIP** $200

Fighter Pilot Set, 1967, Hasbro, working parachute and pack, gold helmet, Mae West vest, green pants, flash light, orange jump suit, black boots, Model No. 7823
EX $400   **NM** $625   **MIP** $1450

Fighter Pilot Set, 1968, Hasbro, reissue, Model No. 7823
EX $400   **NM** $625   **MIP** $1450

Scramble Communications Set, 1965, Hasbro, poncho, field telephone and radio, map w/case, binoculars and wire roll, Model No. 7812
EX $35   **NM** $75   **MIP** $175

Scramble Communications Set, 1967, Hasbro, reissue, Model No. 7812
EX $35   **NM** $75   **MIP** $250

Scramble Crash Helmet, 1964, Hasbro, helmet, face mask, hose, tinted visor, Model No. 7810
EX $65   **NM** $90   **MIP** $125

Scramble Crash Helmet, 1967, Hasbro, reissue, Model No. 7810
EX $65   **NM** $90   **MIP** $225

Scramble Flight Suit, 1964, Hasbro, gray flight suit, Model No. 7808
EX $50   **NM** $225   **MIP** $300

Scramble Flight Suit, 1967, Hasbro, Model No. 7808
EX $50   NM $75   MIP $400

Scramble Parachute Set, 1964, Hasbro, Model No. 7811
EX $20   NM $40   MIP $150

Scramble Parachute Set, 1967, Hasbro, reissue, Model No. 7809
EX $20   NM $40   MIP $250

Scramble Set, 1964, Hasbro, deluxe set, gray flight suit, orange air vest, white crash helmet, pistol belt w/.45 pistol, holster, clipboard, flare gun and parachute w/insert, Model No. 7807
EX $130   NM $210   MIP $900

Survival Life Raft Set, 1964, Hasbro, raft w/oar, flare gun, knife, air vest, first-aid kit, sea anchor and manual, Model No. 7801
EX $75   NM $125   MIP $550

Survival Life Raft Set, 1964, Hasbro, raft w/oar and sea anchor, Model No. 7802
EX $45   NM $90   MIP $325

Vehicle Sets

Crash Crew Fire Truck Set, 1967, Hasbro, includes blue truck and fireproof silver suit, truck has working firehose, Model No. 8040
EX $825   NM $1600   MIP $3400

Official Space Capsule Set, 1966, Hasbro, space capsule, record, space suit, cloth space boots, space gloves, helmet w/visor, Model No. 8020
EX $225   NM $280   MIP $400

Official Space Capsule Set w/Flotation, 1966, Hasbro, Sears Exclusive w/collar, life raft and oars, Model No. 5979
EX $200   NM $325   MIP $700

Spacewalk Mystery, 1969, Hasbro, Model No. 7981
EX $120   NM $265   MIP $450

ACTION SAILOR SERIES
Figure Sets

Action Sailor, 1964, Hasbro, white cap, denim shirt and pants, boots, dog tags, navy manual and insignias, Model No. 7600
EX $140   NM $250   MIP $480

Navy Scuba Set, 1968, Hasbro, Adventure Pack, Model No. 7643-83
EX $320   NM $475   MIP $3575

Talking Action Sailor, 1967, Hasbro, Model No. 7690
EX $200   NM $330   MIP $1250

Talking Landing Signal Officer Set, 1968, Hasbro, Talking Adventure Pack, Model No. 90621
EX $325   NM $350   MIP $3500

Talking Shore Patrol Set, 1968, Hasbro, Talking Adventure Pack, Model No. 90612
EX $200   NM $450   MIP $3500

Uniform/Equipment Sets

Annapolis Cadet, 1967, Hasbro, garrison cap, dress jacket, pants, shoes, sword, scabbard, belt and white M-1 rifle, Model No. 7624
EX $310   NM $390   MIP $1400

Annapolis Cadet, 1968, Hasbro, reissue, Model No. 7624
EX $275   NM $375   MIP $1350

Breeches Buoy, 1967, Hasbro, yellow jacket and pants, chair and pulley, flare gun, blinker light, Model No. 7625
EX $325   NM $425   MIP $1500

Breeches Buoy, 1968, Hasbro, reissue, Model No. 7625
EX $325   NM $425   MIP $1450

Deep Freeze, 1967, Hasbro, white boots, fur parka, pants, snow shoes, ice axe, snow sled w/rope and flare gun, Model No. 7623
EX $220   NM $350   MIP $1400

Deep Freeze, 1968, Hasbro, reissue, Model No. 7623
EX $220   NM $350   MIP $1300

Deep Sea Diver Set, 1965, Hasbro, underwater uniform, helmet, upper and lower plate, sledge hammer, buoy w/rope, gloves, compass, hoses, lead boots and weight belt, Model No. 7620
EX $325   NM $425   MIP $1850

Deep Sea Diver Set, 1968, Hasbro, reissue, Model No. 7620
EX $325   NM $425   MIP $1850

Frogman Scuba Bottoms, 1964, Hasbro, Model No. 7604
EX $20   NM $35   MIP $100

Frogman Scuba Tank Set, 1964, Hasbro, Model No. 7606
EX $25   NM $40   MIP $100

Frogman Scuba Top Set, 1964, Hasbro, Model No. 7603
EX $25   NM $45   MIP $125

Frogman Underwater Demolition Set, 1964, Hasbro, headpiece, face mask, swim fins, rubber suit, scuba tank, depth gauge, knife, dynamite, and manual, Model No. 7602
EX $175   NM $250   MIP $1500

Landing Signal Officer, 1966, Hasbro, jumpsuit, signal paddles, goggles, cloth head gear, headphones, clipboard (complete), binoculars, and flare gun, Model No. 7621
EX $225   NM $350   MIP $575

Navy Attack Helmet Set, 1964, shirt and pants, boots, yellow life vest, blue helmet, flare gun binoculars, signal flags, Model No. 7610
EX $35   NM $75   MIP $150

Navy Attack Life Jacket, 1964, Hasbro, Model No. 7611
EX $20   NM $45   MIP $120

Navy Attack Set, 1964, Hasbro, life jacket, field glasses, blinker light, signal flags, manual, Model No. 7607
EX $60   NM $125   MIP $425

Navy Attack Work Pants Set, 1964, Hasbro, Model No. 7609
EX $25   NM $40   MIP $150

Navy Attack Work Shirt Set, 1964, Hasbro, Model No. 7608
EX $25   NM $40   MIP $175

Navy Basics Set, 1966, Hasbro, Model No. 7628
EX $25   NM $55   MIP $125

Navy Dress Parade Rifle Set, 1965, Hasbro, Model No. 7619
EX $35   NM $65   MIP $125

Navy Dress Parade Set, 1964, Hasbro, billy club, cartridge belt, bayonet and white dress rifle, Model No. 7619
EX $45   NM $80   MIP $175

Navy L.S.O. Equipment Set, 1966, Hasbro, helmet, headphones, signal paddles, flare gun, Model No. 7626
EX $40   NM $80   MIP $150

Navy Life Ring Set, 1966, Hasbro, U.S.N. life ring, helmet sticker, Model No. 7627
EX $25   NM $45   MIP $150

Navy Machine Gun Set, 1965, Hasbro, MG and ammo box, Model No. 7618

EX $40   **NM** $80   **MIP** $175

Sea Rescue Set, 1964, Hasbro, life raft, oar, anchor, flare gun, first-aid kit, knife, scabbard, manual, Model No. 7601

EX $95   **NM** $135   **MIP** $500

Sea Rescue Set, 1966, Hasbro, reissued w/life preserver, Model No. 7622

EX $95   **NM** $135   **MIP** $500

Shore Patrol, 1964, Hasbro, dress shirt, tie and pants, helmet, white belt, .45 and holster, billy club, boots, arm band, sea bag, Model No. 7612

EX $425   **NM** $905   **MIP** $1800

Shore Patrol, 1967, Hasbro, reissued w/radio and helmet and shoes, Model No. 7612

EX $1100 **NM** $2100   **MIP** $3575

Shore Patrol Dress Jumper Set, 1964, Hasbro, Model No. 7613

EX $75   **NM** $125   **MIP** $225

Shore Patrol Dress Pant Set, 1964, Hasbro, Model No. 7614

EX $40   **NM** $75   **MIP** $175

Shore Patrol Helmet and Small Arms Set, 1964, Hasbro, white belt, billy stick, white helmet, .45 pistol, Model No. 7616

EX $40   **NM** $75   **MIP** $150

Shore Patrol Sea Bag Set, 1964, Hasbro, Model No. 7615

EX $25   **NM** $50   **MIP** $125

Vehicle Sets

Official Sea Sled and Frogman Set, 1966, Hasbro, w/out cave, Model No. 8050

EX $150   **NM** $300   **MIP** $550

Official Sea Sled and Frogman Set, 1966, Hasbro, Sears, w/figure and underwater cave, orange scuba suit, fins, mask, tanks, sea sled in orange and black, Model No. 5979

EX $175   **NM** $325   **MIP** $650

ACTION SOLDIER SERIES

Figure Sets

Action Soldier, 1964, Hasbro, fatigue cap, shirt, pants, boots, dog tags, army manual and insignias, M-1 rifle, Model No. 7500

EX $135   **NM** $230   **MIP** $510

Black Action Soldier, 1965, Hasbro, fatigue cap, shirt, pants, boots, dog tags, army manual and insignias, M-1 rifle, Model No. 7900

EX $400   **NM** $700   **MIP** $1950

Canadian Mountie Set, 1967, Hasbro, Sears Exclusive, Model No. 5904

EX $925   **NM** $2000   **MIP** $4300

Desert Patrol Attack Jeep Set, 1967, Hasbro, Desert Fighter figure, jeep w/steering wheel, spare tire, tan tripod, gun and gun mount and ring, black antenna, tan jacket and shorts, socks, goggles, Model No. 8030

EX $400   **NM** $1250   **MIP** $2000

Forward Observer Set, 1966, Hasbro, Sears Exclusive, 51 pieces, Model No. 5969

EX $200   **NM** $375   **MIP** $750

Green Beret, 1966, Hasbro, field radio, green beret, jacket, pants, M-16 rifle, six grenades, camo scarf, belt pistol and holster, Model No. 7536

EX $250   **NM** $510   **MIP** $2700

Green Beret Machine Gun Outpost Set, 1966, Hasbro, Sears Exclusive, two figures, two uniform shirts, two uniform pants, two cartridge belts, two green berets, two dog tags, two pair boots, M-16 rifle, tripod, field radio, bazooka, six bazooka shells, foliage, six tent poles, six grenades, machine gun, ammo box, netting, tent stakes, six plugs, eight rope loops, Model No. 5978

EX $350   **NM** $650   **MIP** $3400

Machine Gun Emplacement Set, 1965, Hasbro, Sears Exclusive, 27 pieces, Model No. 5931

EX $150   **NM** $275   **MIP** $1250

Talking Action Soldier, 1967, Hasbro, Model No. 7590

EX $85   **NM** $135   **MIP** $825

Talking Adventure Pack, Bivouac Equipment, 1967, Hasbro, Model No. 90513

EX $250 NM $300 MIP $2800

Talking Adventure Pack, Command Post Equipment, 1968, Hasbro, Model No. 90517

EX $250 NM $325 MIP $2500

Talking Adventure Pack, Mountain Troop Series, 1967, Hasbro, Model No. 7557-83

EX $325 NM $600 MIP $2950

Talking Adventure Pack, Special Forces Equipment, 1968, Hasbro, Model No. 90532

EX $235 NM $450 MIP $2950

Uniform/Equipment Sets

Adventure Pack w/12 items, 1968, Hasbro, Adventure Pack Footlocker, Model No. 8005.83

EX $75 NM $125 MIP $600

Adventure Pack w/12 items, 1968, Hasbro, Adventure Pack Footlocker, Model No. 8006.83

EX $75 NM $125 MIP $600

Adventure Pack w/14 pieces, 1968, Hasbro, Adventure Pack Footlocker, Model No. 8008.83

EX $75 NM $125 MIP $600

Adventure Pack w/16 items, 1968, Hasbro, Adventure Pack Footlocker, Model No. 8007.83

EX $75 NM $125 MIP $600

Adventure Pack, Army Bivouac Series, 1967, Hasbro, Model No. 7549-83

EX $210 NM $400 MIP $3300

Air Police Equipment, 1964, Hasbro, gray field phone, carbine, white helmet and bayonet, Model No. 7813

EX $40 NM $95 MIP $200

Basic Footlocker, 1964, Hasbro, wood tray w/cardboard wrapper, Model No. 8000

EX $35 NM $75 MIP $125

Bivouac Deluxe Pup Tent Set, 1964, Hasbro, M-1 rifle and bayonet, shovel and cover, canteen and cover, mess kit, cartridge belt, machine gun, tent, pegs, poles, camouflage, sleeping bag, netting, ammo box, Model No. 7513

EX $115 NM $225 MIP $450

Bivouac Machine Gun Set, 1964, Hasbro, machine gun set and ammo box, Model No. 7514

EX $25 NM $40 MIP $125

Bivouac Machine Gun Set, 1967, Hasbro, reissue, Model No. 7514

EX $25 NM $40 MIP $225

Bivouac Sleeping Bag, 1964, Hasbro, zippered bag, Model No. 7515

EX $20 NM $30 MIP $125

Bivouac Sleeping Bag Set, 1964, Hasbro, mess kit, canteen, bayonet, cartridge belt, M-1 rifle, manual, Model No. 7512

EX $25 NM $30 MIP $150

Combat Camouflaged Netting Set, 1964, Hasbro, foliage and posts, Model No. 7511

EX $25 NM $40 MIP $85

Combat Construction Set, 1967, Hasbro, orange safety helmet, work gloves, jack hammer, Model No. 7572

EX $325 NM $400 MIP $575

Combat Demolition Set, 1967, Hasbro, Model No. 7573

EX $65 NM $100 MIP $525

Combat Engineer Set, 1967, Hasbro, pick, shovel, detonator, dynamite, tripod, and transit w/grease gun, Model No. 7571

EX $125 NM $175 MIP $625

Combat Fatigue Pants Set, 1964, Hasbro, Model No. 7504

EX $15 NM $25 MIP $110

Combat Fatigue Shirt Set, 1964, Hasbro, Model No. 7503

EX $20 NM $30 MIP $125

Combat Field Jacket, 1964, Hasbro, Model No. 7505

EX $45 NM $65 MIP $325

Combat Field Jacket Set, 1964, Hasbro, jacket, bayonet, cartridge belt, hand grenades, M-1 rifle, and manual, Model No. 7501

EX $65 NM $100 MIP $525

Combat Field Pack & Entrenching Tool, 1964, Hasbro, Model No. 7506

EX $25 NM $45 MIP $125

Combat Field Pack Deluxe Set, 1964, Hasbro, field jacket, pack, entrenching shovel w/cover, mess kit, first-aid pouch, canteen w/cover, Model No. 7502

EX $75 NM $125 MIP $325

Combat Helmet Set, 1964, Hasbro, w/netting and foliage leaves, Model No. 7507

EX $20 NM $35 MIP $75

Combat Mess Kit, 1964, Hasbro, plate, fork, knife, spoon, canteen, etc., Model No. 7509

EX $20 NM $45 MIP $85

Combat Rifle Set, 1967, Hasbro, bayonet, M-1 rifle, belt and grenades, Model No. 7510

EX $55 NM $100 MIP $325

Combat Sandbags Set, 1964, Hasbro, three bags per set, Model No. 7508

EX $10 NM $40 MIP $85

Command Post Field Radio and Telephone Set, 1964, Hasbro, field radio, telephone w/wire roll and map, Model No. 7520

EX $30 NM $60 MIP $370

Command Post Field Radio and Telephone Set, 1967, Hasbro, reissue, Model No. 7520

EX $35 NM $70 MIP $400

Command Post Poncho, 1964, Hasbro, on card, Model No. 7519

EX $30 NM $45 MIP $225

Command Post Poncho Set, 1964, Hasbro, poncho, field radio and telephone, wire roll, pistol, belt and holster, map and case and manual, Model No. 7517

EX $85 NM $125 MIP $400

Command Post Small Arms Set, 1964, Hasbro, holster and .45 pistol, belt, grenades, Model No. 7518

EX $30 NM $60 MIP $100

Dress Parade Adventure Pack, 1968, Hasbro, Adventure Pack w/37 pieces, Model No. 8009.83

EX $800 NM $1300 MIP $3575

Green Beret and Small Arms Set, 1966, Hasbro, Model No. 7533

EX $85 NM $110 MIP $300

Green Beret and Small Arms Set, 1967, Hasbro, reissue, Model No. 7533

EX $85 NM $100 MIP $425

Green Beret Machine Gun Outpost Set, 1966, Hasbro, Sears Exclusive w/two figures and equipment, Model No. 5978

EX $225   **NM** $450   **MIP** $1500

Heavy Weapons Set, 1967, Hasbro, mortar launcher and shells, M-60 machine gun, grenades, flak jacket, shirt and pants, Model No. 7538

EX $160   **NM** $300   **MIP** $1700

Heavy Weapons Set, 1968, Hasbro, reissue, Model No. 7538

EX $175   **NM** $325   **MIP** $1500

Military Police Duffle Bag Set, 1964, Hasbro, Model No. 7523

EX $25   **NM** $40   **MIP** $85

Military Police Helmet and Small Arms Set, 1964, Hasbro, Model No. 7526

EX $35   **NM** $75   **MIP** $125

Military Police Helmet and Small Arms Set, 1967, Hasbro, reissue, Model No. 7526

EX $35   **NM** $75   **MIP** $250

Military Police Ike Jacket, 1964, Hasbro, jacket w/red scarf and arm band, Model No. 7524

EX $45   **NM** $65   **MIP** $130

Military Police Ike Pants, 1964, Hasbro, matches Ike jacket, Model No. 7525

EX $20   **NM** $30   **MIP** $100

Military Police Uniform Set, 1964, Hasbro, includes Ike jacket and pants, scarf, boots, helmet, belt w/ammo pouches, .45 pistol and holster, billy club, armband, duffle bag, Model No. 7521

EX $400   **NM** $1550   **MIP** $2800

Military Police Uniform Set, 1967, Hasbro, includes green or tan uniform, black and gold MP Helmet, billy club, belt, pistol and holster, MP armband and red tunic, Model No. 7539

EX $380   **NM** $1500   **MIP** $3300

Military Police Uniform Set, 1968, Hasbro, reissue, Model No. 7539

EX $425   **NM** $850   **MIP** $2900

America's *movable* fighting man

Mountain Troops Set, 1964, Hasbro, snow shoes, ice axe, ropes, grenades, camoflage pack, web belt, manual, Model No. 7530

EX $80   **NM** $160   **MIP** $260

Sabotage Set, 1967, Hasbro, dingy and oar, blinker light, detonator w/strap, TNT, wool stocking cap, gas mask, binoculars, green radio and .45 pistol and holster, Model No. 7516

EX $110   **NM** $225   **MIP** $1850

Sabotage Set, 1968, Hasbro, reissued in photo box, Model No. 7516

EX $125   **NM** $250   **MIP** $1700

Ski Patrol Deluxe Set, 1964, Hasbro, white parka, boots, goggles, mittens, skis, poles, and manual, Model No. 7531

EX $170   **NM** $350   **MIP** $1250

Ski Patrol Helmet and Small Arms Set, 1965, Hasbro, Model No. 7527

EX $35   **NM** $75   **MIP** $135

Ski Patrol Helmet and Small Arms Set, 1967, Hasbro, reissue, Model No. 7527

EX $75   **NM** $125   **MIP** $250

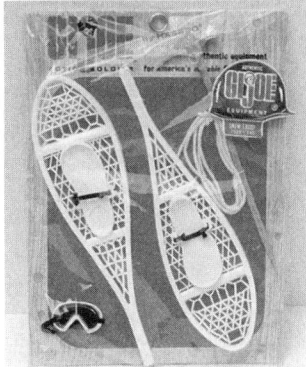

Snow Troop Set, 1966, Hasbro, snow shoes, goggles and ice pick, Model No. 7529

EX $20   **NM** $45   **MIP** $150

Snow Troop Set, 1967, Hasbro, reissue, Model No. 7529

EX $20   **NM** $45   **MIP** $225

Special Forces Bazooka Set, 1966, Hasbro, Model No. 7528

EX $35   **NM** $45   **MIP** $225

Special Forces Bazooka Set, 1967, Hasbro, reissue, Model No. 7528

EX $35   **NM** $45   **MIP** $325

Special Forces Uniform Set, 1966, Hasbro, Model No. 7532

EX $200   **NM** $375   **MIP** $1000

West Point Cadet Uniform Set, 1967, Hasbro, dress jacket, pants, shoes, chest and belt sash, parade hat w/plume, saber, scabbard, and white M-1 rifle, Model No. 7537

EX $240   **NM** $450   **MIP** $1450

West Point Cadet Uniform Set, 1968, Hasbro, reissue, Model No. 7537

EX $250   **NM** $375   **MIP** $1200

Vehicle Sets

Amphibious Duck, 1967, Irwin, 26" long, Model No. 5693

EX $175   **NM** $375   **MIP** $700

Armored Car, 1967, Irwin, friction powered, 20" long, Model No. 5397

EX $150   **NM** $300   **MIP** $500

Helicopter, 1967, Hasbro, Irwin, friction powered, 28" long, Model No. 5395

EX $150   **NM** $300   **MIP** $500

Jet Fighter Plane, 1967, Irwin, friction powered, 30" long, Model No. 5396

EX $225   **NM** $475   **MIP** $800

Military Staff Car, 1967, Irwin, friction powered, 24" long, Model No. 5652

EX $200   **NM** $400   **MIP** $750

Motorcycle and Sidecar, 1967, Irwin, 14" long, khaki, w/decals, Model No. 5651

EX $75   **NM** $150   **MIP** $325

Official Combat Jeep Set, 1965, trailer, steering wheel, spare tire, windshield, cannon, search light, shell, flag, guard rails, tripod, tailgate and hood, w/out Moto-Rev Sound, Model No. 7000

EX $200   **NM** $375   **MIP** $550

Official Jeep Combat Set, 1965, w/Moto-Rev sound, Model No. 7000

EX $225   **NM** $400   **MIP** $650

Personnel Carrier/Mine Sweeper, 1967, Irwin, 26" long, Model No. 5694

EX $300   **NM** $350   **MIP** $700

ACTION SOLDIERS OF THE WORLD

Figure Sets

Australian Jungle Fighter, 1966, Hasbro, action figure w/jacket, shorts, socks, boots, bush hat, belt, "Victoria Cross" medal, knuckle knife, flamethrower, entrenching tool, bush knife and sheath, Model No. 8105

EX $225   **NM** $350   **MIP** $2300

Australian Jungle Fighter, 1966, standard set w/action figure uniform, no equipment, Model No. 8205

EX $150   **NM** $275   **MIP** $1200

British Commando, 1966, Hasbro, deluxe set w/action figure, helmet, night raid green jacket, pants, boots, canteen and cover, gas mask and cover, belt, Sten sub machine gun, gun clip and "Victoria Cross" medal, Model No. 8104

EX $300   **NM** $425   **MIP** $2500

British Commando, 1966, Hasbro, standard set w/no equipment, Model No. 8204

EX $150   **NM** $275   **MIP** $1750

Foreign Soldiers of the World, 1968, Hasbro, Talking Adventure Pack, Model No. 8111-83

EX $810   **NM** $875   **MIP** $5250

French Resistance Fighter, 1966, Hasbro, standard set w/action figure and equipment, Model No. 8203

EX $135   **NM** $250   **MIP** $1300

French Resistance Fighter

French Resistance Fighter, 1966, Hasbro, deluxe set w/figure, beret, short black boots, black sweater, denim pants, "Croix de Guerre" medal, knife, shoulder holster, pistol, radio, submachine gun and grenades, Model No. 8103

EX $250   **NM** $375   **MIP** $2400

German Storm Trooper, 1966, Hasbro, deluxe set w/figure, helmet, jacket, pants, boots, Luger pistol, holster, cartridge belt, cartridges, "Iron Cross" medal, stick grenades, 9mm Schmeisser, field pack, Model No. 8100

EX $300   **NM** $475   **MIP** $2700

German Storm Trooper, 1966, Hasbro, standard set w/no equipment, Model No. 8200

EX $285   **NM** $350   **MIP** $1350

Japanese Imperial Soldier, 1966, Hasbro, deluxe set w/figure, Arisaka rifle, belt, cartridges, field pack, Nambu pistol, holster, bayonet, "Order of the Kite" medal, helmet, jacket, pants, short brown boots, Model No. 8101

EX $450   **NM** $750   **MIP** $2900

Japanese Imperial Soldier, 1966, Hasbro, standard set w/equipment, Model No. 8201

EX $310   **NM** $340   **MIP** $1475

Russian Infantry Man, 1966, Hasbro, standard set w/no equipment, Model No. 8202

EX $350   **NM** $410   **MIP** $1300

Russian Infantry Man, 1966, Hasbro, deluxe set w/action figure, fur cap, tunic, pants, boots, ammo box, ammo rounds, anti-tank grenades, belt, bipod, DP light machine gun, "Order of Lenin" medal, field glasses and case, Model No. 8102

EX $300   **NM** $430   **MIP** $2400

Uniforms of Six Nations, 1967, Hasbro, Model No. 5038

EX $750   **NM** $950   **MIP** $2500

Uniform/Equipment Sets

Australian Jungle Fighter Set, 1966, Hasbro, basic set w/flamethrower, machete, grenades, Victoria Cross medal, shovel, bayonet, Model No. 8305

EX $35   **NM** $60   **MIP** $275

British Commando Set, 1966, Hasbro, Sten submachine gun, gas mask and carrier, canteen and cover, cartridge belt, rifle, "Victoria Cross" medal, manual, Model No. 8304

EX $135   **NM** $210   **MIP** $350

French Resistance Fighter Set, 1966, Hasbro, shoulder holster, Lebel pistol, knife, grenades, radio, 7.65 submachine gun, "Croix de Guerra" medal, counter-intelligence manual, Model No. 8303

EX $35   **NM** $65   **MIP** $285

German Storm Trooper, 1966, Hasbro, Model No. 8300

EX $130   **NM** $180   **MIP** $335

Japanese Imperial Soldier Set, 1966, Hasbro, field pack, Nambu pistol and holster, Arisaka rifle w/bayonet, cartridge belt, "Order of the Kite" medal, counter-intelligence manual, Model No. 8301

EX $180   **NM** $280   **MIP** $650

Russian Infantry Man Set, 1966, Hasbro, DP light machine gun, bipod, field glasses and case, anti-tank grenades, ammo box, "Order of Lenin" medal, counter-intelligence medal, Model No. 8302

EX $180   **NM** $225   **MIP** $330

ADVENTURE TEAM

Figure Sets

Air Adventurer, 1970, Hasbro, orange flight suit, short black boots, insignia, dog tags, revolver, shoulder holster, boots, warranty, club insert, Model No. 7403

EX $125 **NM** $375 **MIP** $400

Air Adventurer, 1974, Hasbro, Kung Fu grip, rifle, orange flight suit w/AT insignia, short black boots, AT Club flyer, boot removal instructions, Model No. 7282

EX $100 **NM** $160 **MIP** $325

Air Adventurer, 1976, Hasbro, life-like body figure, short pants, orange flight suit w/AT insignia, rifle, short black boots, came carded not boxed, w/Kung Fu grip, Model No. 7272 and 7282

EX $80 **NM** $110 **MIP** $215

Black Adventurer, 1970, Hasbro, tan shirt w/AT insignia, tan pants, short black boots, dog tags, shoulder holster w/revolver, AT Club flyer, boot removal instructions, boxed, Model No. 7404

EX $135 **NM** $165 **MIP** $390

Black Adventurer, 1974, Hasbro, Kung Fu grip, tan shirt w/AT insignia, tan pants, short black boots, rifle, paperwork, boxed, Model No. 7283

EX $75 **NM** $165 **MIP** $250

Black Adventurer, 1976, Hasbro, life-like body, Kung Fu grip, tan shirt w/AT insignia, tan pants, short black boots, rifle, paperwork, Model No. 7273

EX $85 **NM** $125 **MIP** $225

Bulletman, 1976, Hasbro, black-painted hair, silver eyes, silver helmet, red body suit w/bullet insignia, black elastic belt, red boots, handle, flight line, Model No. 8026

EX $60 **NM** $100 **MIP** $175

Eagle Eye Black Commando, 1976, Hasbro, Model No. 7278

EX $85 **NM** $125 **MIP** $250

Eagle Eye Land Commander, 1976, Hasbro, either green shirt and pants or camoflaged shirt and pants, AT insignia, short black boots, rifle, eyes move via lever, paperwork, carded, Model No. 7276

EX $65 **NM** $80 **MIP** $150

Eagle Eye Man of Action, 1976, Hasbro, green shirt and pants, AT insignia, rifle, short black boots, eyes move via lever, paperwork, carded, Model No. 7277

EX $65 **NM** $80 **MIP** $165

Intruder Commander, 1976, Hasbro, gold body armor, Model No. 8050

EX $50 **NM** $60 **MIP** $135

Intruder Warrior, 1976, Hasbro, silver body armor, Model No. 8051

EX $50 **NM** $60 **MIP** $175

Land Adventurer, 1970, Hasbro, camoflaged shirt and pants, AT insignia, short black boots, shoulder holster w/revolver, dog tags, paperwork, Model No. 7401

EX $45 **NM** $90 **MIP** $160

Land Adventurer, 1974, Hasbro, Kung Fu grip, camoflaged shirt w/AT insignia, camoflaged pants, short black boots, rifle, paperwork, Model No. 7280

EX $50 **NM** $65 **MIP** $200

Land Adventurer, 1976, Hasbro, life-like body, Kung Fu grip, "New," camoflaged shirt and pants, AT insignia, short black boots, rifle, carded, Model No. 7280

EX $35 **NM** $50 **MIP** $150

Land Adventurer, 1976, Hasbro, life-like body, Kung Fu grip, camoflaged shirt and pants, AT insignia, short

black boots, rifle, carded, Model No. 7270

EX $20 **NM** $50 **MIP** $180

Man of Action, 1970, Hasbro, green shirt and pants, AT insignia, short black boots, dog tags, team inserts, boxed, Model No. 7500

EX $50 **NM** $75 **MIP** $225

Man of Action, 1974, Hasbro, Kung Fu grip, green shirt w/AT insignia, green pants, short black boots, rifle, paperwork, boxed, Model No. 7284

EX $45 **NM** $75 **MIP** $200

Man of Action, 1976, Hasbro, life-like body, Kung Fu grip, green shirt w/AT insignia, green pants, short black boots, rifle, paperwork, carded, Model No. 7274 and 7284

EX $25 **NM** $45 **MIP** $175

Mike Powers/Atomic Man, 1975, Hasbro, figure w/"atomic" flashing eye, arm that spins hand-held helicopter, Model No. 8025

EX $28 **NM** $50 **MIP** $135

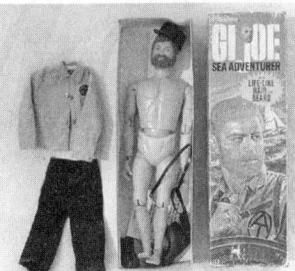

Sea Adventurer, 1970, Hasbro, light blue denim shirt w/AT insignia, dark blue dungarees, short black boots, shoulder holster w/revolver, dog tags, paperwork, Model No. 7402

EX $45 **NM** $95 **MIP** $250

Sea Adventurer, 1974, Hasbro, Kung Fu grip, light blue denim shirt w/AT insignia, dark blue dungarees, short

black boots, rifle, paperwork,
Model No. 7281

EX $55   **NM** $85   **MIP** $200

Sea Adventurer, 1976, Hasbro, life-
like body, Kung Fu grip, light blue
denim shirt w/AT insignia, dark blue
dungarees, short black boots, rifle,
carded, Model No. 7271

EX $40   **NM** $75   **MIP** $250

Sea Adventurer, 1976, Hasbro, life-
like body, Kung Fu grip, light blue
denim shirt w/AT insignia, dark blue
dungarees, short black boots, rifle,
"New," carded, Model No. 7281

EX $55   **NM** $135   **MIP** $295

**Talking Adventure Team Black
Commander,** 1973, Hasbro, green
shirt w/AT insignia, green pants,
short black boots, dog tag, shoulder
holster w/revolver, paperwork,
boxed, Model No. 7406

EX $160   **NM** $490   **MIP** $850

**Talking Adventure Team Black
Commander,** 1974, Hasbro, Kung
Fu grip, green shirt w/AT insignia,
green pants, dog tag, rifle, short
black boots, paperwork, boxed,
Model No. 7291

EX $95   **NM** $365   **MIP** $775

**Talking Adventure Team
Commander,** 1970, Hasbro, two-
pocket green shirt w/AT insignia,
green pants, short black boots,
instructions, dog tag, shoulder
holster w/revolver, w/life-like hair
and beard, Model No. 7400

EX $65   **NM** $140   **MIP** $400

**Talking Adventure Team
Commander,** 1974, Hasbro, Kung
Fu grip, green fatigue shirt w/AT
insignia, green pants, dog tag, short
black boots, rifle, paperwork,
boxed, Model No. 7290

EX $75   **NM** $200   **MIP** $500

Talking Astronaut, 1970, Hasbro,
white jumpsuit w/AT insignia, dog
tag, white boots, Model No. 7405

EX $90   **NM** $175   **MIP** $430

Talking Black Commander, 1976,
Hasbro, life-like body, Kung Fu grip,
green shirt w/AT insignia, green
pants, dog tag, short black boots,
rifle, paperwork, Model No. 7291

EX $135   **NM** $320   **MIP** $625

Talking Commander, 1976, Hasbro,
life-like body, Kung Fu grip, green
shrit w/AT insignia, green pants,
dog tag, short black boots, rifle,
paperwork, Model No. 7290

EX $75   **NM** $115   **MIP** $500

Talking Man of Action, 1970, Hasbro,
green shirt, green pants, short black
boots, hat, dog tags, instructions,
Model No. 7590

EX $75   **NM** $125   **MIP** $350

Talking Man of Action, 1974, Hasbro,
Kung Fu grip, green shirt, green
pants, rifle, dog tags, short black
boots, paperwork, Model No. 7292

EX $75   **NM** $200   **MIP** $650

Talking Man of Action, 1976, Hasbro,
life-like body, Kung Fu grip, green
shirt w/AT insignia, green pants,
dog tag, short black boots, rifle,
paperwork, Model No. 7292

EX $75   **NM** $120   **MIP** $525

Uniform/Equipment Sets

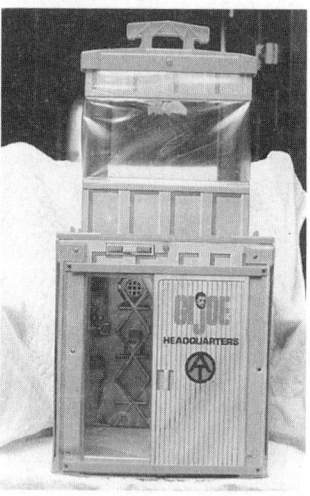

Adventure Team Headquarters Set,
1972, Hasbro, Adventure Team play
set, Model No. 7490

EX $60   **NM** $140   **MIP** $325

Adventure Team Training Center Set,
1973, Hasbro, rifle rack, logs,
barrel, barbed wire, rope ladder,
three tires, two targets, escape

slide, tent and poles, first aid kit,
respirator and mask, snake,
instructions, Model No. 7495

EX $75   **NM** $125   **MIP** $225

Aerial Reconnaissance Set, 1971,
Hasbro, jumpsuit, helmet, aerial
recon vehicle w/built-in camera,
Model No. 7345

EX $75   **NM** $125   **MIP** $242

Attack at Vulture Falls, 1975, Hasbro,
super deluxe set, Model No. 7420

EX $75   **NM** $150   **MIP** $275

Black Widow Rendezvous, 1975,
Hasbro, super deluxe set, Model
No. 7414

EX $125   **NM** $200   **MIP** $350

Buried Bounty, 1975, Hasbro, deluxe
set, Model No. 7328-5

EX $10   **NM** $25   **MIP** $85

Capture of the Pygmy Gorilla Set,
1970, Hasbro, Model No. 7437

EX $100   **NM** $175   **MIP** $485

Challenge of Savage River, 1975,
Hasbro, deluxe set, Model No. 8032

EX $100   **NM** $175   **MIP** $350

Chest Winch Set, 1972, Hasbro,
Model No. 7313

EX $10   **NM** $15   **MIP** $65

Chest Winch Set, 1974, Hasbro,
reissue, Model No. 7313

EX $10   **NM** $15   **MIP** $75

Command Para Drop, 1975, Hasbro,
deluxe set, Model No. 8033

EX $190   **NM** $275   **MIP** $575

Copter Rescue Set, 1973, Hasbro,
blue jumpsuit, red binoculars,
Model No. 7308-6

EX $15   **NM** $20   **MIP** $30

Danger of the Depths Set, 1970,
Hasbro, Model No. 7412

EX $100   **NM** $175   **MIP** $325

Danger Ray Detection, 1975, Hasbro,
magnetic ray detector, solar
communicator w/headphones,
two-piece uniform, instructions
and comic, Model No. 7338-1

EX $45   **NM** $90   **MIP** $225

Dangerous Climb Set, 1973, Hasbro,
Model No. 7309-2

EX $20   **NM** $35   **MIP** $75

Dangerous Mission Set, 1973,
Hasbro, green shirt, pants, hunting
rifle, Model No. 7308-2

EX $20   **NM** $35   **MIP** $75

Demolition Set, 1971, Hasbro,
armored suit, face shield, bomb,
bomb disposal box, extension
grips, Model No. 7370

EX $20   **NM** $45   **MIP** $125

Desert Explorer Set, 1973, Hasbro,
Model No. 7309-5
EX $20   **NM** $40   **MIP** $80

Desert Survival Set, 1973, Hasbro,
Model No. 7308-1
EX $20   **NM** $40   **MIP** $80

Dive to Danger, 1975, Hasbro, Mike
Powers set, orange scuba suit, fins,
mask, spear gun, shark, buoy, knife
and scabbard, mini sled, air tanks,
comic, Model No. 8031
EX $150 **NM** $250   **MIP** $450

Diver's Distress, 1975, Hasbro,
Model No. 7328-6
EX $35   **NM** $70   **MIP** $125

Drag Bike Set, 1971, Hasbro, three-
wheel motorcycle brakes down to
backpack size, Model No. 7364
EX $25   **NM** $65   **MIP** $125

Eight Ropes of Danger Set, 1970,
Hasbro, Model No. 7422
EX $125 **NM** $225   **MIP** $375

Emergency Rescue Set, 1971,
Hasbro, shirt, pants, rope ladder
and hook, walkie talkie, safety belt,
flashlight, oxygen tank, axe, first aid
kit, Model No. 7374
EX $45   **NM** $75   **MIP** $145

Equipment Tester Set, 1972, Hasbro,
Model No. 7319-5
EX $15   **NM** $75   **MIP** $40

Escape Car Set, 1971, Hasbro, Model
No. 7360
EX $30   **NM** $60   **MIP** $85

Escape Slide Set, 1972, Hasbro,
Model No. 7319-1
EX $15   **NM** $25   **MIP** $40

Fangs of the Cobra, 1975, Hasbro,
deluxe set, Model No. 8028-2
EX $125 **NM** $175   **MIP** $235

Fantastic Freefall Set, 1970, Hasbro,
Model No. 7423
EX $125 **NM** $200   **MIP** $345

Fight for Survival Set, 1970, Hasbro,
w/blue parka, Model No. 7431
EX $315 **NM** $570   **MIP** $2610

Fight for Survival Set, 1973, Hasbro,
brown shirt and pants, machete,
Model No. 7308-3
EX $20   **NM** $30   **MIP** $70

**Fight for Survival Set w/Polar
Explorer,** 1969, Hasbro, Model
No. 7982
EX $260 **NM** $475   **MIP** $875

Fire Fighter Set, 1971, Hasbro, Model
No. 7351
EX $20   **NM** $30   **MIP** $55

Flying Rescue Set, 1971, Hasbro,
Model No. 7361
EX $35   **NM** $60   **MIP** $85

Flying Space Adventure Set, 1970,
Hasbro, Model No. 7425
EX $425 **NM** $625   **MIP** $3750

Footlocker, 1974, Hasbro, green
plastic w/cardboard wrapper,
Model No. 8000
EX $35   **NM** $45   **MIP** $200

Green Danger, 1975, Hasbro, Model
No. 7328-4
EX $30   **NM** $75   **MIP** $60

Hidden Missile Discovery Set, 1970,
Hasbro, Model No. 7415
EX $115 **NM** $250   **MIP** $1800

Hidden Treasure Set, 1973, Hasbro,
shirt, pants, pick axe, shovel, Model
No. 7308-5
EX $15   **NM** $25   **MIP** $40

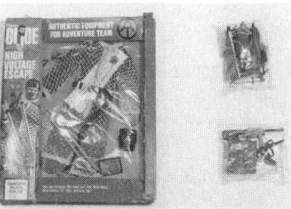

High Voltage Escape Set, 1971,
Hasbro, net, jumpsuit, hat, wrist
meter, wire cutters, wire, warning
sign, Model No. 7342
EX $40   **NM** $75   **MIP** $110

Hurricane Spotter Set, 1971, Hasbro,
slicker suit, rain measure, portable
radar, map and case, binoculars,
Model No. 7343
EX $55   **NM** $110   **MIP** $220

Infiltration, 1971, Hasbro, replaced
Karate set, black pants, black
hooded top, revilver, machine gun,
map, knife and scabbard, radio,
shoulder holster, map case, Model
No. 7372
EX $45   **NM** $90   **MIP** $135

Jaws of Death, 1975, Hasbro, super
deluxe set, Model No. 7421
EX $325 **NM** $500   **MIP** $650

Jettison to Safety, 1975, Hasbro,
infrared terrain scanner, mobile
rocket pack, two-piece flight suit,
instructions and comic, Model
No. 7339-2
EX $85   **NM** $200   **MIP** $275

Jungle Ordeal Set, 1973, Hasbro,
Model No. 7309-3
EX $15   **NM** $25   **MIP** $66

Jungle Survival Set, 1971, Hasbro,
Model No. 7323
EX $15   **NM** $60   **MIP** $180

Karate Set, 1971, Hasbro, Model
No. 7372
EX $35   **NM** $70   **MIP** $210

Laser Rescue Set, 1972, Hasbro,
hand-held laser w/backpack
generator, Model No. 7311
EX $20   **NM** $35   **MIP** $45

Laser Rescue Set, 1974, Hasbro,
reissue, Model No. 7311
EX $20   **NM** $35   **MIP** $100

Life-Line Catapult Set, 1971, Hasbro,
Model No. 7352
EX $15   **NM** $25   **MIP** $85

Long Range Recon, 1975, Hasbro,
deluxe set, Model No. 7328-3
EX $10   **NM** $20   **MIP** $35

Magnetic Flaw Detector Set, 1972,
Hasbro, Model No. 7319-2
EX $10   **NM** $20   **MIP** $56

Mine Shaft Breakout, 1975, Hasbro,
sonic rock blaster, chest winch,
two-piece uniform, netting,
instructions, comic, Model
No. 7339-3
EX $70   **NM** $125   **MIP** $250

Missile Recovery Set, 1971, Hasbro,
Model No. 7340
EX $100 **NM** $200   **MIP** $325

Mystery of the Boiling Lagoon, 1973,
Hasbro, Sears, pontoon boat,
diver's suit, diver's helmet,
weighted belt and boots, depth

gauge, air hose, buoy, nose cone, pincer arm, instructions
EX $150 **NM** $200 **MIP** $295

Night Surveillance, 1975, Hasbro, deluxe set, Model No. 7338-2
EX $65 **NM** $160 **MIP** $165

Peril of the Raging Inferno, 1975, Hasbro, fireproof suit, hood and boots, breathing apparatus, camera, fire extinguisher, detection meter, gaskets, Model No. 7416
EX $85 **NM** $150 **MIP** $275

Photo Reconnaissance Set, 1973, Hasbro, Model No. 7309-4
EX $20 **NM** $30 **MIP** $65

Race for Recovery, 1975, Hasbro, Model No. 8028-1
EX $20 **NM** $35 **MIP** $140

Radiation Detection Set, 1971, Hasbro, jumpsuit w/belt, "uranium ore," goggles, container, pincer arm, Model No. 7341
EX $30 **NM** $50 **MIP** $160

Raging River Dam Up, 1975, Hasbro, Model No. 7339-1
EX $100 **NM** $225 **MIP** $450

Rescue Raft Set, 1971, Hasbro, Model No. 7350
EX $15 **NM** $45 **MIP** $65

Revenge of the Spy Shark, 1975, Hasbro, super deluxe set, Model No. 7413
EX $50 **NM** $175 **MIP** $400

Rock Blaster, 1972, Hasbro, sonic blaster w/tripod, backpack generator, face shield, Model No. 7312
EX $10 **NM** $20 **MIP** $35

Rocket Pack Set, 1972, Hasbro, Model No. 7315
EX $10 **NM** $20 **MIP** $75

Rocket Pack Set, 1974, Hasbro, reissue, Model No. 7315
EX $10 **NM** $20 **MIP** $50

Sample Analyzer Set, 1972, Hasbro, Model No. 7319-3
EX $55 **NM** $155 **MIP** $275

Search for the Abominable Snowman Set, 1973, Hasbro, Sears, white suit, belt, goggles, gloves, rifle, skis and poles, show shoes, sled, rope, net, supply chest, binoculars, Abominable Snowman, comic book, Model No. 7439.16
EX $120 **NM** $185 **MIP** $310

Secret Agent Set, 1971, Hasbro, Model No. 7375
EX $30 **NM** $55 **MIP** $190

Secret Courier, 1975, Hasbro, Model No. 7328-1
EX $45 **NM** $80 **MIP** $135

Secret Mission Set, 1973, Hasbro, Model No. 7309-1
EX $45 **NM** $65 **MIP** $135

Secret Mission Set, 1975, Hasbro, deluxe set, Model No. 8030
EX $65 **NM** $95 **MIP** $200

Secret Mission to Spy Island Set, 1970, Hasbro, comic, inflatable raft w/oar, binoculars, signal light, flare gun, TNT and detonator, wire roll, boots, pants, sweater, black cap, camera, radio w/earphones, .45 submachine gun, Model No. 7411
EX $75 **NM** $125 **MIP** $400

Secret Mountain Outpost, 1975, Hasbro, Model No. 8040
EX $50 **NM** $85 **MIP** $200

Secret Rendezvous Set, 1973, Hasbro, parka, pants, flare gun, Model No. 7308-4
EX $10 **NM** $20 **MIP** $35

Seismograph Set, 1972, Hasbro, Model No. 7319-6
EX $10 **NM** $20 **MIP** $35

Shocking Escape, 1975, Hasbro, escape slide, chest pack climber, jumpsuit w/gloves and belt, high voltage sign, instructions and comic, Model No. 7338-3
EX $125 **NM** $240 **MIP** $525

Signal Flasher Set, 1971, Hasbro, large back pack type signal flash unit, Model No. 7362
EX $20 **NM** $30 **MIP** $66

Sky Dive to Danger, 1975, Hasbro, super deluxe set, Model No. 7440
EX $90 **NM** $150 **MIP** $350

Smoke Jumper Set, 1971, Hasbro, yellow jumpsuit, yellow helmet, chain saw, cutters, flashlight, black tool belt, red fire extinguisher, pliers, ax, Model No. 7371
EX $75 **NM** $100 **MIP** $250

Solar Communicator Set, 1972, Hasbro, Model No. 7314
EX $10 **NM** $20 **MIP** $35

Solar Communicator Set, 1974, Hasbro, reissue, Model No. 7314
EX $10 **NM** $20 **MIP** $95

Sonic Rock Blaster Set, 1972, Hasbro, Model No. 7312
EX $10 **NM** $20 **MIP** $35

Sonic Rock Blaster Set, 1974, Hasbro, reissue, Model No. 7312
EX $10 **NM** $20 **MIP** $35

Special Assignment, 1975, Hasbro, deluxe set, Model No. 8028-3
EX $30 **NM** $55 **MIP** $135

Thermal Terrain Scanner Set, 1972, Hasbro, Model No. 7319-4
EX $25 **NM** $35 **MIP** $50

Three-in-One Super Adventure Set, 1971, Hasbro, Danger of the Depths, Secret Mission to Spy Island and Flying Space Adventure Packs, Model No. 7480
EX $575 **NM** $1050 **MIP** $1300

Three-in-One Super Adventure Set, 1971, Hasbro, Cold of the Arctic, Heat of the Desert and Danger of the Jungle, Model No. 7480
EX $250 **NM** $400 **MIP** $750

Thrust into Danger, 1975, Hasbro, deluxe set, Model No. 7328-2
EX $45 **NM** $55 **MIP** $175

Trouble at Vulture Pass, 1975, Hasbro, Sears Exclusive, super deluxe set, Model No. 59289
EX $75 **NM** $175 **MIP** $325

Turbo Copter Set, 1971, Hasbro, strap-on one man helicopter, Model No. 7363
EX $15 **NM** $35 **MIP** $65

Undercover Agent Set, 1973, Hasbro, trenchcoat and belt, walkie-talkie, Model No. 7309-6
EX $15 **NM** $30 **MIP** $45

Underwater Demolition Set, 1972, Hasbro, hand-held propulsion device, breathing apparatus, dynamite, Model No. 7310
EX $18 **NM** $25 **MIP** $50

Underwater Demolition Set, 1974, Hasbro, reissue, Model No. 7310
EX $10 **NM** $20 **MIP** $75

Underwater Explorer Set, 1971, Hasbro, self propelled underwater device, Model No. 7354
EX $15 **NM** $30 **MIP** $60

Volcano Jumper Set, 1971, Hasbro, jumpsuit w/hood, belt, nylon rope, chest pack, TNT pack, Model No. 7344
EX $45 **NM** $80 **MIP** $250

White Tiger Hunt Set, 1970, Hasbro, hunter's jacket and pants, hat, rifle, tent, cage, chain, campfire, white tiger, comic, Model No. 7436

EX $85   NM $190   MIP $375

Windboat Set, 1971, Hasbro, back pack, sled w/wheels, sail, Model No. 7353

EX $10   NM $25   MIP $65

Winter Rescue Set, 1973, Hasbro, Replaced by Photo Reconnaissance Set, Model No. 7309-4

EX $40   NM $75   MIP $150

Vehicle Sets

Action Sea Sled, 1973, Hasbro, J.C. Penney, 13", Adventure Pack

EX $25   NM $40   MIP $85

Adventure Team Vehicle Set, 1970, Hasbro, Model No. 7005

EX $50   NM $75   MIP $225

All Terrain Vehicle, 1973, Hasbro, 14" vehicle, Model No. 23528

EX $50   NM $75   MIP $125

Amphicat, 1973, Hasbro, Irwin, scaled to fit two figures, Model No. 59158

EX $35   NM $55   MIP $125

Avenger Pursuit Craft, 1976, Hasbro, Sears Exclusive

EX $100   NM $175   MIP $275

Big Trapper, 1976, Hasbro, w/out action figure, Model No. 7498

EX $75   NM $245   MIP $600

Big Trapper Adventure w/Intruder, 1976, Hasbro, w/action figure, Model No. 7494

EX $100   NM $150   MIP $425

Capture Copter, 1976, Hasbro, w/out action figure, Model No. 7480

EX $80   NM $175   MIP $325

Capture Copter Adventure w/Intruder, 1976, Hasbro, w/action figure, Model No. 7481

EX $110   NM $200   MIP $350

Chopper Cycle, 1973, Hasbro, 15" vehicle, J.C. Penney's, Model No. 59114

EX $30   NM $50   MIP $100

Combat Action Jeep, 1973, Hasbro, 18" vehicle, J.C. Penney's, Model No. 59751

EX $50   NM $65   MIP $125

Combat Jeep and Trailer, 1976, Hasbro, Model No. 7000

EX $80   NM $135   MIP $550

Devil of the Deep, 1974, Hasbro, Model No. 7439

EX $80   NM $135   MIP $325

Fantastic Sea Wolf Submarine, 1975, Hasbro, Model No. 7460

EX $60   NM $100   MIP $175

Fate of the Troubleshooter, 1974, Hasbro, includes vehicle, vulture, instructions and comic book, Model No. 7450

EX $85   NM $210   MIP $310

Giant Air-Sea Helicopter, 1973, Hasbro, 28" vehicle, J.C. Penney's, Model No. 59189

EX $50   NM $125   MIP $225

Helicopter, 1973, Hasbro, 14", yellow, w/working winch, Model No. 7380

EX $50   NM $90   MIP $150

Helicopter, 1976, Hasbro, Model No. 7380

EX $50   NM $90   MIP $300

Mobile Support Vehicle Set, 1972, Hasbro, Model No. 7499

EX $130   NM $210   MIP $435

Recovery of the Lost Mummy Adventure Set, 1971, Hasbro, Sears Exclusive

EX $125   NM $250   MIP $575

Sandstorm Survival Adventure, 1974, Hasbro, Model No. 7493

EX $125   NM $200   MIP $335

Search for the Stolen Idol Set, 1971, Hasbro, Model No. 7418

EX $120   NM $225   MIP $400

Secret of the Mummy's Tomb Set, 1970, Hasbro, w/Land Adventurer figure, shirt, pants, boots, insignia, pith helmet, pick, shovel, Mummy's tomb, net, gems, vehicle w/winch, comic, Model No. 7441

EX $265   NM $625   MIP $1600

Sharks Surprise Set w/Sea Adventurer, 1970, Hasbro, Model No. 7442

EX $265   NM $385   MIP $565

Signal All Terrain Vehicle, 1973, Hasbro, J.C. Penney's, 12" vehicle

EX $30   NM $65   MIP $125

Sky Hawk, 1975, Hasbro, 5-3/4' wingspan, Model No. 7470

EX $65   NM $100   MIP $175

Spacewalk Mystery Set w/Astronaut, 1970, Hasbro, Model No. 7445

EX $225   NM $300   MIP $550

Trapped in the Coils of Doom, 1974, Hasbro, J.C. Penney's Exclusive, Model No. 79-59301

EX $250   NM $300   MIP $550

ADVENTURES OF G.I. JOE

Figure Sets

Aquanaut, 1969, Hasbro, Model No. 7910

EX $210   NM $590   MIP $3100

Negro Adventurer, 1969, Hasbro, Sears Exclusive, includes painted hair figure, blue jeans, pullover sweater, shoulder holster and pistol, plus product letter from Sears, Model No. 7905

EX $450   NM $750   MIP $2750

Sharks Surprise Set w/Frogman, 1969, Hasbro, w/figure, orange scuba suit, blue sea sled, air tanks, harpoon, face mask, treasure chest, shark, instructions and comic, Model No. 7980

EX $125   NM $300   MIP $750

Talking Astronaut, 1969, Hasbro, hard-hand figure w/white coveralls w/insignias, white boots, dog tags, Model No. 7615

EX $85   NM $275   MIP $1000

Uniform/Equipment Sets

Adventure Locker, 1969, Hasbro, Footlocker, Model No. 7940

EX $165   NM $400   MIP $450

Aqua Locker, 1969, Hasbro, Footlocker, Model No. 7941

EX $110   NM $180   MIP $325

Astro Locker, 1969, Hasbro, Footlocker, Model No. 7942
EX $90 NM $225 MIP $375

Danger of the Depths Underwater Diver Set, 1969, Hasbro, Model No. 7920
EX $140 NM $275 MIP $500

Eight Ropes of Danger Set, 1969, Hasbro, diving suit, treasure chest, octopus, Model No. 7950
EX $110 NM $225 MIP $525

Fantastic Freefall Set, 1969, Hasbro, includes figure w/parachute and pack, blinker light, air vest, flash light, crash helmet w/visor and oxygen mask, dog tags, orange jump suit, black boots, Model No. 7951
EX $150 NM $325 MIP $675

Flight for Survival Set w/Polar Explorer, 1969, Hasbro, reissue, Model No. 7982.83
EX $150 NM $300 MIP $500

Hidden Missile Discovery Set, 1969, Hasbro, Model No. 7952
EX $70 NM $135 MIP $400

Mouth of Doom Set, 1969, Hasbro, Model No. 7953
EX $125 NM $250 MIP $550

Mysterious Explosion Set, 1969, Hasbro, basic, Model No. 7921
EX $60 NM $180 MIP $425

Perilous Rescue Set, 1969, Hasbro, basic, Model No. 7923
EX $150 NM $300 MIP $500

Secret Mission to Spy Island Set, 1969, Hasbro, basic, Model No. 7922
EX $110 NM $225 MIP $545

Vehicle Sets

Sharks Surprise Set w/Frogman, 1969, Hasbro, Model No. 7980
EX $175 NM $325 MIP $650

Sharks Surprise Set w/out Frogman, 1969, Hasbro, Model No. 7980.83
EX $150 NM $300 MIP $550

Spacewalk Mystery Set w/out Spaceman, 1969, Hasbro, reissue, Model No. 7981.83
EX $150 NM $285 MIP $575

Spacewalk Mystery Set w/Spaceman, 1969, Hasbro, Model No. 7981
EX $175 NM $385 MIP $700

GI JOE ACTION SERIES, ARMY, NAVY, MARINE AND AIR FORCE

Uniform/Equipment Sets

Basic Footlocker, 1965, Hasbro, Model No. 8000
EX $50 NM $75 MIP $175

Footlocker Adventure Pack, 1968, Hasbro, 22 pieces, Model No. 8002.83
EX $70 NM $145 MIP $450

Footlocker Adventure Pack, 1968, Hasbro, 15 pieces, Model No. 8001.83
EX $65 NM $135 MIP $450

Footlocker Adventure Pack, 1968, Hasbro, 16 pieces, Model No. 8000.83
EX $65 NM $135 MIP $450

Footlocker Adventure Pack, 1968, Hasbro, 15 pieces, Model No. 8002.83
EX $65 NM $135 MIP $450

SUPER JOE

Figure Sets

Gor, 1977, Hasbro, Model No. 7510
EX $40 NM $70 MIP $130

Luminos, 1977, Hasbro, Model No. 7506
EX $45 NM $70 MIP $130

Super Joe, 1977, Hasbro, Model No. 7503
EX $25 NM $50 MIP $85

Super Joe (Black), 1977, Hasbro, Model No. 7504
EX $35 NM $65 MIP $125

Super Joe Commander, 1977, Hasbro, Model No. 7501
EX $25 NM $45 MIP $75

The Shield, 1977, Hasbro, Model No. 7505
EX $40 NM $65 MIP $125

Uniform/Equipment Sets

Aqua Laser, 1977, Hasbro, Model No. 7528-1
EX $10 NM $20 MIP $30

Edge of Adventure, 1977, Hasbro, Model No. 7518-2
EX $10 NM $20 MIP $35

Emergency Rescue, 1977, Hasbro, Model No. 7518-3
EX $10 NM $20 MIP $30

Fusion Bazooka, 1977, Hasbro, Model No. 7528-3
EX $10 NM $20 MIP $30

Helipak, 1977, Hasbro, Model No. 7538-2
EX $10 NM $20 MIP $30

Invisible Danger, 1977, Hasbro, Model No. 7518-1
EX $10 NM $20 MIP $35

Magna Tools, 1977, Hasbro, w/uniform and rock-cutting drill and saw, Model No. 7538-1
EX $10 NM $20 MIP $30

Path of Danger, 1977, Hasbro, Model No. 7518-4
EX $10 NM $20 MIP $30

Sonic Scanner, 1977, Hasbro, Model No. 7538-3
EX $10 NM $20 MIP $30

Treacherous Dive, 1977, Hasbro, Model No. 7528-2
EX $10 NM $20 MIP $30

Vehicle Sets

Rocket Command Center, 1977, Hasbro, Super Adventure Set including Gor, Model No. 7571
EX $60 NM $115 MIP $225

Rocket Command Center, 1977,
Hasbro, Model No. 7570

EX $50	NM $100	MIP $200

3-3/4" Figures

SERIES 01, COBRA
Figure Sets

Cobra, 1982, Hasbro, Infantry Soldier,
Model No. 6423

EX $18	NM $26	MIP $175

Cobra Commander, 1982, Hasbro,
mail order; Commanding Leader

EX $65	NM $125	MIP $450

Cobra Officer, 1982, Hasbro, Infantry
Officer, Model No. 6424

EX $18	NM $26	MIP $175

Vehicles/Acessories

**Headquarters Missile-Command
Center**, 1982, Hasbro, w/three
figures: Cobra Commander, Officer,
Troope, Sears Exclusive offered in
1982 Sears Christmas catalog,
Model No. 6200

EX $310	NM $565	MIP $1600

SERIES 01, GI JOE
Figure Sets

Breaker, 1982, Hasbro,
Communications Officer, Model
No. 6403

EX $12	NM $18	MIP $135

Flash, 1982, Hasbro, Laser Rifle
Trooper, Model No. 6406

EX $12	NM $18	MIP $160

Grunt, 1982, Hasbro, Infantry
Trooper, Model No. 6409

EX $10	NM $15	MIP $135

Rock 'n Roll, 1982, Hasbro, Machine
Gunner, Model No. 6408

EX $12	NM $16	MIP $150

Scarlett, 1982, Hasbro, Counter
Intelligence, Model No. 6407

EX $18	NM $30	MIP $450

(KP Photo, Karen O'Brien collection)

Short-Fuze, 1982, Hasbro, Mortar
Soldier, Model No. 6402

EX $12	NM $16	MIP $130

Snake Eyes, 1982, Hasbro,
Commando, Model No. 6404

EX $30	NM $45	MIP $750

Stalker, 1982, Hasbro, Ranger, Model
No. 6401

EX $14	NM $20	MIP $250

Zap, 1982, Hasbro, Bazooka Soldier,
Model No. 6405

EX $15	NM $22	MIP $140

Vehicle Sets

M.O.B.A.T., 1982, Hasbro, Motorized
Battle Tank w/Steeler, Model
No. 6000

EX $14	NM $125	MIP $950

R.A.M., 1982, Hasbro, Rapid Fire
Motorcycle, Model No. 6073

EX $7	NM $25	MIP $250

V.A.M.P., 1982, Hasbro, Multi-
Purpose Attack Vehicle w/Clutch,
Model No. 6050

EX $30	NM $100	MIP $550

Vehicles/Acessories

F.L.A.K., 1982, Hasbro, Attack
Cannon, Model No. 6075

EX $8	NM $25	MIP $100

H.A.L., 1982, Hasbro, Heavy Artillery
Laser w/Grand Slam, Model No. 6052

EX $14	NM $45	MIP $675

J.U.M.P., 1982, Hasbro, Jet Pack
w/Platform, Model No. 6071

EX $14	NM $32	MIP $250

M.M.S., 1982, Hasbro, Mobile Missile
System w/Hawk, Model No. 6054

EX $20	NM $45	MIP $675

SERIES 02, COBRA
Figure Sets

Cobra, 1983, Hasbro, reissue, Model
No. 6423

EX $18	NM $26	MIP $160

Cobra Commander, 1983, Hasbro,
reissue, Model No. 6425

EX $30	NM $40	MIP $550

Cobra Officer, 1983, Hasbro, reissue,
Model No. 6424

EX $18	NM $26	MIP $160

Destro, 1983, Hasbro, Enemy
Weapons Supplier, Model No. 6427

EX $12	NM $16	MIP $325

Major Bludd, 1982, Hasbro, mail
order; mercenary w/card, Model
No. 6426

EX $10	NM $15	MIP $225

Major Bludd, 1983, Hasbro, Model
No. 6426

EX $10	NM $14	MIP $210

Vehicle Sets

Cobra Viper Glider, 1983, Hasbro,
Attack Glider w/Viper, Model
No. 6097

EX $175	NM $225	MIP $780

F.A.N.G., 1983, Hasbro, Fully Armed
Negator Gyro Copter, Model
No. 6077

EX $12	NM $40	MIP $325

H.I.S.S., 1983, Hasbro, High Speed
Sentry Tank w/H.I.S.S., Model
No. 6051

EX $14	NM $55	MIP $590

Vehicles/Acessories

S.N.A.K.E., 1983, Hasbro, One-Man
Battle Armor (white), Model
No. 6083

EX $10	NM $40	MIP $125

SERIES 02, GI JOE
Figure Sets

Airborne, 1983, Hasbro, Helicopter
Assault Trooper, Model No. 6411

EX $10	NM $13	MIP $130

Breaker, 1983, Hasbro, reissue,
Model No. 6403

EX $10	NM $12	MIP $130

Doc, 1983, Hasbro, Medic, Model
No. 6415

EX $15	NM $18	MIP $175

Duke, 1983, Hasbro, mail order;
Master Sergeant

EX $15	NM $22	MIP $125

Flash, 1983, Hasbro, reissue, Model
No. 6406

EX $13	NM $18	MIP $145

Grunt, 1983, Hasbro, reissue, Model
No. 6409

EX $8	NM $12	MIP $130

Gung-Ho, 1983, Hasbro, Marine,
Model No. 6414

EX $10	NM $14	MIP $140

Rock 'n Roll, 1983, Hasbro, reissue,
Model No. 6408

EX $12	NM $16	MIP $135

Scarlett, 1983, Hasbro, reissue, Model No. 6407
EX $15   **NM** $22   **MIP** $340

Short-Fuze, 1983, Hasbro, reissue, Model No. 6402
EX $12   **NM** $15   **MIP** $135

Snake Eyes, 1983, Hasbro, reissue, Model No. 6404
EX $30   **NM** $135   **MIP** $600

Snow Job, 1983, Hasbro, Arctic Trooper, Model No. 6412
EX $15   **NM** $22   **MIP** $130

Stalker, 1983, Hasbro, reissue, Model No. 6401
EX $14   **NM** $20   **MIP** $255

Torpedo, 1983, Hasbro, Navy S.E.A.L., Model No. 6413
EX $12   **NM** $15   **MIP** $210

Tripwire, 1983, Hasbro, Mine Detector, Model No. 6410
EX $10   **NM** $13   **MIP** $175

Zap, 1983, Hasbro, reissue, Model No. 6405
EX $15   **NM** $20   **MIP** $120

Vehicle Sets

A.P.C., 1983, Hasbro, Amphibious Personnel Carrier, Model No. 6093
EX $20   **NM** $50   **MIP** $350

Dragon Fly XH-1, 1983, Hasbro, Assault Copter w/Wild Bill, Model No. 4025
EX $30   **NM** $90   **MIP** $550

Falcon, 1983, Hasbro, Attack Glider w/Grunt, Model No. 6097
EX $100   **NM** $175   **MIP** $590

Polar Battle Bear, 1983, Hasbro, Skimobile, Model No. 6072
EX $12   **NM** $30   **MIP** $250

Sky Striker XP-14F, 1983, Hasbro, F-14 Jet and Parachute w/Ace, Model No. 6010
EX $80   **NM** $145   **MIP** $900

Wolverine, 1983, Hasbro, Armored Missile Vehicle w/Cover Girl, 12 missiles, plastic tow cable, Model No. 6048
EX $35   **NM** $60   **MIP** $460

Vehicles/Acessories

Battle Gear Accessory Pack #1, 1983, Hasbro, Model No. 6088
EX $8   **NM** $13   **MIP** $20

Headquarters Command Center, 1983, Hasbro, Model No. 6020
EX $95   **NM** $125   **MIP** $750

Jump, 1983, Hasbro, Jet Pack and Platform w/Grand Slam, Model No. 6065
EX $12   **NM** $75   **MIP** $475

Pac/Rats Flamethrower, 1983, Hasbro, Remote Control Weapon, Model No. 6086-1
EX $7   **NM** $15   **MIP** $55

Pac/Rats Machine Gun, 1983, Hasbro, Remote Control Weapon, Model No. 6086-2
EX $7   **NM** $15   **MIP** $55

Pac/Rats Missile Launcher, 1983, Hasbro, Remote Control Weapon, Model No. 6086-3
EX $7   **NM** $15   **MIP** $55

Whirlwind, 1983, Hasbro, Twin Battle Gun, Model No. 6074
EX $10   **NM** $25   **MIP** $155

SERIES 03, COBRA
Figure Sets

Baroness, 1984, Hasbro, Intelligence Officer, Model No. 6428
EX $18   **NM** $25   **MIP** $310

Cobra Commander, 1984, Hasbro, mail order; Enemy Leader w/Hood, Model No. 6425
EX $10   **NM** $30   **MIP** $40

Firefly, 1984, Hasbro, Saboteur, Model No. 6432
EX $25   **NM** $40   **MIP** $475

Scrap Iron, 1984, Hasbro, Anti-Armor Specialist, Model No. 6431
EX $12   **NM** $15   **MIP** $120

Storm Shadow, 1984, Hasbro, Ninja, Model No. 6429
EX $35   **NM** $60   **MIP** $475

Vehicle Sets

Rattler, 1984, Hasbro, Ground Attack Jet w/Wild Weasel, Model No. 6027
EX $65   **NM** $175   **MIP** $495

Stinger, 1984, Hasbro, Night Attack Jeep w/Cobra Officer, Model No. 6055
EX $25   **NM** $50   **MIP** $400

Swamp Skier, 1984, Hasbro, Chameleon Vehicle w/Zartan, Model No. 6064
EX $40   **NM** $60   **MIP** $300

Water Moccasin, 1984, Hasbro, Swamp Boat w/Copperhead, Model No. 6058
EX $28   **NM** $50   **MIP** $350

Vehicles/Acessories

A.S.P., 1984, Hasbro, Assault System Pod, Model No. 6070
EX $10   **NM** $15   **MIP** $100

C.L.A.W., 1984, Hasbro, Cobra Covert Light Aerial Weapons, Model No. 6081-1
EX $10   **NM** $25   **MIP** $118

SERIES 03, GI JOE
Figure Sets

Blow Torch, 1984, Hasbro, Flamethrower, Model No. 6421
EX $8   **NM** $12   **MIP** $115

Duke, 1984, Hasbro, First Sergeant, Model No. 6422
EX $18   **NM** $25   **MIP** $415

Mutt, 1984, Hasbro, Dog Handler w/Dog, Model No. 6416
EX $12   **NM** $16   **MIP** $125

Recondo, 1984, Hasbro, Jungle Trooper, Model No. 6420
EX $10   **NM** $14   **MIP** $125

Rip Cord, 1984, Hasbro, H.A.L.O. Jumper, Model No. 6418
EX $12   **NM** $16   **MIP** $125

Roadblock, 1984, Hasbro, Heavy Machine Gunner, Model No. 6419
EX $12   **NM** $16   **MIP** $180

(KP Photo, Karen O'Brien collection)

Spirit, 1984, Hasbro, Tracker w/Eagle, Model No. 6417
EX $15   **NM** $25   **MIP** $125

Vehicle Sets

Killer W.H.A.L.E. Hovercraft, 1984, Hasbro, Armored Hovercraft w/Cutter driver, Model No. 6005
EX $70   **NM** $145   **MIP** $625

(KP Photo, Karen O'Brien collection)

S.H.A.R.C., 1984, Hasbro, Submersible High-Speed Attack & Recon Craft w/Deep Six figure (shown), Model No. 6049
EX $13   NM $42   MIP $300

Sky Hawk, 1984, Hasbro, V.T.O.L. Jet, Model No. 6079
EX $10   NM $25   MIP $80

Slugger, 1984, Hasbro, Self-Propelled Cannon w/Thunder, Model No. 6056
EX $12   NM $38   MIP $260

V.A.M.P. and H.A.L., 1984, Hasbro, Sears exclusive, no figures, Model No. 7444-2
EX $50   NM $215   MIP $1400

V.A.M.P. Mark II, 1984, Hasbro, w/Clutch (tan version) driver, Model No. 7444-1
EX $18   NM $50   MIP $355

Vehicles/Acessories

Battle Gear Accessory Pack #2, 1984, Hasbro, Model No. 6092
EX $8   NM $15   MIP $20

Bivouac, 1984, Hasbro, Battle Station, Model No. 6125-1
EX $12   NM $22   MIP $80

M.A.N.T.A., 1984, Hasbro, mail order; Marine Assault Nautical Air Driven Transport
EX $8   NM $16   MIP $40

Machine Gun Defense Unit, 1984, Hasbro, Battlefield Accessories, Model No. 6129-2
EX $10   NM $18   MIP $50

Missile Defense Unit, 1984, Hasbro, Battlefield Accessories, Model No. 6129-1
EX $10   NM $18   MIP $50

Mortar Defense Unit, 1984, Hasbro, Battlefield Accessories, Model No. 6129-3
EX $10   NM $18   MIP $50

Mountain Howitzer, 1984, Hasbro, Battle Station, Model No. 6125-3
EX $10   NM $16   MIP $60

Watchtower, 1984, Hasbro, Battle Station, Model No. 6125-2
EX $8   NM $22   MIP $65

SERIES 04, COBRA
Figure Sets

Buzzer, 1985, Hasbro, Dreadnok Mercenary, Model No. 6433
EX $8   NM $12   MIP $75

Crimson Guard, 1985, Hasbro, Elite Trooper, Model No. 6450
EX $15   NM $20   MIP $125

Eel, 1985, Hasbro, Frogman, Model No. 6448
EX $14   NM $18   MIP $100

Ripper, 1985, Hasbro, Mercenary, Model No. 6434
EX $8   NM $12   MIP $125

Snow Serpent, 1985, Hasbro, Polar Assault Trooper, Model No. 6449
EX $14   NM $18   MIP $85

Tele-Viper, 1985, Hasbro, Communications Trooper, Model No. 6447
EX $7   NM $10   MIP $65

(KP Photo, Karen O'Brien collection)

Tomax and Xamot, 1985, Hasbro, Crimson Guard Commanders, two blasters, one pulley w/string, Model No. 6063
EX $22   NM $35   MIP $240

Torch, 1985, Hasbro, Mercenary, Model No. 6435
EX $8   NM $12   MIP $90

Vehicle Sets

C.A.T., 1985, Hasbro, Motorized Crimson Attack Tank, Sears exclusive
EX $80   NM $250   MIP $475

Ferret, 1985, Hasbro, All-Terrain Vehicle, Model No. 6069
EX $12   NM $25   MIP $85

Moray, 1985, Hasbro, Cobra Hydrofoil w/Lamprey, Model No. 6024
EX $80   NM $135   MIP $510

Sentry and Missile System, S.M.S., 1985, Hasbro, Sears exclusive, w/H.I.S.S. Tank, Model No. 6686
EX $100   NM $225   MIP $575

Vehicles/Acessories

Cobra Bunker, 1985, Hasbro, Battle Station, Model No. 6125
EX $18   NM $15   MIP $65

Cobra Rifle Range Unit, 1985, Hasbro, Battlefield Accessories, Model No. 6129
EX $12   NM $22   MIP $62

Flight Pod, 1985, Hasbro, Trouble-Bubble, One-Man Bubble Pod, Model No. 6081
EX $12   NM $25   MIP $135

Night Landing, 1985, Hasbro, small boat, two oars, 12mm submachine gun, knife, shovel, radio, .45-cal machine gun, engine, Model No. 6085
EX $12   NM $22   MIP $70

S.N.A.K.E., 1985, Hasbro, One-Man Armored Suit (dark blue), Model No. 6081-2
EX $40   NM $70   MIP $195

SERIES 04, GI JOE
Figure Sets

Airtight, 1985, Hasbro, Hostile Environment Trooper, Model No. 6439
EX $7   NM $10   MIP $85

Alpine, 1985, Hasbro, Mountain Trooper, Model No. 6443
EX $12   NM $15   MIP $150

Barbecue, 1985, Hasbro, Fire Fighter, Model No. 6445
EX $7   NM $10   MIP $125

Bazooka, 1985, Hasbro, Missile Specialist, Model No. 6438
EX $8   NM $12   MIP $125

Dusty, 1985, Hasbro, Desert Trooper, Model No. 6442
EX $15   NM $20   MIP $190

Flint, 1985, Hasbro, Warrant Officer, Model No. 6436

EX $10   **NM** $12   **MIP** $120

Footloose, 1985, Hasbro, Infantry Trooper, Model No. 6444

EX $7   **NM** $10   **MIP** $125

Lady Jaye, 1985, Hasbro, Covert Operations Officer, Model No. 6440

EX $12   **NM** $15   **MIP** $150

Quick Kick, 1985, Hasbro, Silent Weapons Martial Artist, Model No. 6441

EX $7   **NM** $12   **MIP** $125

Shipwreck, 1985, Hasbro, Sailor and Parrot, Model No. 6446

EX $14   **NM** $18   **MIP** $145

Snake Eyes, 1985, Hasbro, Commando and Wolf, Model No. 6437

EX $40   **NM** $45   **MIP** $455

Tripwire, "Listen 'N Fun," 1985, Hasbro, Mine Detector, Model No. 6102

EX $55   **NM** $65   **MIP** $85

Vehicle Sets

A.W.E. Striker, 1985, Hasbro, All-Weather Environment Jeep w/Crankcase driver, Model No. 6053

EX $15   **NM** $150   **MIP** $425

Armadillo Mini Tank, 1985, Hasbro, holds up to three figures, Model No. 6078

EX $5   **NM** $12   **MIP** $70

Bridge Layer Toss 'n Cross, 1985, Hasbro, Bridge Laying Trank w/Toll Booth, Model No. 6023

EX $18   **NM** $75   **MIP** $325

Mauler M.B.T. Tank, 1985, Hasbro, Motorized Battle Tank w/Heavy Metal driver, Model No. 6015

EX $120   **NM** $175   **MIP** $600

Silver Mirage, 1985, Hasbro, Motorcycle w/Sidecar, Model No. 6076

EX $22   **NM** $40   **MIP** $100

Snow Cat, 1985, Hasbro, Snow Half-Track Vehicle w/Frost-Bite, Model No. 6057

EX $25   **NM** $70   **MIP** $275

U.S.S. Flagg, 1985, Hasbro, Aircraft Carrier w/Admiral Keel Haul, Model No. 6001

EX $625   **NM** $850   **MIP** $2500

Vehicles/Acessories

Air Defense, 1985, Hasbro, Battle Station, Model No. 6125-2

EX $5   **NM** $12   **MIP** $40

Ammo Dump, 1985, Hasbro, Battlefield Accessories, Model No. 6129-1

EX $8   **NM** $15   **MIP** $50

Battle Gear Accessory Pack #3, 1985, Hasbro, Model No. 6092

EX $6   **NM** $12   **MIP** $20

Bomb Disposal, 1985, Hasbro, small vehicle, Model No. 6085-2

EX $6   **NM** $16   **MIP** $42

Check Point Alpha, 1985, Hasbro, Battle Station, Model No. 6125-1

EX $8   **NM** $14   **MIP** $60

Forward Observer Unit, 1985, Hasbro, Battlefield Accessories, Model No. 6129-2

EX $6   **NM** $15   **MIP** $40

Parachute Pack, 1985, Hasbro, mail order; HALO parachute pack w/working parachute, available from 1985-89

EX $5   **NM** $12   **MIP** $25

Transportable Tactical Battle Platform, 1985, Hasbro, w/crane, heli-pad, swivel guns and missile launcher, Model No. 6021

EX $40   **NM** $70   **MIP** $300

Weapon Transport, 1985, Hasbro, small vehicle, Model No. 6085-1

EX $5   **NM** $10   **MIP** $40

SERIES 05, COBRA

Figure Sets

B.A.T., 1986, Hasbro, Battle Android Trooper, Model No. 6456

EX $17   **NM** $25   **MIP** $72

Dr. Mindbender, 1986, Hasbro, Master of Mind Control, Model No. 6461

EX $10   **NM** $13   **MIP** $60

Monkeywrench, 1986, Hasbro, Mercenary, Model No. 6460

EX $5   **NM** $8   **MIP** $48

Vipers, 1986, Hasbro, Infantry Trooper, Model No. 6473

EX $14   **NM** $18   **MIP** $58

Zandar, 1986, Hasbro, Zartan's Brother, Mercenary, Model No. 6457

EX $8   **NM** $11   **MIP** $38

Zarana, 1986, Hasbro, Zartan's Sister, Mercenary, w/out earrings, Model No. 6472

EX $6   **NM** $8   **MIP** $40

Zarana, 1986, Hasbro, Reissue w/earrings, Model No. 6472

EX $10   **NM** $14   **MIP** $60

Vehicle Sets

Air Chariot, 1986, Hasbro, w/Serpentor "Cobra Emperor," Model No. 6062

EX $22   **NM** $32   **MIP** $225

Cobra Hydro Sled, 1986, Hasbro, small vehicle, Model No. 6099-2

EX $5   **NM** $11   **MIP** $60

Dreadnok Air Assault, 1986, Hasbro, Sears Exclusive, VTOL and Gyrocopter

EX $165   **NM** $260   **MIP** $925

Dreadnok Ground Assault, 1986, Hasbro, Sears Exclusive, motorcycle and 4WD vehicle

EX $175   **NM** $275   **MIP** $1025

Dreadnok Swampfire, 1986, Hasbro, Air/Swamp Transforming Vehicle w/Color-Change, Model No. 6068

EX $15   **NM** $22   **MIP** $125

Dreadnok Thunder Machine, 1986, Hasbro, compilation vehicle of spare car and truck parts, designed by Destro, w/Thrasher driver, Model No. 6042

EX $24   **NM** $44   **MIP** $350

Night Raven S-3P, 1986, Hasbro, Surveillance Jet w/Drone Pod and Strato Viper pilot, Model No. 6014

EX $60   **NM** $90   **MIP** $725

Stun, 1986, Hasbro, Split Attack Vehicle w/Motor Viper driver, Model No. 6041

EX $15   **NM** $38   **MIP** $305

Vehicles/Acessories

Battle Gear Accessory Pack #4, 1986, Hasbro, Model No. 6096

EX $5   **NM** $10   **MIP** $15

Surveillance Port, 1986, Hasbro, Battle Station, Model No. 6130

EX $10   **NM** $25   **MIP** $135

Terror Drome, 1986, Hasbro, Armored Headquarters w/Firebat Jet and A.V.A.C. pilot, Model No. 6003

EX $210   **NM** $310   **MIP** $1600

SERIES 05, GI JOE

Figure Sets

Beach Head, 1986, Hasbro, Ranger, Model No. 6463

EX $10   **NM** $14   **MIP** $92

Major Matt Mason, Sgt. Storm,
Mattel, 1967-79, 6", $430

Spawn, McFarlane Toys,
1994, 5-1/4, $25

Planet of the Apes, Galen,
Mego, 1973-75, 8", $100

Action Figures

Bob and Doug McKenzie,
Doug Mckenzie, McFarlane Toys,
2000, $15

The Simpsons, Homer, Mattel,
1990, $15

Strawberry Shortcake
(Series 1), Strawberry
Shortcake, Kenner, $80

Transformers (Generation 1,
Series 2), Blaster, Hasbro, 1985, $120

G.I. Joe, 3-3/4" Figures,
Night Force-Lightfoot
(Toys R Us Exclusive).
Hasbro, 1987, $185

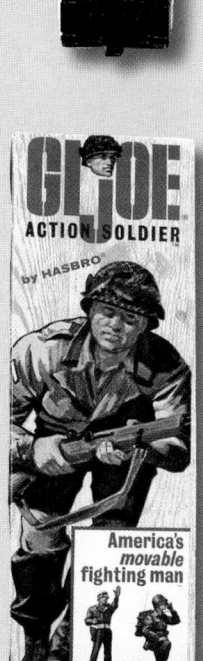

G.I. Joe Action Soldier,
Hasbro, 1964, 12", $450

Cobra Commander, 1982, 3-3/4",
Mail Exclusive, $50

G.I. Joe Attack Glider
Falcon, 1983, $150

G.I. Joe

G.I. Joe, 3-3/4" Figures,
Motorized Battle Wagon,
Hasbro, 1991, $60

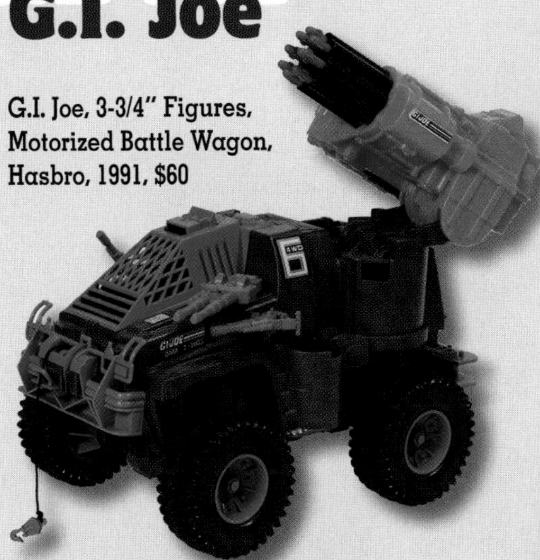

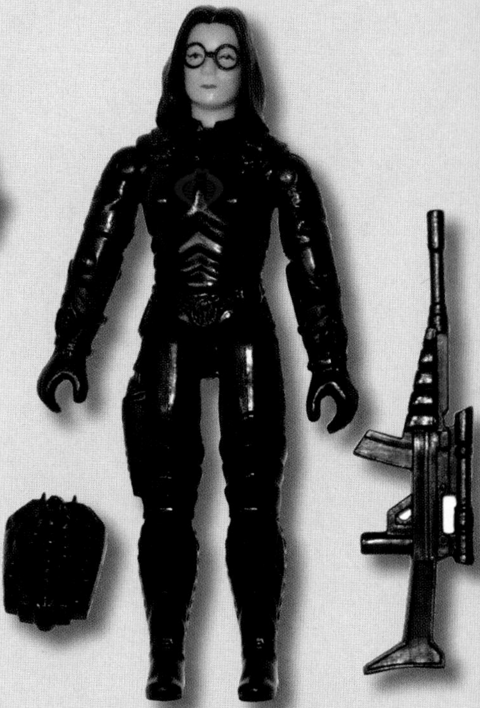

Baroness, 1982, 3-3/4", $275

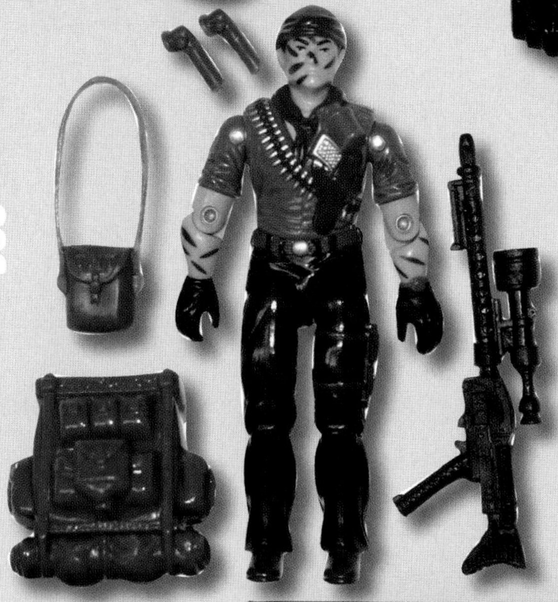

G.I. Joe, 3-3/4" Figures,
Tunnel Rat, #6481, Hasbro,
1987, $70

Cobra Missile
Command
Headquarters,
Sears Exclusive,
1982, $500

Games
Games

The Rebel, Ideal, 1961, $100

Wagon Train, Milton Bradley,
1960, $50

Mod Squad Game, Remco, 1968, $125

Johnny Quest Game,
Transogram, 1964, $500

Six Million Dollar Man,
Parker Bros., 1975, $25

Battle of the Planets,
Milton Bradley, 1979, $35

Hot Wheels

Hot Wheels Heavy Chevy,
Redline, 1970, $180

Hot Wheels '57 Chevy, Redline, 1977, $110

Hot Wheels Boss Hoss,
Redline, 1971, $325

Hot Wheels Classic '57 T-Bird,
Redline, 1969, $190

Hot Wheels Evil Weevil,
Redline, 1971, $250

Hot Wheels Cockney Cab,
Redline, 1971, $150

Hot Wheels Deora,
Redline, 1968, $400

Hot Wheels Custom VW Bug, Redline, 1968, $350

Hot Wheels

Hot Wheels Funny Money, Redline, 1972, $345

Hot Wheels Classic '36 Ford Coupe, Redline, 1969, $190

Hot Wheels Beatnik Bandit, Redline, 1968, $90

Hot Wheels Classic '32 Ford Vicky, Redline, 1969, $150

-391-

Hot Wheels King Kuda, Redline, 1970, $225

Hot Wheels Classic Nomad, Redline, 1970, $125

Hot Wheels Classic '31 Woody, Redline. 1969, $150

Lunch Boxes

Archies, The, Aladdin, 1969, $325

Johnny Lightning, Aladdin, 1970, $250

Snoopy Dome, blue cup in Snoopy's hand,
King Seeley Thermos, $450

Superman, front of box, Adco, 1954, $16,500

Battlestar Galactica, Aladdin, 1978, $275

Star Wars: Return of the Jedi,
King Seeley Thermos, 1983, $150

Man From U.N.C.L.E., The, King Seeley Thermos, 1966, $850

Dr. Seuss, Aladdin, 1970, $525

Get Smart, King Seeley Thermos, 1966, $575

James Bond XX, Ohio Arts, 1969, $300

G.I. Joe, King Seeley Thermos, 1967, $425

Planet of the Apes, Aladdin, 1974, $525

Space Toys

Buck Rogers 25th Century Rocket Pistol
XZ-31, Daisy, 1934, $600

Robert Lilliput, KTA,
1939, 6", $10,000

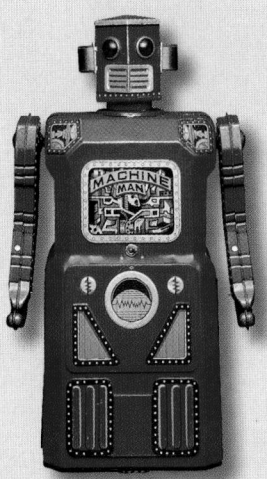

Lost In Space Robot
Remco, 1966, $700

Machine Man,
Masudaya,
1950s, $45,000

Cragston Robot,
1962, 12", $1,800

Tom Corbett Push-Outs Book,
Saalfield, 1952, $100

Chewbacca, Star Wars first series,
Kenner, 3-3/4", $300

Return of the Jedi,
Scout Walker Vehicle,
Kenner, 1983, $55

POTF2-1, R2-D2 w/Holographic Princess Leia,
Hasbro, 1999, $20

Action Figures, 3-3/4"
(Star Wars Series 1),
Ben (Obi-Wan) Kenobi,
Kenner, 1977, $425

Star Wars

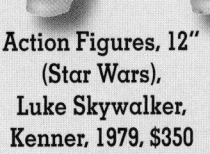

Action Figures, 12"
(Star Wars),
Luke Skywalker,
Kenner, 1979, $350

Bob Fett Doll, Kenner,
13", 1979-1980, $200 loose

Action Figures, 3-3/4" (Star Wars
Series 1), Snaggletooth (blue body –
Sears exclusive), Kenner, 1979, $300

The Empire Strikes Back Carrying Case,
Kenner, 1980, $50

Naboo Fighter, LEGO, 1999, $25

Nylint Payloader No. 1600, 1951-55, $350

Corgi Volkswagen Military
Personnel Carrier, 1964-66, $180

Marx Magnetic Crane and Truck,
1950, $275

Vehicles

Smith-Miller GMC Bank of America, 1949, $600

Structo Wrecker Truck, #822, $450

Tonka Carnation Milk Step Van, 11-3/4", 1954, $600

Marx Carousel Truck, 7-1/2" long, 1967-68, $45

Roy Rogers Toy Cap Pistols,
Kilgore, 1950s, $550

Luca McCain, The Rifleman,
Hartland statue, $610

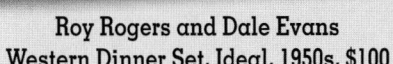

Roy Rogers and Dale Evans
Western Dinner Set, Ideal, 1950s, $100

Johnny Ringo
Gun and Holster Set,
Marx, 1960, $375

The Lone Ranger Rides Again,
Lone Ranger and Tonto,
Gabriel, 1979, 9", $75 each

Mystic Motorcycle Cop,
Marx, 1930s, 9", $400

G.I. Joe and His Jouncing Jeep,
Unique Art, 1940s, $275

Popeye Heavy Hitter, Chein, $6,400

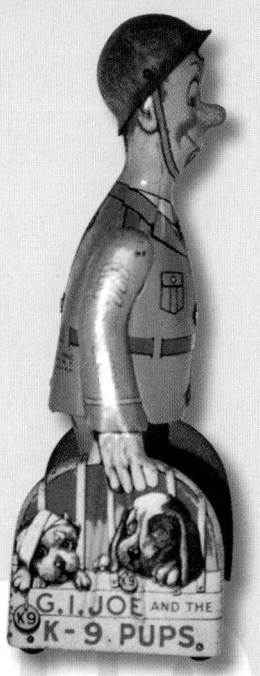

Charlie McCarthy, Marx, 1930s, $700

Mickey Mouse Lionel Circus Train Hand Car,
9" long, $1,500

G.I. Joe and His K-9 Pups

–400–

Dial-Tone, 1986, Hasbro, Communications Expert, Model No. 6471
EX $6 **NM** $10 **MIP** $60

Hawk, 1986, Hasbro, Commander, Model No. 6468
EX $7 **NM** $10 **MIP** $50

Iceberg, 1986, Hasbro, Snow Trooper, Model No. 6466
EX $6 **NM** $8 **MIP** $40

Leatherneck, 1986, Hasbro, Marine Gunner, Model No. 6458
EX $7 **NM** $10 **MIP** $50

Lifeline, 1986, Hasbro, Rescue Trooper, Model No. 6465
EX $8 **NM** $10 **MIP** $65

Low-Light, 1986, Hasbro, Night Spotter, Model No. 6459
EX $10 **NM** $12 **MIP** $68

Mainframe, 1986, Hasbro, Computer Specialist, Model No. 6462
EX $6 **NM** $8 **MIP** $50

Roadblock, 1986, Hasbro, Heavy Machine Gunner, Model No. 6467
EX $8 **NM** $11 **MIP** $50

Sci-Fi, 1986, Hasbro, Laser Trooper, Model No. 6469
EX $7 **NM** $10 **MIP** $45

Sgt. Slaughter, 1986, Hasbro, mail-away, Drill Sergeant
EX $7 **NM** $13 **MIP** $40

Special Missions: Brazil, 1986, Hasbro, Toys R Us set w/five figures: Dial-Tone, Mainframe, Wet-Suit, Leatherneck, and Claymore (this figure's only appearance)
EX $95 **NM** $190 **MIP** $700

The Fridge, 1986, Hasbro, mail order, Physical Training Instructor
EX $8 **NM** $12 **MIP** $25

Wet-Suit, 1986, Hasbro, Navy S.E.A.L., Model No. 6470
EX $10 **NM** $14 **MIP** $65

Vehicle Sets

Conquest X-30, 1986, Hasbro, Super-Sonic Jet w/Slip-Stream pilot, Model No. 6031
EX $30 **NM** $50 **MIP** $300

Devilfish, 1986, Hasbro, High-Speed Attack Boat, Model No. 6066
EX $15 **NM** $20 **MIP** $82

H.A.V.O.C., 1986, Hasbro, Heavy Artillery Vehicle Ordinance Carrier w/Cross-Country driver, Model No. 6030
EX $22 **NM** $48 **MIP** $325

L.V.C. Recon Sled, 1986, Hasbro, Low-Crawl Vehicle Cycle, Model No. 6067
EX $6 **NM** $15 **MIP** $45

Tomahawk, 1986, Hasbro, Troop Transit Helicopter w/Lift-Ticket, Model No. 6022
EX $52 **NM** $75 **MIP** $585

(Karen O'Brien collection)

Triple T (Tag Team Terminator), 1986, Hasbro, one-man tank w/Sgt. Slaughter driver, Model No. 6061
EX $12 **NM** $32 **MIP** $150

Vehicles/Acessories

Outpost Defender, 1986, Hasbro, Battle Station, Model No. 6130
EX $5 **NM** $15 **MIP** $45

SERIES 06, COBRA

Figure Sets

Big Boa, 1987, Hasbro, Troop Trainer, Model No. 6484
EX n/a **NM** $10 **MIP** $45

Cobra Commander, 1987, Hasbro, Cobra Leader w/Battle Armor, Model No. 6474
EX n/a **NM** $10 **MIP** $52

Cobra-La Team, 1987, Hasbro, three-figure set: Nemesis Enforcer, Royal Guard, Golobulus, Model No. 6154
EX n/a **NM** $26 **MIP** $70

Croc Master, 1987, Hasbro, Reptile Trainer, Model No. 6487
EX n/a **NM** $10 **MIP** $43

Crystal Ball, 1987, Hasbro, Hypnotist, Model No. 6479
EX n/a **NM** $6 **MIP** $20

Raptor, 1987, Hasbro, Falconer, Model No. 6485
EX n/a **NM** $10 **MIP** $34

Techno-Viper, 1987, Hasbro, Battlefield Technician, Model No. 6490
EX n/a **NM** $10 **MIP** $42

Vehicle Sets

Buzz Boar, 1987, Hasbro, Underground Attack Vehicle, Model No. 6087-3
EX $7 **NM** $12 **MIP** $35

Dreadnok Air Skiff, 1987, Hasbro, mini-set w/Zanzibar, Model No. 6070
EX $5 **NM** $11 **MIP** $50

Dreadnok Cycle, 1987, Hasbro, Compilation Cycle w/Gunner Station, Model No. 6171
EX $8 **NM** $14 **MIP** $38

Maggot, 1987, Hasbro, three-in-one tank vehicle w/W.O.R.M.S. driver, Model No. 6029
EX $14 **NM** $37 **MIP** $205

Mamba, 1987, Hasbro, Attack Copter w/removable pods w/Gyro-Viper, Model No. 6026
EX $30 **NM** $44 **MIP** $215

Pogo, 1987, Hasbro, Ballistic Battle Ball, Model No. 6170
EX $8 **NM** $11 **MIP** $42

Sea Ray, 1987, Hasbro, Combination Submarine/Jet w/Sea Slug, Model No. 6040
EX $10 **NM** $28 **MIP** $175

Wolf, 1987, Hasbro, Arctic Terrain Vehicle w/Ice Viper, Model No. 6039
EX $13 **NM** $30 **MIP** $110

Vehicles/Acessories

Cobra Jet Pack, 1987, Hasbro, accessory for figures
EX $5 **NM** $8 **MIP** $30

Earth Borer, 1987, Hasbro, Motorized Action Packs, Model No. 6133-3
EX n/a **NM** $5 **MIP** $10

Mountain Climber, 1987, Hasbro, Motorized Action Packs, Model No. 6133-7
EX n/a **NM** $5 **MIP** $10

Pom-Pom Gun Pack, 1987, Hasbro, Motorized Action Packs, Model No. 6133-8
EX n/a **NM** $5 **MIP** $10

Rope Crosser, 1987, Hasbro, Motorized Action Packs, Model No. 6133-5
EX n/a **NM** $5 **MIP** $10

SERIES 06, GI JOE

Figure Sets

Battleforce 2000 Avalanche, 1987, Hasbro, Dominator Snow Vehicle Driver
EX $6 **NM** $10 **MIP** $24

Battleforce 2000 Blaster, 1987, Hasbro, Vindicator Hovercraft pilot
EX $6 **NM** $10 **MIP** $24

Battleforce 2000 Blocker, 1987, Hasbro, four-wheeled driver
EX $6 **NM** $10 **MIP** $24

Battleforce 2000 Dodger, 1987, Hasbro, Marauder Half-Track driver
EX $6   NM $10   MIP $24

Battleforce 2000 Knockdown, 1987, Hasbro, Sky Sweeper Anti-Aircraft operator
EX $6   NM $10   MIP $24

Battleforce 2000 Maverick, 1987, Hasbro, Jet Fighter Pilot
EX $6   NM $10   MIP $24

Chuckles, 1987, Hasbro, Undercover M.P., Model No. 6482
EX n/a   NM $11   MIP $40

Crazy Legs, 1987, Hasbro, Air Assault Trooper, Model No. 6475
EX n/a   NM $8   MIP $28

Falcon, 1987, Hasbro, Green Beret, Model No. 6476
EX n/a   NM $14   MIP $62

Fast Draw, 1987, Hasbro, Mobile Missile Specialist, Model No. 6488
EX n/a   NM $10   MIP $30

Gung-Ho, 1987, Hasbro, Marine in Dress Blues, Model No. 6486
EX n/a   NM $12   MIP $49

Jinx, 1987, Hasbro, Ninja Intelligence Officer, Model No. 6480
EX n/a   NM $10   MIP $65

Law & Order, 1987, Hasbro, M.P. w/Dog, Model No. 6478
EX n/a   NM $12   MIP $45

Outback, 1987, Hasbro, Survivalist, Model No. 6483
EX n/a   NM $10   MIP $50

Psyche-Out, 1987, Hasbro, Deceptive Warfare Trooper, Model No. 6477
EX n/a   NM $18   MIP $25

Sgt. Slaughter's Renegades, 1987, Hasbro, three-figure set: Red Dog, Mercer and Taurus, Model No. 6153
EX n/a   NM $28   MIP $62

Sneak Peek, 1987, Hasbro, Advanced Recon Trooper, Model No. 6491
EX n/a   NM $10   MIP $32

Starduster, 1987, Hasbro, Jet Pack Trooper, mail-in figure through 1991
EX $40   NM $80   MIP $165

Steel Brigade, 1987, Hasbro, Special Forces trooper, mail-in figure through 1994, five versions were produced
EX $12   NM $24   MIP $42

Tunnel Rat, 1987, Hasbro, Underground Explosive Expert, Model No. 6481
EX n/a   NM $8   MIP $70

Vehicle Sets

Anti-Aircraft Gun, 1987, Hasbro, Motorized Action Pack, Model No. 6133-1
EX n/a   NM $5   MIP $10

Coastal Defender, 1987, Hasbro, Mini-Vehicle w/accessories, Model No. 6087-2
EX $5   NM $10   MIP $40

Crossfire-Alfa, 1987, Hasbro, Radio Control Vehicle w/Rumbler, Model No. 6004-1
EX $45   NM $70   MIP $245

Crossfire-Delta, 1987, Hasbro, Radio Control Vehicle w/Rumbler, Model No. 6004-2
EX $45   NM $70   MIP $245

Defiant Space Shuttle Complex, 1987, Hasbro, space shuttle, space station, crawler, Model No. 6002
EX $345   NM $550   MIP $1475

Dominator Snow Tank, 1988, Hasbro, Battleforce 2000
EX $8   NM $13   MIP $65

Eliminator 4WD, 1988, Hasbro, Battleforce 2000
EX $8   NM $13   MIP $65

Helicopter, 1987, Hasbro, Motorized Action Pack, Model No. 6133-2
EX n/a   NM $5   MIP $10

Marauder Motorcycle-Tank, 1988, Hasbro, Battleforce 2000
EX $8   NM $13   MIP $65

Persuader, 1987, Hasbro, Laser Tank w/Backstop, Model No. 6038
EX $9   NM $15   MIP $65

Radar Station, 1987, Hasbro, Motorized Action Pack, Model No. 6133-3
EX n/a   NM $5   MIP $10

Road Toad, 1987, Hasbro, Tow Vehicle w/accessories, Model No. 6087-1
EX $4   NM $7   MIP $15

Rope Walker, 1987, Hasbro, Motorized Action Pack, Model No. 6133-4
EX n/a   NM $5   MIP $10

S.L.A.M., 1987, Hasbro, Strategic Long-Range Artillery Machine, Model No. 6172
EX $6   NM $20   MIP $85

Sky Sweeper Anti-Aircraft Tank, 1988, Hasbro, Battleforce 2000
EX $8   NM $13   MIP $65

Vector Jet, 1988, Hasbro, Battleforce 2000
EX $8   NM $13   MIP $65

Vindicator Hovercraft, 1988, Hasbro, Battleforce 2000
EX $8   NM $13   MIP $65

Vehicles/Acessories

Battle Gear Accessory Pack #5, 1987, Hasbro, Model No. 6677
EX $5   NM $10   MIP $15

Mobile Command Center, 1987, Hasbro, w/Steam-Roller driver, large crane play set, Model No. 6006
EX $60   NM $95   MIP $460

Vehicle Gear Accessory Pack #1, 1987, Hasbro, Model No. 6098
EX n/a   NM $5   MIP $10

SERIES 07, COBRA
Figure Sets

Astro-Viper, 1988, Hasbro, Cobranaut
EX n/a   NM $10   MIP $27

Hydro-Viper, 1988, Hasbro, Underwater Elite Trooper
EX n/a   NM $10   MIP $35

Iron Grenadier, 1988, Hasbro, Destro's Elite Troops
EX n/a   NM $14   MIP $38

Road Pig, 1988, Hasbro, Dreadnok
EX n/a   NM $10   MIP $35

Toxo-Viper, 1988, Hasbro, Hostile Environment
EX n/a   NM $10   MIP $30

Voltar, 1988, Hasbro, Destro's General
EX n/a   NM $7   MIP $20

Vehicle Sets

Cobra Adder, 1988, Hasbro, Twin Missile Launcher
EX $5   NM $8   MIP $40

Cobra B.U.G.G., 1988, Hasbro, w/Secto-Viper driver
EX $35   NM $50   MIP $290

Cobra Battle Barge, 1988, Hasbro, clear labels on retail version, white labels on mail-away version
EX $5   NM $10   MIP $45

Cobra IMP, 1988, Hasbro, w/three two-part missiles & 24 mines (eight mines per missile)
EX $7   NM $10   MIP $34

Cobra Stellar Stiletto, 1988, Hasbro, w/Star-Viper
EX $16   NM $38   MIP $125

Gyrocoptor, 1988, Hasbro, Motorized Vehicle Packs
EX n/a   NM $6   MIP $12

Iron Grenadiers A.G.P. (Anti-Gravity Pods), 1988, Hasbro, w/Nullifier pilot
EX $10   NM $22   MIP $132

Iron Grenadiers D.E.M.O.N., 1988, Hasbro, w/Ferret the driver
EX $14   NM $32   MIP $130

Iron Grenadiers Destro's Despoiler, 1988, Hasbro, w/Destro, gold helmet, black outfit, gold sword
EX $7   **NM** $22   **MIP** $78

Rocket Sled, 1988, Hasbro, Motorized Vehicle Packs
EX n/a   **NM** $6   **MIP** $12

Vehicles/Acessories

Battle Gear Accessory Pack #6, 1988, Hasbro
EX $5   **NM** $10   **MIP** $15

Dreadnok Battle Axe, 1988, Hasbro, Motorized Action Packs
EX n/a   **NM** $6   **MIP** $12

Machine Gun Nest, 1988, Hasbro, Motorized Action Packs
EX n/a   **NM** $6   **MIP** $12

Twin Missile Radar, 1988, Hasbro, Motorized Action Packs
EX n/a   **NM** $6   **MIP** $12

SERIES 07, GI JOE
Figure Sets

Blizzard, 1988, Hasbro, Artic Attack
EX n/a   **NM** $8   **MIP** $25

Budo, 1988, Hasbro, Samuri Warrior
EX n/a   **NM** $7   **MIP** $30

Charbroil, 1988, Hasbro, Flamethrower
EX n/a   **NM** $7   **MIP** $25

Hardball, 1988, Hasbro, Multi-Shot Grenadier
EX n/a   **NM** $6   **MIP** $25

Hit & Run, 1988, Hasbro, Light Infantryman
EX n/a   **NM** $10   **MIP** $40

Lightfoot, 1988, Hasbro, Explosives Expert
EX n/a   **NM** $7   **MIP** $22

Muskrat, 1988, Hasbro, Swamp Fighter
EX n/a   **NM** $7   **MIP** $25

Night Force (Toys R Us Exclusive), 1988, Hasbro, two-figure pack: Psyche-Out and Tunnel Rat
EX n/a   **NM** $55   **MIP** $160

Night Force (Toys R Us Exclusive), 1988, Hasbro, two-figure pack: Outback and Crazylegs
EX n/a   **NM** $48   **MIP** $108

Night Force (Toys R Us Exclusive), 1988, Hasbro, two-figure pack: Lt. Falcon and Sneak Peek
EX n/a   **NM** $65   **MIP** $155

Repeater, 1988, Hasbro, Stedi-Cam Machine Gunner
EX n/a   **NM** $7   **MIP** $25

Shockwave, 1988, Hasbro, S.W.A.T.
EX n/a   **NM** $10   **MIP** $35

Spearhead & Max, 1988, Hasbro, Point Man & Bobcat
EX n/a   **NM** $8   **MIP** $25

Storm Shadow, 1988, Hasbro, Ninja
EX n/a   **NM** $16   **MIP** $55

Super Trooper, 1988, Hasbro, mail-in
EX n/a   **NM** $10   **MIP** $30

Tiger Force Bazooka, 1988, Hasbro, Missile Specialist
EX n/a   **NM** $10   **MIP** $25

Tiger Force Duke, 1988, Hasbro, First Sergeant
EX n/a   **NM** $12   **MIP** $34

Tiger Force Dusty, 1988, Hasbro, Desert Trooper
EX n/a   **NM** $10   **MIP** $26

Tiger Force Flint, 1988, Hasbro, Warrant Officer
EX n/a   **NM** $10   **MIP** $27

Tiger Force Lifeline, 1988, Hasbro, Medic
EX n/a   **NM** $8   **MIP** $27

Tiger Force Roadblock, 1988, Hasbro, Heavy Machine Gunner
EX n/a   **NM** $10   **MIP** $30

Tiger Force Tripwire, 1988, Hasbro, Mine Detector
EX n/a   **NM** $8   **MIP** $27

Vehicle Sets

A.T.V., 1988, Hasbro, Motorized Vehicle Packs
EX n/a   **NM** $7   **MIP** $16

Desert Fox 6-Wheel Drive, 1988, Hasbro, w/Skidmark driver
EX $12   **NM** $30   **MIP** $105

Mean Dog, 1988, Hasbro, w/Wildcard driver
EX $22   **NM** $36   **MIP** $235

Night Blaster, 1988, Hasbro, Night Force, based on 1987 Cobra Maggot
EX $40   **NM** $75   **MIP** $230

Night Raider, 1988, Hasbro, Night Force, based on 1986 Triple T
EX $20   **NM** $40   **MIP** $140

Night Shade, 1988, Hasbro, Night Force, based on 1983 S.H.A.R.C.
EX $22   **NM** $40   **MIP** $140

Night Storm, 1988, Hasbro, Night Force, based on 1987 Persuader
EX $30   **NM** $42   **MIP** $160

Night Striker, 1988, Hasbro, Night Force, based on 1984 W.H.A.L.E.
EX $250   **NM** $285   **MIP** $650

Phantom X-19 Stealth Fighter, 1988, Hasbro, w/Ghostrider pilot
EX $35   **NM** $60   **MIP** $240

R.P.V., 1988, Hasbro, Remot Piloted Vehicle
EX $5   **NM** $16   **MIP** $40

Rolling Thunder, 1988, Hasbro, w/Armadillo driver
EX $48   **NM** $65   **MIP** $240

Scuba Pack, 1988, Hasbro, Motorized Vehicle Packs
EX n/a   **NM** $12   **MIP** $20

Skystorm X-Wing Chopper, 1988, Hasbro, w/Windmill pilot
EX $10   **NM** $28   **MIP** $105

Swampmasher, 1988, Hasbro
EX $6   **NM** $12   **MIP** $42

Tank Car, 1988, Hasbro, Motorized Vehicle Packs
EX n/a   **NM** $10   **MIP** $20

Tiger Cat, 1988, Hasbro, Tiger Force snow vehicle w/Frostbite driver
EX $16   **NM** $34   **MIP** $120

Tiger Fly, 1988, Hasbro, Tiger Force Helicopter w/Recondo
EX $22   **NM** $46   **MIP** $160

Tiger Paw, 1988, Hasbro, Tiger Force 4WD vehicle
EX $12   **NM** $26   **MIP** $60

Tiger Rat, 1988, Hasbro, Tiger Force Airplane w/Skystriker pilot
EX $42   **NM** $62   **MIP** $240

Tiger Shark, 1988, Hasbro, Tiger Force (Water Mocassin) boat
EX $16   **NM** $36   **MIP** $130

Warthog A.I.F.V, 1988, Hasbro, Amphibious Infantry Fighting Vehicle w/Sgt. Slaughter driver
EX $14   **NM** $26   **MIP** $150

Vehicles/Acessories

Double Machine Gun, 1988, Hasbro, Motorized Action Packs
EX n/a   **NM** $5   **MIP** $10

Mine Sweeper, 1988, Hasbro, Motorized Action Packs
EX n/a   **NM** $5   **MIP** $10

Mortar Launcher, 1988, Hasbro, Motorized Action Packs
EX n/a   **NM** $5   **MIP** $10

SERIES 08, COBRA
Figure Sets

Alley Viper, 1989, Hasbro, Cobra Urban Assault
EX n/a   **NM** $14   **MIP** $48

Frag-Viper, 1989, Hasbro, Cobra Grenade Thrower
EX n/a   **NM** $12   **MIP** $30

Gnawgahyde, 1989, Hasbro, Dreadnok Poacher
EX n/a   **NM** $13   **MIP** $40

H.E.A.T. Viper, 1989, Hasbro, Cobra Bazooka Man

EX n/a   **NM** $8   **MIP** $26

Iron Grenadiers Annihilator, 1989, Hasbro, Destro's Elite Trooper

EX n/a   **NM** $8   **MIP** $25

Iron Grenadiers T.A.R.G.A.T., 1989, Hasbro, Trans Atmospheric Rapid Global Assault Trooper

EX n/a   **NM** $7   **MIP** $25

Night-Viper, 1989, Hasbro, Night Fighter

EX n/a   **NM** $13   **MIP** $34

Python Patrol Copperhead, 1989, Hasbro, Swamp Fighter

EX n/a   **NM** $12   **MIP** $35

Python Patrol Crimson Guard, 1989, Hasbro, Elite Trooper

EX n/a   **NM** $12   **MIP** $38

Python Patrol Officer, 1989, Hasbro

EX n/a   **NM** $12   **MIP** $38

Python Patrol Tele-Viper, 1989, Hasbro, Communications

EX n/a   **NM** $9   **MIP** $32

Python Patrol Trooper, 1989, Hasbro, Infantry

EX n/a   **NM** $12   **MIP** $26

Python Patrol Viper, 1989, Hasbro, Assault Trooper

EX n/a   **NM** $12   **MIP** $38

Vehicle Sets

Condor Z25, 1989, Hasbro, w/Aero-Viper pilot

EX $50   **NM** $70   **MIP** $270

Devastator, 1989, Hasbro, Battlefield Robot

EX $4   **NM** $9   **MIP** $22

F.A.N.G. II, 1989, Hasbro

EX $9   **NM** $16   **MIP** $55

H.I.S.S. II, 1989, Hasbro, Cobra Tank w/Track Viper

EX $17   **NM** $32   **MIP** $165

Hovercraft, 1989, Hasbro, Battlefield Robot

EX $5   **NM** $19   **MIP** $22

Iron Grenadiers Darklon's Evader, 1989, Hasbro, w/Darklon

EX $9   **NM** $16   **MIP** $80

Iron Grenadiers Destro's Razorback, 1989, Hasbro, w/Wild Boar

EX $22   **NM** $38   **MIP** $160

Python Patrol ASP, 1989, Hasbro, cannon

EX $15   **NM** $24   **MIP** $63

Python Patrol Conquest, 1989, Hasbro, plane

EX $22   **NM** $32   **MIP** $110

Python Patrol STUN, 1989, Hasbro, tri-wheel vehicle

EX $22   **NM** $32   **MIP** $110

SERIES 08, GI JOE
Figure Sets

Backblast, 1989, Hasbro, Anti-Aircraft Soldier

EX n/a   **NM** $8   **MIP** $24

Battleforce 2000 Dee Jay, 1989, Hasbro, Comm-Tech Trooper

EX n/a   **NM** $6   **MIP** $12

Countdown, 1989, Hasbro, Astronaut

EX n/a   **NM** $8   **MIP** $24

Deep Six, 1989, Hasbro, Deep Sea Diver

EX n/a   **NM** $12   **MIP** $26

Downtown, 1989, Hasbro, Mortar Man

EX n/a   **NM** $6   **MIP** $15

Night Force (Toys R Us Exclusive), 1989, Hasbro, two-figure pack: Muskrat and Spearhead & Max

EX n/a   **NM** $100   **MIP** $150

Night Force (Toys R Us Exclusive), 1989, Hasbro, two-figure pack: Charbroil and Repeater

EX n/a   **NM** $110   **MIP** $210

Night Force (Toys R Us Exclusive), 1989, Hasbro, two-figure pack: Lightfoot and Shockwave

EX n/a   **NM** $100   **MIP** $150

Recoil, 1989, Hasbro, Long Range Recon Patrol

EX n/a   **NM** $8   **MIP** $23

Rock 'N' Roll, 1989, Hasbro, Gatling Gunner

EX n/a   **NM** $8   **MIP** $30

Scoop, 1989, Hasbro, Information Specialist

EX n/a   **NM** $8   **MIP** $24

Slaughter's Marauders Barbecue, 1989, Hasbro, Firefighter

EX n/a   **NM** $10   **MIP** $24

Slaughter's Marauders Footloose, 1989, Hasbro, Infantry Trooper

EX n/a   **NM** $10   **MIP** $24

Slaughter's Marauders Low Light, 1989, Hasbro, Night Spotter

EX n/a   **NM** $10   **MIP** $24

Slaughter's Marauders Mutt & Junkyard, 1989, Hasbro, Animal Control

EX n/a   **NM** $10   **MIP** $24

Slaughter's Marauders Sgt. Slaughter, 1989, Hasbro, Commander

EX n/a   **NM** $12   **MIP** $40

Slaughter's Marauders Spirit & Freedom, 1989, Hasbro, Tracker

EX n/a   **NM** $10   **MIP** $24

Snake Eyes, 1989, Hasbro, Commando

EX n/a   **NM** $14   **MIP** $50

Stalker, 1989, Hasbro, Tundra Ranger

EX n/a   **NM** $8   **MIP** $24

Vehicle Sets

Battleforce 2000 Pulverizer, 1989, Hasbro, mini-tank

EX $5   **NM** $15   **MIP** $50

Crusader Space Shuttle, 1989, Hasbro, w/Avenger aircraft and Payload the pilot

EX $45   **NM** $85   **MIP** $295

Mudfighter, 1989, Hasbro, w/Dogfight driver

EX $8   **NM** $20   **MIP** $105

Night Boomer, 1989, Hasbro, Night Force, based on 1983 Skystriker

EX $180   **NM** $255   **MIP** $495

Night Ray, 1989, Hasbro, Night Force, based on 1985 Cobra Hydrofoil

EX $180   **NM** $210   **MIP** $410

Night Scrambler, 1989, Hasbro, Night Force, based on 1983 APC

EX $60   **NM** $75   **MIP** $225

Radar Rat, 1989, Hasbro, Battlefield Robot

EX $4   **NM** $9   **MIP** $33

Raider, 1989, Hasbro, w/Hot Seat

EX $20   **NM** $32   **MIP** $160

Slaughter's Marauders Armadillo, 1989, Hasbro, tank w/rocket launchers

EX $14   **NM** $22   **MIP** $58

Slaughter's Marauders Equalizer, 1989, Hasbro, tank w/rocket launchers and two laser cannons

EX $28   **NM** $32   **MIP** $110

Slaughter's Marauders Lynx, 1989, Hasbro, tank w/large cannon

EX $22   **NM** $30   **MIP** $105

Thunderclap, 1989, Hasbro, w/Long Range driver

EX $32   **NM** $65   **MIP** $200

Tiger Fish, 1989, Hasbro, Tiger Force (Devil Fish) boat

EX $16   **NM** $25   **MIP** $85

Tiger Sting, 1989, Hasbro, Tiger Force (Vamp Mark II) jeep vehicle

EX $25   **NM** $32   **MIP** $130

Tri-Blaster, 1989, Hasbro, Battlefield Robot

EX $4   **NM** $9   **MIP** $22

SERIES 09, COBRA
Figure Sets

Iron Grenadiers Metal-Head, 1990, Hasbro, Destro's Anti-Tank Specialist and one crazy guy!
EX n/a   NM $9   MIP $28

Iron Grenadiers Undertow, 1990, Hasbro, Destro's Frogman
EX n/a   NM $10   MIP $26

Laser-Viper, 1990, Hasbro, Laser Trooper
EX n/a   NM $9   MIP $28

Night Creeper, 1990, Hasbro, Ninja
EX n/a   NM $10   MIP $32

Range-Viper, 1990, Hasbro, Wilderness Trooper
EX n/a   NM $12   MIP $24

Rock-Viper, 1990, Hasbro, Mountain Trooper
EX n/a   NM $10   MIP $27

S.A.W.-Viper, 1990, Hasbro, Heavy Machine Gunner
EX n/a   NM $10   MIP $30

Sonic Fighters Lampreys, 1990, Hasbro, Amphibious Assault
EX n/a   NM $10   MIP $26

Sonic Fighters Viper, 1990, Hasbro, Infantry
EX n/a   NM $10   MIP $26

Vehicle Sets

Cobra Piranha, 1990, Hasbro, Depth Charge Firing Sea Marauder
EX $6   NM $12   MIP $32

Cobra Rage, 1990, Hasbro
EX $22   NM $32   MIP $95

Hammerhead, 1990, Hasbro, Submersible Sea Tank, six vehicles in one, w/Decimator driver
EX $32   NM $55   MIP $170

Hurricane VTOL, 1990, Hasbro, Vertical Take-off and Landing plane w/Vapor pilot
EX $40   NM $70   MIP $210

Iron Grenadiers Destro's Dominator, 1990, Hasbro, tank converts to helicopter
EX $16   NM $30   MIP $75

Overlord's Dictator, 1990, Hasbro, w/Overlord driver
EX $15   NM $20   MIP $50

SERIES 09, GI JOE
Figure Sets

Ambush, 1990, Hasbro, Concealment Specialist
EX n/a   NM $14   MIP $25

Bullhorn, 1990, Hasbro, Intervention Specialist
EX n/a   NM $12   MIP $26

Captain Grid Iron, 1990, Hasbro, Hand-to-Hand Combat
EX n/a   NM $8   MIP $18

Freefall, 1990, Hasbro, Paratrooper
EX n/a   NM $10   MIP $26

Pathfinder, 1990, Hasbro, Jungle Assault
EX n/a   NM $10   MIP $30

Rampart, 1990, Hasbro, Shoreline Defender
EX n/a   NM $8   MIP $20

Salvo, 1990, Hasbro, Anti-Armor Trooper
EX n/a   NM $10   MIP $30

Sky Patrol Airborne, 1990, Hasbro, Parachute Assembler
EX n/a   NM $23   MIP $42

Sky Patrol Airwave, 1990, Hasbro, Audible Frequency Specialist
EX n/a   NM $23   MIP $42

Sky Patrol Altitude, 1990, Hasbro, Recon Scout
EX n/a   NM $23   MIP $42

Sky Patrol Drop Zone, 1990, Hasbro, Weapons Specialist
EX n/a   NM $23   MIP $42

Sky Patrol Sky Dive, 1990, Hasbro, Leader
EX n/a   NM $23   MIP $42

Sky Patrol Static Line, 1990, Hasbro, Demolitions Expert
EX n/a   NM $18   MIP $32

Sonic Fighters Dial-Tone, 1990, Hasbro, Communications w/sonic backpack
EX n/a   NM $10   MIP $20

Sonic Fighters Dodger, 1990, Hasbro, Heavy Ordinance Operator w/sonic backpack
EX n/a   NM $10   MIP $26

Sonic Fighters Law, 1990, Hasbro, M.P. w/sonic backpack
EX n/a   NM $8   MIP $20

Sonic Fighters Tunnel Rat, 1990, Hasbro, E.O.D. w/sonic backpack
EX n/a   NM $8   MIP $20

Stretcher, 1990, Hasbro, Medical Specialist
EX n/a   NM $10   MIP $25

Sub-Zero, 1990, Hasbro, Winter Operations
EX n/a   NM $10   MIP $20

Topside, 1990, Hasbro, Navy Assault Seaman
EX n/a   NM $6   MIP $22

Vehicle Sets

Avalanche, 1990, Hasbro, w/Cold Front driver
EX $30   NM $52   MIP $145

General, 1990, Hasbro, Mobile Strike Headquarters and Launch Pad w/Major Storm driver
EX $85   NM $125   MIP $325

Hammer, 1990, Hasbro, High-Tech Attack Jeep
EX $25   NM $40   MIP $110

Locust, 1990, Hasbro, Bomb Dropping Assault Copter
EX $10   NM $14   MIP $28

Mobile Battle Bunker, 1990, Hasbro
EX $10   NM $18   MIP $52

Retaliator, 1990, Hasbro, Helicopter w/Updraft the pilot
EX $32   NM $40   MIP $160

Sky Patrol Sky HAVOC, 1990, Hasbro, Heavy Armored Transport vehicle w/hidden scout ship
EX $22   NM $30   MIP $85

Sky Patrol Sky Hawk, 1990, Hasbro, VTOL craft
EX $12   NM $20   MIP $36

Sky Patrol Sky Raven, 1990, Hasbro
EX $90   NM $110   MIP $355

Sky Patrol Sky SHARC, 1990, Hasbro
EX $10   NM $20   MIP $38

SERIES 10, COBRA
Figure Sets

B.A.T., 1991, Hasbro, Battle Android Trooper
EX n/a   NM $11   MIP $20

Cobra Commander w/Eyebrows, 1991, Hasbro, Leader
EX n/a   NM $15   MIP $25

Cobra Commander w/out Eyebrows, 1991, Hasbro, Leader
EX n/a   NM $8   MIP $20

Crimson Guard Immortal, 1991, Hasbro, Elite Trooper
EX n/a   NM $10   MIP $27

Desert Scorpion, 1991, Hasbro, Desert Fighter
EX n/a   NM $10   MIP $27

Eco Warriors Cesspool, 1991, Hasbro, Chief Environmental Operative
EX n/a   NM $7   MIP $14

Eco Warriors Sludge-Viper, 1991, Hasbro, Hazardous Waste
EX n/a   NM $8   MIP $14

Eco Warriors Toxo-Viper, 1991, Hasbro, Hostile Environment
EX n/a   NM $8   MIP $14

Incinerators, 1991, Hasbro, Flamethrowers
EX n/a   NM $10   MIP $18

Snow Serpent, 1991, Hasbro, Snow Trooper
EX n/a   NM $10   MIP $18

Super Sonic Fighters Major Bludd, 1991, Hasbro, Mercenary
EX n/a   NM $6   MIP $12

Super Sonic Fighters Road Pig, 1991, Hasbro, Dreadnok
EX n/a   NM $6   MIP $12

Talking Battle Commanders Cobra Commander, 1991, Hasbro, Cobra Leader
EX n/a   NM $4   MIP $10

Talking Battle Commanders Overkill, 1991, Hasbro, B.A.T. Leader
EX n/a   NM $4   MIP $10

Vehicle Sets

Air Commandos w/Night Vulture, 1991, Hasbro, Air Recon Trooper
EX $16   NM $22   MIP $40

Air Commandos w/Sky Creeper, 1991, Hasbro, Air Recon Leader
EX $14   NM $20   MIP $38

Battle Copter, 1991, Hasbro, w/Interrogator pilot
EX $7   NM $11   MIP $22

Eco Warriors Septic Tank, 1991, Hasbro
EX $10   NM $17   MIP $55

Ice Sabre, 1991, Hasbro
EX $8   NM $12   MIP $32

Paralyzer, 1991, Hasbro
EX $9   NM $12   MIP $35

SERIES 10, GI JOE
Figure Sets

Big Ben, 1991, Hasbro, S.A.S
EX n/a   NM $14   MIP $22

Dusty & Sandstorm, 1991, Hasbro, Desert Trooper
EX n/a   NM $9   MIP $20

Eco Warriors Clean-Sweep, 1991, Hasbro, Anit-Tox Trooper
EX n/a   NM $6   MIP $14

Eco Warriors Flint, 1991, Hasbro, Commander
EX n/a   NM $7   MIP $14

Eco Warriors Ozone, 1991, Hasbro, Ozone Replenisher
EX n/a   NM $6   MIP $14

General Hawk, 1991, Hasbro, Commander
EX n/a   NM $12   MIP $22

Grunt, 1991, Hasbro, Infantry Squad Leader
EX n/a   NM $8   MIP $18

Heavy Duty, 1991, Hasbro, Heavy Ordinance Trooper
EX n/a   NM $8   MIP $20

Lifeline, 1991, Hasbro, Kellogg's mail in, no guns
EX n/a   NM $10   MIP $30

Low-Light, 1991, Hasbro, Night Fighter
EX n/a   NM $8   MIP $20

Mercer, 1991, Hasbro, Mercenary
EX n/a   NM $10   MIP $18

Red Star, 1991, Hasbro, Oktober Guard
EX n/a   NM $12   MIP $20

Sci-Fi, 1991, Hasbro, Directed Energy Expert
EX n/a   NM $9   MIP $18

Snake Eyes, 1991, Hasbro, Commando
EX n/a   NM $10   MIP $27

Super Sonic Fighters Lt. Falcon, 1991, Hasbro, Green Beret
EX n/a   NM $6   MIP $12

Super Sonic Fighters Psyche-Out, 1991, Hasbro, Deceptive Warfare
EX n/a   NM $8   MIP $14

Super Sonic Fighters Rock 'N' Roll, 1991, Hasbro, Machine Gunner
EX n/a   NM $6   MIP $12

Super Sonic Fighters Zap, 1991, Hasbro, Ground Artillery Soldier
EX n/a   NM $6   MIP $12

Talking Battle Commanders General Hawk, 1991, Hasbro, Commander
EX n/a   NM $4   MIP $10

Talking Battle Commanders Stalker, 1991, Hasbro, Ranger
EX n/a   NM $4   MIP $10

Tracker, 1991, Hasbro, S.E.A.L.
EX n/a   NM $10   MIP $20

Vehicle Sets

Air Commandos w/Cloudburst, 1991, Hasbro, Glider Trooper
EX $16   NM $22   MIP $42

Air Commandos w/Skymate, 1991, Hasbro, Glider Trooper, Australian S.A.S.
EX $20   NM $35   MIP $55

Attack Cruiser, 1991, Hasbro, Mobile Attack Vehicle w/Flying Glider Bomb
EX $10   NM $16   MIP $52

Badger, 1991, Hasbro, Attack Jeep
EX $8   NM $14   MIP $40

Battle Copter, 1991, Hasbro, w/Major Altitude pilot
EX $6   NM $11   MIP $22

Brawler, 1991, Hasbro
EX $13   NM $23   MIP $60

Motorized Battle Wagon, 1991, Hasbro
EX $15   NM $23   MIP $60

SERIES 11, COBRA
Figure Sets

Cobra Ninja Viper, 1992, Hasbro, mail-in, w/two swords
EX n/a   NM $40   MIP $58

Destro, 1992, Hasbro, Weapons Supplier
EX n/a   NM $8   MIP $12

Eel, 1992, Hasbro, Underwater Demolitions
EX n/a   NM $8   MIP $12

Evil Headhunters Headman, 1992, Hasbro, Drug Kingpin
EX n/a   NM $8   MIP $12

Evil Headhunters, Headhunters, 1992, Hasbro, Narcotics Guards
EX n/a   NM $8   MIP $12

Firefly, 1992, Hasbro, Saboteur
EX n/a   NM $8   MIP $12

Flak-Viper, 1992, Hasbro, Anti-Aircraft Trooper
EX n/a   NM $8   MIP $12

Ninja Force Dice, 1992, Hasbro, Cobra Ninja Bo Staff
EX n/a   NM $7   MIP $12

Ninja Force Slice, 1992, Hasbro, Cobra Ninja Swordsman
EX n/a   NM $7   MIP $12

Toxo-Zombie, 1992, Hasbro, Toxic Disaster Trooper
EX n/a   NM $8   MIP $12

Vehicle Sets

Air Commandos w/Cobra Air Devil, 1992, Hasbro, Aerobatic Arial Assault Trooper
EX $20   NM $30   MIP $45

Cobra Battle Copter, 1992, Hasbro, w/Heli-Viper
EX $7   NM $13   MIP $22

Cobra Earthquake, 1992, Hasbro, Bulldozer
EX $18   NM $27   MIP $60

Cobra Liquidator A.T.F., 1992, Hasbro, Advanced Tactical Fighter
EX $7   NM $12   MIP $25

Cobra Parasite, 1992, Hasbro, Armored Personnel Carrier w/Catapult launcher
EX $7   NM $12   MIP $30

Cobra Rat, 1992, Hasbro, High-Speed Attack Hovercraft
EX $7   **NM** $10   **MIP** $27

Vehicles/Acessories

Eco Warriors Toxo-Lab, 1992, Hasbro, play set for Eco Warriors
EX $35   **NM** $55   **MIP** $135

SERIES 11, GI JOE
Figure Sets

Barricade, 1992, Hasbro, Bunker Buster
EX n/a   **NM** $8   **MIP** $12

Big Bear, 1992, Hasbro, Oktober Guard Anti-Armor Specialist
EX n/a   **NM** $8   **MIP** $12

D.E.F. Bullet-Proof, 1992, Hasbro, Drug Elimination Force Leader
EX n/a   **NM** $8   **MIP** $12

D.E.F. Cutter, 1992, Hasbro, Vehicle Operations Specialist
EX n/a   **NM** $8   **MIP** $12

D.E.F. Mutt & Junkyard, 1992, Hasbro, K-9
EX n/a   **NM** $8   **MIP** $12

D.E.F. Shockwave, 1992, Hasbro, S.W.A.T.
EX n/a   **NM** $8   **MIP** $12

Duke, 1992, Hasbro, Master Sergeant
EX n/a   **NM** $8   **MIP** $12

Eco-Warriors Barbecue, 1992, Hasbro, Firefighter
EX n/a   **NM** $8   **MIP** $12

Eco-Warriors Deep Six, 1992, Hasbro, Deep Water Specialist
EX n/a   **NM** $8   **MIP** $12

General Flagg, 1992, Hasbro, General
EX n/a   **NM** $8   **MIP** $12

Gung-Ho, 1992, Hasbro, Marine
EX n/a   **NM** $6   **MIP** $10

Ninja Force Dojo, 1992, Hasbro, Silent Weapons
EX n/a   **NM** $7   **MIP** $12

Ninja Force Nunchuk, 1992, Hasbro, Nunchaku Ninja
EX n/a   **NM** $7   **MIP** $12

Ninja Force Storm Shadow, 1992, Hasbro, Leader
EX n/a   **NM** $7   **MIP** $12

Ninja Force T'Jbang, 1992, Hasbro, Ninja Swordsman
EX n/a   **NM** $7   **MIP** $12

Roadblock, 1992, Hasbro, Heavy Machine Gunner, recalled by Hasbro
EX n/a   **NM** $70   **MIP** $220

Wet-Suit, 1992, Hasbro, S.E.A.L.
EX n/a   **NM** $8   **MIP** $12

Wild Bill, 1992, Hasbro, Air Cavalry Scout
EX n/a   **NM** $8   **MIP** $12

Vehicle Sets

AH-74 Desert Apache, 1992, Hasbro, Sonic Fighters
EX $40   **NM** $50   **MIP** $120

Air Commandos w/Spirit, 1992, Hasbro, Air Commandos Leader
EX $13   **NM** $24   **MIP** $38

Barracuda, 1992, Hasbro, One-Man Attack Sub w/Real Diving Action
EX $6   **NM** $12   **MIP** $26

Battle Copter, 1992, Hasbro, w/Ace
EX $7   **NM** $11   **MIP** $23

Eco-Warriors Eco Striker, 1992, Hasbro, All-Terrain Environmental Assault Vehicle
EX $16   **NM** $22   **MIP** $60

Fort America, 1992, Hasbro, Sonic Fighters, Fortress turns into tank
EX $16   **NM** $30   **MIP** $70

Patriot, 1992, Hasbro, Armored Missile Launcher Transport
EX $7   **NM** $14   **MIP** $40

Storm Eagle A.T.F., 1992, Hasbro, Advanced Tactical Fighter
EX $7   **NM** $12   **MIP** $25

Vehicles/Acessories

G.I. Joe Headquarters, 1992, Hasbro, play set w/electronic battle sounds
EX $30   **NM** $45   **MIP** $110

SERIES 12, COBRA
Battle Corps Figure Sets

Alley Viper, #6, 1993, Hasbro, Urban Assault Trooper
EX n/a   **NM** $15   **MIP** $32

Cobra Commander, #24, 1993, Hasbro, Supreme Leader
EX n/a   **NM** $7   **MIP** $16

Cobra Eel, #27, 1993, Hasbro, Underwater Demolitions
EX n/a   **NM** $7   **MIP** $15

Crimson Guard Commander, #23, 1993, Hasbro, Elite Trooper
EX n/a   **NM** $7   **MIP** $15

Dr. Mindbender, #15, 1993, Hasbro, Master of Mind Control
EX n/a   **NM** $7   **MIP** $15

Firefly, #18, 1993, Hasbro, Saboteur
EX n/a   **NM** $7   **MIP** $15

Flak-Viper, #9, 1993, Hasbro, Anti-Aircraft Trooper
EX n/a   **NM** $7   **MIP** $15

Gristle, #32, 1993, Hasbro, Urban Crime Commander
EX n/a   **NM** $7   **MIP** $15

H.E.A.T. Viper, #5, 1993, Hasbro, Hi Explosive Anti-Tank Trooper
EX n/a   **NM** $7   **MIP** $15

Headhunter Stormtrooper, #33, 1993, Hasbro, Elite Urban Crime Guard
EX n/a   **NM** $14   **MIP** $25

Headhunters, #35, 1993, Hasbro, Cobra Street Troopers
EX n/a   **NM** $7   **MIP** $15

Night Creeper Leader, #14, 1993, Hasbro, Ninja Supreme Master
EX n/a   **NM** $7   **MIP** $15

Figure Sets

Ninja Force Night Creeper, 1993, Hasbro, Cobra Ninja
EX n/a   **NM** $7   **MIP** $15

Ninja Force Slice, 1993, Hasbro, Cobra Ninja Swordsman
EX n/a   **NM** $7   **MIP** $15

Ninja Force Zartan, 1993, Hasbro, Master of Disguise
EX n/a   **NM** $7   **MIP** $15

Mail-In Figures

Name Your Own Cobra, 1993, Hasbro, "Create A Cobra" mail-away exclusive
EX $28   **NM** $58   **MIP** $105

Mega Marines/Mega Monsters

Bio-Viper, 1993, Hasbro, Genetically Enhanced Undersea Monster
EX n/a   **NM** $7   **MIP** $15

Cyber-Viper, 1993, Hasbro, Cybernetic Officer
EX n/a   **NM** $13   **MIP** $26

Mega-Viper, 1993, Hasbro, Mega-Monster Trainer
EX n/a   **NM** $13   **MIP** $26

Monstro-Viper, 1993, Hasbro, Mega Monster
EX n/a   **NM** $7   **MIP** $15

Star Brigade Figure Sets

Astro-Viper, #11, 1993, Hasbro, Cobranaut
EX n/a   **NM** $7   **MIP** $15

B.A.A.T., #6, 1993, Hasbro, Battle Armored Android Trooper
EX n/a   **NM** $7   **MIP** $15

Destro, #5, 1993, Hasbro, Cobra-Tech Commander
EX n/a   **NM** $7   **MIP** $15

T.A.R.G.A.T., 1993, Hasbro, Trans Asmospheric Rapid Global Assault Trooper
EX n/a   **NM** $7   **MIP** $15

Vehicle Sets

Battle Corps Cobra Detonator, 1993, Hasbro, w/Nitro-Viper
EX $15   **NM** $25   **MIP** $40

Battle Corps Ice Snake, 1993, Hasbro
EX $5   **NM** $10   **MIP** $15

Ninja Force Battle Ax, 1993, Hasbro, w/Red Ninja driver
EX $8   **NM** $16   **MIP** $38

Star Brigade Cobra Invader, 1993, Hasbro
EX $5   **NM** $10   **MIP** $15

SERIES 12, GI JOE
Battle Corps Figure Sets

Backblast, #22, 1993, Hasbro, Anti-Aircraft Soldier
EX n/a   **NM** $7   **MIP** $15

Barricade, #17, 1993, Hasbro, Bunker Buster
EX n/a   **NM** $7   **MIP** $15

Bazooka, #1, 1993, Hasbro, Missile Specialist
EX n/a   **NM** $7   **MIP** $15

Beach-Head, #4, 1993, Hasbro, Ranger
EX n/a   **NM** $7   **MIP** $15

Bulletproof, #34, 1993, Hasbro, Urban Commander
EX n/a   **NM** $7   **MIP** $15

Colonel Courage, #10, 1993, Hasbro, Strategic Commander
EX n/a   **NM** $7   **MIP** $15

Cross-Country, #2, 1993, Hasbro, Transport Expert
EX n/a   **NM** $7   **MIP** $15

Duke, #19, 1993, Hasbro, Battle Commander
EX n/a   **NM** $7   **MIP** $15

Frostbite, #20, 1993, Hasbro, Arctic Commander
EX n/a   **NM** $7   **MIP** $15

General Flagg, #26, 1993, Hasbro, General
EX n/a   **NM** $7   **MIP** $15

Gung-Ho, #16, 1993, Hasbro, Marine
EX n/a   **NM** $7   **MIP** $15

Iceberg, #3, 1993, Hasbro, Arctic Assault Trooper
EX n/a   **NM** $7   **MIP** $15

Keel-Haul, #21, 1993, Hasbro, Admiral, most have large logo on back, small logo is rare
EX n/a   **NM** $7   **MIP** $15

Law, #28, 1993, Hasbro, M.P.
EX n/a   **NM** $7   **MIP** $15

Leatherneck, #11, 1993, Hasbro, Infantry Training Specialist
EX n/a   **NM** $7   **MIP** $15

Long Arm, #31, 1993, Hasbro, Fire Strike Specialist
EX n/a   **NM** $7   **MIP** $15

Mace, #29, 1993, Hasbro, Undercover Operative
EX n/a   **NM** $7   **MIP** $15

Muskrat, #30, 1993, Hasbro, Heavy Fire Specialist
EX n/a   **NM** $7   **MIP** $15

Mutt & Junkyard, #36, 1993, Hasbro, K-9
EX n/a   **NM** $7   **MIP** $15

Outback, #13a, 1993, Hasbro, Survival Specialist, Eco Warriors version released as Battle Corps instead
EX n/a   **NM** $7   **MIP** $15

Outback, #13b, 1993, Hasbro, Survival Specialist, tan pants, green shirt
EX n/a   **NM** $7   **MIP** $15

Road Block, #7a, 1993, Hasbro, Heavy Machine Gunner, yellow shirt
EX n/a   **NM** $7   **MIP** $15

Road Block, #7b, 1993, Hasbro, Heavy Machine Gunner, blue shirt
EX n/a   **NM** $7   **MIP** $15

Snow Storm, #12a, 1993, Hasbro, High-Tech Snow Trooper, white body w/orange accents
EX n/a   **NM** $7   **MIP** $15

Snow Storm, #12b, 1993, Hasbro, High-Tech Snow Trooper, white body w/blue accents
EX n/a   **NM** $7   **MIP** $15

Wet-Suit, #8, 1993, Hasbro, S.E.A.L.
EX n/a   **NM** $7   **MIP** $15

Wild Bill, #25, 1993, Hasbro, Aero Scout
EX n/a   **NM** $7   **MIP** $15

Figure Sets

Ninja Force Banzai, 1993, Hasbro, Rising Sun Ninja
EX n/a   **NM** $7   **MIP** $15

Ninja Force Bushido, 1993, Hasbro, Snow Ninja
EX n/a   **NM** $7   **MIP** $15

Ninja Force Scarlett, 1993, Hasbro, Counter Intelligence
EX n/a   **NM** $7   **MIP** $15

Ninja Force Snake Eyes, 1993, Hasbro, Covert Mission Specialist
EX n/a   **NM** $7   **MIP** $15

Mail-In Figures

Arctic Commandos, 1993, Hasbro, four-figure pack: Dee-Jay, Snow Serpent, Stalker, Sub-Zero
EX n/a   **NM** $20   **MIP** $42

Copter Pilots, 1993, Hasbro, two-figure pack: Interrogator and Major Altitude
EX n/a   **NM** $11   **MIP** $28

Deep Six, 1993, Hasbro, Deep Sea Diver
EX n/a   **NM** $6   **MIP** $15

General Hawk, 1993, Hasbro, Commander
EX n/a   **NM** $6   **MIP** $12

International Action Force, 1993, Hasbro, four-figure pack: Big Bear, Big Ben, Budo, and Spirit
EX n/a   **NM** $20   **MIP** $42

Rapid Deployment Force, 1993, Hasbro, three-figure pack: Fast Draw, Night Force Repeater, Night Force Shockwave
EX n/a   **NM** $25   **MIP** $40

Mega Marines/Mega Monsters

Blast-Off, 1993, Hasbro, Flame Thrower
EX n/a   **NM** $7   **MIP** $15

Clutch, 1993, Hasbro, Monster Blaster A.P.C.
EX n/a   **NM** $7   **MIP** $15

Gung-Ho, 1993, Hasbro, Commander
EX n/a   **NM** $7   **MIP** $15

Mirage, 1993, Hasbro, Bio-Artillery Expert
EX n/a   **NM** $7   **MIP** $15

Star Brigade Figure Sets

Countdown, #8, 1993, Hasbro, Combat Astronaut
EX n/a   **NM** $6   **MIP** $12

Duke, #2, 1993, Hasbro, Commander
EX n/a   **NM** $6   **MIP** $12

Heavy Duty, #4, 1993, Hasbro, Heavy Ordinance Specialist
EX n/a   **NM** $6   **MIP** $12

Ozone, #10a, 1993, Hasbro, Astro Infantry Trooper, tan suit
EX n/a   **NM** $6   **MIP** $12

Ozone, #10b, 1993, Hasbro, Astro Infantry Trooper, gray suit
EX n/a   **NM** $6   **MIP** $12

Payload, #7a, 1993, Hasbro, Astro Pilot, black suit, green and silver accents
EX n/a   **NM** $6   **MIP** $12

Payload, #7b, 1993, Hasbro, Astro Pilot, black suit, blue and gold accents
EX n/a   **NM** $6   **MIP** $12

Roadblock, #9, 1993, Hasbro, Space Gunner
EX n/a   **NM** $6   **MIP** $12

Robo-JOE, #1, 1993, Hasbro, Jet Tech Ops Expert

EX n/a   NM $6   MIP $12

Rock 'N Roll, #3, 1993, Hasbro, Robo-Gunner

EX n/a   NM $6   MIP $12

Street Fighter Figure Sets

Balrog, #11, 1993, Hasbro, Heavyweight Boxer

EX n/a   NM $7   MIP $15

Blanka, #5, 1993, Hasbro, Jungle Fighter

EX n/a   NM $7   MIP $15

Chun-Li, #4, 1993, Hasbro, Kung-Fu Fighter

EX n/a   NM $7   MIP $15

Dhalsim, #8, 1993, Hasbro, Yoga Fighter

EX n/a   NM $7   MIP $15

Edmond Honda, #7, 1993, Hasbro, Sumo Wrestler

EX n/a   NM $7   MIP $15

Guile, #3, 1993, Hasbro, Special Forces Fighter

EX n/a   NM $7   MIP $15

Ken Masters, #2, 1993, Hasbro, Shotokan Karate Fighter

EX n/a   NM $7   MIP $15

M. Bison, #6, 1993, Hasbro, Grand Master

EX n/a   NM $7   MIP $15

Ryu, #1, 1993, Hasbro, Kung-Fu Fighter

EX n/a   NM $7   MIP $15

Sagat, #12, 1993, Hasbro, Thai Fighter

EX n/a   NM $7   MIP $15

Vega, #10, 1993, Hasbro, Spanish Ninja

EX n/a   NM $7   MIP $15

Zangeif, #9, 1993, Hasbro, Russian Bear Wrestler

EX n/a   NM $7   MIP $15

Street Fighters Vehicle Sets

Beast Blaster, 1993, Hasbro, w/Blanka and Chun-Li

EX $16   NM $26   MIP $65

Crimson Cruiser, 1993, Hasbro, w/M. Bison

EX $6   NM $13   MIP $40

Dragon Fortress, 1993, Hasbro, w/Ken Masters and Ryu

EX $20   NM $32   MIP $80

Sonic Boom, 1993, Hasbro, w/Guile

EX $6   NM $13   MIP $38

Vehicle Sets

Battle Corps Ghoststriker X-16, 1993, Hasbro, w/Ace pilot

EX $22   NM $38   MIP $110

Battle Corps Mudbuster, 1993, Hasbro, All-terrain, 4x4 truck

EX $6   NM $11   MIP $27

Battle Corps Shark 9000, 1993, Hasbro, w/Cutter driver

EX $10   NM $20   MIP $65

Dino-Hunter Mission Play Set, 1993, Hasbro, w/Low-Light and Ambush, Toys R Us Exclusive

EX $45   NM $70   MIP $210

Mega Marines Monster Blaster, 1993, Hasbro, APC

EX $10   NM $20   MIP $60

Ninja Force Ninja Lightning, 1993, Hasbro, Fast Attack Ninja Cycle w/Detachable Sidecar

EX $4   NM $8   MIP $26

Ninja Force Pile Driver, 1993, Hasbro, w/T'Gin-Zu driver

EX $8   NM $16   MIP $38

Star Brigade Armor-Bot, 1993, Hasbro, w/Armor-Tech General Hawk

EX $16   NM $30   MIP $62

Star Brigade Starfighter, 1993, Hasbro, w/Sci-Fi

EX $9   NM $14   MIP $40

SERIES 13, COBRA
Battle Corps Figure Sets

Alley Viper, #7, 1994, Hasbro, Urban Assault Trooper

EX n/a   NM $13   MIP $22

Major Bludd, #11, 1994, Hasbro, Mercenary

EX $5   NM $10   MIP $15

Metal-Head, #4, 1994, Hasbro, Anti-Tank Trooper

EX $5   NM $10   MIP $15

Night Creeper Leader, #13, 1994, Hasbro, Cobra Ninja Supreme Leader

EX $5   NM $10   MIP $15

Viper, #5, 1994, Hasbro, Cobra Infantry Trooper

EX n/a   NM $8   MIP $17

Shadow Ninjas Figure Sets

Night Creeper, #42, 1994, Hasbro, Cobra Ninja

EX $5   NM $10   MIP $15

Slice, #40, 1994, Hasbro, Cobra Ninja Swordsman

EX $5   NM $10   MIP $15

Star Brigade Figure Sets

Carcass, #52, 1994, Hasbro, Alien Destroyer

EX n/a   NM $8   MIP $12

Cobra Blackstar, #25, 1994, Hasbro, Cobra Elite Space Pilot

EX n/a   NM $8   MIP $12

Cobra Commander, #24, 1994, Hasbro, Cobra Supreme Leader

EX n/a   NM $8   MIP $16

Lobotomax, #50, 1994, Hasbro, Stellar Explorer

EX n/a   NM $8   MIP $12

Predacon, #51, 1994, Hasbro, Alien Bounty Hunter

EX n/a   NM $8   MIP $15

Vehicle Sets

Battle Corps Scorpion, 1994, Hasbro, 4WD vehicle

EX $16   NM $19   MIP $27

Star Brigade Cobra Power Fighter, 1994, Hasbro, w/Techno-Viper driver

EX $25   NM $35   MIP $60

SERIES 13, GI JOE
30th Anniversary

Action Marine, 1994, Hasbro, #81047, Marine Corps Commando

EX n/a   NM $5   MIP $9

Action Pilot, 1994, Hasbro, #81046, Air Force Fighter Pilot

EX n/a   NM $5   MIP $9

Action Pilot Astronaut, 1994, Hasbro, astronaut was available in the boxed gift set

EX $5   NM $9   MIP n/a

Action Sailor, 1994, Hasbro, #81048, Navy Frogman

EX n/a   NM $5   MIP $10

Action Soldier, 1994, Hasbro, #81045, U.S. Army Infantryman

EX n/a   NM $5   MIP $10

Battle Corps Figure Sets

Beach-Head, #6, 1994, Hasbro, Ranger

EX n/a   NM $7   MIP $15

Dial-Tone, #2, 1994, Hasbro, Communications Expert

EX n/a   NM $7   MIP $15

Flint, #1, 1994, Hasbro, Desert Paratrooper

EX n/a   NM $7   MIP $15

Ice Cream Soldier, #10, 1994, Hasbro, Flamethrower Commando

EX n/a   NM $7   MIP $15

Lifeline, #8, 1994, Hasbro, Rescue Trooper

EX n/a   NM $7   MIP $15

Shipwreck, #3, 1994, Hasbro, Navy S.E.A.L.
EX n/a   **NM** $7   **MIP** $15

Snow Storm, #12, 1994, Hasbro, High Tech Snow Trooper
EX n/a   **NM** $7   **MIP** $15

Stalker, #9, 1994, Hasbro, Ranger
EX n/a   **NM** $7   **MIP** $15

Windchill, #62, 1994, Hasbro, Blockbuster Driver
EX n/a   **NM** $5   **MIP** $12

Mail-In Figures

Lt. Joseph Colton, G.I. Joe, 1994, Hasbro
EX n/a   **NM** $8   **MIP** $25

Shadow Ninjas Figure Sets

Bushido, #39, 1994, Hasbro, Shadow Ninja
EX n/a   **NM** $7   **MIP** $15

Nunchuk, #41, 1994, Hasbro, Nunchuku Ninja
EX n/a   **NM** $7   **MIP** $15

Snake Eyes, #37, 1994, Hasbro, Covert Mission Specialist
EX n/a   **NM** $7   **MIP** $25

Storm Shadow, #38, 1994, Hasbro, Shadow Ninja Leader
EX n/a   **NM** $7   **MIP** $15

Star Brigade Figure Sets

Countdown, #53, 1994, Hasbro, Combat Astronaut
EX n/a   **NM** $7   **MIP** $15

Duke, #21, 1994, Hasbro, Star Brigade Commander
EX n/a   **NM** $7   **MIP** $15

Effects, #49, 1994, Hasbro, Explosives Expert
EX n/a   **NM** $7   **MIP** $15

Ozone, #54, 1994, Hasbro, Astro-Infantry Trooper
EX n/a   **NM** $7   **MIP** $15

Payload, #26a, 1994, Hasbro, Astro Pilot, black suit, blue and gold accents
EX n/a   **NM** $7   **MIP** $15

Payload, #26b, 1994, Hasbro, Astro Pilot, white suit, red and silver accents
EX n/a   **NM** $7   **MIP** $15

Roadblock, #27, 1994, Hasbro, Space Gunner
EX n/a   **NM** $7   **MIP** $15

Sci-Fi, #22, 1994, Hasbro, Star Brigade Pilot
EX n/a   **NM** $7   **MIP** $15

Space Shot, #23, 1994, Hasbro, Combat Freighter Pilot
EX n/a   **NM** $7   **MIP** $15

Vehicle Sets

Battle Corps Blockbuster, 1994, Hasbro, w/Windmill driver
EX $12   **NM** $22   **MIP** $52

Battle Corps Manta Ray, 1994, Hasbro, wind-up propeller
EX $7   **NM** $13   **MIP** $28

Battle Corps Razor-Blade, 1994, Hasbro, one-man copter
EX $12   **NM** $15   **MIP** $28

Star Brigade Power Fighter, 1994, Hasbro, w/Gears driver
EX $20   **NM** $30   **MIP** $55

SERIES 6 GI JOE

Figure Sets

Steel Brigade, 1987, Hasbro, "gold headed"
EX $70   **NM** $170   **MIP** $250

Collector Editions (1990s to Present)

12" HALL OF FAME

Figure Sets

Ace, Fighter Pilot, 1993, Hasbro, Model No. 6837
EX $5   **NM** $10   **MIP** $15

Cobra Commander, Cobra Leader, 1992, Hasbro, Model No. 6827
EX $6   **NM** $12   **MIP** $20

Destro, Weapons Manufacturer, 1993, Hasbro, Model No. 6839
EX $6   **NM** $12   **MIP** $18

Duke, Combat Camo, 1994, Hasbro, Model No. 6044
EX n/a   **NM** $4   **MIP** $10

Duke, Master Sergeant, 1991, Hasbro, Target Exclusive, Model No. 6019
EX $5   **NM** $10   **MIP** $15

Duke, Master Sergeant, 1992, Hasbro, Model No. 6826
EX $5   **NM** $10   **MIP** $15

Flint, Green Beret, 1994, Hasbro, Model No. 6127
EX $5   **NM** $10   **MIP** $15

Grunt, Infantry Squad Leader, 1993, Hasbro, Model No. 6111
EX n/a   **NM** $3   **MIP** $7

Gung-Ho, Dress Marine, 1993, Hasbro, Model No. 6849
EX $6   **NM** $12   **MIP** $20

Heavy Duty, Heavy Ordinance Specialist, 1993, Hasbro, Model No. 6114
EX n/a   **NM** $4   **MIP** $7

Major Budd, Battle-Pack, 1994, Hasbro, Model No. 6159
EX $5   **NM** $10   **MIP** $15

Martial Arts Specialist, 1995, Hasbro, Kay Bee Exclusive
EX $5   **NM** $10   **MIP** $15

Rapid Fire, Commando, 1993, Hasbro, Model No. 6924
EX $7   **NM** $12   **MIP** $17

Red Beret Commando, 1995, Hasbro, Kay Bee Exclusive
EX n/a   **NM** $5   **MIP** $10

Roadblock, Combat Camo, 1994, Hasbro, Model No. 6049
EX n/a   **NM** $5   **MIP** $10

Rock 'n' Roll, Gatlin' Blastin', 1994, Hasbro, Model No. 6128
EX $5   **NM** $10   **MIP** $15

Rock 'n' Roll, Heavy Weapons Gunner, 1993, Hasbro, Model No. 6128
EX $5   **NM** $10   **MIP** $15

Snake Eyes, Commando, 1992, Hasbro, Model No. 6828
EX $5   **NM** $10   **MIP** $15

Snake-Eyes, Karate Choppin', 1994, Hasbro, Model No. 6089
EX $7   **NM** $12   **MIP** $17

Stalker, Ranger, 1992, Hasbro, Model No. 6829
EX $5   **NM** $10   **MIP** $15

Storm Shadow, Ninja, 1993, Hasbro, Model No. 6848
EX $6   **NM** $12   **MIP** $18

Surveillance Specialist, 1995, Hasbro, Kay Bee Exclusive
EX n/a   **NM** $5   **MIP** $10

Talking Duke, Talking Battle Commander, 1993, Hasbro, Model No. 6117
EX $8   **NM** $12   **MIP** $25

Uniform/Equipment Sets

Air Force Flyer Gear, 1993, Hasbro
EX n/a   **NM** $3   **MIP** $7

Arctic Assault Mission Gear, 1993, Hasbro
EX n/a   **NM** $3   **MIP** $7

Army Boot Camp Gear, 1993, Hasbro
EX n/a   **NM** $3   **MIP** $7

Backpack Missile Blaster, 1993, Hasbro
EX n/a   **NM** $3   **MIP** $7

Cobra Helicopter Attack, 1993, Hasbro, Deluxe Mission Gear
EX n/a   **NM** $3   **MIP** $7

Cobra Infantry Uniform, 1993, Hasbro, mail-in

EX n/a   **NM** $3   **MIP** $7

Deep Water Salvage Mission Gear, 1995, Hasbro

EX n/a   **NM** $3   **MIP** $7

Desert Camo Mission Gear, 1993, Hasbro

EX n/a   **NM** $3   **MIP** $7

Footlocker, 1993, Hasbro, storage for Hall of Fame equipment

EX n/a   **NM** $3   **MIP** $7

GI Joe Infantry Uniform, 1993, Hasbro, mail-in

EX n/a   **NM** $3   **MIP** $7

Green Beret Weapons Arsenal, 1993, Hasbro

EX n/a   **NM** $3   **MIP** $7

High Caliber Weapons Arsenal, 1994, Hasbro, weapons pack

EX n/a   **NM** $3   **MIP** $7

Jungle Patrol Mission Gear, 1993, Hasbro

EX n/a   **NM** $3   **MIP** $7

Light Infantry Mission Gear, 1993, Hasbro

EX n/a   **NM** $3   **MIP** $7

Marine Paris Island Gear, 1993, Hasbro

EX n/a   **NM** $3   **MIP** $7

Mobile Artillery Assault Set, 1993, Hasbro

EX n/a   **NM** $3   **MIP** $7

Mountain Assault Mission Gear, 1993, Hasbro

EX n/a   **NM** $3   **MIP** $7

Navy SEAL Commando, 1993, Hasbro, Deluxe Mission Gear

EX n/a   **NM** $3   **MIP** $7

Navy Shore Patrol Gear, 1993, Hasbro

EX n/a   **NM** $3   **MIP** $7

Ocean Enforcer Mission Gear, 1994, Hasbro

EX n/a   **NM** $3   **MIP** $7

Red Beret Weapons Arsenal, 1993, Hasbro

EX n/a   **NM** $3   **MIP** $7

Red Ninja Mission Gear, 1993, Hasbro

EX n/a   **NM** $3   **MIP** $7

S.W.A.T. Assault Mission Gear, 1993, Hasbro

EX n/a   **NM** $3   **MIP** $7

Smart Gun Blaster, 1993, Hasbro

EX n/a   **NM** $3   **MIP** $7

Star Brigade Astronaut Mission Gear, 1994, Hasbro

EX n/a   **NM** $3   **MIP** $7

Swamp Fighter Mission Gear, 1994, Hasbro

EX n/a   **NM** $3   **MIP** $7

The Ultimate Arsenal, 1993, Hasbro, more than 25 pieces

EX n/a   **NM** $3   **MIP** $7

Underwater Attack Mission Gear, 1993, Hasbro

EX n/a   **NM** $3   **MIP** $7

Urban S.W.A.T., 1994, Hasbro, weapons pack

EX n/a   **NM** $3   **MIP** $7

Vehicle

Jet Pack, 1994, Hasbro

EX $3   **NM** $5   **MIP** $10

Strike Cycle, 1994, Hasbro

EX $3   **NM** $5   **MIP** $10

Vehicles

Rhino G.P.V., 1993, Hasbro, General Purpose Vehicle, 4WD

EX $8   **NM** $15   **MIP** $30

30TH SALUTE SERIES

30th Salute Black Action Soldier, 1994, Hasbro, Model No. 81271

EX $15   **NM** $20   **MIP** $40

35th Anniversary Gift Set, 1999, Hasbro, Then and Now, 1964 figure, 1999 figure, set of two, 1999

EX $10   **NM** $20   **MIP** $40

Action Marine, 1994, Hasbro, Model No. 81047

EX $7   **NM** $12   **MIP** $20

Action Pilot, 1994, Hasbro, Model No. 81046

EX $7   **NM** $12   **MIP** $20

Action Sailor, 1994, Hasbro, Model No. 81048

EX $7   **NM** $12   **MIP** $20

Action Soldier, 1994, Hasbro, Model No. 81045

EX $7   **NM** $12   **MIP** $20

Green Beret Lt. Joseph Colton, 1994, Hasbro, mail order

EX $12   **NM** $15   **MIP** $27

ACTION ASSORTMENT

Adventures of G.I. Joe: Peril of the Raging River, 1999, Hasbro

EX n/a   **NM** $6   **MIP** $12

Delta Force, 1999, Hasbro

EX n/a   **NM** $6   **MIP** $12

Salute to the Millennium Marine, 1999, Hasbro

EX n/a   **NM** $6   **MIP** $12

ALPHA ASSORTMENT

Battle of the Bulge, 2000, Hasbro

EX n/a   **NM** $6   **MIP** $12

Demolitions Expert, 2000, Hasbro

EX n/a   **NM** $6   **MIP** $12

Navy Seal, 2000, Hasbro

EX n/a   **NM** $6   **MIP** $12

WWII Pacific Marine, 2000, Hasbro

EX n/a   **NM** $6   **MIP** $12

ARMED FORCES ASSORTMENT

Army National Guard, 1998, Hasbro

EX n/a   **NM** $6   **MIP** $11

U.S. Air Force Crew Chief, 1998, Hasbro

EX n/a   **NM** $6   **MIP** $11

U.S. Marine Corps Korean Soldier, 1998, Hasbro

EX n/a   **NM** $6   **MIP** $11

U.S. Marine Corps Recruit, 1998, Hasbro

EX n/a   **NM** $6   **MIP** $11

U.S. Navy Serviceman, 1998, Hasbro

EX n/a   **NM** $6   **MIP** $11

ARMED FORCES SERVICE COLLECTION

Police Officer, 1999, Hasbro

EX n/a   **NM** $8   **MIP** $25

U.S. Army Infantry Desert Soldier, 1999, Hasbro

EX n/a   **NM** $8   **MIP** $25

U.S. Army Pacific Forces, 1999, Hasbro

EX n/a   **NM** $8   **MIP** $25

U.S. Army Vietnam Soldiers, 1998, Hasbro

EX n/a   **NM** $8   **MIP** $20

U.S. Navy SEAL, 1999, Hasbro

EX n/a   **NM** $8   **MIP** $20

USAF Fighter Pilot: Korean War, 1999, Hasbro

EX n/a   **NM** $8   **MIP** $20

Vietnam Marine, 1999, Hasbro

EX n/a   **NM** $10   **MIP** $15

ASTRONAUT ASSORTMENT

(Hasbro Photo)

Mercury Astronaut, 1997, Hasbro, in spacesuit and helmet

EX $12   **NM** $22   **MIP** $35

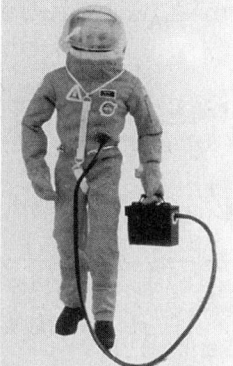

(Hasbro Photo)

Space Shuttle Astronaut, 1997, Hasbro, in orange spacesuit

EX n/a   **NM** $10   **MIP** $20

BRAVO ASSORTMENT

Vietnam Combat Engineer, 2000, Hasbro

EX n/a   **NM** $10   **MIP** $15

Vietnam Jungle Recon Soldier, 2000, Hasbro

EX n/a   **NM** $6   **MIP** $10

CORE FIGURE ASSORTMENT

Adventures of G.I. Joe: Save the Tiger, 1999, Hasbro

EX n/a   **NM** $10   **MIP** $15

G.I. Joe: Challenge at Hawk River, 1999, Hasbro

EX n/a   **NM** $6   **MIP** $10

U.S. Army Nurse: Vietnam, 1999, Hasbro

EX n/a   **NM** $5   **MIP** $12

U.S. Coast Guard Boarding Party, 1999, Hasbro

EX n/a   **NM** $5   **MIP** $10

DELTA ASSORTMENT

Navajo Code Talker, 2000, Hasbro

EX $7   **NM** $15   **MIP** $30

U.S. Marine Dog Unit, 2000, Hasbro

EX $7   **NM** $20   **MIP** $45

ECHO ASSORTMENT

John F. Kennedy, 2000, Hasbro

EX $7   **NM** $10   **MIP** $20

Vietnam Wall, 2000, Hasbro

EX $3   **NM** $7   **MIP** $15

WWI Doughboy, 2000, Hasbro

EX $12   **NM** $20   **MIP** $32

WWII U.S. Army Airborne Normandy, 2000, Hasbro

EX $5   **NM** $15   **MIP** $20

FOREIGN ASSORTMENT

Japanese Zero Pilot, 2000, Hasbro

EX $7   **NM** $15   **MIP** $25

Red Infantry Pilot, 2000, Hasbro

EX $3   **NM** $10   **MIP** $20

FOURTH OF JULY EDITION

(Hasbro Photo)

D-Day Salute, 1997, Hasbro, w/M-1 rifle, pack and camo-net helmet

EX $7   **NM** $12   **MIP** $23

GREATEST HEROES

Buzz Aldrin, 1999, Hasbro

EX $10   **NM** $20   **MIP** $40

(KP Photo)

Lt. Colonel Theodore Roosevelt, 1999, Hasbro, in Spanish-American War uniform, dark blue shirt, tan coat and pants, includes American flag, pistol and other accessories

EX $10   **NM** $20   **MIP** $30

Ted Williams, 1999, Hasbro

EX $7   **NM** $14   **MIP** $28

WWII Flame Thrower Soldier, 1999, Hasbro

EX $7   **NM** $10   **MIP** $18

HISTORICAL COMMANDERS ASSORTMENT

Colin Powell, 1998, Hasbro

EX $10   **NM** $15   **MIP** $30

Dwight Eisenhower, 1997, Hasbro

EX $10   **NM** $15   **MIP** $26

General Patton, 1997, Hasbro

EX $10   **NM** $15   **MIP** $30

Omar Bradley, 1998, Hasbro

EX $10   **NM** $15   **MIP** $26

HOLIDAY SALUTE

(Hasbro)

George Washington, 1998, Hasbro

EX $10   **NM** $15   **MIP** $25

HOLLYWOOD HEROES

Bob Hope, 1998, Hasbro
EX $5   NM $10   MIP $15

MILITARY SPORTS ASSORTMENT

Army Football, 1998, Hasbro
EX $4   NM $9   MIP $18

Navy Football, 1998, Hasbro
EX $3   NM $6   MIP $12

MODERN FORCES ASSORTMENT

82nd Airborne Division, female, 1998, Hasbro
EX n/a   NM $4   MIP $15

Australian O.D.F., 1996, Hasbro
EX n/a   NM $4   MIP $10

Battle of the Bulge, Toys R Us Exclusive, 1996, Hasbro
EX n/a   NM $4   MIP $10

Belgium Para Commando, 1997, Hasbro
EX n/a   NM $4   MIP $10

(Hasbro Photo)

British SAS, 1996, Hasbro, limited edition, w/rifle, helmet and goggles
EX n/a   NM $4   MIP $10

Dress Marine, Toys R Us Exclusive, 1996, Hasbro
EX $4   NM $6   MIP $14

French Foreign Legion Legionnaire, 1997, Hasbro
EX $4   NM $8   MIP $12

U.S. Airborne Ranger HALO Parachutist, 1996, Hasbro
EX $5   NM $9   MIP $16

U.S. Army Coldweather Soldier, 1998, Hasbro
EX $4   NM $8   MIP $12

U.S. Army Drill Sergeant, 1997, Hasbro
EX $5   NM $10   MIP $15

U.S. Army Helicopter Pilot, female, 1997, Hasbro
EX $10   NM $20   MIP $30

(Hasbro Photo)

U.S. Army Infantry Soldier, 1996, Hasbro, limited edition, w/goggles, machine gun, and desert-pattern uniform
EX $4   NM $6   MIP $12

U.S. Army M-1 Tank Commander, 1997, Hasbro
EX $4   NM $8   MIP $15

U.S. Marine Corp Force Recon, 1998, Hasbro
EX $6   NM $12   MIP $25

(Hasbro Photo)

U.S. Marine Corps Sniper, 1996, Hasbro, camouflaged rifle w/scope, camo netting
EX $6   NM $10   MIP $15

U.S. Navy Blue Angel, 1998, Hasbro
EX $6   NM $10   MIP $14

U.S. Navy Flight Deck Fuel Handler, 1997, Hasbro
EX $7   NM $12   MIP $20

PEARL HARBOR COLLECTION

Army Defense Diorama Set, 2000, Hasbro
EX $5   NM $10   MIP $20

Battleship Row Defender, 2000, Hasbro
EX $4   NM $8   MIP $16

Diamond Head Lookout Invasion Alert, 2000, Hasbro
EX $4   NM $6   MIP $12

Hickam Field Army Defender, 2000, Hasbro
EX $4   NM $6   MIP $12

Vicker's Machine Gun, 2000, Hasbro
EX $4   NM $6   MIP $12

Wheeler Field Army Air Corp, 2000, Hasbro
EX $4   NM $6   MIP $16

WWII COMMEMORATIVE FIGURES, TARGET EXCLUSIVE

(Hasbro)

Action Marine, 1995, Hasbro, in camo uniform w/cap, rifle, canteen, grenades and pack
EX $6   NM $12   MIP $20

(Hasbro)

Action Pilot, 1995, Hasbro, khaki uniform, leather jacket and helmet, goggles, bayonet, .45 pistol, dog tags
EX $5   NM $10   MIP $15

(Hasbro)

Action Sailor, 1995, Hasbro, blue uniform, Shore Patrol armband, M-1 rifle, duffle bag

EX $8   **NM** $15   **MIP** $20

Action Soldier, 1995, Hasbro

EX $8   **NM** $10   **MIP** $15

WWII FORCES ASSORTMENT

442nd Americans of Japanese Descent Combat Soldiers, 1998, Hasbro

EX $4   **NM** $8   **MIP** $12

Congressional Medal of Honor, Platoon Sgt. Mitchell Paige, 1998, Hasbro

EX $4   **NM** $8   **MIP** $12

Congressional Medal of Honor, Sgt. Francis S. Currey, 1997, Hasbro

EX $12   **NM** $25   **MIP** $35

Tuskegee B-25 Bomber Pilot, African American, 1997, Hasbro

EX $6   **NM** $12   **MIP** $20

Tuskegee Fighter Pilot, African American, 1997, Hasbro

EX $6   **NM** $12   **MIP** $20

U.S. Air Force B-17 Bomber Crewman, 1998, Hasbro

EX $8   **NM** $10   **MIP** $15

U.S. Navy PT-Boat Commander, 1998, Hasbro

EX $4   **NM** $7   **MIP** $12

Guns

by George H. Newcomb

The first toy guns appeared in the mid-1860s and were made of cast iron. By the end of the 19th century, manufacturers such as Ives, Dent, Grey Iron, Hubley, Stevens, Kilgore, and other companies produced a wide variety of cap guns, figural guns, exploders, peashooters, cap canes, and cap bombs. By 1940, toy guns sported revolving cylinders, nickel finishes, detailed plastic grips, and realistic actions. Such detailed cast-iron guns with names like "Long Tom," "Big Horn," "Peace Maker," "American," and "The Law West of The Pecos" are highly sought after today.

By the late 1940s, young baby boomers were following the adventures of Roy Rogers, Hop-Along Cassidy, The Lone Ranger, Gene Autry, and others on a new medium called television. In the mid-to-late 1950s, TV produced new shows with new heroes like The Cisco Kid, Wyatt Earp, Maverick, Johnny Yuma (The Rebel), Lucas McCain (The Rifleman), Joe Friday (Dragnet), Matt Dillon (Gunsmoke), and more.

Trends

The toy gun market has changed with the rise of eBay and the Internet. The downturn in the economy has caused many collectors to liquidate or trim their collections. The once meteoric rise in values has flattened out somewhat. However, the hobby is still alive and flourishing. There still seems to be a good number of collectible pieces out there at reasonable prices for every level of collector.

Condition and Value

When buying or selling toy guns, the three watchwords of this hobby are CONDITION, RARITY and CONDITION. Mint condition, like new from the factory, and rare items will always retain their value. A cap gun that has been fired, even just once, is no longer in mint condition and cannot be sold as such. A water squirt gun that has fired water is usually prone to rust inside the mechanism. A dart gun without the darts or a big plastic machine gun without the bullets is worth less than one complete with all parts. Every toy gun must be carefully examined and judged by its good and bad points before any determination of value can be made. As with any collectible, the sale price is always determined by what the buyer is willing to pay and the seller accept.

Online Resources

http://www.nicholscapguns.com
The most complete and largest toy gun Web site is run by Mike Nichols, surviving member of the Nichols family. This is a free Web site that provides tons of links to dealers, classifieds, toy gun shows, services, other Web sites and more.

http://www.miniaturearms.com/Marx/MarxMain.html
This Web site specializes in the miniature cap guns made by Marx in the 1950s, 60s and 70s.

Contributor: George H. Newcomb is president of Plymouth Rock Toy Co. Inc., a company he started in 1987 to better pursue his passion of buying and selling antique and collectible toys. Check out their Web site at www.plyrocktoy.com. You can contact George by email at plyrocktoy@aol.com.

NOTE: For Ray Guns see Sci-Fi and Space Toys.

The **Top 10 Guns** in mint condition

1. Hopalong Cassidy Double Holster Set, Wyandotte, 1940s $4,000
2. Man From U.N.C.L.E. THRUSH Rifle, Ideal, 1966 . . . . $3,250
3. Hopalong Cassidy Holster/Gun Set, Schmidt, 1950s $3,000
4. Man From U.N.C.L.E. Attache Case, Ideal, 1965 . . . . $1,650
5. ISA 07-11 Attache Case, Marx, 1965 . . . . $1,650
6. Roy Rogers Double Gun & Holster Set, two 8-1/2″ pistols, Classy, 1950s . . . $1,600
7. Roy Rogers Double Holster Set, two 9″ pistols, Classy, 1950s. $1,550
8. Roy Rogers Double Holster Set, two 10″ pistols, Classy, 1950s. $1,500
9. Maverick Two-Gun Holster Set, 1958 . . . . $1,200
10. Dale Evans D-26 cap pistol, Schmidt, 1950s $1,100

Detective/Spy

Agent Zero M Pocket-Shot, 1965-66, Mattel, plastic jackknife turns into pistol
EX $15   NM $30   MIP $45

Agent Zero M Radio Rifle, 1964, Mattel, plastic, 8-1/2" closed, 22-1/2" open, looks like portable radio
EX $45   NM $90   MIP $150

Agent Zero M Snap-Shot Camera Pistol, 1964, Mattel, plastic, 7-1/2" extended, camera turns into pistol at press of a button
EX $35   NM $60   MIP $90

Agent Zero W Potshot, 1965, Mattel, 3" die-cast potshot derringer, gold finish, has brown vinyl armband holster, holds two Shootin' Shell cartridges, gold buckle w/Agent Zero W logo
EX $30   NM $75   MIP $145

Colt .38 Detective Special, 1959, Hubley, 4-1/2" miniature Colt .38 pistol single shot caps, loads six play bullets w/suspenders chest holster
EX $35   NM $75   MIP $150

Detective Shell Firing Pistol, 1950s, Nichols, 5-1/2" die-cast snub-nose pistol chambers and fires six three-piece cap cartridges, cut-out badge, bullet cartridges, extra red plastic bullet heads
EX $100   NM $175   MIP $325

Dick Cap Pistol, 1950s, Halco, die-cast, 4-1/4" automatic style, side loading w/nickel finish, Model 210A, eagles on grips
EX $25   NM $55   MIP $100

Dick Cap Pistol, 1950s, Hubley, 4-3/4", die-cast automatic, side loading, nickel finish
EX $25   NM $45   MIP $90

Dragnet Badge 714 Detective Special Repeating Revolver, 1955, Knickerbocker, no. 639, plastic cap pistol, 6-3/4", black plastic w/gold "Dragnet" and "714" badge on grip
EX $75   NM $130   MIP $235

Dragnet Badge 714 Triple Fire Comb. Game, 1955, Knickerbocker, tin litho stand-up target has four plastic spinners, includes two 6" black plastic guns, one fires darts, the other cork gun, includes four plastic darts and three corks
EX $90   NM $150   MIP $275

Dragnet Snub Nose Cap Pistol, 1960s, Knickerbocker, plastic/die-cast works, 6-3/4", black plastic w/gold "Dragnet" and "714" badge on grip, on card
EX $35   NM $110   MIP $150

Dragnet Water Gun, 1960s, Knickerbocker, 6" black plastic, .38 Special-style w/gold "714" shield on grip
EX $30   NM $65   MIP $165

Girl From U.N.C.L.E. Garter Holster, 1966, Lone Star, "gang buster" die-cast metal gun fires plastic bullets from metal shells, checker design vinyl holster and bullet pouch, on card
EX $80   NM $145   MIP $225

G-Man Gun Wind-Up Machine Gun, 1948, Marx, 23" tin-litho, red, black, orange and gray litho, round drum magazine, wind-up mechanism makes sparks from muzzle, uses cigarette flint, wooden stock
EX $125   NM $245   MIP $425

ISA 07-11 Attache Case, 1965, Marx, 15" x 10" x 2-1/2", comes w/cap firing pistol and clip, ID card, wallet, cap grenade, badge, passport and secret message sender
EX $525   NM $1050 MIP $1650

James Bond Attache Case, 1966, Multiple Plastics, vinyl-covered cardboard, 9mm automatic Luger, should stock, sight, silencer, belt, secret message coding machine, hidden dagger, wallet, passport, money
EX $300   NM $600   MIP $900

Man From U.N.C.L.E. Attache Case, 1966, Lone Star, vinyl case w/pistol, holster, walkie talkie, cigarette box gun, badge, passport, invisible cartridge pen, handcuffs
EX $265   NM $530   MIP $775

Man From U.N.C.L.E. Illya K. Special Lighter Gun, 1966, Ideal, cigarette lighter gun shoots caps, has radio compartment concealed behind fake cigs, in window box
EX $110   NM $225   MIP $350

Man From U.N.C.L.E. Illya Kuryakin Gun Set, 1966, Ideal, includes clip loading, cap firing plastic pistol, badge, wallet, ID card, in window box
EX $210   NM $420   MIP $650

Man From U.N.C.L.E. Napoleon Solo Gun Set, 1965, Ideal, clip loading, cap firing plastic pistol w/rifle attachments, badge, ID card, in window box
EX $280   NM $560   MIP $875

Man From U.N.C.L.E. Pistol and Holster, 1965, Ideal, 7" long pistol and plastic holster, both w/orange ID sticker
EX $45   NM $90   MIP $135

Man From U.N.C.L.E. Pistol Cane, 1966, Marx, 25" long, cap firing, bullet shooting aluminum cane w/eight bullets and one metal shell, on card
EX $175   NM $350   MIP $550

Man From U.N.C.L.E. Secret Service Pop Gun, 1960s, bagged Luger pop gun on header card w/unlicensed art of Napoleon and Illya
EX $5   NM $12   MIP $25

Man From U.N.C.L.E. Stash Away Guns, 1966, Ideal, three cap firing guns, holsters, two straps, ID card and badge, in window box
EX $210   NM $420   MIP $650

(KP Photo)

Man From U.N.C.L.E. THRUSH Rifle, 1966, Ideal, 36" long
EX $875   NM $1750 MIP $3250

Official Detective Shootin' Shell Snub-Nose .38, 1959, Mattel, .38 die-cast chrome w/brown plastic grips, black vinyl shoulder holster, wallet, badge, ID card, Pistol Range Target and bullets
EX $95   NM $175   MIP $250

Official Detective Shootin' Shell Snub-Nose .38, 1960, Mattel, .38 die-cast 7" chrome finish, gold cylinder, brown plastic grips, Private Detective badge and Shootin' Shell bullets
EX $60   NM $100   MIP $165

Official Dick Tracy Shootin' Shell Snub-Nose .38, 1961, Mattel, die-cast chrome .38 w/brown plastic grips, chrome finish w/Shootin' Shell bullets and Stick-m caps
EX $75   NM $150   MIP $250

Official James Bond 007 Thunderball Pistol, 1985, Wicke, 4-1/2" Walther PPK style, single shot fires plastic caps, Secret Agent ID
EX $20   NM $40   MIP $85

Secret Sam Attache Case, 1965, Topper/Deluxe Reading, 15" x 11" plastic case holds multi-gun that assemble into rifle w/stock, real camera and periscope
EX $150   NM $290   MIP $450

Sharkmatic Cap Gun, 1980s, Edison G., 6" automatic, style pistol, fires "Supermatic System" strip caps
EX $10   NM $15   MIP $20

The Saint Ruger, 1960s, Lone Star, die-cast w/telescopic sight and silencer
EX $50   NM $100   MIP $150

Military/Automatics

7580 UZI Automatic, 1986, Esquire Novelty, 10-1/2", battery-operated, black plastic uses 250-shot roll caps, shoulder strap
EX $20   NM $35   MIP $50

9mm Z-Matic Uzi Cap Gun, 1984, Larami, 8" replica, removeable cap storage magazine, black finish, small orange plug in barrel
EX $5   NM $10   MIP $15

Anti-Aircraft Gun, Marx, mechanical, sparks, tin litho, 16-1/2" long, 1941
EX $50   NM $135   MIP $275

Army .45 Cap Pistol, 1950s, Hubley, 6-1/2" automatic, dark gray finish, white plastic grips, pop-up cap
EX $45   NM $120   MIP $275

Army 45 Automatic, 1959, Nichols, 4-1/4" all metal, side loading automatic, olive
EX $15   NM $25   MIP $50

Army Automatic Pistol, 1950s, Marx, 2-1/2" automatic, (ACP style), black w/white grips, small leather holster w/flaps (Marx Miniature)
EX $10   NM $20   MIP $40

Army Pistol w/Revolving Cylinder, Marx, tin litho
EX $35   NM $60   MIP $125

Army Sparking Pop Gun, 1940-50, Marx
EX $45   NM $75   MIP $150

Automatic Cap Pistol, 1950s, National, 6-1/2" silver finish w/simulated walnut grip
EX $35   NM $65   MIP $90

Automatic Cap Pistol No. 290, Hubley, die-cast, 6-1/2", nickel finish, brown checkered grips, magazine pops up when slider is pulled back
EX $85   NM $190   MIP $340

Burp Gun, 1960s, Marx, 20" battery-operated, green and black plastic
EX $20   NM $35   MIP $75

Desert Patrol Machine Pistol, 1960, Marx, plastic, 11" long
EX $30   NM $45   MIP $75

Falcon Service Automatic, 1950s, Kilgore, Colt .45 cap pistol
EX $8   NM $16   MIP $25

Green Beret Tommy Gun, 1960s, Marx, sparkles, trigger action, on card
EX $35   NM $55   MIP $95

Johnny Seven One Man Army-OMA, 1964, Topper/Deluxe-Reading, 36" multi-purpose seven guns in one, removeable pistol fires caps, rifle fires white plastic bullets, bolt spring fired machine gun "tommy gun" sound, rear launcher fires grenades, forward diff. shell
EX $135   NM $225   MIP $450

M-1 Kadet Training Rifle, 1960s, Parris Arms, 32" wood/metal M-1 carbine, clicker action, metal barrel, trigger guard, bolt
EX $20   NM $35   MIP $50

Matic 45 Cap Gun, 1980s, Edison, 24", plastic gun w/stock, fires "Supermatic System" strip caps
EX $10   NM $15   MIP $20

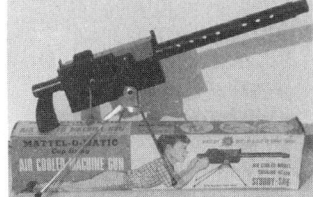

Mattel-O-Matic Air Cooled Machine Gun, 1955, Mattel, 16" machine gun fires perforated roll caps by

cranking handle, plastic w/die-cast, tripod-mounted, plastic/die-cast works, red and black plastic, box
EX $45   NM $85   MIP $125

Mauser Cap Pistol, 1960s, Lone Star, 6-1/4", Mauser style automatic pop up magazine, silver finish, brown plastic grips
EX $20   NM $35   MIP $55

Mini-M.A.G. Combat Gun, Marx, cap pistol, miniature scale, die-cast
EX $20   NM $30   MIP $40

MM Automatic Carbine, 1960s, 24" recoil red slide in muzzle and flashing light, brown and black plastic
EX $15   NM $30   MIP $45

Model 12 SoftAir Gun, 1990, Daisy, machine gun style, loads "SoftAir" pellets in plastic cartridge, 10 rounds, spring fired, can be cocked by barrel grip or bolt
EX $35   NM $50   MIP $85

Molotov Cocktail Tank Buster Cap Bomb, 1964, Maco, 6" plastic and die-cast, insert caps in head and throw
EX $15   NM $25   MIP $45

MP Holster Set, 1950s, Maco, plastic pistol has removeable magazine, loads and ejects bullets, white leather belt and holster
EX $75   NM $120   MIP $225

Mustang Toy Machine Gun, 1958, Buddy L, 25" long chrome and hard plastic paper roll popping gun
EX $75   NM $125   MIP $175

Paratrooper Carbine, 1950s, Maco, 24" carbine, removeable magazine, fires plastic bullets, bayonet and target
EX $95   NM $135   MIP $185

SA Automatic Burp Gun, 1970s, Daisy, 10" w/stock, black plastic, burp-gun style, removeable clip, loads and fires white plastic bullets
EX $20   NM $35   MIP $50

Siren Sparkling Airplane Pistol, Marx, heavy-gauge enamel steel, 9-1/2" wingspan, 7" long
EX $50   NM $75   MIP $100

Sparkling Siren Machine Gun, 1949, Marx, 26" long
EX $45   NM $90   MIP $185

Special Mission Tommy Gun, Marx
EX $20   NM $35   MIP $45

Spitfire Cap Firing Machine Gun, 1950, Buddy L, biped stand attached to muzzle, black plastic stock and grip crank fired paper popper
EX $75   NM $120   MIP $195

Tommy Burp Gun, 1957, Mattel, 17" plastic w/die-cast works, perforated roll caps fired by cranking the handle
EX $90   NM $150   MIP $300

USA Machine Gun, 1950s, Maco, 12" tripod-mounted gun fires plastic bullets, red and yellow plastic
EX $85   NM $145   MIP $225

Wind-Up Burp Gun, 1955, Mattel, plastic/pressed steel, 24", "Grease Gun," fires perforated roll caps, fold-over wire stock, cap storage in magazine, boxed
EX $75   NM $125   MIP $225

Yo Gun, 1960s, 7-1/4", red plastic gun releases yellow plastic ball which snaps back when trigger is pulled, functions like a yo-yo
EX $30   NM $45   MIP $60

Miscellaneous

6 Shot Cap Pistol, Stevens, 6-3/4", six separate triggers revolve to deliver caps to hammer, metal finish
EX $85   NM $150   MIP $300

Airplane Clicker Pistol, 1950s, Palmer Plastics, 4-1/2" yellow and black plane, red pilot and guns
EX $25   NM $45   MIP $65

Atomee Water Pistol, 1960s, Park Plastics, 4-1/4", black plastic
EX $10   NM $20   MIP $35

Automatic Repeater Paper Pop Pistol, 1950s, LMC/Langson Mfg. Co., die-cast, 7-3/4" long
EX $25   NM $55   MIP $125

Automatic Sparkling Pistol, 1960s, Ronson, 6-1/2", plastic/metal, uses cigarette lighter flints to make sparks, available in green-red, yellow-green, red or white colors
EX $15   NM $30   MIP $45

Blastaway Cap Gun, 1960, Marx, die-cast, 50 shooter repeater
EX $25   NM $35   MIP $75

Click Pistol, Marx, pressed steel, 7-3/4" long
EX $20   NM $50   MIP $100

Click Pistol, Marx, tin litho
EX $20   NM $50   MIP $100

Crack Shot Dart Pistol, 1950s, Wyandotte, black plastic, shoots darts at target
EX $10   NM $25   MIP $45

Double Holster Set, 1950s, black leather, large size, steer head conches, lots of red jewels, fringe, holsters only, no guns
EX $75   NM $125   MIP $200

Dynamic Automatic Repeating Bubble Gun, Atomic Industries, 8" black plastic pistol projects bubbles
EX $25   NM $40   MIP $65

Famous Firearms Deluxe Edition Collectors Album, 1959, Marx, set of four rifles, five pistols and four holsters, miniature series, includes: Mare's Laig, Thompson machine gun, Sharps rifle, Winchester saddle rifle, Derringer, .38 snub-nose, Civil War pistol, six shooter/Flint
EX $50   NM $100   MIP $200

Hideaway Derringer, 1950s, Esquire, 3-1/2" single shot, loads solid metal bullet, grip is removeable to store two more bullets, gold finish, white plastic grips
EX $40   NM $95   MIP $125

Johnny Tremain Flintlock Pistol, 1950s, Swansea Industries, cap gun based on Walt Disney character
EX $35   NM $70   MIP $125

Long Tom Dart Gun, 1950s, Wyandotte, 11" pressed steel
EX $35   NM $50   MIP $100

M240 Machine Pistol, 1970s, Marx, black plastic, no caps, pull trigger produces sound
EX $5   NM $12   MIP $20

Marx Miniatures Famous Gun Sets, 1958, Marx, set of four guns, features tommy gun, Civil War revolver, "Mare's Laig" and western saddle rifle
EX $25   NM $50   MIP $100

Marxman Target Pistol, Marx, plastic, 5-1/2" long
EX $35   NM $50   MIP $100

Midget Cap Pistol, 1950s, Hubley, 5-1/2" long, die-cast, all-metal flintlock w/silver finish
EX $20   NM $35   MIP $50

Model No. 25 Pump Action BB Gun, 1960s, Daisy, plastic stock
EX $35   NM $65   MIP $125

Model No. 25 Pump Action BB Gun, 1960s, Daisy, wood stock
EX $35   NM $65   MIP $135

Mountie Automatic Cap Pistol, Kilgore, 6", automatic style w/pop-up magazine, unusual nickel finish, black plastic grips
EX $25   NM $45   MIP $85

Nu-Matic Paper Popper Gun, 1940s, Langson Mfg. Co., pressed steel, 7" squeeze grip trigger, mechanism pops roll of paper (reel at top of gun) to make loud noise, black finish
EX $30   NM $50   MIP $75

P-38 Clicker Pistol, 1950s, Meldon, 7-1/2" black finish, automatic style
EX $35   NM $50   MIP $90

Paper Cracker Rifle, 1940s, Buddy L, 26" steel and machined aluminum mechanism, barrel, trigger and operating lever, uses 1000 shot paper roll, brown plastic stock
EX $95   NM $190   MIP $250

Pirate Cap Pistol, 1939-50, Hubley, 9-1/2" side-by-side flintlock style die-cast frame and cast-iron double hammers and trigger, nickel finish, white plastic grips feature Pirate in red oval
EX $75   NM $165   MIP $300

Potato Gun, 1991, China, Spud Gun, plastic, pneumatic action fires potato pellet from muzzle
EX $3   NM $7   MIP $10

Repeating Cap Pistol, Marx, aluminum
EX $20   NM $30   MIP $50

Revolver Aquila Pop Pistol, 1960s, Spain, 10" green finish, pop gun breaks to cock, fires cork from barrel, sparks from mechanism under barrel
EX $15   NM $30   MIP $60

Sparkling Machine Gun "Sure-Shot," 1950s, T. Cohn, tin litho in red, yellow and blue, turn handle and barrel sparks
EX $30   NM $60   MIP $110

Sparkling Pop Gun, Marx
EX $25   NM $50   MIP $100

Spud Gun, 1950s-60s, Cossman, case aluminum, pneumatic all-metal gun shoots potato pellets
EX $15   NM $35   MIP $50

Spud Gun (Tira Papas), 1960s, Welco, 6" all-metal gun
EX $10   NM $20   MIP $35

Targeteer No. 18 Target Air Pistol, 1949, Daisy, 10" gun metal finish, push barrel to cock, Daisy BB tin w/special BBs, spinner target
EX $50   NM $90   MIP $135

Trooper Cap Pistol, 1950, Hubley, 6-1/2" all metal, pop-up cap magazine, nickel finish, black grips
EX $30   NM $75   MIP $165

Police

.38 Cap Pistol, 1960s, Marx, w/caps and plastic bullets, miniature scale, die-cast
EX $35 **NM** $75 **MIP** $125

Detective Snub-Nose Special, 1950s, Marx, die-cast, 5-3/4" top release break, unusual revolving cylinder, fires Kilgore style disc caps and plastic bullets, chrome finish w/black plastic grips
EX $75 **NM** $90 **MIP** $185

Dick Tracy Click Pistol, 1940s, Marx, w/decal
EX $50 **NM** $120 **MIP** $185

Dick Tracy Sparkling Pop Pistol, 1940s, Marx, tin litho, sparkling action
EX $50 **NM** $135 **MIP** $225

G-Boy Pistol, 1950s, Acme, 7" automatic (ACP) style entire left rear side of gun swings down to load
EX $25 **NM** $50 **MIP** $125

G-Man Automatic Silent Arm Pistol, Marx, tin
EX $35 **NM** $55 **MIP** $100

G-Man Machine Gun, 1940s, Marx, tin litho, wind-up, wood stock, red and yellow litho
EX $65 **NM** $130 **MIP** $225

G-Man Sparkling Sub-Machine Gun, 1950s, Marx, tin litho, wind-up, plastic stock, red and yellow litho
EX $50 **NM** $75 **MIP** $150

Marx Miniatures Detective Set, 1950s, Marx, miniature cap firing brown and gray tommy gun, chrome pistol and holster on card w/wood grain frame border
EX $25 **NM** $45 **MIP** $75

Mountie Automatic Cap Pistol, 1960s, Hubley, die-cast, 7-1/4" automatic style, pop-up lever-release magazine, blue finish
EX $25 **NM** $45 **MIP** $85

Official Dick Tracy Tommy Burst Machine Gun, 1960s, Mattel, 25" Thompson style machine gun fire perforated roll caps, single shot or in full burst when bolt is pulled back, brown plastic stock and black plastic body, lift up rear sight, Dick Tracy decal on stock
EX $100 **NM** $175 **MIP** $350

Peter Gunn Private Eye Revolver & Holster Set, 1959, Esquire, 36" die-cast Remington w/six two-piece bullets, badge and wallet, Peter Gunn business cards, black leather shoulder holster
EX $145 **NM** $275 **MIP** $350

Sheriff Signal Pistol, 1950, Marx, plastic, 5-1/2" long
EX $20 **NM** $30 **MIP** $60

Siren Sparkling Pistol, Marx, tin litho
EX $30 **NM** $50 **MIP** $85

Sparkling "Sure-Shot" Machine Gun, 1950s, T. Cohn, long body tin multicolored red/yellow/blue tin noise making gun, great box graphics show boy shooting sparks as pigtailed blond girl looks
EX $50 **NM** $75 **MIP** $150

Western

2 Guns in 1 Cap Pistol, 1950s, Hubley, die-cast, 8" w/long barrel, twist-off barrels to change from long to short, side loading, white plastic grips
EX $65 **NM** $110 **MIP** $175

45 Smoker, 1950s, Product Engineering, 10" cast aluminum, single cap, shoots talcum-like powder by use of bellows when trigger is pulled, aluminum finish
EX $50 **NM** $90 **MIP** $165

760 Rapid Fire Shotgun Air Rifle, 1960s, Daisy, 31" pump shotgun, gray metal one-piece frame, brown plastic stock and slider grip, fires blast of air
EX $65 **NM** $95 **MIP** $150

Authentic Derringer, 1960, Esquire Novelty, die-cast, 2" cap firing, copper finish, twin swivel barrel
EX $15 **NM** $25 **MIP** $60

Big Horn Cap Pistol, 1950s, Kilgore, 7" die-cast, all-metal revolving cylinder, break-to-front, disk caps, silver finish
EX $80 **NM** $155 **MIP** $225

Billy The Kid Cap Pistol, Stevens, die-cast, 8" long, cap pistol
EX $55 **NM** $110 **MIP** $225

Bobcat Saddle Gun, 1960s, USA, 13-1/2", pull-down cap magazine
EX $50 **NM** $90 **MIP** $150

Bonanza Guns Outfit, 1960s, Marx, 25" cap firing saddle rifle, magazine pulls down to load, 9-1/2" Western pistol fires two-piece Marx shooting bullets, wood plastic stocks and gun metal gray plastic body, tan vinyl holster
EX $85 **NM** $175 **MIP** $350

Bronco Cap Pistol, 1950s, Kilgore, 8-1/2", die-cast, revolving swing-out cylinder fires Kilgore disc caps, silver finish, black plastic "Bronco" grips
EX $65 **NM** $130 **MIP** $225

Buck'n Bronc Marshal Cap Pistol, 1950s, Schmidt, die-cast, 10" long barrel revolver style, lever release, break-to-front, plain silver finish, copper color metal grips
EX $100 **NM** $200 **MIP** $350

Buck'n Bronc Shoot'n Iron, 1950s, Schmidt, die-cast, cap gun, 50-shot repeater, gold finish, copper stag grips
EX $185 **NM** $275 **MIP** $450

Buffalo Bill Stevens, 1940s, Marx, cast-iron, 50 shooter repeater
EX $70 **NM** $110 **MIP** $175

Cap Gun Store Display, 1950s, Nichols, 24" x 14" wood board, derringer and two strips of Nichols bullets
EX $300 **NM** $600 **MIP** $950

Centennial Rifle, Marx, w/big sound
EX $25 **NM** $35 **MIP** $65

Champion Quick Draw Timer Cap Pistol, 1959, Kilgore, silver finish, side loading, wind-up mechanism in grip records elapsed time of draw, black plastic grips
EX $100 **NM** $200 **MIP** $325

Cheyenne Cap Pistol, 1974, Kilgore, 9-3/4" side loading, "Sure-K" plastic stag grips, silver finish
EX $10 **NM** $25 **MIP** $50

Cody Colt Paper Buster Gun, 1950s, Langson Mfg. Co., 7-3/4", paper popper, nickel finish, white plastic steer grips fires Cody Colt ammunition
EX $40 **NM** $80 **MIP** $125

Colt .38 Detective Special, 1959, Hubley, 4-1/2" Colt .38 pistol single shot caps and loads six play bullets w/suspenders chest holster
EX $35 **NM** $75 **MIP** $150

Colt .45 Cap Pistol, 1959, Hubley, die-cast, 13", revolving cylinder produced w/open or closed chamber ends, loads six two-piece cap-firing bullets, white plastic grips, red felt box
EX $125 **NM** $275 **MIP** $450

Cork-Shooting Rifle Parris Arms, 1960s, Marx, wood and steel
EX $25 **NM** $40 **MIP** $60

Cowboy Cap Pistol, 1950s, Hubley, 12", die-cast, swing-out revolving cylinder, release on barrel, gold finish, black plastic steer grips
EX $150 **NM** $300 **MIP** $500

Cowboy Cap Pistol, 1950s, Hubley, die-cast, 12" swing-out revolving cyclinder, release on barrel, nickel or aluminum finish, white plastic steer grips w/black steer head
EX $115 **NM** $235 **MIP** $375

Cowboy Jr. Cap Pistol No. 225, 1950s, Hubley, 9" die-cast, revolving cylinder, side loading, release on barrel, silver finish, white plastic cow grips, lanyard ring and cord

EX $65   **NM** $130   **MIP** $250

Dagger Derringer, 1958, Hubley, 7", unusual over and under pistol has hidden red plastic dagger that slides out from between barrels, rotating barrels load and fire two-piece bullets

EX $55   **NM** $100   **MIP** $165

Dale Evans D-26, 1950s, Classy, initials in butterfly symbol

EX $350   **NM** $600   **MIP** $1100

Dale Evans Holster Set, Classy, brown and yellow leather, white fringe on holsters, stylized blue butterflies are also "DE" logo, if buckled in front, holsters are backwards; holsters only, no guns

EX $100   **NM** $225   **MIP** $400

Davy Crockett Buffalo Rifle, 1950s, Hubley, 25" die-cast and plastic, unusual flintlock style, fires single cap under pan cover, brown plastic stock, ammo storage door in stock

EX $75   **NM** $145   **MIP** $225

Davy Crockett Frontier Fighter Cork Gun, 1950s, Unknown, 21" pop gun shoots cork on string and has cigarette flint mechanism at muzzle that makes sparks when fired, wood stock, leather sling

EX $75   **NM** $150   **MIP** $250

Deputy Cap Pistol, 1950s, Hubley, 10" die-cast, front breaking, release on barrel, ornate scroll work, nickel finish

EX $50   **NM** $125   **MIP** $200

Double Holster Set, 1950s, Classy, imitation alligator-texture brown leather, steer-head conches on holsters, lots of studs, yellow felt backing, holsters only, no guns

EX $150   **NM** $300   **MIP** $500

Double Holster Set, Johnny Ringo, 1960, Marx, 10", two pistols similar to 1860s Remington, fires roll caps by use of a lanyard that is pulled from the bottom of the grip, internal hammer, white plastic horse and steer grips, silver, brown vinyl holster

EX $90   **NM** $150   **MIP** $325

Dyna-Mite Derringer, 1955, Nichols, 3-1/4" die-cast, loads single cap cartridge, silver finish, white plastic grips

EX $15   **NM** $30   **MIP** $45

Dyna-Mite Derringer in Clip, 1950s, Nichols, 3-1/2" die-cast, fires single cap in Nichols cartridge, nickel finish, white plastic grips w/small leather holster

EX $25   **NM** $45   **MIP** $65

Fanner 50 "Swivelshot Trick Holster" Set, 1958, Mattel, die-cast bullet loading Fanner 50, leather swivel style holster, attaches to any belt, gun fires in holster when swiveled, string included for last ditch draw

EX $110   **NM** $225   **MIP** $375

Fanner 50 Cap Pistol, 1960s, Mattel, later version non-revolving cylinder, 11" fires perforated roll caps, black finish, white plastic antelope grips

EX $45   **NM** $90   **MIP** $175

Fanner 50 Cap Pistol Holster Set, 1960s, Mattel, 11" fanner non-revolving cylinder, stag plastic grips, nickel finish, black vinyl "Durahyde" holster

EX $55   **NM** $110   **MIP** $225

Fanner 50 Smoking Cap Pistol, 1957, Mattel, 11" w/revolving cylinder, first version w/grapefruit cylinder does not chamber bullets

EX $125   **NM** $175   **MIP** $300

Fanner 50 Smoking Cap Pistol, 1958, Mattel, 11" w/revolving cylinder, chambers six metal play bullets, die-cast

EX $90   **NM** $175   **MIP** $375

Fastest Gun Electronic Draw Game, 1958, Kilgore, die-cast, wire plug into "Rangers" gun grips, gun that shoots first lights eye of plastic battery-operated steer head, red and blue plastic holsters w/matching cowboy gun grips, plastic belts

EX $90   **NM** $175   **MIP** $300

Flintlock Jr. Cap Pistol, 1955, Hubley, 7-1/2" single shot, double action, brown swirl plastic stock

EX $20   **NM** $45   **MIP** $85

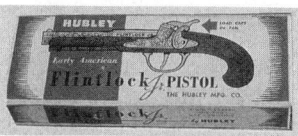

Flintlock Pistol, 1954, Hubley, 9-1/4", two-shot cap shooting single-action double barrel, over and under style, brown swirl plastic stock, nickel finish

EX $40   **NM** $90   **MIP** $155

Frontier Repeating Cap Rifle, 1950s, Hubley, 35-1/4" rifle nickel finish w/brown plastic stock and forestock, blue metal barrel, red plastic choke and front sight, pop down magazine, released by catch in front of trigger, scroll work

EX $75   **NM** $165   **MIP** $225

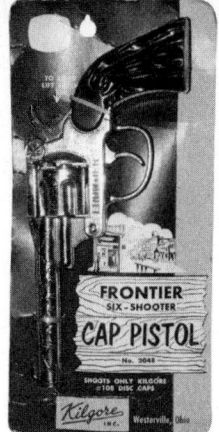

Frontier Six-Shooter Cap Pistol, 1950s, Kilgore, black grips, Model No. 2048

EX $65   **NM** $110   **MIP** $155

Frontier Smoker, 1950s, Product Engineering, 9-1/2" cap pistol, cast aluminum, pop-up magazine shoots white powder from internal bellows, all metal, black grips, silver finish, gold magazine, hammer and trigger

EX $85   **NM** $150   **MIP** $225

Gene Autry 44 Cap Pistol, 1950s, Leslie-Henry, 11" lever release, side loading, long barrel, nickel finish, white plastic horse-head grips

EX $125   **NM** $300   **MIP** $550

Gene Autry 44 Cap Pistol, 1950s, Leslie-Henry, 11" lever release, side loading, long barrel, nickel finish, brown translucent plastic horse-head grips

EX $175   **NM** $450   **MIP** $700

Gene Autry Cap Pistol, 1950s, Leslie-Henry, 9", die-cast, break-to-front lever release, nickel finish, white plastic horse-head grips

EX $100   **NM** $200   **MIP** $425

Gene Autry Cap Pistol, 1950s, Leslie-Henry, 9", die-cast, break-to-front lever release, nickel finish, black plastic horse-head grips

EX $115   **NM** $225   **MIP** $425

Gene Autry Cap Pistol, 1950s, Buzz-Henry, 7-3/4" die-cast, small size, lever release, break-to-front, nickel finish w/extension scroll work, black plastic horse-head grips

EX $115   **NM** $250   **MIP** $450

Gene Autry Cap Pistol, 1950s, Leslie-Henry, 9", die-cast, break-to-front lever release, copper finish, white plastic horse-head grips

EX $125   **NM** $255   **MIP** $475

Gene Autry Champion Single Holster Set, 1940s, M.A. Henry, leather and cardboard, red, yellow and green "jewels," four white wooden bullets, silver buckle

EX $125 **NM** $250 **MIP** $375

Grizzly Cap Pistol, 1950s, Kilgore, 10" revolving cylinder fires disc caps, swing out cylinder, black plastic grips w/grizzly bear

EX $100 **NM** $200 **MIP** $375

Gunfighter Holster Set, 1960s, Lone Star, 9" Frontier Ace, lever release, break-to-front, silver finish, brown plastic grips, white and red leather "Laramie" single holster w/separate belt

EX $60 **NM** $125 **MIP** $250

Gunsmoke Double Holster Set, 1950s, Leslie-Henry, 9" Leslie-Henry guns w/copper steer grips

EX $225 **NM** $475 **MIP** $650

Hawkeye Cap Pistol, 1950s, Kilgore, 4-1/4" all metal, automatic style, side loading, silver finish

EX $20 **NM** $40 **MIP** $75

Historic Guns Derringer, 1974, Marx, Marx Historic Guns series, derringer w/plastic presentation case, 4-1/2" long, on card

EX $15 **NM** $25 **MIP** $30

Hi-Yo Silver Lone Ranger Pistol, 1940s, Marx, tin gun w/decal

EX $60 **NM** $200 **MIP** $325

Hopalong Cassidy Cap Pistol, 1950, G. Schmidt, 9" pull hammer to release, scroll work, nickel finish w/black plastic grips w/white bust of Hopalong Cassidy, Model No. 80-G1140

EX $175 **NM** $400 **MIP** $750

Hopalong Cassidy Double Holster Set, 1940s, Wyandotte, w/two gold guns w/black grips, holster has silver studs w/Hoppy's name in belt

EX $1250 **NM** $2500 **MIP** $4000

Hopalong Cassidy Holster/Gun Set, 1950s, G. Schmidt, black holster, black grips on gun w/bust of Hoppy

EX $1000 **NM** $2000 **MIP** $3000

How the West Was Won Gun Rifle, Marx, deep gray Winchester model w/tan stock, in box

EX $55 **NM** $85 **MIP** $145

Johnny Eagle Red River Bullet Firing, 1965, Topper/Deluxe-Reading, over 12" double-action revolving cylinder pistol, die-cast hammer, trigger, blue plastic overall w/wood plastic grips w/gold horse, side loading, shell ejector, fires two-piece plastic bullets

EX $75 **NM** $100 **MIP** $185

Johnny Ringo Gun & Holster Set, 1960, Marx, die-cast gun, white plastic head grips, vinyl quick draw holster has rawhide tie, gun is fired by lanyard which passes through grip butt and attaches to belt, when pulled lanyard trips internal hammer

EX $90 **NM** $150 **MIP** $325

Johnny Ringo, Adventure of, Gun & Holster, 1960, Esquire Novelty, 10-3/4" long barrel Actoy, friction break, black/gold plastic stag grips, black leather two-gun holster, felt backing, loops hold four to six bullets, silver buckle

EX $250 **NM** $500 **MIP** $750

Johnty West Cowboy Rifle, 1950s, Marx, repeater cap action, winchester-style

EX $35 **NM** $80 **MIP** $155

Lone Ranger 45 Flasher Flashlight Pistol, Marx, in box

EX $60 **NM** $125 **MIP** $200

Lone Ranger Carbine, 1950s, Marx, 26" gray plastic repeater-style rifle has pull down cap magazine, western trim and Lone Ranger signature on stock

EX $75 **NM** $150 **MIP** $225

Lone Ranger Holster, Unknown, 9", leather/pressboard, Hi-Yo Silver and Lone Ranger printed, red jewel, belt loop

EX $50 **NM** $100 **MIP** $200

Lone Ranger Rifle, 1973, Gabriel, 29" long

EX $55 **NM** $100 **MIP** $150

Lone Rider Cap Pistol, 1950s, Buzz-Henry, 8" die-cast, white plastic inset rearing horse grips

EX $40 **NM** $100 **MIP** $175

Longhorn Cap Pistol, 1960, Leslie-Henry, 10" die-cast, release in front of trigger guard, scroll work, white plastic horse head grips, unusual pop-up cap magazine, Model No. 38-G927

EX $85 **NM** $125 **MIP** $200

Mare's Laig Rifle Pistol, 1960, Marx, 13-1/2", plastic, imprinted w/"Official Wanted Dead or Alive" Mare's Laig logo, brown plastic stock

EX $65 **NM** $125 **MIP** $200

Marshal Cap Pistol, 1950s, Halco, 10" revolving cylinder chambers, Nichols-style bullets, white plastic grips w/star ovals

EX $55 **NM** $85 **MIP** $175

Marshal Cap Pistol, 1960, Hubley, 9-3/4" die-cast, side loading, nickel finish w/scrollwork, w/brown and white plastic stag grips w/a clip on left grip, Model No. 24-G1142

EX $35 **NM** $85 **MIP** $125

Marshal Matt Dillon "Gunsmoke" Cap Pistol, 1950s, Halco/Leslie-Henry, 10" pop-up cap magazine, release in front of trigger guard, scroll work, bronze steer-head grips

EX $75 **NM** $150 **MIP** $275

Matt Dillon Marshal Holster Set, Halco/Leslie-Henry, gun and holster set w/jail keys, handcuffs and badge

EX $125 **NM** $225 **MIP** $400

Maverick Cap Pistol, 1960, Leslie-Henry, 9" break-to-front, lever release, nickel finish, Maverick on sides, cream and brown swirl colored grips features notch bar w/extra set of black plastic grips

EX $65 **NM** $175 **MIP** $300

Maverick Derringer, 1958, Leslie-Henry, 3-1/4" w/removeable cap-shooting bullets, tan vinyl holster w/two bullets

EX $35 **NM** $55 **MIP** $95

Maverick Two Gun Holster Set, 1958, Leslie-Henry, 11" x 14" box picutres of James Garner as Maverick, two six-shooters w/individual bullets

EX $400 **NM** $800 **MIP** $1200

Maverick Two Gun Holster Set, 1960, Carnell, 9" break-to-front, lever release, nickel finish, Maverick on sides, cream/brown swirl grips features notch bar, black leather double holster set w/silver plates, studs and white trim, six loops, buckle
EX $225 **NM** $450 **MIP** $750

Model 1860 Cal .44 Cap Pistol, 1959, Hubley, die-cast metal model kit, 13", revolving cylinder w/closed chamber ends, six two-piece bullets, flat aluminum finish, white plastic grips, complete w/wooden display plaque
EX $125 **NM** $275 **MIP** $425

Model 95 Shell Firing Rifle, 1961, Nichols, 35-1/2" rifle uses shell firing cartridges, holds five in removeable magazine and one chamber, lever action ejects cartridges, open frame box holds six bullets and 12 additional red bullet heads
EX $400 **NM** $650 **MIP** $950

Mustang Cap Pistol, 1960s, Kilgore, 9-1/2" chrome finish w/"stag" plastic grips
EX $30 **NM** $65 **MIP** $125

Official Wanted Dead or Alive Mare's Laig Rifle, Marx, 19" bullet loading, cap firing saddle rifle-pistol ejects plastic bullets, w/holster
EX $150 **NM** $275 **MIP** $450

Official Wyatt Earp Buntline Clicker Pistol, Young Premiums, 18-1/2" plastic
EX $50 **NM** $125 **MIP** $210

Panther Pistol, 1958, Hubley, die-cast, 4" derringer-style pistol snaps out from secret spring-loaded wrist holster
EX $85 **NM** $130 **MIP** $185

Pecos Kid Cap Pistol, 1970s, Lone Star, die-cast, 9" silver chrome finish, brown plastic grips, lever release
EX $25 **NM** $55 **MIP** $90

Pepperbox Derringer Cap Pistol, 1960, Lone Star, die-cast, 6-1/4" rotating barrel holds four cap loads, silver finish w/black plastic grips
EX $65 **NM** $90 **MIP** $165

Pinto Cap Pistol, 1950s, Nichols, 3-1/2", miniature w/chrome finish, black plastic grips, flip out cylinder, white plastic "Pinto" holster in leather holster clip
EX $20 **NM** $35 **MIP** $75

Pony Boy Double Holster Set, 1950s, Esquire/Actoy, brown leather double holster w/bucking broncs and studs, cuffs, spurs and spur leathers, guns

are Actoy "Spitfires," die-cast 8-1/2" copper finish, white plastic grips
EX $150 **NM** $300 **MIP** $500

Pony Cap Pistol, 1950s, Actoy, single shot, all-metal, nickel finish w/eagle on grip
EX $35 **NM** $55 **MIP** $100

Ranch Rifle, Marx, plastic, repeater
EX $30 **NM** $45 **MIP** $60

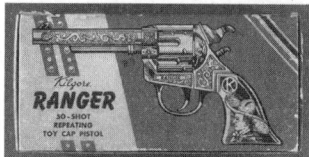

Ranger Cap Pistol, 1950s, Kilgore, 8-1/2" nickel finish, brown swirl plastic grips, spring release on right side, break-to-front
EX $90 **NM** $135 **MIP** $255

Ranger Cap Pistol, 1950s, Leslie-Henry, die-cast, 7-3/4" gun came w/derringer w/removeable cap, shooting bullets, tan vinyl holster w/two bullets
EX $85 **NM** $110 **MIP** $150

Real Texan Outfit w/Nichols Stallion .22, 1950s, Smart Style/Nichols, brown/white leather double holsters have silver conches w/red reflectors, silver horses at top of holster, belt w/three bullet loops, guns are a pair of double action .22s
EX $125 **NM** $250 **MIP** $475

Rebel Holster & Pistol, 1960s, Classy, 12" die-cast long barrel pistol, brown plastic grips, black leather single holster left side, Rebel insignia on holster flap
EX $275 **NM** $450 **MIP** $800

Red Ranger Jr. Cap Pistol, 1950s, Wyandotte, 7-1/2" lever release, break-to-front, silver finish, white plastic horse grips
EX $65 **NM** $100 **MIP** $165

Red Ryder BB Rifle, 1980, Daisy, carved wooden stock
EX $35 **NM** $75 **MIP** $125

Remington .36 Cap Pistol, 1950s, Hubley, 8" long, nickel finish, black plastic grips, revolving cylinder chambers two-piece bullets
EX $85 **NM** $165 **MIP** $275

Rex Trailer Two Gun & Holster Set, 1960, Hubley, 9-1/2" side loading, nickel finish, stag plastic grips, brown textured tooled leather w/white holsters and trim, six bullet loops w/plastic silver bullets, plain buckle
EX $110 **NM** $225 **MIP** $450

Ric-O-Shay .45 Cap Pistol, 1959, Hubley, 13", die-cast, nickel chrome finish, large frame, revolving cylinder, fires rolled caps, chambers brass bullets and fires caps, black plastic grips, makes a twang sound when fired, Model No. 28-G938
EX $85 **NM** $150 **MIP** $300

Ric-O-Shay .45 Cap Pistol Holster Set, Hubley, 13", die-cast, revolving cylinder swings out to chamber six brass bullets, six loaded in gun and 12 on holster, 1" flake in nickel finish at heel, holster black leather w/separate belt, horse-head emblem, rawhide tiedown, Model No. 26-G1141
EX $250 **NM** $400 **MIP** $750

Rifleman Flip Special Cap Rifle, 1959, Hubley, 3' long rifle, resembles classic Winchester w/ring lever, brown plastic stock, pop down cap magazine
EX $160 **NM** $350 **MIP** $500

Rodeo Cap Pistol, 1950s, Hubley, 7-1/2" single shot, white plastic steer grips
EX $20 **NM** $50 **MIP** $100

Roy Rogers Cap Pistol, 1950s, Kilgore, 10" revolving cylinder swings out to load, fires disc caps, white plastic horse-head grips w/"RR" logo
EX $250 **NM** $375 **MIP** $700

Roy Rogers Carbine, 1950s, Marx, 26" gray plastic repeater-style rifle has pull down cap magazine, western trim and Roy Rogers signature on stock
EX $80 **NM** $160 **MIP** $325

Roy Rogers Double Gun & Holster Set, 1950s, Classy, die-cast two 8-1/2" nickel finish pistols w/copper figural grips, holster is brown and black leather w/raised detail, plastic play bullets and leather tie-downs
EX $550 **NM** $1100 **MIP** $1600

Roy Rogers Double Holster Set, 1950s, Keyston Bros./Classy, black and white leather set, silver studs and conches, 9" Roy Rogers pistols w/plain nickel finish and copper figural grips, friction release
EX $525 **NM** $1050 **MIP** $1550

Roy Rogers Double Holster Set, 1950s, Classy, 10" guns w/plain nickel finish and copper grips, lever release, brown and cream leather set, silver studs, gold fleck jewels and four wooden bullets
EX $500 **NM** $1000 **MIP** $1500

Roy Rogers Tiny Tots Double Holster Set, 1950s, Hubley, w/die-cast single shot guns
EX $55 **NM** $100 **MIP** $165

Ruff Rider Western Holster Set, Latco, brown leather double holster, variety of studs and red jewels, 12 plastic silver bullets, tie-downs

EX $110   NM $250   MIP $400

Sheriff's Derringer Pocket Pistol, 1960s, Ohio Art, 3-1/4" silver finish derringer chambers two-piece, Nichols-style cartridge, red plastic grips w/an "A" logo, on card

EX $10   NM $20   MIP $25

Shootin' Shell .45 Fanner Cap Pistol, 1959, Mattel, 12" revolving cylinder pistol shoots Mattel Shootin' Shell cartridges, shell ejector

EX $250   NM $400   MIP $675

Shootin' Shell Buckle Gun, 1958, Mattel, cap and bullet shooting copy of Remington Derringer pops out from belt buckle, two brass cartridges and six bullets

EX $45   NM $85   MIP $135

Shootin' Shell Fanner, 1958, Mattel, 9" die-cast chrome finish, revolving cylinder chambers six Shootin' Shell bullets

EX $100   NM $225   MIP $475

Shootin' Shell Fanner & Derringer Set, 1958, Mattel, small-size Shooting Shell Fanner w/chrome finish, revolving cylinder, chambers six Shootin' Shell bullets, brown leather holster

EX $175   NM $325   MIP $575

Shootin' Shell Fanner Single Holster, 1959, Mattel, cowhide holster takes small-size Shootin' Shell Fanner w/six brass play bullets and tie-downs

EX $175   NM $285   MIP $475

Shootin' Shell Indian Scout Rifle, 1958, Mattel, 29-1/2" plastic/metal Sharps rolling block rifle, chambers two-piece Shootin' Shell bullets, secret compartment in stock for ammo storage, plastic stock and metal barrel

EX $125   NM $275   MIP $425

Shootin' Shell Potshot Remington Derringer, 1959, Mattel, 3" derringer alone (no buckle), on card

EX $35   NM $75   MIP $125

Shootin' Shell Winchester Rifle, Mattel, 26" long

EX $100   NM $165   MIP $225

Showdown Set w/Three Shootin' Shell Guns, 1958, Mattel, 30" single shot rifle w/metal barrel, die-cast w/plastic stock, Shootin' Shell Fanner small size, revolving cylinder, chrome finish and imitation stag plastic grips, tan holster w/bullet loops

EX $500   NM $800   MIP $1300

Side-By Double Barrel Pop Shotgun, 1950s, Marx, 29" long, pressed steel w/plastic stock

EX $20   NM $35   MIP $45

Silver Pony Cap Pistol, 1950s, Nichols, 7-1/2" single shot, silver metal grip and one replacement black plastic grip, silver-nickel finish

EX $35   NM $65   MIP $125

Spitfire Hip Gun No. 100, 1950s, Nichols, 9" cap cartridge loading mini rifle, chrome finish, tan plastic stock

EX $15   NM $30   MIP $55

Spitfire w/Clip, 1950s, Nichols, 9" mini rifle, chrome finish, plastic stock, plastic holders w/two extra cartridges

EX $20   NM $35   MIP $75

Spittin Image Peacemaker BB Pistol, Daisy, 10-1/2" die-cast, spring fired, single action, BBs load into spring fed magazine under barrel

EX $25   NM $60   MIP $120

Stagecoach Pistol, 1950s, Marx, 5" miniature pistol w/plastic box marked "Stagecoach Pistol"

EX $25   NM $45   MIP $75

Stallion .22 Cap Pistol, 1950s, Nichols, 7" revolving cylinder chambers five two-piece cartridges, single action, black plastic stag grips, never came in box

EX $45   NM $85   MIP $175

Stallion .22 Double Action Cap Pistol, 1950s, Nichols, 7" double-action, pull trigger to fire, white plastic grips, nickel finish, cylinder revolves

EX $45   NM $90   MIP $200

Stallion .38 Cap Pistol, 1955, Nichols, 9-1/2", chambers six two-piece cap cartridges, nickel finish, white plastic grips

EX $85   NM $165   MIP $350

Stallion .45 MK I Cap Pistol, 1950, Nichols, die-cast, 12" chrome finish, revolving cylinder, chambers six two-piece bullets, shell ejector, white "pearlescent" plastic grips w/rearing stallion, red jewels and six bullets and Stallion caps

EX $150   NM $300   MIP $500

Stallion .45 MK II Cap Pistol, 1956, Nichols, 12" pistol, chrome finish, revolving cylinder, chambers six two-piece, bullets, shell ejector, extra set of white grips to replace black grips on gun and box of Stallion caps

EX $100   NM $185   MIP $375

Stallion 32 Six Shooter, 1955, Nichols, 8" revolving cylinder chambers six two-piece cartridges, nickel finish, black plastic grips

EX $75   NM $150   MIP $275

Stallion 41-40 Cap Pistol, 1950s, Nichols, 10-1/2" revolving cylinder chrome finish pistol, swing out cylinder that chambers six two-piece cap cartridges, shell ejector, scroll work on frame, cream-purple swirl colored plastic grips

EX $150   NM $375   MIP $500

Susanna 90 12 Shot Cap Pistol, 1980s, Edison, 9" uses ring caps, wind out cylinder, black finish, plastic wood grips

EX $10   NM $15   MIP $25

Tales of Wells Fargo Double Barrel Shotgun, 1950s, Marx, 26"-long double-barrel shotgun, two toy shotgun shells, decal on the butt of the gun, Model No. 44

EX $100   NM $225   MIP $375

Texan .38 Cap Pistol, 1950s, Hubley, 10" long, revolving cylinder gun chambers six solid brass bullets (caps go into cylinder first), top release front break automatically ejects shells, plastic steer grips

EX $100   NM $200   MIP $350

Texan Cap Pistol, 1950s, Hubley, die-cast, nickel finish, white plastic steer grips, star logo on grips

EX $75   NM $150   MIP $300

Texan Dummy Cap Pistol, 1950s, Hubley, cast-iron, 9-1/4", revolving cylinder, lever release, white plastic steer grips, nickel finish, star logo on grip
EX $100 NM $185 MIP $375

Texan Jr. Cap Pistol, 1950s, Hubley, 8", spring button release on side of cylinder, break-to-front, nickel finish white plastic grips w/black steers
EX $75 NM $125 MIP $250

Texan Jr. Cap Pistol, 1954, Hubley, die-cast, release under cylinder, nickel finish, white plastic Longhorn grips
EX $65 NM $110 MIP $225

Texan Jr. Gold Plated Cap Pistol, 1950s, Hubley, die-cast, 9", gold finish w/black longhorn steer grips, break-to-front release from cylinder
EX $95 NM $175 MIP $350

Texas Cap Pistol, 1950s, Long Island Die Casting, die-cast, 8-1/2" friction break, Circle "T" logo, scroll work on barrel
EX $50 NM $100 MIP $200

Texas Ranger Cap Pistol, Leslie-Henry, 8-1/4" die-cast, lever release break to front, nickel finish, scroll work, vasoline-colored plastic grips
EX $85 NM $150 MIP $325

The Plainsman Cap Pistol, 1950s, National Metal & Plastic Toy, 10-1/2" revolving cylinder loads Kilgore-style disk caps, lever holds cylinder forward for loading, scroll work, white plastic grips, Model No. 62-G1101
EX $125 NM $225 MIP $350

Thundergun Cap Pistol, 1950s, Marx, 12-1/2" single action, "Thundercaps" perforated roll cap system, silver finish, brown plastic grips
EX $100 NM $200 MIP $325

Tophand 250 Cap Pistol, 1960, Nichols, 9-1/2" break-to-front, lever release, black finish, brown plastic grips w/a roll of "Tophand 250" caps
EX $35 NM $75 MIP $165

Wagon Train Complete Western Cowboy Outfit, 1960, Halco/Leslie-Henry, plastic flip ring lever rifle and wagon train pistol (late model L-H pistol) and leather holster
EX $110 NM $225 MIP $450

Wagon Train Gun & Holster Set, 1950s, Halco, two 5" plastic guns, vinyl holster w/plastic bullets and metal badge, Model No. 45
EX $25 NM $50 MIP $100

Wanted Dead or Alive Miniature Mare's Laig, 1959, Marx, Marx Miniatures series miniature cap rifle on "wood frame" card
EX $20 NM $40 MIP $65

Wells Fargo Buntline Cap Pistol, 1950s, Actoy, 11" long barrel, break-to-front, cream plastic stag grips
EX $85 NM $160 MIP $325

Western Buntline Pistol, 1963, Haig, 13", pistol fires single caps and/or BBs, BBs are propelled down barrel sleeve by cap explosion
EX $75 NM $130 MIP $165

Western Cap Pistol, 1950s, Hubley, 9" die-cast, friction break, nickel finish w/white plastic steer grips w/black steer, Model No. 33-G1100
EX $40 NM $75 MIP $150

Wild Bill Hickok 44 Cap Pistol Set, 1950s, Leslie-Henry, 11" nickel finish, swing-out side loading action, revolving cylinder chambers six metal bullets, amber plastic horse-head grips, single holster black and brown leather w/silver studs, diamond conches
EX $200 NM $400 MIP $650

Wild Bill Hickok Cap Pistol, 1950s, Leslie-Henry, 10" pop-up cap magazine, release in front of trigger guard, scroll work, translucent brown plastic grips w/oval star inserts
EX $100 NM $200 MIP $375

Wild Bill Hickok Gun & Holster, Leslie-Henry, single gun and holster set
EX $150 NM $300 MIP $450

Wild West Rifle, Marx, 30" long w/sight, cap rifle
EX $40 NM $75 MIP $125

Winchester Saddle Gun Rifle, 1959, Mattel, 33" die-cast and plastic, perforated roll caps and chambers eight play bullets loaded through side door
EX $75 NM $145 MIP $375

Wyatt Earp Buntline Special, 1950s, Hubley, 11" barrel, die-cast, friction break-to-front, white plastic grips, nickel finish
EX $100 NM $250 MIP $375

Wyatt Earp Double Holster Set, 1950s, Hubley, black and white leather holster w/silk screened "Marshal Wyatt Earp" logo, two No. 247 Hubley Wyatt Earp Buntline Specials, 10-3/4" nickel finish, purple swirl grips
EX $250 NM $500 MIP $850

Wyatt Earp Double Holster Set, 1950s, Unknown, medium size, reflectors, black leather w/brown rawhide fringe, holsters only
EX $50 NM $80 MIP $125

Young Buffalo Bill Cowboy Outfit, Halco/Leslie-Henry, black and white leather holster set w/pistol, white grip, holster bands read Texas Ranger
EX $100 NM $200 MIP $325

Zorro Flintock Pistol, 1959, Marx, 11", plastic w/die-cast works
EX $45 NM $80 MIP $140

Zorro Rifle, 1950s, Marx, plastic
EX $60 NM $125 MIP $175

Zorro Rifle, 1958, Daisy, pressed steel barrel w/wood stock, Zorro logo, 25" long
EX $100 NM $200 MIP $300

Lunch Boxes

by Justin Moen

The evolution of the lunch box goes back as far as the mid-19th century, when they primarily consisted of woven baskets with a handle. The wealthy, however, were fortunate enough to have strong, wooden boxes.

From there, the lunch box continued to evolve, and in 1902, the first true kids' lunch box came out. The box was shaped like a picnic basket with pictures of playing children lithographed on its side.

Lunch boxes, as we know them today, have been manufactured since the 1920s, the most desirable of which are those that bear illustrations of popular licensed characters. The first licenced character lunch box was a Mickey Mouse lunch box released in 1935 by Geuder, Paeschke and Frey.

The advent of television in the 1950s launched the lunch box out of the domed steel domain of workers and into the artful boxes generations of kids carried to school every day.

In 1950, Aladdin Industries manufactured the first children's lunch box based on a TV show, Hopalong Cassidy—television Western hero at the time. Debuting in time for back-to-school 1950, 600,000 "Hoppy" boxes were produced and sold for only $2.39 a box.

In 1953, American Thermos, Aladdin's chief competitor, responded by introducing the Roy Rogers box in full-color lithography. Aladdin came back by issuing a new 1954 Hoppy box in full-color litho. The lunch box era had officially begun, so too did the box wars between Aladdin and American Thermos, with occasional challenges from Adco Liberty, Ohio Art, and Okay Industries.

Metal lunch boxes reigned supreme in the 50s, 60s, and 70s. In 1971, however, a concerned group of parents believed that metal lunch boxes could potentially be used as weapons in schoolyard brawls. With petitions signed, they took their case to the Florida State Legislature, and demanded the passage of safety legislation. With legislation passed, other counties in Florida adopted this legislation, which was eventually accepted in other states. And by 1986, Aladdin and American Thermos were producing all of their boxes in plastic.

Today, lunch boxes are generally made of vinyl, with foam insulation, and an aluminum/vinyl interior. These vinyl boxes are usually much better at retaining their temperature, however, they have a tendency to be less rigid or protective.

Trends

High-profile character lunch boxes command the highest prices, and there is no one who commands higher prices than the Man of Steel. The 1954 Superman box by Adco is the Holy Grail of lunch boxes. A Mint condition box can sell for nearly $20,000 in today's market. Other high-profile characters like Underdog, Rocky and Bullwinkle, and Dudley Do-Right have also seen substantial prices, with no signs of letting up anytime soon.

While prices remain strong for high-profile characters, prices for more common or non-character boxes have recently seen a drop in value. However, it is the common or non-character boxes where collectors can use the current drop-off in prices to build their collections. With time and a little patience, an nice collection can be put together and significant value realized as long as a collector is willing to wait out the soft market.

Note: In this price guide, for ease of searching, boxes are listed alphabetically by box composition—plastic, steel, and vinyl.

The **Top 10 LUNCH BOXES** in mint condition

1. Superman, Universal, 1954 . . . . $19,250
2. 240 Robert, Aladdin, 1978 . . . . $5,500
3. Bullwinkle, vinyl, King Seeley Thermos, 1963 . . . . $4,500
4. Toppie Elephant, American Thermos, 1957 . . . . $3,850
5. Underdog, Okay Industries, 1974 . . . . $3,500
6. Bullwinkle & Rocky, Universal, 1962, ... $3,500
7. Dudley Do-Right, Universal, 1962 . . . . $3,450
8. Jetsons Dome, Aladdin, 1963 . . . . $2,650
9. Beatles, Aladdin, 1966 . . . . $2,500
10. Star Trek Dome, Aladdin, 1968 . . . . $2,350

Contributor: Joe Soucy of Seaside Toys specializes in pristine-condition lunch boxes. He can be reached at the Seaside Toy Center, 179 Main St., Westerly, RI, 02891. Tel. (401) 596-0962

Plastic

101 Dalmatians, 1990, Aladdin
  BOX $25   BOTTLE $8
18 Wheeler, 1978, Aladdin
  BOX $40   BOTTLE $10
ALF, 1987, Thermos, red plastic
  BOX $35   BOTTLE n/a
Animalympics Dome, 1979, Thermos
  BOX $40   BOTTLE $10
Astronauts, 1986, Thermos
  BOX $35   BOTTLE $15
Atari Missile Command Dome, 1983, Aladdin
  BOX $55   BOTTLE $10
Back to School, 1980, Aladdin
  BOX $75   BOTTLE $20
Back to the Future, 1989, Thermos
  BOX $45   BOTTLE $15
Bang Bang, 1982, Thermos
  BOX $50   BOTTLE n/a
Barbie w/Hologram Mirror, 1990, Thermos
  BOX $30   BOTTLE $8
Batman (dark blue), 1989, Thermos
  BOX $30   BOTTLE $10
Batman (light blue), 1989, Thermos
  BOX $55   BOTTLE $10
Batman Returns, 1991, Thermos
  BOX $30   BOTTLE $5
Beach Bronto, 1984, Aladdin, no bottle
  BOX $45   BOTTLE n/a
Beach Party (blue/pink), 1988, Deka, w/generic plastic bottle
  BOX $20   BOTTLE $5
Bear w/Heart (3-D), 1987, Servo
  BOX $20   BOTTLE n/a
Beauty & the Beast, 1991, Aladdin
  BOX $30   BOTTLE $7
Bee Gees, 1978, Thermos
  BOX $45   BOTTLE $20
Beetlejuice, 1980, Thermos
  BOX $20   BOTTLE $10

(KP Photo)

Big Jim, 1976, Thermos
  BOX $100   BOTTLE $30
Bozostuffs, 1988, Deka
  BOX $30   BOTTLE $10

C.B. Bears, 1977, Thermos
  BOX $30   BOTTLE n/a
Care Bears, 1986, Aladdin
  BOX $20   BOTTLE $5
Centurions, 1986, Thermos
  BOX $25   BOTTLE $8
Chiclets, 1987, Thermos, no bottle
  BOX $45   BOTTLE n/a
Chipmunks, Alvin and The, 1983, Thermos
  BOX $25   BOTTLE $10
CHiPs, 1977, Thermos
  BOX $65   BOTTLE $20
Cinderella, 1992, Aladdin
  BOX $30   BOTTLE $10
Civil War, The, 1961, Universal, generic "Thermax" bottle
  BOX $200   BOTTLE $25
Colonial Bread Van, 1984, Moldmark Industries
  BOX $65   BOTTLE $20
Crestman Tubular!, 1980, Taiwan
  BOX $55   BOTTLE $20
Days of Thunder, 1988, Thermos
  BOX $35   BOTTLE $10
Deka 4 x 4, 1988, Deka, generic plastic bottle
  BOX $35   BOTTLE $5
Dick Tracy, 1989, Aladdin
  BOX $30   BOTTLE $10
Dino Riders, 1988, Aladdin
  BOX $25   BOTTLE $10
Dinobeasties, 1988, Thermos
  BOX $25   BOTTLE n/a
Dinorocker w/Radio & Headset, 1986, Fundes
  BOX $55   BOTTLE n/a
Disney on Parade, 1970, Aladdin, plastic bottle, glass liner
  BOX $50   BOTTLE $15
Disney's Little Mermaid, 1989, Thermos, w/generic plastic bottle
  BOX $35   BOTTLE $5
Duck Tales (4 X 4/Game), 1986, Aladdin
  BOX $25   BOTTLE $5
Dukes of Hazzard, 1981, Aladdin
  BOX $50   BOTTLE $10
Dukes of Hazzard Dome, 1981, Aladdin
  BOX $75   BOTTLE $10
Dune, 1984, Aladdin
  BOX $60   BOTTLE $20
Dunkin Munchkins, 1972, Thermos
  BOX $30   BOTTLE $15
Ecology Dome, 1980, Thermos
  BOX $45   BOTTLE $20

Ed Grimley, 1988, Aladdin
  BOX $30   BOTTLE $5
EnteBOXann's, 1989, Thermos
  BOX $20   BOTTLE n/a
Ewoks, 1983, Thermos, red box
  BOX $45   BOTTLE $15
Fame, 1972, Thermos
  BOX $50   BOTTLE $15
Fievel Goes West, 1991, Aladdin
  BOX $20   BOTTLE $4
Fire Engine Co. 7, 1985, D.A.S., w/generic plastic bottle
  BOX $30   BOTTLE $5
Fisher-Price Mini Lunch Box, 1962, Fisher-Price, red w/barnyard scenes, matching bottle
  BOX $25   BOTTLE $5
Flash Gordon Dome, 1979, Aladdin
  BOX $75   BOTTLE $20
Flintstones, unknown, premium, Denny's Restaurants
  BOX $35   BOTTLE n/a
Flintstones Kids, 1987, Thermos
  BOX $45   BOTTLE $10
Food Fighters, 1988, Aladdin
  BOX $25   BOTTLE $10
Fraggle Rock, 1987, Thermos
  BOX $35   BOTTLE $7
Frito Lay's, 1982, Thermos, no bottle
  BOX $60   BOTTLE n/a
G.I. Joe (Space Mission), 1989, Aladdin
  BOX $35   BOTTLE $10
G.I. Joe, Live the Adventure, 1986, Aladdin
  BOX $30   BOTTLE $10
Garfield (food fight), 1979, Thermos
  BOX $25   BOTTLE $10
Garfield (lunch), 1977, Thermos
  BOX $25   BOTTLE $10

(KP Photo)

Geoffrey, 1981, Aladdin
  BOX $35   BOTTLE $10
Get Along Gang, 1983, Aladdin
  BOX $15   BOTTLE $5
Ghostbusters, 1986, Deka
  BOX $40   BOTTLE $11

Go Bots, 1984, Thermos
        BOX $30   **BOTTLE** $5
Golden Girls, 1984, Thermos
        BOX $20   **BOTTLE** $5
Goonies, 1985, Aladdin
        BOX $35   **BOTTLE** $10
Gumby, 1986, Thermos
        BOX $65   **BOTTLE** $20
Hot Wheels, 1984, Thermos
        BOX $55   **BOTTLE** $20

(KP Photo)
Howdy Doody Dome, 1977, Thermos
        BOX $90   **BOTTLE** $35
Incredible Hulk Dome, 1980, Aladdin
        BOX $35   **BOTTLE** $10

(KP Photo)
Incredible Hulk, The, 1978, Aladdin,
        plastic bottle
        BOX $40   **BOTTLE** $10
Inspector Gadget, 1983, Thermos
        BOX $30   **BOTTLE** $8
It's Not Just the Bus - Greyhound,
        1980, Aladdin
        BOX $60   **BOTTLE** $20

(KP Photo)
Jabber Jaw, 1977, Thermos
        BOX $60   **BOTTLE** $20

Jetsons (3-D), 1987, Servo
        BOX $75   **BOTTLE** $30
Jetsons (paper picture), 1987, Servo
        BOX $125   **BOTTLE** $30
Jetsons, The Movie, 1990, Aladdin
        BOX $30   **BOTTLE** $15
Kermit the Frog, Lunch w/, 1988,
        Thermos
        BOX $25   **BOTTLE** $5
Kermit's Frog Scout Van, 1989,
        Superseal, no bottle
        BOX $15   **BOTTLE** n/a
Kool-Aid Man, 1986, Thermos
        BOX $20   **BOTTLE** $10
Lisa Frank, 1980, Thermos
        BOX $20   **BOTTLE** $5
Little Orphan Annie, 1973, Thermos
        BOX $70   **BOTTLE** $20
Looney Tunes Birthday Party, 1989,
        Thermos, blue or red
        BOX $25   **BOTTLE** $10
Looney Tunes Dancing, 1977,
        Thermos
        BOX $20   **BOTTLE** $10
Looney Tunes Playing Drums, 1978,
        Thermos
        BOX $35   **BOTTLE** $10
Looney Tunes Tasmanian Devil,
        1988, Thermos, w/generic plastic
        bottle
        BOX $20   **BOTTLE** $10
Los Angeles Olympics, 1984, Aladdin
        BOX $55   **BOTTLE** $5
Lucy's Luncheonette, 1981,
        Thermos, Peanuts characters
        BOX $25   **BOTTLE** $5
Lunch Man w/Radio, 1986, Fun
        Design, w/built-in radio, no bottle
        BOX $40   **BOTTLE** n/a
Lunch 'N Tunes Safari, 1986, Fun
        Design, w/built-in radio, no bottle
        BOX $35   **BOTTLE** n/a
Lunch 'N Tunes Singing Sandwich,
        1986, Fun Design, w/built-in radio,
        no bottle
        BOX $40   **BOTTLE** n/a
Lunch Time w/Snoopy Dome, 1981,
        Thermos
        BOX $30   **BOTTLE** $5
Mad Balls, 1986, Aladdin
        BOX $30   **BOTTLE** $10
Marvel Super Heroes, 1990, Thermos
        BOX $35   **BOTTLE** $10
Max Headroom (Coca-Cola), 1985,
        Aladdin
        BOX $55   **BOTTLE** $25

McDonald's Happy Meal, 1986,
        Fisher-Price
        BOX $25   **BOTTLE** n/a
Menudo, 1984, Thermos
        BOX $15   **BOTTLE** $5
Mickey & Minnie Mouse in Pink Car,
        1988, Aladdin
        BOX $20   **BOTTLE** $5

Mickey Mouse & Donald Duck, 1984,
        Aladdin, dome-style lunchbox
        w/image of Mickey, Minnie, Donald
        and Daisy having a picnic
        BOX $25   **BOTTLE** $5
Mickey Mouse & Donald Duck See-
        Saw, 1986, Aladdin
        BOX $15   **BOTTLE** $5
Mickey Mouse at City Zoo, 1985,
        Aladdin
        BOX $10   **BOTTLE** $5

(KP Photo)
Mickey Mouse Head, 1989, Aladdin
        BOX $25   **BOTTLE** $5
Mickey on Swinging Bridge, 1987,
        Aladdin
        BOX $15   **BOTTLE** $5
Mickey Skateboarding, 1980, Aladdin
        BOX $25   **BOTTLE** $5
Mighty Mouse, 1979, Thermos, light
        blue, Viacom Int'l
        BOX $50   **BOTTLE** $15
Miss Piggy's Safari Van, 1989,
        Superseal, no bottle
        BOX $18   **BOTTLE** n/a

Monster in My Pocket, 1990, Aladdin
    BOX $30   **BOTTLE** $5

Movie Monsters, 1979, Universal
    BOX $35   **BOTTLE** $12

Mr. T, 1984, Aladdin
    BOX $35   **BOTTLE** $10

Munchie Tunes Bear w/Radio, 1986, Fun Design, w/built-in radio
    BOX $35   **BOTTLE** $5

Munchie Tunes Punchie Pup w/Radio, 1986, Fun Design, w/built-in radio
    BOX $40   **BOTTLE** $5

Munchie Tunes Robot w/Radio, 1986, Fun Design, w/built-in radio
    BOX $35   **BOTTLE** $5

Muppets, 1982, Thermos, blue
    BOX $35   **BOTTLE** $5

Muppets Dome, 1981, Thermos, plastic red box w/matching bottle
    BOX $20   **BOTTLE** $5

New Kids on the Block, 1990, Thermos, pink/orange
    BOX $20   **BOTTLE** $5

Nosy Bears, 1988, Aladdin
    BOX $15   **BOTTLE** $5

Official Lunch Football, 1974, unknown, football shaped box, red or brown
    BOX $100   **BOTTLE** n/a

Peanuts, Wienie Roast, 1985, Thermos
    BOX $15   **BOTTLE** $4

Pee Wee's Playhouse, 1987, Thermos, w/generic plastic bottle
    BOX $35   **BOTTLE** $10

Peter Pan Peanut Butter, 1984, Taiwan
    BOX $90   **BOTTLE** $20

Pickle, 1972, Fesco, no bottle
    BOX $140   **BOTTLE** n/a

Popeye & Son, 1987, Servo, plastic red box, flat paper label, w/matching bottle
    BOX $65   **BOTTLE** $12

Popeye & Son (3-D), 1987, Servo, plastic box, red or yellow, w/matching bottle
    BOX $50   **BOTTLE** $12

Popeye Dome, 1979, Aladdin, blue
    BOX $50   **BOTTLE** $15

Popeye, Truant Officer, 1964, King Seeley Thermos, plastic red box, matching metal bottle (Canada)
    BOX $150   **BOTTLE** $35

Punky Brewster, 1984, Deka
    BOX $25   **BOTTLE** $10

Q-Bert, 1983, Thermos, bright yellow
    BOX $20   **BOTTLE** $12

Race Cars, 1987, Servo
    BOX $25   **BOTTLE** n/a

Raggedy Ann & Andy, 1988, Aladdin
    BOX $45   **BOTTLE** $20

Rainbow Bread Van, 1984, Moldmark Industries
    BOX $60   **BOTTLE** $20

Rainbow Brite, 1983, Thermos
    BOX $35   **BOTTLE** $8

Robot Man and Friends, 1984, Thermos
    BOX $25   **BOTTLE** $10

Rocketeer, 1990, Aladdin
    BOX $20   **BOTTLE** $5

Rocky Roughneck, 1977, Thermos
    BOX $25   **BOTTLE** $10

Roller Games, 1989, Thermos
    BOX $30   **BOTTLE** $10

S.W.A.T. Dome, 1975, Thermos
    BOX $70   **BOTTLE** $15

Scooby Doo, 1973, Thermos
    BOX $40   **BOTTLE** $20

Scooby Doo, 1984, Aladdin
    BOX $40   **BOTTLE** $20

Scooby-Doo, A Pup Named, 1988, Aladdin
    BOX $25   **BOTTLE** $10

Sesame Street, 1985, Aladdin/Canada
    BOX $15   **BOTTLE** $5

Shirt Tales, 1981, Thermos
    BOX $18   **BOTTLE** $5

Sky Commanders, 1987, Thermos, generic plastic bottle
    BOX $20   **BOTTLE** $5

Smurfette, 1984, Thermos
    BOX $15   **BOTTLE** $7

Smurfs, 1984, Thermos
    BOX $35   **BOTTLE** $15

Smurfs Dome, 1981, Thermos
    BOX $35   **BOTTLE** $15

Smurfs Fishing, 1984, Thermos
    BOX $20   **BOTTLE** $5

Snak Shot Camera, 1987, Hummer, camera-shaped box, blue or green, w/generic plastic bottle
    BOX $30   **BOTTLE** $2

Snoopy Dome, 1978, Thermos
    BOX $25   **BOTTLE** $5

Snorks, 1984, Thermos
    BOX $12   **BOTTLE** $5

Snow White, 1980, Aladdin
    BOX $45   **BOTTLE** $15

Spare Parts, 1982, Aladdin, w/generic plastic bottle
    BOX $35   **BOTTLE** $10

Sport Billy, 1982, Thermos
    BOX $20   **BOTTLE** $10

Sport Goofy, 1986, Aladdin
    BOX $30   **BOTTLE** $10

Star Com. U.S. Space Force, 1987, Thermos
    BOX $20   **BOTTLE** $10

Star Trek Next Generation, 1988, Thermos, blue box, group picture, matching bottle
    BOX $75   **BOTTLE** $25

Star Trek Next Generation, 1989, Thermos, red box, Picard, Data, Wesley, matching bottle
    BOX $90   **BOTTLE** $20

Star Wars, Droids, 1985, Thermos
    BOX $65   **BOTTLE** $25

Strawberry Shortcake, 1980, Aladdin
    BOX $10   **BOTTLE** $5

Superman II Dome, 1986, Aladdin
    BOX $75   **BOTTLE** $25

Superman, This is a Job For, 1980, Aladdin, no bottle
    BOX $25   **BOTTLE** n/a

Tail Spin, 1986, Aladdin
    BOX $25   **BOTTLE** $10

Tang Trio, 1988, Thermos, red or yellow box w/generic plastic bottle
    BOX $35   **BOTTLE** $5

Teenage Mutant Ninja Turtles, 1990, Thermos, w/generic plastic bottle
    BOX $35   **BOTTLE** $5

Thundarr the Barbarian Dome, 1981, Aladdin, plastic dome box w/matching bottle
    BOX $25   **BOTTLE** $10

Timeless Tales, 1989, Aladdin
    BOX $10   **BOTTLE** $5

Tiny Toon Adventures, 1990, Thermos
    BOX $10   **BOTTLE** $5

Tom & Jerry, 1989, Aladdin
    BOX $30   **BOTTLE** $10

Transformers, 1985, Aladdin
    BOX $75   **BOTTLE** $25

Transformers Dome, 1986, Aladdin/Canada, dome box, generic plastic bottle
    BOX $85   **BOTTLE** $20

Tweety & Sylvester, 1986, Thermos
    BOX $45   **BOTTLE** $20

(KP Photo)

Wayne Gretzky, 1980, Aladdin
BOX $100 BOTTLE $30

Wayne Gretzky Dome, 1980, Aladdin
BOX $120 BOTTLE $30

Where's Waldo, 1990, Thermos
BOX $10 BOTTLE $5

Who Framed Roger Rabbit, 1987, Thermos, red or yellow, w/matching bottle
BOX $25 BOTTLE $10

Wild Fire, 1986, Aladdin
BOX $15 BOTTLE $8

Wizard of Oz, 50th Anniversary, 1989, Aladdin
BOX $60 BOTTLE $20

Woody Woodpecker, 1972, Aladdin, yellow box, red bottle
BOX $50 BOTTLE $40

World Wrestling Federation, 1986, Thermos
BOX $30 BOTTLE $10

Wrinkles, 1984, Thermos
BOX $10 BOTTLE $5

Wuzzles, 1985, Aladdin
BOX $10 BOTTLE $5

Yogi's Treasure Hunt, 1987, Servo, flat paper label, w/matching bottle
BOX $25 BOTTLE $30

Yogi's Treasure Hunt (3-D), 1987, Servo, 3-D box, green or pink, w/matching bottle
BOX $65 BOTTLE $30

Steel

"V," 1984, Aladdin, matching plastic thermos
BOX $225 BOTTLE $75

240 Robert, 1978, Aladdin
BOX $5500 BOTTLE n/a

Action Jackson, 1973, Okay Industries, matching steel bottle
BOX $1500 BOTTLE $650

Adam-12, 1973, Aladdin, matching plastic bottle
BOX $300 BOTTLE $75

(KP Photo)

Addams Family, 1974, King Seeley Thermos, matching plastic bottle
BOX $275 BOTTLE $50

Airline, 1969, Ohio Art, no bottle
BOX $140 BOTTLE n/a

All American, 1954, Universal, steel/glass bottle
BOX $350 BOTTLE $95

America on Parade, 1976, Aladdin, matching plastic bottle
BOX $65 BOTTLE $25

Americana, 1958, King Seeley Thermos, steel/glass bottle
BOX $425 BOTTLE $165

Animal Friends, 1978, Ohio Art, yellow or red background behind name
BOX $60 BOTTLE n/a

Annie Oakley & Tagg, 1955, Aladdin, matching steel bottle
BOX $695 BOTTLE $150

Annie, The Movie, 1982, Aladdin, plastic bottle, shown w/Dukes of Hazzard and Magic Kindon lunch boxes
BOX $65 BOTTLE $25

Apple's Way, 1975, King Seeley Thermos, plastic bottle
BOX $150 BOTTLE $40

Archies, 1969, Aladdin, matching plastic bottle
BOX $300 BOTTLE $75

Astronaut Dome, 1960, King Seeley Thermos, steel/glass bottle
BOX $300 BOTTLE $60

Astronauts, 1969, Aladdin, matching plastic bottle
BOX $225 BOTTLE $65

A-Team, 1985, King Seeley Thermos, plastic bottle
BOX $65 BOTTLE $20

Atom Ant/Secret Squirrel, 1966, King Seeley Thermos, matching steel bottle
BOX $360 BOTTLE $120

Auto Race, 1967, King Seeley Thermos, matching steel bottle
BOX $250 BOTTLE $65

Back in '76, 1975, Aladdin, plastic bottle
BOX $65 BOTTLE $30

Barbie Lunch Kit, 1962, King Seeley Thermos, steel/glass bottle
BOX $300 BOTTLE $90

Basketweave, 1968, Ohio Art, no bottle
BOX $55 BOTTLE n/a

Batman and Robin, 1966, Aladdin, matching steel bottle
BOX $700 BOTTLE $175

Battle Kit, 1965, King Seeley Thermos, matching steel bottle
BOX $275 BOTTLE $65

Battle of the Planets, 1979, King Seeley Thermos, matching plastic bottle, shown w/The Chan Clan and Hot Wheels lunch boxes
BOX $150 BOTTLE $40

Battlestar Galactica, 1978, Aladdin, matching plastic bottle
BOX $175 BOTTLE $30

Beatles, 1966, Aladdin, blue, matching bottle
BOX $2500 BOTTLE $325

Bedknobs & Broomsticks, 1972, Aladdin, plastic bottle
BOX $200 BOTTLE $45

Bee Gees, 1978, King Seeley Thermos, Robin on back, matching plastic bottle
BOX $175 **BOTTLE** $45

Bee Gees, 1978, King Seeley Thermos, Barry on back, matching plastic bottle
BOX $125 **BOTTLE** $45

Bee Gees, 1978, King Seeley Thermos, Maurice on back, matching plastic bottle
BOX $125 **BOTTLE** $45

Berenstain Bears, 1983, American Thermos, matching plastic bottle
BOX $75 **BOTTLE** $30

Betsy Clark, 1976, King Seeley Thermos, blue and yellow
BOX $60 **BOTTLE** $20

Beverly Hillbillies, 1963, Aladdin, matching steel bottle
BOX $325 **BOTTLE** $80

Bionic Woman, w/Car, 1977, Aladdin, plastic bottle
BOX $175 **BOTTLE** $40

Bionic Woman, w/Dog, 1978, Aladdin, matching plastic bottle
BOX $210 **BOTTLE** $40

Black Hole, 1979, Aladdin, matching plastic bottle
BOX $80 **BOTTLE** $40

Blondie, 1969, King Seeley Thermos, matching steel bottle
BOX $275 **BOTTLE** $60

Boating, 1959, American Thermos, matching steel bottle
BOX $400 **BOTTLE** $90

Bobby Sherman, 1972, King Seeley Thermos, matching steel bottle
BOX $250 **BOTTLE** $60

Bonanza, 1963, Aladdin, green rim box, steel bottle
BOX $325 **BOTTLE** $90

Bonanza, 1965, Aladdin, brown rim box, steel bottle
BOX $200 **BOTTLE** $60

Bonanza, 1968, Aladdin, black rim box, steel bottle
BOX $425 **BOTTLE** $100

Bond XX, 1967, Ohio Art, no bottle
BOX $200 **BOTTLE** n/a

Bond XX, 1968, Ohio Art, w/Secret Agent
BOX $275 **BOTTLE** n/a

Boston Bruins, 1973, Okay Industries, steel/glass bottle
BOX $525 **BOTTLE** $250

(Joe Soucy collection)

Bozo the Clown Dome, 1963, Aladdin, steel bottle
BOX $325 **BOTTLE** $80

Brady Bunch, 1970, King Seeley Thermos, matching steel bottle
BOX $475 **BOTTLE** $90

Brave Eagle, 1957, American Thermos, red, blue, gray or green band, matching steel bottle
BOX $300 **BOTTLE** $90

Bread Box Dome, 1968, Aladdin, Campbell's Soup bottle
BOX $375 **BOTTLE** $90

(KP Photo)

Buccaneer Dome, 1957, Aladdin, matching bottle, shown w/Julia lunch box
BOX $375 **BOTTLE** $85

Buck Rogers, 1979, Aladdin, matching plastic bottle
BOX $85 **BOTTLE** $25

Bugaloos, 1971, Aladdin, matching plastic bottle
BOX $250 **BOTTLE** $60

Bullwinkle & Rocky, 1962, Universal, blue box, steel bottle
BOX $3500 **BOTTLE** $1500

Cabbage Patch Kids, 1984, King Seeley Thermos, matching plastic bottle
BOX $50 **BOTTLE** $20

Cable Car Dome, 1962, Aladdin, steel/glass bottle
BOX $475 **BOTTLE** $95

Campbell's Kids, 1973, Okay, matching steel bottle
BOX $195 **BOTTLE** $125

Campus Queen, 1967, King Seeley Thermos, matching steel bottle
BOX $200 **BOTTLE** $65

Canadian Pacific Railroad, 1970, Ohio Art, no bottle
BOX $65 **BOTTLE** n/a

Captain Astro, 1966, Ohio Art, no bottle
BOX $475 **BOTTLE** n/a

Care Bear Cousins, 1985, Aladdin, matching plastic bottle
BOX $50 **BOTTLE** $20

Care Bears, 1984, Aladdin, plastic bottle
BOX $75 **BOTTLE** $20

Carnival, 1959, Universal, matching steel bottle
BOX $675 **BOTTLE** $175

Cartoon Zoo Lunch Chest, 1962, Universal, steel/glass bottle
BOX $475 **BOTTLE** $95

Casey Jones, 1960, Universal, steel dome box, steel/glass bottle
BOX $550 **BOTTLE** $95

(KP Photo)

Chan Clan, The, 1973, King Seeley Thermos, plastic bottle, shown w/Battle of the Planets and Hot Wheels lunch boxes
BOX $175 **BOTTLE** $40

Charlie's Angels, 1978, Aladdin, matching plastic bottle
BOX $200 **BOTTLE** $50

Chavo, 1979, Aladdin, matching plastic bottle
BOX $200 **BOTTLE** $50

Children, Blue, 1974, Okay Industries, plastic bottle

BOX $150   **BOTTLE** $40

Children, Yellow, 1974, Okay Industries, plastic bottle

BOX $225   **BOTTLE** $40

Children's, 1984, Ohio Art, no bottle

BOX $60   **BOTTLE** n/a

Chitty Chitty Bang Bang, 1969, King Seeley Thermos, matching steel bottle

BOX $350   **BOTTLE** $75

Chuck Wagon Dome, 1958, Aladdin, matching bottle

BOX $295   **BOTTLE** $90

Circus Wagon Dome, 1958, King Seeley Thermos, steel/glass bottle

BOX $325   **BOTTLE** $95

(Joe Soucy collection)

Clash of the Titans, 1981, King Seeley Thermos, matching plastic bottle

BOX $125   **BOTTLE** $40

Close Encounters of the Third Kind, 1978, King Seeley Thermos, plastic bottle

BOX $150   **BOTTLE** $40

Color Me Happy, 1984, Ohio Art, no bottle

BOX $300   **BOTTLE** n/a

Corsage, 1958, American Thermos, matching steel bottle

BOX $95   **BOTTLE** $40

Corsage, 1963, American Thermos, matching steel thermos

BOX $95   **BOTTLE** $45

Corsage, 1964, American Thermos, matching steel thermos

BOX $85   **BOTTLE** $40

Corsage, 1970, American Thermos, matching steel thermos

BOX $80   **BOTTLE** $40

(KP Photo)

Cowboy in Africa, Chuck Connors, 1968, King Seeley Thermos, matching steel bottle

BOX $350   **BOTTLE** $75

Cracker Jack, 1969, Aladdin, matching plastic bottle

BOX $125   **BOTTLE** $40

Curiosity Shop, 1972, King Seeley Thermos, matching steel bottle

BOX $125   **BOTTLE** $60

Cyclist Dirt Bike, 1979, Aladdin, plastic bottle

BOX $125   **BOTTLE** $45

Daniel Boone, 1955, Aladdin, matching steel bottle

BOX $525   **BOTTLE** $95

Daniel Boone, 1965, Aladdin, matching steel bottle

BOX $350   **BOTTLE** $90

Dark Crystal, 1982, King Seeley Thermos, matching plastic bottle

BOX $75   **BOTTLE** $25

(Joe Soucy)

Davy Crocket at the Alamo, 1955, Adco

BOX $1800   **BOTTLE** $3500

Davy Crockett, 1955, Holtemp, matching steel bottle (shown)

BOX $375   **BOTTLE** $75

Davy Crockett, 1955, Kruger, no bottle

BOX $900   **BOTTLE** n/a

Davy Crockett/Kit Carson, 1955, Adco Liberty

BOX $350   **BOTTLE** n/a

Debutante, 1958, Aladdin, matching steel bottle

BOX $90   **BOTTLE** $65

Denim Diner Dome, 1975, Aladdin, matching plastic bottle

BOX $95   **BOTTLE** $30

(KP Photo)

Dick Tracy, 1967, Aladdin, matching steel bottle

BOX $450   **BOTTLE** $95

Disco, 1979, Aladdin, matching plastic bottle

BOX $90   **BOTTLE** $45

Disco Fever, 1980, Aladdin, matching plastic bottle

BOX $100   **BOTTLE** $45

(KP Photo)

Disney Express, 1979, Aladdin, matching plastic bottle, shown w/Wonderful World of Disney and Mickey Mouse Club lunch boxes

BOX $75   **BOTTLE** $25

Disney Fire Fighters Dome, 1974, Aladdin, matching plastic bottle

BOX $195   **BOTTLE** $60

Disney on Parade, 1970, Aladdin, matching plastic bottle

BOX $85   **BOTTLE** $45

Disney School Bus Dome, "1960-1968," Aladdin, steel/glass bottle, yellow and orange

BOX $120   **BOTTLE** $40

Disney World, 1970, Aladdin, matching plastic bottle

BOX $75   **BOTTLE** $40

Disney World 50th, "1976," Aladdin, light blue

    BOX $150   **BOTTLE** $40

Disney World 50th, "1976," Aladdin, matching plastic bottle

    BOX $95   **BOTTLE** $40

(KP Photo)

Disney, Wonderful World of Ice, 1982, Aladdin, plastic bottle, shown w/Mickey Mouse Club and Disney Express lunch boxes

    BOX $95   **BOTTLE** $30

Disneyland (Castle), 1957, Aladdin, matching steel bottle

    BOX $550 **BOTTLE** $125

Disneyland (Monorail), 1968, Aladdin, matching steel bottle

    BOX $600 **BOTTLE** $125

(KP Photo)

Disney's Magic Kingdom, 1980, Aladdin, plastic bottle

    BOX $95   **BOTTLE** $40

Disney's Rescuers, The, 1977, Aladdin, plastic bottle

    BOX $125   **BOTTLE** $35

Disney's Robin Hood, 1974, Aladdin, plastic bottle

    BOX $100   **BOTTLE** $30

Donald Duck, 1980, Cheinco, no bottle

    BOX $75   **BOTTLE** n/a

Double Decker, 1970, Aladdin, matching plastic bottle

    BOX $200   **BOTTLE** $50

Dr. Dolittle, 1968, Aladdin, steel/glass bottle

    BOX $300   **BOTTLE** $75

Dr. Seuss, 1970, Aladdin, matching plastic bottle

    BOX $450   **BOTTLE** $75

(KP Photo)

Drag Strip, 1975, Aladdin, matching plastic bottle

    BOX $165   **BOTTLE** $45

Dragon's Lair, 1983, Aladdin, matching plastic bottle

    BOX $75   **BOTTLE** $25

Duchess, 1960, Aladdin, steel/glass bottle

    BOX $125   **BOTTLE** $40

(Joe Soucy collection)

Dudley Do-Right, 1962, Universal, matching steel bottle

    BOX $3450   **BOTTLE** $1450

(KP Photo)

Dukes of Hazzard, 1980, Aladdin, matching plastic bottle, shown w/Annie and Magic Kingdom lunch boxes

    BOX $175   **BOTTLE** $50

Dukes of Hazzard, 1983, Aladdin, matching plastic thermos

    BOX $225   **BOTTLE** $50

Dutch Cottage Dome, 1958, King Seeley Thermos, steel/glass bottle

    BOX $375   **BOTTLE** $95

Dyno Mutt, 1977, King Seeley Thermos, plastic bottle

    BOX $100   **BOTTLE** $40

E.T., The Extra-Terrestrial, 1982, Aladdin, matching plastic bottle

    BOX $100   **BOTTLE** $25

Early West Indian Territory, 1982, Ohio Art, no bottle

    BOX $120   **BOTTLE** n/a

Early West Oregon Trail, 1982, Ohio Art, no bottle

    BOX $120   **BOTTLE** n/a

Early West Pony Express, 1982, Ohio Art, no bottle

    BOX $120   **BOTTLE** n/a

El Chapulin Colorado, 1979, Aladdin, matching plastic thermos

    BOX $95   **BOTTLE** $40

Emergency!, 1973, Aladdin, plastic bottle

    BOX $300   **BOTTLE** $50

Emergency! Dome, 1977, Aladdin, plastic bottle

    BOX $365   **BOTTLE** $50

(Joe Soucy collection)

Evel Knievel, 1974, Aladdin, plastic bottle

    BOX $225   **BOTTLE** $45

Exciting World of Metrics, The, 1976, King Seeley Thermos, plastic bottle

    BOX $60   **BOTTLE** $20

Fall Guy, 1981, Aladdin, matching plastic bottle

    BOX $65   **BOTTLE** $30

Family Affair, 1969, King Seeley Thermos, matching steel bottle

    BOX $325   **BOTTLE** $65

Fat Albert and the Cosby Kids, 1973, King Seeley Thermos, plastic bottle

    BOX $85   **BOTTLE** $30

Fess Parker, 1965, King Seeley Thermos, matching steel bottle

    BOX $325   **BOTTLE** $90

Fireball XL5, 1964, King Seeley Thermos, steel/glass bottle

    BOX $350   **BOTTLE** $85

Firehouse Dome, 1959, American Thermos, steel/glass bottle

    BOX $400   **BOTTLE** $95

Flag, "1973," Ohio Art, no thermos
BOX $90   **BOTTLE** n/a

Flag-O-Rama, 1954, Universal, steel/glass bottle
BOX $475 **BOTTLE** $110

Flintstones, 1962, Aladdin, orange, 1st issue, matching bottle
BOX $550 **BOTTLE** $110

Flintstones, 1964, Aladdin, yellow, 2nd issue, matching bottle
BOX $595 **BOTTLE** $110

Flintstones, 1973, Aladdin, matching plastic bottle
BOX $300   **BOTTLE** $50

(KP Photo)

Flipper, 1966, King Seeley Thermos, matching steel bottle
BOX $350   **BOTTLE** $75

Floral, 1970, Ohio Art, no bottle
BOX $40   **BOTTLE** n/a

Flying Nun, 1968, Aladdin, matching steel bottle
BOX $400   **BOTTLE** $95

Fonz, The, 1978, King Seeley Thermos, plastic bottle
BOX $250   **BOTTLE** $40

Fox and the Hound, 1981, Aladdin, plastic bottle
BOX $85   **BOTTLE** $30

Fraggle Rock, 1984, King Seeley Thermos, matching plastic bottle
BOX $85   **BOTTLE** $30

Fritos, 1975, King Seeley Thermos, generic bottle
BOX $275   **BOTTLE** n/a

Frontier Days, 1957, Ohio Art, no bottle
BOX $350   **BOTTLE** n/a

Frost Flowers, 1962, Ohio Art, no bottle
BOX $70   **BOTTLE** n/a

Fruit Basket, 1975, Ohio Art, no bottle
BOX $45   **BOTTLE** n/a

Funtastic World of Hanna-Barbera, 1971, King Seeley Thermos, Huck Hound, plastic bottle
BOX $300   **BOTTLE** $45

Funtastic World of Hanna-Barbera, 1978, King Seeley Thermos, Flintstones and Yogi, plastic bottle
BOX $325   **BOTTLE** $45

G.I. Joe, 1967, King Seeley Thermos, steel/glass bottle
BOX $350   **BOTTLE** $75

G.I. Joe, 1982, King Seeley Thermos, plastic bottle
BOX $75   **BOTTLE** $25

Gene Autry, 1954, Universal, steel/glass bottle
BOX $1500 **BOTTLE** $225

(KP Photo)

Gentle Ben, 1968, Aladdin, plastic bottle, glass liner, shown here w/Lance Link lunch box
BOX $225   **BOTTLE** $75

(KP Photo)

Get Smart, 1966, King Seeley Thermos, steel/glass bottle
BOX $575   **BOTTLE** $95

Ghostland, 1977, Ohio Art, spinner game, no bottle
BOX $80   **BOTTLE** n/a

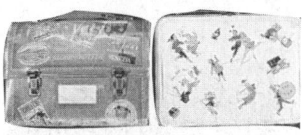

(KP Photo)

Globe-Trotter Dome, 1959, Aladdin, steel dome box, matching steel/glass bottle
BOX $300 **BOTTLE** $120

Gomer Pyle USMC, 1966, Aladdin, matching steel bottle
BOX $450 **BOTTLE** $110

(KP Photo)

Goober and the Ghostchasers/Inch High, 1974, King Seeley Thermos, matching plastic bottle
BOX $90   **BOTTLE** $25

Great Wild West, 1959, Universal, matching steel bottle
BOX $625 **BOTTLE** $225

Green Hornet, 1967, King Seeley Thermos, matching steel bottle
BOX $750 **BOTTLE** $175

(KP Photo)

Gremlins, 1984, Aladdin, matching plastic bottle
BOX $75   **BOTTLE** $35

Grizzly Adams Dome, 1977, Aladdin, plastic bottle
BOX $250   **BOTTLE** $40

Guns of Will Sonnett, The, 1968, King Seeley Thermos, steel/glass bottle
BOX $300   **BOTTLE** $90

Gunsmoke, 1959, Aladdin, plastic bottle
BOX $375   **BOTTLE** $95

Gunsmoke, 1972, Aladdin, mule splashing box w/matching bottle
BOX $300   **BOTTLE** $75

Gunsmoke, 1973, Aladdin, stagecoach box, matching bottle
BOX $325   **BOTTLE** $75

Gunsmoke, Double L Version, 1959, Aladdin, double L error version, matching bottle
BOX $1200   **BOTTLE** $95

(KP Photo)

Gunsmoke, Marshal Matt Dillon, 1962, Aladdin, matching steel bottle
BOX $450   **BOTTLE** $95

(KP Photo)

H.R. Pufnstuf, 1970, Aladdin, matching plastic bottle
BOX $850 **BOTTLE** $110

Hair Bear Bunch, The, 1972, King Seeley Thermos, plastic bottle
BOX $100 **BOTTLE** $35

Hansel and Gretel, 1982, Ohio Art, no bottle
BOX $85 **BOTTLE** n/a

Happy Days, 1977, American Thermos, matching plastic bottle
BOX $250 **BOTTLE** $40

Hardy Boys Mysteries, 1977, King Seeley Thermos, matching plastic bottle
BOX $120 **BOTTLE** $45

Harlem Globetrotters, 1971, King Seeley Thermos, steel bottle, blue or purple uniforms
BOX $225 **BOTTLE** $65

Have Gun Will Travel, 1960, Aladdin, matching bottle, Paladin
BOX $550 **BOTTLE** $100

Heathcliff, 1982, Aladdin, matching plastic bottle
BOX $85 **BOTTLE** $20

Hector Heathcote, 1964, Aladdin, matching steel bottle
BOX $325 **BOTTLE** $90

(KP Photo)

Hee Haw, 1971, King Seeley Thermos, matching steel bottle
BOX $275 **BOTTLE** $75

He-Man & Masters of the Universe, 1984, Aladdin, matching plastic bottle
BOX $95 **BOTTLE** $30

Highway Signs, 1972, Ohio Art, no bottle
BOX $70 **BOTTLE** n/a

(KP Photo)

Hogan's Heroes Dome, 1966, Aladdin, steel/glass bottle
BOX $575 **BOTTLE** $160

Holly Hobbie, 1968, Aladdin, red rim, matching plastic bottle
BOX $65 **BOTTLE** $20

Holly Hobbie, 1973, Aladdin, matching plastic bottle
BOX $65 **BOTTLE** $20

Holly Hobbie, 1979, Aladdin, matching plastic bottle
BOX $65 **BOTTLE** $20

Home Town Airport Dome, 1960, King Seeley Thermos, steel/glass bottle
BOX $1200 **BOTTLE** $275

(KP Photo)

Hong Kong Phooey, 1975, King Seeley Thermos, steel/glass bottle
BOX $275 **BOTTLE** $50

(KP Photo)

Hopalong Cassidy, 1950, Aladdin, red or blue, steel/glass bottle
BOX $400 **BOTTLE** $90

Hopalong Cassidy, 1952, Aladdin, steel bottle
BOX $400 **BOTTLE** $90

Hopalong Cassidy, 1954, Aladdin, black rim, steel/glass bottle, full litho
BOX $525 **BOTTLE** $150

Hot Wheels, 1969, King Seeley Thermos, matching steel bottle
BOX $325 **BOTTLE** $75

How the West Was Won, 1979, King Seeley Thermos, matching plastic bottle
BOX $125 **BOTTLE** $40

Howdy Doody, 1954, Adco Liberty
BOX $950 **BOTTLE** n/a

Huckleberry Hound, 1961, Aladdin, steel/glass bottle
BOX $300 **BOTTLE** $75

Indiana Jones, 1984, King Seeley Thermos, matching plastic bottle
BOX $100 **BOTTLE** $30

Indiana Jones Temple of Doom, 1984, King Seeley Thermos, matching plastic bottle
BOX $100 **BOTTLE** $30

It's About Time Dome, 1967, Aladdin, matching bottle
BOX $375 **BOTTLE** $95

Jack and Jill, 1982, Ohio Art
BOX $400 **BOTTLE** n/a

(Joe Soucy collection)

James Bond 007, 1966, Aladdin, matching steel bottle
> **BOX** $700 **BOTTLE** $150

Jet Patrol, 1957, Aladdin, matching steel bottle
> **BOX** $400 **BOTTLE** $150

Jetsons Dome, 1963, Aladdin, matching bottle
> **BOX** $2650 **BOTTLE** $375

Joe Palooka, 1949, Continental Can, no bottle
> **BOX** $100 **BOTTLE** n/a

(KP Photo)

Johnny Lightning, 1970, Aladdin, plastic bottle
> **BOX** $175 **BOTTLE** $60

Jonathan Livingston Seagull, 1973, Aladdin, matching plastic bottle
> **BOX** $150 **BOTTLE** $50

Jr. Miss, 1956, Aladdin, matching steel bottle
> **BOX** $150 **BOTTLE** $60

Jr. Miss, 1960, Aladdin, steel bottle
> **BOX** $140 **BOTTLE** $50

Jr. Miss, 1962, Aladdin, steel bottle
> **BOX** $225 **BOTTLE** $95

Jr. Miss, 1966, Aladdin, steel and plastic bottle
> **BOX** $150 **BOTTLE** $75

Jr. Miss, 1970, Aladdin, plastic bottle
> **BOX** $120 **BOTTLE** $50

Jr. Miss, 1973, Aladdin, plastic bottle
> **BOX** $95 **BOTTLE** $40

Jr. Miss, 1978, Aladdin, plastic bottle
> **BOX** $95 **BOTTLE** $40

(KP Photo)

Julia, 1969, King Seeley Thermos, matching steel bottle, shown w/Buccaneer Dome lunch box
> **BOX** $195 **BOTTLE** $75

Jungle Book, 1968, Aladdin, matching steel bottle
> **BOX** $275 **BOTTLE** $75

Junior Miss, 1978, Aladdin, matching plastic bottle
> **BOX** $110 **BOTTLE** $40

Kellogg's, 1969, Aladdin, plastic bottle
> **BOX** $325 **BOTTLE** $75

King Kong, 1977, King Seeley Thermos, plastic bottle
> **BOX** $200 **BOTTLE** $40

(Joe Soucy collection)

KISS, 1977, King Seeley Thermos, plastic bottle
> **BOX** $350 **BOTTLE** $50

Knight in Armor, 1959, Universal, matching steel bottle
> **BOX** $1250 **BOTTLE** $300

Knight Rider, 1984, King Seeley Thermos, matching plastic bottle
> **BOX** $95 **BOTTLE** $25

Korg, 1975, King Seeley Thermos, matching plastic bottle
> **BOX** $150 **BOTTLE** $45

Krofft Supershow, 1976, Aladdin, matching plastic bottle
> **BOX** $250 **BOTTLE** $50

Kung Fu, 1974, King Seeley Thermos, matching plastic bottle
> **BOX** $250 **BOTTLE** $40

(KP Photo)

Lance Link, Secret Chimp, 1971, King Seeley Thermos, matching steel bottle, shown here w/Gentle Ben lunch box
> **BOX** $250 **BOTTLE** $75

(KP Photo)

Land of the Giants, 1968, Aladdin, plastic bottle
> **BOX** $325 **BOTTLE** $85

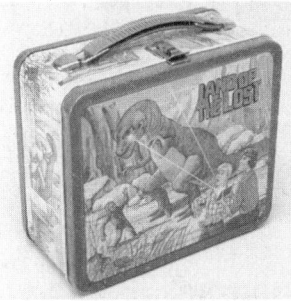

Land of the Lost, 1975, Aladdin, matching plastic bottle
> **BOX** $300 **BOTTLE** $50

Laugh-In (Helmet), 1969, Aladdin, helmet on back, matching plastic bottle
> **BOX** $300 **BOTTLE** $65

Laugh-In (Tricycle), 1969, Aladdin, trike on back, matching plastic bottle
> **BOX** $325 **BOTTLE** $65

Lawman, 1961, King Seeley Thermos, generic bottle
> **BOX** $300 **BOTTLE** $85

Legend of the Lone Ranger, 1980, Aladdin, plastic bottle
> **BOX** $175 **BOTTLE** $45

Lidsville, 1971, Aladdin, matching plastic bottle
> **BOX** $375 **BOTTLE** $65

Little Dutch Miss, 1959, Universal, matching steel bottle
> **BOX** $225 **BOTTLE** $75

Little Friends, 1982, Aladdin, matching plastic bottle
> **BOX** $850 **BOTTLE** $260

Little House on the Prairie, 1978, King Seeley Thermos, matching plastic bottle
> **BOX** $300 **BOTTLE** $45

Little Red Riding Hood, 1982, Ohio Art, no bottle
> **BOX** $60 **BOTTLE** n/a

Lone Ranger, 1955, Adco Liberty, blue band, no bottle

BOX $1150 BOTTLE n/a

Lone Ranger, 1955, Adco Liberty, red rim, no bottle

BOX $900 BOTTLE n/a

Looney Tunes TV Set, 1959, King Seeley Thermos, steel/glass bottle

BOX $350 BOTTLE $95

(Joe Soucy collection)

Lost in Space Dome, 1967, King Seeley Thermos, steel/glass bottle

BOX $950 BOTTLE $100

Ludwig Von Drake, 1962, Aladdin, steel/glass bottle

BOX $350 BOTTLE $90

Luggage Plaid, 1955, Adco Liberty, no bottle

BOX $75 BOTTLE n/a

Luggage Plaid, 1957, Ohio Art, no bottle

BOX $75 BOTTLE n/a

Luggage Tweed, 1957, American Thermos, blue, matching steel bottle

BOX $120 BOTTLE $70

Luggage Tweed, 1957, American Thermos, tan, matching steel bottle

BOX $80 BOTTLE $60

Luggage Tweed, 1957, American Thermos, maroon, matching steel bottle

BOX $140 BOTTLE $70

Magic of Lassie, 1978, King Seeley Thermos, matching plastic bottle

BOX $175 BOTTLE $40

Major League Baseball, 1968, King Seeley Thermos, matching bottle

BOX $225 BOTTLE $55

(Joe Soucy collection)

Man from U.N.C.L.E., 1966, King Seeley Thermos, matching steel bottle

BOX $775 BOTTLE $90

(Joe Soucy collection)

Marvel Super Heroes, 1976, Aladdin, black rim, matching plastic bottle

BOX $125 BOTTLE $45

Mary Poppins, 1965, Aladdin, steel/glass bottle

BOX $250 BOTTLE $75

Masters of the Universe, 1983, Aladdin, matching plastic bottle

BOX $75 BOTTLE $25

Mickey Mouse & Donald Duck, 1954, Adco Liberty, matching steel bottle

BOX $900 BOTTLE $1650

Mickey Mouse Club, 1963, Aladdin, white, matching steel bottle

BOX $375 BOTTLE $90

(KP Photo)

Mickey Mouse Club, 1976, Aladdin, yellow, steel/glass bottle, shown w/Wonderful World of Disney and Mickey Mouse Club lunch boxes

BOX $250 BOTTLE $60

Mickey Mouse Club, 1977, Aladdin, red rim, sky boat, matching bottle

BOX $150 BOTTLE $40

(Joe Soucy collection)

Mickey Mouse School Days, plastic bottle, Mickey as school teacher

BOX $600 BOTTLE $175

Miss America, 1972, Aladdin, matching plastic bottle

BOX $300 BOTTLE $50

Mod Floral Dome, 1975, Okay Industries, matching steel bottle

BOX $400 BOTTLE n/a

Monroes, 1967, Aladdin, matching steel bottle

BOX $450 BOTTLE $110

(KP Photo)

Mork & Mindy, 1979, American Thermos, matching plastic bottle

BOX $175 BOTTLE $45

Mr. Merlin, 1982, King Seeley Thermos, matching plastic bottle

BOX $100 BOTTLE $35

Munsters, 1965, King Seeley Thermos, matching steel bottle

BOX $900 BOTTLE $150

Muppet Babies, 1985, King Seeley Thermos, matching plastic bottle

BOX $75 BOTTLE $20

Muppet Movie, 1979, King Seeley Thermos, plastic bottle

BOX $225 BOTTLE $40

Muppet Show, 1978, King Seeley Thermos, plastic bottle

BOX $125 BOTTLE $30

Muppets, 1979, King Seeley Thermos, back shows Animal, Fozzie or Kermit, matching plastic bottle

BOX $125 BOTTLE $30

My Lunch, 1976, Ohio Art, no bottle

BOX $65 BOTTLE n/a

Nancy Drew, 1978, King Seeley Thermos, plastic bottle

BOX $125 BOTTLE $30

NFL, 1962, Okay, black rim, steel/glass bottle
BOX $350 **BOTTLE** $130

NFL, 1975, King Seeley Thermos, yellow rim, plastic bottle
BOX $175 **BOTTLE** $40

NFL, 1976, King Seeley Thermos, red rim, matching plastic bottle
BOX $175 **BOTTLE** $40

NFL, 1978, King Seeley Thermos, blue rim, matching plastic bottle
BOX $100 **BOTTLE** $40

NFL Quarterback, 1964, Aladdin, matching steel bottle
BOX $450 **BOTTLE** $95

NHL, 1970, Okay Industries, plastic bottle
BOX $600 **BOTTLE** $250

Orbit, 1963, King Seeley Thermos, matching steel bottle
BOX $500 **BOTTLE** $90

(Joe Soucy collection)

Osmonds, The, 1973, Aladdin, matching plastic bottle
BOX $265 **BOTTLE** $45

Our Friends, 1982, Aladdin, matching plastic bottle
BOX $900 **BOTTLE** $350

Pac-Man, 1980, Aladdin, matching plastic bottle
BOX $95 **BOTTLE** $25

Para-Medic, 1978, Ohio Art, no bottle
BOX $75 **BOTTLE** n/a

Partridge Family, 1971, King Seeley Thermos, plastic or steel bottle
BOX $225 **BOTTLE** $60

Pathfinder, 1959, Universal, matching steel bottle
BOX $750 **BOTTLE** $225

Patriotic, 1974, Ohio Art, no bottle
BOX $75 **BOTTLE** n/a

Peanuts, 1966, King Seeley Thermos, orange rim, matching steel bottle (shown)
BOX $275 **BOTTLE** $50

Peanuts, 1973, King Seeley Thermos, red rim psychiatric box, plastic bottle
BOX $125 **BOTTLE** $30

Peanuts, 1976, King Seeley Thermos, red pitching box, plastic bottle
BOX $150 **BOTTLE** $35

Peanuts, 1980, King Seeley Thermos, pitching box, yellow face, green band, matching bottle
BOX $125 **BOTTLE** $35

Pebbles & Bamm-Bamm, 1971, Aladdin, matching plastic bottle
BOX $300 **BOTTLE** $60

Pele, 1975, King Seeley Thermos, matching plastic bottle
BOX $195 **BOTTLE** $45

Pennant, 1950, Ohio Art, basket type box, no bottle
BOX $50 **BOTTLE** n/a

Peter Pan, 1969, Aladdin, matching plastic bottle, Disney
BOX $285 **BOTTLE** $50

Pete's Dragon, 1978, Aladdin, matching plastic bottle
BOX $95 **BOTTLE** $35

Pets 'n Pals, 1961, King Seeley Thermos, matching steel bottle
BOX $250 **BOTTLE** $65

Pigs In Space, 1977, King Seeley Thermos, matching plastic bottle
BOX $75 **BOTTLE** $30

Pink Gingham, 1976, King Seeley Thermos, matching plastic bottle
BOX $60 **BOTTLE** $20

Pink Panther & Sons, 1984, King Seeley Thermos, matching plastic bottle
BOX $100 **BOTTLE** $30

Pinocchio, 1971, Aladdin, plastic bottle
BOX $250 **BOTTLE** $50

(Joe Soucy collection)

Pit Stop, 1968, Ohio Art
BOX $450 **BOTTLE** n/a

Plaid, "1953," Aladdin, gray, matching steel bottle (ultra rare)
BOX $375 **BOTTLE** $120

Plaid, "1955," Aladdin, matching steel bottle
BOX $75 **BOTTLE** $50

Plaid Scotch, "1957," Ohio Art, no bottle
BOX $65 **BOTTLE** n/a

Plaid Scotch, "1964," Ohio Art, no bottle
BOX $65 **BOTTLE** n/a

Plaid Scotch, "1964-1971," Ohio Art, no bottle
BOX $50 **BOTTLE** n/a

Plaid Scotch, 1959, Universal, matching steel bottle
BOX $175 **BOTTLE** $65

Plaid Scotch, 1964, King Seeley Thermos, blue, no bottle
BOX $190 **BOTTLE** n/a

Plaid Scotch, 1974, King Seeley Thermos, green, matching steel bottle
BOX $225 **BOTTLE** $90

Plaid Tweed, "1960," American Thermos, red band, matching steel bottle
BOX $90 **BOTTLE** $40

Plaid Tweed, "1960," American Thermos, green band, matching steel bottle
BOX $90 **BOTTLE** $40

Planet of the Apes, 1974, Aladdin, matching plastic bottle
BOX $475 **BOTTLE** $80

(KP Photo)

Play Ball, 1969, King Seeley Thermos, game on back, steel bottle
BOX $200 **BOTTLE** $55

Police Patrol, 1978, Aladdin, plastic bottle
BOX $300 **BOTTLE** $45

Polly Pal, 1975, King Seeley Thermos, matching plastic bottle
BOX $60 **BOTTLE** $20

Pony Express, 1982, Ohio Art
BOX $90 **BOTTLE** n/a

(Joe Soucy collection)

Popeye, 1962, Universal, "Popeye socks Bluto" box, matching bottle

BOX $900 **BOTTLE** $450

Popeye, 1964, King Seeley Thermos, "Popeye in boat" box w/matching steel bottle

BOX $450 **BOTTLE** $80

Popeye, 1980, Aladdin, "arm wrestling" box, plastic bottle

BOX $200 **BOTTLE** $45

Popples, 1986, Aladdin, plastic bottle

BOX $75 **BOTTLE** $20

Porky's Lunch Wagon Dome, 1959, King Seeley Thermos, steel/glass bottle

BOX $575 **BOTTLE** $95

Pro Sports, 1974, Ohio Art, no bottle

BOX $95 **BOTTLE** n/a

Psychedelic Dome, 1969, Aladdin, plastic bottle

BOX $350 **BOTTLE** $85

Racing Wheels, 1977, King Seeley Thermos, plastic bottle

BOX $150 **BOTTLE** $25

Raggedy Ann & Andy, 1973, Aladdin, plastic bottle

BOX $175 **BOTTLE** $40

Rambo, 1985, King Seeley Thermos, matching plastic bottle

BOX $95 **BOTTLE** $20

(KP Photo)

Rat Patrol, 1967, Aladdin, steel/glass bottle

BOX $400 **BOTTLE** $90

Red Barn Dome, 1957, King Seeley Thermos, closed door version, plain Holtemp bottle

BOX $200 **BOTTLE** $30

Red Barn Dome, 1958, King Seeley Thermos, open door version, matching steel bottle

BOX $150 **BOTTLE** $50

Red Barn Dome, 1972, Thermos, four cutis, matching steel/glass bottle

BOX $150 **BOTTLE** $50

Rifleman, The, 1961, Aladdin, steel/glass bottle

BOX $625 **BOTTLE** $175

Road Runner, 1970, King Seeley Thermos, lavender or purple rim, steel or plastic bottle

BOX $275 **BOTTLE** $75

(KP Photo)

Robin Hood, 1956, Aladdin, matching bottle

BOX $425 **BOTTLE** $120

Ronald McDonald, Sheriff, 1982, Aladdin, plastic bottle

BOX $95 **BOTTLE** $20

Rose Petal Place, 1983, Aladdin, plastic bottle

BOX $75 **BOTTLE** $20

Rough Rider, 1973, Aladdin, plastic bottle

BOX $125 **BOTTLE** $40

Roy Rogers & Dale Double R Bar Ranch, 1953, King Seeley Thermos, steel/glass bottle

BOX $395 **BOTTLE** $75

Roy Rogers & Dale Double R Bar Ranch, 1954, American Thermos, blue or red band, woodgrain tall bottle

BOX $350 **BOTTLE** $95

(KP Photo)

Roy Rogers & Dale Double R Bar Ranch, 1955, American Thermos, eight-scene box, red or blue band, matching bottle

BOX $375 **BOTTLE** $95

(KP Photo)

Roy Rogers & Dale Double R Bar Ranch, 1955, American Thermos, cowhide back box, red or blue band, matching bottle

BOX $350 **BOTTLE** $95

Roy Rogers & Dale on Rail, 1957, American Thermos, silver "only" band, matching bottle

BOX $450 **BOTTLE** $95

(KP Photo)

Roy Rogers Chow Wagon Dome, 1958, King Seeley Thermos, steel/glass bottle

BOX $475 **BOTTLE** $95

Saddlebag, 1977, King Seeley Thermos, generic plastic bottle

BOX $165 **BOTTLE** $40

Satellite, 1958, American Thermos, matching bottle, narrow band

 BOX $400 BOTTLE $60

Satellite, 1960, King Seeley Thermos, steel bottle

 BOX $350 BOTTLE $60

Scooby Doo, 1973, King Seeley Thermos, orange rim, plastic bottle

 BOX $800 BOTTLE $40

Scooby Doo, 1973, King Seeley Thermos, yellow rim, plastic bottle

 BOX $750 BOTTLE $40

Secret Agent T, 1968, King Seeley Thermos, matching bottle

 BOX $325 BOTTLE $75

Secret of NIMH, 1982, Aladdin, plastic bottle

 BOX $60 BOTTLE $30

Secret Wars, 1984, Aladdin, plastic bottle

 BOX $160 BOTTLE $40

See America, 1972, Ohio Art, no bottle

 BOX $75 BOTTLE n/a

Sesame Street, 1983, Aladdin, yellow or green rim, plastic bottle

 BOX $95 BOTTLE $30

Sigmund and the Sea Monsters, 1974, Aladdin, plastic bottle

 BOX $475 BOTTLE $75

Six Million Dollar Man, 1974, Aladdin, plastic bottle

 BOX $200 BOTTLE $40

(Joe Soucy collection)

Six Million Dollar Man, 1978, Aladdin, plastic bottle

 BOX $225 BOTTLE $40

Skateboarder, 1977, Aladdin, plastic bottle

 BOX $150 BOTTLE $40

Sleeping Beauty, 1960, General Steel Ware/Canada, generic steel bottle

 BOX $450 BOTTLE $55

Smokey Bear, 1975, Okay Industries, plastic bottle

 BOX $550 BOTTLE $350

Smurfs, 1983, King Seeley Thermos, blue box, plastic bottle

 BOX $225 BOTTLE $30

Snoopy Dome, 1968, King Seeley Thermos, yellow, "Have Lunch w/Snoopy," matching bottle

 BOX $225 BOTTLE $50

Snow White, Disney, 1975, Aladdin, orange rim, plastic bottle

 BOX $110 BOTTLE $30

Snow White, w/out Game, 1980, Ohio Art, no bottle

 BOX $95 BOTTLE n/a

Space Explorer Ed McCauley, 1960, Aladdin, matching steel bottle

 BOX $475 BOTTLE $150

Space Ship, 1950, unknown, Decoware, dark blue square

 BOX $250 BOTTLE n/a

Space Shuttle Orbiter Enterprise, 1977, King Seeley Thermos, plastic bottle

 BOX $250 BOTTLE $45

Space: 1999, 1976, King Seeley Thermos, plastic bottle

 BOX $250 BOTTLE $40

Speed Buggy, 1974, King Seeley Thermos, red rim, plastic bottle

 BOX $225 BOTTLE $25

Spider-Man & Hulk, 1980, Aladdin, Captain America on back, plastic bottle

 BOX $200 BOTTLE $30

Sport Goofy, 1983, Aladdin, yellow rim, plastic bottle

 BOX $95 BOTTLE $25

Sport Skwirts, 1982, Ohio Art, several variations

 BOX $95 BOTTLE n/a

Sports Afield, 1957, Ohio Art, no bottle

 BOX $275 BOTTLE n/a

(KP Photo)

Star Trek Dome, 1968, Aladdin, matching bottle

 BOX $2350 BOTTLE $450

Star Trek, The Motion Picture, 1980, King Seeley Thermos, matching bottle

 BOX $250 BOTTLE $60

Star Wars, 1978, King Seeley Thermos, cast or stars on band, matching plastic bottle

 BOX $250 BOTTLE $40

Star Wars, Empire Strikes Back, 1980, King Seeley Thermos, swamp scene, plastic bottle

 BOX $250 BOTTLE $40

Star Wars, Empire Strikes Back, 1980, King Seeley Thermos, ship scene, plastic bottle

 BOX $175 BOTTLE $30

Star Wars, Return of the Jedi, 1983, King Seeley Thermos, plastic bottle

 BOX $150 BOTTLE $30

Stars and Stripes Dome, 1970, King Seeley Thermos, matching plastic bottle

 BOX $150 BOTTLE $40

Steve Canyon, 1959, Aladdin, steel/glass bottle

 BOX $450 BOTTLE $150

Strawberry Land, 1985, Aladdin, no bottle

 BOX $150 BOTTLE n/a

Strawberry Shortcake, 1980, Aladdin, plastic bottle

 BOX $100 BOTTLE $15

Strawberry Shortcake, 1981, Aladdin, plastic bottle
BOX $100   BOTTLE $15

Street Hawk, 1985, Aladdin, plastic bottle
BOX $300   BOTTLE $90

Submarine, 1960, King Seeley Thermos, steel/glass bottle
BOX $325   BOTTLE $80

Super Friends, 1976, Aladdin, matching plastic bottle
BOX $150   BOTTLE $40

Super Powers, 1983, Aladdin, plastic bottle
BOX $150   BOTTLE $40

Supercar, 1962, Universal, steel/glass bottle
BOX $400   BOTTLE $150

Superman, 1954, Universal, blue rim
BOX $19250   BOTTLE $250

Superman, 1967, King Seeley Thermos, red rim, "under fire" art on back, matching steel/glass bottle
BOX $1500   BOTTLE $125

Superman, 1978, Aladdin, red rim, Daily Planet Office on back, matching bottle
BOX $250   BOTTLE $50

Tapestry, 1963, Ohio Art, no bottle
BOX $60   BOTTLE n/a

Tarzan, 1966, Aladdin, steel/glass bottle
BOX $325   BOTTLE $65

Teenager, 1957, King Seeley Thermos, generic bottle
BOX $225   BOTTLE $35

Teenager Dome, 1957, King Seeley Thermos, generic bottle
BOX $225   BOTTLE $35

The Incredible Hulk, 1978, Aladdin, matching plastic thermos
BOX $120   BOTTLE $60

Three Little Pigs, 1982, Ohio Art, red rim, generic/plastic bottle
BOX $95   BOTTLE n/a

Thundercats, 1985, Aladdin, plastic bottle
BOX $150   BOTTLE $25

Tom Corbett Space Cadet, "1952," Aladdin, blue or red box, steel/glass bottle
BOX $375   BOTTLE $95

(Joe Soucy collection)

Tom Corbett Space Cadet, 1954, Aladdin, full litho, matching bottle
BOX $625   BOTTLE $110

Toppie Elephant, 1957, American Thermos, yellow, matching bottle
BOX $3850   BOTTLE $800

Track King, 1975, Okay Industries, matching steel bottle
BOX $275   BOTTLE $650

Train, 1971, Ohio Art, no bottle
BOX $45   BOTTLE n/a

Transformers, 1986, Aladdin, red box, matching plastic bottle
BOX $95   BOTTLE $15

Traveler, 1962/64, Ohio Art, blue or brown, no bottle
BOX $85   BOTTLE n/a

Trigger, 1956, King Seeley Thermos, no bottle
BOX $700   BOTTLE n/a

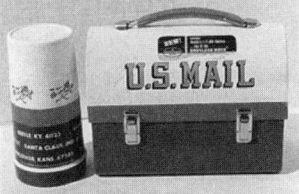

U.S. Mail Dome, 1969, Aladdin, plastic bottle
BOX $175   BOTTLE $45

U.S. Space Corps, 1961, Universal, plastic rocket bottle
BOX $525   BOTTLE $150

UFO, 1973, King Seeley Thermos, plastic bottle
BOX $225   BOTTLE $40

(Joe Soucy collection)

Underdog, 1974, Okay Industries, plastic bottle
BOX $3500   BOTTLE $1250

Universal's Movie Monsters, 1980, Aladdin, plastic bottle
BOX $350   BOTTLE $50

(KP Photo)

Voyage to the Bottom of the Sea, 1967, Aladdin, steel/glass bottle
BOX $750   BOTTLE $175

VW Bus Dome, 1960, Omni, plastic bottle
BOX $850   BOTTLE $220

Wagon Train, 1964, King Seeley Thermos, matching steel bottle
BOX $325   BOTTLE $75

Wags'n Whiskers, 1978, King Seeley Thermos, matching plastic bottle
BOX $95   BOTTLE $25

Wake Up America, 1973, Okay Industries, matching steel bottle
BOX $700   BOTTLE $250

Waltons, The, 1973, Aladdin, plastic bottle
BOX $265   BOTTLE $40

Washington Redskins, 1970, Okay Industries, steel bottle
BOX $375   BOTTLE $140

Wee Pals Kid Power, 1974, American Thermos, matching plastic bottle
BOX $120   BOTTLE $35

Welcome Back Kotter, 1977, Aladdin, flat or embossed face, red rim, matching plastic bottle
BOX $250   BOTTLE $50

Western, 1963, King Seeley Thermos, gear band, steel/glass bottle
BOX $225   BOTTLE $75

Western, 1963, King Seeley Thermos, tan band, steel/glass bottle
BOX $275   BOTTLE $75

(KP Photo)

Wild Bill Hickok, 1955, Aladdin, steel/glass bottle
BOX $400 **BOTTLE** $110

Wild Frontier, 1977, Ohio Art, spinner game on back, no bottle
BOX $90 **BOTTLE** n/a

Wild, Wild West, 1969, Aladdin, plastic bottle
BOX $700 **BOTTLE** $120

Winnie the Pooh, 1976, Aladdin, blue rim, plastic bottle
BOX $325 **BOTTLE** $80

Yankee Doodles, 1975, King Seeley Thermos, plastic bottle
BOX $95 **BOTTLE** $25

(KP Photo)

Yellow Submarine, 1968, King Seeley Thermos, steel/glass bottle
BOX $1300 **BOTTLE** $350

Yogi Bear, 1974, Aladdin
BOX $325 **BOTTLE** $60

Yogi Bear & Friends, 1961, Aladdin, black rim, matching steel bottle
BOX $350 **BOTTLE** $80

Zorro, 1958, Aladdin, black band, steel/glass bottle
BOX $450 **BOTTLE** $120

Zorro, 1966, Aladdin, red band, steel/glass bottle
BOX $650 **BOTTLE** $180

Vinyl

Alice in Wonderland, 1972, Aladdin, matching plastic bottle
BOX $225 **BOTTLE** $45

All American, 1976, Bayville, Styrofoam bottle
BOX $160 **BOTTLE** $20

All Dressed Up, 1970s, Bayville, Styrofoam bottle
BOX $90 **BOTTLE** $20

All Star, 1960, Aladdin
BOX $475 **BOTTLE** $95

Alvin and the Chipmunks, 1963, King Seeley Thermos, matching plastic bottle
BOX $350 **BOTTLE** $140

Annie 1, 1981, Aladdin, matching plastic bottle
BOX $75 **BOTTLE** $20

(KP Photo)

Bach's Lunch, 1975, Volkwein Bros., red Styrofoam bottle
BOX $130 **BOTTLE** $20

Ballerina, 1960s, Universal, black, Thermax bottle
BOX $600 **BOTTLE** $95

Ballerina, 1962, Aladdin, pink, steel/glass bottle
BOX $200 **BOTTLE** $60

Ballet, 1961, Universal, red, plastic generic bottle
BOX $500 **BOTTLE** $20

Banana Splits, 1969, King Seeley Thermos, matching steel/glass bottle
BOX $425 **BOTTLE** $150

(KP Photo)

Barbarino Brunch Bag, 1977, Aladdin, zippered bag, plastic bottle
BOX $300 **BOTTLE** $60

Barbie & Francie, 1965, King Seeley Thermos, black, matching steel/glass bottle
BOX $150 **BOTTLE** $65

(KP Photo)

Barbie & Midge, 1963, King Seeley Thermos, black, matching steel/glass bottle
BOX $150 **BOTTLE** $65

Barbie & Midge Dome, 1964, King Seeley Thermos, matching glass/steel bottle
BOX $530 **BOTTLE** $65

Barbie Softy, 1988, King Seeley Thermos, generic plastic bottle
BOX $45 **BOTTLE** $15

Barbie, World of, 1971, King Seeley Thermos, pink box, matching steel/glass bottle
BOX $130 **BOTTLE** $40

Barbie, World of, 1971, King Seeley Thermos, blue box, matching steel/glass bottle
BOX $100 **BOTTLE** $25

Barnum's Animals, 1978, Adco Liberty, no bottle
BOX $75 **BOTTLE** n/a

(KP Photo)

Beany & Cecil, 1963, King Seeley Thermos, steel/glass bottle, three colors: red, blue and black
BOX $675 **BOTTLE** $150

Beatles, 1965, Air Flite, no bottle
BOX $850 **BOTTLE** n/a

Beatles Brunch Bag, 1966, Aladdin, zippered bag, matching bottle
BOX $650 **BOTTLE** $300

Beatles Kaboodles Kit, 1965, Standard Plastic Products, no bottle
BOX $950 **BOTTLE** n/a

Betsey Clark, 1977, King Seeley Thermos, yellow box, matching plastic bottle
> **BOX** $75 **BOTTLE** $15

Betsey Clark Munchies Bag, 1977, King Seeley Thermos, zippered bag, plastic bottle
> **BOX** $60 **BOTTLE** $10

Blue Gingham Brunch Bag, 1975, Aladdin, zippered box and plastic bottle
> **BOX** $50 **BOTTLE** $30

Bobby Soxer, 1959, Aladdin
> **BOX** $575 **BOTTLE** n/a

(KP Photo)

Boston Red Sox, 1960s, Universal
> **BOX** $90 **BOTTLE** $20

Boy on the Swing, Abeama Industries
> **BOX** $60 **BOTTLE** $20

Buick 1910, 1974, Bayville, Styrofoam bottle
> **BOX** $75 **BOTTLE** $20

Bullwinkle, 1963, King Seeley Thermos, yellow, generic steel bottle
> **BOX** $575 **BOTTLE** $60

Bullwinkle, 1963, King Seeley Thermos, white, steel/glass bottle
> **BOX** $4500 **BOTTLE** $180

Bullwinkle, 1963, King Seeley Thermos, blue, steel/glass bottle
> **BOX** $900 **BOTTLE** $180

Calico Brunch Bag, 1980, Aladdin, zippered bag, plastic bottle
> **BOX** $50 **BOTTLE** $30

Captain Kangaroo, 1964, King Seeley Thermos, steel/glass bottle
> **BOX** $475 **BOTTLE** $95

Captain Marvel Brunch Bag, 1947, red rectangular vinyl w/strap handle
> **BOX** $425 **BOTTLE** $200

Carousel, 1962, Aladdin, matching steel/glass bottle
> **BOX** $375 **BOTTLE** $130

Cars, 1960, Universal
> **BOX** $150 **BOTTLE** n/a

(Joe Soucy collection)

Casper the Friendly Ghost, 1966, King Seeley Thermos, blue box, orange steel bottle
> **BOX** $500 **BOTTLE** $150

Challenger, Space Shuttle, 1986, Babcock, puffy box, no bottle
> **BOX** $275 **BOTTLE** n/a

(KP Photo)

Charlie's Angels Brunch Bag, 1978, Aladdin, zippered bag, plastic bottle
> **BOX** $250 **BOTTLE** $50

(KP Photo)

Coca-Cola, 1947, Aladdin, Styrofoam bottle
> **BOX** $125 **BOTTLE** $20

Coco the Clown, 1970s, Gary, Styrofoam bottle
> **BOX** $90 **BOTTLE** $20

Combo Brunch Bag, 1967, Aladdin, zippered bag, steel/glass bottle
> **BOX** $300 **BOTTLE** $80

Corsage, 1970, King Seeley Thermos, steel/glass bottle
> **BOX** $70 **BOTTLE** $30

Cottage, 1974, King Seeley Thermos
> **BOX** $75 **BOTTLE** n/a

Cowboy, 1960, Universal, plain plastic bottle
> **BOX** $150 **BOTTLE** $20

Dateline Lunch Kit, 1960, Hasbro, blue/pink, no bottle
> **BOX** $250 **BOTTLE** n/a

Dawn, 1971, Aladdin, matching plastic bottle
> **BOX** $140 **BOTTLE** $35

Dawn, 1972, Aladdin, matching plastic bottle
> **BOX** $140 **BOTTLE** $35

Dawn Brunch Bag, 1971, Aladdin, zippered bag, plastic bottle
> **BOX** $180 **BOTTLE** $35

Denim Brunch Bag, 1980, Aladdin, zippered bag, plastic bottle
> **BOX** $80 **BOTTLE** $15

Deputy Dawg, King Seeley Thermos, steel/glass bottle
> **BOX** $525 **BOTTLE** $50

Deputy Dawg, 1964, Thermos, no bottle
> **BOX** $500 **BOTTLE** n/a

Donny & Marie, 1977, Aladdin, long hair version, matching plastic bottle
> **BOX** $135 **BOTTLE** $40

(KP Photo)

Donny & Marie, 1978, Aladdin, short hair version, matching plastic bottle
> **BOX** $140 **BOTTLE** $40

Donny & Marie Brunch Bag, 1977, Aladdin, zippered bag, plastic bottle
> **BOX** $150 **BOTTLE** $40

Dr. Seuss, 1970, Aladdin, plastic bottle
> **BOX** $575 **BOTTLE** $95

Dream Boat, 1960, Feldco, dark brown, Styrofoam bottle
> **BOX** $350 **BOTTLE** $20

Dream Boat, 1960, Feldco, white, Styrofoam bottle
> **BOX** $500 **BOTTLE** $20

Dream Boat, 1960, Feldco, blue, Styrofoam bottle
> **BOX** $700 **BOTTLE** $20

Eats 'n Treats, King Seeley Thermos, blue or pink steel/glass bottle
> **BOX** $175 **BOTTLE** $40

Fess Parker Kaboodle Kit, 1960s, Aladdin, matching steel bottle
> **BOX** $425 **BOTTLE** n/a

Fishing, 1970, Universal, Styrofoam bottle
> **BOX** $75 **BOTTLE** $20

Frog Flutist, 1975, Aladdin, matching plastic bottle
BOX $75 BOTTLE $20

Fun to See 'n Keep Tiger, 1960, unknown, no bottle
BOX $275 BOTTLE n/a

G.I. Joe, 1960s, Hasbro, Styrofoam thermos, Hasbro license
BOX $350 BOTTLE $20

G.I. Joe, 1989, King Seeley Thermos, generic plastic bottle
BOX $55 BOTTLE $10

Gigi, 1962, Aladdin, matching steel/glass bottle
BOX $225 BOTTLE $80

Girl & Poodle, 1960, Universal, styrofoam bottle
BOX $90 BOTTLE $20

Glamour Gal, 1960, Aladdin, steel/glass bottle
BOX $75 BOTTLE $35

Goat Butt Mountain, 1960, Universal, styrofoam bottle
BOX $60 BOTTLE $20

Go-Go Brunch Bag, 1966, Aladdin, plastic bottle
BOX $200 BOTTLE $60

Happy Powwow, 1970s, Bayville, red, blue or yellow, w/Styrofoam bottle
BOX $90 BOTTLE $20

(KP Photo)

Highway Signs Snap Pack, 1988, Avon
BOX $50 BOTTLE n/a

Holly Hobbie, 1972, Aladdin, white bag, matching plastic bottle
BOX $90 BOTTLE $30

I Love a Parade, 1970, Universal, styrofoam bottle
BOX $90 BOTTLE $20

Ice Cream Cone, 1975, Aladdin, matching plastic bottle
BOX $55 BOTTLE $20

It's a Small World, 1968, Aladdin, matching steel/glass bottle
BOX $250 BOTTLE $110

Jonathan Livingston Seagull, 1974, Aladdin, matching plastic bottle
BOX $150 BOTTLE $50

Junior Deb, 1960, Aladdin, steel/glass bottle
BOX $175 BOTTLE $50

Junior Miss Safari, 1962, Prepac, no bottle
BOX $150 BOTTLE n/a

Junior Nurse, 1963, King Seeley Thermos, steel/glass bottle
BOX $320 BOTTLE $90

Kaboodle Kit, 1960s, Aladdin, pink or white, no bottle
BOX $200 BOTTLE n/a

Kewtie Pie, Aladdin, steel/glass bottle
BOX $175 BOTTLE $60

Kodak Gold, 1970s, Aladdin
BOX $60 BOTTLE $20

Kodak II, 1970s, Aladdin
BOX $60 BOTTLE $20

Lassie, 1960s, Universal, Styrofoam bottle
BOX $120 BOTTLE $20

(KP Photo)

Laugh-In, 1960s, "Sock it to Me" brunch bag
BOX $225 BOTTLE $65

L'il Jodie (Puffy), 1985, Babcock
BOX $90 BOTTLE n/a

Linus the Lion-Hearted, 1965, Aladdin, steel/glass bottle
BOX $600 BOTTLE $125

Little Ballerina, 1975, Bayville, styrofoam bottle
BOX $75 BOTTLE $20

Little Old Schoolhouse, 1974, Dart
BOX $80 BOTTLE n/a

Love-Peace, 1972, Aladdin, matching plastic bottle
BOX $120 BOTTLE $45

(KP Photo)

Lunch 'n Munch, 1959, American Thermos, boys on raft, tan, boating bottle
BOX $400 BOTTLE $125

Lunch 'n Munch, 1959, King Seeley Thermos, space theme, red, satellite bottle
BOX $450 BOTTLE $60

Lunch 'n Munch, 1959, American Thermos, boys on raft, red, boating bottle
BOX $525 BOTTLE $125

Lunch 'n Munch, 1959, King Seeley Thermos, space theme, tan, satellite bottle
BOX $450 BOTTLE $60

M.A.S.H., 1981, 20th Century Fox, beige w/red cross and "M.A.S.H." symbols
BOX $100 BOTTLE n/a

Mam'zelle, 1971, Aladdin, light blue, plastic bottle
BOX $150 BOTTLE $60

Mardi-Grass, 1971, Aladdin, matching plastic bottle
BOX $110 BOTTLE $25

Mary Ann, 1960, Aladdin, matching steel/glass bottle
BOX $75 BOTTLE $25

Mary Ann Lunch 'N Bag, 1960, Universal, no bottle
BOX $110 BOTTLE n/a

(KP Photo)

Mary Poppins, 1973, Aladdin, matching plastic bottle
BOX $275 BOTTLE $65

Mary Poppins Brunch Bag, 1966, Aladdin, steel/glass bottle
BOX $225 BOTTLE $50

Mod Miss Brunch Bag, 1969, Aladdin, plastic bottle
    BOX $80   **BOTTLE** $30

(KP Photo)

Monkees, 1967, King Seeley Thermos, matching steel/glass bottle
    BOX $650 **BOTTLE** $125

Moon Landing, 1960, Universal, Styrofoam bottle
    BOX $250   **BOTTLE** $20

Mr. Peanut Snap Pack, 1979, Dart, snap close bag, no bottle
    BOX $90   **BOTTLE** n/a

Mushrooms, 1972, Aladdin, matching plastic bottle
    BOX $60   **BOTTLE** $45

(KP Photo)

New Zoo Revue, 1975, Aladdin, plastic bottle
    BOX $275   **BOTTLE** $60

Pac-Man (Puffy), 1985, Aladdin
    BOX $65   **BOTTLE** n/a

Peanuts, 1967, King Seeley Thermos, red "kite" box, steel/glass bottle
    BOX $175   **BOTTLE** $50

Peanuts, 1969, King Seeley Thermos, red "baseball" box, steel bottle
    BOX $150   **BOTTLE** $50

Peanuts, 1971, King Seeley Thermos, green "baseball" box, steel bottle
    BOX $200   **BOTTLE** $50

Peanuts, 1973, King Seeley Thermos, white "piano" box, steel bottle
    BOX $150   **BOTTLE** $50

Pebbles & Bamm-Bamm, 1973, Aladdin, matching plastic bottle
    BOX $275   **BOTTLE** $55

Penelope & Penny, 1970s, Gary, yellow box w/Styrofoam bottle
    BOX $80   **BOTTLE** $20

Peter Pan, 1969, Aladdin, white box, matching plastic bottle
    BOX $250   **BOTTLE** $65

Pink Panther, 1980, Aladdin, matching plastic bottle
    BOX $225   **BOTTLE** $50

Pony Tail, 1960s, Thermos, white box, original art w/gray border added, no bottle
    BOX $200   **BOTTLE** n/a

Pony Tail, 1965, King Seeley Thermos, white box, fold over lid, steel/glass bottle
    BOX $200   **BOTTLE** $40

Pony Tail Tid-Bit-Kit, 1962, King Seeley Thermos, steel/glass satellite bottle
    BOX $200   **BOTTLE** $40

Ponytails Poodle Kit, 1960, King Seeley Thermos, steel/glass bottle
    BOX $150   **BOTTLE** $20

Princess, 1963, Aladdin, steel/glass bottle
    BOX $190   **BOTTLE** $55

Psychedelic, 1969, Aladdin, yellow, matching steel/glass bottle
    BOX $150   **BOTTLE** $30

(KP Photo)

Pussycats, The, 1968, Aladdin, plastic bottle
    BOX $225   **BOTTLE** $80

Ringling Bros. Circus, 1970, King Seeley Thermos, orange box w/matching steel/glass bottle
    BOX $425 **BOTTLE** $140

Ringling Bros. Circus, 1971, King Seeley Thermos, puffy blue box, steel/glass bottle
    BOX $250   **BOTTLE** $40

Robo Warriors, 1970, unknown, no bottle
    BOX $35   **BOTTLE** n/a

Roy Rogers Saddlebag, 1960, King Seeley Thermos, cream, steel/glass bottle
    BOX $650   **BOTTLE** $95

Roy Rogers Saddlebag, 1960, King Seeley Thermos, brown, steel/glass bottle
    BOX $400   **BOTTLE** $95

Sabrina, 1972, Aladdin, yellow box w/matching plastic bottle
    BOX $230   **BOTTLE** $85

Sesame Street, 1979, Aladdin, orange, matching plastic bottle
    BOX $120   **BOTTLE** $30

Sesame Street, 1981, Aladdin, yellow, matching plastic bottle
    BOX $150   **BOTTLE** $30

(KP Photo)

Shari Lewis, 1963, Aladdin, matching steel/glass bottle
    BOX $475 **BOTTLE** $120

Sizzlers, Hot Wheels, 1971, King Seeley Thermos, matching steel/glass bottle
    BOX $375   **BOTTLE** $60

Skipper, 1965, King Seeley Thermos, steel/glass bottle
    BOX $220   **BOTTLE** $60

Sleeping Beauty, Disney, 1970, Aladdin, white box, matching plastic bottle
    BOX $240   **BOTTLE** $80

Smokey the Bear, 1965, King Seeley Thermos, steel/glass bottle
    BOX $450 **BOTTLE** $110

Snoopy Munchies Bag, 1977, King Seeley Thermos, plastic bottle
    BOX $75   **BOTTLE** $20

Snoopy Softy, 1988, King Seeley Thermos, matching plastic bottle
    BOX $45   **BOTTLE** $20

Snow White, 1975, Aladdin, white box w/matching plastic bottle
    BOX $290   **BOTTLE** $45

Snow White, Disney, 1967, unknown, fold-over lid, tapered box, no bottle
    BOX $400   **BOTTLE** n/a

Soupy Sales, 1966, King Seeley Thermos, blue box, no bottle
    BOX $600   **BOTTLE** n/a

Spirit of '76, unknown, red
    BOX $110   **BOTTLE** n/a

Marx Play Sets

Marx Play Sets

by Justin Moen

Louis Marx and his brother, David, founded Louis Marx and Co. in New York City in 1919. During the company's early years it was not known for creating original toys or generating product designs, but Louis Marx compensated by acting as a "middle man," carefully studying the latest available products, which in turn led him to accurately predict which toys would be successful so his company could manufacture them less expensively than the competition.

No toy best exemplifies the success of this approach better than the yo-yo. Although the yo-yo had already been a popular toy for a number of years, it was Marx's ability to market one of his own at a lower cost that launched the yo-yo into a new stratosphere of popularity. And by the end of the 1920s, Louis Marx and Co. sold nearly 100 million of them.

The Great Depression of course brought tremendous economic hardship and strife to everyone in America…almost everyone that is. Louis Marx and Co. was one of the very few American businesses that actually saw revenue growth during the Great Depression, thanks in large part to mass production and mass marketing through nickel and dime stores for their least expensive products, and through stores like Sears and Montgomery Ward for their most expensive products.

By the 50s Louis Marx and Co. was the largest toy manufacturer in the world, producing a wide variety of toys like: play sets, trains, toy soldiers, tin toys, and toy guns just to name a few.

But the prosperous times of the 20s-50s were all but gone by the 60s, as sales plummeted due in large part to a lack of effective advertising, especially on TV, and a general inability to change with the times, largely ignoring the trend toward electronic toys.

In 1972, at age 76, Louis Marx retired and sold his company to the Quaker Oats Co., owners of Fisher-Price at the time. While the Fisher-Price brand did well, the Marx brand continued to struggle, losing money every year under Quaker Oats. In 1976, Quaker Oats sold its Marx division to British conglomerate Dunbee-Combex-Marx. But a decline in the British economy and high interest rates led to the collapse of Dunbee-Combex-Marx. By 1978 the Marx brand was gone, and Dunbee-Combex-Marx filed for bankruptcy and was liquidated in the early-80s.

The Marx name itself has changed hands several times over the years, but neither of the Marx-branded companies today have any connection to the original Louis Marx and Co.

Although the Marx brand no longer has the presence it once did, the toys produced by Louis Marx and Co. during its golden age are widely sought out by collectors today. The most highly coveted Marx toys are the play sets of the 50s and early-60s, with many of them selling for thousands of dollars each.

But play sets are not the only Marx toys treasured by collectors. The figures that accompanied the play sets are highly desired for their craftsmanship and detail.

The **Top 10 MARX PLAY SETS** in mint condition

1. Johnny Ringo Western Frontier, 1959	$5,200
2. Johnny Tremain Revolutionary War, 1957	$2,750
3. Gunsmoke Dodge City, 1960	$2,200
4. Fire House, 1960s	$2,000
5. Ben Hur, Series 5000, 1959	$1,900
6. Sears Store, 1961	$1,850
7. Civil War Centennial, 1961	$1,800
8. Custer's Last Stand, 1963	$1,800
9. Wagon Train, 1959	$1,800
10. Untouchables, 1961	$1,550

Miniature Play Sets

101 Dalmatians, 1961, "The Barn Scene"
EX $75   **NM** $300   **MIP** $450

101 Dalmatians, 1961, "The Wedding Scene"
EX $75   **NM** $300   **MIP** $450

20 Minutes to Berlin, 1964, 174 hand painted pieces
EX $110   **NM** $320   **MIP** $520

Alice in Wonderland, 1961, new series
EX $100   **NM** $225   **MIP** $350

Attack on Fort Apache, stable, cowboys, Indians, Model No. HK-8078
EX $85   **NM** $225   **MIP** $500

Babes In Toyland, six different scenes, each
EX $25   **NM** $65   **MIP** $125

Battleground, 1963, 170 pieces, Model No. HK-6111
EX $20   **NM** $60   **MIP** $200

Blue and Gray, 1960s, 101 individual pieces, "Featured on T.V.," Model No. HK-6109
EX $95   **NM** $180   **MIP** $350

Border Battle, Mexican-American War set w/plastic Alamo, Mexican and Texan troops, horses and accessories
EX $150   **NM** $365   **MIP** $725

Charge of the Bengal Lancers, British/Turks
EX $125   **NM** $325   **MIP** $500

Charge of the Light Brigade, Sears, 216 pieces, Lancers/Cossacks
EX $175   **NM** $325   **MIP** $400

Charge of the Light Brigade, 2nd version, photo box art, Lancers/Turks
EX $110   **NM** $300   **MIP** $400

Charge of the Light Brigade, smaller version, Lancers/Russians
EX $75   **NM** $225   **MIP** $325

Cinderella, new series
EX $100   **NM** $225   **MIP** $350

Covered Wagon Attack
EX $95   **NM** $200   **MIP** $400

Custer's Last Stand, 1964, 181 pieces
EX $125   **NM** $325   **MIP** $600

Disney 3-in-1 Set, original series
EX $100   **NM** $225   **MIP** $365

Disney Circus Parade, Super Circus performers, Disneykins
EX $85   **NM** $225   **MIP** $350

Disney See and Play Castle, 1st and 2nd series Disneykins, Model No. 48-24388
EX $155   **NM** $360   **MIP** $465

Disney See and Play Doll House, 1st series Disneykins
EX $100   **NM** $265   **MIP** $350

Donald Duck, original series; Donald, Daisy, Louie, Goofy
EX $45   **NM** $100   **MIP** $150

Dumbo's Circus, original series
EX $50   **NM** $100   **MIP** $165

Fairykin, six different, each
EX $30   **NM** $80   **MIP** $125

Fairykin TV Scenes, 12 different, each
EX $8   **NM** $20   **MIP** $30

Fairykin TV Scenes Gift Set, two different, each w/six scenes, each
EX $65   **NM** $165   **MIP** $250

Fairykins 3-in-1 Diorama Set
EX $100   **NM** $265   **MIP** $400

Fairykins Gift Set, 34 in window box
EX $40   **NM** $175   **MIP** $250

Fairykins TV Scenes Boxed Set of Eight
EX $45   **NM** $200   **MIP** $250

Fort Apache, large set, HQ building., cavalry/cowboys/Indians
EX $115   **NM** $295   **MIP** $375

Fort Apache, 1963, 90 pieces, Indians, Model No. HK-7526
EX $55   **NM** $80   **MIP** $185

Guerrilla Warfare, 1960s, Viet Cong
EX $275   **NM** $350   **MIP** $450

Huckleberry Hound Presents, two different, each
EX $75   **NM** $115   **MIP** $175

Invasion Day, 1964, 304 pieces, miniature D-Day Invasion set
EX $70   **NM** $205   **MIP** $450

Jungle, smaller than Jungle Safari
EX $50   **NM** $85   **MIP** $175

Jungle Safari, 260 pieces, hunters/natives
EX $55   **NM** $100   **MIP** $225

Knights and Castle, 1963, 132 pieces, Model No. HK-7563
EX $130   **NM** $200   **MIP** $315

Knights and Castle, 1964, 64 pieces, Model No. HK-7562
EX $95   **NM** $175   **MIP** $275

Knights and Vikings, 1964, 143 pieces
EX $145   **NM** $275   **MIP** $425

Lady and the Tramp, 1961, new series
EX $100   **NM** $225   **MIP** $350

Lost Boys, new series
EX $100   **NM** $225   **MIP** $350

Lost Boys, 1961, second series
EX $40   **NM** $120   **MIP** $200

Ludwig Von Drake, RCA premium set
EX $65   **NM** $130   **MIP** $200

Ludwig Von Drake, 1962, "The Professor Misses"
EX $50   **NM** $100   **MIP** $150

Ludwig Von Drake, 1962, "The Nearsighted Professor"
EX $50   **NM** $115   **MIP** $165

Mickey Mouse and Friends, original series, display box
EX $50   **NM** $100   **MIP** $150

Munchville, vegetable characters
EX $65   **NM** $165   **MIP** $265

Noah's Ark, Ward's version, soft
plastic figures
EX $20   NM $50   **MIP** $85

Noah's Ark, 1968, 100 pieces
EX $28   NM $70   **MIP** $110

Over The Top, World War I, Germans/
Doughboys
EX $200 NM $600   **MIP** $950

Panchito Western, original series,
display box
EX $50   NM $100   **MIP** $150

Pinocchio, six different sets, each
original series, display box
EX $65   NM $165   **MIP** $280

Pinocchio 3-in-1 Set
EX $115 NM $295   **MIP** $450

Quick Draw McGraw, two different, each
EX $75   NM $115   **MIP** $200

Revolutionary War, British/Colonials
EX $95   NM $250   **MIP** $475

Sands of Iwo Jima, 1963, 205 pieces
EX $115 NM $210   **MIP** $325

Sands of Iwo Jima, 1963, 88 pieces
EX $75   NM $145   **MIP** $225

Sands of Iwo Jima, 1964, 296 pieces
EX $150 NM $295   **MIP** $425

See and Play Dollhouse, American
Beauties/Campus Cuties
EX $75   NM $175   **MIP** $350

Sleeping Beauty, 1961, new series
EX $75   NM $175   **MIP** $275

Snow White and the Seven Dwarfs,
original series, display box
EX $50   NM $100   **MIP** $185

Sunshine Farm Set, farmers and
animals
EX $45   NM $115   **MIP** $175

Sword in the Stone, British only
Disney release
EX $310 NM $1050 **MIP** $1560

Ten Commandments, Montgomery
Ward
EX $150 NM $395   **MIP** $600

Three Little Pigs, new series
EX $100 NM $225   **MIP** $350

Tiger Town, 1960s, ENCO-like tigers
EX $75   NM $175   **MIP** $300

Top Cat, three different, each
EX $75   NM $115   **MIP** $200

Troll Village, includes hillside, troll
figures, ox cart, trees, fence
sections and accessories
EX $85   NM $220   **MIP** $360

TV-Tinykins Gift Set, set of 34 figures
EX $115 NM $350   **MIP** $550

TV-Tinykins TV Scenes, 12 different,
each
EX $12   NM $35   **MIP** $50

Western Town, over 170 pieces, hand
painted buildings, stagecoach,
fence sections, figures and
accessories, Model No. 48-24398
EX $55   NM $160   **MIP** $265

Wooden Horse of Troy, British only
issue
EX $175 NM $600   **MIP** $850

Zorro, 1958, painted figures
EX $40   NM $80   **MIP** $125

Play Sets

Adventures of Robin Hood, 1956,
Richard Greene TV series, Model
No. 4722
EX $300 NM $750   **MIP** $1250

Alamo, 1957, only two cannons,
w/metal Alamo, Model No. 3546
EX $100 NM $300   **MIP** $500

Alamo, 1960, for 54mm figures, four
cannons, Model No. 3534
EX $140 NM $250   **MIP** $400

Alamo, 1960, Sears Exclusive, Model
No. 3543
EX $50   NM $140   **MIP** $265

Alaska, 1959, 100 pieces including:
igloos, polar bears, kayak, dog sled
team, litho storefront, prospectors,
just in time for Alaskan statehood,
this is a neat set, Model No. 3707-8
EX $300 NM $650   **MIP** $1000

Alaska, 1960, Model No. 2755-6
EX $250 NM $550   **MIP** $800

American Airlines Astro Jet Port,
1961, Model No. 4821-2
EX $150 NM $250   **MIP** $450

**American Airlines International Jet
Port,** 1960, 98 pieces, Model
No. 4810
EX $150 NM $250   **MIP** $450

Arctic Explorer, 1958, Series 2000,
Model No. 3702
EX $250 NM $475   **MIP** $725

Army Combat Set, 1963, Sears
Exclusive, 411 pieces, Model
No. 4158
EX $100 NM $300   **MIP** $475

Army Combat Training Center, 1958,
Model No. 4153
EX $40   NM $60   **MIP** $95

Army Combat Training Center, 1959,
Model No. 2654
EX $35   NM $55   **MIP** $90

Babyland Nursery, 1955, Model
No. 3379-80
EX $125 NM $225   **MIP** $375

Bar-M Ranch, 1957, Model No. 3956
EX $65   NM $125   **MIP** $200

Battle of Iwo Jima, 1964, 247 pieces,
U.S. and Japanese, Model No. 4147
EX $125 NM $250   **MIP** $425

Battle of Iwo Jima, 1964, 128 pieces,
Sears Exclusive, Model No. 4154
EX $50   NM $110   **MIP** $185

Battle of Little Big Horn, 1972,
includes cavalrymen, Indians,

horses, wagons, totem pole,
tepees, and other accessories,
Model No. 4679MO
EX $140 **NM** $265   **MIP** $425

Battle of the Blue & Gray, Series 2000,
large set, Model No. 4658
EX $250 **NM** $700   **MIP** $1250

Battle of the Blue & Gray, 1959, Series
2000, 54mm, Model No. 4745-6
EX $175 **NM** $375   **MIP** $625

Battle of the Blue & Gray, 1960, Series
1000, small set, no house, Model
No. 2645-6
EX $80 **NM** $240   **MIP** $425

Battle of the Blue & Gray, 1963,
centennial edition, Model No. 4744
EX $200 **NM** $700   **MIP** $1250

Battlefield, 1958, Series 5000, Model
No. 4756
EX $25 **NM** $95   **MIP** $175

Battleground, 1958, largest of military
sets, Model No. 4749-50
EX $155 **NM** $395   **MIP** $660

Battleground, 1959, 180 pieces,
Model No. 4751
EX $40 **NM** $110   **MIP** $190

Battleground, 1960s, U.S. and Nazi
troops, Model No. 4756
EX $45 **NM** $100   **MIP** $165

Battleground, 1962, 200 pieces,
Model No. 4754
EX $40 **NM** $110   **MIP** $195

Battleground, 1965, Montgomery
Ward, Model No. 4139
EX $80 **NM** $240   **MIP** $425

Battleground, 1965, Sears, 160
pieces, Model No. 4150
EX $70 **NM** $210   **MIP** $350

Battleground, 1971, Montgomery
Ward Exclusive, Model No. 4752
EX $100 **NM** $285   **MIP** $465

Battleground Convoy, 1962, Model
No. 3745-6
EX $40 **NM** $125   **MIP** $275

Beach Head Landing Set, U.S. and
Nazi Troops, Model No. 4939
EX $25 **NM** $65   **MIP** $110

Ben Hur, blister card, Model No. 2648
EX $25 **NM** $95   **MIP** $150

Ben Hur, 1959, Series 5000, large set,
Model No. 4701
EX $475 **NM** $1100   **MIP** $1900

Ben Hur, 1959, Series 2000, medium
set, Model No. 4702
EX $255 **NM** $770   **MIP** $1450

Ben Hur, 1959, 132 pieces, Model
No. 4696
EX $185 **NM** $275   **MIP** $525

Big Inch Pipeline, 1963, 200 pieces,
Model No. 6008
EX $85 **NM** $250   **MIP** $400

Big Top Circus, 1952, Model No. 4310
EX $125 **NM** $325   **MIP** $550

Boot Camp, Carry-All, tin box set,
w/tank, half-track, jeep, artillery,
figures and tents, Model No. 4645
EX $35 **NM** $135   **MIP** $215

Boy Scout
EX $115 **NM** $600   **MIP** $925

Boys Camp, 1956, Model No. 4103
EX $130 **NM** $395   **MIP** $650

Cape Canaveral, 1959, Sears set,
Model No. 5963
EX $90 **NM** $325   **MIP** $510

Cape Canaveral, 1960, Series 2000,
Model No. 4524
EX $95 **NM** $195   **MIP** $325

Cape Canaveral Missile Center,
1959, includes four-stage rocket,
missile and launcher, flying saucer
and launcher, scientists, and other
accessories, Model No. 2656
EX $75 **NM** $160   **MIP** $265

Cape Canaveral Missile Center,
1959, Model No. 4528
EX $90 **NM** $240   **MIP** $400

Cape Canaveral Missile Center,
1961, Model No. 4525
EX $65 **NM** $195   **MIP** $310

Cape Canaveral Missile Set, 1958,
Model No. 4526
EX $65 **NM** $225   **MIP** $350

Cape Kennedy Carry All, 1968, tin box
set, Model No. 4625
EX $45 **NM** $65   **MIP** $110

**Captain Gallant of the Foreign
Legion,** 1956, includes foreign
legion soldiers, sheiks, horses,
camel and "Cuffy," a hard-to-find
set, Model No. 4729/4730
EX $210 **NM** $620   **MIP** $1200

Captain Space Solar Academy, 1953,
Model No. 7026
EX $100 **NM** $325   **MIP** $500

Captain Space Solar Port, 1954,
Model No. 7018
EX $75 **NM** $250   **MIP** $425

Castle and Moat Set, Sears Exclusive,
Model No. 4734
EX $65 **NM** $260   **MIP** $400

Cattle Drive, 1972-73, Model No. 3983
EX $70 **NM** $250   **MIP** $385

Civil War Centennial, 1961, Model
No. 5929
EX $400 **NM** $1200   **MIP** $1800

Comanche Pass, 1976, Model No. 3416
EX $30 **NM** $130   **MIP** $225

Complete Happitime Dairy Farm,
Sears, Model No. 5957
EX $85 **NM** $325   **MIP** $510

Complete U.S. Army Training Center, 1954, Model No. 4145

EX $80 NM $210   MIP $350

Construction Camp, 1954, includes trucks, figures, buildings and accessories, Model No. 4439

EX $100 NM $290   MIP $475

Construction Camp, 1956, 54mm, Series 1000, includes: field office building, workmen, heavy duty equipment (friction-power dozer, road roller, high-lift loader), Model No. 4442

EX $120 NM $330   MIP $600

Cowboy And Indian Camp, 1953, Model No. 3950

EX $100 NM $275   MIP $450

Custer's Last Stand, 1956, Series 500, Model No. 4779

EX $110 NM $325   MIP $575

Custer's Last Stand, 1963, Sears, 187 pieces, Model No. 4670

EX $195 NM $1200   MIP $1800

D.E.W. Defense Line Arctic Satellite Base, Model No. 4802

EX $125 NM $300   MIP $500

Daktari, Model No. 3718

EX $100 NM $325   MIP $500

Daktari, 1967, 110 pieces, Model No. 3717

EX $100 NM $300   MIP $525

Daktari, 1967, 140 pieces, Model No. 3720

EX $145 NM $395   MIP $660

Daniel Boone Frontier, 1958, includes covered wagon and horses w/driver, Indians, Frontiersman, and other accessories, Model No. 1393

EX $85 NM $235   MIP $375

Daniel Boone Wilderness Scout, 1964, Model No. 0670

EX $90 NM $225   MIP $385

Daniel Boone Wilderness Scout, 1964, Model No. 0631

EX $85 NM $225   MIP $425

Daniel Boone Wilderness Scout, 1964, Model No. 2640

EX $120 NM $360   MIP $650

Davy Crockett at the Alamo, Model No. 3442

EX $150 NM $360   MIP $650

Davy Crockett at the Alamo, 1955, official Walt Disney, biggest set, Model No. 3544

EX $160 NM $500   MIP $825

Davy Crockett at the Alamo, 1955, official Walt Disney, 100 pieces, first set, Model No. 3530

EX $80 NM $275   MIP $450

D-Day Army Set, U.S. and Nazi troops, Model No. 6027

EX $125 NM $300   MIP $575

Desert Fox, 1966, 244 pieces, Model No. 4177

EX $105 NM $275   MIP $475

Desert Patrol, 1967, U.S. and Nazi troops, Model No. 4174

EX $85 NM $185   MIP $325

Farm Set, Model No. 6006

EX $50 NM $195   MIP $300

Farm Set, Model No. 6050

EX $50 NM $180   MIP $275

Farm Set, 1958, 100 pieces, Series 2000, Model No. 3948

EX $80 NM $250   MIP $400

Farm Set, 1965, 1968-73, w/20" steel barn, 14 farm animals, five sections of fence, four rows of crops, plastic tractor w/seven attachments, farm tools, feed boxes, Model No. 5942

EX $45 NM $160   MIP $250

Farm Set, 1969, deluxe, Model No. 3953

EX $75 NM $225   MIP $375

Fighting Knights Carry All, 1966-68, includes litho walls, plastic towers, metallic and solid color knights, catapults and horses, Model No. 4635

EX $55 NM $140   MIP $200

Fire House, Model No. 4819

EX $225 NM $700   MIP $1100

Fire House, w/two friction vehicles, Model No. 4820

EX $500 NM $1500   MIP $2000

Flintstones, The, 1960s, Bedrock, stone fences, buildings, palm trees, play mat, vehicles, figures, dinosaurs, Model No. 4672

EX $175 NM $250   MIP $575

Fort Apache, Model No. 3616

EX $45 NM $90   MIP $150

Fort Apache, Model No. 6068

EX $40 NM $100   MIP $165

Fort Apache, Sears, Model No. 6059

EX $20 NM $35   MIP $75

Fort Apache, giant set, Model No. 3685

EX $140 NM $425   MIP $700

Fort Apache, Model No. 3681A

EX $35 NM $90   MIP $150

Fort Apache, Model No. 3682

EX $15 NM $50   MIP $85

Fort Apache, 1965, Sears, 335 pieces, Model No. 6063

EX $125 NM $315   MIP $550

Fort Apache, 1965, Sears, 147 pieces

EX $45 NM $120   MIP $225

Fort Apache, 1967, Model No. 3681

EX $55 NM $135   MIP $225

Fort Apache, 1970s, Model No. 4202

EX $25 NM $50   MIP $80

Fort Apache, 1972, Sears, over 100 pieces including: plastic fort, U.S. flag, Indians, tepee, horses, soldiers, cannon, and accessories, Model No. 59093C

EX $45   **NM** $95   **MIP** $160

Fort Apache, 1976, Model No. 3681

EX $50   **NM** $120   **MIP** $210

Fort Apache Carry All, 1967, w/plastic block houses, cowboys, horses and Indians, Model No. 4685

EX $35   **NM** $55   **MIP** $100

Fort Apache Rin Tin Tin, 1956, early, 60mm, Model No. 3627

EX $125   **NM** $300   **MIP** $475

Fort Apache Rin Tin Tin, 1957, 54mm, Model No. 3658

EX $100   **NM** $250   **MIP** $375

Fort Apache Rin Tin Tin, 1958, mixed scale set, Model No. 3957

EX $90   **NM** $275   **MIP** $350

Fort Apache Stockade, 1951, Model No. 3610

EX $70   **NM** $210   **MIP** $350

Fort Apache Stockade, 1953, includes stockade, block house, ladders, cowboys and Indians, Model No. 3612

EX $55   **NM** $160   **MIP** $260

Fort Apache Stockade, 1960, Series 2000, 60mm figures, Model No. 3660

EX $85   **NM** $225   **MIP** $400

Fort Apache Stockade, 1961, Series 5000 includes: cavalry HQ building, stockade fence and gate block houses, cannon, cavarly men and horses, tepee, Indian figures, totem pole, canoe, horses, and other accessories

EX $60   **NM** $170   **MIP** $285

Fort Apache w/Famous Americans, Model No. 3636

EX $55   **NM** $165   **MIP** $270

Fort Dearborn, w/plastic walls, Model No. 3688

EX $80   **NM** $240   **MIP** $400

Fort Dearborn, larger set, Model No. 3514

EX $20   **NM** $60   **MIP** $100

Fort Dearborn, 1952, w/metal walls, Model No. 3510

EX $100   **NM** $255   **MIP** $375

Fort Mohawk, 1958, British, Colonials, Indians, 54mm, Model No. 3751-2

EX $100   **NM** $325   **MIP** $550

Fort Pitt, 1959, Series 1000, 54mm, Model No. 3742

EX $100   **NM** $300   **MIP** $475

Fort Pitt, 1959, Series 750, 54mm, Model No. 3741

EX $65   **NM** $260   **MIP** $400

Four-Level Allstate Service Station, 1962, Model No. 3499

EX $80   **NM** $325   **MIP** $500

Four-Level Parking Garage, Model No. 3511

EX $40   **NM** $200   **MIP** $300

Four-Level Parking Garage, Model No. 3502

EX $40   **NM** $120   **MIP** $200

Freight Trucking Terminal, 1950, plastic trucks, Model No. 5220

EX $30   **NM** $90   **MIP** $150

Freight Trucking Terminal, 1950, friction trucks, Model No. 5422

EX $30   **NM** $90   **MIP** $150

Galaxy Command, 1976, Model No. 4206

EX $25   **NM** $55   **MIP** $90

Gallant Men, official set from TV series, Model No. 4634

EX $70   **NM** $290   **MIP** $450

Gallant Men Army, 1963, U.S. troops, Model No. 4632

EX $65   **NM** $260   **MIP** $400

Gunsmoke Dodge City, 1960, official, Series 2000, 80 pieces including: Gunsmoke characters, town building, ranch house, gold mine, stagecoach, wagon, oxen, horses, cowboys, trees, steers, and other accessories, Model No. 4268

EX $375 **NM** $1300   **MIP** $2200

Happi-time Army and Air Force Training Center, 1954, Sears, 147 pieces, Model No. 4159

EX $50   **NM** $150   **MIP** $250

Happi-time Civil War Centennial, 1962, Sears, Model No. 5929

EX $115   **NM** $455   **MIP** $700

Happi-Time Deluxe Farm Set, 1958, Sears, Series 2000, tin litho barn and silo, Model No. 3949

EX $50   **NM** $150   **MIP** $250

Happi-time Farm Set, Sears, Model No. 3480

EX $35   **NM** $95   **MIP** $150

Happi-Time Farm Set, 1953, Sears, barn, silo, no figures, 60mm animals and implements, Model No. 3940

EX $65   **NM** $150   **MIP** $275

Happi-Time Farm Set, 1958, Sears, Series 2000, 100 pieces, chicken shed, Model No. 3943

EX $65   **NM** $150   **MIP** $260

Happi-Time Farm Set, 1959-60, Sears, Deluxe Platform Farm, barn and two silos on raised platform, two-wheel cart pictured on box never included, Model No. 5931

EX $100   **NM** $225   **MIP** $375

Happi-time Roy Rogers Rodeo Ranch, 1953, Sears, Model No. 3990

EX $90   **NM** $185   **MIP** $350

Heritage Battle of the Alamo, 1972, Heritage Series, Model No. 59091

EX $80   **NM** $240   **MIP** $400

History in the Pacific, 1972-73, Model No. 4164

EX $100   **NM** $285   **MIP** $450

Holiday Turnpike, battery-operated w/HO scale vehicles, Model No. 5230

EX $10   **NM** $30   **MIP** $45

I.G.Y. Arctic Satellite Base, 1959, Series 1000, w/quonset hut, missiles, launchers, explorer figures, eskimo figures, igloos, sleds, animals, weather station, skis, etc, a true "cold war" play set, for sure, Model No. 4800
EX $250   NM $750   MIP $1250

Indian Warfare, Series 2000, Model No. 4778
EX $65   NM $260   MIP $400

International Airport, 1973, terminal, planes, cars, trucks, people, accessories, Model No. 4814
EX $35   NM $75   MIP $150

Irrigated Farm Set, working pump, Model No. 6021
EX $7   NM $20   MIP $35

Johnny Apollo Moon Launch Center, 1970, Model No. 4630
EX $75   NM $150   MIP $275

Johnny Ringo Western Frontier Set, 1959, Series 2000, Model No. 4784
EX $1400 NM $2750   MIP $5200

Johnny Tremain Revolutionary War, 1957, official Walt Disney, Series 1000, Model No. 3401-2
EX $635 NM $1400   MIP $2750

Jungle, metal trading post, Series 500, Model No. 3705
EX $110   NM $325   MIP $550

Jungle, 1960, 48 pieces, Sears, large animals, Model No. 3716
EX $25   NM $95   MIP $150

Jungle Jim, 1957, official, Series 1000, includes: HQ building, hunters, natives, wild animals, thatched huts, log fence, and accessories, Model No. 3705-6
EX $290   NM $875   MIP $1450

King Arthur's Castle Medieval Play Set, 1960s, w/22 knights on horses, benches, working drawbridge, accessories, Model No. 4800
EX $100   NM $200   MIP $325

Knights and Vikings, Model No. 4773
EX $50   NM $90   MIP $150

Knights and Vikings, 1972, Model No. 4743
EX $60   NM $150   MIP $275

Knights and Vikings, 1973, includes plastic castle and mat w/metallic silver knights fighting Vikings, Model No. 4733
EX $65   NM $175   MIP $285

Lazy Day Farm, 1951, Wards, barn, 60mm people, no silos, animals, Model No. 3931
EX $60   NM $150   MIP $250

Lazy Day Farm Set, 1958, Wards, Series 1000, no silo, 54mm people and animals, Model No. 3942
EX $50   NM $150   MIP $250

Lazy Day Farm Set, 1960, Wards, 100 pieces, Model No. 3945
EX $60   NM $165   MIP $275

Little Red School House, 1956, Model No. 3381-2
EX $90   NM $270   MIP $450

Lone Ranger Ranch, 1957, Series 500, includes: Lone Ranger, Tonto, cabin, gateway, cowboys, horses, saddles, Indians, and accessories, Model No. 3969
EX $125   NM $260   MIP $475

Lone Ranger Rodeo Set, 1952-53, Model No. 3696
EX $65   NM $130   MIP $210

Medieval Castle, Sears, w/knights and Vikings, Model No. 4734
EX $100   NM $290   MIP $465

Medieval Castle, w/knights and Vikings, Model No. 4733
EX $60   NM $130   MIP $210

Medieval Castle, w/knights and Vikings, Model No. 4707
EX $45   NM $110   MIP $195

Medieval Castle, 1954, Model No. 4709
EX $35   NM $95   MIP $150

Medieval Castle, 1959, Sears, Series 2000, Model No. 4708
EX $125   NM $350   MIP $600

Medieval Castle, 1960, metallic knights, castle, horses, tree, and catapult, Model No. 4700
EX $80   NM $295   MIP $460

Medieval Castle, 1964, gold knights, moat, Model No. 4704
EX $40   NM $90   MIP $150

Medieval Castle Fort, 1953, included: fortress, figures, horses, cannons, and accessories, Model No. 4709-10
EX $65   NM $150   MIP $260

Midtown Service Station, 1960, electric elevator, pumps w/canopy, attendants, cars, and accessories, Model No. 3420
EX $52   NM $155   MIP $255

Midtown Shopping Center, Model No. 2644
EX $30   NM $90   MIP $150

Military Academy, 1954, w/six generals, Model No. 4718
EX $100   NM $350   MIP $500

Modern Farm Set, 1951, 54mm, Model No. 3931
EX $50   NM $150   MIP $250

Modern Farm Set, 1967, Model No. 3932

EX $65   NM $185   MIP $310

Modern Farm Set, c.1951, metal barn, fence, tractor, animals, Model No. 3925

EX $50   NM $150   MIP $250

Modern Service Center, 1962, Model No. 3471

EX $70   NM $210   MIP $350

Modern Service Station, 1966, plastic building w/gray metal base, plastic vehicles, gas pumps, mechanics and attendants, Model No. 6044

EX $45   NM $115   MIP $190

Navarone Mountain Battleground Set, 1976, included five-level plastic mountain w/two gun emplacements, German troops, ladders, communication and radio benches, tank, landing craft, halftrack, jeep, American soldiers, over 200 pieces, Model No. 3412

EX $45   NM $120   MIP $200

New Car Sales and Service, w/battery powered light, Model No. 3466, 3465

EX $80   NM $295   MIP $460

One Million, B.C., 1970s

EX $50   NM $115   MIP $225

Operation Moon Base, 1962, includes vehicles, moon base structure, space man, moon ship, and accessories, Model No. 4653-4

EX $95   NM $275   MIP $465

Pet Shop, Model No. 4209

EX $60   NM $230   MIP $350

Pet Shop, 1953, includes Shop building, fence, tree, cages, crates, dogs, monkees, rabbits, birds, aquarium, and accessories, Model No. 4209-10

EX $65   NM $240   MIP $365

Prehistoric, 1969, Model No. 3398

EX $35   NM $105   MIP $175

Prehistoric Dinosaur, 1978, Model No. 4208

EX $35   NM $105   MIP $175

Prehistoric Times, Series 500, plain box that reads, "Prehistoric Play Set Complete w/Animals in Natural Setting," Model No. 3389

EX $50   NM $120   MIP $195

Prehistoric Times, Model No. 2650

EX $35   NM $130   MIP $200

Prehistoric Times, Model No. 3388

EX $30   NM $75   MIP $150

Prehistoric Times, Model No. 3391

EX $20   NM $55   MIP $95

Prehistoric Times, 1957, Series 1000, big set, includes: molded terrain base, cavemen, prehistoric animals, palm trees, ferns, tree stumps, and accessories, Model No. 3390

EX $85   NM $230   MIP $400

Prince Valiant Castle, 1954, has figures, Model No. 4706

EX $110   NM $320   MIP $550

Prince Valiant Castle, 1955, Model No. 4705

EX $100   NM $270   MIP $475

Project Apollo Cape Kennedy, Model No. 4523

EX $45   NM $75   MIP $125

Project Apollo Moon Landing, Model No. 4646

EX $55   NM $150   MIP $250

Project Mercury Cape Canaveral, 1959, Model No. 4524

EX $100   NM $270   MIP $450

Raytheon Missile Test Center, 1961, Model No. 603-A

EX $70   NM $180   MIP $325

Real Life Western Wagon, Model No. 4998

EX $15   NM $45   MIP $75

Red River Gang, 1970s, mini set w/cowboys, Model No. 4104

EX $35   NM $105   MIP $175

Revolutionary War, 1950s, Series 1000, includes British Redcoats, stone wall section, shooting cannon, trees, litho building, Revolutionary troops, and more, Model No. 3404
EX $125 **NM** $500 **MIP** $850

Revolutionary War, 1957, Series 500, Model No. 3401
EX $225 **NM** $550 **MIP** $1150

Revolutionary War, 1959, No. 3408, 80 pieces, Sears, Model No. 3408
EX $100 **NM** $390 **MIP** $650

Rex Mars Planet Patrol, Model No. 7040
EX $125 **NM** $310 **MIP** $575

Rex Mars Space Drome, 1954, Model No. 7016
EX $150 **NM** $395 **MIP** $700

Rifleman Ranch, The, 1959, Model No. 3997-8
EX $130 **NM** $455 **MIP** $750

Rin Tin Tin at Fort Apache, 1956, Series 5000, Model No. 3686R
EX $250 **NM** $725 **MIP** $1250

Rin Tin Tin at Fort Apache, 1956, Series 500, 60mm, Model No. 3628
EX $160 **NM** $475 **MIP** $800

Robin Hood Castle, 1956, 60mm, Model No. 4717
EX $175 **NM** $375 **MIP** $660

Robin Hood Castle, 1958, 54mm, Model No. 4718
EX $125 **NM** $325 **MIP** $500

Robin Hood Castle Set, 1950s, Series 1000, 54mm, Model No. 4724
EX $100 **NM** $225 **MIP** $400

Roy Rogers Double R Bar Ranch, 1962, Model No. 3982
EX $100 **NM** $300 **MIP** $525

Roy Rogers Mineral City, 1958, 95 pieces, Model No. 4227
EX $110 **NM** $300 **MIP** $500

Roy Rogers Ranch, 1950s, w/ranch kids, Model No. 3980
EX $200 **NM** $300 **MIP** $525

Roy Rogers Rodeo, 1952, w/fence pieces, Model No. 3689-90
EX $60 **NM** $80 **MIP** $150

Roy Rogers Rodeo Ranch, 54mm, Model No. 3988
EX $90 **NM** $195 **MIP** $345

Roy Rogers Rodeo Ranch, Series 2000, Model No. 3996
EX $130 **NM** $395 **MIP** $650

Roy Rogers Rodeo Ranch, 1952, Model No. 3979
EX $55 **NM** $165 **MIP** $275

Roy Rogers Rodeo Ranch, 1952, 60mm, includes: bunk house, rodeo chute, cowboys, horses, steers, saddles, bridles, fence, and accessories, Model No. 3985
EX $75 **NM** $140 **MIP** $235

Roy Rogers Rodeo Ranch, 1958, Model No. 3986R
EX $250 **NM** $750 **MIP** $1250

Roy Rogers Western Town, official, Series 5000, Model No. 4259
EX $95 **NM** $235 **MIP** $450

Roy Rogers Western Town, Model No. 4216
EX $80 **NM** $240 **MIP** $400

Roy Rogers Western Town, 1952, large set, Mineral City, Model No. 4257-8
EX $160 **NM** $475 **MIP** $800

Sears Store, 1961, Allstate box, Model No. 5490
EX $350 **NM** $1200 **MIP** $1850

Service Station, Model No. 5459
EX $25 **NM** $60 **MIP** $125

Service Station, w/parking garage, includes: service station, cars, attendants, high-level parking garage, Model No. 3485
EX $115 **NM** $325 **MIP** $540

Service Station, w/elevator, Model No. 3495
EX $30 **NM** $90 **MIP** $150

Service Station, deluxe, Model No. 3501
EX $50 **NM** $150 **MIP** $250

Shopping Center, 1962, Model No. 3755-6
EX $40 **NM** $120 **MIP** $200

Silver City Frontier Town, 1955, Model No. 4219-20
EX $50 **NM** $150 **MIP** $250

Silver City Western Town, 1956, has Custer, Boone, Carson, Buffalo Bill, Sitting Bull, Model No. 4220
EX $50 **NM** $150 **MIP** $250

Silver City Western Town (Ward's), 1954, Montgomery Wards Exclusive, Model No. 4256
EX $65 **NM** $150 **MIP** $275

Skyscraper, 1957, working elevator, Model No. 5449-50
EX $155 **NM** $800 **MIP** $1200

Skyscraper (Ward's), 1957, Montgomery Ward's Exclusive, working elevator and light, Model No. 5450
EX $155 **NM** $800 **MIP** $1250

Sons of Liberty, 1972, Sears Exclusive set includes: litho building, plastic figures and accessories, flag and stand, historic booklet, Model No. 4170
EX $55 **NM** $155 **MIP** $260

Star Station Seven, 1978, 32 pieces
EX $10 **NM** $30 **MIP** $50

Strategic Air Command, Model No. 6013
EX $130 **NM** $520 **MIP** $800

Super Circus, 1952, w/character figures, Model No. 4320
EX $75   **NM** $290   **MIP** $450

Super Circus, 1952, over 70 pieces, including big top, Model No. 4319
EX $95   **NM** $245   **MIP** $435

Tactical Air Command, 1970s, Model No. 4106
EX $25   **NM** $50   **MIP** $85

Tales of Wells Fargo, Model No. 4263
EX $80   **NM** $240   **MIP** $450

Tales of Wells Fargo, Series 1000, play set includes Wells Fargo office, western town building, stagecoach, horses and cowboys, Indians, and accessories, Model No. 4264
EX $155   **NM** $465   **MIP** $760

Tales of Wells Fargo, Model No. 4262
EX $150   **NM** $450   **MIP** $750

Tales of Wells Fargo Train Set, 1959, w/electric train, Model No. 54752
EX $240   **NM** $600   **MIP** $800

Tank Battle, 1964, Sears, U.S., Nazi troops, Model No. 6056
EX $40   **NM** $120   **MIP** $200

Tank Battle, 1964, U.S., Nazi troops, Model No. 6060
EX $60   **NM** $120   **MIP** $225

Tom Corbett Space Academy, 1952, No. 7099, nine wall sections and gate
EX $150   **NM** $375   **MIP** $710

Treasure Cove Pirate Set, 1962, Model No. 4597-8
EX $50   **NM** $125   **MIP** $210

Turnpike Service Center, 1961, Model No. 3459-60
EX $100   **NM** $300   **MIP** $500

U.S. Air Force, 1963, Model No. 4807
EX $30   **NM** $90   **MIP** $160

U.S. Armed Forces, Model No. 4151
EX $70   **NM** $210   **MIP** $350

U.S. Armed Forces Training Center, Model No. 4150
EX $50   **NM** $150   **MIP** $265

U.S. Armed Forces Training Center, Marines, soldiers, sailors, airmen, tin litho building, Model No. 4144
EX $40   **NM** $160   **MIP** $250

U.S. Armed Forces Training Center, 1955, Series 500, "Featuring Guided Missiles," and including: HQ building, flag, fence, jet plane, compass, helicopter, Air Force, Navy, Army and Marines figures, Model No. 4149-50
EX $90   **NM** $265   **MIP** $430

U.S. Armed Forces Training Center, 1956, includes barracks, tents, planes, soldiers, Marines, sailors, Air Force personnel, guns, and accessories, Model No. 4158
EX $115   **NM** $340   **MIP** $600

U.S. Army Mobile Set, 1956, flat figures, includes vehicles, Model No. 3655
EX $25   **NM** $75   **MIP** $125

U.S. Army Training Center, Model No. 4153
EX $20   **NM** $60   **MIP** $100

U.S. Army Training Center, Model No. 4122
EX $25   **NM** $60   **MIP** $100

U.S. Army Training Center, Model No. 3378
EX $30   **NM** $65   **MIP** $110

U.S. Army Training Center, Model No. 3146
EX $30   **NM** $55   **MIP** $95

U.S. Army Training Center, 1954, 45mm, includes: HQ building, vehicle, soldiers and accessories, Model No. 4123
EX $30   **NM** $80   **MIP** $130

Untouchables, 1961, 90 pieces including: buildings, figures, guns, street layout, furniture, and accessories, Model No. 4676
EX $325   **NM** $985   **MIP** $1550

Vikings and Knights, Model No. 6053
EX $60   **NM** $180   **MIP** $300

Wagon Train, 1959, official, Series 2000, Model No. 4788
EX $120   **NM** $360   **MIP** $600

Wagon Train, 1959, official, Series 5000, Model No. 4888
EX $275   **NM** $975   **MIP** $1800

Wagon Train, 1960, Series 1000, X Team, Model No. 4805
EX $160   **NM** $480   **MIP** $800

Walt Disney Television Playhouse, 1953, Model No. 4352
EX $120   **NM** $360   **MIP** $600

Walt Disney Television Playhouse, 1953, Peter Pan figures, Model No. 4352
EX $105   **NM** $420   **MIP** $750

Walt Disney Television Playhouse, 1953, Model No. 4350
EX $100   **NM** $300   **MIP** $475

Walt Disney's Zorro, 1958, official, Series 1000, includes buildings, horses, figures and accessories, Model No. 3754
EX $275   **NM** $780   **MIP** $1400

PEZ

Invented in 1948, the PEZ dispenser has been around for 65 years. It is believed the Full Body Santa , Full Body Robot and the 1950s space gun were the first dispensers marketed toward children.

Today, collecting PEZ dispensers is still gaining popularity. It seems more people than ever are interested in these cute character pieces. Attendance at national PEZ conventions is still strong.

The items that seem to sell the best and have the most interest are the contemporary pieces that sell for $5 or less.

Prices and demand for recent additions have held steady while mid-range vintage pieces have softened to a degree. The mid-range pieces, priced from $50-$200, may have come down in price as much as 15-25 percent in some cases. High-end dispensers and related material continue to have strong interest—and selling prices reflect that fact.

Current sales show, without a doubt, it's a buyers market. If you have been collecting the new releases for awhile and have been reluctant to move to the next price plateau, now is a great time to pick up some good deals.

Word of caution: When purchasing vintage PEZ, know what you are buying and, when possible, buy from a reputable dealer. Several fake dispensers have recently been released to unknowing buyers via online auction sites. Dispensers such as Indian Chiefs, One Eye Monsters and Mimic the Monkey, to name a few, have been completely remade and sold as originals. Many of these sales have come from overseas sellers, and the buyer has little recourse once they realize they have been taken. If the deal seems too good to be true, it probably is.

Take the time to read up and understand what the subtle characteristics of a certain dispenser should be. When possible, attend a PEZ convention. There is no substitute for actually seeing a rare old dispenser in person, holding it, and giving it a thorough inspection before making a purchase. It also helps to meet the dealers. Most are well known throughout the hobby, and if there is a problem, they will stand behind what they are selling. A bargain purchased online is no bargain if there is a problem with the dispenser.

PEZ the company continues to stay on top of the latest trends and licenses the hottest properties.New dispensers are added regularly and other lines are retired almost as quickly. Given the short retail lifespan of some of these offerings, speculation would say prices for these short runs will increase in the short term. A set such as the unmasked Incredibles (European edition) is very difficult to find. This set was released in 2004 and now sells in the $75 to $100 range – if you can find them.

The best advice I can give anyone is to not to buy as an investment. Buy only what you like, enjoy your purchase, and have FUN!

Contributor: Shawn Peterson is the author of *Collectors Guide to PEZ: Identification and Price Guide, 3rd Edition* (Krause Publications 2008) and *Warman's PEZ Field Guide, 2nd Edition* (Krause Publications 2009). You may contact him by emailing peterson@pezcandyinc.com.

Bicentennial

Betsy Ross, 1970s, no feet, dark hair and white hat, Bicentennial issue
NM $130 MIP $175

Captain (Paul Revere), 1970s, no feet, blue hat, Bicentennial issue
NM $125 MIP $150

Daniel Boone, 1970s, no feet, light brown hair under dark brown hat, Bicentennial issue
NM $150 MIP $175

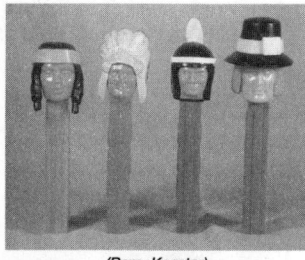

(Barry Koester)

Indian Brave, early 1970s, no feet, small human head, Indian headband w/one feather, Bicentennial issue, shown here w/Indian Chief, Indian Woman, and Pilgrim
NM $150 MIP $200

Indian Chief, 1975, no feet, war bonnet, swirled colors
NM $100 MIP $125

Indian Maiden, 1975, no feet, black hair in braids w/headband
NM $125 MIP $150

Uncle Sam, 1975, no feet, stars and stripes on hat band, white hair and beard, Bicentennial issue
NM $125 MIP $165

Wounded Soldier, 1970s, no feet, white bandage, brown hair, Bicentennial issue
NM $110 MIP $150

Christmas

Angel, 1970s, w/feet, yellow hair and halo
NM $60 MIP $80

Angel, 1970s, no feet, yellow hair and halo
NM $75 MIP $100

Elf, 2002, w/feet, green hat, pointy ears
NM $1 MIP $2

Icee Bear, 1999, w/feet, re-released w/Christmas assortment
NM $1 MIP $3

Polar Bear (Icee Bear), 2002, w/feet, red hat
NM $1 MIP $2

Reindeer, 2002, w/feet, black nose
NM $1 MIP $2

Rudolph, 1970s, no feet, brown deer head, red nose
NM $50 MIP $75

Santa (Full Bodied), 1950s, full body stem w/painted Santa suit and hat
NM $135 MIP $200

Santa A, 1950s, no feet, ivory head w/painted hat
NM $80 MIP $125

Santa B, 1960s, no feet, small head w/flesh painted face, black eyes, red hat
NM $85 MIP $150

Santa C, 1970s, w/feet, removable red hat, white beard
NM $2 MIP $4

(KP Photo, Karen O'Brien collection)

Santa C, 1970s, no feet or w/feet, large head w/white beard, flesh face, red open mouth and hat
NM $7 MIP $12

Santa D, 1990s, w/feet, painted blue eyes
NM $1 MIP $2

(KP Photo, Sharon Bartsch collection)

Santa E, 2000s, w/feet, current version
NM $1 MIP $2

Snowman, 1970s, no feet, black hat, white face
NM $10 MIP $15

Snowman, 2002, w/feet, new scarf and hat
NM $1 MIP $2

Circus

Big Top Elephant, 1970s, no feet, gray-green head, red flat hat
NM $100 MIP $150

Big Top Elephant, 1970s, no feet, orange head w/blue pointed hat
NM $90 MIP $150

Big Top Elephant w/Hair, 1970s, no feet, yellow head and red hair
NM $150 MIP $200

Clown w/Chin, 1970s, no feet, long chin, hat and hair
NM $125 MIP $150

Clown w/Collar, 1960s, no feet, yellow collar, red hair, green hat
NM $50 MIP $70

Giraffe, 1970s, no feet, orange head w/horns, black eyes
NM $125 MIP $175

Gorilla, 1970s, no feet, black head w/red eyes and white teeth
NM $85 MIP $120

Li'l Lion, 1960s, no feet, yellow head w/brown mane
NM $65 MIP $80

Lion w/Crown, 1970s, no feet, black mane, green head w/yellow cheeks and red crown
NM $125 MIP $150

Mimic the Monkey, 1970s, no feet, wearing baseball cap, white eyes
NM $45 MIP $60

Monkey Sailor, 1960s, no feet, cream face, brown hair, white sailor cap, whistlehead
NM $40 MIP $50

Pony-Go-Round, 1970s, no feet, orange head, white harness, blue hair
NM $60 MIP $85

Crazy Fruits

Orange, 1970s, no feet, orange (fruit) head w/face and leaves on top
NM $125 MIP $175

(Barry Koester)

Pear, 1970s, no feet, yellow pear face, green visor
    NM $500   **MIP** $600

Pineapple, 1970s, no feet, pineapple head w/greenery and sunglasses
    NM $2500   **MIP** $3000

Die-Cuts

Bozo the Clown, 1960s, no feet, die-cut Bozo and Butch on stem, no feet, white face, red hair and nose
    NM $150   **MIP** $185

Casper the Friendly Ghost, 1950s, no feet, die-cut
    NM $165   **MIP** $225

Donald Duck Die-Cut, 1960s, no feet, die-cut
    NM $125   **MIP** $175

Easter Bunny, 1950s, no feet, die-cut
    NM $200   **MIP** $250

Mickey Mouse Die-Cut, 1960s, no feet, die-cut stem w/Minnie, painted face
    NM $150   **MIP** $200

Mickey Mouse Die-Cut, 1960s, no feet, die-cut stem w/Minnie, die-cut face mask
    NM $125   **MIP** $150

Disney

Baloo, 1960s, no feet, Jungle Book
    NM $40   **MIP** $60

Baloo, 1960s, w/feet, Jungle Book
    NM $12   **MIP** $25

Bambi, 1970s, w/feet
    NM $30   **MIP** $50

(KP Photo, Karen O'Brien collection)

Best of Pixar, The, 2006, w/feet, Buzz Lightyear (Toy Story), Nemo (Finding Nemo), Mike Wazowski (Monsters, Inc.), Sulley (Monsters Inc.)
    NM $1   **MIP** $2

Bouncer Beagle, 1990s, w/feet, Ducktails
    NM $5   **MIP** $6

Captain Hook, 1960s, no feet, black hair, flesh face winking w/right eye open
    NM $50   **MIP** $75

Cars, 2006, w/feet, Lightning McQueen, Mater the Tow Truck, Sally the Porsche, Doc Hudson
    NM $1   **MIP** $2

Chip, 1970s, w/feet
    NM $40   **MIP** $75

Chip, 1970s, no feet, black top hat, tan head w/white sideburns, brown nose, foreign issue
    NM $80   **MIP** $100

Dalmatian Pup, 1970s, w/feet, white head w/left ear cocked, foreign issue
    NM $35   **MIP** $55

Dewey, 1970s, (Donald Duck's nephew) no feet, blue hat, white head, yellow beak, small black eyes
    NM $20   **MIP** $35

Disney Princesses, 2005, w/feet, Jasmine (Aladdin), Cinderella, Belle (Beauty and the Beast)
    NM $1   **MIP** $2

Disney Princesses, 2006, w/feet, Ariel (Little Mermaid), Aurora (Sleeping Beauty)
    NM $1   **MIP** $2

Disney Princesses, 2007, w/feet, Snow White
    NM $1   **MIP** $2

Donald Duck A, 1960s, no feet, blue hat, one-piece head and bill, open mouth
    NM $12   **MIP** $20

Donald Duck B, 1960s, w/feet, blue hat, white head and hair w/large eyes, removable beak
    NM $1   **MIP** $3

Dopey, 1960s, no feet, flesh colored die-cut face w/wide ears, orange cap
    NM $125   **MIP** $150

Duck Nephews, 1980s, w/feet, (Huey, Dewey or Louie Duck) red, blue, or green stem and matching cap, white head and orange beak
    NM $5   **MIP** $10

Dumbo, 1970s, no feet, gray head w/large ears, red hat
    NM $60   **MIP** $75

Dumbo, 1970s, w/feet, blue head w/large ears, yellow hat
    NM $40   **MIP** $50

Extreme Disney, 2003, w/feet, Mickey Mouse w/ski hat and goggles, Minnie Mouse w/new sunglasses, Daisy Duck w/headphones, Goofy w/headphones, Donald Duck good and mad, Pluto w/bone
    NM $1   **MIP** $2

Goofy A, 1970s, no feet, removable nose, ears, and teeth
    NM $20   **MIP** $30

Goofy B, 1970s, no feet, red hat, painted nose, removable white teeth
    NM $25   **MIP** $35

Goofy C, 1970s, same as version B except teeth are part of head
    NM $15   **MIP** $25

Goofy D, 1980s, w/feet, beige snout, green hat
    NM $1   **MIP** $3

Goofy E, 1990s, w/feet, current
    NM $1   **MIP** $2

Gyro Gearloose, 1990s, w/feet, Ducktails
    NM $5   **MIP** $8

Huey, 1970s, (Donald Duck's nephew) no feet, red hat, white head, yellow beak, small black eyes
    NM $20   **MIP** $35

(KP Photo, Karen O'Brien collection)

Incredibles, The, 2004, w/feet, Mr. Incredible, Elastigirl, Dash, Jack Jack
    NM $1   **MIP** $2

Jiminy Cricket, 1970s, no feet, green hatband and collar, flesh face, black top hat
    NM $150   **MIP** $175

(KP Photo, Sharon Bartsch collection)

Jungle Book 2, 2003, w/feet, Mowgli, Bagherra, Kaa, Shir Kahn, Baloo
    NM $1   **MIP** $3

(KP Photo, Sharon Bartsch collection)

King Louie, 1960s, w/feet, brown hair and "sideburns" over light brown head
NM $40   MIP $50

Li'l Bad Wolf, 1960s, w/feet, black ears, white face, red tongue
NM $30   MIP $45

Li'l Bad Wolf, 1960s, no feet, black ears, white face, red tongue
NM $35   MIP $50

Lion King, 2004, w/feet, Mufasa, Nala, Simba, Pumbaa, Timon
NM $1   MIP $2

Louie, 1970s, (Donald Duck's nephew) no feet, green hat, white head, yellow beak, small black eyes
NM $10   MIP $20

(KP Photo)

Mary Poppins, 1970s, no feet, flesh face, reddish hair, lavender hat
NM $500   MIP $700

Meet the Robinsons, 2007, w/feet, Lewis, Wilber Robinson, Carl the Robot, Bowler Hat Guy
NM $1   MIP $2

Mickey Mouse A, 1970s, no feet, black head and ears, pink face, mask w/cut-out eyes and mouth, nose pokes through mask
NM $10   MIP $15

Mickey Mouse B, 1980s, no feet, painted face, non-painted black eyes and mouth
NM $10   MIP $15

Mickey Mouse C, 1990s, no feet, flesh face, removable nose, painted eyes
NM $10   MIP $15

Mickey Mouse D, 1990s, no feet, flesh face, mask embossed white and black eyes
NM $2   MIP $3

Mickey Mouse E, 1990s, w/feet, flesh face, bulging black and white eyes, oval nose
NM $1   MIP $3

Mowgli, 1960s, no feet, black hair over brown head, Jungle Book
NM $30   MIP $40

Mowgli, 1960s, w/feet, black hair over brown head, Jungle Book
NM $10   MIP $15

Peter Pan, 1960s, no feet, green hat, flesh face, orange hair
NM $150   MIP $175

Pinocchio A, 1960s, no feet, red or yellow cap, pink face, black painted hair
NM $125   MIP $150

Pinocchio B, 1970s, no feet, black hair, red hat
NM $110   MIP $175

Pluto A, 1960s, no feet, yellow head, long black ears, small painted eyes
NM $10   MIP $20

Pluto B, 1970s, w/feet, flat head, movable ears
NM $5   MIP $10

Pluto C, 1980s, w/feet, yellow head, long painted black ears, large white and black decal eyes
NM $1   MIP $3

Pluto D, 1990s, w/feet, large eyes, current
NM $1   MIP $2

Practical Pig A, 1960s, no feet, rounded blue hat, round snout
NM $40   MIP $60

Practical Pig B, 1960s, no feet, crooked blue hat
NM $40   MIP $60

Ratatouille, 2007, w/feet, Remy, Emile, Skinner, Linguini
NM $1   MIP $2

Scrooge McDuck A, 1970s, no feet, white head, yellow beak, black top hat and glasses, white sideburns
NM $15   MIP $25

Scrooge McDuck B, 1970s, w/feet, white head, removable yellow beak, tall black top hat and glasses, large eyes
NM $5   MIP $10

Snow White, 1960s, no feet, flesh face, black hair w/ribbon and matching collar
NM $150   MIP $200

Thumper, 1970s, w/feet, no Disney logo
NM $30   MIP $50

Thumper, 1970s, no feet, orange face
NM $50   MIP $65

Tinkerbell, 1960s, no feet, pale pink stem, white hair, flesh face w/blue and white eyes
NM $150   MIP $175

Webagail or Webby, 1990s, w/feet, Ducktails
NM $2   MIP $4

Winnie the Pooh, 1970s, w/feet, yellow head
NM $50   MIP $60

Winnie the Pooh, 1970s, no feet, European release
NM $60   MIP $75

(KP Photo, Sharon Bartsch collection)

Winnie the Pooh, 2001, w/feet, remakes of originals, Tigger, Piglet, Eeyore, Pooh
NM $1   MIP $2

Winnie the Pooh, 2005, w/feet, Roo, Heffalump
NM $1   MIP $2

Zorro, 1960s, no feet, w/Disney logo
NM $75   MIP $100

Zorro, 1960s, no feet, black mask and hat, no Disney logo
NM $75   MIP $100

Zorro w/Logo, 1960s, no feet, black mask and hat, says "Zorro" on stem
NM $95   MIP $125

Easter

Bunny, 1999
NM $1   MIP $3

Bunny 1990, 1990, w/feet, long ears, white face
NM $1   MIP $2

Bunny A, 1950s, no feet, narrow head and tall ears
NM $175   MIP $200

Bunny B, 1950s, no feet, tall ears and full face, smiling buck teeth
NM $200   MIP $250

(KP Photo, Sharon Bartsch collection)

Bunny D, 1990s, w/feet
    NM $1   **MIP** $2

Bunny E, 2000s, w/feet, painted face, current
    NM $1   **MIP** $2

Bunny w/Fat Ears, 1960s, no feet, wide ear version, assorted colors
    NM $15   **MIP** $30

Bunny w/Fat Ears, 1970s, w/feet, wide ear version
    NM $10   **MIP** $15

Chick in Egg, 1960s, no feet, yellow chick in egg shell, no hat
    NM $75   **MIP** $85

Chick in Egg A, 1970s, no feet, yellow chick in egg shell, red hat
    NM $10   **MIP** $15

Chick in Egg B, 1970s, no feet, red hat, shell thin and flexible
    NM $10   **MIP** $15

Chick in Egg C, 1980s, no feet, red hat, thicker shell
    NM $3   **MIP** $5

(KP Photo, Sharon Bartsch collection)

Chick in Egg C, 1980s, w/feet, red hat
    NM $3   **MIP** $5

Chick in Egg D, 1990s, w/feet, red hat, rounded shell design
    NM $2   **MIP** $4

Chick in Egg E, 2000s, w/feet, red hat, current
    NM $1   **MIP** $2

Duck w/Flower, 1970s, no feet, flower, duck head w/beak, many color combinations
    NM $75   **MIP** $125

(KP Photo, Karen O'Brien collection)

Easter 2004, 2004, w/feet, new sculpts, Chick in Egg, Lamb, Bunny (pink), baby-faced Egg
    NM $1   **MIP** $2

Lamb, 1970s, no feet, white head w/pink bow
    NM $10   **MIP** $15

(KP Photo, Sharon Bartsch collection)

Lamb, 1970s-80s, w/feet
    NM $2   **MIP** $4

Rooster, 1970s, no feet, yellow head, comb and wattle
    NM $75   **MIP** $125

Eerie Spectres

Air Spirit, 1970s, no feet, reddish triangular fish face
    NM $150   **MIP** $200

Diabolic, 1970s, no feet, soft orange monster head
    NM $150   **MIP** $200

Scarewolf, 1970s, no feet, soft head w/orange hair and ears
    NM $150   **MIP** $200

Spook, 1970s, no feet, blue head w/horns, soft head
    NM $150   **MIP** $200

Vamp, 1970s, no feet, light gray head on black collar, green hair and face, red teeth
    NM $150   **MIP** $200

Zombie, 1970s, no feet, burgundy and black soft head
    NM $150   **MIP** $200

Halloween

Black Cat, 2006, w/feet, glow-in-the-dark stem, red collar w/pumpkin
    NM $1   **MIP** $2

Halloween Crystal Series, 1999, w/feet, mail-in series, Happy Henry, Naughty Neil, Slimy Sid, and Polly Pumpkin
    NM $2   **MIP** $4

Halloween Ghosts, 1999, w/feet, non-glowing, Happy Henry, Naughty Neil, Slimy Sid
    NM $1   **MIP** $2

Halloween Glowing Ghosts, 2002, w/feet, glow-in-the-dark, Happy Henry, Naughty Neil, Slimy Sid, Polly Pumpkin
    NM $1   **MIP** $2

Jack-O-Lantern A, 1980s, no feet, green stem, carved face
    NM $10   **MIP** $15

Jack-O-Lantern B, 1980s, black facial features
    NM $1   **MIP** $3

Mr. Ugly, 1970s, no feet, black hair, many color variations
    NM $50   **MIP** $75

Mr. Ugly, 1970s, w/feet
    NM $45   **MIP** $65

Octopus, 1970s, no feet; black; orange or black head
    NM $65   **MIP** $95

One-Eyed Monster, 1970s, w/feet
    NM $55   **MIP** $80

One-Eyed Monster, 1970s, no feet, gorilla head w/one eye missing
    NM $55   **MIP** $80

Skull A, 1970s, w/feet, small white head, black body
    NM $10   **MIP** $15

Skull A, 1970s, no feet, small white head, black dispenser body
    NM $10   **MIP** $15

Skull B, 1970s, no feet, black collar, larger head
    NM $10   **MIP** $15

Skull B, 1980s, w/feet, glow-in-dark version
    NM $2   **MIP** $4

Skull Misfit, 1998, w/feet, mail-in, black head, yellow body
    NM $6   **MIP** $10

Witch 1 Piece, 1950s, no feet, black stem w/witch embossed on stem, orange one-piece head
    NM $150   **MIP** $200

Witch 3-Piece A, 1970s, no feet, chartreuse face, black hair, orange hat
    NM $70   **MIP** $120

Witch 3-Piece B, 1980s, w/feet, red head and hair, green mask, black hat
    NM $3   **MIP** $7

Witch C, 1990s, w/feet, glow-in-the-dark, current
    NM $1   **MIP** $2

Humans

Astronaut A, early 1960s, no feet, helmet, yellow visor, small head
    NM $500   **MIP** $600

Astronaut B, 1970s, no feet, green stem, white helmet, yellow visor, large head

NM $125   **MIP** $175

Cowboy, 1970s, no feet, human head, brown hat

NM $150   **MIP** $200

Emergency Heroes, 2003, w/feet, Army Soldier, Policeman, Scuba Diver, Construction Worker, Police K-9, Policewoman, Nurse, Fireman, Jet Pilot, Fireman and Construction Worker have black variations ($3-5 each)

NM $1   **MIP** $2

Football Player, 1960s, no feet, white stem, red helmet w/white stripe

NM $100   **MIP** $150

Orange County Chopper Set, 2006, w/feet, special edition tin w/Paul Sr., Paul Jr., Mikey

NM $10   **MIP** $20

Pilgrim, 1975, no feet, pilgrim hat, blond hair, hat band

NM $125   **MIP** $160

Pilot, 1970s, no feet, blue hat, gray headphones

NM $150   **MIP** $200

Spaceman, 1950s, no feet, clear helmet over flesh-color head

NM $90   **MIP** $125

Stewardess, 1970s, no feet, light blue flight cap, blonde hair

NM $135   **MIP** $165

Kooky Zoo

Cockatoo, 1970s, no feet, yellow beak and green head, red head feathers

NM $60   **MIP** $85

Cow A, 1970s, no feet, cow head, separate nose

NM $75   **MIP** $95

Cow B, 1970s, no feet, blue head, separate snout, horns, ears and eyes

NM $85   **MIP** $120

Crocodile, 1970s, no feet, dark green head w/red eyes

NM $75   **MIP** $120

Kooky Zoo Crystal Series, 1999, w/feet, "crystal" versions of Blinky Bill, Lion, Gator, Hippo, Elephant

NM $3   **MIP** $6

(KP Photo, Sharon Bartsch collection)

Kooky Zoo Series, late-1990s, w/feet, Blinky Bill the Koala (shown), Lion, Gator (shown), Hippo, Elephant

NM $1   **MIP** $3

Panda A, 1970s, no feet, white head w/black eyes and ears

NM $20   **MIP** $25

Panda A, 1970s, no feet, yellow head w/black eyes and ears

NM $300   **MIP** $350

(KP Photo, Sharon Bartsch collection)

Panda B, 1990s, w/feet, white head w/black eyes and ears

NM $1   **MIP** $3

Panther, 1970s, no feet, blue head w/pink nose

NM $125   **MIP** $175

Puzzy Cat, 1970s, no feet, cat head w/hat

NM $65   **MIP** $95

Raven, 1970s, no feet, black head, short or long beak, glasses

NM $50   **MIP** $75

Yappy Dog, 1970s, no feet, black floppy ears and nose, green or orange head

NM $75   **MIP** $90

Licensed Characters

Arlene, early-1990s, w/feet, 1st series, pink head, Garfield's girlfriend

NM $1   **MIP** $3

Asterix, 1970s, no feet, blue hat w/wings, yellow mustache, European

NM $1500   **MIP** $2000

Asterix (1998 foreign issue), 1998, head different than old

NM $1   **MIP** $3

(KP Photo, Sharon Bartsch collection)

Barney Rubble, 1990s, w/feet, Flintstones, shown w/Pebbles, Dino and Fred

NM $1   **MIP** $2

Bart Simpson, 2000, w/feet

NM $1   **MIP** $2

(KP Photo, Sharon Bartsch collection)

Bob the Builder, 2002, w/feet, four characters: Bob, Wendy, Pilchard and Spud

NM $1   **MIP** $2

Brainy Smurf, 1990s, w/feet, second series

NM $1   **MIP** $2

Bratz, 2005, w/feet, Yasmine, Chloe, Sasha, Jade

NM $1   **MIP** $2

Brutus, 1960s, no feet, black beard and hair

NM $150   **MIP** $175

(KP Photo)

Bullwinkle, 1960s, no feet, brown head, yellow antlers, yellow or brown stem

NM $175   **MIP** $225

Casper the Friendly Ghost, 1950s, no feet, white face

NM $125   **MIP** $175

Chicken Little, 2005, w/feet, Chicken Little, Fish out of Water, Ugly Duckling

NM $1   MIP $2

Dino the Dinosaur, 1990s, w/feet, Flintstones

NM $1   MIP $2

E.T., 2002, w/feet, w/or w/out red hood

NM $2   MIP $4

(KP Photo, Karen O'Brien collection)

Fozzie Bear, 1990s, w/feet, brown head, bow tie, small brown hat

NM $1   MIP $2

Fred Flintstone, 1990s, w/feet, Flintstones

NM $1   MIP $2

(KP Photo, Sharon Bartsch collection)

Garfield, early-1990s, w/feet, 1st series, orange head, smirk, eyes half shut, shown w/other Series 1 releases

NM $1   MIP $2

(KP Photo, Sharon Bartsch collection)

Garfield, late-1990s, w/feet, 2nd series, smiling, eyes wide open

NM $1   MIP $2

Garfield Aviator, late-1990s, w/feet, 2nd series, hat and goggles

NM $1   MIP $2

Garfield Chef, late-1990s, w/feet, 2nd series, chef's hat, smiling

NM $1   MIP $2

Garfield Sleepy, late-1990s, w/feet, 2nd series, night cap

NM $1   MIP $2

Garfield w/Teeth, early-1990s, w/feet, 1st series, orange head, wide painted toothy grin

NM $1   MIP $2

Garfield w/Visor, early-1990s, w/feet, 1st series, orange face, green visor

NM $1   MIP $2

Gargamel, 1990s, w/feet, second series

NM $2   MIP $4

Gonzo, 1990s, w/feet, blue head, yellow eyelids, bow tie

NM $1   MIP $2

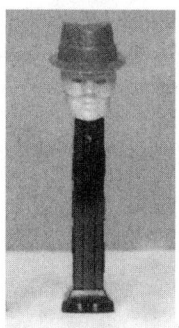

(KP Photo)

Green Hornet, 1960s, no feet, green mask and hat; two hat styles exist

NM $200   MIP $250

Gundam, 2005, w/feet, individually boxed; Gundam RX-78-2, Char's Zaku MS-06S, Zaku II MS-06F, Z'Gock MSM-07

NM $5   MIP $10

Hello Kitty, 2005, w/feet, Aloha Kitty, Hello Kitty w/Rabbit, Hello Kitty, My Melodie

NM $1   MIP $2

Hello Kitty, Crystal, 2005, w/feet, crystal versions: Kuririn, Hello Kitty w/Rabbit, Hello Kitty, My Melodie

NM $2   MIP $4

Hello Kitty, Tin Box Set, 2006, w/feet, crystal versions in tin box

NM $10   MIP $15

(KP Photo, Sharon Bartsch collection)

Homer Simpson, 2000, w/feet, shown w/Maggie, Bart, Lisa, Marge

NM $1   MIP $2

Ice Age 2, 2006, w/feet, Manny the mastadon, Diego the saber toothed tiger, Sid the sloth, Scrat the squirrel

NM $1   MIP $2

Jack-In-The-Box, 1999, w/feet, restaurant premium, three stem colors: yellow, red and blue

NM $4   MIP $10

(KP Photo, Sharon Bartsch collection)

Kermit the Frog, 1990s, w/feet, green head, shown w/Miss Piggy, Gonzo, Fozzie

NM $1   MIP $2

Lisa Simpson, 2000, w/feet

NM $1   MIP $2

Little Orphan Annie, 1982, no feet, light brown hair, flesh face w/black painted features

NM $100   MIP $140

Madagascar, 2005, w/feet, Alex the lion, Marty the zebra, Gloria the hippo

NM $1   MIP $2

Maggie Simpson, 2000, w/feet

NM $1   MIP $2

Marge Simpson, 2000, w/feet

NM $1   MIP $2

Miss Piggy, 1990s, w/feet, pink face, yellow hair

NM $1   MIP $2

Miss Piggy, 1990s, w/eyelashes

NM $10   MIP $15

Miss Piggy B, 1999, w/feet, current version larger ears

NM $1   MIP $2

(KP Photo, Sharon Bartsch collection)

Mr. Bean, 2005, w/feet, European release, Mr. Bean, Irma Gobb, Mini Cooper, Teddy

    NM $2   **MIP** $4

Mueslix, 1970s, no feet, white beard, moustache and eyebrows, European

    NM $2000 **MIP** $2500

Nermal, early-1990s, w/feet, 1st series, gray stem and head

    NM $1   **MIP** $3

Nintendo, Diddy Dong, 1990s, w/feet, yellow stem, red cap

    NM $2   **MIP** $4

Nintendo, Koopa Trooper, 1990s, w/feet, green stem, orange head

    NM $2   **MIP** $4

Nintendo, Mario, 1990s, w/feet, blue stem, red cap

    NM $2   **MIP** $4

Nintendo, Yoshi, 1990s, w/feet, red stem, green head

    NM $2   **MIP** $4

Obelix, 1970s, no feet, red mustache and hair, blue hat, European

    NM $1500 **MIP** $2000

Obelix (1998 foreign issue), 1998, head different than old

    NM $2   **MIP** $3

Odie, late-1990s, w/feet, 2nd series, tongue wagging

    NM $1   **MIP** $2

Olive Oyl, 1960s, no feet, black hair and flesh painted face

    NM $150   **MIP** $200

Open Season, 2006, w/feet, Boog the bear, Elliot the mule deer, McSquizzy the owl, Mr. Weenie the dog

    NM $1   **MIP** $3

Over the Hedge, 2006, w/feet, RJ the racoon, Verne the turtle, Stella the skunk, Hammy the squirrel

    NM $1   **MIP** $2

Papa Smurf, 1980s, original, no feet, white beard, red hat

    NM $10   **MIP** $15

Papa Smurf, 1980s, w/feet, red hat, white beard, blue face

    NM $3   **MIP** $6

Papa Smurf, 1990s, w/feet, second series

    NM $2   **MIP** $4

Pebbles Flintstone, 1990s, w/feet, Flintstones

    NM $1   **MIP** $2

Peter PEZ, 1970s, no feet, blue top hat that says "PEZ," white face, yellow hair

    NM $50   **MIP** $65

(KP Photo, Sharon Bartsch collection)

Peter PEZ, 1993-2001, w/feet, remake

    NM $1   **MIP** $2

(KP Photo, Sharon Bartsch collection)

Pink Panther, 1990s, w/feet, Pink Panther, Inspector Clouseau (shown here), Ant, Aardvark; value for each

    NM $2   **MIP** $4

Pokemon, 2001, w/feet, Pikachu, Meowth, Mew, Psyduck and Kofing; value for each

    NM $1   **MIP** $3

Popeye A, 1950s, no feet, yellow face, painted hat

    NM $125   **MIP** $150

Popeye B, 1960s, no feet, removable white sailor cap

    NM $65   **MIP** $100

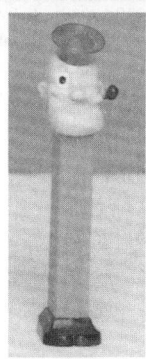

(KP Photo)

Popeye C, 1970s, no feet, one eye painted, removeable pipe and red cap, shown here in stand

    NM $95   **MIP** $150

(KP Photo, Sharon Bartsch collection)

Sesame Street, 2004, w/feet, Bert (shown), Ernie (shown), Zoe, Elmo, Cookie Monster (shown), Big Bird

    NM $1   **MIP** $2

Sesame Street, 35th Anniversary, 2004, w/feet, crystal versions of Cookie Monster, Big Bird and Elmo, each came in own commemorative box

    NM $5   **MIP** $10

Shrek 2, 2004, w/feet, European release, Shrek, Fiona, Donkey, Puss 'n Boots

    NM $1   **MIP** $2

(KP Photo, Karen O'Brien collection)

Shrek the Third, 2007, w/feet, Shrek, Fiona, Donkey, Puss 'n Boots

    NM $1   **MIP** $2

Smurf, 1980s, original, no feet, blue face, white hat

    NM $10   **MIP** $15

Smurf, 1980s, w/feet, blue face, white hat
NM $3   **MIP** $6

Smurf, 1990s, w/feet, second series
NM $1   **MIP** $3

Smurfette, 1980s, original, no feet, blue face, white hat
NM $10   **MIP** $15

Smurfette, 1980s, w/feet, blue face, yellow hair, white hat
NM $3   **MIP** $8

Smurfette, 1990s, w/feet, second series
NM $2   **MIP** $4

Sponge Bob Squarepants, 2004, w/feet, Sponge Bob, Patrick, Squidward
NM $1   **MIP** $3

(KP Photo, Sharon Bartsch collection)

Teenage Mutant Ninja Turtles, 1990s, four different characters, 1st series, shown w/one new series on left
NM $2   **MIP** $3

Teenage Mutant Ninja Turtles, 2005, w/feet, new series, angry faces, Michaelangelo, Raphael, Donatello, Leonardo
NM $1   **MIP** $2

Tweenies, 2002, w/feet, five characters: Jake, Fuzz, Milo, Bella, and Doodles
NM $2   **MIP** $4

Merry Music Makers

Camel, 1980s, w/feet, brown face w/red fez hat
NM $50   **MIP** $65

(KP Photo, Sharon Bartsch collection)

Clown, 1980s, w/feet, green hat, foreign issue (Merry Music Makers)
NM $5   **MIP** $10

(KP Photo, Sharon Bartsch collection)

Coach's Whistle, 1980s, no feet and w/feet, police whistles on top
NM $25   **MIP** $40

Dog, 1980s, no feet and w/feet
NM $20   **MIP** $40

Donkey, 1980s, w/feet, gray head w/pink nose, whistlehead
NM $5   **MIP** $10

Duck, 1980s, no feet, brown head w/yellow beak, whistlehead
NM $30   **MIP** $55

Duck, 1980s, w/feet, brown head w/yellow beak, whistlehead
NM $35   **MIP** $50

Frog, 1980s, no feet, yellow and green head w/black eyes, foreign issue
NM $50   **MIP** $65

Frog, 1980s, w/feet, yellow and green head w/black eyes, foreign issue
NM $45   **MIP** $60

Indian, 1980s, w/feet, black hair and green headband w/feather, foreign issue (Merry Music Makers)
NM $25   **MIP** $40

Koala, 1980s, w/feet, brown head w/a black nose, foreign issue, whistlehead
NM $3   **MIP** $5

Lamb, 1980s, no feet, pink stem, white head, whistle
NM $10   **MIP** $25

Monkey, 1980s, w/feet, whistle head, tan monkey face in brown head, foreign issue
NM $25   **MIP** $40

Parrot, 1980s, w/feet, red hair, yellow beak and green eyes, whistle head
NM $5   **MIP** $10

Penguin, 1980s, w/feet, penguin head w/yellow beak and red hat, foreign issue, whistle head
NM $5   **MIP** $10

(KP Photo, Sharon Bartsch collection)

Pig Whistle, 1980s, w/feet, pink head, whistlehead
NM $60   **MIP** $75

Rhino, 1980s, w/feet, green head, red horn, foreign issue, whistle head
NM $5   **MIP** $10

Rooster, 1980s, no feet, white head, comb
NM $40   **MIP** $65

Tiger, 1980s, w/feet, tiger head w/white snout, whistle head
NM $5   **MIP** $10

MGM

Barney Bear, 1980s, w/feet, brown head, white cheeks and snout, black nose
NM $15   **MIP** $30

Barney Bear, 1980s, no feet, brown head, white cheeks and snout, black nose
NM $30   **MIP** $45

Droopy Dog A, 1980s, w/feet, white face, flesh snout, black movable ears and red hair
NM $10   **MIP** $15

Droopy Dog B, 1992, w/feet, painted ears
NM $5   **MIP** $6

Jerry (Tom & Jerry), 1980s, w/feet, brown face, multiple piece head
NM $8   **MIP** $10

Jerry (Tom & Jerry), 1980s, no feet, rare variation w/brown face, pink lining in ears is removable
NM $200   **MIP** $250

Spike, 1980s, w/feet, brown face, pink snout
NM $5   **MIP** $6

Tom A (Tom & Jerry), 1980s, no feet, gray cat head w/painted black features
NM $25   **MIP** $35

Tom B (Tom & Jerry), 1980s, w/feet, gray cat head w/removable facial features
NM $10   **MIP** $15

Tuffy, 1990s, w/feet, non-U.S. release, similar to Jerry but has gray face rather than Jerry's brown

NM $3   **MIP** $6

Tyke, 1990s, w/feet, brown head

NM $10   **MIP** $25

Miscellaneous

Advertising Regular, 1950s, no feet, no head, advertising printed on side MUST be complete

NM $1500   **MIP** n/a

Arithmetic Regular, 1960s, no feet, headless dispenser w/white top, side of body has openings w/columns of numbers

NM $400   **MIP** $600

Barky Brown, 2005, w/feet, special edition for Australia's Animal Welfare League

NM $10   **MIP** $18

Baseball, 2002, w/feet, Arizona Diamondbacks, LSU (2004), Philadelphia Phillies

NM $10   **MIP** $15

Baseball Dispenser Set, 1960s, no feet, baseball glove w/ball, bat, white home plate marked "PEZ"

NM $350   **MIP** $500

Baseball Glove Only, 1960s, no feet, brown baseball glove w/white ball

NM $150   **MIP** $175

Basketball, 2002-2005, w/feet, Seattle Sonics, Washington Mystics, Connecticut Suns

NM $10   **MIP** $20

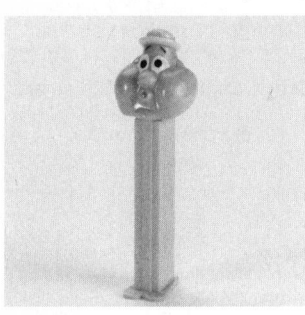

(KP Photo, Sharon Bartsch collection)

Bubbleman, 1996, w/feet, Neon, Crystal, and Glowing varieties

NM $5   **MIP** $9

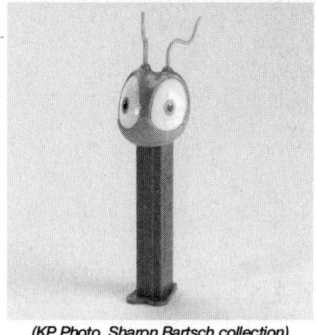

(KP Photo, Sharon Bartsch collection)

Bugz, 2000, w/feet, Jumpin' Jack (grasshopper), Sam Snuffle (fly), Florence Flutterfly (butterfly, shown here), Super Bee (bee), Sweet Ladybird, Clumsy Worm, Baby Bee, Centipede

NM $1   **MIP** $2

Bugz, Crystal, 2002, w/feet, crystal series of all Bugz characters

NM $2   **MIP** $4

Candy Shooter, 1960s, black gun w/PEZ logo on stock

NM $85   **MIP** $135

Candy Shooter, 1960s, red body, white grip, w/German license and double PEZ candy

NM $60   **MIP** $85

Cat w/Derby (Puzzy Cat), 1970s, no feet, blue hat most valuable

NM $80   **MIP** $125

Crazy Animals, 1999, w/feet, Frog, Shark, Octopus, Camel

NM $2   **MIP** $4

Crystal Ball, 2002, w/base, mail-in premium, silver or blue stars

NM $10   **MIP** $15

eBay, 2000, crystal head dispensers, set of four

NM $40   **MIP** $60

eBay Crystal Hearts, 2000, w/feet, yellow, blue, red or green crystal hearts w/eBay logo

NM $5   **MIP** $10

eBay Employee Heart, 2000, w/feet, black stem, white heart, eBay logo

NM $40   **MIP** $60

Elephant, early 1960s, aka Political Elephant, gold or black, one-piece head

NM $3000   **MIP** $10000

Funky Faces, 2003, w/feet, round heads w/13 different expressions: Open Smile, Cool Sunglasses Smile, Nerdy Egghead, Smiley Face, Winking Smiley Face, Kissy Face, Smiling w/Eyelashes, Baby Face, Crying Face, Smiley w/Tongue, Embarassed Face, Angry Face, Toothy Smile

NM $1   **MIP** $2

Katrina PEZ, 2005, w/feet, issued to raise funds for hurricane victims, red stem, white ball w/"Katrina August 29, 2005 10:30 am," Watch for fakes!

NM $50   **MIP** $75

Make-A-Face, 1970s, American card

NM $2500   **MIP** $3000

Make-A-Face, 1970s, German "Super Spiel" card

NM $2500   **MIP** $3000

Make-A-Face, 1970s, no card, feet, oversized head w/18 facial parts

NM $2000   **MIP** $2500

NASCAR Helmets, 2005, w/feet, helmets of drivers: Richard Petty, Rusty Wallace, Kasey Kane, Bobby LaBonte, Tony Stewart, Matt Kenseth, Jeff Gordon

NM $1   **MIP** $2

NCAA Footballs, 2006, w/feet, football w/team logos: Penn State, Georgia, Texas, Florida, Florida State, Michigan, Alabama

NM $1   **MIP** $2

NCAA Footballs, 2007, w/feet, Ohio State, Notre Dame, University of Louisville

NM $1   **MIP** $2

Octopus, 1970s, no feet, red head

NM $70   **MIP** $90

Personalized Regular, 1960s, no feet, no head, paper label for monogramming

NM $125   **MIP** $150

(KP Photo, Sharon Bartsch collection)

Pez-A-Saurs (Dinosaurs), 1993, four different dinosaurs: Hesaur, Shesaur, Flysaur and Isaur
NM $1   MIP $2

Pez-A-Saurs (Dinosaurs), Crystal, 1999, w/feet, mail-in premium
NM $2   MIP $4

Phone, not sold in the U.S.
NM $1   MIP $2

Psychedelic Flower, 1960s, no feet, stem w/decal on side, many color variations
NM $225   MIP $300

Psychedelic Flower, 1998, reproduction
NM $5   MIP $10

(KP Photo)

Psychedelic Hand, 1960s, no feet, decal design on stem, beige or black hands; many color variations, shown w/Psychedelic Flower
NM $150   MIP $225

Psychedelic Hand, 1998, 1998 limited edition, has 1967 copyright date
NM $5   MIP $10

Regular, 1950s, no feet, no head, stem w/top only
NM $80   MIP $125

Regular, 1990s, no feet, no head, stem w/top only; assorted colors; reissues
NM $1   MIP $2

Roman Soldier (1998 foreign issue), 1998, w/feet, Asterix series featured this dispenser and reissues of the 1970s releases
NM $2   MIP $3

(KP Photo, Sharon Bartsch collection)

Sourz, 2002, w/feet, Pineapple (shown), Blue Raspberry, Watermelon (shown), Green Apple
NM $1   MIP $2

Space Gun 1950s, 1950s, various colors
NM $300   MIP $450

Space Gun 1980s, 1980s, red on blister pack
NM $150   MIP $200

Space Gun 1980s, 1980s, silver
NM $85   MIP $125

Space Trooper, 1950s, full bodied robot w/backpack; blue, red, or yellow
NM $150   MIP $250

Space Trooper, 1950s, full bodied robot, gold, "PEZ" on back
NM $1400   MIP $2000

Sports teams, 2000-present, w/feet, professional baseball, basketball, soccer teams
NM $10   MIP $20

USA Hearts, 2002, w/feet, mail-in offer, six different hearts that say "USA"
NM $1   MIP $2

Zielpunkt, 1999, w/feet, from Austrian grocery chain
NM $10   MIP $15

Olympics

Alpine Man, 1972, 1972 Munich Olympics, no feet, green hat w/beige plume, black mustache
NM $2000   MIP $2500

Vucko Wolf, 1984, 1984 Sarajevo Olympics issue, w/feet, gray or brown face
NM $175   MIP $200

Vucko Wolf, 1984, 1984 Sarajevo Olympics issue, w/feet, gray or brown face w/ski hat
NM $200   MIP $250

(Barry Koester)

Vucko Wolf, 1984, 1984 Sarajevo Olympics issue, w/feet, gray or brown face w/bobsled helmet
NM $200   MIP $250

Winter Olympics Snowman, 1976, 1976 Innsbruck, red nose and hat, white head w/arms extended, black eyes, blue smile
NM $300   MIP $350

Peanuts

Charlie Brown, 1990s, w/feet, blue cap, eyes closed
NM $45   MIP $75

Charlie Brown, 1990s, w/feet, blue cap, smile w/red tongue at corner
NM $10   MIP $15

(KP Photo, Sharon Bartsch collection)

Charlie Brown, 1990s, w/feet, crooked smile, blue cap, shown w/Woodstock, Snoopy, Lucy
NM $1   MIP $2

Charlie Brown Cubs, 2001, w/feet, first PEZ Cubs promotion
NM $5   MIP $15

Charlie Brown Yankees, 2003, w/feet, Yankees cap
NM $20   MIP $30

Lucy, 1990s, w/feet, black hair
NM $1   MIP $2

(KP Photo, Sharon Bartsch collection)

Peppermint Patty, 2000, w/feet, green stem, smiling, shown w/Snoopy as Joe Cool and Charlie Brown
NM $1   MIP $2

Snoopy, 1990s, w/feet, w/white head and black ears
NM $1   MIP $2

Snoopy as Joe Cool, 2000, w/feet, black stem, sunglasses
NM $1   MIP $2

Woodstock, 1990s, w/painted feathers
NM $3   MIP $5

Woodstock, 1990s, w/feet, yellow head
NM $1   MIP $2

PEZ Pals

Boy, 1960s, no feet, brown hair
NM $30   MIP $45

Boy w/Cap, 1960s, no feet, white hair, blue cap
NM $85   MIP $125

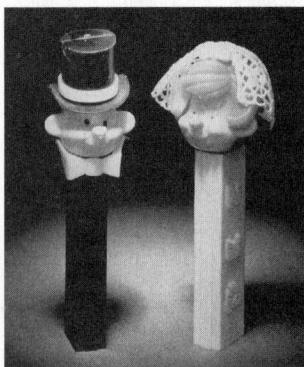

Bride, 1970s, no feet, white veil, light brown, blonde or red hair, shown here w/Groom
NM $1500   MIP $2000

Bride, Limited Edition, 2000s, w/feet, mail-order
NM $10   MIP $20

Doctor, 1970s, no feet, white hair and mustache, gray reflector on white band, black stethoscope
NM $150   MIP $200

Engineer, 1970s, no feet, blue hat
NM $125   MIP $175

Fireman, 1970s, no feet, red hat w/gray #1 insignia
NM $50   MIP $75

Girl, 1970s, no feet, blonde pigtails
NM $25   MIP $35

Girl, 1970s, w/feet, pigtails
NM $4   MIP $8

Groom, 1970s, no feet, black top hat, white bow tie
NM $350   MIP $500

Groom, Limited Edition, 2000s, w/feet, mail-order
NM $10   MIP $15

Knight, 1970s, no feet, gray helmet w/plume
NM $400   MIP $600

Maharajah, 1970s, no feet, green turban w/red inset
NM $60   MIP $85

Mexican, 1960s, no feet, yellow sombrero, black beard and mustache, two earrings
NM $140   MIP $185

Nurse, 1970s, no feet, hair color variations, white nurse's cap
NM $125   MIP $175

Pirate, 1970s, no feet, red cap, patch over right eye
NM $60   MIP $85

Policeman, 1970s, no feet, blue hat w/gray badge
NM $45   MIP $75

Ringmaster, 1970s, no feet, white bow tie, white hat w/red hatband, and black handlebar moustache
NM $250   MIP $350

Sailor, 1960s, no feet, blue hat, white beard
NM $150   MIP $200

Sheik, 1970s, no feet, white head drape, headband
NM $75   MIP $95

Sheriff, 1970s, no feet, brown hat w/badge
NM $125   MIP $175

Premiums

Cocoa Marsh Spaceman, 1950s, no feet, clear helmet on small male head, w/Cocoa Marsh embossed on side
NM $100   MIP $150

Donkey Kong Jr., 1980s, no feet, blond monkey face, dark hair, white cap w/"J" on it, w/box
NM $150   MIP $225

Golden Glow, 1950s, no feet, no head, gold stem and top
NM $80   MIP $125

Hippo, 1970s, no feet, green stem w/"Hippo" printed on side, foreign issue
NM $500   MIP $600

(KP Photo)

Lion's Club Lion, 1962, no feet, stem imprinted "1962 Lion's Club Inter'l Convention," yellow roaring lion head
NM $2000   MIP $3000

Sparefroh (foreign issue), 1970s, no feet, green stem, red triangle hat, coin glued on stem
NM $575   MIP $850

Stand By Me, 1986, dispenser packed w/mini film poster and candy
NM $150   MIP $200

Regulars

(KP Photo)

Witch Regular, 1950s, no feet, orange stem w/black witch graphics, no head
NM $2000   MIP $3500

Sport Toons

Bugs Bunny, 1999
NM $1   MIP $2

Daffy Duck, 1999
NM $1   MIP $2

Sylvester, 1999

    NM $1   **MIP** $2

(KP Photo, Sharon Bartsch collection)

Taz, 1999

    NM $1   **MIP** $2

Tweety, 1999, w/feet, baseball cap

    NM $1   **MIP** $2

Star Wars

Boba Fett, 1999, w/feet, 2nd series

    NM $1   **MIP** $2

C-3PO, 1990s, w/feet, 1st series

    NM $1   **MIP** $2

(KP Photo, Sharon Bartsch collection)

Chewbacca, 1990s, w/feet, 1st series, shown w/other 1st series releases

    NM $1   **MIP** $2

Clone Trooper, 2002, w/feet, 3rd series

    NM $1   **MIP** $2

(KP Photo)

Darth Vader, 1990s, w/feet, 1st series, shown here w/other 1st series releases

    NM $1   **MIP** $2

(KP Photo, Karen O'Brien collection)

Darth Vader, 2000s

    NM $1   **MIP** $2

Death Star, 2005, w/feet, 4th series

    NM $1   **MIP** $2

Emperor Palpatine, 2005, w/feet, 4th series, red cloak

    NM $1   **MIP** $2

Ewok, 1999, w/feet, 2nd series

    NM $1   **MIP** $2

General Grievous, 2005, w/feet, 4th series

    NM $1   **MIP** $2

Jango Fett, 2002, w/feet, 3rd series

    NM $1   **MIP** $2

Luke Skywalker, 1999, w/feet, 2nd series, pilot

    NM $1   **MIP** $2

(KP Photo, Sharon Bartsch collection)

Princess Leia, 1999, w/feet, 2nd series, shown w/Boba Fett and Ewok

    NM $1   **MIP** $2

R2-D2, 2002, w/feet, 3rd series

    NM $1   **MIP** $2

Stormtrooper, 1990s, w/feet, 1st series

    NM $1   **MIP** $2

Wookie Warrior, 2005, w/feet, 4th series

    NM $1   **MIP** $2

Yoda, 1990s, w/feet, 1st series

    NM $1   **MIP** $2

Superheroes

Batgirl, 1970s, Soft Head Superhero, no feet, blue mask, black hair

    NM $120   **MIP** $150

Batman, 1960s, no feet, blue cape, mask and hat

    NM $100   **MIP** $125

Batman, 1970s, Soft Head Superhero, no feet, blue mask

    NM $150   **MIP** $225

Batman, 1970s, w/feet, blue

    NM $3   **MIP** $6

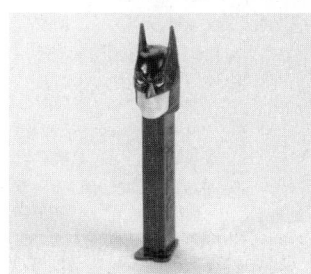

(KP Photo, Sharon Bartsch collection)

Batman, 1990s, w/feet, large ears, dark blue, current

    NM $1   **MIP** $2

Captain America, 1970s, blue mask

    NM $125   **MIP** $150

Captain America, 1970s, no feet, blue cowl, black mask w/white letter A

    NM $150   **MIP** $175

Hulk A, 1970s, no feet, dark green head, black hair

    NM $25   **MIP** $40

Hulk B, 1970s, no feet, light green head, dark green hair

    NM $25   **MIP** $30

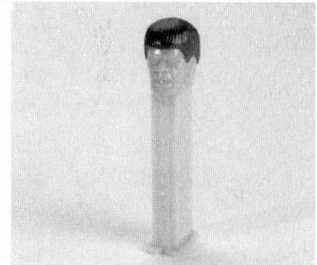

(KP Photo, Sharon Bartsch collection)

Hulk B, 1970s, w/feet, light green head, tall dark green hair

    NM $3   **MIP** $6

Hulk C, 1999, w/teeth

    NM $1   **MIP** $2

Joker, 1970s, Soft Head Superhero, no feet, green painted hair

    NM $150   **MIP** $200

Penguin (Batman villain), 1970s, Soft Head Superhero, no feet, yellow top hat, black painted monocle, whistlehead

    NM $130   **MIP** $175

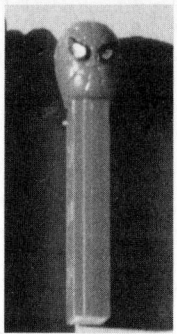

(KP Photo)

Spider-Man A, 1970s, no feet, small head w/black eyes

NM $10   **MIP** $15

(KP Photo, Sharon Bartsch collection)

Spider-Man B, 1980s, w/feet, bigger head

NM $1   **MIP** $2

Spider-Man C, 1990s, w/feet, larger head

NM $1   **MIP** $2

Thor, 1970s, no feet, yellow hair, gray winged helmet

NM $200   **MIP** $275

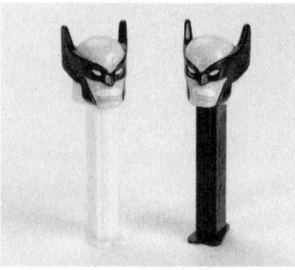

(KP Photo, Sharon Bartsch collection)

Wolverine, 1999, w/feet

NM $1   **MIP** $2

Wonder Woman, 1970s, Soft Head Superhero, no feet, black hair and yellow band w/raised red star

NM $100   **MIP** $150

Wonder Woman, 1970s, no feet, black hair and yellow band w/red star

NM $5   **MIP** $10

(KP Photo, Sharon Bartsch collection)

Wonder Woman, 1990s, w/feet, red stem

NM $1   **MIP** $2

Trucks

Truck A, 1970s, cab, stem body, single rear axle

NM $40   **MIP** $75

Truck B, 1970s, cab, stem body, dual rear axle and dual arch fenders

NM $35   **MIP** $65

(KP Photo, Sharon Bartsch collection)

Truck C, 1980s, cab, stem body, dual rear wheels w/single arch fender, movable wheels

NM $10   **MIP** $15

Truck D, 1990s, cab, stem body, dual rear wheels, single arch fender, nonmovable wheels

NM $1   **MIP** $2

Trucks 2005, 2005, darker cabs and trailers, four different styles

NM $1   **MIP** $2

Walgreens Trucks, 2005, set of two, Walgreens logos

NM $1   **MIP** $2

Wal-Mart Trucks, 2006-07, four different cab styles to collect, white trucks

NM $1   **MIP** $2

Universal Monsters

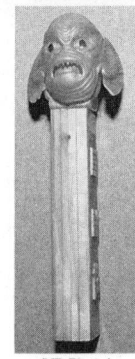

(KP Photo)

Creature From the Black Lagoon, 1960s, no feet, green head and matching stem, w/copyright

NM $250   **MIP** $300

Frankenstein, 1960s, no feet, black hair, gray head

NM $180   **MIP** $225

(Barry Koester)

Wolf Man, 1960s, no feet, black stem, gray head

NM $150   **MIP** $225

Valentine's Day

Boy and Girl PEZ Pals, 1970s, no feet, value for each

NM $25   **MIP** $35

(KP Photo, Sharon Bartsch collection)

Boy and Girl PEZ Pals, 1980s/1990s, w/feet

NM $5   **MIP** $10

Valentine Heart, 1990s, no feet, red stem

NM $1   **MIP** $2

Warner Bros.

Bugs Bunny, w/feet, gray head w/white cheeks
> **NM** $1   **MIP** $1

Bugs Bunny, 1970s, no feet, gray head w/white cheeks
> **NM** $15   **MIP** $20

Cool Cat, 1980, w/feet, orange head, blue snout, black ears
> **NM** $50   **MIP** $75

Daffy Duck A, 1970s, no feet, black head, yellow beak, removable white eyes
> **NM** $10   **MIP** $15

Daffy Duck B, w/feet, black head, yellow beak
> **NM** $3   **MIP** $5

Foghorn Leghorn, 1980s, no feet, brown head, yellow beak, red wattle
> **NM** $75   **MIP** $95

Foghorn Leghorn, 1980s, w/feet, brown head, yellow beak, red wattle
> **NM** $60   **MIP** $85

Henery Hawk, 1980s, w/feet
> **NM** $55   **MIP** $80

Henery Hawk, 1980s, no feet, light brown head, yellow beak
> **NM** $60   **MIP** $95

Looney Tunes Back in Action, 2003, w/feet, European release, Taz, Daffy, Tweety, Bugs, Yosemite Sam
> **NM** $1   **MIP** $2

Merlin Mouse, 1980s, no feet, gray head w/flesh cheeks, green hat
> **NM** $20   **MIP** $35

Merlin Mouse, 1980s, w/feet, gray head w/flesh cheeks, green hat
> **NM** $10   **MIP** $15

Petunia Pig, 1980s, w/or w/out feet, black hair in pigtails
> **NM** $25   **MIP** $35

Road Runner A, 1980s, no feet, purple head, yellow beak
> **NM** $25   **MIP** $35

Road Runner B, 1980s, w/feet, purple head, yellow beak
> **NM** $15   **MIP** $20

(KP Photo, Sharon Bartsch collection)

Speedy Gonzales, w/feet, brown head, yellow sombrero
> **NM** $1   **MIP** $2

Speedy Gonzales, 1970s, no feet, brown head, yellow sombrero
> **NM** $30   **MIP** $45

Sylvester, w/feet, black head, white whiskers, red nose
> **NM** $1   **MIP** $2

Sylvester, 1970s, no feet, black head, white whiskers, red nose
> **NM** $10   **MIP** $15

Tweety Bird, w/feet, painted eyes
> **NM** $1   **MIP** $2

Tweety Bird, 1970s, no feet, painted eyes
> **NM** $15   **MIP** $20

Tweety Bird, 1970s, no feet, removable eyes
> **NM** $15   **MIP** $25

Wile E. Coyote, 1980s, no feet, brown head
> **NM** $60   **MIP** $75

Wile E. Coyote, 1980s, w/feet, brown head
> **NM** $30   **MIP** $40

(KP Photo, Sharon Bartsch collection)

Yosemite Sam, 1990s, w/feet
> **NM** $1   **MIP** $2

Robots

by Justin Pinchot

It is very difficult to pinpoint the allure of vintage toy robots, but alluring they are. And they continue to be extremely popular amongst collectors, commanding real money on the open market – up to high five figures in some cases.

Although robots were alluded to prior to World War II (the word "robot" was first coined in a 1921 stage play called Rossums' Universal Robots - RUR by Karl Capek), our current conception of a toy robot didn't really materialize until just after World War II when Japan was trying to pick itself back up after a devastating loss to the allies.

Following the devastation of World War II, the future was on everyone's mind, including Japanese toymakers. In an effort to capitalize on the idea of the future, and produce a fantasy toy that might be appealing to both boys and girls (both can be seen playing with the toy on the box), a Japanese toy company called KT produced a diminutive, orange robot named "Lilliput Robot." Widely accepted amongst collectors as the first robot toy, Lilliput, aptly named as he is only about 6˝ tall, was fashioned out of stamped and lithographed tin. He was simply designed with rivets and a meter on his chest. With a block head, moveable arms, claw hands and a wind-up pin mechanism in the feet to make him walk, the Lilliput unknowingly started an avalanche of toy robot production from Japan. Robots were produced early on in the U.S. and other countries as well, but the lion's share of robots from the golden age, 1949-1965, were Japanese in origin.

With Japanese toy firms in competition for the American market, new innovations appeared. The use of battery-operated motors with lights, sounds, and actions brought new, complex toys to market, and soon, Japan was the leader in U.S. toy consumption. The era brought present-day collectors a vast array of wonderful, colorful, and whimsical robot toys to collect.

There were almost as many Japanese companies that produced toy robots as there are robot variations. In Japan, postwar toy production was truly a cottage-industry; motors and frames would be delivered to one home for assembly, while other components were assembled at other locations, finally all coming together at the factory where final assembly, touch-up, and packaging took place before export. This sort of production led to robots from different manufacturers resembling one another, sharing the same parts, or robots appearing on the Japanese market for local consumption only differing from U.S. export models in color or lithograph pattern.

As fantasy gave way to actual space travel, robots and space toys gave rise to new reality-based toys of the Apollo era, and production of classic toy robots slowly came to a close. While robots have continued to pop up since that time and often enjoy short resurgences (R2D2 and C3PO of Star Wars fame, the Iron Giant, and most recently Disney's Wall-E), the golden era of robots has tottered off into the sunset, and has been replaced by real life robots from manufacturers like Honda and Sony.

Today, toy robots from the classic era elicit different emotions from different people – some baby boomers collect them for nostalgia, while other younger collectors collect because these items have transcended their original use as toys, and have become art and sculpture. These charming automatons of a bygone era remove us from the "future shock" of the real 21st century – from Blackberries and iPods, corporate dominance and world financial meltdowns, toy robots remind us of a seemingly simpler, gentler time when we dreamt of what the

The **Top 10 ROBOTS** in mint condition

1. Diamond Planet Robot, Yonezawa, 1962 . . . . $50,850
2. Machine Man, Masudaya, 1958 . . . . $45,000
3. Tremendous Mike, Aoshin, 1960 . . . . $25,425
4. Radicon Robot, Masudaya, 1955 . . . . $17,500
5. Chime Trooper, Aoshin, 1955 . . . . $17,500
6. Robot Mighty 8, Masudaya, 1960s $15,000
7. Radar Robot, ("Topolino") Nomura, 1968 . . . . $14,000
8. Astro Scout, Yonezawa, 1963 . . . . $13,560
9. X-27 Explorer, Yonezawa, 1963 . . . . $13,560
10. Robot, Waco ("Hook robot"), 1955 . . . . $13,500

future might be – with robots to do our chores, and jet packs to fly us to work. Toy robots are constant reminders that the "future" was once innocent and exciting.

In the last year, toy robot values have fallen from just a year or two before. Several factors have contributed to the decline; there were two giant auctions held last year featuring hundreds of robots and space toys; the Bob Lesser collection, and the Alan Rosen collection. There were also other smaller auctions of robot and space toys, all sold in a relatively short period of time, essentially saturating the market. Couple this with one of the worst economic climates on record, and it is not hard to understand why prices are down overall. Prices will eventually rise, but now may be a good opportunity to buy that robot or space toy you've always wanted.

Tips for collecting toy robots: they can turn up anywhere; flea markets, yard sales, auctions, the Internet, and the like. Get a good education before spending any money; to realize full value, condition is key. There are many publications (like this one) to help with identification and value

guidelines. Old auction catalogs can also be useful to see past trends and prices. Because speculation can often lead to disappointment when selling, collect only what you love.

Contributor: Justin Pinchot resides near Los Angeles, Calif., and is a lifelong toy collector/dealer specializing in ray guns, robots and space toys from the classic era (1949 – 1964). He owns and operates www.toyraygun.com, an online meeting place for those seeking information on vintage toy ray guns. The Web site also has a trading section with vintage robots, ray guns, and space toys for sale.

Justin has consulted on vintage toys for Antiques Road Show, and writes for several publications on the subject of space toys. He does repairs, restorations, appraisals, and liquidates toy and collectibles estates.

Justin also collects and deals in the very esoteric Baranger Motion window displays, vintage toy trains, 1930s-1950s balloon tire bicycles, 1950s and 60s automobiles, art deco microphones, clocks and wristwatches, and space-related collectibles. Numerous items from his personal collection have appeared in books and museum displays. He is always happy to discuss any of these items, and can be contacted directly through his Web site, www. toyraygun.com.

Advance Toys

Mr. Atom, 1960s, 18", red and silver plastic, battery-operated, "The Electronic Walking Robot… Completely Harmless," according to the box
EX $125   **NM** $250   **MIP** $450

AHI

Lost in Space Robot, 1977, battery-operated, different in design than the Robinson family's companion but desirable, 12"
EX $75   **NM** $125   **MIP** $250

Alps

Cragstan Great Astronaut, 1960s, 11", red tin, battery-operated, w/video scene, key in head
EX $500   **NM** $800   **MIP** $1450

Door Robot, 1958, 9-1/2", tin, battery-operated, remote control, revolving head
EX $725   **NM** $1300   **MIP** $3000

Mechanical Television Spaceman, 1965, wind-up, w/chest scene and antenna, 7"
EX $95   **NM** $185   **MIP** $500

Missle Robot, 1965, battery-operated, lights, walks, then stops while flashing missiles pop out of chest door, plastic head, arms, and feet, 17"
EX $1200 **NM** $2200   **MIP** $4000

Moon Explorer, 1959, battery-operated, lights, walks while clock in chest spins, tin w/plastic head, hands and feet, antenna on/off switch in head, 17-1/2"
EX $700   **NM** $1300   **MIP** $1900

Mr. Robot the Mechanical Brain, 1954, tin wind-up
EX $600   **NM** $1200   **MIP** $1750

Rocketman in Space Armor, 1965, battery-operated w/wired remote, tin w/plastic head that tilts back w/tin astronaut head beneath, lights, walks, missiles eject from back pack, spinning antenna on head, 17"
EX $900 **NM** $2200   **MIP** $4000

Television Space Man, 1959, battery-operated, chest video, key in head operates as antenna, 11"
EX $125   **NM** $250   **MIP** $1200

AN-Japan

Astronaut Robot, 1950s, wind-up, tanks on back, gun in hand, 8"
EX $500   **NM** $1250   **MIP** $2000

Aoshin

Chime Trooper, 1955, wind-up, plays "music," stops and changes direction, VERY rare, 9"
EX $5500 **NM** $8500   **MIP** $17500

Tremendous Mike, 1950s, wind-up, orange or silver body, rotating antenna, chest sparks, 11"
EX $2500 **NM** $4500   **MIP** $25425

Arco

Ro-Gun "It's A Robot," 1984, robot changes into a rifle
EX $11   **NM** $16   **MIP** $25

Asak

Space Guard Pilot, 1975, 8"
EX $20   **NM** $30   **MIP** $45

Asakusa-Japan

Thunder Robot, 1950s, battery-operated, w/antenna and guns in palms of hands, 11"
EX $1300 **NM** $1800   **MIP** $3000

Bandai

Batman, 1960s, battery-operated, juvenile apperance, vinyl and tin, symbol lights in chest, rare, 10"
EX n/a   **NM** n/a   **MIP** n/a

CDI

Star Robot, 1978, battery-operated, knock-off Storm Trooper helmet, chest cannons behind a door, made in Hong Kong, 11"
EX $50   **NM** $150   **MIP** $225

Cragstan

Astronaut, 1961, battery-operated, head-mounted antenna spins, jackhammer gun, barrel chest, 11"
EX $300   **NM** $650   **MIP** $1200

Astronaut, 1962, battery-operated, round chest, laster rifle in right hand, "Cragstan Astronaut" written on waist, 15"
EX $275   **NM** $550   **MIP** $900

Countdown-Y, 1960s, 9"
EX $125   **NM** $175   **MIP** $275

Cragstan Robot, 1962, battery-operated, bump-and-go action, silver body, skirted legs, plastic domed head, 12"
EX $500   **NM** $1100   **MIP** $1800

Cragstan's Mr. Robot, 1960s, battery-operated, red or white body, clear dome head, 10-1/2"
EX $325   **NM** $525   **MIP** $925

Magnor, 1975, 9", plastic
EX $23   **NM** $35   **MIP** $50

Mr. Atomic, 1962, battery-operated, bump-and-go action, built by Yonezawa, 16 lights under plastic dome, silver, 9"
EX $2500 **NM** $3800   **MIP** $6000

Mr. Atomic, 1962, rare, battery-operated, bump-and-go action, built by Yonezawa, 16 lights under plastic dome, blue, 9"
EX $3500 **NM** $5000   **MIP** $7350

Mr. LEM Astronaut Robot, 1970, battery-operated, rotates, 13"
EX $150   **NM** $310   **MIP** $475

Mr. Robot, 1960, battery-operated, skirted legs, "Cragstan Mr. Robot" on chest, red body (white body variation worth 25 percent more), black wrench arms, 12"
EX $600   **NM** $1200   **MIP** $1700

Space Robot Patrol, 1959, friction motor, robot driving red Mercedes convertible, 11" long
EX $350   NM $700   MIP $1200

Talking Robot, 1963, battery-operated voice, friction-motor robot, three functions, says four messages, "Cragstan Talking Robot" on chest, 12"
EX $375   NM $650   MIP $1300

Daiya

Astro Captain, 1970s, wind-up, red/white/blue sparker, NASA on helmet, 6"
EX $35   NM $65   MIP $125

Astronaut, 1963, battery-operated, identical to Cragstan Astronaut, different litho design, laser rifle, 15"
EX $600   NM $1000   MIP $1800

Space Conqueror, 1963, rare green version, tin w/plastic dome and gun, walks w/spinning antenna, then stops and raises flashing ray gun, 12"
EX $1800   NM $2500   MIP $6200

Space Conqueror, 1963, blue version, tin w/plastic dome and gun, walks w/spinning antenna, then stops and raises flashing ray gun, 12"
EX $700   NM $1000   MIP $1800

Durham

Robot 2500, 1970s, battery-operated, "cyclops," 10"
EX $25   NM $45   MIP $65

Dux

Astroman, 1962, battery-operated w/corded remote, green plastic allows view of inner workings, antenna on head, 12"
EX $500   NM $900   MIP $1580

Haji

Space Trooper, 1955, wind-up, human face in helmet, holding rifle across left arm, blue barrel chest, yellow arms and legs
EX $1000   NM $2500   MIP $5876

Hong Kong

Action Robot, 1970s, battery-operated, yellow/blue, multiple functions, 10"
EX $15   NM $35   MIP $55

Radar Hunter, 1970s, wind-up, red/silver or orange, 5"
EX $15   NM $35   MIP $55

Robbie Robot, 1970s, battery-operated, blue/red/yellow, blinks, 9"
EX $25   NM $45   MIP $85

See-Thru Robot, 1970s, battery-operated, clear head and chest w/gears, 10"
EX $125   NM $325   MIP $600

Sounding Robot, 1970s, battery-operated, three push buttons on head, 8"
EX $25   NM $50   MIP $75

Sparking Robot, 1970s, wind-up, black body, 6"
EX $20   NM $35   MIP $50

Star Robot, 1970s, battery-operated, Star Wars Storm Trooper head, 10"
EX $25   NM $45   MIP $70

Horikawa/SH

Astronaut, 1963, battery-operated, human face, opening chest doors w/firing guns, 11"
EX $150   NM $250   MIP $500

Attack Robot, 1962, battery-operated, block head w/mesh eyes, chest doors open and guns fire, 11"
EX $150   NM $300   MIP $450

Attacking Martian, 1964, battery-operated, guns in chest, red mesh eyes, black body, 11"
EX $100   NM $250   MIP $425

Battle Robot, 1962, battery-operated, silver body, round eyes, red lights on head, 11"
EX $200   NM $350   MIP $575

Cosmic Fighter Robot, 1970s, head opens to reveal gunner inside while body spins, 11-1/2"
EX $50   NM $85   MIP $130

Dino Robot, 1960s, battery-operated, head opens to reveal dinosaur, 11"
EX $200   NM $350   MIP $595

Engine Robot, 1968, battery-operated, square chest w/four rotating chest gears, 9"
EX $150   NM $300   MIP $400

Engine Robot, 1970s, battery-operated, 10"
EX $75   NM $150   MIP $350

Excavator Robot, 1960s, battery-operated, w/drill type hands, 10"
EX $275   NM $400   MIP $600

Excavator Robot, 1970s, battery-operated, w/drill-type hands, 10"
EX $60   NM $125   MIP $250

Fighting Martian, 1960s, battery-operated, single gun in chest, moving antennas in shoulders, sounds
EX $150   NM $350   MIP $750

Fighting Robot, 1960s, battery-operated, single chest gun, flashing light on head, "Sounding and lighted rapid fire gun" on box, 11"
EX $150   NM $350   MIP $600

Fighting Space Man, 1962, battery-operated, same toy as Fighting Robot but head has a human face, 11"
EX $200   NM $350   MIP $500

Gear Robot, 1960s, battery-operated, plastic gears in chest, antennae on shoulders, 11-1/2"
EX $225   NM $350   MIP $500

Gear Robot, 1960s, wind-up, visible gears, 9"
EX $125   NM $275   MIP $450

Giant Robot, 1960s, battery-operated, yellow legs, red feet and head, 17"
EX $150   NM $300   MIP $450

Golden Gear Robot, 1960s, gold, battery-operated, w/chest gears and lit dome, 9"
EX $225   NM $500   MIP $700

Launching Robot, 1975, 10"
EX $25   NM $35   MIP $75

Mr. Zerox, 1968, battery-operated, w/blinking chest guns, uses parts from other SH robots, 9-1/2"
EX $100   NM $210   MIP $350

Piston Robot, 1972, battery-operated, lighted pistons in square head, black body, 11"
EX $200   **NM** $450   **MIP** $600

Radar Robot, 1970s, wind up, red body, yellow arms, radar rotates, 6-1/2"
EX $25   **NM** $50   **MIP** $75

Radar Scope Space Scout, 1964, battery-operated, TV screen w/noise, 10"
EX $85   **NM** $200   **MIP** $375

Robot, 1958, battery-operated, early models tin, late models tin and plastic, square chest opens to reveal guns, mesh eyes
EX $250   **NM** $450   **MIP** $550

Silver Ray Secret Weapon Space Scout, 1962, battery-operated, chrome silver body, chest doors open to expose spy camera that transforms to cannons, 9"
EX $275   **NM** $550   **MIP** $700

Sky Robot, 1970s, battery-operated, yellow and red, 8"
EX $20   **NM** $45   **MIP** $65

Smoking Engine Robot, 1970s, battery-operated, piston action, w/sound and smoke, 10"
EX $45   **NM** $85   **MIP** $135

Space Astronaut, 1969, battery-operated, human face, doors open to show chest cannons
EX $85   **NM** $200   **MIP** $350

Space Commander Robot, 1960s, tank type base, bump-and-go motion, w/guns, 10"
EX $500   **NM** $800   **MIP** $1200

Space Explorer Robot, 1960s, battery-operated, drop down chest cover reveals video, 11"
EX $100   **NM** $225   **MIP** $350

Space Fighter, 1960s, battery-operated, w/chest doors and guns, 9"
EX $100   **NM** $225   **MIP** $350

Super Giant (Rotate-a-Matic) Robot, 1970s, battery-operated, w/chest guns, 16"
EX $85   **NM** $150   **MIP** $250

Super Moon Explorer, 1969, battery-operated, torso swivels, plastic arms and feet
EX $100   **NM** $200   **MIP** $300

Super Robot Tank, 1950s, friction powered w/two guns, 9" long
EX $80   **NM** $175   **MIP** $400

Super Space Commander, 1970s, battery-operated, blue body, chest video, 10"
EX $20   **NM** $40   **MIP** $60

Swivel-O-Matic Astronaut, 1960s, battery-operated, black body, 12"
EX $75   **NM** $150   **MIP** $350

Video Robot, 1969, battery-operated, blue body, red feet, simple motion, w/chest video, 9"
EX $75   **NM** $175   **MIP** $350

Ideal

Maxx Steele Robot, 1984, programmable servant, w/charger, 30"
EX $100   **NM** $250   **MIP** $425

Mighty Zogg the Leader Zeroid, 1967, battery-operated, w/Motorific motors, 6"
EX $60   **NM** $100   **MIP** $175

Mr. Machine, 1961, wind-up, w/bell and key, disassembles, 18"
EX $85   **NM** $100   **MIP** $150

Mr. Machine, 1977, wind-up, whistles, does not disassemble, 18"
EX $20   **NM** $40   **MIP** $75

Robert the Robot, 1954, battery-operated, remote "laser gun" styled control attached to toy, 14"
EX $75   **NM** $100   **MIP** $250

Robot Commando, 1961, battery-operated, blue/red, remote control, fires rockets and balls, 19"
EX $75   **NM** $150   **MIP** $350

Zerak the Blue Destroyer Zeroid, 1968, battery-operated, w/Motorific motors, 6"
EX $75   NM $100   MIP $175

Zeroid Alien, 1970, battery-operated, 12"
EX $75   NM $100   MIP $250

ZEROIDS

Zintar the Silver Explorer Zeroid, 1967, battery-operated, w/Motorific motors, 6"
EX $75   NM $100   MIP $175

Zobor the Bronze Transporter Zeroid, 1967, battery-operated, w/Motorific motors, 6"
EX $50   NM $100   MIP $175

Zogg, Zeroid Commander-in-Chief, 1970, battery-operated, 6"
EX $50   NM $100   MIP $175

Irwin

Man From Mars, 1950s, wind-up, yellow body, shooting "space boy," 11"
EX $350   NM $750   MIP $1200

Man From Mars, 1950s, wind-up, red body, "space boy," 11"
EX $125   NM $275   MIP $350

Japan

Answer Game Machine, 1960s, battery-operated, performs math tricks, 14"
EX $350   NM $500   MIP $650

Apollo 2000 Robot, 1960s, battery-operated, red and blue, w/chest guns, 12"
EX $95   NM $175   MIP $300

Apollo 2000X, 1970s, wind-up, blue and red, w/spark, 6"
EX $45   NM $95   MIP $165

Atomic Robot Man, 1948, wind-up, 6"
EX $200   NM $300   MIP $1000

Blink-A-Gear Robot, 1960s, battery-operated, black body, clear plastic front w/gears, 14"
EX $175   NM $500   MIP $750

Construction Robot, 1960s, battery-operated, yellow body w/forklift, 12"
EX $450   NM $1000   MIP $1650

High-Wheel Robot, 1950s, battery-operated, blue body, remote control, 9"
EX $200   NM $350   MIP $550

High-Wheel Ronot, 1950s, wind-up, black body w/chest gears, 9"
EX $125   NM $200   MIP $350

Machine Robot, 1960s, battery-operated, w/shoulder antennae, 11"
EX $145   NM $250   MIP $400

Mars Explorer, 1950s, battery-operated, red body, w/wheels, face doors open, 9-1/2"
EX $450   NM $800   MIP $1100

Mars King, 1960s, battery-operated, w/video, siren and treads, 9"
EX $125   NM $350   MIP $500

Mr. Chief, 1960s, battery-operated, smoking action, 11-1/2"
EX $475   NM $700   MIP $1200

Mr. Patrol, 1960s, battery-operated, meter in chest, 11"
EX $150   NM $350   MIP $575

New Astronaut Robot, 1970s, battery-operated, w/three firing chest guns, 9"
EX $45   NM $85   MIP $135

Piston Robot, 1970s, 10", tin and plastic, battery-operated, lighted chest pistons, 10"
EX $60   NM $110   MIP $225

Piston Robot, 1980s, battery-operated, lighted chest pistons, 10"
EX $35   NM $65   MIP $125

Robot Tank - Mini, battery-operated, w/two guns, 5-1/2"
EX $85   NM $160   MIP $275

Roto-Robot, 1960s, battery-operated, w/chest guns, rotates 360 degrees, 9"
EX $95   NM $185   MIP $250

RX-008 Robot, 1960s, wind-up, w/sparking chest, 5"
EX $150   NM $350   MIP $520

Singing Robot, 1970s, battery-operated, missiles in head, 10"
EX $35   NM $75   MIP $100

Space Explorer Robot, 1950s, wind-up, w/O2 gauge on chest, 9"
EX $450   NM $900   MIP $1200

Space Explorer Robot, 1960s, battery-operated, rotating shoulder antenna, 12"
EX $450   NM $1000   MIP $1650

Space Ranger, 1970s, battery-operated, R/C, fires balls from chest, 10"
EX $50   NM $110   MIP $165

Space Robot X-70, 1960s, battery-operated, lights, noise, and "Tulip Head," 12"

EX $450   **NM** $900   **MIP** $1200

Sparky Robot, 1960s, wind-up, green cylindrical body, 7"

EX $45   **NM** $65   **MIP** $150

Super Astronaut, 1960s, battery-operated, man's face, w/chest guns, 10"

EX $100   **NM** $200   **MIP** $300

Zoomer Robot, 1950s, battery-operated, blue or silver w/red, w/wrench, 7"

EX $295   **NM** $425   **MIP** $700

KTA-Japan

Robot Lilliput, 1949, wind-up, one of the oldest, square "block" head w/yellow litho, "N.P. 5257" on chest, 6"

EX $1500   **NM** $3500   **MIP** $6500

Linemar

Golden Robot, 1958, battery-operated w/corded remote, gold color, smiling, "ROBOT" lights up in chest, 6-1/2"

EX $400   **NM** $650   **MIP** $1630

(Justin Pinchot photo)

Lantern Robot, 1955, battery-operated w/corded remote, holds illuminated lantern, blows smoke from mouth, 8"

EX $800   **NM** $1000   **MIP** $1860

Mechanical Walking Sparking Robot, 1950s, batttery-operated, 6"

EX $250   **NM** $350   **MIP** $550

Spaceman, 1958, battery-operated, small face within helmet, lights up, has gun, 8"

EX $1000   **NM** $2000   **MIP** $3000

Marx

Big Loo, 1963, battery-operated, water squirter, w/rockets and tools, 36"

EX $450   **NM** $1200   **MIP** $1800

Colonel Hap Hazard, 1968, rotating antenna on head, 11"

EX $250   **NM** $475   **MIP** $900

Electric Robot, 1950s, battery-operated, black and red, w/morse code, 15"

EX $95   **NM** $150   **MIP** $300

Frankenstein, 1960s, wind-up walker, 6"

EX $100   **NM** $250   **MIP** $450

Frankenstein Robot, 1968, battery-operated, wired remote control, 14"

EX $575   **NM** $1250   **MIP** $2000

Great Garloo, The, 1962, battery-operated, remote control, monster features, seven movements, popular, 23"

EX $100   **NM** $300   **MIP** $450

Hi-Bouncer Moon Scout, 1968, battery-operated w/corded remote, human face, 11-1/2"

EX $550   **NM** $1200   **MIP** $2000

High Bouncer Moon Scout, 1968, shoots balls from chest, 11"

EX $500   **NM** $1050   **MIP** $2200

Moon Creature, 1968, bug-eyed, mechanical, wind-up, 5-1/2"

EX $95   **NM** $125   **MIP** $275

Mr. Mercury, 1962-64, battery-operated w/corded remote, bending action, "Mr. Mercury" on chest, 14"

EX $275   **NM** $650   **MIP** $900

Mr. Smash, 1970s, wind-up, red body, Martian Mashed Potato promo, 6"

EX $50   **NM** $95   **MIP** $150

Robot and Son, 1956, battery-operated, similar to Marx Robot toy but comes w/small plastic son holding a bar overhead used by Robot to lift him, 15"

EX $75   **NM** $100   **MIP** $200

Rock 'Em, Sock 'Em Robots, 1966-1976, two plastic robots in boxing ring controlled by handles, when one is punched just right his head flies upward on a spring, just plain goofy fun

EX $60   **NM** $120   **MIP** $200

Son of Garloo, 1960s, wind-up, green body, monster walker, 6"

EX $100   **NM** $225   **MIP** $300

Masudaya

Forbidden Planet Robby, 1985, wind-up, 5"

EX $15   **NM** $25   **MIP** $40

Forbidden Planet Robby, 1985, battery-operated, talks, 16"

EX $65   **NM** $125   **MIP** $200

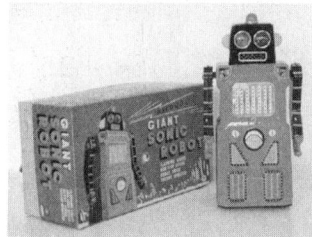

Giant Sonic Robot (Train Robot), 1959, battery-operated, red body, black arms and head, robot makes "trainlike" sound as it rolls along, very hard to find, one of the "Gang of Five," 15"

EX $3800   **NM** $5500   **MIP** $9000

(Sotheby's Photo)

Machine Man, 1950s, battery-operated, the rarest robot from Masudaya's "Gang of Five" series, this robot sold for $42,550 at the Sotheby's auction of the Tin Toy Robot Collection of Matt Wyse in 1996, 15"

EX $10000 NM $20000 MIP $45000

Non-Stop (Lavender) Robot, 1956, battery-operated, part of the skirted "Gang of Five"

EX $2600 NM $3000   MIP $6780

R-35 Robot, 1962, battery-operated, remote-control battery box is red, eyes light up, 8"

EX $175   NM $300   MIP $550

Radicon Robot, 1955, battery-operated, painted a hammer-tone gray/green finish, first true wireless remote-control toy w/stop/start/forward/left/right action, lighted eyes, spinning antenna ears, lighted meter in chest, separate large batter remote w/antenna, both robot and remote take several D cells, very rare robot, 15"

EX $7000 NM $10000 MIP $17500

Robot Mighty 8, 1960s, dark blue metal body, red feet, electric color display on chest

EX $1500 NM $4500   MIP $15000

Robot YM-3, 1985, wind-up, "Lost in Space B9" type, 5"

EX $10   NM $20   MIP $35

Space Commando, 1958, battery-operated w/corded remote, one of a few astronauts produced by Masudaya, poseable head, 7-1/2"

EX $600   NM $1300   MIP $2000

Target Robot, 1958, battery-operated, blue skirted robot w/red target disk in chest, one of the "Gang of Five," 15"

EX $6500 NM $8500   MIP $11000

The Gang of Five, 1997, five mini-robots, Mini Sonic Robot, Mini Target Robot, Mini Machine Man, Mini Non-Stop Lavender Robot, Mini Radicon Robot, 5"

EX $30   NM $50   MIP $80

Mego

Gigantor Robot, 1960s, battery-operated, silver w/white "hands" and red feet, 17"

EX $50   NM $100   MIP $200

Mego-Japan

Krome-Dome Robot, 1960s, plastic, battery-operated, disk-type head opens w/sound, 11"

EX $125   NM $295   MIP $425

Mikes Toy House

Mr. Atomic, 1990s, limited reproduction

EX $95   NM $200   MIP $350

Miscellaneous

Lightning Robot, 1980s, battery-operated, looks like R2D2 w/flashing lights

EX $20   NM $40   MIP $80

Lunar Spaceman, 1978, battery operated, 12"

EX $20   NM $30   MIP $45

Mechanical Interplanetary Explorer, 1950s, wind-up, 8"

EX $180   NM $260   MIP $400

Myrobo, 1970s, battery-operated, 9"

EX $25   NM $35   MIP $55

Raid "Bug" Robot, large, battery-operated, remote control, ad promo, Korea

EX $75   NM $150   MIP $250

Ranger Robot, battery-operated, clear body, w/smoke and sound, Japan, 11"

EX $500   NM $1200   MIP $2250

Zero of Space, 1970s, battery-operated, red and yellow w/visor, w/lights, 14"

EX $100   NM $225   MIP $350

MTU-Korea

Captain the Robot, 1970s, gray wind-up, sparking, 6"

EX $15   NM $35   MIP $50

Naito Shoten

Deep-Sea Robot, 1956, very rare, 8"

EX $800   NM $1525   MIP $3500

N-Japan

Mighty Robot, 1969, wind-up, paddle-feet rotate to move robot forward, sparks in chest

EX $50   NM $100   MIP $150

Robot-7, 1966, wind-up, paddle-feet forward motion

EX $65   NM $125   MIP $225

Wind-Up Walking Robot, 1960s, wind-up sparker, plastic antenna on head, 7"

EX $100   NM $225   MIP $350

Nomura

Musical Drummer Robot, 1955, battery-operated w/lighted eyes, walking motion, lighted chest gel and beating drum, 8"

EX $2000 NM $2500   MIP $9600

Radar Robot (known as "Topolino" robot), 1968, battery-operated w/moving chest gears and lighted scenes in chest windows, plastic arms and two ear antennas

EX $4000 NM $7000   MIP $14000

Nomura/TN

Batman, 1966, battery-operated, walks forward, head lights up, cloth cape w/yellow "Batman" logo stenciled, 12"

EX n/a **NM** n/a **MIP** n/a

Earth Man, 1957, battery-operated w/corded remote, walks and fires his gun, 9"

EX $600 **NM** $1450 **MIP** $2000

Mechanized Robot, 1957, battery-operated; the icon of the hobby, this is based on Robby the Robot from the 1956 film "The Forbidden Planet," 14"

EX $500 **NM** $750 **MIP** $1500

Piston Action Robot, 1958, battery-operated w/corded remote, Robby-like w/pistons moving in clear dome, 11"

EX $500 **NM** $1200 **MIP** $2000

Radar Robot, 1955-58, battery-operated w/corded remote, wrench in right hand, webbed radar dish from back, several color variations, 9"

EX $500 **NM** $1000 **MIP** $1525

(Justin Pinchot photo)

Ratchet Robot, 1957, wind-up, based on Zoomer design, sparks from chest, coiled antenna across head, 7-1/2"

EX $200 **NM** $350 **MIP** $675

Robby Space Patrol, 1957, battery-operated, bump-and-go motion, this is one of the most famous space toys, representing (in an unlicensed way) the robot and his transport vehicle from the 1956 film, "The Forbidden Planet"

EX $1500 **NM** $2000 **MIP** $3800

Robot Tank-Z, 1960s, battery-operated, bump-and-go motion, 10"

EX $150 **NM** $300 **MIP** $500

Space Command Robot, 1950s, wind-up, w/gun in hand, 7-1/2"

EX $375 **NM** $1000 **MIP** $1650

Space Commando, 1956, battery-operated, plastic helmet only part of face visible, laser rifle, 11"

EX $500 **NM** $1000 **MIP** $1550

Tetsujin T-28, 1960s, a series of battery-operated robots based on the popular Japanese character known as "Gigantor" in the U.S., these are rare and very desirable

EX n/a **NM** n/a **MIP** n/a

Walking Mechanical Astroman w/Sparks, 1960s, battery-operated, distinctive red litho w/horizontal lines, body similar to Tetsujin T-28, plastic helmet, human face

EX n/a **NM** n/a **MIP** n/a

Zoomer the Robot, 1954, battery-operated, holding wrench in right hand, eyes glow red, antenna spins, many color variations

EX $250 **NM** $500 **MIP** $750

Orikawa

Mr. Hustler, 1960s, battery-operated, center chest light, 11-1/2"

EX $100 **NM** $225 **MIP** $400

Playing Mantis

Robot B-9, Lost In Space, 1990s, rolling wheels under base, sold individually, part of a series of four Lost-In-Space toys made by Playing Mantis Johnny Lightning, 3"

EX $4 **NM** $8 **MIP** $15

R.M.

Astronaut, 1960s, wind-up, arms move back and forth, red body, human face, 7"

EX $50 **NM** $85 **MIP** $125

Remco

Big Max & His Electronic Conveyor, 1958, battery-operated, w/truck and coins, 8" x 7"

EX $100 **NM** $185 **MIP** $300

Lost in Space Motorized Robot, 1966, battery-operated, black and red body, lights up, arms move, 14"

EX $125 **NM** $250 **MIP** $450

Mr. Brain, 1970, battery-operated, programmable memory, 13"

EX $75 **NM** $150 **MIP** $250

Rudy the Robot, 1967, orange, battery-operated, "He Walks Like a Man!," 16"

EX $75 **NM** $165 **MIP** $375

Rosko

Astronaut, 1962, battery-operated, blue or red litho, uses legs and torso of Nomura Robby series, human face

EX $550 **NM** $1300 **MIP** $2000

Space Conqueror, 1961, battery-operated, blue and yellow litho, copy of Cragstan Astronaut, human face

EX $550 **NM** $1300 **MIP** $2000

S.J.M.

Super Astronaut, 1981, battery-operated, man's face, w/chest guns, 10"

EX $12 **NM** $20 **MIP** $30

Saunders

Marvelous Mike, 1955, battery-operated, plastic robot on yellow tin

Caterpillar bulldozer, rubber treads, 14" long

EX $110   **NM** $225   **MIP** $300

Schaper

Tobor, 1978, black, battery-operated, radio control, 7"

EX $15   **NM** $30   **MIP** $50

SNK

Flashy Jim, 1955, battery-operated, square head, "R7" on chest, walks forward, eyes light up, 7-1/2"

EX $250   **NM** $500   **MIP** $1200

Robbie the Roving Robot, 1956, wind-up, antenna, 7"

EX $450   **NM** $1000   **MIP** $1800

Sparkling Mike Robot, 1957, wind-up, red diamonds in knees, hole in chest shoots sparks, antenna, 7"

EX $150   **NM** $300   **MIP** $550

Sonsco

Space Man, 1958, battery-operated, rifle in right hand, flashlight in left hand, remote w/space scene on it, blue antenna

EX $2000   **NM** $4000   **MIP** $8531

Straco-Japan

Hysterical Robot, 1970s, battery-operated, black body, bump-and-go and laughing actions, 13"

EX $100   **NM** $250   **MIP** $400

SY Japan

Fireman Robot, 1960s, wind-up, "Fire Man" on chest, flapping feet, w/or w/out hat

EX $100   **NM** $200   **MIP** $300

Mechanical Sparking Robot, 1965, keywound, silver w/litho, "W" in chest, flapping feet, 7"

EX $125   **NM** $275   **MIP** $450

Mechanical Walking Space Man, 1962, wind-up, black body, w/floppy arms and forward walking motion, 7-1/2"

EX $150   **NM** $400   **MIP** $700

Mechanical Walking Space Man w/Spark, 1970s, wind-up, silver litho, this variation sparks from chest, 7"

EX $100   **NM** $175   **MIP** $275

The Mego Man, 1960s, wind-up, top hat w/"Mego Man" in hat band, inspiried by Mr. Machine, red laughing face, silver bell in chest

EX $100   **NM** $225   **MIP** $350

Taiyo

Wheel-A-Gear Robot, 1950s, battery-operated, black body, w/mutli-chest gears and pullies, 15"

EX $425   **NM** $600   **MIP** $850

Tomy

Chatbot, 1970s, battery-operated, tape recorder in head, serving tray, speaks, remote control, 8"

EX $30   **NM** $65   **MIP** $110

Omnibot 2000, 1980s, battery-operated, remote control, programmable servant, 24"

EX $175   **NM** $400   **MIP** $675

Verbot, 1984, battery-operated, radio control, programmable, 8"

EX $15   **NM** $35   **MIP** $60

Topper

Boxer Ding-A-Ling, 1970s, battery-operated, orange and blue body

EX $20   **NM** $40   **MIP** $60

Chef Ding-A-Ling, 1970s, battery-operated, red, white and blue body

EX $20   **NM** $40   **MIP** $60

King-Ding Robot, 1970, battery-operated, separate brain robot goes in head, 12"

EX $110   **NM** $275   **MIP** $500

Waco

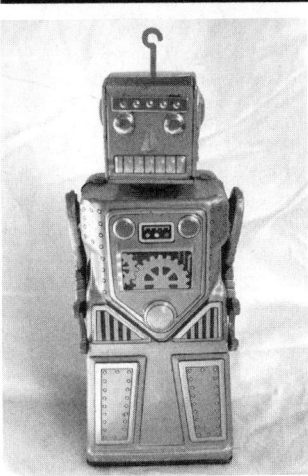

(Justin Pinchot photo)

Robot (known as "HOOK ROBOT"), 1955, tin friction, head moves from side-to-side as it rolls along, dark blue version w/red mouth, light silver-blue version w/silver mouth, 8"

EX $1500   **NM** $2000   **MIP** $13500

Waco-Japan

Laughing Robot, 1960s, battery-operated, mouth opens, laughs loudly, 13"

EX $125   **NM** $275   **MIP** $500

Yanoman

Rendezvous 7.8, 15"

EX $170   **NM** $245   **MIP** $375

Yonezawa

Astro Scout, 1963, crank friction walking motion, rare, 9"

EX $2500   **NM** $5500   **MIP** $13560

Conehead Robot, 1962, wind-up, Robby body and legs, cone-shaped head w/large eyes, 8-1/2"

EX $950   **NM** $1800   **MIP** $7685

Diamond Planet Robot, 1962, wind-up action; rolls forward, arms move up and down, chest meter swings back and forth, sparks in chest gel, very rare toy, 10"

EX $10000   **NM** $18000   **MIP** $50850

Directional Robot, 1963, battery-operated, blue body, head rotates, bump-and-go action, 10"

EX $225   **NM** $650   **MIP** $1500

Eightman, 1966, battery-operated, based on the anime superhero cyborg, rare, 14"

EX $2500   **NM** $5500   **MIP** $10000

Lunar Robot, 1960s, wind-up, sparks, companion to Thunder Robot, 7"

EX $225   **NM** $550   **MIP** $800

Mechanic Robot, 1969, battery-operated, phone dial in chest

EX $65   **NM** $135   **MIP** $250

Mechanical Mighty Robot, 1967, a.k.a. "Athlete Robot" due to its flexing arm motion, wind-up, red tin body, gray plastic head, Model No. 811

EX n/a   **NM** n/a   **MIP** n/a

Modern Robot, 1962, battery-operated, copy of Cragstan Robot w/new litho, "Modern Robot" written on chest

EX $650   **NM** $1400   **MIP** $2000

Mr. Mercury, 1961, battery-operated, believed to be the first model in the series, "Mr. Mercury" across chest, 13"

EX $650 NM $1000 MIP $1600

Robby Robot, 1958, wind-up, wrenches for arms, 8"

EX $600 NM $1500 MIP $2400

Robot Captain, 1968, wind-up, wrenches for arms, 5-1/2"

EX $50 NM $100 MIP $150

Roby Robot, 1960, wind-up, wrenches for arms, black body w/red feet, 8"

EX $800 NM $1750 MIP $2600

Scare Mighty Robot, 1960s, wind-up, red and white, sparking action, 10"

EX $175 NM $550 MIP $1000

Smoking Spaceman, 1960, battery-operated, dark gray metal body, smoke puffs from mouth as robot walks, 12"

EX $600 NM $800 MIP $1200

Space Explorer, 1959, wind-up, astronaut face, oxygen meter in chest, swings arms, 9-1/2"

EX $350 NM $700 MIP $1450

Space Explorer, 1959, battery-operated, TV screen in chest, robot transforms into a TV

EX $350 NM $700 MIP $1300

Space Scout, 1950s, rare, wind-up, w/radiation meter in chest, 10"

EX $1000 NM $2250 MIP $6500

Swinging Baby Robot, 1958, wind-up, clockwork swings the square-head baby, counterweight often missing

EX $295 NM $395 MIP $600

Winky Robot, 1958, wind-up action, walks w/oxygen meter moving back and forth in chest, and spark in mouth, 9"

EX $900 NM $1500 MIP $3000

X-27 Explorer, 1963, crank friction walking motion, rare, 9"

EX $2500 NM $5500 MIP $13560

Yoshiya/KO

Action Planet Robot, 1958, wind-up, Robby look-alike, forward walking, grate over face, black body w/red feet, 8"

EX $100 NM $200 MIP $350

Atom Robot, mid-1960s, wind-up, small skirted robot, bump-and-go action

EX $95 NM $195 MIP $450

Chief Robotman, 1959, battery-operated, bump-and-go motion, two spinning antennae, swinging arms, flashing lights, turning head, skirted robot, 12"

EX $450 NM $900 MIP $1550

Chief Smokey/Mr. Chief, 1959, battery-operated, skirted robot, smokes from head, 12"

EX $450 NM $900 MIP $1500

Jupiter Robot, 1969, wind-up, red body, w/two antennae, sparks, 7"

EX $85 NM $175 MIP $350

Mechanical Space Man Robot, 1950s, wind-up, silver litho, full face showing in helmet, antenna moves as he walks, 6"

EX $100 NM $200 MIP $500

Mighty Robot, 1959, battery-operated, bump-and-go motion, skirted robot,

gray-blue tin body, red plastic arms, clear plastic head, 12"

EX $1800 NM $2500 MIP $4000

Moon Explorer, 1959, wind-up, fixed legs, human-faced astronaut in dome helmet, 7-1/2"

EX $550 NM $1200 MIP $2000

Planet Robot, 1958, battery-operated w/corded remote, just like Action Planet Robot, blue and other color variations, 8"

EX $250 NM $600 MIP $1000

Robby, 1958, wind-up, fixed-legs, red body, plastic dome head, 7"

EX $200 NM $500 MIP $850

Robot Dog, 1956, wind-up, 7" long

EX $250 NM $450 MIP $600

Space Whale, 1957, wind-up, vehicle moves forward when antenna is raised, white and blue litho, google eyes, 7" long

EX $175 NM $285 MIP $600

Sparky Robot, 1954-59, wind-up, silver and red, w/head spring antenna; earliest version all silver from 1954, 7"

EX $275 NM $300 MIP $600

Venus Robot, 1960s, battery-operated, blue/red, remote control, 8"

EX $95 NM $200 MIP $325

Rock 'n' Roll

by Justin Moen

The birth of rock 'n' roll goes back to the rhythm and blues sound that became popular following World War II. Rock pioneers like Bill Haley, Little Richard, Bo Diddley, and Chuck Berry helped put rock music on the map in the early-to-mid-50s.

But it was Elvis Presley who revolutionized the rock sound forever in the late 50s. As a result, Elvis toys, memorabilia, and licensed products became a hot commodity instantly. Elvis products are still highly sought by collectors today.

The King did not have much competition until four lads from Liverpool landed at Kennedy International Airport in February 1964 and swept America and rock music forever. The combination of the Beatles and Elvis had a very strong impact that resonated not only in the music world, but also in the merchandising and collectibles community.

The images of John, Paul, George, and Ringo were very effective in endorsing products. Items like toy guitars, drums, and dolls successfully brought the Beatles to life for young people. Because Beatles memorabilia was produced in abundant quantities, they are not hard to find. But it's memorabilia in the best condition that is treasured by collectors.

Following the success of the Beatles, other talents helped keep rock memorabilia relevant and growing strong. Groups like The Monkees and The Partridge Family enjoyed great exposure on TV, which generated a lot of interest in related memorabilia, especially items featuring The Monkees' Davy Jones and The Partridge Family's David Cassidy.

In the 70s, it was hard rockers KISS that ruled the rock memorabilia world. The KISS name was on almost every major piece of memorabilia you can think of. One of the most notable were a pair of comic books released by Marvel, the first includes red ink mixed with blood donated by members of the band. From 2001-2008, KISS even sold KISS Kaskets (real coffins) on their Web site. Former Pantera guitarist and life-long KISS fan, Dimebag Darrell, was buried in a KISS Kasket following his tragic death in 2004.

Michael Jackson and Madonna memorabilia took over in the 1980s and 1990s, but faded over time. However, Jackson's death in June 2009 has sparked an increase in popularity for his memorabilia.

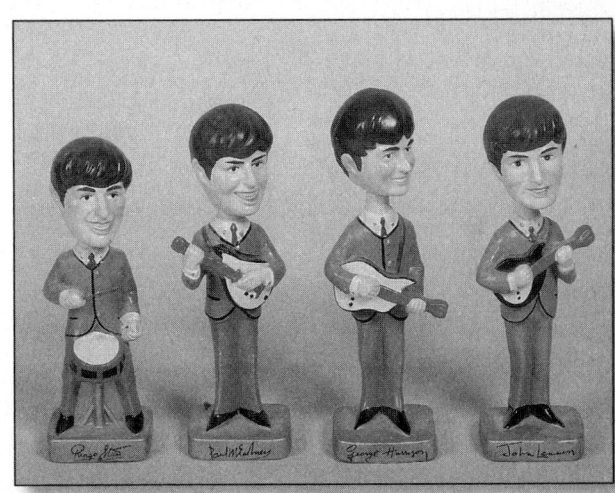

The latest boom in rock toys took place in the late-1990s and early-2000s with the teen pop craze led by the Backstreet Boys and *NSYNC. However, in the last few years the pop-music portion of the market has waned once again—Jackson memorabilia notwithstanding.

Today McFarlane Toys enjoy success with their KISS figures marketed toward older collectors. The company has also released figures of Ozzy Osbourne, Metallica, Rob Zombie, Janis Joplin, and Jim Morrison. Art Asylum even entered the rock 'n' roll toy arena by releasing figures of iconic rap group Run DMC.

The **Top 10 ROCK 'N' ROLL** in mint condition

1. Beatles Banjo, Mastro, 1964 . . . . $800
2. Beatles Bobbin' Head Dolls, set of four, 1960s $750
3. Beatles Guitar, Selcol, 1960s $600
4. Beatles Cartoon Kit, Colorforms, 1966 . . . . $525
5. Beatles Magic Slate, Merit, 1960s $500
6. Beatles Costume, Ben Cooper, 1960s $425
7. Beatles Jr. Guitar, Mastro, 1960s $425
8. Paint Your Own Beatle Kit, Artistic Creations, 1960s $400
9. Yellow Submarine Costume, Collegeville, 1960s $375
10. Paul McCartney Doll, Remco, 1964 . . . . $275

Beatles

ACCESSORIES

Beatles Costume, 1960s, child's costume and mask; John, Paul, George, or Ringo, each
EX $100 NM $200 MIP $425

Paul McCartney Soaky, 1965, red plastic
EX $70 NM $125 MIP $250

Ringo Starr Soaky, 1965, blue plastic
EX $70 NM $125 MIP $275

Yellow Submarine Halloween Costume, 1960s, Blue Meanie costume and mask
EX $100 NM $200 MIP $375

DOLL

George Harrison Doll, 1964
EX $50 NM $100 MIP $275

John Lennon Doll, 1964
EX $50 NM $100 MIP $275

Paul McCartney Doll, 1964
EX $50 NM $100 MIP $275

Ringo Starr Doll, 1964
EX $50 NM $100 MIP $275

TOY

Beatles Cartoon Kit, 1966
EX $150 NM $300 MIP $525

Beatles in Pepperland Puzzles, many variations and sizes, each
EX $35 NM $60 MIP $100

Beatles Jr. Guitar, 1960s, 14" red/pink plastic guitar w/Beatles graphics
EX $100 NM $225 MIP $425

Beatles Magic Slate, British
EX $150 NM $300 MIP $500

Beatles Notebook Binder, 1960s, binder from Beatles Fan Club
EX $50 NM $75 MIP $135

Paint Your Own Beatle Kit, 1960s, oil painting kit; John, Paul, George, or Ringo, each
EX $150 NM $300 MIP $400

Yellow Submarine Water Color Set, 1960s, pictures and paints
EX $40 NM $80 MIP $145

WATCH

Beatles Toy Watches, 1960s, four, tin w/plastic bands, on card
EX $30 NM $75 MIP $150

Elvis Presley

DOLL

Elvis Presley Doll, 1984, 21" tall
EX $50 NM $100 MIP $200

Elvis Presley Doll, 1984, 12" tall
EX $20 NM $40 MIP $80

WATCH

Elvis Presley Wristwatch, 1983, white plastic case, quartz, stainless back, face shows a young Elvis, white vinyl band
EX $25 NM $45 MIP $85

KISS

TOY

KISS Rub n' Play Magic Transfer Set, 1979
EX $20 NM $40 MIP $80

KISS Van Model Kit, 1977
EX $35 NM $70 MIP $140

Michael Jackson

ACCESSORIES

Michael Jackson AM Radio, 1984
EX $12 NM $25 MIP $45

DOLL

Michael Jackson Doll, 1984, several styles
EX $12 NM $25 MIP $50

TOY

Michael's Pets, 1987, plush animals, 10 kinds, each
EX $7 NM $15 MIP $25

Miscellaneous

DOLL

Andy Gibb Doll, 1979, 7" tall
EX $15 NM $30 MIP $60

Boy George Doll, 1980s, 15", polka dot shirt
EX $20 NM $40 MIP $75

Boy George Doll, 1980s, 12", poseable in alphabet shirt
EX $30 NM $60 MIP $120

Cher Doll, 1976, 12", w/growing hair
EX $55 NM $125 MIP $175

Cher Doll, 1976, 12"
EX $50 NM $100 MIP $150

Debby Boone Doll, 10" tall
EX $20 NM $40 MIP $80

Dolly Parton Doll, 1970s, 12" tall
EX $20 NM $40 MIP $80

Toni Tennille Doll, 12" tall
EX $8 NM $15 MIP $30

TOY

Pinky Lee Costume, 1950s, hat, pants, and shirt
EX $35 NM $75 MIP $145

Pinky Lee Xylophone
EX $35 NM $70 MIP $120

Sonny & Cher Play Set, 1976
EX $25 NM $50 MIP $85

Osmonds

DOLL

Donny Osmond Doll, 1976, 12" tall
EX $15 NM $25 MIP $45

Marie Osmond Doll, 1976, 12" tall
EX $10 NM $25 MIP $40

Marie Osmond Modeling Doll, 1976, 30" tall
EX $20 NM $40 MIP $80

TOY

Donny & Marie TV Show Play Set, 1976
EX $15 NM $35 MIP $55

Sci-Fi and Space Toys

Sci-Fi and Space Toys

by Justin Pinchot

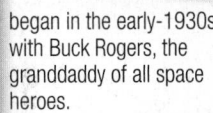

There is little consensus on the origins of Science Fiction among aficionados and devotees of the genre. Some would argue it started in ancient times when man first gazed into the heavens and began to wonder, dream, and create stories of what took place there. Others would say true Science Fiction was not possible until the Middle Ages – the age of science when Copernicus, Galileo, and da Vinci were hypothesizing, observing, or conceptualizing about our place in the universe, and the means to move within it. Still others would assert that Science Fiction, as we know it, did not exist until just after World War II and the dawning of the atomic age. Commercially speaking, however, Science Fiction created, packaged and marketed strictly for mass consumption really

began in the early-1930s with Buck Rogers, the granddaddy of all space heroes.

Buck and friends were an immediate success, first seen in a pulp publication, but soon after in a regular Sunday comic strip, and finally a wildly popular radio show. Daisy, a toy gun company well known for their rugged BB and pop guns, came up with a brilliant idea: they would have the artist of the Buck Rogers comics, Dick Calkins, draw a specifically designed cosmic side arm for our hero, one Daisy could faithfully replicate in the factory for sale to the general public. The idea was the consumer could hold in his hand the very gun he saw in the comics. The concept was a smashing success, so much so that lines formed around the block for consumers to be the first to own the premiere galactic gun, the Buck Rogers XZ-31 Rocket Pistol. Licensed merchandising had arrived, and toy marketing would never be the same.

On the heels of Buck Roger's blockbuster success entered the equally popular Flash Gordon, another space hero created to directly compete with Buck Rogers. Together, Buck Rogers and Flash Gordon ruled the heavens, in the 1930s and 1940s... at least until the wide use and popularity

The **Top 10 SCI-FI / SPACE TOYS** in mint condition

1. Space Patrol Car, Ichico & Yonezawa, c1955 . . . . $39,850
2. Flying Space Saucer, Aoshin, 1950s $26,000
3. Spaceship X-7, Modern Toys, c1953 . . . . $25,000
4. Space Cruiser X-300, Japan, c1955 . . . . $18,000
5. Pyrotomic Disintegrator Space Pistol, Pyro Plastics, c1953 . . . . $10,000
6. ME-56 Mercury Rocket, Daiya Japan, c1953 . . . . $6,500
7. Lost In Space Doll Set, Marusan, 1960s $5,000
8. Marsman Car, Modern Toys, c1953 . . . . $3,500
9. Space Patrol Monorail Set, Toys of Tomorrow, 1950s $3,500
10. Lunar Fleet Base, 1950s $3,200

of TV came in the 1950s, when we saw a whole new crop of space protagonists arrive: Captain Video, Tom Corbett Space Cadet, and the campy Characters of Space Patrol, among others.

Of course each of these shows had numerous products created and marketed for them by a myriad of companies; many of them veterans in the toy business like Marx, but others were unknowns that sprang up to produce one or two obscure items. Today, there are hundreds of these 1950s character space toys for collectors to covet. Then of course we get into Star Trek in the 1960s, and Star Wars in the 1970s, and the collecting possibilities are virtually infinite.

The "space" theme was everywhere in the 1950s, and was so pervasive a toy did not necessarily need a known space hero endorsement to sell – many companies made generic space guns and toys that sold quite well. In fact, many existing western/cowboy toys, a genre almost completely eclipsed by the space phenomenon, were merely re-packaged or redecorated and transformed into "space" toys. In some cases, especially in the cheaper Japanese toys, the western motif was left in place, and a simple rocket or Saturn graphic overlay was added to ride the coattails of the space wave that held the fascination of the nation, indeed the world, at that time.

With ray guns, there are so many generic toys produced, many were simply labeled "space gun," and a staggering number of space toys were marked "Space Patrol," even though they had no association with the television show of the same name.

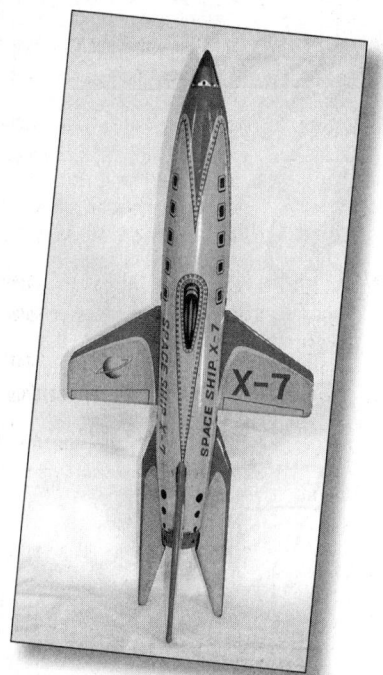

Adding to the angst of today's collectors, back in the day many retailers, to save shelf space, would commonly remove guns or space toys from their factory packaging, discard the boxes, stamp the price mark right on the toys themselves, then place them in bins for sale. This is especially true for smaller toys, often making original boxes or packaging for certain ray guns and space toys so rare their presence will often catapult the value of a toy to the stratosphere, multiplying the loose value exponentially. Although character-related space toys will always be valuable and desirable, it is often the generic space toys, mainly the Japanese lithographed tin toys, that are favorites with sophisticated collectors, and tend to sell for astronomically high prices at auctions, and privately.

Luckily, with franchises like Star Trek and Star Wars, we are assured of the enduring appeal of the theme – and generations of collectors will have endless items to hunt and gather. New or old, sci-fi and space toys are great fun to collect, and there is something for all ages, tastes, and price ranges.

A note on current values: the faltering economy has affected not only housing and grocery prices, but ray gun and space toy values as well. Many toys are trading at 20-40 percent below their value of just two years ago. Conversely, many of the very rare and desirable pieces have continued to hold their value, and in some cases have gone higher as collectors begin to see them not only as coveted examples for their collections, but as a store of value much like gold or commodities. If paper assets can get wiped out overnight, many would rather have a great and rare piece on the shelf they can enjoy, and that also holds its value. The bright side is these tough times have created a great buying opportunity for the general collector.

Contributor: Justin Pinchot is an avid collector of toy space guns. He may be reached through his Web site: www.toyraygun.com.

Alien/Aliens

Alien Blaster Target Game, 1979, set features large free standing cardboard Alien target and plastic dart shooting rifle, gun has large block letters "Alien" on side, based on the movie
EX $65   NM $135   MIP $225

Alien Blaster Target Set, larger set
EX $110   NM $220   MIP $325

Alien Chase Target Set, dart pistol, cardboard target
EX $80   NM $190   MIP $250

Alien Costume, black/white
EX $50   NM $65   MIP $110

Alien Model Kit, 1980s, vinyl, 1/6 scale
EX $60   NM $225   MIP $350

Alien Warrior Model Kit, base and egg
EX $30   NM $40   MIP $60

Aliens Colorforms Set
EX $10   NM $20   MIP $45

Aliens Computer Game, 1985
EX $5   NM $15   MIP $30

Glow Putty, unlicensed art, carded
EX $10   NM $15   MIP $25

Movie Viewer, "Alien Terror" film clip
EX $40   NM $75   MIP $125

Battlestar Galactica

Colorforms Adventure Set, 1978
EX $12   NM $25   MIP $35

Cylon Helmet Radio, 1979
EX $25   NM $50   MIP $85

Cylon Warrior Costume, 1978, boxed
EX $10   NM $15   MIP $35

Galactic Cruiser, 1978, die-cast
EX $5   NM $10   MIP $25

Game of Starfighter Combat, 1978, role playing game
EX $10   NM $17   MIP $30

L.E.M. Lander, 1978, die-cast
EX $5   NM $10   MIP $15

Lasermatic Pistol, 1978
EX $15   NM $35   MIP $60

Lasermatic Rifle, 1978
EX $25   NM $50   MIP $75

Muffit the Daggit Halloween Costume, 1978
EX $10   NM $17   MIP $35

Poster Art Set, 1978
EX $10   NM $15   MIP $25

Puzzles, 1978, The Rag-Tag Fleet, Starbuck, Interstellar Battle, price for each
EX $10   NM $15   MIP $25

Space Alert Game, 1978, hand-held electronic game
EX $10   NM $25   MIP $50

Viper Vertibird, 1979
EX $60   NM $120   MIP $220

Buck Rogers

Buck Rogers and the Children of Hopetown Book, 1979, Little Golden Book
EX $4   NM $7   MIP $15

Buck Rogers in the 25th Century Star Fighter, 1979, vehicle for 3-3/4" figures
EX $20   NM $35   MIP $60

Buck Rogers Sonic Ray Flashlight Gun, 1955, 7-1/4" black, green and yellow plastic w/code signal screw
EX $80   NM $100   MIP $225

Buck Rogers Starfighter, 1980, white body w/yellow plastic wings, amber windows, blue jets, color decal, Buck and Wilma figures, 6-1/2", Model No. 647-A
EX $32   NM $48   MIP $100

Buck Rogers U-235 Atomic Pistol, 1945, 9-1/2" long, pressed steel, makes pop noise and flash in window when trigger is pulled
EX $95   NM $250   MIP $700

Buck Rogers Wristwatch, 1971
EX $50   NM $125   MIP $250

Buck Rogers XXVc Role Playing Game, 1990, numerous game modules, paperback books, comics and a board game sprang from this concept
EX $10   NM $20   MIP $30

Clock, 1990s, wall clock
EX $15   NM $30   MIP $45

Colorforms Set, 1979
EX $10   NM $15   MIP $40

Communicator Set, 1979, w/silver Twiki figure
EX $10   NM $20   MIP $45

Galactic Play Set, 1980s
EX $17   NM $30   MIP $55

Martian Wars Game, 1990s, role playing game expansion set for the Buck Rogers XXVc game
EX $10   NM $20   MIP $35

Official Utility Belt, 1979, in window box, w/decoder glasses, wristwatch, disk-shooting ray gun, intruder detection badge, city decoder map, secret message
EX $20   NM $40   MIP $85

Paint By Number Set, 1980s
EX $15   NM $25   MIP $40

Pendant Watch, 1971
EX $115   NM $200   MIP $300

Pocket Watch, 1971
EX $90   NM $175   MIP $275

Puzzle, 1945, Buck Rogers and His Atomic Bomber, three different each
EX $75   NM $150   MIP $300

Puzzle, 1979, four versions showing TV scenes, each
EX $6   NM $15   MIP $30

Puzzle w/sleeve, 1952, space station scene, 14" x 10"
EX $75   NM $150   MIP $200

Satellite Pioneers Button, 1958, green or blue
EX $20   NM $50   MIP $125

Satellite Pioneers Map of Solar System, 1958
EX $20   NM $40   MIP $85

Satellite Pioneers Membership Card, 1958
EX $30   NM $60   MIP $110

Satellite Pioneers Starfinder, 1958, paper
EX $20   NM $50   MIP $75

Saturn Ring, 1946, red stone, glow-in-the-dark white plastic on crocodile base
EX $150   NM $300   MIP $650

Space Glasses, 1955, No. 1440
EX $40   NM $75   MIP $200

Space Ranger Halolight Ring, 1953
EX $175 NM $500 MIP $750

Space Ranger Kit, 1952, 11" x 15"
premium, envelope w/six punch-
out sheets
EX $50 NM $100 MIP $200

Strato-Kite, 1946
EX $20 NM $35 MIP $75

Super Foto Camera, 1955
EX $40 NM $70 MIP $150

Super Scope Telescope, 1955, No.
1430, 9" plastic telescope
EX $40 NM $70 MIP $150

Super Sonic Ray Gun, 1950, No.
1432, 6-1/4", black w/red and green
knobs on the side
EX $75 NM $100 MIP $150

Toy Watch, 1978
EX $15 NM $30 MIP $60

Two-Way Transceiver, 1948
EX $80 NM $130 MIP $200

View-Master Set, 1979, three-reel
set, in envelope or on blister card
EX $5 NM $7 MIP $10

Walkie Talkies, 1950s
EX $60 NM $150 MIP $200

Captain Midnight

Cup, plastic, 4" tall, "Ovaltine-The
Heart of a Hearty Breakfast"
EX $15 NM $35 MIP $65

Key-O-Matic Code-O-Graph w/Key,
1949, Secret Squadron brass
decoder sets number and letter
combinations
EX $80 NM $185 MIP $325

Captain Video

Captain Video and Ranger Photo,
1950s, premium
EX $25 NM $50 MIP $90

Captain Video Game, 1952
EX $75 NM $150 MIP $250

Captain Video Rite-O-Lite Flashlight
Gun, 1950s, 3" long, red plastic gun
w/bulb, space map, paper,
directions and order form, in
mailing envelope
EX $40 NM $95 MIP $200

Captain Video Rocket Launcher, 1952
EX $65 NM $185 MIP $360

Comic Book, Captain Video No. 1, 1951
EX $100 NM $375 MIP $1000

Flying Saucer Ring, 1950s, w/two
saucers and papers
EX $500 NM $1000 MIP $1500

Galaxy Spaceship Riding Toy, 1950s
EX $250 NM $425 MIP $725

Interplantary Space Men Figures,
1950s, in die-cut box
EX $55 NM $150 MIP $250

Kukla, Fran and Ollie Puppet Show,
1962, cardboard stage, puppets,
props
EX $50 NM $200 MIP $375

Mysto-Coder, 1950s, w/photo
EX $65 NM $200 MIP $400

Rocket Tank, 1952
EX $55 NM $95 MIP $175

Secret Seal Ring, 1950s, w/initials
"CV," gold or copper
EX $250 NM $400 MIP $600

Space Port Play Set, 1950s, all-tin set,
including rocket (not shown)
EX $250 NM $430 MIP $660

Troop Transport Ship, 1950s, in box
EX $55 NM $95 MIP $155

Defenders of the Earth

Gripjaw Vehicle, 1985
EX $11 NM $16 MIP $25

Mongor Figure, 1985
EX $16 NM $23 MIP $35

Puzzle, 1985, frame tray
EX $9 NM $15 MIP $25

Doctor Who

Cyberman Robot Doll, 1970s, 10"
EX $250 NM $350 MIP $550

Dalek Bagatelle, 1976
EX $70 NM $110 MIP $175

Dalek Shooting Game, 1965, 8" x 20",
four-color tin litho stand up target
and generic cork rifle
EX $225 NM $325 MIP $525

Dalek's Oracle Question & Answer
Board Game, 1965, magnetized
Dalek that spins
EX $115 NM $165 MIP $250

Davros Figure, 1986, villain w/left arm
EX $11 NM $16 MIP $45

Doctor Who Card Set, 1970s, 12
octagon cards
EX $14 NM $20 MIP $35

Doctor Who Card Set, 1976, 24 cards
EX $18 NM $26 MIP $45

Doctor Who Trump Card Game, 1970s
EX $9 NM $13 MIP $20

Doctor Who...Dodge the Daleks
Board Game, 1965
EX $120 NM $175 MIP $280

Flash Gordon

Adventure on the Moons of Mongo
Game, 1977
EX $15 NM $25 MIP $40

Arak Figure, 1979, 3-3/4", carded
EX $17 NM $30 MIP $50

Battle Rocket w/Space Probing
Action, 1976
EX $6 NM $10 MIP $20

Beastman Figure, 1979, 3-3/4", carded
EX $15 NM $25 MIP $45

Book Bag, 1950s, 12" wide, three-
color art on flap
EX $17 NM $35 MIP $75

Candy Box, 1970s, eight illustrated
boxes, each
EX $4 NM $10 MIP $20

Dr. Zarkov Figure, 1979, 3-3/4" figure,
on card
EX $15 NM $35 MIP $50

Flash and Ming Button, 1970s, shows
Flash and Ming crossing swords
EX $4 NM $10 MIP $20

Flash Gordon Air Ray Gun, 1950s, 10"
unusual air blaster, handle on top
cocks mechanism, pressed steel
EX $150 NM $225 MIP $450

Flash Gordon and Martian, 1965,
#1450
EX $60 NM $125 MIP $175

Flash Gordon and the Fiery Desert of
Mongo Book, 1948, Big Little Book
EX $30 NM $60 MIP $90

Flash Gordon and the Red Sword Invaders Book, 1945, Big Little Book
EX $30   NM $60   MIP $90

Flash Gordon Costume, 1951
EX $90   NM $145   MIP $250

Flash Gordon Game, 1970s
EX $15   NM $30   MIP $40

Flash Gordon Hand Puppet, 1950s, rubber head
EX $90   NM $145   MIP $250

Flash Gordon in the Jungles of Mongo Book, 1947, Big Little Book
EX $35   NM $65   MIP $95

Flash Gordon Kite, 1950s, 21" x 17", paper
EX $55   NM $90   MIP $135

Flash Gordon Space Water Gun, 1976, water ray gun on illustrated card
EX $10   NM $25   MIP $50

Flash Gordon Three Color Ray Gun, 1976, battery-operated
EX $8   NM $35   MIP $80

Flash Gordon Water Pistol, 1940s, plastic w/whistle in handle, 7-1/2" long
EX $80   NM $175   MIP $350

Flash Gordon Wristwatch, 1979, medium chrome case, back and sweep seconds, Flash in foreground w/city behind
EX $70   NM $115   MIP $175

Flash Gordon, The Movie Buttons, 1980, set of five, each
EX $2   NM $4   MIP $8

Lizard Woman Figure, 1979, 3-3/4", carded
EX $15   NM $25   MIP $40

Medals and Insignia, 1978, set of five on blister card
EX $10   NM $25   MIP $50

Ming Figure, 1979, 3-3/4", carded
EX $12   NM $20   MIP $35

Ming's Space Shuttle
EX $15   NM $25   MIP $50

Pencil Box, 1951
EX $75   NM $150   MIP $225

Puzzle, 1951, frame tray
EX $45   NM $80   MIP $125

Puzzles, 1951, set of three
EX $105   NM $200   MIP $300

Rocket Ship, 1975, 3" die-cast metal
EX $10   NM $20   MIP $35

Rocket Ship, 1979, inflatable, 3' long, w/plastic nose, rocket and gondola attachments
EX $20   NM $40   MIP $60

Solar Commando Set, 1950s
EX $65   NM $115   MIP $175

Space Compass, 1950s, ornately housed compass on illustrated watchband
EX $25   NM $40   MIP $75

Space Water Gun, 1976, water ray gun on illustrated card
EX $6   NM $15   MIP $30

Sunglasses, 1981, plastic w/emblem on bridge, carded
EX $3   NM $5   MIP $10

Three-Color Ray Gun, 1976
EX $8   NM $15   MIP $30

Thun, Lion Man Figure, 1979, 3-3/4", carded
EX $15   NM $25   MIP $45

Two-Way Telephone, 1940s
EX $60   NM $110   MIP $185

View-Master Set, 1963, three reels in envelope
EX $20   NM $35   MIP $60

View-Master Set, 1976, three reels, In the Planet Mongo
EX $6   NM $10   MIP $20

Vultan Figure, 1979, 3-3/4", carded
EX $15   NM $30   MIP $50

Wallet, 1949, w/zipper
EX $70   NM $115   MIP $175

Water Pistol, 1950s, 7-1/2" plastic
EX $155   NM $275   MIP $500

Land of the Giants

Annual Book, 1969, two volumes, set
EX $30   NM $50   MIP $75

Colorforms Set, 1968
EX $30   NM $50   MIP $75

Costumes, 1968, Steve Burton, Giant Witch, or Scientist, each
EX $35   NM $60   MIP $150

Deluxe Numbered Pencil Coloring Set, 1969
EX $60   NM $100   MIP $150

Double Action Bagatelle Game, 1969, pinball game, cardboard back
EX $35   NM $75   MIP $160

Flight of Fear Book, hardcover
EX $8   NM $15   MIP $35

Flying Saucer, 1968, flying disk
EX $60   NM $100   MIP $150

Land of the Giants Book, paperback by Murray Leinster
EX $8   NM $13   MIP $25

Land of the Giants Comic Book #1, 1968
EX $10   NM $15   MIP $30

Land of the Giants Comic Books #2-#5, 1968, each
EX $8   NM $13   MIP $25

Motorized Flying Rocket, 1968, plastic airplane w/motor, LOTG logo on wings
EX $80   NM $130   MIP $200

Movie Viewer, 1968, film strip viewer, on card
EX $25   NM $45   MIP $65

Painting Set, 1969
EX $40   NM $65   MIP $100

Puzzle, 1968, round floor puzzle w/cartoon illustration
EX $35   NM $55   MIP $85

Rub-Ons, 1969
EX $30   NM $50   MIP $75

Shoot & Stick Target Rifle Set, 1968, western rifle w/logo decals
EX $90   NM $145   MIP $225

Signal Ray Space Gun, 1968, ray gun w/logo decals
EX $70   NM $115   MIP $175

Space Sled, 1968, Supercar refitted w/LOTG decals—Mike Mercury still sits behind the wheel
EX $200   NM $350   MIP $525

Spaceship Control Panel, 1968, Firebird 99 dashboard w/a cardboard cut-out of logo on top
EX $200   NM $300   MIP $525

Spindrift Interior Model Kit, 1989, #Sf029, interior for 16" model shell
EX $35   NM $55   MIP $85

Spindrift Toothpick Kit, 1968, box of toothpicks w/a few cardboard pieces to build ship
EX $35 **NM** $60 **MIP** $85

Target Set, 1969, small guns w/darts
EX $60 **NM** $100 **MIP** $160

The Hot Spot Book, paperback, #2 in series, by Leinster
EX $12 **NM** $20 **MIP** $35

Trading Card Wrapper, 1968
EX $60 **NM** $100 **MIP** $160

Trading Cards, 1968, 55 cards
EX $275 **NM** $450 **MIP** $710

Trading Cards, 1968, 55 cards
EX $275 **NM** $450 **MIP** $710

Trading Cards Box, 1968, display box only
EX $395 **NM** $650 **MIP** $1000

Unknown Danger Book, paperback #3 by Leinster
EX $12 **NM** $20 **MIP** $35

View-Master Set, 1968, three reels, first episode
EX $20 **NM** $35 **MIP** $50

Walkie Talkies, 1968, generic walkie talkies w/LOTG decals added
EX $80 **NM** $130 **MIP** $210

Wrist Flashlight, 1968
EX $30 **NM** $50 **MIP** $80

Lost in Space

Chariot Model Kit, figures and motor
EX $625 **NM** $975 **MIP** $1500

Chariot Model Kit, 1987, #SF009, 1:35 scale, w/clear vacuform canopy and dome, plastic body, treads, roof rack
EX $35 **NM** $50 **MIP** $80

Costume, 1965, silver spacesuit w/logo
EX $85 **NM** $150 **MIP** $225

Doll Set, dressed in spacesuits w/their own freezing tubes w/a cardboard insert w/color photos and description
EX $2900 **NM** $3500 **MIP** $5000

Fan Cards, 1960s, promo cards mailed to fans; color photo
EX $20 **NM** $35 **MIP** $60

Fan Cards, 1960s, promo cards mailed to fans; black/white photo
EX $15 **NM** $25 **MIP** $50

Helmet and Gun Set, 1967, child size helmet w/blue flashing light and logo decals, blue and red molded gun
EX $300 **NM** $530 **MIP** $880

Jupiter Model Kit, 1966, large version
EX $425 **NM** $650 **MIP** $1000

Jupiter-2 Model Kit, 2" diameter, solid metal
EX $8 **NM** $13 **MIP** $35

Jupiter-2 Model Kit, 1966, 6" molded in green plastic w/wheels and wind-up motor
EX $425 **NM** $650 **MIP** $1000

Laser Water Pistol, 5" long, first season pistol style
EX $30 **NM** $50 **MIP** $80

Lost In Space 3-D Action Fun Game, 1966, three levels w/small cardboard figures
EX $530 **NM** $785 **MIP** $1250

Note Pad, June Lockhart on front
EX $25 **NM** $40 **MIP** $65

Puzzles, 1966, frame tray; three poses w/Cyclops, 10" x 14"
EX $40 **NM** $65 **MIP** $100

Robot, 1966, 12" high, motorized w/blinking lights
EX $180 **NM** $365 **MIP** $700

Robot, 1968, 6" high w/base
EX $150 **NM** $400 **MIP** $1100

Robot, 1977, 10", plastic w/green dome, battery-operated
EX $85 **NM** $200 **MIP** $325

Robot YM-3, 1985, 4" high, wind-up
EX $20 **NM** $30 **MIP** $50

Robot YM-3, 1986, 16" high, speaks English and Japanese
EX $85 **NM** $150 **MIP** $250

Roto-Jet Gun Set, 1966, TV tie-in, modular gun can be reconfigured into different variations, shoots discs
EX $600 **NM** $1100 **MIP** $2200

Saucer Gun, 1977, disk shooting gun
EX $30 **NM** $60 **MIP** $150

Space Family Robinson Comic Book, 1960s
EX $15 **NM** $25 **MIP** $45

Switch-and-Go Set, 1966, figures, Jupiter and chariot that ran around track
EX $475 **NM** $1000 **MIP** $1800

Trading Cards, 1966, 55 black and white cards, no wrappers or box
EX $100 **NM** $150 **MIP** $300

Tru-Vue Magic Eyes Set, 1967, rectangular reels
EX $30 **NM** $50 **MIP** $80

View-Master Set, 1967, Condemned of Space
EX $25 **NM** $40 **MIP** $65

Walkie Talkies, 1977, small card
EX $30 **NM** $50 **MIP** $85

Miscellaneous

Astro Base, 1960, 22" tall, red/white astronaut base, control panel opens lock door, extends crane and lowers astronaut in scout car
EX $225 **NM** $300 **MIP** $400

Astro Boy Mask/Glasses, 1960s, blue glasses w/Astro boy hair on top
EX $25 **NM** $50 **MIP** $75

Astronaut Costume, 1960
EX $18 **NM** $25 **MIP** $50

Astronaut Costume, 1962
EX $18 **NM** $25 **MIP** $50

Astronaut Space Commander Play Suit, 1950s, green outfit and cap (military style) w/gold piping on collar and pants

EX $35   NM $50   MIP $85

Fireball XL-5 Space City Play Set, 1963, includes ship, base and figures

EX $550 NM $1100   MIP $2200

Fireball XL-5 Spaceship, 1963, plastic, 20" ship w/figures

EX $200 NM $500   MIP $1300

(Justin Pinchot photo)

Marsman Car, 1950s, 5" friction toy finished in turquoise blue w/yellow stars and parachuting astronaut, says "Marsman" across the back, 5"

EX $450 NM $1200   MIP $3500

Martian Bobbing Head, 1960s, 7" tall, blue vinyl martian w/bobbing eyes and exposed brain

EX $23   NM $35   MIP $60

Men into Space Astronaut Space Helmet, 1960s, plastic helmet w/visor

EX $35   NM $50   MIP $80

Moon Space Ship, 1958, battery-operated, cousin of the cancelled Robby Space Patrol, this ship features blue litho and bump-and-go action

EX $600 NM $1300   MIP $2000

Puzzle, 1970, 10" x 14", picture of the moon's surface

EX $14   NM $20   MIP $35

Space Capsule, 1963, battery-operated, blinking nosecone on top, opening panels and spacewalking astronaut, rolling action

EX $220 NM $375   MIP $600

(Justin Pinchot Photo)

Space Patrol Car, 1950s, 8-3/4", exceedingly rare, friction drive, finished in two-tone blue w/block-headed robot driver, flying wing design on side w/"Space Patrol" in red letters, Saturns on hubcaps, 8-3/4"

EX $5000 NM $15000 MIP $39850

Space Safari Planetary Play Set, 1969, four battery operated space vehicles, 3" tall astronaut figures in silver plastic, 2" hard plastic aliens

EX $45   NM $65   MIP $100

Space Station, 1959, battery-operated, circular station w/five animated bays, large satalite dish in center

EX $700 NM $1400   MIP $2250

TV Space Riders Coloring Book, 1952, 14" x 15"

EX $7   NM $12   MIP $25

V-Enemy Visitor Doll, 1984, 12"

EX $16   NM $30   MIP $60

Voyage to the Bottom of the Sea Scout Play Set, 1964, includes mini-sub, sea crawler and divers

EX $250 NM $650   MIP $1300

Voyage to the Bottom of the Sea Seaview Play Set, 1964, includes plastic sub, sea monster and divers

EX $320 NM $675   MIP $1625

Monsters

Creature From the Black Lagoon Aquarium Figure, 1950s, 3-1/2" Lead figure

EX $85   NM $150   MIP n/a

Creature from the Black Lagoon Aquarium Figure, 1971, 6" Moving Figure

EX $150 NM $250   MIP $450

Creature From the Black Lagoon Figure, 1963, 5", hard plastic blue or orange

EX $10   NM $20   MIP $40

Creature From the Black Lagoon Figure, 1973, 5", hard rubber like bendy

EX $40   NM $65   MIP $100

Creature From the Black Lagoon Figure, 1974, 8", plastic, bendable joints

EX $295 NM $425   MIP $700

Creature From the Black Lagoon Halloween Costume, 1973, Child's Mask and Costume

EX $35   NM $80   MIP $120

Creature From the Black Lagoon Motionette, 1992, 24", electric, w/sound

EX $100 NM $200   MIP $350

Creature From the Black Lagoon Motionette, 1992, 17", battery-operated, w/sound

EX $10   NM $15   MIP $30

Creature From the Black Lagoon Robot, 1991, 9", tin/plastic, wind-up

EX $35   NM $65   MIP $110

Creature From the Black Lagoon Soaky, 1963, 10", plastic, bubble bath bottle

EX $35   NM $75   MIP $110

Creature From the Black Lagoon Sparky, 1970s, 3 1/2", plastic, wind-up

EX $10   NM $20   MIP $35

Creature From the Black Lagoon Wiggle Ick Figure, 1960s, 7", rubbery plastic, bobbin' head

EX $50   NM $85   MIP $150

Deadly Grell Figure, 1983, bendable

EX $5   NM $7   MIP $10

Dracula Action Figure, w/Aurora head

EX $65   NM $125   MIP $200

Dracula Glow-in-the-Dark Mini Monsters

EX $23   NM $30   MIP $45

Dwarves of the Mountain Human/ Monster Figure, 1983

EX $5   NM $7   MIP $10

Evil Monster Figure Bugbear & Goblin, 1983, Orcs of the Broken Bone

EX $5   NM $7   MIP $10

Frankenstein Figure, w/Aurora head

EX $65   NM $125   MIP $200

Frankenstein Figure, 1978, poseable, glow-in-the-dark features and removable cloth costumes

EX $23   NM $35   MIP $50

Godzilla Combat Joe Set, 1984, vinyl, w/12" tall Combat Joe figure, poseable

EX $450 NM $650   MIP $1000

Godzilla Figure, 1977, 19" tall

EX $20   NM $30   MIP $60

Godzilla Figure, 1985, 6-1/2" tall, arms, legs and tail movable
EX $5   **NM** $10   **MIP** $20

Godzilla Figure, 1985, 13" tall, arms, legs and tail movable
EX $15   **NM** $23   **MIP** $40

Moon McDare

Action Communication Set, 1966
EX $25   **NM** $35   **MIP** $60

Moon Explorer Set, 1966
EX $35   **NM** $50   **MIP** $85

Moon McDare Figure, 1966, 12" tall astronaut w/blue jumpsuit
EX $55   **NM** $80   **MIP** $150

Moon McDare Space Gun Set, 1966
EX $25   **NM** $50   **MIP** $130

Space Accessory Pack, 1966
EX $25   **NM** $35   **MIP** $75

Space Gun Set, 1966
EX $40   **NM** $80   **MIP** $125

Space Mutt Set, 1966
EX $30   **NM** $45   **MIP** $75

Other Worlds, The

Castle Zendo, 1983
EX $20   **NM** $30   **MIP** $50

Fighting Glowgons Figure Set, 1983
EX $18   **NM** $25   **MIP** $40

Fighting Terrans Figure Set, 1983
EX $20   **NM** $30   **MIP** $50

Kamaro Figure, 1983
EX $8   **NM** $12   **MIP** $18

Sharkoss Figure, 1983
EX $8   **NM** $12   **MIP** $18

Planet of the Apes

Cap Pistol, 1974, Fanner 50
EX $30   **NM** $65   **MIP** $95

Color-Vue Set, 1970s, eight pencils and nine 12" x 13" pictures to color
EX $30   **NM** $45   **MIP** $70

Dr. Zaius Bank, 1967, figural, vinyl, 11"
EX $20   **NM** $30   **MIP** $60

Fun-Doh Modeling Molds, 1974, molds of Zira, Cornelius, Zaius, and Aldo
EX $20   **NM** $30   **MIP** $50

Galen Bank, 1960s
EX $25   **NM** $35   **MIP** $60

Machine Gun, 1974, "Planet of the Apes" sticker on stock, sub-machine gun
EX $40   **NM** $85   **MIP** $125

Planet of the Apes Activity Book, 1974, #C3031
EX $15   **NM** $30   **MIP** $45

Puzzle, 1974, #7512, 224 pieces, 18-1/2" x 13"
EX $5   **NM** $10   **MIP** $15

Puzzle, Battle on Planet of the Apes, 1967, #486-01, 500 pieces, 16" x 20"
EX $7   **NM** $14   **MIP** $20

Puzzle, General Aldo, 1967, #485-05, 96 pieces, 10" x 14"
EX $5   **NM** $10   **MIP** $15

Puzzle, On Patrol, 1967, #486-06, 96 pieces, 10" x 14"
EX $5   **NM** $10   **MIP** $15

Puzzle, The Chase, 1967, #486-02, 500 pieces, 16" x 20"
EX $7   **NM** $14   **MIP** $20

Puzzles, 96-piece canister puzzles, each
EX $7   **NM** $12   **MIP** $25

Rapid Fire Rifle, 1974, "Planet of the Apes" sticker on stock, Winchester mechanism
EX $40   **NM** $85   **MIP** $125

Wagon, friction powered prison wagon
EX $20   **NM** $45   **MIP** $70

Wastebasket, 1967, oval, tin
EX $25   **NM** $35   **MIP** $60

Zaius, Zera, or Cornelius Walkers, 1970s, 3-1/2" plastic, wind-up
EX $20   **NM** $40   **MIP** $80

Rocky Jones, Space Ranger

Pin, Silvercup Bread, 1950s, 1-1/2", photo, "Rocky Jones Space Ranger Silvercup Bread"
EX $10   **NM** $20   **MIP** $35

Rocky Jones, Space Ranger Coloring Book, 1951, 14" x 16"
EX $25   **NM** $50   **MIP** $80

Space Ranger Button, 1954
EX $17   **NM** $35   **MIP** $75

Space Ranger Wings Pin, 1954, gold wings say "Space Ranger" silver ring w/spaceship around it
EX $17   **NM** $40   **MIP** $85

Wristwatch, 1954, in illustrated box
EX $80   **NM** $150   **MIP** $300

Space Guns

4-Barrel Waist Space Dart Gun Belt, 1950s, 11" wide gun system on belt, designed to be worn on waist or chest and aimed w/periscope sight, red plastic belt
EX $45   **NM** $65   **MIP** $150

888 Space Gun, 1955, 3" long, tin, shoots caps, painted blue body and grip w/stars, planets and spaceship, red barrel w/"888" above grip
EX $65   **NM** $125   **MIP** $250

Astro Ray Gun, 1960s, 5-7/8" long, silver finish body w/red, yellow and black detailing, friction sparkling action, single large spark window near muzzle, prominent "Astro Ray Gun" in center of body
EX $15   **NM** $25   **MIP** $50

Astro Ray Gun, 1968, 9" long, friction spark action, tin litho body w/clear red plastic barrel, red on yellow "ASTRO RAY GUN" lettering
EX $25   **NM** $40   **MIP** $75

Astro Ray Laser Lite Beam Dart Gun, 1960s, 10" red and white plastic flashlight lights target w/four darts
EX $70   **NM** $95   **MIP** $200

Astroray Gun, 1960s, 10", tin litho, blue w/red and silver accents, red transparent plastic barrel, Korea, unusual triangular box
EX $20   **NM** $40   **MIP** $65

Astro-Ray Space Gun, 10"
EX $20   **NM** $30   **MIP** $50

Atom Bubble Gun, 1940s, die-cast metal, red tubular barrel w/handle attached, two sets of silver finish fins—at barrel base and muzzle, wire loop projects from muzzle for bubble blowing, handle embossed "Atom Trade Mark"
EX $65   **NM** $85   **MIP** $125

Atom Buster Mystery Gun, 1950s, 11" long yellow plastic gun w/inner bladder, fires blast of air at tissue paper atomic mushroom target, w/instructions, atomic explosion cover art on box
EX $45   **NM** $100   **MIP** $200

Atom Ray Gun, 1949, 5-1/2" long, sleek red body gun of aluminum and brass w/bulbous water reservoir on top of gun, reads "Atom Ray Gun" between two lightning bolts on reservoir
EX $235   **NM** $350   **MIP** $1400

Atomee Water Pistol, 1960s, 4-1/4" black plastic
EX $15   **NM** $25   **MIP** $40

Atomic Disintegrator Ray Gun, 1954, 8" long, die-cast metal w/red plastic handles, ornately embellished w/dials and other equipment outcroppings, drop-down cap magazine shoots caps
EX $125   **NM** $225   **MIP** $550

Atomic Flash Gun, 1955, 7-1/2" long, tin, sparkling action seen through tinted elongated oval plastic muzzle, w/yellow and red on turquoise body w/red lettered "Atomic Flash" over trigger

EX $40   **NM** $80   **MIP** $125

Atomic Gun, 1960s, 5" long, gold, blue, white and red tin litho, friction sparkling action, "Atomic Gun" on body sides

EX $20   **NM** $40   **MIP** $75

Atomic Gun, 1969, 9" long, red, gray and yellow tin litho gun w/plastic muzzle, friction sparkling action, large hollow letter "ATOMIC GUN" on body

EX $15   **NM** $35   **MIP** $70

Atomic Jet Gun, 1954, 8-1/2" long, gold chromed die-cast metal, cap shooting, "Atomic Jet" and large circular "S" logo on grip

EX $300 **NM** $500 **MIP** $2000

Atomic Ray Gun, 1957, 30" long, "Captain Space Solar Scout," blue plastic w/oversized telescope sight flashlight and "electric buzzer" sound

EX $95   **NM** $225   **MIP** $995

Baby Space Gun, 1950s, 6" friction siren and spark action

EX $35   **NM** $60   **MIP** $135

Batman Ray Gun, 1960s, cap pistol w/bat symbol for the sight

EX $35   **NM** $65   **MIP** $140

Battlestar Galactica Lasermatic Pistol, 1978

EX $15   **NM** $30   **MIP** $60

Battlestar Galactica Lasermatic Rifle, 1978

EX $25   **NM** $40   **MIP** $80

Bee-Vo Bell Gun, 1950s, #204, 6-1/2" long, red plastic, fires trapped marble at bell in muzzle, in box

EX $25   **NM** $40   **MIP** $80

Bicycle Water Cannon Ray Gun, 1950s, 10", red plastic, swivel mount attached to bicycle handles, fired by lever

EX $30   **NM** $75   **MIP** $125

Cherilea Space Gun, miniature scale, die-cast

EX $27   **NM** $40   **MIP** $65

Clicker Ray Gun, 1950s, 5" red, blue or gray hard plastic, no boxes, sold loose

EX $15   **NM** $25   **MIP** $50

Clicker Ray Gun, 1960, 9" long, orange or silver

EX $60   **NM** $90   **MIP** $125

Clicker Whistle Ray Gun, 1950s, 5" plastic, blue/green or olive/green swirl plastic, imprinted spacemen and rocket ships, back of gun is a whistle

EX $15   **NM** $25   **MIP** $125

Daisy Rocket Dart Pistol, 1954, 7" long, red, blue and yellow sheet metal gun w/blue body, blue grips w/yellow trim, blue and yellow barrel stripes, same body as Zooka Pop Pistol but w/connecting rob from gun to barrel, and different lithgraphing comes w/ or w/out metal target, w/target MIP $1,000

EX $95   **NM** $175   **MIP** $295

Daisy Zooka Pop Pistol, 1954, 7" long, colorful red, blue and yellow sheet metal gun w/blue body, red grips w/yellow trim and litho star reading "It's a Daisy Play Gun," yellow barrel w/red stripes, and wide red muzzle, handle cock

EX $80   **NM** $175   **MIP** $300

Dan Dare & the Aliens Ray Gun, 1950s, 21", tin litho gun

EX $105 **NM** $175   **MIP** $300

Dune Fremen Tarpel Gun, 1984, 8" long, battery-operated w/internal light, light beam and chirping sound, plastic

EX $25   **NM** $40   **MIP** $70

Dune Sardaukar Laser Gun, 1984, 7" black plastic w/flashing lights, battery-operated

EX $20   **NM** $35   **MIP** $55

Flash-O-Matic, The Safe Gun, 1950s, 7" long red and yellow plastic battery-operated light beam gun

EX $60   **NM** $100   **MIP** $160

Flashy Ray Gun, 1960s, battery-operated, tin litho, machine gun by Nomura of Japan

EX $70   **NM** $140   **MIP** $200

Floating Satellite Target Game, 1958, 6-1/2" x 9", battery-operated, includes a pistol and three rubber tipped darts, a blower supports the styrofoam ball on a column of air and the players shoot darts to knock it down

EX $95   **NM** $150   **MIP** $300

(Justin Pinchot photo)

Ideal 3-Color Gun, 1957, 9" long, w/red, blue, or black body and red trim

EX $65   **NM** $195   **MIP** $350

Jack Dan Space Gun, 1959, 7-1/2" long, in black, red or blue painted die-cast metal cap gun w/"Jack Dan" over trigger

EX $105 **NM** $200   **MIP** $300

Jet Gun, 1957, 6" long, tin, sparkling action, red body w/three small red tinted spark windows near muzzle, grip shows silver-suited astronaut in modern helmet and wording "JET GUN" at top of grip near trigger

EX $35   **NM** $60   **MIP** $130

Jet Jr. Cap Gun, 1950s, 6-1/2" long, fires roll caps, side loading door, silver finish, rear jet "Blast Off Fins"

EX $50   **NM** $100   **MIP** $200

Jet Plane Missile Gun, 1968, jet shaped handgun shoots darts, targets supplied on box back

EX $35   **NM** $60   **MIP** $100

Jupiter 4 Color Signal Gun, 1950s, 9" long black, red and yellow plastic gun that lights up in four colors, red telescoping sight

EX $35   **NM** $55   **MIP** $90

Over and Under Ray Gun, 1960s, 8-1/2" long, red, yellow, white and black tin litho gun w/two over and

under reciprocating plastic muzzles, friction sparkling action
EX $30 **NM** $50 **MIP** $80

Pencil Sharpener Ray Gun, 1950, 3-1/2" plastic ray gun w/removable pencil sharpener, ribbed grip, three rings on barrel, available in red, green, and yellow, 3-1/2"
EX $50 **NM** $85 **MIP** $150

Planet Clicker Bubble Gun, 1953, 8" long, plastic, red body w/yellow accents, dip the barrel in bubble solution and pull trigger to make bubbles and produce click sound, in illustrated box
EX $40 **NM** $65 **MIP** $110

Planet Patrol Saucer Gun, 1950s, w/spaceman motif
EX $40 **NM** $70 **MIP** $120

Pop Gun, 1967, 4-1/2" long red hard plastic gun w/space designs on handle
EX $25 **NM** $35 **MIP** $80

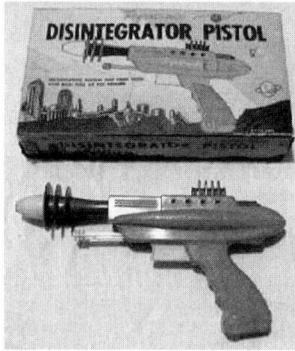

(Justin Pinchot photo)

Pyrotomic Disintegrator Pistol, 1953, 9" clicker gun, all plastic; ringed barrel and plunger reciprocate when trigger is pulled, red/yellow/blue, or copper/silver, 9"
EX $700 **NM** $1600 **MIP** $10000

Radar Gun, 1956, 5-1/2" long, mauve or silver/gray swirl plastic body w/green or yellow spaceman sight and trigger, Saturn and star embossed above grip and "Radar Gun" embossed above that
EX $20 **NM** $35 **MIP** $60

Ranger Gun, 1960s, 15", No. 2057, double-barreled, friction powered, tin litho, camo pattern, white barrels, spark action
EX $50 **NM** $100 **MIP** $150

Ratchet Sound Space Gun, 1950s, 7" long, red plastic w/silver trim, flywheel ratchet on top of gun
EX $30 **NM** $50 **MIP** $80

Ratchet Water Pistol Ray Gun, 1960s, 6-1/2" unusual pull back mechanism loads pistol, ratchet forces water out when trigger is pulled
EX $25 **NM** $40 **MIP** $70

Ray Dart Gun, 1968, 9-1/2" long, blue plastic body w/yellow muzzle, w/three darts, storage compartment in red handle base
EX $15 **NM** $27 **MIP** $55

Ray Gun, 1957, 6-1/2" long, tin, sparkling action w/two red tinted plastic tapered rectangle windows at muzzle, "Ray Gun" in red at top of body w/rocket exhaust encircling green/blue planet against deep blue star studded background
EX $32 **NM** $65 **MIP** $130

Ray Gun Water Pistol, 1950s, 5-1/2" many color variations: green, orange, translucent blue, royal blue, black, yellow and red
EX $10 **NM** $15 **MIP** $30

Razer Ray Gun, 1972, plastic bronze finish body w/five large cooling fins near red plastic barrel, friction sparkling action, chrome finish muzzle tip, "Razer Ray Gun" embossed on rear of barrel
EX $10 **NM** $15 **MIP** $30

Rex Mars Atomix Pistol Flashlight, 1950s, plastic
EX $50 **NM** $80 **MIP** $175

Rex Mars Planet Patrol 45 Caliber Machine Gun, 1950s, 22" long, tin and plastic, wind-up
EX $60 **NM** $150 **MIP** $300

Rex Mars Planet Patrol Space Pistol Arresting Ray, 1950, tin w/red and yellow litho
EX $100 **NM** $200 **MIP** $300

Rex Mars Planet Patrol Super Beam Signal Ray Gun, 1950s, flashlight gun, red plastic, name in grip, clear plastic cap at end of barrel reveals battery compartment, blue trigger
EX $35 **NM** $125 **MIP** $350

Robot Raiders Space Signal Gun, 1980s, 6" long flashlight gun w/interchangeable lenses and click sound
EX $6 **NM** $10 **MIP** $20

Robotech Water Pistol, 1985
EX $6 **NM** $10 **MIP** $20

Rocket Gun, 1958, 7" hard yellow/green plastic w/spring loaded plunger that shoots corks up to 50 feet
EX $10 **NM** $15 **MIP** $30

Rocket Jet Water Pistol, 1957, 5" long, red, orange or yellow clear plastic body, fill plug at top of gun,

large integral gunsight fin at rear, small sight fin at front
EX $12 **NM** $30 **MIP** $60

Rocket Pop Gun, 1955, wood, green and red horizontal striped body w/black tri-fin pump base, cork and string stopper in nose, pump fins into body to make it pop
EX $25 **NM** $40 **MIP** $75

Ro-Gun "It's A Robot," 1984, Shogun-type robot transforms into a rifle, in window box
EX $8 **NM** $13 **MIP** $25

S-58 Space Gun, 1957, 12" long, tin litho, deep metallic blue body w/friction sparkling action, "S-58" on muzzle, w/ringed planet graphic on front sight
EX $35 **NM** $70 **MIP** $135

Satellite & Rocket Pistol, 1960s, 5" long, green plastic gun fires either yellow plastic darts or saucers, on card
EX $12 **NM** $20 **MIP** $60

Secret Squirrel Ray Gun, 1960s
EX $25 **NM** $50 **MIP** $100

Signal Flash Gun, 1957, 6" long, plastic flashlight, black body w/translucent white plastic light housing at muzzle and pearl finish plastic grip plates, modern missile type sight on top of barrel, large "SIGNAL FLASH" above trigger
EX $20 **NM** $40 **MIP** $75

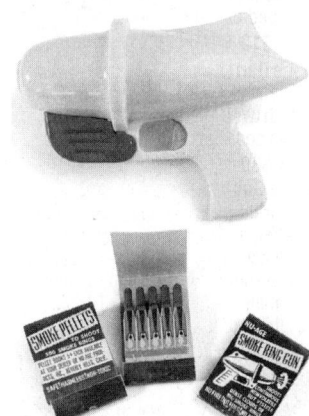

(Justin Pinchot photo)

Smoke Ring Gun, 1950s, large, sleek gray finished breakfront pistol w/red barrel and muzzle ring, used rocket-shaped matches to produce smoke, trigger fired smoke rings, small engraved "Smoke Ring Gun" logo on gunsight fin, rare color variation, all yellow, all red, or combination of both

EX $200 **NM** $300 **MIP** $600

Space Atomic Gun, 1955, 5-1/2" long, tin, sparkling action seen through red tinted plastic window, two-tone blue body w/red/white atomic symbol on grip, "Space Atomic Gun" letters around oval spaceship-and-stars logo above trigger

EX $32 **NM** $65 **MIP** $130

Space Atomic Gun, 1960, 4" long, tin litho, friction sparkling action, silver gray finish w/yellow and red trim, w/"SPACE" on body in white small all caps and large yellow lower caps "atomic gun," small "T/Made in JAPAN" logo above trigger

EX $25 **NM** $40 **MIP** $70

Space Atomic Gun, 1960s, 4" silver, orange/red tin litho, sparking action

EX $25 **NM** $40 **MIP** $70

Space Control Ray Gun, 1956, 5-1/2" long, red plastic w/yellow trigger, clicks

EX $25 **NM** $42 **MIP** $85

Space Control Space Gun, 1954, 3" long, tin sparkling gun w/green body, red sights, decorated all over w/stars and planets, red and yellow "Space Control" letters over trigger and spacemen firing gun and rocket flying overhead on grips

EX $30 **NM** $40 **MIP** $65

Space Dart Gun, 1950s, 4" solid color plastic gun, shoots standard rubber tipped darts

EX $12 **NM** $35 **MIP** $70

Space Dart Gun, 1950s, 6" long, gun has one white side and one black side, both w/star and lightning motif, eight thin cooling fins on barrel

EX $30 **NM** $50 **MIP** $90

Space Gun, 1955, 3-1/4" long, tin, sparkling action, aqua blue body w/red and yellow highlights and "Space" in script lettering over grip, grip shows rocket shooting toward planets, circular San/Japan logo behind trigger

EX $30 **NM** $85 **MIP** $250

Space Gun, 1957, 6" long, tin, sparkling action, metallic teal finish w/red grooves and muzzle, green spaceship on body above "Space Gun," small Daiya logo inside red/yellow burst on grip w/"577001" at bottom of grip

EX $35 **NM** $75 **MIP** $150

Space Gun, 1957, 9" long, friction sparkling action w/three red-tinted plastic spark windows and clear red plastic barrel, body in metallic blue

w/large red "SPACE GUN" letters on yellow background

EX $35 **NM** $65 **MIP** $140

Space Gun, 1957, 7" long, tin w/sparkling action, shows a realistic white rocket blasting off over lunar terrain on side of body and atomic symbol on grip center w/diamond-shaped "SY" logo and "Made in Japan" at bottom of grip

EX $40 **NM** $65 **MIP** $120

Space Gun, 1960, 7" long, tin litho, friction sparkling action, yellow body w/blue and red trim, small Hero Toy logo by trigger

EX $35 **NM** $60 **MIP** $95

Space Gun, 1960s, 8" long, battery-operated, reciprocating barrel shaft has red and blue lenses that flash when fired, makes rat-a-tat noise, large circular "8" over handgrip, winged eagle over trigger, large block letter "SPACE GUN" on barrel

EX $70 **NM** $115 **MIP** $185

Space Gun, 1967, 4" tin litho, friction sparkling action, red body w/blue inset and grips, yellow block letter "SPACE GUN," large yellow and white vertical painted fins, six red-tinted plastic sparkling windows, oval Shudo logo by grip

EX $20 **NM** $35 **MIP** $70

Space Jet Gun, 1957, 9" long, tin, sparkling action w/black body, orange "Space Jet" on body w/orange and red atomic symbol on grip, clear green plastic finned barrel base, clear blue plastic finned muzzle

EX $35 **NM** $60 **MIP** $120

Space Jet Water Pistol, 1957, 4" long, black plastic w/white "Space Jet" lettering and spaceship line art on sides, fill plug in gunsight

EX $15 **NM** $30 **MIP** $65

Space Navigator Gun, 1953, 3-1/2" long, tin, looks like sawed off military .45, colorfully trimmed blue body w/smiling spaceman, blasting winged rocketship and "Space Navigator" logo on grips, planets and star on body

EX $35 **NM** $60 **MIP** $135

Space Outlaw Ray Gun, 1965, 10" long, chrome plated, die-cast metal, recoiling barrel action, "Cosmic," "Sonic," or "Gamma" power levels, large red clear plastic teardrop shaped window

EX $95 **NM** $150 **MIP** $225

Space Pilot Junior Jet Ray Gun, 1960s, friction-powered, gold plastic w/silver and green accents

EX $45 **NM** $90 **MIP** $135

Space Pilot Super-Sonic Gun, 1953, gun flashes red, white, and green light, battery-operated

EX $30 **NM** $60 **MIP** $95

(Justin Pinchot photo)

Space Police/Neutron Blaster Cap Gun, 1958, 7" cast pot-metal chrome-plated cap gun w/removable magazine/sight (very rare box), 7"

EX $275 **NM** $395 **MIP** $3000

Space Rocket Gun, 1950s, 9" gray plastic, modern police-style pistol grip and shell chamber body w/oversized barrel and muzzle sights, spring loaded, shoots rocket projectiles, in box w/two "rockets"

EX $55 **NM** $95 **MIP** $185

Space Scout Spud Gun, 1960s, 7" black and white plastic

EX $15 **NM** $30 **MIP** $50

Space Ship Flashlight Gun, 1950s, 7-1/4", blue plastic ray gun has cockpit w/orange spaceman, nose unscrews for AAA batteries, pulling trigger lights nose and moves guns and spaceman

EX $60 **NM** $150 **MIP** $250

Space Target Game, 1952, 24" tall, metal target w/rubber tipped darts and dart gun to shoot down all the jet rockets and missiles

EX $40 **NM** $80 **MIP** $175

Space Water Gun, 1957, 5-1/2" long, clear red plastic body w/embossed ringed planet and star, four cooling fins at barrel base, hollow telescope sight, yellow plastic trigger, white plastic stopper attached by loop to red knob at gun back

EX $15 **NM** $30 **MIP** $50

Space Water Gun, 1960, 6" long, red transparent plastic, stopper at rear of gun, finned trigger guard, zeppelin-shaped reservoir w/single embossed lightning bolt running its length, tiny "Park Plastics" imprinted along lateral reservoir fin

EX $15 **NM** $25 **MIP** $40

Space Water Pistol, 1976

EX $7 **NM** $10 **MIP** $20

Space X-Ray Gun, 1970s, #46598, 8-1/2" long, plastic, friction sparkling action, same body as Razer Ray Gun but w/more futuristic handgrip and noisemaker at rear, sold in bag w/header card
EX $15   **NM** $25   **MIP** $40

Sparking Atom Buster Pistol, aluminum
EX $30   **NM** $50   **MIP** $85

Sparking Space Gun Rifle
EX $50   **NM** $100   **MIP** $175

Sparkling Machine Gun "Sure-Shot," 1950s, tin litho machine gun sends sparks out of barrel
EX $95   **NM** $125   **MIP** $395

Sparkling Ray Gun, 1976
EX $6   **NM** $10   **MIP** $20

(Justin Pinchot photo)

Sparkling Space Gun, 1953, 2-1/2" tin lithograph friction gun w/rocket, stars and planets on grip, 2-1/2"
EX $100   **NM** $225   **MIP** $395

(Justin Pinchot photo)

Spin Ray Blast Pistol, 1946, 7" cast aluminum beehive design w/red metal propeller that spins when trigger is pulled, 7"
EX $275   **NM** $350   **MIP** $2500

Star Team Ionization Nebulizer, 1969, 9" water gun fires water mist, red, white, blue and black plastic, Star Team decal
EX $30   **NM** $50   **MIP** $85

Strato Gun, 1950s, 9" long, gray finish die-cast, cap firing, internal hammer, top of gun lifts to load
EX $200   **NM** $350   **MIP** $800

Strato Gun, 1950s, 9" long, chrome finish die-cast, red cooling fins, cap firing, internal hammer, top of gun lifts to load
EX $200   **NM** $400   **MIP** $900

Super Sonic Gun, 1957, 9" long, tin, sparkling action w/three red plastic spark windows and clear red plastic barrel, blue body w/red lightning bolt beneath yellow "Super Sonic" on rounded gun body, small ENDOH logo printed above grips
EX $40   **NM** $80   **MIP** $160

Super Sonic Space Gun, 1957, 7-1/2" long, tin litho, metallic gray body w/red gunsight fin, friction siren and sparkling action, large oval center art w/outstanding lunar scene of rockets, mountains and Earth in sky, red helmeted spaceman on grip
EX $40   **NM** $80   **MIP** $160

Super Space Gun, 1960, 6" long, tin litho, friction sparkling action, blue on blue body w/white/yellow/red highlights, large red on white "SUPER SPACE" lettering on side
EX $25   **NM** $50   **MIP** $100

Superior Rocket Gun, 1956, 8" long, dark gray plastic, embossed "Superior Rocket Gun" on grip
EX $30   **NM** $50   **MIP** $85

Tom Corbett Space Cated Atomic Pistol, 1950s, flashlight, battery-operated, "Space Cadet" on handle
EX $100   **NM** $200   **MIP** $450

Tomi Space Gun, 1950s, solid red plastic w/yellow barrel plug, modelled after modern .45 caliber pistol w/rounded reservoir lined w/two horizontal fins over grip; embossed logo and circular Shawnee logos on grip
EX $50   **NM** $90   **MIP** $135

Universe Gun, 1960s, 4" long, blue, yellow and red tin litho gun w/friction sparkling action, large all caps italic "Universe" on body side, sold in bag w/header card
EX $15   **NM** $25   **MIP** $40

Visible Sparkling Ray Gun, 8-1/2" long, plastic, mechanism visible, bagged w/header card
EX $15   **NM** $32   **MIP** $65

Wham-O Air Blaster, 1960s, 10" long plastic gun uses rubber diaphragm to shoot air; styling is reminiscent of Budson Flash Gordon Air Ray Gun
EX $70   **NM** $120   **MIP** $185

X100 Mystery Dart Gun, 1956, 3-3/4" long, yellow or gray plastic gun on cardboard display card, w/two yellow and blue talcum impregnated darts which create a smoke effect when striking any target
EX $25   **NM** $45   **MIP** $125

X-Ray Gun, 1950s, Japan, red see-through plastic, friction toy, sparks
EX $50   **NM** $85   **MIP** $125

Space Patrol

Atomic Pistol Flashlight Gun, 1950s, plastic
EX $85   **NM** $125   **MIP** $250

Cosmic Cap, 1950s
EX $125   **NM** $200   **MIP** $400

Cosmic Gun, 1970, 12" long, plastic, battery-operated w/a small electric motor that runs reciprocating light in clear red plastic barrel, dark blue body, red and orange lettered "COSMIC GUN" decal
EX $35   **NM** $55   **MIP** $90

Cosmic Ray Gun, 1954, 9" long, tin body w/plastic barrel, boldly painted in blue, yellow and red lightning bolts
EX $50   **NM** $90   **MIP** $150

Cosmic Ray Gun #249, 1953, 8" long, plastic, blue body, yellow barrel, red tip, in box showing two space kids in bubble helmets and backpacks shooting at spaceships
EX $40   **NM** $75   **MIP** $135

Cosmic Rocket Launcher Set, 1950s
EX $300   **NM** $525   **MIP** $850

Cosmic Smoke Gun, 1950s, green
EX $100   **NM** $175   **MIP** $395

Cosmic Smoke Gun, 1950s, red
EX $110   **NM** $170   **MIP** $325

Drink Mixer, 1950s, boxed
EX $60   **NM** $100   **MIP** $200

Emergency Kit, 1950s, w/rations, plastic w/yellow insert
EX $600   **NM** $1350   **MIP** $2500

Handbook, 1950s
EX $55   **NM** $125   **MIP** $200

Interplanetary Space Patrol Credits Coins, different denominations and colors: Terra, Moon and Saturn, each
EX $10   **NM** $16   **MIP** $35

Jet Glow Code Belt, 1950s, gold-finish metal, spaceship-shaped buckle, decoder ring behind buckle
EX $120   **NM** $200   **MIP** $375

Lunar Fleet Base, 1950s, premium punch-outs in mailing envelope
EX $500   **NM** $1700   **MIP** $3200

Man From Mars Totem Head Mask, 1950s, paper, several styles
EX $35   **NM** $65   **MIP** $100

Monorail Set, 1950s
EX $1650 NM $2500 MIP $3000

Non-Fall Space Patrol X-16, 1950s
EX $50 NM $150 MIP $300

Outer Space Helmet Mask, 1950s,
paper helmet w/plastic one-way visor
EX $110 NM $170 MIP $300

Project-O-Scope, 1950s, rocket-shaped film viewer w/filmstrips
EX $175 NM $350 MIP $500

Puzzle, 1950s, frame tray w/sleeve
EX $40 NM $75 MIP $175

Rocket Gun and Holster Set, 1950s,
w/darts
EX $200 NM $300 MIP $525

Rocket Gun Set, 1950s, w/darts,
w/out holster
EX $110 NM $185 MIP $360

Rocket Lite Flashlight, 1950s, in box
EX $90 NM $175 MIP $250

Rocket Port Set, 1950s
EX $125 NM $300 MIP $550

Rocket-Shaped Pen, 1950s
EX $120 NM $185 MIP $350

Space Binoculars, 1950s, black
plastic, logo on sides
EX $25 NM $75 MIP $150

Space Binoculars, 1950s, green
plastic, large logo on top, premium
EX $120 NM $190 MIP $300

Space Holster w/Oval Badge, 1950,
w/unmarked blue gun
EX $200 NM $500 MIP $800

**Space Patrol Atomic Flashlight
Pistol**, 1950s, gold/bronze finish
pistol w/seven large cooling fins on
barrel and three smaller ones at
back of gun, large clear plastic
diffuser on muzzle, white "Official
Space Patrol" on handgrip
EX $135 NM $225 MIP $400

Space Patrol Badge, 1950s, plastic,
w/ship and crest
EX $75 NM $150 MIP $300

Space Patrol Badge, 1950s, metal
oval on card
EX $125 NM $300 MIP $500

**Space Patrol Cadet Membership
Card**, 1950s
EX $25 NM $75 MIP $175

Space Patrol Cereal Box, 1953,
Wheat Chex Magic Picture Offer
EX $125 NM $275 MIP $450

Space Patrol Commander Helmet,
1950s, plastic, in box
EX $125 NM $300 MIP $600

Space Patrol Cosmic Glow Ring,
1950s, red and blue
EX $250 NM $400 MIP $750

Space Patrol Cosmic Smoke Gun,
1950s, solid color red or green
plastic w/"Space Patrol" on body
above grip, TV show tie-in, shoots
baking powder, on card
EX $135 NM $375 MIP $750

**Space Patrol Hydrogen Ray Gun
Ring**, 1950s, glow-in-the-dark ring
EX $80 NM $125 MIP $275

Space Patrol Mobile Store Display,
Wheat Chex, 1953
EX $400 NM $1200 MIP $1600

Space Patrol Periscope, 1950s, paper
w/mirrors
EX $75 NM $150 MIP $200

Space Patrol Printing Ring, 1950s
EX $200 NM $400 MIP $600

Space Patrol Wristwatch, 1950s,
illustrated box w/"Terra" compass
EX $200 NM $350 MIP $500

Space-A-Phones, 1950s
EX $175 NM $300 MIP $450

Space:1999

Adventure Play Set, 1976, paper color
and cut-out construction, included
two Eagle Spacecraft, Moonbase
Alpha w/moving antenna, six-
wheeled moon buggy, complete cast
EX $40 NM $55 MIP $85

Astro Popper Gun, 1976, on card
EX $6 NM $10 MIP $20

Astro Popper Gun, 1976, on card
EX $10 NM $15 MIP $45

Colorforms Adventure Set, 1975
EX $10 NM $16 MIP $25

Cut and Color Book, 1975
EX $6 NM $12 MIP $25

Dr. Russell Figure, 1976
EX $17 NM $30 MIP $45

Eagle Freighter, 1975, No. 360, die-cast
EX $25 NM $80 MIP $160

Eagle One Spaceship, 1976
EX $125 NM $325 MIP $525

Eagle Transport, 1975, No. 359,
die-cast
EX $25 NM $55 MIP $110

Eagle Transporter Model Kit, 1976
EX $12 NM $20 MIP $80

Film Viewer TV Set, 1976
EX $8 NM $20 MIP $55

Galaxy Time Meter, 1976
EX $6 NM $10 MIP $20

Puzzle, 1976
EX $8 NM $15 MIP $30

Space Expedition Dart Set, 1976,
carded
EX $6 NM $10 MIP $20

Stamping Set, 1976
EX $8 NM $13 MIP $25

Superscope, 1976
EX $6   NM $10   MIP $18

Utility Belt Set, 1976
EX $12   NM $40   MIP $110

Utility Belt Set, 1976, w/disc shooting stun gun, watch and compass
EX $12   NM $30   MIP $60

Walking Spaceman, 1975
EX $50   NM $175   MIP $425

Zython Figure, 1976
EX $40   NM $80   MIP $100

Spaceships

Eagle Lunar Module, 1960s, 9"
EX $80   NM $115   MIP $185

Friendship 7, 9-1/2", friction
EX $35   NM $50   MIP $80

Inter-Planet Toy Rocketank Patrol, 1950, 10"
EX $30   NM $45   MIP $75

Jupiter Space Station, 1960s, 8"
EX $90   NM $135   MIP $225

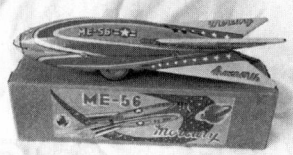

(Justin Pinchot photo)

ME-56 Mercury Rocket, c1953, 10", friction, brightly lithographed in yellow, red and blue, w/die-cut stars for spark action, several slight variations available, 10"
EX $1800 NM $3000   MIP $6500

Mystery Action Satellite, 1950s, battery-operated, puts astronaut in "orbit"
EX n/a   NM $600   MIP $1350

Mystery Spaceship, 1960s, 35mm astronauts and moonmen, rockets, launchers
EX $80   NM $165   MIP $260

Rocket Fighter, 1950s, w/tail fin and sparking action, tin wind-up
EX $250   NM $375   MIP $525

Rocket Fighter Spaceship, 1930s, celluloid window, tin wind-up, 12" long
EX $125   NM $225   MIP $300

Satellite X-107, 1965, 9"
EX $90   NM $130   MIP $200

Sky Patrol Jet, 1960s, 5" x 13" x 5", battery-operated, working taillights
EX $295   NM $425   MIP $650

Solar-X Space Rocket, 15"
EX $45   NM $65   MIP $100

Space Bus, tin helicopter, battery-operated w/wired remote
EX $350   NM $500   MIP $750

(Justin Pinchot photo)

Space Cruiser X-300, c1955, 15" tin lithographed w/sparking friction action, blue or green variations, some w/chrome cap on nose cone, 15"
EX $3500   NM $9000 MIP $18000

Space Pacer, 1978, 7", battery-operated
EX $20   NM $29   MIP $50

Space Survey X-09, battery-operated, tin and plastic flying saucer w/clear bubble
EX $175   NM $375   MIP $550

Space Train, 1950s, 9" long, engine and three metallic cars
EX $18   NM $26   MIP $50

Spaceship, bronze plastic
EX $40   NM $60   MIP $100

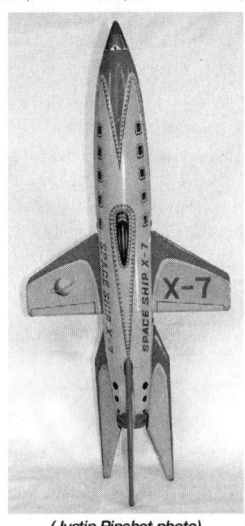

(Justin Pinchot photo)

Spaceship X-7, 1950s, 22-1/2" w/removable center wing and top rear fin, tin friction toy, lithographed in turquoise or silver, both w/red accents, red or black rubber nose cone, sparking action, 22-1/2"
EX $8000   NM $15000 MIP $25000

Super Space Capsule, 1960s, 9-1/2"
EX $70   NM $100   MIP $160

X-3 Rocket Gyro, 1950s
EX $25   NM $35   MIP $60

Star Trek

Action Toy Book, 1976
EX $7   NM $10   MIP $20

Astro-Buzz-Ray Gun, 1967, blue gun w/large yellow barrel and yellow sights, buzzer signal, three color flashing light beam, battery-operated, revolving turret, Spock pictured on box
EX $50   NM $100   MIP $150

Astrocruiser, 1967, movable cannon, fires shells, three military figures, rare
EX $100   NM $200   MIP $325

Beanbag Chair, ST:TMP
EX $25   NM $35   MIP $55

Bowl, ST:TMP, 1979, plastic
EX $3   NM $7   MIP $15

Bridge Punch-Out Book, ST:TMP, 1979
EX $7   NM $10   MIP $25

Bulletin Board, ST:TMP, 1979, w/four pens
EX $6   NM $8   MIP $15

Clock, 1986, white wall clock, red 20th anniversary logo on face, Official Star Trek Fan Club
EX $14   NM $20   MIP $40

Clock, 1989, Enterprise orbiting planet, rectangular
EX $23   NM $33   MIP $60

Colorforms Set, 1975
EX $15   NM $20   **MIP** $50

Comb & Brush Set, 1977, 6" x 3", blue, oval brush
EX $14   NM $20   **MIP** $35

Command Communications Console, 1976, coordinates w/Mego's communicators, lights up
EX $45   NM $100   **MIP** $155

Communicators, 1976, blue plastic walkie talkies
EX $70   NM $125   **MIP** $200

Communicators, 1989, black plastic walkie talkies
EX $35   NM $50   **MIP** $85

Communicators, ST:TMP, 1980, plastic wristband walkie talkies belt pack, battery operated
EX $90   NM $150   **MIP** $250

Controlled Space Flight, 1976, plastic Enterprise, battery operated
EX $80   NM $125   **MIP** $225

Costume, 1979, one-piece outfit, Spock, Kirk, Ilia or Klingon, each
EX $11   NM $16   **MIP** $25

Digital Travel Alarm
EX $15   NM $20   **MIP** $35

Dinnerware Set, ST:TMP, 1979, plate, bowl, glass and cup
EX $15   NM $25   **MIP** $40

Enterprise Make-A-Model, ST:TNG, 1990
EX $4   NM $5   **MIP** $10

Enterprise Model Kit, 1980, #91232/B, Canadian issue, ST:TMP
EX $90   NM $100   **MIP** $150

Enterprise Punch-Out Book, ST:TMP, 1979
EX $9   NM $15   **MIP** $30

Enterprise Wristwatch, ST:TMP
EX $20   NM $30   **MIP** $50

Enterprise Wristwatch, ST:TMP, 1989, gold-plated silver
EX $55   NM $80   **MIP** $125

Enterprise, ST:III, 1984, 4" long, die-cast w/black plastic stand
EX $10   NM $15   **MIP** $30

Enterprise, ST:IV, 1986, 24", silver plastic, inflatable
EX $20   NM $30   **MIP** $45

Enterprise, ST:TMP, 1979, 20" long, white plastic, battery powered lights and sound w/stand
EX $80   NM $120   **MIP** $185

Excelsior, ST:III, 1984, 4" long, die-cast w/black plastic stand
EX $7   NM $10   **MIP** $40

Ferengi Costume, ST:TNG, 1988
EX $7   NM $10   **MIP** $25

Figurine Paint Set, 1979
EX $14   NM $25   **MIP** $40

Flashlight, 1976, battery operated, small phaser shape
EX $6   NM $10   **MIP** $15

Flashlight, ST:TMP, 1979
EX $6   NM $10   **MIP** $15

Giant in the Universe Pop-Up Book, 1977
EX $14   NM $20   **MIP** $35

Golden Trivia Game, 1985
EX $20   NM $30   **MIP** $50

Helmet, 1976, plastic, w/sound and red lights
EX $55   NM $80   **MIP** $130

Inter-Space Communicator, 1974, 6" x 9" box, two yellow and black hand-held devices connected by wire
EX $25   NM $55   **MIP** $90

Kirk & Spock Wristwatch, ST:TMP, LCD rectangular face display, Enterprise on blue face w/Kirk and Spock
EX $25   NM $35   **MIP** $60

Kirk Bank, 1975, 12" plastic
EX $25   NM $35   **MIP** $60

Kirk Costume, 1975, plastic mask, one-piece jumpsuit
EX $9   NM $13   **MIP** $25

Kirk Doll, ST:TMP, shown here w/Spock, 1979, 13" tall, soft body w/plastic head
EX $16   NM $23   **MIP** $50

Kirk or Spock Costumes, 1967, tie-on jumpsuit, mask
EX $11   NM $16   **MIP** $30

Kirk Puzzle, ST:TMP, 1979, 15-piece sliding puzzle
EX $5   NM $7   **MIP** $12

Kite, 1975, TV Enterprise or Spock
EX $14   NM $20   **MIP** $35

Kite, ST:III, 1984, pictures Enterprise
EX $14   NM $20   **MIP** $35

Kite, ST:TMP, 1979, picture of Spock
EX $17   NM $22   **MIP** $38

Klingon Bird of Prey, ST:III, 1984, 3-1/2", die-cast w/black plastic stand
EX $7   NM $10   **MIP** $30

Klingon Costume, 1975, plastic mask, one piece jumpsuit
EX $9   NM $13   **MIP** $30

Klingon Costume, ST:TNG, 1988
EX $7   NM $10   **MIP** $20

Light Switch Cover, 1985, ST:TMP
EX $6   NM $8   **MIP** $15

Magic Slates, 1979, four designs: Spock, Kirk, Kirk and Spock
EX $7   NM $10   **MIP** $20

Make-a-Game Book, 1979
EX $7   NM $10   **MIP** $20

Metal Detector, 1976, U.S.S. Enterprise decal
EX $100   NM $145   **MIP** $225

Mirror, 1966, 2" x 3" metal, w/black and white photo of crew
EX $2   NM $5   MIP $10

Mix 'N Mold, 1975, Kirk, Spock or McCoy, molding compound, paint and brush
EX $35   NM $50   MIP $75

Movie Viewer, 1967, 3" red and black plastic
EX $10   NM $16   MIP $35

Needlepoint Kit, 1980, 14" x 18", "Live Long and Prosper"
EX $16   NM $23   MIP $35

Needlepoint Kit, 1980, Kirk
EX $16   NM $23   MIP $35

Paint-By-Numbers Set, 1972, small
EX $20   NM $35   MIP $55

Paint-By-Numbers Set, 1972, large
EX $35   NM $50   MIP $80

Pen & Poster Kit, 1976, four versions; each
EX $11   NM $16   MIP $30

Pen & Poster Kit, ST:III, 1984, 3-D poster "Search for Spock" w/overlay, 3-D glasses and four felt tip pens
EX $10   NM $20   MIP $40

Pennant, 1982, 12" x 30" triangular, black, yellow and red on white w/"Spock Lives"
EX $6   NM $10   MIP $15

Pennant, 1982, 12" x 30" triangle, The Wrath of Khan
EX $6   NM $10   MIP $15

Pennant, 1988, Paramount Pictures Adventure
EX $6   NM $10   MIP $15

Phaser, 1975, black plastic, shaped like pistol, electronic sound, flashlight projects target
EX $35   NM $100   MIP $200

Phaser Battle Game, 1976, black plastic, 13" high battery-operated electronic target game, LED scoring lights, sound effects and adjustable controls
EX $195   NM $275   MIP $450

Phaser Gun, 1967, Astro Buzz-Ray Gun w/three-color flash beam
EX $80   NM $150   MIP $250

Phaser Gun, ST:III, 1984, white and blue plastic gun w/light and sound effects
EX $35   NM $60   MIP $100

Phaser Gun, ST:TNG, 1988, gray plastic light and sound hand phaser
EX $14   NM $20   MIP $40

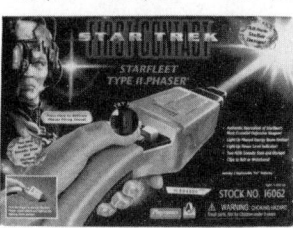

Phaser, ST:FC, 1996, #16062, Starfleet Type II Phaser from film, First Contact
EX $8   NM $16   MIP $25

Pinball Game, ST:TMP, 12", plastic, Kirk or Spock
EX $23   NM $35   MIP $80

Pinball Game, ST:TMP, 1979, electronic
EX $200   NM $350   MIP $650

Pocket Flix, 1978, battery operated movie viewer and film cartridge
EX $18   NM $25   MIP $50

Pop-Up Book, ST:TMP, 1980
EX $10   NM $20   MIP $40

Puzzle, 1974, 150 pieces, Battle on the Planet Romulus
EX $5   NM $10   MIP $15

Puzzle, 1974, 150 pieces, Battle on the Planet Klingon
EX $3   NM $7   MIP $12

Puzzle, 1974, 150 pieces, Kirk and officers beaming down
EX $3   NM $7   MIP $12

Puzzle, 1974, 150 pieces, attempted Hijacking of U.S.S. Enterprise
EX $4   NM $8   MIP $15

Puzzle, 1976, 150 pieces; Kirk, Spock, and McCoy
EX $4   NM $8   MIP $12

Puzzle, 1976, 150 pieces, "Force Field Capture"
EX $4   NM $8   MIP $15

Puzzle, 1978, 8-1/2" x 11" tray, Spock in spacesuit
EX $2   NM $5   MIP $10

Puzzle, 1979, 551 pieces
EX $8   NM $15   MIP $25

Puzzle, 1979, ST:TMP, 50 pieces
EX $3   NM $7   MIP $12

Puzzle, 1979, ST:TMP, 15-piece sliding puzzle
EX $3   NM $7   MIP $12

Puzzle, 1986, 551 pieces, ST:IV, "The Voyage Home"
EX $10   NM $20   MIP $30

Role Playing Game, 2001 Deluxe Edition, Star Trek Basic Set and the Star Trek III Combat Game
EX $20   NM $30   MIP $50

Role Playing Game, 2004 Basic Set, three books outlining Star Trek Universe
EX $7   NM $10   MIP $20

Role Playing Game, Second Deluxe Edition
EX $14   NM $20   MIP $35

Space Design Center, ST:TMP, 1979, blue plastic tray, paints, pens, crayons, project book and crew member cut-outs
EX $70   NM $110   MIP $175

Spock & Enterprise Wristwatch,
ST:TMP, 1986, 20th anniversary,
digital
EX $9   NM $20   MIP $40

Spock Bank, 1975, 12" plastic
EX $25   NM $35   MIP $60

Spock Bop Bag, 1975, plastic,
inflatable
EX $55   NM $80   MIP $125

Spock Chair, ST:TMP, 1979, inflatable
EX $16   NM $23   MIP $40

Spock Costume, 1970s
EX $30   NM $65   MIP $150

Spock Costume, 1973, plastic mask,
one-piece jumpsuit
EX $11   NM $16   MIP $30

Spock Doll, ST:TMP, 1979, 13" tall,
soft body, plastic head
EX $16   NM $25   MIP $50

Spock Ears, ST:TMP, 1979
EX $7   NM $10   MIP $20

Spock Tray, 1979, 17-1/2" metal lap
tray
EX $9   NM $13   MIP $20

Spock Wristwatch, ST:TMP
EX $20   NM $30   MIP $50

Star Trek Cartoon Puzzle, 1978
EX $4   NM $5   MIP $10

Star Trek II U.S.S. Enterprise Ship,
1982, 3" die-cast
EX $9   NM $13   MIP $25

Star Trekulator, 1970s, working
calculator, blue plastic, image of
Kirk in green v-neck shirt on screen
EX $25   NM $50   MIP $75

Super Phaser II Target Game, 1976,
way before Laser Tag you could
shoot Klingon ships or each other
w/phasers
EX $35   NM $80   MIP $125

Telescreen Console Play Set, 1976,
plastic, battery-operated target
game w/light and sound effects
EX $70   NM $100   MIP $160

Tracer Gun, 1966, plastic pistol
w/colored plastic discs
EX $45   NM $65   MIP $135

Tracer Gun, 1966, 6-1/2" plastic firing
tracer gun
EX $40   NM $65   MIP $125

Tracer Scope, 1968, rifle w/disks
EX $50   NM $80   MIP $150

Transporter Room, 1975, play set for
Mego figures, made in England
EX $75   NM $150   MIP $280

Tricorder, 1976, blue plastic tape
recorder, battery operated
w/shoulder strap, 30-minute tape
played "The Menagerie" on one side
and space sounds on the other
EX $70   NM $110   MIP $175

Trillions of Trilligs Pop-Up Book, 1977
EX $16   NM $25   MIP $40

Utility Belt, 1975, black plastic phaser
miniature, tricorder, communicator
and belt w/Star Trek buckle
EX $45   NM $85   MIP $155

Vulcan Shuttle Model Kit, 1980,
#91231, ST:TMP
EX $100   NM $120   MIP $145

Vulcan Shuttle Model Kit, 1984,
#6679, ST:TMP
EX $18   NM $20   MIP $35

Vulcan Shuttle Model Kit, 1984,
#6679, ST:III
EX $20   NM $25   MIP $50

Wastebasket, 1977, black metal
EX $35   NM $50   MIP $80

Wastebasket, ST:TMP, 1979, 13"
high, metal rainbow painting
w/photograph of Enterprise
surrounded by smaller pictures
EX $11   NM $16   MIP $35

Water Pistol, 1976, white plastic,
shaped like U.S.S. Enterprise
EX $20   NM $30   MIP $50

Water Pistol, 1976, white plastic,
shaped like U.S.S. Enterprise
EX $15   NM $30   MIP $60

Water Pistol, ST:TMP, 1979, gray
plastic, early phaser
EX $11   NM $16   MIP $30

Water Pistol, Star Trek:TMP, 1979,
gray plastic, early pistol-grip
phaser design
EX $10   NM $20   MIP $60

Writing Tablet, 1967, 8" x 10"
EX $11   NM $16   MIP $30

Yo-Yo, 1979, ST:TMP, blue sparkle
plastic
EX $10   NM $20   MIP $40

Tom Corbett

Atomic Flashlight Pistol, 1950s,
identical to Space Patrol Atomic
Flashlight Pistol except for body
colors and "Tom Corbett Space
Cadet" printed upside down on
handgrip
EX $135   NM $200   MIP $350

Binoculars
EX $60   NM $100   MIP $150

Coloring Book, 1950s, two versions,
each
EX $25   NM $40   MIP $80

Flash X-1, 1967, 4" long, tin litho,
friction sparkling action, red body
w/blue and yellow inset and grips,
large white "Flash X-1" on body,
four red tinted plastic sparkling
windows
EX $15   NM $25   MIP $75

Flash X-1 Space Gun, 5" long
EX $55   NM $110   MIP $160

**Model Craft Molding and Coloring
Set,** 1950s, various characters
EX $150   NM $350   MIP $500

Official Space Cadet Gun, 1950s,
poorly designed composite rifle
w/modern military plastic stock and
front grip at ends of long tin litho
gun body w/litho bombs and "Ray
Adjuster" scale
EX $135   NM $300   MIP $500

Official Sparking Space Gun, 21" long,
w/numerous apparatus on body
EX $80   NM $150   MIP $250

Polaris Wind-Up Spaceship, 1952,
12" long, blue litho w/yellow, Tom,
Astro and Roger visible in the litho
cockpit
EX $200   NM $375   MIP $600

Portrait Ring, 1950s, premium
EX $20   NM $35   MIP $60

Push-Outs Book, 1952
EX $35   **NM** $65   **MIP** $100

Puzzles, 1950s, frame tray, three versions, each
EX $17   **NM** $30   **MIP** $50

Rocket Scout Ring, 1950s
EX $10   **NM** $20   **MIP** $35

School Bag, 1950s, 15" long, 10" wide, plastic vinyl w/Tom's picture and rocketships on front
EX $25   **NM** $55   **MIP** $85

Signal Siren Flashlight, 1950s
EX $70   **NM** $115   **MIP** $200

Space Academy Play Set, 1950s, #7020
EX $195   **NM** $550   **MIP** $600

Space Academy Play Set, 1952, #7010, 45mm figures
EX $205   **NM** $360   **MIP** $515

Space Cadet Belt, 1950s
EX $65   **NM** $105   **MIP** $175

Space Cadet Gun, 1952, 10-1/2" long, sheet metal clicker based on Flash Gordon Radio repeater molds, red body, blue barrel reads "Space Cadet," handgrips show bust of Tom in front of planet w/rocket ship symbol above
EX $150   **NM** $350   **MIP** $600

Space Gun, 1950s, 9-1/2" long light blue and black sparking
EX $70   **NM** $130   **MIP** $250

Space Suit Ring, 1950s
EX $10   **NM** $16   **MIP** $35

(Justin Pinchot photo)

Tom Corbett Space Cadet Atomic Rifle, 1950s, 25", large plastic clicker rifle in metallic silver, gold or non-metallic robin's egg blue, rings at both ends of barrel, Tom Corbett logo embossed on butt, 25"

EX $200   **NM** $400   **MIP** $1000

Wristwatch, 1950s, round dial, embossed band w/ship and planets, on illustrated rocket shaped card

EX $195   **NM** $250   **MIP** $600

Star Wars

Star Wars

by Mark Bellomo

The foundation of global popular culture was shaken to its core in 1977 when George Lucas released one of the most important films in modern American history: the science fiction space opera, *Star Wars: A New Hope*. Over the past 35+ years, eager fans have popularized Star Wars terms that have been indelibly stamped onto our collective consciousness and even introduced into the American lexicon: words like "light saber," "Jedi Knight," and "droids"; expressions such as "May The Force Be With You," and the moral/psychic concept of "the dark side of the Force."

Little did 20th Century Fox realize the impact that the film would have on children and adult collectors everywhere, and in a brilliant stroke of prescience, Lucas may have subconsciously realized the potential of the *Star Wars* franchise. Lucas alone contracted to retail all sequel and merchandising rights for the film(s).

Kenner toys obtained the rights to produce 3-¾" action figures, playsets, creatures and vehicles based on important scenes from *Star Wars*. The smaller 3 ¾" scale was utilized in direct response to the OPEC oil shortages of the 1970s, shortages that increased the cost of plastic production which was affecting many major toy companies such as Hasbro and Mego. Little would Kenner realize the overwhelming response that their more portable Star Wars figures would attract at retail. Soon after their release, the 3 ¾" action figure format would become the standard in the field: at this smaller size (as opposed to Hasbro's enormous G.I. Joe figures' 11½" or Mego's interchangeable 8" body), characters were easier to produce, simpler to manufacture, could sell higher numbers in order to allow consumers to purchase many more units ("collect them all"), ultimately refreshing sold-out retail pegs much more quickly.

Star Wars figures became a sensation—a phenomenon—in the late 1970s and early 1980s, and the items sold briskly throughout the release of the original trilogy, producing a bevy of toys for each of the three films: *A New Hope (Episode IV)*, *The Empire Strikes Back (Episode V)*, and *The Return of the Jedi (Episode VI)*. A total of 96 figures were available in the original "vintage" line (1977-1985), not including myriad figure variations (telescoping light sabers, vinyl-caped Jawas, etc.), or the Sy Snootles and the Rebo Band three-pack set. The most popular and valuable of these carded figures are the earliest *Star Wars* releases, those figures found on original "12-back cards"—those card backs that showed only the first 12 Star Wars action figures in 1977. Other pricey figures can be found within the final run of the line, 1984/85's "Power of the Force" collection, where figures (both new sculpts and previously released characters) were carded along with a collector's coin. A few of these carded samples are worth thousands of dollars in Mint condition.

Along with the standard 3-¾" figures was a collection of deluxe 12" figures based on more popular characters from the films—these were the very first deluxe 12" action figures made in the likenesses of the most popular characters from the original Star Wars trilogy, and are held in high regard by Star Wars aficionados.

Apart from releasing 96 Star Wars action figures, Kenner crafted five creatures, 31 vehicles (including store exclusives), 13 playsets (again, including exclusives), a few accessories, and seven action figure storage cases. Also adding to the collecting fun were proof-of-purchase mail-aways that children desired: Collector's Action Stands, Survival Kits, Display Arenas, Power of the Force coins, posters, and special bagged figures before their official retail carded release. These special offers added an air of anticipation to the hobby of collecting, and most kids couldn't wait for these packages to arrive in the mail.

Regardless of promotion, mail-away premiums, and large discounts at retail, the vintage Star Wars line was cancelled in 1985 due to poor sales and a shrinking sci-fi marketplace. Sadly, it would be ten very long years before Star Wars collectors would be treated to any new toys.

To much fanfare, Kenner released a new series of Star Wars action figures in 1995, and the "Power of the Force" line (or, as fans dubbed it, the "POTF II" line) was born. Although initially criticized for their bulky statures and poor facial sculpts, the POTF II action figure line lasted five years and yielded many excellent new figures, a

The Top 10 STAR WARS in mint condition

1. Anakin Skywalker, POTF card, Kenner, 1985. . . . . $3,000
2. Jawa, plastic cape, SW card, Kenner, 1978 . . . . $2,700
3. Yak Face, POTF card, Kenner, 1985 . . . . $1,750
4. Boba Fett, Droids card, Kenner, 1985 . . . . $1,400
5. IG-88, 12" figure, ESB box, Kenner, 1982 . . . . $1,150
6. AT-AT Driver, POTF card, Kenner, 1985 . . . . $1,000
7. Boba Fett, 12" figure, ESB box, Kenner, 1982 . . . . $975
8. Han Solo (large head), SW card, Kenner, 1978 . . . . $900
9. Star Wars Early Bird Kit, (four figures total), mail-away, Kenner, 1978 . . . . $850
10. Nitko, POTF card, Kenner, 1985 . . . . $800

slew of unproduced characters, and even improved paint applications, sculpting, and articulation. From 1995-present, Hasbro (the most recent owner of the Star Wars action figure license) has produced many different lines under the Star Wars brand: Shadows of the Empire (1996); Episode I (1999-2002); Power of the Jedi (2000-2002); Star Wars Saga (2002-2004); Clone Wars (2004-2005); Original Trilogy Collection (2004); Revenge of the Sith (2005); The Saga Collection (2006); The 30th Anniversary Collection (2006-2008); The Clone Wars (2008-current); and The Legacy Collection (2008-current).

Star Wars toys are some of the most desirable action figures on the secondary market, and the people who collect them are often the most devoted in the hobby. Vintage figures and vehicles still sealed in their packages command outrageous prices on online auction sites such as eBay and in collectible stores.

Star Wars Trends

The most important aspect of collecting Star Wars action figure product—whether vintage or modern—is the ability of a collector to pursue an education on the subject. With the vast amount of reproduction parts out on the secondary market (and I'm not kidding here… there are THOUSANDS flooding the secondary market), it is essential for aficionados to know exactly what it is they're buying in regard to vintage Star Wars action figures: is this Mint on Sealed Card (MOSC) "plastic-caped" Jawa an authentic specimen or a clever reproduction? If it is a reproduction, I just lost THOUSANDS of dollars… In the lot of 30+ Mint Loose Complete (MLC) vintage Star Wars figures I just bought, are there any reproduction weapons and accessories paired with any of the toys? If so, the value of those action figures just plummeted…

So get yourself an education. The site most die-hards use to distinguish reproduction Star Wars accessories from originals is the magnificent *Imperial Gunnery* located at www.imperialgunnery.com. Here you'll find information on how to determine the difference between the following "repros" and their original counterparts: Imperial Blasters, Rebel Blasters, Palace Blasters, Bespin Blasters, Pilot Blasters, Endor Blasters, Princess Leia Blasters, Jawa Blaster, Bikerscout Blaster, The Rifles Section, The Lightsaber Section, The Staffs / Axes Section, Capes and Cloaks, Helmets and Hoods, Other Weapons, Other Accessories, 12 Inch Figure Accessories, and a set of Repro's F.A.Q's to guide you on your way.

An education about vintage Star Wars figures should also afford collectors the ability to recognize reproduction card backs and bubbles from their more valuable original counterparts. With the obvious quality of modern photocopiers and laser printers, reproduction card backs can be easily manufactured, but the width of the packages' card back, the size of each bubble (they're all just a wee bit different), the images printed on the front

and back of the card (check for pixilation—many of these images are printed from CD or DVD-ROMs), and the small rectangular piece of colored cardboard placed by the figures' feet are all incredibly difficult to EXACTLY reproduce. Your best bet: open your web browser (I prefer Firefox when viewing high-resolution graphics) to eBay, find an AFA (Action Figure Authority)-graded vintage figure in a "Completed Items" search, and compare what you're going to buy with the graded specimen in front of you. Note every detail. If the two don't match, then walk away. Even the most seasoned veterans have been fooled by reproduction items said to be Mint on Sealed Card (MOSC). Or if you'd like to get a head start on educating yourself about Star Wars card back fraud (and variations), check out my pal Gus Lopez's brilliant and informative *Star Wars Collectors Archive* at http://theswca.com.

However, there's also a contrasting opinion about reproduction Star Wars product that many fans espouse. For example, if you're a casual collector who doesn't wish to spend $400-450 for a Mint on Sealed Card (MOSC) Ben (Obi-Wan) Kenobi figure on an original 12-back card from 1978, then simply check eBay for a similar-looking looking-piece, but "custom carded"; "custom carded" is another word for reproduced, where the seller *advertises* the toy as an original 1978 figure mounted on a reproduction card back and bubble. This repro-carded Ben Kenobi on a 12-back card might be obtained for a mere $40. There are many collectors who choose to pick up a full set of all 12 original characters on reproduction 12-back cards for a few hundred dollars, instead of the prohibitively expensive $4,000-4,500 cost of the originals (!).

And in regard to utilizing reproduction weapons with loose Star Wars action figures, you can purchase a set of 30 reproduction accessories for just $19.99. These repro accessory sets include relatively common weapons such as a Stormtrooper's E-11 blaster rifle or Princess Leia's Defender Sporting Blaster Pistol, or much, much rarer pieces. For example, these sets also include Artoo-Detoo's (R2-D2's) green-colored "Pop-Up" lightsaber from the droid's popular Power of the Force (POTF) incarnation or even a reproduction of the super-rare "double-telescoping" lightsaber—since original double-telescoping lightsabers are worth hundreds of dollars each.

As always, your best source of investment—if you can find them inexpensively (let's say… at less than $3-4 each)—is either vintage Mint, Loose, Complete and unpackaged Star Wars toys—which will usually possess a solid return, or the always-hard-to-find and pricey high-grade MISB/MISP (Mint in Factory Sealed Box/Mint in Factory Sealed Package) samples that will garner you the highest profits. Factory-sealed samples of accessories, creatures, figures, playsets, and vehicles are extremely scarce and are highly desirable to every Star Wars aficionado across the galaxy.

STAR WARS
Series 1

(KP Photo)

Ben (Obi-Wan) Kenobi, 1977-78
MNP **$15**   MIP **$425**

Boba Fett, 1979
MNP **$20**   MIP **$650**

C-3PO, 1977-78
MNP **$15**   MIP **$250**

Chewbacca, 1977-78
MNP **$13**   MIP **$250**

Darth Vader, 1977-78
MNP **$16**   MIP **$550**

Death Squad Commander, 1977-78
MNP **$11**   MIP **$200**

Death Star Droid, 1979
MNP **$20**   MIP **$190**

**Early Bird Figures — Luke, Leia,
R2-D2, Chewbacca,** 1977-78
MNP **$150**   MIP **$750**

Greedo, 1979
MNP **$12**   MIP **$220**

(KP Photo)

Hammerhead, 1979
MNP **$11**   MIP **$190**

Han Solo, Large Head, 1977-78
MNP **$22**   MIP **$575**

Han Solo, Small Head, 1977-78
    MNP $26   **MIP $525**

Jawa, Cloth Cape, 1977-78
    MNP $15   **MIP $210**

Jawa, Vinyl Cape, 1977-78
    MNP $300   **MIP $3000**

Luke as X-Wing Pilot, 1979
    MNP $12   **MIP $225**
Luke Skywalker, 1977-78
    MNP $30   **MIP $575**

Luke w/Telescoping Saber, 1977-78
    MNP $600   **MIP $4000**

(KP Photo)
Power Droid, 1979, dark blue body
  w/stocky legs
    MNP $11   **MIP $140**

Princess Leia Organa, 1977-78
    MNP $25   **MIP $525**

R2-D2, 1977-78

    MNP $14   **MIP $250**

(KP Photo)

R5-D4, 1979

    MNP $14   **MIP $225**

Sand People (Tusken Raider), 1977-78

    MNP $16   **MIP $250**

**Snaggletooth, Blue Body, Sears
Exclusive,** 1979

    MNP $125   **MIP $300**

(KP Photo)

Snaggletooth, Red Body, 1979
MNP $8   **MIP** $160

Stormtrooper, 1977-78
MNP $17   **MIP** $270

Walrus Man, 1979
MNP $10   **MIP** $150

EMPIRE STRIKES BACK
Series 2

2-1B, 1981, the medical droid who assists Luke's recovery after his duel w/Vader, in the movie, you actually never see his legs
MNP $10   **MIP** $95

4-LOM, 1982, tan plastic cloak w/brown belt worn over the top, unique blaster rifle
MNP $14   **MIP** $155

(KP Photo)

AT-AT Commander, 1982, available w/Sears Exclusive Hoth Rebel base set, or individually, includes blaster pistol
MNP $10   **MIP** $95

AT-AT Driver, 1981, white and gray uniform, includes blaster rifle
MNP $10   **MIP** $85

(KP Photo)

Bespin Security Guard, Black, 1980, includes blaster pistol
MNP $12   **MIP** $55

Bespin Security Guard, White, 1980, w/blaster pistol
MNP $10   **MIP** $60

Bossk, 1980, includes blaster rifle w/forward grip so rifle body rests against arm
MNP $12   **MIP** $150

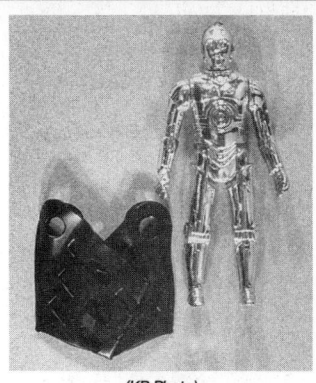

(KP Photo)

C-3PO w/Removable Limbs, 1982, included pouch for Chewbacca to carry the disassembled 3PO
MNP $8   **MIP** $50

Cloud Car Pilot, 1982, white uniform, orange and yellow helmet, style of figure reminiscent of rebel troops
MNP $20   **MIP** $80

(KP Photo)

Dengar, 1980, one of the bounty hunters hired by Vader ("we don't need their scum…"), this figure originally came w/a long rifle
MNP $8   **MIP** $80

FX-7, 1980, also called the "medical droid," this model had a series of spindly arms that pivoted up from the cylindrical body
MNP $10   **MIP** $55

Han in Bespin Outfit, 1981, includes blaster pistol
MNP $10   **MIP** $95

Han in Hoth Gear, 1980, in dark blue parka, khaki pants, includes small blaster pistol
MNP $10   **MIP** $95

Hoth Rebel Soldier, 1980, light brown and off-white uniform, small blaster pistol looking a bit like a Star Trek phaser

| | MNP $8 | MIP $55 |

IG-88, 1980

| | MNP $18 | MIP $150 |

(KP Photo)

Imperial Commander, 1981, the packaging showed General Veers in a green uniform, but the figure was an anonymous black-uniformed officer, some variation in hair color paint exists, included standard-issue Stormtrooper blaster

| | MNP $8 | MIP $65 |

Imperial TIE Fighter Pilot, 1982, black uniform, gray gloves and boots, included gray blaster pistol

| | MNP $12 | MIP $85 |

Lando Calrissian, 1980, two-tone blue clothing w/gray plastic cloak and blaster pistol

| | MNP $12 | MIP $75 |

Leia in Bespin Gown, 1980, brown outfit w/printed plastic cloak, included blaster pistol

| | MNP $26 | MIP $145 |

Leia in Hoth Gear, 1981, white uniform w/light tan vest and brown boots, included small blaster pistol

| | MNP $16 | MIP $110 |

(KP Photo)

Lobot, 1981, includes blaster pistol

| | MNP $10 | MIP $75 |

Luke in Bespin Fatigues, 1980, included blaster pistol and stand-alone lightsaber (not part of the figure)

| | MNP $22 | MIP $175 |

Luke in Hoth Gear, 1982, white uniform w/brown vest and gray boots, included blaster rifle

| | MNP $10 | MIP $115 |

R2-D2 w/Sensorscope, 1982, available first w/Sears Exclusive Hoth Rebel Base play set, or individually, essentially the same as the standard R2, but w/a blue plastic sensorscope that could be raised or lowered from his head

| | MNP $14 | MIP $90 |

Rebel Commander, 1981, off-white uniform, brown boots, blaster rifle

| | MNP $8 | MIP $85 |

Snowtrooper, 1980, plastic cloak along belt, included heavy laser rifle

| | MNP $17 | MIP $125 |

Ugnaught, 1981, w/blue cloth apron and white toolkit

| | MNP $9 | MIP $75 |

Yoda, 1980, w/cloth cloak, plastic belt, brown snake (rare) and walking stick, the plastic accessories were produced in varying colors

| | MNP $22 | MIP $200 |

Yoda, 1981, w/cloth cloak, plastic belt, orange snake (common) and walking stick, the plastic accessories were produced in varying colors

| | MNP $18 | MIP $180 |

Zuckuss, 1982, includes long blaster rifle

| | MNP $10 | MIP $95 |

RETURN OF THE JEDI
Series 3

8D8, 1984

| | MNP $8 | MIP $55 |

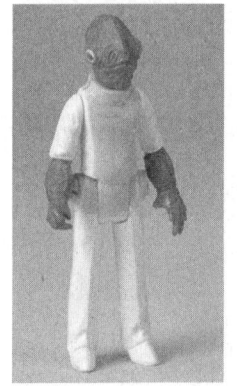

(KP Photo)

Admiral Ackbar, 1983

| | MNP $8 | MIP $35 |

(KP Photo)

AT-ST Driver, 1984

| | MNP $12 | MIP $55 |

(KP Photo)

Bib Fortuna, 1983, "Pay Jabba no bother…" this figure is the original sculpt of Jabba's major domo who was weak-minded enough to allow Luke's Jedi mind trick to work on him

      MNP $10   **MIP $38**

Biker Scout, 1983, short laser pistol

      MNP $20   **MIP $100**

B-Wing Pilot, 1984

      MNP $8   **MIP $35**

Chief Chirpa, 1983

      MNP $10   **MIP $49**

(KP Photo)

Emperor Palpatine, 1984

      MNP $10   **MIP $75**

Emperor's Royal Guard, 1983

      MNP $16   **MIP $55**

(KP Photo)

Gamorrean Guard, 1983

      MNP $10   **MIP $27**

General Madine, 1983

      MNP $8   **MIP $50**

Han in Trenchcoat, 1984

      MNP $12   **MIP $45**

Klaatu, 1984

      MNP $10   **MIP $38**

(KP Photo)

Klaatu in Skiff Guard Outfit, 1983

      MNP $8   **MIP $35**

Lando Calrissian, Skiff Guard Outfit, 1983

      MNP $10   **MIP $47**

(KP Photo)

Leia in Battle Poncho, 1984, green camo pattern cloth poncho, removeable helmet, ammo belt and blaster pistol

      MNP $20   **MIP $55**

Leia in Boushh Disguise, 1983, w/removable helmet and tall gun

      MNP $18   **MIP $50**

Logray, 1983

      MNP $12   **MIP $50**

Luke as Jedi Knight, Blue Saber, 1983

      MNP $32   **MIP $145**

Luke as Jedi Knight, Green Saber, 1983

      MNP $22   **MIP $75**

Lumat, 1984

      MNP $25   **MIP $55**

Nien Nunb, 1983

      MNP $8   **MIP $55**

Nikto, 1984

      MNP $8   **MIP $30**

(KP Photo)

Paploo, 1984

MNP **$25**   MIP **$48**

Prune Face, 1984

MNP **$8**   MIP **$43**

Rancor Keeper, 1984

MNP **$8**   MIP **$39**

Rebel Commando, 1983

MNP **$8**   MIP **$45**

Ree-Yees, 1983

MNP **$8**   MIP **$35**

Squid Head, 1983

MNP **$10**   MIP **$55**

Sy Snootles and the Rebo Band, 1984, three figures: Sy Snootles, Droopy McCool, Max Rebo

MNP **$50**   MIP **$140**

Teebo, 1984

MNP **$12**   MIP **$40**

Weequay, 1984

MNP **$8**   MIP **$49**

Wicket W. Warrick, 1984, w/long staff

MNP **$15**   MIP **$60**

POTF

Amanaman, 1984-85, w/coin

MNP **$90**   MIP **$170**

Anakin Skywalker, 1984-85, w/coin

MNP **$22**   MIP **$2800**

Artoo-Detoo (R2-D2) w/pop-up Lightsaber, 1984-85, w/coin

MNP **$85**   MIP **$140**

AT-AT Driver, 1984-85, w/coin

MNP **$10**   MIP **$575**

(KP Photo)

AT-ST Driver, 1984-85, w/coin

MNP **$12**   MIP **$70**

(KP Photo)

A-Wing Pilot, 1984-85, w/coin

MNP **$55**   MIP **$125**

(KP Photo)

Barada, 1984-85, w/coin

MNP **$40**   MIP **$90**

Ben (Obi-Wan) Kenobi, 1984-85, w/coin

MNP **$13**   MIP **$135**

Biker Scout, 1984-85, w/coin

MNP **$12**   MIP **$200**

(KP Photo)

B-Wing Pilot, 1984-85, w/coin
MNP $8   **MIP $65**

Chewbacca, 1984-85, w/coin
MNP $13   **MIP $120**

Darth Vader, 1984-85, w/coin
MNP $16   **MIP $150**

(KP Photo)

EV-9D9, 1984-85, w/coin
MNP $60   **MIP $130**

Gamorrean Guard, 1984-85, w/coin
MNP $10   **MIP $250**

Han Solo in Carbonite Chamber,
1984-85, w/coin
MNP $80   **MIP $225**

Han Solo in Trench Coat, 1984-85,
w/coin
MNP $50   **MIP $425**

(KP Photo)

Imperial Dignitary, 1984-85, w/coin
MNP $50   **MIP $105**

Imperial Gunner, 1984-85, w/coin
MNP $50   **MIP $110**

Imperial Stormtrooper, 1984-85,
w/coin
MNP $17   **MIP $200**

Jawa, 1984-85, w/coin
MNP $15   **MIP $110**

Lando Calrissian (General Pilot),
1984-85, w/coin
MNP $55   **MIP $95**

**Luke Skywalker (Imperial Stormtrooper
Outfit),** 1984-85, w/coin
MNP $90   **MIP $260**

Luke Skywalker (in Battle Poncho),
1984-85, w/coin
MNP $55   **MIP $115**

Luke Skywalker (Jedi Knight Outfit),
1984-85, w/coin, green lightsaber
MNP $24   **MIP $165**

**Luke Skywalker (X-Wing Fighter
Pilot),** 1984-85, w/coin
MNP $12   **MIP $85**

Lumat, 1984-85, w/coin
MNP $25   **MIP $65**

Nikto, 1984-85, w/coin
MNP $8   **MIP $725**

Paploo, 1984-85, w/coin
MNP $25   **MIP $60**

**Princess Leia Organa (in Combat
Poncho),** 1984-85, w/coin
MNP $16   **MIP $75**

(KP Photo)

Romba, 1984-85, w/coin
MNP $35   **MIP $70**

**See-Threepio C-3PO (Removable
Limbs),** 1984-85, w/coin
MNP $10   **MIP $80**

Teebo, 1984-85, w/coin
MNP $12   **MIP $85**

The Emperor, 1984-85, w/coin, cane
MNP $10   **MIP $110**

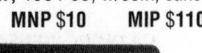

(KP Photo)

Warok, 1984-85, w/coin
MNP $40   **MIP $75**

Wicket W. Warrick, 1984-85, w/coin
> MNP $15   MIP $105

Yak Face, 1984-85, w/coin
> MNP $160   MIP $1150

Yoda, The Jedi Master, 1984-85, w/coin
> MNP $25   MIP $350

DROIDS

A-Wing Pilot, 1985
> MNP $55   MIP $250

Boba Fett, 1985
> MNP $20   MIP $700

C-3PO, 1985, solid, multicolored plastic body (not gold chromed) w/painted eyes
> MNP $90   MIP $175

(KP Photo)

Jann Tosh, 1985
> MNP $20   MIP $60

Jord Dusat, 1985
> MNP $20   MIP $60

(KP Photo)

Kea Moll, 1985, light tan and darker brown clothing, includes blaster pistol
> MNP $35   MIP $85

(KP Photo)

Kez-Iban, 1985, purple body, tan clothing, standard-issue blaster (same as early Stormtroopers)
> MNP $22   MIP $65

(KP Photo)

R2-D2, 1985, simplified body markings and head--same sculpt and legs as regular (vintage) R2, though
> MNP $15   MIP $265

Sise Fromm, 1985, large-headed, green skinned figure w/purple cloth robe
> MNP $142   MIP $255

(KP Photo)

Thall Joben, 1985
> MNP $25   MIP $55

(KP Photo)

Tig Fromm, 1985, blue and gray figure
> MNP $110   MIP $170

Uncle Gundy, 1985, short, portly figure w/white hair and mustache, includes blaster pistol
> MNP $20   MIP $50

EWOKS
Series 5

(KP Photo)

Dulok Scout, 1985, medium-green figure w/club
> MNP $28   MIP $50

(KP Photo)

Dulok Shaman, 1985, bright green figure w/skull-topped staff

MNP $25   MIP $45

(KP Photo)

King Gorneesh, 1985, fearsome bright green figure w/staff

MNP $25   MIP $50

(KP Photo)

Logray, 1985, w/bright blue plastic robe and staff

MNP $25   MIP $50

(KP Photo)

Urgah Lady Gorneesh, 1985, green figure w/red-brown poncho, blue highlights on head and face

MNP $22   MIP $50

(KP Photo)

Wicket, 1985

MNP $40   MIP $100

POTF2-1

(Hasbro Photo)

2-1B Medic Droid, 1997, Series 5

MNP $2   MIP $5

4-LOM, 1997, Series 7

MNP $2   MIP $5

8-D8 Droid, 1998, Series 14

MNP $2   MIP $5

Admiral Ackbar, 1997, Series 7

MNP $2   MIP $5

Admiral Motti, 1999, Series 20

MNP $6   MIP $15

Anakin Skywalker, 1999, Series 17

MNP $2   MIP $8

ASP-7 Droid, 1997, Series 7

MNP $2   MIP $5

AT-ST Driver, 1997, Series 5

MNP $3   MIP $5

Aunt Beru, 1999, Series 17

MNP $3   MIP $7

Bib Fortuna, 1997, Series 6

MNP $2   MIP $5

(Hasbro Photo)

Biggs Darklighter, 1998, Series 11

MNP $3   MIP $5

Boba Fett, 1996, Series 2, variation: half circle one hand, full circle on other hand, scarce $350

MNP $4   MIP $15

(Hasbro Photo)

Bossk, 1997, Series 5

MNP $2   MIP $5

C-3PO, 1995, Series 1

MNP $2   MIP $5

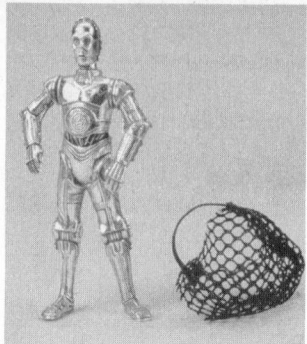

(Hasbro Photo)

C-3PO w/Removable Limbs and Backpack, 1998, Series 13

    MNP $5   MIP $10

C-3PO, Shop Worn, 1999, Series 17

    MNP $2   MIP $5

Cantina Greedo, 1999, Series 18

    MNP $2   MIP $5

Cantina Han Solo, 1999, Series 18

    MNP $2   MIP $5

Captain Piett, 1998, Series 12

    MNP $3   MIP $8

Chewbacca, 1995, Series 1

    MNP $2   MIP $5

Chewbacca (Hoth), 1998, Series 16, w/painted "snow" on face

    MNP $2   MIP $5

Chewbacca as Boushh's Bounty, 1998, Series 15

    MNP $2   MIP $5

Darth Vader, 1995, Series 1, long lightsaber

    MNP $3   MIP $5

Darth Vader, 1998, Series 16, removable cape

    MNP $3   MIP $5

Darth Vader w/Interrogation Droid, 1999, Series 19, Commtech chip version

    MNP $3   MIP $8

(KP Photo)

Darth Vader w/Removable Helmet, 1998, Series 12

    MNP $5   MIP $12

Death Star Gunner, 1996, Series 3

    MNP $3   MIP $5

Death Star Trooper, 1998, Series 15

    MNP $3   MIP $5

Dengar, 1997, Series 7

    MNP $3   MIP $5

Emperor Palpatine, 1997, Series 6, Collection 1

    MNP $2   MIP $5

Emperor Palpatine, 1998, Series 16

    MNP $2   MIP $5

Emperor's Royal Guard, 1997, Series 8

    MNP $2   MIP $5

(Hasbro Photo)

Endor Rebel Soldier, 1998, Series 10

    MNP $2   MIP $5

(Hasbro Photo)

EV-9D9, 1997, Series 9

    MNP $2   MIP $5

(Hasbro Photo)

Gamorrean Guard, 1997, Series 9

    MNP $2   MIP $5

Garindan (Long Snoot), 1997, Series 7

    MNP $2   MIP $5

(KP Photo)

Grand Moff Tarkin, 1997, Series 7, Collection 2

    MNP $2   MIP $5

Greedo, 1996, Series 3, Collection 1

    MNP $2   MIP $5

Han in Bespin Outfit, 1997, Series 8

    MNP $2   MIP $5

Han in Endor Gear, 1997, Series 6, blue pants

    MNP $2   MIP $5

Han in Hoth Gear, 1996, Series 2

    MNP $2   MIP $5

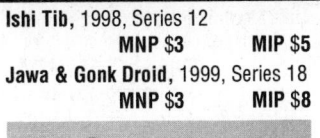

Ishi Tib, 1998, Series 12
MNP $3   MIP $5
Jawa & Gonk Droid, 1999, Series 18
MNP $3   MIP $8

(Hasbro Photo)

(Hasbro Photo)

Lando Calrissian, 1996, Series 2
MNP $2   MIP $5

Leia as Jabba's Prisoner, 1997,
Series 8
MNP $3   MIP $5

(KP Photo)

Han Solo, 1995, Series 1
MNP $2   MIP $5

Jawas, 1996, Series 4
MNP $3   MIP $6

(KP Photo, Karen O'Brien collection)

Han Solo in Carbonite, 1996, Han in
Bespin outfit, frozen in carbonite,
blaster
MNP $2   MIP $5

Hoth Rebel Soldier, 1997, Series 5
MNP $2   MIP $5

(Hasbro Photo)

Lak Sivrak, 1998, Series 11
MNP $3   MIP $8

(Hasbro Photo)

Leia in Ewok Celebration Outfit,
1998, Series 10
MNP $2   MIP $5

Leia w/All-New Likeness, 1998,
Series 13
MNP $2   MIP $5

Lobot, 1998, Series 15
MNP $2   MIP $5

(Hasbro Photo)

(Hasbro Photo)

(Hasbro Photo)

Lando as General, 1998, Series 10
MNP $2   MIP $5

Lando as Skiff Guard, 1997, Series 6
MNP $2   MIP $5

Luke as X-Wing Pilot, 1996, Series 2, short lightsaber
    MNP $2   **MIP $5**

Luke in Bespin Outfit, 1998, Series 10, detachable hand
    MNP $2   **MIP $5**

Luke in Ceremonial Garb, 1997, Series 10, Collection 1
    MNP $2   **MIP $5**

Luke in Dagobah Fatigues, 1996, Series 3, short lightsaber
    MNP $2   **MIP $5**

(Hasbro Photo)

Luke in Hoth Gear, 1997, Series 5, Collection 1
    MNP $2   **MIP $5**

(KP Photo)

Luke in Stormtrooper Disguise, 1996, Series 4
    MNP $2   **MIP $5**

Luke Skywalker, 1995, Series 1, short lightsaber
    MNP $2   **MIP $5**

Luke Skywalker, 1998, Series 16, Flashback photo
    MNP $2   **MIP $5**

Luke Skywalker w/T16, 1999, Series 18
    MNP $2   **MIP $5**

Luke w/Blast Shield Helmet, 1998, Series 13
    MNP $2   **MIP $5**

(Hasbro Photo)

Malakili (Rancor Keeper), 1997, Series 9
    MNP $2   **MIP $5**

Momaw Nadon (Hammerhead), 1996, Series 4, Collection 2
    MNP $2   **MIP $5**

Mon Mothma, 1998, Series 15
    MNP $2   **MIP $5**

(Hasbro Photo)

Nien Nunb, 1997, Series 9
    MNP $2   **MIP $5**

Obi-Wan Kenobi, 1995, Series 1, short lightsaber
    MNP $2   **MIP $5**

Obi-Wan Kenobi, 1998, Series 16
    MNP $2   **MIP $5**

Orrimaarko (Prune Face), 1998, Series 15, w/brown plastic cloak
    MNP $2   **MIP $5**

Ponda Baba, 1997, Series 7, Collection 3, Collection 2
    MNP $2   **MIP $5**

Princess Leia, 1995, Series 1
    MNP $2   **MIP $5**

Princess Leia, 1998, Series 16
    MNP $2   **MIP $5**

Princess Leia Organa, 1997, Series 9
    MNP $2   **MIP $5**

R2-D2, 1995, Series 1
    MNP $2   **MIP $5**

R2-D2, 1998, Series 16
    MNP $2   **MIP $5**

R2-D2 w/Datalink and Sensorscope, 1998, Series 13
    MNP $2   **MIP $5**

R2-D2 w/Holographic Princess Leia, 1999, Series 20
    MNP $3   **MIP $7**

R5-D4, 1996, Series 4
    MNP $2   **MIP $5**

Rebel Fleet Trooper, 1997, Series 7, Collection 1
    MNP $2   **MIP $5**

Ree-Yees, 1998, Series 15
    MNP $3   **MIP $12**

Saelt-Marae (Yak Face), 1997, Series 9
    MNP $3   **MIP $5**

(KP Photo)

Sandtrooper, 1996, Series 3,
w/blaster rifle and backpack
MNP $3   **MIP $5**

(KP Photo)

Snowtrooper, 1997, Series 8
MNP $3   **MIP $5**

Stormtrooper, 1995, Series 1
MNP $3   **MIP $5**

Stormtrooper, 1999, Series 19,
Commtech Chip
MNP $3   **MIP $5**

(KP Photo)

TIE Fighter Pilot, 1996, Series 2,
equipped w/two blaster rifles
MNP $3   **MIP $5**

(KP Photo)

Tusken Raider, 1996, Series 4
MNP $3   **MIP $5**

Ugnaught, 1998, Series 13
MNP $3   **MIP $5**

Weequay Skiff Guard, 1997, Series 7,
Collection 3
MNP $3   **MIP $5**

(Hasbro Photo)

Wicket and Logray, 1998, Series 11
MNP $5   **MIP $8**

Yoda, 1996, Series 2
MNP $3   **MIP $5**

Yoda, 1998, Series 16
MNP $3   **MIP $5**

Zuckuss, 1998, Series 12
MNP $3   **MIP $5**

POTF2-2
Cinema Scene 3-Packs

Cantina Aliens, 1999, Labria, Nabrun
Leids, Takeel
MNP $4   **MIP $10**

Cantina Showdown, 1997, Obi-Wan
Kenobi, Ponda Baba, Dr. Evazan
MNP $4   **MIP $10**

(Karen O'Brien)

Death Star Escape, 1997, Luke and
Han in Stormtrooper Disguise,
Chewbacca
MNP $4   **MIP $10**

Final Jedi Duel, 1998, Darth Vader,
Luke, Emperor Palpatine
MNP $4   **MIP $10**

Jabba the Hutt's Dancers, 1998,
Rystall, Greeata, Lyn Me
MNP $4   **MIP $10**

(KP Photo)

Jabba's Skiff Guards, 1999, Klaatu,
Barada, Nikto, keeping them in-
pack, the box doubles as a diorama
background
MNP $4   **MIP $10**

Jedi Spirits, 1999, Anakin Skywalker,
Yoda, Obi-Wan Kenobi
MNP $3   **MIP $8**

Mynock Hunt, 1998, Han, Leia,
Chewbacca
MNP $8   **MIP $15**

Purchase of the Droids, 1998, Luke,
C-3PO, Uncle Owen
MNP $4   **MIP $10**

Rebel Pilots, 1999, Wedge Antilles, B-
Wing Pilot (Ten Nunb), Y-Wing
Pilot
MNP $6   **MIP $12**

POTF2-3
Complete Galaxy

Dagobah w/Yoda, 1998
MNP $3   **MIP $10**

Death Star w/Darth Vader, 1998
MNP $3   **MIP $10**

Endor w/Wicket, 1998
MNP $3   **MIP $10**

Tatooine w/Luke Skywalker, 1998
MNP $3   **MIP $10**

POTF2-4
Dark Empire

Clone Emperor, 1998
MNP $5   MIP $7

Imperial Sentinel, 1998
MNP $5   MIP $12

Kyle Katarn, 1998
MNP $5   MIP $7

Luke Skywalker (Dark Empire), 1998
MNP $5   MIP $7

Princess Leia Organa Solo, 1998
MNP $5   MIP $7

POTF2-4
Dark Forces

Darktrooper, 1998
MNP $4   MIP $10

POTF2-5
Deluxe

Boba Fett, 1997
MNP $2   MIP $5

Crowd Control Stormtrooper, 1996
MNP $2   MIP $5

Han Solo w/Smuggler's Flight Pack, 1996
MNP $2   MIP $5

Hoth Rebel Soldier w/Anti-Vehicle Laser Canon, 1996
MNP $2   MIP $5

Imperial Probe Droid, 1997
MNP $2   MIP $5

Luke Skywalker's Desert Sport Skiff, 1996
MNP $2   MIP $5

Snowtrooper (Deluxe), 1997, With tripod laser cannon
MNP $2   MIP $5

POTF2-6
Deluxe 2-Packs

Boba Fett vs. IG-88, 1996, packaged w/comic book
MNP $4   MIP $10

Droopy McCool and Barquin D'an, 1998
MNP $5   MIP $10

Leia and Han, 1998
MNP $2   MIP $5

(Hasbro Photo)

Leia and Luke, 1998
MNP $2   MIP $5

Leia and R2-D2, 1998
MNP $2   MIP $5

(Hasbro Photo)

Leia and Wicket the Ewok, 1998
MNP $2   MIP $5

Max Rebo and Doda Bodonawieedo, 1998
MNP $10   MIP $18

Prince Xizor vs. Darth Vader, 1996
MNP $3   MIP $10

Sy Snootles and Joh Yowza, 1998
MNP $5   MIP $10

POTF2-7
Electronic Power F/X

Ben (Obi-Wan) Kenobi, 1997
MNP $2   MIP $5

Darth Vader, 1997
MNP $2   MIP $5

Emporer Palpatine, 1997
MNP $2   MIP $5

Jedi Knight Luke Skywalker, 1997
MNP $2   MIP $5

R2-D2, 1997
MNP $2   MIP $5

POTF2-8
Fan Club Four

AT-AT Driver, 1998
MNP $6   MIP $15

Death Star Droid w/Mouse Droid, 1998
MNP $6   MIP $15

Leia in Hoth Gear, 1998
MNP $5   MIP $12

Pote Snitkin, 1998
MNP $4   MIP $12

POTF2-9
Gunner Stations

Falcon w/Han Solo, 1998
MNP $2   MIP $5

Falcon w/Luke Skywalker, 1998
MNP $2   MIP $5

Tie Fighter w/Darth Vader, 1998
MNP $2   MIP $5

POTF2-10
Heir to the Empire

Grand Admiral Thrawn, 1998
MNP $5   MIP $10

Mara Jade, 1998
MNP $8   MIP $15

Spacetrooper, 1998
MNP $5   MIP $10

POTF2-11
Millennium Minted Coin

C-3PO, 1998, w/Millennium Minted Coin
MNP $4   MIP $7

Chewbacca, 1998, w/Millennium Minted Coin
MNP $4   MIP $7

Emperor Palpatine, 1998, w/Millennium Minted Coin
MNP $4   MIP $7

Han in Bespin Outfit, 1998, w/Millennium Minted Coin
MNP $4   MIP $7

Leia in Endor Gear, 1998, w/Millennium Minted Coin
MNP $54   MIP $7

Luke in Battle Poncho, 1998, w/Millennium Minted Coin
MNP $4   MIP $7

Snowtrooper, 1998, w/Millennium Minted Coin
MNP $4   MIP $7

POTF2-12
Promotional 3" Figures

B'omarr Monk, 1997, Internet exclusive offer, moving spider-like legs and brain encased in plastic bubble
MNP $6   MIP $12

Figrin D'an (Cantina Band Member), 1997, Star Wars Insider magazine exclusive
MNP $3   MIP $8

Han Solo in Stormtrooper Disguise,
1995-96, Kellogg's Fruit Loops
exclusive from August 1995
through December 1996
MNP $2   MIP $5

**Mace Windu Episode I Sneak
Preview,** 1998, Hasbro mail-in
exclusive
MNP $2   MIP $5

Muftak and Kabe, 1997, Internet
exclusive
MNP $3   MIP $8

(KP Photo)

Obi-Wan Kenobi Spirit, 1997, figure
was a mail-in offer from Frito Lay,
made of translucent blue plastic
MNP $2   MIP $4

Oola and Salacious Crumb, 1998, fan
club exclusive
MNP $12   MIP $20

(KP Photo)

**STAP and Battle Droid Episode I
Sneak Preview,** 1998, Hasbro
mail-in exclusive
MNP $8   MIP $14

**Theater Edition Jedi Knight Luke
Skywalker,** 1997, RotJ-SE opening
day exclusive 3/7/97
MNP $3   MIP $25

POTF2-13
Shadows of the Empire

**Chewbacca in Bounty Hunter
Disguise,** 1996
MNP $2   MIP $7

Dash Rendar, 1996
MNP $3   MIP $7

Han in Carbonite, 1996
MNP $2   MIP $7

Leia in Boushh Disguise, 1996
MNP $2   MIP $7

Luke in Imperial Guard Disguise, 1996
MNP $3   MIP $7

Prince Xizor, 1996
MNP $2   MIP $7

POTJ
Collection 1

Anakin Skywalker, Mechanic, 2000,
young Anakin, droid, wrench
MNP $3   MIP $5

Aurra Sing, Bounty Hunter, 2001
MNP $3   MIP $5

Battle Droid, Boomer Damage, 2000,
blaster, power pack
MNP $3   MIP $5

Ben (Obi-Wan) Kenobi, Jedi Knight,
2000, older Ben (ANH), lightsaber
MNP $3   MIP $5

**Chewbacca, Millennium Falcon
Mechanic,** 2001, welder, goggles
MNP $3   MIP $5

Coruscant Guard, 2001, large blaster
rifle
MNP $3   MIP $5

Darth Maul, Final Duel, 2000,
lightsaber, body breaks into two
pieces
MNP $3   MIP $5

Darth Maul, Sith Apprentice, 2001,
lightsaber, tan training attire
MNP $3   MIP $5

Darth Vader, Dagobah, 2000,
lightsaber, removable cape,
detachable head, removable
faceplate reveals Luke's face
MNP $3   MIP $5

Darth Vader, Emperor's Wrath, 2001,
suffering from Jedi lightning 'cause
he won't kill Luke
MNP $3   MIP $5

(KP Photo)

Han Solo, Bespin Capture, 2002,
blaster pistol, cuffs and eight-page
"Jedi Force File"
MNP $3   MIP $5

Han Solo, Death Star Escape, 2001,
blaster, ready to chase the
Stormtroopers
MNP $3   MIP $5

Leia Organa, Bespin Escape, 2001,
blaster
MNP $3   MIP $5

Leia Organa, General, 2000, two
blasters
MNP $3   MIP $5

Luke Skywalker, X-Wing Pilot, 2000,
lightsaber
MNP $3   MIP $5

**Obi-Wan Kenobi, Cold Weather
Gear,** 2001, lightsaber, backpack,
face mask
MNP $3   MIP $5

Obi-Wan Kenobi, Jedi, 2000,
lightsaber, removable cloak, young
Obi-Wan at the end of Episode I
MNP $3   MIP $5

Qui-Gon Jinn, Jedi Training Gear,
2001, lightsaber
MNP $3   MIP $5

Qui-Gon Jinn, Mos Espa Disguise,
2000, gray cloth poncho, lightsaber
MNP $3   MIP $5

R2-D2, Naboo Escape, 2000
MNP $3   MIP $5

Sandtrooper, Tatooine Patrol, 2001,
binoculars, backpack, pistol
MNP $3   MIP $5

POTJ
Collection 2

Battle Droid, Security, 2000, blaster
MNP $3   MIP $5

Bespin Guard, Cloud City Security,
2000
MNP $3   MIP $5

BoShek, 2002, pilot's outfit,
removable helmet
MNP $3   MIP $5

Boss Nass, Gungan Sacred Place,
2000
MNP $3   MIP $5

Chewbacca, Dejarik Champion, 2000
MNP $3   MIP $5

Eeth Koth, Jedi Master, 2001,
lightsaber
MNP $3   MIP $5

(KP Photo)

Ellorrs Madak, Duros, 2001, Fan Choice Figure #1
MNP $3   MIP $5

Fode and Beed, Podrace Announcers, 2000
MNP $3   MIP $5

FX-7, Medical Droid, 2001
MNP $3   MIP $5

Gungan Warrior, 2000, shield, energy weapon
MNP $3   MIP $5

IG-88, Bounty Hunter, 2000
MNP $3   MIP $5

Imperial Officer, 2001, pistol
MNP $3   MIP $5

Jar Jar Binks, Tatooine, 2000
MNP $2   MIP $5

Jek Porkins, Rebel Pilot, 2000, the original "Red Six" himself, removable helmet, "Stay on target!"
MNP $6   MIP $10

K-3PO, Echo Base Protocol Droid, 2000, pouch
MNP $6   MIP $5

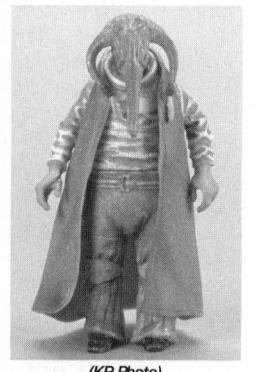

(KP Photo)

Ketwol, 2001
MNP $3   MIP $5

Lando Calrissian, Bespin Escape, 2000, pistol
MNP $3   MIP $5

Mas Amedda, 2000
MNP $3   MIP $5

Mon Calamari Officer, 2000
MNP $3   MIP $5

Obi-Wan Kenobi, Jedi Training Gear, 2001, lightsaber, helmet
MNP $3   MIP $5

Plo Koon, Jedi Master, 2000, lightsaber
MNP $3   MIP $5

Queen Amidala, Royal Decoy, 2001, black outfit
MNP $3   MIP $5

Queen Amidala, Theed Invasion, 2001, red outfit
MNP $3   MIP $5

R2-Q5, Imperial Astromech Droid, 2001
MNP $3   MIP $5

R4-M9, 2001, w/small black droid
MNP $4   MIP $12

Rebel Trooper, Tantive IV Defender, 2001, pistol, removable helmet
MNP $3   MIP $5

Sabe, Queen's Decoy, 2001, blaster pistol
MNP $3   MIP $5

Saesee Tiin, Jedi Master, 2000, lightsaber
MNP $3   MIP $5

Scout Trooper, Imperial Patrol, 2000, biker scout in clean or dirty armor variations, pistol
MNP $4   MIP $5

Sebulba, 2000, removeable helmet, wrench
MNP $3   MIP $5

Shmi Skywalker, 2001
MNP $3   MIP $5

Teebo, 2001, staff
MNP $3   MIP $5

Tessek, 2001, blaster pistol
MNP $3   MIP $5

Tusken Raider, Desert Sniper, 2001, long rifle
MNP $3   MIP $5

Zutton, Snaggletooth, 2001, rifle
MNP $3   MIP $5

POTJ
Deluxe

Amanaman w/Salacious Crumb, 2001
MNP $6   MIP $10

Darth Maul w/Sith Attack Droid
MNP $3   MIP $8

Luke Skywalker in Echo Base Bacta Tank, 2001
MNP $7   MIP $10

Princess Leia w/Sail Barge Cannon, 2001
MNP $3   MIP $8

POTJ
Mega Action

Darth Maul, 2000, Lightsaber Action Moves
MNP $3   MIP $7

Destroyer Droid, Battle Damaged, 2000
MNP $3   MIP $7

Obi-Wan Kenobi, 2000, Lightsaber Battle Moves
MNP $3   MIP $7

POTJ
Multi-Packs

Darth Maul and Darth Vader, 2000, Masters of the Dark Side, lightsabers, base
MNP $4   MIP $8

POTJ
Silver Anniv.

Han Solo and Chewbacca, 2001, Death Star Escape
MNP $4   MIP $8

Luke Skywalker and Princess Leia Organa, 2001, Swing to Freedom
MNP $4   MIP $8

Obi-Wan Kenobi and Darth Vader, 2001, Final Duel
MNP $4   MIP $8

POTJ
Special Edition

Boba Fett, 2000, 300th figure
MNP $5   MIP $10

THE PHANTOM MENACE
Cinema Scene 3-Packs

Mos Espa Encounter, 1999, Sebulba, Jar Jar, Anakin
MNP $4   MIP $10

Tatooine Showdown, 1999, Darth Maul, Qui-Gon, Anakin
MNP $4   MIP $10

Watto's Box, 2000, Watto, Graxol Kelvyyn, Shakka
MNP $5   MIP $12

THE PHANTOM MENACE
Deluxe

(KP Photo)

Darth Maul, 1999
MNP $2   MIP $5

Obi-Wan Kenobi, 1999
MNP $2   MIP $5

Qui-Gon Jinn, 1999
MNP $2   MIP $5

THE PHANTOM MENACE

(KP Photo)

Adi Gallia, 1999, w/removeable cloak and lightsaber
MNP $3   MIP $5

Anakin Skywalker, Mechanic, 2000, includes pit droid figure
MNP $3   MIP $5

Anakin Skywalker, Naboo, 1999, w/removable plastic cloak
MNP $3   MIP $5

Anakin Skywalker, Naboo Pilot, 2000, includes helmet and ship controls
MNP $3   MIP $5

Anakin Skywalker, Tatooine, 1999, w/backpack and blaster pistol
MNP $3   MIP $5

(KP Photo)

Battle Droid w/Federation Issue Blaster, 1999, these droids came in variety of paint finishes--some pristine, others w/battle damage
MNP $3   MIP $5

(KP Photo)

Battle Droid, Battle Damage, 1999, variations on this model include: "star" blast point on chest, silver lines on body, and lighter and darker sand marks
MNP $3   MIP $5

Battle Droid, Security, 2000, fairly plain light tan w/dark brown, includes blaster rifle
MNP $3   MIP $5

Boss Nass, 1999, w/staff
MNP $3   MIP $5

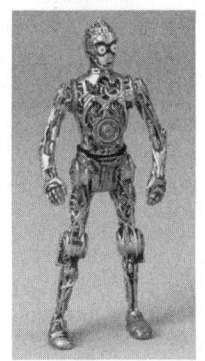

(KP Photo)

C-3PO, 1999, skeletal-looking version of 3PO before he had metal "skin"
MNP $3   MIP $5

(KP Photo)

Captain Panaka, 2000, w/blaster rifle
MNP $3   MIP $5

Captain Tarpals, 1999, w/"electropole" staff
MNP $3   MIP $5

(KP Photo)

Chancellor Valorum, 1999, includes staff
MNP $3   MIP $5

Darth Maul, Jedi Duel, 1999, the first release of a 3-3/4" Darth Maul figure
MNP $5   MIP $5

Darth Maul, Sith Lord, 2000, w/double-edged lightsaber, second stand-alone release of figure
MNP $3   MIP $5

Darth Maul, Tatooine, 1999, w/black cloth cloak--the cloak and other weapons were also available in an accessory set
MNP $2   MIP $5

Darth Sidious, 1999, black-robed figure w/Commtech chip
MNP $3   MIP $5

Darth Sidious, Holograph, 2000, translucent purple figure w/Commtech chip
MNP $3   MIP $5

Destroyer Droid, 1999, includes Commtech chip

MNP $3   **MIP** $5

(KP Photo)

Gasgano, w/Pit Droid, 1999, multi-armed figure packaged w/pit droid and Commtech chip

MNP $3   **MIP** $5

Jar Jar Binks, 1999, figure included Gungan Battle Staff and Commtech chip stand

MNP $2   **MIP** $5

Jar Jar Binks, Naboo Swamp, 2000, specially made to be posed in swimming motion, includes fish

MNP $2   **MIP** $5

(KP Photo)

Ki-Adi-Mundi, 1999, w/lightsaber

MNP $3   **MIP** $5

(KP Photo)

Mace Windu, 1999, w/lightsaber and removeable plastic cloak

MNP $3   **MIP** $5

Mace Windu, Sneak Preview, 1998

MNP $3   **MIP** $5

Naboo Royal Guard, 2000, includes removeable helmet and blaster pistol

MNP $3   **MIP** $5

Naboo Royal Security, 2000, included two blaster rifles

MNP $4   **MIP** $5

Nute Gunray, 1999, includes Commtech chip

MNP $2   **MIP** $5

(KP Photo)

Obi-Wan Kenobi, Jedi Duel, 1999, includes lightsaber

MNP $2   **MIP** $5

Obi-Wan Kenobi, Jedi Knight, 2000, in plain white robe

MNP $2   **MIP** $5

Obi-Wan Kenobi, Naboo, 1999, in dark robe—has two lightsabers, one activated, the other not

MNP $2   **MIP** $5

Ody Mandrell w/Pit Droid, 1999, another two-figure pack w/Commtech chip

MNP $2   **MIP** $5

OOM-9, 1999, yellow markings on head and body, this figure includes binoculars and blaster rifle

MNP $3   **MIP** $5

Padme Naberrie, 1999, figure included viewscreen to watch the pod race

MNP $3   **MIP** $5

(KP Photo)

Pit Droids, 2000, highly-detailed sculpts of the ubiquitous droids seen in Episode 1

MNP $3   **MIP** $5

Queen Amidala, Battle, 2000, in dark robe, includes blaster pistol and grappling hook crossbow

MNP $3   **MIP** $5

Queen Amidala, Coruscant, 1999, in full royal outfit and makeup

MNP $3   **MIP** $5

(KP Photo)

Queen Amidala, Naboo w/Blaster Pistols, 1999, figure included two sleek blaster pistols and Commtech chip stand

MNP $3   **MIP** $5

Qui-Gon Jinn, Jedi Duel, 1999, in plain-colored robe, includes lightsaber

MNP $3   **MIP** $5

Qui-Gon Jinn, Jedi Master, 2000, w/lightsaber and Commtech chip

MNP $3   MIP $5

Qui-Gon Jinn, Naboo, 1999, includes two lightsabers: one activated, the other not

MNP $2   MIP $5

R2-B1 Astromech Droid, 2000, dark blue w/light green body, includes harness pod

MNP $3   MIP $5

(KP Photo)

R2-D2, 1999, w/retractable middle "foot"

MNP $2   MIP $5

Ric Olie, 1999, removeable helmet and two blaster pistols

MNP $2   MIP $5

Rune Haako, 1999, includes Commtech chip

MNP $2   MIP $5

Senator Palpatine, 1999, w/cam droid and Commtech chip

MNP $3   MIP $5

Sio Bibble, 2000, includes blaster pistol and Commtech chip

MNP $8   MIP $14

TC-14, 2000, silver-plated, includes serving tray and Commtech chip

MNP $10   MIP $5

(KP Photo)

Watto, 1999

MNP $3   MIP $5

Yoda, w/Jedi Council Chair, 1999, includes blue chair and Commtech chip

MNP $3   MIP $5

SAGA
Basic

Aayla Secura, Jedi Knight, 2003, platform, blue lightsaber

MNP $3   MIP $5

(KP Photo, Karen O'Brien collection)

Achk Med-Beq, Courscant Outlander Club, 2003

MNP $3   MIP $5

Admiral Ozzel, 2004, Star Destroyer

MNP $3   MIP $5

(KP Photo, Karen O'Brien collection)

Anakin Skywalker, Hangar Duel, 2002, includes two lightsabers, has fighting action

MNP n/a   MIP $5

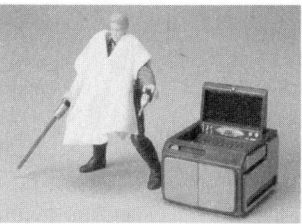

(KP Photo)

Anakin Skywalker, Outland Peasant Disguise, 2002, includes cloak, lightsaber, and cargo

MNP $2   MIP $5

Anakin Skywalker, Secret Ceremony, 2003, flowing robes, mechanical hand

MNP $2   MIP $5

Anakin Skywalker, Tatooine Attack, 2002, mad Anakin, blue lightsaber, Tusken stand

MNP $2   MIP $5

(KP Photo, Karen O'Brien collection)

Ashla & Jempa, Younglings, 2003, two-pack, helmet and blue lightsaber for Ashla and helmet, green lightsaber for Jempa

MNP $4   MIP $10

Ayy Vida, Outlander Nightclub Patron, 2003, barstool and drink

MNP $2   MIP $7

(KP Photo, Karen O'Brien collection)

Bail Organa, Alderaan Senator, 2003, holographic Jedi and projector

MNP $3   MIP $7

Barriss Offee, Luminara Unduli's Padawan, 2003, flowing robes, green lightsaber

MNP $3   MIP $7

(KP Photo)

Battle Droid, Arena Battle, 2002, w/orange laser blast

MNP $3   MIP $7

Boba Fett, Kamino Escape, 2002, two blaster pistols, flame effect, missile pack

MNP $3   MIP $7

Boba Fett, The Pit of Carkoon, 2003, molded engine flames and energy blast, laser rifle

MNP $3   MIP $7

Bossk, Executor Meeting, 2004

MNP $3   MIP $7

C-3PO, Hoth Evacuation, 2004

MNP $3   MIP $7

(KP Photo)

C-3PO, Protocol Droid, 2002, comes w/removeable outer plating and box for storage

MNP $2   MIP $5

C-3PO, Tatooine Ambush, 2003, removable arm, serving tray

MNP $3   MIP $7

Captain Antilles, Tantive IV Invasion, Fan's Choice Figure #5, 2004

MNP $3   MIP $7

Captain Typho, 2002, w/removeable helmet, blaster w/blast effect

MNP $4   MIP $7

Chewbacca, Cloud City, 2002, w/net and C3PO in pieces

MNP $3   MIP $7

(KP Photo, Karen O'Brien collection)

Chewbacca, Mynock Hunt, 2003, crossbow, red bolt, Mynock

MNP $3   MIP $7

(KP Photo)

Clone Trooper, 2002, w/rifle and tripod-style gun, this figure also lacks the painted-on sand and grime that the preview model features

MNP $4   MIP $7

Clone Trooper, Republic Gunship Pilot, 2002, white figure w/yellow stripe on helmet, gun turret attaches to Republic Gunship

MNP $4   MIP $8

Coleman Trebor, Battle of Geonosis, 2003, Jedi knight, green lightsaber

MNP $3   MIP $7

Count Dooku, 2002, includes lightsaber and smaller Darth Sidious hologram figure

MNP $3   MIP $7

Darth Maul, Sith Training, 2002, flowing black robes w/red accents,

double-sided retractable lightsaber, training droid

MNP $3   MIP $7

Darth Maul, Theed Hangar Duel, 2003, two-ended red lightsaber

MNP $3   MIP $7

Darth Tyranus, Geonosian Escape, 2003, flowing robes, red lightsaber, jedi lightning

MNP $3   MIP $7

(KP Photo, Karen O'Brien collection)

Darth Vader, Bespin Duel, 2002, "Luke, I am your father…"

MNP $3   MIP $7

Darth Vader, Death Star Clash, 2003, cloth robe, red lightsaber

MNP $3   MIP $7

Darth Vader, Throne Room Duel, 2003, removable helmet, red lightning

MNP $3   MIP $7

Dengar, Executor Meeting, 2004

MNP $3   MIP $7

Destroyer Droid, Arena Battle, 2002, w/two energy beams

MNP $3   MIP $7

Dexter Jetster, 2002

MNP $3   MIP $7

Djas Puhr, Alien Bounty Hunter, 2002, A New Hope, w/two long pistols

MNP $3   MIP $7

Dutch Vander: Gold Leader, Battle of Yavin, 2004

MNP $3   MIP $7

Eeth Koth, Jedi Master, 2002, green lightsaber

MNP $3   MIP $7

Elan Sleazebaggano, Outlander Nightclub Encounter, 2003, "I do not want to sell you death sticks," bar, death sticks, drink

MNP $3   MIP $7

Emperor, Throne Room, 2003, cane, Jedi lightning

MNP $3   MIP $7

Endor Rebel Soldier, 2002, bearded or non-bearded versions

MNP $3   MIP $7

Ephant Mon, Fan's Choice Figure #3, 2002, w/cane and axe head

MNP $10   MIP $16

General Jan Dodonna, Battle of Yavin, 2004

MNP $3   MIP $7

General Madine, Imperial Shuttle Capture, 2004

MNP $3   MIP $7

(KP Photo)

Geonosian Warrior, 2002, poseable wings

MNP $4   MIP $7

Han Solo, Endor Raid, 2002, w/two detonators and pistol

MNP $3   MIP $7

Han Solo, Endor Strike, 2004, dressed as AT-ST driver

MNP $3   MIP $7

Han Solo, Flight to Alderan, 2003, pistol

MNP $3   MIP $7

(KP Photo, Karen O'Brien collection)

Han Solo, Hoth Rescue, 2003, two versions-blue or brown coat, snow mask, pistol, radio, blue lightsaber

MNP $3   MIP $7

Holographic Luke Skywalker, Jabba's Palace, 2004

MNP $3   MIP $7

(KP Photo, Karen O'Brien collection)

Hoth Trooper, Hoth Evacuation, 2004

MNP $3   MIP $7

Imperial Dignitary Janus Greejatus, Death Star Procession, 2003

MNP $3   MIP $7

(KP Photo, Karen O'Brien collection)

Imperial Officer, 2002, blond or brown hair version, w/laser rifle

MNP $3   MIP $7

Jango Fett, Final Battle, 2002, includes pack, two blasters, and plastic "flame"

MNP $4   MIP $10

(KP Photo)

Jango Fett, Kamino Escape, 2002, w/two pistols, grappling hook, and firing missile pack

MNP $4   MIP $7

Jango Fett, Kamino Escape, 2003, removable helmet, two pistols, string from wrist w/hook, backpack missile

MNP $3   MIP $7

Jango Fett, Slave 1 Pilot, 2002, two silver pistols, can see his face

MNP $3   MIP $7

Jar Jar Binks, Gungan Senator, 2002, w/staff and blue energy bolts

MNP $2   MIP $4

J'Quille, Jabba's Sail Barge, 2004

MNP $3   MIP $7

Ki-Adi Mundi, Jedi Master, 2002, blue lightsaber, deflected energy beam

MNP $3   MIP $7

(KP Photo)

Kit Fisto, Jedi Master, 2002, w/"laser blast" attachment for lightsaber

MNP $3   MIP $7

Klen Blista-Vanee, Imperial Dignitary, 2003

MNP $3   MIP $7

Lama Su w/Clone Youth, 2003, two-pack

MNP $3   MIP $7

Lando Calrissian, Death Star Attack, 2004

MNP $3   MIP $7

Lando Calrissian, Jabba's Sail Barge, 2004

MNP $3   MIP $7

Lott Dod, Neimoidian Senator, 2002, w/tall hat and small holographic Darth Sidious

MNP $3   MIP $7

Lt. Danni Faytonni, Coruscant Outlander Club, 2003, table, drink, pistol

MNP $3   MIP $7

(KP Photo, Karen O'Brien collection)

Luke Skywalker, Bespin Duel, 2002, "Bloody Luke," right hand removable, comes w/antenna
MNP $3   **MIP** $7

Luke Skywalker, Hoth Attack, 2004
MNP $3   **MIP** $7

Luke Skywalker, Jabba's Palace, 2004
MNP $3   **MIP** $7

Luke Skywalker, Tatooine Encounter, 2003, blue lightsaber
MNP $3   **MIP** $7

Luke Skywalker, Throne Room Duel, 2003, green lightsaber, slashing action, causeway breaks - error version has black glove on left hand rather than right
MNP $3   **MIP** $7

(KP Photo)

Luminara Unduli, Jedi Master, 2002, extremely detailed sculpt, figure includes lightsaber w/blaster deflect attachement
MNP $3   **MIP** $7

Mace Windu, Arena Confrontation, 2003, purple lightsaber, flowing robes
MNP $3   **MIP** $7

(KP Photo)

Mace Windu, Geonosian Rescue, 2002, pushing a button on Mace's back moves arm w/lightsaber in a "slashing attack," these newest Star Wars figures probably have the most detail and moving parts of any series yet—and this is just one example
MNP $3   **MIP** $7

Massiff w/Geonosian Warrior, 2002
MNP $3   **MIP** $7

Massiff w/Geonosian Warrior, 2002, includes Geonosian warrior w/Massiff on chain leash
MNP $3   **MIP** $7

(KP Photo, Karen O'Brien collection)

McQuarrie Concept Stormtrooper, Fan Choice Figure #4, 2003, shield, blaster, lightsaber
MNP $6   **MIP** $12

(KP Photo)

Nikto, Jedi Knight, 2002, w/lightsaber and "force blast effect"
MNP $3   **MIP** $7

(KP Photo, Karen O'Brien collection)

Obi Wan Kenobi, Outlander Nightclub Encounter, 2003, bar and drink
MNP $3   **MIP** $7

Obi-Wan Kenobi, Acklay Battle, 2003, w/break-away column, handcuffs, spear, blue lightsaber
MNP $3   **MIP** $7

(KP Photo)

Obi-Wan Kenobi, Coruscant Chase, 2002, w/flying droid that magnetically attaches to Obi-Wan's hand
MNP $3   **MIP** $6

Obi-Wan Kenobi, Jedi Starfighter Pilot, 2002
MNP $3   **MIP** $7

Orn Free Taa, 2002, w/floating camera droid
MNP $3   **MIP** $7

(KP Photo)

Padme Amidala, Arena Escape,
2002, swinging arm w/blaster
pistol and column
MNP $3   **MIP** $7

Padme Amidala, Coruscant Arrival,
2002, pilot outfit w/helmet
MNP $3   **MIP** $7

Padme Amidala, Droid Factory Chase,
2003, platform, white cape, pistol
MNP $3   **MIP** $7

(KP Photo, Karen O'Brien collection)

Padme Amidala, Lars Homestead,
2003, cloak and platform
MNP $3   **MIP** $7

Padme Amidala, Secret Ceremony,
2003, in wedding dress, ornate
railing and flowers
MNP $3   **MIP** $7

Plo Koon, Arena Battle, 2002,
w/lightsaber
MNP $3   **MIP** $7

Princess Leia, Imperial Captive,
2003, pistol and laser rifle
MNP $3   **MIP** $7

Qui-Gon Jinn, Jedi Master, 2002,
better robes
MNP $3   **MIP** $7

R1-G4, Tatooine Transaction, 2004
MNP $3   **MIP** $7

(KP Photo)

R2-D2, Coruscant Sentry, 2002,
w/two plastic assassin bugs,
probably the best R2 sculpt yet,
w/lights and sound, to boot
MNP $3   **MIP** $7

R2-D2, Droid Factory Flight, 2003,
molded energy bolts, string,
retractable side rockets
MNP $3   **MIP** $7

R2-D2, Jabba's Sail Barge, 2004,
w/drink tray
MNP $3   **MIP** $7

Rappertunie, Jabba's Palace, 2004
MNP $3   **MIP** $7

Rebel Fleet Trooper, 2002, red or
black hair version, w/pistol
MNP $3   **MIP** $7

(KP Photo)

Royal Guard, Coruscant Security,
2002, red figure w/staff and blue
"energy bolts"
MNP $3   **MIP** $7

(KP Photo)

Saesee Tiin, Jedi Master, 2002,
w/lightsaber and force-repelled
blast effect
MNP $3   **MIP** $7

(KP Photo)

Shaak Ti, Jedi Master, 2002, w/"blast
effect" lightsaber, very well-
detailed figure
MNP $3   **MIP** $7

(KP Photo, Karen O'Brien collection)

Snowtrooper, The Battle of Hoth,
2003, backpack, laser pistol,
cannon w/missile
MNP $4   **MIP** $7

(KP Photo, Karen O'Brien collection)

SP-4 and JN-66, Research Droids, 2003, SP-4 has spiked head, JN-66 has flat head

MNP $5   **MIP** $7

(KP Photo)

Super Battle Droid, 2002, w/laser blast battle damage and attachments

MNP $3   **MIP** $7

(KP Photo, Karen O'Brien collection)

Supreme Chancellor Palpatine, 2002

MNP $3   **MIP** $7

Tanus Spijek, Jabba's Sail Barge, 2004

MNP $3   **MIP** $7

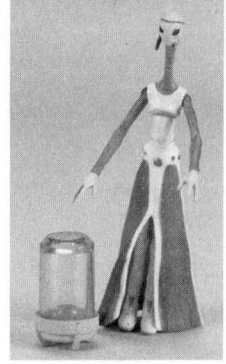

(KP Photo)

Taun We, Kamino Cloner, 2002, w/cloning pod

MNP $3   **MIP** $7

Teebo, Ewok, 2002, w/horn

MNP $3   **MIP** $7

Teemto Pagalies, Pod Racer, 2002, arms in the air, w/droid and engine part

MNP $3   **MIP** $7

TIE Fighter Pilot, Battle of Yavin, 2004

MNP $3   **MIP** $7

Tusken Raider w/Massiff, 2002

MNP $3   **MIP** $7

Tusken Raider, Female w/Tusken Child, 2002, child figure can be freestanding or fit in pack

MNP $6   **MIP** $8

Tusken Raider, Tatooine Camp Ambush, 2003, gaffi stick, platform

MNP $3   **MIP** $7

WA-7, Dexter's Diner, 2003, waitress w/platform and tray

MNP $3   **MIP** $7

Wat Tambor, Geonosis War Room, 2003, mechanical console

MNP $3   **MIP** $7

Watto, Mos Espa Junk Dealer, 2002, wearing hat

MNP $3   **MIP** $7

Yoda & Chian, 2003, two-pack, hoverchair, cane, green lightsaber for Yoda and helmet, blue lightsaber for Chian

MNP $3   **MIP** $7

(KP Photo, Karen O'Brien collection)

Yoda, Battle of Geonosis, 2004, Hall of Fame assortment

MNP $3   **MIP** $6

Yoda, Jedi High Council, 2002, w/elevated chair

MNP $3   **MIP** $7

Yoda, Jedi Master, 2002, includes lightsaber, walking stick, and base

MNP $3   **MIP** $7

(KP Photo)

Zam Wessell, Bounty Hunter, 2002, shorter blaster than preview edition, removable changeling face

MNP $2   **MIP** $6

SAGA Deluxe

(KP Photo, Karen O'Brien collection)

Anakin Skywalker w/Lightsaber Slashing Action, 2002, includes two lightsabers and an easily-sliced Geonosian warrior

MNP $2   MIP $7

Anakin Skywalker, Flipping, 2002, Force Flipping action, lands on his feet

MNP $2   MIP $7

C-3PO and Battle Droid, 2002, interchangable heads

MNP $2   MIP $7

Clone Trooper w/Speeder Bike, 2002, blaster, grenade, removable armor and helmet

MNP $5   MIP $10

Darth Tyranus w/Force Flipping Attack, 2002, like the Obi-Wan version, pushing a button on the launch pad makes Tyranus leap, flip and land on his feet

MNP $2   MIP $7

Geonosian Warrior, 2002, w/insect pod and energy weapon

MNP $3   MIP $7

Jango Fett, Kamino Showdown, 2003, two pistols, jet pack w/missile, column w/flipping base

MNP $3   MIP $7

(KP Photo)

Jango Fett, w/Electronic Attack and Snap-On Armor, 2002, another incredibly detailed Jango figure

MNP $4   MIP $7

(KP Photo)

Mace Windu w/Blast-Apart Battle Droid, 2002, battle droid breaks apart as Mace stikes w/saber

MNP $3   MIP $7

Nexu w/Snapping Jaw and Attack Roar, 2002, well detailed w/snapping jaw and roaring sound

MNP $6   MIP $14

(KP Photo)

Obi-Wan Kenobi w/Force Flipping Attack, 2002, includes platform and launcher that makes Obi-Wan figure flip over and then land on his feet (after a few tries, usually), a neat idea that easily lends itself to "I betcha can't make him land this time" games

MNP $2   MIP $7

Obi-Wan, Kamino Showdown, 2003, flowing robes, blue lightsaber, terrace pieces

MNP $2   MIP $7

Spider Droid, 2003, creepy

MNP $3   MIP $7

Super Battle Droid Builder, 2003, factory to "finish" the SBD

MNP $3   MIP $7

Yoda and Super Battle Droid, 2002, w/Force powers

MNP $3   MIP $8

SAGA
Multi-Packs

Battle of Hoth, 2003, Chewbacca, Princess Leia, Luke Skywalker, R3-A2, Taun Taun, TRU exclusive

MNP $15   MIP $30

Imperial Forces, 2003, AT-ST Driver, Darth Vader, R4-19, Stormtrooper, accessories, TRU exclusive

MNP $18   MIP $25

Ultimate Bounty, 2003, Aurra Sing, Boba Fett, Bossk, IG-88, Swoop Bike, TRU exclusive

MNP $10   MIP $14

SAGA
Screen Scenes

Geonosian War Room No. 1, 2003, Poggle the Lesser, Count Dooku, San Hill

MNP $10   MIP $20

Geonosian War Room No. 2, 2003, Nute Gunray, Passel Argente, Shu Mai

MNP $10   MIP $20

Jedi High Council No. 1, 2003, Mace Windu, Oppo Rancisis, Even Piell

MNP $12   MIP $20

Jedi High Council No. 2, 2003, Yarael Poof, Depa Billaba, Yaddle

MNP $12   MIP $20

Trash Compactor No. 1, 2003, Han and Luke

MNP $6   MIP $12

Trash Compactor No. 2, 2003, Leia and Chewbacca

MNP $6   MIP $12

SAGA
Sneak Preview

(KP Photo)

Clone Trooper, 2002, w/laser rifle and blue "blast" attachment, this model shows painted-on battlefield "dirt" detail

MNP $3   MIP $7

Jango Fett, 2002

MNP $3   MIP $7

R3-T7, 2002, detailed astromech droid w/blue engergy bolts that wrap around body

MNP $3   MIP $7

Zam Wessell, 2002, w/long gun, human face partially covered by scarf

MNP $3   MIP $7

CLONE WARS
Basic

(KP Photo, Karen O'Brien collection)

Anakin Skywalker, Army of the Republic, 2003, two armor pieces, headgear, belt, blue lightsaber

MNP $4 MIP $7

(KP Photo, Karen O'Brien collection)

ARC Trooper, Army of the Republic, 2003, laser rifle

MNP $3 MIP $7

(KP Photo, Karen O'Brien collection)

Asajj Ventress, Sith Apprentice, 2003, two curved-handled red lightsabers, flowing black robes

MNP $3 MIP $7

(KP Photo, Karen O'Brien collection)

Durge, Commander of the Separatist Forces, 2003, laser rifle, pistol, rocket backpack, mace

MNP $6 MIP $10

Mace Windu, General of the Republic Army, 2003, two armor pieces, purple lightsaber

MNP $4 MIP $7

Obi-Wan Kenobi, General of the Republic Army, 2003, belt, backpack, blue lightsaber

MNP $4 MIP $7

Yoda w/Hoverchair, 2003, green lightsaber

MNP $4 MIP $7

CLONE WARS
Deluxe

Clone Trooper w/Speeder Bike, 2003
MNP $5 MIP $10

Destroyer Droid w/Battle Launcher, 2003
MNP $7 MIP $10

Durge w/Swoop Bike, 2003
MNP $8 MIP $14

CLONE WARS
Multi-Packs

Clone Trooper Army (White), 2003, Kneeling Trooper, Prone Trooper, Standing Trooper
MNP $6 MIP $12

Clone Trooper Army w/Clone Captain (Red), 2003, Prone Clone Trooper (Red), Standing Clone Trooper (White), Kneeling Clone Trooper (White)

MNP $6 MIP $12

Clone Trooper Army w/Clone Commander, 2003, Standing Clone Trooper w/Binoculars (Yellow), Standing Clone Trooper (White), Kneeling Clone Trooper (White)
MNP $6 MIP $12

Clone Trooper Army w/Clone Lieutenant (Blue), 2003, Kneeling Trooper, Prone Trooper, Standing Lieutenant (Blue)
MNP $6 MIP $12

Clone Trooper Army w/Clone Sergeant (Green), 2003, Standing Clone Trooper (White), Kneeling Clone Sergeant (Green), Standing Clone Trooper w/Binoculars (White)
MNP $6 MIP $12

Droid Army, 2003, Battle Droid, Super Battle Droid, Destroyer Droid
MNP $5 MIP $10

Jedi Knight Army, 2003, Human Jedi, Rodian Jedi, Twi'lek Jedi
MNP $5 MIP $10

ORIGINAL TRILOGY COLLECTION
Multipacks

Empire Strikes Back, 2004, Wal-Mart Exclusive; Chewbacca, Princess Leia, Han Solo
MNP $6 MIP $15

Endor Ambush, 2004, TRU Exclusive; Han Solo, Endor Rebel Soldier, Wicket, Logray, Biker Scout, Imperial Speeder Bike, Model No. 34515
MNP $12 MIP $20

Naboo Final Combat, 2005, TRU Exclusive; Naboo Palace Guard, Battle Droid, Captain Tarpals, Gungan Soldier, Kaadu
MNP $10 MIP $18

Return of the Jedi, 2004, Wal-Mart Exclusive; Darth Vader, Emperor Palpatine, Stormtrooper
MNP $6 MIP $12

Star Wars, 2004, Wal-Mart Exclusive; Luke Skywalker, Obi-Wan Kenobi, C-3PO, R2-D2
MNP $5 MIP $10

ORIGINAL TRILOGY COLLECTION

Bib Fortuna, 2004, #31, RotJ, w/blaster
MNP $2 MIP $5

Biker Scout, 2004, #11, RotJ, w/blaster
MNP $2 MIP $5

Boba Fett, 2004, #14, RotJ, quick draw
MNP $2 MIP $5

Bossk, 2004, #28, ESB, w/rifle, shoulder strap
MNP $2 MIP $5

C-3PO, 2004, #13, SW, clean
MNP $2 MIP $5

Chewbacca, 2004, #8, ESB, w/welding goggles
MNP $2 MIP $5

Cloud Car Pilot, 2004, #19, ESB, w/blaster, comlink
MNP $2 MIP $5

Darth Vader, 2004, #10, RotJ, w/lightsaber, throws it
MNP $2 MIP $5

Darth Vader, 2004, #34, SW, w/lightsaber
MNP $2 MIP $5

Darth Vader, Hoth, 2004, #29, ESB, w/lightsaber
MNP $2 MIP $5

Gamorrean Guard, 2004, #30, RotJ, w/axe
MNP $2 MIP $5

General Lando Calrissian, 2004, #37, RotJ
MNP $2   MIP $5

General Madine, 2004, #36, RotJ, Battle of Endor, w/baton
MNP $2   MIP $5

Greedo, 2004, #22, SW, w/blaster
MNP $2   MIP $5

Han Solo, 2004, #7, SW, w/blaster
MNP $2   MIP $5

Han Solo AT-ST Driver, 2004, #35, RotJ, Battle of Endor
MNP $2   MIP $5

IG-88, 2004, #27, ESB, w/rifle
MNP $2   MIP $5

Imperial Trooper, 2004, #38, SW, Scanning Crew
MNP $2   MIP $5

Jawa, 2004, #24, SW
MNP $2   MIP $5

Lando Skiff Guard Disguise, 2004, #32, RotJ, w/helmet, blaster pistol, staff
MNP $2   MIP $5

Lobot, 2004, #20, ESB, w/datapad, comlink
MNP $2   MIP $5

Luke Skywalker, 2004, #1, ESB, on Dagobah, w/extra arms
MNP $2   MIP $5

Luke Skywalker Bespin, 2004, #26, ESB, on Bespin
MNP $2   MIP $5

Luke Skywalker Jedi, 2004, #6, RotJ, w/lightsaber
MNP $2   MIP $5

Luke Skywalker X-Wing Pilot, 2004, #5, SW, w/helmet
MNP $2   MIP $5

Obi-Wan Kenobi, 2004, #15, SW, lightsaber, light robes
MNP $2   MIP $5

Obi-Wan Spirit, 2004, #3, ESB, on Dagobah
MNP $2   MIP $5

Princess Leia, 2004, #9, SW, white outfit, w/two blasters
MNP $2   MIP $5

Princess Leia Bespin Gown, 2004, #18, ESB, w/blaster rifle
MNP $2   MIP $5

R2-D2, 2004, #12, SW, clean
MNP $2   MIP $5

R2-D2, 2004, #4, ESB, on Dagobah, dirty, w/sounds
MNP $2   MIP $5

Slave Leia, 2004, #33, RotJ, w/staff
MNP $2   MIP $5

Snowtrooper, 2004, #25, ESB, w/blaster
MNP $2   MIP $5

Stormtrooper, 2004, #16, SW, w/blaster rifle
MNP $2   MIP $5

TIE Fighter Pilot, 2004, #21, SW, w/blaster
MNP $2   MIP $5

Tusken Raider, 2004, #23, SW, w/rifle
MNP $2   MIP $5

Wicket, 2004, #17, RotJ, w/staff
MNP $2   MIP $5

Yoda, 2004, #2, ESB, on Dagobah
MNP $2   MIP $5

ORIGINAL TRILOGY COLLECTION
Transition

Dannik Jerriko, 2005, #1, Cantina Encounter
MNP $7   MIP $15

Feltipern Trevagg, 2005, #6, Cantina Encounter
MNP $7   MIP $15

Myo, 2005, #7, Cantina Encounter
MNP $7   MIP $15

Pablo-Jill, 2005, #1, Geonosis Arena
MNP $7   MIP $12

Queen Amidala, 2005, #4, Celebration Ceremony
MNP $5   MIP $8

Rabe, 2005, #5, Queen's Chambers, w/pistol, TPM
MNP $5   MIP $8

Sly Moore, 2005, #3, Coruscant Senate, AotC
MNP $5   MIP $9

Yarua, 2005, #2, Coruscant Senate, AotC
MNP $5   MIP $18

ORIGINAL TRILOGY COLLECTION
Vintage

Ben (Obi-Wan) Kenobi, 2004, SW card, sealed case
MNP $6   MIP $10

Boba Fett, 2004, RotJ card, sealed case
MNP $6   MIP $12

Chewbacca, 2004, RotJ card, sealed case
MNP $6   MIP $10

Darth Vader, 2004, ESB card, sealed case
MNP $6   MIP $12

Han Solo, 2004, SW card, sealed case
MNP $6   MIP $8

Lando Calrissian, 2004, ESB card, sealed case
MNP $6   MIP $10

Luke Skywalker, 2004, SW card, sealed case
MNP $6   MIP $10

Princess Leia Organa, 2004, SW card, sealed case
MNP $6   MIP $10

See-Threepio (C-3PO), 2004, ESB card, sealed case
MNP $6   MIP $12

Stormtrooper, 2004, RotJ card, sealed case
MNP $6   MIP $15

Yoda, 2004, ESB card, sealed case
MNP $6   MIP $10

REVENGE OF THE SITH
Basic 1

Anakin Skywalker, Battle Damage, 2005, #50, interchangable body parts, cloak, lightsaber
MNP $3   MIP $7

Anakin Skywalker, Lightsaber Attack, 2005, #2, many variations, w/blue lightsaber and Count Dooku's lightsaber
MNP $3   MIP $7

(KP Photo, Karen O'Brien collection)

Anakin Skywalker, Slashing Attack, 2005, #28, fallen to the dark side, cloak, lightsaber
MNP $3   MIP $7

(KP Photo, Karen O'Brien collection)

AT-RT Driver, 2005, #54, w/Missile-Firing Blaster, missile, blaster rifle
MNP $3   MIP $7

Cat Miin, Separatist, 2005, #62, base
MNP $3   MIP $7

Chewbacca, Wookie Rage, 2005, #5, bowcaster
MNP $3   MIP $7

Clone Commander, Battle Gear, 2005, #33, green or red gear variations
MNP $3   MIP $7

(KP Photo, Karen O'Brien collection)

Clone Pilot, Firing Cannon, 2005, #34, white and gray uniform
MNP $4   MIP $7

Clone Trooper, Quick-Draw Attack, 2005, #6, blaster
MNP $4   MIP $7

Clone Trooper, Super Articulation, 2005, #41, blaster, antenna
MNP $4   MIP $7

Commander Bacara, Quick-Draw Attack, 2005, #49, blaster, rifle, fought w/Ki-Adi-Mundi on Mygeeto
MNP $4   MIP $7

Commander Bly, Battle Gear, 2005, #57, rifle, two blasters, fought w/Aayla Secura on Felucia
MNP $4   MIP $7

Commander Gree, Battle Gear, 2005, #59, missile-firing cannon, missile, blaster
MNP $4   MIP $7

(KP Photo, Karen O'Brien collection)

Darth Vader, Lightsaber Attack, 2005, #11, lightsaber, "Lord Vader…rise!"
MNP $3   MIP $7

Destroyer Droid, Firing Arm-Blaster, 2005, #44, two missiles
MNP $3   MIP $7

Emperor Palpatine, Firing Force Lightning, 2005, #12, lightsaber, lightning
MNP $3   MIP $6

General Grievous, Exploding Body, 2005, #36, lightsaber, cloak, blaster
MNP $4   MIP $8

General Grievous, Four Lightsaber Attack, 2005, #9, four lightsabers
MNP $4   MIP $8

Grievous' Bodyguard, Battle Attack, 2005, #60, electrostaff, cloak
MNP $3   MIP $7

Mace Windu, Force Combat, 2005, #10, force lightning, cool purple lightsaber
MNP $3   MIP $6

Mustafar Sentry, Spinning Energy Bolt, 2005, #56, rifle, energy bolt, base
MNP $3   MIP $7

Neimoidian Commander, Separatist Bodyguard, 2005, #63, staff, helmet
MNP $3   MIP $7

Neimoidian Warrior, Neimoidian Weapon Attack, 2005, #42, rifle, helmet
MNP $4   MIP $8

(KP Photo, Karen O'Brien collection)

Obi-Wan Kenobi, Jedi Kick, 2005, #27, lightsaber
MNP $3   MIP $6

Obi-Wan Kenobi, Slashing Attack, 2005, #1, lightsaber
MNP $3   MIP $6

(KP Photo, Karen O'Brien collection)

Obi-Wan Kenobi, w/Pilot Gear, 2005, #55, lightsaber, headgear, cloak
MNP $3   MIP $6

Palpatine, Lightsaber Attack, 2005, #35, base, red lightsaber (blue variations), two heads, two sets of hands
MNP $3   MIP $6

Passel Argente, Separatist Leader, 2005, #61, base
MNP $3   MIP $6

R2-D2, Droid Attack, 2005, #7, w/tools, base
MNP $3   MIP $6

R2-D2, Try Me, 2005, Electronic Light and Sounds, #48
MNP $3   MIP $6

Super Battle Droid, Firing Arm-Blaster, 2005, #4, blaster mounts to right arm
MNP $3   MIP $7

Tarfful, Firing Bowcaster, 2005, #25, bowcaster

MNP $3   MIP $7

Wookie Commando, Kashyyyk Battle Bash, 2005, #58, cannon, missile, bandolier

MNP $3   MIP $7

(KP Photo, Karen O'Brien collection)

Wookie Warrior, Wookie Battle Bash, 2005, #43, shield, blaster, bowcaster, bandolier, missile

MNP $3   MIP $7

Yoda, Firing Cannon, 2005, #3, lightsaber, cannon

MNP $3   MIP $7

Yoda, Spinning Attack, 2005, #26, lightsaber

MNP $3   MIP $7

REVENGE OF THE SITH
Basic 2

Aayla Secura, Jedi Hologram Transmission, 2005, #67, all blue plastic

MNP $4   MIP $8

Aayla Secura, Jedi Knight, 2005, #32, w/lightsaber, base

MNP $3   MIP $7

Agen Kolar, Jedi Master, 2005, #20, w/lightsaber, base

MNP $3   MIP $7

Ask Aak, Senator, 2005, #46, blaster rifle, base

MNP $3   MIP $7

AT-TE Tank Gunner, 2005, #38, blaster pistol, sniper pistol

MNP $4   MIP $8

Bail Organa, Republic Senator, 2005, #15, pistol, base

MNP $3   MIP $7

Battle Droid, Separatist Army, 2005, #17, blaster, base

MNP $3   MIP $7

C-3PO, Protocol Droid, 2005, #18, base, C-3PO finally has his gold coverings

MNP $3   MIP $7

Captain Antilles, Senate Security, 2005, #51, pistol, base

MNP $3   MIP $7

Chancellor Palpatine, Supreme Chancellor, 2005, #14, base, handcuffs

MNP $3   MIP $7

Count Dooku, Sith Lord, 2005, #13, lightsaber (pink or red variations), cloth cape, removable hands, base

MNP $4   MIP $8

Ki-Adi-Mundi, Jedi Master, 2005, #29, lightsaber

MNP $3   MIP $7

Kit Fisto, Jedi Master, 2005, #22, lightsaber, base, removable head

MNP $3   MIP $7

Luminara Unduli, Jedi Master, 2005, #31, lightsaber, base, in Kashyyyk attire

MNP $3   MIP $7

Mas Amedda, Republic Senator, 2005, #40, staff, base, removable tongue

MNP $3   MIP $7

Meena Tills, Senator, 2005, #47, blaster, base

MNP $3   MIP $7

Mon Mothma, Republic Senator, 2005, #24, baton, helmet, base

MNP $2   MIP $6

Padme, Republic Senator, 2005, #19, pistol, base

MNP $3   MIP $7

Plo Koon, Jedi Hologram Transmission, 2005, #66, clear blue plastic, lightsaber, base

MNP $6   MIP $12

Plo Koon, Jedi Master, 2005, #16, lightsaber, base

MNP $3   MIP $7

Polis Massan, Medic, 2005, #39, pistol, headset, base

MNP $3   MIP $7

R4-P17, Rolling Action, 2005, #64, base

MNP $4   MIP $8

Royal Guard, Senate Security, 2005, #23, rifle, pistol, base, cloth cloak

MNP $4   MIP $8

Saesee Tiin, Jedi Master, 2005, #30, lightsaber, base

MNP $3   MIP $7

Shaak Ti, Jedi Master, 2005, #21, lightsaber, datapad, base

MNP $3   MIP $7

Tactical Ops Trooper, Vader's Legion, 2005, #65, blue highlights, blaster, base, removable helmet

MNP $4   MIP $8

Tarkin, Governor, 2005, #45, blaster, base

MNP $4   MIP $8

Utapaun Warrior, Utapaun Security, 2005, #53, shield, staff, base

MNP $4   MIP $8

(KP Photo, Karen O'Brien collection)

Vader's Medical Droid, Chopper Droid, 2005, #37, base

MNP $4   MIP $8

Wookie Heavy Gunner, Blast Attack, 2005, #68

MNP $4   MIP $8

Zett Jukassa, Jedi Padawan, 2005, #52, lightsaber, base, played in the film by Jett Lucas, George's son

MNP $3   MIP $6

REVENGE OF THE SITH
Battle Arena

Senate Chamber, 2005, Palpatine v. Mace Windu

MNP $5   MIP $12

Trade Federation Cruiser, 2005, Count Dooku v. Anakin Skywalker

MNP $5   MIP $12

Utapau Landing Platform, 2005, Obi-Wan Kenobi v. Grievous' Guard

MNP $5   MIP $12

REVENGE OF THE SITH
Deluxe

Anakin Skywalker: Ultimate Villain, 2005, changes to Darth Vader; interchangable limbs and outfits

MNP $22   MIP $40

Clone Trooper, 2005, firing Jet
Backpack; missiles, laser rifle
MNP $4   MIP $7

Clone Troopers, 2005, three per pack;
variations w/two white and one red,
green, or blue trooper
MNP $6   MIP $12

Crab Droid, 2005, moving Legs and
Missile Launcher; missile, used on
Utapau
MNP $4   MIP $8

Darth Vader, 2005, rebuild Darth
Vader, limbs, helmet, swivel table,
chest box, lightsaber
MNP $5   MIP $12

Darth Vader, 2005, Special Edition
500th Figure; Vader's ESB chamber
w/removable helmet
MNP $3   MIP $7

Emperor Palpatine, 2005, changes to
Darth Sideous; jedi lightning, hand
w/lightsaber, left hand, heads
MNP $3   MIP $7

General Grievous, 2005, Secret
Lightsaber Attack; four lightsabers,
cloak, grappling hook
MNP $4   MIP $7

Obi-Wan Kenobi, 2005, Force Jump
Attack; lightsaber, Super Battle
Droid that breaks apart
MNP $4   MIP $7

Spider Droid, 2005, Firing Laser
Action; missile, wind-up walking
action
MNP $4   MIP $7

Stass Allie w/BARC Speeder, 2005,
Exploding Action; Jedi Master
Stass Allie, BARC Speeder
MNP $4   MIP $7

Vulture Droid, 2005, Firing Missile
Launcher; Buzz Droid, movable
wings
MNP $4   MIP $7

Yoda, 2005, Fly Into Battle; lightsaber,
flying Can-Cell native to Kashyyyk
MNP $4   MIP $7

REVENGE OF THE SITH
Evolutions

Anakin Skywalker to Darth Vader,
2005, AotC Anakin, RotS Anakin,
Darth Vader
MNP $10   MIP $20

Clone Trooper to Stormtrooper, 2005,
Clone Trooper (the Clone Wars),
Clone Trooper (Fall of the Republic),
Sandtrooper (the Rebellion)
MNP $12   MIP $25

The Sith, 2005, Darth Maul, Count
Dooku, Emperor Palpatine
MNP $12   MIP $25

REVENGE OF THE SITH
Multipacks

Clone Troopers, 2005, Wal-Mart
Exclusive; three Clone Troopers
w/unique paint design, DVD
Collection
MNP $10   MIP $20

Jedi Knights, 2005, Wal-Mart
Exclusive; Anakin Skywalker, Mace
Windu, Obi-Wan Kenobi, DVD
Collection
MNP $7   MIP $15

Sith Lords, 2005, Wal-Mart Exclusive;
Emperor Palpatine, Count Dooku,
Darth Vader, DVD Collection
MNP $7   MIP $15

REVENGE OF THE SITH
Sneak Peek

General Grievous, 2005, #1,
lightsaber, blaster, cape
MNP $4   MIP $7

R4-G9, 2005, #4, planet hologram
MNP $4   MIP $7

Tion Medon, 2005, #2, staff, rifle
MNP $4   MIP $7

Wookie Warrior, 2005, #3, helmet,
shin guards, rifle, bandolier
MNP $4   MIP $7

SAGA 2006
Basic

(KP Photo, Karen O'Brien collection)

Anakin Skywalker, 2006, #25, Battle
of Coruscant, lightsaber, cloak
MNP $3   MIP $7

AT-AT Driver, 2006, #9, Battle of Hoth,
blaster pistol, base, hologram figure
MNP $3   MIP $7

Aurra Sing, 2006, #70, Wal-Mart
Exclusive, long rifle, pistol, lightsaber
MNP $3   MIP $7

(KP Photo, Karen O'Brien collection)

Barada, 2006, #4, Battle of Carkoon,
blaster, base, hologram figure
MNP $3   MIP $7

Battle Droids, 2006, #62, two battle
droids
MNP $4   MIP $7

Bib Fortuna, 2006, #3, Battle of
Carkoon, base
MNP $3   MIP $7

(KP Photo, Karen O'Brien collection)

Boba Fett, 2006, #6, Battle of Carkoon,
flame exhaust base, blaster,
hologram figure
MNP $3   MIP $7

(KP Photo, Karen O'Brien collection)

C-3PO Ewok Throne, 2006, #42, Battle
of Endor, hologram figure
MNP $5   MIP $10

(KP Photo, Karen O'Brien collection)

C-3PO w/Battle Droid Head, 2006, #17, Battle of Geonosis, base, blaster, "regular" head, hologram figure

MNP $3   MIP $7

Chewbacca w/Electronic C-3PO, 2006, #54, ESB, C-3PO has gone all to pieces

MNP $3   MIP $7

Chewbacca, Boushh Prisoner, 2006, #5, Battle of Carkoon, chain, base, hologram figure

MNP $3   MIP $7

Chief Chirpa, 2006, #39, Battle of Endor, staff, base, hologram figure

MNP $3   MIP $7

Clone Commander Cody, 2006, #24, Battle of Utapau, blaster, helmet, rifle, base, hologram figure

MNP $3   MIP $7

Clone Trooper, 2006, #26, Battle of Utapau, blaster, communications backpack, base, hologram figure

MNP $3   MIP $7

Clone Trooper 442nd Siege Battalion, 2006, #57, blaster, antenna on back

MNP $3   MIP $7

Clone Trooper 5th Fleet Security, 2006, #59, blue stripes, blaster, antenna on back

MNP $3   MIP $7

Clone Trooper Sergeant, 2006, #60, Battle of Geonosis, blaster, base, hologram figure

MNP $3   MIP $7

Clone Trooper Sergeant, 2006, #60, green accents

MNP $3   MIP $7

Combat Engineer Trooper, 2006, #68, removable helmet, black striping on helmet

MNP $3   MIP $7

Commander Appo, 2006, #64, blue shoulder pads

MNP $3   MIP $7

Darth Maul, Holographic, 2006, #48, clear blue plastic, lightsaber, base

MNP $3   MIP $6

Darth Maul, Sith Training, 2006, #53, Battle of Naboo, lightsaber, base, hologram figure

MNP $3   MIP $6

(KP Photo, Karen O'Brien collection)

Darth Vader, 2006, #38, Bespin Confession

MNP $3   MIP $6

(KP Photo, Karen O'Brien collection)

Darth Vader, 2006, #13, Battle of Hoth, helmet, lightsaber, base, hologram figure

MNP $3   MIP $6

(KP Photo, Karen O'Brien collection)

Darth Vader, 2006, #45, Endor Confrontation, lightsaber, base, hologram figure

MNP $4   MIP $7

Death Star Gunner, 2006, #37, Battle of Endor, base, hologram figure

MNP $4   MIP $7

Death Star Trooper, 2006, Battle of Yavin, hologram figure

MNP $4   MIP $7

Dud Bolt and Mars Guo, 2006, #51, Podracer Pilots, Mos Espa, bases, hologram figure

MNP $3   MIP $7

Elite Corps Clone Trooper, 2006, #65, Biker Scout armor in camo pattern

MNP $3   MIP $7

Emperor Palpatine, 2006, #43, Battle of Endor, hologram figure

MNP $3   MIP $7

Firespeeder Pilot, 2006, #22, Battle of Coruscant, helmet, fire supression gear, hologram figure

MNP $4   MIP $8

Foul Moudama, 2006, #29, Clone Wars Battle of Coruscant, character was featured in the animated series, lightsaber, hologram figure

MNP $4   MIP $8

Garindan, 2006, #34, Battle of Tatooine, base, hologram figure

MNP $3   MIP $7

General Grievous, 2006, #30, Battle of Coruscant, lightsaber, electrostaff, base, hologram figure

MNP $4   MIP $8

General Rieekan, 2006, #12, Battle of Hoth, pistol, base, hologram figure

MNP $3   MIP $7

General Veers, 2006, #10, Battle of Hoth, pistol, base, hologram figure

MNP $4   MIP $8

Gragra, 2006, #52, Battle of Naboo

MNP $3   MIP $7

Han Solo, 2006, #35, Battle of Tatooine, blaster, base, hologram figure

MNP $3   MIP $7

(KP Photo, Karen O'Brien collection)

Han Solo w/Carbonite, 2006, #2, Battle of Carkoon, base, force pike, Han in carbonite block, hologram figure

  MNP $3 **MIP $7**

Hem Dazon, 2006, #33, Battle of Tatooine, base, hologram figure
  MNP $3 **MIP $7**

Holographic Clone Commnader Cody, 2006, #56, helmet removable, blaster
  MNP $4 **MIP $8**

Holographic Ki-Adi-Mundi, 2006, #27, Battle of Coruscant, clear blue plastic, lightsaber, base, hologram figure

  MNP $4 **MIP $8**

Holographic Obi-Wan Kenobi, 2006, #63, removable robe, lightsaber
  MNP $4 **MIP $8**

Jango Fett, 2006, #20, Battle of Geonosis, two blasters, jetpack, grappling hook, removable helmet, `base, hologram figure
  MNP $4 **MIP $8**

(KP Photo, Karen O'Brien collection)

Kit Fisto, 2006, #55, bare chested
  MNP $3 **MIP $6**

Kitik Keed'kak, 2006, #71, Wal-Mart exclusive
  MNP $3 **MIP $6**

Labria, 2006, #73, Wal-Mart exclusive, Cantina alien
  MNP $3 **MIP $6**

Luke Skywalker, 2006, #44, Battle of Endor, cammo poncho, helmet, lightsaber, base, hologram figure
  MNP $3 **MIP $6**

Luke Skywalker, 2006, #36, Battle of Tatooine, desert poncho, desert hat, goggles, base, hologram figure
  MNP $3 **MIP $6**

Lushros Dofine, 2006, #23, Battle of Coruscant, datapad, console, base, hologram figure
  MNP $4 **MIP $8**

(KP Photo, Karen O'Brien collection)

Major Bren Derlin, 2006, #8, Battle of Hoth, pistol, base, hologram figure
  MNP $4 **MIP $8**

Moff Jerjerrod, 2006, #40, Battle of Endor, pistol, base, hologram figure
  MNP $4 **MIP $8**

Momaw Nadon, 2006, #30, Battle of Tatooine, staff, bar table, drink, base, hologram figure
  MNP $4 **MIP $8**

(KP Photo, Karen O'Brien collection)

Naboo Soldier, 2006, #50, Battle of Naboo, rifle, base, hologram figure
  MNP $4 **MIP $8**

Nabrun Leids & Kabe, 2006, #72, Wal-Mart exclusive
  MNP $3 **MIP $6**

(KP Photo, Karen O'Brien collection)

Obi-Wan Kenobi, 2006, #47, Battle of Naboo, cloth robe, lightsaber, base, hologram figure
  MNP $3 **MIP $7**

(KP Photo, Karen O'Brien collection)

Obi-Wan Kenobi, 2006, #28, Battle of Coruscant, cloth robe, lightsaber, base, hologram figure
  MNP $3 **MIP $7**

Padme Amidala, 2006, #67, Geonosian Arena
  MNP $3 **MIP $6**

Poggle the Lesser, 2006, #18, Battle of Geonosis, walking stick, base, hologram figure
  MNP $4 **MIP $7**

(KP Photo, Karen O'Brien collection)

Power Droid, 2006, #14, Battle of Hoth, Gonk and Treadwell droids, base, hologram figure

MNP $4   MIP $7

(KP Photo, Karen O'Brien collection)

Princess Leia, Boushh Disguise, 2006, #1, Battle of Carkoon, thermal detonator, removable helmet, staff, base, hologram figure

MNP $3   MIP $7

R2-D2, 2006, #10, Battle of Hoth, rations kit, lantern, base, hologram figure

MNP $3   MIP $7

R4-K5 (Darth Vader's Astromech Droid), 2006, #66, looks like R2's evil twin

MNP $3   MIP $7

R4-M6 (Mace Windu's Astromech Droid), 2006, #74, Wal-Mart exclusive

MNP $3   MIP $7

(KP Photo, Karen O'Brien collection)

R5-D4, 2006, #32, Tatooine, base, hologram figure

MNP $3   MIP $7

R5-J2, 2006, #58

MNP $3   MIP $6

Rebel Trooper, 2006, #46, Battle of Endor, hologram figure

MNP $3   MIP $7

Rep Been, 2006, #49, Battle of Naboo, Gungan record keeper, staff, base, hologram figure

MNP $3   MIP $7

Sandtrooper, 2006, #37, Battle of Tatooine, staff, blaster, base, hologram figure

MNP $3   MIP $7

Scorch Republic Commando, 2006, #21, Expanded Universe, base, hologram figure

MNP $4   MIP $8

Sith Training Darth Maul, 2006, #53, dual-sided lightsaber, training droid

MNP $3   MIP $6

Snowtrooper, 2006, #11, Battle of Hoth, backpack, blaster, base, hologram figure

MNP $4   MIP $8

Sora Bulq, 2006, #15, Battle of Geonosis, lightsaber, base, hologram figure

MNP $3   MIP $7

Sun Fac, 2006, #16, Battle of Geonosis, Geonosian staff and blaster, base, hologram figure

MNP $3   MIP $7

Super Battle Droid, 2006, #61, Battle of Geonosis

MNP $3   MIP $6

Yarael Poof, 2006, #69, Jedi High Council

MNP $3   MIP $7

Yoda, 2006, #19, Battle of Geonosis, lightsaber, cloak, base, hologram figure

MNP $3   MIP $7

SAGA 2006
Exclusive

501st Stormtrooper, 2006, Comic-Con Int'l 2006 exclusive

MNP $8   MIP $15

Astromech Droid Pack Series 1, 2006, R3-T6, R2-C4, R4-A22, R2-Q2, R3-T2, Entertainment Earth exclusive

MNP $25   MIP $50

Astromech Droid Pack Series 2, 2006, R3-Y2, R2-X2, R4-E1, R2-A6, R2-M5, Entertainment Earth exclusive

MNP $25   MIP $50

General Grievous, Demise of Grievous, 2006, Target exclusive, electrostaff, flames from eyes are removable

MNP $4   MIP $10

Infant Leia Organa w/Bail Organa, 2005, Separation of the Twins, Wal-Mart exclusive

MNP $5   MIP $8

Infant Luke Skywalker w/Obi-Wan Kenobi, 2005, Separation of the Twins, Wal-Mart exclusive

MNP $5   MIP $8

Lucas Collector's Set, 2006, George Lucas as Baron Papanoida, Katie Lucas as Chi Eekway, Amanda Lucas as Terr Taneel, and Jett Lucas as Zett Jukassa, StarWarsShop.com exclusive

MNP $10   MIP $20

Shadow Stormtrooper, 2006, Expanded Universe, blaster, StarWarsShop.com exclusive

MNP $6   MIP $12

SAGA 2006
Greatest Battles

(KP Photo, Karen O'Brien collection)

501st Legion Trooper, 2006, #1, Ep:III; this line contains figures repackaged from the RotS line

MNP $3   MIP $7

AT-TE Tank Gunner, 2006, #2, Ep:III

MNP $3   MIP $7

C-3PO, 2006, #3, Ep:III

MNP $3   MIP $6

Clone Commander (Deviss), 2006, #10, Ep:III

MNP $4   MIP $8

Count Dooku, 2006, #4, Ep:III

MNP $3   MIP $6

Emperor Palpatine, 2006, #12, Ep:III

MNP $3   MIP $6

Kit Fisto, 2006, #8, Ep:III

MNP $3   MIP $6

Obi-Wan Kenobi, 2006, #11, Ep:III

MNP $3   MIP $6

Padme, 2006, #6, Ep:III

MNP $3   MIP $6

R2-D2 (Electronic), 2006, #13, Ep:III

MNP $3   MIP $6

R4-G9, 2006, #7, Ep:III
MNP $3   MIP $6

Royal Guard, 2006, #5, Ep:III
MNP $3   MIP $6

Shocktrooper, 2006, #14, Ep:III
MNP $4   MIP $8

Wookie Warrior, 2006, #9, Ep:III
MNP $3   MIP $6

SAGA 2006
Heroes v. Villains

Anakin Skywalker, 2006, #2, Ep:III
MNP $3   MIP $6

Chewbacca, 2006, #7, Ep:III
MNP $3   MIP $6

(KP Photo, Karen O'Brien collection)

Clone Pilot (Shadow Pilot), 2006, #6, Ep:III
MNP $4   MIP $8

Clone Trooper, 2006, #5, Ep:III
MNP $4   MIP $8

Commander Bacara, 2006, #4, Ep:III
MNP $4   MIP $8

Darth Vader, 2006, #1, Ep:III
MNP $3   MIP $6

(KP Photo, Karen O'Brien collection)

Destroyer Droid, 2006, #12, Ep:III
MNP $3   MIP $6

General Grievous, 2006, #9, Ep:III
MNP $3   MIP $6

Mace Windu, 2006, #10, Ep:III
MNP $3   MIP $6

Obi-Wan Kenobi, 2006, #8, Ep:III
MNP $3   MIP $6

R2-D2, 2006, #11, Ep:III
MNP $3   MIP $6

(KP Photo, Karen O'Brien collection)

Yoda, 2006, #3, Ep:III
MNP $3   MIP $6

SAGA 2006
Ultimate Galactic Hunt
"Chase" Figures

Anakin Skywalker, 2006, lightsaber, cloak, silver base, silver hologram figure
MNP $3   MIP $7

AT-AT Driver, 2006, blaster pistol, silver base, silver hologram figure
MNP $5   MIP $10

Boba Fett, 2006, flame base, blaster, silver base, silver hologram figure
MNP $5   MIP $10

Clone Commander Cody, 2006, blaster, helmet, rifle, silver base, silver hologram figure
MNP $3   MIP $7

Darth Vader, 2006, lightsaber, silver base, silver hologram figure
MNP $3   MIP $7

General Grievous, 2006, lightsaber, blaster, staff, silver base, silver hologram figure
MNP $5   MIP $10

Han Solo (Carbonite), 2006, force pike, Han in Carbonite, silver base, silver hologram figure
MNP $5   MIP $10

Obi-Wan Kenobi, 2006, robe, lightsaber, silver base, silver hologram figure
MNP $3   MIP $7

Scorch, 2006, backpack, blaster, silver base, silver hologram figure
MNP $6   MIP $12

Snowtrooper, 2006, backpack, blaster, silver base, silver hologram figure
MNP $4   MIP $8

SAGA 2006
Vintage

Biker Scout, 2006, RotJ, articulated, holster, pistol
MNP $6   MIP $12

George Lucas in Stormtrooper Disguise, 2006, mail-away, removable helmet
MNP $8   MIP $25

Greedo, 2006, SW, pistol
MNP $4   MIP $10

Han Solo in Trench Coat, 2006, RotJ, cloth trench coat, pistol
MNP $4   MIP $10

Luke Skywalker X-Wing Pilot, 2006, SW, removable helmet, lightsaber
MNP $4   MIP $10

Sand People, 2006, SW
MNP $5   MIP $10

TAC (30TH ANNIV. COL.)
Basic-1, Revenge of the Sith

2-1B (Surgical Droid), 2008, #6, display stand
MNP $4   MIP $8

Commander Gree, 2008, #3, blaster, removable helmet, scanners, antenna, display stand
MNP $4   MIP $8

Darth Vader, 2008, #2, lightsaber, display stand
MNP $4   MIP $8

Kashyyk Trooper, 2008, #4, rifle, mask, removable belt, display stand
MNP $4   MIP $8

Mustafar Panning Droid, 2008, #8, platform, lava, bucket, display stand
MNP $4   MIP $8

Obi-Wan Kenobi, 2008, #1, lightsaber, display stand
MNP $4   MIP $8

Tri-Droid, 2008, #7, display stand
MNP $4   MIP $8

TAC (30TH ANNIV. COL.)
Basic-1, RotS

(KP Photo, Karen O'Brien collection)

Airborne Trooper, 2007, #7, blaster rifle, pistol, coin, shoulder pouch, removable helmet, soldier from Commander Cody's 212th Attack Battalion on Utapau

    MNP $4   MIP $8

Concept Stormtrooper, 2007, #9, shield, pistol, lightsaber, coin, based on the conceptual art of Ralph McQuarrie

    MNP $4   MIP $8

Darth Vader, 2007, #1, packaged w/30th Anniv. Coin Album, lightsaber

    MNP $3   MIP $6

(KP Photo, Karen O'Brien collection)

Galactic Marine, 2007, #2, blaster rifle, coin

    MNP $4   MIP $7

Mace Windu, 2007, #6, lightsaber, cloth cloak, coin, Jedi lightning, throne room duel

    MNP $4   MIP $7

Mustafar Lava Miner, 2007, #3, lava scoop, coin

    MNP $4   MIP $7

Obi-Wan Kenobi, 2007, #5, electro staff, blaster, coin, underwater breathing apparatus, from the Battle of Utapau

    MNP $4   MIP $7

(KP Photo, Karen O'Brien collection)

R2-D2, 2007, #4, coin, flame base attaches to Super Battle Droid to recreate the scene in the hangar bay

    MNP $4   MIP $7

(KP Photo, Karen O'Brien collection)

Super Battle Droid, 2007, #8, coin, attached flames courtesy of R2-D2

    MNP $4   MIP $7

TAC (30TH ANNIV. COL.)
Basic-2, The Force Unleashed

Darth Vader (Battle Damage), 2008, #12, lightsaber, helmet, three pieces of armor, display stand

    MNP $4   MIP $8

Emperor's Shadow Guard, 2008, #14, force pike, blade, blaster, cloak, display stand

    MNP $4   MIP $8

Imperial EVO Trooper, 2008, #9, backpack, blaster rifle, two smaller blasters, display stand

    MNP $4   MIP $8

Imperial Jumptrooper, 2008, #10, blaster pistol, display stand

    MNP $4   MIP $8

Juno Eclipse, 2008, #15, blaster, cap, display stand

    MNP $4   MIP $8

Maris Brood, 2008, #11, two lightsabers, display stand

    MNP $4   MIP $8

Rahm Kota, 2008, #13, lightsaber, holster, two capes, chest armor, display stand

    MNP $4   MIP $8

TAC (30TH ANNIV. COL.)
Basic-2, Yavin

Concept Boba Fett, 2007, #15, blaster pistol, flame thrower, additional head, belly blaster, coin

    MNP $8   MIP $15

Death Star Trooper, 2007, #13, blaster pistol, removable helmet, coin

    MNP $4   MIP $8

(KP Photo, Karen O'Brien collection)

Han Solo, 2007, #11, communication headset, blaster pistol, coin

    MNP $4   MIP $7

(KP Photo, Karen O'Brien collection)

Luke Skywalker, 2007, #12, medal, blaster pistol, (Darth Vader's lightsaber hilt), coin

    MNP $4   MIP $7

Rebel Honor Guard, 2007, #10, pistol, staff, removable helmet, coin

    MNP $4   MIP $7

Rebel Pilot Bigs Darklighter, 2007, #14, pistol, removable helmet, coin

    MNP $4   MIP $7

TAC (30TH ANNIV. COL.) Basic-3, A New Hope

Biggs Darklighter, 2007, #17, civilian attire, cape

MNP $3　　　MIP $6

Concept Chewbacca, 2007, #21, pistol, rifle, coin

MNP $4　　　MIP $8

(KP Photo, Karen O'Brien collection)

Darth Vader, 2007, #16, raised left fist

MNP $4　　　MIP $7

Elis Helrot, 2007, #23, bar section, bar base, two bar stools, removable scarf, blaster, drinking glass, coin

MNP $4　　　MIP $8

Jawa & LIN Droid, 2007, #19

MNP $4　　　MIP $7

Luke Skywalker, 2007, #18, w/blue lightsaber

MNP $4　　　MIP $7

M'iiyoom Onith, 2007, #22, bar section, bar base, two bar stools, blaster, drinking glass, coin

MNP $4　　　MIP $8

Stormtrooper, 2007, #20

MNP $4　　　MIP $7

TAC (30TH ANNIV. COL.) Basic-4, Return of the Jedi

Boba Fett; Animated Debut, 2007, #24, blaster, electropole, rangefinder, jet pack, coin

MNP $5　　　MIP $10

C-3PO & Salacious Crumb, 2007, #30, Salacious Crumb, coin

MNP $5　　　MIP $8

Concept Darth Vader, 2007, #28, lightsaber, blaster, cape, alternate mask, coin

MNP $5　　　MIP $10

CZ-4, 2007, #26, coin

MNP $4　　　MIP $8

Hermi Odle, 2007, #29, staff, rags, coin

MNP $12　　　MIP $18

Luke Skywalker; Jedi Knight, 2007, #25, lightsaber, lightsaber hilt, bone, tunic, coin

MNP $4　　　MIP $8

Umpass-Stay, 2007, #27, drum half, drum base, two drum tubes, drumstick, hood, shoulder pads, coin

MNP $4　　　MIP $8

TAC (30TH ANNIV. COL.) Basic-5, Expanded Universe

Anakin Skywalker; Jedi Knight, 2007, #33, right hand, right hand (damaged), lightsaber, coin

MNP $4　　　MIP $8

Concept Starkiller Hero, 2007, #37, lightsaber blade, lightsaber hilt, pistol, goggles, mask/backpack, coin

MNP $4　　　MIP $8

Darth Malak, 2007, #35, lightsaber, lightsaber hilt, cape, removable jaw, coin

MNP $15　　　MIP $25

Darth Revan, 2007, #34, cloak, lightsaber, lightsaber hilt, coin

MNP $30　　　MIP $48

Pre-Cyborg Grievous, 2007, #36, mask, cape, rifle, sword, coin

MNP $14　　　MIP $24

Roron Corobb, 2007, #31, lightsaber, coin

MNP $5　　　MIP $10

Yoda & Kybuck, 2007, #32, Kybuck, lightsaber, bandolier, cloak, coin

MNP $4　　　MIP $8

TAC (30TH ANNIV. COL.) Basic-6, The Empire Strikes Back

4-LOM (Bounty Hunter), 2007, #41, rifle, coin

MNP $4　　　MIP $8

Concept Stormtrooper, 2007, #42, rifle, mask, harness, coin

MNP $5　　　MIP $9

General McQuarrie (Rebel Officer), 2007, #40, blaster pistol, headgear, coin

MNP $4　　　MIP $8

Han Solo; w/Torture Rack, 2007, #38, torture rack, coin

MNP $4　　　MIP $8

Lando Calrissian; Smuggler Outfit, 2007, #39, pistol, coin

MNP $3　　　MIP $7

TAC (30TH ANNIV. COL.) Basic-7, Return of the Jedi

Anakin Skywalker; Jedi Spirit, 2007, #45, lightsaber blade, lightsaber hilt, robe, skirt, coin

MNP $3　　　MIP $6

Concept Han Solo, 2007, #47, lightsaber, lightsaber hilt, blaster, cape, coin

MNP $4　　　MIP $8

R2-D2; w/Cargo Net, 2007, #46, stretcher, cargo net, coin

MNP $4　　　MIP $8

Romba & Graak (Ewok Warriors), 2007, #43, spear, knife, sheath, bow, three arrows, hood, hood w/quiver, coin

MNP $4　　　MIP $8

Tycho Celchu, 2007, #44, cap, helmet, harness, coin

MNP $4　　　MIP $8

TAC (30TH ANNIV. COL.) Basic-7.5, "Repaint" Series

Clone Trooper (7th Legion), 2007, #49, helmet, blaster, coin

MNP $4　　　MIP $8

Clone Trooper (Hawkbat Battalion), 2007, #50, helmet, rifle, poncho, coin

MNP $4　　　MIP $8

Darth Vader (Hologram), 2007, #48, cape, lightsaber, coin

MNP $4　　　MIP $8

Naboo Soldier (Royal Naboo Army), 2007, #52, blaster pistol, helmet, coin

MNP $4　　　MIP $8

Pax Bonkik (Rodanian Podracer Mechanic), 2007, #54, pistol, vest, coin

MNP $4　　　MIP $8

R2-B1 (Astromech Droid), 2007, #51, power harness, coin

MNP $4　　　MIP $8

TAC (30TH ANNIV. COL.) Basic-8, Attack of the Clones

Clone Trooper (Training Fatigues), 2007, #55, seven-piece suit of armor, helmet, rifle, coin

MNP $4　　　MIP $8

Concept Rebel Trooper, 2007, #60, helmet, neck armor, chest armor, pistol, coin

MNP $4　　　MIP $8

Destoyer Droid (Droideka), 2007, #59, energy shield, two blast effects, coin
MNP $4   MIP $8

Jango Fett (Bounty Hunter), 2007, #57, two blasters, jet pack, two shin guards, poncho, helmet, chest armor, belt, coin
MNP $4   MIP $8

Padme Amidala (Naboo Senator), 2007, #56, drinking glass, shawl, scarf, coin
MNP $4   MIP $8

Voolvif Moon (Jedi Master), 2007, #58, lightsaber, coin
MNP $4   MIP $8

TAC (30TH ANNIV. COL.) Saga Legends, "Fan's Choice" (2008)

Commander Neyo, 2008, blaster, harness, coin
MNP $4   MIP $8

Covert Ops Clone Trooper, 2008, blaster, blaster rifle, coin
MNP $4   MIP $8

Shadow Stormtrooper, 2008, blaster, coin
MNP $4   MIP $10

Utapau Shadow Trooper, 2008, blaster, blaster rifle, coin
MNP $5   MIP $12

Zev Senesca, 2008, helmet, pistol, coin
MNP $4   MIP $12

TAC (30TH ANNIV. COL.) Saga Legends, Variations (Waves 1-4)

501st Clone Trooper, 2007, (version II), blaster, coin
MNP $4   MIP $8

Imperial Officer, 2007, (variant head sculpt #3), blaster, coin
MNP $4   MIP $8

Pit Droids, 2007, (orange; w/accessory #2), w/storage locker and coin
MNP $4   MIP $8

Pit Droids, 2007, (brown; w/accessory #2), w/storage locker and coin
MNP $4   MIP $8

Pit Droids, 2007, (white; w/accessory #1), w/power converter and coin
MNP $4   MIP $8

Sandtrooper, 2007, (V: "Dirty" [Sergeant]-body type #2), shoulder pad, blaster, backpack, thermal detonator, lance, coin
MNP $4   MIP $8

Sandtrooper, 2007, (IV: "Clean" [Sergeant]-body type #1), shoulder pad, blaster, backpack, thermal detonator, lance, coin
MNP $4   MIP $8

TAC (30TH ANNIV. COL.) Saga Legends, Wave 1

Battle Droids, 2007, (I: tan [Infantry & Commander]), two blasters, two backpacks, coin
MNP $4   MIP $7

C-3PO, 2007, (w/Battle Droid head), C-3PO head, Battle Droid head, blaster, backpack, coin
MNP $3   MIP $7

Clone Trooper, 2007, (Attack of the Clones), blaster, coin
MNP $3   MIP $7

Darth Maul, 2007, lightsaber, cloak, coin
MNP $3   MIP $7

Darth Vader, 2007, lightsaber, cape, coin
MNP $3   MIP $7

General Grievous, 2007, four lightsabers, coin
MNP $4   MIP $8

R2-D2, 2007, w/electronic lights and sounds, coin
MNP $3   MIP $7

Shocktrooper, 2007, blaster, antenna, coin
MNP $3   MIP $7

Yoda, 2007, lightsaber, cloak, cannon, projectile, coin
MNP $3   MIP $7

TAC (30TH ANNIV. COL.) Saga Legends, Wave 2

501st Clone Trooper, 2007, I, blaster, helmet, shoulder pad, coin
MNP $3   MIP $7

Battle Droids, 2007, (II: maroon [blaster damage and lightsaber damage]), two blasters, two backpacks, coin
MNP $4   MIP $7

Boba Fett, 2007, rifle, jet pack, rangefinder, cape, coin
MNP $3   MIP $7

Chewbacca, 2007, bowcaster, coin
MNP $3   MIP $7

Darth Vader, 2007, (Anakin Skywalker), lightsaber hilt, right hand, right hand w/lightsaber, cloak, coin
MNP $3   MIP $7

Destroyed Droid, 2007, two missiles, coin
MNP $3   MIP $7

Obi-Wan Kenobi, 2007, lightsaber, lightsaber hilt, headgear, cloak, coin
MNP $3   MIP $7

Princess Leia, 2007, (in Boushh Disguise), helmet, staff, thermal detonator, cape, coin
MNP $3   MIP $7

Saesee Tiin, 2007, lightsaber, lightsaber blade, cloak, coin
MNP $3   MIP $7

Sandtrooper, 2007, (I: "Super Dirty" [Sergeant]-body type #1), shoulder pad, blaster, backpack, thermal detonator, lance, coin
MNP $3   MIP $7

TAC (30TH ANNIV. COL.) Saga Legends, Wave 3

Battle Droids, 2007, (III: tan [blaster damage and lightsaber damage]), two backpacks, two blasters, coin
MNP $4   MIP $8

Clone Commander, 2007, (Coruscant), helmet, two blasters, belt, kama (loincloth), shoulder pads, rifle, coin
MNP $4   MIP $8

Clone Trooper Officer, 2007, (Lieutenant), blaster, coin
MNP $4   MIP $8

Clone Trooper Officer, 2007, (Commander), blaster, coin
MNP $4   MIP $8

Clone Trooper Officer, 2007, (Captain), blaster, coin
MNP $4   MIP $8

Darktrooper, 2007, (Fan's Choice #1), canon, jet pack, coin
MNP $5   MIP $10

Imperial Officer, 2007, (variant head sculpt #1), blaster, coin
MNP $4   MIP $8

Pit Droids, 2007, (white; w/accessory #1), w/power converter and coin
MNP $4   MIP $8

Sandtrooper, 2007, (II: "Dirty" [Squad Leader]-body type #1), shoulder pad, blaster, backpack, thermal detonator, lance, coin
MNP $4   MIP $8

TAC (30TH ANNIV. COL.) Saga Legends, Wave 4

Battle Droids, 2007, (IV: tan [dirty and clean]), two backpacks, two blasters, coin
MNP $5   MIP $9

Biker Scout, 2007, blaster, coin
MNP $4   MIP $8

Clone Trooper Officer, 2007, (Sergeant), blaster, coin
MNP $4   MIP $8

Imperial Officer, 2007, (variant head sculpt #2), blaster, coin
MNP $4   MIP $8

Pit Droids, 2007, (brown; w/accessory #1), w/power converter and coin
MNP $4   MIP $8

R4-I9, 2007, w/coin
MNP $4   MIP $8

RA-7, 2007, w/coin
MNP $4   MIP $8

Sandtrooper, 2007, (III: "Clean" [Corporal]-body type #1), shoulder pad, blaster, backpack, thermal detonator, lance, coin
MNP $4   MIP $8

TC-14, 2007, container, serving tray, coin
MNP $4   MIP $8

TAC (30TH ANNIV. COL.) Ultimate Galactic Hunt

Airborne Trooper, 2007, #7, blaster rifle, pistol, pouch, removable helmet, coin
MNP $4   MIP $8

Biggs Darklighter (Rebel Pilot), 2007, #14, pistol, removable helmet, coin
MNP $4   MIP $8

Boba Fett (Animated Debut), 2007, #24, blaster, electropole, rangefinder, jet pack, coin
MNP $5   MIP $10

Concept Boba Fett, 2007, #15, blaster, flamethrower, extra head, belly gun, coin
MNP $7   MIP $12

Concept Chewbacca, 2007, #21, rifle, pistol, coin
MNP $4   MIP $8

Concept Stormtrooper, 2007, #9, shield, pistol, lightsaber, coin
MNP $5   MIP $10

Darth Vader (Sith Lord), 2007, #16, removable helmet, Obi-Wan cloak, lightsaber, coin
MNP $4   MIP $8

Galactic Marine, 2007, #2, blaster rifle, coin
MNP $4   MIP $8

Han Solo (Smuggler), 2007, #11, headset, pistol, coin
MNP $4   MIP $8

Luke Skywalker (Yavin Ceremony), 2007, #12, medal, pistol, lightsaber hilt, coin
MNP $4   MIP $8

Mace Windu, 2007, #6, lightsaber, cloak, lightning
MNP $4   MIP $8

R2-D2, 2007, #4, flame base, coin
MNP $4   MIP $8

VINTAGE 30TH ANNIVERSARY FIGURES (ULTIMATE GALACTIC HUNT)

Bossk (Bounty Hunter), 2007, w/grenade launcher, vintage coin set proof of purchase and redemption form
MNP $4   MIP $8

Han Solo (Hoth Outfit), 2007, w/grenade launcher, vintage coin set proof of purchase and redemption form
MNP $4   MIP $8

IG-88 (Bounty Hunter), 2007, w/grenade launcher, vintage coin set proof of purchase and redemption form
MNP $8   MIP $15

Imperial Stormtrooper (Hoth Battle Gear), 2007, w/grenade launcher, vintage coin set proof of purchase and redemption form
MNP $4   MIP $8

Luke Skywalker (Bespin Fatigues), 2007, w/grenade launcher, vintage coin set proof of purchase and redemption form
MNP $4   MIP $8

Princess Leia Organa (in Combat Poncho), 2007, w/grenade launcher, vintage coin set proof of purchase and redemption form
MNP $4   MIP $8

SAGA LEGENDS, 2008-PRESENT

501st Legion Trooper, 2008, #16, blaster, battle gear
MNP $5   MIP $8

ARC Trooper, 2009, #19, rifle, helmet, shoulder pads, kama (loincloth), battle gear
MNP $5   MIP $8

BARC Trooper, 2009, #18, rifle, antenna, battle gear
MNP $5   MIP $8

Battle Droids, 2009, (tan), #20 (A), two blasters, two backpacks, battle gear
MNP $5   MIP $8

Battle Droids, 2009, (maroon), #20, (B), two blasters, two backpacks, battle gear
MNP $5   MIP $8

C-3PO, 2008, #6, removable arms and head, Ewok throne, two carry poles, and Clone gear
MNP $4   MIP $8

Clone Trooper, 2008, #5, blaster rifle w/Clone gear
MNP $4   MIP $8

Clone Trooper Officer, 2008, (Sergeant [Green]), #12 (C), blaster, battle gear
MNP $4   MIP $8

Clone Trooper Officer, 2008, (Captain [Red]), #12, blaster, battle gear
MNP $4   MIP $8

Clone Trooper Officer, 2008, (Commander [Yellow]), #12 (A), blaster, battle gear
MNP $4   MIP $8

Clone Trooper Officer, 2008, (Lieutenant [Blue]), #12 (B), blaster, battle gear
MNP $4   MIP $8

Darth Maul, 2008, #14, lightsaber, cloak, battle gear
MNP $4   MIP $8

Darth Vader, 2008, #13, lightsaber, cape, battle gear
MNP $4   MIP $8

Darth Vader (Anakin Skywalker), 2008, #3, lightsaber and Clone gear
MNP $4   MIP $8

Destroyer Droid, 2008, #11, two missiles, Clone gear
MNP $4   MIP $8

General Grievous, 2008, #7, lightsaber, blaster, cape, and Clone gear
MNP $4   MIP $8

Jango Fett, 2008, #15, two blasters, jet pack, two shin guards, poncho, helmet, chest armor, belt, battle gear
MNP $4   MIP $8

Mace Windu, 2008, #8, lightsaber, force lightning, Jedi cloak, and Clone gear
MNP $4   MIP $8

Obi-Wan Kenobi, 2008, #4, lightsaber and Clone gear
MNP $4   MIP $8

Plo Koon, 2008, #9, lightsaber and Clone gear
MNP $4   MIP $8

R2-D2, 2008, #1, w/electronic lights and sounds
MNP $4   MIP $8

Shock Trooper, 2008, #17, blaster, antenna, battle gear
MNP $4   MIP $8

Super Battle Droid, 2008, #10, Clone gear
MNP $4   MIP $8

Yoda & Kybuck, 2008, #2, Kybuck, lightsaber, bandolier, cloak, and Clone gear

MNP $4   MIP $8

THE CLONE WARS, 2008-PRESENT

Ahsoka Tano, 2008, #9, Rotta the Huttlet, backpack, lightsaber

MNP $6   MIP $12

Anakin Skywalker, 2008, #1, lightsaber, force effect, force effect launcher, cable w/handles

MNP $4   MIP $7

Asajj Ventress, 2008, #15, two lightsabers, skirt, belt, projector, Count Dooku hologram

MNP $3   MIP $7

Battle Droid, 2008, #7, blaster, blaster cannon, missile, backpack

MNP $3   MIP $7

C-3PO, 2008, #16, "glowing eyes"

MNP $3   MIP $6

Captain Rex, 2008, #4, rifle, two pistols, launcher, missile, missile w/cable, removalbe helmet, shoulder pad

MNP $4   MIP $8

Clone Pilot Odd Ball, 2008, #11, blaster, launcher, rocket

MNP $4   MIP $7

Clone Trooper, 2008, #5, blaster, launcher, rocket

MNP $4   MIP $8

Clone Trooper (212th Attack Battalion), 2008, #19, rocket launcher, rocket, blaster

MNP $4   MIP $8

Clone Trooper (Space Gear), 2008, #21, firing backpack launcher, missile, blaster, pistol

MNP $4   MIP $8

Commander Cody, 2008, #10, blaster, blaster rifle, launcher, missile, missile w/cable, removable helmet

MNP $4   MIP $8

Count Dooku, 2008, #13, lightsaber, cape, projector, Asajj Ventress hologram, right hand, right hand w/Sith lightning

MNP $4   MIP $7

Destroyed Droid, 2008, #17, two missiles and two hip guards

MNP $4   MIP $7

General Grievous, 2008, #6, four lightsabers, pistol, two sets of arms

MNP $4   MIP $8

IG-86 Assassin Droid, 2008, #18, two blasters, backpack

MNP $4   MIP $8

Magnaguard, 2008, #22, launcher, missile, cape, staff

MNP $4   MIP $8

Obi-Wan Kenobi, 2008, #2, lightsaber, jet backpack, missile, alternate head

MNP $4   MIP $7

Padme Amidala (Hooded), 2008, #20, cape, hood, blaster, pistol, belt

MNP $4   MIP $8

Plo Koon, 2008, #14, two lightsabers, lightsaber gaunlet, and two removable hoods (up and down)

MNP $4   MIP $7

R2-D2, 2008, #8, two booster rockets, and three hidden panels

MNP $3   MIP $7

R3-S6 (Goldie), 2008, #23, hidden gadgets and removable middle leg

MNP $4   MIP $8

Super Battle Droid, 2008, #12, two missile launchers and two missiles

MNP $4   MIP $7

Yoda, 2008, #3, lightsaber, gimer stick, firing force blast

MNP $4   MIP $7

THE LEGACY COLLECTION, 2008-PRESENT
Build-A-Droid, Wave 1: Return of the Jedi

Ak-Rev, 2008, (w/R7-Z0 left leg), #5 of 8

MNP $4   MIP $8

Bane Malar, 2008, (w/R7-Z0 body), #7 of 8

MNP $4   MIP $8

Chewbacca, 2008, (w/R4-D6 head and middle leg), #3 of 8

MNP $3   MIP $7

Darth Vader, 2008, (w/R7-Z0 head and middle leg), #8 of 8

MNP $5   MIP $10

Han Solo, 2008, (w/R4-D6 left leg), #1 of 8

MNP $4   MIP $8

Leektar & Nippet, 2008, (w/R4-D6 body), #4 of 8

MNP $5   MIP $10

Luke Skywalker, 2008, (w/R4-D6 right leg), #2 of 8

MNP $5   MIP $10

R4-D6, 2008, ("Build-A-Droid" [packed w/Wave 1 #s 1-4])

MNP $15   MIP n/a

R7-Z0, 2008, ("Build-A-Droid" [packed w/Wave 1 #s 5-8])

MNP $14   MIP n/a

Yarna d'al' Gargan, 2008, (w/R7-Z0 right leg), #6 of 8

MNP $5   MIP $8

THE LEGACY COLLECTION, 2008-PRESENT
Build-A-Droid, Wave 2: Clone Wars

Clone SCUBA Trooper, 2008, (w/R4-J1 head and middle leg), #10

MNP $6   MIP $12

Clone Trooper (Heavy Gunner), 2008, (w/R4-J1 right leg), #16

MNP $7   MIP $12

IG Lancer Droid, 2008, (wR4-J1 body), #13

MNP $4   MIP $8

Mon Calamari Warrior, 2008, (w/R7-T1 body), #14

MNP $4   MIP $8

Obi-Wan Kenobi, 2008, (w/R4-J1 left leg), #9

MNP $3   MIP $7

Padme Amidala, 2008, (w/R7-T1 left leg), #12

MNP $4   MIP $8

Quarren Soldier, 2008, (w/R7-T1 head and middle leg), #15

MNP $4   MIP $8

R4-J1, 2008, ("Build-A-Droid" [packed w/Wave 2 #s 9, 10, 13, and 16])

MNP $16   MIP n/a

R7-T1, 2008, ("Build-A-Droid" [packed w/Wave 2 #s 11, 12, 14, and 15])

MNP $14   MIP n/a

Saesee Tiin, 2008, (w/R7-T1 right leg), #11

MNP $4   MIP $8

THE LEGACY COLLECTION, 2008-PRESENT
Build-A-Droid, Wave 3: Repacks and Repaints

5D6-RA7, 2008, ("Build-A-Droid" [packed w/Wave 3 figures])

MNP $13   MIP n/a

Clone Trooper (Coruscant Landing Platform), 2008, (w/5D6-RA7 body), #17

MNP $5   MIP $10

Count Dooku (Holographic Transmission), 2008, (w/5D6-RA7 right arm), #21

MNP $3   MIP $7

Imperial Engineer (Star Wars: Battlefront II), 2008, (w/5D6-RA7 left arm), #22

    MNP $5   MIP $10

Jodo Kast, 2008, (w/5D6-RA7 head), #18

    MNP $6   MIP $12

Saleucami Trooper, 2008, (w/5D6-RA7 left leg), #20

    MNP $5   MIP $10

Yaddle & Even Piell, 2008, (w/5D6-RA7 right leg), #19

    MNP $8   MIP $12

THE LEGACY COLLECTION, 2008-PRESENT
Build-A-Droid, Wave 4: Revenge of the Sith

Bail Organa, 2008, (w/MB-RA7 right arm), #26

    MNP $5   MIP $10

Breha Organa, 2008, (w/MB-RA7 left leg), #27

    MNP $5   MIP $10

Clone Trooper (327th Star Corps), 2008, (w/MB-RA7 body), #29

    MNP $5   MIP $10

Commander Faie, 2008, (w/MB-RA7 body), #24

    MNP $8   MIP $12

FX-6, 2008, (w/MB-RA7 right leg), #28

    MNP $5   MIP $10

General Grievous, 2008, (w/MB-RA7 head), #25

    MNP $5   MIP $10

MB-RA7, 2008, ("Build-A-Droid" [packed w/Wave 4 figures])

    MNP $13   MIP n/a

Stass Allie, 2008, (w/MB-RA7 left arm), #23

    MNP $4   MIP $8

THE LEGACY COLLECTION, 2008-PRESENT
Droid Factory/ Build-A-Droid "Sneak Preview" Wave

C-3PX figure, 2008, ("Build-A-Droid" from six above)

    MNP $20   MIP n/a

Darth Vader & K-3PX, 2008, (w/C-3PX left arm), #2 of 6

    MNP $7   MIP $11

Han Solo & R-3PO, 2008, (w/C-3PX left leg), #3 of 6

    MNP $7   MIP $11

Kit Fisto & R4-H5, 2008, (w/C-3PX torso), #4 of 6

    MNP $7   MIP $11

Luke Skywalker & R2-D2, 2008, (w/C-3PX right arm), #6 of 6

    MNP $7   MIP $11

Plo Koon & R4-F5, 2008, (w/C-3PX right leg), #1 of 6

    MNP $7   MIP $11

Watto & R2-T0, 2008, (w/C-3PX head), #5 of 6

    MNP $7   MIP $11

VINTAGE 30TH ANNIVERSARY FIGURES (ULTIMATE GALACTIC HUNT)

Bossk (Bounty Hunter), 2007, w/grenade launcher, vintage coin set proof of purchase and redemption form

    MNP $4   MIP $10

Han Solo (Hoth Outfit), 2007, w/grenade launcher, vintage coin set proof of purchase and redemption form

    MNP $4   MIP $10

IG-88 (Bounty Hunter), 2007, w/grenade launcher, vintage coin set proof of purchase and redemption form

    MNP $4   MIP $10

Imperial Stormtrooper (Hoth Battle Gear), 2007, w/grenade launcher, vintage coin set proof of purchase and redemption form

    MNP $5   MIP $12

Luke Skywalker (Bespin Fatigues), 2007, w/grenade launcher, vintage coin set proof of purchase and redemption form

    MNP $4   MIP $10

Princess Leia Organa (in Combat Poncho), 2007, w/grenade launcher, vintage coin set proof of purchase and redemption form

    MNP $4   MIP $10

Action Figures, 12"
STAR WARS

Boba Fett, 1979, Star Wars or Empire Strikes Back box

    MNP $110   MIP $500

C-3PO, 1979

    MNP $35   MIP $145

Chewbacca, 1979

    MNP $55   MIP $185

Darth Vader, 1978

    MNP $55   MIP $300

Han Solo, 1979
MNP $120   MIP $425

Jawa, 1979
MNP $40   MIP $150

Luke Skywalker, 1979
MNP $75   MIP $300

Obi-Wan Kenobi, 1979
MNP $75   MIP $300

Princess Leia Organa, 1979
MNP $75   MIP $220

R2-D2, 1979
MNP $40   MIP $185

Stormtrooper, 1979
MNP $80   MIP $275

EMPIRE STRIKES BACK

Boba Fett, 1979, Empire Strikes Back Box
MNP $110   MIP $875

IG-88, 1980, Empire Strikes Back Box
MNP $150   MIP $490

COLLECTOR'S SERIES

Admiral Ackbar, 1997, Series 4
MNP $5   MIP $12

AT-AT Driver, 1997, ESB Assortment, Service Merchandise exclusive
MNP $5   MIP $10

Boba Fett, 1997, Series 3
MNP $6   MIP $12

C-3PO, 1997, Series 4
MNP $4   MIP $10

Chewbacca, 1997, Series 4
MNP $6   MIP $15

(KP Photo)

Darth Vader, 1996, Series 1
MNP $5   MIP $10

Doikk Na'ts, 1997, w/Fizzz, Wal-Mart exclusive, Cantina Band member
MNP $3   MIP $8

Figrin D'an, 1997, w/Kloo Horn, Wal-Mart exclusive, Cantina Band member
MNP $5   MIP $15

Grand Moff Tarkin and Imperial Gunner, 1997, FAO exclusive
MNP $18   MIP $30

(Hasbro Photo)

Greedo, 1997, SW Assortment, JC Penney exclusive
MNP $4   MIP $10

Han and Luke in Stormtrooper Disguise, 1997, KB exclusive
MNP $16   MIP $30

(KP Photo)

Han Solo, 1996, Series 1, w/blaster
    MNP $5   **MIP $10**

Han Solo in Hoth Gear w/Tauntaun, 1997, TRU exclusive
    MNP $20   **MIP $55**

Ickabel, 1997, w/Fantor, Wal-Mart exclusive, Cantina Band member
    MNP $10   **MIP $20**

Jedi Luke Skywalker and Bib Fortuna, 1997, FAO Schwarz exclusive
    MNP $20   **MIP $40**

Lando Calrissian, 1997, Series 2
    MNP $3   **MIP $7**

Luke Skywalker, 1996, Series 1
    MNP $5   **MIP $10**

Luke Skywalker as X-Wing Pilot, 1996, Series 3
    MNP $5   **MIP $10**

Luke Skywalker in Bespin Fatigues, 1997, Series 2
    MNP $5   **MIP $10**

Luke Skywalker vs. Wampa, 1997, Target exclusive
    MNP $20   **MIP $55**

Nalan, 1997, w/Bandfill, Wal-Mart exclusive, Cantina Band member
    MNP $10   **MIP $20**

(KP Photo, Karen O'Brien collection)

Obi-Wan Kenobi, 1996, Series 1
    MNP $5   **MIP $10**

Obi-Wan Kenobi vs. Darth Vader, 1997, electronic power F/X
    MNP $15   **MIP $30**

Princess Leia, 1997, Series 3
    MNP $5   **MIP $12**

Princess Leia in Ceremonial Gown, 1999, Princess Leia Collection, 1999 Collectors Edition
    MNP $6   **MIP $14**

Sandtrooper, 1997, Diamond exclusive
    MNP $5   **MIP $10**

Stormtrooper, 1997, Series 3
    MNP $6   **MIP $12**

Tech, 1997, w/Ommni Box, Wal-Mart exclusive, Cantina Band member
    MNP $10   **MIP $20**

Tedn, 1997, w/Fantar, Wal-Mart exclusive, Cantina Band
    MNP $10   **MIP $20**

TIE Fighter Pilot, 1997, Series 4
    MNP $5   **MIP $10**

Tusken Raider, 1997, Series 2
    MNP $5   **MIP $12**

ACTION COLLECTION

AT-AT Driver, 1998, Service Merchandise exclusive
    MNP $5   **MIP $10**

Barquin D'an, 1998, ROTJ Assortment
    MNP $4   **MIP $10**

Boba Fett, Electronic, 1998, KB Toys exclusive
    MNP $20   **MIP $38**

C-3PO and R2-D2, 1997, electronic power F/X, TRU exclusive
    MNP $12   **MIP $30**

Chewbacca (Chained), 1998, ROTJ Assortment
    MNP $6   **MIP $12**

Darth Vader, Electronic, 1998, w/removable helmet
    MNP $15   **MIP $35**

Emperor Palpatine, 1998, ROTJ Assortment
    MNP $5   **MIP $10**

Emperor Palpatine and Royal Guard, 1998, electronic power F/X, Target exclusive
    MNP $16   **MIP $38**

Grand Moff Tarkin w/Interrogation Droid, 1998, SW Assortment
    MNP $6   **MIP $12**

Greedo, 1998, fully poseabale, blaster
    MNP $5   **MIP $10**

(KP Photo, Karen O'Brien collection)

Han Solo in Carbonite, 1998, "I know," Target exclusive
    MNP $8   **MIP $12**

Han Solo in Hoth Gear, 1998, ESB Assortment
    MNP $5   **MIP $12**

Jawa, 1998, Trilogy Assortment, light-up eyes
    MNP $4   **MIP $8**

Luke Skywalker (Hoth), Han Solo (Hoth), Snowtrooper, AT-AT Driver, 1998, JC Penny exclusive
    MNP $28   **MIP $50**

Luke Skywalker (Tatooine), Han Solo w/Flight Jacket, Leia as Boushh, 1998, KB exclusive
    MNP $25   **MIP $50**

Luke Skywalker as Jedi Knight, 1998, ROTJ Assortment, fighting the Rancor
    MNP $4   **MIP $10**

Luke Skywalker in Ceremonial Garb, 1998, SW Assortment
    MNP $4   **MIP $10**

Luke Skywalker in Hoth Gear, 1998, ESB Assortment
    MNP $4   **MIP $10**

Princess Leia and R2-D2 as Jabba's Prisoners, 1998, FAO exclusive, Princess Leia Collection
    MNP $14   **MIP $25**

Princess Leia in Hoth Gear, 1998, Service Merchandise exclusive
    MNP $5   **MIP $10**

R2-D2, 1998, Trilogy Assortment
    MNP $4   **MIP $8**

R2-D2 (Detachable Utility Arms), 1998, Wal-Mart exclusive
    MNP $3   **MIP $7**

R5-D4, 1998, Wal-Mart exclusive
    MNP $4   **MIP $10**

Sandtrooper, 1998, w/Imperial Droid
    MNP $6   **MIP $12**

Snowtrooper, 1998, ESB Assortment
    MNP $6   **MIP $12**

Wedge Antilles and Biggs Darklighter, 1998, FAO exclusive, in X-Wing pilot gear

MNP $18   MIP $30

Wicket the Ewok, 1998, Wal-Mart exclusive

MNP $6   MIP $12

Yoda, 1998, Trilogy Assortment

MNP $15   MIP $25

POTF2

Dewback & Sandtrooper, 2000, TRU exclusive

MNP $25   MIP $40

Han Solo w/Magnetic Detonators, 1999, Endor gear, trench coat

MNP $6   MIP $12

Princess Leia w/Chain, 1999, "Slave Leia"

MNP $6   MIP $12

Speeder Bike w/Scout Trooper, 2000, Target exclusive

MNP $22   MIP $35

POTJ

4-LOM, 2000, concussion rifle

MNP $10   MIP $14

Bossk, 2000, blaster rifle

MNP $10   MIP $14

Captain Tarpals & Kaadu, 2000, Target exclusive

MNP $12   MIP $25

Death Star Droid, 2000, w/mouse droid

MNP $8   MIP $12

Death Star Trooper, 2001, w/Imperial blaster

MNP $7   MIP $12

Dengar, 2002, rifle

MNP $8   MIP $14

Han Solo in Stormtrooper Disguise, 2001, blaster

MNP $6   MIP $12

IG-88, 2000, rifle, Imperial blaster

MNP $10   MIP $14

Luke Skywalker & Yoda, 2001, Wal-Mart exclusive, on Dagobah

MNP $7   MIP $14

Luke Skywalker, 100th Figure, 2001

MNP $20   MIP $35

Sith Lords: Darth Vader & Darth Maul, 2001, lightsabers

MNP $14   MIP $25

Speeder Bike w/Luke Skywalker, 2001, Target exclusive

MNP $20   MIP $35

THE PHANTOM MENACE Action Collection

Anakin Skywalker, 1999

MNP $4   MIP $8

Battle Droid, 1999

MNP $6   MIP $12

(KP Photo)

Darth Maul, 1999

MNP $6   MIP $12

Jar Jar Binks, 1999

MNP $5   MIP $12

Obi-Wan Kenobi, 1999

MNP $5   MIP $10

Pit Droid, 1999

MNP $6   MIP $12

(KP Photo)

Qui-Gon Jinn, 1999

MNP $6   MIP $12

R2-A6, 1999

MNP $4   MIP $12

Watto, 1999

MNP $4   MIP $10

THE PHANTOM MENACE Defense of Naboo Two-Pack

Qui-Gon Jinn and Queen Amidala, 2000, Entertainment Earth exclusive

MNP $22   MIP $60

THE PHANTOM MENACE

Anakin Skywalker, w/Theed Hangar Droid, 2000

MNP $4   MIP $10

Aurra Sing, 2000

MNP $10   MIP $20

Battle Droid Commander w/Electrobinoculars, 1999

MNP $6   MIP $12

Boss Nass, 2000

MNP $6   MIP $12

Mace Windu w/Lightsaber, 1999

MNP $6   MIP $12

Qui-Gon Jimm w/Tatooine Poncho, 1999

MNP $4   MIP $10

R2-D2, 1998, Wal-Mart exclusive

MNP $4   MIP $8

Sebulba, w/Chubas, 2000

MNP $5   MIP $10

TC-14 Protocol Droid, Electronic, 1999, KayBee exclusive

MNP $6   MIP $12

THE PHANTOM MENACE Queen Amidala Collection

Padme, Beautiful Braids, 2000

MNP $4   MIP $10

(KP Photo)

Queen Amidala, Hidden Majesty, 1999

MNP $4   MIP $8

Queen Amidala, Royal Elegance, 1999

MNP $4   MIP $8

Queen Amidala, Ultimate Hair, 1999
MNP $4   MIP $8

THE PHANTOM MENACE
Queen Amidala
Collection, 1999 Portrait
Edition

(KP Photo)

Queen Amidala, Black Travel Dress, 1999
MNP $4   MIP $12

Queen Amidala, Red Senate Gown, 1999
MNP $4   MIP $12

THE PHANTOM MENACE
Queen Amidala
Collection, 2000 Portrait
Edition

Queen Amidala, Return to Naboo, 2000
MNP $8   MIP $15

SAGA

(KP Photo)

Anakin Skywalker, 2002, in black robe, includes lightsaber
MNP $5   MIP $10

Anakin Skywalker, Removable Arm, 2003, w/two lightsabers and robotic arm
MNP $6   MIP $12

AT-ST Driver, 2002
MNP $6   MIP $12

Ben Kenobi, A New Hope, 2003
MNP $5   MIP $10

Biker Scout, Battle of Endor, 2003
MNP $8   MIP $16

Clone Commander, Yellow, 2002, KB Toys exclusive
MNP $7   MIP $15

Clone Trooper, 2002, includes blaster rifle
MNP $7   MIP $15

Clone Trooper, Red, 2002, KB Toys exclusive
MNP $7   MIP $15

Count Dooku, 2002
MNP $8   MIP $15

Dengar, 2003
MNP $8   MIP $14

Electronic Jango Fett, 2002
MNP $14   MIP $25

Electronic Obi-Wan Kenobi, 2002
MNP $4   MIP $10

Gammorean Guard, 2003, KB Toys exclusive
MNP $10   MIP $22

Garindan, Long Snoot, 2003
MNP $6   MIP $14

Geonosian Warrior, 2002
MNP $5   MIP $12

Han Solo, w/Taun Taun
MNP $15   MIP $38

Han Solo, 2003
MNP $5   MIP $10

Imperial Officer, 2003
MNP $6   MIP $12

Jango Fett, 2002, deluxe set w/extra accessories
MNP $22   MIP $40

Jawas, 2003, two-pack
MNP $8   MIP $14

Ki-Adi-Mundi, 2002, Star Wars Fan Club exclusive
MNP $10   MIP $22

Lando Calrissian, Skiff Guard, 2003
MNP $7   MIP $14

Leia as Boushh w/Han Solo in Carbonite, 2003, TRU exclusive
MNP $15   MIP $30

Logray & Paploo, Battle of Endor, 2003
MNP $12   MIP $20

Luke Skywalker w/Taun Taun, 2002, Hoth scene, large scale, TRU exclusive
MNP $25   MIP $50

(KP Photo, Karen O'Brien collection)

Luke Skywalker, Jedi Knight, 2003, w/handcuffs and green lightsaber
MNP $6   MIP $10

Mace Windu, Jedi Master, 2002, in light tan cloak, includes lightsaber, TRU exclusive
MNP $6   MIP $10

Obi-Wan Kenobi, 2002, includes lightsaber
MNP $8   MIP $20

(KP Photo, Karen O'Brien collection)

Padme Amidala, 2002
MNP $6   MIP $12

Plo Koon, 2003, Star Wars Fan Club exclusive
MNP $12   MIP $20

Princess Leia on Speeder Bike, Target exclusive
MNP $15   MIP $30

Super Battle Droid, 2002
MNP $7   MIP $12

Yoda, Jedi Master, 2003,
w/hoverchair, green lightsaber, belt
MNP $8   **MIP $15**

Zam Wessell, 2002
MNP $5   **MIP $10**

(KP Photo, Karen O'Brien collection)

Zuckuss, 2003
MNP $6   **MIP $14**

ORIGINAL TRILOGY COLLECTION

Boba Fett, 2004, blue or gray jumpsuit
variations, Model No. 85232
MNP $7   **MIP $15**

Luke Skywalker, 2004, w/lightsaber,
articulated, Model No. 85231
MNP $7   **MIP $15**

Stormtrooper, 2004, w/blaster,
armor, Model No. 85233
MNP $7   **MIP $15**

REVENGE OF THE SITH

Barriss Offee, 2005, lightsaber
MNP $7   **MIP $15**

Chewbacca, 2005, KB Toys Exclusive
MNP $7   **MIP $15**

Clone Trooper, 2005, blaster
MNP $7   **MIP $15**

Darth Sidious, 2005, lightsaber, cloak
w/hood
MNP $7   **MIP $15**

General Grievous, 2005, four
lightsabers, cloak
MNP $24   **MIP $40**

Shaak Ti, 2005, lightsaber
MNP $7   **MIP $15**

Action Figures, 6"

UNLEASHED

Aayla Secura, 2004, EpII:AotC
MNP $6   **MIP $12**

Anakin Skywalker, 2002, EpII:AotC,
two lightsabers
MNP $8   **MIP $15**

Anakin Skywalker, 2005, EpIII:RotS,
Mustafar base, lava
MNP $6   **MIP $12**

Asajj Ventress, 2005, two red
lightsabers
MNP $6   **MIP $12**

Aurra Sing, 2005, bonus figure
MNP $6   **MIP $12**

Boba Fett, 2003, RotJ
MNP $10   **MIP $20**

Bossk, 2004, ESB
MNP $6   **MIP $12**

Chewbacca, 2004, Star Wars
MNP $8   **MIP $15**

Chewbacca, 2006, EpIII:RotS, shield,
blaster
MNP $6   **MIP $12**

Clone Trooper, 2004, EpII:AotC, red
MNP $6   **MIP $12**

Clone Trooper, 2004, EpII:AotC, white
MNP $6   **MIP $12**

(KP Photo, Brian Brogaard collection)

Darth Maul, 2002, EpI:TPM
MNP $8   **MIP $15**

Darth Sidious w/Sith Lightning, 2003,
RotJ
MNP $6   **MIP $12**

Darth Tyranus, 2002, EpII:AotC
MNP $6   **MIP $12**

Darth Vader, 2005, Best Buy exclusive,
repaint of 2005 RotJ model
MNP $6   **MIP $12**

Darth Vader, 2005, RotJ, leaping
down stairs
MNP $6   **MIP $12**

Darth Vader, w/Mask, 2002, ESB:
"I…am your father."
MNP $6   **MIP $12**

Darth Vader, w/out Mask, 2003, RotJ
MNP $6   **MIP $12**

General Grievous, 2005, EpIII:RotS,
two lightsabers, base
MNP $8   **MIP $15**

(KP Photo, Karen O'Brien collection)

Han Solo, 2003, Star Wars, running
up ramp
MNP $12   **MIP $22**

Han Solo Stormtrooper, 2006, Star
Wars
MNP $8   **MIP $15**

Jango and Boba Fett, 2002, EpII:AotC
MNP $9   **MIP $18**

(KP Photo, Karen O'Brien collection)

Luke Skywalker, 2003, RotJ outfit
MNP $8   **MIP $18**

Luke Skywalker, 2004, ESB, X-Wing
Pilot
MNP $6   **MIP $12**

Mace Windu, 2002, EpII:AotC
MNP $6   MIP $12

Obi-Wan Kenobi, 2003, EpII:AotC
MNP $6   MIP $12

Obi-Wan Kenobi, 2005, EpIII:RotS, Mustafar base, lava
MNP $6   MIP $12

Padme Amidala, 2002, two versions
MNP $12   MIP $30

Princess Leia, 2003, RotJ
MNP $12   MIP $42

Shock Trooper, 2006, EpIII:RotS, Clone Trooper on Mustafar
MNP $6   MIP $12

Stormtrooper, 2005, Star Wars
MNP $8   MIP $18

Tusken Raider, 2004, Star Wars
MNP $10   MIP $16

(KP Photo, Brian Brogaard collection)

Yoda, 2003, EpII:AotC
MNP $7   MIP $15

Yoda vs. Sidious, 2005, EpIII:RotS
MNP $6   MIP $12

Battle Packs

Battle Above the Sarlacc, 2006, w/Boba Fett, Han Solo, Lando Calrissian (Skiff Guard), Luke Skywalker, and Weequay
MNP $10   MIP $15

Battle of Geonosis, 2007, w/Aayla Secura, Count Dooku, Jango Fett, Obi-Wan Kenobi, and a Super Battle Droid
MNP $10   MIP $16

Battle of Mygeeto, 2007, w/Clone Commander Bacara, Galactic Marine, Ki-Adi-Mundi, Super Battle Droid, and Tri-Droid
MNP $18   MIP $35

Betrayal on Bespin, 2007, w/Boba Fett, Chewbacca, Darth Vader, Han Solo, and Princess Leia
MNP $12   MIP $22

Capture of Tantive IV, 2007, w/Darth Vader, two Rebel Soldiers, two Stormtroopers
MNP $10   MIP $15

Clone Attack on Coruscant, 2007, w/four Clone Troopers, and one Clone Trooper Commander
MNP $17   MIP $28

Droid Factory Capture, 2007, w/Anakin Skywalker, C-3PO, Destroyer Droid, Jango Fett, and R2-D2
MNP $12   MIP $19

Jedi Training on Dagobah, 2007, w/Luke Skywalker, R2-D2, Spirit of Obi-Wan Kenobi, Spirit of Darth Vader, and Yoda
MNP $10   MIP $22

Jedi vs. Darth Sidious, 2006, w/Agen Kolar, Darth Sidious, Kit Fisto, Mace Windu, and Saesee Tiin
MNP $10   MIP $15

Jedi vs. Darth Sidious, 2007, w/Agen Kolar, Darth Sidious, Kit Fisto, Mace Windu, and Saesee Tiin
MNP $10   MIP $22

Jedi vs. Sith, 2007, w/Anakin Skywalker, Assaj Ventress, General Grievous, Obi-Wan Kenobi, and Yoda
MNP $10   MIP $22

Mace Windu's Attack Battalion (Target Exclusive), 2006, w/Mace Windu, Clone Commander, and three Clone Troopers
MNP $7   MIP $12

Sith Lord Attack, 2006, w/Battle Droid, Battle Droid Security, Darth Maul, Obi-Wan Kenobi, and Qui-Gon Jinn
MNP $10   MIP $15

Skirmish in the Senate (Target Exclusive), 2006, w/Emperor Palpatine, senate pod, two Shock Troopers, and Yoda
MNP $10   MIP $15

The Hunt for Grievous, 2007, w/Captain Fordo, Heavy Gunner

Clone Trooper, and three Clone Troopers
MNP $14   MIP $25

The Hunt for Grievous (Toys R Us Exclusive, 2006, w/Captain Fordo, three Clone Troopers, and one Heavy Gunner Clone Trooper
MNP $10   MIP $20

SAGA LEGENDS, 2008-PRESENT

Clone Attack on Coruscant, 2008, w/four Clone Troopers and one Clone Commander
MNP $12   MIP $22

Hoth Recon Patrol, 2008, w/Chewbacca, Han Solo, Imperial Probe Droid, K-3PO, and R5-M2
MNP $10   MIP $20

Hoth Speeder Bike Patrol, 2008, w/two Biker Scouts and two Speeder Bike vehicles
MNP $14   MIP $22

Jedi Training on Dagobah, 2008, w/Luke Skywalker, R2-D2, Spirit of Obi-Wan Kenobi, Spirit of Darth Vader, and Yoda
MNP $8   MIP $14

Jedi vs. Darth Sidious, 2008, w/Ager Kolar, Darth Sidious, Kit Fisto, Mace Windu, and Saesee Tiin
MNP $8   MIP $14

Millennium Falcon Passengers, 2008, w/C-3PO, Luke Skywalker, Obi-Wan Kenobi, and R2-D2
MNP $8   MIP $14

Scramble on Yavin, 2009, w/R5-K6, Rebel Ground Crew, a Rebel Transport, and Red Leader
MNP $8   MIP $14

Shield Generator Assault, 2008, w/Han Solo, Imperial Officer, R2-D2, and Rebel Trooper (in Biker Scout disguise)
MNP $8   MIP $14

TARGET EXCLUSIVES

Ambush on Ilum, 2007, w/C-3PO, R2-D2, Padme Amidala, and two Chameleon Droids
MNP $10   MIP $19

ARC-170 Elite Squad, 2007, (Aggressive Reconnaissance starfighter), w/two ARC-170 Troopers, an Astromech Droid, and two Clone Trooper Pilots
MNP $16   MIP $25

AT-RT Assault Squad, 2007, w/two AT-RTs, two AT-RTs Drivers, and a Clone Commander
MNP $16   MIP $25

Attack on Kashyyyk, 2007, w/Darth Vader, two Stormtroopers, and two Wookie Warriors
MNP $10   MIP $19

Battle Rancor w/Felucian Rider and Saddle, 2007, w/"Battle Rancor" and Felucian Warrior
MNP $52   MIP $70

Betrayal at Felucia, 2007, w/Aayla Secura, three Clone Troopers, and Commander Bly
MNP $14   MIP $24

Ultimate: The Battle of Endor, 2007, w/AT-ST vehicle, AT-ST Driver, two Biker Scouts, Chewbacca, Han Solo, two Logs, OOchee, two Speeder Bike vehicles, Stormtrooper, and Wicket W. Warrick
MNP $40   MIP $75

Ultimate: The Battle of Hoth, 2007, w/AT-ST vehicle, AT-ST Driver, Han Solo, Hoth Laser Turret, Luke Skywalker, Rebel Officer, Rebel Trooper, and three Snowtroopers
MNP $35   MIP $70

THE CLONE WARS, 2008-PRESENT

AT-TE Assault Squad, 2008, four Clone Trooper figures and accessories
MNP $12   MIP $22

Battle at B'Omarr Monestary, 2008, Anakin Skywalker, Battle Droid, and two STAPs
MNP $12   MIP $22

Battle of Christophsis, 2008, (Ultimate Battle Pack), Target Exclusive, two Clone Troopers, Two Battle Droids, AAT (Armored Assault Tank), Super Battle Droid, Anakin Skywalker, and an AT-AP
MNP $30   MIP $50

Obi-Wan & 212th Attack Batallion, 2008, Target Exclusive, one Clone Trooper Armor, Obi-Wan Kenobi, four 212th Battalion Clone Troopers
MNP $16   MIP $25

Speeder Bike Recon, 2008, two Clone Troopers and Speeder Bikes
MNP $14   MIP $22

Yoda & Coruscant Guard, 2008, Target Exclusive, four Coruscant Guards and Yoda
MNP $14   MIP $22

TOYS R US EXCLUSIVES

Bantha w/Tusken Raiders, 2007, w/Bantha, Tusken Raider (rider), Tusken Raider (w/Massiff), and Tusken Raider Female (w/child)
MNP $28   MIP $45

Hoth Patrol, 2007, w/Luke Skywalker, Tauntaun, and Wampa
MNP $10   MIP $14

STAP Attack, 2007, w/two Battle Droids, two STAP vehicles, and a Super Battle Droid
MNP $12   MIP $20

WAL-MART EXCLUSIVES

Treachery on Saleucami, 2007, w/Clone Trooper, Commander Neyo, and two BARC Speeders
MNP $12   MIP $22

Carrying Cases

EMPIRE STRIKES BACK

(KP Photo)

Darth Vader, 1982
MNP $10   MIP $50

(KP Photo)

Mini Figure, 1980
MNP $11   MIP $55

ORIGINAL TRILOGY COLLECTION

Darth Vader, 2004, vintage-style w/Boba Fett and Stormtrooper, Model No. 85405
MNP $15   MIP $30

RETURN OF THE JEDI

C-3PO, 1983
MNP $12   MIP $40

Darth Vader (w/Three Figs), 1983, w/three figures
MNP $20   MIP $300

Laser Rifle, 1984
MNP $12   MIP $38

REVENGE OF THE SITH

Darth Vader, 2005, Wal-Mart Exclusive; Anakin Skywalker and Clone Trooper included, holds 30 figures, Model No. 85646
MNP $12   MIP $22

STAR WARS

24-Figure, 1978
MNP $18   MIP $55

Coins

2-1B, 1985
MNP $105   MIP n/a

63rd Coin, Lightsaber, 1985
MNP $1200   MIP n/a

Amanaman, 1985
MNP $12   MIP n/a

Anakin Skywalker, 1985
MNP $75   MIP n/a

AT-AT, 1985
MNP $100   MIP n/a

AT-ST Driver, 1985
MNP $15   MIP n/a

A-Wing Pilot, 1985
MNP $25   MIP n/a

Barada, 1985
MNP $12   MIP n/a

Bib Fortuna, 1985
MNP $125   MIP n/a

Biker Scout, 1985
MNP $20   MIP n/a

Boba Fett, 1985
MNP $225   MIP n/a

B-Wing Pilot, 1985
MNP $20   MIP n/a

C-3PO, 1985
    MNP $20   MIP n/a

Chewbacca, 1985
    MNP $20   MIP n/a

Chief Chirpa, 1985
    MNP $50   MIP n/a

Creatures, 1985
    MNP $125   MIP n/a

Darth Vader, 1985
    MNP $35   MIP n/a

Droids, 1985
    MNP $125   MIP n/a

Emperor, 1985
    MNP $30   MIP n/a

Emperor's Royal Guard, 1985
    MNP $80   MIP n/a

EV-9D9, 1985
    MNP $12   MIP n/a

FX-7, 1985
    MNP $190   MIP n/a

Gamorrean Guard, 1985
    MNP $50   MIP n/a

Greedo, 1985
    MNP $190   MIP n/a

Han Hoth, 1985
    MNP $100   MIP n/a

Han in Carbonite, 1985
    MNP $15   MIP n/a

Han Original, 1985
    MNP $190   MIP n/a

Han Rebel (trenchcoat), 1985
    MNP $15   MIP n/a

Hoth Stormtrooper, 1985
    MNP $250   MIP n/a

Imperial Commander, 1985
    MNP $70   MIP n/a

Imperial Dignitary, 1985
    MNP $12   MIP n/a

Imperial Gunner, 1985
    MNP $12   MIP n/a

Jawas, 1985
    MNP $20   MIP n/a

Lando General, 1985
    MNP $12   MIP n/a

Lando w/Cloud City, 1985
    MNP $80   MIP n/a

Logray, 1985
    MNP $50   MIP n/a

Luke Jedi, 1985
    MNP $20   MIP n/a

Luke on Dagobah, 1985
    MNP $150   MIP n/a

Luke Original, 1985
    MNP $100   MIP n/a

Luke Poncho, 1985
    MNP $15   MIP n/a

Luke Stormtrooper, 1985
    MNP $15   MIP n/a

Luke w/Taun Taun, 1985
    MNP $100   MIP n/a

Luke X-Wing, 1985
    MNP $20   MIP n/a

Luke X-Wing, small, 1985
    MNP $60   MIP n/a

Lumat, 1985
    MNP $12   MIP n/a

Millennium Falcon, 1985
    MNP $100   MIP n/a

Obi-Wan Kenobi, 1985
    MNP $30   MIP n/a

Paploo, 1985
    MNP $12   MIP n/a

Princess Leia Rebel Leader (poncho), 1985
    MNP $12   MIP n/a

Princess Leia, Boushh, 1985
    MNP $210   MIP n/a

Princess Leia, Original, 1985
    MNP $115   MIP n/a

R2-D2 Pop-Up Lightsaber, 1985
    MNP $20   MIP n/a

Romba, 1985
    MNP $12   MIP n/a

Sail Skiff, 1985
    MNP $700   MIP n/a

Star Destroyer Commander, 1985
    MNP $70   MIP n/a

Stormtrooper, 1985
    MNP $25   MIP n/a

Teebo, 1985
    MNP $15   MIP n/a

TIE Fighter Pilot, 1985
    MNP $65   MIP n/a

Tusken Raider, 1985
    MNP $170   MIP n/a

Warok, 1985
    MNP $12   MIP n/a

Wicket, 1985
    MNP $12   MIP n/a

Yak Face, 1985
    MNP $110   MIP n/a

Yoda, 1985
    MNP $30   MIP n/a

Zuckuss, 1985
    MNP $210   MIP n/a

Collector Coins

2007 Vintage Coin Set, 2007, w/coins for Bossk (Bounty Hunter), Han Solo (Rebel Leader), IG-88 (Bounty Hunter), Luke Skywalker (Jedi Apprentice), Princess Leia (Rebel General), Snowtrooper (Galactic Empire), and the 2007 Toy Fair
    MNP $8   MIP $14

Toy Fair Exclusive Collector Coin, 2007, from the 2007 International Toy Fair (the value of this toy is in its exclusive packaging)
    MNP $3   MIP $20

Comic Packs

DARK HORSE COMICS

Anakin Skywalker & Assassin Droid, 2007, (Republic), #11
    MNP $5   MIP $10

A'sharad Hett & The Dark Woman, 2007, (Clone Wars), #08
    MNP $5   MIP $10

Baron Fel & Derek "Hobbie" Klivian, 2007, (X-Wing Rogue Squadron), #12
    MNP $7   MIP $14

Clone Commando & Super Battle Droid, 2007, (Star Wars Tales), #16
    MNP $12   MIP $20

Koffi Arana & Bultar Swan, 2007, (Purge), #13
    MNP $5   MIP $10

Leia Organa & Darth Vader, 2007, (Infinites), #09
    MNP $5   MIP $10

Lt. Jundland & Deena Shan, 2007, (Empire), #14
    MNP $5   MIP $10

Mara Jade & Luke Skywalker, 2007, (Heir to the Empire), #10
    MNP $5   MIP $10

Mouse & Basso in Disguise, 2007, (Empire), #15
    MNP $5   MIP $10

Obi-Wan Kenobi & ARC Trooper Alpha, 2007, (Republic), #07
    MNP $5   MIP $10

Quinlan Vos & Vilmarh Grahrk, 2007, (Republic), #05
    MNP $5   MIP $10

INTERNET EXCLUSIVE

Carnor Jax & Kir Kanos, 2007, (Crimson Empire), #01
    MNP $10   MIP $16

MARVEL COMICS

Chewbacca & Han Solo, 2007, (Marvel), #04
    MNP $5   MIP $10

MARVEL COMICS

Darth Vader & Rebel Officer, 2007, (Marvel), #02
MNP $5 MIP $10

Governor Tarkin & Stormtrooper, 2007, (Marvel), #03
MNP $5 MIP $10

Luke Skywalker & R2-D2, 2007, (Marvel), #06
MNP $5 MIP $10

WAL-MART EXCLUSIVES

Boba Fett & RA-7 Droid, 2007, (Marvel)
MNP $8 MIP $12

Commander Keller & Galactic Marine, 2007, (Dark Horse)
MNP $8 MIP $12

Count Dooku & Anakin Skywalker, 2007, (Dark Horse)
MNP $8 MIP $10

Kashyyyk Trooper & Wookie Warrior, 2007, (Dark Horse)
MNP $8 MIP $16

Lando Calrissian & Stormtrooper, 2007, (Marvel)
MNP $5 MIP $10

Obi-Wan Kenobi & Bail Organa, 2007, (Dark Horse), w/Luke and Leia
MNP $15 MIP $26

Commemorative DVD Collections

Commemorative Episode IV DVD Collection (Wal-Mart Exclusive), 2006, w/Darth Vader, Luke Skywalker, and Obi-Wan Kenobi
MNP $4 MIP $10

Commemorative Episode V DVD Collection (Wal-Mart Exclusive), 2006, w/Chewbacca, Han Solo, and Stormtrooper
MNP $4 MIP $10

Commemorative Episode VI DVD Collection (Wal-Mart Exclusive), 2006, w/C-3PO, Emperor Palpatine, Luke Skywalker, and R2-D2
MNP $4 MIP $10

Commemorative Tin Collections

MULTI-PACKS

Episode I, 2007, (The Phantom Menace), w/Darth Maul, Obi-Wan Kenobi, Qui Gon Jinn, and R2-R9
MNP $10 MIP $22

Episode II, 2007, (K-Mart Exclusive), w/Mace Windu, Oppo Rancisis, Sora Bulq, and Zam Wesell
MNP $20 MIP $40

Episode II, 2007, (Attack of the Clones), w/Anakin Skywalker, Count Dooku, Jango Fett, and Clone Trooper
MNP $10 MIP $22

Episode III, 2007, (K-Mart Exclusive), w/Anakin Skywalker, Clone Commander Cody, Clone Pilot, General Grievous
MNP $12 MIP $25

Episode III, 2007, (Revenge of the Sith), w/Anakin Skywalker, AT-RT Driver, Mace Windu, and Yoda
MNP $10 MIP $22

Episode IV, 2007, (A New Hope), w/C-3PO, Darth Vader, Princess Leia, and Sandtrooper
MNP $10 MIP $22

Episode V, 2007, (The Empire Strikes Back), w/Chewbacca, Han Solo, Luke Skywalker, and Snowtrooper
MNP $10 MIP $22

Episode VI, 2007, (K-Mart Exclusive), w/Biker Scout, Darth Vader, Death Star Gunner, R5-J2
MNP $10 MIP $22

Episode VI, 2007, (Return of the Jedi), w/Darth Vader, Princess Leia, Rebel Commando, and Biker Scout
MNP $10 MIP $22

Figrin D'an and the Modal Nodes, 2007, (Wal-Mart Exclusive), w/five of seven character names (as there are seven members of the band): Figrin D'an, Doikk Na'ts, Ickabel G'ont, Tedn Dahai, Tech Mo'r, Nalan Cheel, or Lirin Car'n)
MNP $10 MIP $20

Creatures

STAR WARS

Patrol Dewback, 1978
MNP $20 MIP $85

EMPIRE STRIKES BACK

Hoth Wampa, 1980
MNP $17 MIP $37

(KP Photo)

Tauntaun, Solid Belly, 1980
MNP $15 MIP $40

Tauntaun, Split Belly, 1980
MNP $22 MIP $65

RETURN OF THE JEDI

Rancor, 1983
MNP $30 MIP $85

THE PHANTOM MENACE

(KP Photo)

Kaadu w/Jar Jar Binks, 1999
MNP $2 MIP $5

SAGA

Acklay, Arena Battle Beast, 2002
MNP $15 MIP $30

Reek, Arena Battle Beast, 2002
MNP $15 MIP $30

REVENGE OF THE SITH

Boga and Obi-Wan Kenobi, 2005, lizard rears its front legs, opens its mouth and shakes head
MNP $12 MIP $30

Evolutions (Action Figure Three-Packs)

Anakin Skywalker to Darth Vader, 2008, w/Anakin Skywalker (Jedi Hero), Anakin Skywalker (Clone Wars Commander), and Darth Vader (Evil Sith Lord) figures

MNP $8   MIP $15

Clone Trooper to Stormtrooper, 2008, w/Clone Trooper (Clone Wars), Clone Trooper (The Fall of the Republic), and Sandtrooper (The Rebellion) figures

MNP $8   MIP $15

The Fett Legacy, 2008, w/Mandalore (Knights of the Old Republic), Jango Fett (Attack of the Clones), and Boba Fett (The Empire Strikes Back), figures

MNP $13   MIP $22

The Jedi Legacy, 2008, w/Qui-Gonn (The Phantom Menace), Bultar Swan (Attack of the Clones), and Luke Skywalker (New Jedi Order) figures

MNP $8   MIP $15

The Sith, 2008, w/Darth Maul (The Sith Return), Count Dooku (The Clone Wars), and Emperor Palpatine (The Republic Falls) figures

MNP $8   MIP $15

The Sith Legacy, 2008, w/Darth Bane (The Old Republic), Darth Nihilus (Knights of the Old Republic), and Darth Maul (The Phantom Menace) figures

MNP $14   MIP $26

Vader's Secret Apprentice, 2008, w/Secret Apprentice, Sith Lord, and Jedi Knight figures

MNP $12   MIP $22

Exclusive Figures

THE CLONE WARS, 2008-PRESENT
Mail-Away

Captain Rex, 2008, accessories and display package

MNP $8   MIP $20

THE CLONE WARS, 2008-PRESENT
San Diego Comic-Con/StarWarsShop.com

Clone Trooper (Senate Security), 2008, accessories

MNP $7   MIP $12

THE CLONE WARS, 2008-PRESENT
Target

Commander Fox, 2008, accessories

MNP $14   MIP $30

THE CLONE WARS, 2008-PRESENT
Toys R Us

Holographic General Grievous, 2008, accessories

MNP $4   MIP $8

THE CLONE WARS, 2008-PRESENT
Wal-Mart

Clone Trooper (501st Legion), 2008, accessories

MNP $4   MIP $8

Exclusive Vehicles

SAGA LEGENDS, 2008-PRESENT

A-Wing Starfighter, 2008, (Wal-Mart Exclusive), w/Green Leader (Arvel Crynyd) figure

MNP $15   MIP $30

Dagger Squadron B-Wing Fighter, 2008, (Toys R Us Exclusive), w/360 degree rotating cockpit and Lieutenant Pollard figure

MNP $15   MIP $30

Ecliptic Evader TIE Fighter, 2008, (Previews Exclusive), w/Hobbie Klivian figure

MNP $20   MIP $50

Exclusives

CELEBRATION IV/ CELEBRATION EUROPE

Concept Luke Skywalker, 2007, blaster, lightsaber hilt, lightsaber blade, backpack w/mask, coin

MNP $12   MIP $22

CELEBRATIONS IV/ CELEBRATION EUROPE

Concept R2-D2 & C-3PO, 2007, w/coin

MNP $10   MIP $15

GAMESTOP EXCLUSIVE

Stormtrooper Commander, 2008, blaster, helmet, display stand

MNP $16   MIP $30

MULTI-PACKS

I Am Your Father's Day Gift Pack, 2007, (Wal-Mart Exclusive), w/Darth Vader and Luke Skywalker

MNP $8   MIP $15

Max Rebo Band: Jabba's Entertainers, 2007, (Wal-Mart Exclusive), w/Greeata, Joh Yowza, Lyn Me, Rappertunie, and Rystall

MNP $15   MIP $30

Max Rebo Band: Jabba's Musicians, 2007, (Wal-Mart Exclusive), w/Barquin D'an, Doda Bodonawieedo, Droopy McCool, Max Rebo, and Sy Snootles

MNP $15   MIP $30

Republic Elite Forces: Mandalorians & Clone Troopers, 2007, (Entertainment Earth Exclusive), w/Dred Priest, Isabet Reau, Mij Gilamar, two ARC Troopers, and two Clone Troopers

MNP $30   MIP $65

Republic Elite Forces: Mandalorians & Omega Squad, 2007, (Entertainment Earth Exclusive), w/Llats Ward, Rav Bralor, B'Arin Ampa, and four members of Omega Squad

MNP $38   MIP $75

Star Wars: Battlefront II - Clone Pack, 2007, (Previews Exclusive), w/Clone Engineer, Clone Sharpshooter, Clone Trooper, Galactic Marine, Heavy Trooper, and Jet Trooper

MNP $15   MIP $30

Star Wars: Battlefront II - Droid Pack, 2007, (Previews Exclusive), w/Ammunition Droid, Assassin Battle Droid, Assault Battle Droid, Engineer Battle Droid, Destroyer Droid, Magnaguard Droid, Super Battle Droid

MNP $12   MIP $24

501st Stormtrooper, 2007, (San Diego Comic Con Exclusive)

MNP $6   MIP $12

Demise of General Grievous, (Target Exclusive)

MNP $5   MIP $10

Early Bird (Figures) Kit (Wal-Mart Exclusive), 2005, w/Chewbacca, Luke Skywalker, Princess Leia, and R2-D2

MNP $8   MIP $15

Early Bird Certificate Package (Wal-Mart Exclusive), 2005, w/certificate, display stand, envelope, membership cards (two), stickers

MNP $5   MIP $10

George Lucas; Stormtrooper, (Ultimate Galactic Hunt mail away)

MNP $12   MIP $20

Separation of the Twins; Leia Organa w/Bail Organa, (Wal-Mart Exclusive)

MNP $6   MIP $10

Separation of the Twins; Luke Skywalker w/Obi-Wan Kenobi, (Wal-Mart Exclusive)
MNP $6   MIP $10

Shadow Stormtrooper, (StarWarsShop.com Exclusive)
MNP $6   MIP $14

SAGA LEGENDS, 2008-PRESENT

Disturbance at the Lars Homestead, 2009, (Toys R Us Exclusive), w/Aunt Beru Lars, a Homestead playset w/removalbe roof, Moisture Vaporator, Stormtrooper, Uncle Own Lars, Womp Rat figure
MNP $28   MIP $52

Pit of Carkoon, 2008, (Ultimate Battle Pack; Target Exclusive), w/Boba Fett, Han Solo, Lando Calrissian, Luke Skywalker, the Sarlacc Monster, the Sarlacc Pit, and Skiff vehicle, and Weequay
MNP $38   MIP $70

SAN DIEGO COMIC-CON

Concept Obi-Wan Kenobi & Yoda, 2007, lightsaber, lightsaber hilt, stick, coin
MNP $12   MIP $28

R2-KT, 2007, (Shared Exclusive)
MNP $18   MIP $35

Shadow Scout w/Speeder Bike, 2007, w/blaster and Speeder Bike vehicle
MNP $14   MIP $26

STAR WARS SHOP

Concept General Grievous, 2007, blaster, shield, cape, coin
MNP $10   MIP $20

Shadow Troopers (Jedi-Con 2008), 2007, two blasters, two scout blasters, two helmets, two shoulder pads, and two antennae
MNP $10   MIP $16

TARGET EXCLUSIVES Order 66, Series 1 (2007)

Anakin Skywalker & Airborne Trooper, 2007, #5 of 6
MNP $7   MIP $10

Darth Vader & Commander Bow, 2007, #3 of 6
MNP $8   MIP $12

Emperor Palpatine & Commander Thire, 2007, #1 of 6
MNP $8   MIP $12

Mace Windu & Galactic Marine, 2007, #2 of 6
MNP $7   MIP $10

Obi-Wan Kenobi & AT-RT Driver, 2007, #4 of 6
MNP $7   MIP $10

Yoda & Kashyyyk Trooper, 2007, #6 of 6
MNP $7   MIP $10

TARGET EXCLUSIVES Order 66, Series 2 (2008)

Anakin Skywalker & ARC Trooper, 2008, #2 of 6
MNP $9   MIP $15

Emperor Palpatine & Commander Vill, 2008, #4 of 6
MNP $9   MIP $15

Luminari Unduli & AT-RT Driver, 2008, #5 of 6
MNP $7   MIP $12

Master Sev & ARC Trooper, 2008, #6 of 6
MNP $7   MIP $12

Obi-Wan Kenobi & ARC Trooper Commander, 2008, #1 of 6
MNP $9   MIP $15

Tsui Choi & BARC Trooper, 2008, #3 of 6
MNP $8   MIP $13

WAL-MART

Darth Vader & Incinerator Troopers, 2008, (Wal-Mart), Darth Vader w/two Incinerator (Storm) Troopers
MNP $16   MIP $30

Emperor Palpatine & Shadow Stormtroopers, 2008, (Wal-Mart), Emperor Palpatine w/two Shadow Stormtroopers
MNP $16   MIP $30

K-Mart

SAGA LEGENDS, 2008-PRESENT

Legends of the Saga, 2008, w/Boba Fett, Darth Maul, Darth Vader, Luke Skywalker, and Obi-Wan Kenobi
MNP $8   MIP $16

LEGO Sets

ATTACK OF THE CLONES

Bounty Hunter Pursuit w/Obi-Wan Kenobi, Anakin Skywalker, Zam Wessell, 2002, 7133
MNP $25   MIP $40

Jango Fett, 2002, 8011
MNP $25   MIP $50

Jango Fett's Slave I w/Jango Fett, Boba Fett, 2002, 7153
MNP $70   MIP $160

(KP Photo)

Jedi Duel w/Yoda, Count Dooku, 2002, 7103
MNP $8   MIP $20

Jedi Starfighter w/Obi-Wan Kenobi, R4-P17, 2002, 7143
MNP $12   MIP $30

Republic Gunship w/Jedi Clone Troopers, Battle Droids, Destroyer Droids, 2002, 7163
MNP $95   MIP $200

Super Battle Droid, 2002, 8012
MNP $10   MIP $25

Tusken Raider Encounter w/Anakin Skywalker, two Tusken Raiders, 2002, 7113
MNP $12   MIP $25

EMPIRE STRIKES BACK Mini-Figure Sets

Luke Skywalker, Han Solo, Boba Fett, 2002, 3341
MNP $15   MIP $30

EMPIRE STRIKES BACK

Boba Fett's Slave I, 2002, 7144
MNP $10   MIP $30

Twin-Pod Cloud Car w/Lobot, 1980, 7119
MNP $10   MIP $30

EMPIRE STRIKES BACK Ultimate Collectors Series

Yoda, 1980, 7194
MNP $160   MIP $275

RETURN OF THE JEDI Mini-Figure Sets

Chewbacca, Two Biker Scouts, 3342
MNP $14   MIP $22

RETURN OF THE JEDI

B-Wing at Rebel Control Center w/pilot, droid, mechanic, 7180
MNP $27   MIP $45

Desert Skiff w/Luke Skywalker, Han Solo, 7104
MNP $8   MIP $20

Ewok Attack w/Biker Scout, Stormtrooper, two Ewoks, 7139
MNP $14   MIP $20

Final Duel I w/Emperor, Darth Vader, 7200
MNP $16   MIP $40

Final Duel II w/Luke Skywalker, Imperial Officer, Stormtrooper, 7201
MNP $8   MIP $15

Imperial AT-ST w/Chewbacca, 7127
MNP $15   MIP $30

Imperial Shuttle w/Emperor, Pilot, two Royal Guards, 7166
MNP $45   MIP $80

REVENGE OF THE SITH

ARC-170 Starfighter, 2005, 7259, 396 pieces
MNP $40   MIP $75

Clone Scout Walker, 2005, 7250, 108 pieces, w/Clone Trooper
MNP $28   MIP $42

Clone Turbo Tank, 2005, 7261
MNP $110   MIP $200

Darth Vader Transformation, 2005, 7251, 53 pieces
MNP $14   MIP $30

Droid Tri-Fighter, 2005, 7252, 148 pieces, Buzz Droid
MNP $12   MIP $30

Episode III Collector's Set, 2005, 65771
MNP $80   MIP $105

General Grievous Chase, 2005, 7255, 111 pieces, Grievous on Wheel Bike, Obi-Wan on Boga
MNP $45   MIP $90

STAR WARS
Mini-Figure Sets

Emperor Palpatine, Darth Maul, Darth Vader, 3340
MNP $25   MIP $40

STAR WARS

Darth Vader, 8010
MNP $30   MIP $60

Droid Escape w/R2-D2, C-3PO, 7106
MNP $12   MIP $20

(KP Photo)

Landspeeder w/Luke Skywalker, Obi-Wan Kenobi, 1999, 7110
MNP $15   MIP $25

Millennium Falcon w/Han Solo, Leia, Luke, Chewbacca, R2-D2, C-3PO, 7190
MNP $50   MIP $150

R2-D2, 8009
MNP $12   MIP $35

Rebel Blockade Runner - Tantive IV Corellian Corvette, 10019
MNP $275   MIP $475

TIE Figher w/Pilot, Stormtrooper, 7146
MNP $18   MIP $40

TIE Interceptor, 7181
MNP $250   MIP $675

(LEGO Photo)

X-Wing Fighter, 7140
MNP $30   MIP $50

STAR WARS
Technic

C-3PO, 8007
MNP $25   MIP $70

Stormtrooper, 8008
MNP $25   MIP $50

THE PHANTOM MENACE
Mini-Figure Sets

Command Officer, two Battle Droids, 3343
MNP $8   MIP $13

THE PHANTOM MENACE

Darth Maul (bust), 10018
MNP $300   MIP $550

Droid Fighter, 7111
MNP $8   MIP $26

Flash Speeder w/Royal Naboo Security Force, 7121
MNP $15   MIP $38

Gungan Patrol w/Jar Jar Binks, Gungan Warrior, 7115
MNP $14   MIP $22

Gungan Sub w/Qui-Gon Jinn, Obi-Wan Kenobi, Jar Jar Binks, 1999, 7161
MNP $30   MIP $60

Jedi Defense I w/Obi-Wan Kenobi, two Destroyer Droids, 7203
MNP $12   MIP $24

Jedi Defense II w/Qui-Gon Jinn, two Battle Droids, 7204
MNP $13   MIP $25

Lightsaber Duel w/Qui-Gon Jinn, Darth Maul, 1999, 7101
MNP $8   MIP $18

Mos Espa Podrace w/Padme, Anakin, R2-D2, Qui-Gon, Jar Jar, Sebulba, Gasgano, 7171
MNP $45   MIP $100

(KP Photo)

Naboo Fighter w/Anakin Skywalker, two Battle Droids, 1999, 7141
MNP $20   MIP $40

(KP Photo)

Naboo Swamp w/Qui-Gon Jinn, Jar Jar Binks, two Battle Droids, 1999, 7121
MNP $40   MIP $20

Podracer, 1999, 7131
MNP $15   MIP $30

Sith Infiltrator w/Darth Maul, 7151
MNP $20   MIP $50

Trade Federation MTT, 7184
MNP $60   MIP $100

THE PHANTOM MENACE
Technic

Battle Droid, 8001
MNP $15   MIP $30

Destroyer Droid, 8002
MNP $45   MIP $155

Pit Droid, 8000
MNP $14   MIP $40

Micro Collection

EMPIRE STRIKES BACK

Bespin Control Room, 1982
MNP $25   MIP $40

Bespin Freeze Chamber, 1982
MNP $25   MIP $60

Bespin Gantry, 1982
MNP $15   MIP $40

Bespin World, 1982
MNP $58   MIP $100

Death Star Compactor, 1982
MNP $40   MIP $100

Death Star Escape, 1982
MNP $38   MIP $65

Death Star World, 1982
MNP $80   MIP $150

Hoth Generator Attack, 1982
MNP $22   MIP $40

Hoth Ion Cannon, 1982
MNP $17   MIP $50

Hoth Turret Defense, 1982
MNP $19   MIP $40

Hoth Wampa Cave, 1982
MNP $12   MIP $23

Hoth World, 1982
MNP $60   MIP $120

Imperial TIE Fighter, 1982
MNP $20   MIP $47

Millennium Falcon, 1982
MNP $55   MIP $165

Snowspeeder, 1982
MNP $42   MIP $130

X-Wing Fighter, 1982
MNP $32   MIP $65

Micro Machines

THE PHANTOM MENACE
Deluxe Action Set

Trade Federation MTT/Naboo
Battlefield Mega Deluxe Action
Set, 1999
MNP $3   MIP $8

THE PHANTOM MENACE
Deluxe Platform Action Set

Theed Palace Assault, 1999
MNP $4   MIP $18

THE PHANTOM MENACE
Deluxe Remote Control

Fambaa, 1999
MNP $4   MIP $18

Trade Federation Tank, 1999
MNP $4   MIP $18

THE PHANTOM MENACE
Die-Cast Vehicle

(KP Photo)

Gian Speeder, 1999, a nicely detailed,
heavy model w/pivoting cannon
and slide-open canopy
MNP $3   MIP $8

Republic Cruiser, 1999
MNP $3   MIP $8

Royal Starship, 1999
MNP $3   MIP $8

Sebulba's Podracer, 1999
MNP $3   MIP $8

Sith Infiltrator, 1999
MNP $3   MIP $8

Trade Federation Battleship, 1999
MNP $3   MIP $8

Trade Federation Droid Fighter,
1999, the wings of this model slide
open into "firing" mode
MNP $3   MIP $8

Trade Federation Tank, 1999
MNP $3   MIP $8

THE PHANTOM MENACE
Inside Action Set

Gungan Sub (Bonto)/Otoh Gunga, 1999
MNP $3   MIP $8

(KP Photo)

Jar Jar Binks/Naboo, 1999
MNP $3   MIP $8

THE PHANTOM MENACE
Mini Scene

Destroyer Droid Ambush, 1999
MNP $3   MIP $8

Generator Core Duel, 1999
MNP $3   MIP $8

THE PHANTOM MENACE

Anakin Skywalker's Podracer w/Figure, 1999
MNP $2 MIP $6

Arch Canyon Adventure, 1999
MNP $2 MIP $6

Battle Droid/Trade Federation Droid Control Ship, 1999
MNP $2 MIP $6

Beggar's Canyon Challenge, 1999
MNP $2 MIP $6

Boonta Eve Challenge Deluxe Podracing Track Set, 1999
MNP $2 MIP $6

Build Your Own Podracer Pack I, 1999
MNP $5 MIP $8

Flash Speeder w/Figure, 1999
MNP $2 MIP $6

Gian Speeder & Theed Palace Sneak Preview Set, 1999
MNP $2 MIP $6

Gungan Sub w/Figure, 1999
MNP $2 MIP $6

Mars Guo's Podracer w/Figure, 1999
MNP $2 MIP $6

Naboo Fighter w/Figure, 1999
MNP $2 MIP $6

Podracer Launchers, 1999
MNP $2 MIP $6

Republic Cruiser w/Figure, 1999
MNP $2 MIP $6

Sebulba's Podracer w/Figure, 1999
MNP $2 MIP $6

Trade Federation Droid Fighter w/Figure, 1999
MNP $2 MIP $6

Trade Federation Landing Ship w/Figure, 1999
MNP $2 MIP $6

Trade Federation MTT w/Figure, 1999
MNP $2 MIP $6

Turbo Blast Podracers, 1999
MNP $2 MIP $6

THE PHANTOM MENACE
Platform Action Set

Galactic Dogfight, 1999
MNP $2 MIP $5

Galactic Senate, 1999
MNP $2 MIP $5

Naboo Temple Ruins, 1999
MNP $2 MIP $5

Podrace Arena, 1999
MNP $2 MIP $5

Royal Starship Repair Deluxe Platform Action Set, 1999
MNP $2 MIP $5

Tatooine Desert, 1999
MNP $3 MIP $6

Theed Rapids, 1999
MNP $2 MIP $5

THE PHANTOM MENACE
Podracer Pack I

Boles Roor & Neva Kee, 1999
MNP $3 MIP $8

THE PHANTOM MENACE
Podracer Pack II

Dud Bolt & Mars Guo, 1999
MNP $3 MIP $8

THE PHANTOM MENACE
Podracer Pack III

(KP Photo)

Anakin Skywalker & Ratts Tyerell, 1999
MNP $3 MIP $8

THE PHANTOM MENACE
Podracer Pack IV

Sebulba & Clegg Holdfast, 1999
MNP $3 MIP $8

Mini Rigs

AST-5, 1983
MNP $10 MIP $30

CAP-2 Captivator, 1982, bubble-topped vehicle w/room for one figure, roller wheels on bottom w/tank tread façade and two laser moveable laser cannon in front
MNP $10 MIP $30

Desert Sail Skiff, 1984
MNP $16 MIP $35

Endor Forest Ranger, 1984
MNP $20 MIP $55

INT-4 Interceptor, 1982
MNP $10 MIP $25

ISP-6 Imperial Shuttle Pod, 1983
MNP $30 MIP $55

MLC-3 Mobile Laser Cannon, 1981
MNP $10 MIP $25

(KP Photo)

MTV-7 Multi-Terrain Vehicle, 1981, off-white w/room for one 3-3/4" figure (most likely a snowtrooper, if the box is a guide), features two spring-loaded roller wheels and a pivoting front blaster, the Mini Rigs were, in a way, the first "expanded universe" toys for Star Wars
MNP $10 MIP $32

PDT-8 Personal Deployment Transport, 1981
MNP $12 MIP $35

Radar Laser Cannon, 1982
MNP $10 MIP $30

Tri-Pod Laser Cannon, 1982, cannon w/"ammo box" and three folding legs
MNP $10 MIP $30

Vehicle Maintenance Energizer, 1982, generator for vehicles
MNP $10 MIP $30

Multi-Packs

Astromech Droid Pack Series I (Entertainment Earth Exclusive), 2006, w/R4-A22, R2-C4, R3-T2, R2-Q2, and R3-T6
MNP $16 MIP $30

Astromech Droid Pack Series II (Entertainment Earth Exclusive), 2006, w/R4-E1, R2-X2, R2-M5, R2-A6, and R3-Y2
MNP $16 MIP $30

Lucas Collector Set (StarWarsShop.com Exclusive), 2006, w/Baron Papanoida, Chi Eekway, Terr Taneel, and Zett Jukassa
MNP $6 MIP $20

Value Packs (Wal-Mart Exclusive), 2006, randomly-inserted two-packs
MNP n/a MIP n/a

Play Sets

EMPIRE STRIKES BACK

Cloud City Play Set, Sears Exclusive, 1981
MNP $120   MIP $350

Dagobah, 1982
MNP $25   MIP $100

Darth Vader's Star Destroyer, 1982
MNP $40   MIP $120

Hoth Ice Planet, 1980
MNP $40   MIP $165

Imperial Attack Base, 1980
MNP $25   MIP $90

Rebel Command Center, 1980
MNP $60   MIP $180
Turret and Probot, 1980
MNP $35   MIP $110

EWOKS

Ewoks Treehouse, 1985
MNP $50   MIP $125

POTJ

Carbon-Freezing Chamber, 2000, Star Wars Fan Club exclusive
MNP $22   MIP $50

RETURN OF THE JEDI

Ewok Village, 1983
MNP $100   MIP $230

Jabba the Hutt, 1983
MNP $22   MIP $70

Jabba the Hutt Dungeon, w/EV-9D9, Amanaman, Barada, 1983
MNP $200   MIP $350

Jabba the Hutt Dungeon, w/Nikto, 8D8, Klaatu, 1983, Sears
MNP $32   MIP $85

REVENGE OF THE SITH

Mustafar Final Battle, 2005, w/Anakin Darth Vader and Obi-Wan Kenobi
MNP $32   MIP $65

SAGA

Geonosian Arena, 2002
MNP $20   MIP $55

STAR WARS

Cantina Adventure Set, Sears Exclusive, 1977
MNP $185   MIP $575

Creature Cantina, 1977
MNP $32   MIP $100

Death Star Space Station, 1977
MNP $100   MIP $450

Droid Factory, 1977
MNP $50   MIP $135

Land of the Jawas, 1977
MNP $40   MIP $125

Previews

SAGA LEGENDS, 2008-PRESENT

Crimson Empire: The Crucible, 2008, w/Alum Frost, Carnor Jax, Darth Vader, Emperor Palpatine, Kir Kanos, and Lemmet Tauk
MNP $16   MIP $30

Scene Packs

Death Star Briefing (Internet Exclusive), 2006, w/Admiral Motti, Chief Bast, Colonel Wulf Yularen, Darth Vader, General Tagge, Grand Moff Tarkin, and Officer Cass
MNP $20   MIP $40

Hunt for the Millennium Falcon; Bounty Hunter Pack (Previews Exclusive), 2006, w/Darth Vader, Boba Fett, Bossk, Dengar, 4-LOM, IG-88, Zuckuss
MNP $20   MIP $40

Republic Commando Delta Squad (Internet Exclusive), 2006, w/Delta Three-Eight ("Boss"), Fixer, Scorch, Sev, Sun Fac, and two Geonosian Warriors
MNP $50   MIP $85

Vehicles

Imperial Shuttle (Target Exclusive), 2006, w/Darth Vader and Royal Guard figures, opening cockpit, fold-down ramp, opening wings, and retractable landing gear
MNP $60   MIP $100

SAGA LEGENDS, 2008-PRESENT

Darth Vader's TIE Advanced x1 Starfighter, 2008, w/extendable cannons
MNP $13   MIP $25

Millenium Falcon, 2008, w/Chewbacca and Han Solo (largest Star Wars vehicle made to

date [over 2-1/2' long], a new, updated Falcon)
MNP $75   MIP $150

TIE Fighter, 2008, w/ejecting wing panels
MNP $12   MIP $22

TAC (30TH ANNIV. COL.)

Anakin's Jedi Starfighter, 2008, (Green), w/firing blaster cannons
MNP $12   MIP $25

AT-AP Walker, 2008, w/firing projectile launcher
MNP $10   MIP $22

(KP Photo, Karen O'Brien collection)

Darth Vader's Sith Starfighter, 2007, all black, opening canopy, two missiles
MNP $12   MIP $25

Darth Vader's TIE Advanced x1 Starfighter, 2007, w/extendable cannons
MNP $12   MIP $20

General Grievous' Starfighter, 2008, w/firing projectile launchers
MNP $12   MIP $20

Hailfire Droid, 2007, 32 missiles, oversized wheels
MNP $12   MIP $20

Mace Windu's Jedi Starfighter, 2007, w/spring-open wings
MNP $13   MIP $22

Obi-Wan's Jedi Starfighter, 2007, w/firing blaster cannons
MNP $13   MIP $22

(KP Photo, Karen O'Brien collection)

Saesee Tiin's Jedi Starfighter, 2007, opening cockpit and wings, blast panels
MNP $12   MIP $25

Sith Infiltrator, 2007, w/spring-open wings
MNP $14   MIP $28

Tie Fighter, 2007, opening cockpit, wing panels eject
MNP $12   MIP $25

Trade Federation Armored Assault Tank (AAT), 2007, rotating turret, firing missiles
MNP $15   MIP $25

V-Wing Starfighter, 2007, w/spring-open wings
MNP $12   MIP $24

TAC (30TH ANNIV. COL.)
Target Exclusives

Aayla Secura's Jedi Starfighter, 2008, w/firing blaster cannons
MNP $12   MIP $22

ARC-170 Fighter, 2008, (Clone Wars deco), w/firing blaster cannons
MNP $15   MIP $38

TIE Bomber, 2008, w/TIE Bomber pilot
MNP $18   MIP $40

TAC (30TH ANNIV. COL.)
Toys R Us Exclusives

Elite TIE Interceptor, 2008, w/181st Squadron TIE Pilot
MNP $22   MIP $42

Obi-Wan's Starfighter w/Hyperspace Ring, 2008, w/firing cannons
MNP $16   MIP $35

Y-Wing Fighter, 2008, w/Y-Wing Pilot (Lt. Lepira) and R5-F7 droid
MNP $16   MIP $35

THE CLONE WARS, 2008-PRESENT

Anakin's Modified Jedi Starfighter, 2008, firing torpedo launcher
MNP $14   MIP $32

AT-AP Walker (All-Terrain Attack Pod), 2008, w/firing projectile launcher
MNP $10   MIP $22

AT-TE (All-Terrain Tactical Enforcer), 2008, electronic lights, sounds, and Clone Trooper phrases, w/Clone Trooper figure
MNP $65   MIP $105

General Grievous' Starfighter, 2008, firing projectile launchers
MNP $12   MIP $32

THE CLONE WARS, 2008-PRESENT
Toys R Us

Hailfire Droid, 2008/09, exclusive Clone Wars variant, General Grievous figure and oversized rolling wheels
MNP $13   MIP $32

Homing Spider Droid, 2008, firing laser cannons
MNP $10   MIP $22

Obi-Wan Kenobi's Starfighter, 2008, spring-open wings
MNP $13   MIP $32

Obi-Wan's Delta Starfighter, 2008, which separates into two vehicles
MNP $16   MIP $35

V-19 Torrent Starfighter, 2008, firing blaster cannons
MNP $14   MIP $34

V-Wing Fighter, 2008/09, firing laser cannons and spring-open wings w/exclusive V-Wing Pilot figure
MNP $13   MIP $32

DIE-CAST

Darth Vader's TIE Fighter, 1979
MNP $20   MIP $50

Land Speeder, 1979
MNP $15   MIP $65

Millennium Falcon, 1979
MNP $25   MIP $105

Naboo Starfighter, 1999
MNP $4   MIP $10

Slave I, 1979
MNP $25   MIP $75

Snowspeeder, 1979
MNP $20   MIP $65

Star Destroyer, 1979
MNP $30   MIP $110

TIE Bomber, 1979
MNP $160   MIP $410

TIE Fighter, 1979
MNP $15   MIP $45

Twin-Pod Cloud Car, 1979
MNP $20   MIP $70

X-Wing Fighter, 1979
MNP $17   MIP $70

Y-Wing Fighter, 1979
MNP $25   MIP $90

EXPANDED UNIVERSE

(KP Photo)

Speeder Bike, 1998, based on previous concept drawing for speeder bike, includes figure unique to vehicle, like other Expanded Universe vehicles, fires missile, and outriggers move to sides when in "battle mode"
MNP $3   MIP $8

STAR WARS

Darth Vader's TIE Fighter, 1977, fly-apart panels, battery-powered laser cannon lights up in front
MNP $40   MIP $135

(KP Photo)

Imperial Cruiser, 1982, second version of this vehicle, what was once the compartment for a nine-volt battery was now a "weapons storage bin," this vehicle had no battery-powered sounds, but did have opening doors, rotating turret and antenna and opening tailgate
MNP $28   MIP $75

Imperial TIE Fighter, 1977, fly-apart panels
MNP $30   MIP $125

Imperial Trooper Transport, 1977, first version was a Sears Exclusive, w/battery-powered laser sounds, later model released w/"Empire Strikes Back" didn't include sounds or require battery power
MNP $35   MIP $110

Jawa Sandcrawler, Battery-Operated, 1977, battery-operated
MNP $250   MIP $650

Land Speeder, 1977, retractable hovering wheels, opening hood
MNP $15   MIP $60

Millennium Falcon, 1977
MNP $80   MIP $365

Sonic Land Speeder, JC Penney exclusive, 1977
MNP $130   MIP $450

X-Wing Fighter, 1977, pushing R2 head into vehicle would put foils in "X-wing" position, opening canopy, light-up laser cannon on front
MNP $35   MIP $125

EMPIRE STRIKES BACK

AT-AT, 1981, All-Terrain Armored
Transport

    MNP $95   MIP $250

Rebel Transport, 1980

    MNP $42   MIP $100

(KP Photo)

Scout Walker, 1982, two-legged
vehicle w/"walking" legs operated
by button behind cockpit, a lever
allowed the legs to remain locked
so the vehicle could stand in place,
opening flip-up top to place figures,
and opening turret allowing
stormtroopers to fire weapons

    MNP $22   MIP $55

Slave I, 1980

    MNP $50   MIP $140

Snowspeeder, 1980

    MNP $45   MIP $110

Twin-Pod Cloud Car, 1980

    MNP $35   MIP $95

RETURN OF THE JEDI

B-Wing Fighter, 1984

    MNP $60   MIP $150

Ewok Combat Glider, 1984

    MNP $15   MIP $45

Imperial Shuttle, 1984

    MNP $150   MIP $500

Speeder Bike, 1983

    MNP $14   MIP $45

TIE Interceptor, 1984

    MNP $45   MIP $120

Y-Wing Fighter, 1983

    MNP $55   MIP $160

POTF

Ewok Battle Wagon, 1985

    MNP $90   MIP $210

Imperial Sniper Vehicle, 1985

    MNP $38   MIP $65

One-Man Sand Skimmer, 1985

    MNP $25   MIP $60

Security Scout Vehicle, 1985

    MNP $35   MIP $80

Tatooine Skiff, 1985

    MNP $190   MIP $440

DROIDS

ATL Interceptor, 1985

    MNP $40   MIP $80

A-Wing Fighter, 1983

    MNP $170   MIP $360

Inperial Side Gunner, 1985

    MNP $32   MIP $65

EWOKS

Ewoks Fire Cart, 1985

    MNP $15   MIP $35

Ewoks Woodland Wagon, 1985

    MNP $25   MIP $60

DIE-CAST

Darth Vader's TIE Fighter, 1979

    MNP $20   MIP $50

Land Speeder, 1979

    MNP $15   MIP $65

Millennium Falcon, 1979

    MNP $25   MIP $105

Naboo Starfighter, 1999

    MNP $4   MIP $10

Slave I, 1979

    MNP $25   MIP $75

Snowspeeder, 1979
    MNP $20   **MIP $65**

Star Destroyer, 1979
    MNP $30   **MIP $110**

TIE Bomber, 1979
    MNP $160   **MIP $410**

TIE Fighter, 1979
    MNP $15   **MIP $45**

Twin-Pod Cloud Car, 1979
    MNP $20   **MIP $70**

X-Wing Fighter, 1979
    MNP $17   **MIP $70**

Y-Wing Fighter, 1979
    MNP $25   **MIP $90**

POTF2

Speeder Bike, 1997, includes Scout Trooper figure, bike pieces and trooper fall off when "battle damage" button is pushed on bike
    MNP $10   **MIP $25**

POTJ

B-Wing Fighter, 2001, includes Sullustan Pilot, Target exclusive
    MNP $20   **MIP $50**

Imperial AT-ST & Speeder Bike, 2001, TRU exclusive, Paploo figure
    MNP $18   **MIP $35**

Luke Skywalker's Snowspeeder, 2002, Wal-Mart exclusive, Dack Ralter
    MNP $22   **MIP $40**

Tie Bomber, 2002, Wal-Mart exclusive, Imperial Pilot figure
    MNP $20   **MIP $45**

(KP Photo)

TIE Interceptor, 2002, includes figure, wings pop off simulating battle damage, a Toys R Us exclusive,

these toys are now exclusively found in the secondary market, doubling the price collectors pay to get their hands on one
    MNP $15   **MIP $45**

DIE-CAST

Darth Vader's TIE Fighter, 1979
    MNP $20   **MIP $50**

Land Speeder, 1979
    MNP $15   **MIP $65**

Millennium Falcon, 1979
    MNP $25   **MIP $105**

Naboo Starfighter, 1999
    MNP $4   **MIP $10**

Slave I, 1979
    MNP $25   **MIP $75**

Snowspeeder, 1979
    MNP $20   **MIP $65**

Star Destroyer, 1979
    MNP $30   **MIP $110**

TIE Bomber, 1979
    MNP $160   **MIP $410**

TIE Fighter, 1979
    MNP $15   **MIP $45**

Twin-Pod Cloud Car, 1979
    MNP $20   **MIP $70**

X-Wing Fighter, 1979
    MNP $17   **MIP $70**

Y-Wing Fighter, 1979
    MNP $25   **MIP $90**

THE PHANTOM MENACE
Invasion Force

Armored Scout Tank w/Battle Droid, 1999
    MNP $6   **MIP $15**

Gungan Assault Cannon w/Jar Jar Binks, 1999
    MNP $6   **MIP $12**

Gungan Mini-Sub w/Obi-Wan Kenobi, 1999
    MNP $6   **MIP $15**

THE PHANTOM MENACE

Anakin Skywalker's Podracer, 1999
    MNP $7   **MIP $14**

(KP Photo)

Flash Speeder, 1999, hovercraft much in the style of other Star Wars speeders, shown here w/unloaded gun turret, this model actually fires a missile (a pretty fair distance, too)
    MNP $4   **MIP $10**

Naboo Starfighter, 1999
    MNP $8   **MIP $28**

Sebulba's Pod Racer w/Sebulba, 1999
    MNP $7   **MIP $20**

(KP Photo)

Sith Speeder w/Darth Maul, 1999
    MNP $5   **MIP $15**

STAP w/Battle Droid, 1999
    MNP $4   **MIP $10**

Trade Federation Droid Fighter, 1999
    MNP $5   **MIP $15**

Trade Federation Tank, 1999
    MNP $5   **MIP $15**

THE PHANTOM MENACE
Wal-Mart Exclusive

Ammo Wagon and Falumpaset, 1999
MNP $10   MIP $25

SAGA

(KP Photo)

Anakin Skywalker Speeder, 2002, w/blast-off panels
MNP $3   MIP $10

Anakin Skywalker's Swoop Bike, 2003, w/Anakin figure (showing a lot of teeth)
MNP $3   MIP $10

A-Wing Fighter, 2003, Target exclusive, w/pilot
MNP $12   MIP $25

A-Wing Fighter w/Rebel Pilot, 2003, Target exclusive
MNP $12   MIP $25

Darth Tyranus' Geonosian Speeder Bike, 2003, w/Darth Tyranus figure
MNP $8   MIP $15

Imperial Dogfight Tie Fighter w/Tie Pilot, 2003, KB Toys exclusive
MNP $14   MIP $30

Imperial Shuttle, 2003, FAO Schwarz exclusive
MNP $60   MIP $100

(KP Photo)

Jango Fett's Slave I, 2002, launches four missiles, has more vibrant color as a new ship than it does by the time Boba inherits it
MNP $12   MIP $25

Jedi Starfighter w/Obi-Wan Kenobi, 2002, KB Toys exclusive
MNP $12   MIP $20

Jedi Starfighter, Obi-Wan Kenobi, 2002, no figure
MNP $8   MIP $15

Landspeeder, 2002, TRU exclusive
MNP $7   MIP $15

Luke Skywalker's X-Wing Fighter, 2002, TRU exclusive, R2-D2
MNP $10   MIP $25

Republic Gunship, 2002, fits one pilot, carries troops in main body, pivoting laser cannon
MNP $15   MIP $35

Tie Bomber, 2003, w/pilot
MNP $16   MIP $35

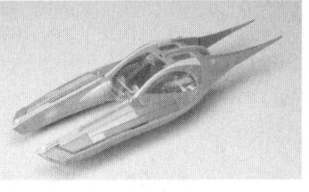

(KP Photo)

Zam Wessell Coruscant Speeder, 2002, w/flexible "crush zones" to emulate Zam's rough landing on Coruscant, a nice-looking vehicle
MNP $3   MIP $10

CLONE WARS

Anakin Skywalker's Jedi Starfighter, 2003, one missile, red droid
MNP $18   MIP $30

Arrmored Assault Tank (AAT), 2003, four missiles
MNP $18   MIP $30

(KP Photo, Karen O'Brien collection)

Command Gunship, 2003
MNP $25   MIP $55

(KP Photo, Karen O'Brien collection)

Geonosian Starfighter w/Pilot, 2003, exclusive Geonosian pilot, one missile
MNP $25   MIP $38

(KP Photo, Karen O'Brien collection)

Hailfire Droid, 2003, 32 red missiles
MNP $16   MIP $30

(KP Photo, Karen O'Brien collection)

Jedi Starfighter, 2003, blue w/yellow droid
MNP $18   MIP $30

ORIGINAL TRILOGY COLLECTION

Millennium Falcon, 2004, laser cannons w/light and sound, Hyperspace light at rear, figures pilot the ship, missile launchers, interior compartments
MNP $35   MIP $75

Slave 1, 2004, w/Boba Fett, Target Exclusive, Model No. 34512
MNP $20   MIP $40

TIE Fighter, 2004, opening cockpit, pilot fits inside, wings pop off
MNP $15   MIP $30

X-Wing Fighter, 2004, wings pop open, cockpit opens, Luke fits inside
MNP $15   MIP $30

Y-Wing Fighter, 2004, w/pilot figure, Toys 'R Us Exclusive, Model No. 34517
MNP $25   MIP $50

REVENGE OF THE SITH

Anakin's Jedi Starfighter, 2005, Sneak Preview, yellow
MNP $10   MIP $25

Anakin's Jedi Starfighter, 2005, w/Anakin Skywalker
MNP $20   MIP $35

ARC-170 Fighter, 2005, Sam's Club Exclusive; includes four figures, ARC Pilot, two Clone Troopers, droid
MNP $30   MIP $65

ARC-170 Fighter, 2005, opening wings, firing cannons
MNP $15   MIP $35

AT-RT, 2005, motorized action, w/driver
MNP $14   MIP $30

AT-RT, 2005, motorized walking action, w/driver and bonus Clone Trooper
MNP $18   MIP $35

BARC Speeder, 2005, w/BARC Trooper and bonus Wookie Warrior, Kohl's Exclusive
MNP $18   MIP $35

BARC Speeder, 2005, w/BARC Trooper, ripcord action
MNP $10   MIP $25

(KP Photo, Karen O'Brien collection)

Droid Tri-Fighter, 2005, buzz droid drop attack
MNP $8   MIP $20

(KP Photo, Karen O'Brien collection)

General Grievous' Wheel Bike, 2005, w/General Grievous, fires missiles
MNP $16   MIP $30

(KP Photo, Karen O'Brien collection)

Obi-Wan Kenobi's Jedi Starfighter, 2005, firing missiles, opening wings, opening cockpit
MNP $12   MIP $25

Plo Koon's Jedi Starfighter, 2005, Target Exclusive
MNP $12   MIP $25

Republic Gunship, 2005, firing blaster cannons
MNP $22   MIP $40

Wookie Flyer, 2005, firing cannon, blades flap, w/Wookie Warrior
MNP $12   MIP $25

SAGA 2006

Anakin's Jedi Starfighter, 2006, firing blaster cannons
MNP $12   MIP $30

(KP Photo, Karen O'Brien collection)

Darth Vader's Tie Advanced X1 Starfighter, 2006
MNP $12   MIP $30

Droid Tri-Fighter, 2006, Buzz Droid Drop Attack
MNP $12   MIP $30

Endor AT-AT, 2006, Toys 'R Us exclusive, w/AT-AT Driver and Biker Scout
MNP $75   MIP $115

Grievous' Wheel Bike, 2006, w/General Grievous
MNP $8   MIP $20

(KP Photo, Karen O'Brien collection)

Kit Fisto's Jedi Starfighter, 2006, Target exclusive
MNP $12   MIP $25

Luke Skywalker's X-Wing, 2006, on Dagobah, covered in moss, large scale, Toys 'R Us Exclusive
MNP $32   MIP $65

(KP Photo, Karen O'Brien collection)

Mace Windu's Jedi Starfighter, 2006, w/firing missiles, purple accents, Target exclusive
MNP $12   MIP $30

Obi-Wan's Jedi Starfighter, 2006, firing blaster cannons
MNP $12   MIP $30

Republic Gunship, 2006, Clone Wars animated version, very cool, very rare
MNP $30   MIP $60

Rogue Two Snowspeeder, 2006, w/Zev Senesca, Target exclusive
MNP $15   MIP $25

Tie Fighter w/Large Scale Wings, 2006, w/Tie Fighter Pilot, Toys 'R Us exclusive
MNP $30   MIP $65

TAC (30TH ANNIV. COL.)

Anakin's Jedi Starfighter, 2008, (Green), w/firing blaster cannons
MNP $12   MIP $25

AT-AP Walker, 2008, w/firing projectile launcher
MNP $10   MIP $22

(KP Photo, Karen O'Brien collection)

Darth Vader's Sith Starfighter, 2007, all black, opening canopy, two missiles
MNP $12   MIP $25

Darth Vader's TIE Advanced x1 Starfighter, 2007, w/extendable cannons
MNP $12   MIP $20

General Grievous' Starfighter, 2008, w/firing projectile launchers
MNP $12   MIP $20

Hailfire Droid, 2007, 32 missiles, oversized wheels
MNP $12   MIP $20

Mace Windu's Jedi Starfighter, 2007,
w/spring-open wings
MNP $13   MIP $22

Obi-Wan's Jedi Starfighter, 2007,
w/firing blaster cannons
MNP $13   MIP $22

(KP Photo, Karen O'Brien collection)

Saesee Tiin's Jedi Starfighter, 2007,
opening cockpit and wings, blast
panels
MNP $12   MIP $25

Sith Infiltrator, 2007, w/spring-open
wings
MNP $14   MIP $28

Tie Fighter, 2007, opening cockpit,
wing panels eject
MNP $12   MIP $25

**Trade Federation Armored Assault
Tank (AAT),** 2007, rotating turret,
firing missiles
MNP $15   MIP $25

V-Wing Starfighter, 2007, w/spring-
open wings
MNP $12   MIP $24

Weapons

Basic Lightsaber, 2007, (various colors)
MNP $7   MIP $15

Clone Trooper Blaster, 2006,
w/electronic lights and sounds
MNP $20   MIP $40

Darth Maul Lightsaber, 2007,
(Double Bladed)
MNP $12   MIP $32

Darth Vader's Lightsaber, 2007,
(Force Action), w/spring-activated
blade
MNP $12   MIP $32

Force Unleashed Lightsaber, 2007,
w/spring-activated blade
MNP $8   MIP $20

General Grievous Blaster, 2007,
(Blue Highlights), w/electronic
lights and sounds
MNP $8   MIP $20

Luke Skywalker's Lightsaber, 2007,
(Force Action), w/spring-activated
blade
MNP $8   MIP $20

Obi-Wan Kenobi's Lightsaber, 2007,
(Force Action), w/spring-activated
blade
MNP $8   MIP $20

Rebel Trooper Blaster, 2007,
w/electronic lights and sounds
MNP $10   MIP $22

Stormtrooper Blaster, 2007,
w/electronic lights and sounds
MNP $10   MIP $25

STAR WARS
Series 1

Han Solo's Laser Pistol, 1977
MNP $50   MIP $175

Inflatable Lightsaber, 1977
MNP $60   MIP $180

Three-Position Laser Rifle, 1980
MNP $90   MIP $300

EMPIRE STRIKES BACK
Series 2

Laser Pistol, 1980
MNP $35   MIP $75

Lightsaber, Red or Green, 1980, red
or green
MNP $35   MIP $65

RETURN OF THE JEDI
Series 3

Biker Scout's Laser Pistol, 1984
MNP $35   MIP $100

Lightsaber, Red or Green, red or
green plastic
MNP $35   MIP $40

DROIDS
Series 5

Droids Lightsaber, 1985
MNP $110   MIP $300

SAGA

Anakin Skywalker Lightsaber, 2002
MNP $12   MIP $30

Count Dooku Lightsaber, 2002
MNP $12   MIP $30

Lightsaber, Blue, 2002
MNP $10   MIP $20

Lightsaber, Green, 2002
MNP $10   MIP $20

Lightsaber, Purple, 2002
MNP $10   MIP $20

Lightsaber, Red, 2002
MNP $10   MIP $20

Obi-Wan Kenobi Lightsaber, 2002
MNP $10   MIP $30

TV Toys

By Justin Moen

Over the years toys and TV have gone together like peanut butter and jelly thanks to licensed merchandising. Licensed toys based on TV shows have been around for more than 60 years, and collectors have become very fond of them ever since.

One of the earliest toys released from TV shows were those based on NBC's *The Howdy Doody Show (1947-1960)* in the 1950s. Releasing toys based on the TV characters of the time are no doubt a very effective way to market both the program and the toys to a target audience. In most cases that target audience is children, who use "pester power" to bug their parents to the point where they finally give in to the child's demands and buy the product the child wants because their favorite characters on TV told them to.

Not long after Howdy Doody saw success in licensed merchandising, TV Westerns like *Gunsmoke* and *Bonanza* realized commercial success with toys from their respective shows, as young boys dreamed of being lawmen or heroes saving the day by bringing down the bad guys.

In the 1960s shows like *The Green Hornet*, *Gilligan's Island*, *Man From U.N.C.L.E*, and *Lost in Space* saw some of the greatest success in licensed merchandising. In the 1970s it was *The Brady Bunch*, *Charlie's Angels*, *The Six Million Dollar Man*, and a host of others that saw great success.

In the 1980s it was *The A-Team*, *Dukes of Hazzard*, and *Knight Rider*. In recent years shows like *The Simpsons*, *X-Files*, and *Family Guy* have represented some of the most popular TV toys on the market. Reader Alert: If you can't find a particular TV toy in this chapter, please check the Contents page and look through the following chapters: Action Figures, Character Toys, Games, Guns, Lunch Boxes, Marx Play Sets, Sci-Fi and Space Toys, View-Master, and Western Toys.

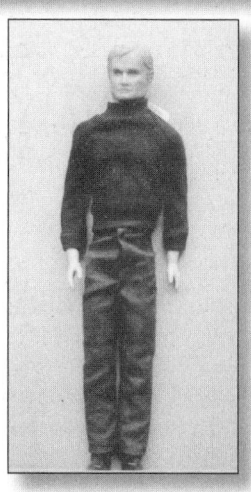

The **Top 10 TV TOYS** in mint condition

1. Green Hornet Dashboard, Remco, 1966. . . . . $2,250
2. Green Hornet Seal Ring, General Mills, 1940. . . . . $1,900
3. Gilligan's Island Trading Cards, Topps, 1965 . . . . $1,550
4. Man From U.N.C.L.E. Counterspy Outfit Store Display, Marx, 1966. . . . . $1,350
5. Gilligan's Island Dip Dots Painting Set, Kenner, 1975. . . . . $1,200
6. Green Hornet Fan Club Photos, Golden Jersey Milk, 1938 . . . . $1,200
7. Man From U.N.C.L.E. Crime Buster Gift Set, Corgi, 1966 . . . . $1,100
8. Howdy Doody Periscope, Wonder Bread, 1950s $1,100
9. Girl From U.N.C.L.E. Doll, Marx, 1967. . . . . $1,000
10. Howdy Doody, Rice Crispies Cereal Box, Kellogg's, 1954 . . . . $1,000

Addams Family

Gomez Hand Puppet, 1965, Ideal
EX $50 **NM** $120 **MIP** $250

Lurch Figure, 1964, Remco
EX $80 **NM** $185 **MIP** $360

Morticia Figure, 1964, Remco
EX $100 **NM** $210 **MIP** $675

Morticia Halloween Costume, 1964, Ben Cooper, painted hair
EX $40 **NM** $100 **MIP** $200

Morticia Halloween Costume, 1964, Ben Cooper, w/hair
EX $60 **NM** $125 **MIP** $250

Morticia Hand Puppet, 1965, Ideal
EX $50 **NM** $130 **MIP** $260

Thing Bank, 1964, plastic, battery-operated
EX $40 **NM** $150 **MIP** $225

Uncle Fester Figure, 1964, Remco
EX $100 **NM** $250 **MIP** $625

Alvin Show

Sliding Squares Game, 1960s, Roalex Co., sliding squares form a variety of "possible" solutions
EX $25 **NM** $45 **MIP** $60

A-Team

A-Team Combat Headquarters Set, 1980s, Galoob, includes 3-3/4" figures of Hannibal, Face, B.A. Baracus, Murdock and gear, including inflatable raft, machine guns, flag, and tent
EX $40 **NM** $85 **MIP** $125

A-Team Rocket Ball Target Set, 1983, gumballs w/gun and target
EX $5 **NM** $10 **MIP** $25

A-Team Shrinky Dinks Set, 1980s
EX $5 **NM** $10 **MIP** $20

Avengers

Shooting Game, 1960s, Merit
EX $10 **NM** $20 **MIP** $45

Steed Sword Stick, 1960s, Lone Star, toy of John Steed's secret cane/sword combo
EX $17 **NM** $35 **MIP** $70

Banana Splits

4 The Banana Splits Puzzle, 1969, Whitman, frame tray
EX $25 **NM** $55 **MIP** $85

Banana Band, 1973, Larami, horn, sax, mouth harp
EX $25 **NM** $60 **MIP** $120

Banana Buggy Model Kit, 1968, Aurora
EX $60 **NM** $200 **MIP** $325

Banana Splits Bingo Costume, 1968, Ben Cooper
EX $60 **NM** $175 **MIP** $300

Banana Splits Doll, 1960s, Sutton, 12" tall, plush Drooper
EX $45 **NM** $95 **MIP** $200

Banana Splits Kut-Up Kit, 1973, Larami
EX $25 **NM** $40 **MIP** $75

Banana Splits Mug, 1969, plastic yellow dog mug
EX $20 **NM** $40 **MIP** $65

Banana Splits Record, 1969, Kellogg's
EX $20 **NM** $90 **MIP** $175

Paint-By-Number Set, 1969, Hasbro
EX $45 **NM** $80 **MIP** $150

Talking Telephone, 1969, Hasbro
EX $75 **NM** $175 **MIP** $350

Beany and Cecil

Beany and Cecil and Their Pals Record Player, 1961, Vanity Fair
EX $80 **NM** $200 **MIP** $375

Beany and Cecil Carrying Case, 1960s, 9" diameter, w/strap, vinyl-covered cardboard
EX $40 **NM** $85 **MIP** $100

Beany and Cecil Gun, 1961, Mattel, w/propeller disks
EX $30 **NM** $150 **MIP** $200

Beany and Cecil Puzzle, 1961, Playskool, wooden frame tray
EX $25 **NM** $65 **MIP** $100

Beany and Cecil Skill Ball, 1960s, colorful tin w/wood frame
EX $30 **NM** $80 **MIP** $125

Beany and Cecil Travel Case, 1960s, 8" tall, round, red vinyl w/zipper and strap
EX $25 **NM** $55 **MIP** $95

Beany and Cecil Travel Case, 1960s, square, 4-1/2" x 3-1/2" x 3" red vinyl, carrying strap, illustrated w/characters
EX $30 **NM** $70 **MIP** $100

Beany and His Magic Set Book, 1953,
Tell-a-Tale Book
EX $10   **NM** $20   **MIP** $55

Beany Doll, 1963, Mattel, 15" tall,
non-talking
EX $45   **NM** $100   **MIP** $165

Beany Figure, 1984, Caltoy, 8" tall
EX $10   **NM** $20   **MIP** $45

Beany Talking Doll, 1950s, Mattel,
17" tall, stuffed cloth, vinyl head
w/pull string
EX $90   **NM** $250   **MIP** $425

Bob Clampetts' Beany Coloring Book,
1960s, Whitman
EX $15   **NM** $75   **MIP** $150

Captain Huffenpuff Puzzle, 1961, large
EX $25   **NM** $85   **MIP** $120

Cecil and His Disguise Kit, 1962,
Mattel, 17" tall plush Cecil
w/disguise wigs, mustaches, etc.
EX $30   **NM** $90   **MIP** $175

Cecil in the Music Box, 1961, Mattel,
jack-in-the-box
EX $90   **NM** $225   **MIP** $375

Cecil Soaky, 8-1/2" tall, plastic
EX $35   **NM** $85   **MIP** $150

Leakin' Lena Boat, 1962, Irwin,
plastic and wood
EX $50   **NM** $115   **MIP** $225

Leakin' Lena Pound 'N Pull Toy,
1960s, Pressman, wood
EX $60   **NM** $125   **MIP** $250

Ben Casey M.D.

Ben Casey Pencils, 1962, Hassenfeld
Bros., 10 red/white pencils on card
EX $15   **NM** $30   **MIP** $70

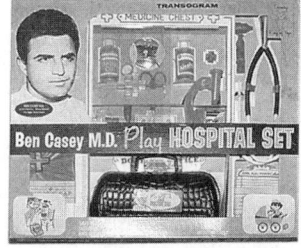

Play Hosptial Set, 1960s,
Transogram, includes doctor bag,
microscope, stethascope and more
EX $50   **NM** $100   **MIP** $175

Beverly Hillbillies

Paper Cut-Outs, 1960s, Whitman,
includes Jed, Jethro, Granny and
Elly May
EX $35   **NM** $80   **MIP** $125

Bewitched

Bewitched Samantha Doll, 1967,
Ideal, 12-1/2" tall
EX $180   **NM** $395   **MIP** $750

Bewitched Tabitha Paper Doll Set,
1966, Magic Wand, 11" cardboard
doll, clothes
EX $30   **NM** $75   **MIP** $150

Bionic Woman

Play-Doh Action Play Set, 1970s,
Kenner, includes molds for making
Play-Doh characters from the

show, three containers of Play-Doh,
plastic mat and six-wheeled vehicle
EX $15   **NM** $25   **MIP** $40

Bozo

Bozo Record Player
EX $20   **NM** $45   **MIP** $90

Bozo the Clown Beach Towel, 1960s,
16" x 24"
EX $8   **NM** $15   **MIP** $35

Bozo the Clown Bendiface, 1970s,
Lakeside, soft rubber face flexes
into different expressions
EX $8   **NM** $16   **MIP** $24

Bozo the Clown Doll, 1970, Mattel, 19"
tall, talks when you pull the cord,
"This is your old pal Bozo!"
EX $25   **NM** $50   **MIP** $85

Bozo the Clown Figure, 1970s, vinyl,
5" tall
EX $5   **NM** $15   **MIP** $30

Bozo the Clown Hand Puppet, 1960s,
Knickerbocker, vinyl head, cloth
outfit, 17" long
EX $15   **NM** $30   **MIP** $45

Bozo the Clown King of the Ring,
1960, Whitman, Tell-A-Tale book
EX $10   **NM** $20   **MIP** $30

**Bozo the Clown Push Button
Marionette,** 1962, Knickerbocker
EX $25   **NM** $45   **MIP** $85

Bozo the Clown Puzzle, 1965,
Whitman, #4516, Model No. 4516
EX $10   **NM** $25   **MIP** $50

Bozo the Clown Slide Puzzle, 1960s
EX $15   **NM** $40   **MIP** $75

Bozo the Clown Soaky, 1960s,
Palmolive
EX $15   **NM** $45   **MIP** $85

Bozo Tricky Trapeze, 1960s, Kohner,
"Push Button Acrobat," red base,
also called "push puppets," two
buttons on either side of the base
are pushed to propel Bozo
EX $15   **NM** $35   **MIP** $65

Tumbling Bozo the Clown, 1971, Sonsco, battery-operated, remote control, cloth outfit, somersaults
EX $15   NM $32   MIP $50

Brady Bunch

Brady Bunch Halloween Costume, 1970s, Collegeville, smock reads "One of The Brady Bunch"
EX $40   NM $90   MIP $150

Brady Bunch Kite Fun Book, 1976, Pacific Gas and Electric
EX $15   NM $35   MIP $75

Brady Bunch Paper Dolls Cut-Out Book, 1973, Whitman
EX $30   NM $85   MIP $150

Brady Bunch Puzzle, frame tray
EX $25   NM $45   MIP $80

Brady Bunch Trading Cards, 1971, Topps, 55 cards
EX $250   NM $525   MIP $775

Kitty Karry-All Doll, 1969, Remco
EX $90   NM $175   MIP $325

Captian Kangaroo

Captain Kangaroo Duck Pin Game, 1950s, Gardner, w/self returning ball
EX $15   NM $35   MIP $75

Captain Kangaroo Presto Slate, 1960s, Fairchild, slate on illustrated card, several versions
EX $12   NM $30   MIP $40

Captain Kangaroo Puzzle, 1960, Whitman, #4446, frame tray, Model No. 4446
EX $10   NM $30   MIP $60

Charlie's Angels

Charlie's Angels Paper Dolls, 1977, Toy Factory, Farrah, Kate or Jaclyn sets, each
EX $20   NM $50   MIP $90

Charlie's Angels Pendant, 1977, Fleetwood Toys, 4" plastic figure of Farrah hangs from pendant
EX $10   NM $25   MIP $45

Farrah Fawcett Doll, 1977, Mattel, 12"
EX $50   NM $125   MIP $200

Farrah Travel Trunk, 1970s, Grand Toys, Canadian toy, box has french language
EX $10   NM $20   MIP $30

Hide-A-Way House, 1970s, Hasbro, revolving five-sided dollhouse for Charlie's Angels figures
EX $50   NM $100   MIP $150

Kate Jackson Doll, 1978, Mattel, 12"
EX $20   NM $45   MIP $90

Kelly Doll, 1977, Hasbro, 8"
EX $12   NM $35   MIP $80

Kris Doll, 1977, Hasbro, 8"
EX $10   NM $30   MIP $70

River Race Outfits, 1977, Palitoy
EX $15   NM $35   MIP $60

Sabrina Doll, 1977, Hasbro, 8"
EX $20   NM $70   MIP $120

Sabrina, Kelly, and Kris Gift Set, 1977, Hasbro
EX $30   NM $70   MIP $145

Slalom Caper Outfits, 1977, Palitoy
EX $10   NM $30   MIP $50

Target Set, 1970s, Placo Toys, includes two safety guns, six safety darts and a knockdown target
EX $20   NM $45   MIP $85

(KP Photo)

Underwater Intrigue Outfits, 1977, Palitoy
EX $10   NM $30   MIP $50

CHiPs

Colorforms Play Set, 1970s, Colorforms
EX $15   NM $30   MIP $55

Free Wheeling Motorcycle, 1970s, Mego, made to fit Mego's 8" figures from the series
EX $15   NM $35   MIP $50

Police Set, 1970s, HG Toys, includes snub-nose revolver, badge, sunglasses (of course!), handcuffs and holster
EX $18   **NM** $32   **MIP** $60

Combat!

Official Play Set, 1960s, Marx, super-cool toy soldier set includes tanks, howitzers, army trucks, tanks, personnel carriers, soldiers and landing craft, this same set was re-packaged in the 1970s w/out the "Combat" TV-show name or tie-in
EX $20   **NM** $40   **MIP** $85

Dobie Gillis

Paint-N-Press Art Set, 1960s, includes watercolors and instructions
EX $5   **NM** $15   **MIP** $25

Dr. Kildare

Dr. Kildare Photo Scrapbook, 1962
EX $10   **NM** $25   **MIP** $50

Dragnet

Dragnet Badge 714, 1955, Knicker-bocker, 2-1/2" bronze finish badge in yellow box w/illustration of Jack Webb, box bottom has ID card
EX $45   **NM** $90   **MIP** $135

Dragnet Badge 714 Target Game, 1950s, includes three guns, corks and darts and litho metal target, $2.98 original price!
EX $30   **NM** $75   **MIP** $150

Dragnet Crime Lab, 1950s, Transogram, "A complete crime detection outfit for the junior detective"
EX $60   **NM** $120   **MIP** $225

Dukes of Hazzard

Daisy's Jeep, 1970s, includes "Dixie," a white and brown CJ5 Jeep and one Daisy Duke figure
EX $15   **NM** $35   **MIP** $50

Family Affair

5 Family Affair Paper Dolls, Whitman
EX $30   **NM** $45   **MIP** $55

Buffy Halloween Costume, 1970, Ben Cooper
EX $20   **NM** $40   **MIP** $80

Buffy Make-Up and Hairstyling Set, 1971, Amsco
EX $20   **NM** $40   **MIP** $80

Buffy w/Mrs. Beasley Dolls, 1967, Mattel, 6" Buffy w/smaller Mrs. Beasley
EX $30   **NM** $65   **MIP** $115

Family Affair Cartoon Kit, 1970, Colorforms
EX $12   **NM** $25   **MIP** $50

Family Affair Puzzle, 1970, Whitman
EX $12   **NM** $30   **MIP** $60

Mrs. Beasley Paper Dolls, 1970s, Whitman, several variations
EX $12   **NM** $30   **MIP** $60

Mrs. Beasley Rag Doll, 1973, Mattel, 14"
EX $12   **NM** $25   **MIP** $45

Talking Mrs. Beasley Doll, 1967, Mattel
EX $50   **NM** $100   **MIP** $225

Flintstones

Baby Puss Figure, 1961, Knicker-bocker, 10" tall, vinyl
EX $35   **NM** $75   **MIP** $135

Bamm-Bamm Bank, 1960s, 11" tall, hard plastic figure sitting on turtle
EX $20   **NM** $45   **MIP** $75

Bamm-Bamm Bubble Pipe, 1963, Transogram, figural pipe on illustrated card
EX $12   **NM** $25   **MIP** $50

Bamm-Bamm Doll, 1962, Ideal, 15" tall
EX $50   **NM** $115   **MIP** $225

Bamm-Bamm Figure, 1970, Dakin, 7" tall
EX $20   **NM** $40   **MIP** $75

Bamm-Bamm Finger Puppet, 1972, Knickerbocker
EX $5   **NM** $15   **MIP** $25

Bamm-Bamm Soaky, 1960s, Purex
EX $20   NM $40   MIP $75

Barney Bank, 1973, solid plastic, Barney holding a bowling ball
EX $15   NM $35   MIP $60

Barney Doll, 1962, 6" tall, soft vinyl doll, movable arms and head
EX $25   NM $45   MIP $80

Barney Figure, 1961, Knickerbocker, 10" tall, vinyl
EX $40   NM $55   MIP $160

Barney Figure, 1970, Dakin, 7-1/4" tall
EX $20   NM $40   MIP $75

Barney Figure, 1986, Flintoys
EX $5   NM $10   MIP $15

Barney Finger Puppet, 1972, Knickerbocker
EX $8   NM $15   MIP $25

Barney Night Light, 1979, Electricord, figural
EX $8   NM $15   MIP $25

Barney Policeman Figure, 1986, Flintoys
EX $4   NM $8   MIP $12

Barney Riding Dino Toy, 1960s, Marx, 8" long, metal and vinyl, wind-up
EX $110   NM $300   MIP $550

Barney Soaky, 1970s, Roclar
EX $10   NM $20   MIP $55

Barney Wind-Up Toy, 1960s, Marx, 3-1/2" tall figure, tin
EX $85   NM $190   MIP $375

Barney's Car, 1986, Flintoys
EX $8   NM $15   MIP $30

Betty Figure, 1961, Knickerbocker, 10" tall, vinyl
EX $50   NM $100   MIP $200

Betty Figure, 1986, Flintoys
EX $4   NM $7   MIP $10

Dino Bank, China, Dino carrying a golf bag
EX $45   NM $95   MIP $185

Dino Bank, 1973, hard vinyl, blue w/Pebbles on his back
EX $18   NM $35   MIP $75

Dino Bath Puppet Sponge, 1973, bath mitt
EX $10   NM $18   MIP $35

Dino Doll, movable head and arms
EX $15   NM $25   MIP $50

Dino Figure, 1970, Dakin, 7-3/4" tall
EX $25   NM $50   MIP $100

Dino Figure, 1986, Flintoys
EX $4   NM $7   MIP $15

Dino Wind-Up Toy, 1960s, Marx, 3-1/2" tall, tin
EX $90   NM $180   MIP $360

Fang Figure, 1970, Dakin, 7" tall
EX $25   NM $50   MIP $95

Flintmobile, 1986, Flintoys
EX $10   NM $18   MIP $40

Flintmobile w/Fred Figure, 1986, Flintoys
EX $18   NM $33   MIP $60

Flintstones Ashtray, 1960, ceramic w/Wilma
EX $25   NM $70   MIP $100

Flintstones Bank, 1971, 19" tall w/Barney and Bamm Bamm
EX $25   NM $50   MIP $85

Flintstones Car, 1964, Remco, battery-operated car w/Barney, Fred, Wilma and Betty
EX $85   NM $200   MIP $385

Flintstones Figure Set, 1981, Spoontiques, eight figures
EX $35   NM $50   MIP $90

Flintstones Figures, 1976, Empire, three-inch solid figures of Fred, Barney, Wilma and Betty
EX $10   NM $40   MIP $85

Flintstones Figures, 1976, Imperial, eight acrylic figures: Fred, Barney, Wilma, Betty, Pebbles, Bamm Bamm, Dino, and Baby Puss
EX $15   NM $35   MIP $65

Flintstones House, 1986, Flintoys
EX $12   NM $25   MIP $35

Flintstones Lamp, 9-1/2" tall, plastic Fred w/lampshade picturing characters
EX $50   NM $120   MIP $210

Flintstones Paint Box, 1961, Transogram
EX $18   NM $35   MIP $60

Flintstones Party Place Set, 1969, Reed, tablecloth, napkins, plates, cups
EX $10   NM $20   MIP $40

Flintstones Roto Draw, 1969, British
EX $30   NM $70   MIP $100

Flintstones Tru-Vue Film Card, 1962, Tru-Vue, #T-37, w/strips of Fred
EX $30   NM $70   MIP $100

Fred Bubble Blowing Pipe, soft vinyl w/curved stem
EX $6   NM $12   MIP $20

Fred Doll, 1960, 13" soft vinyl doll w/movable head
EX $45   NM $100   MIP $225

Fred Doll, 1972, Perfection Plastic, 11" tall
EX $15   NM $35   MIP $60

Fred Figure, 1960, Knickerbocker, 15" tall
EX $40   NM $85   MIP $200

Fred Figure, 1961, Knickerbocker, 10" tall, vinyl
EX $32   NM $75   MIP $150

Fred Figure, 1970, Dakin, 8-1/4" tall
EX $22   NM $45   MIP $85

Fred Figure, 1986, Flintoys
EX $4   NM $8   MIP $12

Fred Finger Puppet, 1972, Knickerbocker
EX $8   NM $15   MIP $22

Fred Flintstone's Bedrock Bank, 1962, Alps, 9", tin and vinyl, battery-operated
EX $175   NM $310   MIP $325

Fred Flintstone's Lithograph Wind-Up, 1960s, Marx, 3-1/2" tall figure, metal
EX $85   NM $170   MIP $385

Fred Gumball Machine, 1960s, plastic, shaped like Fred's head
EX $20   NM $32   MIP $60

Fred Loves Wilma Bank, ceramic
EX $50   NM $110   MIP $185

Fred Night Light, 1970, figural
EX $6   NM $12   MIP $25

Fred Policeman Figure, 1986, Flintoys
EX $4   NM $8   MIP $15

Fred Push Puppet, 1960s, Kohner
EX $10   NM $25   MIP $45

Fred Riding Dino, 1962, Marx, 18" long battery-operated w/Fred in Howdah
EX $175   NM $350   MIP $675

Fred Riding Dino, 1962, Marx, 8" long, tin and vinyl, wind-up
EX $175   NM $350   MIP $675

Great Big Punch-Out Book, 1961, Whitman
EX $20   NM $50   MIP $125

Motorbike, 1986, Flintoys
EX $6   NM $12   MIP $20

Pebbles Bank, 9" tall vinyl w/Pebbles sitting in chair
EX $10   NM $25   MIP $50

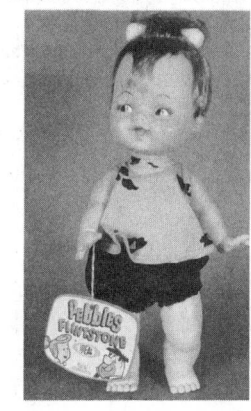

Pebbles Doll, 1963, Ideal, 15" tall
EX $55   NM $115   MIP $225

Pebbles Doll, 1982, Mighty Star, vinyl head, arms and legs, cloth stuffed body 12" tall
EX $15   NM $25   MIP $45

Pebbles Figure, 1970, Dakin, 8" tall w/blonde hair and purple velvet shirt
EX $25   NM $45   MIP $85

Pebbles Finger Puppet, 1972, Knickerbocker
EX $5   NM $13   MIP $20

Pebbles Flintstone Cradle, 1963, Ideal, for a 15" doll
EX $40   NM $75   MIP $150

Pebbles Soaky, 1960s, Purex
EX $20   NM $35   MIP $70

Police Car, 1986, Flintoys
EX $8   NM $15   MIP $30

Wilma Figure, 1961, Knickerbocker, 10" tall, vinyl
EX $50   NM $100   MIP $190

Wilma Figure, 1986, Flintoys
EX $4   NM $7   MIP $15

Wilma Friction Car, 1962, Marx, metal
EX $90   NM $175   MIP $375

Flipper

Flipper Game, 1970s, Koide, Japanese issue
EX $20   NM $40   MIP $65

Flipper Numbered Pencil Coloring Set, 1960s, includes colored pencils, sharpener and pre-sketched pictures to color
EX $10   NM $20   MIP $40

Puncho, 1960s, Coleco, inflatable 40" toy w/weighted bottom, so he appears to be swimming upright in a pool or lake
EX $15   NM $25   MIP $45

Flying Nun

Flying Nun Chalkboard, 1967, Screen Gems
EX $22   NM $45   MIP $80

Flying Nun Doll, 1960s, Hasbro, 4"
EX $22   NM $125   MIP $200

Flying Nun Doll, 1967, Hasbro, 11"
EX $30   NM $85   MIP $175

Flying Nun Halloween Costume, 1967, Ben Cooper
EX $20   NM $60   MIP $100

Flying Nun Paint-By-Number Set, 1960s, Hasbro, two scenes and 10 paint vials
EX $15   NM $30   MIP $60

Flying Nun Paper Doll Set, 1969, Saalfield, five dolls and costumes
EX $16   NM $40   MIP $80

Get Smart

Secret Agent 86 Pen Radio, 1960s, Miner Industries, functioning crystal radio set in shape of pen, included earphone and contact clip, received AM radio stations
EX $20   NM $35   MIP $70

Secret Agent 99 Spy Purse, 1960s, Miner Industries, includes secret compartment, two-way mirror, secret micro-film holder (inside rose), ID card
EX $30   NM $65   MIP $105

Gilligan's Island

Gilligan's Floating Island Play Set, 1977, Playskool
EX $75   NM $190   MIP $350

Gilligan's Island Notepad, 1965, Whitman, Gilligan and Skipper on cover
EX $12   NM $30   MIP $60

Gilligan's Island Trading Cards, 1965, Topps, set of 55 cards
EX $400   NM $800   MIP $1550

New Adventures of Gilligan Dip Dots Painting Set, 1975, Kenner, book w/paints and brush

EX $220 NM $570 MIP $1200

Girl from U.N.C.L.E.

1967 British Annual Book, 1967, World Distributors, hardcover, 95 pages, photo cover

EX $10 NM $30 MIP $60

1968 British Annual Book, 1968, World Distributors, hardcover, 95 pages, photo cover

EX $10 NM $30 MIP $60

1969 British Annual Book, 1969, World Distributors, hardcover, 95 pages, photo cover

EX $10 NM $30 MIP $60

Costume, 1967, Halco, transparent or painted mask, dress-style costume has show logo and silhouette image of Girl spy holding smoking gun, in illustrated window box

EX $55 NM $115 MIP $250

Garter Holster, 1966, Lone Star, metal pistol fires small plastic bullets from metal shells, checker design vinyl holster and bullet pouch, on card

EX $80 NM $175 MIP $350

Girl From U.N.C.L.E. Doll, 1967, Marx, 11" tall w/30 accessories in illustrated box

EX $250 NM $500 MIP $1000

Music from the Television Series, 1966, M.G.M. Records, photo cover shows Stephanie against a wall

EX $9 NM $20 MIP $40

Secret Agent Wristwatch, 1966, Bradley, watch has pink face w/April Dancer image, in case

EX $85 NM $200 MIP $400

Green Acres

2 Magic Stay-On Dolls, 1960s, includes Oliver and Lisa figures, plus complete wardrobes

EX $25 NM $40 MIP $75

Green Hornet

Assistant Badge, 1966, Don Howard Associates

EX $45 NM $95 MIP $200

Bike Badge, 1966, Burry Cookies, premium; w/Vari-Vue flasher

EX $85 NM $175 MIP $350

Black Beauty Balloon Toy, 1966, Oak Rubber

EX $70 NM $145 MIP $275

Black Beauty Slot Car, 1966, Aurora, clear box w/insert

EX $85 NM $175 MIP $400

Black Beauty Slot Car, 1966, BZ Industries, large scale

EX $160 NM $380 MIP $775

Captain Action Flasher Ring, 1966, Vari-Vue, blue

EX $10 NM $18 MIP $30

Captain Action Flasher Ring, 1966, Vari-Vue, chrome

EX $13 NM $25 MIP $40

Charm, 1966, Cracker Jack, hornet-shaped

EX $10 NM $30 MIP $50

Charms, 1966, Folz Vending, hornet-shaped

EX $10 NM $15 MIP $25

Comic Strip Stickers, 1966, Folz Vending, 7" long, from vending machines, each

EX $25 NM $50 MIP $100

Electric Drawing Set, 1966, Lakeside

EX $90 NM $190 MIP $275

Fan Club Photos, 1938, Golden Jersey Milk, set of four; radio premium

EX $400 NM $800 MIP $1250

Flasher Button, 1966, Vari-Vue, pinback, 3"

EX $15 NM $30 MIP $45

Flasher Button, 1966, Vari-Vue, no pinback, 3"

EX $10 NM $20 MIP $35

Flasher Button, 1966, Vari-Vue, no pinback, 7"

EX $25 NM $45 MIP $80

Flasher Rings, 1960s, Vari-Vue, chrome base, each

EX $10 NM $20 MIP $50

Flasher Rings, 1960s, Vari-Vue, blue plastic base, each

EX $5 NM $10 MIP $40

Flashlight Whistle, 1966, Bantamlight

EX $40 NM $90 MIP $175

Frame Tray Puzzles, 1966, Whitman, box of four

EX $40 NM $90 MIP $175

Green Hornet Bendy Figure, 1966, Lakeside

EX $40 NM $80 MIP $175

Green Hornet Bubble Gum Ring, Frito Lay, rubber ring, in cello pack

EX $25 NM $45 MIP $90

Green Hornet Candy/Toy Box, 1966, Phoenix Candy, several variations

EX $40 NM $90 MIP $150

Green Hornet Charm Bracelet, 1966, gold finish chain w/five charms: Hornet, Van, Kato, Pistol, Black Beauty, on 3" x 7-1/2" illustrated card

EX $50 NM $125 MIP $200

Green Hornet Colorforms Set, 1966, Colorforms

EX $60 NM $125 MIP $250

Green Hornet Dashboard, 1966, Remco

EX $300 NM $1000 MIP $2250

Green Hornet Mini Walkie Talkies, 1966, Remco

EX $75 NM $150 MIP $300

Green Hornet Print Putty, 1966, Colorforms

EX $20 NM $50 MIP $95

Green Hornet Seal Ring, 1940, General Mills, cereal premium

EX $225 NM $780 MIP $1900

Green Hornet Soundtrack Record, 1966, 20th Century Fox

EX $25 NM $100 MIP $200

Green Hornet Troll Figure, 1966, Uneeda Wishnik, 7" tall

EX $55 NM $100 MIP $250

Green Hornet Troll Figure, 1966, Damm, 3" tall

EX $45 NM $75 MIP $150

Green Hornet TV Guide, 1966, cover features Van Williams and Bruce Lee

EX $50 NM $125 MIP $250

Green Hornet Utensils, 1966, Imperial Knife, fork and spoon

EX $30 NM $75 MIP $150

Green Hornet Walkie Talkies, 1966, Remco

EX $50 NM $100 MIP $175

Green Hornet Wallet, 1966, green vinyl, Hornet or Kato

EX $25 NM $50 MIP $100

Green Hornet Wrist Radios, 1966, Remco, battery-operated
EX $150   NM $250   MIP $525

Halloween Costume, 1966, Ben Cooper, several variations
EX $100   NM $200   MIP $375

Hand Puppet, 1966, Ideal, w/hat
EX $80   NM $175   MIP $300

Inflatable Raft, 1966, Ideal
EX $160   NM $350   MIP $700

Instant Squeeze Candy, 1966, Dre's Inc., toothpaste-type container w/hornet-shaped plug
EX $40   NM $90   MIP $175

Kite, 1966, Roalex
EX $30   NM $75   MIP $150

Magic Eyes Movie Viewer Slides, 1966, Sawyers
EX $75   NM $150   MIP $300

Magic Rub-On Set, 1966, Whitman
EX $70   NM $150   MIP $275

Magic Slate, 1966, Watkins-Strathmore, three variations
EX $35   NM $90   MIP $175

Mini Movie Viewer, 1966, Acme/Chemtoy, w/filmstrips
EX $50   NM $100   MIP $200

Mini Movie Viewer, 1971, Chemtoy, w/filmstrips
EX $25   NM $45   MIP $90

Numbered Pencil and Paint Set, 1966, Hasbro
EX $75   NM $160   MIP $300

Paint By Number Set, 1966, Hasbro
EX $65   NM $130   MIP $260

Pencil Case, 1966, Hasbro
EX $30   NM $65   MIP $120

Pencils, 1966, Empire Pencil, five on card
EX $30   NM $80   MIP $150

Pennant, 1966, RMS, blue or orange
EX $35   NM $100   MIP $175

Playing Cards, 1966, Ed-U-Cards
EX $10   NM $75   MIP $150

Punch-Out Book, 1966, Whitman
EX $100   NM $200   MIP $375

Secret Agent Badge, 1966, Don Howard Associates
EX $20   NM $35   MIP $65

Stardust Craft Kit, 1966, Hasbro
EX $35   NM $75   MIP $150

The Case of the Disappearing Doctor Book, 1966, Whitman
EX $20   NM $30   MIP $45

Thingmaker Mold and Accessories, 1966, Mattel
EX $100   NM $175   MIP $325

Trading Cards, 1966, Donruss, set of 44
EX $85   NM $100   MIP $325

Trading Cards Display Box, 1966, Donruss
EX $100   NM $250   MIP $500

Trading Cards Wrapper, 1966, Donruss
EX $15   NM $30   MIP $60

Trading Stickers, 1966, Topps, set of 44
EX $85   NM $160   MIP $325

Trading Stickers Display Box, 1966, Topps
EX $100   NM $250   MIP $500

Trading Stickers Wrapper, 1966, Topps
EX $10   NM $25   MIP $50

Wrist Signal Light, 1966, Bantamlight
EX $40   NM $80   MIP $175

Grizzly Adams

Grizzly Adams, 1979, Mattel, 9" figure, w/accessories, #2377
EX $15   NM $30   MIP $45

Nakoma, 1979, Mattel, 9" figure, w/accessories
EX $15   NM $30   MIP $45

Hogan's Heroes

Peri-Peeper, 1977, Continental Plastics, includes Periscope, ID card and pinback button
EX $5   NM $15   MIP $30

Howdy Doody

Cereal Box, 1954, Kellogg's, Rice Krispies, Howdy Mask on back
EX $250   NM $650   MIP $1000

Clarabell Bank, 1976, Strauss, flocked plastic, 9"
EX $20   NM $65   MIP $120

Clarabell Jumping Toy, 1950s, Linemar, 7" tall tin litho, squeeze lever to make figure hop forward and squeak
EX $200   NM $450   MIP $825

Clarabell Marionette, 1950s, Peter Puppet
EX $100   NM $210   MIP $425

Flub-a-Dub Figure, 1950s, TeeVee Toys, 4" x 4" painted plastic, movable mouth
EX $40   NM $90   MIP $150

Flub-a-Dub Flip A Ring Game, 1950s, Flip-A-Ring, 9", ring toss game
EX $25   NM $45   MIP $75

Flub-a-Dub Marionette, 1950s, Peter Puppet
EX $100   NM $225   MIP $450

Flub-a-Dub Puppet, 1950s, Gund
EX $40   NM $75   MIP $150

Howdy Doody Acrobat, 1950s, Arnold, tin, plastic, Howdy swings on high bar
EX $15   NM $25   MIP $60

Howdy Doody Air Doodle Beanie, 1950s, Kellogg's, Rice Krispies premium
EX $75   NM $200   MIP $300

Howdy Doody Air-O-Doodle Circus Train, 1950s, Plasticraft/Kagran, red/yellow plastic train, boat and plane toy on card w/cut out character passengers
EX $40   NM $100   MIP $160

Howdy Doody and Clarabell Book, 1952, Simon and Schuster, Little Golden Book
EX $12   NM $22   MIP $50

Howdy Doody and Clarabell Coloring Book, 1955, Whitman, Model No. 1188
EX $15   NM $75   MIP $185

Howdy Doody and Clarabell Puppet Mitten Kit, 1950s, Connecticut Leather
EX $30   NM $75   MIP $110

Howdy Doody and his Magic Hat Book, 1953, Whitman, Little Golden Book
EX $12   NM $22   MIP $40

Howdy Doody and Mr. Bluster Book, 1954, Whitman, Little Golden Book
EX $10   NM $22   MIP $40

Howdy Doody and the Musical Forest Record, 1950s, RCA, 45 rpm
EX $20   NM $50   MIP $80

Howdy Doody and the Princess Book, 1952, Whitman, Little Golden Book
EX $10   NM $25   MIP $45

Howdy Doody and You Record, 1950s, RCA, 45 rpm
EX $18   NM $40   MIP $65

Howdy Doody Bank, Vandor, ceramic figural head
EX $25   NM $55   MIP $100

Howdy Doody Bank, 1950s, ceramic bank, all color, bust of Howdy
EX $300   NM $500   MIP $900

Howdy Doody Bank, 1950s, 7" tall, ceramic, Howdy riding a pig
EX $70   NM $160   MIP $300

Howdy Doody Bank, 1976, Strauss, flocked plastic, 9"
EX $20   NM $40   MIP $85

Howdy Doody Bubble Pipe, 1950s, Lido, 4" long, Howdy or Clarabell
EX $30   NM $160   MIP $285

Howdy Doody Button, 1949, New York Sunday News, reads "New Color Comic—Sunday News"
EX $30   NM $55   MIP $100

Howdy Doody Coin, 1950s, Kellogg's, plastic, silver, raised bust on Howdy on front
EX $20   NM $40   MIP $75

Howdy Doody Color TV Set, American Plastic, plastic, w/films
EX $130   NM $275   MIP $500

Howdy Doody Coloring Books, 1955, Whitman, boxed set of six
EX $42   NM $150   MIP $300

Howdy Doody Comic Book, 1950, Dell, issue No. 1, January
EX $110   NM $275   MIP $425

Howdy Doody Cookbook, 1952, Welch's
EX $30   NM $110   MIP $225

Howdy Doody Cookie-Go-Round, 1950s, Luce/Krispy Kan, lithographed cookie tin
EX $75   NM $160   MIP $285

Howdy Doody Costume, 1950s, Collegeville
EX $50   NM $100   MIP $200

Howdy Doody Crayon Set, 1950, Milton Bradley, 16 crayons w/pictures
EX $45   NM $100   MIP $200

Howdy Doody Doll, 1950s, 7" tall vinyl squeeze toy, Howdy in blue pants and red shirt
EX $40   NM $90   MIP $170

Howdy Doody Doll, 1950s, Ideal, eyes and mouth move
EX $40   NM $90   MIP $160

Howdy Doody Doll, 1970s, Goldberger, 30", vinyl ventriloquist doll
EX $40   NM $90   MIP $160

Howdy Doody Doll, 1976, Goldberger, 12" vinyl ventriloquist doll
EX $25   NM $50   MIP $110

Howdy Doody Doll, 1988, Applause, 11" cloth doll
EX $10   NM $40   MIP $75

Howdy Doody Dominoes, 1950s
EX $20   NM $40   MIP $80

Howdy Doody Figure, Stahlwood, 5" x 7" rubber squeeze figure on airplane
EX $175   NM $360   MIP $725

Howdy Doody Fingertronic Puppet Theater, 1970s, Sutton
EX $25   NM $45   MIP $85

Howdy Doody Flasher Rings, 1950s, Nabisco, set of eight plastic character rings
EX $90   NM $175   MIP $400

Howdy Doody Flicker Ring, 1950s, Nabisco
EX $10   NM $20   MIP $50

Howdy Doody in Funland Book, 1953, Whitman, Little Golden Book
EX $10   NM $25   MIP $50

Howdy Doody Kiddie Pool, 1950s, Ideal, 40" diameter, yellow/blue vinyl
EX $80   NM $150   MIP $275

Howdy Doody Marionette, 1950s, Peter Puppet
EX $85   NM $190   MIP $375

Howdy Doody Mug, 1950s, Ovaltine, red plastic w/Howdy decal (Be Keen, Drink Chocolate Flavored Ovaltine)
EX $35   NM $50   MIP $100

Howdy Doody Music Box, Vandor, Howdy playing piano
EX $40   NM $55   MIP $90

Howdy Doody Newspaper #1, 1950, Poll Parrot, premium
EX $200   NM $400   MIP $500

Howdy Doody Night Light, 1950s, Leco, figural, Howdy's face
EX $35   NM $75   MIP $140

Howdy Doody Outdoor Sports Box, 1950s, tin litho box w/colorful graphics
EX $30   NM $60   MIP $110

Howdy Doody Paint Set, 1950s, Marx, plaster figures, paint
EX $35   NM $100   MIP $185

Howdy Doody Paint Set, 1950s, Milton Bradley
EX $40   NM $80   MIP $160

Howdy Doody Pencil Case, 1950s, vinyl; smiling Howdy on front
EX $20   NM $90   MIP $160

Howdy Doody Periscope, 1950s, Wonder Bread premium
EX $350   NM $700   MIP $1100

Howdy Doody Phono Doodle, Sharatone Products
EX $120   NM $260   MIP $350

Howdy Doody Pumpmobile, Nylint, tin vehicle
EX $110   NM $275   MIP $525

Howdy Doody Puppet Show Set, 1950s, includes plastic figures of Howdy, Clarabell, Mr. Bluster, Flub, Dilly Dally
EX $80   NM $170   MIP $325

Howdy Doody Puzzle, 1950s, Whitman, frame tray, Howdy Goes Fishing
EX $25   NM $45   MIP $90

Howdy Doody Puzzle Set, 1950s, Milton Bradley, set of three
EX $40   NM $75   MIP $150

Howdy Doody Ranch House Tool Box, 1950s, Liberty Steel, 14" x 6" x 3" illustrated steel box w/handle
EX $45   NM $110   MIP $185

Howdy Doody Salt and Pepper Shakers, 1950s, Peter Puppet, shape of Howdy's head; removable blue vinyl neckerchief
EX $75   NM $160   MIP $300

Howdy Doody Sand Forms, 1952, Ideal/Kagran, on card
EX $40   NM $80   MIP $150

Howdy Doody Songs Record, 1974, Take Two, record, cut-outs, coloring book
EX $20   NM $50   MIP $75

Howdy Doody Sticker Fun Book, 1952, Whitman
EX $15   NM $30   MIP $60

Howdy Doody Swim Ring, 1950s, Ideal, inflatable, 20" diameter
EX $20   NM $40   MIP $75

Howdy Doody Talking Alarm Clock, 1974, Janex
EX $30   NM $90   MIP $185

Howdy Doody Television, 1950s, Lido, filmstrips w/TV box
EX $25   NM $110   MIP $250

Howdy Doody Ukulele, 1950s, Emenee, plastic, white or yellow, 17"
EX $40   NM $65   MIP $110

Howdy Doody Umbrella, 1950s, Holllander, Howdy head for handle
EX $30   NM $80   MIP $160

Howdy Doody Wall Walker, Tigrett
EX $25   NM $50   MIP $100

Howdy Doody Wristwatch, 1950s, Ever Tick/Kagran, glow-in-the-dark
EX $100   NM $300   MIP $600

Howdy Doody Wristwatch, 1954, Ingraham, deep blue band w/blue and white dial showing character faces
EX $140   NM $350   MIP $750

Howdy Doody Xylo-Doodle, 1950s, yellow plastic piano/xylophone w/colorful graphics
EX $75   NM $375   MIP $675

Howdy Doody's Animal Friends Book, 1956, Whitman, Little Golden Book
EX $10   NM $20   MIP $50

Howdy Doody's Circus Book, 1950, Whitman, Little Golden Book
EX $10   NM $20   MIP $50

Howdy Doody's Electric Carnival Game, 1950s, Harett-Gilmar
EX $60   NM $120   MIP $225

Howdy Doody's Laughing Circus Record Set, 1950s, RCA, two 78 rpm records
EX $35   NM $70   MIP $135

Howdy Doody's Lucky Trip Book, 1953, Whitman, Little Golden Book
EX $12   NM $25   MIP $50

Howdy Doody's One-Man Band, Trophy Products/Kagran, musical instruments
EX $100   NM $225   MIP $500

Merchandise Manual, 1954, list of toys
EX $150   NM $450   MIP $650

Merchandise Manual, 1955, list of toys
EX $100   NM $350   MIP $600

Mr. Bluster Bank, 1976, Strauss, flocked plastic, 9"
EX $20   NM $35   MIP $75

Princess Summerfall Winterspring Doll, 1950s, Beehler Arts, 8", hard plastic, braided black hair
EX $100   NM $190   MIP $400

Princess Summerfall Winterspring Sewing Cards, 1950s, Milton Bradley, four cards, thread, plastic needle
EX $30   NM $65   MIP $135

Puppets, 1950s, Gund, Howdy, Bluster, Clarabell, Dilly or Princess
EX $20   NM $50   MIP $90

Sparkle Gun, 1987, Ja-Ru, plastic gun
EX $6   NM $20   MIP $45

Spinning Top, 1970s, Lorenz Bolz, tin top w/characters
EX $30   NM $60   MIP $110

I Dream of Jeannie

I Dream of Jeannie Costume, 1970s, Ben Cooper
EX $8   NM $20   MIP $50

I Dream of Jeannie Doll, 1965, Ideal, 18"
EX $65   NM $165   MIP $300

I Dream of Jeannie Doll, 1977, Remco, 6"
EX $25   NM $50   MIP $110

I Dream of Jeannie Play Set, 1977, Remco, w/6" doll
EX $40   NM $120   MIP $250

I Spy

Official Shoulder Holster Set, 1960s, Ray Line, Inc., includes rapid fire pistol ("shoots more than 50 rounds in one loading"), shoulder holster and ammo
EX $40   NM $65   MIP $95

Jetsons

Elroy Toy, 1963, Transogram
EX $10   NM $20   MIP $40

Jetson Figures, 1990, Applause, 10" tall; Judy, George, Elroy, Rosie, each
EX $50   NM $100   MIP $185

Jetsons Birthday Surprise Book, 1963, Whitman, Tell-A-Tale Book
EX $12   NM $25   MIP $65

Jetsons Colorforms Kit, 1963, Colorforms
EX $40   NM $75   MIP $150

Puzzle, 1962, Whitman, 70 pieces
EX $25   NM $95   MIP $175

Knight Rider

Knight Rider Impossibles Stunt Set, 1982, LJN
EX $45   NM $95   MIP $150

Knight Rider Wrist Communicator, 1982, Larami
EX $10   NM $20   MIP $40

Lassie

Lassie's Pups, 1950s, set including plastic toy dogs, blanket, tub and puppy bed
EX $12   NM $25   MIP $45

Original Lassie Stuffed Toy, 1950s, Smile Novelty Toy Co., reddish-brown and white stuffed toy w/plastic face
EX $40   NM $80   MIP $120

Laugh-In

"Sock It To Me" Plastic Purse, 1970s, yellow w/black lettering and strap
EX $10   **NM** $17   **MIP** $30

Laugh-In Electric Drawing Set, 1960s, Lakeside Toys, included an "electric" drawing set, color pencils, Laugh-In cartoon guides, drawing paper, eraser, sharpener, and instructions
EX $15   **NM** $35   **MIP** $65

Love Boat

Love Boat Play Set, 1970s, boat-shaped dollhouse w/figures of the cast, furniture and accessories, over two feet long
EX $25   **NM** $45   **MIP** $90

Man from U.N.C.L.E.

1966 British Annual, 1966, World Distributors, hardcover, 95 pages, photo cover
EX $20   **NM** $50   **MIP** $75

1967 British Annual Book, 1967, World Distributors, hardcover, 95 pages, photo cover
EX $15   **NM** $35   **MIP** $65

1968 British Annual Book, 1968, World Distributors, hardcover, 95 pages, photo cover
EX $15   **NM** $30   **MIP** $60

1969 British Annual, 1969, World Distributors, hardcover, 95 pages, photo cover
EX $15   **NM** $25   **MIP** $55

Action Figure Apparel Set, 1965, Gilbert, bullet proof vest, three targets, three shells, binoculars, and bazooka
EX $50   **NM** $100   **MIP** $210

Action Figure Armament Set, 1965, Gilbert, for 12" figures: jacket, cap firing pistol w/barrel extension, bipod stand, telescopic sight, grenade belt, binoculars, accessory pouch, and beret
EX $50   **NM** $90   **MIP** $180

Action Figure Arsenal Set #1, 1965, Gilbert, tommy gun, bazooka, three shells, cap firing pistol, and attachments, in shallow window box
EX $40   **NM** $80   **MIP** $175

Action Figure Arsenal Set #2, 1965, Gilbert, cap firing THRUSH rifle w/telescopic sight, grenade belt and four grenades, on wrapped header card
EX $40   **NM** $80   **MIP** $175

Action Figure Jumpsuit Set, 1965, Gilbert, for 12" figures: jumpsuit w/boots, helmet w/chin strap, 28" parachute and pack, cap firing tommy gun w/scope, instructions
EX $50   **NM** $100   **MIP** $225

Action Figure Pistol Conversion Kit, 1965, Gilbert, binoculars and pistol w/attachments, for 12" figures, on wrapped header card
EX $22   **NM** $45   **MIP** $90

Action Figure Scuba Set, 1965, Gilbert, for 12" Gilbert dolls: swim trunks, air tanks, tank bracket, tubes, scuba jacket, and knife
EX $65   **NM** $130   **MIP** $260

Affair of the Gentle Saboteur Book, 1966, Whitman, hardcover
EX $8   **NM** $15   **MIP** $35

Affair of the Gunrunners' Gold Book, 1967, Whitman, hardcover
EX $8   **NM** $15   **MIP** $35

Alexander Waverly Figure, 1966, Marx, blue plastic, 5-3/4" tall, stamped w/character's name and U.N.C.L.E. logo on the bottom of base
EX $8   **NM** $15   **MIP** $30

Arcade Cards, 1960s, postcards w/b/w photo fronts, Napoleon or Illya
EX $5   **NM** $10   **MIP** $30

Attache Case, 1966, Lone Star, small cardboard briefcase, contains die-cast Mauser and parts to assemble U.N.C.L.E. Special
EX $130   **NM** $230   **MIP** $500

Attache Case, British, 1965, Lone Star, 15" x 8" x 2" vinyl case w/a pistol, holster, walkie talkie, cigarette box gun, U.N.C.L.E. badge, international passport, invisible cartridge pen and handcuffs
EX $225   **NM** $450   **MIP** $900

Attache Case, British, 1966, Lone Star, cardboard covered in vinyl, 9mm automatic luger, shoulder stock, sight, silencer, belt, holster, secret wrist holster and pistol that fires cap and cork, grenade, wallet w/passport, play money
EX $250   **NM** $500   **MIP** $950

Bagatelle Game, 1966, Hong Kong, 8" x 14" pinball game
EX $75   **NM** $155   **MIP** $325

Bicycle License Plates, 1967, Marx, four different, metal: Man from U.N.C.L.E., The Girl from U.N.C.L.E., Napoleon Solo, Illya Kuryakin, each
EX $15   **NM** $30   **MIP** $50

Calcutta Affair Book, 1967, Whitman, 254 pages, Big Little Book
EX $10   **NM** $20   **MIP** $45

Candy Cigarette Box, 1966, Cadet Sweets, candy and trading card, illustrated box
EX $25   **NM** $60   **MIP** $125

Candy Cigarette Counter Display Box, 1966, Cadet Sweets, holds 72 candy cigarette boxes, illustrated
EX $30   **NM** $90   **MIP** $200

Coin of El Diablo Affair Book, 1965, Wonder Books, softcover, 48 pages
EX $10   **NM** $20   **MIP** $40

Counter Spy Water Gun, 1960s, Hong Kong, luger water gun w/unlicensed Napoleon Solo illustration header card
EX $5   **NM** $15   **MIP** $40

Counterspy Outfit, 1966, Marx, contains trench coat w/secret pockets, pistol, shoulder holster, launcher barrel, silencer, scope sight, two pair of glasses, beards, eye patch, badge case, etc., in box
EX $125   **NM** $230   **MIP** $485

Counterspy Outfit Store Display, 1966, Marx, 35" x 36" wide cardboard display w/one piece of each item in Counterspy Outfit
EX $320   **NM** $650   **MIP** $1350

Crime Buster Gift Set, 1966, Corgi, set includes Man from U.N.C.L.E. car, James Bond Aston Martin and Batmobile w/Batboat on trailer, in window box

EX $275   NM $525   MIP $1100

Die-Cast Car, 1968, Playart, 2-3/4" long, die-cast metal, metallic purple

EX $90   NM $200   MIP $425

Die-Cast Metal Gun, 1965, Lone Star, die-cast automatic cap pistol w/plastic grips, plus cut-out badge, on card

EX $75   NM $150   MIP $325

Diving Dames Affair Book, 1967, Souvenir Press/England, #10 in series

EX $4   NM $8   MIP $20

Doomsday Affair Book, 1965, Souvenir Press, #2 in series

EX $4   NM $8   MIP $20

Fingerprint Kit, 1966, ink pad, roller, code book, magnifier, fingerprint records and pressure plate, in illustrated window box

EX $125   NM $250   MIP $500

Flicker Ring, 1965, silver plastic ring w/b/w photos, each

EX $10   NM $20   MIP $50

Flicker Ring, 1966, blue plastic w/"changing portrait" of Napoleon or Illya, each

EX $10   NM $20   MIP $40

Foto-Fantastiks Coloring Set, 1965, Eberhard Faber, six colored pencils, paint brush, and six 8" x 10" photos, came in four different versions, each

EX $40   NM $85   MIP $175

Generic Spies Figures, 1966, Marx, six different solid plastic, unpainted figures 5-3/4" tall, each

EX $8   NM $15   MIP $20

Handkerchief, 1966, England, U.N.C.L.E. logo, Illya and Napoleon

EX $30   NM $65   MIP $150

Headquarters Transmitter, 1965, Cragstan, molded gold colored plastic transmitter, amplifier and under cover case, silver ID card, 20-foot wire, in box

EX $80   NM $160   MIP $350

Illya Kuryakin Action Figure, 1965, Gilbert, 12" tall, plastic, black sweater, pants and shoes, spring loaded arm for firing cap pistol, folding badge, ID card and instruction sheet, in photo box

EX $80   NM $225   MIP $425

Illya Kuryakin Action Puppet, 1965, Gilbert, 13" tall, soft vinyl hand puppet of Illya holding a communicator, on 10" x 16" card

EX $80   NM $175   MIP $375

Illya Kuryakin Costume, 1967, Halco, painted mask, rayon costume in three colors showing Illya holding a gun, in illustrated window box

EX $45   NM $90   MIP $200

Illya Kuryakin Figure, 1966, Marx, blue or gray plastic figure, 5-3/4" tall, stamped w/character's name and U.N.C.L.E. logo on the bottom of base

EX $15   NM $40   MIP $80

Illya, That Man From U.N.C.L.E. Book, 1966, Pocket Books, 6" x 9" paperback, 100 pages of David McCallum

EX $10   NM $30   MIP $70

Invisible Writing Cartridge Pen, 1965, Platinum/England, pen, two vials of ink and two invisible ink vials

EX $125   NM $230   MIP $475

Magic Slates, 1965, Watkins-Strathmore, 9" x 14" slate w/two punch-out figures of either Napoleon or Illya, each

EX $45   NM $100   MIP $200

Man from the U.N.C.L.E. Record, 1965, Capitol Records, 45 rpm w/The Man from U.N.C.L.E. theme song and "The Vagabond"

EX $25   NM $60   MIP $120

Man from U.N.C.L.E. and other TV Themes Record, 1965, Metro Records, photo cover, has three songs from U.N.C.L.E. plus theme songs from Dr. Kildare, Mr. Novak, Bonanza and other shows

EX $8   NM $25   MIP $50

Man from U.N.C.L.E. Button, 1965, Button World, 3-1/2" diameter round button w/portrait of Napoleon or Illya, each

EX $10   NM $17   MIP $30

Man from U.N.C.L.E. Card Game, 1966, Japan, small artwork cards in illustrated box

EX $40   NM $75   MIP $160

Man from U.N.C.L.E. Code Board, 1966, chalkboard w/line art illustrations

EX $70   NM $150   MIP $300

Man from U.N.C.L.E. Finger Puppets, 1966, Dean, vinyl; THRUSH agent, Solo, Kuryakin, Waverly and two female agents; window box

EX $140   NM $300   MIP $600

Man from U.N.C.L.E. Playing Cards, 1965, Ed-U-Cards, standard 54-card deck w/action photo illustrations, on card

EX $20   NM $35   MIP $70

Man from U.N.C.L.E. Playing Cards Display Box, 1965, Ed-U-Cards, holds 12 packs

EX $130   NM $250   MIP $525

Man from U.N.C.L.E. Puzzles, 1965, Jaymar, frame tray; three versions; each

EX $25   NM $40   MIP $75

Man from U.N.C.L.E. Record, 1965, Crescendo Records, by the Challengers, cover shows blonde female spy w/gun

EX $5   NM $15   MIP $35

Man from U.N.C.L.E. Record, 1966, Union/Japan, 45 rpm w/photo sleeve

EX $35   NM $75   MIP $150

Man from U.N.C.L.E. Sheet Music, 1964, Hastings Music Corp., six pages, theme song and a brief description of the TV show

EX $15   NM $50   MIP $100

Man from U.N.C.L.E. Trading Cards, 1965, Topps, set of 55 b/w photo cards

EX $45   NM $95   MIP $175

Man from U.N.C.L.E. Trading Cards, 1966, Cadet Sweets, set of 50 cards, color photos, set

EX $22   NM $45   MIP $90

Man from U.N.C.L.E. Trading Cards, 1966, ABC/England, 25 cards

EX $22   NM $45   MIP $90

Mystery Jigsaw Series Puzzles, 1965, Milton Bradley, 14" x 24" puzzle, 250 pieces plus story booklet, The Loyal Groom, The Vital Observation, The Impossible Escape, The Micro-Film Affair, each

EX $25   NM $50   MIP $100

Napoleon Solo Costume, 1965, Halco, transparent plastic "mystery mask," costume has line art shirt, tie, shoulder holster and U.N.C.L.E. logo, in illustrated box
EX $50   **NM** $95   **MIP** $185

Napoleon Solo Credentials and Passport Set, 1965, Ideal, silver ID card, badge, identification wallet, slide window passport, on header card
EX $35   **NM** $65   **MIP** $150

Napoleon Solo Credentials and Secret Message Sender, 1965, Ideal, message sender, badge, and silver ID, on card
EX $40   **NM** $80   **MIP** $175

Napoleon Solo Doll, 1965, Gilbert, 11" tall, plastic, white shirt, black pants and shoes, spring loaded arm for firing cap pistol, folding badge, ID card and instruction sheet
EX $70   **NM** $145   **MIP** $350

Napoleon Solo Figure, 1966, Marx, blue or gray plastic figure, 5-3/4" tall stamped w/character's name and U.N.C.L.E. logo on the bottom of base
EX $15   **NM** $35   **MIP** $80

Pinball Affair Game, 1966, Marx, 12" x 24" tin litho pinball game
EX $75   **NM** $150   **MIP** $300

Pistol Cane Gun, 1966, Marx, 25" long, cap firing, bullet shooting aluminum cane w/eight bullets and one metal shell, on illustrated card
EX $125   **NM** $250   **MIP** $600

Power Cube Affair Book, 1968, Souvenir, #15 in series, British
EX $5   **NM** $10   **MIP** $25

Puzzle, 1966, Milton Bradley, 10" x 19", 100 pieces, Illya's Battle Below
EX $15   **NM** $35   **MIP** $70

Puzzle, 1966, Milton Bradley, 10" x 19", 100 pieces, Illya Crushes THRUSH
EX $15   **NM** $40   **MIP** $70

Puzzles, 1966, England, four 11" x 17" puzzles, each w/340 pieces: The Getaway, Solo in Trouble, The Frogman Affair, Secret Plans, each
EX $40   **NM** $80   **MIP** $165

Secret Agent Wristwatch, 1966, Bradley, gray watch face shows Solo holding a communicator, came w/either plain "leather" or "mod" watch band, in case
EX $115   **NM** $250   **MIP** $500

Secret Code Wheel Pinball, 1966, Marx, 10" x 22" x 6" tin litho pinball game
EX $80   **NM** $170   **MIP** $325

Secret Message Pen, 1966, American Character, 6-1/2" long double tipped pen for writing invisible messages, on header card
EX $100   **NM** $200   **MIP** $325

Secret Print Putty, 1965, Colorforms, putty in a gun shaped container, print paper, display cards of Kuryakin and Solo and a book of spy and weapons illustrations, on card
EX $20   **NM** $45   **MIP** $95

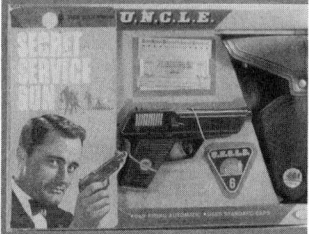

Secret Service Gun, 1965, Ideal, pistol, holster, badge and silver ID card, in window box
EX $160   **NM** $310   **MIP** $650

Secret Service Pop Gun, 1960s, bagged Luger pop gun on header card w/unlicensed illustration of Illya and Napoleon on header
EX $10   **NM** $15   **MIP** $50

Secret Weapon Set, 1965, Ideal, clip loading cap firing pistol, holster, ID wallet, silver ID card, U.N.C.L.E. badge, two demolition grenades and holster, in window box
EX $190   **NM** $400   **MIP** $775

Shirt, 1965, has secret pocket, glow-in-the-dark badge and ID, photo package
EX $190   **NM** $375   **MIP** $725

Shoot Out! Game, 1965, Milton Bradley, skill and action game for two players, plastic marble game in illustrated box
EX $80   **NM** $160   **MIP** $325

Shooting Arcade Game, 1966, Marx, tin litho arcade w/mechanical wind-up THRUSH agent targets for pellet shooting pistol, scope and stock attachments
EX $200   **NM** $400   **MIP** $850

Shooting Arcade Game, 1966, Marx, smaller version w/THRUSH spinner targets
EX $150   **NM** $275   **MIP** $525

Spy Magic Tricks, 1965, Gilbert, mystery gun, Illya playing cards, tricks
EX $125   **NM** $250   **MIP** $525

Television Picture Story Book, 1968, P.B.S. Limited, hardcover, 62 pages, Gold Key reprints
EX $15   **NM** $20   **MIP** $60

THRUSH Agent Figures, 1966, Marx, three different blue plastic figures, 5-3/4" tall stamped w/titles and U.N.C.L.E. logo on the bottom of each base, each
EX $10   **NM** $20   **MIP** $50

THRUSH Ray-Gun Affair Game, 1966, Ideal, four U.N.C.L.E. agent pieces, Area Decoder cards, 3-D THRUSH hideouts, THRUSH vehicles, crayons, dice and a rotating "ray gun," in illustrated box
EX $55   **NM** $110   **MIP** $225

THRUSH-Buster Display Box, 1966, Corgi, large display box w/graphics, holds 12 cars
EX $170   **NM** $330   **MIP** $700

U.N.C.L.E. Badges Store Display, 1965, Lone Star, illustrated card holds 12 triangular black plastic badges w/gold lettering, w/badges
EX $50   **NM** $120   **MIP** $225

McHale's Navy

McHale's Navy Signal Sender, 1960s, Gabriel-Bell, Inc., Megaphone sends amplifies voice, sends light signal and includes a Morse code button
EX $15   **NM** $25   **MIP** $55

Monkees

Flip Movies, 1967, Topps, each
EX $5   **NM** $10   **MIP** $30

Halloween Costumes, 1967, Bland Charnas, each
EX $60   **NM** $125   **MIP** $250

Jigsaw Puzzle, 1967, Fairchild
EX $15   **NM** $25   **MIP** $45

Monkees Dolls, 1967, Remco, 4", rubber, each
EX $35   **NM** $80   **MIP** $175

Monkees Finger Puppets, 1969, Remco
EX $15   **NM** $25   **MIP** $45

Talking Hand Puppet, 1966, Mattel, cloth w/heads of Monkees on fingertips

EX $50   NM $110   MIP $200

Tambourine, 1967, Raybert

EX $45   NM $100   MIP $200

Toy Guitar, 1966, Mattel, 20"

EX $60   NM $125   MIP $250

Toy Guitar, 1966, Mattel, 14", wind-up crank

EX $40   NM $90   MIP $175

Mork and Mindy

Mork and Mindy Colorforms, 1979, Colorforms

EX $10   NM $15   MIP $30

Mr. Ed

Mr. Ed Talking Horse Puppet, 1962, Mattel

EX $40   NM $80   MIP $150

Munsters, The

Grandpa Doll, 1964, Remco

EX $150   NM $325   MIP $610

Herman Munster Doll, 1964, Remco

EX $155   NM $350   MIP $720

Lily Baby Doll, 1965, Ideal, unlicensed "monster baby"

EX $45   NM $85   MIP $170

Lily Doll, 1964, Remco

EX $150   NM $325   MIP $625

Puzzle, 1960s, Whitman, frame tray

EX $30   NM $50   MIP $100

Puzzle, 1965, Whitman, 100 pieces, boxed

EX $35   NM $60   MIP $150

The Last Resort Book, 1964, Whitman

EX $13   NM $30   MIP $50

Partridge Family

David Cassidy Dress-Up Kit, 1972, Colorforms

EX $20   NM $40   MIP $75

Laurie Partridge Doll, 1973, Remco, 20" tall

EX $55   NM $120   MIP $225

Partridge Family Bus, 1973, Remco, plastic, 14" long

EX $65   NM $160   MIP $300

Partridge Family Guitar, 1970s, Carnival, 19" plastic, decal of David Cassidy on body

EX $35   NM $75   MIP $150

Partridge Family Paper Dolls, 1970s, Saalfield, several styles

EX $20   NM $40   MIP $75

Patti Partridge Doll, 1971, Ideal

EX $50   NM $110   MIP $200

Pee Wee Herman

Ball Dart Set

EX $5   NM $10   MIP $15

Billy Baloney Doll, 1988, Matchbox, 18" tall

EX $12   NM $20   MIP $75

Chairry Figure, Matchbox, 15" tall

EX $12   NM $20   MIP $45

Conky Wacky Wind-Up, 1988, Matchbox

EX $3   NM $5   MIP $10

Cowboy Curtis Figure, Matchbox

EX $8   NM $15   MIP $35

Globey w/Randy, 1988, Matchbox

EX $8   NM $15   MIP $40

King of Cartoons Figure, 1988, Matchbox, 5" tall

EX $8   NM $15   MIP $35

Magic Screen Figure, 1988, Matchbox, 5" tall poseable

EX $8   NM $15   MIP $35

Magic Screen Wacky Wind-Up, 1988, Matchbox, 6" tall

EX $3   NM $5   MIP $10

Miss Yvonne Doll, 1988, Matchbox, poseable 5" tall

EX $8   NM $15   MIP $45

Pee Wee Herman Deluxe Colorforms, 1980s, Colorforms

EX $7   NM $10   MIP $35

Pee Wee Herman Doll, 1980s, Matchbox, 15" tall, non talking

EX $10   NM $35   MIP $75

Pee Wee Herman Doll, 1988, Matchbox, poseable 5" tall

EX $4   NM $10   MIP $25

Pee Wee Herman Play Set, 1989, Matchbox, 20" x 28" x 8" for use w/5" figures, Pee Wee's bike, folds into large carrying case

EX $12   NM $28   MIP $60

Pee Wee Herman Slumber Bag, 1988, Matchbox

EX $10   NM $20   MIP $35

Pee Wee Herman Ventriloquist Doll, 1980s, Matchbox

EX $30   NM $65   MIP $135

Pee Wee w/Scooter and Helmet, 1988, Matchbox

EX $4   NM $7   MIP $15

Pee Wee Yo-Yo, 1980s

EX $3   NM $10   MIP $20

Pterri Doll, 1980s, Matchbox, 13" tall
EX $15   NM $25   MIP $45

Pterri Wacky Wind-Ups, 1988, Matchbox
EX $3   NM $5   MIP $10

Reba Figure, 1988, Matchbox, poseable
EX $5   NM $10   MIP $30

Ricardo Figure, 1988, Matchbox
EX $5   NM $10   MIP $30

Vance the Talking Pig Figure, 1987, Matchbox
EX $20   NM $40   MIP $85

Pinky Lee

Pinky Lee Paint Set, 1950s, Gabriel, eight pictures to watercolor
EX $10   NM $20   MIP $33

Toy Medicine Chest, 1950s
EX $10   NM $20   MIP $50

Who Am I? Game, 1950s, based on the TV show
EX $5   NM $15   MIP $25

Rat Patrol

Rat Patrol Diorama Kit, 1960s, Aurora, includes 15 figures, two Rat Patrol Jeeps, one German Panzer Tank, one German Panther Tank, dimensional battlefield w/sandbags, bunkers, dunes and palm trees
EX $20   NM $40   MIP $65

Rocky and Bullwinkle

Bullwinkle and Rocky Clock Bank, 1969, Larami, 4-1/2" tall, plastic
EX $30   NM $60   MIP $120

Bullwinkle and Rocky Movie Viewer, 1960s, #225, red and white plastic viewer w/three movies
EX $25   NM $50   MIP $75

Bullwinkle and Rocky Wastebasket, 1961, 11" tall, metal w/Jay Ward cast pictured
EX $35   NM $65   MIP $135

Bullwinkle Bank, 1960s, 6" tall, glazed china
EX $75   NM $125   MIP $400

Bullwinkle Bank, 1972, Play Pal, 11-1/2", plastic
EX $35   NM $50   MIP $100

Bullwinkle Cartoon Kit, 1962, Colorforms
EX $35   NM $50   MIP $160

Bullwinkle Dinner Set, 1960s, Boonton Molding, plate and cup pictures Bullwinkle and the Cheerios Kid
EX $25   NM $50   MIP $85

Bullwinkle Figure, 1976, Dakin, Cartoon Theater, 7-1/2" tall, plastic
EX $25   NM $50   MIP $90

Bullwinkle Flexy Figure, 1970, Larami
EX $10   NM $35   MIP $75

Bullwinkle for President Bumper Sticker, 1972
EX $10   NM $16   MIP $40

Bullwinkle Jewelry Hanger, 1960s, 5" tall, suction cup on back
EX $15   NM $25   MIP $50

Bullwinkle Magic Slate, 1963
EX $15   NM $40   MIP $85

Bullwinkle Make Your Own Badge Set, 1960s, Larami
EX $20   NM $40   MIP $85

Bullwinkle Paintless Paint Book, 1960, Whitman
EX $15   NM $35   MIP $80

Bullwinkle Spell and Count Board, 1969
EX $12   NM $25   MIP $50

Bullwinkle Stamp Set, 1970, Larami
EX $12   NM $25   MIP $40

Bullwinkle Stickers, 1984, Bullwinkle, Sherman and Peabody, Snidely Whiplash
EX $5   NM $10   MIP $20

Bullwinkle Talking Doll, 1970, Mattel
EX $30   NM $75   MIP $150

Bullwinkle Travel Adventure Board Game, 1960s, Transogram
EX $30   NM $70   MIP $135

Bullwinkle Travel Game, 1971, Larami, magnetic
EX $15   NM $30   MIP $60

Bullwinkle's Circus Time Toy, 1969, Rocky on a circus horse
EX $20   NM $40   MIP $90

Bullwinkle's Circus Time Toy, 1969, Bullwinkle on a elephant
EX $20   NM $40   MIP $90

Bullwinkle's Double Boomerangs, 1969, Larami, set of two on illustrated card
EX $15   NM $25   MIP $50

Dudley Do-Right Figure, 1972, Wham-O, 5" tall, flexible
EX $12   NM $40   MIP $80

Dudley Do-Right Figure, 1976, Dakin, Cartoon Theater
EX $15   NM $40   MIP $85

Dudley Do-Right Puzzle, 1975, Whitman
EX $12   NM $30   MIP $60

Mr. Peabody Bank, 1960s, 6" tall, glazed china
EX $90   NM $190   MIP $385

Mr. Peabody Figure, 1972, Wham-O, 4" tall, flexible
EX $10   NM $30   MIP $70

Natasha Figure, 1972, Wham-O
EX $10   NM $30   MIP $70

Rocky and Bullwinkle Bank, 1960, 5" tall, glazed china
EX $90   NM $190   MIP $385

Rocky and Bullwinkle Presto Sparkle Painting Set, 1962, Kenner, six cartoon pictures and two comic strip panels
EX $30   NM $70   MIP $135

Rocky and Bullwinkle Puzzle, 1972, Whitman, boxed
EX $15   NM $30   MIP $75

Rocky and Bullwinkle Toothpaste Holder, 1960s, glazed china
EX $80   NM $190   MIP $375

Rocky and His Friends Book, 1960s, Whitman, Little Golden Book
EX $20   NM $50   MIP $80

Rocky Bank, 1950s, 5" tall, slot in large tail, glazed china
EX $80   NM $225   MIP $425

Rocky Figure, 1976, Dakin, Cartoon Theater, 6-1/2" tall, plastic
EX $30   NM $60   MIP $125

Rocky Flexy Figure, 1970, Larami
EX $10   NM $25   MIP $50

Rocky Soaky, Colgate-Palmolive, 10-1/2" tall, plastic
EX $15   NM $35   MIP $65

Rocky the Flying Squirrel Coloring Book, 1960, Whitman
EX $20   NM $40   MIP $85

Sherman Figure, 1972, Wham-O, 4" tall, flexible
EX $15   NM $35   MIP $70

Snidely Whiplash Figure, 1972, Wham-O, 5" tall, flexible
EX $15   NM $40   MIP $80

Romper Room

Bop-A-Loop Toy (MIB), Hasbro, shown here w/Romper Room Rhythm set
EX $4   NM $8   MIP $10

Build & Play Discs, Hasbro
EX $3   NM $6   MIP $12

Can You Guess? Wonder Book, Hasbro
EX $2   NM $4   MIP $8

Ceramic Mug – Jack-in-the-Box, Hasbro
EX $5   NM $15   MIP $34

Chalkboard, Hasbro
EX $4   NM $7   MIP $15

Digger the Dog (MIB), Hasbro
EX $5   NM $15   MIP $32

Do Bee Dough Machine, Hasbro
EX $5   NM $15   MIP $34

Do Bee Iron On Transfer, Hasbro
EX $1   NM $3   MIP $5

Do Bee Rider, Hasbro
EX $10   NM $20   MIP $55

Do Bees Little Golden Book of Manners, Hasbro
EX $5   NM $9   MIP $18

Dump Truck (Do Bee hubcaps), Hasbro
EX $2   NM $4   MIP $8

Fitness Fun 45 RPM, Hasbro
EX $2   NM $4   MIP $8

Fun Time Puzzle Clock, Hasbro
EX $3   NM $5   MIP $10

G.E. Show 'N Tell Phonoviewer, Hasbro
EX $8   NM $14   MIP $28

G.E. Show 'N Tell Picturesound Refill Programs (each), Hasbro
EX $1   NM $2   MIP $4

Happy Jack and Mr. Do Bee Hand Puppets, Hasbro
EX $10   NM $20   MIP $40

Happy Jack Magnetic Puzzle, Hasbro
EX $4   NM $8   MIP $16

Happy Jack Punching Clown, Hasbro
EX $5   NM $9   MIP $18

Inchworm, Hasbro, green w/yellow saddle
EX $15   NM $30   MIP $65

Moe the Monkey Game, Hasbro
EX $3   NM $5   MIP $10

Mr. Do Bee Bank, Hasbro
EX $5   NM $15   MIP $35

Mr. Do Bee Miniature Poly-Blocks, Hasbro
EX $3   NM $5   MIP $10

Mr. Stacking Man, Hasbro
EX $4   NM $8   MIP $15

Musical Block Clock, Hasbro
EX $10   NM $20   MIP $45

Musical Jack in the Box, Hasbro
EX $15   NM $35   MIP $75

Official TV Bo Dee Dance Record, Hasbro
EX $4   NM $8   MIP $20

Peg Town Railroad, Hasbro
EX $2   NM $5   MIP $10

Preschool Super Fun Pad, Hasbro
EX $1   NM $3   MIP $6

Rhythm Set, Hasbro
EX $4   NM $9   MIP $22

Sew Easy Sewing Machine, Hasbro
EX $3   NM $6   MIP $12

Snoopy Counting Camera, Hasbro
EX $5   NM $10   MIP $20

Snoopy Play Telephone, Hasbro
EX $3   NM $5   MIP $10

Squirt, Squirt, Squirt the Animals Tub Toy, Hasbro
EX $3   NM $5   MIP $10

Super Mr. Potato Head, Hasbro
EX $3   NM $7   MIP $14

Talk 'N Chalk Board, Hasbro
EX $5   NM $15   MIP $30

Toy Ring – Gold Plated Plastic, Hasbro
EX $10   NM $20   MIP $40

Weebles Playground, Hasbro
EX $22   NM $55   MIP $110

Willie the Weather Man, Hasbro
EX $10   NM $20   MIP $45

Rookies, The

Rookie Chris Figure, 1973, LJN, 8" tall
EX $10   NM $20   MIP $60

Rookie Mike Figure, 1973, LJN, 8" tall
EX $10   NM $20   MIP $60

Rookie Terry Figure, 1973, LJN, 8" tall
EX $10   NM $20   MIP $60

Rookie Willy Figure, 1973, LJN, 8" tall
EX $10   NM $20   MIP $60

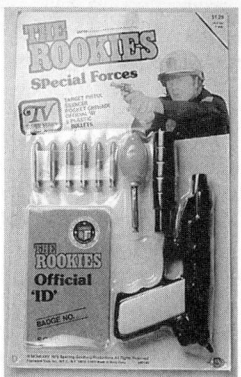

Special Forces Set, 1975, Fleetwood Toys, includes target pistol, silencer, rocket grenade, official ID, and six plastic bullets
EX $15   NM $25   MIP $50

S.W.A.T.

Bullhorn, 1976
EX $15   NM $25   MIP $35

Clicker Gun & Handcuffs Set, 1975, Fleetwood Toys
EX $10   NM $17   MIP $25

Deacon, 1976, LJN, 8" figure
EX $5   NM $12   MIP $35

Hondo, 1976, LJN, 8" figure
EX $5   NM $12   MIP $35

Luca, 1976, LJN, 8" figure
EX $5   NM $12   MIP $35

McCabe, 1976, LJN, 8" figure
EX $5   NM $12   MIP $35

Officer Jim Street, 1976, LJN, 8" figure
EX $5   NM $12   MIP $35

T.J., 1976, LJN, 8" figure
EX $5   NM $12   MIP $35

Van, 1976, LJN, fits 8" figures
EX $15   NM $30   MIP $45

Scooby Doo

Scooby Doo and the Pirate Treasure Book, 1974, Golden, Little Golden Book
EX $5   NM $10   MIP $15

Scooby Doo Hand Puppet, 1970s, Ideal, vinyl head
EX $20   NM $40   MIP $75

Scooby Doo Paint w/Water Book, 1984
EX $5   NM $10   MIP $20

Scooby Doo Squeak Toy, 1970s, Sanitoy, 6" tall
EX $20   NM $35   MIP $50

Sgt. Preston

Sgt. Preston of the Yukon Punch-Out Cards, 1950s, Quaker, "Big Game Trophy" cardboard cut-outs, set of nine
EX $30   NM $100   MIP $175

Six Million Dollar Man

Porta-Communicator, 1970s, Kenner, walkie-talkie device that attaches to Col. Austin like a backpack, you transmit your voice on one end, and it's broadcasted from the receiver on the other, included a 10-foot cord
EX $20   NM $45   MIP $65

Soupy Sales

Soupy Sales Card Game, 1960s, Jaymar, Slap Jack, Old Maid, Funny Rummy, or Hearts/Crazy 8s
EX $20   NM $40   MIP $60

Soupy Sales Doll, 1960s, Remco, 5" doll
EX $40   NM $150   MIP $250

Soupy Sales Doll, 1966, Knicker-bocker, 12" plush, vinyl head
EX $25   NM $60   MIP $150

Starsky & Hutch

Deluxe Police Set, 1970s, HG Toys, includes badges, service revolver, Colt .45, shoulder holster, cuffs, whistle, and poster
EX $30   NM $60   MIP $75

Starsky and Hutch Puzzle, 1970s, HG Toys
EX $15   NM $30   MIP $50

Starsky and Hutch Shoot-Out Target Set, 1970s, Berwick
EX $25   NM $45   MIP $95

Stingray

Puzzle, 1960s, Whitman
EX $10   NM $20   MIP $35

Stingray Atomic Submarine, Doyusha, w/electonic lights and sounds
EX $25   NM $45   MIP $90

Stingray Hand Puppet, Titan, 1960s
EX $7   NM $15   MIP $30

Stingray Hand Puppet, Troy Tempest, 1960s
EX $10   NM $20   MIP $35

Stingray Hand Puppet, X2-Zero, 1960s
EX $12   NM $22   MIP $40

Stingray Underwater Maze Game, 1960s, Transogram
EX $22   NM $40   MIP $70

The Fall Guy

Fall Guy Bounty Hunter HO Scale Race Set, 1970s, Aurora, includes Fall Guy truck, passenger car, figure-eight track
EX $25   **NM** $50   **MIP** $90

Pickup Truck Model Kit, 1980s, MPC
EX $5   **NM** $12   **MIP** $25

Target Shooting Game, 1980s, Arco, targets spin when hit
EX $5   **NM** $12   **MIP** $20

Thunderbirds

"The Mole" Vehicle, Bandai, tracked vehicle w/rotating drill section, from the Gerry Anderson series "Thunderbirds"
EX $14   **NM** $25   **MIP** $45

Underdog

Kite Fun Book, 1970s, Pacific Gas and Electric
EX $10   **NM** $35   **MIP** $85

Puzzle, 1975, Whitman, 100 pieces
EX $10   **NM** $20   **MIP** $30

Underdog Costume, 1969, Ben Cooper
EX $55   **NM** $85   **MIP** $150

Underdog Dot Funnies Kit, 1974, Whitman
EX $10   **NM** $20   **MIP** $40

Underdog Figure, 1976, Dakin, plastic, Cartoon Theater
EX $35   **NM** $100   **MIP** $150

Welcome Back, Kotter

Halloween Costume, 1976, Collegeville, several styles
EX $10   **NM** $20   **MIP** $25

Sweathogs Dolls, 1976, Mattel, Epstein, Washington, Barbarino, Kotter, Horshack; each
EX $10   **NM** $25   **MIP** $60

Sweathogs Grease Machine Cars, 1977, Ahi, 3" long, plastic cars; various styles, each
EX $15   **NM** $30   **MIP** $60

Welcome Back, Kotter Classroom, 1976, Mattel, play set
EX $25   **NM** $45   **MIP** $100

Welcome Back, Kotter Colorforms Set, 1976, Colorforms
EX $10   **NM** $20   **MIP** $50

Winky Dink and You

When Winky Winks at You Record, 1956, Decca
EX $45   **NM** $60   **MIP** $80

Winky Dink Book, 1956, Golden, Little Golden Book
EX $9   **NM** $16   **MIP** $30

Winky Dink Comic Book, 1950s, Dell, #663
EX $20   **NM** $40   **MIP** $90

Winky Dink Costume, 1950s, Halco, No. 642, cloth mask and jumper
EX $10   **NM** $20   **MIP** $40

Winky Dink Magic Crayons, 1960s
EX $20   **NM** $35   **MIP** $50

Winky Dink Official TV Game Kit, 1950s
EX $30   **NM** $50   **MIP** $100

Winky Dink Secret Message Game, 1950s, Lowell
EX $75   **NM** $130   **MIP** $225

Winky Dink Winko Magic Kit, 1950s
EX $20   **NM** $35   **MIP** $50

Vehicles

by Justin Moen

Toy vehicles have been around about as long as the real vehicles themselves. The first toy vehicles were basic, consisting of a small body with no interior. In the early days, especially with die-cast vehicles, impurities in the alloy were common, resulting in the distortion or cracking in the casting. But great improvements were made following World War II that helped bring toy vehicles to greater mainstream popularity.

One of the first enormously popular die-cast vehicles was Lesney's Matchbox vehicles. In fact, they were so popular that "Matchbox" was adopted as a generic term for any die-cast vehicle, no matter the actual manufacturer.

The detail and quality of the toy vehicles continued to improve in the 50s, with more companies like Corgi entering the field, pioneering the use of interiors and clear plastic windows in their models. By the end of the 60s a new player would enter the picture and change the face of toy vehicles forever.

Mattel was already an American toy-making pioneer, having hit the jackpot nearly a decade earlier with the release of the Barbie dolls line in 1959. Mattel co-founder Elliot Handler knew the company had to create new, pocket-size die-cast vehicles that not only looked better than the competition, they had to roll better than the competition, as little had been done over the years to improve the movement of toy vehilces.

Handler hired Fred Adickes to create a design team for the new toy vehicle. Former General Motors stylist Harry Bentley Bradley soon joined the Mattel staff, sketching Handler's visions of what these vehilces should look like.

Engineer Jack Malek believed mandolin string could be used to make the vehicles spin fast and smooth. Engineer Howard Newman went even further by creating a straight-axle suspension that would allow the vehicles to bounce like real ones while rolling smoothly on the mandolin wire.

Designer Rick Irons was responsible for creating the vehicles' package. Contrary to Matchbox, who hid the vehicles in their famous blue-and-yellow boxes, kids would be able to see these new bright-colored vehicles on clear plastic blister packs, with a wave to the top of the card that complemented the iconic flame design. Soon, others like Matchbox and Johnny Lightning would adopt Irons' blister pack concept.

Originally called "California Customs," the brand name was soon changed after Handler saw Harry Bradley's 1964 yellow El Camino and referred to it as one set of "hot wheels."

With a packaged product now in place, it was time to sell Hot Wheels to retail store toy buyers. In a private viewing, Kmart's boys' toy buyer Ken Sanger saw a Hot Wheels car pitted against a Matchbox car down a stretch of track. Impressed, Sanger ordered 50 million Hot Wheels for his store, predicting that Mattel would be able to sell every vehicle it produced. Sanger's prediction proved correct.

In 1968, the first 16 Hot Wheels redlines were released, launching one of the most successful toy lines in history. Today, some 45 years after their debut, over 4 billion Hot Wheels have been produced, with a Hot Wheels car purchased somewhere in the world every six seconds.

But vintage vehicles from Matchbox, Corgi, Dinky, Tonka, Johnny Lightning, and many of the Japanese vehicles are no slouches, as many of these vehicles enjoy enormous popularity in the toy vehicle collecting market.

Contributors: Corgi and Dinky contributor Dr. Douglas Sadecky; Japanese Tin Cars contributor Ron Smith; Structo contributor Randy Prasse; and Mark Rich contributed the Buddy L, Deluxe Reading, Eldon, Gay Toys, Midgetoy, Nylint, Processed Plastic, Remco, Tonka, and Tootsietoy chapters.

The Top 10 VEHICLES in mint condition

1. Hot Wheels Pink Rear-Loading VW Beach Bomb, Mattel, 1969 . . . . $72,000
2. Chrysler Imperial, Japanese Tin Cars, 1962 . . . . $20,000
3. 1956 Ford Two-Door Sedan, Japanese Tin Cars, Marusan $9,000
4. Avro Vulcan Delta Wing Bomber, Dinky, #749, 1955-56 . . . . $6,500
5. Hot Wheels Purple Olds 442, Mattel, 1971 . . . . $5,000
6. Custom T-Bird, Johnny Lightning Topper, 1969 . . . . $5,000
7. Vulcan Bomber, Dinky, 1955-56 . . . . $4,000
8. 1956 Ford Sedan, Japanese Tin Cars, Marusan $4,000
9. Hot Wheels Blue Rodger Dodger, Mattel, 1974 . . . . $3,500
10. Lincoln Continental Mark II, Japanese Tin Cars, Linemar, 1956 . . . . $3,500

Buddy L

AIRPLANES

Brute Good Year Blimp, Buddy L, 5" long; 1976

EX $3   NM $5   MIP $8

Four Motor Air Cruiser, Buddy L, white, red engine cowlings, yellow fuselage and twin tails, four engine monoplane, 27" wingspan; 1952

EX $200   NM $310   MIP $350

Four-Engine Transport, Buddy L, green wings, white engine cowlings, yellow fuselage and twin tails, four engine monoplane, 27" wingspan; 1949

EX $205   NM $300   MIP $405

Transport Airplane, Buddy L, white wings and engine cowlings, red fuselage and twin tails, four engine monoplane, 27" wingspan; 1946

EX $205   NM $310   MIP $410

BUSES

Greyhound, Buddy L, 16-1/2" long, blue and white, key-wound, 1940s

EX $115   NM $200   MIP $450

Greyhound, Buddy L, 7-1/2" long bus, white hubs, 1983

EX $4   NM $8   MIP $25

Greyhound Americruiser, Buddy L, made in Macau; marked 1979

EX $5   NM $10   MIP $18

Greyhound Americruiser, Buddy L, 7-1/2" long; made in Japan, "No. 4950"; 1979

EX $5   NM $10   MIP $18

School Bus, Buddy L, yellow station wagon, "School Bus" roof sign, door "Stop" sign, 1970s

EX $40   NM $75   MIP $275

School Bus, Buddy L, 11-1/4" long; van design w/open side door, chrome-hub whitewall tires, yellow body, orange chassis, 1960s

EX $14   NM $25   MIP $40

School Bus, Buddy L, 9-3/4" long; yellow, open top; 1981

EX $3   NM $5   MIP $10

School Bus, Buddy L, 6-1/2" long; made in Macau; marked 1980

EX $2   NM $4   MIP $10

School Bus, Buddy L, 6-1/2" long; yellow, black front fenders, made in Japan; 1980

EX $3   NM $6   MIP $10

CARS

"CHIPS" Wind & Watch Speedster, Buddy L, motorcycle, motorized, 1981

EX $2   NM $3   MIP $10

"The Rebel" Rev 'Em Up Racer, Buddy L, 8" long, orange "Dukes"-like car w/Confederate flag, various sportscar makes, 1987

EX $4   NM $8   MIP $20

Army Jeep, Buddy L, 5-1/2" long; metal base, plastic body, Army green w/white star on hood and sides; 1979

EX $3   NM $5   MIP $5

Army Staff Car, Buddy L, olive drab body, 15-3/4" long; 1964

EX $100   NM $150   MIP $200

Baha Bronc, Buddy L, 6-1/2" long; white Jeep w/stars/stripes motif, black rollover roof, 1980s

EX $4   NM $9   MIP $17

Big "H" Race Team, Buddy L, 17" long; hot Rod w/two trailers and two Honda motorcycles; 1966-68

EX $35   NM $75   MIP $110

Bloomin' Bus (VW), Buddy L, 10-3/4" long; chartreuse body, white roof and supports; 1969

EX $25   NM $55   MIP $85

Brute '57 Chevy, Buddy L, 5-1/2" long, 1989

EX $2   NM $4   MIP $10

Brute Baby Buggy, Buddy L, 5" long; baby-carriage type vehicle; 1969-70

EX $3   NM $5   MIP $8

Brute Beach Buggy, Buddy L, 5" long; covered dune buggy; 1969-70

EX $3   NM $5   MIP $8

Brute Boss Bug, Buddy L, 5" long; muscle car style; 1970-71

EX $3   NM $5   MIP $8

Brute Fire Buggy, Buddy L, 5" long; ladder truck; 1969-71

EX $3   NM $5   MIP $8

Brute Road Buggy, Buddy L, 5" long; roadster; 1970-71

EX $3   NM $5   MIP $8

Brute Super Bug, Buddy L, 5" long; VW Beetle; 1970-71

EX $3   NM $7   MIP $8

Buddywagen (VW), Buddy L, 10-3/4" long; red body w/white roof, opening side doors, folding seats, sliding sun roof; 1966

EX $30   NM $60   MIP $90

Buddywagen (VW), Buddy L, 10-3/4" long; red body w/white roof, no chrome "V" on front; 1967

EX $30   NM $60   MIP $90

Camaro, Buddy L, 4-1/2" long; plastic, opaque windows, "Camaro" sitcker on sides; 1980

EX $2   NM $6   MIP n/a

Captain America Rocket Bronc, Buddy L, "Super Heroes" series, steel and plastic Bronco, 1980

EX $5   NM $15   MIP $60

Colt Sportsliner, Buddy L, 10-1/4" long; light blue-green open body, white hardtop, pale tan seats and interior; 1968-69

EX $20   NM $45   MIP $65

Colt Sportsliner, Buddy L, 10-1/4" long; red open body, white hardtop; off-white seats and interior; 1967

EX $20   NM $45   MIP $70

Colt Utility Car, Buddy L, light orange body, tan interior, 10-1/4" long; 1968

EX $35   NM $45   MIP $65

Colt Utility Car, Buddy L, 10-1/4" long; red open body, white plastic seats, floor and luggage spade; 1967

EX $20   NM $45   MIP $70

Country Squire Wagon, Buddy L, off-white hood fenders, end gate and roof, brown woodgrain side panels, 15-1/2" long; 1963

EX $85   NM $140   MIP $290

Country Squire Wagon, Buddy L, red hood fenders, end gate and roof, brown woodgrain side panels, 15-1/2" long; 1965

EX $75   NM $115   MIP $150

Deluxe Convertible Coupe, Buddy L, metallic blue enamel front, sides and deck, cream top retracts into rumble seat, 19" long; 1949

EX $310   NM $455   MIP $605

Desert Rat Command Car, Buddy L, 10-1/4" long; tan body, beige interior, black machine gun between seats, whitewall tires; 1967

EX $30   NM $65   MIP $90

Desert Rat Command Car, Buddy L, 10-1/4" long; tan body, beige interior, blackwall tires; 1968

EX $30   NM $65   MIP $90

Dr. Doom Blaster Car, Buddy L, Marvel Super Heroes Secret Wars series, 1984

EX $2   NM $8   MIP $15

Dr. Octopus Blaster Car, Buddy L, Marvel Super Heroes Secret Wars series, 1984

EX $2   NM $8   MIP $15

Formula One Racer, Buddy L, 8" long; blue w/"3" and "STP", 1980s

EX $7   NM $12   MIP $18

Gull Wing Vette, Buddy L, 4" long; "Pace Car" on sides; 1979

EX $6　　NM $12　　MIP $18

Hot Rod, Buddy L, whitewall tires, plastic roof, spare tire in rear (until 1968), various colors; 1965

EX $25　　NM $35　　MIP $60

Hot Rod Woody Station Wagon, Buddy L, Ol' Buddys series, 10-1/2" long; made in Japan, opening driver door and back door, steering; late 1960s

EX $30　　NM $50　　MIP $110

Jr. Buggy Hauler, Buddy L, 12" long; Jeep, Sandpiper dune buggy on trailer; 1971

EX $17　　NM $33　　MIP $50

Jr. Camaro, Buddy L, 9" long; metallic blue body, white racing stripes on hood; 1968

EX $17　　NM $25　　MIP $50

Jr. Flower Power Sportster, Buddy L, purple hood, fenders and body, white roof and supports, white plastic seats, lavender and orange five-petal blossom decals on hood top, roof, and sides, 6" long; 1969

EX $23　　NM $35　　MIP $55

Jr. Mustang, Buddy L, 9" long; whitewall tires; 1971

EX $15　　NM $45　　MIP n/a

Jr. Sportster, Buddy L, blue hood and open body, white hardtop and upper sides, 6" long; 1968

EX $23　　NM $35　　MIP $55

Mr. T Corvette, Buddy L, 5-1/4" long; red plastic w/Mr. T image, 1980s

EX $4　　NM $8　　MIP $12

Police Colt, Buddy L, 10-1/4" long; blue body, white hardtop, "Police 1" on sides; 1968-69

EX $17　　NM $33　　MIP $50

Ski Bus (VW), Buddy L, 10-3/4" long; white body and roof, ski rack, skis and ski poles, two skiers; 1967-68

EX $75　　NM $125　　MIP $300

Sling Shot Race Team, Buddy L, 6-1/2" long; green Jeep w/4" racer on trailer; 1970s

EX $8　　NM $14　　MIP $20

Spiderman Van, Buddy L, "Marvel Super Heroes Secret Wars" series, 1980s

EX $4　　NM $8　　MIP $12

Station Wagon, Buddy L, light blue/green body and roof, 15-1/2" long; 1963

EX $75　　NM $115　　MIP $150

Suburban Wagon, Buddy L, gray/green body and roof, 15-3/4" long; 1964

EX $70　　NM $125　　MIP $160

Suburban Wagon, Buddy L, powder blue or white body and roof, 15-1/2" long; 1963

EX $75　　NM $125　　MIP $160

Thunderbird, Buddy L, 5" long; red body, white top, whitewall tires, 1980s

EX $8　　NM $15　　MIP $25

Town and Country Convertible, Buddy L, maroon front, hood, rear deck and fenders, gray top retracts into rumble seat, 19" long; 1947

EX $300　　NM $450　　MIP $600

Travel Trailer and Station Wagon, Buddy L, red station wagon, two-wheel trailer w/red lower body and white steel camper-style upper body, 27-1/4" long; 1965

EX $155　　NM $230　　MIP $310

VW Bug, Buddy L, 2-1/2" long; red, white-hub tires, 1970s

EX $2　　NM $4　　MIP $8

Wolverine Bike, Buddy L, 3-1/2" long, "Super Heroes" series, w/attached Marvel Wolverine figure

EX $2　　NM $4　　MIP $15

Yellow Taxi w/Skyview, Buddy L, yellow hood, roof and body, red radiator front and fenders, 18-1/2" long; 1948

EX $200　　NM $400　　MIP $600

CONSTRUCTION AND FARM EQUIPMENT

Big Brute Scraper, Buddy L, 15-1/2" long, No. 5164, yellow earthmover, 1970s

EX $5　　NM $10　　MIP $25

Brute Articulated Scooper, Buddy L, 5-1/2" long; yellow, front-loading scoop, articulated frame; 1970

EX $6　　NM $12　　MIP $18

Brute Articulated Scooper, Buddy L, yellow front-loading scoop, cab, articulated frame and rear power unit, black radiator, exhaust, steering wheel and driver's seat, 5-1/2" long; 1970

EX $6　　NM $12　　MIP $18

Brute Double Dump Train (tractor-trailer), Buddy L, 9-1/2" long; yellow, coupled bottom-dumping earth carriers; 1969

EX $8　　NM $17　　MIP $25

Brute Dumping Scraper, Buddy L, 7" long; yellow; 1970

EX $7　　NM $13　　MIP $20

Brute Farm Tractor-n-Cart, Buddy L, 6-1/4" long; blue tractor w/green engine and driver's seat, blue two-wheel open car; 1969

EX $7　　NM $13　　MIP $20

Brute Road Grader, Buddy L, 6-1/2" long; yellow, adjustable blade; 1970

EX $6　　NM $12　　MIP $18

Concrete Mixer, Buddy L, green frame, base, crank, crank handle and bottom of mixing drum, gray hopper and top of drum, 9-5/8" long; 1949

EX $100　　NM $150　　MIP $200

Concrete Mixer w/Motor Sound, Buddy L, green frame, base, crank, crank handle and bottom of mixing drum, gray hopper and top of drum, w/sound when crank rotates drum, 9 5/8" long; 1950

EX $75　　NM $115　　MIP $150

Dandy Digger, Buddy L, yellow seat lower control lever and main boom, black underframe, skids, shovel and arm, 38-1/2" long w/shovel arm extended; 1953

EX $75　　NM $115　　MIP $150

Dandy Digger, Buddy L, yellow seat, lower control lever and main boom, black underframe, skids, shovel, arm and control lever, 38-1/2" long w/shovel arm extended; 1953

EX $75　　NM $115　　MIP $150

Hauling Rig w/Construction Derrick, Buddy L, duo-tone slant design tractor, yellow bumper, lower hood and cab sides, white upper hood and cab, white trailer w/yellow loading ramp, overall 38-1/2" long; 1953

EX $175　　NM $250　　MIP $400

Hauling Rig w/Construction Derrick, Buddy L, yellow tractor unit, green semi-trailer, winch on front of trailer makes sound, 36-3/4" long; 1954

EX $110　　NM $175　　MIP $225

Husky Tractor, Buddy L, bright yellow body and large rear fenders, black engine block, exhaust, steering wheel and driver's seat, 13" long; 1966

EX $50　　NM $80　　MIP $105

Husky Tractor, Buddy L, bright blue body w/white wheels and large rear fenders, black engine block, exhaust, steering wheel and driver's seat, 13" long; 1969

EX $40   NM $60   MIP $80

Husky Tractor, Buddy L, bright yellow body, red large rear fenders and wheels, black engine block, exhaust, steering wheel and driver's seat, 13" long; 1970

EX $30   NM $45   MIP $65

Junior Excavator, Buddy L, red shovel, arm, underframe, control lever and twin skids, yellow boom, rear lever, frame and seat, 28" long; 1945

EX $75   NM $115   MIP $150

Mechanical Crane, Buddy L, orange removable roof, boom, yellow wheels in white rubber crawler treads, olive green enclosed cab and base, hand crank w/rat-tat motor noise, 20" tall; 1952

EX $150   NM $225   MIP $300

Mechanical Crane, Buddy L, orange removable roof, boom and wheels in black cleated rubber crawler treads, olive green enclosed cab and base, hand crank w/rat-tat motor noise, 20" tall; 1950

EX $175   NM $265   MIP $350

Mobile Construction Derrick, Buddy L, orange laticework main mast, swiveling base, yellow latticework boom, gray clamshell bucket, green main platform base, 25-1/2" long w/boom lowered; 1955

EX $160   NM $260   MIP $355

Mobile Construction Derrick, Buddy L, orange laticework main mast, swiveling base, yellow latticework boom, gray clamshell bucket, orange main platform base, 25-1/2" long w/boom lowered; 1956

EX $150   NM $250   MIP $350

Mobile Construction Derrick, Buddy L, orange laticework main mast, swiveling base, yellow latticework boom, green clamshell bucket and main platform base, 25-1/2" long w/boom lowered; 1953

EX $155   NM $250   MIP $355

Mobile Power Digger Unit, Buddy L, clamshell dredge mounted on 10-wheel truck, orange truck, yellow dredge cab on swivel base, 31-3/4" long w/boom lowered; 1955

EX $125   NM $185   MIP $250

Mobile Power Digger Unit, Buddy L, clamshell dredge mounted on six-wheel truck, orange truck, yellow dredge cab on swivel base, 31-3/4" long w/boom lowered; 1956

EX $100   NM $150   MIP $250

Polysteel Farm Tractor, Buddy L, orange molded plastic four-wheel tractor, silver radiator front, head lights, and motor parts, 12" long; 1961

EX $80   NM $120   MIP $155

Pull-n-Ride Horse-Drawn Farm Wagon, Buddy L, red four-wheel steel hopper-body wagon, detailed litho horse, 22-3/4" long; 1952

EX $150   NM $225   MIP $300

Ruff-n-Tuff Tractor, Buddy L, yellow grille, hood and frame, black plastic engine block and driver's seat, 10-1/2" long; 1971

EX $50   NM $75   MIP $100

Scoop-n-Load Conveyor, Buddy L, cream body frame, green loading scoop, black circular crank operates black rubber cleated conveyor belt, "PORTABLE" decal in red, 18" long; 1954

EX $65   NM $105   MIP $140

Scoop-n-Load Conveyor, Buddy L, cream body frame, red loading scoop and chute, bright-plated circular crank operates black rubber cleated conveyor belt, "PORTABLE" decal in white, 18" long; 1955

EX $60   NM $95   MIP $125

Scoop-n-Load Conveyor, Buddy L, cream body frame, red loading scoop and chute, bright-plated circular crank operates black rubber cleated conveyor belt, "PORTABLE" decal in yellow, 18" long; 1956

EX $55   NM $85   MIP $115

Scoop-n-Load Conveyor, Buddy L, cream body frame, green loading scoop, black circular crank operates black rubber cleated conveyor belt, 18" long; 1953

EX $75   NM $115   MIP $150

Scoop-n-Load Conveyor, 1956-57, Buddy L, cream body frame, green loading scoop, black circular crank operates black rubber cleated conveyor belt, "PORTABLE" decal in green, 18" long; 1956-57

EX $50   NM $100   MIP $150

Side Conveyor Load-n-Dump, Buddy L, yellow plastic front end including cab, yellow steel bumper, green frame and dump body, red conveyor frame w/chute, 20-1/2" long; 1953

EX $80   NM $130   MIP $150

Side Conveyor Load-n-Dump, Buddy L, all steel yellow cab, hood, bumper and frame, white dump body and tailgate, red conveyor frame w/chute, 21-1/4" long; 1954

EX $65   NM $100   MIP $135

Side Conveyor Load-n-Dump, Buddy L, all steel yellow cab, hood, bumper and frame, deep blue dump body, white tailgate, red conveyor frame w/chute, 21-1/4" long; 1955

EX $60   NM $95   MIP $125

EMERGENCY VEHICLES

Aerial Ladder and Emergency Truck, Buddy L, red w/white ladders, bumper and steel disc wheels, three eight-rung steel ladders, no rear step, no siren or SIREN decal, 22-1/4" long; 1953

EX $225   NM $345   MIP $450

Aerial Ladder and Emergency Truck, Buddy L, red w/white ladders, bumper and steel disc wheels, three eight-rung steel ladders, 22-1/4" long; 1952

EX $200   NM $300   MIP $400

Aerial Ladder Fire Engine, Buddy L, red tractor, wraparound bumper and semi-trailer, two aluminum 13-rung extension ladders on sides, swivel-base aluminum central ladder, 26-1/2" long; 1960

EX $125   NM $185   MIP $250

Aerial Ladder Fire Engine, Buddy L, red tractor and semi-trailer, white plastic bumper w/integral grille guard, two aluminum 13-rung extension ladders on sides, swivel-base aluminum central ladder, 26-1/2" long; 1961

EX $125   NM $185   MIP $250

Aerial Ladder Fire Engine, Buddy L, red tractor and semi-trailer, chrome one-piece wraparound bumper, slotted grille, two aluminum 13-rung extension ladders on sides, swivel-base aluminum central ladder, 26-1/2" long; 1966

EX $125   NM $185   MIP $250

Aerial Ladder Fire Engine, Buddy L, red cabover-engine tractor and semi-trailer units, two 13-rung white sectional ladders and swivel-mounted aerial ladder w/side rails, 25-1/2" long; 1968

EX $100   NM $150   MIP $200

Aerial Ladder Fire Engine, Buddy L, snub-nose red tractor and semi-trailer, white swivel-mounted aerial ladder w/side rails, two white 13-rung sectional ladders, 27-1/2" long; 1970

EX $100   NM $150   MIP $200

Aerial Ladder Fire Engine (tractor-trailer), Buddy L, 26-1/2" long; chrome one-piece wraparound bumper, slotted grille; 1966-67

EX $40   **NM** $85   **MIP** $125

Aerial Ladder Fire Engine (tractor-trailer), Buddy L, 25-1/2" long; cabover, two 13-rung white sectional ladders, swivel-mounted aerial ladder w/side rails; 1968

EX $35   **NM** $65   **MIP** $100

Aerial Ladder Fire Engine (tractor-trailer), Buddy L, 27-1/2" long; snub-nose cab, white swivel-mounted aerial ladder w/side rails, two white 13-rung sectional ladders; 1970

EX $25   **NM** $50   **MIP** $75

American LaFrance Aero-Chief Pumper, Buddy L, 25-1/2" long; cabover, white underbody, rear step and simulated hose reels, black extension ladders on right side; 1962

EX $40   **NM** $80   **MIP** $200

Brute Fire Pumper, Buddy L, 5-1/4" long; red cabover, two yellow 5-rung sectional ladders on sides; 1969

EX $4   **NM** $8   **MIP** $12

Brute Hook-N-Ladder, Buddy L, red cabover-engine tractor and detachable semi-trailer, white elevating, swveling aerial ladder w/side rails, 10" long; 1969

EX $15   **NM** $30   **MIP** $55

Extension Ladder Fire Truck, Buddy L, red w/silver ladders and yellow removable rider seat, enclosed cab, 35" long; 1945

EX $200   **NM** $300   **MIP** $400

Extension Ladder Rider Fire Truck, Buddy L, duo-tone slant design, tractor has white front, lower hood sides and lower doors, red hood top, cab and frame, red semi-trailer, white ten-rung and eight-rung ladders, 32-1/2" long; 1949

EX $150   **NM** $225   **MIP** $300

Extension Ladder Trailer Fire Truck, Buddy L, red tractor w/enclosed cab, boxy fenders, red semi-trailer w/fenders, two white eight-rung side ladders, 10-rung central extension ladder, 29-1/2" long; 1955

EX $200   **NM** $300   **MIP** $400

Extension Ladder Trailer Fire Truck, Buddy L, red tractor unit and semi-trailer, enclosed cab, two white 13-rung side extension ladders on sides, white central ladder on swivel base, 29-1/2" long; 1956

EX $125   **NM** $185   **MIP** $250

Fire and Chemical Truck, Buddy L, duo-tone slant design, white front, lower hood sides and lower doors, rest is red, bright-metal or white eight-rung ladder on sides, 25" long; 1949

EX $125   **NM** $185   **MIP** $250

Fire Department Emergency Truck, Buddy L, red streamlined body, enclosed cab, chrome one-piece grille, bumper, and headlights, 12-3/4" long; 1953

EX $100   **NM** $150   **MIP** $200

Fire Hose and Water Pumper, Buddy L, red w/two white five-rung ladders, two removable fire extinguishers, enclosed cab, 12-1/2" long; 1950

EX $105   **NM** $155   **MIP** $200

Fire Hose and Water Pumper, Buddy L, red w/two white five-rung ladders, one red/white removable fire extinguisher, enclosed cab, 12-1/2" long; 1952

EX $100   **NM** $150   **MIP** $200

Fire Pumper, Buddy L, 16-1/4" long; red cabover, 11-rung white 10" ladder on each side; 1968

EX $56   **NM** $85   **MIP** $100

Fire Pumper, Buddy L, No. 5311, station wagon design, "Buddy L No. 6" on cab door, siren light, ladder; 1964-65

EX $20   **NM** $40   **MIP** $60

Fire Pumper w/Action Hydrant, Buddy L, red wraparound bumper, hood cab and cargo section, aluminum nine-rung ladders, white hose reel, 15" long; 1960

EX $75   **NM** $115   **MIP** $150

Fire Truck, Buddy L, red w/two white ladders, enclosed cab, bright metal grille and headlights, 25" long; 1948

EX $125   **NM** $200   **MIP** $250

Fire Truck, Buddy L, duo-tone slant design, tractor has white front, lower hood sides and lower doors, red hood top, cab and frame, red semi-trailer, rubber wheels w/black tires, 32-1/2" long; 1953

EX $200   **NM** $300   **MIP** $400

Fire Truck, Buddy L, red w/white ladders, black rubber wheels, enclosed cab, 12" long; 1945

EX $75   **NM** $115   **MIP** $150

GMC Deluxe Aerial Ladder Fire Engine, Buddy L, white tractor and semi-trailer units, golden 13-rung extension ladder on sides, golden central aerial ladder, black and white DANGER battery case w/two flashing lights, 28" long; 1959

EX $225   **NM** $345   **MIP** $450

(Calvin L. Chaussee Photo)

GMC Extension Ladder Trailer Fire Engine, Buddy L, red tractor w/chrome GMC bar grille, red semi-trailer, white 13-rung extension ladders on sides, white swiveling central ladder w/side rails, 27-1/4" long; 1957

EX $110   **NM** $260   **MIP** $405

GMC Fire Pumper w/Horn, Buddy L, red w/aluminum-finish eleven-rung side ladders and white reel of black plastic hose in open cargo section, chrome GMC bar grille, 15" long; 1958

EX $150   **NM** $200   **MIP** $300

GMC Hydraulic Aerial Ladder Fire Engine, Buddy L, red tractor unit w/chrome GMC bar grille, red semi-trailer, white 13-rung extension ladders on sides, white swiveling central ladder, 26-1/2" long; 1958

EX $125   **NM** $185   **MIP** $250

GMC Red Cross Ambulance, Buddy L, all white, removable fabric canopy w/a red cross and "Ambulance" in red, 14-1/2" long; 1960

EX $150   **NM** $250   **MIP** $400

Hydraulic Snorkel Fire Pumper, Buddy L, red cabover-engine and open rear body, white 11-rung 10" ladder on each side, snorkel pod w/solid sides, 21" long; 1969

EX $105   **NM** $155   **MIP** $210

Hydraulic Snorkel Fire Pumper, Buddy L, 21" long; red cabover, white 11-rung 10" ladder on each side; 1969

EX $32   **NM** $65   **MIP** $95

Jr. Fire Emergency Truck, Buddy L, 6-3/4" long; red cabover, wider bumper, four-slot grille w/two square plastic headlights; 1969

EX $8   **NM** $12   **MIP** $20

Jr. Fire Emergency Truck, Buddy L, 6-3/4" long; red cabover, one-piece chrome wraparound narrow bumper, 24-hole grille w/plastic vertical-pair headlights; 1968

EX $8   **NM** $12   **MIP** $20

Jr. Fire Snorkel Truck, Buddy L, 11-1/2" long; red cabover, one-piece chrome wraparound narrow bumper, 24-hole grille w/plastic vertical-pair headlights; 1968

EX $9   **NM** $14   **MIP** $22

Jr. Fire Snorkel Truck, Buddy L, 11-1/2" long; red cabover, wider bumper, four-slot grille w/two square plastic headlights; 1969
EX $9   NM $14   MIP $22

Jr. Hook-n-Ladder Aerial Truck, Buddy L, 17" long; red cabover, one-piece chrome wraparound narrow bumper, 24-hole grille w/plastic vertical-pair headlights; 1968
EX $23   NM $35   MIP $48

Jr. Hook-n-Ladder Aerial Truck, Buddy L, 17" long; red cabover, wider bumper, four-slot grille w/two square plastic headlights; 1969
EX $17   NM $25   MIP $40

Police Squad Truck, Buddy L, yellow front and front fenders, dark blue-green body, yellow fire extinguisher, 21-1/2" long over ladders; 1947
EX $150   NM $300   MIP $550

Police Wrecker, Buddy L, 13-3/4" long; operating boom, front-wheel steering, whitewall tires; 1971
EX $8   NM $17   MIP $25

Police Wrecker, Buddy L, 4-3/4" long; bubble-window cabover; 1970s
EX $3   NM $7   MIP $10

Rear Steer Trailer Fire Truck, Buddy L, red w/two white 10-rung ladders, chrome one-piece grille, headlights and bumper, 20" long; 1952
EX $65   NM $100   MIP $200

Red Cross Ambulance, Buddy L, all white, removable fabric canopy w/a red cross and "Ambulance" in red, 14-1/2" long; 1958
EX $60   NM $95   MIP $125

Rescue Force Ambulance, Buddy L, 12" long; battery-operated, siren; 1993
EX $5   NM $10   MIP $15

Suburban Pumper, Buddy L, red station wagon body, white plastic wraparound bumpers, one-piece grille and double headlights, 15" long; 1964
EX $100   NM $150   MIP $175

Texaco Fire Chief American LaFrance Pumper, Buddy L, promotional piece, red rounded-front enclosed cab and body, white one-piece underbody, running boards and rear step, 25" long; 1962
EX $100   NM $200   MIP $410

Voice-Command Hook-N-Ladder, Buddy L, 23" long; ladder extends to 31" high; battery-operated voice commands and actions
EX $15   NM $25   MIP $35

MISCELLANEOUS

49 LST, Buddy L, Gray landing craft w/swivel guns on deck, opening ramp door, includes tank and army truck
EX $35   NM $75   MIP $95

Fill-R-Up Gas Pump, Buddy L, 7" high; battery operated, ringing bell, price "totals"; 1966-69
EX $6   NM $12   MIP $18

Fill-R-Up Gas Pump, Buddy L, White plastic gas pump, 4" wide, 7" high, 2-3/4" deep, magnetic pump holds to metal vehicles, two "C" batteries power the pump register and bell, according to the 1970 catalog, it "totals price automatically—up to 39 gallons at $9.75"
EX $12   NM $25   MIP $40

Hydraulic Service Lift, Buddy L, 15" long; battery-operated service ramp, steel, push-button w/bell and retractable air hoses; 1967-68
EX $8   NM $17   MIP $25

Jr. Animal Ark, Buddy L, 5" long; 10 pairs of plastic animals; 1970
EX $5   NM $10   MIP $15

Traffic Light, Buddy L, 8" high; plastic, battery-operated, push-button, made in Japan; 1967-69
EX $3   NM $6   MIP $10

Yogi Bear Sit-N-Ride, Buddy L, 22" long, 19" high; plastic Yogi Bear w/green hat on casters, triangular metal handle behind Yogi's head, 1960
EX $50   NM $80   MIP $120

SETS

Amazing Spider-Man Set, Buddy L, four-piece tray set of cycle, helicopter, van and car; 1980
EX $8   NM $14   MIP $20

Army Combination, Buddy L, searchlight repair-it truck, transport truck and howitzer, ammunition conveyor, stake delivery truck, ammo, soldiers; 1956
EX $300 NM $400   MIP $500

Army Commando, Buddy L, 14-1/2" truck, searchlight unit, two-wheel howitzer, soldiers; 1957
EX $125   NM $185   MIP $250

Big "H" Race Team Set, Buddy L, 17", hot rod hauling two motorcycles, 1960s
EX $60   NM $80   MIP $130

Big Brute Freeway, Buddy L, scraper, grader, scooper and dump truck; 1971
EX $30   NM $60   MIP $90

Big Brute Hi-Way, Buddy L, bulldozer, dump truck, yellow four-wheel trailer; 1971
EX $20   NM $40   MIP $60

Big Brute Road, Buddy L, cement mixer truck, scooper, dump truck; 1971
EX $20   NM $40   MIP $60

Brute Fire Department, Buddy L, semi trailer aerial ladder, fire pumper, fire wrecker, tow truck; 1970
EX $17   NM $33   MIP $50

Brute Five-Piece Highway, Buddy L, bulldozer, grader, scraper, dumping scraper and double dump train; 1970
EX $50   NM $80   MIP $105

Brute Fleet, Buddy L, car carrier w/two plastic coupes, dump truck, pickup truck, cement mixer truck, tow truck; 1969
EX $85   NM $130   MIP $175

Brute Fleet, Buddy L, car carrier w/two plastic coupes, dump truck, pickup truck, cement mixer truck, tow truck; 1970
EX $17   NM $56   MIP $50

Brute Hi-Way, Buddy L, bulldozer, grader, scraper, sumping scraper and double dump train; 1970
EX $17   NM $33   MIP $50

Coca-Cola, Buddy L, 10-1/2" trailer truck; three-vehicle set w/tractor-trailer w/clear plastic cover, five cases and hadtruck; delivery truck w/two cases; and forklift truck w/two extra cases; late-1970s
EX $10   NM $18   MIP $35

Coca-Cola Set, Buddy L, includes trailer truck, delivery truck, three extra cases w/bottles, extra handtruck, delivery man, 1981
EX $10   NM $18   MIP $35

Delivery Set Combination, Buddy L, 16-1/2" long Wrigley express truck, 15" long sand and stone dump truck, 14-1/4" long freight conveyor and 14-1/4" long stake delivery truck; 1955
EX $175   NM $265   MIP $350

Deluxe Riding Academy, Buddy L, 18-1/2" long truck; Sears exclusive, red horse truck w/bubbletop, "Riding Academy" on van sides, two horses and two colts, plastic six-piece fense; 1966-69

EX $40 NM $80 MIP $125

Emergency Set, Buddy L, five-piece set w/ladder tractor-trailer, van, helicopter, pickup and ladder/pumper, all red and white, tray display box, 1970s

EX $12 NM $20 MIP $35

Exxon Road Service Set, Buddy L, 11" Exxon tractor-trailer tanker, 4-1/2" Jeep, 5" Wrecker, all white w/Exxon decals, white-hub tires, in tray box w/Exxon tiger, 1976

EX $15 NM $25 MIP $50

Family Camping, Buddy L, Camper/cruiser truck, 15-1/2" long maroon suburban wagon, and brown/light gray/beige folding teepee camping trailer; 1963

EX $60 NM $95 MIP $130

Family Camping, Buddy L, blue camping trailer and suburban wagon, blue camper-n-cruiser; 1964

EX $50 NM $75 MIP $100

Farm Combination, Buddy L, cattle transport stake truck w/six plastic steers, hydraulic farm supplies trailer dump truck, trailer and three farm machines and farm machinery trailer hauler truck; 1956

EX $100 NM $155 MIP $210

Fire Department, Buddy L, aerial ladder fire engine, fire pumper w/action hydrant that squirts water, two plastic hoses, two plastic firemen, fire chief's badge; 1960

EX $125 NM $250 MIP $505

Freight Conveyor and Stake Delivery Truck, Buddy L, blue frame 14-1/4" long conveyor, red, white and yellow body 14-3/4" long truck; 1955

EX $125 NM $185 MIP $250

Friendly Highway, Buddy L, 8-1/2" x 6-3/4" x 2-1/2" box; steel and plastic, includes Texacto Tanker truck; 1980s

EX $8 NM $17 MIP $25

GMC Air Defense, Buddy L, 15" long, GMC army searchlight truck, 15" long, GMC signal corps truck, two four-wheel trailers, plastic soliders; 1957

EX $150 NM $300 MIP $700

GMC Brinks Bank, Buddy L, silver gray, barred windows on sides and in double doors, coin slot and hole in roof, brass padlock w/two keys, pouch, play money, two gray plastic guard figures, 16" long; 1959

EX $305 NM $360 MIP $455

GMC Fire Department, Buddy L, red GMC extension ladder trailer and GMC pumper w/ladders and hose reel, four-wheel red electric searchlight trailer, warning barrier, red plastic helmet, firemen, policeman; 1958

EX $300 NM $500 MIP $750

GMC Highway Maintenance Fleet, Buddy L, orange maintenance truck w/trailer, sand and stone dump truck, scoop-n-load conveyor, sand hopper, steel scoop shovel, four white steel road barriers; 1957

EX $310 NM $505 MIP $710

GMC Livestock, Buddy L, red fenders, hood, cab and frame, white flatbed cargo section , six sections of brown plastic rail fencing, five black plastic steers, 14-1/2" long; 1958

EX $100 NM $200 MIP $500

GMC Western Roundup, Buddy L, blue fenders, hood, cab and frame, white flatbed cargo section, plastic six sections of rail fencing w/swinging gate, rearing and standing horse, cowboys, calf, steer; 1959

EX $100 NM $200 MIP $500

Highway Construction, Buddy L, orange and black bulldozer and driver, truck w/orange pickup body, orange dump truck; 1962

EX $200 NM $300 MIP $400

Highway Maintenance Mechanical Truck & Concrete Mixer, Buddy L, 20" truck plus movable ramp, w/duo-tone slant design, blue lower hood sides, yellow hood top and cab, 10-3/4" blue and yellow mixer, overall 36" long; 1949

EX $160 NM $245 MIP $325

Interstate Highway, Buddy L, orange, parks department dumper, landscape truck, telephone truck, accessories include trees, drums, workmen and traffic cones, scoop shovel; 1959

EX $260 NM $410 MIP $505

Interstate Highway, Buddy L, orange, husky dumper, contractor's truck and ladder, utility truck, plastic pickaxe, spade, shovel, nail keg; 1960

EX $250 NM $350 MIP $500

Jr. Animal Farm, Buddy L, Jr. Giraffe Truck, Jr. Kitty Kennel, Jr. Pony Trailer w/Sportster; 1968

EX $32 NM $63 MIP $95

Jr. Animal Farm, Buddy L, 6-1/2" long Jr. Giraffe Truck, 6-1/4" long Jr. Kitty Kennel, 11-1/4" long Jr. Pony Trailer w/Sportster; 1968

EX $120 NM $185 MIP $250

Jr. Fire Department, Buddy L, 17" long Jr. hook-n-ladder aerial truck, 11-1/2" long Jr. fire snorkel, 6-3/4" long truck, all have four-slot grilles and two square plastic headlights; 1969

EX $120 NM $185 MIP $250

Jr. Fire Department, Buddy L, Jr. Hook-n-Ladder Aerial, Jr. Fire Snorkel, Jr. Fire Emergency Truck w/four-slot grilles and square plastic headlights; 1969

EX $32 NM $63 MIP $95

Jr. Fire Department, Buddy L, 17" long Jr. hook-n-ladder aerial truck, 11-1/2" long Jr. fire snorkel, 6-3/4" long truck, all have 24-hole chrome grilles; 1968

EX $32 NM $63 MIP $95

Jr. Hi-Way, Buddy L, Jr. Scooper Tractor, Jr. Cement Mixer, Jr. Dump Truck; 1969

EX $30 NM $60 MIP $90

Jr. Sportsman, Buddy L, Jr. Camper Pickup, boat trailer and plastic runabout; 1971

EX $17 NM $33 MIP $50

Jr. Sportsman, Buddy L, Jr. camper pickup w/red cab and body and yellow camper, towing 6" plastic runabout on yellow two-wheel boat trailer; 1971

EX $25 NM $50 MIP $105

Loader, Dump Truck, and Shovel, Buddy L, conveyor, blue body sand and gravel dump truck, 8-3/4" long blue-enameled steel scoop shovel; 1955

EX $85 NM $130 MIP $175

Loader, Dump Truck, and Shovel, Buddy L, conveyor, green body sand and gravel dump truck, 8-3/4" long green-enameled steel scoop shovel; 1954

EX $100 NM $150 MIP $200

Lumberjack Set, Buddy L, log hauler, log loader, pickup, lumberjack figure, 1979

EX $10 NM $15 MIP $35

Marvel Super Hero Vehicle Set, Buddy L, Captain America Cycle, Wolverine Helicopter, Doctor Doom Car, Doctor Octopus Van, 1982

EX $10 NM $20 MIP $45

Mechanical Hauling Truck and Concrete Mixer, Buddy L, truck w/duo-tone slant design, red-orange lower hood sides, dark green upper hood, cab, trailer and ramp, 9-5/8" green mixer, gray hopper, 38" long w/ramps; 1950

EX $160 NM $245 MIP $325

Mechanical Hauling Truck and Concrete Mixer, Buddy L, truck w/duo-tone slant design, red/orange lower hood sides, dark green upper hood, cab, ramp, yellow trailer, 9-5/8" green mixer, gray hopper, 38" long w/ramps; 1951

EX $150 NM $225 MIP $300

Pepsi-Cola Set, Buddy L, 10" white tractor-trailer, 4-1/2" white pickup, forklift, w/Pepsi logos and four Pepsi cases, 1976

EX $8 NM $15 MIP $20

Polysteel Farm, Buddy L, blue milkman truck w/rack and nine milk bottles, red and gray milk tanker, orange farm tractor; 1961

EX $70 NM $115 MIP $160

Road Builder, Buddy L, green/white cement mixer truck, yellow/black bulldozer, red dump truck, husky dumper; 1963

EX $200 NM $300 MIP $400

Texaco Highway Truck Stop, Buddy L, 11" tractor-trailer; three-vehicle set w/Texaco Tanker, red/white Jeep and red wrecker; also three attendant figures, two gas pumps w/flexible hoses, made in Japan; late-1970s.

EX $18 NM $36 MIP $55

Warehouse, Buddy L, Coca-Cola truck, two hand trucks, eight cases Coke bottles, store-door delivery truck, lumber, sign, two barrels, forklift; 1958

EX $175 NM $265 MIP $350

Warehouse, Buddy L, Coca-Cola truck, two hand trucks, eight cases Coke bottles, store-door delivery truck, sign, two barrels, forklift; 1959

EX $150 NM $225 MIP $300

Western Roundup, Buddy L, turquoise fenders, hood, cab and frame, white flatbed cargo section, six sections of rail fencing w/swinging gate, rearing and standing horse, cowboys, calf, steer; 1960

EX $175 NM $250 MIP $400

TRUCKS

'01 Buddys Custom Pick-Up Truck, Buddy L, 10" long, pink stripped-down hot rod truck, whitewalls

EX $15 NM $35 MIP $80

Air Force Supply Transport, Buddy L, blue w/blue removable fabric canopy, rubber wheels, decals on cab doors, 14-1/2" long; 1957

EX $95 NM $150 MIP $355

Army Electric Searchlight Unit, Buddy L, shiny olive drab flatbed truck, battery-operated searchlight, 14-3/4" long; 1957

EX $125 NM $230 MIP $330

Army Half-Track and Howitzer, Buddy L, olive drab w/olive drab carriage, 12-1/2" truck, 9-3/4" gun, overall 22-1/2" long; 1953

EX $105 NM $150 MIP $200

Army Half-Track w/Howitzer, Buddy L, olive drab steel, red firing knob on gun, 17" truck, 9-3/4" gun, overall 27" long; 1955

EX $100 NM $150 MIP $200

Army Searchlight Repair-It Truck, Buddy L, shiny olive drab truck and flatbed cargo section, 15" long; 1956

EX $125 NM $175 MIP $225

Army Spotlight Truck, Buddy L, 8" long; 1969

EX $5 NM $9 MIP $12

Army Supply Truck, Buddy L, shiny olive drab truck and removable fabric cover, 14-1/2" long; 1956

EX $100 NM $150 MIP $175

Army Transport, Buddy L, 5" long; bubble-window cabover, "T-415 Transport"; 1970s

EX $3 NM $6 MIP $9

Army Transport w/Howitzer, Buddy L, olive drab steel, 17" truck, 9-3/4" gun, overall 27" long; 1955

EX $150 NM $250 MIP $350

Army Transport w/Howitzer, Buddy L, olive drab steel, re-firing knob on gun, 17" truck, 9-3/4" gun, overall 27" long; 1954

EX $115 NM $175 MIP $230

Army Transport w/Howitzer, Buddy L, olive drab, 12" truck, 9-3/4" gun, overall 28" long; 1953

EX $100 NM $150 MIP $200

Army Transport w/Tank, Buddy L, olive drab, 15-1/2" long truck, 11-1/2" long detachable two-wheel trailer, overall 26-1/2" long, 7-1/2" long tank; 1959

EX $100 NM $150 MIP $200

Army Troop Transport w/Howitzer, Buddy L, dark forest green truck and gun, canopy mixture of greens, 14" long truck, 12" long gun, overall 25-3/4" long; 1965

EX $100 NM $150 MIP $200

Atlas Van Lines, Buddy L, green tractor unit, chrome one-piece toothed grille and headlights, green lower half of semi-trailer van body, cream upper half, silvery roof, 29" long; 1956

EX $200 NM $300 MIP $400

Auto Hauler, Buddy L, 27-5/8" long; blue turbo cab, double-deck trailer, three plastic coupes; 1970s

EX $40 NM $80 MIP $105

Auto Hauler, Buddy L, yellow cabover-engine tractor unit and double-deck semi-trailer, three 8" long vehicles, 25-1/2" long; 1968

EX $75 NM $115 MIP $150

Baggage Rider, Buddy L, duo-tone horizontal design, green bumper, fenders and lower half of truck, white upper half, 28" long; 1950

EX $250 NM $175 MIP $500

Baggage Truck, Buddy L, green hood, fenders, and cab, yellow cargo section, no bumper, 17-1/2" long; 1945

EX $175 NM $265 MIP $350

Big Brute Dumper, Buddy L, yellow cabover-engine, frame and tiltback dump section w/cab shield, striped black and yellow bumper, black grille, 8" long; 1971

EX $50 NM $75 MIP $100

Big Brute Mixer Truck, Buddy L, yellow cabover-engine, body and frame, white plastic mixing drum, white plastic seats, 7" long; 1971

EX $35 NM $50 MIP $70

Big Fella Hydraulic Rider Dumper, Buddy L, duo-tone slant design, yellow front and lower hood, red upper cab, dump body and upper hood, rider seat has large yellow sunburst-style decal, 26-1/2" long; 1950

EX $110 NM $175 MIP $225

Big Mack Dumper, Buddy L, yellow front, hood cab, chassis and tiltback dump section, black plastic bumper, heavy-duty black balloon tires on yellow plastic five-spoke wheels, 20-1/2" long; 1971

EX $26 NM $40 MIP $55

Big Mack Dumper, Buddy L, yellow front, hood cab, chassis and tiltback dump section, black plastic bumper, single rear wheels, 20-1/2" long; 1968

EX $30 NM $45 MIP $60

Big Mack Dumper, Buddy L, yellow front, hood cab, chassis and tiltback dump section, black plastic bumper, 20-1/2" long; 1967

EX $30 NM $45 MIP $60

Big Mack Dumper, Buddy L, off-white front, hood cab and chassis, blue-green tiltback dump section, white plastic bumper, 20-1/2" long; 1964

EX $30 NM $45 MIP $60

Big Mack Hydraulic Dumper, Buddy L, white hood, cab and tiltback dump section w/cab shield, white plastic bumper, short step ladder on each side, 20-1/2" long; 1969
EX $15   **NM** $30   **MIP** $45

Big Mack Hydraulic Dumper, Buddy L, red hood, cab and tiltback dump section w/cab shield, dump body sides have a large circular back, white plastic bumper, short step ladder on each side, 20-1/2" long; 1970
EX $15   **NM** $30   **MIP** $45

Big Mack Hydraulic Dumper, Buddy L, red hood, cab and tiltback dump section w/cab shield, white plastic bumper, short step ladder on each side, 20-1/2" long; 1968
EX $15   **NM** $30   **MIP** $45

Black & Decker Truck, Buddy L, 10-1/2" long; white tractor-trailer, Japan
EX $8   **NM** $12   **MIP** $17

Boat Transport, Buddy L, blue flatbed truck carrying 8" litho metal boat, boat deck white, hull red, truck 15" long; 1959
EX $200   **NM** $450   **MIP** $750

Borden's Milk Delivery Van, Buddy L, 11-1/2" long; white body, sliding side doors, opening rear doors, yellow tray w/six white fillable polyethylene milk bottles w/yellow caps; 1965-67
EX $90   **NM** $185   **MIP** $275

Brute Air Freight Truck, Buddy L, 5" long; blue cabover, "American Airlines Freight System" on doors, "Toys, Handle With Pride" containers in rear, six wheels; 1960s
EX $5   **NM** $10   **MIP** $14

Brute Army Transport, Buddy L, three-axel w/"canvas" cover, 1982
EX $2   **NM** $4   **MIP** $8

Brute Car Carrier (tractor-trailer), Buddy L, 10" long; blue cabover, double-deck trailer, two plastic cars; 1969
EX $7   **NM** $15   **MIP** $22

Brute Cement Mixer, Buddy L, 5-1/4" long, green cabover, yellow drum, 1970s
EX $2   **NM** $4   **MIP** $10

Brute Cement Mixer Truck, Buddy L, 5-1/4" long; blue cabover, white crank rotates drum; 1969
EX $5   **NM** $9   **MIP** $14

Brute Cement Mixer Truck, Buddy L, 5-1/4" long; beige cabover, white plastic mixing drum; 1968
EX $5   **NM** $9   **MIP** $14

Brute Coca-Cola Delivery Truck, Buddy L, 5" long; 1985
EX $3   **NM** $7   **MIP** $10

Brute Dumper, Buddy L, 5" long; red cabover; 1968-69
EX $3   **NM** $7   **MIP** $10

Brute Merry-Go-Round, Buddy L, 5" long; cabover, merry-go-round in rear; 1970s
EX $7   **NM** $15   **MIP** $22

Brute Monkey House, Buddy L, yellow cabover-engine body, red and white awning roof, cage on back, two plastic monkeys, 5" long; 1969
EX $6   **NM** $12   **MIP** $18

Brute Monkey House, Buddy L, yellow cabover-engine body, striped orange and white awning roof, cage on back, two plastic monkeys, 5" long; 1968
EX $6   **NM** $12   **MIP** $18

Brute Pick-Up, Buddy L, 4-3/4" long; 1968-70s
EX $3   **NM** $6   **MIP** $10

Brute Sanitation Truck, Buddy L, 5" long; lime-green cabover; 1968-69
EX $6   **NM** $12   **MIP** $18

Brute Vault Van, Buddy L, 5" long; bank vault truck; 1970s
EX $3   **NM** $5   **MIP** $20

Buddy L Milk Farms Truck, Buddy L, light cream body, red roof, nickel glide headlights, sliding doors, 13" long; 1949
EX $170   **NM** $300   **MIP** $500

Buddy L Milk Farms Truck, Buddy L, white body, black roof, short hood w/black wooden headlights, 13-1/2" long; 1945
EX $150   **NM** $300   **MIP** $450

Buddy L Moving Van, Buddy L, 10-1/2" long; futuristic cabover, white w/Buddy L logo, stripes on moving-van body; 1970s
EX $4   **NM** $8   **MIP** $12

Buddy L Ranch, Buddy L, 13: long, aqua, livestock hauler, "Buddy L Ranch" decal on door, 1960s
EX $20   **NM** $30   **MIP** $55

Cambell's Chunk Soup Semi, Buddy L, 22" long, Sonic Hauler, mail-away promotional
EX $8   **NM** $15   **MIP** $30

Camper, Buddy L, bright medium blue steel truck and camper body, 14-1/2" long; 1964
EX $60   **NM** $95   **MIP** $125

Camper, Buddy L, 5" long; bubble-window cabover, green; 1970s
EX $3   **NM** $5   **MIP** $8

Camper, Buddy L, medium blue truck and back door, white camper body, 14-1/2" long; 1965
EX $50   **NM** $75   **MIP** $100

Camper-N-Cruiser, Buddy L, powder blue pickup truck and trailer, pale blue camper body, 24-1/2" long; 1963
EX $60   **NM** $95   **MIP** $125

Camper-N-Cruiser, Buddy L, bright medium blue camper w/matching boat trailer and 8-1/2" long plastic sport cruiser, overall 27" long; 1964
EX $50   **NM** $75   **MIP** $100

Campers Truck, Buddy L, turquoise pickup truck, pale turquoise plastic camper, 14-1/2" long; 1961
EX $55   **NM** $85   **MIP** $110

Campers Truck w/Boat, Buddy L, green/turquoise pickup truck, lime green camper body, red plastic runabout boat on camper roof, 14-1/2" long; 1962
EX $50   **NM** $100   **MIP** $150

Campers Truck w/Boat, Buddy L, green/turquoise pickup, no side mirror, lime green camper body w/red plastic runabout boat on top, 14-1/2" long; 1963
EX $50   **NM** $100   **MIP** $150

Camping Trailer and Wagon, Buddy L, bright medium blue suburban wagon, matching teepee trailer, overall 24-1/2" long; 1964
EX $60   **NM** $95   **MIP** $125

Canada Dry Delivery Truck, Buddy L, 9-1/2" long; two-tone green, high-window cabover, 10 bottle cases, roll-up side doors, hand truck; 1968-69
EX $10   **NM** $30   **MIP** $60

Cattle Ranch Truck, Buddy L, blue GMC, black stake sides and rear gate, 1950s
EX $70   **NM** $140   **MIP** n/a

Cattle Transport Truck, Buddy L, green and white w/white stake sides, 15" long; 1957
EX $75   **NM** $115   **MIP** $150

Cattle Transport Truck, Buddy L, red w/yellow stake sides, 15" long; 1956
EX $75   **NM** $115   **MIP** $150

Cement Mixer Truck, Buddy L, red body, tank ends, and chute, white water tank, mixing drum and loading hopper, blackwall tires, 15-1/2" long; 1967
EX $38   **NM** $76   **MIP** $115

Cement Mixer Truck, Buddy L, turquoise body, tank ends, and chute, white side ladder, water tank, mixing drum and loading hopper, 16-1/2" long; 1964
EX $60   **NM** $95   **MIP** $125

Cement Mixer Truck, Buddy L, red body, tank ends, and chute, white side ladder, water tank, mixing drum and loading hopper, 15-1/2" long; 1965

EX $60   NM $95   MIP $125

Cement Mixer Truck, Buddy L, red body, tank ends, and chute, white water tank, mixing drum and loading hopper, whitewall tires, 15-1/2" long; 1968

EX $50   NM $75   MIP $100

Cement Mixer Truck, Buddy L, snub-nosed yellow body, cab, frame and chute, white plastic mixing drum, loading hopper and water tank w/yellow ends, 16" long; 1970

EX $35   NM $50   MIP $70

Champion Spark Plugs Semi, Buddy L, 22-1/2" long, electronic voice, lights, sound

EX $3   NM $8   MIP $15

Charles Chip Delivery Truck Van, Buddy L, beige body, potato-chip decal; 1966

EX $45   NM $90   MIP $135

City Baggage Dray, Buddy L, green front, hood, and fenders, non-open doors, yellow stake-side cargo section, No. 839, 19" long, 1934

EX $400   NM $800   MIP $1200

Coca Cola Delivery Truck, Buddy L, 4-3/4" long, cabover truck w/two bottle cases in open compartment, 1970s

EX $2   NM $4   MIP $10

Coca-Cola Bottling Route Truck, Buddy L, bright yellow, w/small metal hand truck, six or eight yellow cases of miniature green Coke bottles, 14-3/4" long; 1955

EX $125   NM $175   MIP $250

Coca-Cola Bottling Route Truck, Buddy L, bright yellow, w/two small metal hand trucks and eight yellow cases of miniature green Coke bottles, 14-3/4" long; 1957

EX $110   NM $175   MIP $225

Coca-Cola Delivery Truck, Buddy L, orange/yellow cab and double-deck, open-side cargo, two small hand trucks, four red and four green cases of bottles, 15" long; 1964

EX $62   NM $100   MIP $130

Coca-Cola Delivery Truck, Buddy L, 9" long; red and white cabover and van body, left side lifts to show bottle cases, hand truck; 1970s

EX $9   NM $18   MIP $30

(KP Photo)

Coca-Cola Delivery Truck, Buddy L, red lower cabover-engine and van body, white upper cab, left side of van lifts to reveal 10 miniature bottle cases, 9-1/2" long; 1971

EX $30   NM $45   MIP $60

Coca-Cola Delivery Truck, Buddy L, orange/yellow cab and double-deck, open-side cargo, two small hand trucks, four red and four green cases of bottles, 15" long; 1963

EX $75   NM $100   MIP $150

Coca-Cola Delivery Truck, Buddy L, orange/yellow cab and double-deck, open-side cargo, two small hand trucks, four red and four green cases of bottles, 15" long; 1960

EX $100   NM $150   MIP $200

Coca-Cola Delivery Truck (tractor-trailer), Buddy L, 14" long; load includes Coke machine and handtruck; 1980s

EX $10   NM $20   MIP $50

Coca-Cola Delivery Truck (tractor-trailer), Buddy L, 10" long; five cases of bottles, handcart; 1980

EX $4   NM $8   MIP $12

Coke Coffee Co. Delivery Truck Van, Buddy L, black lower half of body, orange upper half, roof and sliding side doors; 1966

EX $85   NM $130   MIP $175

Colt Vacationer, Buddy L, 22-1/2" long; blue and white Colt Sportsliner w/trailer carrying red and white plastic 8-1/2" sport cruiser; 1967

EX $42   NM $85   MIP $125

Cook Coffee Van, Buddy L, 11-1/2", orange/ black van, "Cook Coffee" decal, 1960s

EX $50   NM $75   MIP $155

Curtiss Candy Trailer Van, Buddy L, blue tractor and bumper, white semi-trailer van, blue roof, chrome one-piece toothed grille and headlights, white drop-down rear door, 32-3/4" long w/tailgate/ramp lowered; 1955

EX $250   NM $400   MIP $500

Deluxe Auto Carrier, Buddy L, turquoise tractor unit, aluminum loading ramps, three plastic cars, overall 34" long including; 1962

EX $100   NM $175   MIP $250

Deluxe Camping Outfit, Buddy L, turquoise pickup truck and camper, and 8-1/2" long plastic boat on pale turquoise boat trailer, overall 24" long; 1961

EX $60   NM $95   MIP $125

Deluxe Hydraulic Rider Dump Truck, Buddy L, duo-tone slant design, red front and lower hood sides, white upper cab, dump body and chassis, red or black removable rider saddle, 26" long; 1948

EX $175   NM $265   MIP $350

Deluxe Motor Market, Buddy L, duo-tone slant design, red front, curved bumper, lower hood and cab sides, white hood top, body and cab, 22-1/4" long; 1950

EX $250   NM $350   MIP $500

(Joe and Sharon Freed Photo)

Deluxe Rider Delivery Truck, Buddy L, duo-tone horizontal design, gray lower half, blue upper half, red rubber disc wheels, black barrel skid, 22-3/4" long; 1945

EX $135   NM $200   MIP $270

Deluxe Rider Delivery Truck, Buddy L, duo-tone horizontal design, deep blue lower half, gray upper half, red rubber disc wheels, black barrel skid, 22-3/4" long; 1945

EX $135   NM $200   MIP $270

Deluxe Rider Dump Truck, Buddy L, various colors, dual rear wheels, no bumper, 25-1/2" long; 1945

EX $75   NM $115   MIP $150

Double Hydraulic Self-Loader-N-Dump, Buddy L, green front loading scoop w/yellow arms attached to cab sides, yellow hood and enclosed cab, orange frame and wide dump body, 29" long w/scoop lowered; 1956

EX $85   NM $130   MIP $175

Double Tandem Hydraulic Dump and Trailer, Buddy L, truck has red bumper, hood, cab and frame, four-wheel trailer w/red tow and frame, both w/white tiltback dump bodies, 38" long; 1957

EX $85   NM $130   MIP $175

Double-Deck Boat Transport, Buddy L, light blue steel flatbed truck carrying three 8" white plastic boats w/red decks, truck 15" long; 1960

EX $150   NM $250   MIP $400

Dr. Pepper Delivery Truck Van,
Buddy L, white, red and blue; 1966
EX $45   **NM** $90   **MIP** $135

**Dr. Pepper Delivery Truck Van
(tractor-trailer),** Buddy L, 6" long;
bubble-window cabover; 1970s
EX $5   **NM** $10   **MIP** $24

Dump Truck, Buddy L, red hood top and
cab, white or cream dump body and
frame, no bumper, 17-1/2" long; 1945
EX $75   **NM** $115   **MIP** $150

Dump Truck, Buddy L, various colors,
black rubber wheels, 12" long; 1945
EX $50   **NM** $75   **MIP** $100

Dump Truck, Buddy L, 14-1/4" long;
orange, turbine cabover, decal "It
Steers" on driver's window;
late-1960s
EX $6   **NM** $12   **MIP** $18

Dump Truck, Buddy L, duo-tone slant
design, red front, fenders and dump
body, yellow hood top, upper sides,
upper cab and chassis, no bumper,
22-1/2" long; 1948
EX $125   **NM** $185   **MIP** $250

Dumper w/Shovel, Buddy L, turquoise
body, frame and dump section, white
one-piece bumper and grille guard,
large white steel scoop shovel, 15"
long; 1962
EX $75   **NM** $115   **MIP** $150

Dumper w/Shovel, Buddy L, orange
body, frame and dump section,
chrome one-piece grille, no bumper
guard, no side mirror, large white
steel scoop shovel, no spring
suspension, 15-3/4" long; 1965
EX $75   **NM** $115   **MIP** $150

Dumper w/Shovel, Buddy L, medium
green body, frame and dump
section, white one-piece bumper
and grille guard, no side mirror,
large white steel scoop shovel,
spring suspension on front axle
only, 15" long; 1964
EX $75   **NM** $115   **MIP** $150

Dumper w/Shovel, Buddy L, medium
green body, frame and dump section,
white one-piece bumper and grille
guard, no side mirror, large white steel
scoop shovel, 15" long; 1963
EX $75   **NM** $115   **MIP** $150

Dump-n-Dozer, Buddy L, orange
husky dumper truck and orange
flatbed four-wheel trailer carrying
orange bulldozer, 23" long
including trailer; 1962
EX $75   **NM** $115   **MIP** $150

Electric Emergency Unit Truck,
Buddy L, white service truck
w/hoist, door decals, 1950s
EX $40   **NM** $90   **MIP** $200

Farm Bureau Co-op Gas Tanker,
Buddy L, 10" long; red tractor
w/chrome tanker trailer; 1980s
EX $3   **NM** $6   **MIP** $9

Farm Machinery Hauler Trailer Truck,
Buddy L, blue tractor unit, yellow
flatbed semi-trailer, 31-1/2" long;
1956
EX $125 **NM** $185   **MIP** $250

Farm Supplies Automatic Dump,
Buddy L, duo-tone slant design,
blue curved bumper, front, lower
hood sides and cab, yellow upper
hood, cab and rest of body, 22-1/2"
long; 1950
EX $125   **NM** $190   **MIP** $250

Farm Supplies Dump Truck, Buddy L,
duo-tone slant design, red front,
fenders and lower hood sides,
yellow upper hood, cab and body,
22-3/4" long; 1949
EX $125   **NM** $185   **MIP** $250

**Farm Supplies Hydraulic Dump
Trailer,** Buddy L, green tractor unit,
long cream body on semi-trailer, 14
rubber wheels, 26-1/2" long; 1956
EX $100 **NM** $150   **MIP** $200

Fast Delivery Pickup, Buddy L, yellow
hood and cab, red open cargo body,
removable chain across open back,
13-1/2" long; 1949
EX $50   **NM** $100   **MIP** $200

**Finger-Tip Steering Hydraulic
Dumper,** Buddy L, powder blue
bumper, fenders, hood, cab and
frame, white tiltback dump body,
22" long; 1959
EX $75   **NM** $115   **MIP** $150

Fisherman, Buddy L, light tan pickup
truck w/tan steel trailer carrying
plastic 8-1/2" long sport crusier,
overall 24-1/4" long; 1962
EX $80   **NM** $120   **MIP** $160

Fisherman, Buddy L, pale blue/green
station wagon w/four-wheel boat
trailer carrying plastic 8-1/2" long
boat, overall 27-1/2" long; 1963
EX $75   **NM** $115   **MIP** $150

Fisherman, Buddy L, metallic sage
green pickup truck w/boat trailer
carrying plastic 8-1/2" long sport
cruiser, overall 25" long; 1964
EX $70   **NM** $100   **MIP** $140

Fisherman, Buddy L, sage gray/green
and white pickup truck w/steel
trailer carrying plastic 8-1/2" long
sport cruiser, overall 25" long; 1965
EX $65   **NM** $100   **MIP** $135

Flat Tire Wrecker, Buddy L, 16" long,
yellow-cream cab and body, black
boom, tools
EX $45   **NM** $125   **MIP** $260

Flat Tire Wrecker, Buddy L, 16" long;
blue, battery-operated flasher on
roof, spare tire, three polyethylene
tools, boom and winch; 1965
EX $45   **NM** $125   **MIP** $200

**Frederick & Nelson Delivery Truck
Van,** Buddy L, medium green body,
roof and sliding side doors; 1966
EX $125 **NM** $200   **MIP** $275

Freight Delivery Stake Truck, Buddy
L, red hood, bumper, cab and
frame, white cargo section, yellow
three-post, three-slat removable
stake sides, 14-3/4" long; 1955
EX $75   **NM** $125   **MIP** $175

Front Loader Hi-Lift Dump Truck,
Buddy L, red scoop and arms
attached to white truck at rear
fenders, green dump body, 17-3/4"
long w/scoop down and dump body
raised; 1955
EX $85   **NM** $130   **MIP** $175

Giant Hydraulic Dumper, Buddy L, red
bumper, frame, hood and cab, light
tan tiltback dump body and cab shield
23-3/4" long; 1960
EX $125   **NM** $185   **MIP** $250

Giant Hydraulic Dumper, Buddy L,
overall color turquoise, dump lever
has a red plastic tip, 22-3/4" long; 1961
EX $135   **NM** $200   **MIP** $275

Giraffe Truck, Buddy L, 13-1/4" long;
blue hood and white cab roof, open
cargo section, two plastic giraffes;
1968
EX $35   **NM** $70   **MIP** $105

**GMC Air Force Electric Searchlight
Unit,** Buddy L, all blue flatbed, off
white battery-operated searchlight
swivel mount, decals on cab doors,
14-3/4" long; 1958
EX $200   **NM** $300   **MIP** $410

GMC Airway Express Van, Buddy L,
green hood, cab and van body,
latching double rear doors, shiny
metal drum coin bank and metal
hand truck, 17-1/2" long w/rear
doors open; 1957
EX $250 **NM** $350   **MIP** $450

GMC Anti-Aircraft Unit w/Searchlight,
Buddy L, 15" truck w/four-wheel
trailer, battery-operated, over 25-1/4"
long; 1957
EX $240   **NM** $345   **MIP** $460

GMC Army Hauler w/Jeep, Buddy L,
shiny olive drab tractor unit and
flatbed trailer, 10" long jeep, overall
31-1/2" long; 1958
EX $200 **NM** $300   **MIP** $400

GMC Army Transport w/Howitzer, Buddy L, shiny olive drab, 14-1/2" long, truck, overall w/gun 22-1/2" long; 1957

EX $200   NM $300   MIP $400

GMC Brinks Armored Truck Van, Buddy L, silver gray, barred windows on sides and in double doors, coin slot and hole in roof, brass padlock w/two keys, pouch, play money, three gray plastic guard figures, 16" long; 1958

EX $300   NM $350   MIP $450

GMC Coca-Cola Route Truck, Buddy L, orange/yellow, w/two small metal hand trucks and eight cases of miniature green Coke bottles, 14-1/8" long; 1958

EX $200   NM $300   MIP $400

GMC Coca-Cola Route Truck, Buddy L, lime/yellow, w/small metal hand truck and eight cases of miniature green Coke bottles, 14-1/8" long; 1957

EX $200   NM $305   MIP $410

GMC Construction Company Dumper, Buddy L, pastel blue including control lever on left and dump section w/cab shield, hinged tailgate, chrome GMC bar grille, six wheels, 16" long; 1958

EX $200   NM $305   MIP $410

GMC Construction Company Dumper, Buddy L, pastel blue including control lever on left and dump section w/cab shield, hinged tailgate, chrome GMC bar grille, four wheels, 16" long; 1959

EX $150   NM $250   MIP $350

GMC Highway Giant Trailer, Buddy L, blue tractor, blue and white van, chrome GMC bar grille and headlights, blue roof on semi-trailer, white tailgate doubles as loading ramp, 18-wheeler, 31-1/4" long; 1957

EX $250   NM $350   MIP $450

GMC Highway Giant Trailer Truck, Buddy L, blue tractor, blue and white van, chrome GMC bar grille and headlights, blue roof on semi-trailer, white tailgate doubles as loading ramp, 14-wheeler, 30-3/4" long; 1958

EX $200   NM $300   MIP $400

GMC Husky Dumper, Buddy L, red hood, bumper, cab and chassis, chrome GMC bar grille and nose emblem, white oversize dump body, red control lever on right side, 17-1/2" long; 1957

EX $150   NM $250   MIP $350

GMC Self-Loading Auto Carrier, Buddy L, yellow tractor and double-deck semi trailer, three plastic cars, overall 33-1/4" long; 1959

EX $200   NM $300   MIP $410

GMC Signal Corps Unit, Buddy L, both olive drab, 14-1/4" long truck w/removable fabric canopy, 8" long four-wheel trailer; 1957

EX $150   NM $200   MIP $255

Harley-Davidson Semi, Buddy L, 21" long; battery-operated sounds and lights, "Ten-four, good buddy" voice, pressed steel and plastic; 1992

EX $7   NM $15   MIP $25

Hawaiian Punch (tractor-trailer), Buddy L, 10" long, 1980

EX $2   NM $4   MIP $9

Heavy Hauling Dumper, Buddy L, red hood, bumper, cab and frame, cream oversize dump body, hinged tailgate, 21-1/2" long; 1956

EX $75   NM $125   MIP $140

Heavy Hauling Dumper, Buddy L, red hood, bumper, cab and frame, cream tiltback dump body, 20-1/2" long; 1955

EX $75   NM $125   MIP $150

Heavy Hauling Hydraulic Dumper, Buddy L, green hood, cab and frame, cream tiltback dump body, and cab shield, raising dump body almost to vertical, 23" long; 1956

EX $70   NM $105   MIP $200

Heavy Machinery Service Truck, Buddy L, 24" long; green cab and chassis, white body, orange machinery rig, 1950s

EX $150   NM $180   MIP $230

Hershey's Kiss Truck, Buddy L, 4-3/4" long; made in Japan; 1982

EX $3   NM $6   MIP $9

Hertz Auto Hauler, Buddy L, bright yellow tractor and double-deck semi-trailer, three plastic vehicles, 27" long; 1965

EX $100   NM $150   MIP $200

Hertz Auto Hauler (tractor-trailer), Buddy L, 27" long; yellow, double-deck trailer, three plastic vehicles; 1965

EX $67   NM $130   MIP $200

Highway Hawk Trailer Van, Buddy L, bronze cab tractor, chrome metallized plastic bumper, grille, air cleaner and exhaust, 19-3/4" long, 1985

EX $50   NM $80   MIP $100

Highway Maintenance Truck w/Trailer, Buddy L, orange w/black rack of four simulated floodlights behind cab, 19-1/2" long including small two-wheel trailer; 1957

EX $100   NM $150   MIP $200

Hi-Lift Farm Supplies Dump, Buddy L, all steel, red front end including hood and enclosed cab, yellow dump body, cab shield and hinged tailgate, 23-1/2" long; 1954

EX $100   NM $175   MIP $225

Hi-Lift Farm Supplies Dump, Buddy L, red plastic front end including hood and enclosed cab, yellow dump body, cab shield and hinged tailgate, 21-1/2" long; 1953

EX $100   NM $175   MIP $225

Hi-Lift Scoop-n-Dump Truck, Buddy L, blue hood, fenders and cab, yellow front loading scoop and arms attached to fenders, white frame, dump body, cab shield, and running boards, 17-3/4" long; 1957

EX $80   NM $125   MIP $175

Hi-Lift Scoop-n-Dump Truck, Buddy L, orange truck w/deeply fluted sides, dark green scoop on front rises to empty load into hi-lift cream/yellow dump body, 16" long; 1952

EX $85   NM $130   MIP $175

Hi-Lift Scoop-n-Dump Truck, Buddy L, orange truck w/deeply fluted sides, dark green scoop on front rises to empty load into hi-lift light cream dump body, 16" long; 1953

EX $80   NM $125   MIP $175

Hi-Lift Scoop-n-Dump Truck, Buddy L, orange truck w/deeply fluted sides, dark green scoop on front rises to empty load into deep hi-lift slightly orange dump body, 16" long; 1955

EX $30   NM $75   MIP $155

Hi-Lift Scoop-n-Dump Truck, Buddy L, orange hood, fenders and cab, yellow front loading scoop and arms attached to fenders, white frame, dump body and cab shield, 17-3/4" long; 1956

EX $70   NM $135   MIP $145

Hi-Tip Hydraulic Dumper, Buddy L, orange hood, cab and frame, cream tiltback dump body, and cab shield, raising dump body almost to vertical, 23" long; 1957

EX $70   NM $115   MIP $150

Horse Van, Buddy L, 17-1/2" long; maroon pickup cab w/plastic horse van body, w/side and rear ramps, two horses and one colt; 1965-66, see also Deluxe Riding Academy Set

EX $40   NM $80   MIP $160

Horse Van (tractor-trailer), Buddy L, 14-1/2" long; high-window cabover tractor, brown w/white roof, hauls white trailer, side and rear loading ramps, three horses; 1968-69
EX $12   **NM** $23   **MIP** $35

Horse Van (tractor-trailer), Buddy L, 10" long; red, paired circular windows on trailer; 1980
EX $3   **NM** $7   **MIP** $10

Horserack 400, Buddy L, 5" long; bubble-window cabover, red, stake truck back w/two plastic horses; 1970s
EX $4   **NM** $8   **MIP** $12

Husky Dumper, Buddy L, orange wraparound bumper, body, frame and dump section, hinged tailgate, plated dump lever on left side, 15-1/4" long; 1960
EX $75   **NM** $115   **MIP** $150

Husky Dumper, Buddy L, white plastic wraparound bumper, tan body, frame and dump section, hinged tailgate, plated dump lever on left side, 15-1/4" long; 1961
EX $75   **NM** $125   **MIP** $140

Husky Dumper, Buddy L, bright yellow, chrome one-piece bumper, slotted rectangular grille and double headlights, 14-1/2" long; 1966,
EX $25   **NM** $50   **MIP** $75

Husky Dumper, Buddy L, red hood, cab, chassis and dump section, chrome one-piece bumper and slotted grille w/double headlights, 14-1/2" long; 1968
EX $10   **NM** $30   **MIP** $60

Husky Dumper, Buddy L, yellow hood, cab, fram and tiltback dump section w/cab shield, crome one-piece wraparound bumper, 14-1/2" long; 1969
EX $17   **NM** $33   **MIP** $50

Husky Dumper, Buddy L, snub-nose red body, tiltback dump section, cab shield, full-width chrome bumperless grille, deep-tread whitewall tires, 14-1/2" long; 1970
EX $15   **NM** $30   **MIP** $45

Husky Dumper, Buddy L, snub-nose red body, tiltback dump section and cab shield, full-width chrome bumperless grille, white-tipped dump-control lever on left, deep-tread whitewall tires, 14-1/2" long; 1971
EX $15   **NM** $30   **MIP** $45

Hydraulic Auto Hauler w/Four GMC Cars, Buddy L, powder blue GMC tractor, 7" long plastic cars, overall 33-1/2" long including loading ramp; 1958
EX $250   **NM** $350   **MIP** $450

Hydraulic Construction Dumper, Buddy L, bright blue front, cab and chassis, large green dump section w/cab shield, 15-1/2" long; 1964
EX $23   **NM** $46   **MIP** $70

Hydraulic Construction Dumper, Buddy L, bright green front, cab and chassis, large green dump section w/cab shield, 14" long; 1965
EX $23   **NM** $46   **MIP** $70

Hydraulic Construction Dumper, Buddy L, tan/beige front, cab and chassis, large green dump section w/cab shield, 15-1/4" long; 1963
EX $28   **NM** $56   **MIP** $85

Hydraulic Construction Dumper, Buddy L, red front, cab and chassis, large green dump section w/cab shield, 15-1/4" long; 1962
EX $28   **NM** $56   **MIP** $85

Hydraulic Construction Dumper, Buddy L, medium blue front, cab and chassis, large green dump section w/cab shield, 15-1/4" long; 1967
EX $20   **NM** $40   **MIP** $60

Hydraulic Dumper, Buddy L, 20" long; green, white dump body w/opening gate, three axles w/tandem wheels in back, 1950s
EX $50   **NM** $100   **MIP** $220

Hydraulic Dumper, Buddy L, green, plated dump lever on left side, large hooks on left side hold yellow or off-white steel scoop shovel, white plastic side mirro and grille guard, 17" long; 1961
EX $50   **NM** $100   **MIP** $245

Hydraulic Dumper w/Shovel, Buddy L, green, plated dump lever on left side, large hooks on left side hold yellow or off-white steel scoop shovel, 17" long; 1960
EX $120   **NM** $185   **MIP** $250

Hydraulic Farm Supplies Trailer Dumper, Buddy L, 22" long; green tractor, white trailer dump body, 1950s
EX $80   **NM** $100   **MIP** $140

Hydraulic Highway Dumper, Buddy L, orange w/row of black square across scraper edges, one-piece chrome eight-hole grille and double headlights, no scraper blade, 17-3/4" long over blade and raised dump body; 1959
EX $55   **NM** $85   **MIP** $150

Hydraulic Highway Dumper w/Scraper Blade, Buddy L, orange w/row of black square across scraper edges, one-piece chrome eight-hole grille and double headlights, 17-3/4" long over blade and raised dump body; 1958
EX $75   **NM** $115   **MIP** $175

Hydraulic Hi-Lift Dumper, Buddy L, blue hood, fenders, cab, and dump-body supports, white dump body w/cab shield, 22-1/2" long; 1955
EX $45   **NM** $90   **MIP** $175

Hydraulic Hi-Lift Dumper, Buddy L, duo-tone slant design, green hood nose and lower cab sides, remainder white w/chrome grille, enclosed cab, 24" long; 1953
EX $75   **NM** $115   **MIP** $165

Hydraulic Hi-Lift Dumper, Buddy L, green hood, fenders, cab, and dump-body supports, white dump body w/cab shield, three axels, 10 wheels, 22-1/2" long; 1954
EX $85   **NM** $130   **MIP** $185

Hydraulic Husky Dumper, Buddy L, red body, frame, dump section and cab shield, 15-1/4" long; 1962
EX $30   **NM** $60   **MIP** $135

Hydraulic Husky Dumper, Buddy L, red body, white one-piece bumper and grille guard, heavy side braces on dump section, 14" long; 1963
EX $50   **NM** $75   **MIP** $115

Hydraulic Rider Dumper, Buddy L, duo-tone slant design, yellow front and lower hood, red upper cab, dump body and upper hood, 26-1/2" long; 1949
EX $175   **NM** $265   **MIP** $360

Hydraulic Sturdy Dumper, Buddy L, 14-1/2" long; snub-nose green-yellow body and cab; 1970
EX $7   **NM** $15   **MIP** $22

Hydraulic Sturdy Dumper, Buddy L, 14-1/2" long; yellow cab; 1969
EX $20   **NM** $40   **MIP** $60

Hydraulic Sturdy Dumper, Buddy L, 14-1/2" long; lime-green cab, green lever; 1969
EX $20   **NM** $40   **MIP** $60

(Tim Oei Photo)

Hy-Way Maintenance Mechanical Truck and Concrete Mixer, Buddy L, Yellow and dark blue cab, silver wheels, yellow flatbed w/dark blue and yellow mixer, 36" long; 1949

EX $345   NM $550   MIP $700

Ice Truck, Buddy L, 21" long, white and blue-green two-tone cab

EX $70   NM $150   MIP n/a

Jewel Home Service Truck Van, Buddy L, 11-1/2" long; dark brown body, sliding side doors; 1967

EX $42   NM $83   MIP $125

Jewel Home Shopping Truck Van, Buddy L, 11-1/2" long; pale mint green upper body, darker lower half, no sliding doors; 1968

EX $38   NM $76   MIP $115

Jolly Joe Ice Cream Truck, Buddy L, white w/black roof, black tires and wooden wheels, 17-1/2" long; 1947

EX $225   NM $350   MIP $455

Jolly Joe Popsicle Truck, Buddy L, white w/black roof, black tires and wooden wheels, 17-1/2" long; 1948

EX $275   NM $430   MIP $555

Jr. Animal Ark, Buddy L, fuschia lapstrake hull, four black tires, 10 pairs of plastic animals, 5" long; 1970

EX $40   NM $60   MIP $80

Jr. Auto Carrier, Buddy L, 17-1/2" long; blue cabover, double-deck trailer, two plastic cars; 1969

EX $17   NM $33   MIP $50

Jr. Auto Carrier, Buddy L, 15-1/2" long; yellow cabover, double-deck trailer, two red plastic cars; 1967

EX $17   NM $33   MIP $50

Jr. Beach Buggy, Buddy L, 6" long; lime-green Jeep body and surfboard; 1971

EX $5   NM $9   MIP $14

Jr. Beach Buggy, Buddy L, 6" long; yellow Jeep body, rollbar, white plastic surfboard; 1969

EX $5   NM $9   MIP $14

Jr. Buggy Hauler, Buddy L, 12" long; fuschia Jeep body, orange two-wheel trailer w/Sandpiper beach buggy; 1970

EX $12   NM $23   MIP $35

Jr. Camper, Buddy L, 7" long; red pickup, yellow camper; 1971

EX $5   NM $9   MIP $14

Jr. Canada Dry Delivery Truck, Buddy L, 9-1/2" long; green and lime green cabover, hand truck, 10 cases of green bottles; 1968-69

EX $27   NM $53   MIP $80

Jr. Cement Mixer Truck, Buddy L, 7-1/2" long; blue cabover, white mixing drum; 1968-69

EX $6   NM $12   MIP $18

Jr. Dump Truck, Buddy L, 7-1/2" long; red cabover, plastic vertical headlights, 1967

EX $4   NM $8   MIP $12

Jr. Dumper, Buddy L, 7-1/2" long; avocado cabover, four-slot grille; 1969

EX $4   NM $8   MIP $12

Jr. Giraffe Truck, Buddy L, 6-1/2" long; turquoise cabover, plastic giraffe; 1968-69

EX $7   NM $13   MIP $20

Jr. Kitty Kennel, Buddy L, 6-1/4" long; pink cabover, four white plastic cats; 1968-69

EX $7   NM $20   MIP $30

Jr. Sanitation Truck, Buddy L, 10" long; yellow; 1969

EX $6   NM $12   MIP $18

Jr. Sanitation Truck, Buddy L, 10" long; blue cabover, white body; 1968

EX $6   NM $12   MIP $18

Jr. Sportster, Buddy L, 6" long, blue Jeep w/white roof, No. 515

EX $4   NM $8   MIP $30

Jr. Tow Truck, Buddy L, No. 5107; red body, white winch; late-1960s or 1970s

EX $6   NM $12   MIP $18

Jr. Turbine Racer Transport, Buddy L, red truck, "Turbine Transport" on racer lift, w/red racer; 1970s

EX $35   NM $65   MIP $100

Kennel Truck, Buddy L, futuristic cab, pink body, six-section kennel w/dogs

EX $15   NM $35   MIP $80

Kennel Truck, Buddy L, 13-1/4" long; bright blue, clear plastic 12-section kennel w/12 plastic dogs; 1966-67

EX $32   NM $63   MIP $225

Kennel Truck, Buddy L, medium blue pickup body and cab, clear plastic 12-section kennel w/twelve plastic dogs fits in cargo box, 13-1/2" long; 1964

EX $60   NM $90   MIP $225

Kennel Truck, Buddy L, 13-1/4" long; snub-nosed red-orange cab, six-section kennel w/six dogs; 1970

EX $20   NM $40   MIP $60

Kennel Truck, Buddy L, turquoise pickup body and cab, clear plastic 12-section kennel w/twelve plastic dogs fits in cargo box, 13-1/2" long; 1965

EX $60   NM $95   MIP $125

Kennel Truck, Buddy L, 13-1/4" long; red-orange, six-section kennel w/six dogs; 1969

EX $22   NM $43   MIP $65

Kennel Truck, Buddy L, 13-1/4" long; cream yellow; 1968

EX $27   NM $53   MIP $80

Mack Hydraulic Dumper, Buddy L, 20-1/2" long; red cab; 1965

EX $40   NM $80   MIP $160

Mack Hydraulic Dumper, Buddy L, 20-1/2" long; red cab, short step ladder on each side; 1967

EX $33   NM $65   MIP $100

Mack Quarry Dumper, Buddy L, 20-1/2" long; all yellow, 1960s

EX $35   NM $85   MIP $120

Mack Quarry Dumper, Buddy L, 20-1/2" long, orange cab, blue-green tiltback dujmp; 1965

EX $50   NM $100   MIP $150

Mammoth Hydraulic Quarry Dumper, Buddy L, 23" long; green cab, red dump section, black bumper; 1962-63

EX $45   NM $89   MIP $135

Marshall Field's Delivery Truck Van, Buddy L, hunter green body, sliding doors; 1966

EX $42   NM $83   MIP $125

Merry-Go-Round, 1967, Buddy L, red truck w/merry-go-round on flatbed, blackwall tires; 1967, Model No. 5429

EX $50   NM $100   MIP $230

Milkman Truck, Buddy L, light blue hood, cab and flatbed body, white side rails, 14 3" white plastic milk bottles, 14-1/4" long; 1963

EX $85   NM $130   MIP $175

Milkman Truck, Buddy L, deep cream hood, cab and flatbed body, white side rails, 14 3" white plastic milk bottles w/red caps, 14-1/4" long; 1962

EX $50   NM $105   MIP $200

Milkman Truck, Buddy L, light yellow hood, cab and flatbed body, white side rails, 14 3" white plastic milk bottles, 14-1/4" long; 1964

EX $75   NM $125   MIP $155

Milkman Truck, Buddy L, medium blue hood, cab and flatbed body, white side rails, eight 3" white plastic milk bottles, 14-1/4" long; 1961

EX $50   NM $100   MIP $200

Mister Buddy Ice Cream Truck, Buddy L, 11-1/2" long; red plastic underbody; 1966-67

EX $45   NM $89   MIP $135

Mister Buddy Ice Cream Truck, Buddy L, No. 5353, 11-1/2" long; white van, "Mister Buddy Ice Cream" and ice cream cone decoration, pale blue or off-white plastic underbody, spring suspension, window sides, whitewall tires; 1964-65

EX $60   **NM** $140   **MIP** $175

NASA Lowboy and Shuttle, Buddy L, 10-1/2" long; tractor-trailer hauler w/Shuttle Discovery, steel and plastic, made in Japan; 1979-80

EX $7   **NM** $13   **MIP** $20

Ol' Buddys Dump Truck, Buddy L, 10-1/2" long; blue old-fashioned truck, whitewall tires, 1960s

EX $25   **NM** $50   **MIP** $75

Ol' Buddy's Pie Wagon, Buddy L, 10-1/2" long; old-fashioned delivery van; 1970

EX $30   **NM** $65   **MIP** $90

Ol' Buddys Sand Drag'n, Buddy L, 5" long; yellow stripped-down hot rod, whitewall tires, orange seat, 1970s

EX $20   **NM** $35   **MIP** $80

Pan-Am Clipper Cargo, Buddy L, 10-1/2" long; tractor-trailer van truck, luggage truck, lift truck and cargo boxes; 1976

EX $12   **NM** $23   **MIP** $35

Pepsi Delivery Truck, Buddy L, 15" long; blue hood and lower cab, white upper cab, double-deck cargo, two hand trucks, four blue cases of red bottles, four red cases of blue bottles; 1970

EX $20   **NM** $40   **MIP** n/a

Pick-Up, Buddy L, 13" long; stepside, red body, white roof, whitewall tires; mid-1960s

EX $22   **NM** $43   **MIP** $65

Polysteel Boat Transport, Buddy L, medium blue soft plastic body, steel flatbed carrying 8" white plastic runabout boat w/red deck, truck 12-1/2" long; 1960

EX $75   **NM** $115   **MIP** $150

Polysteel Coca-Cola Delivery Truck, Buddy L, yellow plastic truck, slanted bottle racks, eight red Coke cases w/green bottles, small metal hand truck, 12-1/2" long; 1961

EX $50   **NM** $75   **MIP** $100

Polysteel Coca-Cola Delivery Truck, Buddy L, yellow plastic truck, slanted bottle racks, eight green Coke cases w/red bottles, small metal hand truck, 12-1/4" long; 1962

EX $60   **NM** $90   **MIP** $120

Polysteel Dumper, Buddy L, orange plastic body and tiltback dump section w/cab shield, no "Come-Back Motor," no door decals, 13-1/2" long; 1962

EX $20   **NM** $40   **MIP** $80

Polysteel Dumper, Buddy L, medium blue soft molded plastic front, cab and frame, off-white steel dump body w/sides rounded at back, hinged tailgate, 13" long; 1960

EX $20   **NM** $40   **MIP** $80

Polysteel Dumper, Buddy L, orange plastic body and tiltback dump section w/cab shield, "Come-Back Motor," 13" long; 1961

EX $20   **NM** $40   **MIP** $80

Polysteel Dumper, Buddy L, green soft molded plastic front, cab and frame, yellow steel dump body w/sides rounded at back, hinged tailgate, 13" long; 1959

EX $20   **NM** $40   **MIP** $80

Polysteel Highway Transport, Buddy L, red soft plastic tractor, cab roof lights, double horn, radio antenna and side fuel tanks, white steel semi-trailer van, 20-1/2" long; 1960

EX $100   **NM** $150   **MIP** $200

Polysteel Hydraulic Dumper, Buddy L, beige soft molded-plastic front, cab and frame, off-white steel dump section w/sides rounded at rear, 13" long; 1959

EX $60   **NM** $95   **MIP** $125

Polysteel Hydraulic Dumper, Buddy L, red soft molded-plastic front, cab and frame, light green steel dump section w/sides rounded at rear, 13" long; 1960

EX $80   **NM** $120   **MIP** $160

Polysteel Hydraulic Dumper, Buddy L, yellow soft plastic body, frame and tiltback ribbed dump section w/cab shield, 13" long; 1961

EX $75   **NM** $125   **MIP** $150

Polysteel Hydraulic Dumper, Buddy L, red soft plastic body, frame and tiltback ribbed dump section w/cab shield, 13" long; 1962

EX $65   **NM** $100   **MIP** $130

Polysteel Milk Tanker, Buddy L, red soft plastic tractor unit, light blue/gray semi-trailer tank w/red ladders and five dooms, 22" long; 1961

EX $60   **NM** $95   **MIP** $125

Polysteel Milk Tanker, Buddy L, turquoise soft plastic tractor unit, light blue/gray semi-trailer tank w/red ladders and five dooms, 22" long; 1961

EX $60   **NM** $95   **MIP** $125

Polysteel Milkman Truck, Buddy L, light blue soft plastic front, cab and frame, light yellow steel open cargo section w/nine oversized white plastic milk bottles, 11-3/4" long; 1960

EX $65   **NM** $100   **MIP** $130

Polysteel Milkman Truck, Buddy L, light blue soft plastic front, cab and frame, light blue steel open cargo section w/nine oversized white plastic milk bottles, 11-3/4" long; 1961

EX $60   **NM** $95   **MIP** $125

Polysteel Milkman Truck, Buddy L, turquoise soft plastic front, cab and frame, light blue steel open cargo section w/nine oversized white plastic milk bottles w/red caps, 11-3/4" long; 1962

EX $35   **NM** $50   **MIP** $70

Polysteel Supermarket Delivery, Buddy L, medium blue soft molded-plastic front, hood, cab and frame, steel off-white open cargo section, 13" long; 1959

EX $75   **NM** $115   **MIP** $150

Pull-N-Ride Baggage Truck, Buddy L, duo-tone horizontal design, light cream upper half, off-white lower half and bumper, 24-1/4" long; 1953

EX $150   **NM** $225   **MIP** $300

Racing Team, Buddy L, No. 5464; crossed-flag emblem on cab doors, double-deck racer carrier in rear, three racers; 1964-65

EX $30   **NM** $55   **MIP** $85

Raggedy Ann and Andy Camper, Buddy L, 11-1/2" long; van truck, blue w/"Raggedy Ann and Andy Camper" panel decoration, pink interior, whitewall tires; w/Raggedy Ann and Andy figures, dog and boat; 1970s or 1980s

EX $30   **NM** $100   **MIP** $135

Railroad Transfer Rider Delivery Truck, Buddy L, duo-tone horizontal design, yellow upper half, hood top, cab and slatted caro sides, green lower half, small hand truck, two milk cans w/removable lids, 23-1/4" long; 1949

EX $70   **NM** $100   **MIP** $140

Railroad Transfer Store Door Delivery, Buddy L, duo-tone horizontal design, yellow hood top, cab and upper body, red lower half of hood and body, small hand truck, two metal drums w/coin slots, 23-1/4" long; 1950

EX $90   **NM** $135   **MIP** $180

Railway Express Truck, Buddy L, deep green plastic "Diamond T" hood and cab, deep green steel frame and van body w/removable silvery roof, small two-wheel hand truck, steel four-rung barrel skid, 21" long; 1952

EX $200   **NM** $300   **MIP** $400

Railway Express Truck, Buddy L, green plastic hood and cab, green steel high-sides open body, frame and bumper, small two-wheel hand truck, steel four-rung barrel skid, 20-3/4" long; 1953
EX $125 **NM** $185 **MIP** $250

Railway Express Truck, Buddy L, green all-steel hood, cab, frame and high-sides open body, sides have three horizontal slots in upper back corners, 22" long; 1954
EX $75 **NM** $115 **MIP** $150

Ranchero Stake Truck, Buddy L, medium green, white plastic one-piece bumper and grille guard, four-post, four-slat fixed stake sides and cargo section, 14" long; 1963
EX $50 **NM** $75 **MIP** $100

Randy Travis Truck, Buddy L, 20-1/2" long; tractor-trailer, battery-operated sounds, 1990s
EX $8 **NM** $12 **MIP** $20

REA Express Van, Buddy L, 11-1/2" long; same as 1965 but w/side doors embossed "Buddy L" and no suspension; 1966
EX $45 **NM** $90 **MIP** $200

REA Express Van, Buddy L, 11-1/2" long; dark green, "REA Express" and pigeon decoration, sliding side doors, double rear doors, spring suspension; 1964-65
EX $45 **NM** $125 **MIP** $250

Reese's Pieces Semi, Buddy L, 10" long, made in Japan, 1980
EX $6 **NM** $12 **MIP** $25

Repair It Unit Truck, Buddy L, 24"-long wrecker, red cab and chassis, white body, green hoist, spare tire, tools, 1950s
EX $75 **NM** $125 **MIP** $200

Rider Dump Truck, Buddy L, duo-tone horizontal design, yellow hood top, upper cab and upper dump body, red front, hood sides, lower doors and lower dump body, no bumper, 21-1/2" long; 1945
EX $160 **NM** $245 **MIP** $325

Rider Dump Truck, Buddy L, duo-tone horizontal design, yellow hood top, upper cab and upper dump body, red front, hood sides, lower doors and lower dump body, no bumper, 23" long; 1947
EX $75 **NM** $115 **MIP** $150

(Thomas G. Nefos Photo)

Riding Academy Truck, Buddy L, 18-1/2"; blue/green body, white roof over bed, side and rear opening ramps, three plastic horses, "Buddy L" logo on cab doors, "Riding Academy" in white type along sides, No. 5455, 1964
EX $70 **NM** $120 **MIP** $150

Riding Academy Truck, Buddy L, 18-1/2", green hood, cab and van body; white roofs and ramps; three horses, No. 5555, 1972-75
EX $25 **NM** $55 **MIP** $100

Riding Academy Truck, Buddy L, 18-1/2", similar to 1965-67 version, tan body and roof, No. 5455, 1968-69
EX $25 **NM** $75 **MIP** $100

Riding Academy Truck, Buddy L, 18-1/2", similar to 1964 version, maroon body and roof, two white ramps, three horses, 1965-67
EX $40 **NM** $85 **MIP** $125

Riding Academy Truck, Buddy L, 18-1/2", light brown hood and body, tan roof, three horses, No. 5555, 1970-71
EX $25 **NM** $55 **MIP** $100

Rival Dog Food Delivery Van, Buddy L, cream front, cab and boxy van body, metal drum coin bank w/"RIVAL DOG FOOD" label in blue, red, white and yellow, 16-1/2" long; 1956
EX $160 **NM** $245 **MIP** $325

Rockin' Giraffe Truck, Buddy L, 13-1/4" long; blue cab, open cargo, two plastic giraffes; 1967
EX $30 **NM** $125 **MIP** $175

Ruff-n-Tuff Cement Mixer Truck, Buddy L, 16" long; yellow cabover, white plastic water tank; 1971
EX $22 **NM** $43 **MIP** $65

Ruff-n-Tuff Log Truck, Buddy L, 16" long; yellow cabover; 1971
EX $23 **NM** $46 **MIP** $70

Ryder City Special Delivery Truck Van, Buddy L, duo-tone horizontal design, yellow upper half including hood top and cab, brown removable van roof, warm brown front and lower half of van body, 24-1/2" long; 1949
EX $150 **NM** $225 **MIP** $300

Ryder Van Lines Trailer, Buddy L, duo-tone slant design, black front and lower hood sides and doors, deep red hood top, enclosed cab and chassis, 35-1/2" long; 1949
EX $350 **NM** $525 **MIP** $700

Sand and Gravel Rider Dump Truck, Buddy L, duo-tone horizontal design, blue lower half, yellow upper half including hoop top and enclosed cab, 24" long; 1950
EX $100 **NM** $200 **MIP** $700

Sand and Gravel Truck, Buddy L, dark or medium green hood, cab, roof lights and skirted body, white or cream dump section, 13-1/2" long; 1949
EX $65 **NM** $100 **MIP** $200

Sand and Gravel Truck, Buddy L, duo-tone horizontal design, red front, bumper, lower hood, cab sides, chassis and lower dump body sides, white hood top, enclosed cab and upper dump body, 23-3/4" long; 1949
EX $350 **NM** $525 **MIP** $700

Sand Dump Truck, Buddy L, 10-1/2" long; green tractor-trailer, futuristic cabover, 1970s
EX $5 **NM** $10 **MIP** $20

Sand Loader and Dump Truck, Buddy L, duo-tone horizontal design, yellow hood top and upper dump blue cab sides, frame and lower dump body, red loader on dump w/black rubber conveyor belt, 24-1/2" 1950-52
EX $175 **NM** $265 **MIP** $350

Sanitation Service Truck, Buddy L, 17" long; blue cab, white body, two round plastic headlights; 1972
EX $17 **NM** $33 **MIP** $50

Sanitation Service Truck, Buddy L, 16-1/2" long; blue cab, white enclosed dump section, no plastic windows in garbage section; 1968
EX $32 **NM** $85 **MIP** n/a

Sanitation Service Truck, Buddy L, 16-1/2" long; blue cab, white enclosed dump section, plastic windows in garbage section; 1967
EX $32 **NM** $85 **MIP** n/a

Sanitation Truck, Buddy L, 6" long; white and blue; 1970s
EX $3 **NM** $5 **MIP** $8

Sears Roebuck Delivery Truck Van, Buddy L, gray/green and off-white, no side doors; 1967, Model No. *
EX $125 **NM** $200 **MIP** $280

Sears Service Van Truck, Buddy L, 11-1/2" long; gray-green, open side doors, swing-open rear doors; 1967-68
EX $42 **NM** $90 **MIP** $125

Self-Loading Auto Carrier, Buddy L, medium tan tractor unit, three plastic cars, overall 34" long including loading ramp; 1960
EX $85 **NM** $130 **MIP** $175

Self-Loading Boat Hauler, Buddy L, pastel blue tractor and semi-trailer w/three 8-1/2" long boats, overall 26-1/2" long; 1962-63
EX $150 **NM** $225 **MIP** $350

Self-Loading Car Carrier, Buddy L, beige/yellow tractor unit, three plastic cars, overall 33-1/2" long including; 1964

EX $60   NM $95   MIP $125

Self-Loading Car Carrier, Buddy L, lime green tractor unit, three plastic cars, overall 33-1/2" long including; 1963

EX $75   NM $115   MIP $150

Service Wrecker, Buddy L, 14" long; red, black boom; mid-1960s

EX $50   NM $100   MIP $150

Shark Show Truck, Buddy L, 10-1/2" long; green tractor-trailer w/shark and tank, futuristic cabover, 1970s

EX $5   NM $20   MIP $40

Shell Pickup and Delivery, Buddy L, yellow/orange hood and body, open cargo section, three curved slots toward rear in sides, chains across back, red coin-slot oil drum w/Shell emblem and lettering, 13-1/4" long; 1952-53

EX $125   NM $185   MIP $250

Shell Pickup and Delivery, Buddy L, reddish orange hood and body, open cargo section w/solid sides, chain across back, red coin-slot oil drum w/Shell emblem and lettering, 13-1/4" long; 1950

EX $135   NM $200   MIP $275

Sit-N-Ride Truck, Buddy L, 25" long; removable steel seat in dump bed, lever-action dump body; 1965

EX $38   NM $76   MIP $115

Smoke Patrol, Buddy L, 13-1/4" long; lemon-yellow body, six wheels, garden-hose attachment for water cannon; 1970

EX $22   NM $43   MIP $65

Standard Coffee Co. Delivery Truck Van, Buddy L, 11-1/2" long; 1966

EX $40   NM $60   MIP $120

Stor-Dor Delivery, Buddy L, red hood and body, open cargo body w/four horizontal slots in sides, plated chains across open back, 14-1/2" long; 1955

EX $65   NM $100   MIP $175

(Joe and Sharon Freed Photo)

Sunshine Biscuits Van, Buddy L, Dark yellow body, light gray chassis, whitewall tires, Sunshine chef decals along sides, w/Sunshine Biscuits photo decal showing Krispy, Cheez-It crackers and Hydrox and HiHo cookies

EX $145   NM $260   MIP $330

Sunshine Biscuits Van Truck, Buddy L, 11-1/2" long; yellow cabover, sliding side doors, opening rear doors, "Sunshine Biscuits" on panels; 1967-68

EX $60   NM $140   MIP n/a

Super Dog Truck, Buddy L, 6-1/2" long; high-windshield cabover, doghouse w/Snoopy-like dog's head as load; 1970s

EX $6   NM $12   MIP $18

Supermarket Delivery, Buddy L, blue bumper, front, hood, cab and frame, one-piece chrome four-hole grille and headlights, 14-1/2" long; 1956

EX $75   NM $115   MIP $150

Supermarket Delivery, Buddy L, all white w/rubber wheels, enclosed cab, pointed nose, bright metal one-piece grille, 13-3/4" long; 1950

EX $125   NM $185   MIP $250

Surf-N-Turf, Buddy L, yellow Bronco-type beach vehicle w/oversize tires, two removable surf boards, 1970s

EX $30   NM $60   MIP $130

Teepee Camping Trailer and Wagon, Buddy L, maroon suburban wagon, two-wheel teepee trailer and its beige plastic folding tent, overall 24-1/2" long; 1963

EX $75   NM $180   MIP $260

(Calvin L. Chaussee Photo)

Texaco Tank Truck, Buddy L, red steel GMC 550-series blunt-nose tractor and semi-trailer tank, 25" long; 1959

EX $80   NM $125   MIP $400

Texaco Tanker, Promotional Piece, Buddy L, White rounded cabover w/red tanker section, black plastic hose, "Texaco" logo stickers on cab, "Texaco" on tanker sides, 25" long

EX $60   NM $110   MIP $205

Tide Racing Team Truck, Buddy L, 20-1/2" long; Kenworth tractor-trailer, "Ricky Rudd," 1990s

EX $5   NM $8   MIP $12

Tom's Toasted Peanuts Delivery Truck Van, Buddy L, 11-1/2" long; tan body , no sliding doors, blue underbody; 1973

EX $27   NM $53   MIP $80

Trail Boss, Buddy L, 7" long; red, white plastic seat; 1970

EX $4   NM $9   MIP $12

Trail Boss, Buddy L, 7" long; lime green, yellow seat; 1971

EX $4   NM $9   MIP $12

Trailer Van Truck, Buddy L, red tractor and van roof, blue bumper, white semi-trailer van, chrome one-piece toothed grille and headlights, white drop-down rear door, 29" long w/tailgate/ramp lowered; 1956

EX $145   NM $225   MIP $300

Trailer Van w/Tailgate Loader, Buddy L, green high-impacted styrene plastic tractor on steel frame, cream steel detachable semi-trailer van w/green roof and crank operated tailgate, 33" long w/tailgate lowered; 1953

EX $125   NM $185   MIP $250

Trailer Van w/Tailgate Loader, Buddy L, green steel tractor, bumper, chrome one-piece toothed grille and headlights, cream van w/green roof and tailgate loader, 31-3/4" long, w/tailgate down; 1954

EX $125   NM $185   MIP $250

Traveling Zoo Truck, Buddy L, 14" long; snub-nosed yellow cab, six red cages w/six animals; 1970

EX $17   NM $33   MIP $50

Traveling Zoo Truck, Buddy L, 14" long; red pickup, yellow six-copartment cage w/six plastic jungle animals; 1965-67

EX $40   NM $85   MIP $260

Traveling Zoo Truck, Buddy L, 14" long; yellow pickup, six compartments w/animals; 1969

EX $25   NM $50   MIP $75

Turbine Racer Transport, Buddy L, short high-window cabover truck w/platform for hauling red "Turbine" open-cockpit racer, 1960s

EX $12   NM $25   MIP $50

Corgi

AGRICULTURAL

Agricultural Set, 1962-66, 1962-64 issue: No. 55 Fordson Tractor, No. 51 Tipping Trailer, No. 438 Land Rover, No. 101 Flat Trailer w/No. 1487 Milk Churns; 1965-66 issue: No. 60 Fordson Tractor, No. 62 Tipping Trailer, No. 438 Land Rover, red No. 100 Dropside Trailer w/No. 1487 Milk Churns, a difficult set to find, Model No. 22-A
EX $380 NM $1000 MIP $2400

Agricultural Set, 1967-72, No. 69 Massey-Ferguson tractor, No. 62 trailer, No. 438 Land Rover, No. 484 Livestock Truck w/pigs, No. 71 harrow, No. 1490 skip and churns; w/accessories: four calves, farmhand, dog and six sacks, Model No. 5-B
EX $200 NM $400 MIP $700

Agricultural Set, 1978-80, No. 55 Tractor, No. 56 Tipping Trailer, Silo and mustard yellow conveyor, Model No. 42-A
EX $60 NM $90 MIP $130

Beast Carrier Trailer, 1965-71, red chassis, yellow body and tailgate, four plastic calves, red plastic wheels, black rubber tires, Model No. 58-A
EX $24 NM $36 MIP $60

Bedford Articulated Horse Box, 1973-76, cast cab, lower body and three working ramps, yellow interior, plastic upper body, w/horse and Newmarket Racing Stables labels, dark metallic green or light green body w/orange or yellow upper, four horses, Model No. 1104-B
EX $40 NM $80 MIP $120

Berliet Articulated Horse Box, 1976-80, bronze cab and lower semi body, cream chassis, white upper body, black interior, three working ramps, National Racing Stables decals, horse figures, chrome wheels, Model No. 1105-B
EX $30 NM $45 MIP $75

Combine, Tractor and Trailer, 1959-62, set of three: No. 1111 combine, No. 50 Massey-Ferguson tractor, and No. 51 trailer, Model No. 8-A
EX $180 NM $350 MIP $500

Country Farm Set, 1974-75, No. 50 Massey-Ferguson tractor, red No. 62 hay trailer w/load, fences, figures, Model No. 4-B
EX $30 NM $45 MIP $75

Country Farm Set, 1976, same as 4-B but w/out hay load on trailer, Model No. 5-C
EX $30 NM $45 MIP $75

David Brown Combine, 1978-79, No. 55 tractor, red and yellow combines, white JF labels, Model No. 1112-B
EX $30 NM $45 MIP $75

David Brown Tractor, 1977-82, white body w/black/white David Brown No. 1412 labels, red chassis and plastic engine, Model No. 55-B
EX $15 NM $25 MIP $45

David Brown Tractor & Trailer, 1976-79, two-piece set: No. 55 tractor and No. 56 trailer, Model No. 34-A
EX $30 NM $45 MIP $75

Dodge Livestock Truck, 1967-72, tan cab and hood, green body, working tailgate and ramp, five pigs, Model No. 484-A
EX $34 NM $60 MIP $100

Ford 5000 Super Major Tractor, 1967-73, blue body/chassis w/Ford Super Major 5000 decals, gray cast fenders and rear wheels, gray plastic front wheels, black plastic tires, driver, Model No. 67-A
EX $30 NM $45 MIP $75

Ford 5000 Tractor w/Scoop, 1969-72, blue body/chassis, gray fenders, yellow scoop arm and controls, chrome scoop, black control lines, Model No. 74-A
EX $55 NM $80 MIP $180

(KP Photo by Dr. Douglas Sadecky)

Ford Tractor and Beast Carrier, 1966-72, Gift Set included No. 67 Fordson 5000 tractor and No. 58 Beast Carrier, Model No. 1-B
EX $60 NM $90 MIP $190

Ford Tractor and Conveyor, 1966-69, No. 67 tractor, conveyor w/trailer, figures and accessories, Model No. 47-A
EX $60 NM $90 MIP $225

Ford Tractor w/Trencher, 1970-74, blue body/chassis, gray fenders, cast yellow trencher arm and controls, chrome trencher, black control lines, Model No. 72-A
EX $50 NM $75 MIP $190

(KP Photo by Dr. Douglas Sadecky)

Fordson Power Major Halftrack Tractor, 1962-64, blue body/chassis, silver steering wheel, seat and grille, two versions: orange plastic wheels, gray treads, lights in radiator or on sides of radiator, this bizarre little model can be quite difficult to find—especially w/original tracks, Model No. 54-A
EX $90 NM $190 MIP $325

(KP Photo by Dr. Douglas Sadecky)

Fordson Power Major Tractor, 1961-63, blue body/chassis w/Fordson Power Major decals, silver steering wheel, seat, exhaust, grille and lights, the 61-A Four Furrow Plough makes a nice companion piece to the model, Model No. 55-A
EX $45 NM $70 MIP $130

Fordson Power Major Tractor, 1964-66, blue body w/Fordson Power Major decals, driver, blue chassis and steering wheel, silver seat, hitch, exhaust, Model No. 60-A
EX $50 NM $75 MIP $130

Fordson Tractor and Plow, 1961-64, No. 55 Fordson Tractor and No. 56 Four Furrow plow, Model No. 18-A
EX $55 NM $85 MIP $180

Fordson Tractor and Plow, 1964-66, No. 60 tractor and No. 61 four-furrow plow, Model No. 13-A
EX $55 NM $85 MIP $140

Four Furrow Plow, 1961-63, red frame, yellow plastic parts, Model No. 56-A
EX $15 NM $20 MIP $55

Four Furrow Plow, 1964-70, blue frame w/chrome plastic parts, Model No. 61-A
EX $15 NM $20 MIP $40

Jeep FC-150 Pickup w/Conveyor Belt, 1965-69, red body, yellow interior, orange grille, two black rubber belts, shaped wheels, black rubber tires;

accessories include farmland figure and sacks, Model No. 64-A

EX $45   **NM** $100   **MIP** $220

Land Rover & Horse Box, 1968-77, blue/white Land Rover w/horse trailer in two versions: cast wheels (1968-74) and Whizz Wheels (1975-77); accessories include a mare and a foal; value is for each individual complete set, Model No. 15-B

EX $50   **NM** $75   **MIP** $125

Land Rover and Pony Trailer, 1958-62, two versions: green No. 438 Land Rover and a red and black No. 102 Pony trailer (1958-62); tan/cream No. 438 Land Rover and a pony trailer (1963-68); value given is for each individual complete set, Model No. 2-A

EX $50   **NM** $90   **MIP** $220

Massey-Ferguson 165 Tractor, 1966-72, gray engine and chassis, red hood and fenders w/black/white Massey-Ferguson 165 decals, white grille, red cast wheels; makes engine sound, Model No. 66-A

EX $35   **NM** $55   **MIP** $95

(KP Photo by Dr. Douglas Sadecky)

Massey-Ferguson 165 Tractor w/Saw, 1969-73, red hood and fenders, gray engine and seat, cast yellow arm and control, chrome circular saw, Model No. 73-A

EX $55   **NM** $85   **MIP** $200

(KP Photo by Dr. Douglas Sadecky)

Massey-Ferguson 165 Tractor w/Shovel, 1967-73, gray chassis, red hood, fenders and shovel arms, unpainted shovel and cylinder, red cast wheels, black plastic tires,

w/figure, this tractor even featured engine noises, Model No. 69-A

EX $45   **NM** $65   **MIP** $120

Massey-Ferguson 50B Tractor, 1973-77, yellow body, black interior and roof, red plastic wheels w/black plastic tires, windows, Model No. 50-B

EX $15   **NM** $18   **MIP** $75

Massey-Ferguson 65 Tractor, 1959-66, silver metal or plastic steering wheel, seat and grille, red engine hood, red metal or plastic wheels w/black rubber tires, Model No. 50-A

EX $40   **NM** $70   **MIP** $130

Massey-Ferguson 65 Tractor and Shovel, 1960-66, two versions: red bonnet w/either cream or gray chassis, red metal or orange plastic wheels; value is for each, Model No. 53-A

EX $55   **NM** $85   **MIP** $140

Massey-Ferguson Combine, 1959-63, red body w/yellow metal blades, metal tines, black/white decals, yellow metal wheels, Model No. 1111-A

EX $70   **NM** $105   **MIP** $200

Massey-Ferguson Combine, 1968-73, red body, plastic yellow blades, red wheels, Model No. 1111-B

EX $60   **NM** $100   **MIP** $180

Massey-Ferguson Tipping Trailer, 1959-65, two versions: red chassis w/either yellow or gray tipper and tailgate, red metal or plastic wheels, value is for each, Model No. 51-A

EX $10   **NM** $18   **MIP** $40

Massey-Ferguson Tractor and Tipping Trailer, 1959-63, No. 50 tractor and No. 51 trailer, no driver, Model No. 7-A

EX $50   **NM** $75   **MIP** $150

Massey-Ferguson Tractor and Tipping Trailer, 1965, No. 50 Massey-Ferguson tractor w/driver, No. 51 trailer, Model No. 29-A

EX $50   **NM** $100   **MIP** $200

(KP Photo by Dr. Douglas Sadecky)

Massey-Ferguson Tractor w/Fork, 1963-67, red cast body and shovel, arms, cream chassis, red plastic wheels, black rubber tires, Massey-

Ferguson 65 decals, w/driver, Model No. 57-A

EX $60   **NM** $90   **MIP** $150

Massey-Ferguson Tractor w/Shovel, 1974-81, two versions: either yellow and red or red and white body colors; value is for each, Model No. 54-B

EX $20   **NM** $30   **MIP** $50

Massey-Ferguson Tractor w/Shovel & Trailer, 1965-66, No. 54 MF tractor w/driver and shovel, No. 62 trailer, Model No. 32-A

EX $45   **NM** $100   **MIP** $175

Pony Club Set, 1978-80, brown/white No. 421 Land Rover w/Corgi Pony Club labels, horse box, horse and rider, Model No. 47-B

EX $30   **NM** $45   **MIP** $75

Rice Beaufort Double Horse Box, 1969-72, long, blue body and working gates, white roof, brown plastic interior, two horses, cast wheels, plastic tires, Model No. 112-A

EX $15   **NM** $30   **MIP** $50

(KP Photo by Dr. Douglas Sadecky)

Rice Pony Trailer, 1958-65, cast body and chassis w/working tailgate, horse, in six variations, smooth or shaped hubs, cast or wire drawbar, shown here is the harder-to-find two-tone cream/red variation, Model No. 102-A

EX $20   **NM** $30   **MIP** $75

Silo & Conveyor Belt, 1978-80, w/yellow conveyor and Corgi Harvesting Co. label on silo, Model No. 43-A

EX $35   **NM** $50   **MIP** $85

Tandem Disc Harrow, 1967-72, yellow main frame, red upper frame, working wheels linkage, unpainted linkage and cast discs, black plastic tires, Model No. 71-A

EX $15   **NM** $25   **MIP** $55

Tipping Farm Trailer, 1965-72, red working tipper and tailgates, yellow chassis, red plastic wheels, black tires, w/detachable raves, Model No. 62-A

EX $10   **NM** $15   **MIP** $35

Tipping Farm Trailer, 1977-80, cast chassis and tailgate, red plastic tipper and wheels, black tires, in two versions, Model No. 56-B

EX $10   **NM** $15   **MIP** $25

Tractor and Beast Carrier, 1965-66, No. 55 Fordson tractor, figures and No. 58 beast carrier, Model No. 33-A
EX $65   **NM** $100   **MIP** $190

Tractor w/Shovel and Trailer, 1968-73, standard colors, No. 69 Massey-Ferguson Tractor and No. 62 Tipping Trailer, Model No. 9-B
EX $65   **NM** $100   **MIP** $165

AIRCRAFT

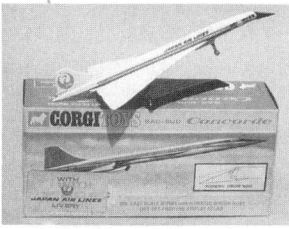

(KP Photo by Dr. Douglas Sadecky)

Concorde-First Issues, 1969-72, Japan Airlines decals, this rare model was probably an import issue, ironically, the real Concorde was never part of the Japan Air Lines, Model No. 653-A
EX $150   **NM** $300   **MIP** $600

Concorde-First Issues, 1969-72, Air Canada decals, (the real Concorde was not a part of Air Canada), Model No. 652-A
EX $80   **NM** $120   **MIP** $250

Concorde-First Issues, 1969-72, Air France decals, Model No. 651-A
EX $50   **NM** $100   **MIP** $170

Concorde-First Issues, 1969-72, BOAC decals, Model No. 650-A
EX $40   **NM** $85   **MIP** $150

Concorde-Second Issues, 1976-82, Air France model on display stand, Model No. 651-B
EX $15   **NM** $30   **MIP** $60

Concorde-Second Issues, 1976-82, BOAC model on display stand, Model No. 650-B
EX $15   **NM** $25   **MIP** $50

Corgi Flying Club Set, 1972-77, blue/orange No. 438 Land Rover w/red dome light, blue trailer w/either orange/yellow or orange/white plastic airplane, Model No. 19-B
EX $24   **NM** $50   **MIP** $100

Flying Club Set, 1978-80, green and white No. 419 Jeep w/Corgi Flying Club labels, green trailer, blue/white airplane, Model No. 49-A
EX $36   **NM** $55   **MIP** $90

Glider Set, 1981-83, two versions: white No. 345 Honda, 1981-82; yellow Honda, 1983, value is for individual complete sets, Model No. 12-C
EX $30   **NM** $45   **MIP** $75

Lunar Bug, 1970-72, white body w/red roof, blue interior and wings, clear and amber windows, red working ramp, Lunar Bug labels, Model No. 806-A
EX $25   **NM** $40   **MIP** $95

NASA Space Shuttle, 1980, white body, two opening hatches, black plastic interior, jets and base, unpainted retracting gear castings, black plastic wheels, w/satellite, Model No. 648-A
EX $30   **NM** $45   **MIP** $75

Stromberg Jet Ranger Helicopter, 1978-79, black body w/yellow trim and interior, clear windows, black plastic rotors, white/blue labels, Model No. 926-A
EX $45   **NM** $65   **MIP** $125

AUTOMOBILE

AMC Pacer, 1977-78, metallic red body, white Pacer X decals, working hatch, clear windows, light yellow interior, chrome bumpers and wheels, Model No. 291-A
EX $15   **NM** $20   **MIP** $50

Aston Martin DB4, 1960-65, red or yellow body w/working hood, detailed engine, clear windows, plastic interior, silver lights, grille, license plate and bumpers, red taillights, rubber tires, smooth, or spun cast spoked wheels; working scoop on early models, Model No. 218-A
EX $45   **NM** $65   **MIP** $150

(KP Photo by Dr. Douglas Sadecky)

Austin A40, 1959-62, one-piece light blue body w/dark blue roof or red body w/black roof and clear windows, smooth or spun hubs, rubber tires, Model No. 216-A
EX $35   **NM** $75   **MIP** $125

Austin A40-Mechanical, 1959-60, friction motor, red body w/black roof, smooth wheels, Model No. 216-M
EX $55   **NM** $125   **MIP** $275

(KP Photo by Dr. Douglas Sadecky)

Austin A60 Driving School, 1964-68, medium blue body w/silver trim, left-hand drive steering wheel, steering control on roof; came w/five language leaflet (US version of No. 236), Model No. 255-A
EX $45   **NM** $65   **MIP** $180

(KP Photo by Dr. Douglas Sadecky)

Austin A60 Motor School, 1964-69, light blue body w/silver trim, red interior, single body casting, right-hand drive steering wheel, two figures, steering control on roof; came w/Highway Patrol leaflet, Model No. 236-A
EX $45   **NM** $65   **MIP** $150

(KP Photo by Dr. Douglas Sadecky)

Austin Cambridge, 1956-61, available in gray, green/gray, silver/green, aqua, green/cream, two-tone green, smooth wheels, shown here w/Austin Cambridge-Mechanical, Model No. 201-A
EX $45   **NM** $90   **MIP** $160

Austin Cambridge-Mechanical, 1956-59, fly-wheel motor, available in orange, cream, light or dark gray, or silver over metallic blue, smooth wheels, Model No. 201M
EX $50   **NM** $120   **MIP** $240

Austin Mini Countryman, 1965-69, turquoise body, jeweled headlights, opening rear doors, chrome roofrack w/two surfboards, shaped or cast wheels, w/surfer figure, Model No. 485-A
EX $55   **NM** $80   **MIP** $160

Austin Mini-Metro, 1981, blue or red body w/plastic interior, working rear hatch and doors, clear windows, folding seats, chrome headlights, orange taillights, black plastic base, grille, bumpers, Whizz Wheels, Model No. 275-B
EX $18   **NM** $27   **MIP** $45

Austin Seven Mini, 1961-67, red, yellow interior, silver bumpers, grille and headlights, orange taillights, Model No. 225-A1
EX $50   **NM** $100   **MIP** $170

Austin Seven Mini, 1961-67, primrose yellow, red interior, rare, Model No. 225-A2, second issue
EX $100   **NM** $200   **MIP** $325

Bentley Continental, 1961-66, two-tone green or black and silver bodies, w/red interior, clear windows, chrome grille and bumpers, jewel headlights, red jeweled taillights, suspension, shaped wheels, gray rubber tires, Model No. 224-A
EX $45   **NM** $65   **MIP** $110

Bentley T Series, 1970-72, red body, cream interior, working hood, trunk and doors, clear windows, folding seats, chrome bumper/grille, jewel headlights, Whizz Wheels, Model No. 274-A
EX $36   **NM** $55   **MIP** $90

Buick and Cabin Cruiser, 1965-68, two versions: light blue or dark metallic blue, No. 245 Buick, red boat trailer, dolphin cabin cruiser w/two figures, Model No. 31-A
EX $80   **NM** $120   **MIP** $280

Buick Riviera, 1964-68, metallic gold, dark blue, pale blue or gold body, red interior, gray steering wheel, and tow hook, clear windshield, chrome grille and bumpers, suspension, Trans-o-lite headlights, spoked wheels and rubber tires, Model No. 245-A
EX $30   **NM** $45   **MIP** $95

Chevrolet Caprice Classic, 1981-82, working doors and trunk, whitewall tires, two versions: light metallic green body w/green interior or silver on blue body w/brown interior, Model No. 325-B
EX $24   **NM** $36   **MIP** $60

(KP Photo by Dr. Douglas Sadecky)

Chevrolet Corvair, 1961-66, either blue or pale-blue body w/yellow interior and working rear hood, detailed engine, clear windows, silver bumpers, headlights and trim, red taillights, rear window blind, smooth or shaped wheels, rubber tires, Model No. 229-A
EX $36   **NM** $55   **MIP** $100

(KP Photo by Dr. Douglas Sadecky)

Chevrolet Impala, 1960-62, pink body, yellow plastic interior, clear windows, silver headlights, bumpers, grille and trim, suspension, die-cast base w/rubber tires; a second version has a blue body w/red or yellow interior and smooth or shaped hubs, Model No. 220-A
EX $50   **NM** $75   **MIP** $135

Chevrolet Impala, 1965-67, tan body, cream interior, gray steering wheel, clear windshields, chrome bumpers, grille, headlights, suspension, red taillights, shaped wheels and rubber tires, Model No. 248-A
EX $50   **NM** $75   **MIP** $125

(KP Photo by Dr. Douglas Sadecky)

Chevrolet Kennel Club Van, 1967-69, white upper, red lower body, working tailgate and rear windows, green interior, four dog figures, kennel club decals; shaped spun or detailed cast wheels, rubber tires, Model No. 486-A
EX $56   **NM** $90   **MIP** $180

Chrysler Imperial Convertible, 1965-66, red body w/gray base, working hood, trunk and doors, golf bag in trunk, detailed engine, clear windshield, aqua interior, driver, chrome bumpers, shaped or cast wheels, Model No. 246-A1
EX $45   **NM** $85   **MIP** $165

Chrysler Imperial Convertible, 1967-68, metallic blue body w/gray base, working hood, trunk and doors, golf bag in trunk, detailed engine, clear windshield, aqua interior, driver, chrome bumpers, shaped or cast wheels, Model No. 246-A2
EX $50   **NM** $120   **MIP** $230

Citroen 2CV Charleston, 1981, yellow/black or maroon/black body versions w/opening hood, Model No. 346-A
EX $15   **NM** $18   **MIP** $30

Citroen DS19, 1957-65, one-piece body in several colors, clear windows, silver lights, grille and bumpers, smooth wheels, rubber tires; colors: red, metallic green w/black roof, yellow w/red roof, Model No. 210-A
EX $56   **NM** $84   **MIP** $140

Citroen Dyane, 1974-78, metallic yellow or green body, black roof and interior, working rear hatch, clear windows, black base and tow bar, silver bumpers, grille and headlights, red taillights, marching duck and French flag decals, suspension, chrome wheels, Model No. 287-A
EX $15   **NM** $18   **MIP** $30

Citroen ID-19 Safari, 1963-65, yellow body w/red/brown or red/green luggage on roof rack, green/brown interior, working hatch, two passengers, Wildlife Preservation decals, Model No. 436-A
EX $40   **NM** $70   **MIP** $140

Citroen Le Dandy Coupe, 1966, metallic maroon body and base, yellow interior, working trunk and two doors, clear windows, plastic interior, folding seats, chrome grille and bumpers, jewel headlights, red taillights, suspension, spoked wheels, rubber tires, Model No. 259-A1
EX $50   **NM** $75   **MIP** $125

(KP Photo by Dr. Douglas Sadecky)

Citroen Le Dandy Coupe, 1967-69, metallic dark blue hood, sides and base, plastic aqua interior, white roof and trunk lid, clear windows, folding seats, chrome grille and bumpers, jewel headlights, red taillights, suspension, spoked wheels, rubber tires, Model No. 259-A2
EX $70   **NM** $105   **MIP** $175

Citroen SM, 1971-75, metallic lime gold w/chrome wheels or mauve body w/spoked wheels, pale blue interior and lifting hatch cover, working rear hatch and two doors, chrome inner doors, window frames, bumpers, grille, amber headlights, red taillights, Whizz Wheels, Model No. 284-A

EX $16   **NM** $24   **MIP** $40

Citroen Tour de France Car, 1970-72, red body, yellow interior and rear bed, clear windshield and headlights, driver, black plastic rack w/four bicycle wheels, swiveling team manager figure w/megaphone in back of car, Paramount and Tour de France decals, Whizz Wheels, Model No. 510-A

EX $40   **NM** $70   **MIP** $160

Citroen Winter Olympics Car, 1967-69, white body, blue roof and hatch, blue interior, red roof rack w/yellow skis, gold sled w/rider, skier, gold Grenoble Olympiade decals on car roof, cast wheels, Model No. 499-A

EX $75   **NM** $200   **MIP** $400

Citroen Winter Sports Safari, 1964-67, white body in three versions: two w/Corgi Ski Club decals and either w/or w/out roof ski rack, or one w/1964 Winter Olympics decals, shaped wheels, Model No. 475-A

EX $60   **NM** $95   **MIP** $180

(KP Photo by Dr. Douglas Sadecky)

Fiat 1800, 1960-63, one-piece body in several colors, clear windows, plastic interior, silver lights, grille and bumpers, red taillights, smooth or shaped wheels, rubber tires, colors: blue body w/light or bright yellow interior, light tan, mustard, light blue or two-tone blue body, Model No. 217-A

EX $24   **NM** $40   **MIP** $90

Fiat 2100, 1961-64, light two-tone mauve body, yellow interior, purple roof, clear windows w/rear blind, silver grille, license plates and bumpers, red taillights, shaped wheels, rubber tires, Model No. 232-A

EX $22   **NM** $33   **MIP** $90

(KP Photo by Dr. Douglas Sadecky)

Ford Consul, 1956-61, one-piece body in several colors, clear windows, silver grille, lights and bumpers, smooth wheels, rubber tires, Model No. 200-A

EX $45   **NM** $90   **MIP** $165

Ford Consul Classic, 1961-65, cream or gold body and base, yellow interior, pink roof, clear windows, gray steering wheel, silver bumpers, grille, opening hood, shaped wheels, Model No. 234-A

EX $35   **NM** $55   **MIP** $90

Ford Consul-Mechanical, 1956-59, same as model 200-A but w/friction motor and blue or green body, Model No. 200-M

EX $55   **NM** $100   **MIP** $225

Ford Cortina Estate Car, 1966-68, 3-1/2" metallic dark blue body and base, brown and cream simulated wood panels, cream interior, chrome bumpers and grille, jewel headlights, shaped wheels, Model No. 440-A

EX $35   **NM** $55   **MIP** $90

Ford Cortina Estate Car, 1966-69, red body and base or metallic charcoal gray body and base, cream interior, chrome bumpers and grille, jewel headlights, shaped wheels, Model No. 491-A

EX $35   **NM** $55   **MIP** $90

Ford Escort 13 GL, 1980, red, blue or yellow body, opening doors, Model No. 334-B

EX $8   **NM** $15   **MIP** $25

Ford Torino Road Hog, 1981, orange-red body, yellow and gray chassis, gold lamps, chrome radiator shell, windows and bumpers, one-piece body, working horn, Model No. 1003-A

EX $15   **NM** $20   **MIP** $35

Ford Zephyr Estate Car, 1960-65, light blue one-piece body, dark blue hood and stripes, red interior, silver bumpers, grille and headlights, red taillights, smooth or shaped wheels, Model No. 424-A

EX $30   **NM** $50   **MIP** $110

(KP Photo by Dr. Douglas Sadecky)

Ghia L64 Chrysler V8, 1963-69, metallic light blue, green, copper or yellow, plastic interior, hood, trunk and two doors working, detailed engine, clear windshield, shaped or detailed cast wheels, Model No. 241-A

EX $25   **NM** $55   **MIP** $120

Ghia-Fiat 600 Jolly, 1963-65, light or dark blue body, red and silver canopy, red seats, two figures, windshield, chrome dash, floor, steering wheel, spun hubs, Model No. 240-A

EX $45   **NM** $85   **MIP** $180

Golden Guinea Set, 1961-63, three vehicle set, gold plated No. 224 Bentley Continental, No. 229 Chevy Corvair and No. 234 Ford Consul, difficult to find w/nice plating and box, includes 1961 Corgi catalog, Model No. 20-A

EX $90   **NM** $175   **MIP** $425

(KP Photo by Dr. Douglas Sadecky)

Hillman Husky, 1956-60, one-piece tan or metallic blue/silver body, clear windows, silver lights, grille and bumpers, smooth wheels, the car on the left is the more rare two-tone version, while the car on the right is the mechanical flywheel version that was only produced for one year in 1959, Model No. 206-A

EX $40   **NM** $80   **MIP** $140

Hillman Husky-Mechanical, 1956-59, same as 206-A but w/friction motor, black base and dark blue, gray or cream body, smooth wheels, Model No. 206-M

EX $50   **NM** $100   **MIP** $200

Hillman Imp, 1963-67, metallic copper, blue, dark blue or gold one-piece bodies, w/white/yellow interior, silver bumpers, headlights, shaped wheels, Model No. 251-A

EX $30   **NM** $45   **MIP** $85

Honda Ballade Driving School, 1982-83, red body/base, tan interior, clear windows, tow hook, mirrors, bumpers, Model No. 273-B

EX $10   **NM** $15   **MIP** $25

Honda Prelude, 1981-82, dark metallic blue body, tan interior, clear windows, folding seats, sunroof, chrome wheels, Model No. 345-B

EX $8   **NM** $15   **MIP** $20

Jaguar 2.4 Litre, 1957-63, one-piece white body w/no interior 1957-59, or yellow body w/red interior 1960-63, clear windows, smooth or shaped hubs, Model No. 208-A

EX $50   **NM** $100   **MIP** $200

(KP Photo by Dr. Douglas Sadecky)

Jaguar 2.4 Litre-Mechanical, 1957-59, same as 208-A but w/friction motor and metallic blue body, Model No. 208-M

EX $60   **NM** $90   **MIP** $225

(KP Photo by Dr. Douglas Sadecky)

Jaguar Mark X Saloon, 1962-67, several different color versions w/working front and rear hood castings, clear windshields, plastic interior, gray steering wheel, shown here in silver and blue versions, pictured at the left are the two suitcases that were included w/each car, shaped wheels, Model No. 238-A

EX $35   **NM** $65   **MIP** $150

Lincoln Continental, 1967-69, metallic gold or light blue body, black roof, maroon plastic interior, working hood, trunk and doors, clear windows; accessories include TV w/picture strips for TV, shaped wheels, Model No. 262-A

EX $60   **NM** $90   **MIP** $190

Mercedes-Benz 220SE Coupe, 1962-64, cream, black or dark red body, red plastic interior, clear windows, working trunk, silver bumpers, grille and plate, spare wheel in boot, shaped wheels, Model No. 230-A

EX $40   **NM** $60   **MIP** $110

(KP Photo by Dr. Douglas Sadecky)

Mercedes-Benz 220SE Coupe, 1967-68, metallic maroon or blue body, cream plastic interior, medium gray base, clear windows, silver bumpers, headlights, grille and license; accessories include plastic luggage and spare wheel in boot, except for different exterior colors and the inclusion of luggage, this was exactly the same car as the 230-A, shaped wheels, Model No. 253-A

EX $40   **NM** $60   **MIP** $110

Mercedes-Benz 240D, 1975-81, silver, blue or copper/beige body, working trunk, two doors, clear windows, plastic interior, two hook, chrome bumpers, grille and headlights, Whizz Wheels, Model No. 285-A

EX $10   **NM** $15   **MIP** $25

Mercedes-Benz 600 Pullman, 1964-69, metallic maroon or maroon body, cream interior and steering wheel, clear windshields, chrome grille, trim and bumpers, working windshield operators; includes instruction sheet, shaped wheels, Model No. 247-A

EX $40   **NM** $65   **MIP** $140

(KP Photo by Dr. Douglas Sadecky)

Morris Cowley, 1959-60, long, one-piece body in several colors, clear windows, silver lights, grille and bumper, smooth wheels, rubber tires, the model on the left is the rare blue version, and the car on the right is the 202-M mechanical flywheel version, Model No. 202-A

EX $45   **NM** $90   **MIP** $165

Morris Cowley-Mechanical, 1956-59, same as 202-A but w/friction motor, available in off-white or green body, smooth wheels, Model No. 202-M

EX $55   **NM** $100   **MIP** $225

Oldsmobile Super 88, 1962-68, three versions: light blue, light or dark metallic blue body w/white stripes, red interior, single body casting, shaped wheels, Model No. 235-A

EX $40   **NM** $60   **MIP** $100

Oldsmobile Toronado, 1967-68, metallic medium or dark blue body, cream interior, one-piece body, clear windshield, chrome bumpers, grille, headlight covers, gray tow hooks, shaped or cast spoked wheels, Model No. 264-A

EX $35   **NM** $55   **MIP** $100

Oldsmobile Toronado, 1968-70, metallic copper, red one-piece body, cream interior, golden jacks, gray tow hook, clear windows, bumpers, grille, headlights, Model No. 276-A

EX $35   **NM** $55   **MIP** $90

Opel Senator Doctor's Car, 1980-81, Model No. 332-B

EX $10   **NM** $15   **MIP** $25

OSI DAF City Car, 1971-74, orange/red body, light cream interior, textured black roof, sliding left door, working hood, hatch and two right doors, Whizz Wheels, Model No. 283-A

EX $18   **NM** $25   **MIP** $45

Plymouth Sports Suburban, 1959-63, dark cream body, tan roof, red interior, die-cast base, red axle, silver bumpers, trim and grille and rubber tires, smoother shaped wheels, Model No. 219-A

EX $40   **NM** $60   **MIP** $110

(KP Photo by Dr. Douglas Sadecky)

Plymouth Sports Suburban, 1963-65, pale blue body w/silver trim, red roof, yellow interior, gray die-cast base w/out rear axle bulge, shaped wheels, Model No. 445-A

EX $40   **NM** $60   **MIP** $110

Plymouth Suburban Mail Car, 1963-66, white upper, blue lower body w/red stripes, gray die-cast base w/out rear axle bulge, silver bumpers and grille, U.S. Mail decals, shaped wheels, Model No. 443-A

EX $55   **NM** $85   **MIP** $140

Rambler Marlin Fastback, 1966-69, red body, black roof and trim, cream interior, clear windshield, folding seats, chrome bumpers, grille and headlights, opening doors, spun or cast wheels, Model No. 263-A

EX $35   **NM** $55   **MIP** $100

Rambler Marlin w/Kayak and Trailer, 1968-69, blue No. 263 Marlin w/roof rack, blue/white trailer, w/two kayaks, the blue Marlin only came w/this set, Model No. 10-A
EX $100   **NM** $150   **MIP** $325

Renault 16, 1969, metallic maroon body, dark yellow interior, chrome base, grille and bumpers, clear windows, opening bonnet and hatch cover, Renault decal, cast wheels, Model No. 260-A
EX $25   **NM** $35   **MIP** $75

Renault 16TS, 1970-72, metallic blue body w/Renault decal on working hatch, clear windows, detailed engine, yellow interior, Model No. 202-B
EX $20   **NM** $25   **MIP** $50

Renault 5TS, 1980-81, light blue body, red plastic interior, dark blue roof, dome light, S.O.S. Medicine lettering, working hatch and two doors, French issue, Model No. 293-A
EX $20   **NM** $35   **MIP** $70

Renault Alpine 5TS, 1980, dark blue body, off white interior, red and chrome trim, clear windows and headlights, gray base and bumpers, black grille, opening doors and hatchback, Model No. 294-A
EX $15   **NM** $25   **MIP** $40

Renault Floride, 1959-65, one-piece dark red, blue or lime green body, clear windows, silver bumper, grille, lights and plates, red taillights, smooth or shaped hubs, rubber tires, Model No. 222-A
EX $35   **NM** $55   **MIP** $110

(KP Photo by Dr. Douglas Sadecky)

Riley Pathfinder, 1956-61, red or dark blue one-piece body, clear windows, silver lights, grille and bumpers, smooth wheels, or spun rubber tires, Model No. 205-A
EX $45   **NM** $90   **MIP** $165

Riley Pathfinder-Mechanical, 1956-59, w/friction motor and either red or blue body, Model No. 205-M
EX $60   **NM** $100   **MIP** $225

Rolls-Royce Corniche, 1979, different color versions w/light brown interior, working hood, trunk and two doors, clear windows,

folding seats, chrome bumpers, Model No. 279-A
EX $10   **NM** $20   **MIP** $40

Rolls-Royce Silver Shadow, 1970, metallic white upper/dusty blue lower body, working hood, trunk and two doors, clear windows, folding seats, chrome bumpers, Golden Jacks wheels, Model No. 273-A
EX $30   **NM** $50   **MIP** $95

Rolls-Royce Silver Shadow, 1971-73, metallic silver upper and metallic blue lower body, light brown interior, may or may not include hole in trunk for spare tire, Whizz Wheels, Model No. 280-A1
EX $25   **NM** $40   **MIP** $65

Rolls-Royce Silver Shadow, 1974-78, metallic blue or gold body, bright blue interior, working hood, trunk and two doors, clear windows, folding seats, spare wheel, Model No. 280-A2
EX $25   **NM** $40   **MIP** $65

Rover 2000, 1963-66, metallic light or medium blue w/red interior or maroon body w/yellow interior, gray steering wheel, clear windshields, shaped wheels, Model No. 252-A
EX $30   **NM** $45   **MIP** $100

Rover 2000TC, 1968-70, metallic olive green or maroon one-piece body, light brown interior, chrome bumpers/grille, jewel headlights, red taillights, Golden Jacks wheels, Model No. 275-A
EX $30   **NM** $45   **MIP** $75

Rover 2000TC, 1971-73, metallic purple body, light orange interior, black grille, one-piece body, amber windows, chrome bumpers and headlights, Whizz Wheels, Model No. 281-A
EX $25   **NM** $35   **MIP** $60

Rover 3500, 1979, three different body and interior versions, plastic interior, opening hood, hatch and two doors, lifting hatch cover, Model No. 338-B
EX $8   **NM** $15   **MIP** $25

(KP Photo by Dr. Douglas Sadecky)

Rover 90, 1956-60, one-piece body, silver headlights, grille and bumpers, smooth wheels, rubber tires; multiple colors available, the car on the left is the rare two-tone color scheme and the vehicle on the right is the mechanical version in metallic green, Model No. 204-A
EX $50   **NM** $90   **MIP** $165

Rover 90-Mechanical, 1956-59, w/friction motor and red, green, gray or metallic green body, Model No. 204-M
EX $60   **NM** $100   **MIP** $225

(KP Photo by Dr. Douglas Sadecky)

Standard Vanguard, 1957-61, one-piece red and pale green body, clear windows, silver lights, grille and bumpers, smooth wheels, rubber tires, pictured w/the 207M, the attractive two-tone 207-A version is on the left, and the mechanical version is on the right, Model No. 207-A
EX $50   **NM** $90   **MIP** $165

Standard Vanguard-Mechanical, 1957-59, w/friction motor and yellow or off-white body w/black or gray base, or cream body w/red roof, Model No. 207-M
EX $55   **NM** $90   **MIP** $180

Studebaker Golden Hawk, 1958-60, one-piece body in blue and gold or white and gold, clear windows, silver lights, grille and bumpers, smooth wheels, rubber tires, Model No. 211-A
EX $55   **NM** $85   **MIP** $140

(KP Photo by Dr. Douglas Sadecky)

Studebaker Golden Hawk, 1960-65, second issue: gold painted body, smoother shaped hubs, the "S" after the catalog number stood for "suspension" which was a new Corgi innovation at the time of the model's release, Model No. 211S
EX $60   **NM** $180   **MIP** $180

Studebaker Golden Hawk-Mechanical, 1958-59, w/friction motor and white body w/gold trim, Model No. 211-M
EX $70   **NM** $105   **MIP** $225

Tour de France Set, 1968-72, white and black body, Renault w/Paramount Film roof sign, rear platform w/cameraman and black camera on tripod, plus bicycle and rider, Model No. 13-B
EX $60   **NM** $90   **MIP** $225

Tour de France Set, 1981-82, w/white No. 373 Peugeot, red and yellow Raleigh and Total logos, Racing cycles, includes manager figures, Model No. 13-C

EX $25   **NM** $45   **MIP** $90

Triumph Acclaim Driving School, 1982, dark yellow body w/black trim, black roof mounted steering wheel steers front wheels, clear windows, mirrors, bumpers, Model No. 277-B

EX $15   **NM** $25   **MIP** $40

Triumph Acclaim Driving School, 1982-83, yellow or red body/base, Corgi Motor School labels, black roof mounted steering wheel steers front wheels, clear windows, Model No. 278-B

EX $15   **NM** $25   **MIP** $50

Triumph Acclaim HLS, 1981-83, metallic peacock blue body/base, black trim, light brown interior, clear windows, mirrors, bumpers, vents, tow hook, Model No. 276-B

EX $15   **NM** $18   **MIP** $30

Triumph Herald Coupe, 1961-66, blue or gold top and lower body, white upper body, red interior, clear windows, silver bumpers, grille, headlights, shaped hubs, Model No. 231-A

EX $35   **NM** $65   **MIP** $110

(KP Photo by Dr. Douglas Sadecky)

Trojan Heinkel, 1962-72, issued in mauve, red, orange or lilac body, plastic interior, silver bumpers and headlights, red taillights, suspension, smooth or detailed cast wheels, Model No. 233-A

EX $35   **NM** $70   **MIP** $130

(KP Photo by Dr. Douglas Sadecky)

Vauxhall Velox, 1956-60, one-piece body in red, cream, yellow or yellow and red body, clear windows, silver

lights, grille and bumpers, smooth wheels, rubber tires, Model No. 203-A

EX $50   **NM** $90   **MIP** $170

Vauxhall Velox-Mechanical, 1956-59, w/friction motor; orange, red, yellow or cream body, Model No. 203-M

EX $60   **NM** $100   **MIP** $225

Volkswagen 1200 Driving School, 1974-75, metallic red or blue body, yellow interior, gold roof mounted steering wheel that steers, silver headlights, red taillights, Model No. 400-A

EX $25   **NM** $35   **MIP** $60

Volkswagen 1500 Karmann-Ghia, 1963-68, cream, red or gold body, plastic interior and taillights, front and rear working hoods, clear windshields, silver bumpers; includes spare wheel and plastic suitcase in trunk, shaped wheels, Model No. 239-A

EX $35   **NM** $55   **MIP** $90

Volkswagen Driving School, 1975-77, metallic blue body, yellow interior, gold roof mounted steering wheel that steers, silver headlights, red taillights, orange cones, Model No. 401-A

EX $25   **NM** $40   **MIP** $75

Volkswagen Polo, 1976-79, apple green or bright yellow body, black DBP and posthorn (German Post Office) labels, off white interior, black dash, Model No. 289-A

EX $25   **NM** $40   **MIP** $65

Volkswagen Polo, 1979-81, metallic light brown body, off-white interior, black dash, clear windows, silver bumpers, grille and headlights, Model No. 302-C

EX $15   **NM** $18   **MIP** $30

Volkswagen Polo Auto Club Car, 1977-79, yellow body, white roof, yellow dome light, ADAC Strassenwacht labels, Model No. 489-B

EX $15   **NM** $25   **MIP** $40

Volkswagen Polo German Auto Club Car, 1977-79, yellow body, off-white interior, black dash, silver bumpers, grille and headlights, white roof, yellow dome light, Model No. 489-A2

EX $25   **NM** $35   **MIP** $60

Volkswagen Polo Mail Car, 1976-80, bright yellow body, black DBP and Posthorn labels, German issue, Model No. 289-B

EX $25   **NM** $35   **MIP** $60

Volvo P-1800, 1962-65, one-piece body light brown, orange-red, pink or dark red body, clear windows, plastic interior, shaped wheels, rubber tires, Model No. 228-A

EX $40   **NM** $70   **MIP** $130

BOAT

(KP Photo by Dr. Douglas Sadecky)

Dolphin Cabin Cruiser, 1965-68, white hull, blue deck plastic boat w/red/white stripe labels, driver, blue motor w/white cover, gray prop, cast trailer w/smooth wheels, rubber tires, Model No. 104-A

EX $24   **NM** $70   **MIP** $130

Fiat X 1/9 & Powerboat, 1979-82, green and white automobile, w/white and gold boat, Carlsberg labels, Model No. 37-B

EX $30   **NM** $45   **MIP** $75

HDL Hovercraft SR-N1, 1960-62, blue superstructure, gray base and deck, clear canopy, red seats, yellow SR-N1 decals, Model No. 1119-A

EX $60   **NM** $90   **MIP** $180

Olds Toronado and Speedboat, 1967-70, blue No. 276 Toronado, blue and yellow boat and chrome trailer, w/swordfish decals and three figures, Model No. 36-A

EX $60   **NM** $90   **MIP** $200

Powerboat Team, 1980-81, white/red No. 319 Jaguar w/red/white boat on silver trailer, Team Corgi Carlsberg, Union Jack and #1 labels on boat, Model No. 38-C

EX $25   **NM** $35   **MIP** $60

BUS

Beep Beep London Bus, 1981, battery-operated working horn, red body, black windows, BTA decals, Model No. 1004-A

EX $26   **NM** $39   **MIP** $65

Green Line Bus, 1983, green body, white interior and stripe, TDK labels, six spoked wheels, Model No. 470-C

EX $10   **NM** $15   **MIP** $25

Inter-City Mini Bus, 1973-79, orange body w/brown interior, clear windows, green/yellow/black decals, Whizz Wheels, Model No. 701-A

EX $8   **NM** $15   **MIP** $25

London Set, 1964-68, No. 418 taxi and No. 468 bus w/policeman, in two versions: "Corgi Toys" on bus (1964-66); "Outspan Oranges" on bus (1967-68); values for each individual complete set, Model No. 35-A

EX $55   **NM** $125   **MIP** $375

London Set, 1971-75, orange No. 226 Mini, Policeman, No. 418 London Taxi and No. 468 Outspan Routemaster bus, Whizz Wheels, Model No. 11-B

EX $50   **NM** $75   **MIP** $180

London Set, 1980-82, No. 425 London Taxi and No. 469 Routemaster B.T.A. bus in two versions: w/mounted Policeman (1980-81); w/out Policeman, (1982-on); value is for each individual complete set, Model No. 11-C

EX $25   **NM** $35   **MIP** $60

London Transport Routemaster Bus, 1964-75, clear windows w/driver and conductor, released w/numerous advertiser logos that sell in a vide range of prices, shaped or cast spoked wheels, Model No. 468-A

EX $35   **NM** $40   **MIP** $75

London Transport Routemaster Bus, 1975, long, clear windows, interior, some models have driver and conductor, released w/numerous advertiser logos, Whizz Wheels, Model No. 469-A

EX $25   **NM** $30   **MIP** $50

Midland Red Express Coach, 1961-62, red one-piece body, black roof w/shaped or smooth wheels, yellow interior, clear windows, silver grille and headlights, two box variations shown in this photo, Model No. 1120-A

EX $70   **NM** $105   **MIP** $225

National Express Bus, 1983, variety of colors and label variations, Model No. 1168-A

EX $8   **NM** $15   **MIP** $25

Open Top Disneyland Bus, 1977-78, yellow body, red interior and stripe, Disneyland labels, eight-spoke wheels or orange body, white interior and stripe, Model No. 470-B

EX $30   **NM** $50   **MIP** $75

Routemaster Bus-Promotionals, 1977, different body and interior versions and promotional labels, Model No. 467-A

EX $15   **NM** $25   **MIP** $40

Silver Jubilee London Transport Bus, 1977, silver body w/red interior, no passengers, labels read "Woolworth Welcomes the World" and "The Queen's Silver," Model No. 471-B

EX $15   **NM** $18   **MIP** $30

CHARACTER

1927 Bentley "World of Wooster," 1967-69, green body, metallic black chassis, cast spoked wheels, figures of Jeeves and Bertie Wooster, Model No. 9004-A

EX $50   **NM** $100   **MIP** $165

Avengers Set, 1966-69, white Lotus, red or green (rare) Bentley; Jonathan Steed and Emma Peel figures w/three umbrellas, Model No. 40-A

EX $260   **NM** $390   **MIP** $800

Basil Brush's Car, 1971-73, red body, dark yellow chassis, gold lamps and dash, Basil Brush figure, red plastic wheels, plastic tires; w/"Laugh Tapes" and soundbox, Basil Brush could be heard laughing w/the aid of laugh tapes and a soundbox that were included w/the car, Model No. 808-A

EX $70   **NM** $105   **MIP** $200

Batbike, 1978-83, black body, one-piece body, black and red plastic parts, gold engine and exhaust pipes, clear windshield, chrome stand, black or white plastic five-spoked wheels, Batman figure and decals, Model No. 268-B

EX $40   **NM** $60   **MIP** $125

Batboat, 1967-72, black plastic boat, red seats, fin and jet, blue windshield, Batman and Robin figures, gold cast trailer, tinplate fin cover, cast wheels, plastic tires, w/plastic tow hook for Batmobile, solid box, Model No. 107-A1

EX $60   **NM** $100   **MIP** $200

Batboat, 1976-80, black plastic boat w/Batman and Robin figures, small Bat logo labels on fin and on side of boat, chain link labels, Whizz Wheels on trailer, window box, Model No. 107-A2

EX $30   **NM** $45   **MIP** $100

Batcopter, 1976-81, black body w/yellow/red/black decals, red rotors, Batman figure, operable winch, Model No. 925-A

EX $30   **NM** $50   **MIP** $100

Batman Set, 1976-81, three vehicle set: No. 267 Batmobile, No. 107 Batboat w/trailer and No. 925 Batcopter, Whizz Wheels on trailer, Model No. 40-B

EX $150   **NM** $300   **MIP** $800

Batmobile, 1966, matte black (rare) or gloss black body, gold hubs, bat logos on door and hubs, maroon interior, black body, plastic rockets, yellow headlights and gold rocket control, blue tinted canopy, working front chain cutter, no tow hook, rubber tires, although it's difficult to tell from this photo, this is the rare first issue matte black finish w/no tow hook version of the famous Batmobile, Model No. 267-A1

EX $200   **NM** $400   **MIP** $850

Batmobile, 1967-72, same as first issue except for gloss black body, gold tow hook, Model No. 267-A2

EX $200   **NM** $300   **MIP** $500

(KP Photo by Dr. Douglas Sadecky)

Batmobile, 1973, chrome hubs w/red bat logos on door, maroon interior, red plastic tires, gold tow hook, plastic rockets, yellow headlight and gold rocket control, tinted blue canopy w/chrome support, chain cutter, made for only one year, this version featured red plastic tires and chrome wheels, also pictured is the back of the rare first-issue window box for this model, Model No. 267-C1

EX $140　**NM** $200　**MIP** $450

Batmobile, 1974-79, chrome hubs w/black plastic tires, red bat logos on door, light red interior, gold tow hook, plastic rockets, yellow headlights and gold rocket control, tinted blue canopy w/chrome support, Model No. 267-C2

EX $80　**NM** $120　**MIP** $200

Batmobile, 1980-81, gloss black body, light red interior, gold tow hook, Whizz Wheels w/eight-spoke chrome hubs, Model No. 267-D

EX $80　**NM** $110　**MIP** $200

Batmobile, Batboat and Trailer, 1967-72, first and second versions: red bat hubs on wheels, 1967-72; red tires and chrome wheels 1972-73, Model No. 3-B1

EX $240　**NM** $360　**MIP** $650

Batmobile, Batboat and Trailer, 1973-81, third and fourth versions: 1973; black tires, labels on boat, 1974-76; chrome wheels, boat labels, Whizz Wheels on trailer, Model No. 3-B2

EX $120　**NM** $175　**MIP** $350

Beatles' Yellow Submarine, 1969, yellow and white hatches, red pinstripes, first issue, rare, Model No. 803-A1

EX $200　**NM** $400　**MIP** $800

Beatles' Yellow Submarine, 1969-70, second issue, yellow and white body, working red hatches w/two Beatles in each, Model No. 803-A2

EX $180　**NM** $250　**MIP** $600

Buck Rogers Starfighter, 1980, white body w/yellow plastic wings, amber windows, blue jets, color decal, Buck and Wilma figures, Model No. 647-A

EX $32　**NM** $48　**MIP** $90

Captain America Jetmobile, 1979-80, 6" white body, metallic blue chassis, black nose cone, red shield and jet, red-white-blue Captain America decals, light blue seats and driver, chrome wheels, red tires, Model No. 263-B

EX $24　**NM** $36　**MIP** $60

Captain Marvel Porsche, 1979-80, white body, gold parts, red seat, driver, red/yellow/blue Captain Marvel decals, black plastic base, gold wheels, Model No. 262-B

EX $20　**NM** $30　**MIP** $60

Chevrolet Charlie's Angels Van, 1977-80, light rose-mauve body w/Charlie's Angels labels, in two versions: either solid or spoked chrome wheels, Model No. 434-B

EX $15　**NM** $30　**MIP** $55

Chevrolet Spider-Van, 1978-80, dark blue body w/Spider-Man decals, in two versions: w/either spoke or solid wheels, Model No. 436-B

EX $26　**NM** $39　**MIP** $65

Chitty Chitty Bang Bang, 1968-72, metallic copper body, dark red interior and spoked wheels, four figures, black chassis w/silver running boards, silver hood, horn, brake, dash, tail and headlights, gold radiator, red and orange wings, handbrake operates side wings, Model No. 266-A

EX $180　**NM** $270　**MIP** $395

Daily Planet Helicopter, 1979-81, red and white body, rocket launcher w/10 spare missiles, Model No. 929-A

EX $24　**NM** $36　**MIP** $60

Daktari Set, 1967-75, two versions: No. 438 Land Rover, green w/black stripes, spun or cast spoke wheels, 1968-73; Whizz Wheels, 1974-75, each set, Model No. 7-B

EX $50　**NM** $75　**MIP** $180

Dick Dastardly's Racing Car, 1973-76, dark blue body, yellow chassis, chrome engine, red wings, Dick and Muttley figures, Model No. 809-A

EX $40　**NM** $60　**MIP** $150

(KP Photo by Dr. Douglas Sadecky)

Dougal's Magic Roundabout Car, 1971-74, yellow body, red interior,

clear windows, dog and snail figures, red wheels w/gold trim, Magic Roundabout labels, Model No. 807-A

EX $70　**NM** $105　**MIP** $190

Drax Jet Helicopter, 1979-81, white body, yellow rotors and fins, yellow/black Drax labels, Model No. 930-A

EX $35　**NM** $75　**MIP** $175

Giant Daktari Set, 1969-73, black and green No. 438 Land Rover, tan No. 503 Giraffe truck, blue and brown No. 484 Dodge Livestock truck, figures, several wheel variations, Model No. 14-B

EX $225　**NM** $350　**MIP** $750

Green Hornet's Black Beauty, 1967-72, black body, green window/interior, two figures, working chrome grille and panels w/weapons, green headlights, red taillights, shaped or cast wheels, Model No. 268-A

EX $175　**NM** $275　**MIP** $550

Hardy Boys' Rolls-Royce, 1970, red body w/yellow hood, roof and window frames, band figures on roof on removable green base, Model No. 805-A

EX $70　**NM** $105　**MIP** $180

Incredible Hulk Mazda Pickup, 1979-80, metallic light brown or copper body, gray or red plastic cage, black interior, Hulk label on hood, chrome wheels; includes green and red Hulk figure, Model No. 264-B

EX $20　**NM** $30　**MIP** $75

(KP Photo by Dr. Douglas Sadecky)

James Bond Aston Martin, 1968-77, metallic silver body, red interior, two figures, working roof hatch, ejector seat, bullet shield and guns, chrome bumpers, spoked wheels, orginally issued in a rare bubble-pack, the subsequent issues were sold in window boxes, on the left, the rare first issue window box; on the right, the more commonly seen version, Model No. 270-A

EX $100　**NM** $150　**MIP** $325

James Bond Aston Martin, 1978, metallic silver body and die-cast base, red interior, two figures, clear windows, passenger seat raises to eject, Model No. 271-B

EX $30　**NM** $45　**MIP** $90

James Bond Aston Martin DB5, 1965-68, metallic gold body, red interior, working roof hatch, clear windows, two figures, left seat ejects, spoked wheels, accessory pack, Model No. 261-A

EX $70 **NM** $150 **MIP** $365

James Bond Aston Martin DB6, 1979, metallic silver body and die-cast base, red interior, two figures, clear windows, passenger seat raises to eject, Model No. 40

EX n/a **NM** n/a **MIP** n/a

(KP Photo by Dr. Douglas Sadecky)

James Bond Citroen 2CV6, 1981-86, dark yellow body and hood, red interior, clear windows, chrome headlights, red taillights, black plastic grille, this model was available in a window box, or the more difficult to find photo box shown here, Model No. 272-A

EX $15 **NM** $35 **MIP** $80

James Bond Lotus Esprit, 1977, white body and base, black windshield, grille and hood panel, white plastic roof device that triggers fins and tail, rockets, Model No. 269-B

EX $30 **NM** $45 **MIP** $110

James Bond Moon Buggy, 1972-73, white body w/blue chassis, amber canopy, yellow tanks, red radar dish, arms and jaws, yellow wheels, Model No. 811-A

EX $175 **NM** $275 **MIP** $475

(KP Photo by Dr. Douglas Sadecky)

James Bond Mustang Mach 1, 1972-73, red and white body w/black hood and opening doors, two wheel variations, because using this model as a Bond vehicle was a last-minute decision, a label was adhered to the right side of the window box, without this label, no one would know this was a James Bond issue, Model No. 391-A

EX $100 **NM** $150 **MIP** $300

James Bond Set, 1979-81, set of three: No. 271 Lotus Esprit, No. 649

Space Shuttle and No. 269 Aston Martin, Model No. 22-B

EX $100 **NM** $200 **MIP** $700

James Bond Space Shuttle, 1979-81, white body w/yellow/black Moonraker labels w/satellite, Model No. 649-A

EX $30 **NM** $50 **MIP** $95

James Bond Toyota 2000GT, 1967-69, white body, black interior w/Bond and female driver, working trunk and gun rack, spoked wheels, plastic tires, accessory pack, Model No. 336-A

EX $115 **NM** $180 **MIP** $375

Kojak's Buick Regal, 1976-81, metallic bronze or light brown body, off-white interior, two opening doors, clear windows, chrome bumpers, grille and headlights, red taillights; accessories include Kojak w/ or w/out hat and Crocker figures, Model No. 290-A

EX $25 **NM** $55 **MIP** $125

Lions of Longleat, 1968-74, black/white No. 438 Land Rover pickup w/lion cages and accessories, two versions: shaped or cast spoked wheels, 1969-73; Whizz Wheels, 1974, Model No. 8-B

EX $60 **NM** $90 **MIP** $200

Magic Roundabout Musical Carousel, 1973, plastic roundabout w/Swiss musical movement, w/Dylan, Rosalie, Paul, Florence and Basil figures, rare, Model No. 852-A

EX $275 **NM** $425 **MIP** $650

Magic Roundabout Playground, 1973, contains No. 851 Train, No. 852 Carousel, six figures, seesaw, park bench, shrubs and fowers, rare, Model No. 853-A

EX $295 **NM** $500 **MIP** $800

Magic Roundabout Train, 1973, red and blue plastic three-piece train; accessories include figures of Mr. Rusty, Basil, Rosaile, Paul and Dougal, Model No. 851-A

EX $70 **NM** $195 **MIP** $350

Man From U.N.C.L.E. THRUSH-Buster, 1966-68, plastic interior, blue windows, two figures, two spotlights, dark metallic blue body, w/3-D Waverly ring, shaped or cast wheels, Model No. 497-A1

EX $80 **NM** $130 **MIP** $325

(KP Photo by Dr. Douglas Sadecky)

Man From U.N.C.L.E. THRUSH-Buster, 1968-69, plastic interior, blue windows, two figures, two spotlights, cream body, w/3-D Waverly ring, cast wheels, rare, Model No. 497-A2

EX $100 **NM** $350 **MIP** $550

Monkeemobile, 1968-70, red body/base, white roof, yellow interior, clear windows, four figures, chrome grille, headlights, engine, orange taillights, Model No. 277-A

EX $145 **NM** $225 **MIP** $400

Mr. McHenry's Trike, 1972-74, red and yellow trike and trailer; accessories include Mr. McHenry and Zebedee figures, Model No. 859-A

EX $70 **NM** $105 **MIP** $175

Muppet Vehicles, Fozzie Bear's Truck, Model No. 2031-A

EX $15 **NM** $30 **MIP** $50

Muppet Vehicles, Animal's Percussion-mobile, Model No. 2033-A

EX $15 **NM** $30 **MIP** $50

Muppet Vehicles, Miss Piggy's Sports Coupe, Model No. 2032-A

EX $15 **NM** $30 **MIP** $50

Muppet Vehicles, Kermit's Car, Model No. 2030-A

EX $15 **NM** $35 **MIP** $60

Noddy's Car, yellow body, red chassis, Noddy alone, closed trunk w/spare wheel, Model No. 804-A

EX $60 **NM** $90 **MIP** $175

Noddy's Car, 1969-71, first issue: yellow body, red chassis and fenders, figures of Noddy, Big-Ears, and black, gray, or light tan face Golliwog, Model No. 801-A1

EX $200 **NM** $400 **MIP** $550

Noddy's Car, 1972-73, second issue: same as first issue except Master Tubby painted light or dark brown is substituted for Golliwog, Model No. 801-A2

EX $100 **NM** $200 **MIP** $350

Penguinmobile, 1979-80, white body, black and white lettering on orange-yellow-blue labels, gold body panels, seats, air scoop, chrome engine, w/penguin figure, Model No. 259-B

EX $20   **NM** $30   **MIP** $65

(KP Photo by Dr. Douglas Sadecky)

Popeye's Paddle Wagon, 1969-72, yellow and white body, red chassis, blue rear fenders, bronze and yellow stacks, white plastic deck, white or yellow rear paddle wheel, blue lifeboat w/Swee' Pea; includes figures of Popeye, Olive Oyl, Bluto and Wimpey, produced for a short period, the colorful Paddle-Wagon had multiple working features and contained all of the main characters, Model No. 802-A

EX $195   **NM** $300   **MIP** $475

Professionals Ford Capri, 1980-82, metallic silver body and base, red interior, black spoiler, grille, bumpers, tow hook and trim, blue windows, chrome wheels; includes figures of Cowley, Bodie and Doyle, Model No. 342-B

EX $30   **NM** $65   **MIP** $150

Saint's Jaguar XJS, 1978-81, white body, red interior, black trim, Saint figure hood label, opening doors, black grille, bumpers and tow hook, chrome headlights, Model No. 320-B

EX $30   **NM** $45   **MIP** $85

(KP Photo by Dr. Doug Sadecky)

Saint's Volvo P-1800, 1965-69, three versions of white one-piece body w/silver trim and different colored Saint decals on hood, driver, (blue hood label is rare $400) pictured here w/the 201-B, note the wheel and hood logo variation between the two cars, shaped or cast wheels, Model No. 258-A

EX $55   **NM** $85   **MIP** $185

Saint's Volvo P-1800, 1970-72, one-piece white body w/red Saint decal on hood, gray base, clear windows, black interior w/driver, Whizz Wheels, Model No. 201-B

EX $55   **NM** $95   **MIP** $225

Silver Jubilee Landau, 1977-80, Landua w/four horses, two footmen, two riders, Queen and Prince figures, and Corgi dog, in two versions, Model No. 41-B

EX $15   **NM** $25   **MIP** $50

Spider-Bike, 1979-83, medium blue body, one-piece body, dark blue plastic front body and seat, blue and red Spider-Man figure, amber or clear windshield, black or white wheels, Model No. 266-B

EX $40   **NM** $60   **MIP** $85

Spider-Buggy, 1979-81, red body, blue hood, clear windows, dark blue dash, seat and crane, chrome base w/bumper and steps, silver headlights; includes Spider-Man and Green Goblin figures, Model No. 261-A

EX $50   **NM** $75   **MIP** $150

Spider-Copter, 1979-81, blue body w/Spider-Man labels, red plastic legs, tongue and tail rotor, black windows and main rotor, Model No. 928-A

EX $30   **NM** $45   **MIP** $85

Spider-Man Set, 1980-81, set of three: No. 266 Spider-Bike, No. 928 Spider-Copter and No. 261 Spider-Buggy, Model No. 23-B

EX $80   **NM** $160   **MIP** $375

Starsky and Hutch Ford Torino, 1977-81, red one-piece body, white trim, light yellow interior, clear windows, chrome bumpers, grille and headlights, orange taillights; includes Starsky, Hutch and Bandit figures, Model No. 292-A

EX $35   **NM** $65   **MIP** $140

Superman Set, 1979-81, set of three: No. 265 Supermobile, No. 925 Daily Planet Helicopter and No. 260 Metropolis Police Car, Model No. 21-C

EX $70   **NM** $120   **MIP** $350

Supermobile, 1979-81, blue body, red, chrome or gray fists, red interior, clear canopy, Superman figure, chrome arms w/removable "striking fists," Model No. 265-A

EX $30   **NM** $45   **MIP** $75

Supervan, 1978-81, silver van w/Superman labels, working rear doors, chrome spoked wheels, two wheel variations, Model No. 435-B

EX $15   **NM** $30   **MIP** $60

Tarzan Set, 1976-78, metallic green No. 421 Land Rover w/trailer and dinghy; cage, five figures and other accessories, Model No. 36-B

EX $100   **NM** $150   **MIP** $285

Vegas Ford Thunderbird, 1980-81, orange/red body and base, black interior and grille, opening hood and trunk, amber windshield, white seats, driver, chrome bumper, Model No. 348-B

EX $25   **NM** $40   **MIP** $85

CIRCUS

Chipperfield Circus Bedford Giraffe Transporter, 1964-71, red "TK" Bedford truck w/blue giraffe box w/Chipperfield decal, two giraffes, shaped, cast spoked or detailed wheels, Model No. 503-A

EX $60   **NM** $90   **MIP** $175

Chipperfield Circus Cage Wagon, 1961-68, red body, yellow chassis, smooth or spun hubs; includes lions, tigers or polar bears, Model No. 1123-A

EX $56   **NM** $84   **MIP** $140

Chipperfield Circus Chevrolet Performing Poodles Van, 1970-72, blue upper body and tailgate, red lower body and base, clear windshield, pale blue interior w/poodles in back and ring of poodles and trainer, plastic tires, cast wheels, Model No. 511-A

EX $160   **NM** $240   **MIP** $500

Chipperfield Circus Crane and Cage, 1970-72, No. 1144 crane truck, cage w/rhinoceros, red and blue trailer w/three animal cages and animals; very rare gift set, Model No. 21-B

EX $400   **NM** $700   **MIP** $2200

Chipperfield Circus Crane and Cage Wagon, 1961-65, No. 1121 crane truck, No. 1123 cage wagon and accessories, Model No. 12-A

EX $150   **NM** $225   **MIP** $425

(KP Photo by Dr. Douglas Sadecky)

Chipperfield Circus Crane Truck, 1960-68, red body, embossed Chipperfield blue logo, tinplate boom, blue wheels, pictured here w/Chipperfield Circus Cage Wagon 1123-A, that included a set of polar bears or lions and their appropriate label transfers, Model No. 1121-A

EX $80   **NM** $120   **MIP** $225

(KP Photo by Dr. Douglas Sadecky)

Chipperfield Circus Horse Transporter, 1962-72, red Bedford "TK" cab, blue upper/red lower horse trailer, three wheel variations; includes six gray or brown horses, Model No. 1130-A

EX $80   **NM** $120   **MIP** $300

(KP Photo by Dr. Douglas Sadecky)

Chipperfield Circus Karrier Booking Office, 1962-64, red body, light blue roof, clear windows, tin lithographed interior, circus decals, smooth or shaped wheels, rubber tires, Model No. 426-A

EX $105   **NM** $165   **MIP** $325

Chipperfield Circus Land Rover and Elephant Cage, 1962-68, red No. 438 Range Rover w/blue tin or plastic canopy, Chipperfields Circus decal on canopy, burnt orange or gray No. 607 elephant cage on red bed trailer, Model No. 19-A

EX $90   **NM** $135   **MIP** $345

(KP Photo by Dr. Douglas Sadecky)

Chipperfield Circus Land Rover Parade Vehicle, 1967-69, red body, yellow interior, blue rear and speakers, revolving clown, chimp figures, Chipperfield labels, w/or w/out tow hooks, shaped wheels, Model No. 487-A

EX $60   **NM** $90   **MIP** $175

Chipperfield Circus Menagerie Transporter, 1968-72, Scammell Handyman MKIII red/blue cab, blue trailer w/three animal cages, two lions, two tigers and two bears, two wheel variations, Model No. 1139-A

EX $120   **NM** $180   **MIP** $400

Chipperfield Circus Scammell Crane Truck, 1969-72, red upper cab and rear body, light blue lower cab, crane base and winch crank housing, red interior, tow hook, jewel headlights, Model No. 1144-A

EX $175   **NM** $275   **MIP** $450

Chipperfield Circus Set, 1st Version, 1963-65, vehicle and accessory set in two versions: w/No. 426 Booking Office, Model No. 23-A1

EX $380   **NM** $600   **MIP** $1800

Chipperfield Circus Set, 2nd Version, 1966, vehicle and accessory set w/#503 Giraffe Truck, Model No. 23-A2

EX $340   **NM** $500   **MIP** $1600

Circus Human Cannonball Truck, 1978-81, red and blue body; w/Marvo figure, Model No. 1163-A

EX $30   **NM** $45   **MIP** $75

Circus Land Rover and Trailer, 1978-81, yellow/red No. 421 Land Rover w/Pinder-Jean Richard decals; accessories include blue loudspeakers and figures, Model No. 30-B

EX $30   **NM** $50   **MIP** $90

Jean Richard Circus Set, 1978-81, yellow and red Land Rover and cage trailer w/Pinder-Jean Richard decals, No. 426 office van and trailer, No. 1163 Human Cannonball truck, ring and cut-out "Big Top" circus tent, Model No. 48-C

EX $90   **NM** $135   **MIP** $300

CLASSICS

1910 Renault 12/16, 1965-69, pale yellow body and spoked wheels, light black chassis, black ragtop, Model No. 9032-A

EX $25   **NM** $50   **MIP** $80

1910 Renault 12/16, 1965-69, light purple body and spoked wheels, light black chassis, Model No. 9031-A

EX $25   **NM** $50   **MIP** $80

(KP Photo by Dr. Douglas Sadecky)

1927 Bentley, 1964-69, red body, metallic black chassis, brown interior, black ragtop, red spoked wheels, driver, the red Bentley is slightly harder to find than the green version, Model No. 9002-A

EX $30   **NM** $60   **MIP** $90

1927 Bentley, 1964-69, green body, metallic black chassis, brown interior, black ragtop, spoked wheels, driver, Model No. 9001-A

EX $35   **NM** $50   **MIP** $75

(KP Photo by Dr. Douglas Sadecky)

Daimler 38 1910, 1964-69, orange-red body, gray and yellow chassis, yellow spoked wheels; w/four figures, Model No. 9021-A

EX $20   **NM** $40   **MIP** $65

Model T Ford, 1964-69, blue body, black chassis, black ragtop, yellow wheels, one figure, Model No. 9013-A

EX $20   **NM** $40   **MIP** $65

Model T Ford, 1964-69, black body and chassis, spoked wheels, two figures, Model No. 9011-A

EX $20   **NM** $40   **MIP** $65

(KP Photo by Dr. Douglas Sadecky)

Model T Ford, 1964-69, yellow body and spoked wheels, black chassis, two figures, Model No. 9012-A

EX $20   **NM** $40   **MIP** $65

Rolls-Royce Silver Ghost, 1966-69, silver body/hood, charcoal and silver chassis, bronze interior, gold lights, box and tank, clear windows, dash lights, radiator, Model No. 9041-A

EX $15   **NM** $30   **MIP** $65

CONSTRUCTION

Allis-Chalmers AFC 60 Fork Lift, 1981, yellow body, white engine hood, w/driver, tan pallets and red containers, Model No. 409-C

EX $15   **NM** $20   **MIP** $45

(KP Photo by Dr. Douglas Sadecky)

Bedford TK Tipper Truck, 1968-72, red cab and chassis w/yellow or silver tipper, side mirrors, Model No. 494-A

EX $25   **NM** $40   **MIP** $85

Berliet Fruehauf Dumper, 1974-76, yellow cab, fenders and dumper; black cab and semi chassis; plastic orange or dark orange dumper body; black interior, Model No. 1102-B

EX $30   **NM** $45   **MIP** $75

(KP Photo by Dr. Douglas Sadecky)

ERF 64G Earth Dumper, 1958-67, red cab, yellow tipper, clear windows, unpainted hydraulic cylinder, spare tire, smooth or shaped wheels, rubber tires, Model No. 458-A

EX $30   **NM** $50   **MIP** $100

Euclid Caterpillar Tractor, 1960-63, TC-12 lime green body w/black or pale gray rubber treads, gray plastic seat, driver figure, controls, stacks, silver grille, painted blue engine sides and Euclid decals, Model No. 1103-A

EX $50   **NM** $100   **MIP** $200

(KP Photo by Dr. Douglas Sadecky)

Euclid TC-12 Bulldozer, 1958-62, lime green body w/black or pale gray treads, silver blade surface, gray plastic seat, controls, and stacks; silver grille and lights, painted blue engine sides, black sheet metal base, rubber treads and Euclid decals, Model No. 1102-A

EX $80   **NM** $150   **MIP** $275

Euclid TC-12 Bulldozer, 1963-66, yellow (more rare) or pale lime-green body, metal control rod, driver, black rubber treads, Model No. 1107-A

EX $80   **NM** $120   **MIP** $250

Ford Transit Tipper, 1983, orange cab and chassis, tan tipper, chrome wheels, Model No. 1121-B

EX $10   **NM** $15   **MIP** $25

Giant Tower Crane, 1981-82, white body, orange cab and chassis, Model No. 1154-B

EX $35   **NM** $50   **MIP** $85

Hyster 800 Stacatruck, 1977, clear windows, black interior w/driver, Model No. 1113-B

EX $35   **NM** $50   **MIP** $85

JCB 110B Crawler Loader, 1976-80, white cab, yellow body, working red shovel, red interior w/driver, clear windows, black treads, JCB labels, Model No. 1110-B

EX $20   **NM** $30   **MIP** $50

Mack-Priestman Crane Truck, 1972-76, red truck, yellow crane cab, red interior, black engine, Hi Lift and Long Vehicle or Hi-Grab labels, Model No. 1154-A

EX $50   **NM** $75   **MIP** $125

Mercedes-Benz Unimog & Dumper, 1969-76, yellow cab and tipper, red fenders and tipper chassis, charcoal gray cab chassis, black plastic mirrors or w/out, Model No. 1145-A

EX $25   **NM** $35   **MIP** $60

Priestman Cub Crane, 1972-74, orange body, red chassis and two-piece bucket, unpainted bucket arms, lower boom, knobs, gears and drum castings, clear window, Hi-Grab labels, Model No. 1153-A

EX $50   **NM** $75   **MIP** $125

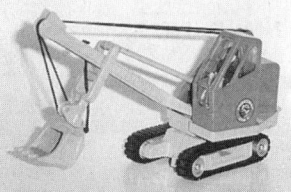

(KP Photo by Dr. Douglas Sadecky)

Priestman Cub Power Shovel, 1963-76, orange upper body and panel, yellow lower body, lock rod and chassis, rubber or plastic treads, pulley panel, gray boom, w/figure of driver, Model No. 1128-A

EX $40   **NM** $60   **MIP** $120

Priestman Shovel and Carrier, 1963-72, No. 1128 cub shovel and No. 1131 low loader machinery carrier,

three wheel variations on 1131, Model No. 27-A

EX $90   **NM** $135   **MIP** $275

Raygo Rascal Roller, 1973-78, dark yellow body, base and mounting, green interior and engine, orange and silver roller mounting and castings, clear windshield, Model No. 459-B

EX $15   **NM** $25   **MIP** $45

Road Repair Unit, 1982, dark yellow Land Rover w/battery hatch and trailer w/red plastic interior w/sign and open panels, stripe and Roadwork labels, Model No. 1007-A

EX $15   **NM** $25   **MIP** $40

Scania Dump Truck, 1983, white cab w/green tipper, black/green Barratt labels, black exhaust and hydraulic cylinders, six-spoked Whizz Wheels, Model No. 1152-B

EX $7   **NM** $15   **MIP** $30

Scania Dump Truck, 1983, yellow truck and tipper w/black Wimpey labels, in two versions: either clear or green windows; six-spoked Whizz Wheels, Model No. 1153-B

EX $7   **NM** $15   **MIP** $30

Skyscraper Tower Crane, 1975-79, red body w/yellow chassis and booms, gold hook, gray loads of block, black/white Skyscraper labels, black tracks, Model No. 1155-A

EX $30   **NM** $45   **MIP** $85

Thwaites Tusker Skip Dumper, 1974-79, yellow body, chassis and tipper, driver and seat, hydraulic cylinder, red wheels, black tires two sizes, name labels, Whizz Wheels, Model No. 403-B

EX $10   **NM** $20   **MIP** $40

Unimog Dump Truck, 1971-73, first issue, blue cab, yellow tipper, fenders and bumpers, metallic charcoal gray chassis, red interior, black mirrors, gray tow hook, Model No. 409-B1

EX $20   **NM** $30   **MIP** $50

Unimog Dump Truck, 1976-77, second issue, yellow cab, chassis, rear frame and blue tipper, fenders and bumpers, red interior, no mirrors, gray tow hook, hydraulic cylinders, Model No. 409-B2

EX $20   **NM** $30   **MIP** $50

Unimog Dumper & Priestman Cub Shovel, 1971-73, standard colors, #1145 Mercedes-Benz Unimog w/Dumper and 1128 Priestman Cub Shovel, Model No. 2-B

EX $70   **NM** $135   **MIP** $225

Volvo Concrete Mixer, 1977-81, yellow or orange cab, red or white mixer w/yellow and black stripes, rear chassis, chrome chute and unpainted hitch casings, Model No. 1156-A

EX $30   **NM** $45   **MIP** $75

Warner & Swasey Crane, 1975-81, yellow cab and body, blue chassis, blue/yellow stripe labels, red interior, black steering wheel, silver knob, gold hook, Model No. 1101-B

EX $30   **NM** $45   **MIP** $75

EMERGENCY

AMC Pacer Rescue Car, 1978-80, chrome roll bars and red roof lights, white w/black engine hood; w/or w/out Secours decal, Model No. 484-B

EX $10   **NM** $15   **MIP** $30

(KP Photo by Dr. Douglas Sadecky)

American LaFrance Ladder Truck, 1968-81, first issue: red cab, trailer, ladder rack and wheels; chrome decks and chassis, yellow plastic three-piece operable ladder, rubber tires, six firemen figures, issued 1968-70; second issue: same as first issue except for unpainted wheels, issued 1970-72; third issue: same as earlier issues except for white decks and chassis, silver wheels, plastic tires, issued 1973-81; later issues only had four firemen and no aerial, Model No. 1143-A

EX $60   **NM** $90   **MIP** $195

(KP Photo by Dr. Douglas Sadecky)

Austin Police Mini Van, 1964-69, dark blue body w/policeman and dog figures, white police decals, opening rear doors, gray plastic antenna, shaped or cast wheels, Model No. 448-A

EX $50   **NM** $75   **MIP** $175

(KP Photo by Dr. Douglas Sadecky)

Bedford Fire Tender, 1956-61, divided windshield, red or green body, each w/different decals, smooth or shaped hubs, Model No. 405-A

EX $60   **NM** $90   **MIP** $175

Bedford Fire Tender, 1960-62, single windshield version, red body w/either black ladders and smooth wheels or unpainted ladders and shaped wheels, Model No. 423-A

EX $60   **NM** $90   **MIP** $160

Bedford Fire Tender-Mechanical, 1956-59, friction motor, red body w/Fire Dept. decals, divided windshield, silver or black ladder, smooth or shaped hubs, Model No. 405M

EX $70   **NM** $115   **MIP** $225

(KP Photo by Dr. Douglas Sadecky)

Bedford Utilecon Ambulance, 1957-60, divided or single windshield, cream body w/red/white/blue decals, smooth wheels, Model No. 412-A

EX $50   **NM** $75   **MIP** $145

Belgian Police Range Rover, 1976-77, white body, working doors, red interior, Belgian Police decal; includes policeman, Emergency signs, Model No. 483-B

EX $22   **NM** $33   **MIP** $55

Bell Rescue Helicopter, 1976-80, two-piece blue body w/working doors, red interior, yellow plastic floats, black rotors, white N428 decals, Model No. 924-A

EX $20   **NM** $30   **MIP** $50

Buick Police Car, 1977-78, metallic blue body w/white stripes and Police decals, chrome light bar w/red lights, orange taillights, chrome-spoked wheels, w/two policemen, Model No. 416-B

EX $18   **NM** $27   **MIP** $45

(KP Photo by Dr. Douglas Sadecky)

Cadillac Superior Ambulance, 1962-68, battery-operated warning lights, red lower/cream upper body or white lower body/blue upper body, shaped or cast wheels, Model No. 437-A

EX $60   **NM** $90   **MIP** $180

Canadian Mounted Police Set, 1978-80, blue No. 421 Land Rover w/Police sign on roof and RCMP decals, No. 102 trailer; includes mounted Policeman, Model No. 45-B

EX $30   **NM** $50   **MIP** $100

Chevrolet Caprice Fire Chief Car, 1982, red body, red-white-orange decals, chrome roof bar, opaque black windows, red dome light, chrome bumpers, grille and headlights, orange taillights, Fire Dept. and Fire Chief decals, chrome wheels; includes working siren and dome light, Model No. 1008-A

EX $28   **NM** $42   **MIP** $70

Chevrolet Caprice Police Car, 1980-81, black body w/white roof, doors and trunk, red interior, silver light bar, Police decals, Model No. 326-A

EX $20   **NM** $30   **MIP** $50

Chevrolet Impala Fire Chief Car, 1963-65, red body, yellow interior, w/four white doors, w/either round shield or rectangular decals on two doors; includes two firemen, shaped wheels, Model No. 439-A

EX $55   **NM** $80   **MIP** $160

(KP Photo by Dr. Douglas Sadecky)

Chevrolet Impala Fire Chief Car, 1965-69, w/Fire Chief decal on hood, yellow interior w/driver, red on white body w/either round or rectangular "Fire Chief" decals on doors, spun or cast spoked wheels, Model No. 482-A

EX $55   **NM** $80   **MIP** $140

(KP Photo by Dr. Douglas Sadecky)

Chevrolet Impala Police Car, 1965-69, black lower body and roof, white upper body, yellow interior w/two policemen, Police and Police Patrol decals on doors and hood, shaped or cast wheels, Model No. 481-A

EX $55   **NM** $80   **MIP** $140

Chevrolet State Patrol Car, 1959-61, black body, State Patrol decals, smooth wheels w/hexagonal panel or raised lines and shaped wheels, yellow plastic interior, gray antenna, clear windows, silver bumpers, grille, headlights and trim, rubber tires, Model No. 223-A

EX $50   **NM** $75   **MIP** $160

Chevrolet Superior Ambulance, 1978-80, white body, orange roof and stripes, two working doors, clear windows, red interior w/patient on stretcher and attendant, Red Cross decals, Model No. 405-B

EX $30   **NM** $45   **MIP** $75

Chopper Squad Helicopter, 1978-79, blue and white body, Sure Rescue decals, Model No. 927-A

EX $20   **NM** $30   **MIP** $50

Chopper Squad Rescue Set, 1978-79, blue No. 919 Jeep w/Chopper Squad decal and red/white boat w/Surf Rescue decal, No. 927 Helicopter, Model No. 35-B

EX $40   **NM** $60   **MIP** $100

Chubb Pathfinder Crash Tender, 1981-83, red body, Emergency Unit decals, working water pump, Model No. 1118-B

EX $45   **NM** $65   **MIP** $110

Chubb Pathfinder Crash Truck, 1974-80, red body w/either "Airport Fire Brigade" or "New York Airport" decals, upper and lower body, gold water cannon unpainted and sirens, clear windshield, yellow interior, black steering wheel, chrome plastic deck, silver lights; w/working pump and siren, Model No. 1103-B

EX $60   **NM** $90   **MIP** $150

(KP Photo by Dr. Douglas Sadecky)

Citroen Alpine Rescue Safari, 1970-72, white body, light blue interior, red roof and rear hatch, yellow or red roof rack and skis, clear windshield, man and dog, gold die-cast bobsled, Alpine Rescue decals, cast wheels, Model No. 513-A

EX $80   **NM** $175   **MIP** $500

Coast Guard Jaguar XJ12C, 1975-77, blue and white body, Coast Guard labels, Model No. 414-B

EX $18   **NM** $27   **MIP** $45

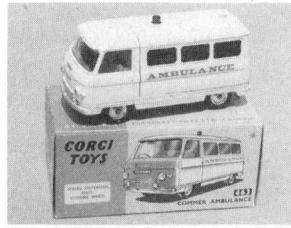

(KP Photo by Dr. Douglas Sadecky)

Commer 3/4-Ton Ambulance, 1964-66, in either white or cream body, red interior, blue dome light, red Ambulance decals, shaped wheels, Model No. 463-A

EX $36   **NM** $55   **MIP** $110

(KP Photo by Dr. Douglas Sadecky)

Commer 3/4-Ton Police Van, 1963-68, battery-operated working dome light, in several color combinations of dark or light metallic blue or green bodies, various foreign issues, the van on the left has "County Police" labels, horizontal cast bars on the rear side windows, and a metallic blue paint finish, the van on the right has an embossed "Police" logo cast in the sides, vertical lines on the rear side windows, and a dark blue paint finish, both models have a battery-operated flashing roof light, shaped wheels, Model No. 464-A

EX $45   **NM** $75   **MIP** $185

Emergency Set, 1976-77, three-vehicle set w/figures and accessories, No. 402 Ford Cortina Police car, No. 921 Police Helicopter, No. 481 Range Rover Ambulance, Model No. 18-B

EX $40   **NM** $60   **MIP** $100

Emergency Set, 1979-81, No. 339 Land Rover Police Car and No. 921 Police Helicopter w/figures and accessories, Model No. 19-C

EX $30   **NM** $50   **MIP** $80

Fire Bug, 1972-73, orange body, Whizz Wheels, Model No. 395-A

EX $20   **NM** $30   **MIP** $50

Ford Cortina Police Car, 1972-76, white body, red or pink and black stripe labels, red interior, folding seats, blue dome light, clear windows, chrome bumpers, Police labels, opening doors, Model No. 402-A

EX $15   **NM** $25   **MIP** $45

Ford Escort Police Car, 1982, blue body and base, tan interior, white doors, blue dome lights, red Police labels, black grille and bumpers, Model No. 297-A

EX $8   **NM** $15   **MIP** $30

(KP Photo by Dr. Douglas Sadecky)

Ford Zephyr Patrol Car, 1960-65, white or cream body, blue and white Police red interior, blue dome light, silver bumpers, the car on the left has the common "Police" label, the car on the right, 419-A2, has the rare Dutch "Politie" label on the hood, smooth or shaped wheels, Model No. 419-A1

EX $35   **NM** $60   **MIP** $130

Ford Zephyr Patrol Car, 1960-65, white or cream body, blue and white Politie/Rijkspolitie decals, red interior, blue dome light, silver bumpers; Dutch import, rare, Model No. 419-A2

EX $75   **NM** $300   **MIP** $500

German Life Saving Set, 1980-82, red/white No. 421 Land Rover and lifeboat, white trailer, German labels, Model No. 33-B

EX $30   **NM** $45   **MIP** $75

HGB-Angus Firestreak, 1980, chrome plastic spotlight and ladders, black hose reel, red dome light, white water cannon, in two interior versions, electronic siren and lights, Model No. 1001-A

EX $35   **NM** $50   **MIP** $85

Hi-Speed Fire Engine, 1975-78, red body, yellow plastic ladder, Model No. 703-A

EX $16   **NM** $24   **MIP** $40

Hughes Police Helicopter, 1975-80, red interior, dark blue rotors, in several international imprints, Netherlands, German, Swiss, in white or yellow, Model No. 921-A

EX $20   **NM** $30   **MIP** $50

(KP Photo by Dr. Douglas Sadecky)

Jaguar 2.4 Litre Fire Chief's Car, 1959-61, red body w/unpainted roof signal/siren, red/white fire and shield decals on doors, in two versions, smooth or spun hubs, Model No. 213-A

EX $60   **NM** $90   **MIP** $160

Jaguar XJ12C Police Car, 1978-80, white body w/blue and pink stripes, light bar w/blue dome light, tan interior, police labels, Model No. 429-A

EX $15   **NM** $28   **MIP** $45

Jet Ranger Police Helicopter, 1980, white body w/chrome interior, red floats and rotors, amber windows, Police labels, Model No. 931-A

EX $25   **NM** $40   **MIP** $65

Mercedes-Benz Ambulance, 1980-81, four different foreign versions, white interior, opening rear and two doors, blue windows and dome lights, chrome bumpers, grille and headlights, various labels; accessories include two attendant figures, Model No. 406-C

EX $15   **NM** $20   **MIP** $35

Mercedes-Benz Ambulance, 1981, white body and base, red stripes and taillights, Red Cross and black and white ambulance labels, open rear door, white interior, no figures, Model No. 407-B

EX $15   **NM** $20   **MIP** $35

Mercedes-Benz Fire Chief, 1982-83, light red body, black base, tan plastic interior, blue dome light, white Notruf 112 labels, red taillights, no tow hook, German export model, Model No. 284-B

EX $15   **NM** $25   **MIP** $40

Mercedes-Benz Police Car, 1975-80, white body w/two different hood versions, brown interior, polizei or police lettering, blue dome light, Model No. 412-B

EX $15   **NM** $18   **MIP** $30

Metropolis Police Car, 1979-81, metallic blue body, off white interior, white roof/stripes, two working doors, clear windows, chrome bumpers, grille and headlights, two roof light bars, City of Metropolis labels, Model No. 260-B

EX $20   **NM** $30   **MIP** $95

Motorway Ambulance, 1973-79, white body, dark blue interior, red-white-black Accident and Red Cross labels, dark blue windows, clear headlights, red die-cast base and bumpers, Model No. 700-A

EX $10   **NM** $15   **MIP** $30

(KP Photo by Dr. Douglas Sadecky)

Oldsmobile Sheriff's Car, 1962-66, black upper body w/white sides, red interior w/red dome light and County Sheriff decals on doors, single body casting, shaped wheels, Model No. 237-A

EX $50   **NM** $75   **MIP** $145

Police Land Rover, 1981, white body, red and blue police stripes, black lettering, open rear door, opaque black windows, blue dome light, working roof light and siren, Model No. 1005-A

EX $15   **NM** $25   **MIP** $50

Police Land Rover and Horse Box, 1978-80, white No. 421 Land Rover w/police labels and mounted policeman, No. 112 Horse Box, Model No. 44-A

EX $30   **NM** $45   **MIP** $75

Police Vigilant Range Rover, 1972-79, white body, red interior, black shutters, blue dome light, two chrome and amber spotlights, black grille, silver headlights, Police labels, w/police figure, Model No. 461-A

EX $25   **NM** $35   **MIP** $60

Porsche 924 Police Car, 1978-80, white body w/different hood and door color versions, blue and chrome light, Polizei white on green panels or Police

labels, "1" or "20" labels, Model No. 430-B

EX $15   **NM** $25   **MIP** $50

Porsche Targa Police Car, 1970-75, white body and base, red doors and hood, black roof and plastic interior also comes w/an orange interior, unpainted siren, Polizei labels, Model No. 509-A

EX $25   **NM** $35   **MIP** $60

Range Rover Ambulance, 1975-77, two different versions of body sides, red interior, raised roof, open upper and lower doors, black shutters, blue dome light, Ambulance label; includes stretcher and two ambulance attendants, Model No. 482-B

EX $20   **NM** $30   **MIP** $50

Renault 5 Police Car, 1978-79, white body, red interior, blue dome light, black hood, hatch and doors w/white Police labels, orange taillights, aerial, Model No. 428-B

EX $15   **NM** $20   **MIP** $35

Renault 5TS, 1977-80, metallic golden orange body, black trim, tan plastic interior, working hatch and two doors, clear windows and headlights, Model No. 293-A

EX $15   **NM** $18   **MIP** $30

Renault 5TS Fire Chief, 1982, red body, tan interior, amber headlights, gray antenna, black/white Sapeurs Pompiers labels, blue dome light, French export issue, Model No. 295-A

EX $15   **NM** $25   **MIP** $40

Riley Pathfinder Police Car, 1958-61, black body w/blue/white Police lettering, unpainted roof sign, gray antenna, smooth or spun wheels, Model No. 209-A

EX $50   **NM** $85   **MIP** $180

Riot Police Quad Tractor, 1977-80, white body and chassis, brown interior, red roof w/white panel, gold water cannons, gold spotlight w/amber lens, Riot Police and No. 6 labels, Model No. 422-B

EX $15   **NM** $20   **MIP** $35

Rover 3500 Police Car, 1980, white body, light red interior, red stripes, white plastic roof sign, blue dome light, red and blue Police and badge label, Model No. 339-B

EX $8   **NM** $15   **MIP** $25

Sikorsky Skycrane Casualty Helicopter, 1975-78, red and white body, black rotors and wheels, orange pipes, working rear hatch, Red Cross decals, Model No. 922-A

EX $15   **NM** $20   **MIP** $40

Simon Snorkel Fire Engine, 1964-76, red body w/yellow interior, two snorkel arms, rotating base, five firemen in cab and one in basket, three styles of wheels, Model No. 1127-A

EX $35   **NM** $55   **MIP** $135

Simon Snorkel Fire Engine, 1977-81, red body w/yellow interior, blue windows and dome lights, chrome deck, black hose reels and hydraulic cylinders, Model No. 1126-B

EX $30   **NM** $45   **MIP** $85

(KP Photo by Dr. Douglas Sadecky)

Sunbeam Imp Police Car, 1968-72, three versions, white or light blue body, tan interior, driver, black or white hood and lower doors, dome light, Police decals, cast spoked wheels, shown here are two color and box variations, Model No. 506-A

EX $25   **NM** $45   **MIP** $105

Volkswagen 1200, 1970-76, seven different color and label versions, plastic interior, one-piece body, silver headlights, red taillights, die-cast base and bumpers, Model No. 383-A2

EX $20   **NM** $45   **MIP** $85

Volkswagen 1200, 1970-76, dark yellow body, white roof, red interior and dome light, unpainted base and bumpers, black and white ADAC Strassenwacht labels, Whizz Wheels, Model No. 383-A1

EX $60   **NM** $90   **MIP** $150

(KP Photo by Dr. Douglas Sadecky)

Volkswagen 1200 Police Car, 1966-69, two different body versions made for Germany, Netherlands and Switzerland, blue dome light in chrome collar, Polizei or Politie decals, note the opening hood and trunk on this attractive car, the front wheels turn via the roof warning light, shaped wheels, Model No. 492-A

EX $40   **NM** $75   **MIP** $140

Volkswagen Police Car/Foreign Issues, 1970-76, five different versions, one-piece body, red interior, dome light, silver headlights, red taillights, clear windows, Whizz Wheels, Model No. 373-A

EX $60   **NM** $90   **MIP** $150

Volkswagen Polo Police Car, 1976-80, white body, green hood and doors, black dash, silver bumpers, grille and headlights, white roof, blue dome light, Model No. 489-A1

EX $15   **NM** $25   **MIP** $40

JEEP

Golden Eagle Jeep, 1979-82, tan and brown or white and gold body, tan plastic top, chrome plastic base, bumpers and steps, chrome wheels, Model No. 441-B

EX $8   **NM** $15   **MIP** $35

Jeep & Horse Box, 1981-83, metallic painted No. 441 Jeep and No. 112 trailer; accessories include girl on pony, three jumps and three hay bales, Model No. 29-C

EX $15   **NM** $30   **MIP** $50

Jeep and Motorcycle Trailer, 1982-83, red working No. 441 Jeep w/two blue/yellow bikes on trailer, Model No. 10-C

EX $15   **NM** $20   **MIP** $45

Jeep CJ-5, 1977-79, dark metallic green body, removable white top, white plastic wheels, spare tire, Model No. 419-B

EX $8   **NM** $15   **MIP** $30

(KP Photo by Dr. Douglas Sadecky)

Jeep FC-150 Covered Truck, 1965-72, four versions: blue body, rubber tires (1965-67); yellow/brown body; rubber tires w/spun hubs (1965-67); blue or yellow/brown body, plastic tires w/cast spoked hubs, the two major color and wheel variations are pictured here, Model No. 470-A

EX $30   **NM** $45   **MIP** $75

Jeep FC-150 Pickup, 1959-65, blue body, clear windows, sheet metal tow hook, in two wheel versions: smooth or shaped wheels, Model No. 409-A

EX $35   **NM** $55   **MIP** $90

(KP Photo by Dr. Douglas Sadecky)

Jeep FC-150 Tower Wagon, 1965-69, metallic green body, yellow interior and basket w/workman figure, clear windows, w/either rubber or plastic tires, this was the updated version of the previously released GS14-A which had a red Jeep, smooth wheels and a lamp post, shaped wheels, Model No. 478-A

EX $40   **NM** $60   **MIP** $100

Off Road Set, 1983, No. 5 label on No. 447 Jeep, blue boat, trailer, Model No. 36-C

EX $15   **NM** $20   **MIP** $50

Renegade Jeep, 1983, dark blue body w/no top, white interior, base and bumper, white plastic wheels and rear mounted spare, Model No. 447-B

EX $8   **NM** $15   **MIP** $35

Renegade Jeep w/Hood, 1983, yellow body w/removable hood, red interior, base, bumper, white plastic wheels, side mounted spare, No. 8, Model No. 448-B

EX $8   **NM** $15   **MIP** $35

Tower Wagon and Lamp Standard, 1961-65, red No. 409 Jeep Tower wagon w/yellow basket, workman figure and lamp post, smooth or shaped wheels, Model No. 14-A

EX $40   **NM** $90   **MIP** $180

LAND ROVER

(KP Photo by Dr. Douglas Sadecky)

Land Rover 109 WB Pickup, 1957-62, yellow, green or metallic blue body, spare wheel on hood, clear windows, sheet metal tow hook, smooth or shaped hubs, rubber tires, Model No. 406-A

EX $45   **NM** $75   **MIP** $130

Land Rover 109WB, 1977-79, working rear doors, tan interior, spare wheel on hood, plastic tow hook, Model No. 421-B

EX $15 **NM** $18 **MIP** $30

Land Rover Breakdown Truck, 1960-65, red body w/silver boom and yellow canopy, revolving spotlight, Breakdown Service labels, smooth or shaped wheels, Model No. 417-A

EX $35 **NM** $60 **MIP** $120

Land Rover Breakdown Truck, 1965-77, red body, yellow canopy, chrome revolving spotlight, Breakdown Service labels, shaped hubs or Whizz Wheels, Model No. 477-A

EX $25 **NM** $50 **MIP** $100

Land Rover w/Canopy, 1963-77, long, one-piece body w/clear windows, plastic interior, spare wheel on hood, issued in numerous colors, w/shaped, cast, or Whizz Wheels, Model No. 438-A

EX $35 **NM** $55 **MIP** $90

(KP Photo by Dr. Douglas Sadecky)

Public Address Land Rover, 1964-66, green No. 438 Land Rover body, yellow plastic rear body and loudspeakers, red interior, clear windows, silver bumper, grille and headlights; includes figure w/microphone and girl figure w/pamphlets, shaped wheels, Model No. 472-A

EX $50 **NM** $75 **MIP** $180

(KP Photo by Dr. Douglas Sadecky)

RAC Land Rover, 1959-64, light or dark blue body, plastic interior and rear cover, gray antenna, RAC and Radio Rescue decals, smooth or shaped wheels, Model No. 416-A

EX $60 **NM** $90 **MIP** $185

Safari Land Rover and Trailer, 1976-80, black and white No. 341 Land Rover in two versions: w/chrome wheels, 1976; w/red wheels, 1977-80; came w/Warden and Lion figures, Model No. 31-B

EX $20 **NM** $30 **MIP** $60

LARGE TRUCK

Bedford Car Transporter, 1957, first issue, black die-cast cab base w/blue "S" cab, yellow semi trailer, blue lettering decals, smooth wheels, RARE, Model No. 1101-A1

EX $100 **NM** $200 **MIP** $375

Bedford Car Transporter, 1957-62, second issue, red cab, pale green upper and blue lower semi-trailer, white decals, working ramps, clear windshield, smooth or shaped wheels, Model No. 1101-A2

EX $70 **NM** $105 **MIP** $200

Bedford Car Transporter, 1962-66, red "TK" cab w/blue lower and light green upper trailer, working ramp, yellow interior, clear windows, white lettering and Corgi dog decals, shaped wheels, Model No. 1105-A

EX $60 **NM** $90 **MIP** $185

(KP Photo by Dr. Douglas Sadecky)

Bedford Carrimore Low Loader, 1958-62, red or yellow "S" cab, metallic blue semi trailer and tailgate; smooth or shaped wheels, Model No. 1100-A

EX $60 **NM** $90 **MIP** $175

(KP Photo by Dr. Douglas Sadecky)

Bedford Carrimore Low Loader, 1963-65, yellow "TK" cab, red trailer w/working ramp, clear windows, red interior, suspension, shaped wheels, rubber tires, Model No. 1132-A

EX $90 **NM** $225 **MIP** $350

(KP Photo by Dr. Douglas Sadecky)

Bedford Milk Tanker, 1962-65, light blue "S" cab and lower semi, white upper tank, w/blue/white milk decals, shaped wheels, rubber tires, Model No. 1129-A

EX $100 **NM** $150 **MIP** $345

Bedford Milk Tanker, 1966-67, light blue "TK" cab and lower semi, white upper tank w/blue/white milk decals, shaped wheels, Model No. 1141-A

EX $110 **NM** $165 **MIP** $395

(KP Photo by Dr. Douglas Sadecky)

Bedford Mobilgas Tanker, 1959-65, red "S" cab and tanker w/Mobilgas decals, shaped wheels, rubber tires, Model No. 1110-A

EX $100 **NM** $150 **MIP** $275

Bedford Mobilgas Tanker, 1965-66, red "TK" cab and tanker w/red, white and blue Mobilgas decals, shaped wheels, rubber tires, Model No. 1140-A

EX $100 **NM** $175 **MIP** $385

Bedford Tanker, 1983, red cab w/black chassis, plastic tank w/chrome catwalk, Corgi Chemco decals, Model No. 1130-B

EX $15 **NM** $20 **MIP** $35

Berliet Container Truck, 1978, blue cab and semi fenders; white cab chassis and semi flatbed; each w/United States Lines label, Model No. 1107-B

EX $30 **NM** $45 **MIP** $75

Berliet Dolphinarium Truck, 1980-83, yellow and blue cab and trailer, clear plastic tank; includes two dolphins and a girl trainer, Model No. 1164-A

EX $56 **NM** $84 **MIP** $175

Berliet Holmes Wrecker, 1975-78, red cab and bed, blue rear body, white chassis, black interior, two gold booms and hooks, yellow dome light, driver, amber lenses and red/white/blue stripes, Model No. 1144-B

EX $30 **NM** $45 **MIP** $75

BL Roadtrain and Trailers, 1981, white and orange cab, dark blue freighter semi body w/Yorkie Chocolate labels and tanker semi body w/Gulf label; includes playmat, Model No. 1002-A
EX $16   NM $24   MIP $40

Car Transporter & Cars, 1970-73, Scammell tri-deck transporter w/six cars: Ford Capri, the Saint's Volvo, Pontiac Firebird, Lancia Fulvia, MGC GT, Marcos 3 Litre, each w/Whizz Wheels; value is for complete set, Model No. 20-B
EX $200   NM $400   MIP $900

Car Transporter and Four Cars, 1963-66, two versions: No. 1105 Bedford TK Transporter w/Fiat 1800, Renault Floride, Mercedes 230SE and Ford Consul, 1963-65; No. 1105 Bedford TK Transporter w/Chevy Corvair, VW Ghia, Volvo P-1800 and Rover 2000, 1966 only; value is for each individual complete set, Model No. 28-A
EX $200   NM $300   MIP $800

Carrimore Car Transporter and Cars, 1966, Ford "H" series Transporter and six cars; there are several car variations; sold by mail order only, Model No. 41-A
EX $240   NM $360   MIP $700

Carrimore Car Transporter and Four Cars, 1957-62, three versions: No. 1101 Bedford Carrimore Transporter w/Riley, Jaguar, Austin Healey and Triumph, 1957-60; No. 1101 Bedford Carrimore Transporter w/four American cars, 1959; No. 1101 Bedford Carrimore Transporter w/Triumph, Mini, Citroen and Plymouth, 1961-62; value is for individual complete sets, Model No. 1-A
EX $300   NM $450   MIP $900

(KP Photo by Dr. Douglas Sadecky)

Ecurie Ecosse Transporter, 1961-65, dark blue body w/either blue or yellow lettering, or metallic light blue body w/red or yellow lettering, working tailgate and sliding door, yellow interior, shaped wheels, rubber tires, Model No. 1126-A
EX $70   NM $105   MIP $245

Ford Aral Tank Truck, 1977-80, light blue cab and chassis, white tanker body, Aral labels, Model No. 1161-A
EX $20   NM $30   MIP $50

Ford Car Transporter, 1976-79, metallic lime green or metallic cab and semi, cream cab chassis, deck and ramp, Model No. 1159-A
EX $20   NM $30   MIP $60

Ford Car Transporter, 1982, white cab, red chassis and trailer, white labels and ramps, Model No. 1170-A
EX $20   NM $30   MIP $50

Ford Covered Semi-Trailer, 1979-80, blue cab and trailer, black cab chassis and trailer fenders, yellow covers, Model No. 1109-B
EX $15   NM $25   MIP $50

Ford Esso Tank Truck, 1976-81, white cab and tank, red tanker chassis and fenders, chrome wheels, Esso labels, Model No. 1157-A
EX $15   NM $30   MIP $60

Ford Express Semi-Trailer, 1965-70, metallic blue cab and trailer, silver roof on trailer, chrome doors marked "Express Service," shaped or detailed cast wheels, figure, Model No. 1137-A
EX $60   NM $110   MIP $225

Ford Exxon Tank Truck, 1976-81, white cab and tank, red tanker chassis and fenders, chrome wheels, Exxon labels, Model No. 1158-A
EX $15   NM $30   MIP $60

Ford Guinness Tanker, 1982, orange, tan, black cab, tan tanker body, Guinness labels, Model No. 1169-A
EX $20   NM $30   MIP $50

Ford Gulf Tank Truck, 1976-78, white cab w/orange chassis, blue tanker body, Gulf labels, chrome wheels, Model No. 1160-A
EX $15   NM $25   MIP $40

Ford Holmes Wrecker, 1967-74, white upper cab, black roof, red rear body and lower cab, mirrors, unpainted or gold booms, two figures, Model No. 1142-A
EX $60   NM $90   MIP $225

Ford Michelin Container Truck, 1981, blue cab and trailer, white cab chassis and trailer fenders, yellow containers; includes Michelin Man figure, Model No. 1108-B
EX $15   NM $25   MIP $60

Ford Transit Wrecker, 1981, white cab and rear body, red roof, silver bed, "24-hour Service" labels, Model No. 1140-B
EX $25   NM $35   MIP $60

Mack Container Truck, 1972-78, yellow cab, red interior, white engine, red suspension, white ACL labels, Model No. 1106-B
EX $30   NM $50   MIP $80

Mack Esso Tank Truck, 1971-75, white cab and tank w/Esso labels, red tank chassis and fenders, Model No. 1152-A
EX $20   NM $40   MIP $90

Mack Exxon Tank Truck, 1974-75, white cab and tank, red tank chassis and fenders, red interior, chrome catwalk, Exxon labels, Model No. 1151-B
EX $15   NM $35   MIP $85

Mack Trans Continental Semi, 1971-73, orange cab body and semi chassis and fenders, metallic light blue semi body, unpainted trailer rests, Model No. 1100-B
EX $35   NM $55   MIP $110

Mercedes-Benz Refrigerator, 1983, yellow cab and tailgate, red semi-trailer, two-piece lowering tailgate and yellow spare wheel base, red interior, clear window, Model No. 1131-B
EX $15   NM $18   MIP $30

Mercedes-Benz Semi-Trailer, 1983, red cab and trailer, black chassis, Model No. 1144-C
EX $15   NM $18   MIP $30

Mercedes-Benz Semi-Trailer Van, 1983, black cab and plastic semi trailer, white chassis and airscreen, red doors, red, blue and yellow stripes, white Corgi lettering, Model No. 1129-B
EX $15   NM $18   MIP $30

Mercedes-Benz Tanker, 1983, two different versions, white cab and tank, green chassis, chrome or black plastic catwalk, red/white/green 7-Up labels or Corgi Chemo labels, Model No. 1167-A
EX $15   NM $18   MIP $30

Mercedes-Benz Tanker, 1983, tan cab, plastic tank body, black chassis, black and red Guinness labels, w/chrome or black plastic catwalk, clear windows, Model No. 1166-A
EX $15   NM $18   MIP $30

Scammell Carrimore Tri-deck Car Transporter, 1970-73, orange lower cab, chassis and lower deck, white upper cab and middle deck, blue top deck, red interior, black hydraulic cylinders, detachable rear ramp, Model No. 1146-A
EX $35   NM $60   MIP $130

Scammell Coop Semi-Trailer Truck, 1970, white cab and trailer fenders, light blue semi-trailer, red interior, gray bumper base, jewel headlights, black hitch lever, spare wheel, Model No. 1151-A

EX $135 **NM** $210 **MIP** $350

Scammell Ferrymasters Semi-Trailer Truck, 1969-72, white cab, red interior, yellow chassis, black fenders, clear windows, jewel headlights, cast step-hub wheels, plastic tires, Model No. 1147-A

EX $60 **NM** $90 **MIP** $150

Scania Bulk Carrier, 1983, white cab, blue and white silos, ladders and catwalk, amber windows, blue British Sugar labels, Whizz Wheels, Model No. 1150-B

EX $7 **NM** $15 **MIP** $30

Scania Bulk Carrier, 1983, white cab, orange and white silos, clear windows, orange screen, black/orange Spillers Flour labels, Whizz Wheels, Model No. 1151-C

EX $7 **NM** $15 **MIP** $30

Scania Container Truck, 1983, yellow truck and box w/red Ryder Truck rental labels, clear windows, black exhaust stack, red rear doors, six-spoke Whizz Wheels, Model No. 1147-B

EX $7 **NM** $15 **MIP** $30

Scania Container Truck, 1983, blue cab w/blue and white box and rear doors, white deck, Securicor Parcels labels, in red or white rear door colors, Model No. 1148-B

EX $7 **NM** $15 **MIP** $30

Scania Container Truck, 1983, white cab and box w/BRS Truck Rental labels, blue windows, red screen, roof and rear doors, Model No. 1149-A

EX $7 **NM** $15 **MIP** $30

Transporter & Six Cars, 1970-73, Scammell transporter w/six cars: No. 180 Mini DeLuxe, No. 204 Mini, No. 339 Mini Rally, No. 201 The Saint's Volvo, No. 340 Sunbeam Imp, No. 378 MGC GT; includes bag of cones and leaflet, Model No. 48-B

EX $250 **NM** $450 **MIP** $900

(KP Photo by Dr. Douglas Sadecky)

Transporter and Six Cars, 1966-69, first issue: No. 1138 Ford 'H' Series Transporter w/six cars, No. 252 Rover

2000, blue No. 251 Hillman Imp, No. 440 Ford Cortina Estate, No. 180 Mini w/'wickerwork', metallic maroon No. 204 Mini, and No. 321 Mini Rally ('1966 Monte Carlo Rally') racing No. 2; second issue: same as first issue except No. 251 Hillman is metallic gold, No. 204 Mini is blue, No. 321 Mini is substituted for No. 333 SUN/RAC Rally Mini w/autographs on roof. The Car Transporter gift sets were a good way for Corgi to get rid of their excess stock of automobile models, Model No. 48-A

EX $225 **NM** $365 **MIP** $850

MILITARY

AMX 30D Recovery Tank, 1976-80, olive body w/black plastic turret and gun, accessories and three figures, Model No. 908-A

EX $35 **NM** $50 **MIP** $80

Army Heavy Equipment Transporter, 1964-65, olive cab and trailer w/white U.S. Army decals w/red or yellow interior and driver, shaped wheels, Model No. 1135-A

EX $70 **NM** $105 **MIP** $325

Army Troop Transporter, 1964-65, olive w/white U.S. Army decals, Model No. 1133-A

EX $70 **NM** $105 **MIP** $190

(KP Photo by Dr. Douglas Sadecky)

Bedford Army Fuel Tanker, 1964-65, olive cab and tanker, w/white "U.S. Army" and "No Smoking" decals, shaped wheels, Model No. 1134-A

EX $140 **NM** $210 **MIP** $395

Bedford Military Ambulance, 1961-64, clear front and white rear windows, olive body w/Red Cross decals, w/or w/out suspension, smooth or shaped wheels, Model No. 414-A

EX $56 **NM** $84 **MIP** $140

Bell Army Helicopter, 1975-80, two-piece olive/tan camouflage body, clear canopy, olive green rotors, U.S. Army decals, Model No. 920-A

EX $24 **NM** $36 **MIP** $60

Bloodhound Launching Ramp, 1959-62, military green ramp, cream platform, Model No. 1116-A

EX $35 **NM** $50 **MIP** $100

Bloodhound Loading Trolley, 1959-62, military green working lift, Model No. 1117-A

EX $40 **NM** $60 **MIP** $100

Bloodhound Missile, 1959-62, white and yellow missile, red rubber nose cone, Model No. 1115-A

EX $70 **NM** $105 **MIP** $175

(KP Photo by Dr. Douglas Sadecky)

Bloodhound Missile and Launching Platform, 1958-61, white and yellow missile, red rubber nose cone; military green ramp, cream platform, Model No. 1108-A

EX $110 **NM** $165 **MIP** $290

Bloodhound Missile on Trolley, 1959-62, white and yellow missile, red rubber nose cone; military green trolley, rubber tires, Model No. 1109-A

EX $120 **NM** $180 **MIP** $300

Centurion Mark III Tank, 1974-78, tan and brown camouflage or olive drab body, rubber tracks; includes 12 shells, Model No. 901-A

EX $30 **NM** $45 **MIP** $75

Centurion Tank and Transporter, 1973-78, No. 901 olive tank and No. 1100 transporter, Model No. 10-B

EX $55 **NM** $80 **MIP** $140

Chieftain Medium Tank, 1974-80, olive drab body, black tracks, Union Jack labels; includes 12 shells, Model No. 903-A

EX $30 **NM** $45 **MIP** $75

Commer Military Ambulance, 1964-66, olive drab body, blue rear windows and dome light, driver, Red Cross decals, shaped wheels, Model No. 354-A

EX $50 **NM** $75 **MIP** $135

Commer Military Police Van, 1964-65, olive drab body, barred rear windows, white MP decals, driver, battery-operated light, shaped wheels, Model No. 355-A

EX $55 **NM** $80 **MIP** $165

(KP Photo by Dr. Douglas Sadecky)

Corporal Missile & Erector Vehicle, 1959-62, white missile, red rubbernose cone, olive green body on erector body, Model No. 1113-A

EX $240 **NM** $275 **MIP** $550

Corporal Missile Launching Ramp, 1960-61, sold in temporary pack, Model No. 1124-A

EX $36 **NM** $55 **MIP** $100

Corporal Missile on Launching Ramp, 1959-62, white missile, red rubbernose cone, Model No. 1112-A

EX $80 **NM** $120 **MIP** $200

Corporal Missile Set, 1959-62, No. 1112 missile and No. 1113 ramp, erector vehicle and No. 1118 army truck, Model No. 9-A

EX $340 **NM** $510 **MIP** $900

Decca Airfield Radar Van, 1959-60, cream body w/four or five orange vertical bands, working rotating scanner and aerial, smooth wheels, Model No. 1106-A

EX $120 **NM** $180 **MIP** $360

Decca Radar Scanner, 1959-60, w/either orange or custard colored scanner frame, silver scanner face, w/gear on base for turning scanner, Model No. 353-A

EX $34 **NM** $51 **MIP** $85

Half Track Rocket Launcher & Trailer, 1975-80, two rocket launchers and single trailer castings, gray plastic roll cage, man w/machine gun, front wheels and hubs, Model No. 907-A

EX $20 **NM** $35 **MIP** $75

International 6x6 Army Truck, 1959-63, olive drab body w/clear windows, red/blue decals, six cast olive wheels w/rubber tires, Model No. 1118-A

EX $70 **NM** $105 **MIP** $225

(KP Photo by Dr. Douglas Sadecky)

Karrier Field Kitchen, 1964-66, olive body, white decals, w/figure, shaped wheels, Model No. 359-A

EX $60 **NM** $90 **MIP** $195

King Tiger Heavy Tank, 1974-78, tan and rust body, working turret and barrel, tan rollers and treads, German labels, Model No. 904-A

EX $30 **NM** $45 **MIP** $75

M60 A1 Medium Tank, 1974-80, green/tan camouflage body, working turret and barrel, green rollers, white decals, Model No. 902-A

EX $30 **NM** $45 **MIP** $75

Military Set, 1975-80, set of three, No. 904 Tiger tank, No. 920 Bell Helicopter, No. 906 Saladin Armored Car, Model No. 17-B

EX $60 **NM** $90 **MIP** $150

Oldsmobile 88 Staff Car, 1964-66, olive drab body, four figures, white decals, shaped wheels, Model No. 358-A

EX $50 **NM** $75 **MIP** $140

RAF Land Rover, 1958-62, blue body and cover, sheet metal rear cover, RAF rondel label, w/or w/out suspension, silver bumper, smooth or shaped wheels, Model No. 351-A

EX $60 **NM** $90 **MIP** $150

RAF Land Rover & Bloodhound, 1958-61, set of three standard colored, No. 351 RAF Land Rover, No. 1115 Bloodhound Missile, No. 1116 Ramp and No. 1117 Trolley, Model No. 4-A

EX $150 **NM** $300 **MIP** $600

RAF Land Rover and Thunderbird Missile, 1958-63, Standard colors, No. 350 Thunderbird Missile on Trolley and No. 351 RAF Land Rover, Model No. 3-A

EX $100 **NM** $150 **MIP** $325

Rocket Age Set, 1959-60, set of eight standard models including: No. 350 Thunderbird Missile on Trolley, No. 351 RAF Land Rover, No. 352 RAF Staff Car, No. 353 Radar Scanner, No. 1106 Decca Radar Van and No.

1108 Bloodhound missile w/ramp, Model No. 6-A

EX $325 **NM** $750 **MIP** $1900

Rocket Launcher and Trailer, 1975-80, steel blue and red launcher, fires rocket, Model No. 907-A

EX $25 **NM** $35 **MIP** $60

Saladin Armored Car, 1974-77, olive drab body, swiveling turret and raising barrel castings, black plastic barrel end and tires, olive cast wheels, w/2 shells, fires shells, Model No. 906-A

EX $30 **NM** $45 **MIP** $75

Sikorsky Skycrane Army Helicopter, 1975-78, olive drab and yellow body w/Red Cross and Army labels, Model No. 923-A

EX $15 **NM** $20 **MIP** $40

Standard Vanguard RAF Staff Car, 1958-62, blue body, RAF labels, smooth or spun wheels, Model No. 352-A

EX $55 **NM** $85 **MIP** $140

SU-100 Medium Tank, 1974-77, olive and cream camouflage upper body, gray lower, working hatch and barrel, black treads, red star and #103 labels; 12 shells included, fires shells, Model No. 905-A

EX $30 **NM** $50 **MIP** $80

Thunderbird Missile and Trolley, 1958-62, ice blue or silver missile, RAF blue trolley, red rubber-nose cone, plastic tow bar, steering front and rear axles, Model No. 350-A

EX $55 **NM** $85 **MIP** $165

Tiger Mark I Tank, 1973-78, tan and green camouflage finish, German emblem, swiveling turret and raising barrel castings, black plastic barrel end, antenna; includes 12 shells, fires shells, Model No. 900-A

EX $30 **NM** $45 **MIP** $75

Tractor, Trailer and Field Gun, 1976-80, tan tractor body and chassis, trailer body, base and opening doors, gun chassis and raising barrel castings, brown plastic interior; 12 shells included, fires shells, Model No. 909-A

EX $30 **NM** $50 **MIP** $80

(KP Photo by Dr. Douglas Sadecky)

Volkswagen Military Personnel Carrier, 1964-66, olive drab body, white decals, driver, shaped wheels, Model No. 356-A

EX $55   **NM** $95   **MIP** $180

MISCELLANEOUS

Service Ramp, 1958-60, metallic blue and silver operable ramp, Model No. 1401-A

EX $30   **NM** $45   **MIP** $95

Shell or BP Garage Gift Set, 1963-65, gas station/garage w/pumps and other accessories including five different cars; in two versions: Shell or B.P., rare; value is for each set, Model No. 25-A

EX $295   **NM** $900   **MIP** $2700

Touring Caravan, 1975-79, white body w/blue trim, white plastic opening roof and door, pale blue interior, red plastic hitch and awning, Model No. 490-B

EX $15   **NM** $25   **MIP** $40

MOTORCYCLE

Cafe Racer Motorcycle, 1983, Model No. 173-A

EX $15   **NM** $18   **MIP** $30

Matra & Motorcycle Trailer, 1980-81, red No. 57 Talbot Matra Rancho w/two yellow and blue bikes on trailer, Model No. 25-C

EX $15   **NM** $20   **MIP** $35

Red Wheelie Motorcycle, 1982, red plastic body and fender w/black/white/yellow decals, black handlebars, kickstand and seat, chrome engine, pipes, flywheel-powered rear wheel, Model No. 171-A

EX $10   **NM** $15   **MIP** $25

Stunt Motorcycle, 1971-72, made for Corgi Rockets race track, gold cycle, blue rider w/yellow helmet, clear windshield, plastic tires, Model No. 681-A

EX $70   **NM** $105   **MIP** $175

White Wheelie Motorcycle, 1982, white body w/black/white police decals, Model No. 172-A

EX $15   **NM** $20   **MIP** $35

RACING

Adams Drag-Star, 1972-74, orange body, red nose, gold engines, chrome pipes and hood panels, Whizz Wheels, Model No. 165-A

EX $20   **NM** $30   **MIP** $45

Adams Probe 16, 1970-73, one-piece body, blue sliding canopy; metallic burgundy, or metallic lime/gold w/and w/out racing stripes, Whizz Wheels, Model No. 384-A

EX $15   **NM** $25   **MIP** $40

All Winners Set, 1966-69, first issue: No. 310 Corvette, No. 312 Jaguar XKE, No. 314 Ferrari 250LM, No. 324 Marcos, No. 325 Mustang; second issue: No. 312 Jaguar XKE, No. 314 Ferrari 250LM, No. 264 Toronado, No. 327 MGB, No. 337 Corvette, Model No. 46-A

EX $100   **NM** $300   **MIP** $650

(KP Photo by Dr. Douglas Sadecky)

Aston Martin DB4, 1962-65, white top w/aqua green sides, yellow plastic interior, three wheel variants, racing Nos. 1, 3 or 7, Model No. 309-A

EX $50   **NM** $75   **MIP** $140

Austin Mini-Metro Datapost, 1982-83, white body, blue roof, hood and trim, red plastic interior, hepolite and #77 decals, working hatch and doors, clear windows, folding seats, chrome headlights, orange taillights, Whizz Wheels, Model No. 281-B

EX $15   **NM** $18   **MIP** $30

Bertone Barchetta Runabout, 1971-73, yellow and black body, black interior, amber windows, die-cast air foil, suspension, red/yellow Runabout decals, Whizz Wheels, Model No. 386-A

EX $15   **NM** $22   **MIP** $45

BMC Mini-Cooper, 1971-74, white body, black working hood, trunk, two doors, red interior, clear windows, orange/black stripes and #177 decals, suspension, Whizz Wheels, Model No. 282-A

EX $30   **NM** $60   **MIP** $125

(KP Photo by Dr. Douglas Sadecky)

BMC Mini-Cooper S "Sun/RAC" Rally Car, 1967, red body, white roof w/six jewel headlights, shaped wheels, RAC Rally and No. 21 decals, Model No. 333-A

EX $90   **NM** $180   **MIP** $425

BMC Mini-Cooper S Rally, 1967-72, red body, white roof, chrome roof rack w/two spare tires, Monte Carlo Rally

and No. 177 decals, w/shaped wheels/rubber tires or cast detailed wheels/plastic tires, Model No. 339-A

EX $40   **NM** $90   **MIP** $180

(KP Photo by Dr. Douglas Sadecky)

BMC Mini-Cooper S Rally Car, 1965-66, red body, white roof, five jewel headlights, Monte Carlo Rally decals w/either No. 52 (1965) or No. 2 (1966); rare w/drivers' autographs on roof, shaped wheels, Model No. 321-A

EX $100   **NM** $275   **MIP** $500

BMW M1, 1981, yellow body, black plastic base, rear panel and interior, white seats, clear windshield, multicolored stripes, lettering and #25 decal, Goodyear label, Model No. 308-B

EX $15   **NM** $20   **MIP** $35

BMW M1 BASF, 1983, red body, white trim w/black/white BASF and No. 80 decals, Model No. 380-B

EX $15   **NM** $18   **MIP** $30

British Leyland Mini 1000, 1978, red interior, chrome lights, grille and bumper, #8 decal; three variations: silver body w/decals, 1978-82; silver body, no decals; orange body w/extra hood stripes, 1983, Model No. 201-C

EX $16   **NM** $24   **MIP** $40

British Racing Cars, 1959-63, set of three cars, three versions: blue No. 152 Lotus, green No. 151 BRM, green No. 150 Vanwall, all w/smooth wheels, 1959; same cars w/shaped wheels, 1960-61; red Vanwall, green BRM and blue Lotus, 1963, each set, Model No. 5-A

EX $140   **NM** $210   **MIP** $500

BRM Racing Car, 1958-65, silver seat, dash and pipes, smooth wheels, rubber tires, in three versions: dark green body, 1958-60; light green body w/driver and various number decals 1961-65; light green body, no driver, smooth or cast spoked wheels, Model No. 152-A

EX $50   **NM** $75   **MIP** $150

Campbell Bluebird, 1960-65, blue body, red exhaust, clear windshield, driver, in two versions: black plastic wheels, 1960; metal wheels and rubber tires, Model No. 153-A

EX $56   **NM** $84   **MIP** $180

Chevrolet Caprice Classic, 1981, white upper body, red sides w/red/white/blue stripes and No. 43 decals, tan interior, STP labels, Model No. 341-B

EX $24   **NM** $36   **MIP** $60

(KP Photo by Dr. Douglas Sadecky)

Citroen DS 19 Rally, 1965-66, light blue body, white roof, yellow interior, four jewel headlights, Monte Carlo Rally and No. 75 decals, w/antenna, shaped wheels, Model No. 323-A

EX $70   **NM** $105   **MIP** $200

Commuter Dragster, 1971-73, maroon body w/Ford Commuter, Union Jack and #2 decals, cast silver engine, chrome plastic suspension and pipes, clear windshield, driver, spoke wheels, Model No. 161-A

EX $30   **NM** $45   **MIP** $75

Cooper-Maserati Racing Car, 1967-69, blue body w/red/white/blue Maserati and #7 decals, unpainted engine and suspension, chrome plastic steering wheel, roll bar, mirrors and pipes, driver, cast eight-spoke wheels, plastic tires, Model No. 156-A

EX $26   **NM** $39   **MIP** $75

Cooper-Maserati Racing Car, 1969-72, yellow/white body w/yellow/black stripe and #3 decals, driver tilts to steer car, cast eight-spoke wheels, Model No. 159-A

EX $18   **NM** $27   **MIP** $65

(KP Photo by Dr. Douglas Sadecky)

Corvette Sting Ray, 1967-69, yellow body, red interior, suspension, No. 13 decals, this car's decorative appearance definitely places it in the 1960s, cast eight-spoke wheels, Model No. 337-A

EX $30   **NM** $65   **MIP** $145

Corvette Sting Ray, 1970-73, metallic gray body w/black hood, Go-Go-Go labels, Whizz Wheels, Model No. 376-A

EX $40   **NM** $65   **MIP** $100

Datsun 240Z, 1973-76, white body w/red hood and roof, No. 46 and John Morton labels, Whizz Wheels, Model No. 396-A

EX $15   **NM** $20   **MIP** $35

Datsun 240Z, 1973-76, red body w/No. 11 and other labels, two working doors, white interior, orange roll bar and tire rack; one version also has East Africa Rally labels, Model No. 394-A

EX $15   **NM** $20   **MIP** $35

Ecurie Ecosse Racing Set, 1961-66, metallic dark or light blue No. 1126 transporter w/three cars in two versions: BRM, Vanwall and Lotus XI, 1961-64; BRM, Vanwall and Ferrari, 1964-66, value is for individual complete set, Model No. 16-A

EX $140   **NM** $275   **MIP** $600

Ferrari 206 Dino, 1969-73, black interior and fins, in either red body w/No. 30 label and gold hubs or Whizz Wheels, or yellow body w/No. 23 label and gold hubs or Whizz Wheels, Model No. 344-A

EX $24   **NM** $36   **MIP** $60

Ferrari 312 B2 Racing Car, 1973-75, red body, white fin, gold engine, chrome suspension, mirrors and wheels, Ferrari and #5 labels, Model No. 152-B

EX $16   **NM** $24   **MIP** $40

(KP Photo by Dr. Douglas Sadecky)

Ferrari Berlinetta 250LM, 1965-72, red body w/yellow stripe, blue windshields, chrome interior, grille and exhaust pipes, detailed engine, #4 Ferrari logo and yellow stripe decals, spoked wheels and spare, rubber tires, Model No. 314-A

EX $30   **NM** $50   **MIP** $110

Ferrari Daytona, 1973-78, white body w/red roof and trunk, black interior, two working doors, amber windows and headlights, No. 81 and other labels, Model No. 323-B

EX $15   **NM** $30   **MIP** $55

Ferrari Daytona, 1979, apple green body, black tow hook, red-yellow-silver-black Daytona #5 and other racing labels, amber windows, headlights, black plastic interior, base, four spoke chrome wheels, Model No. 300-C

EX $15   **NM** $20   **MIP** $35

Ferrari Daytona and Racing Car, 1975-77, blue/yellow No. 323 Ferrari and No. 150 Surtees on yellow trailer, Model No. 29-D

EX $25   **NM** $40   **MIP** $85

Ferrari Daytona JCB, 1973-74, orange body w/No. 33, Corgi and other labels, chrome-spoked wheels, Model No. 324-B

EX $15   **NM** $25   **MIP** $50

Ferrari Racing Car, 1963-72, red body, chrome plastic engine, roll bar and dash, driver, silver cast base and exhaust, Ferrari and No. 36 decals, shaped or cast wheels, Model No. 154-A

EX $24   **NM** $36   **MIP** $85

Fiat X1/9, 1980-81, metallic blue body and base, white Fiat #3, multicolored lettering and stripe labels, black roof, trim, interior, rear panel, grille, bumpers and tow hook, chrome wheels and detailed engine, Model No. 306-B

EX $15   **NM** $20   **MIP** $35

Ford Capri 3 Litre GT, 1973-76, white and black body, racing number 5 label, Model No. 331-A

EX $15   **NM** $20   **MIP** $35

Ford Capri S, 1982, white body, red lower body and base, red interior, clear windshield, black bumpers, grille and tow hook, chrome headlights and wheels, red taillights, #6 and other racing labels, Model No. 312-C

EX $15   **NM** $20   **MIP** $35

Ford Capri Santa Pod Gloworm, 1971-76, white and blue body w/red, white and blue lettering and flag decals, red chassis, amber windows, gold-based black engine, gold scoop, pipes and front suspension, w/driver, plastic wheels, Model No. 163-A

EX $18   **NM** $27   **MIP** $45

Ford GT 70, 1972-73, green and black body, white interior, No. 32 label, Model No. 316-B

EX $10   **NM** $25   **MIP** $45

Grand Prix Racing Set, 1968-72, four vehicle set includes: No. 490 Volkswagen Breakdown Truck w/No. 330 Porsche (1969), Porsche No. 371 (1970-72), No. 155 Lotus, 156 Cooper-Maserati, red trailer, Model No. 12-B

EX $135   **NM** $210   **MIP** $425

Grand Prix Set, 1973, sold by mail order only; kit version of No. 151 Yardley, No. 154 JPS, No. 152 Surtees and No. 153 Surtees, Model No. 30-A

EX $60   **NM** $125   **MIP** $275

Hesketh-Ford Racing Car, 1975-78, white body w/red/white/blue Hesketh, stripe and #24 labels, chrome suspension, roll bar, mirrors and pipes, Model No. 160-A

EX $15   **NM** $18   **MIP** $30

Hillman Hunter, 1969-72, blue body, gray interior, black hood, white roof, unpainted spotlights, clear windshield, red radiator screen, black equipment, Golden Jacks wheels; came w/Kangaroo figure and label sheet, Model No. 302-B

EX $45   **NM** $70   **MIP** $140

(KP Photo by Dr. Douglas Sadecky)

Hillman Imp Rally, 1966, in various metallic body colors, w/cream interior, Monte Carlo Rally and No. 107 decals, shaped wheels, Model No. 328-A

EX $30   **NM** $65   **MIP** $140

Jaguar E Type Competition, 1964-68, gold or chrome plated body, black interior, blue and white stripes and black #2 decals, no top, clear windshield, headlights, w/driver, spoked wheels, Model No. 312-A

EX $45   **NM** $65   **MIP** $150

Jaguar XJS Motul, 1983, black body w/red/white Motul and No. 4, chrome wheels, Model No. 318-B

EX $8   **NM** $15   **MIP** $25

JPS Lotus Racing Car, 1974-77, black body, scoop and wings w/gold John Player Special, Texaco and #1 labels, gold suspension, pipes and wheels, Model No. 190-A

EX $30   **NM** $45   **MIP** $75

Lamborghini Miura, 1973-74, silver body, black interior, yellow/purple stripes and No. 7 label, Whizz Wheels, Model No. 319-B

EX $30   **NM** $45   **MIP** $75

Land Rover and Ferrari Racer, 1963-67, red and tan No. 438 Land Rover and red No. 154 Ferrari F1 on yellow trailer, Model No. 17-A

EX $60   **NM** $100   **MIP** $200

(KP Photo by Dr. Douglas Sadecky)

Lotus Elan S2 Roadster, 1965-67, working hood, plastic interior w/folding seats, shaped wheels and rubber tires, issued in metallic blue, Exxon "I've got a Tiger in my tank" label on trunk, the ordinary model is powder blue, but shown here is the rare white version of the car, Model No. 318-A

EX $30   **NM** $75   **MIP** $140

(KP Photo by Dr. Douglas Sadecky)

Lotus Eleven, 1958-64, red, silver, or light blue/green body, clear windshield and plastic headlights, smooth wheels, rubber tires, racing decals, Model No. 151-A

EX $60   **NM** $95   **MIP** $160

Lotus Racing Car, 1973-82, black body and base, gold cast engine, roll bar, pipes, dash and mirrors, driver, gold cast wheels, in two versions, Model No. 154-B

EX $25   **NM** $35   **MIP** $60

Lotus Racing Set, 1976-79, three versions: "3" on No. 301 Elite and "JPS" on No. 154 Lotus racer; "7" on No. 301 Elite and "JPS" on racer; "7" on No. 301 Elite and "Texaco" on No. 154 Lotus racer; value is for each individual complete set, Model No. 32-B

EX $30   **NM** $45   **MIP** $95

Lotus Racing Team Set, 1966-69, 490 VW Breakdown Truck, red trailer w/#318 Lotus Elan Open Top, #319 Lotus Elan Hard Top, #155 Lotus Climax; includes pack of cones, sheet of racing number labels, Model No. 37-A

EX $125   **NM** $200   **MIP** $475

Lotus-Climax Racing Car, 1964-69, green body and base w/black/white #1 and yellow racing stripe labels, unpainted engine and suspension, w/driver, shaped wheels, Model No. 155-A

EX $25   **NM** $40   **MIP** $85

(KP Photo by Dr. Douglas Sadecky)

Lotus-Climax Racing Car, 1969-72, orange/white body w/black/white stripe and #8 labels, unpainted cast rear wing, cast eight-spoke wheels, w/driver, Model No. 158-A

EX $15   **NM** $25   **MIP** $65

Matra and Racing Car, 1983, black/yellow No. 457 Talbot Matra Rancho and No. 160 Hesketh yellow car w/Team Corgi trailer and labels, Model No. 26-B

EX $15   **NM** $35   **MIP** $65

McLaren M19A Racing Car, 1972-77, white body, orange stripes, chrome engine, exhaust and suspension, black mirrors, driver, Yardley McLaren #55 labels, Whizz Wheels, Model No. 151-B

EX $15   **NM** $25   **MIP** $40

McLaren M23 Racing Car, 1974-77, large 1:18-scale red and white body and wings w/red, white and black Texaco-Marlboro #5 labels, chrome pipes, suspension and mirrors, removable wheels, Model No. 191-A

EX $30   **NM** $70   **MIP** $130

Mercedes-Benz 240D Rally, 1982, cream or tan body, black, red and blue lettering, "dirt," red plastic interior, clear windows, black radiator guard and roof rack, opening doors, racing #5 label, Model No. 291-B

EX $10   **NM** $15   **MIP** $25

(KP Photo by Dr. Douglas Sadecky)

Mercedes-Benz 300SL Coupe, 1959-65, chrome body, red hardtop, red stripe, clear windows, 1959-60 smooth wheels no suspension, 1961-65 racing stripes, Model No. 304-A

EX $45   **NM** $75   **MIP** $165

Mercedes-Benz 300SL Roadster,
1958-66, blue or white body, yellow
interior, plastic interior, smooth,
shaped or cast wheels, racing
stripes and number, driver, Model
No. 303-A

EX $45   **NM** $75   **MIP** $140

Mini-Marcos GT850, 1972-73, white
body, red-white-blue racing stripe
and #7 labels, clear headlights,
Whizz Wheels, opening doors and
hood, Model No. 305-B

EX $20   **NM** $30   **MIP** $50

(KP Photo by Dr. Douglas Sadecky)

Monte Carlo Rally Set, 1965-67, three
vehicle set, No. 326 Citroen, No.
318 Mini and No. 322 Land Rover
rally cars, Model No. 38-A

EX $295   **NM** $450   **MIP** $950

(KP Photo by Dr. Douglas Sadecky)

Morris Mini-Cooper, 1962-65, yellow
or blue body and base and/or hood,
white roof and/or hood, two
versions, red plastic interior, jewel
headlights, flag, numbers decals,
even though there are various paint
and decal versions of this model,
any one of them is valuable, shaped
wheels, Model No. 227-A

EX $80   **NM** $150   **MIP** $345

Morris Mini-Cooper, 1964-65, red
body and base, white roof, yellow
interior, chrome spotlight, No. 37
and Monte Carlo Rally decals,
shaped wheels, Model No. 317-A

EX $60   **NM** $125   **MIP** $265

Mustang Organ Grinder Dragster,
1971-74, yellow body
w/green/yellow name, #39 and
racing stripe labels, black base,
green windshield, red interior, roll
bar, w/driver, Model No. 166-A

EX $20   **NM** $30   **MIP** $50

Porsche 924, 1978-81, red or metallic
light brown or green body, dark red
interior, opening two doors and rear

window, chrome headlights, black
plastic grille, racing No. 2, Model
No. 321-B

EX $10   **NM** $25   **MIP** $50

Porsche Carrera 6, 1967-69, white body,
red or blue trim, blue or amber tinted
engine covers, black interior, clear
windshield and canopy, red jewel
taillights, No. 1 or No. 20 decals, cast
eight-spoke wheels, Model No. 330-A

EX $30   **NM** $45   **MIP** $85

Porsche Carrera 6, 1970-73, white
upper body, red front hood, doors,
upper fins and base, black interior,
purple rear window, tinted engine
cover, racing No. 60 decals, Whizz
Wheels, Model No. 371-A

EX $25   **NM** $35   **MIP** $60

Porsche-Audi 917, 1973-78, white body,
red and black No. 6, L and M, Porsche
Audi and stripe labels or orange body,
orange, two-tone green, white No. 6,
racing driver, Model No. 397-A

EX $15   **NM** $20   **MIP** $35

(KP Photo by Dr. Douglas Sadecky)

Psychedelic Ford Mustang, 1968, light
blue body and base, aqua interior, red-
orange-yellow No. 20 and flower
decals, cast eight-spoke wheels,
plastic tire, Model No. 348-A

EX $30   **NM** $65   **MIP** $130

Quartermaster Dragster, 1971-73,
long, dark metallic green upper
body w/green/yellow/black #5 and
Quartermaster labels, light green
lower body, w/driver, Model
No. 162-A

EX $30   **NM** $45   **MIP** $75

Radio Luxembourg Dragster, 1972-
76, long, blue body w/yellow, white
and blue John Wolfe Racing, Radio
Luxembourg and #5 labels, silver
engine, w/driver, Model No. 170-A

EX $30   **NM** $45   **MIP** $85

Renault 5 Turbo, 1981, bright yellow
body, red plastic interior, black roof
and hood, working hatch and two
doors, black dash, chrome rear
engine, racing #8 Cibie and other
sponsor labels, Model No. 307-B

EX $15   **NM** $18   **MIP** $25

Renault 5 Turbo, 1983, white body,
red roof, red and blue trim painted
on, No. 5 lettering, blue and white
label on windshield, facom decal,
Model No. 381-B

EX $15   **NM** $18   **MIP** $25

Roger Clark's Capri, 1970-72, white
body, black hood, grille and interior,
open doors, folding seats, chrome
bumpers, clear headlights, red
taillights, Racing #73, label sheet,
Whizz Wheels, Model No. 303-B

EX $15   **NM** $25   **MIP** $65

(KP Photo by Dr. Douglas Sadecky)

Rover 2000 Rally, 1965-66, white body,
red interior, black bonnet, No. 21
decal, cast wheels, Model No. 322-A2

EX $55   **NM** $135   **MIP** $295

Rover 2000 Rally, 1965-66, metallic
dark red body, white roof, shaped
wheels, No. 136 and Monte Carlo
Rally decals, Model No. 322-A1

EX $50   **NM** $95   **MIP** $195

Rover 3500 Triplex, 1981, white sides
and hatch, blue roof and hood, red
plastic interior and trim, detailed
engine, red-white-black No. 1 label,
Model No. 340-B

EX $8   **NM** $15   **MIP** $20

Shadow-Ford Racing Car, 1974-76,
black body and base w/white/black
#17, UOP and American flag labels,
cast chrome suspension and pipes,
Embassy Racing label, Model
No. 155-B

EX $10   **NM** $20   **MIP** $50

Shadow-Ford Racing Car, 1974-77,
white body, red stripes, driver,
chrome plastic pipes, mirrors and
steering wheel, in two versions, Jackie
Collins driver figure, Model No. 156-B

EX $10   **NM** $20   **MIP** $45

Silver Streak Jet Dragster, 1973-76,
metallic blue body w/Firestone and
flag labels on tank, silver engine,
orange plastic jet and nose cone,
Model No. 169-A

EX $15   **NM** $25   **MIP** $45

Silverstone Racing Layout, 1963-66,
seven-vehicle set w/accessories;
Vanwall, Lotus XI, Aston Martin,
Mercedes 300SL, BRM, Ford
Thunderbird, Land Rover Truck;
second version has a No. 154
Ferrari substituted for Lotus XI,
rare, Model No. 15-A

EX $400   **NM** $1000   **MIP** $2600

(KP Photo by Dr. Douglas Sadecky)

Simca 1000, 1964-66, chrome plated or blue body, No. 8 and red-white-blue stripe decals, one-piece body, clear windshield, red interior, shaped wheels, Model No. 315-A

EX $30   **NM** $50   **MIP** $105

STP Patrick Eagle Racing Car, 1974-77, red body w/red, white and black STP and #20 labels, chrome lower engine and suspension, black plastic upper engine; includes Patrick Eagle driver figure, Model No. 159-B

EX $20   **NM** $30   **MIP** $50

Sunbeam Imp Rally, 1967-68, metallic blue body w/white stripes, Monte Carlo Rally and No. 77 decals, cast wheels, Model No. 340-A

EX $20   **NM** $60   **MIP** $130

Super Karts, 1982, two carts, orange and blue, Whizz Wheels in front, slicks on rear, silver and gold drivers, Model No. 46-B

EX $15   **NM** $18   **MIP** $30

Surtees TS9 Racing Car, 1972-74, black upper engine, chrome lower engine, pipes and exhaust, driver, Brook Bond Oxo-Rob Walker labels, eight-spoke Whizz Wheels, Model No. 150-A

EX $15   **NM** $20   **MIP** $40

Surtees TS9B Racing Car, 1972-74, red body w/white stripes and wing, black plastic lower engine, driver, chrome upper engine, pipes, suspension, eight-spoke Whizz Wheels, Model No. 153-B

EX $15   **NM** $20   **MIP** $40

Tyrrell P34 Racing Car, 1977, dark blue body and wings w/yellow stripes, #4 and white Elf and Union Jack decals, chrome plastic engine, w/driver in red or blue helmet, Model No. 161-B

EX $20   **NM** $30   **MIP** $55

Tyrrell P34 Racing Car, 1978-79, w/out yellow labels, First National Bank labels, w/driver in red or orange helmet, Model No. 162-B

EX $20   **NM** $30   **MIP** $55

Tyrrell-Ford Racing Car, 1974-78, dark blue body w/blue/black/white Elf and #1 labels, chrome suspension, pipes, mirrors, Jackie Stewart driver figure, Model No. 158-B

EX $18   **NM** $25   **MIP** $50

U.S. Racing Buggy, 1972-74, white body w/red/white/blue stars, stripes and USA #7 labels, red base, gold engine, red plastic panels, driver, Model No. 167-A

EX $18   **NM** $25   **MIP** $50

(KP Photo by Dr. Douglas Sadecky)

Vanwall Racing Car, 1957-65, clear windshield, unpainted dash, silver pipes and decals, smooth or cast detailed spoked wheels, rubber tires, in three versions: green body or red body w/silver or yellow seats, Model No. 150-A

EX $35   **NM** $65   **MIP** $150

Volkswagen 1200 Rally, 1976-77, light blue body, off-white plastic interior, silver headlights, red taillights, suspension, Whizz Wheels, Model No. 384-B

EX $20   **NM** $30   **MIP** $50

(KP Photo by Dr. Douglas Sadecky)

Volkswagen East African Safari, 1965-69, light red body, brown interior, right- or left-hand steering wheel, working front and rear hood, clear windows, spare wheel on roof steers front wheels, jewel headlights, w/rhinoceros figure, although never issued as a gift set, this spectacular little toy could easily have been made into one, a rhinoceros was added as a charging menace to the racing VW, shaped wheels, Model No. 256-A

EX $60   **NM** $130   **MIP** $285

Volkswagen Racing Tender and Cooper, 1967-69, white No. 490 VW breakdown truck w/racing labels, blue No. 156 Cooper on trailer, Model No. 6-B

EX $50   **NM** $95   **MIP** $225

Volkswagen Racing Tender and Cooper Maserati, 1970-71, two versions: tan or white No. 490 VW breakdown truck, and No. 159 Cooper-Maserati on trailer; value is for each set, Model No. 25-B

EX $50   **NM** $100   **MIP** $245

Wild Honey Dragster, 1971-73, yellow body w/red/yellow Wild Honey and Jaguar Powered labels, green windows and roof, black grille, driver, Whizz Wheels, Model No. 164-A

EX $25   **NM** $40   **MIP** $65

SMALL TRUCK

Breakdown Truck, 1975-79, red body, black plastic boom w/gold hook, yellow interior, amber windows, black/yellow decals, Whizz Wheels, Model No. 702-A

EX $15   **NM** $18   **MIP** $40

Commer 3/4-Ton Pickup, 1963-66, red cab w/orange canopy, yellow interior, Trans-o-Lites, shaped wheels, Model No. 465-A

EX $30   **NM** $45   **MIP** $95

Commer 5-Ton Dropside Truck, 1956-62, either blue or red cab, both w/cream rear body, sheet metal tow hook, smooth or shaped wheels, rubber tires, Model No. 452-A

EX $40   **NM** $70   **MIP** $140

Commer 5-Ton Platform Truck, 1957-62, either yellow or metallic blue cab w/silver body, smooth or shaped wheels, Model No. 454-A

EX $40   **NM** $70   **MIP** $140

(KP Photo by Dr. Douglas Sadecky)

Commer Refrigerator Van, 1956-60, either light or dark blue cab (pictured here), both w/cream bodies and red/white/blue Wall's Ice Cream decals, smooth wheels, Model No. 453-A

EX $80   **NM** $120   **MIP** $245

(KP Photo by Dr. Douglas Sadecky)

Constructor Set, 1963-68, one red and one white cab bodies, w/four different interchangeable rear units; van, pickup, milk truck, and ambulance; various accessories include a milkman figure, Model No. 24-A

EX $48   **NM** $80   **MIP** $240

(KP Photo by Dr. Douglas Sadecky)

Dodge Kew Fargo Tipper, 1967-72, white cab and working hood, blue tipper, red interior, clear windows, black hydraulic cylinders, shaped or cast wheels, plastic tires, Model No. 483-A

EX $34   **NM** $51   **MIP** $85

ERF 44G Dropside Truck, 1961-64, yellow cab and chassis, metallic blue bed, smooth or shaped wheels, Model No. 456-A

EX $40   **NM** $70   **MIP** $140

(KP Photo by Dr. Douglas Sadecky)

ERF 44G Moorhouse Van, 1958-60, yellow cab, red body, Moorhouse Lemon Cheese decals, smooth wheels, rubber tires, Model No. 459-A

EX $100   **NM** $150   **MIP** $345

(KP Photo by Dr. Douglas Sadecky)

ERF 44G Platform Truck, 1958-64, light blue cab w/dark blue flatbed body or yellow cab and blue flatbed, smooth hubs, Model No. 457-A

EX $40   **NM** $70   **MIP** $140

ERF Dropside Truck and Trailer, 1960-64, No. 456 truck and No. 101 trailer w/No. 1488 cement sack load and No. 1485 plank load, Model No. 11-A

EX $60   **NM** $90   **MIP** $260

(KP Photo by Dr. Douglas Sadecky)

ERF Neville Cement Tipper, 1959-66, yellow cab, gray tipper, cement decal, plastic or metal filler caps, w/either smooth or shaped wheels, Model No. 460-A

EX $32   **NM** $48   **MIP** $120

Ford Transit Milk Float, 1982, white one-piece body, blue hood and roof, tan interior, chrome and red roof lights, open compartment door and milk cases, Model No. 405-C

EX $15   **NM** $25   **MIP** $40

Mazda 4X4 Open Truck, 1983, blue body, white roof, black windows, no interior, white plastic wheels, Model No. 495-A

EX $15   **NM** $20   **MIP** $35

Mazda B-1600 Pickup Truck, 1975-78, issued in either blue and white or blue and silver bodies w/working tailgate, black interior, chrome wheels, Model No. 493-A

EX $15   **NM** $20   **MIP** $35

Mazda Camper Pickup, 1976-78, red truck and white camper w/red interior and folding supports, Model No. 415-A

EX $15   **NM** $25   **MIP** $50

Mazda Custom Pickup, 1979-80, orange body w/red roof, United States flag label, Model No. 440-B

EX $15   **NM** $18   **MIP** $30

Mazda Motorway Maintenance Truck, 1976-78, deep yellow body w/red base, black interior and hydraulic cylinder, yellow basket w/workman figure, Model No. 413-B

EX $18   **NM** $25   **MIP** $45

Mazda Pickup and Dinghy, 1975-78, two versions: red No. 493 Mazda w/"Ford" labels; or w/"Sea Spray" labels, dinghy and trailer, Model No. 28-A

EX $25   **NM** $35   **MIP** $60

Mercedes-Benz and Caravan, 1975-81, truck and trailer in two versions: w/blue No. 285 Mercedes truck and No. 490 Caravan (1975-79); w/brown No. 285 Mercedes and No. 490 Caravan (1980-81); value is for each set, Model No. 24-B

EX $15   **NM** $30   **MIP** $50

Mercedes-Benz Unimog 406, 1970-76, yellow body, red and green front fenders and bumpers, metallic charcoal gray chassis w/olive or tan rear plastic covers, red interior, Model No. 406-B

EX $18   **NM** $25   **MIP** $50

Mercedes-Faun Street Sweeper, 1980, orange body w/light orange or brown figure, red interior, black chassis and unpainted brushing housing and arm castings, Model No. 1117-B

EX $15   **NM** $25   **MIP** $40

(KP Photo by Dr. Douglas Sadecky)

Milk Truck and Trailer, 1962-66, blue and white ERF No. 456 milk truck w/No. 101 trailer and milk churns, shaped wheels, Model No. 21-A

EX $60   **NM** $130   **MIP** $285

Shelvoke and Drewry Garbage Truck, 1979, long, orange or red cab, silver body w/City Sanitation decals, black interior, grille and bumpers, clear windows, Model No. 1116-B

EX $15   **NM** $25   **MIP** $40

Unimog w/Snowplow (Mercedes-Benz), 1971-76, 6" four different body versions, red interior, cab, rear body, fender-plow mounting, lower and charcoal upper chassis, rear fenders, Model No. 1150-A

EX $30   **NM** $45   **MIP** $75

Volkswagen Breakdown Truck, 1966-72, tan, pea green, or white body, red interior and equipment boxes, clear windshield, chrome tools, spare wheels, red VW emblem, no lettering, shaped or cast wheels, Model No. 490-A

EX $50   **NM** $75   **MIP** $135

Volkswagen Pickup, 1964-66, dark yellow or gold body, red interior and rear plastic cover, silver bumpers and headlights, red VW emblem, shaped wheels, Model No. 431-A

EX $45   **NM** $70   **MIP** $140

SPORTS CAR

Alfa Romeo P33 Pininfarina, 1970-74, white body, gold or black spoiler, red seats, Whizz Wheels, Model No. 380-A

EX $16   **NM** $24   **MIP** $45

Austin Healey, 1956-63, blue body w/cream seats, shaped hubs, rare, Model No. 300-A2

EX $100   **NM** $215   **MIP** $350

(KP Photo by Dr. Douglas Sadecky)

Austin-Healey, 1956-63, cream body w/red seats or red body w/cream seats, smooth or shaped wheels, Model No. 300-A1

EX $50   **NM** $80   **MIP** $165

Beach Buggy & Sailboat, 1971-76, purple No. 381 buggy, yellow trailer and red/white boat, Model No. 26-A

EX $20   **NM** $30   **MIP** $55

Bertone Shake Buggy, 1972-74, clear windows, green interior, gold engine, four variations: yellow upper/white lower body or metallic mauve upper/white lower body w/spoked or solid chrome wheels, Model No. 392-A

EX $15   **NM** $22   **MIP** $45

BMC Mini-Cooper Magnifique, 1966-70, metallic blue or olive green body w/working doors, hood and trunk, clear windows and sunroof, cream interior w/folding seats, jewel headlights, cast wheels, plastic tires, Model No. 334-A

EX $34   **NM** $65   **MIP** $135

BMC Mini-Cooper S, 1972-76, bright yellow body, red plastic interior, chrome plastic roof rack w/two spare wheels, clear windshield, one-piece body, silver grille, bumpers, headlights, red taillights, suspension, Whizz Wheels, Model No. 308-A

EX $45   **NM** $65   **MIP** $130

British Leyland Mini 1000, 1976-78, metallic blue body, working doors, black base, clear windows, white interior, silver lights, grille and bumper, Union Jack decal on roof, Whizz Wheels, Model No. 200-B

EX $18   **NM** $27   **MIP** $75

Chevrolet Astro I, 1969-74, dark metallic green/blue body w/working rear door, cream interior w/two passengers, in two versions: gold wheels w/red plastic hubs or Whizz wheels, Model No. 347-A

EX $18   **NM** $40   **MIP** $85

Chevrolet Camaro SS, 1968-70, metallic gold body w/two working doors, black roof and stripes, red interior, take-off wheels, Model No. 338-A

EX $30   **NM** $45   **MIP** $95

Chevrolet Camaro SS, 1972-73, blue or turquoise body w/white stripe, cream interior, working doors, white plastic top, clear windshield, folding seats, silver air intakes, red taillights, black grille and headlights, suspension, Whizz Wheels, Model No. 304-B

EX $30   **NM** $45   **MIP** $95

(KP Photo by Dr. Douglas Sadecky)

Corvette Sting Ray, 1963-68, metallic silver, bronze (rare) or red body, two working headlights, clear windshield, yellow interior, silver hood panels, four rotating jewel headlights, suspension, chrome bumpers, w/spoked or shaped wheels, rubber tires, the swivelling jeweled headlights and spoked wheels added real pizzaz to this cool toy, Model No. 310-A

EX $60   **NM** $90   **MIP** $175

Corvette Sting Ray, 1970-72, metallic green or metallic red body, yellow interior, black working hood, working headlights, clear windshield, amber roof panel, gold dash, chrome grille and bumpers, decals, gray die-cast base, golden jacks, cast wheels, plastic tires, Model No. 300-B

EX $40   **NM** $90   **MIP** $185

Corvette Sting Ray, 1972, either dark metallic blue or metallic mauve-rose body, chrome dash, Whizz Wheels, Model No. 387-A

EX $40   **NM** $65   **MIP** $100

De Tomaso Mangusta, 1969, white upper/light blue lower body/base, black interior, clear windows, silver engine, black grille, amber headlights, red taillights, gray antenna, spare wheel, gold stripes and black logo decal on hood, suspension, removable gray chassis, Model No. 271-A

EX $32   **NM** $48   **MIP** $100

De Tomaso Mangusta, 1970-73, metallic dark green body w/gold stripes and logo on hood, silver lower body, clear front windows, cream interior, amber rear windows and

headlights, gray antenna, spare wheel, Whizz Wheels, Model No. 203-B

EX $26   **NM** $39   **MIP** $65

Ferrari 308GTS, 1982, red or black body w/working rear hood, black interior w/tan seats, movable chrome headlights, detailed engine, Model No. 378-B

EX $15   **NM** $20   **MIP** $35

Ferrari 308GTS Magnum, 1982, red body w/solid chrome wheels, or four spoked wheels, Model No. 298-A

EX $24   **NM** $36   **MIP** $75

Fiat X1/9, 1975-79, metallic light green or silver body w/black roof, trim and interior, two working doors, rear panel, grille, tow hook and bumpers, detailed engine, suspension, chrome wheels, Model No. 314-B

EX $15   **NM** $20   **MIP** $35

Ford Capri, 1970-72, orange-red or dark red body, gold wheels w/red hubs or Whizz Wheels, two working doors, clear windshield and headlights, black interior, folding seats, black grille, silver bumpers, Model No. 311-A

EX $40   **NM** $80   **MIP** $145

Ford Capri 30 S, 1980-81, silver or yellow body, black markings, opening doors and hatchback, Model No. 343-B

EX $15   **NM** $20   **MIP** $35

Ford Cobra Mustang, 1982, white, black, red and blue body and chassis, Mustang decal, Model No. 370-A

EX $15   **NM** $18   **MIP** $30

Ford Cortina GXL, 1970-73, tan or metallic silver blue body, black roof and stripes, red plastic interior, working doors, clear windshield, Model No. 313-A

EX $30   **NM** $45   **MIP** $75

Ford Mustang Fastback, 1965-66, metallic lilac, metallic dark blue, silver or light green body, w/shaped, spoked, or cast wheels, Model No. 320-A

EX $30   **NM** $70   **MIP** $140

(KP Photo by Dr. Douglas Sadecky)

Ford Mustang Fastback, 1965-69, white body w/double red stripe, blue interior, spun, detailed cast, wire or cast alloy wheels, shown in the foreground of this photo is an unused number sheet to help jazz up the model, Model No. 325-A

EX $30   **NM** $70   **MIP** $140

Ford Mustang Mach 1, 1973-76, green upper body, white lower body and base, cream interior, folding seat backs, chrome headlights and rear bumper, Model No. 329-A

EX $25   **NM** $35   **MIP** $60

Ford Sierra, 1982, many body color versions w/plastic interior, working hatch and two doors, clear windows, folding seat back, lifting hatch cover, Model No. 299-A

EX $8   **NM** $15   **MIP** $25

Ford Sierra and Caravan Trailer, 1983, blue #299 Sierra, two-tone blue/white #490 Caravan, Model No. 1-C

EX $15   **NM** $20   **MIP** $35

Ford Thunderbird 1957, 1982, cream body, dark brown, black or orange plastic hardtop, black interior, open hood and trunk, chrome bumpers, Model No. 801-B

EX $10   **NM** $20   **MIP** $35

Ford Thunderbird 1957, 1983, white body, black interior and plastic top, amber windows, white seats, chrome bumpers, headlights and spare wheel cover, Model No. 810-B

EX $10   **NM** $20   **MIP** $35

(KP Photo by Dr. Douglas Sadecky)

Ford Thunderbird Hardtop, 1959-65, light green body, cream roof, clear windows, silver lights, grille and bumpers, red taillights, rubber tires, smooth or shaped wheels, Model No. 214-A

EX $50   **NM** $80   **MIP** $140

(KP Photo by Dr. Douglas Sadecky)

Ford Thunderbird Hardtop-Mechanical, 1959, same as 214-A but w/friction motor and pink body and black roof, this model is fairly hard to find, smooth wheels, Model No. 214-M

EX $70   **NM** $160   **MIP** $395

Ford Thunderbird Roadster, 1959-65, clear windshield, silver seats, lights, grille and bumpers, red taillights, rubber tires, white body, smooth or shaped wheels, Model No. 215-A

EX $50   **NM** $75   **MIP** $130

(KP Photo by Dr. Douglas Sadecky)

Ghia-Fiat 600 Jolly, 1965-66, dark yellow body, red seats, two figures and a dog, clear windshield, silver bumpers and headlights, red taillights, rare, shaped wheels, Model No. 242-A

EX $80   **NM** $175   **MIP** $365

GP Beach Buggy, 1970-76, metallic blue or orange-red body, two surfboards, flower label, Whizz Wheels, Model No. 381-A

EX $15   **NM** $20   **MIP** $35

Iso Grifo 7 Litre, 1970-73, metallic blue body, light blue interior, black hood and stripe, clear windshield, black dash, folding seats, chrome bumpers, Whizz Wheels, Model No. 301-B

EX $15   **NM** $18   **MIP** $30

Jaguar 1952 XK120 Rally, 1983, cream body w/black top and trim, red interior, Rally des Alps and #414 decals, Model No. 803-A

EX $8   **NM** $15   **MIP** $25

(KP Photo by Dr. Douglas Sadecky)

Jaguar E Type, 1962-64, maroon or metallic dark gray body, tan interior, red and clear plastic removable hardtop, clear windshield, folded top, spun hubs, shaped wheels, Model No. 307-A

EX $45   **NM** $65   **MIP** $140

Jaguar E Type 2+2, 1968-69, red or blue body and chassis, working hood, doors and hatch, black interior w/folding seats, copper engine, pipes and suspension, spoked wheels, Model No. 335-A

EX $40   **NM** $60   **MIP** $130

Jaguar E Type 2+2, 1970-76, in five versions: red or yellow w/nonworking doors; or w/V-12 engine in yellow

body or metallic yellow body, Whizz Wheels, Model No. 374-A

EX $35   **NM** $55   **MIP** $90

Jaguar XJ12C, 1974-79, five different metallic versions, working hood and two doors, clear windows, tow hook, chrome bumpers, grille and headlights, Model No. 286-A

EX $10   **NM** $15   **MIP** $45

Jaguar XJS, 1978-81, metallic burgundy body, tan interior, clear windows, working doors, spoked chrome wheels, Model No. 319-C

EX $10   **NM** $15   **MIP** $25

Jaguar XJS-HE Supercat, 1982-83, black body w/silver stripes and trim, red interior, dark red taillights, light gray antenna, no tow hook, clear windshield, Model No. 314-C

EX $8   **NM** $15   **MIP** $25

Jaguar XK120 Hardtop, 1983, red body, black hardtop, working hood and trunk, detailed engine, cream interior, clear windows, chrome wheels, Model No. 803-B

EX $8   **NM** $15   **MIP** $25

Lamborghini Miura P400, 1970-72, w/red or yellow body, working hood, detailed engine, clear windows, jewel headlights, bull figure, Whizz Wheels, Model No. 342-A

EX $40   **NM** $60   **MIP** $100

Lancia Fulvia Zagato, 1967-69, metallic blue body, metallic green or yellow and black body, light blue interior, working hood and doors, folding seats, amber lights, cast wheels, Model No. 332-A

EX $25   **NM** $35   **MIP** $90

Lancia Fulvia Zagato, 1970-72, orange body, black working hood and interior, Whizz Wheels, Model No. 372-A

EX $15   **NM** $25   **MIP** $40

Lotus Elan S2 Hardtop, 1967-68, cream interior w/folding seats and tan dash, working hood, separate chrome chassis, issued in blue body w/white top or red body w/white top, cast wheels, Model No. 319-A

EX $30   **NM** $45   **MIP** $95

Lotus Elite, 1976-78, red body, white interior, two working doors, clear windshield, black dash, hood panel, grille, bumpers, base and tow hook, Model No. 315-C

EX $15   **NM** $18   **MIP** $35

Lotus Elite 22, 1970-75, dark blue body w/silver trim, Whizz Wheels, Model No. 382-B

EX $15   **NM** $18   **MIP** $35

Marcos 3 Litre, 1970-73, working hood, detailed engine, black interior, Marcos label, Whizz Wheels, issued in orange or metallic blue-green, Model No. 377-A

EX $20 **NM** $30 **MIP** $55

Marcos Mantis, 1971-73, metallic red body, opening doors, cream interior and headlights, silver gray lower body base, bumpers, hood panel, spoked wheels, Model No. 312-B

EX $20 **NM** $35 **MIP** $55

(KP Photo by Dr. Douglas Sadecky)

Marcos Volvo 1800 GT, 1966-69, issued w/either white body w/two green stripes or blue body w/two white stripes, plastic interior w/driver, spoked wheels, rubber tires, the blue version is shown here—the common version is white w/racing stripes, Model No. 324-A

EX $25 **NM** $40 **MIP** $100

Mercedes-Benz 300SC Convertible, 1983, black body, black folded top, white interior, folding seat backs, detailed engine, chrome grille and wheels, lights, bumpers, Model No. 806-B

EX $8 **NM** $12 **MIP** $25

Mercedes-Benz 300SC Hardtop, 1983, maroon body, tan top and interior, open hood and trunk, clear windows, folding seat backs, top w/chrome side irons, Model No. 805-B

EX $8 **NM** $15 **MIP** $25

Mercedes-Benz 300SL, 1982, red body and base, tan interior, open hood and two gullwing doors, black dash, detailed engine, clear windows, chrome bumpers, Model No. 802-B

EX $8 **NM** $15 **MIP** $25

Mercedes-Benz 300SL, 1983, silver body, tan interior, black dash, clear windows, open hood and two gullwing doors, detailed engine, chrome bumpers, Model No. 811-B

EX $8 **NM** $15 **MIP** $25

Mercedes-Benz 350SL, 1972-79, white body, spoke wheels or metallic dark blue body solid wheels, pale blue interior, folding seats, detailed engine, Model No. 393-A

EX $15 **NM** $30 **MIP** $60

Mercedes-Benz C-111, 1971-74, orange main body w/black lower and base, black interior, vents, front and rear grilles, silver headlights, red taillights, Whizz Wheels, Model No. 388-A

EX $15 **NM** $20 **MIP** $45

MG Maestro, 1983, yellow body, black trim, opaque black windows, black plastic grille, bumpers, spoiler, trim and battery hatch, clear headlights, AA Service label, Model No. 1009-A

EX $15 **NM** $20 **MIP** $35

MGA, 1957-65, red or metallic green body, cream seats, black dash, clear windshield, silver bumpers, grille and headlights, smooth or shaped wheels, Model No. 302-A

EX $60 **NM** $90 **MIP** $160

MGB GT, 1967-69, dark red body, pale blue interior, opening hatch and two doors, jewel headlights, chrome grille and bumpers, orange taillights, spoked wheels, w/suitcase, Model No. 327-A

EX $50 **NM** $75 **MIP** $110

MGC GT, 1969, bright yellow body and base, black interior, hood and hatch, folding seats, luggage, jewel headlights, red taillights, spoked wheels, Model No. 345-A

EX $50 **NM** $75 **MIP** $135

MGC GT, 1970-73, red body, black hood and base, black interior, opening hatch and two doors, folding seat backs, luggage, orange taillights, Whizz Wheels, Model No. 378-A

EX $50 **NM** $75 **MIP** $125

Mini Camping Set, 1977-78, cream Mini, w/red/blue tent, grille and two figures, Model No. 38-B

EX $25 **NM** $40 **MIP** $75

Mini-Marcos GT850, 1968-70, metallic maroon body, white name and trim decals, cream interior, open hood and doors, clear windows and headlights, Golden Jacks wheels, Model No. 341-A

EX $30 **NM** $45 **MIP** $75

Minissima, 1975-79, cream upper body, metallic lime green lower body w/black stripe centered, black interior, clear windows, headlights, Model No. 288-A

EX $15 **NM** $20 **MIP** $35

Morris Marina 1.8 Coupe, 1971-73, metallic dark red or lime green body, cream interior, working hood and two doors, clear windshield, chrome grille and bumpers, Whizz Wheels, Model No. 306-A

EX $15 **NM** $30 **MIP** $60

Morris Mini-Cooper Deluxe, 1965-68, black body/base, red roof, yellow and black wicker work decals on sides and rear, yellow interior, gray steering wheel, jewel headlights, shaped or cast wheels, Model No. 249-A

EX $45 **NM** $65 **MIP** $140

(KP Photo by Dr. Douglas Sadecky)

Morris Mini-Minor, 1960-71, light blue or red body w/shaped or smooth wheels, plastic interior, silver bumpers, grille and headlights, Model No. 226-A1

EX $40 **NM** $75 **MIP** $160

Morris Mini-Minor, 1960-71, sky blue body w/shaped and/or smooth wheels, plastic interior, silver bumpers, grille and headlights, rare, Model No. 226-A2

EX $100 **NM** $175 **MIP** $350

Morris Mini-Minor, 1972-73, one-piece body in dark or metallic blue or orange body, plastic interior, silver lights, grille and bumpers, red taillights, Whizz Wheels, Model No. 204-B

EX $30 **NM** $45 **MIP** $75

(KP Photo by Dr. Douglas Sadecky)

NSU Sport Prinz, 1963-66, metallic burgundy or maroon body, yellow interior, one-piece body, silver bumpers, headlights and trim, shaped wheels, Model No. 316-A

EX $30 **NM** $45 **MIP** $95

Pontiac Firebird, 1969-72, metallic silver body and base, red interior, black hood, stripes and convertible top, doors open, clear windows, folding seats, Golden Jacks wheels, or Whizz Wheels, Model No. 343-A

EX $50 **NM** $75 **MIP** $125

(KP Photo by Dr. Douglas Sadecky)

Pop Art Mini-Mostest, 1969, light red body and base, yellow interior, jewel headlights, orange taillights, yellow-blue-purple pop art and "Mostest" decals; very rare, this rare Mini is one of the Holy Grails of any Corgi collection, very few of these cars were produced in 1969, possibly due to the fact that psychedelia had already passed its prime, cast wheels, in the U.K. auctions this car is selling for $3,500-$4,000, Model No. 349-A

EX $1000 **NM** $1500 **MIP** $2700

Porsche 917, 1970-76, red or metallic blue, black or gray base, blue or amber tinted windows and headlights, opening rear hood, headlights, Whizz Wheels, Model No. 385-A

EX $15 **NM** $20 **MIP** $45

Porsche 92 Turbo, 1982, black body w/gold trim, yellow interior, four chrome headlights, clear windshield, taillight-license plate decal, opening doors and hatchback, Model No. 310-B

EX $15 **NM** $20 **MIP** $35

Porsche 924, 1980-81, bright orange body, dark red interior, black plastic grille, multicolored stripes, swivel roof spotlight, Model No. 303-C

EX $10 **NM** $15 **MIP** $25

Porsche Targa 911S, 1970-75, metallic blue, silver-blue or green body, black roof w/or w/out stripe, orange interior, opening hood and two doors, chrome engine and bumpers, Whizz Wheels, Model No. 382-A

EX $25 **NM** $35 **MIP** $60

Reliant Bond Bug 700 E.S., 1971-74, bright orange or lime green body, off white seats, black trim, silver headlights, red taillights, Bug label, Model No. 389-A

EX $15 **NM** $25 **MIP** $50

Renault 11 GTL, 1983, light tan or maroon body and base, red interior, opening doors and rear hatch, lifting hatch cover, folding seats, grille, Model No. 384-C

EX $15 **NM** $25 **MIP** $40

Talbot-Matra Rancho, 1981-84, red and black, green and black or white and blue body, working tailgate and hatch, clear windows, plastic interior, black bumpers, grille and tow hook, Model No. 457-B

EX $10 **NM** $15 **MIP** $25

Toyota 2000 GT, 1970-72, metallic dark blue or purple one-piece body, cream interior, red gear shift and antenna,

two red and two amber taillights, Whizz Wheels, Model No. 375-A

EX $15 **NM** $30 **MIP** $55

Triumph TR2, 1956-59, cream one-piece body w/red seats, light green body w/white or cream seats, clear windshield, silver grille, smooth wheels, Model No. 301-A

EX $70 **NM** $105 **MIP** $185

(KP Photo by Dr. Douglas Sadecky)

Triumph TR3, 1960-62, metallic olive or cream one-piece body, red seats, clear windshield, silver grille, bumpers and headlights, smooth or shaped hubs, Model No. 305-A

EX $60 **NM** $90 **MIP** $150

Volkswagen Polo Turbo, 1982, cream body, red interior w/red and orange trim, working hatch and two door castings, clear windshield, black plastic dash, Model No. 309-B

EX $15 **NM** $18 **MIP** $30

TAXI

Austin London Taxi, 1960-65, black body w/yellow plastic interior, w/or w/out driver, shaped or smooth hubs, rubber tires, Model No. 418-A1

EX $36 **NM** $55 **MIP** $100

Austin London Taxi, 1978-83, black body w/two working doors, light brown interior, Whizz Wheels, Model No. 425-A

EX $15 **NM** $20 **MIP** $35

Austin London Taxi/Reissue, 1971-74, updated version w/Whizz Wheels, black or maroon body, Model No. 418-A2

EX $15 **NM** $20 **MIP** $45

Chevrolet Caprice Taxi, 1979-81, orange body w/red interior, white roof sign, Taxi and TWA decals, Model No. 327-B

EX $20 **NM** $30 **MIP** $50

Chevrolet Impala Taxi, 1960-65, light orange body, base w/hexagonal panel under rear axle and smooth wheels, or two raised lines and shaped wheels, one-piece body, clear windows, plastic interior, silver grille, headlights and bumpers; smooth or shaped spun

wheels w/rubber tires, Model No. 221-A

EX $50 **NM** $80 **MIP** $180

(KP Photo by Dr. Douglas Sadecky)

Chevrolet Impala Yellow Cab, 1965-67, red lower body, yellow upper, red interior w/driver, white roof sign, red decals, shaped or cast wheels, Model No. 480-A

EX $80 **NM** $120 **MIP** $200

Ford Sierra Taxi, 1983, cream body, Model No. 451-A

EX $8 **NM** $15 **MIP** $20

Mercedes-Benz 240D Taxi, 1975-80, orange body, orange interior, black roof sign w/red and white Taxi labels, black on door, Model No. 411-B

EX $15 **NM** $18 **MIP** $30

Peugeot 505 STI, 1981-82, red body and base, red interior, blue-red-white Taxi labels, black grille, bumpers, tow hook, chrome headlights and wheels, opening doors, Model No. 373-B

EX $8 **NM** $15 **MIP** $25

Peugeot 505 Taxi, 1983, cream body, red interior, red, white and blue taxi decals, Model No. 450-B

EX $8 **NM** $15 **MIP** $25

Thunderbird Bermuda Taxi, 1962-65, white body w/blue, yellow or green plastic canopy w/red fringe, yellow interior, driver, yellow and black labels, shaped wheels, Model No. 430-A

EX $50 **NM** $75 **MIP** $155

TRAILER

Dropside Trailer, 1957-65, cream body, red chassis in five versions: smooth wheels 1957-61; shaped wheels, 1962-1965; white body, cream or blue chassis; or silver gray body, blue chassis, each, Model No. 100-A

EX $10 **NM** $21 **MIP** $45

Pennyburn Workmen's Trailer, 1968-69, blue body w/working lids, red plastic interior, three plastic tools, cast wheels, plastic tires, Model No. 109-A

EX $15 **NM** $35 **MIP** $55

(KP Photo by Dr. Douglas Sadecky)

Platform Trailer, 1958-64, in five versions: silver body, blue chassis; silver body, yellow chassis; blue body, red chassis; blue body, yellow chassis, smooth or shaped wheels, Model No. 101-A

EX $10   **NM** $20   **MIP** $45

VANS

(KP Photo by Dr. Douglas Sadecky)

Austin Mini Van, 1964-67, metallic deep green body w/two working rear doors, clear windows, shaped wheels, Model No. 450-A

EX $40   **NM** $60   **MIP** $140

(KP Photo by Dr. Douglas Sadecky)

Bedford AA Road Service Van, 1957-62, dark yellow body in two versions: first version w/divided windshield, smooth wheels, 1957-59 shown; single windshield, 1960-62; shaped wheels, Model No. 408-A

EX $50   **NM** $80   **MIP** $175

(KP Photo by Dr. Douglas Sadecky)

Bedford Corgi Toys Van, 1960-62, Corgi Toys decals, w/either yellow body/blue roof or blue body/yellow roof, smooth or shaped wheels, Model No. 422-A2

EX $60   **NM** $105   **MIP** $295

Bedford Corgi Toys Van, 1962, yellow upper/blue lower body, Corgi Toy decals, rare, Model No. 422-A1

EX $200   **NM** $400   **MIP** $800

Bedford Daily Express Van, 1956-59, dark blue body w/white Daily Express decals, divided windshield, smooth wheels, rubber tires, Model No. 403-A

EX $60   **NM** $90   **MIP** $150

(KP Photo by Dr. Douglas Sadecky)

Bedford Dormobile, 1956-62, two versions and several colors: divided windshield w/cream, green or metallic maroon body; or single windshield w/yellow body/blue roof w/shaped or smooth wheels, pictured here; the 404-A on the left and the 404M on the right w/a mechanical friction motor, Model No. 404-A

EX $50   **NM** $75   **MIP** $140

Bedford Dormobile-Mechanical, 1956-59, friction motor, dark metallic red or turquoise body, smooth wheels, Model No. 404M

EX $60   **NM** $90   **MIP** $180

(KP Photo by Dr. Douglas Sadecky)

Bedford Evening Standard Van, 1960-62, black body/silver roof or black lower body/silver upper body and roof, Evening Standard decals, smooth or spun wheels, Model No. 421-A

EX $55   **NM** $80   **MIP** $160

Bedford KLG Van-Mechanical, 1956-59, w/friction motor, red body w/KLG Spark Plugs decals, smooth hubs, Model No. 403M

EX $70   **NM** $125   **MIP** $285

Chevrolet Coca-Cola Van, 1978-80, red body, white trim, w/Coca Cola logos, Model No. 437-B

EX $15   **NM** $20   **MIP** $40

Chevrolet Rough Rider Van, 1977-78, yellow body w/working rear doors, cream interior, amber windows, Rough Rider decals, Model No. 423-B

EX $15   **NM** $18   **MIP** $30

Chevrolet Vantastic Van, 1977-80, off white body w/Vantastic decals, Model No. 431-B

EX $10   **NM** $15   **MIP** $25

Chevrolet Vantastic Van, 1977-80, black body w/Vantastic decals, Model No. 432-A

EX $10   **NM** $15   **MIP** $25

Commer 3/4-Ton Milk Float, 1964-65, white cab w/light blue body, shaped wheels, Model No. 466-A1

EX $32   **NM** $48   **MIP** $95

Commer 3/4-Ton Milk Float, 1970, white cab w/light blue body, w/CO-OP decals, cast wheels, Model No. 466-A2

EX $40   **NM** $80   **MIP** $190

Commer 3/4-Ton Van, 1970-71, either dark blue body w/green roof and Hammonds decals (1971) or white body w/light blue roof and CO-OP labels (1970), both w/cast wheels w/plastic tires, Model No. 462-A

EX $45   **NM** $90   **MIP** $200

Commer Holiday Mini Bus, 1968-69, white upper body w/orange lower body, white interior, clear windshield, silver bumpers, grille and headlights, Holiday Camp Special decal, roof rack, two working rear doors, w/bathing suits packed in the roof luggage, a trip to the shore was inevitable in this mod van, shaped wheels, Model No. 508-A

EX $30   **NM** $75   **MIP** $160

(KP Photo by Dr. Douglas Sadecky)

Commer Mobile Camera Van, 1967-72, metallic blue lower body and roof rack, white upper body, two working rear doors, black camera on gold tripod, cameraman, shaped or cast wheels, Model No. 479-A

EX $60   **NM** $105   **MIP** $225

(KP Photo by Dr. Douglas Sadecky)

Ford Thames Airborne Caravan,
1962-67, three various color versions of body and plastic interior w/table, white blinds, silver bumpers, grille/ headlights, two doors, shaped wheels, Model No. 420-A

EX $35   **NM** $60   **MIP** $130

(KP Photo by Dr. Douglas Sadecky)

Ford Thames Wall's Ice Cream Van,
1965-68, light blue body, cream pillar, chimes, chrome bumpers/grille, no figures, this won. toy played the Wall's Ice Cream musical tune by turning the hand crank on the rear of the van, shaped wheels, Model No. 474-A

EX $65   **NM** $140   **MIP** $325

Ford Wall's Ice Cream Van, 1965-67, light blue body, dark cream pillars, plastic striped rear canopy, white interior, silver bumpers, grille/head-lights, a sidewalk/street display plus a salesman/small boy dress up this non-musical version of the van, shaped wheels, Model No. 447-A

EX $80   **NM** $160   **MIP** $350

Karrier Bantam Two Ton Van, 1957-60, blue body, red chassis and bed, clear windows, smooth wheels, rubber tires, Model No. 455-A

EX $35   **NM** $55   **MIP** $130

(KP Photo by Dr. Douglas Sadecky)

Karrier Butcher Shop, 1960-64, white body, blue roof, butcher shop interior, Home Service labels, in two versions: w/or w/out suspension, smooth or

spun hubs, note the meat hanging in the side windows, Model No. 413-A

EX $65   **NM** $100   **MIP** $185

(KP Photo by Dr. Douglas Sadecky)

Karrier Dairy Van, 1962-64, light blue body w/Drive Safely on Milk decals, white roof, w/either smooth or shaped wheels, Model No. 435-A

EX $50   **NM** $75   **MIP** $195

(KP Photo by Dr. Douglas Sadecky)

Karrier Lucozade Van, 1958-62, yellow body w/gray rear door, Lucozade decals, rubber tires, w/either smooth or shaped wheels, Model No. 411-A

EX $70   **NM** $120   **MIP** $245

(KP Photo by Dr. Douglas Sadecky)

Karrier Mister Softee Ice Cream Van,
1963-66, cream upper, blue lower body/interior, clear wind., sliding side win., Mister Softee decals, figure ins., shaped wheels, Model No. 428-A

EX $90   **NM** $165   **MIP** $295

(KP Photo by Dr. Douglas Sadecky)

Karrier Mobile Canteen, 1965-66, blue body, white interior, amber windows, roof knob rotates figure, working side

panel counter, Joe's Diner label, in this photo, the model on the left has the common "Joe's Diner" label, while the van on the right (471-A2) features the rare Belgian-issued "patates frites" label, shaped wheels, Model No. 471-A1

EX $60   **NM** $90   **MIP** $150

Karrier Mobile Canteen, 1965-66, blue body, white interior, amber windows, roof knob rotates figure, working side panel counter, Patates Frites label, Belgium issue, shaped wheels, Model No. 471-A2

EX $90   **NM** $150   **MIP** $325

Karrier Mobile Grocery, 1957-61, light green body, grocery store interior, red/white Home Service labels, smooth or spun hubs, rubber tires, Model No. 407-A

EX $70   **NM** $110   **MIP** $185

Radio Roadshow Van, 1982, white body, red plastic roof and rear interior, opaque black windows, red-white-black Radio Tele Luxembourg labels, gray plastic loudspeakers and working radio in van, Model No. 1006-A

EX $25   **NM** $35   **MIP** $60

Security Van, 1976-79, black body, blue mesh windows and dome light, yellow/black Security labels, Whizz Wheels, Model No. 424-B

EX $7   **NM** $15   **MIP** $25

Volkswagen Del. Van, 1962-64, white upper and red lower body, plastic red or yellow interior, silver bumpers/ headlights, red VW emblem, shaped wheels, Model No. 433-A

EX $55   **NM** $85   **MIP** $140

Volkswagen Kombi Bus, 1962-66, off-green upper/olive green lower body, red/yellow interior, silver bumpers/ headlights, red VW emblem, shaped wheels, Model No. 434-A

EX $50   **NM** $75   **MIP** $130

(KP Photo by Dr. Douglas Sadecky)

Volkswagen Tobler Van, 1963-67, light blue body, plastic interior, silver bumpers, Trans-o-lite headlights and roof panel, shaped wheels, rubber tires, Model No. 441-A

EX $55   **NM** $85   **MIP** $160

Deluxe Reading

Crusader 101, 30" long; red plastic open convertible, chrome grille and accents, brown plastic driver, battery-operated remote control; 1964
EX $32   **NM** $63   **MIP** $100

Jimmy Jet, 23" wide, flight simulator, firing missiles, battery light, 1960s
EX $125   **NM** $300   **MIP** $650

Johnny Express Cargo Kit, cargo load for Johnny Express trucks, including four pallets, three barrels, one large crate, two mid-sized crates and eight small crates; 1965 and later
EX $4   **NM** $8   **MIP** $18

Johnny Express Conveyor, 17" long, 11" high; red conveyor-loader, hand-cranked belt, four wheels, for use w/Johnny Express tractor-trailers; 1965 and later
EX $6   **NM** $12   **MIP** $18

Johnny Express Crane, 15" long, 9" high; yellow plastic boom, hand-crank action, sold individually or w/Johnny Express Tractor Trailer; 1965-69
EX $6   **NM** $12   **MIP** $35

Johnny Express Danger Security Cones, set of five cones, 2-3/4" high
EX $40   **NM** $60   **MIP** n/a

Johnny Express Dump Body, 24" long; dumping trailer to go on Johnny Express Tractor Trailer; 1965 and later
EX $25   **NM** $35   **MIP** $45

Johnny Express Fork Lift, 9" long, 7" high; red plastic, sold individually or w/larger trucks; 1965 and later
EX $5   **NM** $9   **MIP** $40

Johnny Express Light and Horn, 1960s set
EX $20   **NM** $30   **MIP** $120

Johnny Express Liquid Tanker, 26" long; tanker body, yellow plastic, for Johnny Express Tractor Trailer, w/open top and valve underneath; 1965 and later
EX $35   **NM** $65   **MIP** $75

Johnny Express Pipe Kit, pipe load for Johnny Express Tractor Trailer; 1965 and later
EX $5   **NM** $9   **MIP** $14

Johnny Express Reefer Van, 24" long; van body w/sliding door, yellow plastic, for Johnny express Tractor Trailer; 1965 and later
EX $18   **NM** $36   **MIP** $55

Johnny Express Tire Kit, set including spare tire, working jack, lug wrench, and tire rack for mounting on the Johnny Express Tractor Trailer; 1965 and later
EX $13   **NM** $26   **MIP** $40

Johnny Express Tractor & Trailer Combination, 33" long; motorized red cabover w/yellow bumpers, black tires, gray wheel hubs, and yellow flat-bed trailer; 1965-69
EX $95   **NM** $152   **MIP** $230

Johnny Express Trooper Carrier, 24" long; trooper carrier w/swiveling gun turret, canvas canopy; 1966-67
EX $18   **NM** $36   **MIP** $55

Johnny Service Body Shop, building, tow truck, car wreck, spare parts
EX $10   **NM** $30   **MIP** $55

Johnny Service Car Wash Set, building and car, 1960s
EX $10   **NM** $25   **MIP** $45

Johnny Seven Armored Battalion, No. 3018; includes Halftrack, Jeep, Cannon, Ammunition Trailer and six white plastic figures, originally in box 22" across; 1964-65
EX $32   **NM** $63   **MIP** $95

Johnny Seven Fire Brigade, No. 3034; includes Chief Car, Pumper Truck, Hook and Ladder Truck, and seven plastic firefighter figures, originally in box 24" across; 1964-65
EX $28   **NM** $56   **MIP** $85

Johnny Seven Service Station, No. 3042; includes Tow Truck, car w/replaceable fender, Service Island, and four plastic service attendant figures, originally in box 31-1/8" across; 1964-65
EX $15   **NM** $36   **MIP** $45

Johnny Seven Speed Set, No. 3050; red sports car, boat trailer and white speedboat, originally in box 31-5/8" across; 1964-65
EX $15   **NM** $30   **MIP** $45

Johnny Seven Task Force, boat set w/PT 109 gun boat w/rocket launcher, 12" long, D-109 Destroyer, U.S. Navy Target Float, 10 figures; 1960s
EX $50   **NM** $100   **MIP** $150

Johnny Speed, red plastic remote-control Corvette-type racer, w/white plastic driver, 22" long; 1968-69
EX $18   **NM** $50   **MIP** $70

Johnny Speed Finish Line, cardboard finish line, flag, judges' stand, 1966
EX $3   **NM** $7   **MIP** $12

Johnny Speed Rally Pack, 17-piece Obstacle Course set
EX $5   **NM** $15   **MIP** $35

Mighty Mo Cannon, 9" diameter plastic wheels
EX $40   **NM** $90   **MIP** n/a

Playmobile, 23" wide, 12" high, driving simulator, wipers, steering wheel
EX $150   **NM** $350   **MIP** $650

PT-109, PT boat w/firing missile, 1963
EX $17   **NM** $25   **MIP** $55

Tiger Cannon, w/plastic wall
EX $30   **NM** $70   **MIP** $200

Tiger Joe, 3' long; remote-control plastic tank, three shells, rotating turret; 1965
EX $50   **NM** $150   **MIP** $300

USA Battlewagon, battery-operated battleship w/missiles, torpedos, landing craft, jet airplane, personnel, 1960s
EX $50   **NM** $100   **MIP** $250

Dinky

AIRCRAFT

A.W. Ensign, 1945-49, A.W. Airliner, silver, G-ADSV, Model No. 62P
EX $65   **NM** $145   **MIP** $175

A.W. Ensign, 1945-49, 40-seat airliner, olive/dark green, G-AZCA, Model No. 62x
EX $95   **NM** $275   **MIP** $350

Airspeed Envoy, 1945-49, light transport, red, G-ATMH, Model No. 62m
EX $50   **NM** $125   **MIP** $200

Amiot 370, 1939-48, Model No. 64a
EX $70   **NM** $130   **MIP** $200

Avro Vulcan Delta Wing Bomber, 1955-56, rare, Model No. 749/992
EX $2000 **NM** $4000   **MIP** $6500

Avro York, 1946-59, silver, G-AGJC, Model No. 70a/704
EX $45   **NM** $155   **MIP** $200

Beechcraft C55 Baron, 1968-76, red or white w/yellow props, N555C, Model No. 715
EX $25   **NM** $60   **MIP** $90

Beechcraft S35 Bonanza, 1965-76, orange and yellow, Model No. 710
EX $20   **NM** $55   **MIP** $80

Beechcraft T42A, 1972-77, Model No. 712
EX $30   **NM** $75   **MIP** $110

Bell 47 Police Helicopter, 1974-80, orange and blue, pilot figure, Model No. 732
EX $15   **NM** $30   **MIP** $55

Bloch 220, 1939-48, Model No. 64b
EX $75   **NM** $150   **MIP** $250

Boeing 737, 1970-75, white, Model No. 717
EX $25   **NM** $50   **MIP** $95

Boeing Flying Fortress, 1945-48, "Long Range Bomber" under wings, Model No. 62g
EX $70   **NM** $135   **MIP** $225

Bristol 173 Helicopter, 1956-63, turquoise, red rotors, G-AUXR, Model No. 715
EX $40   **NM** $70   **MIP** $105

Bristol Blenheim, 1945-48, medium bomber; silver, red, and blue roundels, Model No. 62B
EX $35   **NM** $95   **MIP** $150

Bristol Blenheim, 1946-49, Model No. 62B
EX $60   **NM** $85   **MIP** $160

(KP Photo by Dr. Douglas Sadecky)

Bristol Brittania, 1959-65, silver, blue line, CF-CZA. Canadian Pacific shown, Model No. 998
EX $50   **NM** $250   **MIP** $500

(KP Photo by Dr. Douglas Sadecky)

Caravelle S.E. 210, 1959-62, Model No. 60f/891
EX $45   **NM** $170   **MIP** $250

Clipper III Flying Boat, 1945-49, silver, no registration, Model No. 60w
EX $75   **NM** $175   **MIP** $270

D.H. Albatross, 1945-49, four-engine liner; gray, G-ATPV, Model No. 62R
EX $75   **NM** $170   **MIP** $250

(KP Photo by Dr. Douglas Sadecky)

D.H. Comet Airliner, 1954-65, silver wings, G-ALYX, wingspan 7-1/8", Model No. 702/999
EX $45   **NM** $105   **MIP** $225

D.H. Comet Racer, 1946-49, yellow, G-RACE, Model No. 60g
EX $50   **NM** $110   **MIP** $155

D.H. Sea Vixen, 1960-65, gray, white undersides, Model No. 738
EX $30   **NM** $65   **MIP** $110

Dewoitine D338, 1937-46, Model No. 61a/64
EX $225   **NM** $350   **MIP** $550

Empire Flying Boat, 1945-49, silver, G-ADUV, hollowed out front to hull, Model No. 60r
EX $90   **NM** $175   **MIP** $250

Gloster Javelin, 1956-65, green/gray camouflage, wingspan, 3-1/4", Model No. 735
EX $15   **NM** $50   **MIP** $90

(KP Photo)

Gloster Meteor, 1946-62, silver, RAF roundels, Model No. 70e/732
EX $10   **NM** $25   **MIP** $70

Hawker Harrier, 1970-80, Model No. 722
EX $25   **NM** $65   **MIP** $95

Hawker Hunter, 1955-63, green/gray camouflage, Model No. 736
EX $15   **NM** $45   **MIP** $95

Hawker Hurricane, 1945-49, three-blade prop; red, white, and blue roundels, Model No. 62S
EX $40   **NM** $95   **MIP** $130

Hawker Hurricane IIc, 1972-75, Model No. 718
EX $50   **NM** $95   **MIP** $155

Hawker Siddeley HS 125, 1970-75, working landing gear, Model No. 723/728
EX $25   **NM** $50   **MIP** $80

Hawker Tempest II, 1946-55, silver, RAF roundels, flat spinner, Model No. 70b/730
EX $15   **NM** $45   **MIP** $90

Junkers JU87B Stuka, 1969-80, gray w/yellow nose, gray propeller, detachable bomb, Model No. 721
EX $50   **NM** $85   **MIP** $175

Junkers JU89, 1945-49, high speed monoplane, silver, G-ATBK, Model No. 62Y
EX $70   **NM** $160   **MIP** $225

Lockheed P-80 Shooting Star, 1947-62, silver, USAF stars, Model No. 701/733
EX $10   **NM** $20   **MIP** $50

M.D. F-4 Phantom, 1972-77, Model No. 725/727/73
EX $70   **NM** $125   **MIP** $175

ME Bl 109, 1972-76, motorized, Model No. 726
EX $50   **NM** $100   **MIP** $175

Mercury Seaplane, 1949-57, silver, G-AVKW, Model No. 700
EX $40   **NM** $80   **MIP** $120

Mitsubishi A65M Zero, 1975-78, motorized, Model No. 739
EX $75 **NM** $150 **MIP** $225

MRCA Tornado, 1974-76, "Multi-Role Combat Aircraft," camoflauged, Model No. 729
EX $35 **NM** $90 **MIP** $155

Mystere IV, 1957-63, silver, gold wings, Model No. 60a/800
EX $30 **NM** $75 **MIP** $110

Nord Noratlas, 1960-64, Model No. 804
EX $125 **NM** $250 **MIP** $400

P1B Lightning, 1959-69, silver, RAF roundels, Model No. 737
EX $20 **NM** $55 **MIP** $100

Percival Gull, 1945-48, Light Tourer, light green, Model No. 66c
EX $65 **NM** $125 **MIP** $150

Potez 63, 1939-48, Model No. 64c
EX $150 **NM** $250 **MIP** $400

Republic P47 Thunderbolt, 1975-78, motorized, silver, Model No. 734
EX $75 **NM** $175 **MIP** $250

S.E. Caravelle Airliner, 1962-69, Air France, F-BGNY, starboard wing, Model No. 997
EX $70 **NM** $150 **MIP** $280

Sea King Helicopter, 1971-79, motorized, Model No. 724/736
EX $30 **NM** $60 **MIP** $100

SEPCAT Jaguar, 1973-76, Model No. 731
EX $25 **NM** $70 **MIP** $115

Short Shetland Flying Boat, 1947-49, silver, G-AGVD, Model No. 701
EX $200 **NM** $550 **MIP** $750

Sikorsky S58 Helicopter, 1957-61, Model No. 60d/802
EX $45 **NM** $135 **MIP** $190

Spitfire, 1945-49, silver, large canopy, roundels red, white, and blue, Model No. 62A
EX $30 **NM** $75 **MIP** $125

Spitfire II, 1979, chrome, Model No. 700
EX $65 **NM** $165 **MIP** $250

Spitfire Mk II, 1978-80, non-motorized, tan/green camouflage, Model No. 741
EX $40 **NM** $80 **MIP** $135

(KP Photo by Dr. Douglas Sadecky)

Super G Constellation Lockheed, 1956-63, Wingspan, 7-3/4", Model No. 60c/892
EX $90 **NM** $200 **MIP** $450

Supermarine Spitfire II, 1969-78, motorized, Model No. 719
EX $60 **NM** $95 **MIP** $175

Supermarine Swift, 1955-63, green/gray camouflage, Model No. 734
EX $10 **NM** $45 **MIP** $95

Trident Star Fighter, 1970s, French-made, w/firing Stellar missile, Model No. 362
EX $15 **NM** $30 **MIP** $60

Trident Starfighter, Model No. 285
EX $30 **NM** $55 **MIP** $75

Twin Engined Fighter, 1946-55, silver, no registration, Model No. 70d/731
EX $10 **NM** $25 **MIP** $45

Vautour, 1957-63, Model No. 60b/801
EX $30 **NM** $80 **MIP** $125

Vickers Viking, 1947-63, silver, G-AGOL, flat spinners, Model No. 70c/705
EX $20 **NM** $45 **MIP** $70

(KP Photo by Dr. Douglas Sadecky)

Vickers Viscount, 1956-65, British European Airways, G-AOJA, wingspan 5-7/8", Model No. 708
EX $40 **NM** $125 **MIP** $225

Vickers Viscount, 1956-65, Air France, F-BGNL, Model No. 708
EX $40 **NM** $125 **MIP** $225

Viscount, 1957-60, Model No. 60e/803
EX $75 **NM** $125 **MIP** $175

Vulcan Bomber, 1955-56, silver, RAF roundels, rare, Model No. 749/707/99
EX $500 **NM** $1500 **MIP** $4000

Westland Sikorsky Helicopter, 1957-63, red/cream, G-ATWX, Model No. 716
EX $30 **NM** $75 **MIP** $125

BUSES AND TAXIS

(KP Photo)

Austin Taxi w/Driver, 1951-62, pictured here w/Robot Traffic Signal, 773 (which is 2-3/4" H and approx. $35 MIP), Model No. 40H/254
EX $70 **NM** $145 **MIP** $225

Austin/London Taxi, 1972-79, Model No. 284
EX $25 **NM** $35 **MIP** $75

Autobus Parisien, 1948-51, Model No. F29D
EX $80 **NM** $135 **MIP** $220

Autocar Chausson, 1956-60, Model No. F29F/571
EX $70 **NM** $120 **MIP** $200

B.O.A.C. Coach, 1956-63, dark blue and white w/"BOAC" lettering and symbol in yellow, Model No. 283
EX $55 **NM** $80 **MIP** $160

Continental Touring Coach, 1963-66, Model No. 953
EX $135 **NM** $200 **MIP** $400

Ford Vedette Taxi, 1956-59, Model No. F24XT
EX $60 **NM** $95 **MIP** $150

Observation Coach, 1954-60, Model No. 29F/280
EX $50 **NM** $75 **MIP** $140

Peugeot 404 Taxi, 1967-71, Model No. F1400
EX $50 **NM** $75 **MIP** $100

Plymouth Plaza Taxi, 1960-67, Model No. 266
EX $65 **NM** $100 **MIP** $165

(D. Klein Photo)

Plymouth USA Taxi, 1970s, Model
No. 265
EX $15   NM $70   MIP $140

Routemaster Bus, 1964-80, Tern
Shirts, Model No. 289
EX $75   NM $100   MIP $150

Silver Jubilee Bus, 1977, Model No. 297
EX $25   NM $35   MIP $70

CARS

Alfa Romeo Racing Car, 1954-64,
open Grand Prix race car, white
driver, red body, "8" on side, Model
No. 23P/232
EX $40   NM $85   MIP $170

Aston Martin DB3S, 1956-59, green,
gray, or blue body, white driver,
Model No. 104
EX $60   NM $140   MIP $295

Aston Martin DB5, Model No. 110
EX $25   NM $60   MIP $135

Austin 1800 Taxi, Model No. 282
EX $35   NM $70   MIP $100

Austin A105 Saloon, 1958-63, four-
door sedan, two-tone, Model No. 176
EX $75   NM $150   MIP $250

Austin Atlantic Convertible, 1954-58,
blue, Model No. 106/140A
EX $70   NM $145   MIP $240

Austin Healey "100," 1956-59, Model
No. 109
EX $70   NM $150   MIP $300

Austin Mini-Moke, 1967-75, Model
No. 342
EX $20   NM $35   MIP $60

Austin Somerset, 1954-60, four-door
sedan, no interior, Model No. 161
EX $50   NM $100   MIP $225

Austin Somerset Saloon, 1954-60,
red and yellow body, Model No. 161
EX $150   NM $325   MIP $550

Beach Buggy, Model No. 227
EX $5   NM $20   MIP $40

Big Cat Jaguar, Model No. 219
EX $5   NM $12   MIP $40

Bristol 450, 1956-60, racing car,
green, #27 door decals, black tires,
Model No. 163
EX $50   NM $100   MIP $165

Buick Roadmaster, French Dinky,
Model No. 545
EX $70   NM $130   MIP $200

Cabriolet 404 Peugeot Pininfarina,
Model No. 528
EX $25   NM $100   MIP $200

Cadillac 1962, 1962-69, blue, red
interior, white tires, Model No. 147
EX $50   NM $95   MIP $150

Cadillac Eldorado, 1956-62, Model
No. 131
EX $60   NM $95   MIP $155

Chrysler Royal Saloon, note that
some colors are worth more than
values shown, Model No. 39e
EX $45   NM $150   MIP $300

Chrysler Saratoga, 1961-66, Model
No. F550
EX $70   NM $100   MIP $190

Chrysler Simca 1308/GT, Model
No. 11542
EX $25   NM $60   MIP $120

Citroen 2 CV, 1950, 1952-59, 1959-
63, Model No. F535/24T
EX $50   NM $100   MIP $150

Citroen DS-19, 1959-68, Model
No. F522/24C
EX $60   NM $90   MIP $135

Cooper-Bristol Racer, 1954-64, open
cockpit, driver, green body, Model
No. 233
EX $40   NM $90   MIP $175

Corvette Stingray, Model No. 221
EX $10   NM $25   MIP $75

Cunningham C-5R Racer, Model
No. 133
EX $30   NM $75   MIP $150

Custom Land Rover, Model No. 202
EX $5   NM $15   MIP $60

Custom Stingray, Model No. 206
EX $5   NM $15   MIP $75

Customized Freeway Cruiser, Model
No. 390
EX $5   NM $15   MIP $40

Customized Range Rover, Model
No. 203
EX $5   NM $15   MIP $40

De Tomaso-Mangusta, Model No. 137
EX $5   NM $10   MIP $40

DeSoto Diplomat, 1960-63, orange,
Model No. F545
EX $25   NM $85   MIP $160

DeSoto Diplomat, 1960-63, green,
Model No. F545
EX $70   NM $130   MIP $210

DeSoto Fireflite Sedan, 1958-63,
four-door sedan; gray, green, or
blue body, Model No. 192
EX $50   NM $105   MIP $175

(KP Photo)

Dodge Royal Sedan, 1959-64,
available in various color schemes,
Model No. 191
EX $80   NM $120   MIP $160

Estate Car, 1954-61, Model
No. 27D/344
EX $45   NM $70   MIP $115

Ferrari Racer, Model No. 242
EX $15   NM $30   MIP $65

Fiat 1800 Familiale, 1960-63,
silver/gray station wagon, red
interior, Model No. 548
EX $45   NM $90   MIP $160

Ford Capri, 1969-74, Model No. 165
EX $40   NM $90   MIP $130

Ford Consul Corsair, 1963-69, four-
door sedan, white interior, black
tires, Model No. 130
EX $50   NM $100   MIP $150

Ford Cortina Rally Car, 1967-69,
Model No. 212
EX $35   NM $55   MIP $75

Ford Escort, Model No. 168
EX $30   NM $60   MIP $120

Ford Fairlane, Model No. 149
EX $25   NM $50   MIP $125

Ford Fairlane, 1962-66, pale green,
Model No. 148
EX $60   NM $200   MIP $415

Ford Fairlane, 1962-66, South African
issue, bright blue, Model No. 148
EX $150   NM $300   MIP $700

Ford Fordor Sedan, 1954-59, four-
door sedan, pink and blue color
combination rare, Model No. 170
EX $100   NM $200   MIP $300

Ford GT, 1966-74, white race car,
Model No. 215
EX $20   NM $40   MIP $65

Ford Thunderbird, South African
Issue, blue, Model No. F565
EX $120   NM $250   MIP $600

Ford Thunderbird, 1965-67, (Hong
Kong), Model No. 57/005
EX $50   NM $70   MIP $100

Ford Thunderbird Coupe, Model
No. 1419
EX $25   NM $70   MIP $140

Ford Zephyr Saloon, 1956-60, four-
door sedan, two-tone, black tires,
Model No. 162
EX $50   NM $100   MIP $175

Gabriel's Model T Ford, 1969-71,
yellow and black, driver, "Gabriel"
on doors, open cab, spoked wheels,
Model No. 109
EX $25   NM $50   MIP $80

Hesketh 308E Racing Car, Model No. 222
EX $20   NM $40   MIP $75

Hillman Imp, Model No. 138
EX $50   NM $100   MIP $150

Hillman Minx, Model No. 40f
EX $40   NM $90   MIP $150

Hillman Minx, 1958-61, two-tone, black tires, Model No. 175
EX $50   NM $100   MIP $150

Hudson Commodore Sedan, Hi-Line, Model No. 171
EX $50   NM $200   MIP $400

Hudson Commodore Sedan, cream and blue body, Model No. 171
EX $25   NM $100   MIP $295

Hudson Hornet Sedan, yellow and brown, white tires, Model No. 174
EX $25   NM $90   MIP $185

Humber Hawk, 1959-63, two-tone, Model No. 165
EX $30   NM $80   MIP $150

HWM Racer, Model No. 235
EX $25   NM $70   MIP $140

Jaguar 3.4 Saloon, Model No. 195
EX $25   NM $80   MIP $170

Jaguar D-Type, 1957-65, light blue, white driver, racing car, Model No. 238
EX $60   NM $120   MIP $210

Jaguar E Type, 1962-67, Model No. 120
EX $20   NM $60   MIP $140

Jaguar Mark X, 1962-69, opening trunk, two pieces of luggage, Model No. 142
EX $65   NM $130   MIP $225

Jaguar SS 100 Sports Car, Model No. 38f
EX $30   NM $100   MIP $200

Jaguar XK 120, 1954-62, turquoise, cerise, Model No. 157
EX $80   NM $125   MIP $275

Jaguar XK 120, 1954-62, yellow/gray, Model No. 157
EX $80   NM $125   MIP $275

Jaguar XK 120, 1954-62, white, Model No. 157
EX $120   NM $200   MIP $400

(KP Photo by Dr. Douglas Sadecky)

Jaguar XK 120, 1959-62, gray-green, yellow or red, Model No. 157
EX $95   NM $210   MIP $430

Jensen FF, Model No. 188
EX $15   NM $50   MIP $100

Lamborghini Marzal, Model No. 189
EX $10   NM $20   MIP $60

Lotus F1 Racing Car, Model No. 225
EX $10   NM $20   MIP $40

Lotus Racing Car, 1963-70, Model No. 241
EX $20   NM $30   MIP $60

Maserati Race Car, 1954-64, red, green wheels, white driver, open Grand Prix racer, Model No. 231
EX $60   NM $135   MIP $230

Maserati Sport 2000, 1958, red open racer, white driver, black tires, Model No. 22A
EX $75   NM $150   MIP $215

McLaren M8A Can Am Racer, Model No. 223
EX $10   NM $20   MIP $40

Mercedes 190 SL, Model No. 526
EX $25   NM $100   MIP $200

Mercedes-Benz 250SE, 1968-72, metallic blue, white interior, Model No. 160
EX $20   NM $40   MIP $65

Mercedes-Benz C111, Model No. 224
EX $5   NM $20   MIP $50

MG Midget Sports, U.S. issue, Model No. 129
EX $250   NM $450   MIP $750

MG Midget Sports Car, Model No. 108
EX $25   NM $100   MIP $200

MGB Sports Car, Model No. 113
EX $25   NM $60   MIP $130

Morris Oxford, 1954-60, four-door sedan, Model No. 159
EX $100   NM $200   MIP $375

Mustang Fastback, 1965-73, Model No. 161
EX $35   NM $55   MIP $110

Nash Rambler, Model No. 173
EX $20   NM $70   MIP $175

Packard Clipper Sedan, 1958-63, two-tone, white tires, Model No. 180
EX $50   NM $110   MIP $200

Packard Convertible, Model No. 132
EX $25   NM $80   MIP $180

Packard Super 8 Tourer, Model No. 39a
EX $25   NM $80   MIP $180

Panhard PL17, 1960-68, Model No. F547
EX $45   NM $80   MIP $120

Pathe News Camera Car, 1967-70, Model No. 281
EX $70   NM $105   MIP $230

Peugeot 203 Berline Saloon, Model No. 24r
EX $25   NM $100   MIP $200

Peugeot 403 Sedan, 1959-61, Model No. F521/24B
EX $50   NM $90   MIP $135

Peugeot 404, Model No. 553
EX $60   NM $120   MIP $200

Plymouth Belvedere, Model No. 24D
EX $35   NM $150   MIP $300

Plymouth Estate Car, Model No. 27F
EX $20   NM $70   MIP $140

Plymouth Fury Convertible, Model No. 137G
EX $20   NM $60   MIP $120

Plymouth Fury Sports, 1965-69, Model No. 115
EX $35   NM $55   MIP $85

Plymouth Plaza, 1959-63, white roof, harder-to-find version, Model No. 178
EX $25   NM $150   MIP $300

Plymouth Plaza, 1959-63, white tires, Model No. 178
EX $25   NM $75   MIP $150

Plymouth Stock Car, Model No. 201
EX $10   NM $20   MIP $40

Pontiac Parisienne, Model No. 173
EX $20   NM $50   MIP $100

Porsche 356A, 1958-66, cream, black tires, Model No. 182
EX $50   NM $100   MIP $250

Rambler Cross Country Station Wagon, Model No. 193
EX $20   NM $70   MIP $140

Range Rover, 1970-80, copper; opening doors, hood, and trunk, Model No. 192
EX $15   NM $35   MIP $65

Renault Dauphine, 1959-62, Model No. F524/24E
EX $50   NM $80   MIP $125

Rolls Royce Phantom V, Model No. 194
EX n/a   NM n/a   MIP n/a

Rolls Royce Silver Wraith, 1959-62, Model No. 150
EX $30   NM $65   MIP $125

Rolls-Royce, 1946-50, Model No. 30B
EX $65   NM $100   MIP $140

Rolls-Royce Phantom V, 1962-69, Model No. 198
EX $50   **NM** $75   **MIP** $140

Rover 3500, Model No. 180
EX $5   **NM** $20   **MIP** $60

Simca Chambord, 1959, four-door sedan, two-tone, opening doors, Model No. 24K
EX $50   **NM** $100   **MIP** $150

Singer Gazel, 1959-63, four-door sedan, two-tone, black tires, Model No. 168
EX $50   **NM** $100   **MIP** $150

Singer Vogue, 1962-67, Model No. 145
EX $50   **NM** $75   **MIP** $100

Standard Vanguard, 1954-60, Model No. 153
EX $60   **NM** $85   **MIP** $120

Streamline Racer, harder to find and subsequently, worth more, in red finish, Model No. 23s
EX $20   **NM** $40   **MIP** $80

(KP Photo)

Studebaker Commander, 1959-61, another in the line of French-made Dinky toys, Model No. F24Y/540
EX $75   **NM** $95   **MIP** $170

Studebaker Golden Hawk, 1958-63, green or tan body in two-tone, coupe, white tires, Model No. 169
EX $65   **NM** $115   **MIP** $190

Studebaker Land Cruiser, single color body, Model No. 172
EX $35   **NM** $85   **MIP** $160

Studebaker Land Cruiser, two-toned version, harder-to-find, Model No. 172
EX $25   **NM** $160   **MIP** $345

Studebaker President, Model No. 179
EX $25   **NM** $80   **MIP** $185

Sunbeam Alpine, Model No. 107
EX $30   **NM** $80   **MIP** $175

Sunbeam Rapier Saloon, 1958-63, two-tone, black tires, Model No. 166
EX $50   **NM** $100   **MIP** $150

Triumph 1300, 1967-69, light blue body, red interior, Model No. 162
EX $30   **NM** $65   **MIP** $120

Triumph 1800 Saloon, 1954-60, four-door sedan, baseplate changed in 1958, Model No. 40B/151
EX $65   **NM** $140   **MIP** $210

Triumph 2000, Model No. 135
EX $35   **NM** $60   **MIP** $100

Triumph Spitfire, Model No. 114
EX $20   **NM** $75   **MIP** $150

Triumph TR2, 1956-59, salmon/pink body, blue interior, white driver, Model No. 111
EX $100   **NM** $200   **MIP** $315

(KP Photo)

Triumph TR-2, 1957-60, yellow, pictured here w/773 Robot Traffic Signal, Model No. 105
EX $75   **NM** $120   **MIP** $200

Triumph TR-2, 1957-60, gray, Model No. 105
EX $60   **NM** $85   **MIP** $135

Universal Jeep, green or red body, Model No. 405
EX $25   **NM** $60   **MIP** $135

Vanguard, Model No. 40e
EX $25   **NM** $75   **MIP** $150

Vanwall Race Car, Model No. 239
EX $20   **NM** $60   **MIP** $130

Vauxhall, Model No. 151
EX $20   **NM** $50   **MIP** $100

Volkswagen 1300 Sedan, 1965-76, Model No. 129
EX $20   **NM** $35   **MIP** $90

Volkswagen Karmann-Ghia, 1959-64, red, green, or yellow body, Model No. 24M/187
EX $45   **NM** $80   **MIP** $125

Volkswagen VW 1600 TL, Model No. 163
EX $15   **NM** $40   **MIP** $135

Volkswagen VW Beetle, 1956-70, green, gray, white, or blue body, Model No. 181
EX $35   **NM** $70   **MIP** $165

Volvo 1800S, Model No. 116
EX $20   **NM** $60   **MIP** $120

(KP Photo)

Volvo 265 DL Estate, 1977-79, blue, w/opening rear hatch and brown

plastic interior, black grille, Model No. 122
EX $12   **NM** $22   **MIP** $45

VW Porsche 914, Model No. 208
EX $15   **NM** $30   **MIP** $80

CHARACTER & TV RELATED

"Emergency" Rescue Paramedic Truck, Model No. 267
EX $10   **NM** $45   **MIP** $95

Captain Scarlett Spectrum Pursuit Vehicle, 1968-77, fantasy car from Captain Scarlett and the Mysterons show, antenna, rocket, driver, Model No. 104
EX $150   **NM** $325   **MIP** $550

Gabriel's Model T, Model No. 109
EX $30   **NM** $60   **MIP** $100

Galactic War Chariot, 1979-80, Model No. 361
EX $30   **NM** $45   **MIP** $70

Joe's Car, 1969-75, from the TV show, "Joe 90," Model No. 102
EX $55   **NM** $90   **MIP** $140

Klingon Battle Cruiser, 1976-79, Model No. 357
EX $35   **NM** $55   **MIP** $85

Lady Penelope's Fab 1, 1966-76, shocking pink version, rocket and four missiles, Model No. 100
EX $125   **NM** $225   **MIP** $450

Lady Penelope's Fab 1, 1966-76, pink version, rocket and four missiles, Model No. 100
EX $90   **NM** $145   **MIP** $250

Maximum Security Vehicle, 1968-75, fantasy car from Captain Scarlett and the Mysterons show, white, gullwing doors, cargo, Model No. 105
EX $50   **NM** $100   **MIP** $160

(KP Photo by Dr. Douglas Sadecky)

Parsley's Car Morris Oxford, 1970-72, cut-out stand-up figures of Parsley's friends were included for additional play, Model No. 477

EX $65 **NM** $115 **MIP** $145

Prisoner Mini-Moke, 1967-70, from the TV show, "The Prisoner," Model No. 106

EX $100 **NM** $195 **MIP** $325

Renault Sinpar, 1968-71, Model No. F1406

EX $80 **NM** $135 **MIP** $220

Santa Special Model T Ford, 1964-68, Model No. 485

EX $65 **NM** $100 **MIP** $150

Thunderbirds 2 & 4, 1967-73, spaceship from Thunderbirds show, Model No. 101

EX $110 **NM** $275 **MIP** $400

Tiny's Mini-Moke, 1970-73, Model No. 350

EX $60 **NM** $85 **MIP** $120

(KP Photo)

U.S.S. Enterprise, 1980, Model No. 371/803

EX $45 **NM** $85 **MIP** $135

Zygon Marauder, Model No. 368

EX $20 **NM** $40 **MIP** $60

Zygon War Chariot, Model No. 368

EX $12 **NM** $24 **MIP** $45

CONSTRUCTION

Atlas Digger, Model No. 984

EX $30 **NM** $45 **MIP** $70

Aveling Barford Road Roller, 1954-63, green body, red rollers, Model No. 25P/251

EX $30 **NM** $60 **MIP** $110

Bedford Tipper, orange, Model No. 410

EX $20 **NM** $75 **MIP** $150

Blaw Knox Bulldozer, Model No. 561

EX $45 **NM** $75 **MIP** $125

Coles Crane, Model No. 972

EX $20 **NM** $65 **MIP** $185

Coles Hydra Crane Truck 150T, yellow w/black chassis, swivel crane section w/working boom and hook, working levellers, 210mm, Model No. 980

EX $10 **NM** $40 **MIP** $80

Coles Mobile Crane, 1955-66, Model No. 971

EX $40 **NM** $70 **MIP** $140

Conventry Climax Fork Lift, Model No. 401

EX $15 **NM** $40 **MIP** $80

Conveyancer Fork Lift Truck, includes driver and pallet, rear wheels turn, Model No. 404

EX $20 **NM** $40 **MIP** $60

Dinky Shovel Dozer, yellow body, red-roofed cab, rolling treads, lifting and dumping bucket, Model No. 977

EX $10 **NM** $40 **MIP** $80

Dumper Truck, Model No. 382

EX $5 **NM** $10 **MIP** $20

Eaton Yale Articulated Tractor Shovel, Model No. 973

EX $10 **NM** $40 **MIP** $80

(KP Photo)

Euclid Dump Truck, 1955-69, w/lever-operated tipping bed, part of the "Dinky Supertoys" range, Model No. 965

EX $55 **NM** $80 **MIP** $135

Ford D800 Snow Plow Tipper, blue cab w/opening doors, silver tipping section w/opening tailgate, yellow plow raises and lowers, 194mm, Model No. 439

EX $10 **NM** $40 **MIP** $80

Johnson 2-Ton Dumper, yellow open-cab articulated body w/driver, red tipper section, 106mm, Model No. 430

EX $5 **NM** $30 **MIP** $60

Lorry Mounted Concrete Mixer, Model No. 960

EX $10 **NM** $50 **MIP** $125

Michigan 180-111 Tractor Dozer, yellow body, silver engine, red blade raises and lowers, cab is removeable, Model No. 976

EX $10 **NM** $40 **MIP** $80

Muir Hill Dumper Truck, Model No. 962

EX $15 **NM** $30 **MIP** $60

Muir Hill Loader & Trencher, yellow tractor body w/working loader and backhoe, 163mm, Model No. 967

EX $5 **NM** $30 **MIP** $60

Muir Hill Two-Wheel Loader, 1962-78, Model No. 437

EX $30 **NM** $40 **MIP** $60

Richier Road Roller, 1959-69, Model No. F830

EX $75 **NM** $100 **MIP** $150

Road Grader, 1973-75, yellow and red w/swivel blade, Model No. 963

EX $30 **NM** $45 **MIP** $70

Salev Crane, 1959-61, Model No. F595

EX $65 **NM** $100 **MIP** $175

Simca Tipper Dump Truck, French-made, Model No. 33

EX $30 **NM** $90 **MIP** $180

EMERGENCY VEHICLES

Airport Fire Engine, Model No. 263

EX $10 **NM** $40 **MIP** $100

(KP Photo by Dr. Douglas Sadecky)

Airport Fire Tender w/Flashing Light, 1962-69, Model No. 276

EX $32 **NM** $65 **MIP** $145

Ambulance, Model No. 30F

EX $100 **NM** $160 **MIP** $275

Bedford Fire Escape, 1969-74, Model No. 956

EX $75 **NM** $110 **MIP** $195

(KP Photo by Dr. Douglas Sadecky)

Berliet Fire Pumper, included two detachable hose reels as accessories, French-made Dinky toy, Model No. 32E

EX $75 **NM** $95 **MIP** $260

Citroen DS19 Police Car, 1967-70, Model No. F501

EX $75   **NM** $95   **MIP** $175

Citroen Fire Van, 1959-63, Model No. F25D/562

EX $80   **NM** $110   **MIP** $250

Commer Fire Engine, 1955-69, Model No. 955

EX $60   **NM** $85   **MIP** $135

Convoy Rescue Fire Truck, Model No. 384

EX $5   **NM** $20   **MIP** $40

Crash Squad Set, w/Bell Helicopter and Plymouth Police Car, Model No. 299

EX $10   **NM** $40   **MIP** $80

Daimler Ambulance, Model No. 254

EX $15   **NM** $60   **MIP** $140

(KP Photo by Dr. Douglas Sadecky)

Delahaye Fire Truck, 1955-70, the white tires really enhance this French-made Dinky toy, Model No. F32D/899

EX $120   **NM** $225   **MIP** $425

DeSoto USA Police Car, Model No. 258

EX $20   **NM** $60   **MIP** $160

ERF Fire Tender, red body, removable extending escape ladder w/wheels, Model No. 266

EX $15   **NM** $50   **MIP** $100

Fire Chief Land Rover,

EX $35   **NM** $50   **MIP** $85

Fire Chief's Range Rover, red body, opening hood, tailgate and doors, Model No. 195

EX $5   **NM** $30   **MIP** $60

Fire Engine, Model No. 555

EX $25   **NM** $65   **MIP** $140

Ford Escort Panda Police Car, Model No. 270

EX $5   **NM** $30   **MIP** $60

Ford Police Car, 1960s, Model No. F551

EX $50   **NM** $100   **MIP** $150

Ford Transit Ambulance, Model No. 274

EX $5   **NM** $25   **MIP** $50

Ford Transit Fire Appliance, red w/silver ladder and sliding door, Model No. 286

EX $5   **NM** $25   **MIP** $65

Ford Transit Police Accident Unit, Model No. 269

EX $5   **NM** $30   **MIP** $60

Merryweather Marquis Fire Tender, 1970s, red body w/removeable silver ladder and working fire pump, Model No. 285

EX $5   **NM** $50   **MIP** $100

(KP Photo)

Mersey Tunnel Police Land Rover, 1955-61, Model No. 255

EX $60   **NM** $85   **MIP** $145

Motorway Services Ford Transit Van, 1970s, yellow body w/"Motorway Services" on panel sides, Model No. 417

EX $5   **NM** $25   **MIP** $50

Nash Rambler Canadian Fire Chief's Car, Model No. 257

EX $10   **NM** $40   **MIP** $95

Plymouth Police Car, Model No. 244

EX $5   **NM** $30   **MIP** $85

Plymouth Police Car, 1977-80, Model No. 244

EX $25   **NM** $35   **MIP** $50

Police Accident Unit, Model No. 287

EX $5   **NM** $30   **MIP** $60

Police Land Rover, Model No. 277

EX $5   **NM** $30   **MIP** $60

Police Mini Clubman, 1976, light blue w/opening white doors and "Police" on sides, Model No. 255

EX $5   **NM** $30   **MIP** $60

Police Range Rover, white body, orange stripe on sides, opening hood, doors and tailgate, 109mm, Model No. 254

EX $5   **NM** $30   **MIP** $60

Range Rover Ambulance, 1974-78, opening hood, doors and tailgate, includes patient on stretcher, Model No. 268

EX $25   **NM** $35   **MIP** $50

RCMP Ford Fairlane, Model No. 264

EX $20   **NM** $60   **MIP** $160

Rover 3500 Police, Model No. 264

EX $5   **NM** $30   **MIP** $60

Streamlined Fire Engine, 1946-53, red, Merryweather fire engine, ladder, bell, Model No. 25H/25

EX $60   **NM** $85   **MIP** $175

Streamlined Fire Engine, 1954-62, red, Merryweather fire engine, ladder, bell, Model No. 250

EX $35   **NM** $65   **MIP** $140

(KP Photo)

Superior Cadillac Ambulance, 1971-79, opening rear hatch w/plastic patient on stretcher, regular or speed wheels, Model No. 288

EX $15   **NM** $28   **MIP** $135

Superior Criterion Ambulance, 1962-68, white body, Model No. 263

EX $50   **NM** $75   **MIP** $145

(KP Photo by Dr. Douglas Sadecky)

Superior Criterion Ambulance, 1962-68, the roof beacon warning light actually flashed w/the aid of a small battery, light blue metallic lower and white upper body, Model No. 277

EX $40   **NM** $75   **MIP** $160

USA Police Car (Pontiac), Model No. 251

EX $35   **NM** $50   **MIP** $140

Vauxhall Victor Ambulance, 1964-70, Model No. 278
EX $55   NM $85   MIP $165

Volvo Police Car, 1970s, same body as 265 Estate, but in white w/orange stripes, Model No. 243
EX $5   NM $30   MIP $60

FARM

Convoy Farm Truck, Model No. 381
EX $5   NM $15   MIP $30

David Brown Tractor, 1966-75, Model No. 305
EX $60   NM $120   MIP $200

Field Marshall Tractor, 1953, 1954-65, orange, driver, black tires, Model No. 27N/301
EX $60   NM $85   MIP $175

(KP Photo)

Garden Roller, 1948-54, Model No. 105A
EX $15   NM $25   MIP $45

Halesowen Harvest Trailer, 1949-53, 1954-70, Model No. 27B/320
EX $15   NM $35   MIP $75

Hayrake, 1954-71, Model No. 324
EX $30   NM $40   MIP $60

Leyland 384 Tractor, 1971-78, blue w/blue driver, Model No. 308
EX $45   NM $90   MIP $135

Massey-Harris Manure Spreader, 1949-53, 1954-71, red, Model No. 27C/321
EX $25   NM $50   MIP $75

Massey-Harris Tractor, 1948-53, 1954-71, red w/yellow wheels, brown driver to blue, Model No. 27A/300
EX $60   NM $135   MIP $225

Moto-Cart, 1954-60, Model No. 27G/342
EX $35   NM $50   MIP $75

Wheelbarrow, Model No. 382
EX $10   NM $20   MIP $40

MILITARY

105mm U.S. Howitzer w/Crew, Model No. 609
EX $20   NM $40   MIP $80

10-Ton Army Truck, 1954-63, Model No. 622
EX $20   NM $40   MIP $100

155mm Mobile Gun, Model No. 654
EX $25   NM $50   MIP $100

155mm Self-Propelled Gun, French-made toy, Model No. 813
EX $45   NM $90   MIP $180

1-Ton Cargo Truck, Model No. 641
EX $20   NM $40   MIP $80

25-Pounder Field Gun, Model No. 686
EX $20   NM $40   MIP $85

25-Pounder Field Gun w/Tractor and Trailer, Model No. 697
EX $55   NM $110   MIP $220

25-Pounder Gun Trailer, Model No. 687
EX $15   NM $30   MIP $60

(KP Photo)

5.5 Medium Gun, 1955, Model No. 692
EX $15   NM $30   MIP $50

6-Pounder Anti-Tank Gun, Model No. 625
EX $16   NM $32   MIP $65

7.2 Howitzer, Model No. 693
EX $25   NM $50   MIP $100

88mm Gun, Model No. 656
EX $25   NM $50   MIP $100

AEC Arctic Transport w/Helicopter, Model No. 618
EX $50   NM $85   MIP $165

Alvis Scorpion, 1970s, turret fires plastic shells, includes camo netting, 1:40-scale, Model No. 690
EX $10   NM $40   MIP $80

AML Panhard Armored Car, French-made Dinky Toy, Model No. 814
EX $30   NM $60   MIP $120

AMX 13 T Tank, Model No. 801/80c
EX $35   NM $70   MIP $140

(KP Photo)

AMX Bridge Layer, lever extends folding bridge set on AMX tank chassis, Model No. F883
EX $75   NM $110   MIP $225

(KP Photo)

AMX Tank, Model No. F80C/817
EX $50   NM $75   MIP $100

Armored Car, Model No. 670
EX $25   NM $50   MIP $100

Armored Personnel Carrier, Model No. 676
EX $25   NM $50   MIP $100

(KP Photo)

Armoured Command Vehicle, squared, longer bodied six-wheeled vehicle, shown here w/#641 Cargo Truck, Model No. 677
EX $50   NM $85   MIP $140

Army Covered Wagon, Model No. 623
EX $40   NM $85   MIP $150

Army Field Kitchen Cuisine Roulante, trailer w/two boilers/kettles, stovepipe, spare tire, Model No. 823
EX $30   NM $60   MIP $130

Army Jeep, Model No. 669
EX $20   NM $40   MIP $85

Army Water Tanker, Model No. 643
EX $50   NM $75   MIP $120

Austin Champ, Model No. 674
EX $20   NM $40   MIP $80

Austin Covered Truck, Model No. 30SM/625
EX $85   NM $135   MIP $275

Austin Paramoke, includes parachute, vehicle holder and vehicle, Model No. 601
EX $25   NM $35   MIP $50

Bedford Military Truck, Model No. 25WM/60
EX $80   NM $125   MIP $250

Berliet All Terrain 6x6 Truck, green body w/canopy top over bed, shown here w/80E/819 Howitzer, Model No. 80D/818
EX $40   **NM** $80   **MIP** $170

(KP Photo)

Berliet Missile Launcher, green six-wheeled truck w/Nord R20 winged missile, Model No. 620
EX $75   **NM** $100   **MIP** $175

Berliet Tank Transporter, another French-made Dinky Toy, shown here w/Panhard Armored Car, #815, Model No. 890
EX $65   **NM** $130   **MIP** $250

Berliet Wrecker, crane hook and swivel base, six-wheels, Model No. F826
EX $60   **NM** $120   **MIP** $240

Bren Gun Carrier, green body, working treads, two figures included, 1:32-scale, Model No. 622
EX $25   **NM** $45   **MIP** $85

Bren Gun Carrier and Anti-Tank Gun, includes #622 Bren Gun Carrier w/#625 6-pounder anti-tank gun that fires shells, Model No. 619
EX $35   **NM** $65   **MIP** $110

Centurian Tank, 1954-70, rubber or plastic treads, olive drab, Model No. 651
EX $60   **NM** $110   **MIP** $185

Centurion Tank, rolling rubber treads, swivel turret, raising and lowering gun barrel, Model No. 683
EX $45   **NM** $90   **MIP** $180

Chieftain Tank, 1970s, rolling treads, swivel turret, gun barrel that raises and lowers, white numbers on front, gold square emblem on turret, fires shells, 1:50-scale, Model No. 683
EX $15   **NM** $50   **MIP** $100

Commando Jeep, Model No. 612
EX $25   **NM** $35   **MIP** $70

Commando Squad Gift Set, Model No. 303
EX $25   **NM** $70   **MIP** $140

Convoy Army Truck, green body w/removeable plastic canopy, "Available Later" in 1977 catalog, Model No. 687
EX $5   **NM** $20   **MIP** $40

Cooker Trailer, Model No. 151c
EX $25   **NM** $50   **MIP** $100

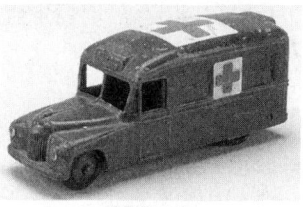

(KP Photo)

Daimler Ambulance, a popular casting available in military and civilian variations, Model No. 30HM/624
EX $80   **NM** $125   **MIP** $250

Dodge Command Car, Model No. F810
EX $40   **NM** $60   **MIP** $90

DUKW Amphibian, green, open-topped body, 1:76-scale, Model No. 681
EX $18   **NM** $55   **MIP** $125

EBR Panhard Armored Car, eight-wheeled vehicle, two sets of road wheels, front and back, w/two sets of floating all-terrain wheels in the center, rotating turret, Model No. 80A/815
EX $30   **NM** $60   **MIP** $120

Ferret Armored Car, green scout car w/open turret, 1:48-scale, Model No. 680
EX $12   **NM** $30   **MIP** $50

Ferret Armoured Car, Model No. 630
EX $25   **NM** $35   **MIP** $50

Field Artillery Tractor, Model No. 688
EX $25   **NM** $50   **MIP** $90

Foden Army Truck, Model No. 668
EX $5   **NM** $30   **MIP** $60

Ford U.S. Army Staff Car, Model No. 170
EX $65   **NM** $130   **MIP** $250

GMC Military Truck, French-made, Model No. 809
EX $50   **NM** $100   **MIP** $225

GMC Tanker, Model No. F823
EX $125   **NM** $250   **MIP** $500

Hanomag Tank Destroyer, German Hanomag half-track w/pivoting anti-tank gun that fires plastic shells, 1:35-scale, Model No. 694
EX $10   **NM** $40   **MIP** $80

Honest John Missile Launcher, green truck w/rubber-band powered plastic missile, Model No. 665
EX $45   **NM** $90   **MIP** $195

Jeep, French-made, Model No. 80b
EX $30   **NM** $60   **MIP** $140

Jeep, Model No. 153a
EX $25   **NM** $50   **MIP** $100

Jeep, Model No. F816
EX $50   **NM** $75   **MIP** $115

Jeep avec Canon de 106, French-made, Model No. 829
EX $25   **NM** $50   **MIP** $100

Jeep Hotchkiss-Willys, French-made, Model No. 816
EX $25   **NM** $50   **MIP** $120

Jeep w/Rocket Launcher, French-made, Model No. 828
EX $35   **NM** $75   **MIP** $160

Land Rover Bomb Disposal Unit, 1976, green Land-Rover Safari w/orange quarter panels, blue dome light and "Explosive Disposal" sign on roof, has opening doors and hood, and includes remote bomb-finding tank, 1:42-scale, Model No. 604

EX $20 **NM** $40 **MIP** $80

Leopard Recovery Tank, 1970s, green w/rolling treads, pivoting boom, raising and lowering blade, West German Bundeswehr markings, 1:50-scale, Model No. 699

EX $15 **NM** $50 **MIP** $100

Leopard Tank, swivel turret, pivoting gun fires plastic shells, West German Army markings, Model No. 692

EX $15 **NM** $50 **MIP** $100

Light Dragon Field Gun Set, Model No. 162

EX $75 **NM** $150 **MIP** $300

Light Dragon Tractor, Model No. 162a

EX $40 **NM** $80 **MIP** $150

Light Tank, green, metal treads, rolling tread wheels, Model No. 152A

EX $50 **NM** $100 **MIP** $200

Light Tank Set, Model No. 152

EX $125 **NM** $250 **MIP** $500

M3 Halftrack, olive body, working treads, AA gun in turret, Model No. 822

EX $50 **NM** $100 **MIP** $225

Medium Artillery Tractor, part of the Dinky Supertoys line, this model was 5-1/2" long, shown here at

bottom w/#622 truck at top, Model No. 689

EX $25 **NM** $50 **MIP** $120

Mercedes-Benz Military Unimog, French-made toy, dark olive w/canopy top over bed, shown here w/823 Field Kitchen trailer, Model No. 821

EX $30 **NM** $60 **MIP** $130

Military Ambulance, Model No. F80F/820

EX $50 **NM** $75 **MIP** $100

Military Ambulance, Red Cross decals and opening rear doors, Model No. 626

EX $25 **NM** $45 **MIP** $75

(KP Photo by Dr. Douglas Sadecky)

Missile Erecting Vehicle, 1959, w/Corporal Missile and Launching Platform, Model No. 666

EX $100 **NM** $155 **MIP** $350

(KP Photo by Dr. Douglas Sadecky)

Missile Servicing Platform, 1960, this vehicle made a nice companion to the 666 Missile Erecting Vehicle, a nicely detailed toy that had a short production run, Model No. 667

EX $95 **NM** $130 **MIP** $270

Obusier 155mm Cannon, French Dinky toy, four-wheeled chassis under cannon, Model No. 80E/819

EX $40 **NM** $80 **MIP** $160

RAF Pressure Refueller, dark gray body, part of the Dinky Supertoys line, 5-1/2" long, shown here (top) in photo w/#661 recovery tractor, Model No. 642

EX $40 **NM** $80 **MIP** $190

(KP Photo)

Reconnaisance Car, this model was produced in pre- and post-war periods, Model No. 152B

EX $40 **NM** $60 **MIP** $120

(KP Photo)

Recovery Tractor, 1957, tow hook has working reel, Model No. 661

EX $60 **NM** $90 **MIP** $165

Scout Car, open-turret scout car, shown here at right w/#601 Austin Para-Moke, 2-5/8", Model No. 673

EX $5 **NM** $40 **MIP** $80

Sinpar 4x4 Military Police Vehicle, Model No. 815

EX $60 **NM** $120 **MIP** $200

Stalwart Load Carrier, Model No. 682

EX $10 **NM** $30 **MIP** $60

Static 88mm Gun w/Crew, includes shells and three soldiers, Model No. 662

EX $10   **NM** $40   **MIP** $80

Stiker Anti-Tank Vehicle, angluar armored vehicle w/five-missile launcher that fires all rockets individually or at once

EX n/a   **NM** n/a   **MIP** n/a

Tank Transporter, Model No. 660

EX $75   **NM** $100   **MIP** $175

Tank Transporter and Centurion Tank, 1956-64, includes #660 Tank Transporter w/#651 Centurion Tank, shown here w/single box for tank, Model No. 698

EX $85   **NM** $165   **MIP** $295

Tank Transporter w/Chieftain Tank, Model No. 616

EX $20   **NM** $60   **MIP** $140

Task Force Set, Model No. 677

EX $20   **NM** $50   **MIP** $100

Three Ton Army Wagon, 1954-63, Model No. 621

EX $50   **NM** $85   **MIP** $125

U.S. Jeep w/105mm Howitzer Set, includes firing gun, Model No. 615

EX $20   **NM** $50   **MIP** $100

VW KDF (Kubelwagen) and PAK Anti-Tank Gun, excellent two-piece set-the gun actually fires plastic shells, Model No. 617

EX $20   **NM** $50   **MIP** $100

MISCELLANEOUS

(KP Photo by Dr. Douglas Sadecky)

Healey Sports Boat on Trailer, 1960-62, Model No. 796

EX $25   **NM** $35   **MIP** $70

Land Rover, 1954-71, red, orange or green open body, plastic driver, Model No. 340

EX $100   **NM** $200   **MIP** $300

Land Rover Trailer, Model No. 341

EX $15   **NM** $40   **MIP** $80

Large Trailer, Model No. 428

EX $15   **NM** $25   **MIP** $50

Loading Ramp for Pullmore Car Transporter, Model No. 994

EX $10   **NM** $20   **MIP** $50

MOTORCYCLES AND CARAVANS

4-Berth Caravan w/Transparent Roof, 1963-69, Model No. 188

EX $25   **NM** $45   **MIP** $85

(KP Photo by Dr. Douglas Sadecky)

A.A. Motorcycle Patrol, 1946-64, the decal on the sidecar changed depending in which country the motorcycle was sold, Model No. 270/44B

EX $30   **NM** $45   **MIP** $95

Caravan, postwar, Model No. 30G

EX $40   **NM** $60   **MIP** $85

Caravan, 1956-64, Model No. 190

EX $30   **NM** $45   **MIP** $70

Caravane Caravelair

EX $75   **NM** $150   **MIP** $250

Police Motorcycle Patrol, 1946-53, Model No. 42B

EX $30   **NM** $45   **MIP** $80

Police Motorcyclist, 1946-48, Model No. 37B

EX $30   **NM** $45   **MIP** $100

Touring Secours Motorcycle Patrol, 1960s, Swiss version, Model No. 271

EX $70   **NM** $110   **MIP** $200

SHIPS

Coastguard Amphibious Missile Launch, white-hulled amphibious vehicle launches missiles from hood, 155mm, Model No. 674

EX $5   **NM** $20   **MIP** $40

Cunard White-Star No 534 Queen Mary, Model No. 52

EX $25   **NM** $50   **MIP** $100

MK 1 Corvette, white, black and gray camo hull, gray conning tower, brown deck, Model No. 671

EX $5   **NM** $20   **MIP** $40

Motor Patrol Boat, Model No. 1050

EX $5   **NM** $20   **MIP** $40

OSA Missile Boat, white and black, fires four missiles, runs on concealed wheels, Model No. 672

EX $5   **NM** $20   **MIP** $40

RAF Air/Sea Rescue Launch, black hull, orange cabin, silver deck, includes figure and raft, Model No. 678

EX $5   **NM** $20   **MIP** $40

Submarine Chaser, 1976, white and gray w/launching depth charges, Model No. 673

EX $5   **NM** $20   **MIP** $40

TRUCKS

A.E.C. Hoynor Transporter, 1969-75, Model No. 974

EX $60   **NM** $90   **MIP** $150

A.E.C. Shell Chemicals Tanker, Model No. 991

EX $35   **NM** $80   **MIP** $230

B.E.V. Truck, 1954-60, Model No. 14A/400

EX $15   **NM** $30   **MIP** $75

Bedford Garbage Truck, brown, Model No. 252

EX $15   **NM** $50   **MIP** $100

Berliet Flat Truck w/Container, French-made, Model No. 34b

EX $30   **NM** $60   **MIP** $125

Berliet Transformer Carrier, 1961-65, Model No. F898

EX $100   **NM** $200   **MIP** $450

Big Bedford, maroon, fawn, Model No. 408/922

EX $80   **NM** $120   **MIP** $200

Big Bedford, blue, yellow, Model No. 408/922

EX $90   **NM** $135   **MIP** $210

Breakdown Lorry, 1954-64, "Dinky Service," white cab, blue boom, Model No. 25x/430

EX $80   **NM** $150   **MIP** $275

Chevrolet El Camino, 1961-68, Model No. 449

EX $35   **NM** $65   **MIP** $160

Citroen Milk Truck, 1961-65, Model No. F586
EX $145   NM $275   MIP $600

Citroen Wrecker, 1959-71, Model No. F35A/582
EX $75   NM $120   MIP $250

Covered Wagon, green, gray, Model No. 25B
EX $65   NM $115   MIP $160

Covered Wagon, Carter Paterson, Model No. 25B
EX $150   NM $300   MIP $750

Dodge Rear Tipping Wagon, Model No. 424
EX $30   NM $60   MIP $100

Electric Articulated Vehicle, Model No. 30W/421
EX $60   NM $85   MIP $120

Esso Gas Tanker, Model No. 442
EX $40   NM $90   MIP $200

(KP Photo)

Foden Diesel 8-Wheel Wagon, 1948-52, dark cab and bed, red fenders and chassis, various color variations were available, pictured here is the first-version cab updated in 1952, part of the Dinky Supertoy range, Model No. 501
EX $160   NM $220   MIP $450

Foden Flat Truck w/Tailboard 1, red/black, Model No. 503/903
EX $140   NM $210   MIP $450

Foden Flat Truck w/Tailboard 1, gray/blue, Model No. 503/903
EX $140   NM $210   MIP $450

Foden Flat Truck w/Tailboard 2, blue/yellow, orange or blue, Model No. 503/903
EX $90   NM $150   MIP $275

Foden Mobilgas Tanker, 1954-57, Model No. 941
EX $145   NM $350   MIP $750

Foden Regent Tanker, Model No. 942
EX $135   NM $300   MIP $550

Fordson Thames Flat Truck, 1954-60, green or red body, flatbed truck, Model No. 422
EX $40   NM $80   MIP $135

Forward Control Wagon, 1948-53, Model No. 25R
EX $45   NM $65   MIP $90

Guy Flat Truck, common variations, Model No. 513
EX $80   NM $250   MIP $500

Guy Flat Truck w/Tailboard, 1956-58, blue cab and chassis, orange flatbed, Model No. 433
EX $75   NM $160   MIP $250

Guy Truck, "Eveready" decals, Model No. 918
EX $80   NM $200   MIP $440

Guy Warrior 4 Ton, 1958-64, Model No. 431
EX $150   NM $270   MIP $700

Guy Warrior Snow Plow, Model No. 958
EX $60   NM $150   MIP $300

Hindle Smart Helecs, Model No. 30w
EX $20   NM $50   MIP $100

Horse Box, Model No. 981
EX $30   NM $60   MIP $160

(KP Photo by Dr. Douglas Sadecky)

Johnston Road Sweeper, 1970s, as the toy was pushed forward, a spring coil turned the brushes in a sweeping motion, Model No. 449/451
EX $25   NM $50   MIP $85

Leland Tanker, Corn Products
EX $700   NM $1200   MIP $3000

Leland Tanker, 1963-69, Shell/BP, Model No. 944
EX $125   NM $215   MIP $480

(KP Photo)

Leyland Cement Wagon, 1956-59, one of Dinky's foreign vehicles, this toy was made in Argentina, Model No. 419/933
EX $90   NM $130   MIP $225

Leyland Comet Lorry, 1956-59, stake truck, gray tires, blue cab and chassis, yellow stakes, Model No. 417
EX $75   NM $190   MIP $325

Leyland Comet Truck, 1956-59, open hauler w/tailgate, gray tires, green cab and chassis, orange bed, Model No. 418
EX $75   NM $150   MIP $225

Leyland Eight-Wheeled Test Chassis, 1964-69, Model No. 936
EX $65   NM $125   MIP $230

Leyland Octapus Flat Truck w/Chassis, 1964-66, Model No. 935
EX $500   NM $1000   MIP $1600

Leyland Octopus Esso Tanker, Model No. 943
EX $100   NM $300   MIP $600

Market Gardeners Wagon, yellow, Model No. 25F
EX $65   NM $115   MIP $160

(KP Photo by Dr. Douglas Sadecky)

McLean Tractor-Trailer, 1961-67, Model No. 948
EX $95   NM $190   MIP $300

Midland Bank, 1966-68, Model No. 280
EX $60   NM $85   MIP $120

(KP Photo)

Mighty Antar w/Propeller, 1959-64, the propeller included w/this model is made of plastic, Model No. 986
EX $150   NM $300   MIP $450

Motor Truck, red, blue, Model No. 22C
EX $150   NM $350   MIP $650

Motor Truck, red, green, blue, Model No. 22C
EX $80   NM $120   MIP $200

National Benzole Tanker, Model No. 443
EX $30   NM $80   MIP $175

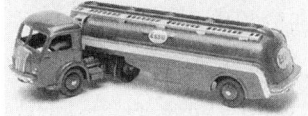

(KP Photo)

Panhard Esso Tanker, 1954-59, French-made, part of the Dinky Supertoys line, Model No. F32C
EX $75 NM $120 MIP $220

Panhard Kodak Semi Trailer, 1952-54, Model No. F32AJ
EX $140 NM $250 MIP $450

Panhard SNCF Semi Trailer, 1954-59, Model No. F32AB
EX $100 NM $165 MIP $280

Petrol Wagon, Power, Model No. 25D
EX $150 NM $300 MIP $500

(KP Photo by Dr. Douglas Sadecky)

Pinder Circus Peugeot and Caravan, 1969-71, the Peugeot and Caravan are the only other vehicles produced in the Pinder Circus livery by Dinky, it would have been interesting to see what other circus vehicles would have been produced had sales been better, French-made, Model No. 882
EX $225 NM $475 MIP $950

(KP Photo by Dr. Douglas Sadecky)

Pinder Circus Truck and Wagon, 1969-71, French-made, this photo shows the animals and decorative labels still in the package, Model No. 881
EX $200 NM $400 MIP $800

Pullmore Car Transporter, light blue, Model No. 583
EX $55 NM $110 MIP $230

(KP Photo by Dr. Douglas Sadecky)

Pullmore Car Transporter w/994 Loading Ramp, 1954-63, the 784 loading ramp cam separately

packaged in the Transporter box and was used to unload the cars, Model No. 982
EX $85 NM $140 MIP $260

Renault Estafette, Model No. F561
EX $50 NM $85 MIP $150

Simca Glass Truck, gray, green, Model No. F33C/579
EX $75 NM $120 MIP $170

Simca Glass Truck, yellow, green, Model No. F33C/579
EX $100 NM $150 MIP $250

Studebaker Mobilgas Tanker, 1954-61, Model No. 440
EX $70 NM $100 MIP $190

Thames Flat Truck, 1951-60, Model No. 422/30R
EX $45 NM $75 MIP $110

(KP Photo by Dr. Douglas Sadecky)

Unic Auto Transporter, 1959-68, French-made, part of the Supertoys line, ramp raises and lowers w/a lever on the side of the trailer, Model No. F39A/984
EX $100 NM $200 MIP $300

Unic Bucket Truck, 1957-65, Model No. F38A/895
EX $75 NM $120 MIP $225

Willeme Log Truck, 1956-71, Model No. F36A/897
EX $75 NM $120 MIP $200

(KP Photo)

Willeme Semi Trailer Truck, 1959-71, another French-made Dinky toy, Model No. F36B/896
EX $95 NM $140 MIP $235

VANS

(KP Photo by Dr. Douglas Sadecky)

ABC-TV Mobile Control Room, 1962-69, a camera and cameraman was also included w/this van, Model No. 987
EX $75 NM $160 MIP $280

(KP Photo by Dr. Douglas Sadecky)

ABC-TV Transmitter Van, 1962-69, this was the companion vehicle to the #987 ABC TV Mobile Control Room, Model No. 988
EX $80 NM $160 MIP $300

Austin Van, 1954-56, Shell/BP, Model No. 470
EX $60 NM $110 MIP $180

Austin Van, 1955-63, Nestle's, Model No. 471
EX $60 NM $110 MIP $180

Austin Van, 1957-60, Raleigh, Model No. 472
EX $60 NM $110 MIP $180

(KP Photo by Dr. Douglas Sadecky)

BBC TV Extending Mast Vehicle, 1959-64, Model No. 969
EX $60 NM $125 MIP $230

(KP Photo by Dr. Douglas Sadecky)

BBC-TV Camera Truck, 1959-64, Model No. 968

EX $60   NM $125   MIP $230

BBC-TV Control Room, 1959-64, Model No. 967

EX $60   NM $125   MIP $230

Bedford 10 cwt Van, Ovaltine, Model No. 481

EX $25   NM $100   MIP $200

Bedford 10 CWT. "Kodak" Van, 1954-56, yellow/orange body, "Kodak Cameras & Film" on sides, Model No. 480

EX $50   NM $125   MIP $220

Bedford AA Van, Model No. 412

EX $5   NM $30   MIP $60

Bedford CA Van, 1956-58, "Dinky Toys" on sides, orange and yellow, Model No. 482

EX $100   NM $275   MIP $425

Bedford Van, 1955-59, Heinz, Model No. 923

EX $100   NM $165   MIP $420

Citroen Breakdown Truck, Model No. 582

EX $100   NM $200   MIP $300

Citroen Cibie Delivery Van, 1960-63, Model No. F561

EX $90   NM $150   MIP $350

Citroen Police Van, Model No. 566

EX $120   NM $240   MIP $360

Electric Dairy Van, Model No. 490

EX $45   NM $90   MIP $130

Ford Transit Van, 1978-80, Model No. 417

EX $15   NM $20   MIP $30

Guy Van, Spratts, Model No. 514

EX $135   NM $300   MIP $625

Guy Van, Lyons, Model No. 514

EX $275   NM $550   MIP $1600

(KP Photo)

Guy Van, Slumberland, Model No. 514

EX $145   NM $315   MIP $625

Mini Minor Van, Joseph Mason Paints, Model No. 274

EX $150   NM $300   MIP $600

Mini Minor Van, 1960s, R.A.C., Model No. 273

EX $65   NM $115   MIP $150

Royal Mail Bedford Van, Model No. 410

EX $5   NM $15   MIP $40

(KP Photo by Dr. Douglas Sadecky)

Royal Mail Van, 1955-61, Model No. 260

EX $50   NM $100   MIP $150

Saviem Race Horse Van, 1969-71, Model No. F571

EX $125   NM $225   MIP $400

Telephone Service Van, Model No. 261

EX $25   NM $75   MIP $150

Trojan Dunlop Van, 1952-57, Model No. 31B/451

EX $70   NM $110   MIP $185

Trojan OXO Van, 1953, dark blue, Model No. 31D

EX $85   NM $210   MIP $320

Doepke

Adams Road Grader, 1948-56,
26" long, yellow, #2006; 1948-56,
Model No. 2006
EX $210 **NM** $295 **MIP** $395

Adams Road Grader, 1948-56,
26" long, orange, #2006; 1948-56,
Model No. 2006
EX $140 **NM** $255 **MIP** $355

**American LaFrance Aerial Ladder
Truck,** 1950-52, 33-1/2" long, red,
#2008; 1950-52, Model No. 2008
EX $245 **NM** $325 **MIP** $400

**American LaFrance Improved Aerial
Ladder Truck,** 1953-56, 33-1/2"
long, red, w/outriggers and cast
aluminum ladder, #2014; 1953-56,
Model No. 2014
EX $290 **NM** $375 **MIP** $450

American LaFrance Pumper, 1951-
56, 19" long, red, #2010; 1951-56,
Model No. 2010
EX $200 **NM** $340 **MIP** $425

**American LaFrance Searchlight
Truck,** 1955-56, white w/battery-
operated search light, #2023; 1955-
56, Model No. 2023
EX $950 **NM** $1650 **MIP** $2100

Barber-Greene Bucket Loader, on
wheels, 22" long, green, #2013,
Model No. 2013
EX $325 **NM** $400 **MIP** $525

Barber-Greene Bucket Loader, 1946-
50, on tracks, 18" tall, early model
w/swivel chute, green, #2001;
1946-50, Model No. 2001
EX $430 **NM** $510 **MIP** $625

Barber-Greene Bucket Loader, 1946-
50, on tracks, 18" tall, later model
w/out swivel chute, green, #2001;
1946-50, Model No. 2001
EX $250 **NM** $375 **MIP** $500

Barber-Greene Bucket Loader, 1946-
50, on tracks; 18" tall, later model
w/out swivel chute, orange, #2001;
1946-50, Model No. 2001
EX $350 **NM** $425 **MIP** $550

Bulldozer, 1952-56, 15" long, yellow,
#2012; 1952-56, Model No. 2012
EX $425 **NM** $550 **MIP** $650

Clark Airport Tractor and Trailers Set,
1954-56, 26-1/2" long; three
pieces: red tractor, green trailer,
yellow trailer, #2015; 1954-56,
Model No. 2015
EX $375 **NM** $450 **MIP** $550

Euclid Truck, 1950-56, 27" long, olive-
green, #2009; 1950-56, Model
No. 2009
EX $250 **NM** $330 **MIP** $425

Euclid Truck, 1950-56, 27" long,
forest green, #2009; 1950-56,
Model No. 2009
EX $225 **NM** $325 **MIP** $400

Euclid Truck, 1950-56, 27" long,
orange, #2009; 1950-56, Model
No. 2009
EX $225 **NM** $300 **MIP** $375

Heiliner Scraper, 1951-56, 29" long,
red, #2011; 1951-56, Model
No. 2011
EX $295 **NM** $300 **MIP** $375

Jaeger Concrete Mixer, 1947-49, 15"
long, yellow w/black drum, #2002;
1947-49, Model No. 2002
EX $225 **NM** $310 **MIP** $450

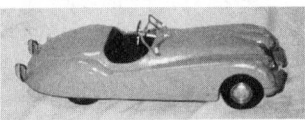

Jaguar, 1955-56, 18" long, kit or built,
light blue or red, #2018; 1955-56,
Model No. 2018
EX $450 **NM** $550 **MIP** $650

MG Auto, 1954-56, 15-1/2" long, kit,
aluminum body; red, yellow, or gray
primer, #2017; 1954-56, Model
No. 2017
EX $300 **NM** $415 **MIP** $490

Unit Crane, 1949-54, 11" long, w/out
boom, orange, w/finger wheel,
#2007; 1949-54, Model No. 2007
EX $200 **NM** $325 **MIP** $400

Unit Crane, 1949-54, 11" long, w/out
boom, orange, w/out finger wheel,
#2007; 1949-54, Model No. 2007
EX $225 **NM** $300 **MIP** $375

Wooldridge Earth Hauler, 1946-49,
25", yellow, #2000; 1946-49, Model
No. 2000
EX $200 **NM** $325 **MIP** $450

Eldon Industries

Air Force Fighter Jet, 21" long; gray plastic jet w/bomb underneath, 1960s
EX $50   **NM** $80   **MIP** $120

Auto Ferry, 16" long, 7" wide, plastic ferry w/retractable ramps, plastic cars
EX $50   **NM** $100   **MIP** n/a

Clipper Ship, 21" long, 15" tall; three masts, two life boats, turning rudder; 1960s
EX $25   **NM** $40   **MIP** $60

Command Cassette Dump Truck, battery-operated, yellow/orange, programmable w/cassettes, 1971
EX $4   **NM** $8   **MIP** $15

Computer Truck, futuristic cab, programming dial, battery-operated movement
EX $5   **NM** $10   **MIP** $18

Dump Truck, 15-3/4" long; white and yellow plastic dump truck w/red dumping body, whitewall tires; mid-1960s
EX $13   **NM** $18   **MIP** $30

Dump Truck, 18" long; Euclid-type dump truck, lever-activated dumping; 1960s
EX $10   **NM** $20   **MIP** $40

Fire Engine Pumper, 16" long; removable ladder, rubber hose, water tank, pump, two firemen, Big Poly series, 1960
EX $35   **NM** $75   **MIP** $200

Fire Pumper Truck, 15" long; red and silver plastic, water-squirting action; 1960s
EX $15   **NM** $25   **MIP** $35

Ford Econoline, two-tone blue plastic, side gate, 1963
EX $12   **NM** $22   **MIP** $35

Hot Road Roadster, 13" long, red plastic, battery-operated wheels, headlights and blower, 1952
EX $20   **NM** $40   **MIP** $70

Hot Rod, 14" long; red plastic body, black seats, chromed engine; early-1960s
EX $12   **NM** $23   **MIP** $35

House Trailer Hauler, 14-1/2" long; light blue tractor and house trailer w/white roof and door; 1950s
EX $20   **NM** $30   **MIP** $45

Navy Convair Tradewinds 880 Seaplane, 20" long, 22" wingspan, w/Jeep, rocket launcher, soldiers
EX $75   **NM** $125   **MIP** n/a

Pick-Up, 15" long, large red plastic truck, black tires, chromed hubs and grille unit, issued individually or w/white trailer to haul the Hot Rod; early 1960s
EX $15   **NM** $30   **MIP** $45

Power Shovel, 8" high cab, 24" long w/shovel extended; red swiveling body, working shovel bucket, gray tread, 1960s
EX $30   **NM** $60   **MIP** $95

Quarry Dump Truck, 30" long, orange 10-wheel tractor-trailer
EX $25   **NM** $35   **MIP** $65

Ride 'Em Fire Engine, 27" long; red plastic riding truck, six wheels, red steering wheel emerging from cab roof, working siren, raising and extending ladder on swivel base, and two hoses; 1960
EX $42   **NM** $83   **MIP** $125

Service Panel Truck, 10" long; yellow plastic body, red opening rear gate and hood, also other colors, removable ladder on roof; 1950s
EX $15   **NM** $24   **MIP** $35

Service Panel Truck, 10" long; opening rear gate and hood, removable ladder on roof; 1950s
EX $10   **NM** $18   **MIP** $28

Touch Command Car, 14" long; red plastic Corvette, battery-operated, remote-control w/air pressure; 1968-69
EX $6   **NM** $12   **MIP** $18

Touch Command Corvette Sting Ray, 13-1/2" long; red car w/darkened windows; battery-operated, six-way remote control; 1960s
EX $8   **NM** $14   **MIP** $25

Tow Truck, 21" long; white hard "Fortiflex" plastic, silver plastic winch and rails, red flasher on cab roof, silver grille unit and rear tow bar, six black tires, two metal cranks control boom height and hauling hood; 1960s
EX $25   **NM** $50   **MIP** $75

Tow Truck, green/white cab, yellow towing body, 1962
EX $12   **NM** $23   **MIP** $35

Truck Transport Set, truck hauler in red hard "Fortiflex" plastic, tractor-trailer, black tires, load of small plastic dump, stake, pickup and wrecker trucks; 1960
EX $30   **NM** $60   **MIP** $90

USAF F-100 Jet, 12-1/2" long; retractable landing gear, firing missile, 1970s
EX $20   **NM** $50   **MIP** n/a

USAF Missile Launcher Truck and Trailer, 20" long; "USAF" on cab doors, antenna on roof; flatbed w/white and red platform w/trigger for launching white missile w/red nose cone, Air Force emblems on missile's wings; 1950s
EX $100   **NM** $225   **MIP** $300

Water Tanker Truck, 10" long; red soft plastic cab and chassis, white plastic tanker body and tire/axle units, opening at tank top for water and seven-hold trough in rear for dampening roads; 1960
EX $15   **NM** $30   **MIP** $45

Gay Toys

AMC Pacer, 5" long; whitewall tires
EX $5   NM $10   MIP $15

Amphicat, 8-1/2" long; polyethylene, six-wheel all-terrain vehicle, snap-in interior, steering gear, chromed front, and rear lights; early 1970s
EX $3   NM $7   MIP $10

Back-Hoe Truck, 14" long; cabover w/snap-in grille and steering wheel, oversize tires, lever-controlled hoe; early 1970s
EX $3   NM $7   MIP $10

Baha Jeep, polyethylene Jeepster w/balloon tires, chromed hubs, hood decal; early 1970s
EX $2   NM $4   MIP $7

Beach Buggy, 8-1/2" long; polyethylene Jeep w/striped canopy, flower decal on hood, chromed headlights, bumpers, and wheel hubs; early-1970s
EX $8   NM $18   MIP $25

Big Mac Earth Scraper, 14" long; two-piece yellow scraper w/lever-controlled action, swiveling tractor w/chromed grille; early-1970s
EX $6   NM $12   MIP $18

Camper Trailer, 9" long, yellow plastic
EX $21   NM $35   MIP n/a

Camper Van, 7" long; red van, skylight roof, white interior, whitewall tires
EX $3   NM $6   MIP $9

Cement Mixer, 14" long; cabover w/interior detail and snap-in grille and steering wheel, revolving and dumping mixing drum, oversize tires, polyethylene; early-1970s
EX $4   NM $8   MIP $12

Chevy Camaro, 7" long, plastic
EX $5   NM $8   MIP $15

Chevy Corvette, No. 7951; 18" long; T-roof, white interior, chrome hubs; 1970s
EX $5   NM $8   MIP $15

Chevy Corvette Convertible, 7-1/2" long; various colors, white interior, white-line tires, 1970s styling
EX $3   NM $6   MIP $10

Chevy Impala Highway Patrol, 11" long, plastic, whitewalls
EX $9   NM $15   MIP n/a

Chevy Luv Truck, 10-1/2" long, orange, yellow rollbar, 1970s-80s
EX $11   NM $18   MIP $24

Cobra Mustang, 10-1/2" long, plastic, "Cobra" decal on hood, 1984
EX $12   NM $24   MIP n/a

Dirt Demon, 18" long; pickup w/rollbar; 1970s
EX $5   NM $8   MIP $15

Dukes of Hazzard's General Lee, Dodge Charger, 12" long; 1980s
EX $12   NM $18   MIP $25

Dump Truck, 9" long, Mack-type cab w/heavy-duty dump body, three axles
EX $3   NM $7   MIP $10

Dump Truck, 7-3/4" long; Ford-type cab, heavy-duty dumping body, white-line tires, 1970s
EX $2   NM $4   MIP $8

Dump Truck, 20-1/2" long; Euclid-type, yellow body, black tires w/white hubs; 1970s
EX $10   NM $15   MIP $20

Dump Truck, 12" long; cabover w/interior details, chromed hubs and grille, hinged dump, oversize tires, polyethylene; late-1960s-70s
EX $2   NM $4   MIP $7

Dune Buggy, 8"; polyethylene dune buggy, contrasting canopy, w/chromed headlights, rear motor, and hub caps; early-1970s
EX $10   NM $18   MIP $22

Farm Tractor, 11" long; red and white body, white scoop, black tires; 1970s
EX $9   NM $14   MIP $20

Fire Ladder Truck, 9" long; red plastic w/white ladder base and yellow ladder, black tires, cabover design, separate grille; 1960s
EX $4   NM $8   MIP $15

Fire Truck, 4" long, Ford, 1960s
EX $4   NM $8   MIP $15

Fire Truck, 12" long; cabover design, oversized balloon tires, snap-in grille, steering wheel, hose reel and nozzle; late-1960s-70s
EX $3   NM $7   MIP $10

Ford Bronco, 7" long; pickup, opening tail gate, Bronco logo, white-line tires
EX $30   NM $70   MIP n/a

Ford Bronco, 12" long; black tires w/white hubs, white grille and roof, tan/yellow body and interior; 1970s
EX $50   NM $100   MIP $250

Ford Bronco 4X4 Trail Buster, 12" long, black and yellow, 1970
EX $30   NM $50   MIP n/a

Ford GT, 10" long; polyethylene, clear windshields, chromed motor visible through rear panel, gold lettering, chromed wheel details, early-1970s
EX $15   NM $25   MIP n/a

Ford Mustang, 4" long, one-piece toy, 1960s
EX $4   NM $8   MIP n/a

Ford Mustang Racecar, 10" long, red plastic w/white interior, "Ford" sticker, "33" on sides and hood, 1970s
EX $8   NM $15   MIP n/a

Ford Pinto, orange w/"The Dukes of Hazzard" style Confederate flag; 1980s
EX $7   NM $13   MIP $20

Ford Pinto, 10-1/2" long; no decals, black tires w/white hubs; 1970s
EX $10   NM $18   MIP $24

Ford Ranchero, 4" long; 1960s
EX $2   NM $4   MIP $7

Ford Street "T," polyethylene hot rod Model T coupe, chromed motor and wheel discs, headlights and front bumper; early-1970s
EX $4   NM $15   MIP $22

Gaymaster Dragster, 7-1/2" long, exposed engine and pipes, black body w/white roof, 1960s-70s
EX $20   NM $35   MIP n/a

Gulf Oil Truck, 7" long, cabover, "Gulf" sticker
EX $4   NM $8   MIP $12

Hardee's NASCAR No. 28, 11-3/4" long; Cale Yarborough, 1980s
EX $10   NM $15   MIP $22

Hardee's Speedway Crew, set w/12" orange wrecker and 12" white No. 28 "Cale Yarborough" stock car, in open window box
EX $12   NM $20   MIP $35

Harry Gant Stock Car, 12" long, white w/decals
EX $10   NM $17   MIP n/a

Hot Rod, 6-1/2" long, red body, white engine w/pipes, black wheels
EX $5   NM $10   MIP n/a

Indy Racer, 6" long, "Gay Special '5'" sticker, plastic driver
EX $5   NM $10   MIP $16

Jeep w/Canopy, 8-1/2" long, blue body w/white interior, striped canopy, silver-hubbed black tires, also other color combinations
EX $5   NM $10   MIP n/a

Maverick, race car with lift-off body, roll bars; early-1970s
EX $4   NM $8   MIP $12

Mercury Cougar, 11" long; chromed bumpers, clear windshields, chrome-detailed tires, in red, blue or green polyethylene; early-1970s
EX $5   NM $10   MIP $15

Mountain Dew Stock Car, 16" long, "Darrell Waltrip," early-1980s
EX $12 **NM** $25 **MIP** n/a

Mustang, 4" long, simple single-mold toy, 60 or 70s
EX $1 **NM** $3 **MIP** n/a

Police Three-Wheeler, 8" long, "Gay Police," red and white, siren light, steering wheel
EX $15 **NM** $30 **MIP** n/a

Puddle Jumper, polyethylene open-top dune buggy, "Puddle 77 Jumper" on hood, roll bar, chromed headlights, rear motor and wheel hubs; early 1970s
EX $3 **NM** $7 **MIP** $10

Pumper, 4" long; single-mold pumper truck, black plastic wheel-axle units; 1960s
EX $3 **NM** $5 **MIP** $8

Race Team Set, "R&D Speed Shop" Oldsmobile station wagon towing green racer on trailer, 1960s
EX $14 **NM** $25 **MIP** $35

Richard Petty Racer, 11" long; blue plastic, white-hub tires, "STP" and "Richard Petty 43"
EX $20 **NM** $30 **MIP** $40

Road Runner Camper, tan camper, white top and interior, black tires w/white hubs; 1970s
EX $10 **NM** $17 **MIP** $25

Rodeo Riders, 22" long; orange/yellow tractor-trailer w/two black horses
EX $7 **NM** $12 **MIP** $16

Rough Riders Pickup Truck and Trailer, 11-1/2" truck, 7" trailer; "Rough Riders" stickers on truck and horse-trailer sides, truck tires black w/white hubs, plastic horse
EX $10 **NM** $15 **MIP** $22

School Bus, 9" long; "Gay School Bus" on sides, chrome grille, yellow body; 1960s
EX $10 **NM** $18 **MIP** $25

School Bus, 9" long "School Bus" on sides, chrome grille, yellow body; 1960s
EX $8 **NM** $12 **MIP** $20

School Bus Set, bus w/"School Bus" on sides, chromed grille, issued w/a child shelter, stop sign and three school figures; early-1970s
EX $10 **NM** $15 **MIP** $25

Sports Cycle, red plastic, blue wheels and seats, 1970s
EX $20 **NM** $35 **MIP** $55

Texaco Star Racer, 17-3/4" long; white plastic open-cockpit racer, "Texaco Star" on sides and spoiler; 1970s
EX $5 **NM** $10 **MIP** $15

Tractor Loader, farm tractor w/lever-controlled front scoop and lifting and dumping action; early-1970s
EX $4 **NM** $8 **MIP** $12

Triumph Wedge TR7, 15"; convertible, "The Wedge" decal, Goodyear tires, 1970s
EX $25 **NM** $55 **MIP** n/a

U.S. Air Force Fighter, 13-1/2" long; 12" wingspan; Army-green single prop airplane, clear plastic cockpit cover
EX $3 **NM** $6 **MIP** $10

U.S. Mail Three-Wheeler, 7" long, 6" tall, blue and white, steering wheel turns front wheel, removalbe rear compartment cover
EX $20 **NM** $35 **MIP** n/a

VW Bug, 11" long, black tires w/white wheels, red body, white chassis
EX $8 **NM** $15 **MIP** n/a

VW Camper, 6-1/2" long; "Gay Camper" decals on doors, opening side doors, interior plastic table and seats; early-1960s
EX $25 **NM** $35 **MIP** $45

VW Hot Rod, 9" long; yellow body, exposed white rear engine, single driver seat, white-hub tires
EX $4 **NM** $8 **MIP** $15

Wrecker, cabover w/interior design, snap-in grille, working crane w/tow rope, oversize tires, polyethylene; early-1970s
EX $3 **NM** $7 **MIP** $10

Wrecker, 7" long, blue cab/chassis, yellow body
EX $4 **NM** $8 **MIP** n/a

Yard Tractor, 6-1/4" long tractor alone; polyethylene tractor, plow, mower, wagon, w/snap-in hood, steering wheel, seats and wheel hubs; early-1970s
EX $2 **NM** $4 **MIP** $8

YF-12A Flying Sword Interceptor, red USAF jet, blue plastic figures, missiles, 1960s
EX $20 **NM** $35 **MIP** $55

Hot Wheels Redlines

'31 Doozie, 1977, orange, tan top, brown fenders, Model No. 9649
EX $25   **NM** $40   **MIP** $75

'56 Hi Tail Hauler, 1977, orange, redline, two black plastic motorcycles, Model No. 9647
EX $30   **NM** $50   **MIP** $85

'57 Chevy, 1977, red, yellow and white tampo, "57 Chevy," Model No. 9638
EX $40   **NM** $80   **MIP** $110

Alive '55, 1973, assorted, Model No. 6968
EX $135   **NM** $155   **MIP** $550

Alive '55, 1974, blue, Model No. 6968
EX $70   **NM** $175   **MIP** $460

Alive '55, 1974, green, Model No. 6968
EX $35   **NM** $75   **MIP** $150

Alive '55, 1977, chrome, redlines, green and yellow tampo, Model No. 9210
EX $30   **NM** $50   **MIP** $70

(KP Photo)

Ambulance, 1970, met. blue, white back w/red cross and blue light on top, "Heavyweights" series, Model No. 6451
EX $30   **NM** $60   **MIP** $100

(KP Photo)

American Hauler, 1976, blue cab, white plastic box, American-flag-style tampo, "American Hauler," Model No. 9118
EX $15   **NM** $30   **MIP** $50

(KP Photo)

American Tipper, 1976, red metal cab, white plastic tipper bed, American flag tampo, "American Tipper," Model No. 9089
EX $30   **NM** $50   **MIP** $85

(KP Photo)

American Victory, 1975, light blue, American flag tampo, "9" on sides, silver interior, exposed silver engine, Model No. 7662
EX $15   **NM** $25   **MIP** $50

(KP Photo)

AMX/2, 1971, dark met. red, rear engine covers lift up, metal chassis, Model No. 6460
EX $40   **NM** $55   **MIP** $150

Aw Shoot, 1976, tank, olive drab, Model No. 9243
EX $20   **NM** $40   **MIP** $65

(KP Photo)

Backwoods Bomb, 1975, blue body w/green and yellow tampo on sides, plastic camper shell on bed, "Keep On Camping," silver base, Model No. 7670
EX $30   **NM** $70   **MIP** $120

Baja Bruiser, 1974, orange, stars and stripes side tampo, "Firestone," "Cragar," and "Ford," Model No. 8258
EX $20   **NM** $40   **MIP** $120

Baja Bruiser, 1974, yellow, blue in tampo, Model No. 8258
EX $175   **NM** $550   **MIP** $1200

Baja Bruiser, 1974, yellow, magenta in tampo, Model No. 8258
EX $175   **NM** $450   **MIP** $1200

Baja Bruiser, 1976, light green, Model No. 8258
EX $200   **NM** $700   **MIP** $1000

Baja Bruiser, 1977, blue, redline or blackwall, Model No. 8258
EX $20   **NM** $40   **MIP** $70

(KP Photo)

Beatnik Bandit, 1968, met. blue, tan interior, clear bubble, exposed engine, Model No. 6217
EX $20   **NM** $30   **MIP** $90

(KP Photo)

Boss Hoss, 1970, chrome, black stripes on top, Club Kit, black number "9" in white circle on side, Model No. 6499
EX $80   **NM** $100   **MIP** $350

(KP Photo)

Boss Hoss, 1971, met. green, black "8" in white circle on side, exposed engine, Model No. 6406
EX $75   **NM** $150   **MIP** $325

(KP Photo)

Brabham-Repco F1, 1969, met. green, long tailpipes on silver engine, black "1" in white circle on side, blue-tinted windows, Model No. 6264

EX $10   **NM** $30   **MIP** $80

(KP Photo)

Breakaway Bucket, 1974, dark blue, orange tampo w/yellow designs, Model No. 8262

EX $45   **NM** $125   **MIP** $175

(KP Photo)

Bugeye, 1971, red, black interior, hood lifts to expose engine, Model No. 6178

EX $15   **NM** $30   **MIP** $120

Bugeye, 1971, magenta, white interior, Model No. 6178

EX $20   **NM** $35   **MIP** $120

Buzz Off, 1973, assorted, Model No. 6976

EX $115   **NM** $175   **MIP** $500

Buzz Off, 1974, blue, Model No. 6976

EX $30   **NM** $45   **MIP** $115

Buzz Off, 1977, gold plated, redline or blackwall, Model No. 6976

EX $15   **NM** $30   **MIP** $50

(KP Photo)

Bye-Focal, 1971, met. green, opening hood, bifocals and "Bye Focal" on side, Model No. 6187

EX $50   **NM** $140   **MIP** $375

Carabo, 1970, assorted met. colors, opening doors, black painted chassis, Model No. 6420

EX $20   **NM** $60   **MIP** $140

(KP Photo)

Carabo, 1974, light green w/blue and red stripes, opening gull-wing style doors, Model No. 7617

EX $30   **NM** $65   **MIP** $120

Carabo, 1974, yellow, Model No. 7617

EX $275   **NM** $850   **MIP** $1300

(KP Photo)

Cement Mixer, 1970, "Heavyweights" series, met. green, orange plastic cement mixer, Hot Wheels logo, Model No. 6452

EX $20   **NM** $60   **MIP** $120

(KP Photo)

Chaparral 2G, 1969, white, back opens to expose metal engine, Model No. 6256

EX $30   **NM** $40   **MIP** $150

Chevy Monza, 1977, chrome, yellow and black tampo, Model No. 9202

EX $15   **NM** $30   **MIP** $40

Chevy Monza 2+2, 1975, light green enamel w/"Monza" rally stripes on hood and roof, black plastic interior, Model No. 7671

EX $125   **NM** $350   **MIP** $800

Chevy Monza 2+2, 1975, orange enamel finish, "Monza" rally stripes on hood and roof, Model No. 7671

EX $20   **NM** $40   **MIP** $100

Chief's Special Cruiser, 1975, red, redline, Model No. 7665

EX $30   **NM** $50   **MIP** $100

(KP Photo)

Classic '31 Ford Woody, 1969, met. red, metal engine, Model No. 6251

EX $35   **NM** $75   **MIP** $150

(KP Photo)

Classic '32 Ford Vicky, 1969, met. gold, metal engine, black roof, Model No. 6250

EX $30   **NM** $65   **MIP** $150

(KP Photo)

Classic '36 Ford Coupe, 1969, red, opening back reveals rumble seat, black roof, Model No. 6253

EX $45   **NM** $90   **MIP** $190

Classic '36 Ford Coupe, 1969, blue, Model No. 6253

EX $25   **NM** $50   **MIP** $100

(KP Photo)

Classic '57 T-Bird, 1969, met. orange, hood opens to reveal engine, Model No. 6252
EX $30   **NM** $65   **MIP** $190

(KP Photo)

Classic Cord, 1971, met. green, opening hood, detachable plastic soft-top roof (often missing), Model No. 6472
EX $250 **NM** $500   **MIP** $1500

(KP Photo)

Classic Nomad, 1970, met. aqua, opening hood, metal engine, Model No. 6404
EX $30   **NM** $60   **MIP** $125

(KP Photo)

Cockney Cab, 1971, blue, British flag tampo on rear, "Cockney Cab," Model No. 6466
EX $30   **NM** $80   **MIP** $150

(KP Photo)

Cool One, 1976, magenta body, "Cool One" letting on front, lightning tampo on body, available as blackwalls variation, Model No. 9120
EX $30   **NM** $60   **MIP** $80

Corvette Stingray, 1976, red body, red, white, yellow and blue tampo, Model No. 9241
EX $30   **NM** $60   **MIP** $120

(KP Photo)

Custom AMX, 1969, met. green, hood lifts to expose engine, Model No. 6267
EX $45   **NM** $65   **MIP** $275

(KP Photo)

Custom Barracuda, 1968, met. green, hood opens to reveal metal engine, Model No. 6211
EX $40   **NM** $150   **MIP** $550

(KP Photo)

Custom Camaro, 1968, met. orange, black roof, opening hood, Model No. 6208
EX $75   **NM** $200   **MIP** $600

Custom Camaro, 1968, white enamel--an almost mythical car, and apparently none "in-pack," Model No. 6208
EX $1000 **NM** $2000   **MIP** n/a

(KP Photo)

Custom Charger, 1969, assorted body colors, white plastic interior, opening hood, Model No. 6268
EX $75   **NM** $150   **MIP** $700

(KP Photo)

Custom Continental Mark III, 1969, met. pink, opening hood, metal engine, Model No. 6266
EX $75   **NM** $150   **MIP** $450

(KP Photo)

Custom Corvette, 1968, met. orange, opening hood, assorted interior color, Model No. 6215
EX $35   **NM** $125   **MIP** $350

(KP Photo)

Custom Cougar, 1968, met. green, opening hood, black interior, Model No. 6205
EX $35   **NM** $125   **MIP** $475

(KP Photo)

Custom Eldorado, 1968, met. green, black interior, black top, opening hood, Model No. 6218
EX $15   **NM** $65   **MIP** $250

(KP Photo)

Custom Firebird, 1968, met. orange, metal engine, opening hood, Model No. 6212
EX $30   **NM** $80   **MIP** $325

(KP Photo)

Custom Fleetside, 1968, met. purple, black roof, opening bed cover, Model No. 6213

EX $50   **NM** $100   **MIP** $300

(KP Photo)

Custom Mustang, 1968, assorted, Model No. 6206

EX $35   **NM** $150   **MIP** $450

(KP Photo)

Custom Mustang, 1968, assorted w/open hood scoops or louvered windows, Model No. 6206

EX $200   **NM** $600   **MIP** $2200

(KP Photo)

Custom Police Cruiser, 1969, black and white paint scheme on a Plymouth w/"Police" and star tampos, red dome light, a nice companion car to the 6469 Fire Chief Cruiser, Model No. 6269

EX $30   **NM** $90   **MIP** $250

(KP Photo)

Custom T-Bird, 1968, met. brown, opening hood, metal engine, Model No. 6207

EX $30   **NM** $55   **MIP** $250

(KP Photo)

Custom VW Bug, 1968, met. aqua, oversized engine, sunroof, Model No. 6220

EX $80   **NM** $155   **MIP** $350

(KP Photo)

Demon, 1970, blue, exposed engine, called "Prowler" in 1973, Model No. 6401

EX $15   **NM** $25   **MIP** $100

(KP Photo)

Deora, 1968, assorted, Model No. 6210

EX $15   **NM** $50   **MIP** $400

(KP Photo)

Double Header, 1973, green, blue-tinted windshield, Model No. 5880

EX $100 **NM** $150   **MIP** $500

(KP Photo)

Double Vision, 1973, met. green, flip-up plastic canopy over the seats, rear engine, Model No. 6975

EX $70   **NM** $175   **MIP** $450

Double Vision, 1973, orange, white interior, blue-tinted windows, Model No. 6975

EX $100 **NM** $200   **MIP** $480

(KP Photo)

Dump Truck, 1970, metal cab and chassis, unpainted base, plastic dump truck bed, "Heavyweights" series, 1970-72, Model No. 6453

EX $30   **NM** $55   **MIP** $110

(KP Photo)

Dune Daddy, 1973, green, blue-tinted windshield, white interior, Model No. 6967

EX $50   **NM** $110   **MIP** $340

Dune Daddy, 1975, light green w/60s-style daisy tampos on hood, Model No. 6967

EX $25   **NM** $50   **MIP** $95

Dune Daddy, 1975, orange body w/60s-style flowers on hood, Model No. 6967

EX $150 **NM** $300   **MIP** $575

El Rey Special, 1974, light blue w/orange tampos, unpainted metal base, Model No. 8273

EX $175 **NM** $600   **MIP** $1100

El Rey Special, 1974, light green, Model No. 8273

EX $30   **NM** $75   **MIP** $130

El Rey Special, 1974, dark blue, Model No. 8273

EX $100   **NM** $225   **MIP** $700

(KP Photo)

El Rey Special, 1974, green, yellow and red "Dunlop," number "1" tampos, silver metal base, Model No. 8273

EX $25   **NM** $60   **MIP** $130

Emergency Squad, 1975, red body, yellow and white side tampos, silver plastic base, very much in the mold of the paramedic vehicle used on the TV show, "Emergency!," Model No. 7650

EX $10   **NM** $20   **MIP** $70

(KP Photo)

Evil Weevil, 1971, met. blue, black "8" inside white circle, sunroof, blue-tinted windows, Model No. 6471

EX $60   **NM** $100   **MIP** $250

(KP Photo)

Ferrari 312P, 1970, gold chrome, back opens to expose metal engine, black "60" in white circles, Model No. 6417

EX $20   **NM** $40   **MIP** $80

Ferrari 312P, 1973, red, back opens to expose metal engine, black "60" in white circles, Model No. 6973

EX $140   **NM** $280   **MIP** $600

Ferrari 512S, 1972, blue, opening rear hood and cockpit, Model No. 6022

EX $75   **NM** $150   **MIP** $250

(KP Photo)

Ferrari 512S, 1972, met. magenta, opening rear hood and cockpit, Model No. 6021

EX $40   **NM** $125   **MIP** $250

(KP Photo)

Fire Chief Cruiser, 1970, red Plymouth Fury, matches Custom Police Cruiser, #6269, Model No. 6469

EX $20   **NM** $40   **MIP** $100

(KP Photo)

Fire Engine, 1970, met. red cab, black ladder, rear is red plastic, white hoses, "Heavyweights" series, Model No. 6454

EX $40   **NM** $85   **MIP** $175

Fire-Eater, 1977, blue-tinted window, blue plastic hoses, Model No. 9640

EX $10   **NM** $20   **MIP** $50

(KP Photo)

Ford J-Car, 1968, met. aqua, back opens to reveal metal engine, Model No. 6214

EX $15   **NM** $30   **MIP** $90

(KP Photo)

Ford MK IV, 1969, red, back opens to reveal metal engine, Model No. 6257

EX $15   **NM** $25   **MIP** $100

Formula 5000, 1976, white race car, metal chassis, Model No. 9119

EX $20   **NM** $35   **MIP** $60

Formula P.A.C.K., 1976, black race car, Model No. 9037

EX $20   **NM** $40   **MIP** $65

(KP Photo)

Fuel Tanker, 1971, white cab and chassis, plastic fuel tanker section, removable fuel hoses, "Heavyweights" series, Model No. 6018

EX $30   **NM** $95   **MIP** $210

(KP Photo)

Funny Money, 1972, gray armored car body on funny car chassis, orange plastic bumper (usually missing), "Funny Money" labels, Model No. 6005

EX $70   **NM** $95   **MIP** $345

Funny Money, 1974, plum w/floral tampo, Model No. 7621

EX $30   **NM** $60   **MIP** $175

Funny Money, 1977, gray body, white "Brink's" on sides, body lifts open, Model No. 7621

EX $25   **NM** $40   **MIP** $80

GMC Motor Home, 1977, orange, blue-tinted windows, Model No. 9645

EX $200   **NM** $400   **MIP** n/a

(KP Photo)

Grass Hopper, 1971, met. red, shown w/out white plastic canopy, Model No. 6461
EX $20   **NM** $60   **MIP** $125

(KP Photo)

Grass Hopper, 1974, light green, engine, orange and blue side tampo, blue-tinted windshield, Model No. 7622
EX $25   **NM** $50   **MIP** $120

Grass Hopper, 1975, light green, no engine, Model No. 7622
EX $45   **NM** $100   **MIP** $240

Gremlin Grinder, 1975, green, blue-tinted windows, yellow, orange and black tampo, exposed engine, Model No. 7652
EX $20   **NM** $40   **MIP** $100

(KP Photo)

Gremlin Grinder, 1976, chrome, orange, black and green tampo, exposed engine, Model No. 9201
EX $20   **NM** $40   **MIP** $60

(KP Photo)

Gun Bucket, 1976, olive-green body, white "Army" star and number tampos on hood, black plastic anti-aircraft gun and treads, Model No. 9090
EX $20   **NM** $40   **MIP** $60

Gun Slinger, 1975, olive, Model No. 7664
EX $15   **NM** $30   **MIP** $80

(KP Photo)

Hairy Hauler, 1971, assorted, w/lifting front canopy, exposed engine, Model No. 6458
EX $25   **NM** $50   **MIP** $110

(KP Photo)

Heavy Chevy, 1970, chrome, Club Kit, black stripes, Model No. 6189
EX $70   **NM** $80   **MIP** $350

Heavy Chevy, 1970, assorted, exposed engine, Model No. 6408
EX $55   **NM** $80   **MIP** $180

Heavy Chevy, 1974, light green, Model No. 7619
EX $350   **NM** $700   **MIP** $1100

Heavy Chevy, 1974, yellow, exposed engine, orange and red side tampo, "7," Model No. 7619
EX $45   **NM** $90   **MIP** $200

Heavy Chevy, 1977, chrome, redline or blackwall, Model No. 9212
EX $35   **NM** $75   **MIP** $115

(KP Photo)

Hiway Robber, 1973, red, black interior, exposed engine, Model No. 6979
EX $75   **NM** $120   **MIP** $350

(KP Photo)

Hood, The, 1971, met. light green, exposed engine, black interior, Model No. 6175
EX $40   **NM** $75   **MIP** $250

(KP Photo)

Hot Heap, 1968, met. yellow, white interior, exposed engine, Model No. 6219
EX $20   **NM** $40   **MIP** $130

(KP Photo)

Ice T, 1971, yellow, w/"Ice T" on plastic roof, Model No. 6184
EX $30   **NM** $55   **MIP** $230

(KP Photo)

Ice T, 1973, body in assorted colors, black plastic interior, plastic roof (mostly in white), silver base, blackwall wheels variations also produced at the same time, Model No. 6980
EX $95   **NM** $175   **MIP** $550

Ice T, 1974, light green, Model No. 6980
EX $25   **NM** $50   **MIP** $95

Ice T, 1974, yellow w/hood tampo, Model No. 6980

EX $150   **NM** $300   **MIP** $600

Indy Eagle, 1969, gold, Model No. 6263

EX $75   **NM** $100   **MIP** $350

(KP Photo)

Indy Eagle, 1969, assorted colors w/tinted plastic windshield and silver rear engine and tailpipes, Model No. 6263

EX $15   **NM** $25   **MIP** $110

Inferno, 1976, yellow drag racer, exposed engine, Model No. 9186

EX $30   **NM** $55   **MIP** $80

(KP Photo)

Jack Rabbit Special, 1970, white, blue stripe, clear windshield, Model No. 6421

EX $15   **NM** $40   **MIP** $100

Jack-in-the-Box Promotion, 1970, white, Jack Rabbit w/decals, Model No. 6421

EX $150   **NM** $250   **MIP** $350

(KP Photo)

Jet Threat, 1971, met. yellow, blue-tinted windshield, Model No. 6179

EX $40   **NM** $95   **MIP** $225

Jet Threat, 1973, light blue, blue-tinted windshield "SHELL" promo

EX $30   **NM** $95   **MIP** $140

Jet Threat II, 1976, plum w/yellow flames, blue-tinted windshield, exposed engine, Model No. 8235

EX $20   **NM** $45   **MIP** $65

Khaki Kooler, 1976, khaki body, "Military Police," black interior,

smoke-colored windshield, Model No. 9183

EX $15   **NM** $30   **MIP** $55

King Kuda, 1970, chrome, Club Kit, exposed engine, Model No. 6411

EX $70   **NM** $90   **MIP** $350

(KP Photo)

King 'Kuda, 1970, met. green, exposed engine, blue-tinted windshield, Model No. 6411

EX $45   **NM** $100   **MIP** $225

(KP Photo)

Large Charge, 1975, green, red and yellow tampos, blue-tinted windows, Model No. 8272

EX $20   **NM** $40   **MIP** $80

Letter Getter, 1977, U.S. Mail truck, white, Model No. 9643

EX $225   **NM** $450   **MIP** n/a

(KP Photo)

Light My Firebird, 1970, convertible in assorted finishes, decal number on doors, exposed silver engine in front, brown plastic interior, Model No. 6412

EX $30   **NM** $75   **MIP** $175

(KP Photo)

Lola GT 70, 1969, dark green, opening rear, clear windows, Model No. 6254

EX $20   **NM** $35   **MIP** $100

(KP Photo)

Lotus Turbine, 1969, met. brown, blue-tinted windshield, Model No. 6262

EX $20   **NM** $35   **MIP** $130

Lowdown, 1976, light blue, "Flyin' Low," Model No. 9185

EX $30   **NM** $35   **MIP** $75

Mantis, 1970, assorted, exposed engines, Model No. 6423

EX $25   **NM** $35   **MIP** $180

Maserati Mistral, 1969, assorted, Model No. 6277

EX $25   **NM** $50   **MIP** $500

(KP Photo)

Maxi Taxi, 1976, Oldsmobile 442 body, yellow w/checkerboard and "Maxi Taxi" tampo, black plastic interior, Model No. 9184

EX $25   **NM** $50   **MIP** $100

(KP Photo)

McClaren M6A, 1969, orange, blue-tinted windshield, Model No. 6255

EX $20   **NM** $45   **MIP** $150

(KP Photo)

Mercedes 280SL, 1969, red, opening hood, metal engine, blue-tinted windows, Model No. 6275

EX $25   **NM** $40   **MIP** $130

Mercedes 280SL, 1973, assorted, Model No. 6962

EX $90   **NM** $150   **MIP** $600

Mercedes C-111, 1972, assorted, Model No. 6169

EX $60   **NM** $125   **MIP** $300

Mercedes C-111, 1973, assorted, Model No. 6978

EX $175   **NM** $325   **MIP** $1000

(KP Photo)

Mercedes C-111, 1974, red, w/stars and stripes tampo, Model No. 6978

EX $20   **NM** $45   **MIP** $110

Mercedes-Benz 280SL, 1969, met. blue, blue-tinted windows, opening hood, metal engine, Model No. 6275

EX $30   **NM** $35   **MIP** $110

Mighty Maverick, 1970, assorted, opening hood, black plastic spoiler, Model No. 6414

EX $65   **NM** $130   **MIP** $200

Mighty Maverick, 1975, blue, orange, yellow and white tampo, blue-tinted windows, Model No. 7653

EX $25   **NM** $60   **MIP** $160

(KP Photo)

Mighty Maverick, 1976, chrome, yellow and blue tampo, blue-tinted windows, "Super Chromes" series, Model No. 9209

EX $25   **NM** $50   **MIP** $100

(KP Photo)

Mod-Quad, 1970, met. red, black interior, four metal engines, top opens, Model No. 6456

EX $20   **NM** $40   **MIP** $140

Mongoose, 1973, blue w/red stickers, Model No. 6970

EX $250   **NM** $650   **MIP** $1300

(KP Photo)

Mongoose Funny Car, 1970, red, opening body, white, blue and yellow tampo, Model No. 6410

EX $65   **NM** $75   **MIP** $190

(KP Photo)

Mongoose II, 1971, met. blue, opening body, Model No. 5954

EX $55   **NM** $125   **MIP** $350

Mongoose Rail Dragster, 1971, blue, two pack, w/Snake Rail, Model No. 5952

EX $75   **NM** $100   **MIP** $1250

Monte Carlo Stocker, 1975, yellow, blue-tinted windows, black interior, Model No. 7660

EX $10   **NM** $35   **MIP** $70

(KP Photo)

Motocross I, 1975, red plastic seat and tank, unpainted gray die-cast body, Model No. 7668

EX $45   **NM** $100   **MIP** $225

(KP Photo)

Moving Van, 1970, met. blue, white trailer, "Heavyweights" series, Model No. 6455

EX $40   **NM** $60   **MIP** $110

Mustang Stocker, 1975, yellow w/red in tampo, Model No. 9203

EX $100   **NM** $375   **MIP** $650

Mustang Stocker, 1975, yellow w/magenta and orange tampo w/"Ford" and "450 HP," Model No. 7664

EX $50   **NM** $145   **MIP** $300

Mustang Stocker, 1975, white, Model No. 7664

EX $175   **NM** $650   **MIP** $1000

Mustang Stocker, 1976, chrome, Model No. 9203

EX $60   **NM** $120   **MIP** $180

Mustang Stocker, 1977, chrome, redline or blackwall, Model No. 9203

EX $25   **NM** $55   **MIP** $80

(KP Photo)

Mutt Mobile, 1971, met. red, dogs in back, Model No. 6185

EX $80   **NM** $145   **MIP** $350

Neet Streeter, 1976, blue, red and white roof stripes, Model No. 9244

EX $25   **NM** $50   **MIP** $85

(KP Photo)

Nitty Gritty Kitty, 1970, gold chrome, metal engine, blue-tinted windows, Model No. 6405

EX $50   **NM** $100   **MIP** $300

(KP Photo)

Noodle Head, 1971, assorted, opening headlight cover, Model No. 6000

EX $30   **NM** $50   **MIP** $250

Odd Job, 1973, red, white topper, exposed engine, Model No. 6981

EX $100   **NM** $200   **MIP** $450

(KP Photo)

Odd Rod, 1977, yellow plastic bucket around seats, clear plastic hood w/flame graphics, Model No. 9642

EX $25   **NM** $50   **MIP** $90

Odd Rod, 1977, plum, blackwall or redline, Model No. 9642

EX $150   **NM** $300   **MIP** $500

Olds 442, 1971, assorted, Model No. 6467

EX $100   **NM** $200   **MIP** $1000

(KP Photo)

Open Fire, 1972, met. red, modified AMC Gremilin, oversized engine and six wheels, Model No. 5881

EX $75   **NM** $150   **MIP** $300

(KP Photo)

Paddy Wagon, 1970, blue, w/plastic covering over bed, Model No. 6402

EX $15   **NM** $30   **MIP** $90

Paddy Wagon, 1973, blue, Model No. 6966

EX $30   **NM** $45   **MIP** $190

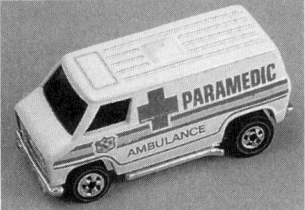

(KP Photo)

Paramedic, 1975, white w/yellow and red stripes and "Paramedic" lettering, Model No. 7661

EX $20   **NM** $40   **MIP** $85

(KP Photo)

Peepin' Bomb, 1970, met. yellow, clear windshield, exposed engine, Model No. 6419

EX $15   **NM** $30   **MIP** $80

Peepin' Bomb, 1973, red, exposed engine, blue-tinted windshield

EX $35   **NM** $70   **MIP** $125

(KP Photo)

Pit Crew Car, 1971, white, opening trunk w/tool box, Model No. 6183

EX $70   **NM** $100   **MIP** $325

(KP Photo)

Poison Pinto, 1976, light green body, skull and crossbones, "Poison Pinto" tampo, late-era redlines, Model No. 9240

EX $25   **NM** $50   **MIP** $75

Police Cruiser, 1973, white Olds 442, "Police" labels on doors, opening hood and red dome light on roof, Model No. 6963

EX $100   **NM** $225   **MIP** $550

Police Cruiser, 1974, white, "State Police, Law Enforcement" decal on doors, Model No. 6963

EX $30   **NM** $65   **MIP** $150

Police Cruiser, 1977, white Olds 442 w/black doors, yellow police tampos on doors, non-opening hood, blue light, Model No. 6963

EX $15   **NM** $30   **MIP** $50

(KP Photo)

Porsche 911, 1975, yellow, w/blue and red stripes on hood and roof, Model No. 7648

EX $40   **NM** $65   **MIP** $130

Porsche 911, 1976, chrome, red and green tampo, black interior, Model No. 9206

EX $20   **NM** $40   **MIP** $80

Porsche 917, 1970, silver, clear windshield, opening back, Model No. 6416

EX $20   **NM** $40   **MIP** $80

Porsche 917, 1973, red, opening back, blue-tinted windshield, Model No. 6972

EX $100   **NM** $250   **MIP** $600

Porsche 917, 1974, red, Model No. 6972

EX $125   **NM** $250   **MIP** $500

Porsche 917, 1974, orange, Model No. 6972

EX $20   **NM** $50   **MIP** $100

(KP Photo)

Power Pad, 1970, met. red, clear windshield, black interior, exposed engine, shown w/out camper, Model No. 6459

EX $30   **NM** $75   **MIP** $125

Prowler, 1973, assorted, Model No. 6965

EX $150 **NM** $300 **MIP** $800

Prowler, 1974, light green, Model No. 6965

EX $175 **NM** $525 **MIP** $900

Prowler, 1974, orange w/demon flame tampo on roof (which makes sense, considering this car was known as "The Demon" in its previous incarnation in 1970,) unpainted metal base, Model No. 6965

EX $25 **NM** $50 **MIP** $125

Prowler, 1976, chrome, yellow and red flames, devil tampo, exposed engine, Model No. 9207

EX $40 **NM** $65 **MIP** $85

(KP Photo)

Python, 1968, met. red, black top, exposed engine, Model No. 6216

EX $20 **NM** $40 **MIP** $120

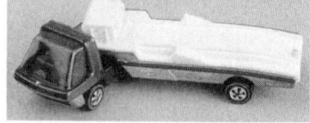

(KP Photo)

Racer Rig, 1971, red/white, "Heavyweights" series, Model No. 6194

EX $60 **NM** $130 **MIP** $300

Ramblin' Wrecker, 1975, white, "Larry's 24 Hour Towing," blue lift, Model No. 7659

EX $25 **NM** $40 **MIP** $100

(KP Photo)

Ranger Rig, 1975, medium green w/yellow lettering and design, Model No. 7666

EX $20 **NM** $45 **MIP** $100

Rash 1, 1974, green, blue-tinted windshield, yellow and white tampo, exposed engine, Model No. 7616

EX $20 **NM** $55 **MIP** $120

Rash I, 1974, blue, Model No. 7616

EX $225 **NM** $500 **MIP** $900

Rear Engine Mongoose, 1972, red, Model No. 5699

EX $90 **NM** $150 **MIP** $450

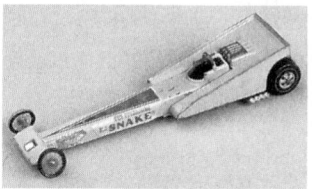

(KP Photo)

Rear Engine Snake, 1972, yellow, blue w/red stars tampo, Model No. 5856

EX $60 **NM** $120 **MIP** $400

(KP Photo)

Red Baron, 1970, red, cross on helmet, Model No. 6400

EX $20 **NM** $45 **MIP** $155

(KP Photo)

Red Baron, 1973, red, note no Iron Cross on the helmet, Model No. 6964

EX $30 **NM** $50 **MIP** $170

Road King Truck, 1974, yellow cab and trailer w/metal chassis, tilting dumper section, availabe in set only, Model No. 7615

EX $375 **NM** $750 **MIP** n/a

Rock Buster, 1976, chrome dune buggy w/black plastic rollcage and interior, racing graphics on hood and sides, Model No. 9507

EX $25 **NM** $55 **MIP** n/a

Rock Buster, 1976, yellow, Model No. 9088

EX $20 **NM** $30 **MIP** $50

(KP Photo)

Rocket-Bye-Baby, 1971, met. yellow, metal rocket on top, Model No. 6186

EX $60 **NM** $120 **MIP** $300

(KP Photo)

Rodger Dodger, 1974, magenta Dodge Challenger, flame tampos on hood and roof, exposed silver engine, red plastic exhaust pipes, Model No. 8259

EX $30 **NM** $80 **MIP** $200

Rodger Dodger, 1974, blue, Model No. 8259

EX $1500 **NM** $2500 **MIP** $3500

Rodger Dodger, 1977, gold plated, blackwall or redline, Model No. 8259

EX $20 **NM** $45 **MIP** $80

(KP Photo)

Rolls-Royce Silver Shadow, 1969, silver, opening hood shows detailed engine, Model No. 6276

EX $10 **NM** $20 **MIP** $70

(KP Photo)

Sand Crab, 1970, red, black interior, clear windshield, Model No. 6403

EX $20 **NM** $30 **MIP** $100

Sand Drifter, 1975, green, Model No. 7651

EX $150   NM $300   MIP $625

(KP Photo)

Sand Drifter, 1975, yellow, flame tampo on hood, black plastic interior and covering over bed, Model No. 7651

EX $10   NM $25   MIP $55

(KP Photo)

Sand Witch, 1973, green, blue-tinted windshield, opening rear hood, Model No. 6974

EX $75   NM $150   MIP $300

(KP Photo)

S'Cool Bus, 1971, yellow, lift-up funny car body, silver chassis, "Heavyweights" series, Model No. 6468

EX $250   NM $400   MIP $2200

(KP Photo)

Scooper, 1971, met. green, yellow scoop and rear, Model No. 6193

EX $50   NM $100   MIP $220

(KP Photo)

Seasider, 1970, met. light green, exposed engine, plastic boat, Model No. 6413

EX $60   NM $80   MIP $200

(KP Photo)

Second Wind, 1977, white w/yellow and red striping, number "5" on hood, Model No. 9644

EX $30   NM $80   MIP $300

(KP Photo)

Shelby Turbine, 1969, met. Purple, Model No. 6265

EX $25   NM $30   MIP $110

(KP Photo)

Short Order, 1971, blue, extending plastic tailgate, exposed engine, Model No. 6176

EX $25   NM $75   MIP $200

(KP Photo)

Show Hoss II, 1977, yellow funny car Mustang II body lifts up over silver base, black plastic rollcage, redline or blackwalls versions available, Model No. 9646

EX $25   NM $35   MIP $90

Show-Off, 1973, orange, exposed engine, blue-tinted windows, Model No. 6982

EX $125   NM $275   MIP $500

Side Kick, 1972, met. green, exposed engine, Model No. 6022

EX $75   NM $100   MIP $225

(KP Photo)

Silhouette, 1968, body in assorted colors, plastic dome canopy over seats, exposed front engine, Model No. 6209

EX $15   NM $25   MIP $85

Sir Sidney Roadster, 1974, light green, Model No. 8261

EX $200   NM $425   MIP $725

(KP Photo)

Sir Sidney Roadster, 1974, orange body w/brown plastic roof and exposed silver engine, red flame tampos, silver metal base, Model No. 8261

EX $180   NM $380   MIP $575

Sir Sidney Roadster, 1974, yellow, red flames, exposed engine, brown top, Model No. 8261

EX $25   NM $50   MIP $90

(KP Photo)

Six Shooter, 1971, met. blue, exposed engines, blue-tinted windshield, six wheels, Model No. 6003

EX $35   NM $85   MIP $275

(KP Photo)

Sky Show Fleetside (Aero Launcher), 1970, met. blue, orange plastic ramp, Model No. 6436

EX $175 **NM** $350 **MIP** n/a

Snake, 1973, white/yellow, Model No. 6969

EX $300 **NM** $750 **MIP** $1300

(KP Photo)

Snake Funny Car, 1970, yellow, body opens, metal engine, Model No. 6409

EX $45 **NM** $110 **MIP** $500

Snake II, 1971, white, Model No. 5953

EX $60 **NM** $90 **MIP** $315

(KP Photo)

Snake Rail Dragster, 1971, white, exposed engine, part of a two-pack w/blue Mongoose Rail, Model No. 5951

EX $75 **NM** $100 **MIP** $1250

(KP Photo)

Snorkel, 1971, assorted, Model No. 6020

EX $30 **NM** $90 **MIP** $475

(KP Photo)

Special Delivery, 1971, blue, exposed engines, U.S. Mail tampo, Model No. 6006

EX $50 **NM** $70 **MIP** $250

(KP Photo)

Splittin' Image, 1969, met. orange, clear windows, exposed engine, Model No. 6261

EX $15 **NM** $25 **MIP** $115

(KP Photo)

Spoiler Sport, 1977, light green van, tropical island scene on side panels, Model No. 9641

EX $25 **NM** $45 **MIP** $80

Staff Car, 1976, Olds 442 casting in olive drab, "Staff Car U.S. Army" on doors, Model No. 9521

EX $350 **NM** $700 **MIP** n/a

Steam Roller, 1974, white body w/red white and blue graphics, seven stars on front, Model No. 8260

EX $125 **NM** $300 **MIP** $550

(KP Photo)

Steam Roller, 1974, white body, stars and stripes tampo, three stars reversed out of red stripe on hood;

the more common model, Model No. 8260

EX $25 **NM** $50 **MIP** $90

Street Rodder, 1976, black, flames, exposed engine, clear windshield, Model No. 9242

EX $40 **NM** $55 **MIP** $100

Street Snorter, 1973, light green, blue-tinted windows, Model No. 6971

EX $95 **NM** $200 **MIP** $450

Street Snorter, 1973, assorted, Model No. 6971

EX $90 **NM** $180 **MIP** $600

(KP Photo)

Strip Teaser, 1971, blue, opening back, exposed engine, Model No. 6188

EX $45 **NM** $75 **MIP** $275

Strip Teaser, 1973, blue, exposed engine, driver area opens to reveal black interior, SHELL promo

EX $75 **NM** $125 **MIP** $160

Sugar Caddy, 1971, assorted, exposed engine, Model No. 6418

EX $30 **NM** $75 **MIP** $250

Super Van, 1975, black body, chrome plastic base, red and yellow flames, Model No. 7649

EX $30 **NM** $80 **MIP** $180

(KP Photo)

Super Van, 1975, blue body, yellow flames, Model No. 7649

EX $35 **NM** $70 **MIP** $130

Superfine Turbine, 1973, red, exposed engine, black interior, Model No. 6004

EX $180 **NM** $425 **MIP** $950

Sweet 16, 1973, red, exposed engine, trunk opens to expose spare, Model No. 6007

EX $165 **NM** $225 **MIP** $550

(KP Photo)

Swingin' Wing, 1970, met. red, blue-tinted windows, Model No. 6422
EX $15 **NM** $30 **MIP** $70

(KP Photo)

T-4-2, 1971, met. yellow, black top, exposed metal engines, blue-tinted windows, Model No. 6177
EX $10 **NM** $30 **MIP** $80

(KP Photo)

Team Trailer, 1971, white/red, detailed plastic interior and opening door on trailer, "Heavyweights" series, Model No. 6019
EX $75 **NM** $100 **MIP** $325

(KP Photo)

TNT-Bird, 1970, met. green, white stripe, blue-tinted windshield, exposed engine, Model No. 6407
EX $40 **NM** $85 **MIP** $155

(KP Photo)

Top Eliminator, 1974, blue lift-up funny car body on silver chassis, green, light tan, and orange "Hot Wheels" tampo w/stripes on sides, Model No. 7630
EX $30 **NM** $80 **MIP** $145

(KP Photo)

Torero, 1969, gold chrome, opening hood, clear windows, white interior, Model No. 6260
EX $15 **NM** $25 **MIP** $100

(KP Photo)

Torino Stocker, 1975, red, blue-tinted windshield, black interior, Model No. 7647
EX $30 **NM** $65 **MIP** $115

(KP Photo)

Tough Customer, 1975, olive, w/rotating turret and white numbering tampos, Model No. 7655
EX $15 **NM** $30 **MIP** $60

(KP Photo)

Tow Truck, 1970, assorted, "Heavyweights" series, Model No. 6450
EX $25 **NM** $50 **MIP** $125

(KP Photo)

Tri-Baby, 1970, blue, interesting engine casting under opening rear hood, Model No. 6424
EX $25 **NM** $55 **MIP** $110

T-Totaller, 1977, black, redlines, six-pack only, red body common $25, Model No. 9648
EX $200 **NM** $500 **MIP** n/a

Turbofire, 1969, met. yellow, opening rear, clear windshield, Model No. 6259
EX $10 **NM** $20 **MIP** $110

(KP Photo)

Twin Mill, 1969, met. aqua, clear windows, two exposed engines, Model No. 6258
EX $15 **NM** $25 **MIP** $110

Twin Mill, 1973, met. red, blue-tinted windshield, two exposed engines, "SHELL" promo
EX $40 **NM** $90 **MIP** $165

Twin Mill II, 1976, orange, two engines, blue-tinted windows, blue, white and red tampo, Model No. 8240
EX $20 **NM** $30 **MIP** $45

Vega Bomb, 1975, green, Model No. 7658
EX $350 **NM** $700 **MIP** $1250

(KP Photo)

Vega Bomb, 1975, orange, this model is right on the cusp of the Redlines era—blackwall versions (like this one as #7654) were becoming a more common sight, Model No. 7658

EX $35   **NM** $65   **MIP** $120

(KP Photo)

Volkswagen, 1974, orange enamel, bug graphic on roof, Model No. 7620

EX $25   **NM** $65   **MIP** $145

Volkswagen, 1974, orange w/stripes on roof, Model No. 7620

EX $225   **NM** $475   **MIP** $900

(KP Photo)

Volkswagen Beach Bomb, 1969, surf boards on side raised panels, Model No. 6274

EX $200   **NM** $400   **MIP** $1200

Volkswagen Beach Bomb, 1969, surf boards in rear window, Model No. 6274

EX n/a   **NM** $72000   **MIP** n/a

(KP Photo)

Warpath, 1975, white, stars and stripes tampo, opening plastic engine covers, Model No. 7654

EX $30   **NM** $75   **MIP** $115

(KP Photo)

Waste Wagon, 1971, met. yellow, orange receptacle, "Heavyweights" series, Model No. 6192

EX $50   **NM** $100   **MIP** $210

(KP Photo)

What-4, 1971, met. green, blue-tinted windshield, Model No. 6001

EX $15   **NM** $35   **MIP** $145

(KP Photo)

Whip Creamer, 1970, met. yellow, clear slide-back plastic canopy, Model No. 6457

EX $25   **NM** $55   **MIP** $100

Winnipeg, 1974, yellow body, orange spoiler, blue and orange tampo, Model No. 7618

EX $50   **NM** $100   **MIP** $210

Xploder, 1973, red, black interior, blue-tinted windows, Model No. 6977

EX $100   **NM** $150   **MIP** $500

Z Whiz, 1977, gray body, orange and yellow tampo, Model No. 9639

EX $20   **NM** $35   **MIP** $70

Z Whiz, 1977, white, redline, Model No. 9639

EX $1000   **NM** $2000   **MIP** n/a

Japanese Tin Cars

(Ron Smith)

Agajanian Racer No.98, 1950s, friction, "Y" Co., 18" (J286)
   EX $900 **NM** $1600 **MIP** $3300

(Ron Smith)

Aston-Martin DB5, 1960s, (James Bond), friction, Gilbert, 11-1/2" (J1)
   EX $90 **NM** $300 **MIP** $600

(Ron Smith)

Aston-Martin DB6, 1960s, friction, Asahi Toy Co., 11" (J2)
   EX $200 **NM** $400 **MIP** $600

(Ron Smith)

Atom Car, 1950s, Yonezawa, 17" (J284)
   EX $600 **NM** $1200 **MIP** $2700

BMW Coupe, 1960s, Yonezawa, 11" tan, battery-operated
   EX $50 **NM** $105 **MIP** $200

(Ron Smith)

Buick, 1959, friction, T.N., 11" (J8)
   EX $90 **NM** $200 **MIP** $400

(Ron Smith)

Buick Century, 1958, friction, Yonezawa, 12" (J6)
   EX $400 **NM** $800 **MIP** $1800

(Ron Smith)

Buick Century, 1958, friction, Bandai, 8" (J7)
   EX $65 **NM** $85 **MIP** $185

Buick Convertible, 1959, 11", orange/yellow, friction, dog and driver figures
   EX $100 **NM** $275 **MIP** $350

Buick Fire Department Car, 1961, 16", red, friction, working wipers, revolving emergency light
   EX $80 **NM** $150 **MIP** $265

(Ron Smith)

Buick Futuristic LeSabre, 1950s, friction, Yonezawa, 7-1/2" (J276)
   EX $300 **NM** $600 **MIP** $1200

Buick HT Convertible, 1959, Linemar, 9-1/2" red/white, friction
   EX $50 **NM** $105 **MIP** $150

(Ron Smith)

Buick Roadmaster, 1955, friction, Yoshiya, 11" (J5)
   EX $125 **NM** $350 **MIP** $700

Buick Special, 1955, 8-1/2", two-tone blue, battery-operated, working headlights
   EX $55 **NM** $122 **MIP** $175

Buick Station Wagon, 1959, Yonezawa, 9", two-tone green, friction, HT or Convertible
   EX $50 **NM** $105 **MIP** $150

(Ron Smith)

Buick Wildcat, 1963, friction, Ichiko, 15" (J13)
   EX $300 **NM** $650 **MIP** $1300

(Ron Smith)

Cadillac, 1950, battery-operated, Marusan, 11" (J18)
   EX $400 **NM** $1000 **MIP** $2200

(Ron Smith)

Cadillac, 1952, friction, Alps, 11-1/2" (J20)
   EX $250 **NM** $600 **MIP** $1200

Cadillac, 1954, battery-operated, Joustra, 12" (J23)
   EX $150 **NM** $300 **MIP** $600

Cadillac, 1960, black, Marusan, 12" (J27A), Model No. J27A
   EX $300 **NM** $800 **MIP** $1500

(Ron Smith)

Cadillac, 1967, friction, K.O., 10-1/2" (J34)
   EX $65 **NM** $150 **MIP** $300

(Ron Smith)

Cadillac Convertible, 1960, friction, Bandai, 12" (J25)
   EX $60 **NM** $100 **MIP** $200

Cadillac Fleetwood, 1961, friction, SSS, 17-1/2" (J29)

EX $200 **NM** $450 **MIP** $975

Cadillac Four-Door Sedan, 1951, Marusan, 12-1/2", gray, black, white, or red, friction

EX $400 **NM** $900 **MIP** $1800

Cadillac Four-Door Sedan, 1951, Marusan, 12-1/2", gray, battery-operated, remote control, working headlights

EX $600 **NM** $1500 **MIP** $3000

(Ron Smith)

Cadillac Four-Door Sedan, 1960, Yonezawa, 18" black or maroon, friction, shown is a customized convertible

EX $300 **NM** $630 **MIP** $900

Cadillac Police Car, 1962, Ichiko, 6-1/2" black/white, friction w/siren

EX $30 **NM** $50 **MIP** $80

(Ron Smith)

Champion No. 15 Racer, 1950, friction, German, 18" (J289)

EX $800 **NM** $1400 **MIP** $2600

(Ron Smith)

Champion No. 42 Racer, 1950, friction, Gem France, 18" (J288)

EX $600 **NM** $1200 **MIP** $2400

(Ron Smith)

Champion No. 98 Racer, 1950s, friction, "Y" Co., 18" (J287)

EX $600 **NM** $1200 **MIP** $2400

(Ron Smith)

Chevrolet, 1954, friction, Marusan, 11" (J49)

EX $300 **NM** $600 **MIP** $1300

(Ron Smith)

Chevrolet, 1955, battery-operated, Marusan, 10-3/4" (J50)

EX $600 **NM** $1100 **MIP** $2200

(Ron Smith)

Chevrolet, 1960, friction, Marusan, 11-1/2" (J60)

EX $200 **NM** $450 **MIP** $900

(Ron Smith)

Chevrolet, 1962, friction, unknown manufacturer, 11" (J65)

EX $300 **NM** $600 **MIP** $1200

Chevrolet Bel Air, 1954, Marusan and Linemar, 11", gray/black, friction

EX $400 **NM** $600 **MIP** $1200

Chevrolet Bel Air, 1954, Marusan and Linemar, 11", rare orange/yellow, friction

EX $400 **NM** $600 **MIP** $1200

Chevrolet Bel Air, 1955, Asahi Toy, 7" light green, friction

EX $50 **NM** $105 **MIP** $130

Chevrolet Camaro, 1967, battery-operated, T.N., 14" (J46)

EX $125 **NM** $200 **MIP** $400

(Ron Smith)

Chevrolet Camaro Rusher, 1971, battery-operated, Taiyo, 9-1/2" (J48)

EX $10 **NM** $20 **MIP** $25

(Ron Smith)

Chevrolet Corvette, 1953, friction, Bandai, 7" (J37)

EX $90 **NM** $110 **MIP** $200

(Ron Smith)

Chevrolet Corvette, 1958, friction, Yonezawa, 9-1/2" (J38)

EX $200 **NM** $300 **MIP** $600

(Ron Smith)

Chevrolet Corvette, 1964, battery-operated, Ichida, 12" (J41)

EX $75 **NM** $125 **MIP** $300

(Ron Smith)

Chevrolet Corvette, 1968, battery-operated, Taiyo, 9-1/2" (J42)
EX $20   **NM** $30   **MIP** $40

Chevrolet Corvette Coupe, 1963, 12", metallic red or white, battery-operated, working headlights
EX $180   **NM** $420   **MIP** $600

Chevrolet Hardtop, 1959, red w/white top; 1960s, 10", Model No. J59A
EX $90   **NM** $150   **MIP** $325

Chevrolet Highway Patrol Car, 1959, ASC, 10", black/white, friction
EX $55   **NM** $125   **MIP** $150

Chevrolet HT, 1959, 7", green, friction
EX $20   **NM** $30   **MIP** $65

(Ron Smith)

Chevrolet Impala, 1963, friction, T.N., 18" (J66)
EX $200   **NM** $300   **MIP** $600

(Ron Smith)

Chevrolet Impala Convertible, 1961, friction, Bandai, 11" (J63)
EX $100   **NM** $275   **MIP** $500

Chevrolet Impala HT, 1960, Alps, 9", red/white, friction
EX $105   **NM** $200   **MIP** $400

(Ron Smith)

Chevrolet Impala Sedan, 1961, friction, Bandai, 11" (J62)
EX $100   **NM** $300   **MIP** $400

(Ron Smith)

Chevrolet Secret Agent, 1962, battery-operated, unknown manufacturer, 14" (J64)
EX $50   **NM** $100   **MIP** $200

(Ron Smith)

Chevrolet Sedan/Convertible/Wagon, 1959, friction, SY, 11-1/2" (J59)
EX $400   **NM** $600   **MIP** $1200

Chevrolet Station Wagon/Sedan/Convertible, 1958, friction, Bandai, 8" (J57)
EX $50   **NM** $75   **MIP** $150

(Ron Smith)

Chrylser Imperial Convertible or Sedan, 1959, friction, Bandai, 8" (J74)
EX $50   **NM** $100   **MIP** $150

(Ron Smith)

Chrysler, 1955, friction, Yonezawa, 8" (J71)
EX $100   **NM** $200   **MIP** $300

(Ron Smith)

Chrysler, 1958, battery-operated, unknown manufacturer, 13" (J73)
EX $300   **NM** $400   **MIP** $800

(Ron Smith)

Chrysler Imperial, 1962, 16", friction, black, red (white: add 20 percent to value)
EX $3000   **NM** $12000   **MIP** $20000

Chrysler New Yorker, 1957, 6-1/2", red/black, friction
EX $25   **NM** $60   **MIP** $85

Chrysler New Yorker, 1957, friction, Alps, 14" (J72)
EX $600   **NM** $1500   **MIP** $2500

Chrysler Orion Convertible, 1953, 6-1/2", blue/green, friction
EX $25   **NM** $60   **MIP** $85

Citroen 2 CV, 1960, friction, Daiya, 8" (J269A)
EX $100   **NM** $150   **MIP** $275

Citroen DS 19 Sedan/Wagon/Convertible, 1960, friction, Bandai, 12" (J68)
EX $300   **NM** $600   **MIP** $1200

Cunningham Roadster, 1950s, 7-1/2", light blue, friction
EX $40   **NM** $100   **MIP** $160

DeSoto, 1950s, 6", green, friction
EX $20   **NM** $45   **MIP** $65

DeSoto, 1950s, Asahi Toy, 8", green, friction
EX $40   NM $90   MIP $125

Dodge Charger Sonic Car, 1966, 16", red, battery-operated
EX $90   NM $150   MIP $275

Dodge Four-Door HT, 1958, 8-1/2", orange/white, friction
EX $55   NM $125   MIP $175

(Ron Smith)

Dodge Pickup, 1959, friction, unknown manufacturer, 18-1/2" (J84)
EX $300   NM $600   MIP $1200

(Ron Smith)

Dodge Sedan, 1958, friction, T.N., 11" (J82)
EX $300   NM $600   MIP $1200

Dodge Two-Door HT, 1959, 9", blue/white, friction
EX $135   NM $315   MIP $450

Dream Car, friction, "Y" Co., 17" (J278A)
EX $1000 NM $2000   MIP $4000

(Ron Smith)

Edsel Convertible/Sedan, 1958, friction, Haji, 10-1/2" (J86)
EX $300   NM $600   MIP $1250

(Ron Smith)

Edsel Hardtop, 1958, friction, Asahi, 10-3/4" (J91)
EX $150   NM $300   MIP $600

(Ron Smith)

Edsel Station Wagon, 1958, friction, T.N., 11" (J89)
EX $150   NM $200   MIP $400

(Ron Smith)

Edsel Wagon, 1958, friction, Haji, 10-1/2" (J87)
EX $200   NM $300   MIP $400

Electrospecial No. 21, battery-operated, "Y" Co., 10" (J290)
EX $300   NM $900   MIP $1800

Ferrari Berlinetta 250 LeMans, 1960s, Asahi Toy, 11", red, friction
EX $70   NM $90   MIP $125

(Ron Smith)

Ford, 1960, friction, Haji, 11" (J119)
EX $100   NM $200   MIP $375

(Ron Smith)

Ford Ambulance, 1955, friction, Bandai, 12" (J98)
EX $150   NM $200   MIP $250

Ford Convertible, 1955, Haji, 6-1/2", two-tone blue or red/white, friction
EX $50   NM $75   MIP $125

(Ron Smith)

Ford Convertible, 1955, friction, Bandai, 12" (J100)
EX $225   NM $450   MIP $900

(Ron Smith)

Ford Convertible, 1956, friction, Haji, 11-1/2" (J102)
EX $400   NM $850   MIP $1600

Ford Convertible, 1957, HTC, 12", orange/pink, friction
EX $90   NM $150   MIP $225

(Ron Smith)

Ford Country Sedan, 1961, friction, Bandai, 10-1/2" (J120)
EX $100   NM $160   MIP $225

(Ron Smith)

Ford Country Sedan, 1962, friction, Asahi, 12" (J121)
EX $400   NM $600   MIP $1200

Ford Country Squire Wagon, 1965, 9", white, friction
EX $30   NM $70   MIP $100

Ford Fairlane 500 HT, 1957, ToyMaster, 9-1/2", green/yellow, friction
EX $30   **NM** $60   **MIP** $90

Ford Fairlane Hardtop/Convertible, 1958, friction, Sankei Gangu, 9" (J114)
EX $200   **NM** $400   **MIP** $650

(Ron Smith)

Ford Fairlane Sedan, 1957, friction, Ichiko, 10" (J105)
EX $100   **NM** $200   **MIP** $300

Ford Falcon, 1960s, Marusan, 9", red/white, friction
EX $20   **NM** $40   **MIP** $75

Ford Fire Chief Car, 1963, Taiyo, 12-1/2", red, battery-operated
EX $23   **NM** $40   **MIP** $60

(Ron Smith)

Ford Galaxie Hardtop, 1965, friction, MT, 11" (J125)
EX $200   **NM** $400   **MIP** $800

Ford Gyron, 1960, Ichida, red/black, friction
EX $45   **NM** $100   **MIP** $170

Ford Gyron, 1960, Ichida, 11", red/black, remote control, battery-operated
EX $100   **NM** $200   **MIP** $300

Ford Gyron, 1960, Ichida, 11", red/white, battery-operated
EX $135   **NM** $315   **MIP** $450

(Ron Smith)

Ford Hardtop, 1957, friction, T.N., 12" (J106)
EX $150   **NM** $300   **MIP** $600

(Ron Smith)

Ford Hardtop, 1964, friction, Ichiko, 13" (J122)
EX $200   **NM** $300   **MIP** $600

Ford HT Convertible, 1958, 9-1/2", blue/white, battery-operated
EX $85   **NM** $195   **MIP** $275

Ford HT Convertible, 1958, 11", orange/white, battery-operated
EX $60   **NM** $140   **MIP** $200

Ford HT Convertible, 1959, 11", blue/white, red/white, or green/white, battery-operated
EX $70   **NM** $160   **MIP** $225

Ford Model-T, 9", red, hard top, friction
EX $25   **NM** $50   **MIP** $85

Ford Model-T, 9", black, open top, friction
EX $25   **NM** $55   **MIP** $75

(Ron Smith)

Ford Mustang Fastback, 1965, friction, Bandai, 11" (J139)
EX $45   **NM** $65   **MIP** $90

(Ron Smith)

Ford Mustang Fastback, 1966, friction, T.N., 17" (J143)
EX $100   **NM** $150   **MIP** $250

Ford Mustang GT, 1965, 15-1/2", red, friction
EX $85   **NM** $195   **MIP** $250

Ford Mustang Hardtop/Convertible, 1965, friction/battery-operated, Bandai, 11" (J140)
EX $75   **NM** $125   **MIP** $150

(Ron Smith)

Ford Panel Truck, 1955, "Flowers," friction, Bandai, 12" (J99)
EX $250   **NM** $500   **MIP** $1000

(Ron Smith)

Ford Pickup, 1955, friction, Bandai, 12" (J96)
EX $150   **NM** $300   **MIP** $400

(Ron Smith)

Ford Retractable, 1959, friction, T.N., 11" (J117)
EX $80   **NM** $100   **MIP** $150

(Ron Smith)

Ford Sedan, 1949, wind-up, Guntherman, 11" (J93)
EX $150   **NM** $300   **MIP** $400

Ford Sedan, 1951, 7", tan, battery-operated
EX $30   **NM** $70   **MIP** $100

(Ron Smith)

Ford Sedan, 1956, friction, Marusan, 13" (J103)
EX $2000 **NM** $4000   **MIP** $9000

(Ron Smith)

Ford Sedan/Convertible/Wagon/ Pickup, 1957, friction, Joustra, 12" (J107)
EX $150 NM $200 MIP $275

(Ron Smith)

Ford Station Wagon, 1955, friction, Bandai, 12" (J97)
EX $150 NM $250 MIP $300

Ford Station Wagon, 1959, 10-1/2", green/white, friction
EX $40 NM $90 MIP $125

(Ron Smith)

Ford Station Wagon, 1959, friction, T.N., 12" (J116)
EX $100 NM $150 MIP $200

Ford Stock Car, 1963, Taiyo, 10-1/2", red/silver/blue, friction
EX $15 NM $30 MIP $60

(Ron Smith)

Ford Taunus 17M, 1960s, friction, Bandai, 8" (J145)
EX $40 NM $60 MIP $110

Ford Thunderbird, 1955, friction, Bandai, 7" (J126A)
EX $40 NM $60 MIP $80

(Ron Smith)

Ford Thunderbird, 1956, battery-operated, T.N., 11" (J129)
EX $200 NM $300 MIP $400

(Ron Smith)

Ford Thunderbird, 1956, friction, T.N., 11" (J127)
EX $200 NM $250 MIP $300

(Ron Smith)

Ford Thunderbird, 1963, battery-operated, Yonezawa, 11" (J134)
EX $80 NM $100 MIP $150

Ford Thunderbird Convertible, 1955, 8", orange, friction
EX $45 NM $60 MIP $80

(Ron Smith)

Ford Thunderbird Hardtop, 1964, friction, Asahi, 12" (J136)
EX $150 NM $250 MIP $500

(Ron Smith)

Ford Thunderbird Hardtop, 1965, friction, Bandai, 10-3/4" (J138)
EX $75 NM $150 MIP $300

Ford Thunderbird HT Convertible, 1962, Yonezawa, 11-1/2", red, battery-operated
EX $105 NM $245 MIP $350

(Ron Smith)

Ford Thunderbird HT Convertible, 1964, Ichiko, 15-1/2", red, working side windows, friction
EX $120 NM $275 MIP $600

(Ron Smith)

Ford Thunderbird Retractable, 1963, battery-operated, Yonezawa, 11" (J134)
EX $70 NM $90 MIP $110

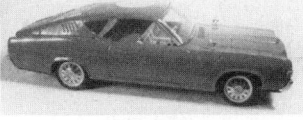
(Ron Smith)

Ford Torino, 1968, friction, S.T., 16" (J126)
EX $200 NM $400 MIP $1000

Ford Two-Door HT, 1956, Ichiko, 10", two-tone blue or orange/white, friction
EX $165 NM $385 MIP $550

Ford Two-Door Sedan, 1956, Marusan, 13", orange/white or blue/white
EX $2000 NM $4000 MIP $9000

(Ron Smith)

Ford Wagon, 1956, friction, Nomura, 10-1/2" (J104)
EX $125 NM $225 MIP $300

Ford Yellow Cab, 1952, Marusan, 10-1/2", yellow, friction, working money meter
EX $200 NM $400 MIP $600

Futuristic Buick LeSabre, 1951, Yonezawa, 7-1/2", black, friction
EX $240 NM $560 MIP $800

GM Gas Turbine Firebird II, 1956, Asahi, 8-1/2", red, friction (J281)
EX $200 NM $400 MIP $800

Jaguar XKE Convertible, 1950s, Tomiyama, 12", white, friction

EX $200 **NM** $350 **MIP** $475

Jaguar XKE Convertible, 1960s, friction, T.T., 10-1/2" (J155)

EX $75 **NM** $150 **MIP** $325

Jaguar XKE Coupe, 1960s, 10-1/2", red, friction

EX $50 **NM** $75 **MIP** $120

Jeep Station Wagon, 1950s, Yonezawa, 7-1/2", two-tone brown, friction

EX $100 **NM** $210 **MIP** $350

Kaiser Darren Convertible, 1950s, 6-1/2", red, friction

EX $30 **NM** $70 **MIP** $100

(Ron Smith)

Lincoln, 1956, friction, Ichiko, 16-1/2" (J165)

EX $200 **NM** $400 **MIP** $800

(Ron Smith)

Lincoln, 1964, friction, unknown manufacturer, 10-1/2" (J169)

EX $90 **NM** $175 **MIP** $300

(Ron Smith)

Lincoln Continental Mark II, 1956, friction, Linemar, 12" (J164)

EX $800 **NM** $1800 **MIP** $3500

(Ron Smith)

Lincoln Continental Mark III Convertible, 1959, friction, Bandai, 12" (J166)

EX $90 **NM** $125 **MIP** $225

(Ron Smith)

Lincoln Continental Mark III Sedan, 1959, friction, Bandai, 12" (J167)

EX $90 **NM** $125 **MIP** $175

(Ron Smith)

Lincoln Hardtop/Convertible, 1960, friction, Yonezawa, 11" (J168)

EX $75 **NM** $125 **MIP** $250

Lincoln Premiere Two-Door HT, 1956, 7-1/2", orange, friction

EX $30 **NM** $70 **MIP** $90

(Ron Smith)

Lincoln Sedan, 1955, friction, Yonezawa, 12" (J163)

EX $600 **NM** $1500 **MIP** $3000

(Ron Smith)

Mazda Auto Tricycle, 1950s, friction, Bandai, 8" (J274)

EX $200 **NM** $400 **MIP** $800

Mercedes 220-S, 1961, 12", black, jack-up feature, friction

EX $75 **NM** $175 **MIP** $250

Mercedes 300 SL Coupe, 1955, 9", metallic red, opening gull-wing doors, battery-operated

EX $105 **NM** $245 **MIP** $350

Mercedes Convertible, 1950s, Alps, 9", red, friction

EX $105 **NM** $245 **MIP** $350

Mercedes Convertible, 1960s, HTC, 8", red, opening door w/swing-out driver, friction

EX $45 **NM** $105 **MIP** $150

(Ron Smith)

Mercedes-Benz 219 Convertible, 1960s, friction, Bandai, 8" (J177)

EX $50 **NM** $90 **MIP** $150

(Ron Smith)

Mercedes-Benz 219 Sedan, 1960s, friction, Bandai, 8" (J176)

EX $50 **NM** $80 **MIP** $150

(Ron Smith)

Mercury Cougar Hardtop, 1967, friction, Asakusa Toys, 15" (J197)

EX $200 **NM** $450 **MIP** $950

(Ron Smith)

Mercury Hardtop, 1956, friction, Alps, 9-1/2" (J193)

EX $600 **NM** $800 **MIP** $2200

(Ron Smith)

Mercury Hardtop, 1958, friction, Yonezawa, 11-1/2" (J195)
EX $300 **NM** $400   **MIP** $600

Midget Special No. 6, friction, "Y" Co., 7" (J291)
EX $200 **NM** $400   **MIP** $900

Oldsmobile, 1952, friction, "Y" Co., 11" (J207A)
EX $150 **NM** $350   **MIP** $500

Oldsmobile, 1958, Asahi Toy, 12", gold/black, friction
EX $540 **NM** $1260   **MIP** $1800

(Ron Smith)

Oldsmobile Convertible/Sedan/ Wagon, 1961, friction, Yonezawa, 12" (J214)
EX $150 **NM** $300   **MIP** $600

Oldsmobile Highway Patrol Car, 1959, Ichiko, 12-1/2", black/white, friction, working speed meter on trunk
EX $75   **NM** $175   **MIP** $250

Oldsmobile Rally Car, 1961, Asahi Toy, 15", red, friction
EX $55   **NM** $125   **MIP** $175

(Ron Smith)

Oldsmobile Sedan, 1956, friction, Ichiko/Kanto, 10-1/2" (J208)
EX $400 **NM** $600   **MIP** $1200

(Ron Smith)

Oldsmobile Sedan, 1958, friction, A.T.C., 12" (J210)
EX $200 **NM** $300   **MIP** $600

Oldsmobile Station Wagon, 1958, 7-1/2", red/black, friction
EX $30   **NM** $60   **MIP** $90

Oldsmobile Super 88, 1956, Modern Toys, 14", orange, battery-operated, working headlights and signal lights
EX $200 **NM** $400   **MIP** $600

(Ron Smith)

Oldsmobile Super 88 Sedan, 1956, friction, Masudaya, 16" (J209)
EX $150 **NM** $200   **MIP** $400

(Ron Smith)

Oldsmobile Toronado, 1966, battery-operated, Bandai, 11" (J215)
EX $65   **NM** $100   **MIP** $125

(Ron Smith)

Oldsmobile Toronado, 1968, friction, Ichiko, 17-1/2" (J216)
EX $200 **NM** $300   **MIP** $400

(Ron Smith)

Oldsmobile Two-Door HT, 1959, Ichiko, 12-1/2", two-tone blue, two-tone green, or brown/white, friction
EX $135 **NM** $315   **MIP** $450

Packard Convertible/Sedan, 1953, friction, Alps, 16" (J222)
EX $600 **NM** $1500   **MIP** $3000

(Ron Smith)

Packard Hawk Convertible, 1957, battery-operated, Schuco, 10-3/4" (J223)
EX $300 **NM** $500   **MIP** $1000

Plymouth Convertible, 1959, Asahi Toy, 11", red/white, friction
EX $330 **NM** $770   **MIP** $1200

(Ron Smith)

Plymouth Fury Hardtop, 1957, friction, "Y" Co., 11-1/2" (J226)
EX $300 **NM** $400   **MIP** $800

(Ron Smith)

Plymouth Fury/Sedan/Wagon/Conv., 1958, friction, Bandai, 8" (J227)
EX $75   **NM** $90   **MIP** $165

(Ron Smith)

Plymouth Hardtop, 1956, battery-operated, Alps, 12" (J225)
EX $300 **NM** $400   **MIP** $600

(Ron Smith)

Plymouth Hardtop, 1956, friction, unknown manufacturer, 8-1/2" (J224)

EX $80   **NM** $100   **MIP** $150

(Ron Smith)

Plymouth Hardtop, 1959, friction, A.T.C., 10-1/2" (J228)

EX $200   **NM** $400   **MIP** $850

Plymouth HT, 1956, Alps, 8-1/2", two-tone green, friction

EX $165   **NM** $300   **MIP** $450

(Ron Smith)

Plymouth Sedan, 1961, friction, Ichiko, 12" (J230)

EX $200   **NM** $600   **MIP** $950

(Ron Smith)

Plymouth Station Wagon, 1961, friction, Ichiko, 12" (J231)

EX $150   **NM** $300   **MIP** $600

(Ron Smith)

Plymouth T.V. Car, 1961, battery-operated, Ichiko, 12" (J232)

EX $300   **NM** $800   **MIP** $1200

(Ron Smith)

Pontiac, 1954, friction, Minister, 11" (J218A)

EX $10   **NM** $15   **MIP** $20

(Ron Smith)

Pontiac Firebird, 1967, friction, Bandai, 10" (J220)

EX $30   **NM** $55   **MIP** $80

(Ron Smith)

Pontiac Firebird, 1967, friction, Akasura, 15-1/2" (J219)

EX $350   **NM** $800   **MIP** $1500

Pontiac Four-Door HT, 1958, Asahi Toy, 8", green/pink, friction

EX $45   **NM** $105   **MIP** $150

Porsche 911 Rally, 1960s, 11", red, friction

EX $70   **NM** $160   **MIP** $225

Porsche 914 Rally, 1960s, Daiya, 9", blue, battery-operated

EX $25   **NM** $55   **MIP** $75

(Ron Smith)

Porsche Speedster, 1950s, battery-operated, Distler, 10-1/2" (J235)

EX $200   **NM** $300   **MIP** $600

Porsche Speedster, 1950s, battery-operated, Distler, 10-1/2" (J235)

EX $200   **NM** $300   **MIP** $600

(Ron Smith)

Rambler Rebel Station Wagon, 1960s, friction, Bandai, 12" (J240)

EX $60   **NM** $150   **MIP** $200

Renault, 1960, friction, Bandai, 7-1/2" (J241)

EX $60   **NM** $90   **MIP** $150

Rolls Royce, 1960, friction, T.N., 10-1/2" (J239)

EX $200   **NM** $400   **MIP** $800

(Ron Smith)

Rolls Royce Silver Coupe Convertible, 1960, friction, Bandai, 12" (J236)

EX $100   **NM** $150   **MIP** $300

(Ron Smith)

Rolls Royce Silver Sedan Coupe,
1960s, friction, Bandai, 12" (J237)
EX $100 **NM** $150 **MIP** $250

(Ron Smith)

Studebaker, 1954, friction, Yoshiya,
9" (J243)
EX $150 **NM** $225 **MIP** $450

(Ron Smith)

Studebaker Avanti, 1960s, friction,
Bandai, 8" (J242)
EX $90 **NM** $150 **MIP** $250

Studebaker Coupe, 1953, 9", yellow,
friction, working wipers
EX $45 **NM** $100 **MIP** $175

Studebaker Lark, 1950s, 5-1/2", blue,
friction SSS
EX $20 **NM** $45 **MIP** $65

(Ron Smith)

Volkswagen, 1960s, battery-
operated, Bandai, 11" (J264)
EX $75 **NM** $125 **MIP** $200

(Ron Smith)

Volkswagen Convertible, 1950,
friction, T.N., 9-1/2" (J258)
EX $100 **NM** $150 **MIP** $250

(Ron Smith)

Volkswagen Convertible, 1960s,
battery-operated, Bandai, 11" (J260)
EX $110 **NM** $200 **MIP** $450

(Ron Smith)

Volkswagen Karmann-Ghia, 1960,
friction, Bandai, 7" (J252), add $50
for convertible
EX $100 **NM** $200 **MIP** $450

Volkswagen Micro-Bus, 1960s,
orange w/white top; 1960s (J256),
9-1/2", Model No. J256
EX $70 **NM** $150 **MIP** $300

(Ron Smith)

Volkswagen w/or w/out Sun Roof,
1960s, friction, Bandai, 15" (J265)
EX $90 **NM** $120 **MIP** $250

Volvo, 1950s, 5-1/2", red, friction SSS
EX $20 **NM** $40 **MIP** $80

(Ron Smith)

Volvo, 1950s, wind-up, Sweden, 11"
(J265A)
EX $600 **NM** $900 **MIP** $1500

Volvo PV-544, 1950s, HoKu, 7-1/2",
black, friction
EX $100 **NM** $200 **MIP** $350

VW Convertible, 1950s, 9-1/2", dark
blue, maroon, or light metallic blue,
friction w/battery-operated engine
light
EX $85 **NM** $195 **MIP** $275

VW Rabbit Rally Team Car, 1970s,
Asahi Toy, 8", yellow, battery-operated
EX $20 **NM** $45 **MIP** $65

VW Sedan, 1950s, 7-1/2", gray, oval
window, friction
EX $45 **NM** $105 **MIP** $150

Zephyr Deluxe Convertible, 1950s,
11", maroon/yellow/blue, friction
EX $120 **NM** $280 **MIP** $400

Johnny Lightning/Topper

(KP Photo)

'32 Roadster, 1969, varied color body, rumble seat in back flips up, this model has missing windshield, common to play worn examples

EX $25   **NM** $60   **MIP** $150

A.J. Foyt Indy Special, 1970, blackwall tires

EX $40   **NM** $60   **MIP** $250

(KP Photo, Tom Michael collection)

Al Unser Indy Special, 1970, chrome blue finish, Lightning number "2" decal, blackwall tires

EX $100   **NM** $200   **MIP** $500

Baja, 1970

EX $45   **NM** $125   **MIP** $200

(KP Photo, Tom Michael collection)

Big Rig, 1971, originally included add on extras called "Customs"; prices reflect fully accessorized car, called the "Track Bac" in the 1970 Topper Toys catalog

EX $65   **NM** $150   **MIP** $275

Bubble, 1970, jet powered

EX $45   **NM** $75   **MIP** $150

(Photo courtesy Dennis Seleman)

Bug Bomb, 1970, various chromed color schemes, two silver engines, blackwall tires, this example is missing the rear engine

EX $40   **NM** $90   **MIP** $240

Condor, 1970, blackwall tires

EX $150   **NM** $200   **MIP** $1200

Custom Camaro, 1968-69, prototype, only one known to exist

EX n/a   **NM** $6000   **MIP** n/a

Custom Charger, 1968-69, prototype, only one known to exist, a version of this car was released by Playing Mantis as part of the "Lost Toppers" series

EX n/a   **NM** $6000   **MIP** n/a

Custom Continental, 1968-69, prototype, only six known to exist, another casting re-released by Playing Mantis

EX n/a   **NM** $4000   **MIP** n/a

Custom Dragster, 1969, w/out canopy

EX $35   **NM** $75   **MIP** $125

Custom Dragster, 1969, mirror finish

EX $150   **NM** $250   **MIP** $1000

(KP Photo)

Custom Dragster, 1969, version w/a plastic canopy, Topper-style redlines wheels, unpainted base, while versions were made w/out a canopy, the example here is simply missing one

EX $60   **NM** $150   **MIP** $200

Custom El Camino, 1969, w/sealed doors

EX $110   **NM** $300   **MIP** $550

(Photo courtesy Dennis Seleman)

Custom El Camino, 1969, w/opening doors, surfboards on back, Topper-style redlines wheels

EX $150   **NM** $275   **MIP** $475

Custom El Camino, 1969, mirror finish

EX $200   **NM** $350   **MIP** $1125

Custom Eldorado, 1969, w/sealed doors

EX $200   **NM** $450   **MIP** $1000

Custom Eldorado, 1969, w/opening doors

EX $150   **NM** $275   **MIP** $350

Custom Ferrari, 1969, w/opening doors, mirror finish

EX $300   **NM** $450   **MIP** $1000

(KP Photo)

Custom Ferrari, 1969, w/sealed doors

EX $40   **NM** $80   **MIP** $130

Custom Ferrari, 1969, w/opening doors

EX $150   **NM** $275   **MIP** $500

Custom GTO, 1969, mirror finish

EX $200   **NM** $475   **MIP** $1200

Custom GTO, 1969, w/sealed doors

EX $200   **NM** $450   **MIP** $1700

Custom GTO, 1969, w/opening doors

EX $200   **NM** $450   **MIP** $1500

Custom Mako Shark, 1969, w/sealed doors

EX $40   **NM** $75   **MIP** $225

(Photo Courtesy Dennis Seleman)

Custom Mako Shark, 1969, w/opening doors, mirror finish

EX $200   **NM** $500   **MIP** $2000

Custom Mako Shark, 1969, w/opening doors

EX $125   **NM** $350   **MIP** $500

Custom Mustang, 1968-69, prototype, only one known to exist
EX n/a   NM $6000   MIP n/a

Custom Spoiler, 1970, blackwall tires
EX $35   NM $75   MIP $160

Custom T-Bird, 1969, w/opening doors
EX $100   NM $250   MIP $475

Custom T-Bird, 1969, mirror finish
EX $200   NM $450   MIP $5000

Custom T-Bird, 1969, w/sealed doors
EX $150   NM $300   MIP $700

Custom Toronado, 1969, w/opening doors
EX $225   NM $400   MIP $1000

Custom Toronado, 1969, mirror finish
EX $450   NM $650   MIP $2000

Custom Toronado, 1969, w/sealed doors
EX $300   NM $500   MIP $1500

Custom Turbine, 1969, red, black, white painted interior
EX $50   NM $150   MIP $200

(KP Photo, Tom Michael collection)

Custom Turbine, 1969, w/unpainted interior, Topper redline-style wheels
EX $30   NM $60   MIP $125

Custom Turbine, 1969, mirror finish
EX $150   NM $225   MIP $550

Custom XKE, 1969, w/opening doors, mirror finish
EX $300   NM $450   MIP $800

(KP Photo, Tom Michael collection)

Custom XKE, 1969, w/sealed doors, unpainted base, full window plastic all-around, opening hood, blackwall tires
EX $35   NM $80   MIP $110

(KP Photo, Tom Michael collection)

Custom XKE, 1969, w/opening doors, unpainted base, opening hood, blackwall tires
EX $150   NM $275   MIP $500

Double Trouble, 1970, blackwall tires
EX $75   NM $180   MIP $1500

Flame Out, 1970, blackwall tires
EX $60   NM $150   MIP $350

Flying Needle, 1970, jet powered
EX $45   NM $125   MIP $225

(KP Photo)

Frantic Ferrari, 1970, unpainted base, silver exposed engine, various finishes
EX $35   NM $55   MIP $110

Glasser, 1970, jet powered
EX $40   NM $85   MIP $150

Hairy Hauler, 1971, Came w/add-on extras called "Customs;" prices reflect fully accessorized cars
EX $65   NM $150   MIP $275

Jumpin' Jag, 1970, blackwall tires
EX $35   NM $80   MIP $175

(KP Photo)

Leapin' Limo, 1970, blackwall tires, large silver and black plastic engine, example here shows Topper packaging, duplicated to an extent by Playing Mantis w/the Commemorative series
EX $50   NM $125   MIP $400

Mad Maverick, 1970, blackwall tires
EX $75   NM $150   MIP $450

Monster, 1970, jet powered
EX $40   NM $74   MIP $150

Movin' Van, 1970, blackwall tires
EX $35   NM $65   MIP $90

(KP Photo, Tom Michael collection)

Nucleon, 1970, blackwall tires
EX $40   NM $85   MIP $220

Parnelli Jones Indy Special, 1970, blackwall tires
EX $40   NM $85   MIP $250

Pipe Dream, 1971, came w/add-on extras called "Customs"; prices reflect fully accessorized cars
EX $65   NM $150   MIP $275

(KP Photo, Tom Michael collection)

Sand Stormer, 1970, blackwall tires
EX $25   NM $45   MIP $100

Sand Stormer, 1970, black roof, blackwall tires
EX $50   NM $100   MIP $200

Screamer, 1970, jet powered
EX $45   NM $75   MIP $200

Sling Shot, 1970, blackwall tires
EX $50   NM $95   MIP $250

Smuggler, 1970, blackwall tires
EX $35   NM $75   MIP $150

(KP Photo)

Stiletto, 1970, blackwall tires, various paint schemes, the example shown is pretty rough, the casting was re-released by Playing Mantis as part of the "Topper Series"
EX $60   NM $85   MIP $300

TNT, 1970, blackwall tires
EX $40   NM $75   MIP $175

Triple Threat, 1970, blackwall tires
EX $40   NM $90   MIP $200

Matchbox
KING-SIZE

K1-1, Hydraulic Shovel, 1960, yellow body and front loader, no plastic windows, no interior, gray plastic wheels
EX $30 **NM** $65 **MIP** $95

(KP Photo by Dr. Douglas Sadecky)

K1-2, Foden Tipper Truck, 1964, red cab and chassis, orange dumper bed w/"Hoveringham" decals or labels on sides, red plastic wheels w/removable black plastic tires, blue plastic windows, no interior, axle suspension system to roll over bumps, silver metal horns on cab, 4-1/2"
EX $20 **NM** $45 **MIP** $75

K1-3, O & K Excavator, 1970, red body w/silver excavator arm, red hubs w/eight black plastic removable tires, "MH6," "O&K" and white stripe labels on sides, 4-15/16"
EX $15 **NM** $25 **MIP** $50

K2-1, Dumper Truck, 1960, blocky red body and chassis w/open cab, gray or black plastic tires on green metal hubs, "Muir-Hill" decals
EX $25 **NM** $45 **MIP** $90

(KP Photo by Dr. Douglas Sadecky)

K2-2, KW-Dart Dump Truck, 1964, yellow articulated body w/silver trim on engine and hood, red hubs w/removable black plastic tires, "KW-Dart" decals w/arrow graphic, no window plastic, 5-5/8"
EX $30 **NM** $65 **MIP** $110

K2-3, Scammell Heavy Wreck Truck, 1969, white or gold body w/red plastic hubs and black removable wheels, silver metal hooks, red

towing arm, silver horns on cab roof, "Esso" labels on doors, 4-3/4"
EX $20 **NM** $40 **MIP** $75

(KP Photo by Dr. Douglas Sadecky)

K3-1, Caterpillar Bulldozer, 1960, yellow body w/green rubber treads and unpainted metal or yellow or red plastic roller wheels, cast tow hook, red-painted engine
EX $25 **NM** $50 **MIP** $90

(KP Photo by Dr. Douglas Sadecky)

K3-2, Hatra Tractor Shovel, 1965, orange-red body w/articulating center and lifting loader, blue-tinted plastic windows, "Hatra" decals on sides of cab, red hubs w/black plastic removable tires, 6"
EX $36 **NM** $65 **MIP** $110

K3-3, Massey-Ferguson Tractor and Trailer, 1970, red cab and hood w/gray engine and base, yellow hubs w/removable black plastic tires, white grille, green plastic windows, trailer w/yellow chassis, red dumper bed, yellow hubs w/black removable tires, set measures 8"
EX $17 **NM** $35 **MIP** $80

(KP Photo)

K4-1, International Tractor, 1960, red body w/"McCormick International" and "B-250" decals, green, red or orange hubs w/black plastic removable tires, 2-7/8"
EX $25 **NM** $40 **MIP** $75

(KP Photo by Dr. Douglas Sadecky)

K4-2, GMC Tractor w/Hopper Train, 1967, red tractor w/two silver hopper trailers, red plastic hubs w/black plastic removable wheels, opening chutes, "Fruehauf" decals on each trailer, set measures 11-1/4"
EX $55 **NM** $90 **MIP** $150

(KP Photo)

K4-3, Leyland Tipper, 1969, red cab and chassis, silver dumper bed, red hubs w/black plastic removable tires, (duals in rear), "Wates" and "LE Transport" labels most common, amber plastic windows, yellow plastic interior, 4-1/2", some hard-to-find models w/green cabs exist, but have approx. $300 MIP values, other models include orange cabs w/green dumper beds
EX $15 **NM** $25 **MIP** $50

(KP Photo by Dr. Douglas Sadecky)

K5-1, Tipper Truck, 1961, yellow body, silver-painted grille, silver metal or red plastic hubs w/black tires, "Foden" decal on sides of hood, 4-1/4", first-version siver-hub models about $80 MIP
EX $25 **NM** $50 **MIP** $80

(KP Photo)

K5-2, Racing Car Transporter, 1967, medium-green body, cream plastic interior, clear plastic windows and skylights, red plastic hubs w/black removable tires, decals on sides show racing car graphic w/"Racing Transporter," "BP," and "LeMans, Sebring, Silverstone, Nurburgring," silver metal base, opening tailgate reveals tilting ramp and space for two racing cars, 5", this model entered the King-Size line, after being number M-6 in the Major Packs series

EX $25   **NM** $50   **MIP** $85

K6-1, Allis-Chalmers Earth Scraper, 1961, orange scraper w/silver metal or red plastic hubs and black plastic tires, adjustable scaper bed w/springs (sometimes missing) "Allis-Chalmers" decals, 5-7/8"

EX $45   **NM** $80   **MIP** $130

(KP Photo)

K6-2, Mercedes-Benz "Binz" Ambulance, 1967, white body w/blue plastic windows and dome light, black base, red cross decal on hood and shield decals on opening doors, opening rear hatch w/white plastic patient and red plastic blanket, silver hubs w/black plastic tires, silver metal grille and bumpers, "True Guide" steering, 4-1/8"

EX $15   **NM** $25   **MIP** $60

(KP Photo by Dr. Douglas Sadecky)

K7-1, Curtiss-Wright Rear Dumper, 1961, yellow articulated body w/silver metal hubs and black plastic tires, tilting dumper bed, "Curtiss-Wright" decals, red-painted engine block, 5-3/4"

EX $40   **NM** $80   **MIP** $125

K7-2, SD Refuse Truck, 1967, red cab and chassis, silver rear refuse unit, "Cleansing Service" decals or labels, red plastic wheels w/black plastic tires, cream-colored plastic interior, clear plastic windows, 4-5/8"

EX $15   **NM** $25   **MIP** $45

(KP Photo by Dr. Douglas Sadecky)

K8-1, Prime Mover and Transporter w/Caterpillar Tractor, 1962, orange body and trailer, yellow "Laing" decals, metal towhook, unpainted metal or red plastic wheels w/black plastic tires, yellow tractor w/green treads and no blade, set measures 12-1/2"

EX $125 **NM** $180 **MIP** $275

K8-2, Car Transporter, 1967, green or yellow cab, orange or yellow trailer, orange or red plastic wheels w/black plastic tires, "Car Auction Collection" and "Farnborough Meashan" decals on trailer, 8-1/2"

EX $25   **NM** $45   **MIP** $85

K8-3, Caterpillar Traxcavator, 1970, various versions of shades of yellow cab, orange shovel and arms, figure, yellow or black wheels w/green or black treads, "available mid-1970" in catalog, 4-1/4"

EX $15   **NM** $25   **MIP** $50

K9-1, Diesel Road Roller, 1962, green body, red metal rollers, gray or red driver, red "Aveling Barford" decals on sides w/white reversed type, 3-3/4"

EX $35   **NM** $65   **MIP** $95

(KP Photo)

K9-2, Claas Combine Harvester, 1967, green or red body, red or yellow reels, "Claas" decals or labels, yellow plastic wheels w/black plastic tires, 5-1/2"

EX $22   **NM** $40   **MIP** $80

K10-1, Aveling-Barford Tractor Shovel, 1963, light-blue body and shovel, red seat, w/or w/out air filter, unpainted metal or red plastic wheels w/black plastic tires, 4-1/8"

EX $30   **NM** $60   **MIP** $90

K10-2, Pipe Truck, 1967, yellow cab and trailer chassis, black house-shaped decal on cab doors, gray plastic pipes, red plastic wheels w/black plastic tires, later issues had Superfast wheels and pink cab and chassis, 8"

EX $20   **NM** $50   **MIP** $100

(KP Photo)

K11-1, Fordson Tractor and Trailer, 1963, blue tractor body and trailer chassis, light-gray trailer bed, orange metal or plastic wheels w/black plastic tires, 6-1/4"

EX $25   **NM** $45   **MIP** $80

K11-2, DAF Car Transporter, 1969, metallic blue cab w/gold trailer or yellow cab w/orange and yellow trailer, DAF labels, red plastic wheels w/black plastic tires or Superfast Wheels, 9"

EX $20   **NM** $50   **MIP** $85

(KP Photo by Dr. Douglas Sadecky)

K12-1, Heavy Breakdown Wreck Truck, 1963, green body, yellow boom, w/or w/out roof lights, unpainted metal or red plastic wheels w/black plastic tires, 4-3/4"

EX $25   **NM** $50   **MIP** $85

(KP Photo)

K12-2, Scammell Crane Truck, 1970, yellow cab and crane, red plastic wheels w/black plastic tires or orange body and crane w/Superfast wheels, 6"

EX $20   **NM** $35   **MIP** $60

(KP Photo by Dr. Douglas Sadecky)

K13-1, Ready-Mix Concrete Truck,
1963, orange body and mixer
w/unpainted metal or red plastic
wheels w/black plastic tires, green
plastic windows, no interior,
"Readymix" or "RMC" decals on
mixer barrel, 4-1/2"

EX $25   **NM** $50   **MIP** $80

(KP Photo by Dr. Douglas Sadecky)

K14-1, Taylor Jumbo Crane, 1964,
yellow body and crane, green
windows, red or yellow weight box,
red plastic wheels w/black plastic
tires, 5-1/4"

EX $18   **NM** $30   **MIP** $60

(KP Photo)

K15-1, Merryweather Fire Engine,
1964, red body, gray extending
ladder, red plastic wheels w/black
plastic tires or Superfast wheels,
6-1/8"

EX $25   **NM** $45   **MIP** $75

(KP Photo by Dr. Douglas Sadecky)

**K16-1, Dodge Tractor w/Twin
Tippers,** 1966, green cab and trailer
chassis, yellow dumps, Dodge
Trucks decals, red plastic wheels
w/black plastic tires; later issues
had yellow cab w/blue dump and
Superfast wheels, 11-7/8"

EX $65   **NM** $135   **MIP** $185

(KP Photo by Dr. Douglas Sadecky)

K17-1, Low Loader w/Bulldozer,
1967, green Ford cab and trailer,
red plastic wheels w/black plastic
tires, red Case bulldozer body,
yellow roof and blade, green treads,
"Laing" or "Taylor Woodrow"
decals or labels, later issues had
Superfast wheels and lime-green
cab and trailer, 9-1/2"

EX $60   **NM** $90   **MIP** $150

K18-1, Articulated Horse Box, 1967,
red Dodge cab w/tan trailer, clear
windows on trailer, gray ramp, four
white horses, red plastic wheels
w/black plastic tires, later issues
had Superfast wheels, 6-5/8"

EX $35   **NM** $55   **MIP** $100

K19-1, Scammell Tipper Truck, 1967,
red cab and yellow dump, red
plastic wheels w/black plastic tires
or Superfast wheels, 4-3/4"

EX $20   **NM** $35   **MIP** $60

K20-1, Tractor Transporter, 1968, red
Ford cab and trailer, red plastic
wheels w/black plastic tires, green
plastic windows, three blue tractors
w/yellow wheels, later issues had
Superfast wheels, 9"

EX $65   **NM** $100   **MIP** $150

K21-1, Mercury Cougar, 1968, gold
body, red or white interior,
unpainted metal wheels w/black
plastic tires, 4-1/8", shown in blue
in 1968 catalog, announcing model
would be available mid-year

EX $25   **NM** $50   **MIP** $75

K22-1, Dodge Charger, 1969, dark-
blue body, light-blue interior,
unpainted metal wheels w/black
plastic tires w/"True Guide"
steering, 4-1/2", shown in 1969
catalog, announcing available mid-
year

EX $25   **NM** $50   **MIP** $75

(KP Photo)

K23-1, Mercury Police Car, 1969, white
body, red interior, blue dome lights,
police labels, unpainted metal wheels
w/black plastic tires w/"True Guide"
steering or Superfast wheels, 4-3/8",
introduced in 1969 catalog as being
available mid-year

EX $20   **NM** $35   **MIP** $50

K24-1, Lamborghini Miura, 1969, red
body, white interior, unpainted
metal wheels w/black plastic tires
and "True Guide" steering, many
color and wheel variations exist, 4"

EX $20   **NM** $35   **MIP** $55

Matchbox

REGULAR WHEELS

1-1RW, Road Roller, 1953, one of the first Matchbox offerings, this model had a "steamroller"-style large-roofed cab that matched the large toy produced by Lesney, green paint on body can vary in shade, red metal wheels and rollers

EX $40   NM $75   MIP $125

1-2RW, Diesel Road Roller, 1955, second in the series, but first w/a smaller cab, roller attachment a little more snug than the first version, red metal wheels and roller, driver available in light and dark tan variations, gold-painted upright tow hook, 2-1/4"

EX $30   NM $60   MIP $100

1-3RW, Road Roller, 1958, third in the series, this casting kept the driver, but changed the tow hook at rear of the tractor, it still featured red metal wheels and rollers, 2-1/4"

EX $45   NM $70   MIP $95

(KP Photo)

1-4RW, Diesel Road Roller, 1962, green w/orange/red plastic wheels, open window on cab behind driver, tow hook on back. 2-5/8", "Aveling Barford Road Roller" on base near rear wheels

EX $12   NM $30   MIP $60

(KP Photo, George Cuhaj collection)

1-5RW, Mercedes-Benz Truck, 1968, light pea-green, w/orange or yellow plastic canopy, truck could be

hitched to a matching trailer, released the same year, 3"

EX $5   NM $12   MIP $20

2-1RW, Dumper, 1953, this first version featured a gold-painted front grille on a green body w/red dump bed, 1-1/2"

EX $25   NM $60   MIP $100

(KP Photo by Dr. Douglas Sadecky)

2-2RW, Dumper, 1957, second casting is larger than first, w/less painted detail, first issue w/metal wheels, second w/gray plastic wheels, green body, red dumper bed, 2", pictured here w/2-3RW Muir-Hill Dumper

EX $25   NM $60   MIP $90

(KP Photo, George Cuhaj collection)

2-3RW, Dumper, 1961, short, blocky cab w/"Laing" or "Muir-Hill" decal on right-hand door, red cab w/pea-green dumper bed, black plastic wheels, 2-1/8", although the cab is different, this model is very similar to the K-2 dumper released one year earlier, "Muir-Hill" decal versions can have about $100 MIP value

EX $12   NM $22   MIP $45

(KP Photo, George Cuhaj collection)

2-3RW, Dumper, 1961, another view of 2-3RW, also simply called "Dumper" in Matchbox 1966 catalog

EX $12   NM $22   MIP $45

(KP Photo, George Cuhaj collection)

2-4RW, Mercedes-Benz Trailer, 1968, pea-green trailer released same year as Mercedes-Benz Truck, 1-5RW, also came w/orange or yellow canopy, 3-1/2"

EX $5   NM $10   MIP $20

(KP Photo by Dr. Douglas Sadecky)

3-1RW, Cement Mixer, 1953, another early Matchbox, this model mirrors one of Lesney's first larger die-cast toys, variations seem to exist in castings, earlier models measure slightly larger at 1-3/4" length than the later ones, coming in at 1-1/2" length, orange metal or gray plastic wheels

EX $25   NM $60   MIP $120

(KP Photo, Tom Michael collection)

3-2RW, Bedford Tipper Truck, 1961, available in red and maroon dumper variations, as well as gray and black plastic wheels, 2-1/2"

EX $10   NM $25   MIP $60

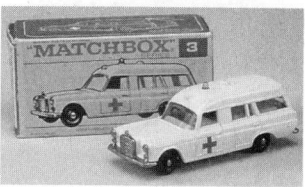

(KP Photo)

3-3RW, Mercedes-Benz "Binz" Ambulance, 1968, white or cream body w/Red Cross label or decal and plastic patient on stretcher, this

was a smaller version of the K-6 ambulance released one year earlier, 2-7/8", unpainted base w/textured surface along sides and near back tailgate
EX $10   **NM** $18   **MIP** $35

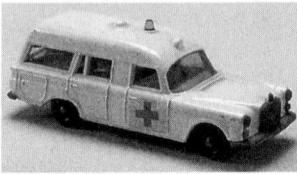

(KP Photo)

3-3RW, Mercedes-Benz "Binz" Ambulance, 1968, variation photo showing cream paint and decal version of Mercedes ambulance
EX $10   **NM** $18   **MIP** $30

(KP Photo)

4-1RW, Tractor, 1954, red Massey-Harris tractor body and fenders; a small version of larger Lesney Massey-Harris toy tractor
EX $35   **NM** $65   **MIP** $125

4-2RW, Massey-Harris Tractor, 1957, red w/no fenders, an update on the previous model, metal wheel and gray plastic wheel variations, some casting variations w/1-1/2" and 1-3/4" lengths
EX $30   **NM** $65   **MIP** $100

(KP Photo)

4-3RW, Triumph Motorcycle w/Sidecar, 1960, light metallic blue w/24-spoke silver wheels and black tires, 2-1/8"
EX $17   **NM** $40   **MIP** $100

(KP Photo, George Cuhaj collection)

4-3RW, Triumph Motorcycle w/Sidecar, 1960, another view of the Triumph Motorcycle w/Sidecar
EX $17   **NM** $40   **MIP** $100

(KP Photo, George Cuhaj collection)

4-4RW, Dodge Stake Truck, 1967, yellow cab and body w/green plastic stakes, a popular model, Matchbox made many toy trucks w/this Dodge cab style, 2-7/8", models w/blue-green stakes, a very slight color difference, can have about $150 MIP value
EX $10   **NM** $18   **MIP** $27

5-1RW, Double Decker Bus, 1954, first of Matchbox's London Buses, this one featured decals that read "Buy Matchbox Series" on the side, 2"
EX $20   **NM** $45   **MIP** $100

(KP Photo, Tom Michael collection)

5-2RW, Double Decker Bus, 1958, second London Bus, casting slightly larger, at 2-1/4" length, "No. 5" cast into front of bus, no interior, available w/metal and gray plastic wheels, w/a variety of decals
EX $30   **NM** $60   **MIP** $120

5-3RW, Routemaster London Bus, 1961, red, w/gray or black plastic wheels, "Visco-Static" decal most common, no interior in bus, major change from last model: a wider front grille, w/cast headlights on front fenders
EX $20   **NM** $40   **MIP** $70

(KP Photo)

5-4RW, Routemaster London Bus, 1965, red body, white plastic interior-first Matchbox model bus to feature one, like 5-3RW, the "Visco-Static" decals and labels are the most common, 2-3/4"
EX $8   **NM** $15   **MIP** $30

(KP Photo)

6-1RW, Quarry Truck, 1954, orange body w/gray dumper bed, no interior, most commonly seen w/metal wheels, crimped or rounded axles, 2-1/4"
EX $20   **NM** $50   **MIP** $100

6-2RW, Quarry Truck, 1959, yellow body, black plastic wheels most common, red, white and black decal on cab doors, cab extends the full width of the front of truck, appears first in 1959 catalog w/black plastic wheels
EX $15   **NM** $35   **MIP** $75

(KP Photo)

6-3RW, Euclid 10-Wheel Quarry Truck, 1964, yellow body, no decals, exposed engine shows on casting, partial cab does not extend across body of truck, 2-5/8"

EX $7   **NM** $15   **MIP** $30

(KP Photo, George Cuhaj collection)

6-4RW, Ford Pickup, 1969, red, w/white plastic camper top and white or silver plastic front grille, featured "Autosteer," a Matchbox innovation making its appearance in the 1969 catalog, that "turns the front wheels in either direction by simple pressure," 2-3/4"

EX $10   **NM** $20   **MIP** $30

(KP Photo by Dr. Douglas Sadecky)

7-1RW, Horse-Drawn Milk Float, 1954, orange wagon body, white painted driver, brown horse, available w/metal spoked or gray solid plastic wheels, 2-1/4"

EX $45   **NM** $75   **MIP** $125

(KP Photo, George Cuhaj collection)

7-2RW, Ford Anglia, 1961, light blue body, no interior, gray, silver or black plastic wheels, silver painted grille, bumper and headlights, 2-5/8", black-painted baseplate, tow hook, gray plastic wheel versions, about $110 MIP; silver plastic wheel versions, about $55 MIP, thanks to the film, "Harry Potter and the Chamber of Secrets," (2002) interest in these models has increased

EX $25   **NM** $60   **MIP** $95

(KP Photo by Dr. Douglas Sadecky)

7-2RW, Ford Anglia, 1961, a view of a gray-plastic-wheel version of the Ford Anglia, a harder-to-find variation

EX $30   **NM** $60   **MIP** $110

(KP Photo, Tom Michael collection)

7-3RW, Ford Refuse Truck, 1967, red body, gray and silver dumper section, tilts together when dumped, no interior, black plastic wheels, green window plastic, 3"

EX $10   **NM** $18   **MIP** $30

(KP Photo)

8-1RW, Caterpillar Tractor, 1955, yellow or orange w/cast driver, silver-painted grille, unpainted roller wheels for treads, 1-1/2", fully exposed engine under hood, note: orange variation harder to find, MIP value can reach over $200; yellow versions w/painted drivers also about $200 MIP

EX $20   **NM** $40   **MIP** $85

8-2RW, Caterpillar Tractor, 1959, yellow, different casting w/engine partially covered by hood, and cast "roller wheels" between two actual turning metal wheels, driver cast w/toy, 1-3/4", green or gray rubber treads

EX $25   **NM** $65   **MIP** $90

8-3RW, Caterpillar Crawler Tractor, 1961, yellow body w/cast driver, metal or plastic tread wheels, very similar to previous casting, models w/silver plastic roller wheels about $100 MIP

EX $20   **NM** $40   **MIP** $65

(KP Photo, Tom Michael collection)

8-4RW, Caterpillar Crawler Tractor, 1965, yellow, cast w/out driver, black plastic roller wheels, 2"

EX $12   **NM** $22   **MIP** $35

(KP Photo, George Cuhaj collection)

8-5RW, Ford Mustang Fastback, 1966, white, w/red interior and tow hook, black plastic tires on silver wheels, unique steering lever on driver's side allows front wheels to turn left or right, 2-7/8", orange versions are quite rare, about $500 MIP

EX $12   **NM** $30   **MIP** $55

(KP Photo)

9-1RW, Fire Escape, 1955, red w/cast driver, metal wheels, gold-painted trim, 2-1/4", no front bumper in casting

EX $20   **NM** $45   **MIP** $90

(KP Photo)

9-2RW, Fire Escape, 1957, red, cast w/driver, metal wheels most common, versions w/gray plastic wheels about $400 MIP, front bumper included in casting, 2-1/4"

EX $20   **NM** $45   **MIP** $90

(KP Photo)

9-3RW, Merryweather Marquis Fire Engine, 1959, red body w/cab, gold ladder, black plastic wheels (first versions had gray plastic wheels), ladder colors can vary, 2-5/8", simply called "Fire Truck" in 1966 catalog

EX $20   **NM** $55   **MIP** $70

(KP Photo, Tom Michael collection)

9-4RW, Boat and Trailer, 1967, plastic blue and white boat w/blue die-cast trailer, black plastic wheels, first time a stand-alone trailer makes appearance in regular wheels line

EX $10   **NM** $20   **MIP** $35

(KP Photo)

10-1RW, Mechanical Horse and Trailer, 1955, red, three-wheeled cab and gray stake-style trailer, metal wheels, 3"

EX $55   **NM** $70   **MIP** $95

(KP Photo by Dr. Douglas Sadecky)

10-2RW, Mechanical Horse and Trailer, 1957, second casting of Scammell Scarab, red three-wheeled cab and light-tan stake-style trailer w/fenders, grille can be painted or unpainted, metal wheels, 3", appears first in 1957 catalog/flyer

EX $40   **NM** $60   **MIP** $95

(KP Photo)

10-3RW, Sugar Container Truck, 1962, blue Foden truck body w/"Tate & Lyle" decal, w/silver, gray, or black plastic wheels (shown), popular Foden cab design, 2-5/8"

EX $25   **NM** $50   **MIP** $80

(KP Photo, George Cuhaj collection)

10-3RW, Sugar Container Truck, 1962, another view of 10-3RW, showing decal from back of truck

(KP Photo, John Brown Sr. collection)

10-4RW, Pipe Truck, 1967, red Leyland die-cast body, silver grille and baseplate, gray plastic pipes.

"Ergomatic Cab" written on baseplate, 3", the Ergomatic cab was a new feature on large British trucks, including Leyland and AEC, beginning in the mid-60s, so this model reflected the latest advance at time of release

EX $10   **NM** $17   **MIP** $35

11-1RW, Road Tanker, 1955, yellow or red ERF truck body, metal wheels, "Esso" decal on rear of tank, 2", painted side gas tanks, crimped axles

EX $40   **NM** $75   **MIP** $115

11-2RW, Road Tanker, 1959, red ERF truck body, metal wheels, gray or black plastic wheels, variations include silver painted side gas tanks and grilles, slightly larger casting, 2-1/2"

EX $35   **NM** $60   **MIP** $100

(KP Photo)

11-3RW, Jumbo Crane, 1965, yellow, red plastic hook, large black plastic wheels in front near cab, small in back, some w/red counterweights, 3"

EX $8   **NM** $15   **MIP** $30

(KP Photo, John Brown Sr. collection)

11-4RW, Scaffold Truck, mid-1969, Mercedes-Benz truck, silver body w/yellow plastic scaffold sections in stake-style bed, "Builders Supply Company" decal on side, 2-5/8", released late in 1969, just before transition to Superfast

EX $8   **NM** $12   **MIP** $25

(KP Photo, John Brown Sr. collection)

12-1RW, Land Rover, 1957, dark green body w/tan driver, metal wheels, no real windshield, just a low flat piece of the casting appearing where the base of a windshield would be, slight casting variations, some 1-5/8" length, later editions, 1-3/4" length, silver-painted grille

EX $15 **NM** $40 **MIP** $85

(KP Photo)

12-2RW, Land Rover, 1960, dark green, black or gray plastic wheels (black more common), open cab, model shown has bent windshield, "Land-Rover Series II" on black baseplate

EX $15 **NM** $40 **MIP** $75

(KP Photo)

12-3RW, Safari Land Rover, 1965, dark green or blue body, plastic luggage on top, white interior, white tow hook, black plastic baseplate, first issue of the Safari Land Rover, says "Land Rover Safari" on base, 2-3/4"

EX $8 **NM** $20 **MIP** $35

(KP Photo)

12-3RW, Safari Land Rover, 1967, medium-blue body, light reddish-brown plastic luggage, white plastic interior and tow hook, black plastic

baseplate w/"Land Rover Safari," second issue of same casting in blue

EX $8 **NM** $15 **MIP** $25

(KP Photo)

13-1RW, Wreck Truck, 1955, tan Bedford truck w/red tow hook and scaffold, metal wheels, silver-painted grille and bumper, 2-1/4"

EX $35 **NM** $50 **MIP** $75

13-2RW, Wreck Truck, 1958, tan Bedford body, red boom section, metal or gray plastic wheels, no interior, slightly smaller than previous casting at 2"

EX $40 **NM** $60 **MIP** $90

(KP Photo, George Cuhaj collection)

13-3RW, Wreck Truck, 1961, red body w/metal or plastic tow hook, and gray or black plastic wheels, decal on side of truck says "A.A. & R.A.C. Matchbox Garages Breakdown Service," silver trim on front grille

EX $18 **NM** $45 **MIP** $110

(KP Photo, George Cuhaj collection)

13-4RW, Wreck Truck, 1966, dodge Wreck Truck w/yellow cab, green tow bed, red plastic hook, clear red plastic cab light, BP decals or labels, 3", black plastic wheels, variations w/colors reversed, (green cab and yellow body) are extremely rare, "Dodge Wreck Truck" on green base near rear wheels

EX $12 **NM** $20 **MIP** $45

(KP Photo)

14-1RW, Ambulance, 1956, cream painted body, metal wheels, Red Cross decal, word "Ambulance" cast in raised letters along side of vehicle, 2"

EX $20 **NM** $45 **MIP** $85

(KP Photo, John Brown Sr. collection)

14-2RW, Ambulance, 1958, Daimler w/cream or off-white body w/metal or gray plastic wheels, Red Cross decal, slightly larger casting at 2-1/4", word "Ambulance" cast in raised letters

EX $22 **NM** $60 **MIP** $90

(KP Photo, George Cuhaj collection)

14-3RW, Lomas Ambulance, 1962, white body w/black plastic wheels and "LCC Ambulance" decals, 2-5/8", referred to simply as "Ambulance" in catalog, "LCC" is an abbreviation for the "London County Council," responsible for designing and building ambulances in the 1950s and 1960s to its own specifications, later adapted by Daimler and other companies

EX $10 **NM** $20 **MIP** $45

(KP Photo, George Cuhaj collection)

14-4RW, Iso Grifo, 1968, dark blue, almost purple body, light blue plastic interior and tow hook, opening doors, 3", in 1968 catalog, "available in early 1968," steering wheel on right-hand side, black tires on silver wheels, textured baseplate

EX $10   **NM** $17   **MIP** $35

(KP Photo, George Cuhaj collection)

14-4RW, Iso Grifo, detail photo: shows white tow hook and driver's side door open to British-style steering wheel arrangement

(KP Photo, George Cuhaj collection)

15-1RW, Prime Mover Truck, 1956, orange body, silver grille and trim, metal wheels, harder to find editions: yellow body w/metal wheels and orange w/gray plastic wheels

EX $22   **NM** $45   **MIP** $70

(KP Photo)

15-2RW, Atlantic Prime Mover, 1959, orange body, black plastic wheels, spare tire in bed of truck, no interior

EX $25   **NM** $45   **MIP** $95

(KP Photo)

15-3RW, Dennis Refuse Truck, 1963, blue body, gray dumper section, red and white decals or labels say "Cleansing Service," and have cross-in-shield design at center, black plastic knobby wheels, no interior, 2-1/2"

EX $7   **NM** $14   **MIP** $30

(KP Photo, George Cuhaj collection)

15-4RW, Volkswagen 1500 Saloon, 1968, white Volkswagen Beetle body w/"137" decals or labels, black tires on silver wheels, 2-7/8"

EX $12   **NM** $20   **MIP** $40

(KP Photo)

16-1RW, Transporter Trailer, 1956, tan, flat bodied trailer w/ramp and non-skid surface for vehicles, one axle and metal wheels in front near towbar, two axles w/metal wheels on back near ramp, 3", ramp fold up onto trailer body

EX $17   **NM** $30   **MIP** $60

(KP Photo by Dr. Douglas Sadecky)

16-2RW, Atlantic Transporter, 1960, orange trailer body, black plastic wheels, four axles; two at front near

drawbar, two at back near ramp, non-skid tire tracks on trailer, pictured here w/15-2RW Atlantic Prime Mover

EX $12   **NM** $20   **MIP** $40

(KP Photo, George Cuhaj collection)

16-3RW, "Mountaineer" Dump Truck w/Snowplough, 1964, gray cab and body w/orange dumper section, snowplow on front w/orange and white striped decal, black plastic wheels, 3", gray plastic wheel version about twice MIP value

EX $18   **NM** $30   **MIP** $50

(KP Photo, George Cuhaj collection)

16-3RW, "Mountaineer" Dump Truck w/Snowplough, 1964, another view of Mountaineer Dump Truck w/raised dumper bed

(KP Photo, John Brown Sr. collection)

16-4RW, Case Bulldozer, 1969, red body w/yellow blade and cab, 2-1/2"

EX $9   **NM** $18   **MIP** $30

17-1RW, Removals Van, 1956, green, blue or dark red body, metal wheels, "Matchbox Removals Service" decal, green more common color

EX $15   **NM** $60   **MIP** $100

(KP Photo by Dr. Douglas Sadecky)

17-2RW, Removals Van, 1958, green body, w/"Matchbox Removals Service" decal on sides, metal or gray plastic wheels
EX $35   **NM** $75   **MIP** $125

(KP Photo)

17-3RW, Metropolitan Taxi, 1960, dark red w/gray or silver plastic wheels, gray more common, silver can have $130+ MIP value, gray-wheel values shown
EX $25   **NM** $40   **MIP** $80

(KP Photo)

17-4RW, 8-Wheel Tipper, 1963, red Foden body, orange dumper section, black plastic wheels, no interior, 3", "Hoveringham" decal on tipper, a "little brother" to the 8-Wheel Tipper K-1 in the King Size line
EX $9   **NM** $18   **MIP** $40

(KP Photo)

17-4RW, 8-Wheel Tipper, 1963, another view of Foden 8-Wheel Tipper, w/hinged gate at back opening when dumper section is tilted up
EX $9   **NM** $18   **MIP** $37

(KP Photo)

17-5RW, Horse Box, 1969, red body, green plastic box w/gray door
EX $4   **NM** $7   **MIP** $20

(KP Photo)

18-1RW, Bulldozer, 1956, yellow body, tow hook, red blade, metal roller wheels, driver in hat cast as part of toy
EX $18   **NM** $35   **MIP** $85

18-2RW, Bulldozer, 1958, yellow body, tow hook, yellow blade, driver cast into body, metal roller wheels, engine partially covered on side
EX $18   **NM** $45   **MIP** $100

(KP Photo)

18-3RW, Caterpillar Bulldozer, 1961, yellow body, tow hook, yellow blade, driver cast into body, metal or black plastic rollers
EX $18   **NM** $40   **MIP** $80

18-4RW, Caterpillar Crawler Bulldozer, 1964, yellow body, curving tow hook, no driver, black plastic roller wheels
EX $7   **NM** $18   **MIP** $40

(KP Photo, George Cuhaj collection)

18-5RW, Field Car, 1969, yellow body, white plastic interior, generally red wheels w/black plastic tires, many collectors consider this vehicle to be an International Scout model, and in fact the side view bears close resemblance
EX $7   **NM** $11   **MIP** $25

(KP Photo, George Cuhaj collection)

18-5RW, Field Car, 1969, view of rear of Field Car, showing spare and tow hook

(KP Photo)

19-1RW, MG TC Sports Car, 1956, white or cream body w/metal wheels, painted driver, silver grille
EX $45   **NM** $70   **MIP** $150

19-2RW, MG "A" Sports Car, 1958, white body, metal or gray plastic wheels, painted driver, can have rounded or crimped axles, silver-painted grille and headlights, 2-1/4"
EX $58   **NM** $85   **MIP** $150

(KP Photo)

19-3RW, Aston Martin Racer, 1961, green body, white or gray driver, 24-spoke wheels w/black plastic tires, variable number decals on body

EX $30   **NM** $60   **MIP** $120

(KP Photo)

19-4RW, Lotus Racing Car, 1966, green or orange body, white plastic driver, yellow wheels w/black plastic tires, No. "3" decal or label, 2-3/4", green pictured in 1966 catalog, but orange variation included in G-4 Racetrack Set that same year

EX $11   **NM** $22   **MIP** $40

(KP Photo)

20-1RW, Heavy Lorry, 1956, dark red ERF truck body, metal or gray plastic wheels, no interior, dropside stake bed appearance w/fuel tanks along sides, can have silver-painted grille, some casting variations, 2-1/4" and 2-5/8"

EX $18   **NM** $40   **MIP** $80

20-2RW, Transport Truck, 1959, ERF dropside truck w/dark blue body, gray or black plastic wheels, "Ever Ready For Life" decal along stake sides, model also called "Heavy Lorry" in 1959 catalog

EX $22   **NM** $55   **MIP** $100

(KP Photo by Dr. Douglas Sadecky)

20-3RW, Taxi Cab, 1965, Chevrolet Impala Taxi Cab w/yellow body, red

or white plastic interior, (red is harder to find) black plastic wheels, 3"

EX $11   **NM** $18   **MIP** $35

(KP Photo)

21-1RW, Bedford Coach, 1956, light pea-green body w/red and yellow "London to Glasgow" decals above windows, metal wheels

EX $22   **NM** $50   **MIP** $100

(KP Photo, George Cuhaj collection)

21-2RW, Bedford Coach, 1958, light or dark green body w/red and yellow "London to Glasgow" decal above windows, metal or gray plastic wheels, "Bedford Duple Luxury Coach" on black base, 2-1/2", silver painted grille and front bumper, no interior

EX $25   **NM** $50   **MIP** $100

(KP Photo by Dr. Douglas Sadecky)

21-3RW, Milk Delivery Truck, 1961, commer truck w/light green body, white or cream plastic cargo and gray or black plastic wheels, 2-1/4", cow or milk bottle decal on cab doors, both variations shown here

EX $20   **NM** $35   **MIP** $70

(KP Photo, George Cuhaj collection)

21-4RW, Foden Concrete Truck, 1969, yellow Foden cab and plastic mixer w/orange body, dark green plastic windows, eight black plastic wheels, 3", worm-gear under second set of wheels turns mixer as truck rolls forward

EX $5   **NM** $9   **MIP** $22

(KP Photo)

22-1RW, Vauxhall Cresta, 1956, red body w/white roof, no interior, metal wheels, silver-painted grille and bumpers, tow hook

EX $25   **NM** $40   **MIP** $80

(KP Photo by Dr. Douglas Sadecky)

22-2RW, Vauxhall Cresta, 1958, different casting than previous version, longer, more "Chevy-like" body w/low tailfins and wraparound front and rear windshields, many paint variations exist, some pushing MIP price well into the hundreds of dollars, can have gray or black plastic wheels or metal wheels

EX $30   **NM** $72   **MIP** $150

(KP Photo, George Cuhaj collection)

22-3RW, Pontiac Grand Prix, 1964, red body, black plastic wheels, gray plastic interior and tow hook, 3", opening doors, "Pontiac G.P. Sports Coupe" on black painted baseplate
EX $12   **NM** $22   **MIP** $45

23-1RW, Caravan, 1956, pale blue body, metal wheels, 2-1/2", no number cast on base.
EX $17   **NM** $30   **MIP** $75

23-2RW, Trailer, 1958, pale blue-green or lime-green body, metal or gray plastic wheels, number 23 cast on base
EX $22   **NM** $40   **MIP** $75

(KP Photo by Dr. Douglas Sadecky)

23-3RW, Bluebird Dauphine Trailer, 1960, metallic tan or green body, opening door, no interior or plastic windows, black or gray plastic wheels, variations w/green bodies are hard to find, and can be quite valuable, more common tan variation prices given below
EX $25   **NM** $40   **MIP** $85

(KP Photo)

23-4RW, Trailer Caravan, 1966, yellow or pink body, black plastic wheels, white plastic interior, 3", pink more common beginning in 1968 and after, yellow version about $45 MIP value
EX $9   **NM** $17   **MIP** $30

24-1RW, Hydraulic Excavator, 1956, yellow or orange body w/metal wheels; larger two at rear and smaller at front, figure cast as part of body, front dumping bucket
EX $18   **NM** $40   **MIP** $75

24-2RW, Hydraulic Excavator, 1959, yellow body, black or gray plastic

wheels, larger at rear or cab, smaller in front near dumper bucket, figure cast in piece, 2-5/8"
EX $17   **NM** $28   **MIP** $45

(KP Photo, George Cuhaj collection)

24-3RW, Rolls-Royce Silver Shadow, 1967, deep red sedan body, white plastic interior, opening trunk, silver wheels w/black plastic tires, clear plastic windshield and windows, unpainted silver metal grille, headlights and front bumper, 3", black baseplate w/"A" near front axle
EX $7   **NM** $11   **MIP** $25

(KP Photo, George Cuhaj collection)

24-3RW, Rolls-Royce Silver Shadow, 1967, view of opening trunk on Rolls

(KP Photo)

25-1RW, Bedford Dunlop Van, 1956, dark blue Bedford panel van, w/yellow "Dunlop" decals on sides, no interior or plastic windows
EX $18   **NM** $50   **MIP** $100

(KP Photo by Dr. Douglas Sadecky)

25-2RW, Volkswagen Sedan, 1960, Volkswagen 1200 Sedan, blue-silver body, gray plastic wheels, opening rear engine hood, green or clear plastic windows, black base
EX $45   **NM** $75   **MIP** $125

(KP Photo, George Cuhaj collection)

25-3RW, Petrol Tanker, 1964, yellow Bedford cab, green body, white tanker w/"BP" decal, cab tilts to reveal white plastic interior, black plastic wheels, 3", called "B.P. Tanker" in 1966 catalog, blue versions w/"Aral" decals on tanker section harder to find, about $200 MIP
EX $8   **NM** $20   **MIP** $35

(KP Photo)

25-4RW, Ford Cortina, 1968, light brown body, cream-colored plastic interior and tow hook, black plastic wheels, "Auto-Steer," textured pattern on unpainted baseplate near front and rear axles, opening doors, 2-5/8", yellow roof rack included in 1969 G-4 Race'n Rally Gift Set
EX $8   **NM** $20   **MIP** $30

(KP Photo, Tom Michael collection)

26-1RW, Ready Mixed Concrete Lorry, 1957, orange ERF cab and body w/silver-painted grille and side gas tanks, metal or gray plastic wheels, 1-3/4", metal mixer section, four wheels

EX $18   **NM** $45   **MIP** $80

(KP Photo, George Cuhaj collection)

26-2RW, Ready-Mix Concrete Truck, 1961, orange die-cast Foden cab and body w/plastic orange mixer section, gray or black plastic wheels, 2-1/2", six wheels, says "Foden Cement Mixer" on base

EX $9   **NM** $19   **MIP** $40

(KP Photo, George Cuhaj collection)

26-3RW, GMC Tipper Truck, 1968, red cab w/green plastic windows, silver-gray tipper bed, green chassis, black plastic wheels w/duals at rear, 2-5/8", 1968 catalog shows subhead "Available early 1968" and model w/yellow tipper bed

EX $6   **NM** $10   **MIP** $25

(KP Photo, George Cuhaj collection)

26-3RW, GMC Tipper Truck, 1968, view showing tilting cab and green engine block underneath

(KP Photo)

27-1RW, Bedford Low Loader, 1956, green Bedford cab w/silver trim, tan trailer, metal wheels, 3", no windows or interior

EX $28   **NM** $60   **MIP** $125

27-2RW, Bedford Low Loader, 1958, green Bedford cab w/silver trim, tan trailer, metal or gray plastic knobby wheels, slightly larger casting at 3-3/4" length, no windows or interior

EX $30   **NM** $90   **MIP** $175

(KP Photo, John Brown Sr. collection)

27-3RW, Cadillac Sixty Special, 1960, silver-gray or silver-purple Cadillac body w/cream or pink colored roof, plastic windows, no interior and gray or black plastic wheels, red base, tow hook, red-painted taillights and silver-painted trim

EX $28   **NM** $55   **MIP** $125

(KP Photo, George Cuhaj collection)

27-4RW, Mercedes 230SL, 1966, white Mercedes convertible w/red plastic interior, opening doors, black plastic wheels, tow hook, 2-3/4", "Available early 1966" in catalog

EX $7   **NM** $20   **MIP** $35

(KP Photo, George Cuhaj collection)

27-4RW, Mercedes 230SL, 1966, rear view of Mercedes convertible showing opening doors and tow hook

(KP Photo by Dr. Douglas Sadecky)

28-1RW, Bedford Compressor Lorry, 1956, orange or yellow Bedford cab and chassis w/Caterpillar-type compressor engine on back, painted-silver grille and trim, 1-3/4", metal wheels, pictured here w/28-2RW Thames Compressor Truck

EX $30   **NM** $60   **MIP** $90

(KP Photo, John Brown Sr. collection)

28-2RW, Ford Thames Compressor Lorry, 1959, yellow Ford Thames truck cab and chassis w/black plastic wheels, no interior or window plastic, silver headlights and grille

EX $25   **NM** $40   **MIP** $75

(KP Photo, George Cuhaj collection)

28-3RW, Mark Ten Jaguar, 1964, light metallic brown body w/opening hood, black plastic wheels, black-painted base, engine can be painted the same as body color or left unpainted, 2-3/4", white plastic interior, clear window plastic, tow hook

EX $15   **NM** $25   **MIP** $45

(KP Photo, George Cuhaj collection)

28-4RW, Mack Dump Truck, 1969, orange Mack truck body w/orange dumper bed, black plastic tires on orange or yellow wheels, 2-5/8", green window plastic, unpainted base
EX $7　　**NM** $18　　**MIP** $25

(KP Photo, George Cuhaj collection)

28-4RW, Mack Dump Truck, 1969, view of operating dumper bed, this model first appears in the 1969 1st edition catalog

(KP Photo)

29-1RW, Bedford Milk Delivery Van, 1956, tan body w/white plastic milk bottles and boxes, silver trim, metal or gray plastic wheels, no interior or window plastic, 2-1/4"
EX $20　　**NM** $50　　**MIP** $100

(KP Photo, George Cuhaj collection)

29-2RW, Austin A55 Cambridge, 1961, medium green body w/light green roof, gray or black plastic wheels, green window plastic, no interior, black-painted base w/tow hook, 2-1/2"
EX $17　　**NM** $30　　**MIP** $70

(KP Photo, John Brown Sr. collection)

29-3RW, Fire Pumper, 1966, red LaFrance fire engine body, white plastic ladders along sides, unpainted base and trim, green window plastic, no interior, blue dome light, black plastic wheels, 3", w/or w/out "Denver" decal
EX $6　　**NM** $15　　**MIP** $30

(KP Photo, George Cuhaj collection)

30-1RW, Ford Prefect, 1956, light sage-green or light brown body w/metal or gray plastic wheels, (light blue harder to find, $200 or more MIP), no window plastic or interior, silver-painted grille, headlights and bumpers, red-painted taillights, tow hook, black-painted base, 2-3/8"
EX $15　　**NM** $40　　**MIP** $80

(KP Photo, George Cuhaj collection)

30-2RW, Magirus-Deutz Crane Truck, 1961, silver cab and truck body w/orange boom section and gray or black plastic wheels, hook can be metal or plastic, black-painted baseplate under front cab section, 2-3/8"
EX $17　　**NM** $30　　**MIP** $60

(KP Photo, George Cuhaj collection)

30-3RW, 8-Wheel Crane, 1965, medium-dark green body w/eight

black plastic wheels, orange crane section, yellow plastic hook, 3"
EX $5　　**NM** $11　　**MIP** $25

(KP Photo)

31-1RW, American Ford Station Wagon, 1957, yellow body w/metal or gray plastic wheels, silver painted bumpers and headlights, no interior or window plastic, 2-5/8", appears brown in 1957 leaflet catalog
EX $15　　**NM** $50　　**MIP** $100

(Photo by Dr. Douglas Sadecky)

31-2RW, Ford Fairlane Station Wagon, 1960, mint green w/pink-white roof, gray or black plastic wheels, silver-painted trim, tow hook, yellow-painted versions are harder to find, and can bring higher MIP values (up to $300), two box variations shown
EX $22　　**NM** $60　　**MIP** $110

(KP Photo)

31-3RW, Lincoln Continental, 1964, dark blue or mint-green body, white plastic interior, clear window glass, opening trunk, 3"
EX $10　　**NM** $25　　**MIP** $40

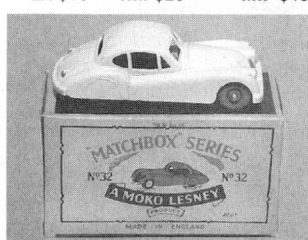

(KP Photo by Dr. Douglas Sadecky)

32-1RW, Jaguar XK140 Coupe, 1957, body w/metal or gray plastic wheels, 2-3/8", called "Fixed Head Coupe" in 1957 catalog/flyer, silver-painted grille, red-painted taillights

EX $30   **NM** $50   **MIP** $100

(KP Photo, John Brown Sr. collection)

32-2RW, E-Type Jaguar, 1962, metallic red body, spoked wheels w/gray or black tires, green or clear window plastic, 2-5/8", white plastic interior

EX $20   **NM** $40   **MIP** $80

(KP Photo)

32-2RW, Leyland Petrol Tanker, 1968, medium-green Ergomatic cab and chassis, eight black plastic wheels, white tanker section, "BP" decals or labels, silver or white plastic grille and bumper, 3", a blue and white version w/"Aral" labels is harder to find, and can have $120 or more MIP value, "Available early 1968" in catalog

EX $5   **NM** $12   **MIP** $25

(KP Photo by Dr. Douglas Sadecky)

33-1RW, Ford Zodiac, 1957, a variety of body colors exist for this model: blue, dark green, blue-green, silver, tan, orange, and turquoise, dark green and tan and orange models more common, w/around $80-$90 MIP values, 2-5/8"

EX $25   **NM** $45   **MIP** $80

(KP Photo, George Cuhaj collection)

33-2RW, Ford Zephyr 6, 1962, blue-green body, white plastic interior, gray or black plastic wheels, silver front grille and headlights, slight tailfins, black painted base, 2-1/2", some models w/black wheels have a lighter blue-green color than earlier versions

EX $10   **NM** $15   **MIP** $30

(KP Photo, George Cuhaj collection)

33-3RW, Lamborghini Miura, 1969, yellow or gold body w/red or cream plastic interior, 2-3/4", silver wheels w/black plastic tires, opening doors, gold cars w/cream interiors (as shown in 1969 catalog) have high MIP values, around $250

EX $4   **NM** $12   **MIP** $25

(KP Photo, John Brown Sr. collection)

34-1RW, Volkswagen Microvan, 1957, blue panel van body, no interior, "Matchbox International Express" yellow type decal on sides, w/silver-painted bumper and headlights, 2-1/4", mostly found w/metal or gray plastic wheels, decal on side w/"Matchbox International Express" in yellow lettering

EX $30   **NM** $50   **MIP** $100

(KP Photo)

34-2RW, Volkswagen Camping Car, 1962, light sea-green body, gray or black plastic wheels, opening side doors, top window plastic, camper section interior, 2-5/8"

EX $25   **NM** $50   **MIP** $100

(KP Photo)

34-3RW, Volkswagen Camper, 1967, silver body w/opening camper section doors, orange plastic interior, yellow window plastic, raised roof w/windows and top window plastic, black plastic wheels, 2-5/8"

EX $10   **NM** $20   **MIP** $50

34-3SF, Chevy Pro Stocker, 1981, white body w/blue "34" lightning design

EX $3   **NM** $6   **MIP** $12

(KP Photo)

34-3RW, Volkswagen Camper, 1967, another view of the Volkswagen Camper

EX $10   **NM** $18   **MIP** $45

(KP Photo)

34-4RW, Volkswagen Camper, 1969, silver body, opening doors to camper section, slightly raised roof w/window plastic on top but no windows, orange plastic interior, black plastic wheels, interestingly, the size of this vehicle remained the same since the 1962 release at 2-5/8", makes first appearance in 1969 catalog

EX $11   **NM** $17   **MIP** $40

(Photo by Dr. Douglas Sadecky)

35-1RW, Marshall Horse Box, 1957, red ERF cab w/silver-painted grille and headlights, brown horse box w/opening side door, metal and gray plastic wheels most common, 2-1/8"

EX $15   **NM** $30   **MIP** $80

(KP Photo)

35-2RW, Snow-Trac Tractor, 1964, red body w/unpainted base, six black tread roller wheels, green window plastic, 2-1/4", white or gray treads, some versions have "Snow-Trac" cast in side of tractor, (as seen in 1968 and 1969 catalogs) others have decal, and some variations have neither, (as seen in the 1966 catalog)

EX $9   **NM** $17   **MIP** $40

(KP Photo)

35-2RW, Snow-Trac Tractor, 1964, a plain-sided variation of the Snow-Trac in the condition many of us find them-w/out treads

(KP Photo, George Cuhaj collection)

36-1RW, Austin A 50, 1957, blue-green body, no interior, metal or gray plastic wheels, silver-painted grille, headlights and bumper, tow bar, 2-3/8"

EX $20   **NM** $35   **MIP** $75

36-2RW, Lambretta Motorscooter w/Sidecar, 1961, dark or light metallic green body, black plastic wheels

EX $30   **NM** $65   **MIP** $150

(KP Photo, George Cuhaj collection)

36-3RW, Opel Diplomat, 1966, gold body, black-painted metal base, white plastic interior and tow hook, opening hood, silver or gray plastic motor, 2-3/4", pictured in elusive sea-green in 1966 catalog w/caption "Available mid 1966," these (possibly) first versions are rarely seen

EX $5   **NM** $10   **MIP** $25

(KP Photo, George Cuhaj collection)

36-1RW, Opel Diplomat, 1966, a view of Opel Diplomat w/open hood and silver engine

37-1RW, Coca-Cola Lorry, 1956, yellow-orange truck w/Coca-Cola decals on sides and back of truck, metal or gray plastic wheels, 2-1/4", no step on the running board on cab, silver-painted trim on running boards, grille, some versions have "uneven" loads of cast Coca-Cola cases (as seen in 1957 flyer) in the bed of the truck, these typically run about $150 MIP, "Even" load versions in gray plastic wheels comparable MIP price, even-load metal wheel version prices shown below

EX $30   **NM** $55   **MIP** $110

(KP Photo by Dr. Douglas Sadecky)

37-2RW, Coca-Cola Lorry, 1960, yellow body, black baseplate, "even" cast crate load on bed, Coca-Cola decals on sides and back, 2-1/4", gray or black plastic wheels

EX $25   **NM** $40   **MIP** $95

(KP Photo, John Brown Sr. collection)

37-3RW, Cattle Truck, 1966, yellow Dodge cab and chassis, gray plastic cattle box, originally included two white plastic steers, 2-1/2", introduced in 1966 catalog as a new model, but hadn't yet replaced the #37 Coca-Cola truck in the line-up

EX $5   **NM** $10   **MIP** $20

38-1RW, Refuse Wagon, 1957, silver-gray or dark gray cab and almost tanker-truck-shaped rounded-top bed and "Cleansing Department" decals, metal or gray plastic wheels, 1957 flyer shows model painted green and w/out the decals, casting variations must account for size difference: 2-1/8" and 2-1/2" lengths

EX $18   **NM** $45   **MIP** $85

(KP Photo)

38-2RW, Vauxhall Victor Estate Car, 1963, yellow station wagon w/opening rear hatch, gray, silver or black plastic tires, red or green plastic interiors, clear plastic windows. 2-1/2"

EX $10   **NM** $25   **MIP** $50

(KP Photo, George Cuhaj collection)

38-3RW, Honda Motorcycle w/Trailer, 1967, blue-silver Honda motorcycle w/kickstand and orange or yellow trailer, trailer may or may not included labels or decals 3", as w/many motorcycle-related toys, these fairly common models are increasing in value

EX $12   **NM** $25   **MIP** $40

38-4SF, Camper, 1980, red Ford Courier w/tan camper top

EX $3   **NM** $7   **MIP** $15

(KP Photo, John Brown Sr. collection)

39-1RW, "Zodiac" Convertible, 1957, pink body, turquoise interior, driver, tow hook, metal, gray or silver plastic wheels, casting variations: model can measure 2-5/8" or 2-1/2", silver-painted grille, gray-painted headlights, red-painted taillights, light green baseplate

EX $27   **NM** $68   **MIP** $100

(KP Photo by Dr. Douglas Sadecky)

39-2RW, Pontiac Convertible, 1962, purple Pontiac convertible body w/gray or silver plastic wheels; yellow body w/gray, silver or black plastic wheels, yellow w/black plastic wheels is most common, around $55 MIP, purple version w/silver plastic wheels is hard to find 2-3/4", yellow w/gray or silver wheels prices shown below

EX $28   **NM** $55   **MIP** $110

(KP Photo)

39-3RW, Ford Tractor, 1967, blue Ford tractor body w/yellow die-cast hood, yellow wheels w/black plastic tires, 2-1/8", tow hook, versions of this tractor exist in all-blue, being part of the King Size K-20 set

EX $10   **NM** $20   **MIP** $30

(KP Photo, John Brown Sr. collection)

40-1RW, Bedford 7-Ton Tipper, 1957, red Bedford cab and chassis, tan dumper bed, metal or gray plastic wheels, silver painted trim, casting variations: size varies between 2-1/8" and 2-1/4", shown in all-green color in 1957 flyer

EX $20   **NM** $40   **MIP** $80

(KP Photo, Tom Michael collection)

40-2RW, Long Distance Bus, 1961, blue-silver coach body w/tailfins at rear, 3", green window plastic, silver-painted grille, w/gray, silver or black plastic wheels, (gray or silver-wheel versions about $55 MIP value) black-wheel version values given below

EX $7   **NM** $15   **MIP** $28

(KP Photo)

40-3RW, Hay Trailer, 1967, blue die-cast trailer body w/yellow die-cast stake-ends, often missing, yellow plastic wheels w/black plastic tires, 3-3/8"

EX $3   **NM** $8   **MIP** $15

(KP Photo by Dr. Douglas Sadecky)

41-1RW, "D" Type Jaguar, 1957, green D-type body, metal driver in later catalogs, but not in 1957 flyer, "41" decal, metal or gray plastic tires, 2-1/4", photo shows 41-1RW

and second release w/a larger casting, 41-2R

EX $25   **NM** $60   **MIP** $100

41-2RW, Jaguar Racing Car ("D"-Type), 1961, second issue of car featured a green body and tan driver, but came in a variety of wheel types, from more common gray and silver plastic wheels to rare spoked versions and black plastic wheels

EX $30   **NM** $75   **MIP** $150

(KP Photo, George Cuhaj collection)

41-3RW, Ford G.T., 1966, generally white Ford G.T. bodies w/yellow plastic wheels and black plastic tires, clear window plastic, blue rally stripe on hood w/"6" or "9" reversed in white, visible rear engine, 2-5/8", "Available early 1966" in 1966 catalog, black base, red plastic interior, versions w/differently-colored wheels or bodies are hard to find

EX $15   **NM** $30   **MIP** $45

(KP Photo by Dr. Douglas Sadecky)

42-1RW, Bedford "Evening News" Van, 1957, mustard-yellow Bedford panel van body w/die-cast billboard on roof and red decal "First With The News" in white type, "Evening News" on panel side of van and "Football Results" in red type decals on each door, metal, gray or black plastic wheels, (gray and black shown), 2-1/4"

EX $17   **NM** $40   **MIP** $95

(KP Photo, George Cuhaj collection)

42-2RW, Studebaker Station Wagon, 1965, blue body w/blue or light blue sliding roof, white plastic interior and tow hook, clear window plastic, white

plastic dog and hunter figure included w/original (often missing), 3"
EX $15　　**NM** $30　　**MIP** $60

(KP Photo, George Cuhaj collection)

42-2RW, Studebaker Station Wagon, 1965, another view, showing the sliding rear roof of the Studebaker Station Wagon, 42-2RW

(KP Photo, George Cuhaj collection)

42-3RW, Iron Fairy Crane, 1969-70, red body, yellow crane arm, yellow plastic hook and seat, black plastic wheels, 3", introduced in 1970 catalog, as a "non-Superfast" toy
EX $5　　**NM** $11　　**MIP** $20

(KP Photo, George Cuhaj collection)

43-1RW, Hillman "Minx," 1958, blue body, light gray roof, no window plastic or interior, silver-painted grille, metal or gray plastic wheels, 2-1/2", first appears in 1958 catalog
EX $15　　**NM** $45　　**MIP** $80

(KP Photo, John Brown Sr. collection)

43-2RW, Aveling-Barford Tractor Shovel, 1962, yellow tractor body w/cast yellow or red driver and yellow or red bucket, black wheels, 2-5/8", all yellow versions can have $140 MIP value, model prices for

yellow w/red bucket and yellow w/red driver shown
EX $15　　**NM** $30　　**MIP** $55

(KP Photo, George Cuhaj collection)

43-3RW, Pony Trailer, 1968, yellow body w/clear window plastic on sides and top, gray/brown plastic door, black plastic wheels, two white plastic horses, 2-5/8"
EX $8　　**NM** $11　　**MIP** $30

(KP Photo, John Brown Sr. collection)

44-1RW, Rolls Royce Silver Cloud, 1958, blue metallic Rolls Royce body, metal, gray or silver plastic wheels, crimped axles, no interior, no window plastic, silver-painted grille and bumpers, 2-5/8"
EX $18　　**NM** $35　　**MIP** $80

(KP Photo, George Cuhaj collection)

44-2RW, Rolls Royce, 1962, metallic tan or metallic silver/gray body, opening trunk, black plastic wheels, white plastic interior, clear window plastic, black base, silver-painted grille, 2-7/8"
EX $12　　**NM** $20　　**MIP** $40

(KP Photo, George Cuhaj collection)

44-3RW, Refrigerator Truck, 1967, red GMC cab and chassis, green refrigerator box, green window plastic, black plastic wheels, opening rear door on box, 3"
EX $5　　**NM** $12　　**MIP** $20

(KP Photo, George Cuhaj collection)

44-3RW, Refrigerator Truck, 1967, another view showing box of refrigerator truck

(KP Photo, George Cuhaj collection)

45-1RW, Vauxhall "Victor," 1958, yellow body, silver-painted headlights and grille, can have no windows, clear or green plastic windows, no interior, metal, gray, silver or black plastic wheels, 2-3/8"
EX $18　　**NM** $40　　**MIP** $85

(KP Photo by Dr. Douglas Sadecky)

45-1RW, Vauxhall "Victor", 1958, Vauxhall Victor models can include green or clear plastic windows, as this one does

(KP Photo)

45-2RW, Ford Corsair, 1965, cream-yellow body, red plastic interior and tow hook, gray or black plastic wheels, silver-painted grille and headlights, green plastic roof rack and boat (not shown), 2-5/8", gray-wheeled versions may have higher MIP values

EX $6   **NM** $12   **MIP** $30

(KP Photo, George Cuhaj collection)

46-1RW, Morris Minor 1000, 1958, dark blue or dark green body, metal or gray plastic wheels, black base, no interior, no plastic windows, 2", dark blue w/gray plastic wheels harder to find, w/higher MIP values

EX $45   **NM** $65   **MIP** $125

(KP Photo by Dr. Douglas Sadecky)

46-2RW, Pickford's Removal Van, 1960, dark blue or green body, silver-painted grille, no interior, no plastic windows, gray, silver or black plastic wheels, 2-5/8", decals can have two or three lines, many variations of this model exist, although versions w/two-line decals seem hard to find, bumping up the MIP price from what is shown here

EX $18   **NM** $40   **MIP** $80

(KP Photo, George Cuhaj collection)

46-3RW, Mercedes 300SE, 1968, medium blue or green body, white plastic interior, opening doors and trunk, black plastic wheels, unpainted base extends to bumpers and front grille, 2-7/8"

EX $9   **NM** $18   **MIP** $30

(KP Photo)

46-3RW, Mercedes 300SE, 1968, another view of the 46-3RW Mercedes showing opening doors and trunk

(KP Photo by Dr. Douglas Sadecky)

47-1RW, Trojan "Brooke Bond" Van, 1958, red body, metal or gray plastic wheels, decals on van box read "Brooke Bond Tea," tea leaf decal on each door, silver-painted headlights, 2-1/4"

EX $20   **NM** $45   **MIP** $95

(KP Photo, John Brown Sr. collection)

47-2RW, Commer Ice Cream Van, 1963, blue, cream or metallic blue body w/white plastic interior, clear plastic windows and black plastic wheels, 2-1/4", color and decal variations change MIP values considerably, metallic blue versions w/square roof decals are more rare than cream-colored models w/plain (non-striped) side decals

EX $20   **NM** $45   **MIP** $75

(KP Photo, George Cuhaj collection)

47-3RW, DAF Tipper Container Truck, 1969, green or silver-gray cab and chassis, yellow tipper bed w/removable gray top, red plastic grille and baseplate under cab, black plastic wheels, 3", makes first appearance in 1969 catalog, green version higher MIP value, about $50

EX $5   **NM** $12   **MIP** $25

(KP Photo, George Cuhaj collection)

47-3RW, DAF Tipper Container Truck, 1969, another view of truck w/raised tipper bed

(KP Photo, Tom Michael collection)

48-1RW, "Meteor" Sports Boat on Trailer, 1958, blue and yellow plastic boat w/slight rise for windshield, black die-cast trailer, metal or gray plastic wheels, 2-3/4"

EX $25   **NM** $40   **MIP** $70

48-2RW, Sports-Boat and Trailer, 1961, plastic red and white boat w/gold or silver outboard motor, blue die-cast trailer, gray or black plastic wheels, 3-1/2", boat can come w/red deck and white hull or white deck and red hull

EX $12   **NM** $25   **MIP** $60

(KP Photo, John Brown Sr. collection)

48-3RW, Dumper Truck, 1967, red Dodge cab, chassis and dumper bed, silver plastic baseplate, bumper and front grille, black plastic wheels, 3"

EX $7   **NM** $20   **MIP** $40

(KP Photo)

49-1RW, Army Half-Track, 1958, dark olive-green w/star-in-circle U.S. insignia on hood, no interior, metal, gray or black plastic wheels and rollers, gray treads 2-1/2", known as Army Half-Track and Military Personnel Carrier, this toy stayed in the 1-75 lineup for many years

EX $18   **NM** $30   **MIP** $70

(KP Photo, George Cuhaj collection)

49-2RW, Mercedes Unimog, 1967, two color variations, one tan and blue and the other blue and red, green plastic windows, yellow plastic wheels w/black plastic tires, silver-painted grille, tow hook cast, 2-1/2"

EX $8   **NM** $20   **MIP** $35

49-2SF, Chop Suey Chopper, 1973, magenta body w/red handle bars

EX $4   **NM** $7   **MIP** $18

(KP Photo, George Cuhaj collection)

49-2RW, Mercedes Unimog, 1967, another view of the Mercedes Unimog, blue and red variation

(KP Photo by Dr. Douglas Sadecky)

50-1RW, Commer Pickup, 1958, tan or red and gray body, w/metal, gray or black plastic wheels, 2-1/2", silver-painted grille and headlights

EX $35   **NM** $70   **MIP** $125

(KP Photo, John Brown Sr. collection)

50-2RW, John Deere-Lanz Tractor, 1964, a view of the gray-tire version of the John Deere-Lanz tractor-a very detailed model

(KP Photo)

50-2RW, John Deere-Lanz Tractor, 1964, green body, yellow plastic wheels, gray or black plastic tires, cast tow hook, 2-1/8", after John Deere acquired the German manufacturer Lanz in the 1950s, a variety of toy manufacturers, including Matchbox, produced models of this tractor, photo shows black-tire version tractor w/51-2RW Tipping Trailer, note: gray-tire

versions have slightly higher MIP value, about $55

EX $14   **NM** $20   **MIP** $40

50-3RW, Kennel Truck, 1969, dark green die-cast body, white or silver plastic grille, green window plastic, truck bed partitioned into four sections, to hold one plastic dog each (included), clear plastic canopy over truck bed, "Auto-Steer" front wheels, black plastic wheels, 2-3/4"

EX $12   **NM** $30   **MIP** $50

51-1RW, Albion "Portland Cement" Lorry, 1958, yellow Albion truck cab and chassis, two decal variations: "Portland Cement" and "Blue Circle Portland Cement," metal, gray, silver or black plastic wheels, silver-painted trim, tan-painted cement bag load on flatbed, no interior, no window plastic, 2-1/2", silver plastic wheel versions have about $150 MIP values

EX $18   **NM** $40   **MIP** $80

(KP Photo)

51-2RW, Tipping Trailer, 1964, green body, yellow wheels, tilting bed, black or gray plastic tires, three yellow barrels, 2-5/8"

EX $8   **NM** $12   **MIP** $20

(KP Photo, George Cuhaj collection)

51-3RW, 8-Wheel Tipper, 1969, orange or yellow Ergomatic AEC cab and chassis w/silver-gray tipper bed, eight black plastic wheels, green plastic windows, no interior, "Douglas" or "Pointer" labels on the sides of tipper bed, 3", orange models w/"Douglas" appear to have higher MIP values, about $40

EX $9   **NM** $16   **MIP** $30

51-3RW, 8-Wheel Tipper, 1969, another view of Tipper truck w/bed tilted, as w/all miniature construction toys, finding these models in pristine shape can be a bit of a hunt

52-1RW, Maserati 4CLT Racecar, 1958, yellow or red body w/spoked wheels and black tires or solid black plastic wheels, open cockpit w/driver, mostly seen w/"52" decal, 2-3/8", silver-painted grille

EX $25   **NM** $50   **MIP** $100

52-2RW, BRM Racing Car, 1965, blue or red body, white plastic driver, yellow wheels, black plastic tires, 2-3/4", generally carries no. "5" decals on hood and sides

EX $10   **NM** $20   **MIP** $40

53-1RW, Aston Martin, 1958, light green or red body, metal or gray plastic wheels, no interior, no plastic windows, 2-1/2", silver-painted grille

EX $22   **NM** $55   **MIP** $100

53-2RW, Mercedes-Benz 220SE, 1963, red or maroon body, opening doors, white plastic interior, clear plastic windows, 2-3/4", silver, gray or black plastic wheels

EX $10   **NM** $30   **MIP** $55

53-3RW, Ford Zodiac Mk. IV, 1968, blue-silver body, opening hood, white plastic interior, clear plastic windows, black plastic wheels, 2-3/4"

EX $3   **NM** $6   **MIP** $15

53-3RW, Ford Zodiac Mk. IV, 1968, view of Ford Zodiac w/opened hood, showing silver plastic engine and a spare tire tucked in front, opening doors and hoods were always favorite features

54-1RW, Army Saracen Carrier, 1958, olive-green "turtle-shaped" body, six black plastic wheels, rotating turret on top, 2-1/4", one of Matchbox's first military vehicle releases, like rescue and construction vehicles, military toys tend to be in rough shape, so finding mint or MIP examples can be a little tough

EX $8   **NM** $25   **MIP** $50

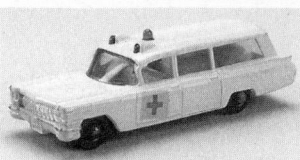

54-2RW, S&S Cadillac Ambulance, 1965, white Cadillac ambulance body w/red cross decal or label, blue plastic windows, detailed white plastic interior, black plastic wheels, silver-painted grille, red plastic dome lights, 2-7/8"

EX $15   **NM** $30   **MIP** $50

55-1RW, D.U.K.W. Amphibian, 1958, olive-green body, metal, gray or black plastic wheels, 2-3/4", another in the early military grouping of Matchbox vehicles

EX $15   **NM** $40   **MIP** $80

55-2RW, Ford Fairlane Police Car, 1963, dark or light blue Ford Fairlane w/white plastic interior, clear plastic windows, red dome light, silver-painted grille, black plastic wheels, dark blue version is harder to find; about $300 MIP, light blue values shown

EX $22   **NM** $50   **MIP** $100

55-3RW, Ford Galaxie Police Car, 1966, white body, white plastic interior w/molded figure, black plastic wheels, red, white and blue stars-in-shield decals, unpainted base, red dome light

EX $20   **NM** $35   **MIP** $60

(KP Photo)

55-4RW, Mercury Police Car, 1969, white Mercury sedan w/white plastic interior, featuring two officers, silver hubs w/black plastic tires, blue dome light, clear plastic windows, unpainted base, "Auto-Steer" front wheels, 3-1/16", a new model, this police car was released at the same time as a Mercury station wagon, #73, both share auto-steer feature and a baseplate, reading "55 or 73"

EX $20   **NM** $30   **MIP** $50

(KP Photo)

56-1RW, Trolley Bus, 1958, red double-decker body w/sloped front, no interior; six metal, gray, or black plastic wheels, "Drink Peardrax" decals on sides, flat trolley poles on roof, "OXO" decal on front, 2-5/8", note that MIP metal wheel versions have sold for $250, common prices for gray and black wheel versions shown

EX $20   **NM** $45   **MIP** $80

(KP Photo, George Cuhaj collection)

56-2RW, Fiat 1500, 1965, pea-green Fiat 1500 sedan w/dark or light brown plastic luggage on roof, red plastic interior, silver-painted grille and headlight details, black plastic wheels, 2-5/8", black plastic base, red versions of this car were included w/the G-1 Service Station Gift Set, and are tough to find,

usually over $100 mint value, standard green values shown

EX $4   **NM** $9   **MIP** $20

(KP Photo, George Cuhaj collection)

57-1RW, Wolseley 1500, 1958, pale green body, no plastic windows, no interior, silver-painted grille, bumpers and headlights, red-painted taillights, black-painted base, 2-1/8"

EX $20   **NM** $35   **MIP** $70

57-1SF, Land Rover Fire Truck, 1970, red body w/"Kent Fire Brigade" decals

EX $18   **NM** $40   **MIP** $75

(KP Photo by Dr. Douglas Sadecky)

57-2RW, Chevrolet Impala, 1961, medium-blue body w/light-blue top, cast tow hook, clear plastic windows, no interior, silver, gray or black plastic wheels

EX $25   **NM** $50   **MIP** $110

(KP Photo, George Cuhaj collection)

57-3RW, Land Rover Fire Truck, 1966, red Land Rover body w/"Kent Fire Brigade" and fire department insignia decals on sides, blue plastic windows and dome light, white plastic ladder (removable) on top, black plastic wheels, 2-1/2"

EX $6   **NM** $11   **MIP** $25

(KP Photo)

58-1RW, British European Airways Coach, 1958, rounded metal blue bus body, no plastic windows, no interior, gray plastic wheels, "British European Airways" decals, 2-1/2"

EX $30   **NM** $50   **MIP** $85

(KP Photo, John Brown Sr. collection)

58-2RW, Drott Excavator, 1962, red or orange body, silver-painted motors on some red variations, orange motor on some orange models, 2-5/8"

EX $15   **NM** $35   **MIP** $60

(KP Photo, John Brown Sr. collection)

58-3RW, DAF Girder Truck, 1968, cream-colored cab and chassis, red plastic grille, green plastic windows, no interior, "Available mid-1968" in 1968 catalog, black plastic wheels, 12 red plastic girders, 3"

EX $4   **NM** $9   **MIP** $20

(KP Photo, John Brown Sr. collection)

59-1RW, Ford "Singer" Van, 1958, light green Ford Thames van w/"Singer" decals on panel sides and "S" logo decals on doors, no plastic windows, no interior, silver-painted grille, gray plastic wheels, 2-1/8", dark green models seem hard to find, about $250 MIP

EX $35 **NM** $55 **MIP** $100

(KP Photo)

59-2RW, Ford Fairlane Fire Chief Car, red Ford Fairlane casting (same as 55-2RW Ford Fairlane police car) black or silver plastic wheels, white plastic interior, clear plastic windows

EX $25 **NM** $45 **MIP** $80

(KP Photo, Tom Michael collection)

59-3RW, Ford Galaxie Fire Chief Car, 1966, red Ford Galaxie body, white plastic interior w/figure cast as part of interior (like police car version) unpainted base and metal grille and headlight section, fire chief decals or labels on side doors and hood, clear plastic windows, white plastic tow hook, blue plastic dome light, 2-7/8"

EX $12 **NM** $30 **MIP** $50

(KP Photo, George Cuhaj collection)

60-1RW, Morris J2 Pick-Up Truck, 1958, blue pick-up body, gray, silver or black plastic tires, "Builders Supply Company" decals on sides, silver-painted grille, no plastic windows, no interior, 2-1/4"

EX $18 **NM** $35 **MIP** $60

(KP Photo, George Cuhaj collection)

60-2RW, Site Hut Truck, 1967, blue Leyland Ergomatic cab and flatbed chassis, silver plastic grille and headlights, blue plastic windows, no interior, black plastic wheels, plastic yellow hut on back w/green roof, 2-1/2"

EX $5 **NM** $12 **MIP** $20

(KP Photo, George Cuhaj collection)

61-1RW, Ferret Scout Car, 1959, olive-green, open-cockpit armored car body, tan-colored driver, four black plastic wheels, (one spare on side), 2-1/4"

EX $9 **NM** $20 **MIP** $50

(KP Photo)

61-2, Alvis Stalwart, 1967, white body w/green plastic windows and green or yellow wheels w/black plastic tires, plastic canopy over bed (not shown), no interior, 2-5/8", yellow wheels are less common and have approx. $75 MIP values

EX $9 **NM** $25 **MIP** $40

(KP Photo)

62-1RW, General Service Lorry, 1959, olive-green body w/six black plastic wheels, no plastic windows, no interior

EX $20 **NM** $32 **MIP** $70

(KP photo by Dr. Douglas Sadecky)

62-2RW, TV Service Van, 1963, cream colored body w/"Rentaset" or "Radio Rentals" decals on sides, red plastic accessories: antenna, three TV sets and ladder, no interior, 2-1/2"

EX $20 **NM** $50 **MIP** $100

(KP Photo)

62-3RW, Mercury Cougar, 1969, lime-green Mercury Cougar body w/unpainted base, silver wheels w/removable black plastic tires (like other Mercury models in the line), opening doors, red plastic interior, "auto-steer" front wheels, tow hook, 3"

EX $12 **NM** $20 **MIP** $35

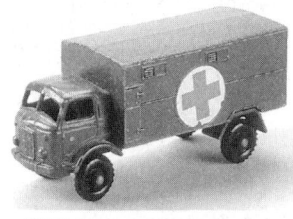

(KP Photo, George Cuhaj collection)

63-1RW, Service Ambulance, 1959, olive green truck-ambulance chassis, black plastic wheels, no interior, no plastic windows, red cross decals on sides

EX $8 **NM** $30 **MIP** $60

(KP Photo)

63-2RW, Fire Fighting Crash Tender, 1964, block-shaped red body w/white plastic ladder (missing in this photo) and white plastic lettering on sides, no plastic windows, no interior, black plastic wheels, 2-3/8"

EX $12   **NM** $30   **MIP** $50

(KP Photo, George Cuhaj collection)

63-2RW, Fire Fighting Crash Tender, 1964, view of the detailed casting on rear of vehicle

(KP Photo, George Cuhaj collection)

63-3RW, Dodge Crane Truck, 1969, yellow Dodge cab and chassis, red or yellow plastic hook, black grille and headlights, green plastic windows, no interior, six black plastic wheels, swivelling crane section, 3"

EX $6   **NM** $10   **MIP** $20

(KP Photo, George Cuhaj collection)

64-1RW, Scammell Breakdown Lorry, 1959, olive green body, box

cab, green, silver or gray hook, six black plastic wheels

EX $25   **NM** $45   **MIP** $75

(KP Photo, George Cuhaj collection)

64-2RW, M.G. 1100, 1966, green car body, white plastic interior w/driver in front and dog peeking out of rear window, clear plastic windows, black plastic wheels, unpainted base, white plastic tow hook, 2-5/8"

EX $5   **NM** $10   **MIP** $17

(KP Photo, George Cuhaj collection)

64-2RW, M.G. 1100, 1966, view of the M.G. and collie peeking out from window, matchbox included dogs in many later regular wheels models—a fun addition

(KP Photo by Dr. Douglas Sadecky)

65-RW, Jaguar 3.4 Litre, 1959, blue body, no interior, no plastic windows, gray plastic wheels, silver-painted grille, shown here w/65-2RW Jaguar 3.8 Litre Sedan

EX $18   **NM** $35   **MIP** $70

(KP Photo, George Cuhaj collection)

65-2RW, Jaguar 3.8 Litre Sedan, 1962, red body, opening hood, silver-painted grille and headlights, gray, silver or black plastic wheels, green plastic windows, no interior, 2-5/8"

EX $11   **NM** $25   **MIP** $50

(KP Photo, George Cuhaj collection)

65-2RW, Jaguar 3.8 Litre Sedan, 1962, view of gray-wheeled model w/open hood-a favorite feature

(KP Photo)

65-3RW, Combine Harvester, 1967, red Claas combine w/yellow plastic grain reel and yellow wheels w/removable black plastic tires, 3", a popular casting for Matchbox, matching the King-Size model (K-9) version

EX $12   **NM** $20   **MIP** $40

(KP Photo by Dr. Douglas Sadecky)

66-1RW, Citroen DS19, 1959, yellow body, silver-painted grille, no window plastic, no interior, gray or silver plastic wheels

EX $28   **NM** $60   **MIP** $110

(KP Photo by Dr. Douglas Sadecky)

66-2RW, Harley-Davidson Motorcycle w/Sidecar, 1962, gold metallic body w/spoked wheels, 2-5/8", this piece has escalated in value due to Matchbox and Harley-Davidson collector cross-over

EX $65   **NM** $95   **MIP** $160

(KP Photo, George Cuhaj collection)

66-3RW, Greyhound Bus, 1967, silver-gray body, "Greyhound" decals or labels, yellow plastic windows, white plastic interior, black plastic wheels, 3"

EX $10   **NM** $20   **MIP** $40

(KP Photo)

67-1RW, Saladin Armoured Car, 1959, olive-green body, rotating turret six black plastic wheels, 2-1/4"

EX $11   **NM** $25   **MIP** $50

(KP Photo, George Cuhaj collection)

67-2RW, Volkswagen 1600 TL, 1967, red body, white interior, unpainted base running up into headlights, clear window plastic, opening doors, 2-11/16", one version w/snap-on plastic roof rack was included w/Race'n Rally G-4 gift set, harder to find

EX $11   **NM** $20   **MIP** $40

(KP Photo, George Cuhaj collection)

67-2RW, Volkswagen 1600 TL, 1967, another view of the car showing opening doors and interior

(KP Photo, George Cuhaj collection)

68-1RW, Austin Mark II Radio Truck, 1959, olive-green body, no window plastic, no interior, black plastic wheels

EX $18   **NM** $35   **MIP** $65

(KP Photo, George Cuhaj collection)

68-2RW, Mercedes Coach, 1966, white and blue-green or white and orange body, clear window plastic, white plastic interior, black plastic wheels, 2-7/8", blue-green version harder-to-find w/approximately $130 MIP values, more common orange-version values shown

EX $7   **NM** $15   **MIP** $25

(KP Photo by Dr. Douglas Sadecky)

69-1RW, Commer 30 CWT Nestlé's Van, 1959, dark red or red van w/Nestlé's decals on panel sides, sliding doors, no window plastic, no interior, silver-painted grille, gray plastic wheels

EX $22   **NM** $40   **MIP** $90

(KP Photo, George Cuhaj collection)

69-2RW, Hatra Tractor Shovel, 1965, yellow or orange body w/black plastic removable tires, hubs can be yellow or red, 3-1/8"

EX $11   **NM** $25   **MIP** $50

(KP Photo, George Cuhaj collection)

70-1RW, Ford Thames Estate Car, 1959, pale blue and yellow van-shaped body w/clear or green plastic windows, no interior, silver-painted grille, gray, silver or black plastic wheels

EX $12   **NM** $25   **MIP** $50

(KP Photo, John Brown Sr. collection)

70-2RW, Grit Spreader, 1966, red Ford cab and chassis, yellow hopper section, green plastic windows, no interior, black plastic wheels, silver metal grille, gray or black plastic "pulls" that open bottom chute, 2-5/8"

EX $7   **NM** $9   **MIP** $20

(KP Photo)

71-1RW, Service Water Truck, 1959, olive-green truck chassis w/water tank on back, black plastic wheels, spare black plastic tire behind cab, no plastic windows, no interior

EX $28   **NM** $40   **MIP** $75

(KP Photo, George Cuhaj collection)

71-2RW, Jeep Pick-Up Truck, 1964, red body, opening doors, black partial base, black plastic wheels, clear plastic windows, silver-painted grille, 2-5/8", early models came w/green plastic interior (shown in 1964 catalog) and are hard to find, about $175 MIP, white plastic interior more common; prices shown

EX $12   **NM** $25   **MIP** $50

(KP Photo, George Cuhaj collection)

71-2RW, Jeep Pick-Up Truck, 1964, another view of Jeep Pick-Up Truck showing opening doors

(KP Photo, George Cuhaj collection)

71-3RW, Ford Heavy Wreck Truck, 1969, red cab, green plastic windows and dome light, red plastic hook, black plastic wheels, "Esso" label, white grille extending from white base w/"1968" date, 3", a nice, hefty model

EX $12   **NM** $20   **MIP** $50

(KP Photo by Dr. Douglas Sadecky)

72-1RW, Fordson Major Tractor, 1959, blue tractor w/gray or black plastic tires, and orange hubs in rear and in variations, on front,

silver-painted grille, 2", gray-tire version and black-tire version w/box variations shown

EX $18   **NM** $30   **MIP** $75

(KP Photo, George Cuhaj collection)

72-1RW, Fordson Major Tractor, 1959, another variation of the Fordson tractor w/orange hubs and black tires, front and rear, this is the version of the tractor that appeared in its last catalog appearance in 1966

EX $18   **NM** $30   **MIP** $75

(KP Photo, George Cuhaj collection)

72-2RW, Standard Jeep, 1967, yellow body w/upright windshield, black base, red plastic interior and tow hook, black plastic removable tires over yellow hubs, spare tire on back, 2-3/8"

EX $12   **NM** $20   **MIP** $40

73-1RW, RAF Refueller Truck, 1960, blue body w/RAF decal on top of truck behind cab, no plastic windows, no interior, gray plastic wheels

EX $20   **NM** $45   **MIP** $90

(KP Photo)

73-2RW, Ferrari Racing Car, 1962, red racing car body w/"73" and Ferrari decals on sides, spoked wheels, white or gray plastic driver, 2-5/8"

EX $20   **NM** $30   **MIP** $70

(KP Photo)

73-3RW, Mercury Commuter, 1969, another view of the Mercury station wagon, showing the two dogs peeking out of the back window

(KP Photo)

73-3RW, Mercury Commuter, 1969, lime green body w/clear plastic windows, white plastic interior (including two dogs peeking out of the back), black plastic removable tires w/silver hubs, "Auto-Steer" front steering, 3-1/16"

EX $9   **NM** $15   **MIP** $30

(KP Photo)

74-1, Mobile Refreshment Bar, 1960, silver trailer body w/opening sides and plastic interior, "Refreshments" decals below side openings, silver or gray plastic wheels, medium-blue baseplate models about $190 MIP, 2-5/8", common prices w/lighter blue bases shown below

EX $28   **NM** $60   **MIP** $120

Matchbox
SUPERFAST

(KP Photo, George Cuhaj collection)

1-1SF, Mercedes Truck, 1970, gold-colored body, orange plastic tarp cover, green window plastic, narrow transitional Superfast wheels, silver plastic grille and half-baseplate, tow hook cast w/body, 3"

EX $4   **NM** $15   **MIP** $30

(KP Photo, Tom Michael collection)

1-2SF, Mod Rod, 1971, yellow body, amber window plastic, exposed silver-plastic engine in back, red or black Superfast wheels, "wildcat" label on hood, 2-7/8"

EX $12   **NM** $18   **MIP** $25

(KP Photo)

1-3SF, Dodge Challenger, 1976, red or blue body, white or red plastic interior, black wheels, plastic air scoops on hood, blue-tinted windshield plastic, white plastic roof, 2-7/8"

EX $6   **NM** $10   **MIP** $20

(KP Photo)

1-4SF, Dodge Challenger, 1982, yellow body, gray base, "Toyman" tampos, black plastic roof

EX $3   **NM** $6   **MIP** $9

2-1SF, Mercedes Trailer, 1970, gold-colored body w/orange plastic canopy, thin transitional wheels, 3-1/2"

EX $6   **NM** $14   **MIP** $25

2-2SF, Hot Rod Jeep, 1971, pink or red body, exposed silver plastic engine w/black plastic exhaust pipes, white plastic seats, lime-green base and bumpers, 2-5/16"

EX $5   **NM** $9   **MIP** $20

(KP Photo)

2-3SF, Hovercraft, 1976, metallic green hovercraft body w/light brown plastic base and thin "hidden wheels" beneath, 3-1/6"

EX $2   **NM** $4   **MIP** $8

(KP Photo)

3-1SF, Mercedes-Benz "Binz" Ambulance, 1970, white body w/opening hatch and patient on stretcher, red cross labels, blue window plastic, white plastic interior, thin transitional wheels, (later issued w/thicker wheels as part of TP-10 Two-Pack), 2-7/8"

EX $7   **NM** $20   **MIP** $45

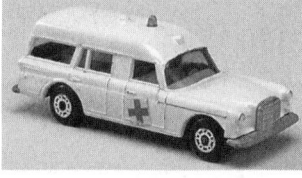

(KP Photo)

3-1SF, Mercedes-Benz "Binz" Ambulance, view of wider-wheel version w/out opening rear hatch, included as part of TP-10

(KP Photo)

3-2SF, Monterverdi Hai, 1973, orange body w/number "3" label on hood, blue window plastic, thick black wheels, opening doors, 3"

EX $5   **NM** $7   **MIP** $15

(KP Photo)

3-2SF, Monterverdi Hai, 1974, another view of the Monterverdi Hai showing opening doors

(KP Photo, Tom Michael collection)

3-3SF, Porsche Turbo, 1979, charcoal-gray, red or white exterior w/rally number "14," plastic interior can be yellow, tan or brown, plastic tow hook, opening doors

EX $2   **NM** $3   **MIP** $7

(KP Photo)

4-1SF, Stake Truck, 1970, yellow, or orange-yellow cab and chassis w/green window plastic, no interior, green plastic stake-side cargo area, silver metal base, grille and headlights, 2-7/8"

EX $5   **NM** $10   **MIP** $25

(KP Photo, Tom Michael collection)

4-2SF, Gruesome Twosome, 1971, gold or red w/cream interiors and pink or purple window plastic, two exposed engines, unpainted base, 2-7/8"

EX $4   **NM** $8   **MIP** $15

(KP Photo, Tom Michael collection)

4-3SF, Pontiac Firebird, 1975, blue body w/silver plastic interior, amber window plastic, unpainted base and bumpers, 2-7/8"

EX $4   **NM** $8   **MIP** $15

(KP Photo)

4-4SF, '57 Chevy, 1981, red or light purple w/unpainted or black base, opening hood w/silver plastic engine underneath

EX $4   **NM** $8   **MIP** $15

(KP Photo)

5-1SF, Lotus Europa, 1970, pink or blue body, white plastic interior, opening doors, 2-7/8", thin or thick Superfast wheels, blue model shown in 1970 catalog, but pink was advertised afterward until model removed from lineup

EX $5   **NM** $10   **MIP** $25

(KP Photo, Tom Michael collection)

5-1SF, Lotus Europa, 1970, the pink version of the Lotus Europa, here w/thin wheels, this color variation also comes w/wide wheels, and generally seems more common

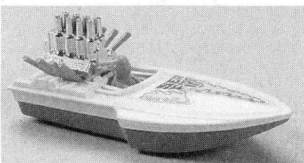

(KP Photo, John Brown Sr. collection)

5-2SF, Seafire, 1976, white body w/"Seafire" label on front, blue base, blue or orange driver, exposed silver plastic engine w/red plastic exhaust pipes, this casting has been used many times by Matchbox, returning in 5-Packs in the 1990s

EX $3   **NM** $7   **MIP** $12

(KP Photo)

6-1SF, Ford Pick-Up Truck, 1970, red body, white plastic camper top, silver or white plastic grille, 2-3/4", black or charcoal base

EX $12   **NM** $25   **MIP** $50

(KP Photo, Tom Michael collection)

6-2SF, Mercedes Tourer, 1973, orange or yellow 350SL body w/black plastic top, amber windows, light yellow or cream plastic interior, 3", unpainted base, later models in light or dark red w/white plastic roof, or red or metallic blue w/no roof

EX $3   **NM** $7   **MIP** $14

7-1SF, Ford Refuse Truck, 1970, red-orange cab w/gray plastic and silver metal garbage dumper bed, 3", the same model as the old regular-

wheels version, just w/thin or thick Superfast wheels

EX $4   **NM** $12   **MIP** $25

(KP Photo, Tom Michael collection)

7-2SF, Hairy Hustler, 1973, bronze body, w/amber windows, number "5" racing labels on front and side, or white body w/checkered labels on hood and roof, and red stripes on fenders, black metal base

EX $5   **NM** $10   **MIP** $15

(KP Photo, John Brown Sr. collection)

7-3SF, Volkswagen Golf, 1977, lime green, dark green, yellow or red body, amber window plastic, black plastic, detachable surf boards on roof rack, yellow plastic interior, black or charcoal base, tow hook

EX $4   **NM** $7   **MIP** $12

8-1SF, Ford Mustang Fastback, 1970, white, red or orange-red body, white or red plastic interior (red is harder-to-find), tow hook, 2-7/8", red models w/red plastic interiors are the most rare, selling for around $375 MIB

EX $65   **NM** $80   **MIP** $150

(KP Photo)

8-2SF, Wildcat Dragster, 1971, orange or pink body w/silver engine protruding from hood, and "Wild Cat" labels on sides, tow hook, 2-7/8", this is the same casting used on the Mustang Fastback model 8-1SF

EX $8   **NM** $12   **MIP** $25

(KP Photo)

8-3SF, De Tomasa Pantera, 1975, white body w/"8" labels, blue base, red plastic interior, or blue body, tempo "17," black base, 3"

EX $3   **NM** $5   **MIP** $10

(KP Photo)

8-3SF, De Tomasa Pantera, 1975, a view of the blue version of the Pantera w/the "17" tempo

EX $3   **NM** $5   **MIP** $10

9-1SF, Boat and Trailer, 1970, blue die-cast boat trailer w/thin Superfast wheels and plastic blue and white boat, 3-1/2"

EX $4   **NM** $12   **MIP** $25

(KP Photo)

9-2SF, AMX Javelin, 1972, lime-green or blue body (blue included w/Twin-Pack #3, Javelin and Pony Trailer), black or silver plastic air scoop, light yellow or white plastic interior, opening doors, tow hook, 3-1/16"

EX $3   **NM** $9   **MIP** $15

(KP Photo, Tom Michael collection)

9-3SF, Ford Escort RS 2000, 1979, white body w/Ford and Shell rally labels, clear window plastic, black base, tan plastic interior

EX $3   **NM** $5   **MIP** $8

10-1SF, Pipe Truck, 1970, red or orange cab and chassis, gray or yellow plastic pipes, thin or wide Superfast wheels, silver grille, green window plastic, 3", red models about $35 MIB, orange model values shown below

EX $10   **NM** $18   **MIP** $35

(KP Photo, Tom Michael collection)

10-2SF, Piston Popper, 1973, blue or yellow Mustang Mach I body w/silver Rola-Matic engine w/red plastic pistons that move as car is rolled along, yellow plastic interior, unpainted base, 2-7/8"

EX $3   **NM** $9   **MIP** $15

(KP Photo)

10-3SF, Plymouth Gran Fury Police Car, 1979, black and white w/"Metro Police" on doors and hood, blue police lights on roof, amber or blue window plastic, unpainted or silver base, introduced in 1979/80 catalog, it hadn't yet replaced Piston Popper in the lineup

EX $4   **NM** $8   **MIP** $12

(KP Photo, George Cuhaj collection)

11-3SF, Scaffold Truck, 1970, silver Mercedes-Benz truck w/red plastic base and grille, yellow plastic scaffold sections in back, "Builders Supply Company" labels on sides of truck, green window plastic, no interior, 2-5/8"

EX $7   **NM** $12   **MIP** $20

(KP Photo)

11-2SF, Flying Bug, 1973, red metallic Volkswagen Beetle w/Iron Cross label on hood, oversized face w/silver helmet peeking up from car, opaque windows, tailwing and yellow plastic jet engine section on back, silver or unpainted base, 2-7/8"

EX $4   **NM** $11   **MIP** $20

(KP Photo)

11-3SF, Car Transporter, 1978, orange body w/black base and light tan/cream car carrying section w/red, yellow and blue plastic cars, dark blue window plastic, no interior

EX $4   **NM** $10   **MIP** $14

(KP Photo, Tom Michael collection)

11-4SF, Cobra Mustang, 1982, orange body w/opening hood, chrome interior, yellow windows, "The Boss" in white lettering on sides, number "5" on roof, another in the many variations of the old "Boss Mustang" casting

EX $2   **NM** $4   **MIP** $10

(KP Photo)

12-1SF, Safari Land Rover, 1970, gold body w/white plastic interior, red-brown plastic luggage, tow hook, thin Superfast wheels, 2-3/4", blue versions of this model exist as Superfasts, but are extremely rare, so prices shown are for gold models only

EX $8   **NM** $20   **MIP** $40

(KP Photo, John Brown Sr. collection)

12-2SF, Setra Coach, 1971, metallic yellow and white or burgundy and white w/clear or green window plastic, white plastic interior, unpainted base, 3"

EX $3   **NM** $7   **MIP** $15

(KP Photo, John Brown Sr. collection)

12-3SF, Big Bull, 1975, orange bulldozer body and rollers, green base and blade, silver plastic engine and trim, 2-1/2"

EX $3   **NM** $8   **MIP** $12

(KP Photo)

12-4SF, Citroen CX Station Wagon, 1980, blue body w/cream or light yellow plastic interior, clear or blue window plastic, unpainted or silver base

EX $2   **NM** $5   **MIP** $10

13-1SF, Wreck Truck, 1970, yellow Dodge cab and tow boom w/green bed, "BP" labels on sides, thin Superfast wheels, red window plastic and dome light, no interior, red plastic tow hook, 3", this is another transitional model that is becoming hard to find

EX $30   **NM** $60   **MIP** $110

(KP Photo, Tom Michael collection)

13-2SF, Baja Buggy, 1972, lime green body, orange plastic interior, no window plastic, thick Superfast wheels, flower label on hood, silver plastic engine w/orange plastic exhaust pipes, 2-5/8"

EX $4   **NM** $8   **MIP** $14

(KP Photo)

13-3SF, Snorkel Fire Engine, 1977, red body w/blue or amber window plastic, yellow or white snorkel section, unpainted metal base, models w/amber-colored window plastic tend to have higher MIP prices, about $15, this fire engine first appeared in the 1977 catalog w/a white snorkel as a new model to watch for, not yet replacing Baha Buggy in the lineup

EX $3   **NM** $7   **MIP** $12

(KP Photo)

14-1SF, Iso Grifo, 1970, dark or medium blue w/thin Superfast wheels, light blue or white plastic interior, unpainted base, 3"

EX $6   **NM** $15   **MIP** $30

(KP Photo)

14-2SF, Mini-Ha-Ha, 1976, red body w/blue opaque window plastic, silver plastic rotary engine protruding through hood, large rear wheels, head w/pilot's helmet showing through roof, circular British RAF side labels on doors

EX $3   **NM** $8   **MIP** $17

15-1SF, Volkswagen 1500, 1970, white, cream or red body w/white plastic interior, tow hook, unpainted base, "137" labels on doors, 2-7/8"

EX $7   **NM** $20   **MIP** $40

(KP Photo)

15-2SF, Fork Lift Truck, 1973, red body w/larger wheels at front, gray or yellow plastic lifting forks on yellow metal or unpainted track, "Lansing Bagnall" or "Hi-Lift" side labels, unpainted, black or green base, 2-3/4"

EX $3   **NM** $6   **MIP** $15

(KP Photo)

15-3SF, Hi Ho Silver, 1981, silver Volkswagen Beetle (same casting as "Volks Dragon") w/"Hi Ho Silver" and "31" tempo, black base, clear window plastic, red plastic interior, 2-5/8", having "31" on the roof is an interesting choice of graphic, considering it was the same vehicle casting as the 31-2SF

EX $4   **NM** $7   **MIP** $12

(KP Photo by Dr. Douglas Sadecky)

16-1SF, Case Bulldozer, 1970, red w/yellow engine, cab and blade and green or black rubber tracks, 2-1/2", this model was released at the same time as the Superfast line-notice that the box has "speed lines" just like the other models

EX $5   **NM** $10   **MIP** $20

(KP Photo)

16-2SF, Badger, 1974, block, metallic bronze-red body w/surface detail tools, ladders, etc., and plastic "Rola-Matic" radar, green window plastic, no interior, six thick wheels, 2-3/4", later editions in olive-green were included as part of TP-14 Two-Pack

EX $4   **NM** $7   **MIP** $12

(KP Photo, Tom Michael collection)

16-3SF, Pontiac Firebird, 1981, metallic light or dark tan, Firebird tempo on hood, light tan plastic interior

EX $3   **NM** $7   **MIP** $12

17-1SF, Horse Box, 1971, red or orange AEC Ergomatic cab w/green or gray plastic horse box, gray or mustard door, and two white plastic horses, 2-7/8"

EX $6   **NM** $13   **MIP** $25

(KP Photo, John Brown Sr. collection)

17-2SF, The Londoner, 1973, red body w/"Berger Paints" or "Swinging London Carnaby Street" side labels (most common), white plastic interior, no window plastic,

3", there are many color and label variations of this model, some limited runs that command MIP values over $200, however, prices shown are for the common red-colored "Berger" and "Swinging London" versions

EX $3   **NM** $8   **MIP** $12

(KP Photo, Tom Michael collection)

17-2SF, The Londoner, 1973, the "Swinging London" version of the The Londoner bus

(KP Photo, Tom Michael collection)

18-1SF, Field Car, 1970, yellow body w/tan plastic roof, white plastic interior, no window plastic, unpainted base, spare tire, tow hook, thin or thick wheels, 2-7/8", other variations as part of Two-Packs in the 1970s, included orange w/checked hood label and black plastic roof, olive green w/light-tan plastic roof and hood label, red with light-tan plastic roof and "44" hood label-almost all w/black plastic interiors, white editions are harder to find, about $250-300 in MIP condition, prices shown reflect the more common models listed

EX $7   **NM** $12   **MIP** $25

(KP Photo, Tom Michael collection)

18-1SF, Field Car, variation w/dark yellow-orange body, black interior, base and roof, part of Two Pack (TP-8), w/Honda motorcycle

(KP Photo)

18-2SF, Hondarora, 1975, red or orange body w/silver or black forks and black seat are the most common, some w/gas-tank labels, some w/out, olive-drab military models were part of the TP-11 set w/the olive-drab field car, 2-1/2"

EX $5   **NM** $10   **MIP** $15

19-1SF, Lotus Racing Car, 1970, dark metallic purple, white plastic driver, wide Superfast wheels, "3" decal on sides, 2-3/4"

EX $15   **NM** $30   **MIP** $60

(KP Photo, Tom Michael collection)

19-2SF, Road Dragster, 1971, red or metallic pink body w/unpainted base, exposed silver plastic engine, white plastic interior, wide wheels, clear window plastic, "8" labels on hood and roof, 3", some models have "Wynns" or scorpion labels and are pink or orange-red and harder to find, about $80 MIP

EX $5   **NM** $10   **MIP** $20

(KP Photo)

19-3SF, Cement Truck, 1977, red cab and chassis, unpainted metal base, green window plastic, no interior, yellow plastic mixer, w/or w/out black or red stripes, 3"

EX $3   **NM** $8   **MIP** $13

(KP Photo)

20-1SF, Lamborghini Marzal, 1970, pink or dark red w/amber window plastic, white plastic interior and thin wheels; or pink or orange-pink w/thick wheels, 2-3/4"

EX $8   **NM** $15   **MIP** $25

(KP Photo, Tom Michael collection)

20-2SF, Police Patrol: Site Engineer, 1977, orange body w/rotating orange dome light, "Site Engineer" labels on doors, plain metal base, part of #13 Construction Gift Pack

EX $5   **NM** $8   **MIP** $14

(KP Photo)

20-2SF, Police Patrol: Paris-Dakar Rallye, 1983, gold body w/black and white checkered label and "Securitie-Rallye Paris Dakar 83" on sides, black base, red rotating dome light

EX $5   **NM** $9   **MIP** $13

(KP Photo)

20-2SF, Police Patrol: County Sheriff, 1982, white body w/blue doors and roof, star design on hood and doors, "County Sheriff" in blue type on sides, blue rotating dome light

EX $3   **NM** $5   **MIP** $8

20-2SF, Police Patrol: British Police, 1983, white body w/yellow and black/white checkered "Police" labels on sides, blue rotating dome light, black base

EX $4   **NM** $8   **MIP** $12

(KP Photo)

20-2SF, Police Patrol, 1975, white Range Rover w/orange stripe "Police" label, frosted window plastic and blue or orange revolving police light (part of the Rola-Matics series), 2-7/8", other models include orange Site Engineer from Gift Pack #13, olive-drab military ambulance model, and orange Paris-Dakar model, each w/approximately $25-$35 MIP value, common white model values given below

EX $4   **NM** $10   **MIP** $20

(KP Photo)

21-1SF, Foden Concrete Truck, 1971, yellow cab, orange truck bed w/yellow plastic mixer, eight thin wheels, 3"

EX $8   **NM** $20   **MIP** $40

(KP Photo)

21-2SF, Rod Roller, 1973, yellow body w/red plastic seat, star and flames

label on hood, (later editions w/out black plastic roller wheels, some w/red or metallic red hubs on rear, black plastic steering lever, 2-1/2"

EX $5   **NM** $12   **MIP** $20

(KP Photo)

21-3SF, Renault 5TL, 1979, yellow, blue, white or silver-gray body, clear or amber window plastic, tan or red plastic interior, tow hook, 2-1/2", some yellow models have "Le Car" tempo

EX $2   **NM** $6   **MIP** $10

(KP Photo)

22-1SF, Pontiac Grand Prix, 1970, purple body, thin wheels, silver grille and black base, 3"

EX $12   **NM** $60   **MIP** $125

(KP Photo, Tom Michael collection)

22-2SF, Freeman Inter-City Commuter, 1971, purple-red body w/white plastic interior, clear window plastic, unpainted base, some w/side labels, 3"

EX $3   **NM** $8   **MIP** $15

(KP Photo)

22-3SF, Blaze Buster, 1976, red body w/yellow or black plastic ladder, silver plastic interior, amber window plastic, black or silver base,

3-1/16", black-ladder versions about $25 MIP value

EX $2   **NM** $5   **MIP** $13

(KP Photo)

22-4SF, 4 x 4 Big Foot, 1982, silver body, white plastic camper top, blue window plastic, black base, "Big Foot" and "26" tempos on sides and hood

EX $2   **NM** $5   **MIP** $12

23-1SF, Volkswagen Camper, 1970, blue or orange body w/plastic orange lift-up top reveals white plastic interior, amber or clear window plastic, some models w/sailboat labels on sides, 2-5/8", military olive-drab versions w/out lift-up camper top were included as ambulances w/TP-12 Two-Pack

EX $9   **NM** $22   **MIP** $45

(KP Photo)

23-2SF, Atlas Tipper, 1976, blue body w/orange or silver tipper section, wide wheels, amber or clear window plastic, silver or gray plastic interior, 2-3/4", later versions available w/red body

EX $1   **NM** $5   **MIP** $12

(KP Photo, Tom Michael collection)

23-3SF, Ford Mustang GT-350, 1981, white body, blue Shelby stripes, exposed engine in front, "GT 350" on sides

EX $5   **NM** $12   **MIP** $25

(KP Photo)

24-1SF, Rolls-Royce Silver Shadow, 1970, metallic red body, white plastic interior, clear window plastic, opening trunk, silver metal grille and headlights, black or silver base, 3"

EX $5   **NM** $12   **MIP** $25

(KP Photo)

24-2SF, Team Matchbox, 1973, metallic green, red or orange body, "8" or "44" label (included w/TP-9, Field Car and Racing Car Two-Pack), white plastic driver, 2-7/8"

EX $1   **NM** $4   **MIP** $9

(KP Photo, John Brown Sr. collection)

24-3SF, Diesel Shunter, 1979, dark green and red or yellow and red body, no window plastic, labels read "Rail Freight" or "D1496-RF"

EX $2   **NM** $4   **MIP** $8

(KP Photo)

25-1SF, Ford Cortina GT, 1970, metallic tan or blue body, white plastic interior, opening doors, tow hook, 2-5/8", metallic tan versions, the first of the transitional Superfast models,

are harder-to-find and have approximately $70-$80 MIP values

EX $8   **NM** $20   **MIP** $40

(KP Photo)

25-2SF, Mod Tractor, 1973, metallic purple body, black base, some w/"V" cast on fenders, some w/out, silver plastic exposed engine, yellow plastic seat, 2-1/4"

EX $3   **NM** $6   **MIP** $12

(KP Photo, John Brown Sr. collection)

25-3SF, Flat Car and Container, 1979, black or charcoal flat car w/tan or red plastic container w/"NYK Worldwide Service" labels

EX $1   **NM** $3   **MIP** $5

26-1SF, GMC Tipper Truck, 1970, red tipping cab, green engine and base, silver dump bed, green window plastic, no interior, 2-5/8"

EX $5   **NM** $12   **MIP** $25

(KP Photo, Tom Michael collection)

26-2SF, Brown Sugar, 1973, the "Brown Sugar" version of the Big Banger w/brown body, large silver engine w/black scoop and yellow and red "Brown Sugar" labels

(KP Photo, Tom Michael collection)

26-2SF, Big Banger, 1973, red w/dark-blue window plastic, no interior, large silver plastic engine and exhaust pipes, "Big Banger" side labels, 3", later versions were brown w/"Brown Sugar" side labels or white w/"Cosmic Blues" tempo
EX $4 **NM** $9 **MIP** $18

26-3SF, Site Dumper, 1977, yellow body w/yellow or red dumper bed, or orange body w/silver-gray dumper bed, no window plastic, black or brown base, black plastic interior
EX $3 **NM** $6 **MIP** $13

(KP Photo)

27-1SF, Mercedes 230SL, 1970, yellow convertible body w/black plastic interior, or white body w/red plastic interior, clear window plastic, silver base, thin wheels, 2-3/4"
EX $8 **NM** $20 **MIP** $40

(KP Photo, Tom Michael collection)

27-2SF, Lamborghini Countach, 1973, pale-orange body w/"3" label on hood, or red-orange w/"8" tempo and stripes, silver or gray plastic interior, amber or blue window plastic, opening rear hood, 3"
EX $3 **NM** $7 **MIP** $14

(KP Photo)

28-1SF, Mack Dump Truck, 1970, light green body and dumper bed, silver

base, wide wheels, no interior, amber window plastic, 2-5/8", olive-drab versions were released w/Case bulldozer in TP-16 Two-Pack
EX $6 **NM** $12 **MIP** $25

(KP Photo)

28-2SF, Stoat, 1973, metallic bronze-tan body w/rotating (Rola-Matic) soldier holding binoculars, black base, wide wheels, 2-5/8", olive-green versions w/all-black wheels were included in TP-13 Two-Pack along w/an olive version of 73-2SF Weasel armored vehicle
EX $3 **NM** $10 **MIP** $17

(KP Photo, Tom Michael collection)

28-3SF, Lincoln Continental Mk V, 1979, red body, white plastic roof, light-yellow or gray interior, silver base, first introduced in the 1979/80 catalog, this model had not yet replaced the Stoat in the lineup, but was due to be "available in your shops later this year"
EX $3 **NM** $6 **MIP** $10

(KP Photo)

29-1SF, Fire Pumper, 1970, red body, blue window plastic and dome light, white plastic ladders and reels, silver base, thin wheels, 3"
EX $12 **NM** $32 **MIP** $70

(KP Photo, Tom Michael collection)

29-2SF, Racing Mini, 1971, orange-red body w/yellow "29" labels, clear window plastic, white plastic interior, unpainted silver-gray base and grille, 2-1/4", also included w/TP-6 Two-Pack
EX $5 **NM** $11 **MIP** $20

(KP Photo)

29-3SF, Shovel-Nose Tractor, 1977, yellow body w/silver or black plastic engine and interior, shovel can be red or black plastic, 2-7/8", lime green models w/yellow plastic shovels are harder to find, about $65 MIP value, models w/yellow body, black plastic and stripes (as shown) were included in the G-5 Giftset in the 1979/80 catalog, orange models w/red plastic shovels, also about $65 MIP value
EX $5 **NM** $8 **MIP** $16

(KP Photo)

30-1SF, 8-Wheel Crane, 1970, red w/gold crane section, red plastic hook, no window plastic, yellow plastic hook, 3"
EX $10 **NM** $20 **MIP** $45

(KP Photo, Tom Michael collection)

30-2SF, Beach Buggy, 1971, pink body w/yellow "spatter paint," white or yellow plastic interior and side tanks, no window plastic, 2-9/16", white interior versions have approximately $20 MIP value

EX $4   **NM** $7   **MIP** $12

(KP Photo)

30-3SF, Swamp Rat, 1977, squared-boat body w/olive-green deck, tan plastic hull, rotating striped army gunner (Rola-Matic), "Swamp Rat" labels, 3-1/16"

EX $3   **NM** $7   **MIP** $13

31-1SF, Lincoln Continental, 1970, lime-green body w/thin wheels, opening trunk, clear window plastic, white plastic interior, 3"

EX $12   **NM** $20   **MIP** $50

31-2SF, Volksdragon, 1972, red Volkswagen Beetle body w/clear window plastic, white or yellow plastic interior, silver plastic engine, "eyes" label, unpainted base, 2-5/8"

EX $6   **NM** $10   **MIP** $16

(KP Photo, John Brown Sr. collection)

31-3SF, Caravan, 1978, white body w/amber or blue window plastic, some w/orange stripe w/white reversed bird graphic label, unpainted base, light-yellow plastic interior, 2-3/4"

EX $1   **NM** $5   **MIP** $10

(KP Photo)

32-1SF, Leyland Petrol Tanker, 1970, green cab and chassis, white tank, "BP" labels, thin wheels, blue or

amber window plastic, no interior, chrome plastic base, 3"

EX $8   **NM** $14   **MIP** $30

(KP Photo, Tom Michael collection)

32-2SF, Maserati Bora, 1973, magenta body w/yellow plastic interior, clear window plastic, opening doors, "8" stripe label on hood, lime green, dark green or unpainted base, 3"

EX $3   **NM** $7   **MIP** $13

(KP Photo)

32-3SF, Field Gun, 1978, olive-green w/black plastic barrel that fired shells attached to sprue on tan plastic base with soldiers, 3", an interesting piece, in that it included a diarama with the toy, Field Gun was removable from base

EX $3   **NM** $6   **MIP** $14

(KP Photo, George Cuhaj collection)

33-1SF, Lamborghini Miura, 1970, gold body, opening doors, white plastic interior, thin wheels, unpainted base, 2-3/4"

EX $7   **NM** $12   **MIP** $30

(KP Photo)

33-2SF, Datsun 126X, 1973, yellow body w/silver plastic interior, orange base, opening rear hood, amber window plastic, 3", some

versions have black and red flame tempo detail on hood and roof

EX $1   **NM** $4   **MIP** $8

(KP Photo)

33-3SF, Police Motorcycle, 1978, white motorcycle w/blue plastic policeman rider, silver plastic engine, "Police" on saddlebags, silver or black wire spoked wheels, 2-7/8", models included w/the K-71 Porsche Polizei set had green plastic riders and detailing

EX $3   **NM** $8   **MIP** $15

34-1SF, Formula 1 Racing Car, 1970, magenta or yellow body, white plastic driver, silver plastic engine, wide wheels, "16" striped label on hood, clear windshield plastic, 2-7/8"

EX $5   **NM** $8   **MIP** $14

(KP Photo, Tom Michael collection)

34-2SF, Vantastic, 1976, earlier and harder-to-find release w/out the exposed engine, number "34" appears on hood

(KP Photo, Tom Michael collection)

34-2SF, Vantastic, 1976, modified orange Ford Mustang body, white plastic interior, blue window plastic, early models w/large silver plastic engine, later models w/closed hood, white base, 2-7/8"

EX $2   **NM** $6   **MIP** $12

(KP Photo)

34-3SF, Chevy Pro Stocker, 1981, white body w/blue "34" lightning design

EX $3   **NM** $6   **MIP** $12

(KP Photo, George Cuhaj collection)

35-1SF, Merryweather Marquis Fire Engine, 1970, red body, blue window plastic, gray plastic reels and instrument panel, white plastic ladder, blue dome lights, "London Fire Service" labels, narrow or wide tires, 3", this model was also included w/TP-2 Two-Pack (900 Range), a modified casting was later used for 63-5SF Snorkel Fire Engine

EX $8   **NM** $15   **MIP** $30

(KP Photo, Tom Michael collection)

35-2SF, Fandango, 1975, white body w/red plastic interior, "35" label w/stripe on hood, rotating (Rola-Matic) fan behind driver, clear window plastic, 3", also red body w/red or white plastic interiors, a later release, versions w/white body and red interior and a number "6" label are harder to find, and about $40 MIP

EX $3   **NM** $6   **MIP** $10

(KP Photo, Tom Michael collection)

36-1SF, Opel Diplomat, 1970, metallic green-gold color, opening hood, thin wheels, 2-3/4"

EX $6   **NM** $16   **MIP** $30

(KP Photo, Tom Michael collection)

36-2SF, Hot Rod Draguar, 1971, metallic red or purple body w/white or light yellow plastic interior, clear bubble window plastic, large silver engine, wide wheels, 2-7/8"

EX $5   **NM** $11   **MIP** $20

(KP Photo, Tom Michael collection)

36-3SF, Formula 5000, 1977, orange w/blue label number "3" and blue plastic driver, or red w/"Texaco" and "Champion" labels and yellow plastic driver, 2-7/8"

EX $1   **NM** $4   **MIP** $10

37-1SF, Cattle Truck, 1970, yellow Dodge cab and chassis, green plastic windows, no interior, gray-brown plastic stake-side bed w/two white plastic cows, 2-1/2"

EX $6   **NM** $13   **MIP** $25

(KP Photo, Tom Michael collection)

37-2SF, Scoopa Coopa, 1973, blue or pink body w/yellow plastic interior, amber plastic windshield, unpainted base, 2-7/8", pink models have a daisy-shaped sticker on the roof section, and were shown first in the 1976 catalog

EX $5   **NM** $11   **MIP** $20

(KP Photo)

37-3SF, Skip Truck, 1977, red cab and chassis, clear or amber plastic windows, yellow bucket, white plastic interior, 2-3/4"

EX $2   **NM** $6   **MIP** $12

38-1SF, Honda Motorcycle w/Trailer, 1970, yellow motorcycle trailer w/thin wheels and "Honda" labels, green or pink motorcycle, silver spokes, 3"

EX $7   **NM** $11   **MIP** $25

(KP Photo)

38-2SF, Stingeroo, 1973, purple chopper-style bike w/cream-colored plastic horse head on seat, two wide wheels in rear, one solid wheel in front, purple plastic forks, silver plastic engine, 3-1/8"

EX $6   **NM** $10   **MIP** $22

(KP Photo)

38-3SF, Armored Jeep, 1977, dark olive-drab w/white star emblem on hood, black base and grille, black plastic gun on back (swivels), all-black wide wheels

EX $4   **NM** $7   **MIP** $12

(KP Photo)

38-4SF, Camper, 1980, red Ford body w/tan camper top

EX $3   **NM** $7   **MIP** $15

(KP Photo)

39-1SF, Ford Tractor, 1970, blue body w/yellow hood and wheels or all-blue body (included w/K-20 Tractor Transporter), 2-1/8", this was another regular-wheels holdover into the Superfast era

EX $7   **NM** $16   **MIP** $25

(KP Photo)

39-2SF, Clipper, 1973, metallic magenta body w/light metallic green base, yellow plastic interior, flip-up cockpit, and "clicking" exhaust pipes that moved up and down as the car rolled along, one of the first in the Rola-Matics series, 3"

EX $3   **NM** $7   **MIP** $12

(KP Photo)

39-4SF, Rolls-Royce Mark II, 1979, silver body w/red plastic interior or metallic red body w/yellow plastic interior, clear window plastic, opening doors, unpainted base, silver grille and headlights, introduced in the 1979/80 catalog,

but had not replaced Clipper in the 1-75 lineup

EX $2   **NM** $5   **MIP** $12

(KP Photo)

40-1SF, Hay Trailer, 1970, blue w/yellow wheels and stakeside attachments, 3-3/8", another holdover from the regular wheels series, this model was replaced in 1972

EX $3   **NM** $8   **MIP** $12

(KP Photo, Tom Michael collection)

40-2SF, Guildsman, 1972, pink w/white plastic interior and light green window plastic, star and flames label on hood; or, red body w/white plastic interior w/amber window plastic and "40" label on hood (first appears in 1976 catalog), 3"

EX $4   **NM** $8   **MIP** $16

(KP Photo, John Brown Sr. collection)

40-3SF, Horse Box, 1978, orange cab and chassis, no interior, green window plastic, cream-colored plastic box w/light brown door, two white plastic horses, 2-7/8", this model was reissued in the 1990s w/green and blue color variations

EX $2   **NM** $6   **MIP** $12

(KP Photo)

41-1SF, Ford GT, 1970, white or red w/red plastic interior, blue stripe and number "6" label on hood, thin or wide wheels

EX $8   **NM** $15   **MIP** $30

(KP Photo, Tom Michael collection)

41-2SF, Siva Spyder, 1973, red body w/cream-colored plastic interior, black segment wraps behind cabin, wide wheels, clear window plastic, 3", blue versions w/stars and stripes label motif available in 1976 catalog

EX $3   **NM** $7   **MIP** $15

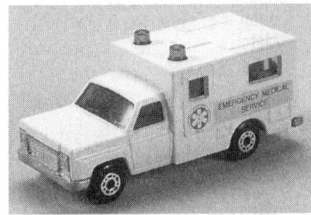

(KP Photo, John Brown Sr. collection)

41-3SF, Ambulance, 1979, white body, blue window plastic and dome lights, opening rear doors, unpainted base, white plastic interior, "Emergency Medical Service" or "Ambulance" w/red cross labels, 2-1/2"

EX $3   **NM** $6   **MIP** $12

42-1SF, Iron Fairy Crane, 1971, red w/open cab (no window plastic) yellow plastic interior, yellow crane section w/yellow plastic hook, wide wheels, 3", continued as a regular wheels model, but only for the 1970 catalog, then converted to Superfast

EX $15   **NM** $25   **MIP** $45

(KP Photo, Tom Michael collection)

42-2SF, Tyre Fryer, 1973, light or dark-blue body, open cockpit, yellow plastic seat, large silver plastic engine behind driver, large Superfast wheels in rear, wide wheels in front, 3"

EX $2　　**NM** $6　　**MIP** $15

(KP Photo, John Brown Sr. collection)

42-3SF, Mercedes Container Truck, 1978, red cab and chassis, blue window plastic, no interior, unpainted or black base, plastic container w/"SeaLand," "NYK" or "Matchbox" labels, 3"

EX $3　　**NM** $6　　**MIP** $12

(KP Photo)

42-4SF, '57 T-Bird, 1981, red body, white interior, clear windshield, silver metal base

EX $3　　**NM** $6　　**MIP** $12

(KP Photo)

42-4SF, '57 T-Bird, 1982, later version w/black body, red interior, yellow windshield, plain base

EX $1　　**NM** $3　　**MIP** $7

(KP Photo)

43-1SF, Pony Trailer, 1970, yellow body w/green base, clear window plastic, two white plastic horses, narrow wheels, brown plastic door, 2-5/8", orange version w/horse label included w/TP-3 Two-Pack

EX $5　　**NM** $10　　**MIP** $25

(KP Photo, Tom Michael collection)

43-2SF, Dragon Wheels, 1973, green Volkswagen Beetle funny-car body hinged to silver plastic and metal base, "Dragon Wheels" labels on sides, 2-7/8"

EX $4　　**NM** $12　　**MIP** $20

(KP Photo, John Brown Sr. collection)

43-3SF, Steam Loco, 1979, red and black body, red base, "4345" labels on sides, 2-11/16"

EX $1　　**NM** $3　　**MIP** $6

(KP Photo, Tom Michael collection)

44-1SF, Refrigerator Truck, 1970, yellow GMC cab and chassis w/red refrigeration box, green window plastic, 3", the first release in 1970 was painted like the regular wheels version w/red cab and chassis and green refrigeration box, these are hard to find and command approximately $145 MIP values

EX $7　　**NM** $20　　**MIP** $45

(KP Photo)

44-2SF, Boss Mustang, 1973, yellow body w/opening black hood, silver plastic interior, amber plastic window, unpainted base, 3"

EX $5　　**NM** $10　　**MIP** $15

(KP Photo, John Brown Sr. collection)

44-3SF, Passenger Coach, 1979, red body, cream-colored plastic top, green window plastic, black base, "431 & 432" or "GWR" labels, 2-7/8"

EX $3　　**NM** $6　　**MIP** $12

(KP Photo, Tom Michael collection)

45-1SF, Ford Group Six, 1970, metallic green body w/white plastic interior, silver plastic engine, clear window plastic and number "7" label; or red body w/amber-colored windows and number "45" labels, 3"

EX $4　　**NM** $10　　**MIP** $22

(KP Photo)

45-2SF, B.M.W. 3.0 CSL, 1975, orange body w/opening doors, yellow plastic interior, amber or blue plastic windows, silver base, "BMW" label on hood, 2-7/8"

EX $3　　**NM** $7　　**MIP** $15

(KP Photo)

46-1SF, Mercedes 300SE, 1970, gold or blue body, white plastic interior, opening trunk, (some early models w/opening doors, too) thin wheels, unpainted base, grille and headlights, 2-7/8", blue models are hard to find and may command MIP values of $100 or more, olive-drab staff car versions as part of TP-14 Two-Pack set, about $20 in NM condition

EX $6   **NM** $20   **MIP** $40

(KP Photo, Tom Michael collection)

46-2SF, Stretcha Fetcha, 1973, white w/blue windows, white plastic interior, red base, "Ambulance" red cross labels, wide wheels, opening rear hatch, 2-3/4"

EX $3   **NM** $7   **MIP** $15

(KP Photo)

46-3SF, Ford Tractor & Harrow, 1979, blue Ford tractor w/cab, no window plastic, gray engine block and base, black wheels w/or w/out orange-yellow painted hubs, yellow plastic disk or harrow included (not shown), also included w/hay trailer in TP-11 Two-Pack

EX $1   **NM** $6   **MIP** $14

(KP Photo)

46-4SF, Hot Chocolate, 1982, metallic brown and black funny car body w/white stripe, this car was an update on the "Dragon Wheels" funny car

EX $3   **NM** $6   **MIP** $12

47-1SF, DAF Tipper Container Truck, 1970, silver-green cab and chassis, plastic tipping box w/removable top, red plastic grille and partial base, green plastic windows, no interior, 3", a Superfast update of the regular wheels model

EX $6   **NM** $14   **MIP** $30

(KP Photo, Tom Michael collection)

47-2SF, Beach Hopper, 1973, blue w/pink "spatter" paint, brown plastic interior, tan plastic driver that "hops" as car moves along (a Rola-Matic model), wide wheels, sun label on hood, 2-5/8"

EX $2   **NM** $7   **MIP** $14

(KP Photo)

47-3SF, Pannier Locomotive, 1979, green body, "GWR" labels, metallic brown base

EX $2   **NM** $5   **MIP** $8

(KP Photo)

47-4SF, Jaguar SS, 1982, red body, silver grille, headlights and windshield, light-brown plastic interior, wide wheels

EX $2   **NM** $6   **MIP** $12

48-1SF, Dumper Truck, 1970, blue Dodge cab and chassis, yellow dumper bed, green plastic windows, no interior, silver plastic grille, bumper and partial base, 3", a Superfast version of the 48-3RW regular wheels model

EX $10   **NM** $18   **MIP** $32

(KP Photo, John Brown Sr. collection)

48-2SF, Pi-Eyed Piper, 1973, blue body, oversized plastic engine on hood, number "8" label on roof, silver exhaust pipes along sides, no interior, blue plastic windows, 2-1/2"

EX $5   **NM** $8   **MIP** $20

(KP Photo)

48-3SF, Sambron Jack Lift, 1978, yellow body w/yellow plastic lifting forks, no window plastic, 3-1/16"

EX $2   **NM** $4   **MIP** $10

(KP Photo, Tom Michael collection)

49-1SF, Unimog, 1970, blue or metallic blue-green w/red base, green plastic windows, wide wheels, 2-1/2", another update of a regular wheels model, in the 1-75 lineup until 1973, an olive-drab version w/a plastic container for artillery shells in the bed was part of the TP-13 Two-Pack in 1979

EX $10   **NM** $15   **MIP** $30

(KP Photo)

49-2SF, Chop Suey, 1973, magenta body w/red handlebars

49-3SF, Crane Truck, 1977, yellow body w/swiveling crane section, extendable crane arm, red plastic hook, six wide wheels, 3"

EX $3   **NM** $6   **MIP** $12

50-1SF, Kennel Truck, 1970, dark-green Ford truck body, w/four white plastic dogs and clear plastic canopy over bed, green plastic window, no interior, thin wheels, 2-3/4"

EX $12   **NM** $25   **MIP** $40

(KP Photo, Tom Michael collection)

50-2SF, Articulated Truck, 1973, short yellow cab w/green plastic windows and blue trailer w/yellow plastic chassis, wide wheels, 3", some have arrow labels, some do not, notice the difference in the wheels on the trailer

EX $3   **NM** $6   **MIP** $12

(KP Photo, George Cuhaj collection)

51-1SF, 8-Wheel Tipper, 1971, yellow AEC cab and chassis, silver tipper bed, green plastic windows, no interior, "Pointer" labels, silver grille and headlights and partial base, 3"

EX $8   **NM** $18   **MIP** $40

(KP Photo)

51-2SF, Citroen SM, 1973, dark red metallic body, opening doors, unpainted base, white plastic interior and tow hook, clear plastic windows, 2-7/8", in 1976, the paint scheme changed to blue w/a red stripe and number "8" on roof

EX $4   **NM** $7   **MIP** $12

(KP Photo)

51-3SF, Combine Harvester, 1979, red w/yellow reel and auger, black Superfast wheels, Superfast wheels w/yellow hubs or regular wheels, 2-7/8"

EX $1   **NM** $3   **MIP** $7

(KP Photo)

52-1SF, Dodge Charger Mk III, 1970, metallic red or metallic lime-green body w/black plastic interior, lift-up canopy, wide wheels, 3"

EX $4   **NM** $7   **MIP** $18

(KP Photo)

52-2SF, Police Launch, 1977, white body w/blue plastic base and two blue plastic officers, labels on sides read "Police," silver metal horns on cabin roof, dark-blue plastic windows, thin wheels, 3-1/16"

EX $1   **NM** $4   **MIP** $10

(KP Photo, Tom Michael collection)

53-1SF, Ford Zodiac Mk IV, 1970, metallic green body, opening hood, silver engine w/spare tire, white plastic interior, clear plastic windows, 2-3/4"

EX $7   **NM** $14   **MIP** $30

(KP Photo, Tom Michael collection)

53-2SF, Tanzara, 1973, orange body, amber or green plastic windows, opening rear hood shows silver plastic engine, wide wheels, silver plastic interior, unpainted base, 3", models in 1976 had a bicentennial color scheme; white w/red and blue stripes and number "53" on hood

EX $2   **NM** $6   **MIP** $12

(KP Photo)

53-3SF, Wild Life Truck, 1973, yellow body, red plastic windows, "Ranger" label on hood w/elephant illustration, silver plastic grille, wide wheels, red plastic lion circles in truck bed as it is pushed along (Rola-Matic), no interior, clear plastic canopy over truck bed

EX $4   **NM** $10   **MIP** $25

(KP Photo)

53-3SF, CJ6 Jeep, 1978, red or green body, tan plastic roof, yellow plastic interior, unpainted metal base

EX $3   **NM** $6   **MIP** $12

(KP Photo by Dr. Douglas Sadecky)

54-1SF, Cadillac Ambulance, 1970, white body, blue plastic windows, white plastic interior, red cross labels, white or silver-painted grille, narrow wheels, 2-7/8"

EX $25   **NM** $40   **MIP** $75

(KP Photo, Tom Michael collection)

54-2SF, Ford Capri, 1971, red w/black hood or all pink w/white plastic interior, unpainted base, opening hood, wide wheels, 2-7/8", all-red models were included w/boat and trailer in TP-5 Two-Pack starting in 1977

EX $2   **NM** $5   **MIP** $11

(KP Photo)

54-3SF, Personnel Carrier, 1978, olive-green w/tan plastic troops and gun, black base, wide wheels, 3"

EX $3   **NM** $7   **MIP** $12

(KP Photo, Tom Michael collection)

55-1SF, Police Car, 1970, white Mercury sedan, clear windows, white plastic interior w/molded figures, police label on hood, shield labels on doors, blue or red dome light, thin wheels, 3-1/16"

EX $8   **NM** $20   **MIP** $40

(KP Photo, Tom Michael collection)

55-2SF, Mercury Police Car, 1971, white station wagon body w/blue or red dome lights, thin or wide wheels, unpainted base and grille, clear plastic windows, 3-1/16", early versions had shield labels on doors and "Police" label on hood, versions from 1973 to 1975 had only arrow-shaped red "Police" label, this car was a minor casting variation of the Mercury Commuter 73-1SF

EX $7   **NM** $15   **MIP** $27

(KP Photo, Tom Michael collection)

55-3SF, Hellraiser, 1976, white body w/red plastic interior, silver plastic rear engine, clear windshield, wide wheels, stars and stripes label on hood, or, blue body and white plastic interior, stars and stripes label, 3"

EX $2   **NM** $5   **MIP** $12

(KP Photo, Tom Michael collection)

55-4SF, Ford Cortina 1600 GL, 1979, metallic gold w/clear plastic

windows, opening doors, unpainted base, red plastic interior, introduced in 1979/80 catalog, but not yet part of the 1-75 lineup

EX $2   **NM** $6   **MIP** $10

(KP Photo, George Cuhaj collection)

56-1SF, BMC 1800 Pininfarina, 1970, metallic gold or orange body, thin or wide wheels, opening doors, clear plastic windows, unpainted base, white plastic interior, 2-3/4", later models modified the casting of the rear wheel wells to accommodate the wider Superfast wheels that became standard by 1973, this was a new model in the 1-75 lineup, not an adapted regular wheels casting like many others in 1970, orange body versions about $16 MIP

EX $4   **NM** $10   **MIP** $20

(KP Photo)

56-2SF, Hi-Tailer, 1975, white body w/yellow or blue plastic driver, silver plastic rear engine, red, white and blue striped label w/"5, Team Matchbox and MB," 3"

EX $2   **NM** $6   **MIP** $13

56-3SF, Mercedes 450 SEL, 1979, blue body, opening doors, light-yellow plastic interior, clear plastic windows, unpainted base

EX $1   **NM** $3   **MIP** $8

(KP Photo)

57-1SF, Land Rover Fire Truck, 1970, red body w/"Kent Fire Brigade" decals

EX $25   **NM** $60   **MIP** $110

(KP Photo)

57-2SF, Eccles Caravan, 1970, cream or light-yellow trailer body w/four thin wheels, stripe and flower label on sides, red or orange plastic roof, green or light-yellow plastic interior, 3-1/16", like many models, the Eccles Caravan continued on in a Two-Pack set, the TP-4 Holiday Set

EX $4   **NM** $10   **MIP** $20

(KP Photo)

58-1SF, DAF Girder Truck, 1970, off-white or lime-green cab and chassis, red plastic girders, red plastic grille and partial base, green window plastic, no interior, 3", off-white versions aren't real common and have approximately $65 MIP value

EX $6   **NM** $15   **MIP** $40

(KP Photo, Tom Michael collection)

58-2SF, Woosh-N-Push, 1973, yellow body w/open cockpit, red plastic interior, silver plastic exhaust, number "2" label on back of roof; or metallic red body, cream plastic interior, number "8" label w/stars and stripes on roof (1976 version), 3"

EX $2   **NM** $6   **MIP** $12

(KP Photo)

58-3SF, Faun Dumper, 1977, yellow body and dumper bed, black base, red plastic windows, 2-3/4"

EX $1   **NM** $6   **MIP** $10

(KP Photo, Tom Michael collection)

59-1SF, Ford Galaxie Fire Chief Car, 1970, red body, white plastic interior and tow hook, clear plastic windows, thin wheels, shield labels on doors, blue dome light, 2-7/8", oddly, this model dropped from the lineup for one year and returned, briefly, for 1972

EX $12   **NM** $22   **MIP** $50

59-2SF, Mercury Fire Chief Car, 1971, red sedan body w/white plastic interior (early versions w/two figures), unpainted base, blue dome light, thin or wide wheels, shield and fire chief labels or fire helmet labels, also included in TP-10 Two-Pack w/a dual dome light arrangement

EX $4   **NM** $10   **MIP** $20

(KP Photo, Tom Michael collection)

59-3SF, Planet Scout, 1976, metallic green w/lime-green or red w/yellow body, silver plastic interior, yellow plastic windows, wide wheels, 2-3/4"

EX $2   **NM** $4   **MIP** $8

(KP Photo)

60-1SF, Truck w/Site Office, 1970, blue Leyland truck w/Ergomatic cab, yellow plastic hut w/green plastic roof, thin wheels, green plastic windows, silver plastic grille and partial base, 2-1/2"

EX $6   **NM** $12   **MIP** $28

60-2SF, Lotus Super Seven, 1972, orange or yellow body w/unpainted base, black plastic interior, clear plastic windshield, ghost and flame label on hood, or checker pattern w/"60" along length of car, 2-7/8"

EX $5   **NM** $9   **MIP** $16

60-3SF, Holden Pick-Up, 1978, red w/yellow plastic motorcycles in bed and yellow plastic interior, unpainted base, checkered label w/"500" on hood, 3-1/16"

EX $4   **NM** $7   **MIP** $14

(KP Photo)

60-4SF, Piston Popper, 1982, yellow body w/"Piston Popper" on hood and number "60" on sides, unpainted metal base, red Rola-Matic pistons like the earlier version

EX $2   **NM** $5   **MIP** $10

(KP Photo, George Cuhaj collection)

61-1SF, Alvis Stalwart, 1970, white body, w/yellow plastic canopy (not shown) green plastic wheels w/removable black tires, "BP Exploration" labels on sides, 2-5/8", olive-green versions were included w/TP-16 Two-Pack in 1979

EX $9   **NM** $17   **MIP** $30

(KP Photo)

61-2SF, Blue Shark, 1972, blue body w/unpainted base, white plastic driver, silver plastic rear engine, black plastic exhaust pipes, clear plastic windshield, "86" or Scorpion label (harder to find, about $50 MIP), 3"

EX $3   **NM** $9   **MIP** $17

(KP Photo)

61-3SF, Wreck Truck, 1979, red truck body, black base, red plastic windows and dome lights, no interior, white towing arms w/red plastic hooks

EX $3   **NM** $6   **MIP** $12

(KP Photo)

62-1SF, Mercury Cougar, 1970, lime-green body w/red plastic interior and tow hook, opening doors, 3"

EX $9   **NM** $16   **MIP** $45

62-2SF, Rat Rod Dragster, 1971, light-green body, clear plastic windows, red plastic interior, exposed engine through hood, "Rat Rod" labels on sides, 3", a reworking of the Mercury Cougar casting

EX $5   **NM** $8   **MIP** $18

(KP Photo, Tom Michael collection)

62-2SF, Renault 17TL, 1974, red body w/opening doors, white plastic interior, blue plastic windows, some w/stripe and number "6" label, some w/out, 3", a version w/"Fire" labels was included in the G-12 Rescue Gift Set in the 1977 catalog

EX $2   **NM** $5   **MIP** $12

(KP Photo, Tom Michael collection)

62-3SF, Chevy Corvette, 1982, black body w/yellow and orange stripes running from hood to trunk, white plastic interior, plain base w/side-pipes

EX $2   **NM** $5   **MIP** $8

(KP Photo)

62-1SF, Dodge Crane Truck, 1970, yellow body w/rotating crane section, yellow plastic hook, black base, green plastic windows, no interior, 3"

EX $6   **NM** $11   **MIP** $25

(KP Photo)

63-2SF, Freeway Gas Tanker, 1974, short red cab w/black base and wide wheels, white plastic tanker trailer w/red chassis, "Burmah" labels on tanker section, 3-1/8", also available in yellow and white Shell versions, blue and white Aral versions and red and white Chevron version (part of TP-17 Two-Pack), as with regular wheels editions, the German-issue Aral version is harder to find, about $25 MIP, there is also an olive-green version w/TP-14 w/"High Octane" labels on the sides

EX $2   **NM** $6   **MIP** $12

(KP Photo, Tom Michael collection)

63-2SF, Freeway Gas Tanker, 1974, a view showing the more popular edition w/the "Burmah" labels and red cab

64-1SF, MG 1100, 1970, blue body, white plastic interior w/dog and driver, tow hook, thin wheels, silver base, 2-5/8"

EX $9   **NM** $22   **MIP** $40

(KP Photo, Tom Michael collection)

64-2SF, Slingshot Dragster, 1972, pink or blue body w/dual silver plastic engines and red exhaust pipes, label on hood w/number "9" and flames, white plastic driver, 3"

EX $4   **NM** $7   **MIP** $15

(KP Photo, Tom Michael collection)

64-3SF, Fire Chief Car, 1976, red body w/blue plastic windows, silver air scoops on hood, silver base, "Fire Chief" labels w/shield on sides, 3"

EX $3   **NM** $5   **MIP** $12

(KP Photo)

64-4SF, Caterpillar Bulldozer, 1981, yellow die-cast body w/yellow plastic blade and unpainted base and engine, cab can be tan or black, and later models have "CAT" and "C" logos on sides near cab

EX $2   **NM** $6   **MIP** $12

(KP Photo, John Brown Sr. collection)

64-4SF, Caterpillar Bulldozer, the black cab and "CAT" logos appeared on later versions of the bulldozer

(KP Photo)

65-1SF, Combine Harvester, red w/yellow plastic reel and front wheels w/removable black plastic tires, 3", this model was another holdover from the regular wheels lineup, first introduced in 1967, but remaining until 1973

EX $3   **NM** $7   **MIP** $12

(KP Photo)

65-2SF, Saab Sonnet, 1974, blue body w/plastic lift-up rear hatch, light-yellow plastic interior, wide wheels, unpainted base, 2-7/8"

EX $4   **NM** $7   **MIP** $15

(KP Photo, Tom Michael collection)

65-3SF, Airport Coach, 1978, version w/red body, white top and "Qantas" labels

(KP Photo, Tom Michael collection)

65-3SF, Airport Coach, 1978, version w/red body, white top and "TWA" labels

(KP Photo, Tom Michael collection)

65-3SF, Airport Coach, 1978, metallic blue body, white roof, yellow plastic windows, off-white interior, "British Airways," "American Airlines" or "Lufthansa" labels on sides are most common, 3-1/16", German versions w/"Schulbus" labels are harder to find, about $45 MIP, other variations include: red body, white top w/"TWA" or "Qantas" labels

EX $4   **NM** $6   **MIP** $13

(KP Photo by Dr. Douglas Sadecky)

66-1SF, Greyhound Bus, 1971, silver w/yellow plastic windows, thin wheels, blue and white Greyhound labels on sides, 3", shown here in an interesting blister-pack/box combo that Matchbox tried out in the late 1960s and early 1970s, MIP value approximately $60 for this combo, regular MIP values shown

EX $15   **NM** $30   **MIP** $60

(KP Photo, Tom Michael collection)

66-2SF, Mazda RX 500, 1972, early releases were orange w/white base, opening rear engine hood, silver plastic interior w/purple windows, 2-7/8", later versions were red w/white base and racing tempo "77" on hood w/yellow windows

EX $3   **NM** $5   **MIP** $12

(KP Photo)

66-3SF, Ford Transit, 1978, orange truck w/dropside bed and plastic cargo crates, unpainted base, blue/green plastic windows, light-yellow plastic interior, 2-3/4"

EX $4   **NM** $7   **MIP** $12

(KP Photo)

67-1SF, Volkswagen 1600 TL, 1970, orange or purple body, opening doors, white plastic interior, clear windows, unpainted base, thin or wide wheels (wide wheels version included in G-2 Transporter Gift Set), 2-11/16"

EX $15   **NM** $30   **MIP** $50

(KP Photo, Tom Michael collection)

67-2SF, Hot Rocker, 1973, Ford Capri body w/open hood and oversized "hopping" engine (part of Rola-Matics series), wide wheels, unpainted base, available in lime-green and red paint variations, 3"

EX $3   **NM** $5   **MIP** $12

(KP Photo, Tom Michael collection)

67-3SF, Datsun 260Z, 1979, pinkish-red or silver body w/yellow plastic or red interior, opening doors, black base, 3", silver model has red and black stripes on sides and hood w/"Datsun 2+2" in black type

EX $3   **NM** $6   **MIP** $10

(KP Photo, Tom Michael collection)

68-1SF, Porsche 910, 1970, red body w/thin or wide wheels, cream or light-yellow plastic interior, clear windows, number "68" label on hood, 3"

EX $8   **NM** $12   **MIP** $20

(KP Photo)

68-2SF, Cosmobile, 1976, blue or red body, silver plastic trim and interior, yellow base, wide wheels, 2-7/8"

EX $2   **NM** $5   **MIP** $8

(KP Photo)

68-3SF, Chevy Van, 1979, orange w/blue and red stripes along sides, blue plastic windows, silver base

EX $1   **NM** $4   **MIP** $7

(KP Photo, George Cuhaj collection)

69-1SF, Rolls-Royce Coupe, 1970, blue or gold body, clear windshield, brown plastic interior, thin wheels, opening trunk, tow hook, 3-1/16"

EX $6   **NM** $13   **MIP** $35

(KP Photo, Tom Michael collection)

69-2SF, Turbo Fury, 1973, red body, clear windshield, number "69" label on hood, white plastic driver, fans on rear of car rotate when pushed (Rola-Matics series), and front of vehicle same style as Blue Shark, 3"

EX $4   **NM** $9   **MIP** $16

(KP Photo, Tom Michael collection)

69-3SF, Security Truck, 1979, red armored truck w/white "Wells Fargo" type on sides, blue windows and dome light, unpainted base, wide wheels, white roof, 2-7/8"

EX $5   **NM** $9   **MIP** $14

70-1SF, Grit Spreader, 1971, red Ford cab and chassis, yellow hopper section, no interior, thin wheels, green windows, 2-5/8"

EX $5   **NM** $12   **MIP** $25

(KP Photo)

70-2SF, Dodge Dragster, 1972, pink funny-car Dodge Charger body, silver engine, black or unpainted base, red plastic struts to hold body, snake labels along sides, 3"

EX $10   **NM** $20   **MIP** $40

70-3SF, Self-Propelled Gun, 1977, green w/black plastic gun that fires and recoils while rolled along (Rola-Matics series), tan treads, black roller wheels, 2-5/8"

EX $2   **NM** $4   **MIP** $8

(KP Photo, Tom Michael collection)

70-4SF, Ferrari 308 GTB, 1981, red, may or may not have "Ferrari" on sides and emblem on hood, black base

EX $2   **NM** $4   **MIP** $6

71-1SF, Ford Heavy Wreck Truck, 1970, red cab and towing crane, red plastic hook, white bed w/"Esso" labels on sides, green windows and dome light, white grille, 3", olive-green versions w/all-black wheels were included in 1978's TP-16 Two-Pack

EX $11   **NM** $22   **MIP** $45

(KP Photo)

71-2SF, Jumbo Jet, 1973, motorcycle w/blue seat and handlebars, black roller-style wheels, silver plastic engine, red elephant head on handlebars, 2-3/4"

EX $6   **NM** $9   **MIP** $18

(KP Photo, Tom Michael collection)

71-3SF, Cattle Truck, 1978, red or metallic gold w/plastic yellow or cream stake bed, black plastic cattle, blue or green windows, 2-7/8", also included in the 1979 TP-19 Two-Pack in red w/a matching trailer and plastic cattle

EX $2   **NM** $5   **MIP** $8

72-1SF, Standard Jeep, 1970, yellow body w/red plastic seats, black bumpers, spare tire on back, 2-3/8", an update of the 72-2RW Standard

Jeep, but in this case the spare couldn't actually be used

EX $10 **NM** $20 **MIP** $30

(KP Photo)

72-2SF, SRN Hovercraft, 1972, white top w/black plastic base and "SRN6" w/British flag labels on sides, red plastic propeller, thin wheels in underside of hull, blue plastic windows, 3-1/16"

EX $2 **NM** $4 **MIP** $8

(KP Photo)

72-3SF, Bomag Road Roller, 1979, yellow body w/red plastic interior and engine, black plastic roller, silver or yellow hubs, introduced in 1979/80 catalog, but hadn't yet replaced the SRN Hovercraft in the 1-75 lineup

EX $1 **NM** $4 **MIP** $10

(KP Photo)

72-4SF, Maxi Taxi, 1982, yellow Ford Capri body w/Rola-Matic engine that hops when car is moved, an update of the Hot Rocker model, checkered taxi tampos and rates on sides, "Maxi Taxi" on roof, black base

EX $1 **NM** $4 **MIP** $8

(KP Photo, Tom Michael collection)

73-1SF, Mercury Commuter, 1973, view of red model, w/roof rack grooves, red paint scheme, wide wheels and label on hood

(KP Photo)

73-1SF, Mercury Commuter, 1970, metallic lime-green body w/thin wheels, clear windows, white plastic interior w/dogs looking out the back, unpainted base, 3-1/16", by 1972, this car had changed to red w/a bull's head label on the hood and luggage rack grooves on the roof, w/approximately $16 MIP value, prices for green model shown

EX $6 **NM** $14 **MIP** $25

(KP Photo)

73-1SF, Mercury Commuter, view showing back of car, w/dogs still making an appearance out the back window

(KP Photo)

73-2SF, Weasel, 1973, medium metallic green armored vehicle w/black turret that turns as the car is rolled (Rola-Matics series), wide wheels, all-black or w/silver hubs, 2-7/8", olive-green versions were issued as part of TP-13 Two-Pack

EX $2 **NM** $5 **MIP** $10

74-1SF, Daimler Bus, 1970, red or pink body, white plastic interior, thin or wide wheels, "Esso Extra Petrol" and Esso logo labels on sides, 3"

EX $10 **NM** $15 **MIP** $30

(KP Photo, Tom Michael collection)

74-2SF, Toe Joe, 1974, metallic lime-green body w/green plastic towing arms and red plastic hooks, yellow windows, unpainted base, 3", versions w/yellow bodies and red towing arms w/black plastic hooks were included w/the Racing Mini in TP-6 Two-Pack

EX $3 **NM** $6 **MIP** $17

(KP Photo, Tom Michael collection)

74-3SF, Mercury Cougar Villager, 1979, lime-green or blue body, pale yellow interior, unpainted base, opening tailgate, 3-1/16"

EX $2 **NM** $5 **MIP** $11

(KP Photo)

75-1SF, Ferrari Berlinetta, 1970, red w/white plastic interior, thin wheels, unpainted base, 2-7/8", some early models were produced in green, echoing the regular wheels editions, but they are rare and can have $350 MIP values

EX $20 **NM** $40 **MIP** $75

Midgetoy

JUMBO SERIES, 6" VEHICLES

American LaFrance Pumper Truck, Midgetoy, red w/silver detailing and decals; 1970s-80s
EX $7	**NM** $12	**MIP** $25

Mobile Artillery, Midgetoy, Army green, w/silver detailing, 1970s-80s
EX $6	**NM** $12	**MIP** $20

Oil Tanker, Midgetoy, white-green, "Midgetoy Oil Co.," painted details; 1970s-80s
EX $10	**NM** $15	**MIP** $37

Scenicruiser Bus, Midgetoy, two-tone paint, "Midgetoy Bus Line"; 1970s-80s
EX $8	**NM** $15	**MIP** $30

JUNIOR SERIES, 2-1/2" TO 3" VEHICLES

Army Jeep, Midgetoy, Army green, black plastic tires; 1960s-70s
EX $3	**NM** $6	**MIP** $9

Bus, Midgetoy, 3" long, Greyhound type
EX $4	**NM** $9	**MIP** $12

Camper, Midgetoy, Ford pickup w/die-cast camper body; 1970s-80s
EX $15	**NM** $22	**MIP** n/a

Corvette Stingray, Midgetoy, various colors but often orange; 1971-80s
EX $1	**NM** $2	**MIP** $4

Ford Mustang, Midgetoy, 1970s-80s
EX $1	**NM** $2	**MIP** $4

Ford Pickup, Midgetoy, 1971 Ford model, white or other color; 1970s-80s
EX $2	**NM** $3	**MIP** $5

Ford Torino, Midgetoy, various colors but often orange; 1971-80s
EX $1	**NM** $2	**MIP** $4

Ford Torino Fire Chief Car, Midgetoy, red, cast-in flasher lights; 1970s-80s
EX $4	**NM** $9	**MIP** $12

Hot Rod, Midgetoy, Ford V-8 design, open cockpit, black plastic tires, decals and/or painted headlights; 1970s-80s
EX $2	**NM** $4	**MIP** $6

Hot Rod, Midgetoy, Ford V-8 design, open cockpit, black plastic tires, single-color paint; 1960s
EX $3	**NM** $4	**MIP** $8

Indy Race Car, Midgetoy, open cockpit, Kurtis Kraft race car, black plastic tires, decals and/or painted highlights; 1970s-80s
EX $3	**NM** $6	**MIP** $12

Indy Race Car, Midgetoy, open cockpit, Kurtis Kraft design race car, black plastic tires, single-color paint; 1960s-70s
EX $6	**NM** $9	**MIP** $13

MG Sports Roadster, Midgetoy, open-top sports car, black plastic tires, single-color paint; 1960s
EX $6	**NM** $9	**MIP** $13

MG Sports Roadster, Midgetoy, open-top sports car, black plastic tires, decals and/or painted highlights; 1960s-80s
EX $3	**NM** $6	**MIP** $9

Sunbeam Racer, Midgetoy, land-speed race car, black plastic tires, decals and/or painted highlights; 1960s-80s
EX $3	**NM** $8	**MIP** $12

Volkswagen Beetle, Midgetoy, black plastic tires, no decals or masking; 1960s-80s
EX $8	**NM** $15	**MIP** $20

Volkswagen Beetle, Midgetoy, various colors, black plastic tires, decals and/or painted detailing; 1970s-80s
EX $8	**NM** $15	**MIP** $20

Wrecker Truck, Midgetoy, cabover, metal boom w/hook, black plastic tires; 1960s-70s
EX $4	**NM** $8	**MIP** $12

PEE-WEE SERIES, 2" VEHICLES

American LaFrance Fire Truck, Midgetoy, 1969-80s
EX $1	**NM** $1	**MIP** $2

Ford GT, Midgetoy, 1969-80s
EX $1	**NM** $1	**MIP** $2

Gas Pumps, Midgetoy, 1-3/4" across, plastic
EX $1	**NM** $1	**MIP** $2

Hot Rod, Midgetoy, 1969-80s
EX $1	**NM** $1	**MIP** $2

Jeep, Midgetoy, 1969-80s
EX $1	**NM** $1	**MIP** $2

MG Sports Roadster, Midgetoy, 1969-80s
EX $1	**NM** $1	**MIP** $2

Motorboat, Midgetoy, 2-1/4", plastic
EX $1	**NM** $1	**MIP** $2

Open-Cockpit Racer, Midgetoy, 1960s-70s
EX $1	**NM** $1	**MIP** $2

Utility Trailer, Midgetoy, 1-1/2"
EX $1	**NM** $2	**MIP** $3

TRACTOR-TRAILERS

Aerial Fire Truck, Midgetoy, 8" long; Chevy cab, cast-in ladder on trailer, 1960s-80s
EX $12	**NM** $24	**MIP** $35

Oil Tanker, Midgetoy, 8" long; Chevy cab, "Midgetoy Oil Co." decal on tanker trailer
EX $12	**NM** $25	**MIP** $40

Oil Tanker, Midgetoy, 8" long; Chevy cab, plain paint w/out masking or decals, 1960s-80s
EX $12	**NM** $20	**MIP** $30

Shipping Van, Midgetoy, 8" long; Chevy ab, "Midgetoy Van Lines, Inc." decal on van box
EX $12	**NM** $25	**MIP** $40

Shipping Van, Midgetoy, 8" long; Chevy cab, plain paint w/out masking or decals, 1960s-80s
EX $12	**NM** $20	**MIP** $30

Nylint

No. 1000, Deliverall, 1946-51, wind-up; three-wheeled scooter w/large cargo box; white, yellow, red, blue and black; rare
EX $100   NM $300   MIP $600

No. 1100, Big Dig, regular version
EX $50   NM $115   MIP $225

No. 1100, Elgin Street Sweeper, 1950-52, wind-up; yellow w/red and black highlights; white plastic driver; bottom and side brooms rotate
EX $50   NM $175   MIP $350

No. 1101, Big Dig, 1967-70, re-design of No. SR1100 to look like Tonka's Mighty Cranes; orange, yellow and black w/yellow plastic track wheels
EX $50   NM $100   MIP $200

No. 1200, Lawn and Garden Set, 1965, new number; same as No. 7000
EX $50   NM $125   MIP $250

No. 1200, Pumpmobile, 1950-52, wind-up; Howdy Doody cowboy-like figure (unlicensed), yellow, red and blue
EX $100   NM $300   MIP $600

No. 1210, Aerial Ladder Fire Truck, 1968-74, red w/white ladders and black handwheels; Nylint's first large fire truck
EX $75   NM $140   MIP $275

No. 1211, Aerial Ladder Fire Truck, 1975-, second version of No. 1210 (less steel)
EX $50   NM $100   MIP $200

No. 1300, Tournarocker, 1951-52, first version; open tractor w/driver; orange (1951) or mustard yellow (1952); scale model of a machine by R. G. Letourneau
EX $50   NM $150   MIP $300

No. 1300, Tournarocker, 1953-54, second version; closed cab, no driver, grille plate on front, larger 3-3/4" wheels; all yellow; also by R.G. Letourneau
EX $75   NM $125   MIP $250

No. 1300, Tournarocker, 1955-57, third version; embossed grille details, larger 3-3/4" wheels; all yellow (1955), orange and yellow (1956-57); also by R.G. Letourneau
EX $75   NM $125   MIP $250

No. 1310, Backhoe, 1968-73, yellow backhoe on rubber crawler tracks w/black base
EX $75   NM $140   MIP $275

No. 1400, Road Grader, 1951, first version; small wheels and steel grille plate; orange
EX $75   NM $125   MIP $250

No. 1400, Road Grader, 1954-58, third version; embossed grille, large 3-3/4" wheels; orange (1954-55), yellow (1956-58)
EX $50   NM $175   MIP $350

No. 1400, Road Grader, 1952-53, second version; larger 3-3/4" wheels and grille plate; orange
EX $50   NM $175   MIP $350

No. 1410, Hopper Dump, 1968-69, regular single-trailer version; yellow w/black dump doors
EX $75   NM $150   MIP $300

No. 1420, Twin Hopper Dump Truck, 1967, Sears exclusive; yellow semi tractor pulling two hopper dump trailers, black dump doors and operating levers
EX $125   NM $225   MIP $450

No. 1500, Tournahopper, 1952-53, first version; grille plate on front of closed tractor; yellow w/black decals; replica of a R.G. Letourneau machine
EX $75   NM $175   MIP $350

No. 1500, Tournahopper, 1954-56, second version; embossed front, 3-3/4" wheels; yellow (1954-55), orange (1956). After 1953, these are replicas of Letourneau-Westinghouse machines
EX $75   NM $175   MIP $350

No. 1600, Payloader, 1951, tan
EX $50   NM $175   MIP $350

No. 1600, Payloader, 1956-58, light green and yellow
EX $50   NM $175   MIP $350

No. 1600, Payloader, 1958, yellow
EX $50   NM $175   MIP $350

(Calvin Chausse)

No. 1600, Payloader, 1951-55, red and yellow
EX $50   NM $175   MIP $350

No. 1600, Payloader, 1958, dark green
EX $50   NM $175   MIP $350

No. 1610, Bronco Police Car, 1968, white Ford Bronco w/lights and black trim
EX $35   NM $75   MIP $150

No. 1700, Tournahauler, 1956, fourth version; light green
EX $50   NM $125   MIP $250

No. 1700, Tournahauler, 1954-55, third version; dark green embossed grille
EX $50   NM $125   MIP $250

No. 1700, Tournahauler, 1953, first version; yellow
EX $100   NM $200   MIP $400

No. 1700, Tournahauler, 1953-54, second version dark green w/grille plate
EX $50   NM $125   MIP $250

No. 1710, Bronco Petmobile, 1968-70s, dark blue Ford Bronco, white plastic cage for dogs
EX $40   NM $115   MIP $225

No. 1800, Traveloader, 1953-55, first version w/smaller blades on front feeder belt (1953); second version w/larger blades (1954-55); both versions orange w/black decals, black belts on front feeder, black rear conveyor belt
EX $75   NM $125   MIP $250

No. 1810, Twister Exploration Car, 1969-73, yellow and black; Nylint's version of Tonka's Crater Crawler
EX $25   NM $100   MIP $200

No. 1900, Tournaractor, 1954-55, yellow and black w/4-7/16" wheels; by J.D. Adams
EX $50   NM $175   MIP $350

No. 1910, Hot Rod, 1969-72
EX $25   NM $40   MIP $75

No. 2000, Speed Swing Loader, 1955-58, orange or yellow; by Pettibone-Mulliken Co. orange and black (1955), yellow and black (1956-58)
EX $50   NM $125   MIP $250

No. 2010, Elevating Scraper, 1969-73, two-wheel tractor w/large earthmover w/rubber belt, pan scraper trailer (looked like a Caterpillar earthmover)
EX $75   NM $200   MIP $400

No. 2050, Jumbo Street Roller, 1971-77, roller in front, wheels in back; large red roller in front and red operator's cab (1971); yellow and black (1972-77)
EX $50   NM $100   MIP $200

No. 2070, Bobcat Loader, 1970-, yellow and black trim
EX $35   NM $65   MIP $125

No. 2100, Tournadozer, 1956-59, orange w/black seat and motor; first version w/larger 4-7/16" wheels (1956)
EX $75   NM $150   MIP $300

No. 2200, Michigan Shovel (crane), 1955-65, 10 wheels, clamshell bucket, single headlights, grille plate, steering (1955-56); six wheels, single or dual headlights, embossed front grille or grille plate (1956-60); no steering, grille sticker (1961-63); magnet added to bucket but only drop-down outriggers (1964-65); only Nylint toy to have real rubber tires through its first 10 years

EX $50　**NM** $150　**MIP** $300

No. 2201, Michigan Shovel (crane), 1966-73, redesigned version (made to look like Tonka mobile crane); clamshell bucket; this toy continued w/number changes until the mid-1980s

EX $50　**NM** $150　**MIP** $300

No. 2300, Elgin Street Sweeper, 1956-57, battery-operated version, closed cab; yellow cab roof, red/yellow body (1956); red cab roof, yellow body (1957)

EX $50　**NM** $175　**MIP** $350

No. 2310, Beach Buggy, 1969-72

EX $25　**NM** $40　**MIP** $75

No. 2400, Electronic Cannon Truck, 1957-59, w/yellow radar antenna and four rockets

EX $75　**NM** $150　**MIP** $300

No. 2400, Electronic Cannon Truck, 1956, no radar antenna; four red/black-tipped rockets; Nylint's second battery-operated toy

EX $75　**NM** $150　**MIP** $300

No. 2410, Bronco Bobcat, 1969-72, dark red Bronco w/white top and larger wheels

EX $35　**NM** $85　**MIP** $175

No. 2500, Telescopic Crane, 1957-60, red w/yellow boom, four-wheel steering, extendable boom

EX $100　**NM** $150　**MIP** $300

No. 2500, Telescopic Crane, 1957-60, green w/white boom for 1959 NY Toy Fair (won award for toy of the year); rare

EX $150　**NM** $225　**MIP** $450

No. 2600, Missile Launcher, 1957-60, blue-gray, white radar antenna, white missiles w/black tips

EX $50　**NM** $125　**MIP** $250

No. 2600, Missile Launcher, 1959, orange, white radar antenna, white missiles w/black tips

EX $100　**NM** $175　**MIP** $350

No. 2700, Uranium Hauler, 1958-59, olive drab hydraulic bumper, yellow/black front guard

EX $50　**NM** $125　**MIP** $250

No. 2800, Guided Missile Carrier, 1958-59, first version (1958), non-firing missiles

EX $75　**NM** $125　**MIP** $250

No. 2800, Guided Missile Carrier, 1958-59, later version (through 1960), firing cone of missiles, side-mounted forklift w/red/yellow pallet, white missile w/red fins and red nose cone

EX $75　**NM** $125　**MIP** $250

No. 2900, Junior Jack Hammer, 1958-59, w/air compressor package that connected to toy w/4' rubber hose; Nylint's first plastic toy; red/black jackhammer, yellow/red/black compressor box

EX $50　**NM** $125　**MIP** $250

No. 3000, Grader-Loader, 1959-62, first version w/remote bucket release (1959 only); yellow, black bucket; first Nylint construction toy to have plastic tractor wheels (to keep shipping weight low)

EX $75　**NM** $150　**MIP** $300

No. 3100, Payloader Tractor-Shovel, 1959-62, first version yellow w/levers in cab (1959 only); red/yellow w/levers in cab (1959-60); w/out levers (1961-62); less than 1,300 made, replica of Hough machine; all toys had steel track base and rubber tracks

EX $75　**NM** $175　**MIP** $350

No. 3200, Power & Light Lineman Truck, 1959-61, yellow cab and flasher light, orange trailer, black rear hoist w/tools, rope, yellow spool of wire, two stained poles; orange w/yellow cab and flasher light, orange trailer, yellow wire spool

EX $75　**NM** $175　**MIP** $350

No. 3300, Power & Light Posthole Digger Truck, 1959-61, orange, yellow cab roof, orange trailer, yellow posthole assembly and tool box cover, plastic tools, four wooden phone poles

EX $75　**NM** $175　**MIP** $350

No. 3400, Highway Emergency Unit Truck, 1959-63, large cabover Ford wrecker, white w/red cab roof, red dolly and wrecker boom; later versions w/out boom hoist (only hook hoist); w/whitewall tires and tilt cab w/motor (1963 only)

EX $50　**NM** $150　**MIP** $300

No. 3500, Countdown Rocket Launcher, 1959-61, three rockets (Atlas, Jupiter, Thor) in various colors; gray gantry crane, dark blue base w/yellow, black, or red countdown dial; last Nylint toy from the 1950s and second plastic toy

EX $50　**NM** $125　**MIP** $250

No. 3600, Ford Rapid Delivery Truck, 1960-62, dark blue cabover Ford truck w/white stake racks and working lift gate, tilt cab w/motor; first Nylint toy of 1960s

EX $75　**NM** $175　**MIP** $300

No. 3700, Street Sprinkler Truck, 1960-61, white tank truck, operating nozzles on front bumper, tilt cab

EX $75　**NM** $175　**MIP** $350

No. 3800, Ford Sales & Service, 1960-61, aqua green w/utility rack and ladder

EX $50　**NM** $175　**MIP** $350

No. 3900, Ford Platform Tilt Truck, 1960, metallic blue, white cab roof w/tilt cab, narrow side panels on rear bed

EX $75　**NM** $175　**MIP** $350

No. 3900, Platform Dump Truck, 1961, yellow, white cab roof, narrow side panels on rear bed; last truck to feature tilt cab

EX $75　**NM** $175　**MIP** $350

No. 4000, Ford Speedway Truck w/Racer, 1960-63, dark tan pickup w/white top and trailer and race car

EX $75　**NM** $140　**MIP** $275

No. 4100, Ford Pickup & U-Haul Box Trailer, 1961-66, orange pickup, white cab roof, orange trailer w/white/cream top and opening rear door; trucks made before 1965 have two-piece front grille (trucks from 1965-66 w/one-piece front grille/bumper and I-beam suspension)

EX $75　**NM** $175　**MIP** $350

No. 4200, Bulldozer, 1961-70, all yellow w/rear chain winch (1961-65); yellow w/orange winch (1967-70); black plastic motor

EX $50　**NM** $150　**MIP** $300

No. 4200, Bulldozer, 1967-72, orange w/towbar instead of winch (1967-70); yellow w/towbar (1971-72)

EX $50　**NM** $125　**MIP** $250

No. 4300, Ford U-Haul Rental Fleet, 1960s, includes orange Ford pickup, orange U-Haul van and orange U-Haul open trailer; pickup has two-piece front grille bumper (1961-64), one-piece bumper and I-beam suspension (1965)

EX $75　**NM** $225　**MIP** $450

No. 4400, Camper Pickup, 1961-63, red Ford pickup truck w/two-piece front grille/bumper, white topper camper, two green air mattresses

EX $50   NM $125   MIP $250

No. 4500, Ranch Truck, 1961-64, light blue Ford stake truck, two-piece front grille/bumper, white stake racks, round decals on doors

EX $50   NM $100   MIP $200

(Thomas G. Nefos)

No. 4501, Chase and Sanborne Stake Truck, 1964, same as No. 4500 but w/coffee boxes (add 75 percent premium if present)

EX $75   NM $175   MIP $350

No. 4502, Boysen Paints Stake Truck, 1964, same as No. 4500

EX $75   NM $200   MIP $400

No. 4600, Construction Four-Wheel Platform Dump

EX $100   NM $150   MIP $225

No. 4600, Hydraulic Dump, 1961-66, same as No. 2700 but orange w/yellow/black decals, front grille guard in yellow/black, hollow plastic wheels

EX $50   NM $125   MIP $250

No. 4700, Happy Acres Truck w/Horses, 1961-63, same as No. 4500 but red truck w/white stakes, large picture decal on doors

EX $75   NM $150   MIP $300

No. 4800, U-Haul Van, 1961, closed trailer, orange and cream, U-Haul decals

EX $50   NM $100   MIP $200

No. 4900, U-Haul Van, 1961, open trailer, orange and cream, U-Haul decals

EX $50   NM $100   MIP $200

No. 5000, Dump Truck w/Cement Mixer, 1962-66, yellow truck w/round decal on doors and two-piece front grille/bumper (1962-64); yellow/green truck w/special decal on mixer (1965); yellow body, green dump box, large N logo decal on doors (1966); cement mixer is always yellow

EX $75   NM $200   MIP $400

No. 5100, Dump Truck, 1962-66, red truck, yellow dump box, two-piece grille/bumper (1962-64); red/yellow truck, one-piece grille/bumper

(1965); light green truck, white dump box, one-piece grille/bumper (1966)

EX $50   NM $140   MIP $275

No. 5200, Econoline Pickup Truck, 1962-72, dual headlights (1962); teardrop headlights (1963-72); red/white truck (1962-65); yellow w/black roof (1966-72)

EX $50   NM $125   MIP $250

No. 5201, Western Auto Econoline Pickup, 1964, rare

EX $75   NM $225   MIP $450

No. 5300, Custom Camper Econoline Pickup Truck, 1962-66, aqua green truck and plastic camper w/opening windows and rear door, slide-out steps under rear door

EX $50   NM $125   MIP $250

No. 5301, Trailblazer Camper, 1969-72, green and white Econoline camper

EX $35   NM $65   MIP $125

No. 5302, Philco Radio Camper

EX $75   NM $325   MIP $650

No. 5400, Custom Camper on Pickup Truck w/Boat, 1962-65, w/red and green sailboat on trailer

EX $75   NM $175   MIP $350

No. 5500, Pepsi Delivery Truck, 1962-67, red, white and blue Ford C-600 truck w/decals, six cases of Pepsi and hand truck

EX $50   NM $225   MIP $450

No. 5600, Farm Set, 1962-64, w/light blue/white No. 4500 Stake Truck, light blue/white No. 5200 Econoline Pickup Truck and other assorted pieces

EX $75   NM $175   MIP $350

No. 5700, Construction Set, 1962-64, orange No. 5000 Dump and Cement Mixer w/yellow drum, Econoline Pickup Truck and Open Stake Trailer; rare

EX $100   NM $300   MIP $600

No. 5800, Ford Econoline Van, 1963-64, purple w/white decals; dark pink or maroon (1964 only)

EX $50   NM $175   MIP $350

No. 5801, U-Haul Van, 1966-67, orange Ford Econoline, white U-Haul decals

EX $50   NM $200   MIP $400

No. 5802, Admiral TV Van, 1966, Ford Econoline w/decals on both sides and all doors; special premium available through Admiral TV delaers, very rare

EX $75   NM $325   MIP $650

No. 5803, Culligan Water Van, 1966, dark blue Ford Econoline w/white top and Culligan decals on sides and doors; very rare

EX $75   NM $275   MIP $550

No. 5900, Race Team, 1963-66, Ford Econoline w/race car (white and other colors) and red trailer

EX $50   NM $175   MIP $350

No. 600, Amazing Car, 1946-49, wind-up; green or blue; box commands a premium (contains operating instructions)

EX $75   NM $150   MIP $300

No. 600, Amazing Car, 1946-49, wind-up; red; box commands a premium (contains operating instructions)

EX $50   NM $125   MIP $250

No. 6000, American Oil Emergency Truck, 1963-69, red Ford Econoline Wrecker, white boom, w/or w/out American Oil decals

EX $50   NM $150   MIP $300

No. 6001, JC Penney Wrecker, 1966, light blue Ford Econoline Wrecker w/white boom; available only form the JC Penney's wishbook

EX $75   NM $250   MIP $500

No. 6100, Hydraulic Dump Truck, 1963-70, beige truck w/red dump box; two-piece grille/bumper (1963-64); one-piece grille bumper (1965-70)

EX $75   NM $150   MIP $300

No. 6200, Kennel Truck, 1963-69, pink Ford Econoline, plastic dog cage in back, 12 dogs (12 different breeds); paper band around cage featuring the dog breeds on it (1964 only)

EX $175   NM $265   MIP $525

No. 6300, Horse Van Semi Truck, 1963-67, brownish-gold truck, white doors, decals, four horses and ponies; two-piece grille/bumper on front (1963-64); one-piece grille/bumper (1965-67); light blue and white truck (1967 only)

EX $50   NM $175   MIP $350

No. 6500, Payloader, 1963-66, red and yellow

EX $50   NM $100   MIP $200

No. 6600, Mobile Home Semi Truck, 1964, aqua blue cab w/white or light tan roof, nine pieces of furniture, two-piece grille/bumper on front, round "6600" decal on cab doors

EX $75   NM $300   MIP $600

No. 6601, Mobile Home Trailer, 1965, aqua blue or turquoise w/white or light tan top, 27 pieces of furniture, one-piece grille/bumper on front, round "6601" decal on cab doors

EX $75   **NM** $300   **MIP** $600

No. 6602, Mobile Home Trailer, 1966, dark blue cab w/white top, no extras, large "N" logo on cab doors

EX $75   **NM** $325   **MIP** $650

No. 6603, Mobile Home Trailer, 1964-66, American Transit Mobile Home Movers and other variations

EX $100   **NM** $350   **MIP** $700

No. 6700, Ambulance, 1964-67, white Ford Econoline Van w/red crosses on sides and doors; included stretcher, interior seats, red flasher light

EX $50   **NM** $150   **MIP** $300

No. 6800, Jalopy, 1964-78, Ford hot rod in red w/white top or light blue w/white top (1964); also No. 6801 w/seats, available in same colors as 1964 version (1965-68); No. 6802 purple and white (1969-71); No. 6803 neon green top and purple body (1972-78)

EX $25   **NM** $150   **MIP** $300

No. 6900, Airport Courtesy Van, 1964, Ford Econoline Van, yellow w/Holiday Inn decals on sides and doors; rare

EX $75   **NM** $350   **MIP** $700

No. 700, Lift Truck (fork lift), 1946-49, red and yellow; box commands a premium (contains operating instructions)

EX $75   **NM** $125   **MIP** $250

No. 700, Lift Truck (fork lift), 1946-49, green and yellow; box commands a premium (contains operating instructions)

EX $75   **NM** $140   **MIP** $275

No. 7000, Lawn and Garden Set, 1964, dark green Econoline Pickup w/white roof; included lawn mower and other garden equipment

EX $50   **NM** $150   **MIP** $300

No. 7100, Fun on Farm Econoline Truck Set, 1964-65, 29 pieces Ford Econoline Pickup w/farm family, farming items, plus small cans of paint to customize your farm family

EX $50   **NM** $175   **MIP** $350

No. 7200, Happy Ranchers Set, 1964, Stake Truck w/Open Stake Trailer, both light blue and white

EX $75   **NM** $175   **MIP** $350

No. 7300, Army Ambulance, 1965, olive drab Ford Econoline Van, stretcher, red cross decals on sides and doors, red flasher light on top

EX $50   **NM** $175   **MIP** $350

No. 7408, Suburban Fire Department Set, 1966-70, red Ford Econoline Pumper Fire Truck, Fire Rescue Econoline Van, Fire Chief's Bronco; Rescue Van and Fire Chief's Bronco available only in this set

EX $75   **NM** $225   **MIP** $450

No. 7800, Race Team, 1965-69, white Econoline Pickup, red trailer, white race car

EX $50   **NM** $150   **MIP** $300

No. 7900, Road Grader, 1965-68, yellow and black

EX $25   **NM** $100   **MIP** $200

No. 7910, Road Grader, 1969, yellow w/larger wheels

EX $40   **NM** $65   **MIP** $125

No. 800, Scootscycle/Servicecycle, 1946-51, wind-up; red, blue, yellow or black; rare

EX $75   **NM** $225   **MIP** $450

No. 8000, Pony Farm Van Set, white Ford Econoline Pick,up, green cab top, large green/white Pony Farm decal on sides, four ponies

EX $75   **NM** $175   **MIP** $350

No. 8001, Gambles Stores Pickup, 1966, white Ford Econoline w/green top

EX $75   **NM** $175   **MIP** $350

No. 8100, Suburban Fire Pumper, 1965-70, Ford Econoline Pumper fire Truck w/water cannon; a garden hose could be connected to the cannon to shoot water; hard to find in good condition since the pressure from the garden hose usually blew up the truck

EX $50   **NM** $150   **MIP** $300

No. 8200, Ford Bronco, 1965-69, listed in the 1965 catalog as a Roustabout but was changed to a Bornco right after the catalog was printed

EX $50   **NM** $140   **MIP** $275

No. 8300, Texaco Service Van, 1965, red Ford Econoline Van, white decals, red flasher light

EX $50   **NM** $200   **MIP** $400

No. 8400, U-Haul Cube Van, 1966-67, five-ton cube van

EX $50   **NM** $175   **MIP** $350

No. 8401, Hertz Rental Truck, 1967, same as No. 8400 but exclusive to Sears; yellow cab, black base, silver cargo box, Hertz decals; rare

EX $85   **NM** $250   **MIP** $500

(Ron O'Brien)

No. 8410, U-Haul Truck & Trailer, 1974, orange and white truck, trailer

EX $100   **NM** $150   **MIP** $200

No. 8411, U-Haul Truck, 1975, Chevy, orange and white cab, silver box, opening rear door

EX $100   **NM** $125   **MIP** $175

(Thomas G. Nefos)

No. 8600, Vacationer Set, 1966-70, blue and white Ford Bronco and camper trailer

EX $50   **NM** $150   **MIP** $300

No. 8700, Truck and Horse Trailer, 1966-70, Ford Bronco, two-axle horse trailer w/yellow top

EX $50   **NM** $145   **MIP** $285

No. 8800, Safari Hunt Set, 1966-71, Ford Bronco w/white top, cage trailer w/wild animals; cage has door, trailer has slide-out ramp and winch for loading

EX $75   **NM** $200   **MIP** $400

No. 8900, Car Carrier, 1967-77, yellow car carrier; three cars (1967-68); two cars (1969-77); several color variations for cars

EX $50   **NM** $150   **MIP** $300

No. 900, Power Pony, 1949, light tan, black, yellow; three-wheeled pony performed tricks; rare

EX $100   **NM** $250   **MIP** $500

No. 9000, Jungle Wagon, 1966-72, two-tone green Ford Econoline w/cages to transport wild animals

EX $45   **NM** $140   **MIP** $275

No. 9100, Stake Pickup Truck, 1966-69, light blue and white Ford Econoline stake truck

EX $35   **NM** $125   **MIP** $250

No. 9200, Big Haul Dump, 1966-68, yellow and black, reminiscent of Tonka's Mighty Dump Truck

EX $45   **NM** $125   **MIP** $250

No. 9201, Big Haul Dump, 1969-72, same as No. 9200 but larger wheels

EX $45   **NM** $125   **MIP** $250

No. 9300, Tin Lizzy Hot Rod Pickup, 1967-72, red and other colors
EX $35   NM $100   MIP $200

No. 9400, Truck and U-Haul Trailer, 1967-68, Ford Econoline Pickup and open trailer, orange and white
EX $50   NM $140   MIP $275

No. 9401, Truck and Haul-It Trailer, 1969, rare; knock-off of U-Haul Trailer w/similar decals
EX $50   NM $175   MIP $350

No. 9500, Sportster, 1967-69, pink Ford Bronco
EX $45   NM $140   MIP $275

No. 9600, Race Team, 1967-69, Ford Econline Pikup and trailer w/race car, red and white
EX $40   NM $140   MIP $275

No. 9700, Sportsman Set, 1967-69, truck w/boat and trailer; white and other colors
EX $50   NM $140   MIP $275

No. 9800, Hydraulic Big Haul Dump Truck, 1967-68, orange and black
EX $35   NM $140   MIP $275

No. 9801, Hydraulic Big Haul Dump Truck, 1969-73, orange and black, new tires
EX $35   NM $140   MIP $275

No. 9900, Farm Set, 1968-71, one of four farm sets made by Nylint; included light blue and white Ford Bronco, Ford Econoline Pickup, Stake Truck and trailer
EX $75   NM $175   MIP $350

No. SR1000/5465, U-Haul Van Set, 1962, Sears exclusive; orange and white Ford Pickup, U-Haul Van (closed type), and trailer w/race car
EX $75   NM $200   MIP $400

No. SR1100, Big Dig Shovel, 1964-65, Sears exclusive; orange and black, all steel except for rubber tracks; later versions (non-exclusives) available in orange yellow and black while track wheels were yellow plastic
EX $50   NM $140   MIP $275

No. SR1200/5439, Lawn and Garden Set, 1964-65, Sears exclusive
EX $50   NM $175   MIP $350

ABC-Olympics Truck, 1980, 21" long GMC tractor-trailer, "ABC Sports ... 1980 Winter Games," sports-center interior
EX $5   NM $10   MIP $20

Classic Twin Boom Wrecker, 1999, "Nylint Towing Service," plastic figure included, 1999
EX $15   NM $24   MIP $40

Classic Twin Boom Wrecker, 1999, "Nylint Towing Service," plastic figure included
EX $15   NM $24   MIP $40

Coca-Cola Tanker, 1980s, 26" long, 1980s
EX $45   NM $80   MIP n/a

Freightliner Trans Tanker, 25" long, "Gas A Haul" on tanker
EX $16   NM $25   MIP $50

Hard Hat Cement Mixer, 1990s, pressed-steel and plastic, rotating tumbler, late 1990s
EX $8   NM $14   MIP $25

Hard Hat Construction Set, 1990s, includes dump truck, plastic trailer, end loader, late 1990s
EX $18   NM $27   MIP $40

Hard Hat Contractors Dump and Trailer, 1990s, pressed-steel tractor, plastic dumping trailer, late 1990s
EX $20   NM $45   MIP $60

Hard Hat Log Truck, 1990s, pressed-steel cab, plastic trailer w/three plastic logs, Hard Hat Construction series, late 1990s
EX $12   NM $22   MIP $50

Hard Hat Snow Plow & Dump Truck, 1999, orange dump truck w/silver plow, Hard Hat Road Team series, 1999
EX $15   NM $24   MIP $40

Jimmy Dean Truck, 24-3/4" long tractor-trailer, "Silver Knight"
EX $8   NM $14   MIP $26

Keebler Delivery Truck, 1988, 10" long, 1988
EX $7   NM $14   MIP $20

Louis Rich Truck, 21" long GMC tractor-trailer
EX $8   NM $14   MIP $24

MAC Tools Truck, 21" long GMC tractor-trailer
EX $10   NM $15   MIP $32

Mr. Goodwrench Truck, 1980s, 21" long GMC tractor-trailer, 1980s
EX $8   NM $12   MIP $27

NAPA Auto Parts Truck, 1980s, 21" long GMC tractor-trailer
EX $5   NM $10   MIP $15

NAPA City Delivery Truck, 10" long
EX $5   NM $8   MIP $17

Northup King Pick-Up, 1970s, Chevy, 1970s
EX $8   NM $10   MIP $22

Outbounder, 1980s, 17" long, motor home/camper, 1980s
EX $5   NM $8   MIP $17

Pillsbury Doughboy Sound Machine, 1999, 20" long, engine/horn sound, headlights, "Honk if you love The Doughboy," 1999
EX $14   NM $30   MIP $55

Rainbow Bread Truck, 1980s, 21" long GMC tractor-trailer, 1980s
EX $15   NM $33   MIP $55

Stanley Truck, 1980s, 21" long GMC tractor-trailer, "Stanley Helps You Do Things Right," 1980s
EX $12   NM $24   MIP $40

Steel Classics Wrecker, 1980, 12" long, 1980
EX $5   NM $8   MIP $15

Twister, 1970s, 10-1/2" long, all-terrain vehicle w/center pivot, 1970s
EX $10   NM $15   MIP $38

U-Haul Box Truck, 1980s, 16" long, 1980s
EX $18   NM $28   MIP $40

U-Haul Truck and Trailer, 1970s, 12" truck and 8-1/2" trailer, 1970s
EX $15   NM $30   MIP $55

Wheel Horse Truck, 21" long GMC tractor-trailer, "Wheel Horse Lawn and Garden Tractors"
EX $18   NM $28   MIP $43

White Sales Pick-Up, 1970s, Chevy, "White Sales Services Parts," 1970s
EX $15   NM $22   MIP $42

Processed Plastic/ Tim-Mee Toys

"Soupercharged" Airplane, 12" wingspan; four free-turning props, "Soupercharged" sticker, cast in beef, ham, and soup; 1960s
EX $7   NM $12   MIP $18

ABCD TV Blimp, 9" long; white blimp, "ABCD TV" on sides, on hauling platform
EX $10   NM $18   MIP $25

Apollo Moon Rocket, 14-1/2" tall, multi-stage rocket, 1960s
EX $10   NM $20   MIP $45

Armored Car, 7" long; rear-mounted swiveling cannon atop Army green armored vehicle, black plastic tires
EX $5   NM $8   MIP $15

Armored Car, 5-1/2" long; center-mounted turret, light Army green, four black-rubber tires
EX $20   NM $35   MIP $40

Armored Truck, 6" long, American LaFrance style
EX $4   NM $7   MIP n/a

Army C-130 Cargo Plane, 24-1/2" long, 26-1/2" wingspan, four-prop, 1960s
EX $15   NM $35   MIP n/a

Army Helicopter, 9" long, green
EX $20   NM $50   MIP n/a

Army Jeep, 7" long, folding-down windshield, mounted machine gun in rear
EX $5   NM $12   MIP n/a

Army Jeep and Howitzer, 9-1/2" long; "Tim-Mee Toys" Army green Jeep, 5-1/4" long; w/snugly fitting driver, snap-in steering wheel, towing cannon, 4-1/4" long, both toys w/black rubber tires; 1960s
EX $6   NM $12   MIP $18

Army Jeep and Howitzer, 9-1/2" long; "Tim-Mee Toys," w/black plastic tires
EX $4   NM $8   MIP $14

Army Tank, 14-1/2" long, cast-in treads, green, 1960s
EX $20   NM $30   MIP n/a

Army Tank, 14" long, cast-in treads, opening hatch, tan plastic
EX $8   NM $15   MIP n/a

Army Tank, 6-1/2" long, cast-in treads, revolving turret, green
EX $3   NM $5   MIP $20

Army Tow Truck and Trailer, truck 9-1/4" long, trailer 7-3/4" long
EX $25   NM $40   MIP n/a

Army Troop Carrier, 7-1/2" long, three-axel, 2-1/2-ton truck, "canvas" cover in rear, plastic tires
EX $8   NM $16   MIP n/a

Beach Runner, 10" long; red car chassis w/10" blue and white upper body that snaps out to become power boat
EX $6   NM $8   MIP $15

Bi-Plane, 4" long, 6" wingspan, British SPAD XIII
EX $8   NM $16   MIP n/a

Bi-Plane, 4" long, 6" wingspan, German Fokker D-VII
EX $8   NM $16   MIP n/a

Boat and Trailer Set, plastic station wagon, 7-1/4" long, separate top and bottom moldings, black plastic tires on metal axles, "Bear Lake Lodge" stickers, hauling plastic trailer w/motor boat; early 1970s
EX $20   NM $40   MIP $60

Cadillac Eldorado, 9-1/4" long, white w/red interior, white steering wheel, chrome hubs
EX $15   NM $35   MIP n/a

Can-Am Challenge Race Car, 11" long; red body, white steering wheel and driver's head, chromed engine pipes and rearviews, "Can Am Challenger" sticker on hood
EX $15   NM $25   MIP $35

Chevy Camaro, 10-1/4" long; T-top, popped engine, flames on hood, chrome hubs on black wheels
EX $8   NM $12   MIP $20

Chevy Camaro, 9" long; black roof, green body, popped/chromed engine, spoiler, late 1960s modeling
EX $20   NM $40   MIP $60

Chevy Camaro, 9-1/4" long; tan body and interior, chromed hubs, 1960s
EX $8   NM $12   MIP $20

Chevy Chevette, 8" long, Rally Couple hatchback, white w/red chassis/interior or vice versa, opening rear gate, 1970s
EX $10   NM $20   MIP n/a

Chevy Corvette, T-roof, clear windshields, purple body, red-stripe tires, late 1960s modeling
EX $10   NM $20   MIP $25

Chevy Flatbed Truck, 4" long; 1950s-style, blue plastic w/windows not cut out, simple rolling toy; 1960s
EX $3   NM $8   MIP n/a

Chevy Hi-Rider, 9" long; yellow pickup truck, chromed grille and rear bumper, orange rollbar and interior, opening rear gate w/"Chevrolet,"

"Hi-Rider 4WD" stickers on doors, oversize tires; 1980s
EX $5   NM $9   MIP $15

Chevy Nomad Station Wagon, 4" long; 1950s-style, blue plastic w/windows not cut out, simple rolling toy; 1960s
EX $3   NM $8   MIP n/a

Clipper Sailing Ship, 21" long, 15" tall; brown ship, three masts, white sails, two lifeboats, turning rudder, weighted keel; 1960s
EX $30   NM $45   MIP $60

Convertible, 4" long; 1950s-style red Cadillac w/finned fenders, open top, simple rolling toy; 1960s
EX $3   NM $8   MIP n/a

Dodge Charger Fire Chief, 12"; opening hood w/chromed engine
EX $35   NM $55   MIP n/a

Dodge Charger Police Chief, 12"; opening hood w/chromed engine
EX $35   NM $55   MIP n/a

Dragster, 20" long; stretch dragster, black plastic, chrome engine and pipes, "Top Eliminator" stickers
EX $8   NM $12   MIP $20

Dump Truck, 12-1/4" long; chrome grille, clear windshield, whitewall tires; 1950s to early 1960s
EX $10   NM $18   MIP $30

Dump Truck, 6-1/2" long, red and blue, black rubber tires
EX $5   NM $10   MIP n/a

Dump Truck, 7-1/4" long; Chevy cabover w/roof lights, black spoked tires, heavy-duty dumping body
EX $3   NM $7   MIP $10

Dump Truck, 7" long; rounded-top cabover, tilting heavy-duty dump body; 1950s or 1960s
EX $3   NM $7   MIP $10

Dump Truck, 10" long, hard plastic, rubber tires, 1950s
EX $15   NM $30   MIP $55

Eureka Hauler, 22" long; tractor-trailer, orange cab w/white interior and chromed grille, white trailer w/"Eureka Vacuum Cleaners" panels; 1980s
EX $12   NM $25   MIP $30

Fighter Plane, 4" long, 6" wingspan; World War I biplane, "Nieuport 17C," plastic pilot
EX $8   NM $15   MIP $25

Ford Car, 8-1/2" long; red plastic w/"The Dukes of Hazzard" style Confederate flag stickers; 1980s
EX $15   NM $30   MIP $40

Ford Hot Rod, 5" long; plastic body in various colors w/red plastic driver, chrome engine and dual exhaust pipes
EX $10   NM $15   MIP $25

Ford Mustang, 11" long, "State Police" and "Highway Patrol" stickers, siren lights, whitewalls, plastic windows
EX $20   NM $40   MIP $90

GMC Pickup Truck w/Camper, 13" long, green truck, white camper, "GMC" on front and fender, 1960s
EX $10   NM $22   MIP n/a

Honda ATC Three-Wheeler, 9" long; red and white plastic, "ATC" on tank, black balloon tires
EX $20   NM $45   MIP $60

Honda Trail Bike, 8-1/2" long; "Honda" sticker, various colors, chromed engine, black plastic tires
EX $6   NM $12   MIP $18

Houseboat, 12" long, "Princess Pat"
EX $5   NM $10   MIP $18

Indy Race Car, 12-1/2" long; moveable front air fins and rear spoiler; 1970s
EX $5   NM $11   MIP $16

Indy Race Car, 9" long; open-cockpit racer, tail fin, red plastic w/yellow steering wheel and chrome pipes, "98" on decal
EX $8   NM $16   MIP n/a

Indy Racer, 8"; open-cockpit racer, "500 Special" sticker
EX $12   NM $35   MIP n/a

Mercedes 190SL Convertible, 7" long, plastic windshield, separately cast driver, black "spoke" wheels
EX $20   NM $40   MIP n/a

Mighty Mite Big Rig, 22" long, 18-wheeler, box trailer w/Eureka Mighty Mite vacuum cleaner advertisement
EX $3   NM $5   MIP $15

Motorboat, 7-1/4" long; snap-together open-top motorboat w/plastic motor clear windshield; 1960s or 1970s
EX $7   NM $10   MIP $18

Passenger Jet, 12" wingspan, 12" length, fuselage top opens
EX $7   NM $14   MIP n/a

Pontiac Firebird, 17-1/2" long; red or gray plastic, interior details; 1970s
EX $15   NM $30   MIP n/a

Racer, 8" long, smooth nose, rubber tires, "7" on rear sides, separately cast driver
EX $10   NM $20   MIP n/a

Racer, 7-3/4" long; open cockpit race car w/separately-cast driver, "7" cast into long nose, "700 Special" sticker; 1960s or 1970s
EX $9   NM $18   MIP $27

Renault Sedan, 4-1/4" long; simple rolling toy, modeled on 1950s Renault; 1960s or 1970s
EX $5   NM $10   MIP n/a

Rocket Launcher, scaled for Tim-Mee toy soldiers
EX $20   NM $45   MIP n/a

Seaplane, 8" long; red and white plastic seaplane, wheels under pontoons, propeller
EX $5   NM $9   MIP $14

Shur Fine Truck and Trailer, 21" long, red cabover, white trailer w/"Shur Fine" on doors and "Shur Fine Quality Foods" on sides
EX $14   NM $26   MIP $38

Snowmobile, 11" long, "Ski-bob" sticker, clear windshield, late 1960s
EX $20   NM $35   MIP n/a

Space Shuttle Columbia, 9" long; white and red Space Shuttle, "NASA" on wings, "Columbia, United States" sticker on sides; 1980s
EX $3   NM $8   MIP $12

Station Wagon, 8" long; red body, blue chassis, 1960s
EX $10   NM $30   MIP n/a

Station Wagon, 4" long; 1950s-style Chevy station wagon, simple rolling toy; 1960s or 1970s
EX $3   NM $5   MIP n/a

Submarine, 10" long; hard plastic, "X-13 USN," w/plastic on base, two red missiles, periscope, radar dish
EX $25   NM $40   MIP $60

Thunderhauler, 22" long; black tractor-trailer, batter-operated horn; 1980s
EX $8   NM $20   MIP $25

Troop Hauler, 7" long; Army-green plastic truck w/"canvas" cover, three axles, six plastic tires
EX $10   NM $20   MIP $25

VW Bug, VW hot rod w/popped and chromed engine, oversize rear tires; 1970s
EX $6   NM $10   MIP $18

VW Bug, 7"; red plastic body, black wheels
EX $8   NM $15   MIP n/a

VW Pickup, 4-1/4" long; Army-green body, black plastic tires, "1234" license plates; 1960s
EX $9   NM $15   MIP $25

Wrecker, scaled for Tim-Mee toy soldiers
EX $15   NM $30   MIP $55

Remco

Barney's Auto Factory, battery-operated auto factory, makes red plastic car, 1960s
EX $20   NM $50   MIP $120

Barney's Tow Truck Factory, set for constructing red plastic tow truck, 1964
EX $20   NM $50   MIP $100

Barracuda Atomic Sub, No. 578, motorized, missile launchers, torpdedoes, 25-man crew, nuclear reactor
EX $60   NM $120   MIP $340

Big Caesar Motorized Roman Warship, Roman galley w/oars, soldiers, catapults, chariots, horses, 1963
EX $100   NM $200   MIP $550

Bulldog Tank, 16" long; plastic tank, metal underside, four shells, remote-control firing; 1960s
EX $15   NM $30   MIP $160

Casey's Automatic Car Wash, 14" wide, w/cars 2-3/4" long, 1963
EX $35   NM $70   MIP $175

Caterpillar Tractor, 8" long; 1986
EX $5   NM $8   MIP $11

Coca-Cola Set, window box set w/pickup, car, tractor-trailer, Coca-Cola cases; 1989
EX $7   NM $12   MIP $20

Coca-Cola Tractor-Trailer, 10-1/2" long, red and white, steel and plastic, six bottle cases in trailer, 1980s
EX $4   NM $9   MIP $15

Corvette, 6" long, plastic, red and black plastic, 1988
EX $1   NM $2   MIP n/a

Duffy's Daredevils, play set featuring plastic red convertible, car launcher, ramp, hoops of "fire" and barrels for auto thrill show; 1965
EX $7   NM $15   MIP $25

Dump Truck, 16" long, heavy-duty quarry dumper, steel, yellow enamel, 1980s
EX $4   NM $12   MIP $35

Fess Parker "Daniel Boone" Trail Blazer Cannon, 16" long, 1964
EX $40   NM $70   MIP $140

Fighting Lady Battleship, 36" long; depth charges, 5" plane, 7-1/2" small boat
EX $25   NM $55   MIP $125

Firebird "99," 13" across; battery-operated steering wheel and dashboard, w/windshield, speedometer, ignition key; 1963-64
EX $22   NM $43   MIP $65

Flying Dutchman Antique Car, battery-operated "U-Control," #611, 1970s
EX $10   NM $35   MIP $125

Gallant Gladiator Roman Warship, No. 522, Roman galley w/oars, 1963
EX $100   NM $160   MIP $300

Giant Hamilton's Invaders, play set w/tank, helicopter, mosquito jeep, figures, alien invaders, 1960s
EX $150   NM $300   MIP $550

Jeep, 7-1/2" long; pink molded plastic, marketed as Heidi's Jeep, Pocketbook Dolls series, 1960s
EX $10   NM $20   MIP $30

Johnny Reb Cannon, brown and black plastic, cannonballs
EX $40   NM $80   MIP $350

Loader, "Real Steel," yellow frontloader, oversize tires, 1980s
EX $1   NM $2   MIP $5

Long John, 4" long; large red plastic fire truck w/white ladders, 1960s
EX $30   NM $40   MIP $75

Midget Motors Mighty Mike Jeep, 5-1/2" long; battery-operated Jeep, white w/black tires and exposed engine, sold individually and w/Midget Motors Mighty Mike Action Sets; late 1960s
EX $15   NM $25   MIP $50

Mighty Magee Aircraft Carrier, 18" long, w/pursuit planes, bombers, tow truck and plane launcher, 1963
EX $20   NM $35   MIP $90

Mighty Matilda Aircraft Carrier, play set includes planes, helicopters, lifeboats and other plastic pieces; #720M0
EX $50   NM $140   MIP $275

Mighty Mike Astro Train Gift Set, mobile helicopter launcher, hauling submarine trailer and robot carrier, 1960s
EX $10   NM $20   MIP $30

Mighty Mike Dump Truck Skyway Set, 1960s
EX $8   NM $15   MIP $30

Mighty Mike Motorized Truck, six-wheel truck w/interchangeable, snap-on bodies; late 1960s
EX $8   NM $15   MIP $30

Mini Tru-Smoke 4-in-1 Trailer Set, motorized cab w/four trailer backs
EX $10   NM $18   MIP $35

Monkeemobile, die-cast, white plastic roof, chrome engine, Hong Kong, 1970
EX $12   NM $35   MIP n/a

Movieland Drive-In Theatre, five tin cars, drive-in theatre w/screen, signs, filmstrips, 1959
EX $50   NM $80   MIP $150

Mr. Kelly's Automatic Car Wash, 27" long; battery-operated working car wash w/see-through roof, two cars, wax cans, towels, sponges and free-standing sign; 1963-64
EX $28   NM $80   MIP $300

Pepsi Set, "Heavy Metal" semi truck, pickup, Pepsi crates, pop machine, two figures, also in "Tuff Ones" packaging
EX $4   NM $8   MIP $14

Putty Cat Wrecker, "Real Steel," working bom, off-road tires, 1980s
EX $1   NM $2   MIP $5

Rat Patrol Jeep Set, "Mighty Mike" jeep, trailer, skyway
EX $40   NM $80   MIP $200

Sanitation Truck, 13" long; "Save Our Planet," metal and plastic; early 1990s
EX $5   NM $10   MIP $15

Seaview, yellow, "Voyage to the Bottom of the Sea" TV submarine, 1960s
EX $75   NM $125   MIP $35

Shark, 19" long; plastic, billed as "Battery Driven U-Control Racing Car," orange plastic body, white side pipes, chromed grille, black tires with chromed hubs; 1961 and later
EX $10   NM $40   MIP $90

Showboat, 1962, play set includes the pink riverboat and scripts and scenes for four productions: Wizard of Oz, Heidi, Pinocchio and Cinderella, 1962
EX $50   NM $95   MIP $175

Sky Diver, jet plane play set, w/white jet, parachuting sky diver, ejection seat, motorized tow tractor, battery-operated
EX $75   NM $150   MIP $250

Stubby Camper, 23" long; plastic, blue cab, white camper w/rear slide-up door; 1973
EX $7   NM $13   MIP $20

Supercar, Gerry Anderson TV-show ship, red plastic, battery-operated, figure of Mercury inside, 1960s
EX $100   NM $200   MIP n/a

Swamp Buggy, 12" long; battery-operated plastic pontoon, yellow and red w/white plastic rider; 1968
EX $4   NM $15   MIP $22

Thimble City Services Station, includes police and fire vehicles, tow truck, four passenger cars
EX $60   NM $85   MIP $140

Smith-Miller

EMERGENCY VEHICLES

"L" Mack Aerial Ladder, Smith-Miller, red w/gold lettering; polished aluminum surface, SMFD decals on hood and trailer sides, six-wheeler; 1950

EX $375 NM $475 MIP $795

TRUCKS

"B" Mack Associated Truck Lines, Smith-Miller, red cab, polished aluminum trailer, decals on trailer sides, six-wheel tractor, eight-wheel trailer; 1954

EX $500 NM $850 MIP $1200

"B" Mack Blue Diamond Dump, Smith-Miller, all white truck w/blue decals, hydraulic piston, 10-wheeler; 1954

EX $600 NM $950 MIP $1300

"B" Mack Lumber Truck, Smith-Miller, yellow cab and timber deck, three rollers, loading bar and two chains, six-wheeler, load of nine timbers; 1954

EX $450 NM $650 MIP $1000

"B" Mack Orange Dump Truck, Smith-Miller, construction orange all over, no decals, hydraulic piston, 10-wheeler; 1954

EX $650 NM $1150 MIP $1650

"B" Mack P.I.E., Smith-Miller, red cab, polished trailer, six-wheel tractor, eight-wheel trailer; 1954

EX $375 NM $600 MIP $850

"B" Mack Searchlight, Smith-Miller, dark red paint schemes, fully rotating and elevating searchlight, battery-operated; 1954

EX $500 NM $775 MIP $1100

"B" Mack Silver Streak, Smith-Miller, yellow cab, unpainted, unpolished trailer sides, "Silver Streak" decal on both sides, six-wheel tractor, eight-wheel trailer; 1954

EX $450 NM $775 MIP $1050

"B" Mack Watson Bros., Smith-Miller, yellow cab, polished aluminum trailer, decals on trailer sides and cab doors, 10-wheel tractor, eight-wheel trailer; 1954

EX $650 NM $1100 MIP $1500

"L" Mack Army Materials Truck, Smith-Miller, Army green, flatbed w/dark green canvas, 10-wheeler, load of three wood barrels, two boards, large and small crate; 1952

EX $375 NM $500 MIP $750

"L" Mack Army Personnel Carrier, Smith-Miller, all Army green, wood sides, Army seal on door panels, military star on roof, 10-wheeler; 1952

EX $375 NM $500 MIP $750

"L" Mack Bekins Van, Smith-Miller, white, covered w/"Bekins" decals, six-wheel tractor, four-wheel trailer; 1953

EX $1000 NM $1650 MIP $2000

"L" Mack Blue Diamond Dump, Smith-Miller, white cab, white dump bed, blue fenders and chassis, hydraulically operated, 10-wheeler; 1952

EX $425 NM $750 MIP $1050

"L" Mack International Paper Co., Smith-Miller, white tractor cab, "International Paper Co." decals, six-wheel tractor, four-wheel trailer; 1952

EX $375 NM $650 MIP $900

"L" Mack Lyon Van, Smith-Miller, silver gray cab, dark blue fenders and frame, silver gray van box w/blue "Lyon" decal, six-wheeler; 1950

EX $425 NM $800 MIP $1100

"L" Mack Material Truck, Smith-Miller, light metallic green cab, dark green fenders and frame, wood flatbed, six-wheeler, load of two barrels and six timbers; 1950

EX $400 NM $600 MIP $875

"L" Mack Merchandise Van, Smith-Miller, red cab, black fenders and frame, "Smith-Miller" decals on both sides of van box, double rear doors, six-wheeler; 1951

EX $425 NM $695 MIP $1000

"L" Mack Mobil Tandem Tanker, Smith-Miller, all red cab, "Mobilgas" and "Mobiloil" decals on tank sides, six-wheel tractor, six-wheel trailer; 1952

EX $450 NM $725 MIP $1000

"L" Mack Orange Hydraulic Dump, Smith-Miller, orange cab, orange dump bed, hydraulic, 10-wheeler, may or may not have "Blue Diamond" decals; 1952

EX $850 NM $1500 MIP $1950

"L" Mack Orange Materials Truck, Smith-Miller, all orange, flatbed w/canvas, 10-wheeler, load of three barrels, two boards, large and small crate; 1952

EX $400 NM $650 MIP $900

"L" Mack P.I.E., Smith-Miller, all red tractor, polished aluminum trailer, "P.I.E." decals on sides and front,

six-wheel tractor, eight-wheel trailer; 1950

EX $395 NM $550 MIP $850

"L" Mack Sibley Van, Smith-Miller, dark green cab, black fenders and frame, dark green van box w/"Sibley's" decal in yellow on both sides, six-wheeler; 1950

EX $850 NM $1375 MIP $1850

"L" Mack Tandem Timber, Smith-Miller, red/black cab, six-wheeler, load of six wood lumber rollers, two loading bars, four chains and 18 or 24 boards; 1950

EX $400 NM $600 MIP $725

"L" Mack Tandem Timber, Smith-Miller, two-tone green cab, six-wheeler, load of six wood lumber rollers, two loading bars, four chains, and 18 timbers; 1953

EX $400 NM $700 MIP $1000

"L" Mack Telephone Truck, Smith-Miller, all dark or two-tone green truck, "Bell Telephone System" decals on truck sides, six-wheeler; 1952

EX $475 NM $750 MIP $975

"L" Mack West Coast Fast Freight, Smith-Miller, silver w/red/black or silver cab and chassis, "West Coast-Fast Freight" decals on sides of box, six-wheeler; 1952

EX $475 NM $775 MIP $1000

Chevrolet Arden Milk Truck, Smith-Miller, red cab, white wood body, four-wheeler; 1945

EX $275 NM $465 MIP $800

Chevrolet Bekins Van, Smith-Miller, blue die-cast cab, all-white trailer, 14-wheeler; 1945

EX $275 NM $350 MIP $750

Chevrolet Coca-Cola Truck, Smith-Miller, red cab, wood body painted red, four-wheeler; 1945

EX $300 NM $600 MIP $850

Chevrolet Flatbed Tractor-Trailer, Smith-Miller, unpainted wood trailer, unpainted polished cab, 14-wheeler; 1945

EX $250 NM $300 MIP $500

Chevrolet Heinz Grocery Truck, Smith-Miller, yellow cab, load of four waxed cases; 1946

EX $225 NM $325 MIP $475

Chevrolet Livestock Truck, Smith-Miller, polished, unpainted tractor cab and trailer; 1946

EX $175 NM $275 MIP $375

Chevrolet Lumber, Smith-Miller, green cab, load of 60 polished boards and two chains; 1946
EX $150   **NM** $195   **MIP** $275

Chevrolet Lyons Van, Smith-Miller, blue cab, silver trailer; 1946
EX $165   **NM** $325   **MIP** $500

Chevrolet Material Truck, Smith-Miller, green cab, no side rails, load of three barrels, two cases and 18 boards; 1946
EX $135   **NM** $185   **MIP** $225

Chevrolet Stake, Smith-Miller, yellow tractor cab
EX $185   **NM** $250   **MIP** $425

Chevrolet Transcontinental Vanliner, Smith-Miller, blue tractor cab, white trailer, "Bekins" logos and decals on trailer sides; 1946
EX $200   **NM** $350   **MIP** $495

Chevrolet Union Ice Truck, Smith-Miller, blue cab, white body, load of eight waxed blocks of ice; 1946
EX $300   **NM** $495   **MIP** $800

GMC Arden Milk Truck, Smith-Miller, red cab, white-painted wood body w/red stakes, four-wheeler; 1947
EX $200   **NM** $425   **MIP** $650

GMC Bank of America Truck, Smith-Miller, dark brownish green cab and box, "Bank of America" decal on box sides, four-wheeler; 1949
EX $150   **NM** $375   **MIP** $600

GMC Be Mac Tractor-Trailer, Smith-Miller, red cab, plain aluminum frame, "Be Mac Transport Co." in white letters on door panels, 14-wheeler; 1949
EX $250   **NM** $350   **MIP** $700

GMC Bekins Vanliner, Smith-Miller, blue cab, metal trailer painted white, 14-wheeler; 1947
EX $175   **NM** $275   **MIP** $425

GMC Coca-Cola Truck, Smith-Miller, red cab, yellow wood body, four-wheeler, load of 16 Coca-Cola cases; 1947
EX $500   **NM** $700   **MIP** $895

GMC Coca-Cola Truck, Smith-Miller, all-yellow truck, red Coca-Cola decals, five-spoke hubs, four-wheeler, load of six cases each w/24 plastic bottles; 1954
EX $500   **NM** $800   **MIP** n/a

GMC Drive-O, Smith-Miller, red cab, red dump body, runs forward and backward w/handturned control at end of 5-1/2' cable, six-wheeler; 1949
EX $175   **NM** $300   **MIP** $450

(Larry Planer collection)

GMC Dump Truck, Smith-Miller, all-red truck, six-wheeler; 1950
EX $150   **NM** $275   **MIP** $450

GMC Emergency Tow Truck, Smith-Miller, white cab, red body and boom, "Emergency Towing Service" on body side panels, four-wheeler; 1953
EX $185   **NM** $250   **MIP** $400

GMC Furniture Mart, Smith-Miller, blue cab, off-white body, "Furniture Mart, Complete Home Furnishings" markings on body sides, four-wheeler; 1953
EX $275   **NM** $325   **MIP** $400

GMC Heinz Grocery Truck, Smith-Miller, yellow cab, wood body, six-wheeler; 1947
EX $250   **NM** $325   **MIP** $450

GMC Highway Freighter Tractor-Trailer, Smith-Miller, red tractor cab, hardwood bed on trailer w/full length wood fences, "Fruehauf" decal on trailer, 14-wheeler; 1948
EX $150   **NM** $210   **MIP** $325

GMC Kraft Foods, Smith-Miller, yellow cab, yellow steel box, large "Kraft" decal on both sides, four-wheeler; 1948
EX $300   **NM** $500   **MIP** $600

GMC Lumber Tractor-Trailer, Smith-Miller, metallic blue cab and trailer, three rollers and two chains, 14-wheeler; 1949
EX $185   **NM** $250   **MIP** $350

GMC Lumber Truck, Smith-Miller, green cab, six-wheeler; 1947
EX $300   **NM** $750   **MIP** $1200

GMC Lyons Van Tractor-Trailer, Smith-Miller, blue tractor cab, "Lyons Van" decals on both sides, fold down rear door, 14-wheeler; 1948
EX $200   **NM** $350   **MIP** $400

GMC Machinery Hauler, Smith-Miller, construction orange, two loading ramps, 10-wheeler; 1953
EX $200   **NM** $325   **MIP** $425

GMC Machinery Hauler, Smith-Miller, construction orange cab and lowboy trailer, "Fruehauf" decal on gooseneck, 13-wheeler; 1949
EX $150   **NM** $225   **MIP** $335

GMC Machinery Hauler, Smith-Miller, construction orange cab and lowboy trailer, "Fruehauf" decal on gooseneck, 13-wheeler; 1949
EX $150   **NM** $225   **MIP** $335

GMC Marshall Field's & Co. Tractor-Trailer, Smith-Miller, dark green cab and trailer, double rear doors, never had Smith-Miller decals, 10-wheeler; 1949
EX $295   **NM** $395   **MIP** $500

GMC Material Truck, Smith-Miller, green cab, wood body, six-wheeler, load of three barrels, three cases and 18 boards; 1947
EX $115   **NM** $250   **MIP** $350

GMC Material Truck, Smith-Miller, yellow cab, natural finish hardwood bed and sides, four-wheeler, load of four barrels and two timbers; 1949
EX $125   **NM** $250   **MIP** $375

GMC Mobilgas Tanker, Smith-Miller, red cab and tanker trailer, large "Mobilgas," "Mobiloil" emblems on sides and rear panel of tanker, 14-wheeler; 1949
EX $200   **NM** $300   **MIP** $500

GMC Oil Truck, Smith-Miller, orange cab, rear body unpainted, six-wheeler, load of three barrels; 1947
EX $115   **NM** $220   **MIP** $375

GMC P.I.E., Smith-Miller, red cab, polished aluminum box trailer, double rear doors, "P.I.E." decals on sides and front panels, 14-wheeler; 1949
EX $170   **NM** $350   **MIP** $475

GMC People's First National Bank and Trust Co., Smith-Miller, dark brownish green cab and box, "People's First National Bank and Trust Co." decals on box sides; 1951
EX $165   **NM** $250   **MIP** $385

GMC Rack Truck, Smith-Miller, red or yellow cab, natural finish wood deck, red stake sides, six-wheeler; 1948

EX $135 **NM** $200   **MIP** $650

GMC Redwood Logger Tractor-Trailer, Smith-Miller, green or maroon cab, unpainted aluminum trailer w/four hardwood stakes, load of three cardboard logs; 1948

EX $365 **NM** $585   **MIP** $700

GMC Rexall Drug Truck, Smith-Miller, orange cab and closed steel box body, "Rexall" logo on both sides and on front panel of box, four-wheeler; 1948

EX $500 **NM** $750   **MIP** $1000

GMC Scoop Dump, Smith-Miller, rack and pinion dump w/a scoop, five-spoke wheels, six-wheeler; 1954

EX $400 **NM** $800   **MIP** $1000

GMC Searchlight Truck, Smith-Miller, four-wheel truck pulling four-wheel trailer, color schemes vary, "Hollywood Film Ad" on truck body side panels; 1953

EX $300 **NM** $500   **MIP** $695

GMC Silver Streak, Smith-Miller, unpainted polished cab and trailer, wrap around sides and shield, some had tail gate; 1950

EX $200 **NM** $350   **MIP** $600

GMC Sunkist Special Tractor-Trailer, Smith-Miller, cherry/maroon tractor cab, natural mahogany trailer bed, 14-wheeler; 1947

EX $165 **NM** $275   **MIP** $475

GMC Super Cargo Tractor-Trailer, Smith-Miller, silver gray tractor cab, hardwood bed on trailer w/red wraparound side rails, 14-wheeler, load of 10 barrels; 1948

EX $150 **NM** $225   **MIP** $395

GMC Timber Giant, Smith-Miller, green or maroon cab, unpainted aluminum trailer w/four hardwood stakes, load of three cardboard logs; 1948

EX $175 **NM** $285   **MIP** $495

GMC Tow Truck, Smith-Miller, white cab, red body and boom, five spoke cast hubs, "Emergency Towing Service" on body side panels, four-wheeler; 1954

EX $95 **NM** $135   **MIP** $200

GMC Transcontinental Tractor-Trailer, Smith-Miller, red tractor cab, hardwood bed on trailer w/full length wood fences, "Fruehauf" decal on trailer, 14-wheeler; 1948

EX $150 **NM** $210   **MIP** $325

GMC Triton Oil Truck, Smith-Miller, blue cab, mahogany body unpainted, six-wheeler, load of three Triton Oil drums (banks) and side chains; 1947

EX $115 **NM** $185   **MIP** $265

GMC U.S. Treasury Truck, Smith-Miller, gray cab and box, "U.S.Treasury" insignia and markings on box sides, four-wheeler; 1952

EX $235 **NM** $325   **MIP** $475

Structo

Standard Steam Shovel, 1948, orange, 20.5L x 6.25W x 7.75H, wooden wheels w/out tracks, Model No. 100

EX $25   **NM** $35   **MIP** $125

Heavy Duty Steam Shovel, 1948, blue, 21.5L x 6.25W x 7.75H, rubber tracks, Model No. 105

EX $35   **NM** $55   **MIP** $150

Dump Truck, 1948, red, 20L x 6.75W x 6.25H, long bullet headlights, Model No. 200

EX $35   **NM** $65   **MIP** $150

Aerial Fire Truck, 1948, red, 24L x 6.75W x 6.25H, one raising/two side ladders and bell on hood, Model No. 250

EX $55   **NM** $75   **MIP** $275

Machinery Truck & Steam Shovel, 1948, orange and blue, 21.5L x 6.75W x 6.25H, comes 2/#105 steam shovel and loading ramp, Model No. 402

EX $55   **NM** $95   **MIP** $275

Standard Steam Shovel, 1949, orange, 20.5L x 6.25W x 7.75H, wooden wheels w/out tracks, Model No. 100

EX $35   **NM** $55   **MIP** $150

Heavy Duty Steam Shovel, 1949, blue, 21.5L x 6.25W x 7.75H, rubber tracks, Model No. 105

EX $35   **NM** $55   **MIP** $150

Dump Truck, 1949, red, 20L x 6.75W x 6.25H, long bullet headlights, Model No. 200

EX $35   **NM** $65   **MIP** $150

Aerial Fire Truck, 1949, red, 24L x 6.75W x 6.25H, one raising, two side ladders and bell on hood, Model No. 250

EX $55   **NM** $75   **MIP** $275

Machinery Truck & Steam Shovel, 1949, orange and blue, 21.5L x 6.75W x 6.25H, comes w/#105 steam shovel and loading ramp, Model No. 402

EX $55   **NM** $95   **MIP** $275

Standard Steam Shovel, 1950, orange, 20.5L x 6.25W x 7.75H, wooden wheels w/out tracks, Model No. 100

EX $25   **NM** $35   **MIP** $125

Heavy Duty Steam Shovel, 1950, blue, 21.5L x 6.25W x 7.75H, rubber tracks, Model No. 105

EX $35   **NM** $55   **MIP** $150

Dump Truck, 1950, red, 20L x 6.75W x 6.25H, long bullet headlights, Model No. 200

EX $35   **NM** $65   **MIP** $150

Aerial Fire Truck, 1950, red, 24L x 6.75W x 6.25H, one raising/two side ladders and bell on hood, Model No. 250

EX $55   **NM** $75   **MIP** $275

Machinery Truck & Steam Shovel, 1950, orange and blue, 21.5L x 6.75W x 6.25H, comes w/#105 steam shovel and loading ramp, Model No. 402

EX $55   **NM** $95   **MIP** $275

Heavy Duty Steam Shovel, 1951-52, blue, 21.5L x 6.25W x 7.75H, Model No. 105

EX $35   **NM** $55   **MIP** $150

Dump Truck, 1951-52, red, 20L x 6.75W x 6.25H, w/plastic fireball motor under the hood, Model No. 200

EX $35   **NM** $65   **MIP** $150

Aerial Fire Truck, 1951-52, red, 24L x 6.75W x 6.25H, w/plastic fireball motor under the hood, Model No. 250

EX $55   **NM** $75   **MIP** $275

Road Grader, 1951-52, orange, 18L x 7W x 7.5H, w/plastic fireball motor under the hood, Model No. 300

EX $35   **NM** $65   **MIP** $150

Machinery Truck & Steam Shovel, 1951-52, orange and blue, 21.5L x 6.75W x 6.25H, w/plastic fireball motor under the hood, Model No. 402

EX $55   **NM** $95   **MIP** $275

Utility (Garbage) Truck, 1951-52, red and blue, 21.5L x 6.5W x 7.5H, w/plastic fireball motor under the hood, Model No. 500

EX $55   **NM** $95   **MIP** $275

(Randy Prasse Photo)

Motor Express Truck, 1951-52, gray and orange, 12.75L x 5.5W x 5H, cast cab "Freeport Motor Express" decals, Model No. 601

EX $35   **NM** $55   **MIP** $200

(Calvin Chaussee Photo)

Package Delivery Truck, 1951-52, orange and green, 13L x 5.5W x 5H, cast cab, tail gate w/chain, Model No. 603

EX $35   **NM** $65   **MIP** $200

Shovel Dump Truck, 1951-52, orange and blue, 12.75L x 5.5W x 5H, cast cab, dump box, Model No. 605

EX $35   **NM** $65   **MIP** $200

(Randy Prasse Photo)

Machinery Truck, 1951-52, orange and blue, 12.75L x 5.5W x 5H, w/loading ramp and chain winch, Model No. 607

EX $35   **NM** $75   **MIP** $275

Transport Trailer, 1951-52, blue and red, 21.5L x 5.5W x 7.5H, blue cast cab w/red trailer, no hubcaps, Model No. 700

EX $55   **NM** $75   **MIP** $275

Steel Cargo Trailer, 1951-52, blue and red, 20.75L x 5.5W x 5.5H, blue cast cab w/red trailer, no hubcaps, Model No. 702

EX $55   **NM** $75   **MIP** $250

Overland Freight Trailer, 1951-52, blue and orange, 20.75L x 5.5W x 5.5H, blue cast cab w/orange stake trailer, Model No. 704

EX $65   **NM** $95   **MIP** $275

Combination w/Two Trailers, 1951-52, blue cast cab w/#702 and 704 trailers, Model No. 706

EX $75   **NM** $150   **MIP** $300

Barrel Truck, 1951-52, red and blue, 12.75L x 5.5W x 5H, wind-up motor and two oil can banks, Model No. 811

EX $55   **NM** $75   **MIP** $250

Wrecker Truck, 1951-52, red and gray, 12.25L x 5.5W x 5.25H, wind-up motor and chain winch, Model No. 822

EX $35   **NM** $65   **MIP** $200

Hi-Lift Dump Truck, 1951-52, red and blue, 12.5L x 5.5W x 5.25H, wind-up motor w/scissors lift box, Model No. 844
EX $35 **NM** $65 **MIP** $200

Gasoline Truck, 1951-52, red and red, 13.5L x 5.5W x 5H, wind-up motor, Model No. 866
EX $55 **NM** $95 **MIP** $275

Steam Shovel (New Design), 1953, blue, 26.5L x 6.5W x 8H, new design, two cranks, Model No. 105
EX $25 **NM** $55 **MIP** $150

Dump Truck, 1953, red, 20L x 6.75W x 6.25H, w/plastic fireball motor under the hood, Model No. 200
EX $35 **NM** $65 **MIP** $200

Road Grader, 1953, orange, 18L x 7W x 7.5H, w/plastic fireball motor under the hood, Model No. 300
EX $25 **NM** $55 **MIP** $150

Rocker, 1953, red, 20L x 6.25W x 6.5H, w/plastic fireball motor under the hood, Model No. 310
EX $25 **NM** $55 **MIP** $150

Bottom Dump, 1953, orange, 21.5L x 6.5W x 6.5H, w/plastic fireball motor under the hood, Model No. 320
EX $25 **NM** $55 **MIP** $150

Scraper, 1953, red, 22L x 7W x 6.5H, w/plastic fireball motor under the hood, Model No. 330
EX $25 **NM** $55 **MIP** $150

End Loader, 1953, orange, 15.25L x 6.25W x 6.75H, w/plastic fireball motor under the hood, Model No. 340
EX $25 **NM** $55 **MIP** $150

Machinery Truck & Steam Shovel, 1953, orange and blue, 21.5L x 6.75W x 6.25H, comes w/#105 steam shovel & loading ramp, Model No. 402
EX $55 **NM** $125 **MIP** $275

Utility (Garbage) Truck, 1953, red and white, 21.5L x 6.5W x 7.5H, w/plastic fireball motor under the hood, Model No. 500
EX $55 **NM** $95 **MIP** $275

(Randy Prasse Photo)

Motor Express Truck, 1953, white and red, 12.75L x 5.5W x 5H, cast cab "Freeport Motor Express" decals, Model No. 601
EX $35 **NM** $65 **MIP** $200

Package Delivery Truck, 1953, white and orange, 13L x 5.5W x 5H, cast cab, tail gate w/chain, w/hubcaps, Model No. 603
EX $35 **NM** $65 **MIP** $200

Shovel Dump Truck, 1953, white and blue, 12.75L x 5.5W x 5H, cast cab, dump box, w/hubcaps, Model No. 605
EX $35 **NM** $65 **MIP** $200

Transport Trailer, 1953, white and red, 21.5L x 5.5W x 7.5H, w/hubcaps, Model No. 700
EX $55 **NM** $75 **MIP** $275

Steel Cargo Trailer, 1953, white and red, 20.75L x 5.5W x 5.5H, w/hubcaps and loading ramp, Model No. 702
EX $55 **NM** $75 **MIP** $250

Grain Trailer, 1953, white and orange, 20.75L x 5.5W x 5.5H, replaced freight trailer, sliding rear door, Model No. 704
EX $65 **NM** $95 **MIP** $225

Cattle Trailer, 1953, white and red, 21.5L x 5.5W x 7.5H, no loading ramp or animals, Model No. 708
EX $75 **NM** $150 **MIP** $300

(Randy Prasse Photo)

Barrel Truck, 1953, red and blue, 12.75L x 5.5W x 5H, wind-up motor and oil can bank, Model No. 811
EX $55 **NM** $75 **MIP** $250

Wrecker Truck, 1953, white and orange, 12.25L x 5.5W x 5.25H, wind-up motor and chain winch, Model No. 822
EX $35 **NM** $65 **MIP** $200

Hi-Lift Dump Truck, 1953, white and red, 12.5L x 5.5W x 5.25H, wind-up motor w/scissors lift box, Model No. 844
EX $35 **NM** $65 **MIP** $200

Gasoline Truck, 1953, red and red, 13.5L x 5.5W x 5H, wind-up motor, Model No. 866
EX $55 **NM** $95 **MIP** $275

Steam Shovel, 1954, blue, 26.5L x 6.5W x 8H, two cranks and rubber tracks, Model No. 105
EX $25 **NM** $55 **MIP** $150

Dump Truck, 1954, red, 20L x 6.75W x 6.25H, w/plastic fireball motor under the hood, Model No. 200
EX $35 **NM** $65 **MIP** $200

Road Grader, 1954, orange, 18L x 7W x 7.5H, w/plastic fireball motor under the hood, Model No. 300
EX $25 **NM** $55 **MIP** $150

Rocker, 1954, red, 20L x 6.25W x 6.5H, w/plastic fireball motor under the hood, Model No. 310
EX $25 **NM** $55 **MIP** $150

Bottom Dump, 1954, orange, 21.5L x 6.5W x 6.5H, w/plastic fireball motor under the hood, Model No. 320
EX $25 **NM** $55 **MIP** $150

Scraper, 1954, red, 22L x 7W x 6.5H, w/plastic fireball motor under the hood, Model No. 330
EX $25 **NM** $55 **MIP** $150

End Loader, 1954, orange, 15.25L x 6.25W x 6.75H, w/plastic fireball motor under the hood, Model No. 340
EX $50 **NM** $100 **MIP** $150

Machinery Truck & Steam Shovel, 1954, orange and blue, 26.5L x 6.75W x 14.25H, comes w/#105 steam shovel and loading ramp, Model No. 402
EX $75 **NM** $150 **MIP** $250

Utility (Garbage) Truck, 1954, red and white, 21.5L x 6.5W x 7.5H, w/plastic fireball motor under the hood, Model No. 500
EX $55 **NM** $95 **MIP** $275

(Randy Prasse Photo)

Package Delivery Truck, 1954, white and orange, 13L x 5.5W x 5H, cast cab, tail gate w/chain, w/hubcaps, Model No. 603
EX $75 **NM** $150 **MIP** $350

Shovel Dump Truck, 1954, white and blue, 12.75L x 5.5W x 5H, cast cab, dump box, w/hubcaps, Model No. 605
EX $35 **NM** $65 **MIP** $200

Machinery Truck, 1954, white and blue, 12.75L x 5.5W x 5H, rare, made only in 1954, hubcaps, loading ramp, Model No. 607
EX $35 **NM** $65 **MIP** $200

Barrel Truck, 1954, white and red, 12.75L x 5.5W x 5H, rare, made only in 1954, replaced #811, no wind-up, Model No. 609
EX $35 **NM** $75 **MIP** $275

Transport Trailer, 1954, white and red, 21.5L x 5.5W x 7.5H, w/hubcaps, Model No. 700

EX $55   **NM** $75   **MIP** $275

Steel Cargo Trailer, 1954, white and red, 20.75L x 5.5W x 5.5H, w/hubcaps and loading ramp, Model No. 702

EX $55   **NM** $75   **MIP** $250

Grain Trailer, 1954, white and orange, 20.75L x 5.5W x 5.5H, sliding rear door, Model No. 704

EX $55   **NM** $75   **MIP** $250

Auto Transport, 1954, white and red, 27L x 5.5W x 6.75H, w/four die-cast cars and loading ramp, Model No. 706

EX $55   **NM** $95   **MIP** $275

Cattle Trailer, 1954, white and red, 21.5L x 5.5W x 7.5H, no loading ramp or animals, Model No. 708

EX $55   **NM** $95   **MIP** $275

Wrecker Truck, 1954, white and orange, 12.25L x 5.5W x 5.25H, wind-up motor and chain winch, Model No. 822

EX $35   **NM** $65   **MIP** $200

(Randy Prasse Photo)

Hi-Lift Dump Truck, 1954, white and red, 12.5L x 5.5W x 5.25H, wind-up motor w/scissors lift box, Model No. 844

EX $35   **NM** $65   **MIP** $200

(Randy Prasse Photo)

Gasoline Truck, 1954, red and red, 13.5L x 5.5W x 5H, wind-up motor, Model No. 866

EX $55   **NM** $95   **MIP** $275

Tow Truck (Fix-It), 1954, red and red, 11.75L x 5.5W x 6H, w/mini tool set, new pressed steel cab design, Model No. 910

EX $25   **NM** $55   **MIP** $150

Telephone Truck (Fix-It), 1954, green, 12L x 5.5W x 5.25H, w/mini tool set, new pressed steel cab design, Model No. 920

EX $25   **NM** $55   **MIP** $150

Freight Trailer, 1954, red and red, 17.75L x 5W x 4.5H, new pressed steel cab design, Model No. 930

EX $55   **NM** $75   **MIP** $200

Log Trailer, 1954, orange and orange, 17.75L x 5W x 4.5H, w/five wooden logs, Model No. 940

EX $35   **NM** $55   **MIP** $150

Caddy Sedan, 1954, various, 6.25L x 2.5W x 2H, same scale as appear on auto transport set, Model No. 20

EX $5   **NM** $15   **MIP** $40

Pick-Up Truck, 1954, various, 6.5L x 2.5W x 2.25H, same scale as appears on auto transport set, Model No. 21

EX $5   **NM** $15   **MIP** $40

Wrecker Truck, 1954, various, 7.5L x 2.5W x 2.25H, same scale #21 pick-up but w/cast tow boom arm, Model No. 30

EX $15   **NM** $25   **MIP** $60

8-Wheel Transport Truck, 1954, orange, 7.25L x 2.5W x 2.25H, also in 1957 as six-wheeled, red version in farm set, Model No. 40

EX $15   **NM** $25   **MIP** $100

Dump Truck, 1954, green and orange, 8.25L x 2.5W x 2.5H, spring dump action, Model No. 50

EX $15   **NM** $25   **MIP** $100

4 Pc. Truck Assortment, 1954, one each: #21, #30, #40, #50, Model No. 90

EX $55   **NM** $95   **MIP** $200

Dump Truck, 1954, green and orange, 10.25L x 3.25W x 3.5H, spring dump action, Model No. 75

EX $25   **NM** $35   **MIP** $115

Stake Truck, 1954, green and orange, 9.25L x 3.25W x 3.25H, removable stake panels, Model No. 76

EX $25   **NM** $35   **MIP** $115

Lumber Truck, 1954, red and blue, 10.5L x 3.5W x 3.25H, w/ five wooden logs, Model No. 77

EX $25   **NM** $35   **MIP** $115

3 Pc. Truck Assortment, 1954, one each: #75, #76, #77, Model No. 91

EX $75   **NM** $105   **MIP** $300

Motor Express Truck, 1954, yellow and blue, 12.5L x 5.25W x 4.5H, stake truck w/"S" grille cab, Model No. 150

EX $35   **NM** $55   **MIP** $150

Machinery Hauling Truck, 1954, red and yellow, 12.5L x 5.5W x 4H, flatbed w/winch and "S" grille cab, Model No. 151

EX $55   **NM** $75   **MIP** $200

Semi Trailer Freight Truck, 1955, yellow and red, 17L x 4.5W x 4.5H, same trailer as #930 w/"S" grille cab, Model No. 155

EX $55   **NM** $75   **MIP** $150

Semi Trailer Lumber Truck, 1955, green and orange, 17L x 4.5W x 4.5H, w/three wooden logs and "S" grille cab, Model No. 156

EX $55   **NM** $75   **MIP** $150

Auto Haulaway, 1955, blue and orange, 25L x 4.5W x 6.5H, w/two cars, loading ramp and "S" grille cab, Model No. 175

EX $75   **NM** $95   **MIP** $200

Steam Shovel, 1955, orange, 26.5L x 6.5W x 8H, two cranks and rubber tracks, Model No. 105

EX $25   **NM** $55   **MIP** $150

Dump Truck, 1955, yellow and red, 20L x 6.75W x 6.25H, spring dump action, Model No. 201

EX $25   **NM** $55   **MIP** $125

Hydraulic Lift Dump Truck, 1955, green and orange, 21L x 8W x 7H, hydraulic dump lift arm on dump box, Model No. 250

EX $55   **NM** $75   **MIP** $200

Hook and Ladder Truck, 1955, red, 33.25L x 6.75W x 7H, w/raising and two ladders, cast metal siren on roof, Model No. 260

EX $55   **NM** $75   **MIP** $200

Road Grader, 1955, orange, 18L x 7W x 7.5H, w/plastic fireball motor under the hood, Model No. 300

EX $25   **NM** $55   **MIP** $125

Rocker, 1955, green, 20L x 6.25W x 6.5H, w/plastic fireball motor under the hood, Model No. 310

EX $25   **NM** $55   **MIP** $125

Earth Mover, 1955, orange, 21.5L x 6.5W x 6.5H, w/plastic fireball motor under the hood, Model No. 320

EX $25   **NM** $55   **MIP** $125

Scraper, 1955, red, 22L x 7W x 6.5H, w/plastic fireball motor under the hood, Model No. 330

EX $25   **NM** $55   **MIP** $125

End Loader, 1955, orange, 15.25L x 6.25W x 6.75H, w/plastic fireball motor under the hood, Model No. 340

EX $25   **NM** $55   **MIP** $125

3 Pc. Truck Assortment, 1955, one each: #105, #201, $300, Model No. 325

EX $75 **NM** $155 **MIP** $350

Steam Shovel & Machinery Truck, 1955, green and orange, 26.5L x 6.5W x 14.25H, w/plastic fireball motor under the hood, Model No. 403

EX $55 **NM** $95 **MIP** $250

Utility (Garbage) Truck, 1955, blue and gray, 21.5L x 6.5W x 7.5H, w/plastic fireball motor under the hood, Model No. 500

EX $55 **NM** $95 **MIP** $275

Shovel Dump Truck, 1955, chrome and orange, 12.75L x 6W x 6.25H, same as #605 from past years, mag wheels, Model No. 606

EX $35 **NM** $55 **MIP** $150

Hi-Lift Dump Truck, 1955, chrome and green, 12.5L x 6W x 5H, same as #844 from past years, mag wheels, Model No. 644

EX $35 **NM** $55 **MIP** $150

Steel Cargo Trailer, 1955, white and red, 25.5L x 5.5W x 5.5H, shown in catalog w/yellow cab but have not been seen, Model No. 702

EX $55 **NM** $75 **MIP** $150

Grain Trailer, 1955, white and orange, 20.75L x 5.5W x 5.5H, shown in catalog w/green cab but have not been seen, Model No. 704

EX $55 **NM** $75 **MIP** $150

Deluxe Auto Transport, 1955, chrome and yellow, 27L x 6W x 6.75H, w/four die-cast cars and loading ramp, Model No. 706

EX $55 **NM** $75 **MIP** $150

(Randy Prasse Photo)

Deluxe Moving Van, 1955, chrome and yellow, 24L x 6W x 8.5H, w/loading ramp, Model No. 710

EX $55 **NM** $95 **MIP** $250

Deluxe Cattle Transport, 1955, chrome and green, 24L x 6W x 8.5H, w/loading ramp and metal farm animals, Model No. 712

EX $55 **NM** $95 **MIP** $250

Timber Toter, 1955, chrome and green, 21L x 6W x 6H, w/six wooden logs and chains, Model No. 714

EX $35 **NM** $75 **MIP** $150

10 Pc. Truck Assortment, 1955, two cabs plus one each #702, #706, #714, cattle trailer, Model No. 725

EX $100 **NM** $200 **MIP** $450

Wrecker Truck, 1955, white and orange, 12L x 5.5W x 5.25H, shown in catalog w/green cab but have not been seen, Model No. 822

EX $35 **NM** $55 **MIP** $150

Tow Truck (Fix-It), 1955, red and red, 11.75L x 5.5W x 6H, w/mini tool set, Model No. 910

EX $25 **NM** $55 **MIP** $150

Telephone Truck (Fix-It), 1955, green, 12L x 5.5W x 5.25H, w/mini tool set, Model No. 920

EX $25 **NM** $55 **MIP** $150

Freight Trailer, 1955, yellow and red, 17.75L x 5W x 4.5H, Model No. 930

EX $55 **NM** $75 **MIP** $200

Log Trailer, 1955, green and orange, 17.75L x 5W x 4.5H, w/five wooden logs, Model No. 940

EX $35 **NM** $55 **MIP** $150

Package Delivery Truck, 1955, yellow and green, 13L x 5.5W x 4.75H, w/tailgate and chains, Model No. 911

EX $35 **NM** $55 **MIP** $150

Gasoline Truck, 1955, red and yellow, 13.5L x 5W x 4.5H, non-wind-up model, Model No. 912

EX $55 **NM** $75 **MIP** $200

Barrel Truck, 1955, yellow and red, 12.75L x 5.5W x 5H, non-wind-up model, no oil can bank, Model No. 913

EX $55 **NM** $75 **MIP** $200

Transport Trailer, 1955, yellow and red, 21L x 5W x 7.75H, new pressed steel cab design, Model No. 950

EX $55 **NM** $75 **MIP** $200

Cattle Trailer, 1955, green and orange, 21L x 5W x 7.75H, new pressed steel cab design, Model No. 960

EX $55 **NM** $75 **MIP** $200

Dump Truck, 1956-57, gold and blue, 10.25L x 3.25W x 3.5H, spring dump action, Model No. 75

EX $25 **NM** $35 **MIP** $115

Stake Truck, 1956-57, gold and green, 9.25L x 3.25W x 3.25H, removable stake panels, Model No. 76

EX $25 **NM** $35 **MIP** $115

Lumber Truck, 1956-57, red and blue, 10.5L x 3.5W x 3.25H, w/five wooden logs, Model No. 77

EX $25 **NM** $35 **MIP** $115

3 Pc. Truck Assortment W/Garage, 1956-57, one each: #75, #76, #77 w/garage storage box, Model No. 92

EX $75 **NM** $105 **MIP** $300

Motor Express Truck, 1956-57, yellow and blue, 12.5L x 5.25W x 4.5H, stake truck w/"S" grille cab, Model No. 150

EX $35 **NM** $55 **MIP** $150

Machinery Hauling Truck, 1956-57, red and yellow, 12.5L x 5.5W x 4H, flatbed w/winch and "S" grille cab, Model No. 151

EX $35 **NM** $75 **MIP** $140

Semi Trailer Freight Truck, 1956-57, yellow and red, 17L x 4.5W x 4.5H, same trailer as #930 w/"S" grille cab, Model No. 155

EX $55 **NM** $75 **MIP** $150

Auto Haulaway, 1956-57, blue and orange, 25L x 4.5W x 6.5H, w/two cars, loading ramp and "S" grille cab, Model No. 175

EX $75 **NM** $95 **MIP** $200

Clam Bucket, 1956-57, yellow and green, 16.75L x 7W x 7.25H, Model No. 101

EX $25 **NM** $55 **MIP** $150

Heavy Duty Steam Shovel, 1956-57, green and orange, 26.5L x 7W x 6.75H, two cranks and rubber tracks, Model No. 106

EX $25 **NM** $55 **MIP** $150

Dump Truck, 1956-57, green and orange, 20L x 6.75W x 6.25H, spring dump action, Model No. 201

EX $25 **NM** $55 **MIP** $125

Hydraulic Lift Dump Truck, 1956-57, yellow and green, 21L x 8W x 7H, hydraulic dump lift arm on dump box, Model No. 250

EX $55 **NM** $75 **MIP** $200

Hook and Ladder Truck, 1956-57, red, 33.25L x 6.75W x 7H, w/raising and two ladders, cast metal siren on roof, Model No. 260

EX $55 **NM** $75 **MIP** $200

Ready Mix Concrete Truck, 1956-57, red and yellow, 21.5L x 7.5W x 9.25H, w/gear on barrel, driven by axle, Model No. 271

EX $35 **NM** $75 **MIP** $200

Mobile Steam Shovel Unit, 1956-57, green and yellow, 32.5L x 6.75W x 8H, half-track truck w/steam shovel on back, Model No. 272

EX $75 **NM** $125 **MIP** $275

Road Grader, 1956-57, green, 18L x 7W x 7.5H, w/plastic fireball motor under the hood, Model No. 300

EX $25 **NM** $55 **MIP** $150

Rocker Dump, 1956-57, green, 20L x 6W x 6.5H, rubber tracks on tractor, dumps to the rear, Model No. 311

EX $25   **NM** $55   **MIP** $150

Earth Mover, 1956-57, orange, 22L x 6.5W x 6.5H, same tractor as #311, bottom panels open to dump, Model No. 321

EX $25   **NM** $55   **MIP** $150

Scraper, 1956-57, orange, 22L x 7W x 6.5H, w/plastic fireball motor under the hood, Model No. 330

EX $25   **NM** $55   **MIP** $150

End Loader, 1956-57, green, 15.25L x 6W x 6.75H, w/plastic fireball motor under the hood, Model No. 340

EX $25   **NM** $55   **MIP** $150

Clam Bucket and Machinery Truck, 1956-57, yellow and green, 32L x 7.25W x 13.75H, w/plastic fireball motor under the hood, Model No. 404

EX $55   **NM** $95   **MIP** $250

Utility (Garbage) Truck, 1956-57, blue and gray, 21.5L x 6.5W x 7.5H, w/plastic fireball motor under the hood, Model No. 500

EX $55   **NM** $75   **MIP** $200

Shovel Dump Truck, 1956-57, green and yellow, 12.75L x 6W x 5H, w/mag wheels, Model No. 606

EX $55   **NM** $75   **MIP** $150

Hi-Lift Dump Truck, 1956-57, chrome and blue, 12.5L x 6W x 5H, same as #644 from 1955 only blue dump box, Model No. 644

EX $35   **NM** $55   **MIP** $150

Trailer Truck, 1956-57, chrome and red, 24.5L x 6W x 5.5H, same as #702 but w/chrome cab and lift gate, Model No. 705

EX $55   **NM** $95   **MIP** $250

Deluxe Auto Transport, 1956-57, chrome and yellow, 27L x 6W x 6.75H, w/four die-cast cars and loading ramp, Model No. 706

EX $55   **NM** $75   **MIP** $150

Deluxe Moving Van, 1956-57, chrome and blue, 24L x 6W x 8.5H, w/loading ramp and mini grocery freight, Model No. 710

EX $55   **NM** $75   **MIP** $250

Western Auto Moving Van, 1956-57, chrome and white, 24L x 6W x 8.5H, private label, same body as #710 deluxe moving van, red doors, Model No. 711

EX $75   **NM** $95   **MIP** $275

(Randy Prasse Photo)

Deluxe Cattle Transport, 1956-57, chrome and green, 24L x 6W x 8.5H, w/loading ramp and metal farm animals, Model No. 712

EX $55   **NM** $95   **MIP** $250

(Randy Prasse Photo)

Timber Toter, 1956-57, chrome and green, 21L x 6W x 6H, w/six wooden logs and chains, Model No. 714

EX $35   **NM** $75   **MIP** $150

Wrecker Truck, 1956-57, white and orange, 12L x 5.5W x 5.25H, wind-up, Model No. 822

EX $35   **NM** $55   **MIP** $150

Freight Hauler, 1956-57, blue and yellow, 20.5L x 5.25W x 5.5H, w/grocery freight, Model No. 935

EX $55   **NM** $75   **MIP** $150

Transport Truck, 1956-57, red and yellow, 21L x 5W x 7.5H, Model No. 950

EX $55   **NM** $75   **MIP** $150

Cattle Transport, 1956-57, green and orange, 21L x 5W x 7.75H, Model No. 960

EX $55   **NM** $75   **MIP** $150

Tow Truck (Fix-It), 1956-57, blue and blue, 11.75L x 5.5W x 6H, w/mini tool set, Model No. 910

EX $25   **NM** $55   **MIP** $150

Package Delivery Truck, 1956-57, blue and yellow, 13L x 5.5W x 4.75H, w/tailgate and chains, Model No. 911

EX $35   **NM** $55   **MIP** $150

Gasoline Truck, 1956-57, blue and yellow, 13.5L x 5W x 4.5H, Model No. 912

EX $55   **NM** $75   **MIP** $200

Barrel Truck, 1956-57, yellow and red, 12.75L x 5.5W x 5H, non-wind-up model, no oil can bank, Model No. 913

EX $55   **NM** $75   **MIP** $200

Telephone Truck (Fix-It), 1956-57, blue, 12L x 5.5W x 5.25H, w/mini tool set, Model No. 920

EX $25   **NM** $55   **MIP** $150

3 Pc. Truck Assortment, 1956-57, various, one each: #106, #201, #300, Model No. 326

EX $75   **NM** $125   **MIP** $300

5 Pc. Turnpike Builder Set, 1956-57, various, one each: #321, #340, #404 combo, Model No. 327

EX $75   **NM** $155   **MIP** $300

32 Pc. Big Job Transcontinental Set, 1956-57, various, two cabs plus one each #702, #706, #714, cattle trailer, Model No. 726

EX $155   **NM** $275   **MIP** $600

17 Pc. Coast To Coast Fleet, 1956-57, various, two cars plus lumber trailer, #175, #935, #950; two cars, Model No. 925

EX $125   **NM** $255   **MIP** $600

15 Pc. Farm Set, 1958, various, caddy, dump, pick-up/horse trailer, six-wheel transport, Model No. 93

EX $75   **NM** $125   **MIP** $275

3 Pc. Truck Assortment w/Garage, 1958, various, one each; dump, log and stake truck, Model No. 94

EX $75   **NM** $125   **MIP** $275

Pick-Up Truck w/Horse Van, 1958, blue and yellow, 10.5L x 2.5W x 3H, includes two plastic horses, Model No. 100

EX $55   **NM** $75   **MIP** $150

Power Shovel, 1958, orange, 26.5L x 7W x 6.75H, two cranks and rubber tracks, Model No. 106

EX $25   **NM** $55   **MIP** $125

Heavy Duty Dump Truck, 1958, blue and orange, 20L x 6.75W x 6.25H, spring dump action plus red light on roof, Model No. 200

EX $35   **NM** $75   **MIP** $200

Dump w/Front-End Loader, 1958, yellow and blue, 23L x 6.75W x 6.25H, spring loaded dump w/front loader bucket, Model No. 202

EX $55   **NM** $95   **MIP** $250

Pick-Up Truck, 1958, red and yellow, 19.25L x 6.5W x 6H, includes mini grocery freight, Model No. 210

EX $55   **NM** $75   **MIP** $150

Air Force Truck, 1958, blue and red, 17.25L x 7.25W x 8H, includes soldiers and canvas top, spare tires on side, Model No. 212

EX $75   **NM** $95   **MIP** $200

Farm Truck & Trailer, 1958, blue and yellow, 28L x 6W x 6.25H, pick-up w/pick-up box trailer and plastic farm animals, Model No. 213

EX $55   **NM** $75   **MIP** $150

Towing & Service Truck, 1958, green and orange, 17.5L x 6W x 7.5H, same as #210 but w/tow set-up and red light on roof, Model No. 214

EX $55   NM $75   MIP $150

Hydraulic Lift Dump Truck, 1958, orange and green, 21L x 8W x 7H, hydraulic dump lift arm on dump box, Model No. 250

EX $55   NM $75   MIP $150

Double Hydraulic Load & Dump, 1958, black and yellow, 24.5L x 7.75W x 7H, hydraulic dump lift arm on dump box and front bucket, Model No. 252

EX $75   NM $95   MIP $200

Hook and Ladder Truck, 1958, red, 33.5L x 6W x 7H, w/raising and two ladders, cast metal siren on roof, Model No. 261

EX $75   NM $95   MIP $250

Pumper Fire Truck W/Light, 1958, red, 22.75L x 7.25W x 7H, pumps water through truck and hydrant, flashing light, Model No. 262

EX $55   NM $75   MIP $200

Hydraulic Hook & Ladder Truck, 1958, red, 33.25L x 6.75W x 7H, w/raising and two ladders, red flashing light on roof, Model No. 266

EX $75   NM $95   MIP $250

Mobile Communications Center, 1958, red and blue, 20L x 6.25W x 6.25H, includes antenna tower and morse code buttons, Model No. 270

EX $55   NM $95   MIP $300

Ready Mix Concrete Truck, 1958, green and orange, 21.5L x 7.5W x 9.25H, w/gear on barrel, driven by axle, Model No. 271

EX $35   NM $75   MIP $200

Mobile Power Shovel Unit, 1958, green and yellow, 32.5L x 6.75W x 8H, half-track truck w/steam shovel on back, Model No. 272

EX $75   NM $125   MIP $275

Deluxe Cattle Transport, 1958, yellow and brown, 25.75L x 6.25W x 8.5H, includes plastic farm animals, Model No. 275

EX $55   NM $95   MIP $250

Deluxe Road Grader, 1958, orange, 18.75L x 7.25W x 7.5H, w/plastic fireball motor under the hood, Model No. 301

EX $25   NM $55   MIP $150

Deluxe Rocker Dump, 1958, orange, 20.25L x 6.25W x 6.5H, w/plastic fireball motor under the hood, Model No. 312

EX $25   NM $55   MIP $150

Deluxe Earth Mover, 1958, orange, 22L x 6.5W x 6.5H, w/plastic fireball motor under the hood, Model No. 322

EX $25   NM $55   MIP $150

Combination, 1958, green and orange, 32L x 7.5W x 6.75H, #106 power shovel and machinery hauling low-boy, Model No. 405

EX $75   NM $155   MIP $300

5 Pc. Highway Builder Set, 1958, various, one each: #106, #201, #300 plus two metal road signs, Model No. 510

EX $75   NM $155   MIP $300

17 Pc. USA Combat Convoy Set, 1958, green, transport, searchlight and missle trucks w/soldiers, Model No. 520

EX $175   NM $250   MIP $600

Big Job Transcontinental Fleet, 1958, various, two cabs plus one each trailers: steel, auto, freight, cattle, Model No. 540

EX $125   NM $255   MIP $600

12 Pc. US Highway Set, 1958, orange, dump, grader, maintenance, pick-up plus eight road signs, Model No. 550

EX $125   NM $255   MIP $600

6 Pc. Fire Department, 1958, red and white, pumper, hook and ladder, ambulance, road signs, Model No. 570

EX $155   NM $275   MIP $600

Deluxe Auto Transport, 1958, chrome and yellow, 27L x 6W x 6.75H, w/two cars, one truck and loading ramp, Model No. 707

EX $55   NM $75   MIP $125

(Randy Prasse Photo)

Gold Plated Cadillac, 1958, gold, 6.75L x 2.25W x 2H, same as used on car carriers, 50th anniversary decal on roof

EX $25   NM $55   MIP $200

Deluxe Moving Van, 1958, chrome and blue, 31L x 6W x 8.5H, w/loading ramp and mini grocery freight, Model No. 710

EX $55   NM $75   MIP $250

Timber Toter, 1958, chrome and blue, 21L x 6W x 6.25H, w/six wooden logs and chains, Model No. 714

EX $35   NM $75   MIP $150

USA Transport Truck, 1958, green, 12.5L x 5.25W x 7.5H, w/canvas top, Model No. 905

EX $35   NM $55   MIP $150

USA Guided Missile Launcher, 1958, green, 12.75L x 5.25W x 6H, w/two plastic missiles, Model No. 906

EX $35   NM $75   MIP $200

USA Searchlight Truck, 1958, green, 12.75L x 5.25W x 7.25H, w/battery-operated searchlight, Model No. 907

EX $35   NM $75   MIP $200

Gasoline Truck, 1958, blue and yellow, 13.5L x 5W x 4.5H, Model No. 912

EX $55   NM $75   MIP $200

Hi-Lift Dump Truck, 1958, blue and yellow, 12L x 5.25W x 5.75H, w/scissors lift mechanism, Model No. 914

EX $35   NM $55   MIP $150

Trailer W/Mechanical Lift, 1958, blue and yellow, 50.75L x 5.5W x 5.75H, mechanical lift gate w/mini grocery freight, Model No. 936

EX $55   NM $95   MIP $250

Farm Truck, 1958, green and red, 13L x 5.75W x 4.5H, w/plastic farm animals, Model No. 938

EX $55   NM $75   MIP $150

(Randy Prasse Photo)

Highway Maintenance Service, 1958, orange and green, 12L x 4.5W x 7H, w/lift/swivel boom arm, Model No. 939

EX $55   NM $75   MIP $200

Hydraulic Dump Trailer, 1958, yellow and green, 20.5L x 5.5W x 5.75H, w/hydraulic lift arm on trailer dump, Model No. 941

EX $55   NM $95   MIP $200

Parcel Service Truck, 1958, yellow and green, 12.25L x 5.25W x 7H, w/mini grocery freight, Model No. 942

EX $35   NM $55   MIP $150

US Mail Truck, 1958, blue and red, 12.25L x 5.25W x 6.5H, Model No. 943

EX $35   NM $55   MIP $150

Farm Trailer Truck, 1958, blue and red, 20.5L x 5.5W x 5.5H, w/plastic animals and loading ramp, Model No. 945

EX $55   **NM** $95   **MIP** $200

Auto Haulaway, 1958, yellow and red, 21.5L x 4.5W x 6.5H, smaller model w/two cars and loading ramp, Model No. 946

EX $55   **NM** $75   **MIP** $150

Refrigerated Express Truck, 1958, yellow and brown, 21L x 5W x 7.5H, transport trailer w/refrigerator unit on front, Model No. 951

EX $55   **NM** $95   **MIP** $250

Cattle Transport, 1958, green and orange, 21L x 5W x 7.5H, w/plastic farm animals, Model No. 961

EX $55   **NM** $95   **MIP** $200

Ride 'Em Dump Truck, 1958, blue and yellow, 20.5L x 7.75W x 10.25H, w/seat and steering wheel, Model No. 990

EX $55   **NM** $75   **MIP** $250

Ride 'Em Air Force Jeep, 1958, blue and red, 25.5L x 11W x 14.5H, w/steering wheel and fold-down windshield, Model No. 995

EX $75   **NM** $95   **MIP** $275

Kitchen-Laundry Ensemble, 1959, pink and gray, nine-piece 1/4-scale set, Model No. 50

EX $75   **NM** $125   **MIP** $300

Counter-Top Cabinet, 1959, pink and gray, 7L x 7.75W x 13H, cabinet doors open, includes pots and pans, Model No. 2

EX $15   **NM** $25   **MIP** $100

Built-In Cooking Range, 1959, pink and gray, 7L x 7.75W x 13H, plastic burners on top, cabinets open, pots and pans, Model No. 4

EX $15   **NM** $25   **MIP** $100

Corner Counter-Top Cabinet, 1959, pink and gray, 12L x 9.75W x 13H, two lazy susan shelves, drawer opens, pots and pans, Model No. 6

EX $15   **NM** $25   **MIP** $100

Built-In Double Sink, 1959, pink and gray, 7L x 7.75W x 13H, works w/water, battery-operated, Model No. 8

EX $15   **NM** $25   **MIP** $100

Automatic Under Counter Dishwasher, 1959, pink and gray, 7L x 7.75W x 13H, works w/water, battery-operated, Model No. 10

EX $15   **NM** $25   **MIP** $100

Combination Refrigerator/Freezer, 1959, pink and gray, 7.25L x 7.75W x 13H, swing out shelves, freezer drawer, plastic food, Model No. 12

EX $15   **NM** $25   **MIP** $100

Built-In Double Oven, 1959, pink and gray, 7.25L x 7.75W x 13H, battery-operated, rotisserie in top oven unit, Model No. 14

EX $15   **NM** $25   **MIP** $100

Washer-Dryer Combination, 1959, pink and gray, 7.25L x 8W x 10H, washes and spins, battery-operated, Model No. 16

EX $15   **NM** $25   **MIP** $100

Dump Truck, 1959, copper and cream, 10.75L x 4.5W x 4.5H, Model No. 70

EX $35   **NM** $75   **MIP** $150

Dump Truck, 1959, blue and yellow, 9L x 3.5W x 3.5H, Model No. 75

EX $35   **NM** $75   **MIP** $150

Stake Truck, 1959, copper and cream, 9.25L x 3.25W x 3H, Model No. 76

EX $35   **NM** $75   **MIP** $150

Air Force Radar Truck, 1959, blue and red, 12L x 5.25W x 12.5H, scarce, radar dish on roof of box, two plastic soldiers, Model No. 102

EX $75   **NM** $125   **MIP** $300

Dump Truck, 1959, black and yellow, 15.75L x 6.75W x 6.75H, red roof and plastic "S" grille, no windshield, Model No. 201

EX $35   **NM** $75   **MIP** $150

Fleetside Pick-Up, 1959, copper and cream, 14.5L x 6W x 6H, six mini grocery box play freight, Model No. 202

EX $35   **NM** $75   **MIP** $150

Guided Missile Launcher, 1959, red and silver, 12.25L x 5.25W x 10.25H, plastic missile launcher on bed, metal "S" grille, Model No. 203

EX $55   **NM** $95   **MIP** $200

Mechanical Hydraulic Dump, 1959, red and white, 12.25L x 5.25W x 5.5H, scarce, hydraulic cylinder controls dump box, Model No. 204

EX $55   **NM** $125   **MIP** $250

Bulldozer, 1959, copper and cream, 11.75L x 7W x 6.75H, cream blade, yellow wheels and motor, also on #502 set, Model No. 205

EX $25   **NM** $55   **MIP** $125

The Camper, 1959, red and white, 21.75L x 4.5W x 6.75H, canvas cover on truck, convertible boat and trailer, Model No. 206

EX $35   **NM** $75   **MIP** $200

Farm Pick-Up And Trailer, 1959, yellow and blue, 27.5L x 6.25W x 6H, seven plastic animals included, Model No. 213

EX $55   **NM** $95   **MIP** $150

Double Hydraulic Load & Dump, 1959, copper and yellow, 23.75L x 7.75W x 6.75H, yellow bucket dumps over top into dump box, Model No. 252

EX $35   **NM** $75   **MIP** $150

Deluxe Road Grader, 1959, copper and yellow, 18.75L x 7.25W x 7.5H, copper w/yellow wheels and engine, Model No. 301

EX $25   **NM** $55   **MIP** $125

Power Shovel, 1959, copper, 26.5L x 7W x 6.75H, rubber tracks, Model No. 302

EX $25   **NM** $55   **MIP** $150

Emergency Fire Patrol Searchlight Unit, 1959, white and red, 19.5L x 5.75W x 7.5H, white trailer w/red battery-operated searchlight unit, Model No. 303

EX $25   **NM** $55   **MIP** $150

Cattle Transport, 1959, red and white, 21.25L x 5.25W x 7.5H, Structo Farms decals on white trailer, Model No. 304

EX $35   **NM** $75   **MIP** $150

Deluxe Rocker Dump, 1959, copper and cream, 20.25L x 6.25W x 6.5H, bronze dump, cream tractor w/yellow wheels and motor, Model No. 312

EX $25   **NM** $55   **MIP** $125

Highway Truck Assortment, 1959, varies, 13-piece set, includes #70, #76 plus six-wheel truck, log truck and signs, Model No. 400

EX $95   **NM** $155   **MIP** $300

Deluxe Auto Transport, 1959, green and yellow, 31.5L x 5.5W x 6.75H, two cars, one truck w/loading ramp, plastic "S" grille, Model No. 401

EX $35   **NM** $75   **MIP** $150

Army Troop Transport, 1959, green, 18.75L x 6.75W x 9H, canvas top w/"USA" printed, four plastic soldiers, Model No. 412

EX $35   **NM** $95   **MIP** $250

Hydraulic Sanitation Truck, 1959, blue and white, 18L x 6W x 7.5H, hydraulic cylinder controls dump box, Model No. 454

EX $55   **NM** $95   **MIP** $200

Deluxe Hydraulic Dumper, 1959, copper and yellow, 20.5L x 8W x 7H, hydraulic cylinder controls dump box, Model No. 500

EX $35   **NM** $55   **MIP** $150

Stock Farm Set, 1959, red and white, 15L x 6W x 7.25H, stake truck w/cattle loading ramp and four plastic horses, Model No. 501
EX $55 **NM** $75 **MIP** $200

Tilt-Top Trailer Truck w/Dozer, 1959, yellow and green, 20.25L x 7.5W x 6H, dozer is copper w/yellow plastic wheels and engine, Model No. 502
EX $55 **NM** $95 **MIP** $200

Mobile Outer Space Launcher, 1959, red and blue, 19.5L x 6W x 12.75H, scarce, two plastic missiles launch, launcher swivels, Model No. 503
EX $95 **NM** $155 **MIP** $300

Deluxe Moving Van, 1959, yellow and red, 26.25L x 6W x 8.5H, red cab w/bulb horn on roof, Model No. 504
EX $55 **NM** $95 **MIP** $250

Ride-er Dump Truck, 1959, blue and yellow, 20L x 7.75W x 10H, metal seat in dump box, bulb horn on steering wheel, Model No. 505
EX $35 **NM** $55 **MIP** $200

Air Force Anti-Aircraft Set, 1959, red and blue, scarce, canvas covered truck, missile launcher, searchlight, Model No. 506
EX $75 **NM** $125 **MIP** $300

Deluxe Camper w/Boat & Trailer, 1959, red and white, 29L x 6W x 6H, red truck w/white roof, battery-operated boat motor, Model No. 601
EX $55 **NM** $95 **MIP** $275

Mobile Anti-Missile Unit, 1959, blue and yellow, 27L x 7.5W x 11.25H, scarce, battery-operated spotlight and missile launcher on trailer, Model No. 620
EX $75 **NM** $125 **MIP** $300

Ready-Mix Concrete Truck, 1959, copper and cream, 20.75L x 7.5W x 9.25H, gear powered barrel, runs off axle, Model No. 700
EX $55 **NM** $75 **MIP** $150

Pumper Fire Truck, 1959, red and red, 20L x 7.25W x 6H, open cab, plastic "S" grille, sprays water through hose, Model No. 701
EX $55 **NM** $95 **MIP** $200

Deluxe Power Wrecker, 1959, blue and white, 23L x 7W x 9.25H, battery-operated winch and lights, Model No. 702
EX $75 **NM** $95 **MIP** $250

Timber Toter, 1959, red and blue, 21.5L x 4.75W x 5.25H, five wooden logs and load chains, Model No. 714
EX $35 **NM** $55 **MIP** $150

Explorer Vanguard Tracking Station, 1959, red, 7.75L x 4.5W x 10H,

scarce, various buttons, globe revolves in TV screen, Model No. 801
EX $95 **NM** $155 **MIP** $300

Boat w/Play Motor, 1959, red and white, 9.5L x 3W x 2.5H, boat only, from #206 set, convertible boat and motor, Model No. 802
EX $55 **NM** $75 **MIP** $150

Boat w/Outboard Motor, 1959, red and white, 13.25L x 4W x 3.25H, boat only, from #601 set, convertible boat and motor, Model No. 803
EX $55 **NM** $75 **MIP** $150

Highway Builder Set, 1959, varies, 11-piece set includes #201, #205, #302, road signs, plastic workers, Model No. 900
EX $95 **NM** $155 **MIP** $350

Hydraulic Hook & Ladder, 1959, red and red, 31L x 6.25W x 7.25H, open cab, plastic "S" grille, metal ladders, Model No. 901
EX $55 **NM** $95 **MIP** $250

Mobile Crane, 1959, green and yellow, 19.25L x 6.25W x 7.25H, battery-operated boom and cab, Model No. 902
EX $55 **NM** $95 **MIP** $250

Ride-er Fire Truck, 1959, red and white, 25.5L x 10.5W x 12.75H, crank siren on hood, trunk opens, Model No. 925
EX $55 **NM** $75 **MIP** $200

Tree Trimming Truck, 1959, copper and green, 12L x 4.25W x 12.5H, green boom arm and basket, Model No. 939
EX $35 **NM** $75 **MIP** $150

Ride-er Air Force Jeep, 1959, blue and red, 25.75L x 10.25W x 18H, missile launcher and missiles on hood, trunk opens, Model No. 950
EX $55 **NM** $75 **MIP** $275

Fire Department Set, 1959, red and white, three-piece set, includes #701, #901, #303 (minus searchlight unit), Model No. 975
EX $95 **NM** $175 **MIP** $350

Kitchen Ensemble, 1960, pink and gray, individual appliances still available, see 1959 for values
EX $15 **NM** $50 **MIP** $75

Kitchen Ensemble, 1960, pink and gray, three-piece set, includes #8, #12, #4-1959 models, Model No. 23
EX $55 **NM** $95 **MIP** $250

Kitchen-Laundry Ensemble, 1960, pink and gray, five-piece set,

includes #8, #12, #4, #10, #16-1959 models, Model No. 25
EX $75 **NM** $125 **MIP** $275

Deluxe Kitchen-Laundry Ensemble, 1960, pink and gray, seven-piece set, includes #8, #12, #4, #10, #14, #16, #2-1959 models, Model No. 27
EX $95 **NM** $155 **MIP** $350

All-In-One Wild Animal Set, 1960, pink, blue, yellow, 5.5L x 4W x 2H, smaller animals fit inside larger animals, Model No. 105
EX $15 **NM** $25 **MIP** $60

Hammer Tower, 1960, yellow and red, 6.5L x 4.75W x 9H, scarce, hammer button and marbles shoot up through tower, Model No. 110
EX $55 **NM** $75 **MIP** $150

Auto Elevator, 1960, red and yellow, 9L x 3.5W x 9H, scarce, plastic parking garage, crank release car down ramp, Model No. 111
EX $75 **NM** $125 **MIP** $250

Jack And Jill Pump, 1960, copper and yellow, 8L x 4.25W x 11.25H, scarce, plastic marble toy, Structo pre-school series, Model No. 112
EX $55 **NM** $95 **MIP** $250

Concrete Mixer, 1960, copper and yellow, 6.25L x 5.5W x 13.25H, scarce, plastic cement mixer w/clear barrel w/marbles, Model No. 114
EX $55 **NM** $95 **MIP** $250

School Bus, 1960, yellow, 5.5L x 4W x 12H, scarce, plastic, hinged school bus w/blocks, pull toy, Model No. 115
EX $95 **NM** $125 **MIP** $300

Pickup And Delivery, 1960, metallic green, 14L x 5.75W x 6.5H, whitewall tires, plastic horn on roof, Model No. 207
EX $35 **NM** $75 **MIP** $150

Dumper, 1960, copper, 11.5L x 5.5W x 6H, whitewall tires, plastic horn on roof, Model No. 209
EX $35 **NM** $75 **MIP** $150

Bulldozer, 1960, yellow, 11.75L x 7W x 6.75H, black tires and motor, blade tips up, Model No. 210
EX $25 **NM** $55 **MIP** $125

Camper, 1960, teal and red, 23.25L x 4.5W x 6.5H, red and white canvas over truck bed, boat and trailer, Model No. 211
EX $35 **NM** $75 **MIP** $200

Cabin Cruiser, 1960, red and white, 12L x 4W x 3H, plastic hull, wooden deck and cabin, battery-operated motor, Model No. 212
EX $35 **NM** $75 **MIP** $200

Road Grader, 1960, yellow, 18.75L x 7.25W x 7.5H, black tires and motor, scraper blade lifts w/levers, Model No. 301

EX $55   NM $75   MIP $150

Power Shovel, 1960, yellow, 26.5L x 7W x 6.75H, black rubber tracks, Model No. 305

EX $55   NM $75   MIP $150

Livestock Truck, 1960, red and white, 14.75L x 6W x 7.25H, white plastic stake panels and two plastic animals, Model No. 306

EX $55   NM $75   MIP $150

Earth Mover, 1960, yellow, 21.5L x 6.5W x 6H, black tires and motor, Model No. 322

EX $55   NM $75   MIP $150

Timber Toter, 1960, copper, 20.75L x 5.5W x 5.5H, plastic mirrors and horn, five wooden logs and chains, Model No. 323

EX $35   NM $55   MIP $150

Auto Transport, 1960, metallic green, 22L x 5.5W x 6.5H, four metal cars plus loading ramp, Model No. 402

EX $35   NM $55   MIP $150

Cattle Transport, 1960, red and white, 21.25L x 5.5W x 7.5H, plastic mirrors, windshield wipers and horn, Model No. 403

EX $35   NM $55   MIP $150

Hydraulic Dumper, 1960, metallic green, 14.75L x 6.25W x 6.5H, plastic mirrors, windshield wipers and horn, Model No. 404

EX $35   NM $55   MIP $150

Machinery Hauler, 1960, copper, 19.5L x 7.5W x 6.5H, includes #210 dozer, Model No. 509

EX $35   NM $75   MIP $200

Stock Farm Set, 1960, red and white, 14.75L x 6W x 7.25H, stake truck w/cattle loading ramp and four plastic horses, Model No. 510

EX $55   NM $75   MIP $150

Deluxe Camper, 1960, gold, 27.5L x 6W x 6.5H, #207 truck plus #212 boat on trailer, Model No. 602

EX $35   NM $55   MIP $200

Pumper, 1960, white, 19.75L x 7.25W x 6H, scarce, open cab, operating water tank and hose, Model No. 603

EX $75   NM $95   MIP $275

Ready Mix Concrete Truck, 1960, teal and white, 16L x 7.5W x 9H, axle driven gear operates barrel, Model No. 604

EX $35   NM $55   MIP $150

Ride-er Dump Truck, 1960, blue and white, 20L x 7.75W x 10H, metal seat in dump box and bulb horn on steering wheel, Model No. 605

EX $55   NM $75   MIP $200

Mobile Crane, 1960, copper and yellow, 19.25L x 6.25W x 7.25H, half-track w/single-driver cab, Model No. 800

EX $55   NM $75   MIP $200

Power Wrecker, 1960, blue and white, 23L x 7W x 9.25H, battery-operated winch and lights, Model No. 802

EX $55   NM $95   MIP $250

Hydraulic Hook & Ladder, 1960, red and red, 31L x 6.25W x 7.25H, open cab, two metal ladders, hydraulic lift ladder, Model No. 901

EX $55   NM $75   MIP $200

Highway Builder Set, 1960, copper, includes #209, #210, #305 plus road barricade, Model No. 903

EX $95   NM $155   MIP $300

Transcontinental Express Fleet, 1960, varies, 20-piece set includes auto transport, express, steel trailer, Model No. 904

EX $95   NM $155   MIP $350

Transcontinental Express Semi, 1960, blue and silver, 26L x 6W x 8.5H, unpainted aluminum trailer w/blue decals, Model No. 905

EX $55   NM $75   MIP $200

Ride-er Fire Truck, 1960, red and white, 25.5L x 10.5W x 12.75H, crank siren on hood, trunk opens, Model No. 925

EX $55   NM $75   MIP $200

Die-Cast Dump Truck, 1961, varies, 7.25L x 2.5W x 2.25H, packaged on bubble pack for in-store display, Model No. 79

EX $15   NM $35   MIP $125

Rampside Pick-Up, 1961, copper, 10.5L x 4.5W x 5H, plastic bed liner and drop-down door in side of bed, Model No. 195

EX $25   NM $55   MIP $150

Camper, 1961, metallic green, 21.5L x 4.5W x 5H, rampside truck towing boat and trailer, Model No. 202

EX $35   NM $55   MIP $150

Bulldozer, 1961, yellow, 11L x 6.5W x 6.5H, rubber tracks, Model No. 206

EX $25   NM $55   MIP $150

Dispatch Truck, 1961, metallic green, 13L x 5.25W x 5H, similar to 1950s barrel truck, plastic mirrors, wipers, and horns, Model No. 208

EX $35   NM $55   MIP $150

Road Grader, 1961, yellow, 18.75L x 7W x 7.5H, plastic tires, Model No. 301

EX $15   NM $35   MIP $125

Wrecker, 1961, white, 12L x 5.75W x 6.5H, crank-operated winch, plastic mirrors, wipers, and horns, Model No. 302

EX $35   NM $75   MIP $150

Airlines Lift Truck, 1961, copper and white, 12.5L x 5.25W x 7H, lever lifts cargo box w/scissors lift mechanism, Model No. 303

EX $35   NM $75   MIP $150

Power Shovel, 1961, yellow, 26.5L x 7.5W x 7H, rubber tracks, Model No. 305

EX $35   NM $75   MIP $150

Livestock Truck, 1961, red and white, 14.5L x 6.25W x 7.5H, stake truck w/two plastic animals, Model No. 306

EX $35   NM $75   MIP $150

Fire Rescue Truck, 1961, red, 12L x 5.75W x 5.25H, plastic hose reel w/braided hose, two ladders, Model No. 307

EX $35   NM $55   MIP $150

Deluxe Dump Truck, 1961, metallic green, 11.75L x 5.5W x 5.75H, lever operates dump box, Model No. 309

EX $35   NM $55   MIP $150

Timber Toter, 1961, metallic green, 23L x 5.5W x 6H, six wooden logs and chains, Model No. 406

EX $25   NM $55   MIP $125

Hydraulic Dumper, 1961, metallic green, 13.75L x 5.5W x 6.25H, hydraulic cylinder controls dump box, Model No. 407

EX $35   NM $55   MIP $150

Auto Transport, 1961, copper, 22L x 5.5W x 7H, includes one car and one truck plus loading ramp, Model No. 502

EX $35   NM $55   MIP $150

Cattle Transport, 1961, green and white, 23.5L x 6.5W x 8H, white trailer w/green doors, Model No. 503

EX $35   NM $55   MIP $125

Deluxe Transport, 1961, red and white, 23.5L x 6.5W x 8H, North American Vanlines decals on trailer, Model No. 504

EX $35   NM $75   MIP $200

Hydraulic Sanitation Truck, 1961, white, 18L x 6W x 8H, all white design, Model No. 606

EX $55   NM $95   MIP $200

Ride-er Wrecker Truck, 1961, copper and white, 23.5L x 7.75W x 10.25H, metal seat and crank-operated boom in box, Model No. 607

EX $35   **NM** $75   **MIP** $200

Ready-Mix Concrete Truck, 1961, red and white, 15.5L x 7.75W x 9H, axle driven gear operates barrel, Model No. 609

EX $35   **NM** $75   **MIP** $200

Mobile Crane, 1961, yellow, 15.5L x 6.5W x 7.25H, double cranks control crane arm and clam bucket, Model No. 700

EX $55   **NM** $75   **MIP** $200

Pumper, 1961, red, 19.5L x 7.25W x 6.5H, operating water tank and hose, two ladders, Model No. 708

EX $55   **NM** $75   **MIP** $200

Aerial Hook & Ladder, 1961, red, 30.75L x 6.25W x 6.25H, two metal ladders, crank-operated lift ladder, Model No. 902

EX $55   **NM** $75   **MIP** $200

Highway Builder Set, 1961, copper, includes #206, #305, #309 plus road barricade, Model No. 905

EX $95   **NM** $155   **MIP** $350

Transcontinental Express Fleet, 1961, varies, 25-piece set includes auto transport, express, cattle trailers, Model No. 906

EX $125   **NM** $155   **MIP** $400

Construction And Paving Set, 1961, varies, four-piece set includes #309, #609, #700 plus barricade, Model No. 907

EX $75   **NM** $155   **MIP** $300

Ride-er Fire Truck, 1961, red and white, 25.5L x 10.5W x 12.75H, crank siren on hood, trunk opens, Model No. 925

EX $55   **NM** $95   **MIP** $300

Little Miss Structo Washer/Dryer, 1962, teal, 7.25L x 8W x 10H, washes and spins, battery-operated, Model No. 16

EX $15   **NM** $35   **MIP** $100

Rampside Pick-Up, 1962, red, 10.5L x 4.5W x 5H, plastic bed liner and drop-down door in side of bed, Model No. 195

EX $35   **NM** $55   **MIP** $150

School Bus, 1962, yellow, 10.5L x 4.75W x 5H, steel body, plastic mirrors, wipers and horn, Model No. 196

EX $35   **NM** $75   **MIP** $200

Fisherman, 1962, blue, 21.5L x 4.5W x 5H, rampside truck towing boat and trailer, Model No. 202

EX $50   **NM** $75   **MIP** $200

Camper, 1962, green and yellow, 10.5L x 4.5W x 6.5H, rampside truck w/plastic camper in bed of truck, Model No. 203

EX $55   **NM** $75   **MIP** $150

Hi-Lift Bulldozer, 1962, yellow, 11.25L x 5.75W x 3.75H, rubber tracks, lever controls bucket, Model No. 207

EX $25   **NM** $50   **MIP** $150

Wrecker, 1962, white, 12L x 5.75W x 6.5H, crank-operated winch, plastic mirrors, wipers, and horns, Model No. 302

EX $50   **NM** $75   **MIP** $200

American Airlines Sky Chef, 1962, blue and white, 12.5L x 5.25W x 7H, lever lifts cargo box w/scissors lift mechanism, Model No. 303

EX $75   **NM** $100   **MIP** $225

Deluxe Camper, 1962, green and yellow, 21.5L x 4.5W x 6.5H, #203 plus boat and trailer, Model No. 304

EX $75   **NM** $100   **MIP** $225

Power Shovel, 1962, yellow, 26.5L x 7.5W x 7H, rubber tracks, Model No. 305

EX $25   **NM** $75   **MIP** $150

Fire Rescue Truck, 1962, red, 12L x 5.75W x 5.25H, plastic hose reel w/braided hose, two ladders, Model No. 307

EX $25   **NM** $75   **MIP** $150

Deluxe Dump Truck, 1962, yellow and red, 11.75L x 5.5W x 5.75H, lever operates dump box, Model No. 309

EX $25   **NM** $75   **MIP** $150

Sportsman, 1962, red and white, 13.25L x 5.25W x 5.5H, scarce, white plastic "Sportsman" camper top, Model No. 311

EX $75   **NM** $150   **MIP** $350

Livestock Truck, 1962, red and white, 14.75L x 6.25W x 5.5H, white metal stake panels, Model No. 312

EX $50   **NM** $75   **MIP** $200

Road Grader, 1962, yellow, 19L x 7.5W x 8H, covered cab, plated blade, black plastic tires, Model No. 400

EX $25   **NM** $35   **MIP** $125

Giant Bulldozer, 1962, orange, 11.5L x 7W x 5H, levers operate blade, rubber tracks, Model No. 405

EX $35   **NM** $55   **MIP** $150

Timber Toter, 1962, red, 23L x 5.5W x 6H, six wooden logs and chains, Model No. 406

EX $25   **NM** $55   **MIP** $125

Hydraulic Dumper, 1962, green, 13.75L x 5.5W x 6.25H, hydraulic cylinder controls dump box, Model No. 407

EX $35   **NM** $55   **MIP** $150

Ready Mix Concrete Truck, 1962, red and white, 15.5L x 6.75W x 7.25H, axle driven gear operates barrel, Model No. 408

EX $35   **NM** $75   **MIP** $200

Nationwide Rental Truck & Trailer, 1962, green and yellow, 21L x 5.75W x 5.5H, scarce, same design as #311 plus tow behind trailer, Model No. 500

EX $75   **NM** $125   **MIP** $300

Dump Truck and Sandloader, 1962, yellow and red, 21.5L x 5.5W x 8.25H, crank-operated conveyer belt takes sand up to truck, Model No. 501

EX $55   **NM** $75   **MIP** $200

Auto Transport, 1962, yellow and green, 22L x 5.5W x 7H, two metal cars, one metal truck plus loading ramp, Model No. 502

EX $35   **NM** $75   **MIP** $200

Cattle Transport, 1962, yellow and green, 23.5L x 5.5W x 8H, green trailer w/yellow doors, Model No. 503

EX $35   **NM** $55   **MIP** $150

Farm Stake Truck & Horse Trailer, 1962, red and white, 23.25L x 6.25W x 6H, same as #312 plus tow behind trailer and four animals, Model No. 507

EX $35   **NM** $55   **MIP** $150

Deluxe Van Truck, 1962, blue and white, 25.5L x 6.5W x 8.5H, structo express w/rocketship on decals, Model No. 600

EX $35   **NM** $75   **MIP** $200

Hydraulic Sanitation Truck, 1962, gray and white, 18L x 6W x 8H, w/manual lift arm that dumps into body, Model No. 606

EX $55   **NM** $75   **MIP** $200

Ride-er Wrecker Truck, 1962, red and yellow, 23.5L x 7.5W x 10.25H, metal seat and crank-operated tow boom in box, Model No. 607

EX $55   **NM** $95   **MIP** $200

Grading Service Set, 1962, yellow and red, 25L x 6W x 5.75H, same truck as in #501 set plus #207 bulldozer on trailer, Model No. 701

EX $75   **NM** $95   **MIP** $200

Pumper, 1962, red, 19.5L x 7.25W x 6.5H, operating water tank and hose, two ladders, Model No. 708

EX $55   **NM** $75   **MIP** $200

Mobile Crane, 1962, yellow, 15.5L x 6.5W x 7.25H, double cranks control crane arm and clam bucket, Model No. 800

EX $55   **NM** $75   **MIP** $200

Giant Bulldozer Truck & Trailer, 1962, orange, 29L x 7.25W x 6.25H, Structo Construction Co. on decals, Model No. 850

EX $55   **NM** $75   **MIP** $200

Aerial Hook & Ladder, 1962, red, 30.75L x 6.25W x 6.25H, two metal ladders, crank-operated lift ladder, Model No. 902

EX $55   **NM** $75   **MIP** $200

Ride-er Fire Truck, 1962, red and white, 25.5L x 10.5W x 12.75H, crank siren on hood, trunk opens, Model No. 925

EX $55   **NM** $95   **MIP** $300

Nationwide Rental Truck & Trailer Set, 1962, green and yellow, scarce, same as #500 set plus larger open trailer, Model No. 904

EX $95   **NM** $155   **MIP** $400

Air Terminal Service Set, 1962, red and white, includes #195, #303, #307, Model No. 908

EX $95   **NM** $155   **MIP** $300

Highway Builder Set, 1962, varies, includes #207, #501 plus sand hopper and one barricade, Model No. 913

EX $95   **NM** $155   **MIP** $300

Farm Set, 1962, varies, includes #507, pick-up and trailer similar to nationwide set, Model No. 914

EX $55   **NM** $95   **MIP** $250

Road Builder Set, 1962, red and yellow, same as #913 set plus #400, Model No. 915

EX $125   **NM** $175   **MIP** $350

Paving Department, 1962, varies, same as #913 but #408 replaces sand loader trailer, Model No. 916

EX $125   **NM** $175   **MIP** $350

Little Miss Structo Washer/Dryer, 1963, teal, 7.25L x 8W x 10H, washes and spins, battery-operated, Model No. 16

EX $15   **NM** $35   **MIP** $100

Sand Hopper, 1963, chartreuse, 8.25L x 6W x 12H, goes w/construction sets, Model No. 190

EX $15   **NM** $25   **MIP** $100

Rampside Pick-Up, 1963, red, 10.5L x 4.5W x 5H, plastic bed liner and drop-down door in side of bed, Model No. 194

EX $35   **NM** $55   **MIP** $150

School Bus, 1963, yellow, 10.5L x 4.75W x 5H, steel body, plastic mirrors, wipers and horn, Model No. 196

EX $55   **NM** $95   **MIP** $200

The Army Cub, 1963, army green, 10.75L x 5W x 4.75H, windshield and tailgate raise and lower, yellow seat, no doors, Model No. 200

EX $25   **NM** $55   **MIP** $150

Camper, 1963, teal, 10.5L x 4.5W x 6.5H, rampside truck w/plastic camper in bed of truck, Model No. 203

EX $55   **NM** $75   **MIP** $150

Fisherman, 1963, teal, 21.5L x 4.5W x 5H, rampside truck towing boat and trailer, Model No. 204

EX $55   **NM** $75   **MIP** $200

Hi-Lift Bulldozer, 1963, chartreuse, 11.25L x 5.75W x 4H, scarce chartreuse color - only used in 1963 production year, Model No. 207

EX $55   **NM** $75   **MIP** $200

Cub Pick-Up, 1963, light blue, 10.75L x 5W x 5H, white plastic convertible roof, doors open, Model No. 250

EX $35   **NM** $55   **MIP** $150

Dump Truck, 1963, green, 11.75L x 5.5W x 5.75H, new cab - over design, plus steering wheel and seat detail, Model No. 300

EX $35   **NM** $55   **MIP** $150

Wrecker, 1963, white, 13L x 5.25W x 5.5H, door windows and interior detail, black metal boom arm, Model No. 301

EX $35   **NM** $55   **MIP** $150

Power Shovel, 1963, chartreuse, 26.5L x 7.25W x 7H, scarce chartreuse color - only used in 1963 production year, Model No. 305

EX $55   **NM** $75   **MIP** $200

Fire Rescue Truck, 1963, red, 12L x 5.75W x 5.25H, plastic hose reel w/braided hose, two ladders, Model No. 307

EX $35   **NM** $55   **MIP** $150

Pick-Up Truck, 1963, red, 13.25L x 5.25W x 5.5H, Model No. 311

EX $35   **NM** $55   **MIP** $125

Livetstock Truck, 1963, blue and white, 14.75L x 6.25W x 5.5H, white metal stake panels, Model No. 314

EX $35   **NM** $55   **MIP** $150

Cub Station Wagon, 1963, teal and white, 10.75L x 5W x 5H, same body as #250 but white plastic roof cover whole body, Model No. 325

EX $35   **NM** $55   **MIP** $150

The Cub Set, 1963, teal and white, 10.75L x 5W x 5H, converts to three variations w/#250 and #325 roofs, Model No. 350

EX $55   **NM** $95   **MIP** $200

Road Grader, 1963, chartreuse, 19L x 7.5W x 8H, scarce chartreuse color - only used in 1963 production year, Model No. 400

EX $55   **NM** $75   **MIP** $200

(Randy Prasse Photo)

Hydraulic Dumper, 1963, red, 13.75L x 5.5W x 6.25H, hydraulic cylinder controls dump box, Model No. 401

EX $35   **NM** $55   **MIP** $150

Auto Transport, 1963, metallic gold, 22L x 5.5W x 7H, one metal car, one metal truck plus loading ramp, Model No. 402

EX $35   **NM** $55   **MIP** $150

Cub Station Wagon & Horse Trailer, 1963, teal and white, 20.5L x 5.25W x 6H, same as #190 plus two wheel horse trailer and two horses, Model No. 403

EX $55   **NM** $75   **MIP** $200

Deluxe Camper, 1963, blue and white, 20L x 5W x 5H, same as #190 plus boat and trailer, Model No. 404

EX $35   **NM** $55   **MIP** $125

Giant Bulldozer, 1963, chartreuse, 11.5L x 7W x 5H, scarce chartreuse color - only used in 1963 production year, Model No. 405

EX $55   **NM** $95   **MIP** $200

Timber Toter, 1963, red, 23L x 5.5W x 6H, six wooden logs and chains, Model No. 406

EX $25   **NM** $35   **MIP** $125

Ready-Mix Concrete Truck, 1963, green and chartreuse, 15.5L x 6.75W x 7.25H, axle driven gear operates barrel, Model No. 408

EX $35   **NM** $55   **MIP** $150

Dump Truck and Sandloader, 1963, green and chartreuse, 21.5L x 5.5W x 8.25H, crank-operated conveyer belt takes sand up to truck, Model No. 409

EX $55   **NM** $75   **MIP** $200

Nationwide Rental Truck & Trailer, 1963, green and yellow, 21L x

5.75W x 5.5H, scarce, same design as #311 plus tow behind trailer, Model No. 500

EX $75   **NM** $125   **MIP** $300

Cattle Transport, 1963, red and red, 22.25L x 6.5W x 8H, new cab - over design, plus steering wheel and seat detail, Model No. 503

EX $35   **NM** $55   **MIP** $150

Deluxe Van Truck, 1963, red and white, 25.5L x 6.5W x 8.5H, white trailer w/red doors, Model No. 601

EX $35   **NM** $55   **MIP** $150

Hydraulic Sanitation Truck, 1963, blue and white, 18L x 6W x 8H, w/manual lift arm that dumps into body, Model No. 602

EX $35   **NM** $75   **MIP** $200

Hydraulic Trailer Dump, 1963, chartreuse, 20.75L x 6.25W x 5.75H, scarce chartreuse color - only used in 1963 production year, Model No. 603

EX $75   **NM** $95   **MIP** $250

Ride-er Dump Truck, 1963, red and white, 20L x 7.75W x 10.25H, metal seat in dump box, Model No. 605

EX $55   **NM** $75   **MIP** $200

Mobile Crane, 1963, chartreuse, 15.5L x 6.5W x 7.25H, scarce chartreuse color - only used in 1963 production year, Model No. 801

EX $55   **NM** $75   **MIP** $200

Aerial Hook & Ladder, 1963, red and red, 30.75L x 6.25W x 6.25H, two metal ladders, crank-operated lift ladder, Model No. 902

EX $55   **NM** $75   **MIP** $200

Nationwide Rental Truck & Trailer Set, 1963, green and yellow, scarce, same as #500 set plus larger open trailer, Model No. 904

EX $95   **NM** $155   **MIP** $400

Highway Builder Set, 1963, varies, includes #190 and #409, Model No. 913

EX $95   **NM** $155   **MIP** $300

Farm Set, 1963, teal and white, includes #314 w/trailer and #403, Model No. 914

EX $55   **NM** $95   **MIP** $250

Army Engineer's Set, 1963, army green, includes #190, #400, #409, all in army green, Model No. 915

EX $75   **NM** $125   **MIP** $300

Paving Department, 1963, varies, includes #190, #305, #400, #401, #408, Model No. 916

EX $125   **NM** $175   **MIP** $350

Ride-er Doodle Bug, 1963, yellow, 25.5L x 10.25W x 12.75H, same as ride-er fire truck from 1962, Model No. 925

EX $55   **NM** $95   **MIP** $250

Pickup, 1964, red and yellow, 8.75L x 3.5W x 3.5H, metal w/rubber tires, Model No. 100

EX $15   **NM** $25   **MIP** $100

Fire Rescue Truck, 1964, red, 8.75L x 3.5W x 3.5H, two plastic ladders, Model No. 105

EX $25   **NM** $35   **MIP** $125

Wrecker Truck, 1964, white and gray, 9.25L x 3.5W x 3.5H, w/metal tow boom and hook, Model No. 110

EX $15   **NM** $25   **MIP** $100

Vista Dome Army Truck, 1964, army green, 8.75L x 3.5W x 4H, clear plastic cover over bed, two plastic soldiers, Model No. 115

EX $15   **NM** $25   **MIP** $100

Vista Dome Livestock Truck, 1964, blue and yellow, 8.75L x 3.5W x 4H, clear plastic cover over bed, two plastic animals, Model No. 120

EX $15   **NM** $35   **MIP** $100

Automatic Dump Truck, 1964, copper, 8.75L x 3.5W x 4H, spring dump mechanism, Model No. 125

EX $15   **NM** $35   **MIP** $100

Vista Dome Kennel Truck, 1964, teal and yellow, 8.75L x 3.5W x 4H, clear plastic cover over bed, six plastic dogs, Model No. 130

EX $25   **NM** $35   **MIP** $100

Rampside Pick-Up, 1964, copper, 10.5L x 4.5W x 5H, plastic bed liner and drop-down door in side of bed, Model No. 194

EX $35   **NM** $55   **MIP** $150

The Army Cub, 1964, army green, 10.75L x 5W x 4.75H, tailgate and windshield raises and lowers, Model No. 200

EX $35   **NM** $55   **MIP** $150

Camper, 1964, teal and teal, 10.5L x 4.5W x 6.5H, plastic camper in truck bed, Model No. 203

EX $55   **NM** $75   **MIP** $200

Fisherman, 1964, teal and red, 20L x 4.5W x 6H, rampside pick-up towing plastic boat on trailer, Model No. 204

EX $55   **NM** $75   **MIP** $200

Hi-Lift Bulldozer, 1964, yellow and black, 11.25L x 5.75W x 4H, metal levers operate the bucket, Model No. 207

EX $15   **NM** $35   **MIP** $100

Cub Pick-Up, 1964, blue and white, 20.75L x 5W x 6H, white plastic convertible roof covers cab, doors open, Model No. 250

EX $15   **NM** $35   **MIP** $100

Dump Truck, 1964, green, 11.75L x 5.5W x 5.75H, cab-over design, plus steering wheel and seat detail, Model No. 300

EX $35   **NM** $55   **MIP** $150

Wrecker, 1964, white and black, 13.25L x 5.25W x 5.5H, door windows and interior detail, black metal boom arm, Model No. 301

EX $35   **NM** $55   **MIP** $150

Power Shovel, 1964, yellow, 26.5L x 7.25W x 7H, rubber tracks, two cranks operate boom and bucket, Model No. 305

EX $35   **NM** $55   **MIP** $150

Fire Rescue Truck, 1964, red, 12L x 5.75W x 5.25H, plastic hose reel w/braided hose, two ladders, Model No. 307

EX $35   **NM** $55   **MIP** $150

Pick-Up Truck, 1964, red, 13.25L x 5.25W x 5.5H, plastic window, yellow interior, whitewall tires, Model No. 311

EX $35   **NM** $55   **MIP** $125

Livestock Truck, 1964, blue and white, 14.75L x 6.25W x 5.5H, white metal stake panels, two plastic cows, Model No. 314

EX $35   **NM** $55   **MIP** $150

Vista Dome Troop Carrier, 1964, army green, 13.25L x 5.25W x 5.5H, clear plastic cover over bed, eight plastic soldiers, Model No. 315

EX $35   **NM** $55   **MIP** $150

Cub Station Wagon, 1964, teal and white, 10.75L x 5W x 5H, white plastic convertible roof cover body, doors open, Model No. 325

EX $35   **NM** $55   **MIP** $150

The Cub Set, 1964, teal and white, 10.75L x 5W x 5H, converts to three variations w/#250 and #325 roofs, Model No. 350

EX $55   **NM** $95   **MIP** $200

Road Grader, 1964, orange, 19L x 7.5W x 8.25H, plated scraper blade, black plastic wheels, and engine, Model No. 400

EX $15 **NM** $35 **MIP** $125

Hydraulic Dumper, 1964, copper, 13.75L x 5.5W x 6.25H, hydraulic cylinder controls dump box, Model No. 401

EX $25 **NM** $35 **MIP** $125

Auto Transport, 1964, red and yellow, 22L x 5.5W x 7H, includes one metal car and one metal truck and loading ramp, Model No. 402

EX $35 **NM** $55 **MIP** $150

Cub Station Wagon w/Horse Trailer, 1964, teal and white, 20.5L x 5.25W x 6H, #325 cub station wagon and trailer, two plastic horses, Model No. 403

EX $35 **NM** $55 **MIP** $150

Station Wagon w/Boat & Trailer, 1964, blue and red, 20L x 5W x 5H, cub station wagon (#325) towing plastic boat on trailer, Model No. 404

EX $55 **NM** $75 **MIP** $150

Giant Bulldozer, 1964, orange and black, 11.5L x 7W x 5H, blade raises and lowers w/lever controls, Model No. 405

EX $35 **NM** $55 **MIP** $125

Ready-Mix Concrete Truck, 1964, red and yellow, 15.5L x 6.75W x 7.25H, axle driven gear operates barrel, Model No. 408

EX $35 **NM** $55 **MIP** $150

U.S. Army Missile Launcher, 1964, army green, 17.25L x 6.5W x 7H, missile launcher on back, three missiles, two outriggers, Model No. 410

EX $35 **NM** $55 **MIP** $150

Army Engineers Dump & Sand Loader, 1964, army green, 21.5L x 5.5W x 8.25H, includes four plastic soldiers, Model No. 411

EX $35 **NM** $55 **MIP** $150

Vista Dome Horse Van, 1964, metallic gold, 21.75L x 5.5W x 6H, ramp on side and back of trailer, four plastic horses, Model No. 412

EX $35 **NM** $55 **MIP** $125

Cattle Transport, 1964, red and red, 22.25L x 6.5W x 8H, Model No. 503

EX $35 **NM** $55 **MIP** $125

Deluxe Van Truck, 1964, red and white, 25.5L x 6.5W x 8.5H, white trailer w/red doors, Model No. 601

EX $35 **NM** $55 **MIP** $150

Hydraulic Sanitation Truck, 1964, gray and white, 18L x 6W x 8H, w/manual lift arm that dumps into body, Model No. 602

EX $35 **NM** $75 **MIP** $200

Hydraulic Trailer Dump Truck, 1964, gray and orange, 20.75L x 6.25W x 5.75H, also available as "Scotch-O-Lass" private label-add $50, Model No. 603

EX $55 **NM** $75 **MIP** $150

Ride-er Dump Truck, 1964, red and white, 20L x 7W x 10.25H, metal seat in dump box, Model No. 605

EX $55 **NM** $75 **MIP** $200

Mobile Crane, 1964, orange, 15.5L x 6.5W x 7.25H, cranks control the boom and clam bucket, swivels, Model No. 801

EX $55 **NM** $75 **MIP** $200

Aerial Hook & Ladder, 1964, red and red, 30.75L x 6.25W x 6.25H, two metal ladders, crank-operated lift ladder, Model No. 902

EX $55 **NM** $75 **MIP** $200

Highway Builder Set, 1964, varies, includes #207, #300, sand hopper, sand loader, and barricade, Model No. 913

EX $95 **NM** $155 **MIP** $300

Farm Set, 1964, teal and white, five-piece set includes #314 and trailer, #250 cub pick-up and trailer, Model No. 914

EX $55 **NM** $95 **MIP** $250

U.S. Army Combat Set, 1964, army green, includes #315 and searchlight, #410, eight plastic soldiers, Model No. 920

EX $75 **NM** $95 **MIP** $300

Ride-er Doodle Bug, 1964, yellow, 25.5L x 10.25W x 12.75H, Model No. 925

EX $55 **NM** $95 **MIP** $250

Pick-Up Truck, 1965, teal and white, 8.75L x 3.5W x 3.5H, metal w/rubber tires, Model No. 100

EX $15 **NM** $25 **MIP** $100

Fire Rescue Truck, 1965, red, 8.75L x 3.5W x 3.5H, two plastic ladders, Model No. 105

EX $25 **NM** $35 **MIP** $125

Wrecker Truck, 1965, red and white, 9.25L x 3.5W x 3.5H, w/metal tow boom and hook, Model No. 110

EX $15 **NM** $25 **MIP** $100

Vista Dome Army Truck, 1965, army green, 8.75L x 3.5W x 4H, clear plastic cover over bed, two plastic soldiers, Model No. 115

EX $15 **NM** $25 **MIP** $100

Automatic Dump Truck, 1965, green and yellow, 8.75L x 3.5W x 4H, spring dump mechanism, Model No. 125

EX $15 **NM** $35 **MIP** $100

Vista Dome Kennel Truck, 1965, blue and white, 8.75L x 3.5W x 4H, clear plastic cover over bed, six plastic dogs, Model No. 130

EX $25 **NM** $35 **MIP** $100

Cement Mixer, 1965, red and white, 8.75L x 3.5W x 5H, axle driven gear operates barrel, Model No. 136

EX $25 **NM** $35 **MIP** $125

Road Grader, 1965, orange and black, 11.75L x 4W x 4H, new z-z-z sound when unit rolls, no batteries, Model No. 140

EX $15 **NM** $35 **MIP** $100

Van Truck, 1965, red and white, 16.5L x 4W x 5H, red Structo Van Line decals on side, Model No. 145

EX $25 **NM** $35 **MIP** $125

Cattle Truck, 1965, green and white, 16.5L x 4W x 5H, white plastic insert panels in side of trailer, Model No. 150

EX $25 **NM** $35 **MIP** $125

Kompak Assortment, 1965, varies, three-piece set includes #100, #105, #110, Model No. 170

EX $55 **NM** $75 **MIP** $200

Contractor Set, 1965, varies, three-piece set includes #125, #136, #140, Model No. 180

EX $55 **NM** $75 **MIP** $200

Rampside Pick-Up, 1965, copper, 10.5L x 4.5W x 5H, plastic bed liner and drop-down door in side of bed, Model No. 194

EX $15 **NM** $35 **MIP** $125

The Army Cub, 1965, army green, 10.75L x 5W x 4.75H, tailgate and windshield raises and lowers, Model No. 200

EX $35 **NM** $55 **MIP** $150

Camper, 1965, teal and white, 10.5L x 4.5W x 6.5H, plastic camper in truck bed, Model No. 203

EX $35 **NM** $55 **MIP** $150

Fisherman, 1965, teal and red, 20L x 4.5W x 5H, rampside pick-up towing plastic boat on trailer, Model No. 204

EX $35 **NM** $55 **MIP** $150

Hi-Lift Bulldozer, 1965, yellow and black, 11.25L x 5.75W x 4H, metal levers operate the bucket, Model No. 207

EX $15 **NM** $35 **MIP** $100

Cub Pick-Up, 1965, blue and white, 20.75L x 5W x 6H, white plastic convertible roof covers cab, doors open, Model No. 250

EX $15   **NM** $35   **MIP** $100

Wrecker Truck, 1965, white and red, 10.75L x 4.75W x 5.75H, red convertible roof, seats and metal boom arm, Model No. 251

EX $35   **NM** $55   **MIP** $150

Riding Academy, 1965, teal and teal, 20L x 4.75W x 6H, #250 cub pick-up plus horse trailer, two plastic horses, Model No. 252

EX $35   **NM** $55   **MIP** $150

Dump Truck, 1965, metallic green, 11.75L x 5.5W x 5.75H, cab - over design, plus steering wheel and seat detail, Model No. 300

EX $25   **NM** $35   **MIP** $125

Wrecker Truck, 1965, white and red, 12.5L x 5.25W x 6.25H, red light on roof (non-operable), red metal boom arm, Model No. 302

EX $35   **NM** $55   **MIP** $150

Camper w/Boat & Trailer, 1965, teal and red, 20L x 4.5W x 6.5H, #203 w/plastic boat on trailer, Model No. 304

EX $35   **NM** $55   **MIP** $150

Power Shovel, 1965, orange, 26.5L x 7.25W x 7H, rubber tracks, two cranks operate boom and bucket, Model No. 305

EX $25   **NM** $35   **MIP** $125

Fire Rescue Truck, 1965, red, 13.25L x 5.75W x 5.75H, red light on roof (non-operable), two metal ladders, Model No. 308

EX $35   **NM** $55   **MIP** $150

Livestock Truck, 1965, blue and white, 14.75L x 6.25W x 5.5H, white stakes, five-piece plastic fence, four animals, Model No. 310

EX $35   **NM** $55   **MIP** $150

Vista Dome Troop Carrier, 1965, army green, 13.25L x 5.25W x 5.75H, clear plastic cover over bed, eight plastic soldiers, Model No. 315

EX $35   **NM** $55   **MIP** $150

Cub Station Wagon, 1965, teal and white, 10.75L x 5W x 5H, white plastic convertible roof cover body, doors open, Model No. 325

EX $50   **NM** $75   **MIP** $100

Road Grader, 1965, orange, 19L x 7.5W x 8.25H, plated scraper blade, black plastic wheels, and engine, Model No. 400

EX $15   **NM** $35   **MIP** $100

Hydraulic Dump Truck, 1965, red, 14L x 5.5W x 6.25H, hydraulic cylinder controls dump box, Model No. 401

EX $15   **NM** $35   **MIP** $100

Station Wagon w/Boat & Trailer, 1965, blue and red, 20L x 5W x 5H, cub station wagon (#325) towing plastic boat on trailer, Model No. 404

EX $25   **NM** $55   **MIP** $125

Giant Bulldozer, 1965, orange and black, 11.5L x 7W x 5H, blade raises and lowers w/lever controls, Model No. 405

EX $15   **NM** $35   **MIP** $100

Timber Toter, 1965, red and red, 23L x 6W x 5H, five wooden logs plus chains, Model No. 406

EX $15   **NM** $35   **MIP** $125

U.S. Army Missile Launcher, 1965, army green, 17.25L x 6.5W x 7H, missile launcher on back, three missiles, two outriggers, Model No. 410

EX $35   **NM** $55   **MIP** $125

Vista Dome Horse Van, 1965, teal and teal, 21.75L x 5.5W x 6H, ramp on side and back of trailer, four-piece fence, four plastic horses, Model No. 412

EX $35   **NM** $55   **MIP** $125

Car Carrier, 1965, teal and teal, 22L x 6W x 7H, new, two plastic cars (T-Birds) and loading ramp, Model No. 413

EX $35   **NM** $55   **MIP** $150

Hydraulic Dump Truck, 1965, gray and orange, 14L x 5.5W x 6.25H, hydraulic cylinder controls dump box, Model No. 425

EX $35   **NM** $55   **MIP** $125

Cement Mixer, 1965, gray and orange, 14L x 6.75W x 5.25H, axle driven gear operates barrel, Model No. 450

EX $35   **NM** $55   **MIP** $125

Livestock Set, 1965, teal and white, 22.25L x 6.5W x 8H, white insert panels in side of trailer, five-piece fence and four animals, Model No. 505

EX $35   **NM** $55   **MIP** $150

Van Truck, 1965, red and white, 22L x 6.5W x 8H, red Structo Van Line decals on side, Model No. 506

EX $35   **NM** $55   **MIP** $125

Deluxe Van Truck, 1965, red and white, 25.5L x 6W x 8.75H, white trailer w/red doors, Model No. 601

EX $35   **NM** $55   **MIP** $150

Hydraulic Trailer Dump Truck, 1965, gray and orange, 20.75L x 5.75W x 5.75H, also available as "Scotch-O-Lass" private label - add $50, Model No. 603

EX $55   **NM** $75   **MIP** $150

Hydraulic Sanitation Truck, 1965, gray and white, 18L x 6W x 8H, w/manual lift arm that dumps into body, Model No. 604

EX $35   **NM** $75   **MIP** $200

Ride-er Dump Truck, 1965, teal and white, 20L x 7W x 10.25H, metal seat in dump box, Model No. 605

EX $55   **NM** $75   **MIP** $200

Weekender, 1965, teal and white, 12L x 5.75W x 7H, canvas awning, white plastic interior, Model No. 700

EX $35   **NM** $55   **MIP** $150

U.S. Mail Van, 1965, white and blue, 12L x 5.75W x 6.5H, includes two plastic mail bags, Model No. 710

EX $35   **NM** $55   **MIP** $150

Mobile Crane, 1965, orange, 16.5L x 5.5W x 7H, cranks control the boom and clam bucket, swivels, Model No. 801

EX $35   **NM** $55   **MIP** $150

Aerial Hook & Ladder, 1965, red and red, 30.75L x 6.25W x 6.25H, two metal ladders, crank-operated lift ladder, Model No. 900

EX $35   **NM** $75   **MIP** $150

Highway Builder Set, 1965, varies, includes #207, #300, sand hopper, sand loader, and barricade, Model No. 913

EX $95   **NM** $155   **MIP** $300

Highway Builder Set Showcase Display, 1965, rare, boxed set for dealer trade show and store display, Model No. 9130

EX n/a   **NM** n/a   **MIP** $500

Farm Set, 1965, teal and white, five-piece set includes #310 and trailer, #250 cub pick-up and trailer, Model No. 914

EX $55   **NM** $95   **MIP** $250

Farm Set Showcase Display, 1965, rare, boxed set for dealer trade show and store display, Model No. 9140

EX n/a   **NM** n/a   **MIP** $500

U.S. Army Combat Set, 1965, army green, includes #315 and searchlight, #410, eight plastic soldiers, Model No. 920

EX $75   **NM** $95   **MIP** $300

U.S. Army Combat Set Showcase Display, 1965, rare, boxed set for dealer trade show and store display, Model No. 9201

EX n/a   **NM** n/a   **MIP** $500

Ride-er Doodle Bug, 1965, teal and white, 25.5L x 10.25W x 12.75H, Model No. 925

EX $55   **NM** $95   **MIP** $250

Pickup Truck, 1966, teal, 8.75L x 3.5W x 3.5H, Kom-pak design, Model No. 100

EX $15   **NM** $25   **MIP** $60

Fire Rescue Truck, 1966, red, 8.75L x 3.5W x 3.5H, Kom-pak design w/two ladders, Model No. 105

EX $25   **NM** $55   **MIP** $125

Wrecker Truck, 1966, yellow and red, 9.25L x 3.5W x 3.5H, Kom-pak design w/red boom arm, Model No. 110

EX $15   **NM** $25   **MIP** $60

Army Troop Carrier, 1966, army green, 8.75L x 3.5W x 4H, Kom-pak design w/clear plastic cover $2 soldiers, Model No. 115

EX $15   **NM** $25   **MIP** $60

All Steel Dump Truck, 1966, gray and orange, 8.75L x 3.5W x 4H, Kom-pak design, Model No. 125

EX $15   **NM** $25   **MIP** $60

Kennel Truck, 1966, teal and white, 8.75L x 3.5W x 4H, Kom-pak design w/clear cover and six dogs, Model No. 130

EX $15   **NM** $25   **MIP** $100

Cement Mixer, 1966, gray and orange, 9.75L x 4W x 4.5H, Kom-pak design w/dumping barrel, Model No. 136

EX $15   **NM** $25   **MIP** $60

Road Grader, 1966, orange, 11.75L x 5W x 4.75H, Kom-pak design, Model No. 140

EX $15   **NM** $25   **MIP** $60

Van Truck, 1966, red and white, 16.5L x 4W x 5.25H, Kom-pak design, Model No. 145

EX $25   **NM** $35   **MIP** $100

Cattle Truck, 1966, teal and white, 16.5L x 4W x 5.25H, Kom-pak design white insert panels in side of trailer, Model No. 150

EX $25   **NM** $35   **MIP** $100

Contractor Set, 1966, gray and orange, three-piece Kom-pak set includes #125, #136, #140, Model No. 180

EX $55   **NM** $75   **MIP** $150

Rampside Pick-Up, 1966, red, 10.5L x 4.5W x 5H, plastic bed liner and drop-down door in side of bed, Model No. 194

EX $25   **NM** $35   **MIP** $100

The Army Cub, 1966, army green, 10.75L x 5W x 4.75H, tailgate and windshield raises and lowers, Model No. 200

EX $35   **NM** $55   **MIP** $125

Camper, 1966, light blue and white, 10.5L x 4.5W x 6.5H, plastic camper in truck bed, Model No. 203

EX $35   **NM** $55   **MIP** $150

Fisherman, 1966, light blue and red, 20L x 4.5W x 5H, rampside pick-up towing plastic boat on trailer, Model No. 204

EX $35   **NM** $55   **MIP** $150

Hi-Lift Bulldozer, 1966, orange and black, 11.25L x 5.75W x 4H, metal levers operate the bucket, Model No. 207

EX $25   **NM** $35   **MIP** $100

Wrecker Truck, 1966, white and black, 10.75L x 4.75W x 5.75H, black convertible roof and boom, red seat, Model No. 251

EX $35   **NM** $55   **MIP** $150

Riding Academy, 1966, teal and teal, 18L x 4.75W x 6H, #194 rampside pick-up plus horse trailer, two plastic horses, Model No. 254

EX $35   **NM** $55   **MIP** $150

Dump Truck, 1966, red, 11.75L x 5.5W x 5.75H, spring dump mechanism, Model No. 300

EX $25   **NM** $35   **MIP** $125

Power Shovel, 1966, orange, 26.5L x 7.25W x 7H, rubber tracks, two cranks operate boom and bucket, Model No. 305

EX $25   **NM** $35   **MIP** $125

Livestock Truck Set, 1966, teal and white, 14.75L x 6.25W x 5.5H, white stakes, five-piece plastic fence, two plastic cows, Model No. 310

EX $35   **NM** $55   **MIP** $150

Wrecker, 1966, white and red, 12.5L x 5.25W x 6.25H, red light on roof (non-operable), red interior and boom, Model No. 312

EX $35   **NM** $55   **MIP** $125

Fire Rescue Truck, 1966, red, 12.75L x 5.75W x 5.75H, red light on roof (non-operable) three ladders, sim. hose reel, Model No. 313

EX $35   **NM** $55   **MIP** $150

Vista Dome Troop Carrier, 1966, army green, 13.25L x 5.25W x 5.75H, clear plastic cover over bed, six plastic soldiers, Model No. 315

EX $35   **NM** $55   **MIP** $150

Dump Truck, 1966, green and yellow, 13.5L x 5.5W x 5.75H, lever action dump box, Model No. 316

EX $25   **NM** $35   **MIP** $100

Station Wagon, 1966, teal and white, 10.75L x 5W x 5H, white plastic convertible roof cover body, doors open, Model No. 325

EX $15   **NM** $35   **MIP** $100

Road Grader, 1966, orange, 19L x 7.5W x 8.25H, plated scraper blade, black plastic wheels and engine, Model No. 400

EX $15   **NM** $35   **MIP** $100

Giant Bulldozer, 1966, orange and black, 11.5L x 7W x 5H, blade raises and lowers w/lever controls, Model No. 405

EX $15   **NM** $35   **MIP** $125

Timber Toter, 1966, red and red, 23L x 6W x 5H, six wooden logs and chains, Model No. 406

EX $15   **NM** $35   **MIP** $125

Vista Dome Horse Van, 1966, metallic blue, 21.75L x 6W x 6H, two ramp doors and two horses, two colts, Model No. 417

EX $35   **NM** $55   **MIP** $125

Car Carrier, 1966, gray and yellow, 22.25L x 6W x 7H, three plastic cars (Mustangs & T-Birds) loading ramp, Model No. 418

EX $35   **NM** $55   **MIP** $150

Hydraulic Dump Truck, 1966, metallic blue, 13.75L x 5.5W x 6.25H, same body style as #316 but w/hydraulic dump control, Model No. 419

EX $35   **NM** $55   **MIP** $125

Hydraulic Dump Truck, 1966, gray and orange, 13.75L x 5.5W x 6.25H, hydraulic cylinder dumps box, POW-R-R-R sound, Model No. 425

EX $35   **NM** $55   **MIP** $125

Cement Mixer, 1966, gray and orange, 15.5L x 6.75W x 5.25H, axle driven gear operates barrel, POW-R-R-R sound, Model No. 450

EX $35   **NM** $55   **MIP** $125

Bulldozer & Earth Mover, 1966, green and yellow, 25.5L x 7.5W x 7H, combination bulldozer towing bottom dump earth mover unit, Model No. 460

EX $55   **NM** $75   **MIP** $150

Bulldozer & Scraper, 1966, green and yellow, 25.5L x 7.5W x 7H, combination bulldozer towing scraper unit, Model No. 461

EX $55   NM $75   MIP $150

Livestock Van, 1966, teal and white, 22.25L x 6.5W x 8H, white insert panels in side of trailer, five-piece fence, and four animals, Model No. 505

EX $35   NM $55   MIP $150

Van Truck, 1966, dark. blue and light blue, 22L x 6.5W x 8H, scarce two-tone blue color combination, Model No. 506

EX $35   NM $55   MIP $150

Hydraulic Sanitation Truck, 1966, gray and white, 18L x 6W x 8H, manual lift bucket dumps into body, POW-R-R-R sound, Model No. 604

EX $35   NM $55   MIP $150

Ride-er Dump Truck, 1966, white and green, 20L x 7W x 10.25H, metal seat in dump box, Model No. 605

EX $55   NM $75   MIP $200

Deluxe Van Truck, 1966, red and silver, 24L x 6W x 8.75H, unpainted steel trailer w/"Structo Freught Lines" decal, Model No. 609

EX $35   NM $55   MIP $150

Hydraulic Trailer Dump Truck, 1966, gray and orange, 21.5L x 5.75W x 5.75H, turbine cab, hydraulic controlled dump, Model No. 610

EX $35   NM $55   MIP $125

Weekender, 1966, teal and white, 12L x 5.75W x 7H, canvas awning, white plastic interior, Model No. 700

EX $35   NM $55   MIP $150

U.S. Mail Van, 1966, blue and white, 12L x 5.75W x 6.5H, includes two cloth mail bags, Model No. 710

EX $35   NM $55   MIP $150

Ice Cream Truck, 1966, white and teal, 12L x 6W x 6.5H, scarce, bell rings as truck moves, built-in coolers, and detail, Model No. 712

EX $55   NM $75   MIP $250

Police Emergency Truck, 1966, blue and white, 12L x 6W x 7.5H, bell rings as truck moves, three ladders, hose reel, Model No. 716

EX $55   NM $75   MIP $150

Mobile Crane, 1966, orange, 16.5L x 5.5W x 7H, cranks control the boom and clam bucket, swivels, Model No. 801

EX $35   NM $55   MIP $150

Aerial Hook & Ladder, 1966, red and white, 29.25L x 6.25W x 6.25H, two metal ladders, crank-operated lift ladder, Model No. 901

EX $55   NM $75   MIP $200

Highway Builder Set, 1966, green and yellow, four-piece set, includes #207, #316, sand hopper, and sand loader, Model No. 910

EX $95   NM $155   MIP $300

Display For Highway Set, 1966, rare, boxed set for dealer trade show and store display, Model No. 9101

EX n/a   NM n/a   MIP $500

Ride-er Chief's Car, 1966, red and white, 25.5L x 10.25W x 12.75H, bell rings when string is pulled, Model No. 921

EX $75   NM $95   MIP $250

Farm Set, 1966, green and yellow, five-piece set includes #194 and trailer, #310 and trailer, four animals, Model No. 937

EX $75   NM $95   MIP $250

Display For Farm Set, 1966, rare, boxed set for dealer trade show and store display, Model No. 9371

EX n/a   NM n/a   MIP $500

State Fair Set, 1966, metallic blue, four-piece set includes #203, #310, #417, six animals, Model No. 952

EX $95   NM $155   MIP $300

Display For State Fair Set, 1966, rare, boxed set for dealer trade show and store display, Model No. 9521

EX n/a   NM n/a   MIP $500

Pickup, 1967, green, 8.75L x 3.5W x 3.5H, Kom-pak design, Model No. 101

EX $15   NM $25   MIP $60

Wrecker Truck, 1967, white and gray, 9.25L x 3.5W x 3.5H, Kom-pak design w/red boom arm, Model No. 112

EX $15   NM $25   MIP $60

Fire Rescue Truck, 1967, red, 8.75L x 3.5W x 3.5H, Kom-pak design w/two ladders, Model No. 121

EX $25   NM $35   MIP $125

Green Beret Truck, 1967, green, 8.75L x 3.5W x 4H, Kom-pak design w/clear plastic cover $2 soldiers, Model No. 126

EX $25   NM $35   MIP $125

Kennel Truck, 1967, yellow, 8.75L x 3.5W x 4H, Kom-pak design w/clear cover and six dogs, Model No. 137

EX $15   NM $25   MIP $60

Steel Dump Truck, 1967, gray and orange, 8.75L x 3.5W x 4H, Kom-pak design, Model No. 141

EX $15   NM $25   MIP $60

Cement Mixer, 1967, gray and orange, 9.75L x 4W x 4.5H, Kom-pak design w/dumping barrel, Model No. 153

EX $15   NM $25   MIP $60

Tractor Trailer Truck, 1967, red and silver, 16.5L x 4W x 5.25H, Kom-pak design, no decals on trailer, Model No. 160

EX $25   NM $35   MIP $125

Mobile Merry-Go-Round Truck, 1967, yellow and red, 9.25L x 4.25W x 5.75H, scarce, Kom-pak design, circus carousel spins when truck moves, Model No. 174

EX $55   NM $75   MIP $200

Kenya Karryall, 1967, green and yellow, 9.25L x 4.25W x 4.25H, scarce, Kom-pak design, four cages w/four hand-painted wild animals, Model No. 176

EX $55   NM $75   MIP $200

Sanitation Truck, 1967, gray and white, 11.5L x 3.5W x 5H, Kom-pak design, bucket dumps into body, Model No. 178

EX $25   NM $35   MIP $125

Road Grader, 1967, orange, 11.75L x 5W x 4.75H, Kom-pak design, Model No. 183

EX $15   NM $25   MIP $60

Contractor Set, 1967, gray and orange, three-piece set includes #141, #153, #183, Model No. 192

EX $55   NM $75   MIP $200

Highway Department Set, 1967, red and yellow, four-piece set includes emergency, dump, wrecker, and pickup trucks, Model No. 197

EX $55   NM $75   MIP $200

Wrecker Truck, 1967, white and black, 10.75L x 4.75W x 5.75H, black convertible roof and boom, red seat, Model No. 205

EX $35   NM $55   MIP $125

Fisherman, 1967, white and red, 20L x 5W x 4.75H, jeep towing plastic boat and trailer, no doors on jeep, Model No. 210

EX $35   NM $55   MIP $150

Rampside Pick-Up, 1967, red, 10.5L x 4.5W x 5H, plastic bed liner and drop-down door in side of bed, Model No. 230

EX $25   NM $35   MIP $100

Camper Truck, 1967, light blue and dark blue, 10.5L x 4.5W x 6.5H, dark blue rampside truck w/light blue plastic cover, Model No. 235

EX $15   NM $25   MIP $60

Livestock Truck, 1967, red and yellow, 14.75L x 3.25W x 5.5H, yellow metal panels, Model No. 260

EX $15   NM $25   MIP $60

Sanitation Truck, 1967, green and white, 18L x 6W x 8H, lever action trash bucket dumps into box, Model No. 266

EX $25   NM $35   MIP $100

Dump Truck, 1967, red, 13.5L x 5.5W x 5.75H, lever controls dump action, Model No. 303

EX $15   NM $25   MIP $100

Hydraulic Dump Truck, 1967, red and yellow, 13.5L x 5.5W x 6.25H, hydraulic controlled dump box, Model No. 309

EX $25   NM $35   MIP $125

Hydraulic Dump Truck, 1967, yellow and green, 12L x 6W x 6H, turbine cab. hydraulic controlled dump, Model No. 319

EX $25   NM $35   MIP $125

Vista Dome Horse Van, 1967, metallic gold, 21.75L x 6W x 6H, two ramp doors and two horses, two colts, Model No. 322

EX $35   NM $55   MIP $125

Car Carrier, 1967, red and yellow, 22.25L x 6W x 7H, three plastic cars (Mustangs & T-Birds) loading ramp, Model No. 331

EX $35   NM $55   MIP $150

Livestock Van, 1967, teal and white, 21.25L x 7.75W x 5.75H, turbine cab, white panels on side of trailer, Model No. 344

EX $25   NM $35   MIP $125

Timber Toter, 1967, red and red, 20.75L x 6.5W x 5.5H, turbine cab., five wooden logs and chains, Model No. 360

EX $25   NM $35   MIP $100

Snorkel Utility Truck, 1967, green and yellow, 21L x 6.5W x 5.5H, hydraulic snorkel book and plastic bucket, outriggers, Model No. 380

EX $35   NM $55   MIP $150

Aerial Hook & Ladder, 1967, red and red, 29.25L x 6.25W x 6.25H, two metal ladders, crank-operated lift ladder, Model No. 381

EX $35   NM $55   MIP $150

Wrecker Truck, 1967, white, 12.5L x 5.25W x 6.25H, red light (non-operable) on roof, POW-R-R-R sound, Model No. 415

EX $25   NM $35   MIP $125

Hydraulic Dump Truck, 1967, gray and yellow, 12.75L x 6W x 6H, hydraulic dump box, POW-R-R-R sound, Model No. 423

EX $25   NM $35   MIP $125

Cement Mixer, 1967, gray and orange, 16.5L x 6.5W x 7.5H, axle driven gear operates barrel, POW-R-R-R sound, Model No. 432

EX $25   NM $35   MIP $125

Fire Rescue Truck, 1967, red, 12.75L x 5.75W x 5.75H, turbine cab. lever operated ladder, Model No. 453

EX $25   NM $35   MIP $125

Snorkel Fire Truck, 1967, red, 21L x 6.5W x 8H, same design as #380, Model No. 466

EX $35   NM $55   MIP $150

Hydraulic Sanitation Truck, 1967, gray and white, 16.5L x 5.75W x 7.75H, manual lift bucket dumps into body, POW-R-R-R sound, Model No. 474

EX $25   NM $35   MIP $125

Tractor Trailer Truck, 1967, red and red, 21.25L x 7.75W x 5.75H, turbine cab. red, white and blue "Structo" decal on trailer, Model No. 483

EX $25   NM $35   MIP $125

Auto Transporter, 1967, red and yellow, 28.25L x 5.75W x 5.5H, large, open car carrier, ramps adjust, three plastic cars, Model No. 492

EX $55   NM $75   MIP $200

Hi-Lift Bulldozer, 1967, orange and black, 11.25L x 5.75W x 4H, metal levers operate the bucket, Model No. 501

EX $25   NM $35   MIP $100

Giant Bulldozer, 1967, orange and black, 11.5L x 7W x 5H, blade raises and lowers w/lever controls, Model No. 514

EX $25   NM $35   MIP $125

Road Grader, 1967, orange, 19L x 7.5W x 8H, plated scraper blade, black plastic wheels and engine, Model No. 527

EX $15   NM $35   MIP $125

Bulldozer & Earth Mover, 1967, green and yellow, 24.5L x 6.5W x 5.75H, combination bulldozer towing bottom dump earth mover unit, Model No. 574

EX $35   NM $55   MIP $150

Weekender, 1967, teal, 12L x 5.75W x 6.5H, molded built-in refrigerator and sink detail, Model No. 708

EX $35   NM $55   MIP $150

Police Emergency Truck, 1967, blue and white, 12L x 6W x 7.5H, bell rings as truck moves, three ladders, hose reel, Model No. 727

EX $35   NM $55   MIP $150

Highway Builder Set, 1967, green and yellow, four-piece set includes #183, #303, #501 and sand hopper, Model No. 909

EX $55   NM $75   MIP $200

Heavy Construction Set, 1967, red and yellow, four-piece set includes #303, #432, #514 and barricade, Model No. 941

EX $55   NM $75   MIP $200

Pickup, 1968, teal, 8.75L x 3.5W x 3.5H, Kom-pak design, Model No. 101

EX $15   NM $25   MIP $60

Wrecker Truck, 1968, white and red, 9.25L x 3.5W x 3.5H, Kom-pak design w/red boom arm, Model No. 112

EX $15   NM $25   MIP $60

Fire Rescue Truck, 1968, red, 8.75L x 3.5W x 3.5H, Kom-pak design w/two ladders, Model No. 121

EX $25   NM $35   MIP $100

Kennel Truck, 1968, yellow, 8.75L x 3.5W x 4H, Kom-pak design w/clear cover and six dogs, Model No. 137

EX $25   NM $35   MIP $100

Steel Dump Truck, 1968, red and yellow, 8.75L x 3.5W x 4H, Kom-pak design, Model No. 141

EX $15   NM $25   MIP $60

Cement Mixer, 1968, gray and orange, 9.75L x 4W x 4.5H, Kom-pak design w/dumping barrel, Model No. 153

EX $15   NM $25   MIP $60

Tractor Trailer Truck, 1968, red and silver, 16.5L x 4W x 5.25H, Kom-pak design, w/"National Freight Lines" decal on trailer, Model No. 160

EX $25   NM $55   MIP $125

Kom-pak Pony Van, 1968, teal and teal, 16.5L x 3.5W x 4.5H, clear roof on trailer w/coral and three ponies, Model No. 163

EX $25   NM $35   MIP $125

Mobile Merry-Go-Round Truck, 1968, yellow and red, 9.25L x 4.25W x 5.75H, scarce, Kom-pak design, circus carousel spins when truck moves, Model No. 174

EX $55   NM $75   MIP $200

Air Force Truck, 1968, blue, 8.75L x 3.5W x 4H, scarce, Kom-pak design w/clear cover on bed, four blue soldiers, Model No. 175

EX $55   **NM** $75   **MIP** $150

Kenya Karryall, 1968, green and yellow, 9.25L x 4.25W x 4.25H, scarce, Kom-pak design, four cages w/four hand-painted wild animals, Model No. 176

EX $55   **NM** $75   **MIP** $200

Sanitation Truck, 1968, gray and white, 11.5L x 3.5W x 5H, Kom-pak design, bucket dumps into body, Model No. 178

EX $25   **NM** $35   **MIP** $100

Kom-pak Sandy, 1968, green and yellow, 8.75L x 3.5W x 3.5H, Kom-pak design w/plastic sand hopper, Model No. 184

EX $25   **NM** $35   **MIP** $100

Kom-pak Contractor Set, 1968, green and yellow, four-piece set includes #153, #183, #184, Model No. 193

EX $55   **NM** $75   **MIP** $150

Kom-pak Animal Set, 1968, teal and white, four-piece set includes #137, #163, six dogs, four ponies, and fence coral, Model No. 196

EX $35   **NM** $55   **MIP** $150

Wrecker Truck, 1968, white and black, 10.75L x 4.75W x 5.75H, black convertible roof and boom, red seat, Model No. 205

EX $35   **NM** $55   **MIP** $125

Sea Sprite, 1968, white and red, 23.5L x 5W x 5.25H, jeep towing "Johnson Reveler" model boat on trailer, Model No. 211

EX $35   **NM** $55   **MIP** $150

Rampside Pick-Up, 1968, red, 10.5L x 4.5W x 5H, plastic bed liner and drop-down door in side of bed, Model No. 230

EX $25   **NM** $35   **MIP** $100

Camper Truck, 1968, light blue and dark blue, 10.5L x 4.5W x 6.5H, dark blue rampside truck w/light blue plastic camper, Model No. 235

EX $15   **NM** $25   **MIP** $60

Livestock Truck, 1968, red and yellow, 14.75L x 3.25W x 5.5H, yellow metal panels, Model No. 260

EX $15   **NM** $25   **MIP** $60

Wrecker Truck, 1968, red, 15L x 5.5W x 6.25H, white boom arm, red light (non-operable) on roof, Model No. 264

EX $35   **NM** $55   **MIP** $125

Sanitation Truck, 1968, green and white, 18L x 6W x 8H, lever action trash bucket dumps into box, Model No. 266

EX $25   **NM** $35   **MIP** $100

Hydraulic Sanitation Truck, 1968, gray and white, 16.5L x 5.75W x 7.75H, manual lift bucket dumps into body, Model No. 268

EX $35   **NM** $55   **MIP** $150

Cement Mixer, 1968, red and yellow, 16.5L x 6.5W x 7.5H, axle driven gear operates barrel, Model No. 270

EX $35   **NM** $55   **MIP** $125

Hydraulic Cement Mixer, 1968, green and yellow, 16.5L x 6.5W x 7.5H, same as #270 but w/hydraulic dump action on barrel, Model No. 271

EX $35   **NM** $55   **MIP** $125

Dump Truck, 1968, red, 13.5L x 5.5W x 5.75H, lever controls dump action, Model No. 303

EX $15   **NM** $35   **MIP** $100

Super Sandy Set, 1968, yellow and green, 13.5L x 5.5W x 5.75H, dump truck and large plastic sand hopper, Model No. 306

EX $25   **NM** $55   **MIP** $125

Hydraulic Dump Truck, 1968, red and yellow, 13.5L x 5.5W x 6.25H, hydraulic controlled dump box, Model No. 309

EX $15   **NM** $35   **MIP** $100

Hydraulic Dump Truck, 1968, yellow and green, 12L x 6W x 6H, turbine cab. hydraulic controlled dump, Model No. 319

EX $25   **NM** $55   **MIP** $125

Vista Dome Horse Van, 1968, metallic gold, 21.75L x 6W x 6H, two ramp doors and two horses, two colts, Model No. 322

EX $35   **NM** $55   **MIP** $125

Car Carrier, 1968, red and yellow, 22.25L x 6W x 7H, three plastic cars (Mustangs and T-Birds) loading ramp, Model No. 331

EX $35   **NM** $55   **MIP** $150

Livestock Van, 1968, teal and white, 21.25L x 7.75W x 5.75H, turbine cab. white panels on side of trailer, Model No. 344

EX $25   **NM** $35   **MIP** $125

Timber Toter, 1968, blue and blue, 20.75L x 6.5W x 5.5H, turbine cab, five wooden logs and chains, Model No. 360

EX $25   **NM** $35   **MIP** $100

Snorkel Utility Truck, 1968, green and yellow, 21L x 6.5W x 5.5H, hydraulic snorkel book and plastic bucket, outriggers, Model No. 380

EX $35   **NM** $55   **MIP** $150

Aerial Hook & Ladder, 1968, red and red, 29.25L x 6.25W x 6.25H, two metal ladders, crank lift ladder "9" decal on side, Model No. 381

EX $35   **NM** $55   **MIP** $150

Police Emergency Truck, 1968, blue and white, 12L x 6W x 7.5H, bell rings as truck moves, three ladders, hose reel, Model No. 727

EX $35   **NM** $55   **MIP** $150

Wrecker Truck, 1968, white, 12.5L x 5.25W x 6.25H, red light (non-operable) on roof, POW-R-R-R sound, Model No. 415

EX $25   **NM** $35   **MIP** $125

Hydraulic Dump Truck, 1968, gray and orange, 12.75L x 6W x 6H, hydraulic dump box, POW-R-R-R sound, Model No. 423

EX $25   **NM** $35   **MIP** $125

Fire Rescue Truck, 1968, red, 12.75L x 5.75W x 5.75H, turbine cab, lever-operated ladder, Model No. 453

EX $25   **NM** $55   **MIP** $125

Snorkel Fire Truck, 1968, red, 21L x 6.5W x 8H, same design as #380, Model No. 466

EX $35   **NM** $55   **MIP** $150

Tractor Trailer Truck, 1968, red and red, 21.25L x 7.75W x 5.75H, turbine cab. red, white and blue "Structo" decal on trailer, Model No. 483

EX $25   **NM** $55   **MIP** $100

Auto Transporter, 1968, red and yellow, 28.25L x 5.75W x 5.5H, large, open car carrier, ramps adjust, three plastic cars, Model No. 492

EX $55   **NM** $75   **MIP** $200

Road Grader, 1968, orange, 11.75L x 5W x 4.75H, Kom-pak design, Model No. 183

EX $15   **NM** $25   **MIP** $60

Hi-Lift Bulldozer, 1968, orange and black, 11.25L x 5.75W x 4H, metal levers operate the bucket, Model No. 501

EX $25   **NM** $35   **MIP** $100

Giant Bulldozer, 1968, orange and black, 11.5L x 7W x 5H, blade raises and lowers w/lever controls, Model No. 514

EX $25   **NM** $35   **MIP** $100

Road Grader, 1968, orange, 19L x 7.5W x 8H, plated scraper blade, black plastic wheels and engine, Model No. 527

EX $15 **NM** $25 **MIP** $100

Bulldozer & Earth Mover, 1968, green and yellow, 24.5L x 6.5W x 5.75H, combination bulldozer towing bottom dump earth mover unit, Model No. 574

EX $35 **NM** $55 **MIP** $150

Sand Master Set, 1968, yellow, 17.5L x 9W x 15H, plastic sand hopper w/rubber conveyor belt, Model No. 580

EX $15 **NM** $35 **MIP** $100

Roadbuilder Set, 1968, yellow and green, #580 set and #303 dump truck, Model No. 905

EX $55 **NM** $75 **MIP** $150

Highway Builder Set, 1968, yellow and green, four-piece set includes #183, #306 set, #501, Model No. 932

EX $55 **NM** $75 **MIP** $200

Heavy Construction Set, 1968, red and yellow, four-piece set includes #270, #303, #514 and barricade, Model No. 941

EX $55 **NM** $75 **MIP** $200

Rough Rider Pick-Up Truck, 1969, yellow, 9.25L x 4W x 4H, hurricanes design w/open bed, Model No. 801

EX $15 **NM** $25 **MIP** $60

Minuteman Tow Truck, 1969, dark orange, 9.25L x 4W x 4H, hurricanes design w/crank-operated tow rope, Model No. 812

EX $15 **NM** $25 **MIP** $60

Waggin' Wagon Kennel Truck, 1969, yellow, 9.25L x 4W x 4H, hurricanes design w/clear kennel and six dogs, Model No. 837

EX $15 **NM** $25 **MIP** $60

Dump Truck, 1969, dark orange and white, 10.5L x 4W x 4.25H, hurricanes design, Model No. 841

EX $15 **NM** $25 **MIP** $60

Cement Mixer, 1969, dark orange and white, 9.5L x 4W x 4.25H, hurricanes design w/axle driven barrel, Model No. 853

EX $15 **NM** $25 **MIP** $60

Livestock Truck, 1969, teal and white, 9.5L x 4.25W x 4H, hurricanes design w/white stake panels and five animals, Model No. 870

EX $15 **NM** $25 **MIP** $60

Merry-Go-Round, 1969, yellow and red, 9.5L x 4.25W x 5.75H, hurricanes design w/carousel, Model No. 874

EX $25 **NM** $35 **MIP** $100

Snorkel Fire Truck, 1969, red and white, 9.5L x 4W x 5.25H, hurricanes design w/white plastic snorkel arm and bucket, Model No. 878

EX $15 **NM** $35 **MIP** $100

Hydraulic Dump Truck, 1969, dark orange and white, 12.25L x 5.5W x 6.25H, thunderbolt design w/steer-o-matic front wheels, Model No. 626

EX $25 **NM** $35 **MIP** $100

Cement Mixer, 1969, dark orange and white, 12.25L x 7W x 7H, thunderbolt design w/steer-o-matic front wheels, Model No. 632

EX $25 **NM** $35 **MIP** $100

Fire Rescue Truck, 1969, red and white, 12.5L x 6W x 6.5H, thunderbolt design w/steer-o-matic front wheels, Model No. 653

EX $25 **NM** $35 **MIP** $100

Scamp, 1969, gold and white, 9.5L x 4.5W x 5.25H, sport model design w/5" blond doll, Model No. 744

EX $25 **NM** $35 **MIP** $100

Sea Sprite, 1969, blue and red, 23L x 5.5W x 5.25H, sport model design w/"Johnson Reveler" boat in tow, Model No. 755

EX $25 **NM** $35 **MIP** $100

Boog-A-Loo, 1969, pink and white, 9.5L x 4.5W x 5H, sport model design w/5" blond doll, Model No. 766

EX $25 **NM** $35 **MIP** $100

Tractor Trailer Truck, 1969, white and red, 16.5L x 4.25W x 5.5H, Kom-pak design w/red trailer, and white doors, Model No. 160

EX $25 **NM** $35 **MIP** $100

Pony Van, 1969, lime green, 16.5L x 3.25W x 5H, Kom-pak design w/clear roof on trailer and three colts, Model No. 163

EX $25 **NM** $35 **MIP** $100

Kom-pak Sandy, 1969, green and yellow, 9L x 5.25W x 8.5H, Kom-pak design, Model No. 184

EX $25 **NM** $35 **MIP** $100

Rampside Pick-Up, 1969, gold and white, 10.5L x 4.75W x 5.25H, typhoons design w/white plastic bed liner, Model No. 230

EX $25 **NM** $35 **MIP** $100

Camper Truck, 1969, gold and white, 10.5L x 5W x 6.5H, typhoons design w/white plastic camper in bed, Model No. 235

EX $25 **NM** $35 **MIP** $100

Sanitation Truck, 1969, gray and white, 16.5L x 6W x 7.5H, typhoons design w/lever action, Model No. 269

EX $25 **NM** $35 **MIP** $100

Cement Mixer, 1969, red and yellow, 14.5L x 7W x 7.5H, typhoons design w/axle driven barrel, Model No. 270

EX $25 **NM** $35 **MIP** $100

Wrecker Truck, 1969, yellow and red, 12.5L x 6W x 6.25H, typhoons design w/red tow boom, and crank winch, Model No. 277

EX $25 **NM** $35 **MIP** $100

Dump Truck, 1969, red, 13.5L x 6W x 5.5H, typhoons design w/lever action dump box, Model No. 303

EX $25 **NM** $35 **MIP** $100

Dump Truck, 1969, gray and orange, 13L x 5.5W x 6H, typhoons design w/spring action dump box, Model No. 311

EX $25 **NM** $35 **MIP** $100

Hydraulic Dump Truck, 1969, yellow and green, 13L x 6W x 6H, typhoons design w/hydraulic dump box, Model No. 319

EX $25 **NM** $35 **MIP** $100

Vista Dome Horse Van, 1969, metallic gold, 22L x 5.5W x 6.5H, typhoons design w/four horses, Model No. 322

EX $25 **NM** $35 **MIP** $100

Car Carrier, 1969, red and yellow, 22.5L x 5.5W x 5.5H, typhoons design w/three plastic cars (Mustangs/T-Birds) ramp, Model No. 331

EX $25 **NM** $35 **MIP** $100

Livestock Van, 1969, teal and white, 21.75L x 5.5W x 7.5H, typhoons design w/fifth wheel detail, Model No. 344

EX $25 **NM** $35 **MIP** $100

Timber Toter, 1969, red and red, 21.75L x 5.5W x 6.5H, typhoons design w/six wooden logs and chain, Model No. 361

EX $25 **NM** $35 **MIP** $100

Tractor Trailer Truck, 1969, red and red, 22L x 5.5W x 8H, typhoons design, Model No. 373

EX $25 **NM** $35 **MIP** $100

Snorkel Utility Truck, 1969, green and yellow, 17.5L x 6W x 9H, typhoons design w/white boom and plastic bucket, Model No. 380

EX $25 **NM** $35 **MIP** $100

Aerial Hook & Ladder, 1969, red and red, 30.25L x 5.5W x 7H, typhoons design w/crank-operated extension ladder, Model No. 381
EX $25   **NM** $35   **MIP** $100

Snorkel Fire Truck, 1969, red, 17.5L x 5.75W x 9H, typhoons design, Model No. 385
EX $25   **NM** $35   **MIP** $100

Road Grader, 1969, orange, 11.75L x 5W x 6H, black plastic wheels and motor, Model No. 183
EX $15   **NM** $25   **MIP** $60

Super Sandy Set, 1969, green and yellow, 13.5L x 9.5W x 13H, #303 dump truck plus plastic sand hopper, Model No. 306
EX $25   **NM** $35   **MIP** $100

Hi-Lift Bulldozer, 1969, orange and black, 12L x 6W x 6.5H, metal levers operate the bucket, Model No. 501
EX $25   **NM** $35   **MIP** $100

Giant Bulldozer, 1969, red and yellow, 12L x 6.75W x 7H, blade raises and lowers w/lever controls, Model No. 514
EX $25   **NM** $35   **MIP** $100

Road Grader, 1969, orange, 19L x 7.5W x 8H, plated scraper blade, black plastic wheels, and engine, Model No. 527
EX $25   **NM** $35   **MIP** $100

Sand Master Set, 1969, yellow, 17.5L x 9W x 15H, plastic sand hopper w/rubber conveyor belt, Model No. 580
EX $15   **NM** $35   **MIP** $100

Roadbuilder Set, 1969, yellow and green, #580 set and #303 dump truck, Model No. 905
EX $55   **NM** $75   **MIP** $150

Highway Builder Set, 1969, green and yellow, four-piece set includes #183, #306 set, #501, Model No. 932
EX $55   **NM** $75   **MIP** $150

Animal Set, 1969, yellow and green, two-piece set contains #837 and #870, Model No. 961
EX $32   **NM** $55   **MIP** $125

Hurricane Contractor Set, 1969, dark orange and white, two-piece set contains #841 and #853 plus sand hopper and signs, Model No. 965
EX $25   **NM** $35   **MIP** $125

Typhoon Construction Set, 1969, gray and orange, three-piece set including #270, #311, #501, Model No. 966
EX $55   **NM** $75   **MIP** $150

Dig 'N Dump Set, 1970-71, orange and white, 20L x 3.25W x 4.25H, road tow'ds design w/shovel and dual dump boxes in tow, Model No. 280
EX $15   **NM** $25   **MIP** $60

Pipe-Layer Set, 1970-71, blue and white, 20L x 3.25W x 4.25H, road tow'ds design w/grab bucket and dual trailers in tow, Model No. 285
EX $15   **NM** $25   **MIP** $60

Bridge Set, 1970-71, yellow and white, 22.25L x 3.5W x 5.5H, road tow'ds design w/stake truck, two trailers, and four-piece bridge, Model No. 290
EX $15   **NM** $25   **MIP** $60

Steerable Rough Rider Pickup, 1970-71, blue and white, 9.25L x 4W x 4H, steerable stormers design, Model No. 420
EX $15   **NM** $25   **MIP** $60

Steerable Minuteman Wrecker, 1970-71, lime green and white, 9.25L x 4W x 4H, steerable stormers design w/white metal boom, Model No. 428
EX $15   **NM** $25   **MIP** $60

Steerable Waggin' Wagon, 1970-71, blue and white, 9.25L x 4W x 4H, steerable stormers design w/clear kennel, and six dogs, Model No. 437
EX $15   **NM** $25   **MIP** $60

Steerable Dump Truck, 1970-71, gold and white, 10.5L x 4W x 4.25H, steerable stormers design, Model No. 441
EX $15   **NM** $25   **MIP** $60

Steerable Livestock Truck, 1970-71, gold and white, 9.5L x 4.25W x 4.25H, steerable stormers design w/stake sides, and four animals, Model No. 471
EX $15   **NM** $25   **MIP** $60

Steerable Snorkel Truck, 1970-71, red and white, 9.5L x 4W x 5.5H, steerable stormers design w/white plastic snorkel, Model No. 478
EX $15   **NM** $25   **MIP** $60

Steerable Stubby Wrecker, 1970-71, gold and white, 11L x 5.5W x 7H, steerable thunderbolt design w/"Road Tug" decal on side, Model No. 615
EX $15   **NM** $25   **MIP** $60

Steerable Hydraulic Dump Truck, 1970-71, orange and white, 13.25L x 5.5W x 6.25H, steerable thunderbolt design, Model No. 626
EX $15   **NM** $25   **MIP** $60

Steerable Cement Mixer, 1970-71, orange and white, 12.25L x 7W x 7.5H, steerable thunderbolt design, Model No. 632
EX $15   **NM** $25   **MIP** $60

Steerable Hydraulic Dump Truck, 1970-71, blue and white, 13.25L x 5.5W x 6.25H, steerable thunderbolt design, Model No. 640
EX $15   **NM** $25   **MIP** $60

Steerable Fire Rescue Truck, 1970-71, red, 12.5L x 6W x 6.5H, steerable thunderbolt design, Model No. 653
EX $15   **NM** $25   **MIP** $60

Steerable Timber Toter, 1970-71, lime green and white, 21.75L x 5.5W x 6.5H, steerable thunderbolt design w/six wooden logs, and chains, Model No. 661
EX $15   **NM** $35   **MIP** $100

Steerable Tractor Trailer, 1970-71, orange and orange, 22L x 5.5W x 8H, steerable thunderbolt design, Model No. 673
EX $25   **NM** $35   **MIP** $100

Steerable Hook & Ladder Truck, 1970-71, red and red, 17.5L x 6W x 7.25H, steerable thunderbolt design, Model No. 681
EX $25   **NM** $35   **MIP** $100

Scamp Sportster, 1970-71, gold and white, 9.5L x 4.5W x 5.25H, sport model design w/5" blond female doll, Model No. 744
EX $15   **NM** $35   **MIP** $100

Sea Sprite, 1970-71, blue and red, 23L x 5.5W x 5.25H, sport model design w/"Johnson Reveler" boat in tow, Model No. 755
EX $25   **NM** $35   **MIP** $100

Race-A-Roo, 1970-71, gold and white, 9.5L x 4.5W x 5H, sport model design w/5" white male doll, Model No. 760
EX $25   **NM** $35   **MIP** $100

Boog-A-Loo, 1970-71, pink and white, 9.5L x 4.5W x 5H, sport model design w/5" blond doll, Model No. 766
EX $25   **NM** $35   **MIP** $100

Lad-A-Bout, 1970-71, lime green and white, 9.5L x 4.5W x 5.25H, sport model design w/5" black male doll, Model No. 769
EX $35   **NM** $55   **MIP** $150

Sand-Grenade Dune Buggy, 1970-71, red and black, 9.5L x 4.5W x 5H, sport model design w/dual rear mag wheels, Model No. 777

EX $35　**NM** $55　**MIP** $125

Rough Rider Pickup, 1970-71, yellow, 9.25L x 4W x 4H, hurricanes design w/open bed, Model No. 801

EX $15　**NM** $25　**MIP** $100

Minuteman Tow Truck, 1970-71, dark orange, 9.25L x 4W x 4H, hurricanes design w/crank-operated tow rope, Model No. 812

EX $15　**NM** $25　**MIP** $100

Camper Truck, 1970-71, lime green and white, 9.25L x 4.25W x 5H, hurricane design w/white plastic camper, Model No. 835

EX $15　**NM** $25　**MIP** $100

Waggin' Wagon Kennel Truck, 1970-71, yellow, 9.25L x 4W x 4H, hurricanes design w/clear kennel and six dogs, Model No. 837

EX $25　**NM** $35　**MIP** $100

Dump Truck, 1970-71, dark orange and white, 10.5L x 4W x 4.25H, hurricanes design, Model No. 841

EX $15　**NM** $25　**MIP** $60

Cement Mixer, 1970-71, dark orange and white, 9.5L x 4W x 4.25H, hurricanes design w/axle driven barrel, Model No. 853

EX $15　**NM** $25　**MIP** $60

Livestock Truck, 1970-71, green and white, 9.5L x 4.25W x 4H, hurricanes design w/white stake panels and five animals, Model No. 870

EX $15　**NM** $25　**MIP** $60

Snorkel Fire Truck, 1970-71, red and white, 9.5L x 4W x 5.25H, hurricanes design w/white plastic snorkel arm, and bucket, Model No. 878

EX $15　**NM** $25　**MIP** $60

Cement Mixer, 1970-71, red and yellow, 14.5L x 7W x 7.5H, typhoons design w/axle driven barrel, Model No. 270

EX $15　**NM** $25　**MIP** $60

Dump Truck, 1970-71, red, 13.5L x 6W x 5.5H, typhoons design w/lever action dump box, Model No. 303

EX $15　**NM** $25　**MIP** $60

Hydraulic Dump Truck, 1970-71, yellow and green, 13L x 6W x 6H, typhoons design w/hydraulic dump box, Model No. 319

EX $15　**NM** $25　**MIP** $60

Vista Dome Horse Van, 1970-71, metallic gold, 22L x 5.5W x 6.5H, typhoons design w/four horses, Model No. 322

EX $15　**NM** $25　**MIP** $60

Car Carrier, 1970-71, red and yellow, 22.5L x 5.5W x 5.5H, typhoons design w/three plastic cars (Mustangs/T-Birds) ramp, Model No. 331

EX $25　**NM** $35　**MIP** $100

Snorkel Utility Truck, 1970-71, green and yellow, 17.5L x 6W x 9H, typhoons design w/white boom and plastic bucket, Model No. 380

EX $25　**NM** $35　**MIP** $125

Snorkel Fire Truck, 1970-71, red, 17.5L x 5.75W x 9H, typhoons design, Model No. 385

EX $25　**NM** $35　**MIP** $125

Tractor Trailer Truck, 1970-71, white and red, 16.5L x 4.25W x 5.5H, Kom-pak design w/red trailer, and white doors, Model No. 160

EX $35　**NM** $55　**MIP** $125

Pony Van, 1970-71, lime green, 16.5L x 3.25W x 5H, Kom-pak design w/clear roof on trailer and three colts, Model No. 163

EX $35　**NM** $55　**MIP** $125

Road Grader, 1970-71, lime green and yellow, 11.75L x 5W x 6H, black plastic wheels and motor, Model No. 183

EX $15　**NM** $25　**MIP** $60

Hi-Lift Bulldozer, 1970-71, lime green and yellow, 12L x 6W x 6.5H, metal levers operate the bucket, Model No. 501

EX $15　**NM** $25　**MIP** $60

Giant Bulldozer, 1970-71, lime green and yellow, 12L x 6.75W x 7H, blade raises and lowers w/lever controls, Model No. 514

EX $15　**NM** $35　**MIP** $100

Kom-pak Sandy, 1970-71, green and yellow, 9L x 5.25W x 8.5H, Kom-pak design, Model No. 184

EX $15　**NM** $25　**MIP** $60

Super Sandy Set, 1970-71, green and yellow, 13.5L x 9.5W x 13H, #303 dump truck plus plastic sand hopper, Model No. 306

EX $25　**NM** $35　**MIP** $100

Sand Master Set, 1970-71, yellow, 17.5L x 9W x 15H, plastic sand hopper w/rubber conveyor belt, Model No. 580

EX $25　**NM** $35　**MIP** $100

Highway Builder Set, 1970-71, green and yellow, four-piece set includes #183, #306 set, #501, Model No. 932

EX $55　**NM** $75　**MIP** $150

Steerable Stormer Construction Set, 1970-71, yellow, #441 steer-o-matic dump, sand hopper and 10-piece road sign set, Model No. 955

EX $55　**NM** $75　**MIP** $150

Hurricane Construction Set, 1970-71, orange and white, three-piece set including #841, sand hopper, and 10-piece road sign set, Model No. 965

EX $35　**NM** $55　**MIP** $125

Monster Machine, 1971, green, 2.75L x 3.5W x 3H, two-wheeled design w/exposed "Chrome" engine, Model No. 215

EX $5　**NM** $15　**MIP** $40

Panic Panel, 1971, orange, 2.75L x 3.5W x 3H, two-wheeled design w/panel wagon sides, Model No. 216

EX $5　**NM** $15　**MIP** $40

Weird Wagon, 1971, red, 2.75L x 3.5W x 3H, two-wheeled design w/WV bug style, Model No. 217

EX $5　**NM** $15　**MIP** $40

Buzzin' Buggy, 1971, yellow, 2.75L x 3.5W x 3H, two-wheeled design w/open dune buggy style, Model No. 218

EX $5　**NM** $15　**MIP** $40

Monster Machine, 1972, green, 2.75L x 3.5W x 3H, two-wheeled design w/exposed "Chrome" engine, Model No. 215

EX $5　**NM** $15　**MIP** $40

Panic Panel, 1972, orange, 2.75L x 3.5W x 3H, two-wheeled design w/panel wagon sides, Model No. 216

EX $5　**NM** $15　**MIP** $40

Weird Wagon, 1972, red, 2.75L x 3.5W x 3H, two-wheeled design w/WV bug style, Model No. 217

EX $5　**NM** $15　**MIP** $40

Buzzin' Bugggy, 1972, yellow, 2.75L x 3.5W x 3H, two-wheeled design w/open dune buggy style, Model No. 218

EX $5　**NM** $15　**MIP** $40

Giant 24-Pack Assortment, 1972, 17.75L x 16.5W x 16.5H, all four weird wheels designs in a store display - 24 cars total, Model No. 219

EX n/a　**NM** n/a　**MIP** $200

Triple Terrific 3 Pack, 1972, 14L x 5W x 5H, one each #215, #216, #217 in a three-pack store display box, Model No. 220

EX n/a　**NM** n/a　**MIP** $125

Brain Barrel, 1972, brown, 2.75L x 3.5W x 3H, two-wheeled design w/brown "Wooden" barrel and bald driver, Model No. 250
EX $5   **NM** $15   **MIP** $40

Loonie Looper, 1972, yellow and orange, 2.75L x 3.5W x 3H, two-wheeled design w/airplane styling including propeller, Model No. 251
EX $5   **NM** $15   **MIP** $40

Litter Picker, 1972, chrome and orange, 2.75L x 3.5W x 3H, two-wheeled design w/trash can style, Model No. 252
EX $5   **NM** $15   **MIP** $40

Triple Terrific 3 Pack, 1972, 14L x 5W x 5H, one each #250, #251, #252 in a three-pack store display box, Model No. 262
EX n/a   **NM** n/a   **MIP** $125

Big 2-Dozen Assortment, 1972, 17.75L x 14.75W x 16.5H, all three weird wheels designs in a store display - 24 cars total, Model No. 265
EX n/a   **NM** n/a   **MIP** $200

Giant Gantry Crane, 1972, yellow, 32.5L x 12.25W x 14H, hand crank pulley system w/crane mechanism, Model No. 555
EX $25   **NM** $35   **MIP** $125

Kom-pak Sandy, 1972, yellow, 9L x 5.25W x 8.5H, sand hopper and dump truck, Model No. 184
EX $15   **NM** $25   **MIP** $60

Sand Loader, 1972, yellow, 9.5L x 5W x 9.5H, small sand hopper w/conveyor, Model No. 560
EX $15   **NM** $25   **MIP** $60

Sand Set, 1972, yellow, 9.75L x 5W x 9.5H, #560 unit plus sand hopper unit, Model No. 579
EX $25   **NM** $55   **MIP** $125

Sand Master Set, 1972, yellow, 14.5L x 4.5W x 15H, plastic sand hopper w/rubber conveyor belt, Model No. 580
EX $25   **NM** $35   **MIP** $100

Contractor Set, 1972, yellow, combination of #579 set and #184 set plus 10 street signs, Model No. 967
EX $55   **NM** $75   **MIP** $150

Boon Dock'r, 1972, red and green, 23L x 5.5W x 5.25H, sport model design w/buggy towing boat & trailer, Model No. 758
EX $15   **NM** $25   **MIP** $60

Dirt Tracker, 1972, white and black, 10L x 4.5W x 5H, sport model design w/dual wheels #1 logo and flags on doors, Model No. 770
EX $15   **NM** $25   **MIP** $60

American Rev-O-Lution, 1972, white and black, 10L x 4.5W x 5H, sport model design w/american flag on doors, Model No. 775
EX $15   **NM** $25   **MIP** $60

Sand-Grenade Dune Buggy, 1972, red and black, 9.5L x 4.5W x 5H, sport model design w/dual rear mag wheels, Model No. 777
EX $15   **NM** $25   **MIP** $60

Blacktop Bandit, 1972, plum and black, 10L x 4.5W x 5H, sport model design w/dragster styling, Model No. 780
EX $15   **NM** $25   **MIP** $60

Speedway Series Wrecker, 1972, purple, 9.25L x 4W x 4H, same as hurricane design #428 w/speedway decals, Model No. 845
EX $15   **NM** $25   **MIP** $60

Speedway Series Ambulance, 1972, white, 9.25L x 4W x 4H, similar to hurricane design w/first aid decals, Model No. 855
EX $15   **NM** $25   **MIP** $60

Speedway Series Pacer, 1972, green, 9.25L x 4W x 4H, same as hurricane design #801 w/speedway decals, Model No. 865
EX $15   **NM** $25   **MIP** $60

Road Boss Vista Dome Horse Van, 1972, orange, 22L x 5.5W x 6H, w/chrome stacks and air horn detail plus four black horses, Model No. 324
EX $15   **NM** $25   **MIP** $60

Road Boss Hydraulic Dump, 1972, orange, 13.25L x 5.25W x 6.25H, w/chrome stacks and air horn detail, Model No. 327
EX $15   **NM** $25   **MIP** $60

Road Boss Timber Toter, 1972, orange, 21.75L x 5.5W x 6.5H, w/chrome stacks and air horn detail, Model No. 328
EX $15   **NM** $25   **MIP** $60

Road Boss Tractor Trailer Truck, 1972, orange, 22L x 5.5W x 8H, w/chrome stacks and air horn detail, Model No. 329
EX $15   **NM** $25   **MIP** $60

Road Boss Car Carrier, 1972, orange, 22.5L x 5.5W x 5.5H, w/chrome stacks and air horn detail plus three cars, Model No. 335
EX $15   **NM** $25   **MIP** $60

Steerable Stubby Wrecker, 1972, gold and white, 11L x 5.5W x 7H, thunderbolt design, w/black tow boom, Model No. 615
EX $15   **NM** $25   **MIP** $60

Steerable Cement Mixer Truck, 1972, gold and white, 12.25L x 7W x 7.5H, thunderbolt design, axle drives barrel, Model No. 634
EX $15   **NM** $25   **MIP** $60

Steerable Hydraulic Dump Truck, 1972, blue and white, 13.25L x 5.5W x 6.25H, thunderbolt design, Model No. 640
EX $15   **NM** $25   **MIP** $60

Steerable Fire Rescue Truck, 1972, red, 12.5L x 6W x 6.5H, thunderbolt design, w/two ladders and extension ladder, Model No. 653
EX $15   **NM** $25   **MIP** $60

Dump Truck, 1972, yellow, 13.5L x 6W x 5.5H, typhoon design, Model No. 303
EX $15   **NM** $25   **MIP** $60

Vista Dome Horse Van, 1972, metallic gold, 22L x 5.5W x 6H, typhoon design w/three plastic cars and ramp, Model No. 320
EX $15   **NM** $25   **MIP** $60

Car Carrier, 1972, red and yellow, 22.5L x 5.5W x 6H, typhoon design w/three plastic cars and ramp, Model No. 330
EX $15   **NM** $25   **MIP** $60

Aerial Hook & Ladder, 1972, red and red, 17.5L x 6W x 7.25H, typhoon design w/two ladders and extension ladder, Model No. 381
EX $15   **NM** $25   **MIP** $60

Dig'n Dump, 1972, orange and white, 20L x 3.25W x 4.25H, road tow'ds design w/shovel and dual dump boxes in tow, Model No. 280
EX $15   **NM** $25   **MIP** $60

Pipe-Layer Set, 1972, blue and white, 20L x 3.25W x 4.25H, road tow'ds design w/grab bucket and dual trailers in tow, Model No. 285
EX $15   **NM** $25   **MIP** $60

Bridge Set, 1972, yellow and white, 22.25L x 3.5W x 5.5H, road tow'ds design w/stake truck, two trailers, and four-piece bridge, Model No. 290
EX $15   **NM** $25   **MIP** $60

Road Grader, 1972, yellow, 11.75L x 5W x 6H, black plastic wheels and motor, Model No. 183
EX $15   **NM** $25   **MIP** $60

Hi-Lift Bulldozer, 1972, yellow, 12L x 6W x 6.5H, metal levers operate the bucket, Model No. 501
EX $15   **NM** $25   **MIP** $60

Giant Bulldozer, 1972, yellow, 12L x 6.75W x 7H, blade raises and lowers w/lever controls, Model No. 514
EX $15   NM $25   MIP $60

Steerable Rough Rider Pickup, 1972, blue and white, 9.25L x 4W x 4H, steerable stormers design, Model No. 420
EX $15   NM $25   MIP $60

Steerable Minuteman Wrecker, 1972, lime green and white, 9.25L x 4W x 4H, steerable stormers design w/white metal boom, Model No. 428
EX $15   NM $25   MIP $60

Steerable Camper Truck, 1972, red and white, 9.25L x 4.25W x 5H, steerable stormers design w/white plastic camper, Model No. 435
EX $15   NM $25   MIP $60

Steerable Waggin' Wagon, 1972, blue and white, 9.25L x 4W x 4H, steerable stormers design w/waggin' wagon treatment, Model No. 437
EX $15   NM $25   MIP $60

Steerable Dump Truck, 1972, gold and white, 10.5L x 4W x 4.25H, steerable stormers design, Model No. 441
EX $15   NM $25   MIP $60

Rough Rider Pickup, 1972, yellow, 9.25L x 4W x 4H, hurricanes design, Model No. 801
EX $10   NM $20   MIP $30

Camper Truck, 1972, orange and white, 9.25L x 4.25W x 5H, hurricanes design, Model No. 835
EX $15   NM $25   MIP $60

Waggin' Wagon, 1972, lime green and white, 9.25L x 4W x 4H, hurricanes design w/clear cover, and six dogs, Model No. 837
EX $15   NM $25   MIP $60

Tractor-Trailer Truck, 1972, blue and silver, 16.5L x 4.25W x 5.5H, hurricanes design w/structo van lines on trailer, Model No. 861
EX $15   NM $25   MIP $60

Livestock Truck, 1972, blue and white, 9.5L x 4.25W x 4H, hurricanes design w/white panels and five animals, Model No. 870
EX $15   NM $25   MIP $60

Kom-pak Sandy, 1973, yellow and orange, 8.5L x 5.5W x 9.5H, sand hopper and dump truck, Model No. 184
EX $15   NM $25   MIP $60

Sand Master Set, 1973, yellow and orange, 14.5L x 4.5W x 15H, plastic sand hopper w/rubber conveyor belt, Model No. 580
EX $15   NM $25   MIP $60

Vacation Set, 1973, orange and green, 22L x 5.75W x 10H, includes #758 and #835, Model No. 962
EX $25   NM $55   MIP $125

Contractor Set, 1973, yellow and orange, combination of #580 set and #184 set plus 10 street signs, Model No. 967
EX $35   NM $55   MIP $125

Speedway Midget Race Hauler, 1973, red and black, 10.5L x 4W x 4H, flatbed w/race car, Model No. 842
EX $25   NM $55   MIP $125

Speedway Wrecker, 1973, purple, 9.25L x 4W x 4H, same as hurricane design #428 w/speedway decals, Model No. 845
EX $15   NM $25   MIP $60

Speedway Ambulance, 1973, white, 9.25L x 4W x 4H, similar to hurricane design w/first aid decals, Model No. 855
EX $15   NM $25   MIP $60

Speedway Pacer, 1973, green, 9.25L x 4W x 4H, same as hurricane design #801 w/speedway decals, Model No. 865
EX $15   NM $25   MIP $60

Speedway Water Tanker, 1973, blue and white, 9.25L x 4W x 4.5H, white plastic water tank on back, Model No. 868
EX $15   NM $25   MIP $60

Boon Dock'r, 1973, orange and green, 23L x 5.5W x 5.25H, sport model design w/buggy towing boat and trailer, Model No. 758
EX $15   NM $25   MIP $60

Scorpion, 1973, pink and white, 10L x 4.5W x 5.75H, new design for 1973, Model No. 763
EX $15   NM $25   MIP $60

Top Chopper, 1973, lime green and orange, 10L x 4.5W x 5.75H, new design for 1973, Model No. 765
EX $15   NM $25   MIP $60

Propur-T, 1973, blue and white, 10L x 4.5W x 5.75H, new design for 1973, Model No. 768
EX $15   NM $25   MIP $60

Dirt Tracker, 1973, yellow and black, 10L x 4.5W x 5H, sport model design w/dual wheels #1 logo and flags on doors, Model No. 770
EX $15   NM $25   MIP $60

American Rev-O-Lution, 1973, white and black, 10L x 4.5W x 5H, sport model design w/American flag on doors, Model No. 775
EX $15   NM $25   MIP $60

Blacktop Bandit, 1973, yellow and black, 10L x 4.5W x 5H, sport model design w/dragster styling, Model No. 780
EX $15   NM $25   MIP $60

Road Boss Pipeline Transport, 1973, blue and yellow, 21.75L x 5.5W x 6.5H, w/chrome stacks and air horn detail, same as #328, Model No. 323
EX $15   NM $25   MIP $60

Road Boss Vista-Dome Horse Van, 1973, blue and yellow, 22L x 5.5W x 6H, w/chrome stacks and air horn detail, four black horses, Model No. 324
EX $15   NM $25   MIP $60

Road Boss Hydraulic Dump, 1973, blue and yellow, 13.25L x 5.5W x 6.25H, w/chrome stacks and air horn detail, Model No. 327
EX $15   NM $25   MIP $60

Road Boss Timber Toter, 1973, blue and yellow, 21.75L x 5.5W x 6.5H, w/chrome stacks and air horn detail, same as #323, Model No. 328
EX $15   NM $25   MIP $60

Road Boss Tractor Trailer Truck, 1973, blue and yellow, 22L x 5.5W x 8H, w/chrome stacks and air horn detail, Model No. 329
EX $15   NM $25   MIP $60

Road Boss Car Carrier, 1973, blue and yellow, 22.5L x 5.5W x 5.5H, w/chrome stacks and air horn detail plus three cars, Model No. 335
EX $15   NM $25   MIP $60

Typhoon Dump Truck, 1973, yellow, 13.5L x 6W x 5.5H, typhoon design, Model No. 303
EX $15   NM $25   MIP $60

Typhoon Hydraulic Dump, 1973, blue and white, 13L x 6W x 6H, typhoon design w/turbine cab, Model No. 311
EX $15   NM $25   MIP $60

Vista Dome Horse Van, 1973, metallic gold, 22L x 5.5W x 6H, typhoon design w/four plastic horses, Model No. 320
EX $15   NM $25   MIP $60

Typhoon Cement Mixer, 1973, blue and white, 13.5L x 6.75W x 7.5H, typhoon design w/turbine cab, Model No. 325
EX $15   NM $25   MIP $60

Typhoon Car Carrier, 1973, red and yellow, 22.5L x 5.5W x 6H, typhoon design w/three plastic cars and ramp, Model No. 330
EX $15   NM $25   MIP $60

Typhoon Fire Rescue Truck, 1973, red, 12.5L x 6W x 6.5H, typhoon design w/three ladders, Model No. 353

EX $15   NM $25   MIP $60

Typhoon Emergency Truck, 1973, white, 12.5L x 6W x 6.5H, typhoon design w/one red ladder on top, Model No. 358

EX $15   NM $25   MIP $60

Steerable Stubby Wrecker, 1973, gold and white, 11L x 5.5W x 7H, thunderbolt design, w/black tow boom, Model No. 615

EX $15   NM $25   MIP $60

Road Grader, 1973, yellow, 11.75L x 5W x 6H, "Structo 11" stencilled in black on blade, Model No. 183

EX $15   NM $25   MIP $60

Hi-Lift Bulldozer, 1973, yellow, 12L x 6W x 6.5H, "Structo 11" stencilled in black on blade, Model No. 501

EX $15   NM $25   MIP $60

Giant Bulldozer, 1973, yellow, 12L x 6.75W x 7H, "Structo 11" stencilled in black on blade, Model No. 514

EX $15   NM $25   MIP $60

Rough Rider Pickup, 1973, yellow, 9.25L x 4W x 4H, hurricanes design, Model No. 801

EX $15   NM $25   MIP $60

Camper Truck, 1973, orange and white, 9.25L x 4.25W x 5H, hurricanes design, Model No. 835

EX $15   NM $25   MIP $60

Waggin' Wagon, 1973, lime green and white, 9.25L x 4W x 4H, hurricanes design w/clear cover, and six dogs, Model No. 837

EX $15   NM $25   MIP $60

Dump Truck, 1973, gold and white, 10.75L x 4W x 4.25H, "Structo 841" stencilled on side of dump box, Model No. 841

EX $15   NM $25   MIP $60

Tractor-Trailer Truck, 1973, blue and silver, 16.5L x 4.25W x 5.5H, hurricanes design w/Structo Van Lines on trailer, Model No. 861

EX $15   NM $25   MIP $60

Livestock Truck, 1973, blue and white, 9.5L x 4.25W x 4H, hurricanes design w/white panels and five animals, Model No. 870

EX $15   NM $25   MIP $60

Monster Machine, 1973, green, 2.75L x 3.5W x 3H, two-wheeled design w/exposed "Chrome" engine, Model No. 215

EX $15   NM $25   MIP $60

Panic Panel, 1973, orange, 2.75L x 3.5W x 3H, two-wheeled design w/panel wagon sides, Model No. 216

EX $15   NM $25   MIP $60

Weird Wagon, 1973, red, 2.75L x 3.5W x 3H, two-wheeled design w/WV bug style, Model No. 217

EX $15   NM $25   MIP $60

Buzzin' Buggy, 1973, yellow, 2.75L x 3.5W x 3H, two-wheeled design w/open dune buggy style, Model No. 218

EX $15   NM $25   MIP $60

Giant 24-Pack Assortment, 1973, 17.75L x 16.5W x 16.5H, all four weird wheels designs in a store display - 24 cars total, Model No. 219

EX n/a   NM n/a   MIP $200

Triple Terrific 3 Pack, 1973, 14L x 5W x 5H, one each #215, #216, #217 in a three-pack store display box, Model No. 220

EX n/a   NM n/a   MIP $125

Brain Barrel, 1973, brown, 2.75L x 3.5W x 3H, two-wheeled design w/brown "Wooden" barrel and bald driver, Model No. 250

EX $5   NM $15   MIP $40

Loonie Looper, 1973, yellow and orange, 2.75L x 3.5W x 3H, two-wheeled design w/airplane styling including propeller, Model No. 251

EX $5   NM $15   MIP $40

Litter Picker, 1973, white and orange, 2.75L x 3.5W x 3H, two-wheeled design w/ trash can style w/propeller, Model No. 252

EX $5   NM $15   MIP $40

Triple Terrific 3 Pack, 1973, 14L x 5W x 5H, one each #250, #251, #252 in a three-pack store display box, Model No. 262

EX n/a   NM n/a   MIP $125

Big 2-Dozen Assortment, 1973, 17.75L x 14.75W x 16.5H, all three weird wheels designs in a store display - 24 cars total, Model No. 265

EX n/a   NM n/a   MIP $200

Giant Gantry Crane, 1973, yellow, 32.5L x 12.25W x 14H, hand crank pulley system w/crane mechanism, Model No. 555

EX $25   NM $35   MIP $100

Motorized Giant Gantry Crane, 1973, blue and yellow, 32.5L x 12.25W x 14H, motor operates all action, battery-operated, Model No. 558

EX $25   NM $35   MIP $100

Tonka

MIGHTY-TONKA TOYS

Backhoe, 1968-70s, Tonka, 21" long; swiveling body, rubber treads, yellow hoe
EX $25   NM $65   MIP $150

Bottom Dump, 1971, Tonka, 34" long; No. 3938, green tractor-trailer; 1971 and later
EX $40   NM $85   MIP $260

Bulldozer, 1968-70s, Tonka, 12-3/8" long; No. 3906, lever-adjusted blade, sun umbrella over seat
EX $10   NM $22   MIP $65

Bulldozer, 1970s, Tonka, 17" long; yellow, "Turbo-Diesel," cage over seat
EX $8   NM $17   MIP $50

Car Carrier, 1967-69, Tonka, 34-1/4" long; No. 3990, carries Mini-Tonka load of two Jeep Pickups and one Wagoneer
EX $60   NM $85   MIP $210

Car Carrier, 1970, Tonka, 34-1/4" long; No. 2990, in 1968 changes to No. 3990, carries Mini-Tonka load of one Jeep Pickup and two Volkswagens
EX $60   NM $85   MIP $195

Car Carrier, 1971, Tonka, 21-1/8" long; No. 3950, green, six wheels, 1971 and later
EX $30   NM $65   MIP $195

Cement Mixer, 1968-70s, Tonka, 19" long; "Turbo-Diesel," yellow, white drums
EX $20   NM $45   MIP $75

Cement Mixer, 1971, Tonka, 21-1/8" long; No. 3950, green, six wheels, 1971 and later
EX $25   NM $100   MIP $220

Clam, 1965, Tonka, 25" long, 18" high; No. 2905, yellow
EX $12   NM $28   MIP $85

Crane, 1965-70s, Tonka, 30" long, 20" high; No. 2940, yellow, black boom w/clam, also called Mobile Crane, in 1968 becomes No. 3940
EX $25   NM $35   MIP $50

Custom Van, 1970s, Tonka, open top, sliding door; late 1970s
EX $3   NM $7   MIP $20

Dump, 1964-70s, Tonka, 18-1/2" long; No. 900, becomes No. 2900 in 1965, then No. 3900 in 1968
EX $5   NM $10   MIP $30

Forklift, 1976, Tonka, yellow, No. 3989
EX $10   NM $25   MIP $75

Grader, 1972, Tonka, 24-3/4" long; No. 3945, orange; 1972 and later
EX $10   NM $30   MIP $50

Hard Hat, 1960s, Tonka, No. 4999; plastic hard hat, sold individually or w/sets of Mighty-Tonka toys; late 1960s
EX $5   NM $10   MIP $15

Hydraulic Dump, 1971, Tonka, 18-1/2" long; No. 3902, orange; 1971 and later
EX $85   NM $175   MIP $260

Loader, 1967-70s, Tonka, 1907/8" long; No. 2920, later 3920, lever-operated bucket
EX $12   NM $25   MIP $80

Loadmaster, 1971, Tonka, 18" high; No. 4002, sand loader for dump trucks, green and black; 1971 and later
EX $10   NM $20   MIP $30

Lowboy (Tractor-Trailer), 1968-70s, Tonka, "Mighty Diesel," yellow
EX $15   NM $30   MIP $45

Mobile Shovel, 1967-70, Tonka, 23" long; box-shaped cab, rubber treads, handgrip on shovel handle
EX $20   NM $40   MIP $60

Motor Home, 1973, Tonka, 22-3/4" long; No. 3885, Winnebago recreational vehicle, swiveling seats, shock-absorbing bumpers, fold-back top, two 6" dolls and dog; 1973 and later
EX $15   NM $30   MIP $60

Off-Road Adventure Buggy, 1970s, Tonka, changeable tires, jack; late 1970s
EX $7   NM $13   MIP $20

Rescue Vehicle, 1974-79, Tonka, 18" long; also Rescue Van, white van w/orange top, removable stretcher, driver, nurse and patient
EX $20   NM $40   MIP $60

Roller, 1971, Tonka, 16" long; No. 3910, road-roller; 1971 and later
EX $22   NM $50   MIP $100

School Bus, 1970s, Tonka, 19" long; yellow, van design, white plastic hubs, open top
EX $7   NM $15   MIP $22

Scraper, 1967-70s, Tonka, 27-1/4" long; No. 2935, becomes No. 3935 in 1968, fills, hauls, dumps
EX $130   NM $260   MIP $400

Scraper-Dozer, 1967-69, Tonka, 30" long; dozer w/swivel-attached scraper end
EX $40   NM $79   MIP $120

Shovel, 1965-69, Tonka, 29" long; No. 2930, yellow, handgrip on shovel lever, becomes No. 3930 in 1968
EX $42   NM $83   MIP $125

Shovel, 1970, Tonka, 29" long; No. 3930, lime green; 1970 and later
EX $15   NM $30   MIP $45

Wrecker, 1969-70, Tonka, 17-1/4" long; No. 3915, white, dual hoists
EX $32   NM $70   MIP $95

Wrecker, 1971, Tonka, 17-1/4" long; No. 3915, orange body, white cab and hoists; 1971 and later
EX $28   NM $56   MIP $85

MINI-TONKA TOYS

Allied Van (Tractor-Trailer), 1965-69, Tonka, 16" long; No. 98, orange, high-window cabover, "Allied Van Lines," rear doors open, becomes No. 1098 in 1968
EX $35   NM $69   MIP $105

Apple Peeler, 1971, Tonka, 7" long; No. 1335, hot rod panel truck
EX $6   NM $12   MIP $20

Beach Buggy, 1965-66, Tonka, 6-1/2" long; No. 42, tan Jeep, balloon tires
EX $3   NM $7   MIP $18

Beach Buggy, 1967, Tonka, 6-1/2" long; No. 42, brown Jeep, balloon tires, white canopy
EX $3   NM $7   MIP $18

Beach Buggy (Jeep), 1969-70, Tonka, 6-1/2" long; No. 1042, purple w/white canopy, wide balloon tires
EX $3   NM $6   MIP $25

Beach Buggy (Jeep), 1971, Tonka, 6-1/2" long; No. 1042, purple w/yellow canopy, wide balloon tires; 1971 and later
EX $3   NM $6   MIP $25

Bell System Truck, 1970s-80s, Tonka, 5-1/2" long; boom lift, white cab, six wheels, No. 55010 on bottom
EX $5   NM $10   MIP $15

Bell System Van, 1979, Tonka, 5" long; white van, w/blue-yellow side panels
EX $2   NM $4   MIP $8

Bone Bruzzer, 1972, Tonka, No. 1020, orange Jeep w/roll bars
EX $3   NM $6   MIP $9

Camper, 1963-64, Tonka, 9-1/2" long; No. 70, red-pink Jeep pickup w/white camper
EX $6   NM $12   MIP $25

Camper, 1965, Tonka, 9-1/2" long; No. 70, tan pickup, white camper
EX $5   NM $10   MIP $25

Camper, 1967, Tonka, 9-1/2" long; No. 70, brown body, white camper
EX $5   NM $10   MIP $25

Camper, 1968-70, Tonka, 9-1/2" long; No. 1070, purple pickup w/camper
EX $10   NM $15   MIP $25

Car Carrier (Tractor-Trailer), 1964-70, Tonka, 18-1/2" long; No. 96, green tall windshield cabover, green trailer, two plastic Sting Rays, becomes No. 1096 in 1968
EX $28   NM $56   MIP $85

Car Carrier (Tractor-Trailer), 1978, Tonka, 20" long; white and orange
EX $7   NM $13   MIP $25

Cement Truck or Cement Mixer, 1964-70, Tonka, 9-1/2" long; No. 77, originally called simply Mixer, red Jeep truck w/white, crank-turned mixer assembly, lever-tilting body, becomes No. 1077 in 1968
EX $13   NM $26   MIP $40

Chevron Package Delivery Truck, Tonka, 20"-long tractor-trailer, No. 2165, 1980s
EX $10   NM $15   MIP $55

Crane Truck, 1973, Tonka, 12" long; No. 1099, mobile crane w/hook
EX $4   NM $8   MIP $35

Datsun, 1974, Tonka, No. 1029
EX $9   NM $19   MIP $28

Dump, 1963, Tonka, 9-1/2" long; No. 60, all red Jeep truck, lever-operated dump bed
EX $9   NM $19   MIP $90

Dump, 1964, Tonka, 9-1/2" long, No. 60, green body, yellow dump bed
EX $9   NM $19   MIP $90

Dump, 1965-70, Tonka, 9-1/2" long; No. 60, red w/yellow dump bed, becomes No. 1060 in 1968
EX $8   NM $17   MIP $25

Farmer Charmer, 1971, Tonka, 8-1/2" long; No. 1225, "Super Thrust" in 1971, turbo cab, purple pickup; 1971 and later
EX $5   NM $10   MIP $15

Fire Chief, 1967-69, Tonka, 9-1/8" long; No. 66, Jeep Wagoneer, all red, "Fire Chief" on door, flasher, becomes No. 1066 in 1968
EX $8   NM $17   MIP $25

Fire Chief, 1970, Tonka, 9-1/8" long; No. 1066, Jeep Wagoneer, red body and white roof, "Fire Chief" on door, flasher; 1970 and later
EX $7   NM $13   MIP $20

Fire Fighter, 1966-70, Tonka, 9-3/4" long; No. 72, red and white, detachable ladders, flasher, becomes No. 1072 in 1968
EX $7   NM $13   MIP $20

Fire Fighter, 1971, Tonka, 8-7/8" long; No. 1255, "Super Thrust" in 1971, turbo cab, removable ladders; 1971 and later
EX $5   NM $10   MIP $15

Fixer Mixer, 1971, Tonka, 8-7/8" long; No. 1249, "Super Thrust" in 1971, turbo cab, yellow cement mixer; 1971 and later
EX $5   NM $11   MIP $20

Fun Buggy, 1969-70s, Tonka, 7" long; No. 1010, roll bar, issued w/removable top in at least 1969, various colors
EX $3   NM $6   MIP $25

Grader, 1964-69, Tonka, 10-3/4" long; No. 76, yellow, originally had black stripes on blade, open cab, yellow hubs, becomes No. 1076 in 1968
EX $5   NM $9   MIP $14

Grader, 1970, Tonka, 10-3/4" long; No. 1076, lime green, metal hubs; 1970 and later
EX $5   NM $9   MIP $14

Hi-Way Patrol, 1965-70, Tonka, 9-1/8" long; No. 64, black and white police Jeep Wagoneer w/flasher, becomes No. 1064 in 1968
EX $15   NM $30   MIP $55

Honey Bucket, 1972, Tonka, No. 1025, yellow jeep, blue top
EX $3   NM $6   MIP $12

Hoot 'N Hauler, 1971, Tonka, 8-7/8" long; No. 1230, "Super Thrust" in 1971; turbo cabover, dump truck; 1971 and later
EX $5   NM $9   MIP $14

Hot Hauler, 1971, Tonka, 7" long; No. 1330, yellow, hot rod pickup
EX $5   NM $15   MIP $20

Jeep Commander, 1965-69, Tonka, 6-1/2" long; No. 40, Army green, w/canopy, becomes No. 1040 in 1968
EX $7   NM $13   MIP $20

Jeep Dispatcher, 1965, Tonka, 6-1/8" long; No. 30, green, open top
EX $7   NM $13   MIP $50

Jeep Dispatcher, 1965-70, Tonka, 6-1/8" long; No. 30, blue, becomes No. 1030 in 1968
EX $5   NM $10   MIP $40

Jeep Wagoneer, 1965-66, Tonka, 9-1/2" long; No. 62, turquoise station wagon
EX $12   NM $23   MIP $35

Lightning Bugs, 1972, Tonka, No. 1165, Volkswagen, yellow hubs, chromed rear engines; 1972 and later
EX $6   NM $12   MIP $20

Litter Bug, 1971, Tonka, 9-1/2" long; No. 1260, "Super Thrust" in 1971, turbo cab, garbage truck
EX $5   NM $11   MIP $16

Livestock Van (Tractor-Trailer), 1964-66, Tonka, 16" long; No. 90, red w/white trailer sides; high-window cabover, opening rear doors
EX $15   NM $30   MIP $45

Loader, 1969-70s, Tonka, 10-1/2" long; No. 1087, yellow, movable scoop, metal hubs
EX $5   NM $8   MIP $12

Luv Bug, 1971, Tonka, 8-5/8" long; No. 1160, Volkswagen
EX $6   NM $12   MIP $18

Mini-Bucket, 1971, Tonka, 7" long; No. 1349, hot rod, single bucket seat
EX $5   NM $11   MIP $20

Mixer, 1964, Tonka, 9-5/8" long: No. 1977, Jeep truck cab, rotating plastic mixer section and hopper, tilting bed
EX $10   NM $20   MIP $30

Motor Mover (Tractor-Trailer), 1971, Tonka, 18-5/8" long: No. 1275, "Super Thrust" in 1971, turbo cab car carrier, two plastic Corvettes; 1971 and later
EX $15   NM $25   MIP $35

Pacer Police Car, 1970s, Tonka, 9" long; white, flasher bar on roof, chromed bumpers, white plastic hubs
EX $9   NM $19   MIP $30

Pickup, 1963-70, Tonka, 9-1/8" long; introduced as No. 50 in 1963, becomes No. 1050 in 1968, all red Jeep truck, snap-open tailgate
EX $8   NM $16   MIP $100

Pickup and Horse Trailer, 1967-70, Tonka, 14-3/4" long; No. 82, blue Jeep Pickup, white horse trailer, horses, becomes No. 1082 in 1968
EX $17   NM $33   MIP $150

Pony Puller, 1972, Tonka, 14-1/8" long; No. 1265, pink bubble-window pickup w/white horse trailer; 1972 and later
EX $7   NM $13   MIP $22

Road Paver, 1973, Tonka, 9-1/2" long; No. 1095, green paver w/plastic "asphalt" road; 1973 and later
EX $20   NM $40   MIP $60

Road Roller, 1972, Tonka, No. 1083, 1972 and later
EX $5   NM $10   MIP $15

Rollin' On (Tractor-Trailer), 1970s, Tonka, 16" long; blue bubble-window cab, white van trailer w/large "Rollin' On" panels
EX $5   NM $10   MIP $15

Ruff Rider, 1970, Tonka, 6-1/8" long; No. 1045, green, open top, six wheels
EX $4   NM $8   MIP $12

Sanitary Service, 1968-70, Tonka, 9-1/2" long; No. 1084, blue tall-windshield cabover, lever-controlled white dump body
EX $15   NM $30   MIP $45

Scamper Camper, 1971, Tonka, 8-5/8" long; No. 1250, "Super Thrust" in 1971, green bubble-window cabover, green camper w/opening white door; 1971 and later
EX $5   NM $9   MIP $20

Scotts Pick-Up, 1979, Tonka, 8-1/2" long; green and white pickup, "Scotts" in oval
EX $3   NM $6   MIP $9

Scraper, 1969-70s, Tonka, 14" long; No. 1091, yellow, metal hubs
EX $7   NM $13   MIP $20

Side Winder (Volkswagen), 1970, Tonka, wind-up key decal
EX $6   NM $12   MIP $18

Snow Seekers, 1970, Tonka, 16-7/8" long: No. 1081, originally called "Wagoneer and Snowmobile," yellow Wagoneer w/trailer and snowmobile; 1970, 1974 and later
EX $17   NM $33   MIP $50

Snowmobile, 1970s, Tonka, 7" long; from Wagoneer set
EX $7   NM $13   MIP $20

Stake Crate, 1971, Tonka, 8-7/8" long: No. 1245, "Super Thrust" in 1971, turbo cab, stake truck; 1971 and later
EX $4   NM $8   MIP $12

Stake Truck, 1963, Tonka, 9-3/4" long; No. 56, blue Jeep body and stakes, lever-raised dump stake body
EX $13   NM $26   MIP $40

Stake Truck, 1964-70, Tonka, 9-3/4" long; No. 56, blue Jeep truck, white stakes, became No. 1056 in 1968
EX $8   NM $20   MIP $25

Stanley Home Products Truck (Tractor-Trailer), 1970s-80s, Tonka, 16" long; white van body w/opening rear doors, bubble-window cabover, "Stanhome" stickers
EX $5   NM $11   MIP $16

Start Cart, 1971, Tonka, 9" long; No. 1235, "Super Thrust" in 1971, turbo cab, wrecker; 1971 and later
EX $4   NM $8   MIP $16

Sun Seeker, 1972, Tonka, No. 1079; Bone Bruzzer w/orange trailer and Tiny-Tonka dune buggy; 1972 and later
EX $7   NM $13   MIP $20

Thunder Hubs, 1971, Tonka, 7" long; No. 1325, hot rod convertible coupe
EX $5   NM $10   MIP $20

Track Duster, 1972, Tonka, No. 1345, blue and orange, Mack-type hot rod truck w/rear water tank; 1972
EX $6   NM $12   MIP $18

Trencher, 1969, Tonka, 18" long; No. 1089, yellow w/black backhoe, metal hubs
EX $7   NM $13   MIP $20

Trencher, 1970, Tonka, 18" long; No. 1089, lime green w/black backhoe, metal hubs; 1970 and later
EX $5   NM $10   MIP $18

Twinkle Toes, 1970, Tonka, 8-5/8" long; Volkswagen, foot-shaped yellow "Twinkle Toes" decal on doors
EX $5   NM $11   MIP $20

Van (Tractor-Trailer), 1964, Tonka, 16" long; No. 86, blue tall-windshield cabover, white van trailer w/"Tonka"
EX $17   NM $33   MIP $50

Van (Tractor-Trailer), 1965-66, Tonka, 16" long; No. 86, blue cabover, white van trailer w/"Mini-Tonka"
EX $12   NM $23   MIP $35

Volkswagen, 1970, Tonka, 8-5/8" long; No. 1158, assorted colors, previously grouped as Regular Tonka by Tonka Corp.; 1970 and later
EX $10   NM $30   MIP n/a

Wagoneer and Snowmobile, 1970-71, Tonka, 16-7/8" long; No. 1081, yellow Jeep Wagoneer w/trailer, yellow plastic snowmobile
EX $40   NM $80   MIP $135

Wagoneer and Trailer, 1965-69, Tonka, 17-1/2" long; No. 80, red Jeep Wagoneer w/trailer, yellow plastic Sting Ray, becomes No. 1080 in 1968
EX $48   NM $96   MIP $145

Wrecker, 1963-70, Tonka, 9-1/2" long; No. 68, white Jeep truck, red boom, lever-operated winch, becomes No. 1068 in 1968
EX $12   NM $23   MIP $75

REGULAR TONKA

"V" Blade Snow Plow, 1957, Tonka, 9" wide; No. AC-308, orange Hi-Way blade w/mounting bracket, large "V" shape
EX n/a   NM n/a   MIP n/a

3-in-1 Hi-Way Service Truck, 1957, Tonka, 13" long; No. 44, orange, w/two snowblades
EX $275   NM $400   MIP $700

5th Wheel Trailer, 1974-75, Tonka, 14" pickup w/19" trailer; open-top trailer attaches to bed of white Styleside pickup; camper
EX $23   NM $46   MIP $70

Aerial Ladder, 1955, Tonka, 32-1/2" long; No. 700-4, red w/aluminum ladder, "MFD" decals
EX $100   NM $300   MIP $450

Aerial Ladder, 1956, Tonka, 32-1/2" long; No. 700, red, 36" fully extendable aluminum ladder, rotating base, "TFD" decals, two extra ladders
EX $150   NM $300   MIP $450

Aerial Ladder, 1960-61, Tonka, 32-1/2" long; No. 48, red w/aluminum ladder, "TFD" decals
EX $125   NM $250   MIP $450

Aerial Ladder, 1962, Tonka, No. 1348
EX $100   NM $150   MIP $350

Aerial Ladder, 1964, Tonka, No. 998, two auxiliary ladders
EX $50   NM $75   MIP $100

Aerial Ladder, 1972, Tonka, No. 2960, not tractor-trailer, open cab; 1972 and later
EX $12   NM $23   MIP $35

Aerial Ladder (Tractor-Trailer), 1965-70s, Tonka, 28-3/4" long; No. 998 in 1965, red, "glassed-in" cabover, "T.F.D." on sides, becomes No. 2998 in 1968
EX $25   NM $50   MIP $75

(Harvey K Rainess)

Aerial Ladder Semi Fire Truck, 1954, Tonka, 32-1/2" long; No. 700
EX $175   NM $260   MIP $450

Aerial Ladder Truck, 1963, Tonka, No. 1348
EX $100   NM $150   MIP $200

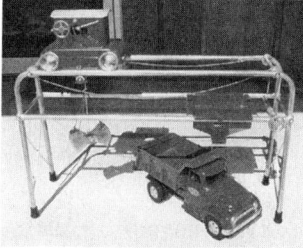

(KP Photo)

Aerial Sand Loader Set, 1955, Tonka, 25-1/2" long; No. 825-5, Loader and Dump Truck
EX $275   NM $425   MIP $875

Air Express Truck, 1959, Tonka, No. 16, dark blue body, square box bed, whitewall tires, "Air Express" decals on sides, plastic windshield, opening rear doors

  EX $350 **NM** $425 **MIP** $700

Air Force Ambulance, 1965-66, Tonka, 14" long; No. 402, blue pickup w/"USAF" on doors, red cross on hood, troop canopy over bed

  EX $45 **NM** $95 **MIP** $135

Air Force Jeep, 1965-68, Tonka, 10-1/2" long; No. 252 in 1965, blue w/"USAF," becomes No. 2252 in 1968

  EX $10 **NM** $20 **MIP** $30

Airlines Luggage Service, 1962, Tonka, 16-5/8" long; No. 420

  EX $100 **NM** $250 **MIP** $400

Airport Service Set, 1963, Tonka, No. 2100

  EX $150 **NM** $225 **MIP** $300

Alley Gater, 1972, Tonka, No. 2310, red and white open boat w/wheels

  EX $7 **NM** $13 **MIP** $20

Allied Moving Van, 1957, Tonka, 24" long; No. 38, orange cab and box trailer, "Allied Van Lines" decals

  EX n/a **NM** n/a **MIP** n/a

(KP Photo)

Allied Van, 1961, Tonka, 21-1/4" long; No. 39, orange cab and trailer w/"Allied Van Lines" decals, black bumper on cab, blackwall tires on cab and trailer

  EX $120 **NM** $250 **MIP** $450

Allied Van, 1962, Tonka, No. 739

  EX $125 **NM** $250 **MIP** $350

Allied Van, 1963, Tonka, No. 739

  EX $118 **NM** $175 **MIP** $235

Allied Van Lines, 1955, Tonka, 23-3/4" long; No. 400-5, orange tractor/trailer

  EX $100 **NM** $200 **MIP** $300

Allied Van Lines, 1964, Tonka, No. 739, black knob on door

  EX $75 **NM** $125 **MIP** $175

Allied Van Lines Semi, 1950, Tonka, 23-1/2" long; No. 400

  EX $175 **NM** $260 **MIP** $400

Back Hoe, 1963, Tonka, 17-1/8" long; No. 422

  EX $100 **NM** $175 **MIP** $350

Backhoe, 1963-65, Tonka, 17" long; No. 422, yellow truck cab, body, and backhoe, w/red rear seat

  EX $28 **NM** $65 **MIP** $90

Backhoe, 1970s, Tonka, yellow swivel body, black boom and scoop, six wheels

  EX $17 **NM** $33 **MIP** $50

Backhoe, 1971, Tonka, green; 1971 and later

  EX $17 **NM** $33 **MIP** $50

Bell System Truck, 1978, Tonka, lift truck, white cab roof

  EX $7 **NM** $13 **MIP** $20

Big Mike Dual Hydraulic Dump Truck, 1957, Tonka, 14" long; No. 43, twin hydraulic mechanisms lift dump bed

  EX $325 **NM** $595 **MIP** $1000

Big Mike Dual Hydraulic Dump Truck, 1958, Next Generation Cars, Tonka, No. 45, orange Hi-Way dump w/"V" snow plow, and "twin hydraulic action"

  EX $375 **NM** $675 **MIP** $1000

Boat Service Truck, 1961, Tonka, 23-1/2" long; No. 117, 1961 only, included blue fleetside pickup truck w/white cab roof, silver hubs, whitewall tires, blue trailer w/three plastic boats stacked horizontally

  EX $100 **NM** $250 **MIP** $450

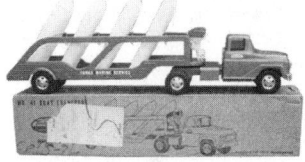

(KP Photo)

Boat Transport, 1960, Tonka, 28" long; No. 41, blue truck w/semi-trailer, four plastic boats stacked virtually upright, w/bar at the front for two outboard motors

  EX $250 **NM** $450 **MIP** $850

Boat Transport Truck, 1961, Tonka, 28" long; No. 41, blue truck w/semi-trailer, four plastic boats stacked virtually upright, w/bar at the front for two outboard motors

  EX $150 **NM** $300 **MIP** $650

Bottom Dump (Tractor-Trailer), 1965-69, Tonka, No. 910 in 1965, yellow, "glassed-in" cabover, five-position dump action, became No. 2910 in 1968

  EX $38 **NM** $76 **MIP** $115

Bulldozer, 1960, Tonka, 8-7/8" long; No. 10, plated roller wheels only in 1960, black rubber treads, three-position blade

  EX $75 **NM** $125 **MIP** $200

Bulldozer, 1962, Tonka

  EX $50 **NM** $75 **MIP** $100

Bulldozer, 1962-70s, Tonka, 8-7/8" long; No. 300 in 1962, yellow, adjustable blade, becomes No. 2300 in 1968

  EX $13 **NM** $26 **MIP** $40

Bulldozer, 1963, Tonka, No. 300

  EX $55 **NM** $82 **MIP** $110

Bulldozer, 1970s, Tonka, "Tonka Trax," plastic rollover cage

  EX $7 **NM** $13 **MIP** $20

Camper, 1962, Tonka, 14" long; No. 530

  EX $75 **NM** $150 **MIP** $250

Camper, 1962-65, Tonka, 14-5/8" long; No. 530, blue/turquoise Styleside Pickup w/white camper

  EX $60 **NM** $120 **MIP** $180

Camper, 1963, Tonka, No. 530

  EX $25 **NM** $38 **MIP** $50

Camper, 1965-66, Tonka, 14-5/8" long; No. 530, black pickup, white camper

  EX $42 **NM** $83 **MIP** $125

(KP Photo)

Camper, 1968, Tonka, No. 1070, Jeep Gladiator truck body, magenta, w/white camper top, the pattern for these trucks is the same as the No. 70 models dating from 1963, but color changes and line expansion forced Tonka to add more two more digits to the stock number

  EX $15 **NM** $30 **MIP** $50

Camper, 1972, Tonka, No. 255, red truck, white camper

  EX $8 **NM** $17 **MIP** $40

Canadian Tire Jeep, 1972, Tonka, red and white Jeep, oversized tires, "To Years of Service, 1922-1972" on hood

  EX $10 **NM** $20 **MIP** $30

Car Carrier, 1960, Tonka, 29" long; No. 40, yellow cab w/trailer includes three plastic 1960 Ford Falcon cars, moveable ramp for loading and unloading

EX $100 **NM** $225 **MIP** $450

Car Carrier, 1961, Tonka, 29" long; No. 40, yellow cab and trailer includes three plastic cars

EX $100 **NM** $250 **MIP** $450

Car Carrier, 1962, Tonka, No. 840

EX $100 **NM** $150 **MIP** $300

Car Carrier, 1963, Tonka, No. 840

EX $42 **NM** $63 **MIP** $85

Car Carrier, 1965-68, Tonka, 27" long; No. 840, "glassed-in" cabover, yellow, trailer w/circular openings on sides, lever-operated loading ramp, three plastic cars; made first appearance in 1965 catalog; becomes No. 2840 in 1968

EX $42 **NM** $83 **MIP** $125

Car Carrier (Tractor-Trailer), 1969-70s, Tonka, 27-1/2" long; No. 2850, yellow, trailer sides w/four larger openings, lever-operated ramp, two plastic cars

EX $22 **NM** $43 **MIP** $65

Car Quest Pickup, 1970s, Tonka, 14-1/2" long; white Styleside, "Car Quest Auto Parts Stores" red and blue decals

EX $8 **NM** $17 **MIP** $30

Cargo King Truck, 1957, Tonka, 23-1/2" long; No. 30, red cab, open aluminum box, "Cargo King" decals

EX n/a **NM** n/a **MIP** n/a

(Mark McManus)

Carnation Milk Step Van, 1954, Tonka, 11-3/4" long; No. 750

EX $200 **NM** $400 **MIP** $600

Carnation Milk Truck, 1955, Tonka, 11-3/4" long; No. 750-5, white Divco-style delivery truck w/Carnation Milk decals on panel sides, sliding front door, opening rear door

EX $200 **NM** $400 **MIP** $600

(KP Photo)

Cement Mixer, 1960, Tonka, 15-1/2" long; No. 120, red body, plastic mixer and hopper, tilting bed, blackwall tires

EX $100 **NM** $150 **MIP** $300

Cement Mixer, 1961, Tonka, 15-1/2" long; No. 120, red body, plastic mixer and hopper, tilting bed, adjustable chute for cement, mixer geared to turn as truck moves

EX $100 **NM** $150 **MIP** $300

Cement Mixer, 1962, Tonka, No. 620

EX $85 **NM** $150 **MIP** $300

Cement Mixer, 1963, Tonka, No. 620

EX $75 **NM** $125 **MIP** $250

Cement Mixer, 1965-70, Tonka, 14" long; No. 6320, red "glassed-in" cabover and chassis, white drum, becomes No. 2620 in 1968

EX $15 **NM** $30 **MIP** $100

Cement Mixer, 1971, Tonka, 14" long; No. 2620, yellow-orange, w/white drum; 1971 and later

EX $12 **NM** $23 **MIP** $80

Chevron Tanker, Tonka, 16"-long pickup, plastic serviceman, barrels

EX $8 **NM** $12 **MIP** $30

Crane and Clam, 1947, Tonka, 24" long; No. 150

EX $135 **NM** $200 **MIP** $350

Crater Crawler, 1970-71, Tonka, 11-7/16" long; No. 2546, metallic blue and white, bubble top, oversize tires; 1970-71

EX $8 **NM** $17 **MIP** $50

Deluxe Fisherman, 1960, Tonka, No. 130, new boat and trailer for this year (trailer stayed in lineup until the 1970s), blue "Fisherman" pickup w/white cab roof and white topper, larger white and red plastic boat on blue trailer w/working winch

EX $150 **NM** $350 **MIP** $550

Deluxe Fisherman, 1961, Tonka, 27-5/8" long in total; No. 130, same as previous year's model, that is, a fleetside pickup w/topper, but this time in red and white rather than blue and white

EX $150 **NM** $350 **MIP** $550

Deluxe Sportman, 1959, Tonka, No. 22, blue pickup truck w/white cab roof, whitewall tires, silver rims, boat trailer w/plastic boat

EX $150 **NM** $325 **MIP** $500

Deluxe Sportman, 1960, Tonka, No. 22, blue pickup truck w/white cab roof, whitewall tires, silver rims, boat trailer w/plastic boat

EX $100 **NM** $250 **MIP** $400

Deluxe Sportman, 1961, Tonka, 22-3/4" long; No. 22, blue pickup truck w/white cab roof, whitewall tires, silver rims, boat trailer w/plastic boat

EX $100 **NM** $200 **MIP** $450

Deluxe Sportsman w/Boat Trailer, 1958, Next Generation Cars, Tonka, 22-3/4" long; No. 34, red truck w/white cab roof, red trailer w/plastic fishing boat and attachable motor

EX $150 **NM** $325 **MIP** $750

Dozer Packer, 1962, Tonka, 18-1/4" long total; No. 524, Packer has 11 tires, sold only in 1962

EX $100 **NM** $250 **MIP** $400

Dozer Packer, 1963, Tonka, No. 524, yellow

EX $200 **NM** $300 **MIP** $400

Drag, 1963, Tonka, No. 514

EX $60 **NM** $90 **MIP** $120

Dragline, 1959, Tonka, 20" long; No. 14, yellow, rolling treads, working scoop that rotates on base, bucket actually scoops, black nylon cord "cables" control bucket

EX $100 **NM** $175 **MIP** $375

Dragline, 1961, Tonka, 18" high, 18" long; No. 14, yellow, black bucked, rubber treads

EX $100 **NM** $150 **MIP** $250

Dragline, 1962, Tonka, No. 514

EX $150 **NM** $225 **MIP** $300

Dragline, 1966, Tonka, 20-1/2" long; No. 514, yellow, "Dragline" in large letters, oval Tonka emblem, swivel body, rubber treads, black boom and dragging scoop, becomes No. 612 in 1966

EX $48 **NM** $96 **MIP** $145

Dragline & Trailer, 1959, Tonka, 26-1/4" long; No. 44, lime-green cab and loboy trailer, lime-green dragline

EX $150 **NM** $275 **MIP** $400

Dump (Tailgate), 1965, Tonka, 13-3/8" long; No. 406, light orange, white cab roof, reinforced dump body w/opening tailgate

EX $40 **NM** $80 **MIP** $120

Dump (Tailgate), 1966, Tonka, 13-3/8" long; No. 406, tan, white cab roof, reinforced dump body w/opening tailgate
EX $35   **NM** $65   **MIP** $100

Dump (Tailgate), 1967, Tonka, 13-3/8" long; No. 406, red w/green-blue dump body
EX $28   **NM** $56   **MIP** $85

Dump (Tailgate), 1968, Tonka, 14" long; No. 2406, red w/green dump, new cab w/slanted roof
EX $20   **NM** $40   **MIP** $60

Dump (Tailgate), 1969-70s, Tonka, 13-1/2" long; No. 2465, red "glassed-in" cabover w/yellow dump body
EX $7   **NM** $15   **MIP** $22

Dump and Sand Loader, 1965, Tonka, 23-3/4" long; No. 616, all red w/yellow dump body, tailgate dump w/conveyor
EX $50   **NM** $100   **MIP** $150

Dump and Sand Loader, 1965-68, Tonka, 24-1/8" long; No. 616, dump No. 315 w/conveyor, all red w/yellow dump body
EX $40   **NM** $79   **MIP** $120

Dump and Sand Loader, 1968-70, Tonka, No. 2315 dump w/conveyor, all red except yellow dump body, new cab
EX $32   **NM** $63   **MIP** $140

(KP Photo)

Dump Truck, 1949, Tonka, 12" long; No. 180
EX $100   **NM** $175   **MIP** $375

Dump Truck, 1955, Tonka, 13" long; No. 180-5, red cab, green dump body
EX $100   **NM** $150   **MIP** $350

Dump Truck, 1956, Tonka, 13" long: No. 180-6, red cab, green dump bed
EX $100   **NM** $150   **MIP** $350

Dump Truck, 1957, Tonka, 13" long; No. 06, red cab w/green dump bed
EX n/a   **NM** n/a   **MIP** n/a

Dump Truck, 1958, Next Generation Cars, Tonka, 13-1/2" long; No. 06, red cab w/green dump bed, two-position tailgate
EX $100   **NM** $150   **MIP** $300

Dump Truck, 1960, Tonka, 13-1/2" long: No. 06, silver five-spoke hubs, red cab, plastic windshield, opening tailgate on dumper bed
EX $35   **NM** $75   **MIP** $150

Dump Truck, 1961, Tonka, 13-1/2" long; No. 06, red truck w/blue-green dump bed, plastic windshield
EX $75   **NM** $100   **MIP** $250

Dump Truck, 1962, Tonka, No. 406, 1962
EX $75   **NM** $150   **MIP** $275

Dump Truck, 1963, Tonka, No. 406
EX $45   **NM** $68   **MIP** $90

Dump Truck, 1964, Tonka, 13-1/2" long; No. 315
EX $40   **NM** $60   **MIP** $90

Dump Truck, 1964-65, Tonka, 13-5/16" long; No. 315, orange-red, dump body w/out tailgate
EX $15   **NM** $30   **MIP** $55

Dump Truck, 1966-67, Tonka, 13-5/16" long; No. 315, red cab, yellow dump body, dump body w/out tailgate
EX $15   **NM** $30   **MIP** $55

Dump Truck, 1968-69, Tonka, 13-7/8" long; No. 2315, red and yellow, new cab w/slanted windshield, lever operated
EX $12   **NM** $23   **MIP** $35

Dump Truck, 1970, Tonka, 13-7/8" long; No. 2315, orange; 1970 and later
EX $10   **NM** $20   **MIP** $35

Dump Truck, 1990s, Tonka, 50th anniversary, red w/green dump body
EX $15   **NM** $25   **MIP** $55

Dump Truck & Sand Loader, 1963, Tonka, No. 616, yellow
EX $100   **NM** $150   **MIP** $235

Dump Truck & Sandloader, 1964, Tonka, No. 616, orange and yellow
EX $75   **NM** $125   **MIP** $175

Dump Truck and Sand Loader, 1962, Tonka, No. 616
EX $100   **NM** $200   **MIP** $300

Dump Truck w/Sandloader, 1961, Tonka, 23-1/4" long; No. 116
EX $100   **NM** $175   **MIP** $395

Dune Buggy, 1968-70s, Tonka, 10-7/8" long, 8-1/4" wide; No. 2445, red Jeep w/white canopy and interior, folding windshield, removable top, oversize tires, "Dune Buggy" on front fenders; originally came w/chain for towing, expeditions, etc.
EX $10   **NM** $20   **MIP** $35

Dune Buggy, 1970s, Tonka, 10-7/8" long; No. 2445, yellow Jeep w/white canopy
EX $8   **NM** $16   **MIP** $24

Express Truck, 1950, Tonka, 13-1/2" long; No. 185
EX $200   **NM** $450   **MIP** $900

Falcon, 1960s, Tonka, 8" long; plastic, sold separately and w/car carriers
EX $4   **NM** $8   **MIP** $12

(Ron O'Brien)

Farm Stake and Horse Trailer, 1959-61, Tonka, 21-3/4" long; No. 35, tan farm stake truck w/white stakes, white two-horse trailer, two plastic horses
EX $125   **NM** $180   **MIP** $350

Farm Stake and Horse Trailer, 1962, Tonka, No. 735
EX $75   **NM** $125   **MIP** $225

Farm Stake Truck, 1956, Tonka, 13-1/2" long; No. 925-6, white cab and flatbed section w/six blue removeable stake sections
EX $125   **NM** $260   **MIP** $410

Farm Stake Truck, 1957, Tonka, 13-1/2" long; No. 04, white truck w/six removable blue stake panels
EX $190   **NM** $375   **MIP** $480

Farm Stake Truck, 1958, Next Generation Cars, Tonka, No. 04, "Tonka Farms" bull decal on sides, green truck w/white removeable stake panels
EX $100   **NM** $150   **MIP** $300

Farm Stake Truck, 1960, Tonka, 14" long; No. 04, turquoise truck w/six white removeable rack sections, whitewall tires, five-spoke silver hubs, plastic windshield
EX $100   **NM** $200   **MIP** $325

Farm Stake Truck, 1961, Tonka, 14" long; No. 04, blue truck w/six white removeable rack sections, whitewall tires, five-spoke silver hubs, plastic windshield
EX $85   **NM** $175   **MIP** $370

Farm Stake Truck, 1962, Tonka, No. 404
EX $50   **NM** $95   **MIP** $150

Farm Stake Truck, 1963, Tonka, No. 404
EX $60   **NM** $90   **MIP** $150

(KP Photo)

Farm Stake w/Two Horse Trailer,
1958, Next Generation Cars, Tonka,
21-3/4" long; No. 35, green farm
stake truck w/white stakes, white
two-horse trailer, two plastic horses
EX $125 **NM** $250 **MIP** $450

Fisherman, Tonka, No. 110, 14" long,
red and white
EX $25 **NM** $50 **MIP** $125

Fisherman Pick-Up, 1960, Tonka, 14"
long; No. 110, blue and white two-
tone body and topper, opening
tailgate, topper w/"Fisherman" decal
EX $100 **NM** $175 **MIP** $375

Forklift w/Container, 1970s, Tonka,
12-1/2" long; w/pallet and box;
mid-1970s
EX $10 **NM** $20 **MIP** $30

Gasoline Truck, 1957, Tonka, 15"
long; No. 16, red tanker truck
w/"Gasoline" decals
EX $350 **NM** $525 **MIP** $1000

Gasoline Truck, 1958, Next
Generation Cars, Tonka, No. 33,
hinged back door, "Gasoline"
decals, hose and nozzle
EX $350 **NM** $500 **MIP** $900

Giant Dozer, 1961, Tonka, 12-1/2"
long; No. 118, a king-sized version
of the regular dozer
EX $70 **NM** $100 **MIP** $250

Giant Dozer, 1962, Tonka, No. 618
EX $100 **NM** $150 **MIP** $200

Giant Dozer, 1963, Tonka, No. 536
EX $110 **NM** $160 **MIP** $225

Giant Dozer, 1964-65, Tonka, 12-3/8"
long; No. 536, Army green
EX $25 **NM** $50 **MIP** $75

Giant Dozer, 1965-67, Tonka, 12-3/8"
long; No. 537, yellow
EX $20 **NM** $40 **MIP** $60

Grader, 1955, Tonka, 17" long; No.
600-5, orange, blade adjustable,
working steering
EX $75 **NM** $125 **MIP** $200

Grader, 1965-66, Tonka, 17-1/8" long;
No. 510, yellow, metal hubs
EX $22 **NM** $43 **MIP** $65

Grader, 1967-70s, Tonka, 17-1/2"
long; No. 510, yellow, lever
steering, yellow plastic hubs,
becomes No. 2510 in 1968
EX $13 **NM** $26 **MIP** $40

Grading Service Truck, 1962, Tonka,
No. 834
EX $125 **NM** $250 **MIP** $350

**Grading Service Truck, Trailer and
Bulldozer,** 1961, Tonka, 25-1/2"
long total; No. 134, includes yellow
dump truck w/red dumper bed,

yellow trailer and bulldozer w/three-
position blade
EX $100 **NM** $150 **MIP** $350

Grain Hauler, 1955, Tonka, 23-1/2"
long; No. 550-5, red cab w/silver
steel box, decals
EX $90 **NM** $135 **MIP** $280

Grain Hauler Semi, 1952, Tonka, 22-
1/4" long; No. 550
EX $125 **NM** $180 **MIP** $350

Green Giant Transport, 1956, Tonka,
23-1/2" long; No. 650-6, white tractor/
trailer, refrigerated, "Green Giant"
decals
EX $155 **NM** $350 **MIP** $600

Green Giant Transport Semi, 1953,
Tonka, 22-1/4" long; No. 650, white
cab and trailer w/Green Giant logo
decals
EX $150 **NM** $300 **MIP** $500

(Ron O'Brien)

Green Giant Utility Truck, 1953, Tonka,
white w/"Green Giant" labels, 1954
wheels on model in photo
EX $85 **NM** $175 **MIP** $300

(KP Photo)

Hi-Way Hydraulic Dump Truck, 1956,
Tonka, 13" long; No. 980-6, orange
w/yellow decals
EX $130 **NM** $280 **MIP** $395

(KP Photo)

Hi-Way Patrol, 1965-70, Tonka,
9-1/8" long; No. 64, Jeep Wagoneer
body, black w/white roof, red dome
light, opening tailgate, "Hi-Way

Patrol" decals on doors, becomes
No. 1964 in 1968
EX $20 **NM** $40 **MIP** $80

Hi-Way Service Truck, 1958, Next
Generation Cars, Tonka, No. 41,
orange dump truck w/two-position
tailgate, drop side bed, scraper
blade and plastic road signs
EX $100 **NM** $200 **MIP** $400

Horse Van, 1965-67, Tonka, 12-3/4"
long; No. 430, green truck w/horse-
carrier body, two horses, ramp gate
EX $17 **NM** $33 **MIP** $50

Horse Van, 1968-70, Tonka, 13-1/4"
long; No. 2430, new cab w/slanted
windshield, green, open-top horse
compartment, two plastic horses
EX $15 **NM** $30 **MIP** $45

Houseboat Set, 1961, Tonka, 29" long
total; No. 136, includes red and
white "Fisherman" pickup w/red
tilt-bed boat trailer and plastic
(floating) houseboat
EX $200 **NM** $400 **MIP** $800

Hydraulic Aerial Ladder, 1958, Next
Generation Cars, Tonka, No. 48,
bright red cab and trailer
w/extending ladder to 36"
EX $35 **NM** $75 **MIP** $150

Hydraulic Aerial Ladder Truck, 1957,
Tonka, 32" long; No. 48, red
w/aluminum ladder, "TFD" decals
EX $200 **NM** $300 **MIP** $500

Hydraulic Dump, 1962, Tonka, No. 520
EX $75 **NM** $100 **MIP** $220

Hydraulic Dump, 1965-67, Tonka,
13-3/8" long; No. 520, blue w/white
cab roof, "Hydraulic" decals on doors
EX $25 **NM** $50 **MIP** $75

Hydraulic Dump, 1968-70s, Tonka,
13-7/8" long; No. 2520, becomes
No. 2480 in 1969, blue, white roof,
new cab w/slanting windshield
EX $23 **NM** $46 **MIP** $90

Hydraulic Dump (Tailgate), 1969,
Tonka, 13-1/2" long; No. 2585,
"glassed-in" cabover, orange cab
and dumping body, hydraulic
action, tailgate
EX $30 **NM** $56 **MIP** $85

Hydraulic Dump (Tailgate), 1970,
Tonka, 13-1/2" long; No. 2585,
"glassed-in" cabover, lime-green
cab and dumping body, hydraulic
action, tailgate; 1970 and later
EX $32 **NM** $46 **MIP** $70

Hydraulic Dump Truck, 1957, Tonka,
13" long; No. 20, two-position
tailgate, hydraulic cylinder controls
dump bed
EX n/a **NM** n/a **MIP** n/a

Hydraulic Dump Truck, 1958, Next Generation Cars, Tonka, No. 20, dark gold body, working dumper w/lever and hydraulic lifter, plastic windshield
EX $125 NM $175 MIP $275

Hydraulic Dump Truck, 1960, Tonka, No. 20, dark gold body, working dumper w/lever and hydraulic lifter, two-position tailgate on dumper
EX $75 NM $150 MIP $300

(KP Photo)

Hydraulic Dump Truck, 1961, Tonka, 13-1/2" long; No. 20, dark gold body, working dumper w/lever and hydraulic lifter, two-position tailgate on dumper
EX $75 NM $110 MIP $250

Hydraulic Dump Truck, 1963, Tonka, No. 520
EX $45 NM $68 MIP $90

Hydraulic Dump Truck, 1965, Tonka, 13-3/8".long; No. 520, blue cab w/white roof, blue dumper bed
EX $35 NM $60 MIP $82

Jeep & Horse Trailer, 1964, Tonka, 19-1/4" long total; No. 525, two horses
EX $45 NM $68 MIP $135

Jeep Commander, 1964, Tonka, 10-1/2" long; No. 304, canvas top
EX $30 NM $50 MIP $75

Jeep Commander, 1964-69, Tonka, 10-1/2" long, Army green, "canvas" canopy top, No. 2304, 1968
EX $7 NM $13 MIP $25

Jeep Dispatcher, 1962, Tonka, 9-3/4" long; No. 200, light blue w/white plastic interior, folding windshield
EX $20 NM $40 MIP $60

Jeep Dispatcher, 1963, Tonka, No. 200
EX $30 NM $50 MIP $75

Jeep Dispatcher, 1963-65, Tonka, 9-3/4" long; No. 200, turquoise
EX $9 NM $19 MIP $60

Jeep Dispatcher, 1970, Tonka, 9-3/4" long; No. 2200, lime green
EX $5 NM $10 MIP $60

Jeep Pumper, 1963, Tonka, 10-3/4" long; No. 425
EX $100 NM $175 MIP $400

Jeep Pumper, 1963-65, Tonka, 10-3/4" long; No. 425, red, hose connector, removable ladder
EX $67 NM $132 MIP $200

Jeep Pumper, 1964, Tonka, No. 425, black steering wheel
EX $100 NM $150 MIP $275

Jeep Runabout, 1962-68, Tonka, 24-1/4" long; No. 516, blue Jeep Dispatcher w/boat trailer and red/white motorboat, becomes No. 2516 in 1968
EX $17 NM $33 MIP $50

Jeep Runabout, 1963, Tonka, No. 516, trailer and boat
EX $50 NM $100 MIP $300

Jeep Runabout, Trailer and Boat, 1960s, Tonka, No. 2516, blue Jeep and trailer, red and white boat
EX $35 NM $70 MIP $200

Jeep Runabout, Trailer, Boat, 1962, Tonka, 25-5/8" long total; No. 516
EX $50 NM $150 MIP $350

Jeep Surrey, 1963, Tonka, No. 350
EX $50 NM $75 MIP $100

Jeep Surrey, Fringe Top, 1962, Tonka, 10-1/2" long; No. 350
EX $42 NM $83 MIP $175

(KP Photo)

Jeep Universal, 1962, Tonka, No. 249
EX $75 NM $125 MIP $175

Jeep Wrecker, 1964, Tonka, 11" long; No. 375,
EX $40 NM $85 MIP $125

Jeep Wrecker, 1965, Tonka, 11" long; No. 375, white, black boom;
EX $25 NM $50 MIP $75

Jeep Wrecker w/Plow, 1965-69, Tonka, 12-3/8" long; No. 435, white jeep, flasher, black winch and snow plow, becomes No. 2435 in 1968
EX $25 NM $50 MIP $75

Jeep Wrecker w/Plow, 1970, Tonka, 12-3/8" long; No. 2435, blue w/orange plow and winch
EX $20 NM $50 MIP $150

Jeepster Convertible Sedan, 1969, Tonka, 13" long; No. 2245, red, black plastic removable top
EX $12 NM $23 MIP $45

Jeepster Convertible Sedan, 1970-71, Tonka, 13" long; No. 2245, red Jeepster, white plastic canopy
EX $12 NM $23 MIP $45

Jeepster Pickup, 1969-70, Tonka, 13" long; No. 2230, light green w/black roof
EX $15 NM $30 MIP $100

Jeepster Runabout, 1969-70, Tonka, 27-1/4" long; No. 2460, yellow Jeepster and boat trailer w/red and white boat
EX $17 NM $40 MIP $170

Jeepster Runabout, 1971, Tonka, 27-1/4" long; No. 2460, light blue Jeepster and trailer, blue and white boat
EX $15 NM $35 MIP $170

Jeepster Sport Convertible, 1969, Tonka, 13" long; No. 2240, blue, removable top
EX $12 NM $23 MIP $35

Jeepster w/Boat & Trailer, 1974, Tonka, No. 2460, blue jeep body w/white interior, blue trailer, blue and white plastic boat
EX $40 NM $75 MIP $92

Jet Delivery Truck, 1962, Tonka, 14" long; No. 410, 1962 only
EX $200 NM $350 MIP $850

Jolly Green Giant Special, 1960-61, Tonka, 14" long; white w/green stake racks, "Green Giant Company" decal on doors
EX $150 NM $300 MIP $450

Life Guard Jeep, 1968, Tonka, 9-3/4"
long; No. 2306, orange, flasher,
rescue raft on top
EX $15 **NM** $30 **MIP** $60

Life Guard Jeep, 1969, Tonka, 9-3/4"
long; No. 2306, red, yellow rescue
raft on top
EX $15 **NM** $30 **MIP** $60

Lift Truck and Trailer, 1948, Tonka,
No. 200
EX $200 **NM** $350 **MIP** $600

(KP Photo)

Livestock Hauler Semi, 1952, Tonka,
22-1/4" long; No. 500
EX $125 **NM** $160 **MIP** $350

Livestock Van, 1955, Tonka, 24" long;
No. 500-5, red, tractor/trailer has
slits
EX $110 **NM** $200 **MIP** $350

Livestock Van, 1957, Tonka, 24" long;
No. 36, red cab and trailer w/slits,
tailgate loading ramp
EX n/a **NM** n/a **MIP** n/a

Livestock Van, 1958, Next Generation
Cars, Tonka, No. 36, red cab and
trailer w/opening rear ramp and
floating suspension
EX $175 **NM** $250 **MIP** $450

Loader, 1962, Tonka, No. 402, yellow
and green
EX $40 **NM** $60 **MIP** $80

Loader, 1963, Tonka, No. 352
EX $40 **NM** $60 **MIP** $80

Loader, 1963-69, Tonka, 11-3/4" long;
No. 352, yellow, rubber treads,
lever-tripped dumping action,
becomes No. 2352 in 1968
EX $15 **NM** $30 **MIP** $60

Loader, 1970, Tonka, 11-3/4" long;
No. 2352, lime green; 1970 and
later
EX $9 **NM** $19 **MIP** $50

Loading Tractor, 1949, Tonka, 10-1/2"
long; No. 190
EX n/a **NM** n/a **MIP** n/a

Logger, 1957, Tonka, 23-3/4" long;
No. 14, red cab, aluminum frame,
nine round logs, chains
EX n/a **NM** n/a **MIP** n/a

Logger, 1959, Tonka, No. 07, single-
axel trailer w/square logs
EX $100 **NM** $200 **MIP** $550

Logger [Tonka Logger], 1956, Tonka,
23-1/2" long; No. 575-6, red cab,
logging trailer includes nine sanded
dowel logs, silver five-hole hubs
EX $130 **NM** $240 **MIP** $360

Logger Semi, 1953, Tonka, No. 575,
wood flatbed
EX $125 **NM** $180 **MIP** $350

Logger Semi, 1953, Tonka, 22-1/4"
long; No. 575
EX $125 **NM** $180 **MIP** $350

Lowboy and Bulldozer, 1960, Tonka,
26-1/4" long; No. 125, light green cab,
trailer, and bulldozer, solid rubber
tires w/out hubs on rear of trailer,
bulldozer w/three-position blade
EX $190 **NM** $375 **MIP** $675

Lowboy and Dozer, 1974, Tonka, No.
2831, red tractor and lowboy
w/orange dozer
EX $17 **NM** $33 **MIP** $70

Lumber Truck, 1955, Tonka, 18-3/4"
long; No. 850-5, red cab, aluminum
flatbed, six-wheel, square lumber
pieces
EX $175 **NM** $260 **MIP** $400

Lumber Truck, 1956, Tonka, 18-3/4"
long; No. 850-6, red cab, aluminum
flatbed, square lumber pieces
EX $130 **NM** $225 **MIP** $360

Lumber Truck, 1957, Tonka, 18" long;
No. 22, bronze cab, aluminum
flatbed, square lumber pieces
EX n/a **NM** n/a **MIP** n/a

Military Jeep, Tonka, No. 2205, green
w/"canvas" cover
EX $5 **NM** $10 **MIP** $50

Military Jeep & Box Trailer, 1964,
Tonka, 19-3/8" overall; No. 384
EX $50 **NM** $75 **MIP** $175

Military Jeep Universal, 1963-65,
Tonka, 10-1/2" long; No. 251, Army
green, no canopy
EX $8 **NM** $16 **MIP** $24

Military Jeep Universal, 1964, Tonka,
No. 251
EX $35 **NM** $55 **MIP** $75

Military Tractor, 1964, Tonka,
No. 250, black seat
EX $55 **NM** $70 **MIP** $100

(KP Photo)

Minute Maid Van, 1955, Tonka,
14-1/2" long; No. 725-5, white truck
w/Minute Maid Orange Juice
graphics and opening rear doors
EX $275 **NM** $650 **MIP** $950

Mobile Clam, 1961, Tonka, 27-1/4"
long; No. 142, orange cab, flatbed
section and crane cab, floating rear
wheels, operating "clam" style
bucket (still in use on later "Mighty
Tonka" models), that tripped open
when pulled to top of crane boom
EX $100 **NM** $250 **MIP** $450

Mobile Clam, 1962, Tonka, No. 942
EX $100 **NM** $150 **MIP** $320

Mobile Clam, 1963, Tonka, No. 942
EX $75 **NM** $112 **MIP** $150

Mobile Clam, 1964, Tonka, No. 942,
yellow
EX $50 **NM** $75 **MIP** $100

Mobile Dragline, 1960, Tonka,
No. 135, orange cab, flatbed section
and crane cab w/black boom and
bucket, bucket operates w/cords
and levers, and swivels on base
attached to truck
EX $100 **NM** $250 **MIP** $450

Motor Boat, 1960s, Tonka, 13" long;
plastic, sold separately and w/boat
carriers and trailers
EX $5 **NM** $10 **MIP** $15

Nationwide Moving Van, 1958, Next
Generation Cars, Tonka, 24-1/4"
long; No. 39, long white cab and
trailer w/full-width doors
EX $250 **NM** $475 **MIP** $800

No. 0250 Tractor, 1963, Tonka,
No. 250, yellow w/red seat
EX $75 **NM** $112 **MIP** $150

Parcel Delivery Truck, 1957, Tonka,
12" long; No. 10, bronze, Divco-
style delivery van, "Parcel Delivery"
decals
EX $200 **NM** $350 **MIP** $500

Parcel Delivery Van, 1954, Tonka,
11-3/4" long; No. 750
EX $200 **NM** $300 **MIP** $500

Pickup, 1962, Tonka, No. 302, red
body w/silver hubs, white cab roof,
opening tailgate
EX $95 **NM** $150 **MIP** $250

Pickup, 1963, Tonka, No. 302
EX $35   **NM** $52   **MIP** $70

(KP Photo)

Pickup, 1967, Tonka, 12-3/4" long; No. 302, all red body, opening tailgate, five-spoke silver hubcaps
EX $35   **NM** $55   **MIP** $76

Pickup, 1990s, Tonka, 50th anniversary, blue stepside
EX $25   **NM** $50   **MIP** $75

Pickup & Trailer, 1962, Tonka, No. 528
EX $50   **NM** $75   **MIP** $150

(KP Photo)

Pickup and Horse Trailer, 1965, Tonka, 14-3/4" long; No. 82, Blue Jeep Gladiator truck w/white horse trailer w/clear plastic dome roof, includes two plastic horses
EX $30   **NM** $55   **MIP** $110

Pickup and Trailer, 1960, Tonka, No. 28, bronze pickup towing stakeside trailer w/white plastic steer in back, end panel in trailer lifts out
EX $100   **NM** $150   **MIP** $300

Pickup Truck, 1955, Tonka, 12-3/4" long; No. 880-5, red pickup
EX $125   **NM** $280   **MIP** $450

(KP Photo)

Pickup Truck, 1956, Tonka, 13-3/4" long; No. 880-6, dark blue body, opening tailgate w/securing chain
EX $150   **NM** $350   **MIP** $650

Pickup Truck, 1957, Tonka, 12-1/2" long; No. 02, dark blue, opening tailgate w/chains
EX $100   **NM** $200   **MIP** $600

Pickup Truck, 1958, Next Generation Cars, Tonka, 12-3/4" long; No. 02, dark blue body, opening tailgate, trailer hitch, plastic windshield
EX $100   **NM** $240   **MIP** $300

Pickup Truck, 1960, Tonka, No. 02, bronze body, whitewall tires, solid silver hubs, opening tailgate, trailer hitch, plastic windshield
EX $100   **NM** $200   **MIP** $375

Pickup Truck, 1961, Tonka, 12-3/4" long; No. 02, bronze body, whitewall tires, solid silver hubs, opening tailgate, plastic windshield
EX $100   **NM** $190   **MIP** $320

Pickup Truck, 1962-66, Tonka, 12-3/4" long; No. 302, stepside, red body, white cab roof
EX $20   **NM** $40   **MIP** $200

Pickup Truck, 1967, Tonka, 12-3/4" long; No. 302, all red
EX $20   **NM** $40   **MIP** $200

Pickup Truck, 1968-69, Tonka, 13-1/2" long; No. 2302, all red, stepside w/rounded rear fenders, spoked metal hubs, new cab w/slanted windshield
EX $17   **NM** $33   **MIP** $150

Pickup w/Box Trailer, 1957, Tonka, 20-1/2" long; No. 26, dark blue No. 02 pickup, dark blue No. AC-310 box trailer
EX n/a   **NM** n/a   **MIP** n/a

Pickup w/Stake Trailer and Animal, 1957, Tonka, 20-1/2" long; No. 28, blue No. 02 Pickup and red No. AC-312 stake trailer, plastic animal
EX $150   **NM** $250   **MIP** $400

Pickup w/Stake Trailer and Animal, 1958, Next Generation Cars, Tonka, No. 28, dark blue pickup, red stake trailer, plastic livestock animal, stake tailgate on trailer lifts out
EX $125   **NM** $175   **MIP** $350

Police Jeep, 1965, Tonka, 10-1/2" long; No. 325, white Jeep, black and white canopy, flasher on hood, originally called Jeep Police Car
EX $28   **NM** $56   **MIP** $85

Police Jeep, 1966, Tonka, 10-1/2" long; No. 325, white Jeep, all black canopy, flasher on hood
EX $28   **NM** $56   **MIP** $85

Power Boom Loader, 1960, Tonka, 18-1/2" long; No. 115, 1960 only, blue flatbed truck w/working clamp and winch to pick up logs, pipe, etc, whitewall tires, plastic windshield
EX $300   **NM** $650   **MIP** $1000

Pumper, 1963, Tonka, No. 926
EX $60   **NM** $90   **MIP** $120

Pumper, 1965-68, Tonka, 15-1/2" long; No. 926, "glassed-in" cabover, red, hydrant, becomes No. 2926 in 1968
EX $23   **NM** $46   **MIP** $70

Pumper, 1969-70s, Tonka, 17-1/8" long; No. 2820, long LaFrance-style cab, hydrant, shoots water stream
EX $15   **NM** $30   **MIP** $45

Pumper Truck, 1962, Tonka, No. 926
EX $100   **NM** $150   **MIP** $300

Ramp Hoist, 1963, Tonka, 19-1/4" long; No. 640, red and white
EX $175   **NM** $350   **MIP** $1100

Ramp Hoist, 1964, Tonka, No. 640, park green and white, very rare
EX $300   **NM** $650   **MIP** n/a

Ranchero, 1960s, Tonka, 8" long; plastic, sold separately and w/car carriers
EX $5   **NM** $10   **MIP** $15

Rescue Squad, 1960, Tonka, 13-3/4" long; No. 105, white truck body w/square box bed, silver siren on driver's side of hood, red dome light, Civil Defence "CD" decals on doors, "Rescue Squad" w/red cross decals on back, red plastic boat attached w/rubber straps on top, removeable ladder
EX $100   **NM** $250   **MIP** $450

Rescue Squad Truck, 1956, Tonka, 11-3/4" long; included w/Tonka Fire Dept. Set
EX $120   **NM** $260   **MIP** $400

Rescue Squad Truck, 1957, Tonka, 12" long; No. 24, white Divco-style van, "Rescue Squad" decals, sliding side door, opening rear doors
EX n/a   **NM** n/a   **MIP** n/a

Rescue Van, 1955, Tonka
EX $200   **NM** $450   **MIP** $800

Road Builder Set, 1954, Tonka, No. 775, Road Grader, Semi T&T Crane and Dump Truck, five pieces
EX $350   **NM** $525   **MIP** $900

Road Grader, 1953, Tonka, 17" long; No. 600

EX $50 **NM** $75 **MIP** $100

Road Grader, 1956, Tonka, 17" long; No. 600-6, orange, steerable front wheels, tilting and rotating blade, floating rear wheels

EX $75 **NM** $125 **MIP** $200

(KP Photo)

Road Grader, 1958 Next Generation Cars, Tonka, No. 12, orange body w/rotating and tilting blade, working steering, floating rear wheels

EX $75 **NM** $112 **MIP** $150

Road Grader, 1961, Tonka, 17" long; No. 12, yellow cab and body w/steerable front wheels, tilting and rotating scraper blade, and floating rear wheels

EX $75 **NM** $100 **MIP** $200

Road Grader, 1962, Tonka, No. 512

EX $45 **NM** $68 **MIP** $90

Road Grader, 1963, Tonka, No. 512, red clearance lights

EX $80 **NM** $120 **MIP** $160

Road Grader (All-Weather), 1957, Tonka, 13" long; No. 12, orange, yellow Hi-Way decals

EX n/a **NM** n/a **MIP** n/a

Robin Hood Flour Truck, 1956, Tonka, white box truck w/"Robin Hood Flour" panel sides

EX n/a **NM** $2000 **MIP** n/a

Sanitary Service, 1967-69, Tonka, 16" long; No. 690, "glassed-in" cabover, dark blue cab, white garbage dump body, becomes No. 2690 in 1968

EX $23 **NM** $46 **MIP** $70

Sanitary Service, 1970, Tonka, 16" long; No. 2690, light blue cabover, white dumping body with blue gate

EX $20 **NM** $40 **MIP** $60

Sanitary Truck, 1959, Tonka, square back

EX $450 **NM** $700 **MIP** $1000

(KP Photo)

Sanitary Truck, 1960, Tonka, No. 140, hydraulic

EX $350 **NM** $550 **MIP** $900

(Patrick O'Neil)

Sanitary Truck, 1961, Tonka, 19-1/2" long; No. 140, white cab and rounded garbage section, swinging rear door, hopper bucket raises up to drop garbage in truck

EX $400 **NM** $700 **MIP** $1500

Scraper Blade, 1957, Tonka, 7" wide; No. AC-306, orange Hi-Way blade w/mounting bracket

EX n/a **NM** n/a **MIP** n/a

Serv-I-Car, 1962, Tonka, 9-1/8" long; No. 201, three-wheeled cart w/small dump bed, white

EX $75 **NM** $125 **MIP** $200

(KP Photo)

Service Truck, 1959-60, Tonka, 12-3/4" long; No. 01, blue body, square box bed w/"Tonka Service" decals, whitewall tires, solid silver hubs, removeable aluminum ladder, plastic windshield

EX $100 **NM** $150 **MIP** $350

Servi-I-Car, 1963, Tonka, No. 201

EX $55 **NM** $82 **MIP** $110

Shovel, 1957, Tonka, 15" long; No. 08, orange, rubber treads

EX n/a **NM** n/a **MIP** n/a

Shovel, 1965-68, Tonka, 20" long, 15" high; No. 526, yellow, lever-scoop w/handgrip, becomes No. 2536 in 1968

EX $25 **NM** $50 **MIP** $75

Shovel, 1970, Tonka, 24-1/2" long, No. 2720, yellow swivel body, six tires; 1970 and later

EX $15 **NM** $30 **MIP** $45

Shovel and Carry-All (Loboy), 1955, Tonka, 33" long; No. 120-5, red tractor, blue loboy, red shovel w/rubber treads

EX $150 **NM** $300 **MIP** $450

Shovel and Carry-All (Loboy), 1956, Tonka, 33" long; No. 120-6, red cab, blue loboy, red shovel w/rubber treads

EX $188 **NM** $280 **MIP** $475

Shovel and Carry-All Trailer, 1957, Tonka, 32" long; No. 40, orange cab and loboy, orange shovel, yellow decals

EX n/a **NM** n/a **MIP** n/a

Shovel and Carry-All Trailer, 1958, Next Generation Cars, Tonka, No. 43, orange cab and loboy trailer, orange steam shovel w/black rubber treads

EX $200 **NM** $300 **MIP** $500

Snorkel Pumper, 1969-70s, Tonka, 17-1/8" long; No. 2950, hand-operated aerial platform rising to 28" high, hydrant, 14" hose, long LaFrance-type cab

EX $12 **NM** $27 **MIP** $35

Sportsman, 1958, Next Generation Cars, Tonka, 12-3/4" long; No. 05, dark blue body, box camper top, opening tailgate, trailer hitch

EX $150 **NM** $225 **MIP** $450

(KP Photo)

Sportsman, 1959, Tonka, No. 05, tan body, box camper top, whitewall tires, solid silver hubs, white plastic boat attaches to topper w/rubber straps

EX $100 **NM** $175 **MIP** $350

Sportsman, 1960-61, Tonka, 12-3/4" long; No. 05, tan box pickup w/white boat strapped to top, silver disk wheels, whitewall tires

EX $100 **NM** $175 **MIP** $250

Sportsman, 1962, Tonka, No. 405

EX $75 **NM** $100 **MIP** $200

Sportsman w/Box Trailer, 1958, Next Generation Cars, Tonka, No. 29, dark blue Sportsman, dark blue trailer w/opening tailgate
EX $150 **NM** $225 **MIP** $400

Stake Jumper, 1971, Tonka, 13" long; No. 2447, lime green Jeepster w/oversized tires; 1971 and later
EX $12 **NM** $25 **MIP** $35

Stake Pickup, 1962, Tonka, 12-5/8" long; No. 308
EX $40 **NM** $80 **MIP** $120

Stake Pickup, 1963, Tonka, No. 308
EX $50 **NM** $95 **MIP** $150

Stake Pickup, 1964-65, Tonka, 12-3/4" long, No. 308, light blue, white roof
EX $25 **NM** $50 **MIP** $75

Stake Pickup & Horse Trailer, 1963, Tonka, 21-3/4" long overall; No. 625
EX $75 **NM** $125 **MIP** $175

Stake Pickup & Trailer, 1964, Tonka, 21-5/8" long; No. 504
EX $50 **NM** $75 **MIP** $185

Stake Pickup and Trailer, 1965-66, Tonka, 21-5/8" long; No. 504, stake pickup w/stake trailer, light blue, white cab roof, animals
EX $32 **NM** $63 **MIP** $95

Stake Trailer, 1957, Tonka, 5-1/2" long; No. AC-312, red stake trailer, sold as accessory, originally retailed for $1.98
EX $15 **NM** $30 **MIP** $45

Stake Truck, 1955, Tonka, 16-1/2" long; No. 860-5, red truck w/eight green stakes, six-wheel
EX $175 **NM** $360 **MIP** $500

Stake Truck, 1956, Tonka, 13" long; No. 991, red w/eight removeable stake sides
EX $150 **NM** $250 **MIP** $460

Stake Truck, 1964, Tonka, No. 404, red w/red stakes
EX $70 **NM** $120 **MIP** $425

Standard Oil Co. Wrecker Special, 1960, Tonka
EX $200 **NM** $400 **MIP** $600

Star Kist Van, 1954, Tonka, 14-1/2" long; No. 725
EX $250 **NM** $575 **MIP** $950

Steam Shovel, 1947, Tonka, 20-3/4" long; No. 100
EX $135 **NM** $200 **MIP** $350

Stearn Shovel Deluxe, 1949, Tonka, 22" long; No. 100
EX $100 **NM** $250 **MIP** $400

Steel Carrier Semi, 1950, Tonka, 22" long; No. 145
EX $125 **NM** $200 **MIP** $350

(KP Photo)

Steel Carrier Truck, 1954, Tonka, No. 145, orange cab, green open box trailer, yellow "Steel Carrier" decals
EX $100 **NM** $185 **MIP** $380

Sting Ray, 1960s, Tonka, 6-1/2" long; plastic, sold separately and w/car carriers
EX $4 **NM** $8 **MIP** $12

Stock Farm, 1957, Tonka, No. B-202, No. 32 Stock Rack truck, six farm animals, wooden corral
EX n/a **NM** n/a **MIP** n/a

Stock Rack Truck, 1958, Next Generation Cars, Tonka, No. 32, white cab and chassis, tall, removeable red stake sections
EX $100 **NM** $225 **MIP** $300

Stock Rack Truck w/Animals, 1957, Tonka, 16-1/4" long; No. 32, blue truck w/red stock rack, three plastic animals
EX $175 **NM** $365 **MIP** $650

Stump Jumper, 1970s, Tonka, 13" long; No. 2447, red, "Stump Jumper" sticker; green in 1972, purple in 1973
EX $10 **NM** $20 **MIP** $30

Stump Jumper, 1971, Tonka, 13" long; No. 2447, lime-green Jeepster w/oversize tires, white canopy
EX $12 **NM** $18 **MIP** $30

Styleside Pickup, 1967, Tonka, 14-1/8" long; No. 360, brown, white cab roof
EX $17 **NM** $33 **MIP** $50

Styleside Pickup, 1968, Tonka, 14-9/16" long; No. 2360, maroon w/white cab roof, new cab w/slanted windshield
EX $13 **NM** $26 **MIP** $40

Styleside Pickup, 1969-70, Tonka, 14-9/16" long; No. 2360, purple w/white cab roof
EX $13 **NM** $26 **MIP** $40

Styleside Pickup, 1971, Tonka, 14-9/16" long; No. 2360, orange, white black cab roof; 1971 and later
EX $9 **NM** $18 **MIP** $26

Style-Side Pickup, 1963, Tonka, 14" long; No. 354
EX $40 **NM** $60 **MIP** $125

Style-Side Pickup & Stake Trailer, 1963, Tonka, 22-3/4" long total; No. 522
EX $75 **NM** $125 **MIP** $250

(Mark McManus)

Suburban Pumper, 1956, Tonka, 17" long; No. 950-6, includes toy hydrant that attaches to garden hose, two 6" black hoses, removeable ladder
EX $120 **NM** $230 **MIP** $350

Suburban Pumper, 1957, Tonka, 17" long; No. 46, red pumper, hydrant attaches to garden hose, two black hoses, one 36" hose, ladder
EX n/a **NM** n/a **MIP** n/a

(Harvey K Rainess)

Suburban Pumper, 1958, Next Generation Cars, Tonka, No. 46, red truck w/hydrant that connects to garden hose, black hoses, whitewall tires
EX $175 **NM** $225 **MIP** $450

(Harvey K Rainess)

Suburban Pumper, 1960, Tonka, No. 46, red, hydrant connects to garden hose, black hoses, whitewall tires
EX $100 **NM** $250 **MIP** $350

Super Tanker, Tonka, No. 2975, red cab, yellow plastic tanker trailer
EX $20 **NM** $45 **MIP** $120

Tandem No. 36 Tandem Air Express, 1959, Tonka, w/trailer, 24" long
EX $325 **NM** $650 **MIP** $1000

Tandem No. 40 Car Carrier, 1959, Tonka
EX $100 **NM** $300 **MIP** $500

Tandem No. 41 Boat Transport, 1959, Tonka, 38" long
EX $250 **NM** $350 **MIP** $700

Tandem No. 42 Hydraulic Land Rover, 1959, Tonka, 15" long
EX $550 **NM** $825 **MIP** $1700

Tandem Platform Stake, 1959, Tonka, 28-1/4" long; No. 30, bronze, whitewall tires on truck and trailer
EX $100 **NM** $200 **MIP** $400

Tanker, 1960, Tonka, 28" long; No. 145, first Tonka w/major use of plastic
EX $100 **NM** $350 **MIP** $550

(Harvey K Rainess)

Tanker, 1961, Tonka, 28" long; No. 145, red w/"Texaco" decals, dual rear wheels
EX $100 **NM** $250 **MIP** $350

Terminal Train, 1963, Tonka, 33-5/8" long; No. 720, total, 15 suitcases
EX $105 **NM** $175 **MIP** $300

Thunderbird Express, 1957, Tonka, 24" long; No. 34, white semi tractor/trailer w/Thunderbird decal
EX $150 **NM** $400 **MIP** $600

Thunderbird Express, 1958 Next Generation Cars, Tonka, No. 37, white cab and freight trailer w/fold-down wheels and opening rear doors
EX $150 **NM** $300 **MIP** $600

Thunderbird Express, 1960, Tonka, No. 37, red cab w/white roof, red trailer w/white stripe and "Thunderbird" decal, floating tandem dual wheels on trailer
EX $150 **NM** $350 **MIP** $550

Timber (Logger) Truck, 1960, Tonka, No. 08, red cab, aluminum bed, includes square and round sanded "logs"
EX $150 **NM** $225 **MIP** $300

Tonka "Cargo King," 1956, Tonka, 23-1/2" long; No. 550-6, red cab, open-top silver trailer, opening rear door
EX $145 **NM** $230 **MIP** $355

(KP Photo)

Tonka Toy Transport Van, 1949, Tonka, 22-1/4" long; No. 140
EX $175 **NM** $300 **MIP** $500

Tractor, 1962, Tonka, 8-5/8" long; No. 250
EX $50 **NM** $75 **MIP** $100

Tractor and Carry-All Trailer, 1949, Tonka, No. 170, w/No. 150 Crane and Clam
EX $200 **NM** $300 **MIP** $525

Tractor and Carry-All Trailer, 1949, Tonka, No. 120, w/No. 50 Steam Shovel
EX $155 **NM** $280 **MIP** $475

Tractor and Carry-All Trailer, 1949, Tonka, No. 125, w/No. 100 Steam Shovel
EX $150 **NM** $250 **MIP** $550

Tractor and Wagon, 1973, Tonka, 21" long; No. 2710, green tractor, four-wheel wagon, yellow hubs
EX $8 **NM** $16 **MIP** $24

Tractor w/Trencher, 1975, Tonka, 21" long; No. 2525, farm tractor w/scoop and backhoe
EX $5 **NM** $17 **MIP** $25

Tractor-Carry-All Trailer, 1949, Tonka, 30-1/2" long; No. 130
EX $100 **NM** $150 **MIP** $350

Trailer, 1955, Tonka, No. 65, stake side
EX $30 **NM** $45 **MIP** $60

Trailer Fleet Set, 1953, Tonka, No. 675, two tractors (five interchangeable trailers), per set
EX $450 **NM** $680 **MIP** $975

(KP Photo)

Trencher, 1963, Tonka, 18-1/4" long; No. 534
EX $40 **NM** $75 **MIP** $150

Trencher, 1963-70s, Tonka, 18-1/4" long; No. 534, yellow, rubber tread, lever-operated front bucket, pivoting hoe, becomes No. 2534 in 1968
EX $9 **NM** $18 **MIP** $45

Trencher & LoBoy, 1963, Tonka, 28-1/2" long total; No. 1001
EX $75 **NM** $112 **MIP** $150

Troop Carrier, 1964, Tonka, 14" long; No. 380
EX $70 **NM** $100 **MIP** $150

Troop Carrier, 1965, Tonka, 14" long; No. 380, Army green Styleside pickup w/"canvas" cover
EX $18 **NM** $36 **MIP** $55

Utility Dump, 1961, Tonka, 12-1/2" long; No. 301, revised Golf Club Tractor; 1961 only
EX $100 **NM** $150 **MIP** $300

Utility Hauler, 1950, Tonka, 12" long; No. 175
EX $100 **NM** $150 **MIP** $300

Utility Truck, 1954, Tonka, No. 175, orange cab w/green utility (slit) bed
EX $110 **NM** $275 **MIP** $425

Utility Truck, 1958, Next Generation Cars, Tonka, No. 03, red cab, aluminum flatbed
EX $100 **NM** $150 **MIP** $300

Volkswagen, 1965-75, Tonka, 8-5/8" long; No. 150 yellow, No 152 blue, No. 153 green, No 156 red, VW "beetle"
EX $8 **NM** $16 **MIP** $24

Volkswagen, 1967, Tonka, 8-5/8" long; No. 150 black, No. 152 blue, No. 154 green, and No. 156 maroon
EX $8 **NM** $16 **MIP** $70

Volkswagen, 1969, Tonka, 8-5/8" long; No. 1158, various colors, reclassified by Tonka Corp. in 1970, see Mini-Tonka listing
EX $8 **NM** $16 **MIP** $24

Wrecker, 1949, Tonka, 12-1/2" long; No. 250
EX $125 **NM** $250 **MIP** $375

Wrecker, 1953, Tonka, blue w/red boom, chain, hook
EX $125 **NM** $200 **MIP** $350

Wrecker, 1954, Tonka, red cab, white bed, red boom, chain and hook
EX $100 **NM** $300 **MIP** $500

Wrecker, 1956, Tonka, 12" long; No. 996, white body, silver five-hole hubs, red dome light, "MM" decal on sides, working winch
EX $100 **NM** $300 **MIP** $500

Wrecker, 1956, Tonka, 12" long; No. 960-6, white body, silver five-hole hubs, red dome light, "AAA" decal on sides, working winch, rare
EX $390 **NM** $525 **MIP** $800

Wrecker, 1957, Tonka, 12-1/2" long; No. 18, white w/black boom, "AA" decals
EX $75 **NM** $200 **MIP** n/a

Wrecker, 1958-61, Tonka, No. 18, white, "AA" decals, black boom w/chain and hook, red dome light, whitewall tires, plastic windshield; 13-1/4" long
EX $75 **NM** $150 **MIP** $300

Wrecker, 1962, Tonka, No. 518, black boom
EX $50 **NM** $120 **MIP** $150

Wrecker, 1962-67, Tonka, 14-1/4" long; No. 518, white, red boom, flasher light
EX $42 **NM** $83 **MIP** $125

(KP Photo)

Wrecker, 1963-64, Tonka, No. 518, red boom, "AAA" on doors

EX $45   NM $85   MIP $150

Wrecker, 1968-70, Tonka, 14-5/8" long; No. 2518, white, new cab w/slanted windshield, red boom, "24 Hr. Service"

EX $30   NM $59   MIP $100

Wrecker, 1970s, Tonka, 14" long; 4x4 "24 Hr. Towing" truck, green, oversize tires; 1970s or 1980s

EX $12   NM $23   MIP $35

Wrecker, 1971, Tonka, 14-5/8" long; No. 2518, orange w/white winch, new cab w/slanted windshield; 1971 and later

EX $27   NM $55   MIP $80

TINY-TONKA TOYS

Aerial Ladder, Tonka, No. 1962, 22" long

EX $8   NM $15   MIP $30

Aerial Ladder (Tire Truck, Tractor-Trailer), 1968-70s, Tonka, ladder raises, swivels, also removable ladders, Model No. 675

EX $12   NM $23   MIP $35

Ambulance, 1970s, Tonka, white van, "Ambulance," Fire Dept. set

EX $5   NM $9   MIP $14

Banana Wheeler, 1973, Tonka, yellow hot rod, oversize tires, Model No. 788

EX $3   NM $7   MIP $15

Bottom Dump (Tractor-Trailer), 1969-70s, Tonka, dumps, spreads; Model No. 655

EX $5   NM $9   MIP $14

Car Carrier (Tractor-Trailer), 1968-70s, Tonka, steel body, plastic cars, Model No. 635

EX $7   NM $15   MIP $45

Carnation Milk Tanker, 1970s, Tonka, six-wheel tanker, red w/silver tank, "Milk is a Natural"

EX $7   NM $13   MIP $20

Cement Mixer, 1968-70s, Tonka, yellow w/red rotating and tilting drum, Model No. 575

EX $4   NM $8   MIP $12

Dozer, 1969-70s, Tonka, yellow, black treads, blade raises, Model No. 495

EX $3   NM $5   MIP $40

Draggin' Wagon, 1970-71, Tonka, "Crazy A's" hot rod, purple convertible sedan, Model No. 452

EX $5   NM $10   MIP $15

Dump, 1968-70s, Tonka, red cab, yellow dump box raises, Model No. 535

EX $5   NM $10   MIP $22

Dump Stake, 1969-70, Tonka, blue cab, white stake box raises, Model No. 527

EX $3   NM $7   MIP $10

Dump Stake, 1971, Tonka, blue cab, yellow stake box, Model No. 527

EX $3   NM $7   MIP $10

Fire Chief, 1970s, Tonka, red van w/window sides, Fire Dept. set

EX $4   NM $8   MIP $12

Frantic Flivver, 1970, Tonka, "Crazy A's" hot rod, black body w/orange-red running boards/fenders, Model No. 458

EX $5   NM $10   MIP $35

Fun-Buggy, 1969, Tonka, orange dune buggy, roll bar, Model No. 500

EX $3   NM $5   MIP $12

Fun-Buggy, 1969, Tonka, purple dune buggy, removable white top, Model No. 503

EX $3   NM $5   MIP $12

Fun-Buggy, 1970, Tonka, orange dune buggy, removable white top; 1970 and later, Model No. 500

EX $2   NM $4   MIP $10

Fun-Buggy, 1973, Tonka, yellow w/white top, Model No. 503

EX $2   NM $4   MIP $10

Hot Horse Mustang, 1974, Tonka, Powered Scrambler series

EX $4   NM $8   MIP $15

Hot Trike, 1972, Tonka, red and blue three-wheeler, Model No. 750

EX $2   NM $4   MIP $6

Hub Heater, 1974, Tonka, Powered Scrambler series, yellow body, flames on door

EX $4   NM $8   MIP $15

Lemon Wheeler, 1970s, Tonka, yellow hot rod, oversize tires

EX $3   NM $7   MIP $12

Lightning Rod, 1971, Tonka, Powered Scrambler series, orange body

EX $4   NM $8   MIP $15

Loader, 1969, Tonka, rubber treads, lever-operated scoop, yellow, Model No. 521

EX $3   NM $6   MIP $12

Loader, 1970, Tonka, rubber treads, lever-operated scoop, lime green; 1970 and later, Model No. 521

EX $3   NM $5   MIP $8

Lowboy and Dozer (Tractor-Trailer), 1969-70s, Tonka, hauls Tiny-Tonka Dozer, Model No. 695

EX $4   NM $8   MIP $45

Minnie Winnie, 1973, Tonka, pickup w/white Winnebago camper body, Model No. 800

EX $5   NM $10   MIP $15

Mod Rod, 1970-71, Tonka, "Crazy A's" hot rod, yellow convertible coupe, Model No. 450

EX $3   NM $7   MIP $20

Pickup, 1968-70, Tonka, red w/white interior, Model No. 515

EX $9   NM $18   MIP $45

Pickup, 1971, Tonka, orange, Model No. 515

EX $4   NM $8   MIP $25

Pumper, 1968-70s, Tonka, red fire truck, removable white ladders, Model No. 595

EX $7   NM $13   MIP $20

Rat-a-Tat-Tat, 1971, Tonka, black hot rod sedan, Model No. 434

EX $6   NM $10   MIP $25

Rumble Bee, 1971, Tonka, hot rod coupe w/rumble seat, Model No. 436

EX $4   NM $8   MIP $12

Sand Piper, 1972, Tonka, green and yellow three-wheeler, Model No. 755

EX $2   NM $4   MIP $12

Sand Roamer, 1972, Tonka, pink dune buggy w/white canopy, oversize tires, Model No. 765

EX $2   NM $4   MIP $7

Sanitary Service (Garbage Truck), 1968-70s, Tonka, blue cab, white body, Model No. 615

EX $5   NM $10   MIP $45

School Bus, 1970, Tonka, yellow van, "Tonka School District"; 1970 and later, Model No. 580

EX $4   NM $8   MIP $12

Scorcher, 1970-71, Tonka, "Crazy A's" hot rod pickup, Model No. 454

EX $3   NM $7   MIP $35

Shell Oil Truck, 1970s, Tonka, yellow, "Shell" on tanker body

EX $3   NM $6   MIP $9

Smart Cart, 1971, Tonka, blue hot rod coupe, orange fenders, Model No. 432

EX $3   NM $10   MIP $20

Snap Dragon (Van), 1970, Tonka, green, "Snap Dragon" decal; early 1970 and later, Model No. 585

EX $5   NM $11   MIP $16

Station Wagon, 1969, Tonka, blue van w/window sides, Model No. 529

EX $5   NM $10   MIP $15

Stinger, 1970, Tonka, "Crazy A's" hot rod, green convertible sedan, Model No. 456

EX $3   NM $7   MIP $15

Sun Buggy, 1972, Tonka, blue dune buggy w/oversized tires, Model No. 760

EX $2   NM $4   MIP $7

Taxi, 1971, Tonka, orange hot rod sedan, Model No. 438

EX $3   NM $7   MIP $15

Track Blaster, 1971, Tonka, Powered Scrambler series, blue body

EX $4   NM $8   MIP $15

Van, 1969, Tonka, "Tiny Van," orange, Model No. 531

EX $5   NM $11   MIP $25

Wrecker, 1969-70s, Tonka, blue w/red lever-operated winch, Model No. 555

EX $5   NM $10   MIP $40

YKK Zipper Van (Tractor-Trailer), 1960s, Tonka, white, van trailer w/"YKK World's Largest Zipper Manufacturer"

EX $25   NM $50   MIP $75

TONKA-TOTES

Beach Buzzer, 1971, Tonka, 2-1/4" long; No. 169, pink hot rod

EX $2   NM $3   MIP $5

Bug Blaster, 1970, Tonka, 2-1/2" long; No. 175, VW; 1970 and later

EX $2   NM $5   MIP $9

Construction Helmet, 1970s, Tonka, No. 4999, early 1970s

EX $3   NM $6   MIP $9

Double Deuce, 1970, Tonka, 3" long; No. 181, hot rod; 1970 and later

EX $2   NM $3   MIP $5

Dune Duster, 1970, Tonka, 2-13/16" long; No. 179, rear-engine buggy; 1970 and later

EX $2   NM $3   MIP $5

Gremlin, 1972, Tonka, No. 160, green

EX $2   NM $3   MIP $5

Hemi-Hauler, 1970, Tonka, No. 110, 3-1/4" long; yellow, rear-engine; 1970 and later

EX $2   NM $3   MIP $5

Launcher and Turn-Around Ramp, 1970, Tonka

EX $2   NM $3   MIP $5

Pocket Rocket Launcher, 1971, Tonka, 5-1/4" long

EX $2   NM $3   MIP $5

Quicker-Mixer, 1970, Tonka, 3-1/8" long; No. 114, cement mixer, six-wheel; 1970 and later

EX $2   NM $3   MIP $5

Racing Helmet, 1970s, Tonka, No. 4950, early 1970s

EX $2   NM $3   MIP $5

Salt Flat Racer, 1972, Tonka, No. 162, racer w/streamlined fenders

EX $2   NM $3   MIP $5

Scream 'n Demon, 1970, Tonka, No. 117, race car; 1970 and later

EX $2   NM $3   MIP $5

Strip Whip, 1971, Tonka, 3-1/4" long; No. 165, thin-bodied racer; 1971 and later

EX $2   NM $3   MIP $5

Super Snoot, 1971, Tonka, 2-3/4" long; No. 167, wedge-bodied; 1971 and later

EX $2   NM $3   MIP $5

Thumper Dumper, 1970, Tonka, 3-1/16" long; No. 112, dump truck, six-wheel; 1970 and later

EX $2   NM $3   MIP $5

Tonka-Bronc, 1971, Tonka, 2-7/8" long; No. 171, hot rod, blue

EX $2   NM $3   MIP $5

Wicked Wrecker, 1970, Tonka, 3-9/16" long; No. 116, wreck truck, six-wheel; 1970 and later

EX $2   NM $3   MIP $5

Tootsietoy

AIRPLANES

Atlantic Clipper, 2" long, mini series
EX $5   NM $10   MIP $20

Beechcraft Bonanza, orange, front propellor
EX $15   NM $25   MIP $35

Boeing Stratocruiser
EX $20   NM $40   MIP $110

Crusader, Model No. 719
EX $25   NM $65   MIP $75

Curtis P-40, light green, Model No. 721
EX $120   NM $250   MIP $525

DC-4 Supermainliner
EX $15   NM $30   MIP $50

Dirigible, 4" long, reissue of prewar Navy Zeppelin, silver paint, "U.S.N. Los Angeles," 1953
EX $50   NM $110   MIP $180

Dirigible U.S.N. Los Angeles, silver, Model No. 1030
EX $40   NM $60   MIP $90

F-22 Fighter, Hard Body Series, 1990s
EX $2   NM $4   MIP $15

F-94 Starfire, green, four engines; 1970s
EX $10   NM $15   MIP $35

Helicopter, die-cast and plastic, three blades 6" long; 1970s
EX $6   NM $9   MIP $12

KOP-1 USN
EX $20   NM $30   MIP $60

Low Wing Plane, miniature Piper Cub, Model No. 106
EX $20   NM $30   MIP $50

Navion, red, front propellor
EX $10   NM $20   MIP $35

Navy Jet, red; 1970s
EX $5   NM $10   MIP $30

Navy Jet Cutlass, red w/silver wings
EX $10   NM $15   MIP $30

Northrop F5A, U.S. fighter Jet; 1970s
EX $2   NM $4   MIP $5

P-38 Fighter Plane, 9-3/4" wingspan; 1950
EX $40   NM $60   MIP $110

P80 Panther Shooting Star
EX $25   NM $35   MIP $70

Piper Cub, blue, front propellor
EX $10   NM $20   MIP $30

S-58 Sikorsky Helicopter, 1970s
EX $15   NM $30   MIP $50

Snow Skids Airplane, rotating prop, 4" wingspan
EX $40   NM $60   MIP $85

Top Wing Plane, miniature, Model No. 107
EX $20   NM $30   MIP $50

Tri-Motor Plane, three propellors, Model No. 04649
EX $50   NM $85   MIP $150

TWA Electra, two engines, propellors, Model No. 125
EX $10   NM $20   MIP $45

Waco Bomber, blue base/silver top or silver base, Model No. 718
EX $50   NM $80   MIP $150

AUTOS.

Army Jeep, 5" long, upright windshield, protruding steering wheel
EX $7   NM $15   MIP $35

Chrysler New Yorker, 6", open front fenders, closed rear, 1950s
EX $12   NM $20   MIP $60

Ford Bronco, 4" long, single-molding plastic tires, 1980s
EX $1   NM $2   MIP $8

Jeep Cherokee 4X4, 5-1/2" long, plastic body and chassis/interior, various colors, 1980s
EX $4   NM $10-   MIP n/a

Jumbo Sedan, 6" long, 1948 streamlined sedan
EX $12   NM $25   MIP n/a

Jungle Cage Hitch Up, blue Jeepster w/green/white cage, tiger inside, 1969
EX $8   NM $15   MIP $30

Lincoln w/U-Haul Trailer, Hitch-Up series, Midget scale, early-1970s
EX $8   NM $16   MIP $30

U-Haul Trim Line Trailer & Car, white hub tires, dual axel trailer, 1970s
EX $3   NM $6   MIP $12

BOATS AND SHIPS

Battleship, Sea Power series, metal and plastic, "145" on side, late-1970s
EX $2   NM $4   MIP $18

Cargo Ship, Sea Power series, metal and plastic, late-1970s
EX $2   NM $4   MIP $18

Carrier, silver, Model No. 1036
EX $15   NM $25   MIP $40

Submarine, Sea Power series, black, metal and plastic, late-1970s
EX $2   NM $4   MIP $18

BUSES

Bus, 4" long, Toughs series, "bus" on plastic underside, white hub tires
EX $1   NM $3   MIP $6

Cross Country Bus
EX $30   NM $45   MIP $65

GMC Greyhound Bus, blue/silver, 6"; 1948-55, Model No. 3571
EX $20   NM $35   MIP $55

Greyhound Scenicruiser Bus, 6" bus, raised upper deck, lower body painted silver, middle section and lower roof painted blue, roof top painted cream, 1955-69
EX $17   NM $33   MIP $50

School Bus, 3-1/2" long, HO series, yellow w/black line down side
EX $100   NM $230   MIP n/a

School Bus, "Buzy Bee Bus," white hub tires; 1970s
EX $2   NM $5   MIP $7

Twin Coach Bus, red w/black tires, 3" long; 1950
EX $20   NM $35   MIP $55

CANNONS AND TANKS

Army Tank, miniature
EX $5   NM $10   MIP $25

Four Wheel Cannon, 4" long; 1950s
EX $10   NM $20   MIP $45

Long Range Cannon, Model No. 4642
EX $7   NM $10   MIP $30

Six-Wheel Army Cannon, 1950s
EX $10   NM $20   MIP $50

CARS

Auburn Roadster, red, white rubber wheels, Model No. 1016
EX $15   NM $30   MIP $45

Austin Healey 3000, 5" long, model kit in clear plastic cover on card, die-cast toy w/wheels, axles, decals and plastic pieces; 1961
EX $50   NM $100   MIP $170

Austin-Healey, light brown roadster; 6" long; 1956
EX $20   NM $30   MIP $60

Baggage Car, Model No. 1101
EX $10   NM $15   MIP $30

Baja Runabout, Midget, 2-1/4"; 1960s-70s
EX $1   NM $2   MIP $3

Bandito, Super Slicks series, 4-1/4" long, gold hardtop hot rod, side-panel stickers, chrome-hub wheels, 1971-76
EX $3   NM $5   MIP $8

Bluebird Daytona Race Car
EX $20   NM $35   MIP $65

Boat Tail Roadster, red roadster, 6" long, Model No. 233
EX $20   NM $35   MIP $55

Buckin' Bronco, Hitch-Up series, Ford Bronco, white hub tires, 1970s
EX $6   NM $14   MIP $28

Buick Brougham, tan/black, Model No. 6003
EX $20 **NM** $35 **MIP** $70

Buick Coupe, 4" long, Model No. 6002
EX $20 **NM** $35 **MIP** $50

Buick Estate Wagon, yellow and maroon w/black wheels, 6" long; 1948
EX $20 **NM** $35 **MIP** $50

Buick Experimental Car, blue w/black wheels, detailed tin bottom, 6" long; 1954
EX $10 **NM** $25 **MIP** $85

Buick LaSabre, red open top, black wheels, 6" long; 1951
EX $25 **NM** $45 **MIP** $70

Buick Roadmaster, blue w/black wheels, four-door; 1949
EX $25 **NM** $40 **MIP** $65

Buick Roadster, yellow open top, black wheels, 4" long, 1947-49
EX $20 **NM** $40 **MIP** $65

Buick Sedan, 6" long, Model No. 6004
EX $25 **NM** $35 **MIP** $55

Buick Special, 4" long; 1947, Model No. 103
EX $50 **NM** $75 **MIP** $100

Buick Station Wagon, green w/yellow top, black wheels, 6" long; 1954
EX $10 **NM** $20 **MIP** $45

Buick Touring Car, Model No. 6005
EX $50 **NM** $75 **MIP** $110

Cadillac, HO series, blue car/white top, 2" long; 1960
EX $10 **NM** $20 **MIP** $30

Cadillac 60, red-orange w/black wheels, four-door; 1948
EX $20 **NM** $40 **MIP** $60

Cadillac 62, red-orange w/white top, black wheels, four-door, 6" long; 1954
EX $20 **NM** $35 **MIP** $120

Cadillac Brougham, Model No. 6103
EX $40 **NM** $60 **MIP** $85

Cadillac Coupe, blue/tan, black wheels, Model No. 6102
EX $40 **NM** $60 **MIP** $85

Cadillac Eldorado, Midget series, 2-5/8" long, 1960s-70s
EX $2 **NM** $3 **MIP** n/a

Cadillac Sedan, white rubber wheels, Model No. 6104
EX $40 **NM** $60 **MIP** $85

Car and Cabin Cruiser, Midget series combination, 5-1/2" long, Cadillac Eldorado hauls trailer w/plastic Cabin Cruiser, 1969
EX $6 **NM** $9 **MIP** $12

Cheetah, Midget series, 2" long, different numbers on hood, 1960s
EX $2 **NM** $3 **MIP** n/a

Chevrolet Ambulance, 4" long
EX $15 **NM** $20 **MIP** $35

Chevrolet Bel Air, yellow w/black wheels, 3" long; 1955
EX $15 **NM** $30 **MIP** $50

Chevrolet Brougham, Model No. 6203
EX $40 **NM** $60 **MIP** $85

Chevrolet Coupe, Model No. 6202
EX $20 **NM** $35 **MIP** $90

Chevrolet Coupe, various colors, 3", Model No. 231
EX $8 **NM** $15 **MIP** $55

Chevrolet Fleetline, 1950 style, various colors, black wheels, 3" long; 1951-54
EX $10 **NM** $17 **MIP** $25

Chevrolet Roadster, Model No. 6201
EX $20 **NM** $35 **MIP** $90

Chevrolet Sedan, Model No. 6204
EX $20 **NM** $35 **MIP** $75

Chevrolet Touring Car, Model No. 6205
EX $60 **NM** $150 **MIP** $200

Chevy Corvette, 4" long, 1953 styling, black rubber wheels, 1955-69
EX $10 **NM** $24 **MIP** $35

Chrysler Convertible, green w/black wheels, 4" long; 1947-49
EX $20 **NM** $30 **MIP** $45

Chrysler Convertible, blue-green w/black wheels, 4" long; 1960
EX $8 **NM** $14 **MIP** $22

Chrysler Experimental Roadster, 4" long, various colors, open top, black wheels
EX $13 **NM** $26 **MIP** $40

Chrysler New Yorker, blue w/black wheels, four-door, 6" long; 1953
EX $25 **NM** $35 **MIP** $55

Chrysler Windsor Convertible, black wheels, 6" long; 1950
EX $50 **NM** $90 **MIP** $120

Classic Series 1906 Cadillac or Studebaker, green and black, spoke wheels
EX $5 **NM** $10 **MIP** $15

Classic Series 1907 Stanley Steamer, yellow and black, spoke wheels; 1960-65
EX $5 **NM** $10 **MIP** $15

Classic Series 1912 Ford Model T, black w/red seats, spoke wheels
EX $5 **NM** $10 **MIP** $15

Classic Series 1919 Stutz Bearcat, black and red, solid wheels
EX $5 **NM** $10 **MIP** $15

Classic Series 1929 Ford Model A, blue and black, black tread wheels; 1960-65
EX $5 **NM** $10 **MIP** $15

Convertible, 3" long, single-seat 1939-style generic convertible, various body colors, black rubber tires, axle ends visible outside closed fenders, 1947-52
EX $9 **NM** $14 **MIP** $20

Corvair, red, 4" long; 1960s
EX $30 **NM** $55 **MIP** $75

Corvette Roadster, blue open top, black wheels, 4" long; 1954-55
EX $15 **NM** $25 **MIP** $35

Coupe, 3" long, 1939/40-style generic coupe, various body colors, black rubber tires, axle ends visible outside closed fenders, 1947-52
EX $13 **NM** $27 **MIP** $35

Desert Fox, Super Slicks series, 4-1/4" long; purple open-top hot rod, side panel stickers, chrome-hub tires, 1971-76
EX $3 **NM** $5 **MIP** $8

DeSoto Airflow, green w/white wheels, Model No. 0118
EX $20 **NM** $35 **MIP** $60

Doodlebug, same as Buick Special
EX $50 **NM** $75 **MIP** $100

Dune Buggy, White plastic top, white hub tires, 3-1/4" long; 1970s
EX $2 **NM** $4 **MIP** $6

Dune Buggy, Hitch-Up series, red dune buggy, 3-3/4" long; w/white plastic top and surfboards, white hub tires, front hitch for hauling, 1970s
EX $2 **NM** $4 **MIP** $10

Dune Buster, Super Slicks series, 4-14" long, green hot rod, roof sticker, chrome-hub tires, 1971-76
EX $3 **NM** $5 **MIP** $8

Ferrari Lancia Race Car, red or dark green racer, 5" long, w/silver grille, no racing number, plastic driver's head, plastic tires, 1964-67
EX $10 **NM** $20 **MIP** $30

Ferrari Racer, red w/gold driver, black wheels, 6" long; 1956
EX $30 **NM** $40 **MIP** $65

Ford B Hot Rod, 1960s
EX $5 **NM** $10 **MIP** $20

Ford Bronco, 4" long, white-hub tires, 1970s
EX $4 **NM** $10 **MIP** $15

Ford Bronco and Horse Trailer, black "Bronco Ranch" Bronco, white-hub tires, brown "Rodeo Team" trailer, plastic horse, 1970s
EX $10 **NM** $15 **MIP** $20

Ford Convertible Sedan, red w/black wheels, 3" long; 1949
EX $10   NM $20   MIP $35

Ford Coupe, Midget series, 2-3/4" long, model of 1940 Ford coupe, 1960s
EX $1   NM $2   MIP n/a

Ford Customline, blue w/black wheels; 1955
EX $15   NM $20   MIP $30

Ford Fairlane 500 Convertible, two-door 1957 convertible, 3" long, painted red, blue or green, molded front windshield, open wheel wells, patterned plastic tires
EX $6   NM $12   MIP $18

Ford Falcon, two-door 1960 sedan, 3" long, painted red, blue or orange, open wheel wells, patterned plastic tires, 1961-69
EX $4 NM $8 MIP $12

Ford GT, Midget, 2-1/8"; 1960s-70s
EX $1   NM $2   MIP n/a

Ford LTD, blue w/black wheels, 4" long; 1969
EX $8   NM $12   MIP $20

Ford Mainliner, red w/black wheels, four-door, 3" long; 1952
EX $10   NM $20   MIP $30

Ford Model A Coupe, blue w/white wheels, Model No. 4655
EX $25   NM $35   MIP $50

Ford Model A Sedan, green w/black wheels, Model No. 6665
EX $25   NM $35   MIP $50

Ford Model A Sedan, 4-1/2" long, green body, black chassis, oversize silver-hub tires, Collector's Customized Model A Series, 1974
EX $5   NM $8   MIP $12

Ford Model A Wagon, 4-1/2" long, brown body, black chassis, woodside styling, oversize silver-hub tires, Collector's Customized Model A Series, 1974
EX $5   NM $8   MIP $12

Ford Mustang, Midget series, 2-1/8" long, 1960s-70s
EX $1   NM $2   MIP n/a

Ford Mustang w/Boat Trailer, Midget series combination, 4-1/2" long; Mustang hauling trailer w/Chris-Craft Boat, 1966
EX $6   NM $10   MIP $15

Ford Ranch Wagon, red w/yellow top, four-door, 3" long; 1954
EX $15   NM $20   MIP $35

Ford Ranch Wagon, green w/yellow top, four-door, 4" long; 1954
EX $15   NM $25   MIP $35

Ford Ranch Wagon, four-door 1960 station wagon, 3" long, painted

blue, open wheel wells, patterned plastic tires, 1962-67
EX $6   NM $10   MIP $20

Ford Roadster, powder blue w/open top, white wheels, Model No. 0116
EX $25   NM $40   MIP $60

Ford Sedan, various colors, four-door, 3" long; 1949
EX $6   NM $15   MIP $35

Ford Station Wagon, powder blue w/white top, black wheels, 6" long; 1959
EX $15   NM $20   MIP $35

Ford Station Wagon, blue w/black wheels, 3" long; 1960
EX $20   NM $40   MIP $60

Ford Station Wagon, red w/white top, black wheels, four-door, 6" long; 1962
EX $25   NM $40   MIP $55

Ford Thunderbird, two-door 1955 coupe, 4" long; open wheel wells, fin-style rear fenders, open wheel wells, patterned plastic tires, 1960-67
EX $4   NM $10   MIP $24

Ford Thunderbird (1967), Midget, 2-3/8"; 1960s
EX $1   NM $2   MIP n/a

Ford Tourer, open top, red w/silver spoke wheels, Model No. 4570
EX $20   NM $30   MIP $45

Ford V-8 Hotrod, red w/open top, black wheels, open silver motor, 6" long; 1940
EX $15   NM $25   MIP $35

Ford w/Trailer, blue sedan, white rubber wheels, Model No. 1043
EX $50   NM $75   MIP $130

Gremlin, Hitch-Up series, 4" long, "Gremlin" decal, 1970s
EX $3   NM $5   MIP $8

Hot Rod, Midget series, 2" long; 1960s
EX $1   NM $2   MIP $4

Hot Rod Model B, single-seat Ford hot rod, 3" long, painted red, blue or green, detailed engine, exposed plastic tires, 1961-69
EX $4   NM $8   MIP $12

Hot Rod Wagon, Hitch-Up series, "Bimini Buggy," white hub tires, 1970s
EX $2   NM $4   MIP $6

Indy Race Car, Midget series, 2-3/8" long, 1960s
EX $1   NM $2   MIP n/a

Insurance Patrol, miniature, Model No. 104
EX $15   NM $25   MIP $35

International Station Wagon, red/yellow, 3" long, 1947-52, Model No. 239
EX $8   NM $30   MIP $50

International Station Wagon, 4" long, rubber wheels; 1940s
EX $25   NM $50   MIP $50

Jaguar Formula D, Midget series, 2-1/2" long, 1960s
EX $2   NM $3   MIP n/a

Jaguar Type D, green w/black wheels, 3" long; 1957
EX $10   NM $15   MIP $25

Jaguar XK 120 Roadster, green open top, black wheels, 3" long
EX $10   NM $15   MIP $25

Jaguar XK 140 Coupe, blue w/black wheels, 6" long
EX $8   NM $17   MIP $25

Kaiser Sedan, blue w/black wheels, 6" long; 1947
EX $25   NM $45   MIP $55

Lancia Racer, dark green w/black wheels, 6" long; 1956
EX $30   NM $50   MIP $75

Large Bluebird Racer, green w/yellow solid wheels, Model No. 4666
EX $20   NM $40   MIP $60

LaSalle Convertible, rubber wheels, Model No. 0714
EX $80   NM $200   MIP $300

LaSalle Convertible Sedan, rubber wheels, Model No. 0715
EX $80   NM $200   MIP $300

LaSalle Coupe, rubber wheels, Model No. 0712
EX $150 NM $300   MIP $350

LaSalle Sedan, red w/black rubber wheels, 3" long, Model No. 230
EX $15   NM $20   MIP $30

LaSalle Sedan, rubber wheels, Model No. 0713
EX $140 NM $200   MIP $275

Limousine, blue w/silver spoke wheels; prewar, Model No. 4528
EX $20   NM $40   MIP $65

Lincoln Capri, red w/yellow top, black wheels, two-door, 6" long
EX $20   NM $35   MIP $50

Maserati Race Car, dark green or red race car, 5" long, w/silver grille and black racing number on white background, driver's head of plastic, 1962-67
EX $10   NM $20   MIP $30

Mercedes 190 SL Coupe, powder blue w/black wheels, 6" long; 1956
EX $15   NM $25   MIP $40

Mercedes Convertible, Midget series, 2-3/8" long; 1960s
EX $1   NM $2   MIP n/a

Mercury, red w/black wheels, four-door, 4" long; 1952
EX $15   NM $20   MIP $40

Mercury Custom, blue w/black wheels, four-door, 4" long; 1949
EX $15   NM $30   MIP $40

MG, Midget series, 2-1/4" long, 1960s
EX $2   NM $4   MIP $18

MG TF Roadster, blue open top, black wheels, 3" long; 1954
EX $10   NM $15   MIP $30

MG TF Roadster, red open top, black wheels, 6" long; 1954
EX $15   NM $25   MIP $45

Monza, Midget series, 2-1/4" long; 1970s
EX $1   NM $2   MIP n/a

Nash Metropolitan Convertible, red w/black tires; 1954
EX $25   NM $35   MIP $60

Observation Car, Model No. 1103
EX $10   NM $15   MIP $30

Offenhauser Racer, dark blue w/black wheels, 4" long; 1947
EX $10   NM $20   MIP $35

Oldsmobile 88 Convertible, yellow w/black wheels, 4" long; 1949
EX $15   NM $25   MIP $35

Oldsmobile 88 Convertible, bright green w/black wheels, 6" long; 1959
EX $20   NM $25   MIP $40

Oldsmobile 98, various colors, open fenders, black wheels, 4" long; 1955-60
EX $20   NM $25   MIP $45

Oldsmobile 98, various colors, skirted fenders, black wheels, 4" long; 1955-60
EX $20   NM $25   MIP $40

Oldsmobile 98 Staff Car
EX $20   NM $25   MIP $45

Oldsmobile Brougham, Model No. 6303
EX $25   NM $35   MIP $50

Oldsmobile Coupe, Model No. 6302
EX $25   NM $35   MIP $50

Oldsmobile Sedan, Model No. 6304
EX $25   NM $35   MIP $50

Oldsmobile Touring, Model No. 6305
EX $25   NM $35   MIP $50

Open Touring, green convertible, white wheels, 3", Model No. 232
EX $25   NM $35   MIP $45

Packard, white body w/blue top, black wheels, four-door, 6" long; 1956
EX $12   NM $25   MIP $35

Panzer Wagon, Super Slicks series, 4-1/4" long, red hot rod w/rear engine, hood sticker, chrome-hub tires, 1971-76
EX $3   NM $5   MIP $8

Pie Wagon, Super Slicks series, 4-1/4" long, pink hardtop hot rod, roof sticker, chrome-hub tires, 1971-76
EX $3   NM $5   MIP $8

Plymouth, dark blue w/black wheels, two-door, 3" long; 1957
EX $10   NM $15   MIP $20

Plymouth Belvedere, Plymouth 1957 model, 3" long; two-door hardtop, blue or red, open wheel wells, patterned plastic tires, 1959-69
EX $6   NM $12   MIP $18

Plymouth Sedan, blue w/black wheels, four-door, 3" long; 1950
EX $15   NM $20   MIP $30

Pontiac, Midget series, 2-3/8" long; 1970s
EX $1   NM $2   MIP n/a

Pontiac Fire Chief, red w/black wheels, 4" long; 1950
EX $12   NM $25   MIP $50

Pontiac Sedan, green w/black wheels, two-door, 4" long; 1950
EX $10   NM $20   MIP $45

Pontiac Star Chief, red w/black wheels, four-door, 4" long; 1959
EX $10   NM $20   MIP $40

Porsche, Midget series, 2-3/8" long; 1960s
EX $1   NM $2   MIP n/a

Porsche Roadster, red w/open top, black wheels, two-door, 6" long; 1956
EX $10   NM $25   MIP $40

Racer, orange w/black wheels, open cockpit, 3" long; 1950s-60s
EX $10   NM $15   MIP $30

Racer, miniature, Model No. 1110
EX $15   NM $40   MIP $50

Rambler Wagon, dark green w/yellow top, black wheels, yellow interior; 1960s
EX $15   NM $25   MIP $35

Rambler Wagon, blue w/black wheels, 4" long; 1960s styling; 1961-63
EX $8   NM $15   MIP $35

Roadster, miniature, Model No. 102
EX $15   NM $25   MIP $40

Roadster, Model No. 6001
EX $50   NM $100   MIP $140

Roadster, Midget series, 2-1/8" long; 1960s
EX $1   NM $2   MIP n/a

Sedan, Model No. 6-04
EX $50   NM $100   MIP $135

Sedan, miniature, Model No. 103
EX $20   NM $25   MIP $40

Station Wagon, red w/tan upper, 3", Model No. 239
EX $15   NM $35   MIP $55

Stingin' Bug, VW Beetle, white plastic interior, "Stingin' Bug" sticker on doors, white-hub tires, 1970s
EX $3   NM $5   MIP $7

Studebaker Coupe, green w/black wheels, 3" long; 1947
EX $25   NM $35   MIP $50

Studebaker Lark Convertible, two-door 1960 convertible, 3" long; painted teal green, green, yellow, blue or red, molded front windshield, open wheel wells, patterned plastic tires, 1960-69
EX $4   NM $8   MIP $25

Tank Car, miniature, Model No. 105
EX $20   NM $25   MIP $40

Thunderbird Coupe, blue w/black wheels, 3" long; 1955
EX $15   NM $20   MIP $30

Thunderbird Coupe, powder blue w/black wheels, 4" long; 1955
EX $15   NM $30   MIP $40

Toronado, Midget series, 2-3/4" long, 1970s
EX $1   NM $2   MIP n/a

Torpedo Sedan, red, Model No. 1018
EX $20   NM $30   MIP $50

Triumph, two-seat 1956 sports car, 3" long; painted green, red, blue, yellow or orange, bucket seats, oval grille, plastic tires, 1963-69
EX $4   NM $8   MIP $12

Triumph TR 3 Roadster, black wheels, 3" long; 1956
EX $4   NM $8   MIP $12

Twin Shaft, Super Slicks series, 4-1/4" long; blue bubble-top hot rod, side-panel stickers, chrome-hub tires, 1971-76
EX $4   NM $7   MIP $14

Volkswagen, two-door 1954 VW, 3" long, painted copper, red, yellow or green, open wheel wells, plastic tires, 1960-69
EX $5   NM $10   MIP $15

Volkswagen Rabbit, Midget series, 2-1/4" long, 1970s
EX $2   NM $3   MIP n/a

Volkswagen Rabbit, 4-3/4" long; opening rear gate, hood and side decals, 1970s
EX $3   NM $6   MIP $10

VW Bug, lime green w/black tread wheels, 3" long; 1960
EX $10   NM $20   MIP $35

VW Bug, "Stingin' Bug," white hub tires; 1970s

EX $3   NM $5   MIP $7

VW Bug, metallic gold w/black tread wheels, 6" long; 1960

EX $15   NM $25   MIP $30

VW Rabbit, opening rear gate, hood and side decals, 4-3/4"; 1970s

EX $3   NM $6   MIP $10

Wedge Dragster, Midget series, 2-5/8" long, 1960s-70s

EX $1   NM $3   MIP n/a

Wheelie Wagon, blue pickup, 3-7/8" long; white plastic interior, "Wheelie Wagon" stickers, white hub tires, 1970s

EX $2   NM $3   MIP $5

EMERGENCY VEHICLES

Ambulance Van, white, "Ambulance" decal, white hub tires, 1970s

EX $2   NM $4   MIP $7

American LaFrance Ladder Truck, Collector series, 4-1/8" long; chromed plastic ladder, 1967-69

EX $3   NM $5   MIP $89

American LaFrance Pumper, red, 3" long; 1954

EX $15   NM $20   MIP $35

American LaFrance Snorkel Fire Truck, Collector Series, 4-1/8" long; red, 1967-60

EX $3   NM $6   MIP $9

Chevrolet Ambulance, yellow, red cross on top, 4" long; 1950

EX $15   NM $25   MIP $40

Chevrolet Ambulance, army green, red cross on roof top, army star on top of hood, 4" long; 1950

EX $15   NM $25   MIP $50

Fire Chief Pickup, Hitch-Up series scale, 3-3/4" long; pickup truck, white hub tires, "Fire Chief" decal, 1970s

EX $2   NM $4   MIP $6

Fire Hook and Ladder, red/blue w/side ladders, Model No. 4652

EX $25   NM $40   MIP $50

Fire Water Tower Truck, blue/orange, red water tower, Model No. 4653

EX $30   NM $60   MIP $80

Graham Ambulance, white w/red cross on sides, Model No. 0809

EX $40   NM $95   MIP $125

Graham Wrecker, red/black; rubber wheels, Model No. 0806

EX $50   NM $110   MIP $150

Hoky Smoky, 6" long, Playmates serie, red fire truck, Little People-type

fireman, trailer w/dalmatian, purple tires, 1967-69

EX $10   NM $15   MIP $22

Hook and Ladder, Road Haulers series, 7-1/4" long, red die-cast body, white plastic interior and ladder assembly, white-hub tires, 1970s

EX $5   NM $10   MIP $15

Hook and Ladder, red and silver; white rubber wheels, Model No. 236

EX $15   NM $30   MIP $45

Hook and Ladder, #1040, Model No. 1040

EX $20   NM $25   MIP $40

Hose Wagon, red, black rubber wheels, postwar, Model No. 238

EX $20   NM $25   MIP $40

Insurance Patrol, w/driver, Model No. 1042

EX $25   NM $40   MIP $60

Insurance Patrol, red, white wheels, prewar, Model No. 237

EX $25   NM $30   MIP $45

Insurance Patrol, red, black rubber wheels, postwar, Model No. 237

EX $20   NM $25   MIP $40

Ladder Fire Truck, Midget scale, swiveling ladder, 3-1/2" long; 1960s

EX $4   NM $8   MIP $12

Ladder Fire Truck, swiveling white plastic ladder, 7-1/4"; 1970s

EX $8   NM $12   MIP $15

Lincoln Wrecker, sedan w/wrecker hook

EX $200   NM $425   MIP $600

Mack L-Line Fire Pumper, red w/ladders on sides

EX $35   NM $65   MIP $75

Mack L-Line Hook & Ladder, 9" long, late-1940s, extending ladder

EX $15   NM $30   MIP $75

Mack L-Line Hook and Ladder, red w/silver ladder

EX $35   NM $65   MIP $75

Mercury Fire Chief Car, red w/black wheels, 4" long; 1949

EX $25   NM $35   MIP $50

Pumper Fire Truck, Hitch-Up series scale, 3-3/4" long; two removable plastic ladders, white hub tires, 1970s

EX $3   NM $5   MIP $7

Rescue Truck, Hitch-Up series scale, 3-5/8" long, die-cast and plastic, white hub tires, "Emergency" decal, 1970s

EX $2   NM $4   MIP $7

FARM AND CONSTRUCTION EQUIPMENT

Caterpillar Bulldozer, yellow, 6" long

EX $25   NM $45   MIP $55

Caterpillar Scraper, yellow w/black wheels, silver blade, 6" long; 1956

EX $15   NM $25   MIP $40

Caterpillar Tractor, miniature, Model No. 108

EX $15   NM $25   MIP $35

Cement Truck, Road Haulers series, 6" long; die-cast cab, two-color plastic drum assembly, white plastic interior, white-hub tires; 1970s

EX $5   NM $9   MIP $14

D7 Crawler w/Blade, 1:50 scale, die-cast; 1956

EX $20   NM $35   MIP $55

D8 Crawler w/Blade, 1:87 scale, die-cast

EX $20   NM $30   MIP $45

Dozer, Construction Rigs series, 5-1/2" long, yellow die-cast tractor, black treads, plastic blade, 1970s

EX $1   NM $2   MIP $5

Earth Mover, Midget series, 2-1/2" long, 1960s

EX $2   NM $3   MIP n/a

Farm Tractor, w/driver, Model No. 4654

EX $60   NM $100   MIP $145

Farm Tractor and Spreader, green, white hub tires on tractor, white plastic steering wheel, early-1970s

EX $5   NM $10   MIP $20

Farm Tractor and Trailer, die-cast tractor w/hay trailer, 4-1/4" long, 1968-69

EX $3   NM $7   MIP $15

Farm Tractor and Trailer Hitch-Up, red tractor and trailer, plastic cow, 1980s

EX $2   NM $4   MIP $6

Ford Tractor, red w/loader, die-cast, 7" long, 1955-60

EX $20   NM $40   MIP $70

Grader, 1:50 scale; 1956, 6"

EX $20   NM $30   MIP $50

Heavy Duty Hydraulic Crane, Mobile crane, 4" long, w/telescoping boom and rotating cab, 1968-69

EX $4   NM $8   MIP $12

Heavy Duty Power Shovel, Mobile shovel, operating boom and rotating cab, 1968-69

EX $4   NM $8   MIP $12

International Tractor

EX $10   NM $15   MIP $25

Loader, Construction Rigs series, 5-1/2" long, yellow tractor w/plastic front scoop, black plastic tires, 1970s
EX $15   NM $2   MIP $12

Power Shovel, red four-axle truck w/plastic hydraulic shovel body, issued in window box, 1969
EX $7   NM $12   MIP $16

Road Builder, tractor-trailer, 5" long, long-nose truck hauls flatbed trailer and Michigan Earth Mover, 1969
EX $2   NM $4   MIP $8

Roller, Construction Rigs series, 5" long, yellow die-cast body, yellow plastic front roller, 1970s
EX $1   NM $2   MIP $5

Super Tractor, Super Tootsietoys series, 6-3/4" long; 1966-68
EX $5   NM $10   MIP $15

SETS

Box Trailer and Road Scraper Set, w/driver on road scraper
EX $75   NM $130   MIP $250

Car Fleet, blister card eight-piece set, cars and boat trailers in Midget series scale, 1969
EX $16   NM $20   MIP $25

Car Fleet, blister card eight-piece set, cars, racer trailer, boat trailer, Midget series scale, 1967
EX $16   NM $20   MIP $27

Cheerios Tootsietoy Box, 1950s cereal box offer on side, 1950s
EX $80   NM $100   MIP $120

Construction Set, five Midget-series vehicles including machinery hauler, earth mover, scraper, 1969
EX $5   NM $10   MIP $20

Contractor Set, pickup truck w/three wagons, Model No. 0191
EX $50   NM $100   MIP $130

Farm Set, blister card four-piece set, tractor, trailer and implements, 1969
EX $8   NM $10   MIP $14

Fire Station Set, Midget series scale pumper, jeep, fire chief car and badge, 1967
EX $10   NM $14   MIP $18

Flash Gordon Play Set, spaceships, 3-1/8" figures of Gordon, Dale Arden, Ming, 1978, Model No. 1793
EX $15   NM $20   MIP $40

Four-Car Transport Set, flatbed trailer carries cars, Model No. 0190X
EX $50   NM $90   MIP $135

Freight Train, five-piece set, Model No. 0194
EX $35   NM $60   MIP $80

Grand Prix #1687 Set, seven vehicles; 1969
EX $50   NM $95   MIP $150

Jam Pac, boxed 10-car Midget series set, 1969
EX $10   NM $20   MIP $35

Jam Pac, 12-piece Midget series set; 1967
EX $12   NM $24   MIP $30

Jam Pac, blister card six-car Midget series set, late 1970s
EX $6   NM $10   MIP $15

Jam Pac, blister card five-car Midget series set, 1981
EX $5   NM $8   MIP $12

Jam Pac, Midget series 10-car sets, 1966
EX $10   NM $20   MIP $27

Keep On Trucking, log, hauling and "Keep on Trucking" moving van tractor-trailers in tray box, 1981
EX $8   NM $10   MIP $15

Little Toughs Boat Set, blistercard w/Baha Buggy, blue/white boat and orange trailer, 197
EX $5   NM $10   MIP $15

Milk Trailer Set, tractor w/three milk tankers, Model No. 0192
EX $50   NM $100   MIP $200

Motorcycle w/Truck and Trailer Set, #1456, Collector Series window box, 4-1/2" long, Jeep pickup w/trailer and silver Honda motorcycle, 1968-69
EX $10   NM $15   MIP $22

Passenger Train, five-piece set, Model No. 0193
EX $40   NM $60   MIP $100

Playtime Set, six cars, two trucks, two planes
EX $200   NM $500   MIP $850

Road Construction Assortment, Caterpillar Bulldozer, Caterpillar Road Grader, Mack Dump Truck, Mack Machinery Hauler, six yellow road signs, full-color box, 1956-58
EX $100   NM $175   MIP $250

Road Racing Set, slot car set, two die-cast Corvair Monza racers, trestles, transformer, 1963
EX $35   NM $45   MIP $55

Task Force 88, five metal and plastic battleships
EX $5   NM $15   MIP $40

Tractor w/Scoop Shovel and Wagon, red w/silver scoop, flatbed trailer; 1946-52
EX $125   NM $185   MIP $250

U-Haul Hitch Up, 7-1/2" long, Jeep truck w/U-Haul trailer, six pieces of plastic furniture, 1969
EX $8   NM $13   MIP $18

SPACESHIPS

Flash Gordon Spaceship, 1970s
EX $3   NM $8   MIP $12

Space Ship, 4" long, reissue of Buck Rogers Flash Blast Attack Ship w/two-pod design, silver paint, U.S. Air Force insignia, 1958-59
EX $30   NM $50   MIP n/a

Space Ship, 4" long, reissue of Buck Rogers Venus Duo Destroyer, silver w/U.S. Air Force insignia, 1958-59
EX $30   NM $50   MIP n/a

Space Ship, 60, 120, 4" long, reissue of Buck Rogers Battle Cruiser, silver paint, U.S. Air Force insignia, 1958-59, Model No. 260
EX $30   NM $50   MIP n/a

Spaceship, 5-1/4" long, red metal top, white plastic bottom, six side windows, 1970s
EX $1   NM $3   MIP $8

Spaceship, 4" long, bus-type space transport w/three side windows, blue metal top, white plastic lower portion, red plastic forward windows, 1970s
EX $1   NM $3   MIP $8

TRAILERS

Boat Trailer, two-wheel
EX $10   NM $15   MIP $20

Horse Trailer, red w/white top, two-wheel, black tread wheels
EX $10   NM $15   MIP $20

House Trailer, powder blue w/black wheels, two-wheel, door opens, 6" long
EX $15   NM $30   MIP $40

Restaurant Trailer, yellow w/black tread wheels, two-wheel, open sides
EX $30   NM $40   MIP $65

Small House Trailer, two-wheel, three side windows, 1935
EX $30   NM $45   MIP $65

U-Haul Trailer, red w/black tread wheels, two-wheel, U-Haul logo on sides
EX $10   NM $15   MIP $30

TRAINS

Borden's Milk Tank Car, yellow; red base, Model No. 1093
EX $15   NM $20   MIP n/a

Box Car, "Southern," Model No. 1089
EX $15   NM $20   MIP n/a

Caboose, red, Model No. 1095
EX $10   NM $15   MIP n/a

Coal Car, red, Model No. 1090
EX $10   NM $15   MIP n/a

Diesel Train, Midget series scale, 13"
long; complete w/engine, three box
cars, one caboose, early-1970s
EX $10   NM $15   MIP $25

Log Car, silver w/red wheels; logs
chained on, Model No. 1092
EX $10   NM $15   MIP n/a

Oil Tank Car, silver top, red base,
"Sinclair," Model No. 1094
EX $15   NM $20   MIP n/a

Pennsylvania Engine, red/silver
EX $20   NM $30   MIP n/a

Refrigerator Car, yellow ochre, red
base, black roof, Model No. 1088
EX $10   NM $15   MIP n/a

Santa Fe Engine, black/silver
EX $15   NM $20   MIP n/a

Stock Car, red, Model No. 1091
EX $10   NM $15   MIP n/a

Wrecking Crane, green crane on silver
flatbed car w/red wheels, Model
No. 1087
EX $20   NM $30   MIP n/a

TRUCKS

All Across America Moving Van,
10" long, die-cast tractor, blue
plastic trailer w/"All Across
America...Keep On Truckin'"
EX $8   NM $12   MIP $18

Amoco Aviation Tanker Truck,
4" long, Toughs series, white hub
wheels, 1980s
EX $1   NM $3   MIP $6

Army Jeep, windshield up, 6" long;
1950s
EX $15   NM $25   MIP $40

Army Jeep CJ3, extended back,
windshield down, 4" long; 1950
EX $10   NM $15   MIP $35

Army Jeep CJ3, no windshield, 3"
long; 1950
EX $10   NM $15   MIP $40

Army Rocket Launcher, tractor-
trailer, plastic rocket; late-1950s
EX $50   NM $75   MIP $100

Army Supply Truck, w/driver, Model
No. 4634
EX $25   NM $40   MIP $55

Auto Transport, Collector Series
tractor-trailer, 5" long; red Ford or
Chevy tractor w/yellow two-level
hauler, w/two Triumphs, 1967
EX $5   NM $9   MIP $25

Auto Transport, Road Haulers series
tractor-trailer, 8-1/2" long, die-cast
cab w/white plastic interior and
grille hauls yellow plastic hauler for

Midget series cars, white-hub tires,
1970s
EX $4   NM $8   MIP $12

Auto Transport, tractor-trailer, 8-3/4"
long, Hendrickson tractor pulls
polypropylene hauler w/lowering
ramp, and three Midget series cars,
1969
EX $6   NM $12   MIP $18

Bimini Buggy, hot rod bus, white
plastic interior and exposed engine,
"Bimini Buggy" stickers on sides,
white-hub tires, 1970s
EX $2   NM $4   MIP $6

Box Truck, red w/white wheels,
3" long, Model No. 234
EX $15   NM $20   MIP $30

Buick Delivery Van, Model No. 6006
EX $25   NM $35   MIP $50

Cadillac Delivery Van, Model
No. 6106
EX $25   NM $35   MIP $50

Carousel and Transport Unit, tractor-
trailer, 4-1/2" long, Chevy or Ford
truck hauls flatbed trailer w/plastic
carousel, 1968
EX $5   NM $9   MIP $14

CB Super Wheeler Express, 8-3/4"
long semi truck, metal and plastic
cab, plastic-top box trailer, white
hub tires, 1970s
EX $7   NM $15   MIP n/a

Cherry Picker, Super Tootsietoys
series, 8" long; Ford Pickup truck
w/cherry-picker snorkel mounted
in truck bed, 1966
EX $7   NM $15   MIP $22

Chevrolet Cameo Pickup, green
w/black wheels, 4" long; 1956
EX $15   NM $25   MIP $40

Chevrolet Delivery Van, Model
No. 6206
EX $25   NM $35   MIP $50

Chevrolet El Camino, red, 6" long,
various colors, 1960s
EX $10   NM $18   MIP $35

**Chevrolet El Camino Camper and
Boat,** blue body w/red camper,
black/white boat on top of camper
EX $25   NM $35   MIP $85

Chevrolet Panel Truck, light green
w/black wheels, 4" long; 1950
EX $25   NM $30   MIP $40

Chevrolet Panel Truck, green, closed
front fenders, 3" long; 1950s
EX $10   NM $20   MIP $30

Chevrolet Panel Truck, green, front
fenders opened, 3" long; 1950s
EX $8   NM $17   MIP $25

Chevy El Camino, Midget series,
2-5/8" long, 1960s
EX $2   NM $4   MIP n/a

Civilian Jeep, blue w/black tread
wheels, 6" long; 1960
EX $15   NM $20   MIP $35

Civilian Jeep, red, open top, black
wheels, 4" long; 1950
EX $15   NM $20   MIP $35

Civilian Jeep, burnt orange, open top,
black wheels, 3" long; 1950
EX $10   NM $15   MIP $30

CJ3 Army Jeep, open top, no steering
wheel cast on dashboard, 3" long;
1950
EX $10   NM $15   MIP $30

CJ5 Jeep, red w/black tread wheels,
windshield up, 6" long; 1960s
EX $15   NM $20   MIP $30

CJ5 Jeep, red w/black tread wheels,
windshield up, 6" long; 1950s
EX $15   NM $25   MIP $35

Coast to Coast Van, 9" long
EX $40   NM $75   MIP $125

Dean Van Lines, tractor-trailer; 1950-56
EX $35   NM $75   MIP $100

Delivery Van, "Wild Wagon," white
hub tires, 3-7/8" long; 1970s
EX $3   NM $4   MIP $5

Diamond T K5 Dump Truck, yellow
cab and chassis, green dump body,
6" long
EX $25   NM $35   MIP $50

Diamond T K5 Semi, red tractor and
light green closed trailer
EX $25   NM $45   MIP $55

Diamond T Metro Van, powder blue,
6" long
EX $35   NM $75   MIP $100

Diamond T Tow Truck, red w/silver
tow bar
EX $25   NM $35   MIP $55

Dodge D100 Panel, green and yellow,
6" long
EX $18   NM $36   MIP $55

Dodge Pickup, lime green, 4" long
EX $8   NM $16   MIP $40

Double Bottom-Dumper Truck, tractor-
trailer, 8-1/4" long, Hendrickson truck
pulls two die-cast bottom-dumper
transport units, w/three-position
lever for dumping, 1969
EX $5   NM $11   MIP $30

Dump Truck, Road Haulers series,
6-1/4" long; die-cast cab and chassis,
white plastic interior, plastic dump
body, white hub tires; 1970s
EX $4   NM $8   MIP $12

Federal Express Van, 3-3/4" long, Toughs series, 1970s
EX $2   NM $5   MIP $10

Ford Bronco, "Buckin' Bronco," white hub tires; 1969-70s
EX $6   NM $14   MIP $28

Ford C600 Oil Tanker, bright yellow, 3" long
EX $10   NM $15   MIP $20

Ford C600 Oil Tanker, red, 6" long; 1962
EX $15   NM $30   MIP $40

Ford Dump Truck, 2-3/8" long, red w/silver grille and dump body, 1960 styling, HO-scale Pocket Series, 1962
EX $30   NM $70   MIP $120

Ford Econoline Pickup, red; 1962
EX $15   NM $25   MIP $35

Ford Econoline Pickup Truck, cabover pickup 6" long; hidden axles, plastic "Tootsietoy" tires, 1962-69
EX $7   NM $18   MIP $25

Ford F1 Pickup, various colors, open tailgate, 3" long; 1949
EX $8   NM $15   MIP $35

Ford F1 Pickup, various colors, closed tailgate, 3" long; 1949
EX $8   NM $15   MIP $35

Ford F6 Oil, orange, 4" long; 1949
EX $10   NM $15   MIP $25

Ford F6 Oil Tanker, red w/Texaco, Sinclair, Shell or Standard on sides, 6" long; 1949
EX $25   NM $50   MIP $100

Ford F6 Pickup, red, 4" long; 1949
EX $15   NM $25   MIP $40

Ford F600 Army Anti-Aircraft Gun, tractor-trailer flatbed, guns on flatbed
EX $20   NM $30   MIP $45

Ford F600 Army Radar, tractor-trailer flatbed, yellow radar unit on flatbed, 6" long; 1955
EX $10   NM $20   MIP $45

Ford F600 Army Stake Truck, tractor-trailer box, army star on top of trailer box roof and "U.S. Army" on sides, 6" long; 1955
EX $25   NM $40   MIP $55

Ford F600 Stake Truck, light green, 6" long; 1955
EX $15   NM $25   MIP $35

Ford Model A Pickup, 4-1/2" long, blue w/white canopy, black chassis, oversize wheels, Collector's Customized Model A Series, 1974
EX $5   NM $8   MIP $12

Ford Pickup Truck, Ford 1957 model truck, 3" long; covered-over rear window, patterned plastic tires, 1968-69
EX $4   NM $8   MIP $12

Ford Styleside Pickup, orange, 3" long; 1957
EX $10   NM $15   MIP $30

Ford Tanker Truck, Midget series 2-1/2" long; 1960s-70s
EX $2   NM $3   MIP n/a

Ford Tow Truck, Midget series, 2-3/8" long; 1960s
EX $1   NM $2   MIP n/a

Hendrickson Cement Truck, Collector series, 3" long; red body and chassis, silver tank, yellow plastic drum, 1967-69
EX $4   NM $8   MIP $12

Hendrickson Dump Truck, Collector series, 3" long; red cab and chassis, green heavy-duty dump body, 1967-69
EX $4   NM $8   MIP $12

Horse Trailer, Road Haulers series tractor-trailer, 8-1/4" long, die-cast cab w/white plastic interior and grille, orange plastic horse trailer w/lowering gate, six plastic horses, white hub tires, 1970s
EX $5   NM $10   MIP $15

Hot Rod Truck, Midget series, 1-7/8" long; 1960s
EX $2   NM $3   MIP n/a

Houseboat and Transporter, tractor-trailer, 4-1/4" long; Ford or Chevy truck hauls flatbed trailer w/House Boat, 1969
EX $5   NM $11   MIP $20

Hudson Pickup, red, 4" long; 1947-49
EX $35   NM $70   MIP n/a

International Bottle Truck, various colors, 1940s
EX $15   NM $30   MIP $65

International Car Transport Truck, red tractor, orange double-deck trailer w/cars
EX $35   NM $50   MIP $70

International Gooseneck Trailer, orange tractor and flatbed trailer
EX $30   NM $40   MIP $55

International K1 Oil Truck, green, comes w/oil brands on sides, 6" long
EX $12   NM $23   MIP $35

International K1 Panel Truck, various colors, 4" long, 1948-49
EX $20   NM $30   MIP $55

International RC180 Grain Semi, green tractor and red trailer
EX $30   NM $50   MIP $70

International Sinclair Oil Truck, 6" long, 1949, Model No. 1006
EX $15   NM $35   MIP $100

International Standard Oil Truck, 6" long, Model No. 1006
EX $35   NM $75   MIP $100

Jeep and Racer, Midget series combination, 4-1/2" long, Jeep w/trailer and Midget Racer, 1968-69
EX $2   NM $4   MIP $8

Jeep CJ5, Midget series, 2-1/8" long, 1960s-70s
EX $1   NM $2   MIP $35

Jeep Delivery Truck, Midget series, trailer hitch, 1960s
EX $1   NM $2   MIP $4

Jeep Panel Truck/Land Rover, Midget series, 2-3/8"; 1960s
EX $4   NM $8   MIP n/a

Jeep Pickup, Hitch-Up series, 3-5/8" long; die-cast and plastic, white hub tires, 1970s
EX $2   NM $3   MIP $5

Jeep Pickup, die-cast and plastic, white hub tires, 3-5/8" long; 1970s
EX n/a   NM n/a   MIP $35

Jeep Pickup, Midget series, 2-1/8" long; late 1960s
EX $2   NM $3   MIP n/a

Jeep Pickup Truck, Midget series, 2-1/4" long; 1960s
EX $2   NM $3   MIP n/a

Jeep Pickup w/U-Haul Trailer, Midget series combination, 4-1/2" long, 1967
EX $2   NM $3   MIP n/a

Jeep Truck w/Honda Motorcycle, Midget series combination, 4-1/2" long; Jeep truck w/trailer, chromed motorcycle, 1968-69
EX $3   NM $7   MIP n/a

Jeepster, Hitch-Up series, 3-7/8" long, "Jumpin Jeeper," white hub tires, 1970s
EX $2   NM $5   MIP $15

Jeepster, bright yellow w/open top, black wheels, 3" long; 1947
EX $10   NM $15   MIP $35

Jumbo Pickup, 6" long, 1940s, often silver, Model No. 1019
EX $10   NM $30   MIP n/a

Kennel Truck, Super Tootsietoy series, 8" long; Ford Pickup w/clear plastic dome over truck bed, partitioned to hold four dogs, 1967
EX $8   NM $17   MIP $25

Livestock Transporter, tractor-trailer, 4-1/4" long; Ford or Chevy tractor

hauls trailer w/two horses and two cattle, 1969
EX $7 **NM** $13 **MIP** $20

Log Truck, tractor-trailer, 4-1/4" long; Ford or Chevy truck w/logger trailer, three natural-finish logs, 1967-69
EX $10 **NM** $20 **MIP** $30

Logger, Road Haulers series tractor-trailer, 7-1/2" long; die-cast cab w/white plastic interior, die-cast trailer w/three wood logs, white-hub tires, 1970s
EX $5 **NM** $10 **MIP** $15

Mack Anti-Aircraft Gun, Model No. 4643
EX $25 **NM** $40 **MIP** $55

Mack B-Line Cement Truck, red truck w/yellow cement mixer; 1955
EX $20 **NM** $35 **MIP** $55

Mack B-Line Log Hauler, red cab, trailer w/load of logs; 1940s
EX $15 **NM** $35 **MIP** $135

Mack B-Line Oil Tanker, red tractor and trailer, "Mobil"
EX $15 **NM** $35 **MIP** $75

Mack B-Line Stake Trailer, red tractor, orange closed trailer; 1955
EX $20 **NM** $35 **MIP** $55

Mack Coal Truck, "City Fuel Company," 10 wheels, Model No. 0804
EX $60 **NM** $120 **MIP** $175

Mack L-Line Dump Truck, yellow cab and chassis, light green dump body, 6" long; 1947
EX $8 **NM** $15 **MIP** $55

Mack L-Line Semi and Stake Trailer, red tractor and trailer
EX $25 **NM** $50 **MIP** $125

Mack L-Line Semi-Trailer, red tractor cab, silver semi-trailer, "Gerard Motor Express" on sides
EX $60 **NM** $115 **MIP** $145

Mack L-Line Stake Truck, red w/silver bed inside
EX $25 **NM** $35 **MIP** $55

Mack L-Line Tow Truck, red w/silver tow bar
EX $8 **NM** $15 **MIP** $55

Mack Milk Truck, "Tootsietoy Dairy," one-piece cab, Model No. 0805
EX $50 **NM** $110 **MIP** $175

Mack Oil Tanker, "DOMACO" on side of tanker, Model No. 0802
EX $60 **NM** $100 **MIP** $155

Mack Stake Trailer-Truck, enclosed cab, open stake trailer, "Express" on sides of trailer, Model No. 0801
EX $50 **NM** $90 **MIP** $120

Mack Trailer-Truck, open cab, Model No. 4670
EX $50 **NM** $85 **MIP** $110

Mack Transport, red, open cab w/flatbed trailer, Model No. 190
EX $60 **NM** $150 **MIP** $200

Mack Van Trailer-Truck, enclosed cab and box trailer, Model No. 0803
EX $50 **NM** $100 **MIP** $140

Mack Wrigley's Spearmint Gum Truck, 4", green w/white rubber wheels, red hubs, Model No. 0810
EX $70 **NM** $150 **MIP** $225

Mobil Gas Tanker, tractor-trailer, 4-1/4" long; Ford or Chevy tractor hauling red tanker body w/"Mobil" sticker on sides, 1960s-70s
EX $8 **NM** $17 **MIP** $25

Mobile Gas Tanker, 9", 1960s
EX $15 **NM** $30 **MIP** n/a

Model T Pick-up, 3", black, spoked metal wheels, Model No. 4610
EX $25 **NM** $40 **MIP** $50

Oil Tanker, orange, four caps on top of tanker, 3" long, postwar, Model No. 235
EX $10 **NM** $15 **MIP** $25

Oil Tanker, blue and silver, two caps on top of tanker, 3" long, Model No. 235
EX $13 **NM** $26 **MIP** $40

Oldsmobile Delivery Van, Model No. 6306
EX $25 **NM** $35 **MIP** $50

Pickup, "wheelie Wagon," white hub tires, 3-7/8" long; 1970s
EX $3 **NM** $4 **MIP** $5

RC Cola Truck, blue cab, white box trailer, 1980s
EX $2 **NM** $5 **MIP** $10

Rodeo Cowboy, Toughs series Chevy, trailer and brown plastic horse, 1981
EX $3 **NM** $5 **MIP** $10

Royal Crown Cola Truck, 6" long, red cab, white plastic body w/transparent hinged side over soda-bottle decal, two plastic soda cases, "Me and My RC," 1970s
EX $5 **NM** $10 **MIP** $15

Safari Hunt, Midget series combination, 5-1/4" long, Jeep Panel Truck hauls plastic animal cage trailer w/giraffe, elephant, and hippo, 1968-69
EX $5 **NM** $15 **MIP** $30

Sanitation Truck, Road Haulers series, 6-1/2" long, die-cast cab and chassis, white plastic interior and dumping body, white-hub tires, 1970s
EX $4 **NM** $8 **MIP** $12

Shell Oil Truck, Hitch-Up scale, "Shell" decal, white hub tires, 1970
EX $3 **NM** $5 **MIP** $7

Shell Oil Truck, 6" long, rounded 1950s Ford style
EX $10 **NM** $20 **MIP** n/a

Shell Oil Truck, yellow/silver, 6", white rubber wheels, 1940s, Model No. 1009
EX $20 **NM** $40 **MIP** $75

Shuttle Truck, Midget series, usually green, 2-1/4" long; 1960s
EX $1 **NM** $2 **MIP** n/a

Sinclair Oil Truck, 6" long; green/silver, 1950s, Model No. 1007
EX $15 **NM** $50 **MIP** $75

Stake Truck, miniature, Model No. 109
EX $25 **NM** $40 **MIP** $55

Standard Oil Truck, red/silver; 6", white rubber wheels, 1940s, Model No. 1006
EX $25 **NM** $60 **MIP** $75

Super Camper, Super Tootsietoy series, 8-1/2" long; Ford Pickup truck w/removable camper
EX $7 **NM** $15 **MIP** $11

Super Dump Truck, Super Tootsietoy series, 9-3/8" long, blue Ford or GMC truck w/yellow operating dump, 1966-68
EX $5 **NM** $10 **MIP** $15

Super Tow Truck, Super Tootsietoy series, 8-1/2" long, Ford or GMC truck w/red cab, white rear tow assembly w/windup winch and tow hook, 1966-68
EX $7 **NM** $15 **MIP** $22

Super U-Haul Truck, Super Tootsietoy series, 8-1/2" long; Ford truck w/U-Haul body, 1966
EX $8 **NM** $17 **MIP** $25

Texaco Oil Truck, red/silver; 6", white rubber wheels, 1940s, Model No. 1008
EX $20 **NM** $40 **MIP** $75

Texaco Oil Truck, 6" long, rounded 1950s Ford style
EX $10 **NM** $20 **MIP** n/a

Tootsietoy Dairy, semi trailer truck, Model No. 0805
EX $75 **NM** $110 **MIP** $140

Tootsietoy Oil Tanker, red cab, silver tanker, "Tootsietoy Line" on side; 1950s
EX $60 **NM** $95 **MIP** $125

Turnpike Auto Transport, Midget scale, two cars, 5" long; 1960s-70s
EX n/a **NM** n/a **MIP** n/a

View-Master

by Mary Ann Sell

History

Initially designed to be sold in camera, drug and gift stores, View-Master has been in continuous production since 1939. View-Master reels were introduced at the 1939 New York World's Fair and at the 1940 Golden Gate Exposition in San Francisco. From there, the titles spread out to include a host of scenic attractions featuring everything from Crater Lake, Ore., to Miami Beach, Fla.

In the early-1940s, film and paper were scarce, and View-Master production all but halted due to the onset of World War II. However, a large contract to produce airplane and ship identification and range estimation reels saved the product from potential oblivion. Millions of reels were produced and used by GIs, along with thousands of Model B (round) View-Master viewers.

Although scenic reels were View-Master's forte, the company decided to spread out a bit in the late 1940s and produced a series of children's fairy-tale reels. These single-sleeved reels were identified with the prefix "FT." Clay figure models were initially produced by Lee Green Studios in Hollywood and later at the View-Master art studios in Portland, Ore. Dozens of reel titles were produced using the great diorama effect created by tabletop photography.

Keeping ahead of the competition, View-Master purchased the assets of its main rival, Tru-Vue, in 1951. This acquisition resulted in obtaining the license to use Disney characters, previously held by Tru-Vue. Since that time, the company has produced many Disney and other cartoon/character favorites. Some of these were produced as clay figures, others were drawn as stereo cells, and still others were created using actual products in the reel set up, as was the case with Barbie and G.I. Joe.

From 1946-2002, the fundamental design of the View-Master viewer had remained the same. The basic principal is you insert a View-Master reel vertically into the slot at the top of the viewer and pull a lever to advance the scene. All reels produced—from 1939 through today—can be viewed in any viewer. In 2003, Fisher-Price, the current manufacturer of View-Master, introduced a new viewer where the reel is inserted horizontally, rather than vertically.

In the late 1980s and early 1990s, View-Master developed character viewers (Mickey Mouse, Big Bird, Batman, Casper, etc), but these were short-lived and abandoned in favor of colorful versions of regular production viewers. New viewers come in a wide variety of colors and many gift sets feature viewers with colorful graphics and logos. New titles are always being added

The **Top 10 VIEW-MASTER** in mint condition

1. John F. Kennedy's Trip to Ireland	$500
2. Girl Scouts Serve Their Country	$250
3. House of Wax (Movie Preview Reel)	$250
4. It Came From Outer Space (Movie Preview Reel)	$250
5. Barbie Advertising Reel (Vintage Dresses)	$175
6. Son of Sinbad (Movie Preview Reel)	$150
7. Taza, Son of Cochise (Movie Preview Reel)	$150
8. The Maze (Movie Preview Reel)	$150
9. They Called Him Hondo (Movie Preview Reel)	$150
10. Jesse James v. The Daltons (Movie Preview Reel)	$150

to the line and a special line of educational titles is made under the Discovery Kids banner. Many retail outlets carry Discovery and children's titles today both through on-line and in retail stores.

Pricing

Condition determines value. As with any other paper collectible, it is important that View-Master reels be free of mold, mildew, brown foxing spots, etc. Reels missing scenes are virtually worthless. Those reels with paper blisters (caused by heat/moisture) are valued at less than 1/4 of mint reels. Three-reel packets need to be complete with outer color envelope, three reels, and inner story booklet, if indicated. Any part of the packet or booklet that is torn or damaged drops the value of the set. Adjust prices accordingly. Prices shown here are for MIP—Mint in Package—examples. Those in excellent condition command about 85 percent of the MIP price.

Trends: Sci-Fi and TV/Movie titles tend to sell high—scenic and cartoon titles are a little lower than in previous years. Some images on the reels have "gone magenta," meaning the film has turned red. This is a result of the type of film used. Usually all issues of that packet are red. One good example is the clay figure packet of Dracula. It is important to note this problem when considering condition.

Since the death of Michael Jackson in June 2009, "Thriller" reels and gift sets have started demanding high prices with the gift sets selling for $100 or more.

Collector Groups: At present, there are no collector groups solely dedicated to View-Master; however, there is a national organization devoted to 3-D collectibles. This is the National Stereoscopic Association and can be found on the Web at www.stereoview.org. And there is a Yahoo group dedicated to View-Master hosted by the contributor to this section. Every year the NSA hosts an annual convention and many View-Master products can be found at these events.

Other on-line resources: The View-Master home page, featuring historic View-Master information is http://www.cinti.net:/~vmmasell/

Contributor: This information is developed and written by View-Master collector/historian Mary Ann Sell. For more information turn to Mary Ann's View-Master Home Page www.cinti.net/~vmmasell/

Fisher-Price-official corporate View-Master page is www.fisher-price.com/us/view-master/

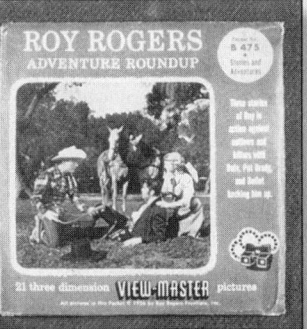

(Mary Ann Sell)

(KP Photo)

$1,000,000 Duck, Model No. B506
  NM $7 **MIP** $10

101 Dalmatians, Model No. B532
  NM $3 **MIP** $5

101 Dalmatians, Model No. 3014
  NM $3 **MIP** $5

**1939 New York World's Fair
(Single Reel),** Model No. 87
  NM $10 **MIP** $25

**1939 New York World's Fair
(Single Reel),** Model No. 86
  NM $10 **MIP** $25

**1939 New York World's Fair
(Single Reel),** Model No. 88
  NM $5 **MIP** $10

**1939 New York World's Fair
(Single Reel),** Model No. 89
  NM $5 **MIP** $10

**1940 Golden Gate International Expo
(Single Reel),** Model No. 58
  NM $5 **MIP** $15

**1940 Golden Gate International Expo
(Single Reel),** Model No. 57
  NM $12 **MIP** $35

**1940 Golden Gate International Expo
(Single Reel),** Model No. 59
  NM $5 **MIP** $15

**1940 Golden Gate International Expo
(Single Reel),** Model No. 56
  NM $12 **MIP** $35

**1962 Seattle World's Fair
(Four Reels),** Model No. A272
  NM $20 **MIP** $50

**1962 Seattle World's Fair
(Single Reel),** Model No. A2726
  NM $7 **MIP** $15

**1962 Space Needle U.S.A.
(Single Reel),** Model No. A2725
  NM $7 **MIP** $15

**1970s America's Cup (ABC's
WW/Sports),** Model No. B937
  NM $25 **MIP** $45

20,000 Leagues Under the Sea,
1954, Model No. B370
  NM $10 **MIP** $25

Adam & the Ants, Model No. BD199
  NM $25 **MIP** $50

Adam-12, Model No. B593
  NM $10 **MIP** $12

Addams Family, Model No. B486
  NM $75 **MIP** $100

Adventures of Morph, Model No. BD205
  NM $7 **MIP** $8

Aesop's Fables, clay figure, Model
No. B309
  NM $8 **MIP** $15

Aladdin, Model No. 3088
  NM $3 **MIP** $4

Alex, Model No. BD265
  NM $10 **MIP** $15

ALF, Model No. 4082
  NM $5 **MIP** $15

Alice in Wonderland, Model No. B360
  NM $8 **MIP** $12

An American Tail II, Model No. 4111
  NM $5 **MIP** $6

Annie, Model No. N3
  NM $6 **MIP** $12

Annie Oakley, Model No. B470
  NM $12 **MIP** $25

Apple's Way, Model No. B558
  NM $12 **MIP** $14

Arabian Nights, clay figure, Model
No. B335
  NM $8 **MIP** $15

Archie, Model No. B574
  NM $10 **MIP** $15

Arena (Movie Preview Reel)
  NM $50 **MIP** $75

Aristocats, The, 1970s, Model No. B365
  NM $5 **MIP** $10

Astrix & Cleopatra, Model No. B457
  NM $16 **MIP** $25

A-Team, Model No. 4045
  NM $10 **MIP** $25

**Auto Racing, Phoenix 200 (ABC's
WW/Sports),** Model No. B948
  NM $25 **MIP** $35

Babar the Elephant, Model No. B419
  NM $10 **MIP** $18

Babes in Toyland, Model No. B375
  NM $21 **MIP** $25

Backyardigans, Model No. H9696
  NM $2 **MIP** $5

**Bad News Bears in "Breaking
Training,"** 1977, Model No. H77
  NM $7 **MIP** $8

Bambi, clay figure, Model No. B400
  NM $5 **MIP** $8

Banana Splits, Model No. B502
  NM $10 **MIP** $20

Bananaman, Model No. BD239
  NM $9 **MIP** $10

Barbie and the Rockers, Model
No. 4071
  NM $7 **MIP** $10

Barbie Custom Advertising Reel,
1960s, only used to promote Barbie
dresses
  NM $125 **MIP** $175

Barbie Dolls of the World, Model
No. 36338
  NM $2 **MIP** $7

Barbie Prom Date, Model No. 35428
  NM $3 **MIP** $5

**Barbie Special Pink Viewer Set;
Regular Viewer in Barbie Pink,**
Model No. 1998
  NM $7 **MIP** $10

**Barbie Special Pink Viewer Set;
Supershow Viewer in Barbie Pink;
Target Exc,** Model No. 1998
  NM $12 **MIP** $30

Barbie's Around the World Trip,
Model No. B500
  NM $20 **MIP** $25

Barbie's Great American Photo Race,
Model No. B576
  NM $20 **MIP** $35

**Batman - The Animated Series
(Blister Pack),** blister pack, three
reel, Model No. 3086
  NM $2 **MIP** $4

Batman (Adam West), original
envelope package, three reel, Model
No. B492
  NM $10 **MIP** $25

Batman (Adam West), (Blister Pack),
blister pack, three reel, Model
No. BB492
  NM $13 **MIP** $15

Batman (Blister Pack), Model No. 1086
  NM $5 **MIP** $8

Batman Returns (Blister Pack), blister pack, three reel, Model No. 4137
> **NM** $7   **MIP** $8

Batman, The Perfect Crime (Blister Pack), 1976, blister pack, three reel, Model No. 4011
> **NM** $7   **MIP** $8

Battle Beyond the Stars, original envelope package, three reel, Model No. L16
> **NM** $15   **MIP** $25

Battle of the Planets (Blister Pack), blister pack, three reel, Model No. BD185
> **NM** $13   **MIP** $15

Beauty & the Beast (Blister Pack), blister pack, three reel, Model No. 3079
> **NM** $2   **MIP** $4

Bedknobs & Broomsticks, original envelope package, three reel, Model No. B366
> **NM** $5   **MIP** $10

Beetlejuice, Model No. 1074
> **NM** $10   **MIP** $25

Beetlejuice (Blister Pack), blister pack, three reel, Model No. 1074
> **NM** $10   **MIP** $25

Benji, Superstar (Blister Pack), blister pack, three reel, Model No. 4018
> **NM** $5   **MIP** $6

Benji's Very Own Christmas, original envelope package, three reel, Model No. J51
> **NM** $7   **MIP** $8

Bertha, blister pack, three reel, Model No. BD259
> **NM** $7   **MIP** $8

Best of Barbie, Model No. M8970
> **NM** $2   **MIP** $5

Beverly Hillbillies, 1963, original envelope package, three reel, Model No. B570
> **NM** $12   **MIP** $30

Big Blue Marble, original envelope package, three reel, Model No. B587
> **NM** $10   **MIP** $12

Black Beauty, original envelope package, three reel, Model No. D135
> **NM** $9   **MIP** $10

Black Hole, viewer and reel set
> **NM** n/a   **MIP** $60

Black Hole, blister pack, three reel, Model No. BK035
> **NM** $7   **MIP** $12

Black Hole, 1979, original envelope package, three reel, Model No. K35
> **NM** $15   **MIP** $18

Blue's Clues, Model No. 73059
> **NM** $2   **MIP** $6

Bollie & Billie, blister pack, three reel, Model No. BD207
> **NM** $7   **MIP** $8

Bonanza, original envelope package, three reel, Model No. B471
> **NM** $10   **MIP** $25

Bonanza, blister pack, three reel, Model No. BB487
> **NM** $10   **MIP** $20

Bonanza (w/out Pernell Roberts), original envelope package, three reel, Model No. B487
> **NM** $30   **MIP** $35

Bozo, blister pack, three reel, Model No. BD1484
> **NM** $13   **MIP** $15

Brady Bunch, original envelope package, three reel, Model No. B568
> **NM** $20   **MIP** $25

Brave Eagle, original envelope package, three reel, Model No. B466
> **NM** $21   **MIP** $25

Bravestar, blister pack, three reel, Model No. BD272
> **NM** $9   **MIP** $10

Buck Rogers, 1979, original envelope package, three reel, Model No. L15
> **NM** $7   **MIP** $10

Buckaroo Banzai, blister pack, three reel, Model No. 4056
> **NM** $10   **MIP** $25

Buffalo Bill, Jr., original envelope package, three reel, Model No. B464
> **NM** $18   **MIP** $25

Buffalo Bill, Jr., 1955, original envelope package, three reel, Model No. 965abc
> **NM** $21   **MIP** $25

Bugs Bunny, 1959, original envelope package, three reel, Model No. B531
> **NM** $9   **MIP** $10

Bugs Bunny & Tweety, blister pack, three reel, Model No. 1077
> **NM** $2   **MIP** $3

Bugs Bunny and Elmer Fudd (Single Reel), 1951, original envelope package, one reel, Model No. 800
> **NM** $7   **MIP** $8

Bugs Bunny, Big Top Bunny, original envelope package, three reel, Model No. B549
> **NM** $5   **MIP** $6

Bugs Bunny/Road Runner Show, original envelope package, three reel, Model No. M10
> **NM** $3   **MIP** $4

(KP Photo)

Bullwinkle, original envelope package, three reel, Model No. B515
> **NM** $12   **MIP** $20

Button Moon, blister pack, three reel, Model No. BD212
> **NM** $7   **MIP** $8

Can't Stop the Music, original envelope package, three reel, Model No. L1
> **NM** $17   **MIP** $20

Captain America, original envelope package, three reel, Model No. H43
> **NM** $4   **MIP** $5

Captain Kangaroo, original envelope package, three reel, Model No. 755abc
> **NM** $14   **MIP** $16

Captain Kangaroo, original envelope package, three reel, Model No. B560
> **NM** $10   **MIP** $12

Captain Kangaroo Show, original envelope package, three reel, Model No. B565
> **NM** $10   **MIP** $12

Care Bears, blister pack, three reel, Model No. BD264
> **NM** $5   **MIP** $10

Cars, Model No. H0703
> **NM** $2   **MIP** $5

Cartoon Carnival w/Supercar, original envelope package, three reel, Model No. B521
> **NM** $40   **MIP** $60

Casimir Costureiro, blister pack, three reel, Model No. BD171
> **NM** $7   **MIP** $8

Casper the Friendly Ghost, original envelope package, three reel, Model No. B533
> **NM** $5   **MIP** $6

Casper the Friendly Ghost, 1988, blister pack, three reel, Model No. BB533
> **NM** $5   **MIP** $6

Cat from Outer Space, 1970s, original envelope package, three reel, Model No. J22

    NM $7   **MIP** $10

Centurions, blister pack, three reel, Model No. 1057

    NM $3   **MIP** $4

Charge at Feather River, The (Movie Preview Reel), Movie Preview Reel

    NM $75   **MIP** $100

Charlie Brown Christmas

    NM $2   **MIP** $5

Charlie Brown, Bon Voyage, original envelope package, three reel, Model No. L2

    NM $6   **MIP** $12

Charlie Brown, It's a Bird, original envelope package, three reel, Model No. B556

    NM $6   **MIP** $12

Charlie Brown, It's Your First Kiss, 1980s, blister pack, three reel, Model No. 1039

    NM $10   **MIP** $15

Charlotte's Web, original envelope package, three reel, Model No. B321

    NM $5   **MIP** $6

Chip 'n Dale Rescue Rangers, blister pack, three reel, Model No. 3075

    NM $4   **MIP** $5

CHiPs, 1980, original envelope package, three reel, Model No. L14

    NM $13   **MIP** $15

Cinderella, Model No. B318

    NM $5   **MIP** $8

Cinderella (Single Reel), 1953, original envelope package, one reel, Model No. FT5

    NM $1   **MIP** $2

Cisco Kid (Single Reel), original envelope package, one reel, Model No. 960

    NM $2   **MIP** $4

City Beneath the Sea, original envelope package, three reel, Model No. B496

    NM $20   **MIP** $35

Clifford the Big Red Dog, Model No. C7174

    NM $2   **MIP** $5

Close Encounters of the Third Kind, original envelope package, three reel, Model No. J47

    NM $15   **MIP** $20

Cowboy Stars, original envelope package, three reel, Model No. B461

    NM $21   **MIP** $25

Curiosity Shop, original envelope package, three reel, Model No. B564

    NM $10   **MIP** $12

Curious George, Model No. 2015

    NM $6   **MIP** $12

Daktari, original envelope package, three reel, Model No. B498

    NM $10   **MIP** $13

Dale Evans, original envelope package, three reel, Model No. 944abc

    NM $26   **MIP** $33

Dale Evans, original envelope package, three reel, Model No. B463

    NM $23   **MIP** $30

Danger Mouse, blister pack, three reel, Model No. BD214

    NM $15   **MIP** $18

Dangerous Mission (Movie Preview Reel), Movie Preview Reel

    NM $75   **MIP** $100

Daniel Boone, original envelope package, three reel, Model No. B479

    NM $15   **MIP** $20

Dark Crystal, blister pack, three reel, Model No. 4036

    NM $7   **MIP** $15

Dark Shadows, original envelope package, three reel, Model No. B503

    NM $30   **MIP** $65

Davy Crockett, original envelope package, three reel, Model No. 935abc

    NM $64   **MIP** $75

Dempsey & Makepeace, blister pack, three reel, Model No. BD244

    NM $7   **MIP** $8

Dennis the Menace, blister pack, three reel, Model No. 1065

    NM $2   **MIP** $3

Dennis the Menace, original envelope package, three reel, Model No. B539

    NM $3   **MIP** $4

Deputy Dawg, original envelope package, three reel, Model No. B519

    NM $30   **MIP** $50

Devil's Canyon (Movie Preview Reel), Movie Preview Reel

    NM $75   **MIP** $100

Dick Tracy, 1990, blister pack, three reel, Model No. 4105

    NM $7   **MIP** $10

Dick Turpin, blister pack, three reel, Model No. BD188

    NM $9   **MIP** $10

Dinosaurs (Disney TV Show), blister pack, three reel, Model No. 4138

    NM $4   **MIP** $7

(KP Photo)

Discovery Channel Space Images, 1997, in plastic case/envelope w/relief of Shuttle and planet Saturn

    NM $3   **MIP** $7

Disneyland, Adventureland, Model No. A177

    NM $6   **MIP** $25

Disneyland, Fantasyland, Model No. A178

    NM $6   **MIP** $25

Disneyland, Frontierland, Model No. A176

    NM $6   **MIP** $25

(Mary Ann Sell)

Disneyland, Main Street U.S.A., Model No. A175

NM $6   MIP $25

Disneyland, New Orleans Square, Model No. A180

NM $6   MIP $25

Disneyland, Tomorrowland, Model No. A179

NM $6   MIP $25

Donald Duck, 1973, original envelope package, three reel, Model No. B525

NM $7   MIP $8

Dora's World Adventure, Model No. L2208

NM $2   MIP $5

Dr. Shrinker & Wonderbug, original envelope package, three reel, Model No. H2

NM $10   MIP $14

Dr. Who, blister pack, three reel, Model No. BD216

NM $35   MIP $50

Dr. Who, blister pack, three reel, Model No. BD187

NM $35   MIP $50

Dracula, 1976, original envelope package, three reel, Model No. B324

NM $13   MIP $15

Drums of Tahiti (Movie Preview Reel), Movie Preview Reel

NM $75   MIP $100

Duck Tales, blister pack, three reel, Model No. 3055

NM $4   MIP $5

Dukes of Hazzard, original envelope package, three reel, Model No. L17

NM $10   MIP $12

Dukes of Hazzard #2, original envelope package, three reel, Model No. M19

NM $10   MIP $12

Dukes of Hazzard 2, blister pack, three reel, Model No. 4000

NM $10   MIP $12

Dukes of Hazzard Canister Gift Set, 1981

NM $20   MIP $35

Dumbo, blister pack, three reel, Model No. BD1474

NM $9   MIP $10

Dumbo, original envelope package, three reel, Model No. J60

NM $7   MIP $8

Dune, blister pack, three reel, Model No. 4058

NM $7   MIP $12

E.T. (Reissued), blister pack, three reel, Model No. 4117

NM $3   MIP $6

E.T. The Extra-Terrestrial, 1982, original envelope package, three reel, Model No. N7

NM $15   MIP $18

E.T., More Scenes from, blister pack, three reel, Model No. 4001

NM $15   MIP $18

Eight is Enough, original envelope package, three reel, Model No. K76

NM $13   MIP $15

Electra Woman & Dyna Girl, 1977, original envelope package, three reel, Model No. H3

NM $9   MIP $18

Elmo Wants to Play, blister pack, three reel, Model No. 4125

NM $2   MIP $3

Emergency, original envelope package, three reel, Model No. B597

NM $10   MIP $12

Emil, blister pack, three reel, Model No. BD122

NM $10   MIP $12

Expo 67 Montreal, Model No. A074

NM $12   MIP $20

Expo 67 Montreal, Model No. A073

NM $12   MIP $20

Expo 67 Montreal, Model No. A071

NM $12   MIP $20

Expo 70 Osaka

NM $20   MIP $40

Expo 74 Spokane, single reel 1-6, each

NM $5   MIP $10

Fabeltjes Krant, blister pack, three reel, Model No. BD251

NM $10   MIP $12

Family Affair, original envelope package, three reel, Model No. B571

NM $21   MIP $25

Family Matters, blister pack, three reel, Model No. 4118

NM $4   MIP $8

Fang Face, original envelope package, three reel, Model No. K66

NM $5   MIP $6

Fantastic Four, 1979, blister pack, three reel, Model No. K36

NM $9   MIP $10

Fantastic Voyage, 1968, original envelope package, three reel, Model No. B546

NM $10   MIP $20

Fat Albert & Cosby Kids, original envelope package, three reel, Model No. B554

NM $5   MIP $6

Ferdy, blister pack, three reel, Model No. BD269

NM $9   MIP $10

Fiddler on the Roof, original envelope package, three reel, Model No. B390

NM $21   MIP $25

Finding Nemo, Model No. C7157

NM $2   MIP $5

Flash Gordon in the Planet Mongo, 1963, original envelope package, three reel

NM $21   MIP $25

Flight to Tangier (Movie Preview Reel), Movie Preview Reel

NM $75   MIP $100

Flintstone Kids, blister pack, three reel, Model No. 1066

NM $2   MIP $4

Flintstones, blister pack, three reel, Model No. 1080

NM $2   MIP $3

(KP Photo)

Flintstones, 1962, original envelope package, three reel, Model No. L6

NM $10   MIP $12

(KP Photo)

Flintstones: Pebbles and Bamm-Bamm, 1964, original picture envelope, three reel
    NM $7   **MIP** $14

Flipper, original envelope package, three reel, Model No. B485
    NM $10   **MIP** $12

Flipper, blister pack, three reel, Model No. BB480
    NM $10   **MIP** $12

Flying Kiwi, blister pack, three reel, Model No. BD189
    NM $10   **MIP** $12

Flying Nun, original envelope package, three reel, Model No. B495
    NM $21   **MIP** $25

Fonz, The, blister pack, three reel, Model No. BJ013
    NM $7   **MIP** $8

For the Love of Benji, original envelope package, three reel, Model No. H54
    NM $7   **MIP** $16

Fort Ti (Movie Preview Reel), Movie Preview Reel
    NM $75   **MIP** $100

Fox & Hound, original envelope package, three reel, Model No. L29
    NM $7   **MIP** $8

Fox & the Hound, The (Disney), 1980, blister pack, three reel, Model No. 3000
    NM $4   **MIP** $5

Fraggle Rock, blister pack, three reel, Model No. 1067
    NM $4   **MIP** $5

Fraggle Rock, blister pack, three reel, Model No. 4053
    NM $4   **MIP** $8

Frankenstein, 1976, original envelope package, three reel, Model No. B323
    NM $13   **MIP** $15

French Line, The (Movie Preview Reel), Movie Preview Reel
    NM $75   **MIP** $100

Full House, blister pack, three reel, Model No. 4119
    NM $6   **MIP** $12

G.I. Joe, 1974, original envelope package, three reel, Model No. B585
    NM $13   **MIP** $25

Garfield, original envelope package, three reel, Model No. L28
    NM $3   **MIP** $4

Gene Autry (Single Reel), original envelope package, one reel, Model No. 950
    NM $2   **MIP** $3

Gene Autry, "The Kidnapping" (Single Reel), 1953, original envelope package, one reel, Model No. 951
    NM $2   **MIP** $3

Ghostbusters, The Real, blister pack, three reel, Model No. 1062
    NM $4   **MIP** $6

Gil & Julie, blister pack, three reel, Model No. BD225
    NM $7   **MIP** $8

Girl Scouts Serve Their Country, Model No. 401
    NM $100   **MIP** $250

Glass Web (Movie Preview Reel), Movie Preview Reel
    NM $75   **MIP** $100

Godzilla, 1978, blister pack, three reel, Model No. J23
    NM $13   **MIP** $15

Gold Cup Hydroplane Races (ABC's WW/Sports), original envelope package, three reel, Model No. B945
    NM $24   **MIP** $30

Goldilocks, Model No. B317
    NM $7   **MIP** $10

Goldilocks and the Three Bears (Single Reel), 1946, original envelope package, one reel, Model No. FT6
    NM $1   **MIP** $2

Goonies, blister pack, three reel, Model No. 4064
    NM $50   **MIP** $100

Great Muppet Caper, original envelope package, three reel, Model No. M7
    NM $5   **MIP** $15

Green Hornet, original envelope package, three reel, Model No. B488
    NM $30   **MIP** $60

Gremlins, blister pack, three reel, Model No. 4055
    NM $7   **MIP** $12

Grimm's Fairy Tales, clay figure, Model No. B312
    NM $7   **MIP** $12

Grizzly Adams, original envelope package, three reel, Model No. J10
    NM $9   **MIP** $10

Gulliver's Travels, Model No. B374
    NM $10   **MIP** $15

Gun Fury (Movie Preview Reel), Movie Preview Reel
    NM $75   **MIP** $100

Gunsmoke, original envelope package, three reel, Model No. B589
    NM $21   **MIP** $25

Hair Bear Bunch, original envelope package, three reel, Model No. B552
    NM $7   **MIP** $8

Hammerman, blister pack, three reel, Model No. 1081
    NM $3   **MIP** $6

Hammerman, MC Hammer, Model No. 1061
    NM $6   **MIP** $12

Handy Manny, Model No. M733G
    NM $2   **MIP** $5

Hannah Lee (Movie Preview Reel), Movie Preview Reel
    NM $75   **MIP** $100

Hans Christian Andersen Fairy Tales, clay figure, Model No. B305
    NM $7   **MIP** $9

Happy Birthday Bugs Bunny, Model No. 1072
    NM $2   **MIP** $4

Happy Days, original envelope package, three reel, Model No. J13
    NM $7   **MIP** $8

Happy Days, 1974, original envelope package, three reel, Model No. B586
    NM $9   **MIP** $10

Happy Days, 1981, blister pack, three reel, Model No. BB586
    NM $7   **MIP** $8

Hardy Boys, original envelope package, three reel, Model No. B547
    NM $9   **MIP** $12

Harry Potter - Belgium Version, Model No. 73999
    NM $12   **MIP** $25

Harry Potter Sorcerer's Stone Part 1, Model No. 73632
    NM $4   **MIP** $8

Harry Potter Sorcerer's Stone Part 2, Model No. 73633
    NM $4   **MIP** $8

Harry Potter Sorcerer's Stone Part 3, Model No. 73634
    NM $4   **MIP** $8

Hawaii Five-O, 1972, original envelope package, three reel, Model No. B590
    NM $17   **MIP** $20

Heidi, Model No. B425
    NM $6   **MIP** $10

Herbie Rides Again, original envelope package, three reel, Model No. B578
    NM $7   **MIP** $8

Here's Lucy, original envelope package, three reel, Model No. B588
    NM $43   **MIP** $50

(KP Photo)

Holly Hobbie, 1976, "Classic Tales" series, picture envelope and booklet, three reels
    NM $6   **MIP** $13

Hopalong Cassidy (Single Reel), original envelope package, one reel, Model No. 955
    NM $2   **MIP** $3

Hopalong Cassidy (Single Reel), original envelope package, one reel, Model No. 956
    NM $2   **MIP** $3

House of Wax (Movie Preview Reel), Movie Preview Reel
    NM $150   **MIP** $250

Howard the Duck, blister pack, three reel, Model No. 4073
    NM $50   **MIP** $100

Huckleberry Finn, original envelope package, three reel, Model No. B343
    NM $5   **MIP** $8

Huckleberry Hound & Yogi Bear, 1960, original envelope package, three reel, Model No. B512
    NM $4   **MIP** $5

I Go Pogo, original envelope package, three reel, Model No. L32
    NM $7   **MIP** $15

Ice Age 2 - The Meltdown
    NM $2   **MIP** $5

Ice Age 3 - Dawn of the Dinosaurs
    NM $2   **MIP** $5

Inferno (Movie Preview Reel), Movie Preview Reel
    NM $75   **MIP** $100

Inspector Gadget, blister pack, three reel, Model No. BD232
    NM $7   **MIP** $10

International Moto-Cross (ABC's WW/Sports), original envelope package, three reel, Model No. B946
    NM $15   **MIP** $30

International Swimming & Diving Meet (ABC's WW/Sports), original envelope package, three reel, Model No. B936
    NM $60   **MIP** $70

Ironman, original envelope package, three reel, Model No. H44
    NM $3   **MIP** $5

Isis, 1976, original envelope package, three reel, Model No. T100
    NM $10   **MIP** $12

Island at Top of the World, original envelope package, three reel, Model No. B367
    NM $21   **MIP** $25

It Came From Outer Space (Movie Preview Reel), Movie Preview Reel
    NM $220   **MIP** $250

Jack & the Beanstalk, clay figure, Model No. B314
    NM $7   **MIP** $9

Jack and the Beanstalk (Single Reel), 1951, original envelope package, one reel, Model No. FT3
    NM $1   **MIP** $2

James Bond, Live & Let Die, original envelope package, three reel, Model No. B393
    NM $15   **MIP** $30

James Bond, Live & Let Die, 1973, blister pack, three reel, Model No. BB393
    NM $17   **MIP** $20

James Bond, Moonraker, 1979, original envelope package, three reel, Model No. K68
    NM $15   **MIP** $25

Jaws 3-D, blister pack, three reel, Model No. 4041
    NM $4   **MIP** $6

Jem, 1986, blister pack, three reel, Model No. 1059
    NM $6   **MIP** $7

Jesse James vs. The Daltons (Movie Preview Reel), Movie Preview Reel
    NM $100   **MIP** $130

Jetsons, original envelope package, three reel, Model No. L27
    NM $5   **MIP** $6

Jim Henson's Muppet Movie, original envelope package, three reel, Model No. K27
    NM $4   **MIP** $7

Jimbo and the Jet Set, blister pack, three reel, Model No. BD261
    NM $7   **MIP** $8

Joe 90, original envelope package, three reel, Model No. B456
    NM $50   **MIP** $70

Joe Forrester, original envelope package, three reel, Model No. BB454
    NM $9   **MIP** $10

John F. Kennedy's Trip to Ireland, Model No. 1305
    NM $200   **MIP** $500

Johnny Mocassin, original envelope package, three reel, Model No. B468
    NM $21   **MIP** $25

Johnny Mocassin, 1960s, original envelope package, three reel, Model No. 937abc
    NM $21   **MIP** $25

Julia, original envelope package, three reel, Model No. B572
    NM $15   **MIP** $25

Jungle Book, Model No. B363
    NM $7   **MIP** $11

Jurassic Park, blister pack, three reel, Model No. 4150
    NM $7   **MIP** $10

King Kong, original envelope package, three reel, Model No. B392
    NM $5   **MIP** $6

Kiss Me Kate (Movie Preview Reel), Movie Preview Reel
    NM $75   **MIP** $100

Knight Rider, blister pack, three reel, Model No. 4054
    NM $5   **MIP** $8

Korg 70,000 B.C., original envelope package, three reel, Model No. B557
    NM $10   **MIP** $15

Kung Fu, original envelope package, three reel, Model No. B598
    NM $13   **MIP** $15

Kung-Fu Panda, Model No. N1780
    NM $2   **MIP** $5

Lancelot Link Secret Chimp, original envelope package, three reel, Model No. B504
    NM $21   **MIP** $25

Land of the Giants, original envelope package, three reel, Model No. B494
    NM $20   **MIP** $30

Land of the Lost, 1977, original envelope package, three reel, Model No. B579
    NM $10   **MIP** $25

Land of the Lost 2, original envelope package, three reel, Model No. H1
    NM $10   **MIP** $25

Larry the Lamb, blister pack, three reel, Model No. BD190
    NM $7   **MIP** $8

Lassie & Timmy, original envelope package, three reel, Model No. B472

NM $13   **MIP** $15

Lassie Look Homeward, original envelope package, three reel, Model No. B480

NM $9   **MIP** $10

Lassie Rides the Log Flume, original envelope package, three reel, Model No. B489

NM $13   **MIP** $15

Last Starfighter, The, blister pack, three reel, Model No. 4057

NM $5   **MIP** $10

Laugh-In, original envelope package, three reel, Model No. B497

NM $13   **MIP** $20

Laverne & Shirley, original envelope package, three reel, Model No. J20

NM $5   **MIP** $10

Legend of Indiana Jones, blister pack, three reel, Model No. 4092

NM $5   **MIP** $6

Legend of the Lone Ranger, original envelope package, three reel, Model No. L26

NM $7   **MIP** $8

Legend of the Lone Ranger, blister pack, three reel, Model No. 4033

NM $6   **MIP** $10

Les Maitres Du Temps, blister pack, three reel, Model No. BD203

NM $7   **MIP** $8

Little Einsteins, Model No. L7863

NM $2   **MIP** $5

Little League World Series (ABC's WW/Sports), original envelope package, three reel, Model No. B940

NM $43   **MIP** $50

Little Mermaid, blister pack, three reel, Model No. 3078

NM $2   **MIP** $4

Little Mermaid - TV Show, blister pack, three reel, Model No. 3089

NM $2   **MIP** $4

Little Red Hen/Thumbelina/Pied Piper, 1957, original envelope package, three reel, Model No. B319

NM $7   **MIP** $8

Little Red Riding Hood, clay figure, Model No. B310

NM $5   **MIP** $7

(KP Photo)

Little Yellow Dinosaur, The, 1971, original picture envelope, three reel

NM $6   **MIP** $11

Lone Ranger, original envelope package, three reel, Model No. B465

NM $21   **MIP** $25

Lone Ranger, The, original envelope package, three reel, Model No. 962abc

NM $21   **MIP** $25

(KP Photo)

Lone Ranger, The Legend, tie-in w/the movie, original picture envelope, three reels

NM $10   **MIP** $17

Lost in Space, original envelope package, three reel, Model No. B482

NM $40   **MIP** $60

Lost Treasures of the Amazon (Movie Preview Reel), Movie Preview Reel

NM $75   **MIP** $100

Love Bug, The, 1968, original envelope package, three reel, Model No. B501

NM $9   **MIP** $12

Lucky Luke vs. The Daltons, original envelope package, three reel, Model No. B455

NM $21   **MIP** $25

M*A*S*H, blister pack, three reel, Model No. BJ011

NM $9   **MIP** $10

M*A*S*H, original envelope package, three reel, Model No. J11

NM $9   **MIP** $10

Magic Roundabout, The, original envelope package, three reel, Model No. B441

NM $13   **MIP** $15

Maja the Bee, blister pack, three reel, Model No. BD182

NM $7   **MIP** $10

Man from U.N.C.L.E., original envelope package, three reel, Model No. B484

NM $20   **MIP** $25

(Mary Ann Sell)

Mannix, original envelope package, three reel, Model No. BB450

NM $21   **MIP** $25

Mary Poppins, blister pack, three reel, Model No. BB372

NM $7   **MIP** $8

(Mary Ann Sell)

Mary Poppins, 1964, original envelope package, three reel, Model No. B376

NM $7   **MIP** $8

Mask, blister pack, three reel, Model No. 1056

NM $4   **MIP** $8

Maze, The (Movie Preview Reel), Movie Preview Reel

NM $128   **MIP** $150

Metal Mickey, blister pack, three reel, Model No. BD217

NM $7   **MIP** $8

Meteor, original envelope package, three reel, Model No. K46
NM $9 **MIP** $10

Michael, original envelope package, three reel, Model No. D122
NM $20 **MIP** $25

Michael Jackson's Thriller, blister pack, three reel, Model No. 4047
NM $6 **MIP** $18

(Mary Ann Sell)

Mickey Mouse, 1958, original envelope package, three reel, Model No. B528
NM $5 **MIP** $10

Mickey Mouse - Clock Cleaners, original envelope package, three reel, Model No. B551
NM $9 **MIP** $30

Mickey Mouse Club, original envelope package, three reel, Model No. 865abc
NM $21 **MIP** $25

(Mary Ann Sell)

Mickey Mouse Club Mouseketeers, 1956, original envelope package, three reel, Model No. B524
NM $21 **MIP** $25

Mickey Mouse Jubilee, 1980s, blister pack, three reel, Model No. J29
NM $9 **MIP** $10

Mighty Mouse, 1958, original envelope package, three reel, Model No. B526
NM $17 **MIP** $20

Mighty Mouse, 1970s, blister pack, three reel, Model No. BB526
NM $4 **MIP** $5

Miss Sadie Thompson (Movie Preview Reel), Movie Preview Reel
NM $75 **MIP** $100

(Mary Ann Sell)

Mission Impossible, original envelope package, three reel, Model No. B505
NM $20 **MIP** $25

(Mary Ann Sell)

Mod Squad, original envelope package, three reel, Model No. B478
NM $16 **MIP** $20

Money From Home (Movie Preview Reel), Movie Preview Reel
NM $75 **MIP** $100

(Mary Ann Sell)

Monkees, original envelope package, three reel, Model No. B493
NM $12 **MIP** $30

Monsters vs. Aliens
NM $2 **MIP** $5

Monsters, Inc., Model No. C7170
NM $2 **MIP** $5

Mork & Mindy, 1978, original envelope package, three reel, Model No. K67
NM $7 **MIP** $8

Movie Stars I (Single Reel), original envelope package, one reel, Model No. 740
NM $13 **MIP** $15

Movie Stars II (Single Reel), original envelope package, one reel, Model No. 741
NM $13 **MIP** $15

Movie Stars III (Single Reel), original envelope package, one reel, Model No. 742
NM $13 **MIP** $15

Mr. Magoo, 1977, original envelope package, three reel, Model No. H56
NM $6 **MIP** $10

Munch Bunch, blister pack, three reel, Model No. BD197
NM $7 **MIP** $8

(Mary Ann Sell)

Munsters, original envelope package, three reel, Model No. B481
NM $75 **MIP** $100

Muppet Movie, Scenes From The, blister pack, three reel, Model No. 4005
NM $4 **MIP** $8

Muppets Audition Night, blister pack, three reel, Model No. 4003
NM $4 **MIP** $8

Muppets Audition Night, The, original envelope package, three reel, Model No. L9
NM $4 **MIP** $8

Muppets Go Hawaiian, The, original envelope package, three reel, Model No. L25
NM $4 **MIP** $8

Muppets, Meet Jim Henson's, original envelope package, three reel, Model No. K26

NM $4   **MIP** $8

Muppets, The, blister pack, three reel, Model No. BK026

NM $4   **MIP** $8

Nanny & The Professor, original envelope package, three reel, Model No. B573

NM $30   **MIP** $35

NCAA Track & Field Championships (ABC's WW/Sports), original envelope package, three reel, Model No. B935

NM $40   **MIP** $60

Nebraskan, The (Movie Preview Reel), Movie Preview Reel

NM $75   **MIP** $100

New Mickey Mouse Club, original envelope package, three reel, Model No. H9

NM $5   **MIP** $8

New Zoo Revue, original envelope package, three reel, Model No. B566

NM $13   **MIP** $15

New Zoo Revue 2, original envelope package, three reel, Model No. B567

NM $13   **MIP** $15

Ni Hao, Kai, Lan

NM $2   **MIP** $5

Old Surehand, original envelope package, three reel, Model No. B443

NM $30   **MIP** $40

(Mary Ann Sell)

One of Our Dinosaurs Is Missing, original envelope package, three reel, Model No. B377

NM $10   **MIP** $12

Oregon Centennial Exposition (1959), Model No. A0250

NM $35   **MIP** $75

Orm & Cheap, blister pack, three reel, Model No. BD266

NM $10   **MIP** $12

Partridge Family, blister pack, three reel, Model No. BB5924

NM $17   **MIP** $20

Partridge Family, 1971, original envelope package, three reel, Model No. B569

NM $17   **MIP** $20

(KP Photo)

Partridge Family, 1971, Talking View-Master reels, original envelope package, three reel

NM $22   **MIP** $27

Pee-Wee's Playhouse, 1988, blister pack, three reel, Model No. 4074

NM $10   **MIP** $25

Pendelton Round-Up (ABC's WW/Sports), original envelope package, three reel, Model No. B943

NM $30   **MIP** $35

Perishers, The, blister pack, three reel, Model No. BD184

NM $6   **MIP** $8

Peter Pan, Disney's, original envelope package, three reel

NM $5   **MIP** $6

Pete's Dragon, original envelope package, three reel, Model No. H38

NM $7   **MIP** $8

Pink Panther, original envelope package, three reel, Model No. J12

NM $5   **MIP** $6

Pink Panther, 1970s, blister pack, three reel, Model No. BJ012

NM $4   **MIP** $5

Pinky Lee's 7 Days (Single Reel), original envelope package, one reel, Model No. 750

NM $21   **MIP** $25

Pinocchio, clay figure, Model No. B311

NM $8   **MIP** $12

Pippi Longstocking, original envelope package, three reel, Model No. B322

NM $13   **MIP** $15

Pippi Longstocking, original envelope package, three reel, Model No. D113

NM $13   **MIP** $15

Planet of the Apes, blister pack, three reel, Model No. BB507

NM $30   **MIP** $35

Planet of the Apes, 1967, original envelope package, three reel, Model No. B507

NM $30   **MIP** $35

Pluto, blister pack, three reel, Model No. 3013

NM $4   **MIP** $7

Pluto, original envelope package, three reel, Model No. B529

NM $9   **MIP** $10

Pluto, blister pack, three reel, Model No. BB529

NM $4   **MIP** $7

Polly in Portugal, original envelope package, three reel, Model No. B442

NM $26   **MIP** $30

Polly in Venice, original envelope package, three reel, Model No. D100

NM $17   **MIP** $20

Popeye, 1962, original envelope package, three reel, Model No. B516

NM $6   **MIP** $8

Popeye Talking View-Master Set, 1983, original envelope package, three reel

NM $9   **MIP** $10

Popeye's Fun, original envelope package, three reel, Model No. B527

NM $7   **MIP** $10

Portland Bill, blister pack, three reel, Model No. BD226

NM $10   **MIP** $12

Poseidon Adventure, original envelope package, three reel, Model No. B391

NM $21   **MIP** $25

Postman Pat, blister pack, three reel, Model No. BD218

NM $7   **MIP** $10

Power Rangers, Model No. 36870

NM $2   **MIP** $6

Princess & the Frog

NM $2   **MIP** $5

Pumcki, blister pack, three reel, Model No. BD220

NM $7   **MIP** $8

Punky Brewster, 1984, blister pack, three reel, Model No. 4068

NM $7   **MIP** $8

(Mary Ann Sell)

Quick Draw McGraw, 1960s, three reels
    NM $7   **MIP** $15

Raggedy Ann & Andy, Model No. B406
    NM $9   **MIP** $15

Ratatouille, Model No. L5994
    NM $2   **MIP** $5

Red Riding Hood (Single Reel), 1950, original envelope package, one reel, Model No. FT1
    NM $2   **MIP** $3

Rescuers, The, original envelope package, three reel, Model No. H26
    NM $5   **MIP** $8

Rescuers, The, blister pack, three reel, Model No. BH026
    NM $5   **MIP** $8

Return to Witch Mountain, original envelope package, three reel, Model No. J25
    NM $10   **MIP** $15

Rin-Tin-Tin, original envelope package, three reel, Model No. B467
    NM $13   **MIP** $15

Rin-Tin-Tin, 1955, original envelope package, three reel, Model No. 930abc
    NM $13   **MIP** $15

Robin Hood, 1954, original envelope package, three reel
    NM $21   **MIP** $25

Robin Hood Meets Friar Tuck, 1956, original envelope package, three reel, Model No. B373
    NM $17   **MIP** $20

Rocketeer, The, blister pack, three reel, Model No. 4115
    NM $7   **MIP** $8

Roland Rat Superstar, blister pack, three reel, Model No. BD240
    NM $7   **MIP** $8

Romper Room, original envelope package, three reel, Model No. K20
    NM $7   **MIP** $8

Rookies, The, 1975, original envelope package, three reel, Model No. BB452
    NM $13   **MIP** $15

Roy Rogers, original envelope package, three reel, Model No. B462
    NM $21   **MIP** $25

(KP Photo)

Roy Rogers, original envelope package, three reel, Model No. B475
    NM $21   **MIP** $25

Roy Rogers, original envelope package, three reel, Model No. 948abc
    NM $21   **MIP** $25

Roy Rogers (Single Reel), original envelope package, one reel, Model No. 945
    NM $2   **MIP** $3

Rudolph, 2004, Reel & Viewer Set: Target Exclusive, Rankin Bass Version
    NM $10   **MIP** $20

(KP Photo)

Rudolph the Red-Nosed Reindeer, 1955, definitely based on the Little Golden Book, the puppets even look like the illustrations, interesting, considering these reels were created about 10 years before the Rankin/Bass animated special, includes picture envelope and three reels
    NM $10   **MIP** $17

Rugrats, Model No. 36343
    NM $2   **MIP** $4

Run Joe Run, 1974, original envelope package, three reel, Model No. B594
    NM $13   **MIP** $15

Rupert the Bear, blister pack, three reel, Model No. BD109
    NM $12   **MIP** $15

S.W.A.T., 1975, original envelope package, three reel, Model No. BB453
    NM $10   **MIP** $12

Sangaree (Movie Preview Reel), Movie Preview Reel
    NM $75   **MIP** $100

Scooby Doo, blister pack, three reel, Model No. 1079
    NM $2   **MIP** $5

Scooby Doo, original envelope package, three reel, Model No. B553
    NM $4   **MIP** $5

Search, original envelope package, three reel, Model No. B591
    NM $17   **MIP** $20

Sebastian, original envelope package, three reel, Model No. D101
    NM $26   **MIP** $30

Sebastian, original envelope package, three reel, Model No. B452
    NM $26   **MIP** $30

Second Chance (Movie Preview Reel), Movie Preview Reel
    NM $75   **MIP** $100

Secret Squirrel & Atom Ant, original envelope package, three reel, Model No. B535
    NM $9   **MIP** $12

Secret Valley, blister pack, three reel, Model No. BD208
    NM $10   **MIP** $12

Sesame Street - Follow That Bird, blister pack, three reel, Model No. 4066
    NM $4   **MIP** $5

Sesame Street - People in Your Neighborhood, blister pack, three reel, Model No. 4049
    NM $4   **MIP** $5

Sesame Street - People in Your Neighborhood, original envelope package, three reel, Model No. M12
NM $4   MIP $5

Sesame Street Alphabet, blister pack, three reel, Model No. 4051
NM $2   MIP $5

Sesame Street Baby Animals, blister pack, three reel, Model No. 4072
NM $4   MIP $5

Sesame Street Circus Fun, blister pack, three reel, Model No. 4097
NM $4   MIP $5

Sesame Street Counting, blister pack, three reel, Model No. 4050
NM $4   MIP $5

Sesame Street Goes on Vacation, blister pack, three reel, Model No. 4077
NM $4   MIP $5

Sesame Street Goes Western, blister pack, three reel, Model No. 4085
NM $4   MIP $5

Sesame Street Nursery Rhymes, blister pack, three reel, Model No. 4083
NM $4   MIP $5

Sesame Street Shapes, Colors, blister pack, three reel, Model No. 4052
NM $4   MIP $5

Sesame Street Visits the Zoo, blister pack, three reel, Model No. 4017
NM $4   MIP $5

Shaggy D.A., original envelope package, three reel, Model No. b368
NM $10   MIP $12

Shazam, original envelope package, three reel, Model No. B550
NM $5   MIP $7

Shoe People, The, blister pack, three reel, Model No. BD270
NM $10   MIP $12

Siegfried & Roy, Model No. 73930
NM $6   MIP $12

Sigmund & the Sea Monsters (Correct Issue Numbers), original envelope package, three reel, Model No. B595
NM $15   MIP $18

Sigmund & the Sea Monsters (Wrong Issue Number), original envelope package, three reel, Model No. B559
NM $15   MIP $18

Silverhawks, blister pack, three reel, Model No. 1058
NM $4   MIP $5

Six Million Dollar Man, 1974, original envelope package, three reel, Model No. B556
NM $15   MIP $25

Sleeping Beauty, clay figure, Model No. B308
NM $5   MIP $7

Sleeping Beauty, Disney's, original envelope package, three reel, Model No. B308
NM $4   MIP $5

Smith Family, The, original envelope package, three reel, Model No. B490
NM $10   MIP $30

Smokey Bear, Model No. B404
NM $10   MIP $20

Smuggler, blister pack, three reel, Model No. BD194
NM $7   MIP $8

Smurf, Baby, blister pack, three reel, Model No. BD246
NM $7   MIP $8

Smurf, Flying, original envelope package, three reel, Model No. N1
NM $4   MIP $5

Smurf, Traveling, original envelope package, three reel, Model No. N2
NM $4   MIP $5

Smurfs, blister pack, three reel, Model No. BD172
NM $5   MIP $6

Snoopy and the Red Baron, 1980s, blister pack, three reel, Model No. B544
NM $7   MIP $8

Snorkes, blister pack, three reel, Model No. BD250
NM $8   MIP $10

Snow White, clay figure, Model No. B300
NM $7   MIP $9

Snow White & the Seven Dwarfs, original envelope package, three reel, Model No. K69
NM $7   MIP $8

Snow White (Single Reel), 1946, original envelope package, one reel, Model No. FT4
NM $3   MIP $4

Snowman, blister pack, three reel, Model No. BD262
NM $7   MIP $8

Son of Sinbad (Movie Preview Reel), Movie Preview Reel
NM $128   MIP $150

Space Mouse, original envelope package, three reel, Model No. B509
NM $10   MIP $20

Space: 1999, blister pack, three reel, Model No. BD150
NM $21   MIP $20

Space: 1999, 1975, original envelope package, three reel, Model No. BB451
NM $21   MIP $20

Spider-Man, original envelope package, three reel, Model No. K31
NM $8   MIP $9

Spider-Man, 1978, original envelope package, three reel, Model No. H11
NM $10   MIP $15

Spider-Man, 1980s, blister pack, three reel, Model No. BH011
NM $7   MIP $8

SpongeBob, Model No. C7177
NM $2   MIP $5

Star Trek - The Motion Picture, original envelope package, three reel, Model No. K57
NM $10   MIP $12

Star Trek - The Next Generation, blister pack, three reel, Model No. 4095
NM $10   MIP $20

Star Trek - Wrath of Khan, original envelope package, three reel, Model No. M38
NM $10   MIP $12

Star Trek (Cartoon Series), original envelope package, three reel, Model No. B555
NM $9   MIP $10

(KP Photo)

Star Trek (TV Series), "Omega Glory," 1968, original envelope package, three reel, Model No. B499
NM $17   MIP $20

Steve Canyon, 1959, original envelope package, three reel, Model No. B582
NM $64   MIP $75

Stranger Wore a Gun, The (Movie Preview Reel), Movie Preview Reel
NM $75   MIP $100

Superman, blister pack, three reel, Model No. 1064
NM $4   **MIP** $5

Superman, blister pack, three reel, Model No. BJ78
NM $5   **MIP** $6

Superman - The Movie, original envelope package, three reel, Model No. J78
NM $10   **MIP** $20

Superman (Cartoon), original envelope package, three reel, Model No. B584
NM $4   **MIP** $5

Superman II, original envelope package, three reel, Model No. L46
NM $17   **MIP** $25

Superman III, blister pack, three reel, Model No. 4044
NM $7   **MIP** $15

Superstar Barbie, Model No. J070
NM $7   **MIP** $15

Surf's Up, Model No. L6984
NM $2   **MIP** $5

Tailspin, blister pack, three reel, Model No. 3081
NM $4   **MIP** $5

Tarzan, original envelope package, three reel, Model No. B580
NM $9   **MIP** $10

Tarzan (Single Reel), original envelope package, one reel, Model No. 975
NM $4   **MIP** $5

Tarzan Finds a Son (Single Reel), 1955, original envelope package, one reel, Model No. 976A
NM $3   **MIP** $4

Tarzan of the Apes, 1955, original envelope package, three reel, Model No. 976abc
NM $21   **MIP** $25

Taza, Son of Cochise (Movie Preview Reel), Movie Preview Reel
NM $128   **MIP** $150

Teenage Mutant Ninja Turtles, blister pack, three reel, Model No. 1073
NM $2   **MIP** $5

Teenage Mutant Ninja Turtles - Movie II, blister pack, three reel, Model No. 4114
NM $3   **MIP** $7

Teenage Mutant Ninja Turtles - Movie III, blister pack, three reel, Model No. 4149
NM $2   **MIP** $5

Teenage Mutant Ninja Turtles - The Movie, blister pack, three reel, Model No. 4109
NM $3   **MIP** $5

Telecat, blister pack, three reel, Model No. BD243
NM $7   **MIP** $8

Terrahawks, blister pack, three reel, Model No. BD230
NM $10   **MIP** $20

They Called Him Hondo (Movie Preview Reel), Movie Preview Reel
NM $128   **MIP** $150

Thomas the Tank Engine, Model No. C7161
NM $2   **MIP** $5

Thomas the Tank Engine, blister pack, three reel, Model No. BD238
NM $6   **MIP** $10

Thor, original envelope package, three reel, Model No. H39
NM $2   **MIP** $5

Those Redheads from Seattle (Movie Preview Reel), Movie Preview Reel
NM $75   **MIP** $100

Three Little Pigs, clay figure, Model No. B307
NM $7   **MIP** $9

Thunderbirds, original envelope package, three reel, Model No. B453
NM $43   **MIP** $50

Time Tunnel, 1966, original envelope package, three reel, Model No. B491
NM $20   **MIP** $35

Tiny Toon Adventures, blister pack, three reel, Model No. 1076
NM $2   **MIP** $5

Tiswas, blister pack, three reel, Model No. BD205
NM $7   **MIP** $8

Toby Tyler, original envelope package, three reel, Model No. B476
NM $30   **MIP** $35

Tom & Jerry (Single Reel), 1956, original envelope package, Model No. 810
NM $2   **MIP** $3

Tom & Jerry, Two Musketeers, 1956, original envelope package, three reel, Model No. B511
NM $9   **MIP** $15

Tom Corbett, Secret from Space, original envelope package, three reel, Model No. B581
NM $21   **MIP** $25

Tom Corbett, Space Cadet, 1954, original envelope package, three reel, Model No. 970abc
NM $21   **MIP** $25

Tom Sawyer, original envelope package, three reel, Model No. B340
NM $7   **MIP** $8

Tom Thumb, original envelope package, three reel, Model No. D123
NM $13   **MIP** $15

Top Cat, blister pack, three reel, Model No. BB513
NM $13   **MIP** $15

Top Cat, original envelope package, three reel, Model No. B513
NM $13   **MIP** $15

Tournament of Thrills (ABC's WW/Sports), original envelope package, three reel, Model No. B947
NM $30   **MIP** $35

Toy Story 2, Model No. C7167
NM $2   **MIP** $5

Tripods, The, blister pack, three reel, Model No. BD242
NM $10   **MIP** $12

Tron, original envelope package, three reel, Model No. M37
NM $8   **MIP** $10

TV Shows at Universal Studios, original envelope package, three reel, Model No. B477
NM $26   **MIP** $30

TV Stars I (Single Reel), original envelope package, one reel, Model No. 745
NM $15   **MIP** $18

TV Stars II (Single Reel), original envelope package, one reel, Model No. 746
NM $15   **MIP** $18

TV Stars III (Single Reel), original envelope package, one reel, Model No. 747
NM $15   **MIP** $18

Tweety & Sylvester, original envelope package, three reel, Model No. J28
NM $3   **MIP** $4

Tweety & Sylvester, blister pack, three reel, Model No. BD1161
NM $7   **MIP** $8

Twice Upon a Time, blister pack, three reel, Model No. 4043
    NM $3   **MIP** $4

U.F.O., original envelope package, three reel, Model No. B417
    NM $38   **MIP** $45

Ulysses 31, blister pack, three reel, Model No. BD198
    NM $7   **MIP** $8

Veggie Tales - Madame Blueberry, Model No. 73992
    NM $6   **MIP** $12

Victor & Maria, blister pack, three reel, Model No. BD224
    NM $7   **MIP** $10

Voyage to the Bottom of the Sea, original envelope package, three reel, Model No. B483
    NM $10   **MIP** $15

Wall-E, Model No. N9918
    NM $2   **MIP** $5

Walt Disney Presents, Model No. B315
    NM $7   **MIP** $10

Waltons, The, blister pack, three reel, Model No. BB596
    NM $10   **MIP** $12

Waltons, The, 1972, original envelope package, three reel, Model No. B596
    NM $10   **MIP** $15

Welcome Back Kotter, original envelope package, three reel, Model No. J19
    NM $10   **MIP** $12

Where the Wild Things Are
    NM $2   **MIP** $5

Who Framed Roger Rabbit, blister pack, three reel, Model No. 4086
    NM $8   **MIP** $16

(KP Photo)

Wild Animals of Africa, 1960, original picture envelope showing giraffes, three-reel set
    NM $5   **MIP** $11

Wild Bill Hickcock & Jingles, original envelope package, three reel, Model No. B473
    NM $26   **MIP** $30

Willo the Wisp, blister pack, three reel, Model No. BD215
    NM $7   **MIP** $8

Wind in the Willows, blister pack, three reel, Model No. BD231
    NM $7   **MIP** $8

Wind in the Willows, blister pack, three reel, Model No. 4084
    NM $7   **MIP** $10

Wings of the Hawk (Movie Preview Reel), Movie Preview Reel
    NM $128   **MIP** $150

Winnetou, blister pack, three reel, Model No. BB731
    NM $21   **MIP** $25

Winnetou, original envelope package, three reel, Model No. B728
    NM $26   **MIP** $30

Winnetou, blister pack, three reel, Model No. BB7284
    NM $21   **MIP** $25

Winnetou & Halfblood Apache, original envelope package, three reel, Model No. B728
    NM $26   **MIP** $30

Winnie the Pooh & The Blustery Day, original envelope package, three reel, Model No. K37
    NM $7   **MIP** $8

Wiz, The, 1978, original envelope package, three reel, Model No. J14
    NM $17   **MIP** $20

Wizard of Oz, blister pack, three reel, Model No. BD267
    NM $7   **MIP** $8

Wizard of Oz, 1957, original envelope package, three reel, Model No. FT45abc
    NM $13   **MIP** $15

Wombles, The, blister pack, three reel, Model No. BD131
    NM $7   **MIP** $8

Wombles, The, original envelope package, three reel, Model No. D131
    NM $13   **MIP** $15

Wonder Pets, Model No. M1355
    NM $2   **MIP** $5

(KP Photo)

Wonderful World of Disney, includes three reels: Pinocchio, Lady & The Tramp, Snow White
    NM $8   **MIP** $15

Woody Woodpecker, 1955, original envelope package, three reel, Model No. B522
    NM $13   **MIP** $15

Woody Woodpecker Pony Express Ride (Single Reel), 1951, original envelope package, one reel, Model No. 820
    NM $3   **MIP** $4

Western Toys

By Mark Bellomo

The success of nearly every modern toy line is in no small way dependent upon a well-developed media tie-in. Which raises the question: how will the most iconic Western toys in the hobby—those toys derived from the revered "Big Four" Western brands (Gene Autry, Hopalong Cassidy, the Lone Ranger, and Roy Rogers)—survive in a secondary market flooded with resurrected toy franchises from the 1980s or the massively successful modern superhero genre?

The solution rests in the hands of the companies who currently own these licenses: Gene Autry Entertainment (Gene Autry), Sagebrush Entertainment (Hopalong Cassidy), the Classic Media Corporation (Lone Ranger), and Roy Rogers Jr. (Roy Rogers). These companies must build brand awareness with their current audience while indoctrinating new fans along the way.

Why is it so difficult for our favorite Western brands to capture the attention of the American collective consciousness? Furthermore, if the height of the genre's popularity occurred in the 1940s and 1950s, these former fans are of retirement age: so then, why aren't these aficionados returning to their beloved childhood hobby?

Beyond the lack of interest evidenced by many Baby Boomers, the shortage of contemporary brand awareness is definitely hurting the hobby. From the Great Train Robbery (1903) to the brilliant films directed by John Ford and Howard Hawkes to the outstanding Spaghetti Westerns of the 1960s and 1970s, modern American children are not replacing the fans of Westerns who've retired, passed on, or have left the hobby because of the lack of disposable income due to the global economic crisis. Diehard fans simply must pass their love of the genre on to their children and grandchildren. Due to these numerous obstacles, the prices of many pieces of Western memorabilia have certainly decreased; some toys, quite dramatically. Even the premiere pieces of any Western line in dead mint condition—those "Holy Grails" so-to-speak—have also declined in value. For instance, let's regard the single most prestigious piece of Western toy memorabilia that exists in any high-end collection: the Hopalong Cassidy Roller Stakes produced by the Rollfast [Bicycle] Company.

At one time, these magnificently-constructed Hoppy Roller Skates were a quick sell at $1,000+ for a Mint in Box, Mint Condition pair with the oft-broken spurs totally intact, the quality leather straps completely un-cracked, with the [rarely] included skate key and impossible-to-find instruction booklet, and with all of the delicate paint applications and intricate decorations unblemished. I currently witnessed a set of these roller skates in this aforementioned condition sell for a mere $735. That's $735 for one of THE premiere Western toys of all time—and $265 less than its suggested guide value. It appears that the competition for these toys is not as fierce as it once was.

Like the honorable, steadfast Western heroes of old—things are certainly not the way they used to be… even on the secondary market. However, it is our responsibility and duty as stalwart collectors of Western memorabilia to usher new fans into our hobby. So then, take a family member or close friend to view the sophisticated new Lone Ranger film. Instead of letting your grandchildren watch modern cartoons, follow up your trip to the theater with a DVD viewing of some episodes of the classics Lone Ranger television series (1949-1957) featuring Clayton Moore and Jay Silverheels. If you have a teenager in the family, pick up some trade paperbacks that collect the spectacular (and adult-themed) issues of Dynamite Entertainment's award-winning, ongoing Lone Ranger comic book series (2006-present).

And no matter what, please support the hobby any way you can, Ke-mo sah-be.

The Top 10 WESTERN TOYS in mint condition

1. Hopalong Cassidy Rollerskates, Rollfast, 1950s $800
2. Wagon Train Complete Western Outfit, Leslie Henry, 1950s $590
3. Hopalong Cassidy Cap Gun, Wyandotte, 1950s $575
4. Hopalong Cassidy Radio, Arvin, 1950s $525
5. Roy Rogers Toy Chest, 1950s $475
6. Harland Figures, Bill Longley – The Texan, 1959 . . . . $460
7. Hopalong Cassidy metal figures, Timpo, 1950s $400
8. Hartland Figures, Bat Masterson, 1950s $390
9. Lone Ranger Record Player, Decca, 1950s $325
10. Bonanza Outfit, Marx, 1960s $315

Annie Oakley

Annie Oakley w/Tagg and Lofty Cut-Out Dolls, 1955, Whitman, paper dolls
EX $20   NM $35   MIP $50

Cut-Out Dolls, 1956, Watkins-Strathmore, paper dolls, Model No. 1822
EX $20   NM $45   MIP $80

Cut-Out Dolls, 1958, Whitman, paper dolls
EX $20   NM $35   MIP $50

Girl's Outfit, 1950s, Pla-Master, red w/yellow fringe and four pictures (Gail Davis?)
EX $40   NM $85   MIP $140

Holster Set, 1950s, Daisy, leather holsters and cap pistols
EX $100   NM $185   MIP $300

Puzzle, 1955, Milton Bradley, boxed jigsaw puzzle
EX $5   NM $10   MIP $30

Sewing Set, 1950s, Pressman
EX $25   NM $45   MIP $65

Sharpshooter Book, 1956, Golden, Little Golden Books
EX $10   NM $20   MIP $30

Sparkle Picture Craft, 1950s, Gabriel
EX $20   NM $30   MIP $45

Bonanza

Ben Cartwright and His Horse, 1966, American Character, plastic figures
EX $60   NM $140   MIP $275

Bonanza Four-in-One Wagon, 1960s, American Character
EX $75   NM $150   MIP $300

Bonanza Outfit, 1960s, Marx, set containing: single holster; cap firing bullet shooting pistol; cap shooting repeating saddle rifle, plastic bullets
EX $150   NM $300   MIP $450

Foto Fantastiks Photo Coloring Set, 1960s, Eberhard Faber
EX $40   NM $75   MIP $150

Hoss Cartwright and his Horse, 1966, American Character, plastic figures
EX $60   NM $140   MIP $275

Hoss Range Pistol, 1960s, Marx, carded plastic gun
EX $35   NM $65   MIP $125

Little Joe Cartwright Figure, 1966, American Character, 6" figure
EX $60   NM $140   MIP $275

Mustang, American Character, the outlaw's horse
EX $25   NM $50   MIP $100

Outlaw Figure, 1966, American Character
EX $40   NM $80   MIP $160

Palomino, American Character, Ben's horse
EX $25   NM $50   MIP $100

Pinto, American Character, Little Joe's horse
EX $25   NM $50   MIP $100

Puzzle, 1960s, Saalfield, frame tray
EX $20   NM $40   MIP $75

Puzzle, 1964, Milton Bradley
EX $10   NM $20   MIP $40

Stallion, American Character, Hoss's horse
EX $25   NM $50   MIP $100

Woodburning Set, 1960s, ATF Toys
EX $65   NM $125   MIP $250

Daniel Boone

Card Game, 1965, Ed-U-Cards
EX $7   NM $10   MIP $15

Figure, 1964, Remco, 5" tall, hard plastic body, vinyl head, cloth coonskin cap and long rifle
EX $35   NM $90   MIP $160

Film Viewer, 1964, Acme, w/two arms
EX $7   NM $10   MIP $20

Inflatable Toy, 1965, Multiple Toymakers
EX $25   NM $50   MIP $75

Davy Crockett

3-D Moving Picture and Viewer, 1950s, Armour-Cloverbloom Margarine, premium cardboard viewer w/3-D cards
EX $40   NM $80   MIP $150

Alamo Construction Set, 1950s, Practi-Cole
EX $40   NM $75   MIP $150

Auto-Magic Picture Gun, 1950s, Stephens, projection gun w/films
EX $40   NM $75   MIP $150

Baby Davy Crockett Doll, 1950s, Spunky, 8" tall vinyl squeeze toy
EX $20   NM $40   MIP $75

Davy Crockett and His Horse Figures, 1950s, Ideal, plastic
EX $30   NM $50   MIP $150

Dispatch Case, 1950s, Neptune Plastics, vinyl pouch, yellow graphics
EX $15   NM $30   MIP $65

Doll, 1950s, 8", hard plastic, sleepy eyes, leather clothes, two rifles, hat
EX $60   NM $130   MIP $250

Doll, 1973, Exel, Legends of the West series, 9-1/2"
EX $30   NM $55   MIP $95

Frontier Rifle, 1950s, Marx, 32" rifle
EX $40   NM $75   MIP $150

Frontier Target Game, American Toys, tin litho dartboard
EX $35   NM $75   MIP $130

Frontierland Pencil Case, 1950s, Hassenfeld Bros., cardboard
EX $45   NM $75   MIP $100

Frontierland Pioneer Scout Outfit, 1950s, Eddy, costume set
EX $50   NM $100   MIP $250

Guitar, 1950s, Peter Puppet Playthings, 24" long, wood
EX $80   NM $175   MIP $350

Iron-Ons, 1950s, Vogart, three transfers on sheet
EX $15   NM $35   MIP $50

Magic Paint w/Water Pictures, 1950s, Artcraft, construction and art set w/Frontierland fort
EX $75   NM $150   MIP $275

Offical Davy Crockett Color TV Set, 1950s, Lido, plastic viewer, four films
EX $75   NM $150   MIP $275

Official Davy Crockett Belt, 1950s, on card
EX $35   NM $80   MIP $150

Official Davy Crockett Tool Kit, 1950s, Liberty Steel Chest, w/tools
EX $75   NM $175   MIP $250

Pocket Knife, 1950s, Disney, single blade, 2", yellow
EX $20   NM $40   MIP $75

Pony Express Bank, 1950s, Randing, brown and white cloth pouch w/lock and key
EX $15   NM $30   MIP $50

Push Puppet, 1950s, Kohner Bros.
EX $30   NM $65   MIP $100

Puzzle, 1950s, Marx, Seige on the Fort
EX $15   NM $40   MIP $60

Puzzle, 1955, Whitman, 11-1/4" x 15"
EX $15   NM $40   MIP $60

Ride-On Bouncing Horse, 1950s, Rich Toys, 37" x 31", white plastic w/black and yellow saddle
EX $75   NM $150   MIP $275

Ring, 1950s, bronze-colored
EX $40   NM $50   MIP $60

Sand Pail, 1950s, Ohio Art, tin litho
EX $20   NM $35   MIP $85

Suspenders, 1950s, tan w/Crockett graphics
EX $25   NM $50   MIP $90

Travel Bag, 1950s, Neevel, 6-1/2" x 12" x 10" heavy cardboard w/brass hinges and plastic handle
EX $30   NM $75   MIP $130

Wallet, 1950s, Walt Disney, red vinyl w/faux fur
EX $20   NM $45   MIP $80

Wood Burning Set, 1950s, American Toy & Furniture
EX $10   NM $25   MIP $50

Gene Autry

Frame Tray Puzzle, 1950s, Whitman, wood
EX $15   NM $21   MIP $45

Gene Autry Drum Set, 1940s, Colmor
EX $100   NM $175   MIP $300

Gene Autry Guitar, 1950s, Emenee, plastic
EX $65   NM $125   MIP $225

Gene Autry Jump-Up Book, 1955, Adprint Limited London
EX $30   NM $52   MIP $82

Gene Autry Ranch Outfit, 1940s, Henry, dress-up kit w/holster and gun
EX $100   NM $175   MIP $285

Gene Autry's Champion Slate, 1950s, Lowe
EX $15   NM $26   MIP $55

Gene Autry's Stencil Book, 1950s
EX $15   NM $31   MIP $55

Spurs, 1960s, Leslie-Henry, metal spur w/leather back "Gene Autry" signature burned into the leather
EX $40   NM $100   MIP $185

Stringless Marionette, 1950s, National Mask & Puppet, 14-1/2" tall
EX $75   NM $125   MIP $175

Gunsmoke

Coloring Book, 1950s, Whitman
EX $10   NM $20   MIP $45

Gunsmoke Puzzle, 1950s, Whitman, boxed
EX $18   NM $33   MIP $55

Gunsmoke Puzzle, 1958, Whitman, frame tray
EX $19   NM $34   MIP $60

Marshal Matt Dillon's Gunsmoke Play Set, 1958, Multiple, red, yellow, and blue plastic characters, jailhouse, wagon, guns, hats and accessories
EX $40   NM $85   MIP $125

Hartland Figures

Annie Oakley and Target, 1950s, Hartland, 9" plastic rider w/horse, #823, tan horse, white hat, black pistol, black saddle
EX $160   NM $340   MIP $600

Bat Masterson, 1950s, Hartland, 9" figure only, w/hat, gun, cane
EX $250   NM $550   MIP $950

Bill Longley - The Texan, 1959, Hartland, #827, 9" plastic rider w/horse
EX $250   NM $600   MIP $1100

Brave Eagle and White Cloud, 1950s, Hartland, 9" plastic rider w/horse
EX $150   NM $300   MIP $450

Bret Maverick, 1950s, Hartland, #762, 9" plastic figure, long light blue jacket, light blue hat, two pistols
EX $160   NM $320   MIP $620

Bret Maverick, 1960s, Hartland, #862, 9" plastic rider w/horse
EX $150   NM $310   MIP $500

Buffalo Bill, 1950s, Hartland, #819, 9" plastic rider w/horse, hat, two pistols
EX $160   NM $280   MIP $550

Cheyenne, 1950s, Hartland, #818, 9" plastic rider w/horse
EX $100   NM $180   MIP $340

Cheyenne, 1960s, Hartland, 9" plastic rider w/horse
EX $80   NM $170   MIP $280

Chief Brave Eagle, 1950s, Hartland, #812, white horse, headdress, saddle blanket, bow, knife
EX $80   NM $220   MIP $370

Chief Thunderbird and Horse, 1950s, Hartland, #813, black/white horse, saddle blanket, tomahawk, spear, knife, headdress
EX $120   NM $250   MIP $400

Clay Holister Gunfighter, 1950s, Hartland, #763, figure only, two guns, black hat
EX $140   NM $250   MIP $400

Cochise, 1950s, Hartland, 9" plastic rider w/horse, saddle blanket, rifle
EX $120   NM $220   MIP $370

Col. Ronald Mackenzie, 1959, Hartland, #829, 9" plastic rider w/horse
EX $250   NM $550   MIP $1000

Cowgirl, 1960s, Hartland, #802, 9" plastic rider w/horse, jade green w/tan pants or red shirt w/white pants
EX $100   NM $170   MIP $320

Dale Evans, 1950s, Hartland, 9" plastic rider w/horse
EX $100   NM $220   MIP $400

Davy Crockett, 1950s, Hartland, 9" plastic rider w/horse
EX $110   NM $190   MIP $330

General Robert E. Lee, 1950s, Hartland, #808, w/horse

(Traveller), confederate flag, saddle, and sword
EX $120   NM $220   MIP $380

George Washington and Ajax, 1950s, Hartland, plastic rider w/horse, flag, hat
EX $100   NM $220   MIP $330

Gil Favor from Rawhide, 1950s, Hartland, #831, w/horse, saddle, hat, gun; 9" figure has dark blue pants, light blue shirt and yellow vest
EX $230   NM $400   MIP $750

Hoby Gilman, 1960s, Hartland, #825, 9" plastic rider w/horse
EX $100   NM $190   MIP $330

Jim Bowie and Blaze, 1950s, Hartland, #817, 9" plastic rider w/horse, long rifle, knife
EX $160   NM $400   MIP $820

Jim Hardie, 1950s, Hartland, #864, 9" plastic rider w/horse
EX $100   NM $190   MIP $330

Johnny Yuma - The Rebel, 1961, Hartland, #832, 9" plastic rider w/horse
EX $100   NM $190   MIP $330

Josh Randall, 1959, Hartland, #828, 9" plastic rider w/horse
EX $100   NM $190   MIP $330

Lone Ranger, 1950s, Hartland, #801, 9" plastic rider w/horse, hat
EX $110   NM $220   MIP $400

Lone Ranger, 1960s, Hartland, 9" plastic rider w/horse, hat
EX $90   NM $170   MIP $370

Lucas McCain, 1960s, Hartland, #826, 9" plastic rider w/horse
EX $130   NM $270   MIP $510

Major Seth Adams of Wagon Train and Horse, 1950s, Hartland, #824, horse and rider, red shirt, gray vest, yellow pants
EX $170   NM $290   MIP $500

Marshal Matt Dillon, 1950s, Hartland, 9" plastic rider w/horse
EX $120   NM $220   **MIP** $350

Marshal Matt Dillon, 1960s, Hartland, 9" plastic rider w/horse
EX $120   NM $200   **MIP** $350

Paladin, 1950s, Hartland, #822, 9" plastic rider w/horse
EX $110   NM $180   **MIP** $270

Paladin, 1960s, Hartland, 9" plastic rider w/horse
EX $80   NM $160   **MIP** $250

Roy Rogers and Trigger, 1950s, Hartland, #806, 9" plastic rider w/horse, hat, two pistols
EX $120   NM $300   **MIP** $550

Roy Rogers and Trigger, 1960s, Hartland, 9" plastic rider w/horse, hat, two pistols
EX $120   NM $250   **MIP** $270

Tom Jeffords, 1950s, Hartland, #821, 9" plastic rider w/horse, hat, rifle
EX $80   NM $150   **MIP** $330

Tonto, 1950s, Hartland, 9" plastic rider w/horse, knife
EX $110   NM $180   **MIP** $350

Tonto, 1960s, Hartland, 9" plastic rider w/horse, knife
EX $80   NM $150   **MIP** $290

Ward Bond, 1960s, Hartland, #824, 9" plastic rider w/horse
EX $90   NM $180   **MIP** $330

Wyatt Earp, 1950s, Hartland, #809, 9" plastic rider w/horse
EX $110   NM $180   **MIP** $350

Wyatt Earp, 1960s, Hartland, 9" plastic rider w/horse
EX $90   NM $160   **MIP** $220

Have Gun, Will Travel

Have Gun, Will Travel Play Set, 1958, Prestige
EX $20   NM $50   **MIP** $100

Have Gun, Will Travel Slate, 1960s
EX $10   NM $25   **MIP** $50

Holster Set, 1960s, Halco, double-rig holsters, two Henry cap guns, belt, canteen, 18 bullets, calling cards
EX $150   NM $300   **MIP** $550

Paladin Checkers, 1960s, Ideal, carded
EX $25   NM $50   **MIP** $75

Paladin Western Outfit, 1959, Ben Cooper, mask, vest
EX n/a   NM $65   **MIP** $150

Hopalong Cassidy

Automatic Television Set, 1950s, Automatic Toy
EX $60   NM $100   **MIP** $200

Bar 20 Ranch Badge, 1950s
EX $25   NM $50   **MIP** $75

Bar Twenty Shooting Game, 1950s, Chad Valley
EX $50   NM $100   **MIP** $250

Bread Wrapper, 1950s, Butternut, 14" x 23"
EX $50   NM $70   **MIP** $95

Canvas School Bag, 1950s
EX $25   NM $50   **MIP** $150

Cap Gun, 1950s, Wyandotte, 7", silver metal w/white handles, Hoppy pictured on sides
EX $150   NM $300   **MIP** $600

Chinese Checkers, 1950, Milton Bradley
EX $60   NM $130   **MIP** $225

Coloring Outfit, 1950s, Transogram
EX $35   NM $75   **MIP** $150

Compass Hat Ring, 1950s, brass, features "HC" on one side and "20" on other; compass on top
EX $195   NM $250   **MIP** $300

Crayon and Stencil Set, 1950s, Transogram
EX $35   NM $75   **MIP** $150

Frame Tray Puzzle, 1950s, Whitman
EX $10   NM $20   **MIP** $40

Hopalong Canasta, 1950s, Pacific Playing Card
EX $55   NM $100   **MIP** $250

Hopalong Cassidy Figure, 1950s, Ideal, plastic figure of Hoppy w/Topper
EX $40   NM $65   **MIP** $150

Lasso Game, 1950s, Transogram
EX $35   NM $75   **MIP** $150

Mechanical Shooting Gallery, 1950s, Automatic Toy
EX $75   NM $150   **MIP** $350

Original Hopalong Pogo Stick, 1950s
EX $50   NM $100   **MIP** $225

Picture Gun and Theatre, 1950s, Stephens Products, projects film, Hoppy decals on sides, includes film, gun, cardboard stage
EX $75   NM $150   **MIP** $225

Pony Express Toss Game, 1950s, Transogram
EX $30   NM $45   **MIP** $70

Puzzles, 1950s, Milton Bradley, boxed set of three
EX $30   NM $50   **MIP** $100

Radio, 1950s, Arvin, red metal case, embossed image of Hoppy and topper on front
EX $200   NM $450   **MIP** $600

Roller Skates, Rollfast
EX $200   NM $500   **MIP** $1000

Stationery, 1950s, Whitman
EX $20   NM $50   **MIP** $100

Topper Rocking Horse, 1950s, Rich Toys, plastic/wood
EX $65   NM $125   MIP $250

Western Series, 1950s, Timpo, British set of seven metal figures
EX $100   NM $250   MIP $475

Wrist Cuffs, 1950s
EX $55   NM $100   MIP $250

How the West Was Won

Dakota Figure, 1978, Mattel
EX $10   NM $25   MIP $45

How the West Was Won Action Play Set, 1977, Timpo
EX $10   NM $25   MIP $40

Lone Wolf Figure, 1978, Mattel, #2369, 9-1/2" tall
EX $10   NM $20   MIP $50

Puzzle, 1978, HG Toys, boxed jigsaw puzzle
EX $5   NM $7   MIP $15

Zeb Macahan Figure, 1978, Mattel
EX $10   NM $25   MIP $60

Lone Ranger

Coloring Book, 1975, Whitman, #1010
EX $8   NM $15   MIP $25

Electric Drawing Set, 1960s, Lakeside
EX $5   NM $10   MIP $20

Flashlight Ring, 1948, premium
EX $45   NM $90   MIP $175

Hand Puppet, 1940s, cloth body, blue and white polka-dot shirt w/bells in both hands
EX $40   NM $90   MIP $160

Lone Ranger and Tonto Target Set, 1970s, Multiple Toymakers, 3" figures w/horses, guns, darts
EX $15   NM $35   MIP $65

Pencil Box, 1940s, American Pencil, snap close, 8-1/2" long
EX $20   NM $40   MIP $75

Record Player, 1940s, Dekka, 12" x 10" x 6" wooden box w/burned in illustrations, leather strap
EX $100   NM $225   MIP $450

Sheriff Jail Keys, 1945, Esquire Novelty, on ring, came on card w/cut-out Sheriff card, 5"
EX $30   NM $63   MIP $125

Tonto Indian Outfit, 1950s, Esquire, costume set
EX $50   NM $100   MIP $350

Miscellaneous Characters

Bat Masterson Holster Set, 1950s, Carnell, holster, belt, cane, yellow and black vest
EX $75   NM $200   MIP $350

Buck Jones Rangers Cowboy Suit, 1930s, Yankiboy, costume set
EX $60   NM $200   MIP $500

Buffalo Bill Puzzle, 1956, Built-Rite, frame tray
EX $10   NM $20   MIP $35

Cheyenne Book, 1958, Whitman, Little Golden Book
EX $6   NM $13   MIP $24

Cheyenne Little Golden Record, 1950s, 45 rpm
EX $7   NM $15   MIP $25

Cheyenne Puzzle, 1957, Milton Bradley, frame tray
EX $12   NM $25   MIP $45

Cisco Kid Official Holster Set, 1950s, white and black leather double holster rig, no guns
EX $150   NM $300   MIP $450

Cisco Kid Puzzle Set, 1950s, Saalfield, set of three puzzles
EX $30   NM $50   MIP $70

Johnny Moccasin View-Master Reels, 1957, Sawyers, set of three reels, booklet
EX $20   NM $45   MIP $60

Johnny Ringo Hand Puppet, 1950s, Tops in Toys, 15" full body puppet, vinyl head
EX $65   NM $100   MIP $200

Kit Carson Holster Set, 1950s, brown leather double holster rig, no guns
EX $100   NM $200   MIP $300

Laramie Cowboy Holster Set, 1960s, Clarke Bros., double rig, "Laramie" on each holster
EX $85   NM $185   MIP $410

Maverick Oil Painting by Numbers Set, 1960s, Hassenfeld Bros., image of James Garner as Bret Maverick on front
EX $25   NM $45   MIP $70

Red Ranger Ride 'Em Cowboy, 1950s, Wyandotte, mechanical bucking horse and rider on half-circle base
EX $75   NM $140   MIP $220

Rin-Tin-Tin Magic Slate, 1950s, Whitman
EX $10   NM $20   MIP $30

Rin-Tin-Tin Ring, 1955, Nabisco, plastic, Nabisco Rice Honeys premium

EX $8   **NM** $15   **MIP** $24

Rin-Tin-Tin Rusty Costume, 1950s, Ben Cooper

EX $25   **NM** $40   **MIP** $85

Straight Arrow Target Game, 1949, Novel Novelties, tin litho target w/crossbow

EX $40   **NM** $75   **MIP** $150

Wagon Train Complete Western Outfit, 1950s, Leslie Henry, set contains: leather double holster, two spurs, two gauntlets, cap pistol, derringer, 50-shot repeater rifle

EX $200 **NM** $450   **MIP** $750

Wild Bill Hickok and Jingles Puzzle Set, 1950s, Built-Rite, set of four

EX $25   **NM** $50   **MIP** $75

Wild Bill Hickok Treasure Map/Guide, 1950s, Kellogg's, cereal premium

EX $40   **NM** $65   **MIP** $90

Red Ryder

Corral Bagatelle Game, 1940s, Gotham

EX $25   **NM** $45   **MIP** $75

Frame Tray Puzzle, 1951, Jaymar, Red Ryder or Little Beaver

EX $5   **NM** $10   **MIP** $20

Little Beaver Archery Set, 1951, cardboard target

EX $10   **NM** $20   **MIP** $30

Little Beaver Coloring Book, 1956, Whitman

EX $5   **NM** $10   **MIP** $25

Pop-Um Shooting Game, 1940s, Daisy

EX $30   **NM** $50   **MIP** $150

Whirli-Crow Game, 1940s, Daisy

EX $30   **NM** $50   **MIP** $100

Roy Rogers

Alarm Clock, 1950s, Ingraham, square ivory-color case, full-color graphics, 4"

EX $153   **NM** $315   **MIP** $440

Crayon Set, 1950s, Standard Toykraft

EX $35   **NM** $52   **MIP** $110

Dale Evans Wristwatch, 1951, Ingraham, Dale inside upright horseshoe, tan background, chrome case, black leather band

EX $61   **NM** $157   **MIP** $325

Deputy Badge, 1950s

EX $25   **NM** $50   **MIP** $75

Fix-It Chuck Wagon and Jeep, 1950s, Ideal, set w/two horses, four figures, Nellybelle, accessories

EX $71   **NM** $157   **MIP** $330

Give-A-Show Projector, 1960s, Kenner, projector w/slides

EX $25   **NM** $52   **MIP** $82

Horeshoe Set, Ohio Art, tin litho

EX $40   **NM** $105   **MIP** $275

Horsedrawn Wagon Pull Toy, 1950s, Hill, wood w/paper litho, 18"

EX $56   **NM** $105   **MIP** $275

Horseshoe Set, 1950s, rubber horseshoes and pegs

EX $30   **NM** $52   **MIP** $143

Nodder, Japanese, composition, blue shirt, white hat and pants and red bandana and boots

EX $10   **NM** $25   **MIP** $50

Play Set, 1950s, Amsco, cardboard w/magnetic figures

EX $51   **NM** $210   **MIP** $440

Puzzle, 1950s, frame tray

EX $20   **NM** $36   **MIP** $50

Ranch Lantern, 1950s, Ohio Art, tin litho, battery-operated

EX $56   **NM** $135   **MIP** $275

Rodeo Board Game, 1949, Rogden, four games in one

EX $102   **NM** $147   **MIP** $220

Rodeo Sticker Fun Book, 1953, Whitman

EX $35   **NM** $57   **MIP** $121

Roy Rogers & Dale Evans Coloring Book, 1975, Whitman

EX $10   **NM** $21   **MIP** $33

Roy Rogers & Dale Evans Paper Dolls, 1954, Whitman

EX $35   **NM** $57   **MIP** $88

Roy Rogers & Dale Evans Western Dinner Set, 1950s, Ideal, utensils in 14" x 24" box

EX $35   **NM** $68   **MIP** $104

Stagecoach, 1950s, Ideal, plastic w/two harnessed horses, Roy, and accessories, 14"

EX $25   **NM** $70   **MIP** $135

Toy Chest, 1950s, 17" x 17" x 12" w/Roy and Bullet graphics

EX $178   **NM** $315   **MIP** $550

Toy Football, 1950s, white vinyl w/logo

EX $20   **NM** $42   **MIP** $66

Trigger Rocking Horse, 1950s, Bell Toys, wood w/metal seat

EX $51   **NM** $105   **MIP** $220

Trigger Trotter, 1950s, pogo stick

EX $153   **NM** $236   **MIP** $330

Truck, 1950s, Marx, tin litho, red, yellow and blue, 14"

EX $95   **NM** $175   **MIP** $300

Tom Mix

Magnet Ring, 1947, Ralston, Ralston cereal premium, brass w/silver magnet

EX $12   **NM** $25   **MIP** $65

Sheriff's Badge, Dobie County, 1940s, Ralston, Ralston Straight Shooters Club premium from Tom Mix radio show, 2-1/4" tall, metal

EX $15   **NM** $25   **MIP** $50

Zorro

"Color" TV Set, 1958, Walt Disney Productions, small plastic TV w/paper scrolls

EX $12   **NM** $25   **MIP** $50

Bean Bag & Dart Set, 1950s, Walt Disney Productions, two games in one

EX $10   **NM** $20   **MIP** $30

Book Bag, 1950s, National Leather Mfg. Co., white and black w/Zorro on rearing Tornado

EX $45   **NM** $90   **MIP** $140

Costume, 1957, Ben Cooper, plastic mask, hat, costume
EX $35   **NM** $70   **MIP** $100

Costume - Complete Playsuit, 1950s, Ben Cooper, six-piece costume set: hat, mask, shirt, pants, belt, cape
EX $50   **NM** $125   **MIP** $225

Dart Rifle Target Set, 1960s
EX $40   **NM** $70   **MIP** $175

Dominoes, 1950s, Halsam, #650
EX $25   **NM** $45   **MIP** $65

Fencing Set, 1950s, swords, masks, face guards
EX $45   **NM** $75   **MIP** $165

Figurine, 1958, Enesco, ceramic, 5-3/4" tall
EX $45   **NM** $100   **MIP** $175

Flashlight, 1950s, Bantamlight, plastic w/Zorro logo and image of him on rearing Tornado
EX $15   **NM** $30   **MIP** $45

Gloves (Children's), 1950s, Wells Lamont/Walt Disney, black gloves w/white gauntlets that have Zorro image and logo, 8-1/2" long
EX $15   **NM** $30   **MIP** $60

Hand Puppet, 1958, Gund, vinyl and fabric, 9-1/4" tall
EX $25   **NM** $50   **MIP** $75

Holster Set, 1950s, Daisy, w/leather cuffs
EX n/a   **NM** n/a   **MIP** n/a

Magic Slate, 1958, Walt Disney Productions
EX $10   **NM** $22   **MIP** $45

Official Zorro Action Set, 1950s, Marx, costume and weapons set
EX $75   **NM** $150   **MIP** $350

Paint by Number Set, Hasbro, canvas and paints
EX $35   **NM** $60   **MIP** $85

Pencil by Number Set, 1960s
EX $35   **NM** $60   **MIP** $80

Pencil Case, 1960s, Hasbro, vinyl/cardboard
EX $15   **NM** $35   **MIP** $60

Puzzle, 1958, Jaymar, boxed jigsaw puzzle, pictures Zorro and Monasterio duelling
EX $10   **NM** $20   **MIP** $40

Spanish Play Set, 1965, released during the show's syndicated TV run, mask, two cuffs, holster, photo of Zorro dueling w/Monasterio
EX $25   **NM** $55   **MIP** $85

Spring Action Target, 1950s, Knickerbocker
EX $45   **NM** $75   **MIP** $150

Target Shoot, 1950s, gun w/soldier targets
EX $40   **NM** $75   **MIP** $150

Velvet Pait Set, 1966, Hasbro, by numbers on velvet, #2821
EX $15   **NM** $30   **MIP** $45

Wallet, 1957, Walt Disney Productions, white vinyl w/red interior, snap closure, another model is in white vinyl
EX $10   **NM** $20   **MIP** $35

Walt Disney's The Adventures of Zorro, 1958, Golden, Big Golden Book
EX $10   **NM** $20   **MIP** $30

Walt Disney's Zorro, 1958, Little Golden Book
EX $5   **NM** $7   **MIP** $15

Walt Disney's Zorro, 1958, Golden, Golden Book
EX $5   **NM** $10   **MIP** $25

Watch, 1960s, U.S. Time, "Zorro" on face
EX $12   **NM** $25   **MIP** $75

Zorro and Horse Set, 1950s, Lido, small plastic figure and horse
EX $15   **NM** $25   **MIP** $50

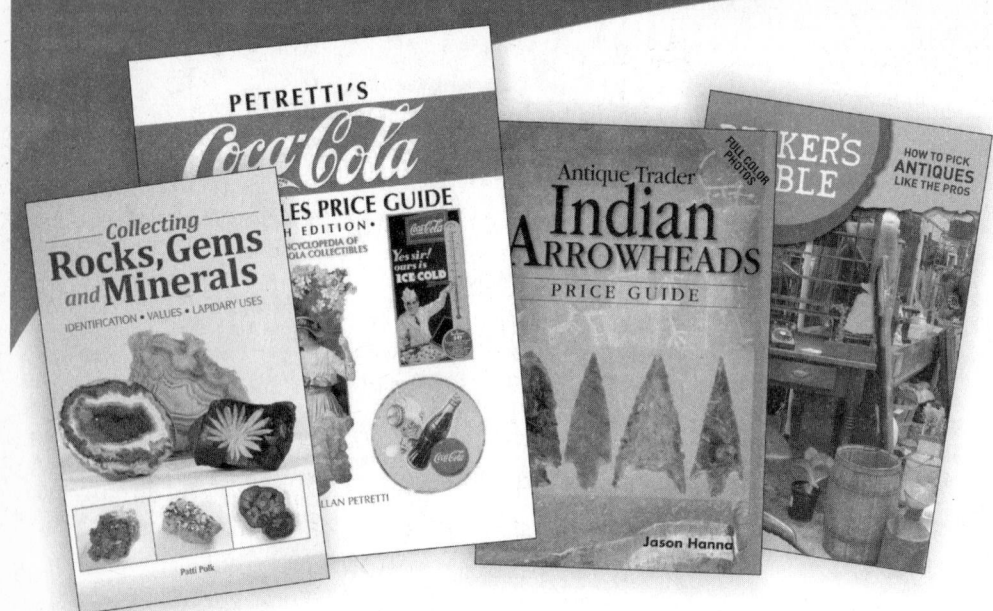